The New Penguin Dictionary of *Quotations*

The New Penguin Dictionary of
Quotations

Robert Andrews

**with the assistance of
Kate Hughes**

PENGUIN BOOKS

PENGUIN BOOKS

Published by the Penguin Group
Penguin Books Ltd, 80 Strand, London WC2R 0RL, England
Penguin Group (USA) Inc., 375 Hudson Street, New York, New York 10014, USA
Penguin Group (Canada), 90 Eglinton Avenue East, Suite 700, Toronto, Ontario, Canada M4P 2Y3
(a division of Pearson Penguin Canada Inc.)
Penguin Ireland, 25 St Stephen's Green, Dublin 2, Ireland
(a division of Penguin Books Ltd)
Penguin Group (Australia), 250 Camberwell Road, Camberwell, Victoria 3124, Australia
(a division of Pearson Australia Group Pty Ltd)
Penguin Books India Pvt Ltd, 11 Community Centre, Panchsheel Park, New Delhi – 110 017, India
Penguin Group (NZ), 67 Apollo Drive, Mairangi Bay, Auckland 1310, New Zealand
(a division of Pearson New Zealand Ltd)
Penguin Books (South Africa) (Pty) Ltd, 24 Sturdee Avenue, Rosebank, Johannesburg 2196, South Africa

Penguin Books Ltd, Registered Offices: 80 Strand, London WC2R 0RL, England

www.penguin.com

First published 2006
1

Set in PostScript TheAntiquaB5 and TheSans
Typeset by Rowland Phototypesetting Ltd, Bury St Edmunds, Suffolk
Printed in Finland by WS Bookwell

ISBN-13: 978–0–140–29267–1
ISBN-10: 0–140–29267–5

To my parents

Contents

Preface

The New Penguin Dictionary of Quotations puts the best and the best-remembered sayings and writings of all time in their historical context. The speakers and writers are presented alphabetically, but under each name the quotes are ordered chronologically, according to when each was first uttered, written or recorded (the exceptions are entries under the headings Advertising Slogans, Anonymous, Hymns and Carols, Nursery Rhymes and Political Slogans, which are arranged alphabetically). Brief biographical sketches are given for each person quoted, and contextual information is supplied where necessary or helpful for appreciating the significance of a quote. This may range from naming the speaker of words quoted from a play or novel, to summarizing the circumstances or incident to which the words refer. So, for example, Shakespeare's lines, 'Out, vile jelly! / Where is thy lustre now?' make little sense if it's not clear that these are words spoken by Cornwall on gouging out Gloucester's eyes in *King Lear*. Biblical extracts too have most impact when the setting is understood: the stark prophecy 'His hand will be against every man, and every man's hand against him' refers to Abraham's son Ishmael, who would later be banished to the desert and become the archetypal outcast.

The citations provide the information needed both to identify the source of a quote and to locate it for further research. Details of modern publications are given where the original writings and speeches were not published during or shortly after the lifetime of their originators (nearly all letters and journals fall into this category). Quotes which are better known in their non-English form are given in the original language, accompanied by an English translation. Dates of translation are supplied when these are significantly later than the first writing or utterance of the words, and translators are named when it is necessary to distinguish one version from others, or when the translator is well known or appears elsewhere in the anthology. Lines from songs or films appear under the names with which they are most associated, usually the singer or actor who has made them famous, though in all cases the original writers are credited.

The chronological sequence and biographical and contextual notes help to put familiar and not so familiar quotes in a new light. Products of specific times and circumstances, quotations constitute a continuum with the past, and are gateways into our cultural history. They tell us as much about the things people have chosen to remember and repeat, as they preserve (in the words of Isaac d'Israeli) 'the wisdom of the wise, and the experience of ages'. They can also be capsules of humour, fragments associated with great historical moments, or simply the pithy elegance of a few well-chosen words that have never been bettered. Some have been passed down through generations to become embedded in our cultural heritage, while others may have a more ephemeral existence.

Attitudes to the art of quotation have shifted over the years. In centuries past, such learned essayists as Francis Bacon and Michel de Montaigne could embellish their works with a rich mixture of borrowed aphorisms and observations, usually uncited, which their readers were expected to recognize, while in the eighteenth century Samuel Johnson was able to declare: 'Classical quotation is the *parole* of literary men all over the world.' Only a few years after, however, Ralph Waldo Emerson – himself not shy of borrowing copiously from the literary canon – could write: 'I hate quotation. Tell me what you know.' As Evelyn Waugh later expressed it: 'In the dying world I come from quotation is a national vice. It used to be the classics, now it's lyric verse.' More recently, the power of the media has fostered the growth of sound-bites, especially in the political context. Often these turn out to be hostages to fortune – sound-bites can bite back, as was the case with John Major's 'Back to Basics' speech or George Bush's 'Read my lips – no new taxes'. More generally, it would be well for all quotations to be accompanied by a health warning. Robertson Davies commented: 'To be apt in quotation is a splendid and dangerous gift. Splendid, because it ornaments a man's speech with other men's jewels; dangerous, for the same reason.' But perhaps the most comprehensive caveat came from Henry W. Fowler, writing about 'literary or decorative quotation' in *A Dictionary of Modern English Usage* (1925): 'A writer expresses himself in words that have been used before because they give his meaning better than he can give it himself, or because they are beautiful or witty, or because he expects them to touch a chord of association in his reader, or because he wishes to show that he is learned or well read. Quotations due to the last motive are invariably ill advised; the discerning reader detects it & is contemptuous; the undiscerning is perhaps impressed, but even then is at the same time repelled, pretentious quotations being the surest road to tedium.' No such danger resides in the *reading* of quotations, however, and I hope the reader will derive as much amusement, delight and surprise in perusing this collection as we have done from its compilation.

Kate Hughes has collaborated with me on various quotation anthologies in the past, and has undertaken much of the original research and editing for this book. Her input is immense and my gratitude is boundless. Special thanks are also due to Richard Davoll and Dr Margaret Jones, who energetically performed miracles of painstaking research in libraries and online. Other contributors who lent their time and enthusiasm are Quinn Andrews, Booker Forte, Charles Lewsen and Jo Morgan. The past input of Philip Krynsky is also gratefully acknowledged. Thanks too to all at Penguin for supporting this project and to Sarah Waldram for copy-editing.

A

Chinua Achebe
(b. 1930)
Nigerian novelist

Originally named Albert Chinualumogo. His books deal with the impact of European colonialism on Africa, and with post-colonial African politics. Among the most notable are his first, Things Fall Apart *(1958), and* Anthills of the Savannah *(1987).*

1 For I do honestly believe that in the fat-dripping, gummy, eat-and-let-eat régime just ended – a régime which inspired the common saying that a man could only be sure of what he had put away safely in his gut or, in language ever more suited to the times, 'you chop, me self I chop, palaver finish'; a régime in which you see a fellow cursed in the morning for stealing a blind man's stick and later in the evening saw him again mounting the altar of the new shrine in the presence of all the people to whisper into the ear of the chief celebrant – in such a régime, I say, you died a good death if your life had inspired someone to come forward and shoot your murderer in the chest – without asking to be paid.
A Man of the People, ch. 13 (1966). In this closing sentence of the book, the narrator (Odili Samalu) refers to the end of the repressive régime of Chief Nanga.

Dean Acheson
(1893–1971)
US politician

A Democrat, he was adviser to four presidents. As Secretary of State under TRUMAN *(1949–53), he was instrumental in implementing the Marshall Aid Plan to Europe and the Truman Doctrine, and in the formation of NATO.*

1 Great Britain has lost an Empire and has not yet found a role.
Speech at US Military Academy, West Point, 5 December 1962, publ. in *Vital Speeches* (1963)

2 The first requirement of a statesman is that he be dull. This is not always easy to achieve.
Quoted in the *Observer* 21 June 1970

3 A memorandum is written not to inform the reader but to protect the writer.
Quoted in the *Wall Street Journal* 8 September 1977

Lord Acton
(1834–1902)
English historian

John Emerich Edward Dalberg, first Baron Acton. A prominent Liberal and Roman Catholic (who opposed the doctrine of papal infallibility), he was appointed Professor of Modern History at Cambridge in 1895, and founded the Cambridge Modern History *series, editing the first two volumes.*

1 Every thing secret degenerates, even the administration of justice; nothing is safe that does not show how it can bear discussion and publicity.
Letter, 23 January 1861, publ. in *Lord Acton and his Circle* (ed. Abbot Gasquet, 1906)

2 Power tends to corrupt, and absolute power corrupts absolutely. Great men are almost always bad men.
Letter to Bishop Mandell Creighton, 3 April 1887, publ. in *The Life and Letters of Mandell Creighton*, vol. 1, ch. 13 (ed. Louise Creighton, 1904). WILLIAM PITT THE ELDER had previously stated, in a speech to the House of Lords, 9 January 1770: 'Unlimited power is apt to corrupt the minds of those who possess it.' More recently, J. K. GALBRAITH wrote, 'In the United States, though power corrupts, the expectation of power paralyzes.'

Douglas Adams
(1952–2001)
British author

He attracted a huge following with The Hitch Hiker's Guide to the Galaxy, *a satirical science-fiction series originally broadcast on radio in 1978. It subsequently became a book and was adapted for television, stage, film and a computer game.*

1 Don't panic.
The Hitch Hiker's Guide to the Galaxy, Preface and passim (1979). The words are inscribed in 'large friendly letters' on the cover of the (fictional) book, 'The Hitch Hiker's Guide to the Galaxy'. The same words were also a catch-phrase of the excitable Corporal Jones (played by Clive Dunn) in the TV series *Dad's Army* (1968–77).

2 This must be Thursday. I never could get the hang of Thursdays.
Arthur Dent, ibid., ch. 2. Said on the day that he learns that his house is about to be demolished and the world is going to end. The line was voted the most popular in the *Hitch Hiker* series.

3 I think you ought to know I'm feeling very depressed.
Marvin the robot, ibid., ch. 11. The first words in the book spoken by this prototype for a new generation of robots with 'Genuine People Personalities'. Adams claimed he based

Marvin's character on Andrew Marshall, the comedy writer, though he also acknowledged the influence of Eeyore in *Winnie-the-Pooh*.

4 Life . . . don't talk to me about Life.
Marvin, ibid., ch. 11

5 I've been ordered to take you down to the bridge. Here I am, brain the size of a planet and they ask me to take you down to the bridge. Call that job satisfaction? 'Cos I don't.
Marvin, ibid., ch. 11

6 The Answer to the Great Question . . . Of Life, the Universe and Everything . . . Is . . . Forty-two.
The computer Deep Thought, ibid., ch. 27

7 So long, and thanks for all the fish.
The dolphins' farewell message to humanity, in *So Long, and Thanks for All the Fish*, ch. 31 (fourth book in the *Hitch Hiker's Guide to the Galaxy* series, 1984)

Franklin Pierce Adams
(1881–1960)
US journalist and humorist

A byword in the 1930s, '40s and '50s for wit and erudition, he set a precedent for the contemporary newspaper column with 'The Conning Tower', which appeared in the Herald Tribune *1913–37.*

1 Years ago we discovered the exact point, the dead center of middle age. It occurs when you are too young to take up golf and too old to rush up to the net.
Nods and Becks, 'Valentine' (1944)

2 Too much Truth
Is uncouth.
Ibid., 'From the New England Primer'

3 The trouble with this country is that there are too many politicians who believe, with a conviction based on experience, that you can fool all of the people all of the time.
Ibid., 'Baseball Note'. The allusion is to the famous saying credited to both Abraham Lincoln (see ABRAHAM LINCOLN 33) and PHINEAS BARNUM.

Gerry Adams
(b. 1948)
Irish politician

President of Sinn Féin, he was elected to the Northern Ireland Assembly in 1982 and became MP for Belfast West in 1983, though refusing to take his seat at Westminster. He was a principal negotiator in the IRA ceasefire (1994–6) and the Good Friday peace agreement (1999).

1 He [David Trimble] is a man I can do business with; he is a man I have to do business with; and he is a man who I will do business with. This is more important than the personalities involved.
Quoted in the *Guardian* 11 September 1998. Referring to his meeting with the Ulster Unionist leader, the first time Unionist and Sinn Féin leaders had met since 1922.

Henry Brooks Adams
(1838–1918)
US historian

A member of one of Boston's most influential families – grandson of John Quincy Adams and great-grandson of JOHN ADAMS, *both US presidents. He wrote novels and historical works, but is best remembered for his autobiography,* The Education of Henry Adams *(1907).*

1 Politics, as a practise, whatever its professions, has always been the systematic organization of hatreds.
The Education of Henry Adams, ch. 1 (1907)

2 All experience is an arch to build upon.
Ibid., ch. 6

3 A friend in power is a friend lost.
Ibid., ch. 7. Referring to the rupture with Senator Charles Sumner.

4 Chaos often breeds life, when order breeds habit.
Ibid., ch. 16

5 A teacher affects eternity; he can never tell where his influence stops.
Ibid., ch. 20

6 One friend in a lifetime is much; two are many; three are hardly possible. Friendship needs a certain parallelism of life, a community of thought, a rivalry of aim.
Ibid., ch. 20

7 Practical politics consists in ignoring facts.
Ibid., ch. 24

8 America has always taken tragedy lightly. Too busy to stop the activity of their twenty-million-horse-power society, Americans ignore tragic motives that would have overshadowed the Middle Ages; and the world learns to regard assassination as a form of hysteria, and death as neurosis, to be treated by a rest-cure.
Ibid., ch. 28

9 Power is poison. Its effect on Presidents had always been tragic.

Ibid., ch. 28. Adams explained, 'No mind is so well balanced as to bear the strain of seizing unlimited force without habit or knowledge of it; and finding it disputed with him by hungry packs of wolves and hounds whose lives depend on snatching the carrion.' The passage refers to THEODORE ROOSEVELT.

10 Modern politics is, at bottom, a struggle not of men but of forces.

Ibid., ch. 28

John Adams
(1735–1826)
US statesman and president

A leading Boston lawyer, he was one of the prime movers in the struggle against the British, and helped draft the Declaration of Independence. In 1789 he became Vice-President under GEORGE WASHINGTON, *whom he succeeded as President in 1796.*

1 I always consider the settlement of America with reverence and wonder, as the opening of a grand scene and design in providence, for the illumination of the ignorant and the emancipation of the slavish part of mankind all over the earth.

Notes for a Dissertation on the Canon and Feudal Law (1765), publ. in *The Works of John Adams*, vol. 3 (ed. Charles Francis Adams, 1851)

2 There is danger from all men. The only maxim of a free government ought to be to trust no man living with power to endanger the public liberty.

Notes for an Oration at Braintree, Massachusetts, Spring 1772, publ. in *Diary and Autobiography of John Adams*, vol. 2 (ed. L. H. Butterfield, 1961)

3 A government of laws, and not of men.

The Novanglus Papers, publ. in the *Boston Gazette* no. 7 (1774), repr. in *The Works of John Adams*, vol. 4 (ed. Charles Francis Adams, 1851). This phrase, incorporated by Adams into the Massachusetts Constitution (1780), was attributed by him to the English political theorist and republican, James Harrington (1611–77), whose actual words (in *Oceana*, 1656) were, 'the empire of laws and not of men'.

4 The happiness of society is the end of government.

Thoughts on Government (1776), ibid., vol. 4. The purpose of government to secure the pursuit of happiness is one of the 'self-evident truths' enshrined in the Declaration of Independence.

5 I agree with you that in politics the middle way is none at all.

Letter, 23 March 1776, publ. in *Papers of John Adams*, third series, vol. 4 (ed. R. J. Taylor, 1979)

6 I must study politics and war that my sons may have liberty to study mathematics and philosophy.

Letter to his wife Abigail Adams, 12 May 1780, publ. in *The Adams Family Correspondence*, vol. 3 (ed. L. H. Butterfield, 1973)

7 Remember, democracy never lasts long. It soon wastes, exhausts, and murders itself. There never was a democracy yet that did not commit suicide.

Letter, 15 April 1814, publ. in *The Works of John Adams*, vol. 6 (ed. Charles Francis Adams, 1851)

Sarah Flower Adams
See HYMNS AND CAROLS 59

Harold Adamson
(1906–80)
US songwriter

He provided Broadway and Hollywood musicals with numerous successful songs, working with jazz composers to produce such standards as 'Manhattan Serenade' (1948). He wrote lyrics for films including Gentlemen Prefer Blondes *(1953).*

1 Comin' in on a wing and a pray'r.

'Comin' in on a Wing and a Pray'r' (song, 1943). The phrase is said to have originated from a pilot's radioed words while attempting a landing with a damaged plane.

Joseph Addison
(1672–1719)
English essayist and playwright

Having made his name with such patriotic poetical works as The Campaign *(1704), he contributed to* RICHARD STEELE'S *Tatler, and with Steele went on to launch the* Spectator *in 1711, with the declared aim to 'enliven morality with wit and to temper wit with morality'. His tragedy* Cato *(1713) brought further success. He was satirized as 'Atticus' by Pope (see* ALEXANDER POPE 149, 150).

1 And, pleased th'Almighty's orders to perform,
Rides in the whirlwind and directs the storm.

The Campaign, ll. 291–2 (1704). Referring to John Churchill, the Duke of Marlborough, victor at the Battle of Blenheim.

2 For wheresoe'er I turn my ravished eyes,
Gay gilded scenes and shining prospects rise,

Poetic fields encompass me around,
And still I seem to tread on classic ground.
'Letter from Italy', publ. in *Remarks on Several Parts of Italy* (1705)

3 There is not a more unhappy being than a super-annuated idol.
Spectator, no. 73, 24 May 1711

4 It is very wonderful to see persons of the best sense passing away a dozen hours together in shuffling and dividing a pack of cards, with no other conversation but what is made up of a few game phrases, and no other ideas but those of black or red spots ranged together in different figures.
Spectator, no. 93, 16 June 1711

5 There is no defence against reproach but obscurity; it is a kind of concomitant to greatness, as satires and invectives were an essential part of a Roman triumph.
Spectator, no. 101, 26 June 1711

6 Authors have established it as a kind of rule, that a man ought to be dull sometimes; as the most severe reader makes allowances for many rests and nodding-places in a voluminous writer.
Spectator, no. 124, 23 July 1711

7 What sculpture is to a block of marble, education is to a human soul.
Spectator, no. 215, 6 November 1711

8 Admiration is a very short-lived passion that immediately decays upon growing familiar with its object, unless it be still fed with fresh discoveries, and kept alive by a new perpetual succession of miracles rising up to its view.
Spectator, no. 256, 24 December 1711

9 These widows, Sir, are the most perverse creatures in the world.
Spectator, no. 335, 25 March 1712. Sir Roger de Coverley is speaking.

10 Mirth is like a flash of lightning, that breaks through a gloom of clouds, and glitters for a moment; cheerfulness keeps up a kind of daylight in the mind, and fills it with a steady and perpetual serenity.
Spectator, no. 381, 17 May 1712

11 Wide and undetermined prospects are as pleasing to the fancy as the speculations of eternity or infinitude are to the understanding.
Spectator, no. 412, 23 June 1712

12 There is not a sight in nature so mortifying as that of a distracted person, when his imagination is troubled, and his whole soul disordered and confused: Babylon in ruins is not so melancholy a spectacle.
Spectator, no. 421, 3 July 1712. The passage may well have been the inspiration for words written by the dandy and companion to BYRON, Scrope Berdmore Davies (1783–1852), in a letter of May 1835 to Thomas Raikes, describing his own condition: 'Babylon in all its desolation is a sight not so awful as that of the human mind in ruins.' Raikes attributed his friend's 'excitement' to the effects of 'the brandy-bottle'.

13 The spacious firmament on high,
With all the blue ethereal sky,
And spangled heavens, a shining frame,
Their great original proclaim.
'Ode', in the *Spectator* no. 465, 23 August 1712

14 Our disputants put me in mind of the scuttlefish, that when he is unable to extricate himself, blackens the water about him until he becomes invisible.
Spectator, no. 476, 5 September 1712

15 If we may believe our logicians, man is distinguished from all other creatures by the faculty of laughter. He has a heart capable of mirth, and naturally disposed to it.
Spectator no. 494, 26 September 1712

16 Husband a lie, and trump it up in some extraordinary emergency.
Spectator, no. 507, 11 October 1712

17 'Tis not in mortals to command success,
But we'll do more, Sempronius, we'll deserve it.
Cato, Act 1, Sc. 2 (1713). Spoken by Portius. 'Curse on the stripling! ... ambitiously sententious,' responds his father, Sempronius.

18 Young men soon give, and soon forget, affronts;
Old age is slow in both.
Syphax, ibid., Act 2, Sc. 5

19 The woman that deliberates is lost.
Marcia, ibid., Act 4, Sc. 1

20 What pity is it
That we can die but once to serve our country!
Ibid., Act 4, Sc. 2. Cato speaks over the body of his son Marcus.
See NATHAN HALE 1.

21 From hence, let fierce contending nations know
What dire effects from civil discord flow.
Lucius, ibid., Act 5, Sc. 4

22 We are always doing, says he, 'something for

posterity, but I would fain see posterity do something for us.'

Spectator, no. 583, 20 August 1714. In the style of an old fellow of a college, articulating the feelings of 'most people'.

23 There is nothing more requisite in business than dispatch.

The Drummer, Act 5, Sc. 1 (1716)

24 No oppression is so heavy or lasting as that which is inflicted by the perversion and exorbitance of legal authority.

Interesting Anecdotes, Memoirs, Allegories, Essays, and Poetical Fragments, 'The Cruelty of Parental Tyranny' (1794)

25 See in what peace a Christian can die.

Dying words, quoted in *Conjectures on Original Composition*, by EDWARD YOUNG (1759, ed. Edith Morley, 1918)

George Ade
(1866–1944)
US humorist and playwright

A columnist on the Chicago Morning News *(later the* Record*), he published his pieces in* Fables in Slang *(1899) and* Forty Modern Fables *(1901). He also wrote plays and light operas, notably* The Sultan of Sulu *(1902).*

1 After being turned down by numerous publishers, he had decided to write for posterity.

Fables in Slang, 'The Fable of the Bohemian who Had Hard Luck' (1899). Referring to the 'main Bohemian'.

2 The time to enjoy a European tour is about three weeks after you unpack.

Forty Modern Fables, 'The Hungry Man from the Bird Center' (1901)

3 The cocktail is a pleasant drink;
It's mild and harmless – I don't think.
When you've had one, you call for two,
And then you don't care what you do.

'R-e-m-o-r-s-e', in *The Sultan of Sulu*, Act 2 (1902). The song of Ki-Ram.

4 Those dry Martinis did the work for me;
Last night at twelve I felt immense,
Today I feel like thirty cents.
My eyes are bleared, my coppers hot,
I'll try to eat, but I cannot.
It is no time for mirth and laughter,
The cold, gray dawn of the morning after.

'R-e-m-o-r-s-e', ibid.

Alfred Adler
(1870–1937)
Austrian psychiatrist

A founder member of the Vienna Psychoanalytic Society, he introduced the concept of the inferiority complex in 1907 and developed his own school of Individual Psychology from 1911. The Neurotic Character (1912) was his first and most significant book.

1 The truth is often a terrible weapon of aggression. It is possible to lie, and even to murder, for the truth.

The Problems of Neurosis, ch. 2 (1929)

2 It is always easier to fight for one's principles than to live up to them.

Quoted in *Alfred Adler: Apostle of Freedom*, ch. 5 (1939) by Phyllis Bottome. The words were famously recalled by ADLAI STEVENSON in a speech in New York, 27 August 1952.

Polly Adler
(1900–62)
US brothel-keeper

A New York 'madam' in the 1920s and '30s, she retired in 1945. Her memoirs were filmed in 1964.

1 A House is Not a Home.

Title of memoirs (1954)

2 What it comes down to is this: the grocer, the butcher, the baker, the merchant, the landlord, the druggist, the liquor dealer, the policeman, the doctor, the city father and the politician – these are the people who make money out of prostitution, these are the real reapers of the wages of sin.

Ibid., ch. 9

Theodor W. Adorno
(1903–69)
German philosopher, sociologist and musicologist

A member of the Frankfurt School of philosophy, he was associated with the Frankfurt Institute for Social Research from 1928 before fleeing the Nazis to the USA. He returned to Frankfurt to assume the post of Director of the Institute (1958–69). His publications include The Dialectic of Enlightenment *(1947).*

1 Technology is making gestures precise and brutal, and with them men. It expels from movements all hesitation, deliberation, civility.

Minima Moralia, pt 1, 'Do Not Knock' (1951, transl. 1978)

2 True thoughts are those alone which do not understand themselves.
Ibid., pt 3, 'Monograms'

3 Culture is only true when implicitly critical, and the mind which forgets this revenges itself in the critics it breeds. Criticism is an indispensable element of culture.
Prisms, 'Cultural Criticism and Society' (1967)

Advertising slogans
See also NEWS OF THE WORLD 1.

1 Access – your flexible friend.
Access credit card, 1980s

2 American Express? That'll do nicely, sir.
American Express credit card, 1970s

3 An ace caff with quite a nice museum attached.
Victoria and Albert Museum, London, 1989, by Saatchi and Saatchi advertising agency. The most visible feature of a marketing drive spearheaded by museum director Elisabeth Esteve-Coll, the advertisement created great negative publicity by suggesting that culture took second place at the museum.

4 Australians wouldn't give a XXXX for anything else.
Castlemaine lager, from 1986, by Saatchi and Saatchi advertising agency

5 Can you tell Stork from butter?
Stork margarine, 1950s

6 Cool as a mountain stream.
Consulate menthol cigarettes, 1960s

7 Even your closest friends won't tell you.
Listerine mouthwash, 1920s. The campaign, which focused on halitosis, ran in the USA from 1922 mainly in women's magazines. It hugely boosted sales of the product, giving birth to the technique of playing on people's neuroses by inventing unheard of complaints. It was subsequently widely copied, and the 'halitosis influence' became part of standard advertising jargon (discussed in *The Mirror Makers: A History of American Advertising*, 1984, by Stephen Fox).

8 Full of Eastern promise.
Fry's Turkish Delight, from 1950s

9 Go to work on an egg.
British Egg Marketing Board, from 1957. Claimed to have been written by FAY WELDON.

10 Guinness is good for you.
Guinness beer, credited to Oswald Greene in 1929, in *The Book of Guinness Advertising*, ch. 4 (1985) by Brian Sibley. Other slogans famously associated with Guinness include 'Guinness Gives You Strength' (also from 1929), which first appeared as 'Guinness Is So Strengthening' and was accompanied by an image of a workman carrying a girder on his fingertips, and 'My Goodness, My Guinness', which was devised by DOROTHY L. SAYERS, then an advertising copywriter.

11 Heineken refreshes the parts other beers cannot reach.
Heineken lager, from 1970s

12 I'm Mandy, fly me.
TWA, 1975. The words, spoken by an air hostess, were a target of feminists and the title of a hit song by the band 10cc in 1976.

13 I'm only here for the beer.
Double Diamond beer, from 1971. Credited to Ros Levenstein.

14 It could be you.
National Lottery, from November 1994

15 It's finger lickin' good.
Kentucky Fried Chicken, from 1950s

16 It's good to talk.
British Telecom, from 1994, later changed to 'It's good to listen.'

17 Just when you thought it was safe to go back in the water.
Publicity tag-line for *Jaws 2* (film, 1978)

18 Labour isn't working.
British Conservative Party slogan, 1978–9. A 1999 survey in *Campaign* ranked the poster on which it appeared, designed by the Saatchi and Saatchi advertising agency, as the most memorable of the century, and it was cited as instrumental in the downfall of JAMES CALLAGHAN's Labour government.

19 Let the train take the strain.
British Rail, from 1970s

20 Let your fingers do the walking.
Yellow Pages telephone book, from 1960s in USA and Britain

21 A Mars a day helps you work, rest and play.
Mars bar, from 1960s

22 A million housewives every day
Pick up a tin of beans and say
Beanz Meanz Heinz!
Heinz Baked Beans, from 1967, credited to Maurice Drake

23 The mint wth the hole.
Polo mints, from 1940s, also used in the USA for Life-Savers, 1920s

24 Nice one, Cyril.
Wonderloaf bread, 1972. The phrase was adopted by supporters of Tottenham Hotspur football club referring to Cyril

Knowles, and was the title of a song recorded by the 'Cockerel Chorus' in 1973.

25 Put a tiger in your tank.
Esso petrol, 1960s

26 Say it with flowers.
Slogan for the Society of American Florists, from 1917. Ascribed to Patrick O'Keefe, an advertising agent.

27 Snap! Crackle! Pop!
Kellogg's Rice Krispies, from 1920s

28 Sssch . . . you know who.
Schweppes drinks, 1960s

29 Tell Sid.
British Gas, 1986, advertising shares at privatization, devised by the Saatchi and Saatchi advertising agency

30 Things go better with Coke.
Coca-Cola, from 1960s

31 Top people take *The Times*.
The Times, from 1959

32 *Vorsprung durch Technik.*
[Progress through technology.]
Audi cars, from 1980s

33 We are the Ovaltineys,
Happy girls and boys.
'We are the Ovaltineys' (song), promoting the drink Ovaltine, from 1930s

34 You're never alone with a Strand.
Strand cigarettes, 1960. The music backing the advertisement was later released as a record called 'The Lonely Man Theme'.

35 Wouldn't it be nice if all cities were like Milton Keynes?
For Milton Keynes, 1990s

Æ
(1867–1935)
Irish poet and essayist

Pseudonym of George William Russell. He was prominent in the Irish literary revival and edited the Irish Homestead *(1905–23) and* Irish Statesman *(1923–30). His poems, plays and other writings were inspired by mysticism and magic.*

1 In ancient shadows and twilights
Where childhood had strayed,
The world's great sorrows were born
And its heroes were made.
In the lost boyhood of Judas
Christ was betrayed.
'Germinal' (1931), repr. in *Selected Poems by Æ* (1935)

Aeschylus
(*c.* 525–456 BC)
Athenian dramatist

One of the key founders of the Greek dramatic tradition, he wrote plays which deal with moral and political issues. Only seven of the seventy-odd works ascribed to him survive, including The Persians *and the* Oresteia. *According to tradition, he died when an eagle, mistaking his bald head for a stone, dropped a tortoise upon it to break the shell.*

1 He who learns must suffer. And even in our sleep pain that cannot forget falls drop by drop upon the heart, and in our own despite, against our will, comes wisdom to us by the awful grace of God.
Agamemnon, ll. 177–83 (first of the *Oresteia* trilogy, *c.* 458 BC, transl. EDITH HAMILTON, 1937). Spoken by the Chorus. The passage was quoted by ROBERT F. KENNEDY in a speech on the death of MARTIN LUTHER KING, 4 April 1968.

2 For not many men, the proverb saith,
Can love a friend whom fortune prospereth
Unenvying; and about the envious brain
Cold poison clings, and doubles all the pain
Life brings him.
Agamemnon, ibid., ll. 832–6 (transl. Gilbert Murray, 1920). See GORE VIDAL 5.

3 Against a spike
Kick not, for fear it pain thee if thou strike.
Aigisthos, ibid., ll. 1623–4. Some translations give the more colloquial 'Do not kick against the pricks' (see BIBLE, NEW TESTAMENT: ACTS 14). The words sum up one of the play's major themes, that of helplessness and submission in the face of life's savage struggle.

4 In every tyrant's heart there springs in the end
This poison, that he cannot trust a friend.
Prometheus Bound, ll. 226–7 (*c.* 478 BC, transl. Gilbert Murray, 1931). Spoken by Prometheus.

5 By Time and Age full many things are taught.
Prometheus, ibid., l. 981

6 It is not the oath that makes us believe the man, but the man the oath.
Fragments, no. 385 (transl. M. H. Morgan)

Aesop's Fables
(6th century BC)

According to tradition, Aesop was a slave living on the island of Samos, but he may have been a legendary figure. His name and reputation were well known from the 5th century BC, and the first known collection of the Fables *dates from around a century later. Most of the morals were added subsequently.*

1 The fly sat upon the axle-tree of the chariot-wheel and said, What a dust do I raise!
Fables, 'The Fly on the Wheel' (transl. FRANCIS BACON in his essay 'Of Vain-Glory')

2 Never trust the advice of a man in difficulties.
Ibid., 'The Fox and the Goat'. Moral of tale.

3 Familiarity breeds contempt.
Ibid., 'The Fox and the Lion'. Moral of tale.

4 Put your shoulder to the wheel.
Hercules, ibid., 'Hercules and the Wagoner'

5 The gods help them that help themselves.
Ibid., 'Hercules and the Wagoner'. Moral of tale.

6 Do not count your chickens before they are hatched.
Ibid., 'The Milkmaid and Her Pail'. Moral of tale.

7 Appearances often are deceiving.
Ibid., 'The Wolf in Sheep's Clothing'. Moral of tale.

8 No act of kindness, no matter how small, is ever wasted.
Ibid., 'The Lion and the Mouse'. Moral of tale.

9 Slow and steady wins the race.
Ibid., 'The Hare and the Tortoise'. Moral of tale.

James Agate
(1877–1947)
British drama critic

An exacting drama critic of The Sunday Times from 1923 until his death, he was also an assiduous diary-writer. His journals were published in the nine-part Ego (1935–49).

1 The Englishman can get along with sex quite perfectly so long as he can pretend that it isn't sex but something else.
Journal entry, 14 October 1932, publ. in Ego (1935)

2 Shaw's plays are the price we pay for Shaw's prefaces.
Journal entry, 10 March 1933, ibid.

3 I was asked to-night why I refuse to have truck with intellectuals after business hours. But of course I won't. 1. I am not an intellectual. Two minutes' talk with Aldous Huxley, William Glock, or any of the New Statesman crowd would expose me utterly. 2. I am too tired after my day's work to man the intellectual palisade. 3. When my work is finished I want to eat, drink, smoke, and relax. 4. I don't know very much, but what I do know I know better than anybody, and I don't want to argue about it. I know

what I think about an actor or an actress, and am not interested in what anybody else thinks. My mind is not a bed to be made and re-made.
Journal entry, 9 June 1943, publ. in Ego 6 (1946)

Spiro T. Agnew
(1918–96)
US politician, vice-president

Elected Republican Governor of Maryland as a liberal and anti-racist in 1966, he later adopted a more conservative position and was Vice-President under RICHARD NIXON 1969–73. He resigned after charges of tax evasion were brought against him.

1 I didn't say I wouldn't go into ghetto areas. I've been in many of them and to some extent I would have to say this: If you've seen one city slum you've seen them all.
Speech in Detroit, 18 October 1968, quoted in the Detroit Free Press 19 October 1968

2 A spirit of national masochism prevails, encouraged by an effete corps of impudent snobs who characterize themselves as intellectuals.
Speech in New Orleans, 19 October 1969, publ. in Collected Speeches of Spiro Agnew (1971). The aphorism 'An intellectual is a man who doesn't know how to park a bike' is ascribed to Agnew.

3 Ultraliberalism today translates into a whimpering isolationism in foreign policy, a mulish obstructionism in domestic policy, and a pusillanimous pussyfooting on the critical issue of law and order.
Speech at Springfield, Illinois, 10 September 1970, ibid.

Jonathan Aitken
(b. 1942)
British businessman and politician

Formerly a journalist, he was elected a Conservative MP in 1974 and rose to be Chief Secretary to the Treasury (1994–5). Allegations about his business dealings in 1998 resulted in a conviction for perjury and perverting the course of justice, for which he served a prison sentence.

1 If it falls to me to start a fight to cut out the cancer of bent and twisted journalism in our country with the simple sword of truth and the trusty shield of British fair play, so be it, I am ready for the fight.
Remark, 10 April 1995, quoted in the Guardian 11 April 1995. Referring to libel writs issued against the Guardian and the World in Action television programme over allegations of fraudulent business dealings with the Saudi royal family.

2 As far as the physical miseries go, I am sure I will

cope. I lived at Eton in the 1950s and I know all about life in uncomfortable quarters.

Quoted in the *Daily Express* 19 January 1999. On his probable imprisonment. See EVELYN WAUGH 6.

Anna Akhmatova
(1889–1966)
Russian poet

Originally Anna Andreyevna Gorenko. A member of the Acme-ist group, she was silenced for the predominantly Christian tone of Anno Domini *(1922), but rehabilitated in 1956. Later works include* Requiem *(1940) and* Poem without a Hero *(1940–62).*

1 It was a time when only the dead
smiled, happy in their peace.

Requiem, Introduction (written 1935–40, transl. 1985). Akhmatova's long poem about the Stalinist purges – during which her only son was arrested – was not published until 1963 in West Germany, and not in its entirety in the Soviet Union until 1987.

2 Stars of Death stood over us,
and innocent Russia squirmed
under the bloody boots,
under the wheels of black Marias.

Ibid. Final words of introduction.

3 The triumphs of a mysterious non-meeting are desolate ones; unspoken phrases, silent words.

Two Poems, no. 2 (1956, transl. 1965)

Zoë Akins
(1886–1958)
US playwright

Although she also wrote screenplays, she is best known for her work for the theatre, including the comedies Daddy's Gone A-Hunting *(1921) and* The Greeks Had a Word For It *(1930) and a dramatization of* The Old Maid *by* EDITH WHARTON *(1935).*

1 The Greeks Had a Word For It.

Title of play (1930). The word in question is said to have been *hetaera* ('strumpet'). In a passage deleted from the play's final script, one of the characters states, 'Even the Anglo-Saxons have a word for her sort, and it's usually spelt with a dash.' The words of the play's title appear in the final version.

Alain
(1868–1951)
French philosopher

Pseudonym of Émile-Auguste Chartier. Taking his pen-name from a medieval French poet, he wrote over 5,000 essays, or Propos, *written in a lucid, terse style with a strong anti-idealist theme.*

1 It is the human condition to question one god after another, one appearance after another, or better, one apparition after another, always pursuing the truth of the imagination, which is not the same as the truth of appearance.

Les Dieux, Introduction (*The Gods* 1934, transl. 1988)

2 Nothing is more dangerous than an idea, when you have only one idea.

Propos sur la religion, no. 74 (1938)

Edward Albee
(b. 1928)
US playwright

Though such early plays as The Zoo Story *(1959) labelled him as an exponent of the Theatre of the Absurd, he is chiefly known for the naturalistic* Who's Afraid of Virginia Woolf? *(1962, filmed 1966), a harsh portrayal of married life.*

1 What I wanted to get at is the value difference between pornographic playing-cards when you're a kid, and pornographic playing-cards when you're older. It's that when you're a kid you use the cards as a substitute for a real experience, and when you're older you use real experience as a substitute for the fantasy.

The Zoo Story (1959). Spoken by Jerry.

2 Who's Afraid of Virginia Woolf?

Title of play (1962). The words are sung by Martha to the tune of 'Who's Afraid of the Big Bad Wolf?'

3 I have a fine sense of the ridiculous, but no sense of humor.

Martha, in *Who's Afraid of Virginia Woolf?,* Act 1 (1962)

4 Martha, won't you show her where we keep the . . . euphemism?

George, ibid., Act I, after a guest, Honey, states 'I want to put some powder on my nose.'

Amos Bronson Alcott
(1799–1888)
US educational and social reformer

He was a renowned teacher, and was one of the leading members of the New England Transcendentalists. He was the father of LOUISA M. ALCOTT.

1 The true teacher defends his pupils against his own personal influence. He inspires self-distrust. He

guides their eyes from himself to the spirit that quickens him. He will have no disciple.
Orphic Sayings, 'The Teacher', publ. in the *Dial* July 1840

2 That is a good book which is opened with expectation and closed with profit.
Table Talk, bk 1, 'Books' (1877)

3 One must be a wise reader to quote wisely and well.
Ibid., 'Quotation'

Louisa May Alcott
(1832–88)
US author

The daughter of A. BRONSON ALCOTT, *she achieved great success with her novels of family life, which became children's classics, notably* Little Women *(1868) and its sequel* Good Wives *(1869).*

1 Housekeeping ain't no joke.
Little Women, ch. 11 (1868). The cook Hannah's favourite maxim.

2 People don't have fortunes left them in that style nowadays; men have to work and women to marry for money. It's a dreadfully unjust world.
Meg, ibid., ch. 15

3 Love is a great beautifier.
Good Wives, ch. 1 (1869)

4 It takes two flints to make a fire.
Laurie, ibid., ch. 16

5 What *do* girls do who haven't any mothers to help them through their troubles?
Jo March, ibid., ch. 23

Richard Aldington
(1892–1962)
British author

A leading Imagist poet, translator, critic and editor, he established his name with Death of a Hero *(1929), a novel that drew on his experiences of the horrors of the First World War. He also produced controversial biographies of* D. H. LAWRENCE *(1950) and* T. E. LAWRENCE *(1955).*

1 Patriotism is a lively sense of collective responsibility. Nationalism is a silly cock crowing on its own dunghill and calling for larger spurs and brighter beaks. I fear that nationalism is one of England's many spurious gifts to the world.
The Colonel's Daughter, pt 1, ch. 6 (1931). Spoken by Purfleet.

2 Pure scholarship, like pure science and art, is entirely useless. That is why it is admirable, a demonstration that civilised man is neither an animal nor a savage nor a peasant, for whom nothing exists but what is immediately useful.
Life for Life's Sake, ch. 5 (1941)

3 Certainly, truth prevails in the long run, but only when it is too late to have any real influence on affairs.
Ibid., ch. 10

Brian Aldiss
(b. 1925)
British science fiction writer

He is a prolific writer of 'classic' as well as experimental science fiction works, of which The Helliconia Trilogy *(1982–5) is among the most prominent.* Billion-Year Spree *(1973, rev. 1986 as* Trillion-Year Spree*) is a history of the genre.*

1 Science fiction is no more written for scientists than ghost stories are written for ghosts.
Penguin Science Fiction, Introduction (1962)

2 The bombs were only
In his head
On his memorial tree
A joker wrote
KEEP VIOLENCE IN THE MIND
WHERE IT BELONGS
Barefoot in the Head, 'Charteris' (1969). Closing lines of book.

Henry Aldrich
(1648–1710)
English scholar and churchman

He was Dean of Christ Church, Oxford, from 1689 and Vice-Chancellor of the university. He wrote works on logic, composed and adapted songs, and is said to have designed the chapel of Trinity College and All Saints' Church, Oxford.

1 If all be true that I do think,
There are five reasons we should drink:
Good wine – a friend – or being dry –
Or lest we should be by and by –
Or any other reason why.
'Reasons For Drinking' (1689)

Thomas Bailey Aldrich
(1836–1907)
US author and editor

The writer of numerous works of fiction and poetry, he was Editor of the Atlantic Monthly *1881–90. 'Though I am not genuine Boston,' he said of himself, 'I am Boston-plated.'*

1 Books that have become classics – books that have had their day and now get more praise than perusal – always remind me of retired colonels and majors and captains who, having reached the age limit, find themselves retired on half pay.
Ponkapog Papers, 'Leaves from a Notebook' (1903)

2 Civilization is the lamb's skin in which barbarism masquerades.
Ibid.

Cecil Frances Alexander
See HYMNS AND CAROLS 8, 70, 84

Alfonso X
(1221–84)
King of Castile and León

Acceding in 1252, he was known as 'the Wise' for his active interest in poetry, history and astronomy. He made his court a great cultural centre and did much to promote Castilian as the literary language of Spain.

1 If the Lord Almighty had consulted me before embarking upon Creation, I should have recommended something simpler.
Attributed remark, on hearing an explanation of the Ptolemaic system of astronomy. Alfonso enlisted Jewish and Arab astronomers to prepare the 'Alfonsine Tables' of planetary movements.

Nelson Algren
(1909–81)
US author

He was known as 'the poet of the Chicago slums' for such uncompromising works as The Man with the Golden Arm *(1949) and* A Walk on the Wild Side *(1956), both of which were filmed. His affair with* SIMONE DE BEAUVOIR *inspired her novel* The Mandarins *(1956).*

1 A Walk on the Wild Side.
Title of novel (1956, filmed 1962). 'Take a Walk on the Wild Side' was the title of one of the biggest-selling records of LOU REED, in 1973.

2 Never play cards with a man called Doc. Never eat at a place called Mom's. Never sleep with a woman whose troubles are worse than your own. Never let nobody talk you into shaking another man's jolt. And never you cop another man's plea. I've tried 'em all and I know. They don't work.
Cross-Country Kline advising Dove Linkhorn, in *A Walk on the Wild Side*, pt 3 (1956)

3 The avocation of assessing the failures of better men can be turned into a comfortable livelihood, providing you back it up with a Ph.D.
Interview in *Writers at Work* (first series, ed. Malcolm Cowley, 1958)

4 I went out there [Hollywood] for a thousand a week, and I worked Monday, and I got fired Wednesday. The guy that hired me was out of town Tuesday.
Ibid.

5 The hard necessity of bringing the judge on the bench down into the dock has been the peculiar responsibility of the writer in all ages of man.
Preface added in 1961 to his prose-poem *Chicago: City on the Make* (1951)

Muhammad Ali
(b. 1942)
US boxer

Originally Cassius Clay, he changed his name in 1964 when he joined the Nation of Islam. He won the World Heavyweight title in 1964, 1974 and 1978 (the only boxer to be world champion three times), but was stripped of his title in 1967 for refusing to be drafted to the Vietnam War.

1 I am the greatest.
Slogan used from 1961. In his autobiography, *The Greatest*, ch. 4 (1975), Ali describes the origin of his famous brag in Las Vegas in June 1961: 'Before the fight, for the first time I'd talk openly about beating my opponent . . . I kept calling out "I'm the greatest! I can't be beat!" I'd seen good fighters carry on bloody brawls with hardly anybody caring which one won or lost. At least now they were interested in my fight, even if they wanted me to lose.'

2 At home I am a nice guy: but I don't want the world to know. Humble people, I've found, don't get very far.
Sunday Express 13 January 1963

3 Float like a butterfly, sting like a bee.
Quoted in *The Story of Cassius Clay*, ch. 8 (1964) by George Edward Sullivan. Ali's catchphrase is said to have originated with his aide Drew 'Bundini' Brown.

4 It's just a job. Grass grows, birds fly, waves pound the sand. I beat people up.
New York Times 6 April 1977

Dave Allen
(1936–2005)
Irish comedian

Born David Tynan O'Mahoney. After a spell as a journalist in Dublin, he moved to London where he became a stand-up comic. He is remembered for the laid-back, story-telling style on his television shows 1968–94.

1 May your god go with you.
Sign-off line ending every show

Fred Allen
(1894–1957)
US radio comic

Originally John Florence Sullivan. Influencing a generation of radio and television performers with his dry wit and laconic style, he is most remembered for The Fred Allen Show *(1939–49), for which he wrote almost all of the episodes.*

1 California is a fine place to live – if you happen to be an orange.
American Magazine December 1945

2 An advertising agency is 85 per cent confusion and 15 per cent commission.
Treadmill to Oblivion, pt 2 (1954)

3 We are living in the machine age. For the first time in history the comedian has been compelled to supply himself with jokes and comedy material to compete with the machine. Whether he knows it or not, the comedian is on a treadmill to oblivion.
Ibid., pt 4

4 Hollywood is a place where people from Iowa mistake each other for stars.
Quoted in *No People Like Show People*, ch. 8 (1951) by Maurice Zolotow

5 Committee – a group of men who individually can do nothing but as a group decide that nothing can be done.
Attributed

Woody Allen
(b. 1935)
US film-maker

Originally Allen Stewart Konigsberg. Stand-up comedian and TV scriptwriter turned film-maker, he stars in most of his own films, which developed from farces such as Sleeper *(1973) to convoluted tales of sexual neurosis set in New York, notably* Annie Hall *(1977). See also* DIANE KEATON 1.

1 Some guy hit my fender the other day, and I said unto him, 'Be fruitful, and multiply.' But not in those words.
Comedy routine at Chicago night-club, March 1964, recorded on *Woody Allen*, 'Private Life' (album, 1964). Woody Allen's first live recorded monologue describes an acting class rehearsing a play where Allen takes the part of God, and, as he recounts, 'it was method acting, so two weeks beforehand I started to live the part offstage'. See BIBLE, OLD TESTAMENT: GENESIS 5.

2 I had a rough marriage ... It was partially my fault that we got a divorce. I had a lousy attitude toward her. For the first year of our marriage, I tended to place my wife underneath a pedestal all the time. We used to argue and fight and finally we decided we should either take a vacation or get a divorce. We discussed it very maturely and we decided on the divorce because we felt we had a limited amount of money to spend. A vacation in Bermuda is over in two weeks but a divorce is something that you always have.
Ibid., 'My Marriage'. Allen's accounts of the break-up of his first marriage to Harlene Rosen in 1962 and the repeated jokes at her expense in his comedy acts eventually led her to sue him for a million dollars in 1967; they settled out of court and did not meet again, according to *The Woody Allen Companion*, ch. 4 (1993) by Stephen Spignesi.

3 Is sex dirty? Only if it's done right.
Everything You Always Wanted to Know About Sex (But Were Afraid to Ask) (film, 1972, written and directed by Woody Allen). 'Chapter' title. See DAVID REUBEN 1.

4 I'm not the heroic type. I was beaten up by Quakers.
Sleeper (film, 1973, screenplay by Woody Allen and Marshall Brickman, directed by Woody Allen). Spoken by Miles Monroe (Woody Allen).

5 My brain ... it's my second favorite organ.
Miles Monroe, ibid.

6 I don't want to achieve immortality through my work ... I want to achieve it through not dying.
Quoted in *Woody Allen and his Comedy*, ch. 12 (1975) by Eric Lax

7 The important thing, I think, is not to be bitter. If it turns out that there is a God, I don't think that he's evil. But the worst thing you can say about him is that he's basically an underachiever. After all, you know, there are worse things in life than death.
Love and Death (film, 1975, written and directed by Woody Allen). Spoken by Boris Grushenko (Woody Allen).

8 Some men are heterosexual, and some men are homosexual, and some men don't think about sex at all. They become lawyers.
Boris Grushenko, ibid.

9 To me nature is ... spiders and bugs, and big fish eating little fish, and plants eating plants, and

animals eating . . . It's like an enormous restaurant, that's the way I see it.
Boris Grushenko, ibid.

10 I want to tell you a terrific story about oral contraception. I asked this girl to sleep with me and she said 'no'.
Quoted in *Woody Allen: Clown Prince of American Humor*, ch. 2 (1975) by B. Adler and J. Feinman

11 It [bisexuality] immediately doubles your chances for a date on Saturday night.
New York Times 1 December 1975

12 It's not that I'm afraid to die, I just don't want to be there when it happens.
Kleinman, in 'Death (A Play)' publ. in *Without Feathers* (1976)

13 The chief problem about death, incidentally, is the fear that there may be no afterlife – a depressing thought, particularly for those who have bothered to shave. Also, there is the fear that there is an afterlife but no one will know where it's being held.
'The Early Essays', ibid. In the film *Love and Death*, there is the line, 'I don't believe in an afterlife although I'm bringing a change of underwear.'

14 Money is better than poverty, if only for financial reasons.
'The Early Essays', ibid.

15 If only God would give me some clear sign! Like making a large deposit in my name at a Swiss bank.
'Selections from the Allen Notebooks', ibid.

16 Hey, don't knock masturbation! It's sex with someone I love.
Annie Hall (film, 1977, screenplay by Woody Allen and Marshall Brickman, directed by Woody Allen). Spoken by Alvy Singer (Woody Allen).

17 I don't wanna live in a city where the only cultural advantage is that you can make a right turn on a red light.
Alvy Singer, ibid. Comparing Los Angeles unfavourably to Manhattan.

18 I was depressed . . . I was suicidal; as a matter of fact, I would have killed myself but I was in analysis with a strict Freudian and if you kill yourself they make you pay for the sessions you miss.
Alvy Singer, ibid. The gag can also be heard on *The Nightclub Years*, 'Second Marriage' (album, 1968), a live recording of a stand-up routine in San Francisco.

19 I was thrown out of NYU my freshman year . . . for cheating on my metaphysics final. You know, I

looked within the soul of the boy sitting next to me.
Alvy Singer, ibid. In performance in front of a college audience.

20 In Beverly Hills . . . they don't throw their garbage away. They make it into television shows.
Alvy Singer, ibid.

21 Life is divided up into the horrible and the miserable.
Alvy Singer, ibid.

22 A relationship, I think, is like a shark, you know? It has to constantly move forward or it dies. And I think what we got on our hands is a dead shark.
Alvy Singer, ibid. On the end of his affair with Annie Hall (played by DIANE KEATON).

23 That [sex] was the most fun I've ever had without laughing.
Alvy Singer, ibid.

24 I finally had an orgasm and my doctor told me it was the wrong kind.
Manhattan (film, 1979, screenplay by Woody Allen and Marshall Brickman, directed by Woody Allen). Spoken by Polly (Tisa Farrow).

25 More than any other time in history, mankind faces a crossroads. One path leads to despair and utter hopelessness. The other, to total extinction. Let us pray we have the wisdom to choose correctly.
Side Effects, 'My Speech to the Graduates' (1980)

26 You can't control life. It doesn't wind up perfectly. Only . . . only art you can control. Art and masturbation. Two areas in which I am an absolute expert.
Stardust Memories (film, 1980, written and directed by Woody Allen). Spoken by Sandy Bates (Woody Allen).

27 Child molestation is a touchy subject . . . Read the papers! Half the country's doing it!
Hannah and Her Sisters (film, 1986, written and directed by Woody Allen). Spoken by Mickey Sachs (Woody Allen). Allen caused controversy in 1993 when a relationship with Soon-Yi Previn, the adopted daughter of Mia Farrow, led to accusations of child abuse and a court case over custody of their children. He married Soon-Yi in 1997.

28 Life doesn't imitate art, it imitates bad television.
Husbands and Wives (film, 1992, written and directed by Woody Allen). Spoken by Rain (Juliette Lewis).

Salvador Allende
(1908–73)
Chilean statesman and president

A founder of the Chilean Socialist Party, he became President in 1970. His nationalization of US-owned copper mines was the prelude to CIA involvement in the coup of 1973, in which he died.

1 Our Vietnam is neither in Moscow, nor in Peking, Havana or Belgrade. It is in Chile.
Quoted in the *Observer* 1 November 1970

William Allingham
(1824–89)
Irish poet and editor

He published two volumes of verse in the 1850s and succeeded William Froude as Editor of Dublin's Fraser's Magazine *in 1874. His* Diary *(1907) was edited by his wife, the illustrator Helen Paterson.*

1 Up the airy mountain,
Down the rushy glen,
We daren't go a-hunting
For fear of little men.
'The Fairies', publ. in *Day and Night Songs* (1855)

2 A man who keeps a diary pays
Due toll to many tedious days;
But life becomes eventful – then
His busy hand forgets the pen.
Most books, indeed, are records less
Of fulness than of emptiness.
Journal entry, 24–28 March 1864, publ. in *A Diary*, ch. 6 (ed. H. Allingham and D. Radford, 1907)

3 Poor Paddy of all Christian men I think
On basest food pours down the vilest drink.
Lawrence Bloomfield, ch. 12, ll. 296–7 (1864). These two lines, as Allingham proudly noted in his diary, were quoted by WILLIAM GLADSTONE – an advocate of Irish Home Rule – in the House of Commons, 30 May 1864, with reference to a proposed alteration of spirit duties.

Lisa Alther
(b. 1944)
US novelist

Her ribald feminist tales include Kinflicks *(1976),* Original Sins *(1981) and* Bedrock *(1990).*

1 I happen to feel that the degree of a person's intelligence is directly reflected by the number of con-

flicting attitudes she can bring to bear on the same topic.
Ginny Babcock, in *Kinflicks*, ch. 7 (1976)

Robert Altman
(b. 1922)
US film-maker

He made his name with the antiwar comedy M*A*S*H *(1970) and went on to direct* McCabe and Mrs Miller *(1971),* Nashville *(1976) and* The Player *(1992), among other films.*

1 What is a cult? It just means not enough people to make a minority.
Interview in the *Guardian* 11 April 1981

Ferdinand Alvarez de Toledo, Duke of Alva
(1508–82)
Spanish general

A general at twenty-six and commander-in-chief at thirty, he is remembered for his brutal suppression of the revolt against Spanish rule in the Netherlands in 1567.

1 I have tamed men of iron in my day, shall I not easily crush these men of butter?
Quoted in *The Rise of the Dutch Republic*, vol. 2 (1889), by J. L. Motley. Alleged reply to the Duchess of Parma on his appointment as Governor-General of the Netherlands, 1567.

Leo Amery
(1873–1955)
British politician

A Conservative MP from 1911, he was a fierce critic of the Munich Agreement and was instrumental in bringing down the government of NEVILLE CHAMBERLAIN *in 1940. He served as Secretary of State for India and Burma 1940–45.*

1 Speak for England.
Said in House of Commons, 2 September 1939, quoted in *My Political Life*, vol. 3 (1955). The exhortation was addressed to MP Arthur Greenwood, Deputy Leader of the Labour Party, who was about to speak on the situation in Europe, a day after the Nazi invasion of Poland and on the eve of the declaration of war on Germany by Britain and France. The MP Robert Boothby is also credited with the words.

2 I will quote certain other words. I do it with great reluctance, because I am speaking of those who are old friends and associates of mine, but they are words which, I think, are applicable to the present situation. This is what Cromwell said to the Long Parliament when he thought it was no longer fit to

conduct the affairs of the nation: 'You have sat too long here for any good you have been doing. Depart, I say, and let us have done with you. In the name of God, go.'

Speech to House of Commons, 7 May 1940, publ. in *The Penguin Book of Twentieth-Century Speeches* (ed. Brian MacArthur, 1999). Amery was addressing NEVILLE CHAMBERLAIN's government, blamed for the failed policy of appeasement to Germany and now faced with the German invasion of Norway. Chamberlain resigned 10 May, to be replaced by WINSTON CHURCHILL. See OLIVER CROMWELL 6.

Henri-Frédéric Amiel
(1821–81)
Swiss philosopher and poet

A professor of aesthetics and of moral philosophy at the Académie in Geneva, he wrote articles and poetry, but is best known for his diaries, published posthumously as Journal Intime *(1882–4).*

1 *Action is but coarsened thought* – thought become concrete, obscure, and unconscious.

Journal entry, 30 December 1850, publ. in *Journal Intime* (1882, transl. Mrs Humphry Ward, 1892)

2 An error is the more dangerous in proportion to the degree of truth which it contains.

Ibid., 12 November 1852

3 It is by teaching that we teach ourselves, by relating that we observe, by affirming that we examine, by showing that we look, by writing that we think, by pumping that we draw water into the well.

Ibid., 27 October 1853

4 The man who insists upon seeing with perfect clearness before he decides, never decides. Accept life, and you must accept regret.

Ibid., 17 December 1856

5 Our systems, perhaps, are nothing more than an unconscious apology for our faults – a gigantic scaffolding whose object is to hide from us our favourite sin.

Ibid., 13 August 1865

6 Cleverness is serviceable for everything, sufficient for nothing.

Ibid., 16 February 1868

(Sir) Kingsley Amis
(1922–95)
British novelist and poet

He won acclaim for his first novel Lucky Jim *(1954, filmed 1957), a satire on provincial academic life. Later novels include* The Old Devils *(1986). He once commented, 'If you can't annoy somebody, there's little point in writing.' He was the father of* MARTIN AMIS.

1 We men have got love well weighed up; our stuff
Can get by without it.
Women don't seem to think that's good enough;
They will write about it.

'A Bookshop Idyll', publ. in *A Case of Samples* (1956)

2 Women are really much nicer than men:
No wonder we like them.

'A Bookshop Idyll', ibid.

3 More will mean worse.

Encounter July 1960. On the expansion of higher education in Britain, attacking the notion that 'there are thousands of young people about who are capable of benefiting from university training, but have somehow failed to find their way there.'

4 Outside every fat man there was an even fatter man trying to close in.

One Fat Englishman, ch. 3 (1963). Spoken by Roger Micheldene, 'a shortish fat Englishman of forty' and the book's protagonist, here musing over a particularly heavy lunch. Earlier versions of the remark exist: see CYRIL CONNOLLY 18 and GEORGE ORWELL 6.

5 He was of the faith chiefly in the sense that the church he currently did not attend was Catholic.

Ibid., ch. 8

6 Growing older, I have lost the need to be political, which means, in this country, the need to be left. I am driven into grudging toleration of the Conservative Party because it is the party of non-politics, of resistance to politics.

Sunday Telegraph 2 July 1967

7 Death has got something to be said for it:
There's no need to get out of bed for it;
Wherever you may be,
They bring it to you, free.

'Delivery Guaranteed' (1979), publ. in *Collected Poems* (1944–79). In his novel *Money* (1984), Kingsley's son MARTIN AMIS wrote: 'Addictions do come in handy sometimes: at least you have to get out of bed for them.'

8 If there's one word that sums up everything that's gone wrong since the War, it's Workshop.
Jake's Thing, ch. 14 (1979). Spoken by Jake, who added: '. . . After Youth, that is.'

9 Alun's life was coming to consist more and more exclusively of being told at dictation speed what he knew.
The Old Devils, ch. 7, sect. 1 (1986). Of author and 'professional Welshman' Alun Weaver.

10 It is not extraordinary that the extraterrestrial origin of women was a recurrent theme of science fiction, though I have never seen their imperfect grasp of their native language put forward as one more piece of evidence.
The King's English: A Guide to Modern English Usage, 'Womanese' (1997)

Martin Amis
(b. 1949)
British author

Son of KINGSLEY AMIS, *he writes novels in which, in his words, 'everyone has a bad time'. His scabrous wit and American literary influences are evident in such works as* The Rachel Papers *(1973),* Money *(1984) and* The Information *(1995).*

1 Making lots of money – it's not that hard, you know. It's overestimated. Making lots of money is a breeze. You watch.
Money (1984)

2 And being rich is about acting too, isn't it? A style, a pose, an interpretation that you force upon the world? Whether or not you've made the stuff yourself, you have to set about pretending that you merit it, that money chose right in choosing you, and that you'll do right by money in your turn.
Ibid.

3 Style is not neutral; it gives moral directions.
Novelists in Interview (ed. John Haffenden, 1985)

4 Weapons are like money; no one knows the meaning of *enough*.
Einstein's Monsters, Introduction (1987)

5 For myself and my loved ones, I want the heat, which comes at the speed of light. I don't want to have to hang about for the blast, which idles along at the speed of sound.
Ibid., Introduction

6 The literary interview won't tell you what a writer is like. Far more compellingly, to some, it will tell you what a writer is like to interview.
Observer 30 August 1987, repr. in *Visiting Mrs Nabokov*, 'John Updike' (1993)

7 And meanwhile time goes about its immemorial work of making everyone look and feel like shit.
London Fields, ch. 2 (1989)

8 Class! Yes, it's still here. Terrific staying power, and against the historical odds. What is it with that old, old crap? The class system just doesn't know when to call it a day. Even a nuclear holocaust, I think, would fail to make that much of a dent in it.
Ibid., ch. 2

9 These days he [Richard Tull] smoked and drank largely to solace himself for what drinking and smoking had done to him – but smoking and drinking had done a lot to him, so he drank and smoked a lot.
The Information, pt 1 (1995)

10 Never trust a poet who can drive. Never trust a poet at the wheel. If he can drive, distrust the poems.
Ibid., pt 1

Cleveland Amory
(1917–98)
US author

He wrote social histories and animal stories, and was founder (1967) and President of the animal welfare organization Fund for Animals.

1 The New England conscience . . . does not stop you from doing what you shouldn't – it just stops you from enjoying it.
New York 5 May 1980

Hans Christian Andersen
(1805–73)
Danish author

Although he was an acknowledged novelist and travel writer, he is best known for his series of Fairy Tales *written for children (1835–72).*

1 The Emperor's New Clothes.
Title of story in *Fairy Tales* (1835)

2 But the Emperor has nothing on at all!
'The Emperor's New Clothes', ibid. Spoken by the little child.

3 But what did he see in the clear stream below? His own image; no longer a dark, grey bird, ugly and disagreeable to look at, but a graceful and beautiful

swan. To be born in a duck's nest, in a farmyard, is of no consequence to a bird, if it is hatched from a swan's egg.

'The Ugly Duckling', in *Fairy Tales* (1844)

Gerry Anderson

(b. 1929)

British programme-maker for children's TV

Together with his wife Sylvia Anderson, he created some of the classic puppet programmes for children's TV of the 1960s, including Supercar *(1961–2),* Thunderbirds *(1965–6) and* Captain Scarlet *(1967).*

1 Thunderbirds are go!

Thunderbirds (TV puppet series, 1965–6, created by Gerry and Sylvia Anderson, written by the Andersons et al.)

Ian Anderson

(b. 1947)

British rock musician

He was singer and leader of the blues and heavy rock band Jethro Tull, whose albums Aqualung *(1971) and* Thick as a Brick *(1972) gained them a large following.*

1 A lot of pop music is about stealing pocket money from children.

Rolling Stone 30 November 1989

Maxwell Anderson

(1888–1959)

US playwright

His writings include the verse-play Elizabeth the Queen *(1930), the screenplay for* All Quiet on the Western Front *(1930) and the prose satire* Both Your Houses *(1933).*

1 But it's a long, long while
From May to December;
And the days grow short
When you reach September.

'September Song' (song, written with Kurt Weill) in *Knickerbocker Holiday* (stage musical, 1938). Among the singers associated with the number are BING CROSBY, FRANK SINATRA and, most famously, MAURICE CHEVALIER in the musical *Pepe* (1960).

Maxwell Anderson

(1888–1959)

Laurence Stallings

(1894–1968)

US playwrights

Stallings worked on numerous film screenplays from 1925 to 1954, but achieved greatest success for his collaboration with Anderson in the play What Price Glory? *(1924).*

1 What Price Glory?

Title of anti-First World War play (1924, filmed 1926 and 1952)

Robert Anderson

(b. 1917)

US playwright

His first and most successful play, Tea and Sympathy *(1953, filmed 1956), was followed by lesser Broadway hits such as* You Know I Can't Hear You When the Water's Running *(1967).*

1 All you're supposed to do is every once in a while give the boys a little tea and sympathy.

Tea and Sympathy, Act 1 (1957). Bill gives advice about not getting too involved with schoolchildren.

(Sir) James Anderton

(b. 1932)

British senior police officer

Chief Constable of Greater Manchester Police 1976–91, he has been involved in a range of Christian and philanthropic causes, often attracting criticism for his outspoken comments.

1 Everywhere I go I see increasing evidence of people swirling about in a human cesspit of their own making.

On AIDS, quoted in the *Guardian* 12 December 1986

2 God works in mysterious ways. Given my love of God and my belief in God and in Jesus Christ, I have to accept that I may well be used by God in this way.

Radio interview, 18 January 1987, quoted in the *Daily Telegraph* 19 January 1987. Referring to the possibility that he might have prophetic powers.

Giulio Andreotti

(b. 1919)

Italian politician and prime minister

A leading member of the Christian Democrat party throughout the post-war period, he was several times Prime Minister between 1972 and 1992.

1 Power tires only those who do not have it.
Quoted in the *Independent on Sunday* 5 April 1992. Reply when asked how his party had endured in government for so long.

(Dame) Julie Andrews
(b. 1935)
British actress and singer

Having made an impact in Broadway musicals including My Fair Lady *(1956) and* Camelot *(1960), she went on to star in the films* Mary Poppins *(1964) and* The Sound of Music *(1965).*

1 Just a spoonful of sugar helps the medicine go down.
'A Spoonful of Sugar' (song, written by Richard and Robert Sherman), in *Mary Poppins* (film musical, 1964, screenplay by Bill Walsh and Don Da Gradi based on the Mary Poppins books by P. L. Travers, directed by Robert Stevenson). Julie Andrews played the title role in the film.

2 Supercalifragilisticexpialidocious!
Even though the sound of it is something quite atrocious!
If you say it loud enough you'll always sound precocious.
Supercalifragilisticexpialidocious!
'Supercalifragilisticexpialidocious!', ibid.

Maya Angelou
(b. 1928)
US author and poet

Active in the black civil rights movement of the 1950s and '60s, she chronicled her 'roller coaster of a life' in several volumes of autobiography, the first part of which, I Know Why the Caged Bird Sings *(1970), was an instant success. She is also a prolific poet. See also* PAUL LAURENCE DUNBAR 1.

1 Children's talent to endure stems from their ignorance of alternatives.
I Know Why the Caged Bird Sings, ch. 17 (1969)

2 The quality of strength lined with tenderness is an unbeatable combination, as are intelligence and necessity when unblunted by formal education.
Ibid., ch. 29

3 At fifteen life had taught me undeniably that surrender, in its place, was as honorable as resistance, especially if one had no choice.
Ibid., ch. 31

4 The fact that the adult American Negro female emerges a formidable character is often met with amazement, distaste and even belligerence. It is seldom accepted as an inevitable outcome of the struggle won by survivors, and deserves respect if not enthusiastic acceptance.
Ibid., ch. 34

5 My life has been one great big joke,
A dance that's walked
A song that's spoke,
I laugh so hard I almost choke
When I think about myself.
'When I Think About Myself', publ. in *Just Give Me a Cool Drink of Water 'fore I Diiie* (1971)

6 For Africa to me ... is more than a glamorous fact. It is a historical truth. No man can know where he is going unless he knows exactly where he has been and exactly how he arrived at his present place.
Quoted in the *New York Times* 16 April 1972. Angelou lived and worked in Ghana and Egypt 1962–6.

7 Life loves the liver of it.
Interview, 1977, repr. in *Conversations with Maya Angelou* (ed. Jeffrey M. Elliot, 1989)

8 You may write me down in history
With your bitter, twisted lies,
You may trod me in the very dirt
But still, like dust, I'll rise.
'Still I Rise', publ. in *And Still I Rise* (1978)

9 I love to see a young girl go out and grab the world by the lapels. Life's a bitch. You've got to go out and kick ass.
Interview, 1986, repr. in *Conversations with Maya Angelou* (ed. Jeffrey M. Elliot, 1989)

10 We allow our ignorance to prevail upon us and make us think we can survive alone, alone in patches, alone in groups, alone in races, even alone in genders.
Address at Centenary College of Louisiana, March 1990, publ. in the *New York Times* 11 March 1990

11 A rose by any other name may smell as sweet, but a woman called by a devaluing name will only be weakened by the misnomer.
Wouldn't Take Nothing for my Journey Now, 'In All Ways a Woman' (1993)

Paul Anka
See FRANK SINATRA 3

Anne, Princess Royal of Great Britain and Northern Ireland
(b. 1950)

Only daughter of ELIZABETH II, *she is patron of over eighty charities and is also a skilled horsewoman, representing Britain in the 1976 Olympics.*

1 It could be said that the AIDS pandemic is a classic own-goal scored by the human race against itself.
Quoted in the *Daily Telegraph* 27 January 1988

2 The very idea that all children want to be cuddled by a complete stranger I find utterly amazing.
Quoted in the *Observer* 27 December 1998. Referring to her public duties visiting children.

Anonymous

1 Adieu, adieu, kind friends, adieu, adieu, adieu,
I can no longer stay with you.
I'll hang my harp on a weeping willow tree,
And may the world go well with thee.
'There's a Tavern in the Town', refrain

2 Alas, my love! ye do me wrong
To cast me off discourteously:
And I have loved you so long,
Delighting in your company.
. . .
Greensleeves was all my joy,
Greensleeves was my delight;
Greensleeves was my heart of gold,
And who but Lady Greensleeves.
'Greensleeves', st. 1 and refrain, publ. in *A Handful Of Pleasant Delights* (1584) by Clement Robinson. The song is traditionally ascribed to HENRY VIII, supposedly written for Anne Boleyn.

3 And this is law, I will maintain,
Unto my dying day, sir,
That whosoever king shall reign,
I will be the Vicar of Bray, sir!
'The Vicar of Bray', publ. in the *British Musical Miscellany*, vol. 1 (1734)

4 Are we downhearted? No!
Expression used by British soldiers during the First World War

5 *Ave Caesar, morituri te salutant.*
[Hail Caesar, those who are about to die salute you.]
Gladiators saluting the Roman Emperor in the arena, before commencing the contest, quoted in *Lives of the Caesars*, 'Claudius', by Suetonius

6 *Ave Maria, gratia plena, Dominus tecum: Bene-dicta tu in mulieribus, et benedictus fructus ventris tui, Jesus.*
[Hail Mary, full of grace, the Lord is with thee: Blessed art thou among women, and blessed is the fruit of thy womb, Jesus.]
'Ave Maria', also known as 'The Angelic Salutation' (6th century). See BIBLE, NEW TESTAMENT: LUKE 1, 2.

7 Begone, dull Care! I prithee begone from me!
Begone, dull Care! Thou and I shall never agree.
Traditional ballad, publ. in *The Buck's Delight* (1798). An earlier version appears in the *Musical Companion*, pt 2 (1687) by John Playford as 'Begone, old Care, and I prithee be gone from me,/ For i'faith, old Care, thee and I shall never agree.'

8 *Ça ira.*
[Things will work out.]
Adopted by French revolutionaries in the late 1780s. A favourite phrase of BENJAMIN FRANKLIN.

9 A camel is a horse designed by a committee.
Late 20th-century saying

10 The Campbells are comin'! Oho! Oho!
Scottish song, probably dating from the suppression of the Jacobite rebellion by the Duke of Argyll in 1715

11 Careless talk costs lives.
Ministry of Information slogan, July 1940, quoted in *Keep Smiling Through: The Home Front 1939–1945*, 'Don't Fence Me In' (1976) by Susan Briggs. The government's poster campaign to persuade people not to betray the war effort through gossip was illustrated with memorable cartoons by Fougasse. Other slogans included 'Tittle-tattle lost the battle', 'Walls have ears' and, in the USA, 'Loose talk costs lives'.

12 Christmas is coming, the geese are getting fat,
Please to put a penny in the old man's hat;
If you haven't got a penny, a ha'penny will do,
If you haven't got a ha'penny, God bless you!
Beggar's rhyme

13 The Cloud of Unknowing.
Title of mystical prose work (14th century)

14 Coughs and sneezes spread diseases. Trap the germs in your handkerchief.
British government health slogan (1942), quoted in *Second World War Posters* (1972) by J. Darracott and B. Loftus

15 Crabbed age and youth cannot live together:
Youth is full of pleasance, age is full of care;
Youth like summer morn, age like winter weather;
Youth like summer brave, age like winter bare.
The Passionate Pilgrim, no. 12 (1599). Sometimes attributed to WILLIAM SHAKESPEARE.

16 The difficult we do immediately; the impossible takes a little longer.

US Armed Forces' slogan. The words are said to be an interpretation of a remark ascribed to Charles Alexandre de Calonne (1734–1802) during the French Revolution: *Madame, si c'est possible, c'est fait; impossible? cela se fera* ('Madam, if it is possible, consider it done; the impossible? that will be done').

17 Do not fold, spindle or mutilate.

Instruction on punched cards (found in this form in the 1950s, and in differing forms from the 1930s)

18 Don't die of ignorance.

Slogan in publicity campaign to promote AIDS awareness, 1987

19 *E pluribus unum.*
[Out of many, one.]

Motto for the Seal of the United States, adopted 20 June 1782, recommended by JOHN ADAMS, BENJAMIN FRANKLIN and THOMAS JEFFERSON 10 August 1776, and proposed by Swiss artist Pierre Eugene du Simitière. It had earlier appeared on the title page of the *Gentleman's Journal* January 1692. See also VIRGIL 49.

20 *Et in Arcadia ego.*
[I too am in Arcadia.]

Tomb inscription, appearing in classical paintings by Guercino and Poussin, among others. The words probably mean that even the most ideal earthly lives are mortal. Arcadia, a mountainous region in the central Peloponnese, Greece, was supposedly the rustic abode of Pan, depicted in literature and art as a land of innocence and ease; it was also the title of PHILIP SIDNEY's pastoral romance (1590).

21 Every country has its own constitution; ours is absolutism moderated by assassination.

Anonymous Russian, quoted in *Political Sketches of the State of Europe 1814–1867* (1868) by Ernst Friedrich Herbert, Count Münster, a Hanoverian diplomat

22 Everyman, I will go with thee, and be thy guide,
In thy most need to go by thy side.

Everyman, Act 1, ll. 522–3 (*c.* 1509–19). Spoken by Knowledge.

23 Expletive deleted.

Transcripts of taped conversations of President NIXON, September 1972–April 1973, publ. in *The Presidential Transcripts* (1974). The tapes, which were played for the judicial committee of the House of Representatives 30 April 1974, were edited transcripts of meetings between Nixon and his advisers in the Oval Office over a period of seven months. Public reaction seemed more shocked by the sleazy language used by the President and his inner circle than by the revelations of Nixon appearing to condone corrupt practices.

24 Flashed from his bed the electric tidings came,

'He is no better, he is much the same.'

Parody by a Dublin undergraduate *c.* 1871 of the style of poet laureate ALFRED AUSTIN, describing the illness of the Prince of Wales (later Edward VII)

25 Frankie and Albert were lovers, O Lordy, how they could love.
Swore to be true to each other, true as the stars above;
He was her man, but he done her wrong.

'Frankie and Albert' (ballad), probably 19th-century. Later known as 'Frankie and Johnny'.

26 From ghoulies and ghosties and long-leggety beasties
And things that go bump in the night,
Good Lord, deliver us!

'The Cornish or West Country Litany', quoted in *Polperro Proverbs and Others*, 'Pokerwork Panels' (1926) by Francis T. Nettleinghame

27 *Gaudeamus igitur,*
Juvenes dum sumus
Post jucundam juventutem,
Post molestam senectutem,
Nos habebit humus.
[Let us live, then, and be glad,
While joys of youth are 'fore us;
After youthful pastime had,
After old age, hard and sad,
Earth will slumber o'er us.]

Medieval students' song, 13th-century, revised in the 18th century

28 Give me a child for the first seven years, and you may do what you like with him afterwards.

Jesuit maxim. See MURIEL SPARK 4.

29 Give me that old-time religion,
It's good enough for me.

'Old Time Religion' (gospel song, *c.* 1891)

30 Go down, Moses,
Way down in Egypt land,
Tell old Pharaoh
To let my people go.

'Go Down, Moses' (spiritual song). See BIBLE, OLD TESTAMENT: EXODUS 10.

31 God gave Noah the rainbow sign don't you see,
God gave Noah the rainbow sign, no more water but fire next time.

'God gave Noah the rainbow sign', negro spiritual collected in 1929

32 Hear no evil, see no evil, speak no evil.

These words are said to be the legend carved over the door

of the Sacred Stable, Nikko, Japan (17th century), relating to the 'Three Wise Monkeys'. Similar phrases are to be found in all cultures, in English the closest and earliest in the work by Brian Melbancke, *Philotimus: The War Betwixt Nature and Fortune* (1583): 'Thus you are hearing, and seeing and saying nothing.'

33 Heaven is the place where the donkey at last catches up with the carrot.

Anonymous, 20th century

34 Here lies a poor woman who always was tired,
For she lived in a place where help wasn't hired.
Her last words on earth were, Dear friends I am going
Where washing ain't done nor sweeping nor sewing,
And everything there is exact to my wishes,
For there they don't eat and there's no washing of dishes . . .
Don't mourn for me now, don't mourn for me never,
For I'm going to do nothing for ever and ever.

Epitaph in churchyard, Bushey, Hertfordshire, now destroyed. JAMES AGATE, in a journal entry 14 March 1933, described the 'poor woman' as a 'self-deceiver', surmising that 'anybody meeting her in Heaven will find her scrubbing marble and dusting porphyry with a new-born gleam in her old eye'.

35 Here men from the planet Earth first set foot upon the Moon, July 1969 A.D. We came in peace for all mankind.

Moon plaque, inscribed by the astronauts NEIL ARMSTRONG, Michael Collins and Edwin 'Buzz' Aldrin, and by President NIXON.

36 Hogamus, higamous
Man is polygamous
Higamus, hogamous
Woman monogamous.

The lines have been variously attributed to WILLIAM JAMES, DOROTHY PARKER and GERTRUDE STEIN, and were supposedly inspired by a dream: the dreamer awoke to jot down the profound insight received, and found that these were the lines written on the paper in the morning.

37 How different, how very different from the home life of our own dear Queen!

Comment (probably apocryphal) overheard at a performance of *Antony and Cleopatra* with SARAH BERNHARDT as Cleopatra, quoted in *A Laugh a Day* (1924) by Irvin S. Cobb

38 I'm a Celebrity, Get Me Out of Here.

Title of TV show (ITV, from 2002)

39 I don't like the family Stein!

There is Gert, there is Ep, there is Ein.
Gert's writings are punk,
Ep's statues are junk,
Nor can anyone understand Ein.

A 'low-brow American limerick current in the 20s', according to *The Long Weekend: A Social History of Great Britain 1918–1939*, ch.12 (1940) by ROBERT GRAVES and Alan Hodge. Another version, noted in *Einstein*, ch. 18 (1973) by R. W. Clark, runs, 'Three wonderful people called Stein;/There's Gert and there's Ep and there's Ein./Gert writes in blank verse,/Ep's sculptures are worse,/And nobody understands Ein.' Clark is unable to find a source for this, though suggests it may have been inspired by 'Precious Steins', a piece of verse which appeared in *Punch* 11 September 1929. The sculptor Jacob Epstein obtained three sittings for a bust of ALBERT EINSTEIN at Roughton Heath, Norfolk, where Einstein stayed for a month in September 1933 prior to leaving for the USA. Neither, as far as is known, had any dealings with GERTRUDE STEIN.

40 I feel no pain dear mother now
But oh, I am so dry!
O take me to a brewery
And leave me there to die.

Nineteenth-century parody of EDWARD FARMER 1

41 I hate mankind, for I think myself one of the best of them, and I know how bad I am.

A 'foreign friend' of SAMUEL JOHNSON, quoted in *Life of Samuel Johnson, LL.D.*, February 1776 (1791) by JAMES BOSWELL

42 I wooed her in the wintertime
And in the summer too.
And the only, only thing that I did that was wrong
Was to keep her from the foggy, foggy dew.

'The Foggy, Foggy Dew', traditional English song

43 If you can remember the 1960s you can't have been there.

Origin untraced

44 In affectionate remembrance of English cricket, which died at the Oval on 29 August, 1882. Deeply lamented by a large circle of sorrowing friends and acquaintances. RIP. NB The body will be cremated and the ashes taken to Australia.

Notice in the *Sporting Times* 2 September 1882 after the England cricket team's defeat by Australia. The 'Ashes' is the name given to the trophy played for in Test matches between England and Australia.

45 In necessary things, unity; in disputed things, liberty; in all things, charity.

Variously ascribed. The formulation was used as a motto by the English Nonconformist clergyman RICHARD BAXTER.

46 It became necessary to destroy the town to save it.
Unnamed US army major, quoted in the *New York Times* 8 February 1968. The report concerned the battle for Ben Tre during the Tet offensive in Vietnam.

47 It's not the bullet with my name on it that worries me. It's the one that says 'To whom it may concern'.
Belfast resident, quoted in the *Guardian* 16 October 1991

48 It's the same the whole world over,
It's the poor wot gets the blame,
It's the rich wot gets the pleasure,
Ain't it all a bloomin' shame?
'She Was Poor, But She Was Honest', English music-hall song (c. 1915), sung to a pre-1914 melody and popularized by soldiers in the First World War. See also ANONYMOUS 85.

49 John Brown's body lies a-moldering in the grave,
His soul is marching on.
'John Brown's Body' (song, c. 1861). Attributed to Thomas Brigham Bishop (1835–1905), who claimed to have written verses for a song entitled 'He's Gone to Be a Soldier in the Army of the Lord' in 1858; subsequently, having visited Harper's Ferry after JOHN BROWN's raid in 1859, he wrote new verses to his song, one of which was 'John Brown's body lies a-molderin' in the grave'. Other attributions to this song include Henry Howard Brownell and Charles Sprague Hall. After abolitionist John Brown was hanged 2 December 1859, his name became a rallying cry among the Unionist armies.

50 Know thyself.
Inscription on the Oracle of Apollo at Delphi, Greece (6th century BC). The words are traditionally ascribed to the 'Seven Sages' or 'Seven Wise Men' of ancient Greece, and specifically to SOLON of Athens (c. 640–c. 558 BC).

51 *L'amour est aveugle; l'amitié ferme les yeux.*
[Love is blind; friendship closes its eyes.]
The words can be found in Theocritus (3rd century BC), and in CHAUCER's *Merchant's Tale*

52 The law locks up both man and woman
Who steals the goose from off the common;
But lets the greater felon loose
Who steals the common from the goose.
Popular rhyme, c. 1800

53 A liberal is a socialist with a wife and two children.
Thought to have been coined in the 1930s, quoted in ALISTAIR COOKE's *Letter From America* BBC Radio 4, 8 April 1990

54 Lizzie Borden took an axe
And gave her mother forty whacks;

When she saw what she had done,
She gave her father forty-one.
Ballad (late 19th century). The quatrain refers to the famous case of Lizzie Borden, tried for the murder of her father and step-mother on 4 August 1892, in Fall River, Massachusetts. Though she was found innocent, there were many who contested the verdict, occasioning a prodigious output of articles and books.

55 Love me little, love me long,
Is the burden of my song.
'Love Me Little' (1569–70). The lines appeared in various literary works of the period.

56 The lower organs of the Party in Britain must make still greater efforts to penetrate the backward parts of the proletariat.
Supposedly a directive from the Communist Party in Moscow, quoted in *Rebel with a Cause* (1990) by H. J. Eysenck

57 Miss Buss and Miss Beale
Cupid's darts do not feel.
How different from us,
Miss Beale and Miss Buss.
Nineteenth-century popular rhyme satirizing Dorothea Beale and Frances Buss, respectively the Principal of Cheltenham Ladies' College and the founder and headmistress of the North London Collegiate School. Both were pioneers of girls' education and, as members of the Kensington Society, supporters of women's suffrage.

58 Monday's child is fair in face,
Tuesday's child is full of grace,
Wednesday's child is full of woe,
Thursday's child has far to go,
Friday's child is loving and giving,
Saturday's child works hard for its living;
And a child that is born on a Christmas day,
Is fair and wise, good and gay.
Traditions, Legends, Superstitions, and Sketches of Devonshire, vol. 2 (ed. Anna E. K. S. Bray, 1838). The last lines are more commonly recited: 'But the child that is born on the Sabbath day/Is bonny and blithe and good and gay.'

59 *Mundus mihi crucifixus est.*
[The world is my crucifix.]
Motto of the Carthusian Order in the Middle Ages

60 My name is George Nathaniel Curzon,
I am a most superior person.
My cheek is pink, my hair is sleek,
I dine at Blenheim twice a week.
Of LORD CURZON, publ. in *The Masque of Balliol* (c. 1870), in *The Balliol Rhymes* (ed. W. G. Hiscock, 1939)

61 The nature of God is a circle of which the centre is everywhere and the circumference is nowhere.

Supposedly traced to a lost treatise of Empedocles, quoted in the *Roman de la Rose*, and by St Bonaventura in *Itinerarium Mentis in Deum*, ch. 5 (both 13th century)

62 *Nil carborundum illegitimi.*
[Don't let the bastards grind you down.]

British army motto 1939–45, in *A Dictionary of Catchphrases* (second edn, 1983) by Eric Partridge. The expression was current among army intelligence, gradually becoming more widespread in the army, chiefly among officers.

63 Not So Much A Programme, More A Way Of Life

Title of comedy series on television (BBC, 1964–5). The programme was a successor to the satirical series *That Was The Week That Was* (1962–3), using a similar format and with DAVID FROST as anchorman. It consisted of interviews and discussion around topical subjects.

64 O Death, thou comest when I had thee least in mind.

Everyman, Act 1, l. 119 (*c*. 1509–19). Spoken by Everyman.

65 O Death, where is thy sting-a-ling-a-ling,
O Grave, thy victor-ee?
The bells of hell go ting-a-ling-a-ling,
For you but not for me.

'The Bells of Hell' (song, 1914–18). Sung to the tune of 'She Only Answered "Ting-a-ling-a-ling" ', which itself is believed to be founded on an old Salvation Army song. See BIBLE, NEW TESTAMENT: 1 CORINTHIANS 46.

66 *O Fortuna,*
velut luna
statu variabilis,
semper crescis
aut decrescis;
vita detestabilis
nunc obdurat
et tunc curat
ludo mentis aciem,
egestatem,
potestatem
dissolvit ut glaciem.
[O Fortune,
Like the moon
You are changeable,
Ever waxing
And waning;
Hateful life
First oppresses
And then soothes
As fancy takes it;
Poverty

And power
It melts them like ice.]

Carmina Burana (*The Songs of Beuren*), 'Carmina Moralia et Satirica', no. 17 (12th century). Set to music by Carl Orff in 1937, together with a selection of other songs from this source.

67 O God, if there be a God, save my soul, if I have a soul!

Prayer of a common soldier before the battle of Blenheim (1704), quoted in *Apologia Pro Vita Sua*, pt 3 (1864) by JOHN HENRY NEWMAN

68 Oh, Paddy dear! and did ye hear the news that's goin' round?
The shamrock is forbid by law to grow on Irish ground!
No more St. Patrick's day we'll keep; his colour can't be seen,
For there's a cruel law against the wearin' o' the green!
I met with Napper Tandy, and he took me by the hand,
And he said, 'How's poor old Ireland, and how does she stand?'
She's the most distressful country that ever yet was seen,
For they're hanging men and women for the wearin' o' the green.

'The Wearin' o' the Green' (song, *c*. 1795). The United Irishmen, formed in 1791 in opposition to British rule, wore the shamrock as their emblem. After their defeat in 1798, the British declared the wearing of green illegal and a capital offence, since when the colour green has become a symbol of allegiance to Irish nationalism. Napper Tandy was a leader of the United Irishmen.

69 O Western wind, when wilt thou blow,
The small rain down can rain?
Christ, if my love were in my arms
And I in my bed again!

'O Western Wind' (*c*. 1530), also known as 'Absence'

70 O ye'll tak' the high road, and I'll tak' the low road,
And I'll be in Scotland afore ye,
But me and my true love will never meet again,
On the bonnie, bonnie banks o' Loch Lomon'.

'Loch Lomon'' (traditional Scottish song). The words have been attributed to Lady John Scott (1810–1900), who adapted a broadside by Sanderson of Edinburgh (1838). The above version is thought to have first appeared in print in *Poets and Poetry of Scotland* (1876).

71 Oh give me a home where the buffalo roam,
Where the deer and the antelope play,

Where never is heard a discouraging word
And the skies are not cloudy all day.
'Home on the Range' (*c.* 1873). The official song of the state of Kansas, and sometimes credited to Brewster Higley (1823–1911).

72 Once again we stop the mighty roar of London's traffic . . .
In Town Tonight (BBC radio series, 1933–60). The words opened this topical weekly magazine programme presented by Lionel Gamlin, which included live outside-broadcasts in central London as well as studio interviews.

73 The only reason I might go to the funeral is to make absolutely sure that he's dead.
An 'eminent editor', referring to press baron Lord Beaverbrook, quoted in *Anatomy of Britain Today*, ch. 9 (1965) by Anthony Sampson

74 The opera ain't over till the fat lady sings.
Attributed to sports commentator Dan Cook in the *Washington Post* 13 June 1978, but already current before then. An older version was: 'Church ain't out till the fat lady sings', from the American South.

75 Over-paid, over-sexed and over here.
Referring to US troops stationed in Britain during the Second World War.

76 *Per ardua ad astra.*
[Through struggle to the stars.]
Motto of the Mulvany family, quoted and translated by RIDER HAGGARD in *The People of the Mist*, ch. 1 (1894). Used as the motto of the RAF, having been proposed by J. S. Yule in 1912 and approved by King GEORGE V in 1913.

77 Please don't shoot the piano player.
Printed notice in bars in the American West. OSCAR WILDE noted while touring America *c.* 1881, that he had seen in a dancing saloon the notice: 'Please do not shoot the pianist. He is doing his best.' He commented: 'I was struck with this recognition of the fact that bad art merits the penalty of death, and I felt that in this remote city, where the aesthetic applications of the revolver were clearly established in the case of music, my apostolic task would be much simplified, as indeed it was.' (*Impressions of America*, 'Leadville', 1906)

78 Please to remember the fifth of November,
Gunpowder, treason and plot.
We know no reason why gunpowder treason
Should ever be forgot.
Traditional rhyme on the Gunpowder Plot to blow up Parliament in 1605, often now sung 'Remember, remember . . .'

79 Politics is show business for ugly people.
The line is associated with the US broadcaster Jim Hightower, but unverified

80 *Post coitum omne animal triste.*
[After coition every animal is sad.]
Sometimes attributed to 2nd-century Greek physician Galen. One version adds: '. . . *praeter mulierem gallumque*' ('. . . except the woman and the cock').

81 The quick brown fox jumps over the lazy dog.
Practice sentence used in typing, employing every letter of the alphabet; said to derive from *c.* 1867

82 Rest in peace. The mistake shall not be repeated.
Inscription on the cenotaph at Hiroshima, Japan, 1945

83 See the happy moron,
He doesn't give a damn,
I wish I were a moron,
My God! perhaps I am!
Rhyme, early 20th century

84 She's gone with the wraggle-taggle gypsies, O!
'The Wraggle-Taggle Gypsies' (song, *c.* 1720), publ. in *Tea Table Miscellany* (1740)

85 She was poor, but she was honest,
Victim of the squire's whim:
For he wooed and he seduced her,
And she had a child by him.
'She Was Poor, But She Was Honest', English music-hall song (*c.* 1915), sung to a pre-1914 melody and popularized by soldiers in the First World War. See also ANONYMOUS 48.

86 *Sic transit gloria mundi.*
[Thus passes the glory of the world.]
Said during the coronation of a new Pope, used from 1409, but earlier in origin. See also THOMAS À KEMPIS 2.

87 *Si monumentum requiris, circumspice.*
[If you would see his monument, look around.]
Sir Christopher Wren's epitaph, attributed to his son, inscribed on his tomb in St Paul's Cathedral, London

88 Some talk of Alexander, and some of Hercules,
Of Hector and Lysander, and such great names as
   these,
But of all the world's great heroes,
There's none that can compare,
With a tow, row row row, row row row,
To the British Grenadiers!
'The British Grenadiers' (song, *c.* 1750)

89 Sumer is icumen in,
Lhude sing cuccu!
Groweth sed, and bloweth med,
And springth the wude nu –
Sing cuccu!
'Cuckoo Song' (*c.* 1250). The oldest documented British song

is still sung annually at Reading Abbey, where it was written. See EZRA POUND 7.

90 Swing low, sweet chariot –
Comin' for to carry me home;
I looked over Jordan and what did I see?
A band of angels comin' after me –
Comin' for to carry me home!

'Swing Low, Sweet Chariot' (spiritual, *c.* 1850). The gospel song was adopted as an anthem by the supporters of the England rugby team in the late 1980s, apparently first sung by an appreciative section of the crowd when three tries scored by Chris Oti, a black player making his debut at Twickenham, helped to give England a massive win over Ireland in March 1988.

91 There is no such thing as a free lunch.

Popularized in the 1960s, the words have no known source, though have been ascribed to an Italian immigrant outside New York's Grand Central Station in ALISTAIR COOKE'S *America* (Epilogue, 1973). 'Free lunches' appeared in the US in the 1840s with the advent of the new drinking saloons which sold lager beer when it first became widely available, chiefly in Milwaukee. The expression appears in *The Moon is a Harsh Mistress*, ch. 11 (1966) by Robert A. Heinlein, but has become most closely associated with the economist MILTON FRIEDMAN, who made it the title of a book in 1975.

92 'Tis the gift to be simple,
'Tis the gift to be free,
'Tis the gift to come down
Where we ought to be.

'Simple Gifts' (Shaker song, *c.* 1848)

93 Tom Pierce, Tom Pierce, lend me your grey mare
All along, down along, out along, lee,
For I want for to go to Widdicombe Fair,
Wi' Bill Brewer, Jan Stewer, Peter Gurney, Peter
   Davy,
Dan'l Whiddon, Harry Hawk,
Old Uncle Tom Cobbleigh and all,
Uncle Tom Cobbleigh and all.

'Widdicombe Fair' (traditional ballad)

94 Turn again Whittington,
Lord Mayor of London.

Traditional refrain of Bow Bells, as heard by Dick Whittington in the tale. Richard Whittington, son of a London mercer, was mayor of London three times.

95 *Ubi libertas, ibi patria.*
[Where liberty dwells there is my country.]

Latin motto, adopted by ALGERNON SIDNEY (*c.* 1640) and later by US patriot and orator JAMES OTIS

96 The water is wide, I cannot get o'er
And neither have I wings to fly.

Give me a boat that can carry two,
And both shall row, my love and I.

'The Water is Wide', st. 1 (song). Also known as 'O Waly, Waly'.

97 We shall overcome, we shall overcome,
We shall overcome some day.
Oh, deep in my heart I do believe
We shall overcome some day.

This 19th-century song was adapted as a Baptist hymn by C. Albert Tindley in 1901, and revived in the 1940s by black tobacco workers in Charleston, South Carolina, and by the civil rights movement in the 1960s.

98 We're here
Because
We're here
Because
We're here
Because we're here.

'We're Here Because', First World War soldiers' marching song, sung to the tune of 'Auld Lang Syne'

99 Were You There When They Crucified My Lord?

Title of spiritual (*c.* 1865)

100 Who Dares Wins.

Motto of the Special Air Services from 1941. In *The SAS at War: 1941–1945*, ch. 1 (1991) by Anthony Kemp, the motto is ascribed to David Stirling (1915–90) who created the SAS in 1941.

101 Yankee Doodle came to town
Riding on a pony;
Stuck a feather in his cap
And called it Macaroni.

'Yankee Doodle' (song, *c.* 1755). A 'macaroni' was the slang name for a dandy in the 18th century.

102 You should try everything once, except incest and folk-dancing.

Twentieth-century saying

103 Your country needs you.

First World War recruiting slogan, from 1914

Jean Anouilh

(1910–87)
French playwright

His plays which, he declared, present a 'great thirst for purity', include the fantasy Thieves' Carnival *(1938), the historical drama* Becket *(1959) and his re-workings of Greek myths,* Antigone *(1944) and* Medea *(1946).*

1 However tight I shut my eyes, there will always

be a stray dog somewhere in the world who'll stop me being happy.

La Sauvage, Act 3 (1938; *Restless Heart*). Thérèse's last speech in the play.

2 It is restful, tragedy, because one knows that there is no more lousy hope left. You know you're caught, caught at last like a rat with all the world on its back. And the only thing left to do is shout – not moan, or complain, but yell out at the top of your voice.

Antigone (1944). Spoken by The Chorus.

3 To say yes, you have to sweat and roll up your sleeves and plunge both hands into life up to the elbows. It's easy to say no, even if it means dying.

Creon, ibid.

4 It takes a certain courage and a certain greatness to be truly base.

Ardèle, Act 1 (1947). Spoken by Le Général.

5 There is love of course. And then there's life, its enemy.

Le Général, ibid., Act I

6 Poor little men, poor little cocks! As soon as they're old enough, they swell their plumage to be conquerors . . . If they only knew that it's enough to be just a little bit wounded and sad in order to obtain everything without fighting for it.

Cécile (1951). Spoken by Araminthe.

7 Everything ends this way in France. Weddings, christenings, duels, burials, swindlings, affairs of state – everything is a pretext for a good dinner.

Monsieur Orlas, ibid.

8 Every man thinks God is on his side. The rich and powerful know he is.

The Lark (1953, adapted by LILLIAN HELLMAN, 1955). Spoken by Charles. See also ROGER DE BUSSY-RABUTIN 3 and VOLTAIRE 7.

9 Saintliness is also a temptation.

Becket, Act 3 (1959). Spoken by Thomas à Becket.

Susan Brownell Anthony
(1820–1906)
US social reformer and feminist

Founder of the Women's State Temperance Society of New York (1852), and co-founder, with ELIZABETH CADY STANTON, of the National American Woman Suffrage Association (1869), she was the first woman to be represented on US currency.

1 The true Republic: men, their rights and nothing more; women, their rights and nothing less.

Motto printed on the front of her newspaper, *The Revolution*, from 1868

2 Join the union, girls, and together say *Equal Pay for Equal Work*.

The Revolution 18 March 1869

3 Suffrage is the pivotal right.

'The Status of Women, Past, Present and Future' publ. in *Arena* May 1897

Minna Antrim
(*c.* 1856–1950)
US epigrammist

1 A fool bolts pleasure, then complains of moral indigestion.

Naked Truth and Veiled Allusions (1901)

2 When a woman is very, very bad, she is awful, but when a man is correspondingly good, he is weird.

Ibid.

3 A homely face and no figure have aided many women heavenward.

Ibid.

4 An epigram is a flashlight of a truth; a witticism, truth laughing at itself.

Ibid.

5 Man forgives women anything save the wit to outwit him.

Ibid.

6 To be loved is to be fortunate, but to be hated is to achieve distinction.

Ibid.

7 The 'Green-Eyed Monster' causes much woe, but the absence of this ugly serpent argues the presence of a corpse whose name is Eros.

Ibid.

8 Experience is a good teacher, but she sends in terrific bills.

Ibid.

9 Between flattery and admiration there often flows a river of contempt.

Ibid.

Apelles

(*c.* 352–308 BC)
Greek artist

Considered one of the most progressive artists of his day, he was court painter to Alexander the Great and Ptolemy I. None of his work survives.

1 *Nulla dies sine linea.*
[No day without a line.]
Motto, attributed. Apelles apparently attached great value to the drawing of outlines, practising every day. A longer version of his motto is quoted by PLINY THE ELDER in *Natural History*, bk 35, sect. 36: *Numquam tam occupatum diem agendi, ut non lineam ducendo exercet artem* ('Don't have a day so busy that you can't exercise your art by drawing a line'). According to ERASMUS, the words were: *Nulla dies abeat, quin linea ducta supersit* (similarly translated).

Guillaume Apollinaire

(1880–1918)
French poet and critic

Originally Guillaume Apollinaris de Kostrowitzky. Born in Italy of Polish descent, he settled in Paris in 1900 where he became a leading figure of the Dada movement and is said to have coined the term 'surrealism'. He died of wounds in the First World War.

1 I love men, not for what unites them, but for what divides them, and I want to know most of all what gnaws at their hearts.
Mercure de France no. 331, 1 April 1911, repr. in *Anecdotiques* (1926)

2 Memories are hunting horns
Whose notes die on the wind.
'Hunting Horns' ('Cors de Chasse'), st. 3, publ. in *Alcools* (1913)

3 You cannot carry around on your back the corpse of your father. You leave him with the other dead. You remember him, miss him, speak of him with admiration. And if you became a father yourself, you cannot expect one of your children to split in two for the sake of your corpse.
The Cubist Painters, 'On Painting', sect. 1 (1913, transl. 1944)

4 Without poets, without artists, men would soon weary of nature's monotony. The sublime idea men have of the universe would collapse with dizzying speed. The order which we find in nature, and which is only an effect of art, would at once vanish. Everything would break up in chaos. There would be no seasons, no civilization, no thought, no humanity; even life would give way, and the impotent void would reign everywhere.
Ibid., 'On Painting', sect. 5

5 A structure becomes architectural, and not sculptural, when its elements no longer have their justification in nature.
Ibid., 'New Painters'

Thomas Appleton

(1812–84)
US author and philanthropist

Dubbed by RALPH WALDO EMERSON the 'king of clubs', he was a prominent member of Boston's literary circle, known as a bon viveur, wit and patron of the arts.

1 Good Americans, when they die, go to Paris.
Quoted in *The Autocrat of the Breakfast-Table*, ch. 6 (1858) by OLIVER WENDELL HOLMES SR. The saying is quoted by OSCAR WILDE in *The Picture of Dorian Gray*, ch. 3 (1891) and *A Woman of No Importance*, Act 1 (1893).

2 A Boston man is the east wind made flesh.
Attributed

Saint Thomas Aquinas

(*c.* 1225–74)
Italian theologian and philosopher

The most influential of the Scholastic philosophers, he wrote hymns, theological treatises and a series of commentaries on ARISTOTLE, whose philosophy he aimed to reconcile with Christian dogma. His teachings ('Thomism') came to underpin Roman Catholic doctrine.

1 *Pange, lingua, gloriosi*
Corporis mysterium,
Sanguinisque pretiosi,
Quem in mundi pretium
Fructus ventris generosi
Rex effudit gentium.
[Sing, my tongue, the Saviour's glory,
Of His flesh the mystery sing;
Of the blood, all price exceeding,
Shed by our immortal king,
Destined, for the world's redemption,
From a noble womb to spring.]
'Pange, lingua, gloriosi', st. 1 (hymn, 1264)

2 *Tantum ergo sacramentum*
Veneremur cernui;
Et antiquum documentum
Novo cedat ritui.
[Down in adoration falling,

Lo! the sacred Host we hail,
Lo! o'er ancient forms departing
Newer rites of grace prevail.]
'Pange, lingua, gloriosi', st. 5

3 *O salutaris hostia,*
Quae coeli pandis ostium,
Bella premunt hostilia,
Da robur, fer auxilium.
[O saving victim opening wide
The gate of heaven to all below.
Our foes press on from every side;
Thine aid supply, Thy strength bestow.]
'Verbum supernum', st. 5 (hymn, 1264)

4 In the intellect things even of contrary natures
cease to be contraries: for white and black are not
contraries in the intellect, since they do not exclude
one another, in fact rather do they follow from one
another, seeing that by understanding the one we
understand the other.
Summa contra gentiles, bk 2, ch. 55 (c. 1258–64)

5 Three things are required for any war to be just.
The first is the authority of the sovereign on whose
command war is waged . . . Secondly, a just cause is
required, namely that those who are attacked are
attacked because they deserve it on account of some
wrong they have done . . . Thirdly, the right intention of those waging war is required, that is, they
must intend to promote the good and to avoid evil.
Summa theologiae, pt 2, Question 40, Article 1 (1265–73)

6 For it is necessary in every practical science to
proceed in a composite (i.e. deductive) manner. On
the contrary in speculative science, it is necessary
to proceed in an analytical manner by breaking
down the complex into elementary principles.
Commentary to *Nicomachean Ethics*, bk 1, ch. 2, Lecture 3
(1271). The passage has been summarized: 'Practical sciences
proceed by building up; theoretical sciences by resolving into
components.'

7 All that I have written seems to me like straw
compared to what has now been revealed to me.
Now I await the end of my life.
Attributed remark following a vision he had during mass on
6 December 1273

Arabian Nights

Also known as The Thousand and One Nights, *the tales are of*
uncertain date, first mentioned in a 9th-century fragment,
and thought to be a composite work from Indian, Persian,
Arabic and Greek sources, augmented over the centuries. It is
structured as a series of stories related nightly by Shahrazad
(Scheherezade) as a ploy to postpone her execution.

1 Open Sesame.
'Ali Baba and the Forty Thieves'. Magic formula to open the
door to the robbers' cave. In RICHARD BURTON's translation
(1885–8), the words are 'Open Simsim', using the Arabic word
for 'sesame'.

2 Who will exchange old lamps for new lamps?
'Aladdin, or The Wonderful Lamp'. Spoken by Maghrabi, the
magician, and commonly quoted 'New lamps for old'.

Yasser Arafat
(1929–2004)
Palestinian leader

Having helped found the resistance group Al Fatah in the late
1950s, he gained control of the Palestine Liberation Organiz-
ation in 1969. He was elected President of the Palestinian
National Council in 1996.

1 Palestine is the cement that holds the Arab world
together, or it is the explosive that blows it apart.
Time 11 November 1974

Louis Aragon
(1897–1982)
French poet

Originally Louis Andrieux. With ANDRÉ BRETON *he founded*
the Surrealist review Littérature *(1919) to promote the same*
'passionate and unruly use of stupefying images' that charac-
terized his poetry. He became a Communist after visiting
Russia in 1930.

1 No more painters, no more scribblers, no more
musicians, no more sculptors, no more religions, no
more royalists, no more radicals, no more imperial-
ists, no more anarchists, no more socialists, no more
communists, no more proletariat, no more democrats, no more republicans, no more bourgeois, no
more aristocrats, no more arms, no more police, no
more nations, an end at last to all this stupidity,
nothing left, nothing at all, nothing, nothing.
'Manifesto of the Dada Movement' read out at the second
Dada event, 5 February 1920, Salon des Indépendents, Paris,
repr. in *The History of Surrealism*, ch. 3 (1964) by Maurice
Nadeau

2 There are strange flowers of reason to match each
error of the senses.
Paris Peasant, 'Preface to a Modern Mythology' (1926)

3 We know that the nature of genius is to provide
idiots with ideas twenty years later.
Treatise on Style, pt 1, 'The Pen' (1928)

4 O months of blossoming, months of
    transfigurations,
May without cloud and June stabbed to the heart,
I shall not ever forget the lilacs or the roses
Nor those the spring has kept folded away apart.
'Les Lilas et les roses', publ. in *Le Crève-Coeur* (1940)

Diane Arbus
(1923–71)
US photographer

*She is best remembered for her monochrome images of
strange or unusual subjects from the streets of New York and
other US cities in the 1960s. In the view of* NORMAN MAILER,
*'Giving a camera to Diane Arbus is like putting a live grenade
in the hands of a child.'*

1 There's a quality of legend about freaks. Like a
person in a fairy tale who stops you and demands
that you answer a riddle. Most people go through
life dreading they'll have a traumatic experience.
Freaks were born with their trauma. They've already
passed their test in life. They're aristocrats.
From classes given in 1971, publ. in *Diane Arbus: An Aperture
Monograph* (1972)

2 A photograph is a secret about a secret. The more
it tells you the less you know.
Quoted in *Diane Arbus: A Biography*, Preface (1985) by Patricia
Bosworth

John Arbuthnot
(1667–1735)
Scottish physician and author

*He was physician to Queen Anne, but won more lasting fame
as a satirist and close friend of* JONATHAN SWIFT *and* ALEX-
ANDER POPE. *His* History of John Bull *(1712) popularized the
image of John Bull as the archetypal Englishman.*

1 One of the new terrors of death.
Quoted in *Life of Pope*, ch. 3 (1853, vol. 1 of *The Poetical Works
of Pope*) by Robert Carruthers. Referring to Edmund Curll
(or Curle), publisher of brief biographies of eminent people
following their death.

2 All political parties die at last of swallowing their
own lies.
Attributed, in *Life of Emerson*, ch. 7 (1888) by Richard Garnett

Jeffrey Archer
(b. 1940)
British author, businessman and politician

*Baron Archer of Weston-super-Mare. He was a Conservative
MP 1969–74 and Deputy Chairman of the Conservative Party
in 1985, and is the author of numerous bestselling novels. In
2000 he was given a four-year sentence for perjury. Gyles
Brandreth called him 'a modern day Toad of Toad Hall . . .
historic, but disaster-prone'.*

1 I was unemployed with debts of £400,000. I know
what unemployment is like and a lot of it is getting
off your backside and finding a job.
Quoted in the *Observer* 13 October 1985

2 I was allowed to ring the bell for five minutes until
everyone was in assembly. It was the beginning of
power.
Daily Telegraph 16 March 1988. On his schooldays.

3 If I am given the privilege of becoming the first
democratically elected Lord Mayor I'll never write
another book.
Independent 21 March 1998

4 I'm down to my last hundred million.
Quoted in the *Guardian* 28 September 1998. Said when he
was reduced to selling his Andy Warhol collection.

The Archers
British soap opera on BBC radio

*The world's longest-running radio serial started in 1951, and
its tales of village life continue to draw a strong audience
today. Episodes were written first by Edward J. Mason and
Geoffrey Webb; John Keir Cross took over Webb's place on the
latter's death in 1962, and different writers were later used.*

1 An everyday story of country folk.
Introduction to each episode, publ. in *The Archers: The First
Thirty Years* (ed. William Smethurst, 1980). After a trial week's
broadcast in 1950, the series began 1 January 1951 with this
preamble. It continued: 'The Archers are country folk –
farmers . . . children of the soil, and like most work-a-day folk
they have their joys and troubles, their ups and downs . . .'

Archimedes
(c. 287–212 BC)
Greek mathematician and inventor

*Based in Syracuse, Sicily, he is credited with Archimedes' screw,
a device for raising water, and Archimedes' principle, which
established a law for fluid displacement. He famously contributed to the defence of Syracuse during the Second Punic War,
but was killed when the city fell to the besieging Roman forces.*

1 *Eureka!*
[I have found it!]

Quoted in *De Architectura*, bk 9, Introduction, sect. 10 (1st century BC) by Vitruvius Pollio. According to legend, this was the exclamation of Archimedes as he ran naked in the street, after he had stepped into a bath and realized that his theory of water displacement might allow him to discover whether a metal was pure gold or alloyed with silver, thereby fulfilling a request by his patron Hieron II of Syracuse.

2 Give me a place to stand and I will move the earth.

Quoted in *Synagoge*, bk 8, Proposition 10, sect. 11 (*c.* 340) by Pappus of Alexandria. On his discovery of the laws of leverage, as deduced purely from geometry.

3 Do not disturb my circles.

Attributed last words. On the capture of Syracuse, the Roman general Marcellus had apparently ordered that the mathematician's life be spared, but a Roman soldier who encountered Archimedes sitting on the ground drawing geometric diagrams in the dirt was provoked to wrath by his words and slew him. Also quoted: 'Wait until I have finished my problem' and 'Stand away, fellow, from my diagram.'

Hannah Arendt

(1906–75)
German-born US political philosopher

A refugee from the Nazis, she was active in Jewish organizations in New York from the 1940s, and in 1951 published The Origins of Totalitarianism, *which related the development of totalitarianism to the anti-Semitism, nationalism and imperialism of the 19th century.*

1 Totalitarianism is never content to rule by external means, namely, through the state and a machinery of violence; thanks to its peculiar ideology and the role assigned to it in this apparatus of coercion, totalitarianism has discovered a means of dominating and terrorizing human beings from within.

The Origins of Totalitarianism, ch. 10, sect. 1 (1951)

2 Wherever the relevance of speech is at stake, matters become political by definition, for speech is what makes man a political being.

The Human Condition, Prologue (1958)

3 The human condition is such that pain and effort are not just symptoms which can be removed without changing life itself; they are the modes in which life itself, together with the necessity to which it is bound, makes itself felt. For mortals, the 'easy life of the gods' would be a lifeless life.

Ibid., 'Labor', ch. 16

4 Man cannot be free if he does not know that he is subject to necessity, because his freedom is always won in his never wholly successful attempts to liberate himself from necessity.

Ibid., 'Labor', ch. 16

5 The fearsome, word-and-thought-defying *banality of evil.*

Eichmann in Jerusalem, ch. 15 (1963)

6 It is in the very nature of things human that every act that has once made its appearance and has been recorded in the history of mankind stays with mankind as a potentiality long after its actuality has become a thing of the past.

Ibid., Epilogue

7 No cause is left but the most ancient of all, the one, in fact, that from the beginning of our history has determined the very existence of politics, the cause of freedom versus tyranny.

On Revolution, Introduction (1963)

8 What makes it so plausible to assume that hypocrisy is the vice of vices is that integrity can indeed exist under the cover of all other vices except this one. Only crime and the criminal, it is true, confront us with the perplexity of radical evil; but only the hypocrite is really rotten to the core.

Ibid., ch. 2, sect. 5

9 Economic growth may one day turn out to be a curse rather than a good, and under no conditions can it either lead into freedom or constitute a proof for its existence.

Ibid., ch. 6

10 It is well known that the most radical revolutionary will become a conservative the day after the revolution.

New Yorker 12 September 1970

11 Under conditions of tyranny it is far easier to act than to think.

Quoted in *A Certain World*, 'Tyranny' (1970) by W. H. AUDEN

12 It is a secret from nobody that the famous random event is most likely to arise from those parts of the world where the old adage 'There is no alternative to victory' retains a high degree of plausibility.

Crises of the Republic, 'On Violence', sect. 1 (1972)

13 The Third World is not a reality but an ideology.

Ibid., 'On Violence', sect. 1

Ludovico Ariosto
(1474–1533)
Italian poet and playwright

The author of satires and Latin verse, he won greatest renown for his epic Orlando Furioso *(1516, rev. 1521 and 1532), which narrated the legends of Roland and is regarded as the finest literary work of the Italian Renaissance.*

1 Nature cast him, and then broke the mould.
Orlando Furioso, canto 10, st. 84 (1516, rev. 1521, 1532). Referring to Zerbino (son of the king of Scotland).

2 Though he was on the water, he could not extinguish the flames; though he changed his location, he could not change his state of mind.
Ibid., canto 28, st. 89. Referring to Rodomont.

Aristophanes
(c. 450–c. 388 BC)
Greek dramatist

The eleven plays that survive of around forty he is thought to have written are boisterous comic satires directed at the radical teachings of SOCRATES *(in* The Clouds), *the power of women* (Lysistrata) *and the military ambitions of the war party in Athens (*The Babylonians), *among other targets.*

1 You've already
Whatever else a demagogue requires.
A brutal voice, low birth, an agora training;
Why you've got all one wants for public life.
The Knights, ll. 217–19 (424 BC). Demosthenes addresses a sausage-seller.

2 This Second Logic then, I mean the Worse one,
They teach to talk unjustly, and – prevail.
The Clouds, ll. 114–15 (423 BC). Spoken by Strepsiades.

3 The wise learn many things from their enemies.
The Birds, l. 375 (414 BC). Spoken by Epops (Hoopoe).

4 What about 'Cloud-cuckoo-land'?
Ibid., l. 819. Peisthetaerus suggests a name for the capital city of the birds.

5 Democracy,
What will you bring us to at last, I wonder,
If voting Gods elect a clown like this!
Ibid., ll. 1570–2. Poseidon addresses the God of the Triballians.

6 There is nothing so resistless as a woman in her
ire,
She is wilder than a leopard, she is fiercer than a
fire.
Lysistrata, ll. 1014–15 (411 BC). The men's chorus.

7 But *he* was contented here, is contented there.
The Frogs, l. 84 (405 BC). Dionysus refers to SOPHOCLES, in Hades ('here'), having been on earth ('there').

8 Brekekekex koax koax.
Ibid., l. 212 and passim. The chorus of frogs.

9 Where most I prosper, there's my fatherland.
Hermes, in *Plutus*, l. 1151 (388 BC)

Aristotle
(384–322 BC)
Greek philosopher

He studied under PLATO, *was tutor to Alexander the Great, and established his own 'peripatetic' school in the Athenian Lyceum (335 BC). His treatises on logic, metaphysics, ethics, politics, biology, physics and astronomy were rediscovered in the Middle Ages through the work of Muslim and Jewish scholars.*

1 All men by nature desire to know.
Metaphysics, bk 1, ch. 1. Opening words of book.

2 Every art and every inquiry, and similarly every action and choice, is thought to aim at some good; and for this reason the good has rightly been declared to be that at which all things aim.
Nicomachean Ethics, bk 1, ch. 1. Opening words of book.

3 Yet it would perhaps be thought to be better, indeed to be our duty, for the sake of maintaining the truth even to destroy what touches us closely, especially as we are philosophers; for, while both are dear, piety requires us to honour truth above our friends.
Ibid., bk 1, ch. 6. Aristotle, who spent twenty years at PLATO's Academy as pupil and teacher, referred to his philosophical colleagues as 'friends'. The allusion to Plato and his school has traditionally been inferred here, giving rise to the popular misquotation: 'Plato is dear to me, but dearer still is truth.'

4 If happiness is activity in accordance with virtue, it is reasonable that it should be in accordance with the highest virtue.
Ibid., bk 1, ch. 7

5 The life of money-making is one undertaken under compulsion, and wealth is evidently not the good we are seeking; for it is merely useful and for the sake of something else.
Ibid., bk 1, ch. 7

6 Human good turns out to be activity of soul in accordance with virtue, and if there are more than one virtue, in accordance with the best and most complete. But we must add 'in a complete life'. For

one swallow does not make a summer, nor does one day; and so too one day, or a short time, does not make a man blessed and happy.

Ibid., bk 1, ch. 7

7 What the statesman is most anxious to produce is a certain moral character in his fellow citizens, namely a disposition to virtue and the performance of virtuous actions.

Ibid., bk 1, ch. 9

8 None of the moral virtues arises in us by nature; for nothing that exists by nature can form a habit contrary to its nature ... Neither by nature, then, nor its contrary do the virtues arise in us; rather we are adapted by nature to receive them, and are made perfect by habit.

Ibid., bk 2, ch. 1

9 The man who is angry at the right things and with the right people, and, further, as he ought, when he ought, and as long as he ought, is praised.

Ibid., bk 4, ch. 5

10 Happiness is thought to depend on leisure; for we are busy that we may have leisure, and make war that we may live in peace.

Ibid., bk 10, ch. 7

11 Beauty is a matter of size and order.

Poetics, ch. 7

12 The poet's function is to describe, not the thing that has happened, but a kind of thing that might happen, i.e. what is possible as being probable or necessary.

Ibid., ch. 9

13 Poetry is something more philosophical and of graver import than history, since its statements are of the nature rather of universals, whereas those of history are singulars.

Ibid., ch. 9

14 A likely impossibility is always preferable to an unconvincing possibility.

Ibid., ch. 24

15 Hence it is evident that the state is a creation of nature, and that man is by nature a political animal.

Politics, bk 1, ch. 2 (transl. BENJAMIN JOWETT, 1885, rev. W. D. Ross, 1921). See also KARL MARX 8.

16 Whosoever is delighted in solitude is either a wild beast or a god.

Ibid., bk 1, ch. 2 (transl. FRANCIS BACON in *Essays*, 'Of Friendship', 1597–1625). FRIEDRICH NIETZSCHE wrote: 'To live alone one must be an animal or a god – says Aristotle. There is yet a third case: one must be both – a *philosopher*' (*Twilight of the Idols*, 'Maxims and Arrows', aph. 3, 1889).

17 Nature does nothing in vain.

Ibid., Introduction, bk 1, ch. 2 (transl. BENJAMIN JOWETT, 1885, rev. W. D. Ross, 1921)

18 Men always want more and more without end; for it is of the nature of desire to be unlimited, and most men live only for the gratification of it. The beginning of reform is not so much to equalize property as to train the nobler sort of natures not to desire more, and to prevent the lower from getting more; that is to say, they must be kept down, but not ill-treated.

Ibid., bk 2, ch. 7

19 A state exists for the sake of a good life, and not for the sake of life only: if life only were the object, slaves and brute animals might form a state ... Nor does a state exist for the sake of alliance and security from injustice, nor yet for the sake of exchange and mutual intercourse ... Whereas, those who care for good government take into consideration virtue and vice in states. Whence it may be further inferred that virtue must be the care of a state which is truly so called, and not merely enjoys the name.

Ibid., bk 3, ch. 9

20 The best political community is formed by citizens of the middle class, and ... those states are likely to be well-administered in which the middle class is large, and stronger if possible than both the other classes, or at any rate than either singly; for the addition of the middle class turns the scale, and prevents either of the extremes from being dominant.

Ibid., bk 4, ch. 11

21 Inferiors revolt in order that they may be equal, and equals that they may be superior. Such is the state of mind which creates revolutions.

Ibid., bk 5, ch. 2

22 They [youths] are fond of fun and therefore witty, wit being well-bred insolence.

Rhetoric, bk 2, ch. 12

23 To the query, 'What is a friend?' his reply was 'A single soul dwelling in two bodies.'

Quoted in *Lives of Eminent Philosophers*, 'Aristotle', bk 5, sect. 20, by Diogenes Laertius

24 No great genius has ever existed without some touch of madness.

Attributed by SENECA in *Moral Essays*, 'De Tranquillitate Animi' ('On Tranquillity of Mind'), sect. 17, subsect. 10. A similar dictum is attributed to Aristotle by CICERO (in *Tusculanae Disputationes*) and PLUTARCH (in *Life of Lysander*); the origin may be a passage in Aristotle's *Problemata*, bk 30: 'Why is it that all those who have become eminent in philosophy or poetry or the arts are clearly of an atrabilious [melancholy] temperament?'

Giorgio Armani

(b. 1935)

Italian fashion designer

Presenting collections from the mid-1970s, he is known for his elegant, minimalist style. In his own words, 'I was the first to soften the image of men, and harden the image of women.'

1 I would like to be remembered as the person who created a modern elegance.

Interview in the *Guardian* 4 February 1995

Simon Armitage

(b. 1963)

British poet

A public poet with a colloquial style, he has published Zoom *(1989),* Kid *(1992) and* The Dead Sea Poems *(1995), and the novel* Little Green Man *(2001) among other works.*

1 The North, where England tucks its shirt in its underpants.

All Points North, 'Where You're At' (1998)

2 Drugs is
your own tattoos coming alive on your skin,
opening a door and letting a light in
is what drugs is.

Ibid., 'Saturday Night'

3 And a well-shod president walks to the camera
   to say why
we should put in the boot,
and when that happens, a well-dressed prime
   minister
usually follows suit.

Killing Time (1999)

4 Then the Chinese whisper of a countdown
   spreads across the crowd,
first to be lit by a century's morning,

mad to say they were there and then when the
   moment came,
wild for the starlight that passes for meaning.

Ibid.

Harry Armstrong

(1879–1951)

US songwriter

1 There's an old mill by the stream,
Nellie Dean!
Where we used to sit and dream,
Nellie Dean!
And the waters as they flow
Seem to murmur soft and low.
You're my heart's desire.
I love you,
Nellie Dean! Sweet Nellie Dean!

'Nellie Dean' (vaudeville song, 1905)

Louis Armstrong

(1900–71)

US jazz musician

Nicknamed Satchmo ('Satchel Mouth'), he was famous for his gravelly voice, big smile and improvisatory solos with his 'Hot Five' and 'Hot Seven' ensembles (1925–8). He is said to have invented the 'scat' style of singing.

1 Hello, Dolly, well, hello Dolly –
It's so nice to have you back where you belong.

'Hello, Dolly' (song, written by Jerry Herman), in *Hello, Dolly* (stage musical 1964, filmed 1969). In the original stage production, the number was sung by Carol Channing, though it is most associated with Armstrong, who performed it in the film version.

2 And I think to myself
What a wonderful world.

'What a Wonderful World' (song, written by George David Weiss and George Douglas), on the album *What a Wonderful World* (1967)

3 If you still have to ask . . . shame on you.

On being asked what jazz is, quoted in *Louis*, 'Ambassadors of Jazz' (1971, rev. 1975) by Max Jones and John Chilton. Many versions of the riposte exist, along the lines of 'If you have to ask what jazz is, you'll never know', and variously attributed.

4 All music is folk music, I ain't never heard no horse sing a song.

Quoted in the *New York Times* 7 July 1971. The words have also been attributed to blues guitarist Big Bill Broonzy.

Neil Armstrong
(b. 1930)
US astronaut

Commander of the Apollo 11 moon mission in 1969, he was the first person to set foot on the moon.

1 Houston, Tranquility Base here. The Eagle has landed.

Radio message to earth announcing the first manned moon landing, 20 July 1969, quoted in the *Washington Post* 21 July 1969. The message was transmitted as the lunar module 'Eagle' touched down in the Sea of Tranquillity. The words have also been attributed to 'Buzz' Aldrin (Edwin Eugene Aldrin Jr), a fellow crew-member and the second man on the moon.

2 That's one small step for a man, one giant leap for mankind.

Quoted in the *New York Times* 21 July 1969. On his first steps on the moon's surface, 10.56 p.m. (EDT), 20 July 1969. Armstrong's message – possibly garbled or obscured by static – was originally reported 'one small step for man, one giant leap for mankind'.

Robert Armstrong
(1890–1973)
US screen actor

Originally Donald Robert Smith. A character actor associated with action roles, he is mostly remembered as the film producer who brought the ape to New York in King Kong *(1932).*

1 Oh no, it wasn't the airplanes. It was beauty killed the beast.

King Kong (film, 1933, screenplay by James Creelman and Ruth Rose based on a story by Merian Cooper and Edgar Wallace, directed by Merian Cooper and Ernest Schoedsack). Last lines of film, spoken by Carl Denham (Robert Armstrong).

(Sir) Robert Armstrong
(b. 1927)
British civil servant

Baron Armstrong of Ilminster. Secretary of the Cabinet (1979–87) and Head of the Civil Service (1981–7) in the Thatcher government, he played a prominent role during the 'Spycatcher' affair in 1987.

1 It contains a misleading impression, not a lie. It was being economical with the truth.

Remark to Supreme Court, New South Wales, 18 November 1986, quoted in the *Daily Telegraph* 19 November 1986. Referring to a letter written by Armstrong when the British government was attempting to suppress publication of the book *Spycatcher* by ex-secret service agent Peter Wright. As Armstrong made clear, he was quoting EDMUND BURKE in *Two Letters on Proposals for Peace* (1796): 'Falsehood and delusion are allowed in no case whatsoever: But, as in the exercise of all the virtues, there is an economy of truth.' Tory minister ALAN CLARK echoed the words when he admitted he had been 'economical with the *actualité*' when discussing his role in the Matrix Churchill arms-to-Iraq affair in 1990. See also MARK TWAIN 12.

Mary Arnim
(1866–1941)
New Zealand-born British novelist

Mary Annette, Countess von Arnim. The cousin of KATHERINE MANSFIELD, *she married a Prussian count and her life on his Pomeranian estate formed the basis of her most successful book,* Elizabeth and Her German Garden *(1898), written under the pseudonym Elizabeth.*

1 I suppose the fact is that no friendship can stand the breakfast test ... Who can begin conventional amiability the first thing in the morning? It is the hour of savage instincts and natural tendencies; it is the triumph of the Disagreeable and the Cross. I am convinced that the Muses and the Graces never thought of having breakfast anywhere but in bed.

Elizabeth and Her German Garden, 'September 15th' (1898)

Peter Arno
(1904–68)
US cartoonist

Originally Curtis Arnoux Peters. From the 1920s until his death he was associated with the New Yorker *magazine, where his quirky cartoons gently satirized café society.*

1 Well, back to the old drawing board.

Caption to cartoon in the *New Yorker*, repr. in *Peter Arno's Cartoon Revue* (1942). The words are spoken by the designer of a plane just crashed.

(Sir) Edwin Arnold
(1832–1904)
British journalist and poet

After spending five years teaching in India, he returned to England to work at the Daily Telegraph, *becoming editor in 1863. He achieved success with his verse epic on the life and teachings of the Buddha,* The Light of Asia *(1879).*

1 One can be a soldier without dying, and lover without sighing.

Adzuma, Act 2, Sc. 5 (1893). Spoken by Sakamune.

Matthew Arnold
(1822–88)
English poet and critic

The son of THOMAS ARNOLD, *he made his mark as a poet with such works as 'The Scholar-Gipsy' and 'Dover Beach', and published several distinguished works of criticism. 'I am a Liberal,' he asserted, 'yet I am a Liberal tempered by experience, reflection, and renouncement, and I am, above all, a believer in culture.'*

1 France, famed in all great arts, in none supreme.
'To a Republican Friend – Continued', publ. in *The Strayed Reveller and Other Poems* (1849)

2 Come, dear children, let us away;
Down and away below!
'The Forsaken Merman', ibid. Opening lines of poem.

3 Where great whales come sailing by,
Sail and sail, with unshut eye,
Round the world for ever and aye.
'The Forsaken Merman', st. 4, ibid.

4 Yet they, believe me, who await
No gifts from chance, have conquered fate.
'Resignation', ll. 247–8, ibid.

5 Be neither saint- nor sophist-led, but be a man!
Empedocles on Etna, Act 1, Sc. 2, l. 136, publ. in *Empedocles on Etna and Other Poems* (1852). Spoken by Empedocles.

6 Thou hast no *right* to bliss.
Ibid., Act 1, Sc. 2, l. 160. Empedocles addresses Pausanias.

7 Man errs not that he deems
His welfare his true aim,
He errs because he dreams
The world does but exist that welfare to bestow.
Empedocles, ibid., Act 1, Sc. 2, ll. 172–5

8 Each new man strikes root into a far fore-time.
Empedocles, ibid., Act 1, Sc. 2, l. 191

9 We do not what we ought;
What we ought not, we do;
And lean upon the thought
That chance will bring us through.
Empedocles, ibid., Act 1, Sc. 2, ll. 237–40

10 Nature, with equal mind,
Sees all her sons at play;
Sees man control the wind,
The wind sweep man away.
Empedocles, ibid., Act 1, Sc. 2, ll. 257–60

11 Is it so small a thing
To have enjoyed the sun,
To have lived light in the spring,
To have loved, to have thought, to have done.
Empedocles, ibid., Act 1, Sc. 2, ll. 397–400

12 Come to me in my dreams, and then
By day I shall be well again!
For then the night will more than pay
The hopeless longing of the day.
'Longing', st. 1, publ. in *Empedocles on Etna and Other Poems* (1852) Later published as 'Faded Leaves', no. 5, in *Poems* (second series, 1855)

13 But each day brings its petty dust
Our soon-choked souls to fill,
And we forget because we must,
And not because we will.
'Absence', st. 3, ibid.

14 Yes! in the sea of life enisled,
With echoing straits between us thrown,
Dotting the shoreless watery wild,
We mortal millions live *alone*.
'To Marguerite – Continued', st. 1, ibid.

15 A God, a God their severance ruled!
And bade betwixt their shores to be
The unplumbed, salt, estranging sea.
'To Marguerite – Continued', st. 4, ibid.

16 And sigh that one thing only has been lent
To youth and age in common – discontent.
'Sonnet', st. 4, ibid., later titled 'Youth's Agitations' in *New Poems* (1867)

17 Resolve to be thyself: and know, that he
Who finds himself, loses his misery.
'Self-Dependence', st. 8, ibid. Last lines of poem.

18 Still bent to make some port he knows not
    where,
Still standing for some false impossible shore.
'A Summer Night', ll. 68–9, ibid.

19 But often in the world's most crowded streets,
But often, in the din of strife,
There rises an unspeakable desire
After the knowledge of our buried life.
'The Buried Life', ll. 45–8

20 We cannot kindle when we will
The fire that in the heart resides,
The spirit bloweth and is still,
In mystery our soul abides.
'Morality', st. 1, ibid.

21 Curled minion, dancer, coiner of sweet words!
'Sohrab and Rustum', l. 458, publ. in *Poems* (1853). Spoken by Rustum.

22 Truth sits upon the lips of dying men.
'Sohrab and Rustum', l. 656, ibid. Spoken by Sohrab.

23 Hark! ah, the nightingale!
The tawny-throated!
Hark! from that moonlit cedar what a burst!
What triumph! Hark – what pain!
'Philomela', ll. 1–4, ibid.

24 Eternal passion!
Eternal pain!
'Philomela', ll. 31–2, ibid.

25 Her cabined ample spirit,
It fluttered and failed for breath.
To-night it doth inherit
The vasty hall of death.
'Requiescat', st. 4, ibid.

26 Go, for they call you, shepherd, from the hill.
'The Scholar-Gipsy', ibid. Opening line of poem.

27 All the live murmur of a summer's day.
'The Scholar-Gipsy', st. 2, ibid.

28 Tired of knocking at preferment's door.
'The Scholar-Gipsy', st. 4, ibid.

29 Light half-believers of our casual creeds,
Who never deeply felt, nor clearly willed,
Whose insight never has borne fruit in deeds,
Whose vague resolves never have been fulfilled.
'The Scholar-Gipsy', st. 18, ibid.

30 With close-lipped patience for our only friend,
Sad patience, too near neighbour to despair.
'The Scholar-Gipsy', st. 20, ibid.

31 This strange disease of modern life,
With its sick hurry, its divided aims.
'The Scholar-Gipsy', st. 21, ibid.

32 Still nursing the unconquerable hope,
Still clutching the inviolable shade.
'The Scholar-Gipsy', st. 22, ibid.

33 I am past thirty, and three parts iced over.
Letter, 12 February 1853, publ. in *The Letters of Matthew Arnold to Arthur Hugh Clough* (ed. H. F. Lowry, 1932)

34 Sanity – that is the great virtue of the ancient literature; the want of that is the great defect of the modern, in spite of its variety and power.
Poems, Preface (second edn, 1854)

35 For rigorous teachers seized my youth,
And purged its faith, and trimmed its fire,
Showed me the high, white star of truth,
There bade me gaze, and there aspire.
'Stanzas from the Grande Chartreuse', st. 12 (1855), repr. in *New Poems* (1867)

36 Wandering between two worlds, one dead,
The other powerless to be born,
With nowhere yet to rest my head,
Like these, on earth I wait forlorn.
'Stanzas from the Grande Chartreuse', st. 15, ibid.

37 Unquiet souls!
In the dark fermentation of earth,
In the never idle workshop of nature,
In the eternal movement,
Ye shall find yourselves again!
'Haworth Churchyard', ll. 134–8 (1855), rev. in *Collected Poems* (1877). Closing lines of poem.

38 The grand style arises in poetry, when a noble nature, poetically gifted, treats with simplicity or with severity a serious subject.
'On Translating Homer: Last Words', lecture in Oxford, 30 November 1861, publ. 1862

39 Like driftwood spars, which meet and pass
Upon the boundless ocean plain,
So on the sea of life, alas!
Man meets man – meets and quits again.
'The Terrace at Berne', st. 11, written 1863, publ. in *New Poems* (1867)

40 Beautiful city! so venerable, so lovely, so unravaged by the fierce intellectual life of our century, so serene! . . . Home of lost causes, and forsaken beliefs, and unpopular names, and impossible loyalties!
Essays in Criticism, Preface (first series, 1865). Referring to Oxford, where Arnold was Professor of Poetry at the university 1857–67; see also quote 42.

41 I am bound by my own definition of criticism: *a disinterested endeavour to learn and propagate the best that is known and thought in the world.*
Ibid., 'The Function of Criticism at the Present Time'

42 And that sweet city with her dreaming spires,
She needs not June for beauty's heightening.
'Thyrsis', st. 2, publ. in *New Poems* (1867). Referring to Oxford.

43 So have I heard the cuckoo's parting cry,
From the wet field, through the vexed
   garden-trees,
Come with the volleying rain and tossing breeze:

'The bloom is gone, and with the bloom go I.'
'Thyrsis', st. 6, ibid.

44 Yes, thou art gone! and round me too the night
In ever-nearing circle weaves her shade.
'Thyrsis', st. 14, ibid. Referring to A. H. CLOUGH, the 'Thyrsis' of the poem's title.

45 The sea is calm tonight.
The tide is full, the moon lies fair
Upon the Straits; on the French coast, the light
Gleams, and is gone; the cliffs of England stand,
Glimmering and vast, out in the tranquil bay.
'Dover Beach', st. 1, ibid. Opening lines.

46 The sea of faith
Was once, too, at the full, and round earth's shore
Lay like the folds of a bright girdle furled.
But now I only hear
Its melancholy, long, withdrawing roar,
Retreating, to the breath
Of the night-wind, down the vast edges drear
And naked shingles of the world.
'Dover Beach', st. 3, ibid.

47 Ah, love, let us be true
To one another! for the world, which seems
To lie before us like a land of dreams,
So various, so beautiful, so new,
Hath really neither joy, nor love, nor light,
Nor certitude, nor peace, nor help for pain;
And we are here as on a darkling plain
Swept with confused alarms of struggle and flight,
Where ignorant armies clash by night.
'Dover Beach', st. 4, ibid.

48 Creep into thy narrow bed,
Creep, and let no more be said!
'The Last Word', ibid. Opening lines.

49 Let the long contention cease!
Geese are swans, and swans are geese.
Let them have it how they will!
Thou art tired; best be still.
'The Last Word', st. 2, ibid.

50 Our society distributes itself into Barbarians, Philistines and Populace; and America is just ourselves with the Barbarians quite left out, and the Populace nearly.
Culture and Anarchy, Preface (1869)

51 The pursuit of perfection, then, is the pursuit of sweetness and light ... He who works for sweetness

and light united, works to make reason and the will of God prevail.
Ibid., ch. 1. See JONATHAN SWIFT 2.

52 The men of culture are the true apostles of equality.
Ibid., ch. 1

53 One has often wondered whether upon the whole earth there is anything so unintelligent, so unapt to perceive how the world is really going, as an ordinary young Englishman of our upper class.
Ibid., ch. 2

54 The working class ... is now issuing from its hiding-place to assert an Englishman's heaven-born privilege of doing as he likes, and is beginning to perplex us by marching where it likes, meeting where it likes, bawling what it likes, breaking what it likes.
Ibid., ch. 3

55 Hebraism and Hellenism – between these two points of influence moves our world.
Ibid., ch. 4. For Arnold, 'The governing idea of Hellenism is spontaneity of consciousness; that of Hebraism, strictness of conscience.'

56 Culture, the acquainting ourselves with the best that has been known and said in the world, and thus with the history of the human spirit.
Literature and Dogma, Preface (1873). In Culture and Anarchy, Arnold wrote: 'Culture, then, is a study of perfection, and perfection which insists on becoming something rather than in having something, in an inward condition of the mind and spirit, not in an outward set of circumstances.'

57 The true meaning of religion is thus, not simply morality, but morality touched by emotion.
Ibid., ch. 1, sect. 2

58 Conduct is three-fourths of our life and its largest concern.
Ibid., ch. 1, sect. 3

59 At the present moment two things about the Christian religion must surely be clear to anybody with eyes in his head. One is, that men cannot do without it; the other, that they cannot do with it as it is.
God and the Bible, Preface (1875)

60 Bald as the bare mountain tops are bald, with a baldness which is full of grandeur.
Preface to Poems of Wordsworth (1879), repr. in Essays in Criticism (second series, 1888)

61 The man Shelley, in very truth, is not entirely

sane, and Shelley's poetry is not entirely sane either. The Shelley of actual life is a vision of beauty and radiance, indeed, but availing nothing, effecting nothing. And in poetry, no less than in life, he is 'a beautiful and ineffectual angel, beating in the void his luminous wings in vain'.

Essays in Criticism, 'Shelley' (second series, 1888). Closing words of review first published 1886. Arnold was quoting himself from another essay collected in this volume, 'Byron'. He was appalled at what he considered the depravity of SHELLEY's personal life: 'What a set! what a world! ... One ... feels sickened for ever of the subject of irregular relations.'

Thomas Arnold
(1795–1842)
English scholar and educator

In 1828 he became Headmaster of Rugby School and gradually raised it to the rank of a great public school. His methods, such as the use of prefects, and aims, principally that of 'moulding gentlemen', were adopted by many secondary schools after his death. He was the father of MATTHEW ARNOLD.

1 My object will be, if possible, to form Christian men, for Christian boys I can scarcely hope to make.

Letter, 2 March 1828, publ. in *The Life and Correspondence of Thomas Arnold, DD*, vol. 1, ch. 2 (ed. Arthur Penrhyn Stanley, 1845). Written on his appointment as Headmaster of Rugby School.

2 What we must look for here is, 1st, religious and moral principles; 2ndly, gentlemanly conduct; 3rdly, intellectual ability.

Address to Rugby School, quoted ibid., ch. 3

3 Rather than have [science] the principal thing in my son's mind, I would gladly have him think that the sun went round the earth, and that the stars were so many spangles set in the bright blue firmament.

Letter, 9 May 1836, ibid., vol. 2. Referring to the teaching of Physical Science. Arnold welcomed that his children be well versed in science only if 'in due subordination to the fulness and freshness of their knowledge on moral subjects'.

Sophie Arnould
(1740–1802)
French actress and operatic soprano

Famous as a singer, lover and wit, she debuted in 1757 to great acclaim. She retired from performing in 1778, but continued to generate scandal for her affairs and her distinguished admirers.

1 They give themselves to God when the devil will no longer have them.

Quoted in *Sophie Arnould: Actress and Wit*, ch. 4 (1898) by Robert B. Douglas. Referring to nuns.

Antonin Artaud
(1896–1948)
French theatre producer, actor and theorist

The anarchistic principles of his Theatre of Cruelty, which aimed to attack the complacency of the audience, were expounded in his Manifesto of the Theatre of Cruelty *(1932 and 1933) and* The Theatre and Its Double *(1938). His best known acting role was as Marat in Abel Gance's film* Napoléon *(1927).*

1 If I commit suicide, it will not be to destroy myself but to put myself back together again. Suicide will be for me only one means of violently reconquering myself, of brutally invading my being, of anticipating the unpredictable approaches of God. By suicide, I reintroduce my design in nature, I shall for the first time give things the shape of my will.

'On Suicide' (1925), repr. in *Artaud Anthology* (ed. Jack Hirschman, 1965)

2 *Theatre of cruelty* means a theatre difficult and cruel for myself first of all. And, on the level of performance, it is not the cruelty we can exercise upon each other by hacking at each other's bodies, carving up our personal anatomies, or, like Assyrian emperors, sending parcels of human ears, noses, or neatly detached nostrils through the mail, but the much more terrible and necessary cruelty which things can exercise against us. We are not free. And the sky can still fall on our heads. And the theatre has been created to teach us that first of all.

The Theatre and Its Double, ch. 1 (1938, transl. 1958)

3 All true language
is incomprehensible,
Like the chatter
of a beggar's teeth.

'Ci-Gît' (1947), repr. in *Selected Writings*, pt 36 (ed. SUSAN SONTAG, 1976)

4 Where there is a stink of shit
there is a smell of being.

To Have Done with the Judgment of God, 'The Pursuit of Fecality' (1947)

5 No one has ever written, painted, sculpted, modelled, built, or invented except literally to get out of hell.

Van Gogh, the Man Suicided by Society (1947)

6 Tragedy on the stage is no longer enough for me, I shall bring it into my own life.

Quoted in *Memories for Tomorrow*, pt. 2 'The Grenier des Grands-Augustins' (1972) by Jean-Louis Barrault

George Asaf
(1880–1951)
British songwriter

1 What's the use of worrying?
It never was worthwhile,
So, pack up your troubles in your old kit-bag,
And smile, smile, smile.

'Pack up your Troubles' (song, 1915, with music by Felix Powell)

Lord (Paddy) Ashdown
(b. 1941)
British politician

Jeremy John Durham Ashdown, Baron Ashdown of Norton-sub-Hamden. Having served with the Royal Marines and in the diplomatic service, he was elected as a Liberal MP in 1983 and was leader of the amalgamated Liberal and Social Democrat (later Liberal Democrat) Party 1988–99.

1 Politics is about putting yourself in a state of grace.

Daily Telegraph 16 September 1992

2 Lord, make my words sweet and reasonable. For some day I may have to eat them.

Speech at Liberal Party Conference, Brighton, broadcast on *Radio 5 Live* 24 September 1998

Daisy Ashford
(1881–1972)
British writer

An irrepressible story-teller, she was said to have dictated her first tale aged four, but stopped writing altogether at the age of thirteen. Shortly before marrying, she discovered the manuscript of a high-society romance she had written when she was nine, which was published as The Young Visiters *(1919).*

1 Mr Salteena was an elderly man of 42 and was fond of asking people to stay with him.

The Young Visiters, 'Quite a Young Girl' (1919). Opening words of book (which is subtitled *Mr Salteena's Plan*), describing Alfred Salteena, the less attractive of Ethel Monticue's two suitors.

2 I am not quite a gentleman but you would hardly notice it but cant be helped anyhow.

Mr Salteena, ibid.

3 You look rarther rash my dear your colors dont quite match your face but never mind.

Mr Salteena, 'survaying' Ethel, ibid., 'Starting Gaily'

4 Bernard always had a few prayers in the hall and some whiskey afterwards as he was rarther pious.

Ibid., 'The First Evening'

5 My own idear is that these things are as piffle before the wind.

The Earl of Clincham, ibid., 'The Chrystal Palace'

6 Taking the bull by both horns he kissed her violently on her dainty face. My bride to be he murmered several times.

Ibid., 'A Proposale'. Bernard's proposal to Ethel.

7 Her name was called Lady Helena Herring and her age was 25 and she mated well with the earl.

Ibid., 'How It Ended'

Ashurnasirpal II
(reigned 883–859 BC)
King of Assyria

A brilliant general and administrator, he consolidated the conquests of his father, Tukulti-Ninurta II, and laid the basis of a new Assyrian empire. The details of his reign are known almost entirely from his own inscriptions and the reliefs in the ruins of his palace at Calah (now Nimrud, Iraq).

1 The supreme, the merciless, the destroyer of opposition, the exalted King, the shepherd, the protector of the quarters of the world, the King the word of whose mouth destroys mountains and seas, who by his lordly attack has forced mighty and merciless Kings from the rising of the sun to the setting of the same to acknowledge one supremacy.

Cuneiform inscription on alabaster relief from palace at Nimrud (Iraq), 9th century BC, exhibited in Bristol City Museum

Isaac Asimov
(1920–92)
Russian-born US author

A pioneering figure in science fiction and also a distinguished biochemist, he is principally known for his collection of short stories I, Robot *(1950), and* The Foundation Trilogy *(1951–3).*

1 Let's start with the three fundamental Rules of Robotics . . . We have: one, a robot may not injure a human being, or, through inaction, allow a human

being to come to harm. Two, a robot must obey the orders given it by human beings except where such orders would conflict with the First Law. And three, a robot must protect its own existence as long as such protection does not conflict with the First or Second Laws.

'Runaround' (1942), repr. in *I, Robot* (1950). Spoken by Powell. According to Asimov, who called the formulation his most important contribution to science fiction, later adopted by other writers on robots, this passage contains the first recorded use of the term, 'Robotics' (discussed in his essay 'My Robots' in *Robot Visions*, 1993).

2 Science fiction writers foresee the inevitable, and although problems and catastrophes may be inevitable, solutions are not.

'How Easy to See the Future' (1975), repr. in *Asimov on Science Fiction* (1981)

3 It is change, continuing change, inevitable change, that is the dominant factor in society today. No sensible decision can be made any longer without taking into account not only the world as it is, but the world as it will be ... This, in turn, means that our statesmen, our businessmen, our everyman must take on a science fictional way of thinking.

'My Own View', publ. in *The Encyclopedia of Science Fiction* (ed. Robert Holdstock, 1978)

Elizabeth Asquith
(1897–1945)

The daughter of HERBERT ASQUITH, *she married Prince Antoine Bibesco, a Romanian diplomat, in 1919 and subsequently wrote novels, plays and poetry.*

1 Kitchener is a great poster.

Quoted by HERBERT ASQUITH, in *More Memories*, ch. 6 (1933) by Margot Asquith. The quote is often misattributed to MARGOT ASQUITH, as in *Kitchener: Portrait of an Imperialist*, ch. 14 (1980) by Sir Philip Magnus, where the quote appears in the form, 'If Kitchener was not a great man, he was, at least, a great poster.'

Herbert Asquith
(1852–1928)
British statesman

Soon after entering parliament as a Liberal MP in 1886, he served as Home Secretary and then Chancellor of the Exchequer. He was Prime Minister 1908–16 but was ousted as leader of the wartime coalition by LLOYD GEORGE's *wing of the party.*

1 Happily there seems to be no reason why we should be anything more than spectators.

Letter, 24 July 1914, quoted in *Asquith*, ch. 20 (1964) by ROY JENKINS. Referring to the approaching war.

2 Youth would be an ideal state if it came a little later in life.

Quoted in the *Observer* 15 April 1923

3 It is fitting that we should have buried the Unknown Prime Minister by the side of the Unknown Soldier.

Quoted in *The Unknown Prime Minister*, ch. 32, sect. 2 (1955) by Robert Blake. Referring to Andrew Bonar Law, Prime Minister 1922–3. Bonar Law was the first prime minister to be buried in Westminster Abbey since GLADSTONE in 1898, though it was contrary to his own wishes. Blake comments, 'Asquith certainly intended no compliment by this remark, but Bonar Law would not have resented it. He cared little enough for fame in his own lifetime, still less for the verdict of posterity.'

4 Nothing is so demoralising to the tone of public life, or so belittling to the stature of public men, as the atmosphere of a Coalition.

Fifty Years of Parliament, vol. 2, pt 6, ch. 2 (1926)

Margot Asquith
(1864–1945)
British socialite

Second wife of HERBERT ASQUITH, *she was a renowned wit and society hostess. She published three volumes of revelatory autobiography (1920–43) and an autobiographical novel* Octavia *(1928). As* DOROTHY PARKER *quipped, 'The affair between Margot Asquith and Margot Asquith will live as one of the prettiest love stories in all literature.'*

1 One can only influence the strong characters in life, not the weak; and it is the height of vanity to suppose that you can make an honest man of anyone.

The Autobiography of Margot Asquith, vol. 1, ch. 7 (1920)

2 The first element of greatness is fundamental humbleness (this should not be confused with servility); the second is freedom from self; the third is intrepid courage, which, taken in its widest interpretation, generally goes with truth; and the fourth – the power to love – although I have put it last, is the rarest.

Ibid., vol. 1, ch. 8

3 From the happy expression on their faces you might have supposed that they welcomed the war. I have met with men who loved stamps, and stones,

and snakes, but I could not imagine any man loving war.

Ibid., vol. 2, ch. 7 (1922). On the crowds outside Downing Street 3 August 1914, the eve of Britain's declaration of war against Germany.

4 He could not see a belt without hitting below it.

Quoted by Mark Bonham Carter in the Introduction to Margot Asquith's *Autobiography* (1962 edn, first publ. 1920). Of DAVID LLOYD GEORGE.

5 No, no, Jean. The *t* is silent, as in *Harlow*.

Quoted in *Great Tom: Notes Towards a Definition of T.S. Eliot*, ch. 7 (1973) by T. S. Matthews. Said to the actress Jean Harlow, who had been mispronouncing her name. The anecdote is remembered by Emily Hale, a friend of T. S. ELIOT.

Mary Astell
(1668–1731)
English author and feminist

Hailed today as one of the first feminists, she was also one of the earliest woman philosophers of the early modern period. Her outspoken beliefs concerning marriage and the education of women appeared in A Serious Proposal to the Ladies *(1694, 1697) and other works, which were mostly published anonymously though her authorship was widely known.*

1 Happy am I who out of danger sit,
Can see and pity them who wade through it;
Need take no thought my treasure to dispose,
What I ne'er had I cannot fear to lose:
Nor am concerned with what I must wear or buy,
To show my plenty and my vanity.

'Awake my lute', publ. in *A Collection of Poems Humbly Presented . . . to the Lord Archbishop of Canterbury* (1689)

2 Fetters of gold are still fetters, and the softest lining can never make them so easy as liberty.

An Essay in Defence of the Female Sex (1696)

3 To be thoroughly sensible of the capacity of the mind, to discern precisely its bounds and limits and to direct our studies and inquiries accordingly, to know what is to be known, and to believe what is to be believed is the property of a wise person.

A Serious Proposal to the Ladies, pt 2, ch. 3 (1697)

4 If absolute sovereignty be not necessary in a state, how comes it to be so in a family?

Some Reflections upon Marriage, Preface (1700, rev. 1706)

5 If all men are born free, how is it that all women are born slaves?

Ibid., Preface

6 But if marriage be such a blessed state, how comes it, may you say, that there are so few happy marriages? Now in answer to this, it is not to be wondered that so few succeed, we should rather be surprised to find so many do, considering how imprudently men engage, the motives they act by, and the very strange conduct they observe throughout.

Ibid., Preface

7 How can a woman scruple entire subjection, how can she forbear to admire the worth and excellency of the superior sex, if she at all considers it? Have not all the great actions that have been performed in the world been done by men? Have not they founded empires and overturned them? Do not they make laws and continually repeal and amend them? Their vast minds lay kingdoms waste, no bounds or measures can be prescribed to their desires. War and peace depend on them; they form cabals and have the wisdom and courage to get over all the rubs, the petty restraints which honour and conscience may lay in the way of their desired grandeur. What is it they cannot do? They make worlds and ruin them, form systems of universal nature and dispute eternally about them; their pen gives worth to the most trifling controversy; nor can a fray be inconsiderable if they have drawn their swords in it.

Ibid.

(Sir) Jacob Astley
(1579–1652)
English soldier

He served the Royalist cause with distinction during the Civil War, and commanded the infantry at Edgehill (1642). He also fought at Newbury (1643) and Naseby (1645).

1 O Lord! thou knowest how busy I must be this day: if I forget thee, do not thou forget me.

Attributed prayer uttered before the Battle of Edgehill, 23 October 1642, in the English Civil War

Nancy Astor
(1879–1964)
US-born British politician

In 1919 she was the first woman to take her seat in the House of Commons, succeeding her husband as Conservative MP for Plymouth. Generally considered a wit, she was portrayed as a 'sort of V-2 rocket' by her husband.

1 I married beneath me – all women do.

Attributed, speech at Oldham, 1951, also quoted in *Dictionary of National Biography*

2 The penalty of success is to be bored by people who snub you.
Quoted in the *Sunday Express* 12 January 1956

Brooks Atkinson
(1894–1984)
US critic and essayist

Drama critic of the New York Times *(1925–42 and 1946–60), he published collections of essays and articles, as well as histories of the theatre.*

1 After each war there is a little less democracy to save.
Once Around the Sun, '7 January' (1951)

2 The virtue of the camera is not the power it has to transform the photographer into an artist, but the impulse it gives him to keep on looking.
Ibid., '28 August'

Charles Atlas
(1893–1972)
Italian-born US bodybuilder

Originally Angelo Siciliano. With his business partner Charles P. Roman, he devised and ran a highly successful mail-order bodybuilding programme during the 1920s, and he was subsequently dubbed 'America's Most Perfectly Developed Man'.

1 You too can have a body like mine.
Quoted in *The Life and Times of Charles Atlas*, pt 1 (1942) by Charles Gaines. The slogan was coined by Atlas's partner, Charles Roman *c.* 1929.

(Sir) David Attenborough
(b. 1926)
British naturalist and broadcaster

Inspired by the 'splendour and fecundity of the natural world', he began filming wildlife in exotic locations for the BBC series Zoo Quest *(1954–64). His documentary series include* Life on Earth *(1979) and* The Life of Mammals *(2002).*

1 We can now manipulate images to such an extraordinary degree that there is no lie you can't tell.
Quoted in the *Observer* 18 October 1998

2 One cannot get bored by a bluebell.
Quoted in *The Times* 22 April 2000

Clement Attlee
(1883–1967)
British politician and prime minister

First Earl Attlee. He was the first Labour prime minister to hold an absolute majority in the House of Commons. His premiership (1945–51) saw the initiation of the welfare state and the nationalization of major industries. See ANEURIN BEVAN 5, WINSTON CHURCHILL 51, 60 AND 61.

1 Few thought he was even a starter
There were many who thought themselves smarter
But he ended PM
CH and OM
An earl and a knight of the garter.
Quoted in *Attlee*, ch. 29 (1982) by Kenneth Harris. Describing himself in a letter to his brother Tom Attlee, 8 April 1956, shortly before being enrolled as a Knight of the Garter.

2 [Russian Communism is] the illegitimate child of Karl Marx and Catherine the Great.
Speech at Aarhus University, Denmark, 11 April 1956, quoted in *The Times* 12 April 1956

3 Democracy means government by discussion, but it is only effective if you can stop people talking.
Speech at Oxford, 14 June 1957, quoted in *The Times* 15 June 1957

Margaret Atwood
(b. 1939)
Canadian novelist, poet and critic

Described by MICHAEL ONDAATJE *as 'the quiet Mata Hari, the mysterious violent figure . . . who pits herself against the ordered, too-clean world like an arsonist', she has been influenced by feminism and science fiction in her novels, which include* The Handmaid's Tale *(1986) and* The Blind Assassin *(2001).*

1 Everyone thinks writers must know more about the inside of the human head, but that is wrong. They know less, that's why they write. Trying to find out what everyone else takes for granted.
Dancing Girls, 'Lives of the Poets' (1977)

2 The beginning of Canadian cultural nationalism was not 'Am I really that oppressed?' but 'Am I really that boring?'
Interview with JOYCE CAROL OATES (1978), repr. in *Conversations*, 'Dancing On the Edge Of the Precipice' (ed. Earl G. Ingersoll, 1990)

3 We yearned for the future. How did we learn it, that talent for insatiability?
The Handmaid's Tale, ch. 1 (1986)

4 As all historians know, the past is a great darkness, and filled with echoes. Voices may reach us from it; but what they say to us is imbued with the obscurity of the matrix out of which they come; and try as we may, we cannot always decipher them precisely in the clearer light of our day.
Ibid., 'Historical Note'

5 All fathers . . . are invisible in daytime; daytime is ruled by mothers. But fathers come out at night. Darkness brings home the fathers, with their real, unspeakable power. There is more to them than meets the eye.
Cat's Eye, ch. 31 (1989)

John Aubrey
(1626–97)
English antiquary and biographer

He distinguished himself by his discovery and survey of the site of Avebury (1660–70), and is remembered for his detailed biographies of prominent Englishmen, including some of the leading figures of his day, not published until 1813.

1 How these curiosities would be quite forgot, did not such idle fellows as I am put them down.
Brief Lives, 'Venetia Digby' (written from 1667)

2 He [THOMAS HOBBES] had read much, if one considers his long life; but his contemplation was much more than his reading. He was wont to say that if he had read as much as other men he should have known no more than other men.
Ibid., 'Thomas Hobbes'

3 His [JOHN MILTON's] complexion exceeding fair – he was so fair that they called him the lady of Christ's College.
Ibid., 'John Milton'

4 Sir Walter, being strangely surprised and put out of his countenance at so great a table, gives his son a damned blow over the face. His son, as rude as he was, would not strike his father, but strikes over the face the gentleman that sat next to him and said 'Box about: 'twill come to my father anon.'
Ibid., 'Sir Walter Raleigh'

W. H. Auden
(1907–73)
Anglo-American poet

Wystan Hugh Auden. A member of the movement of left-wing literati during the 1930s, he was, according to PERCY WYND-HAM LEWIS, *'all ice and woodenfaced acrobatics'. He estab-lished his reputation with* Look Stranger! *(1936) and* Spain *(1937) before emigrating to the USA in 1939. He also wrote plays, libretti and literary criticism.*

1 Let us honour if we can
The vertical man,
Though we value none
But the horizontal one.
Poems, Epigraph (1930)

2 Harrow the house of the dead; look shining at
New styles of architecture, a change of heart.
'Sir, No Man's Enemy', publ. ibid.

3 Private faces in public places
Are wiser and nicer
Than public faces in private places.
The Orators, Epigraph (1932)

4 This is the Night Mail crossing the border,
Bringing the cheque and the postal order,
Letters for the rich, letters for the poor,
The shop at the corner, the girl next door.
Pulling up Beattock, a steady climb:
The gradient's against her, but she's on time.
Past cotton-grass and moorland border,
Shovelling white steam over her shoulder.
Night Mail, sect. 1 (1936). Opening lines of poem written as a commentary for a Post Office film.

5 And none will hear the postman's knock
Without a quickening of the heart.
For who can bear to feel himself forgotten?
Ibid. Concluding lines.

6 And make us as Newton was, who in his garden
    watching
The apple falling towards England, became aware
Between himself and her of an eternal tie.
'O Love, the Interest Itself', publ. in *Look, Stranger!* (1936). *Falling Towards England* was the title of the second volume of CLIVE JAMES's 'unreliable memoirs' (1985).

7 A shilling life will give you all the facts.
Title and first line of poem, ibid.

8 The desires of the heart are as crooked as
    corkscrews,
Not to be born is the best for man.
'Death's Echo', publ. in *Spain* (1937). The second line echoes SOPHOCLES 11.

9 To-morrow for the young the poets exploding
    like bombs,
The walks by the lake, the weeks of perfect
    communion;
To-morrow the bicycle races

Through the suburbs on summer evenings. But
  to-day the struggle.
'Spain', st. 23, ibid.

10 The stars are dead. The animals will not look.
We are left alone with our day, and the time is
  short, and
History to the defeated
May say Alas but cannot help nor pardon.
'Spain', st. 26, ibid.

11 'I'll love you, dear, I'll love you
Till China and Africa meet
And the river jumps over the mountain
And the salmon sing in the street,

'I'll love you till the ocean
Is folded and hung up to dry
And the seven stars go squawking
Like geese about the sky.'
'As I Walked Out One Evening', publ. in *Another Time* (1940)

12 'O plunge your hands in water,
Plunge them in up to the wrist;
Stare, stare in the basin
And wonder what you've missed.

'The glacier knocks in the cupboard,
The desert sighs in the bed,
And the crack in the tea-cup opens
A lane to the land of the dead.'
'As I Walked Out One Evening', ibid.

13 When he laughed, respectable senators burst
  with laughter,
And when he cried the little children died in the
  streets.
'Epitaph on a Tyrant', ibid. The lines may have been inspired
by a description of William of Orange (WILLIAM III): see
JOHN LOTHROP MOTLEY 1.

14 He was my North, my South, my East and West,
My working week and my Sunday rest,
My noon, my midnight, my talk, my song;
I thought that love would last for ever: I was
  wrong.
'Funeral Blues', ibid. The poem was recited during the funeral
scene in the film *Four Weddings and A Funeral* (1994).

15 For one who lived among enemies so long:
If often he was wrong and at times absurd,
To us he is no more a person
Now but a whole climate of opinion.
'In Memory of Sigmund Freud', st. 17, ibid.

16 Mad Ireland hurt you into poetry.

Now Ireland has her madness and her weather
  still.
'In Memory of W. B. Yeats', pt 2, ibid.

17 For poetry makes nothing happen: it survives
In the valley of its saying where executives
Would never want to tamper.
'In Memory of W. B. Yeats', pt 2, ibid.

18 Earth, receive an honoured guest:
William Yeats is laid to rest.
Let the Irish vessel lie
Emptied of its poetry.
'In Memory of W. B. Yeats', pt 3, ibid.

19 In the nightmare of the dark
All the dogs of Europe bark,
And the living nations wait,
Each sequestered in its hate.
'In Memory of W. B. Yeats', pt 3, ibid.

20 Intellectual disgrace
Stares from every human face.
'In Memory of W. B. Yeats', pt 3, ibid.

21 Lay your sleeping head, my love,
Human on my faithless arm.
'Lay your sleeping head, my love', ibid. Opening lines.

22 But in my arms till break of day
Let the living creature lie,
Mortal, guilty, but to me
The entirely beautiful.
'Lay your sleeping head, my love', ibid.

23 About suffering they were never wrong,
The Old Masters: how well they understood
Its human position; how it takes place
While someone else is eating or opening a window
  or just walking dully along.
'Musée des Beaux Arts', ibid. Opening lines.

24 I and the public know
What all schoolchildren learn,
Those to whom evil is done
Do evil in return.
'September 1, 1939', st. 2, ibid.

25 We must love one another or die.
'September 1, 1939', st. 8, ibid. Auden later repudiated the line,
insisting that it be altered for a 1955 anthology to 'We must
love one another and die'. He referred to the poem as 'the
most dishonest poem I have ever written'.

26 Blessed Cecilia, appear in visions
To all musicians, appear and inspire:
Translated Daughter, come down and startle

Composing mortals with immortal fire.
'Anthem for St Cecilia's Day', pt. 1, publ. in *New Year Letter* (in USA *The Double Man*) (1941)

27 To the man-in-the-street, who, I'm sorry to say,
Is a keen observer of life,
The word 'Intellectual' suggests straight away
A man who's untrue to his wife.
'New Year Letter', note to l. 1277, ibid.

28 At Dirty Dick's and Sloppy Joe's
We drank our liquor straight,
Some went upstairs with Margery,
And some, alas, with Kate.
'The Sea and the Mirror', pt 2, 'Master and Boatswain', publ. in *For the Time Being* (1944)

29 Thou shalt not sit
With statisticians nor commit
A social science.
'Under Which Lyre', st. 27, written 1946, publ. in *Nones* (1951)

30 Criticism should be a casual conversation.
Notebook entry, November 16, 1946, publ. in *The Table Talk of W.H. Auden* (comp. Alan Ansen, ed. Nicholas Jenkins, 1990)

31 Sob, heavy world,
Sob as you spin
Mantled in mist, remote from the happy.
'The Dirge', publ. in *The Age of Anxiety* (1947)

32 The detective must be either the official representative of the ethical or the exceptional individual who is in a state of grace.
'The Guilty Vicarage' (1948), repr. in *The Dyer's Hand*, pt 3 (1962)

33 Routine, in an intelligent man, is a sign of ambition.
'The Life of That-There Poet', publ. in the *New Yorker* 26 April 1958

34 What reverence is rightly paid
To a Divinity so odd
He lets the Adam whom he made
Perform the Acts of God?
'Friday's Child', publ. in *Homage to Clio* (1960)

35 It is a sad fact about our culture that a poet can earn much more money writing or talking about his art than he can by practising it.
The Dyer's Hand, Foreword (1962). Opening words.

36 Some books are undeservedly forgotten; none are undeservedly remembered.
Ibid., pt 1, 'Reading'

37 No poet or novelist wishes he were the only one who ever lived, but most of them wish they were the only one alive, and quite a number fondly believe their wish has been granted.
Ibid., pt 1, 'Writing'

38 It takes little talent to see clearly what lies under one's nose, a good deal of it to know in which direction to point that organ.
Ibid., pt 1, 'Writing'

39 Fame often makes a writer vain, but seldom makes him proud.
Ibid., pt 1, 'Writing'

40 When I find myself in the company of scientists, I feel like a shabby curate who has strayed by mistake into a drawing room full of dukes.
Ibid., pt 2, 'The Poet & the City'. Auden had specialized in science at Oxford University before switching to English.

41 A man has his distinctive personal scent which his wife, his children and his dog can recognize. A crowd has a generalized stink. The public is odourless.
Ibid., pt 2, 'The Poet & the City'

42 Between friends differences in taste or opinion are irritating in direct proportion to their triviality.
Ibid., pt 3, 'Hic et Ille', sect. D

43 Among those whom I like or admire, I can find no common denominator, but among those whom I love, I can: all of them make me laugh.
Ibid., pt 7, 'Notes on the Comic'

44 A verbal art like poetry is reflective; it stops to think. Music is immediate, it goes on to become.
Ibid., pt 8, 'Notes on Music and Opera'

45 God bless the U.S.A., so large,
So friendly, and so rich.
'On the Circuit', publ. in *About the House* (1965). Concluding lines of poem.

46 Some thirty inches from my nose
The frontier of my Person goes,
And all the untilled air between
Is private pagus or demesne.
Stranger, unless with bedroom eyes
I beckon you to fraternize,
Beware of rudely crossing it:
I have no gun, but I can spit.
'Prologue: the Birth of Architecture: Postscript', ibid.

47 Healing,
Papa would tell me,
'is not a science,

but the intuitive art
of wooing Nature.'

'The Art of Healing', written 1969, publ. in *Collected Poems* (1976)

48 Of course, Behaviourism 'works'. So does torture. Give me a no-nonsense, down-to-earth behaviourist, a few drugs, and simple electrical appliances, and in six months I will have him reciting the Athanasian Creed in public.

A Certain World, 'Behaviourism' (1970)

49 All sin tends to be addictive, and the terminal point of addiction is what is called damnation.

Ibid., 'Hell'

50 Proper names are poetry in the raw. Like all poetry they are untranslatable.

Ibid., 'Names, Proper'

51 As a poet there is only one political duty, and that is to defend one's language against corruption. When it is corrupted, people lose faith in what they hear and this leads to violence.

Quoted in the *Observer* 31 October 1971

52 You will be a poet because you will always be humiliated.

Quoted by STEPHEN SPENDER in journal entry, 11 April 1979, publ. in his *Journals 1939–1983* (1985). Spender was reminiscing on his first meeting with Auden at Oxford. In his memoir *World Within World* (1951), Spender quoted Auden: 'Art is born of humiliation.' See also EDWARD DAHLBERG 4.

53 My face looks like a wedding-cake left out in the rain.

Quoted in *W.H. Auden*, pt 2, ch. 6 (1981) by Humphrey Carpenter

Saint Augustine
(354–430)
Christian theologian

As recounted in his autobiographical Confessions, *he led a dissolute life until his conversion to Christianity at the age of thirty-two. Ordained as a priest, he became Bishop of Hippo, in North Africa, 396–410. He defended Christianity against heretical beliefs in* City of God *(413–26), among other writings. See also* SAINT CYPRIAN 1.

1 I went to Carthage, where I found myself in the midst of a hissing cauldron of lust.

Confessions, bk 3, ch. 1 (written 397–8, transl. R. S. Pine-Coffin, 1961). Also translated 'To Carthage then I came . . .', as recalled in T. S. ELIOT's *The Waste Land*, pt 3 (1922).

2 Give me chastity and continency – but not yet.

Ibid., bk 8, ch. 7. The prayers of the young Augustine, recalled in later life.

3 *Tolle lege, tolle lege.*
[Take it and read, take it and read.]

Ibid., bk 8, ch. 12. The refrain of a child overheard by Augustine, which, he believed, 'could only be a divine command to open my book of Scripture and read the first passage on which my eyes should fall.' The passage was *Romans* 13:13–14 (see BIBLE, NEW TESTAMENT: ROMANS 40).

4 I have learnt to love you late, Beauty at once so ancient and so new! [*Pulchritudo tam antiqua et tam nova.*]

Ibid., bk 10, ch. 27

5 You command me to be continent. Give me the grace to do as you command, and command me to do what you will!

Ibid., bk 10, ch. 29

6 Total abstinence is easier to many than perfect moderation.

On the Good of Marriage, ch. 21 (401)

7 Two cities have been formed by two loves: the earthly by the love of self, even to the contempt of God; the heavenly by the love of God, even to the contempt of self.

City of God, bk 14, ch. 28 (413–26)

8 *Audi partem alteram.*
[Hear the other side.]

De Duabus Animabus contra Manicheos, ch. 14, sect. 2

9 *Roma locuta est. Causa finita est.*
[Rome has spoken. The case is concluded.]

Attributed. The words are a misquotation of a passage from a sermon preached at Carthage in September 417 (*Sermones*, no. 131, Benedictine edn), referring to a synodical dispute: 'The dispute is finished. Would that the error might be finished sometime as well.' The summary has often been cited as an argument for the dogma of papal infallibility, though Augustine's writings did not support this.

Augustus
(63 BC–14 AD)
Roman emperor

Gaius Julius Caesar Octavianus. The adopted son of JULIUS CAESAR, *he defeated Mark Antony at Actium in 31 BC and took the title Augustus ('venerable'). The 'Augustan Age' over which he presided as emperor was marked by general prosperity, literary achievements and the consolidation of Rome's provinces.*

1 Quintilius Varus, give me back my legions!

Quoted in *Lives of the Caesars*, 'Augustus', sect. 23 (2nd century AD, transl. ROBERT GRAVES) by Suetonius. This was reportedly the emperor's constant lament (while beating his head against the door), referring to the disastrous loss of three legions under Varus in Germany (9 AD).

2 *Festina lente.*

[More haste less speed.]

Quoted by Suetonius, ibid., 'Augustus', sect. 25. Greek proverb often repeated by Augustus, also translated 'Make haste slowly'.

3 I found Rome built of bricks; I leave her clothed in marble.

Quoted by Suetonius, ibid., 'Augustus', sect. 28

Daw Aung San Suu Kyi
(b. 1945)
Burmese opposition leader

The daughter of General Aung San, the architect of Burmese independence, she co-founded in 1988 the National League for Democracy. Although her party won the 1990 elections, she was held under house arrest by the military junta.

1 It may take time and it won't be easy. But what's ten years?

Sunday Telegraph 4 April 1999. Referring to her persecution by the government of Myanmar (Burma), and her hopes to re-establish democracy there.

Marcus Aurelius
(121–80)
Roman emperor and philosopher

Marcus Aurelius Antoninus. His time as emperor (161–80) was beset with internal disturbances and constant wars. The twelve books of Meditations, *written in Greek, revealed his Stoic philosophy, and were published after his death.*

1 This being of mine, all there is of it, consists of flesh, breath, and the ruling part.

Meditations, bk 2, sect. 2

2 Perform every action as though it were your last.

Ibid., bk 2, sect. 2

3 Remember how often you have postponed minding your interest, and let slip those opportunities the gods have given you. It is now high time to consider what sort of world you are part of, and from what kind of governor of it you are descended; that you have a set period assigned you to act in, and unless you improve it to brighten and compose your thoughts, it will quickly run off with you, and be lost beyond recovery.

Ibid., bk 2, sect. 4

4 Life is but a campaign, or course of travels, and after-fame is oblivion.

Ibid., bk 2, sect. 17

5 Never throw away your legs, to stand upon crutches.

Ibid., bk 3, sect. 5

6 The world is all transformation, and life is opinion.

Ibid., bk 4, sect. 3

7 To understand the true quality of people, you must look into their minds, and examine their pursuits and aversions.

Ibid., bk 4, sect. 38

8 Time is like a rapid river, and a rushing torrent of all that comes and passes. A thing is no sooner well come, but it is past.

Ibid., bk 4, sect. 43

9 Whatever happens is as common and well known as a rose in the spring, or an apple in the autumn.

Ibid., bk 4, sect. 44

10 A man that has done a kindness never proclaims it, but does another as soon as he can, just like a vine that bears again the next season.

Ibid., bk 5, sect. 6

11 There is nothing happens to any person but what was in his power to go through with.

Ibid., bk 5, sect. 18

12 Life is but a sort of exhalation of the blood, and a little breathing in of air.

Ibid., bk 6, sect. 15

13 That which is not good for the bee-hive cannot be good for the bees.

Ibid., bk 6, sect. 54

14 It is the privilege of human nature to love those that disoblige us.

Ibid., bk 7, sect. 22

15 Happiness has very few wants.

Ibid., bk 7, sect. 67

16 To retract or mend a fault at the admonition of a friend in no way hurts your liberty, for it is still your own activity which . . . makes you see mistakes.

Ibid., bk 8, sect. 16

17 Do not despise death, but accept it willingly; look upon it as part of the product of nature, and one of those things which providence has been pleased to order.
Ibid., bk 9, sect. 3

18 Omissions no less than commissions are often part of injustice.
Ibid., bk 9, sect. 5

19 Let it be your constant method to look into the design of people's actions, and see what they would be at, as often as it is practicable; and to make this custom the more significant, practise it first upon yourself.
Ibid., bk 10 sect. 37

Jane Austen
(1775–1817)
English novelist

During a brief writing career, she produced six of the greatest novels in the English language. Her sheltered life as an unmarried rector's daughter did not hinder her sharply satirical observations on the manners of the wealthy middle classes and provincial high society of her day. She wrote of herself: 'I think I may boast myself to be, with all possible vanity, the most unlearned and uninformed female who ever dared to be an authoress.'

1 What dreadful hot weather we have! It keeps me in a continual state of inelegance.
Letter to her sister Cassandra, 18 September 1796, publ. in *Jane Austen's Letters* (ed. R. W. Chapman, 1952)

2 I do not want people to be very agreeable, as it saves me the trouble of liking them a great deal.
Letter to her sister Cassandra, 24 December 1798, ibid.

3 A person and face, of strong, natural, sterling insignificance, though adorned in the first style of fashion.
Sense and Sensibility, vol. 2, ch. 11 (1811)

4 It is not time or opportunity that is to determine intimacy; it is disposition alone. Seven years would be insufficient to make some people acquainted with each other, and seven days are more than enough for others.
Marianne, ibid., vol. 2, ch. 12

5 It is a truth universally acknowledged, that a single man in possession of a good fortune must be in want of a wife.
Pride and Prejudice, ch. 1 (1813). Opening words of book.

6 You mistake me, my dear. I have a high respect for your nerves. They are my old friends. I have heard you mention them with consideration these twenty years at least.
Ibid., ch. 1. Mr Bennet answers Mrs Bennet's accusation that her husband has 'no compassion on my poor nerves'.

7 She was a woman of mean understanding, little information, and uncertain temper. When she was discontented, she fancied herself nervous. The business of her life was to get her daughters married; its solace was visiting and news.
Ibid., ch. 1. Referring to Mrs Bennet.

8 A person who can write a long letter with ease, cannot write ill.
Miss Bingley, ibid., ch. 10

9 Nothing is more deceitful than the appearance of humility. It is often only carelessness of opinion, and sometimes an indirect boast.
Mr Darcy, ibid., ch. 10

10 Nobody can tell what I suffer! But it is always so. Those who do not complain are never pitied.
Mrs Bennet, ibid., ch. 20

11 Unhappy as the event must be ... we may draw from it this useful lesson: that loss of virtue in a female is irretrievable; that one false step involves her in endless ruin; that her reputation is no less brittle than it is beautiful; and that she cannot be too much guarded in her behaviour towards the undeserving of the other sex.
Mary Bennet, ibid., ch. 47. On the elopement of Lydia Bennet with Wickham.

12 For what do we live, but to make sport for our neighbours, and laugh at them in our turn?
Mr Bennet, ibid., ch. 57

13 An engaged woman is always more agreeable than a disengaged. She is satisfied with herself. Her cares are over, and she feels that she may exert all her powers of pleasing without suspicion. All is safe with a lady engaged; no harm can be done.
Mansfield Park, ch. 5 (1814). Spoken by Henry Crawford.

14 We do not look in great cities for our best morality.
Edmund Bertram, ibid., ch. 9

15 It will, I believe, be everywhere found, that as the clergy are, or are not what they ought to be, so are the rest of the nation.
Edmund Bertram, ibid., ch. 9

16 It is indolence ... indolence and love of ease;

a want of all laudable ambition, of taste for good company, or of inclination to take the trouble of being agreeable, which make men clergymen. A clergyman has nothing to do but be slovenly and selfish; read the newspaper, watch the weather, and quarrel with his wife. His curate does all the work and the business of his own life is to dine.
Mary Crawford, ibid., ch. 11

17 Where an opinion is general, it is usually correct.
Mary Crawford, ibid., ch. 11

18 Shakespeare one gets acquainted with without knowing how. It is a part of an Englishman's constitution. His thoughts and beauties are so spread abroad that one touches them everywhere; one is intimate with him by instinct.
Henry Crawford, ibid., ch. 34

19 Let other pens dwell on guilt and misery. I quit such odious subjects as soon as I can, impatient to restore everybody, not greatly in fault themselves, to tolerable comfort, and to have done with all the rest.
Ibid., ch. 48

20 A real, honest, old-fashioned boarding-school, where a reasonable amount of accomplishments were sold at a reasonable price, and where girls might be sent to be out of the way, and scramble themselves into a little education, without any danger of coming back prodigies.
Emma, ch. 3 (1816). Referring to Mrs Goddard's school.

21 One half of the world cannot understand the pleasures of the other.
Ibid., ch. 9

22 The truth is, that in London it is always a sickly season. Nobody is healthy in London, nobody can be.
Mr Woodhouse, ibid., ch. 12

23 With men he can be rational and unaffected, but when he has ladies to please, every feature works.
John Knightley, ibid., ch. 13. Describing Mr Elton.

24 Human nature is so well disposed towards those who are in interesting situations, that a young person, who either marries or dies, is sure of being kindly spoken of.
Ibid., ch. 22

25 There is safety in reserve, but no attraction. One cannot love a reserved person.
Frank Churchill, ibid., ch. 24. Emma replies, 'Not till the

reserve ceases towards one's self; and then the attraction may be the greater.'

26 It may be possible to do without dancing entirely. Instances have been known of young people passing many, many months successively without being at any ball of any description, and no material injury accrue either to body or mind; but when a beginning is made – when the felicities of rapid motion have once been, though slightly, felt – it must be a very heavy set that does not ask for more.
Ibid., ch. 29

27 The post-office had a great charm at one period of our lives. When you have lived to my age, you will begin to think letters are never worth going through the rain for.
John Knightley, ibid., ch. 34

28 Business, you know, may bring money, but friendship hardly ever does.
John Knightley, ibid., ch. 34

29 One has not great hopes from Birmingham. I always say there is something direful in the sound.
Mrs Elton, ibid., ch. 36

30 What should I do with your strong, manly, spirited sketches, full of variety and glow? – How could I possibly join them on to the little bit (two inches wide) of ivory on which I work with so fine a brush, as produces little effect after much labour?
Letter to her nephew James Edward Austen, 16 December 1816, publ. in Jane Austen's Letters (ed. R. W. Chapman, 1952)

31 Single women have a dreadful propensity for being poor – which is one very strong argument in favour of matrimony.
Letter, 13 March 1817, ibid.

32 Although our productions have afforded more extensive and unaffected pleasure than those of any other literary corporation in the world, no species of composition has been so much decried ... 'And what are you reading, Miss –?' 'Oh! it is only a novel!' replies the young lady; while she lays down her book with affected indifference, or momentary shame. 'It is only Cecilia, or Camilla, or Belinda'; or, in short, only some work in which the greatest powers of the mind are displayed, in which the most thorough knowledge of human nature, the happiest delineation of its varieties, the liveliest effusions of

wit and humour, are conveyed to the world in the best chosen language.
Northanger Abbey, ch. 5 (1818)

33 Oh! who can ever be tired of Bath?
Catherine Morland, ibid., ch. 10

34 History, real solemn history, I cannot be interested in . . . I read it a little as a duty; but it tells me nothing that does not either vex or weary me. The quarrels of popes and kings, with wars and pestilences in every page; the men all so good for nothing, and hardly any women at all, it is very tiresome.
Catherine Morland, ibid., ch. 14

35 A woman, especially, if she have the misfortune of knowing anything, should conceal it as well as she can.
Ibid., ch. 14

36 My idea of good company . . . is the company of clever, well-informed people who have a great deal of conversation; that is what I call good company.
Persuasion, ch. 16 (1818). Spoken by Anne. Mr Elliot replies: 'that is not good company; that is the best.'

37 One does not love a place the less for having suffered in it, unless it has been all suffering, nothing but suffering.
Anne, ibid., ch. 20

38 All the privilege I claim for my own sex (it is not a very enviable one, you need not covet it) is that of loving longest, when existence or when hope is gone.
Anne, ibid., ch. 23

Paul Auster
(b. 1947)
US author

The New York Trilogy (1987) established him as an experimental writer on the themes of modern city life. Other works include Leviathan *(1992) and* Timbuktu *(1999).*

1 We construct a narrative for ourselves, and that's the thread that we follow from one day to the next. People who disintegrate as personalities are the ones who lose that thread.
Interview in *The Sunday Times* 16 April 1989

2 Our lives don't really belong to us, you see – they belong to the world, and in spite of our efforts to make sense of it, the world is a place beyond our understanding.
Interview 1989/90, publ. in *The Red Notebook* (1995)

Alfred Austin
(1835–1913)
English poet

He inherited money which enabled him to become a man of letters, publishing twenty volumes of poetry 1871–1908. He was appointed poet laureate in 1896, to general mockery: see ANONYMOUS 24.

1 Show me your garden and I shall tell you what you are.
The Garden That I Love (1905)

Tex Avery
(1907–80)
US animator

Originally Frederick Bean. He created such cartoon characters as Bugs Bunny and Daffy Duck, which appeared on television and in the films King Size Canary *(1947) and* Bad Luck Blackie *(1949), among other classics.*

1 Th-th-th-th-that's all, folks!
Looney Tunes/Merrie Melodies (Warner Brothers cartoons, 1935–65). The sign-off line by Porky Pig (created and voiced by Mel Blanc from 1938) was also used to close various other Warner Brothers cartoons, and was affectionately reprised at the end of the 1972 film *What's Up Doc?* (see below). Porky Pig first appeared in the *Looney Tunes* cartoon *I Haven't Got A Hat* (1935).

2 Eh, what's up Doc?
Ibid. Bugs Bunny's running gag. The rabbit made his first appearance in a Warner Brothers Looney Tunes cartoon in 1937, voiced by Mel Blanc. In 1940 Tex Avery gave him his name (after West Coast mobster Bugsy Siegel) and his famous catchphrase, and directed the first official Bugs Bunny cartoon, *A Wild Hare* (1940). 'What's Up Doc?' was also the title of Peter Bogdanovich's screwball comedy with Barbra Streisand and Ryan O'Neal (1972).

Reverend W. Awdry
(1911–97)
British writer of children's books

Wilbert Vere Awdry, a country clergyman 1936–65, wrote the Thomas the Tank Engine *series of stories for children, the first of which appeared in 1945, and which have since gathered a huge following.*

1 You've a lot to learn about trucks, little Thomas. They are silly things and must be kept in their place. After pushing them about here for a few weeks

you'll know almost as much about them as Edward. Then you'll be a Really Useful Engine.
Thomas the Tank Engine, 'Thomas and the Trucks' (1946). Spoken by the Fat Controller.

Hoyt Axton
(1938–99)
US rock musician

A composer of songs for Glen Campbell, RINGO STARR *and the group Steppenwolf, among many others, he also recorded his own material in the 1970s.*

1 God damn the pusher man.
'The Pusher' (song) on the album *Steppenwolf* (1968) by Steppenwolf. The anti-drug anthem, which featured in Dennis Hopper's film *Easy Rider* (1969), was banned on the radio.

(Sir) Alan Ayckbourn
(b. 1939)
British playwright

Prolific and master farceur of what he terms 'inspired nonsense', he depicts middle-class suburban life with acid wit in such plays as The Norman Conquests *(1975).*

1 The only thing for old age is a brave face, a good tailor and comfortable shoes.
Table Manners, Act 2, Sc. 1 (first of *The Norman Conquests* trilogy, 1975). Spoken by Reg.

2 Where's the romance gone? Destroyed by cynics and liberationalists . . . Forget the flowers, the chocolates, the soft word – rather woo her with a self-defence manual in one hand and a family planning leaflet in the other.
Round and Round the Garden, Act 1, Sc. 1 (third of *The Norman Conquests* trilogy, 1975). Spoken by Norman.

3 This place, you tell them you're interested in the arts, you get messages of sympathy.
Chorus of Disapproval, Act 2 (1986). Spoken by Dafydd.

(Sir) A. J. Ayer
(1910–89)
British philosopher

Alfred Jules Ayer. His first book Language, Truth and Logic *(1936), which expounded the theory of logical positivism as associated with the Vienna Circle, was iconoclastic and influential. He was Wykeham Professor of Logic at Oxford (1959–78).*

1 The traditional disputes of philosophers are, for the most part, as unwarranted as they are unfruitful.
Language, Truth and Logic, ch. 1 (1936). Opening sentence of book.

2 If science can be said to be blind without philosophy, it is true also that philosophy is virtually empty without science.
Ibid., ch. 8

3 No moral system can rest solely on authority.
Humanist Outlook, Introduction (1968). In a later essay, Ayer wrote, 'To say that authority, whether secular or religious, supplies no ground for morality is not to deny the obvious fact that it supplies a sanction.' ('The Meaning of Life', 1988)

4 There never comes a point where a theory can be said to be true. The most that one can claim for any theory is that it has shared the successes of all its rivals and that it has passed at least one test which they have failed.
Philosophy in the Twentieth Century, ch. 4 (1982)

5 It seems that I have spent my entire time trying to make life more rational and that it was all wasted effort.
Quoted in the *Observer* 17 August 1986

Dan Aykroyd
(b. 1950)
Canadian actor and comic

Born Daniel Agraluscarsacra. He developed his writing and performing skills on the TV show Saturday Night Live *before co-starring in* The Blues Brothers *(1980) and the* Ghostbusters *films (1984, 1989 and 1998).*

1 They're not going to catch us. We're on a mission from God.
Elwood (Dan Aykroyd), in *The Blues Brothers* (film, 1980, screenplay by John Landis and Dan Aykroyd, directed by John Landis)

Pam Ayres
(b. 1947)
British writer of humorous verse

Composer of comic verse since the 1970s, she also writes books for children, and performs monologues.

1 I'm glad tomorrow's Thursday,
'Cause with a bit of luck,
As far as I remember,
That's the day they pass the buck.
'The Bunny Poem', publ. in *Some of Me Poetry* (1976)

2 Oh, I wish I'd looked after me teeth,
And spotted the perils beneath,

All the toffees I chewed,
And the sweet sticky food,
Oh, I wish I'd looked after me teeth.
'Oh, I wish I'd looked after me teeth', ibid.

3 I see the Time and Motion clock,
Is sayin' nearly noon,
I 'spec me squirt of water,
Will come flyin' at me soon,
And then me spray of pellets,
Will nearly break me leg,
And I'll bite the wire nettin'
And lay one more bloody egg.
'The Battery Hen', ibid.

4 Medicinal discovery,
It moves in mighty leaps,
It leapt straight past the common cold
And gave it us for keeps.
'Oh no, I got a cold', ibid.

W. E. Aytoun
(1813–65)
Scottish poet

William Edmonstoune Aytoun. He contributed to Blackwood's Magazine *and wrote parodies of contemporary poets, but was most popular for his* Lays of the Scottish Cavaliers *(1849) and* Ballads of Scotland *(1858).*

1 News of battle! News of battle!
Hark. 'Tis ringing down the street
And the archways and the pavement
Bear the clang of hurrying feet.
News of battle. Who has brought it?
'Edinburgh After Flodden', publ. in *Lays of the Scottish Cavaliers* (1849)

2 The deep, unutterable woe
Which none save exiles feel.
'The Island of the Scots', ibid.

B

Lauren Bacall
(b. 1924)
US screen actress

Billed as 'slinky, sultry and sensational', she co-starred with her husband HUMPHREY BOGART *in a succession of hit films including* The Big Sleep *(1946) and* Key Largo *(1948).*

1 Anybody got a match?
To Have and Have Not (film, 1944, screenplay by Jules Furthman and WILLIAM FAULKNER, based on ERNEST HEMINGWAY's 1937 novel of the same name, directed by Howard Hawks). Lauren Bacall's screen-debut line, in the role of Marie ('Slim') Browning. The film is remembered for the on- and off-screen romance between Bogart and Bacall which resulted in marriage the following year.

2 You know you don't have to act with me, Steve. You don't have to say anything, and you don't have to do anything. Not a thing. Oh, maybe just whistle. You know how to whistle, don't you, Steve? You just put your lips together, and blow.
Ibid. Marie addresses Harry ('Steve') Morgan (Humphrey Bogart).

Gaston Bachelard
(1884–1962)
French scientist, philosopher and literary theorist

He belonged to the 'criticism of science' school, believing that reverie and imagination were as important as observation and analysis for the understanding of reality. Major works include The Psychoanalysis of Fire *(1938) and* The Right to Dream *(1970).*

1 Man is a creation of desire, not a creation of need.
The Psychoanalysis of Fire, ch. 2, 'Fire and Reverie' (1938)

2 If I were asked to name the chief benefit of the house, I should say: the house shelters daydreaming, the house protects the dreamer, the house allows one to dream in peace.
The Poetics of Space, ch. 1, 'The House' (1958)

3 Reverie is not a mind vacuum. It is rather the gift of an hour which knows the plenitude of the soul.
The Poetics of Reverie, ch. 2, sect. 3 (1960)

4 The words of the world want to make sentences.
Ibid., ch. 5, sect. 4

Francis Bacon
(1561–1626)
English philosopher, essayist and statesman

Baron Verulam, later Viscount St Albans. He became Lord Chancellor in 1618, but was forced to resign in 1621 after charges of corruption. His main works include Essays *(1597–1625),* The Advancement of Learning *(1604) and* Novum Organum *(1620). 'If parts allure thee, think how Bacon shined,/ The wisest, brightest, meanest of mankind,'* ALEXANDER POPE *wrote. See also* ARISTOTLE 16, LORD MACAULAY 25, IZAAK WALTON 15.

1 I have as vast contemplative ends, as I have moderate civil ends; for I have taken all knowledge to be my province.
Letter 'To My Lord Treasurer Burghley', 1592, publ. in *The Letters and Life of Francis Bacon*, vol. 1 (ed. J. Spedding, 1861)

2 For also knowledge itself is a power.
Meditationes Sacrae, 'Of Heresies' (1597; *Religious Meditations*)

3 What is truth? said jesting Pilate; and would not stay for an answer.
Essays, 'Of Truth' (1597–1625). Opening words of essay, alluding to a passage in the Bible in which Pilate questions Jesus before the crucifixion (see BIBLE, NEW TESTAMENT: JOHN 61). In the Apocryphal Gospel of Nicodemus 3:10–14, the conversation is continued: 'Jesus said, Truth is from heaven. Pilate said, Therefore truth is not on earth. Jesus saith to Pilate, Believe that truth is on earth among those who, when they have the power of judgment, are governed by truth and form right judgment.'

4 The inquiry of truth, which is the love-making, or wooing of it, the knowledge of truth, which is the presence of it, and the belief of truth, which is the enjoying of it, is the sovereign good of human nature.
Ibid., 'Of Truth'

5 It is a pleasure to stand upon the shore, and to see ships tossed upon the sea: a pleasure to stand in the window of a castle, and to see a battle and the adventures thereof below: but no pleasure is comparable to standing upon the vantage ground of truth.
Ibid., 'Of Truth'. Bacon's free translation of Lucretius: see LUCRETIUS 3.

6 It is as natural to die as to be born; and to a little infant, perhaps, the one is as painful as the other.
Ibid., 'Of Death'

7 All colours will agree in the dark.
Ibid., 'Of Unity in Religion'

8 Revenge is a kind of wild justice, which the more a man's nature runs to, the more ought law to weed it out.
Ibid., 'Of Revenge'

9 A man that studieth revenge keeps his own wounds green.
Ibid., 'Of Revenge'

10 Prosperity is the blessing of the Old Testament; adversity is the blessing of the New.
Ibid., 'Of Adversity'

11 The pencil of the Holy Ghost hath laboured more in describing the afflictions of Job than the felicities of Solomon.
Ibid., 'Of Adversity'

12 Prosperity doth best discover vice, but adversity doth best discover virtue.
Ibid., 'Of Adversity'

13 Nakedness is uncomely, as well in mind as body, and it addeth no small reverence to men's manners and actions if they be not altogether open . . . Therefore set it down: That a habit of secrecy is both politic and moral.
Ibid., 'Of Simulation and Dissimulation'. See also WILLIAM HAZLITT 34.

14 He that hath wife and children hath given hostages to fortune; for they are impediments to great enterprises, either of virtue or mischief. Certainly the best works, and of greatest merit for the public, have proceeded from the unmarried, or childless men.
Ibid., 'Of Marriage and Single Life'

15 Wives are young men's mistresses, companions for middle age, and old men's nurses.
Ibid., 'Of Marriage and Single Life'

16 The rising unto place is laborious, and by pains men come to greater pains; and it is sometimes base, and by indignities men come to dignities. The standing is slippery, and the regress is either a downfall, or at least an eclipse, which is a melancholy thing.
Ibid., 'Of Great Place'

17 It is a strange desire to seek power and to lose liberty, or to seek power over others and to lose power over a man's self.
Ibid., 'Of Great Place'

18 Mahomet made the people believe that he would call a hill to him, and from the top of it offer up his prayers for the observers of his law. The people

assembled; Mahomet called the hill to come to him again and again; and when the hill stood still, he was never a whit abashed, but said, 'If the hill will not come to Mahomet, Mahomet will go to the hill.'
Ibid., 'Of Boldness'. Referring to a tradition relating to Muhammad. 'So,' Bacon, explained, 'these men, when they have promised great matters, and failed most shamefully (yet if they have the perfection of boldness), they will but slight it over, and make a turn, and no more ado.' This is the first appearance of the proverb in English.

19 If a man be gracious and courteous to strangers, it shows he is a citizen of the world, and that his heart is no island cut off from other lands, but a continent that joins to them.
Ibid., 'Of Goodness, and Goodness of Nature'

20 Money is like muck, not good except it be spread.
Ibid., 'Of Seditions and Troubles'

21 I had rather believe all the fables in the legend, and the Talmud, and the Alcoran, than that this universal frame is without a mind; and, therefore, God never wrought miracle to convince atheism, because his ordinary works convince it.
Ibid., 'Of Atheism'

22 A little philosophy inclineth man's mind to atheism, but depth in philosophy bringeth men's minds about to religion.
Ibid., 'Of Atheism'

23 There is a superstition in avoiding superstition, when men think to do best if they go furthest from the superstition formerly received.
Ibid., 'Of Superstition'

24 Travel, in the younger sort, is a part of education, in the elder, a part of experience. He that travelleth into a country before he hath some entrance into the language, goeth to school, and not to travel.
Ibid., 'Of Travel'. Opening words of essay.

25 As the births of living creatures, at first, are ill-shapen: so are all *Innovations*, which are the births of time.
Ibid., 'Of Innovations'. In his *Annotations to Bacon* (c. 1798), WILLIAM BLAKE irascibly commented on this passage: 'What a cursed fool is this, Ill Shapen! Are infants or small plants ill shapen because they are not yet come to their maturity? What a contemptible fool is this Bacon!'

26 He that will not apply new remedies, must expect new evils: for time is the greatest innovator: and if time, of course, alter things to the worse, and

wisdom and counsel shall not alter them to the better, what shall be the end?
Ibid., 'Of Innovations'

27 For a crowd is not company; and faces are but a gallery of pictures; and talk but a tinkling cymbal, where there is no love.
Ibid., 'Of Friendship'. See BIBLE, NEW TESTAMENT: 1 CORIN-THIANS 29.

28 There is as much difference between the counsel that a friend giveth, and that a man giveth himself, as there is between the counsel of a friend and of a flatterer. For there is no such flatterer as is a man's self.
Ibid., 'Of Friendship'

29 Cure the disease and kill the patient.
Ibid., 'Of Friendship'

30 Neither will it be that a people overlaid with taxes should ever become valiant and martial.
Ibid., 'Of the True Greatness of Kingdoms and Estates'

31 There is nothing makes a man suspect much, more than to know little.
Ibid., 'Of Suspicion'

32 Discretion of speech is more than eloquence, and to speak agreeably to him with whom we deal is more than to speak in good words, or in good order.
Ibid., 'Of Discourse'

33 Men of age object too much, consult too long, adventure too little, repent too soon, and seldom drive business home to the full period, but content themselves with a mediocrity of success.
Ibid., 'Of Youth and Age'

34 Houses are built to live in, and not to look on: therefore let use be preferred before uniformity, except where both may be had.
Ibid., 'Of Building'

35 God Almighty first planted a garden; and, indeed, it is the purest of human pleasures; it is the greatest refreshment to the spirits of man.
Ibid., 'Of Gardens'

36 Read not to contradict and confute; nor to believe and take for granted; nor to find talk and discourse; but to weigh and consider.
Ibid., 'Of Studies'

37 Some books are to be tasted, others to be swallowed, and some few to be chewed and digested.
Ibid., 'Of Studies'

38 Reading maketh a full man; conference a ready man; and writing an exact man.
Ibid., 'Of Studies'

39 Histories make men wise; poets witty; the mathematics subtle; natural philosophy deep; moral grave; logic and rhetoric able to contend.
Ibid., 'Of Studies'

40 I do not believe that any man fears to be dead, but only the stroke of death.
Ibid., 'An Essay on Death'

41 If a man will begin with certainties, he shall end in doubts; but if he will be content to begin with doubts, he shall end in certainties.
The Advancement of Learning, bk 1, ch. 5, sect. 8 (1605)

42 Poesy ... was ever thought to have some participation of divineness, because it doth raise and erect the mind, by submitting the shows of things to the desires of the mind; whereas reason doth buckle and bow the mind unto the nature of things.
Ibid., bk 2, ch. 4, sect. 2

43 They are ill discoverers that think there is no land, when they can see nothing but sea.
Ibid., bk 2, ch. 7, sect. 5

44 Words are the tokens current and accepted for conceits, as moneys are for values.
Ibid., bk 2, ch. 16, sect. 3

45 But men must know, that in this theatre of man's life it is reserved only for God and angels to be lookers on.
Ibid., bk 2, ch. 20, sect. 8

46 We are much beholden to Machiavel and others, that write what men do, and not what they ought to do.
Ibid., bk 2, ch. 21, sect. 9

47 For it is not possible to join serpentine wisdom with the columbine innocency, except men know exactly all the conditions of the serpent: his baseness and going upon his belly, his volubility and lubricity, his envy and sting, and the rest; that is, all forms and natures of evil: for without this, virtue lieth open and unfenced.
Ibid., bk 2, ch. 21, sect. 9. Bacon was referring to Jesus's words to the Apostles: see BIBLE, NEW TESTAMENT: MATTHEW 74.

48 All good moral philosophy is but a handmaid to religion.
Ibid., bk 2, ch. 22, sect. 14

49 It is as hard and severe a thing to be a true politician as to be truly moral.
Ibid., bk 2, ch. 23, sect. 13

50 As for the philosophers, they make imaginary laws for imaginary commonwealths; and their discourses are as the stars, which give little light, because they are so high.
Ibid., bk 2, ch. 23, sect. 49

51 For rightly is truth called the daughter of time, not of authority.
Novum Organum, bk 1, aph. 84 (1620)

52 It is well to mark the force, virtue and consequences of discoveries, and these occur nowhere more manifestly than in ... the arts ... of printing, of gunpowder and the mariner's compass. For these three have changed the face and condition of things all over the world ... so that no government, no sect, no star seems to have exercised greater power and influence over human affairs than these mechanical discoveries.
Ibid., bk 1, aph. 129

53 The empire of man over things is founded on the arts and sciences alone, for nature is only governed by obeying her.
Ibid., bk 1, aph. 129

54 Truth will sooner come out from error than from confusion.
Ibid., bk 2, aph. 20

55 Age appears to be best in four things: old wood best to burn; old wine to drink; old friends to trust; and old authors to read.
Apophthegms New and Old, no. 97 (1624). Quoting Alonso of Aragon.

56 For my name and memory I leave it to men's charitable speeches, and to foreign nations, and the next ages.
Last will, 19 December 1625, publ. in Works of Francis Bacon, vol. 3 (1765)

57 But thus you see we maintain a trade, not for gold, silver, or jewels; nor for silks; nor for spices; nor any other commodity of matter; but only for God's first creature, which was light: to have light, I say, of the growth of all parts of the world.
New Atlantis, sect. 14 (1627)

Roger Bacon
(c. 1220–c. 1292)
English philosopher and scientist

Studying and teaching in Oxford and Paris, he became a Franciscan friar in 1257, and embarked on an encyclopedia of the sciences in 1266, producing the Opus Maius, Opus Minus *and* Opus Tertium. *He later spent a period in prison, though was dubbed the 'Doctor Admirabilis' on his death.*

1 If in other sciences we should arrive at certainty without doubt and truth without error, it behoves us to place the foundations of knowledge in mathematics.
Opus Majus, pt 1, ch. 4 (1267)

(Sir) Robert Baden-Powell
(1857–1941)
English soldier and founder of the Boy Scouts

First Baron Baden-Powell. He served with the British army in Africa, where he won distinction for his 217-day defence of Mafeking against a Boer army (1899–1900). He founded the Boy Scout movement in England in 1907, and, with his sister, the Girl Guides in 1910.

1 The scouts' motto is founded on my initials, it is: BE PREPARED, which means, you are always to be in a state of readiness in mind and body to do your DUTY.
Scouting for Boys, pt 1 (1908)

George F. Baer
(1842–1914)
US railroad magnate

As President of the Reading Railroad and a leading business tycoon, he came to prominence during the 1902 miners' strike in West Virginia and Pennsylvania, when he infuriated President THEODORE ROOSEVELT *by his refusal to negotiate.*

1 The rights and interests of the laboring man will be protected and cared for, not by the labor agitators, but by the Christian men to whom God in His infinite wisdom has given control of the property interests of the country.
Open letter to the Press, August–October 1902, during the Pennsylvania miners' strike

Joan Baez
(b. 1941)
US singer

Prominent in the American folk revival of the early 1960s, she was also associated with the protest movement, performing frequently at rallies and festivals. Her albums include Any Day Now *(1968) and* Diamonds and Rust *(1975).*

1 The only thing that's been a worse flop than the organization of nonviolence has been the organization of violence.
Daybreak, 'What Would You Do If?' (1970)

2 I've never had a humble opinion in my life. If you're going to have one, why bother to be humble about it?
International Herald Tribune 2 December 1992

Walter Bagehot
(1826–77)
English economist and critic

Trained as a barrister, he became joint editor of The National Review *with* R. H. HUTTON *in 1855, then edited* The Economist *(1860–77). He wrote literary and biographical studies, and the influential* The English Constitution *(1867) and* Physics and Politics *(1872).*

1 The habit of common and continuous speech is a symptom of mental deficiency. It proceeds from not knowing what is going on in other people's minds.
'Hartley Coleridge' (1852), repr. in *Literary Studies*, vol. 1 (1878)

2 A schoolmaster should have an atmosphere of awe, and walk wonderingly, as if he was amazed at being himself.
'Hartley Coleridge', ibid.

3 A constitutional statesman is in general a man of common opinions and uncommon abilities.
'The Character of Sir Robert Peel' (1856), repr. in *Estimates of Some Englishmen and Scotchmen* (1858)

4 Poverty is an anomaly to rich people. It is very difficult to make out why people who want dinner do not ring the bell.
'The Waverley Novels' (1858), repr. in *Literary Studies*, vol. 1 (1878)

5 A slight daily unconscious luxury is hardly ever wanting to the dwellers in civilisation; like the gentle air of a genial climate, it is a perpetual minute enjoyment.
'The Waverley Novels', ibid.

6 The most intellectual of men are moved quite as much by the circumstances which they are used to as by their own will. The active voluntary part of a man is very small, and if it were not economised by a sleepy kind of habit, its results would be null.
The English Constitution, no. 1 ('The Cabinet') (1867)

7 Under a Presidential government, a nation has, except at the electing moment, no influence; it has not the ballot-box before it; its virtue is gone, and it must wait till its instant of despotism again returns.
Ibid., no. 1

8 The best reason why monarchy is a strong government, is, that it is an intelligible government. The mass of mankind understand it, and they hardly anywhere in the world understand any other.
Ibid., no. 2 ('The Monarchy')

9 It is often said that men are ruled by their imaginations; but it would be truer to say they are governed by the weakness of their imaginations.
Ibid., no. 2

10 A *family* on the throne is an interesting idea ... It brings down the pride of sovereignty to the level of petty life.
Ibid., no. 2

11 The women – one half the human race at least – care fifty times more for a marriage than a ministry.
Ibid., no. 2

12 A princely marriage is the brilliant edition of a universal fact, and, as such, it rivets mankind.
Ibid., no. 2

13 Royalty is a government in which the attention of the nation is concentrated on one person doing interesting actions. A republic is a government in which that attention is divided between many, who are all doing uninteresting actions. Accordingly, so long as the human heart is strong and the human reason weak, royalty will be strong because it appeals to diffused feeling, and republics weak because they appeal to the understanding.
Ibid., no. 2

14 Its mystery is its life. We must not let in daylight upon magic.
Ibid., no. 3 ('The Monarchy [continued]'). Referring to the British monarchy.

15 The Sovereign has, under a constitutional monarchy such as ours, three rights – the right to be consulted, the right to encourage, the right to warn. And a king of great sense and sagacity would want no others.
Ibid., no. 3. ('The Monarchy [continued]'). Bagehot construed the formula, 'I do not oppose, it is my duty not to oppose; but observe that I warn,' as a notional statement by a British constitutional sovereign.

16 A severe though not unfriendly critic of our institutions said that 'the *cure* for admiring the House of Lords was to go and look at it.'
Ibid., no. 4 ('The House of Lords')

17 An ambassador is not simply an agent; he is also a spectacle.
Ibid., no. 4

18 A bureaucracy is sure to think that its duty is to augment official power, official business, or official members, rather than to leave free the energies of mankind; it overdoes the quantity of government, as well as impairs its quality. The truth is, that a skilled bureaucracy ... is, though it boasts of an appearance of science, quite inconsistent with the true principles of the art of business.
Ibid., no. 4 ('On Changes of Ministry')

19 It has been said, not truly, but with a possible approximation to truth, 'that in 1802 every hereditary monarch was insane'.
Ibid., no.46 ('Its Supposed Checks and Balances')

20 Where great questions end, little parties begin.
Ibid., no. 8 ('The Prerequisites of Cabinet Government')

21 'Public opinion', nowadays, is the opinion of the bald-headed man at the back of the omnibus.
Ibid., no. 8. See LORD BOWEN 1.

22 What impresses men is not mind, but the results of mind.
Ibid., no. 8

23 The apparent rulers of the English nation are like the most imposing personages of a splendid procession: it is by them the mob are influenced; it is they whom the spectators cheer. The real rulers are secreted in second-rate carriages; no one cares for them or asks about them, but they are obeyed implicitly and unconsciously by reason of the splendour of those who eclipsed and preceded them.
Ibid., no. 8

24 Our law very often reminds one of those outskirts of cities where you cannot for a long time tell how the streets come to wind about in so capricious and serpent-like a manner. At last it strikes you that they grew up, house by house, on the devious tracks of the old green lanes; and if you follow on to the existing fields, you may often find the change half complete.
Ibid., no. 9 ('History and the Effects of That History')

25 In every particular state of the world, those nations which are strongest tend to prevail over

the others; and in certain marked peculiarities the strongest tend to be the best.
Physics and Politics, ch. 2, sect. 1 (1872)

26 History is strewn with the wrecks of nations which have gained a little progressiveness at the cost of a great deal of hard manliness, and have thus prepared themselves for destruction as soon as the movements of the world gave a chance for it.
Ibid., ch. 2, sect. 2

27 The best history is but like the art of Rembrandt; it casts a vivid light on certain selected causes, on those which were best and greatest; it leaves all the rest in shadow and unseen.
Ibid., ch. 2, sect. 2

28 In early times every sort of advantage tends to become a military advantage; such is the best way, then, to keep it alive. But the Jewish advantage never did so; beginning in religion, contrary to a thousand analogies, it remained religious. *For* that we care for them; *from* that have issued endless consequences.
Ibid., ch. 2, sect. 2

29 So long as war is the main business of nations, temporary despotism – despotism during the campaign – is indispensable.
Ibid., ch. 2, sect. 3

30 Progress would not have been the rarity it is if the early food had not been the late poison.
Ibid., ch. 2, sect. 3

31 War both needs and generates certain virtues; not the highest, but what may be called the preliminary virtues, as valour, veracity, the spirit of obedience, the habit of discipline. Any of these, and of others like them, when possessed by a nation, and no matter how generated, will give them a military advantage, and make them more likely to *stay* in the race of nations.
Ibid., ch. 2, sect. 3

32 The whole history of civilisation is strewn with creeds and institutions which were invaluable at first, and deadly afterwards.
Ibid., ch. 2, sect. 3

33 One of the greatest pains to human nature is the pain of a new idea.
Ibid., ch. 5, sect. 1

34 The most melancholy of human reflections, perhaps, is that, on the whole, it is a question whether the benevolence of mankind does most good or harm.
Ibid., ch. 5, sect. 2

Enid Bagnold
(1889–1981)
British novelist and playwright

She adapted several of her own novels into plays, the best known of which, the horseracing tale National Velvet *(1935), was also filmed in 1944. Her last play,* The Chalk Garden *(1955), was her most successful.*

1 Judges don't age. Time decorates them.
The Chalk Garden, Act 2 (1955). Spoken by the Judge.

2 The theatre is a gross art, built in sweeps and over-emphasis. Compromise is its second name.
Autobiography, ch. 3 (1969)

3 Sex – the great inequality, the great miscalculator, the great Irritator.
Ibid., ch. 6

David Bailey
(b. 1938)
British photographer

The 'personification of the photographer as pop hero', in the words of GEORGE MELLY, *he specialized in fashion pictures, making an icon of the model Jean Shrimpton.*

1 All that Swinging Sixties nonsense, we all thought it was passé at the time.
Interview in *The Face* December 1984

2 It takes a lot of imagination to be a good photographer. You need less imagination to be a painter, because you can invent things. But in photography everything is so ordinary; it takes a lot of looking before you learn to see the ordinary.
Ibid.

3 I never cared for fashion much, amusing little seams and witty little pleats: it was the girls I liked.
Independent 5 November 1990

Philip James Bailey
(1816–1902)
English poet

According to W. E. AYTOUN, *he was the father of the 'Spasmodic' school of poetry, characterized by overblown feeling and extravagant language. His fame rests principally on* Festus, *a blank verse epic based on the Faust legend, first published in 1839 and frequently revised.*

1 America, thou half-brother of the world;
With something good and bad of every land.
Festus, 'The Surface' (1839–89). Spoken by Festus.

(Dame) Beryl Bainbridge
(b. 1934)
British author

Her richly ironic comedies, which she calls 'horror stories told like everyday gossip', include The Dressmaker *(1973) and* An Awfully Big Adventure *(1989). She has been the author most often shortlisted for the Booker Prize without having won it.*

1 It never ceases to puzzle me that, while men and women's bodies fit jigsaw tight in an altogether miraculous way their minds remain wretchedly unaligned.
Evans, in *The Birthday Boys*, 'Petty Officer (Taff) Evans, June 1910' (1991)

2 When passion is mutual, there is always the danger of the fire burning to ashes.
Master Georgie, plate 4, 'August 1854: Concert Party at Varna' (1998)

3 Women are programmed to love completely, and men are programmed to spread it around. We are fools to think it's any different.
Sunday Times 1 November 1998

4 The older one becomes the quicker the present fades into sepia and the past looms up in glorious technicolour.
Observer 27 December 1998

5 You've got to learn to speak properly. You don't take people seriously who speak badly.
Sunday Times 7 March 1999. Bainbridge renounced her own Liverpool accent.

James Baker
(b. 1930)
US politician

A shrewd political manager for the Republican party, he was REAGAN's *Chief of Staff (1981–5) and successfully oversaw* GEORGE BUSH's *presidential campaign. He was appointed Secretary of State in 1989 and in 1992 once again served as White House Chief of Staff.*

1 Who could not be moved by the sight of that poor, demoralized rabble, outwitted, outflanked, out-maneuvered by the US military? Yet, given time, I think the press will bounce back.
Quoted in the *Guardian* 26 March 1991. Referring to the media pack during the Gulf War.

Kenneth Baker
(b. 1934)
British politician

Baron Baker of Dorking. Elected Conservative MP in 1968, he rose to become Secretary of State for the Environment (1985–6) and Education (1986–9). He was Chairman of the Conservative Party (1989–90) and Home Secretary (1990–2).

1 He has conferred on the practice of vacillation the aura of statesmanship.
Daily Telegraph 11 October 1989. Referring to SDP leader David Owen.

Nicholson Baker
(b. 1957)
US author

He said of his books, 'I got rid of the plot', and his off-beat fiction typically eschews action and character as well, in favour of detailed observation and dialogue.

1 Shoes are the first adult machines we are given to master.
The Mezzanine, ch. 2 (1988)

2 In my case, adulthood itself was not an advance, although it was a useful waymark.
Ibid., ch. 3

3 Footnotes are the finer-suckered surfaces that allow tentacular paragraphs to hold fast to the wider reality of the library.
Ibid., ch. 14, footnote

Russell Baker
(b. 1925)
US journalist

Known for his 'Observer' column in the New York Times, *he has satirized politicians, bureaucrats and the excesses of America. Time summarized him as 'funny, but full of the pain and absurdity of the age'.*

1 Inanimate objects are classified scientifically into three major categories – those that don't work, those that break down and those that get lost.
New York Times 18 June 1968

2 In America nothing dies easier than tradition.
New York Times 14 May 1991

Mikhail Bakunin
(1814–76)
Russian political theorist

As one of the guiding lights of the anarchist movement, he was exiled to Siberia in 1855 following his participation in the German revolutionary movement, but escaped, arriving in England in 1861. He was expelled from the Communist Party in 1872.

1 The passion for destruction is also a creative passion.
'Die Reaktion in Deutschland' ('Reaction in Germany') (1842), repr. in *Selected Writings* (ed. Arthur Lehning, 1973). These final words in Bakunin's article, which was written under the pseudonym Jules Elysard, quickly became adopted as an anarchist slogan.

2 The State . . . is the most flagrant negation, the most cynical and complete negation of humanity.
Federalism, Socialism and Anti-Theologism (1868)

3 Idealism is the despot of thought, just as politics is the despot of will.
A Circular Letter to My Friends in Italy (1871)

4 Does it follow that I reject all authority? Perish the thought. In the matter of boots, I defer to the authority of the bootmaker.
God and the State (1871)

5 I am truly free only when all human beings, men and women, are equally free. The freedom of other men, far from negating or limiting my freedom, is, on the contrary, its necessary premise and confirmation.
Ibid.

6 The first revolt is against the supreme tyranny of theology, of the phantom of God. As long as we have a master in heaven, we will be slaves on earth.
Ibid.

7 Freedom, morality, and the human dignity of the individual consists precisely in this; that he does good not because he is forced to do so, but because he freely conceives it, wants it, and loves it.
Ibid.

8 To revolt is a natural tendency of life. Even a worm turns against the foot that crushes it. In general, the vitality and relative dignity of an animal can be measured by the intensity of its instinct to revolt.
The International and Karl Marx (1872)

James Baldwin
(1924–87)
US author

Brought up in poverty in Harlem where most of his works are set, he later lived in Paris. His autobiographical first novel, Go Tell It On the Mountain *(1953), and others such as* Giovanni's Room *(1956) and* Another Country *(1962) were bleak depictions of sexual and racial relationships.*

1 The American ideal, after all, is that everyone should be as much alike as possible.
'The Harlem Ghetto' (1948) , repr. in *Notes of a Native Son*, pt 2 (1955)

2 It is only in his music, which Americans are able to admire because a protective sentimentality limits their understanding of it, that the Negro in America has been able to tell his story.
'Many Thousands Gone' (1951), ibid.

3 Any writer, I suppose, feels that the world into which he was born is nothing less than a conspiracy against the cultivation of his talent.
Notes of a Native Son, 'Autobiographical Notes' (1955)

4 Children have never been very good at listening to their elders, but they have never failed to imitate them. They must, they have no other models.
'Fifth Avenue, Uptown: a letter from Harlem' (1960), repr. in *Nobody Knows My Name* (1961)

5 American history is longer, larger, more various, more beautiful, and more terrible than anything anyone has ever said about it.
'A Talk To Teachers' (1963), repr. in *The Price of the Ticket* (1985)

6 It comes as a great shock around the age of five, six or seven to discover that the flag to which you have pledged allegiance, along with everybody else, has not pledged allegiance to you. It comes as a great shock to see Gary Cooper killing off the Indians and, although you are rooting for Gary Cooper, that the Indians are you.
Speech to Cambridge Union, Cambridge University, 17 February 1965, quoted in the *New York Times* 7 March 1965

7 If they take you in the morning, they will be coming for us that night.
'Open Letter to my Sister, Angela Davis', publ. in the *New York Review of Books* 7 January 1971

8 You know, it's not the world that was my oppressor, because what the world does to you, if

the world does it to you long enough and effectively enough, you begin to do to yourself.
In conversation with NIKKI GIOVANNI, London, 4 November 1971, publ. in *A Dialogue* (1973)

9 He may be a very nice man. But I haven't got the time to figure that out. All I know is, he's got a uniform and a gun and I have to relate to him that way. That's the only way to relate to him because one of us may have to die.
Ibid. Referring to the police.

10 Whereas England may have been doomed to civilize the world, no power under heaven can civilize England.
The Devil Finds Work, ch. 2 (1976)

11 The condition that is now called gay was then called queer. The operative word was *faggot* and, later, pussy, but those epithets really had nothing to do with the question of sexual preference: You were being told simply that you had no balls.
'Freaks and the American Ideal of Manhood', publ. in *The Price of the Ticket*, 'Here Be Dragons' (1985)

Stanley Baldwin
(1867–1947)
British statesman

First Earl of Bewdley. Serving three times as Conservative Prime Minister (1923–4, 1924–9 and 1935–7) he opposed the rearmament of Britain against the rise of HITLER, *which precipitated his resignation. Lord Beaverbrook called him a 'well-meaning man of indifferent judgement'. See also* WINSTON CHURCHILL 47 *and* RUDYARD KIPLING 81.

1 A platitude is simply a truth repeated until people get tired of hearing it.
Speech to House of Commons, 29 May 1924, quoted in the *Observer* 1 June 1924

2 I hate elections, but you have got to have them; they are medicine.
Quoted in the *Observer* 11 October 1931

3 I think it is well also for the man in the street to realize that there is no power on earth that can protect him from being bombed. Whatever people may tell him, the bomber will always get through. The only defence is in offence, which means that you have to kill more women and children more quickly than the enemy if you want to save yourselves.
Speech to House of Commons, 10 November 1932, publ. in *The Penguin Book of Twentieth-Century Speeches* (ed. Brian MacArthur, 1999). Baldwin's ambiguous speech strengthened the public mood against rearmament.

4 Let us never forget this – since the day of the air the old frontiers are gone. When you think of the defence of England you no longer think of the chalk cliffs of Dover; you think of the Rhine. That is where our frontier lies.
Speech to House of Commons, 30 July 1934, publ. in *Hansard*

5 Do not run up your nose dead against the Pope or the NUM!
Quoted in *The Art of Memory*, 'Iain Macleod' (1982) by Lord [R. A. B.] Butler

A. J. Balfour
(1848–1930)
British politician and prime minister

Arthur James Balfour, first Earl of Balfour. He entered parliament as a Conservative MP in 1874. While Prime Minister (1902–5) he initiated the entente cordiale with France, and as Foreign Secretary (1916–19) he was responsible for the Balfour Declaration (see below).

1 His Majesty's Government view with favour the establishment in Palestine of a national home for the Jewish people, and will use their best endeavours to facilitate the achievement of this object, it being clearly understood that nothing shall be done which may prejudice the civil and religious rights of existing non-Jewish communities in Palestine, or the rights and political status enjoyed by Jews in any other country.
Letter to Lord Rothschild, 2 November 1917, publ. in *The Middle East Conflict: Notes and Documents (1915–1967)*. The document, which became known as the 'Balfour Declaration', represented a commitment of British support for a Jewish national home in Palestine, though the original wording suggested by Chaim Weizmann, on behalf of the Political Committee of the Zionist Organization (which Rothschild represented), was that the government should recognize Palestine as 'the national home of the Jewish people'.

2 The General Strike has taught the working classes more in four days than years of talking could have done.
Speech, 7 May 1926, quoted in the *Observer* 14 November 1926. Five days after the speech, the Trades Unions Congress was forced to call off the General Strike, which, though bringing the country to a virtual standstill, was unable to prevent volunteers from manning essential services.

3 Biography should be written by an acute enemy.
Quoted in the *Observer* 30 January 1927

Hugo Ball
(1886–1927)
German Dadaist poet

Along with RICHARD HUELSENBECK *he was in 1916 the co-founder of Dada in Zurich, where he performed the first 'sound poem' dressed in cardboard tubes and a cape.*

1 We should burn all libraries and allow to remain only that which everyone knows by heart. A beautiful age of the legend would then begin.
Journal entry, 9 January 1917, publ. in *Flight out of Time: A Dada Diary* (1927)

2 The symbolic view of things is a consequence of long absorption in images. Is sign language the real language of Paradise?
Journal entry, 8 April 1917, ibid.

John Ball
(d. 1381)
English priest and agitator

A renowned preacher, he was excommunicated in 1376 for his views on ecclesiastical poverty and social equality, and executed for his part in the Peasants' Revolt.

1 When Adam delved and Eve span,
Who was then the gentleman?
Attributed. Verse preached to rebels at Blackheath, outside London, 12 June 1381, during the Peasants' Revolt. The lines, which have been traced back to c. 1340, are said to have breathed 'a spirit fatal to the whole system of the Middle Ages' (*A Short History of the English People*, 1874, by J. R. Green).

J. G. Ballard
(b. 1930)
British author

James Graham Ballard. He typically portrays apocalyptic visions in his science fiction. His experimental novel Crash *(1973) was filmed in 1996, as was his more mainstream autobiographical novel* Empire of the Sun *(1984) in 1988.*

1 A car crash harnesses elements of eroticism, aggression, desire, speed, drama, kinaesthetic factors, the stylizing of motion, consumer goods, status – all these in one event. I myself see the car crash as a tremendous sexual event really: a liberation of human and machine libido (if there is such a thing).
Interview in *Penthouse* September 1970

2 Everything is becoming science fiction. From the margins of an almost invisible literature has sprung the intact reality of the 20th century.
'Fictions of Every Kind', publ. in *Books and Bookmen* February 1971. Ballard continued: 'Even the worst science fiction is better ... than the best conventional fiction. The future is a better key to the present than the past.'

3 The car as we know it is on the way out. To a large extent, I deplore its passing, for as a basically old-fashioned machine, it enshrines a basically old-fashioned idea: freedom. In terms of pollution, noise and human life, the price of that freedom may be high, but perhaps the car, by the very muddle and confusion it causes, may be holding back the remorseless spread of the regimented, electronic society.
'The Car, The Future', publ. in *Drive* Autumn 1971

4 Science and technology multiply around us. To an increasing extent they dictate the languages in which we speak and think. Either we use those languages, or we remain mute.
Crash, Introduction to French edn (1974)

5 A widespread taste for pornography means that nature is alerting us to some threat of extinction.
Myths of the Near Future, 'News from the Sun' (1982)

6 I would sum up my fear about the future in one word: *boring*. And that's my one fear: that everything has happened; nothing exciting or new or interesting is ever going to happen again ... the future is just going to be a vast, conforming *suburb of the soul*.
Interview, 30 October 1982, publ. in *Re/Search* no. 8/9 1984

7 'Responsible' TV is far more dangerous than the most mindless entertainment. At its worst, American TV merely trivializes the already trivial, while British TV consistently trivializes the serious.
The Atrocity Exhibition: With Author's Annotations, 'Love and Napalm: Export USA', annotation (1993, original text publ. 1970, rev. 1990)

Whitney Balliet
(b. 1926)
US author

He was a long-serving jazz critic for the New Yorker *and published collections of pieces on jazz musicians.*

1 The Sound of Surprise.
Title of book on jazz (1959)

2 A critic is a bundle of biases held loosely together by a sense of taste.
Dinosaurs in the Morning, Introductory note (1962)

Honoré de Balzac
(1799–1850)
French novelist

A highly prolific writer, he achieved his first great success with Les Chouans (1829), part of an ambitious series of works entitled La Comédie humaine, a historical and social portrait of France.

1 Hatred is a tonic, it makes one live, it inspires vengeance; but pity kills, it makes our weakness weaker.
La Peau de chagrin, ch. 1 (1831; *The Wild Ass's Skin*)

2 Despotism accomplishes great things illegally; liberty doesn't even go to the trouble of accomplishing small things legally.
Ibid., ch. 3

3 Man is neither good nor bad; he is born with instincts and abilities.
La Comédie humaine, vol. 1, Foreword (1842; *The Human Comedy*)

4 Manners are the hypocrisy of a nation.
Journal entry 1911, quoted by ANDRÉ GIDE in his *Journals 1889–1949* (ed. Justin O'Brien, 1951)

Lester Bangs
(1948–82)
US rock journalist

He was the first to popularize the term 'heavy metal' and his magazine Creem became the model for punk-rock and heavy-metal fanzines. From 1976 he worked in New York, contributing to Village Voice.

1 The first mistake of Art is to assume that it's serious.
Who Put the Bomp Winter/Spring 1971

2 The ultimate sin of any performer is contempt for the audience.
Village Voice 29 August 1977

3 At its best New Wave/punk represents a fundamental and age-old Utopian dream: that if you give people the license to be as outrageous as they want in absolutely any fashion they can dream up, *they'll be creative about it,* and do something good besides.
New Musical Express 24 December 1977

4 I think that if most guys in America could some-how get their fave-rave poster girl in bed and have total license to do whatever they wanted with this legendary body for one afternoon, at least 75 percent of the guys in the country would elect to beat her up.
Quoted in *Sound Effects: Youth, Leisure and the Politics of Rock,* ch. 10 (1979) by Simon Frith

Tallulah Bankhead
(1903–68)
US actress

Notorious for her extravagant personality, 'more of an act than an actress' in the words of one critic, she appeared in plays, on radio and in films, most famously in HITCHCOCK's Lifeboat *(1944). See also LILLIAN HELLMAN 6.*

1 There is less in this than meets the eye.
Quoted in *Shouts and Murmurs,* ch. 4 (1922) by ALEXANDER WOOLLCOTT. Remark to Woollcott, referring to a revival of MAETERLINCK's play *Aglavaine and Selysette.*

2 I'm as pure as the driven slush.
Quoted in the *Saturday Evening Post* 12 April 1947

3 Let's not quibble! I'm the foe of moderation, the champion of excess. If I may lift a line from a die-hard whose identity is lost in the shuffle, 'I'd rather be strongly wrong than weakly right.'
Tallulah, ch. 4 (1952)

4 Cocaine habit-forming? Of course not. I ought to know. I've been using it for years.
Ibid., ch. 4. This was, she said, the riposte she used to shock people when taking throat-lozenges; apart from on one occasion, she claimed never to have used cocaine 'except medicinally'.

5 I've tried several varieties of sex. The conventional position makes me claustrophobic and the others give me a stiff neck or lockjaw.
Quoted in *Miss Tallulah Bankhead* (1972) by Lee Israel

Nancy Banks-Smith
British columnist

She is a TV reviewer for the Guardian *of many years' standing, known for her acute critiques and wry digressions.*

1 In my experience, if you have to keep the lavatory door shut by extending your left leg, it's modern architecture.
Guardian 20 February 1979

2 Anthropology is the science which tells us that

people are the same the whole world over – except when they are different.
Quoted in the *Guardian* 21 July 1988

[Imamu] Amiri Baraka
(b. 1934)
US poet and playwright

Known as LeRoi Jones until 1967, when he converted to Islam. A confrontational writer of verse collections including The Dead Lecturer *(1964) and plays such as* Dutchman *(1964), he has been active in black arts and community organizations from the late 1960s.*

1 Lately, I've become accustomed to the way
The ground opens up and envelops me
Each time I go out to walk the dog.
'Preface to a Twenty Volume Suicide Note', publ. in *Preface to a Twenty Volume Suicide Note* (1961). Opening lines of poem.

2 A man is either free or he is not. There cannot be any apprenticeship for freedom.
'Tokenism', publ. in *Kulchur* spring 1962

3 You can't steal nothing from a white man, he's already stole it, he owes you anything you want, even his life. All the stores will open if you will say the magic words. The magic words are: Up against the wall motherfucker this is a stick-up!
'Black People!' (1967), repr. in *Black Magic* (1969). The poem/manifesto was read out by the judge at Baraka's trial for illegal arms possesion in Newark, July 1967, with the obscenities omitted. Baraka was involved with the anarchist group Up Against the Wall Motherfucker.

4 When I die, the consciousness I carry I will to black people. May they pick me apart and take the useful parts, the sweet meat of my feelings. And leave the bitter bullshit rotten white parts alone.
'leroy', publ. in *Black Magic* (1969)

5 James Brown and Frank Sinatra are two different quantities in the universe. They represent two different experiences of the world.
Interview in *The Americans*, 'Is Democracy a White Man's Word?' (1970) by DAVID FROST

Anna Laetitia Barbauld
(1743–1825)
English poet and editor

Her writings for children include Hymns in Prose for Children *(1781). She also published poetry and essays, and edited and annotated* British Novelists *(1810).*

1 Beware, lest in the worm you crush
A brother's soul you find.
'The Mouse's Petition', st. 9, publ. in *Poems* (1773)

2 When, one by one, those ties are torn,
And friend from friend is snatched forlorn,
When man is left alone to mourn,
Ah then, how easy 'tis to die!
'A Thought on Death', st. 3, written 1814, first publ. 1821, repr. in *The Poems of Anna Laetitia Barbauld* (ed. W. McCarthy and E. Kraft, 1994)

Daniel Barenboim
(b. 1942)
Argentinian-born Israeli pianist, conductor

He was made Director of the Chicago Symphony Orchestra in 1991 and the Berlin Staatsoper in 1992, and Chief Conductor for Life of the Staatskapelle, Berlin in 2000. He was married to the cellist Jacqueline du Pré.

1 Every great work of art has two faces, one toward its own time and one toward the future, toward eternity.
International Herald Tribune 20 January 1989

Pat Barker
(b. 1943)
British novelist

She is best known for her First World War trilogy consisting of Regeneration *(1991),* The Eye in the Door *(1993) and* The Ghost Road *(1995).*

1 Even the living were only ghosts in the making.
Lieutenant Billy Prior, in *The Ghost Road*, pt 1, ch. 3 (1995)

Djuna Barnes
(1892–1982)
US author, poet and columnist

She produced influential works of Modernist fiction including Ladies Almanack *(1928), a satire of literary lesbians, and her masterpiece,* Nightwood *(1936). She was admired by* T. S. ELIOT, *who jibed: 'She's always pissing on the parade.'*

1 After all, it is not where one washes one's neck that counts but where one moistens one's throat.
'Greenwich Village As It Is' (1916), repr. in *Djuna Barnes's New York* (1989)

2 The heart of the jealous knows the best and most satisfying love, that of the other's bed, where the rival perfects the lover's imperfections.
Nightwood, ch. 5 (1936). Spoken by the Doctor.

Julian Barnes
(b. 1946)
British novelist

He won acclaim for Metroland *(1981), his first novel, and Flaubert's* Parrot *(1984), an ironic and witty tribute to his acknowledged influence Flaubert. Later works include* A History of the World in 10½ Chapters *(1989) and* Cross Channel *(1996), a collection of short stories.*

1 Why does the writing make us chase the writer? Why can't we leave well alone? Why aren't the books enough?
The narrator (Geoffrey Braithwaite), in *Flaubert's Parrot*, ch. 1 (1984)

2 I don't care much for coincidences. There's something spooky about them: you sense momentarily what it must be like to live in an ordered, God-run universe, with Himself looking over your shoulder and helpfully dragging coarse hints about a cosmic plan.
Ibid., ch. 5. The narrator adds: 'One way of legitimising coincidences, of course, is to call them ironies. That's what smart people do.'

3 The greatest patriotism is to tell your country when it is behaving dishonourably, foolishly, viciously.
Ibid., ch. 10

4 The writer must be universal in sympathy and an outcast by nature: only then can he see clearly.
Ibid., ch. 10

5 It's a sort of primitive law of survival – find someone worse off than yourself and beside them you will blossom.
Stuart, in *Talking it Over*, ch. 2 (1991)

6 And my conclusion was this: that as you go on living with someone, you slowly lose the power to make them happy, while your capacity to hurt them remains undiminished. And vice versa, of course.
Mme Wyatt, ibid., ch. 15

7 Love is only what people agree exists, what they agree to put a notional value on. Nowadays it's prized as a commodity by almost everyone. Only not by me. If you ask me, I think love is trading artificially high. One of these days the bottom is going to fall out of love.
Stuart, ibid., ch. 16

8 We have moved into an era when 'character' is a misleading concept. Character has been replaced by ego, and the exercise of authority as a reflection of character has been replaced by the psychopathic retention of power by all possible means and in mockery of all implausibilities.
Solinsky, in *Porcupine* (1992)

9 Women have traditionally accommodated themselves to men's needs. Men's needs being, of course, double. You put us on a pedestal in order to look up our skirts.
Martha, in *England, England*, pt 1, 'Others May Like' (1998)

William Barnes
(1801–86)
English clergyman and poet

His poems concentrate on domestic themes and his native Dorset, and include Hwomely Rhymes *(1859), written in local dialect, and* Poems of Rural Life in Common English *(1868).*

1 An' there vor me the apple tree
Do leän down low in Linden Lea.
'My Orcha'd in Linden Lea', publ. in *Hwomely Rhymes* (1859). The poem was set to music by Ralph Vaughan Williams in 1901.

Natalie Clifford Barney
(1876–1972)
US-born French author

As a wealthy heiress, she established a literary circle in her adopted home in Paris, where she lived from 1902, attracting such figures as EZRA POUND. *Her open lesbianism provoked controversy, but her publications were infrequent and had a limited circulation.*

1 Renouncement: the heroism of mediocrity.
Quoted in *Adam*, no. 299, 'Gods' (1962)

2 If we keep an open mind, too much is likely to fall into it.
Quoted ibid., 'Samples from Almost Illegible Notebooks'

3 To be one's own master is to be the slave of self.
Quoted ibid., 'Samples from Almost Illegible Notebooks'

4 Most virtue is a demand for greater seduction.
Quoted ibid., 'My Country 'tis of Thee'

5 How many inner resources one needs to tolerate a life of leisure without fatigue.
Quoted in *The Amazon of Letters*, ch. 10 (1976) by George Wickes

6 Fatalism is the lazy man's way of accepting the evitable.
Quoted ibid.

Phineas T. Barnum
(1810–91)
US showman

After managing a museum in New York, where he introduced 'freak shows', he established 'the greatest show on earth' in 1871, which included midgets and a menagerie of circus animals, with whom he toured America in a hundred-carriage train. See also ABRAHAM LINCOLN 33.

1 Every crowd has a silver lining.
Attributed

2 There's a sucker born every minute.
Attributed. Barnum doubted ever having uttered these words, though he conceded he may have said, 'The people like to be humbugged.' In A. H. Saxon's biography, *P.T. Barnum: The Legend and the Man* (1989), it is claimed that the phrase, 'There's a sucker born every minute, but none of them ever die', originated with a notorious con-man known as 'Paper Collar Joe' (real name Joseph Bessimer), and was later falsely ascribed to Barnum by show-biz rival Adam Forepaugh in a newspaper interview; Barnum never took pains to deny it, and even thanked Forepaugh for the free publicity.

(Sir) J. M. Barrie
(1860–1937)
British playwright

James Matthew Barrie. Described by MRS PATRICK CAMPBELL *as 'a little child whom the Gods have whispered to', he continually returned to the themes of childhood and disenchantment with the adult world. He achieved success with his plays* Quality Street *(1901) and* The Admirable Crichton *(1902), but is best remembered for* Peter Pan *(1904).*

1 In dinner talk it is perhaps allowable to fling any faggot rather than let the fire go out.
Tommy and Grizel, ch. 3 (1900)

2 I am not young enough to know everything.
The Admirable Crichton, Act 1 (performed 1902, publ. 1914). Spoken by Ernest.

3 His lordship may compel us to be equal upstairs, but there will never be equality in the servants' hall.
Crichton, ibid., Act 1

4 That is ever the way. 'Tis all jealousy to the bride and good wishes to the corpse.
Quality Street, Act 1 (1902). Spoken by Miss Susan.

5 When the first baby laughed for the first time, the laugh broke into a thousand pieces and they all went skipping about, and that was the beginning of fairies. And now when every new baby is born its first laugh becomes a fairy. So there ought to be one fairy for every boy or girl.
Peter Pan, Act 1 (performed 1904, published 1928). Spoken by Peter.

6 Every time a child says 'I don't believe in fairies' there is a fairy somewhere that falls down dead.
Peter, ibid., Act 1

7 To die will be an awfully big adventure.
Peter, ibid., Act 3. Closing words of act.

8 [Charm is] a sort of bloom on a woman. If you have it, you don't need to have anything else; and if you don't have it, it doesn't much matter what else you have.
What Every Woman Knows, Act 1 (performed 1908, publ. 1918). Spoken by Maggie Wylie.

9 There are few more impressive sights in the world than a Scotsman on the make.
David Wylie, ibid., Act 2

10 I've sometimes thought ... that the difference between us and the English is that the Scotch are hard in all other respects but soft with women, and the English are hard with women but soft in all other respects.
Maggie Wylie, ibid., Act 2

11 You've forgotten the grandest moral attribute of a Scotsman ... that he'll do nothing which might damage his career.
John Shand, ibid., Act 2

12 Every man who is high up likes to think he has done it all himself; and the wife smiles, and lets it go at that. It's our only joke. Every woman knows that.
Maggie Shand, ibid., Act 4

13 One's religion is whatever he is most interested in, and yours is Success.
The Twelve-Pound Look (1910). Kate to Sir Harry Sims.

14 Ambition – it is the last infirmity of noble minds.
Sir Harry Sims (quoting from his morning paper), ibid.

15 Someone said that God gave us memory so that we might have roses in December.
Rectorial address at St Andrew's University, 3 May 1922, publ. in *Courage* (1922)

16 Never ascribe to an opponent motives meaner than your own.
Ibid.

17 We are all failures – at least, all the best of us are.
Ibid.

18 You must have been warned against letting the golden hours slip by. Yes, but some of them are golden only because we let them slip.
Ibid.

Ethel Barrymore
(1879–1959)
Anglo-American actress

As the sister of actors John and Lionel Barrymore she was one of the 'Fabulous Barrymores'. Her stage roles in The Second Mrs Tanqueray *(1924) and* The Corn is Green *(1942) helped to establish her as 'the first lady of the American theater'.*

1 For an actress to be a success, she must have the face of Venus, the brains of a Minerva, the grace of Terpsichore, the memory of a Macaulay, the figure of Juno, and the hide of a rhinoceros.
Quoted in *The Theatre in the Fifties* (1953) by George Jean Nathan

2 I never let them [audiences] cough. They wouldn't dare.
New York Post 7 June 1956

Don Barthelme
(1931–89)
US author

He employed a collage effect in his minimalist short stories, such as Come Back, Dr Caligari *(1964) and* City Life *(1970), and his novels, for example* Snow White *(1967).*

1 The distinction between children and adults, while probably useful for some purposes, is at bottom a specious one, I feel. There are only individual egos, crazy for love.
'Me and Miss Mandible', publ. in *Come Back, Dr Caligari* (1964). Spoken by the narrator (Joseph).

Roland Barthes
(1915–80)
French semiologist

He was one of France's leading post-war critics whose writings on literature and semiotics demystified the language of mass culture and helped to establish structuralism and the New Criticism. Mythologies *(1957),* Death of the Author *(1968) and* S/Z *(1970) are among his most influential publications.*

1 What I claim is to live to the full the contradiction of my time, which may well make sarcasm the condition of truth.
Mythologies, Preface (1957, transl. 1972)

2 What the public wants is the image of passion, not passion itself.
Ibid., 'The World of Wrestling'

3 The face of Garbo is an Idea, that of Hepburn an Event.
Ibid., 'The Face of Garbo'

4 Through the mythology of Einstein, the world blissfully regained the image of knowledge reduced to a formula.
Ibid., 'The Brain of Einstein'

5 I think that cars today are almost the exact equivalent of the great Gothic cathedrals: I mean the supreme creation of an era, conceived with passion by unknown artists, and consumed in image if not in usage by a whole population which appropriates them as a purely magical object.
Ibid., 'The New Citroën'

6 Myth is neither a lie nor a confession: it is an inflexion.
Ibid., 'Myth Today: Reading and Deciphering Myth'

7 Once the Author is removed, the claim to decipher a text becomes quite futile. To give a text an Author is to impose a limit on that text, to furnish it with a final signifier, to close the writing.
Image-Music-Text, 'The Death of the Author' (1966, transl. 1978)

8 There is only one way left to escape the alienation of present day society: *to retreat ahead of it.*
The Pleasure of the Text, 'Modern' (1975)

9 The bastard form of mass culture is humiliated repetition . . . always new books, new programmes, new films, news items, but always the same meaning.
Ibid., 'Modern'

10 Language is legislation, speech is its code. We do not see the power which is in speech because we forget that all speech is a classification, and that all classifications are oppressive.
Inaugural lecture, Collège de France, 7 January 1977, publ. in *Barthes: Selected Writings* (ed. SUSAN SONTAG, 1982)

11 Literature is *without proofs*. By which it must be understood that it cannot prove, not only *what* it says, but even that it is worth the trouble of saying it.
'Deliberation' (1979), ibid.

Bernard Baruch

(1870–1965)
US financier

He was instrumental in drafting the economic sections of the Treaty of Versailles (1919) and was an adviser to ROOSEVELT *and* CHURCHILL *during the Second World War. He later served on the UN Atomic Energy Commission (1946–51).*

1 Let us not be deceived – we are today in the midst of a cold war. Our enemies are to be found abroad and at home.
Speech to South Carolina Legislature, 16 April 1947, quoted in the *New York Times* 17 April 1947. A year later Baruch told the Senate War Investigating Committee, 'We are in the midst of a cold war which is getting warmer.' Baruch claimed the expression had been suggested to him by his speechwriter, the former editor of the *New York World* Herbert Bayard Swope.

2 To me, old age is always fifteen years older than I am.
Quoted in the *Observer* 21 August 1955

3 A political leader must keep looking over his shoulder all the time to see if the boys are still there. If they aren't still there, he's no longer a political leader.
Quoted in obituary, *New York Times* 21 June 1965

Jacques Barzun

(b. 1907)
US scholar

Influential in the development of higher education in America, he advocated a broad approach rather than specialization. He published widely on the humanities.

1 Whoever wants to know the heart and mind of America had better learn baseball, the rules and realities of the game.
God's Country and Mine, ch. 8 (1954)

2 Teaching is not a lost art, but the regard for it is a lost tradition.
Newsweek 5 December 1955

Frédéric Bastiat

(1801–50)
French political economist

He was an advocate of freedom of choice, private property, free markets and limited government. Major works include Economic Sophisms *(1845) and* Economic Harmonies *(1850).*

1 Government is the great fiction, through which everybody endeavors to live at the expense of everybody else.
Essays on Political Economy, pt 3, 'Government' (1846)

Augusto Roa Bastos

(1917–2005)
Paraguayan novelist

His works, including the novel Son of Man *(1960) and his masterpiece* I The Supreme *(1974), deal largely with Paraguayan history. He lived in exile in Buenos Aires 1947–70.*

1 The things that have come into being change continually. The man with a good memory remembers nothing because he forgets nothing.
I The Supreme (1974, transl. 1986)

2 Anyone who attempts to relate his life loses himself in the immediate. One can only speak of another.
Ibid.

Georges Bataille

(1897–1962)
French novelist and critic

He founded the influential journal Critique *in 1946 and remained its editor until his death. His works emphasize the themes of atheism, mysticism, and freedom through excess rather than self-denial. He wrote in English under the name of Lord Auch.*

1 Intellectual despair results in neither weakness nor dreams, but in violence . . . It is only a matter of knowing how to give vent to one's rage; whether one only wants to wander like madmen around prisons, or whether one wants to overturn them.
'The "Lugubrious Game"' (1929), repr. in *Visions of Excess: Selected Writings 1927–1939* (ed. Allan Stoekl, 1985)

2 Eroticism is assenting to life even in death.
Eroticism, Introduction (1957)

3 Beauty is desired in order that it may be befouled; not for its own sake, but for the joy brought by the certainty of profaning it.
Ibid., ch. 13

4 I believe that truth has only one face: that of a violent contradiction.
The Deadman, Preface (1967)

H. E. Bates
(1905–74)
British author

Herbert Ernest Bates. A master of the short story and a prolific novelist, he wrote of rural England, as in The Darling Buds of May *(1958, televised 1980s).*

1 Perfick!
A Breath of French Air, ch. 1 (1959). Spoken by Pop Larkin.

Katharine Lee Bates
(1859–1929)
US author and academic

She taught at Wellesley College, Massachusetts, 1886–1925, and was a prolific author of poetry, travel books and children's books. She is best remembered for the words of the national hymn 'America the Beautiful' (1895).

1 America! America!
God shed His grace on thee
And crown thy good with brotherhood
From sea to shining sea!
'America the Beautiful', st. 1, publ. in *The Congregationalist* (1895), repr. in *America the Beautiful and Other Poems* (1911). The words were set to a tune by Samuel Ward, 'Materna' (1882).

Kathy Bates
(b. 1948)
US actress

On the stage she made an impact with Frankie and Johnny in the Clair de Lune *(1987), while her films have included* Misery *(1990) and* Diabolique *(1996).*

1 I'm your number-one fan.
Misery (film, 1990, screenplay by WILLIAM GOLDMAN based on 1987 short story by Stephen King, directed by Rob Reiner). Spoken by Annie Wilkes (Kathy Bates).

Charles Baudelaire
(1821–67)
French poet

A leading French Symbolist, he foreshadowed much modern poetry in his subject matter, which often focused on the perverse or grotesque. His translations of the works of EDGAR ALLAN POE *became classics.* Les Fleurs du mal *(1857) was his only volume of verse. His debauched excesses contributed to his early death.*

1 To be just, that is to say, to justify its existence, criticism should be partial, passionate and political, that is to say, written from an exclusive point of view, but a point of view that opens up the widest horizons.
Salon de 1846, sect. 1, publ. in *Curiosités esthétiques* (1868)

2 There are as many kinds of beauty as there are habitual ways of seeking happiness.
Ibid., sect. 2. Baudelaire may have been recalling a footnote in STENDHAL's *Histoire de la peinture en Italie*, ch. 110 (1816): *'La beauté est l'expression d'une certaine manière habituelle de chercher le bonheur'* ('Beauty is the expression of a certain habitual manner of seeking happiness').

3 All forms of beauty, like all possible phenomena, contain an element of the eternal and an element of the transitory – of the absolute and of the particular.
Ibid., sect. 18

4 The life of our city is rich in poetic and marvellous subjects. We are enveloped and steeped as though in an atmosphere of the marvellous; but we do not notice it.
Ibid., sect. 18

5 A frenzied passion for art is a canker that devours everything else.
L'Ecole païenne (1852), repr. in *Oeuvres complètes*, vol. 2 (ed. Yves-Gérard le Dantec, rev. Claude Pichois, 1976)

6 What is exhilarating in bad taste is the aristocratic pleasure of giving offence.
Intimate Journals, 'Squibs', sect. 18 (written 1855–66, publ. 1930, transl. CHRISTOPHER ISHERWOOD)

7 The son will run away from the family not at eighteen but at twelve, emancipated by his gluttonous precocity; he will fly not to seek heroic adventures, not to deliver a beautiful prisoner from a tower, not to immortalize a garret with sublime thoughts, but to found a business, to enrich himself and to compete with his infamous papa.
Ibid., 'Squibs', sect. 22

8 The dandy should aspire to be uninterruptedly sublime. He should live and sleep in front of a mirror.
Ibid., 'My Heart Laid Bare', sect. 27

9 There are in every man, always, two simultaneous allegiances, one to God, the other to Satan. Invocation of God, or Spirituality, is a desire to climb higher; that of Satan, or animality, is delight in descent.
Ibid., 'My Heart Laid Bare', sect. 41

10 On the day when a young writer corrects his first

proof-sheet he is as proud as a schoolboy who has just got his first dose of pox.
Ibid., 'My Heart Laid Bare', sect. 71

11 Theory of the true civilization. It is not to be found in gas, or steam, or table-turning. It consists in the diminution of the traces of original sin.
Ibid., 'My Heart Laid Bare', sect. 81

12 The more a man cultivates the arts the less he fornicates. A more and more apparent cleavage occurs between the spirit and the brute.
Ibid., 'My Heart Laid Bare', sect. 93

13 For the merchant, even honesty is a financial speculation.
Ibid., 'My Heart Laid Bare', sect. 97

14 The world only goes round by misunderstanding.
Ibid., 'My Heart Laid Bare', sect. 99

15 I have cultivated my hysteria with delight and terror. Now I suffer continually from vertigo, and today, 23rd of January, 1862, I have received a singular warning, I have felt the wind of the wing of madness pass over me.
Ibid., 'My Heart Laid Bare', sect. 109

16 The man who says his evening prayer is a captain posting his sentinels. He can sleep.
Ibid., 'My Heart Laid Bare', sect. 116

17 *Hypocrite lecteur – mon semblable – mon frère!*
[Hypocrite reader – my second self – my brother!]
Les Fleurs du mal, Preface: 'Au Lecteur' (1857; *The Flowers of Evil*). The line is quoted by T. S. ELIOT in *The Waste Land* (1922).

18 The poet is like the prince of the clouds
Who haunts the tempest and laughs at the archer;
Exiled on the ground in the midst of jeers,
His giant's wings prevent him from walking.
'L'Albatros', st. 4, publ. ibid., 'Spleen et Idéal'

19 If photography is allowed to stand in for art in some of its functions it will soon supplant or corrupt it completely thanks to the natural support it will find in the stupidity of the multitude. It must return to its real task, which is to be the servant of the sciences and the arts, but the very humble servant, like printing and shorthand which have neither created nor supplanted literature.
Salon de 1859, sect. 2, publ. in *Curiosités esthétiques* (1868)

20 Poetry and progress are like two ambitious men who hate one another with an instinctive hatred,

and when they meet upon the same road, one of them has to give place.
Ibid., sect. 2

21 I consider it useless and tedious to represent what *exists*, because nothing that *exists* satisfies me. Nature is ugly, and I prefer the monsters of my fancy to what is positively trivial.
Ibid., sect. 3

22 Alas! Man's vices, horrible as they may seem, contain the proof . . . of his thirst for the infinite.
Les Paradis artificiels, 'The Poem of Hashish', ch. 1 (1860)

23 Any man who refuses to accept the conditions of human life sells his soul.
Ibid., 'The Poem of Hashish', ch. 5

24 It is the hour to be drunken! To escape being the martyred slaves of time, be ceaselessly drunk. On wine, on poetry, or on virtue, as you wish.
'Enivrez-vous' (1864), repr. in *Petits poèmes en prose* (1869)

25 I have to confess that I had gambled on my soul and lost it with heroic insouciance and lightness of touch. The soul is so impalpable, so often useless, and sometimes such a nuisance, that I felt no more emotion on losing it than if, on a stroll, I had mislaid my visiting card.
'Le Joueur généreux' ('The Generous Gambler', 1864), ibid.

26 Genius is no more than childhood recaptured at will, childhood equipped now with man's physical means to express itself, and with the analytical mind that enables it to bring order into the sum of experience, involuntarily amassed.
Le Peintre de la vie moderne ('The Painter of Modern Life'), sect. 3, publ. in *L'Art romantique* (1869)

27 For the perfect idler, for the passionate observer it becomes an immense source of enjoyment to establish his dwelling in the throng, in the ebb and flow, the bustle, the fleeting and the infinite. To be away from home and yet to feel at home anywhere; to see the world, to be at the very centre of the world, and yet to be unseen of the world, such are some of the minor pleasures of those independent, intense and impartial spirits, who do not lend themselves easily to linguistic definitions. The observer is a prince enjoying his incognito wherever he goes.
Ibid., sect. 3

28 Modernity is the transient, the fleeting, the contingent; it is one half of art, the other being the eternal and the immovable.
Ibid., sect. 4

29 Dandyism is the last flicker of heroism in decadent ages ... Dandyism is a setting sun; like the
declining star, it is magnificent, without heat and
full of melancholy. But alas! the rising tide of
democracy, which spreads everywhere and reduces
everything to the same level, is daily carrying away
these last champions of human pride, and submerg-
ing, in the waters of oblivion, the last traces of these
remarkable myrmidons.
Ibid., sect. 9

30 Everything that is beautiful and noble is the
product of reason and calculation.
Ibid., sect. 11

31 Nature ... is nothing but the inner voice of self-
interest.
Ibid., sect. 11

32 All fashions are charming, or rather relatively
charming, each one being a new striving, more or
less well conceived, after beauty, an approximate
statement of an ideal, the desire for which constantly teases the unsatisfied human mind.
Ibid., sect. 11

33 We all have the republican spirit in our veins,
like syphilis in our bones. We are democratized and
venerealized.
Sur la Belgique, Epilogue, publ. in Oeuvres complètes, vol. 2
(ed. Yves-Gérard le Dantec, rev. Claude Pichois, 1976). The
uncompleted work is also known as Pauvre Belgique.

34 Il faut épater le bourgeois.
[You must shock the bourgeois.]
Attributed

Jean Baudrillard
(b. 1929)
French semiologist

His postmodernist theories on the consumer society, media,
art and metaphysics are laid out in In the Shadow of Silent
Majorities (1978) and Simulations and Simulacra (1981) among
other titles. The New York Times called him 'the sharp-
shooting Lone Ranger of the post-Marxist left'.

1 Cities are ... distinguished by the catastrophic
forms they presuppose and which are a vital part of
their essential charm. New York is King Kong, or
the blackout, or vertical bombardment: Towering
Inferno. Los Angeles is the horizontal fault, California breaking off and sliding into the Pacific:
Earthquake.
Fatal Strategies, 'Ecstasy And Inertia' (1983)

2 The very definition of the real becomes: that of
which it is possible to give an equivalent reproduction ... The real is not only what can be reproduced, but that which is always already reproduced.
The hyperreal.
Simulations, pt 2, 'The Hyperrealism of Simulation' (1983)

3 If you are prepared to accept the consequences of
your dreams ... then you must still regard America
today with the same naive enthusiasm as the generations that discovered the New World.
America, 'Utopia Achieved' (1986)

4 What you have to do is enter the fiction of
America, enter America as fiction. It is, indeed, on
this fictive basis that it dominates the world.
Ibid., 'Astral America'

5 It is always the same: once you are liberated, you
are forced to ask who you are.
Ibid., 'Astral America'

6 With the truth, you need to get rid of it as soon
as possible and pass it on to someone else. As with
illness, this is the only way to be cured of it. The
person who keeps truth in his hands has lost.
Cool Memories, ch. 1 (1987)

7 The sad thing about artificial intelligence is that
it lacks artifice and therefore intelligence.
Ibid., ch. 4

8 Information can tell us everything. It has all the
answers. But they are answers to questions we have
not asked, and which doubtless don't even arise.
Ibid., ch. 5

9 Everywhere one seeks to produce meaning, to
make the world signify, to render it visible. We are
not, however, in danger of lacking meaning; quite
the contrary, we are gorged with meaning and it is
killing us.
The Ecstasy of Communication, 'Seduction, or the Superficial
Abyss' (1987)

L. Frank Baum
(1856–1919)
US author

He wrote books for adults, such as The Last Egyptian (1908),
but is principally known for The Wonderful Wizard of Oz
(1900), a tale for children, with many sequels.

1 The road to the City of Emeralds is paved with
yellow brick, so you cannot miss it.
The Wonderful Wizard of Oz, ch. 2 (1900). Spoken by the Witch

of the North. The words do not appear thus in the film (1939), which features the song, 'Follow the Yellow Brick Road'.

Vicki Baum
(1888–1960)
Austrian-born US novelist

Originally Vicki Hedvig. Her principal achievement was the novel Grand Hotel *(1930), whose success as a play in New York (1931) allowed her to emigrate to America. It was later filmed with* GRETA GARBO *in the main role.*

1 The events that happen to people in a big hotel do not constitute entire human destinies, complete and rounded off. They are fragments merely, scraps, pieces. The people behind its doors may signify much or little. They may be rising or falling in the scale of life. Prosperity and disaster may be parted by no more than the thickness of a wall. The revolving door twirls around, and what passes between arrival and departure is nothing complete in itself.
Grand Hotel (1930)

2 Marriage always demands the greatest understanding of the art of insincerity possible between two human beings.
And Life Goes On (1932)

Richard Baxter
(1615–91)
English Nonconformist cleric

A Puritan sympathizer during the Civil War and a royal chaplain at the Restoration, he was driven out of the Church of England by the Act of Uniformity in 1662. His major work was The Reformed Pastor *(1656).*

1 I preached as never sure to preach again,
And as a dying man to dying men.
'Love Breathing Thanks and Praise', publ. in *Poetical Fragments* (1681)

Stephen Bayley
(b. 1951)
British design critic

Founder and chief executive (1981–90) of the Design Museum, he left his job as creative director of the Millennium Dome in 1999 after political disagreements.

1 Where *do* architects and designers get their ideas? The answer, of course, is mainly from other architects and designers, so is it mere casuistry to distinguish between tradition and plagiarism?
Commerce and Culture, ch. 3 (1989)

2 Taste is a merciless betrayer of social and cultural attitudes. Thus, while anybody will tell you as much (and perhaps more than) you want to know about their triumphs in bed and at the bank, it is taste that gets people's nerves tingling.
Taste, pt 1, 'Taste: The Story of an Idea' (1991)

3 Viewed holistically, interior design is a travesty of the architectural process and a frightening condemnation of the credulity, helplessness and gullibility of the most formidable consumers – the rich.
Ibid., pt 2, 'Interiors: Vacuums of Taste'

4 Alas, in a culture that encourages feeble-minded political correctness, great monuments and great works of art are not to be expected.
Independent 17 January 1998. Referring to the influence of focus groups on the Millennium Dome project, of which he was creative director.

Thomas Bayly
(1797–1839)
English song-writer, poet and playwright

He was principally known for his light verse and also wrote plays, for example Perfection *(1830).*

1 Oh! no! we never mention her,
Her name is never heard;
My lips are now forbid to speak
That once familiar word.
'Oh! No! We Never Mention Her', publ. in *Songs, Ballads, and Other Poems* (ed. Helena Bayly, 1844)

André Bazin
(1918–58)
French film critic

As co-founder in 1951 of Europe's most influential film periodical, Les Cahiers du cinéma, *he was called the 'spiritual father of the New Wave'.*

1 The cinema gives us a substitute world which fits our desires.
Quoted in *The New Wave*, ch. 7 (1976) by James Monaco. The words appear in the closing credits of JEAN-LUC GODARD's film *Le Mépris* (1963).

BBC [British Broadcasting Corporation]

1 Nation shall speak peace unto nation.
Motto from 1927, devised by Montague John Rendall (1862–1950), a schoolmaster and member of the first BBC Board of

Governors. Probably inspired by BIBLE, OLD TESTAMENT: ISAIAH 6 also (*Micah* 4:3). See also RUDYARD KIPLING 64.

Aubrey Beardsley
(1872–98)
English illustrator and writer

An influential figure in the aesthetic movement of the 1890s, he made his name with his black and white drawings on erotic and fantastic subjects, for example his illustrations of OSCAR WILDE's Salome (1894) and BEN JONSON's Volpone (1898).

1 No language is rude that can boast polite writers.
The Story of Venus and Tannhäuser or Under the Hill, Dedicatory epistle (1907)

2 In the present age, alas! our pens are ravished by unlettered authors and unmannered critics, that make a havoc rather than a building, a wilderness rather than a garden. But, alack! what boots it to drop tears upon the preterit?
Ibid., Dedicatory epistle

Pierre de Beaumarchais
(1732–99)
French dramatist

A courtier and watchmaker for Louis XV, he achieved success for his plays, notably The Barber of Seville (1775) and The Marriage of Figaro (1784), both of which recounted the exploits of Figaro, a clever servant.

1 These days, what isn't worth saying is sung.
Le Barbier de Séville, Act 1, Sc. 2 (1775; *The Barber of Seville*). Spoken by Figaro.

2 I hasten to laugh at everything for fear of being obliged to weep at it.
Figaro, ibid. See also BYRON 121.

3 Drinking when we are not thirsty and making love at any time, madam, is all that distinguishes us from the other animals.
Le Mariage de Figaro, Act 2, Sc. 21 (1784; *The Marriage of Figaro*). Spoken by Antonio.

Francis Beaumont
(c. 1584–1616)
English poet and playwright

He is best known for his collaborations with JOHN FLETCHER, with whom he shared home and belongings. The Woman Hater (1607) and The Knight of the Burning Pestle (1609) are plays attributed to his hand alone.

1 What things have we seen,
Done at the Mermaid! heard words that have been

So nimble, and so full of subtle flame,
As if that every one from whence they came,
Had meant to put his whole wit in a jest,
And had resolved to live a fool, the rest
Of his dull life.
'Letter to Ben Jonson', ll. 43–9, written 1602, publ. in *Poems* (1640)

2 Here are sands, ignoble things,
Dropt from the ruined sides of kings;
Here's a world of pomp and state,
Buried in dust, once dead by fate.
'On the Tombs in Westminster', ibid. Closing lines. Beaumont himself was eventually buried in Westminster Abbey.

Francis Beaumont
(c. 1584–1616)
John Fletcher
(1579–1625)
English playwrights
See also JOHN FLETCHER

1 Young maids were as cold as cucumbers, and much of that complexion!
Cupid's Revenge, Act 1, Sc. 1, l. 133 (1615). Spoken by Nisus.

Cesare Beccaria
(1735–94)
Italian jurist and philosopher

He is best known for On Crimes and Punishments (1764), published anonymously, which denounced torture and capital punishment in favour of education and other preventative measures.

1 Happy is the nation without a history.
On Crimes and Punishments, Introduction (1764). See CHARLES DE MONTESQUIEU 4.

Samuel Beckett
(1906–89)
Irish playwright and novelist

A major influence on absurdist and postmodern literature, he portrayed the human condition in comic but bleakly pessimistic terms, as in the plays Waiting for Godot (1953) and Endgame (1957). Most of his later works were written both in French and English.

1 I shall state silences more competently than ever a better man spangled the butterflies of vertigo.
Dream of Fair to Middling Women (written 1932, publ. 1992). Spoken by Belacqua.

2 Nothing to be done.
Waiting for Godot, Act 1 (1952). These opening words (by Estragon) are repeated in the play.

3 There's man all over for you, blaming on his boots the fault of his feet.
Vladimir, ibid., Act 1

4 Estragon: Charming spot. Inspiring prospects. Let's go.
Vladimir: We can't.
Estragon: Why not?
Vladimir: We're waiting for Godot.
Ibid., Act 1. The exchange is repeated several times during the play.

5 The tears of the world are a constant quality. For each one who begins to weep, somewhere else another stops. The same is true of the laugh.
Pozzo, ibid., Act 1

6 Let us not then speak ill of our generation, it is not any unhappier than its predecessors. Let us not speak well of it either. Let us not speak of it at all.
Pozzo, ibid., Act 1

7 Nothing happens, nobody comes, nobody goes, it's awful!
Estragon, ibid., Act 1

8 Don't touch me! Don't question me! Don't speak to me! Stay with me!
Estragon, ibid., Act 2

9 We always find something, eh Didi, to give us the impression we exist?
Estragon, ibid., Act 2

10 We all are born mad. Some remain so.
Estragon, ibid., Act 2

11 I can't go on. I'll go on.
The Unnamable (1952). Closing words of book.

12 But we breathe, we change! We lose our hair, our teeth! Our bloom! Our ideals!
Endgame (1958). Spoken by Hamm.

13 Nothing is funnier than unhappiness, I grant you that ... Yes, yes, it's the most comical thing in the world.
Nell, ibid.

14 The bastard! He doesn't exist!
Hamm, ibid. Hamm's exclamation after attempting to pray. Clov replies: 'Not yet.'

15 Let me go to hell, that's all I ask, and go on cursing them there, and them look down and hear me, that might take some of the shine off their bliss.
From an Abandoned Work (1958). The narrator speaks of his parents.

16 Just under the surface I shall be, all together at first, then separate and drift, through all the earth and perhaps in the end through a cliff into the sea, something of me. A ton of worms in an acre, that is a wonderful thought, a ton of worms, I believe it.
Ibid.

17 To find a form that accommodates the mess, that is the task of the artist now.
Conversation with Tom Driver, 1961, quoted in *Samuel Beckett, a Biography* ch. 21 (1978) by Deirdre Bair

18 What do I know of man's destiny? I could tell you more about radishes.
'Enough', publ. in *No's Knife* (1967)

19 Personally I have no bone to pick with graveyards, I take the air there willingly, perhaps more willingly than elsewhere, when take the air I must.
First Love (1970)

20 I couldn't have done it otherwise. Gone on, I mean. I could not have gone through the awful wretched mess of life without having left a stain upon the silence.
Quoted in *Samuel Beckett, a Biography*, ch. 26 (1978) by Deirdre Bair. Variations of this remark were made on different occasions.

21 Birth was the death of him.
'A Piece of Monologue', publ. in *Three Occasional Pieces* (1982)

22 Ever tried. Ever failed. No matter. Try again. Fail again. Fail better.
Worstward Ho (1984)

23 Make sense who may. I switch off.
Bam, in *What Where* (1984)

Thomas Becon
(1512–67)
English cleric

Chaplain to Thomas Cranmer, he was committed to the Tower of London (1553–4) as a 'seditious preacher', but was reinstated in 1558.

1 For commonly, wheresoever God buildeth a church, the devil will build a chapel just by.
Catechism (1560). See DANIEL DEFOE 4, MARTIN LUTHER 6. The words are also associated with the prelate (later Archbishop of Canterbury) Richard Bancroft (1544–1610), in a ser-

mon in 1588: 'Where Christ erecteth his Church, the devil in the same churchyard will have his chapel.'

2 When the wine is in, the wit is out.
Ibid.

(Sir) Thomas Beecham
(1879–1961)
British conductor

He introduced Diaghilev's Ballets Russes to London (1911) and founded the Royal Philharmonic Orchestra (1947). He was famous for his 'Lollipop' encores and for his forthright pronouncements.

1 All the arts in America are a gigantic racket run by unscrupulous men for unhealthy women.
Quoted in the *Observer* 5 May 1946

2 The English may not like music, but they absolutely love the noise it makes.
Quoted in the *New York Herald Tribune* 9 March 1961

3 Composers should write tunes the chauffeurs and errand boys can whistle.
Quoted in the *New York Times* 9 March 1961

4 Great music is that which penetrates the ear with facility and leaves the memory with difficulty. Magical music never leaves the memory.
Quoted in *The Sunday Times* 16 September 1962

5 Like two skeletons copulating on a corrugated tin roof.
Quoted in *Beecham Stories* (1978) by Harold Atkins and Archie Newman. Referring to the sound of the harpsichord. Another version likens it to 'a bird-cage played with toasting forks'.

6 Madam, you have between your legs an instrument capable of giving pleasure to thousands – and all you can do is scratch it.
Attributed remark to a cellist. Also quoted '. . . the most sensitive instrument known to man . . .'

Henry Ward Beecher
(1813–87)
US clergyman, editor and writer

The brother of HARRIET BEECHER STOWE, he won a huge following for his sermons, in which he condemned slavery and advocated women's rights. His reputation was damaged by accusations of adultery, though his guilt was never proved.

1 When a nation's young men are conservative, its funeral bell is already rung.
Proverbs From Plymouth Pulpit (1887)

2 In things pertaining to enthusiasm, no man is

sane who does not know how to be insane on proper occasions.
Ibid.

Max Beerbohm
(1872–1956)
British essayist and caricaturist

He was a drama critic and the author of numerous witty collections of essays and caricatures and one novel, Zuleika Dobson *(1911), a parody of Oxford life.* SHAW *called him 'the incomparable Max', while* WILDE *remarked, 'the gods have bestowed on Max the gift of eternal old age'.*

1 The Non-Conformist Conscience makes cowards of us all.
'King George the Fourth', publ. in *The Yellow Book*, vol. 3 (1894)

2 There is always something rather absurd about the past.
'1880', ibid., vol. 4 (1895)

3 To give an accurate and exhaustive account of that period would need a far less brilliant pen than mine.
'1880', ibid., vol. 4. Of the 1880s.

4 Most women are not so young as they are painted.
'A Defence of Cosmetics', ibid., vol. 4

5 I was a modest, good-humoured boy. It is Oxford that has made me insufferable.
More, 'Going Back to School' (1899)

6 As a teacher, as a propagandist, Mr Shaw is no good at all, even in his own generation. But as a personality, he is immortal.
'A Cursory Conspectus of G.B.S.', written 1901, publ. in *Around Theatres* (1924). Closing words of essay.

7 The most perfect caricature is that which, on a small surface, with the simplest means, most accurately exaggerates, to the highest point, the peculiarities of a human being, at his most characteristic moment in the most beautiful manner.
'The Spirit of Caricature', written 1901, publ. in *A Variety of Things* (1928)

8 The dullard's envy of brilliant men is always assuaged by the suspicion that they will come to a bad end.
Zuleika Dobson, ch. 4 (1911)

9 You will find that the woman who is really kind

to dogs is always one who has failed to inspire sympathy in men.
Ibid., ch. 6

10 She was one of the people who say 'I don't know anything about music really, but I know what I like.'
Ibid., ch. 9. Of Zuleika Dobson.

11 One might well say that mankind is divisible into two great classes: hosts and guests.
'Hosts and Guests', publ. in *And Even Now* (1920)

12 To say that a man is vain means merely that he is pleased with the effect he produces on other people. A conceited man is satisfied with the effect he produces on himself.
'Quia Imperfectum', ibid.

13 It seems to be a law of nature that no man, unless he has some obvious physical deformity, ever is loth to sit for his portrait.
'Quia Imperfectum', ibid.

Ethel Lynn Beers
(1827–79)
US poet

She contributed stories and verses to magazines, especially the New York Ledger *and published* All Quiet Along the Potomac and Other Poems *in 1879.*

1 All quiet along the Potomac to-night,
No sound save the rush of the river,
While soft falls the dew on the face of the dead,
The picket's off duty forever.
'The Picket Guard', st. 6 (1861), repr. in *All Quiet Along the Potomac and Other Poems* (1879). The words are based on the dispatches regularly sent by George Brinton McClellan during the Civil War.

Ludwig van Beethoven
(1770–1827)
German composer

Preeminently an instrumental composer, and of prodigious output despite increasing deafness, he bridged the classical and romantic movements.

1 Art! Who understands it, with whom can one speak concerning this great goddess!
Letter to author Bettina von Arnim, 11 August 1810, publ. in *Beethoven's Letters* (ed. A. Eaglefield-Hull, 1926)

2 I maintain that an artist should not be shabbily treated. For alas! sad to relate, however glittering his fame may seem on the surface, yet the artist is not allowed to be Jupiter's guest in Olympia every day.
Letter, 5 June 1822, publ. in *The Letters of Beethoven*, vol. 2 (ed. Emily Anderson, 1961)

3 *Muss es sein? Es muss sein.*
[Must it be? It must be.]
String Quartet in F Major, Opus 135, Epigraph to fourth movement (1826). The movement was entitled 'Der schwer gefasste Entschluss', or 'The Decision Taken with Difficulty'. 'Es muss sein' was one of Beethoven's favourite phrases.

Isabella Beeton
(1836–65)
English writer on domestic science

She became celebrated through her Book of Household Management *(1861), which covered all aspects of domestic science.*

1 I have always thought that there is no more fruitful source of family discontent than a housewife's badly-cooked dinners and untidy ways.
Book of Household Management, Preface (1861)

2 A place for everything and everything in its place.
Ibid., ch. 2, sect. 55. The maxim was already known, and had appeared in Frederick Marryat's novel *Masterman Ready* (1842).

3 First, catch your hare.
Attributed. This famously difficult first stage of a recipe does not appear in Mrs Beeton's *Book of Household Management* (1861), and was already proverbial when the work was published. A similar phrase, 'Take your hare when it is cased [skinned] . . .', formed part of a recipe in *The Art of Cookery Made Plain and Easy* (1747) by Hannah Glasse.

Brendan Behan
(1923–64)
Irish playwright

A supporter of Irish Nationalism, he incorporated his prison experience into his first play The Quare Fellow *(1954). His heavy drinking limited his creative output, though his play* The Hostage *(1958) and autobiographical novel* Borstal Boy *(1958) were acclaimed.*

1 He was born an Englishman and remained one for years.
The Hostage, Act 1 (1958). Pat refers to Monsewer, who later 'found out he was an Irishman'.

2 Pat: He was an Anglo-Irishman.
Meg: In the blessed name of God, what's that?
Pat: A Protestant with a horse.
Ibid. Referring to Monsewer.

3 When I came back to Dublin, I was court-martialled in my absence, and sentenced to death in my absence, so I said they could shoot me in my absence.

Pat, ibid. Referring to his experiences in the IRA.

4 All publicity is good, except an obituary notice.

Quoted in the *Sunday Express* 5 January 1964

5 I am a daylight atheist.

Quoted in *Sacred Monsters*, 'Rousting in Dublin' (1988) by Daniel Farson. The comment was made by Rae Jeffs, publicist and assistant to Behan.

6 One drink is too many for me and a thousand not enough.

Ibid., 'Rousting in Dublin'

Aphra Behn
(1640–89)
English playwright

Considered the first professional female writer, she wrote a number of popular plays involving intrigue, as well as one novel, Oroonoko, The History of the Royal Slave *(c. 1678), based on her acquaintance with an enslaved negro prince in Surinam, where she was brought up. While in Antwerp, she worked as a spy for* CHARLES II.

1 There is no sinner like a young saint.

The Rover, pt 1, Act 1 (1681). Spoken by Willmore.

2 Variety is the soul of pleasure, a good unknown; and we want faith to find it.

Willmore, ibid., pt 2, Act 1

3 Money speaks sense in a language all nations understand.

Willmore, ibid., pt 2, Act 3

4 A brave world, Sir, full of religion, knavery, and change: we shall shortly see better days.

The Roundheads, Act 1, Sc. 1 (1682). Spoken by Corporal Right.

5 He that will live in this world must be endowed with the three rare qualities of dissimulation, equivocation, and mental reservation.

Lambert, ibid., Act 1, Sc. 2

6 Love ceases to be a pleasure, when it ceases to be a secret.

The Lover's Watch, 'Four O'Clock, General Conversation' (1686)

7 All I ask, is the privilege for my masculine part the poet in me ... If I must not, because of my sex, have this freedom ... I lay down my quill and you shall hear no more of me.

The Lucky Chance, Preface (1686)

8 Oh, what a dear ravishing thing is the beginning of an Amour!

The Emperor of the Moon, Act 1, Sc. 1 (1687). Spoken by Bellemante.

Harry Belafonte
(b. 1927)
US singer and civil rights activist

Known as the 'King of Calypso' in the late 1950s, he had hits with 'Banana Boat Song' (1956) and 'Mary's Boy Child' (1957), and later became committed to the advancement of black culture.

1 You can cage the singer but not the song.

International Herald Tribune 3 October 1988. Referring to the arts in South Africa.

Gertrude Bell
(1868–1926)
British archaeologist and diplomat

Her explorations in the Middle East on the eve of the First World War led to her appointment to the Mesopotamia Expeditionary Force in Basra and Baghdad. There, she continued her archaeological research and contributed to the inception of the modern state of Iraq.

1 When you have drunk the milk of the naga [mother camel] over the camp fire of Abu Tayyi you are baptised of the desert and there is no other salvation for you.

Letter to her father, Hugh Bell, 4 February 1914, publ. in *The Letters of Gertrude Bell*, vol. 1 (ed. Lady Florence Bell, 1927)

2 When people talk of our muddling through it throws me into a passion. Muddle through! why yes so we do – wading through blood and tears that need never have been shed.

Letter to her stepmother, Florence Bell, 27 April 1916, ibid. Referring to 'the co-ordinating of Arab politics and the creation of an Arabian policy', which Bell believed had been poorly managed by the War Office.

3 The real difficulty under which we labour here is that we don't know, and I suppose can't know till the end of the war, exactly what we intend to do in this country. You are continually confronted with that uncertainty. Can you persuade people to take your side when you are not sure in the end whether you'll be there to take theirs?

Letter to Hugh and Florence Bell, 15 July 1916, ibid. Speaking of Iraq, from which British forces had expelled the Ottoman administration during the First World War. In 1920 the country was placed under a League of Nations mandate to be administered by the British, remaining such until 1932.

4 It is almost impossible to believe that a few years ago the human race was more or less governed by reason and considered consequences, before it did things ... At the back of my mind I have a feeling that we people of the war can never return to complete sanity. The shock has been too great; we're unbalanced.

Letter to Hugh Bell, 16 January 1923, ibid. Speaking of the excavation at Niffar (ancient Nippur): 'You see in section age after age of civilization extending over a period of three or four thousand years. It's amazing and rather horrible to be brought face to face with millenniums of human effort and then to consider what a mess we've made of it.'

(Sir) Tim Bell
(b. 1941)
British advertising executive

As a specialist in public relations, he was the original 'spin doctor' and midwife of the general election victory by MARGARET THATCHER in 1979, when he was Managing Director at Saatchi and Saatchi, the Conservative Party's publicity agency.

1 I'd rather be called a spin doctor than a hidden persuader. Actually I rather like the term. After all, doctors are qualified professionals, and putting the right spin on things is exactly what we do.

PR Week 13 October 1995. *The Hidden Persuaders* (1973) was a book by VANCE PACKARD about the manipulative methods of the advertising industry.

2 Don't write a press release when a good leak will do.

Remark at Marketing Society lunch, 8 December 1995, quoted in *Campaign* 5 January 1996. Bell added, 'The truth is that a strong story placed in the newspaper, picked up by everybody else will actually have more impact than an advertising campaign.'

Hilaire Belloc
(1870–1953)
British author

A devout Roman Catholic, he was the author of travel books, historical studies and satirical novels, though probably best known for his Cautionary Tales *(1907). He was a lifelong friend of* G. K. CHESTERTON, *who illustrated his books, the pair said to be 'two buttocks of one bum'.*

1 Child! do not throw this book about;
Refrain from the unholy pleasure
Of cutting all the pictures out!

Preserve it as your chiefest treasure.
The Bad Child's Book of Beasts, Dedication (1896)

2 Oh! Let us never, never doubt
What nobody is sure about!
'The Microbe', publ. in *More Beasts for Worse Children* (1897)

3 And always keep a-hold of Nurse
For fear of finding something worse.
'Jim', publ. in *Cautionary Tales for Children* (1907)

4 Is there no Latin word for Tea? Upon my soul, if I had known that I would have let the vulgar stuff alone.
On Nothing, 'On Tea' (1908)

5 It is the best of all trades to make songs, and the second best to sing them.
On Everything, 'On Song' (1909)

6 From quiet homes and first beginning,
Out to the undiscovered ends,
There's nothing worth the wear of winning,
But laughter and the love of friends.
'Dedicatory Ode', publ. in *Verses* (1910)

7 I am living in the Midlands
That are sodden and unkind.
'The South Country', ibid.

8 Balliol made me, Balliol fed me,
Whatever I had she gave me again;
And the best of Balliol loved and led me,
God be with you, Balliol men.
'To the Balliol Men Still in Africa', ibid. Closing lines.

9 Remote and ineffectual Don
That dared attack my Chesterton.
'Lines to a Don', ibid.

10 I said to Heart, 'How goes it?' Heart replied:
'Right as a Ribstone Pippin!' But it lied.
'The False Heart', ibid.

11 It is sometimes necessary to lie damnably in the interests of the nation.
Letter to G. K. CHESTERTON, 12 December 1917, quoted in *Life of Hilaire Belloc*, ch. 16 (1957) by Robert Speaight. Belloc was a zealous propagandist during the First World War.

12 When I am dead, I hope it may be said:
'His sins were scarlet, but his books were read.'
'On His Books', publ. in *Sonnets and Verse* (1923). See BIBLE, OLD TESTAMENT: ISAIAH 4.

13 The Devil, having nothing else to do,
Went off to tempt My Lady Poltagrue.
My Lady, tempted by a private whim,

To his extreme annoyance, tempted him.
'On Lady Poltagrue', ibid.

14 I'm tired of Love; I'm still more tired of Rhyme.
But Money gives me pleasure all the time.
'Fatigue', ibid.

15 Do you remember an Inn,
Miranda?
Do you remember an Inn?
And the tedding and the spreading
Of the straw for a bedding,
And the fleas that tease in the High Pyrenees
And the wine that tasted of the tar?
'Tarantella', publ. in *Sonnets and Verse* (1923). Opening lines.

16 Strong brother in God and last companion,
Wine.
'Heroic Poem upon Wine', publ. in *Short Talks with the Dead* (1926)

17 Like many of the Upper Class
He liked the Sound of Broken Glass.
'About John', publ. in *New Cautionary Tales* (1930)

Saul Bellow
(1915–2005)
US novelist

A leading figure in post-war American fiction, he typically set his novels and short stories in Chicago, with Jewish intellectuals as protagonists. Notable works are Herzog *(1964) and* Humboldt's Gift *(1975).*

1 Everybody knows there is no fineness or accuracy of suppression; if you hold down one thing, you hold down the adjoining.
The Adventures of Augie March, ch. 1 (1953)

2 As for types like my own, obscurely motivated by the conviction that our existence was worthless if we didn't make a turning point of it, we were assigned to the humanities, to poetry, philosophy, painting – the nursery games of humankind, which had to be left behind when the age of science began. The humanities would be called upon to choose a wallpaper for the crypt, as the end drew near.
Ibid., ch. 6

3 I think that New York is not the cultural center of America, but the business and administrative center of American culture.
BBC radio interview, publ. in the *Listener* 22 May 1969

4 No one is stirred to the bowels by Europe of the ancient parapets. A huge force has lost its power over the imagination. This force began to weaken in the fifties, and by the sixties it was entirely gone.
'My Paris' (1983), repr. in *It All Adds Up* (1994)

5 But now the moronic inferno had caught up with me. My elegant carmy shimmering silver motor tureen ... was mutilated.
Humboldt's Gift (1975). Spoken by the narrator.

6 There are evils ... that have the ability to survive identification and go on for ever ... money, for instance, or war.
The Dean's December, ch. 13 (1982). Spoken by Albert Corde.

7 Psycho-analysis pretends to investigate the Unconscious. The Unconscious by definition is what you are not conscious of. But the Analysts already know what's in it – they should, because they put it all in beforehand.
Albert Corde, ibid., ch. 18

8 In the greatest confusion there is still an open channel to the soul. It may be difficult to find because by midlife it is overgrown, and some of the wildest thickets that surround it grow out of what we describe as our education. But the channel is always there, and it is our business to keep it open, to have access to the deepest part of ourselves.
The Closing of the American Mind, Foreword (1987) by Allan Bloom

9 There were two varieties of truth, one symbolized by the Tree of Knowledge, the other by the Tree of Life, one the truth of striving and the other the truth of receptivity. Knowledge divorced from life equals sickness.
More Die of Heartbreak, ch. 1 (1987)

10 If you think that historical forces are sending everybody straight to hell you can either go resignedly with the procession or hold out, and hold out not from pride or other personal motives, but from admiration and love for human abilities and powers to which, without exaggeration, the words 'miracle' and 'sublimity' can be applied.
Ibid., ch. 2

11 Everything has to be tried out. Funnily enough, the same mind that takes in 'Dallas' or rap music is also accessible to Homer and Shakespeare.
It All Adds Up, 'Mozart: an Overture' (1994)

12 Human character is smaller now, people don't have durable passions; they've replaced passions

with excitement. But this won't give you love as strong as death.
Quoted in the *Guardian* 10 September 1997

Robert Benchley
(1889–1945)
US humorous writer

A drama critic, sketchwriter and editor for Vanity Fair *and the* New Yorker, *he was a founder member of the Algonquin Round Table, a New York dinner club of literati and wits.*

1 One square foot less and it would be adulterous.
Quoted in the *New Yorker* 5 January 1946. Referring to the office he shared with DOROTHY PARKER, who echoed this remark in an interview in 1956: 'He [Robert Benchley] and I had an office so tiny that an inch smaller and it would have been adultery.'

2 A dog teaches a boy fidelity, perseverance, and to turn around three times before lying down.
Quoted in *Artemus Ward, His Book*, Introduction (1964 edn)

3 In America there are two classes of travel – first class and with childen.
Quoted in *The Algonquin Wits* (ed. Robert E. Drennan 1968)

4 Anyone can do any amount of work, provided it isn't the work he is supposed to be doing.
Ibid. Benchley's own method is also quoted in the book: 'I do most of my work sitting down. That's where I shine.'

5 Streets flooded. Please advise.
Ibid. Telegram on arrival at Venice.

6 It took me fifteen years to discover that I had no talent for writing, but I couldn't give it up because by that time I was too famous.
Quoted in *Robert Benchley*, ch. 1 (1955) by Nathaniel Benchley

Ruth Benedict
(1887–1948)
US anthropologist

Her studies of primitive societies led her to argue for cultural relativity and against the imposition of cultural values. Patterns of Culture *(1964) is regarded as her most important work.*

1 No man ever looks at the world with pristine eyes. He sees it edited by a definite set of customs and institutions and ways of thinking.
Patterns of Culture, ch. 1 (1934)

2 Racism is an *ism* to which everyone in the world today is exposed; for or against, we must take sides.

And the history of the future will differ according to the decision which we make.
Race: Science and Politics, ch. 1 (1940)

Stephen Vincent Benét
(1898–1943)
US poet and author

He published numerous novels and short stories on themes of American history, but is chiefly known for his long poem on the Civil War John Brown's Body *(1928).*

1 I have fallen in love with American names,
The sharp, gaunt names that never get fat,
The snakeskin titles of mining claims,
The plumed war-bonnet of Medicine Hat,
Tucson and Deadwood and Lost Mule Flat.
'American Names', st. 1 (1927) repr. in *America in Poetry* (ed. Charles Sullivan, 1988)

2 I shall not rest quiet in Montparnasse.
I shall not lie easy at Winchelsea.
You may bury my body in Sussex grass,
You may bury my tongue at Champmédy.
I shall not be there, I shall rise and pass. Bury my
    heart at Wounded Knee.
Ibid., st. 7. Wounded Knee, a creek in South Dakota, was site of the last major battle of the Indian Wars, 1890. *Bury My Heart at Wounded Knee* was the title of a history of the Indian wars by Dee Brown (1970).

David Ben Gurion
(1886–1973)
Israeli statesman

Born in Poland, he became an active Zionist and emigrated to Palestine in 1906. In 1930 he was elected leader of the Mapai (Labour) party, and in 1948 became Israel's first Prime Minister, serving two terms 1948–63.

1 In Israel, in order to be a realist you must believe in miracles.
Interview on CBS-TV, 5 October 1956

Walter Benjamin
(1892–1940)
German critic and philosopher

Considered one of Germany's most original modern critics, he incorporated Marxism and Jewish mysticism into his essays and aphorisms. He moved to Paris in 1933, where he committed suicide after a failed attempt to escape the Nazi occupation.

1 Opinions are to the vast apparatus of social existence what oil is to machines: one does not go up to

a turbine and pour machine oil over it; one applies a little to hidden spindles and joints that one has to know.

One-Way Street, 'Filling Station' (1928)

2 Work on good prose has three steps: a musical stage when it is composed, an architectonic one when it is built, and a textile one when it is woven.

Ibid., 'Caution: Steps'

3 Genuine polemics approach a book as lovingly as a cannibal spices a baby.

Ibid., 'Post No Bills: The Critic's Technique in Thirteen Theses'

4 The art of the critic in a nutshell: to coin slogans without betraying ideas. The slogans of an inadequate criticism peddle ideas to fashion.

Ibid., 'Post No Bills: The Critic's Technique in Thirteen Theses'

5 Books and harlots have their quarrels in public.

Ibid., 'No. 13'

6 Truth wants to be startled abruptly, at one stroke, from her self-immersion, whether by uproar, music or cries for help.

Ibid., 'Technical Aid'

7 Quotations in my work are like wayside robbers who leap out armed and relieve the stroller of his conviction.

Ibid., 'Hardware'

8 Of all the ways of acquiring books, writing them oneself is regarded as the most praiseworthy method ... Writers are really people who write books not because they are poor, but because they are dissatisfied with the books which they could buy but do not like.

'Unpacking my Library' (1931) repr. in *Illuminations* (1961, ed. Hannah Arendt, 1968)

9 The destructive character lives from the feeling, not that life is worth living, but that suicide is not worth the trouble.

'The Destructive Character' (1931), repr. in *One-Way Street and Other Writings* (1978)

10 Boredom is the dream bird that hatches the egg of experience. A rustling in the leaves drives him away.

'The Storyteller', sect. 8 (1936), repr. in *Illuminations* (1961, ed. Hannah Arendt, 1968)

11 Death is the sanction of everything the storyteller can tell. He has borrowed his authority from death.

Ibid., sect. 11

Tony Benn
(b. 1925)
British politician

Originally Anthony Wedgwood Benn. A committed parliamentary radical who is also a staunch traditionalist, he was a Labour MP 1950–60 and 1963–2001. He held various government posts, though was defeated in bids for leadership of the party. HAROLD MACMILLAN *thought that he 'immatures with age'.*

1 The House of Lords is the British Outer Mongolia for retired politicians.

Quoted in the *Observer* 4 February 1962. Comment made during his campaign to disclaim his hereditary peerage. In his *Diaries 1963–67*, Benn states the words came from a speech made in San Francisco in 1961, and were also used by the Russian former Prime Minister Molotov. Benn was always relieved to have escaped the Lords, though he was, he said, 'not a reluctant peer but a persistent commoner'.

2 Britain today is suffering from galloping obsolescence.

Speech, 31 January 1963, publ. in the *Observer* 2 February 1963

3 We thought we could put the economy right in five years. We were wrong. It will probably take ten.

Speech at Bristol, 18 April 1968, quoted in *The Times* 19 April 1968. Benn was then Minister of Technology.

4 The Marxist analysis has got nothing to do with what happened in Stalin's Russia: it's like blaming Jesus Christ for the Inquisition in Spain.

Quoted in the *Observer* 27 April 1980

5 A holy war with atom bombs could end the human family for ever. I say this as a socialist whose political commitment owes much more to the teachings of Jesus – without the mysteries within which they are presented – than to the writings of Marx whose analysis seems to lack an understanding of the deeper needs of humanity.

Arguments for Democracy, ch. 7 (1981)

6 For those without personal wealth or political authority a trade union card and a ballot paper are the only two routes to political power.

Ibid., ch. 9

7 I did not enter the Labour Party forty-seven years ago to have our manifesto written by Dr Mori, Dr Gallup and Mr Harris.

Guardian 13 June 1988

8 A faith is something you die for, a doctrine is

something you kill for. There is all the difference in the world.

BBC Television broadcast, 11 April 1989

9 It's the same each time with progress. First they ignore you, then they say you're mad, then dangerous, then there's a pause and then you can't find anyone who disagrees with you.

Quoted in the *Observer* 6 October 1991

Alan Bennett

(b. 1934)

British playwright

At the heart of the satire boom in the 1960s, he was a contributor to the revue Beyond the Fringe *(1960–1) and achieved further success with his first stage play* Forty Years On *(1969). Later plays include* The Madness of George III *(1991).*

1 Life, you know, is rather like opening a tin of sardines. We are all of us looking for the key.

'Sermon', in *Beyond the Fringe* (revue, 1960–1), publ. in *From Fringe to Flying Circus*, ch. 1 (1980) by Roger Wilmut. Bennett first wrote the sketch in 1956 for a concert organized with Russell Harty at Oxford University. 'It took about half an hour to write, and was, I suppose, the most profitable half-hour's work I've ever done. Once I had hit on the form I used to be able to run up sermons for all sorts of occasions.'

2 Memories are not shackles, Franklin, they are garlands.

Forty Years On, Act 2 (1969). Spoken by the Headmaster.

3 Never read the Bible as if it means something. Or at any rate don't *try* and mean it. Nor prayers. The liturgy is best treated and read as if it's someone announcing the departure of trains.

Journal entry, 30 June 1984, publ. in *Writing Home, Diaries 1980–1990* (1994)

4 The majority of people perform well in a crisis and when the spotlight is on them; it's on the Sunday afternoons of this life, when nobody is looking, that the spirit falters.

Journal entry, 13 October 1984, ibid.

5 When people are on their best behaviour they aren't always at their best.

'Dinner at Noon', broadcast April 1988 in BBC series *Byline*, ibid.

6 Biography is all about cutting people down to size. Getting an unruly quart into a pint pot.

Quoted in *Beyond the Fringe . . . and Beyond*, pt 4 (1989) by Ronald Bergan

7 Definition of a classic: a book everyone is assumed to have read and often thinks they have.

Independent on Sunday 27 January 1991

8 To be heir to the throne is not a position: it is a predicament.

The Madness of George III, pt 2, 'Carlton House' (1991). In the film adaptation (*The Madness of King George*, 1995), the words are: 'To be Prince of Wales is not a position. It is a predicament.' Spoken by the Prince of Wales.

9 I generally assume that childhoods more or less ended with the First World War – halcyon childhoods certainly – and that most of them since have been the 'forgotten boredom' of Larkin's poem 'Coming'. Anyone born after 1940 got the Utility version, childhood according to the Authorized Economy Standard.

Writing Home, 'Bad John' (1994)

Arnold Bennett

(1867–1931)

British novelist

He set much of his best work in the Potteries region of his boyhood, notably Anna of the Five Towns *(1902) and* The Old Wives' Tale *(1908). He also wrote for the theatre and was an influential reviewer, called by* WYNDHAM LEWIS *'the Hitler of the book-racket'.*

1 To the artist is sometimes granted a sudden, transient insight which serves in this matter for experience. A flash, and where previously the brain held a dead fact, the soul grasps a living truth! At moments we are all artists.

Journal entry, 18 March 1897, publ. in *The Journals of Arnold Bennett* (1932)

2 The traveller, however virginal and enthusiastic, does not enjoy an unbroken ecstasy. He has periods of gloom, periods when he asks himself the object of all these exertions, and puts the question whether or not he is really experiencing pleasure. At such times he suspects that he is not seeing the right things, that the characteristic, the right aspects of these strange scenes are escaping him. He looks forward dully to the days of his holiday yet to pass, and wonders how he will dispose of them. He is disgusted because his money is not more, his command of the language so slight, and his capacity for enjoyment so limited.

Journal entry, 25 October 1897, ibid.

3 Essential characteristic of the really great novelist: a Christ-like, all-embracing compassion.
Journal entry, 25 October 1897, ibid.

4 A cause may be inconvenient, but it's magnificent. It's like champagne or high heels, and one must be prepared to suffer for it.
The Title, Act 1 (1918). Spoken by Hildegarde Culver.

5 Being a husband is a whole-time job. That is why so many husbands fail. They can't give their entire attention to it.
Arthur Culver, ibid., Act 1

6 Examine the Honours List and you can instantly tell how the Government feels in its inside. When the Honours List is full of rascals, millionaires, and – er – chumps, you may be quite sure that the Government is dangerously ill.
Arthur Culver, ibid., Act 1

7 Journalists say a thing that they know isn't true, in the hope that if they keep on saying it long enough it will be true.
Arthur Culver, ibid., Act 1

8 Literature's always a good card to play for Honours. It makes people think that Cabinet ministers are educated.
Hildegarde Culver, ibid., Act 1

9 A test of a first-rate work, and a test of your sincerity in calling it a first-rate work, is that you finish it.
Things that Have Interested Me, 'Finishing Books' (first series, 1921)

10 The price of justice is eternal publicity.
Ibid., 'Secret Trials' (second series, 1923)

11 Good taste is better than bad taste, but bad taste is better than no taste, and men without individuality have no taste – at any rate no taste that they can impose on their publics.
Evening Standard 21 August 1930

Jill Bennett
(1931–90)
British actress

Having gained her first success in ANOUILH*'s* Dinner With the Family *(1957), she performed in many plays by her husband* JOHN OSBORNE, *such as* West of Suez *(1971) and* Watch It Come Down *(1976).*

1 Never marry a man who hates his mother, because he'll end up hating you.
Quoted in the *Observer* 12 September 1982

Tony Bennett
(b. 1926)
US singer

Originally Anthony Dominick Benedetto. He established his reputation with a series of hit singles in the 1950s and '60s, and recorded more jazz-orientated songs in the 1970s.

1 I left my heart in San Francisco
High on a hill it calls to me.
'I Left My Heart in San Francisco' (song, 1954, written by Douglas Cross). Recorded by Bennett in 1962, the song became his signature tune.

Connie Bensley
(b. 1929)
British poet

Her sharp and satirical poetry, which focuses on the everyday, appears in the collections Moving In *(1984) and* Choosing To Be a Swan *(1994).*

1 I sing the love homeopathic:
it cures you before very long.
You just take a speck
of that pain-in-the-neck
and let it dissolve on your tongue.
'A Cure for Love', publ. in *Choosing To Be a Swan* (1994)

A. C. Benson
(1862–1925)
British author

Arthur Christopher Benson. Master of Magdalene College, Cambridge (1915–25) , he was a prolific writer of essays, novels, literary criticism and biographies, but was best known for his poems and hymns.

1 Land of hope and glory, mother of the free,
How shall we extol thee who are born of thee?
Wider still and wider shall thy bounds be set;
God who made thee mighty, make thee mightier yet.
'Land of Hope and Glory', written for the finale of Elgar's *Coronation Ode* (1902) for Edward VII

Jeremy Bentham
(1748–1832)
English philosopher, political theorist and jurist

A thorough-going utilitarian, he applied scientific values to ethics, pleasure and pain, and believed that laws should serve socially useful ends. He founded University College, London, where his clothed skeleton may still be seen.

1 The said truth is that it is the greatest happiness of the greatest number that is the measure of right and wrong.
A Fragment on Government (1776). The formula was repeated with minor variations in Bentham's later writings. He credited the originator of this definition as either clergyman and scientist Joseph Priestley (1733–1804) or Italian legal reformer CESARE BECCARIA. See also FRANCIS HUTCHESON 2.

2 The principle of asceticism never was, nor ever can be, consistently pursued by any living creature. Let but one tenth part of the inhabitants of the earth pursue it consistently, and in a day's time they will have turned it into a Hell.
An Introduction to the Principles of Morals and Legislation, ch. 2 (1789)

3 All punishment is mischief: all punishment in itself is evil.
Ibid., ch. 13

4 The question is not, Can they *reason*? nor, can they *talk*? but, can they suffer?
Ibid., ch. 17. Referring to animals.

5 *Natural rights* is simple nonsense: natural and imprescriptible rights, rhetorical nonsense – nonsense upon stilts.
Anarchical Fallacies: an Examination of the Declarations of Rights Issued During the French Revolution, article 2 (written c. 1791–5, publ. 1816)

Edmund Clerihew Bentley
(1875–1956)
British novelist and journalist

A close friend of G. K. CHESTERTON, he wrote and gave his name to brief, humorous verse biographies known as 'clerihews'. He worked at the Daily Telegraph *for twenty-two years, and as a writer of detective stories, he is best known for* Trent's Last Case *(1913).*

1 Sir Humphry Davy
Abominated gravy.
He lived in the odium

Of having discovered Sodium.
Biography for Beginners, 'Sir Humphry Davy' (1905)

2 Sir Christopher Wren
Said, 'I am going to dine with some men.
If anybody calls
Say I am designing St Paul's.'
Ibid., 'Sir Christopher Wren'

3 Between what matters and what seems to matter, how should the world we know judge wisely?
Trent's Last Case, ch. 1 (1913). Opening words.

4 George the Third
Ought never to have occurred.
One can only wonder
At so grotesque a blunder.
More Biography, 'George the Third' (1929)

Lloyd Bentsen
(1921–2006)
US politician

He was the Democratic vice-presidential candidate in 1988 and Secretary of the Treasury (1993–4) under President CLINTON.

1 Senator, I served with Jack Kennedy. I knew Jack Kennedy. Jack Kennedy was a friend of mine. Senator, you're no Jack Kennedy.
TV Vice-presidential debate, 6 October 1988, publ. in *Lend Me Your Ears,* pt 4 (ed. William Safire, 1992). Bentsen was responding to the assertion by DAN QUAYLE that he possessed 'as much experience in the Congress as Jack Kennedy had when he sought the presidency'. Safire calls the riposte 'the most effective single punch in the history of televised presidential debates'.

Nicolai A. Berdyaev
(1874–1948)
Russian philosopher

He founded the Academy of Philosophy and Religion in Berlin in 1922 (transferred in 1924 to Paris). As a leader of the Christian existentialist school, he was a consistent critic of Russian communism. His books include The Meaning of History *(1923).*

1 In sex we have the source of man's true connection with the cosmos and of his servile dependence. The categories of sex, male and female, are cosmic categories, not merely anthropological categories.
The Meaning of the Creative Act (1916)

2 We find the most terrible form of atheism, not in the militant and passionate struggle against the idea of God himself, but in the practical atheism of everyday living, in indifference and torpor. We often

encounter these forms of atheism among those who are formally Christians.

Truth and Revelation (1953)

John Berger

(b. 1926)

British author and critic

An uncompromising Marxist-influenced critic, he has written extensively on culture and society, as in Ways of Seeing *(1972). His novels include* G *(1972) and the trilogy* Into Their Labours *(1991), which charts peasant life in France.*

1 Nothing fortuitous happens in a child's world. There are no accidents. Everything is connected with everything else and everything can be explained by everything else . . . For a young child everything that happens is a necessity.

A Fortunate Man (1967)

2 Is boredom anything less than the sense of one's faculties slowly dying?

Ibid.

3 Nakedness reveals itself. Nudity is placed on display . . . The nude is condemned to never being naked. Nudity is a form of dress.

Ways of Seeing, ch. 3 (1972)

4 A peasant becomes fond of his pig and is glad to salt away its pork. What is significant, and is so difficult for the urban stranger to understand, is that the two statements are connected by an *and* and not by a *but*.

About Looking, 'Why Look at Animals?' (1980)

5 The zoo cannot but disappoint. The public purpose of zoos is to offer visitors the opportunity of looking at animals. Yet nowhere in a zoo can a stranger encounter the look of an animal. At the most, the animal's gaze flickers and passes on. They look sideways. They look blindly beyond.

Ibid., 'Why Look at Animals?'

6 The camera relieves us of the burden of memory. It surveys us like God, and it surveys for us. Yet no other god has been so cynical, for the camera records in order to forget.

Ibid., 'Uses of Photography'

7 One can say of language that it is potentially the only human home, the only dwelling place that cannot be hostile to man.

And Our Faces, My Heart, Brief As Photos, pt 2 (1984)

8 Emigration, forced or chosen, across national frontiers or from village to metropolis, is the quintessential experience of our time.

Ibid., pt 2

9 Autobiography begins with a sense of being alone. It is an orphan form.

'Mother' (1986), repr. in *Keeping a Rendezvous* (1992)

10 What makes shit such a universal joke is that it's an unmistakeable reminder of our duality, of our soiled nature and of our will to glory. It is the ultimate *lèse-majesté*.

'Muck and Its Entanglements' (1989), ibid.

11 Compassion has no place in the natural order of the world which operates on the basis of necessity. Compassion opposes this order and is therefore best thought of as being in some way supernatural.

Guardian 19 December 1991

Ingmar Bergman

(b. 1918)

Swedish stage and film writer-director

Often bleak in outlook and preoccupied with guilt, repression and loneliness, his films include The Seventh Seal *(1956),* The Virgin Spring *(1959) and the more optimistic and autobiographical* Fanny and Alexander *(1982).*

1 Today the individual has become the highest form and the greatest bane of artistic creation. The smallest wound or pain of the ego is examined under the microscope as if it were of eternal importance. The artist considers his isolation, his subjectivity, his individualism almost holy. Thus we finally gather in one large pen, where we stand and bleat about our loneliness without listening to each other and without realizing that we are smothering each other to death.

The Seventh Seal (film, 1956, written and directed by Ingmar Bergman). Spoken introduction.

2 My basic view of things is – not to have any basic view of things.

Interview in *Bergman on Bergman*, 'Solna, 25 June 1968' (1970)

Ingrid Bergman

(1915–82)

Swedish screen actress

A hugely popular romantic star from 1939, she won an Oscar for Gaslight *(1944), but was ostracized from Hollywood after her affair with the director Roberto Rossellini in 1949.*

1 Play it, Sam. Play 'As Time Goes By'.
Casablanca (film, 1942, screenplay Julius and Philip Epstein, and Howard Koch, from the unproduced play by Murray Burnett and Joan Alison; directed by Michael Curtiz). Ilsa Lund (Ingrid Bergman) makes the request to the piano player Sam (Dooley Wilson). Later in the film, Rick Blaine (Humphrey Bogart) repeats the request: 'You played it for her, you can play it for me. If she can stand it, I can. Play it!' (usually misquoted 'Play it again Sam', the title of WOODY ALLEN's 1972 film). For the song, see HERMAN HUPFELD 1.

Henri Bergson
(1859–1941)
French philosopher

His most famous work Creative Evolution *(1907) rejected Darwinism in favour of the concept of the* élan vital, *or creative impulse. His writings influenced* MARCEL PROUST *and* GEORGE BERNARD SHAW.

1 To perceive means to immobilize ... we seize, in the act of perception, something which outruns perception itself.
Matter and Memory, ch. 4, sect. 4 (1896)

2 Intelligence ... is the faculty of making artifical objects, especially tools to make tools.
Ibid., 'Summary and Conclusion', sect. 9

3 An absolute can only be given in an *intuition*, while all the rest has to do with *analysis*. We call intuition here the *sympathy* by which one is transported into the interior of an object in order to coincide with what there is unique and consequently inexpressible in it. Analysis, on the contrary, is the operation which reduces the object to elements already known.
Metaphysics, Introduction (1903)

4 The present contains nothing more than the past, and what is found in the effect was already in the cause.
Creative Evolution, ch. 1, sect. 1 (1907)

Steven Berkoff
(b. 1937)
British playwright, actor and director

Having formed the London Theatre Group in 1968, he embarked on a series of adaptations of classic dramas. His own radical, sometimes brutal plays, in which he often acts, include East *(1975) and* Greek *(1979).*

1 Wake up, you git, we need a war ...
Establish once again our might and strength
Shake our old mane, out fly the moths

Oh God, I start to feel myself again
Now where is this damn Falkland Isle?
Sink the Belgrano (1987). Spoken by Maggot Scratcher.

2 That just ain't cricket, is it dear?
Or they may say, and it will be true,
Britain does not rule the waves
She simply waives the bloody rules!
Command, ibid.

Irving Berlin
(1888–1989)
US songwriter

Originally Israel Baline. He was a pivotal figure in US popular music, already established as a composer when 'Alexander's Ragtime Band' was a hit in 1911. He received a presidential citation as composer of patriotic songs in 1954. 'Irving Berlin has no place in American music,' Jerome Kern asserted, 'Irving Berlin is American music.'

1 From the mountains to the prairies,
To the oceans white with foam,
God bless America,
My home sweet home!
'God Bless America' (song, written 1917, recorded 1938). This unofficial national anthem, originally written for the Broadway show, *Yip Yip Yaphank* (1918), is said to have provoked Woody Guthrie to compose 'This Land Is Your Land': see WOODY GUTHRIE 2.

2 The song is ended (but the melody lingers on).
'The Song Is Ended (But the Melody Lingers On)' (song) in *Will O' the Whispers* (stage musical, 1927). Sung by Jack 'Whispering' Smith in the show, the song was popularized by Ruth Etting, and re-released in 1948 by Nellie Lutcher.

3 I'm puttin' on my top hat,
Tyin' up my white tie,
Brushin' off my tails.
'Top Hat, White Tie and Tails' (song) in *Top Hat* (film, 1935). The song was performed by Fred Astaire.

4 Heaven – I'm in Heaven –
And my heart beats so that I can hardly speak;
And I seem to find the happiness I seek
When we're out together dancing cheek to cheek.
'Cheek to Cheek' (song), ibid. Written for Ginger Rogers and Fred Astaire.

5 There may be trouble ahead,
But while there's moonlight and music and love
    and romance,
Let's face the music and dance.
'Let's Face the Music and Dance' (song), in *Follow the Fleet* (film, 1936). The song was a hit for Fred Astaire.

6 I'm dreaming of a white Christmas,
Just like the ones I used to know.
'White Christmas' (song), in *Holiday Inn* (film, 1942). First recorded by BING CROSBY, the song was featured again in the film *White Christmas* (1954), and recorded by artists as diverse as FRANK SINATRA (1944), Mantovani (1952) and the Drifters (1954). Crosby's sales alone exceeded 25 million.

7 There's no business like show business.
'There's No Business Like Show Business' (song), in *Annie Get Your Gun* (musical show 1946, filmed 1949). Sung by Ethel Merman on Broadway and by Betty Hutton in the film version, the title was borrowed for the 1954 movie in which MARILYN MONROE sang Berlin's 'Heat Wave'.

8 Anything you can do, I can do better,
I can do anything better than you.
'Anything You Can Do' (song), ibid.

9 Everybody ought to have a lower East Side in their life.
Vogue 1 November 1962

(Sir) Isaiah Berlin
(1909–97)
Latvian-born British philosopher

Regarded as one of the leading liberal thinkers of his generation, he was Professor of Social and Political Theory at Oxford (1957–67). Among his major works on political philosophy are Karl Marx *(1939),* Historical Inevitability *(1954) and* The Age of Enlightenment *(1956).*

1 Injustice, poverty, slavery, ignorance – these may be cured by reform or revolution. But men do not live only by fighting evils. They live by positive goals, individual and collective, a vast variety of them, seldom predictable, at times incompatible.
'Political Ideas in the Twentieth Century' (1950), repr. in *Four Essays on Liberty* (1969)

2 A great man need not be morally good, or upright, or kind, or sensitive, or delightful, or possess artistic or scientific talent. To call someone a great man is to claim that he has intentionally taken (or perhaps could have taken) a large step, one far beyond the normal capacities of men, in satisfying, or materially affecting, central human interests.
'Chaim Weizmann' (1958), repr. in *Personal Impressions* (1981)

3 It is only a very vulgar historical materialism that denies the power of ideas, and says that ideals are mere material interests in disguise. It may be that, without the pressure of social forces, political ideas are stillborn: what is certain is that these forces,

unless they clothe themselves in ideas, remain blind and undirected.
'Two Concepts of Liberty' (1958), repr. in *Four Essays on Liberty* (1969)

4 One belief, more than any other, is responsible for the slaughter of individuals on the altars of the great historical ideals . . . the belief that somewhere, in the past or in the future, in divine revelation or in the mind of an individual thinker, in the pronouncements of history or science, or in the simple heart of an uncorrupted good man, there is a final solution.
'Two Concepts of Liberty', ibid.

5 Scepticism, driven to extremes, defeats itself by becoming self-refuting.
Four Essays on Liberty, Introduction (1969)

Georges Bernanos
(1888–1948)
French novelist and political writer

A Roman Catholic polemicist, he wrote in support of royalism and, in A Diary of My Times *(1938), against Franco. His novels include* The Star of Satan *(1926) and* The Diary of a Country Priest *(1936).*

1 The wish to pray is a prayer in itself . . . God can ask no more than that of us.
The Diary of a Country Priest, ch. 4 (1936)

2 Faith is not a thing which one 'loses', we merely cease to shape our lives by it.
Ibid., ch. 4

3 Hell is not to love any more, madame. Not to love any more!
The priest, ibid., ch. 5

4 No one ever discovers the depths of his own loneliness.
Ibid., ch. 7

5 Civilization exists precisely so that there may be no masses but rather men alert enough never to constitute masses.
The Last Essays of Georges Bernanos, 'Why Freedom?' (1955)

Friedrich von Bernhardi
(1849–1930)
German soldier and author

He became commander of the Seventh Army corps in 1909 and wrote on military subjects.

1 The inevitableness, the idealism, and the blessing

of war, as an indispensable and stimulating law of development, must be repeatedly emphasized.
Germany and the Next War, ch. 1 (1912). This book, translated and widely diffused in cheap editions, did much to exacerbate anti-German sentiments before and during the First World War.

Sarah Bernhardt
(1844–1923)
French stage actress

Originally Henriette Rosine Bernard. The most celebrated actress of her day and known as the 'Divine Sarah', she founded the Théâtre Sarah Bernhardt in 1899, and continued to act after a leg amputation in 1914.

1 On the stage one needs long arms; it is better to have them too long than too short. An artiste with short arms can never, never make a fine gesture.
My Double Life: Memoirs of Sarah Bernhardt, ch. 9 (1907)

2 We must live for the few who know and appreciate us, who judge and absolve us, and for whom we have the same affection and indulgence. The rest I look upon as a mere crowd, lively or sad, loyal or corrupt, from whom there is nothing to be expected but fleeting emotions, either pleasant or unpleasant, which leave no trace behind them.
The Memoirs of Sarah Bernhardt, ch. 9 (1977 edn)

Leonard Bernstein
(1918–90)
US composer and conductor

An accomplished composer in both the classical and modern idiom, he was also a popular and flamboyant conductor. His compositions include symphonies and the musical West Side Story *(1957).*

1 Technique is communication: the two words are synonymous in conductors.
The Times 27 June 1989

Yogi Berra
(b. 1925)
US baseball player

Lawrence Peter Berra. He held many world championship titles during his career as catcher with the New York Yankees and Mets (1946–65), and was famous for his malapropisms.

1 It ain't over till it's over.
Attributed

Chuck Berry
(b. 1926)
US rock musician

One of the first rock and roll stars to attract a large teenage following, he was a major influence on British and US rock bands of the 1960s. According to JOHN LENNON, *'if you tried to give rock 'n' roll another name, you might call it Chuck Berry.'*

1 Roll over, Beethoven,
And tell Tchaikovsky the news.
'Roll Over, Beethoven' (song, 1956)

2 Hail, hail rock 'n' roll,
Deliver me from the days of old.
'School Days' (song, 1957)

3 Go Johnny go!
'Johnny B. Goode' (song, 1958). *Go Johnny Go* was the title of a rock and roll film in 1959, in which Berry appeared.

John Berryman
(1914–72)
US poet

He established his reputation with Homage to Mistress Bradstreet *(1956) but is remembered chiefly for his* Dream Songs. *An alcoholic, he committed suicide by jumping into the Mississippi River.*

1 We must travel in the direction of our fear.
'A Point of Age', publ. in *Poems* (1942)

2 Life, friends, is boring. We must not say so.
After all, the sky flashes, the great sea yearns,
we ourselves flash and yearn,
and moreover my mother told me as a boy
(repeatedly) 'Ever to confess you're bored
means you have no
Inner Resources'. I conclude now I have no
inner resources, because I am heavy bored.
77 Dream Songs, no. 14 (1964)

3 The world is gradually becoming a place
Where I do not care to be any more.
His Toy, His Dream, His Rest, no. 149 (1968). The lines were incorporated into the final version of the *Dream Songs* (1969)

4 The artist is extremely lucky who is presented with the worst possible ordeal which will not actually kill him. At that point, he's in business.
Interview in *Paris Review*, winter 1972, repr. in *Writers at Work* (fourth series, ed. George Plimpton, 1976)

Mary McLeod Bethune

(1875–1955)
US academic

She was founder and president of the National Council of Negro Women (1935–49) and advised the New Deal administration of FRANKLIN D. ROOSEVELT *on minority issues.*

1 The true worth of a race must be measured by the character of its womanhood.
Address to Chicago Women's Federation, 3 June 1933, publ. in *Black Women in White America*, 'A Century of Progress of Negro Women' (ed. Gerda Lerner, 1972)

(Sir) John Betjeman

(1906–84)
British poet

Quintessentially English and a champion of tradition, he mingled satire with humour and nostalgia. His verse autobiography Summoned by Bells *(1960) was an instant success and he was appointed Poet Laureate in 1972. His mother-in-law Lady Chetwode said of him: 'We invite people like that to tea, but we don't marry them.'*

1 Oh! Chintzy, chintzy cheeriness,
Half dead and half alive!
'Death in Leamington', publ. in *Mount Zion* (1931)

2 Broad of Church and broad of mind,
Broad before and broad behind,
A keen ecclesiologist,
A rather dirty Wykehamist.
'The Wykehamist', ibid. Opening lines.

3 Ghastly Good Taste, or a depressing story of the rise and fall of English architecture.
Title of book (1933)

4 He rose, and he put down *The Yellow Book*.
He staggered – and, terrible-eyed,
He brushed past the palms on the staircase
And was helped to a hansom outside.
'The Arrest of Oscar Wilde at the Cadogan Hotel', st. 9, publ. in *Continual Dew* (1937). Closing lines of poem.

5 Come, friendly bombs, and fall on Slough!
It isn't fit for humans now,
There isn't grass to graze a cow.
Swarm over, Death!
'Slough', st. 1, ibid. Betjeman made no secret of his antipathy towards modern architecture and town planning.

6 When Captain Webb the Dawley man,
Captain Webb from Dawley,
Came swimming along the old canal
That carried the bricks to Lawley.

Swimming along –
Swimming along –
Swimming along from Severn,
And paying a call at Dawley Bank while swimming along to Heaven.
'A Shropshire Lad', st. 1, publ. in *Old Lights for New Chancels* (1940)

7 Sand in the sandwiches, wasps in the tea,
Sun on our bathing-dresses heavy with the wet,
Squelch of the bladder-wrack waiting for the sea,
Fleas round the tamarisk, an early cigarette.
'Trebetherick', st. 1

8 Gracious Lord, oh bomb the Germans.
Spare their women for Thy Sake,
And if that is not too easy
We will pardon Thy Mistake.
But gracious Lord, whate'er shall be,
Don't let anyone bomb me.
'In Westminster Abbey', st. 2, ibid.

9 Keep our Empire undismembered
Guide our Forces by Thy Hand,
Gallant blacks from far Jamaica,
Honduras and Togoland;
Protect them Lord in all their fights,
And, even more, protect the whites.
'In Westminster Abbey', st. 3, ibid.

10 Think of what our Nation stands for,
Books from Boots' and country lanes,
Free speech, free passes, class distinction,
Democracy and proper drains.
'In Westminster Abbey', st. 4, ibid.

11 For me, at any rate, England stands for the Church of England, eccentric incumbents, oil-lit churches, Women's Institutes, modest village inns, arguments about cow parsley on the altar, the noise of mowing machines on Saturday afternoons, local newspapers, local auctions, the poetry of Tennyson, Crabbe, Hardy and Matthew Arnold, local talent, local concerts, a visit to the cinema, branch-line trains, light railways, leaning on gates and looking across fields.
BBC broadcast, 25 February 1943, publ. in *Coming Home* as 'Coming Home' (1997)

12 Miss J. Hunter Dunn, Miss J. Hunter Dunn,
Furnish'd and burnish'd by Aldershot sun,
What strenuous singles we played after tea,
We in the tournament – you against me!
'A Subaltern's Love-song', st. 1, publ. in *New Bats in Old Belfries* (1945)

13 I have a Vision of the Future, chum.
The workers' flats in fields of soya beans
Tower up like silver pencils, score on score.
'The Planster's Vision', ibid.

14 And is it true? And is it true,
This most tremendous tale of all,
Seen in a stained-glass window's hue,
A Baby in an ox's stall?
The Maker of the stars and sea
Become a Child on earth for me?
'Christmas', st. 6, publ. in A Few Late Chrysanthemums (1954)

15 Phone for the fish-knives, Norman
As Cook is a little unnerved;
You kiddies have crumpled the serviettes
And I must have things daintily served.
'How to Get on in Society', ibid. Opening lines of poem.

16 Still they stand, the churches of England, their
towers grey above billowy globes of elm trees, the
red cross of St George flying over their battlements,
the Duplex Envelope System employed for collections, schoolmistresses at the organ, incumbent in
the chancel, scattered worshippers in the nave, Tortoise stove slowly consuming its ration as the
familiar seventh-century phrases come echoing
down arcades of ancient stone.
English Parish Churches, Introduction (1958)

17 The dread of beatings! Dread of being late!
And, greatest dread of all, the dread of games!
Summoned by Bells, ch. 7 (1960)

18 We spray the fields and scatter
The poison on the ground
So that no wicked wild flowers
Upon our farm be found.
'Harvest Hymn', publ. in High and Low (1966)

19 All concrete sheds around us
And Jaguars in the yard,
The telly lounge and deep-freeze
Are ours from working hard.
'Harvest Hymn', ibid.

Aneurin Bevan
(1897–1960)
British politician

*Known as Nye Bevan. He served as Labour MP for Ebbw Vale
1929–60. As Minister of Health (1945–51), he established the
National Health Service, resigning in protest against proposed
charges. A brilliant orator, though also a 'merchant of discour-*
tesy' for WINSTON CHURCHILL, *he inspired a 'Bevanite' faction of the party.*

1 Freedom is the by-product of economic surplus.
Quoted in *Aneurin Bevan*, vol. 1, ch. 3 (1962) by MICHAEL
FOOT. Remark often repeated by Bevan from the 1920s.

2 The worst thing I can say about democracy is that
it has tolerated the Right Honourable Gentleman
[Neville Chamberlain] for four and a half years.
Speech to House of Commons, 23 July 1929, publ. in *Hansard*.
Bevan did not hide his poor opinion of CHAMBERLAIN. 'He
has the lucidity which is the by-product of a fundamentally
sterile mind,' he wrote. 'He does not have to struggle ...
with the crowded pulsations of a fecund imagination. On the
contrary he is almost devoid of imagination.'

3 Fascism is not in itself a new order of society. It is
the future refusing to be born.
Remark, July 1940, quoted in *Aneurin Bevan*, vol. 1, ch. 10
(1962) by MICHAEL FOOT

4 His ear is so sensitively attuned to the bugle note
of history that he is often deaf to the more raucous
clamour of contemporary life. The seven-league
tempo of his imagination hastens him on to the
'sunny uplands' of the future, but he is apt to forget
that the slow steps of humanity must travel every
inch of the weary road that leads there.
Remark made in late 1940, ibid., vol. 1, ch. 10. Referring to
WINSTON CHURCHILL.

5 He seems determined to make a trumpet sound
like a tin whistle.
Of CLEMENT ATTLEE in remark in 1945, quoted ibid., vol. 1,
ch. 14. Referring to Attlee's playing a subordinate role to
ANTHONY EDEN when the two were delegated to represent
Britain at the UN conference in San Francisco. Attlee, according to Bevan, had 'consistently underplayed his position and
opportunities ... He brings to the fierce struggle of politics
the tepid enthusiasm of a lazy summer afternoon at a cricket
match.'

6 This island is made mainly of coal and surrounded by fish. Only an organizing genius could
produce a shortage of coal and fish at the same time.
Speech at Blackpool, 24 May 1945, quoted in the *Daily Herald*
25 May 1945. Bevan's speech was made on the day that CHUR-
CHILL announced the dissolution of the wartime coalition
and the formation of a Conservative 'caretaker' government
in the wake of VE Day. The Conservatives were to be ejected
from office two months later when Labour won a landslide
victory.

7 No amount of cajolery, and no attempts at ethical
or social seduction, can eradicate from my heart a

deep burning hatred for the Tory Party ... So far as I am concerned they are lower than vermin.

Speech at Manchester, 4 July 1948, quoted in *The Times* 5 July 1948. Bevan was referring to the social policies of the Conservative Party, which 'condemned millions of first-class people to semi-starvation'. His invective, which formed part of a speech to inaugurate the National Health Service, provoked outrage in the press and embarrassment within his own party.

8 He is a man suffering from petrified adolescence.

Of WINSTON CHURCHILL, quoted in *Aneurin Bevan*, ch. 11 (1953) by Vincent Brome

9 We know what happens to people who stay in the middle of the road. They get run over.

Quoted in the *Observer* 6 December 1953

10 I know that the right kind of leader for the Labour Party is a kind of desiccated calculating machine.

Speech to Tribune Group at Labour Party Conference, 29 September 1954, quoted in *Aneurin Bevan*, vol. 2, ch. 11 (1973) by MICHAEL FOOT. The remark was taken as referring to HUGH GAITSKELL, though Bevan later denied this.

11 If we complain about the tune, there is no reason to attack the monkey when the organ grinder is present.

Speech to House of Commons, 16 May 1957, publ. in *Hansard*. Bevan was referring to Foreign Minister Selwyn Lloyd and Prime Minister HAROLD MACMILLAN, blaming the latter for the Suez fiasco the previous autumn. Though Macmillan, as Chancellor of the Exchequer, had no direct involvement in foreign affairs during the crisis, he had advocated a strong response to Nasser's nationalization of the canal.

12 If you carry this resolution you will send Britain's Foreign Secretary naked into the conference chamber.

Speech at Labour Party Conference, Brighton 3 October 1957, quoted in the *Daily Herald* 4 October 1957. As Shadow Foreign Secretary under GAITSKELL's leadership of the party, Bevan spoke in opposition to a motion in favour of unilateral nuclear disarmament.

13 The Prime Minister has an absolute genius for putting flamboyant labels on empty luggage.

Queen's Speech debate in House of Commons, 3 November 1959, quoted in *Aneurin Bevan*, vol. 2, ch. 16 (1973) by MICHAEL FOOT. Referring to HAROLD MACMILLAN.

14 I read the newspapers avidly. It is my one form of continuous fiction.

The Times 29 March 1960

15 He is a man walking backwards with his face to the future.

Quoted in *The Fine Art of Political Wit*, ch. 9 (1964) by Leon Harris. Referring to Sir Walter Elliot, the Conservative Minister of Agriculture.

16 The purpose of getting power is to be able to give it away.

Quoted in *Aneurin Bevan*, vol. 2, ch. 1 (1962) by MICHAEL FOOT. Frequently said by Bevan.

17 You're not an MP, you're a gastronomic pimp.

Quoted ibid., vol. 2, ch. 6. Said to a colleague who complained of attending too many public dinners.

(Sir) William Beveridge

(1879–1963)

British economist

Baron Beveridge. He was Director of the London School of Economics (1919–37). In 1942 he produced the Beveridge Report, a scheme of comprehensive social insurance that was the blueprint for the British welfare state.

1 The object of government in peace and in war is not the glory of rulers or of races, but the happiness of the common man.

Social Insurance and Allied Services, pt 7 (1942)

2 The adventure of full employment in a free society is not like the directed flight of an aircraft on a beam. It is a voyage among shifting and dangerous currents. All that can be done is to see that the craft is well found, and that the pilot has all the necessary controls, and the instruments to guide his use of them.

Full Employment in a Free Society, pt 4 (1944)

3 Ignorance is an evil weed, which dictators may cultivate among their dupes, but which no democracy can afford among its citizens.

Ibid., pt 4

Ernest Bevin

(1881–1951)

British politician

He was a veteran trades union campaigner and a Labour MP from 1940. As Foreign Secretary (1945–51) he was one of the architects of the Organization for European Economic Cooperation (1948) and NATO (1949). A. J. P. TAYLOR commented, 'He objected to ideas only when others had them.'

1 The most conservative man in the world is the

British Trade Unionist when you want to change him.

Speech to Trades Union Congress, Edinburgh, 8 September 1927, publ. in the *Report of Proceedings of the Trades Union Congress* (1927)

2 My [foreign] policy is to be able to take a ticket at Victoria Station and go anywhere I damn well please.

Quoted in the *Spectator* 20 April 1951

Bhagavad-Gita

Composed in Sanskrit between the 2nd century BC and the 2nd century AD, the 'Song of God' consists of a dialogue between Prince Arjuna and his charioteer Krishna, an incarnation of Vishnu, on the eve of a great battle. It forms part of Book 6 of the Mahabharata. The translation used here is by R. C. Zaehner (1966).

1 Who thinks that he can be a slayer,
Who thinks that he is slain,
Both these have no [right] knowledge:
He slays not, is not slain.
Never is he born nor dies;
Never did he come to be, nor will he ever come to
   be again:
Unborn, eternal, everlasting he – primeval:
He is not slain when the body is slain.

ch. 2, v. 19–20. The words of Krishna.

2 As a man casts off his worn-out clothes
And takes on other new ones [in their place],
So does the embodied soul cast off his worn-out
   bodies
And enters others new.
He cannot be cut by sword,
Nor burnt by fire;
The waters cannot wet him,
Nor the wind dry him up.

Krishna, ch. 2, v. 22–3

3 For sure is the death of all that comes to birth,
Sure the birth of all that dies.
So in a matter that no one can prevent
Thou hast no cause to grieve.

Krishna, ch. 2, v. 27

4 Work alone is thy proper business,
Never the fruits [it may produce];
Let not your motive be the fruit of work,
Nor your attachment to [mere] worklessness.

Krishna, ch. 2, v. 47

5 Stand fast in Yoga, surrendering attachment.

Krishna, ch. 2, v. 48

6 And when he draws in on every side
His senses from their proper objects,
As a tortoise might its limbs,
Firm-stablished is the wisdom of such a man.

Krishna, ch. 2, v. 58

7 From food [all] contingent beings are born,
And food from rain;
And rain derives from sacrifice,
And sacrifice from works [*karma*].

Krishna, ch. 3, v. 14

8 In all the senses passion and hate
Are seated, [turned] to their proper objects:
Let none fall victim to their power,
For these are brigands on his road.

Krishna, ch. 3, v. 34

9 Better one's own duty [*dharma*] to perform,
   though void of merit,
Than to do another's well.

ch. 3, v. 35. Krishna's words are repeated in ch. 18, v. 47.

10 Exalted are the senses, or so they say;
Higher than they the mind;
Yet higher than the mind is soul.

Krishna, ch. 3, v. 42

11 The integrated man, renouncing the fruit of
   works,
Gains an abiding peace:
The man not integrated, whose works are
   prompted by desire,
Holds fast to fruits and thus remains enslaved.

Krishna, ch. 5, v. 12

12 In all contingent beings indifferent am I;
None do I hate and none do I fondly love;
But those who commune with me in love's
   devotion
[Abide] in Me, and I in them.

Krishna, ch. 9, v. 29

13 Son of Pritha, behold my forms
In their hundreds and their thousands;
How various are they, how divine,
How many-hued and multiform!

Krishna, ch. 11, v. 5

14 If in [bright] heaven together should arise
The shining brilliance of a thousand suns,

Then would that [perhaps] resemble
The brilliance of that God so great of Self.

ch. 11, v. 12. Krishna's words were recalled by J. ROBERT OPPENHEIMER on witnessing the explosion of the first atomic bomb in New Mexico, 16 July 1945, quoted in *Lawrence and Oppenheimer* (1969) by N. P. Davis.

15 Time am I, wreaker of the world's destruction.

Krishna, ch. 11, v. 32. A variation of the words was recalled, as above, by J. ROBERT OPPENHEIMER in New Mexico, 1945: 'I am become Death, the destroyer of worlds.'

16 Do works for Me, make Me thy highest goal,
Be loyal in love to Me,
Cast off [all other] attachments,
Have no hatred for any being at all:
For all who do thus shall come to Me.

ch. 11, v. 55

17 In the region of the heart of all
Contingent beings dwells the Lord,
Twirling them hither and thither by his uncanny
    power
[Like puppets] fixed in a machine.

ch. 18, v. 61

The Bible

The Old Testament, also known as the Hebrew Bible, was compiled from various Jewish sources from about 1200 BC, and was translated from Hebrew into Greek in the 3rd to 2nd centuries BC. The New Testament was written in Greek and Aramaic at the beginning of the Christian period. SAINT JEROME *produced the Latin Vulgate edition (c. 382–405), which became the official version used by the Roman Catholic Church, translated into English in the Rheims (New Testament, 1592) and Douay (Old Testament, 1609) editions. The Authorized, or King James version was commissioned by* JAMES I *for use by the Church of England (1611). Various modernizations were made in the 20th century but the King James version has remained popular and is the one used here – see* LORD MACAULAY 8. *The Apocrypha consists of books considered uncanonical by some parts of the Church, though still suitable for instruction.*

THE OLD TESTAMENT

The First Book of Moses,
called Genesis

1 In the beginning God created the heaven and the earth.

And the earth was without form, and void; and darkness was upon the face of the deep. And the Spirit of God moved upon the face of the waters.

And God said, Let there be light: and there was light.

Genesis 1:1–3

2 And God saw that it was good.

Genesis 1:10. The words are repeated in several other verses of the chapter.

3 And God said, Let us make man in our image, after our likeness: and let them have dominion over the fish of the sea, and over the fowl of the air, and over the cattle, and over all the earth, and over every creeping thing that creepeth upon the earth.

Genesis 1:26

4 So God created man in his own image, in the image of God created he him; male and female created he them.

Genesis 1:27

5 Be fruitful, and multiply, and replenish the earth, and subdue it: and have dominion over the fish of the sea, and over the fowl of the air, and over every living thing that moveth upon the earth.

Genesis 1:28. God's words to the first man and woman.

6 Behold, I have given you every herb bearing seed, which is upon the face of all the earth, and every tree, in the which is the fruit of a tree yielding seed; to you it shall be for meat.

Genesis 1:29. In a later context, God told the disgraced Adam, 'and thou shalt eat the herb of the field.' (*Genesis* 3:18)

7 And the Lord God formed man of the dust of the ground, and breathed into his nostrils the breath of life; and man became a living soul.

Genesis 2:7

8 And out of the ground made the Lord God to grow every tree that is pleasant to the sight, and good for food; the tree of life also in the midst of the garden, and the tree of knowledge of good and evil.

And a river went out of Eden to water the garden.

Genesis 2:9–10

9 Of every tree of the garden thou mayest freely eat:

But of the tree of the knowledge of good and evil, thou shalt not eat of it: for in the day that thou eatest thereof thou shalt surely die.

Genesis 2:16–17. God's injunction to Adam.

10 It is not good that the man should be alone; I will make him an help meet for him.

Genesis 2:18

11 And out of the ground the Lord God formed every

beast of the field, and every fowl of the air; and brought them unto Adam to see what he would call them: and whatsoever Adam called every living creature, that was the name thereof.

And Adam gave names to all cattle, and to the fowl of the air, and to every beast of the field.

Genesis 2:19–20

12 And the Lord God caused a deep sleep to fall upon Adam, and he slept: and he took one of his ribs, and closed up the flesh instead thereof;

And the rib, which the Lord God had taken from man, made he a woman, and brought her unto the man.

Genesis 2:21–22. The creation of Eve.

13 And Adam said, This is now bone of my bones, and flesh of my flesh: she shall be called Woman, because she was taken out of Man.

Genesis 2:23

14 Therefore shall a man leave his father and his mother, and shall cleave unto his wife: and they shall be one flesh.

Genesis 2:24. Similar wording appears in Ephesians 5:31: 'For this cause shall a man leave his father and mother, and shall be joined unto his wife, and they two shall be one flesh.'

15 And they were both naked, the man and his wife, and were not ashamed.

Genesis 2:25

16 Now the serpent was more subtil than any beast of the field which the Lord God had made.

Genesis 3:1. See JOHN MILTON 167.

17 Then your eyes shall be opened, and ye shall be as gods, knowing good and evil.

Genesis 3:5. The serpent's temptation, spoken to Eve.

18 And when the woman saw that the tree was good for food, and that it was pleasant to the eyes, and a tree to be desired to make one wise, she took of the fruit thereof, and did eat, and gave also unto her husband with her; and he did eat.

Genesis 3:6

19 And the eyes of them both were opened, and they knew that they were naked; and they sewed fig leaves together, and made themselves aprons.

Genesis 3:7. 'Aprons' is rendered as 'breeches' in the Geneva Bible (1560), for which it is also known as the 'Breeches Bible'.

20 The woman whom thou gavest to be with me, she gave me of the tree, and I did eat.

Genesis 3:12. Adam's explanation to God for eating from the forbidden tree.

21 And the Lord God said unto the woman, What is this that thou hast done? And the woman said, The serpent beguiled me, and I did eat.

Genesis 3:13

22 And the Lord God said unto the serpent, Because thou hast done this, thou art cursed above all cattle, and above every beast of the field; upon thy belly shalt thou go, and dust shalt thou eat all the days of thy life.

Genesis 3:14

23 I will greatly multiply thy sorrow and thy conception; in sorrow thou shalt bring forth children; and thy desire shall be to thy husband, and he shall rule over thee.

Genesis 3:16. God's judgement on Eve.

24 In the sweat of thy face shalt thou eat bread, till thou return unto the ground; for out of it wast thou taken: for dust thou art, and unto dust shalt thou return.

Genesis 3:19. God's curse on Adam.

25 And Abel was a keeper of sheep, but Cain was a tiller of the ground.

Genesis 4:2

26 Am I my brother's keeper?

Genesis 4:9. Cain's response on being asked the whereabouts of Abel, whom he has slain.

27 My punishment is greater than I can bear.

Genesis 4:13. Cain's lament after God has cursed him.

28 And the Lord set a mark upon Cain, lest any finding him should kill him.

Genesis 4:15

29 And Cain went out from the presence of the Lord, and dwelt in the land of Nod, on the east of Eden.

Genesis 4:16

30 And all the days of Methuselah were nine hundred sixty and nine years: and he died.

Genesis 5:27

31 There were giants in the earth in those days; and also after that, when the sons of God came in unto the daughters of men, and they bare children to them, the same became mighty men which were of old, men of renown.

Genesis 6:4. The extra-canonical Book of Enoch records the tradition that angels descended from heaven and fathered offspring by mortal women.

32 And the rain was upon the earth forty days and forty nights.
Genesis 7:12

33 And they went in unto Noah into the Ark, two and two of all flesh, wherein is the breath of life.

And they that went in, went in male and female of all flesh, as God had commanded him.
Genesis 7:15–16

34 For the imagination of man's heart is evil from his youth.
Genesis 8:21

35 While the earth remaineth, seedtime and harvest, and cold and heat, and summer and winter, and day and night shall not cease.
Genesis 8:22. God's promise on the safe delivery of Noah's ark.

36 Every moving thing that liveth shall be meat for you; even as the green herb have I given you all things.
Genesis 9:3

37 Whoso sheddeth man's blood, by man shall his blood be shed: for in the image of God made he man.
Genesis 9:6

38 I do set my bow in the cloud, and it shall be for a token of a covenant between me and the earth.

And it shall come to pass, when I bring a cloud over the earth, that the bow shall be seen in the cloud.
Genesis 9:13–14

39 And Cush begat Nimrod: he began to be a mighty one in the earth.

He was a mighty hunter before the Lord: wherefore it is said, Even as Nimrod the mighty hunter before the Lord.
Genesis 10:8–9. This part of Noah's genealogy has given rise to the name 'Nimrod' for any outstanding hunter.

40 Therefore is the name of it called Babel; because the Lord did there confound the language of all the earth.
Genesis 11:9

41 Abram dwelled in the land of Canaan, and Lot dwelled in the cities of the plain, and pitched his tent toward Sodom.

But the men of Sodom were wicked and sinners before the Lord exceedingly.
Genesis 13:12–13. The cities of Sodom and Gomorrah were

eventually subjected to a rain of 'brimstone and fire' by God (Genesis 19:24).

42 And thou shalt go to thy fathers in peace; thou shalt be buried in a good old age.
Genesis 15:15. God's encouragement to Abraham. See also BIBLE, OLD TESTAMENT: 1 CHRONICLES 3.

43 His hand will be against every man, and every man's hand against him.
Genesis 16:12. The prophecy spoken to Hagar, the handmaiden of Abraham, of their unborn son Ishmael. He was banished into the desert, and is traditionally regarded as the father of the Arab nation.

44 Thy name shall be Abraham; for a father of many nations have I made thee.
Genesis 17:5. Abraham had previously been referred to in *Genesis* as Abram; his new name, a dialectal variant, is explained in relation to 'ab-hamôn, 'father of many'.

45 And I will establish my covenant between me and thee and thy seed after thee in their generations for an everlasting covenant, to be a God unto thee, and to thy seed after thee.

And I will give unto thee, and to thy seed after thee, the land wherein thou art a stranger, all the land of Canaan, for an everlasting possession; and I will be their God.
Genesis 17:7–8

46 Thou shalt keep my covenant therefore, thou, and thy seed after thee in their generations.

This is my covenant, which ye shall keep, between me and you and thy seed after thee; Every man child among you shall be circumcised.
Genesis 17:9–10

47 But his wife looked back from behind him, and she became a pillar of salt.
Genesis 19:26. Lot's wife turns to contemplate the destruction of Sodom and Gomorrah.

48 My son, God will provide himself a lamb for a burnt offering.
Genesis 22:8. Abraham answers Isaac's question: 'Where is the lamb for a burnt offering?'

49 Esau was a cunning hunter, a man of the field; and Jacob was a plain man, dwelling in tents.
Genesis 25:27

50 And he [Esau] sold his birthright unto Jacob.

Then Jacob gave Esau bread and pottage of lentiles; and he did eat and drink, and rose up, and went his way: thus Esau despised his birthright.
Genesis 25:33–4. The expression 'selleth his birthright for a

mess of pottage' comes from the chapter heading in the Geneva Bible (1560).

51 Behold, Esau my brother is a hairy man, and I am a smooth man.

Genesis 27:11. Jacob explains to his mother Rebekah how the blind Isaac might discover the ploy of his pretending to be Esau.

52 And he dreamed, and behold a ladder set up on the earth, and the top of it reached to heaven: and behold the angels of God ascending and descending on it.

Genesis 28:12. Jacob's vision at Bethel, as he slept on a pillow of stone.

53 I will not let thee go, except thou bless me.

Genesis 32:26. Jacob addresses the angel with whom he has wrestled at the ford of Jabbok, and who gives him the name Israel.

54 Now Israel loved Joseph more than all his children, because he was the son of his old age: and he made him a coat of many colours.

Genesis 37:3

55 Behold, this dreamer cometh.

Genesis 37:19. The words of Joseph's jealous brothers, before they cast him into a pit.

56 And they took him, and cast him into a pit: and the pit was empty, there was no water in it.

Genesis 37:24. Stripped of his coat, Joseph is cast into a pit by his brothers.

57 And Onan knew that the seed should not be his; and it came to pass, when he went in unto his brother's wife, that he spilled it on the ground, lest that he should give seed to his brother.

Genesis 38:9. Onan, son of Judah, refuses to follow the local tradition which requires him to impregnate his elder brother's widow, for which he is slain by God. The passage has been interpreted as a biblical condemnation of masturbation, though it is more likely that Onan was punished for not fulfilling his family obligations, and in any case the term 'spilling seed' probably refers to coitus interruptus.

58 And take your father and your households, and come unto me: and I will give you the good of the land of Egypt, and ye shall eat the fat of the land.

Genesis 45:18. Pharaoh's words to Joseph.

59 Unstable as water, thou shalt not excel.

Genesis 49:4. Jacob, before his death, referring to his eldest son Reuben.

60 His eyes shall be red with wine, and his teeth white with milk.

Genesis 49:12. Jacob referring to his son Judah, a 'lion's whelp'.

The Second Book of Moses, called Exodus

1 She took for him an ark of bulrushes, and daubed it with slime and with pitch, and put the child therein.

Exodus 2:3. Moses is concealed by his mother, 'a daughter of Levi'.

2 Who made thee a prince and a judge over us?

Exodus 2:14. A 'man of the Hebrews' rebuts a rebuke by Moses.

3 I have been a stranger in a strange land.

Exodus 2:22. Moses refers to his time in Egypt, explaining the name of his son, Gershom, meaning 'sojourner'.

4 And the angel of the Lord appeared unto him [Moses] in a flame of fire out of the midst of a bush: and he looked, and, behold, the bush burned with fire, and the bush was not consumed.

Exodus 3:2

5 Draw not nigh hither: put off thy shoes from off thy feet, for the place whereon thou standest is holy ground.

Exodus 3:5. God speaks to Moses from the burning bush.

6 And I am come down to deliver them out of the hand of the Egyptians, and to bring them up out of that land unto a good land and a large, unto a land flowing with milk and honey; unto the place of the Canaanites, and the Hittites, and the Amorites, and the Perizzites, and the Hivites, and the Jebusites.

Exodus 3:8. God directs Moses to deliver Israel. A 'land flowing with milk and honey' is also described in Exodus 33:3 and Jeremiah 11:5.

7 I AM THAT I AM.

Exodus 3:14. God's words to Moses.

8 Thus shalt thou say unto the children of Israel, the Lord God of your fathers, the God of Abraham, the God of Isaac, and the God of Jacob, hath sent me unto you: this is my name for ever, and this is my memorial unto all generations.

Exodus 3:15

9 O my Lord, I am not eloquent, neither heretofore, nor since thou hast spoken unto thy servant: but I am slow of speech, and of a slow tongue.

Exodus 4:10. Moses pleads his unsuitability to deliver the children of Israel.

10 Let my people go.

Exodus 5:1. The plea of Aaron and Moses to Pharaoh.

11 And I will harden Pharaoh's heart, and multiply my signs and my wonders in the land of Egypt.

Exodus 7:3. God promises to support Moses.

12 Take thy rod, and cast it before Pharaoh, and it shall become a serpent.

Exodus 7:9. God's instruction to Aaron, to show a miracle, which Pharaoh's magicians were able to imitate, though 'Aaron's rod swallowed up their rods'.

13 Stretch out thine hand toward heaven, that there may be darkness over the land of Egypt, even darkness which may be felt.

Exodus 10:21. God commands Moses to create a plague of darkness, which lasts three days, though 'all the children of Israel had light in their dwellings'.

14 Your lamb shall be without blemish, a male of the first year: ye shall take it out from the sheep, or from the goats:

And ye shall keep it up until the fourteenth day of the same month: and the whole assembly of the congregation of Israel shall kill it in the evening.

And they shall take of the blood, and strike it on the two side posts and on the upper door post of the houses, wherein they shall eat it.

Exodus 12:5–7. Instructions for the Passover.

15 And they shall eat the flesh in that night, roast with fire, and unleavened bread; and with bitter herbs they shall eat it.

Eat not of it raw, nor sodden at all with water, but roast with fire; his head with his legs, and with the purtenance thereof.

And ye shall let nothing of it remain until the morning; and that which remaineth of it until the morning ye shall burn with fire.

And thus shall ye eat it; with your loins girded, your shoes on your feet, and your staff in your hand; and ye shall eat it in haste: it is the Lord's passover.

Exodus 12:8–11.

16 For I will pass through the land of Egypt this night, and will smite all the firstborn in the land of Egypt, both man and beast; and against all the gods of Egypt I will execute judgment: I am the Lord.

Exodus 12:12

17 And the blood shall be to you for a token upon the houses where ye are: and when I see the blood, I will pass over you, and the plague shall not be upon you to destroy you, when I smite the land of Egypt.

Exodus 12:13

18 And this day shall be unto you for a memorial; and ye shall keep it a feast to the Lord throughout your generations; ye shall keep it a feast by an ordinance for ever.

Exodus 12:14. The institution of the Passover.

19 Seven days shall ye eat unleavened bread.

Exodus 12:15

20 And the Egyptians were urgent upon the people, that they might send them out of the land in haste; for they said, We be all dead men.

Exodus 12:33. Following the slaying of the firstborn, the Egyptians are anxious to let the children of Israel go.

21 And the Lord went before them by day in a pillar of a cloud, to lead them the way; and by night in a pillar of fire, to give them light.

Exodus 13:21

22 And the children of Israel went into the midst of the sea upon the dry ground: and the waters were a wall unto them on their right hand, and on their left.

Exodus 14:22. The crossing of the Red Sea.

23 The Lord is a man of war.

Exodus 15:3. The song of Moses and the children of Israel after their safe passage.

24 Would to God we had died by the hand of the Lord in the land of Egypt, when we sat by the flesh pots, and when we did eat bread to the full.

Exodus 16:3. The complaint of the Israelites in the wilderness of Sin.

25 I am the Lord thy God, which have brought thee out of the land of Egypt, out of the house of bondage.

Thou shalt have no other gods before me.

Thou shalt not make unto thee any graven image, or any likeness of any thing that is in heaven above, or that is in the earth beneath, or that is in the water under the earth:

Thou shalt not bow down thyself to them, nor serve them: for I the Lord thy God am a jealous God, visiting the iniquity of the fathers upon the children unto the third and fourth generation of them that hate me;

And showing mercy unto thousands of them that love me, and keep my commandments.

Thou shalt not take the name of the Lord thy God

in vain; for the Lord will not hold him guiltless that taketh his name in vain.

Remember the sabbath day, to keep it holy.

Six days shalt thou labour, and do all thy work:

But the seventh day is the sabbath of the Lord thy God: in it thou shalt not do any work, thou, nor thy son, nor thy daughter, thy manservant, nor thy maidservant, nor thy cattle, nor thy stranger that is within thy gates:

For in six days the Lord made heaven and earth, the sea, and all that in them is, and rested the seventh day: wherefore the Lord blessed the sabbath day, and hallowed it.

Honour thy father and thy mother: that thy days may be long upon the land which the Lord thy God giveth thee.

Thou shalt not kill.

Thou shalt not commit adultery.

Thou shalt not steal.

Thou shalt not bear false witness against thy neighbour.

Thou shalt not covet thy neighbour's house, thou shalt not covet thy neighbour's wife, nor his manservant, nor his maidservant, nor his ox, nor his ass, nor any thing that is thy neighbour's.

Exodus 20:2–17. The Ten Commandments, as given to Moses on Mount Sinai. They are also laid out in *Deuteronomy* 5:6– 21, with slight variations. Different religious communities vary in their enumeration, though most recognize the same contents.

26 And if thou wilt make me an altar of stone, thou shalt not build it of hewn stone: for if thou lift up thy tool upon it, thou hast polluted it.

Exodus 20:25

27 He that smiteth a man, so that he die, shall be surely put to death.

Exodus 21:12

28 He that curseth his father, or his mother, shall surely be put to death.

Exodus 21:17

29 And if any mischief follow, then thou shalt give life for life,

Eye for eye, tooth for tooth, hand for hand, foot for foot,

Burning for burning, wound for wound, stripe for stripe.

Exodus 21:23–5

30 Thou shalt not suffer a witch to live.

Exodus 22:18

31 I have seen this people, and, behold, it is a stiffnecked people.

Exodus 32:9. God's judgement on the children of Israel after they have worshipped a golden calf.

32 Who is on the Lord's side? let him come unto me.

Exodus 32:26. Moses addresses the idolatrous children of Israel.

33 Thou canst not see my face: for there shall no man see me, and live.

Exodus 33:20. God rejects Moses' request to 'shew me thy glory'.

34 Behold, there is a place by me, and thou shalt stand upon a rock:

And it shall come to pass, while my glory passeth by, that I will put thee in a clift of the rock, and will cover thee with my hand while I pass by:

And I will take away mine hand, and thou shalt see my back parts: but my face shall not be seen.

Exodus 33:21–3

The Third Book of Moses, called Leviticus

1 Whatsoever parteth the hoof, and is clovenfooted, and cheweth the cud, among the beasts, that shall ye eat.

Leviticus 11:3

2 And the swine, though he divide the hoof, and be clovenfooted, yet he cheweth not the cud; he is unclean to you.

Leviticus 11:7

3 But the goat, on which the lot fell to be the scapegoat, shall be presented alive before the Lord, to make an atonement with him, and to let him go for a scapegoat into the wilderness.

Leviticus 16:10

4 Thou shalt love thy neighbour as thyself.

Leviticus 19:18. The words, here referring only to 'the children of thy people', are also ascribed to both Jesus and Paul on various occasions in the New Testament.

5 If a man also lie with mankind, as he lieth with a woman, both of them have committed an abomination: they shall surely be put to death; their blood shall be upon them.

Leviticus 20:13

The Fourth Book of Moses, called Numbers

1 He shall separate himself from wine and strong drink, and shall drink no vinegar of wine, or vinegar of strong drink, neither shall he drink any liquor of grapes, nor eat moist grapes, or dried.

Numbers 6:3. The vow of a Nazarite (one who has dedicated himself to special sacred service).

2 All the days of the vow of his separation there shall no razor come upon his head: until the days be fulfilled, in the which he separateth himself unto the Lord, he shall be holy, and shall let the locks of the hair of his head grow.

Numbers 6:5

3 The Lord bless thee, and keep thee:
The Lord make his face shine upon thee, and be gracious unto thee:
The Lord lift up his countenance upon thee, and give thee peace.

Numbers 6:24–6. The form of blessing the people, ordained by God to be used by 'Aaron and . . . his sons'.

4 He whom thou blessest is blessed, and he whom thou cursest is cursed.

Numbers 22:6. Balak's message to Balaam, requesting his aid against the Israelites.

5 Let me die the death of the righteous.

Numbers 23:10. The words of Balaam, referring to the Israelites.

6 God is not a man, that he should lie; neither the son of man, that he should repent: hath he said, and shall he not do it? or hath he spoken, and shall he not make it good?

Numbers 23:19. The words of Balaam.

7 What hath God wrought!

Numbers 23:23. These words of Balaam were used by Samuel Morse in the first telegraph message, sent from Washington DC to Baltimore, 24 May 1844.

8 How goodly are thy tents, O Jacob, and thy tabernacles, O Israel!

Numbers 24:5. Balaam addresses the children of Israel.

9 I shall see him, but not now: I shall behold him, but not nigh: there shall come a Star out of Jacob, and a Sceptre shall rise out of Israel, and shall smite the corners of Moab, and destroy all the children of Sheth.

Numbers 24:17. Balaam's words have been taken as a prophecy of a great future king of Israel, referring either to David or the Messiah.

10 Be sure your sin will find you out.

Numbers 32:23. Moses addresses the Reubenites and Gadites.

11 So ye shall not pollute the land wherein ye are: for blood it defileth the land: and the land cannot be cleansed of the blood that is shed therein, but by the blood of him that shed it.

Numbers 35:33

The Fifth Book of Moses, called Deuteronomy

1 I call heaven and earth to witness against you this day.

Deuteronomy 4:26. Moses addresses the Israelites.

2 For the Lord thy God is a jealous God among you.

Deuteronomy 6:15. The words are also found in *Exodus* 20:5, referring to the commandment: 'Thou shalt not make unto thee any graven image' (see EXODUS 25).

3 Ye shall not tempt the Lord your God.

Deuteronomy 6:16. The words are recalled by Jesus: see MATTHEW 17.

4 For thou art an holy people unto the Lord thy God: the Lord thy God hath chosen thee to be a special people unto himself, above all people that are upon the face of the earth.

Deuteronomy 7:6. Moses addresses the Israelites.

5 Man doth not live by bread only, but by every word that proceedeth out of the mouth of the Lord doth man live.

Deuteronomy 8:3. These are probably the words recalled in *Matthew* (see MATTHEW 16).

6 For the Lord thy God bringeth thee into a good land, a land of brooks of water, of fountains and depths that spring out of valleys and hills;
A land of wheat, and barley, and vines, and fig trees, and pomegranates; a land of oil olive, and honey;
A land wherein thou shalt eat bread without scarceness, thou shalt not lack any thing in it; a land whose stones are iron, and out of whose hills thou mayest dig brass.

Deuteronomy 8:7–9

7 If there arise among you a prophet, or a dreamer of dreams, and giveth thee a sign or a wonder,
And the sign or the wonder come to pass, whereof he spake unto thee, saying, Let us go after other

gods, which thou hast not known, and let us serve them;

Thou shalt not hearken unto the words of that prophet, or that dreamer of dreams.

Deuteronomy 13:1–3

8 For the poor shall never cease out of the land: therefore I command thee, saying, Thou shalt open thine hand wide unto thy brother, to thy poor, and to thy needy, in thy land.

Deuteronomy 15:11

9 When a man hath taken a new wife, he shall not go out to war, neither shall he be charged with any business: but he shall be free at home one year, and shall cheer up his wife which he hath taken.

Deuteronomy 24:5

10 Cursed be he that removeth his neighbour's landmark. And all the people shall say, Amen.

Deuteronomy 27:17. See also PROVERBS 67.

11 The Lord will smite thee with the botch of Egypt, and with the emerods, and with the scab, and with the itch, whereof thou canst not be healed.

Deuteronomy 28:27. Emerods are piles.

12 And thou shalt become an astonishment, a proverb, and a byword, among all nations whither the Lord shall lead thee.

Deuteronomy 28:37. In *1 Kings* 9:7, God warns Solomon that Israel would be 'a proverb and a byword among all people' should it ignore the commandments and statutes.

13 The secret things belong unto the Lord our God: but those things which are revealed belong unto us and to our children for ever.

Deuteronomy 29:29

14 I have set before you life and death, blessing and cursing: therefore choose life, that both thou and thy seed may live.

Deuteronomy 30:19

15 Be strong and of a good courage, fear not, nor be afraid of them: for the Lord thy God, he it is that doth go with thee; he will not fail thee, nor forsake thee.

Deuteronomy 31:6. Similar words recur in *Deuteronomy* 31:7 and 31:23, and *Joshua* 1:9.

16 Give ear, O ye heavens, and I will speak; and hear, O earth, the words of my mouth.

My doctrine shall drop as the rain, my speech shall distil as the dew, as the small rain upon the tender herb, and as the showers upon the grass.

Deuteronomy 32:1–2. The song of Moses.

17 He found him in a desert land, and in the waste howling wilderness; he led him about, he instructed him, he kept him as the apple of his eye.

Deuteronomy 32:10. Moses recalls God's treatment of Jacob.

18 Thou art waxen fat, thou art grown thick, thou art covered with fatness.

Deuteronomy 32:15

19 Blessed of the Lord be his land, for the precious things of heaven, for the dew, and for the deep that coucheth beneath.

Deuteronomy 33:13

20 Thy shoes shall be iron and brass; and as thy days, so shall thy strength be.

Deuteronomy 33:25. Moses blesses Asher.

The Book of Joshua

1 And it came to pass, when the people heard the sound of the trumpet, and the people shouted with a great shout, that the wall fell down flat, so that the people went up into the city, every man straight before him, and they took the city.

And they utterly destroyed all that was in the city, both man and woman, young and old, and ox, and sheep, and ass, with the edge of the sword.

Joshua 6:20–1. The destruction of Jericho.

2 So the Lord was with Joshua; and his fame was noised throughout all the country.

Joshua 6:27

3 Let them live; but let them be hewers of wood and drawers of water unto all the congregation.

Joshua 9:21. Referring to the Gibeonites, condemned to perpetual bondage.

4 I am going the way of all the earth.

Joshua 23:14. Joshua, 'waxed old and stricken in age', announces he will shortly die. Also translated 'the way of all flesh'.

The Book of Judges

1 I will not drive them out from before you; but they shall be as thorns in your sides, and their gods shall be a snare unto you.

Judges 2:3. An angel rebukes the children of Israel for not having completed the settlement of the promised lands. See also 2 CORINTHIANS 15.

2 And the anger of the Lord was hot against Israel, and he delivered them into the hands of spoilers.

Judges 2:14. God's wrath against the Israelites after they had forsaken his worship.

3 Then Jael Heber's wife took a nail of the tent, and took an hammer in her hand, and went softly unto him, and smote the nail into his temples, and fastened it into the ground: for he was fast asleep and weary. So he died.

Judges 4:21. The slaying of Sisera, the Canaanite general, by Jael. The incident is described more graphically in the Song of Deborah, *Judges* 5:25–7.

4 The inhabitants of the villages ceased, they ceased in Israel, until that I Deborah arose, that I arose a mother in Israel.

Judges 5:7. Part of the Song of Deborah, thought to be the oldest extant Israelite poem.

5 Awake, awake, Deborah: awake, awake, utter a song: arise, Barak, and lead thy captivity captive, thou son of Abinoam.

Judges 5:12. The words 'thou hast led captivity captive' occur in *Psalms* 68:18.

6 Why abodest thou among the sheepfolds, to hear the bleatings of the flocks?

Judges 5:16

7 He asked water, and she gave him milk; she brought forth butter in a lordly dish.

Judges 5:25. Jael's hospitality to Sisera before slaying him.

8 For they had golden earrings, because they were Ishmaelites.

Judges 8:24

9 Then said they unto him, Say now Shibboleth: and he said Sibboleth: for he could not frame to pronounce it right. Then they took him, and slew him at the passages of Jordan.

Judges 12:6. The Ephraimites are challenged by the Gileadites and revealed by their mispronunciation. 'Shibboleth' (an ear of corn) has subsequently come to mean a distinguishing custom, doctrine or phrase.

10 Out of the eater came forth meat, and out of the strong came forth sweetness.

Judges 14:14. The riddle of Samson, put to guests at his wedding feast, referring to the carcass of a lion in which he found 'a swarm of bees and honey'. The prize was 'thirty sheets and thirty change of garments'.

11 If ye had not plowed with my heifer, ye had not found out my riddle.

Judges 14:18. Samson addresses the men who had persuaded his wife to divulge the answer to his riddle.

12 With the jawbone of an ass, heaps upon heaps, with the jaw of an ass have I slain a thousand men.

Judges 15:16. Samson recounts his slaughter of the Philistines.

13 The Philistines be upon thee, Samson.

Judges 16:9, 12, 14 and 20. Delilah's warning to test whether Samson still has his strength.

14 But the Philistines took him [Samson], and put out his eyes, and brought him down to Gaza, and bound him with fetters of brass, and he did grind in the prison house.

Judges 16:21

15 In those days there was no king in Israel, but every man did that which was right in his own eyes.

Judges 17:6. The words are repeated in *Judges* 21:25, the last verse of the book.

16 And all the people arose as one man.

Judges 20:8. The Israelites rise against Gibeah.

The Book of Ruth

1 Intreat me not to leave thee, or to return from following after thee: for whither thou goest, I will go; and where thou lodgest, I will lodge: thy people shall be my people, and thy God my God.

Ruth 1:16. Ruth addresses her mother-in-law Naomi.

2 Go not empty unto thy mother-in-law.

Ruth 3:17. The words of Boaz to Ruth.

The First Book of Samuel

1 The Lord called Samuel: and he answered, Here am I.

1 Samuel 3:4

2 Speak, Lord; for thy servant heareth.

1 Samuel 3:9. Eli advises Samuel how to respond to God's call.

3 Be strong, and quit yourselves like men, O ye Philistines, that ye be not servants unto the Hebrews, as they have been to you: quit yourselves like men, and fight.

1 Samuel 4:9

4 And she named the child I-chabod, saying, The glory is departed from Israel.

1 Samuel 4:21. Referring to the wife of Phinehas, after the ark of God is taken by the Philistines. The name means '[there is] no glory'.

5 Is Saul also among the prophets?

1 Samuel 10:11. The words of old acquaintances of Saul who now see him prophesy.

6 And all the people shouted, and said, God save the king.

1 Samuel 10:24. Saul is acclaimed as first king of Israel.

7 The Lord hath sought him a man after his own

heart, and the Lord hath commanded him to be captain over his people.

1 Samuel 13:14. Samuel refers to Saul's replacement, David.

8 Every man's sword was against his fellow.

1 Samuel 14:20. See also EZEKIEL 7.

9 Hath the Lord as great delight in burnt offerings and sacrifices, as in obeying the voice of the Lord? Behold, to obey is better than sacrifice, and to hearken than the fat of rams.

For rebellion is as the sin of witchcraft, and stubbornness is as iniquity and idolatry.

1 Samuel 15:22–3. Samuel rebukes Saul's disobedience.

10 Look not on his countenance, or on the height of his stature; because I have refused him: for the Lord seeth not as man seeth; for man looketh on the outward appearance, but the Lord looketh on the heart.

1 Samuel 16:7. God warns Samuel not to mistake his choice for the new king of Israel.

11 Now he was ruddy, and withal of a beautiful countenance, and goodly to look to. And the Lord said, Arise, anoint him: for this is he.

1 Samuel 16:12. David is acknowledged to be king of Israel.

12 I know thy pride, and the naughtiness of thine heart.

1 Samuel 17:28. David is rebuked by his brother Eliab for abandoning his flock.

13 Let no man's heart fail because of him; thy servant will go and fight with this Philistine.

1 Samuel 17:32. David offers to fight Goliath.

14 David said moreover, The Lord that delivered me out of the paw of the lion, and out of the paw of the bear, he will deliver me out of the hand of this Philistine. And Saul said unto David, Go, and the Lord be with thee.

1 Samuel 17:37

15 And he took his staff in his hand, and chose him five smooth stones out of the brook.

1 Samuel 17:40

16 The soul of Jonathan was knit with the soul of David, and Jonathan loved him as his own soul.

1 Samuel 18:1

17 Saul hath slain his thousands, and David his ten thousands.

1 Samuel 18:7. Said by the women of Israel after David killed Goliath.

18 Behold, I have played the fool, and have erred exceedingly.

1 Samuel 26:21. Saul acknowledges his folly to David.

The Second Book of Samuel

1 The beauty of Israel is slain upon thy high places: how are the mighty fallen!

2 Samuel 1:19. David laments the death of Saul and Jonathan at the battle of Gilboa. See also 2 SAMUEL 4 AND 6.

2 Tell it not in Gath, publish it not in the streets of Askelon; lest the daughters of the Philistines rejoice, lest the daughters of the uncircumcised triumph.

2 Samuel 1:20. David's lament.

3 Saul and Jonathan were lovely and pleasant in their lives, and in their death they were not divided: they were swifter than eagles, they were stronger than lions.

2 Samuel 1:23. David's lament.

4 How are the mighty fallen in the midst of the battle!

2 Samuel 1:25. See also 2 SAMUEL 1 AND 6.

5 I am distressed for thee, my brother Jonathan: very pleasant hast thou been unto me: thy love to me was wonderful, passing the love of women.

2 Samuel 1:26

6 How are the mighty fallen, and the weapons of war perished!

2 Samuel 1:27. See also 2 SAMUEL 1 AND 4.

7 Tarry at Jericho until your beards be grown.

2 Samuel 10:5. David instructs his two servants whom Hanun has half-shaved. The words also appear in *1 Chronicles* 19:5.

8 But the poor man had nothing, save one little ewe lamb.

2 Samuel 12:3. The parable of the ewe lamb.

9 Thou art the man.

2 Samuel 12:7. Nathan identifies David as the villain of his parable.

10 For we needs must die, and are as water spilt on the ground, which cannot be gathered up again; neither doth God respect any person.

2 Samuel 14:14. The woman of Tekoah speaks to King David.

11 Come out, come out, thou bloody man, and thou man of Belial.

2 Samuel 16:7. Shimei curses David.

12 O my son Absalom, my son, my son Absalom!

would God I had died for thee, O Absalom, my son, my son!

2 Samuel 18:33. David's lament for Absalom, his favourite son, killed by Joab.

13 David the son of Jesse . . . the sweet psalmist of Israel.

2 Samuel 23:1

The First Book of the Kings

1 He said moreover, I have something to say unto thee. And she said, Say on.

1 Kings 2:14. Exchange between Adonijah and Bath-sheba.

2 And Judah and Israel dwelt safely, every man under his vine and under his fig tree, from Dan even to Beer-sheba, all the days of Solomon.

1 Kings 4:25. The words 'From Dan even to Beer-sheba' also appear in *Judges* 20:1.

3 And he spake three thousand proverbs: and his songs were a thousand and five.

1 Kings 4:32. Referring to Solomon.

4 And there came of all people to hear the wisdom of Solomon, from all kings of the earth, which had heard of his wisdom.

1 Kings 4:34

5 But king Solomon loved many strange women.

1 Kings 11:1. According to *1 Kings* 11:3, Solomon had 'seven hundred wives, princesses, and three hundred concubines'.

6 And Solomon slept with his fathers.

1 Kings 11:43. The death of Solomon.

7 My father hath chastised you with whips, but I will chastise you with scorpions.

1 Kings 12:11. The response of Rehoboam to the plea of the Israelites for their yoke to be lightened, as advised by 'the young men that were grown up with him', and in opposition to his father's advisers.

8 To your tents, O Israel: now see to thine own house, David.

1 Kings 12:16. The Israelites reject the harsh rule of Rehoboam.

9 And the ravens brought him bread and flesh in the morning, and bread and flesh in the evening; and he drank of the brook.

1 Kings 17:6. Referring to Elijah.

10 How long halt ye between two opinions?

1 Kings 18:21. Elijah addresses the Israelites.

11 Cry aloud: for he is a god; either he is talking, or

he is pursuing, or he is in a journey, or peradventure he sleepeth, and must be awaked.

1 Kings 18:27. Elijah mocks the prophets of Baal, who have been given a bullock to worship.

12 There is a sound of abundance of rain.

1 Kings 18:41. Elijah announces to Ahab the end of a drought.

13 And he girded up his loins, and ran before Ahab.

1 Kings 18:46. Referring to Elijah.

14 But the Lord was not in the wind: and after the wind an earthquake; but the Lord was not in the earthquake:

And after the earthquake a fire; but the Lord was not in the fire: and after the fire a still small voice.

1 Kings 19:11–12

15 Hast thou found me, O mine enemy?

1 Kings 21:20. Ahab addresses Elijah.

16 I saw all Israel scattered upon the hills, as sheep that have not a shepherd.

1 Kings 22:17. Micaiah's prophecy to Ahab.

17 Put this fellow in the prison, and feed him with bread of affliction and with water of affliction, until I come in peace.

1 Kings 22:27. Ahab's command regarding Micaiah, who has prophesied Ahab's doom.

The Second Book of the Kings

1 Behold, there appeared a chariot of fire, and horses of fire . . . and Elijah went up by a whirlwind into heaven.

2 Kings 2:11

2 And he took the mantle of Elijah.

2 Kings 2:13. Elijah had cast his mantle upon Elisha in *1 Kings* 19:19, as a symbol of his prophetic office, thereby anointing him as his successor.

3 There came forth little children out of the city, and mocked him, and said unto him, Go up, thou bald head; go up, thou bald head.

And he turned back, and looked on them, and cursed them in the name of the Lord. And there came forth two she bears out of the wood, and tare forty and two children of them.

2 Kings 2:23–4. Referring to Elisha.

4 There is death in the pot.

2 Kings 4:40. Said by the sons of the prophets, referring to poisonous herbs in a meal prepared for them, which Elisha makes harmless.

5 Let him come now to me, and he shall know that there is a prophet in Israel.

2 Kings 5:8. Elisha invites Namaan to come to him to be cured of leprosy.

6 Is thy servant a dog, that he should do this great thing?

2 Kings 8:13. Hazael questions Elisha's prophecy that Hazael will ravage Israel.

7 What hast thou to do with peace? turn thee behind me.

2 Kings 9:18 and 19. Jehu addresses Joram's messenger.

8 The driving is like the driving of Jehu the son of Nimshi; for he driveth furiously.

2 Kings 9:20. The report of Joram's watchman, observing Jehu from afar.

9 Who is on my side? who? And there looked out to him two or three eunuchs.

2 Kings 9:32. The appeal of Jehu for help to slay Jezebel.

10 Now, behold, thou trustest upon the staff of this bruised reed, even upon Egypt, on which if a man lean, it will go into his hand, and pierce it: so is Pharaoh king of Egypt unto all that trust on him.

2 Kings 18:21

11 Set thine house in order, for thou shalt die, and not live.

2 Kings 20:1. Isaiah's prophecy to Hezekiah (see also *Isaiah* 38:1).

12 Then he turned his face to the wall, and prayed unto the Lord.

2 Kings 20:2. Hezekiah's response to Isaiah's prophecy.

The First Book of the Chronicles

1 O give thanks unto the Lord; for he is good; for his mercy endureth for ever.

1 Chronicles 16:34. David's psalm of thanksgiving.

2 For we are strangers before thee, and sojourners, as were all our fathers: our days on the earth are as a shadow, and there is none abiding.

1 Chronicles 29:15. David's thanksgiving.

3 And he died in a good old age, full of days, riches, and honour.

1 Chronicles 29:28. Referring to David. See also GENESIS 42.

The Second Book of the Chronicles

1 For the eyes of the Lord run to and fro throughout the whole earth, to shew himself strong in the behalf of them whose heart is perfect toward him. Herein thou hast done foolishly: therefore from henceforth thou shalt have wars.

2 Chronicles 16:9. The words of Hanani the seer to Asa, king of Judah.

The Book of Nehemiah

1 They which builded on the wall, and they that bare burdens, with those that laded, every one with one of his hands wrought in the work, and with the other hand held a weapon.

For the builders, every one had his sword girded by his side, and so builded.

Nehemiah 4:17–18. The rebuilding of the wall around Jerusalem.

2 Go your way, eat the fat, and drink the sweet, and send portions unto them for whom nothing is prepared: for this day is holy unto our Lord.

Nehemiah 8:10

3 But thou art a God ready to pardon, gracious and merciful, slow to anger, and of great kindness.

Nehemiah 9:17

The Book of Esther

1 And the king loved Esther above all the women, and she obtained grace and favour in his sight more than all the virgins.

Esther 2:17. Referring to King Ahasuerus.

2 There was great mourning among the Jews, and fasting, and weeping, and wailing; and many lay in sackcloth and ashes.

Esther 4:3. The response to Haman's decree ordering the Jews to be put to death.

3 What shall be done unto the man whom the king delighteth to honour?

Esther 6:6. King Ahasuerus addresses Haman.

The Book of Job

1 There was a man in the land of Uz, whose name was Job; and that man was perfect and upright, and one that feared God, and eschewed evil.

Job 1:1

2 And the Lord said unto Satan, Whence comest thou? Then Satan answered the Lord, and said, From going to and fro in the earth, and from walking up and down in it.

Job 1:7. The exchange is repeated in 2:2.

3 Doth Job fear God for nought?

Job 1:9. Satan addresses God.

4 Naked came I out of my mother's womb, and naked shall I return thither.

Job 1:21. These words of Job are almost identical to ones used in AESOP'S FABLES, no. 120 (6th century BC).

5 The Lord gave, and the Lord hath taken away; blessed be the name of the Lord.

Job 1:21

6 Skin for skin, yea, all that a man hath will he give for his life.

Job 2:4. The words of Satan.

7 Dost thou still retain thine integrity? curse God, and die.

Job 2:9. Job's wife addresses Job, who is wracked by 'sore boils from the sole of his foot unto his crown'.

8 Let the day perish wherein I was born, and the night in which it was said, There is a man child conceived.

Job 3:3. A similar imprecation appears in *Jeremiah* 20:14-15.

9 For now should I have lain still and been quiet, I should have slept: then had I been at rest,
With kings and counsellors of the earth, which built desolate places for themselves.

Job 3:13–14. Job regrets his survival at birth.

10 There the wicked cease from troubling; and there the weary be at rest.
There the prisoners rest together; they hear not the voice of the oppressor.
The small and great are there; and the servant is free from his master.

Job 3:17–19. The solaces of death.

11 Wherefore is light given to him that is in misery, and life unto the bitter in soul;
Which long for death, but it cometh not; and dig for it more than for hid treasures;
Which rejoice exceedingly, and are glad, when they can find the grave?

Job 3:20–2

12 Shall mortal man be more just than God? shall a man be more pure than his maker?

Job 4:17. The words of a spirit in the vision of Eliphaz.

13 Yet man is born unto trouble, as the sparks fly upward.

Job 5:7. The words of Eliphaz to Job.

14 At destruction and famine thou shalt laugh:
neither shalt thou be afraid of the beasts of the earth.
For thou shalt be in league with the stones of the field: and the beasts of the field shall be at peace with thee.

Job 5:22–3. The benefits of God's protection.

15 Is there not an appointed time to man upon earth? are not his days also like the days of an hireling?

Job 7:1. Job speaks.

16 When I lie down, I say, When shall I arise, and the night be gone? and I am full of tossings to and fro unto the dawning of the day.

Job 7:4

17 My days are swifter than a weaver's shuttle, and are spent without hope.
O remember that my life is wind.

Job 7:6–7. Job laments his suffering.

18 As the cloud is consumed and vanisheth away: so he that goeth down to the grave shall come up no more.
He shall return no more to his house, neither shall his place know him any more.

Job 7:9–10

19 Therefore I will not refrain my mouth; I will speak in the anguish of my spirit; I will complain in the bitterness of my soul.

Job 7:11. Job voices his complaint.

20 My bed shall comfort me, my couch shall ease my complaint.

Job 7:13

21 The just upright man is laughed to scorn.

Job 12:4

22 But ask now the beasts, and they shall teach thee; and the fowls of the air, and they shall tell thee:
Or speak to the earth, and it shall teach thee: and the fishes of the sea shall declare unto thee.

Job 12:7–8

23 With the ancient is wisdom; and in length of days understanding.

Job 12:12

24 But ye are forgers of lies, ye are all physicians of no value.
O that ye would altogether hold your peace! And it should be your wisdom.

Job 13:4–5. Job reproves his friends.

25 Man that is born of a woman is of few days,
and full of trouble.
He cometh forth like a flower, and is cut down: he
fleeth also as a shadow, and continueth not.
Job 14:1–2. See also BOOK OF COMMON PRAYER 88.

26 As the waters fail from the sea, and the flood
decayeth and drieth up:
So man lieth down, and riseth not: till the heavens
be no more, they shall not awake, nor be raised
out of their sleep.
Job 14:11–12

27 If a man die, shall he live again? all the days of
my appointed time will I wait, till my change
come.
Job 14:14

28 Miserable comforters are ye all.
Job 16:2. Job rejects the arguments of his friends.

29 My bone cleaveth to my skin and to my flesh,
and I am escaped with the skin of my teeth.
Job 19:20. Job asks pity of his friends.

30 Oh that my words were now written! Oh that
they were printed in a book!
That they were graven with an iron pen and lead
in the rock for ever!
Job 19:23–4. Job laments his sorry state.

31 For I know that my redeemer liveth, and that he
shall stand at the latter day upon the earth:
And though after my skin worms destroy this
body, yet in my flesh shall I see God.
Job 19:25–6. Job confirms his belief in the resurrection.

32 He hath swallowed down riches, and he shall
vomit them up again: God shall cast them out of
his belly.
Job 20:15. Zophar describes 'the portion of the wicked'.

33 Suffer me that I may speak; and after that I
have spoken, mock on.
Job 21:3. Job addresses his friends.

34 But where shall wisdom be found? and where is
the place of understanding?
Man knoweth not the price thereof; neither is it
found in the land of the living.
Job 28:12–13

35 No mention shall be made of coral, or of pearls:
for the price of wisdom is above rubies.
The topaz of Ethiopia shall not equal it, neither
shall it be valued with pure gold.
Job 28:18–19. See also PROVERBS 16.

36 I was eyes to the blind, and feet was I to the lame.
Job 29:15. Job recalls his past life.

37 I am a brother to dragons, and a companion to
owls.
Job 30:29. Job describes his outcast state.

38 Days should speak, and multitude of years
should teach wisdom.
But there is a spirit in man: and the inspiration of
the Almighty giveth them understanding.
Great men are not always wise: neither do the
aged understand judgment.
Job 32:7–9. Elihu, a young man, criticizes Job and his 'very
old' companions.

39 Therefore doth Job open his mouth in vain; he
multiplieth words without knowledge.
Job 35:16

40 Then the Lord answered Job out of the
whirlwind, and said,
Who is this that darkeneth counsel by words
without knowledge?
Gird up now thy loins like a man.
Job 38:1–3

41 When the morning stars sang together, and all
the sons of God shouted for joy.
Job 38:7

42 Hitherto shalt thou come, but no further: and
here shall thy proud waves be stayed.
Job 38:11. God tells of how he 'shut up the sea with doors'.

43 Hath the rain a father? or who hath begotten
the drops of dew?
Job 38:28. God challenges Job to accept his omnipotence.

44 Canst thou bind the sweet influences of
Pleiades, or loose the bands of Orion?
Job 38:31

45 Behold, I am vile; what shall I answer thee? I
will lay mine hand upon my mouth.
Job 40:4. Job abases himself before God's rebuke.

46 Behold now behemoth, which I made with
thee; he eateth grass as an ox.
Job 40:15. The 'behemoth' described by God (referred to by
JOHN MILTON and JAMES THOMSON) is usually taken to be
a hippopotamus.

47 Canst thou draw out leviathan with an hook?
Job 41:1. The creature – also mentioned in *Psalms* 74:14,
PSALMS 109 and ISAIAH 36 – may be a whale, sea-serpent
or crocodile, and the name has been used to describe any
powerful creature living in the sea, or a ship. For THOMAS

HOBBES, it represented the absolute political state. See also JOHN MILTON 157.

48 So the Lord blessed the latter end of Job more than his beginning.
Job 42:12

The Book of Psalms

1 Blessed is the man that walketh not in the counsel of the ungodly, nor standeth in the way of sinners, nor sitteth in the seat of the scornful.
Psalms 1:1

2 Why do the heathen rage, and the people imagine a vain thing?
Psalms 2:1

3 Blessed are all they that put their trust in him.
Psalms 2:12

4 Lord, lift thou up the light of thy countenance upon us.
Psalms 4:6

5 I will both lay me down in peace, and sleep.
Psalms 4:8. 'I will lay me down in peace, and take my rest' in Book of Common Prayer, *Psalms* 4:9.

6 Out of the mouth of babes and sucklings hast thou ordained strength because of thine enemies, that thou mightest still the enemy and the avenger.
Psalms 8:2

7 When I consider thy heavens, the work of thy fingers, the moon and the stars, which thou hast ordained;
What is man, that thou art mindful of him? and the son of man, that thou visitest him?
For thou hast made him a little lower than the angels, and hast crowned him with glory and honour.
Psalms 8:3–5. See JOSH BILLINGS 1.

8 How long wilt thou forget me, O Lord? for ever? how long wilt thou hide thy face from me?
Psalms 13:1

9 The fool hath said in his heart, There is no God.
Psalms 14:1. The words are repeated in 53:1.

10 Lord, who shall abide in thy tabernacle? who shall dwell in thy holy hill?
Psalms 15:1

11 He that sweareth to his own hurt, and changeth not.

He that putteth not out his money to usury, nor taketh reward against the innocent. He that doeth these things shall never be moved.
Psalms 15:4–5

12 The lines are fallen unto me in pleasant places; yea, I have a goodly heritage.
Psalms 16:6. Referring to property boundaries.

13 The Lord is my rock, and my fortress, and my deliverer; my God, my strength, in whom I will trust; my buckler, and the horn of my salvation, and my high tower.
Psalms 18:2

14 And he rode upon a cherub, and did fly: yea, he did fly upon the wings of the wind.
Psalms 18:10

15 The heavens declare the glory of God; and the firmament sheweth his handywork.
Day unto day uttereth speech, and night unto night sheweth knowledge.
There is no speech nor language, where their voice is not heard.
Psalms 19:1–3

16 Their line is gone out through all the earth, and their words to the end of the world. In them hath he set a tabernacle for the sun,
Which is as a bridegroom coming out of his chamber, and rejoiceth as a strong man to run a race.
Psalms 19:4–5

17 The fear of the Lord is clean, enduring for ever: the judgments of the Lord are true and righteous altogether.
More to be desired are they than gold, yea, than much fine gold: sweeter also than honey and the honeycomb.
Psalms 19:9–10

18 Who can understand his errors? cleanse thou me from secret faults.
Psalms 19:12

19 Let the words of my mouth, and the meditation of my heart, be acceptable in thy sight, O Lord, my strength, and my redeemer.
Psalms 19:14

20 Some trust in chariots, and some in horses: but we will remember the name of the Lord our God.
Psalms 20:7

21 Thou hast given him his heart's desire, and hast
not withholden the request of his lips.

Psalms 21:2

22 My God, my God, why hast thou forsaken me?
Why art thou so far from helping me, and from
the words of my roaring?

*Psalms 22:1. This psalm of David was recited by Jesus on the
cross: see* MATTHEW 171.

23 I am poured out like water, and all my bones
are out of joint: my heart is like wax; it is
melted in the midst of my bowels.

Psalms 22:14

24 The Lord is my shepherd; I shall not want.
He maketh me to lie down in green pastures: he
leadeth me beside the still waters.

Psalms 23:1–2

25 Yea, though I walk through the valley of the
shadow of death, I will fear no evil: for thou art
with me; thy rod and thy staff they comfort me.

Psalms 23:4

26 Thou preparest a table before me in the
presence of mine enemies: thou anointest my
head with oil; my cup runneth over.

Psalms 23:5

27 Surely goodness and mercy shall follow me all
the days of my life: and I will dwell in the house
of the Lord for ever.

Psalms 23:6

28 The earth is the Lord's, and the fulness thereof;
the world, and they that dwell therein.
For he hath founded it upon the seas, and
established it upon the floods.

*Psalms 24:1–2. The words are recalled in the New Testament:
see* 1 CORINTHIANS 26.

29 Lift up your heads, O ye gates; and be ye lift up,
ye everlasting doors; and the King of glory shall
come in.
Who is this King of glory? The Lord strong and
mighty, the Lord mighty in battle.

Psalms 24:7–8

30 Remember not the sins of my youth, nor my
transgressions.

Psalms 25:7

31 Redeem Israel, O God, out of all his troubles.

Psalms 25:22

32 The Lord is my light and my salvation; whom

shall I fear? the Lord is the strength of my life;
of whom shall I be afraid?

Psalms 27:1. The Latin phrase, Dominus illuminatio mea *('The
Lord is my light'), as found in the Vulgate edition of the Bible,
is the motto of Oxford University.*

33 Teach me thy way, O Lord, and lead me in a
plain path, because of mine enemies.

Psalms 27:11

34 I had fainted, unless I had believed to see the
goodness of the Lord in the land of the living.

Psalms 27:13

35 The Lord is my strength and my shield; my
heart trusted in him, and I am helped.

Psalms 28:7

36 Weeping may endure for a night, but joy
cometh in the morning.

Psalms 30:5

37 I am forgotten as a dead man out of mind: I am
like a broken vessel.

Psalms 31:12

38 Thou shalt keep them secretly in a pavilion
from the strife of tongues.

Psalms 31:20. Referring to those who fear and trust in God.

39 When I kept silence, my bones waxed old
through my roaring all the day long.

Psalms 32:3

40 Be ye not as the horse, or as the mule, which
have no understanding: whose mouth must be
held in with bit and bridle, lest they come near
unto thee.

Psalms 32:9

41 Praise the Lord with harp: sing unto him with
the psaltery and an instrument of ten strings.
Sing unto him a new song; play skilfully with a
loud noise.

Psalms 33:2–3

42 O taste and see that the Lord is good: blessed is
the man that trusteth in him.

Psalms 34:8

43 How excellent is thy loving kindness, O God!
therefore the children of men put their trust
under the shadow of thy wings.

Psalms 36:7

44 Fret not thyself because of evildoers, neither be
thou envious against the workers of iniquity.

Psalms 37:1

45 But the meek shall inherit the earth; and shall delight themselves in the abundance of peace.
Psalms 37:11. See also MATTHEW 22.

46 I have been young, and now am old; yet have I not seen the righteous forsaken, nor his seed begging bread.
Psalms 37:25

47 I have seen the wicked in great power, and spreading himself like a green bay tree.
Psalms 37:35

48 Mark the perfect man, and behold the upright: for the end of that man is peace.
Psalms 37:37

49 Lord, make me to know mine end, and the measure of my days, what it is; that I may know how frail I am.
Psalms 39:4

50 Surely every man walketh in a vain shew: surely they are disquieted in vain: he heapeth up riches, and knoweth not who shall gather them.
Psalms 39:6

51 I am a stranger with thee, and a sojourner, as all my fathers were.
O spare me, that I may recover strength, before I go hence, and be no more.
Psalms 39:12–13

52 Yea, mine own familiar friend, in whom I trusted, which did eat of my bread, hath lifted up his heel against me.
Psalms 41:9

53 As the hart panteth after the water brooks, so panteth my soul after thee, O God.
My soul thirsteth for God, for the living God: when shall I come and appear before God?
Psalms 42:1–2. In the Book of Common Prayer, the lines are: 'Like as the hart desireth the water-brooks: so longeth my soul after thee, O God./My soul is a thirst for God, yea, even for the living God.' See also NAHUM TATE 3.

54 Why art thou cast down, O my soul? And why art thou disquieted in me?
Psalms 42:5

55 Deep calleth unto deep at the noise of thy waterspouts; all thy waves and thy billows are gone over me.
Psalms 42:7

56 Yea, for thy sake are we killed all the day long; we are counted as sheep for the slaughter.
Psalms 44:22

57 I speak of the things which I have made touching the king: my tongue is the pen of a ready writer.
Psalms 45:1

58 God is our refuge and strength, a very present help in trouble.
Therefore will not we fear, though the earth be removed, and though the mountains be carried into the midst of the sea.
Psalms 46:1–2

59 O clap your hands, all ye people; shout unto God with the voice of triumph.
Psalms 47:1

60 God is gone up with a shout, the Lord with the sound of a trumpet.
Psalms 47:5. In the Book of Common Prayer, the words are: 'God is gone up with a merry noise: and the Lord with the sound of the trump.'

61 For every beast of the forest is mine, and the cattle upon a thousand hills.
I know all the fowls of the mountains: and the wild beasts of the field are mine.
Psalms 50:10–11

62 Wash me throughly from mine iniquity, and cleanse me from my sin.
For I acknowledge my transgressions: and my sin is ever before me.
Against thee, thee only, have I sinned, and done this evil in thy sight.
Psalms 50:2–4

63 Behold, I was shapen in iniquity; and in sin did my mother conceive me.
Psalms 51:5

64 Purge me with hyssop, and I shall be clean: wash me, and I shall be whiter than snow.
Psalms 51:7. Probably referring to *Origanum maru* (Syrian marjoram), not European hyssop. See BIBLE: VULGATE 1.

65 The sacrifices of God are a broken spirit: a broken and a contrite heart, O God, thou wilt not despise.
Psalms 51:17

66 Oh that I had wings like a dove! for then would I fly away, and be at rest.
Psalms 55:6. The words were adapted by William Bartholo-

mew as 'Hear My Prayer' and set to music by Mendelssohn: 'O for the wings of a dove!/Far away would I rove!'

67 For it was not an enemy that reproached me; then I could have borne it: neither was it he that hated me that did magnify himself against me; then I would have hid myself from him:
But it was thou, a man mine equal, my guide, and mine acquaintance.
We took sweet counsel together, and walked unto the house of God in company.
Psalms 55:12–14

68 The words of his mouth were smoother than butter, but war was in his heart: his words were softer than oil, yet were they drawn swords.
Psalms 55:21. '. . . softer than butter' is the more familiar version in the Book of Common Prayer.

69 The wicked are estranged from the womb: they go astray as soon as they be born, speaking lies.
Their poison is like the poison of a serpent: they are like the deaf adder that stoppeth her ear;
Which will not hearken to the voice of charmers, charming never so wisely.
Psalms 58:3–5

70 Deliver me from the workers of iniquity, and save me from bloody men.
Psalms 59:2

71 They return at evening: they make a noise like a dog, and go round about the city.
Behold, they belch out with their mouth: swords are in their lips: for who, say they, doth hear?
Psalms 59:6–7

72 Moab is my washpot; over Edom will I cast out my shoe: Philistia, triumph thou because of me.
Psalms 60:8. David cites the lands bordering Israel, at various times enemies or tributaries. The words are repeated in Psalm 108:9.

73 Hear my cry, O God; attend unto my prayer.
From the end of the earth will I cry unto thee, when my heart is overwhelmed: lead me to the rock that is higher than I.
For thou hast been a shelter for me, and a strong tower from the enemy.
I will abide in thy tabernacle for ever: I will trust in the covert of thy wings. Selah.
Psalms 61:1–4

74 My soul thirsteth for thee, my flesh longeth for thee in a dry and thirsty land, where no water is.
Psalms 63:1

75 Thou visitest the earth, and waterest it: thou greatly enrichest it with the river of God, which is full of water: thou preparest them corn, when thou hast so provided for it.
Thou waterest the ridges thereof abundantly: thou settlest the furrows thereof: thou makest it soft with showers: thou blessest the springing thereof.
Thou crownest the year with thy goodness; and thy paths drop fatness.
Psalms 65:9–11. In the version in the Book of Common Prayer, the last words are 'thy clouds drop fatness'.

76 Thou broughtest us into the net; thou laidst affliction upon our loins.
Thou hast caused men to ride over our heads; we went through fire and through water: but thou broughtest us out into a wealthy place.
Psalms 66:11–12

77 God be merciful unto us, and bless us; and cause his face to shine upon us;
That thy way may be known upon earth, thy saving health among all nations.
Let the people praise thee, O God; let all the people praise thee.
Psalms 67:1–3

78 Sing unto God, sing praises to his name: extol him that rideth upon the heavens by his name JAH, and rejoice before him.
Psalms 68:4

79 Let them be blotted out of the book of the living, and not be written with the righteous.
Psalms 69:28

80 I am as a wonder unto many; but thou art my strong refuge.
Psalms 71:7. The version in the Book of Common Prayer reads: 'I am become as it were a monster unto many: but my sure trust is in thee.' (Psalms 71:6)

81 Cast me not off in the time of old age: forsake me not when my strength faileth.
Psalms 71:9

82 They that dwell in the wilderness shall bow before him; and his enemies shall lick the dust.
Psalms 72:9

83 I have considered the days of old, the years of ancient times.
I call to remembrance my song in the night: I

commune with mine own heart: and my spirit made diligent search.

Psalms 77:5–6

84 Give ear, O my people, to my law: incline your ears to the words of my mouth.
I will open my mouth in a parable: I will utter dark sayings of old:
Which we have heard and known, and our fathers have told us.

Psalms 78:1–3

85 And might not be as their fathers, a stubborn and rebellious generation; a generation that set not their heart aright, and whose spirit was not steadfast with God.

Psalms 78:8

86 Though he had commanded the clouds from above, and opened the doors of heaven,
And had rained down manna upon them to eat, and had given them of the corn of heaven.
Man did eat angels' food: he sent them meat to the full.

Psalms 78:23–5

87 Then the Lord awaked as one out of sleep, and like a mighty man that shouteth by reason of wine.
And he smote his enemies in the hinder parts: he put them to a perpetual reproach.

Psalms 78:65–66

88 How amiable are thy tabernacles, O Lord of hosts!
My soul longeth, yea, even fainteth for the courts of the Lord: my heart and my flesh crieth out for the living God.
Yea, the sparrow hath found an house, and the swallow a nest for herself, where she may lay her young, even thine altars, O Lord of hosts, my King, and my God.

Psalms 84:1–3

89 They go from strength to strength, every one of them in Zion appeareth before God.

Psalms 84:7. Referring to the blessed.

90 A day in thy courts is better than a thousand. I had rather be a doorkeeper in the house of my God, than to dwell in the tents of wickedness.

Psalms 84:10

91 Mercy and truth are met together; righteousness and peace have kissed each other.

Truth shall spring out of the earth; and righteousness shall look down from heaven.

Psalms 85:10–11

92 For a thousand years in thy sight are but as yesterday when it is past, and as a watch in the night.

Psalms 90:4. See 2 PETER 5.

93 The days of our years are threescore years and ten; and if by reason of strength they be fourscore years, yet is their strength labour and sorrow; for it is soon cut off, and we fly away.

Psalms 90:10

94 So teach us to number our days, that we may apply our hearts unto wisdom.

Psalms 90:12

95 Thou shalt not be afraid for the terror by night; nor for the arrow that flieth by day;
Nor for the pestilence that walketh in darkness; nor for the destruction that wasteth at noonday.
A thousand shall fall at thy side, and ten thousand at thy right hand; but it shall not come nigh thee.

Psalms 91:5–7

96 For he shall give his angels charge over thee, to keep thee in all thy ways.
They shall bear thee up in their hands, lest thou dash thy foot against a stone.

*Psalms 91:11–12. The words are recalled by the devil himself in *Matthew* 4:6 and *Luke* 4:10–11.*

97 The righteous shall flourish like the palm tree: he shall grow like a cedar in Lebanon.
Those that he planted in the house of the Lord shall flourish in the courts of our God.
They shall still bring forth fruit in old age; they shall be fat and flourishing.

Psalms 92:12–14

98 O come, let us sing unto the Lord: let us make a joyful noise to the rock of our salvation.
Let us come before his presence with thanksgiving, and make a joyful noise unto him with psalms.

*Psalms 95:1–2. The psalm, known as *Venite, Exultemus Domino* from the first words of the Vulgate version, is a canticle at Morning Prayer.*

99 For the Lord is a great God, and a great King above all gods.
In his hand are the deep places of the earth: the strength of the hills is his also.

The sea is his, and he made it: and his hands formed the dry land.

Psalms 95:3–5

100 Give unto the Lord the glory due unto his name: bring an offering, and come into his courts.
O worship the Lord in the beauty of holiness: fear before him, all the whole earth.

Psalms 96:8–9

101 The Lord reigneth; let the earth rejoice; let the multitude of isles be glad thereof.

Psalms 97:1

102 O sing unto the Lord a new song; for he hath done marvellous things.

Psalms 98:1

103 Make a joyful noise unto the Lord, all ye lands.
Serve the Lord with gladness: come before his presence with singing.
Know ye that the Lord he is God: it is he that hath made us, and not we ourselves; we are his people, and the sheep of his pasture.

Psalms 100:1–3. The psalm, known as *Jubilate Deo* from the first words of the Vulgate version (see BIBLE, VULGATE: 3), is a canticle in the BOOK OF COMMON PRAYER, 'Morning Prayer'.

104 I am like a pelican of the wilderness: I am like an owl of the desert.
I watch, and am as a sparrow alone upon the house top.

Psalms 102:6–7

105 For as the heaven is high above the earth, so great is his mercy toward them that fear him.

Psalms 103:11

106 As for man, his days are as grass: as a flower of the field, so he flourisheth.
For the wind passeth over it, and it is gone; and the place thereof shall know it no more.

Psalms 103:15–16

107 He causeth the grass to grow for the cattle, and herb for the service of man: that he may bring forth food out of the earth;
And wine that maketh glad the heart of man, and oil to make his face to shine, and bread which strengtheneth man's heart.
The trees of the Lord are full of sap; the cedars of Lebanon, which he hath planted;

Where the birds make their nests: as for the stork, the fir trees are her house.

Psalms 104:14–17

108 He appointed the moon for seasons: the sun knoweth his going down.
Thou makest darkness, and it is night: wherein all the beasts of the forest do creep forth.

Psalms 104:19–20

109 O Lord, how manifold are thy works! in wisdom hast thou made them all: the earth is full of thy riches.
So is this great and wide sea, wherein are things creeping innumerable, both small and great beasts.
There go the ships: there is that leviathan, whom thou hast made to play therein.
These wait all upon thee; that thou mayest give them their meat in due season.

Psalms 104:24–7

110 He sent a man before them, even Joseph, who was sold for a servant:
Whose feet they hurt with fetters: he was laid in iron.

Psalms 105:17–18. In the BOOK OF COMMON PRAYER, the last words of verse 18 are rendered, 'the iron entered into his soul', a mistranslation from the Hebrew in the Latin Vulgate edition. See MARGARET THATCHER 11.

111 For he satisfieth the longing soul, and filleth the hungry soul with goodness.
Such as sit in darkness and in the shadow of death, being bound in affliction and iron

Psalms 107:9–10. See LUKE 6 for an echo of the wording in verse 10.

112 Their soul abhorreth all manner of meat: and they draw near unto the gates of death.

Psalms 107:18. The version in the BOOK OF COMMON PRAYER has the phrase 'at death's door'.

113 They that go down to the sea in ships, that do business in great waters;
These see the works of the Lord, and his wonders in the deep.

Psalms 107:23–4

114 They reel to and fro, and stagger like a drunken man, and are at their wit's end.

Psalms 107:27. Referring to sailors.

115 The Lord said unto my Lord, Sit thou at my

right hand, until I make thine enemies thy footstool.

Psalms 110:1

116 The fear of the Lord is the beginning of wisdom.

Psalms 111:10

117 Not unto us, O Lord, not unto us, but unto thy name give glory, for thy mercy, and for thy truth's sake.

Psalms 115:1. The opening words of this psalm are better known in the Latin version: see VULGATE 5.

118 Their idols are silver and gold, the work of men's hands.
They have mouths, but they speak not: eyes have they, but they see not:
They have ears, but they hear not: noses have they, but they smell not:
They have hands, but they handle not: feet have they, but they walk not: neither speak they through their throat.

Psalms 115:4–7. The verses are repeated in Psalm 135:15–17.

119 I believed, therefore have I spoken: I was greatly afflicted:
I said in my haste, All men are liars.

Psalms 116:10–11

120 Precious in the sight of the Lord is the death of his saints.

Psalms 116:15

121 The stone which the builders refused is become the head stone of the corner.
This is the Lord's doing; it is marvellous in our eyes.
This is the day which the Lord hath made; we will rejoice and be glad in it.

Psalms 118:22–4. Verse 22 is recalled by Jesus in *Matthew* 21:42.

122 Blessed be he that cometh in the name of the Lord.

Psalms 118:26

123 Thy word is a lamp unto my feet, and a light unto my path.

Psalms 119:105. 'Thy word is a lantern unto my feet' in the Book of Common Prayer version.

124 My soul hath long dwelt with him that hateth peace.
I am for peace: but when I speak, they are for war.

Psalms 120:6–7

125 I will lift up mine eyes unto the hills, from whence cometh my help.

My help cometh from the Lord, which made heaven and earth.
He will not suffer thy foot to be moved: he that keepeth thee will not slumber.
Behold, he that keepeth Israel shall neither slumber nor sleep.
The Lord is thy keeper: the Lord is thy shade upon thy right hand.
The sun shall not smite thee by day, nor the moon by night.

Psalms 121:1–6

126 The Lord shall preserve thy going out and thy coming in from this time forth, and even for evermore.

Psalms 121:8

127 I was glad when they said unto me, Let us go unto the house of the Lord.
Our feet shall stand within thy gates, O Jerusalem.

Psalms 122:1–2

128 Pray for the peace of Jerusalem: they shall prosper that love thee.
Peace be within thy walls, and prosperity within thy palaces.
For my brethren and companions' sakes, I will now say, Peace be within thee.

Psalms 122:6–8

129 Turn again our captivity, O Lord, as the streams in the south.
They that sow in tears shall reap in joy.
He that goeth forth and weepeth, bearing precious seed, shall doubtless come again with rejoicing, bringing his sheaves with him.

Psalms 126:4–6

130 Except the Lord build the house, they labour in vain who build it: except the Lord keep the city, the watchman waketh but in vain.

Psalms 127:1

131 As arrows are in the hand of a mighty man; so are children of the youth.
Happy is the man that hath his quiver full of them: they shall not be ashamed, but they shall speak with the enemies in the gate.

Psalms 127:4–5

132 Thy wife shall be as a fruitful vine by the sides of thine house: thy children like olive plants round about thy table.

Psalms 128:3

133 Many a time have they afflicted me from my youth: yet they have not prevailed against me.
The plowers plowed upon my back: they made long their furrows.

Psalms 129:2–3

134 Out of the depths have I cried unto thee, O Lord.
Lord, hear my voice: let thine ears be attentive to the voice of my supplications.

Psalms 130:1–2. See VULGATE 6.

135 Surely I will not come into the tabernacle of my house, nor go up into my bed;
I will not give sleep to mine eyes, or slumber to mine eyelids.

Psalms 132:3–4. The words of verse 4 are echoed in Proverbs 6:4.

136 Behold, how good and how pleasant it is for brethren to dwell together in unity!

Psalms 133:1

137 O give thanks unto the Lord; for he is good: for his mercy endureth for ever.

Psalms 136:1

138 By the rivers of Babylon, there we sat down, yea, we wept, when we remembered Zion.

Psalms 137:1

139 For there they that carried us away captive required of us a song; and they that wasted us required of us mirth, saying, Sing us one of the songs of Zion.
How shall we sing the Lord's song in a strange land?

Psalms 137:3–4

140 If I forget thee, O Jerusalem, let my right hand forget her cunning.
If I do not remember thee, let my tongue cleave to the roof of my mouth; if I prefer not Jerusalem above my chief joy.

Psalms 137:5–6

141 O Lord, thou hast searched me, and known me.
Thou knowest my downsitting and mine uprising, thou understandest my thought afar off.

Psalms 139:1–2

142 Such knowledge is too wonderful for me; it is high, I cannot attain unto it.

Psalms 139:6

143 Whither shall I go from thy spirit? or whither shall I flee from thy presence?

If I ascend up into heaven, thou art there: if I make my bed in hell, behold, thou art there.
If I take the wings of the morning, and dwell in the uttermost parts of the sea;
Even there shall thy hand lead me, and thy right hand shall hold me.

Psalms 139:7–10

144 I will praise thee; for I am fearfully and wonderfully made.

Psalms 139:14

145 Let the wicked fall into their own nets, whilst that I withal escape.

Psalms 141:10. In the BOOK OF COMMON PRAYER, *the wording is 'Let the ungodly fall into their own nets together: and let me ever escape them.'* (Psalms 141:11)

146 The Lord upholdeth all that fall: and raiseth up all those that be bowed down.

Psalms 145:14. SAMUEL BECKETT *took the title of his radio play,* All That Fall *(1957), from this verse.*

147 Put not your trust in princes.

Psalms 146:3

148 He telleth the number of the stars; he calleth them all by their names.

Psalms 147:4

149 Praise the Lord from the earth, ye dragons, and all deeps:
Fire, and hail; snow, and vapours; stormy wind fulfilling his word.

Psalms 148:7–8

150 Let the saints be joyful in glory: let them sing aloud upon their beds.
Let the high praises of God be in their mouth, and a two-edged sword in their hand;
To execute vengeance upon the heathen, and punishments upon the people;
To bind their kings with chains, and their nobles with fetters of iron;
To execute upon them the judgment written: this honour have all his saints. Praise ye the Lord.

Psalms 149:5–9

151 Praise him upon the loud cymbals: praise him upon the high-sounding cymbals.
Let every thing that hath breath praise the Lord. Praise ye the Lord.

Psalms 150:5–6. The final verses of Psalms.

The Book of Proverbs

1 A wise man will hear, and will increase learning;

and a man of understanding shall attain unto wise counsels:

To understand a proverb, and the interpretation; the words of the wise, and their dark sayings.

The fear of the Lord is the beginning of knowledge: but fools despise wisdom and instruction.

Proverbs 1:5–7

2 My son, if sinners entice thee, consent thou not.

Proverbs 1:10

3 Wisdom crieth without; she uttereth her voice in the streets:

She crieth in the chief place of concourse, in the openings of the gates: in the city she uttereth her words, saying,

How long, ye simple ones, will ye love simplicity? and the scorners delight in their scorning, and fools hate knowledge?

Proverbs 1:20–2

4 My son, despise not the chastening of the Lord; neither be weary of his correction:

For whom the Lord loveth he correcteth; even as a father the son in whom he delighteth.

Proverbs 3:11–12. See PROVERBS 31 and HEBREWS 8.

5 Her ways are ways of pleasantness, and all her paths are peace.

Proverbs 3:16. Referring to Wisdom.

6 Wisdom is the principal thing; therefore get wisdom: and with all thy getting get understanding.

Proverbs 4:7

7 But the path of the just is as the shining light, that shineth more and more unto the perfect day.

The way of the wicked is as darkness: they know not at what they stumble.

Proverbs 4:18–19

8 For the lips of a strange woman drop as an honeycomb, and her mouth is smoother than oil:

But her end is bitter as wormwood, sharp as a two-edged sword.

Her feet go down to death; her steps take hold on hell.

Proverbs 5:3–5

9 Let thy fountain be blessed: and rejoice with the wife of thy youth.

Let her be as the loving hind and pleasant roe; let

her breasts satisfy thee at all times; and be thou ravished always with her love.

Proverbs 5:18–19

10 Go to the ant, thou sluggard; consider her ways, and be wise.

Proverbs 6:6. See SAMUEL JOHNSON 21.

11 How long wilt thou sleep, O sluggard? when wilt thou arise out of thy sleep?

Yet a little sleep, a little slumber, a little folding of the hands to sleep:

So shall thy poverty come as one that travelleth, and thy want as an armed man.

Proverbs 6:9–11

12 These six things doth the Lord hate: yea, seven are an abomination unto him:

A proud look, a lying tongue, and hands that shed innocent blood,

An heart that deviseth wicked imaginations, feet that be swift in running to mischief,

A false witness that speaketh lies, and he that soweth discord among brethren.

Proverbs 6:16–19

13 Can a man take fire in his bosom, and his clothes not be burned?

Can one go upon hot coals, and his feet not be burned?

So he that goeth in to his neighbour's wife; whosoever toucheth her shall not be innocent.

Proverbs 6:27–9

14 I have perfumed my bed with myrrh, aloes, and cinnamon.

Come, let us take our fill of love until the morning: let us solace ourselves with loves.

Proverbs 7:17–18. The words of the 'loud and stubborn' harlot to the 'young man void of understanding'.

15 He goeth after her straightway, as an ox goeth to the slaughter.

Proverbs 7:22. The young man yields to the 'fair speech' of the harlot.

16 For wisdom is better than rubies; and all the things that may be desired are not to be compared to it.

Proverbs 8:11. See also JOB 35.

17 Wisdom hath builded her house, she hath hewn out her seven pillars.

Proverbs 9:1. T. E. LAWRENCE called his memoir The Seven Pillars of Wisdom.

18 Stolen waters are sweet, and bread eaten in secret is pleasant.

Proverbs 9:17. Speech of 'a foolish woman' to 'him that wanteth understanding'.

19 A wise son maketh a glad father: but a foolish son is the heaviness of his mother.

Proverbs 10:1

20 The rich man's wealth is his strong city: the destruction of the poor is their poverty.

Proverbs 10:15

21 A false balance is abomination to the Lord: but a just weight is his delight.

Proverbs 11:1

22 Where no counsel is, the people fall: but in the multitude of counsellors there is safety.

Proverbs 11:14

23 He that is surety for a stranger shall smart for it.

Proverbs 11:15

24 As a jewel of gold in a swine's snout, so is a fair woman which is without discretion.

Proverbs 11:22

25 He that trusteth in his riches shall fall.

Proverbs 11:28

26 A virtuous woman is a crown to her husband: but she that maketh ashamed is as rottenness in his bones.

Proverbs 12:4

27 A righteous man regardeth the life of his beast: but the tender mercies of the wicked are cruel.

Proverbs 12:10

28 Hope deferred maketh the heart sick: but when the desire cometh, it is a tree of life.

Proverbs 13:12

29 The way of transgressors is hard.

Proverbs 13:15

30 The desire accomplished is sweet to the soul.

Proverbs 13:19

31 He that spareth his rod hateth his son: but he that loveth him chasteneth him betimes.

Proverbs 13:24. See also PROVERBS 4 and HEBREWS 8.

32 Even in laughter the heart is sorrowful; and the end of that mirth is heaviness

Proverbs 14:13

33 The prudent man looketh well to his going.

Proverbs 14:15

34 In all labour there is profit: but the talk of the lips tendeth only to penury.

Proverbs 14:23

35 Righteousness exalteth a nation: but sin is a reproach to any people.

Proverbs 14:34

36 A soft answer turneth away wrath: but grievous words stir up anger.

Proverbs 15:1

37 A merry heart maketh a cheerful countenance: but by sorrow of the heart the spirit is broken.

Proverbs 15:13. See also PROVERBS 47.

38 Better is a dinner of herbs where love is, than a stalled ox and hatred therewith.

Proverbs 15:17

39 A man hath joy by the answer of his mouth: and a word spoken in due season, how good is it!

Proverbs 15:23

40 A good report maketh the bones fat.

Proverbs 15:30

41 Pride goeth before destruction, and an haughty spirit before a fall.

Proverbs 16:18. Familiarly quoted 'Pride goeth before a fall'.

42 Pleasant words are as an honeycomb, sweet to the soul, and health to the bones.

Proverbs 16:24

43 The hoary head is a crown of glory, if it be found in the way of righteousness.

Proverbs 16:31

44 He that is slow to anger is better than the mighty; and he that ruleth his spirit than he that taketh a city.

Proverbs 16:32

45 Children's children are the crown of old men; and the glory of children are their fathers.

Proverbs 17:6

46 He that repeateth a matter separateth very friends.

Proverbs 17:9

47 A merry heart doeth good like a medicine: but a broken spirit drieth the bones.

Proverbs 17:22. See also PROVERBS 37.

48 Even a fool, when he holdeth his peace, is

counted wise: and he that shutteth his lips is esteemed a man of understanding.

Proverbs 17:28

49 The spirit of a man will sustain his infirmity; but a wounded spirit who can bear?

Proverbs 18:14

50 A brother offended is harder to be won than a strong city: and their contentions are like the bars of a castle.

Proverbs 18:19

51 Whoso findeth a wife findeth a good thing, and obtaineth favour of the Lord.

Proverbs 18:22

52 The poor useth intreaties; but the rich answereth roughly.

Proverbs 18:23

53 A man that hath friends must shew himself friendly: and there is a friend that sticketh closer than a brother.

Proverbs 18:24

54 Wealth maketh many friends; but the poor is separated from his neighbour.

Proverbs 19:4

55 Many will intreat the favour of the prince: and every man is a friend to him that giveth gifts.

Proverbs 19:6

56 He that hath pity upon the poor lendeth unto the Lord.

Proverbs 19:17

57 Wine is a mocker, strong drink is raging: and whosoever is deceived thereby is not wise.

Proverbs 20:1

58 It is an honour for a man to cease from strife: but every fool will be meddling.

Proverbs 20:3

59 Even a child is known by his doings, whether his work be pure, and whether it be right.

Proverbs 20:11

60 The hearing ear, and the seeing eye, the Lord hath made even both of them.

Proverbs 20:12

61 It is naught, it is naught, saith the buyer: but when he is gone his way, then he boasteth.

Proverbs 20:14

62 It is better to dwell in a corner of the housetop, than with a brawling woman in a wide house.

Proverbs 21:9. The words are echoed in 25:24.

63 A good name is rather to be chosen than great riches.

Proverbs 22:1

64 Train up a child in the way he should go: and when he is old, he will not depart from it.

Proverbs 22:6

65 The rich ruleth over the poor, and the borrower is servant to the lender.

Proverbs 22:7

66 Foolishness is bound in the heart of a child; but the rod of correction shall drive it far from him.

Proverbs 22:15

67 Remove not the ancient landmark, which thy fathers have set.

Proverbs 22:28. The words are repeated in 23:10 ('Remove not the old landmark'); see also DEUTERONOMY 10.

68 Wilt thou set thine eyes upon that which is not? for riches certainly make themselves wings; they fly away as an eagle toward heaven.

Proverbs 23:5

69 Be not among winebibbers; among riotous eaters of flesh:

For the drunkard and the glutton shall come to poverty: and drowsiness shall clothe a man with rags.

Proverbs 23:20–1

70 Look not thou upon the wine when it is red, when it giveth his colour in the cup, when it moveth itself aright.

At the last it biteth like a serpent, and stingeth like an adder.

Thine eyes shall behold strange women, and thine heart shall utter perverse things.

Proverbs 23:31–3

71 Through wisdom is an house builded; and by understanding it is established:

And by knowledge shall the chambers be filled with all precious and pleasant riches.

A wise man is strong; yea, a man of knowledge increaseth strength.

Proverbs 24:3–5

72 If thou faint in the day of adversity, thy strength is small.
Proverbs 24:10

73 The heaven for height, and the earth for depth, and the heart of kings is unsearchable.
Proverbs 25:3

74 A word fitly spoken is like apples of gold in pictures of silver.
Proverbs 25:11

75 Confidence in an unfaithful man in time of trouble is like a broken tooth, and a foot out of joint.
Proverbs 25:19

76 If thine enemy be hungry, give him bread to eat; and if he be thirsty, give him water to drink:
For thou shalt heap coals of fire upon his head, and the Lord shall reward thee.
Proverbs 25:21–2. The passage is recalled in *Romans* 12:20.

77 As cold waters to a thirsty soul, so is good news from a far country.
Proverbs 25:25

78 It is not good to eat much honey: so for men to search their own glory is not glory.
Proverbs 25:27

79 Answer a fool according to his folly, lest he be wise in his own conceit.
Proverbs 26:5

80 As a dog returneth to his vomit, so a fool returneth to his folly.
Proverbs 26:11

81 Seest thou a man wise in his own conceit? there is more hope of a fool than of him.
Proverbs 26:12

82 Where no wood is, there the fire goeth out: so where there is no talebearer, the strife ceaseth.
Proverbs 26:20

83 Whoso diggeth a pit shall fall therein: and he that rolleth a stone, it will return upon him.
Proverbs 26:27. See also ECCLESIASTES 32.

84 Boast not thyself of to morrow; for thou knowest not what a day may bring forth.
Proverbs 27:1

85 Faithful are the wounds of a friend; but the kisses of an enemy are deceitful.
Proverbs 27:6

86 Better is a neighbour that is near than a brother far off.
Proverbs 27:10

87 A continual dropping in a very rainy day and a contentious woman are alike.
Proverbs 27:15

88 Iron sharpeneth iron; so a man sharpeneth the countenance of his friend.
Proverbs 27:17

89 The wicked flee when no man pursueth: but the righteous are bold as a lion.
Proverbs 28:1

90 He that maketh haste to be rich shall not be innocent.
Proverbs 28:20

91 He that rebuketh a man afterwards shall find more favour than he that flattereth with the tongue.
Proverbs 28:23

92 He that trusteth in his own heart is a fool.
Proverbs 28:26

93 He that giveth unto the poor shall not lack.
Proverbs 28:27

94 A fool uttereth all his mind: but a wise man keepeth it in till afterwards.
Proverbs 29:11

95 Where there is no vision, the people perish.
Proverbs 29:18. JOHN F. KENNEDY quoted this passage on the eve of his assassination in Dallas, Texas.

96 Remove far from me vanity and lies: give me neither poverty nor riches; feed me with food convenient for me.
Proverbs 30:8. The prayer of Agur, son of Jakeh.

97 There be three things which are too wonderful for me, yea, four which I know not:
The way of an eagle in the air; the way of a serpent upon a rock; the way of a ship in the midst of the sea; and the way of a man with a maid.
Proverbs 30:18–19. Agur's prayer.

98 Such is the way of an adulterous woman; she eateth, and wipeth her mouth, and saith, I have done no wickedness.
Proverbs 30:20. Agur's prayer.

99 Give strong drink unto him that is ready to perish, and wine unto those that be of heavy hearts.

Let him drink, and forget his poverty, and
   remember his misery no more.

Proverbs 31:6–7. The words of king Lemuel, following the
prophecy taught to him by his mother.

100 Who can find a virtuous woman? for her price
   is far above rubies.

Proverbs 31:10

101 Strength and honour are her clothing; and she
   shall rejoice in time to come.
She openeth her mouth with wisdom; and in her
   tongue is the law of kindness.
She looketh well to the ways of her household, and
   eateth not the bread of idleness.
Her children arise up, and call her blessed; her
   husband also, and he praiseth her.

Proverbs 31:25–8. Attributes of 'the virtuous woman', as
described by Lemuel.

Ecclesiastes; or, The Preacher

1 Vanity of vanities, saith the Preacher, vanity of
vanities; all is vanity.

Ecclesiastes 1:2. The words, which summarize the main theme
of this book – the futility of human endeavour – are repeated
throughout *Ecclesiastes*. See BIBLE, VULGATE 7.

2 What profit hath a man of all his labour which he
taketh under the sun?
   One generation passeth away, and another generation cometh: but the earth abideth for ever. The
sun also ariseth, and the sun goeth down, and
hasteth to the place where he arose.

Ecclesiastes 1:3–5. ERNEST HEMINGWAY took the title of his
book *The Sun Also Rises* (1926) from this passage.

3 All the rivers run into the sea; yet the sea is not
full; unto the place from whence the rivers come,
thither they return again.

Ecclesiastes 1:7

4 All things are full of labour; man cannot utter it:
the eye is not satisfied with seeing, nor the ear filled
with hearing.

Ecclesiastes 1:8

5 The thing that hath been, it is that which shall be;
and that which is done is that which shall be done:
and there is no new thing under the sun.

Ecclesiastes 1:9

6 I have seen all the works that are done under the
sun; and, behold, all is vanity and vexation of spirit.

Ecclesiastes 1:14

7 That which is crooked cannot be made straight:
and that which is wanting cannot be numbered.

Ecclesiastes 1:15

8 For in much wisdom is much grief: and he that
increaseth knowledge increaseth sorrow.

Ecclesiastes 1:18

9 I said of laughter, It is mad: and of mirth, What
doeth it?

Ecclesiastes 2:2

10 The wise man's eyes are in his head; but the fool
walketh in darkness: and I myself perceived also
that one event happeneth to them all.

Ecclesiastes 2:14

11 To every thing there is a season, and a time to
   every purpose under the heaven:
A time to be born, and a time to die; a time to
   plant, and a time to pluck up that which is
   planted;
A time to kill, and a time to heal; a time to break
   down, and a time to build up;
A time to weep, and a time to laugh; a time to
   mourn, and a time to dance;
A time to cast away stones, and a time to gather
   stones together; a time to embrace, and a time
   to refrain from embracing;
A time to get, and a time to lose; a time to keep,
   and a time to cast away;
A time to rend, and a time to sew; a time to keep
   silence, and a time to speak;
A time to love, and a time to hate; a time of war,
   and a time of peace.

Ecclesiastes 3:1–8. The lines were set to music by PETE SEEGER
in his song 'Turn! Turn! Turn!', a hit for The Byrds in 1966.

12 Wherefore I praised the dead which are already
dead more than the living which are yet alive.
   Yea, better is he than both they, which hath not
yet been, who hath not seen the evil work that is
done under the sun.

Ecclesiastes 4:2–3. *Evil Under the Sun* is the title of a crime
thriller by AGATHA CHRISTIE (1941). The words recur elsewhere in *Ecclesiastes*.

13 Two are better than one; because they have a
good reward for their labour.
   For if they fall, the one will lift up his fellow: but
woe to him that is alone when he falleth; for he
hath not another to help him up.
   Again, if two lie together, then they have heat:
but how can one be warm alone?
   And if one prevail against him, two shall with-

stand him; and a threefold cord is not quickly broken.

Ecclesiastes 4:9–12. See EPIC OF GILGAMESH 3.

14 Better is a poor and a wise child than an old and foolish king, who will no more be admonished.

Ecclesiastes 4:13

15 God is in heaven, and thou upon earth: therefore let thy words be few.

Ecclesiastes 5:2

16 The sleep of a labouring man is sweet, whether he eat little or much: but the abundance of the rich will not suffer him to sleep.

Ecclesiastes 5:12

17 A good name is better than precious ointment.

Ecclesiastes 7:1

18 Sorrow is better than laughter: for by the sadness of the countenance the heart is made better.

The heart of the wise is in the house of mourning; but the heart of fools is in the house of mirth.

Ecclesiastes 7:3–4. *The House of Mirth* is the title of the novel which established EDITH WHARTON (1905).

19 For as the crackling of thorns under a pot, so is the laughter of the fool: this also is vanity.

Ecclesiastes 7:6

20 Better is the end of a thing than the beginning thereof.

Ecclesiastes 7:8

21 Be not hasty in thy spirit to be angry: for anger resteth in the bosom of fools.

Ecclesiastes 7:9

22 In the day of prosperity be joyful, but in the day of adversity consider.

Ecclesiastes 7:14

23 Be not righteous over much; neither make thyself over wise: why shouldest thou destroy thyself?

Ecclesiastes 7:16

24 For there is not a just man upon earth, that doeth good, and sinneth not.

Ecclesiastes 7:20

25 Lo, this only have I found, that God hath made man upright; but they have sought out many inventions.

Ecclesiastes 7:29

26 There is no man that hath power over the spirit to retain the spirit; neither hath he power in the day of death: and there is no discharge in that war;

neither shall wickedness deliver those that are given to it.

Ecclesiastes 8:8

27 Then I commended mirth, because a man hath no better thing under the sun, than to eat, and to drink, and to be merry: for that shall abide with him of his labour the days of his life, which God giveth him under the sun.

Ecclesiastes 8:15. See also ISAIAH 31, LUKE 36, 1 CORINTHIANS 39.

28 For to him that is joined to all the living there is hope: for a living dog is better than a dead lion.

Ecclesiastes 9:4

29 Whatsoever thy hand findeth to do, do it with thy might; for there is no work, nor device, nor knowledge, nor wisdom, in the grave, whither thou goest.

Ecclesiastes 9:10

30 The race is not to the swift, nor the battle to the strong, neither yet bread to the wise, nor yet riches to men of understanding, nor yet favour to men of skill; but time and chance happeneth to them all.

Ecclesiastes 9:11

31 Dead flies cause the ointment of the apothecary to send forth a stinking savour: so doth a little folly him that is in reputation for wisdom and honour.

Ecclesiastes 10:1

32 He that diggeth a pit shall fall into it.

Ecclesiastes 10:8. See also PROVERBS 83.

33 By much slothfulness the building decayeth; and through idleness of the hands the house droppeth through.

Ecclesiastes 10:18

34 A feast is made for laughter, and wine maketh merry: but money answereth all things.

Ecclesiastes 10:19

35 Curse not the king, no not in thy thought; and curse not the rich in thy bedchamber: for a bird of the air shall carry the voice, and that which hath wings shall tell the matter.

Ecclesiastes 10:20

36 Cast thy bread upon the waters: for thou shalt find it after many days.

Ecclesiastes 11:1

37 He that observeth the wind shall not sow; and he that regardeth the clouds shall not reap.

Ecclesiastes 11:4

38 In the morning sow thy seed, and in the evening withhold not thine hand: for thou knowest not whether shall prosper, either this or that, or whether they both shall be alike good.

Ecclesiastes 11:6

39 Rejoice, O young man, in thy youth; and let thy heart cheer thee in the days of thy youth, and walk in the ways of thine heart, and in the sight of thine eyes: but know thou, that for all these things God will bring thee into judgment.

Ecclesiastes 11:9

40 Remember now thy Creator in the days of thy youth, while the evil days come not, nor the years draw nigh, when thou shalt say, I have no pleasure in them;
While the sun, or the light, or the moon, or the stars, be not darkened, nor the clouds return after the rain:
    In the day when the keepers of the house shall tremble, and the strong men shall bow themselves, and the grinders cease because they are few, and those that look out of the windows be darkened,
    And the doors shall be shut in the streets, when the sound of the grinding is low, and he shall rise up at the voice of the bird, and all the daughters of music shall be brought low.

Ecclesiastes 12:1–4

41 Also when they shall be afraid of that which is high, and fears shall be in the way, and the almond tree shall flourish, and the grasshopper shall be a burden, and desire shall fail: because man goeth to his long home, and the mourners go about the streets:
    Or ever the silver cord be loosed, or the golden bowl be broken, or the pitcher be broken at the fountain, or the wheel broken at the cistern.
Then shall the dust return to the earth as it was: and the spirit shall return unto God who gave it.

Ecclesiastes 12:5–7

42 The words of the wise are as goads, and as nails fastened by the masters of assemblies.

Ecclesiastes 12:11

43 Of making many books there is no end; and much study is a weariness of the flesh.

Ecclesiastes 12:12

44 Let us hear the conclusion of the whole matter: Fear God, and keep his commandments: for this is the whole duty of man.

For God shall bring every work into judgment, with every secret thing, whether it be good, or whether it be evil.

Ecclesiastes 12:13–14. Closing words of *Ecclesiastes*.

The Song of Solomon

1 The song of songs, which is Solomon's.

Song of Solomon 1:1. The book, also known as the 'Canticle of Canticles' or 'Song of Songs' (i.e. the most excellent song), is of unknown authorship, unconnected with Solomon, the poet, sage and king of Israel.

2 Let him kiss me with the kisses of his mouth: for
    thy love is better than wine.
Because of the savour of thy good ointments thy
    name is as ointment poured forth, therefore do
    the virgins love thee.

Song of Solomon 1:2–3

3 I am black, but comely, O ye daughters of
    Jerusalem, as the tents of Kedar, as the curtains
    of Solomon.

Song of Solomon 1:5. The Latin words – *Nigra sum, sed hermosa* – are found inscribed below icons of the cult of the Black Madonna in some Mediterranean countries.

4 A bundle of myrrh is my wellbeloved unto me;
    he shall lie all night betwixt my breasts.

Song of Solomon 1:13

5 I am the rose of Sharon, and the lily of the
    valleys.

Song of Solomon 2:1

6 He brought me to the banqueting house, and his
    banner over me was love.

Song of Solomon 2:4

7 Stay me with flagons, comfort me with apples:
    for I am sick of love.

Song of Solomon 2:5

8 Rise up, my love, my fair one, and come away.
For, lo, the winter is past, the rain is over and
    gone;
The flowers appear on the earth; the time of the
    singing of birds is come, and the voice of the
    turtle is heard in our land.

Song of Solomon 2:10–12

9 Take us the foxes, the little foxes, that spoil the
    vines: for our vines have tender grapes.

Song of Solomon 2:15. LILLIAN HELLMAN's play *The Little Foxes* (1939) portrays the rise of a rapacious class of southern industrialists.

10 My beloved is mine, and I am his: he feedeth among the lilies.

Until the day break, and the shadows flee away, turn, my beloved, and be thou like a roe or a young hart upon the mountains of Bether.

Song of Solomon 2:16–17. 'Until the day break, and the shadows flee away' is repeated in 4:6. See also SONG OF SOLOMON 30.

11 By night on my bed I sought him whom my soul loveth: I sought him, but I found him not.

Song of Solomon 3:1

12 Behold, thou art fair, my love; behold, thou art fair; thou hast doves' eyes within thy locks: thy hair is as a flock of goats, that appear from mount Gilead.

Song of Solomon 4:1

13 Thy lips are like a thread of scarlet, and thy speech is comely: thy temples are like a piece of a pomegranate within thy locks.

Song of Solomon 4:3

14 Thy neck is like the tower of David builded for an armoury, whereon there hang a thousand bucklers, all shields of mighty men.

Song of Solomon 4:4. 'Tower of David' may refer to a siege tower.

15 Thy two breasts are like two young roes that are twins, which feed among the lilies.

Song of Solomon 4:5. Similar imagery is used in SONG OF SOLOMON 25.

16 Thou art all fair, my love; there is no spot in thee.

Song of Solomon 4:7

17 A garden inclosed is my sister, my spouse; a spring shut up, a fountain sealed.

Song of Solomon 4:12

18 Awake, O north wind; and come, thou south; blow upon my garden, that the spices thereof may flow out. Let my beloved come into his garden, and eat his pleasant fruits.

Song of Solomon 4:16

19 I sleep, but my heart waketh: it is the voice of my beloved that knocketh, saying, Open to me, my sister, my love, my dove, my undefiled: for my head is filled with dew, and my locks with the drops of the night.

Song of Solomon 5:2

20 My beloved put in his hand by the hole of the door, and my bowels were moved for him.

Song of Solomon 5:4

21 My beloved is white and ruddy, the chiefest among ten thousand.

His head is as the most fine gold, his locks are bushy, and black as a raven.

His eyes are as the eyes of doves by the rivers of waters, washed with milk, and fitly set.

His cheeks are as a bed of spices, as sweet flowers: his lips like lilies, dropping sweet smelling myrrh.

His hands are as gold rings set with the beryl: his belly is as bright ivory overlaid with sapphires.

His legs are as pillars of marble, set upon sockets of fine gold: his countenance is as Lebanon, excellent as the cedars.

His mouth is most sweet: yea, he is altogether lovely. This is my beloved, and this is my friend, O daughters of Jerusalem.

Song of Solomon 5:10–16

22 Who is she that looketh forth as the morning, fair as the moon, clear as the sun, and terrible as an army with banners?

Song of Solomon 6:10

23 Return, return, O Shulamite; return, return, that we may look upon thee.

Song of Solomon 6:13. The term *Shulamite* has been variously interpreted, and may refer to the name of a goddess, or mean 'perfect one' (from the same root as *shalom*, 'peace').

24 How beautiful are thy feet with shoes, O prince's daughter! The joints of thy thighs are like jewels, the work of the hands of a cunning workman.

Song of Solomon 7:1

25 Thy navel is like a round goblet, which wanteth not liquor: thy belly is like an heap of wheat set about with lilies.

Thy two breasts are like two young roes that are twins.

Song of Solomon 7:2–3

26 Thy neck is as a tower of ivory; thine eyes like the fishpools in Heshbon, by the gate of Bath-rabbim: thy nose is as the tower of Lebanon which looketh toward Damascus.

Thine head upon thee is like Carmel, and the hair of thine head like purple; the king is held in the galleries.

How fair and how pleasant art thou, O love, for
delights!

Song of Solomon 7:4–6

27 Like the best wine for my beloved, that goeth
down sweetly, causing the lips of those that are
asleep to speak.

Song of Solomon 7:9

28 Set me as a seal upon thine heart, as a seal
upon thine arm: for love is strong as death;
jealousy is cruel as the grave: the coals thereof
are coals of fire, which hath a most vehement
flame.

Song of Solomon 8:6

29 Many waters cannot quench love, neither can
the floods drown it: if a man would give all the
substance of his house for love, it would utterly
be contemned.

Song of Solomon 8:7

30 Make haste, my beloved, and be thou like to a
roe or to a young hart upon the mountains of
spices.

Song of Solomon 8:14. Closing words of book. See also SONG
OF SOLOMON 10.

The Book of the Prophet Isaiah

1 The ox knoweth his owner, and the ass his
master's crib: but Israel doth not know, my
people doth not consider.

Isaiah 1:3

2 And the daughter of Zion is left as a cottage in a
vineyard, as a lodge in a garden of cucumbers, as
a besieged city.

Isaiah 1:8

3 Bring no more vain oblations; incense is an
abomination unto me; the new moons and
sabbaths, the calling of assemblies, I cannot
away with; it is iniquity, even the solemn
meeting.

Isaiah 1:13. The 'word of the lord' to the 'rulers of Sodom' and
'people of Gomorrah' (intending Jerusalem).

4 Though your sins be as scarlet, they shall be as
white as snow; though they be red like crimson,
they shall be as wool.

Isaiah 1:18

5 How is the faithful city become an harlot! it was
full of judgment; righteousness lodged in it; but
now murderers.

Thy silver is become dross, thy wine mixed with
water:

Thy princes are rebellious, and companions of
thieves: every one loveth gifts, and followeth
after rewards.

Isaiah 1:21–3

6 They shall beat their swords into plowshares,
and their spears into pruninghooks: nation shall
not lift up sword against nation, neither shall
they learn war any more.

Isaiah 2:4. The words also appear in *Micah* 4:3, and the reverse
injunction is made in *Joel* 3:10 ('Beat your plowshares into
swords . . .'). 'Study War No More' is the title of a well-known
African-American spiritual. See also BBC 1, which is thought
to have been inspired from this verse.

7 What mean ye that ye beat my people to pieces,
and grind the faces of the poor?

Isaiah 3:15. The 'Lord God of hosts' rebukes the oppressors of
Jerusalem and Judah.

8 Because the daughters of Zion are haughty, and
walk with stretched forth necks and wanton
eyes, walking and mincing as they go, and
making a tinkling with their feet:

Therefore the Lord will smite with a scab the
crown of the head of the daughters of Zion, and
the Lord will discover their secret parts.

Isaiah 3:16–17

9 My wellbeloved hath a vineyard in a very
fruitful hill.

Isaiah 5:1

10 And he looked for judgment, but behold
oppression; for righteousness, but behold a cry.

Isaiah 5:7

11 Woe unto them that join house to house, that
lay field to field, till there be no place, that they
may be placed alone in the midst of the earth!

Isaiah 5:8

12 Woe unto them that rise up early in the
morning, that they may follow strong drink;
that continue until night, till wine inflame
them!

Isaiah 5:11

13 Woe unto them that call evil good, and good
evil; that put darkness for light, and light for
darkness; that put bitter for sweet and sweet for
bitter!

Isaiah 5:20

14 I saw also the Lord sitting upon a throne, high
and lifted up, and his train filled the temple.

Above it stood the seraphims: each one had six
wings; with twain he covered his face, and with
twain he covered his feet, and with twain he did
fly.

And one cried unto another, and said, Holy, holy,
holy, is the Lord of hosts: the whole earth is full
of his glory.

Isaiah 6:1–3

15 Woe is me! for I am undone; because I am a man
of unclean lips, and I dwell in the midst of a people
of unclean lips: for mine eyes have seen the King,
the Lord of hosts.

Isaiah 6:5

16 Also I heard the voice of the Lord, saying, Whom
shall I send, and who will go for us? Then said I,
Here am I; send me.

Isaiah 6:8

17 Lord, how long?

Isaiah 6:11. Isaiah asks how long the chastisement of the
people will last. God replies, 'Until the cities be wasted without inhabitant, and the houses without man, and the land be
utterly desolate, and the Lord have removed men far away,
and there be a great forsaking in the midst of the land.'

18 Therefore the Lord himself shall give you a sign;
Behold, a virgin shall conceive, and bear a son, and
shall call his name Immanuel.

Isaiah 7:14. See also MATTHEW 2.

19 Butter and honey shall he eat, that he may know
to refuse the evil, and choose the good.

Isaiah 7:15

20 The people that walked in darkness have seen a
great light: they that dwell in the land of the
shadow of death, upon them hath the light
shined.

Thou hast multiplied the nation, and not increased
the joy: they joy before thee according to the joy
in harvest, and as men rejoice when they divide
the spoil.

For thou hast broken the yoke of his burden, and
the staff of his shoulder, the rod of his
oppressor, as in the day of Midian.

Isaiah 9:2–4

21 For unto us a child is born, unto us a son is
given: and the government shall be upon his
shoulder: and his name shall be called

Wonderful, Counsellor, The mighty God, The
everlasting Father, The Prince of Peace.

Of the increase of his government and peace there
shall be no end.

Isaiah 9:6–7

22 The zeal of the Lord of hosts will perform this.

Isaiah 9:7

23 And there shall come forth a rod out of the
stem of Jesse, and a Branch shall grow out of his
roots:

And the spirit of the Lord shall rest upon him, the
spirit of wisdom and understanding, the spirit of
counsel and might, the spirit of knowledge and
of the fear of the Lord.

Isaiah 11:1–2

24 The wolf also shall dwell with the lamb, and the
leopard shall lie down with the kid; and the calf
and the young lion and the fatling together; and
a little child shall lead them.

Isaiah 11:6

25 And the cow and the bear shall feed; their
young ones shall lie down together: and the lion
shall eat straw like the ox.

And the sucking child shall play on the hole of the
asp, and the weaned child shall put his hand on
the cockatrice' den.

They shall not hurt nor destroy in all my holy
mountain: for the earth shall be full of the
knowledge of the Lord, as the waters cover the
sea.

Isaiah 11:7–9

26 Behold, God is my salvation; I will trust, and
not be afraid: for the Lord JEHOVAH is my
strength and song; he also is become my
salvation.

Therefore with joy shall ye draw water out of the
wells of salvation.

Isaiah 12:2–3

27 But wild beasts of the desert shall lie there; and
their houses shall be full of doleful creatures;
and owls shall dwell there, and satyrs shall
dance there.

And the wild beasts of the islands shall cry in their
desolate houses, and dragons in their pleasant
palaces.

Isaiah 13:21–2. God warns of the destruction of Babylon.

28 Thy pomp is brought down to the grave, and

the noise of thy viols: the worm is spread under thee, and the worms cover thee.

How art thou fallen from heaven, O Lucifer, son of the morning! how art thou cut down to the ground, which didst weaken the nations!

Isaiah 14:11–12. God warns of the destruction of Babylon.

29 Babylon is fallen, is fallen; and all the graven images of her gods he hath broken unto the ground.

Isaiah 21:9. Prophecy of the capture of Babylon by Cyrus, supposed to be spoken by the watchman. See also REVELATION 36.

30 Watchman, what of the night? Watchman, what of the night?

The watchman said, The morning cometh, and also the night.

Isaiah 21:11–12

31 Let us eat and drink; for to morrow we shall die.

Isaiah 22:13. Almost the same words are found in the New Testament: see 1 CORINTHIANS 39. *Both passages are frequently confused with* Ecclesiastes 8:15 (ECCLESIASTES 27).

32 Who hath taken this counsel against Tyre, the crowning city, whose merchants are princes, whose traffickers are the honourable of the earth?

Isaiah 23:8

33 And in this mountain shall the Lord of hosts make unto all people a feast of fat things, a feast of wines on the lees, of fat things full of marrow, of wines on the lees well refined.

Isaiah 25:6

34 He will swallow up death in victory; and the Lord God will wipe away tears from off all faces.

Isaiah 25:8. See also 1 CORINTHIANS 46, REVELATION 24 AND 50.

35 We have been with child, we have been in pain, we have as it were brought forth wind.

Isaiah 26:18

36 In that day the Lord with his sore and great and strong sword shall punish leviathan the piercing serpent, even leviathan that crooked serpent; and he shall slay the dragon that is in the sea.

Isaiah 27:1. For other references to leviathan, see JOB 47 *and* PSALMS 109.

37 For precept must be upon precept, precept upon precept; line upon line, line upon line; here a little, and there a little.

Isaiah 28:10. The words, referring to the teaching of know-

ledge and doctrine, are echoed in verse 13. See also EDMUND BURKE 60.

38 We have made a covenant with death, and with hell are we at agreement.

Isaiah 28:15. The boast of the people of Ephraim.

39 They are drunken, but not with wine; they stagger, but not with strong drink.

Isaiah 29:9

40 For the Egyptians shall help in vain, and to no purpose: therefore have I cried concerning this, Their strength is to sit still.

Isaiah 30:7

41 And though the Lord give you the bread of adversity, and the water of affliction, yet shall not thy teachers be removed into a corner any more, but thine eyes shall see thy teachers.

Isaiah 30:20

42 And thine ears shall hear a word behind thee, saying, This is the way, walk ye in it, when ye turn to the right hand, and when ye turn to the left.

Isaiah 30:21

43 And a man shall be as an hiding place from the wind, and a covert from the tempest; as rivers of water in a dry place, as the shadow of a great rock in a weary land.

Isaiah 32:2

44 The sword of the Lord is filled with blood, it is made fat with fatness, and with the blood of lambs and goats, with the fat of the kidneys of rams.

Isaiah 34:6

45 And thorns shall come up in her palaces, nettles and brambles in the fortresses thereof: and it shall be an habitation of dragons, and a court for owls.

Isaiah 34:13. The fate of Zion's enemies.

46 The wilderness and the solitary place shall be glad for them; and the desert shall rejoice, and blossom as the rose.

Isaiah 35:1. Interpreted as referring to the flourishing of Christ's kingdom.

47 Then the eyes of the blind shall be opened, and the ears of the deaf shall be unstopped.

Then shall the lame man leap as an hart, and the tongue of the dumb sing: for in the wilderness shall waters break out, and streams in the desert.

Isaiah 35:5–6

48 And the ransomed of the Lord shall return, and come to Zion with songs and everlasting joy upon their heads: they shall obtain joy and gladness, and sorrow and sighing shall flee away.

Isaiah 35:10

49 Lo, thou trusteth in the staff of this broken reed, on Egypt; whereon if a man lean, it will go into his hand, and pierce it: so is Pharoah king of Egypt to all that trust in him.

Isaiah 36:6

50 I shall go softly all my years in the bitterness of my soul.

Isaiah 38:15. The words of Hezekiah on his delivery from sickness.

51 Comfort ye, comfort ye my people, saith your God.
Speak ye comfortably to Jerusalem, and cry unto her, that her warfare is accomplished, that her iniquity is pardoned: for she hath received of the Lord's hand double for all her sins.

Isaiah 40:1–2

52 The voice of him that crieth in the wilderness, Prepare ye the way of the Lord, make straight in the desert a highway for our God.

Isaiah 40:3. This passage, like many others in *Isaiah*, has been taken as a prophecy of John the Baptist's message. See MATTHEW 7.

53 Every valley shall be exalted, and every mountain and hill shall be made low: and the crooked shall be made straight, and the rough places plain:
And the glory of the Lord shall be revealed, and all flesh shall see it together: for the mouth of the Lord hath spoken it.

Isaiah 40:4–5

54 The voice said, Cry. And he said, What shall I cry? All flesh is grass, and all the goodliness thereof is as the flower of the field:
The grass withereth, the flower fadeth: because the spirit of the Lord bloweth upon it: surely the people is grass.

Isaiah 40:6–7. The words are recalled in the New Testament: see 1 PETER 2.

55 O Zion, that bringest good tidings, get thee up into the high mountain; O Jerusalem, that bringest good tidings, lift up thy voice with strength; lift it up, be not afraid; say unto the cities of Judah, Behold your God!

Isaiah 40:9

56 He shall feed his flock like a shepherd: he shall gather the lambs with his arm, and carry them in his bosom, and shall gently lead those that are with young.

Isaiah 40:11

57 Behold, the nations are as a drop of a bucket, and are counted as the small dust of the balance: behold, he taketh up the isles as a very little thing.

Isaiah 40:15

58 Have ye not known? have ye not heard? hath it not been told you from the beginning? have ye not understood from the foundations of the earth?

Isaiah 40:21

59 But they that wait upon the Lord shall renew their strength; they shall mount up with wings as eagles; they shall run, and not be weary; and they shall walk, and not faint.

Isaiah 40:31

60 The isles saw it and feared; the ends of the earth were afraid, drew near, and came.
They helped every one his neighbour; and every one said to his brother, Be of good courage.

Isaiah 41:5–6. On the might of God.

61 A bruised reed shall he not break, and the smoking flax shall he not quench; he shall bring forth judgment unto truth.

Isaiah 42:3. Interpreted as referring to Christ's meekness.

62 Woe unto him that striveth with his Maker! Let the potsherd strive with the potsherds of the earth. Shall the clay say to him that fashioneth it, What makest thou? Or thy work, He hath no hands?

Isaiah 45:9. See also ROMANS 26.

63 Verily thou art a God that hidest thyself, O God of Israel, the Saviour.

Isaiah 45:15

64 Behold, I have refined thee, but not with silver; I have chosen thee in the furnace of affliction.

Isaiah 48:10. God's favour towards his chosen people.

65 O that thou hadst hearkened to my commandments! then had thy peace been as a

river, and thy righteousness as the waves of the sea.

Isaiah 48:18

66 There is no peace, saith the Lord, unto the wicked.

Isaiah 48:22. Also in *Isaiah* 57:21.

67 Can a woman forget her sucking child, that she should not have compassion on the son of her womb? yea, they may forget, yet will I not forget thee.

Isaiah 49:15. God's promise to Zion.

68 I gave my back to the smiters, and my cheeks to them that plucked off the hair: I hid not my face from shame and spitting.

Isaiah 50:6

69 How beautiful upon the mountains are the feet of him that bringeth good tidings, that publisheth peace.

Isaiah 52:7

70 Thy watchmen shall lift up the voice; with the voice together shall they sing: for they shall see eye to eye, when the Lord shall bring again Zion.

Isaiah 52:8

71 Who hath believed our report? and to whom is the arm of the Lord revealed?

Isaiah 53:1

72 For he shall grow up before him as a tender plant, and as a root out of a dry ground: he hath no form nor comeliness; and when we shall see him, there is no beauty that we should desire him.

He is despised and rejected of men; a man of sorrows, and acquainted with grief: and we hid as it were our faces from him; he was despised, and we esteemed him not.

Surely he hath borne our griefs, and carried our sorrows: yet we did esteem him stricken, smitten of God, and afflicted.

Isaiah 53:2–4. The passage is traditionally considered to foretell Christ's passion.

73 But he was wounded for our transgressions, he was bruised for our iniquities: the chastisement of our peace was upon him; and with his stripes we are healed.

All we like sheep have gone astray; we have turned every one to his own way; and the Lord hath laid on him the iniquity of us all.

Isaiah 53:5–6

74 He was oppressed, and he was afflicted, yet he opened not his mouth: he is brought as a lamb to the slaughter, and as a sheep before her shearers is dumb, so he openeth not his mouth.

Isaiah 53:7. Similar wording is used in *Acts* 8:32.

75 He hath poured out his soul unto death: and he was numbered with the transgressors; and he bare the sin of many, and made intercession for the transgressors.

Isaiah 53:12

76 Ho, every one that thirsteth, come ye to the waters.

Isaiah 55:1

77 For my thoughts are not your thoughts, neither are your ways my ways, saith the Lord.

For as the heavens are higher than the earth, so are my ways higher than your ways, and my thoughts than your thoughts.

Isaiah 55:8–9

78 Instead of the thorn shall come up the fir tree, and instead of the brier shall come up the myrtle tree: and it shall be to the Lord for a name, for an everlasting sign that shall not be cut off.

Isaiah 55:13

79 The righteous perisheth, and no man layeth it to heart: and merciful men are taken away, none considering that the righteous is taken away from the evil to come.

Isaiah 57:1

80 I create the fruit of the lips; Peace, peace to him that is far off, and to him that is near, saith the Lord; and I will heal him.

Isaiah 57:19

81 Their feet run to evil, and they make haste to shed innocent blood: their thoughts are thoughts of iniquity; wasting and destruction are in their paths.

Isaiah 59:7. Referring to evil-doers.

82 Arise, shine; for thy light is come, and the glory of the Lord is risen upon thee.

For, behold, the darkness shall cover the earth, and gross darkness the people: but the Lord shall arise upon thee, and his glory shall be seen upon thee.

And the Gentiles shall come to thy light, and kings to the brightness of thy rising.

Isaiah 60:1–3

83 A little one shall become a thousand, and a small one a strong nation.

Isaiah 60:22

84 Give unto them beauty for ashes, the oil of joy for mourning, the garment of praise for the spirit of heaviness.

Isaiah 61:3. The benefits of God's blessing.

85 I have trodden the winepress alone; and of the people there was none with me: for I will tread them in mine anger, and trample them in my fury; and their blood shall be sprinkled upon my garments, and I will stain all my raiment.
For the day of vengeance is in mine heart, and the year of my redeemed is come.

Isaiah 63:3–4. The 'grapes of wrath' passage probably inspired the words of the 'Battle Hymn of the Republic' (1862): see JULIA WARD HOWE 1.

86 But we are all as an unclean thing, and all our righteousnesses are as filthy rags; and we all do fade as a leaf; and our iniquities, like the wind, have taken us away.

Isaiah 64:6

87 Stand by thyself, come not near to me; for I am holier than thou.

Isaiah 65:5. The words of 'rebellious' Jews.

88 For, behold, I create new heavens and a new earth: and the former shall not be remembered, nor come into mind.

Isaiah 65:17. 'A new heaven and a new earth' are referred to in *Revelation* 21:1.

89 And it shall come to pass, that from one new moon to another, and from one sabbath to another, shall all flesh come to worship before me, saith the Lord.
And they shall go forth, and look upon the carcases of the men that have transgressed against me: for their worm shall not die, neither shall their fire be quenched; and they shall be an abhorring unto all flesh.

Isaiah 66:23–4. According to scholars, these final verses of *Isaiah* are among the few biblical passages on which a doctrine of hellfire can be based.

The Book of the Prophet Jeremiah

1 Be astonished, O ye heavens, at this, and be horribly afraid.

Jeremiah 2:12

2 They were as fed horses in the morning: every one neighed after his neighbour's wife.

Jeremiah 5:8. Referring to the corruption of morals in Jerusalem.

3 But this people hath a revolting and a rebellious heart; they are revolted and gone.

Jeremiah 5:23. Referring to the Israelites.

4 As a cage is full of birds, so are their houses full of deceit: therefore they are become great, and waxen rich.

Jeremiah 5:27

5 A wonderful and horrible thing is committed in the land;
The prophets prophesy falsely, and the priests bear rule by their means; and my people love to have it so: and what will ye do in the end thereof?

Jeremiah 5:30–1

6 They have healed also the hurt of the daughter of my people slightly, saying, Peace, peace; when there is no peace.

Jeremiah 6:14. The words recur in *Jeremiah* 8:11.

7 Thus saith the Lord, Stand ye in the ways, and see, and ask for the old paths, where is the good way, and walk therein, and ye shall find rest for your souls.

Jeremiah 6:16

8 The harvest is past, the summer is ended, and we are not saved.

Jeremiah 8:20

9 Is there no balm in Gilead; is there no physician there? Why then is not the health of the daughter of my people recovered?

Jeremiah 8:22. The region of Gilead, east of the Jordan River, was famous for the balm produced there (also mentioned in *Genesis* 37:25).

10 Let not the wise man glory in his wisdom, neither let the mighty man glory in his might, let not the rich man glory in his riches:
But let him that glorieth glory in this, that he understandeth and knoweth me.

Jeremiah 9:23–4

11 Can the Ethiopian change his skin, or the leopard his spots? then may ye also do good, that are accustomed to do evil.

Jeremiah 13:23

12 O Lord, though our iniquities testify against us, do thou it for thy name's sake: for our

backslidings are many; we have sinned against thee.

Jeremiah 14:7

13 She hath given up the ghost; her sun is gone down while it was yet day.

Jeremiah 15:9. Referring to Jerusalem.

14 Woe is me, my mother, that thou hast borne me a man of strife and a man of contention to the whole earth!

Jeremiah 15:10

15 I sat not in the assembly of the mockers, nor rejoiced; I sat alone because of thy hand: for thou has filled me with indignation.

Jeremiah 15:17

16 The heart is deceitful above all things, and desperately wicked: who can know it?

Jeremiah 17:9

17 As the partridge sitteth on eggs, and hatcheth them not; so he that getteth riches, and not by right, shall leave them in the midst of his days, and at his end shall be a fool.

Jeremiah 17:11

18 For thus saith the Lord, Behold, I will make thee a terror to thyself, and to all thy friends.

Jeremiah 20:4

19 O earth, earth, earth, hear the word of the Lord.

Jeremiah 22:29

20 And seekest thou great things for thyself? seek them not: for, behold, I will bring evil upon all flesh, saith the Lord: but thy life will I give unto thee for a prey in all places whither thou goest.

Jeremiah 45:5

The Lamentations of Jeremiah

1 How doth the city sit solitary, that was full of people! how is she become as a widow! she that was great among the nations, and princess among the provinces, how is she become tributary!

Lamentations 1:1. Opening words of book, referring to Jerusalem.

2 Is it nothing to you, all ye that pass by? behold, and see if there be any sorrow like unto my sorrow.

Lamentations 1:12

3 And I said, My strength and my hope is perished from the Lord:

Remembering mine affliction and my misery, the wormwood and the gall.

Lamentations 3:18–19

4 It is good for a man that he bear the yoke in his youth.

Lamentations 3:27

5 O Lord, thou hast seen my wrong: judge thou my cause.

Lamentations 3:59

The Book of the Prophet Ezekiel

1 Their appearance and their work was as it were a wheel in the middle of a wheel.

Ezekiel 1:16. The prophet's vision of the four wheels. The image is repeated in Ezekiel 10:10.

2 The days are prolonged, and every vision faileth.

Ezekiel 12:22. An Israelite proverb.

3 As is the mother, so is her daughter.

Ezekiel 16:44. A proverb.

4 The fathers have eaten sour grapes, and the children's teeth are set on edge.

Ezekiel 18:2. Proverbial reproach by God concerning the land of Israel, also in Jeremiah 31:29.

5 For the king of Babylon stood at the parting of the way, at the head of the two ways, to use divination: he made his arrows bright, he consulted with images, he looked in the liver.

Ezekiel 21:21

6 The hand of the Lord was upon me, and carried me out in the spirit of the Lord, and set me down in the midst of the valley which was full of bones,

And caused me to pass by them round about: and behold, there were very many in the open valley; and lo, they were very dry.

And he said unto me, Son of man, can these bones live? And I answered, O Lord God, thou knowest.

Again he said unto me, Prophesy upon these bones, and say unto them, O ye dry bones, hear the word of the Lord.

Ezekiel 37:1–4. The verses were the inspiration for 'Them Dry Bones', a spiritual first recorded in 1927.

7 And I will call for a sword against him throughout all my mountains, saith the Lord God: every man's sword shall be against his brother.

Ezekiel 38:21. God prophesies the time when Gog, of the land of Magog, shall come against Israel. See also 1 SAMUEL 8.

The Book of Daniel

1 Children in whom was no blemish, but well favoured, and skilful in all wisdom, and cunning in knowledge, and understanding science, and such as had ability in them to stand in the king's palace.

Daniel 1:4. Of the Israelite children taken into captivity in Babylon by King Nebuchadnezzar.

2 Thou, O king, sawest, and behold a great image. This great image, whose brightness was excellent, stood before thee; and the form thereof was terrible.

This image's head was of fine gold, his breast and his arms of silver, his belly and his thighs of brass,

His legs of iron, his feet part of iron and part of clay.

Daniel 2:31–3. Daniel explains Nebuchadnezzar's dream.

3 To you it is commanded, O people, nations, and languages,

That at what time ye hear the sound of the cornet, flute, harp, sackbut, psaltery, dulcimer, and all kinds of music, ye fall down and worship the golden image that Nebuchadnezzar the king hath set up:

And whoso falleth not down and worshippeth shall the same hour be cast into the midst of a burning fiery furnace.

Daniel 3:4–6. The words of a herald to the court of Nebuchadnezzar.

4 Shadrach, Meshach, and Abed-nego, ye servants of the most high God, come forth, and come hither.

Daniel 3:26. Nebuchadnezzar commands the companions of Daniel to emerge from the furnace.

5 And he was driven from men, and did eat grass as oxen, and his body was wet with the dew of heaven, till his hairs were grown like eagles' feathers, and his nails like birds' claws.

Daniel 4:33. The legend of the madness and exile of Nebuchadnezzar (Nebuchadnezzar II) was probably transferred to him from the career of his successor, Nabonidus (father of Belshazzar).

6 Belshazzar the king made a great feast to a thousand of his lords, and drank wine before the thousand.

Daniel 5:1

7 In the same hour came forth fingers of a man's hand, and wrote over against the candlestick upon the plaister of the wall of the king's palace.

Daniel 5:5. The phrase 'the writing on the wall' derives from this passage.

8 And this is the writing that was written, MENE, MENE, TEKEL, UPHARSIN.

Daniel 5:25. Daniel's explication of the writing on the wall.

9 Thou art weighed in the balances, and art found wanting.

Daniel 5:27. Daniel interprets for Belshazzar the meaning of *tekel*.

10 According to the law of the Medes and Persians, which altereth not.

Daniel 6:8 and 12. Referring to the decree of Darius the Median that condemned Daniel to the lions' den.

11 Then the king commanded, and they brought Daniel, and cast him into the den of lions.

Daniel 6:16

12 I beheld till the thrones were cast down, and the Ancient of days did sit, whose garment was white as snow, and the hair of his head like the pure wool: his throne was like the fiery flame, and his wheels as burning fire.

A fiery stream issued and came forth from behind him: thousand thousands ministered unto him, and ten thousand times ten thousand stood before him: the judgment was set, and the books were opened.

Daniel 7:9–10. The first of Daniel's apocalyptic visions.

13 I saw in the night visions, and, behold, one like the Son of man came with the clouds of heaven, and came to the Ancient of days, and they brought him near before him.

Daniel 7:13. Daniel's vision.

14 But thou, O Daniel, shut up the words, and seal the book, even to the time of the end: many shall run to and fro, and knowledge shall be increased.

Daniel 12:4

Hosea

1 Like people, like priest.

Hosea 4:9

2 For they have sown the wind, and they shall reap the whirlwind.

Hosea 8:7. A prophecy against idolators.

3 Ye have plowed wickedness, ye have reaped iniquity; ye have eaten the fruit of lies.

Hosea 10:13

4 I drew them with cords of a man, with bands of love.

Hosea 11:4. God recalls his past favour towards Israel.

5 He is a merchant, the balances of deceit are in his hand: he loveth to oppress.
Hosea 12:7. Referring to Ephraim.

6 I have multiplied visions, and used similitudes, by the ministry of the prophets.
Hosea 12:10

Joel

1 Hear this, ye old men, and give ear, all ye inhabitants of the land. Hath this been in your days, or even in the days of your fathers?
Tell ye your children of it, and let your children tell their children, and their children another generation.
Joel 1:2–3

2 That which the palmerworm hath left hath the locust eaten; and that which the locust hath left hath the cankerworm eaten; and that which the cankerworm hath left hath the caterpiller eaten.
Joel 1:4

3 Blow ye the trumpet in Zion, and sound an alarm in my holy mountain: let all the inhabitants of the land tremble: for the day of the Lord cometh, for it is nigh at hand.
Joel 2:1

4 And I will restore to you the years that the locust hath eaten, the cankerworm, and the caterpiller, and the palmerworm, my great army which I sent among you.
Joel 2:25

5 And it shall come to pass afterward, that I will pour out my spirit upon all flesh; and your sons and your daughters shall prophesy, your old men shall dream dreams, your young men shall see visions.
Joel 2:28

6 Put ye in the sickle, for the harvest is ripe: come, get you down; for the press is full, the fats overflow; for their wickedness is great.
Multitudes, multitudes in the valley of decision: for the day of the Lord is near in the valley of decision.
Joel 3:13–14

Amos

1 Can two walk together, except they be agreed?
Amos 3:3

2 Shall a trumpet be blown in the city, and the people not be afraid? shall there be evil in a city, and the Lord hath not done it?
Amos 3:6

3 I have overthrown some of you, as God overthrew Sodom and Gomorrah, and ye were as a firebrand plucked out of the burning: yet have ye not returned unto me, saith the Lord.
Amos 4:11

4 But let judgment run down as waters, and righteousness as a mighty stream.
Amos 5:24. The passage was quoted by Martin Luther King: see MARTIN LUTHER KING 17.

Jonah

1 Now the Lord had prepared a great fish to swallow up Jonah. And Jonah was in the belly of the fish three days and three nights.
Jonah 1:17

Micah

1 But thou, Beth-lehem Ephratah, though thou be little among the thousands of Judah, yet out of thee shall he come forth unto me that is to be ruler in Israel; whose goings forth have been from of old, from everlasting.
Micah 5:2. The passage has been interpreted to foretell the birth of Christ in Bethlehem.

2 He hath shewed thee, O man, what is good; and what doth the Lord require of thee, but to do justly, and to love mercy, and to walk humbly with thy God?
Micah 6:8

3 Trust ye not in a friend, put ye not confidence in a guide: keep the doors of thy mouth from her that lieth in thy bosom.
Micah 7:5

4 For the son dishonoureth the father, the daughter riseth up against her mother, the daughter in law against her mother in law: a man's enemies are the men of his own house.
Micah 7:6

Nahum

1 Woe to the bloody city! it is all full of lies and robbery; the prey departeth not;
The noise of a whip, and the noise of the rattling

of the wheels, and of the prancing horses, and of the jumping chariots.

Nahum 3:1–2. Referring to the destruction of Nineveh.

Habakkuk

1 I will stand upon my watch, and set me upon the tower, and will watch to see what he will say unto me, and what I shall answer when I am reproved.

And the Lord answered me, and said, Write the vision, and make it plain upon tables, that he may run that readeth it.

Habakkuk 2:1–2

2 But the Lord is in his holy temple: let all the earth keep silence before him.

Habakkuk 2:20

Zephaniah

1 Woe to her that is filthy and polluted, to the oppressing city!

Zephaniah 3:1. Referring to Jerusalem.

Haggai

1 Ye have sown much, and bring in little; ye eat, but ye have not enough; ye drink, but ye are not filled with drink; ye clothe you, but there is none warm; and he that earneth wages earneth wages to put it into a bag with holes.

Haggai 1:6. The prophet describes the destitution of the people returned from exile.

Zechariah

1 Your fathers, where are they? and the prophets, do they live for ever?

Zechariah 1:5. Addressing the people of Judah, returned from exile.

2 These are they whom the Lord hath sent to walk to and fro through the earth.

Zechariah 1:10. The vision of the horsemen.

3 I have spread you abroad as the four winds of the heaven.

Zechariah 2:6

4 For who hath despised the day of small things?

Zechariah 4:10

5 Rejoice greatly, O daughter of Zion; shout, O daughter of Jerusalem: behold, thy King cometh unto thee: he is just, and having salvation;

lowly, and riding upon an ass, and upon a colt the foal of an ass.

Zechariah 9:9. The words are recalled in *Matthew* 21:5, referring to Christ's entry into Jerusalem: 'Tell ye the daughter of Sion, shout, Behold, thy King cometh unto thee, meek, and sitting upon an ass, and a colt the foal of an ass.'

6 Turn you to the strong hold, ye prisoners of hope: even to day do I declare that I will render double unto thee.

Zechariah 9:12

7 And I said unto them, If ye think good, give me my price; and if not, forbear. So they weighed for my price thirty pieces of silver.

Zechariah 11:12. The words prefigure those in *Matthew* 26:15; see MATTHEW 154.

Malachi

1 Have we not all one father? hath not one God created us? why do we deal treacherously every man against his brother, by profaning the covenant of our fathers?

Malachi 2:10

2 Behold, I will send my messenger, and he shall prepare the way before me: and the Lord, whom ye seek, shall suddenly come to his temple, even the messenger of the covenant, whom ye delight in: behold, he shall come, saith the Lord of hosts.

But who may abide the day of his coming? and who shall stand when he appeareth? for he is like a refiner's fire, and like fullers' soap.

Malachi 3:1–2

3 For, behold, the day cometh, that shall burn as an oven; and all the proud, yea, and all that do wickedly, shall be stubble: and the day that cometh shall burn them up, saith the Lord of hosts, that it shall leave them neither root nor branch.

But unto you that fear my name shall the Sun of righteousness arise with healing in his wings; and ye shall go forth, and grow up as calves of the stall.

Malachi 4:1–2

THE BIBLE: APOCRYPHA

1 Esdras

1 The first wrote, Wine is the strongest.

The second wrote, The king is strongest.

The third wrote, Women are strongest: but above all things Truth beareth away the victory.

1 Esdras 3:10–12. The 'three young men' of the bodyguard of Darius, king of the Persians, compete for his favour.

2 O ye men, how exceeding strong is wine! it causeth all men to err that drink it:

It maketh the mind of the king and of the fatherless child to be all one; of the bondman and of the freeman, of the poor man and of the rich:

It turneth also every thought into jollity and mirth, so that a man remembereth neither sorrow nor debt:

And it maketh every heart rich, so that a man remembereth neither king nor governor.

1 Esdras 3:18–21. The first bodyguard speaks.

3 And when they are in their cups, they forget their love both to friends and brethren, and a little after draw out swords:

But when they are from the wine, they remember not what they have done.

1 Esdras 3:22–3

4 By this also ye must know that women have dominion over you: do ye not labour and toil, and give and bring all to the woman?

Yea, a man taketh his sword, and goeth his way to rob and to steal, to sail upon the sea and upon rivers;

And looketh upon a lion, and goeth in the darkness; and when he hath stolen, spoiled, and robbed, he bringeth it to his love.

1 Esdras 4:22–4. The third bodyguard, Zorobabel, addresses King Darius.

5 Great is Truth, and mighty above all things.

1 Esdras 4:41. The cry of the people following the speech of the king's third bodyguard. See VULGATE 15.

2 Esdras

1 Then had I pity upon your mournings, and gave you manna to eat; so ye did eat angels' bread.

2 Esdras 1:19

2 For their sakes I made the world: and when Adam transgressed my statutes, then was decreed that now is done.

Then were the entrances of this world made narrow, full of sorrow and travail: they are but few and evil, full of perils, and very painful.

For the entrances of the elder world were wide and sure, and brought immortal fruit.

If then they that live labour not to enter these strait and vain things, they can never receive those that are laid up for them.

2 Esdras 7:11–14

3 For the world hath lost his youth, and the times begin to wax old.

2 Esdras 14:10

4 Come hither, and I shall light a candle of understanding in thine heart, which shall not be put out.

2 Esdras 14:25

Tobit

1 Be not greedy to add money to money: but let it be as refuse in respect of our child.

For that which the Lord hath given us to live with doth suffice us.

Tobit 5:18–19. The words of Anna to Tobit, after he has dispatched their son to Media.

Judith

1 She rose where she had fallen down, and called her maid, and went down into the house, in the which she abode in the sabbath days, and in her feast days,

And pulled off the sackcloth which she had on, and put off the garments of her widowhood, and washed her body all over with water, and anointed herself with precious ointment, and braided the hair of her head, and put on a tire upon it, and put on her garments of gladness.

Judith 10:2–3. Judith prepares to enter the Assyrian camp.

2 Her sandals ravished his eyes, her beauty took his mind prisoner, and the fauchion passed through his neck.

Judith 16:9. The song of Judith, describing her slaying of Holofernes. A 'fauchion' is a broad-bladed sword.

The Wisdom of Solomon

1 For the ear of jealousy heareth all things: and the noise of murmurings is not hid.

Wisdom of Solomon 1:10

2 For our time is a very shadow that passeth away; and after our end there is no returning: for it is fast sealed, so that no man cometh again.

Wisdom of Solomon 2:5

3 Let us crown ourselves with rosebuds, before they be withered.

Wisdom of Solomon 2:8

4 For God created man to be immortal, and made him to be an image of his own eternity.

Nevertheless through envy of the devil came death into the world: and they that do hold of his side do find it.

Wisdom of Solomon 2:23–4

5 But the souls of the righteous are in the hand of God, and there shall no torment touch them.

In the sight of the unwise they seemed to die: and their departure is taken for misery,

And their going from us to be utter destruction: but they are in peace.

For though they be punished in the sight of men, yet is their hope full of immortality.

And having been a little chastised, they shall be greatly rewarded: for God proved them, and found them worthy for himself.

Wisdom of Solomon 3:1–5

6 And in the time of their visitation they shall shine, and run to and fro like sparks among the stubble.

Wisdom of Solomon 3:7

7 For honourable age is not that which standeth in length of time, nor that is measured by number of years.

But wisdom is the gray hair unto men, and an unspotted life is old age.

Wisdom of Solomon 4:8–9

8 For the bewitching of naughtiness doth obscure things that are honest; and the wandering of concupiscence doth undermine the simple mind.

He, being made perfect in a short time, fulfilled a long time.

Wisdom of Solomon 4:12–13

9 And as a ship that passeth over the waves of the water, which when it is gone by, the trace thereof cannot be found, neither the pathway of the keel in the waves;

Or as when a bird hath flown through the air, there is no token of her way to be found, but the light air being beaten with the stroke of her wings, and parted with the violent noise and motion of them, is passed through, and therein afterwards no sign where she went is to be found;

Or like as when an arrow is shot at a mark, it parteth the air, which immediately cometh together again, so that a man cannot know where it went through:

Even so we in like manner, as soon as we were born, began to draw to our end, and had no sign of virtue to shew; but were consumed in our own wickedness.

Wisdom of Solomon 5:10–13

10 For the hope of the ungodly is like dust that is blown away with the wind; like a thin froth that is driven away with the storm; like as the smoke which is dispersed here and there with a tempest, and passeth away as the remembrance of a guest that tarrieth but a day.

Wisdom of Solomon 5:14

11 For all men have one entrance into life, and the like going out.

Wisdom of Solomon 7:6

12 For wisdom is more moving than any motion: she passeth and goeth through all things by reason of her pureness.

For she is the breath of the power of God, and a pure influence flowing from the glory of the Almighty: therefore can no defiled thing fall into her.

For she is the brightness of the everlasting light, the unspotted mirror of the power of God, and the image of his goodness.

And being but one, she can do all things: and remaining in herself, she maketh all things new: and in all ages entering into holy souls, she maketh them friends of God, and prophets.

For God loveth none but him that dwelleth with wisdom.

Wisdom of Solomon 7:24–8

13 She preserved the first formed father of the world, that was created alone, and brought him out of his fall,

And gave him power to rule all things.

Wisdom of Solomon 10:1–2. Describing how Wisdom granted power to Adam.

14 For the whole world before thee is as a little grain of the balance, yea, as a drop of the morning dew that falleth down upon the earth.

Wisdom of Solomon 1:22

The Wisdom of Jesus the Son of Sirach, or Ecclesiasticus

1 Who can number the sand of the sea, and the drops of rain, and the days of eternity?
Who can find out the height of heaven, and the breadth of the earth, and the deep, and wisdom?
Ecclesiasticus 1:2–3

2 My son, if thou come to serve the Lord, prepare thy soul for temptation.
Ecclesiasticus 2:1

3 For gold is tried in the fire, and acceptable men in the furnace of adversity.
Ecclesiasticus 2:5

4 He that forsaketh his father is as a blasphemer; and he that angereth his mother is cursed of God.
Ecclesiasticus 3:16

5 My son, go on with thy business in meekness; so shalt thou be beloved of him that is approved.
The greater thou art, the more humble thyself, and thou shalt find favour before the Lord.
Many are in high place, and of renown: but mysteries are revealed unto the meek.
Ecclesiasticus 3:17–19

6 Seek not out the things that are too hard for thee, neither search the things that are above thy strength.
Ecclesiasticus 3:21

7 Be not curious in unnecessary matters: for more things are shewed unto thee than men understand.
Ecclesiasticus 3:23

8 Be not as a lion in thy house, nor frantick among thy servants.
Ecclesiasticus 4:30

9 Winnow not with every wind, and go not into every way: for so doth the sinner that hath a double tongue.
Ecclesiasticus 5:9

10 Honour and shame is in talk: and the tongue of man is his fall.
Ecclesiasticus 5:13

11 Be not ignorant of any thing in a great matter or a small.
Ecclesiasticus 5:15

12 Sweet language will multiply friends: and a fairspeaking tongue will increase kind greetings.
Ecclesiasticus 6:5

13 If thou wouldest get a friend, prove him first, and be not hasty to credit him.
Ecclesiasticus 6:7

14 Separate thyself from thine enemies, and take heed of thy friends.
Ecclesiasticus 6:13

15 A faithful friend is a strong defence: and he that hath found such an one hath found a treasure.
Ecclesiasticus 6:14

16 A faithful friend is the medicine of life; and they that fear the Lord shall find him.
Ecclesiasticus 6:16

17 And if thou seest a man of understanding, get thee betimes unto him, and let thy foot wear the steps of his door.
Ecclesiasticus 6:36

18 Miss not the discourse of the elders: for they also learned of their fathers, and of them thou shalt learn understanding, and to give answer as need requireth.
Ecclesiasticus 8:9

19 Open not thine heart to every man, lest he requite thee with a shrewd turn.
Ecclesiasticus 8:19

20 Use not much the company of a woman that is a singer, lest thou be taken with her attempts.
Ecclesiasticus 9:4

21 Forsake not an old friend; for the new is not comparable to him: a new friend is as new wine; when it is old, thou shalt drink it with pleasure.
Ecclesiasticus 9:10

22 Pride is hateful before God and man: and by both doth one commit iniquity.
Ecclesiasticus 10:7

23 The physician cutteth off a long disease; and he that is to day a king to morrow shall die.
For when a man is dead, he shall inherit creeping things, beasts, and worms.
Ecclesiasticus 10:10–11

24 The bee is little among such as fly; but her fruit is the chief of sweet things.
Ecclesiasticus 11:3

25 Many kings have sat down upon the ground;

and one that was never thought of hath worn the crown.

Ecclesiasticus 11:5

26 Judge none blessed before his death: for a man shall be known in his children.

Ecclesiasticus 11:28. Similar ideas have been expressed by various classical writers, including AESCHYLUS *and* SOLON.

27 Never trust thine enemy: for like as iron rusteth, so is his wickedness.
Though he humble himself, and go crouching, yet take good heed and beware of him, and thou shalt be unto him as if thou hadst wiped a lookingglass, and thou shalt know that his rust hath not been altogether wiped away.

Ecclesiasticus 12:10–11

28 Who will pity a charmer that is bitten with a serpent?

Ecclesiasticus 12:13

29 He that toucheth pitch shall be defiled therewith; and he that hath fellowship with a proud man shall be like unto him.

Ecclesiasticus 13:1

30 Have no fellowship with one that is mightier and richer than thyself: for how agree the kettle and the earthen pot together? For if the one be smitten against the other, it shall be broken.

Ecclesiasticus 13:2

31 If thou be invited of a mighty man, withdraw thyself, and so much the more will he invite thee.
Press thou not upon him, lest thou be put back; stand not far off, lest thou be forgotten.

Ecclesiasticus 13:9–10

32 Every beast loveth his like, and every man loveth his neighbour.
All flesh consorteth according to kind, and a man will cleave to his like.

Ecclesiasticus 13:15–16

33 All flesh waxeth old as a garment: for the covenant from the beginning is, Thou shalt die the death.

Ecclesiasticus 14:17

34 Praise is not seemly in the mouth of a sinner, for it was not sent him of the Lord.
For praise shall be uttered in wisdom, and the Lord will prosper it.

Ecclesiasticus 15:9–10

35 For in the division of the nations of the whole earth he set a ruler over every people; but Israel is the Lord's portion:
Whom, being his firstborn, he nourisheth with discipline, and giving him the light of his love doth not forsake him.
Therefore all their works are as the sun before him, and his eyes are continually upon their ways.

Ecclesiasticus 17:17–19

36 Be not made a beggar by banqueting upon borrowing, when thou hast nothing in thy purse: for thou shalt lie in wait for thine own life, and be talked on.

Ecclesiasticus 18:33

37 He that contemneth small things shall fall by little and little.

Ecclesiasticus 19:1

38 The fool saith, I have no friends, I have no thank for all my good deeds, and they that eat my bread speak evil of me.

Ecclesiasticus 20:16

39 To slip upon a pavement is better than to slip with the tongue: so the fall of the wicked shall come speedily.

Ecclesiasticus 20:18

40 An unseasonable tale will always be in the mouth of the unwise.

Ecclesiasticus 20:19

41 All wickedness is but little to the wickedness of a woman: let the portion of a sinner fall upon her.

Ecclesiasticus 25:19

42 As the climbing up a sandy way is to the feet of the aged, so is a wife full of words to a quiet man.

Ecclesiasticus 25:20

43 The discourse of fools is irksome.

Ecclesiasticus 27:13

44 The talk of him that sweareth much maketh the hair stand upright; and their brawls make one stop his ears.

Ecclesiasticus 27:14

45 The stroke of the whip maketh marks in the flesh: but the stroke of the tongue breaketh the bones.

Many have fallen by the edge of the sword: but not so many as have fallen by the tongue.
Ecclesiasticus 28:17–18

46 Better is the life of a poor man in a mean cottage, than delicate fare in another man's house.
Ecclesiasticus 29:22

47 Better is the poor, being sound and strong of constitution, than a rich man that is afflicted in his body.
Health and good estate of body are above all gold, and a strong body above infinite wealth.
Ecclesiasticus 30:14–15

48 The gladness of the heart is the life of man, and the joyfulness of a man prolongeth his days.
Love thine own soul, and comfort thy heart, remove sorrow far from thee: for sorrow hath killed many, and there is no profit therein.
Ecclesiasticus 30:22–3

49 Envy and wrath shorten the life, and carefulness bringeth age before the time.
Ecclesiasticus 30:24

50 A cheerful and good heart will have a care of his meat and diet.
Ecclesiasticus 30:25

51 Eat, as it becometh a man, those things which are set before thee; and devour not, lest thou be hated.
Leave off first for manners' sake; and be not unsatiable, lest thou offend.
Ecclesiasticus 31:16–17

52 Wine is as good as life to a man, if it be drunk moderately: what life is then to a man that is without wine? for it was made to make men glad.
Ecclesiasticus 31:27

53 Let thy speech be short, comprehending much in few words; be as one that knoweth and yet holdeth his tongue.
Ecclesiasticus 32:8

54 In all thy works keep to thyself the preeminence; leave not a stain in thine honour.
Ecclesiasticus 33:22

55 Whoso regardeth dreams is like him that catcheth at a shadow, and followeth after the wind.
Ecclesiasticus 34:2

56 Honour a physician with the honour due unto him for the uses which ye may have of him: for the Lord hath created him.
For of the most High cometh healing, and ye shall receive honour of the king.
The skill of the physician shall lift up his head: and in the sight of great men he shall be in admiration.
Ecclesiasticus 38:1–3

57 The Lord hath created medicines out of the earth: and he that is wise will not abhor them.
Was not the water made sweet with wood, that the virtue thereof might be known?
Ecclesiasticus 38:4–5

58 He that sinneth before his Maker, let him fall into the hand of the physician.
Ecclesiasticus 38:4

59 Weep bitterly, and make great moan, and use lamentation, as he is worthy, and that a day or two, lest thou be evil spoken of: and then comfort thyself for thy heaviness.
For of heaviness cometh death, and the heaviness of the heart breaketh strength.
Ecclesiasticus 38:17–18

60 The wisdom of a learned man cometh by opportunity of leisure: and he that hath little business shall become wise.
Ecclesiasticus 38:24

61 How can he get wisdom that holdeth the plough, and that glorieth in the goad, that driveth oxen, and is occupied in their labours, and whose talk is of bullocks?
Ecclesiasticus 38:25

62 O death, how bitter is the remembrance of thee to a man that liveth at rest in his possessions, unto the man that hath nothing to vex him, and that hath prosperity in all things: yea, unto him that is yet able to receive meat!
O death, acceptable is thy sentence unto the needy, and unto him whose strength faileth, that is now in the last age, and is vexed with all things, and to him that despaireth, and hath lost patience!
Ecclesiasticus 41:1–2

63 Let us now praise famous men, and our fathers that begat us.
Ecclesiasticus 44:1

64 There be of them, that have left a name behind them, that their praises might be reported.
And some there be, which have no memorial; who are perished, as though they had never been; and are become as though they had never been born; and their children after them.

Ecclesiasticus 44:8–9

65 Their bodies are buried in peace; but their name liveth for evermore.

Ecclesiasticus 44:14. See RUDYARD KIPLING 85.

The Second Book of the Maccabees

1 It is a foolish thing to make a long prologue, and to be short in the story itself.

2 Maccabees 2:32

2 For as it is hurtful to drink wine or water alone; and as wine mingled with water is pleasant, and delighteth the taste: even so speech finely framed delighteth the ears of them that read the story. And here shall be an end.

2 Maccabees 15:39. The final verse of the book and of the Apocrypha.

THE NEW TESTAMENT

The Gospel According to St Matthew

1 And she shall bring forth a son, and thou shalt call his name JESUS: for he shall save his people from their sins.

Matthew 1:21

2 Behold, a virgin shall be with child, and shall bring forth a son, and they shall call his name Emmanuel, which being interpreted is, God with us.

Matthew 1:23. The verse alludes to a former prophecy: see ISAIAH 18.

3 Where is he that is born King of the Jews? for we have seen his star in the east, and are come to worship him.

Matthew 2:2. Spoken by the 'wise men from the east'.

4 And when they were come into the house, they saw the young child with Mary his mother, and fell down, and worshipped him: and when they had opened their treasures, they presented unto him gifts; gold, and frankincense, and myrrh.

Matthew 2:11

5 In Rama was there a voice heard, lamentation, and weeping, and great mourning, Rachel weeping for her children, and would not be comforted, because they are not.

Matthew 2:18. Alluding to a prophecy in *Jeremiah* 31:15: 'A voice was heard in Ramah, lamentation, and bitter weeping; Rahel weeping for her children refused to be comforted for her children, because they were not.' The words were taken to foretell the slaughter of the innocents by Herod.

6 Repent ye: for the kingdom of heaven is at hand.

Matthew 3:2. The preaching of John the Baptist.

7 The voice of one crying in the wilderness, Prepare ye the way of the Lord, make his paths straight.

Matthew 3:3. Alluding to a former prophecy: see ISAIAH 52.

8 And the same John had his raiment of camel's hair, and a leathern girdle about his loins; and his meat was locusts and wild honey.

Matthew 3:4

9 O generation of vipers, who hath warned you to flee from the wrath to come?

Matthew 3:7. John the Baptist rebukes the Pharisees and Sadducees who have come to be baptized.

10 And now also the axe is laid unto the root of the trees: therefore every tree which bringeth not forth good fruit is hewn down, and cast into the fire.

Matthew 3:10

11 I indeed baptize you with water unto repentance: but he that cometh after me is mightier than I, whose shoes I am not worthy to bear: he shall baptize you with the Holy Ghost, and with fire.

Matthew 3:11

12 I have need to be baptized of thee, and comest thou to me?

Matthew 3:14. The words of John the Baptist to Jesus.

13 Lo, the heavens were opened unto him, and he saw the Spirit of God descending like a dove, and lighting upon him.

Matthew 3:16

14 This is my beloved Son, in whom I am well pleased.

Matthew 3:17. A 'voice from heaven' following the baptism of Jesus by John the Baptist.

15 And when he had fasted forty days and forty nights, he was afterward an hungred.

Matthew 4:2

16 Man shall not live by bread alone, but by every word that proceedeth out of the mouth of God.

Matthew 4:4. Alluding to a prophecy (see DEUTERONOMY 5),

Jesus replies to the devil in the wilderness, after he is tempted to turn stones to bread.

17 Thou shalt not tempt the Lord thy God.
Matthew 4:7. The words of Jesus to the devil; see DEU-TERONOMY 3.

18 Again, the devil taketh him up into an exceeding high mountain, and sheweth him all the kingdoms of the world, and the glory of them;
And saith unto him, All these things will I give thee, if thou wilt fall down and worship me.
Matthew 4:8–9

19 Get thee hence, Satan: for it is written, Thou shalt worship the Lord thy God, and him only shalt thou serve.
Matthew 4:10. See also MATTHEW 115.

20 Then the devil leaveth him, and, behold, angels came and ministered unto him.
Matthew 4:11

21 Follow me, and I will make you fishers of men.
Matthew 4:19. Jesus addresses Peter and Andrew.

22 Blessed are the poor in spirit: for theirs is the kingdom of heaven.
Blessed are they that mourn: for they shall be comforted.
Blessed are the meek: for they shall inherit the earth.
Blessed are they which do hunger and thirst after righteousness: for they shall be filled.
Blessed are the merciful: for they shall obtain mercy.
Blessed are the pure in heart: for they shall see God.
Blessed are the peacemakers: for they shall be called the children of God.
Blessed are they which are persecuted for righteousness' sake: for theirs is the kingdom of heaven.
Blessed are ye, when men shall revile you, and persecute you, and shall say all manner of evil against you falsely, for my sake.
Matthew 5:3–11. The Beatitudes, from the Sermon on the Mount. Many have antecedents in the Old Testament, such as the third beatitude (see PSALMS 45).

23 Ye are the salt of the earth: but if the salt have lost his savour, wherewith shall it be salted?
Matthew 5:13

24 Ye are the light of the world.
Matthew 5:14

25 A city that is set on an hill cannot be hid.
Neither do men light a candle, and put it under a bushel, but on a candlestick; and it giveth light unto all that are in the house.
Let your light so shine before men, that they may see your good works, and glorify your Father which is in heaven.
Matthew 5:14–16. See also *Mark* 4:21 and *Luke* 11:33.

26 Think not that I am come to destroy the law, or the prophets: I am not come to destroy, but to fulfil.
Matthew 5:17

27 Agree with thine adversary quickly, whiles thou art in the way with him; lest at any time the adversary deliver thee to the judge, and the judge deliver thee to the officer, and thou be cast into prison.
Verily I say unto thee, Thou shalt by no means come out thence, till thou hast paid the uttermost farthing.
Matthew 5:25–6

28 Whosoever looketh on a woman to lust after her hath committed adultery with her already in his heart.
Matthew 5:28

29 And if thy right eye offend thee, pluck it out, and cast it from thee: for it is profitable for thee that one of thy members should perish, and not that thy whole body should be cast into hell.
And if thy right hand offend thee, cut it off, and cast it from thee: for it is profitable for thee that one of thy members should perish, and not that thy whole body should be cast into hell.
Matthew 5:29–30. The words of verse 29 are echoed in *Matthew* 18:9.

30 But I say unto you, Swear not at all; neither by heaven; for it is God's throne:
Nor by the earth; for it is his footstool: neither by Jerusalem; for it is the city of the great King.
Neither shalt thou swear by thy head, because thou canst not make one hair white or black.
Matthew 5:34–6

31 Let your communication be, Yea, yea; Nay, nay: for whatsoever is more than these cometh of evil.
Matthew 5:37. See also NEW TESTAMENT: JAMES 16.

32 Ye have heard that it hath been said, An eye for an eye, and a tooth for a tooth:
But I say unto you, That ye resist not evil: but whosoever shall smite thee on thy right cheek, turn to him the other also.

And if any man will sue thee at the law, and take away thy coat, let him have thy cloak also.

And whosoever shall compel thee to go a mile, go with him twain.

Give to him that asketh thee, and from him that would borrow of thee turn not thou away.

Matthew 5:38–42

33 Ye have heard that it hath been said, Thou shalt love thy neighbour, and hate thine enemy.

But I say unto you, Love your enemies, bless them that curse you, do good to them that hate you, and pray for them which despitefully use you, and persecute you.

Matthew 5:43–4

34 He maketh his sun to rise on the evil and on the good, and sendeth rain on the just and on the unjust.

Matthew 5:45

35 Be ye therefore perfect, even as your Father which is in heaven is perfect.

Matthew 5:48

36 Therefore when thou doest thine alms, do not sound a trumpet before thee, as the hypocrites do in the synagogues and in the streets, that they may have glory of men. Verily I say unto you, They have their reward.

But when thou doest alms, let not thy left hand know what thy right hand doeth:

That thine alms may be in secret: and thy Father which seeth in secret himself shall reward thee openly.

Matthew 6:2–4

37 But when ye pray, use not vain repetitions, as the heathen do: for they think that they shall be heard for their much speaking.

Matthew 6:7

38 After this manner therefore pray ye: Our Father which art in heaven, Hallowed be thy name.

Thy kingdom come. Thy will be done in earth, as it is in heaven.

Give us this day our daily bread.

And forgive us our debts, as we forgive our debtors.

And lead us not into temptation, but deliver us from evil: For thine is the kingdom, and the power, and the glory, for ever. Amen.

Matthew 6:9–13. The Lord's Prayer. In *Luke* 11:4, the words are 'And forgive us our sins; for we also forgive every one that is indebted to us.' For the most common form, 'forgive us our trespasses . . .', see BOOK OF COMMON PRAYER 7.

39 Lay not up for yourselves treasures upon earth, where moth and rust doth corrupt, and where thieves break through and steal:

But lay up for yourselves treasures in heaven, where neither moth nor rust doth corrupt, and where thieves do not break through nor steal.

Matthew 6:19–20

40 For where your treasure is, there will your heart be also.

Matthew 6:21. See also *Luke* 12:34.

41 If therefore the light that is in thee be darkness, how great is that darkness!

Matthew 6:23. See also *Luke* 11:34–6.

42 No man can serve two masters: for either he will hate the one, and love the other; or else he will hold to the one, and despise the other. Ye cannot serve God and mammon.

Matthew 6:24

43 Take no thought for your life, what ye shall eat, or what ye shall drink; nor yet for your body, what ye shall put on. Is not the life more than meat, and the body than raiment?

Behold the fowls of the air: for they sow not, neither do they reap, nor gather into barns; yet your heavenly Father feedeth them. Are ye not much better than they?

Matthew 6:25–6

44 Which of you by taking thought can add one cubit unto his stature?

Matthew 6:27

45 Consider the lilies of the field, how they grow; they toil not, neither do they spin:

And yet I say unto you, That even Solomon in all his glory was not arrayed like one of these.

Matthew 6:28–9

46 O ye of little faith.

Matthew 6:30. The first example in the New Testament of this declamation by Jesus.

47 Take therefore no thought for the morrow: for the morrow shall take thought for the things of itself. Sufficient unto the day is the evil thereof.

Matthew 6:34

48 Judge not, that ye be not judged.

Matthew 7:1

49 Why beholdest thou the mote that is in thy

brother's eye, but considerest not the beam that is in thine own eye?
Matthew 7:3

50 Give not that which is holy unto the dogs, neither cast ye your pearls before swine, lest they trample them under their feet, and turn again and rend you.
Matthew 7:6

51 Ask, and it shall be given you; seek, and ye shall find; knock, and it shall be opened unto you:

For every one that asketh receiveth; and he that seeketh findeth; and to him that knocketh it shall be opened.
Matthew 7:7–8

52 Or what man is there of you, whom if his son ask bread, will he give him a stone?
Matthew 7:9

53 Therefore all things whatsoever ye would that men should do to you, do ye even so to them: for this is the law and the prophets.
Matthew 7:12. The 'Golden Rule', as it has become known, is more familiarly rendered 'Do unto others as you would have others do unto you', or more simply 'Do as you would be done by'. In *Luke* 6:31 the words are 'As ye would that men should do to you, do ye also to them likewise.'

54 Enter ye in at the strait gate: for wide is the gate, and broad is the way, that leadeth to destruction, and many there be which go in thereat:

Because strait is the gate, and narrow is the way, which leadeth unto life, and few there be that find it.
Matthew 7:13–14

55 Beware of false prophets, which come to you in sheep's clothing, but inwardly they are ravening wolves.
Matthew 7:15

56 By their fruits ye shall know them.
Matthew 7:20. See also MATTHEW 90.

57 Therefore whosoever heareth these sayings of mine, and doeth them, I will liken him unto a wise man, which built his house upon a rock:

And the rain descended, and the floods came, and the winds blew, and beat upon that house; and it fell not: for it was founded upon a rock.
Matthew 7:24–5. The last parable of the Sermon on the Mount.

58 Every one that heareth these sayings of mine,

and doeth them not, shall be likened unto a foolish man, which built his house upon the sand.
Matthew 7:26

59 Lord, I am not worthy that thou shouldest come under my roof.
Matthew 8:8. The words of a centurion who has requested that Jesus heal his servant.

60 There shall be weeping and gnashing of teeth.
Matthew 8:12. Jesus, referring to 'the children of the kingdom . . . cast out into outer darkness.' The same words are used in the parable of the talents, in *Matthew* 25:30, said of the 'unprofitable servant'.

61 The foxes have holes, and the birds of the air have nests; but the Son of man hath not where to lay his head.
Matthew 8:20

62 Let the dead bury their dead.
Matthew 8:22. Jesus admonishes a disciple who had asked to bury his father before following him.

63 And his disciples came to him, and awoke him, saying, Lord, save us: we perish.

And he saith unto them, Why are ye fearful, O ye of little faith? Then he arose, and rebuked the winds and the sea; and there was a great calm.

But the men marvelled, saying, What manner of man is this, that even the winds and the sea obey him!
Matthew 8:25–7

64 Why eateth your Master with publicans and sinners?
Matthew 9:11

65 They that be whole need not a physician, but they that are sick.
Matthew 9:12

66 I am not come to call the righteous, but sinners to repentance.
Matthew 9:13. The words also appear in *Luke* 5:32.

67 Can the children of the bridechamber mourn, as long as the bridegroom is with them?
Matthew 9:15. Jesus explains to the disciples of John why his own disciples did not fast.

68 Neither do men put new wine into old bottles: else the bottles break, and the wine runneth out, and the bottles perish: but they put new wine into new bottles, and both are preserved.
Matthew 9:17. See also *Mark* 2:22 and *Luke* 5:37–8.

69 The maid is not dead, but sleepeth.

Matthew 9:24. Jesus refers to the daughter of Jairus, identified as such in *Mark* where, in 5:39, the words are 'The damsel is not dead . . .'

70 The harvest truly is plenteous, but the labourers are few.

Matthew 9:37. Jesus refers to the lack of proselytizers among the multitude, shortly before sending forth his apostles. Also in *Luke* 10:2, 'The harvest truly is great . . .'

71 Go rather to the lost sheep of the house of Israel.

Matthew 10:6. Jesus commands the apostles to direct their preaching to the Israelites rather than the gentiles. The expression is repeated in *Matthew* 15:24.

72 Heal the sick, cleanse the lepers, raise the dead, cast out devils: freely ye have received, freely give.

Matthew 10:8

73 And whosoever shall not receive you, nor hear your words, when ye depart out of that house or city, shake off the dust of your feet.

Matthew 10:14

74 Behold, I send you forth as sheep in the midst of wolves: be ye therefore wise as serpents, and harmless as doves.

Matthew 10:16. See also FRANCIS BACON 47 and LUKE 25.

75 And ye shall be hated of all men for my name's sake: but he that endureth to the end shall be saved.

Matthew 10:22

76 The disciple is not above his master, nor the servant above his lord.

Matthew 10:24

77 The very hairs of your head are all numbered.

Matthew 10:30

78 Think not that I am come to send peace on earth: I came not to send peace, but a sword.

Matthew 10:34

79 And a man's foes shall be they of his own household.

Matthew 10:36

80 He that findeth his life shall lose it: and he that loseth his life for my sake shall find it.

Matthew 10:39. Similar words are used in *Matthew* 16:25, *Luke* 9:24, *Luke* 17:33 and *John* 12:25.

81 Art thou he that should come, or do we look for another?

Matthew 11:3. John the Baptist's disciples question Jesus.

82 What went ye out into the wilderness to see? A reed shaken with the wind?

But what went ye out for to see? A man clothed in soft raiment? behold, they that wear soft clothing are in kings' houses.

But what went ye out for to see? A prophet? yea, I say unto you, and more than a prophet.

Matthew 11:7–9

83 He that hath ears to hear, let him hear.

Matthew 11:15. Jesus addresses the multitude. In *Matthew* 13:9, his words are 'Who hath ears to hear, let him hear.'

84 We have piped unto you, and ye have not danced; we have mourned unto you, and ye have not lamented.

Matthew 11:17. The words of the 'children sitting in the markets' to whom Jesus likens this generation.

85 Wisdom is justified of her children.

Matthew 11:19

86 I thank thee, O Father, Lord of heaven and earth, because thou hast hid these things from the wise and prudent, and hast revealed them unto babes.

Matthew 11:25

87 Come unto me, all ye that labour and are heavy laden, and I will give you rest.

Take my yoke upon you, and learn of me; for I am meek and lowly in heart: and ye shall find rest unto your souls.

For my yoke is easy, and my burden is light.

Matthew 11:28–30

88 He that is not with me is against me; and he that gathereth not with me scattereth abroad.

Matthew 12:30

89 All manner of sin and blasphemy shall be forgiven unto men: but the blasphemy against the Holy Ghost shall not be forgiven unto men.

Matthew 12:31

90 Either make the tree good, and his fruit good; or else make the tree corrupt, and his fruit corrupt: for the tree is known by his fruit.

Matthew 12:33. See also MATTHEW 56.

91 O generation of vipers, how can ye, being evil, speak good things? for out of the abundance of the heart the mouth speaketh.

Matthew 12:34

92 Every idle word that men shall speak, they shall give account thereof in the day of judgment.

For by thy words thou shalt be justified, and by thy words thou shalt be condemned.

Matthew 12:36–7

93 An evil and adulterous generation seeketh after a sign.

Matthew 12:39. The words of Jesus to the Pharisees who 'would see a sign', echoed in 16:4.

94 Behold, a greater than Solomon is here.

Matthew 12:42

95 Behold, a sower went forth to sow;

And when he sowed, some seeds fell by the way side, and the fowls came and devoured them up:

Some fell upon stony places, where they had not much earth: and forthwith they sprung up, because they had no deepness of earth:

And when the sun was up, they were scorched; and because they had no root, they withered away.

And some fell among thorns; and the thorns sprung up, and choked them:

But other fell into good ground, and brought forth fruit, some an hundredfold, some sixtyfold, some thirtyfold.

Matthew 13:3–8

96 Blessed are your eyes, for they see: and your ears, for they hear.

Matthew 13:16

97 The care of this world, and the deceitfulness of riches, choke the word.

Matthew 13:22. Jesus explains the parable of the sower.

98 The kingdom of heaven is like to a grain of mustard seed, which a man took, and sowed in his field:

Which indeed is the least of all seeds: but when it is grown, it is the greatest among herbs, and becometh a tree, so that the birds of the air come and lodge in the branches thereof.

Matthew 13:31–2. The words recall *Daniel* 4:11–12 and 20–1.

99 The kingdom of heaven is like unto a merchant man, seeking goodly pearls:

Who, when he had found one pearl of great price, went and sold all that he had, and bought it.

Matthew 13:45–6

100 Is not this the carpenter's son?

Matthew 13:55. The words of the 'astonished' countrymen of Jesus, on seeing him teach in the synagogue.

101 A prophet is not without honour, save in his own country, and in his own house.

Matthew 13:57

102 Give me here John Baptist's head in a charger.

Matthew 14:8. The daughter of Herodias (Salome) – 'being before instructed of her mother' – demands John the Baptist's

head on a flat dish ('charger'), as a reward for having danced at Herod's birthday.

103 And he commanded the multitude to sit down on the grass, and took the five loaves, and the two fishes, and looking up to heaven, he blessed, and brake, and gave the loaves to his disciples, and the disciples to the multitude.

And they did all eat, and were filled: and they took up of the fragments that remained twelve baskets full.

And they that had eaten were about five thousand men, beside women and children.

Matthew 14:19–21. The miracle of the loaves and fishes ('the feeding of the five thousand'). See also JOHN 25.

104 And in the fourth watch of the night Jesus went unto them, walking on the sea.

And when the disciples saw him walking on the sea, they were troubled, saying, It is a spirit; and they cried out for fear.

Matthew 14:25–6

105 Be of good cheer; it is I; be not afraid.

Matthew 14:27. Jesus reassures the disciples when they see him walking on the water.

106 O thou of little faith, wherefore didst thou doubt?

Matthew 14:31. Jesus addresses Peter after he has saved him from drowning.

107 And when the men of that place [Gennesaret] had knowledge of him, they sent out into all that country round about, and brought unto him all that were diseased;

And besought him that they might only touch the hem of his garment: and as many as touched were made perfectly whole.

Matthew 14:35–6

108 Not that which goeth into the mouth defileth a man; but that which cometh out of the mouth, this defileth a man.

Matthew 15:11

109 Let them alone: they be blind leaders of the blind. And if the blind lead the blind, both shall fall into the ditch.

Matthew 15:14. Jesus refers to the Pharisees.

110 Truth, Lord: yet the dogs eat of the crumbs which fall from their masters' table.

Matthew 15:27. The words of the woman of Canaan to Jesus.

111 The Pharisees also with the Sadducees came, and

tempting desired him that he would shew them a sign from heaven.

He answered and said unto them, When it is evening, ye say, It will be fair weather: for the sky is red.

And in the morning, It will be foul weather to day: for the sky is red and lowring. O ye hypocrites, ye can discern the face of the sky; but can ye not discern the signs of the times?

Matthew 16:1–3. See also *Luke* 12:54–6.

112 Thou art the Christ, the Son of the living God.
Matthew 16:16. Peter answers Jesus' question, 'Whom say ye that I am?'

113 And I say also unto thee, That thou art Peter, and upon this rock I will build my church; and the gates of hell shall not prevail against it.
Matthew 16:18. Jesus renames the apostle Simon after the Greek word, *petros*, 'stone' or 'rock'.

114 And I will give unto thee the keys of the kingdom of heaven.
Matthew 16:19

115 Get thee behind me, Satan: thou art an offence unto me: for thou savourest not the things that be of God, but those that be of men.
Matthew 16:23. Jesus rebukes Peter, after he has suggested that Jesus not go into Jerusalem to meet his fate. See also MATTHEW 19.

116 Except ye be converted, and become as little children, ye shall not enter into the kingdom of heaven.
Matthew 18:3

117 Whoso shall receive one such little child in my name receiveth me.

But whoso shall offend one of these little ones which believe in me, it were better for him that a millstone were hanged about his neck, and that he were drowned in the depth of the sea.
Matthew 18:5–6

118 For where two or three are gathered together in my name, there am I in the midst of them.
Matthew 18:20. See also BOOK OF COMMON PRAYER 24.

119 Then came Peter to him, and said, Lord, how oft shall my brother sin against me, and I forgive him? till seven times?

Jesus saith unto him, I say not unto thee, Until seven times: but, Until seventy times seven.
Matthew 18:21–2

120 What therefore God hath joined together, let not man put asunder.
Matthew 19:6. Jesus answers the Pharisees who have asked him whether divorce is lawful. The words are incorporated into the marriage ceremony: see BOOK OF COMMON PRAYER 85.

121 If thou wilt be perfect, go and sell that thou hast, and give to the poor, and thou shalt have treasure in heaven.
Matthew 19:21. Jesus addresses the rich young man who wants to follow him.

122 It is easier for a camel to go through the eye of a needle, than for a rich man to enter into the kingdom of God.
Matthew 19:24

123 With men this is impossible; but with God all things are possible.
Matthew 19:26. Jesus refers to his assertion that the rich shall not be saved. In *Luke* 1:37, the angel tells Mary, 'For with God nothing shall be impossible.'

124 But many that are first shall be last; and the last shall be first.
Matthew 19:30

125 Thou hast made them equal unto us, which have borne the burden and heat of the day.
Matthew 20:12. The parable of the labourers.

126 Is thine eye evil, because I am good?
Matthew 20:15

127 And Jesus went into the temple of God, and cast out all them that sold and bought in the temple, and overthrew the tables of the moneychangers.
Matthew 21:12. See also JOHN 14.

128 My house shall be called the house of prayer; but ye have made it a den of thieves.
Matthew 21:13. Recalling *Jeremiah* 7:11.

129 And all things, whatsoever ye shall ask in prayer, believing, ye shall receive.
Matthew 21:22. See also MARK 12

130 For many are called, but few are chosen.
Matthew 22:14. The parable of the marriage of the king's son; Jesus speaks similar words at the end of the parable of the labourers (*Matthew* 20:16).

131 Render therefore unto Caesar the things which are Caesar's; and unto God the things that are God's.
Matthew 22:21

132 For in the resurrection they neither marry, nor

are given in marriage, but are as the angels of God in heaven.

Matthew 22:30

133 Thou shalt love the Lord thy God with all thy heart, and with all thy soul, and with all thy mind.

This is the first and great commandment.

And the second is like unto it, Thou shalt love thy neighbour as thyself.

On these two commandments hang all the law and the prophets.

Matthew 22:37–40

134 And whosoever shall exalt himself shall be abased; and he that shall humble himself shall be exalted.

Matthew 23:12. See also *Luke* 14:11 and 18:14.

135 Ye blind guides, which strain at a gnat, and swallow a camel.

Matthew 23:24. Jesus admonishes the scribes and Pharisees.

136 Woe unto you, scribes and Pharisees, hypocrites! For ye are like unto whited sepulchres, which indeed appear beautiful outward, but are within full of dead men's bones, and of all uncleanness.

Matthew 23:27

137 O Jerusalem, Jerusalem, thou that killest the prophets, and stonest them which are sent unto thee, how often would I have gathered thy children together, even as a hen gathereth her chickens under her wings, and ye would not!

Matthew 23:37

138 Take heed that no man deceive you.

For many shall come in my name, saying, I am Christ; and shall deceive many.

Matthew 24:4–5. Jesus addresses his disciples on the Mount of Olives.

139 And ye shall hear of wars and rumours of wars: see that ye be not troubled: for all these things must come to pass, but the end is not yet.

For nation shall rise against nation, and kingdom against kingdom: and there shall be famines, and pestilences, and earthquakes, in divers places.

All these are the beginning of sorrows.

Matthew 24:6–8. Jesus foretells to his disciples the signs of the end of the world.

140 When ye therefore shall see the abomination of desolation, spoken of by Daniel the prophet, stand in the holy place, (whoso readeth, let him understand).

Matthew 24:15. *Daniel* 12:11 speaks of 'the abomination that maketh desolate'.

141 For as the lightning cometh out of the east, and shineth even unto the west; so shall also the coming of the Son of man be.

For wheresoever the carcase is, there will the eagles be gathered together.

Matthew 24:27–8

142 Immediately after the tribulation of those days shall the sun be darkened, and the moon shall not give her light, and the stars shall fall from heaven, and the powers of the heavens shall be shaken:

And then shall appear the sign of the Son of man in heaven: and then shall all the tribes of the earth mourn, and they shall see the Son of man coming in the clouds of heaven with power and great glory.

And he shall send his angels with a great sound of a trumpet, and they shall gather together his elect from the four winds, from one end of heaven to the other.

Matthew 24:29–31. The signs of the day of judgement to come.

143 Heaven and earth shall pass away, but my words shall not pass away.

Matthew 24:35

144 Then shall two be in the field; the one shall be taken, and the other left.

Matthew 24:40. Jesus refers to those who are selected at the day of judgement.

145 Watch therefore: for ye know not what hour your Lord doth come.

Matthew 24:42

146 Then shall the kingdom of heaven be likened unto ten virgins, which took their lamps, and went forth to meet the bridegroom.

And five of them were wise, and five were foolish.

Matthew 25:1–2. The parable of the ten virgins.

147 Well done, thou good and faithful servant: thou hast been faithful over a few things, I will make thee a ruler over many things: enter thou into the joy of thy lord.

Matthew 25:21. The parable of the talents; the words are also spoken in verse 23.

148 For unto every one that hath shall be given, and he shall have abundance; but from him that hath not shall be taken away even that which he hath.

Matthew 25:29. Spoken by the lord to his servants in the

parable of the talents. See also *Matthew* 13:12, where the words are spoken directly by Jesus to the disciples.

149 And before him shall be gathered all nations: and he shall separate them one from another, as a shepherd divideth his sheep from the goats:

And he shall set the sheep on his right hand, but the goats on the left.

Matthew 25:32–3

150 For I was an hungred, and ye gave me meat: I was thirsty, and ye gave me drink: I was a stranger, and ye took me in:

Naked, and ye clothed me: I was sick, and ye visited me: I was in prison, and ye came unto me.

Matthew 25:35–6

151 Inasmuch as ye have done it unto one of the least of these my brethren, ye have done it unto me.

Matthew 25:40

152 To what purpose is this waste?

Matthew 26:8. The disciples' response to the anointment of Jesus with 'very precious ointment'.

153 For ye have the poor always with you; but me ye have not always.

Matthew 26:11

154 And [Judas] said unto them, What will ye give me, and I will deliver him unto you? And they covenanted with him for thirty pieces of silver.

Matthew 26:15. See ZECHARIAH 7.

155 My time is at hand.

Matthew 26:18

156 Verily I say unto you, that one of you shall betray me.

Matthew 26:21

157 Lord, is it I?

Matthew 26:22. The disciples ask which of them will betray Jesus.

158 The Son of man goeth as it is written of him: but woe unto that man by whom the Son of man is betrayed! it had been good for that man if he had not been born.

Matthew 26:24

159 And as they were eating, Jesus took bread, and blessed it, and brake it, and gave it to the disciples, and said, Take, eat; this is my body.

And he took the cup, and gave thanks, and gave it to them, saying, Drink ye all of it;

For this is my blood of the new testament, which is shed for many for the remission of sins.

Matthew 26:26–8. The words are cited in the Prayer of Consecration in the service of Holy Communion in the BOOK OF COMMON PRAYER.

160 Verily I say unto thee, That this night, before the cock crow, thou shalt deny me thrice.

Matthew 26:34. Jesus foretells Peter's denial (see MATTHEW 167).

161 O my Father, if it be possible, let this cup pass from me.

Matthew 26:39. Jesus prays in Gethsemane.

162 What, could ye not watch with me one hour?

Matthew 26:40. Jesus rebukes Peter for sleeping while Jesus prayed.

163 Watch and pray, that ye enter not into temptation: the spirit indeed is willing, but the flesh is weak.

Matthew 26:41. See OVID 18.

164 Behold, the hour is at hand, and the Son of man is betrayed into the hands of sinners.

Matthew 26:45

165 And forthwith he [Judas] came to Jesus, and said, Hail, master; and kissed him.

Matthew 26:49. Christ is betrayed with a kiss.

166 Put up again thy sword into his place: for all they that take the sword shall perish with the sword.

Matthew 26:52. Jesus commands his follower (named as Peter in *John* 18:10) not to resist his arrest.

167 Then began he to curse and to swear, saying, I know not the man. And immediately the cock crew.

Matthew 26:74. Peter's third denial (see MATTHEW 160).

168 He [Pilate] took water, and washed his hands before the multitude, saying, I am innocent of the blood of this just person: see ye to it.

Matthew 27:24

169 Then answered all the people, and said, His blood be on us, and on our children.

Matthew 27:25

170 He saved others; himself he cannot save.

Matthew 27:42. The chief priests mock Jesus on the cross.

171 And about the ninth hour Jesus cried with a loud voice, saying *Eli, Eli, lama sabachthani?* that is to say, My God, my God, why hast thou forsaken me?

Matthew 27:46. See PSALMS 22.

172 Go ye therefore, and teach all nations, baptizing

them in the name of the Father, and of the Son, and of the Holy Ghost:

Teaching them to observe all things whatsoever I have commanded you: and, lo, I am with you alway, even unto the end of the world. Amen.

Matthew 28:19–20. Jesus, risen from the cross, addresses his disciples in the final verses of the book.

The Gospel According to St Mark

1 Arise, and take up thy bed, and walk.
Mark 2:9

2 The sabbath was made for man, and not man for the sabbath.
Mark 2:27

3 If a house be divided against itself, that house cannot stand.
Mark 3:25

4 My name is Legion: for we are many.
Mark 5:9. Spoken by the man possessed, in the country of the Gadarenes.

5 And Jesus, immediately knowing in himself that virtue had gone out of him, turned him about in the press, and said, Who touched my clothes?
Mark 5:30

6 He hath done all things well: he maketh both the deaf to hear, and the dumb to speak.
Mark 7:37

7 I see men as trees, walking.
Mark 8:24. The words of a blind man cured by Jesus.

8 For what shall it profit a man, if he shall gain the whole world, and lose his own soul?
Mark 8:36. The words of Jesus appear in *Matthew* 16:26 as 'For what is a man profited . . .'

9 If thou canst believe, all things are possible to him that believeth.
Mark 9:23. Jesus' words to the father of a sick child.

10 Lord, I believe; help thou mine unbelief.
Mark 9:24. Said by the father of the sick child.

11 Suffer the little children to come unto me, and forbid them not: for of such is the kingdom of God.
Mark 10:14

12 For verily I say unto you, That whosoever shall say unto this mountain, Be thou removed, and be thou cast into the sea; and shall not doubt in his heart, but shall believe that those things which he saith shall come to pass; he shall have whatsoever he saith.

Therefore I say unto you, What things soever ye desire, when ye pray, believe that ye receive them, and ye shall have them.

Mark 11:23–4. Jesus' address to his disciples is similarly related in *Matthew* 21 (see MATTHEW 129); the words also recall *Matthew* 17:20.

13 Beware of the scribes, which love to go in long clothing, and love salutations in the marketplaces,

And the chief seats in the synagogues, and the uppermost rooms at feasts:

Which devour widows' houses, and for a pretence make long prayers: these shall receive greater damnation.
Mark 12:38–40

14 And there came a certain poor widow, and she threw in two mites, which make a farthing.
Mark 12:42

15 Watch ye therefore: for ye know not when the master of the house cometh, at even, or at midnight, or at the cockcrowing, or in the morning.

Lest coming suddenly he find you sleeping.

And what I say unto you I say unto all, Watch.
Mark 13:35–7

16 Go ye into all the world, and preach the gospel to every creature.
Mark 16:15. Jesus commands the apostles after his resurrection.

The Gospel According to St Luke

1 Hail, thou that art highly favoured, the Lord is with thee: blessed art thou among women.
Luke 1:28. The words of the Archangel Gabriel to the Virgin Mary. Based on these verses, the Latin 'Ave Maria' ('Hail Mary'), also known as the 'Angelic Salutation', appeared in liturgies from around the 6th century. See ANONYMOUS 6.

2 Blessed art thou among women, and blessed is the fruit of thy womb.
Luke 1:42. Elizabeth, mother-to-be of John the Baptist, addresses Mary; the passage was incorporated into the 'Ave Maria' by the 11th century.

3 My soul doth magnify the Lord,
And my spirit hath rejoiced in God my Saviour.
For he hath regarded the low estate of his
   handmaiden: for, behold, from henceforth all
   generations shall call me blessed.
Luke 1:46–8. The 'Magnificat', or the 'Song of the Blessed Virgin Mary', found in the BOOK OF COMMON PRAYER,

'Evening Prayer'. Some scholars have argued that this canticle was a song of Elizabeth, mother of John the Baptist and kinswoman of Mary. See also BIBLE: VULGATE 9.

4 He hath shewed strength with his arm; he hath scattered the proud in the imagination of their hearts.
He hath put down the mighty from their seats, and exalted them of low degree.
He hath filled the hungry with good things; and the rich he hath sent empty away.

Luke 1:51–3, ibid.

5 Blessed be the Lord God of Israel; for he hath visited and redeemed his people.

Luke 1:68. The prophecy of the priest Zechariah (or Zacharias), father of John the Baptist.

6 Through the tender mercy of our God; whereby the dayspring from on high hath visited us,
To give light to them that sit in darkness and in the shadow of death, to guide our feet into the way of peace.

Luke 1:78–9. See PSALMS 111.

7 And it came to pass in those days, that there went out a decree from Caesar Augustus, that all the world should be taxed.

Luke 2:1

8 And she brought forth her firstborn son, and wrapped him in swaddling clothes, and laid him in a manger; because there was no room for them in the inn.

Luke 2:7

9 And there were in the same country shepherds abiding in the field, keeping watch over their flock by night.
And, lo, the angel of the Lord came upon them, and the glory of the Lord shone round about them: and they were sore afraid.

Luke 2:8–9

10 Fear not: for, behold, I bring you good tidings of great joy, which shall be to all people.

Luke 2:10. The words of the angel Gabriel to the shepherds.

11 Glory to God in the highest, and on earth peace, good will toward men.

Luke 2:14. The words of 'a multitude of the heavenly host'.

12 Lord, now lettest thou thy servant depart in peace, according to thy word:
For mine eyes have seen thy salvation,
Which thou hast prepared before the face of all people;

A light to lighten the Gentiles, and the glory of thy people Israel.

Luke 2:29–32. The words of Simeon on seeing the infant Jesus have become known as the Song of Simeon, or the 'Nunc dimittis', after the opening words in the Latin Vulgate edition (see BIBLE: VULGATE 10). Simeon had been promised that 'he should not see death, before he had seen the Lord's Christ'. The words are also found in the BOOK OF COMMON PRAYER, 'Evening Prayer'.

13 How is it that ye sought me? wist ye not that I must be about my Father's business?

Luke 2:49. The twelve-year-old Jesus answers his parents' concerns after they found him debating with the doctors in the temple.

14 And Jesus increased in wisdom and stature, and in favour with God and man.

Luke 2:52

15 Do violence to no man, neither accuse any falsely; and be content with your wages.

Luke 3:14. John the Baptist advises the soldiers who seek guidance.

16 And the devil, taking him [Jesus] up into an high mountain, shewed unto him all the kingdoms of the world in a moment of time.

Luke 4:5

17 Ye will surely say unto me this proverb, Physician, heal thyself: whatsoever we have heard done in Capernaum, do also here in thy country.

Luke 4:23. Jesus preaches to the people of Nazareth.

18 No man also having drunk old wine straightway desireth new: for he saith, The old is better.

Luke 5:39

19 But woe unto you that are rich! for ye have received your consolation.
Woe unto you that are full! for ye shall hunger.
Woe unto you that laugh now! for ye shall mourn and weep.
Woe unto you, when all men shall speak well of you! For so did their fathers to the false prophets.

Luke 6:24–6

20 Give, and it shall be given unto you; good measure, pressed down, and shaken together, and running over, shall men give into your bosom. For with the same measure that ye mete withal it shall be measured to you again.

Luke 6:38

21 Her sins, which are many, are forgiven; for she loved much.

Luke 7:47. Jesus refers to the 'sinner' who has washed and anointed his feet, sometimes taken to be Mary Magdalene.

22 Thy faith hath saved thee; go in peace.

Luke 7:50

23 For nothing is secret, that shall not be made manifest; neither any thing hid, that shall not be known and come abroad.

Luke 8:17

24 No man, having put his hand to the plough, and looking back, is fit for the kingdom of God.

Luke 9:62

25 Go your ways: behold, I send you forth as lambs among wolves.

Carry neither purse, nor scrip, nor shoes: and salute no man by the way.

Luke 10:3–4. Jesus sends forth his disciples to preach the word. See also MATTHEW 74.

26 The labourer is worthy of his hire.

Luke 10:7. Jesus instructs his disciples to accept any hospitality offered to them.

27 I beheld Satan as lightning fall from heaven.

Luke 10:18

28 Blessed are the eyes which see the things that ye see:

For I tell you, that many prophets and kings have desired to see those things which ye see, and have not seen them; and to hear those things which ye hear, and have not heard them.

Luke 10:23–4

29 A certain man went down from Jerusalem to Jericho, and fell among thieves, which stripped him of his raiment, and wounded him, and departed, leaving him half dead.

Luke 10:30. The parable of the good Samaritan.

30 And by chance there came down a certain priest that way: and when he saw him, he passed by on the other side.

Luke 10:31

31 But a certain Samaritan, as he journeyed, came where he was: and when he saw him, he had compassion on him.

Luke 10:33

32 Go, and do thou likewise.

Luke 10:37. Jesus exhorts a lawyer to emulate the good Samaritan.

33 But Martha was cumbered about much serving, and came to him, and said, Lord, dost thou not care that my sister hath left me to serve alone? bid her therefore that she help me.

And Jesus answered and said unto her, Martha, Martha, thou art careful and troubled about many things:

But one thing is needful: and Mary hath chosen that good part, which shall not be taken away from her.

Luke 10:40–2. Martha, sister of Lazarus and Mary of Bethany, is the patron saint of good housewives.

34 When a strong man armed keepeth his palace, his goods are in peace:

But when a stronger than he shall come upon him, and overcome him, he taketh from him all his armour wherein he trusted, and divideth his spoils.

Luke 11:21–2

35 Woe unto you, lawyers! for ye have taken away the key of knowledge: ye entered not in yourselves, and them that were entering in ye hindered.

Luke 11:52

36 And I will say to my soul, Soul, thou hast much goods laid up for many years; take thine ease, eat, drink, and be merry.

Luke 12:19. The parable of the rich man. See also ECCLESIASTES 27.

37 Thou fool, this night thy soul shall be required of thee.

Luke 12:20. God's words to the rich man in the parable.

38 Let your loins be girded about, and your lights burning.

Luke 12:35

39 For unto whomsoever much is given, of him shall be much required: and to whom men have committed much, of him they will ask the more.

Luke 12:48

40 The father shall be divided against the son, and the son against the father; the mother against the daughter, and the daughter against the mother; the mother in law against her daughter in law, and the daughter in law against her mother in law.

Luke 12:53. Jesus warns of the dissension to come as a result of his ministry.

41 Friend, go up higher.

Luke 14:10. Jesus suggests how the humble may be rewarded.

42 Go out quickly into the streets and lanes of the

city, and bring in hither the poor, and the maimed, and the halt, and the blind.

Luke 14:21. The master instructs his servant in the parable of the great supper.

43 For which of you, intending to build a tower, sitteth not down first, and counteth the cost, whether he have sufficient to finish it?

Luke 14:28. Jesus warns his disciples to weigh the costs of following him.

44 Rejoice with me; for I have found my sheep which was lost.

Luke 15:6. The parable of the lost sheep.

45 A certain man had two sons:

And the younger of them said to his father, Father, give me the portion of goods that falleth to me. And he divided unto them his living.

And not many days after the younger son gathered all together, and took his journey into a far country, and there wasted his substance with riotous living.

Luke 15:11–13. The parable of the prodigal son.

46 Bring hither the fatted calf, and kill it; and let us eat, and be merry.

Luke 15:23

47 For this my son was dead, and is alive again; he was lost, and is found.

Luke 15:24. The words are echoed in verse 32.

48 Son, thou art ever with me, and all that I have is thine.

Luke 15:31. The father of the prodigal son reassures his loyal elder son.

49 I cannot dig; to beg I am ashamed.

Luke 16:3. The parable of the unjust steward.

50 The children of this world are in their generation wiser than the children of light.

Luke 16:8

51 He that is faithful in that which is least is faithful also in much: and he that is unjust in the least is unjust also in much.

Luke 16:10

52 There was a certain rich man, which was clothed in purple and fine linen, and fared sumptuously every day:

And there was a certain beggar named Lazarus, which was laid at his gate, full of sores,

And desiring to be fed with the crumbs which fell from the rich man's table: moreover the dogs came and licked his sores.

Luke 16:19–21. The parable of the rich glutton and Lazarus the beggar.

53 And it came to pass, that the beggar died, and was carried by the angels into Abraham's bosom.

Luke 16:22

54 Between us and you there is a great gulf fixed: so that they which would pass from hence to you cannot; neither can they pass to us, that would come from thence.

Luke 16:26. The words of Abraham in heaven to the rich man in hell.

55 Arise, go thy way: thy faith hath made thee whole.

Luke 17:19. Jesus addresses a healed leper. 'Thy faith hath made thee whole' also appears in *Mark* 5:34 and *Luke* 8:48.

56 The kingdom of God cometh not with observation:

Neither shall they say, Lo here! or, lo there! for, behold, the kingdom of God is within you.

Luke 17:20–1. Jesus answers the Pharisees.

57 Remember Lot's wife.

Luke 17:32

58 God, I thank thee, that I am not as other men are, extortioners, unjust, adulterers, or even as this publican.

Luke 18:11. The prayer of the Pharisee, in the parable of the Pharisee and the publican.

59 God be merciful to me a sinner.

Luke 18:13. The prayer of the publican, in the parable of the Pharisee and the publican.

60 Out of thine own mouth will I judge thee, thou wicked servant.

Luke 19:22. The parable of the ten pieces of money.

61 If these should hold their peace, the stones would immediately cry out.

Luke 19:40. Jesus answers the Pharisees who have asked him to restrain his disciples.

62 If thou hadst known, even thou, at least in this thy day, the things which belong unto thy peace! but now they are hid from thine eyes.

Luke 19:42. The words of Jesus on seeing Jerusalem.

63 For he is not a God of the dead, but of the living: for all live unto him.

Luke 20:38

64 In your patience possess ye your souls.

Luke 21:19. Jesus warns his disciples of the hardships they face.

65 And he shall shew you a large upper room furnished: there make ready.

Luke 22:12. Jesus instructs Peter and John to prepare for the Passover.

66 For whether is greater, he that sitteth at meat, or he that serveth? is not he that sitteth at meat? but I am among you as he that serveth.

Luke 22:27

67 Nevertheless, not my will, but thine, be done.

Luke 22:42

68 Daughters of Jerusalem, weep not for me, but weep for yourselves, and for your children.

Luke 22:38. Jesus addresses a lamenting crowd.

69 For if they do these things in a green tree, what shall be done in the dry?

Luke 23:31

70 And when they were come to the place, which is called Calvary, there they crucified him, and the malefactors, one on the right hand, and the other on the left.

Luke 23:33

71 Father, forgive them; for they know not what they do.

Luke 23:34. The words of Jesus at his crucifixion.

72 If thou be Christ, save thyself and us.

Luke 23:39. The words of one of the 'malefactors' crucified alongside Jesus.

73 Lord, remember me when thou comest into thy kingdom.

Luke 23:42. The words of one of the 'malefactors' to Jesus on the cross.

74 To day shalt thou be with me in paradise.

Luke 23:43. Jesus responds to the 'malefactor' who has asked to be remembered in heaven.

75 And it was about the sixth hour, and there was a darkness over all the earth until the ninth hour.

And the sun was darkened, and the veil of the temple was rent in the midst.

Luke 23:44–5

76 Father, into thy hands I commend my spirit.

Luke 23:46. The words of Jesus also appear in the Book of Common Prayer, *Psalms* 31:6.

77 He gave up the ghost.

Luke 23:46. Of Jesus. See JOHN 69.

78 He was a good man, and a just.

Luke 23:50. Referring to Joseph of Arimathaea.

79 Why seek ye the living among the dead?

Luke 24:5. The words of two angels ('men . . . in shining garments') at the empty sepulchre.

80 And their words seemed to them as idle tales, and they believed them not.

Luke 24:11. The reaction to news of the empty tomb, brought by Mary Magdalene, Joanna and Mary, mother of James.

81 Did not our heart burn within us, while he talked with us by the way, and while he opened to us the scriptures?

Luke 24:32. The disciples recognize the resurrected Jesus.

82 The Lord is risen indeed.

Luke 24:34. The report of the two disciples.

The Gospel According to St John

1 In the beginning was the Word, and the Word was with God, and the Word was God.

John 1:1

2 All things were made by him; and without him was not any thing made that was made.

John 1:3

3 And the light shineth in darkness; and the darkness comprehended it not.

John 1:5

4 There was a man sent from God, whose name was John.

John 1:6

5 He was not that Light, but was sent to bear witness of that Light.

That was the true Light, which lighteth every man that cometh into the world.

John 1:8–9

6 He was in the world, and the world was made by him, and the world knew him not.

John 1:10

7 And the Word was made flesh, and dwelt among us, (and we beheld his glory, the glory as of the only begotten of the Father,) full of grace and truth.

John 1:14

8 No man hath seen God at any time.

John 1:18

9 I baptize with water: but there standeth one among you, whom ye know not;

He it is, who coming after me is preferred before me, whose shoe's latchet I am not worthy to unloose.

John 1:26–7. The words of John the Baptist.

10 Behold the Lamb of God, which taketh away the sin of the world.

John 1:29. John the Baptist hails Jesus with words also used in 1:36.

11 Can there any good thing come out of Nazareth?

John 1:46. Nathanael questions the authenticity of Jesus.

12 Woman, what have I to do with thee? mine hour is not yet come.

John 2:4. Jesus addresses his mother, Mary, who has told him there is no wine at the wedding feast.

13 When the ruler of the feast had tasted the water that was made wine, and knew not whence it was: (but the servants which drew the water knew;) the governor of the feast called the bridegroom,

And saith unto him, Every man at the beginning doth set forth good wine; and when men have well drunk, then that which is worse: but thou hast kept the good wine until now.

John 2:9–10

14 And when he had made a scourge of small cords, he drove them all out of the temple, and the sheep, and the oxen; and poured out the changers' money, and overthrew the tables.

John 2:15. See also MATTHEW 127.

15 Except a man be born again, he cannot see the kingdom of God.

John 3:3. Jesus addresses the Pharisee Nicodemus, reiterating in 3:7: 'Marvel not that I said unto thee, Ye must be born again.'

16 Except a man be not born of water and of the Spirit, he cannot enter into the kingdom of God.

That which is born of the flesh is flesh; and that which is born of the Spirit is spirit.

John 3:5–6

17 The wind bloweth where it listeth, and thou hearest the sound thereof, but canst not tell whence it cometh, and whither it goeth: so is every one that is born of the Spirit.

John 3:8

18 For God so loved the world, that he gave his only begotten Son, that whosoever believeth in him should not perish, but have everlasting life.

John 3:16

19 And this is the condemnation, that light is come into the world, and men loved darkness rather than light, because their deeds were evil.

John 3:19

20 Whosoever drinketh of this water shall thirst again:

But whosoever drinketh of the water that I shall give him shall never thirst; but the water that I shall give him shall be in him a well of water springing up into everlasting life.

John 4:13–14. Jesus addresses the woman of Samaria.

21 But the hour cometh, and now is, when the true worshippers shall worship the Father in spirit and in truth: for the Father seeketh such to worship him.

God is a Spirit: and they that worship him must worship him in spirit and in truth.

John 4:23–4

22 Except ye see signs and wonders, ye will not believe.

John 4:48. The words of Jesus to the nobleman who asks that his son be healed.

23 He was a burning and a shining light: and ye were willing for a season to rejoice in his light.

John 5:35. Referring to John the Baptist.

24 Search the scriptures; for in them ye think ye have eternal life: and they are they which testify of me.

John 5:39

25 Gather up the fragments that remain, that nothing be lost.

John 6:12. Jesus instructs his disciples at the feeding of the five thousand. See also MATTHEW 103.

26 I am the bread of life: he that cometh to me shall never hunger; and he that believeth on me shall never thirst.

John 6:35

27 It is the spirit that quickeneth; the flesh profiteth nothing: the words that I speak unto you, they are spirit, and they are life.

John 6:63

28 Judge not according to the appearance, but judge righteous judgment.

John 7:24

29 Never man spake like this man.

John 7:46. The officers explain to the chief priests and Pharisees why they have not arrested Jesus.

30 Master, this woman was taken in adultery, in the very act.

John 8:4. The scribes and Pharisees question Jesus on the law commanding an adulteress to be stoned.

31 He that is without sin among you, let him first cast a stone at her.

John 8:7

32 When Jesus had lifted up himself, and saw none but the woman, he said unto her, Woman, where are those thine accusers? hath no man condemned thee?

She said, No man, Lord. And Jesus said unto her, Neither do I condemn thee: go, and sin no more.

John 8:10–11

33 I am the light of the world: he that followeth me shall not walk in darkness, but shall have the light of life.

John 8:12

34 And ye shall know the truth, and the truth shall make you free.

John 8:32. These words of Jesus are inscribed on the wall of the main lobby at the CIA headquarters, Langley, Virginia.

35 Ye are of your father the devil, and the lusts of your father ye will do. He was a murderer from the beginning, and abode not in the truth, because there is no truth in him. When he speaketh a lie, he speaketh of his own: for he is a liar, and the father of it.

John 8:44. Jesus addresses sceptical Jews, in a passage from which derives the term 'father of lies' for the devil.

36 Verily, verily, I say unto you, If a man keep my saying, he shall never see death.

John 8:51

37 I must work the works of him that sent me, while it is day: the night cometh, when no man can work.

John 9:4

38 Whether he be a sinner or no, I know not: one thing I know, that, whereas I was blind, now I see.

John 9:25. A blind man healed by Jesus answers the Pharisees.

39 Verily, verily, I say unto you, I am the door of the sheep.

All that ever came before me are thieves and robbers: but the sheep did not hear them.

I am the door: by me if any man enter in, he shall be saved, and shall go in and out, and find pasture.

John 10:7–9. The parable of the good shepherd.

40 I am the good shepherd: the good shepherd giveth his life for the sheep.

John 10:11

41 The hireling fleeth, because he is an hireling, and careth not for the sheep.

John 10:13

42 And other sheep I have, which are not of this fold: them also I must bring, and they shall hear my voice; and there shall be one fold, and one shepherd.

John 10:16

43 I am the resurrection, and the life: he that believeth in me, though he were dead, yet shall he live.

John 11:25. Jesus speaks to Martha at Bethany.

44 Jesus wept.

John 11:35. The shortest verse in the Bible describes Jesus' response to the death of Lazarus, whom he subsequently raised from the dead.

45 Yet a little while is the light with you. Walk while ye have the light, lest darkness come upon you: for he that walketh in darkness knoweth not whither he goeth.

John 12:35

46 That thou doest, do quickly.

John 13:27. Jesus speaks to Judas Iscariot.

47 A new commandment I give unto you, That ye love one another; as I have loved you, that ye also love one another.

John 13:34. Jesus repeats in *John* 15:12, 'This is my commandment, That ye love one another, as I have loved you.'

48 Lord, whither goest thou?

John 13:36. The words, spoken here by Peter and repeated in *John* 16:5, are best known in the Latin form: see BIBLE, VULGATE 11. Jesus replies, 'Whither I go, thou canst not follow me now; but thou shalt follow me afterwards.'

49 In my Father's house are many mansions: if it were not so, I would have told you. I go to prepare a place for you.

John 14:2. Jesus comforts his disciples.

50 I am the way, the truth, and the life: no man cometh unto the Father, but by me.

John 14:6

51 Have I been so long time with you, and yet hast thou not known me, Philip?

John 14:9

52 Peace I leave with you, my peace I give unto you: not as the world giveth, give I unto you. Let not your heart be troubled, neither let it be afraid.
John 14:27

53 I am the true vine, and my Father is the husbandman.
John 15:1

54 Greater love hath no man than this, that a man lay down his life for his friends.
John 15:13. Jesus addresses the disciples in the 'farewell discourse'. See also JAMES JOYCE 29 and JEREMY THORPE 1.

55 Ye have not chosen me, but I have chosen you.
John 15:16

56 A little while, and ye shall not see me: and again, a little while, and ye shall see me, because I go to the Father.
John 16:16

57 A woman when she is in travail hath sorrow, because her hour is come: but as soon as she is delivered of the child, she remembereth no more the anguish, for joy that a man is born into the world.
John 16:21

58 Ask, and ye shall receive, that your joy may be full.
John 16:24

59 These things I have spoken unto you, that in me ye might have peace. In the world ye shall have tribulation: but be of good cheer; I have overcome the world.
John 16:33. Jesus addresses the disciples in the 'farewell discourse'.

60 Put up thy sword into the sheath: the cup which my father hath given me, shall I not drink it?
John 18:11. Jesus restrains Peter.

61 Pilate saith unto him, What is truth?
John 18:38. In the Apocryphal Gospel of Nicodemus 3:10–14, the conversation is continued: 'Jesus said, Truth is from heaven. Pilate said, Therefore truth is not on earth. Jesus saith to Pilate, Believe that truth is on earth among those who, when they have the power of judgment, are governed by truth and form right judgment.' See FRANCIS BACON 3.

62 Now Barabbas was a robber.
John 18:40. The mob had asked that Barabbas be released instead of Jesus.

63 Behold the man!
John 19:5. Pontius Pilate presents Jesus, wearing a crown of thorns and purple robe, to the chief priests. The words are best known in the Latin form: see VULGATE 12.

64 Crucify him, crucify him.
John 19:6. The cry of the chief priests and officers.

65 JESUS OF NAZARETH THE KING OF THE JEWS.
John 19:19. The sign hung on the cross by Pontius Pilate.

66 What I have written I have written.
John 19:22. Disregarding the objections of the chief priests, Pontius Pilate confirms the sign he has hung on the cross.

67 He saith unto his mother, Woman, behold thy son!
  Then saith he to the disciple, Behold thy mother!
John 19:26–7. Jesus speaks to his mother and 'the disciple . . . whom he loved' (John).

68 I thirst.
John 19:28

69 When Jesus therefore had received the vinegar, he said, It is finished: and he bowed his head, and gave up the ghost.
John 19:30. See LUKE 77, VULGATE 13.

70 The first day of the week cometh Mary Magdalene early, when it was yet dark, unto the sepulchre, and seeth the stone taken away from the sepulchre.
John 20:1

71 Woman, why weepest thou? whom seekest thou?
John 20:15. Jesus appears to Mary Magdalene.

72 Touch me not.
John 20:17. Jesus' words to Mary Magdalene are best known in their Latin form: see BIBLE, VULGATE 14.

73 Except I shall see in his hands the print of the nails, and put my finger into the print of the nails, and thrust my hand into his side, I will not believe.
John 20:25. Thomas doubts the resurrection.

74 Be not faithless, but believing.
John 20:27. Jesus addresses Thomas.

75 Thomas answered and said unto him, My Lord and my God.
John 20:28

76 Thomas, because thou hast seen me, thou hast believed: blessed are they that have not seen, and yet have believed.
John 20:29

77 Feed my sheep.
John 21:16. The words of Jesus to Peter are repeated in verse 17 (in verse 15 the words are 'Feed my lambs').

78 Lord, thou knowest all things; thou knowest I love thee.

John 21:17. Spoken by Peter.

The Acts of the Apostles

1 It is not for you to know the times or the seasons which the Father hath put in his own power.

Acts 1:7. Said by Jesus before his ascension.

2 Ye men of Galilee, why stand ye gazing up into heaven?

Acts 1:11. Two angels address the apostles after Christ's ascension.

3 And when the day of Pentecost was fully come, they [the apostles] were all with one accord in one place.

And suddenly there came a sound from heaven as of a rushing mighty wind, and it filled all the house where they were sitting.

Acts 2:1–2

4 And there appeared unto them cloven tongues like as of fire, and it sat upon each of them.

And they were all filled with the Holy Ghost, and began to speak with other tongues, as the Spirit gave them utterance.

Acts 2:3–4

5 And all that believed were together, and had all things common;

And sold their possessions and goods, and parted them to all men, as every man had need.

Acts 2:44–5

6 Silver and gold have I none; but such as I have give I thee.

Acts 3:6. Peter heals a lame beggar.

7 And he leaping up stood, and walked, and entered with them into the temple, walking, and leaping, and praising God.

Acts 3:8

8 Neither was there any among them that lacked: for as many as were possessors of lands or houses sold them, and brought the prices of the things that were sold,

And laid them down at the apostles' feet: and distribution was made unto every man according as he had need.

Acts 4:34–5. Referring to the early Christian community.

9 It is not reason that we should leave the word of God, and serve tables.

Acts 6:2. The apostles delegate to 'seven men of honest report' the task of providing for their material needs.

10 Then they cried out with a loud voice, and stopped their ears, and ran upon him with one accord,

And cast him out of the city, and stoned him: and the witnesses laid down their clothes at a young man's feet, whose name was Saul.

Acts 7:57–8. The stoning of Stephen.

11 Thy money perish with thee, because thou hast thought that the gift of God may be purchased with money.

Acts 8:20. Peter rejects the offer of money by Simon Magus in return for the power of the Holy Ghost. The term 'simony' for the buying or selling of ecclesiastical privileges derives from this episode.

12 And Saul, yet breathing out threatenings and slaughter against the disciples of the Lord, went unto the high priest.

Acts 9:1

13 Saul, Saul, why persecutest thou me?

Acts 9:4. A voice from heaven calls to Saul (St Paul) on his way to Damascus. The words are repeated in 26:14.

14 It is hard for thee to kick against the pricks.

Acts 9:5. The words of Jesus to Saul. See also AESCHYLUS 3.

15 Arise, and go into the street which is called Straight.

Acts 9:11. God instructs Ananias to find Saul.

16 And immediately there fell from his eyes as it had been scales.

Acts 9:18. Saul is cured of his blindness.

17 What God hath cleansed, that call not thou common.

Acts 10:15. A voice from heaven reassures Peter that he can eat what God has provided.

18 Of a truth I perceive that God is no respecter of persons.

Acts 10:34. Said by Peter of the centurion Cornelius, a convert. Similar wording is found in *Romans* 2:11: 'There is no respect of persons with God.'

19 The gods are come down to us in the likeness of men.

Acts 14:11. The people of Lystra acclaim the miraculous healing of a cripple by Paul.

20 Sirs, why do ye these things? We also are men of like passions with you.

Acts 14:15. Paul and Barnabas upbraid the people of Lystra for their 'vanities'.

21 Wherefore my sentence is, that we trouble not them, which from among the Gentiles are turned to God:

But that we write unto them, that they abstain from pollutions of idols, and from fornication, and from things strangled, and from blood.

Acts 15:19–20. The ruling of James on whether believers should be circumcised.

22 Sirs, what must I do to be saved?

Acts 16:30. Paul and Silas are questioned by their jailer.

23 Certain lewd fellows of the baser sort.

Acts 17:5. Referring to a mob raised by the Jews at Thessalonica, where Paul is preaching in the synagogue.

24 These that have turned the world upside down are come hither also.

Acts 17:6. Referring to Paul and Silas.

25 For all the Athenians and strangers which were there spent their time in nothing else, but either to tell, or to hear some new thing.

Acts 17:21

26 Ye men of Athens, I perceive that in all things ye are too superstitious.

Acts 17:22. Paul addresses the Athenians.

27 For as I passed by, and beheld your devotions, I found an altar with this inscription, TO THE UNKNOWN GOD. Whom therefore ye ignorantly worship, him declare I unto you.

Acts 17:23

28 God that made the world and all things therein, seeing that he is Lord of heaven and earth, dwelleth not in temples made with hands.

Acts 17:24. See also 2 CORINTHIANS 6.

29 For in him we live, and move, and have our being; as certain also of your own poets have said, For we are also his offspring.

Acts 17:28. Paul's allusion is probably to the poet Aratus (fl. c. 315–c. 245 BC) of Soli in Cilicia, whose line 'For we are also his offspring' appears in the opening invocation to Zeus in *Phaenomena*, the poem on astronomy for which he is best remembered. The words also appear in *Hymn to Zeus* by the Stoic philosopher Cleanthes (c. 330–c. 232 BC).

30 He said unto them, Have ye received the Holy Ghost since ye believed? And they said unto him, We have not so much as heard whether there be any Holy Ghost.

Acts 19:2. Paul communes with disciples in Ephesus.

31 Great is Diana of the Ephesians.

Acts 19:28 and 34. The cry of the people of Ephesus against Paul and his Christian followers.

32 Behold, I go bound in the spirit unto Jerusalem, not knowing the things that shall befall me there:

Save that the Holy Ghost witnesseth in every city, saying that bonds and afflictions abide me.

Acts 20:22–3. Paul was later arrested in Jerusalem.

33 I have shewed you all things, how that so labouring ye ought to support the weak, and to remember the words of the Lord Jesus, how he said, It is more blessed to give than to receive.

Acts 20:35. Paul addresses the Elders of Ephesus before his departure.

34 I am a man which am a Jew of Tarsus, a city in Cilicia, a citizen of no mean city.

Acts 21:39. Paul identifies himself to the chief captain after his arrest.

35 And the chief captain answered, With a great sum obtained I this freedom. And Paul said, But I was free born.

Acts 22:28

36 God shall smite thee, thou whited wall: for sittest thou to judge me after the law, and commandest me to be smitten contrary to the law?

Acts 23:3. Paul addresses the high priest Ananias, who has ordered him to be struck.

37 Revilest thou God's high priest?

Acts 23:4. The Jews respond to Paul's effrontery towards Ananias.

38 And herein do I exercise myself, to have always a conscience void of offence toward God, and toward men.

Acts 24:16. Paul defends himself against his accusers.

39 Go thy way for this time; when I have a convenient season, I will call for thee.

Acts 24:25. The governor Felix dismisses Paul.

40 I appeal unto Caesar.

Acts 25:11. Paul addresses the Roman Procurator Festus.

41 Hast thou appealed unto Caesar? unto Caesar shalt thou go.

Acts 25:12

42 Paul, thou art beside thyself; much learning doth make thee mad.
Acts 26:24. Said by Festus.

43 None of these things are hidden from him; for this thing was not done in a corner.
Acts 26:26. Paul declares that his case is already known to King Agrippa.

44 Almost thou persuadest me to be a Christian.
Acts 26:28. Agrippa speaks to Paul.

45 For the heart of this people is waxed gross, and their ears are dull of hearing, and their eyes have they closed; lest they should see with their eyes, and hear with their ears, and understand with their heart, and should be converted.
Acts 28:27. Referring to the Jews in Rome who reject Paul's preaching, quoting *Isaiah* 6:10. See also *Matthew* 13:15, *Mark* 4:12 and *John* 12:40.

The Epistle of Paul the Apostle to the Romans

1 For God is my witness, whom I serve with my spirit in the gospel of his Son, that without ceasing I make mention of you always in my prayers.
Romans 1:9

2 I am debtor both to the Greeks, and to the Barbarians; both to the wise, and to the unwise.
Romans 1:14

3 Professing themselves to be wise, they became fools.
Romans 1:22. Referring to the Gentiles.

4 Who changed the truth of God into a lie, and worshipped and served the creature more than the Creator, who is blessed for ever. Amen.
Romans 1:25

5 For this cause God gave them up unto vile affections: for even their women did change the natural use into that which is against nature:
   And likewise also the men, leaving the natural use of the woman, burned in their lust one toward another; men with men working that which is unseemly, and receiving in themselves that recompence of their error which was meet.
Romans 1:26–7

6 Therefore thou art inexcusable, O man, whosoever thou art that judgest: for wherein thou judgest another, thou condemnest thyself; for thou that judgest doest the same things.
Romans 2:1

7 To them who by patient continuance in well doing seek for glory and honour and immortality, eternal life.
Romans 2:7

8 For when the Gentiles, which have not the law, do by nature the things contained in the law, these, having not the law, are a law unto themselves.
Romans 2:14

9 Yea, let God be true, but every man a liar.
Romans 3:4

10 For all have sinned, and come short of the glory of God.
Romans 3:23

11 Because the law worketh wrath: for where no law is, there is no transgression.
Romans 4:15. The doctrine of justification by faith; see also JAMES 8.

12 Who against hope believed in hope, that he might become the father of many nations, according to that which was spoken, So shall thy seed be.
Romans 4:18. Referring to Abraham. 'So shall thy seed be' appears in *Genesis* 15:5.

13 But where sin abounded, grace did much more abound.
Romans 5:20. 'Grace Abounding' was the title of JOHN BUNYAN's spiritual autobiography (1666).

14 Like as Christ was raised up from the dead by the glory of the Father, even so we also should walk in newness of life.
Romans 6:4

15 For he that is dead is freed from sin.
   Now if we be dead with Christ, we believe that we shall also live with him:
   Knowing that Christ being raised from the dead dieth no more; death hath no more dominion over him.
Romans 6:7–9

16 For the wages of sin is death; but the gift of God is eternal life through Jesus Christ our Lord.
Romans 6:23

17 For I know that in me (that is, in my flesh,) dwelleth no good thing: for to will is present with me; but how to perform that which is good I find not.
   For the good that I would I do not: but the evil which I would not, that I do.
Romans 7:18–19. See also OVID 12.

18 O wretched man that I am! who shall deliver me from the body of this death?
Romans 7:24

19 For they that are after the flesh do mind the things of the flesh; but they that are after the Spirit the things of the Spirit.

For to be carnally minded is death; but to be spiritually minded is life and peace.
Romans 8:5–6

20 The Spirit itself beareth witness with our spirit, that we are the children of God:

And if children, then heirs; heirs of God, and joint-heirs with Christ.
Romans 8:16–17

21 For we know that the whole creation groaneth and travaileth in pain together until now.
Romans 8:22

22 And we know that all things work together for good to them that love God.
Romans 8:28

23 If God be for us, who can be against us?
Romans 8:31

24 Who shall lay any thing to the charge of God's elect? It is God that justifieth.
Romans 8:33

25 For I am persuaded, that neither death, nor life, nor angels, nor principalities, nor powers, nor things present, nor things to come,

Nor height, nor depth, nor any other creature, shall be able to separate us from the love of God, which is in Christ Jesus our Lord.
Romans 8:38–9

26 Nay but, O man, who art thou that repliest against God? Shall the thing formed say to him that formed it, Why hast thou made me thus?

Hath not the potter power over the clay, of the same lump to make one vessel unto honour, and another unto dishonour?
Romans 9:20–1. See also ISAIAH 62, also *Isaiah* 29:16.

27 For who hath known the mind of the Lord?
Romans 11:34

28 I beseech you therefore, brethren, by the mercies of God, that ye present your bodies a living sacrifice, holy, acceptable unto God, which is your reasonable service.
Romans 12:1

29 Let love be without dissimulation. Abhor that which is evil; cleave to that which is good.
Romans 12:9

30 Be kindly affectioned one to another with brotherly love; in honour preferring one another.
Romans 12:10

31 Rejoice with them that do rejoice, and weep with them that weep.
Romans 12:15

32 Be of the same mind one toward another. Mind not high things, but condescend to men of low estate. Be not wise in your own conceits.
Romans 12:16

33 Dearly beloved, avenge not yourselves, but rather give place unto wrath: for it is written, Vengeance is mine; I will repay, saith the Lord.
Romans 12:19. St Paul refers to *Deuteronomy* 32:35: 'To me belongeth vengeance, and recompence.' See also *Hebrews* 10:30.

34 Be not overcome of evil, but overcome evil with good.
Romans 12:21

35 Let every soul be subject unto the higher powers. For there is no power but of God: the powers that be are ordained of God.
Romans 13:1

36 For rulers are not a terror to good works, but to the evil. Wilt thou then not be afraid of the power? do that which is good, and thou shalt have praise of the same.
Romans 13:3

37 Render therefore to all their dues: tribute to whom tribute is due; custom to whom custom; fear to whom fear; honour to whom honour.

Owe no man any thing, but to love one another: for he that loveth another hath fulfilled the law.
Romans 13:7–8

38 Love worketh no ill to his neighbour: therefore love is the fulfilling of the law.
Romans 13:10

39 Now it is high time to awake out of sleep: for now is our salvation nearer than when we believed.

The night is far spent, the day is at hand: let us therefore cast off the works of darkness, and let us put on the armour of light.
Romans 13:11–12

40 Let us walk honestly, as in the day; not in rioting

and drunkenness, not in chambering and wantonness, not in strife and envying.

But put ye on the Lord Jesus Christ, and make not provision for the flesh, to fulfil the lusts thereof.

Romans 13:13–14. This was a passage on which St Augustine alighted, a key factor in his conversion from a life of dissipation: see also ST AUGUSTINE 3.

41 Him that is weak in the faith receive ye, but not to doubtful disputations.

For one believeth that he may eat all things: another, who is weak, eateth herbs.

Romans 14:1–2

42 One man esteemeth one day above another: another esteemeth every day alike. Let every man be fully persuaded in his own mind.

Romans 14:5

43 For none of us liveth to himself, and no man dieth to himself.

Romans 14:7

44 Salute one another with an holy kiss. The churches of Christ salute you.

Romans 16:16

The First Epistle of Paul the Apostle to the Corinthians

1 For the preaching of the cross is to them that perish foolishness; but unto us which are saved it is the power of God.

1 Corinthians 1:18

2 For after that in the wisdom of God the world by wisdom knew not God, it pleased God by the foolishness of preaching to save them that believe.

For the Jews require a sign, and the Greeks seek after wisdom:

But we preach Christ crucified, unto the Jews a stumblingblock, and unto the Greeks foolishness.

1 Corinthians 1:21–3

3 But God hath chosen the foolish things of the world to confound the wise; and God hath chosen the weak things of the world to confound the things which are mighty.

1 Corinthians 1:27

4 But as it is written, Eye hath not seen, nor ear heard, neither have entered into the heart of man, the things which God hath prepared for them that love him.

1 Corinthians 2:9. Paul probably alludes to *Isaiah* 64:4: 'For since the beginning of the world men have not heard, nor perceived by the ear, neither hath the eye seen, O God, beside thee, what he hath prepared for him that waiteth for him.'

5 I have planted, Apollos watered; but God gave the increase.

1 Corinthians 3:6. Apollos was an Alexandrian Jew active as a Christian evangelist in Ephesus and Achaia.

6 Every man's work shall be made manifest: for the day shall declare it, because it shall be revealed by fire; and the fire shall try every man's work of what sort it is.

1 Corinthians 3:13

7 Let no man deceive himself. If any man among you seemeth to be wise in this world, let him become a fool, that he may be wise.

For the wisdom of this world is foolishness with God.

1 Corinthians 3:18–19

8 Let a man so account of us, as of the ministers of Christ, and stewards of the mysteries of God.

1 Corinthians 4:1

9 For we are made a spectacle unto the world, and to angels, and to men.

1 Corinthians 4:9

10 We are made as the filth of the world, and are the offscouring of all things unto this day.

1 Corinthians 4:13

11 Absent in body, but present in spirit.

1 Corinthians 5:3

12 Know ye not that a little leaven leaveneth the whole lump?

Purge out therefore the old leaven, that ye may be a new lump, as ye are unleavened. For even Christ our passover is sacrificed for us:

Therefore let us keep the feast, not with old leaven, neither with the leaven of malice and wickedness; but with the unleavened bread of sincerity and truth.

1 Corinthians 5:6–8

13 What? know ye not that your body is the temple of the Holy Ghost which is in you, which ye have of God, and ye are not your own?

1 Corinthians 6:19

14 Let the husband render unto the wife due benevolence: and likewise also the wife unto the husband.

The wife hath not power of her own body, but the

husband: and likewise also the husband hath not power of his own body, but the wife.

1 Corinthians 7:3–4

15 I say therefore to the unmarried and widows, It is good for them if they abide even as I.

But if they cannot contain, let them marry: for it is better to marry than to burn.

1 Corinthians 7:8–9

16 For the fashion of this world passeth away.

1 Corinthians 7:31

17 But he that is married careth for the things that are of the world, how he may please his wife.

1 Corinthians 7:33

18 Knowledge puffeth up, but charity edifieth.

1 Corinthians 8:1

19 But meat commendeth us not to God: for neither, if we eat, are we the better; neither, if we eat not, are we the worse.

1 Corinthians 8:8

20 Wherefore, if meat make my brother to offend, I will eat no flesh while the world standeth, lest I make my brother to offend.

1 Corinthians 8:13

21 For though I be free from all men, yet have I made myself servant unto all, that I might gain the more.

1 Corinthians 9:19

22 I am made all things to all men, that I might by all means save some.

1 Corinthians 9:22

23 Know ye not that they which run in a race run all, but one receiveth the prize? So run, that ye may obtain.

1 Corinthians 9:24

24 Wherefore let him that thinketh he standeth take heed lest he fall.

1 Corinthians 10:12

25 All things are lawful for me, but all things are not expedient: all things are lawful for me, but all things edify not.

1 Corinthians 10:23

26 For the earth is the Lord's, and the fulness thereof.

1 Corinthians 10:26. See also PSALMS 28, also *Psalms* 50:12 and 89:11.

27 Doth not even nature itself teach you, that, if a man have long hair, it is a shame unto him?

But if a woman have long hair, it is a glory to her: for her hair is given her for a covering.

1 Corinthians 11:14–15

28 Now there are diversities of gifts, but the same Spirit.

And there are differences of administrations, but the same Lord.

And there are diversities of operations, but it is the same God which worketh all in all.

But the manifestation of the Spirit is given to every man to profit withal.

1 Corinthians 12:4–7

29 Though I speak with the tongues of men and of angels, and have not charity, I am become as sounding brass, or a tinkling cymbal.

And though I have the gift of prophecy, and understand all mysteries, and all knowledge; and though I have all faith, so that I could remove mountains, and have not charity, I am nothing.

And though I bestow all my goods to feed the poor, and though I give my body to be burned, and have not charity, it profiteth me nothing.

1 Corinthians 13:1–3

30 Charity suffereth long, and is kind; charity envieth not; charity vaunteth not itself, is not puffed up.

Doth not behave itself unseemly, seeketh not her own, is not easily provoked, thinketh no evil;

Rejoiceth not in iniquity, but rejoiceth in the truth;

Beareth all things, believeth all things, hopeth all things, endureth all things.

Charity never faileth.

1 Corinthians 13:4–8

31 When I was a child, I spake as a child, I understood as a child, I thought as a child: but when I became a man, I put away childish things.

1 Corinthians 13:11

32 For now we see through a glass, darkly; but then face to face: now I know in part; but then shall I know even as also I am known.

1 Corinthians 13:12

33 And now abideth faith, hope, charity, these three; but the greatest of these is charity.

1 Corinthians 13:13

34 For if the trumpet give an uncertain sound, who shall prepare himself to the battle?
1 Corinthians 14:8

35 Let all things be done decently and in order.
1 Corinthians 14:40

36 And last of all he was seen of me also, as of one born out of due time.

For I am the least of the apostles, that am not meet to be called an apostle, because I persecuted the church of God.

But by the grace of God I am what I am.
1 Corinthians 15:8–10

37 If in this life only we have hope in Christ, we are of all men most miserable.

But now is Christ risen from the dead, and become the firstfruits of them that slept.

For since by man came death, by man came also the resurrection of the dead.

For as in Adam all die, even so in Christ shall all be made alive.
1 Corinthians 15:19–22

38 The last enemy that shall be destroyed is death.
1 Corinthians 15:26

39 If after the manner of men I have fought with beasts at Ephesus, what advantageth it me, if the dead rise not? let us eat and drink; for to morrow we die.
1 Corinthians 15:32. See also ISAIAH 31.

40 Be not deceived: evil communications corrupt good manners.
1 Corinthians 15:33

41 There is one glory of the sun, and another glory of the moon, and another glory of the stars: for one star differeth from another star in glory.
1 Corinthians 15:41

42 So also is the resurrection of the dead. It is sown in corruption; it is raised in incorruption.
1 Corinthians 15:42

43 There is a natural body, and there is a spiritual body.
1 Corinthians 15:44

44 The first man is of the earth, earthy: the second man is the Lord from heaven.

As is the earthy, such are they also that are earthy: and as is the heavenly, such are they also that are heavenly.
1 Corinthians 15:47–8

45 Behold, I shew you a mystery; We shall not all sleep, but we shall all be changed,

In a moment, in the twinkling of an eye, at the last trump: for the trumpet shall sound, and the dead shall be raised incorruptible, and we shall be changed.

For this corruptible must put on incorruption, and this mortal must put on immortality.
1 Corinthians 15:51–3

46 Death is swallowed up in victory.

O death, where is thy sting? O grave, where is thy victory?
1 Corinthians 15:54–5. See also ISAIAH 34 and ANONYMOUS 66.

47 Watch ye, stand fast in the faith, quit you like men, be strong.
1 Corinthians 16:13

48 If any man love not the Lord Jesus Christ, let him be Anathema Maranatha.
1 Corinthians 16:22. The Aramaic *maranatha*, probably a liturgical expression, has been translated 'Our Lord, come!'

The Second Epistle of Paul the Apostle to the Corinthians

1 Not that we are sufficient of ourselves to think any thing as of ourselves; but our sufficiency is of God;

Who also hath made us able ministers of the new testament; not of the letter, but of the spirit: for the letter killeth, but the spirit giveth life.
2 Corinthians 3:5–6

2 For if that which is done away was glorious, much more that which remaineth is glorious.

Seeing then that we have such hope, we use great plainness of speech.
2 Corinthians 3:11–12

3 But we have this treasure in earthen vessels, that the excellency of the power may be of God, and not of us.
2 Corinthians 4:7

4 We are troubled on every side, yet not distressed; we are perplexed, but not in despair.
2 Corinthians 4:8

5 For the things which are seen are temporal; but the things which are not seen are eternal.
2 Corinthians 4:18

6 For we know that if our earthly house of this

tabernacle were dissolved, we have a building of God, an house not made with hands, eternal in the heavens.

2 Corinthians 5:1. See also ACTS 28.

7 For we walk by faith, not by sight.

2 Corinthians 5:7

8 Now then we are ambassadors for Christ.

2 Corinthians 5:20

9 For he saith, I have heard thee in a time accepted, and in the day of salvation have I succoured thee: behold, now is the accepted time; behold, now is the day of salvation.

2 Corinthians 6:2

10 Giving no offence in any thing, that the ministry be not blamed:

But in all things approving ourselves as the ministers of God, in much patience, in afflictions, in necessities, in distresses,

In stripes, in imprisonments, in tumults, in labours, in watchings, in fastings;

By pureness, by knowledge, by longsuffering, by kindness, by the Holy Ghost, by love unfeigned,

By the word of truth, by the power of God, by the armour of righteousness on the right hand and on the left,

By honour and dishonour, by evil report and good report: as deceivers, and yet true;

As unknown, and yet well known; as dying, and, behold, we live; as chastened, and not killed;

As sorrowful, yet alway rejoicing; as poor, yet making many rich; as having nothing, and yet possessing all things.

2 Corinthians 6:3–10

11 Every man according as he purposeth in his heart, so let him give; not grudgingly, or of necessity: for God loveth a cheerful giver.

2 Corinthians 9:7

12 Though I be rude in speech, yet not in knowledge.

2 Corinthians 11:6

13 For ye suffer fools gladly, seeing ye yourselves are wise.

2 Corinthians 11:19

14 I speak as concerning reproach, as though we had been weak. Howbeit whereinsoever any is bold, (I speak foolishly,) I am bold also.

Are they Hebrews? so am I. Are they Israelites? so am I. Are they the seed of Abraham? so am I.

Are they ministers of Christ? (I speak as a fool) I am more; in labours more abundant, in stripes above measure, in prisons more frequent, in deaths oft.

Of the Jews five times received I forty stripes save one.

Thrice was I beaten with rods, once was I stoned, thrice I suffered shipwreck, a night and a day I have been in the deep;

In journeyings often, in perils of waters, in perils of robbers, in perils by mine own countrymen, in perils by the heathen, in perils in the city, in perils in the wilderness, in perils in the sea, in perils among false brethren;

In weariness and painfulness, in watchings often, in hunger and thirst, in fastings often, in cold and nakedness.

2 Corinthians 11:21–7

15 There was given to me a thorn in the flesh, the messenger of Satan to buffet me, lest I should be exalted above measure.

2 Corinthians 12:7. See also JUDGES 1.

16 My strength is made perfect in weakness.

2 Corinthians 12:9. God's words of comfort to Paul.

17 Therefore I take pleasure in infirmities, in reproaches, in necessities, in persecutions, in distresses for Christ's sake: for when I am weak, then am I strong.

2 Corinthians 12:10

18 In the mouth of two or three witnesses shall every word be established.

2 Corinthians 13:1

The Epistle of Paul the Apostle to the Galatians

1 And when James, Cephas, and John, who seemed to be pillars, perceived the grace that was given unto me, they gave to me and Barnabas the right hands of fellowship.

Galatians 2:9

2 There is neither Jew nor Greek, there is neither bond nor free, there is neither male nor female: for ye are all one in Christ Jesus.

Galatians 3:28

3 But now, after that ye have known God, or rather are known of God, how turn ye again to the weak and beggarly elements, whereunto ye desire again to be in bondage?

Galatians 4:9

4 Christ is become of no effect unto you, whosoever of you are justifed by the law; ye are fallen from grace.
Galatians 5:4

5 For, brethren, ye have been called unto liberty; only use not liberty for an occasion to the flesh, but by love serve one another.
Galatians 5:13

6 For the flesh lusteth against the Spirit, and the Spirit against the flesh: and these are contrary the one to the other: so that ye cannot do the things that ye would.
Galatians 5:17

7 But the fruit of the Spirit is love, joy, peace, long-suffering, gentleness, goodness, faith,
Meekness, temperance: against such there is no law.
Galatians 5:22–3

8 Bear ye one another's burdens, and so fulfil the law of Christ.
For if a man think himself to be something, when he is nothing, he deceiveth himself.
But let every man prove his own work, and then shall he have rejoicing in himself alone, and not in another.
For every man shall bear his own burden.
Galatians 6:2–5

9 Be not deceived; God is not mocked: for whatsoever a man soweth, that shall he also reap.
Galatians 6:7

10 And let us not be weary in well doing: for in due season we shall reap, if we faint not.
Galatians 6:9

11 Ye see how large a letter I have written unto you with mine own hand.
Galatians 6:11

The Epistle of Paul the Apostle to the Ephesians

1 Unto me, who am less than the least of all saints, is this grace given, that I should preach among the Gentiles the unsearchable riches of Christ.
Ephesians 3:8

2 For this cause I bow my knees unto the Father of our Lord Jesus Christ,
Of whom the whole family in heaven and earth is named,

That he would grant you, according to the riches of his glory, to be strengthened with might by his Spirit in the inner man.
Ephesians 3:14–16

3 That Christ may dwell in your hearts by faith; that ye, being rooted and grounded in love,
May be able to comprehend with all saints what is the breadth, and length, and depth, and height;
And to know the love of Christ, which passeth knowledge, that ye might be filled with all the fulness of God.
Ephesians 3:17–19

4 Now unto him that is able to do exceeding abundantly above all that we ask or think, according to the power that worketh in us,
Unto him be glory in the church by Christ Jesus throughout all ages, world without end. Amen.
Ephesians 3:20–1

5 I therefore, the prisoner of the Lord, beseech you that ye walk worthy of the vocation wherewith ye are called.
Ephesians 4:1

6 That we henceforth be no more children, tossed to and fro, and carried about with every wind of doctrine, by the sleight of men, and cunning craftiness, whereby they lie in wait to deceive.
Ephesians 4:14

7 Wherefore putting away lying, speak every man truth with his neighbour: for we are members one of another.
Ephesians 4:25

8 Be ye angry, and sin not: let not the sun go down upon your wrath.
Ephesians 4:26

9 Let no man deceive you with vain words: for because of these things cometh the wrath of God upon the children of disobedience.
Ephesians 5:6

10 And be not drunk with wine, wherein is excess; but be filled with the Spirit;
Speaking to yourselves in psalms and hymns and spiritual songs, singing and making melody in your heart to the Lord.
Ephesians 5:18–19

11 Wives, submit yourselves unto your own husbands, as unto the Lord.
For the husband is the head of the wife, even as

Christ is the head of the church: and he is the saviour of the body.

Therefore as the church is subject unto Christ, so let the wives be to their own husbands in every thing.

Ephesians 5:22–4

12 Husbands, love your wives, even as Christ also loved the church, and gave himself for it;

That he might sanctify and cleanse it with the washing of water by the word,

That he might present it to himself a glorious church, not having spot, or wrinkle, or any such thing; but that it should be holy and without blemish.

So ought men to love their wives as their own bodies. He that loveth his wife loveth himself.

Ephesians 5:25–8

13 Children, obey your parents in the Lord: for this is right.

Ephesians 6:1. See also COLOSSIANS 6.

14 And, ye fathers, provoke not your children to wrath.

Ephesians 6:4. The injunction is repeated in *Colossians* 3:21: 'Fathers, provoke not your children to anger, lest they be discouraged.'

15 Put on the whole armour of God, that ye may be able to stand against the wiles of the devil.

Ephesians 6:11. See also EPHESIANS 17.

16 For we wrestle not against flesh and blood, but against principalities, against powers, against the rulers of the darkness of this world, against spiritual wickedness in high places.

Ephesians 6:12. The words were adopted by WILLIAM BLAKE as an epigraph to *The Four Zoas* (c. 1800).

17 Wherefore take unto you the whole armour of God, that ye may be able to withstand in the evil day, and having done all, to stand.

Stand therefore, having your loins girt about with truth, and having on the breastplate of righteousness;

And your feet shod with the preparation of the gospel of peace;

Above all, taking the shield of faith, wherewith ye shall be able to quench all the fiery darts of the wicked.

And take the helmet of salvation, and the sword of the Spirit, which is the word of God.

Ephesians 6:13–17

The Epistle of Paul the Apostle to the Philippians

1 For to me to live is Christ, and to die is gain.

Philippians 1:21

2 For I am in a strait betwixt two, having a desire to depart, and to be with Christ; which is far better:

Nevertheless to abide in the flesh is more needful for you.

Philippians 1:23–4

3 Let this mind be in you, which was also in Christ Jesus:

Who, being in the form of God, thought it not robbery to be equal with God:

But made himself of no reputation, and took upon him the form of a servant and was made in the likeness of men:

And being found in fashion as a man, he humbled himself, and became obedient unto death, even the death of the cross.

Wherefore God also hath highly exalted him, and given him a name which is above every name:

That at the name of Jesus every knee should bow, of things in heaven, and things in earth, and things under the earth;

And that every tongue should confess that Jesus Christ is Lord, to the glory of God the Father.

Philippians 2:5–11. The interpretation of this early Christian hymn has been the subject of intense debate over its intended meaning.

4 Wherefore, my beloved, as ye have always obeyed, not as in my presence only, but now much more in my absence, work out your own salvation with fear and trembling.

Philippians 2:12

5 Though I might also have confidence in the flesh. If any other man thinketh that he hath whereof he might trust in the flesh, I more:

Circumcised the eighth day, of the stock of Israel, of the tribe of Benjamin, an Hebrew of the Hebrews; as touching the law, a Pharisee;

Concerning zeal, persecuting the church; touching the righteousness which is in the law, blameless.

Philippians 3:4–6

6 Brethren, I count not myself to have apprehended: but this one thing I do, forgetting those things which are behind, and reaching forth unto those things which are before,

I press toward the mark for the prize of the high calling of God in Christ Jesus.

Philippians 3:13–14

7 For many walk, of whom I have told you often, and now tell you even weeping, that they are the enemies of the cross of Christ:

Whose end is destruction, whose God is their belly, and whose glory is in their shame, who mind earthly things.

Philippians 3:18–19

8 Rejoice in the Lord alway: and again I say, Rejoice.

Philippians 4:4

9 And the peace of God, which passeth all understanding, shall keep your hearts and minds through Christ Jesus.

Philippians 4:7. Similar wording is found in the Book of Common Prayer (BOOK OF COMMON PRAYER 67).

10 Whatsoever things are true, whatsoever things are honest, whatsoever things are just, whatsoever things are pure, whatsoever things are lovely, whatsoever things are of good report; if there be any virtue, and if there be any praise, think on these things.

Philippians 4:8

11 For I have learned, in whatsoever state I am, therewith to be content.

Philippians 4:11

12 I can do all things through Christ which strengtheneth me.

Philippians 4:13

The Epistle of Paul the Apostle to the Colossians

1 For by him were all things created, that are in heaven, and that are in earth, visible and invisible, whether they be thrones, or dominions, or principalities, or powers.

Colossians 1:16

2 Beware lest any man spoil you through philosophy and vain deceit, after the tradition of men, after the rudiments of the world, and not after Christ.

Colossians 2:8

3 Touch not; taste not; handle not.

Colossians 2:21

4 Set your affection on things above, not on things on the earth.

Colossians 3:2

5 Where there is neither Greek nor Jew, circumcision nor uncircumcision, Barbarian, Scythian, bond nor free: but Christ is all, and in all.

Colossians 3:11

6 Husbands, love your wives, and be not bitter against them.

Colossians 3:19. See also EPHESIANS 12.

7 And whatsoever ye do, do it heartily, as to the Lord, and not unto men.

Colossians 3:23. See also EPHESIANS 12.

8 Let your speech be alway with grace, seasoned with salt, that ye may know how ye ought to answer every man.

Colossians 4:6

9 Luke, the beloved physician.

Colossians 4:14. Referring to Luke, Paul's 'fellow worker' and the patron saint of artists and physicians.

The First Epistle of Paul the Apostle to the Thessalonians

1 Remembering without ceasing your work of faith, and labour of love.

1 Thessalonians 1:3

2 And that ye study to be quiet, and to do your own business, and to work with your own hands, as we commanded you.

1 Thessalonians 4:11

3 But I would not have you to be ignorant, brethren, concerning them which are asleep.

1 Thessalonians 4:13. Referring to the dead.

4 For yourselves know perfectly that the day of the Lord so cometh as a thief in the night.

1 Thessalonians 5:2. See REVELATION 40, also *2 Peter* 3:10.

5 For they that sleep sleep in the night; and they that be drunken are drunken in the night.

But let us, who are of the day, be sober, putting on the breastplate of faith and love; and for an helmet, the hope of salvation.

1 Thessalonians 5:7–8

6 Prove all things; hold fast that which is good.

1 Thessalonians 5:21

The Second Epistle of Paul the Apostle to the Thessalonians

1 For even when we were with you, this we commanded you, that if any would not work, neither should he eat.

2 Thessalonians 3:10

The First Epistle of Paul the Apostle to Timothy

1 Neither give heed to fables and endless genealogies.

1 Timothy 1:4

2 But we know that the law is good, if a man use it lawfully;

Knowing this, that the law is not made for a righteous man, but for the lawless and disobedient, for the ungodly and for sinners, for unholy and profane, for murderers of fathers and murderers of mothers, for manslayers,

For whoremongers, for them that defile themselves with mankind, for mensteelers, for liars, for perjured persons, and if there be any other thing that is contrary to sound doctrine.

1 Timothy 1:8–10

3 Christ Jesus came into the world to save sinners; of whom I am chief.

1 Timothy 1:15

4 Let the woman learn in silence with all subjection.

But I suffer not a woman to teach, nor to usurp authority over the man, but to be in silence.

For Adam was first formed, then Eve.

And Adam was not deceived, but the woman being deceived was in the transgression.

Notwithstanding she shall be saved in childbearing, if they continue in faith and charity and holiness with sobriety.

1 Timothy 2:11–15

5 If a man desire the office of a bishop, he desireth a good work.

A bishop then must be blameless, the husband of one wife, vigilant, sober, of good behaviour, given to hospitality, apt to teach;

Not given to wine, no striker, not greedy of filthy lucre; but patient, not a brawler, not covetous;

One that ruleth well his own house, having his children in subjection with all gravity;

(For if a man know not how to rule his own house, how shall he take care of the church of God?).

1 Timothy 3:1–5. The expression 'greedy of filthy lucre' is also used in 3:8, and 'filthy lucre' further occurs in *Titus* 1:7 and 1:11

6 For every creature of God is good, and nothing to be refused, if it be received with thanksgiving:

For it is sanctified by the word of God and prayer.

1 Timothy 4:4–5

7 Refuse profane and old wives' fables, and exercise thyself rather unto godliness.

For bodily exercise profiteth little: but godliness is profitable unto all things, having promise of the life that now is, and of that which is to come.

1 Timothy 4:7–8

8 Let no man despise thy youth.

1 Timothy 4:12

9 But if any provide not for his own, and specially for those of his own house, he hath denied the faith, and is worse than an infidel.

1 Timothy 5:8

10 And withal they learn to be idle, wandering about from house to house; and not only idle, but tattlers also and busybodies, speaking things which they ought not.

1 Timothy 5:13. Referring to widows who remarry.

11 Drink no longer water, but use a little wine for thy stomach's sake and thine often infirmities.

1 Timothy 5:23

12 For we brought nothing into this world, and it is certain we can carry nothing out.

1 Timothy 6:7

13 The love of money is the root of all evil.

1 Timothy 6:10

14 Fight the good fight of faith, lay hold on eternal life.

1 Timothy 6:12

15 Charge them that are rich in this world, that they be not highminded, nor trust in uncertain riches, but in the living God, who giveth us richly all things to enjoy;

That they do good, that they be rich in good works, ready to distribute, willing to communicate.

1 Timothy 6:17–18

16 O Timothy, keep that which is committed to thy

trust, avoiding profane and vain babblings, and oppositions of science falsely so called.

1 Timothy 6:20. 'Profane and vain babblings' are also mentioned in *2 Timothy* 2:16.

The Second Epistle of Paul the Apostle to Timothy

1 For God hath not given us the spirit of fear; but of power, and of love, and of a sound mind.

2 Timothy 1:7

2 And if a man also strive for masteries, yet is he not crowned, except he strive lawfully.

2 Timothy 2:5

3 Study to shew thyself approved unto God, a workman that needeth not to be ashamed.

2 Timothy 2:15

4 All scripture is given by inspiration of God, and is profitable for doctrine, for reproof, for correction, for instruction in righteousness:

That the man of God may be perfect, throughly furnished unto all good works.

2 Timothy 3:16–17

5 Preach the word; be instant in season, out of season; reprove, rebuke, exhort with all long-suffering and doctrine.

2 Timothy 4:2

6 I have fought a good fight, I have finished my course, I have kept the faith.

2 Timothy 4:7

7 Alexander the coppersmith did me much evil: the Lord reward him according to his works.

2 Timothy 4:14

8 At my first answer no man stood with me, but all men forsook me: I pray God that it may not be laid to their charge.

Notwithstanding the Lord stood with me, and strengthened me; that by me the preaching might be fully known, and that all the Gentiles might hear: and I was delivered out of the mouth of the lion.

2 Timothy 4:16–17

The Epistle of Paul to Titus

1 The Cretians are alway liars, evil beasts, slow bellies.

Titus 1:12. Cited by St Paul, the remark has been attributed to the 6th-century-BC Cretan seer Epimenides. With Paul's following comment, 'This witness is true', this passage has become celebrated as a paradox.

2 Unto the pure all things are pure: but unto them that are defiled and unbelieving is nothing pure; but even their mind and conscience is defiled.

Titus 1:15

The Epistle of Paul the Apostle to the Hebrews

1 Are they not all ministering spirits, sent forth to minister for them who shall be heirs of salvation?

Hebrews 1:14. Referring to angels.

2 For every one that useth milk is unskilful in the word of righteousness: for he is a babe.

But strong meat belongeth to them that are of full age, even those who by reason of use have their senses exercised to discern both good and evil.

Hebrews 5:13–14

3 And almost all things are by the law purged with blood; and without shedding of blood is no remission.

Hebrews 9:22

4 It is a fearful thing to fall into the hands of the living God.

Hebrews 10:31

5 Faith is the substance of things hoped for, the evidence of things not seen.

Hebrews 11:1

6 These all died in faith, not having received the promises, but having seen them afar off, and were persuaded of them, and embraced them, and confessed that they were strangers and pilgrims on the earth.

Hebrews 11:13

7 Wherefore seeing we also are compassed about with so great a cloud of witnesses, let us lay aside every weight, and the sin which doth so easily beset us, and let us run with patience the race that is set before us,

Looking unto Jesus the author and finisher of our faith; who for the joy that was set before him endured the cross, despising the shame, and is set down at the right hand of the throne of God.

Hebrews 12:1–2

8 For whom the Lord loveth he chasteneth, and scourgeth every son whom he receiveth.

Hebrews 12:6. See PROVERBS 4 AND 31, also *Deuteronomy* 8:5.

9 But ye are come unto mount Sion, and unto the

city of the living God, the heavenly Jerusalem, and to an innumerable company of angels,

To the general assembly and church of the first-born, which are written in heaven, and to God the Judge of all, and to the spirits of just men made perfect.

Hebrews 12:22–3

10 For our God is a consuming fire.

Hebrews 12:29

11 Let brotherly love continue.

Be not forgetful to entertain strangers: for thereby some have entertained angels unawares.

Hebrews 13:1–2. The allusion may be to the account of Lot's hospitality to angels at Sodom, in *Genesis* 19.

12 The Lord is my helper, and I will not fear what men shall do unto me.

Hebrews 13:6

13 Jesus Christ the same yesterday, and to day, and for ever.

Hebrews 13:8

14 For here have we no continuing city, but we seek one to come.

Hebrews 13:14

15 But to do good and to communicate forget not: for with such sacrifices God is well pleased.

Hebrews 13:16

The General Epistle of James

1 But let patience have her perfect work, that ye may be perfect and entire, wanting nothing.

If any of you lack wisdom, let him ask of God, that giveth to all men liberally, and upbraideth not; and it shall be given him.

James 1:4–5

2 Let him ask in faith, nothing wavering. For he that wavereth is like a wave of the sea driven with the wind and tossed.

For let not that man think that he shall receive any thing of the Lord.

A double minded man is unstable in all his ways.

James 1:6–8

3 Blessed is the man that endureth temptation: for when he is tried, he shall receive the crown of life.

James 1:12

4 Every good gift and every perfect gift is from above, and cometh down from the Father of lights, with whom is no variableness, neither shadow of turning.

James 1:17

5 Let every man be swift to hear, slow to speak, slow to wrath:

For the wrath of man worketh not the righteousness of God.

James 1:19–20

6 But be ye doers of the word, and not hearers only, deceiving your own selves.

For if any be a hearer of the word, and not a doer, he is like unto a man beholding his natural face in a glass:

For he beholdeth himself, and goeth his way, and straightway forgetteth what manner of man he was.

James 1:22–4

7 Pure religion and undefiled before God and the Father is this, To visit the fatherless and widows in their affliction, and to keep himself unspotted from the world.

James 1:27

8 Even so faith, if it hath not works, is dead, being alone.

Yea, a man may say, Thou hast faith, and I have works: shew me thy faith without thy works, and I will shew thee my faith by my works.

Thou believest that there is one God; thou doest well: the devils also believe, and tremble.

But wilt thou know, O vain man, that faith without works is dead?

James 2:17–20. The verses have been taken to argue against the doctrine of justification by faith; see also ROMANS 11.

9 The tongue is a little member, and boasteth great things. Behold, how great a matter a little fire kindleth!

James 3:5

10 But the tongue can no man tame; it is an unruly evil, full of deadly poison.

James 3:8

11 Out of the same mouth proceedeth blessing and cursing. My brethren, these things ought not so to be.

Doth a fountain send forth at the same place sweet water and bitter?

James 3:10–11. On the notion that Christians can bless God yet curse men.

12 This wisdom descendeth not from above, but is earthly, sensual, devilish.

For where envying and strife is, there is confusion and every evil work.

But the wisdom that is from above is first pure, then peaceable, gentle, and easy to be intreated, full of mercy and good fruits, without partiality, and without hypocrisy.

James 3:15–17

13 Submit yourselves therefore to God. Resist the devil, and he will flee from you.

James 4:7

14 For what is your life? It is even a vapour, that appeareth for a little time, and then vanisheth away.

James 4:14

15 Behold, we count them happy which endure. Ye have heard of the patience of Job.

James 5:11

16 Let your yea be yea; and your nay, nay; lest ye fall into condemnation.

James 5:12. The words were first uttered by Jesus: see MATTHEW 31, also *2 Corinthians* 1:17.

17 The effectual fervent prayer of a righteous man availeth much.

James 5:16

The First Epistle General of Peter

1 Wherefore gird up the loins of your mind, be sober, and hope to the end for the grace that is to be brought unto you at the revelation of Jesus Christ.

1 Peter 1:13

2 Being born again, not of corruptible seed, but of incorruptible, by the word of God, which liveth and abideth for ever.

For all flesh is as grass, and all the glory of man as the flower of grass. The grass withereth, and the flower thereof falleth away.

But the word of the Lord endureth for ever.

1 Peter 1:23–5. See ISAIAH 54.

3 But ye are a chosen generation, a royal priesthood, an holy nation, a peculiar people; that ye should shew forth the praises of him who hath called you out of darkness into his marvellous light.

1 Peter 2:9

4 Dearly beloved, I beseech you as strangers and pilgrims, abstain from fleshly lusts, which war against the soul.

1 Peter 2:11

5 Submit yourselves to every ordinance of man for the Lord's sake: whether it be to the king, as supreme;

Or unto governors.

1 Peter 2:13–14

6 Honour all men. Love the brotherhood. Fear God. Honour the king.

1 Peter 2:17

7 Whose adorning let it not be that outward adorning of plaiting the hair, and of wearing of gold, or of putting on of apparel;

But let it be the hidden man of the heart, in that which is not corruptible, even the ornament of a meek and quiet spirit, which is in the sight of God of great price.

1 Peter 3:3–4

8 Likewise, ye husbands, dwell with them according to knowledge, giving honour unto the wife, as unto the weaker vessel.

1 Peter 3:7

9 But the end of all things is at hand: be ye therefore sober, and watch unto prayer.

1 Peter 4:7

10 And above all things have fervent charity among yourselves: for charity shall cover the multitude of sins.

1 Peter 4:8. The words 'shall hide a multitude of sins' appear in *James* 5:20.

11 Be sober, be vigilant; because your adversary the devil, as a roaring lion, walketh about, seeking whom he may devour:

Whom resist steadfast in the faith.

1 Peter 5:8–9. The words also appear in the BOOK OF COMMON PRAYER, *Compline*.

The Second Epistle General of Peter

1 For we have not followed cunningly devised fables, when we made known unto you the power and coming of our Lord Jesus Christ, but were eye-witnesses of his majesty.

2 Peter 1:16

2 Ye do well that ye take heed, as unto a light that shineth in a dark place, until the day dawn, and the day star arise in your hearts.

2 Peter 1:19

3 The Lord knoweth how to deliver the godly out of

temptations, and to reserve the unjust unto the day of judgment to be punished:

But chiefly them that walk after the flesh in the lust of uncleanness, and despise government. Presumptuous are they, selfwilled, they are not afraid to speak ill of dignities.

2 Peter 2:9–10

4 The dog is turned to his own vomit again; and the sow that was washed to her wallowing in the mire.

2 Peter 2:22. Referring to a proverb (PROVERBS 80).

5 But, beloved, be not ignorant of this one thing, that one day is with the Lord as a thousand years, and a thousand years as one day.

The Lord is not slack concerning his promise, as some men count slackness; but is longsuffering to us-ward, not willing that any should perish, but that all should come to repentance.

2 Peter 3:8–9. See PSALMS 92.

The First Epistle General of John

1 If we say that we have no sin, we deceive ourselves, and the truth is not in us.

1 John 1:8

2 My little children, these things write I unto you, that ye sin not. And if any man sin, we have an advocate with the Father, Jesus Christ the righteous:

And he is the propitiation for our sins: and not for ours only, but also for the sins of the whole world.

1 John 2:1–2

3 Who is a liar but he that denieth that Jesus is the Christ? He is antichrist, that denieth the Father and the Son.

1 John 2:22

4 But whoso hath this world's good, and seeth his brother have need, and shutteth up his bowels of compassion from him, how dwelleth the love of God in him?

1 John 3:17

5 Beloved, believe not every spirit, but try the spirits whether they are of God: because many false prophets are gone out into the world.

1 John 4:1

6 Beloved, let us love one another: for love is of God; and every one that loveth is born of God, and knoweth God.

He that loveth not knoweth not God; for God is love.

1 John 4:7–8

7 There is no fear in love; but perfect love casteth out fear: because fear hath torment. He that feareth is not made perfect in love.

1 John 4:18

8 If a man say, I love God, and hateth his brother, he is a liar: for he that loveth not his brother whom he hath seen, how can he love God whom he hath not seen?

1 John 4:20

9 Little children, keep yourselves from idols. Amen.

1 John 5:21. Closing words of book.

The General Epistle of Jude

1 These filthy dreamers defile the flesh, despise dominion, and speak evil of dignities.

Jude verse 8. Referring to false teachers. The words recall 2 PETER 3.

2 These are spots in your feasts of charity, when they feast with you, feeding themselves without fear: clouds they are without water, carried about of winds; trees whose fruit withereth, without fruit, twice dead, plucked up by the roots;

Raging waves of the sea, foaming out their own shame; wandering stars, to whom is reserved the blackness of darkness for ever.

Jude verses 12–13. Recalling the extra-canonical Book of Enoch, in which fallen angels were condemned to share the underworld with disobedient stars.

3 These are murmurers, complainers, walking after their own lusts; and their mouth speaketh great swelling words, having men's persons in admiration because of advantage.

Jude verse 16

The Revelation of St John
the Divine

1 Behold, he cometh with clouds; and every eye shall see him, and they also which pierced him: and all kindreds of the earth shall wail because of him. Even so, Amen.

I am Alpha and Omega, the beginning and the ending, saith the Lord, which is, and which was, and which is to come, the Almighty.

Revelation 1:7–8. See also REVELATION 57.

2 What thou seest, write in a book, and send it unto the seven churches which are in Asia.
Revelation 1:11

3 And I turned to see the voice that spake with me. And being turned, I saw seven golden candlesticks;
And in the midst of the seven candlesticks one like unto the Son of man, clothed with a garment down to the foot, and girt about the paps with a golden girdle.
Revelation 1:12–13

4 His head and his hairs were white like wool, as white as snow; and his eyes were as a flame of fire;
And his feet like unto fine brass, as if they burned in a furnace; and his voice as the sound of many waters.
And he had in his right hand seven stars: and out of his mouth went a sharp two-edged sword: and his countenance was as the sun shineth in his strength.
And when I saw him, I fell at his feet as dead. And he laid his right hand upon me, saying unto me, Fear not; I am the first and the last.
Revelation 1:14–17

5 Write the things which thou hast seen, and the things which are, and the things which shall be hereafter.
Revelation 1:19

6 I know thy works, and thy labour, and thy patience, and how thou canst not bear them which are evil: and thou hast tried them which say they are apostles, and are not, and hast found them liars:
And hast borne, and hast patience, and for my name's sake hast laboured, and hast not fainted.
Nevertheless I have somewhat against thee, because thou hast left thy first love.
Revelation 2:2–4. The message to the 'angel of the church of Ephesus'.

7 To him that overcometh will I give to eat of the tree of life, which is in the midst of the paradise of God.
Revelation 2:7

8 Be thou faithful unto death, and I will give thee a crown of life.
Revelation 2:10

9 And he shall rule them with a rod of iron; as the vessels of a potter shall they be broken to shivers: even as I received of my father.

And I will give him the morning star.
Revelation 2:27–8. The message to the 'angel of the church in Thyatira'.

10 He that overcometh, the same shall be clothed in white raiment; and I will not blot out his name out of the book of life, but I will confess his name before my Father, and before his angels.
Revelation 3:5

11 I know thy works, that thou art neither cold nor hot: I would thou wert cold or hot.
So then because thou art lukewarm, and neither cold nor hot, I will spew thee out of my mouth.
Revelation 3:15–16. Addressed to the Christians of Laodicea (Asia Minor), the passage has given rise to the term 'Laodicean' to describe anyone lukewarm or uncommitted in religion or politics.

12 Behold, I stand at the door, and knock: if any man hear my voice, and open the door, I will come in to him, and will sup with him, and he with me.
Revelation 3:20

13 And before the throne there was a sea of glass like unto crystal: and in the midst of the throne, and round about the throne, were four beasts full of eyes before and behind.
And the first beast was like a lion, and the second beast like a calf, and the third beast had a face as a man, and the fourth beast was like a flying eagle.
Revelation 4:6–7. The symbols of the four evangelists – a lion for Mark, a calf for Luke, a man for Matthew and an eagle for John – are derived from this passage. Similar imagery appears in *Ezekiel* 1:5–10 and in extra-canonical works, probably derived from Babylonian sources.

14 And the four beasts had each of them six wings about him; and they were full of eyes within: and they rest not day and night, saying, Holy, holy, holy, Lord God Almighty, which was, and is, and is to come.
Revelation 4:8

15 Thou art worthy, O Lord, to receive glory and honour and power: for thou hast created all things, and for thy pleasure they are and were created.
Revelation 4:11

16 And I saw in the right hand of him that sat on the throne a book written within and on the backside, sealed with seven seals.
And I saw a strong angel proclaiming with a loud voice, Who is worthy to open the book, and to loose the seals thereof?
Revelation 5:1–2

17 And I beheld, and, lo, in the midst of the throne and of the four beasts, and in the midst of the elders, stood a Lamb as it had been slain, having seven horns and seven eyes, which are the seven Spirits of God sent forth into all the earth.
Revelation 5:6

18 And I saw, and behold a white horse: and he that sat on him had a bow; and a crown was given unto him: and he went forth conquering, and to conquer.
Revelation 6:2

19 And I looked, and behold a pale horse: and his name that sat on him was Death, and Hell followed with him. And power was given unto them over the fourth part of the earth, to kill with sword, and with hunger, and with death, and with the beasts of the earth.
Revelation 6:8

20 And I beheld when he had opened the sixth seal, and, lo, there was a great earthquake; and the sun became black as sackcloth of hair, and the moon became as blood;

And the stars of heaven fell unto the earth, even as a fig tree casteth her untimely figs, when she is shaken of a mighty wind.

And the heaven departed as a scroll when it is rolled together; and every mountain and island were moved out of their places.
Revelation 6:12–14. The words recall *Isaiah 34:4.*

21 Hurt not the earth, neither the sea, nor the trees, till we have sealed the servants of our God in their foreheads.
Revelation 7:3. An angel's exhortation to the four angels at the corners of the earth.

22 After this I beheld, and, lo, a great multitude, which no man could number, of all nations, and kindreds, and people, and tongues, stood before the throne, and before the Lamb, clothed with white robes, and palms in their hands.
Revelation 7:9

23 And one of the elders answered, saying unto me, What are these which are arrayed in white robes? and whence came they?

And I said unto him, Sir, thou knowest. And he said to me, These are they which came out of great tribulation, and have washed their robes, and made them white in the blood of the Lamb.
Revelation 7:13–14

24 They shall hunger no more, neither thirst any more; neither shall the sun light on them, nor any heat.

For the Lamb which is in the midst of the throne shall feed them, and shall lead them unto living fountains of waters: and God shall wipe away all tears from their eyes.
Revelation 7:16–17. See also ISAIAH 34 and REVELATION 50.

25 And when he had opened the seventh seal, there was silence in heaven about the space of half an hour.
Revelation 8:1

26 And the name of the star is called Wormwood: and the third part of the waters became wormwood; and many men died of the waters, because they were made bitter.
Revelation 8:11

27 And the fifth angel sounded, and I saw a star fall from heaven unto the earth: and to him was given the key of the bottomless pit.
Revelation 9:1

28 And in those days shall men seek death, and shall not find it; and shall desire to die, and death shall flee from them.
Revelation 9:6

29 And I went unto the angel, and said unto him, Give me the little book. And he said unto me, Take it, and eat it up; and it shall make thy belly bitter, but it shall be in thy mouth sweet as honey.

And I took the little book out of the angel's hand, and ate it up; and it was in my mouth sweet as honey: and as soon as I had eaten it, my belly was bitter.
Revelation 10:9–10

30 And there appeared a great wonder in heaven; a woman clothed with the sun, and the moon under her feet, and upon her head a crown of twelve stars.
Revelation 12:1. An alternative reading has suggested '. . . a woman clothed, with the sun and the moon under her feet . . .' (with altered punctuation).

31 And there was war in heaven: Michael and his angels fought against the dragon; and the dragon fought and his angels,

And prevailed not; neither was their place found any more in heaven.

And the great dragon was cast out, that old serpent, called the Devil, and Satan, which deceiveth the whole world: he was cast out into the earth, and his angels were cast out with him.

Revelation 12:7–9

32 And they worshipped the dragon which gave power unto the beast: and they worshipped the beast, saying, Who is like unto the beast? who is able to make war with him?

Revelation 13:4

33 And he causeth all, both small and great, rich and poor, free and bond, to receive a mark in their right hand, or in their foreheads:

And that no man might buy or sell, save he that had the mark, or the name of the beast, or the number of his name.

Revelation 13:16–17

34 Here is wisdom. Let him that hath understanding count the number of the beast: for it is the number of a man; and his number is Six hundred threescore and six.

Revelation 13:18. The man referred to is usually identified as the Roman Emperor Nero, who persecuted the Christians for the great fire which destroyed much of Rome (for which he himself was the most obvious suspect) in AD 64, and whose name in Hebrew letters has a numerological value of 666.

35 And I heard a voice from heaven, as the voice of many waters, and as the voice of a great thunder: and I heard the voice of harpers harping with their harps.

Revelation 14:2

36 Babylon is fallen, is fallen, that great city, because she made all nations drink of the wine of the wrath of her fornication.

Revelation 14:8. The words, which echo ISAIAH 29, are taken to prophesy the fall of Rome.

37 If any man worship the beast and his image, and receive his mark in his forehead, or in his hand,

The same shall drink of the wine of the wrath of God, which is poured out without mixture into the cup of his indignation; and he shall be tormented with fire and brimstone in the presence of the holy angels, and in the presence of the Lamb:

And the smoke of their torment ascendeth up for ever and ever: and they have no rest day nor night, who worship the beast and his image, and whosoever receiveth the mark of his name.

Revelation 14:9–11. The words of the third angel.

38 Blessed are the dead which die in the Lord from henceforth: Yea, saith the Spirit, that they may rest from their labours; and their works do follow them.

Revelation 14:13

39 And I saw as it were a sea of glass mingled with fire: and them that had gotten the victory over the beast, and over his image, and over his mark, and over the number of his name, stand on the sea of glass, having the harps of God.

Revelation 15:2

40 Behold, I come as a thief.

Revelation 16:15. Referring to Christ. See 1 THESSALONIANS 4, also *Revelation* 3:3.

41 And he gathered them together into a place called in the Hebrew tongue Armageddon.

Revelation 16:16. Referring to Christ.

42 I will shew unto thee the judgment of the great whore that sitteth upon many waters.

Revelation 17:1. An angel shows John an image of Babylon, taken to represent the Roman empire.

43 I saw a woman sit upon a scarlet coloured beast, full of names of blasphemy, having seven heads and ten horns.

And the woman was arrayed in purple and scarlet colour, and decked with gold and precious stones and pearls, having a golden cup in her hand full of abominations and filthiness of her fornication:

And upon her forehead was a name written, MYSTERY, BABYLON THE GREAT, THE MOTHER OF HARLOTS AND ABOMINATIONS OF THE EARTH.

And I saw the woman drunken with the blood of the saints, and with the blood of the martyrs of Jesus: and when I saw her, I wondered with great admiration.

Revelation 17:3–6

44 And I saw heaven opened, and behold a white horse; and he that sat upon him was called Faithful and True, and in righteousness he doth judge and make war.

His eyes were as a flame of fire, and on his head were many crowns; and he had a name written, that no man knew, but he himself.

And he was clothed with a vesture dipped in blood: and his name is called The Word of God.

And the armies which were in heaven followed him upon white horses, clothed in fine linen, white and clean.

And out of his mouth goeth a sharp sword, that with it he should smite the nations: and he shall rule them with a rod of iron: and he treadeth the winepress of the fierceness and wrath of Almighty God.

And he hath on his vesture and on his thigh a name written, KING OF KINGS, AND LORD OF LORDS.
Revelation 19:11–16

45 And I saw an angel come down from heaven, having the key of the bottomless pit and a great chain in his hand.

And he laid hold on the dragon, that old serpent, which is the Devil, and Satan, and bound him a thousand years.

And cast him into the bottomless pit, and shut him up, and set a seal upon him, that he should deceive the nations no more, till the thousand years should be fulfilled: and after that he must be loosed a little season.
Revelation 20:1–3

46 And when the thousand years are expired, Satan shall be loosed out of his prison,

And shall go out to deceive the nations which are in the four quarters of the earth, Gog and Magog, to gather them together to battle: the number of whom is as the sand of the sea.
Revelation 20:7–8. Gog and Magog are also mentioned in Ezekiel 38.

47 And I saw the dead, small and great, stand before God; and the books were opened: and another book was opened, which is the book of life: and the dead were judged out of those things which were written in the books, according to their works.
Revelation 20:12

48 And the sea gave up the dead which were in it; and death and hell delivered up the dead which were in them: and they were judged every man according to their works.
Revelation 20:13

49 And I saw a new heaven and a new earth: for the first heaven and the first earth were passed away; and there was no more sea.

And I John saw the holy city, new Jerusalem, coming down from God out of heaven, prepared as a bride adorned for her husband.
Revelation 21:1–2

50 And God shall wipe away all tears from their eyes; and there shall be no more death, neither sorrow, nor crying, neither shall there be any more pain: for the former things are passed away.
Revelation 21:4. See also ISAIAH 34 and REVELATION 24.

51 And he that sat upon the throne said, Behold, I make all things new. And he said unto me, Write: for these words are true and faithful.
Revelation 21:5

52 And the building of the wall of it was of jasper: and the city was pure gold, like unto clear glass.

And the foundations of the wall of the city were garnished with all manner of precious stones. The first foundation was jasper; the second, sapphire; the third, a chalcedony; the fourth, an emerald;

The fifth, sardonyx; the sixth, sardius; the seventh, chrysolyte; the eighth, beryl; the ninth, a topaz; the tenth, a chrysoprasus; the eleventh, a jacinth; the twelfth, an amethyst.

And the twelve gates were twelve pearls; every several gate was of one pearl: and the street of the city was pure gold, as it were transparent glass.
Revelation 21:18–21

53 And he shewed me a pure river of water of life, clear as crystal, proceeding out of the throne of God and of the Lamb.
Revelation 22:1

54 And there shall be no night there; and they need no candle, neither light of the sun; for the Lord God giveth them light: and they shall reign for ever and ever.
Revelation 22:5

55 Behold, I come quickly.
Revelation 22:7. The words also appear in 22:12 and 22:20.

56 He that is unjust, let him be unjust still: and he which is filthy, let him be filthy still: and he that is righteous, let him be righteous still; and he that is holy, let him be holy still.
Revelation 22:11

57 I am Alpha and Omega, the beginning and the end, the first and the last.
Revelation 22:13. See REVELATION 1, also Revelation 21:6.

58 Blessed are they that do his commandments, that they may have right to the tree of life, and may enter in through the gates into the city.

For without are dogs, and sorcerers, and whoremongers, and murderers, and idolaters, and whosoever loveth and maketh a lie.

I Jesus have sent mine angel to testify unto you these things in the churches. I am the root and the offspring of David, and the bright and morning star.

And the Spirit and the bride say, Come. And let him that heareth say, Come. And let him that is athirst come. And whosoever will, let him take the water of life freely.

Revelation 22:14–17

59 He which testifieth these things saith, Surely I come quickly. Amen. Even so, come, Lord Jesus.

The grace of our Lord Jesus Christ be with you all. Amen.

Revelation 22:20–1. The closing verses of the New Testament.

BIBLE: THE VULGATE

1 *Asperges me hyssopo, et mundabor; lavabis me, et super nivem dealbabor.*
[Thou shalt sprinkle me with hyssop, and I shall be cleansed: thou shalt wash me, and I shall be made whiter than snow.]

Psalms 50:9. See BIBLE, OLD TESTAMENT: PSALMS 64.

2 *Cantate Domino canticum novum, quia mirabilia fecit.*
[Sing ye to the Lord a new canticle: because he hath done wonderful things.]

Psalms 97:1 (98:1 in Authorized version)

3 *Jubilate Deo, omnis terra, servite Domino in laetitia.*
[Sing joyfully to God, all the earth; serve ye the Lord with gladness.]

Psalms 99:2 (100:2 in Authorized version)

4 *Beatus vir qui timet Dominum, in mandatis ejus volet nimis!*
[Blessed is the man that feareth the Lord: he shall delight exceedingly in his commandments.]

Psalms 111:1 (112:1 in Authorized version)

5 *Non nobis, Domine, non nobis, sed nomini tuo da gloriam.*
[Not to us, O Lord, not to us; but to thy name give glory.]

Psalms 113, pt 2:1. See BIBLE, OLD TESTAMENT: PSALMS 117.

6 *De profundis clamavi ad te, Domine; Domine, exaudi vocem meam.*
[Out of the depths have I cried unto thee, O Lord; Lord, hear my voice.]

Psalms 129:1–2. See BIBLE, OLD TESTAMENT: PSALMS 134.

7 *Vanitas vanitatum, dixit Ecclesiastes; vanitas vanitatum, et omnia vanitas.*

[Vanity of vanities, said Ecclesiastes; vanity of vanities; all is vanity.

Ecclesiastes 1:2. See BIBLE, OLD TESTAMENT: ECCLESIASTES 1.

8 *Benedicite, omnia opera Domini, Domino, laudate et superexaltate eum in secula.*
[All ye works of the Lord, bless the Lord: praise and exalt him above all for ever.]

Daniel 3:57. See BOOK OF COMMON PRAYER 12.

9 *Magnificat anima mea Dominum, et exsultavit spiritus meus in Deo salvatore meo.*
[My soul doth magnify the Lord; and my spirit hath rejoiced in God my Saviour.]

Luke 1:46–7. See BIBLE, NEW TESTAMENT: LUKE 3.

10 *Nunc dimittis servum tuum, Domine, secundum verbum tuum in pace.*
[Now thou dost dismiss thy servant, O Lord, according to thy word in peace.]

Luke 2:29. See BIBLE, NEW TESTAMENT: LUKE 12.

11 *Quo vadis?*
[Whither goest thou?]

John 16:5. See BIBLE, NEW TESTAMENT: JOHN 48.

12 *Ecce homo.*
[Behold the Man.]

John 19:5. See BIBLE, NEW TESTAMENT: JOHN 63.

13 *Consummatum est.*
[It is consummated.]

John 19:30. See BIBLE, NEW TESTAMENT: JOHN 69.

14 *Noli me tangere.*
[Do not touch me.]

John 20:17. See BIBLE, NEW TESTAMENT: JOHN 72.

15 *Magna est veritas, et praevalet.*
[Great is truth, and it prevails.]

3 Esdras 4:41. See APOCRYPHA, 1 ESDRAS 5.

Georges Bidault
(1899–1983)
French resistance leader and statesman

He headed the National Council of Resistance in 1943, and was Prime Minister in 1946, 1949–50, and 1958. Opposed to DE GAULLE's Algerian policy, he was charged with treason and went into exile 1962–8.

1 The weak have one weapon: the errors of those who think they are strong.

Quoted in the *Observer* 15 July 1962

Ambrose Bierce
(1842–c. 1914)
US journalist and author

A Civil War veteran, he wrote sardonic short stories. His Demon's Dictionary *(1875) was followed by his best-known work, the misanthropic* Devil's Dictionary, *published in instalments 1881–1906. He vanished while fighting in the Mexican Revolution. See also* WILLIAM WORDSWORTH 83.

1 Abstainer, *n.* A weak person who yields to the temptation of denying himself a pleasure.
The Devil's Dictionary (1881–1906)

2 Absurdity, *n.* A statement of belief manifestly inconsistent with one's own opinion.
Ibid.

3 Acquaintance, *n.* A person whom we know well enough to borrow from, but not well enough to lend to.
Ibid.

4 Admiration, *n.* Our polite recognition of another's resemblance to ourselves.
Ibid.

5 Age, *n.* That period of life in which we compound for the vices that we still cherish by reviling those that we have no longer the enterprise to commit.
Ibid.

6 Alliance, *n.* In international politics, the union of two thieves who have their hands so deeply inserted in each other's pocket that they cannot separately plunder a third.
Ibid.

7 Ambition, *n.* An overmastering desire to be vilified by enemies while living and made ridiculous by friends when dead.
Ibid.

8 Architect, *n.* One who drafts a plan of your house, and plans a draft of your money.
Ibid.

9 Backbite, *v.t.* To speak of a man as you find him when he can't find you.
Ibid.

10 Bore, *n.* A person who talks when you wish him to listen.
Ibid.

11 Bride, *n.* A woman with a fine prospect of happiness behind her.
Ibid.

12 Compromise, *n.* Such an adjustment of conflicting interests as gives each adversary the satisfaction of thinking he has got what he ought not to have, and is deprived of nothing except what was justly his due.
Ibid.

13 Consul, *n.* In American politics, a person who having failed to secure an office from the people is given one by the Administration on condition that he leave the country.
Ibid.

14 Consult, *v.t.* To seek another's approval of a course already decided on.
Ibid.

15 Corporation, *n.* An ingenious device for obtaining individual profit without individual responsibility.
Ibid.

16 Cynic, *n.* A blackguard whose faulty vision sees things as they are, not as they ought to be.
Ibid.

17 Deliberation, *n.* The act of examining one's bread to determine which side it is buttered on.
Ibid.

18 Destiny, *n.* A tyrant's authority for crime and a fool's excuse for failure.
Ibid.

19 Dog, *n.* A kind of additional or subsidiary Deity designed to catch the overflow and surplus of the world's worship.
Ibid.

20 Duty, *n.* That which sternly impels us in the direction of profit, along the line of desire.
Ibid.

21 Education, *n.* That which discloses to the wise and disguises from the foolish their lack of understanding.
Ibid.

22 Egotist, *n.* A person of low taste, more interested in himself than in me.
Ibid.

23 Enthusiasm, *n.* A distemper of youth, curable by small doses of repentance in connection with outward applications of experience.
Ibid.

24 Faith, *n.* Belief without evidence in what is told

by one who speaks without knowledge, of things without parallel.
Ibid.

25 Friendless, *adj.* Having no favors to bestow. Destitute of fortune. Addicted to utterance of truth and common sense.
Ibid.

26 Future, *n.* That period of time in which our affairs prosper, our friends are true and our happiness is assured.
Ibid.

27 History, *n.* An account mostly false, of events mostly unimportant, which are brought about by rulers mostly knaves, and soldiers mostly fools.
Ibid.

28 Incompatibility, *n.* In matrimony a similarity of tastes, particularly the taste for domination.
Ibid.

29 Laziness, *n.* Unwarranted repose of manner in a person of low degree.
Ibid.

30 Marriage, *n.* The state or condition of a community consisting of a master, a mistress and two slaves, making in all, two.
Ibid.

31 Opiate, *n.* An unlocked door in the prison of Identity. It leads into the jail yard.
Ibid.

32 Patience, *n.* A minor form of despair disguised as a virtue.
Ibid.

33 Prejudice, *n.* A vagrant opinion without visible means of support.
Ibid.

34 Sabbath, *n.* A weekly festival having its origin in the fact that God made the world in six days and was arrested on the seventh.
Ibid.

35 The covers of this book are too far apart.
One-sentence book review, quoted in *Bitter Bierce* (1929) by C. H. Grattan

Steve Biko
(1946–77)
South African anti-apartheid activist

Founder and leader of the Black Consciousness Movement in South Africa, he became President of the Black People's Convention in 1972. Banned from political activity in 1973, he was killed in police custody.

1 The philosophy of Black Consciousness therefore expresses group pride and the determination of the black to rise and attain the envisaged self . . . At the heart of this kind of thinking is the realization by blacks that the most potent weapon in the hands of the oppressor is the mind of the oppressed.
'Black Consciousness and the Quest for a True Humanity', publ. in *Black Theology: the South African Voice* (ed. Basil Moore, 1973)

2 Whites must be made to realize that they are only human, not superior. Same with blacks. They must be made to realize that they are also human, not inferior.
Quoted in the *Boston Globe* 26 October 1977

3 You are either alive and proud or you are dead, and when you are dead, you can't care anyway. And your method of death can itself be a politicizing thing . . . So if you can overcome the personal fear of death . . . then you're on the way.
Interview, publ. in *New Republic* 7 January 1978

Josh Billings
(1818–85)
US humorist

Pseudonym of Henry Wheeler Shaw. One of the most successful of the 'cracker-barrel' philosophers in vogue following the American Civil War, he used 'rustic' spellings and grammar to convey his homespun wisdom, published in his columns in the New York Weekly from 1865.

1 Man was kreated a little lower than the angells and has bin gittin a little lower ever sinse.
Josh Billings, His Sayings, ch. 28 (1865). See BIBLE, OLD TESTAMENT: PSALMS 7.

2 We hate those who will not take our advise, and despise them who do.
Ibid., ch. 28

3 About the only difference between the poor and the ritch, is this, the poor *suffer* mizery, while the ritch hav tu *enjoy* it.
Ibid., ch. 71

4 Tew bring up a child in the wa he should go –
travel that wa yourself.
Ibid., ch. 78. See BIBLE, OLD TESTAMENT: PROVERBS 64.

Laurence Binyon
(1869–1943)
British poet

His collections include Lyric Poems *(1894) and* Odes *(1901).*
He is best remembered for his poem 'For the Fallen'. He was
Professor of Poetry at Harvard (1933–4).

1 They shall grow not old, as we that are left grow
old:
Age shall not weary them, nor the years condemn.
At the going down of the sun and in the morning
We will remember them.
'For the Fallen' (1914), repr. in *Collected Poems* (1931). The
lines, which were set to music by Elgar, are inscribed on war
memorials throughout Britain and the Commonwealth.

Lord Birkenhead
See F. E. SMITH

William Norman Birkett
(1883–1962)
British lawyer

Baron Birkett of Ulveston. A Liberal MP (1923–4 and 1929–31),
he established his reputation as counsel in murder trials and
was prominent in the summing up of the Nuremberg Trials
(1945–6). He was Lord Justice of Appeal 1950–7.

1 I do not object to people looking at their watches
when I am speaking. But I strongly object when they
start shaking them to make certain they are still
going.
Quoted in the *Observer* 30 October 1960

Augustine Birrell
(1850–1933)
British essayist and politician

A lawyer and a Liberal MP, he was Chief Secretary for Ireland
(1907–16), resigning when he was held responsible for allowing
the Easter Rising to take place. His essays were collected in
Obiter Dicta *(1884 and 1887).*

1 That great dust-heap called 'history'.
Obiter Dicta, 'Carlyle' (first series, 1884)

2 Reading is not a duty, and has consequently no
business to be made disagreeable.
Ibid., 'The Office of Literature' (second series, 1887)

Elizabeth Bishop
(1911–79)
US poet

Having grown up in New England and Nova Scotia, she lived
for sixteen years in Brazil, the subject of much of her poetry.
She received the Pulitzer Prize in 1956 for her first two collec-
tions North and South *(1946) and* Cold Spring *(1955).*

1 The armored cars of dreams, contrived to let us
do
so many a dangerous thing.
'Sleeping Standing Up', st. 2, publ. in *Poems: North and South*
(1946)

2 Topography displays no favorites; North's as
near as West.
More delicate than the historians' are the
map-makers' colors.
'The Map', ibid.

3 Should we have stayed at home and thought of
here?
Where should we be today?
Is it right to be watching strangers in a play
in this strangest of theatres?
'Questions of Travel', st. 2, publ. in *Questions of Travel* (1965)

4 What childishness is it that while there's breath
of life
in our bodies, we are determined to rush
to see the sun the other way around?
'Questions of Travel', st. 2, ibid.

5 The art of losing isn't hard to master;
so many things seem filled with the intent
to be lost that their loss is no disaster.
'One Art', publ. in *Geography III* (1976)

Otto von Bismarck
(1815–98)
Prussian statesman

The 'Iron Chancellor' masterminded the rise of Prussia and of
modern Germany, on behalf of Wilhelm I and his son,
Wilhelm II. Authoritarian in domestic policy, he largely pur-
sued pacific aims in Europe, though VICTORIA *branded him*
'the most mischievous and dangerous person alive'.

1 The great questions of the day will not be decided
by speeches and the resolutions of the majorities
. . . but by iron and blood.
Speech in Berlin, 29 September 1862, quoted in *Bismarck: the*
Man and the Statesman (1955) by A. J. P. TAYLOR, ch. 3. 'Iron
and blood' (or 'blood and iron') was one of Bismarck's favourite expressions.

2 *Die Politik ist keine exacte Wissenschaft.*
[Politics is not an exact science.]
Speech to Prussian legislature, 18 December 1863, quoted in *Bismarck*, bk 3, ch. 6 (1926) by Emil Ludwig

3 The secret of politics? Make a good treaty with Russia.
Remark, 1863, quoted in *Bismarck: the Man and the States-man*, ch. 7 (1955) by A. J. P. TAYLOR

4 *Die Politik ist die Lehre vom Möglichen.*
[Politics is the art of the possible.]
Remark, 11 August 1867, quoted in *Complete Works*, vol. 7 (1924)

5 Germany has no interest in the Eastern Question that was worth the healthy bones of a single Pomeranian grenadier.
Speech to Reichstag, 14 May 1872, quoted in *Bismarck: the Man and the Statesman*, ch. 7 (1955) by A. J. P. TAYLOR

6 Whoever speaks of Europe is wrong: it is a geographical expression.
Marginal comment on a letter from the Russian Chancellor Gorchakov, November 1876, attributed

7 I am bored; the great things are done. The German *Reich* is made.
Remark, c. 1888, quoted in *Bismarck: the Man and the Statesman*, ch. 4 (1955) by A. J. P. TAYLOR

8 A statesman cannot create anything himself. He must wait and listen until he hears the steps of God sounding through events; then leap up and grasp the hem of his garment.
Quoted ibid., ch. 5. The remark was quoted by HELMUT KOHL to MIKHAIL GORBACHEV during a meeting in the Caucasus to discuss German reunification, July 1990.

Conrad Black
(b. 1944)
Canadian-born British newspaper proprietor

Baron Black of Crossharbour. He spent thirty years building up the Hollinger media empire, and was owner of the Telegraph *newspaper group 1986–2004.*

1 My experience with journalists authorizes me to record that a very large number of them are ignorant, lazy, opinionated, intellectually dishonest and inadequately supervised hacks.
Testimony to Canadian Senate Committee, quoted in the *Chicago Tribune* 6 March 1994. Black noted in his autobiography, 'one of the greatest myths of the industry: that journalists are essential to producing a newspaper.'

Valentine Blacker
(1778–1823)
English soldier and historian

He served as a soldier in India and later became Surveyor-General of India. He published a history of the Mahratta War (1817–19) in 1821.

1 Put your trust in God, my boys, and keep your powder dry!
'Colonel Oliver's Advice, an Orange Ballad', publ. in *Ballads of Ireland* (ed. Edward Hayes, 1856). OLIVER CROMWELL supposedly uttered the words as his troops were about to cross a stream to attack the enemy.

(Sir) William Blackstone
(1723–80)
English jurist

A barrister, judge and later an MP, he delivered the first lectures on law ever given in a university, which became the basis for his Commentaries on the Laws of England *(1765–69), for years the most influential legal textbook in England and North America.*

1 Man was formed for society.
Commentaries on the Laws of England, Introduction, sect. 2 (1765)

2 The Royal Navy of England hath ever been its greatest defence and ornament; it is its ancient and natural strength; the floating bulwark of the island.
Ibid., bk 1, ch. 13

3 It is better that ten guilty persons escape than that one innocent suffer.
Ibid., bk 4, ch. 27

Cherie Blair
(b. 1954)
British lawyer

Also known as Cherie Booth. The wife of TONY BLAIR, *she is a specialist in employment law and a judge.*

1 I'm not Superwoman ... The reality of my daily life is that I am juggling a lot of balls in the air ... and sometimes some of the balls get dropped. There just aren't enough hours in the day.
Speech, 10 December 2002, publ. in the *Daily Telegraph* 11 December 2002. Explaining her error of judgement in enlisting the help of Peter Foster, the boyfriend of her personal adviser Carol Caplin and a convicted fraudster, as an agent to buy property in Bristol.

Tony Blair
(b. 1953)
British politician and prime minister

Elected leader of the Labour Party in 1994, he achieved a land-slide victory in the 1997 general election, becoming the youngest prime minister since 1812. He was re-elected in 2001 and 2005. See SUN 9.

1 Labour is the party of law and order in Britain today. Tough on crime and tough on the causes of crime.
Speech at Labour Party Conference, Brighton, 30 September 1993, quoted in *The Times* 1 October 1993. Speaking as Shadow Home Secretary.

2 The art of leadership is saying no, not saying yes. It is very easy to say yes.
Quoted in the *Mail on Sunday* 2 October 1994

3 Ask me my three main priorities for Government, and I tell you: education, education and education.
Speech at Labour Party Conference, Blackpool, 1 October 1996, quoted in *The Times* 2 October 1996. The wording is said to have been inspired by a speech by NELSON MANDELA.

4 People everywhere ... kept faith with Princess Diana. They liked her, they loved her, they regarded her as one of the people. She was the People's Princess, and that is how she will stay, how she will remain in our hearts and our memories forever.
Speech at Sedgefield, 31 August 1997, quoted in *The Times* 1 September 1997. Blair had been informed of DIANA's death a few hours previously.

5 This is not a time for soundbites. We've left them at home. I feel the hand of history upon our shoulders.
Press conference in Belfast, Radio 5 Live, 7 April 1998. The Prime Minister had arrived in Northern Ireland as the peace discussions appeared to be on the brink of collapse. Blair also used the phrase 'hand of history' on the occasion of the opening of the Northern Ireland Assembly at Stormont Castle, 2 December 1999, the day when the Republic of Ireland dropped its constitutional claim over Northern Ireland.

6 In these past few days, the irresistible force, the political will, has met the immovable object, the legacy of the past, and we have moved it.
Speech at Stormont, 10 April 1998, quoted in *The Times* 11 April 1998. Blair was celebrating Senator George Mitchell's announcement of the signing of the Good Friday Agreement after twenty-two months of negotiation.

7 My friends! The class war is over.
Speech to Labour Party Conference, Bournemouth, 1 October 1999, quoted in *The Times* 2 October 1999

8 This is not a battle between the United States of America and terrorism but between the free and democratic world and terrorism. We therefore here in Britain stand shoulder to shoulder with our American friends in this hour of tragedy and we, like them, will not rest until this evil is driven from our world.
Quoted in *The Times* 12 September 2001. Speaking in the wake of the terrorist attacks of '9/11'.

9 The state of Africa is a scar on the conscience of the world.
Speech at Labour Party Conference, Brighton, 2 October 2001, quoted in *The Times* 3 October 2001

10 The dossier concludes that Iraq has chemical and biological weapons, that Saddam has continued to produce them, that he has military plans for the use of chemical and biological weapons which could be activated within 45 minutes.
Speech to House of Commons, 24 September 2002, quoted in *The Times* 25 September 2002. Referring to the dossier on Iraq's military capability, drawn up by MI6. On 12 October 2004, Jack Straw announced in the House of Commons that John Scarlett, head of MI6, had formally withdrawn this statement.

11 The defining characteristic of the modern world is insecurity.
Quoted in the *Scotsman* 1 January 2003

12 The moral case against war has a moral answer: it is the moral case for removing Saddam ... I ask the marchers to understand this: I do not seek unpopularity as a badge of honour. But sometimes it is the price of leadership and the cost of conviction.
Speech at Labour Party Conference, Glasgow, 15 February 2003, quoted in the *Observer* 16 February 2003

William Blake
(1757–1827)
English poet, painter and engraver

A largely ignored visionary of the English Romantic movement, he was branded by the London Examiner *'an unfortunate lunatic whose personal inoffensiveness secures him from confinement'. With his wife Catherine Boucher, he illustrated and independently published all his major works of lyrical and epic poetry.*

1 Piping down the valleys wild,
Piping songs of pleasant glee,
On a cloud I saw a child,
And he laughing said to me:

'Pipe a song about a Lamb!'
So I piped with merry cheer.
'Piper, pipe that song again;'
So I piped: he wept to hear.
Songs of Innocence, Introduction, sts 1–2 (1789)

2 In futurity
I prophetic see
That the earth from sleep
(Grave the sentence deep)
Shall arise and seek
For her maker meek;
And the desert wild
Become a garden mild.
Ibid., 'The Little Girl Lost', sts 1–2

3 Little Lamb, who made thee?
Dost thou know who made thee?
Gave thee life, and bid thee feed
By the stream and o'er the mead;
Gave thee clothing of delight,
Softest clothing, woolly, bright.
Ibid., 'The Lamb', st. 1

4 To Mercy, Pity, Peace, and Love
All pray in their distress;
And to these virtues of delight
Return their thankfulness.
Ibid., 'The Divine Image', st. 1

5 For Mercy has a human heart,
Pity a human face,
And Love, the human form divine,
And Peace, the human dress.
Ibid., 'The Divine Image', st. 3. See also WILLIAM BLAKE 63.

6 And all must love the human form,
In heathen, turk, or jew;
Where Mercy, Love, and Pity dwell
There God is dwelling too.
Ibid., 'The Divine Image', st. 5

7 When my mother died I was very young,
And my father sold me while yet my tongue
Could scarcely cry ''weep! 'weep! 'weep! 'weep!'
So your chimneys I sweep, and in soot I sleep.
Ibid., 'The Chimney Sweeper', st. 1

8 'I have no name:
'I am but two days old.'
What shall I call thee?
'I happy am,
'Joy is my name.'
Sweet joy befall thee!
Ibid., 'Infant Joy', st. 1

9 The sun descending in the west,
The evening star does shine;
The birds are silent in their nest,
And I must seek for mine.
Ibid., 'Night', st. 1

10 The moon like a flower
In heaven's high bower,
With silent delight
Sits and smiles on the night.
Ibid., 'Night', st. 1

11 When the voices of children are heard on the
green
And laughing is heard on the hill,
My heart is at rest within my breast
And everything else is still.
Ibid., 'Nurse's Song', st. 1

12 Can I see another's woe,
And not be in sorrow too?
Can I see another's grief,
And not seek for kind relief?
Ibid., 'On Another's Sorrow', st. 1

13 But to go to school in a summer morn,
O! it drives all joy away;
Under a cruel eye outworn,
The little ones spend the day
In sighing and dismay.
Ibid., 'The School Boy', st. 2

14 My mother bore me in the southern wild,
And I am black, but O! my soul is white;
White as an angel is the English child,
But I am black, as if bereaved of light.
Ibid., 'The Little Black Boy', st. 1

15 Does the eagle know what is in the pit?
Or wilt thou go ask the mole?
Can wisdom be put in a silver rod?
Or love in a golden bowl?
The Book of Thel, plate i, 'Thel's Motto' (1789)

16 Without contraries is no progression. Attraction
and repulsion, reason and energy, love and hate, are
necessary to human existence.
The Marriage of Heaven and Hell, plate 3 (c. 1790–3)

17 Energy is Eternal Delight.
Ibid., plate 4: 'The Voice of the Devil'

18 The reason Milton wrote in fetters when he wrote
of angels and God, and at liberty when of devils and

hell, is because he was a true poet, and of the devil's party without knowing it.

Ibid., plate 6: 'The Voice of the Devil', note

19 The road of excess leads to the palace of wisdom.

Ibid., plate 7: 'Proverbs of Hell'

20 He who desires but acts not, breeds pestilence.

Ibid., plate 7: 'Proverbs of Hell'

21 A fool sees not the same tree that a wise man sees.

Ibid., plate 7: 'Proverbs of Hell'

22 He whose face gives no light, shall never become a star.

Ibid., plate 7: 'Proverbs of Hell'

23 Eternity is in love with the productions of time.

Ibid., plate 7: 'Proverbs of Hell'

24 The hours of folly are measured by the clock; but of wisdom, no clock can measure.

Ibid., plate 7: 'Proverbs of Hell'

25 No bird soars too high, if he soars with his own wings.

Ibid., plate 7: 'Proverbs of Hell'

26 If the fool would persist in his folly he would become wise.

Ibid., plate 7: 'Proverbs of Hell'

27 Prisons are built with stones of law, brothels with bricks of religion.

Ibid., plate 8: 'Proverbs of Hell'

28 The pride of the peacock is the glory of God.
The lust of the goat is the bounty of God.
The wrath of the lion is the wisdom of God.
The nakedness of woman is the work of God.

Ibid., plate 8: 'Proverbs of Hell'

29 One thought fills immensity.

Ibid., plate 8: 'Proverbs of Hell'

30 Always be ready to speak your mind, and a base man will avoid you.

Ibid., plate 8: 'Proverbs of Hell'

31 Think in the morning. Act in the noon. Eat in the evening. Sleep in the night.

Ibid., plate 9: 'Proverbs of Hell'

32 The tygers of wrath are wiser than the horses of instruction.

Ibid., plate 9: 'Proverbs of Hell'

33 You never know what is enough unless you know what is more than enough.

Ibid., plate 9: 'Proverbs of Hell'

34 The weak in courage is strong in cunning.

Ibid., plate 9: 'Proverbs of Hell'

35 When thou seest an eagle, thou seest a portion of genius; lift up thy head!

Ibid., plate 9: 'Proverbs of Hell'

36 Improvement makes straight roads; but the crooked roads without improvement are roads of genius.

Ibid., plate 10: 'Proverbs of Hell'

37 Sooner murder an infant in its cradle than nurse unacted desires.

Ibid., plate 10: 'Proverbs of Hell'

38 If the doors of perception were cleansed every thing would appear to man as it is, infinite.

Ibid., plate 14: 'A Memorable Fancy'. *The Doors of Perception* was the title of ALDOUS HUXLEY's essay on his experience with mescaline (1954); the 1960s rock group The Doors also reputedly took their name from Blake's aphorism. Blake continued, 'For man has closed himself up, till he sees all things thro' narrow chinks of his cavern.'

39 The man who never alters his opinion is like standing water, and breeds reptiles of the mind.

Ibid., plate 19: 'A Memorable Fancy'. The words of a harper 'on a pleasant bank beside a river by moonlight'.

40 Opposition is true friendship.

Ibid., plate 20: 'A Memorable Fancy'. The line is deleted in some copies of the work.

41 One law for the lion and ox is oppression.

Ibid., plate 24: 'A Memorable Fancy'

42 I told my love, I told my love,
I told her all my heart,
Trembling, cold, in ghastly fears –
Ah, she doth depart.

Manuscript Notebook, 'Poems and Fragments', no. 2 (c. 1793), publ. in *Complete Writings* (ed. Geoffrey Keynes, 1957)

43 Love to faults is always blind,
Always is to joy inclined,
Lawless, winged, and unconfined,
And breaks all chains from every mind.

Ibid., 'Poems and Fragments', no. 29: 'How to Know Love from Deceit'

44 Abstinence sows sand all over
The ruddy limbs and flaming hair,

But desire gratified
Plants fruits of life and beauty there.

Ibid., 'Poems and Fragments', no. 40

45 He who binds to himself a joy
Does the winged life destroy;
But he who kisses the joy as it flies
Lives in eternity's sun rise.

Ibid., 'Poems and Fragments', no. 43: 'Eternity'

46 What is it men in women do require?
The lineaments of gratified desire.
What is it women do in men require?
The lineaments of gratified desire.

Ibid., 'Poems and Fragments', no. 46: 'The Question Answered'. In a previous entry (no. 41), Blake wrote: 'In a wife I would desire/What in whores is always found –/The lineaments of gratified desire.'

47 Her whole life is an epigram, smack-smooth
     and nobly penned,
Plaited quite neat to catch applause with a sliding
     noose at the end.

Ibid., 'Poems and Fragments', no. 57. An alternative version has the wording 'smack, smooth and neatly penned'.

48 The moment of desire! the moment of desire!
     The virgin
That pines for man shall awaken her womb to
     enormous joys
In the secret shadows of her chamber: the youth
     shut up from
The lustful joy shall forget to generate and create
     an amorous image
In the shadows of his curtains and in the folds of
     his silent pillow.

Visions of the Daughters of Albion, plate 7 (1793). Oothoon's lament.

49 Hear the voice of the Bard!
Who present, past, and future, sees;
Whose ears have heard
The Holy Word
That walked among the ancient trees.

Songs of Experience, 'Introduction', st. 1 (1794)

50 Love seeketh not itself to please,
Nor for itself hath any care,
But for another gives its ease,
And builds a Heaven in Hell's despair.

Ibid., 'The Clod and the Pebble', st. 1. Drafts of this poem and most of the following entries from Songs of Experience appear in Blake's Notebook (c. 1793).

51 Love seeketh only self to please,
To bind another to its delight,

Joys in another's loss of ease,
And builds a Hell in Heaven's despite.

Ibid., 'The Clod and the Pebble', st. 3

52 O Rose, thou art sick!
The invisible worm
That flies in the night,
In the howling storm,
Has found out thy bed
Of crimson joy:
And his dark secret love
Does thy life destroy.

Ibid., 'The Sick Rose'

53 Little Fly,
Thy summer's play
My thoughtless hand
Has brushed away.

Ibid., 'The Fly', st. 1

54 Tyger! Tyger! burning bright
In the forests of the night,
What immortal hand or eye
Could frame thy fearful symmetry?

Ibid., 'The Tyger', st. 1. The same lines appear in st. 6, but with 'dare' instead of 'could'.

55 When the stars threw down their spears,
And watered heaven with their tears,
Did he smile his work to see?
Did he who made the Lamb make thee?

Ibid., 'The Tyger', st. 5

56 Ah, Sun-flower, weary of time,
Who countest the steps of the sun,
Seeking after that sweet golden clime
Where the traveller's journey is done:
Where the youth pined away with desire,
And the pale virgin shrouded in snow
Arise from their graves, and aspire
Where my sun-flower wishes to go.

Ibid., 'Ah! Sun-flower'

57 I wander through each chartered street,
Near where the chartered Thames does flow,
And mark in every face I meet
Marks of weakness, marks of woe.

Ibid., 'London', st. 1. In Blake's Notebook, 'dirty' replaces 'chartered' in lines 1 and 2.

58 In every cry of every man,
In every infant's cry of fear,
In every voice, in every ban,
The mind-forged manacles I hear.

Ibid., 'London', st. 2

59 But most through midnight streets I hear
How the youthful harlot's curse
Blasts the new born infant's tear,
And blights with plagues the marriage hearse.

Ibid., 'London', st. 4

60 Pity would be no more
If we did not make somebody poor;
And Mercy no more could be
If all were as happy as we.

Ibid., 'The Human Abstract', st. 1. In Blake's Notebook, the draft of this poem is entitled 'The Human Image'.

61 My mother groaned! my father wept.
Into the dangerous world I leapt:
Helpless, naked, piping loud:
Like a fiend hid in a cloud.

Ibid., 'Infant Sorrow', st. 1

62 I was angry with my friend:
I told my wrath, my wrath did end.
I was angry with my foe:
I told it not, my wrath did grow.

Ibid., 'A Poison Tree', st. 1

63 Cruelty has a human heart,
And jealousy a human face;
Terror the human form divine,
And secrecy the human dress.
The human dress is forged iron,
The human form a fiery forge,
The human face a furnace sealed,
The human heart its hungry gorge.

Ibid., 'A Divine Image'. Though etched on a copper plate (c. 1794) in Blake's usual manner, this poem does not appear in any copy of the Songs of Experience, and so was probably rejected by him. See also WILLIAM BLAKE 5.

64 What is grand is necessarily obscure to weak men. That which can be made explicit to the idiot is not worth my care.

Letter, 23 August 1799, publ. in The Letters of William Blake (ed. Geoffrey Keynes, 1956). Addressed to the Reverend Dr Trusler, author of The Way to Be Rich and Respectable, who had suggested that Blake needed somebody to elucidate his ideas.

65 Fun I love, but too much fun is of all things the most loathsome. Mirth is better than fun, and happiness is better than mirth.

Ibid., 23 August 1799

66 I see every thing I paint in this world, but everybody does not see alike. To the eyes of a miser a guinea is more beautiful than the sun, and a bag worn with the use of money has more beautiful proportions than a vine filled with grapes.

Ibid., 23 August 1799

67 The tree which moves some to tears of joy is in the eyes of others only a green thing that stands in the way. Some see nature all ridicule and deformity . . . and some scarce see nature at all. But to the eyes of the man of imagination, nature is imagination itself.

Ibid., 23 August 1799

68 For a tear is an intellectual thing,
And a sigh is the sword of an Angel King,
And the bitter groan of a martyr's woe
Is an arrow from the Almighty's bow.

Poems from the Pickering Manuscript, 'The Grey Monk', st. 8 (c. 1803). Spoken by the Monk. The stanza was incorporated into Blake's Jerusalem, ch. 3, plate 52 (1804–20).

69 To see a world in a grain of sand
And a heaven in a wild flower,
Hold infinity in the palm of your hand
And eternity in an hour.

Ibid., 'Auguries of Innocence', ll. 1–4

70 A robin red breast in a cage
Puts all Heaven in a rage.

Ibid., 'Auguries of Innocence', ll. 5–6

71 A dog starved at his master's gate
Predicts the ruin of the state.

Ibid., 'Auguries of Innocence', ll. 9–10

72 Each outcry of the hunted hare
A fibre from the brain does tear.
A skylark wounded in the wing,
A cherubim does cease to sing.

Ibid., 'Auguries of Innocence', ll. 13–16

73 A truth that's told with bad intent
Beats all the lies you can invent.

Ibid., 'Auguries of Innocence', ll. 53–4

74 Man was made for joy and woe;
And when this we rightly know
Through the world we safely go.
Joy and woe are woven fine,
A clothing for the soul divine.

Ibid., 'Auguries of Innocence', ll. 56–60

75 The strongest poison ever known
Came from Caesar's laurel crown.

Ibid., 'Auguries of Innocence', ll. 97–8

76 The harlot's cry from street to street
Shall weave old England's winding sheet.
Ibid., 'Auguries of Innocence', ll. 115–16

77 Every night and every morn
Some to misery are born.
Every morn and every night
Some are born to sweet delight.
Some are born to sweet delight,
Some are born to endless night.
Ibid., 'Auguries of Innocence', ll. 119–24

78 God appears and God is Light
To those poor souls who dwell in night,
But does a human form display
To those who dwell in realms of day.
Ibid., 'Auguries of Innocence', ll. 129–32. Closing lines of poem.

79 O why was I born with a different face?
Why was I not born like the rest of my race?
When I look, each one starts! when I speak, I
   offend;
Then I'm silent and passive and lose every friend.
Letter, 16 August 1803, publ. in *The Letters of William Blake*
(ed. Geoffrey Keynes, 1956). The first line also appears in
'Mary', st. 6, a poem from the *Pickering Manuscript* (c. 1803).

80 And did those feet in ancient time
Walk upon England's mountains green?
And was the holy Lamb of God
On England's pleasant pastures seen?
And did the countenance divine
Shine forth upon our clouded hills?
And was Jerusalem builded here
Among these dark Satanic mills?
Bring me my bow of burning gold:
Bring me my arrows of desire:
Bring me my spear: O clouds unfold!
Bring me my chariot of fire.
I will not cease from mental fight,
Nor shall my sword sleep in my hand,
Till we have built Jerusalem
In England's green and pleasant land.
Milton, plate 1, Preface (1804–8). The lines are better known
as 'Jerusalem', set to music by Hubert Parry in 1916.

81 O God, protect me from my friends, that they
   have not power over me.
Thou hast given me power to protect myself from
   thy bitterest enemies.
Ibid., bk 1, plate 9. Palamabron's prayer has numerous antecedents in diverse languages: ELIZABETH I is quoted: 'There
is an Italian proverb which saith, "From my enemy let me
defend myself; but from a pretensed friend, good Lord deliver
me."' (*Elizabeth I and Her Parliament*, ch. 4, 1957, by J. E. Neale)

82 Poetry fettered fetters the human race. Nations
are destroyed or flourish in proportion as their
poetry, painting and music are destroyed or
flourish! The primeval state of man was wisdom, art
and science.
Jerusalem, plate 3: 'To the Public' (1804–20)

83 He who would do good to another must do it in
   minute particulars:
General good is the plea of the scoundrel,
   hypocrite, and flatterer,
For art and science cannot exist but in minutely
   organized particulars.
Ibid., ch. 3, plate 55. See EDMUND BURKE 13, to which Blake
may have been referring.

84 What is a wife and what is a harlot? What is a
   church and what
Is a theatre? are they two and not one? can they
   exist separate?
Are not religion and politics the same thing?
   Brotherhood is religion,
O demonstrations of reason dividing families in
   cruelty and pride!
Ibid., ch. 3, plate 57. The words of the 'great voice of the
Atlantic . . . Weeping over his children'.

85 Embraces are cominglings from the head even
   to the feet,
And not a pompous high priest entering by a
   secret place.
Ibid., ch. 3, plate 69

86 England! awake! awake! awake!
Jerusalem thy sister calls!
Why wilt thou sleep the sleep of death,
And close her from thy ancient walls?
Ibid., ch. 3, plate 77: 'To the Christians'

87 Degrade first the arts if you'd mankind degrade.
Annotations to JOSHUA REYNOLDS's *Discourses* (c. 1808),
publ. in *Complete Writings* (ed. Geoffrey Keynes, 1957). The
'Advice of the Popes who succeeded the Age of Rafael'.

88 The foundation of empire is art and science.
Remove them or degrade them, and the empire is
no more. Empire follows art and not vice versa as
Englishmen suppose.
Annotations to JOSHUA REYNOLDS's *Discourses*, ibid.

89 To generalize is to be an idiot. To particularize
is the alone distinction of merit. General knowledges are those knowledges that idiots possess.
Annotations to JOSHUA REYNOLDS's *Discourses*, ibid. Commenting on a biographical note describing Reynolds as a
'great generalizer'.

90 Thy friendship oft has made my heart to ache:
Do be my enemy for friendship's sake.

Manuscript Notebook (1808–11), no. 39, publ. in *Complete Writings* (ed. Geoffrey Keynes, 1957). Addressed to Blake's patron William Hayley.

91 The errors of a wise man make your rule
Rather than the perfections of a fool.

Ibid., no. 61

92 Great things are done when men and
    mountains meet;
This is not done by jostling in the street.

Ibid., no. 64

93 Men are admitted into Heaven not because they have curbed and governed their passions or have no passions, but because they have cultivated their understandings. The treasures of Heaven are not negations of passion, but realities of intellect, from which all the passions emanate uncurbed in their eternal glory. The fool shall not enter into Heaven let him be ever so holy. Holiness is not the price of entrance into Heaven.

A Vision of the Last Judgment (1810), from the Notebook, publ. in *Complete Writings* (ed. Geoffrey Keynes, 1957)

94 Thinking as I do that the Creator of this world is a very cruel being, and being a worshipper of Christ, I cannot help saying: 'the Son, O how unlike the Father!' First God Almighty comes with a thump on the head. Then Jesus Christ comes with a balm to heal it.

A Vision of the Last Judgment, ibid.

95 'What,' it will be questioned, 'When the sun rises, do you not see a round disc of fire somewhat like a guinea?' O no, no, I see an innumerable company of the heavenly host crying 'Holy, Holy, Holy is the Lord God Almighty.'

A Vision of the Last Judgment, ibid. See BIBLE, OLD TESTAMENT: ISAIAH 14.

96 The vision of Christ that thou dost see
Is my vision's greatest enemy:
Thine has a great hook nose like thine
Mine has a snub nose like to mine.

The Everlasting Gospel, sect. a, ll. 1–4 from the *Notebook* (c. 1818), published in *Complete Writings* (ed. Geoffrey Keynes, 1957)

97 Both read the Bible day and night,
But thou read'st black where I read white.

The Everlasting Gospel, sect. a, ll. 13–14, ibid.

98 This life's dim windows of the soul
Distorts the heavens from pole to pole
And leads you to believe a lie
When you see with, not through, the eye.

The Everlasting Gospel, sect. d, ll. 103–6, ibid.

99 I am sure this Jesus will not do
Either for Englishman or Jew.

The Everlasting Gospel, sect. f, ll. 1–2, ibid.

100 Truly, my Satan, thou art but a dunce,
And dost not know the garment from the man.
Every harlot was a virgin once.

The Gates of Paradise, Epilogue, ll. 1–3 (c. 1818)

101 The Classics! It is the Classics, and not Goths nor monks, that desolate Europe with wars.

On Homer's Poetry and On Virgil (etched c. 1820), publ. in *Complete Writings* (ed. Geoffrey Keynes, 1957)

102 The Goddess Fortune is the devil's servant, ready to kiss any one's arse.

Notes on Illustrations to Dante, no. 16, 'The Goddess Fortune' (1825–7)

103 God keep me from the divinity of yes and no too, the yea nay creeping Jesus, from supposing up and down to be the same thing as all experimentalists must suppose.

Letter, 12 April 1827, publ. in *The Letters of William Blake* (ed. Geoffrey Keynes, 1956)

Maurice Blanchot
(1907–2003)
French literary theorist

After wartime renunciation of Fascism, he became a man of letters. His critical works include The Space of Literature *(1955) and his novels* Death Sentence *(1948) and* The Last Man *(1957).*

1 To write is to make oneself the echo of what cannot cease speaking.

The Space of Literature, ch. 1, 'The Essential Solitude' (1955, transl. 1982)

Alan Bleasdale
(b. 1946)
British playwright and novelist

He won a large audience on TV for the series The Boys from the Blackstuff *(1982) and* GBH *(1991), both set in his native Liverpool, and for his adaptation of* Oliver Twist *(1999).*

1 Gizza job, go on, gizzit!

Yosser Hughes, in *The Boys from the Blackstuff* (TV series, 1983). The catchphrase is usually quoted, 'gissa job!'

Hans Blix

(b. 1928)

Swedish politician and diplomat

He became Sweden's Foreign Minister in 1978 and was Director General of the International Atomic Energy Agency 1981–97, when he was in charge of overseeing inspections of Iraq's nuclear programme. He returned to inspect in 2002–3.

1 We have now been there for some two months and been covering the country in ever wider sweeps and we haven't found any smoking guns.
Guardian 10 January 2003. The phrase 'smoking gun', referring to incriminating evidence, was popularized when the Watergate tapes were made public.

Karen Blixen

See ISAK DINESEN

Alexander Blok

(1880–1921)

Russian poet

Considered the leading Russian Symbolist, he took the 1917 Revolution as inspiration for his masterpiece The Twelve *(1918), though he later became disillusioned with the Bolshevik régime.* TROTSKY *commented: 'Certainly Blok was not one of us, but he came towards us. And that is what broke him.'*

1 O Russia! O my wife! Our long and narrow
Road lies clear though distressed.
Our road with an old Tatar freedom's arrow
Has deeply pierced our breast.
On the Field of Kulikovo, st. 2 (1908, transl. 1966). Recalling the Russian victory over the Tatars in 1380.

2 Ah, a bitter bitterness,
A sweet life we've won,
With a tattered overcoat
And an Austrian gun.
The Twelve, sect. 3 (1918, transl. 1948). The poem describes the experiences of twelve guards during the October Revolution.

3 Like the dog, stands the bourgeois, hungry,
A silent question to the sky;
The old world, like a homeless mongrel,
With tail between its legs stands by.
Ibid., sect. 9

4 On they march with sovereign tread,
With a starving dog behind,
With a blood-red flag ahead –
In the storm where none can see,
From the rifle bullets free,
Gently walking on the snow,

Where like pearls the snowflakes glow,
Marches rose-crowned in the van
Jesus Christ, the Son of Man.
Ibid., sect. 12. Last lines of poem.

Allan Bloom

(1930–92)

US academic and author

A Professor of Philosophy and Political Science whose writings have stoked debate about the state of America, he called himself 'the corrosive force that appeals to liberals'. The Closing of the American Mind (1987) is a critique of the education system.

1 Only Socrates knew, after a lifetime of unceasing labor, that he was ignorant. Now every high-school student knows that. How did it become so easy?
The Closing of the American Mind, Introduction (1987)

2 The most important function of the university in an age of reason is to protect reason from itself.
Ibid., pt 3, 'From Socrates' *Apology* to Heidegger's *Rektoratsrede'* (1987)

Harold Bloom

(b. 1930)

US literary critic

He has taught continuously at Yale University since 1955 while retaining his independence of the academic world, which he sees as dominated 'by fools, knaves, charlatans and bureaucrats'.

1 The Anxiety of Influence.
Title of book (1973). Bloom's most influential work used Freudian concepts to postulate an unconscious literary battle between generations of poets and authors.

Léon Blum

(1872–1950)

French statesman

The first Socialist (and the first Jewish) prime minister of France, he presided over the Popular Front coalition government in 1936–7, was imprisoned during the Second World War, and was premier again in 1946 and 1948.

1 When a woman is twenty, a child deforms her; when she is thirty, he preserves her; and when forty, he makes her young again.
On Marriage, ch. 6 (1907)

Robert Bly
(b. 1926)
US poet and author

His magazine The Fifties *(later* The Sixties *and* The Seventies*)
published lesser known European and South American poets.
The first book of his own poetry,* Silence in the Snowy Fields,
appeared in 1962.

1 Every modern male has, lying at the bottom of his
psyche, a large, primitive being covered with hair
down to his feet. Making contact with this Wild Man
is the step the Eighties male or the Nineties male
has yet to take. That bucketing-out process has yet
to begin in our contemporary culture.
Iron John, ch. 1, 'Finding Iron John' (1990)

Ivan Boesky
(b. 1937)
US financier

*The best known of Wall Street arbitrageurs, he was fined $100
million for insider dealing in 1986 and served a prison
sentence.*

1 Greed is all right, by the way ... I think greed is
healthy. You can be greedy and still feel good about
yourself.
Commencement Address, School of Business Administration,
University of California, Berkeley, 18 May 1986. Boesky's
words were later picked up in Oliver Stone's film, *Wall Street*
(1987), spoken by Gordon Gekko (played by MICHAEL DOUG-
LAS): 'Greed is good. Greed is right. Greed clarifies, cuts
through, and captures. Greed has marked the upward surge
of mankind.' Boesky himself was later convicted of conspiring
to file false documents with the federal government, involving insider trading violations.

Boethius
(c. 475–524)
Roman philosopher and statesman

*Serving under Emperor Theodoric, he was falsely accused of
treason and imprisoned. While awaiting his execution, he
wrote* The Consolation of Philosophy, *which became one of
the most widely read books in medieval times. He was also an
authority on music.*

1 Of all fortune's blows, the unhappiest aspect of
misfortune is to have known happiness.
De Consolatione Philosophiae, bk 2, ch. 4. See also DANTE 11.

Louise Bogan
(1897–1970)
US poet and critic

Poetry editor for the New Yorker *(1931–69), she published six
volumes of her own verse, as well as the highly regarded*
Achievement in American Poetry 1900–1950 *(1951).*

1 Women have no wilderness in them,
They are provident instead,
Content in the tight hot cell of their hearts
To eat dusty bread.
'Women', st. 1, publ. in *Body of this Death* (1923)

2 The intellectual is a middle-class product; if he is
not born into the class he must soon insert himself
into it, in order to exist. He is the fine nervous flower
of the bourgeoisie.
'Some Notes on Popular and Unpopular Art' (1943), repr. in
Selected Criticism: Poetry and Prose (1955)

Humphrey Bogart
(1899–1957)
US screen actor

He gave birth to the 'Bogie' cult with High Sierra *and* The
Maltese Falcon *(both 1941). With his fourth wife* LAUREN
BACALL, *he co-starred in* To Have and Have Not *(1944) and*
The Big Sleep *(1946). See also* INGRID BERGMAN 1, RAYMOND
CHANDLER 1.

1 Of all the gin joints in all the towns all over the
world, she walks into mine.
Casablanca (film, 1942, screenplay by Julius Epstein, Philip
Epstein and Howard Koch, from the play *Everybody Goes to
Rick's* by Murray Burnett and Joan Alison; directed by Michael
Curtiz). Spoken by Rick Blaine (Humphrey Bogart).

2 Here's looking at you, kid.
Rick Blaine, ibid. Toast addressed to Ilsa Lund (Ingrid
Bergman).

3 I'm not fighting for anything anymore, except
myself. I'm the only cause I'm interested in.
Rick Blaine, ibid. Bogart's words are echoed in another speech
by him in John Huston's film *Key Largo* (1948), where he says:
'I fight nobody's battles but my own', and also recall a similar
statement by CLARK GABLE as Rhett Butler in *Gone With the
Wind* (1939).

4 I'm no good at being noble, but it doesn't take
much to see that the problems of three little people
don't amount to a hill o' beans in this crazy world.
Someday you'll understand that.
Rick Blaine, ibid. Spoken in the final scenes of the film to Ilsa
Lund (Ingrid Bergman), escaping from Casablanca with her
husband.

5 Louis, I think this is the beginning of a beautiful friendship.
Ibid. Addressed to Cpt. Louis Renault (Claude Rains) in the film's closing line.

6 Tennis, anyone?
Attributed sole line in first speaking part for the theatre, though denied by Bogart. In contrast to his later cynical film roles, his early parts on stage were as romantic leads; as critic David Thomson commented, 'He was from the upper classes, and he usually played young men who asked girls for tennis.'

Niels Bohr
(1885–1962)
Danish physicist

He founded and directed the Institute of Theoretical Physics in Copenhagen 1920–62, produced a new model of atomic structure, and contributed to the development of quantum physics.

1 An expert is a man who has made all the mistakes which can be made in a very narrow field.
Quoted in *The Harvest of a Quiet Eye* (1977) by Alan L. Mackay

Nicolas Boileau-Despréaux
(1636–1711)
French poet and critic

A champion of classical standards in drama and poetry, he became known for his satirical attacks on public figures, particularly the clergy. L'Art poétique (1674) embodies his critical precepts.

1 Rash author, 'tis a vain presumptuous crime
To undertake the sacred art of rhyme.
L'Art poétique, canto 1, ll. 1–2 (1674; *The Art of Poetry*)

2 No one who cannot limit himself has ever been able to write.
Ibid., canto 1, l. 63

3 At last came Malherbe, the first in France
To give to verse a smooth cadence.
Ibid., canto 1, ll. 131–2. François Malherbe (1555–1628) exercised a profound influence on French verse, initiating a reaction against the florid Baroque poetry of his day in favour of a clear, neo-classical style.

4 However big the fool, there is always a bigger fool to admire him.
Ibid., canto 1, l. 232

5 Of every four words I write, I strike out three.
Satire, no. 2, l. 53 (1666)

6 Gold lends a touch of beauty even to the ugly.
Ibid., no. 8, l. 209

7 But satire, ever moral, ever new,
Delights the reader, and instructs him too.
Ibid., no. 8, ll. 257–8

Henry St. John, Viscount Bolingbroke
(1678–1751)
English politician and author

A passionate Tory propagandist who became a government minister in 1710, he was exiled 1715–25 and devoted much of the remainder of his life to combating ROBERT WALPOLE. His historical and philosophical writings include Reflections upon Exile *(1716).*

1 Truth lies within a little and certain compass, but error is immense.
Reflections Upon Exile (1716)

2 The greatest art of a politician is to render vice serviceable to the cause of virtue.
Remark, *c.* 1728, quoted in *Anecdotes, Observations, and Characters, of Books and Men*, sect. 1 (1820) by Joseph Spence

3 Faction is to party what the superlative is to the positive: party is a political evil and faction is the worst of all parties.
The Patriot King (written 1738, publ. 1749)

4 They maintained the dignity of history.
On the Study and Use of History, Letter 5 (1752). Referring to THUCYDIDES and XENOPHON.

5 Nations, like men, have their infancy.
Ibid., Letter 5

Robert Bolt
(1924–95)
British playwright

He achieved major success with his play A Man for All Seasons *(1960), and wrote the screenplay for the film (1967). He also wrote the screenplays of* Lawrence of Arabia *(1962),* Dr Zhivago *(1965) and* The Mission *(1986).*

1 Morality's *not* practical. Morality's a gesture. A complicated gesture learned from books.
A Man for All Seasons, Act 2 (1960).Spoken by Sir Thomas More. See also ROBERT WHITTINGTON 1.

2 The nobility of England, my lord, would have snored through the Sermon on the Mount.
Sir Thomas More, ibid., Act 2

3 The law is not a 'light' for you or any man to see by; the law is not an instrument of any kind. The

law is a causeway upon which so long as he keeps to it a citizen may walk safely.
Sir Thomas More, ibid., Act 2

Napoléon Bonaparte
See NAPOLEON I

The Book of Common Prayer
(1662)

The official service book of the Church of England and the Anglican communion was first produced under Archbishop Thomas Cranmer in 1549 and made compulsory by the Act of Uniformity in the same year. A revision was authorized in 1662, which is still used today alongside modern alternatives. See also THE MISSAL.

1 It hath been the wisdom of the Church of England, ever since the first compiling of her Public Liturgy, to keep the mean between the two extremes, of too much stiffness in refusing, and of too much easiness in admitting any variation from it.
The Preface. Opening words of Preface.

2 There was never any thing by the wit of man so well devised, or so sure established, which in continuance of time hath not been corrupted.
Concerning the Service of the Church

3 Dearly beloved brethren, the Scripture moveth us in sundry places to acknowledge and confess our manifold sins and wickedness; and that we should not dissemble nor cloke them before the face of Almighty God our heavenly Father; but confess them with an humble, lowly, penitent, and obedient heart.
Morning Prayer. Also said at Evening Prayer.

4 We have erred and strayed from thy ways like lost sheep, We have followed too much the devices and desires of our own hearts.
Ibid., 'General Confession'. Also said at Evening Prayer. P. D. JAMES took the title of her crime novel *Devices and Desires* (1989) from this passage.

5 We have left undone those things which we ought to have done, And we have done those things which we ought not to have done. And there is no health in us.
Ibid., 'General Confession'. Also said at Evening Prayer.

6 O Lord, have mercy upon us miserable offenders; Spare thou them, O God, which confess their faults, Restore thou them that are penitent, According to thy promises declared unto mankind in Christ Jesu

our Lord: And grant, O most merciful Father, for his sake, That we may hereafter live a godly, righteous, and sober life.
Ibid., 'General Confession'. Also said at Evening Prayer.

7 And forgive us our trespasses, As we forgive them that trespass against us.
Ibid., 'The Lord's Prayer'. Also said at Evening Prayer. For the rest of the Lord's Prayer, see BIBLE, NEW TESTAMENT: MATTHEW 38.

8 Glory be to the Father, and to the Son: and to the Holy Ghost;
As it was in the beginning, is now, and ever shall be: world without end. Amen.
Ibid., 'Gloria Patri'

9 We praise thee, O God: we acknowledge thee to be the Lord.
All the earth doth worship thee: the Father everlasting.
To thee all Angels cry aloud: the Heavens and all the Powers therein.
To thee Cherubin, and Seraphin: continually do cry,
Holy, Holy, Holy: Lord God of Sabaoth.
Ibid., 'Te Deum Laudamus'. Traditionally sung on occasions of public rejoicing, the Latin hymn of thanksgiving was said to have been improvised antiphonally by St Ambrose and ST AUGUSTINE at the latter's baptism, though scholars in the 20th century have attributed it to the Greek bishop and theologian Nicetas (died c. 414).

10 The noble army of Martyrs: praise thee.
Ibid., 'Te Deum Laudamus'

11 When thou hadst overcome the sharpness of death: thou didst open the kingdom of heaven to all believers.
Ibid., 'Te Deum Laudamus'

12 O all ye Works of the Lord, bless ye the Lord: praise him, and magnify him for ever.
Ibid., 'Benedicite, Omnia Opera'

13 O all ye Green Things upon the Earth, bless ye the Lord: praise him, and magnify him for ever.
Ibid., 'Benedicite, Omnia Opera'

14 O ye Seas and Floods, bless ye the Lord: praise him, and magnify him for ever.
O ye Whales, and all that move in the Waters, bless ye the Lord: praise him, and magnify him for ever.
Ibid., 'Benedicite, Omnia Opera'

15 I believe in God the Father Almighty, Maker of heaven and earth:

And in Jesus Christ his only Son our Lord, Who was conceived by the Holy Ghost, Born of the Virgin Mary, Suffered under Pontius Pilate, Was crucified, dead, and buried: He descended into hell; The third day he rose again from the dead; He ascended into heaven, And sitteth on the right hand of God the Father Almighty; From thence he shall come to judge the quick and the dead.

I believe in the Holy Ghost; The holy Catholic Church; The Communion of Saints; The Forgiveness of sins; The Resurrection of the body, And the life everlasting. Amen.

Ibid., 'The Apostles' Creed'. Also said at Evening Prayer.

16 Give peace in our time, O Lord.

Ibid., versicle. Also said at Evening Prayer.

17 O God, make clean our hearts within us.

Ibid., versicle. Also said at Evening Prayer.

18 O God, who art the author of peace and lover of concord, in knowledge of whom standeth our eternal life, whose service is perfect freedom: Defend us thy humble servants in all assaults of our enemies.

Ibid., 'Second Collect, for Peace'

19 Grant that this day we fall into no sin, neither run into any kind of danger.

Ibid., 'Third Collect, for Grace'

20 In Quires and Places where they sing, here followeth the Anthem.

Ibid., rubric

21 Endue her plenteously with heavenly gifts; grant her in health and wealth long to live.

Ibid., 'A Prayer for the Queen's Majesty'. Also said at Evening Prayer.

22 Almighty God, the fountain of all goodness.

Ibid., 'A Prayer for the Royal Family'. Also said at Evening Prayer.

23 Pour upon them the continual dew of thy blessing.

Ibid., 'A Prayer for the Clergy and People'. Also said at Evening Prayer.

24 Almighty God, who hast given us grace at this time with one accord to make our common supplications unto thee; and dost promise that when two or three are gathered together in thy Name thou wilt grant their requests: Fulfil now, O Lord, the desires and petitions of thy servants, as may be most expedient for them.

Ibid., 'A Prayer of Saint Chrysostom'. Also said at Evening Prayer. See BIBLE, NEW TESTAMENT, MATTHEW 118.

25 O God, from whom all holy desires, all good counsels, and all just works do proceed: Give unto thy servants that peace which the world cannot give.

Evening Prayer, 'The Second Collect'

26 Lighten our darkness, we beseech thee, O Lord; and by thy great mercy defend us from all perils and dangers of this night.

Evening Prayer, 'The Third Collect, for Aid against all Perils'

27 Whosoever will be saved: before all things it is necessary that he hold the Catholic Faith.

At Morning Prayer, 'Quicunque vult'. The Athanasian Creed, attributed to Athanasius, bishop of Alexandria (d. 373), but probably dating from later.

28 We worship one God in Trinity, and Trinity in Unity;

Neither confounding the Persons: nor dividing the Substance.

Ibid., 'Quicunque vult'

29 There are not three incomprehensibles, nor three uncreated: but one uncreated, and one incomprehensible.

Ibid., 'Quicunque vult'

30 So the Father is God, the Son is God: and the Holy Ghost is God.

And yet they are not three Gods: but one God.

Ibid., 'Quicunque vult'

31 Perfect God, and perfect Man: of a reasonable soul and human flesh subsisting;

Equal to the Father, as touching his Godhead: and inferior to the Father, as touching his Manhood.

Ibid., 'Quicunque vult'

32 Have mercy upon us miserable sinners.

The Litany

33 Remember not, Lord, our offences, nor the offences of our forefathers; neither take thou vengeance of our sins: spare us, good Lord, spare thy people, whom thou hast redeemed with thy most precious blood, and be not angry with us for ever.

Ibid.

34 From all blindness of heart; from pride, vain-glory, and hypocrisy; from envy, hatred, and malice, and from all uncharitableness,

Good Lord, deliver us.

Ibid.

35 From fornication, and all other deadly sin; and from all the deceits of the world, the flesh, and the devil,

Good Lord, deliver us.

Ibid.

36 From battle and murder, and from sudden death,

Good Lord, deliver us.

Ibid.

37 That it may please thee to give and preserve to our use the kindly fruits of the earth, so as in due time we may enjoy them,

We beseech thee to hear us, good Lord.

Ibid.

38 Receive our humble petitions

Prayers and Thanksgivings, Prayer

39 We humbly beseech thee for all sorts and conditions of men; that thou wouldest be pleased to make thy ways known unto them, thy saving health unto all nations.

Ibid., 'A Collect or Prayer for all Conditions of Men'

40 That all who profess and call themselves Christians may be led into the way of truth.

Ibid., 'A Collect or Prayer for all Conditions of Men'

41 We commend to thy fatherly goodness all those, who are any ways afflicted or distressed in mind, body, or estate; that it may please thee to comfort and relieve them, according to their several necessities, giving them patience under their sufferings, and a happy issue out of all their afflictions.

Ibid., 'A Collect or Prayer for all Conditions of Men'

42 We bless thee for our creation, preservation, and all the blessings of this life; but above all for thine inestimable love in the redemption of the world by our Lord Jesus Christ, for the means of grace, and for the hope of glory.

Thanksgivings, 'A General Thanksgiving'

43 Give us grace that we may cast away the works of darkness, and put upon us the armour of light, now in the time of this mortal life.

Collects, 'The First Sunday in Advent'

44 Blessed Lord, who hast caused all holy Scriptures to be written for our learning: Grant that we may in such wise hear them, read, mark, learn, and inwardly digest them.

Ibid., 'The Second Sunday in Advent'

45 Have mercy upon all Jews, Turks, Infidels, and Heretics, and take from them all ignorance, hardness of heart, and contempt of thy word; and so fetch them home, blessed Lord, to thy flock, that they may be saved among the remnant of the true Israelites.

Ibid., 'Good Friday'

46 Grant, we beseech thee, merciful Lord, to thy faithful people pardon and peace, that they may be cleansed from all their sins, and serve thee with a quiet mind.

Ibid., 'The Twenty-first Sunday after Trinity'

47 Lord, we beseech thee to keep thy household the Church in continual godliness.

Ibid., 'The Twenty-second Sunday after Trinity'

48 Stir up, we beseech thee, O Lord, the wills of thy faithful people; that they, plenteously bringing forth the fruit of good works, may of thee be plenteously rewarded.

Ibid., 'The Twenty-fifth Sunday after Trinity'. The last Sunday before Advent (five weeks before Christmas) is known as 'Stir-Up Sunday' after this collect, and is the customary day for preparing Christmas puddings.

49 Almighty God, unto whom all hearts be open, all desires known, and from whom no secrets are hid: Cleanse the thoughts of our hearts by the inspiration of thy Holy Spirit, that we may perfectly love thee, and worthily magnify thy holy Name.

Holy Communion, 'The Collect'

50 I the Lord thy God am a jealous God, and visit the sins of the fathers upon the children unto the third and fourth generation of them that hate me.

Ibid., 'Ten Commandments'

51 I believe in one God the Father Almighty, Maker of heaven and earth, And of all things visible and invisible:

And in one Lord Jesus Christ, the only-begotten Son of God, Begotten of his Father before all worlds, God of God, Light of Light, Very God of very God, Begotten, not made, Being of one substance with the Father, By whom all things were made.

Ibid., 'The Nicene Creed'. The so-called Nicene Creed was first thought to have been an enlargement of the Creed of Nicaea (325), but modern scholarship suggests that it was an independent document issued at the Council of Constantinople in 381, based on a pre-existing baptismal creed.

52 And I believe in the Holy Ghost, The Lord and giver of life, Who proceedeth from the Father and the Son, Who with the Father and the Son together is worshipped and glorified, Who spake by the Prophets. And I believe in one Catholic and Apostolic Church.
Ibid., 'The Nicene Creed'. The *Filioque* clause' ('and the son') has always been rejected by the Eastern churches as an unauthorized insertion and a theological error.

53 Let us pray for the whole state of Christ's Church Militant here in earth.
Ibid., 'Prayer for the Church Militant'

54 And we most humbly beseech thee of thy goodness, O Lord, to comfort and succour all them, who in this transitory life are in trouble, sorrow, need, sickness, or any other adversity.
Ibid., 'Prayer for the Church Militant'

55 That under her [the Queen] we may be godly and quietly governed: And grant unto her whole Council, and to all that are put in authority under her, that they may truly and indifferently minister justice.
Ibid., 'Prayer for the Church Militant'

56 Draw near with faith, and take this holy Sacrament to your comfort; and make your humble confession to Almighty God, meekly kneeling upon your knees.
Ibid., 'The Invitation'

57 We do earnestly repent, And are heartily sorry for these our misdoings; The remembrance of them is grievous unto us; The burden of them is intolerable.
Ibid., 'General Confession'

58 Hear what comfortable words our Saviour Christ saith unto all that truly turn to him.
Ibid., preamble to 'Comfortable Words'

59 Lift up your hearts.
Ibid., versicle

60 It is meet and right so to do.
Ibid., response

61 It is very meet, right, and our bounden duty, that we should at all times and in all places, give thanks unto thee, O Lord, Holy Father, Almighty, Everlasting God.
Ibid., response

62 Almighty God, our heavenly Father, who of thy tender mercy didst give thine only Son Jesus Christ

to suffer death upon the cross for our redemption; who made there (by his one oblation of himself once offered) a full, perfect, and sufficient sacrifice, oblation, and satisfaction, for the sins of the whole world.
Ibid., 'Prayer of Consecration'

63 Who, in the same night that he was betrayed, took Bread; and, when he had given thanks, he brake it, and gave it to his disciples, saying, Take, eat; this is my Body which is given for you: Do this in remembrance of me. Likewise after supper he took the Cup; and, when he had given thanks, he gave it to them, saying, Drink ye all of this; for this is my Blood of the New Testament, which is shed for you and for many for the remission of sins: Do this, as oft as ye shall drink it, in remembrance of me.
Ibid., 'Prayer of Consecration'

64 Although we be unworthy, through our manifold sins, to offer unto thee any sacrifice, yet we beseech thee to accept this our bounden duty and service; not weighing our merits, but pardoning our offences.
Ibid., 'Prayer of Oblation'

65 We are very members incorporate in the mystical body of thy Son, which is the blessed company of all faithful people; and are also heirs through hope of thy everlasting kingdom.
Ibid., 'Second Prayer of Oblation'

66 Glory be to God on high, and in earth peace, good will towards men. We praise thee, we bless thee, we worship thee, we glorify thee, we give thanks to thee for thy great glory, O Lord God heavenly King, God the Father Almighty.
Ibid., 'Gloria'

67 The peace of God, which passeth all understanding, keep your hearts and minds in the knowledge and love of God, and of his Son Jesus Christ our Lord.
Ibid., blessing. See also BIBLE, NEW TESTAMENT: PHILIPPIANS 9.

68 Dost thou, in the name of this Child, renounce the devil and all his works, the vain pomp and glory of the world, with all covetous desires of the same, and the carnal desires of the flesh, so that thou wilt not follow nor be led by them?
Public Baptism of Infants. To the godparents.

69 O merciful God, grant that the old Adam in this

Child may be so buried, that the new man may be raised up in him.
Public Baptism of Infants

70 He shall not be ashamed to confess the faith of Christ crucified, and manfully to fight under his banner against sin, the world, and the devil.
Ibid.

71 An outward and visible sign of an inward and spiritual grace given unto us.
A Catechism. The meaning of the word 'sacrament'.

72 Children being now come to the years of discretion.
The Order of Confirmation, Preface

73 Lord, hear our prayers.
And let our cry come unto thee.
The Order of Confirmation, versicle and response

74 If any of you know cause, or just impediment, why these two persons should not be joined together in holy Matrimony, ye are to declare it. This is the first [second, or third] time of asking.
Solemnization of Matrimony, The Banns of Marriage

75 Dearly beloved, we are gathered together here in the sight of God, and in the face of this Congregation, to join together this man and this woman in holy Matrimony.
Ibid., Exhortation

76 Which holy estate Christ adorned and beautified with his presence, and first miracle that he wrought, in Cana of Galilee; and is commended of Saint Paul to be honourable among all men: and therefore is not by any to be enterprised, nor taken in hand, unadvisedly, lightly, or wantonly, to satisfy men's carnal lusts and appetites, like brute beasts that have no understanding; but reverently, discreetly, advisedly, soberly, and in the fear of God; duly considering the causes for which Matrimony was ordained.
Ibid., Exhortation

77 First, It was ordained for the procreation of children, to be brought up in the fear and nurture of the Lord, and to the praise of his holy Name.
Ibid., Exhortation

78 Secondly, It was ordained for a remedy against sin, and to avoid fornication; that such persons as have not the gift of continency might marry, and keep themselves undefiled members of Christ's body.
Ibid., Exhortation

79 Thirdly, It was ordained for the mutual society, help, and comfort, that the one ought to have of the other, both in prosperity and adversity.
Ibid., Exhortation

80 Therefore if any man can shew any just cause, why they may not lawfully be joined together, let him now speak, or else hereafter for ever hold his peace.
Ibid., Exhortation

81 Wilt thou have this woman to thy wedded wife, to live together after God's ordinance in the holy estate of Matrimony? Wilt thou love her, comfort her, honour, and keep her, in sickness and in health; and, forsaking all other, keep thee only unto her, so long as ye both shall live?
Ibid., Betrothal

82 Wilt thou have this man to thy wedded husband, to live together after God's ordinance in the holy estate of Matrimony? Wilt thou obey him, and serve him, love, honour, and keep him, in sickness and in health; and, forsaking all other, keep thee only unto him, so long as ye both shall live?
Ibid., Betrothal

83 I *N*. take thee *N*. to my wedded husband, to have and to hold from this day forward, for better for worse, for richer for poorer, in sickness and in health, to love, cherish, and to obey, till death us do part, according to God's holy ordinance; and thereto I give thee my troth.
Ibid., Betrothal. 'N' refers to 'name', standing for the Latin *nomen*. The groom promises only 'to love and to cherish' and ends with the words 'I plight thee my troth.'

84 With this ring I thee wed, with my body I thee worship, and with all my worldly goods I thee endow.
Ibid., Wedding

85 Those whom God hath joined together let no man put asunder.
Ibid., Priest's Declaration. Taken from the words of Jesus: see
BIBLE, NEW TESTAMENT: MATTHEW 120.

86 I pronounce that they be man and wife together.
Ibid., Minister's Declaration

87 Peace be to this house, and to all that dwell in it.
The Visitation of the Sick

88 Man that is born of woman hath but a short time to live, and is full of misery. He cometh up, and is cut down, like a flower; he fleeth as it were a shadow, and never continueth in one stay.
The Burial of the Dead. The words are derived from the Old Testament: see BIBLE, OLD TESTAMENT: JOB 25.

89 In the midst of life we are in death.
Ibid.

90 We therefore commit his body to the ground; earth to earth, ashes to ashes, dust to dust; in sure and certain hope of the Resurrection to eternal life.
Ibid., Interment

91 We therefore commit his body to the deep, to be turned into corruption, looking for the resurrection of the body, (when the Sea shall give up her dead,) and the life of the world to come.
Forms of Prayer to be Used at Sea, 'At the Burial of their Dead at Sea'

92 Come, Holy Ghost, our souls inspire,
And lighten with celestial fire.
Thou the anointing Spirit art,
Who dost thy seven-fold gifts impart.
The Ordering of Priests, 'Veni, Creator Spiritus'

93 Holy Scripture containeth all things necessary to salvation.
Articles of Religion, no. 6

94 The laws of the Realm may punish Christian men with death, for heinous and grievous offences.
Ibid., no. 37

95 It is lawful for Christian men, at the commandment of the Magistrate, to wear weapons, and serve in the wars.
Ibid., no. 37

96 The Lord almighty grant us a quiet night and a perfect end.
Compline (added to Book of Common Prayer in 1928)

97 Keep me as the apple of an eye
Hide me under the shadow of thy wings.
Ibid., responsary

98 Preserve us O Lord while waking, and guard us while sleeping, that awake we may watch with Christ, and asleep we may rest in peace.
Ibid.

99 Be present, O merciful God, and protect us through the silent hours of this night, so that we who are wearied by the changes and chances of this fleeting world, may repose upon thy eternal changelessness; through Jesus Christ our Lord.
Ibid.

Daniel J. Boorstin
(1914–2004)
US historian

Professor of American History at Chicago University 1944–69, he authored A History of the United States *(1980) and* The Americans *trilogy (1965–73) among other works. He was Librarian of Congress 1975–87.*

1 The celebrity is a person who is known for his well-knownness.
The Image, ch. 2 (1961)

2 We read advertisements ... to discover and enlarge our desires. We are always ready – even eager – to discover, from the announcement of a new product, what we have all along wanted without really knowing it.
Ibid., ch. 5

John Wilkes Booth
(1838–65)
US actor and assassin

A popular actor of his day, he was a strong suppporter of the Southern cause. He assassinated President ABRAHAM LINCOLN, *and was himself shot after escaping to Virginia.*

1 *Sic semper tyrannis!* The South is avenged.
Quoted in the *New York Times* 15 April 1865. Said to have been his words after shooting President LINCOLN. *Sic semper tyrannis* ('Thus always to tyrants') is the motto of the state of Virginia.

William Booth
(1829–1912)
English evangelist and founder of the Salvation Army

After experiencing a religious conversion at the age of fifteen, he founded the Christian Mission in 1865, which became the Salvation Army in 1878. His wife and children were also prominent in the organization.

1 A population sodden with drink, steeped in vice, eaten up by every social and physical malady, these are the denizens of Darkest England amidst whom my life has been spent.
In Darkest England, and the Way Out, pt 1, ch. 1 (1890)

2 To get a man soundly saved it is not enough to put on him a pair of new breeches, to give him regular work, or even to give him a University edu-

cation. These things are all outside a man, and if the inside remains unchanged you have wasted your labour. You must in some way or other graft upon the man's nature a new nature, which has in it the element of the Divine.

Ibid., pt 1, ch. 5

Jorge Luis Borges
(1899–1986)
Argentinian author

One of the foremost Latin American writers of modern times, he is considered the progenitor of the 'magic realist' school. From 1923 he published poems and essays, and from 1941 collections of stories, notably The Aleph *(1949) and* Dreamtigers *(1960).*

1 I thought that a man can be the enemy of other men, of the moments of other men, but not of a country: not of fireflies, words, gardens, streams of water, sunsets.

Ficciones, 'The Garden of Forking Paths' (1944, transl. 1962)

2 The truth is that we live out our lives putting off all that can be put off; perhaps we all know deep down that we are immortal and that sooner or later all men will do and know all things.

Ibid., 'Funes the Memorious'

3 Like all writers, he [Jaromir Hladik] measured the achievements of others by what they had accomplished, asking of them that they measure him by what he envisaged or planned.

Ibid., 'The Secret Miracle'

4 Universal history is the history of a few metaphors.

Other Inquisitions, 'Pascal's Sphere' (1952)

5 Every writer 'creates' his own precursors. His work modifies our conception of the past, as it will modify the future.

Ibid., 'Kafka and his Precursors'

6 Literature is not exhaustible, for the sufficient and simple reason that a single book is not. A book is not an isolated entity: it is a narration, an axis of innumerable narrations. One literature differs from another, either before or after it, not so much because of the text as for the manner in which it is read.

Ibid., 'For Bernard Shaw'

7 To fall in love is to create a religion that has a fallible god.

Ibid., 'The Meeting in a Dream'

8 Time is the substance from which I am made. Time is a river which carries me along, but I am the river; it is a tiger that devours me, but I am the tiger; it is a fire that consumes me, but I am the fire.

Ibid., 'A New Refutation of Time'

9 Each man is given, in dreams, a little personal eternity which allows him to see the recent past and the near future.

'Nightmares' (1976), publ. in Seven Nights (1980)

10 The Falklands thing was a fight between two bald men over a comb.

Time 14 February 1983

George Borrow
(1803–81)
English traveller and author

He spent five years in Spain and Portugal, as narrated in the two books which made him famous, The Zincali *(1841) and* The Bible in Spain *(1843). In these, and the loosely autobiographical* Lavengro *(1851) and* The Romany Rye *(1857), he described his encounters with Romany culture.*

1 Next to the love of God, the love of country is the best preventive of crime.

The Bible in Spain, ch. 4 (1843)

2 I am invariably of the politics of the people at whose table I sit, or beneath whose roof I sleep.

Ibid., ch. 16

3 If you must commit suicide ... always contrive to do it as decorously as possible; the decencies, whether of life or of death, should never be lost sight of.

Lavengro, ch. 23 (1851). Spoken by an 'elderly individual'.

4 There's night and day, brother, both sweet things; sun, moon, and stars, brother, all sweet things; there's likewise a wind on the heath. Life is very sweet, brother; who would wish to die?

Jasper, ibid., ch. 25

5 I learnt ... to fear God, and to take my own part.

Ibid., ch. 86. The expression of Isopel Berners recurs in the book and in its sequel The Romany Rye (1857).

6 Youth will be served, every dog has his day, and mine has been a fine one.

The landlord, ibid., ch. 92

Pierre Bosquet

(1810–61)

French general

He served in the army for nineteen years in Algeria and in the Crimean War. In 1855 he became a Marshal.

1 *C'est magnifique, mais ce n'est pas la guerre.*
[It is magnificent, but it is not war.]

Quoted in *The Reason Why*, ch. 12 (1953) by Cecil Woodham-Smith. Referring to the charge of the Light Brigade at Balaclava, Crimea, 25 October 1854. DISRAELI told the House of Commons that this military fiasco was 'a feat of chivalry, fiery with consummate courage, and bright with flashing courage'. The London *Times* correspondent, W. H. RUSSELL, called it a 'glorious catastrophe'. See TENNYSON 140–5.

John Collins Bossidy

(1860–1928)

US oculist and Harvard alumnus

He practised as an eye surgeon in Boston, rising to become chief surgeon of the eye department at the City Hospital.

1 And this is good old Boston,
The home of the bean and the cod,
Where the Lowells talk to the Cabots,
And the Cabots talk only to God.

Toast at the Holy Cross College alumni dinner, Harvard University, Cambridge, Massachusetts, 1910

Jacques-Bénigne Bossuet

(1627–1704)

French ecclesiastic and theologian

He was appointed to the Chapel Royal in 1662, and was tutor to the Dauphin. Best known for his funeral orations, he also wrote a number of theological works.

1 *Ah! la perfide Angleterre.*
[Ah! faithless England.]

First sermon on the feast of the Circumcision, in *Oeuvres de Bossuet*, vol. 1 (1816). The words have also been attributed to NAPOLEON.

James Boswell

(1740–95)

Scottish lawyer and author

His best-selling Account of Corsica *(1768) was based on his European travels. In London, he joined the leading literary set. His* Life of Samuel Johnson *(1791) established him as one of the greatest biographers of all time. See* LORD MACAULAY 18.

1 My mind was, as it were, strongly impregnated with the Johnsonian aether.

Life of Samuel Johnson LL.D., 1 July 1763 (1791)

2 I am, I flatter myself, completely a citizen of the world. In my travels through Holland, Germany, Switzerland, Italy, Corsica, France, I never felt myself from home.

Journal entry, 14 August 1773, publ. in *Journal of a Tour to the Hebrides* (ed. Frederick A. Pottle, 1936)

3 I have thought of a pulley to raise me gradually; but that would give me pain, as it would counteract my natural inclination. I would have something that can dissipate the *vis inertiae* and give elasticity to the muscles ... We can heat the body, we can cool it; we can give it tension or relaxation; and surely it is possible to bring it into a state in which rising from bed will not be a pain.

Life of Samuel Johnson LL.D., 19 September 1777 (1791)

4 For my own part I think no innocent species of wit or pleasantry should be suppressed: and that a good pun may be admitted among the smaller excellencies of lively conversation.

Ibid., 19 June 1784

5 I find I *journalize* too tediously. Let me try to abbreviate.

Journal entry, 20 August 1792, publ. in *Boswell: The Great Biographer* (ed. Marlies K. Danziger and Frank Brady, 1989)

Pierre Boulez

(b. 1925)

French composer and conductor

An advocate of the 20th-century repertoire, he was conductor of the New York Philharmonic Orchestra (1971–8) and the BBC Symphony Orchestra (1971–5). His reputation as a composer was established with Le Marteau sans Maître *(1954).*

1 Revolutions are celebrated when they are no longer dangerous.

Guardian 13 January 1989. Referring to the bicentenary celebrations of the French Revolution.

(Sir) Harold Boulton

(1859–1935)

British songwriter and philanthropist

As well as writing songs, he published several song collections. With James Granville he founded the Federation of Working Men's Social Clubs, of which he was President 1895–1930.

1 While the moon her watch is keeping
All through the night;

While the weary world is sleeping,
All through the night;
O'er thy spirit gently stealing,
Visions of delight revealing,
Breathes a pure and holy feeling,
All through the night.
'All Through the Night' (song, 1884). Translated from the Welsh.

2 Speed, bonnie boat, like a bird on the wing,
Onward! the sailors cry;
Carry the lad that's born to be King
Over the sea to Skye.
'Skye Boat Song' (song, 1884)

Francis William Bourdillon
(1852–1921)
English poet and scholar

He edited poems and chronicles from Old French and published thirteen volumes of his own verse. His most famous work is 'The Night Has a Thousand Eyes' (1878).

1 The night has a thousand eyes,
And the day but one;
Yet the light of the bright world dies,
With the dying sun.
The mind has a thousand eyes,
And the heart but one;
Yet the light of a whole life dies,
When love is done.
'The Night Has a Thousand Eyes', publ. in *Among the Flowers* (1878). The words 'Night hath a thousand eyes' have been attributed to JOHN LYLY, though have not been found among his works.

Paul Bourget
(1852–1935)
French novelist and critic

Such novels as Le Disciple *(1889) are distinguished by their psychological insights. He became better known for his works of criticism, for example* Pages de doctrine et de critique *(1912).*

1 One must live the way one thinks or end up thinking the way one has lived.
Le Démon de midi, 'Conclusion' (1914)

Boutros Boutros-Ghali
(b. 1922)
Egyptian politician and diplomat

While Minister of State for Foreign Affairs (1977–91), he was a member of the diplomatic mission that resulted in the Camp David Agreement between Egypt and Israel (1978). He was Secretary-General of the United Nations 1992–6, the first Arab and first African to hold the post.

1 When I have tense relations with my wife, we speak Arabic. When we talk business, then we speak English. And when our relationship is better, then we talk French.
Quoted in the *Mail on Sunday* 15 November 1998

Thomas Bowdler
(1754–1825)
English doctor and editor

He produced a series of edited versions of famous works in a form deemed suitable to be read aloud to families, most notably his Family Shakespeare *(1818). The term* bowdlerize *was current by 1838.*

1 Those expressions are omitted which can not with propriety be read aloud in the family.
Family Shakespeare, Preface (1818)

E. E. Bowen
(1836–1901)
English schoolteacher

Edward Ernest Bowen. He was Master at Harrow School (1859–1901) and wrote on military and theological topics.

1 Forty years on, when afar and asunder
Parted are those who are singing today.
'Forty Years On', written 1872, publ. in *Harrow Songs and Other Verses* (1886). Harrow School song.

2 Forty years on, growing older and older,
Shorter in wind, as in memory long,
Feeble of foot, and rheumatic of shoulder
What will it help you that once you were strong?
Ibid., chorus

Elizabeth Bowen
(1899–1973)
Anglo-Irish novelist

She set her novels and short stories in the milieu she knew best: the country houses of the Anglo-Irish and the homes of London's polite society. The works include The Death of the Heart *(1938) and* The Heat of the Day *(1949).*

1 There is no end to the violations committed by children on children, quietly talking alone.
The House in Paris, pt 1, ch. 2 (1935)

2 Intimacies between women go backwards, begin-

ning with revelations and ending up in small talk without loss of esteem.
The Death of the Heart, pt 2, ch. 1 (1938)

3 Only in a house where one has learnt to be lonely does one have this solicitude for *things*. One's relation to them, the daily seeing or touching, begins to become love, and to lay one open to pain.
Ibid., pt 2, ch. 2

4 The heart may think it knows better: the senses know that absence blots people out. We really have no absent friends. The friend becomes a traitor by breaking, however unwillingly or sadly, out of our own zone: a hard judgment is passed on him, for all the pleas of the heart.
Ibid., pt 2, ch. 2

5 Pity the selfishness of lovers: it is brief, a forlorn hope; it is impossible.
Ibid., pt 2, ch. 4

6 Nobody can be kinder than the narcissist while you react to life in his own terms.
Ibid., pt 3, ch. 3

7 The charm, one might say the genius of memory, is that it is choosy, chancy, and temperamental: it rejects the edifying cathedral and indelibly photographs the small boy outside, chewing a hunk of melon in the dust.
Vogue 15 September 1955

Lord Bowen
(1835–94)
English judge

Charles Synge Christopher Bowen, Baron Bowen of Colwood. He achieved fame as junior counsel in the Tichborne Case (1871–4) and rose to become a Lord Justice of Appeal.

1 The man on the Clapham omnibus.
McQuire v. Western Morning News, publ. in *Law Reports* (1903). See WALTER BAGEHOT 21.

David Bowie
(b. 1947)
British rock musician

Originally David Jones. At the height of his success during the glam-rock era of the 1970s, he was known for his theatrical performances and space-age lyrics. His biggest-selling albums include Ziggy Stardust *(1972) and* Heroes *(1977).*

1 Ground control to Major Tom.
'Space Oddity' (song) on the album *Man of Words, Man of Music* (1969)

2 I think that we have created a new kind of person in a way. We have created a child who will be so exposed to the media that he will be lost to his parents by the time he is twelve.
Quoted in *Melody Maker* 22 January 1972

3 Yes, I believe very strongly in fascism ... People have always responded with greater efficiency under a regimental leadership. A liberal wastes time saying, 'Well, now, what ideas have you got?' Show them what to do, for God's sake. If you don't, nothing will get done. I can't stand people just hanging about.
Interview, February 1976, repr. in *Bowie In His Own Words*, 'Politics' (ed. Miles, 1980). Bowie had earlier voiced similar opinions in an interview in August 1975, though he later dismissed his remarks as 'glib, theatrical observations', calling himself 'apolitical'.

4 We can be heroes
Just for one day.
'Heroes' (song) on the album *Heroes* (1977)

(Sir) Maurice Bowra
(1898–1971)
British scholar

Professor of Poetry (1946–51) and Vice Chancellor (1951–4) at Oxford, he wrote widely on classical literature and ancient and modern poetry, as in Greek Lyric Poetry *(1936) and* Poetry and Politics, 1900–1960 *(1966).*

1 I'm a man more dined against than dining.
Quoted in *Summoned by Bells*, ch. 9 (1960) by JOHN BETJEMAN. See WILLIAM SHAKESPEARE: KING LEAR 28.

Boy George
(b. 1961)
British singer

Originally George O'Dowd. With his glamorous looks, cross-dressing and openly gay image, he led his band Culture Club to a string of chart successes in the 1980s.

1 Sex has never been an obsession with me. It's just like eating a bag of crisps. Quite nice, but nothing marvellous.
Quoted in the *Sun* 21 October 1982

2 In England, glamour's in the gutter, it's everywhere, anywhere you want to find it.
Interview in *Smash Hits* 23 December 1982

3 If you have to be in a soap opera try not to get the worst role.
Interview in *The Face* December 1984

William Boyd
(b. 1952)
British novelist

Having spent his early years in Ghana, he often used an African setting for his novels, among which are A Good Man in Africa *(1981) and* Brazzaville Beach *(1990).*

1 We all want to be happy, and we're all going to die ... You might say those are the only two unchallengeably true facts that apply to every human being on this planet.
Stars and Bars, pt 2, ch. 6 (1984). Spoken by Loomis Gage.

Charles Boyer
(1899–1978)
French actor

After moving to Hollywood in 1929, he became known as the screen's 'great lover' playing romantic roles in Mayerling *(1937) and* Algiers *(1938).*

1 Come with me to the Casbah.
Attributed. The words have been ascribed to Boyer in the film *Algiers* (1938), but do not appear in it.

Malcolm Bradbury
(1932–2000)
British author

Closely involved since 1970 with the creative writing programme at the University of East Anglia, he was one of the principal exponents of the satirical 'campus novel', as in Eating People Is Wrong *(1959) and* The History Man *(1975).*

1 I like the English. They have the most rigid code of immorality in the world.
Eating People is Wrong, ch. 5 (1959). Spoken by Herr Schumann.

2 Reading someone else's newspaper is like sleeping with someone else's wife. Nothing seems to be precisely in the right place, and when you find what you are looking for, it is not clear then how to respond to it.
Stepping Westward, bk 1, ch. 1 (1965). Spoken by Dr Jochum.

3 The English are polite by telling lies. The Americans are polite by telling the truth.
Dr Bernard Froelich, ibid., bk 2, ch. 5

4 A conventional good read is usually a bad read, a relaxing bath in what we know already. A true good read is surely an act of innovative creation in which we, the readers, become conspirators.
The Sunday Times 29 November 1987

Ray Bradbury
(b. 1920)
US science fiction author

He took the genre of science fiction to a wider audience in such novels as Fahrenheit 451 *(1953). His short-story collection* The Martian Chronicles *(1950) is accounted a classic.*

1 I don't try to describe the future. I try to prevent it.
Quoted by Arthur C. Clarke in the *Independent* 16 July 1992

Mary Elizabeth Braddon
(1837–1915)
English author

Her first published novel, Lady Audley's Secret *(1862), was an instant success, its mix of crime and intrigue in high society making it a classic of Victorian 'sensation' fiction.*

1 Let any man make a calculation of his existence, subtracting the hours in which he has been *thoroughly* happy – really and entirely at his ease, without one *arrière pensée* to mar his enjoyment – without the most infinitesimal cloud to overshadow the brightness of his horizon. Let him do this, and surely he will laugh in utter bitterness of soul when he sets down the sum of his felicity, and discovers the pitiful smallness of the amount.
Lady Audley's Secret, ch. 25 (1862). Spoken by Robert Audley.

2 There can be no reconciliation where there is no open warfare. There must be a battle, a brave boisterous battle, with pennants waving and cannon roaring, before there can be peaceful treaties and enthusiastic shaking of hands.
Ibid., ch. 32

F. H. Bradley
(1846–1924)
British philosopher

Francis Herbert Bradley. As an exponent of the absolute Idealist school, he opposed the utilitarian theories of JOHN STUART MILL *and others, notably in* Appearance and Reality *(1893). He drew on the ideas of* KANT *and* HEGEL *and was an influence on G. E. Moore and* BERTRAND RUSSELL.

1 Metaphysics is the finding of bad reasons for what

we believe upon instinct; but to find these reasons is no less an instinct.
Appearance and Reality, Preface (1893)

2 The world is the best of all possible worlds, and everything in it is a necessary evil.
Ibid., Preface. See JAMES BRANCH CABELL 1 and VOLTAIRE 13.

3 *Eclecticism*. Every truth is so true that any truth must be false.
Aphorisms, no. 6 (1930)

4 There are persons who, when they cease to shock us, cease to interest us.
Ibid., no. 20

5 The secret of happiness is to admire without desiring. And that is not happiness.
Ibid., no. 33

Omar Bradley
(1893–1981)
US general

He commanded the US First Army in the Normandy invasion (1944) and was first Permanent Chairman of US Joint Chiefs of Staff 1949–53.

1 We have grasped the mystery of the atom and rejected the Sermon on the Mount . . . The world has achieved brilliance without wisdom, power without conscience. Ours is a world of nuclear giants and ethical infants.
Armistice Day speech, 1948, publ. in *Collected Writings*, vol. 1 (1967)

2 The wrong war, at the wrong place, at the wrong time, and with the wrong enemy.
Speech to Senate Committees on Armed Services and Foreign Relations, 15 May 1951, publ. in *The Military Situation in the Far East*, 'Senate Hearings' (1951). Bradley was giving testimony before a Senate enquiry into General MACARTHUR's proposal to carry the Korean conflict into China; Bradley opposed the scheme, arguing that 'Red China is not the powerful nation seeking to dominate the world'.

3 I am convinced that the best service a retired general can perform is to turn in his tongue along with his suit, and to mothball his opinions.
Armed Forces Day address, quoted in the *New York Times* 17 May 1959

John Bradshaw
(1602–59)
English lawyer

He rose to be President of the Parliamentary Commission which tried and sentenced CHARLES I in 1649, for which he was later branded a regicide. Opposed to CROMWELL's Protectorate, he retired from politics in 1654.

1 Rebellion to tyrants is obedience to God.
Inscription at Bradshaw's final burial place near Martha Bay, Jamaica. Bradshaw was originally buried in Westminster Abbey, but his remains, along with those of OLIVER CROMWELL and Henry Ireton, were dug up and hanged at Tyburn in 1660. Similar sayings have been attributed to both BENJAMIN FRANKLIN and THOMAS JEFFERSON, and the words appeared on Jefferson's seal.

Anne Bradstreet
(c. 1612–72)
English poet

Brought up in a Puritan household, she emigrated with her family to New England in 1630. Her first volume of verse, The Tenth Muse, *was published without her knowledge in London in 1650.*

1 I am obnoxious to each carping tongue
Who says my hand a needle better fits,
A poet's pen, all scorn, I should thus wrong;
For such despite they cast on female wits:
If what I do prove well, it won't advance,
They'll say it's stolen, or else it was by chance.
'The Prologue', publ. in *The Tenth Muse Lately Sprung Up in America* (1650). The volume appeared in America in a revised and expanded form as *Several Poems Compiled with Great Variety of Wit and Learning* (1678).

2 Youth is the time of getting, middle age of improving, and old age of spending.
Meditations Divine and Moral, no. 3 (1664)

Marlon Brando
(1924–2004)
US actor

A 'method' actor of brooding intensity, he took Broadway by storm in A Streetcar Named Desire *(1947), and won Oscars in the films* On the Waterfront *(1954) and* The Godfather *(1972). Bertolucci called him 'an angel as a man, a monster as an actor'. See also* GEORGE GLASS 1.

1 What've ya got?
The Wild One (film, 1953, screenplay by John Paxton from a story by Mick Rooney, directed by Laslo Benedek). Spoken by

Johnny (Marlon Brando), on being asked what he is rebelling against.

2 You don't understand! I could have had class! I could have been a contender! I could have been somebody!

On The Waterfront (film, 1954, screenplay by Budd Schulberg, directed by Elia Kazan). Spoken by Terry Mallon (Marlon Brando), the lines are addressed to Mallon's brother (Rod Steiger) whom he blamed for his failed boxing career. The screenplay was based on a series of Pulitzer Prize-winning articles called 'Crime on the Waterfront' by Malcolm Johnson, publ. in the *New York Sun* November–December 1948.

3 Acting is the expression of a neurotic impulse. It's a bum's life ... The principal benefit acting has afforded me is the money to pay for my psychoanalysis.

Quoted in *Marlon Brando: The Only Contender*, ch. 13 (1985) by Gary Carey

4 It is a simple fact that all of us use the techniques of acting to achieve whatever ends we seek ... Acting serves as the quintessential social lubricant and a device for protecting our interests and gaining advantage in every aspect of life.

The Technique of Acting, Introduction (1988) by Stella Adler

5 Mr Dean appears to be wearing my last year's wardrobe and using my last year's talent ...

Quoted in *James Dean in his Own Words*, 'The Things They Said ... About Jimmy' (ed. Mick St Michael, 1989). Referring to James Dean; an intense rivalry is said to have existed between the two actors.

6 I have the eyes of a dead pig.

Screen International 18 January 1991

Pierre de Brantöme
(c. 1540–1614)
French courtier, soldier and author

Pierre de Bourdeille, Abbé de Brantöme. He spent much of his life at the courts of Marguerite de Valois, Charles IX and Henri III, and soldiered throughout Europe. His memoirs paint an authentic if sometimes unreliable portrait of the age.

1 When a woman wants a man and lusts after him, the lover need not bother to conjure up opportunities, for she will find more in an hour than we men could think of in a century.

Vies des dames galantes, 'First Essay' (*Lives of the Courtesans*, written from c. 1594, publ. 1659)

Georges Braque
(1882–1963)
French artist

Initially influenced by the Impressionists and the Fauvists, he became one of the main pioneers of Cubism after 1907, working closely with PICASSO. *He specialized in still lifes, and provided sets for Diaghilev in the 1920s.*

1 One must not imitate what one wants to create.

'Thoughts and Reflections on Painting', publ. in *Nord-Sud* December 1910, transl. 1945, repr. in *Le Jour et la Nuit* (1952)

2 To work from nature is to improvise.

'Thoughts and Reflections on Painting', ibid.

3 The senses deform, the mind forms. Work to perfect the mind. There is no certitude but in what the mind conceives.

'Thoughts and Reflections on Painting', ibid.

4 'The only valid thing in art is that which cannot be explained,' I once wrote. I still feel this very strongly. To explain away the mystery of a great painting – if such a feat were possible – would do irreparable harm, for whenever you explain or define something you substitute the explanation or the definition for the real thing ... Believe me, there are certain mysteries, certain secrets in my own work which even I don't understand nor do I try to do so ... Mysteries have to be respected if they are to retain their power. Art disturbs: science reassures.

Observer 1 December 1957

Wernher von Braun
(1912–77)
German-born US rocket engineer

After developing V-2 rockets for Germany in the Second World War he moved to the USA to work on the project that launched the first American satellite Explorer 1, in 1958. He later helped develop the Saturn rocket used in the Apollo 8 moon landing in 1969.

1 Don't tell me that man doesn't belong out there [space]. Man belongs wherever he wants to go – and he'll do plenty well when he gets there.

Time 17 February 1958

Richard Brautigan
(1935–84)
US novelist and poet

Lacking conventional plot and character development, his novels A Confederate General from Big Sur *(1965) and* Trout

Fishing in America *(1967) established him as a cult figure of the late 1960s.*

1 If you get hung up on everybody else's hang-ups, then the whole world's going to be nothing more than one huge gallows.
The Abortion: An Historical Romance 1966 (1970)

Bertolt Brecht
(1898–1956)
German dramatist and poet

One of Germany's foremost dramatists and a committed Marxist, he collaborated with Kurt Weill to produce The Threepenny Opera *in 1928. Most of his best work was composed during exile from* HITLER's *Germany (1933–48), including* Mother Courage *(1941) and* The Caucasian Chalk Circle *(1944).*

1 Oh, the shark has pretty teeth, dear –
And he shows them pearly white –
Just a jackknife has Macheath, dear –
And he keeps it out of sight.
'The Ballad of Mac the Knife', in *The Threepenny Opera*, Prologue (1928)

2 Suppose, for instance, a man sees another man standing on the corner with a stump for an arm; the first time he may be shocked enough to give him tenpence, but the second time it will be only fivepence, and if he sees him a third time he'll hand him over to the police without batting an eyelid.
Peachum, ibid., Act 1, Sc. 1

3 Food is the first thing. Morals follow on.
Ibid., Act 2, Sc. 6, 'What Keeps Mankind Alive?' Also translated as 'Food first, then morality.'

4 For once you must try not to shirk the facts:
Mankind is kept alive by bestial acts.
Ibid., Act 2, Sc. 6

5 The law was made for one thing alone, for the exploitation of those who don't understand it, or are prevented by naked misery from obeying it.
Peachum, ibid., Act 3, Sc. 7

6 What's breaking into a bank compared with founding a bank?
Mac, ibid., Act 3, Sc. 9

7 You don't need to pray to God any more when there are storms in the sky, but you do have to be insured.
The Mother, Sc. 10 (1932). Spoken by Pelagea Vlasova.

8 Don't be afraid of death so much as an inadequate life.
Ibid.

9 Let nothing be called natural
In an age of bloody confusion,
Ordered disorder, planned caprice,
And dehumanized humanity, lest all things
Be held unalterable!
The Exception and the Rule, Prologue (1937)

10 Literary works cannot be taken over like factories, or literary forms of expression like industrial methods. Realist writing, of which history offers many widely varying examples, is likewise conditioned by the question of how, when and for what class it is made use of.
'The Popular and the Realistic' (written 1938, publ. 1958), repr. in *Brecht on Theatre* (ed. and transl. John Willett, 1964)

11 The world of knowledge takes a crazy turn
When teachers themselves are taught to learn.
The Life of Galileo, Sc. 6 (1939, transl. HOWARD BRENTON)

12 Unhappy the land that is in need of heroes.
Galileo, ibid., Sc. 13. Responding to Andrea's remark, 'Unhappy the land that has no heroes.'

13 Science knows only one commandment – contribute to science.
Andrea, ibid., Sc. 14

14 What they could do with round here is a good war. What else can you expect with peace running wild all over the place? You know what the trouble with peace is? No organization.
Mother Courage and Her Children, Sc. 1 (1939). Spoken by the Sergeant.

15 War is like love, it always finds a way.
The Chaplain, ibid., Sc. 6

16 No one can be good for long if goodness is not in demand.
The Good Woman of Setzuan, Sc. 1a (1941). Spoken by First God.

17 Mixing one's wines may be a mistake, but old and new wisdom mix admirably.
The Caucasian Chalk Circle, Prologue (1944). Spoken by the Singer.

18 Berlin, an etching by Churchill, after an idea by Hitler.
Journal entry, 27 October 1948, publ. in *Arbeitsjournal*, vol. 2 (1973)

19 We need a type of theatre which not only releases

the feelings, insights and impulses possible within the particular historical field of human relations in which the action takes place, but employs and encourages those thoughts and feelings which help transform the field itself.

'A Short Organum for the Theatre', para. 35 (1949), repr. in *Brecht on Theatre* (ed. and transl. John Willett, 1964)

Howard Brenton
(b. 1942)
David Hare
(b. 1947)
British playwrights

Brenton is known for his provocative politicized plays such as The Churchill Play *(1974) and* The Romans in Britain *(1980). He has collaborated with David Hare on* Pravda *(1985) and with Tariq Ali on* Moscow Gold *(1990). See also* DAVID HARE.

1 The press and politicians. A delicate relationship. Too close, and danger ensues. Too far apart and democracy itself cannot function without the essential exchange of information. Creative leaks, a discreet lunch, interchange in the Lobby, the art of the unattributable telephone call, late at night.

Quince, in *Pravda*, Act 1, Sc. 4 (1985)

Jimmy Breslin
(b. 1929)
US journalist and author

The voice of New York's Irish-American working class, he was prominent in the New Journalism of the 1970s. He has written fiction and biographies but is best known for his newspaper columns.

1 Rage is the only quality which has kept me, or anybody I have ever studied, writing columns for newspapers.

The Times 9 May 1990

Robert Bresson
(1907–99)
French film-maker

He won international acclaim with the austere, introspective films The Ladies of the Bois de Boulogne *(1945) and* Diary of a Country Priest *(1951). Before turning to film he studied painting which, he said, 'taught me to make not beautiful images but necessary ones'.*

1 Model. Two mobile eyes in a mobile head, itself on a mobile body.

Notes on the Cinematographer, 'On Automatism' (1975)

2 Films can only be made by by-passing the will of those who appear in them, using not what they do, but what they are.

The Times 1 November 1990

André Breton
(1896–1966)
French Surrealist author

Having been a leader of the Dadaists in 1916, he became one of the founders of the Surrealist movement, publishing the Surrealist Manifesto *in 1924. His novel* Nadja *was published in 1928 and his collected poems in 1948.*

1 Surrealism, n. Pure psychic automatism, by which it is intended to express, whether verbally or in writing, or in any other way, the real process of thought. Thought's dictation, free from any control by the reason, independent of any aesthetic or moral preoccupation.

Manifesto of Surrealism (1924)

2 It is living and ceasing to live that are imaginary solutions. Existence is elsewhere.

Ibid. See RIMBAUD 14 and V. S. PRITCHETT 4.

3 To speak of God, to think of God, is in every respect to show what one is made of ... *I have always wagered against God* and I regard the little that *I have won* in this world as simply the outcome of this bet. However paltry may have been the stake (my life) I am conscious of having won to the full. Everything that is doddering, squint-eyed, vile, polluted and grotesque is summoned up for me in that one word: God!

Footnote, ibid.

4 The approval of the public is to be avoided like the plague. It is absolutely essential to keep the public from *entering* if one wishes to avoid confusion. I must add that the public must be kept panting in expectation at the gate by a system of challenges and provocations.

Second Manifesto of Surrealism (1930)

Nicholas Breton
(c. 1553–c. 1626)
English poet and author

He wrote diverse religious and pastoral verse, pamphlets and other prose works. The Passionate Shepherd *(1604) helped to make him one of the most popular lyrical poets of his day, though most of his other writings have been forgotten.*

1 I wish my deadly foe no worse
Than want of friends and empty purse.
A Farewell to Town (1577)

2 Thus much for thy assurance know;
A hollow friend is but a hellish foe.
The Mother's Blessing (1602–3)

3 We rise with the lark and go to bed with the lamb.
The Court and Country, para. 8 (1618)

Robert Bridges
(1844–1930)
British poet

Having studied and practised medicine, he published his first volume of Poems *in 1873, and soon after devoted himself entirely to poetry and the study of prosody. He also wrote plays and works of criticism, and was a champion of* GERALD MANLEY HOPKINS. *He was made Poet Laureate in 1913. See also* HYMNS AND CAROLS 6, 72.

1 When first we met we did not guess
That Love would prove so hard a master.
'Triolet', written 1873, publ. in *Shorter Poems*, bk 1, no. 16 (1890)

2 When men were all asleep the snow came flying,
In large white flakes falling on the city brown,
Stealthily and perpetually settling and loosely
    lying,
Hushing the latest traffic of the drowsy town.
'London Snow', ibid., bk 3, no. 2. Opening lines of poem.

3 I love all beauteous things,
I seek and adore them;
God hath no better praise,
And man in his hasty days
Is honoured for them.
'I Love All Beauteous Things', st. 1, ibid., bk 4, no. 1

4 The storm is over, the land hushes to rest:
The tyrannous wind, its strength fordone,
Is fallen back in the west
To couch with the setting sun.
'The storm is over', ibid., bk 4, no. 23. Opening lines of poem.

5 Man's mind that hath this earth for home
Hath too its far-spread starry dome
Where thought is lost in going free,
Prison'd but by infinity.
'The Excellent Way', publ. in *October and Other Poems*, no. 20 (1920). Opening lines of poem.

John Bright
(1811–89)
English radical politician

A Quaker, he favoured free trade, abhorred inequality, and was a founder-member of the Anti-Corn Law League in 1838. Having helped to secure the passage of the Reform Bill of 1867, he served in GLADSTONE's *cabinets but broke with him over Irish Home Rule.*

1 If this phrase of the 'balance of power' is to be always an argument for war, the pretext for war will never be wanting, and peace can never be secure.
Speech to House of Commons, 31 March 1854, publ. in *The History of the Origin of the War with Russia* (1855)

2 The Angel of Death has been abroad throughout the land; you may almost hear the beating of his wings.
Speech to House of Commons, 23 February 1855, publ. in *The Penguin Book of Historic Speeches* (ed. Brian MacArthur, 1995). Appealing for an armistice in the Crimean War, which Bright fiercely opposed.

3 England is the mother of Parliaments.
Speech at Birmingham, 18 January 1865, publ. in *The Times* 19 January 1865

4 My opinion is that the Northern states will manage somehow to muddle through.
Quoted in *Reminiscences*, vol. 1, ch. 5 (1899) by Justin McCarthy. Bright was a vigorous supporter of the LINCOLN government.

5 He is a self-made man who worships his creator.
Attributed. Referring to BENJAMIN DISRAELI.

Jean-Anthelme Brillat-Savarin
(1755–1826)
French jurist and gastronome

A deputy at the States-General of 1789, he was forced to flee the country during the Terror, returning to France in 1796, where he was a judge during NAPOLEON's *consulate. His popular* Physiologie du goût *was a compendium of anecdotes and witty observations to do with the culinary arts.*

1 Tell me what you eat: I will tell you what you are.
La Physiologie du goût, Introduction, aph. 4 (*The Physiology of Taste*, 1826). The title of the work has also been translated *The Philosopher in the Kitchen* (by Anne Drayton, 1970). See LUDWIG FEUERBACH 3.

2 The discovery of a new dish does more for human happiness than the discovery of a star.
Ibid., Introduction, aph. 9

3 The most indispensable quality in a cook is punctuality; it is also that of a guest.
Ibid., Introduction, aph. 16

Vera Brittain
(1896–1970)
British author and pacifist

Her experiences as a nurse in the First World War, recounted in Testament of Youth *(1933), helped to shape her life-long commitment to pacifism, which she interpreted from a feminist perspective. She was the mother of* SHIRLEY WILLIAMS.

1 All that a pacifist can undertake – but it is a very great deal – is to refuse to kill, injure or otherwise cause suffering to another human creature, and untiringly to order his life by the rule of love though others may be captured by hate.
'What Can We Do In Wartime?' (1939), repr. in *Wartime Chronicle: Vera Brittain's Diary 1939–1945* (1989)

2 Politics are usually the executive expression of human immaturity.
The Rebel Passion, ch. 1 (1964)

Benjamin Britten
(1913–76)
British composer

Baron Britten of Aldeburgh. He wrote mainly for the voice, notably for Peter Pears as in Peter Grimes *(1945). Other works include the orchestral* The Young Person's Guide to the Orchestra *(1946) and the opera* Billy Budd *(1951).*

1 It is cruel, you know, that music should be so beautiful. It has the beauty of loneliness & of pain: of strength & freedom. The beauty of disappointment & never-satisfied love. The cruel beauty of nature, and everlasting beauty of monotony.
Letter, 29 June 1937, publ. in *Letters from a Life: Letters and Diaries of Benjamin Britten*, vol. 1, 'A Working Life' (1991). Britten wrote this whilst listening to the 'Abschied', the finale of Mahler's song cycle *Das Lied von der Erde*.

Hermann Broch
(1886–1951)
Austrian novelist

He is known for his multidimensional and innovative novels, for example The Sleepwalkers *(trilogy, 1931–2), which charts the disintegration of 19th-century European society. Imprisoned by the Nazis, he emigrated to America in 1940.*

1 No one's death comes to pass without making some impression, and those close to the deceased inherit part of the liberated soul and become richer in their humaneness.
The Spell, ch. 2 (1976, transl. 1987)

2 The world has always gone through periods of madness so as to advance a bit on the road to reason.
The doctor, ibid. ch. 11

Joseph Brodsky
(1940–96)
Russian-born US poet and critic

Composed in both Russian and English, his poetry deals with loss and exile, influenced by his imprisonment and then banishment from the Soviet Union in 1972. His collections include The End of a Beautiful Era *(1977) and* To Urania *(1984).*

1 The real history of consciousness starts with one's first lie.
'Less Than One', sect. 1 (1976), repr. in *Less Than One: Selected Essays* (1986)

2 For aesthetics is the mother of ethics ... Were we to choose our leaders on the basis of their reading experience and not their political programs, there would be much less grief on earth.
'Uncommon Visage', Nobel Prize acceptance speech, 1987, publ. in *On Grief and Reason* (1996)

3 After all, it is hard to master both life and work equally well. So if you are bound to fake one of them, it had better be life.
Interview in *Writers at Work* (eighth series, ed. George Plimpton, 1988)

Alexander Brome
(1620–66)
English poet

He was a Royalist poet who penned satires against the Rump Parliament, and composed numerous other songs, epistles and elegies. He also translated HORACE *and wrote a comedy,* The Cunning Lovers *(1654).*

1 I have been in love, and in debt, and in drink,
This many and many a year.
'The Mad Lover', publ. in *Songs and Other Poems* (second edn, 1664). Opening lines of poem.

Jacob Bronowski
(1908–74)
British scientist and author

A popularizer of science and the history of thought, he published The Common Sense of Science *(1951) and* The Western

Intellectual Tradition *(1960), and presented the TV series* The Ascent of Man *in 1973.*

1 Man masters nature not by force but by understanding. This is why science has succeeded where magic failed: because it has looked for no spell to cast over nature.
'The Creative Mind', lecture at the Massachusetts Institute of Technology, 26 February 1953, publ. in *Science and Human Values*, sect. 4 (1961)

2 Has there ever been a society which has died of dissent? Several have died of conformity in our lifetime.
'The Sense of Human Dignity', lecture at the Massachusetts Institute of Technology, 19 March 1953, ibid., sect. 5

3 Science has nothing to be ashamed of even in the ruins of Nagasaki. The shame is theirs who appeal to other values than the human imaginative values which science has evolved.
Ibid., sect. 11

4 No science is immune to the infection of politics and the corruption of power.
Encounter July 1971

5 That is the essence of science: ask an impertinent question, and you are on the way to a pertinent answer.
The Ascent of Man, ch. 4 (1973)

6 One aim of the physical sciences has been to give an exact picture of the material world. One achievement of physics in the twentieth century has been to prove that that aim is unattainable.
Ibid., ch. 11

Anne Brontë
(1820–49)
English novelist and poet

With her brother and sisters (see below), she was brought up in the Haworth parsonage in Yorkshire, and contributed verse to the pseudonymous Poems by Currer, Ellis and Acton Bell *published in 1846. She wrote two novels:* Agnes Grey *(1847) and* The Tenant of Wildfell Hall *(1848).*

1 All true histories contain instruction; though, in some, the treasure may be hard to find, and when found, so trivial in quantity that the dry, shrivelled kernel scarcely compensates for the trouble of cracking the nut.
Agnes Grey, ch. 1 (1847). Opening words.

Charlotte Brontë
(1816–55)
English novelist and poet

She was the longest-lived of the Brontë sisters, and the most prolific, achieving considerable success with her three novels Jane Eyre *(1847),* Shirley *(1849) and* Villette *(1853). She married in 1854 and died from complications during pregnancy.*

1 I like high life. I like its manners, its splendours, its luxuries, the beings which move in its enchanted sphere. I like to consider the habits of those beings, their way of thinking, speaking, acting. Let fools talk about the artificial, voluptuous, idle existence spun out by dukes, lords, ladies, knights and esquires of high degree. Such cant is not for me. I despise it.
'High Life in Verdopolis', written 1834, publ. in *The Early Writings of Charlotte Brontë*, vol. 2, pt 2 (ed. Christine Alexander, 1991)

2 We wove a web in childhood,
A web of sunny air;
We dug a spring in infancy
Of water pure and fair;
We sowed in youth a mustard seed,
We cut an almond rod;
We are now grown up to riper age –
Are they withered in the sod?
'We wove a web in childhood', written 1835, publ. in *Saul and Other Poems* (1913). The poem is also known as 'Retrospection'.

3 The human heart has hidden treasures,
In secret kept, in silence sealed;
The thoughts, the hopes, the dreams, the pleasures,
Whose charms were broken if revealed.
'Evening Solace', st. 1, written 1837–8, publ. in *Poems by Currer, Ellis and Acton Bell* (1846)

4 Conventionality is not morality. Self-righteousness is not religion. To attack the first is not to assail the last. To pluck the mask from the face of the Pharisee is not to lift an impious hand to the Crown of Thorns.
Jane Eyre, Preface (1847)

5 Consistency, madam, is the first of Christian duties.
Ibid., ch. 4. Spoken by Mr Brocklehurst to Mrs Reed.

6 It is in vain to say human beings ought to be satisfied with tranquillity: they must have action; and they will make it if they cannot find it.
Ibid., ch. 12

7 Women are supposed to be very calm generally:

but women feel just as men feel; they need exercise for their faculties, and a field for their efforts as much as their brothers do; they suffer from too rigid a restraint, too absolute a stagnation, precisely as men would suffer; and it is narrow-minded in their more privileged fellow creatures to say that they ought to confine themselves to making puddings and knitting stockings, to playing on the piano and embroidering bags. It is thoughtless to condemn them, or laugh at them, if they seek to do more or learn more than custom has pronounced necessary for their sex.
Ibid., ch. 12

8 If you are cast in a different mould to the majority, it is no merit of yours: Nature did it.
Mr Rochester, ibid., ch. 14

9 Feeling without judgement is a washy draught indeed; but judgement untempered by feeling is too bitter and husky a morsel for human deglutition.
Ibid., ch. 21

10 You – poor and obscure, and small and plain as you are – I entreat to accept me as a husband.
Ibid., ch. 23. Mr Rochester's first proposal to Jane.

11 Prejudices, it is well known, are most difficult to eradicate from the heart whose soil has never been loosened or fertilized by education; they grow there, firm as weeds among stones.
Ibid., ch. 29

12 One does not jump, and spring, and shout hurrah! at hearing one has got a fortune, one begins to consider responsibilities, and to ponder business; on a base of steady satisfaction rise certain grave cares, and we contain ourselves, and brood over our bliss with a solemn brow.
Ibid., ch. 33

13 Reader, I married him.
Ibid., ch. 38. Opening words of chapter, referring to Rochester; it is described as 'a quiet wedding'.

14 Of late years, an abundant shower of curates has fallen upon the north of England.
Shirley, ch. 1 (1849). Opening words.

15 Misery generates hate: these sufferers hated the machines which they believed took their bread from them; they hated the buildings which contained those machines; they hated the manufacturers who owned those buildings.
Ibid., ch. 2. Referring to the Luddite rioters. 'Misery generates

hate' is the epigram on the title page of the Beveridge Report, Full Employment in a Free Society (1944).

16 All men, taken singly, are more or less selfish; and taken in bodies they are intensely so.
Ibid., ch. 10

17 But this I know; the writer who possesses the creative gift owns something of which he is not always master – something that at times strangely wills and works for itself ... If the result be attractive, the world will praise you, who little deserve praise; if it be repulsive, the same world will blame you, who almost as little deserve blame.
Preface to Wuthering Heights (1850) by EMILY BRONTË.

Emily Brontë
(1818–48)
English novelist and poet

Considered the most passionate of the Brontë sisters, she is generally reckoned the greater poet. Her one novel, Wuthering Heights *(1847), which vividly evoked the Yorkshire Moors where the family lived, was poorly received; she died of tuberculosis soon after its publication.*

1 Cold in the earth – and fifteen wild Decembers,
From those brown hills, have melted into spring:
Faithful, indeed, is the spirit that remembers
After such years of change and suffering!
'Remembrance', st. 3, publ. in *Poems by Currer, Ellis and Acton Bell* (1846)

2 Sweet Love of youth, forgive, if I forget thee,
While the world's tide is bearing me along;
Other desires and other hopes beset me,
Hopes which obscure, but cannot do thee wrong!
'Remembrance', st. 4, ibid.

3 Love is like the wild rose-briar;
Friendship like the holly-tree.
The holly is dark when the rose-briar blooms,
But which will bloom most constantly?
'Love is like the wild rose-briar', st. 1, publ. in *Wuthering Heights and Agnes Grey* (1850). The poem is also known as 'Love and Friendship'.

4 No coward soul is mine,
No trembler in the world's storm-troubled sphere:
I see Heaven's glories shine,
And faith shines equal, arming me from fear.
'No coward soul is mine', st. 1, written 1846, ibid. Charlotte noted that this was the last poem her sister ever wrote (although three years before her death). The poem is also known as 'Last Lines'.

5 Vain are the thousand creeds
That move men's hearts, unutterably vain;
Worthless as withered weeds,
Or idlest froth amid the boundless main.
'No coward soul is mine, st. 2, ibid.

6 Proud people breed sad sorrows for themselves.
Wuthering Heights, ch. 7 (1847). Spoken by Nelly.

7 If all else perished, and *he* remained, I should still
continue to be; and if all else remained, and he were
annihilated, the universe would turn to a mighty
stranger. I should not seem a part of it ... My love
for Heathcliff resembles the eternal rocks beneath
– a source of little visible delight, but necessary.
Nelly, I *am* Heathcliff – he's always, always in my
mind – not as a pleasure, any more than I am always
a pleasure to myself – but as my own being.
Catherine, ibid., ch. 9

8 The tyrant grinds down his slaves – and they don't
turn against him, they crush those beneath them.
Heathcliff, ibid. ch. 11

9 Having levelled my palace, don't erect a hovel and
complacently admire your own charity in giving me
that for a home.
Heathcliff's words to Catherine, ibid. ch. 11

Rupert Brooke
(1887–1915)
British poet

*The most dashing of the Georgian poets, he came to symbolize
the golden youth sacrificed in the First World War after his
death from blood poisoning en route to the Dardanelles.* F. R.
LEAVIS *summarized his verse as 'rather like Keats's vulgarity
with a Public School accent'. See* FRANCES CORNFORD 2.

1 Oh! Death will find me, long before I tire
Of watching you.
'Sonnet', publ. in *Poems* (1911). Opening lines of poem.

2 Breathless, we flung us on the windy hill,
Laughed in the sun, and kissed the lovely grass.
'The Hill', ibid. Opening lines of poem

3 God! I will pack, and take a train,
And get me to England once again!
For England's the one land, I know,
Where men with Splendid Hearts may go;
And Cambridgeshire, of all England,
The shire for Men who Understand.
'The Old Vicarage, Grantchester', st. 4, publ. in *1914 and Other
Poems* (1915)

4 For Cambridge people rarely smile,
Being urban, squat, and packed with guile.
'The Old Vicarage, Grantchester', st. 4, ibid.

5 The women there do all they ought;
The men observe the Rules of Thought.
They love the Good; they worship Truth;
They laugh uproariously in youth;
(And when they get to feeling old,
They up and shoot themselves, I'm told) ...
'The Old Vicarage, Grantchester', st. 5, ibid. Of the people of
Grantchester, outside Cambridge.

6 Stands the Church clock at ten to three?
And is there honey still for tea?
'The Old Vicarage, Grantchester', st. 5, ibid. Concluding lines
of poem.

7 And I shall find some girl perhaps,
And a better one than you,
With eyes as wise, but kindlier,
And lips as soft, but true,
And I daresay she will do.
'The Chilterns', st. 8, ibid. Final stanza of poem.

8 Fish say, they have their Stream and Pond;
But is there anything Beyond?
'Heaven', ibid.

9 One may not doubt that, somehow, Good
Shall come of Water and of Mud;
And, sure, the reverent eye must see
A Purpose in Liquidity.
'Heaven', ibid.

10 But somewhere, beyond Space and Time,
Is wetter water, slimier slime!
And there (they trust) there swimmeth One
Who swam ere rivers were begun,
Immense, of fishy form and mind,
Squamous, omnipotent, and kind.
'Heaven', ibid.

11 The cool kindliness of sheets, that soon
Smooth away trouble; and the rough male kiss
Of blankets.
'The Great Lover', ibid.

12 If I should die, think only this of me:
That there's some corner of a foreign field
That is for ever England.
'The Soldier', ibid. Opening lines of poem. Brooke is buried
on the island of Skyros, Greece.

13 Now, God be thanked Who has matched us with
His hour,

And caught our youth, and wakened us from
    sleeping,
With hand made sure, clear eye, and sharpened
    power,
To turn, as swimmers into cleanness leaping.
'Peace', st. 1, ibid. Opening lines of poem.

14 And all the little emptiness of love!
'Peace', st. 1, ibid.

Anita Brookner
(b. 1938)
British novelist and art historian

*An expert on 18th-century painting, she is more widely known
for her fiction, including* Hôtel du Lac *(1984) and* Visitors
(1997).

1 She was a handsome woman of forty-five and
would remain so for many years.
Hôtel du Lac, ch. 4 (1984)

2 Good women always think it is their fault when
someone else is being offensive. Bad women never
take the blame for anything.
Ibid., ch. 7

3 Time misspent in youth is sometimes all the freedom one ever has.
A Misalliance, ch. 10 (1986). Spoken by Blanche Vernon.

4 It will be a pity if women in the more conventional mould are to be phased out, for there will
never be anyone to go home to.
A Friend From England, ch. 10 (1987). Spoken by Rachel.

Gwendolyn Brooks
(1917–2000)
US poet

*In 1950 she was the first black author to be awarded the
Pulitzer Prize, for her poetry collection,* Annie Allen *(1949). As
with her first volume,* A Street in Bronzeville *(1945), this dealt
principally with the lives of the urban black poor.*

1 Abortions will not let you forget.
You remember the children you got that you did
    not get.
'The Mother', publ. in *A Street in Bronzeville* (1945)

Jack Brooks
(1912–71)
British songwriter and composer

*A prolific lyricist from the 1940s until the early '60s, he wrote
material for* BING CROSBY *and* FRED ALLEN, *among others.
'That's Amore' was a hit for Dean Martin in 1953.*

1 A four-legged friend, a four-legged friend
He'll never let you down
He's honest and faithful right up to the end
That wonderful one-two-three-four-legged friend.
'Four-Legged Friend' (song), sung to his horse Trigger by Roy
Rogers in the film *Son of Paleface* (1952)

Mel Brooks
(b. 1926)
US film-maker and actor

*An irreverent gag-writer and script-doctor turned director of
his own screenplays, he excelled in brash bad taste. The Producers (1968) was followed by the spoofs* Blazing Saddles *(1974)
and* Silent Movie *(1976), among others.*

1 Springtime for Hitler and Germany,
Winter for France and Poland.
'Springtime for Hitler', in *The Producers* (film, 1968, written
and directed by Mel Brooks). The song was the centrepiece of
the musical of the same name staged by 'the producers' to
guarantee a loss.

2 How could this happen? I was so careful. I picked
the wrong play, the wrong director, the wrong cast.
Where did I go right?
Max Bialystock (Zero Mostel), ibid.

3 Let's face it, sweetheart, without Jews, fags, and
Gypsies, there is no theatre.
To Be or Not To Be (film, 1983, screenplay by Thomas Meehan
and Ronny Graham, directed by Alan Johnson). Spoken by
Frederick Bronski (Mel Brooks).

Lord Brougham
(1778–1868)
Scottish lawyer, politician and journalist

*Henry Peter Brougham, 1st Baron Brougham and Vaux. He
became a prominent member of the Whig opposition, later
serving under Earl Grey as Lord Chancellor. A co-founder of
the* Edinburgh Review, *he wrote numerous books, essays and
articles.*

1 Education makes a people easy to lead, but diffi-

cult to drive; easy to govern but impossible to enslave.

Speech to House of Commons, 29 January 1828, publ. in *Hansard*

2 Look out, gentlemen, the schoolmaster is abroad! And I trust to him armed with his primer, against the soldier in full military array.

Speech to House of Commons, 29 January 1828, publ. in *Hansard*. Brougham is said to have used the words 'The schoolmaster is abroad!' on previous occasions.

3 The great unwashed.

Attributed

Heywood Broun
(1888–1939)
US journalist and novelist

He is chiefly remembered for his columns 'It Seems to Me' in the Tribune *and* World *in the 1920s and 'Shoot the Works' in the* New Republic *from 1935 until his death.*

1 The tragedy of life is not that man loses, but that he almost wins.

Pieces of Hate, and Other Enthusiasms, 'Sport for Art's Sake' (1922)

2 Just as every conviction begins as a whim so does every emancipator serve his apprenticeship as a crank. A fanatic is a great leader who is just entering the room.

New York World 6 February 1928

3 A technical objection is the first refuge of a scoundrel.

New Republic 15 December 1937

Craig Brown
(b. 1957)
British journalist

A specialist in parody and satire, he writes for Private Eye *and the* Daily Telegraph, *sometimes in the guise of Bel Littlejohn or Wallace Arnold.*

1 Journalism could be described as turning one's enemies into money.

Daily Telegraph 28 September 1990

2 The most common form of parody is, of course, self-parody. It is a disease to which every columnist is prone, for it is always easier to reassemble the usual range of columnar emotions – outrage, pity, etc. – than to feel them afresh.

Spectator 22 November 1999

3 A satirist is a humorist who wants to be a politician. Deep down, he believes that the Kingdom of Sense is at hand, and that a dig in the ribs might make it come to pass.

Guardian 25 January 2003

H. Rap Brown
(b. 1943)
US radical and author

Originally Hubert Gerold Brown. A black activist, he was chairman of the Student Nonviolent Coordinating Committee (SNCC) in Alabama and expressed his inflammatory views in Die Nigger Die *(1969). While imprisoned for robbery in New York (1971–6), he converted to Islam, changing his name to Jamil Abdullah al-Amin.*

1 Violence is as American as cherry pie.

Press conference at SNCC, Washington DC, 27 July 1967, quoted in the *Evening Star* 27 July 1967

James Brown
(b. 1933)
US soul singer

The 'Godfather of Soul' grew up in rural poverty on a diet of gospel. His charismatic stage act was captured on the album Live at the Apollo *(1962), which sold a million copies, unprecedented for an album by a black artist.*

1 I feel good, I knew that I would, now.

'I Got You (I Feel Good)' (song, 1965, written by Ted Wright), on the album *I Got You (I Feel Good)* (1966). Brown had produced a version of the song, called 'I Found You', for Yvonne Fair in 1962.

2 It's a man's world, but it wouldn't be nothing without a woman or a girl.

'It's a Man's Man's Man's World' (song, 1966, written with Betty Newsome), on the album *It's a Man's Man's Man's World* (1966). An earlier version of the song, titled 'It's a Man's World', was recorded in 1964 but not released.

3 Say it loud! I'm black and I'm proud!

'Say it Loud! I'm Black and I'm Proud!' (song, 1968, written with Alfred Ellis) on the album *Say it Loud! I'm Black and I'm Proud!* (1969)

John Brown
(1800–59)
US abolitionist

A passionate opponent of slavery, he fought various campaigns against the Federal government with his own militia. After seizing the arsenal at Harper's Ferry, he was captured by forces led by ROBERT E. LEE, *and tried and hanged at Charlestown, Virginia. See also* ANONYMOUS 49.

1 I, John Brown, am now quite certain that the crimes of this guilty land will never be purged away but with blood.

Last statement, written on the day of his execution, 2 December 1859, quoted in *John Brown and His Men*, ch. 12 (1894) by R. J. Hinton

Lew Brown

See BUDDY DE SYLVA AND LEW BROWN

Thomas Brown

(1663–1704)

English satirist

His fame rests on his adaptation of an epigram by MARTIAL, *while a student at Oxford (see below). He later moved to London, where he translated and wrote scurrilous lampoons and satires of ephemeral interest.*

1 I do not love thee, Dr Fell.
The reason why I cannot tell;
But this I know, and know full well,
I do not love thee, Dr Fell.

'I do not love thee, Dr Fell'. The lines supposedly came about when Brown, a student at Christ Church, Oxford, was called before the dean, Dr John Fell, to explain his errant behaviour. The dean agreed to stay Brown's expulsion if he could translate *ex tempore* Martial's epigram beginning 'I like you not, Sabidius' (see MARTIAL 3). Brown was permitted to stay. In an alternative version, the third line reads, 'But this alone I know full well'.

Charles Farrar Browne

See ARTEMUS WARD

(Sir) Thomas Browne

(1605–82)

English author and physician

He practised as a doctor in Norwich from 1637. Religio Medici, an examination of his faith, was circulated privately until published in an authorized edition in 1643. Hydriotaphia, or Urn Burial (1658), is both archaeological treatise and discourse on death and transience, and The Garden of Cyrus (1658) is a history of gardens interwoven with numerological theory.

1 At my devotion I love to use the civility of my knee, my hat, and hand.

Religio Medici, pt 1, sect. 3 (1643; *A Doctor's Religion*)

2 A man may be in as just possession of truth as of a city, and yet be forced to surrender.

Ibid., pt 1, sect. 6

3 I love to lose myself in a mystery, to pursue my reason to an *O altitudo!*

Ibid., pt 1, sect. 9

4 We carry with us the wonders we seek without us: there is all Africa and her prodigies in us.

Ibid., pt 1, sect. 15

5 In brief, all things are artificial, for nature is the art of God.

Ibid., pt 1, sect. 16

6 Obstinacy in a bad cause is but constancy in a good.

Ibid., pt 1, sect. 25

7 Persecution is a bad and indirect way to plant religion.

Ibid., pt 1, sect. 25

8 Not wrung from speculations and subtleties, but from common sense, and observation; not picked from the leaves of any author, but bred among the weeds and tares of mine own brain.

Ibid., pt 1, sect. 36. Referring to his objection to a proposition by SAINT AUGUSTINE.

9 I am not so much afraid of death, as ashamed thereof; 'tis the very disgrace and ignominy of our natures, that in a moment can so disfigure us that our nearest friends, wife, and children, stand afraid and start at us.

Ibid., pt 1, sect. 40

10 He forgets that he can die who complains of misery, we are in the power of no calamity, while death is in our own.

Ibid., pt 1, sect. 44

11 There is no road or ready way to virtue.

Ibid., pt 1, sect. 53

12 All places, all airs make unto me one country: I am in England, everywhere, and under any meridian.

Ibid., pt 2, sect. 1

13 But how shall we expect charity towards others, when we are uncharitable to our selves? Charity begins at home, is the voice of the world; yet is every man his greatest enemy, and as it were his own executioner.

Ibid., pt 2, sect. 4. See JOHN DONNE 52.

14 I could be content that we might procreate like trees, without conjunction, or that there were any way to perpetuate the world without this trivial and vulgar way of coition.
Ibid., pt 2, sect. 9. See MARTIN LUTHER 8.

15 Sure there is music even in the beauty, and the silent note which Cupid strikes, far sweeter than the sound of an instrument. For there is music wherever there is a harmony, order or proportion; and thus far we may maintain the music of the spheres; for those well-ordered motions, and regular paces, though they give no sound unto the ear, yet to the understanding they strike a note most full of harmony.
Ibid., pt 2, sect. 9

16 We all labour against our own cure, for death is the cure of all diseases.
Ibid., pt 2, sect. 9

17 For the world, I count it not an inn, but an hospital, and a place not to live, but to die in.
Ibid., pt 2, sect. 11

18 There is surely a piece of divinity in us, something that was before the elements, and owes no homage unto the sun.
Ibid., pt 2, sect. 11

19 We term sleep a death ... by which we may be literally said to die daily ... *in fine*, so like death, I dare not trust it without my prayers, and an half adieu unto the world, and take my farewell in a colloquy with God.
Ibid., pt 2, sect. 12

20 That unextinguishable laugh in heaven.
The Garden of Cyrus, ch. 2 (1658)

21 Life itself is but the shadow of death, and souls departed but the shadows of the living: all things fall under this name. The sun itself is but the dark simulacrum, and light but the shadow of God.
Ibid., ch. 4

22 All things began in order, so shall they end, and so shall they begin again; according to the ordainer of order and mystical mathematics of the city of heaven.
Ibid., ch. 5

23 Though Somnus in Homer be sent to rouse up Agamemnon, I find no such effects in these drowsy approaches of sleep. To keep our eyes open longer were but to act our Antipodes. The huntsmen are up in America, and they are already past their first sleep in Persia. But who can be drowsy at that hour which freed us from everlasting sleep? Or have slumbering thoughts at that time, when sleep itself must end, and as some conjecture all shall awake again?
Ibid., ch. 5

24 With rich flames and hired tears they solemnized their obsequies.
Hydriotaphia (*Urn Burial*), ch. 3 (1658). Referring to rural burial practices.

25 Men have lost their reason in nothing so much as their religion, wherein stones and clouts make martyrs.
Ibid., ch. 4

26 Were the happiness of the next world as closely apprehended as the felicities of this, it were a martyrdom to live.
Ibid., ch. 4

27 The long habit of living indisposeth us for dying.
Ibid., ch. 5

28 But to subsist in bones, and be but pyramidally extant, is a fallacy in duration.
Ibid., ch. 5

29 Generations pass while some trees stand, and old families last not three oaks.
Ibid., ch. 5

30 To be nameless in worthy deeds exceeds an infamous history.
Ibid., ch. 5

31 But the iniquity of oblivion blindly scattereth her poppy, and deals with the memory of men without distinction to merit of perpetuity.
Ibid., ch. 5

32 Man is a noble animal, splendid in ashes, and pompous in the grave.
Ibid., ch. 5

33 He who discommendeth others obliquely commendeth himself.
Christian Morals, pt 1, sect. 34 (1716)

Elizabeth Barrett Browning
(1806–61)
English poet

She was already an acclaimed poet when she met ROBERT BROWNING *in 1845. The two married in secret the following year and lived in Italy until her death. 'Sonnets from the Portuguese' (1850) and* Aurora Leigh *(1856) confirmed her poetic reputation.*

1 Eve is a twofold mystery.
'The Poet's Vow', pt 1, st. 1 publ. in *The Seraphim and Other Poems* (1838). Opening words of poem.

2 At painful times, when composition is impossible and reading is not *enough*, grammars and dictionaries are excellent for *distraction*.
Letter to author and playwright Mary Russell Mitford, April 1839, publ. in *Elizabeth Barrett to Miss Mitford* (ed. Betty Miller, 1954)

3 What is genius – but the power of expressing a new individuality?
Letter to Mary Russell Mitford, 14 January 1843, ibid.

4 I tell you, hopeless grief is passionless.
'Grief', publ. in *Poems* (1844). Opening line of poem.

5 Experience, like a pale musician, holds
A dulcimer of patience in his hand.
'Perplexed Music', ibid. Opening lines of poem.

6 Thou large-brained woman and large-hearted
  man,
Self-called George Sand!
'To George Sand, A Desire', ibid.

7 'Yes,' I answered you last night,
'No,' this morning, Sir, I say.
Colours seen by candle-light,
Will not look the same by day.
'The Lady's "Yes"', st. 1, ibid.

8 Blessings on thee, dog of mine,
Pretty collars make thee fine,
Sugared milk make fat thee!
Pleasures wag on in thy tail –
Hands of gentle motion fail
Nevermore to pat thee!
'To Flush, My Dog', st. 16, ibid.

9 And lips say 'God be pitiful',
Who ne'er said, 'God be praised'.
'The Cry of the Human', st. 1, ibid.

10 But the child's sob curses deeper in the silence
Than the strong man in his wrath!
'The Cry of the Children', st. 13, ibid. Closing lines of poem.

11 If thou must love me, let it be for nought
Except for love's sake only. Do not say,
'I love her for her smile . . . her look . . . her way
Of speaking gently . . . for a trick of thought
That falls in well with mine, and, certes, brought

A sense of pleasant ease on such a day' –
For these things in themselves, Beloved, may
Be changed, or change for thee – and love so
  wrought,
May be unwrought so.
'Sonnets from the Portuguese', no. 14, publ. in *Poems* (1850)

12 How do I love thee? Let me count the ways.
I love thee to the depth and breadth and height
My soul can reach, when feeling out of sight
For the ends of Being and Ideal Grace.
I love thee to the level of every day's
Most quiet need, by sun and candle-light.
I love thee freely, as men strive for Right;
I love thee purely, as they turn from Praise;
I love thee with a passion put to use
In my old griefs, and with my childhood's faith;
I love thee with a love I seemed to lose
With my lost saints, – I love thee with the breath,
Smiles, tears, of all my life! – and, if God choose,
I shall but love thee better after death.
'Sonnets From the Portuguese', no. 43, ibid.

13 Women know
The way to rear up children (to be just),
They know a simple, merry, tender knack
Of tying sashes, fitting baby-shoes,
And stringing pretty words that make no sense,
And kissing full sense into empty words.
Aurora Leigh, bk 1, ll. 47–52 (1857)

14 The works of women are symbolical.
We sew, sew, prick our fingers, dull our sight,
Producing what? A pair of slippers, sir,
To put on when you're weary – or a stool
To stumble over and vex you . . . 'curse that stool!'
Or else at best, a cushion, where you lean
And sleep, and dream of something we are not,
But would be for your sake. Alas, alas!
This hurts most, this . . . that, after all, we are paid
The worth of our work, perhaps.
Ibid., bk 1, ll. 456–65

15 Books, books, books!
I had found the secret of a garret-room
Piled high with cases in my father's name;
Piled high, packed large, – where, creeping in and
  out
Among the giant fossils of my past,
Like some small nimble mouse between the ribs
Of a mastodon, I nibbled here and there
At this or that box, pulling through the gap,
In heats of terror, haste, victorious joy,

The first book first. And how I felt it beat
Under my pillow, in the morning's dark,
An hour before the sun would let me read!
My books!
Ibid., bk. 1, ll. 831–43

16 What's this, Aurora Leigh,
You write so of the poets and not laugh?
Those virtuous liars, dreamers after dark,
Exaggerators of the sun and moon,
And soothsayers in a tea-cup? I write so
Of the only truth-tellers, now left to God, –
The only speakers of essential truth,
Opposed to relative, comparative,
And temporal truths; the only holders by
His sun-skirts, through conventional grey glooms;
The only teachers who instruct mankind,
From just a shadow on a charnel-wall.
Ibid., bk. 1, ll. 853–64

17 Girls blush, sometimes, because they are alive,
Half wishing they were dead to save the shame.
The sudden blush devours them, neck and brow;
They have drawn too near the fire of life, like
    gnats,
And flare up bodily, wings and all. What then?
Who's sorry for a gnat . . . or girl?
Ibid., bk 2, ll. 691–706

18 For 'tis not in mere death that men die most.
Ibid., bk 3, l. 12

19 I think it frets the saints in heaven to see
How many desolate creatures on the earth
Have learnt the simple dues of fellowship
And social comfort, in a hospital.
Ibid., bk 3, ll. 1121–4

20 We all have known
Good critics, who have stamped out poet's hopes;
Good statesmen, who pulled ruin on the state;
Good patriots, who, for a theory, risked a cause;
Good kings, who disembowelled for a tax;
Good Popes, who brought all good to jeopardy;
Good Christians, who sat still in easy-chairs;
And damned the general world for standing up. –
Now, may the good God pardon all good men!
Ibid., bk 4, ll. 498–506

21 He, in his developed manhood, stood,
A little sunburnt by the glare of life.
Ibid., bk 4, ll. 1139–40. Referring to Aurora's cousin, Romney
Leigh.

22 What is art,
But life upon the larger scale, the higher,
When, graduating up in a spiral line
Of still expanding and ascending gyres,
It pushes toward the intense significance
Of all things, hungry for the Infinite?
Art's life, and where we live, we suffer and toil.
Ibid., bk 4, ll. 1151–7

23 Let no one till his death
Be called unhappy. Measure not the work
Until the day's out and the labour done;
Then bring your gauges.
Ibid., bk. 5, ll. 76–9. See SOLON 1.

24 Nay, if there's room for poets in this world
A little overgrown (I think there is),
Their sole work is to represent the age,
Their age, not Charlemagne's, – this live, throbbing
    age.
That brawls, cheats, maddens, calculates, aspires,
And spends more passion, more heroic heat,
Betwixt the mirrors of its drawing-rooms,
Than Roland with his knights.
Ibid., bk 5, ll. 199–206

25 Whoso loves
Believes the impossible.
Ibid., bk. 5, ll. 408–9

26 And trade is art, and art's philosophy,
In Paris.
Ibid., bk 6, ll. 96–7

27 Since when was genius found respectable?
Ibid., bk 6, l. 275

28 Earth's crammed with heaven,
And every common bush afire with God:
But only he who sees, takes off his shoes;
The rest sit round it, and pluck blackberries,
And daub their natural faces unaware
More and more, from the first similitude.
Ibid., bk 7, ll. 820–5

29 A woman cannot do the thing she ought,
Which means whatever perfect thing she can,
In life, in art, in science, but she fears
To let the perfect action take her part
And rest there: she must prove what she can do
Before she does it, – prate of woman's rights,
Of woman's mission, woman's function, till
The men (who are prating, too, on their side)
    cry,

'A woman's function plainly is . . . to talk.'
Poor souls, they are very reasonably vexed!
Ibid., bk 8, ll. 914–23

30 What monster have we here?
A great Deed at this hour of day?
A great just Deed – and not for pay?
Absurd, – or insincere.
'A Tale of Villafranca', st. 4, publ. in *Poems Before Congress*
(1860)

Robert Browning
(1812–89)
English poet

*Characterized by dramatic monologues and protagonists
based on obscure literary and historical figures, much of his
best work appeared in pamphlets 1841–6. Later collections
include* Dramatis Personae *(1864) and* The Ring and the Book
*(1868–9). A literary circle grew around his home in Florence,
where he lived with* ELIZABETH BARRETT BROWNING.

1 Autumn wins you best by this its mute
Appeal to sympathy for its decay.
Paracelsus, pt 1, ll. 25–6 (1835). The words of Paracelsus.

2 Measure your mind's height by the shade it
casts!
Ibid., pt 3, l. 821. Festus addresses Paracelsus.

3 I give the fight up: let there be an end,
A privacy, an obscure nook for me.
I want to be forgotten even by God.
Ibid., pt 5, ll. 363–5

4 The year's at the spring
And day's at the morn;
Morning's at seven;
The hillside's dew-pearled;
The lark's on the wing;
The snail's on the thorn;
God's in his heaven –
All's right with the world!
Pippa Passes, pt 1 ('Morning') (1841). Pippa's song.

5 In the morning of the world,
When earth was nigher heaven than now.
Ibid., pt 3 ('Evening'). Pippa's song.

6 All service ranks the same with God –
With God, whose puppets, best and worst,
Are we: there is no last nor first.
Ibid., pt 4 ('Night'). Closing lines of work.

7 Boot, saddle, to horse, and away!
'Boot and Saddle', refrain, publ. in *Dramatic Lyrics* (1842).

The third of Browning's 'Cavalier Tunes', first titled 'My Wife
Gertrude'.

8 That's my last Duchess painted on the wall,
Looking as if she were alive.
'My Last Duchess', ibid. Opening lines of poem.

9 I gave commands;
Then all smiles stopped together.
'My Last Duchess', ibid. The Duke of Ferrara orders his wife's
murder.

10 Rats!
They fought the dogs and killed the cats,
And bit the babies in the cradles,
And ate the cheeses out of the vats,
And licked the soup from the cooks' own ladles,
Split open the kegs of salted sprats,
Made nests inside men's Sunday hats,
And even spoiled the women's chats
By drowning their speaking
With shrieking and squeaking
In fifty different sharps and flats.
'The Pied Piper of Hamelin', st. 2, ibid.

11 I sprang to the stirrup, and Joris, and he;
I galloped, Dirck galloped, we galloped all three.
'How They Brought the Good News from Ghent to Aix', publ.
in *Dramatic Romances and Lyrics* (1845). Opening lines of
poem.

12 Just for a handful of silver he left us,
Just for a riband to stick in his coat.
'The Lost Leader', st. 1, ibid. Referring to WILLIAM WORDS-
WORTH.

13 We that had loved him so, followed him,
honoured him,
Lived in his mild and magnificent eye,
Learned his great language, caught his clear
accents,
Made him our pattern to live and to die!
'The Lost Leader', st. 1, ibid.

14 Shakespeare was of us, Milton was for us,
Burns, Shelley, were with us – they watch from
their graves!
'The Lost Leader', st. 1, ibid.

15 Let him never come back to us!
There would be doubt, hesitation and pain,
Forced praise on our part – the glimmer of
twilight,
Never glad confident morning again!
'The Lost Leader', st. 2, ibid.

16 Oh, to be in England
Now that April's there,
And whoever wakes in England
Sees, some morning, unaware,
That the lowest boughs and the brushwood sheaf
Round the elm-tree bole are in tiny leaf,
While the chaffinch sings on the orchard bough
In England – now!
'Home Thoughts, From Abroad', st. 1, ibid.

17 That's the wise thrush; he sings each song twice
over,
Lest you should think he never could recapture
The first fine careless rapture!
'Home Thoughts, From Abroad', st. 2, ibid.

18 And then how I shall lie through centuries,
And hear the blessed mutter of the mass,
And see God made and eaten all day long,
And feel the steady candle-flame, and taste
Good strong thick stupefying incense-smoke!
'The Bishop Orders His Tomb at Saint Praxed's Church', ll. 80–
4, ibid.

19 What's a man's age? He must hurry more, that's
all;
Cram in a day, what his youth took a year to hold.
'The Flight of the Duchess', sect. 17, ibid.

20 Nay but you, who do not love her,
Is she not pure gold, my mistress?
'Song', ibid. Opening lines of poem.

21 Let's contend no more, Love
Strive nor weep:
All be as before, Love,
– Only sleep!
'A Woman's Last Word', st. 1, publ. in *Men and Women*, vol. 1
(1855)

22 Where the apple reddens
Never pry –
Lest we lose our Edens,
Eve and I.
'A Woman's Last Word', st. 5, ibid.

23 If you get simple beauty and nought else,
You get about the best thing God invents.
'Fra Lippo Lippi', ll. 217–18, ibid.

24 For, don't you mark? We're made so that we
love
First when we see them painted, things we have
passed
Perhaps a hundred times nor cared to see;

And so they are better, painted – better to us,
Which is the same thing. Art was given for that.
'Fra Lippo Lippi', ll. 300–4, ibid.

25 What of soul was left, I wonder, when the
kissing had to stop?
'A Toccata of Galuppi's', st. 14, ibid.

26 I and my mistress, side by side,
Shall be together, breathe and ride,
So, one day more am I deified.
Who knows but the world may end tonight?
'The Last Ride Together', st. 2, ibid.

27 It was roses, roses, all the way.
'The Patriot', ibid. Opening line of poem.

28 Truth that peeps
Over the glasses' edge when dinner's done.
'Bishop Blougram's Apology', ll. 17–18, ibid.

29 How can we guard our unbelief,
Make it bear fruit to us? – the problem here.
Just when we are safest, there's a sunset-touch,
A fancy from a flower-bell, someone's death,
A chorus-ending from Euripides.
'Bishop Blougram's Apology', ll. 180–4, ibid.

30 The grand Perhaps! We look on helplessly,
There the old misgivings, crooked questions are.
'Bishop Blougram's Apology', ll. 190–1, ibid.

31 Our interest's on the dangerous edge of
things.
The honest thief, the tender murderer,
The superstitious atheist.
'Bishop Blougram's Apology', ll. 395–7, ibid. These lines were
suggested by GRAHAM GREENE as the epigraph he would
choose for all of his novels.

32 The aim, if reached or not, makes great the life:
Try to be Shakespeare, leave the rest to fate!
'Bishop Blougram's Apology', ll. 492–3, ibid.

33 No, when the fight begins within himself,
A man's worth something.
'Bishop Blougram's Apology', ll. 693–4, ibid.

34 Ah, did you once see Shelley plain,
And did he stop and speak to you
And did you speak to him again?
How strange it seems and new!
'Memorabilia', ibid. Opening lines.

35 Well, less is more, Lucrezia.
'Andrea del Sarto', l. 78, ibid., vol. 2 (1855). See LUDWIG MIES
VAN DER ROHE 1.

36 Ah, but a man's reach should exceed his grasp,
Or what's a heaven for?
'Andrea del Sarto', ll. 97–8, ibid.

37 'Tis not what man Does which exalts him, but
    what man Would do!
'Saul', st. 18, ibid.

38 Your ghost will walk, you lover of trees,
(If our loves remain)
In an English lane,
By a cornfield-side a-flutter with poppies.
'De Gustibus', ibid. Opening lines of poem.

39 What I love best in all the world
Is a castle, precipice-encurled,
In a gash of the wind-grieved Apennine.
'De Gustibus', st. 2, ibid.

40 Open my heart and you will see,
Graved inside of it, 'Italy'.
'De Gustibus', st. 2, ibid. See MARY I 1.

41 Others mistrust and say, 'But time escapes:
Live now or never!'
He said, 'What's time? Leave Now for dogs and
    apes!
Man has Forever.'
'A Grammarian's Funeral', ll. 81–4, ibid.

42 Give me the keys. I feel for the common chord
    again,
Sliding by semitones, till I sink to the minor, – yes,
And I blunt it into a ninth, and I stand on alien
    ground,
Surveying awhile the heights I rolled from into the
    deep;
Which, hark, I have dared and done, for my
    resting-place is found,
The C Major of this life: so, now I will try to sleep.
'Abt Vogler', st. 12, publ. in *Dramatis Personae* (1864)

43 Grow old along with me!
The best is yet to be,
The last of life, for which the first was made:
Our times are in His hand
Who saith 'A whole I planned,
Youth shows but half; trust God: see all nor be
    afraid!'
'Rabbi Ben Ezra', st. 1, ibid.

44 What I aspired to be,
And was not, comforts me.
'Rabbi Ben Ezra', st. 7, ibid.

45 Stung by the splendour of a sudden thought.
'A Death in the Desert', l. 59, ibid.

46 Progress, man's distinctive mark alone,
Not God's, and not the beasts': God is, they are,
Man partly is and wholly hopes to be.
'A Death in the Desert', ll. 586–8, ibid.

47 We loved, sir – used to meet:
How sad and bad and mad it was –
But then, how it was sweet!
'Confessions', ibid. Closing lines of poem.

48 Fear death? – to feel the fog in my throat,
The mist in my face,
When the snows begin.
'Prospice', ibid. Opening lines.

49 I was ever a fighter, so – one fight more,
The best and the last!
I would hate that death bandaged my eyes, and
    forbore,
And bade me creep past.
No! let me taste the whole of it, fare like my peers
The heroes of old,
Bear the brunt, in a minute pay glad life's arrears
Of pain, darkness and cold.
'Prospice', ibid.

50 O lyric Love, half angel and half bird
And all a wonder and a wild desire.
The Ring and the Book, bk 1 ('The Ring and the Book'), ll. 1391–2
(1868–9)

51 Go practise if you please
With men and women: leave a child alone
For Christ's particular love's sake!
Ibid., bk 3 ('The Other Half-Rome'), ll. 88–90

52 Everyone soon or late comes round by Rome.
Ibid., bk 5 ('Count Guido Franceschini'), l. 296

53 That's all we may expect of man, this side
The grave: his good is – knowing he is bad.
Ibid., bk 6 ('Giuseppe Caponsacchi'), ll. 143–4

54 Faultless to a fault.
Ibid., bk 9 ('Juris Doctor Johannes-Baptista Bottinius'), l. 1177.
Describing Pompilia.

55 What I call God,
And fools call Nature.
Ibid., bk 10 ('The Pope'), ll. 1073–4

56 There's a new tribunal now
Higher than God's – the educated man's!
Ibid., bk 10 ('The Pope'), ll. 1976–7

57 Inscribe all human effort with one word,
Artistry's haunting curse, the Incomplete!
Ibid., bk 11 ('Guido'), ll. 1560–1

58 You never know what life means till you die:
Even throughout life, 'tis death that makes life
   live,
Gives it whatever the significance.
Ibid., bk 11 ('Guido'), ll. 2375–7

59 It is the glory and good of Art,
That Art remains the one way possible
Of speaking truth, to mouths like mine at least.
Ibid., bk 12 ('The Book and the Ring'), ll. 842–4

60 Ignorance is not innocence but sin.
The Inn Album, canto 5 (1875)

61 What Youth deemed crystal, Age finds out was
   dew.
'Jochanan Hakkadosh', st. 101, publ. in *Jocoseria* (1883)

62 Never the time and the place
And the loved one all together!
'Never the Time and the Place', ibid. Opening lines of poem.

63 One who never turned his back but marched
   breast forward,
Never doubted clouds would break,
Never dreamed, though right were worsted, wrong
   would triumph,
Held we fall to rise, are baffled to fight better,
Sleep to wake.
'Epilogue', st. 3, publ. in *Asolando* (1889)

Lenny Bruce
(1925–66)
US satirical comedian

*Originally Leonard Alfred Schneider. He built up a cult follow-
ing with his darkly satirical routines, which were often considered offensive. He was imprisoned for obscenity in 1961 and
banned from entering Britain in 1963.*

1 A lot of people say to me, 'Why did you kill Christ?'
'I dunno ... it was one of those parties, got out of
hand, you know.' We killed him because he didn't
want to become a doctor, that's why we killed him.
The Essential Lenny Bruce, 'The Jews' (ed. John Cohen, 1967)

2 All my humor is based upon destruction and
despair. If the whole world were tranquil, without
disease and violence, I'd be standing on the bread-
line right in back of J. Edgar Hoover.
Ibid. The words also appear as the book's epigraph.

3 Satire is tragedy plus time. You give it enough

time, the public, the reviewers will allow you to
satirize it. Which is rather ridiculous, when you
think about it.
Ibid.

4 The liberals can understand everything but
people who don't understand them.
Ibid., 'Politics'

5 I'll die young but it's like kissing God.
Quoted in *Playpower*, ch. 4 (1970) by Richard Neville. On his
drug addiction; Bruce died from a drugs overdose.

Beau Brummell
(1778–1840)
English dandy

*George Bryan Brummell. Known as a wit and fastidious
dresser, his friendship with the Prince of Wales (later George IV)
helped to elevate him to the role of high arbiter of fashion.
He squandered his fortune through extravagant gambling,
however, and ended his days in a charitable institution in
France.*

1 Alvanley, who's your fat friend?
Remark to Lord Alvanley, London, July 1813, quoted in *Life of
George Brummell*, vol. 1, ch. 19 (1844) by Capt. Jesse. Referring
to the Prince Regent, later George IV, who had snubbed Brummell at a reception in the Argyle Rooms. The quarrel between
the two, which probably arose as a result of Brummell's jibes
about Mrs Fitzherbert, the Prince's mistress, precipitated
Brummell's downfall and exile.

Frank Bruno
(b. 1961)
British boxer

*He became WBC world heavyweight champion in 1995 but
was defeated by Mike Tyson the following year, after which he
became a popular media figure.*

1 Know what I mean, 'Arry?
Often repeated remark to the sports commentator Harry Carpenter in TV interviews, from 1980s

2 Boxing is just show business with blood.
Guardian 19 November 1991

Giordano Bruno
(1548–1600)
Italian philosopher

*He entered the Dominican order c. 1565, but his unorthodox
views, particularly his advocacy of the Copernican model of
the universe, forced him to flee Italy in 1578. After his return,
he was arrested by the Inquisition in 1593 and burned at the
stake.*

1 The universe is then one, infinite, immobile ... It is not capable of comprehension and therefore is endless and limitless, and to that extent infinite and indeterminable, and consequently immobile.
Cause, Principle, and Unity, 'Fifth Dialogue' (1584). The words of Teofilo.

2 The beginning, middle, and end of the birth, growth, and perfection of whatever we behold is from contraries, by contraries, and to contraries; and whatever contrarity is, there is action and reaction, there is motion, diversity, multitude, and order, there are degrees, succession and vicissitude.
The Expulsion of the Triumphant Beast, 'First Dialogue', sect. 1 (1584)

3 There is in the universe neither centre nor circumference.
On the Infinite Universe and Worlds, 'Fifth Dialogue' (1584)

4 We delight in one knowable thing, which comprehends all that is knowable; in one apprehensible, which draws together all that can be apprehended; in a single being that includes all, above all in the one which is itself the all.
Ibid., Teofilo, in 'Fifth Dialogue'

5 It may be you fear more to deliver judgment upon me than I fear judgment.
Quoted in *Life of Giordano Bruno*, ch. 11 (1887) by I. Frith. Addressed to the inquisitors who had condemned him to death.

William Jennings Bryan
(1860–1925)
US politician

Elected as a Democrat to Congress in 1890, he ran unsuccessfully for president in 1896, 1900 and 1908. He was known for his pacifism and liberal views, though gained notoriety for his espousal of creationism in the Scopes trial of 1925.

1 The humblest citizen of all the land, when clad in the armor of a righteous cause, is stronger than all the hosts of error.
Speech at Democratic Convention, Chicago, 8 July 1896, publ. in *Speeches of William Jennings Bryan*, vol. 1 (1909)

2 Burn down your cities and leave our farms, and your cities will spring up again as if by magic; but destroy our farms and the grass will grow in the streets of every city in the country.
Speech at Democratic Convention, Chicago, 8 July 1896, ibid.

3 You shall not press down upon the brow of labor this crown of thorns, you shall not crucify mankind upon a cross of gold.
Ibid. Concluding words. The speech has come to be known as the 'Cross of Gold' speech for this widely-quoted attack on the primacy of gold as the backing for currency. Bryan's eloquent performance secured for him the Democratic presidential nomination.

4 If that vital spark that we find in a grain of wheat can pass unchanged through countless deaths and resurrections, will the spirit of man be unable to pass from this body to another?
Speech at Lincoln, Nebraska, 2 December 1906, quoted in the *Nebraska State Journal* 3 December 1906, ibid.

William Cullen Bryant
(1794–1878)
US poet and editor

He came to notice with his blank-verse poem Thanatopsis, *written when he was seventeen. Like much of his later work, this contained sensuous evocations of nature, particularly as experienced in his native Massachusetts. For fifty years he edited the New York* Evening Post.

1 So live, that when thy summons comes to join
The innumerable caravan which moves
To that mysterious realm, where each shall take
His chamber in the silent halls of death,
Thou go not, like the quarry-slave at night,
Scourged to his dungeon, but, sustained and
    soothed
By an unfaltering trust, approach thy grave,
Like one that wraps the drapery of his couch
About him, and lies down to pleasant dreams.
Thanatopsis, ll. 73–81 (1817)

James Bryce
(1838–1922)
British historian, politician and diplomat

Regius Professor of Civil Law at Oxford (1870–93) and a Liberal MP (1880–1907), he was instrumental in establishing a Ministry of Education in Britain. He was Ambassador to the United States (1907–13), where he was already well known for his study of the US Constitution, The American Commonwealth *(1888).*

1 There is a hearty Puritanism in the view of human nature which pervades the instrument of 1787. It is the work of men who believed in original sin, and were resolved to leave open for transgressors no door which they could possibly shut.
The American Commonwealth, vol. 1, ch. 26 (1888). Referring to the US constitution. Bryce was here agreeing with the opinion of one – unnamed – who said that 'the American

Government and Constitution are based on the theology of Calvin and the philosophy of Hobbes.'

2 No wonder that, when a political career is so precarious, men of worth and capacity hesitate to embrace it. They cannot afford to be thrown out of their life's course by a mere accident.
Ibid., vol. 2, ch. 58

Bill Bryson
(b. 1951)
US author and journalist

As well as his best-selling travel books such as Notes from a Small Island *(1995), he has published* Mother Tongue *(1990), on the English language, and* A Short History of Nearly Everything *(2003), on science.*

1 There are things you just can't do in life. You can't beat the phone company, you can't make a waiter see you until he's ready to see you, and you can't go home again.
The Lost Continent: Travels in Small Town America, ch. 2 (1989)

2 The average Southerner has the speech patterns of someone slipping in and out of consciousness. I can change my shoes and socks faster than most people in Mississippi can speak a sentence.
Ibid., ch. 7

3 It is an interesting experience to become acquainted with a country through the eyes of the insane, and, if I may say so, a particularly useful grounding for life in Britain.
Notes from a Small Island, ch. 5 (1995)

4 The only thing special about the atoms that make you is that they make you. That is, of course, the miracle of life.
A Short History of Nearly Everything, Introduction (2003)

John Buchan
(1875–1940)
British author and statesman

Baron Tweedsmuir. MP for the Scottish Universities (1927–35) and Governor General of Canada (1935–40), he was also a prolific writer of thrillers, of which The Thirty-Nine Steps *(1915) is considered his best.*

1 Every man at the bottom of his heart believes that he is a born detective.
The Power-House, ch. 2 (1916). Spoken by Leithen.

2 An atheist is a man who has no invisible means of support.
Quoted in *On Being a Real Person*, ch. 10 (1943) by H. E. Fosdick

Patrick Buchanan
(b. 1938)
US journalist and politician

Host of the radio show Buchanan & Co, *he was speechwriter and senior adviser to* RICHARD NIXON *(1969–74) and an unsuccessful candidate for the Republican presidential nomination in 1992 and 1996. Representing the Reform Party, he made another bid for president in 2000.*

1 Anti-Catholicism is the anti-semitism of the intellectual.
Observer 15 December 1991. Peter Viereck, in *Shame and Glory of the Intellectuals*, ch.3 (1953) had earlier written: 'Catholic-baiting is the anti-Semitism of the liberals.'

2 If America does not wish to end her days in the same nursing home as Britannia she had best end this geo-babble about new world orders. Our war, the Cold War, is over. It is time for America to come home.
Observer 15 December 1991

3 Listen, my friend, I've just come back from Mississippi and over there when you talk about the West Bank they think you mean Arkansas.
Spectator 13 March 1992

Robert Buchanan
(1841–1901)
Scottish poet, novelist and playwright

Arriving in London from Edinburgh in 1860, he tackled numerous different forms of verse, drama and fiction with only sporadic success. London Poems *(1866) was one of his most enduring works, evoking the capital's squalor.*

1 The Fleshly School of Poetry.
Title of article in *The Contemporary Review* October 1871. Referring to the Pre-Raphaelite poets. The article, in which Buchanan (under the pseudonym Thomas Maitland) criticized the 'morbid deviation from the healthy forms of life' in the poetry of ROSSETTI, SWINBURNE and others, was later expanded and published as a pamphlet (1872). Rossetti responded with 'The Stealthy School of Criticism' (1871), and Swinburne also penned a defence in *Under the Microscope* (1872).

2 She just wore
Enough for modesty – no more.
White Rose and Red, pt 1, sect. 5, ll. 60–1 (1873)

3 The sweet post-prandial cigar.
'De Berny', publ. in *Poetical Works*, 'London Poems' (1884)

Frank Buchman
(1878–1961)
US evangelist

He is principally known as the founder of the nondenominational Moral Rearmament Movement at Oxford in 1921, which after the First World War became more politically oriented and opposed to Communism.

1 I thank heaven for a man like Adolf Hitler, who built a front line of defense against the anti-Christ of Communism.
Interview in the *New York World-Telegram* 25 August 1936

2 There is enough in the world for everyone's need, but not enough for everyone's greed.
Remaking the World (1947)

Georg Büchner
(1813–37)
German dramatist

His three plays, Danton's Death *(1835),* Leonce and Lena *(1836) and* Woyzeck *(1836), proved a powerful influence on German theatre in the 1890s and on 20th-century Expressionism.*

1 The revolution is like Saturn, it eats its children.
Danton's Death, Act 1 (1835). Spoken by Danton.

Art Buchwald
(b. 1925)
US humorist

Arthur Buchwald. Known for his 'Art Buchwald' column, syndicated worldwide, he was hailed by DEAN ACHESON *as 'the greatest satirist since Pope and Swift' and was celebrated as the 'court jester of Washington society'.*

1 If you attack the establishment long enough and hard enough, they will make you a member of it.
International Herald Tribune 24 May 1989

Gesualdo Bufalino
(1920–96)
Sicilian author

'Discovered' by his fellow Sicilian author Leonardo Sciascia, he published his first book, The Plague Sower *(1981), late in life, though it was written long before. He won the Strega Prize for* Night's Lies *in 1988.*

1 Don't forget that even our most obscene vices nearly always bear the seal of sullen greatness.
Guardian 21 May 1992. Speaking of the Sicilian character.

George-Louis Leclerc, Comte de Buffon
(1707–88)
French naturalist

After visiting Italy and England, he was appointed keeper of the Royal Botanical Gardens, in which capacity he wrote his monumental Histoire naturelle, générale et particulière *(1749–84), a comprehensive work on natural history.*

1 *Le style c'est l'homme même.*
[Style is the man himself.]
Discours sur le style, inaugural address to the Académie Française, Paris, 25 August 1753

2 Genius is only a greater aptitude for patience.
Quoted in *Voyage à Montbard* (1803) by Hérault de Séchelles

Charles Bukowski
(1920–94)
US author and poet

He gained a cult following for his poetry, short stories and novels, sardonic tales of survival in a down-and-out society. Works include Flower, Fist and Bestial Wail *(1959) and* Tales of Ordinary Madness *(1967).*

1 A man does not get old because he nears death; a man gets old because he can no longer see the false from the good.
Letter, early 1962, publ. in *Screams from the Balcony: Selected Letters* (ed. Seamus Cooney, 1993)

2 Show me a man who lives alone and has a perpetually clean kitchen, and 8 times out of 9 I'll show you a man with detestable spiritual qualities.
Tales of Ordinary Madness, 'Too Sensitive' (1967)

3 You begin saving the world by saving one man at a time; all else is grandiose romanticism or politics.
Ibid., 'Too Sensitive'

4 Almost everybody is born a genius and buried an idiot.
Notes of a Dirty Old Man (1969)

5 If you want to know who your friends are, get yourself a jail sentence.
Ibid.

6 Sexual intercourse is kicking death in the ass while singing.
Ibid.

7 An intellectual is a man who says a simple thing in a difficult way; an artist is a man who says a difficult thing in a simple way.
Ibid.

8 There's always somebody about to ruin your day, if not your life.
Pulp, ch. 28 (1994). Narrated by Nicky Belane.

Prince Bernhard von Bülow
(1849–1929)
German diplomat and politician

He was appointed to the Foreign Department by Wilhelm II in 1897. As Chancellor (1900–9), he pursued an aggressive foreign policy with some success, but eventually fell out with Wilhelm and resigned.

1 We desire to throw no one into the shade, but we also demand our own place in the sun.
Speech to Reichstag, 6 December 1897, publ. in *Graf Bülows Reden* (1903). The phrase 'place in the sun' was used on diverse occasions by Bülow and Wilhelm II.

Edward Bulwer-Lytton
(1803–73)
English author and politician

First Baron Lytton. He produced a string of popular novels, plays and verse works in a variety of genres, including The Last Days of Pompeii *(1834), a historical romance. He entered parliament twice, first in 1831 as a Liberal, then twenty years later as a Tory.*

1 Rank is a great beautifier.
The Lady of Lyons, Act 2, Sc. 1 (1838). Spoken by Melnotte.

2 Beneath the rule of men entirely great
The pen is mightier than the sword.
Richelieu, Act 2, Sc. 2 (1839). Spoken by Richelieu.

3 In the lexicon of youth, which Fate reserves
For a bright manhood, there is no such word
As – *fail*!
Richelieu, ibid., Act 2, Sc. 2

4 Happy is the man who hath never known what it is to taste of fame – to have it is a purgatory, to want it is a Hell!
The Last of the Barons, bk 5, ch. 1 (1843)

Alfred Bunn
(*c.* 1796–1860)
English theatrical manager and librettist

Nicknamed 'Poet Bunn', he was manager of Drury Lane and Covent Garden theatres 1833–48, staged English operas and wrote occasional verse.

1 I dreamt that I dwelt in marble halls
With vassals and serfs at my side.
'The Gipsy Girl's Dream' (song), in *The Bohemian Girl*, Act 2 (1843)

Basil Bunting
(1900–85)
British poet

Influenced by EZRA POUND *and the Imagists, he established his reputation with the lyrical* Briggflatts *(1966), a semi-autobiographical poem which portrays his native Northumberland.*

1 To appreciate present conditions
collate them with those of antiquity.
'Chomei at Toyama' (written 1932), publ. in *Active Anthology* (ed. EZRA POUND, 1933)

2 Can a moment of madness make up for an age of consent?
'The Well of Lycopolis', pt 3, written 1935, publ. in *Poems* (1950)

3 Man's life so little worth,
do we fear to take or lose it?
No ill companion on a journey, Death
lays his purse on the table and opens the wine.
'The Spoils' (1951), repr. in *Loquitur* (1965). Opening lines of poem.

4 Sooner or later we must absorb Islam if our own culture is not to die of anemia.
Preface to *Arabic and Persian Poems* (1970) by Omar Pound

Luis Buñuel
(1900–83)
Spanish film-maker

He collaborated with SALVADOR DALÍ *on his first films* Un Chien andalou *(1928) and* L'Age d'or *(1930), both of which caused a sensation. Later films include* Los Olvidados *(1950),* Belle de jour *(1967) and* The Discreet Charm of the Bourgeoisie *(1972).*

1 Work's a curse, Saturno. I say to hell with the work you have to do to earn a living! That kind of work does us no honour; all it does is fill up the bellies of

the pigs who exploit us. But the work you do because you like to do it, because you've heard the call, you've got a vocation – that's ennobling! We should all be able to work like that. Look at me, Saturno – I don't work. And I don't care if they hang me, I *won't* work! Yet I'm alive! I may live badly, but at least I don't have to work to do it!

Tristana (film, 1970, written and directed by Luis Buñuel). Spoken by Don Lope (Fernando Rey). Buñuel's screenplay was derived from the novel of the same name by Benito Pérez Galdós, but where Galdós criticized his character for laziness, Buñuel praised him.

2 You have to begin to lose your memory, if only in bits and pieces, to realize that memory is what makes our lives. Life without memory is no life at all, just as an intelligence without the possibility of expression is not really an intelligence. Our memory is our coherence, our reason, our feeling, even our action. Without it, we are nothing.

My Last Breath, ch. 1 (1983). 'I can only wait for the final amnesia,' Buñuel wrote, 'the one that can erase an entire life.'

3 Tobacco and alcohol, delicious fathers of abiding friendships and fertile reveries.

Ibid., ch. 6

4 God and Country are an unbeatable team; they break all records for oppression and bloodshed.

Ibid., ch. 14

5 A paranoiac . . . like a poet, is born, not made.

Ibid., ch. 18

John Bunyan

(1628–88)

English preacher and author

Having joined an Independent church in Bedford in 1653, he was imprisoned for preaching (1660–72), during which time he wrote Grace Abounding *(1666). While in prison for a second term, he began work on* The Pilgrim's Progress *(1678), a Christian allegory that was an instant success; a second part followed in 1684.*

1 I have sometimes seen more in a line of the Bible than I could well tell how to stand under, and yet at another time the whole Bible hath been to me as dry as a stick.

Grace Abounding to the Chief of Sinners, para. 4 (1666)

2 Some said, John, print it; others said, Not so: Some said, It might do good; others said, No.

The Pilgrim's Progress, pt 1, 'The Author's Apology for His Book' (1678)

3 As I walked through the wilderness of this world.

Ibid., pt 1. Opening words.

4 The name of the slough was Despond.

Ibid., pt 1. Referring to the 'miry slough' in which Christian and Pliable waded.

5 For it is a hard matter for a man to go down into the Valley of Humiliation, as thou art now, and to catch no slip by the way.

Ibid., pt 1

6 At the town there is a fair kept, called Vanity Fair. It is kept all the year long: it beareth the name of Vanity Fair, because the town where it is kept is lighter than vanity.

Ibid., pt 1. See BIBLE, OLD TESTAMENT: ECCLESIASTES 1.

7 Hanging is too good for him.

Ibid., pt 1. The words of Mr Cruelty, a juror, at the trial of Faithful.

8 Yet my great-grandfather was but a water-man, looking one way, and rowing another: and I got most of my estate by the same occupation.

By-ends, in ibid., pt 1. The image also occurs in the works of PLUTARCH and ROBERT BURTON, among others.

9 Now there was, not far from the place where they lay, a castle, called Doubting Castle, the owner whereof was Giant Despair.

Ibid., pt 1

10 They went then till they came to the Delectable Mountains.

Ibid., pt 1

11 A man that could look no way but downwards, with a muckrake in his hand.

Ibid., pt 2 (1684). See THEODORE ROOSEVELT 6.

12 One leak will sink a ship: and one sin will destroy a sinner.

The Interpreter, ibid., pt 2

13 He that is down needs fear no fall,
He that is low no pride.
He that is humble ever shall
Have God to be his guide.

Ibid., pt 2. The song of the shepherd boy.

14 Who would true valour see,
Let him come hither:
One here will constant be,
Come wind, come weather.
There's no discouragement
Shall make him once relent

His first avowed intent
To be a pilgrim.
Ibid., pt 2. See HYMNS AND CAROLS 36.

15 Whoso beset him round
With dismal stories,
Do but themselves confound –
His strength the more is.
Ibid., pt 2

16 Then fancies fly away,
He'll fear not what men say;
He'll labour night and day
To be a pilgrim.
Ibid., pt 2

17 My sword I give to him that shall succeed me in
my pilgrimage, and my courage and skill to him
that can get it.
Ibid., pt 2. Valiant-for-Truth makes his farewell.

Samuel Dickinson Burchard
(1812–91)
US clergyman

*He was pastor of Houston Street Presbyterian church in New
York 1839–79.*

1 We are Republicans and don't propose to leave our
party and identify ourselves with the party whose
antecedents are rum, Romanism, and rebellion.
Speech in New York, 29 October 1884, quoted in the *New
York World* 30 October 1884. Speaking for a deputation of
clergymen, Burchard welcomed Republican presidential candidate James G. Blaine with these words, alluding to a previous remark by James Garfield about the Democrats in 1876.
Blaine's failure to disown the slur probably cost him the
election.

Julie Burchill
(b. 1960)
British journalist and author

Starting in journalism with the New Musical Express, *she went
on to co-found the* Modern Review, *and has subsequently
worked as a contentious columnist on various newspapers.
She has also published novels.*

1 A good part – and definitely the most fun part –
of being a feminist is about frightening men.
Time Out 16 November 1989

2 Punk, far from being a peasants' revolt, was just
another English spectacle, like the Royal Wedding:

a chance for us to congratulate ourselves on our
talent for tableaux.
Modern Review Autumn 1991

3 She [Princess DIANA] showed the House of Windsor up for what it was: a dumb, numb dinosaur,
lumbering along in a world of its own, gorged sick
on arrogance and ignorance.
Guardian 2 September 1997

4 The Age of Diana has not ended but has rather
just begun. Frozen forever at the height of her
beauty, compassion and power by death, she will
be the mourner at every royal wedding and the
blushing bride at every Coronation.
Diana, Foreword (1998)

5 A wedding is a funeral which masquerades as a
feast. And the greater the pageantry, the deeper the
savagery.
Diana, ch. 1 (1998)

Anthony Burgess
(1917–93)
British author and critic

*John Anthony Burgess Wilson. With an inexhaustible intellect,
he wrote novels, memoirs, biographies, reviews and libretti,
but is chiefly known for* A Clockwork Orange *(1962, filmed
1971), a disturbing and violent vision of the future.*

1 I've always felt that English women had to be
approached in a sisterly manner, rather than an
erotic manner.
The Times 27 July 1988

2 The trouble began with Forster. After him it was
considered ungentlemanly to write more than five
or six novels.
Guardian 24 February 1989. Burgess himself wrote more than
twenty novels.

3 We are supposed to be the children of Seth; but
Seth is too much of an effete nonentity to deserve
ancestral regard. No, we are the sons of Cain, and
with violence can be associated the attacks on
sound, stone, wood and metal that produced civilisation.
Book review in the *Observer* 26 November 1989

4 Novelists are perhaps the last people in the world
to be entrusted with opinions. The nature of a novel
is that it has no opinions, only the dialectic of contrary views, some of which, all of which, may be
untenable and even silly. A novelist should not be

too intelligent either, although ... he may be permitted to be an intellectual.
You've Had Your Time, ch. 2 (1990)

Gelett Burgess
(1866–1951)
US humorist and illustrator

His works include books on Goops (bad-mannered children), and he is credited with enlarging the English language with words such as 'blurb'.

1 I never saw a Purple Cow,
I never hope to see one;
But I can tell you, anyhow,
I'd rather see than be one!
'The Purple Cow' (1895), publ. in *The Burgess Nonsense Book* (1914)

2 Ah, yes, I wrote the 'Purple Cow' –
I'm sorry, now, I wrote it!
But I can tell you, anyhow,
I'll kill you if you quote it.
'Cinq Ans Après', publ. in *The Burgess Nonsense Book* (1914)

3 To appreciate nonsense requires a serious interest in life.
The Romance of the Commonplace, 'The Sense of Humor' (1916)

Edmund Burke
(1729–97)
Anglo-Irish politician and political philosopher

In Parliament from 1765, he opposed the government's stance towards the American colonies, and served in Whig governments 1782–3. His speeches and writings have profoundly influenced political and constitutional debate. 'Almost alone in England,' wrote MATTHEW ARNOLD, 'he brings thought to bear upon politics, he saturates politics with thought.' See also THOMAS PAINE 15.

1 A good parson once said that where mystery begins religion ends. Cannot I say, as truly at least, of human laws, that where mystery begins justice ends?
A Vindication of Natural Society (1756), repr. in *The Writings and Speeches of Edmund Burke*, vol. 1 (ed. Paul Langford, 1997)

2 Beauty in distress is much the most affecting beauty.
A Philosophical Enquiry into the Origin of our Ideas of the Sublime and Beautiful, Introduction (1757), ibid., vol. 1

3 No passion so effectually robs the mind of all its powers of acting and reasoning as fear.
A Philosophical Enquiry into the Origin of our Ideas of the Sublime and Beautiful, pt 2, sect. 2, ibid., vol. 1

4 Custom reconciles us to everything.
A Philosophical Enquiry into the Origin of our Ideas of the Sublime and Beautiful, pt 4, sect. 18, ibid., vol. 1

5 Laws, like houses, lean on one another.
Tracts Relating to Popery Laws, ch. 3, sect. 1 (1765), ibid., vol. 9 (1991)

6 It is a general popular error to suppose the loudest complainers for the public to be the most anxious for its welfare.
Observations on a late Publication on the Present State of the Nation (1769), ibid., vol. 2

7 A strenuous resistance to every appearance of lawless power; a spirit of independence carried to some degree of enthusiasm; an inquisitive character to discover, and a bold one to display, every corruption and every error of government; these are the qualities which recommend a man to a seat in the House of Commons.
Thoughts on the Cause of the Present Discontents, speech, 23 April 1770, ibid., vol. 2

8 When bad men combine, the good must associate; else they will fall, one by one, an unpitied sacrifice in a contemptible struggle.
Thoughts on the Cause of the Present Discontents, ibid., vol. 2. The article argues the need for political parties.

9 Public life is a situation of power and energy; he trespasses against his duty who sleeps upon his watch, as well as he that goes over to the enemy.
Thoughts on the Cause of the Present Discontents, speech, 23 April 1770, ibid., vol. 2

10 It is the nature of all greatness not to be exact.
First Speech on Conciliation with America: American Taxation, House of Commons, 19 April 1774, ibid., vol. 2

11 To tax and to please, no more than to love and to be wise, is not given to men.
First Speech on Conciliation with America: American Taxation, ibid., vol. 2

12 Your representative owes you, not his industry only, but his judgement; and he betrays instead of serving you if he sacrifices it to your opinion.
Speech to the Electors of Bristol, 3 November 1774, ibid., vol. 3 (1996)

13 Parliament is not a *congress* of ambassadors from different and hostile interests; which interests each

must maintain, as an agent and advocate, against other agents and advocates; but parliament is a *deliberative* assembly of *one* nation, with *one* interest, that of the whole; where, not local purposes, not local prejudices ought to guide, but the general good, resulting from the general reason of the whole. You choose a member indeed; but when you have chosen him, he is not a member of Bristol, but he is a member of *parliament*.
Speech to the Electors of Bristol, ibid., vol. 3

14 I have in general no very exalted opinion of the virtue of paper government.
Second Speech on Conciliation with America: The Thirteen Resolutions, House of Commons, 22 March 1775, ibid., vol. 3

15 Young man, there is America, which at this day serves for little more than to amuse you with stories of savage men and uncouth manners.
Second Speech on Conciliation with America: The Thirteen Resolutions, ibid., vol. 3

16 A people who are still, as it were, but in the gristle, and not yet hardened into the bone of manhood.
Second Speech on Conciliation with America: The Thirteen Resolutions, ibid., vol. 3. Referring to English colonists.

17 The use of force alone is but *temporary*. It may subdue for a moment; but it does not remove the necessity of subduing again: and a nation is not governed, which is perpetually to be conquered.
Second Speech on Conciliation with America: The Thirteen Resolutions, ibid., vol. 3

18 All Protestantism, even the most cold and passive, is a sort of dissent. But the religion most prevalent in our northern colonies is a refinement on the principle of resistance; it is the dissidence of dissent, and the Protestantism of the Protestant religion.
Second Speech on Conciliation with America: The Thirteen Resolutions, ibid., vol. 3

19 I do not know a method of drawing up an indictment against a whole people.
Second Speech on Conciliation with America: The Thirteen Resolutions, ibid., vol. 3

20 The march of the human mind is slow.
Second Speech on Conciliation with America: The Thirteen Resolutions, ibid., vol. 3

21 All government, indeed every human benefit and enjoyment, every virtue and every prudent act, is founded on compromise and barter. We balance inconveniences; we give and take; we remit some rights, that we may enjoy others; and, we choose rather to be happy citizens, than subtle disputants.
Second Speech on Conciliation with America: The Thirteen Resolutions, ibid., vol. 3

22 Slavery they can have anywhere. It is a weed that grows in every soil.
Second Speech on Conciliation with America: The Thirteen Resolutions, ibid., vol. 3

23 Magnanimity in politics is not seldom the truest wisdom; and a great empire and little minds go ill together.
Second Speech on Conciliation with America: The Thirteen Resolutions, ibid., vol. 3

24 In effect, to follow, not to force the public inclination; to give a direction, a form, a technical dress, and a specific sanction, to the general sense of the community, is the true end of legislature.
Letter to the Sheriffs of Bristol, 3 April 1777, ibid., vol. 3

25 Among a people generally corrupt, liberty cannot long exist.
Letter to the Sheriffs of Bristol, ibid., vol. 3

26 It is the interest of the commercial world that wealth should be found everywhere.
Letter on the Trade of Ireland, 23 April 1778, ibid., vol. 9 (1991)

27 In doing good, we are generally cold, and languid, and sluggish; and of all things afraid of being too much in the right. But the works of malice and injustice are quite in another style. They are finished with a bold, masterly hand; touched as they are with the spirit of those vehement passions that call forth all our energies, whenever we oppress and persecute.
Speech at Bristol, Previous to the Election, 9 September 1780, ibid., vol. 3 (1996)

28 A rapacious and licentious soldiery.
Speech on Fox's India Bill, House of Commons, 1 December 1783, ibid., vol. 5 (1981). Referring to troops authorized by Warren Hastings, then Governor-General of Bengal, to make personal searches of women.

29 The people never give up their liberties except under some delusion.
Speech at County Meeting of Buckinghamshire, 1784, attributed

30 An event has happened, upon which it is difficult to speak, and impossible to be silent.
Speech at Westminster Hall, 5 May 1789, publ. in *Speeches . . . in the Trial of Warren Hastings*, vol. 2 (ed. Edward A. Bond, 1859). Referring to the impeachment of WARREN HASTINGS on charges of corruption.

31 Circumstances . . . give in reality to every political principle its distinguishing colour and discriminating effect. The circumstances are what render every civil and political scheme beneficial or noxious to mankind.

Reflections on the Revolution in France (1790), repr. in *The Writings and Speeches of Edmund Burke*, vol. 8 (ed. Paul Langford, 1989)

32 Flattery corrupts both the receiver and the giver.

Reflections on the Revolution in France, ibid., vol. 8

33 The effect of liberty to individuals is that they may do what they please: we ought to see what it will please them to do, before we risk congratulations.

Reflections on the Revolution in France, ibid., vol. 8

34 Whenever our neighbour's house is on fire, it cannot be amiss for the engines to play a little on our own.

Reflections on the Revolution in France, ibid., vol. 8

35 A state without the means of some change is without the means of its conservation.

Reflections on the Revolution in France, ibid., vol. 8

36 People will not look forward to posterity, who never look backward to their ancestors.

Reflections on the Revolution in France, ibid., vol. 8

37 I thought ten thousand swords must have leaped from their scabbards to avenge even a look that threatened her with insult. But the age of chivalry is gone. That of sophisters, economists and calculators has succeeded; and the glory of Europe is extinguished forever.

Reflections on the Revolution in France, ibid., vol. 8. Referring to MARIE-ANTOINETTE.

38 In the groves of their academy, at the end of every vista, you see nothing but the gallows.

Reflections on the Revolution in France, ibid., vol. 8. Referring to the aftermath of the French Revolution.

39 To make us love our country, our country ought to be lovely.

Reflections on the Revolution in France, ibid., vol. 8

40 Kings will be tyrants from policy, when subjects are rebels from principle.

Reflections on the Revolution in France, ibid., vol. 8

41 Learning will be cast into the mire, and trodden down under the hoofs of a swinish multitude.

Reflections on the Revolution in France, ibid., vol. 8

42 Society is indeed a contract . . . It is a partnership in all science; a partnership in all art; a partnership in every virtue, and in all perfection. As the ends of such a partnership cannot be obtained in many generations, it becomes a partnership not only between those who are living, but between those who are living, those who are dead, and those who are to be born.

Reflections on the Revolution in France, ibid., vol. 8

43 Whilst shame keeps its watch, virtue is not wholly extinguished in the heart; nor will moderation be utterly exiled from the minds of tyrants.

Reflections on the Revolution in France, ibid., vol. 8

44 Nobility is a graceful ornament to the civil order. It is the Corinthian capital of polished society.

Reflections on the Revolution in France, ibid., vol. 8

45 Superstition is the religion of feeble minds.

Reflections on the Revolution in France, ibid., vol. 8

46 He that wrestles with us strengthens our nerves, and sharpens our skill. Our antagonist is our helper. This amicable conflict with difficulty helps us to an intimate acquaintance with our object, and compels us to consider it in all its relations. It will not suffer us to be superficial.

Reflections on the Revolution in France, ibid., vol. 8

47 If the people are happy, united, wealthy, and powerful, we presume the rest. We conclude that to be good from whence good is derived.

Reflections on the Revolution in France, ibid., vol. 8

48 Nothing turns out to be so oppressive and unjust as a feeble government.

Reflections on the Revolution in France, ibid., vol. 8

49 When the leaders choose to make themselves bidders at an auction of popularity, their talents, in the construction of the state, will be of no service. They will become flatterers instead of legislators; the instruments, not the guides, of the people.

Reflections on the Revolution in France, ibid., vol. 8

50 Those who have been once intoxicated with power, and have derived any kind of emolument from it, even though but for one year, never can willingly abandon it. They may be distressed in the midst of all their power; but they will never look to anything but power for their relief.

A Letter to a Member of the National Assembly, 19 January 1791, ibid., vol. 8

51 Men are qualified for civil liberty in exact proportion to their disposition to put moral chains

upon their own appetites; in proportion as their love to justice is above their rapacity; in proportion as their soundness and sobriety of understanding is above their vanity and presumption; in proportion as they are more disposed to listen to the counsels of the wise and good, in preference to the flattery of knaves.

A Letter to a Member of the National Assembly, ibid., vol. 8

52 Old religious factions are volcanoes burnt out.

Speech on the Petition of the Unitarians, 11 May 1792, repr. in *Works*, vol. 5 (1812)

53 There is but one law in the world, namely, that law which governs all law: the law of our Creator, the law of humanity, justice, equity, the law of nature and of nations.

Speech at Westminster Hall, London, 28 May 1794, publ. in *The Writings and Speeches of Edmund Burke*, vol. 7 (ed. Paul Langford, 2000)

54 The cold neutrality of an impartial judge.

'Translator's Preface' to *Address to His Constituents* by J. P. Brissot (1794), repr. ibid., vol. 8 (1989)

55 Nothing is so fatal to religion as indifference which is, at least, half infidelity.

Letter, 29 January 1795, publ. ibid., vol. 9 (1991)

56 Somebody has said, that a king may make a nobleman but he cannot make a gentleman.

Letter, 29 January 1795, ibid., vol. 9

57 The great must submit to the dominion of prudence and of virtue, or none will long submit to the dominion of the great.

Letter, 26 May 1795, ibid., vol. 9

58 And having looked to government for bread, on the very first scarcity they will turn and bite the hand that fed them. To avoid that evil, government will redouble the causes of it; and then it will become inveterate and incurable.

Thoughts and Details on Scarcity, pamphlet, November 1795, ibid., vol. 9. Cautioning against the 'attempt to feed the people out of the hands of the magistrates'.

59 Under the pressure of the cares and sorrows of our mortal condition, men have at all times, and in all countries, called in some physical aid to their moral consolations – wine, beer, opium, brandy, or tobacco.

Thoughts and Details on Scarcity, ibid., vol. 9

60 It cannot at this time be too often repeated; line upon line; precept upon precept; until it comes into the currency of a proverb, *To innovate is not to reform*.

A Letter to a Noble Lord (1796), ibid., vol. 9. See BIBLE, OLD TESTAMENT, ISAIAH 37.

61 Mere parsimony is not economy . . . Expense, and great expense, may be an essential part in true economy.

A Letter to a Noble Lord (1796), ibid. vol. 9

62 It is, generally, in the season of prosperity that men discover their real temper, principles, and designs.

Letters . . . on the Proposals for Peace, with the Regicide Directory of France, Letter 1 (1796), ibid., vol. 9

63 We must not always judge of the generality of the opinion by the noise of the acclamation.

Letters . . . on the Proposals for Peace, with the Regicide Directory of France, Letter 1, ibid., vol. 9

64 Ambition can creep as well as soar.

Letters . . . on the Proposals for Peace, with the Regicide Directory of France, Letter 3 (1797), ibid., vol. 9

65 Burke said there were Three Estates in Parliament; but, in the Reporters' Gallery yonder, there sat a Fourth Estate more important far than they all.

Heroes and Hero-Worship, 'The Hero as Man of Letters' (1841) by THOMAS CARLYLE. See also LORD MACAULAY 14.

66 The only thing necessary for the triumph of evil is for good men to do nothing.

Attributed. Ascribed in various forms to Burke, though never found in his writings; possibly it is a distillation of a passage in *Thoughts on the Cause of the Present Discontents* (1770).

Johnny Burke

(1908–64)
US songwriter

In the late 1930s and '40s, he wrote a number of hit songs in collaboration with the composer Jimmy Van Heusen, many of them for films starring BING CROSBY.

1 Every time it rains, it rains
Pennies from heaven.
Don't you know each cloud contains
Pennies from heaven?

'Pennies from Heaven' (song, 1936, with music by Arthur Johnston)

Fanny Burney
(1752–1840)
English author

Also known as Madame d'Arblay, after her marriage to a French refugee officer. Her first and best novel, Evelina (1778), published anonymously, relates a provincial girl's experiences in the city. Her diaries and letters paint a vibrant portrait of the age.

1 O! how short a time does it take to put an end to a woman's liberty!
Journal entry, 20 July 1768, publ. in *Early Journals and Letters of Fanny Burney*, vol. 1 (ed. L. E. Troide, 1988). Referring to a wedding.

2 For my part, I confess I seldom listen to the players: one has so much to do, in looking about and finding out one's acquaintance, that, really, one has no time to mind the stage . . . One merely comes to meet one's friends, and show that one's alive.
Evelina, Letter 20 (1778). Spoken by Mr Lovel.

3 Deviations from common rules, when they proceed from genius, are not merely pardonable, but admirable.
Cecilia, bk 1, ch. 2 (1782). Spoken by Mr Monckton.

4 Travelling is the ruin of all happiness! There's no looking at a building here after seeing Italy.
Mr Meadows, ibid., bk 4, ch. 6

5 My pleasure, therefore, is become my business, and my business my pleasure.
Belfield, ibid., bk 9, ch. 3

6 A little alarm now and then keeps life from stagnation.
Camilla, bk 3, ch. 11 (1796). Spoken by Mrs Arlbery.

Robert Burns
(1759–96)
Scottish poet

The 'national bard of Scotland', he was acclaimed as 'a heaven-taught ploughman'. He enjoyed literary fame with his first volume of verse published in 1786, unusual for poetry using the Scots vernacular. After two failed farming ventures he became an excise officer in 1791. His fame rests equally on his songs, many of which were adaptations of traditional airs. See LORD BYRON 40.

1 But I gae mad at their grimaces,
Their sighin', cantin', grace-proud faces,
Their three-mile prayers, an' half-mile graces.
'To the Rev. John M'Math' (written 1785), publ. in *Reliques of Robert Burns* (ed. Robert H. Cromek, 1808). Referring to members of the Scottish kirk.

2 A fig for those by law protected!
Liberty's a glorious feast!
Courts for cowards were erected,
Churches built to please the priest.
'The Jolly Beggars: a Cantata', also called 'Love and Liberty', final chorus (written c. 1785, publ. 1799), repr. in *Poetical Works*, vol. 2 (ed. William Scott Douglas, 1891)

3 Life is all a variorum,
We regard not how it goes;
Let them cant about decorum
Who have characters to lose!
'The Jolly Beggars: a Cantata', ibid.

4 Till tired at last wi' mony a farce,
They set them down upon their arse
An' there began a lang digression
About the lords o' the creation.
'The Twa Dogs', ll. 43–6, publ. in *Poems, Chiefly in the Scottish Dialect* (1786)

5 When up they gat an' shook their lugs,
Rejoiced they were na men, but dogs;
An' each took off his several way,
Resolved to meet some ither day.
'The Twa Dogs', ll. 235–8, ibid.

6 O thou, my Muse! guid, auld Scotch Drink!
Whether thro' wimplin worms thou jink,
Or, richly brown, ream owre the brink,
In glorious faem,
Inspire me, till I lisp an' wink,
To sing thy name!
'Scotch Drink', st. 2, ibid.

7 Scotland, my auld, respected mither!
'The Author's Earnest Cry and Prayer', st. 31, ibid.

8 Freedom and whisky gang thegither!
'The Author's Earnest Cry and Prayer', st. 31, ibid.

9 Here, some are thinkan on their sins,
An' some upo' their claes;
Ane curses feet that fyl'd his shins,
Anither sighs an' prays.
'The Holy Fair', st. 10, ibid.

10 Leeze me on drink! it gies us mair
Than either school or college:
It kindles wit, it waukens lear,
It pangs us fou o' knowledge.
Be't whisky-gill or penny-wheep,
Or ony stronger potion,

It never fails, on drinkin deep,
To kittle up our notion.
'The Holy Fair', st. 19, ibid.

11 O thou! whatever title suit thee!
Auld Hornie, Satan, Nick, or Clootie.
'Address to the Deil', st. 1, ibid.

12 Some rhyme a neebor's name to lash;
Some rhyme (vain thought!) for needfu' cash;
Some rhyme to court the countra clash,
An' raise a din;
For me, an aim I never fash;
I rhyme for fun.
'To J.S. [James Smith]', st. 5, ibid.

13 But facts are cheels that winna ding,
An' downa be disputed.
'A Dream', st. 4, ibid. Alan L. Mackay, in *Harvest of a Quiet
Eye* (1977), offers the translation: 'Facts are entities which
cannot be manipulated or disputed.'

14 All in this mottie, misty clime,
I backward mus'd on wasted time,
How I had spent my youthfu' prime,
An' done nae-thing,
But stringing blethers up in rhyme
For fools to sing.
'The Vision', st. 4, ibid.

15 The healsome porritch, chief of Scotia's food.
'The Cotter's Saturday Night', st. 11, ibid.

16 From scenes like these, old Scotia's grandeur
   springs,
That makes her loved at home, revered abroad:
Princes and lords are but the breath of kings,
'An honest man's the noblest work of God.'
'The Cotter's Saturday Night', st. 19, ibid. In the first edition,
Burns had misquoted 'noble work', later corrected. See ALEX-
ANDER POPE 139.

17 Wee, sleeket, cowran, tim'rous beastie,
O, what a panic's in thy breastie!
Thou need na start awa sae hasty,
Wi' bickering brattle!
I wad be laith to rin an' chase thee,
Wi' murd'ring pattle!
'To a Mouse', st. 1, ibid.

18 I'm truly sorry Man's dominion
Has broken Nature's social union,
An' justifies that ill opinion,
Which makes thee startle,

At me, thy poor, earth-born companion,
An' fellow-mortal!
'To a Mouse', st. 2, ibid.

19 The best laid schemes o' mice and men
Gang aft agley;
An' lea'e us nought but grief an' pain,
For promis'd joy!
'To a Mouse', st. 7, ibid.

20 Nature's law,
That man was made to mourn.
'Man Was Made to Mourn', st. 4, ibid.

21 Man's inhumanity to Man
Makes countless thousands mourn!
'Man was Made to Mourn', st. 7, ibid.

22 Wee, modest, crimson-tipped flow'r,
Thou's met me in an evil hour;
For I maun crush amang the stoure
Thy slender stem:
To spare thee now is past my pow'r,
Thou bonie gem.
'To a Mountain Daisy', st. 1, ibid. Opening lines.

23 O wad some pow'r the giftie gie us
To see oursels as others see us!
It wad frae monie a blunder free us,
And foolish notion.
'To a Louse', st. 8, ibid.

24 Gie me ae spark o' Nature's fire,
That's a' the learning I desire;
Then tho' I drudge thro' dub an' mire
At pleugh or cart,
My Muse, tho' hamely in attire,
May touch the heart.
'Epistle to John L–k [John Laphraik]', st. 13, ibid.

25 For thus the royal mandate ran,
When first the human race began,
'The social, friendly, honest man,
Whate'er he be,
'Tis he fulfils great Nature's plan,
And none but he.'
'To the Same' ['Second Epistle to John Lapraik'], st. 15, ibid.

26 O ye wha are sae guid yoursel,
Sae pious and sae holy,
Ye've nought to do but mark and tell
Your neebour's fauts and folly!
'Address to the Unco Guid, or the Rigidly Righteous', st. 1,
ibid. (1787 edn)

27 Ye high, exalted, virtuous dames,

Tied up in godly laces,
Before ye gie poor Frailty names,
Suppose a change o' cases;
A dear-loved lad, convenience snug,
A treacherous inclination –
But, let me whisper i' your lug,
Ye're aiblins nae temptation.
'Address to the Unco Guid, or the Rigidly Righteous', st. 6, ibid.

28 Then gently scan your brother man,
Still gentler sister woman;
Tho' they may gang a kennin wrang,
To step aside is human.
'Address to the Unco Guid, or the Rigidly Righteous', st. 7, ibid.

29 Fair fa' your honest, sonsie face,
Great chieftain o' the puddin'-race!
'To a Haggis', st. 1, ibid. Opening lines.

30 John Barleycorn was a hero bold,
Of noble enterprise,
For if ye do but taste his blood,
'Twill make your courage rise.
'John Barleycorn', st. 13, ibid. Burns popularized the figure of John Barleycorn – a traditional personification of malt liquor – in various works: see quote 46.

31 There's nought but care on ev'ry han',
In ev'ry hour that passes, O:
What signifies the life o' man,
An' 'twere for the lasses, O.
Green grow the rashes, O;
Green grow the rashes, O;
The sweetest hours that e'er I spend,
Are spent among the lasses, O.
'Green Grow the Rashes', st. 1 and chorus, ibid.

32 Auld nature swears, the lovely dears
Her noblest work she classes, O,
Her prentice han' she tried on man,
An' then she made the lasses, O.
'Green Grow the Rashes', st. 5, ibid.

33 My heart's in the Highlands, my heart is not
    here;
My heart's in the Highlands a-chasing the deer –
A-chasing the wild deer, and following the roe:
My heart's in the Highlands, wherever I go.
'My Heart's in the Highlands', st. 1, publ. in Johnson's Scots Musical Museum, vol. 3 (1790). The lines are based on 'The Strong Walls of Derry', a traditional song.

34 Farewell to the Highlands, farewell to the
    North –

The birth place of valour, the country of worth:
Wherever I wander, wherever I rove,
The hills of the Highlands for ever I love.
'My Heart's in the Highlands', st. 2, ibid., vol. 3

35 John Anderson my jo, John,
When we were first acquent;
Your locks were like the raven,
Your bonie brow was brent;
But now your brow is beld, John,
Your locks are like the snaw;
But blessings on your frosty pow,
John Anderson my jo!
'John Anderson my Jo', st. 1, ibid., vol. 3

36 Had we never loved sae kindly,
Had we never loved sae blindly,
Never met – or never parted –
We had ne'er been broken-hearted!
'Ae Fond Kiss, and Then We Sever', st. 4, ibid., vol. 4 (1792).
WALTER SCOTT described these lines – addressed to 'Clarinda' (Agnes Maclehose), parting for the West Indies – as 'worth a thousand romances', and BYRON chose the stanza as the motto for his poem, 'The Bride of Abydos'.

37 Ye banks and braes o' bonie Doon,
How can ye bloom sae fresh and fair!
How can ye chant, ye little birds,
And I sae weary fu' o' care!
'The Banks o' Doon', st. 1, ibid., vol. 4. An earlier version of the song starts: 'Ye flowery banks o' bonie Doon,/How can ye bloom sae fair!'

38 The English steel we could disdain,
Secure in valour's station;
But English gold has been our bane –
Such a parcel of rogues in a nation!
'Such a Parcel of Rogues in a Nation', st. 2, ibid., vol. 4

39 Flow gently, sweet Afton, among thy green
    braes,
Flow gently, sweet river, the theme of my lays;
My Mary's asleep by thy murmuring stream,
Flow gently, sweet Afton, disturb not her dream.
'Afton Water', st. 6, ibid., vol. 4

40 I've seen sae mony changefu' years,
On earth I am a stranger grown;
I wander in the ways of men,
Alike unknowing and unknown.
'Lament for James, Earl of Glencairn', st. 5, publ. in Poems, Chiefly in the Scottish Dialect (1793 edn)

41 Ah, gentle dames! it gars me greet,
To think how mony counsels sweet,

How mony lengthened, sage advices,
The husband frae the wife despises!
'Tam o' Shanter', ll. 33–6, ibid.

42 And at his elbow, Souter Johnny,
His ancient, trusty, drouthy crony;
Tam lo'ed him like a vera brither –
They had been fou for weeks thegither!
'Tam o' Shanter', ll. 41–4, ibid.

43 Kings may be blest, but Tam was glorious.
O'er a' the ills o' life victorious!
'Tam o' Shanter', ll. 57–8, ibid.

44 But pleasures are like poppies spread,
You seize the flower, its bloom is shed;
Or like the snow falls in the river,
A moment white – then melts for ever.
'Tam o' Shanter', ll. 59–62, ibid.

45 Nae man can tether time or tide.
'Tam o' Shanter', l. 67, ibid.

46 Inspiring bold John Barleycorn!
What dangers thou canst make us scorn!
Wi' tippenny, we fear nae evil;
Wi' usquabae, we'll face the devil!
'Tam o' Shanter', ll. 105–8, ibid. 'Usquabae' or 'usquebae' is
the Gaelic word for whisky.

47 Some hae meat and canna eat,
And some wad eat that want it;
But we hae meat, and we can eat,
And sae the Lord be thanket.
'The Selkirk Grace', also known as the 'Kirkcudbright Grace'
(c. 1793), attributed to Burns, publ. in Poetical Works, vol. 2
(ed. William Scott Douglas, 1891)

48 Should auld acquaintance be forgot
And never brought to mind?
Should auld acquaintance be forgot,
And auld lang syne?
For auld lang syne, my jo,
For auld lang syne,
We'll tak' a cup o' kindness yet,
For auld lang syne.
'Auld Lang Syne', st. 1 and chorus, written 1788, publ. in John-
son's Scots Musical Museum, vol. 5 (1796). Burns referred to
the song as an old fragment he had discovered and adapted,
though the tune with which it is now associated is different
from the original air, which he called mediocre. 'Auld Lang
Syne' means 'old long since' or 'long ago'.

49 O my luve's like a red, red rose
That's newly sprung in June;

O my luve's like the melodie
That's sweetly played in tune.
'A Red, Red Rose', st. 1 and 5, ibid.

50 Till a' the seas gang dry, my dear,
And the rocks melt wi' the sun:
O I will love thee still, my dear,
While the sands o' life shall run.
'A Red, Red Rose', st. 3, ibid.

51 The golden hours, on angel wings,
Flew o'er me and my dearie;
For dear to me, as light and life,
Was my sweet Highland Mary.
'Highland Mary', st. 2, publ. in A Select Collection of Original
Scottish Airs for the Voice, vol. 2 (ed. George Thomson, 1799)

52 For a' that, and a' that,
Our toils obscure and a' that,
The rank is but the guinea's stamp –
The man's the gowd for a' that!
'For A' That and A' That', st. 1, written 1795, publ. 1800, repr.
in Poetical Works, vol. 2 (ed. William Scott Douglas, 1891)

53 A man's a man, for a' that.
'For A' That and A' That', st. 2, ibid.

Edgar Rice Burroughs
(1875–1950)
US author

His series of Tarzan *books, the first of which appeared in 1914,
led to films, radio programmes and comic strips. He also wrote
science fiction and other adventure stories.*

1 Me Tarzan, you Jane.
Attributed to Tarzan. In Burroughs' book Tarzan of the Apes
(1914), Tarzan's words are: 'I am Tarzan of the Apes. I want
you. I am yours. You are mine' (ch. 18). In the movie, Tarzan
the Ape Man (1932), Johnny Weissmuller, as Tarzan, never
utters the words, 'Me Tarzan, you Jane'.

William Burroughs
(1914–97)
US author

*Associated with the Beats in the 1950s, he frankly depicted a
heroin addict's life in* Junkie *(1953) and* The Naked Lunch
(1959). Other works such as The Soft Machine *(1961) helped to
establish his cult status.*

1 A junky runs on junk time. When his junk is cut
off, the clock runs down and stops. All he can do is
hang on and wait for non-junk time to start.
Junkie, ch. 10 (1953)

2 1. Never give anything away for nothing.

2. Never give more than you have to give (always catch the buyer hungry and always make him wait).

3. Always take everything back if you possibly can.

The Naked Lunch, Introduction (1959). The basic principles of dealing heroin.

3 Junk is the ideal product ... the ultimate merchandise. No sales talk necessary. The client will crawl through a sewer and beg to buy.

Ibid., Introduction

4 America is not a young land: it is old and dirty and evil before the settlers, before the Indians. The evil is there waiting.

Ibid. Opening chapter (untitled)

5 A *functioning* police state needs no police.

Ibid., 'Benway'. Spoken by Dr Benway.

6 The face of 'evil' is always the face of total need.

'Deposition: Testimony Concerning a Sickness' (1960), repr. as Introduction to *The Naked Lunch* (1962 edn)

7 Man is an artifact designed for space travel. He is not designed to remain in his present biologic state any more than a tadpole is designed to remain a tadpole.

The Adding Machine, 'Civilian Defense' (1985)

8 Kerouac opened a million coffee bars and sold a million pairs of Levis to both sexes. Woodstock rises from his pages.

Ibid., 'Remembering Jack Kerouac'

9 In deep sadness there is no place for sentimentality.

Queer, ch. 8 (1985)

Robert Burton
(1577–1640)
English scholar, clergyman and author

Attached to Christ Church, Oxford, from 1599, he was the author of The Anatomy of Melancholy *(1621), a compendium of medical knowledge and psychological observations. The work had an enduring influence, claimed by* SAMUEL JOHNSON *to be the only book that ever took him out of bed two hours sooner than he wished to rise.*

1 All my joys to this are folly,
Naught so sweet as melancholy.

The Anatomy of Melancholy, 'The Author's Abstract' (1621). See also JOHN FLETCHER 7.

2 They lard their lean books with the fat of others' works.

Ibid., 'Democritus to the Reader'

3 All poets are mad.

Ibid., 'Democritus to the Reader'

4 Every man hath a good and a bad angel attending on him in particular all his life long.

Ibid., pt 1, sect. 2, member 1, subsect. 2

5 Idleness is an appendix to nobility.

Ibid., pt 1, sect. 2, member 2, subsect. 6

6 I may not here omit those two main plagues, and common dotages of human kind, wine and women, which have infatuated and besotted myriads of people. They go commonly together.

Ibid., pt 1, sect. 2, member 3, subsect. 13

7 One was never married, and that's his hell; another is, and that's his plague.

Ibid., pt 1, sect. 2, member 4, subsect. 7

8 Almost in every kingdom the most ancient families have been at first princes' bastards.

Ibid., pt 2, sect. 2, member 1, subsect. 1

9 All places are distant from heaven alike.

Ibid., pt 2, sect. 3, member 4, subsect. 1

10 Tobacco, divine, rare, superexcellent tobacco, which goes far beyond all the panaceas, potable gold, and philosophers' stones, a sovereign remedy to all diseases ... but as it is commonly abused by most men, which take it as tinkers do ale, 'tis a plague, a mischief, a violent purger of goods, lands, health; hellish, devilish and damned tobacco, the ruin and overthrow of body and soul.

Ibid., pt 2, sect. 4, member 2, subsect. 1

11 One religion is as true as another.

Ibid., pt 3, sect. 4, member 2, subsect. 1

12 A good conscience is a continual feast.

Ibid., pt 3, sect. 4, member 2, subsect. 3

13 Be not solitary, be not idle.

Ibid., pt 3, sect. 4, member 2, subsect. 6. Closing words. See SAMUEL JOHNSON 125.

George Bush
(b. 1924)
US politician and president

Director of the CIA 1976–7, he served as Republican Vice-President under RONALD REAGAN *1981–8, whom he succeeded as president 1989–93. He is the father of* GEORGE W. BUSH.

1 The vision thing.
Time 26 January 1987. Speaking of his long-term policies.

2 Let the others have the charisma. I've got the class.
Comment in California during presidential campaign, quoted in the *Guardian* 3 December 1988

3 The Congress will push me to raise taxes and I'll say no, and they'll push, and I'll say no, and they'll push me again. And I'll say to them: 'Read my lips: no new taxes.'
Acceptance speech for presidential nomination, Republican National Convention, New Orleans, 18 August 1988, quoted in the *New York Times* 19 August 1988. PEGGY NOONAN was mainly responsible for the speech, though the expression 'Read my lips' has been in general usage since the 1970s or earlier. Bush eventually raised taxes.

4 I want a kinder, gentler nation.
Acceptance speech, 18 August 1988, ibid. Similar words were spoken by CHARLIE CHAPLIN at the end of *The Great Dictator* (1940), when he urged: 'More than cleverness, we need kindness and gentleness.'

5 I will keep America moving forward, always forward – for a better America, for an endless enduring dream and a thousand points of light.
Acceptance speech, 18 August 1988, ibid. The phrase 'a thousand points of light', written for Bush by speechwriter PEGGY NOONAN, was used on various occasions during the 1988 presidential campaign. The words are not original, echoing similar phrases by CHARLES DICKENS and THOMAS WOLFE, among others. As president, Bush initiated a 'Points of Light' reform programme in June 1989.

6 We can see a new world coming into view. A world in which there is the very real prospect of a new world order.
Speech, quoted in the *New York Times* 7 March 1991

George W. Bush
(b. 1946)
US politician and president

George Walker Bush. The son of GEORGE BUSH, *he was elected US President in 2000 and 2004. His 'war against terror' led to the American invasions of Afghanistan in 2001 and Iraq in 2003.*

1 We'll let our friends be the peacemakers and the great country called America will be the peacemakers.
Speech at Houston, Texas, 6 September 2000, quoted in *George W. Bushisms* (ed. Jacob Weisberg, 2001)

2 Freedom itself was attacked this morning by a faceless coward and freedom will be defended. Make no mistake, the United States will hunt down and punish those responsible for these cowardly acts.
Speech, 11 September 2001, quoted in the *Daily Telegraph* 12 September 2001. On the terrorist attacks of '9/11'.

3 This crusade, this war on terrorism is going to take a while. And the American people must be patient. I'm going to be patient. But I can assure the American people I am determined, I'm not going to be distracted, I will keep my focus to make sure that not only are these brought to justice, but anybody who's been associated will be brought to justice. Those who harbor terrorists will be brought to justice. It is time for us to win the first war of the 21st century decisively, so that our children and our grandchildren can live peacefully into the 21st century.
Press conference, Washington DC, 16 September 2001, on www.whitehouse.gov

4 I have opinions of my own – strong opinions – but I don't always agree with them.
Quoted in *The Times* 19 January 2002

5 States like these, and their terrorist allies, constitute an axis of evil, arming to threaten the peace of the world. By seeking weapons of mass destruction, these regimes pose a grave and growing danger.
State of the Union address, 31 January 2002, publ. in the *Washington Times* 1 February 2002. Referring to Iran, Iraq and North Korea. Bush's speechwriter on this occasion was David Frum.

6 The problem with the French, is that they don't have a word for entrepreneur.
Quoted in *The Times* 9 July 2002. Discussing the decline of the French economy, as related by SHIRLEY WILLIAMS.

7 In cells and camps, terrorists are plotting further destruction, and building new bases for their war against civilization. And our greatest fear is that terrorists will find a shortcut to their mad ambitions when an outlaw regime supplies them with the technologies to kill on a massive scale. In one place – in one regime – we find all these dangers, in their most lethal and aggressive forms.
Address to United Nations, New York, 12 September 2002, publ. in the *Guardian* 13 September 2002. Referring to SADDAM HUSSEIN's regime in Iraq. 'The first time we may be completely certain he has nuclear weapons is when, God forbids, he uses one,' Bush declared.

8 I earned capital in the campaign, political capital, and now I intend to spend it. It is my style.
Remark, 4 November 2004, quoted in the *New York Times* 5 November 2004. After winning the presidential election.

Roger, Comte de Bussy-Rabutin
(1618–93)
French soldier and author

He caused a scandal in 1665 when his witty tales about ladies at court, Histoire amoureuse des Gaules, *were printed without his consent. He was the cousin of Madame de Sévigné, and after his disgrace the two kept up a celebrated correspondence.*

1 Love comes from blindness, friendship from knowledge.
Histoire Amoureuse des Gaules, 'Maximes d'amour' (1665)

2 Absence is to love what wind is to fire; it extinguishes the small, it enkindles the great.
Ibid., 'Maximes d'amour'. See LA ROCHEFOUCAULD 24.

3 As you know, God is generally on the side of the big squadrons against the small ones.
Letter, 18 October 1677, publ. in *Letters*, vol. 4 (1697). See also JEAN ANOUILH 8 and VOLTAIRE 7.

Ralph Butler
British songwriter

1 The sun has got its hat on
Hip hip hip hooray
The sun has got its hat on
And it's coming out to play.
'The Sun Has Got Its Hat On' (song, 1932, with music by Noel Gay). The song was sung by Jack Hulbert in 1932, and was a hit for Jonathan King in 1971.

2 Run, rabbit, run, rabbit, run, run, run.
Run, rabbit, run, rabbit, run, run, run.
Bang, bang, bang, bang, goes the farmer's gun,
Run, rabbit, run, rabbit, run, run, run.
'Run Rabbit Run!' (song) in *The Little Dog Laughed* (musical show, 1939, with music by Noel Gay). The song was performed by BUD FLANAGAN, who starred alongside the Crazy Gang and the Hoffman Sisters. The song and show were a smash hit during the 'phoney war' (1939–40).

Samuel Butler
(1612–80)
English poet and satirist

His burlesque poem, Hudibras (1663–78), *an attack on the pretensions of Puritanism, met with immense success, though he died in poverty. Other works satirized the Royal Academy*

and contemporary theatre, and he also wrote prose 'characters'.

1 For rhetoric, he could not ope
His mouth, but out there flew a trope.
Hudibras, pt 1, canto 1, ll. 81–2 (1663)

2 A Babylonish dialect
Which learned pedants much affect.
Ibid., pt 1, canto 1, ll. 93–4

3 In mathematics he was greater
Than Tycho Brahe, or Erra Pater:
For he, by geometric scale,
Could take the size of pots of ale;
Resolve, by sines and tangents straight,
If bread and butter wanted weight;
And wisely tell what hour o' th' day
The clock doth strike, by algebra.
Ibid., pt 1, canto 1, ll. 119–26

4 For every why he had a wherefore.
Ibid., pt 1, canto 1, l. 132. See WILLIAM SHAKESPEARE: THE COMEDY OF ERRORS 2.

5 He knew what's what, and that's as high
As metaphysic wit can fly.
Ibid., pt 1, canto 1, ll. 149–50

6 Such as take lodgings in a head
That's to be let unfurnished.
Ibid., pt 1, canto 1, ll. 159–60

7 And prove their doctrine orthodox,
By apostolic blows and knocks.
Ibid., pt 1, canto 1, ll. 215–16

8 Compound for sins they are inclined to
By damning those they have no mind to.
Ibid., pt 1, canto 1, ll. 213–14

9 For rhyme the rudder is of verses,
With which like ships they steer their courses.
Ibid., pt 1, canto 1, ll. 457–8

10 A skilful leech is better far
Than half a hundred men of war.
Ibid., pt 1, canto 2, ll. 245–6

11 And bid the devil take the hin'most.
Ibid., pt 1, canto 2, l. 633. ROBERT BURNS wrote, in his poem 'To a Haggis', st. 3: 'Then, horn for horn, they stretch an strive:/Deil tak the hindmost, on they drive.'

12 Cleric before, and Lay behind;
A lawless linsey-woolsey brother,
Half of one order, half another.
Ibid., pt 1, canto 3, ll. 1226–8

13 Learning, that cobweb of the brain,
Profane, erroneous, and vain.
Ibid., pt 1, canto 3, ll. 1339–40

14 She that with poetry is won,
Is but a desk to write upon.
Ibid., pt 2, canto 1, ll. 591–2 (1664)

15 Love is a boy, by poets styled,
Then spare the rod and spoil the child.
Ibid., pt 2, canto 1, ll. 843–4

16 What makes all doctrines plain and clear?
About two hundred pounds a year.
And that which was proved true before
Prove false again? Two hundred more.
Ibid., pt 3, canto 1, ll. 1277–80 (1678)

17 He that complies against his will
Is of his own opinion still.
Ibid., pt 3, canto 3, ll. 547–8

18 Neither have they hearts to stay,
Nor wit enough to run away.
Ibid., pt 3, canto 3, ll. 569–70

Samuel Butler

(1835–1902)
English author

Having quarrelled with his father, a clergyman, he emigrated to New Zealand (1859–64), but returned to find success with Erewhon *(1872), a Utopian satire. His autobiographical novel* The Way of All Flesh *(1903) is considered his masterpiece. He also painted, composed and translated.*

1 The want of money is the root of all evil.
Erewhon, ch. 20 (1872). A paraphrase of BIBLE, NEW TESTA-MENT: TIMOTHY 13, the aphorism has also been credited to MARK TWAIN.

2 A hen is only an egg's way of making another egg.
Life and Habit, ch. 8 (1877)

3 It was very good of God to let Carlyle and Mrs Carlyle marry one another and so make only two people miserable instead of four, besides being very amusing.
Letter, 21 November 1884, publ. in *Letters Between Samuel Butler and E.M.A. Savage 1871–1885* (1935). The quote has been erroneously ascribed to TENNYSON.

4 Life is like playing a violin solo in public and learning the instrument as one goes on.
Speech at Somerville Club, London, 27 February 1895, publ. in *Samuel Butler's Notebooks* (1951)

5 All animals, except man, know that the principal business of life is to enjoy it.
The Way of All Flesh, ch. 19 (1903)

6 The advantage of doing one's praising for oneself is that one can lay it on so thick and exactly in the right places.
Ibid., ch. 34

7 The best liar is he who makes the smallest amount of lying go the longest way.
Ibid., ch. 39

8 A man's friendships are, like his will, invalidated by marriage – but they are also no less invalidated by the marriage of his friends.
Ibid., ch. 75

9 Life is one long process of getting tired.
Notebooks, ch. 1, 'Life', no. 7 (1912)

10 Life is the art of drawing sufficient conclusions from insufficient premises.
Ibid., ch. 1, 'Life', no. 9

11 All progress is based upon a universal innate desire on the part of every organism to live beyond its income.
Ibid., ch. 1, 'Life', no. 16

12 Is life worth living? This is a question for an embryo not for a man.
Ibid., ch. 1, 'Is Life Worth Living?'

13 When the righteous man turneth away from his righteousness that he hath committed and doeth that which is neither lawful nor quite right, he will generally be found to have gained in amiability what he has lost in holiness.
Ibid., ch. 2, 'Counsels of Imperfection', no. 9

14 Virtue knows that it is impossible to get on without compromise, and tunes herself, as it were, a trifle sharp to allow for an inevitable fall in playing.
Ibid., ch. 2, 'Vice and Virtue', no. 1

15 The healthy stomach is nothing if it is not conservative. Few radicals have good digestions.
Ibid., ch. 6, 'Indigestion'

16 Man is the only animal that can remain on friendly terms with the victims he intends to eat until he eats them.
Ibid., ch. 6, 'Assimilation and Persecution'

17 Arguments are like fire-arms which a man may keep at home but should not carry about with him.
Ibid., ch. 10, 'The Art of Propagating Opinion'

18 An apology for the Devil – it must be remembered that we have only heard one side of the case. God has written all the books.
Ibid., ch. 14, 'An Apology for the Devil'

19 The great pleasure of a dog is that you may make a fool of yourself with him and not only will he not scold you, but he will make a fool of himself too.
Ibid., ch. 14, 'Dogs'

20 It is tact that is golden, not silence.
Ibid., ch. 14, 'Silence and Tact'

21 The public buys its opinions as it buys its meat, or takes in its milk, on the principle that it is cheaper to do this than to keep a cow. So it is, but the milk is more likely to be watered.
Ibid., ch. 16, 'Public Opinion'

22 Men are seldom more commonplace than on supreme occasions.
Ibid., ch. 17, 'Supreme Occasions'

23 There is no such source of error as the pursuit of absolute truth.
Ibid., ch. 19, 'Truth', no. 3

24 I do not mind lying, but I hate inaccuracy.
Ibid., ch. 19, 'Falsehood', no. 4

25 Logic is like the sword – those who appeal to it, shall perish by it.
Ibid., ch. 20, 'Logic and Faith'

26 It is not the church in a village that is the source of the mischief, but the rectory.
Ibid., ch. 21, 'Christianity', no. 3

27 Science, after all, is only an expression for our ignorance of our own ignorance.
Ibid., ch. 21, 'Personified Science'

28 We all like to forgive, and love best not those who offend us least, nor who have done most for us, but those who make it most easy for us to forgive them.
Ibid. ch. 22, 'Amendes Honorables'

29 There is nothing which at once affects a man so much and so little as his own death.
Ibid., ch. 23, 'The Defeat of Death'

30 The world will only, in the end, follow those who have despised as well as served it.
Ibid., ch. 24, 'The World'

31 The three most important things a man has are,

briefly, his private parts, his money, and his religious opinions.
Further Extracts from the Notebooks, 'Volume I (1874–1883, revised 1891–1897' (ed. A. T. Bartholomew, 1934)

William Butler
(1535–1618)
English physician

Called the 'Aesculapius of our age' by THOMAS FULLER, *he was known as an eccentric practitioner.*

1 Doubtless God could have made a better berry, but doubtless God never did.
Quoted in *The Compleat Angler*, pt 1, ch. 5 (third edn, 1661) by Izaak Walton. Referring to strawberries. See IZAAK WALTON 11.

Henry James Byron
(1834–84)
English dramatist

A specialist in burlesque theatre and pantomime (to which he contributed the characters of Buttons and Widow Twankey), he enjoyed success with such productions as The Lancashire Lass *(1867) and* Our Boys *(1875).*

1 Life's too short for chess.
Our Boys, Act 1 (1875). Spoken by Talbot Champneys.

Lord Byron
(1788–1824)
English poet

George Gordon, 6th Baron Byron. One of the greatest English Romantic poets and an enduring symbol of European liberalism, he acquired instant fame with the publication in 1812 of the first two cantos of Childe Harold. *He spent most of his adult life in Italy and died of fever while on a military campaign in Greece. His friend* THOMAS MOORE *regretted 'the temptation, never easily resisted by him, of displaying his wit at the expense of his character'. See also* CAROLINE LAMB 1, LORD MACAULAY 17, P. B. SHELLEY 22.

1 Friendship is Love without his wings!
'L'Amitié est L'Amour Sans Ailes', written 1806, publ. in *Poetical Works* (ed. Frederick Page, 1904)

2 Still I can't contradict, what so oft has been said,
'Though women are angels, yet wedlock's the
    devil.'
'To Eliza', st. 4, publ. in *Fugitive Pieces* (1806)

3 When Love's delirium haunts the glowing mind,

Limping Decorum lingers far behind.
'Answer To Some Elegant Verses Sent By A Friend', publ. in
Hours of Idleness (1807)

4 I'll publish, right or wrong:
Fools are my theme, let satire be my song.
English Bards and Scotch Reviewers, ll. 5–6 (1809)

5 'Tis pleasant, sure, to see one's name in print;
A book's a book, although there's nothing in't.
Ibid., ll. 51–2

6 A man must serve his time to every trade
Save censure – critics all are ready made.
Ibid., ll. 63–4

7 With just enough of learning to misquote.
Ibid., l. 66. Referring to critics.

8 Who, both by precept and example, shows
That prose is verse, and verse is merely prose,
Convincing all by demonstration plain,
Poetic souls delight in prose insane;
And Christmas stories tortured into rhyme,
Contain the essence of the true sublime.
Ibid., ll. 241–6. Of WILLIAM WORDSWORTH.

9 Let simple Wordsworth chime his childish verse,
And brother Coleridge lull the babe at nurse.
Ibid., ll. 917–18

10 I swims in the Tagus all across at once, and I rides
on an ass or a mule, and swears Portuguese, and
have got a diarrhoea and bites from the mosquitoes.
But what of that? Comfort must not be expected by
folks that go a pleasuring.
Letter, 16 July 1809, publ. in *Byron's Letters and Journals*, vol. 1
(ed. Leslie A. Marchand, 1973)

11 I see not much difference between ourselves &
the Turks, save that we have foreskins and they
none, that they have long dresses and we short, and
that we talk much and they little. In England the
vices in fashion are whoring & drinking, in Turkey,
sodomy and smoking.
Letter, 3 May 1810, ibid., vol. 1

12 I begin to find out that nothing but virtue will
do in this damned world. I am tolerably sick of vice
which I have tried in its agreeable varieties, and
mean on my return to cut all my dissolute acquaintance and leave off wine and 'carnal company', and
betake myself to politics and decorum.
Letter, 5 May 1810, ibid., vol. 1. For the opposite view, see
quote 42.

13 I will trouble you no more except to state that all

climates and nations are equally interesting to me;
that mankind are everywhere despicable in different absurdities; that the farther I proceed from your
country the less I regret leaving it.
Letter from Constantinople, 23 June 1810, ibid., vol. 1

14 I am so convinced of the advantages of looking
at mankind instead of reading about them, and of
the bitter effects of staying at home with all the
narrow prejudices of an islander, that I think there
should be a law amongst us to set our young men
abroad for a term among the few allies our wars
have left us.
Letter to his mother, 14 January 1811, ibid, vol. 2 (1973)

15 Nothing so fretful, so despicable as a scribbler,
see what *I* am, and what a parcel of scoundrels I
have brought about my ears, and what language
I have been obliged to treat them with to deal with
them in their own way; – all this comes of
authorship.
Letter to his half-sister, Augusta Leigh, 2 September 1811, ibid.
vol. 2. 'To withdraw *myself* from *myself* . . . has ever been my
sole, my entire, my sincere motive in scribbling at all,' Byron
later wrote in a journal entry (27 November 1813).

16 There is something pagan in me that I cannot
shake off. In short, I deny nothing, but doubt
everything.
Letter, 4 December 1811, ibid., vol. 2

17 Vexed with mirth the drowsy ear of night.
Childe Harold's Pilgrimage, canto 1, st. 2 (1812)

18 The laughing dames in whom he did delight,
Whose large blue eyes, fair locks, and snowy hands,
Might shake the saintship of an anchorite.
Ibid., canto 1, st. 11

19 Ancient of days! august Athena! where,
Where are thy men of might? thy grand in soul?
Gone – glimmering through the dream of things
    that were.
Ibid., canto 2, st. 2

20 Hereditary bondsmen! know ye not
Who would be free themselves must strike the
    blow?
Ibid., canto 2, st. 76

21 What is the worst of woes that wait on age?
What stamps the wrinkle deeper on the brow?
To view each loved one blotted from life's page,
And be alone on earth, as I am now.
Ibid., canto 2, st. 98

22 A land of meanness, sophistry and mist.
Each breeze from foggy mount and marshy plain
Dilutes with drivel every drizzly brain.
The Curse of Minerva, ll. 138–40 (1812). Of Scotland.

23 I awoke one morning and found myself famous.
Journal entry after publication of cantos 1 and 2 of *Childe Harold's Pilgrimage* in 1812, quoted in *Life of Byron*, ch. 14 (1830) by THOMAS MOORE

24 Are we aware of our obligations to a mob? It is the mob that labour in your fields and serve in your houses – that man your navy, and recruit your army – that have enabled you to defy the world, and can also defy you when neglect and calamity have driven them to despair. You may call the people a mob; but do not forget that a mob too often speaks the sentiments of the people.
Maiden speech to the House of Lords, 27 February 1812, publ. in *Lord Byron: The Complete Miscellaneous Prose*, 'Speeches (1812–1813)' (ed. Andrew Nicholson, 1991). Referring to the Luddite machine-wreckers.

25 It is true from early habit, one must make love mechanically as one swims; I was once very fond of both, but now as I never swim unless I tumble into the water, I don't make love till almost obliged.
Letter, 10 September 1812, publ. in *Byron's Letters and Journals*, vol. 2 (ed. Leslie Marchand, 1973)

26 A woman should never be seen eating or drinking, unless it be lobster salad and champagne, the only true feminine and becoming viands.
Letter, 25 September 1812, ibid., vol. 2

27 My Princess of Parallelograms.
Letter to Lady Melbourne, 18 October 1812, ibid., vol. 2. Referring to Annabella Milbanke, Byron's future wife and a keen amateur mathematician. Byron explained: 'Her proceedings are quite rectangular, or rather we are two parallel lines prolonged to infinity side by side but never to meet.'

28 The great object in life is Sensation – to feel that we exist, even though in pain; it is this 'craving void' which drives us to gaming, to battle, to travel, to intemperate but keenly felt pursuits of every description whose principal attraction is the agitation inseparable from their accomplishment.
Letter to Annabella Milbanke, 6 September 1813, ibid., vol. 3 (ed. Leslie Marchand, 1974). The 'craving void' was described by ALEXANDER POPE in *Epistle from Eloisa to Abelard* l. 94.

29 We have progressively improved into a less spiritual species of tenderness – but the seal is not yet fixed though the wax is preparing for the impression.
Letter, 14 October 1813, ibid., vol. 3. Of his dealings with Lady Frances Webster.

30 And yet a little *tumult*, now and then, is an agreeable quickener of sensation; such as a revolution, a battle, or an *aventure* of any lively description.
Journal entry, 22 November 1813, ibid., vol. 3

31 A Republic! Look in the history of the Earth … To be the first man – not the Dictator, not the Sylla, but the Washington or the Aristides, the leader in talent and truth – is next to the Divinity!
Journal entry, 23 November 1813, ibid., vol. 3

32 A mistress never is nor can be a friend. While you agree, you are lovers; and when it is over, anything but friends.
Journal entry, 24 November 1813, ibid., vol. 3. See also quote 137.

33 If I am a fool, it is, at least, a doubting one; and I envy no one the certainty of his self-approved wisdom.
Journal entry, 27 November 1813, ibid., vol. 3

34 All are inclined to believe what they covet, from a lottery-ticket up to a passport to Paradise.
Journal entry, 27 November 1813, ibid., vol. 3

35 The reason that adulation is not displeasing is that, though untrue, it shows one to be of consequence enough, in one way or other, to induce people to lie.
Journal entry, 28 November 1813, ibid., vol. 3

36 I by no means rank poetry high in the scale of intelligence – this may look like affectation but it is my real opinion. It is the lava of the imagination whose eruption prevents an earthquake.
Letter to Annabella Milbanke, 29 November 1813, ibid., vol. 3

37 I shall soon be six-and-twenty. Is there anything in the future that can possibly console us for not being always *twenty-five*?
Journal entry, 1 December 1813, ibid., vol. 3

38 When one subtracts from life infancy (which is vegetation), sleep, eating and swilling, buttoning and unbuttoning – how much remains of downright existence? The summer of a dormouse.
Journal entry, 7 December 1813, ibid., vol. 3

39 I only go out to get me a fresh appetite for being alone.
Journal entry, 12 December 1813, ibid., vol. 3

40 What an antithetical mind! – tenderness, roughness – delicacy, coarseness – sentiment, sensuality – soaring and grovelling, dirt and deity – all mixed up in that one compound of inspired clay!
Journal entry, 13 December 1813, ibid., vol. 3. Referring to ROBERT BURNS.

41 A true voluptuary will never abandon his mind to the grossness of reality. It is by exalting the earthly, the material, the *physique* of our pleasures, by veiling these ideas, by forgetting them altogether, or, at least, never naming them hardly to one's self, that we alone can prevent them from disgusting.
Journal entry, 13 December 1813, ibid., vol. 3

42 Every day confirms my opinion on the superiority of a vicious life – and if virtue is not its own reward I don't know any other stipend annexed to it.
Letter, 18 December 1813, ibid., vol. 3

43 Oh! too convincing – dangerously dear –
In woman's eye the unanswerable tear!
The Corsair, canto 2, st. 15 (1814)

44 Yes – one – the first – the last – the best –
The Cincinnatus of the West,
Whom envy dared not hate,
Bequeathed the name of Washington,
To make man blush there was but one!
Ode to Napoleon Buonaparte, st. 19 (1814). Referring to GEORGE WASHINGTON.

45 I have simplified my politics into an utter detestation of all existing governments; and, as it is the shortest and most agreeable and summary feeling imaginable, the first moment of an universal republic would convert me into an advocate for single and uncontradicted despotism. The fact is, riches are power, and poverty is slavery all over the earth, and one sort of establishment is no better, nor worse, for a *people* than another.
Journal entry, 16 January 1814, publ. in *Byron's Letters and Journals*, vol. 3 (ed. Leslie Marchand, 1974)

46 Is there any thing beyond? – *who* knows? *He* that can't tell. Who tells there *is*? He who don't know. And when shall he know? Perhaps, when he don't expect it, and generally when he don't wish it. In this last respect, however, all are not alike; it depends a good deal upon education, something upon nerves and habits – but most upon digestion.
Journal entry, 18 February 1814, ibid., vol. 3

47 Last night, *party* at Lansdowne-House. Tonight, *party* at Lady Charlotte Greville's – deplorable waste of time, and something of temper. Nothing imparted – nothing acquired – talking without ideas – if any thing like *thought* in my mind, it was not on the subjects on which we were gabbling. Heigho! – and in this way half London pass what is called life.
Journal entry, 22 March 1814, ibid., vol. 3

48 Shakespeare's name, you may depend on it, stands absurdly too high and will go down.
Letter to JAMES HOGG, 24 March 1814, publ. in *Selected Letters and Journals*, vol. 4 (ed. Leslie A. Marchand, 1974). In a letter to the publisher John Murray (14 July 1821), Byron later wrote of Shakespeare: 'I look upon him to be the *worst* of models – though the most extraordinary of writers.'

49 My great comfort is, that the temporary celebrity I have wrung from the world has been in the very teeth of all opinions and prejudices. I have flattered no ruling powers; I have never concealed a single thought that tempted me.
Letter to THOMAS MOORE, 9 April 1814, ibid., vol. 4)

50 I am acquainted with no *im*material sensuality so delightful as good acting.
Letter 8 May [?] 1814, ibid., vol. 4

51 I have great hopes that we shall love each other all our lives as much as if we had never married at all.
Letter to Annabella Milbanke, 5 December 1814, ibid., vol. 4. Annabella married Byron a month later, but left him after a year.

52 She walks in beauty, like the night
Of cloudless climes and starry skies;
And all that's best of dark and bright
Meet in her aspect and her eyes:
Thus mellowed to that tender light
Which heaven to gaudy day denies.
'She Walks in Beauty', st. 1, publ. in *Hebrew Melodies* (1815)

53 Like other parties of the kind, it was first silent, then talky, then argumentative, then disputatious, then unintelligible, then altogethery, then inarticulate, and then drunk. When we had reached the last step of this glorious ladder, it was difficult to get down again without stumbling.
Letter to THOMAS MOORE, 31 October 1815, ibid., vol. 4

54 Once more upon the waters! yet once more!
And the waves bound beneath me as a steed
That knows his rider. Welcome to their roar!
Childe Harold's Pilgrimage, canto 3, st. 2 (1816)

55 Years steal
Fire from the mind as vigour from the limb;
And life's enchanted cup but sparkles near the
   brim.
Ibid., canto 3, st. 8

56 On with the dance! let joy be unconfined;
No sleep till morn, when Youth and Pleasure meet
To chase the glowing hours with flying feet.
Ibid., canto 3, st. 22. Describing the grand ball in Brussels
interrupted by the start of the Battle of Waterloo.

57 To fly from, need not be to hate, mankind:
All are not fit with them to stir and toil,
Nor is it discontent to keep the mind
Deep in its fountain, lest it overboil.
Ibid., canto 3, st. 69

58 I live not in myself, but I become
Portion of that around me; and to me
High mountains are a feeling, but the hum
Of human cities torture.
Ibid., canto 3, st. 72

59 In solitude, where we are *least* alone.
Ibid., canto 3, st. 90

60 And hiving wisdom with each studious year,
In meditation dwelt, with learning wrought,
And shaped his weapon with an edge severe,
Sapping a solemn creed with solemn sneer.
Ibid., canto 3, st. 107. Referring to EDWARD GIBBON.

61 I have not loved the world, nor the world me;
I have not flattered its rank breath, nor bowed
To its idolatries a patient knee.
Ibid., canto 3, st. 113

62 I stood
Among them, but not of them; in a shroud
Of thoughts which were not their thoughts.
Ibid., canto 3, st. 113

63 Eternal spirit of the chainless mind!
Brightest in dungeons, Liberty! thou art.
'Sonnet on Chillon', publ. in *The Prisoner of Chillon, and Other
Poems* (1816). Opening lines of poem.

64 Sleep hath its own world,
And a wide realm of wild reality.
And dreams in their development have breath,
And tears, and tortures, and the touch of joy.
'The Dream', sect. 1, ibid.

65 The mind can make
Substance, and people planets of its own

With beings brighter than have been, and give
A breath to forms which can outlive all flesh.
Ibid., sect. 1

66 For in itself a thought,
A slumbering thought, is capable of years,
And curdles a long life into one hour.
Ibid., sect. 1

67 Long shall we seek his likeness, long in vain,
And turn to all of him which may remain,
Sighing that Nature formed but one such man,
And broke the die – in moulding Sheridan!
Monody on the Death of Sheridan, ll. 115–18 (1816), repr. in
Works (1831). Last lines. Compare ARIOSTO 1.

68 Constancy . . . that small change of love, which
people exact so rigidly, receive in such counterfeit
coin, and repay in baser metal.
Letter to THOMAS MOORE, 17 November 1816, publ. in *Byron's
Letters and Journals*, vol. 5 (ed. Leslie A. Marchand, 1976)

69 Sorrow is knowledge: they who know the most
Must mourn the deepest o'er the fatal truth,
The Tree of Knowledge is not that of Life.
Manfred, Act 1, Sc. 1 (1817). Manfred's opening speech. This
speech was considered by NIETZSCHE to be 'immortal', for
stating the terrible fact that a man might bleed to death
through the truth that he recognizes. See GÉRARD DE
NERVAL 3.

70 So, we'll go no more a-roving
So late into the night,
Though the heart be still as loving,
And the moon be still as bright.
For the sword outwears its sheath,
And the soul wears out the breast.
And the heart must pause to breathe
And love itself have rest.
'So We'll Go No More A-Roving', written 1817, publ. in *Poetical
Works* (ed. Frederick Page, 1904)

71 Here's a sigh to those who love me,
And a smile to those who hate;
And, whatever sky's above me,
Here's a heart for every fate.
To Thomas Moore, st. 2 (1818), repr. in *Life of Byron* (1830) by
THOMAS MOORE

72 But I hate things *all fiction* . . . there should
always be some foundation of fact for the most airy
fabric – and pure invention is but the talent of a
liar.
Letter to publisher John Murray, 2 April 1817, publ. in *Byron's
Letters and Journals*, vol. 5 (ed. Leslie A. Marchand, 1976)

73 One certainly has a soul; but how it came to

allow itself to be enclosed in a body is more than I can imagine. I only know if once mine gets out, I'll have a bit of a tussle before I let it get in again to that of any other.

Letter to THOMAS MOORE, 11 April 1817, ibid., vol. 5

74 Opinions are made to be changed – or how is truth to be got at?

Letter to John Murray, 9 May 1817, ibid., vol. 5

75 So much alarmed that she is quite alarming,
All giggle, blush, half pertness, and half pout.

Beppo, st. 39 (1818)

76 I love the language, that soft bastard Latin,
Which melts like kisses from a female mouth,
And sounds as if it should be writ on satin
With syllables which breathe of the sweet South.

Ibid., st. 44. Of Italian.

77 I like the taxes, when they're not too many;
I like a seacoal fire, when not too dear;
I like a beef-steak, too, as well as any;
Have no objection to a pot of beer;
I like the weather, when it is not rainy,
That is, I like two months of every year.

Ibid., st. 48. Of England.

78 Our standing army, and disbanded seamen,
Poor's rate, reform, my own, the nation's debt,
Our little riots just to show we are free men,
Our trifling bankruptcies in the Gazette,
Our cloudy climate, and our chilly women,
All these I can forgive, and those forget,
And greatly venerate our recent glories,
And wish they were not owing to the Tories.

Ibid., st. 49

79 I stood in Venice, on the Bridge of Sighs;
A palace and a prison on each hand.

Childe Harold's Pilgrimage, canto 4, st. 1 (1818). Opening lines of canto. Byron described Venice as 'the greenest island of my imagination' in a letter of 17 November 1816.

80 Italia! oh Italia! thou who hast
The fatal gift of beauty.

Ibid., canto 4, st. 42. A loose translation of the sonnet 'Italia' by the 17th-century Italian poet Vincenzo da Filicaja.

81 Thy decay
Is still impregnate with divinity.

Ibid., canto 4, st. 55. Referring to Italy.

82 Oh Rome! my country! city of the soul!
The orphans of the heart must turn to thee.

Ibid., canto 4, st. 78

83 Yet, Freedom! yet thy banner, torn, but flying,
Streams like the thunderstorm *against* the wind.

Ibid., canto 4, st. 98

84 Of its own beauty is the mind diseased,
And fevers into false creation.

Ibid., canto 4, st. 122

85 Time, the avenger! unto thee I lift
My hands, and eyes, and heart, and crave of thee a gift.

Ibid., canto 4, st. 130

86 He heard it, but he heeded not – his eyes
Were with his heart, and that was far away;
He recked not of the life he lost nor prize,
But where his rude hut by the Danube lay,
There were his young barbarians all at play,
There was their Dacian mother – he, their sire,
Butchered to make a Roman holiday.

Ibid., canto 4, st. 141. Describing the death of a gladiator.

87 There is a pleasure in the pathless woods,
There is a rapture on the lonely shore,
There is society, where none intrudes,
By the deep sea, and music in its roar:
I love not man the less, but nature more.

Ibid., canto 4, st. 178

88 Thou glorious mirror, where the Almighty's form
Glasses itself in tempests; in all time, –
Calm or convulsed, in breeze, or gale, or storm,
Icing the pole, or in the torrid clime
Dark-heaving – boundless, endless, and sublime,
The image of eternity, the throne
Of the invisible.

Ibid., canto 4, st. 183. Describing the sea.

89 And Coleridge, too, has lately taken wing,
But like a hawk encumbered with his hood, –
Explaining metaphysics to the nation –
I wish he would explain his explanation.

Don Juan, canto 1, Dedication, st. 2 (1819)

90 But – Oh! ye lords of ladies intellectual,
Inform us truly, have they not hen-pecked you all?

Ibid., canto 1, st. 22

91 What men call gallantry, and gods adultery,
Is much more common where the climate's sultry.

Ibid., canto 1, st. 63

92 This is the patent age of new inventions
For killing bodies, and for saving souls,

All propagated with the best intentions.
Ibid., canto 1, st. 132

93 Man's love is of man's life a thing apart,
'Tis woman's whole existence.
Ibid., canto 1, st. 194. Julia's letter from a convent.

94 So for a good old-gentlemanly vice,
I think I must take up with avarice.
Ibid., canto 1, st. 216

95 There's nought, no doubt, so much the spirit
calms
As rum and true religion.
Ibid., canto 2, st. 34

96 All who joy would win
Must share it – happiness was born a twin.
Ibid., canto 2, st. 172

97 Let us have wine and women, mirth and
laughter,
Sermons and soda-water the day after.
Ibid., canto 2, st. 178

98 Man, being reasonable, must get drunk;
The best of life is but intoxication.
Ibid., canto 2, st. 179

99 This sort of adoration of the real
Is but a heightening of the 'beau ideal'.
Ibid., canto 2, st. 211

100 'Tis the perception of the beautiful,
A fine extension of the faculties,
Platonic, universal, wonderful,
Drawn from the stars, and filtered through the
skies,
Without which life would be extremely dull.
Ibid., canto 2, st. 212

101 Many are poets but without the name,
For what is poesy but to create
From overfeeling good or ill; and aim
At an external life beyond our fate,
And be the new Prometheus of new men.
The Prophecy of Dante, canto 4, ll. 10–14 (1819)

102 An exile, saddest of all prisoners,
Who has the whole world for a dungeon strong,
Seas, mountains, and the horizon's verge for bars.
Ibid., canto 4, ll. 131–3

103 I am sure my bones would not rest in an English
grave, or my clay mix with the earth of that country.
I believe the thought would drive me mad on my
death-bed could I suppose that any of my friends
would be base enough to convey my carcass back to
your soil. I would not even feed her worms if I could
help it.
Letter to publisher John Murray, 7 June 1819, publ. in Byron's
Letters and Journals, vol. 6 (ed. Leslie Marchand, 1976). After
Byron's death from a fever in Greece, his body was brought
back to England where it was interred together with his ancestors near his home at Newstead Abbey, having been refused
burial at Westminster Abbey.

104 A Turkish bath – that marble paradise of sher-
bert and sodomy.
Letter to John Murray, 12 August 1819, ibid., vol. 6

105 My time has been passed viciously and agreeably; at thirty-one so few years months days hours
or minutes remain that 'Carpe Diem' is not enough.
I have been obliged to crop even the seconds – for
who can trust to tomorrow?
Letter, 20 August 1819, ibid., vol. 6. See HORACE 24.

106 There is no freedom in Europe – that's certain
– it is besides a worn out portion of the globe.
Letter, 3 October 1819, ibid., vol. 6

107 As to 'Don Juan', confess . . . that it is the sublime
of that there sort of writing; it may be bawdy, but is
it not good English? It may be profligate, but is it
not life, is it not the thing? Could any man have
written it who has not lived in the world? and tooled
in a post-chaise? in a hackney coach? in a gondola?
against a wall? in a court carriage? in a vis à vis? on
a table? and under it?
Letter written from Venice, 26 October 1819, ibid., vol. 6

108 The reading or non-reading a book will never
keep down a single petticoat.
Letter, 29 October 1819, ibid., vol. 6.

109 What should I have known or written had I been
a quiet, mercantile politician or a lord in waiting? A
man must travel, and turmoil, or there is no
existence.
Letter to THOMAS MOORE, 31 August 1820, ibid., vol. 7 (ed.
Leslie A. Marchand, 1977)

110 The French courage proceeds from vanity; the
German from phlegm; the Turkish from fanaticism
& opium; the Spanish from pride; the English from
coolness; the Dutch from obstinacy; the Russian
from insensibility – but the Italian from anger.
Letter to publisher John Murray, 31 August 1820, ibid., vol. 7

111 Such writing is a sort of mental masturbation –
he is always f-gg-g his imagination – I don't mean
that he is indecent but viciously soliciting his own
ideas into a state which is neither poetry nor any-

thing else but a Bedlam vision produced by raw pork and opium.

Letter to publisher John Murray, 9 November 1820, ibid., vol. 7. Referring to KEATS. Byron had previously called Keats's work 'the Onanism of poetry', but later retracted his attack, limiting his criticism to the younger poet's style.

112 In her first passion woman loves her lover,
In all the others all she loves is love.

Don Juan, canto 3, st. 3 (1821)

113 All tragedies are finished by a death,
All comedies are ended by a marriage.

Ibid., canto 3, st. 9

114 Wives in their husbands' absences grow subtler,
And daughters sometimes run off with the butler.

Ibid., canto 3, st. 22

115 Dreading that climax of all human ills
The inflammation of his weekly bills.

Ibid., canto 3, st. 35

116 Though sages may pour out their wisdom's treasure,
There is no sterner moralist than pleasure.

Ibid., canto 3, st. 65

117 He lied with such a fervour of intention –
There was no doubt he earned his laureate pension.

Ibid., canto 3, st. 80

118 The isles of Greece, the isles of Greece!
Where burning Sappho loved and sung.
Where grew the arts of war and peace,
Where Delos rose, and Phoebus sprung!
Eternal summer gilds them yet,
But all, except their sun, is set.

Ibid., canto 3, st. 86, 'The Isles of Greece' (song), verse 1

119 The mountains look on Marathon –
And Marathon looks on the sea;
And musing there an hour alone,
I dreamed that Greece might still be free.

Ibid., 'The Isles of Greece' (song), verse 3

120 But words are things, and a small drop of ink,
Falling like dew, upon a thought, produces
That which makes thousands, perhaps millions, think.

Ibid., canto 3, st. 88

121 And if I laugh at any mortal thing,
'Tis that I may not weep.

Ibid., canto 4, st. 4. See also BEAUMARCHAIS 2.

122 That all-softening, overpowering knell,
The tocsin of the soul – the dinner-bell.

Ibid., canto 5, st. 49

123 All farewells should be sudden, when forever.

Sardanapalus, Act 5, Sc. 1 (1821). Spoken by Sardanapalus.

124 If I don't write to empty my mind, I go mad. As to that regular, uninterrupted love of writing ... I do not understand it. I feel it as a torture, which I must get rid of, but never as a pleasure. On the contrary, I think composition a great pain.

Letter to THOMAS MOORE, 2 January 1821, publ. in *Byron's Letters and Journals*, vol. 8 (ed. Leslie A. Marchand, 1978)

125 Out of chaos God made a world, and out of high passions comes a people.

'Ravenna Journal', 5 January 1821, ibid., vol. 8. Byron was describing the nationalist ferment in Italy, in which he himself played an active part.

126 The king-times are fast finishing. There will be blood shed like water, and tears like mist; but the peoples will conquer in the end. I shall not live to see it, but I foresee it.

'Ravenna Journal', 13 January 1821, ibid., vol. 8

127 Shelley is truth itself – and honour itself – notwithstanding his out-of-the-way notions about religion.

Letter, 2 June 1821, ibid., vol. 8

128 I can never get people to understand that poetry is the expression of *excited passion*, and that there is no such thing as a life of passion any more than a continuous earthquake, or an eternal fever. Besides, who would ever *shave* themselves in such a state?

Letter to THOMAS MOORE, 5 July 1821, ibid., vol. 8. Of the reactions of an American visitor who was 'somewhat too full of poesy and "entusymusy"'.

129 Reviews and magazines are at best ephemeral & superficial reading – who thinks of the grand article of last year in any given review?

Letter to John Murray, 24 September 1821, ibid., vol. 8. Requesting Murray not to trouble the poet with reviews of his work, Byron added, 'My feelings are like the dead, who know nothing and feel nothing of all or aught that is said or done in their regard.'

130 America is a model of force and freedom &

moderation – with all the coarseness and rudeness of its people.

Letter, 12 October 1821, ibid., vol. 8

131 In general I do not draw well with literary men – not that I dislike them, but I never know what to say to them after I have praised their last publication.

'Detached Thoughts (1821–2)', no. 53, ibid., vol. 9 (1979)

132 Posterity will ne'er survey
A nobler grave than this:
Here lie the bones of Castlereagh:
Stop, traveller, and piss.

'Epitaph for Castlereagh', written 1822, publ. in *Poetical Works* (ed. Frederick Page, 1904). Robert Stewart, Viscount Castlereagh, a Tory foreign secretary, was held responsible for many of his government's repressive measures abroad; he committed suicide 12 August 1822.

133 The angels were all singing out of tune,
And hoarse with having little else to do,
Excepting to wind up the sun and moon
Or curb a runaway young star or two.

The Vision of Judgment, st. 2 (1822)

134 He seems
To have seen better days, as who has not
Who has seen yesterday?

Werner, or, The Inheritance, Act 1, Sc. 1 (1822). Gabor's aside referring to Werner.

135 I would rather . . . have a nod from an American, than a snuff-box from an emperor.

Letter to THOMAS MOORE, 8 June 1822, publ. in *Byron's Letters and Journals*, vol. 9 (ed. Leslie A. Marchand, 1979)

136 I have had, and may have still, a thousand friends, as they are called, in life, who are like one's partners in the waltz of this world – not much remembered when the ball is over, though very pleasant for the time.

Letter to MARY SHELLEY, 16 November [?] 1822, ibid., vol. 10 (1980)

137 I have always laid it down as a maxim – and found it justified by experience – that a man and a woman make far better friendships than can exist between two of the same sex – but *then* with the condition that they never have made or are to make love to each other.

Letter, 1 December 1822, ibid., vol. 10. Byron echoed this notion in *Don Juan*: 'No friend like to a woman earth discovers,/So that you have not been nor will be lovers.' (canto 14, st. 93). See also quote 32.

138 The 'good old times' – all times when old are good –
Are gone.

The Age of Bronze, st. 1 (1823). Opening lines of poem.

139 While Franklin's quiet memory climbs to heaven,
Calming the lightning which he thence had riven,
Or drawing from the no less kindled earth
Freedom and peace to that which boasts his birth.

Ibid., st. 5

140 While Washington's a watchword, such as ne'er
Shall sink while there's an echo left to air.

Ibid., st. 5

141 Proud Wellington, with eagle beak so curled,
That nose, the hook where he suspends the world!

Ibid., st. 13

142 For what were all these country patriots born?
To hunt, and vote, and raise the price of corn?

Ibid., st. 14

143 A lady of a 'certain age,' which means
Certainly aged.

Don Juan, canto 6, st. 69 (1823)

144 'Let there be light!' said God, and there was light!
'Let there be blood!' says man, and there's a sea!

Ibid., canto 7, st. 41

145 The drying up a single tear has more
Of honest fame, than shedding seas of gore.

Ibid., canto 8, st. 3

146 Without, or with, offence to friends or foes,
I sketch your world exactly as it goes.

Ibid., canto 8, st. 89

147 War's a brain-spattering, windpipe-slitting art.

Ibid., canto 9, st. 4

148 Though her years were waning,
Her climacteric teased her like her teens.

Ibid., canto 10, st. 47

149 Alas! how deeply painful is all payment!

Ibid, canto 10, st. 79

150 When Bishop Berkeley said 'there was no matter',
And proved it – 'twas no matter what he said.

Ibid., canto 11, st. 1

151 And, after all, what is a lie? 'Tis but
The truth in masquerade.
Ibid., canto 11, st. 37

152 'Tis strange the mind, that very fiery particle,
Should let itself be snuffed out by an article.
Ibid., canto 11, st. 60. Referring to KEATS.

153 Of all the barbarous middle ages, that
Which is most barbarous is the middle age
Of man! it is – I really scarce know what;
But when we hover between fool and sage,
And don't know justly what we would be at –
A period something like a printed page,
Black letter upon foolscap, while our hair
Grows grizzled, and we are not what we were.
Ibid., canto 12, st. 1

154 O gold! I still prefer thee unto paper,
Which makes bank credit like a bark of vapour.
Ibid., canto 12, st. 4

155 Yes! ready money *is* Aladdin's lamp.
Ibid., canto 12, st. 12

156 Now hatred is by far the longest pleasure;
Men love in haste, but they detest at leisure.
Ibid., canto 13, st. 6

157 I should be very willing to redress
Men's wrongs, and rather check than punish
  crimes,
Had not Cervantes, in that all too true tale
Of Quixote, shown how all such efforts fail.
Ibid., canto 13, st. 8

158 Cervantes smiled Spain's chivalry away.
Ibid., canto 13, st. 11

159 The English winter – ending in July,
To recommence in August.
Ibid., canto 13, st. 42

160 Society is now one polished horde,
Formed of two mighty tribes, the *Bores* and *Bored*.
Ibid., canto 13, st. 95

161 But as to women, who can penetrate
The real sufferings of their she condition?
Man's very sympathy with their estate
Has much of selfishness and more suspicion.
Their love, their virtue, beauty, education,
But form good housekeepers, to breed a nation.
Ibid., canto 14, st. 24

162 Of all the horrid, hideous notes of woe,
Sadder than owl-songs or the midnight blast,
Is that portentous phrase, 'I told you so,'

Uttered by friends, those prophets of the past.
Ibid., canto 14, st. 50

163 Romances I ne'er read like those I have seen.
Ibid., canto 14, st. 80

164 Firmness yclept in heroes, kings and seamen,
That is, when they succeed; but greatly blamed
As *obstinacy*, both in men and women,
Whene'er their triumph pales, or star is tamed –
And 'twill perplex the casuist in morality
To fix the due bounds of this dangerous quality.
Ibid., canto 14, st. 89. In stanza 90, Byron added: 'Had Buona-
parte won at Waterloo,/It had been firmness; now 'tis perti-
nacity.'

165 'Tis strange, – but true; for truth is always
   strange;
Stranger than fiction.
Ibid., canto 14, st. 101

166 Sublime tobacco! which from east to west
Cheers the tar's labour or the Turkman's rest.
The Island, canto 2, st. 19 (1823)

167 I always looked to about thirty as the barrier
of any real or fierce delight in the passions, and
determined to work them out in the younger ore
and better veins of the mine, and I flatter myself
(perhaps) that I have pretty well done so, and now
the dross is coming.
Letter, 18 January 1823, publ. in *Byron's Letters and Journals*,
vol. 10 (ed. Leslie A. Marchand, 1980). Byron had earlier
expressed the same sentiment to THOMAS MOORE, to whom
he wrote (2 February 1818): 'I will work the mine of my youth
to the last vein of the ore, and then – good night. I have lived,
and am content.'

168 Sincerity may be humble, but she cannot be
servile.
Letter to STENDHAL, 29 May 1823, ibid., vol. 10

169 The dead have been awakened – shall I sleep?
The world's at war with tyrants – shall I crouch?
The harvest's ripe – and shall I pause to reap?
I slumber not; the thorn is in my couch;
Each day a trumpet soundeth in mine ear,
Its echo in my heart.
'Journal in Cephalonia', 19 June 1823, ibid., vol. 9 (ed. Leslie A.
Marchand, 1979). Opening entry of journal written during
Byron's final mission to aid the Greek revolt.

170 All present life is but an interjection,
An 'Oh!' or 'Ah!' of joy or misery,

Or a 'Ha! ha!' or 'Bah!' – a yawn, or 'Pooh!'
Of which perhaps the latter is most true.
Don Juan, canto 15, st. 1 (1824)

171 Between two worlds life hovers like a star,
'Twixt night and morn, upon the horizon's verge.
Ibid., canto 15, st. 99

172 Nothing can confound
A wise man more than laughter from a dunce.
Ibid., canto 16, st. 88

C

James Branch Cabell
(1879–1958)
US novelist and essayist

He was highly regarded in his day for his romantic and satirical novels, set in the fantasy medieval world of Poictesme (pronounced Pwahtem). The most popular, Jurgen (1919), was considered pornographic by some.

1 The optimist proclaims that we live in the best of all possible worlds; and the pessimist fears this is true.
The Silver Stallion, bk 4, ch. 26 (1926). Spoken by Coth of the Rocks. See F. H. BRADLEY 2 and VOLTAIRE 13.

Lord Caccia
(1905–90)
British diplomat

He was British Ambassador in the USA (1956–62) and head of the Diplomatic Service 1964–5.

1 If you are to stand up for your Government you must be able to stand up to your Government.
Quoted in *Anatomy of Britain*, ch. 17 (1965). Said while British ambassador in Washington.

Irving Caesar
(1895–1996)
US songwriter

He was a Tin Pan Alley composer of more than 1,000 published songs, most famously 'Tea for Two' (1924), 'Crazy Rhythm' (1928) and 'Swanee' (1936). 'Sometimes I write lousy, but always fast,' he said.

1 Picture you upon my knee,
Just tea for two and two for tea.
'Tea for Two' (song, 1925). Caesar claimed that he composed the song in less than five minutes (though he also admitted it might have taken him as long as fifteen).

Julius Caesar
(c. 100–44 BC)
Roman general and statesman

Gaius Julius Caesar. He conquered Gaul (58–50 BC), invaded Britain (55 and 54 BC), and defeated Pompey in the Civil War (49–45 BC). After a period in Egypt, where he fathered a son by Cleopatra, he returned to Rome as dictator in 46 BC. He was assassinated by Brutus and Cassius, members of the republican faction.

1 *Gallia est omnis divisa in partes tres.*
[All Gaul is divided into three parts.]
De Bello Gallico (*The Gallic War*), bk 1, sect. 1 (52–50 BC). First line of the book – indelibly associated with the study of Latin at school.

2 It is not these well-fed long-haired men that I fear, but the pale and the hungry-looking.
Quoted in *Parallel Lives*, 'Antony', sect. 11 by PLUTARCH. See WILLIAM SHAKESPEARE: JULIUS CAESAR 6.

3 Caesar's wife must be above suspicion.
Remark, *c.* 62 BC, quoted ibid., 'Caesar', sect. 10. Caesar's explanation to the court for divorcing Pompeia, his second wife who was accused of adultery. He took the action, he said, not because he believed her guilty, but because her veracity had been questioned.

4 The Ides of March have come.
Quoted ibid., 'Caesar', sect. 63. Recalling the warning of a soothsayer, on his way to the forum on 15th March 44 BC, the day of his assassination. See WILLIAM SHAKESPEARE: JULIUS CAESAR 1.

5 *Iacta alea est.*
[The die is cast.]
Quoted in *Lives of the Caesars*, 'Julius Caesar', sect. 32 (AD 120, transl. ROBERT GRAVES) by Suetonius. Caesar's words in 49 BC on crossing the Rubicon, a small stream that separated Cisalpine Gaul from Italy. By so doing, he provoked the start of the first Civil War that left Caesar ruler of the Roman world.

6 *Veni, vidi, vici.*
[I came, I saw, I conquered.]
Quoted ibid., 'Julius Caesar', sect. 37. Inscribed on a wagon in the triumphal procession following Caesar's victory over Pharnaces at Zela, Asia Minor, in 47 BC.

7 *Et tu, Brute.*
[And you too, Brutus.]
Attributed. Caesar's reproach on seeing that his friend Brutus was one of his assassins is supposed to have been uttered in Greek. In *Lives of the Caesars*, 'Julius Caesar', sect. 82 (AD 120) by Suetonius, the words are quoted: 'You, too, my child?'

John Cage
(1912–92)
US composer

A pupil of Schoenberg (for whom he was 'not a composer, but an inventor – of genius'), he used new methods of notation, invented the 'prepared' piano and was a pioneer of aleatory (chance) music.

1 I have nothing to say
and I am saying it
and that is poetry.
'Lecture on Nothing', publ. in *Silence* (1961)

2 There is no such thing as silence.
'Everything We Do Is Music', interview (1968), repr. in *Conversing with Cage*, 'His Own Music (to 1970)' (ed. Richard Kostelanetz, 1988). Cage claimed his silent piece, *4'33"*, to be his personal favourite: 'It has three movements and in all of these movements there are no sounds. I wanted my work to be free of my own likes and dislikes, because I think music should be free of the feelings of the composer.' (Interview in the *Soho Weekly News* 12 September 1974)

James Cagney
(1899–1986)
US screen actor

Shooting to fame as the feisty gangster in the seminal film The Public Enemy *(1931), he was in demand for the next thirty years, showing his versatility in such films as* A Midsummer Night's Dream *(1935) and* Yankee Doodle Dandy *(1942).*

1 You dirty, double-crossing rat.
Blonde Crazy (film, 1931, screenplay by Kubec Glasmon and John Bright, directed by Roy Del Ruth). Spoken by Bert Harris (James Cagney), the words were popularized and shortened to 'You dirty rat', which Cagney, in his autobiography *Cagney by Cagney* (1976), stridently denied ever having uttered. In the film *Taxi!* (1932), Cagney's character, Matt Nolan, says: 'Come out and take it you dirty, yellow-bellied rat . . .' *Blonde Crazy* was released in the UK with the title *Larceny Lane*.

Sammy Cahn
(1913–93)
US songwriter

Originally Samuel Cohen. He collaborated with Jule Styne on films and Broadway musicals, including Three Coins in the Fountain *(1954), and later with Jimmy Van Heusen, with whom he wrote 'All the Way' (1957), 'High Hopes' (1959), and 'Call Me Irresponsible' (1963).*

1 Give me five minutes more,
Only five minutes more,
Let me stay,
Let me stay in your arms.
'Five Minutes More' (song, 1946, with music by Jule Styne). The song was recorded by FRANK SINATRA.

2 Love and marriage, love and marriage
Go together like a horse and carriage
Dad was told by mother
You can't have one without the other.
'Love and Marriage' (song, with music by Jimmy Van Heusen)

from the TV musical *Our Town* (1955). The song was first aired by FRANK SINATRA, for whom it was a million-seller.

James M. Cain

(1892–1977)
US novelist

Subscribing to the 'hard-boiled' school of American fiction, he is noted for such works as The Postman Always Rings Twice *(1934) and* Mildred Pierce *(1941), both of which became film classics.*

1 The Postman Always Rings Twice.

Title of novel (1934, filmed 1946 and 1981)

(Sir) Michael Caine

(b. 1933)
British actor

Originally Maurice Micklewhite. A prolific performer on stage and screen, he is famous for his roles in the films The Ipcress File *(1965),* Alfie *(1966) and* Cider House Rules *(2000). He is, he says, 'every bourgeois's nightmare – a Cockney with intelligence and a million dollars'.*

1 Not many people know that.

Catch-phrase and book title (1984). Caine's catch-phrase, which found its way into his films and was made the title of an 'Almanac of Amazing Information' compiled by him, is said to have been his comment when habitually offering information garnered from *The Guinness Book of Records*.

2 My name is Michael Caine.

Attributed. Much mimicked, the line was said to have originated with Peter Sellers.

Pedro Calderón de la Barca

(1600–81)
Spanish dramatist and poet

Writing plays for the court from 1623, he produced over a hundred works, among them Life is a Dream *(1635) and* The Mayor of Zalamea *(c. 1640). He was ordained in 1651, and appointed honorary chaplain to Philip IV in 1663.*

1 What is life? A frenzy. What is life? An illusion, a shadow, a fiction. And the greatest good is trivial; for all life is a dream and all dreams are dreams.

La vida es sueño, 'Segunda jornada', ll. 2182–7 (1635; *Life is a Dream*). Spoken by Sigismundo.

Charles Calhoun

See BILL HALEY 2, 3

Caligula

(AD 12–41)
Roman emperor

Gaius Caesar Germanicus. Nicknamed 'Caligula', or 'Little Boot' by the soldiers of his father, Tiberius. Emperor from AD 37, he was renowned for his cruelty and excesses, which famously included bestowing a consulship on his horse. He was murdered by his Praetorian guard.

1 Make him feel that he is dying!

Quoted in *Lives of the Caesars*, 'Gaius Caligula', sect. 30 (AD 120, transl. ROBERT GRAVES) by Suetonius

2 I wish all you Romans had only one neck!

Quoted ibid., 'Gaius Caligula', sect. 30

James Callaghan

(1912–2005)
British politician and prime minister

Leonard James Callaghan, Baron Callaghan of Cardiff. Elected Labour MP in 1945, he held posts as Home and Foreign Secretary before becoming Prime Minister (1976–9). His government fell after a series of strikes had paralysed essential services. See ROY JENKINS 1.

1 I don't think other people in the world would share the view there is mounting chaos.

Interview at London Airport, 10 January 1979, quoted in the *Sun* 11 January 1979. Callaghan was returning from the Guadeloupe Summit conference after the Labour Party's policy of cooperation with the unions had been torn apart by a wave of strikes – the so-called 'winter of discontent' (see below). See SUN 1 for its famous headline paraphrase.

2 I had known it was going to be a 'winter of discontent'.

Quoted in the *Daily Telegraph* 9 February 1979. The New Year had seen a succession of labour disputes, with hospitals picketed and refuse piled in the streets. Callaghan's failure to control the unions led directly to MARGARET THATCHER's election victory later that year and to a subsequent raft of legislation designed to limit their power. See WILLIAM SHAKESPEARE: RICHARD III 1.

3 You may never reach the promised land, but you can certainly march towards it.

Quoted by his daughter, Baroness Jay, in tribute addressed to House of Lords, 4 April 2005, publ. in *Hansard* (Lords), col. 474

Callimachus
(c. 305–240 BC)
Alexandrian poet and scholar

Based at the great library of Alexandria, he wrote prolifically, becoming one of the most influential poets of late antiquity and the model for OVID *and* CATULLUS. *His epigrams and elegies are especially esteemed.*

1 I wept as I remembered how often you and I
Had tired the sun with talking and sent him down
   the sky.
'Heraclitus' (transl. WILLIAM JOHNSON CORY, 1858). Addressed to the poet Heraclitus of Halicarnassus, on the news of his death.

Italo Calvino
(1923–85)
Italian author and critic

Early novels, including his first, A Path to the Nest of Spiders *(1947), are naturalistic, while later books, such as* If on a Winter's Night a Traveller *(1979) are 'magic realist' in style. 'He is far too intelligent to become really cerebral,'* URSULA LE GUIN *commented.*

1 It is not the voice that commands the story: it is the ear.
Invisible Cities (1972). Spoken by Marco Polo.

2 The catalogue of forms is endless: until every shape has found its city, new cities will continue to be born. When the forms exhaust their variety and come apart, the end of cities begins.
Invisible Cities (1972)

3 The universe will express itself as long as somebody will be able to say 'I read, therefore it writes.'
If on a Winter's Night a Traveller, pt 8, 'From the Diary of Silas Flannery' (1979)

4 Everything can change, but not the language that we carry inside us, like a world more exclusive and final than one's mother's womb.
'By Way of an Autobiography' (1980), repr. in *The Literature Machine* (1987)

5 A classic is a book that has never finished saying what it has to say.
'Why Read the Classics?' (1981), ibid. One of a series of definitions of a 'classic'.

Hélder Câmara
(1909–99)
Brazilian cleric

A pioneer of Latin America's liberation theology movement, he was known as the 'red bishop' for his outspoken criticism of Brazil's military dictatorship. He was Archbishop of Olinda and Recife 1964–85.

1 When I feed the poor, I am called a saint. When I ask why the poor have no food, I am called a communist.
Remark in 1964, quoted in the *Western Catholic Reporter* 6 September 1999. Various versions of this saying exist.

Pierre, Baron de Cambronne
(1770–1842)
French general

He accompanied NAPOLEON *to Elba, commanded the army when the emperor took Paris in 1815 and was taken prisoner at Waterloo later that year.*

1 The Guards die, but do not surrender.
Attributed. Reply to a call for his troops to surrender at Waterloo, later denied by him.

2 *Merde!*
[Shit!]
Attributed. Reply when asked to surrender at Waterloo, and known as the 'mot de Cambronne'. VICTOR HUGO alludes to it in *Les Misérables*, vol. 1, bk 2, ch. 15 (1862), as *'le plus beau mot qu'un français ait répété'* ('the finest reply that a Frenchman ever made').

William Camden
(1551–1623)
English historian and antiquary

The author of Britannia *(1586), the first comprehensive topographical survey of England, he was a pioneer of historical methodology, hailed by* SPENSER *as 'the nurse of antiquity/ And lantern unto late succeeding age'.*

1 My friend, judge not me,
Thou seest I judge not thee.
Betwixt the stirrup and the ground
Mercy I asked, mercy I found.
Remains Concerning Britain, 'Epitaph for a Gentleman falling off his horse' (1605)

James Cameron

(1911–85)
British journalist

He made his name as a freelance journalist, addressing issues of war and social justice with integrity and wit. He also wrote and presented TV shows such as Men of Our Time *(1963).*

1 Now, standing up unsteadily from the sea, was the famous Mushroom ... It climbed like a fungus; it looked like a towering mound of firm cream shot with veins and rivers of wandering red; it mounted tirelessly through the clouds as though it were made of denser, solider stuff, as no doubt it was. The only similes that came to mind were banal: a sundae, red ink in a pot of distemper. From behind me I heard a frenetic ticking of typewriters; very soon I found I was fumbling with my own. The reportage had begun. Many of us will never live it down.
Point of Departure, ch. 3 (1967). On the first atomic-bomb test on the Bikini atoll, July 1946.

Donald Cammell

(1934–96)
British film-maker

He made his directorial debut in Performance *(1971), a psychedelic psychodrama for which he is chiefly remembered. He also directed* White of the Eye *(1987) and* Wild Side *(1995).*

1 Comical little geezer. You'll look funny when you're fifty.
Performance (film, 1971, screenplay by Donald Cammell, directed by Donald Cammell and Nicolas Roeg). Spoken by Chas (James Fox) to Turner (Mick Jagger).

2 I know how you do it. I know a thing or two about performing my boy, I can tell you. The only performance that makes it, that really makes it, that makes it all the way, is the one that achieves madness.
Turner (Mick Jagger), ibid. The words were inspired by the writings of ANTONIN ARTAUD.

Jane Montgomery Campbell

See HYMNS AND CAROLS 86

Mrs Patrick Campbell

(1865–1940)
British actress

Originally Beatrice Stella Tanner. Described by YEATS *as possessing 'an ego like a raging tooth', she came to notice with her performance in* The Second Mrs Tanqueray *(1893).* SHAW, *with whom she formed a lasting friendship, created the part of Eliza Doolittle for her in* Pygmalion *(1914).*

1 To be made to hold his tongue is the greatest insult you can offer him – though he might be ready with a poker to make you hold yours.
Of GEORGE BERNARD SHAW, in *My Life and Some Letters*, ch. 16 (1922)

2 The deep, deep peace of the double-bed after the hurly-burly of the chaise-longue.
Quoted in *While Rome Burns*, 'The First Mrs. Tanqueray' (1934) by ALEXANDER WOOLLCOTT. Discussing the benefits of her recent marriage. Woollcott remarked of Mrs Campbell: 'Her failure to be polite took on the proportions of a magnificent gesture.'

3 Does it *really* matter what these affectionate people do – so long as they don't do it in the streets *and frighten the horses!*
Quoted in *Mrs Patrick Campbell*, ch. 15 (1961) by Alan Dent. Referring to rumours of a homosexual liaison between two actors. The words are quoted in various forms, commonly 'I don't mind where people make love ...', and 'My dear, I don't care what they do ...'

Thomas Campbell

(1777–1844)
Scottish poet

He is remembered for The Pleasures of Hope *(1799), a verse portrait of the human condition, the ballad 'Lord Ullin's Daughter' (1809), and several patriotic war songs. With others, he launched a campaign to found the University of London. His diffidence caused Walter Scott to write: 'He is afraid of the shadow that his own fame casts before him.'*

1 'Tis distance lends enchantment to the view,
And robes the mountain in its azure hue.
The Pleasures of Hope, pt 1, ll. 7–8 (1799)

2 What millions died that Caesar might be great!
Ibid., pt 2, l. 174

3 O Star-eyed Science! hast thou wandered there,
To waft us home the message of despair?
Ibid., pt 2, ll. 325–6

4 What though my wingèd hours of bliss have
    been,
Like angel-visits, few and far between?
Ibid., pt 2, ll. 375–6. The image is borrowed from the Scottish poet Robert Blair (1699–1746): 'The good he scorned/Stalked off reluctant, like an ill-used ghost,/Not to return; or if it did, its visits/Like those of angels, short, and far between.' (*The Grave*, ll. 586–9, 1743)

5 O leave this barren spot to me!
Spare, woodman, spare the beechen tree.
'The Beech-Tree's Petition', st. 1 (1801), publ. in *The Poetical Works of Thomas Campbell* (ed. Rev. Alfred W. Hill, 1875)

6 Ye mariners of England,
That guard our native seas;
Whose flag has braved, a thousand years,
The battle and the breeze!
'Ye Mariners of England', st. 1 (1801), ibid.

7 To-morrow let us do or die!
Gertrude of Wyoming, pt 3, st. 37 (1809)

8 To live in hearts we leave behind
Is not to die.
Hallowed Ground (1825)

9 The popularity of that baby-faced boy, who possessed not even the elements of a good actor, was a hallucination in the public mind, and a disgrace to our theatrical history.
Life of Mrs Siddons, ch. 18 (1834). Referring to the child actor, 'Master Betty'. William Henry West Betty (1791–1874) had been taken up by the fashionable world, playing the roles of Romeo, Hamlet and Richard III at the age of twelve. The craze lasted two years, to the despair of many, including LEIGH HUNT, who was eventually able to write in a contemporary newspaper: 'The charm of novelty has at length broken . . . and the town is just now somewhat in the position of the husband who, after passing the honeymoon with a beautiful but childish woman, finds his reason once more returning and is content to sit down and ask why he has been pleased.'

10 Now Barabbas was a publisher.
Quoted in *A Publisher and his Friends*, vol. 1, ch. 14 by SAMUEL SMILES (1891). The words are also ascribed to BYRON. See BIBLE, NEW TESTAMENT: JOHN 62.

Thomas Campion
(1567–1620)
English poet and musician

A composer and lyricist of note, he wrote for the lute, publishing his songs in four Books of Airs *(1601–17). His theories on rhyme were expounded in* Observations in the Art of English Poesy *(1602). He practised as a physician from 1606.*

1 My sweetest Lesbia, let us live and love,
And though the sager sort our deeds reprove,
Let us not weigh them. Heaven's great lamps do dive
Into their west, and straight again revive,
But soon as once set is our little light,
Then must we sleep one ever-during night.
A Book of Airs, no. 1 ('My sweetest Lesbia') (1601). A translation of CATULLUS 6.

2 Never weather-beaten sail more willing bent to shore.
Two Books of Airs, 'First Book' no. 11 ('Never weather-beaten sail') (c. 1613)

3 The summer hath his joys,
And winter his delights;
Though love and all his pleasures are but toys,
They shorten tedious nights.
The Third Book of Airs, no. 12 ('Now winter nights enlarge') (1617)

4 Never love unless you can
Bear with all the faults of man.
Ibid., no. 27 ('Never love unless you can')

5 There is a garden in her face
Where roses and white lilies grow;
A heavenly paradise is that place
Wherein all pleasant fruits do flow.
The Fourth Books of Airs, no. 7 ('There is a garden in her face'), st. 1 (c. 1617)

Albert Camus
(1913–60)
French-Algerian philosopher and author

His works principally deal with l'homme révolté *(the misfit), as in the essay 'The Myth of Sisyphus' (1942) and his first novel* The Outsider *(1942), both of which explore the absurdity of man's situation. Later novels include* The Plague *(1947) and* The Fall *(1956).*

1 An intellectual is someone whose mind watches itself. I like this, because I am happy to be both halves, the watcher and the watched. 'Can they be brought together?' This is a practical question. We must get down to it. 'I despise intelligence' really means: 'I cannot bear my doubts.'
Journal entry, May 1936, publ. in *Carnets 1935–1942* (1962; *Notebooks*, transl./ed. Philip Thody, 1963)

2 Culture: the cry of men in face of their destiny.
Journal entry, June 1937, ibid.

3 There is but one truly serious philosophical problem and that is suicide. Judging whether life is or is not worth living amounts to answering the fundamental question of philosophy. All the rest – whether or not the world has three dimensions, whether the mind has nine or twelve categories – comes afterwards. These are games.
The Myth of Sisyphus, 'Absurdity and Suicide' (1942, transl. 1955). Opening sentences.

4 At any street corner the feeling of absurdity can strike any man in the face.
Ibid., 'Absurd Walls'

5 The struggle itself towards the heights is enough to fill a man's heart. One must imagine Sisyphus happy.
Ibid., 'The Myth of Sisyphus'. Closing words of book.

6 Mother died today. Or, maybe, yesterday; I can't be sure.
Meursault, in *L'Étranger*, pt 1, ch. 1 (*The Outsider*, 1942). Opening words of book.

7 If Christianity is pessimistic as to man, it is optimistic as to human destiny. Well, I can say that, pessimistic as to human destiny, I am optimistic as to man.
Address to monks of Latour-Maubourg, 1948, publ. in *Resistance, Rebellion and Death*, 'The Unbeliever and Christians' (1961)

8 Man is the only creature who refuses to be what he is.
The Rebel, Introduction (1951)

9 What is a rebel? A man who says no.
Ibid., ch. 1. Opening words of chapter.

10 All modern revolutions have ended in a reinforcement of the power of the state.
Ibid., ch. 3, 'State Terrorism and Irrational Terror'

11 Every revolutionary ends by becoming either an oppressor or a heretic.
Ibid., ch. 3, 'Rebellion and Revolution'

12 In the midst of winter, I finally learned that there was in me an invincible summer.
Summer, 'Return to Tipasa' (*L'Été*, 1954)

13 I sometimes think of what future historians will say of us. A single sentence will suffice for modern man: he fornicated and read the papers.
The Fall (1956). Spoken by the narrator (Jean-Baptiste Clamence).

14 You know what charm is: a way of getting the answer yes without having asked any clear question.
Ibid.

15 Men are never convinced of your reasons, of your sincerity, of the seriousness of your sufferings, except by your death. So long as you are alive, your case is doubtful; you have a right only to their scepticism.
Ibid.

16 Martyrs, *cher ami*, must choose between being forgotten, mocked, or made use of. As for being understood – never!
Ibid.

17 I'll tell you a great big secret, *mon cher*. Don't wait for the Last Judgment. It takes place every day.
Ibid.

18 Ah, *mon cher*, for anyone who is alone, without God and without a master, the weight of days is dreadful.
Ibid.

19 I have always denounced terrorism. I must also denounce a terrorism which is exercised blindly, in the streets of Algiers for example, and which some day could strike my mother or my family. I believe in justice, but I shall defend my mother above justice.
Debate at University of Stockholm, 1957, quoted in *Camus, A Biography*, ch. 45 (1979) by Herbert R. Lottman. Camus provoked much criticism with his remarks, taken as a betrayal of the struggle for Algerian independence.

20 We come into the world laden with the weight of an infinite necessity.
Resistance, Rebellion and Death, 'Reflections on the Guillotine' (1961)

21 The more I produce the less I am certain. On the road along which the artist walks, night falls ever more densely. Finally he dies blind.
Undated letter, quoted in *Camus: A Biography*, ch. 43 (1979) by Herbert R. Lottman

Elias Canetti
(1905–94)
Bulgarian author and philosopher

His only novel Die Blendung *(1936, translated as both* Auto da Fé *and* The Tower of Babel*) charts the destruction of a reclusive sinologist, while his greatest work* Crowds and Power *(1960) focuses on his central preoccupation, the psychology of crowds.*

1 Justice begins with the recognition of the necessity of sharing. The oldest law is that which regulates it, and this is still the most important law today and, as such, has remained the basic concern of all movements which have at heart the community of human activities and of human existence in general.
Crowds and Power, 'Distribution and Increase' (1960)

2 Whether or not God is dead: it is impossible to keep silent about him who was there for so long.
The Secret Heart Of The Clock: Notes, Aphorisms, Fragments 1973–1985, '1973' (1991)

3 There is no doubt: the study of man is just beginning, at the same time that his end is in sight.
Ibid., '1980'

George Canning

(1770–1827)

English statesman and author

He entered parliament as a Tory in 1793, and was Foreign Secretary (1807–10 and 1822–7) and Prime Minister for four months in 1827. His verses, satires and parodies, published in his journal The Anti-Jacobin *and elsewhere, earned him many enemies.*

1 A steady patriot of the world alone,
The friend of every country but his own.
'The New Morality', ll. 113–14 (1798), repr. in *Poetry of the Anti-Jacobin* (1799). Referring to the radical ideology of the Jacobins. See BENJAMIN DISRAELI 52, W. S. GILBERT 32.

2 Give me the avowed, the erect, the manly foe,
Bold I can meet – perhaps may turn his blow;
But of all plagues, good heaven, thy wrath can send,
Save, save, oh! save me from the candid friend.
'The New Morality', ll. 207–10, ibid.

3 Away with the cant of 'measures, not men!' – the idle supposition that it is the harness and not the horses that draw the chariot along! No, Sir, if the comparison must be made, if the distinction must be taken, men are everything, measures comparatively nothing.
'On the Army Estimates', speech to House of Commons, 8 December 1802, publ. in *The Speeches of the Right Honourable George Canning*, vol. 2 (ed. R. Therry, 1828)

4 Intimately concerned as we are with the system of Europe, it does not follow that we are therefore called upon to mix ourselves on every occasion, with a restless and meddling activity, in the concerns of the nations which surround us.
Speech at Plymouth, 28 October 1823, ibid., vol. 6, Addenda

5 In matter of commerce the fault of the Dutch
Is offering too little and asking too much.
The French are with equal advantage content,
So we clap on Dutch bottoms just twenty per cent.
Canning's 'rhyming despatch', sent to the British minister in the Netherlands, 31 January 1826, publ. in *Canning: Politician and Statesman*, ch. 9 (1976) by Peter Dixon. The letter, sent in code, served to remind Charles Bagot of proposed reprisals against the Dutch for refusing to sign a trade treaty.

6 I called the New World into existence, to redress the balance of the Old.
Speech, 12 December 1826, publ. in *The Speeches of the Right Honourable George Canning*, vol. 6 (ed. R. Therry, 1828). Referring to Canning's policy of recognizing the independence of Spain's former colonies in the New World, thereby preventing French influence in the zone: 'I resolved that if France had Spain, it should not be Spain *"with the Indies"*.'

Eric Cantona

(b. 1966)

French footballer

A skilful forward and an idol for a generation of fans, he played for Manchester United 1993–7, and has since embarked on an acting career.

1 When the seagulls follow the trawler, it is because they think sardines will be thrown into the sea.
Quoted in the *Independent* 1 April 1995, after he had won his appeal against a prison sentence for his conviction for assault on a hostile fan in January. 'Seagulls follow the trawler' was taken as the name of a sports discussion programme on BBC Radio 4 in 1999.

Cao Yu

(1910–96)

Chinese dramatist

Originally Wan Jiabao. China's foremost 20th-century playwright, he took as his theme the corruption of society, producing his best known work Thunderstorm *in 1935.*

1 Art for art's sake is a philosophy of the well-fed.
Observer 13 April 1980

Karel Čapek

(1890–1938)

Czech writer

He is best remembered for the play R.U.R. (Rossum's Universal Robots) *(1920), in which he coined the word 'robot' (derived from the Czech word for forced labour). With his brother Josef, he wrote the comic satire* The Insect Play *(1921).*

1 Man will never be enslaved by machinery if the man tending the machine be paid enough.
Quoted in obituary in the *News Chronicle* 27 December 1938

Al Capone

(1899–1947)

US gangster

'Neapolitan by birth and Neanderthal by instinct', Alphonse Capone, aka Scarface, was America's most famous gangster, allegedly earning $30 million a year during the Prohibition period. He was eventually gaoled in 1931 for tax evasion.

1 My rackets are run on strictly American lines and they're going to stay that way.

Interview, *c.* 1930, publ. in *Cockburn Sums Up*, 'Mr Capone, Philosopher' (1981) by Claud Cockburn

2 Virgin territory for whorehouses.

Quoted in *The Bootleggers*, ch. 16 (1961) by Kenneth Allsop. Referring to suburban Chicago.

Truman Capote

(1924–84)

US author

Originally Truman Streckfus Presons. A versatile writer, he is remembered for his first novel Other Voices, Other Rooms *(1948), the novella* Breakfast at Tiffany's *(1958), and* In Cold Blood *(1966) which he termed a non-fiction novel.* GORE VIDAL *observed: 'He has made lying an art. A minor art.'*

1 That isn't writing at all – it's typing.

Quoted in the *New Republic* 9 February 1959. Remark in TV discussion, referring to the Beat novelists.

2 Venice is like eating an entire box of chocolate liqueurs at one go.

Quoted in the *Observer* 26 November 1961

3 Even an attorney of moderate talent can postpone doomsday year after year, for the system of appeals that pervades American jurisprudence amounts to a legalistic wheel of fortune, a game of chance, somewhat fixed in the favor of the criminal, that the participants play interminably.

In Cold Blood, ch. 4 (1966)

4 Failure is the condiment that gives success its flavor.

'Self-Portrait' (1972), repr. in *A Capote Reader* (1987)

5 Anyone who is consistently consistent has a head made of biscuit.

Ibid.

6 When God hands you a gift, he also hands you a whip; and the whip is intended solely for self-flagellation.

Music for Chameleons, Preface (1980)

7 It's like a jumble of huts in a jungle somewhere. I don't understand how you can live there. It's really, completely dead. Walk along the street, there's nothing moving. I've lived in small Spanish fishing villages which were literally sunny all day long everyday of the week, but they weren't as boring as Los Angeles.

Conversations With Truman Capote, ch. 7, 'Hollywood' (ed. Lawrence Grobel, 1985). Referring to Los Angeles.

Al Capp

(1909–79)

US cartoonist

Originally Alfred Caplin. He introduced the comic strip featuring the hillbilly character Li'l Abner and friends to the New York Mirror *in 1934. Its popularity ensured that it ran for more than forty years.*

1 A product of the untalented, sold by the unprincipled to the utterly bewildered.

Quoted in the *National Observer* 1 July 1963. Referring to abstract art.

Francesco Caracciolo

(1752–99)

Neapolitan naval commander

He fought with the British in the American War of Independence and commanded the Bourbon navy under Ferdinand IV of Naples. Having joined the pro-French Parthenopean Republic, he was hanged by NELSON *as a traitor.*

1 In England there are sixty different religions, and only one sauce.

Attributed

Peire Cardenal

(c. 1180–1272)

French troubadour poet

The author of seventy songs, he was satirically critical of the crusade against the Albigensians and of contemporary morals.

1 If some beggar steals a bridle
he'll be hung by a man who's stolen a horse.
There's no surer justice in the world than that
which makes the rich thief hang the poor one.

'Las amairitz, qui encolpar las vol', publ. in *Songs of the Troubadours* (ed. and transl. Anthony Bonner, 1972)

Neville Cardus

(1889–1975)

British journalist and critic

He wrote mainly for the Manchester Guardian *which he joined in 1916 as music critic, and he later also became responsible for the paper's cricket coverage.*

1 It is far more than a game, this cricket. It somehow holds the mirror up to English nature. We are not hypocrites, but we try to make the best of things of contrary appeal.
English Cricket (1945)

2 Such reproductions may not interest the reader; but after all, this is my autobiography, not his; he is under no obligation to read further in it; he was under none to begin . . . A modest or inhibited auto-biography is written without entertainment to the writer and read with distrust by the reader.
Autobiography, pt 1 (1947)

Thomas Carew

(*c.* 1595–*c.* 1640)

English poet

A cavalier poet, he was a member of a literary circle that included BEN JONSON *and* EDMUND WALLER. *He wrote the masque* Coelum Britannicum, *performed before* CHARLES I *in 1634, and love poems such as 'The Rapture'.*

1 Here lies a king, that ruled as he thought fit
The universal monarchy of wit.
 'An Elegy upon the Death of the Dean of St Paul's, Dr John Donne', publ. in *Poems* (1633)

2 Give me more love or more disdain;
The torrid or the frozen zone
Bring equal ease unto my pain;
The temperate affords me none.
'Mediocrity in Love Rejected', st. 1, publ. in *Poems* (1640)

3 Ask me no more where Jove bestows,
When June is past, the fading rose;
For in your beauty's orient deep
These flowers, as in their causes, sleep.
'A Song', st. 1, ibid.

George Carey

(b. 1935)

British ecclesiastic, Archbishop of Canterbury

Formerly a theology lecturer, he was primate of the Church of England (1991–2002), during which time he drew some criticism for his liberal and modernizing tendencies.

1 I believe with all my heart that the Church of Jesus Christ should be a Church of blurred edges.
Independent 15 July 1992

Henry Carey

(*c.* 1687–1743)

English poet, playwright and songwriter

Remembered chiefly for his ballads, he also provided words and music for a number of farces, and published Poems on Several Occasions *in 1713. Despite his popularity, he lived his life in poverty and committed suicide.*

1 Of all the girls that are so smart,
There's none like pretty Sally,
She is the darling of my heart,
And she lives in our alley.
'Sally in our Alley', st. 1 (1729)

2 God save our gracious king!
Long live our noble king!
God save the king!
'God Save the King', st. 1 (song, *c.* 1740). The words were attributed to Carey by his son, but his authorship has not been authenticated; the anthem has also been attributed to Dr John Bull (d. 1628), an organist at Antwerp Cathedral. Its first public performance is thought to have been when Carey sang it during a dinner in 1740 in honour of Admiral Edward Vernon who had captured the Spanish harbour of Porto Bello (then in Colombia, now Panama) during the War of Jenkins' Ear. The words and music were published in the *Gentleman's Magazine* October 1745 (the tune was adopted by Germany and Denmark before the end of the 18th century, and has also been used in Sweden, Switzerland, Liechtenstein and the United States).

3 Send him victorious,
Happy and glorious,
Long to reign over us:
God save the king!
Ibid., st. 1

4 Confound their politics,
Frustrate their knavish tricks.
Ibid., st. 2

John Carey

(b. 1934)

British author and critic

Professor of English at Oxford 1976–2001 and principal book reviewer for The Sunday Times *since 1977, he has written works on* MILTON, THACKERAY, DONNE *and* WILLIAM GOLDING.

1 A blank helpless sort of face, rather like a rose just before you drench it with DDT.

Sunday Times 20 September 1981. Referring to photographs of society figure Lady Diana Cooper.

2 It follows that, if society wants to be civilized, it must establish conditions favourable to the preservation of the gifted few.

The Intellectuals and the Masses, ch. 4 (1992)

Peter Carey
(b. 1943)
Australian author

His novels, which include Bliss *(1981), set in the world of advertising in which he formerly worked, and* Oscar and Lucinda *(1988), combine fantasy, comedy and history.*

1 We're built, as a nation, on the grounds of a concentration camp. It's like saying 'OK, here's Auschwitz. Here's where we'll start our country.'

Interview in *City Limits* 7 April 1988

Jane Welsh Carlyle
(1801–66)

Though bolstered by a strong mutual affection, her marriage to THOMAS CARLYLE *was fraught with quarrels and misunderstanding. She was famed as a letter-writer, numbering many eminent Victorians among her correspondents.*

1 Oh Lord! if you but knew what a brimstone of a creature I am behind all this beautiful amiability.

Letter, 29 February 1836, quoted in *I Too Am Here: Selections from the Letters of Jane Welsh Carlyle*, Introduction (1977) by Alan and Mary McQueen Simpson

2 If they had said that the sun or the moon had gone out of the heavens, it could not have struck me with the idea of a more awful and dreary blank in creation than the words: 'Byron is dead!'

Letter to THOMAS CARLYLE, 20 May 1824, publ. in *The Collected Letters of Thomas and Jane Welsh Carlyle*, vol. 3 (ed. C. R. Sanders et al., 1970)

3 When one has been threatened with a great injustice, one accepts a smaller as a favour.

Journal entry, 21 November 1855, publ. in *Letters and Memorials*, vol. 2 (ed. J. A. Froude, 1883)

4 Blessed be the inventor of photography! I set him above even the inventor of chloroform! It has given more positive pleasure to poor suffering humanity than anything else that has 'cast up' in my time or is like to – this art by which even the 'poor' can possess themselves of tolerable likenesses of their absent dear ones. And mustn't it be acting favourably on the morality of the country?

Letter, 21 October 1859, ibid., vol. 3, publ. in *Letters and Memorials*, vol. 3 (ed J. A. Froude, 1883), Lettter 213

5 My dear, if Mr Carlyle's digestion had been stronger, there is no saying what he might have been!

Letter, May [?] 1866, publ. in *Autobiography and Letters of Mrs Margaret Oliphant*, 'Letters' (ed. A. L. Coghill, 1899). In response to a remark by MARGARET OLIPHANT that 'Mr Carlyle seemed the only virtuous philosopher we had'.

Thomas Carlyle
(1795–1881)
Scottish essayist and historian

One of the most influential thinkers of his day, he emphasized the importance of the individual in effecting social change, as reflected in his lectures, On Heroes, Hero-Worship, and the Heroic in History *(1840), and in his biography of* FREDERICK THE GREAT *(1858–65). Other major works include a study of the French Revolution (1837) and* Past and Present *(1843), which argued the need for strong leadership in society.*

1 They raise their minds by brooding over and embellishing their sufferings, from one degree of fervid exaltation and dreary greatness to another, till at length they run amuck entirely, and whoever meets them would do well to run them thro' the body.

Letter, 28 January 1821, publ. in *Collected Letters of Thomas and Jane Welsh Carlyle*, vol. 1 (ed. C. R. Sanders et al., 1970). Referring to the Romantic poets.

2 A terrible, beetle-browed, mastiff-mouthed, yellow-skinned, broad-bottomed, grim-taciturn individual; with a pair of dull-cruel-looking black eyes, and as much parliamentary intellect and silent-rage in him . . . as I have ever seen in any man.

Letter to his brother, 24 June 1824, publ. in *New Letters of Thomas Carlyle* (ed. Alexander Carlyle, 1904). Referring to DANIEL WEBSTER.

3 His cardinal sin is that he wants *will*; he has no resolution, he shrinks from pain or labour in any of its shapes. His very attitude bespeaks this: he never straightens his knee joints, he stoops with his fat ill-shapen shoulders, and in walking he does not tread but shovel and slide.

Letter to his brother, 24 June 1824, following Carlyle's first encounter with SAMUEL TAYLOR COLERIDGE, publ. in *Collected Letters of Thomas and Jane Welsh Carlyle*, vol. 3 (ed. C. R. Sanders et al., 1970)

4 A well-written life is almost as rare as a well-spent one.
'Jean Paul Friedrich Richter' (1827), repr. in *Critical and Miscellaneous Essays*, vol. 1 (1838)

5 No sooner does a great man depart, and leave his character as public property, than a crowd of little men rushes towards it. There they are gathered together, blinking up to it with such vision as they have, scanning it from afar, hovering round it this way and that, each cunningly endeavouring, by all arts, to catch some reflex of it in the little mirror of himself.
'Jean Paul Friedrich Richter', ibid.

6 The three great elements of modern civilization, gunpowder, printing, and the Protestant religion.
'The State of German Literature' (1827), ibid. Carlyle referred to an earlier statement by Bacon (see FRANCIS BACON 52).

7 We were wise indeed, could we discern truly the signs of our own time; and by knowledge of its wants and advantages, wisely adjust our own position in it.
'Signs of the Times' (1829), ibid., vol. 2 (1838). See BIBLE, NEW TESTAMENT: MATTHEW 111.

8 Men are to be guided only by their self-interests. Good government is a good balancing of these; and, except a keen eye and appetite for self-interest, requires no virtue in any quarter. To both parties it is emphatically a machine: to the discontented, a 'taxing-machine'; to the contented, a 'machine for securing property'. Its duties and its faults are not those of a father, but of an active parish-constable.
'Signs of the Times', ibid.

9 When we can drain the ocean into mill-ponds, and bottle up the force of gravity, to be sold by retail in gas jars; then may we hope to comprehend the infinitudes of man's soul under formulas of profit and loss; and rule over this too, as over a patent engine, by checks, and valves, and balances.
'Signs of the Times', ibid.

10 This we take it is the grand characteristic of our age. By our skill in mechanism, it has come to pass, that in the management of external things we excel all other ages; while in whatever respects the pure moral nature, in true dignity of soul and character, we are perhaps inferior to most civilised ages.
'Signs of the Times', ibid.

11 For the 'superior morality', of which we hear so much, we too would desire to be thankful: at the same time, it were but blindness to deny that this 'superior morality' is properly rather an 'inferior criminality', produced not by greater love of virtue, but by greater perfection of police; and of that far subtler and stronger police, called public opinion.
'Signs of the Times', ibid.

12 To reform a world, to reform a nation, no wise man will undertake; and all but foolish men know, that the only solid, though a far slower reformation, is what each begins and perfects on *himself*.
'Signs of the Times', ibid.

13 One seems to believe almost all that they believe; and when they stop short and call it a religion, and you pass on, and call it only a reminiscence of one, should you not part with the kiss of peace?
Letter to JOHN STUART MILL, 10 September 1833, publ. in *Letters of Thomas Carlyle* (ed. Alexander Carlyle, 1923). Referring to the Unitarians, following a meeting with RALPH WALDO EMERSON.

14 No man who has once heartily and wholly laughed can be altogether irreclaimably bad.
Sartor Resartus, bk 1, ch. 4 (1833–4)

15 He who first shortened the labour of copyists by device of movable types was disbanding hired armies, and cashiering most kings and senates, and creating a whole new democratic world: he had invented the art of printing.
Ibid., bk 1, ch. 5. The opinion of Teufelsdröckh.

16 Man is a tool-using animal ... Without tools he is nothing, with tools he is all.
Teufelsdröckh, ibid., bk 1, ch. 5. BENJAMIN FRANKLIN was quoted as defining man as a tool-making animal in BOSWELL's *Life of Johnson* (7 April 1778).

17 Lives the man that can figure a naked Duke of Windlestraw addressing a naked House of Lords? Imagination, choked as in mephitic air, recoils on itself, and will not forward with the picture.
Ibid., bk 1, ch. 9

18 It were a real increase of human happiness, could all young men from the age of nineteen be covered under barrels, or rendered otherwise invisible; and there left to follow their lawful studies and callings, till they emerged, sadder and wiser, at the age of twenty-five.
Ibid., bk 2, ch. 4. Teufelsdröckh disclaims this opinion, but agrees that: 'as young ladies are, to mankind, precisely the most delightful in those years; so young gentlemen do then attain their maximum of detestability.'

19 Sarcasm I now see to be, in general, the language of the Devil; for which reason I have long since as good as renounced it.
Teufelsdröckh, ibid., bk 2, ch. 4

20 The Everlasting No.
Ibid., bk 7. Title of ch. 6. The title of ch. 9 is 'The Everlasting Yea'.

21 Not on morality, but on cookery, let us build our stronghold: there brandishing our frying-pan, as censer, let us offer sweet incense to the Devil, and live at ease on the fat things *he* has provided for his elect!
Teufelsdröckh, ibid., bk 2, ch. 7

22 Man's unhappiness, as I construe, comes of his greatness; it is because there is an Infinite in him, which with all his cunning he cannot quite bury under the Finite.
Teufelsdröckh, ibid., bk 2, ch. 9

23 Foolish soul! What act of legislature was there that *thou* shouldst be happy? A little while ago thou hadst no right to *be* at all.
Teufelsdröckh, ibid., bk 2, ch. 9

24 What are your historical Facts; still more your biographical? Wilt thou know a man . . . by stringing-together beadrolls of what thou namest Facts?
Teufelsdröckh, ibid., bk 2, ch. 10. However, in a letter (29 April 1836) to R. W. EMERSON, Carlyle wrote: 'I grow daily to honour facts more and more, and theory less and less. A fact, it seems to me, is a great thing – a sentence printed, if not by God, then at least by the Devil.'

25 In a symbol there is concealment and yet revelation: here therefore, by silence and by speech acting together, comes a double significance . . . In the symbol proper, what we can call a symbol, there is ever, more or less distinctly and directly, some embodiment and revelation of the Infinite; the Infinite is made to blend itself with the Finite, to stand visible, and as it were, attainable there. By symbols, accordingly, is man guided and commanded, made happy, made wretched.
Teufelsdröckh, ibid., bk 3, ch. 3

26 Good breeding . . . differs, if at all, from high breeding only as it gracefully remembers the rights of others, rather than gracefully insists on its own rights.
Teufelsdröckh, ibid., bk 3, ch. 6

27 That monstrous tuberosity of civilised life, the capital of England.
Teufelsdröckh, ibid., bk 3, ch. 6

28 Foolish Rumour babbles not of what is done, but of what was misdone or undone; and foolish History (ever, more or less, the written epitomised synopsis of Rumour) knows so little that were not as well unknown.
History of the French Revolution, vol. 1, pt 1, bk 2, ch. 1 (1837). See also quote 31.

29 France was long a 'despotism tempered by epigrams'; and now, it would seem, the epigrams have got the upper hand.
Ibid., vol. 1, pt 1, bk 2, ch. 4

30 A whiff of grapeshot.
Ibid., vol. 1, pt 1, bk 5, ch. 3. Referring to a remark made by NAPOLEON, who suppressed a royalist rising in Paris in October 1795 by ordering the republican troops under his command to shoot into the crowd. Napoleon's reference was to 'salve de canons'. Later in the chapter Carlyle observes, 'The whiff of grapeshot can, if needful, become a blast and tempest.'

31 History, a distillation of rumour.
Ibid., vol. 1, pt 1, bk 7, ch. 5. See quote 28.

32 O seagreen Incorruptible.
Ibid., vol. 1, pt 2, bk 4, ch. 4. Referring to ROBESPIERRE, who was known as 'The Incorruptible'.

33 Under all speech that is good for anything there lies a silence that is better. Silence is deep as Eternity; speech is shallow as Time.
'Sir Walter Scott' (1838), repr. in *Critical and Miscellaneous Essays*, vol. 4 (1839)

34 No man lives without jostling and being jostled; in all ways he has to *elbow* himself through the world, giving and receiving offence.
'Sir Walter Scott', ibid.

35 A man willing to work, and unable to find work, is perhaps the saddest sight that fortune's inequality exhibits under this sun.
Chartism, ch. 4 (1839)

36 Worship is transcendent wonder.
On Heroes and Hero-Worship, Lecture 1 ('The Hero as Divinity') (1841)

37 No sadder proof can be given by a man of his own littleness than disbelief in great men.
Ibid., Lecture 1

38 Thought once awakened does not again slumber; unfolds itself into a System of Thought; grows, in

man after man, generation after generation, till its full stature is reached, and *such* System of Thought can grow no farther, but must give place to another.
Ibid., Lecture 1

39 No great man lives in vain. The history of the world is but the biography of great men.
Ibid., Lecture 1. In 'On History' (1830), Carlyle wrote: 'History is the essence of innumerable biographies.'

40 The greatest of faults, I should say, is to be conscious of none.
Ibid., Lecture 2 ('The Hero as Prophet')

41 The Persians are called the French of the East; we will call the Arabs Oriental Italians. A gifted noble people; a people of wild strong feelings, and of iron restraint over these: the characteristic of noble-mindedness, of genius.
Ibid., Lecture 2

42 The true university of these days is a collection of books.
Ibid., Lecture 5 ('The Hero as Man of Letters')

43 Scepticism, as I said, is not intellectual only; it is moral also; a chronic atrophy and disease of the whole soul. A man lives by believing something; not by debating and arguing about many things.
Ibid., Lecture 5

44 Figure him there, with his scrofulous diseases, with his great greedy heart, and unspeakable chaos of thoughts; stalking mournful as a stranger in this Earth; eagerly devouring what spiritual thing he could come at: school-languages and other merely grammatical stuff, if there were nothing better! The largest soul that was in all England.
Ibid., Lecture 5. Referring to SAMUEL JOHNSON.

45 Adversity is sometimes hard upon a man; but for one man who can stand prosperity, there are a hundred that will stand adversity.
Ibid., Lecture 5

46 We call it a Society; and go about professing openly the totalest separation, isolation. Our life is not a mutual helpfulness; but rather, cloaked under due laws-of-war, named 'fair competition' and so forth, it is a mutual hostility.
Past and Present, bk 3, ch. 2 (1843)

47 Cash-payment is not the sole nexus of man with man.
Ibid., bk 3, ch. 9. Carlyle made a previous reference to cash payment as 'the sole nexus of man to man' in *Chartism*, ch. 6 (1839). See also quote 48.

48 Cash-payment never was, or could except for a few years be, the union-bond of man to man. Cash never yet paid one man fully his deserts to another; nor could it, nor can it, now or henceforth to the end of the world.
Ibid., bk 3, ch. 10

49 A man perfects himself by working. Foul jungles are cleared away, fair seed-fields rise instead, and stately cities; and withal the man himself first ceases to be a jungle, and foul unwholesome desert thereby . . . The man is now a man.
Ibid., bk 3, ch. 11

50 Captains of industry.
Ibid., title of bk 4, ch. 4. Carlyle's thesis was: 'The leaders of industry, if industry is ever to be led, are virtually captains of the world.'

51 In the long-run every government is the exact symbol of its people, with their wisdom and unwisdom; we have to say, Like people like government.
Ibid., bk 4, ch. 4

52 Little other than a redtape talking-machine, and unhappy bag of parliamentary eloquence.
Latter-Day Pamphlets, no. 1 ('The Present Time') (1850). Referring to himself.

53 Respectable Professors of the Dismal Science, soft you a little.
Ibid., no. 1. Addressing professors of political economy.

54 Alas, all the world is a 'republic of the mediocrities', and always was.
Letter to RALPH WALDO EMERSON, 13 May 1853, publ. in *The Correspondence of Emerson and Carlyle* (ed. Joseph Slater, 1964). The phrase 'republic of the mediocrities' has not been traced.

55 I never had, and have now (if it were possible) less than ever, the least hope in 'Universal Suffrage' under any of its modifications: and, if it were not that in certain deadly maladies of the body politic, a burning crisis may be considered as beneficent, I should much prefer Tzarism itself, or Grand-Turkism itself, to the sheer anarchy (as I reckon it sadly to be) which is got by 'Parliamentary Eloquence', Free Press and the counting of heads.
Letter to the exiled Russian revolutionary ALEXANDER HERZEN, 13 April 1855, quoted in *The Romantic Exiles*, Appendix B (1933) by E. H. CARR

56 'Genius' (which means transcendent capacity of taking trouble, first of all).
The History of Friedrich II of Prussia, Called Frederick the Great, bk 4, ch. 3 (1858–65). See also BUFFON 2.

57 I don't pretend to understand the universe – it's a great deal bigger than I am.

Quoted by WILLIAM ALLINGHAM in journal entry, 28 December 1868, publ. in *A Diary*, ch. 10 (ed. H. Allingham and D. Radford, 1907)

Stokely Carmichael

(b. 1941)

US political activist

Trinidadian by birth, he was at the forefront of civil rights movements throughout the 1960s, though he publicly broke with the Black Panthers in 1968. He later changed his name to Kwame Touré.

1 This is the 27th time I have been arrested – I ain't going to jail no more. I ain't going to jail no more. Every courthouse in Mississippi ought to be burned down to get rid of the dirt. We want Black Power!

Speech from steps of courthouse in Greenwood, Mississippi, 17 June 1966, quoted in the *New York Times* 17 June 1966. The slogan 'Black Power' (uttered five times by Carmichael) was taken up by the gathered crowd, who were participating in the James Meredith March from Memphis to Jackson to promote black voting. MARTIN LUTHER KING, also on the march, expressed his unease at the slogan and encouraged instead 'Freedom Now', though by the end of the march this had been eclipsed by Carmichael's more inflammatory call. Carmichael was responsible for popularizing the slogan and published a book with that title in 1967 (see below).

2 Those of us who advocate Black power are quite clear in our own minds that a 'non-violent' approach to civil rights is an approach black people cannot afford and a luxury white people do not deserve.

Black Power, ch. 2 (written with Charles Vernon Hamilton, 1967)

Andrew Carnegie

(1835–1919)

US industrialist and philanthropist

Investments in railways and steel established him as one of America's leading industrial magnates. A firm believer in the social obligations of wealth, he founded numerous trusts and cultural, educational and scientific institutes in the USA and Scotland.

1 We accept and welcome . . . as conditions to which we must accommodate ourselves, great inequality of environment; the concentration of business, industrial and commercial, in the hands of a few; and the law of competition between these, as being not only beneficial, but essential for the future progress of the race.

The Gospel of Wealth (1889)

2 This, then, is held to be the duty of the man of wealth: First, to set an example of modest, unostentatious living, shunning display or extravagance; to provide moderately for the legitimate wants of those dependent upon him; and, after doing so, to consider all surplus revenues which come to him simply as trust funds, which he is called upon to administer, and strictly bound as a matter of duty to administer in the manner which, in his judgment, is best calculated to produce the most beneficial results for the community – the man of wealth thus becoming the mere trustee and agent for his poorer brethren, bringing to their service his superior wisdom, experience and ability to administer, doing for them better than they would or could do for themselves.

Ibid.

3 The day is not far distant when the man who dies leaving behind him millions of available wealth, which was free for him to administer during life, will pass away 'unwept, unhonored, and unsung', no matter to what uses he leave the dross which he cannot take with him. Of such as these the public verdict will then be: 'The man who dies thus rich dies disgraced.' Such, in my opinion, is the true gospel concerning wealth, obedience to which is destined some day to solve the problem of the rich and the poor.

Ibid.

4 I can't afford to pay them any other way.

Quoted in *Life of Andrew Carnegie*, vol. 1, ch. 15, sect. 2 (1932) by Burton J. Hendrick. Replying to a banker's question, 'How can you afford to pay your men so well?'

5 Mr Morgan buys his partners; I grow my own.

Quoted ibid., vol. 1, ch. 15, sect. 2. Referring to the banker J. P. Morgan's habit of incorporating men who had made brilliant careers in other houses.

6 I would as soon leave my son a curse as the almighty dollar.

Inscription in album, quoted ibid., vol. 1, ch. 17

Dale Carnegie
(1888–1955)
US writer and lecturer

A pioneer in the field of public speaking, he went on to found numerous branches of the Dale Carnegie Institute for Effective Speaking and Human Relations.

1 How to Win Friends and Influence People.
Title of book (1936)

E. H. Carr
(1892–1982)
British author and academic

Edward Hallett Carr. He worked in the Foreign Office before becoming Assistant Editor of The Times *(1941–6). His magnum opus was* A History of Soviet Russia 1917–29 *(14 vols, 1950–78).*

1 History begins when men begin to think of the passage of time in terms not of natural processes – the cycle of the seasons, the human life-span – but of a series of specific events in which men are consciously involved and which they can consciously influence.
What Is History?, Lecture 6 (1961)

J. L. Carr
(1912–94)
British novelist

James Lloyd Carr. For many years a teacher, he encapsulated English provincial life in such novels as The Harpole Report *(1972) and* A Month in the Country *(1980), while his* Dictionary of Extraordinary Cricketers *(1977) has also become a minor classic.*

1 A school is not a factory. Its raison d'être is to provide opportunity for experience.
The Harpole Report, ch. 6 (1972)

2 You have not had thirty years' experience ... You have had one year's experience thirty times.
Ibid., ch. 21

Lewis Carroll
(1832–98)
English author and mathematician

Real name Charles Lutwidge Dodgson. A fellow of mathematics at Christ Church, Oxford, he produced several mathematical textbooks, but is far better known for his Alice *stories, written down at the insistence of the children to whom they were first related (1865 and 1871), and the long nonsense poem,* The

Hunting of the Snark *(1876). He was also passionately interested in photography.*

1 All in the golden afternoon
Full leisurely we glide.
Alice's Adventures in Wonderland, Introduction, st. 1 (1865). Describing the boating expedition on 4 July 1862 when Carroll narrated the story of *Alice's Adventures Underground* (later renamed *Alice's Adventures in Wonderland*) to the three daughters of Henry George Liddell, Dean of Christ Church.

2 What is the use of a book without pictures or conversations?
Ibid., ch. 1. Alice's reflection on looking at the book her sister is reading.

3 Curiouser and curiouser!
Alice, ibid., ch. 2. On eating the cake marked 'Eat Me', and growing taller.

4 How doth the little crocodile
Improve his shining tail,
And pour the waters of the Nile
On every golden scale!
How cheerfully he seems to grin,
How neatly spreads his claws,
And welcomes little fishes in,
With gently smiling jaws!
Ibid., ch. 2. A parody of ISAAC WATTS 4.

5 'I'll be judge, I'll be jury,'
Said cunning old Fury:
'I'll try the whole cause, and condemn you to death.'
Ibid., ch. 3. The mouse's tale.

6 I know who I *was* when I got up this morning, but I think I must have been changed several times since then.
Alice, ibid., ch. 5

7 I can't explain *myself*, I'm afraid, Sir, because I'm not myself, you see.
Alice, ibid., ch. 5. 'I don't see,' replies the Caterpillar.

8 'You are old, Father William,' the young man said,
'And your hair has become very white;
And yet you incessantly stand on your head –
Do you think, at your age, it is right?'
Ibid., ch. 5. Alice recites a parody of ROBERT SOUTHEY 5.

9 'I have answered three questions, and that is enough,'
Said his father, 'Don't give yourself airs!

Do you think I can listen all day to such stuff?
Be off, or I'll kick you downstairs!'
Ibid., ch. 5. A continuation of Southey's parody.

10 'If everybody minded their own business,' the
Duchess said, in a hoarse growl, 'the world would
go round a deal faster than it does.'
Ibid., ch. 6

11 Speak roughly to your little boy,
And beat him when he sneezes:
He only does it to annoy,
Because he knows it teases.
Ibid., ch. 6. The Duchess's lullaby is a parody of a poem
attributed to both G. W. Langford, and David Bates, a Philadelphia broker. In Bates's *The Eolian* (1849), the poem appears
including the following verse: 'Speak gently to the little
child!/Its love be sure to gain;/Teach it in accents soft and
mild;/It may not long remain.'

12 Twinkle, twinkle, little bat!
How I wonder what you're at!
Up above the world you fly,
Like a teatray in the sky.
Ibid., ch. 7. Carroll's burlesque of the well-known rhyme (see
NURSERY RHYMES 41) may have referred to a professor of
mathematics at Oxford nicknamed 'The Bat', probably from
his tendency when lecturing to soar above the heads of his
listeners.

13 The Queen had only one way of settling all difficulties, great or small. 'Off with his head!' she said
without even looking around.
The Queen of Hearts, ibid., ch. 8

14 Tut, tut, child! Everything's got a moral, if you
can only find it.
The Duchess, ibid., ch. 9

15 Take care of the sense and the sounds will take
care of themselves.
Ibid., ch. 9. One of the Duchess's morals, an allusion to the
proverb ascribed to William Lowndes (1652–1724), Secretary
to the Treasury, in LORD CHESTERFIELD's letters: 'Take care
of the pence, for the pounds will take care of themselves'
(6 November 1747 and 5 February 1750).

16 Reeling and Writhing, of course, to begin with,
and then the different branches of Arithmetic –
Ambition, Distraction, Uglification, and Derision.
Ibid., ch. 9. The Mock Turtle describes 'the regular course'
taken by him at his 'school in the sea'.

17 'Will you walk a little faster?' said a whiting to a
snail,

'There's a porpoise close behind us, and he's
treading on my tail.'
Ibid., ch. 10. The Mock Turtle's song.

18 Will you, won't you, will you, won't you, will
you join the dance?
Will you, won't you, will you, won't you, won't you
join the dance?
Ibid., ch. 10. The Mock Turtle's song (chorus).

19 Beautiful Soup, so rich and green,
Waiting in a hot tureen!
Who for such dainties would not stoop?
Soup of the evening, beautiful Soup!
Ibid., ch. 10. The Mock Turtle sings 'Turtle Soup'.

20 'Write that down,' the King said to the jury; and
the jury eagerly wrote down all three dates on their
slates, and then added them up, and reduced the
answer to shillings and pence.
Ibid., ch. 11

21 Begin at the beginning, and go on till you come
to the end: then stop.
Ibid., ch. 12. The King of Hearts instructs the White Rabbit to
read the evidence against Alice.

22 Who cares for *you*? You're nothing but a pack of
cards!
Ibid., ch. 12. Alice, grown to her full size, answers the sentence
of death declared by the Queen of Hearts.

23 Yet what are all such gaieties to me
Whose thoughts are full of indices and surds?
'Four Riddles', no. 1, (1869), repr. in *Phantasmagoria and Other
Poems* (1919). The lines form part of a cross 'light' in a Double
Acrostic.

24 We are but older children, dear,
Who fret to find our bedtime near.
Through the Looking-Glass, Introduction, st. 4 (1871)

25 'The horror of that moment,' the King went on,
'I shall never, *never* forget!'
'You will, though,' the Queen said, 'if you don't
make a memorandum of it.'
Ibid., ch. 1

26 'Twas brillig, and the slithy toves
Did gyre and gimble in the wabe:
All mimsy were the borogoves,
And the mome raths outgrabe.
'Jabberwocky', st. 1, ibid., ch. 1. This opening stanza of Carroll's
nonsense poem first appeared in a private periodical which
he wrote and illustrated in 1855, aged 23. Calling it a 'stanza
of Anglo-Saxon poetry', Carroll interpreted the words and
gave the literal 'translation' as follows: 'It was evening, and

the smooth active badgers were scratching and boring holes in the hill-side; all unhappy were the parrots; and the grave turtles squeaked out.'

27 Beware the Jabberwock, my son!
The jaws that bite, the claws that catch!
Beware the Jubjub bird, and shun
The frumious Bandersnatch!
'Jabberwocky', st. 2, ibid., ch. 1. The Jubjub and Bandersnatch also occur in Carroll's poem, *The Hunting of the Snark* (1876).

28 One, two! One, two! And through and through
The vorpal blade went snicker-snack!
He left it dead, and with its head
He went galumphing back.
'And hast thou slain the Jabberwock?
Come to my arms, my beamish boy!
O frabjous day! Callooh! Callay!'
He chortled in his joy.
'Jabberwocky', sts 5–6, ibid., ch. 1

29 Curtsey while you're thinking what to say. It saves time.
The Red Queen, ibid., ch. 2

30 Now, *here,* you see, it takes all the running *you* can do, to keep in the same place. If you want to get somewhere else, you must run at least twice as fast as that!
The Red Queen, ibid., ch. 2

31 Speak in French when you can't think of the English for a thing – turn out your toes as you walk – and remember who you are!
The Red Queen, ibid., ch. 2

32 Contrariwise, if it was so, it might be; and if it were so, it would be; but as it isn't, it ain't. That's logic.
Tweedledee, ibid., ch. 4

33 The Walrus and the Carpenter
Were walking close at hand;
They wept like anything to see
Such quantities of sand:
'If this were only cleared away,'
They said, 'it would be grand!'
'The Walrus and the Carpenter', st. 4, ibid., ch. 4. Carroll's poem satirized THOMAS HOOD's little-known poem, 'Dream of Eugene Aram'.

34 'The time has come,' the Walrus said,
'To talk of many things:
Of shoes – and ships – and sealing wax –
Of cabbages – and kings –

And why the sea is boiling hot –
And whether pigs have wings.'
'The Walrus and the Carpenter', st. 11, ibid., ch. 4

35 'I'm very brave generally,' he went on in a low voice: 'only today I happen to have a headache.'
Tweedledum, ibid., ch. 4

36 The rule is, jam tomorrow and jam yesterday – but never jam *today*.
The White Queen, ibid., ch. 5

37 It's a poor sort of memory that only works backwards.
The White Queen, ibid., ch. 5

38 'One *can't* believe impossible things.'
   'I daresay you haven't had much practice,' said the Queen. 'When I was your age, I always did it for half-an-hour a day. Why, sometimes I've believed as many as six impossible things before breakfast.'
Alice and the White Queen, ibid., ch. 5. In a letter in 1864, Carroll wrote: 'If you set to work to believe everything, you will tire out the muscles of your mind, and then you'll be so weak you won't be able to believe the simplest true things.'

39 'When *I* use a word,' Humpty Dumpty said, in rather a scornful tone, 'it means just what I choose it to mean – neither more nor less.'
Ibid., ch. 6. 'The question is,' said Alice, 'whether you *can* make words mean so many different things.' 'The question is,' said Humpty Dumpty, 'which is to be master – that's all.'

40 I feel faint – Give me a ham sandwich!
The White King, ibid., ch. 7

41 It's as large as life, and twice as natural!
Haigha describing Alice, ibid., ch. 7

42 If you'll believe in me, I'll believe in you. Is that a bargain?
The Unicorn to Alice, ibid., ch. 7

43 So, having no reply to give
To what the old man said,
I cried, 'Come, tell me how you live!'
And thumped him on the head.
The White Knight's song, ibid., ch. 8. The song, an extension of an earlier poem by Carroll, 'Upon the Lonely Moor' (1856), is a parody of WORDSWORTH's *Resolution and Independence*, which includes the lines: 'My question eagerly I did renew,/ How is it that you live, and what is it you do?'

44 She's in that state of mind that she wants to deny *something* – only she doesn't know what to deny!
The White Queen, referring to Alice, ibid., ch. 9

45 Then fill up the glasses with treacle and ink,
Or anything else that is pleasant to drink:
Mix sand with the cider, and wool with the wine –
And welcome Queen Alice with ninety-times-nine!
Ibid., ch. 9

46 Still she haunts me, phantomwise.
Alice moving under skies
Never seen by waking eyes.
Ibid., Epilogue, st. 4

47 'What's the good of Mercator's North Poles and
Equators,
Tropics, Zones and Meridian Lines?'
So the Bellman would cry: and the crew would
reply
'They are merely conventional signs!'
The Hunting of the Snark, 'Fit the Second' ('The Bellman's Speech'), st. 3 (1876)

48 But oh, beamish nephew, beware of the day,
If your Snark be a Boojum! For then
You will softly and suddenly vanish away,
And never be met with again!
Ibid., 'Fit the Third' ('The Baker's Tale'), st. 10

49 It is this, it is this that oppresses my soul,
When I think of my uncle's last words:
And my heart is like nothing so much as a bowl
Brimming over with quivering curds!
Ibid., 'Fit the Third', st. 11

50 They sought it with thimbles, they sought it
with care;
They pursued it with forks and hope;
They threatened its life with a railway-share;
They charmed it with smiles and soap.
Ibid., 'Fit the Fifth' ('The Beaver's Lesson'), st. 1. The lines also make up the opening stanza of Fits 6, 7 and 8.

51 He thought he saw an Elephant,
That practised on a fife:
He looked again, and found it was
A letter from his wife.
'At length I realise,' he said,
'The bitterness of life!'
Sylvie and Bruno, ch. 5 (1889)

Johnny Carson
(1925–2005)
US chat-show host and comedian

After presenting his own shows on television and hosting the game show Who Do You Trust? *(1957–62), he took over* The Tonight Show, *hosting it for the next thirty years.*

1 Heeeeere's Johnny!
Spoken by Ed McMahon introducing *The Tonight Show Starring Johnny Carson* (US TV variety show, 1962–92). The intro was often copied, and was famously – and manically – mimicked by Jack Nicholson's character (Jack Torrance) in *The Shining* (film, 1980).

Rachel Carson
(1907–64)
US marine biologist and author

Through her books, notably The Sea Around Us *(1951) and* Silent Spring *(1962), she increased public awareness of the dangers of environmental pollution, which in turn led to US legislation on the use of pesticides.*

1 The sea lies all about us . . . In its mysterious past it encompasses all the dim origins of life and receives in the end, after, it may be, many transmutations, the dead husks of that same life. For all at last returns to the sea – to Oceanus, the ocean river, like the ever-flowing stream of time, the beginning and the end.
The Sea Around Us, pt 3, ch. 14 (1951)

2 Under the philosophy that now seems to guide our destinies, nothing must get in the way of the man with the spray gun.
Silent Spring, ch. 7 (1962)

3 Over increasingly large areas of the United States, spring now comes unheralded by the return of the birds, and the early mornings are strangely silent where once they were filled with the beauty of bird song.
Ibid., ch. 8

4 The 'control of nature' is a phrase conceived in arrogance, born of the Neanderthal age of biology and the convenience of man.
Ibid., ch. 17

Angela Carter
(1940–92)
British author

Her considerable output of fiction combined eroticism, feminism and fantasy. Publications include the stories 'The Magic Toyshop' (1967) and 'The Company of Wolves' (1977), for which she also wrote the screenplays, and the novels Nights at the Circus *(1984) and* Wise Children *(1991).*

1 Midnight, and the clock strikes. It is Christmas Day, the werewolves' birthday, the door of the sol-

stice still wide enough open to let them all slink through.

'The Company of Wolves', publ. in *The Bloody Chamber and Other Stories* (1979)

2 Never stray from the path, never eat a windfall apple and never trust a man whose eyebrows meet in the middle.

'The Company of Wolves', ibid.

3 Pornographers are the enemies of women only because our contemporary ideology of pornography does not encompass the possibility of change, as if we were the slaves of history and not its makers . . . Pornography is a satire on human pretensions.

The Sadeian Woman, 'Polemical Preface' (1979)

4 The bed is now as public as the dinner table and governed by the same rules of formal confrontation.

Ibid., 'Speculative Finale'

5 If *Miss* means respectably unmarried, and *Mrs.* respectably married, then *Ms.* means nudge, nudge, wink, wink.

'The Language of Sisterhood', publ. in *The State of the Language* (ed. Leonard Michaels and Christopher Ricks, 1980)

6 It's one of the scars in our culture that we have too high an opinion of ourselves. We align ourselves with the angels instead of the higher primates.

Marxism Today January 1985

7 The adjective 'post-modernist' really means 'mannerist'. Books about books is fun but frivolous.

Novelists in Interview (ed. John Haffenden, 1985)

8 Just because we're sisters under the skin doesn't mean we've got much in common.

Guardian 25 October 1990

9 Comedy is tragedy that happens to *other* people.

Wise Children, ch. 4 (1991)

Henry Carter
(d. 1806)

1 True patriots we; for be it understood
We left our country for our country's good.

Prologue to celebrate the opening of the first playhouse in Sydney, New South Wales, 16 January 1796, in which most of the actors were former convicts. Carter is described as 'a gentleman of Leicester'. The verse has also been attributed to George Barrington (1755–1810), a celebrated pickpocket before his transportation to Botany Bay.

Jimmy Carter
(b. 1924)
US politician and president

From a farming background, he rose to become Democratic Governor of Georgia (1970–4) and US President (1977–81). His failure to bring home hostages held in Iran contributed to his defeat by RONALD REAGAN *in the 1980 election. He won the Nobel Prize for Peace in 2002.*

1 I've looked on a lot of women with lust. I've committed adultery in my heart many times. This is something God recognizes I will do – and I have done it – and God forgives me for it.

Interview in *Playboy* November 1976. The remark caused widespread surprise when it was published at the height of the presidential campaign in which he stood against GERALD FORD. Carter's wife Rosalynn remarked simply, 'Jimmy talks too much . . .' See BIBLE: NEW TESTAMENT: MATTHEW 28

2 I thought a lot about our nation and what I should do as president. And Sunday night before last, I made a speech about two problems of our country – energy and malaise.

Speech at Bardstown, Kentucky, 31 July 1979, publ. in *Public Papers of the Presidents of the United States* (1979). The speech to which Carter referred, broadcast 15 July from the White House, did not include the word 'malaise', though Carter's identification of these two issues provoked much discussion.

Sydney Carter
(1915–2004)
British poet and songwriter

He wrote for FLANDERS AND SWANN *and was the author of folk and protest songs as well as popular hymns.*

1 Dance then wherever you may be,
I am the Lord of the Dance, said he,
And I'll lead you all, wherever you may be
And I'll lead you all in the dance, said he.

'Lord of the Dance' (song), publ. in *Nine Carols or Ballads* (1967)

2 One more step along the world I go,
One more step along the world I go,
From the old things to the new
Keep me travelling along with You.

'One More Step Along the World I Go' (hymn, 1971)

Barbara Cartland

(1901–2000)

British novelist

Hailed 'the queen of romantic fiction', she sold over 650 million copies of her 623 books, whose sheer number enabled her to claim the longest entry in Who's Who. *She was famous for her pink chiffon, extravagant false eyelashes and traditional views on romance.*

1 The great majority of people in England and America are modest, decent and pure-minded and the amount of virgins in the world today is stupendous.

Interview in *Speaking Frankly* (1978) by Wendy Leigh. But on another occasion, Cartland was reported as saying: 'Only the English and the Americans are improper. East of Suez everyone wants a virgin.'

2 The right diet directs sexual energy into the parts that matter.

Quoted in the *Observer* 11 January 1981

3 France is the only place where you can make love in the afternoon without people hammering on your door.

Quoted in the *Guardian* 24 December 1984

Raymond Carver

(1939–88)

US poet and short story writer

Identified with the 'dirty realism' school, he established his reputation with Will You Please Be Quiet, Please? *(1976), followed by* Cathedral *(1984). Jay Mcinerney suggested: 'The trout in Carver's streams were apt to be pollution-deformed mutants, the romance of drinking replaced by the dull grind of full-time alcoholism.'*

1 Writers don't need tricks or gimmicks or even necessarily need to be the smartest fellows on the block. At the risk of appearing foolish, a writer sometimes needs to be able to just stand and gape at this or that thing – a sunset or an old shoe – in absolute and simple amazement.

'On Writing', publ. in *Fires* (1985)

Joyce Cary

(1888–1957)

British author

He is best remembered for his trilogies dealing with art and politics, and especially for The Horse's Mouth *(1944), a picaresque portrait of a disreputable artist.* V. S. PRITCHETT *called him 'the chameleon among contemporary novelists'.*

1 Sara could commit adultery at one end and weep for her sins at the other, and enjoy both operations at once.

The Horse's Mouth, ch. 8 (1944). Spoken by the narrator (Gulley Jimson).

2 God is a character, a real and consistent being, or He is nothing. If God did a miracle He would deny His own nature and the universe would simply blow up, vanish, become nothing.

Interview in *Writers at Work* (first series, ed. Malcolm Cowley, 1958)

Pablo Casals

(1876–1973)

Spanish cellist, conductor and composer

Called by Rostropovich 'the greatest name in cello history', he is famous for his interpretations of Bach, especially the cello suites. He founded the Barcelona Orchestra in 1919 and conducted it until 1936 when, in protest against the Franco regime, he moved to France.

1 I go back to Bach as a sick dog instinctively grubs at the roots and herbs that are its right medicine.

Quoted in the *Observer* 27 November 1921

2 It [the cello] is like a beautiful woman who has not grown older, but younger with time, more slender, more supple, more graceful.

Quoted in *Time* 29 April 1957

(Sir) Roger Casement

(1864–1916)

Colonial administrator and Irish nationalist

An Ulster Protestant by birth, he gained his knighthood after denouncing cruelty and exploitation while consul in the Congo and Brazil. In Ireland, his efforts to enlist German support for the Easter Rising in 1916 resulted in his execution for high treason.

1 It is a strange, strange fate, and now as I stand face to face with death I feel just as if they were going to kill a boy. For I feel like a boy – and my hands so free from blood that I cannot comprehend how anyone wants to hang me.

Letter, August 1916, quoted in *The Lives of Roger Casement*, ch. 30 (1976) by B. L. Reid. Casement's final letter was written from his condemned cell in Pentonville Prison, London; he was hanged after attempting, with German help, to overthrow British rule in Ireland. From an incomplete copy: the original was destroyed by the prison authorities.

William Casey

(1913–87)

US lawyer and intelligence chief

As RONALD REAGAN*'s Director of the CIA (1981–7), he intensified the agency's anti-communist activities. Investigations into his role in the Iran-Contra affair were interrupted by his death.*

1 I pass the test that says a man who isn't a socialist at 20 has no heart, and a man who is a socialist at 40 has no head.

Quoted in obituary, *Washington Post* 7 May 1987. The saying has also been attributed to French socialist politician and premier Aristide Briand.

Neal Cassady

(1926–68)

US author

An outlaw hero of the Beat generation, he was mythologized as Dean Moriarty ('the holy con man with the shining mind') in KEROUAC*'s* On the Road. *Fragments of autobiography and his correspondence have been published in* The First Third and Other Writings *(1971) and* Grace Beats Karma *(1993).*

1 Art is good when it springs from necessity. This kind of origin is the guarantee of its value; there is no other.

Letter to JACK KEROUAC, 7–8 January 1948, quoted in *Memory Babe*, ch. 5, sect. 5 (1983) by Gerald Nicosia

2 Billboards, billboards, drink this, eat that, use all manner of things, EVERYONE, the best, the cheapest, the purest and most satisfying of all their available counterparts. Red lights flicker on every horizon, airplanes beware; cars flash by, more lights. Workers repair the gas main. Signs, signs, lights, lights, streets, streets.

'Leaving LA by Train at Night, High . . .', publ. in *The First Third and Other Writings* (1971)

(Sir) Hugh Casson

(1910–99)

British architect

After directing the architecture at the Festival of Britain (1948–51), he was Professor of Interior Design at the Royal College of Art (1953–75) and President of the Royal Academy (1976–84).

1 The British love permanence more than they love beauty.

Quoted in the *Observer* 14 June 1964

Ted Castle

(1907–79)

British journalist

Baron Castle of Islington. The husband of Labour politician Barbara Castle, he was Editor of Picture Post *(1944–52) and an alderman of the Greater London Council (1964–70).*

1 In Place of Strife.

White Paper on industrial relations, 17 January 1969. The title was suggested to Employment Secretary Barbara Castle by her husband, as recalled in *The Barbara Castle Diaries*, 15 January 1969 (1984). It was probably inspired by ANEURIN BEVAN's book setting out his political credo, *In Place of Fear* (1952).

Fidel Castro

(b. 1926)

Cuban revolutionary and president

He established a Communist regime in Cuba after ousting President Batista in 1959. Surviving the US-backed Bay of Pigs invasion in 1961 and the Cuban Missile Crisis of 1962, he became president in 1976.

1 History will absolve me.

Last words of speech during trial, 16 October 1953, publ. in *The Penguin Book of Twentieth-Century Speeches* (ed. Brian MacArthur, 1999). Castro had led an unsuccessful assault on the Moncada barracks in July 1953. Sentenced to fifteen years' imprisonment, he was released within a year under an amnesty, returning from exile in 1956 and assuming power soon after. The words *La historia me absolverá* were the title of a revolutionary pamphlet published during the struggle.

2 I feel my belief in sacrifice and struggle getting stronger. I despise the kind of existence that clings to the miserly trifles of comfort and self-interest. I think that a man should not live beyond the age when he begins to deteriorate, when the flame that lighted the brightest moment of his life has weakened.

Letter written from a prison cell on the island of Pines, 19 December 1953, publ. in *Diary of the Cuban Revolution* (1980) by Carlos Franqui

3 I began revolution with 82 men. If I had [to] do it again, I do it with 10 or 15 and absolute faith. It does not matter how small you are if you have faith and plan of action.

New York Times 22 April 1959

Willa Cather

(1876–1947)

US author

Called 'the most sensuous of writers' by REBECCA WEST, *she portrayed the frontier life in Nebraska of her childhood in her novels and stories, of which* O Pioneers! *(1913) and* My Antonia *(1918) are judged her finest achievements.*

1 The history of every country begins in the heart of a man or a woman.
O Pioneers!, pt 1, ch. 5 (1913)

2 There are only two or three human stories, and they go on repeating themselves as fiercely as if they had never happened before.
Ibid., pt 2, ch. 4

3 I like trees because they seem more resigned to the way they have to live than other things do.
Marie, ibid., pt 2, ch. 8

4 Artistic growth is, more than it is anything else, a refining of the sense of truthfulness. The stupid believe that to be truthful is easy; only the artist, the great artist, knows how difficult it is.
The Song of the Lark, pt 6, ch. 11 (1915)

5 Art, it seems to me, should simplify ... finding what conventions of form and what detail one can do without and yet preserve the spirit of the whole – so that all that one has suppressed and cut away is there to the reader's consciousness as much as if it were in type on the page.
'On the Art of Fiction', written 1920, publ. in On Writing (1949)

6 When kindness has left people, even for a few moments, we become afraid of them as if their reason had left them. When it has left a place where we have always found it, it is like shipwreck; we drop from security into something malevolent and bottomless.
My Mortal Enemy (1926)

7 Oh, the Germans classify, but the French arrange!
Death Comes for the Archbishop, Prologue (1927)

8 Only solitary men know the full joys of friendship. Others have their family; but to a solitary and an exile his friends are everything.
Shadows on the Rock, bk 3, ch. 5 (1931). Spoken by Father Hector Saint-Cyr.

9 The world has a habit of being in a bad way from time to time, and art has never contributed anything to help matters – except escape.
'Four Letters: Escapism', written 1936, publ. in On Writing (1949)

10 Give the people a new word and they think they have a new fact.
'Four Letters: Escapism', ibid.

Marcus Porcius Cato
(Cato the Elder)

(234–149 BC)

Roman statesman

Also known as Cato the Censor, he was a strict upholder of traditional values against what he saw as the corrupting influence of Greek custom. He fought in Spain and Greece, and served as censor, or senior magistrate, in 184 BC. One of his few surviving works, De agri cultura *(c. 160 BC), a treatise on farming, is the oldest extant Latin prose work. See* SALLUST 1.

1 It is a hard matter, my fellow citizens, to argue with the belly, since it has no ears.
Quoted in Parallel Lives, 'Marcus Cato', sect. 8, by PLUTARCH

2 I would much rather have men ask why I have no statue than why I have one.
Quoted ibid., 'Marcus Cato', sect. 19

3 *Delenda est Carthago.*
[Carthage must be destroyed.]
Quoted ibid., 'Marcus Cato', sect. 27. The words are supposed to have been repeated by Cato at the end of every speech he made in the senate following his visit to Carthage in c. 153 BC, which convinced him of the military threat posed by the city. It was eventually destroyed by Rome at the end of the Third Punic War in 146 BC.

4 Grasp the subject, the words will follow.
Quoted in Ars Rhetorica, 'De Inventione' (4th century) by Caius Julius Victor

Catullus

(c. 84–c. 54 BC)

Roman poet

Gaius Valerius Catullus. Regarded as the greatest lyric poet of ancient Rome, he composed epigrams, elegies and love poems, including those recording his infatuation with 'Lesbia'. Other poems were addressed to JULIUS CAESAR *and other personages of the day, whom he scurrilously lampooned.*

1 To whom am I to present my pretty new book, freshly smoothed off with dry pumice stone? To

you, Cornelius: for you used to think that my trifles were worth something, long ago.
Carmina, no. 1, ll. 1–4

2 May it . . . live and last for more than one century.
Ibid., no. 1, l. 10

3 *Lugete, O Veneres Cupidinesque,*
Et quantum est hominum venustiorum.
Passer mortuus est meae puellae,
Passer, deliciae meae puellae.
[Ye Cupids, droop each little head,
Nor let your wings with joy be spread:
My Lesbia's favourite bird is dead,
Whom dearer than her eyes she loved.]
Ibid., no. 3, ll. 1–4 (transl. BYRON, in *Hours of Idleness*, 1807). Referring to Lesbia, pseudonym for Clodia Metelli, the inspiration of much of Catullus's poetry. Opening lines of poem.

4 Now having passed the gloomy bourne
From whence he never can return.
Ibid., no. 3, ll. 11–12 (transl. BYRON)

5 But these things are past and gone.
Ibid., no. 4, l. 25

6 *Vivamus, mea Lesbia, atque amemus,*
Rumoresque senum severiorum
Omnes unius aestimemus assis.
Soles occidere et redire possunt:
Nobis cum semel occidit brevis lux
Nox est perpetua una dormienda.
[Let us live my Lesbia, and love, and value at one farthing all the talk of crabbed old men. Suns may set and rise again. For us, when the short light has once set, remains to be slept the sleep of one unbroken night.]
Ibid., no. 5, ll. 1–6

7 Give me a thousand kisses, then a hundred, then another thousand, then a second hundred, then yet another thousand, then a hundred.
Ibid., no. 5, ll. 7–10

8 *Paene insularum, Sirmio, insularumque*
ocelle.
[Sirmio, bright eye of peninsulas and islands.]
Ibid., no. 31, ll. 1–2. Catullus's father owned a villa at Sirmio, on Lake Garda.

9 Ah, what is more blessed than to put cares away, when the mind lays by its burden, and tired with labour of far travel we have come to our own home and rest on the couch we have longed for?
Ibid., no. 31, ll. 7–10

10 For there is nothing more silly than a silly laugh.
Ibid., no. 39, l. 16

11 Now spring brings back balmy warmth.
Ibid., no. 46, l. 1

12 Catullus gives you warmest thanks,
And he the worst of poets ranks;
As much the worst of bards confessed,
As you of advocates the best.
Ibid., no. 49, ll. 4–7 (transl. Sir William Marris). Addressed to CICERO.

13 What is given by the gods more desirable than the fortunate hour?
Ibid., no. 62, l. 30

14 *Sed mulier cupido quod dicit amanti,*
in vento et rapida scribere oportet aqua.
[What a woman says to her ardent lover should be written in wind and running water.]
Ibid., no. 70, ll. 3–4. A similar image has been found in a fragment by SOPHOCLES.

15 It is difficult suddenly to lay aside a
    long-cherished love.
Ibid., no. 76, l. 13

16 *Si vitam puriter egi.*
[If I have led a pure life.]
Ibid., no. 76, l. 19

17 *Odi et amo: quare id faciam, fortasse requiris.*
Nescio, sed fieri sentio et excrucior.
[I hate and love. Why I do so, perhaps you ask. I know not, but I feel it, and I am in torment.]
Ibid., no. 85

18 *Atque in perpetuum, frater, ave atque vale.*
[And forever, O my brother, hail and farewell.]
Ibid., no. 101, l. 10. 'Frater Ave atque Vale' is the title of a poem by LORD TENNYSON.

19 *At non effugies meos iambos.*
[But you shall not escape my iambics.]
Fragment, no. 1, publ. in *Carmina* (Loeb edn, 2000)

(Sir) Bernard Caulfield
(1914–94)
British lawyer

He held the position of Judge of the High Court of Justice 1968–81.

1 Is Jeffrey Archer in need of cold, unloving, rubber-insulated sex? . . . Remember Mary Archer in the witness box. Your vision of her will probably never disappear. Has she elegance? Has she fragrance?

Would she have – without the strain of this trial – a radiance?

Quoted in *The Times* 24 July 1987. Summary at libel case between JEFFREY ARCHER and the *News of the World* 23 July 1987. Archer, who had been implicated in a scandal involving a call girl, won the case and £500,000 damages, though in 1999 it emerged that he had asked a friend to commit perjury at the trial to protect his cover.

Charles Causley
(1917–2003)
British poet

His poetry, written for both children and adults, evokes Cornwall, where he lived and worked for much of his life, and often deals with contemporary concerns in traditional form.

1 Timothy Winters comes to school
With eyes as wide as a football-pool,
Ears like bombs and teeth like splinters:
A blitz of a boy is Timothy Winters.

'Timothy Winters', publ. in *Union Street* (1957)

2 They are waiting for me somewhere beyond
Eden Rock.

'Eden Rock', publ. in *Field of Vision* (1988)

Constantine Cavafy
(1863–1933)
Greek poet

Konstantínos Pétrou Kaváfis. He spent most of his life in Alexandria, the inspiration for much of his verse, which was championed by LAWRENCE DURRELL, among others. Sceptical and anti-conformist in tone, his poems often had a homosexual theme, and were written in a mixture of formal and demotic Greek.

1 But Argos can do without the house of Atreus.
Ancient houses are not eternal.

'When the Watchman Saw the Light' (1900), repr. in *Collected Poems* (ed. George Savidis, transl. 1975)

2 What are we waiting for, assembled in the
forum?
The barbarians are due here today.

'Waiting for the Barbarians' (1904), ibid. Opening lines of poem.

3 Now, what's going to happen to us without the
barbarians?
Those people were a kind of solution.

'Waiting for the Barbarians', ibid.

4 You won't find a new country, won't find
another shore.

This city will always pursue you.

'The City' (1910), ibid.

5 As you set out for Ithaka
hope your road is a long one,
full of adventure, full of discovery.

'Ithaka' (1911), ibid. Opening lines of poem.

Edith Cavell
(1865–1915)
British nurse

A heroine of the First World War, she was executed for assisting Allied soldiers to escape to the Netherlands from German-occupied Belgium.

1 Standing, as I do, in view of God and eternity, I realise that patriotism is not enough. I must have no hatred or bitterness towards anyone.

Quoted in *The Times* 23 October 1915. The words, often erroneously claimed to be Cavell's last, were spoken in conversation with her chaplain 11 October 1915, the eve of her execution in Brussels.

Paul Celan
(1920–70)
German poet

Pseudonym of Paul Antschel. Though he lived in France from 1948, he was one of the foremost poets of post-Second World War German literature. His work is allusive, and informed by his experience as a Jew in a forced labour camp. He committed suicide.

1 Black milk of daybreak we drink you at night
we drink you at noon death is a master from
Germany
we drink you at sundown and in the morning we
drink and we drink you
death is a master from Germany his eyes are blue
he strikes you with leaden bullets his aim is true.

'Death Fugue', publ. in *Mohn und Gedächtnis* (1952, transl. Michael Hamburger, 1988)

Louis-Ferdinand Céline
(1894–1961)
French author

Originally Louis Ferdinand Destouches. Trained and practising as a doctor, he was recognized as a great innovator of 20th-century literature, though criticized for his misanthropy and obscenity, and for his anti-Semitic pamphlets. His best-known novel is the autobiographical Journey to the End of the Night *(1932).*

1 To philosophize is only another way of being afraid and leads hardly anywhere but to cowardly make-believe.

Journey to the End of the Night (1932). The words of the narrator (Ferdinand Bardamu).

2 To hell with reality! I want to die in music, not in reason or in prose.

Letter, 30 June 1947, publ. in *Critical Essays on Louis-Ferdinand Céline* (ed. William K. Buckley, 1989)

3 Life is filigree work ... What is written clearly is not worth much, it's the transparency that counts.

Féerie pour une autre fois (1952), quoted in *Céline*, ch. 8 (1975) by Patrick McCarthy

4 Experience is a dim lamp, which only lights the one who bears it.

Interview in *Writers at Work* (third series, ed. George Plimpton, 1967)

Miguel de Cervantes
(1547–1616)
Spanish author

Miguel de Cervantes Saavedra. His fame rests chiefly on Don Quixote de la Mancha *(2 vols, 1605 and 1615), the tale of an addled and idealistic knight and his earthy and cynical companion Sancho Panza. It was an immediate success, and a seminal influence on the development of the novel. See* LORD BYRON 158.

1 You are a king by your own fireside, as much as any monarch in his throne.

Don Quixote de la Mancha, pt 1, Preface (1605, transl. Peter Motteux, 1712)

2 And for the citation of so many authors, it is the easiest thing in nature. Find out one of these books with an alphabetical index, and without any farther ceremony, remove it verbatim into your own ... there are fools enough to be thus drawn into an opinion of the work; at least, such a flourishing train of attendants will give your book a fashionable air, and recommend it for sale.

Ibid., pt 1, Preface. Probably alluding to Lope de Vega's book, *El Peregrino y el Isidro*, which included a list of cited authors in alphabetical order.

3 Every man is the son of his own works.

Ibid., pt 1, bk 1, ch. 4. Spoken by Don Quixote.

4 Pray look better, Sir ... those things yonder are no giants, but windmills.

Sancho Panza, ibid., pt 1, bk 1, ch. 8

5 There is nothing so subject to the inconstancy of fortune as war.

Don Quixote, ibid., pt 1, bk 1, ch. 8

6 I had rather munch a crust of brown bread and an onion in a corner, without any more ado or ceremony, than feed upon turkey at another man's table, where one is fain to sit mincing and chewing his meat an hour together, drink little, be always wiping his fingers and his chops, and never dare to cough nor sneeze, though he has never so much a mind to it, nor do a many things which a body may do freely by one's self.

Sancho Panza, ibid., pt 1, bk 2, ch. 3

7 The eyes those silent tongues of love.

Ibid., pt 1, bk 2, ch. 3, 'Antonio's Amorous Complaint'

8 He ... had a face like a blessing.

Ibid., pt 1, bk 2, ch. 4. Peter's description of the shepherd and scholar Chrysostome (Grisóstomo).

9 A man must eat a peck of salt with his friend, before he knows him.

Sancho Panza, ibid., pt 1, bk 3, ch. 1

10 Does the devil possess you? You're leaping over the hedge before you come at the stile.

Sancho Panza to Don Quixote, ibid., pt 1, bk 3, ch. 4

11 *El Caballero de la Triste Figura.*
[The Knight of the Woeful Figure.]

Ibid., pt 1, bk 3, ch. 5 and *passim* . Sancho Panza's appellation for Don Quixote, also translated as 'The Knight of the Doleful Countenance' and 'The Knight of the Sorrowful Countenance'.

12 I believe there's no proverb but what is true; they are all so many sentences and maxims drawn from experience, the universal mother of sciences.

Don Quixote, ibid., pt 1, bk 3, ch. 7

13 To withdraw is not to run away, and to stay is no wise action, when there's more reason to fear than to hope.

Sancho Panza, ibid., pt 1, bk 3, ch. 9

14 It is the only comfort of the miserable to have partners in their woes.

Don Quixote, ibid., pt 1, bk 3, ch. 10

15 Mere flim-flam stories, and nothing but shams and lies.

Ibid., pt 1, bk 3, ch. 11. Sancho Panza describes Don Quixote's 'bragging and bouncing'.

16 It is ill talking of halters in the house of a man that was hanged.

Sancho Panza, ibid., pt 1, bk 3, ch. 11

17 Delay always breeds danger; and to protract a great design is often to ruin it.
Don Quixote, ibid., pt 1, bk 4, ch. 2

18 It is said of love that it sometimes goes, sometimes flies; runs with one, walks gravely with another; turns a third into ice, and sets a fourth in a flame: it wounds one, another it kills: like lightning it begins and ends in the same moment: it makes that fort yield at night which it besieged but in the morning; for there is no force able to resist it.
Leonela (Camilla's maid), ibid., pt 1, bk 4, ch. 7

19 That which cost little is less valued.
Camilla, quoting a proverb, ibid., pt 1, bk 4, ch. 7

20 One who has not only the four S's, which are required in every good lover, but even the whole alphabet; as for example ... agreeable, bountiful, constant, dutiful, easy, faithful, gallant, honourable, ingenious, kind, loyal, mild, noble, officious, prudent, quiet, rich, secret, true, valiant, wise; the X indeed, is too harsh a letter to agree with him, but he is young and zealous for your honour and service.
Leonela, ibid., pt 1, bk 4, ch. 7. The 'four S's' were 'sightly, sprightly, sincere and secret'.

21 Virtue is the truest nobility.
Dorothea, ibid., pt 1, bk 4, ch. 9

22 For a man to attain to an eminent degree in learning costs him time, watching, hunger, nakedness, dizziness in the head, weakness in the stomach, and other inconveniences.
Don Quixote, ibid., pt 1, bk 4, ch. 11

23 The bow cannot always stand bent, nor can human frailty subsist without some lawful recreation.
The Canon, ibid., pt 1, bk 4, ch. 21

24 Miracle me no miracles.
Sancho Panza, ibid., pt 2, bk 5, ch. 3 (1615, transl. Peter Motteux, 1712)

25 Every man is as heaven made him, and sometimes a great deal worse.
Sancho Panza, ibid., pt 2, bk 5, ch. 4

26 Thou camest out of thy mother's belly without government, thou hast lived hitherto without government, and thou mayest be carried to thy long home without government, when it shall please the Lord. How many people in this world live without government, yet do well enough, and are well looked upon?
Teresa Panza (Sancho's wife), ibid., pt 2, bk 5, ch. 5

27 There's no sauce in the world like hunger.
Teresa Panza, ibid., pt 2, bk 5, ch. 5. This well-honed proverb was attributed to SOCRATES by CICERO in De Finibus bk 2, sect. 90.

28 Our greatest foes, and whom we must chiefly combat, are within.
Don Quixote, ibid., pt 2, bk 5, ch. 8

29 Truth indeed rather alleviates than hurts, and will always bear up against falsehood, as oil does above water.
ibid., pt 2, bk 5, ch. 10

30 Well, there is a remedy for all things but death, which will be sure to lay us flat one time or other.
Sancho Panza, ibid., pt 2, bk 5, ch. 10

31 Modesty, it is a virtue not often found among poets, for almost every one of them thinks himself the greatest in the world.
Don Quixote, ibid., pt 2, bk 5, ch. 18

32 He [Don Quixote] is mad past recovery, but yet he has lucid intervals.
Don Lorenzo, ibid., pt 2, bk 5, ch. 18

33 If you are ambitious of climbing up to the difficult, and in a manner inaccessible, summit of the Temple of Fame, your surest way is to leave on one hand the narrow path of poetry, and follow the narrower track of knight-errantry, which in a trice may raise you to an imperial throne.
Ibid., pt 2, bk 5, ch. 18. 'With these words', Cervantes continues, 'Don Quixote seemed to have summed up the whole evidence of his madness.'

34 My old grannum (rest her soul) was wont to say, there were but two families in the world, have-much and have-little.
Sancho Panza, ibid., pt 2, bk 5, ch. 20

35 Death eats up all things, both the young lamb and old sheep; and I have heard our parson say, death values a prince no more than a clown; all's fish that comes to his net; he throws at all, and sweeps stakes; he's no mower that takes a nap at noon-day, but drives on, fair weather or foul, and cuts down the green grass as well as the ripe corn: he's neither squeamish nor queasy-stomached, for he swallows without chewing, and crams down all things into his ungracious maw; and though you can see no belly he has, he has a confounded dropsy,

and thirsts after men's lives, which he guggles down like mother's milk.
Sancho Panza, ibid., pt 2, bk 5, ch. 20

36 Love and war are the same thing, and stratagems and policy are as allowable in the one as in the other.
Don Quixote, ibid., pt 2, bk 5, ch. 21

37 A private sin is not so prejudicial in this world, as a public indecency.
Don Quixote, ibid., pt 2, bk 5, ch. 22

38 What I say is, patience, and shuffle the cards.
Durandarte, ibid., pt 2, bk 5, ch. 23

39 Tell me thy company, and I'll tell thee what thou art.
Ibid., pt 2, bk 5, ch. 23. Sancho Panza quotes a proverb.

40 One of the most considerable advantages the great have over their inferiors is to have servants as good as themselves.
Don Quixote, ibid., pt 2, bk 5, ch. 31

41 Hold you there, neither a strange hand nor my own, neither heavy nor light shall touch my bum.
Sancho Panza, ibid., pt 2, bk 6, ch. 2

42 A blot in thy scutcheon to all futurity.
Ibid., pt 2, bk 6, ch. 2. Merlin's nymph attempts to shame Sancho for his quailing at the prospect of receiving three thousand three hundred lashes.

43 It is a dainty thing to command, though it were but a flock of sheep.
Sancho Panza, ibid., pt 2, bk 6, ch. 9

44 When the severity of the law is to be softened, let pity, not bribes, be the motive.
Ibid., pt 2, bk 6, ch. 9. Don Quixote's advice to Sancho Panza.

45 By such innovations are languages enriched, when the words are adopted by the multitude, and naturalized by custom.
Ibid., pt 2, bk 6, ch. 10. Don Quixote refers to the use of the polite word 'eruct' as opposed to the more common 'belch'.

46 I condemn not the use of proverbs, but it is most certain, that such a confusion and hodge-podge of them, as you throw out and drag in by the hair together, make conversation fulsome and poor.
Don Quixote, ibid., pt 2, bk 6, ch. 10

47 Alas! all music jars when the soul's out of tune.
Altisidora, ibid., pt 2, bk 6, ch. 11

48 Man appoints, and God disappoints.
Sancho Panza, ibid., pt 2, bk 6, ch. 22

49 Now blessings light on him that first invented this same sleep: it covers a man all over, thoughts and all, like a cloak; it is meat for the hungry, drink for the thirsty, heat for the cold, and cold for the hot. It is the current coin that purchases all the pleasures of the world cheap; and the balance that sets the king and the shepherd, the fool and the wise-man even. There is only one thing … that I dislike in sleep; it is that it resembles death; there's very little difference between a man in his first sleep, and a man in his last sleep.
Sancho Panza, ibid., pt 2, bk 6, ch. 35

50 There's no taking trout with dry breeches.
Sancho Panza, ibid., pt 2, bk 6, ch. 38

51 It is the maddest trick a man can ever play in his whole life, to let his breath sneak out of his body without any more ado, and without so much as a rap over the pate, or a kick of the guts; to go out like the snuff of a farthing candle, and die merely of the mulligrubs, or the sullens.
Ibid., pt 2, bk 6, ch. 41. Spoken by Sancho Panza to the dying Don Quixote.

52 There is a strange charm in the thoughts of a good legacy, or the hopes of an estate, which wondrously removes or at least alleviates the sorrow that men would otherwise feel for the death of friends.
Ibid., pt 2, bk 6, ch. 41

53 Nor has his death the world deceived
Less than his wondrous life surprised;
For if he like a madman lived
At least he like a wise one died.
Ibid., pt 2, bk 6, ch. 41. Don Quixote's epitaph.

54 With one foot already in the stirrup.
Los Trabajos de Persiles y Sigismunda, Preface (The Labours of Persiles and Sigismunda, 1617). Referring to Cervantes' own imminent demise: he died three days after writing this dedication.

Marc Chagall
(1889–1985)
French artist

His rich colours and dream-like poetic images, often inspired by folklore, placed him in the avant-garde of 20th-century art. Born in Belorussia, he lived in Russia, France and the United States.

1 When I am finishing a picture I hold some God-made object up to it – a rock, a flower, the branch

of a tree or my hand – as a kind of final test. If the painting stands up beside a thing man cannot make, the painting is authentic. If there's a clash between the two, it is bad art.

Saturday Evening Post 2 December 1962

Joseph Chamberlain
(1836–1914)
English politician

Elected a Liberal MP in 1876, he was dedicated to social reform but broke with GLADSTONE *over Irish Home Rule, and subsequently led the Liberal Unionists. As Colonial Secretary (1895–1903), he campaigned for preferential trading links within the British empire.*

1 The day of small nations has long passed away. The day of Empires has come.

Speech in Birmingham, 12 May 1904, quoted in *The Times* 13 May 1904

2 Provided that the City of London remains, as it is at present, the clearing-house of the world, any other nation may be its workshop.

Speech at the Guildhall, London, 19 January 1904, publ. in *The Times* 20 January 1904

3 Learn to think Imperially.

Speech at the Guildhall, ibid. Paraphrasing the words of ALEXANDER HAMILTON: 'Learn to think continentally.'

Neville Chamberlain
(1869–1940)
British politician and prime minister

The son of JOSEPH CHAMBERLAIN, *he was Prime Minister of a coalition government 1937–40. Though party to the Munich Agreement (1938), he reversed his policy of appeasement on* HITLER's *invasion of Czechoslovakia in 1939.* LLOYD GEORGE *claimed that he viewed foreign policy 'through the wrong end of a municipal drainpipe'. See also* ANEURIN BEVAN 2.

1 How horrible, fantastic, incredible it is that we should be digging trenches and trying on gas masks here because of a quarrel in a faraway country between people of whom we know nothing.

BBC radio broadcast, 27 September 1938, quoted in *The Times* 28 September 1938. On Germany's annexation of the Sudetenland, Czechoslovakia, shortly before Chamberlain left for Munich to confer with HITLER, MUSSOLINI and Daladier.

2 My good friends, this is the second time in our history that there has come back from Germany to Downing Street peace with honour. I believe it is peace for our time. We thank you from the bottom of our hearts. And now I recommend you to go home and sleep quietly in your beds.

Speech at Downing Street, 30 September 1938, publ. in *The Penguin Book of Twentieth-Century Speeches* (ed. Brian MacArthur, 1999). Chamberlain had returned the previous day from Munich, where it was agreed that the Sudetenland should be transferred to Germany while guaranteeing Czechoslovakia's remaining frontiers. Chamberlain's words are often misquoted 'peace in our time' (see BOOK OF COMMON PRAYER 16). See also BENJAMIN DISRAELI 53, LORD JOHN RUSSELL.

3 This morning the British Ambassador in Berlin handed the German Government a final Note stating that, unless we heard from them by 11 o'clock that they were prepared at once to withdraw their troops from Poland, a state of war would exist between us. I have to tell you now that no such undertaking has been received, and that consequently this country is at war with Germany.

BBC radio broadcast, 3 September 1939 on the declaration of war, ibid.

4 Whatever may be the reason, whether it was that Hitler thought he might get away with what he had got without fighting for it, or whether it was that after all the preparations were not sufficiently complete – however, one thing is certain: he missed the bus.

Speech to Conservative and Unionist Associations, Central Hall, London, 4 April 1940, quoted in *The Times* 5 April 1940. Chamberlain referred to the postponement of Hitler's attack on the Western Front, the anxious period known as the 'Phoney War'. Five days later, German troops invaded Denmark and Norway, followed shortly after by the invasion of the Netherlands, Belgium, Luxembourg and France, and the start of the Battle of Britain.

Sébastien-Roch Nicolas Chamfort
(1741–94)
French author and wit

Already established as a playwright, he supported the Jacobins at the outbreak of the French Revolution but grew disenchanted by the Reign of Terror and joined the Moderates. He was denounced by the Committee of General Safety and took his own life. His Pensées (1796) have remained popular.

1 Most of those who make collections of verse or epigram are like men eating cherries or oysters: they choose out the best at first, and end by eating all.

Pensées, maximes et anecdotes, vol. 1, no. 2 (1796; *Maxims and Considerations*)

2 Philosophy, like medicine, has plenty of drugs, few good remedies, and hardly any specific cures.
Ibid., vol. 1, no. 17

3 Eminence without merit earns deference without esteem.
Ibid., vol. 1, no. 60

4 Of all days, the day on which one has not laughed is the one most surely wasted.
Ibid., vol. 1, no. 80

5 There are certain times when public opinion is the worst of all opinions.
Ibid., vol. 1, no. 92

6 Living is a sickness to which sleep provides relief every sixteen hours. It's a palliative. The remedy is death.
Ibid., vol. 1, no. 113

7 It is commonly supposed that the art of pleasing is a wonderful aid in the pursuit of fortune; but the art of being bored is infinitely more successful.
Ibid., vol. 1, no. 116

8 It must be admitted that there are some parts of the soul which we must entirely *paralyse* before we can live happily in this world.
Ibid., vol. 1, no. 124

9 Some things are easier to legalize than to legitimate.
Ibid., vol. 1, no. 134

10 Preoccupation with money is the great test of small natures, but only a small test of great ones.
Ibid., vol. 1, no. 164

11 Sometimes apparent resemblances of character will bring two men together and for a certain time unite them. But their mistake gradually becomes evident, and they are astonished to find themselves not only far apart, but even repelled, in some sort, at all their points of contact.
Ibid., vol. 1, no. 166

12 The art of the parenthesis is one of the greatest secrets of eloquence in Society.
Ibid., vol. 1, no. 243

13 Nature never said to me: *Do not be poor*; still less did she say: *Be rich*; her cry to me was always: *Be independent*.
Ibid., vol. 1, no. 281

14 Scandal is an importunate wasp, against which we must make no movement unless we are quite sure that we can kill it; otherwise it will return to the attack more furious than ever.
Ibid., vol. 2, no. 302

15 Man may aspire to virtue, but he cannot reasonably aspire to truth.
Ibid., vol. 2, no. 342

16 A man is not necessarily intelligent because he has plenty of ideas, any more than he is a good general because he has plenty of soldiers.
Ibid., vol. 2, no. 446

17 Only the history of free peoples is worth our attention; the history of men under a despotism is merely a collection of anecdotes.
Ibid. vol. 2, no. 487

18 Paris: a city of pleasures and amusements where four-fifths of the people die of grief.
Ibid., vol. 2, no. 496

19 I have three kinds of friends: those who love me, those who pay no attention to me, and those who detest me.
Quoted in LICHTENBERG's *Aphorisms*, 'Notebook K', aph. 53 (written 1765–99, transl. 1990)

20 Be my brother, or I will kill you.
Quoted in *Complete Works*, vol. 1, 'Note on the Life and Writings of Chamfort' (transl. P. R. Anguis, 1824). Chamfort's interpretation of the revolutionary slogan 'Fraternity or death!'

Raymond Chandler
(1888–1959)
US author

Regarded as the 'pick of the hard-boiled mystery scribblers', he was largely responsible for elevating the pulp detective novel into a successful literary genre. Many of his books have been filmed, including The Big Sleep *(1939),* Farewell My Lovely *(1940) and* The Long Goodbye *(1953), all featuring the detective Philip Marlowe.*

1 I don't mind if you don't like my manners. They're pretty bad. I grieve over them on the long winter evenings.
The Big Sleep, ch. 3 (1939). Spoken by Philip Marlowe. In the film version (1946), Marlowe, played by HUMPHREY BOGART, says, 'I don't mind if you don't like my manners. I don't like 'em myself . . .'

2 What did it matter where you lay once you were dead? In a dirty sump or in a marble tower on top of a high hill? You were dead, you were sleeping the big sleep, you were not bothered by things like that.

Oil and water were the same as wind and air to you.
Ibid., ch. 32

3 It was a blonde. A blonde to make a bishop kick a hole in a stained-glass window.
Farewell My Lovely, ch. 13 (1940). Philip Marlowe meets Helen Grayle.

4 She [Helen Grayle] gave me a smile I could feel in my hip pocket.
Ibid., ch. 18

5 I needed a drink, I needed a lot of life insurance, I needed a vacation, I needed a home in the country. What I had was a coat, a hat and a gun.
Philip Marlowe, ibid., ch. 34. The words have been parodied many times, memorably by CHARLES BUKOWSKI in *Pulp*, ch. 8 (1994): 'I needed a vacation. I needed 5 women. I needed to get the wax out of my ears. My car needed an oil change. I'd failed to file my damned income tax . . . I hadn't laughed in six years. I tended to worry when there was nothing to worry about. And when there was something to worry about, I got drunk.'

6 Down these mean streets a man must go who is not himself mean, who is neither tarnished nor afraid . . . He is the hero, he is everything. He must be a complete man and a common man and yet an unusual man. He must be, to use a rather weathered phrase, a man of honor, by instinct, by inevitability, without thought of it, and certainly without saying it. He must be the best man in his world and a good enough man for any world.
'The Simple Art of Murder' (1944), repr. in *Pearls Are a Nuisance* (1950). The opening words of this article – which defended detective fiction as a genre requiring 'writers with tough minds and a cool spirit of detachment' – inspired plenty of pastiches, and the title of a collection of Chandler's writings, *Down These Mean Streets a Man Must Go* (1963) by Philip Durham. The phrase 'mean streets', however, had been in use since the 19th century to describe tough life in the city, and was borrowed by MARTIN SCORSESE as the title of his 1973 film about petty criminality in the Bronx.

7 The English may not always be the best writers in the world, but they are incomparably the best dull writers.
'The Simple Art of Murder', ibid.

8 If my books had been any worse, I should not have been invited to Hollywood, and . . . if they had been any better, I should not have come.
Letter to *Atlantic Monthly*, 12 December 1945, repr. in *Raymond Chandler Speaking* (ed. Dorothy Gardiner and Kathrine S. Walker, 1962). Chandler's letter was responding to criticism of his article, 'Writers in Hollywood'.

9 Would you convey my compliments to the purist who reads your proofs and tell him or her that I write in a sort of broken-down patois which is something like the way a Swiss waiter talks, and that when I split an infinitive, God damn it, I split it so it will stay split, and when I interrupt the velvety smoothness of my more or less literate syntax with a few sudden words of bar-room vernacular, that is done with the eyes wide open and the mind relaxed but attentive. The method may not be perfect, but it is all I have.
Letter to *Atlantic Monthly* editor Edward Weeks, 18 January 1948, repr. ibid. The letter produced a comic sequel in which Chandler composed a poem to the proof-reader, a certain Margaret Mutch, titled 'Lines to a Lady with an Un-split Infinitive', in which she was made to reproach him: 'Though you went to Yale, your grammar is frail/She snarled as she jabbed his eye./Though you went to Princeton I never winced on/Such a horrible relative clause!'

10 I used to like this town . . . Los Angeles was just a big dry sunny place with ugly homes and no style, but good-hearted and peaceful . . . Now . . . we've got the big money, the sharpshooters, the percentage workers, the fast dollar boys, the hoodlums out of New York and Chicago and Detroit – and Cleveland. We've got the flash restaurants and night clubs they run, and the hotels and apartment houses they own, and the grifters and con men and female bandits that live in them. The luxury trades, the pansy decorators, the Lesbian dress designers, the riff-raff of a big hardboiled city with no more personality than a paper cup.
The Little Sister, ch. 26 (1949). Spoken by Philip Marlowe.

11 I guess God made Boston on a wet Sunday.
Letter, 21 March 1949, publ. in *The Selected Letters of Raymond Chandler* (ed. Frank MacShane, 1981). Chandler was referring to a novel by J. P. Marquand, *Point of No Return*, which he had just finished reading, in which the portrait of Boston reminded him of 'a steel engraving with no color at all'.

12 Alcohol is like love. The first kiss is magic, the second is intimate, the third is routine. After that you take the girl's clothes off.
The Long Goodbye, ch. 4 (1954). Spoken by Terry Lennox.

13 You can always tell a detective on TV. He never takes his hat off.
Playback, ch. 14 (1958). Spoken by Philip Marlowe.

Coco Chanel

(1883–1971)

French couturière

Originally Gabrielle Bonheur Chanel. Described by PICASSO *as 'the woman with the most sense in Europe', she introduced designs which combined comfort with elegance. Her domination of Parisian haute couture extended to a successful range of perfumes.*

1 Fashion is made to become unfashionable.

Life 19 August 1957

2 Elegance does not consist in putting on a new dress.

Quoted in *Coco Chanel: Her Life, Her Secrets*, ch. 21 (1971) by Marcel Haedrich

3 Fashion is architecture: it is a matter of proportions.

Ibid., ch. 21

4 Innovation! One cannot be forever innovating. I want to create classics.

Ibid., ch. 21

Charlie Chaplin

(1889–1977)

British comic actor and film-maker

The greatest of the silent film stars, he combined pathos with clowning in the role of the self-styled 'little fellow'. From 1919, he directed all his films, including The Kid *(1921),* The Goldrush *(1925) and* Modern Times *(1936). 'Charlie Chaplin's genius was in comedy,' his second wife Lita Chaplin declared. 'He has no sense of humour, particularly about himself.'*

1 All I need to make a comedy is a park, a policeman and a pretty girl.

My Autobiography, ch. 10 (1964)

2 The basic essential of a great actor is that he loves himself in acting.

Ibid., ch. 16

3 The saddest thing I can imagine is to get used to luxury.

Ibid., ch. 22

4 I remain just one thing, and one thing only – and that is a clown. It places me on a far higher plane than any politician.

Quoted in the *Observer* 17 June 1960

5 Life is a tragedy when seen in close-up, but a comedy in long-shot.

Quoted in obituary, *Guardian* 28 December 1977

Arthur Chapman

(1873–1935)

US journalist

He worked on a number of newspapers in Chicago, Denver and New York as editor and staff writer.

1 Out where the handclasp's a little stronger,
Out where the smile dwells a little longer,
That's where the West begins.

'Out Where the West Begins', st. 1, publ. in Out *Where the West Begins* (1917)

George Chapman

(c. 1559–1634)

English dramatist, poet and translator

He published poetry from 1593, and wrote extensively for the theatre, enjoying success with Bussy D'Ambois *(1607) and* The Widow's Tears *(1612), among other tragedies. His translation of* HOMER *long remained the standard English version, and was an inspiration for* KEATS.

1 For one heat, all know, doth drive out another,
One passion doth expel another still.

Monsieur d'Olive, Act 5, Sc. 1, ll. 8–9 (1606). Vandome proposes to distract the countess Marcellina from her melancholy.

2 Pure innovation is more gross than error.

Bussy D'Ambois, Act 1, Sc. 2, l. 38 (1607). Spoken by King Henry.

3 Who to himself is law, no law doth need,
Offends no law, and is a king indeed.

Ibid., Act 2, Sc. 1, ll. 203–4. Bussy d'Ambois vindicates himself before Henry III of France, after killing two men in a quarrel.

4 And let a scholar all earth's volumes carry,
He will be but a walking dictionary:
A mere articulate clock.

The Tears of Peace, ll. 530–2 (1609)

5 We have watered our horses in Helicon.

May-Day, Act 3, Sc. 3, l. 8 (1611). Lodovico refers to the mountain-range in Boeotia (central Greece), sacred to the Muses. The line has often appeared with 'houses' printed for 'horses'.

6 I know an Englishman,
Being flattered, is a lamb; threatened, a lion.

Alphonsus, Emperor of Germany, Act 1, Sc. 2, ll. 208–9 (1654). The Archbishop of Cologne refers to the proposal to make Richard, Earl of Cornwall, Holy Roman Emperor. The ascription of the play to Chapman has been questioned.

John Jay Chapman
(1862–1933)
US author and lawyer

As a lawyer, he campaigned against corruption in politics and business. His prolific writings included biography, essays, and plays for adults and children. Causes and Consequences *(1898)* and Practical Agitation *(1898) stressed the duty of individuals to take a stand on social issues.*

1 All progress is experimental.
Practical Agitation (1898) ch. 1

2 Wherever you see a man who gives someone else's corruption, someone else's prejudice as a reason for not taking action himself, you see a cog in The Machine that governs us.
Ibid., ch. 1

3 Good government is the outcome of private virtue.
Ibid., ch. 2

4 Everybody in America is soft, and hates conflict. The cure for this, both in politics and social life, is the same – hardihood. Give them raw truth.
Ibid., ch. 2

Charles I
(1600–49)
King of Great Britain and Ireland

Authoritarian in style and a firm believer in the divine right of kings, he reigned from 1625, ruling without parliament 1629–40. Following the rebellion of the Long Parliament (1642), he enjoyed initial successes in the Civil War, but was eventually captured, tried and executed. See ANDREW MARVELL 1.

1 Never make a defence or apology before you be accused.
Letter to Lord Wentworth, 3 September 1636, publ. in *The Letters of King Charles I* (ed. Sir Charles Petrie, 1935). Wentworth, later Earl of Strafford, was the king's Chief Counsellor.

2 Truly I desire their [the people's] liberty and freedom as much as anybody whomsoever; but I must tell you their liberty and freedom consists in having of government, those laws by which their life and their goods may be most their own. It is not for having a share in government, Sir, that is nothing pertaining to them. A subject and a sovereign are clear different things ... Sirs, it was for this that now I am come here. If I would have given way to an arbitrary way, for to have all laws changed according to the power of the sword, I needed not to have come here; and therefore I tell you (and I pray God it be not laid to your charge) that I am the Martyr of the people.
Speech on the scaffold, 30 January 1649, quoted in *The Trial of Charles I*, ch. 8, sect. 5 (1964) by C. V. Wedgwood. The king's speech was published as a pamphlet immediately after his execution.

3 I go from a corruptible to an incorruptible Crown, where no disturbance can be, no disturbance in the world.
Speech on the scaffold, ibid.

Charles II
(1630–85)
King of Great Britain and Ireland

The son of CHARLES I, *he returned from exile to accept the throne in 1660. His reign was characterized by a loosening of the restrictions imposed under the Commonwealth, and the 'merry monarch' is best remembered for his womanizing and his patronage of the arts and sciences. See also* LORD ROCHESTER 1, 14.

1 It is upon the navy under the good Providence of God that the safety, honour, and welfare of this realm do chiefly depend.
'Articles of War', Preamble, quoted in *The Naval Side of British History*, pt 1, ch. 8 (1952) by Sir Geoffrey Callender

2 Do not let poor Nelly starve.
Quoted in *History of England*, vol. 1, ch. 4 (1849) by THOMAS MACAULAY. Spoken on the king's deathbed, referring to his mistress, NELL GWYN. Following his wishes, Charles's brother and successor James II ensured that Gwyn's debts were paid and that she received a sizeable pension.

3 He had been, he said, a most unconscionable time dying; but he hoped that they would excuse it.
Quoted ibid., vol. 1, ch. 4. Words spoken on his deathbed.

Charles V
(1500–58)
King of Spain and Holy Roman Emperor

He came into a vast inheritance on assuming the Spanish throne (1516) and becoming Holy Roman Emperor (1520). Much of his reign was taken up with rivalry with Francis I of France, and in combating the rise of Protestantism. He abdicated in 1556.

1 Name me an Emperor who was ever struck by a cannonball.
Attributed retort to his military commanders before the Battle of Mühlberg, 23 April 1547

2 I speak Spanish to God, Italian to women, French to men and German to my horse.
Attributed

Charles, Prince of Wales
(b. 1948)

Invested Prince of Wales in 1969, he is founder of the Prince's Trust charity and has particular interests in architecture and organic farming. Married to Lady Diana Spencer (see Princess DIANA) *in 1981, he was divorced in 1996.*

1 Whatever 'in love' means.
BBC interview, 24 February 1981. Reply when asked on his engagement to Princess DIANA if he was in love. See CAROL ANN DUFFY 2.

2 It looks as if we may be presented with a kind of vast municipal fire station . . . I would understand better this type of high-tech approach if you demolished the whole of Trafalgar Square, but what is proposed is like a monstrous carbuncle on the face of a much loved and elegant friend.
Speech to Royal Institute of British Architects, Hampton Court, 30 May 1984, quoted in *The Times* 31 May 1984. Charles was referring to a proposed extension to London's National Gallery – a design which, in the ensuing furore, was rejected in favour of a more classical structure. Charles's words may have been inspired by a passage recently written by Princess Diana's step-mother, Raine Spencer, in *The Spencers on Spas* (1983): 'Alas, for our towns and cities. Monstrous carbuncles of concrete have erupted in gentle Georgian squares.' In January 2000, Charles called the Millennium Dome at Greenwich a 'monstrous blancmange'.

3 I rather feel that deep in the soul of mankind there is a reflection as on the surface of a mirror, of a mirror-calm lake, of the beauty and harmony of the universe . . . So much depends, I think, on how each one of us is introduced to and made aware of that reflection within us.
Speech in Prince George, British Columbia, 4 May 1986, quoted in *The Prince of Wales: a Biography*, ch. 20 (1994) by Jonathan Dimbleby

4 You have to give this much to the Luftwaffe: when it knocked down our buildings it did not replace them with anything more offensive than rubble. We did that.
Speech at Mansion House, London, 1 December 1987, quoted in *The Times* 2 December 1987

5 Perhaps we just have to accept it as God's will that the unorthodox individual is doomed to years of frustration, ridicule and failure in order to act his role in the scheme of things.
Quoted in the *Independent* 8 November 1998

6 I thought the British people were supposed to be compassionate. I don't see much of it . . . All my life, people have been telling me what to do. I'm tired of it. My private life has become an industry. People are making money out of it.
Interview, 1998, quoted in the *Observer* 27 February 2005. The comments, referring to Charles's relationship with Camilla Parker-Bowles, were made to BBC royal correspondent Gavin Hewitt.

7 People seem to think they can all be pop stars, high court judges, brilliant TV personalities or infinitely more competent heads of state without ever putting in the necessary work or having natural ability.
Private memo, March 2003, quoted in the *Daily Express* 19 November 2004. The memo, which was aired during an employment tribunal in November 2004, provoked criticism by Labour Minister of Education Charles Clarke, who argued: 'Everybody has a field marshal's baton in their knapsack.'

Pierre Charron
(1541–1603)
French philosopher

One of the most influential thinkers of the 17th century, he was a disciple of MONTAIGNE *and, like him, a pronounced sceptic. He was renowned as a preacher to Margaret, Queen of Navarre, and published a number of ethical and theological tracts.*

1 *La vraie science et le vrai étude de l'homme, c'est l'homme.*
[The true science and study of man, is man himself.]
De la Sagesse, bk 1, Preface (1601; *Of Wisdom*). See ALEXANDER POPE 127.

François-René de Chateaubriand
(1768–1848)
French author and diplomat

Escaping the French Revolution, he spent time in America and England, returning to Paris in 1800 to work as a journalist and write books. Under NAPOLEON *and* LOUIS XVIII, *he was ambassador to Rome, Berlin and London. His novels and memoirs had a great impact on the French Romantics.*

1 An original writer is not one who imitates no one, but one whom no one can imitate.
Le Génie du Christianisme, pt 2, bk 1, ch. 3 (1802; *The Genius of Christianity*)

Thomas Chatterton
(1752–70)
English poet

An early Romantic hero, he composed medieval poems which he ascribed to a fictitious 15th-century monk. Although HORACE WALPOLE *was initially deceived, the forgery was revealed and Chatterton, destitute, committed suicide. See* WILLIAM WORDSWORTH 47.

1 Since we can die but once, what matters it,
If rope or garter, poison, pistol, sword,
Slow-wasting sickness, or the sudden burst
Of valve arterial in the noble parts
Curtail the miseries of human life?
Though varied is the cause, the effect's the same:
All to one common dissolution tends.
'Sentiment', written January 1770, a few months before he took a fatal dose of arsenic, publ. in *The Complete Works of Thomas Chatterton*, vol. 1 (ed. Donald S. Taylor and Benjamin B. Hoover, 1971)

2 It is my pride, my damned, native, unconquerable pride, that plunges me into distraction. You must know that 19/20th of my composition is pride – I must either live a slave, a servant; to have no will of my own, no sentiments of my own which I may freely declare as such; – or die – perplexing alternative!
Letter, February/March 1770, ibid., vol. 1

3 There is a time for all things – except marriage my dear.
Letter, 9 April 1770, ibid., vol. 1. Reply to a note from an admirer, who had bid him be patient, 'for there is a time for all things'.

4 The author who invents a title well
Will always find his covered dullness sell.
'The Art of Puffing', written 22 July 1770, first publ. 1803, repr. in *Poems* (ed. Walter W. Skeat, 1890)

Bruce Chatwin
(1940–89)
British author

An expert in modern art, he wrote books which combine fiction, history, travel and philosophy. All show an interest in nomads and the dispossessed.

1 Music is a memory bank for finding one's way about the world.
The Songlines, ch. 21 (1987). The words of Arkady. Songlines are the invisible pathways that cover Australia and which the Aborigines believe mark ancestral and personal territory.

Geoffrey Chaucer
(c. 1343–1400)
English poet

Having fought in France, he married into the family of John of Gaunt (1366), and undertook several diplomatic missions to the Continent, including Italy. The influence of Boccaccio is evident in The Parlement of Foules *and* Troilus and Criseyde. *From the 1380s, he was chiefly occupied with his greatest work,* The Canterbury Tales, *which recounted stories told by a group of pilgrims, and was unfinished. See* JOHN DRYDEN 75, JOHN LYDGATE 1.

1 Soun ys noght but eyr ybroken,
And every speche that ys spoken,
Lowd or pryvee, foul or fair,
In his substaunce ys but air;
For as flaumbe is but lyghted smoke,
Ryght soo soun ys air ybroke.
The House of Fame, bk 2, ll. 765–70 (1374–85, Riverside edn, ed. F. N. Robinson, rev. Larry D. Benson, 1987). Spoken by the eagle.

2 Venus clerk, Ovide,
That hath ysowen wonder wide
The grete god of Loves name.
Ibid., bk 3, ll. 1487–9. OVID is said to have been Chaucer's favourite Roman poet.

3 Hard is the hert that loveth nought
In May, whan al this mirth is wrought.
The Romaunt of the Rose, ll. 85–6 (c. 1380, Riverside edn, ed. F. N. Robinson, rev. Larry D. Benson, 1987)

4 For nakid as a worm was she.
Ibid., l. 454. Referring to Poverty.

5 The lyf so short, the craft so long to lerne,
Th' assay so hard, so sharp the conquerynge,
The dredful joye, alwey that slit so yerne;
Al this mene I by love.
The Parlement of Foules, 'The Proem' (1380–6, Riverside edn, ed. F. N. Robinson, rev. Larry D. Benson, 1987). Opening lines. See HIPPOCRATES 1, SENECA 18.

6 For out of olde feldes, as men seyth,
Cometh al this newe corn from yer to yere;
And out of olde bokes, in good feyth,
Cometh al this newe science that men lere.
Ibid., ll. 22–5

7 For thogh I wepe of teres ful a tyne,
Yet may that wo myn herte nat confounde;
Your semy voys that ye so smal out twyne
Maketh my thoght in joye and blis habounde.
So curtaysly I go, with love bounde,
That to myself I sey, in my penaunce,

'Suffyseth me to love you, Rosemounde,
Thogh ye to me ne do no daliaunce.'

'To Rosemounde', st. 2 (*c*. 1385, Riverside edn, ed. F. N. Robinson, rev. Larry D. Benson, 1987)

8 Thou mayst allone here wepe and crye and knele,
But love a womman that she woot it nought,
And she wol quyte it that thow shalt nat fele;
Unknowe, unkist, and lost, that is unsought.

Troilus and Criseyde, bk 1, ll. 806–9 (*c*. 1385, Riverside edn, ed. F. N. Robinson, rev. Larry D. Benson, 1987). Spoken by Pandarus.

9 Ye knowe ek, that in forme of speche is chaunge
Withinne a thousand yeer, and wordes tho
That hadden pris, now wonder nyce and straunge
Us thinketh hem, and yet thei spake hem so,
And spedde as wel in love as men now do;
Ek for to wynnen love in sondry ages,
In sondry londes, sondry ben usages.

Ibid., bk 2, ll. 22–8

10 For which he wex a litel reed for shame,
Whan he the peple upon him herde cryen,
That to byholde it was a noble game,
How sobrelich he caste doun his yën.
Criseÿda gan al his chere aspien,
And leet it so softe it in hire herte synke,
That to hireself she seyde, 'Who yaf me drinke?'

Ibid., bk 2, ll. 645–51

11 For of fortunes sharpe adversitee
The worste kynde of infortune is this,
A man to han ben in prosperitee,
And it remembren, whan it passed is.

Pandarus, ibid., bk 3, ll. 1625–8. The same thought appears in *Consolation of Philosophy* by Boethius (see BOETHIUS 1), translated by Chaucer: 'For in all adversitee of fortune, the most unsely kinde of contrarious fortune is to han been weleful.' See also DANTE 11.

12 And, for ther is so gret diversite
In Englissh and in writyng of oure tonge.

Ibid., bk 5, ll. 1793–4

13 O yonge fresshe folkes, he or she,
In which that love up groweth with youre age,
Repeyreth hom fro worldly vanyte,
And of youre herte up casteth the visage
To thilke God that after his ymage
Yow made, and thynketh al nys but a faire
This world, that passeth soone as floures faire.

Ibid., bk 5, ll. 1835–41

14 Ther is game noon
That fro my bokes maketh me to goon,
But yt be seldom on the holyday,
Save, certeynly, whan that the month of May
Is comen, and that I here the foules synge,
And that the floures gynnen for to sprynge,
Farewel my bok and my devocioun!

The Legende of Good Women, 'The Prologue' ll. 33–9 (*c*. 1385, Riverside edn, ed. F. N. Robinson, rev. Larry D. Benson, 1987)

15 Whan Zephirus eek with his sweete breeth,
Inspired hath in every holt and heeth
The tendre croppes, and the yonge sonne
Hath in the Ram his halve cours yronne,
And smale foweles maken melodye,
That slepen al the nyght with open ye,
(So priketh hem Nature in hir corages);
Thanne longen folk to goon on pilgrimages.

The Canterbury Tales, 'The General Prologue', ll. 5–12 (*c*. 1387–1400, Riverside edn, ed. F. N. Robinson, rev. Larry D. Benson, 1987)

16 And though that he were worthy, he was wys,
And of his port as meeke as is a mayde.
He nevere yet no vileynye ne sayde
In al his lyf unto no maner wight;
He was a verray parfit, gentil knyght.

Ibid., 'The General Prologue', ll. 68–72. Describing the Knight.

17 He was as fressh as is the month of May.

Ibid., 'The General Prologue', l. 92. Referring to the Knight's Squire.

18 A Clerk ther was of Oxenford also,
That unto logyk hadde longe ygo.
As leene was his hors as is a rake,
And he nas nat right fat, I undertake,
But looked holwe, and therto sobrely.

Ibid., 'The General Prologue', ll. 285–9

19 For hym was levere have at his beddes heed,
Twenty bookes, clad in blak or reed,
Of Aristotle and his philosophie,
Than robes riche, or fithele, or gay sautrie:
But al be that he was a philosophre,
Yet hadde he but litel gold in cofre.

Ibid., 'The General Prologue', ll. 293–8. Referring to the Clerk of Oxenford; the last couplet alludes to the 'philosophy' of alchemy.

20 Nowher so bisy a man as he ther nas,
And yet he semed bisier than he was.

Ibid., 'The General Prologue', ll. 321–2. Referring to the Sergeant of the Lawe.

21 She was a worthy womman al hir lyve:
Housbondes at chirche dore she hadde fyve,
Withouten oother compaignye in youthe –
But thereof nedeth nat to speke as nowthe.
Ibid., 'The General Prologue', ll. 459–62. Of the Wife of Bath.

22 But Cristes loore and his apostles twelve
He taughte, but first he folwed it hymselve.
Ibid., 'The General Prologue', ll. 527–8. Referring to the Parson.

23 Wel loved he garleek, oynons, and eek lekes,
And for to drynken strong wyn, reed as blood;
Thanne wolde he speke, and crie as he were wood.
And whan that he wel dronken hadde the wyn,
Than wolde he speke no word but Latyn.
Ibid., 'The General Prologue', ll. 634–8. Describing the Summoner.

24 And thus, with feyned flaterye and japes,
He made the person and the peple his apes.
Ibid., 'The General Prologue', ll. 705–6. Describing the Pardoner.

25 And therfore, at the kynges court, my brother,
Ech man for hymself, ther is noon oother.
Ibid., 'The Knight's Tale', ll. 1181–2. Spoken by Arcite.

26 The bisy larke, messager of day,
Salueth in hir song the morwe gray.
Ibid., 'The Knight's Tale', ll. 1491–2

27 The smylere with the knyf under the cloke.
Ibid., 'The Knight's Tale', l. 1999

28 What is this world? what asketh men to have?
Now with his love, now in his colde grave
Allone, withouten any compaignye.
Ibid., 'The Knight's Tale', ll. 2777–9. Spoken by Arcite.

29 This world nys but a thurghfare ful of wo,
And we been pilgrymes, passynge to and fro.
Deeth is an ende of every worldly soore.
Ibid., 'The Knight's Tale', ll. 2847–9. Spoken by Egeus.

30 So was hir joly whistle wel ywet.
Ibid., 'The Reeve's Tale', l. 4155. Referring to the miller's wife who, like her husband, is drunk.

31 She is mirour of alle curteisye.
Ibid., 'The Man of Law's Tale', l. 166. Describing 'the Emperour's doghter, dame Custance'.

32 Paraventure in thilke large book,
Which that men clepe the hevene ywriten was
With sterres, whan that he his birthe took,
That he for love sholde han his deeth, allas!
For in the sterres, clerer than is glas,

Is writen, God woot, whoso koude it rede,
The deeth of every man, withouten drede.
Ibid., 'The Man of Law's Tale', ll. 190–6

33 Experience, though noon auctoritee
Were in this world, is right ynogh for me
To speke of wo that is in mariage.
Ibid., 'The Wife of Bath's Prologue'. Opening lines.

34 But, Lord Crist! whan that it remembreth me
Upon my yowthe, and on my jolitee,
It tikleth me aboute myn herte roote.
Unto this day it dooth myn herte boote
That I have had my world as in my tyme.
But age, allas! that al wole envenyme
Hath me biraft my beautee and my pith;
Lat go, farewel, the devel go therwith!
The flour is goon, ther is namoore to telle,
The bren, as I best kan, now moste I selle.
Ibid., 'The Wife of Bath's Prologue', ll. 469–78

35 By God, in erthe I was his purgatorie,
For which I hope his soule be in glorie!
Ibid., 'The Wife of Bath's Prologue', ll. 489–90. The Wife of Bath speaks of her fourth husband.

36 That he is gentil that dooth gentil dedis.
Ibid., 'The Wife of Bath's Tale', l. 1170. Citing SENECA and BOETHIUS.

37 O stormy peple! unsad, and evere untrewe!
Ay undiscreet and chaungynge as a fane,
Delitynge evere in rumbul that is newe;
For lyk the moone ay wexe ye and wane!
Ibid., 'The Clerk's Tale', ll. 995–8

38 Ye archewyves, stondeth at defense,
Syn ye be strong as is a greet camaille;
Ne suffreth nat that men yow doon offense.
Ibid., 'Lenvoy de Chaucer', ll. 1995–8

39 Ther nys no werkman, whatsoevere he be,
That may bothe werke wel and hastily;
This wol be doon at leyser parfitly.
Ibid., 'The Merchant's Tale', ll. 1832–4. Spoken by Januarie.

40 Love wol nat been constreyned by maistrye.
When maistrie comth, the God of Love anon
Beteth his wynges, and farewel, he is gon!
Love is a thyng as any spirit free.
Wommen, of kynde, desiren libertee,
And nat to been constreyned as a thral;
And so doon men, if I sooth seyen shal.
Ibid., 'The Franklin's Tale', ll. 764–70

41 She moorneth, waketh, wayleth, fasteth, pleyneth;
Desir of his presence hire so distreyneth,
That al this wyde world she sette at noght.
Ibid., 'The Franklin's Tale', ll. 819–20. Dorigen pines for her absent husband.

42 'Allas!' quod she, 'that evere this sholde happe!
For wende I nevere by possibilitee,
That swich a monstre or merveille myghte be;
It is agayns the proces of nature.'
Ibid., 'The Franklin's Tale', ll. 1342–5. Dorigen's reaction on seeing that Aurelius has made all the rocks disappear from Brittany's coast.

43 O wombe! O bely! O stynkyng cod,
Fulfilled of dong and of corrupcioun!
At either ende of thee foul is the soun.
How greet labour and cost is thee to fynde!
Ibid., 'The Pardoner's Tale', ll. 534–7

44 O dronke man, disfigured is thy face,
Sour is thy breeth, foul artow to embrace.
Ibid., 'The Pardoner's Tale', ll. 551–2

45 'By God,' quod he, 'for pleynly, at a word,
Thy drasty rymyng is nat worth a toord!'
Ibid., 'Sir Thopas', ll. 929–30

46 And what is bettre than wisedoom? Womman.
And what is bettre than a good womman? Nothyng.
Ibid., 'The Tale of Melibee', l. 1107. Spoken by Prudence.

47 Ful wys is he that kan hymselven knowe!
Ibid., 'The Monk's Tale', l. 2139

48 Mordre wol out; that se we day by day.
Ibid., 'The Nun's Priest's Tale', l. 3052. Proverbial expression spoken by Chauntecleer. In 'The Prioress's Tale', there is a similar line: 'Mordre wol out, certeyn, it wol nat faille' (l. 576).

49 For whan a man hath over-greet a wit,
Ful oft hym happeth to mysusen it.
Ibid., 'The Canon's Yeoman's Prologue', ll. 648–9

50 Certes, they been lyk to houndes, for an hound whan he comth by the roser, or by othere bushes, though he may nat pisse, yet wole he heve up his leg and make a contenaunce to pisse.
Ibid., 'The Parson's Tale: Sequitur de Luxuria', sect. 855. Referring to 'thise olde dotardes holours [lechers]' who 'wol ... kisse, though they may nat do'.

John Cheever
(1912–82)
US author

Called 'the Chekhov of the suburbs' for his portraits of middle-class life in New England, he was a regular contributor to the New Yorker. *His best known novels are* The Wapshot Chronicle *(1957) and* The Wapshot Scandal *(1964).*

1 When the beginnings of self-destruction enter the heart it seems no bigger than a grain of sand.
Journal entry, 1952, publ. in *John Cheever: The Journals*, 'The Late Forties and the Fifties' (ed. Robert Gottlieb, 1991)

2 I do not understand the capricious lewdness of the sleeping mind.
Journal entry, 1955, ibid.

3 Then it is dark; it is a night where kings in golden suits ride elephants over the mountains.
'The Country Husband', publ. in *The Stories of John Cheever* (1978)

Anton Chekhov
(1860–1904)
Russian dramatist and author

Anton Pavlovich Chekhov. Relying on mood and character rather than narrative, his plays and short stories use realism to probe the psychological dramas of the Russian middle classes. He published short stories after 1888, but is best known for such plays as The Three Sisters *(1901) and* The Cherry Orchard *(1904).*

1 Medicine is my lawful wife and literature is my mistress. When I get tired of one of them I spend the night with the other. Though it's disorderly it's not so dull, and besides, neither really loses anything from my infidelity.
Letter to his publisher, 11 September 1888, publ. in *Letters of Chekhov* (transl. Constance Garnett, 1920). Chekhov graduated as a doctor in 1884 and regarded medicine as his primary calling, though he only practised sporadically.

2 My holy of holies is the human body, health, intelligence, talent, inspiration, love and the most absolute freedom – freedom from violence and lying, whatever the forms they may take.
Letter, 4 October 1888, ibid.

3 Brevity is the sister of talent.
Letter, 11 April 1889, ibid. It has been said that all of Chekhov's best work is an illustration of this dictum.

4 I'm in mourning for my life.
The Seagull, Act 1 (1896). Masha's first words in the play, in answer to the question, 'Why do you always wear black?'

5 We don't have to depict life as it is, or as it ought to be, but as we see it in our dreams.

Ibid., Act 1. The playwright Trepliov defends his work.

6 Women don't forgive failure.

Trepliov, ibid., Act 2

7 A subject for a short story: a young girl, like you, has lived beside a lake from childhood. She loves the lake as a seagull does, and she's happy and free as a seagull. But a man chances to come along, sees her, and having nothing better to do, destroys her, just like this seagull here.

Ibid., Act 2. Trigorin is speaking to Nina. Trepliov has earlier shot a seagull and laid it at Nina's feet, as a symbol of his ruined hopes.

8 A woman can only become a man's friend in three stages: first, she's an agreeable acquaintance, then a mistress, and only after that a friend.

Uncle Vanya, Act 2 (1897). Spoken by Astrov. Vanya (Voinitsky) replies: 'That's a crude sort of philosophy.'

9 Man must work by the sweat of his brow whatever his class, and that should make up the whole meaning and purpose of his life and happiness and contentment.

Three Sisters, Act 1 (1901). Spoken by Irena.

10 The whole of Russia is our orchard.

The Cherry Orchard, Act 2 (1904). Spoken by Trofimov.

11 It's perfectly clear that to begin to live in the present, we must first atone for our past and be finished with it, and we can only atone for it by suffering, by extraordinary, unceasing exertion.

Trofimov, ibid., Act 2

Mary Bokin Chesnut
(1823–86)
US diarist

Married to a Southern senator who played an active role in the formation of the Confederacy, she is remembered for A Diary from Dixie *(1905), an important historical source for the Civil War.*

1 I think this journal will be disadvantageous for me, for I spend my time now like a spider spinning my own entrails.

Journal entry, 14 March 1861, publ. in *A Diary from Dixie* (1905)

2 We are scattered, stunned, the remnant of heart left alive in us filled with brotherly hate. We sit and wait until the drunken tailor who rules the United States issues a proclamation and defines our anomalous position.

Journal entry, 16 May 1865, ibid. The 'drunken tailor' was President Andrew Johnson, LINCOLN's Vice-president and successor, who was proprietor of a tailor shop in Tennessee before entering politics.

Lord Chesterfield
(1694–1773)
English statesman and man of letters

Philip Dormer Stanhope, fourth earl of Chesterfield. Ambassador at the Hague 1728–32 and Lord Lieutenant of Ireland 1745–6, he is remembered as the literary patron who failed to support Johnson (see SAMUEL JOHNSON 25, 26*), and for his elegant letters of advice to his son and godson.* VOLTAIRE *described him as the 'only Englishman who ever argued for the art of pleasing as the first duty of life'.*

1 If you can once engage people's pride, love, pity, ambition (or whatever is their prevailing passion) on your side, you need not fear what their reason can do against you.

Letter, 8 February 1746, publ. in *Letters to His Son* (1774)

2 Custom has made dancing sometimes necessary for a young man; therefore mind it while you learn it, that you may learn to do it well, and not be ridiculous, though in a ridiculous act.

Letter, 9 October 1746, ibid.

3 There is nothing that people bear more impatiently, or forgive less, than contempt: and an injury is much sooner forgotten than an insult.

Letter, 9 October 1746, ibid.

4 Courts and camps are the only places to learn the world in.

Letter, 2 October 1747, ibid.

5 Take the tone of the company that you are in, and do not pretend to give it.

Letter, 16 October 1747, ibid.

6 I recommend to you to take care of the minutes; for hours will take care of themselves.

Letter, 6 November 1747, ibid.

7 Speak of the moderns without contempt, and of the ancients without idolatry.

Letter, 22 February 1748, ibid. Chesterfield elaborated: 'We are really so prejudiced by our educations, that, as the ancients deified their heroes, we deify their madmen.'

8 Vice, in its true light, is so deformed, that it shocks

us at first sight; and would hardly ever seduce us, if it did not at first wear the mask of some virtue.
Letter, 22 February 1748, ibid.

9 Never seem wiser, nor more learned, than the people you are with. Wear your learning, like your watch, in a private pocket: and do not merely pull it out and strike it; merely to show that you have one.
Letter, 22 February 1748, ibid.

10 In my mind, there is nothing so illiberal, and so ill-bred, as audible laughter.
Letter, 9 March 1748, ibid. In a letter to his godson, 12 December 1765, Chesterfield wrote: 'Observe it, the vulgar often laugh, but never smile, whereas well-bred people often smile, and seldom or never laugh. A witty thing never excited laughter, it pleases only the mind and never distorts the countenance.'

11 I am convinced that a light supper, a good night's sleep, and a fine morning, have sometimes made a hero of the same man, who, by an indigestion, a restless night, and rainy morning, would have proved a coward.
Letter, 26 April 1748, ibid.

12 Manners must adorn knowledge, and smooth its way through the world.
Letter, 1 July 1748, ibid.

13 Women are only children of a larger growth ... A man of sense only trifles with them, plays with them, humours and flatters them, as he does with a sprightly and forward child; but he neither consults them about, nor trusts them with, serious matters.
Letter, 5 September 1748, ibid. See JOHN DRYDEN 20.

14 Women who are either indisputably beautiful, or indisputably ugly, are best flattered upon the score of their understandings; but those who are in a state of mediocrity are best flattered upon their beauty, or at least their graces.
Letter, 5 September 1748, ibid.

15 To have frequent recourse to narrative betrays great want of imagination.
Letter, 19 October 1748, ibid.

16 In the case of scandal, as in that of robbery, the receiver is always thought as bad as the thief.
Letter, 19 October 1748, ibid.

17 Any affectation whatsoever in dress implies, in my mind, a flaw in the understanding.
Letter, 30 December 1748, ibid.

18 No man tastes pleasures truly, who does not earn them by previous business; and few people do business well, who do nothing else.
Letter, 7 August 1749, ibid.

19 The world can doubtless never be well known by theory: practice is absolutely necessary; but surely it is of great use to a young man, before he sets out for that country, full of mazes, windings, and turnings, to have at least a general map of it, made by some experienced traveller.
Letter, 30 August 1749, ibid.

20 A constant smirk upon the face, and a whiffling activity of the body, are strong indications of futility.
Letter, 30 August 1749, ibid.

21 Whoever is in a hurry, shows that the thing he is about is too big for him.
Letter, 30 August 1749, ibid.

22 If ever a man and his wife, or a man and his mistress, who pass nights as well as days together, absolutely lay aside all good breeding, their intimacy will soon degenerate into a coarse familiarity, infallibly productive of contempt or disgust.
Letter, 3 November 1749, ibid.

23 Style is the dress of thoughts; and let them be ever so just, if your style is homely, coarse, and vulgar, they will appear to as much disadvantage, and be as ill received, as your person, though ever so well-proportioned, would if dressed in rags, dirt, and tatters.
Letter, 24 November 1749, ibid.

24 Most people have ears, but few have judgment; tickle those ears, and depend upon it you will catch their judgments, such as they are.
Letter, 9 December 1749, ibid.

25 He makes people pleased with him by making them first pleased with themselves.
Letter, 18 January 1750, ibid. Speaking of the 'agreeable, well-bred man'.

26 Dispatch is the soul of business; and nothing contributes more to dispatch than method.
Letter, 5 February 1750, ibid.

27 Modesty is the only sure bait when you angle for praise.
Letter, 17 May 1750, ibid.

28 The heart never grows better by age; I fear rather worse, always harder. A young liar will be an old

one, and a young knave will only be a greater knave as he grows older.
Letter, 17 May 1750, ibid.

29 Most people enjoy the inferiority of their best friends.
Letter, 9 July 1750, ibid.

30 Let blockheads read what blockheads wrote.
Letter, 1 November 1750, ibid.

31 As fathers commonly go, it is seldom a misfortune to be fatherless; and considering the general run of sons, as seldom a misfortune to be childless.
Letter, 15 July 1751, ibid.

32 It is commonly said, and more particularly by Lord Shaftesbury, that ridicule is the best test of truth; for that it will not stick where it is not just. I deny it. A truth learned in a certain light, and attacked in certain words, by men of wit and humour, may, and often doth, become ridiculous, at least so far, that the truth is only remembered and repeated for the sake of the ridicule.
Letter, 6 February 1752, ibid. Lord Shaftesbury wrote: 'How comes it to pass, then, that we appear such cowards in reasoning, and are so afraid to stand the test of ridicule?' (A Letter Concerning Enthusiasm, sect. 2, 1708)

33 Our prejudices are our mistresses; reason is at best our wife, very often heard indeed, but seldom minded.
Letter, 13 April 1752, ibid.

34 Most maxim-mongers have preferred the prettiness to the justness of a thought, and the turn to the truth; but I have refused myself to everything that my own experience did not justify and confirm.
Letter, 15 January 1753, ibid.

35 I look upon indolence as a sort of *suicide*; for the man is effectually destroyed, though the appetites of the brute may survive.
Letter, 26 February 1754, ibid.

36 The only solid and lasting peace between a man and his wife is, doubtless, a separation.
Letter, 1 September 1763, ibid.

37 In matters of religion and matrimony I never give any advice; because I will not have anybody's torments in this world or the next laid to my charge.
Letter, 12 October 1765, publ. in *Lord Chesterfield's Letters to His Godson*, Appendix (ed. Earl of Carnarvon, 1889)

38 Wit is so shining a quality that everybody admires it; most people aim at it, all people fear it, and few love it unless in themselves. A man must have a good share of wit himself to endure a great share of it in another.
Letter, 18 December 1765, ibid., no. 136

39 Religion is by no means a proper subject of conversation in a mixed company.
Letter, May 1766, ibid., no. 142

40 Lord Tyrawley and I have been dead these two years, but we don't choose to have it known.
Quoted by SAMUEL JOHNSON, in *Life of Samuel Johnson, LL.D.*, 3 April 1773 (1791) by JAMES BOSWELL

41 The pleasure is momentary, the position ridiculous, and the expense damnable.
Attributed, referring to sex

G. K. Chesterton
(1874–1936)
British author

An exuberant personality, he wrote poetry in both ballad and comic form, as well as social and literary criticism. His most popular works of fiction are the tales of the priest-sleuth Father Brown (1911–35). GEORGE BERNARD SHAW *described Chesterton's 'resolute conviviality' as 'about as genial as an auto da fé of teetotallers'.*

1 Fools! For I also had my hour;
One far fierce hour and sweet:
There was a shout about my ears,
And palms before my feet.
'The Donkey', publ. in *The Wild Knight and Other Poems* (1900)

2 My country, right or wrong is a thing that no patriot would think of saying except in a desperate case. It is like saying 'My mother, drunk or sober.'
The Defendant, 'Defence of Patriotism' (1901). See STEPHEN DECATUR 1, CARL SCHURZ 1.

3 All slang is metaphor, and all metaphor is poetry.
Ibid., 'Defence of Slang'

4 There is no such thing on earth as an uninteresting subject; the only thing that can exist is an uninterested person.
Heretics, ch. 3 (1905)

5 Happiness is a mystery, like religion, and should never be rationalised.
Ibid., ch. 7

6 The artistic temperament is a disease that affects amateurs ... Artists of a large and wholesome vitality get rid of their art easily, as they breathe easily

or perspire easily. But in artists of less force, the thing becomes a pressure, and produces a definite pain, which is called the artistic temperament.
Ibid., ch. 17

7 Youth is the period in which a man can be hopeless. The end of every episode is the end of the world. But the power of hoping through everything, the knowledge that the soul survives its adventures, that great inspiration comes to the middle-aged.
Charles Dickens, 'The Boyhood of Dickens' (1906)

8 The lunatic is the man who lives in a small world but thinks it is a large one; he is the man who lives in a tenth of the truth, and thinks it is the whole.
Ibid., 'Dickens and America'

9 An adventure is only an inconvenience rightly considered. An inconvenience is only an adventure wrongly considered.
All Things Considered, 'On Running After One's Hat' (1908)

10 Cruelty is, perhaps, the worst kind of sin. Intellectual cruelty is certainly the worst kind of cruelty.
Ibid., 'Conceit and Caricature'

11 A new philosophy generally means in practice the praise of some old vice.
Ibid., 'The Methuselahite'

12 It is not funny that anything else should fall down; only that a man should fall down ... Why do we laugh? Because it is a gravely religious matter: it is the Fall of Man. Only man can be absurd: for only man can be dignified.
Ibid., 'Spiritualism'

13 What people call impartiality may simply mean indifference, and what people call partiality may simply mean mental activity.
Ibid., 'The Error of Impartiality'

14 We call a man a bigot or a slave of dogma because he is a thinker who has thought thoroughly and to a definite end.
Ibid., 'The Error of Impartiality'

15 Man is an exception, whatever else he is. If he is not the image of God, then he is a disease of the dust. If it is not true that a divine being fell, then we can only say that one of the animals went entirely off its head.
Ibid., 'Wine When it is Red'

16 The man who throws a bomb is an artist, because he prefers a great moment to everything.
The Man Who Was Thursday, ch. 1 (1908). Spoken by Gregory.

17 The most dangerous criminal now is the entirely lawless modern philosopher. Compared to him, burglars and bigamists are essentially moral men.
Policeman, *ibid.*, ch. 4

18 Thieves respect property. They merely wish the property to become their property that they may more perfectly respect it.
Policeman, *ibid.*, ch. 4

19 Tradition means giving votes to the most obscure of all classes – our ancestors. It is the democracy of the dead. Tradition refuses to submit to the small and arrogant oligarchy of those who merely happen to be walking around.
Orthodoxy, ch. 4 (1908)

20 The perplexity of life arises from there being too many interesting things in it for us to be interested properly in any of them.
Tremendous Trifles, 'The Secret of a Train' (1909)

21 Art consists of limitation ... The most beautiful part of every picture is the frame.
Ibid., 'The Toy Theatre'

22 The whole object of travel is not to set foot on foreign land; it is at last to set foot on one's own country as a foreign land.
Ibid., 'The Riddle of the Ivy'

23 The only way of catching a train I have ever discovered is to miss the train before.
Ibid., 'The Prehistoric Railway Station'

24 The Christian ideal has not been tried and found wanting. It has been found difficult; and left untried.
What's Wrong With the World, pt 1, ch. 5 (1910)

25 If a thing is worth doing, it is worth doing badly.
Ibid., pt 4, ch. 14

26 For the great Gaels of Ireland
Are the men that God made mad,
For all their wars are merry
And all their songs are sad.
Ballad of the White Horse, bk 2 (1911)

27 Among the Very Rich you will never find a really generous man, even by accident. They may give their money away, but they will never give themselves away; they are egoistic, secretive, dry as old bones. To be smart enough to get all that money you must be dull enough to want it.
A Miscellany of Men, 'A Miscellany of Men' (1912). In *The Wisdom of Father Brown*, 'Paradise of Thieves' (1914), Muscari

observes: 'To be clever enough to get all that money, one must be stupid enough to want it.'

28 And Noah he often said to his wife when he sat
   down to dine,
'I don't care where the water goes if it doesn't get
   into the wine.'
'Wine and Water', publ. in *The Flying Inn*, ch. 5 (1914)

29 They haven't got no noses
The fallen sons of Eve;
Even the smell of roses
Is not what they supposes;
But more than mind discloses
And more than men believe.
'The Song of Quoodle', ibid., ch. 15

30 And goodness only knowses
The Noselessness of Man.
'The Song of Quoodle', ibid.

31 Tea, although an Oriental,
Is a gentleman at least;
Cocoa is a cad and coward,
Cocoa is a vulgar beast.
'Song of Right and Wrong', ibid., ch. 18

32 The rolling English drunkard made the rolling
   English road.
A reeling road, a rolling road, that rambles round
   the shire.
'The Rolling English Road', ibid., ch. 21

33 But there is good news yet to hear and fine
   things to be seen
Before we go to Paradise by way of Kensal Green.
Ibid. Closing lines of poem. London's Kensal Green Cemetery
holds many of Britain's illustrious dead.

34 Journalism largely consists in saying 'Lord Jones
Dead' to people who never knew that Lord Jones
was alive.
The Wisdom of Father Brown, 'The Purple Wig' (1914). Spoken
by Mr Finn.

35 Are they clinging to their crosses, F. E. Smith?
'Antichrist', publ. in *Poems* (1915). Referring to F. E. Smith (Lord
Birkenhead) pontificating on the Welsh Disestablishment Bill.

36 Strong gongs groaning as the guns boom far,
Don John of Austria is going to the war.
'Lepanto', ibid. Don John, brother of Philip II of Spain, commanded the combined Spanish, Venetian and Papal fleets
which defeated the Turks at Lepanto in 1571.

37 They have given us into the hand of new
   unhappy lords,

Lords without anger and honour, who dare not
   carry their swords.
They fight by shuffling papers; they have bright
   dead alien eyes;
They look at our labour and laughter as a tired
   man looks at flies.
'The Secret People', ibid.

38 But we are the people of England; and we have
   not spoken yet.
Smile at us, pay us, pass us. But do not quite
   forget.
Ibid. Closing lines of poem.

39 They died to save their country and they only
saved the world.
'English Graves', publ. in *The Ballad of St Barbara* (1922)

40 It is as healthy to enjoy sentiment as to enjoy
jam.
Generally Speaking, 'On Sentiment' (1928)

41 A puritan is a person who pours righteous indignation into the wrong things.
New York Times 21 November 1930

42 Democracy means government by the uneducated, while aristocracy means government by the
badly educated.
New York Times 1 February 1931

43 There is nothing the matter with Americans
except their ideals. The real American is all right; it
is the ideal American who is all wrong.
New York Times 1 February 1931

44 The disadvantage of men not knowing the past
is that they do not know the present. History is a
hill or high point of vantage, from which alone men
see the town in which they live or the age in which
they are living.
All I Survey, 'On St George Revivified' (1933)

45 It isn't that they can't see the solution. It is that
they can't see the problem.
The Scandal of Father Brown, 'Point of a Pin' (1935)

46 Boyhood is a most complex and incomprehensible thing. Even when one has been through it, one
does not understand what it was. A man can never
quite understand a boy, even when he has been the
boy.
Autobiography, ch. 3 (1936)

47 There is no better test of a man's ultimate

chivalry and integrity than how he behaves when he is wrong.

The Common Man, 'The Real Dr Johnson' (1950)

48 A stiff apology is a second insult . . . The injured party does not want to be compensated because he has been wronged; he wants to be healed because he has been hurt.

Ibid., 'The Real Dr Johnson'

49 Ten thousand women marched through the streets of London saying: 'We will not be dictated to', and then went off to become stenographers.

Quoted in *G. K. Chesterton*, ch. 1 (1986) by M. Ffinch. Referring to early feminists.

50 Am in Market Harborough. Where ought I to be?

Attributed telegram to wife in London. In his *Autobiography*, ch. 16 (1936), Chesterton wrote: 'I cannot remember whether this story is true; but it is not unlikely, or, I think, unreasonable.'

Maurice Chevalier
(1888–1972)
French singer and actor

He first appeared in the Folies Bergères (1909–13), and later had a film career spanning three decades. 'Paris has two monuments,' JEAN COCTEAU declared, 'the Eiffel tower and Maurice Chevalier.'

1 Thank heaven for little girls!
For little girls get bigger every day.

'Thank Heaven for Little Girls' (song, written by ALAN JAY LERNER with music by Frederick Loewe) in *Gigi* (film, 1958)

2 Old age isn't so bad when you consider the alternative.

New York Times 9 October 1960. Remark on his seventy-second birthday.

Chiang Kai-shek
(1887–1975)
Chinese politician and president

He established himself as president 1928–38 and 1943–9. After the Communist takeover in 1949 he fled to Taiwan where he remained as president until his death.

1 If one does not act, one cannot understand.

China's Destiny, ch. 6 (1943)

Lydia Maria Child
(1802–80)
US abolitionist, author and editor

Following a meeting with WILLIAM LLOYD GARRISON *in 1831, she dedicated herself to Abolitionism, editing the* National Anti-Slavery Standard *(1841–3) and supporting the Underground Railroad, which aided fugitive slaves. She also wrote historical novels.*

1 Who does not see that the American people are walking over a subterranean fire, the flames of which are fed by slavery?

An Appeal on Behalf of that Class of Americans Called Africans, ch. 4 (1833)

2 I have lost the power of looking merely on the surface. Everything seems to me to come from the Infinite, to be filled with the Infinite, to be tending toward the Infinite. Do I see crowds of men hastening to extinguish a fire? I see not merely uncouth garbs, and fantastic, flickering lights, of lurid hue, like a trampling troop of gnomes – but straightway my mind is filled with thoughts about mutual helpfulness, human sympathy, the common bond of brotherhood, and the mysteriously deep foundations on which society rests; or rather, on which it now reels and totters.

Letter, 19 August 1841, publ. in *Letters from New York*, vol. 1 (1843). Describing street life in New York.

3 The nearer society approaches to divine order, the less separation will there be in the characters, duties, and pursuits of men and women. Women will not become less gentle and graceful, but men will become more so. Women will not neglect the care and education of their children, but men will find themselves ennobled and refined by sharing those duties with them; and will receive, in return, co-operation and sympathy in the discharge of various other duties, now deemed inappropriate to women. The more women become rational companions, partners in business and in thought, as well as in affection and amusement, the more highly will men appreciate home.

Letter, January 1843, ibid., vol. 1

Erskine Childers
(1870–1922)
British-born Irish nationalist and author

Robert Erskine Childers. The writer of the spy story The Riddle of the Sands *(1903) was elected to the Irish Assembly as a Sinn Féin deputy in 1921. After the establishment of the Irish Free*

State, he fought in the Civil War and was captured and executed.

1 The Riddle of the Sands.
Title of book (1903)

2 It all seems perfectly simple and inevitable, like lying down after a long day's work.
Letter to his wife, 24 November 1922, quoted in *Peace By Ordeal*, pt 6, ch. 1 (1962) by Frank Pakenham. Of his pending execution, which took place two hours later.

3 Come closer, boys. It will be easier for you.
Quoted in *The Zeal of the Convert*, ch. 26 (1976) by Burke Wilkinson. Spoken to the firing squad before his execution, 24 November 1922. Childers was granted an hour's postponement to see the sun rise, and shook hands with each member of the squad.

Jacques Chirac
(b. 1932)
French politician and president

Twice Prime Minister (1974–6 and 1986–8), he re-established the Gaullist Party (RPR) and was elected President in 1995 and 2002.

1 I am not prepared to accept the economics of a housewife.
Quoted in the *Sunday Times* 27 December 1987. Referring to MARGARET THATCHER. On a later occasion, Chirac extolled the virtues of 'the woman of the old days, who works hard, serves the men at their meals, never sits at table with them, and does not talk.' (*Daily Telegraph* 7 February 1998)

Noam Chomsky
(b. 1928)
US linguist and political analyst

From the mid-1950s he developed a revolutionary and influential theory of linguistics known as transformational-generative grammar, which he described in Syntactic Structures *(1957). He has been a strong critic of US foreign policy in numerous books and essays.*

1 Colorless green ideas sleep furiously.
Syntactic Structures, ch. 2 (1957). Example of a sentence which is 'grammatical' without being 'meaningful'. Chomsky gave the following example of a sentence lacking both meaning and correct grammatical structure: 'Furiously sleep ideas green colorless.'

2 The intellectual tradition is one of servility to power, and if I didn't betray it I'd be ashamed of myself.
Interview on *The Late Show*, BBC2, 25 November 1992. Responding to an accusation of betrayal by ARTHUR SCHLESINGER JR.

3 If we don't believe in freedom of expression for people we despise, we don't believe in it at all.
Ibid.

Agatha Christie
(1890–1976)
British mystery writer

Her whodunnits, many of which have been filmed, have sold more than 100 million copies, while her play The Mousetrap *(1952) holds a world record for the longest continuous run at one theatre. She described herself as 'a sausage machine, a perfect sausage machine'.*

1 These little grey cells. It is 'up to them' – as you say over here.
The Mysterious Affair at Styles, ch. 10 (1920). Spoken by Hercule Poirot. Christie's first detective novel introduced both Belgian sleuth Hercule Poirot and Poirot's famous reference to the efficacy of brain-power – the 'little grey cells' – to solve mysteries, a faith he drew attention to in almost every subsequent appearance.

2 Every murderer is probably somebody's old friend. You cannot mix up sentiment and reason.
Poirot, ibid., ch. 11

3 Crime is terribly revealing. Try and vary your methods as you will, your tastes, your habits, your attitude of mind, and your soul is revealed by your actions.
The ABC Murders, ch. 17 (1936). Spoken by Poirot.

4 There is nothing so dangerous for anyone who has something to hide as conversation! . . . A human being, Hastings, cannot resist the opportunity to reveal himself and express his personality which conversation gives him. Every time he will give himself away.
Poirot, ibid., ch. 31

5 An archaeologist is the best husband any woman can have: the older she gets, the more interested he is in her.
Attributed remark referring to her own second husband Sir Max Mallowan, quoted in news report 9 March 1954 but later denied by her

Ivan Chtcheglov
(b. 1934)
French political theorist

His reputation rests largely on his essay 'Formulary for a New Urbanism' (written under his pseudonym Gilles Ivain), a seminal work on architecture and urban life for the Situationist group Lettriste Internationale (1952–7).

1 A mental disease has swept the planet: banalization . . . Presented with the alternative of love or a garbage disposal unit, young people of all countries have chosen the garbage disposal unit.
'Formulary for a New Urbanism' (1958), repr. in *Situationist International Anthology* (ed. Ken Knabb, 1981)

Caryl Churchill
(b. 1938)
British playwright

To date, her greatest success is a satire on high finance, Serious Money *(1986), written in rhyming couplets. Other plays include* Top Girls *(1982) and* The Skriker *(1994).*

1 Zac: The IMF is not a charity.
It has to insist on absolute austerity.
Nigel: Absolutely. It can't be namby pamby.
These countries must accept restricted diets.
The governments must explain, if there are food riots,
That paying the western banks is the priority.
Serious Money, Act 2 (1987)

2 There's ugly greedy and sexy greedy, you dope.
At the moment you're ugly which is no hope.
If you stay ugly, god knows what your fate is.
But sexy greedy *is* the late eighties.
Starr, ibid.

Charles Churchill
(1731–64)
English poet and clergyman

His sharply satiric verse targeted London actors and acting in The Rosciad *(1761),* SAMUEL JOHNSON *in* The Ghost *(1763) and* TOBIAS SMOLLETT *and other critics of* JOHN WILKES *in* The Duellist *(1764). Ordained as a priest in 1756, he left the Church in 1763.*

1 Learned without sense, and venerably dull.
The Rosciad, l. 592 (1761). Referring to Irish playwright and actor, Arthur Murphy.

2 Prudent dullness marked him for a mayor.
Ibid., l. 596

3 Where he falls short, 'tis Nature's fault alone;
Where he succeeds, the merit's all his own.
Ibid., ll. 1025–6

4 Who often, but without success, have prayed
For apt Alliteration's artful aid.
The Prophecy of Famine, ll. 85–6 (1763)

5 And adepts in the speaking trade

Keep a cough by them ready made.
The Ghost, bk 2, ll. 545–6 (1763)

6 Just to the windward of the law.
Ibid., bk 3, l. 56

7 A joke's a very serious thing.
Ibid., bk 4, l. 1386

8 Though by whim, envy, or resentment led,
They damn those authors whom they never read.
The Candidate, ll. 57–8 (1764)

9 Be England what she will,
With all her faults, she is my country still.
The Farewell, ll. 27–8 (1764). See also WILLIAM COWPER 33 for a later rendering of this sentiment.

10 Little do such men know the toil, the pains,
The daily, nightly racking of the brains,
To range the thoughts, the matter to digest,
To cull fit phrases, and reject the rest.
Gotham, bk 2, ll. 11–14 (1764)

Frank E. Churchill
(1901–42)
US composer

He joined Walt Disney studios in 1930 and composed for the Silly Symphonies *in the 1930s,* Snow White and the Seven Dwarfs *(1937),* Dumbo *(1941) and* Bambi *(1942).*

1 Who's afraid of the big bad wolf?
'Who's Afraid of the Big Bad Wolf?' (song, 1933, probably written in collaboration with Ann Ronell). See also EDWARD ALBEE 2.

Jennie Jerome Churchill
(1854–1921)
Anglo-American society figure

The mother of WINSTON CHURCHILL, *a noted beauty and society hostess, she was responsible for introducing women for the first time to the Conservative Party's Primrose League.*

1 I shall never get used to not being the most beautiful woman in the room. It was an intoxication to sweep in and know every man had turned his head. It kept me in form.
Quoted in *Jennie*, ch. 30 (1969) by Anita Leslie. Remark on her sixtieth birthday.

(Sir) Winston Churchill

(1874–1965)

British statesman and author

Hailed by Henry 'Chips' Channon as the 'saviour of the civilized world' and credited with a 'hundred horse-power mind' by STANLEY BALDWIN, *he led the wartime coalition government as Prime Minister 1940–5, and regained the premiership in 1951. His writings include* The Second World War *(1948–54) and* A History of the English-Speaking Peoples *(1956–8). See* ADOLF HITLER 13; ED MURROW 2.

1 Nothing in life is so exhilarating as to be shot at without result.

The Malakand Field Force (1898)

2 Fanaticism is not the cause of war. It is the means which helps savage peoples to fight.

The River War (1899)

3 It cannot in the opinion of His Majesty's Government be classified as slavery in the extreme acceptance of the word without some risk of terminological inexactitude.

Speech to House of Commons, 22 February 1906, publ. in *Hansard*. Referring to the position of indentured Chinese labourers working in the Rand mines in the Transvaal, South Africa. Churchill made the speech soon after assuming office as Under-Secretary for the Colonies. Of his last phrase, JOSEPH CHAMBERLAIN commented: 'Eleven syllables, many of them of Latin or Greek derivation, when one good English word, a Saxon word of a single syllable, would do!'

4 Don't talk to me about naval tradition. It's nothing but rum, sodomy and the lash.

Remark made in 1911, quoted in *Former Naval Person*, ch. 1 (1968) by Sir Peter Gretton

5 He is one of those orators of whom it was well said, 'Before they get up, they do not know what they are going to say; when they are speaking, they do not know what they are saying; and when they have sat down, they do not know what they have said.'

Speech to House of Commons, 20 December 1912, publ. in *Hansard*. Referring to naval commander Lord Charles Beresford.

6 Business carried on as usual during alterations on the map of Europe.

Speech at Guildhall, London, 9 November 1914, publ. in *Complete Speeches*, vol. 3 (ed. Robert Rhodes James, 1974). On the self-adopted 'motto' of the British people at the start of the First World War.

7 Remember, we are confronted with a foe who would without the slightest scruple extirpate us, man, woman and child, by any method open to him if he had the opportunity. We are fighting a foe who would not hesitate one moment to obliterate every single soul in this great country this afternoon if it could be done by pressing a button. We are fighting a foe who would think as little of that as a gardener would think of smoking out a wasps' nest.

Speech in Dundee, 5 June 1915, publ. in *The Speeches of Winston Churchill* (ed. David Cannadine, 1990). The speech was made shortly before Churchill's resignation from the Admiralty for his failed Dardanelles policy.

8 Anyone can rat, but it takes a certain amount of ingenuity to re-rat.

Remark in 1923, quoted in *Irrepressible Churchill* (1966) by Kay Halle. Churchill was referring to his own rejoining the Conservative Party, having earlier left it to join the Liberals.

9 I decline utterly to be impartial as between the fire brigade and the fire.

Speech to House of Commons, 7 July 1926, publ. in *Hansard*. Churchill was replying to complaints of bias while editing the *British Gazette* during the General Strike, when he referred to the strikers as 'the enemy'.

10 It is a good thing for an uneducated man to read books of quotations ... The quotations, when engraved upon the memory, give you good thoughts. They also make you anxious to read the authors and look for more.

My Early Life, ch. 9 (1930)

11 The War was decided in the first twenty days of fighting, and all that happened afterwards consisted in battles which, however formidable and devastating, were but desperate and vain appeals against the decision of Fate.

Preface to *Liaison 1914* (1930) by E. L. Spears. Of the First World War.

12 I remember, when I was a child, being taken to the celebrated Barnum's circus, which contained an exhibition of freaks and monstrosities, but the exhibit on the programme which I most desired to see was the one described as 'The Boneless Wonder'. My parents judged that that spectacle would be too revolting and demoralizing for my youthful eyes, and I have waited 50 years to see the boneless wonder sitting on the Treasury Bench.

Speech to House of Commons, 28 January 1931, publ. in *Hansard*. Of Labour Prime Minister Ramsay MacDonald.

13 It is alarming and also nauseating to see Mr Gandhi, a seditious Middle Temple lawyer, now posing as a fakir of a type well-known in the East, strid-

ing half-naked up the steps of the Viceregal Palace, while he is still organising and conducting a defiant campaign of civil disobedience, to parley on equal terms with the representative of the King Emperor.
Speech at Winchester House, Epping, 23 February 1931, publ. in *The Speeches of Winston Churchill* (ed. David Cannadine, 1990). Referring to GANDHI's release from prison in India to discuss political devolution with the Viceroy.

14 India is an abstraction ... India is no more a political personality than Europe. India is a geographical term. It is no more a united nation than the Equator.
Speech at Royal Albert Hall, 18 March 1931, quoted in *Maxims and Reflections* (ed. Colin Coote, 1947)

15 So they go on in strange paradox, decided only to be undecided, resolved to be irresolute, adamant for drift, solid for fluidity, all-powerful to be impotent.
Speech to House of Commons, 12 November 1936, publ. in *The Speeches of Winston Churchill* (ed. David Cannadine, 1990). Referring to the government of STANLEY BALDWIN.

16 Dictators ride to and fro upon tigers which they dare not dismount. And the tigers are getting hungry.
Letter, 11 November 1937, publ. in *Step By Step* (1937). Churchill was quoting a 'Hindustani' proverb, though it is cited as Chinese in the *Concise Oxford Dictionary of Proverbs* (ed. John Simpson, 1982).

17 All is over. Silent, mournful, abandoned, broken, Czechoslovakia recedes into darkness ... We have sustained a defeat without a war.
Speech to House of Commons, 5 October 1938, publ. in *The Speeches of Winston Churchill* (ed. David Cannadine, 1990). On the German annexation of the Sudetenland, in Czechoslovakia.

18 I cannot forecast to you the action of Russia. It is a riddle wrapped in a mystery inside an enigma.
Radio broadcast, 1 October 1939, publ. in *Winston S. Churchill: His Complete Speeches, 1897–1963*, vol. 6 (ed. Robert Rhodes James, 1974). Churchill added: 'But perhaps there is a key ... Russian national interest.'

19 I have nothing to offer but blood, toil, tears and sweat.
Speech to House of Commons, 13 May 1940, ibid. Churchill's maiden speech as Prime Minister.

20 You ask, What is our policy? I will say: It is to wage war, by sea, land, and air, with all our might and with all the strength that God can give us: to wage war against a monstrous tyranny, never surpassed in the dark, lamentable catalogue of human crime. That is our policy. You ask, What is our aim? I can answer in one word: Victory – victory at all costs, victory in spite of all terror; victory, however long and hard the road may be; for without victory there is no survival.
Speech to House of Commons, 13 May 1940, ibid.

21 We shall go on to the end, we shall fight in France, we shall fight on the seas and oceans, we shall fight with growing confidence and growing strength in the air, we shall defend our island, whatever the cost may be, we shall fight on the beaches, we shall fight on the landing grounds, we shall fight in the fields and in the streets, we shall fight in the hills; we shall never surrender.
Speech to House of Commons, 4 June 1940, following the retreat from Dunkirk, ibid. Churchill continued, in what may have been a coded appeal to the USA: 'And even if, which I do not for a moment believe, this island or a large part of it were subjugated and starving, then our Empire beyond the seas, armed and guarded by the British Fleet, would carry on the struggle, until in God's good time the new world, with all its power and might, steps forth to the rescue and the liberation of the old.'

22 Let us therefore brace ourselves to our duties, and so bear ourselves that if the British Empire and its Commonwealth last for a thousand years, men will still say, 'This was their finest hour.'
Speech to House of Commons, 18 June 1940, announcing the fall of France and the start of the 'Battle of Britain', ibid. Two days later, a week after German troops had entered Paris, France concluded an armistice with Germany.

23 Never in the field of human conflict was so much owed by so many to so few.
Speech to House of Commons, 20 August 1940, ibid. Referring to the pilots who repulsed the German Luftwaffe during the Battle of Britain.

24 *Nous attendons l'invasion promise de longue date. Les poissons aussi.*
[We are waiting for the long-promised invasion. So are the fishes.]
Radio broadcast to the French people, 21 October 1940, publ. in *Into Battle* (1941)

25 Here is the answer which I will give to President Roosevelt ... Give us the tools and we will finish the job.
Radio broadcast, 9 February 1941, publ. in *Winston S. Churchill: His Complete Speeches, 1897–1963*, vol. 6 (ed. Robert Rhodes James, 1974). The Lend Lease Bill, which allowed the president to sell, lend or lease material to countries whose defence was important to the USA, was then being debated by Congress; it was signed a month later.

26 The British nation is unique in this respect. They are the only people who like to be told how bad things are, who like to be told the worst.
Speech to House of Commons, 10 June 1941, publ. in *Hansard*

27 If Hitler invaded hell I would make at least a favourable reference to the devil in the House of Commons.
Comment to Churchill's private secretary, John Colville, 21 June 1941, regarding British support for Communist Russia, as recounted in *The Second World War*, vol. 3 ('The Grand Alliance'), ch. 20 (1950)

28 All his usual formalites of perfidy were observed with scrupulous technique.
Radio broadcast, 21 June 1941. Of HITLER's invasion of Russia.

29 Do not let us speak of darker days; let us rather speak of sterner days. These are not dark days: these are great days – the greatest days our country has ever lived.
Speech at Harrow School, 29 October 1941, publ. in *Winston S. Churchill: His Complete Speeches, 1897–1963*, vol. 6 (ed. Robert Rhodes James, 1974)

30 When we consider the resources of the United States and the British Empire compared to those of Japan, when we remember those of China, which has so long and valiantly withstood invasion and when also we observe the Russian menace which hangs over Japan, it becomes still more difficult to reconcile Japanese action with prudence or even with sanity. What kind of a people do they think we are?
Speech to Joint Session of US Congress, 26 December 1941, ibid. Britain and the USA had declared war on Japan 8 December 1941, following the surprise attack on Pearl Harbor, Hawaii. Japanese forces rapidly advanced into US and British possessions in the Pacific and Asian mainland; Hong Kong surrendered on Christmas Day, 1941.

31 When I warned them [the French Government] that Britain would fight on alone whatever they did, their generals told their Prime Minister and his divided Cabinet, 'In three weeks England will have her neck wrung like a chicken.' Some chicken! Some neck!
Speech to Canadian Parliament, Ottawa, 30 December 1941, ibid.

32 Now this is not the end. It is not even the beginning of the end. But it is, perhaps, the end of the beginning.
Speech at Lord Mayor's Day Luncheon, Mansion House, 10 November 1942, publ. in *The End of the Beginning* (1943). Churchill was referring to the Eighth Army's victory against

Rommel at El Alamein. See quote 48, also CHARLES DE TALLEYRAND 1.

33 We mean to hold our own. I have not become the King's First Minister in order to preside over the liquidation of the British Empire.
Speech at Lord Mayor's Day Luncheon, Mansion House, 10 November 1942, ibid.

34 The problems of victory are more agreeable than the problems of defeat, but they are no less difficult.
Speech to House of Commons, 11 November 1942, publ. in *Hansard*

35 We make this wide encircling movement in the Mediterranean, having for its primary object the recovery of the command of that vital sea, but also having for its object the exposure of the under-belly of the Axis, especially Italy, to heavy attack.
Speech to House of Commons, 11 November 1942, ibid. The words are the origin of the phrase 'the soft under-belly of the Axis'.

36 National compulsory insurance for all classes for all purposes from the cradle to the grave.
Radio broadcast, 21 March 1943, publ. in *Complete Speeches*, vol. 7 (ed. Robert Rhodes James, 1974)

37 There is no finer investment for any community than putting milk into babies.
Radio broadcast, 21 March 1943, ibid.

38 The empires of the future are the empires of the mind.
Speech at Harvard, 6 September 1943, publ. in *Onwards to Victory* (1944)

39 We shape our buildings: thereafter they shape us.
Speech in London, 28 October 1943, on the rebuilding of the House of Commons after bomb damage, quoted in *Time* 12 September 1960

40 Neither the sure prevention of war, nor the continuous rise of world organization will be gained without what I have called the fraternal association of the English-speaking peoples. This means a special relationship between the British Commonwealth and Empire and the United States.
Speech at Westminster College, Fulton, Missouri, 5 March 1946, publ. in *Winston S. Churchill: His Complete Speeches, 1897–1963*, vol. 7 (ed. Robert Rhodes James, 1974)

41 A shadow has fallen upon the scenes so lately lighted by the Allied victory ... From Stettin in the Baltic to Trieste in the Adriatic, an iron curtain has descended across the Continent.
Speech at Westminster College, Fulton, Missouri, 5 March

1946, ibid. The phrase 'iron curtain' was not original: Churchill had also used the phrase in early 1946 in a telegram to President TRUMAN, and the words had earlier been used by JOSEPH GOEBBELS in the Nazi propaganda weekly *Das Reich* 23 February 1945: 'Should the German people lay down their arms, the Soviets ... would occupy all eastern and southeastern Europe together with the greater part of the Reich. Over all this territory, which with the Soviet Union included, would be of enormous extent, an iron curtain [*ein eiserner Vorhang*] would at once descend.' In fact 'iron curtain' had been used with reference to Communism from 1920 or earlier, while the geographical area from Stettin to Trieste had already been defined by FRIEDRICH ENGELS in an article for the *New York Daily Tribune* in 1853: 'It would appear that the natural frontier of Russia runs from Dantzic or perhaps Stettin to Trieste.'

42 No one pretends that democracy is perfect or all-wise. Indeed, it has been said that democracy is the worst form of Government except all those other forms that have been tried from time to time.
Speech to House of Commons, 11 November 1947, publ. in *Hansard*

43 The English never draw a line without blurring it.
Speech to House of Commons, 16 November 1948, ibid.

44 Moral of the Work. In war: resolution. In defeat: defiance. In victory: magnanimity. In peace: goodwill.
Epigraph in each volume of *The Second World War* (1948–54). Churchill had first conceived his 'moral' shortly after the end of the First World War.

45 I felt as if I were walking with destiny, and that all my past life had been but a preparation for this hour and this trial. Eleven years in the political wilderness had freed me from ordinary Party antagonisms. My warnings over the last six years had been so numerous, so detailed, and were now so terribly vindicated, that no one could gainsay me. I could not be reproached either for making the war or with want of preparation for it. I thought I knew a good deal about it all, and I was sure I should not fail. Therefore, although impatient for the morning, I slept soundly and had no need for cheering dreams. Facts are better than dreams.
The Second World War, vol. 1 ('The Gathering Storm'), bk 2, ch. 17 (1948). On assuming the office of prime minister in 1940.

46 Thus, then, on the night of the tenth of May, at the outset of this mighty battle, I acquired the chief power in the State, which henceforth I wielded in ever-growing measure for five years and three

months of world war, at the end of which time, all our enemies having surrendered unconditionally or being about to do so, I was immediately dismissed by the British electorate from all further conduct of their affairs.
Ibid., vol. 1, bk 2, ch. 17. Though re-elected prime minister in 1951, Churchill never forgot what he considered a slight by the electorate.

47 The candle in that great turnip has gone out.
Quoted in journal entry, 17 August 1950, publ. in *Diaries and Letters 1945–62* (1968) by HAROLD NICOLSON. Referring to STANLEY BALDWIN, as related by Patrick Leigh Fermor.

48 It may almost be said, 'Before Alamein we never had a victory. After Alamein we never had a defeat.'
The Second World War, vol. 4, ch. 33 (1951)

49 Without tradition, art is a flock of sheep without a shepherd. Without innovation, it is a corpse.
Address to Royal Academy of Arts, quoted in *Time* 11 May 1954

50 Better to jaw-jaw than to war-war.
Remark at the White House, 26 June 1954, quoted in the *New York Times* 27 June 1954. The words were reported with slight variations in different newspapers, and also within the same edition of the *New York Times*.

51 He is a modest little man who has a good deal to be modest about.
Quoted in the *Chicago Sunday Tribune Magazine of Books* 27 June 1954. Referring to CLEMENT ATTLEE.

52 A fanatic is one who can't change his mind and won't change the subject.
Quoted in the *New York Times* 5 July 1954

53 I am prepared to meet my Maker. Whether my Maker is prepared for the great ordeal of meeting me is another matter.
Remark on his seventy-fifth birthday, 30 November 1951, quoted in *Winston Churchill: His Wit and Wisdom*

54 I have never accepted what many people have kindly said – namely, that I inspired the nation ... It was the nation and the race dwelling all round the globe that had the lion's heart. I had the luck to be called upon to give the roar. I also hope that I sometimes suggested to the lion the right place to use his claws.
Speech at Westminster Hall, 30 November 1954, quoted in *The Times* 1 December 1954

55 This is the sort of English up with which I will not put.
Quoted in *The Complete Plain Words*, 'The Handling of Words' by Ernest Gowers (1954). Said to be a marginal comment by

Churchill against a sentence that clumsily avoided ending with a preposition.

56 Dead birds don't fall out of nests.

Response to a colleague who told him his flies were open, quoted in *The Lyttelton–Hart-Davis Letters*, vol. 2 (ed. Rupert Hart-Davis, 1979)

57 In defeat unbeatable: in victory unbearable.

Quoted in *Ambrosia and Small Beer*, ch. 5 (1964) by Edward Marsh. Referring to VISCOUNT MONTGOMERY.

58 I have taken more out of alcohol than alcohol has taken out of me.

Quoted in *By Quentin Reynolds*, ch. 11 (1964) by Quentin Reynolds

59 The ability to foretell what is going to happen tomorrow, next week, next month, and next year. And to have the ability afterwards to explain why it didn't happen.

Quoted in *The Churchill Wit* (1965) by Bill Adler. Describing the qualifications desirable in a prospective politician.

60 A sheep in sheep's clothing.

Quoted in *The Way the Wind Blows*, ch. 6 (1976) by Lord Home. Said to refer to CLEMENT ATTLEE, though Churchill is later said to have claimed he had used the words to describe Labour Prime Minister Ramsay MacDonald. The phrase had also been used by the critic and essayist Sir Edmund Gosse of the 'woolly-bearded poet' Sturge Moore, quoted in *Under the Bridge* (1943) by Ferris Greenslet.

61 An empty taxi arrived at 10 Downing Street, and when the door was opened Attlee got out.

Attributed. Kenneth Harris writes (in *Attlee*, ch. 16, sect. 2, 1982) that Churchill's private secretary John Colville repeated this remark to Churchill, who, clearly discomfited and 'after an awful pause', replied: 'Mr Attlee is an honourable and gallant gentleman, and a faithful colleague who served his country well at the time of her greatest need. I should be obliged if you would make it clear whenever an occasion arises that I would never make such a remark about him, and that I strongly disapprove of anybody who does.' However, when Colville suggested that ATTLEE be invited to join Churchill's dining club, Churchill replied, 'I think not. He is an admirable character, but not a man with whom it is agreeable to dine.'

Galeazzo Ciano

(1903–44)

Italian politician

The Conte di Cortelazzo was son-in-law of MUSSOLINI and a leading Fascist. Minister of Foreign Affairs from 1936. He openly opposed Italy's alliance with Germany and was later tried for treason by the pro-Mussolini faction and executed.

1 Victory has a hundred fathers but defeat is an orphan.

Journal entry, 9 September 1942, publ. in *Diario 1939–1943* (1946). JOHN F. KENNEDY is said to have made the same remark in the wake of the Bay of Pigs invasion in April 1961. The original Italian (*nessuno vuole riconoscere l'insuccesso*) is more literally translated: 'No one wants to recognize failure.'

Colley Cibber

(1671–1757)

English actor-manager, playwright and poet

Closely associated with the Theatre Royal in London's Drury Lane, he was poet laureate for twenty-seven years and generally considered one of the worst incumbents of that office. He was depicted as king of the Dunces by ALEXANDER POPE in The Dunciad.

1 You know, one had as good be out of the world, as out of the fashion.

Love's Last Shift, Act 2, Sc. 1 (1696). Spoken by Narcissa. The proverb has been dated back to 1639.

2 Prithee don't screw your wit beyond the compass of good manners.

Narcissa, ibid., Act 2, Sc. 1

3 Possession is eleven points in the law.

Woman's Wit, Act 1 (1697). Spoken by Young Rakish.

4 Our hours in love have wings; in absence, crutches.

Xerxes, Act 4, Sc. 3 (1699). Spoken by Tamira.

5 Off with his head – so much for Buckingham.

Richard III, Act 4, Sc. 3 (adapted from Shakespeare, 1700). Spoken by Richard. See SHAKESPEARE: RICHARD III 11.

6 Tea! Thou soft, thou sober, sage, and venerable liquid, thou innocent pretence for bringing the wicked of both sexes together in a morning; thou female tongue-running, smile-smoothing, heart-opening, wink-tipping cordial, to whose glorious insipidity I owe the happiest moment of my life, let me fall prostrate thus, and . . . adore thee.

The Lady's Last Stake, Act 1, Sc. 1 (1708). Spoken by Lord George, whose 'happiest moment' was sipping tea in the company of Lady Gentle.

7 Thou strange piece of wild nature!

Lord Wronglove to Lord George, ibid., Act 1, Sc. 1

Marcus Tullius Cicero
(106–43 BC)
Roman orator and philosopher

Having distinguished himself in the case against the corrupt Verres, he became consul in 64 BC and succeeded in foiling the conspiracy by Catiline. His most famous works include De Oratore *(55 BC), on oratory, and the* Philippics *(43 BC), speeches against Antony which led to Cicero's downfall and murder.*

1 *Civis Romanus sum.*
[I am a Roman citizen.]
In Verrem, Speech 5, sect. 147 (70 BC)

2 How long, Catiline, will you abuse our patience?
In Catilinam, Speech 1, sect. 1 (63 BC). Opening words of speech.

3 *O tempora! O mores!*
[Oh the times! Oh the customs!]
Ibid., Speech 1, sect. 1

4 *O fortunatam natam me consule Romam!*
[Happy Rome, born in my consulship!]
De Consulatu Suo (62–60 BC). Quoted by JUVENAL in *Satires*, bk 10, l. 122, as an example of Cicero's lack of poetic style.

5 It is that which is far the best and the most desirable for all who are sound and good and prosperous; it is 'Peace with Honour' [*cum dignitate otium*].
Pro Publio Sestio, sect. 98 (56 BC). Translators have disagreed over the interpretation of the words '*cum dignitate otium*'.

6 I prefer tongue-tied knowledge to ignorant loquacity.
De Oratore, bk 3, sect. 142 (55 BC)

7 Laws are silent in times of war.
Pro Milone, sect. 11 (52 BC)

8 *Cui bono?*
[To whose good?]
Ibid., sect. 32. Quoting the tribune L. Cassius Longinus, when urging the jury how to vote. The phrase is sometimes misapplied to mean 'what's the good?'

9 Since an intelligence common to us all makes things known to us and formulates them in our minds, honorable actions are ascribed by us to virtue, and dishonorable actions to vice; and only a madman would conclude that these judgments are matters of opinion, and not fixed by nature.
De Legibus, bk 1, sect. 45 (52–45 BC)

10 *Salus populi suprema lex esto.*
[Let the good of the people be the highest law.]
Ibid., bk 3, sect. 8

11 There were poets before Homer.
Brutus, sect. 71 (46 BC)

12 There is nothing so absurd but some philosopher has said it.
De Divinatione, bk 2, sect. 119 (45 BC)

13 *Summum bonum.*
[The highest good.]
De Officiis, bk 1, sect. 5 (45 BC)

14 Justice consists in doing no injury to men; decency in giving them no offence.
Ibid., bk 1, sect. 99

15 I would rather be wrong with Plato ... than be right with these men.
Tusculanae Disputationes, bk 1, sect. 39 (45 BC). Referring to the Pythagoreans.

16 I never heard of an old man forgetting where he had buried his money! Old people remember what interests them: the dates fixed for their lawsuits, and the names of their debtors and creditors.
De Senectute, sect. 20 (44 BC)

17 No one is so old as to think he cannot live one more year.
Ibid., sect. 24

18 The sinews of war, a limitless supply of money.
Fifth Philippic, ch. 2, sect. 5 (44–43 BC)

E. M. Cioran
(1911–95)
Romanian-born author and philosopher

Emil Mihai Cioran. The 'last of the moralists' lived in Paris from 1937 onwards, where he found a congenial home for his ideas, which he regarded as both a continuation and negation of Nietzsche's philosophy.

1 Reason is a whore, surviving by simulation, versatility, and shamelessness.
The Temptation to Exist, 'Rages and Resignations: Luther' (1956)

2 Much more than our other needs and endeavours, it is sexuality that puts us on an even footing with our kind: the more we practise it, the more we become like everyone else: it is in the performance of a reputedly bestial function that we prove our status as citizens: nothing is more *public* than the sexual act.
Ibid.,'Rages and Resignations: Gogol'

3 We derive our vitality from our store of madness.
Ibid., 'The Temptation to Exist'

4 A civilization is destroyed only when its gods are destroyed.
Le Mauvais démiurge, 'The New Gods' (1969; *The New Gods*)

5 There is no means of *proving* it is preferable to be than not to be.
Ibid., 'Strangled Thoughts', sect. 1

6 What we want is not freedom but its appearances. It is for these simulacra that man has always striven. And since freedom, as has been said, is no more than a *sensation*, what difference is there between being free and believing ourselves free?
Ibid., sect. 3

7 We would not be interested in human beings if we did not have the hope of someday meeting someone worse off than ourselves.
Ibid., sect. 3

8 It is not worth the bother of killing yourself, since you always kill yourself *too late*.
The Trouble with Being Born, ch. 2 (1973)

9 Progress is the injustice each generation commits with regard to its predecessors.
Ibid., ch. 8

10 One does not inhabit a country; one inhabits a language. That is our country, our fatherland – and no other.
Anathemas and Admirations, 'On the Verge of Existence' (1986). This recalls a remark made by ALBERT CAMUS in his *Notebooks*: 'Yes, I have a fatherland: the French language.'

11 The fact that life has no meaning is a reason to live – moreover, the only one.
Ibid., 'Fractures'

Bob Clampett
(1913–84)
US animator

He began animating for the Warner Brothers' Looney Tunes series in the early 1930s and went on to direct cartoons such as the surreal Porky in Wackyland *(1938) and the slapstick* Big Snooze *(1946).*

1 I tawt I taw a puddy tat a-cweepin' up on me.
Tweety, in *Looney Tunes/Merrie Melodies* (Warner Brothers cartoon, 1944–60s). Created by Bob Clampett, voiced by Mel Blanc, the little yellow canary first appeared in the Warners' *Merrie Melodies* cartoon *Birdy and the Beast* (1944), soon to be chased by the lisping cat Sylvester, whose own favourite line was 'Suffering Succotash!'

John Clare
(1793–1864)
English poet

He was hailed as a 'peasant poet' following the publication of Poems Descriptive of Rural Life and Scenery *(1820). Beset by poor health and mental illness, he entered Northampton Asylum in 1837, where he spent the rest of his life.*

1 He falls as dead and kicked by boys and men
Then starts and grins and drives the crowd again
Till kicked and torn and beaten out he lies
And leaves his hold and cackles, groans and dies.
'Badger', written *c.* 1837, publ. in *Selected Poems and Prose* (ed. Geoffrey Summerfield, 1967). Closing lines of sonnet sequence, originally untitled.

2 I am – yet what I am, none cares or knows;
My friends forsake me like a memory lost:
I am the self-consumer of my woes.
'I Am', written 1848, ibid. Opening lines of poem.

3 I long for scenes where man has never trod
A place where woman never smiled or wept
There to abide with my Creator God
And sleep as I in childhood sweetly slept,
Untroubling and untroubled where I lie
The grass below, above, the vaulted sky.
'I Am', ibid. Closing lines of poem.

Edward Hyde, Earl of Clarendon
(1609–74)
English statesman and historian

A lawyer, he headed the Royalist party in the House of Commons until the outbreak of the Civil War, and became Lord Chancellor in 1658. His daughter secretly married James, Duke of York, later James II.

1 He had a head to contrive, a tongue to persuade, and a hand to execute any mischief.
The History of the Rebellion and Civil Wars in England, vol. 3, bk 7, sect. 84 (1704). Referring to the parliamentarian John Hampden.

Alan Clark
(1928–99)
British politician and historian

Notorious for his rakish womanizing, he was the son of KENNETH CLARK, *a Conservative MP, and Minister of State for Defence (1989–92). He was also noted as a military historian* (Donkeys, *1961, and* Aces High, *1973) and diarist. See also* (SIR) ROBERT ARMSTRONG 1.

1 Most of them are buffers, or demi-buffers, or *buffers-aspirant*. They amount to nothing.
Journal entry, 18 November 1986, publ. in *Diaries* (1993). Referring to backbenchers in the House of Commons.

2 There are no true friends in politics. We are all sharks circling, and waiting, for traces of blood to appear in the water.
Journal entry, 30 November 1990, publ. ibid. Clark was musing on the 'descending parabola' of his political career.

3 We all know the principal preoccupation of politicians is how they can do down their colleagues so that they can advance their own careers.
Interview with John Humphrys in *On the Ropes*, BBC Radio 4, 16 May 1995. Clark was explaining how the main regret of his political career was not destabilizing his boss at the Ministry of Defence, Tom King.

4 Dear boy, I can hardly close the door.
Quoted in the *Observer* 27 December 1998. On being asked if he had any 'skeletons in his cupboard'.

Kenneth (Lord) Clark
(1903–83)
British art historian

An expert on the Italian Renaissance, he was director of the National Gallery (1934–45), wrote popular works on art and presented the TV series based on his book Civilisation *(1969).*

1 Opera, next to Gothic architecture, is one of the strangest inventions of Western man. It could not have been foreseen by any logical process.
Civilisation, ch. 9 (1969)

Karl von Clausewitz
(1780–1831)
Prussian soldier and strategist

He was a chief of staff in the army during the Waterloo campaign and was appointed Director of the Prussian Army School. His influential treatise On War *(1833) advocated a concept of total war.*

1 War is nothing but the continuation of policy with other means.
Vom Kriege, Author's note (1833; *On War*). The notion is expressed in variant forms in different parts of the book.

Henry Clay
(1777–1852)
US statesman

Representative for Kentucky in Congress from 1811, and senator 1831–42 and 1849–52, he advocated war against Britain in 1812

and earned the soubriquets 'The Great Pacificator' and 'The Great Compromiser' for his measures designed to reconcile the northern and southern states.

1 Sir, if you wish to avoid foreign collision you had better abandon the ocean.
Speech to the House of Representatives, 22 January 1812, publ. in *The Life, Correspondence and Speeches of Henry Clay*, vol. 5 (ed. Calvin Colton, 1864)

2 I know no allegiance to any one section – East, North, West, or South. And I know ... of but two sovereignties to whom I owe allegiance – the one the Union, and the other my own State.
Speech to the Senate, 14 February 1850, ibid., vol. 6 (ed. Calvin Colton, 1864)

3 As for me, I would rather be right than be President.
Quoted by Representative William Springer, publ. in *The Life of Thomas Brackett Reed*, ch. 21 (1914) by Samuel W. McCall. Clay was twice an unsuccessful candidate for president, in 1832 and 1844.

Eldridge Cleaver
(1935–98)
US black leader and author

A follower of MALCOLM X, *he was Minister of Information for the Black Panthers and ran the party's headquarters in Algiers, where he had fled after a shoot-out in 1968. He returned to New York in 1975, a born-again Christian.*

1 I, for one, do not think homosexuality is the latest advance over heterosexuality in the scale of human evolution. Homosexuality is a sickness, just as are baby-rape or wanting to become head of General Motors.
Soul on Ice, pt 2, 'Notes on a Native Son' (1968)

2 Every time I embrace a black woman I'm embracing slavery, and when I put my arms around a white woman, well, I'm hugging freedom. The white man forbade me to have the white woman on pain of death ... I will not be free until the day I can have a white woman in my bed.
Lazarus, ibid., 'The Allegory of the Black Eunuchs'

3 It's been said that today, you're part of the solution or you're part of the problem. There is no more middle ground.
'Stanford Speech', San Francisco, 1 October 1968, publ. in *Post Prison Writings and Speeches* (ed. Robert Scheer, 1969)

John Cleese
(b. 1939)
British comic actor and author

He made his name in Monty Python's Flying Circus (1969–74) and subsequently co-wrote and starred in Fawlty Towers (1975, 1979) and the film A Fish Called Wanda (1988). See also MONTY PYTHON'S FLYING CIRCUS.

1 Don't mention the war.
Fawlty Towers, 'The Germans' (TV series, 1975, co-written with Connie Booth). Basil Fawlty, on the impending arrival of German guests.

2 So Harry says, 'You don't like me any more. Why not?' And he says, 'Because you've got so terribly pretentious.' And Harry says, 'Pretentious? *Moi?*'
Mr Johnson, chatting to Sybil, ibid., 'The Psychiatrist' (1979)

3 He's from Barcelona.
Basil or Sybil apologizing for Manuel, ibid. (various episodes). Manuel's most quoted remark is 'Qué?'.

Georges Clemenceau
(1841–1929)
French statesman

Known as 'The Tiger', he held two terms as premier (1906–9, 1917–20), and presided at the peace talks in Versailles (1919). He founded several journals including L'Aurore (1897).

1 War is too important a matter to be left to the military.
Quoted in *Soixante années d'histoire française,* 'Clemenceau' (1886) by G. Suarez. Also attributed to Aristide Briand and TALLEYRAND.

2 My home policy: I wage war; my foreign policy: I wage war. All the time I wage war! The Russians betray us, I continue to wage war. Rumania is forced to capitulate: I continue to wage war, and I will continue to the very end.
Speech to Chamber of Deputies, 8 March 1918, publ. in *Discours de guerre* (1968). Clemenceau was about to confront the Ludendorff offensive of March–July 1918, which pushed deep into the Allied lines and was only halted when Foch's counter-offensive eventually drove the German army back behind its own border and led to the armistice.

3 Yes, we have won the war, and not without difficulty. But now we must win the peace, and perhaps that will be harder.
Remark to General J. H. H. Mordacq, 11 November 1918 (Armistice Day), quoted in *The Tiger,* ch. 16 (1976). Clemenceau expressed the idea on different occasions, and it has also been quoted in a simplified form from a speech at Verdun, 20 July 1919: 'It is easier to make war than to make peace.'

4 America is the only nation in history which miraculously has gone directly from barbarism to degeneration without the usual interval of civilization.
Attributed, in the *Saturday Review of Literature* 1 December 1945

Grover Cleveland
(1837–1908)
US politician and president

His independence of the Democratic party machine gained him a reputation for integrity. The only US President to serve two non-consecutive terms of office, he pursued moderate reform in his first term (1885–9), but struggled against economic depression during his second term (1893–7).

1 There is no calamity which a great nation can invite which equals that which follows a supine submission to wrong and injustice, and the consequent loss of national self-respect and honor, beneath which are shielded and defended a people's safety and greatness.
Speech to Congress, 17 December 1895, publ. in *Grover Cleveland: a Study in Courage,* ch. 34, sect. 3 (1932, rev. 1966) by Allan Nevins. Referring to the Venezuelan Boundary Dispute with Great Britain.

Harlan Cleveland
(b. 1918)
US government official and diplomat

He was Assistant Secretary for International Organization Affairs under JOHN F. KENNEDY (1961–5) and Ambassador to NATO (1965–9).

1 The revolution of rising expectations.
'Reflections on the Revolution of Rising Expectations', speech at Colgate University, 1949, quoted in *The New Language of Politics* (1972) by William Safire. The phrase was echoed in the title of a later speech that Cleveland delivered to the UN in 1954: 'The Evolution of Rising Responsibilities'.

Jimmy Cliff
(b. 1948)
Jamaican reggae singer

Originally James Chambers. The first reggae superstar, he had worldwide success with the song 'Wonderful World, Beautiful People' (1969) and in the film The Harder They Come (1972).

1 So as sure as the sun will shine
I'm going to get my share now, what's mine
And then the harder they come, the harder they fall

One and all.
'The Harder They Come' (song, 1970) written and performed by Cliff in *The Harder They Come* (film, 1972), in which he starred as Ivan, a small-time hood. The song was a hit for Desmond Dekker in 1970.

2 Many rivers to cross
But I can't seem to find my way over.
'Many Rivers to Cross' (song, 1970), ibid.

Bill Clinton
(b. 1946)
US politician and president

Democratic Governor of Arkansas 1979–81 and 1983–92, he was President 1993–2001. Though he played a significant role in the 1995 Bosnian settlement, his reputation was damaged by the 'Zippergate' sex scandal, and he narrowly escaped impeachment in 1998. See HENRY KISSINGER 8.

1 When I was in England I experimented with marijuana a time or two, and I didn't like it. I didn't inhale.
Remark during TV debate with Jerry Brown, a rival candidate for the Democratic Party nomination, quoted in the *New York Times* 30 March 1992. Under close questioning to ascertain whether the two men had ever broken state, federal or international laws, Clinton admitted his misdemeanour while a Rhodes Scholar at Oxford University.

2 Indeed I did have a relationship with Ms Lewinsky that was not appropriate. In fact it was wrong. It constituted a critical lapse in judgment and a personal failure on my part for which I am solely and completely responsible . . . Even presidents have private lives.
Broadcast to the nation, 17 August 1998, publ. in the *Daily Telegraph* 19 August 1998. See also MONICA LEWINSKY 1

3 It depends upon what the meaning of the word 'is' means. If 'is' means is, and never has been, that's one thing. If it means, there is none, that was a completely true statement.
Answer to grand jury, broadcast on CNN, 21 September 1998. Clinton was attempting to justify his earlier statement, 'There is no sex of any kind, in any manner, shape or form, with Ms Lewinsky.'

Hillary Clinton
(b. 1947)
US lawyer and First Lady

Wife of BILL CLINTON, *she became the first First Lady to be elected to the Senate (2000).*

1 It takes a village to raise a child.
Speech at Democratic National Convention, Chicago, 26 August 1996. The African proverb was adopted by Hillary Clinton as the motto for her drive to encourage community awareness. Her book, *It Takes a Village: And Other Lessons Children Teach Us* (1996), which discusses family issues and social policies, topped the *New York Times* non-fiction bestseller list in its first week of publication.

2 The great story here . . . is this vast right-wing conspiracy that has been conspiring against my husband since the day he announced for president.
NBC Today, 27 January 1998. On 'Zippergate' and the accusations of adultery and perjury made against BILL CLINTON.

Robert Clive
(1725–74)
British soldier and colonial administrator

Baron Clive of Plassey. In the service of the East India Company, he won victories against French and Indian forces, culminating in the Battle of Plassey (1757), which gave him control over Bengal. In 1767, he faced corruption charges in England, committing suicide soon after his eventual acquittal.

1 It appears I am destined for something; I will live.
Attributed comment in Madras, 1744, after the pistol with which he intended to shoot himself would not fire on two attempts. Thirty years later, at the end of a glorious career, he succeeded in taking his life by stabbing himself.

2 My God, Mr Chairman, at this moment I stand astonished at my own moderation!
Speech to a select committee of the House of Commons, March 1773, quoted in *Life of Robert, First Lord Clive*, ch. 29 (1848) by G. R. Glieg. Clive was defending himself against charges of embezzlement.

Arthur Hugh Clough
(1819–61)
English poet

His verse, most of which was published posthumously, expressed the moral concerns and spiritual doubts of the mid-Victorian era. His early death was the result of contracting malaria in Italy, and he was the subject of the elegy 'Thyrsis' by MATTHEW ARNOLD.

1 Grace is given of God, but knowledge is bought in the market.
The Bothie of Tober-na-Vuolich, pt 4, l. 159 (1848)

2 The world that we live in,
Whithersoever we turn, still is the same narrow crib;
'Tis but to prove limitation, and measure a cord, that we travel;

Let who would 'scape and be free go to his
  chamber and think;
'Tis but to change idle fancies for memories
  wilfully falser;
''Tis but to go and have been.' – Come, little bark!
  let us go.
'Amours de Voyage', canto 1, publ. in *Poems* (1862)

3 Thou shalt not kill; but need'st not strive
Officiously to keep alive.
'The Latest Decalogue', publ. in *Poems, with a Memoir* (1862)

4 Do not adultery commit;
Advantage rarely comes of it.
'The Latest Decalogue', ibid.

5 Thou shalt not covet; but tradition
Approves all forms of competition.
'The Latest Decalogue', ibid.

6 Say not the struggle nought availeth
The labour and the wounds are vain,
The enemy faints not, nor faileth,
And as things have been, things remain.
'Say not the struggle nought availeth', st. 1, ibid.

7 If hopes were dupes, fears may be liars.
'Say not the struggle nought availeth', st. 2, ibid.

8 And almost every one when age,
Disease, or sorrows strike him,
Inclines to think there is a God,
Or something very like Him.
Dipsychus, Sc. 6, ll. 182–5 (1865). Spoken by Spirit.

Kurt Cobain
(1967–94)
US rock musician

*He was lead singer, guitarist and writer with Nirvana, the
leading and most influential 'grunge' band of the 1990s. Beset
with drugs problems, he shot himself at his home in Seattle.*

1 I found it hard, it was hard to find,
Oh well, whatever, never mind.
'Smells Like Teen Spirit' (song) on the album *Nevermind* (1991)
by Nirvana

2 Teenage angst has paid off well,
Now I'm bored and old.
'Serve the Servants' (song) on the album *In Utero* (1993) by
Nirvana

William Cobbett
(1762–1835)
English journalist and reformer

*A champion of traditional agrarian values, he campaigned
against injustice and corrupt commercial interests in his journal, the* Political Register *(1802–35). He was elected to Parliament in 1832. His most famous book,* Rural Rides *(1830),
consists of observations from his many tours of the
countryside.*

1 The very hirelings of the press, whose trade it is
to buoy up the spirits of the people . . . have uttered
falsehoods so long, they have played off so many
tricks, that their budget seems, at last, to be quite
empty.
'The Last Ten Years', publ. in the *Political Register* 4 January
1812

2 Nouns of number, or multitude, such as *Mob,
Parliament, Rabble, House of Commons, Regiment,
Court of King's Bench, Den of Thieves*, and the like.
English Grammar, Letter 17 (1817)

3 It is no small mischief to a boy, that many of
the best years of his life should be devoted to the
learning of what can never be of any real use to
any human being. His mind is necessarily rendered
frivolous and superficial by the long habit of attach-
ing importance to *words* instead of *things*; to *sound*
instead of sense.
'To Mr Benbow' (1817), repr. in *The Opinions of William Cobbett*, ch. 16 (ed. G. D. H. and Margaret Cole, 1944)

4 Women are a sisterhood. They make common
cause in behalf of the sex; and, indeed, this is natural
enough, when we consider the vast power that the
law gives us over them.
Advice to Young Men and to Young Women, Letter 4 ('To a
Husband') (1829)

5 Perhaps there are none more lazy, or more truly
ignorant, than your everlasting readers.
Ibid., Letter 5 ('To a Father'). Cobbett added: 'With regard to
young women, everlasting book-reading is absolutely a *vice*.'

Richard Cobden
(1804–65)
English politician

*As one of the foremost advocates of free trade in Britain, he
led, from 1838, the Anti-Corn-Law League to a successful repeal
of the Corn Laws in 1846.*

1 I can prove that we advocate nothing but what is
agreeable to the highest behests of Christianity. To

buy in the cheapest market, and sell in the dearest.
Speech to the House of Commons, 27 February, 1846, publ. in *Speeches on Questions of Public Policy by Richard Cobden, MP*, vol. 1, Speech 21 (ed. John Bright and James E. Thorold Rogers, 1870). Referring to the Corn Laws, which were repealed three months later.

2 If you want to give a guarantee for peace, and, as I believe, the surest guarantee for progress and freedom, lay down this principle, and act on it, that no foreign state has a right by force to interfere with the domestic concerns of another state, even to confer a benefit on it, with its own consent.
Speech to House of Commons, 28 June 1850, ibid., vol. 2, Speech 10

3 The progress of freedom depends more upon the maintenance of peace, the spread of commerce, and the diffusion of education, than upon the labours of cabinets or foreign offices.
Speech to House of Commons, 28 June 1850, ibid.

4 I believe it has been said that one copy of *The Times* contains more useful information than the whole of the historical works of Thucydides.
Speech at Manchester Athenaeum, 1850, attributed

Eddie Cochran
(1938–60)
US rock musician

One of the giants of rock 'n' roll, he recorded the classics 'C'mon Everybody' (1959) and 'Three Steps to Heaven' (1960). He was killed in a car accident while on a British tour.

1 There ain't no cure for the summertime blues.
'Summertime Blues' (song, 1958, co-written with Cochran's manager, Jerry Capeheart) on the album *Swinging To My Baby* (1960)

Claud Cockburn
(1904–81)
British author and journalist

As a journalist he was called by MALCOLM MUGGERIDGE *'the most perfect specimen of the genus ever to exist'. He was correspondent for the* Daily Worker *and founded the left-wing newsletter* The Week *(1933).*

1 Small earthquake in Chile. Not many dead.
Suggestion for a headline in *The Times* c. 1929, quoted in *In Time of Trouble*, ch. 10 (1956). As Cockburn (then working as a sub-editor on the paper) explained: 'For further entertainment in the long evenings, someone had invented a game – a competition with a small prize for the winner – to see who could write the dullest headline. It had to be a genuine headline, that is to say one which was actually printed in the next morning's newspaper. I won it only once with a headline which announced: "Small Earthquake in Chile. Not many dead." ' There is no trace of this headline having been printed.

Jarvis Cocker
(b. 1963)
British rock musician

With his wry, down-to-earth humour, he led his band Pulp to success in the 1990s with the albums His 'N' Hers *(1994) and* Different Class *(1995).*

1 You'll never live like common people,
you'll never do what common people do,
you'll never fail like common people,
you'll never watch your life slide out of view
and dance and drink and screw
because there's nothing else to do.
'Common People' (song) on the album *Different Class* (1995) by Pulp

2 Is this the way they say the future's meant to feel?
Or just 20,000 people standing in a field.
And I don't quite understand just what this feeling is.
But that's okay 'cos we're all sorted out for E's & wizz.
'Sorted for E's & Wizz', ibid.

Jean Cocteau
(1889–1963)
French author and film-maker

Inspired by Diaghilev's phrase 'Étonne-moi', he was in the forefront of most of the avant-garde movements of the first half of the 20th century, working as a poet, librettist, novelist, actor, film director, critic and painter.

1 Art is science made clear.
'Le Coq et l'Arlequin' (1918), later publ. in *Le Rappel à l'ordre* (1926), repr. in *Collected Works*, vol. 9 (1950)

2 Tact in audacity consists in knowing how far we may go too far.
'Le Coq et l'Arlequin', ibid.

3 The worst tragedy for a poet is to be admired through being misunderstood.
'Le Coq et l'Arlequin', ibid.

4 What the public criticizes in you, cultivate. It is you.
'Le Coq et l'Arlequin', ibid.

5 If it has to choose who is to be crucified, the crowd will always save Barabbas.

'Le Coq et l'Arlequin', ibid. Barabbas was the thief and insurrectionary leader reprieved at Christ's crucifixion, following the custom at Passover (Matthew 27).

6 The Louvre is like the morgue; one goes there to identify one's friends.

'Le Secret professionnel' (1922), later publ. in *Le Rappel à l'ordre* (1926), repr. ibid.

7 I am a lie who always speaks the truth.

Opéra, 'Le Paquet rouge' (1925). Similarly, in his *Journals* (1956), Cocteau wrote, 'The matters I relate/Are true lies.'

8 Living is a horizontal fall.

Opium (1930)

9 Victor Hugo was a madman who believed himself to be Victor Hugo.

Ibid. Quoting himself from a previous occasion.

10 Poetry is indispensable – if I only knew what for.

Quoted in *The Necessity of Art*, ch. 1 (1959) by ERNST FISCHER

11 A film is a petrified fountain of thought.

Esquire February 1961

George M. Cohan
(1878–1942)
US songwriter, playwright and producer

Steeped in vaudeville and theatre from an early age, he is credited with creating the first American musical, Little Johnny Jones, *in 1903. The musical* Yankee Doodle Dandy *(1942), titled after one of his songs, was the story of his life, with* JAMES CAGNEY *in the lead role.*

1 I'm a Yankee Doodle Dandy,
A Yankee Doodle do or die;
A real live nephew of my Uncle Sam's,
Born on the fourth of July.

'Yankee Doodle Dandy' (song), in *Little Johnny Jones* (show, 1904). Cohan claimed his own birthday was 4 July, though sceptics have suggested it was actually 3 July.

2 Give my regards to Broadway,
Remember me to Herald Square,
Tell all the gang at Forty-second Street
That I will soon be there.

'Give my Regards to Broadway' (song), ibid. The song was one of a series of compositions on the theme of Broadway, though at the time of writing, Cohan was just twenty-six, and very much an outsider. In 1959, a statue of him was erected on Broadway.

3 Over there, over there,
Send the word, send the word over there

That the Yanks are coming, the Yanks are coming,
The drums rum-tumming everywhere.
So prepare, say a prayer,
Send the word, send the word to beware.
We'll be over, we're coming over
And we won't come back till it's over, over there.

'Over There' (song, 1917). The song quickly became established as an upbeat patriotic classic, called by WOODROW WILSON 'a genuine inspiration to all American manhood'.

Leonard Cohen
(b. 1934)
Canadian singer, poet and novelist

The 'Bard of the Bedsits' has published volumes of poetry since 1956, releasing the first of his many sombre albums, Songs of Leonard Cohen, *in 1967. He has published two novels:* The Favourite Game *(1963) and* Beautiful Losers *(1966).*

1 Let judges secretly despair of justice: their verdicts will be more acute. Let generals secretly despair of triumph; killing will be defamed. Let priests secretly despair of faith: their compassion will be true.

The Spice-Box Of Earth, 'Lines From My Grandfather's Journal' (1961)

2 History is a needle
for putting men asleep
anointed with the poison
of all they want to keep.

'On Hearing A Name Long Unspoken', st. 3, publ. in *Flowers For Hitler* (1964)

3 I don't consider myself a pessimist at all. I think of a pessimist as someone who is waiting for it to rain. And I feel completely soaked to the skin.

Quoted in the *Independent on Sunday* 2 May 1993

(Sir) Edward Coke
(1552–1634)
English jurist

He was the brutal prosecutor of the earls of Essex and Southampton and Sir WALTER RALEGH, *but later became a staunch defender of the common law against the royal prerogative, and was largely responsible for drafting the Petition of Right in 1628.*

1 How long soever it hath continued, if it be against reason, it is of no force in law.

The First Part of the Institutes of the Laws of England, bk 1, ch. 10, sect. 80 (1628)

2 Reason is the life of the law, nay the common law

itself is nothing else but reason ... The law, which is the perfection of reason.
Ibid., bk 2, ch. 6, sect. 138

3 For a man's house is his castle, *et domus sua cuique est tutissimum refugium* [and each man's home is his safest refuge].
The Third Part of the Institutes of the Laws of England, ch. 73 (1644)

Frank Moore Colby
(1865–1925)
US editor and essayist

He wrote for encyclopaedias throughout his life and edited the New International Year Book *from 1898 until his death. He also contributed widely and wittily to diverse magazines.*

1 Men will confess to treason, murder, arson, false teeth, or a wig. How many of them will own up to a lack of humor?
The Colby Essays, vol. 1, 'Satire and Teeth' (1926)

2 Persecution was at least a sign of personal interest. Tolerance is composed of nine parts of apathy to one of brotherly love.
Ibid., 'Trials of an Encyclopedist'

Dean Henry Cole
(1500–80)
English prelate

Dean of St Paul's 1556–8, he preached at Cranmer's execution and was a supporter of MARY I. *He was committed to the Tower of London in 1560 and Fleet prison in 1561.*

1 Ignorance is the mother of devotion.
'Disputation with the Papists at Westminster', 31 March 1559

Hartley Coleridge
(1796–1849)
English poet and author

David Hartley Coleridge. The eldest son of SAMUEL TAYLOR COLERIDGE, *he taught, contributed to literary journals and wrote sonnets showing the influence of* WILLIAM WORDSWORTH.

1 But what is Freedom? Rightly understood,
A universal licence to be good.
'Liberty', publ. in Poems, Songs and Sonnets (1833)

Samuel Taylor Coleridge
(1772–1834)
English poet and critic

He had a small but significant poetic output, most notably Lyrical Ballads *(1798), co-written with* WILLIAM WORDSWORTH. *His lectures and essays established him as the greatest literary critic of his day, though his bouts of ill health precipitated an enduring addiction to opium.* CHARLES LAMB *called him 'an archangel a little damaged'. See also* THOMAS CARLYLE 3, LEIGH HUNT 11, CHARLES LAMB 9, P. B. SHELLEY 49.

1 Tell me, on what holy ground
May domestic peace be found?
Halcyon daughter of the skies,
Far on fearful wings she flies,
From the pomp of sceptered state,
From the rebel's noisy hate,
In a cottaged vale she dwells
Listening to the Sabbath bells!
'Domestic Peace', written 1794, publ. in Poems (1796). Opening lines of poem.

2 Poor little foal of an oppressed race!
I love the languid patience of thy face.
'To a Young Ass', written 1794, ibid. Opening lines of poem.

3 O! the one life within us and abroad,
Which meets all motion and becomes its soul,
A light in sound, a sound-like power in light,
Rhythm in all thought, and joyance everywhere –
Methinks, it should have been impossible
Not to love all things in a world so filled.
'The Eolian Harp', ll. 26–31, written 1795, ibid.

4 In Xanadu did Kubla Khan
A stately pleasure-dome decree:
Where Alph, the sacred river, ran
Through caverns measureless to man
Down to a sunless sea.
Kubla Khan, ll. 1–5 (written 1797–9, publ. 1816). The poem, begun in the summer of 1797 according to the Preface (the date has been disputed) and originally subtitled 'A Vision in a Dream', was supposedly written under the influence of an opium dream; the visionary state was interrupted by 'a person on business from Porlock' and thus was left forever unfinished. Xanadu – now known as Shangdu – was the site of Kublai Khan's summer residence in South-East Mongolia.

5 A savage place! as holy and enchanted
As e'er beneath a waning moon was haunted
By woman wailing for her demon-lover!
Ibid., ll. 14–16

6 And 'mid this tumult Kubla heard from far

Ancestral voices prophesying war!
Ibid., ll. 29–30

7 It was a miracle of rare device,
A sunny pleasure-dome with caves of ice!
Ibid., ll. 35–6

8 A damsel with a dulcimer
In a vision once I saw:
It was an Abyssinian maid.
And on her dulcimer she played,
Singing of Mount Abora.
Ibid., ll. 37–41

9 Could I revive within me
Her symphony and song,
To such a deep delight 'twould win me,
That with music loud and long,
I would build that dome in air,
That sunny dome! those caves of ice!
And all who heard should see them there,
And all should cry, Beware! Beware!
His flashing eyes, his floating hair!
Weave a circle round him thrice,
And close your eyes with holy dread,
For he on honey-dew hath fed,
And drunk the milk of Paradise.
Ibid., ll. 42–54. Closing lines of poem.

10 Forth from his dark and lonely hiding-place,
(Portentous sight!) the owlet Atheism,
Sailing on obscene wings athwart the noon,
Drops his blue-fringed lids, and holds them close,
And hooting at the glorious sun in Heaven,
Cries out, 'Where is it?'
Fears in Solitude, ll. 81–6 (1798)

11 The frost performs its secret ministry,
Unhelped by any wind. The owlet's cry
Came loud – and hark, again! loud as before.
The inmates of my cottage, all at rest,
Have left me to that solitude, which suits
Abstruser musings.
Frost at Midnight, ll. 1–6 (1798)

12 Sea, and hill, and wood,
With all the numberless goings-on of life,
Inaudible as dreams!
Ibid., ll. 11–13

13 Therefore all seasons shall be sweet to thee,
Whether the summer clothe the general earth
With greenness, or the redbreast sit and sing
Betwixt the tufts of snow on the bare branch
Of mossy apple-tree, while the nigh thatch

Smokes in the sun-thaw; whether eave-drops
   fall
Heard only in the trances of the blast,
Or if the secret ministry of frost
Shall hang them up in silent icicles
Quietly shining to the quiet moon.
Ibid., ll. 65–74

14 It is an ancient Mariner,
And he stoppeth one of three.
'By thy long grey beard and glittering eye,
Now wherefore stopp'st thou me?'
The Rime of the Ancient Mariner, pt 1, st. 1 (1798). Opening
lines of poem.

15 The Wedding-Guest he beat his breast,
Yet he cannot choose but hear;
And thus spake on that ancient man,
The bright-eyed Mariner.
Ibid., pt 1, st. 10

16 And now there came both mist and snow,
And it grew wondrous cold:
And ice, mast-high, came floating by,
As green as emerald.
Ibid., pt 1, st. 13

17 At length did cross an Albatross,
Thorough the fog it came;
As if it had been a Christian soul,
We hailed it in God's name.
Ibid., pt 1, st. 16

18 'God save thee, ancient Mariner!
From the fiends, that plague thee thus! –
Why look'st thou so?' – With my cross-bow
I shot the Albatross.
Ibid., pt 1, st. 20. The Ancient Mariner confesses that he has
killed the albatross, a 'pious bird of good omen'.

19 The fair breeze blew, the white foam flew,
The furrow followed free;
We were the first that ever burst
Into that silent sea.
Ibid., pt 2, st. 5

20 As idle as a painted ship
Upon a painted ocean.
Ibid., pt 2, st. 8

21 Water, water, everywhere,
And all the boards did shrink;
Water, water, everywhere
Nor any drop to drink.
Ibid., pt 2, st. 9

22 Yea, slimy things did crawl with legs
Upon the slimy sea.
Ibid., pt 2, st. 10

23 Ah! well a-day! what evil looks
Had I from old and young!
Instead of the cross, the Albatross
About my neck was hung.
Ibid., pt 2, st. 14

24 With throats unslaked, with black lips baked,
We could nor laugh nor wail;
Through utter drought all dumb we stood!
I bit my arm, I sucked the blood,
And cried, A sail! a sail!
Ibid., pt 3, st. 4

25 Her lips were red, her looks were free,
Her locks were yellow as gold:
Her skin was white as leprosy,
The nightmare Life-in-Death was she,
Who thicks man's blood with cold.
Ibid., pt 3, st. 11. Describing the crew aboard the skeleton-ship.

26 I fear thee, ancient Mariner!
I fear thy skinny hand!
And thou art long, and lank, and brown,
As is the ribbed sea-sand.
Ibid., pt 4, st. 1. The words of the Wedding-Guest. Coleridge
acknowledges a debt to WORDSWORTH for the last two lines.

27 Alone, alone, all, all alone,
Alone on a wide wide sea!
And never a saint took pity on
My soul in agony.
Ibid., pt 4, st. 3

28 An orphan's curse would drag to hell
A spirit from on high;
But oh! more horrible than that
Is a curse in a dead man's eye!
Ibid., pt 4, st. 9

29 O happy living things! no tongue
Their beauty might declare:
A spring of love gushed from my heart,
And I blessed them unaware.
Ibid., pt 4, st. 14. The Mariner's blessing of the creatures of
the sea causes the albatross to fall from his neck.

30 Oh Sleep! it is a gentle thing,
Beloved from pole to pole!
To Mary Queen the praise be given!
She sent the gentle sleep from Heaven,
That slid into my soul.
Ibid., pt 5, st. 1

31 The man hath penance done,
And penance more will do.
Ibid., pt 5, st. 26

32 Like one, that on a lonesome road
Doth walk in fear and dread,
And having once turned round walks on,
And turns no more his head;
Because he knows, a frightful fiend
Doth close behind him tread.
Ibid., pt 6, st. 10

33 I pass, like night, from land to land;
I have strange power of speech.
Ibid., pt 7, st. 17

34 That moment that his face I see,
I know the man that must hear me:
To him my tale I teach.
Ibid., pt 7, st. 17

35 O Wedding-Guest! this soul hath been
Alone on a wide wide sea:
So lonely 'twas, that God himself
Scarce seemed there to be.
Ibid., pt 7, st. 19

36 Farewell, farewell! but this I tell
To thee, thou Wedding-Guest!
He prayeth well, who loveth well
Both man and bird and beast.
He prayeth best, who loveth best
All things both great and small;
For the dear God who loveth us,
He made and loveth all.
Ibid., pt 7, sts 22–3

37 He went like one that hath been stunned,
And is of sense forlorn:
A sadder and a wiser man,
He rose the morrow morn.
Ibid., pt 7, st. 25. Closing lines of poem.

38 Her silken robe, and inner vest,
Dropt to her feet, and full in view,
Behold! her bosom and half her side –
A sight to dream of, not to tell!
O shield her! Shield sweet Christabel!
Christabel, pt 1, ll. 250–4 (written 1798–1800, publ. 1816)

39 Alas! they had been friends in youth;
But whispering tongues can poison truth;
And constancy lives in realms above;
And life is thorny; and youth is vain;
And to be wroth with one we love

Doth work like madness in the brain.
Ibid., pt 2, ll. 408–13

40 Swans sing before they die – 'twere no bad
   thing
Should certain persons die before they sing.
'On a Bad Singer' (1800), repr. in *Poetical Works* (1828)

41 What is an epigram? a dwarfish whole,
Its body brevity, and wit its soul.
'What is an epigram?' (1802), repr. in *Poetical Works*, epigram
33 (ed. James Dyke Campbell, 1893)

42 I see them all so excellently fair,
I see, not feel, how beautiful they are!
Dejection: An Ode, st. 2 (1802), repr. in *Sibylline Leaves* (1817)

43 I may not hope from outward forms to win
The passion and the life, whose fountains are
   within.
Ibid., st. 3

44 O Lady! we receive but what we give,
And in our life alone does Nature live:
Ours is her wedding garment, ours her shroud!
Ibid., st. 4

45 Ah! from the soul itself must issue forth
A light, a glory, a fair luminous cloud
Enveloping the Earth.
Ibid., st. 4

46 Joy, Lady! is the spirit and the power,
Which wedding Nature to us gives in dower,
A new Earth and new Heaven,
Undreamt of by the sensual and the proud –
Joy is the sweet voice, Joy the luminous cloud –
We in ourselves rejoice!
And thence flows all that charms or ear or sight,
All melodies the echoes of that voice,
All colours a suffusion from that light.
Ibid., st. 5

47 But now afflictions bow me down to earth:
Nor care I that they rob me of my mirth;
But oh! each visitation
Suspends what nature gave me at my birth,
My shaping spirit of Imagination.
Ibid., st. 6

48 Hence, viper thoughts, that coil around my
   mind,
Reality's dark dream!
Ibid., st. 7

49 Where the reading of novels prevails as a habit,
it occasions in time the entire destruction of the
powers of the mind; it is such an utter loss to the
reader, that it is not so much to be called pass-time
as kill-time.
Lectures on Shakespeare and Milton, Lecture 1 (delivered winter 1811–12, publ. 1856)

50 Reviewers are usually people who would have
been poets, historians, biographers, &c., if they
could; they have tried their talents at one or at the
other, and have failed; therefore they turn critics.
Ibid., Lecture 1

51 Readers may be divided into four classes:
1. Sponges, who absorb all they read, and return it
   nearly in the same state, only a little dirtied.
2. Sand-glasses, who retain nothing, and are
   content to get through a book for the sake of
   getting through the time.
3. Strain-bags, who retain merely the dregs of what
   they read.
4. Mogul diamonds, equally rare and valuable, who
   profit by what they read, and enable others to
   profit by it also.
Ibid., Lecture 2

52 My case is a species of madness, only that it is a
derangement of the *Volition*, & not of the intellectual faculties.
Letter, 26 April 1814, publ. in *The Collected Letters of Samuel
Taylor Coleridge*, vol. 3 (ed. E. L. Griggs, 1959). Referring to his
addiction to laudanum.

53 Every reform, however necessary, will by weak
minds be carried to an excess, which will itself need
reforming.
Biographia Literaria, ch. 1 (1817)

54 Until you understand a writer's ignorance, presume yourself ignorant of his understanding.
Ibid., ch. 12

55 The primary imagination I hold to be the living
power and prime agent of all human perception,
and as a repetition in the finite mind of the eternal
act of creation in the infinite I AM.
Ibid., ch. 13

56 That willing suspension of disbelief for the
moment, which constitutes poetic faith.
Ibid., ch. 14. W. H. AUDEN commented: 'I cannot accept the
doctrine that in poetry there is a "suspension of belief". A
poet must never make a statement simply because it sounds
poetically exciting; he must also believe it to be true.' (*A
Certain World*, 'Writing', 1970)

57 A poem is that species of composition, which is

opposed to works of science, by proposing for its *immediate* object pleasure, not truth; and from all other species (having *this* object in common with it) it is discriminated by proposing to itself such delight from the *whole*, as is compatible with a distinct gratification from each component *part*.
Ibid., ch. 14

58 The greatest genius, that perhaps human nature has yet produced, our *myriad-minded* Shakespeare.
Ibid., ch. 15. In a footnote, Coleridge states that *myriad-minded* is a phrase 'borrowed from a Greek monk, who applies it to a Patriarch of Constantinople'.

59 No man was ever yet a great poet, without being at the same time a profound philosopher.
Ibid., ch. 15

60 In poetry, in which every line, every phrase, may pass the ordeal of deliberation and deliberate choice, it is possible, and barely possible, to attain that *ultimatum* which I have ventured to propose as the infallible test of a blameless style; namely: its *untranslatableness* in words of the same language without injury to the meaning.
Ibid., ch. 22

61 To most men, experience is like the stern lights of a ship, which illumine only the track it has passed.
Table Talk, 1820, publ. in *Letters and Conversations of S. T. Coleridge*, vol. 1, 'Thomas Allsop' (1836)

62 Humour is consistent with pathos, whilst wit is not.
Table Talk, 1821, ibid.

63 Dew-drops are the gems of morning,
But the tears of mournful eve!
Where no hope is, life's a warning
That only serves to make us grieve,
When we are old:
That only serves to make us grieve
With oft and tedious taking-leave,
Like some poor nigh-related guest,
That may not rudely be dismist;
Yet hath outstayed his welcome while,
And tells the jest without the smile.
'Youth and Age', ll. 39–49, written 1823, publ. in *Poetical Works* (1834)

64 To see him act is like reading Shakespeare by flashes of lightning.
'Table Talk', 27 April 1823, publ. in *Specimens of the Table Talk of Samuel Taylor Coleridge* (ed. Henry Nelson Coleridge, 1835). Referring to the actor Edmund Kean.

65 I wish our clever young poets would remember my homely definitions of prose and poetry; that is, prose = words in their best order; – poetry = the *best* words in the best order.
'Table Talk', 12 July 1827, ibid.

66 The man's desire is for the woman; but the woman's desire is rarely other than for the desire of the man.
'Table Talk', 23 July 1827, ibid. Also attributed to MADAME DE STAËL 4.

67 I do not call the sod under my feet my country; but language – religion – government – blood – identity in these makes men of one country.
'Table Talk', 27 May 1830, ibid.

68 Intense study of the Bible will keep any writer from being *vulgar*, in point of style.
'Table Talk', 14 June 1830, ibid.

69 In politics, what begins in fear usually ends in folly.
'Table Talk', 5 October 1830, ibid.

70 The three great ends which a statesman ought to propose to himself in the government of a nation, are, – 1. Security to possessors; 2. Facility to acquirers; and, 3. Hope to all.
'Table Talk', 25 June 1831, ibid.

71 Look through the whole history of countries professing the Romish religion, and you will uniformly find the leaven of this besetting and accursed principle of action – that the end will sanction any means.
'Table Talk', 6 August 1831, ibid.

72 Rights! There are no rights whatever without corresponding duties. Look at the history of the growth of our constitution, and you will see that our ancestors never upon any occasion stated, as a ground for claiming any of their privileges, an abstract right inherent in themselves; you will nowhere in our parliamentary records find the miserable sophism of the Rights of Man.
'Table Talk', 20 November 1831 ibid.

73 A religion, that is, a true religion, must consist of ideas and facts both; not of ideas alone without facts, for then it would be mere philosophy; – nor of facts alone without ideas, of which those facts are symbols, or out of which they arise, or upon which they are grounded: for then it would be mere history.
'Table Talk', 3 December 1831, ibid.

74 How inimitably graceful children are in general before they learn to dance!
'Table Talk', 1 January 1832, ibid.

75 The principle of the Gothic architecture is infinity made imaginable.
'Table Talk', 29 June 1833, ibid.

76 Some men are like musical glasses; to produce their finest tones, you must keep them wet.
'Table Talk', 20 January 1834, ibid.

77 Exclusively of the abstract sciences, the largest and worthiest portion of our knowledge consists of aphorisms: and the greatest and best of men is but an aphorism.
Aids to Reflection, 'Introductory Aphorisms', aph. 27 (1825)

78 He who begins by loving Christianity better than truth, will proceed by loving his own sect or church better than Christianity, and end in loving himself better than all.
Ibid., 'Moral and Religious Aphorisms', aph. 25

79 And though thou notest from thy safe recess
Old friends burn dim, like lamps in noisome air,
Love them for what they are; nor love them less,
Because to thee they are not what they were.
'Duty Surviving Self-Love', written 1826, publ. in Poetical Works (1828)

80 Summer has set in with its usual severity.
Quoted by CHARLES LAMB in letter, 9 May 1826, publ. in Letters of Charles Lamb, vol. 2 (ed. Alfred Ainger, 1888)

81 And the Devil did grin, for his darling sin
Is pride that apes humility.
'The Devil's Thoughts', publ. in Poetical Works, vol. 2 (1828). The poem was written jointly with ROBERT SOUTHEY. The original version appeared in 1799, with the lines: 'And he grinned at the sight, for his favourite vice/Is pride, that apes humility.'

82 I counted two and seventy stenches,
All well defined, and several stinks!
'Cologne', written 1828, publ. in Poetical Works (1834). Referring to 'Köhln, a town of monks and bones'.

83 Beneath this sod
A poet lies, or that which once seemed he.
O, lift one thought in prayer for S.T.C.;
That he who many a year with toil of breath
Found death in life, may here find life in death!
'Epitaph', written 1833, ibid.

Colette
(1873–1954)
French author

Born Sidonie Gabrielle Colette. Her series of Claudine novels (1900–3) was written in collaboration with her first husband Gauthier-Villars under his pen name, Willy. She later established a reputation in her own right with Chéri (1920), Gigi (1945) and La Chatte (1953).

1 Nothing ages a woman like living in the country.
Music Hall Sidelights, 'On Tour' (1913)

2 Is suffering so very serious? I have come to doubt it. It may be quite childish, a sort of undignified pastime – I'm referring to the kind of suffering a man inflicts on a woman or a woman on a man. It's extremely painful. I agree that it's hardly bearable. But I very much fear that this sort of pain deserves no consideration at all. It's no more worthy of respect than old age or illness.
'Break of Day' (1928), repr. in Earthly Paradise, pt 4, 'The South of France' (ed. Robert Phelps, 1966)

3 It is wise to apply the oil of refined politeness to the mechanism of friendship.
The Pure and the Impure, ch. 9 (1933, transl. 1966)

4 Just as delicate fare does not stop you from craving for saveloys, so tried and exquisite friendship does not take away your taste for something new and dubious.
Chambre d'hôtel, 'The Rainy Moon' (1940)

5 Don't ever wear artistic jewelry; it wrecks a woman's reputation.
Gigi (1944, transl. 1953). Spoken by Aunt Alicia. When asked (by Gilberte) 'What is an artistic jewel?' Aunt Alicia replies: 'It all depends. A mermaid in gold, with eyes of chrysoprase. An Egyptian scarab. A large engraved amethyst. A not very heavy bracelet said to have been chased by a master-hand. A lyre or star, mounted as a brooch. A studded tortoise. In a word, all of them frightful. Never wear baroque pearls, not even as hat-pins. Beware, above all things, of family jewels!'

Jesse Collings
(1831–1920)
English politician

A reforming Mayor of Birmingham, he was elected to parliament in 1880, and made important contributions to education and improving the lot of agricultural workers.

1 Three acres and a cow.
Political slogan, 1880s, referring to proposals for smallholdings and allotments for agricultural workers. The phrase was already in current usage and has been attributed to JOSEPH

CHAMBERLAIN, but it is said to have been suggested by Eli Hamshire, a rustic philosopher who actually farmed three acres and included the words in letters written to Chamberlain and Collings. The words have also been attributed to JEREMY BENTHAM. They were later associated with G. K. CHESTERTON's doctrine of 'distributism'.

R. G. Collingwood
(1889–1943)
British philosopher and historian

Robin George Collingwood. Professor of Philosophy at Oxford (1934–41), he argued that philosophy can only be understood within a historical framework. He was also an authority on Roman Britain.

1 Like other revolutionaries I can thank God for the reactionaries. They clarify the issue.
An Autobiography, ch. 6 (1939)

2 A man ceases to be a beginner in any given science and becomes a master in that science when he has learned that . . . he is going to be a beginner all his life.
The New Leviathan, pt 1, ch. 1, aph. 46 (1942)

3 Knowing yourself means knowing what you can do; and since nobody knows what he can do until he tries, the only clue to what man can do is what man has done. The value of history, then, is that it teaches us what man has done and thus what man is.
The Idea of History, Introduction (1946)

Charles Collins
(1874–1926)
British songwriter

He was a successful writer of lively singalong music hall songs for a variety of performers. See also FRED W. LEIGH 3 AND 4.

1 Any old iron, any old iron,
Any any old old iron?
You look neat
Talk about a treat,
You look dapper from your napper to your feet.
'Any Old Iron' (music hall song, 1911, written with E. A. Sheppard and Fred Terry). The song has been recorded by Harry Champion, Chas & Dave, Ted Heath, Stanley Holloway, Davy Jones and Peter Sellers, among others. The second line is often rendered 'Any any any old iron?'

Wilkie Collins
(1824–89)
English novelist

Considered the progenitor of the modern mystery novel, he was a rival and good friend of CHARLES DICKENS. His most enduring works, The Woman in White *(1860) and* The Moonstone *(1868), were the archetypes of innumerable followers in the genre.*

1 Any woman who is sure of her own wits is a match at any time for a man who is not sure of his own temper.
The Woman in White, 'The Second Epoch' (1860). Marian Halcombe's journal entry for 19 June.

2 Mind rules the world. But what rules the mind? The body . . . lies at the mercy of the most omnipotent of all potentates – the Chemist.
Count Fosco, ibid., 'The Third Epoch'

3 I haven't much time to be fond of anything. But when I *have* a moment's fondness to bestow, most times . . . the roses get it.
The Moonstone, 'First Period', ch. 12 (1868). Spoken by Sergeant Cuff.

William Collins
(1721–59)
English poet

He is best known for his Odes, which prefigured Romantic themes. Apart from his Persian Eclogues (1742), little of his meagre output was well received during his lifetime; he entered a mental asylum in 1754 and died in poverty.

1 How sleep the brave, who sink to rest,
By all their country's wishes blest!
'Ode Written in the Beginning of the Year 1746', st. 1, publ. in *Odes on Several Descriptive and Allegorical Subjects* (1746)

2 By fairy hands their knell is rung,
By forms unseen their dirge is sung;
There Honour comes, a pilgrim grey,
To bless the turf that wraps their clay,
And Freedom shall a-while repair,
To dwell a weeping hermit there!
'Ode Written in the Beginning of the Year 1746', st. 2, ibid.

George Colman the Younger
(1762–1836)
English playwright

He was a popular writer of comedies, comic operas, satirical dramas and scurrilous verse. Most of his plays were performed in the Little Theatre, London, the management of which he took over from his father, George Colman the Elder, also a successful playwright.

1 What a recreation it is to be in love! It sets the heart aching so delicately, there's no taking a wink of sleep for the pleasure of the pain.
The Mountaineers, Act 1, Sc.1 (1793). Spoken by Kilmallock.

2 And, on the label of the stuff,
He wrote this verse;
Which one would think was clear enough,
And terse:
When taken,
To be well shaken.
'The Newcastle Apothecary', publ. in *Broad Grins* (1802)

3 Says he, 'I am a handsome man, but I'm a gay deceiver.'
Song ('The Unfortunate Miss Bailey'), in *Love Laughs at Locksmiths*, Act 2 (1802)

C. C. Colton
(1780–1832)
English author and clergyman

Charles Caleb Colton. He lived in America and Paris where he won and lost fortunes through gambling, and finally committed suicide. He is best known for Lacon *(1820), a collection of aphorisms.*

1 None are so fond of secrets as those who do not mean to keep them.
Lacon, vol. 1, no. 40 (1820)

2 When you have nothing to say, say nothing.
Ibid., vol. 1, no. 183. In his preface to vol. 1, Colton writes: 'Justice to my readers compels me to admit that I write because I have nothing to do; justice to myself induces me to add that I will cease to write the moment I have nothing to say.'

3 It is always safe to learn, even from our enemies; seldom safe to venture to instruct, even our friends.
Ibid., vol. 1, no. 286

4 Applause is the spur of noble minds, the end and aim of weak ones.
Ibid., vol. 1, no. 324

5 If you would be known, and not know, vegetate in a village; if you would know, and not be known, live in a city.
Ibid., vol. 1, no. 334

Padraic Colum
(1881–1972)
Irish author, playwright and poet

One of the founders of the Abbey theatre in Dublin, he wrote poetry, essays, folk romances and epic tales. He lived in the USA after 1914.

1 She stepped away from me and she moved
    through the fair
And fondly I watched her go here and go there,
Then she went her way homeward with one star
    awake,
As the swan in the evening moves over the lake.
'She Moved Through the Fair', st. 2, publ. in *Wild Earth* (1907). This song is often cited as 'traditional', the confusion possibly arising from the fact that it was set to a mixolydian melody based on a traditional Gaelic air by the collector/arranger Herbert Hughes.

Betty Comden
(b. 1915)
Adolph Green
(1915–2002)
US librettists, lyricists and screenwriters

During a fifty-year career the duo was associated with a string of Broadway hits. With Gene Kelly they made the films On The Town *(1949),* Singin' In The Rain *(1952) and* It's Always Fair Weather *(1955).*

1 New York, New York – a helluva town,
The Bronx is up but the Battery's down,
And people ride in a hole in the ground:
New York, New York – it's a helluva town.
'New York, New York' (song from the stage musical *On The Town*, 1944, filmed 1949). The song opens the story, which follows the adventures of a group of sailors on shore leave in New York.

2 The party's over, it's time to call it a day.
'The Party's Over' (song, with music by Jule Styne), in *The Bells are Ringing* (stage musical 1956, filmed 1960)

Alex Comfort
(1920–2000)
British sexologist, author and poet

He was the author of Sex and Society *(1963),* The Anxiety Makers *(1967) and* The Joy of Sex *(1972), his most famous work, dubbed the 'Kama Sutra for the coffee table'.*

1 The Joy of Sex.
Book title (1972)

Ivy Compton-Burnett
(1884–1969)
British novelist

Her stylized novels rely heavily on dialogue to portray the internal wranglings of upper-class Victorian and Edwardian families. Titles include Pastors and Masters *(1925) and* Mother and Son *(1950).*

1 Well, of course, people are only human. But it really does not seem much for them to be.
A Family and a Fortune, ch. 2 (1939). Spoken by Dudley Gaveston.

2 We must use words as they are used or stand aside from life.
Mother and Son, ch. 9 (1955). Spoken by Julius Hume.

3 There is danger in courage. Cowardice is a power for good. We hardly know what it prevents.
The Last and First, ch. 6 (1971). Spoken by Angus.

Confucius
(551–497 BC)
Chinese sage

Having worked in government, he later became an itinerant philosopher. His teachings, collected by his pupils after his death as the Analects, *became the basis of Confucianism.*

1 [The good man] does not grieve that other people do not recognize his merits. His only anxiety is lest he should fail to recognize theirs.
Analects of Confucius, bk 1, no. 16 (transl. Arthur Waley, 1938)

2 He who rules by moral force is like the pole-star, which remains in its place while all the lesser stars do homage to it.
Ibid., bk 2, no. 1

3 At fifteen I set my heart upon learning. At thirty, I had planted my feet firm upon the ground. At forty, I no longer suffered from perplexities. At fifty, I knew what were the biddings of heaven. At sixty I heard them with a docile ear. At seventy, I could follow the dictates of my own heart: for what I desired no longer overstepped the boundaries of right.
Ibid., bk 2, no. 4

4 Behave in such a way that your father and mother have no anxiety about you, except concerning your health.
Ibid., bk 2, no. 6

5 He who by reanimating the old can gain knowledge of the new is fit to be a teacher.
Ibid., bk 2, no. 11

6 [The true gentleman] does not preach what he practises till he has practised what he preaches.
Ibid., bk 2, no. 13

7 He who learns but does not think, is lost. He who thinks but does not learn is in great danger.
Ibid., bk 2, no. 15

8 When you know a thing, to recognize that you know it, and when you do not know a thing, to recognize that you do not know it. That is knowledge.
Ibid., bk 2, no. 17

9 What is over and done with, one does not discuss. What has already taken its course, one does not criticize; what already belongs to the past, one does not censure.
Ibid., bk 3, no. 21

10 The good man rests content with his goodness; he that is merely wise pursues goodness in the belief that it pays to do so.
Ibid., bk 4, no. 2

11 He does not mind not being in office; all he minds about is whether he has qualities that entitle him to office. He does not mind failing to get recognition; he is too busy doing the things that entitle him to recognition.
Ibid., bk 4, no. 14

12 In the presence of a good man, think all the time how you may learn to equal him. In the presence of a bad man, turn your gaze within!
Ibid., bk 4, no. 17

13 While father and mother are alive, a good son does not wander far afield; or if he does so, goes only where he has said he was going.
Ibid., bk 4, no. 19

14 It is always better for a man to know the age of his parents. In the one case such knowledge will be a comfort to him; in the other, it will fill him with a salutary dread.
Ibid., bk 4, no. 21

15 Those who err on the side of strictness are few indeed!
Ibid., bk 4, no. 23

16 A gentleman covets the reputation of being slow in word but prompt in deed.
Ibid., bk 4, no. 24

17 Moral force never dwells in solitude; it will always bring neighbours.
Ibid., bk 4, no. 25

18 When natural substance prevails over ornamentation, you get the boorishness of the rustic. When ornamentation prevails over natural substance, you get the pedantry of the scribe. Only when ornament and substance are duly blended do you get the true gentleman.
Ibid., bk 6, no. 16

19 To prefer it is better than only to know it. To delight in it is better than merely to prefer it.
Ibid., bk 6, no. 18

20 The man who was ready to 'beard a tiger or rush a river' without caring whether he lived or died – that sort of man I should not take. I should certainly take someone who approached difficulties with due caution and who preferred to succeed by strategy.
Ibid., bk 7, no. 10. In answer to the question, 'Supposing you had command of the Three Hosts [the whole army], whom would you take to help you?'

21 He who seeks only coarse food to eat, water to drink and a bent arm for a pillow, will without looking for it find happiness to boot. Any thought of accepting wealth and rank by means that I know to be wrong is as remote from me as the clouds that float above.
Ibid., bk 7, no. 15

22 If we really wanted goodness, we should find that it was at our very side.
Ibid., bk 7, no. 29

23 I have never yet seen anyone whose desire to build up his moral power was as strong as sexual desire.
Ibid., bk 9, no. 17. The same idea is expressed in bk 15, no. 12.

24 To go too far is as bad as not to go far enough.
Ibid., bk 11, no. 15

25 Culture is just as important as inborn qualities; and inborn qualities, no less important than culture. Remove the hairs from the skin of the tiger or panther, and what is left looks just like the hairless hide of a dog or sheep.
Ibid., bk 12, no. 8

26 The essence of the gentleman is that of wind; the essence of small people is that of grass. And when a wind passes over the grass, it cannot choose but bend.
Ibid., bk 12, no. 19

27 When the near approve and the distant approach.
Ibid., bk 13, no. 16. On good government.

28 Imperturbable, resolute, tree-like, slow to speak – such a one is near to goodness.
Ibid., bk 13, no. 27

29 It is possible to be a true gentleman and yet lack goodness. But there has never yet existed a good man who was not a gentleman.
Ibid., bk 14, no. 7

30 So long as the ruler loves ritual, the people will be easy to handle.
Ibid., bk 14, no. 44

31 He who will not worry about what is far off will soon find something worse than worry close at hand.
Ibid., bk 15, no. 11

32 The demands that a gentleman makes are upon himself; those that a small man makes are upon others.
Ibid., bk 15, no. 20

33 Tzu-kung asked saying, Is there any single saying that one can act upon all day and every day? The Master said, Perhaps the saying about consideration: 'Never do to others what you would not like them to do to you.'
Ibid., bk 15, no. 23. 'The Golden Rule', see also BIBLE, NEW TESTAMENT: MATTHEW 53

34 When everyone dislikes a man, enquiry is necessary; when everyone likes a man, enquiry is necessary.
Ibid., bk 15, no. 27

35 Goodness is more to the people than water and fire. I have seen men lose their lives when 'treading upon' water and fire; but I have never seen anyone lose his life through 'treading upon' goodness.
Ibid., bk 15, no. 34

36 It is only the very wisest and the very stupidest who do not change.
Ibid., bk 17, no. 3

37 He who is courteous is not scorned, he who is broad wins the multitude, he who is of good faith is trusted by the people, he who is diligent succeeds

in all he undertakes, he who is clement can get service from the people.

Ibid., bk 17, no. 6. Referring to the five things necessary for goodness: courtesy, breadth, good faith, diligence and clemency.

38 One who has reached the age of forty and is still disliked will be so till the end.

Ibid., bk 17, no. 26

39 The faults of a gentleman are like eclipses of the sun or moon. If he does wrong, everyone sees it. When he corrects his fault, every gaze is turned up towards him.

Ibid., bk 19, no. 21

40 He who does not understand the will of Heaven cannot be regarded as a gentleman. He who does not know the rites cannot take his stand. He who does not understand words, cannot understand people.

Ibid., bk 20, no. 3

William Congreve
(1670–1729)
English dramatist and poet

An outstanding writer of the comedy of manners, whose 'every sentence is replete with sense and satire', according to WIL-LIAM HAZLITT, *he achieved success with his first play,* The Old Bachelor *(1693). Later works include a tragedy,* The Mourning Bride *(1697), and his masterpiece,* The Way of the World *(1700).*

1 Ah! Madam . . . you know everything in the world but your own perfections, and you only know not those, because 'tis the top of perfection not to know them.

Incognita (1692). Spoken by Aurelian.

2 In my conscience I believe the baggage loves me, for she never speaks well of me herself, nor suffers anybody else to rail at me.

The Old Bachelor, Act 1, Sc. 1 (1693). Bellmour refers to Belinda.

3 I find we are growing serious, and then we are in great danger of being dull.

Araminta, ibid., Act 2, Sc. 2. The conversation turns on the subject of love.

4 Eternity was in that moment.

Bellmour, ibid., Act 4, Sc. 2. On the kiss he has received from Laetitia.

5 Thus grief still treads upon the heels of pleasure: Married in haste, we may repent at leisure.

Sharper, ibid., Act 5, Sc. 1. To which Setter replies, 'Some by

experience find those words misplaced:/At leisure married, they repent in haste.'

6 Courtship to marriage, as a very witty prologue to a very dull play.

Belinda, ibid., Act 5, Sc. 1

7 It is the business of a comic poet to paint the vices and follies of humankind.

The Double Dealer, Epistle Dedicatory (1693)

8 Retired to their tea, and scandal, according to their ancient custom after dinner.

Mellefont, ibid., Act 1, Sc. 1. Speaking of the women who have retired after dinner at Lord Touchwood's house.

9 There is nothing more unbecoming a man of quality than to laugh; Jesu, 'tis such a vulgar expression of the passion! Everybody can laugh.

Lord Froth, ibid., Act 1, Sc. 1

10 No mask like open truth to cover lies, As to go naked is the best disguise.

Maskwell, ibid., Act 5, Sc. 1

11 Women are like tricks by sleight of hand, Which, to admire, we should not understand.

Love for Love, Act 4, Sc. 1 (1695). Spoken by Valentine.

12 Ay, 'tis well enough for a servant to be bred at an university, but the education is a little too pedantic for a gentleman.

Tattle, ibid., Act 5, Sc. 1

13 Music has charms to sooth a savage breast, To soften rocks, or bend a knotted oak.

The Mourning Bride, Act 1, Sc. 1 (1697). Opening lines of play, spoken by Almeria.

14 Heaven has no rage like love to hatred turned, Nor Hell a fury, like a woman scorned.

Zara, ibid., Act 3, Sc. 8. Concluding lines of play.

15 They come together like the coroner's inquest, to sit upon the murdered reputations of the week.

The Way of the World, Act 1, Sc. 1 (1700). Fainall refers to his wife and others of the 'cabal' who meet to talk scandal three times a week.

16 A wit should no more be sincere than a woman constant; one argues a decay of parts, as t'other of beauty.

Witwoud, ibid., Act 1, Sc. 1

17 O the pious friendships of the female sex!

Fainall, ibid., Act 2, Sc. 1. Mrs Marwood replies: 'More tender, more sincere, and more enduring than all the vain and empty vows of men, whether professing love to us, or mutual faith to one another.'

18 A little disdain is not amiss; a little scorn is alluring.
Lady Wishfort, ibid., Act 3, Sc. 1

19 If there's delight in love, 'tis when I see
That heart which others bleed for, bleed for me.
Song sung by Mrs Hodgson, ibid., Act 3, Sc. 1

20 I nauseate walking; 'tis a country diversion; I loathe the country and everything that relates to it.
Mrs Millamant, ibid., Act 4, Sc. 1

21 Let us never visit together, nor go to a play together, but let us be very strange and well-bred; let us be as strange as if we had been married a great while, and as well-bred as if we were not married at all.
Mrs Millamant, ibid., Act 4, Sc. 1

22 If I continue to endure you a little longer, I may by degrees dwindle into a wife.
Mrs Millamant to Mirabell, ibid., Act 4, Sc. 1

23 Thou art a retailer of phrases, and dost deal in remnants of remnants, like a maker of pincushions.
Witwoud to Petulant, ibid., Act 4, Sc. 1

24 Oh, she is the antidote to desire.
Ibid., Act 4, Sc. 1. Waitwell refers to Lady Wishfort.

25 Invention flags, his brain goes muddy,
And black despair succeeds brown study.
An Impossible Thing, st. 3 (1720)

James Connell
(1852–1929)
Irish journalist and social activist

He worked as a docker in Dublin, moved to London and entered journalism, writing for the newspaper the Labour Leader, *and was secretary of the Workingmen's Legal Aid Society (1909–29).*

1 The people's flag is deepest red,
It shrouded oft our martyred dead.
'The Red Flag', publ. in *Justice* (1889). Inspired by the London dock strike of 1889 and the rise of trade unionism, and written on a train between Charing Cross and New Cross, the song became an anthem of the international Labour movement. It was originally sung to the tune of 'The White Cockade', and subsequently to the tune of 'Tannenbaum'.

2 Though cowards flinch and traitors sneer,
We'll keep the red flag flying here.
'The Red Flag', ibid.

3 Oh we hate the cruel tiger
And hyena and jackal
But the false and dirty blackleg
Is the vilest beast of all.
Broadsheet, Dublin transport strike, 1913

Cyril Connolly
(1903–74)
British critic

A fastidious wit, he founded and edited the literary magazine Horizon *(1939–50). His essays, reflections and aphorisms were published in* Enemies of Promise *(1938) and* The Unquiet Grave *(1944).*

1 Green leaves on a dead tree is our epitaph – green leaves, dear reader, on a dead tree.
'The Journal of Cyril Connolly 1928–1937', publ. in *Journal and Memoir* by David Pryce-Jones (1983). Pryce-Jones chose these words for his book's epigraph.

2 A best-seller is the golden touch of mediocre talent.
'The Journal of Cyril Connolly 1928–1937', ibid. See LOGAN PEARSALL SMITH 12.

3 Idleness [is] only a coarse name for my infinite capacity for living in the present.
'The Journal of Cyril Connolly 1928–1937', ibid.

4 Destroy him as you will, the bourgeois always bounces up – execute him, expropriate him, starve him out *en masse*, and he reappears in your children.
Quoted in the *Observer* 7 March 1937

5 I shall christen this style the Mandarin, since it is beloved by literary pundits, by those who would make the written word as unlike as possible to the spoken one. It is the style of all those writers whose tendency is to make their language convey more than they mean or more than they feel, it is the style of most artists and all humbugs and one which is always menaced by a puritan opposition.
Enemies of Promise, pt 1, ch. 2 (1938, rev. 1948). Connolly referred to a style of English prose popularized by authors such as JOSEPH ADDISON – who was 'responsible for many of the evils from which English prose has since suffered. He made prose artful and whimsical, he made it sonorous when sonority was not needed, affected when it did not require affectation.'

6 Literature is the art of writing something that will be read twice; journalism what will be grasped at once.
Ibid., pt 1, ch. 3

7 As repressed sadists are supposed to become policemen or butchers so those with an irrational fear of life become publishers.
Ibid., pt 2, ch. 10

8 Whom the gods wish to destroy they first call promising.
Ibid., pt 2, ch. 13

9 There is no more sombre enemy of good art than the pram in the hall.
Ibid., pt 2, ch. 14

10 All charming people have something to conceal, usually their total dependence on the appreciation of others.
Ibid., pt 2, ch. 16

11 Were I to deduce any system from my feelings on leaving Eton, it might be called *The Theory of Permanent Adolescence*. It is the theory that the experiences undergone by boys at the great public schools, their glories and disappointments, are so intense as to dominate their lives and to arrest their development. From these it results that the greater part of the ruling class remains adolescent, school-minded, self-conscious, cowardly, sentimental, and in the last analysis homosexual.
Ibid., pt 3, ch. 24

12 Perfect fear casteth out love.
Quoted in obituary notice in the *Observer* 1 December 1974, by Philip Toynbee, to whom Connolly made this remark during the Blitz. See BIBLE, NEW TESTAMENT: 1 JOHN 7.

13 The more books we read, the clearer it becomes that the true function of a writer is to produce a masterpiece and that no other task is of any consequence.
The Unquiet Grave, pt 1 (1944, rev. 1951). Opening words of book, which was published under the pen-name 'Palinurus'.

14 Slums may well be breeding-grounds of crime, but middle-class suburbs are incubators of apathy and delirium.
Ibid., pt 1

15 No city should be too large for a man to walk out of in a morning.
Ibid., pt 1

16 Civilization is an active deposit which is formed by the combustion of the Present with the Past. Neither in countries without a Present nor in those without a Past is it to be encountered.
Ibid., pt 2. Connolly continued: 'Proust in Venice, Matisse's birdcages overlooking the flower market at Nice, Gide on the 17th-century quais of Toulon, Lorca in Granada, Picasso by Saint-Germain-des-Prés: there lies civilization and for me it can exist only under those liberal regimes in which the Present is alive and therefore capable of assimilating the Past.'

17 The goal of every culture is to decay through over-civilization; the factors of decadence – luxury, scepticism, weariness and superstition – are constant. The civilization of one epoch becomes the manure of the next.
Ibid., pt 2

18 Imprisoned in every fat man a thin one is wildly signalling to be let out.
Ibid., pt 2. The remark had been used earlier by GEORGE ORWELL 6; for a later variant see KINGSLEY AMIS 4.

19 The true index of a man's character is the health of his wife.
Ibid., pt 2

20 We are all serving a life-sentence in the dungeon of self.
Ibid., pt 2

21 Our memories are card indexes consulted and then returned in disorder by authorities whom we do not control.
Ibid., pt 3

22 The boredom of Sunday afternoon, which drove de Quincey to drink laudanum, also gave birth to surrealism: hours propitious for making bombs.
Ibid., pt 3

23 It is closing time in the gardens of the West and from now on an artist will be judged only by the resonance of his solitude or the quality of his despair.
Horizon December 1949

James Connolly
(1870–1916)
Irish syndicalist and Republican leader

Having helped found the Irish Socialist Republican Party (1896) and, in New York (1902–10), the Industrial Workers of the World ('Wobblies'), he established the Irish Labour Party with James Larkin in 1912. He was shot for his part in the Easter Rising of 1916.

1 Just as it is true that a stream cannot rise above its source, so it is true that a national literature cannot rise above the moral level of the social conditions of the people from whom it derives its inspiration.
Labour in Irish History, Foreword (1910)

2 Without the power of the Industrial Union behind it, Democracy can only enter the State as the victim enters the gullet of the Serpent.
The Re-Conquest of Ireland, ch. 9 (1915)

3 Ireland, as distinct from her people, is nothing to me; and the man who is bubbling over with love and enthusiasm for 'Ireland', and can yet pass unmoved through our streets and witness all the wrong and the suffering, the shame and the degradation wrought upon the people of Ireland – yea, wrought by Irishmen upon Irish men and women, without burning to end it, is, in my opinion, a fraud and a liar in his heart, no matter how he loves that combination of chemical elements he is pleased to call Ireland.
Labour in Ireland, Epigraph (1916)

Joseph Conrad

(1857–1924)

Polish-born English novelist

Born Teodor Józef Konrad Korzeniowski. The son of a Polish nationalist, he worked on merchant ships from 1876 and became a British subject in 1886. His adventurous tales were often set in the tropics and contained a strong moral element. Ford Madox Ford deemed him the most 'absolutely passionate man-of-action become conscious man-of-letters' he had ever known.

1 Any work that aspires, however humbly, to the condition of art should carry its justification in every line.
The Nigger of the Narcissus, Preface (1897). Opening words. Conrad continued, 'Art itself may be defined as a single-minded attempt to render the highest kind of justice to the visible universe, by bringing to light the truth, manifold and one, underlying its every aspect.'

2 There is nothing more enticing, disenchanting, and enslaving than the life at sea.
Lord Jim, ch. 2 (1900)

3 Hang ideas! They are tramps, vagabonds, knocking at the back-door of your mind, each taking a little of your substance, each carrying away some crumb of that belief in a few simple notions you must cling to if you want to live decently and would like to die easy!
Marlow, ibid., ch. 5

4 A word carries far – very far – deals destruction through time as the bullets go flying through space.
Marlow, ibid., ch. 15

5 A man that is born falls into a dream like a man who falls into the sea. If he tries to climb out into the air as inexperienced people endeavour to do, he drowns.
Marlow, ibid., ch. 20

6 Going home must be like going to render an account.
Marlow, ibid., ch. 21

7 You shall judge of a man by his foes as well as by his friends.
Marlow, ibid., ch. 34

8 The conquest of the earth, which mostly means the taking it away from those who have a different complexion or slightly flatter noses than ourselves, is not a pretty thing when you look into it too much.
The Heart of Darkness, ch. 1 (1902). Spoken by Marlow.

9 The horror! The horror!
Ibid., ch. 3. Kurtz's dying words.

10 Mistah Kurtz – he dead.
The manager's boy, ibid., ch. 3

11 Droll thing life is – that mysterious arrangement of merciless logic for a futile purpose. The most you can hope from it is some knowledge of yourself – that comes too late – a crop of unextinguishable regrets.
Marlow, ibid., ch. 3

12 I have wrestled with death. It is the most unexciting contest you can imagine. It takes place in an impalpable greyness, with nothing underfoot, with nothing around, without spectators, without clamour, without glory, without the great desire of victory, without the great fear of defeat.
Marlow, ibid., ch. 3

13 I remember my youth and the feeling that will never come back any more – the feeling that I could last for ever, outlast the sea, the earth, and all men; the deceitful feeling that lures us on to joys, to perils, to love, to vain effort – to death; the triumphant conviction of strength, the heat of life in the handful of dust, the glow in the heart that with every year grows dim, grows cold, grows small, and expires – and expires, too soon, too soon – before life itself.
Youth (1902). Spoken by Marlow.

14 A puff of wind, a puff faint and tepid and laden with strange odours of blossoms, of aromatic wood, comes out the still night – the first sigh of the East on my face. That I can never forget. It was impal-

pable and enslaving, like a charm, like a whispered promise of mysterious delight ... The mysterious East faced me, perfumed like a flower, silent like death, dark like a grave.

Marlow, ibid. Of the East, Conrad wrote, 'I have seen its secret places and have looked into its very soul . . .'

15 An artist is a man of action, whether he creates a personality, invents an expedient, or finds the issue of a complicated situation.

The Mirror of the Sea, ch. 9 (1906)

16 The sea has never been friendly to man. At most it has been the accomplice of human restlessness.

Ibid., ch. 35. In ch. 36, Conrad writes: 'The sea – this truth must be confessed – has no generosity. No display of manly qualities – courage, hardihood, endurance, faithfulness – has ever been known to touch its irresponsible consciousness of power.'

17 The terrorist and the policeman both come from the same basket. Revolution, legality – counter-moves in the same game; forms of idleness at bottom identical.

The Secret Agent, ch. 4 (1907). Spoken by the Professor.

18 Words, as is well known, are the great foes of reality.

Under Western Eyes, Prologue to pt 1 (1911). Spoken by the narrator.

19 I take it that what all men are really after is some form or perhaps only some formula of peace.

The narrator, ibid., Prologue to pt 1

20 A man's real life is that accorded to him in the thoughts of other men by reason of respect or natural love.

The narrator, ibid., pt 1, ch. 1

21 They talk of a man betraying his country, his friends, his sweetheart. There must be a moral bond first. All a man can betray is his conscience.

Razumov, ibid., pt 1, ch. 2

22 The scrupulous and the just, the noble, humane, and devoted natures; the unselfish and the intelligent may begin a movement – but it passes away from them. They are not the leaders of a revolution. They are its victims.

The narrator, ibid., pt 2, ch. 3

23 The belief in a supernatural source of evil is not necessary; men alone are quite capable of every wickedness.

The 'dame de compagnie', ibid., pt 2, ch. 4

24 Perhaps life is just that ... a dream and a fear.

Razumov, ibid., pt 4, ch. 2

25 Truth of a modest sort I can promise you, and also sincerity. That complete, praiseworthy sincerity which, while it delivers one into the hands of one's enemies, is as likely as not to embroil one with one's friends.

A Personal Record, 'A Familiar Preface' (1912)

26 Criticism, that fine flower of personal expression in the garden of letters.

Ibid., 'A Familiar Preface'

27 All ambitions are lawful except those which climb upward on the miseries or credulities of mankind. All intellectual and artistic ambitions are permissible, up to and even beyond the limit of prudent sanity. They can hurt no one.

Ibid., 'A Familiar Preface'

28 What is a novel if not a conviction of our fellow-men's existence strong enough to take upon itself a form of imagined life clearer than reality and whose accumulated verisimilitude of selected episodes puts to shame the pride of documentary history?

Ibid., ch. 1

29 Only in men's imagination does every truth find an effective and undeniable existence. Imagination, not invention, is the supreme master of art as of life.

Ibid., ch. 1

30 It is a maudlin and indecent verity that comes out through the strength of wine.

Ibid., ch. 6

Shirley Conran
(b. 1932)
British designer and journalist

The first woman editor of the Observer Colour Magazine *(1964–9), she became a bestseller with her* Superwoman *series (1974–7, 1990), and her novels, including* Lace *(1982).*

1 Life is too short to stuff a mushroom.

Superwoman, Epigraph (1975)

2 First things first, second things never.

Family motto, ibid., 'How to be a Working Wife and Mother'

3 Women want men to change, but they don't. Men want women to stay the same, but they can't.

Quoted in *The Times* 23 December 2000

John Constable

(1776–1837)

English painter

For such well known works as 'The Haywain' (1821) and his views of Salisbury Cathedral, he was hailed as 'the most genuine painter of English landscape' by his friend and biographer C. R. Leslie.

1 There is nothing ugly; *I never saw an ugly thing in my life*: for let the form of an object be what it may, – light, shade, and perspective will always make it beautiful.

Quoted in *Memoirs of the Life of John Constable, R.A.*, ch. 17 (1843) by C. R. Leslie

Benjamin Constant

(1767–1830)

Swiss-born French politician and author

Henri-Benjamin Constant de Rebecque. After siding with the French revolutionaries, he opposed NAPOLEON BONAPARTE *and went into exile in 1803. His best known novel* Adolphe *(1816) was largely based on his long liaison with* MADAME DE STAËL.

1 Art for art's sake, with no purpose, for any purpose perverts art. But art achieves a purpose which is not its own.

Journal entry, 11 February 1804, publ. in *Journaux intimes* (1952). 'Art for art's sake' became an oft-repeated slogan. The French philosopher Victor Cousin (1792–1867) said in a lecture at the Sorbonne in 1818, 'We must have religion for religion's sake, morality for morality's sake, as with art for art's sake . . . the beautiful cannot be the way to what is useful, or to what is good, or to what is holy; it leads only to itself' (*Du vrai, du beau, et du bien*, pt 2, 1853). See also HOWARD DIETZ 1.

Constantine the Great

(c. 288–337)

Roman emperor

Flavius Valerius Constantinus. He was western emperor from 312 and sole emperor from 324. Ascribing his success to his Christian faith, he ended the persecution of Christians. In 330 he founded Constantinople as the imperial capital.

1 *In hoc signo vinces.*
[By this sign you will conquer.]

Quoted in *Life of Constantine*, bk 1, ch. 28 (c. 340) by Eusebius. According to this source, the words were part of a vision in which a Christian sign appeared to Constantine before his battle against his brother-in-law Maxentius at the Milvian Bridge, outside Rome, in 312; Constantine's victory allowed him to become western emperor.

Eliza Cook

(1818–89)

English poet

Her verse, once popular for its domestic themes and simple patriotism, was largely ignored in later years, following her lengthy retirement from the world forced by ill health. Her weekly periodical, Eliza Cook's Journal *(1849–54) was also widely read.*

1 Better build schoolrooms for 'the boy'
Than cells and gibbets for 'the man'.

'A Song for the Ragged Schools', st. 12 (1853)

2 For a glorious charter, deny it who can,
Is breathed in the words 'I'm an Englishman.'

'The Englishman', st. 4, publ. in *Poems and Songs* (1892). Closing lines of poem.

James Cook

(1728–79)

English sailor and explorer

With his ship Endeavour *he sailed to the Pacific (1768–71), charted New Zealand and surveyed Australia, claiming it for Great Britain. On a subsequent expedition, he was killed in an altercation with Hawaiians.*

1 From what I have said of the natives of New Holland they may appear to some to be the most wretched people upon earth; but in reality they are far more happier than we Europeans, being wholly unacquainted not only with the superfluous, but with the necessary conveniencies so much sought after in Europe; they are happy in not knowing the use of them.

Journal entry, 23 August 1770, publ. in *The Journals of Captain James Cook on His Voyages of* Discovery, vol. 1 (ed. J. C. Beaglehole, 1955). Referring to Australia, then named New Holland.

Peter Cook

(1937–95)

British comedian

After the success of Beyond the Fringe *(1959–64), he collaborated with Dudley Moore in the TV series* Not Only . . . But Also *(1965–71) and co-founded the satirical magazine* Private Eye.

1 I go to the theatre to be entertained. I don't want to see plays about rape, sodomy and drug addiction – I can get all that at home.

Cartoon caption in the *Observer* 8 July 1962. The joke also appeared in the revue *Beyond the Fringe*, and has been credited to ALAN BENNETT.

Robin Cook

(1946–2005)
British politician

Originally Robert Cook. He became a Labour MP in 1974, Foreign Secretary in 1997 and Leader of the House of Commons in 2001, resigning from that post in 2003 over the government's policy on Iraq.

1 Our foreign policy must have an ethical dimension and must support the demands of other peoples for the democratic rights on which we insist for ourselves.
Statement on assuming post of Foreign Secretary, 12 May 1997, quoted in *The Times* 13 May 1997

2 Chicken Tikka Massala is now a true British national dish, not only because it is the most popular, but because it is a perfect illustration of the way Britain absorbs and adapts external influences.
Speech to the Social Market Foundation, London, quoted in the *Guardian* 19 April 2001. Other reports quote the words '. . . Britain's true national dish'.

Alistair Cooke

(1908–2004)
British-born US broadcaster and journalist

An urbane observer on current affairs in America, he published several books on his subject and broadcast the weekly Letter from America *on BBC radio (1946–2004).*

1 Cocktail music he accepts as audible wallpaper.
'The Innocent American', publ. in *Holiday* July 1962. The words are often misquoted 'Canned music is like audible wallpaper.'

2 All Presidents start out to run a crusade but after a couple of years they find they are running something less heroic and much more intractable: namely the presidency.
Radio broadcast, 1963, publ. in *Talk About America*, ch. 31 (1968)

Sam Cooke

(1931–64)
US soul musician

His gospel-influenced vocal style and strong commercial appeal made him a major figure in soul music, inspiring numerous covers of such songs as 'You Send Me' (1957), 'Only Sixteen' (1959) and 'Bring it on Home to Me' (1963).

1 Don't know much about history
Don't know much about biology.
'Wonderful World' (song, 1960). In *A Change is Gonna Come:*

Music, Race & the Soul of America (1998) by Craig Werner, the author makes this comment on the lines: 'The cliché's worth a second thought. Because, if there are two things that a black man in pop music needed to encourage the white audience to forget, they were history and biology, at least the parts involving skin color and sexuality.'

2 It's been a long time coming
But I know a change is gonna come.
'A Change is Gonna Come' (song) on the album *Ain't That Good News* (1964). Partly modelled on BOB DYLAN's 'Blowin' in the Wind', the song assumed almost anthemic importance during the rise of the Black Consciousness movement. It was extensively covered, most famously by Otis Redding.

Charles Horton Cooley

(1864–1929)
US sociologist

In 1905 he co-founded the American Sociological Society and became its president in 1918. Stressing the interrelations between indivduals and society, his books blended social psychology, history and philosophy.

1 The imaginations which people have of one another are the *solid facts* of society.
Human Nature and the Social Order, ch. 3 (1902)

2 The mind is not a hermit's cell, but a place of hospitality and intercourse.
Ibid., ch. 3

3 We are ashamed to seem evasive in the presence of a straightforward man, cowardly in the presence of a brave one, gross in the eyes of a refined one, and so on. We always imagine, and in imagining share, the judgments of the other mind.
Ibid., ch. 5

4 We are born to action; and whatever is capable of suggesting and guiding action has power over us from the first.
Ibid., ch. 9

5 Every general increase of freedom is accompanied by some degeneracy, attributable to the same causes as the freedom.
Ibid., ch. 12

Calvin Coolidge

(1872–1933)
US politician and president

As Republican president (1923–9) with the slogan 'Keep Cool with Coolidge', he was noted for non-interference in business, industry and foreign affairs. Modest and frugal throughout his life, he was equally known for his dullness. H. L. MENCKEN *concluded: 'He had no ideas, but was not a nuisance.' See also* DOROTHY PARKER 12.

1 There is no right to strike against the public safety by anybody, anywhere, any time.
Telegram to Samuel Gompers, President of American Federation of Labor, 14 September 1919, quoted in *Have Faith in Massachusetts* (1919). Coolidge, then Governor of Massachusetts, was referring to a strike by the Boston police.

2 Civilization and profits go hand in hand.
Speech in New York, 27 November 1920, quoted in the *New York Times* 28 November 1920

3 After all, the chief business of the American people is business.
Speech to the Society of American Newspaper Editors, Washington DC, 17 January 1925, publ. in *Foundations of the Republic* (1926)

4 Well, they hired the money, didn't they?
Attributed comment in 1925 to US ambassador to France on a proposal to restructure European war debts, quoted in *The Wit and Wisdom of Calvin Coolidge* (ed. John H. McKee, 1933). Coolidge's biographer, Claud M. Fuess, failed to find any evidence that Coolidge spoke these words, though his wife observed, 'I don't know whether he said it, but it is just what he might have said.'

5 I do not choose to run for President in nineteen twenty-eight.
Statement to reporters, Rapid City, South Dakota, 2 August 1927, quoted in the *New York Times* 3 August 1927. The words were said to have been written out and handed to the assembled journalists, in what was taken to be a perfect illustration of Coolidge's legendary taciturnity. Regarding this, one Washington hostess is supposed to have commented: 'Every time he opens his mouth, a moth flies out.'

James Fenimore Cooper
(1789–1851)
US novelist

Regarded as the first great American novelist, he began writing adventure stories in 1820, the best known of which is The Last of the Mohicans *(1826), one of his 'Leatherstocking' tales of frontier life. He later wrote political satires and* The American Democrat *(1838), an acute analysis of political life.*

1 The tendency of democracies is, in all things, to mediocrity.
The American Democrat, 'On the Disadvantages of Democracy' (1838)

2 It is a besetting vice of democracies to substitute public opinion for law. This is the usual form in which masses of men exhibit their tyranny.
Ibid., 'On the Disadvantages of Democracy'

3 The demagogue is usually sly, a detractor of others, a professor of humility and disinterestedness, a great stickler for equality as respects all above him, a man who acts in corners, and avoids open and manly expositions of his course, calls blackguards gentlemen, and gentlemen folks, appeals to passions and prejudices rather than to reason, and is in all respects, a man of intrigue and deception, of sly cunning and management.
Ibid., 'On Demagogues'

4 It is a misfortune that necessity has induced men to accord greater license to this formidable engine, in order to obtain liberty, than can be borne with less important objects in view; for the press, like fire, is an excellent servant, but a terrible master.
Ibid., 'On the Press'

Tommy Cooper
(1922–84)
British comedian

With his trademark red fez, he was the comedian's comedian, enjoying success in variety and his own TV series from the 1950s. He died on stage during a live TV transmission.

1 Just like that!
Catch-phrase and title of autobiography (1975)

Wendy Cope
(b. 1945)
British poet

She gained a wide readership for her wry and parodic verse with her first volume, Making Cocoa for Kingsley Amis *(1986), consolidating her success with* Serious Concerns *(1992) and* If I Don't Know *(2001).*

1 I used to think all poets were Byronic.
They're mostly wicked as a ginless tonic
And wild as pension plans.
'Triolet', publ. in *Making Cocoa for Kingsley Amis* (1986)

2 The Thames runs, bones rattle, rats creep;
Tiresias fancies a peep –
A typist is laid,
A record is played –
Wei la la. After that it gets deep.
'Waste Land Limericks', ibid.

3 Bloody men are like bloody buses –
You wait for about a year
And as soon as one approaches your stop
Two or three others appear.
'Bloody Men', publ. in *Serious Concerns* (1992). The men/buses

analogy had been current for some time: newspaper editor Wendy Henry was quoted in the *Observer* 30 January 1983: 'Men are like buses. If you miss one, there's always another round the corner. But don't get caught at the wrong stop.'

4 They say that men suffer,
As badly, as long.
I worry, I worry,
In case they are wrong.
'I Worry', ibid.

5 I think it's a question which particularly arises over women writers: whether it's better to have a happy life or a good supply of tragic plots.
Independent 9 March 1992

6 Hope is a long leash,
drawn in slowly.
'After Prague', publ. in *If I Don't Know* (2001)

Aaron Copland
(1900–90)
US composer

Originally Aaron Kaplan. Early pieces influenced by STRAVINSKY *were a fusion of classical and jazz styles. Later works such as the ballet* Billy the Kid *(1938) and* Appalachian Spring *(1944) drew on the American folk tradition.*

1 The whole problem can be stated quite simply by asking, 'Is there a meaning to music?' My answer to that would be, 'Yes'. And 'Can you state in so many words what the meaning is?' My answer to that would be, 'No'.
What to Listen for in Music, ch. 2 (1939)

2 Music is in a continual state of becoming.
Music and Imagination: The Charles Eliot Norton Lectures 1951/2, Introduction (1952)

3 Listening is its own reward; there are no prizes to be won, no contests of creative listening. But I hold that person fortunate who has the gift, for there are few pleasures in art greater than the secure sense that one can recognise beauty when one comes upon it.
Ibid., pt 1, ch. 1

4 The greatest moments of the human spirit may be deduced from the greatest moments in music.
'Music as an Aspect of the Human Spirit' (radio broadcast, 1954), publ. in *Man's Right to Knowledge* (second series, 1955)

Francis Ford Coppola
(b. 1939)
US film-maker

He won universal acclaim for the epic Mafia drama The Godfather *(1972), which he co-wrote and directed, and its two sequels. Other films include* Apocalypse Now *(1979) and* The Cotton Club *(1984).*

1 If anything in this life is certain, if history has taught us anything, it's that everyone can be killed.
The Godfather Part II (film, 1974, screenplay by Francis Ford Coppola and Mario Puzo, directed by Francis Ford Coppola). Spoken by Michael Corleone (Al Pacino).

2 Charlie don't surf.
Apocalypse Now (film, 1979, screenplay by John Milius and Francis Ford Coppola, produced and directed by Francis Ford Coppola). Spoken by Colonel Kilgore (Robert Duvall), referring to the Viet Cong. The film's title, credited to John Milius, was derived from a badge popular with hippies in the 1960s, 'Nirvana Now'.

3 Nothing else in the world smells like that . . . I love the smell of napalm in the morning . . . It smells like victory.
Colonel Kilgore (Robert Duvall), ibid.

Pierre Corneille
(1606–84)
French dramatist

Considered the creator of French classical tragedy, he took Paris by storm with Le Cid *in 1637, though it was suppressed for departing from the conventions of the genre. Other successful works included* Horace *(1640),* Cinna *(1641) and* Polyceute *(1643), and the comedy* Le Menteur *(The Liar, 1643).*

1 Too little honour would spring from such a
   victory:
To win without risk is to triumph without glory.
Le Cid, Act 2, Sc. 2 (1637). Spoken by Don Gomès (the Count).

2 *Faites votre devoir et laissez faire aux dieux.*
[Do your duty, and leave the outcome to the Gods.]
Horace, Act 2, Sc. 8 (1640). Spoken by Old Horace.

F. M. Cornford
(1874–1943)
British academic and author

Francis Macdonald Cornford. Professor of Ancient Philosophy at Cambridge University (1931–9), he was a leading Platonic scholar, and published mainly on the ancient Greeks.

1 Every public action, which is not customary, either is wrong, or, if it is right, is a dangerous precedent.

It follows that nothing should ever be done for the first time.
Microcosmographia Academica, ch. 7 (1908)

2 Propaganda is that branch of the art of lying which consists in very nearly deceiving your friends without quite deceiving your enemies.
Ibid., Preface (1928 edn)

Frances Cornford
(1886–1960)
British poet

Granddaughter of CHARLES DARWIN *and wife of* F. M. CORN-FORD, *she published the first of her traditional volumes of poetry in* Poems *(1910).*

1 O why do you walk through the fields in gloves,
Missing so much and so much?
O fat white woman whom nobody loves,
Why do you walk through the fields in gloves,
When the grass is soft as the breast of doves
And shivering sweet to the touch?
'To a Fat Lady Seen from a Train', publ. in *Poems* (1910)

2 A young Apollo, golden-haired,
Stands dreaming on the verge of strife,
Magnificently unprepared
For the long littleness of life.
'Youth', ibid. Of RUPERT BROOKE.

Gregory Corso
(1930–2001)
US poet

Based in San Francisco, from 1956 he was one of the most anarchic of the Beat poets. His numerous collections include Gasoline *(1958) and* Earth Egg *(1974).*

1 I HATE OLD POETMEN!
Especially old poetmen who retract
who consult other old poetmen
who speak their youth in whispers,
saying: – I did those then
but that was then
that was then –
'I Am 25', publ. in *Gasoline* (1958)

2 Must one keep home to keep Rome Rome?
'How One Looks At It', publ. in *Long Live Man* (1962)

William Johnson Cory
(1823–92)
English schoolteacher and poet

Born William Johnson. He was Assistant-Master at Eton (1845–72) and wrote poems and translations from the classics. His only verse collection was Ionica *(1858).*

1 They told me, Heraclitus, they told me you were dead;
They brought me bitter news to hear and bitter tears to shed.
I wept as I remembered how often you and I
Had tired the sun with talking and sent him down the sky.
'Heraclitus', publ. in *Ionica* (1858). The lines are translated from an epigram by CALLIMACHUS addressed to the poet Heraclitus of Halicarnassus, on the news of his death.

2 Jolly boating weather,
And a hay harvest breeze.
'Eton Boating Song', publ. in *Eton Scrap Book* (1865)

Billy Cotton
(1899–1969)
British bandleader

He formed his own band in 1924 which toured from the 1930s. His Billy Cotton Bandshow, *broadcast on radio and television (1949–68), became a national institution.*

1 Wakey wakey!
Standard show opener, from 1940s. The catch-phrase originated in a Sunday morning live radio show. In Cotton's words: 'The boys had been sitting up all night in third-class railway carriages. When we broke before the actual performance they just slumped where they were. I came into the studio only a few minutes before the red light was due to go on, and they were slouched around like a lot of tired giraffes. "Oi, come on," I said. "*Wakey Wakey!*" It worked, and everybody got so cheerful that the producer said that we could well start the actual show with it. And that was the beginning of Wakey Wakey.' (*I Did It My Way*, ch. 10, 1970)

Émile Coué
(1857–1926)
French psychologist

He studied pharmacy before taking up hypnosis and psychotherapy. Believing in autosuggestion and the dominant role of the patient in healing, he established a clinic in Nancy in 1910.

1 Every day, in every way, I'm getting better and better.

De la suggestion et de ses applications (1915). Proposed formula to be repeated by patients.

Douglas Coupland
(b. 1961)
Canadian author

His novel Generation X *(1991) lent its name to the sub-culture of disaffected twenty-somethings whose lives it chronicled. Other works, such as* Microserfs *(1995) and* Polaroids from the Dead *(1996), describe the 'accelerated culture' of our times.*

1 McJob: A low-pay, low-prestige, low-dignity, low-benefit, no-future job in the service sector.

Generation X, 'The Sun is Your Enemy' (1991). Marginal note.

Victor Cousin
See BENJAMIN CONSTANT 1

(Sir) Noël Coward
(1899–1973)
British actor, playwright and composer

Blessed, in his own words, with 'a talent to amuse', he was a sophisticated and versatile performer, and the writer of the classic comedy plays Hay Fever *(1925),* Private Lives *(1930, filmed 1931) and* Blithe Spirit *(1941, filmed 1945). He also wrote numerous musicals and revues, and wrote, produced and acted in films.*

1 Poor little rich girl,
You're a bewitched girl,
Better beware!

'Poor Little Rich Girl' (song) in *On With the Dance* (musical revue, 1925)

2 I'll see you again,
Whenever Spring breaks through again.

'I'll See You Again' (song) in *Bitter Sweet*, Act 1, Sc. 2 (1929). Carl sings the lines in the play.

3 Very flat, Norfolk.

Private Lives, Act 1 (1930). Spoken by Amanda.

4 Extraordinary how potent cheap music is.

Amanda, ibid., Act 1. Often quoted 'Strange how potent cheap music is', after the version used in the 1930 recording of the play (spoken by Gertrude Lawrence).

5 Elyot: It doesn't suit women to be promiscuous.
Amanda: It doesn't suit men for women to be promiscuous.

Ibid., Act 2

6 Certain women should be struck regularly, like gongs.

Elyot, ibid., Act 3

7 In Bengal to move at all
Is seldom, if ever, done,
But mad dogs and Englishmen
Go out in the midday sun.

'Mad Dogs and Englishmen' (song, 1930)

8 Bright young people,
Gay to the utmost degree.
We play funny jokes
On more dignified folks
And laugh with extravagant glee.
We give lovely parties that last through the
   night,
I dress as a woman and scream with delight,
We wake up at lunch time and find we're still
   tight.
What could be duller than that?

'Bright Young People' (song, 1930)

9 Let's drink to our sons who made part of the pattern and to our hearts that died with them. Let's drink to the spirit of gallantry and courage that made a strange Heaven out of unbelievable Hell, and let's drink to the hope that one day this country of ours, which we love so much, will find dignity and greatness and peace again.

Cavalcade, pt 3, Sc. 1 (1932). Jane toasts New Year's Eve with Robert, in last speech of play.

10 Blues, nothing to win or to lose.
It's getting me down.
Blues, I've got those weary Twentieth Century
   Blues.

'Twentieth Century Blues' (song) ibid., pt 3, Sc. 2

11 Mad about the boy,
I know it's stupid to be mad about the boy,
I'm so ashamed of it
But must admit
The sleepless nights I've had about the boy.
On the Silver Screen
He melts my foolish heart in every single scene.

'Mad About the Boy' (song) in *Words and Music* (musical revue, 1932)

12 Don't put your daughter on the stage,
Mrs Worthington,
Don't put your daughter on the stage.

'Mrs Worthington' (song, 1935, with music by COLE PORTER). Noël Coward sang the song in the original recording.

13 The stately Homes of England,
How beautiful they stand,
To prove the upper classes
Have still the upper hand.
'The Stately Homes of England' (song) in *Operette* (musical show, 1938). See FELICIA HEMANS 1 and QUENTIN CRISP 6.

14 Please do not think that I criticize or cavil
At a genuine urge to roam,
But why oh why do the wrong people travel
When the right people stay back home?
'Why Do the Wrong People Travel?' (song) in *Sail Away* (musical show, 1962)

Abraham Cowley
(1618–67)
English poet and essayist

He published his first volume of verse, Poetical Blossom, *aged fifteen, and later explored metaphysical forms. He is best known for his Pindaric odes and the epic poem 'Davideis' (1656).* JOSEPH ADDISON *wrote of him: 'He more had pleased us, had he pleased us less.'*

1 Lukewarmness I account a sin,
As great in love as in religion.
'The Request', st. 4, publ. in *The Mistress* (1647)

2 The world's a scene of changes, and to be
Constant, in Nature were inconstancy.
'Inconstancy', ibid.

3 Love in her sunny eyes does basking play;
Love walks the pleasant mazes of her hair;
Love does on both her lips for ever stray;
And sows and reaps a thousand kisses there.
In all her outward parts Love's always seen;
But, oh, he never went within.
'The Change', ibid., st. 1

4 Well then; I now do plainly see
This busy world and I shall ne'er agree;
The very honey of all earthly joy
Does of all meats the soonest cloy,
And they (methinks) deserve my pity,
Who for it can endure the stings,
The crowd, and buzz, and murmurings
Of this great hive, the city.
'The Wish', ibid., st. 1

5 Ye fields of Cambridge, our dear Cambridge, say,
Have ye not seen us walking every day?
Was there a tree about which did not know

The love betwixt us two?
'On the Death of Mr William Hervey', st. 6, publ. in *Poems*, 'Miscellanies' (1656)

6 Poet and Saint! to thee alone are given
The two most sacred names of earth and Heaven.
'On the Death of Mr Crashaw', ibid. Opening lines of poem.

7 Hail, Bard triumphant! and some care bestow
On us, the Poets Militant below!
'On the Death of Mr Crashaw', ibid.

8 The thirsty earth soaks up the rain,
And drinks, and gapes for drink again.
The plants suck in the earth, and are
With constant drinking fresh and fair.
'Drinking', publ. in *Poems*, 'Anacreontics' (1656)

9 Fill all the glasses there, for why
Should every creature drink but I,
Why, man of morals, tell me why?
'Drinking', ibid.

10 Life is an incurable disease.
'To Dr Scarborough', st. 6, publ. in *Poems*, 'Pindaric Odes' (1656)

11 Nothing so soon the drooping spirits can raise
As praises from the men, whom all men praise.
'Ode Upon Occasion of a Copy of Verses of My Lord Broghill's', st. 4, publ. in *Verses Written upon Several Occasions* (1663)

12 God the first garden made, and the first city Cain.
'The Garden', st. 3, publ. in *Essays in Verse and Prose* (1668). See also WILLIAM COWPER 32.

Hannah Cowley
(1743–1809)
English playwright

One of the earliest English female playwrights, she wrote a series of successful comedies of manners for the London stage, most notably The Belle's Stratagem *(1780).*

1 The charms of women were never more powerful, never inspired such achievements, as in those immortal periods, when they could neither read nor write.
Who's the Dupe?, Act 1, Sc. 3 (1779). Spoken by Gradus.

2 But what is woman? – only one of Nature's agreeable blunders.
Granger, ibid., Act 2, Sc. 2

3 Five minutes! Zounds! I have been five minutes too late all my life-time!
The Belle's Stratagem, Act 1, Sc. 1 (1780). Spoken by Saville's servant.

4 O Lord! your wise men are the greatest fools upon earth; they reason about their enjoyments, and analyse their pleasures, whilst the essence escapes.
Flutter, ibid., Act 4, Sc. 1

William Cowper

(1731–1800)

English poet

His output ranged from the intensely religious verse he contributed to Olney Hymns *(1779) to the humorous ballad 'The Diverting History of John Gilpin' (1783), and the rural themes of* The Task *(1785). His quiet life in the country was interrupted by bouts of mental illness.*

1 Man disavows, and Deity disowns me:
Hell might afford my miseries a shelter;
Therefore hell keeps her ever-hungry mouths all
Bolted against me.
'Lines Written During a Period of Insanity', ll. 9–12 (written c. 1774), publ. in *Memoir* (ed. Cox, 1816)

2 Oh! for a closer walk with God,
A calm and heav'nly frame.
'Walking with God', publ. in *Olney Hymns*, bk 1, no. 3 (1779)

3 There is a fountain filled with blood
Drawn from Emmanuel's veins;
And sinners, plunged beneath that flood,
Lose all their guilty stains.
'Praise for the Fountain Opened', ibid., bk 1, no. 79

4 And Satan trembles when he sees
The weakest saint upon his knees.
'Exhortation to Prayer', ibid., bk 2, no. 60

5 God moves in a mysterious way,
His wonders to perform;
He plants his footsteps in the sea,
And rides upon the storm.
'Light Shining Out of Darkness', ibid., bk 3, no. 15

6 Behind a frowning providence
He hides a smiling face.
'Light Shining Out of Darkness', ibid.

7 Candid and generous and just,
Boys care but little whom they trust,
An error soon corrected –
For who but learns in riper years,
That man, when smoothest he appears,
Is most to be suspected?
'Friendship', ll. 19–24 (written 1781), publ. in *Poems*, vol. 2 (1800)

8 A fretful temper will divide
The closest knot that may be tied,

By ceaseless sharp corrosion;
A temper passionate and fierce
May suddenly your joys disperse
At one immense explosion.
'Friendship', ll. 61–6, ibid.

9 A man renowned for repartee
Will seldom scruple to make free
With friendship's finest feeling,
Will thrust a dagger at your breast,
And say he wounded you in jest,
By way of balm for healing.
'Friendship', ll. 91–6, ibid.

10 The man that hails you Tom or Jack,
And proves by thumps upon your back
How he esteems your merit,
Is such a friend, that one had need
Be very much his friend indeed
To pardon or to bear it.
'Friendship', ll. 169–74, ibid.

11 Thus happiness depends, as nature shows,
Less on exterior things than most suppose.
'Table Talk', ll. 246–7, publ. in *Poems* (1782)

12 Freedom has a thousand charms to show,
That slaves, howe'er contented, never know.
'Table Talk', ll. 260–1, ibid.

13 Manner is all in all, whate'er is writ,
The substitute for genius, sense, and wit.
'Table Talk', ll. 542–3, ibid.

14 Then Pope, as harmony itself exact,
In verse well discipined, complete, compact,
Gave virtue and morality a grace,
That, quite eclipsing pleasure's painted face,
Levied a tax of wonder and applause,
Even on the fools that trampled on their laws.
But he (his musical finesse was such,
So nice his ear, so delicate his touch)
Made poetry a mere mechanic art;
And every warbler has his tune by heart.
'Table Talk', ll. 646–55, ibid.

15 Remorse, the fatal egg by pleasure laid
In every bosom where her nest is made.
'The Progress of Error', ll. 239–40, ibid.

16 How much a dunce that has been sent to roam
Excels a dunce that has been kept at home.
'The Progress of Error', ll. 415–16, ibid.

17 So may the ruffian, who with ghostly glide,
Dagger in hand, steals close to your bedside;

Not he, but his emergence forced the door,
He found it inconvenient to be poor.
'Charity', ll. 188–9, ibid.

18 Once more I would adopt the graver style –
A teacher should be sparing of his smile.
'Charity', ll. 489–90, ibid.

19 'Tis hard if all is false that I advance –
A fool must now and then be right, by chance.
'Conversation', ll. 95–6, ibid.

20 A tale should be judicious, clear, succinct;
The language plain, and incidents well linked;
Tell not as new what ev'ry body knows,
And, new or old, still hasten to a close.
'Conversation', ll. 235–8, ibid.

21 The pipe, with solemn interposing puff,
Makes half a sentence at a time enough;
The dozing sages drop the drowsy strain,
Then pause, and puff – and speak, and pause
    again.
'Conversation', ll. 245–8, ibid.

22 Pernicious weed! whose scent the fair annoys,
Unfriendly to society's chief joys.
'Conversation', ll. 251–2, ibid. Of tobacco.

23 I cannot talk with civet in the room,
A fine puss-gentleman that's all perfume.
'Conversation', ll. 283–4, ibid.

24 He likes the country, but in truth must own,
Most likes it, when he studies it in town.
'Retirement', ll. 573–4, ibid.

25 'Tis easy to resign a toilsome place,
But not to manage leisure with a grace.
'Retirement', ll. 621–2, ibid.

26 Till authors hear at length, one general cry,
Tickle and entertain us, or we die.
The loud demand, from year to year the same,
Beggars invention and makes fancy lame,
Till farce itself, most mournfully jejune,
Calls for the kind assistance of a tune;
And novels (witness every month's review)
Belie their name, and offer nothing new.
'Retirement', ll. 707–14, ibid.

27 I am monarch of all I survey,
My right there is none to dispute.
'Verses Supposed to be Written by Alexander Selkirk', ll. 1–2,
ibid.

28 Oh, solitude! where are the charms
That sages have seen in thy face?
'Verses Supposed to be Written by Alexander Selkirk', ll. 5–6,
ibid.

29 Religion! what treasure untold
Resides in that heavenly word!
'Verses Supposed to be Written by Alexander Selkirk', ll. 25–
6, ibid.

30 The poplars are felled, farewell to the shade
And the whispering sound of the cool colonnade.
'The Poplar-Field', st. 1 (1784), publ. in *Poems*, vol. 2 (1800)

31 Mr Grenville squeezed me by the hand again,
kissed the ladies, and withdrew. He kissed likewise
the maid in the kitchen, and seemed upon the whole
a most loving, kissing, kind-hearted gentleman.
Letter, 29 March 1784, publ. in *Letters and Prose Writings of
William Cowper*, vol. 2 (ed. James King and Charles Ryskamp,
1981)

32 God made the country, and man made the
    town.
The Task, bk 1 ('The Sofa'), l. 749, publ. in *Poems* (1785). See
also ABRAHAM COWLEY 12.

33 England, with all thy faults, I love thee still –
My country!
Ibid., bk 2 ('The Time-piece'), ll. 206–7, ibid. See also CHARLES
CHURCHILL 9.

34 There is a pleasure in poetic pains
Which only poets know.
Ibid., bk 2, ll. 285–6

35 O, popular applause! what heart of man
Is proof against thy sweet, seducing charms?
Ibid., bk 2, ll. 481–2

36 Variety's the very spice of life
That gives it all its flavour.
Ibid., bk 2, ll. 606–7

37 Domestic happiness, thou only bliss
Of Paradise that has survived the fall!
Ibid., bk 3 ('The Garden'), ll. 41–2

38 Defend me, therefore, common sense, say I,
From reveries so airy, from the toil
Of dropping buckets into empty wells,
And growing old in drawing nothing up!
Ibid., bk 3, ll. 187–90

39 Such was thy wisdom, Newton, childlike sage!
Sagacious reader of the works of God,
And in his word sagacious.
Ibid., bk 3, ll. 252–4

40 Detested sport,
That owes its pleasures to another's pain:
That feeds upon the sobs and dying shrieks
Of harmless nature.
Ibid., bk 3, ll. 326–9. Referring to hunting.

41 Now stir the fire, and close the shutters fast,
Let fall the curtains, wheel the sofa round,
And, while the bubbling and loud-hissing urn
Throws up a steamy column, and the cups,
That cheer but not inebriate, wait on each,
So let us welcome peaceful evening in.
Ibid., bk 4 ('The Winter Evening'), ll. 36–41

42 I crown thee king of intimate delights,
Fire-side enjoyments, home-born happiness,
And all the comforts that the lowly roof
Of undisturbed retirement, and the hours
Of long uninterrupted evening, know.
Ibid., bk 4, ll. 139–43

43 Drink, and be mad, then; 'tis your country
bids!
Gloriously drunk, obey th' important call!
Ibid., bk 4, ll. 509–10

44 There is in souls a sympathy with sounds;
And, as the mind is pitched, the ear is pleased
With melting airs, or martial, brisk, or grave:
Some chord in unison with what we hear
Is touched within us, and the heart replies.
Ibid., bk 6 ('The Winter Walk at Noon'), ll. 1–5

45 Knowledge, a rude unprofitable mass,
The mere materials with which wisdom builds,
Till smoothed and squared and fitted to its place,
Does but encumber whom it seems to enrich.
Knowledge is proud that he has learned so much;
Wisdom is humble that he knows no more.
Ibid., bk 6, ll. 92–7

46 Nature is but a name for an effect,
Whose cause is God.
Ibid., bk 6, ll. 223–4

47 The parson knows enough who knows a Duke.
'Tirocinium', l. 403, publ. in Poems (1785)

48 John Gilpin kissed his loving wife;
O'erjoyed was he to find
That, though on pleasure she was bent,
She had a frugal mind.
'The Diverting History of John Gilpin', st. 8, ibid.

49 Forced from home, and all its pleasures,
Afric's coast I left forlorn;

To increase a stranger's treasures,
O'er the raging billows borne.
Men from England bought and sold me,
Paid my price in paltry gold;
But, though theirs they have enrolled me,
Minds are never to be sold.
'The Negro's Complaint', st. 1 (1788), publ. in Poems, vol. 1
(1800)

50 I pity them greatly, but I must be mum,
For how could we do without sugar and rum?
'Pity for Poor Africans', st. 2 (1788), ibid.

George Crabbe
(1754–1832)
English poet

Supported by EDMUND BURKE, he achieved success with 'The
Village' (1783), a harsh depiction of rural life. One of the twenty-
four verse tales in The Borough (1810) was the basis of BEN-
JAMIN BRITTEN's opera, Peter Grimes.

1 The cold charities of man to man.
The Village, bk 1, l. 245 (1783)

2 Our farmers round, well pleased with constant
gain,
Like other farmers, flourish and complain.
The Parish Register, pt 1, 'Baptisms', ll. 273–4 (1807)

3 With awe, around these silent walks I tread;
These are the lasting mansions of the dead.
The Library, ll. 105–6 (1808)

4 Fashion, though Folly's child, and guide of fools,
Rules e'en the wisest, and in learning rules.
Ibid., ll. 167–8

5 While the town small-talk flows from lip to lip;
Intrigues half-gathered, conversation-scraps,
Kitchen-cabals, and nursery-mishaps.
The Borough, Letter 3 ('The Vicar'), ll. 70–2 (1810)

6 Habit with him was all the test of truth,
'It must be right: I've done it from my youth.'
Ibid., Letter 3 ('The Vicar'), ll. 138–9

7 Secrets with girls, like loaded guns with boys,
Are never valued till they make a noise.
Tales of the Hall, 'The Maid's Story', ll. 84–5 (1819)

Hart Crane
(1899–1932)
US poet

Influenced by RIMBAUD *and* T. S. ELIOT, *he is remembered principally for* The Bridge *(1930), a wide-ranging and epic portrait of American culture. He committed suicide.*

1 Cowslip and shad-blow, flaked like tethered foam
Around bared teeth of stallions, bloomed that
    spring
When first I read thy lines, rife as the loam
Of prairies, yet like breakers cliffward leaping!
'Cape Hatteras', publ. in *The Bridge*, sect. 4 (1930). Addressed to WALT WHITMAN.

2 yes, Walt,
Afoot again, and onward without halt, –
Not soon, nor suddenly, – no, never to let go
My hand
in yours,
Walt Whitman –
so –
'Cape Hatteras', ibid. Final lines of poem.

3 And through that cordage, threading with its call
One arc synoptic of all tides below –
Their labyrinthine mouths of history
Pouring reply as though all ships at sea
Complighted in one vibrant breath made cry, –
'Make thy love sure – to weave whose song we
    ply!'
'Atlantis', publ. in *The Bridge* sect. 8 (1930)

4 We left the haven hanging in the night –
Sheened harbor lanterns backward fled the keel.
Pacific here at time's end, bearing corn. –
Eyes stammer through the pangs of dust and steel.
'Atlantis', ibid.

Stephen Crane
(1871–1900)
US author, poet and journalist

Considered the frst modern American writer, he published in 1895 both The Black Riders, *a volume of verse, and* The Red Badge of Courage, *a classic novel of the Civil War. He was also renowned for his short stories, many of them inspired by his work as a war correspondent.*

1 They were going to look at war, the red animal
war – war, the blood-swollen god.
The Red Badge of Courage, ch. 3 (1895)

2 A man said to the universe:
'Sir, I exist!'

'However,' replied the universe,
'The fact has not created in me
a sense of obligation.'
War is Kind & Other Lines, no. 21 (1899)

3 Every sin is the result of a collaboration.
Attributed

Adelaide Crapsey
(1878–1914)
US poet

Her poetry was written during the last year of her life, mostly in the cinquain verse form which she devised, comprising five unrhyming lines of two, four, six, eight and two syllables.

1 These be
Three silent things:
The falling snow ... the hour
Before the dawn ... the mouth of one
Just dead.
'Triad', publ. in *Verse* (1915)

Richard Crashaw
(c. 1613–49)
English poet

He is best known for his religious poems, often employing flamboyant imagery. He also wrote secular verse in Latin and English. He lived in France from 1644, where he converted to Catholicism, and died in Italy.

1 *Nympha pudica Deum vidit, et erubuit.*
[The chaste nymph saw God, and blushed.]
'Aquae in vinum versae', publ. in *Epigrammata Sacra* (1634). Translated by DRYDEN as, 'The conscious water saw its God, and blushed.'

2 I would be married, but I'd have no wife,
I would be married to a single life.
'On Marriage', publ. in *Steps to the Temple* (1648)

3 By all the eagle in thee, all the dove.
'The Flaming Heart upon the Book of Saint Teresa', l. 95, publ. in *Sacred Poems* (1652)

4 And when life's sweet fable ends,
Soul and body part like friends;
No quarrels, murmurs, no delay;
A kiss, a sigh, and so away.
'Temperance', ibid.

Marcus Licinius Crassus

(c. 108–53 BC)

Roman political leader

A powerful landowner in Rome, he gained prestige for his part in suppressing the revolt of Spartacus (71 BC), and was a member of the First Triumvirate with JULIUS CAESAR *and Pompey (60 BC).*

1 Those who aim at great deeds should also suffer greatly.

Quoted in *Parallel Lives*, ch. 26, by PLUTARCH

Mandell Creighton

(1843–1901)

English prelate and historian

Professor of Ecclesiastical History at Cambridge (1884–91) and Bishop of Peterborough in 1891, he published works on English history.

1 No people do so much harm as those who go about doing good.

Quoted in *The Life and Letters of Mandell Creighton*, vol. 2, ch. 14 (ed. Louise Creighton, 1904)

Quentin Crisp

(1908–99)

British author and raconteur

Originally Dennis Pratt. Following the success of his witty autobiography The Naked Civil Servant *(1968), he moved permanently to New York. He continued to write and give public performances.*

1 Vice is its own reward. It is virtue which, if it is to be marketed with consumer appeal, must carry Green Shield stamps.

The Naked Civil Servant, ch. 2 (1968)

2 The poverty from which I have suffered could be diagnosed as 'Soho' poverty. It comes from having the airs and graces of a genius and no talent.

Ibid., ch. 7

3 To know all is not to forgive all. It is to despise everybody.

Ibid., ch. 11

4 There was no need to do any housework at all. After the first four years the dirt doesn't get any worse.

Ibid., ch. 15

5 Life was a funny thing that happened to me on the way to the grave.

Ibid., ch. 18

6 I became one of the stately homos of England.

Ibid., ch. 24. Alluding to Noël Coward's song and Felicia Heman's poem. See NOËL COWARD 13 and FELICIA HEMANS 1.

7 An autobiography is an obituary in serial form with the last instalment missing.

Ibid., ch. 29

8 The very purpose of existence is to reconcile the glowing opinion we have of ourselves with the appalling things that other people think about us.

How to Become a Virgin, ch. 2 (1981)

9 It is explained that all relationships require a little give and take. This is untrue. Any partnership demands that we give and give and give and at the last, as we flop into our graves exhausted, we are told that we didn't give enough.

Ibid., ch. 4

10 Living *en famille* provides the strongest motives for rudeness combined with the maximum opportunity for displaying it.

Manners from Heaven, ch. 2 (1984)

11 Manners are love in a cool climate.

Ibid., ch. 2

12 A gentleman doesn't pounce . . . he glides.

Ibid., ch. 6

13 The formula for achieving a successful relationship is simple: you should treat all disasters as if they were trivialities but never treat a triviality as if it were a disaster.

Ibid., ch. 7

14 The time comes for everyone to do deliberately what he used to do by mistake . . . If you are effeminate by nature, you have to find some way of telling the world that you know you are, otherwise they keep telling you.

Quoted in obituary, *The Times* 22 November 1999

Julian Critchley

(1930–2000)

British politician

His sceptical, often maverick political views ensured that he remained an outsider at Westminster, where he was Conservative MP for Aldershot (1970–97), though his newspaper columns and books have kept him in the public eye.

1 The only safe pleasure for a parliamentarian is a bag of boiled sweets.
Listener 10 June 1982. *A Bag of Boiled Sweets* was the title of Critchley's memoirs (1994).

2 She has been beastly to the Bank of England, has demanded that the BBC 'set its house in order' and tends to believe the worst of the Foreign and Commonwealth Office. She cannot see an institution without hitting it with her handbag.
Quoted in *The Times* 21 June 1982. Referring to MARGARET THATCHER.

Croesus
(d. *c.* 547 BC)
Lydian king

The last King of Lydia, he was famed for his great wealth. Having overrun the Greeks of mainland Ionia (on the west coast of Anatolia), he waged war against Persia, supposedly after misinterpreting a Delphic oracle, and was defeated and imprisoned by Cyrus the Great in 546 BC.

1 In peace children bury fathers, but in war fathers bury sons. It must have been heaven's will that this should happen.
Quoted in *The Histories*, bk 1, sect. 87 by HERODOTUS. Spoken to the Persian king, Cyrus.

Richmal Crompton
(1890–1969)
British author

Originally Richmal Crompton Lamburn. She made her name with the schoolboy character William Brown, who appeared in magazines from 1919 and in thirty-eight books, starting with Just–William (1922).

1 I'll thcream and thcream and thcream till I'm thick.
Still–William, ch. 8 (1925). Spoken by Violet Elizabeth Bott, who demands that William 'play houth' with her. She is renowned for her scream: in *William–In Trouble* it would 'have put a factory siren to shame' and was 'guaranteed to reduce anyone within ten yards of it to quite an expensive nervous breakdown'.

2 I like you better than *any* insect, Joan.
William, ibid., ch. 14. William explains his intention to marry Joan, the girl next door, as long as he wasn't expected 'to talk a lot of soppy stuff'.

3 There's Conservatives an' they want to make things better by keepin' 'em jus' like what they are now. An' there's Lib'rals an' they want to make things better by alterin' them jus' a bit, but not so's anyone'd notice, an' there's communists an' they want to make things better by killin' everyone but themselves.
William the Bad, ch. 3 (1930). Spoken by Henry.

Oliver Cromwell
(1599–1658)
English soldier and politician

A leading Puritan in Parliament, he became the commander of the anti-Royalist forces during the Civil War, training the New Model Army and winning victories at Edgehill (1642), Marston Moor (1644) and Naseby (1645). He was Lord Protector of England 1653–8.

1 A few honest men are better than numbers.
Letter, September 1643, publ. in *Oliver Cromwell's Letters and Speeches*, vol. 1, no. 16 (ed. THOMAS CARLYLE, second edn, 1846)

2 I would rather have a plain, russet-coated captain, that knows what he fights for, and loves what he knows, than that which you call 'a gentleman' and is nothing else.
Letter, September 1643, ibid., vol. 1, no. 16

3 Do not trust to that, for these very persons would shout as much if you and I were going to be hanged.
Quoted in *Writings and Speeches of Oliver Cromwell*, vol. 2, 'The Campaign in Scotland' (ed. W. C. Abbott, 1939). Comment to Colonel John Lambert and Colonel Richard Ingoldsby, Northampton, July [?] 1650, on the cheering crowds during their ride north.

4 I beseech you, in the bowels of Christ, think it possible you may be mistaken.
Letter to the General Assembly of the Scottish Kirk, 3 August 1650, publ. in *Oliver Cromwell's Letters and Speeches*, no. 136 (ed. THOMAS CARLYLE, 1845)

5 It is high time for me to put an end to your sitting in this place, which you have dishonoured by your contempt of all virtue, and defiled by your practice of every vice; ye are a factious crew, and enemies to all good government ... Ye have no more religion than my horse; gold is your God ... I command ye therefore, upon the peril of your lives, to depart immediately out of this place; go, get you out! Make haste! Ye venal slaves be gone! So! Take away that shining bauble there, and lock up the doors. In the name of God, go!
Speech, 20 April 1653, dismissing the 'rump' of the Long Parliament, publ. in *The Penguin Book of Historic Speeches* (ed. Brian MacArthur, 1995). Cromwell later justified his action: 'When I was there, I did not think to have done this. But perceiving the Spirit of God so strong upon me, I would not

consult flesh and blood.' The move was a popular one in the nation, inspiring the ditty: 'Brave Oliver came to the House like a sprite,/His fiery face struck the Speaker dumb;/ "Begone," said he, "you have sat long enough,/Do you think to sit here till Doomsday come?"' – quoted in *History of England*, bk 4, ch. 4 (1927) by G. M. Trevelyan. Some sources quote Cromwell saying: 'Take away that fool's bauble!' See also LEO AMERY 2.

6 Necessity hath no law.

Speech to Parliament, 12 September 1654, quoted in *Oliver Cromwell's Letters and Speeches* (ed. THOMAS CARLYLE, 1845). The proverb has a lineage extending as far back as PLUTARCH.

7 Weeds and nettles, briars and thorns, have thriven under your shadow; dissettlement and division, discontentment and dissatisfaction, together with real dangers to the whole has been more multiplied within these five months of your sitting, than in some years before.

Quoted in *Writings and Speeches*, vol. 3, ch. 12 (ed. W. C. Abbott, 1945). On dissolving the First Protectoral Parliament, 22 January 1655.

8 Mr Lely, I desire you would use all your skill to paint my picture truly like me, and not flatter me at all; but remark all these roughnesses, pimples, warts, and everything as you see me, otherwise I will never pay a farthing for it.

Remark to painter Sir Peter Lely, c. 1657, quoted in *Anecdotes of Painting in England*, vol. 3, ch. 1 (1763) by HORACE WALPOLE. Usually quoted 'warts and all'.

9 No man rises so high as he knows not whither he goes.

Quoted in *Essays in English History*, 'Cromwell and the Historians' (1976) by A. J. P. Taylor

10 Cruel necessity.

Remark, 1649, quoted in *Anecdotes, Observations, and Characters, of Books and Men*, sect. 7 (1820) by Joseph Spence. Cromwell's words upon paying his last respects (anonymously) to CHARLES I after his execution.

11 It is not my design to drink or to sleep, but my design is to make what haste I can to be gone.

Last words, quoted in *Cromwell: Our Chief of Men*, ch. 23 (1973) by Antonia Fraser

Bing Crosby
(1903–77)
US singer and actor

Hugely popular throughout a career spanning fifty years, he was known for his rich, crooning voice and roles in such light comedies as the Road to . . . *comedy series and* High Society *(1956). See* IRVING BERLIN 6.

1 He was an average guy who could carry a tune.

Suggested epitaph for himself, in *Newsweek* 24 October 1977

Tony Crosland
(1918–77)
British politician

Considered Labour's leading intellectual in his time, he became an MP in 1950 and was author of the influential analysis of his party's role, The Future of Socialism *(1956). He died suddenly ten months after becoming Foreign Secretary.*

1 If it's the last thing I do, I'm going to destroy every fucking grammar school in England. And Wales. And Northern Ireland.

Quoted in *Tony Crosland*, ch. 16 (1982) by Susan Crosland. Said to his wife c. 1965, when Crosland was Secretary for Education and Science. 'The school system in Britain remains the most divisive, unjust, and wasteful of all aspects of social equality,' he wrote in *The Future of Socialism*.

Richard Crossman
(1907–74)
British politician

Elected Labour MP for Coventry East in 1945, he held cabinet posts in the government of HAROLD WILSON. *He is chiefly remembered for his detailed political diary, published posthumously. His colleague Bessie Braddock described him as 'a man of many opinions, most of them of short duration'.*

1 My Minister's room is like a padded cell, and in certain ways I am like a person who is suddenly certified a lunatic and put safely into this great, vast room, cut off from real life and surrounded by male and female trained nurses and attendants. When I am in a good mood they occasionally allow an ordinary human being to come in and visit me; but they make sure that I behave right, and that the other person behaves right; and they know how to handle me. Of course, they don't behave *quite* like nurses because the Civil Service is profoundly deferential – 'Yes, Minister! No, Minister! If you wish it, Minister!'

Journal entry, 22 October 1964, publ. in *The Crossman Diaries* (1979). Written after Crossman's first week in the Cabinet as Minister of Housing, the passage may have been the inspiration for the title of the TV series by ANTONY JAY and JONATHAN LYNN, *Yes, Minister* (1980–5), depicting a minister's relationship with the Civil Service.

Aleister Crowley

(1875–1947)

British occultist

An accomplished chess-master and mountaineer, he founded a system of beliefs based on what he called Thelema ('The Will') and others termed witchcraft. He wrote widely on this as well as yoga, astrology and the tarot. He was dubbed by the press, 'The Wickedest Man in the World'.

1 Do what thou wilt shall be the whole of the law.

The Book of the Law, ch. 1, verse 40 (1909). The words also appear in the book's preliminary 'Comment', and are repeated throughout Crowley's works, as representing the key to his philosophy. It recalls SAINT AUGUSTINE's 'Love and do what you will' (*Dilige et quod vis fac*), and Rabelais (see RABELAIS 7).

2 Ordinary morality is only for ordinary people.

The Confessions of Aleister Crowley, ch. 22 (1929; 1970 edn)

3 The pious pretence that evil does not exist only makes it vague, enormous and menacing.

Ibid., ch. 33

Robert Crumb

(b. 1943)

US cartoonist

One of America's most influential comic-book artists in the 1960s, he depicted a hippy subculture of political emancipation and sexual freedom. His Zap *(from 1967) is regarded as the first underground comic book.*

1 Keep on truckin' . . . truckin' on down the line . . . hey, hey, hey
I said keep on truckin' . . . truckin' my blues away.

Caption to cartoon, in *Zap Comix* no. 1 (1967), repr. in *R. Crumb's Head Comix* (1968, rev. 1988). The cartoon showed various large-booted characters walking through the city. 'Keep on truckin'' became one of the key hippy slogans of the 1960s and '70s, and was the subject of litigation proceedings over copyright ownership.

Ralph Cudworth

(1617–88)

English theologian and philosopher

A fellow and Professor of Hebrew at Cambridge, he is best remembered for The True Intellectual System of the Universe *(1678), a sprawling and unfinished work which argued against Hobbesian materialism. A fragment of it was published posthumously as* Treatise Concerning Eternal and Immutable Morality *(1731).*

1 Now all the knowledge and wisdom that is in creatures, whether angels or men, is nothing else but a participation of that one eternal, immutable and increated wisdom of God, or several signatures of that one archetypal seal, or like so many multiplied reflections of one and the same face, made in several glasses, whereof some are clearer, some obscurer, some standing nearer, some further off.

Treatise Concerning Eternal and Immutable Morality, bk 1, ch. 3, sect. 7 (1731)

2 Truth is the most unbending and uncompliable, the most necessary, firm, immutable, and *adamantine* thing in the world.

Ibid., bk 4, ch. 5, sect. 3

3 The true knowledge or science which exists nowhere but in the mind itself, has no other entity at all besides intelligibility; and therefore whatsoever is clearly intelligible, is absolutely true.

Ibid., bk 4, ch. 5, sect. 7

E. E. Cummings

(1894–1962)

US poet

Edward Estlin Cummings. He won international acclaim with The Enormous Room *(1922), an account of his wartime internment in France, but is now chiefly known for his poetry, either satirical or lyrical and set out in unorthodox typography.*

1 Humanity i love you because
when you're hard up you pawn your
intelligence to buy a drink

'La Guerre no. 2', publ. in *XLI Poems* (1925)

2 It is with roses and locomotives (not to mention acrobats Spring electricity Coney Island the 4th of July the eyes of mice and Niagara Falls) that my 'poems' are competing.

is 5, Foreword (1926)

3 next to of course god america i
love you land of the pilgrims and so forth oh
say can you see by the dawn's early my
country 'tis of centuries come and go
and are no more what of it we should worry
in every language even deafanddumb
thy sons acclaim your glorious name by gorry
by jing by gee by gosh by gum

'next to of course god america i', ibid.

4 The tabloid newspaper actually means to the typical American of the era what the Bible is popularly supposed to have meant to the typical Pilgrim Father: *viz.* a very present help in times of trouble, plus a means of keeping out of trouble via harmless,

since vicarious, indulgence in the pomps and vanities of this wicked world.
'The Tabloid Newspaper' (1926), repr. in *A Miscellany* (ed. George J. Firmage, 1958)

5 America makes prodigious mistakes, America has colossal faults, but one thing cannot be denied: America is always on the move. She may be going to Hell, of course, but at least she isn't standing still.
'Why I Like America' (1927), ibid.

6 a politician is an arse upon which everyone has sat except a man.
1 x 1, 'No. 10' (1944)

7 pity this busy monster, manunkind, not. Progress is a comfortable disease.
Ibid., 'No. 14'

8 We doctors know a hopeless case if – listen: there's a hell of a good universe next door; let's go.
Ibid., 'No. 14'

9 when man determined to destroy himself he picked the was of shall and finding only why smashed it into because
Ibid., 'No. 26'

10 anyone lived in a pretty how town (with up so floating many bells down) spring summer autumn winter he sang his didn't he danced his did.
50 Poems, 'No. 29' (1949)

11 It takes three to make a child.
'Jottings' (1951), publ. in *A Miscellany* (ed. George J. Firmage, 1958)

12 Knowledge is a polite word for dead but not buried imagination.
'Jottings', ibid.

13 for whatever we lose (like a you or a me) it's always ourselves we find in the sea
'maggie and milly and molly and may', publ. in *95 Poems* (1958)

14 The sensual mysticism of entire vertical being.
Quoted in *Architectural Digest* September 1986. Referring to New York City.

William Thomas Cummings
(1903–45)
US priest

An army chaplain, he was captured during the Second World War in the Philippines, where he died.

1 There are no atheists in the foxholes.
Sermon, Bataan (1942), quoted in *I Saw the Fall of the Philippines*, ch. 1 (1943) by Carlos P. Romulo. The Bataan Peninsula saw ferocious fighting when it was heroically defended for three months by US and Filipino forces. Its capture by the Japanese in April 1942 was followed by the notorious 'Bataan death march', in which thousands died.

Mario Cuomo
(b. 1932)
US politician

A Democrat, he held office as Governor of New York (1983–94) and was regarded as a potential presidential nominee in 1984, 1988 and 1992.

1 You campaign in poetry. You govern in prose.
New Republic 8 April 1985

Marie Curie
(1867–1934)
Polish-born French physicist

Originally Maria Sklodowska. From 1891 she studied in Paris, where she married Pierre Curie. Together they worked on radioactivity and discovered the elements polonium and radium. She won the Nobel Prize for Physics in 1903 (with Pierre Curie and Henri Becquerel) and for Chemistry in 1911.

1 In science, we must be interested in things, not in persons.
Quoted in *Madame Curie*, ch. 16 (1937, transl. 1943) by Ève Curie

Gaius Scribonius Curio
(d. 53 BC)
Roman statesman and orator

He was consul in 76 BC, governor of Macedonia, and the first Roman general to reach the Danube. He was implacably opposed to JULIUS CAESAR.

1 He is every woman's man and every man's woman.
Quoted in *Lives of the Caesars*, 'Julius', sect. 52, by Suetonius. Referring to JULIUS CAESAR.

John Philpot Curran
(1750–1817)
Irish lawyer and politician

He was called to the Bar in Dublin in 1775 where he gained a reputation for his ready wit and championship of civil liberties. He defended the leaders of the Society of United Irishmen and opposed the Act of Union (1800).

1 The condition upon which God hath given liberty to man is eternal vigilance; which condition if he break, servitude is at once the consequence of his crime, and the punishment of his guilt.
Speech in Dublin, 10 July 1790, publ. in *Speeches of the Right Hon. John Philpot Curran* (ed. Thomas Davis, 1847). On the right of election of the Lord Mayor of Dublin. GEORGE ORWELL wrote, in *The Road to Wigan Pier*, ch. 4 (1937): 'I sometimes think that the price of liberty is not so much eternal vigilance as eternal dirt.'

Edwina Currie
(b. 1946)
British politician and author

She became Conservative MP for Derbyshire South in 1983, and was Minister for Women's Health (1986–8). Since losing her seat in 1997, she has established herself as a novelist and radio presenter on Radio 5 Live.

1 Most of the egg production in this country sadly is now infected with salmonella.
TV interview, 3 March 1988. Currie's statement led to a national outcry and her resignation a fortnight later.

Richard Curtis
(b. 1956)
British screenwriter

An accomplished comedy writer, he co-wrote the Blackadder *(1984–9) and* Mr. Bean *(1989–95) TV series for Rowan Atkinson, and for the cinema scripted* Four Weddings and a Funeral *(1994) and* Notting Hill *(1999).*

1 So basically you're saying marriage is just a way of getting out of an embarrassing pause in conversation.
Four Weddings and a Funeral (film, 1994, screenplay by Richard Curtis, directed by Mike Newell). Spoken by Charles (Hugh Grant); Gareth answers, 'Yup. The definitive ice-breaker.'

2 It's pretty easy. Just say 'I do' whenever anyone asks you a question.
Carrie (Andie MacDowell), ibid.

Lord Curzon
(1859–1925)
British politician

Described by LLOYD GEORGE *as 'a supreme civil servant' and by* MAX BEERBOHM *as 'Britannia's butler', he was Viceroy of India 1898–1905, and Foreign Secretary in the Conservative government (1919–24). See* ANONYMOUS 61.

1 Dear me, I never knew that the lower classes had such white skins.
Attributed in *Superior Person*, ch. 12 (1969) by Kenneth Rose. The words were supposedly said by Curzon when touring the lines as a member of the War Cabinet during the First World War, when he saw troops bathing in beer kegs.

2 Not even a public figure. A man of no experience. And of the utmost insignificance.
Of STANLEY BALDWIN, quoted in *Curzon: the Last Phase*, ch. 12 (1934) by HAROLD NICOLSON. Curzon is supposed to have made the remark on hearing that Baldwin had become Prime Minister in 1923, a post Curzon himself had long aspired to. His rancour was suggested in a remark attributed to Baldwin when PM: 'I met Curzon in Downing Street, from whom I got the sort of greeting a corpse would give to an undertaker.'

Saint Cyprian
(c. 200–258)
Christian ecclesiastic

Thascius Caecilius Cyprianus. Two years after converting, he became Bishop of Carthage (c. 248), and the leader of Christians in Africa. Following the Decian persecution, he set historic guidelines for readmitting apostates into the church. He was martyred during a later period of persecution.

1 There can be no salvation to any except in the Church.
Epistle to Pomponius, Concerning Some Virgins (c. 249). The words were quoted by SAINT AUGUSTINE and often attributed to him.

2 He can no longer have God for his father, who has not the Church for his mother.
Concerning the Unity of the Church, sect. 6 (251). The treatise confirmed the primacy of the see of Peter in Rome over all other churches.

Savinien Cyrano de Bergerac
(1619–55)
French author and playwright

He fell under the influence of the philosopher Pierre Gassendi, whose Epicurean ideas about science, religion and free will were incorporated in Cyrano's works. He was said to have fought more than a thousand duels on account of his pro-digious nose.

1 A large nose is the mark of a witty, courteous, affable, generous, and liberal man.
The Other World: States and Empires of the Moon, ch. 8 (1656). Spoken by a 'lunarian'. The 'lunarian' inhabitants of the moon tell the time by using a natural sundial composed of their long noses, which project their shadows onto the 'dial' of their teeth. The speech was taken almost verbatim by EDMOND ROSTAND in his 1897 dramatization of Cyrano's life, *Cyrano de Bergerac*, Act 1, Sc. 4.

2 Luckless is the country in which the symbols of procreation are the objects of shame, while the agents of destruction are honoured! And yet you call that member your pudendum, or shameful part, as if there were anything more glorious than creating life, or anything more atrocious than taking it away.
A 'lunarian', ibid., ch. 8

D

D:Ream
British pop group

1 Things can only get better.
'Things Can Only Get Better' (song, 1993, written by Peter Cunnah, with music by Jamie Petrie). Sung by Cunnah, the song was released in 1993, topped the charts when remixed in 1994, and re-entered the top twenty after it was chosen as New Labour's election anthem in 1997.

Edward Dahlberg
(1900–77)
US author and critic

His travels as a hobo formed the basis for his first novels. In later life, he became something of a 'literary Jeremiah', attacking American materialism.

1 Genius, like truth, has a shabby and neglected mien.
Alms for Oblivion, 'For Sale' (1964)

2 The earnings of a poet could be reckoned by a metaphysician rather than a bookkeeper.
Ibid., 'For Sale'

3 What most men desire is a virgin who is a whore.
Reasons of the Heart, 'On Lust' (1965)

4 To write is a humiliation.
The Carnal Myth, Introduction (1968). See W. H. AUDEN 52.

Daily Express

1 It's that man again . . . !
Headline, 2 May 1939, referring to HITLER. The acronym ITMA was the title of a weekly satire on BBC radio (1939–49) starring Tommy Handley.

Daily Mirror

1 Whose finger do you want on the trigger?
Headline, 21 September 1951. Warning against voting the Conservative Party into power in the coming general election.

Dalai Lama (Tenzin Gyatso)

(b. 1935)
Spiritual and temporal leader of Tibet

He assumed his role as Dalai Lama in 1940. After he and his followers were forced to flee Tibet after an unsuccessful uprising against the occupying Chinese forces in 1959, he set up a government-in-exile in Dharamsala, India.

1 I have done nothing, really nothing for world peace. The only thing I do for peace is talk about it a great deal.

Interview in the *Sunday Telegraph* 9 August 1998

Richard J. Daley

(1902–76)
US politician

Richard Joseph Daley. One of the last of the big city bosses, he was Democratic Mayor of Chicago from 1955 until his death. The efficient operation of the so-called 'Daley Machine' is said to have ensured JOHN F. KENNEDY's *victory in the presidential election of 1960.*

1 The policeman isn't there to create disorder; the policeman is there to preserve disorder.

Quoted in *Don't Make No Waves: Don't Back No Losers* (1975) by Milton N. Rakove. Remark to the press, referring to the riots during the Democratic Convention in 1968. Daley was well known for his malapropisms. Others include: 'Ladies and gentlemen of the League of Women Voters' and 'It is amazing what they will be able to do once they get the atom harassed.'

Salvador Dalí

(1904–89)
Spanish artist

He became the highest-profile member of the Paris Surrealists which he joined in 1928, though they later spurned him. 'The Persistence of Memory' (better known as 'Limp Watches', 1931) is probably the best-known example of his dream-like juxtapositions. For ANDRÉ BRETON, *'Dalí is like a man who hesitates between talent and genius, or, as one might once have said, between vice and virtue.'*

1 Picasso is Spanish, I am too. Picasso is a genius. I am too. Picasso will be seventy-two and I about forty-eight. Picasso is known in every country of the world; so am I. Picasso is a Communist; I am not [*moi non plus*].

Lecture in Madrid, 12 October 1951, quoted in *Dalí*, ch. 12 (1992) by Meredith Etherington Smith. Dalí's lecture contained an apology to the Spanish Left who had branded him a coward and renegade during the Spanish Civil War, and a condemnation of PICASSO's espousal of Communism and his absence

from Spain. The final words are more familiarly quoted: 'Neither am I.'

2 There is only one difference between a madman and me. I am not mad.

Journal entry, May 1952, publ. in *Diary of a Genius* (1966)

3 Don't bother about being modern. Unfortunately it is the one thing that, whatever you do, you cannot avoid.

Journal entry, 15 July 1952, ibid.

4 I seated ugliness on my knee, and almost immediately grew tired of it.

Journal entry, 1 August 1953, ibid. Dalí's words echo those of Rimbaud: see RIMBAUD 14.

5 I have a Dalinian thought: the one thing the world will never have enough of is the outrageous.

Journal entry, 30 August 1953, ibid.

6 In order to acquire a growing and lasting respect in society, it is a good thing, if you possess great talent, to give, early in your youth, a very hard kick to the right shin of the society that you love. After that, be a snob.

Journal entry, 11 May 1956, ibid.

7 Take me, I am the drug; take me, I am hallucinogenic.

Dalí by Dalí, 'The Hallucogenic Dalí' (1970)

8 Those who do not want to imitate anything, produce nothing.

Ibid., 'The Futuristic Dalí'

9 This grandiose tragedy that we call modern art.

Ibid., 'The Futuristic Dalí'

10 *Le surréalisme, c'est moi.*
[I am surrealism.]

Quoted in *Surrealist Art*, ch. 5 (1969) by Saranne Alexandrian

Daniel Daly

(1874–1937)
Gunnery sergeant, US Marines

1 Come on you sons of bitches! Do you want to live for ever?

Attributed, at Belleau Wood, 4 June 1918. See also FREDERICK THE GREAT 1.

Mary Daly
(b. 1928)
US theologian and author

Her books, for example The Church and the Second Sex *(1968)* and Beyond God the Father *(1973), address the male bias in the Roman Catholic church from a feminist viewpoint.*

1 If God is male, then male is God. The divine patriarch castrates women as long as he is allowed to live on in the human imagination.
Beyond God the Father, ch. 1 (1973)

2 A woman's asking for equality in the church would be comparable to a black person's demanding equality in the Ku Klux Klan.
The Church and the Second Sex, New Autobiographical Preface (1975 edn)

Serge Daney
(1944–92)
French film critic

Regarded as one of France's greatest film critics, he was Editor of Cahiers du Cinéma *(1973–81), and contributed film columns to* Libération *during the 1980s.*

1 In an age of synthetic images and synthetic emotions, the chances of an accidental encounter with reality are remote indeed.
'Falling out of Love', publ. in *Sight and Sound* July 1992

Samuel Daniel
(c. 1562–1619)
English poet and dramatist

The writer of court masques, verse dramas and histories, he was praised for his sonnet sequence, Delia *(1592), and the poem, 'Musophilus' (1599). His essay,* A Defence of Rime *(1603), was a response to* THOMAS CAMPION*'s criticism of rhymed verse.*

1 Care-charmer Sleep, son of the sable Night,
Brother to Death, in silent darkness born:
Relieve my languish, and restore the light,
With dark forgetting of my care's return,
And let the day be time enough to mourn
The shipwreck of my ill adventured youth:
Let waking eyes suffice to wail their scorn,
Without the torment of the night's untruth.
Delia, Sonnet 45 (1592)

2 Fond man, Musophilus, that thus dost spend
In an ungrateful art thy dearest days,

Tiring thy wits and toiling to no end,
But to attain that idle smoke of praise.
'Musophilus', ll. 1–4, publ. in *Poetical Essays* (1599)

3 And who, in time, knows whither we may vent
The treasure of our tongue, to what strange shores
This gain of our best glory shall be sent,
T' enrich unknowing nations with our stores?
What worlds in th' yet unformed Occident
May come refined with th' accents that are ours?
Ibid., ll. 957–62

4 Custom that is before all law, Nature that is above all art.
A Defence of Rime (1603)

Dante Alighieri
(1265–1321)
Italian poet

Responsible for establishing Italian as a literary language, he wrote La Vita Nuova *(The New Life, c. 1293) and studies of philosophy and politics. His chief work was* La Divina Commedia *(The Divine Comedy, completed 1321), an epic in which he himself was the protagonist, visiting Hell and Purgatory, in the company of* VIRGIL*, and Paradise, guided by Beatrice, the idealized love of his life. Embroiled in the factional conflict engulfing his native city of Florence, he died in exile.*

1 *Nel mezzo del cammin di nostra vita,*
Mi ritrovai per una selva oscura,
Che la diritta via era smarrita.
[Midway along the journey of our life
I woke to find myself in a dark wood,
for I had wandered off from the straight path.]
The Divine Comedy, 'Inferno', canto 1, ll. 1–3 (c. 1307–21, transl. Mark Musa, 1971). Opening lines of work.

2 You are my teacher, the first of all my authors,
and you alone the one from whom I took
the noble style that was to bring me honour.
Ibid., 'Inferno', canto 1, ll. 85–7. Dante addresses Virgil.

3 I am the way into the doleful city.
I am the way into eternal grief,
I am the way to a forsaken race.
Ibid., 'Inferno', canto 3, ll. 1–3. Inscription at the entrance to Hell.

4 *Lasciate ogni speranza voi ch'entrate!*
[Abandon every hope, all you who enter.]
Ibid., 'Inferno', canto 3, l. 9. Inscription at the entrance to Hell.

5 Here sighs and cries and shrieks of lamentation
echoed throughout the starless air of Hell;
at first these sounds resounding made me weep:

tongues confused, a language strained in
    anguish
with cadences of anger, shrill outcries
and raucous groans that joined with sounds of
    hands,
raising a whirling storm that turns itself
forever through that air of endless black,
like grains of sand swirling when a whirlwind
    blows.
Ibid., 'Inferno', canto 3, ll. 22–30. Of the Vestibule to Hell.

6 This wretched state of being
is the fate of those sad souls who lived a life
but lived it with no blame and with no praise.
Ibid., 'Inferno', canto 3, ll. 34–6. Virgil describes the souls of
the Futile, in the Vestibule to Hell.

7 The world will not record their having been
    there;
Heaven's mercy and its justice turn from them.
Let's not discuss them; look and pass them by.
Virgil, ibid., 'Inferno', canto 3, ll. 49–51. Referring to the souls
of the Futile.

8 I saw the shade of the one who must have been
the coward who had made the great refusal [il
    gran rifiuto].
Ibid., 'Inferno', canto 3, ll. 59–60. Referring to one of the
Futile, possibly Pontius Pilate.

9 Onorate l'altissimo poeta;
L'ombra sua torna, ch'era dipartita.
[Now let us honour our illustrious poet,
his shade that left is now returned to us.]
Ibid., 'Inferno', canto 4, ll. 80–1. Addressed to Virgil, in Limbo.

10 The infernal storm, eternal in its rage,
sweeps and drives the spirits with its blast;
it whirls them, lashing them with punishment.
When they are swept back past their place of
    judgment
then come the shrieks, laments, and anguished
    cries;
there they blaspheme God's almighty power.
Ibid., 'Inferno', canto 5, ll. 31–6. Of the whirlwind of the Lustful, in the second circle of Hell.

11 Nessun maggior dolore,
Che ricordarsi del tempo felice
Nella miseria.
[There is no greater pain
than to remember, in our present grief,
past happiness.]
Francesca da Rimini, ibid., 'Inferno', canto 5, ll. 121–3. See also
BOETHIUS 1, CHAUCER 11, TENNYSON 37.

12 Medusa, come, we'll turn him into stone,
they shouted all together glaring down,
'how wrong we were to let off Theseus lightly!'
Ibid., canto 9, ll. 52–4. The three Furies threaten Dante at the
gates of Dis, the Infernal City.

13 Is this really you, here, Ser Brunetto?
Ibid., 'Inferno', canto 15, l. 30. Dante's words on meeting Brunetto Latini among the 'Sodomites' in the seventh circle of
Hell. A Florentine statesman and scholar, Latini was a close
friend and mentor of Dante in his youth.

14 Considerate la vostra semenza:
Fatti non foste a viver come bruti,
Ma per seguir virtute e conoscenza.
[Consider what you came from: you are Greeks!
you were not born to live like mindless brutes
but to follow paths of excellence and knowledge.]
Ibid., 'Inferno', canto 26, ll. 118–20. Ulysses, in Hell, repeats
his exhortation to his fellows on their last, disastrous voyage
beyond the pillars of Hercules.

15 I did not weep, I turned to stone inside.
Ibid., 'Inferno', canto 33, l. 49. Ugolino looks on the faces of
his two young sons, with whom he was starved to death in
the Tower of Hunger at Pisa.

16 E quindi uscimmo a riveder le stelle.
[And we came out to see once more the stars.]
Ibid., 'Inferno', canto 34, l. 139. Final line of the 'Inferno'; each
of the books of the Divine Comedy closes with a reference to
the stars.

17 O dignity of conscience, noble, chaste,
how one slight fault can sting you into shame!
Ibid., 'Purgatory', canto 3, ll. 8–9

18 The more one learns,
the more one comes to hate the waste of time.
Virgil, ibid., 'Purgatory', canto 3, ll. 77–8

19 Wait until she shall make it clearer – she,
the light between truth and intelligence.
Ibid., 'Purgatory', canto 6, ll. 44–5. Virgil refers to Beatrice.

20 Your earthly fame is but a gust of wind
that blows about, shifting this way and that,
and as it changes quarter, changes name.
Oderisi of Gubbio, ibid., 'Purgatory', canto 11, ll. 100–2

21 O race of men, born to fly heavenward,
how can a breath of wind make you fall back?
Ibid., 'Purgatory', canto 12, ll. 95–6

22 You are free subjects of a greater power,
a nobler nature that creates your mind,

and over this the spheres have no control.
Ibid., 'Purgatory', canto 16, ll. 79–81. Marco the Lombard addresses Dante and Virgil.

23 O power of fantasy that steals our minds
from things outside, to leave us unaware,
although a thousand trumpets may blow loud –
what stirs you if the senses show you nothing?
Light stirs you, formed in Heaven, by itself,
or by His will Who sends it down to us.
Ibid., 'Purgatory', canto 17, ll. 13–18

24 'I am,' she sang, 'the sweet Siren, I am,
whose song beguiles the sailors in mid-sea,
enticing them, inviting them to joy!
My singing made Ulysses turn away
from his desired course; who dwells with me
seldom departs, I satisfy so well.'
Ibid., 'Purgatory', canto 19, ll. 19–24. Sung by the Siren to Dante in his dream.

25 If anyone should want to know my name,
I am called Leah. And I spend all my time
weaving garlands of flowers with my fair hands,
to please me when I stand before the mirror;
my sister Rachel sits all the day long
before her own, and never moves away.
She loves to contemplate her lovely eyes;
I love to use my hands to adorn myself:
her joy is in reflection, mine in act.
Ibid., 'Purgatory', canto 27, ll. 100–8. Leah and Rachel traditionally stood for the active and the contemplative life.

26 Men che dramma
Di sangue m'è rimaso,
Che no tremi;
Conosco i segni dell' antica fiamma.
[Not one drop of blood
is left inside my veins that does not throb:
I recognize signs of the ancient flame.]
Ibid., 'Purgatory', canto 30, ll. 46–8. Dante recognizes Beatrice.

27 The glory of the One Who moves all things
penetrates all the universe, reflecting
in one part more and in another less.
Ibid., 'Paradiso', canto 1, ll. 1–3. Opening invocation.

28 And you will know how salty is the taste
of others' bread, how hard the road that takes
you down and up the stairs of others' homes.
Ibid., 'Paradiso', canto 17, ll. 58–60. Cacciaguida, Dante's great-great-grandfather, predicts years of exile.

29 Ora conosce quanto caro costa
non seguir Cristo, per l' esperienza
di questa dolce vita e de l'opposta.
[And now he knows from living this sweet life,
and having lived its opposite, how dear
it costs a man to fail to follow Christ.]
Ibid., 'Paradiso', canto 20, ll. 46–8. Referring to the Emperor Trajan who, despite dying a pagan, has reached Paradise by means of divine dispensation.

30 But like a wheel in perfect balance turning,
I felt my will and my desire impelled
by the love that moves the sun and the other stars.
[l'amor che muove il sole e l'altre stelle.]
Ibid., 'Paradiso', canto 33, ll. 143–5. Closing lines of the Divine Comedy.

Joe Darion
(1917–2001)
US songwriter

He was the lyricist for a number of Broadway musical shows in the 1960s, most successful of which was Man of La Mancha *(1965).*

1 To dream the impossible dream,
To reach the unreachable star!
'The Impossible Dream' (song, 1965, music by Mitch Leigh). Sung by Simon Gilbert, the song was dubbed onto the film *Man of La Mancha* (1972, adapted from the 1965 musical play by Darion and Mitch Leigh) for Peter O'Toole, in the role of Don Quixote, to mime to.

Charles Brace Darrow
(1889–1967)
US inventor

When Parker Bros rejected his game Monopoly, *he produced and marketed it himself. Parker Bros subsequently took up the option in 1935, since when over 200 million sets in twenty-six languages have been sold.*

1 Go to jail. Go directly to jail. Do not pass Go. Do not collect $200.
Instruction in *Monopoly* (1933). The board-game was devised by Darrow c. 1931, adapted from *The Landlord's Game* invented by Joanna Pitman in 1904.

Clarence Darrow
(1857–1938)
US lawyer and author

As a leading defence counsel he opposed capital punishment, Prohibition and segregation. His most famous cases were those of EUGENE DEBS, *who called the Pullman Strike (1894), and the so-called 'monkey trial' of John T. Scopes (1925).*

1 I do not pretend to know where many ignorant men are sure – that is all that agnosticism means.

Speech at Dayton, Tennessee, 13 July 1925, quoted in *The World's Most Famous Court Trial* ch. 4 (1925). Darrow was defending John Thomas Scopes, on trial for teaching Darwinism. Scopes was found guilty, though the decision was later overturned by the State Supreme Court.

2 When I was a boy I was told that anybody could become President. I'm beginning to believe it.

Quoted in *Clarence Darrow for the Defence*, ch. 6 (1941) by Irving Stone

Charles Darwin
(1809–82)
English naturalist

The observations made on an expedition to South America and the Pacific Ocean aboard HMS Beagle (1831–6) formed the basis of his theory of organic evolution, which he presented in 1859 and published in The Origin of Species *(1859). 'Darwinism' was further developed in later works, notably* The Descent of Man *(1871).*

1 Without speculation there is no good and original observation.

Letter to A. R. Wallace, 22 December 1857, publ. in *The Life and Letters of Charles Darwin*, (ed. Francis Darwin, 1887). Wallace was then working on a theory of natural selection similar to Darwin's.

2 Nothing is easier than to admit in words the truth of the universal struggle for life, or more difficult – at least I have found it so – than constantly to bear this conclusion in mind. Yet unless it be thoroughly engrained in the mind, I am convinced that the whole economy of nature, with every fact on distribution, rarity, abundance, extinction, and variation, will be dimly seen or quite misunderstood.

The Origin of Species, ch. 3 (1859)

3 From the war of nature, from famine and death, the most exalted object which we are capable of conceiving, namely, the production of the higher animals, directly follows. There is grandeur in this view of life, with its several powers, having been breathed into a few forms or into one; and that, whilst this planet has gone cycling on according to the fixed law of gravity, from so simple a beginning endless forms most beautiful and most wonderful have been, and are being, evolved.

Ibid., ch. 14. Closing words of book.

4 The highest possible stage in moral culture is when we recognize that we ought to control our thoughts.

The Descent of Man, ch. 4 (1871)

5 A hairy quadruped, furnished with a tail and pointed ears, probably arboreal in its habits.

Ibid., ch. 21. Referring to the ancestry of humankind, according to Darwin's theory. 'For my own part,' he wrote, 'I would as soon be descended from that heroic little monkey ... or that old baboon ... as from a savage who delights to torture his enemies, offers up bloody sacrifices, practises infanticide without remorse, treats his wives like slaves, knows no decency, and is haunted by the grossest superstitions.'

6 Man with all his noble qualities, with sympathy which feels for the most debased, with benevolence which extends not only to other men but to the humblest living creature, with his god-like intellect which has penetrated into the movements and constitution of the solar system – with all these exalted powers – man still bears in his bodily frame the indelible stamp of his lowly origin.

Ibid., ch. 21. Closing words of book.

(Sir) Francis Darwin
(1848–1925)
British botanist

He is known for his publications relating to his father, CHARLES DARWIN, *as well as for his work on vegetable physiology.*

1 In science the credit goes to the man who convinces the world, not to the man to whom the idea first occurs.

'Francis Galton', First Galton Lecture before the Eugenics Society, publ. in *Eugenics Review* April 1914

René Daumal
(1908–44)
French poet and critic

He was co-founder in 1928 of Le Grand Jeu, *both a review and a quasi-mystical group. His posthumous fame rests primarily on his novels,* A Night of Serious Drinking *(1938) and* Mount Analogue *(1952).*

1 It is still not enough for language to have clarity and content ... it must also have a goal and an imperative. Otherwise from language we descend to chatter, from chatter to babble and from babble to confusion.

A Night of Serious Drinking, Foreword (1938)

2 Each time dawn appears, the mystery is there in its entirety.

'Poetry Black, Poetry White' (1942), repr. in *The Powers of the Word* (ed./transl. Mark Polizzotti, 1991). *Chaque fois que l'aube paraît* was the title given to a posthumous anthology of Daumal's writings.

Hal David
(b. 1921)
US lyricist

Dating from 1957, his writing partnership with Burt Bacharach was one of the most successful in modern popular music, producing a string of hits, notably for Dionne Warwick.

1 Raindrops keep falling on my head.

'Raindrops Keep Falling on my Head' (song, 1969, with music by Burt Bacharach). Sung by B. J. Thomas in the film *Butch Cassidy and the Sundance Kid*, the Oscar-winning song was a hit for Sacha Distel in 1970.

Andrew Davies
(b. 1936)
British screenwriter

He has made skilful TV adaptations of classic novels, including Pride and Prejudice *(1995),* Wives and Daughters *(1999) and* Daniel Deronda *(2002).*

1 Tolstoy got it all wrong. It's the unhappy marriages that are boringly similar to each other; it's the happy ones that are so extraordinary and eccentric and unlike anyone else's.

Independent 7 August 1989. See LEO TOLSTOY 7.

2 You might say that, my dear: I couldn't possibly comment.

House of Cards (TV series, 1992, written by Andrew Davies, based on the original novel by Michael Dobbs). Spoken by Francis Urquhart (Ian Richardson) to the journalist Mattie Storin (Susannah Harker).

Jack Davies
(1913–94)
Ken Annakin
(b. 1914)
British screenwriter and British director

Davies was a comedy scriptwriter for Will Hay, Norman Wisdom and the 'Doctor' series of films. Annakin is better known as the director of such films as Swiss Family Robinson *(1960) and* Those Magnificent Men in Their Flying Machines *(1965).*

1 Those magnificent men in their flying machines,

or How I flew from London to Paris in 25 hours and 11 minutes.

Title of film (1965, screenplay by Jack Davies and Ken Annakin, directed by Ken Annakin). The film, for which the eponymous song was penned, was a comic account of the first London–Paris air race at the beginning of the 20th century.

(Sir) John Davies
(1569–1626)
English poet and lawyer

Called to the bar in 1595, he composed poetry throughout his career, which included serving as Attorney-General in Ireland (from 1606) and in the Irish and English parliaments. 'Orchestra' (1596) is a poem in praise of dancing and 'Nosce Te Ipsum' ('Know Thyself', 1599) addresses philosophy and cosmology.

1 This wondrous miracle did Love devise,
For dancing is love's proper exercise.

Orchestra, st. 185 (1596)

2 I know my life's a pain and but a span;
I know my sense is mocked in every thing:
And to conclude, I know myself a man,
Which is a proud, and yet a wretched thing.

Nosce Te Ipsum, st. 45 (1599)

Ray Davies
(b. 1944)
British rock musician

Co-founder and leader of the Kinks (from 1964), he contributed perceptive, witty and elegiac lyrics to such hits as 'Sunny Afternoon' (1966) and 'Waterloo Sunset' (1967). He has also written for film, the stage and television.

1 One week he's in polka dots, the next week he's
  in stripes,
'Cos he's a dedicated follower of fashion.

'Dedicated Follower of Fashion' (song), on the album *Kinks Kontroversy* (The Kinks, 1966)

2 As long as I gaze on Waterloo sunset, I am in
  paradise.

'Waterloo Sunset' (song), on the album *Something Else* (The Kinks, 1967)

Robertson Davies
(1913–95)
Canadian novelist and journalist

Described as 'Jane Austen reworking Rabelais', he is known for his articles written under the pseudonym Samuel Marchbanks, and for his tales of provincial life, the Deptford Trilogy *(1970–5) and the Cornish Trilogy (1981–8).*

1 To be apt in quotation is a splendid and dangerous gift. Splendid, because it ornaments a man's speech with other men's jewels; dangerous, for the same reason.
'Dangerous Jewels' (1960), repr. in *The Enthusiasms of Robertson Davies* (1990). 'Too much traffic with a quotation book begets a conviction of ignorance in a sensitive reader,' Davies noted. 'Not only is there a mass of quotable stuff he never quotes, but an even vaster realm of which he has never heard.'

2 If we seek the pleasures of love, passion should be occasional, and common sense continual.
'The Pleasures of Love' (1961), ibid.

3 Canada is not really a place where you are encouraged to have large spiritual adventures.
'The Table Talk of Robertson Davies', ibid.

4 Nothing is so easy to fake as the inner vision.
Saraceni, in *What's Bred in the Bone*, pt 4, 'What Would Not Out of the Flesh?' (1985)

W. H. Davies
(1871–1940)
British poet and author

William Henry Davies. He published numerous collections of verse, but his most successful work was an account of his itinerant life, Autobiography of a Super-tramp *(1906).*

1 What is this life if, full of care,
We have no time to stand and stare?
'Leisure', publ. in *Songs of Joy* (1911)

2 And hear the pleasant cuckoo, loud and long –
The simple bird that thinks two notes a song.
'April's Charms', publ. in *Child Lovers* (1916)

3 Girls scream,
Boys shout;
Dogs bark,
School's out.
'School's Out', publ. in *The Poems of W.H. Davies* (1934)

Angela Davis
(b. 1944)
US philosopher and political activist

Combining an academic career with a commitment to black rights, she gained international publicity in 1970 when she was acquitted of charges of supplying guns for the murder of a judge.

1 No potential victim of the fascist terror should be without the knowledge that the greatest menace to racism and fascism is unity!
If they come in the morning..., pt 2, 'Political Prisoners, Prisons and Black Liberation' (1971)

Bette Davis
(1908–89)
US screen actress

Originally Ruth Elizabeth Davis. She played strong, independent roles for more than five decades, memorably opposite Joan Crawford in Whatever Happened to Baby Jane? *(1962). Jack L. Warner remembered her as 'an explosive little broad with a straight left'.*

1 Oh, Jerry, don't let's ask for the moon – we have the stars.
Now, Voyager (film, 1942, screenplay by Casey Robinson based on the 1941 novel by Olive Higgins Prouty, directed by Irving Rapper). Spoken by Charlotte Vale (Bette Davis). The film's title is taken from WALT WHITMAN's *Leaves of Grass* (1855).

2 What a dump!
Beyond the Forest (film, 1949, screenplay by Leonore Coffee based on a novel by Stuart Engstrand, directed by King Vidor). Spoken by Rosa Moline (Bette Davis), referring to her small-town Wisconsin home which she dreams of escaping. According to Davis, the line is 'the only claim to fame that the film had or ever will have.' The words were famously quoted in EDWARD ALBEE's *Who's Afraid of Virginia Woolf?* (1962); in the film version of this (1966), Martha (Elizabeth Taylor) mimics Bette Davis's voice.

3 Fasten your seat belts. It's going to be a bumpy night.
All About Eve (film, 1950, written and directed by Joseph L. Mankiewicz). Spoken by Margo Channing (Bette Davis), bracing herself for a party.

4 To look back is to relax one's vigil.
The Lonely Life, ch. 1 (autobiography, 1962)

5 I see – she's the original good time that was had by all.
Attributed in *Parade* 15 February 1981. Referring to a starlet.

Sammy Davis Jr
(1925–90)
US entertainer

A 'one-eyed Jewish Negro', as he described himself, he was an accomplished singer, tap dancer, musician, mime and comedian. He starred in Broadway musicals such as Mr. Wonderful *(1956) and appeared in films.*

1 Being a star has made it possible for me to get

insulted in places where the average Negro could never hope to go and get insulted.
Yes I Can, pt 3, ch. 23 (1965)

Thomas Osborne Davis
(1814–45)
Irish poet and nationalist

He was one of the founders of the literary Young Ireland movement and of their organ, the Nation *newspaper (1842), to which he contributed articles, essays and poems.*

1 And then I prayed I yet might see,
Our fetters rent in twain,
And Ireland, long a province, be
A nation once again.
'A Nation Once Again', publ. in *National and Historical Ballads, Songs, and Poems* (1846)

2 Come in the evening, or come in the morning,
Come when you're looked for, or come without
  warning.
'The Welcome', st. 1, ibid.

Richard Dawkins
(b. 1941)
British biologist and author

The Selfish Gene (1976) was the first of a series of books which helped to explain and popularize sociobiology from a Darwinian perspective. In 1995 he became the first Professor of Public Understanding of Science at Oxford.

1 Much as we might wish to believe otherwise, universal love and the welfare of the species as a whole are concepts which simply do not make evolutionary sense.
The Selfish Gene, ch. 1 (1976)

2 They are in you and in me; they created us, body and mind; and their preservation is the ultimate rationale for our existence – they go by the name of genes, and we are their survival machines.
Ibid., ch. 2

3 Natural selection, the blind, unconscious, automatic process which Darwin discovered, and which we now know is the explanation for the existence and apparently purposeful form of all life, has no purpose in mind. It has no mind and no mind's eye. It does not plan for the future. It has no vision, no foresight, no sight at all. If it can be said to play the role of the watchmaker in nature, it is the *blind* watchmaker.
The Blind Watchmaker, ch. 1 (1986)

4 The essence of life is statistical improbability on a colossal scale.
Ibid., ch. 11

5 The universe we observe has precisely the properties we should expect if there is, at bottom, no design, no purpose, no evil and no good, nothing but blind, pitiless indifference . . . DNA neither cares nor knows. DNA just is. And we dance to its music.
River Out of Eden, ch. 4 (1995)

6 We are going to die, and that makes us the lucky ones. Most people are never going to die because they are never going to be born.
Unweaving the Rainbow, ch. 1 (1998). Opening lines of book.

7 If we want to sustain the planet into the future, the first thing we must do is stop taking advice from nature. Nature is a short-term Darwinian profiteer.
Observer 21 May 2000. Open letter to Prince Charles in response to his Reith Lecture.

Christopher Dawson
(1889–1970)
British historian

An esteemed Catholic scholar, he published works on European history, culture and religion, including The Age of the Gods *(1928) and* Religion and Culture *(1948).*

1 As soon as men decide that all means are permitted to fight an evil, then their good becomes indistinguishable from the evil that they set out to destroy.
The Judgement of the Nations, ch. 1 (1942)

Lord Dawson of Penn
(1864–1945)
British physician

Bertrand Edward Dawson, Viscount Dawson of Penn. Physician to several members of the British royal family, he helped to draw up a white paper for the inception of the National Health Service in 1944.

1 The King's life is moving peacefully towards its close.
Bulletin on the eve of the king's death, 20 January 1936, in *King George V*, ch. 1 (1983) by Kenneth Rose. The wording was supposedly drafted on a menu card at Buckingham Palace.

Doris Day
(b. 1922)
US singer and actor

Born Doris Kappelhoff. She began singing in the 1930s and made her film debut in Romance on the High Seas *(1948), later appearing in numerous light comedies and musicals.*

1 Que sera, sera,
Whatever will be, will be,
The future's not ours to see,
Que sera, sera,
What will be, will be.
'Whatever Will Be, Will Be', refrain (song, written by Jay Livingston and Ray Evans) in ALFRED HITCHCOCK's film *The Man Who Knew Too Much* (1956). In its Italian form, *Che sara sara* is the motto of the Russells (the dukes of Bedford), as mentioned in DICKENS' *Hard Times* (1854), spoken by James Harthouse: 'There's an English family with a charming Italian motto. What will be, will be. It's the only truth going!' (bk 2, ch. 2).

Dorothy Day
(1897–1980)
US reformer and author

A socialist, pacifist and Catholic convert, she co-founded the Catholic Worker *in 1933 and established the Catholic Worker movement, which aided victims of the Depression.*

1 All our talks about peace and the weapons of the spirit are meaningless unless we try in every way to embrace *voluntary poverty* and not work in any position, any job that contributes to war . . . We must give up our place in this world, sacrifice children, family, wife, mother, and embrace poverty, and then we will be laying down life itself.
Journal entry, 7 May 1948, publ. in *On Pilgrimage* (1948)

2 To go on picket lines to protest discrimination in housing, to protest the draft, is one of the works of mercy which include 'rebuking the sinner, enlightening the ignorant, counseling the doubtful'. But I confess I always do these things in fear and trembling.
Journal entry, 1 September 1948, ibid.

3 The best thing to do with the best things in life is to give them up.
Quoted in *Time* 29 December 1975

(Sir) Robin Day
(1915–2000)
British journalist and broadcaster

Known for his formidable interviewing techniques, he presented on BBC television Panorama *(1967–72) and* Question Time *(1979–89), and on radio* The World at One *(1979–87).*

1 Television thrives on unreason, and unreason thrives on television. It strikes at the emotions rather than the intellect.
Financial Times 8 November 1989

Cecil Day Lewis
(1904–72)
British poet

Initially associated with W. H. AUDEN *and his circle, he later became more of an Establishment figure. He was Professor of Poetry at Oxford (1951–6) and appointed Poet Laureate in 1968.*

1 Desire is a witch
And runs against the clock.
It can unstitch
The decent hem
Where space tacks on to time;
It can unlock
Pandora's privacies.
Transitional Poem, pt 2, sect. 15 (1929)

2 With me, my lover makes
The clock assert its chime:
But when she goes, she takes
The mainspring out of time.
Ibid., pt 3, sect. 27

3 Tempt me no more; for I
Have known the lightning's hour,
The poet's inward pride,
The certainty of power.
The Magnetic Mountain, sect. 24 (1933)

4 You that love England, who have an ear for her music,
The slow movement of clouds in benediction,
Clear arias of light thrilling over her uplands,
Over the chords of summer sustained peacefully.
Ibid., sect. 32

5 We'd like to fight but we fear defeat,
We'd like to work but we're feeling too weak,
We'd like to be sick but we'd get the sack,
We'd like to behave, we'd like to believe,
We'd like to love, but we've lost the knack.
Ibid., sect. 33

6 It is the logic of our times,
No subject for immortal verse –
That we who lived by honest dreams
Defend the bad against the worse.

'Where are the War Poets?', publ. in *Word Over All* (1943)

7 How selfhood begins with a walking away,
And love is proved in the letting go.

'Walking Away', publ. in *The Gate* (1962). Last lines of poem.

Simone de Beauvoir
(1908–86)
French philosopher and author

A celebrated feminist and existentialist, she had a long association with JEAN-PAUL SARTRE, with whom she founded the review Les Temps modernes *(1945). Her book* The Second Sex *(1949) became a classic feminist text.*

1 It is not in giving life but in risking life that man is raised above the animal; that is why superiority has been accorded in humanity not to the sex that brings forth but to that which kills.

The Second Sex, bk 1, pt 2, ch. 1 (1949)

2 One is not born, but rather becomes, a woman.

Ibid., bk 2, pt 4, ch. 1. ANDREA DWORKIN was perhaps alluding to de Beauvoir's famous statement when she wrote: 'Woman is not born: she is made. In the making, her humanity is destroyed. She becomes symbol of this, symbol of that: mother of the earth, slut of the universe; but she never becomes herself because it is forbidden for her to do so.' (*Pornography*, ch. 4, 1981)

3 To *make* oneself an object, to *make* oneself passive, is a very different thing from *being* a passive object.

Ibid., bk 2, pt 4, ch. 3

4 Sex pleasure in woman ... is a kind of magic spell; it demands complete abandon; if words or movements oppose the magic of caresses, the spell is broken.

Ibid., bk 2, pt 4, ch. 3

5 Between women love is contemplative; caresses are intended less to gain possession of the other than gradually to re-create the self through her; separateness is abolished, there is no struggle, no victory, no defeat; in exact reciprocity each is at once subject and object, sovereign and slave; duality become mutuality.

Ibid., bk 2, pt 4, ch. 4

6 Since it is the Other within us who is old, it is natural that the revelation of our age should come to us from outside – from others. We do not accept it willingly.

The Coming of Age, pt 2, ch. 5 (1970)

7 It is old age, rather than death, that is to be contrasted with life. Old age is life's parody, whereas death transforms life into a destiny: in a way it preserves it by giving it the absolute dimension ... Death does away with time.

Ibid., Conclusion

Louis de Bernières
(b. 1951)
British novelist

His stories are concerned with issues of freedom, power and ideology, as in Captain Corelli's Mandolin *(1994). Among his other books are* Señor Vivo and the Coca Lord *(1992) and* Red Dog *(2001).*

1 A guilty man wishes only to be understood, because to be understood is to appear to be forgiven.

Captain Corelli's Mandolin, ch. 10 (1994). Spoken by Carlo.

2 It's a fact of life that the honour of a family derives from the conduct of its women. I don't know why this is, and possibly matters are different elsewhere. But we live here, and I note the fact scientifically in the same way that I observe that there is snow on Mt Aenos in January and that we have no rivers.

Dr Iannis, ibid., ch. 47

3 Italians always act without thinking, it's the glory and the downfall of your civilisation. A German plans a month in advance what his bowel movements will be at Easter, and the British plan everything in retrospect, so it always looks as though everything occurred as they intended. The French plan everything whilst appearing to be having a party, and the Spanish ... well, God knows.

Dr Iannis to Captain Corelli, ibid., ch. 49

4 Every Greek, man, woman, and child, has two Greeks inside. We even have technical terms for them. They are a part of us, as inevitable as the fact that we all write poetry and the fact that every one of us thinks that he knows everything that there is to know.

Ibid., ch. 49. The two types, Iannis explained, correspond to the 'Hellene' and the 'Romoi'.

5 God is an oppressor, He is incapable of human sympathy; behind a smiling face He hides an evil heart.

Introduction to *The Book of Job*, (1998)

6 The real index of civilisation is when people are kinder than they need be.
'The Turks Are So Wonderful With Children', publ. in the *Guardian* 1 January 2000. Spoken by Robert.

Edward De Bono
(b. 1933)
British psychologist

His concept of 'lateral thinking' as a creative approach to problem solving was first propounded in The Use of Lateral Thinking *(1967) and has since been widely used in business and management studies.*

1 Some people are aware of another sort of thinking which ... leads to those simple ideas that are obvious only after they have been thought of ... the term 'lateral thinking' has been coined to describe this other sort of thinking; 'vertical thinking' is used to denote the conventional logical process.
The Use of Lateral Thinking, Foreword (1967)

2 Unhappiness is best defined as the difference between our talents and our expectations.
Quoted in the *Observer* 12 June 1977

Guy Debord
(1931–94)
French philosopher

A leading figure of the Situationist movement, he dealt with the interplay of modernity, capitalism and everyday life. His main work is The Society of the Spectacle *(1967). See also* MARSHALL MCLUHAN 3.

1 Boredom is always counter-revolutionary. Always.
'The Bad Old Days Will End' (1963), repr. in *The Incomplete Works of the Situationist International* (ed. Christopher Gray, 1974)

2 In societies where modern conditions of production prevail, all of life presents itself as an immense accumulation of *spectacles*. Everything that was directly lived has moved away into a representation.
The Society of the Spectacle, ch. 1, sect. 1 (1967)

3 Tourism, human circulation considered as consumption ... is fundamentally nothing more than the leisure of going to see what has become banal.
Ibid., ch. 7, sect. 168

4 Ideas improve. The meaning of words participates in the improvement. Plagiarism is necessary. Progress implies it. It embraces an author's phrase, makes use of his expressions, erases a false idea, and replaces it with the right idea.
Ibid., ch. 8, sect. 207

5 Young people everywhere have been allowed to choose between love and a garbage disposal unit. Everywhere they have chosen the garbage disposal unit.
The Incomplete Works of the Situationist International, 'Formula for a New City' (ed. Christopher Gray, 1974)

6 Quotations are useful in periods of ignorance or obscurantist beliefs.
Panegyric, pt 1 (first volume of autobiography, 1989)

De Bussy-Rabutin
See BUSSY-RABUTIN

Malcolm de Chazal
(1902–81)
French author

From semi-isolation on Mauritius he wrote his major work Sens plastique *(1946), which described the sexual act as a mediator between birth and death and caused a sensation when published in Paris.*

1 The idealist walks on tiptoe, the materialist on his heels.
Sens plastique, vol. 2 (1946)

Madame de Cornuel
(1605–94)
French society hostess

Anne Bigot de Cornuel. She hosted a famous salon for wits and intellectuals in Paris.

1 No man is a hero to his valet.
Attributed. See G. W. F. HEGEL 13.

Marquis de Custine
(1790–1857)
French traveller and author

Astolphe Louis Léonard. The first openly homosexual member of French high society, he wrote travel books on Italy, Germany, England and Spain, but is principally known for his Empire of the Czar *(1839).*

1 I do not believe I am exaggerating in affirming that the empire of Russia is a country whose inhabitants are the most miserable on earth, because

they suffer at one and the same time the evils of barbarism and of civilization.

Empire of the Czar: A Journey Through Eternal Russia, ch. 37 (1839)

2 Nations have always good reasons for being what they are, and the best of all is that they cannot be otherwise.

Ibid., ch. 37

Eugene Debs

(1855–1926)

US trade unionist and political leader

President of the American Railway Union from 1893, he stood as Socialist candidate for the US presidency five times 1900–20. Hearing him speak, said Art Young, was 'to listen to a hammer riveting a chamber in Hell for the oppressors of the poor'.

1 When great changes occur in history, when great principles are involved, as a rule the majority are wrong.

Speech in Cleveland, Ohio, 11 September 1918, publ. in *Eugene V. Debs Speaks* (ed. Jean Y. Tussey, 1970). Debs was defending himself against charges of violating the 1917 Espionage Act, for which he was found guilty and sentenced to ten years in jail. He was pardoned by the incoming President Harding in 1921.

2 While there is a lower class, I am in it, while there is a criminal element, I am of it, and while there is a soul in prison, I am not free.

Speech from the dock at Cleveland, Ohio, 14 September 1918, publ. in *The Penguin Book of Twentieth-Century Speeches* (ed. Brian MacArthur, 1999)

Stephen Decatur

(1779–1820)

US naval commander

He achieved fame in the Tripolitan War by setting fire to a captured US frigate (1804), and by forcing the Dey of Algiers to sign a treaty revoking demands for tribute (1815). He also distinguished himself in the War of 1812 against Britain.

1 Our country! In her intercourse with foreign nations, may she always be in the right; but our country, right or wrong.

Toast, April 1816, quoted in *Life of Stephen Decatur*, ch. 14 (1846) by Alexander Slidell Mackenzie. The toast was proposed at a banquet in Norfolk, Virginia, to celebrate Decatur's victory over Algerian 'Barbary pirates'. See also G. K. CHESTERTON 2 and CARL SCHURZ 1.

Daniel Defoe

(1660–1731)

English journalist, author and poet

Born Daniel Foe. His poem The True-Born Englishman *(1701), a defence of William III, brought him royal favour, though he was imprisoned for his satirical pamphlet,* The Shortest Way With Dissenters *(1702). He wrote and published* The Review *(1704–13), and contributed to many other periodicals, but is best remembered today for* Robinson Crusoe *(1719) and* Moll Flanders *(1722), considered the first novels in English.*

1 We loved the doctrine for the teacher's sake.

'The Character of the Late Dr Samuel Annesley' (1697), publ. in *A True Collection of the Writings of the Author of The True Born Englishman* (1703)

2 The best of men cannot suspend their fate:
The good die early, and the bad die late.

'The Character of the Late Dr Samuel Annesley', ibid.

3 The soul is placed in the body like a rough diamond, and must be polished, or the lustre of it will never appear.

An Essay Upon Projects, 'Of Academies: An Academy for Women' (1697)

4 Wherever God erects a house of prayer,
The Devil always builds a chapel there;
And 'twill be found, upon examination,
The latter has the largest congregation.

The True Born Englishman, pt 1, ll. 1–4 (1701), repr. in *Works of Daniel Defoe*, vol. 3 (1843). See also THOMAS BECON 1, MARTIN LUTHER 6.

5 From this amphibious ill-born mob began
That vain, ill-natured thing, an Englishman.

The True Born Englishman, pt 1, ll. 132–3, ibid.

6 The royal refugee our breed restores
With foreign courtiers and with foreign whores,
And carefully repeopled us again,
Throughout his lazy, long, lascivious reign.

The True Born Englishman, pt 1, ll. 233–6, ibid. Referring to CHARLES II.

7 Wealth, howsoever got, in England makes
Lords of mechanics, gentlemen of rakes;
Antiquity and birth are needless here;
'Tis impudence and money makes a peer.

The True Born Englishman, pt 1, ll. 360–3, ibid.

8 Great families of yesterday we show,
And lords, whose parents were the Lord knows who.

The True Born Englishman, pt 1, ll. 374–5, ibid.

9 In their religion they are so uneven,
That each man goes his own by-way to heaven.
The True Born Englishman, pt 2, ll. 102–3, ibid.

10 And of all plagues with which mankind are
cursed,
Ecclesiastic tyranny's the worst.
The True Born Englishman, pt 2, ll. 299–300, ibid.

11 Alas the Church of England! What with Popery on
one hand, and schismatics on the other, how has
she been crucified between two thieves!
The Shortest Way with the Dissenters (pamphlet, 1702), ibid.

12 Nature has left this tincture in the blood,
That all men would be tyrants if they could.
The History of the Kentish Petition, Addenda (1712–13), ibid.

13 He bid me observe it, and I should always find,
that the calamities of life were shared among the
upper and lower part of mankind; but that the
middle station had the fewest disasters.
Robinson Crusoe (1719). The advice of Robinson Crusoe's
father.

14 For never man had a more faithful, loving, sincere servant than Friday was to me; without passions, sullenness or designs, perfectly obliged and
engaged; his very affections were tied to me, like
those of a child to a father; and I dare say, he would
have sacrificed his life for the saving mine, upon
any occasion whatsoever.
Ibid. Crusoe refers to his 'man Friday'.

Lee De Forest
(1873–1961)
US physicist and inventor

*Following his invention of the Audion vacuum tube in 1906,
he made significant contributions to the development of radio
and telephone, as well as radar, television and computers.*

1 You have debased [my] child … You have made
him a laughing-stock of intelligence … a stench in
the nostrils of the gods of the ionosphere.
Speech to National Association of Broadcasters, quoted in
obituary in *Time* 7 July 1961

Edgar Degas
(1834–1917)
French painter and sculptor

*A painter of classical and historical subjects in the orthodox
tradition, he turned to group portraits of jockeys, musicians
and theatre hands in the 1860s, becoming well known for his
studies of ballet dancers.*

1 What a delightful thing is the conversation of
specialists! One understands absolutely nothing
and it's charming.
Quoted by Daniel Halévy, 31 January 1892, in *Degas Letters*,
Appendix (ed. Marcel Guerin, 1947)

Charles De Gaulle
(1890–1970)
French general and president

*Having directed the Free French movement from Britain dur-
ing the Second World War, he led the provisional French
government (1944–6) and was architect and first president of
the Fifth Republic (1959–69). He bequeathed to France 'Gaull-
ism' as a political philosophy, and the Gaullist party.* HAROLD
MACMILLAN *said he was 'alleged to have the rigidity of a
poker without its occasional warmth'.*

1 Nothing strengthens authority so much as silence.
Quoted in *The Art of Living*, 'The Art of Leadership' (1940) by
ANDRÉ MAUROIS

2 France has lost a battle. But France has not lost
the war!
Speech in London, broadcast 18 June 1940, publ. in *Speeches
of General de Gaulle* (1941). De Gaulle's famous words were
not part of the official typescript for this speech, and not
issued in written form until the following month.

3 Since they whose duty it was to wield the sword
of France have let it fall shattered to the ground, I
have taken up the broken blade.
Speech, 13 July 1940, publ. in *Discours et messages* (1942)

4 *Maintenant elle est comme les autres.*
[Now she is like everybody else.]
Remark at the funeral of his handicapped daughter, Anne,
1948, quoted in *De Gaulle*, ch. 8 (1965) by Jean Lacouture.
De Gaulle was devoted to his daughter, who had Down's
Syndrome. 'Without Anne,' he explained, 'perhaps I should
not have done all that I have done. She made me understand
so many things. She gave me so much heart and spirit.'

5 The French will only be united under the threat
of danger. How else can one govern a country that
produces 246 different kinds of cheese?
Speech, 1951, quoted in *Les Mots du Général* (ed. Ernest Mignon, 1962)

6 *Je vous ai compris.*
[I have understood you.]
Speech at Algiers, 4 June 1958, publ. in *Discours et messages*,
vol. 3 (1970). De Gaulle was addressing French settlers, whose
interests were threatened by Algerian nationalists. He was
granted emergency powers to resolve the crisis.

7 Old France, weighed down with history, pros-

trated by wars and revolutions, endlessly vacillating from greatness to decline, but revived, century after century, by the genius of renewal!
War Memoirs, vol. 3, ch. 7 (1959)

8 In the tumult of men and events, solitude was my temptation; now it is my friend. What other satisfaction can be sought once you have confronted History?
Ibid., vol. 3, ch. 7

9 Politics are too serious a matter to be left to the politicians.
Quoted in *Attlee: A Prime Minister Remembers*, ch. 4 (1961) by Francis Williams. De Gaulle was responding to CLEMENT ATTLEE's remark that 'De Gaulle is a very good soldier and a very bad politician.'

10 *Vive le Québec libre!*
[Long live free Quebec!]
Speech at Montreal, 24 July 1967, publ. in *Speeches of General de Gaulle* (1970). His rallying call aroused controversy for appearing to advocate the cause of Quebec separatists.

11 I respect only those who resist me; but I cannot tolerate them.
Quoted in the *New York Times Magazine* 12 May 1968

12 No country without an atom bomb could properly consider itself independent.
Quoted in the *New York Times Magazine* 12 May 1968

13 One does not arrest Voltaire.
Quoted in *Encounter* June 1975. Referring to the inflammatory Communist activities of JEAN-PAUL SARTRE during the 1960s.

14 *On n'est pas là pour rigoler.*
[We are not here to laugh.]
Attributed, on frequent occasions

Thomas Dekker
(c. 1572–c. 1632)
English dramatist

A vivid portrayer of London life, he wrote The Shoemaker's Holiday *(1600) and collaborated with various playwrights, for example* THOMAS MIDDLETON *in* The Honest Whore *(1604) and* The Roaring Girl *(c. 1610).*

1 Work apace, apace, apace, apace;
Honest labour bears a lovely face.
'Sweet Content' (song), in *Patient Grissil*, Act 2, Sc. 1 (1603)

2 Golden slumbers kiss your eyes,
Smiles awake you when you rise:
Sleep, pretty wantons, do not cry,

And I will sing a lullaby:
Rock them, rock them, lullaby.
Lullaby, ibid., Act 4, Sc. 2. The words were set to a traditional melody, and were adapted by PAUL MCCARTNEY in 1970 ('Golden Slumbers', by The Beatles).

3 The best of men
That e'er wore earth about him, was a sufferer,
A soft, meek, patient, humble, tranquil spirit,
The first true gentleman that ever breathed.
The Honest Whore, pt 1, Act 5, Sc. 2 (1604, written with THOMAS MIDDLETON). Spoken by Candido.

4 The principle is old, but true as fate,
Kings may love treason, but the traitor hate.
Duke of Milan, ibid., pt 1, Act 4, Sc. 4. The same notion was expressed by SAMUEL DANIEL in *Tragedy of Cleopatra* (1594), and the words 'I love treason but hate a traitor' were earlier ascribed to JULIUS CAESAR in PLUTARCH's *Parallel Lives*.

F. W. de Klerk
(b. 1936)
South African politician and president

Frederik Willem de Klerk. As President (1989–94), he began the process of dismantling apartheid, lifting the ban on the African National Congress and releasing NELSON MANDELA *from prison in 1990. He served as Vice-President in the Mandela administration (1994–6).*

1 Today we have closed the book on apartheid.
Quoted in the *Independent* 19 March 1992. Referring to the results of the referendum endorsing his proposals for constitutional and political reform.

Willem De Kooning
(1904–97)
Dutch-born US artist

By the 1950s he was a key figure of the Abstract Expressionist movement in New York. A superb draughtsman, he alternated between the abstract and figurative, as in the Woman *series (1950–3).*

1 Whatever an artist's personal feelings are, as soon as an artist fills a certain area on the canvas or circumscribes it, he becomes historical. He acts from or upon other artists.
'A Desperate View', paper delivered to friends in New York, 18 February 1949, publ. in *William de Kooning* (1968) by Thomas B. Hess

2 If you pick up some paint with your brush and make somebody's nose with it, this is rather ridiculous when you think of it, theoretically or

philosophically. It's really absurd to make an image, like a human image, with paint, today.

'Painting As Self Discovery', interview 30 December 1960, publ. in *Location* Spring 1963 as 'Content Is A Glimpse...', quoted in *William de Kooning* (1988) by Diane Waldman

Eugène Delacroix

(1798–1863)

French artist

The pre-eminent Romantic painter in France, he specialized in large-scale historical subjects and scenes from literature. He exhibited his first masterpiece, Dante and Virgil in Hell, *in 1822; later works included* Massacre of Chios *(1824) and* Liberty Leading the People *(1830).*

1 When one yields oneself completely to one's soul, it opens itself to one, and then it is that the capricious thing allows one the greatest of good fortunes ... that of sympathizing with others, of studying itself, of painting itself constantly in its works.

Journal entry, 14 May 1824, publ. in *The Journal of Eugène Delacroix* (transl. 1937)

2 What makes men of genius, or rather, what they make, is not new ideas, it is that idea – possessing them – that what has been said has still not been said enough.

Ibid., 15 May 1824

3 I live in company with a body, a silent companion, exacting and eternal. He it is who notes that individuality which is the seal of the weakness of our race. My soul has wings, but the brutal jailer is strict.

Ibid., 4 June 1824

4 A taste for simplicity cannot endure for long.

Ibid., 1847

5 Real beauty in the arts is eternal and would be accepted at all periods; but it wears the dress of its century: something of that dress clings to it, and woe to the works which appear in periods when the general taste is corrupted!

Ibid., 12 October 1859

Walter de la Mare

(1873–1956)

British poet and novelist

He was placed by DYLAN THOMAS *in a compartment marked 'Subtlety and Sensitivity. Perishable With Care,' but admired by* AUDEN *for the 'graceful architecture of his stanzas'. His lyrical writing reflects his preoccupation with fantasy and the imaginative world of childhood.*

1 Softly along the road of evening,
In a twilight dim with rose,
Wrinkled with age, and drenched with dew,
Old Nod, the shepherd, goes.

'Nod', st. 1, publ. in *The Listeners* (1912)

2 Very old are the woods;
And the buds that break
Out of the brier's boughs,
When March winds wake,
So old with their beauty are.

'All That's Past', ibid. Opening lines of poem.

3 Oh, no man knows
Through what wild centuries
Roves back the rose.

'All That's Past', ibid.

4 'Is there anybody there?' said the Traveller,
Knocking on the moonlit door;
And his horse in the silence champed the grasses
Of the forest's ferny floor.

'The Listeners', ibid.

5 'Tell them I came, and no one answered,
That I kept my word,' he said.

'The Listeners', ibid.

6 Rest, rest – there is no rest,
Until the quiet grave
Comes with its narrow arch
The heart to save
From life's long cankering rust.

'Home', ibid.

7 Who said, 'Peacock Pie'?
The old King to the sparrow:
Who said, 'Crops are ripe'?
Rust to the harrow.

'The Song of the Mad Prince', publ. in *Peacock Pie: a Book of Rhymes* (1913). Opening lines of poem.

8 A face peered. All the grey night
In chaos of vacancy shone;
Nought but vast Sorrow was there –
The sweet cheat gone.

'The Ghost', publ. in *Motley and Other Poems* (1918). *The Sweet Cheat Gone* was the title of the 1930 English translation of vol. 11 of *Remembrance of Things Past* by MARCEL PROUST.

9 Look thy last on all things lovely,
Every hour. Let no night
Seal thy sense in deadly slumber
Till to delight

Thou have paid thy utmost blessing;
Since that all things thou wouldst praise
Beauty took from those who loved them
In other days.
'Fare Well', ibid.

10 How shall I know that the end of things is
   coming?
The drummers will be drumming; the fiddlers at
   their thrumming;
Nuns at their beads; the mummers at their
   mumming;
Heaven's solemn Seraph stoopt weary o'er his
   summing;
The palsied fingers plucking, the way-worn feet
   numbing –
And the end of things coming.
'A Sign', publ. in *The Veil and Other Poems* (1921)

11 Hi! handsome hunting man
Fire your little gun.
Bang! Now the animal
Is dead and dumb and done.
'Hi!', publ. in *Poems for Children* (1930)

12 In the long drouth of life,
Its transient wilderness,
The mindless euthanasia of a kiss
Reveals that in
An instant's beat
Two souls in flesh confined
May yet in an immortal freedom meet.
'The Kiss' (1947), repr. in *Inward Companion: Poems* (1950)

Shelagh Delaney
(b. 1939)
British playwright

She is principally known for A Taste of Honey *(1958), which earned her the title of 'Angry Young Woman'. She has also written screenplays.*

1 Women never have young minds. They are born three thousand years old.
A Taste of Honey, Act 1, Sc. 2 (1959). Spoken by Jo's boyfriend.

Don DeLillo
(b. 1936)
US author

A leading exponent of the postmodern novel, he writes oblique analyses of contemporary US society which focus on subcultures such as American football in End Zone *(1972) and baseball in* Underworld *(1999).*

1 People stress the violence. That's the smallest part of it. Football is brutal only from a distance. In the middle of it there's a calm, a tranquility. The players accept pain. There's a sense of order even at the end of a running play with bodies strewn everywhere. When the systems interlock, there's a satisfaction to the game that can't be duplicated. There's a harmony.
End Zone, ch. 28 (1972). Spoken by Emmett Creed.

2 I've come to think of Europe as a hardcover book, America as the paperback version.
The Names, ch. 1 (1982). Spoken by Owen Brademas.

3 Men with secrets tend to be drawn to each other, not because they want to share what they know but because they need the company of the like-minded, the fellow afflicted.
Libra, pt 1, '17 April' (1988). Spoken by Walter Everett Jr.

4 There's never a dearth of reasons to shoot at the President.
Larry Parmenter, ibid., pt 1, '26 April'

5 A conspiracy is everything that ordinary life is not. It's the inside game, cold, sure, undistracted, forever closed off to us. We are the flawed ones, the innocents, trying to make some rough sense of the daily jostle. Conspirators have a logic and a daring beyond our reach. All conspiracies are the same taut story of men who find coherence in some criminal act.
Ibid., pt 2 'In Dallas'

6 That's the thing about baseball ... You do what they did before you. That's the connection you make. There's a whole long line. A man takes his kid to a game and thirty years later this is what they talk about when the poor old mutt's wasting away in the hospital.
Underworld, 'Prologue, The Triumph of Death' (1997). Spoken by Bill Waterson.

7 If you know you're worth nothing, only a gamble with death can gratify your vanity.
Narrator, ibid., pt 2, 'Elegy for Left Hand Alone, Mid-1980s–Early 1990s', ch. 8

Lothar de Maizière
(b. 1940)
German lawyer and politician

Leader of the Christian Democratic Union (1989–90), he became the first democratically elected premier of East Ger-

many in 1990 and as such negotiated the country's unification with West Germany.

1 The era of long parades past an official podium filled with cold faces is gone. Celebrating is now a right, not a duty.
Speech, 1 May 1990, quoted in the *Independent* 5 May 1990. Said while East German prime minister, referring to the fall of Communism.

Paul de Man
(1919–83)
Belgian-born US literary critic

He taught at various universities including Yale, where he became a leading advocate of deconstruction. His essays were published in Blindness and Insight *(1971) and* Allegories of Reading *(1979).*

1 The critical method which denies literary modernity would appear – and even, in certain respects, would be – the most modern of critical movements.
'Literary History and Literary Modernity', lecture, September 1969, publ. in *Blindness and Insight* (1971, rev. 1983)

2 Literature . . . is condemned (or privileged) to be forever the most rigorous and, consequently, the most reliable of terms in which man names and transforms himself.
Allegories Of Reading, pt 1, ch. 1, 'Semiology And Rhetoric' (1979)

3 Death is a displaced name for a linguistic predicament.
Quoted in *Signs of the Times*, ch. 4 (1991) by DAVID LEHMAN. Lehman called this 'the ultimate statement of the deconstructive credo'.

Cecil B. De Mille
(1881–1959)
US film-maker

Cecil Blount De Mille. Called 'the director to end all directors', he became known for spectacular epics, for example The Ten Commandments *(1923, remade 1956) and* The Greatest Show on Earth *(1952).*

1 What I have crossed out I didn't like. What I haven't crossed out I am dissatisfied with.
Note attached to rejected script, attributed

Demosthenes
(c. 384–22 BC)
Greek orator

A leader of the democratic faction in Athens, he argued for resistance to the ambitions of Macedonia under Philip II and Alexander the Great in his Philippics *and* Olynthiacs, *which helped to establish him as the greatest of Greek orators.*

1 A man is his own easiest dupe, for what he wishes to be true he generally believes to be true.
Third Olynthiac, sect. 19 (349 BC)

2 There is one safeguard known generally to the wise, which is an advantage and security to all, but especially to democracies as against despots. What is it? Distrust.
Second Philippic, sect. 24 (344 BC)

Jack Dempsey
(1895–1983)
US boxer

Born William Harrison Dempsey. Nicknamed 'the Manassa Mauler', he was world heavyweight champion 1919–26. His 1921 title fight was the first to amass a million dollars from the gate.

1 Honey, I just forgot to duck.
Quoted in *Dempsey*, ch. 24 (1977) by Jack and Barbara P. Dempsey. This celebrated remark made to his wife after losing a title fight in 1926 was famously repeated by RONALD REAGAN to NANCY REAGAN after John Hinckley III's assassination attempt on the president, 30 March 1981.

(Sir) John Denham
(1615–69)
Irish poet

Trained as a lawyer, he translated VIRGIL's Aeneid *and composed verse and the historical tragedy* The Sophy *(1641). He specialized in the heroic couplet and evocations of landscape, as in* Cooper's Hill *(1642).*

1 Can knowledge have no bound, but must advance
So far, to make us wish for ignorance?
Cooper's Hill (1642)

2 Thames, the most loved of all the ocean's sons,
By his old sire to his embraces runs,
Hasting to pay his tribute to the sea,
Like mortal life to meet eternity.
Ibid.

3 Such is our pride, our folly, or our fate,

That few but such as cannot write, translate.

'To Sir Richard Fanshawe upon his translation of *Il Pastor Fido*', ll. 1–2 (1648). The poem continues: 'Nor ought a genius less than his that writ/Attempt translation.' (ll. 9–10)

Robert De Niro
(b. 1943)
US screen actor

Favouring tough, working-class roles, and closely associated with the films of MARTIN SCORSESE, *he has starred in* Mean Streets *(1973),* The Deerhunter *(1978) and* Raging Bull *(1980).*

1 They're all animals anyway. All the criminals come out at night. Whores, skunk pussies, buggers, queens, fairies, dopers, junkies, sick, venal. Someday a *real* rain will come and wash all this scum off the streets.

Taxi Driver (film, 1976, screenplay by Paul Schrader, directed by Martin Scorsese). Voiceover by Travis Bickle (Robert De Niro).

2 You talkin' to me?

Travis Bickle, ibid.

3 Better to be a king for a night than a schmuck for a lifetime.

The King of Comedy (film, 1983, screenplay by Paul Zimmerman, directed by Martin Scorsese). Spoken by Rupert Pupkin (Robert De Niro).

John Dennis
(1657–1734)
English playwright and critic

Expelled from Cambridge University for stabbing a fellow student, he had an unsuccessful career as a dramatist but became established as a literary critic. His writings include The Grounds of Criticism in Poetry *(1704).*

1 A man who could make so vile a pun would not scruple to pick a pocket.

Quoted in *The Gentleman's Magazine*, vol. 51, editorial note (1781)

2 Damn them! They will not let my play run, but they steal my thunder!

Quoted in *Handy-Book of Literary Curiosities*, 'Thunder, Steal my' (1893) by William S. Walsh. Remark on hearing the thunder effects he had devised for his own failed play, *Appius and Virginia*, used in a production of *Macbeth*. ALEXANDER POPE wrote of Dennis in *The Dunciad*, bk 2, ll. 223–6: 'To move, to raise, to ravish every heart,/With Shakespeare's nature, or with Jonson's art,/Let others aim: 'Tis yours to shake the soul/ With thunder rumbling from the mustard bowl.' As Pope noted, 'The old way of making thunder and mustard were the same.'

Gérard Depardieu
(b. 1948)
French actor

He has appeared in over seventy films, including Jean de Florette *(1986),* Cyrano de Bergerac *(1990), and* Le Tartuffe *(1984), which he directed himself.*

1 I learnt to be in the light. The stage is like a cage of light. People are no longer afraid of you – they are the ones out there in the dark, watching.

Quoted in *Depardieu*, ch. 3 (1991) by Marianne Gray. Describing how acting saved him from a life of crime.

Thomas De Quincey
(1785–1859)
English author and critic

One of the foremost critics of the English Romantic movement, he contributed numerous insightful essays to the leading magazines of the day, mostly on literary subjects, but was best known for his autobiographical Confessions of an English Opium-Eater *(1822). He lived for many years in the Lake District.*

1 In many walks of life, a conscience is a more expensive encumbrance than a wife or a carriage.

Confessions of an English Opium-Eater, 'Preliminary Confessions' (1822)

2 It was a Sunday afternoon, wet and cheerless: and a duller spectacle this earth of ours has not to show than a rainy Sunday in London.

Ibid., pt 2. Recalling the day in 1804 when he first took opium.

3 Thou hast the keys of Paradise, O just, subtle, and mighty opium!

Ibid., pt 2

4 Tea, though ridiculed by those who are naturally of coarse nerves, or are become so from wine-drinking, and are not susceptible of influence from so refined a stimulant, will always be the favourite beverage of the intellectual.

Ibid., pt 2

5 Books, we are told, propose to *instruct* or to *amuse*. Indeed! . . . The true antithesis to knowledge in this case is not *pleasure*, but *power*. All that is literature seeks to communicate power; all that is not literature, to communicate knowledge.

'Letters to a Young Man whose Education has been Neglected', no. 3 ('On Languages'), publ. in the *London Magazine* March 1823, repr. in *The Works of Thomas de Quincey*, vol. 3 (ed. Frederick Burwick, 2000). De Quincey, who in a footnote credited WORDSWORTH with formulating this distinction, explained 'literary power' as 'the case in which I should be made to feel vividly, and with a vital consciousness, emotions which ordinary life rarely or never supplies occasions for exciting, and which had previously lain unawakened, and hardly within the dawn of consciousness'.

6 For if once a man indulges himself in murder, very soon he comes to think little of robbing; and from robbing he comes next to drinking and Sabbath-breaking, and from that to incivility and procrastination.
'Second Paper on Murder Considered As One of the Fine Arts', publ. in *Blackwood's Edinburgh Magazine*, November 1839, ibid., vol. 11 (ed. Julian North, 2000)

7 I have generally found that, if you are in quest of some certain escape from Philistines of whatsoever class – sheriff-officers, bores, no matter what – the surest refuge is to be found amongst hedgerows and fields, amongst cows and sheep.
Confessions of an English Opium-Eater (1856 edn)

8 If in this world there is one misery having no relief, it is the pressure on the heart from the *Incommunicable*. And if another Sphinx should arise to propose another enigma to man – saying, What burden is that which only is insupportable by human fortitude? I should answer at once – *It is the burden of the Incommunicable.*
Ibid.

John Derek
(1926–98)
US actor and director

Born Derek Harris. A leading man in the 1940s and '50s, he later turned to photography and directing films.

1 Live fast, die young and have a good-looking corpse.
Knock On Any Door (film, 1949, screenplay by Daniel Taradash and John Monks Jr, based on Willard Motley's novel, directed by Nicholas Ray). Spoken by Nick Romano (John Derek).

Jacques Derrida
(1930–2004)
Algerian-born French literary theorist

He introduced the theory of deconstruction into literary criticism in the paper 'Structure, Sign, and Play' (1966) and such books as Speech and Writing *(1967).*

1 Writing in the common sense is the dead letter, it is the carrier of death. It exhausts life.
Of Grammatology, pt 1, ch. 1 (1967, rev. 1998)

2 There is nothing outside of the text.
Ibid., pt 2, ch. 2

3 Were I not so frequently associated with this adventure of deconstruction, I would risk, with a smile, the following hypothesis: America *is* deconstruction ... [The United States] is that historical space which today, in all its dimensions and through all its power plays, reveals itself as being undeniably the most sensitive, receptive, or responsive space of all to the themes and effects of deconstruction.
Mémoirs: for Paul de Man (1989). Written shortly after the death of the critic PAUL DE MAN in 1983.

Marquis de Sade
(1740–1814)
French author

Donatien Alphonse François, comte de Sade. He spent most of his life mired in controversy for his licentiousness and the sexual perversity of his writings, for example The 120 Days of Sodom *(1784) and* Justine *(1791). Many of his books were written in prison and he died in an insane asylum.*

1 There is no more lively sensation than that of pain; its impressions are certain and dependable, they never deceive as may those of the pleasure women perpetually feign and almost never experience.
Justine, ou les malheurs de la vertu (1791; *The Misfortunes of Virtue*). Spoken by Clément.

2 I've already told you: the only way to a woman's heart is along the path of torment. I know none other as sure.
Oxtiern, ou les malheurs du libertinage, Act 2, Sc. 1 (1791). Spoken by Oxtiern.

3 It is only by enlarging the scope of one's tastes and one's fantasies, by sacrificing everything to pleasure, that that unfortunate individual called man, thrown despite himself into this sad world, can succeed in gathering a few roses among life's thorns.
La Philosophie dans le boudoir, 'To Libertines' (1795; *Philosophy in the Bedroom*)

4 Ah, Eugénie, have done with virtues! Among the sacrifices that can be made to those counterfeit divinities, is there one worth an instant of the pleasures one tastes in outraging them?
Dolmancé, ibid., 'Dialogue the Third'

5 Cruelty is simply the energy in a man civilization has not yet altogether corrupted.
Dolmancé, ibid., 'Dialogue the Third'

6 Nature has not got two voices, you know, one of them condemning all day what the other commands.
Dolmancé, ibid., 'Dialogue the Fifth'

7 I don't know what the heart is, not I: I only use the word to denote the mind's frailties.
Dolmancé, ibid., 'Dialogue the Fifth'

8 Get it into your head once and for all, my simple and very fainthearted fellow, that what fools call *humaneness* is nothing but a weakness born of fear and egoism; that this chimerical virtue, enslaving only weak men, is unknown to those whose character is formed by stoicism, courage, and philosophy.
Dolmancé, ibid., 'Dialogue the Seventh'

9 They declaim against the passions without bothering to think that it is from their flame philosophy lights its torch.
L'Histoire de Juliette, ou les prospérités du vice, pt 1 (1797; *Juliette*). Spoken by Delbène.

10 To judge from the notions expounded by theologians, one must conclude that God created most men simply with a view to crowding hell.
Juliette, ibid., pt 2

Ferdinand de Saussure
(1857–1913)
Swiss linguist

Considered the founder of modern linguistics, he conceived of language as a socially contextualized system, paving the way for Structuralism. A Course in General Linguistics (1916) was compiled from his lecture notes after his death.

1 Language furnishes the best proof that a law accepted by a community is a thing that is tolerated and not a rule to which all freely consent.
Course in General Linguistics, pt 1, ch. 2, sect. 1 (1916). 'Of all social institutions,' de Saussure continued, 'language is least amenable to initiative. It blends with the life of society, and the latter, inert by nature, is a prime conservative force.'

2 A linguistic system is a series of differences of sound combined with a series of differences of ideas.
Ibid., pt 2, ch. 4, sect. 4

René Descartes
(1596–1650)
French philosopher and mathematician

He made significant advances in the fields of analytic geometry, algebra and optics, and has been called the father of modern philosophy. His theories were based on the acceptance of certain a priori truths, dualism and what he called 'methodic doubt', as laid out in Discourse on Method (1637) and Meditations (1641).

1 It is well to know something of the manners of various peoples, in order more sanely to judge our own, and that we do not think that everything against our modes is ridiculous, and against reason, as those who have seen nothing are accustomed to think.
Le Discours de la méthode, pt 1 (1637; *Discourse on Method*)

2 One cannot conceive anything so strange and so implausible that it has not already been said by one philosopher or another.
Ibid., pt 2

3 *Cogito, ergo sum.*
[I think, therefore I am.]
Ibid., pt 4. The work was written first in French (where the words are *Je pense, donc je suis*), then Latin.

4 I could not possibly exist with the nature I actually have, that is, one endowed with the idea of God, unless there really is a God; the very God, I mean, of whom I have an idea.
Meditationes, 'Third Meditation' (1641; *Meditations*)

Camille Desmoulins
(1760–94)
French revolutionary and journalist

He emerged as an effective pamphleteer and orator during the French Revolution, exhorting the mob to storm the Bastille and becoming a leader, with Danton, of the moderate faction within the Jacobin party. He was guillotined with Danton on the orders of ROBESPIERRE.

1 Clemency is also a revolutionary measure.
Speech to a crowd outside the Palais Royal, Paris, 14 July 1789, recalled by Desmoulins in his newspaper *Le Vieux Cordelier* 5 January 1794

2 I am thirty-three – the age of the good *Sans-culotte* Jesus; an age fatal to revolutionists.
Quoted in *History of the French Revolution*, bk 6, ch. 2 (1837) by THOMAS CARLYLE. Answer to the Revolutionary Tribunal, Paris, 2 April 1794, on the eve of his execution.

Buddy De Sylva
(1895–1950)
Lew Brown
(1893–1958)
US songwriters

De Sylva (originally George Gard De Sylva) and Brown caught the spirit of the jazz age with such songs as 'Black Bottom' and 'The Birth of the Blues' (1926). De Sylva later became a film producer and was co-founder of Capitol records.

1 The moon belongs to everyone,
The best things in life are free.
'The Best Things in Life are Free' (song, 1927, with music by Ray Henderson)

Helene Deutsch
(1884–1982)
Polish-born US psychiatrist

A pupil of FREUD, *she broke new ground with her work on the female libido. Among her major works is* The Psychology of Women *(1944–5).*

1 After all, the ultimate goal of all research is not objectivity, but truth.
The Psychology of Women, vol. 1, Preface (1944)

2 All observations point to the fact that the intellectual woman is masculinized; in her, warm, intuitive knowledge has yielded to cold unproductive thinking.
Ibid., vol. 1, ch. 8

3 The embattled gates to equal rights indeed opened up for modern women, but I sometimes think to myself: 'That is not what I meant by freedom – it is only "social progress."
Confrontations With Myself, ch. 1 (1973)

Miguel de Unamuno
See UNAMUNO

Robert Devereux
See EARL OF ESSEX

Bernard DeVoto
(1897–1955)
US historian and critic

Winning acclaim for Mark Twain's America *(1932), he continued his historical studies with a trilogy on the American*

West. *He wrote the 'Easy Chair' comment column in* Harper's Magazine *from 1935.*

1 The trouble with the sacred Individual is that he has no significance, except as he can acquire it from others, from the social whole.
Harper's Magazine May 1941

2 You can no more keep a martini in the refrigerator than you can keep a kiss there. The proper union of gin and vermouth is a great and sudden glory; it is one of the happiest marriages on earth, and one of the shortest-lived. The fragile tie of ecstasy is broken in a few minutes, and thereafter there can be no remarriage.
Harper's Magazine December 1949

Peter De Vries
(1910–93)
US author

Underpinned by his Dutch Calvinist upbringing, his humour is displayed in such novels as The Tunnel of Love *(1954) and* Slouching Towards Kalamazoo *(1983), depictions of the affluent American middle-classes.*

1 Gluttony is an emotional escape, a sign something is eating us.
Comfort Me With Apples, ch. 15 (1956). Spoken by Crystal.

2 You can make a sordid thing sound like a brilliant drawing-room comedy. Probably a fear we have of facing up to the real issues. Could you say we were guilty of Noel Cowardice?
Narrator, ibid.

3 It is the final proof of God's omnipotence that he need not exist in order to save us.
The Mackerel Plaza, ch. 1 (1958). This aphorism by the Reverend Andrew Mackerel 'seemed to his hearers so much better than anything Voltaire had said on the subject that he was given an immediate hike in pay and invited out to more dinners than he could possibly eat'. See VOLTAIRE 30.

4 Everybody hates me because I'm so universally liked.
The Vale of Laughter, pt 1, ch. 1 (1967). Narrated by Joe Sandwich.

5 We must love one another, yes, yes, that's all true enough, but nothing says we have to like each other. It may be the very recognition of all men as our brothers that accounts for the sibling rivalry, and even enmity, we have toward so many of them.
The Glory of the Hummingbird, ch. 1 (1974). Opening sentences of book, narrated by Jim Tickler.

Lord Dewar

(1864–1930)

British industrialist

Thomas, Lord Dewar of Homestall. He was Managing Director of Scotch Whisky Brands and published books of his epigrammatic humour.

1 [There are] only two classes of pedestrians in these days of reckless motor traffic – the quick, and the dead.

Quoted in *Looking Back on Life*, ch. 28 (1933) by George Robey

Sergei Diaghilev

(1872–1929)

Russian impresario

With the Ballets Russes, the company he co-founded in Paris in 1909, he revolutionized the conventions of ballet by integrating music, costume and design. His greatest successes include The Firebird, Petruschka *and* The Rite of Spring, *all by* STRAVINSKY.

1 *Étonne-moi.*
[Astonish me.]

Quoted in *Journals of Jean Cocteau*, ch. 1 (ed. Wallace Fowlie, 1956). Said in Paris, 1912, to JEAN COCTEAU, who had complained that he was not getting enough artistic notice.

Diana, Princess of Wales

(1961–97)

Originally Lady Diana Frances Spencer. Married to CHARLES, PRINCE OF WALES *1981–96, she focused world attention on the issues of AIDS and landmines. Her death in a car accident gave rise to unprecedented national mourning.*

1 I don't even know how to use a parking meter, let alone a phone box.

Quoted in *The Times* 22 August 1994. Said to Richard Kay, royal correspondent for the *Daily Mail*, on allegations that she had pestered art dealer Oliver Hoare with telephone calls.

2 When I see them around all the time, it is like being raped.

Quoted in the *Guardian* 6 April 1995. Referring to press photographers.

3 I'd like to be a queen of people's hearts, in people's hearts, but I don't see myself being Queen of this country.

Interview on *Panorama*, BBC1, 20 November 1995, publ. in *The Times* 21 November 1995

4 She won't go quietly, that's the problem. I'll fight to the end.

Ibid. Speaking of herself.

5 There were three of us in this marriage.

Ibid. Referring to Prince Charles's relationship with Camilla Parker-Bowles.

6 You are going to get a big surprise with the next thing I do.

Quoted in the *Observer* 20 July 1997. Remark to reporters while holidaying on Mohamed al-Fayed's yacht at St Tropez.

7 I touch people. I think everyone needs that. Placing a hand on a friend's face means making contact.

Interview in *Le Monde* 27 August 1997

Porfirio Diaz

(1830–1915)

Mexican soldier and president

As President (1877–80 and 1884–1911), he established a strong centralized government and encouraged foreign investment. He was toppled by a coup in 1911 and died in exile.

1 Poor Mexico, so far from God and so close to the United States.

Attributed. The words are also attributed to AMBROSE BIERCE.

Thomas Dibdin

(1771–1841)

English playwright, songwriter and actor

The son of the actor and songwriter Charles Dibdin, he composed a vast number of songs, as well as writing plays, pantomimes and operas. He also acted and managed various London theatres.

1 Oh! what a snug little island,
A right little, tight little island!
All the globe round, none can be found
So happy as this little island.

'The Tight Little Island' (song), in *The British Taft* (musical play, 1797)

Philip K. Dick

(1928–82)

US science fiction writer

Exploring standard science fiction ideas with offbeat humour, his novels and short stories such as Do Androids Dream of Electric Sheep? *(1968, filmed as* Blade Runner *1982) have generated a cult following.*

1 Reality is that which, when you stop believing in it, doesn't go away.

Definition given in 1972, quoted by Dick in 'How to Build a Universe That Doesn't Fall Apart Two Days Later' (1978), publ. in *I Hope I Shall Arrive Soon* (1986)

2 Science fiction writers, I am sorry to say, really do not know anything. We can't talk about science, because our knowledge of it is limited and un-official, and usually our fiction is dreadful.
'How to Build a Universe That Doesn't Fall Apart Two Days Later', ibid.

3 The basic tool for the manipulation of reality is the manipulation of words. If you can control the meaning of words, you can control the people who must use the words.
'How to Build a Universe That Doesn't Fall Apart Two Days Later', ibid.

Charles Dickens

(1812–70)

English novelist

Working as a journalist, he began writing stories from 1833 that were serialized in magazines and quickly gained a wide readership. His major works, which frequently highlighted social injustice, include Oliver Twist *(1837–9),* David Copper-field *(1849–50) and* Great Expectations *(1860–1). His public readings were also immensely popular.*

1 It is strange with how little notice, good, bad, or indifferent, a man may live and die in London.
Sketches by Boz, 'Characters', ch. 1 (1833–6)

2 Minerva House ... was 'a finishing establishment for young ladies', where some twenty girls of the ages from thirteen to nineteen inclusive, acquired a smattering of everything and a knowledge of nothing.
Ibid., 'Tales', ch. 3

3 Mr Blotton had no hesitation in saying, that ... he had used the word ['humbug'] in its Pickwickian sense.
The Pickwick Papers, ch. 1 (1836–7). Mr Pickwick, in response, 'begged it to be at once understood, that his own observations had been merely intended to bear a Pickwickian con-struction'.

4 Great men are seldom over scrupulous in the arrangement of their attire.
Ibid., ch. 2

5 'Philosopher, sir?'
'An observer of human nature, sir,' said Mr Pickwick.
Ibid., ch. 2. Exchange between Mr Pickwick and a stranger (Alfred Jingle).

6 Kent, sir – everybody knows Kent – apples, cher-ries, hops, and women.
Jingle, ibid., ch. 2. Dickens spent much of his life in Kent, and

lived on the North Kent coast while writing the early chapters of *The Pickwick Papers*.

7 There are very few moments in a man's existence, when he experiences so much ludicrous distress, or meets with so little charitable commiseration, as when he is in pursuit of his own hat.
Ibid., ch. 4

8 I wants to make your flesh creep.
The fat boy, ibid., ch. 8

9 Take example by your father, my boy, and be very careful o' widders all your life, specially if they've kept a public house, Sammy.
Mr Weller, ibid., ch. 20

10 Why, I think he's the wictim o' connubiality, as Blue Beard's domestic chaplain said, with a tear of pity, ven he buried him.
Mr Weller, ibid., ch. 20

11 It's a wery remarkable circumstance, sir, that poverty and oysters always seem to go together.
Sam Weller, ibid., ch. 22

12 Dumb as a drum with a hole in it.
Sam Weller, ibid., ch. 25

13 Ven you're a married man, Samivel, you'll under-stand a good many things as you don't understand now; but vether it's worth while goin' through so much, to learn so little, as the charity-boy said ven he got to the end of the alphabet, is a matter o' taste. *I* rayther think it isn't.
Mr Weller, ibid., ch. 27

14 Eccentricities of genius, Sam.
Mr Pickwick, ibid., ch. 30. Describing the behaviour of medical students.

15 Yes, I have a pair of eyes, and that's just it. If they wos a pair o' patent double million magnifyin' gas microscopes of hextra power, p'raps I might be able to see through a flight o' stairs and a deal door; but bein' only eyes, you see, my wision's limited.
Sam Weller, ibid., ch. 34

16 *We* know, Mr Weller – we, who are men of the world – that a good uniform must work its way with the women, sooner or later.
The gentleman in blue, ibid., ch. 37

17 It is the fate of most men who mingle with the world and attain even the prime of life, to make many real friends, and lose them in the course of nature. It is the fate of all authors or chroniclers to create imaginary friends, and lose them in the

course of art. Nor is this the full extent of their misfortunes; for they are required to furnish an account of them besides.
Ibid., ch. 57

18 Please, sir, I want some more.
Oliver Twist, ch. 2 (1837–9). Oliver, suffering from slow starvation in the workhouse, asks for more food.

19 Among his intimate friends he was better known by the sobriquet of 'the artful Dodger'.
Ibid., ch. 8

20 There is a passion *for hunting something* deeply implanted in the human breast.
Ibid., ch. 10. Referring to chasing pickpockets.

21 I never see any difference in boys. I only know two sorts of boys. Mealy boys, and beef-faced boys.
Mr Grimwig, ibid., ch. 14

22 It opens the lungs, washes the countenance, exercises the eyes, and softens down the temper; so cry away.
Mr Bumble to Mrs Bumble, ibid., ch. 37. Mr Bumble was 'pleased and exalted' by tears: 'Like washable beaver hats that improve with rain, his nerves were rendered stouter and more vigorous by showers of tears.'

23 If the law supposes that, the law is a ass – a idiot.
Mr Bumble, ibid., ch. 51

24 He had but one eye, and the popular prejudice runs in favour of two.
Nicholas Nickleby, ch. 4 (1838–9). Referring to the schoolmaster Wackford Squeers.

25 Subdue your appetites, my dears, and you've conquered human natur'.
Mr Squeers, ibid., ch. 5

26 There are only two styles of portrait painting; the serious and the smirk.
Miss La Creevy, ibid., ch. 10

27 A man in public life expects to be sneered at – it is the fault of his elewated sitiwation, and not of himself.
Mr Kenwigs, ibid., ch. 14

28 It is a pleasant thing to reflect upon, and furnishes a complete answer to those who contend for the gradual degeneration of the human species, that every baby born into the world is a finer one than the last.
Ibid., ch. 36

29 Bring in the bottled lightning, a clean tumbler, and a corkscrew.
The gentleman in the small-clothes, ibid., ch. 49

30 She is come at last – at last – and all is gas and gaiters!
The gentleman in the small-clothes, ibid., ch. 49

31 Fan the sinking flame of hilarity with the wing of friendship; and pass the rosy wine.
The Old Curiosity Shop, ch. 7 (1840–1). Spoken by Dick Swiveller.

32 If there were no bad people there would be no good lawyers.
Sampson Brass, ibid., ch. 56

33 It was a maxim with Foxey – our revered father, gentlemen – 'Always suspect everybody.' That's the maxim to go through life with!
Sampson Brass, ibid., ch. 66

34 Father Time is not always a hard parent, and, though he tarries for none of his children, often lays his hand lightly upon those who have used him well; making them old men and women inexorably enough, but leaving their hearts and spirits young and in full vigour. With such people the grey head is but the impression of the old fellow's hand in giving them his blessing, and every wrinkle but a notch in the quiet calendar of a well-spent life.
Barnaby Rudge, ch. 2 (1841)

35 A lady of what is commonly called an uncertain temper – a phrase which being interpreted signifies a temper tolerably certain to make everybody more or less uncomfortable.
Ibid., ch. 7. Referring to Martha Varden.

36 To be shelterless and alone in the open country, hearing the wind moan and watching for day through the whole long weary night; to listen to the falling rain, and crouch for warmth beneath the lee of some old barn or rick, or in the hollow of a tree; are dismal things – but not so dismal as the wandering up and down where shelter is, and beds and sleepers are by thousands; a houseless rejected creature.
Ibid., ch. 18

37 There are strings in the human heart that had better not be wibrated.
Sim Tappertit, ibid., ch. 22

38 Oh gracious, why wasn't I born old and ugly?
Miss Miggs, ibid., ch. 70

39 The men who learn endurance, are they who call the whole world, brother.

Mr Haredale, ibid., ch. 79

40 The bright old day now dawns again; the cry
  runs through the land,
In England there shall be dear bread – in Ireland,
  sword and brand;
And poverty, and ignorance, shall swell the rich
  and grand,
So, rally round the rulers with the gentle iron
  hand,
Of the fine old English Tory days;
Hail to the coming time!

'The Fine Old English Gentleman' (1841), repr. in *The Poems and Verse of Charles Dickens* (ed. F. G. Kitton, 1903)

41 It [Washington DC] is sometimes called the City of Magnificent Distances, but it might with greater propriety be termed the City of Magnificent Intentions ... Spacious avenues, that begin in nothing, and lead nowhere; streets, mile-long, that only want houses, roads, and inhabitants; public buildings that need but a public to be complete; and ornaments of great thoroughfares, which only lack great thoroughfares to ornament – are its leading features.

American Notes, ch. 8 (1842)

42 They are so filthy and bestial that no honest man would admit one into his house for a water-closet doormat.

Comment on the US press while on an American tour, March 1842, quoted in *Dickens*, ch. 8 (1949) by Hesketh Pearson

43 I am quite serious when I say that I do not believe there are, on the whole earth besides, so many intensified bores as in these United States. No man can form an adequate idea of the real meaning of the word, without coming here.

Comment while on an American tour, March 1842, quoted ibid.

44 Oh! but he was a tight-fisted hand at the grindstone, Scrooge! a squeezing, wrenching, grasping, scraping, clutching, covetous old sinner! Hard and sharp as flint, from which no steel had ever struck out generous fire; secret, and self-contained, and solitary as an oyster.

A Christmas Carol, 'First Stave' (1843)

45 Bah! Humbug!

Ibid., 'First Stave'. Scrooge's customary exclamation.

46 I am the Ghost of Christmas Past.

Ibid., 'Second Stave'. The first of the three spirits presents himself to Scrooge. The other two are the ghosts of Christmas Present and Christmas Yet To Come.

47 Any man may be in good spirits and good temper when he's well dressed. There ain't much credit in that.

Martin Chuzzlewit, ch. 5 (1843–4). Spoken by Mark Tapley.

48 With affection beaming in one eye, and calculation shining out of the other.

Ibid., ch. 8. Referring to Mrs Todgers.

49 Here's the rule for bargains: 'Do other men, for they would do you.' That's the true business precept.

Jonas Chuzzlewit, ibid., ch. 11

50 All their cares, hopes, joys, affections, virtues, and associations seemed to be melted down into dollars. Whatever the chance contributions that fall into the slow cauldron of their talk, they made the gruel thick and slab with dollars. Men were weighed by their dollars, measures gauged by their dollars; life was auctioneered, appraised, put up, and knocked down for its dollars. The next respectable thing to dollars was any venture having their attainment for its end. The more of that worthless ballast, honour and fair-dealing, which any man cast overboard from the ship of his Good Nature and Good Intent, the more ample stowage-room he had for dollars. Make commerce one huge lie and mighty theft. Deface the banner of the nation for an idle rag; pollute it star by star; and cut out stripe by stripe as from the arm of a degraded soldier. Do anything for dollars! What is a flag to *them*!

Ibid., ch.16. Referring to a company of New Yorkers.

51 I believe no satirist could breathe this air. If another Juvenal or Swift could rise up among us tomorrow, he would be hunted down. If you have any knowledge of our literature, and can give me the name of any man, American born and bred, who has anatomised our follies as a people, and not as this or that party; and who has escaped the foulest and most brutal slander, the most inveterate hatred and intolerant pursuit; it will be a strange name in my ears, believe me.

Mr Bevan, ibid., ch. 16. On the United States.

52 Change begets change. Nothing propagates so fast. If a man habituated to a narrow circle of cares and pleasures, out of which he seldom travels, step beyond it, though for never so brief a space, his departure from the monotonous scene on which he

has been an actor of importance would seem to be the signal for instant confusion . . . The mine which Time has slowly dug beneath familiar objects is sprung in an instant; and what was rock before, becomes but sand and dust.

Ibid., ch. 18

53 Rich folks may ride on camels, but it ain't so easy for 'em to see out of a needle's eye. That is my comfort, and I hope I knows it.

Mrs Gamp, ibid., ch. 25. See BIBLE, NEW TESTAMENT: MATTHEW 122.

54 She's the sort of woman one would almost feel disposed to bury for nothing: and do it neatly, too!

Mould, ibid., ch. 25. Referring to Mrs Gamp.

55 He'd make a lovely corpse.

Mrs Gamp, ibid., ch. 25. Mrs Gamp, the 'night-nurse', refers to her patient.

56 Charity begins at home, and justice begins next door.

Tigg, ibid., ch. 27

57 A man who could build a church, as one may say, by squinting at a sheet of paper.

Ibid., ch. 31. Referring to Mr Pecksniff, an architect.

58 Our fellow-countryman is a model of a man, quite fresh from Natur's mould!

Elijah Pogram, ibid., ch. 34. Referring to Mr Chollop, an American.

59 Home is a name, a word, it is a strong one; stronger than magician ever spoke, or spirit ever answered to, in the strongest conjuration.

Ibid., ch. 35

60 The words she spoke of Mrs Harris, lambs could not forgive . . . nor worms forget!

Mrs Gamp, ibid., ch. 49. Referring to Betsey Prigg.

61 O let us love our occupations,
Bless the squire and his relations,
Live upon our daily rations,
And always know our proper stations.

The Chimes, 'Second Quarter' (1844). Lines set to music by Lady Bowley for the men and boys in the village to sing.

62 Oh the nerves, the nerves; the mysteries of this machine called man! Oh the little that unhinges it, poor creatures that we are!

Alderman Cute, ibid., 'Third Quarter'

63 Cows are my passion.

Dombey and Son, ch. 21 (1846–8). Spoken by Mrs Skewton.

64 Vices are sometimes only virtues carried to excess!

Mr Morfin, ibid., ch. 58

65 Barkis is willin'.

David Copperfield, ch. 5 (1849–50). Message of proposal to Clara Peggotty carried by David Copperfield on behalf of Mr Barkis. 'When a man says he's willin',' Barkis explains in ch. 8, '. . . it's as much as to say, that a man's waitin' for a answer.' Clara becomes Mrs Barkis.

66 Experientia does it – as papa used to say.

Mrs Micawber, ibid., ch. 11. See TACITUS 12.

67 Annual income twenty pounds, annual expenditure nineteen nineteen six, result happiness. Annual income twenty pounds, annual expenditure twenty pounds ought and six, result misery.

Mrs Micawber, ibid., ch. 12

68 We are so very 'umble.

Uriah Heep, ibid., ch. 17

69 It was as true as taxes is. And nothing's truer than them.

Mr Barkis, ibid., ch. 21. See also BENJAMIN FRANKLIN 16.

70 What a world of gammon and spinnage it is, though, ain't it!

Miss Mowcher, ibid., ch. 22

71 Accidents will occur in the best-regulated families; and in families not regulated by that pervading influence which sanctifies while it enhances . . . in short, by the influence of Woman, in the lofty character of Wife, they may be expected with confidence, and must be borne with philosophy.

Mr Micawber, ibid., ch. 28. See JOHN WILSON 2

72 This is a London particular . . . A fog, miss.

Bleak House, ch. 3 (1852–3). Mr Guppy addresses Esther Summerson.

73 Keep out of Chancery . . . It's being ground to bits in a slow mill; it's being roasted at a slow fire; it's being stung to death by single bees; it's being drowned by drops; it's going mad by grains.

Mr Krook (reporting Tom Jarndyce), ibid., ch. 5

74 Not to put too fine a point upon it.

Ibid., ch. 11. The expression was 'a favourite apology for plain-speaking with Mr Snagsby, which he always offers with a sort of argumentative frankness'.

75 I don't know nothink.

Jo, ibid., ch. 16

76 It's my old girl that advises. She has the head.

But I never own to it before her. Discipline must be maintained.
Mr Bagnet, ibid., ch. 27

77 It is a melancholy truth that even great men have their poor relations.
Ibid., ch. 28

78 The one great principle of the English law is, to make business for itself.
Ibid., ch. 39. Dickens continued: 'There is no other principle distinctly, certainly, and consistently maintained through all its narrow turnings. Viewed by this light it becomes a coherent scheme, and not the monstrous maze the laity are apt to think it. Let them but once clearly perceive that its grand principle is to make business for itself at their expense, and surely they will cease to grumble.'

79 Now, what I want is, Facts. Teach these boys and girls nothing but Facts. Facts alone are wanted in life. Plant nothing else, and root out everything else. You can only form the minds of reasoning animals upon Facts: nothing else will ever be of any service to them. This is the principle on which I bring up my own children, and this is the principle on which I bring up these children. Stick to Facts, sir!
Hard Times, bk 1, ch. 1 (1854). Opening lines, spoken by Mr Gradgrind, described in ch. 2 as 'a man of realities. A man of facts and calculations'.

80 It was not a bosom to repose upon, but it was a capital bosom to hang jewels upon.
Little Dorrit, bk 1, ch. 21 (1855–7). Describing Mrs Merdle.

81 There's mile-stones on the Dover road!
Ibid., bk 1 ch. 23. This 'inexorable and awful statement' by Mr F.'s Aunt was issued with 'mortal hostility towards the human race'.

82 I revere the memory of Mr F. as an estimable man and most indulgent husband, only necessary to mention Asparagus and it appeared or to hint at any little delicate thing to drink and it came like magic in a pint bottle it was not ecstasy but it was comfort.
Flora Finching, ibid., bk 1, ch. 24

83 Father is rather vulgar, my dear. The word papa, besides, gives a pretty form to the lips. Papa, potatoes, poultry, prunes, and prism, are all very good words for the lips, especially prunes and prism. You will find it serviceable, in the formation of a demeanour, if you sometimes say to yourself in company – on entering a room, for instance – papa, potatoes, poultry, prunes and prism, prunes and prism.
Mrs General, ibid., bk 2, ch. 5

84 I have known a vast quantity of nonsense talked about bad men not looking you in the face. Don't trust that conventional idea. Dishonesty will stare honesty out of countenance any day in the week, if there is anything to be got by it.
Hunted Down, ch. 2 (1859). The words of the narrator (Mr Sampson).

85 It was the best of times, it was the worst of times, it was the age of wisdom, it was the age of foolishness, it was the epoch of belief, it was the epoch of incredulity, it was the season of Light, it was the season of Darkness, it was the spring of hope, it was the winter of despair, we had everything before us, we had nothing before us, we were all going direct to Heaven, we were all going direct the other way.
A Tale of Two Cities, bk 1, ch. 1 (1859). Opening lines. The novel, set in the period of the French Revolution, begins in the year 1775.

86 A wonderful fact to reflect upon, that every human creature is constituted to be that profound secret and mystery to every other.
Ibid., bk 1, ch. 3

87 It is a far, far better thing that I do, than I have ever done; it is a far, far better rest that I go to than I have ever known.
Ibid., bk 3, ch. 15. Sydney Carton's thoughts on the scaffold are the closing words of the book.

88 In the little world in which children have their existence, whosoever brings them up, there is nothing so finely perceived and so finely felt, as injustice.
Great Expectations, ch. 8 (1860–1)

89 What larks!
Joe Gargery, ibid., ch. 57

90 There is in the Englishman a combination of qualities, a modesty, an independence, a responsibility, a repose, combined with an absence of everything calculated to call a blush into the cheek of a young person, which one would seek in vain among the Nations of the Earth.
Our Mutual Friend, bk 1, ch. 11 (1864–5). Spoken by Mr Podsnap.

91 Recollect, we must scrunch or be scrunched.
Mr Boffin, ibid., bk 3, ch. 5

92 I want to be something so much worthier than the doll in the doll's house.

Bella, ibid., bk 4, ch. 5

93 It was a good thing to have a couple of thousand people all rigid and frozen together, in the palm of one's hand.

Quoted in *Dickens: A Biography*, ch. 11 (1988) by Fred Kaplan. Referring to reading in public.

Emily Dickinson
(1830–86)
US poet

Living most of her life in seclusion in Amherst, Massachusetts, she wrote prolifically from around 1850, though few of her poems were published during her lifetime. Most of her work was untitled and undated, and was unconventional and aphoristic in style.

1 Success is counted sweetest
By those who ne'er succeed.
To comprehend a nectar
Requires sorest need.

'Success is counted sweetest', st. 1 (written 1859, publ. 1878), repr. in *The Complete Poems*, no. 67 (Harvard *variorum* edn, ed. Thomas H. Johnson, 1955)

2 Surgeons must be very careful
When they take the knife!
Underneath their fine incisions
Stirs the Culprit – *Life!*

'Surgeons must be very careful' (written *c*. 1859, publ. 1891), ibid., no. 108

3 To fight aloud is very brave –
But *gallanter*, I know
Who charge within the bosom
The Cavalry of Woe –

'To fight aloud is very brave' (written *c*. 1859, publ. 1891), ibid., no. 126

4 'Faith' is a fine invention
When Gentlemen can *see* –
But *Microscopes* are prudent
In an Emergency.

' "Faith" is a fine invention' (written *c*. 1860, publ. 1891), ibid., no. 185

5 I like a look of Agony,
Because I know it's true –
Men do not sham Convulsion,
Nor simulate, a Throe –

'I like a look of Agony', st. 1 (written *c*. 1861, publ. 1890), ibid., no. 241

6 'Hope' is the thing with feathers –
That perches in the soul –
And sings the tunes without the words –
And never stops – at all –

' "Hope" is the thing with feathers', st. 1 (written *c*. 1861, publ. 1891), ibid., no. 254

7 There's a certain Slant of light,
Winter Afternoons –
That oppresses, like the Heft
Of Cathedral Tunes –

'There's a certain Slant of light', st. 1 (written *c*. 1861, publ. 1890), ibid., no. 258. The word 'heft' was changed to read 'weight' in the first edition of Dickinson's verse, edited in 1890 by THOMAS WENTWORTH HIGGINSON and Mabel Loomis Todd.

8 Nods from the Gilded pointers –
Nods from the Seconds slim –
Decades of Arrogance between
The Dial life –
And Him –

'A Clock stopped' (written *c*. 1861, publ. 1896), ibid., no. 287

9 How dreary – to be – Somebody!
How public – like a frog –
To tell one's name – the livelong June –
To an admiring Bog!

'I'm Nobody! Who are you?', st. 2 (written *c*. 1861, publ. 1896), ibid., no. 288

10 Some keep the Sabbath going to Church –
I keep it, staying at Home –
With a Bobolink for a Chorister –
And an Orchard, for a Dome –

'Some keep the Sabbath going to Church', st. 1 (written *c*. 1860, publ. 1864), ibid., no. 324

11 After great pain, a formal feeling comes –
The Nerves sit ceremonious, like Tombs –

'After great pain, a formal feeling comes', st. 1 (written *c*. 1862, publ. 1929), ibid., no. 341

12 This is the Hour of Lead –
Remembered, if outlived,
As Freezing persons, recollect the Snow –
First – Chill – then Stupor – then the letting go –

'After great pain, a formal feeling comes', st. 3, ibid., no. 341

13 Heaven is so far of the Mind
That were the Mind dissolved –
The Site – of it – by Architect
Could not again be proved –

'Heaven is so far of the Mind' (written *c*. 1862, publ. 1929), ibid., no. 370

14 What Soft – Cherubic Creatures –
These Gentlewomen are –
One would as soon assault a Plush –
Or violate a Star –

'What Soft Cherubic Creatures', st. 1 (written c. 1862, publ. 1896), ibid., no. 401

15 Much Madness is divinest Sense –
To a discerning Eye –
Much Sense – the starkest Madness –

'Much Madness is divinest Sense' (written c. 1862, publ. 1890), ibid., no. 435

16 Assent – and you are sane –
Demur – you're straightway dangerous –
And handled with a Chain –

'Much Madness is divinest Sense', ibid., no. 435

17 This is my letter to the World
That never wrote to Me –
The simple News that Nature told –
With tender Majesty.

'This is my letter to the World', st. 1 (written c. 1862, publ. 1890), ibid., no. 441

18 The Brain – is wider than the Sky –
For – put them side by side –
The one the other will contain
With ease – and You – beside –

'The Brain is wider than the Sky' (written c. 1862, publ. 1896), ibid., no. 632

19 I cannot live with You –
It would be Life –
And Life is over there –
Behind the Shelf

'I cannot live with You' (written c. 1862, publ. 1890), ibid., no. 640

20 I dwell in Possibility –
A fairer House than Prose –
More numerous of Windows –
Superior – for Doors –

'I dwell in Possibility' (written c. 1862, publ. 1929), ibid., no. 657

21 The Soul unto itself
Is an imperial friend –
Or the most agonizing Spy –
An Enemy – could send –

'The Soul unto itself' (written c. 1862, publ. 1891), ibid., no. 683

22 Will you tell me my fault, frankly as to yourself, for I had rather wince, than die. Men do not call the surgeon to commend the bone, but to set it, Sir, and fracture within is more critical.

Letter to THOMAS WENTWORTH HIGGINSON, July 1862, publ. in The Life and Letters of Emily Dickinson, pt 2 (1924) by Martha Dickinson Bianchi. Dickinson had sent four poems to Higginson, an author, critic, and retired Unitarian minister, in April 1862, and the correspondence continued until her death. Higginson, in the role of literary mentor, eventually cooperated in producing a volume of her poems in 1890, though only after making significant textual changes.

23 I had no portrait, now, but am small, like the wren; and my hair is bold, like the chestnut burr; and my eyes, like the sherry in the glass, that the guest leaves.

Letter to THOMAS WENTWORTH HIGGINSON, July 1862, ibid.

24 Because I could not stop for Death –
He kindly stopped for me –
The Carriage held but just Ourselves –
And Immortality.

'Because I could not stop for Death' (written c. 1863, publ. 1890), repr. in The Complete Poems, no. 712 (Harvard variorum edn, ed. Thomas H. Johnson, 1955)

25 Remorse – is Memory – awake –
Her Parties all astir –
A Presence of Departed Acts –
At window – and at Door –

'Remorse is Memory awake' (written c. 1863, publ. 1891), ibid., no. 744

26 Of Consciousness, her awful Mate
The Soul cannot be rid –
As easy the secreting her
Behind the Eyes of God.

'Of Consciousness, her awful Mate' (written c. 1864, publ. 1945), ibid., no. 894

27 Faith – is the Pierless Bridge
Supporting what We see
Unto the Scene that We do not –

'Faith is the Pierless Bridge' (written c. 1864, publ. 1929), ibid., no. 915

28 His Labor is a Chant –
His Idleness – a Tune –
Oh, for a Bee's experience
Of Clovers, and of Noon!

'His Feet Are shod with Gauze', st. 2 (written c. 1864, publ. 1890), ibid., no. 916

29 Death is a Dialogue between
The Spirit and the Dust.

'Death is a Dialogue between' (written c. 1864, publ. 1890), ibid., no. 976

30 Nature, like Us is sometimes caught
Without her diadem.
'The Sky is low the Clouds are mean', st. 2 (written *c.* 1866, publ. 1890), ibid., no. 1075

31 If I read a book [and] it makes my whole body so cold no fire ever can warm me, I know *that* is poetry. If I feel physically as if the top of my head were taken off, I know *that* is poetry. These are the only way I know it. Is there any other way?
Quoted by THOMAS WENTWORTH HIGGINSON in letter to his wife, 16 August 1870, publ. in *Letters of Emily Dickinson*, vol. 2, ch. 9 (ed. Thomas H. Johnson, 1958). Recording Dickinson's words at his first meeting with her.

32 A word is dead
When it is said,
Some say.
I say it just
Begins to live
That day.
'A word is dead' (written *c.* 1872, publ. 1894), repr. in *The Complete Poems*, no. 1212 (Harvard *variorum* edn, ed. Thomas H. Johnson, 1955)

33 There is no Frigate like a Book
To take us Lands away
Nor any Coursers like a Page
Of prancing Poetry.
'There is no Frigate Like a Book' (written *c.* 1873, publ. 1894), ibid., no. 1263

34 To see the Summer Sky
Is Poetry, though never in a Book it lie –
True Poems flee –
'To See the Summer Sky' (written *c.* 1879, publ. 1945), ibid., no. 1472

35 The abdication of Belief
Makes the Behavior small –
Better an ignis fatuus
Than no illume at all.
'Those – Dying Then', st. 2 (written *c.* 1882, publ. 1945), ibid., no. 1551

36 Witchcraft was hung, in History,
But History and I
Find all the Witchcraft that we need
Around us, every Day –
'Witchcraft was hung, in History', (written *c.* 1883, publ. 1945), ibid., no. 1583

37 No Life can pompless pass away –
The lowliest career

To the same Pageant wends its way
As that exalted here –
'No Life can pompless pass away' (written *c.* 1884, publ. 1891), ibid., no. 1626

38 The Pedigree of Honey
Does not concern the Bee –
A Clover, any time, to him,
Is Aristocracy –
'The Pedigree of Honey', version 2 (written *c.* 1884, publ. 1890), ibid., no. 1627

39 His mind of man, a secret makes
I meet him with a start
He carries a circumference
In which I have no part.
'His mind of man, a secret makes' (undated, publ. 1914), ibid., no. 1663

40 The gleam of an heroic Act
Such strange illumination
The Possible's slow fuse is lit
By the Imagination.
'The gleam of an heroic Act' (undated, publ. 1914), ibid., no. 1687

41 Parting is all we know of heaven,
And all we need of hell.
'My life closed twice before its close', st. 2 (undated, publ. 1896), ibid., no. 1732

42 The distance that the dead have gone
Does not at first appear –
Their coming back seems possible
For many an ardent year.
'The distance that the dead have gone' (undated, publ. 1896), ibid., no. 1742

43 I must go in, the fog is rising.
Attributed last words, quoted in *The Life and Letters of Emily Dickinson*, pt 1, ch. 8 (1924) by Martha Dickinson Bianchi. Apparently this was 'a pencilled note'.

John Dickinson
(1732–1808)
US statesman and essayist

His Letters from a Farmer in Pennsylvania *(1767–8) rallied opposition to the duties imposed by the Townshend Acts, and he was later a conservative member of the Continental Congress (1774–6) and a signatory to the US Constitution (1787).*

1 Then join hand in hand, brave Americans all!
By uniting we stand, by dividing we fall!
'The Liberty Song', publ. in the *Boston Gazette* 18 July 1768. 'United we stand, divided we fall!' was a motto of the American revolutionaries. The journalist and poet George Pope

Morris wrote, in 'Flag of Our Union' (*Poems*, 1853): '"United we stand, divided we fall!" – It made and preserves a nation!' The words are also found as the moral of one of AESOP'S FABLES, 'The Four Oxen and the Lion'.

2 Our cause is just. Our union is perfect.
Declaration Setting Forth the Causes and Necessity of Taking Up Arms (pamphlet, 1775)

Denis Diderot
(1713–84)
French philosopher, author and critic

As chief editor of the Encyclopédie *(1751–76), he enlisted some of the great thinkers of the day to create one of the key texts of the Enlightenment. He authored numerous novels, plays and philosophical works, and was imprisoned for* Lettre sur les aveugles *(1749).*

1 From fanaticism to barbarism is only one step.
Essai sur le mérite et la vertue, 'A Mon Frère' (1745; *Essay on Merit and Virtue*). Diderot's essay is a loose translation of Shaftesbury's *Inquiry Concerning Virtue* (1699).

2 I can be expected to look for truth but not to find it.
Pensées philosophiques, no. 29 (1746; *Philosophic Thoughts*)

3 No man has received from nature the right to give orders to others. Freedom is a gift from heaven, and every individual of the same species has the right to enjoy it as soon as he is in enjoyment of his reason.
Encyclopedia, vol. 1, 'Political Authority' (1751)

4 There are three principal means of acquiring knowledge available to us: observation of nature, reflection, and experimentation. Observation collects facts; reflection combines them; experimentation verifies the result of that combination. Our observation of nature must be diligent, our reflection profound, and our experiments exact. We rarely see these three means combined; and for this reason, creative geniuses are not common.
Pensées sur l'interprétation de la nature, no. 15 (1753; *On the Interpretation of Nature*)

5 In order to shake a hypothesis, it is sometimes not necessary to do anything more than push it as far as it will go.
Ibid., no. 50

6 The following general definition of an animal: a system of different organic molecules that have combined with one another, under the impulsion of a sensation similar to an obtuse and muffled sense of touch given to them by the creator of matter as a whole, until each one of them has found the most suitable position for its shape and comfort.
Ibid., no. 51

7 It is not human nature we should accuse but the despicable conventions that pervert it.
Discours sur la poésie dramatique (1758; *On Dramatic Poetry*)

8 Poetry must have something in it that is barbaric, vast and wild.
Ibid.

9 Genius is present in every age, but the men carrying it within them remain benumbed unless extraordinary events occur to heat up and melt the mass so that it flows forth.
Ibid.

10 Shakespeare's fault is not the greatest into which a poet may fall. It merely indicates a deficiency of taste.
Ibid.

11 *Mes pensées, ce sont mes catins.*
[My ideas are my whores.]
Le Neveu de Rameau (written 1762, publ. 1821; *Rameau's Nephew*)

12 There is no more inequality between the different stations in life than there is among the different characters in a comedy: the end of the play finds all the players once again in a common position, and the brief period for which their play lasted did not and could not convince any two of them that one was really above or below the other.
Encyclopedia, vol. 15, 'Society' (1765)

13 Do you see this egg? With this you can topple every theological theory, every church or temple in the world.
Le Rêve de d'Alembert, 'Conversation between d'Alembert and Diderot' (written 1769, publ. 1830; *D'Alembert's Dream*)

14 All abstract sciences are nothing but the study of relations between signs.
Dr Théophile de Bordeu, ibid.

15 There is no kind of harassment that a man may not inflict on a woman with impunity in civilized societies.
On Women (1772)

16 *L'esprit de l'escalier.*
[Staircase wit.]
Paradox on Acting (written 1773–8, publ. 1830; *Paradoxe sur le comédien*). Referring to the witty remarks one might have uttered, only thought of after having left the drawing-room.

17 The philosopher has never killed any priests, whereas the priest has killed a great many philosophers.
Observations on the Drawing Up of Laws (written 1774, publ. 1921)

18 Morals are in all countries the result of legislation and government; they are not African or Asian or European: they are good or bad.
Ibid.

19 There is only one passion, the passion for happiness.
Eléments de physiologie, 'Will, Freedom' (notes written 1774–80, publ. 1875–7; *Elements of Physiology*)

20 Genius always presupposes some disorder in the machine.
Ibid., 'Diseases'

21 *Le monde est la maison du fort.*
[The world is the house of the strong.]
Ibid., 'Conclusion'

22 There is not a Musselman alive who would not imagine that he was performing an action pleasing to God and his Holy Prophet by exterminating every Christian on earth, while the Christians are scarcely more tolerant on their side.
Conversations with a Christian Lady (1777)

23 The most dangerous madmen are those created by religion, and ... people whose aim is to disrupt society always know how to make good use of them on occasion.
Ibid.

24 The blood of Jesus Christ can cover a multitude of sins, it seems to me.
Madame de Maréchale, ibid.

25 *Le premier pas vers la philosophie, c'est l'incré.*
[The first step towards philosophy is incredulity.]
Attributed, variously claimed to be last words, or remark during his last conversation

Joan Didion
(b. 1934)
US essayist

Her essay collections Slouching Towards Bethlehem *(1968) and* The White Album *(1979) chronicled the transformation of American society during the 1960s and '70s.*

1 Most of our platitudes notwithstanding, self-deception remains the most difficult deception. The tricks that work on others count for nothing in that very well-lit back alley where one keeps assignations with oneself: no winning smiles will do here, no prettily drawn lists of good intentions.
'On Self-Respect' (1961), repr. in *Slouching Towards Bethlehem* (1968)

2 California is a place in which a boom mentality and a sense of Chekhovian loss meet in uneasy suspension; in which the mind is troubled by some buried but ineradicable suspicion that things had better work here, because here, beneath that immense bleached sky, is where we run out of continent.
'Notes From a Native Daughter' (1965), ibid.

3 When we start deceiving ourselves into thinking not that we want something or need something, not that it is a pragmatic necessity for us to have it, but that it is a *moral imperative* that we have it, then is when we join the fashionable madmen, and then is when the thin whine of hysteria is heard in the land, and then is when we are in bad trouble.
'On Morality' (1965), ibid.

4 We are well advised to keep on nodding terms with the people we used to be, whether we find them attractive company or not. Otherwise they turn up unannounced and surprise us, come hammering on the mind's door at 4am of a bad night and demand to know who deserted them, who betrayed them, who is going to make amends. We forget all too soon the things we thought we could never forget.
'On Keeping a Notebook' (1966), ibid.

5 Writers are always selling somebody out.
Slouching Towards Bethlehem, Preface (1968)

6 Many people I know in Los Angeles believe that the Sixties ended abruptly on August 9, 1969, ended at the exact moment when word of the murders on Cielo Drive traveled like brushfire through the community, and in a sense this is true. The tension broke that day. The paranoia was fulfilled.
'The White Album: A Chronicle of Survival in the Sixties' (1979), repr. in *The White Album* (1979). Referring to the Charles Manson murders.

Marlene Dietrich
(1901–92)
German-born US actress and entertainer

Originally Maria Magdalene Dietrich. One of the most glamorous and sensual of film icons, she starred in the German film

The Blue Angel *(1930) and in Hollywood films such as* Blonde Venus *(1932). She later became a cabaret star.*

1 Falling in love again,
I never wanted to
What am I to do?
I can't help it.
'Falling in Love Again' (song, written by Fredrich Hollander and Sammy Lerner from German lyrics by Robert Liebmann) in the film *The Blue Angel* (1930)

2 In Europe it doesn't matter if you're a man or a woman. We make love with anyone we find attractive.
Remark, 1930, quoted in *Dietrich*, ch. 5 (1992) by Donald Spoto. Addressed to a woman fellow passenger who had declined Marlene's advances. The actor was on a ship making her first voyage to America.

3 It took more than one man to change my name to Shanghai Lily.
Shanghai Express (film, 1932, screenplay by Jules Furthman based on a story by Harry Hervey, directed by Josef von Sternberg). Spoken by Shanghai Lily (Marlene Dietrich).

4 A country without bordels is like a house without bathrooms.
Marlene Dietrich's ABC, 'Bordel' (1962)

5 Most people who make movies are in real life a bitter disappointment. I, on the other hand, am so much better in real life.
Said to critic Sheridan Morley, quoted by him in *The Sunday Times* 24 May 1992

Howard Dietz
(1896–1983)
US songwriter and publicist

Director of advertising and publicity for Metro-Goldwyn-Mayer film studios 1919–57, he later wrote Broadway musicals and revues.

1 *Ars gratia artis.*
[Art for art's sake.]
Motto of MGM studios, adopted in the 1930s. Dietz was responsible for devising MGM's 'roaring lion' trademark and accompanying motto. The phrase 'Art for art's sake' was not new, however: see BENJAMIN CONSTANT 1.

Wentworth Dillon
(c. 1633–85)
Irish poet and translator

Fourth Earl of Roscommon. His translation of HORACE*'s Ars Poetica (1680) and his* Essay on Translated Verse *(1684) established him as a fastidious writer and critic. He founded a*

literary society, and was an early admirer of MILTON*'s* Paradise Lost.

1 Choose an author as you choose a friend.
Essay on Translated Verse, l. 96 (1684)

2 Immodest words admit of no defence,
For want of decency is want of sense.
Ibid., ll. 113–14

3 The multitude is always in the wrong.
Ibid., l. 183

Isak Dinesen
(1885–1962)
Danish author

Pen name of Baroness Karen Blixen, born Karen Christence Dinesen. She lived on a coffee plantation in Kenya 1914–31, and later published Seven Gothic Tales *(1934) and her autobiography* Out of Africa *(1937, filmed 1985).*

1 What is life, when you come to think upon it, but a most excellent, accurately set, infinitely complicated machine for turning fat playful puppies into old mangy blind dogs, and proud war horses into skinny nags, and succulent young boys, to whom the world holds great delight and terrors, into old weak men, with running eyes, who drink ground rhino-horn? What is man, when you come to think upon him, but a minutely set, ingenious machine for turning, with infinite artfulness, the red wine of Shiraz into urine?
Mira, in *Seven Gothic Tales*, 'The Dreamers' (1934)

2 If I know a song of Africa – I thought – of the giraffe, and the African new moon lying on her back, of the ploughs in the fields, and the sweaty faces of the coffee-pickers, does Africa know a song of me?
Out of Africa, pt 1, 'A Gazelle' (1937). The book's title derives from Pliny the Elder; see PLINY THE ELDER 5.

3 The true aristocracy and the true proletariat of the world are both in understanding with tragedy. To them it is the fundamental principle of God, and the key – the minor key – to existence. They differ in this way from the bourgeoisie of all classes, who deny tragedy, who will not tolerate it, and to whom the word tragedy means in itself unpleasantness.
Ibid., pt 3, 'A Fugitive Rests on the Farm'

Diogenes of Sinope

(c. 410–c. 320 BC)

Greek philosopher and moralist

Called 'the Cynic' for his role as inspiration to the Cynics, a sect that spurned luxury, he was said to have lived in a tub. According to tradition, he searched Athens with a lantern in daylight in search of an honest man.

1 Of what use is a philosopher who doesn't hurt anybody's feelings?
Fragment 10, publ. in *Herakleitos & Diogenes*, pt 2 (transl. Guy Davenport, 1976)

2 The art of being a slave is to rule one's master.
Fragment 20, ibid., pt 2

3 In a rich man's house there is no place to spit but his face.
Fragment 56, ibid., pt 2

4 Why not whip the teacher when the pupil misbehaves?
Fragment 99, ibid., pt 2

5 Discourse on virtue and they pass by in droves, whistle and dance the shimmy, and you've got an audience.
Fragment 102, ibid., pt 2

6 Yes . . . that you stand out of my sun a little.
Quoted in *Parallel Lives*, 'Alexander' by PLUTARCH. Reply to Alexander the Great, who had asked him if he wanted anything.

Christian Dior

(1905–57)

French couturier

He founded his own Paris house in 1945 and shocked the public with the extravagant designs of his New Look in 1947. He later devised the 'H' and 'A' line, and 'discovered' YVES SAINT LAURENT.

1 Women are most fascinating between the ages of thirty-five and forty, after they have won a few races and know how to pace themselves. Since few women ever pass forty, maximum fascination can continue indefinitely.
Collier's Magazine 10 June 1955

2 The maintenance of the tradition of fashion is in the nature of an act of faith. In a century which attempts to tear the heart out of every mystery, fashion guards its secret well, and is the best possible proof that there is still magic abroad.
Dior By Dior, pt 4, ch. 19 (1957)

Walt Disney

(1901–66)

US animator and film-maker

Having created Mickey Mouse in 1927 and Donald Duck in 1936, he produced the first full-length colour cartoon film, Snow White and the Seven Dwarfs *in 1937. 'Disney has the best casting,'* ALFRED HITCHCOCK *once remarked. 'If he doesn't like an actor, he just tears him up.'*

1 Dream, diversify – and never miss an angle.
Quoted in *The Disney Studio Story*, Introduction (1988) by Richard Holliss and Brian Sibley

Benjamin Disraeli

(1804–81)

English statesman and author

First earl of Beaconsfield. The leading force in the revitalized Conservative Party after 1867, he was Prime Minister in 1868 and 1874–80. His second term was marked by imperial expansion and the coronation of Queen VICTORIA *as Empress of India in 1876. He also wrote successful political novels. See* JOHN BRIGHT 5.

1 Grief is the agony of an instant: the indulgence of grief the blunder of a life.
Vivian Grey, bk 6, ch. 7 (1826). Spoken by Beckendorf.

2 In politics experiments mean revolutions.
The Voyage of Captain Popanilla, ch. 4, footnote (1828 edn)

3 A good eater must be a good man, for a good eater must have a good digestion, and a good digestion depends upon a good conscience.
The Young Duke, bk 1, ch. 14 (1831)

4 The age of chivalry is past. Bores have succeeded to dragons.
May Dacre, ibid., bk 2, ch. 5

5 A want of tact is worse than a want of virtue. Some women, it is said, work on pretty well without the last: I never knew one who did not sink, who ever dared to sail without the other.
Ibid., bk 2, ch. 9

6 Take a pair of pistols and a pack of cards, a cookery book and a set of new quadrilles; mix them up with half an intrigue and a whole marriage, and divide them into three equal portions.
Ibid., bk 3, ch. 1. Mrs Dallington Vere quotes a recipe for writing a novel.

7 Read no history: nothing but biography, for that is life without theory.
Contarini Fleming, pt 1, ch. 23 (1832). Spoken by Peter Winter.

8 The practice of politics in the East may be defined by one word: dissimulation.

Ibid., pt 5, ch. 10. Spoken by 'a Frank experienced in the Turkish character'.

9 I never offered an opinion till I was sixty, and then it was one which had been in our family for a century.

The Rise of Iskander, ch. 8 (1833). Spoken by the Old Turk.

10 Though I sit down now, the time will come when you will hear me.

Maiden speech in House of Commons, 7 December 1837, publ. in *Selected Speeches of the Late Right Honourable the Earl of Beaconsfield*, vol. 2, 'Irish Election Petitions' (ed. T. E. Kebbel, 1882). Closing words of speech. T. E. Kebbel commented on Disraeli's performance: 'That in some way or another the speaker, before he had done, succeeded in making himself ridiculous is a fact too well attested to be doubted.'

11 Let us consider Ireland ... You have a starving population, an absentee aristocracy, and an alien Church; and in addition the weakest executive in the world. That is the Irish question.

Speech to House of Commons, 16 February 1844, publ. in *Speeches on the Conservative Policy of the Last Thirty Years*, 'State of Ireland' (ed. John F. Bulley, 1869)

12 That doctrine [of peace at any price] has done more mischief than any I can well recall that have been afloat in this country. It has occasioned more wars than any of the most ruthless conquerors. It has disturbed and nearly destroyed that political equilibrium so necessary to the liberties and the welfare of the world.

Speech to House of Lords, 24 April 1844

13 No Government can be long secure without a formidable Opposition. It reduces their supporters to that tractable number which can be managed by the joint influences of fruition and hope. It offers vengeance to the discontented, and distinction to the ambitious; and employs the energies of aspiring spirits, who otherwise may prove traitors in a division or assassins in a debate.

Coningsby, bk 2, ch. 1 (1844)

14 Youth is a blunder; Manhood a struggle; Old Age a regret.

Sidonia, ibid., bk 3, ch. 1

15 Genius, when young, is divine.

Sidonia, ibid., bk 3, ch. 1

16 It seems to me a barren thing, this Conservatism,

an unhappy cross-breed, the mule of politics that engenders nothing.

Lyle, ibid., bk 3, ch. 5. See IGNATIUS DONNELLY 1.

17 I have been ever of opinion that revolutions are not to be evaded.

Sidonia, ibid., bk 4, ch. 11

18 Man is made to adore and to obey: but if you will not command him, if you give him nothing to worship, he will fashion his own divinities, and find a chieftain in his own passions.

Sidonia, ibid., bk 4, ch. 13

19 It was not reason that besieged Troy; it was not reason that sent forth the Saracen from the desert to conquer the world; that inspired the crusades; that instituted the monastic orders; it was not reason that produced the Jesuits; above all, it was not reason that created the French Revolution. Man is only great when he acts from the passions; never irresistible but when he appeals to the imagination.

Sidonia, ibid., bk 4, ch. 13

20 Life is too short to be little. Man is never so manly as when he feels deeply, acts boldly, and expresses himself with frankness and with fervour.

Ibid., bk 7, ch. 2

21 Nature, like man, sometimes weeps from gladness.

Ibid., bk 7, ch. 5. Describing summer showers.

22 The right honourable gentleman caught the Whigs bathing, and walked away with their clothes. He has left them in the full enjoyment of their liberal positions, and he is himself a strict conservative of their garments.

Speech to House of Commons, 28 February 1845, publ. in *Selected Speeches of the Late Right Honourable the Earl of Beaconsfield*, vol. 1, 'Opening of Letters' (ed. T. E. Kebbel, 1882). Referring to the embracing of Whig policies on free trade by Robert Peel, prime minister and fellow Tory.

23 Protection is not a principle, but an expedient.

Speech to House of Commons, 17 March 1845, ibid., vol. 1, 'Agricultural Distress'. Disraeli said exactly the opposite in a speech two years earlier, 25 April 1843.

24 A Conservative government is an organised hypocrisy.

Speech to House of Commons, 17 March 1845, ibid., vol. 1, 'Agricultural Distress'. Closing words of speech, on the abandonment of Prime Minister Sir Robert Peel's protectionist policies on which his government had been elected.

25 It is well-known what a middleman is: he is a

man who bamboozles one party and plunders the other.
Speech, 11 April 1845, ibid., vol. 1, 'Maynooth'

26 Things must be done by parties, not by persons using parties as tools.
Letter, 17 December 1845, publ. in *Benjamin Disraeli, Letters*, vol. 4 (ed. M. G. Wiebe, 1989). Referring to the tactics of Prime Minister Sir Robert Peel on the issue of the Irish Famine.

27 In great cities men are brought together by the desire of gain. They are not in a state of co-operation, but of isolation, as to the making of fortunes; and for all the rest they are careless of neighbours. Christianity teaches us to love our neighbour as ourself; modern society acknowledges no neighbour.
Sybil, or: The Two Nations, bk 2, ch. 5 (1845). Spoken by Stephen Morley.

28 Two nations between whom there is no intercourse and no sympathy; who are as ignorant of each other's habits, thoughts, and feelings, as if they were dwellers in different zones, or inhabitants of different planets . . . The rich and the poor.
Stephen Morley, ibid., bk 2, ch. 5

29 Toryism will yet rise from the tomb over which Bolingbroke shed his last tear, to bring back strength to the Crown, liberty to the subject, and to announce that power has only one duty – to secure the social welfare of the People.
Ibid., bk 4, ch. 14

30 Frank and explicit . . . that is the right line to take when you wish to conceal your own mind and to confuse the minds of others.
The gentleman in Downing Street, ibid., bk 6, ch. 1

31 We live in an age when to be young and to be indifferent can be no longer synonymous. We must prepare for the coming hour. The claims of the Future are represented by suffering millions; and the Youth of a Nation are the trustees of Posterity.
Ibid., bk 6, ch. 13. Closing words of novel.

32 That fatal drollery called a representative government.
Tancred, bk 2, ch. 13 (1847). Spoken by Tancred.

33 We moralise among ruins, it is always when the game is played, that we discover the cause of the result.
Ibid., bk 5, ch. 5. A few lines further, Disraeli writes: 'Men moralise among ruins, or, in the throng and tumult of successful cities, recall past visions of urban desolation for prophetic warning.'

34 London is a modern Babylon.
Ibid., bk 5, ch. 5

35 My objection to Liberalism is this – that it is the introduction into the practical business of life of the highest kind – namely, politics – of philosophical ideas instead of political principles.
Speech to House of Commons, 5 June 1848, publ. in *Hansard*, vol. 99, col. 396–7

36 Coalitions although successful, have always found this, that their triumph has been short. This too I know, that England does not love coalitions.
Speech to House of Commons, 16 December 1852, publ. in *Selected Speeches of the Late Right Honourable the Earl of Beaconsfield* (ed. T. E. Kebbel, 1882)

37 Finality is not the language of politics.
Speech to House of Commons, 28 February 1859, publ. in *Speeches on the Conservative Policy of the Last Thirty Years*, 'The Reform Bill of 1859' (ed. John F. Bulley, 1869)

38 The question is this: Is man an ape or an angel? My Lord, I am on the side of the angels. I repudiate with indignation and abhorrence the contrary view, which is, I believe, foreign to the conscience of humanity.
Speech at Diocesan Conference, Oxford, 25 November 1864, publ. in *Selected Speeches of the Late Right Honourable the Earl of Beaconsfield*, vol. 2, 'Church Policy' (ed. T. E. Kebbel, 1882)

39 Assassination has never changed the history of the world.
Speech to House of Commons, 1 May 1865, publ. in *Hansard*, vol. 178, col. 1246. Referring to the assassination of ABRAHAM LINCOLN.

40 We authors, Ma'am . . .
Quoted in *Disraeli*, ch. 22 (1993) by Stanley Weintraub. Said in 1868, prefacing a remark to Queen VICTORIA, as reported by Lady Palmerston. Disraeli had recently presented Victoria with a collected edition of his novels, and she had given him a signed copy of her best-selling *Leaves from the Journal of Our Life in the Highlands*.

41 The divine right of kings may have been a plea for feeble tyrants, but the divine right of government is the key-stone of human progress, and without it government sinks into police and a nation is degraded into a mob.
Lothair, Preface (1870)

42 The pursuit of science leads only to the insoluble.
Cardinal Grandison, ibid., ch.17

43 A Protestant, if he wants aid or advice on any matter, can only go to his solicitor.
Ibid., ch. 18

44 When a man fell into his anecdotage it was a sign for him to retire from the world.
Ibid., ch. 28

45 Books are fatal: they are the curse of the human race. Nine-tenths of existing books are nonsense, and the clever books are the refutation of that nonsense. The greatest misfortune that ever befell man was the invention of printing.
Mr Phoebus, ibid., ch. 29

46 My idea of an agreeable person is a person who agrees with me.
Hugo Bohun, ibid., ch. 41

47 Religion is civilisation, the highest; it is a reclamation of man from savageness by the Almighty.
Cardinal Grandison, ibid., ch. 48

48 Increased means and increased leisure are the two civilizers of man.
Speech at Manchester Free Trade Hall, 3 April 1872, publ. in *Selected Speeches of the Late Right Honourable the Earl of Beaconsfield*, vol. 2, 'Conservative Principles' (ed. T. E. Kebbel, 1882)

49 You behold a range of exhausted volcanoes. Not a flame flickers on a single pallid crest.
Speech at Manchester Free Trade Hall, 3 April 1872, ibid., vol. 2. Referring to the government Treasury Bench. EDMUND BURKE had previously described old religious factions as 'volcanoes burnt out' (speech, 11 May 1792).

50 A University should be a place of light, of liberty, and of learning.
Speech to House of Commons, 11 March 1873, ibid., vol. 2, 'Irish University Education Bill'

51 An author who speaks about his own books is almost as bad as a mother who talks about her own children.
Speech, Glasgow, 19 November 1873, quoted in *The Times* 20 November 1873. Spoken on his inauguration as Lord Rector of Glasgow University.

52 Cosmopolitan critics, men who are the friends of every country save their own.
Speech at Guildhall, London, 9 November 1877, quoted in *The Times* 10 November 1877. See also GEORGE CANNING 1 and W. S. GILBERT 32.

53 Lord Salisbury and myself have brought you back peace – but a peace I hope with honour.
Speech to crowds at Downing Street, 16 July 1878, quoted in *Disraeli*, ch. 27 (1993) by Stanley Weintraub. The address was made on Disraeli's return from the Congress of Berlin, convened to resolve the 'Eastern Question'. GEORGE BERNARD SHAW made a humorous reference to these words in his play *Caesar and Cleopatra* (1898). See also NEVILLE CHAMBERLAIN 2, LORD JOHN RUSSELL 1.

54 A sophistical rhetorician, inebriated with the exuberance of his own verbosity, and gifted with an egotistical imagination that can at all times command an interminable and inconsistent series of arguments to malign an opponent and to glorify himself.
Speech in Knightsbridge, London, 27 July 1878, quoted in *The Times* 29 July 1878, referring to GLADSTONE. On another occasion, Disraeli said of Gladstone, 'He has not a single redeeming defect.'

55 Everyone likes flattery; and when you come to Royalty you should lay it on with a trowel.
Remark to MATTHEW ARNOLD, *c.* 1880, quoted in *Collections and Recollections*, ch. 23 (1898) by G. W. E. Russell

56 Next to knowing when to seize an opportunity, the most important thing in life is to know when to forego an advantage.
The Infernal Marriage, pt 3, ch. 1 (1881). Spoken by Tiresias.

57 I have climbed to the top of the greasy pole.
Quoted in *The Life of Benjamin Disraeli*, vol. 4, ch. 16 (1916) by W. F. Monypenny and G. E. Buckle. Remark to friends on becoming prime minister.

58 I am dead: dead, but in the Elysian fields.
Quoted ibid., vol. 5, ch. 13 (1920). Referring to his elevation to the House of Lords.

59 There are three kinds of lies: lies, damned lies and statistics.
Quoted by MARK TWAIN in his *Autobiography*, ch. 29 (1924, rev. Charles Neider, 1959). The words have never been found among Disraeli's works; they have also been attributed to his old adversary HENRY LABOUCHERE.

60 Yes, I am a Jew, and when the ancestors of the right honourable gentleman were brutal savages in an unknown island, mine were priests in the temple of Solomon.
Quoted in *The Fine Art of Political Wit*, ch. 4 (1964) by Leon Harris. Disraeli's attributed reply to a taunt by Irish political leader Daniel O'Connell recalls the reputed remonstrance of a senator of German extraction by Senator Judah P. Benjamin of Louisiana (1811–84): 'The gentleman will please remember that when his half-civilized ancestors were hunting the wild boar in the forests of Silesia, mine were the princes of the earth.'

61 When I meet a man whose name I can't remem-

ber, I give myself two minutes, then if it is a hopeless case I always say, 'And how is the old complaint?'
Quoted ibid., ch. 4. Also attributed to LORD PALMERSTON.

62 No it is better not. She would only ask me to take a message to Albert.
Quoted in *Disraeli*, ch. 32 (1966) by Robert Blake. Remark on hearing that Queen VICTORIA wished to see him during his last illness.

63 The Church of England is the Tory Party at prayer.
Attributed. Among Disraeli's biographers, Robert Blake has been unable to confirm that Disraeli ever wrote or spoke these words, while Stanley Weintraub calls this 'a wry saying' of the time with which Disraeli agreed.

Isaac D'Israeli
(1766–1848)
English author

The father of BENJAMIN DISRAELI, *he wrote novels, but was best known for his commentaries and criticism, notably in the six-volume* Curiosities of Literature *(1791–1834).*

1 The wisdom of the wise, and the experience of ages, may be preserved by quotation.
Curiosities of Literature, 'Quotation' (1791–1834)

Mort Dixon
(1892–1956)
US songwriter

A leading lyricist of popular songs of the 1920s and '30s, he collaborated with Ray Henderson, Harry Woods and ALLIE WRUBEL, *among others, on such hits as 'Bye Bye Blackbird' (1926) and 'You're My Everything' (1931).*

1 Bye bye blackbird.
'Bye Bye Blackbird' (song, 1926, with music by Ray Henderson)

2 I'm looking over a four leaf clover
That I overlooked before.
'I'm Looking Over a Four Leaf Clover' (song, 1927, with music by Harry Woods)

Milovan Djilas
(1911–95)
Yugoslav political leader and author

A leading partisan in the Second World War and subsequently a minister in Tito's cabinet, he was made President of the Federal People's Assembly in 1953, but his criticism of the Communist Party caused him to lose his post and leave the Party.

1 The Party line is that there is no Party line.
Comment, November 1951, quoted in *Disputed Barricade*,

ch. 15 (1957) by Fitzroy Maclean. On reforms of the Yugoslavian Communist Party.

2 The terrible thing is that one cannot be a Communist and not let oneself in for the shameful act of recantation. One cannot be a Communist and preserve an iota of one's personal integrity.
Encounter December 1979

3 Normal life cannot sustain revolutionary attitudes for long.
Guardian 9 April 1990

(Henry) Austin Dobson
(1840–1921)
English poet and author

A careful versifier who popularized the French triolet and rondeau forms in English, he later turned to writing studies of 18th-century literary figures, such as FIELDING, STEELE *and* GOLDSMITH.

1 Time goes, you say? Ah, no!
Alas, Time stays, *we* go.
'The Paradox of Time', st. 1 (1875), repr. in *Collected Poems* (1923). A variation on 'Amour de Marie' (1555) by PIERRE DE RONSARD: 'Le temps s'en va, le temps s'en va, ma dame!/Las! le temps non: mais nous, nous en allons!'

2 The ladies of St James's!
They're painted to the eyes;
Their white it stays for ever,
Their red it never dies.
'The Ladies of St James's', st. 4 (1883), repr. in *At the Sign of the Lyre* (1889)

E. L. Doctorow
(b. 1931)
US novelist

Edgar Lawrence Doctorow. Blending fact with invention and using a range of genres, his books include Ragtime *(1975) and* Billy Bathgate *(1989).*

1 There is no longer any such thing as fiction or nonfiction; there's only narrative.
New York Times Book Review 27 January 1988

2 It's like driving a car at night. You never see further than your headlights, but you can make the whole trip that way.
Interview in *Writers at Work* (eighth series, ed. George Plimpton, 1988). Discussing his writing technique.

3 Like art and politics, gangsterism is a very important avenue of assimilation into society.
International Herald Tribune 1 October 1990

4 The radical's role is to propose intolerable ideas, and to be sacrificed for them, so that subsequent generations can absorb them as privileges.
Interview in the *Guardian* 4 June 1994

Ken Dodd
(b. 1929)
British comic

Primarily a stand-up comedian, he has appeared in variety and pantomime and on television and radio since his debut in 1954.

1 The trouble with Freud is that he never played the Glasgow Empire Saturday night.
'The Laughter Makers', TV interview, quoted in *The Times* 7 August 1965

2 If I get a hard audience they are not going to get away until they laugh. Those seven laughs a minute – I've got to have them.
Daily Telegraph 20 September 1990

J. P. Donleavy
(b. 1926)
Irish-American author

James Patrick Donleavy. The Ginger Man (1955) was the first of a series of bawdy picaresque novels, mostly set in Ireland.

1 But Jesus, when you don't have any money, the problem is food. When you have money, it's sex. When you have both, it's health, you worry about getting ruptured or something. If everything is simply jake then you're frightened of death.
The Ginger Man, ch. 5 (1955). Spoken by O'Keefe.

2 When I die I want to decompose in a barrel of porter and have it served in all the pubs in Dublin.
Sebastian Dangerfield, ibid. ch. 31

3 Writing is turning one's worst moments into money.
Playboy May 1979. He has repeated the aphorism on various occasions.

John Donne
(c. 1572–1631)
English poet and divine

His use of elaborate conceits in his devotional, philosophical and love poetry place him among the greatest of the metaphysical poets. A convert from Catholicism, in 1621 he became Dean of St Paul's, where he was celebrated for his sermons. See THOMAS CAREW 1, IZAAK WALTON 1.

1 I wonder by my troth, what thou and I
Did, till we loved? Were we not weaned till then?
But sucked on country pleasures, childishly?
Or snorted we in the seven sleepers' den?
Songs and Sonnets, 'The Good-Morrow', written *c.* 1592–1614, publ. in *Poems* (1633). Opening lines of poem.

2 And now good morrow to our waking souls,
Which watch not one another out of fear;
For love, all love of other sights controls,
And makes one little room an everywhere.
Songs and Sonnets, 'The Good-Morrow', st. 2, ibid.

3 Go, and catch a falling star,
Get with child a mandrake root,
Tell me, where all past years are,
Or who cleft the devil's foot,
Teach me to hear mermaids singing,
Or to keep off envy's stinging,
And find
What wind
Serves to advance an honest mind.
Songs and Sonnets, 'Song (Go, and catch a falling star)', st. 1, ibid.

4 I have done one braver thing
Than all the worthies did,
And yet a braver thence doth spring,
Which is, to keep that hid.
Songs and Sonnets, 'The Undertaking', st. 1, ibid.

5 Busy old fool, unruly Sun,
Why dost thou thus,
Through windows and through curtains call on us?
Must to thy motions lovers' seasons run?
Songs and Sonnets, 'The Sun Rising', st. 1, ibid.

6 Love, all alike, no season knows, nor clime,
Nor hours, days, months, which are the rags of time.
Songs and Sonnets, 'The Sun Rising', st. 1, ibid.

7 Shine here to us, and thou art everywhere;
This bed thy centre is, these walls thy sphere.
Songs and Sonnets, 'The Sun Rising', st. 3, ibid.

8 For God's sake hold your tongue, and let me love.
Songs and Sonnets, 'The Canonization', ibid. Opening line of poem.

9 I am two fools, I know,
For loving, and for saying so
In whining poetry.
Songs and Sonnets, 'The Triple Fool', ibid. Opening lines of poem.

10 Sweetest love, I do not go
For weariness of thee,
Nor in hope the world can show
A fitter love for me;
But since that I
Must die at last, 'tis best,
To use my self in jest
Thus by feigned deaths to die.
Songs and Sonnets, 'Song (Sweetest love, I do not go)', st. 1,
ibid.

11 When I died last, and, dear, I die
As often as from thee I go,
Though it be but an hour ago,
And lovers' hours be full eternity.
Songs and Sonnets, 'The Legacy', ibid. Opening lines.

12 Oh do not die, for I shall hate
All women so, when thou art gone.
Songs and Sonnets, 'A Fever', ibid. Opening lines.

13 Twice or thrice had I loved thee,
Before I knew thy face or name;
So in a voice, so in a shapeless flame,
Angels affect us oft, and worshipped be.
Songs and Sonnets, 'Air and Angels', ibid. Opening lines.

14 'Tis true, 'tis day; what though it be?
O wilt thou therefore rise from me?
Why should we rise, because 'tis light?
Did we lie down because 'twas night?
Songs and Sonnets, 'Break of Day', ibid. Opening lines.

15 All kings, and all their favourites,
All glory of honours, beauties, wits,
The sun itself, which makes times, as they pass,
Is elder by a year, now, than it was
When thou and I first one another saw:
All other things to their destruction draw,
Only our love hath no decay;
This, no tomorrow hath, nor yesterday,
Running it never runs from us away,
But truly keeps his first, last, everlasting day.
Songs and Sonnets, 'The Anniversary', st. 1, ibid.

16 Let us love nobly, and live, and add again
Years and years unto years, till we attain
To write threescore: this is the second of our
   reign.
Songs and Sonnets, 'The Anniversary', st. 3, ibid. Closing lines
of poem.

17 Mark but this flea, and mark in this,
How little that which thou deny'st me is;
It sucked me first, and now sucks thee,

And in this flea, our two bloods mingled be;
Thou know'st that this cannot be said
A sin, nor shame, nor loss of maidenhead,
Yet this enjoys before it woo,
And pampered swells with one blood made of two
And this, alas, is more than we would do.
Songs and Sonnets, 'The Flea', st. 1, ibid.

18 'Tis the year's midnight, and it is the day's.
Songs and Sonnets, 'A Nocturnal upon St Lucy's Day', ibid.
Opening line.

19 The world's whole sap is sunk:
The general balm th' hydroptic earth hath drunk.
Songs and Sonnets, 'A Nocturnal upon St Lucy's Day', st. 1,
ibid.

20 Come live with me, and be my love,
And we will some new pleasures prove
Of golden sands, and crystal brooks,
With silken lines, and silver hooks.
Songs and Sonnets, 'The Bait', st. 1, ibid. See also CHRIS-
TOPHER MARLOWE 1 and WALTER RALEGH 5.

21 As virtuous men pass mildly away,
And whisper to their souls to go,
Whilst some of their sad friends do say
The breath goes now, and some say no.
Songs and Sonnets, 'Valediction: Forbidding Mourning', st. 1,
ibid.

22 'Twere profanation of our joys
To tell the laity our love.
Songs and Sonnets, 'Valediction: Forbidding Mourning', st. 2,
ibid.

23 Dull sublunary lovers' love
(Whose soul is sense) cannot admit
Absence, because it doth remove
Those things which elemented it.
Songs and Sonnets, 'Valediction: Forbidding Mourning', st. 4,
ibid.

24 If they be two, they are two so
As stiff twin compasses are two,
Thy soul, the fixed foot, makes no show
To move, but doth, if the other do.
Songs and Sonnets, 'Valediction: Forbidding Mourning', st. 7,
ibid.

25 So must pure lovers' souls descend
T'affections, and to faculties,
Which sense may reach and apprehend,
Else a great prince in prison lies.
Songs and Sonnets, 'The Ecstasy', ll. 65–8, ibid.

26 I long to talk with some old lover's ghost,
Who died before the god of love was born.
Songs and Sonnets, 'Love's Deity', ibid. Opening lines.

27 To rage, to lust, to write to, to commend,
All is the purlieu of the god of love.
Songs and Sonnets, 'Love's Deity', st. 3, ibid.

28 So, so, break off this last lamenting kiss,
Which sucks two souls, and vapours both away.
Songs and Sonnets, 'The Expiration', ibid. Opening lines.

29 Love built on beauty, soon as beauty, dies.
Elegies, no. 2 ('The Anagram'), l. 27, written *c.* 1593–6, ibid.

30 No spring, nor summer beauty hath such grace,
As I have seen in one autumnal face.
Elegies, no. 9 ('The Autumnal'), ll. 1–2, ibid. This may have been written later than Donne's other Elegies, possibly *c.* 1605.

31 Love was as subtly catched as a disease;
But being got it is a treasure sweet,
Which to defend is harder than to get:
And ought not be profaned on either part,
For though 'tis got by *chance*, 'tis kept by *art*.
Elegies, no. 15 ('The Expostulation'), ll. 66–70, ibid. Last lines of poem, whose authorship has been questioned.

32 By our first strange and fatal interview,
By all desires which thereof did ensue.
Elegies, no. 16 ('On His Mistress'), written *c.* 1593–6, publ. in *Poems* (1635). Opening lines of poem.

33 Whoever loves, if he do not propose
The right true end of love, he's one that goes
To sea for nothing but to make him sick.
Elegies, no. 18 ('Love's Progress'), written *c.* 1593–6, publ. in *Poems* (1669). Opening lines of poem.

34 The straight Hellespont between
The Sestos and Abydos of her breasts.
Elegies, no. 18 ('Love's Progress'), ll. 60–1, ibid. In classical mythology, Sestos and Abydos lay on either side of the Hellespont (the Dardanelles), and were the homes of the doomed lovers Hero and Leander.

35 Licence my roving hands, and let them go,
Before, behind, between, above, below.
O my America, my new found land,
My kingdom, safeliest when with one man manned.
Elegies, no. 19 ('To His Mistress Going to Bed'), ll. 25–8, ibid. An alternative version has the second line, 'Behind, before, above, between, below.'

36 Full nakedness! All joys are due to thee,
As souls unbodied, bodies unclothed must be,
To taste whole joys.
Elegies, no. 19 ('To His Mistress Going to Bed'), ll. 33–5, ibid.

37 Sir, more than kisses, letters mingle souls;
For, thus friends absent speak.
'Verse Letter to Sir Henry Wotton', written *c.* 1597–8, publ. in *Poems* (1633). Opening lines.

38 And seeing the snail, which everywhere doth roam,
Carrying his own house still, still is at home,
Follow (for he is easy paced) this snail,
Be thine own palace, or the world's thy gaol.
'Verse Letter to Sir Henry Wotton', ll. 49–52, ibid.

39 Let me arrest thy thoughts; wonder with me,
Why plowing, building, ruling and the rest,
Or most of those arts, whence our lives are blest,
By cursed *Cain's* race invented be,
And blest *Seth* vexed us with astronomy.
'The Progress of the Soul', st. 52, written 1601, ibid.

40 Reason is our soul's left hand, faith her right,
By these we reach divinity.
'Verse Letter to the Countess of Bedford', written *c.* 1607–8, ibid.

41 I would not that death should take me asleep. I would not have him merely seize me, and only declare me to be dead, but win me, and overcome me. When I must shipwreck, I would do it in a sea, where mine impotency might have some excuse; not in a sullen weedy lake, where I could not have so much as exercise for my swimming.
Letter, September 1608, publ. in *Complete Poetry and Selected Prose* (ed. John Hayward, 1929)

42 At most, the greatest persons are but great wens, and excrescences; men of wit and delightful conversation, but as moles for ornament, except they be so incorporated into the body of the world that they contribute something to the sustentation of the whole.
Letter, September 1608, ibid.

43 Whensoever any affliction assails me, me thinks I have the keys of my prison in mine own hand, and no remedy presents itself so soon to my heart, as mine own sword. Often meditation of this hath won me to a charitable interpretation of their action, who die so: and provoked me a little to watch and exagitate their reasons, which pronounce so peremptory judgements upon them.
Biathanatos, Preface (written *c.* 1608, publ. 1646)

44 Contemplative and bookish men must of necess-

ity be more quarrelsome than others, because they contend not about matter of fact, nor can determine their controversies by any certain witnesses, nor judges. But as long as they go towards peace, that is truth, it is no matter which way.

Biathanatos, Preface, ibid.

45 I am a little world made cunningly
Of elements, and an angelic sprite.

Holy Sonnets, no. 5 ('I am a little world'), written *c.* 1609, publ. in *Poems* (1635)

46 Death, be not proud, though some have called thee
Mighty and dreadful, for thou art not so,
For, those whom thou think'st thou dost overthrow,
Die not, poor death, nor yet canst thou kill me.

Holy Sonnets, no. 6 ('Death, be not proud'), ibid., publ. in *Poems* (1633)

47 One short sleep past, we wake eternally,
And death shall be no more; death, thou shalt die.

Holy Sonnets, no. 6 ('Death, be not proud'), ibid.

48 Take me to you, imprison me, for I
Except you enthral me, never shall be free,
Nor ever chaste, except you ravish me.

Holy Sonnets, no. 10 ('Batter my heart, three-personed God'), ibid. Last lines of sonnet.

49 And new philosophy calls all in doubt,
The element of fire is quite put out;
The sun is lost, and th'earth, and no man's wit
Can well direct him where to look for it.

An Anatomy of the World: The First Anniversary, ll. 205–8 (1611)

50 Wicked is not much worse than indiscreet.

Ibid., l. 338

51 We are all conceived in close prison; in our mothers' wombs, we are close prisoners all; when we are born, we are born but to the liberty of the house; prisoners still, though within larger walls; and then all our life is but a going out to the place of execution, to death.

Sermon, 28 March 1619, publ. in *Eighty Sermons*, no. 27 (1640)

52 But I do nothing upon myself, and yet am mine own executioner.

Devotions upon Emergent Occasions, Meditation 12 (1624). See THOMAS BROWNE 13.

53 When one man dies, one chapter is not torn out of the book, but translated into a better language.

Ibid., Meditation 17

54 God employs several translators; some pieces are translated by age, some by sickness, some by war, some by justice.

Ibid., Meditation 17

55 No man is an island entire of itself; every man is a piece of the continent, a part of the main; if a clod be washed away by the sea, Europe is the less, as well as if a promontory were, as well as if a manor of thy friends or of thine own were; any man's death diminishes me because I am involved in mankind; and therefore never send to know for whom the bell tolls; it tolls for thee.

Ibid., Meditation 17. In a letter of September 1608, Donne wrote: 'To be no part of any body, is to be nothing.'

56 I throw myself down in my chamber, and I call in and invite God and his angels thither, and when they are there, I neglect God and his angels for the noise of a fly, for the rattling of a coach, for the whining of a door.

Sermon, 12 December 1626, publ. in *Eighty Sermons*, no. 80 (1640)

57 Poor intricated soul! Riddling, perplexed, labyrinthical soul!

Sermon, 25 January 1628/9, ibid., no. 48

58 He must pull out his own eyes, and see no creature, before he can say, he sees no God; he must be no man, and quench his reasonable soul, before he can say to himself, there is no God.

Sermon, 13 April 1628, ibid., no. 23

59 Humiliation is the beginning of sanctification.

Sermon, 25 December 1629, ibid., no. 7

Ignatius Donnelly
(1831–1901)
US politician and author

A Radical Republican in Congress 1863–9, he won a wide readership for his speculative writings, notably Atlantis *(1882) and* The Great Cryptogram *(1888), which expounded his notion that* FRANCIS BACON *wrote many of the works ascribed to* SHAKESPEARE.

1 The Democratic Party is like a mule. It has neither pride of ancestry nor hope of posterity.

Speech to Minnesota State Legislature, 13 September 1860, attributed. See BENJAMIN DISRAELI 16.

Ariel Dorfman
(b. 1942)
Chilean author

Forced into exile by the 1973 military coup in Chile, he expressed his revulsion at political oppression in his novels and plays, notably Death and the Maiden *(1991, filmed 1995).*

1 The enemy is inside, and we find it hard to distinguish him from some of our innermost thoughts and nurturings.
The Empire's Old Clothes, 'Conclusion' (1983)

(Sir) Reginald Dorman-Smith
(1899–1977)
British politician

Conservative MP for Petersfield, Hampshire (1935–46), he was Minister for Agriculture and Fisheries (1939–40) and Governor of Burma (1941–6).

1 Let 'Dig for Victory' be the motto of every one with a garden and of every able-bodied man and woman capable of digging an allotment in their spare time.
Radio broadcast, 3 October 1939, quoted in *The Times* 4 October 1939

John Dos Passos
(1896–1970)
US novelist

Praised by Edmund Wilson as 'perhaps the first really important writer to have succeeded in using colloquial American', he described the disillusionment of war and the failings of materialism in his novels, which include Three Soldiers *(1921) and the trilogy* USA *(1930–6).*

1 The only man that gets anything out of capitalism is a crook, an' he gets to be a millionaire in short order . . .
42nd Parallel, 'Mac' (first title in the *USA* trilogy, 1930). Spoken by Tim O'Hara.

2 People don't choose their careers; they are engulfed by them.
New York Times 25 October 1959

Fyodor Dostoyevsky
(1821–81)
Russian novelist

He excelled in social and psychological portraits in such works as Crime and Punishment *(1866),* The Idiot *(1868) and The Brothers Karamazov *(1879–80). Much of his life was spent in* poverty, and he served a prison sentence for political dissidence.*

1 Sarcasm: the last refuge of modest and chaste-souled people when the privacy of their soul is coarsely and intrusively invaded.
Notes from Underground, pt 2, ch. 6 (1864)

2 Power is given only to those who dare to lower themselves and pick it up. Only one thing matters, one thing; to be able to dare!
Crime and Punishment, pt 5, ch. 4 (1866, transl. 1991). 'I wanted to *make the dare*,' Raskolnikov explains to Sonya, 'and so I killed someone . . .'

3 A real gentleman, even if he loses everything he owns, must show no emotion. Money must be so far beneath a gentleman that it is hardly worth troubling about.
The Gambler, ch. 2 (1866)

4 The cleverest of all, in my opinion, is the man who calls himself a fool at least once a month.
'Bobok', first publ. in *A Writer's Diary* (1873). Spoken by Ivan Ivanovich.

5 If one were to destroy mankind's faith in its own immortality, there would instantly grow enfeebled within it not only love but every vital force for the continuation of universal life.
The Brothers Karamazov, bk 2, ch. 6 (1879–80, transl. 1993). Spoken by Miusov.

6 Beauty is not only a terrifying thing – it is also a mysterious one. In it the Devil struggles with God, and the field of battle is the hearts of men.
Mitya, ibid., bk 3, ch. 3

7 Imagine that you yourself are erecting the edifice of human fortune with the goal of, at the finale, making people happy, of at last giving them peace and quiet, but that in order to do it it would be necessary and unavoidable to torture to death only one tiny little creature, that same little child that beat its breast with its little fist, and on its unavenged tears to found that edifice, would you agree to be the architect on those conditions?
Ivan Karamazov, ibid., bk 5, ch. 4

8 If the Devil doesn't exist and, consequently, man has created him, he has created him in his own image and likeness.
Ivan Karamazov, ibid., bk 5, ch. 4

9 There is for man no preoccupation more constant or more nagging than, while in a condition of free-

dom, quickly to find someone to bow down before.
Ibid., bk 5, ch. 5. Ivan Karamazov reports the words of the Grand Inquisitor.

10 The human race fails to accept its prophets and does them to death, but men love their martyrs and honour those whom they have martyred.
Father Zossima, ibid., bk 6, ch. 3, sect. h

11 Who does not desire the death of his father?
Ivan Fyodorovich, ibid., bk 12, ch. 5

12 Much is said to you about your education, but a beautiful, sacred memory like that, one preserved from childhood, is possibly the very best education of all. If he gathers many such memories in his life, a man is saved from it all. And even if only one good memory remains within our hearts, then even it may serve some day for our salvation.
Alyosha Karamazov, ibid., 'Epilogue', sect. 3

13 We have all come out of Gogol's 'Overcoat'.
Attributed. 'The Overcoat' (1824), by NIKOLAI GOGOL, has been called the most influential short story ever on account of its early naturalistic style. The saying has also been attributed to TURGENEV.

(Lord) Alfred Douglas
(1870–1945)
British poet

Noted as a sonnet-writer, he was the beloved 'Bosie' of OSCAR WILDE, whose libel case against Douglas's father, the Marquess of Queensberry, led to Wilde's downfall. Wilde dedicated his De Profundis to him.

1 I am the Love that dare not speak its name.
'Two Loves' (1894). Concluding line of poem contributed by Douglas to the undergraduate magazine The Chameleon December 1894. During the first trial of OSCAR WILDE for 'indecent acts' (Regina v. Wilde and Taylor, 30 April 1895), Wilde responded to questioning about the meaning of these words with a statement that, in the words of MAX BEERBOHM, provoked 'a tremendous burst of applause' from the public gallery: ' "The Love that dare not speak its name" in this century is such a great affection of an elder for a younger man as there was between David and Jonathan, such as Plato made the very basis of his philosophy, and such as you find in the sonnets of Michelangelo and Shakespeare. It is that deep, spiritual affection that is as pure as it is perfect ... It is in this century misunderstood ... and on account of it I am placed where I am now.' (Quoted in Oscar Wilde, ch. 18, 1987, by Richard Ellmann)

Keith Douglas
(1920–44)
British poet

One of the few British poets associated with the Second World War, he served as a tank commander in North Africa and died in action in Normandy.

1 Remember me when I am dead
And simplify me when I'm dead.
'Simplify me when I'm dead', written 1941, publ. in Collected Poems (1951)

2 Under the parabola of a ball,
a child turning into a man,
I looked into the air too long.
The ball fell in my hand, it sang
in the closed fist: Open Open
Behold a gift designed to kill.
'How to Kill', written 1943, publ. in Alamein to Zem Zem (1946)

3 The weightless mosquito touches
her tiny shadow on the stone,
and with how like, how infinite
a lightness, man and shadow meet.
They fuse. A shadow is a man
when the mosquito death approaches.
'How to Kill', ibid.

4 For here the lover and killer are mingled
who had one body and one heart.
And death, who had the soldier singled
has done the lover mortal hurt.
'Vergissmeinnicht', written 1943, ibid.

5 If at times my eyes are lenses
through which the brain explores
constellations of feeling
my ears yielding like swinging doors
admit princes to the corridors
into the mind, do not envy me.
I have a beast on my back.
'Bête Noire', written 1944, publ. in Collected Poems (1951)

Michael Douglas
(b. 1944)
US screen actor

Son of Kirk Douglas, he co-produced One Flew Over the Cuckoo's Nest (1975) and starred in Wall Street and Fatal Attraction (both 1987). See also IVAN BOESKY 1.

1 Lunch is for wimps.
Wall Street (film, 1987, screenplay by Oliver Stone and Stanley Weiser, directed by Oliver Stone). Spoken by Gordon Gekko (Michael Douglas).

Norman Douglas

(1868–1952)

British author

His best-known novel, the symposium-like South Wind *(1917), reflects his diverse interests – art, ethics, food and religion – which are also aired in his travel books* Siren Land *(1911) and* Old Calabria *(1915).*

1 You can tell the ideals of a nation by its advertisements.

South Wind, ch. 7 (1917). Spoken by Don Francesco.

2 Shall I give you my recipe for happiness? I find everything useful and nothing indispensable. I find everything wonderful and nothing miraculous. I reverence the body. I avoid first causes like the plague.

Mr Keith, ibid., ch. 18

3 Many a man who thinks to found a home discovers that he has merely opened a tavern for his friends.

Mr Keith, ibid. ch. 24

4 I wish the English still possessed a shred of the old sense of humour which Puritanism, and dyspepsia, and newspaper reading, and tea-drinking have nearly extinguished.

Ibid., ch. 32

5 To find a friend one must close one eye. To keep him – two.

An Almanac (1941)

(Sir) Alec Douglas-Home

(1903–95)

British politician and prime minister

Baron Home of the Hirsel. Elected Conservative MP in 1931, he became Prime Minister in 1963 but lost the 1964 general election to HAROLD WILSON. *He was Foreign Secretary 1970–4.*

1 As far as [being] the fourteenth earl is concerned, I suppose Mr Wilson, when you come to think of it, is the fourteenth Mr Wilson.

Television interview, 21 October 1963, quoted in the *Daily Telegraph* 22 October 1963. Home succeeded his father as the 14th Earl of Home in 1951.

2 There are two problems in my life. The political ones are insoluble and the economic ones are incomprehensible.

Quoted in the *New York Times* 9 January 1964

Frederick Douglass

(*c.* 1817–95)

US abolitionist

Born into slavery, he became a fervent abolitionist, gaining support through his autobiography (1845) and his anti-slavery newspaper (1847–60). He became the first African-American to hold high office in the US government, as adviser to President LINCOLN *during the Civil War.*

1 For it is not light that is needed, but fire; it is not the gentle shower, but thunder. We need the storm, the whirlwind, and the earthquake. The feeling of the nation must be quickened; the conscience of the nation must be roused; the propriety of the nation must be startled; the hypocrisy of the nation must be exposed; and its crimes against God and man must be proclaimed and denounced.

'The Meaning of July Fourth for the Negro', speech at Rochester, New York, 5 July 1852, publ. in *The Life and Writings of Frederick Douglass*, vol. 2 (ed. Philip S. Foner, 1950)

2 What, to the American slave, is your Fourth of July? I answer: A day that reveals to him, more than all other days in the year, the gross injustice and cruelty to which he is the constant victim. To him your celebration is a sham.

'The Meaning of July Fourth for the Negro', ibid., vol. 2

3 If there is no struggle there is no progress. Those who profess to favor freedom and yet deprecate agitation, are men who want crops without plowing up the ground, they want rain without thunder and lightning. They want the ocean without the awful roar of its many waters. This struggle may be a moral one, or it may be a physical one, and it may be both moral and physical, but it must be a struggle. Power concedes nothing without a demand. It never did and it never will.

'West India Emancipation', speech at Canandaigua, New York, 4 August 1857, ibid., vol. 2

4 Where justice is denied, where poverty is enforced, where ignorance prevails, and where any one class is made to feel that society is in an organized conspiracy to oppress, rob, and degrade them, neither persons nor property will be safe.

Speech, Washington DC, April 1886, ibid., vol. 4. The speech marked the 24th anniversary of emancipation in the District of Columbia.

Lorenzo Dow

(1777–1834)
US evangelist

Known as 'Crazy Dow' and self-styled as a 'cosmopolite', he travelled widely preaching Methodism, but was never ordained in the Methodist church.

1 You will be damned if you do – And you will be damned if you don't.
Reflections on the Love of God, ch. 6 (1836)

Coleman Dowell

(1925–85)
US novelist, playwright and lyricist

His novels dealing with sexual obsession and homosexuality include One of the Children is Crying *(1968) and* White on Black on White *(1983). His plays include* Eve of the Green Grass *(1963).*

1 Being is a fiction invented by those who suffer from becoming.
Mrs October Was Here, pt 3, 'Tasmania, Now' (1973). Entry in Mrs October's journals.

Ernest Dowson

(1867–1900)
English poet

Associated with the fin-de-siècle 'Decadent' group, he wrote sensuous and melancholy verse, much of it dedicated to the love of his life, a waitress whom he met when she was 12. He died consumptive, alcoholic and debt-ridden.

1 I have been faithful to thee, Cynara! in my
	fashion.
'*Non sum qualis eram bonae sub regno Cynarae*', refrain, publ. in *Verses* (1896). The Latin title ('I am not as I was when dear Cinara was my queen') is from Horace (see HORACE 47), but the poem is more popularly known simply as 'Cynara'.

2 I cried for madder music and for stronger wine,
But when the feast is finished and the lamps
	expire,
Then falls thy shadow, Cynara! the night is thine.
'*Non sum qualis eram bonae sub regno Cynarae*', st. 4, ibid.

3 They are not long, the days of wine and roses:
Out of a misty dream
Our path emerges for a while, then closes
Within a dream.
'*Vitae Summa Brevis Spem Nos Vetat Incohare Longam*', st. 2, ibid.

(Sir) Arthur Conan Doyle

(1859–1930)
British author

His Sherlock Holmes stories (from 1887) established the genre of detective fiction. He also wrote tales of adventure, notably The White Company *(1891) and* The Lost Valley *(1912), and books on spiritualism.*

1 London, that great cesspool into which all the loungers and idlers of the Empire are irresistibly drained.
A Study in Scarlet, pt 1, ch. 1 (1887). Narrated by Dr Watson.

2 I consider that a man's brain originally is like a little empty attic, and you have to stock it with such furniture as you choose.
Sherlock Holmes, ibid., pt 1, ch. 2. Holmes made a similar comparison in 'The Five Orange Pips' (1892): 'A man should keep his little brain attic stocked with all the furniture that he is likely to use, and the rest he can put away in the lumber room of his library, where he can get it if he wants it.'

3 Depend upon it there comes a time when for every addition of knowledge you forget something that you knew before. It is of the highest importance, therefore, not to have useless facts elbowing out the useful ones.
Sherlock Holmes, ibid., pt 1, ch. 2

4 From a drop of water a logician could infer the possibility of an Atlantic or a Niagara without having seen or heard of one or the other.
Sherlock Holmes, ibid., pt 1, ch. 2

5 One's ideas must be as broad as Nature if they are to interpret Nature.
Sherlock Holmes, ibid., pt 1, ch. 5

6 Where there is no imagination there is no horror.
Sherlock Holmes, ibid., pt 1, ch. 5

7 My mind rebels at stagnation. Give me problems, give me work, give me the most abstruse cryptogram, or the most intricate analysis, and I am in my own proper atmosphere. I can dispense then with artificial stimulants. But I abhor the dull routine of existence. I crave for mental exaltation.
The Sign of Four, ch. 1 (1890). Spoken by Sherlock Holmes.

8 Detection is, or ought to be, an exact science, and should be treated in the same cold and unemotional manner. You have attempted to tinge it with romanticism, which produces much the same effect as if you worked a love-story or an elopement into the fifth proposition of Euclid.
Ibid., ch. 1. Dr Watson, to whom Holmes addresses these

words, had written what he called 'a small brochure, with the somewhat fantastic title of "A Study in Scarlet"' – the name of the tale in which Conan Doyle first introduced Sherlock Holmes.

9 Some facts should be suppressed, or, at least, a just sense of proportion should be observed in treating them.
Sherlock Holmes, ibid., ch. 1

10 I never guess. It is a shocking habit – destructive to the logical faculty.
Sherlock Holmes, ibid., ch. 1

11 A client is to me a mere unit, a factor in a problem.
Sherlock Holmes, ibid., ch. 2

12 The most winning woman I ever knew was hanged for poisoning three little children for their insurance-money, and the most repellent man of my acquaintance is a philanthropist who has spent nearly a quarter of a million upon the London poor.
Sherlock Holmes, ibid., ch. 2

13 There is nothing more unaesthetic than a policeman.
Thaddeus Sholto, ibid., ch. 4

14 How often have I said to you that when you have eliminated the impossible, whatever remains, *however improbable*, must be the truth?
Sherlock Holmes to Watson, ibid., ch. 6

15 It is a capital mistake to theorize before one has data.
The Adventures of Sherlock Holmes, 'Scandal in Bohemia' (1892). Spoken by Sherlock Holmes. In *A Study in Scarlet*, ch. 3, Holmes states: 'It is a capital mistake to theorize before you have all the evidence. It biases the judgement.'

16 It is quite a three-pipe problem, and I beg that you won't speak to me for fifty minutes.
Sherlock Holmes to Dr Watson, ibid., 'The Red-Headed League'. Holmes smoked a 'black clay pipe'.

17 Life is infinitely stranger than anything which the mind of man could invent. We would not dare to conceive the things which are really merely commonplaces of existence. If we could fly out of that window hand in hand, hover over this great city, gently remove the roofs and peep in at the queer things which are going on, the strange coincidences, the planning, the cross-purposes, the wonderful chain of events, working through generations and leading to the most *outré* results, it would make

all fiction with its conventionalities and foreseen conclusions most stale and unprofitable.
Sherlock Holmes, ibid., 'A Case of Identity'

18 It has long been an axiom of mine that the little things are infinitely the most important.
Sherlock Holmes, ibid., 'A Case of Identity'

19 I can never bring you to realize the importance of sleeves, the suggestiveness of thumb-nails, or the great issues that may hang from a boot-lace.
Sherlock Holmes to Watson, ibid., 'A Case of Identity'

20 Philosophy, astronomy, and politics were marked at zero, I remember. Botany variable, geology profound as regards the mud stains from any region within fifty miles of town, chemistry eccentric, anatomy unsystematic, sensational literature and crime records unique, violin player, boxer, swordsman, lawyer, and self-poisoner by cocaine and tobacco.
Ibid., 'The Five Orange Pips'. Dr Watson lists the limits of Sherlock Holmes's knowledge and character.

21 When a doctor does go wrong he is the first of criminals. He has nerve and he has knowledge.
Sherlock Holmes, ibid., 'The Adventure of the Speckled Band'

22 Violence does, in truth, recoil upon the violent, and the schemer falls into the pit which he digs for another.
Sherlock Holmes, ibid., 'The Adventure of the Speckled Band'. Holmes has just driven a poisonous snake to return fatally upon its owner, Dr Grimesby Roylott.

23 It is my belief, Watson, founded upon my experience, that the lowest and vilest alleys of London do not present a more dreadful record of sin than does the smiling and beautiful countryside.
Sherlock Holmes, ibid., 'The Adventure of the Copper Beeches'

24 'Is there any point to which you would wish to draw my attention?'
'To the curious incident of the dog in the night-time.'
'The dog did nothing in the night-time.'
'That was the curious incident,' remarked Sherlock Holmes.
The Memoirs of Sherlock Holmes, 'Silver Blaze' (1893). Exchange between Sherlock Holmes and Inspector Gregory. *The Curious Incident of the Dog in the Night-time* is the title of a best-selling novel by Mark Haddon (2003).

25 The Napoleon of crime.
Ibid., 'The Final Problem'. Sherlock Holmes's description of his arch-enemy, 'ex-Professor Moriarty of mathematical celebrity'.

26 You mentioned your name as if I should recognise it, but I assure you that, beyond the obvious facts that you are a bachelor, a solicitor, a Freemason, and an asthmatic, I know nothing whatever about you.

The Return of Sherlock Holmes, 'The Adventure of the Norwood Builder' (1904). Holmes addresses a new client (John MacFarlane).

27 You will, I am sure, agree with me that ... if page 534 only finds us in the second chapter, the length of the first one must have been really intolerable.

The Valley of Fear, pt 1, ch. 1 (1915). Spoken by Sherlock Holmes.

28 The vocabulary of 'Bradshaw' is nervous and terse, but limited. The selection of words would hardly lend itself to the sending of general messages.

Sherlock Holmes, ibid., pt 1, ch. 1. Watson had suggested Bradshaw, the railway timetable, as containing the key to decipher a code; Holmes opted instead for *Whitaker's Almanack*.

29 Mediocrity knows nothing higher than itself, but talent instantly recognizes genius.

Sherlock Holmes, ibid., pt 1, ch. 1

30 But here, unless I am mistaken, is our client.

His Last Bow, 'The Adventure of Wisteria Lodge', ch. 1 (1917). Spoken by Sherlock Holmes.

31 All other men are specialists, but his specialism is omniscience.

Sherlock Holmes, ibid., 'The Adventure of the Bruce-Partington Plans'. Referring to his brother, Mycroft.

32 Of all ruins that of a noble mind is the most deplorable.

Sherlock Holmes, ibid., 'The Adventure of the Dying Detective'. The words recall those of the conversationalist and dandy Scrope Berdmore Davies (c. 1783–1852), who wrote: 'Babylon in all its desolation is a sight not so awful as that of the human mind in ruins.' (letter, 25 May 1835)

33 Holmes: I followed you.
Watson: I saw no one.
Holmes: That is what you may expect to see when I follow you.

Ibid., 'The Adventure of the Devil's Foot'

34 Good old Watson! You are the one fixed point in a changing age.

Sherlock Holmes, ibid., 'His Last Bow'

35 Matilda Briggs ... was a ship which is associated with the giant rat of Sumatra, a story for which the world is not yet prepared.

The Case-Book of Sherlock Holmes, 'The Adventure of the Sussex Vampire' (1927). Spoken by Sherlock Holmes.

36 Elementary, my dear Watson!

Attributed. The famous exclamation is not found in any of the original Sherlock Holmes tales, though the great detective does utter 'Elementary' to Watson in 'The Crooked Man' (in *The Memoirs of Sherlock Holmes*, 1894). The phrase appears in the closing lines of the first Sherlock Holmes 'talkie', *The Return of Sherlock Holmes* (1929), and became popularized with subsequent film versions of the stories with Basil Rathbone in the leading role. Other celebrated misquotations include Holmes urging, 'Quick, Watson, the needle!'

Roddy Doyle
(b. 1958)
Irish novelist

A teacher who turned to writing plays and novels about the inner life of Dublin, he won praise for The Commitments *(1987), first of the Barrytown trilogy, and* Paddy Clarke Ha Ha Ha *(1993).*

1 The Irish are the niggers of Europe, lads. An' Dubliners are the niggers of Ireland ... An' the northside Dubliners are the niggers o' Dublin. – Say it loud, I'm black an' I'm proud.

The Commitments (1987). Spoken by Jimmy Rabbitte. See JAMES BROWN 3.

Margaret Drabble
(b. 1939)
British novelist

Her novels, including The Radiant Way *(1987) and* The Gates of Ivory *(1991), explore the everyday experience and ideas of educated middle-class women.*

1 The more unhappy I was the more I wrote: grief and words were to me inseparably connected, and I could see myself living out that maxim of literary criticism which claims that rhyme and metre are merely ways of regularizing and making tolerable despair.

The Waterfall (1969). The words of the narrator (Jane Gray).

2 England's not a bad country. It's just a mean, cold, ugly, divided, tired, clapped-out, post-imperial, post-industrial slag-heap covered in polystyrene hamburger cartons.

A Natural Curiosity (1989). Spoken by Alix.

3 You learn to put your emotional luggage where it will do some good, instead of using it to shit on other people, or blow up aeroplanes.

Quoted in the *Observer* 6 October 1991

(Sir) Francis Drake
(1540–96)
English navigator

Privateer, trader and slaver, he was the first Briton to circum-navigate the world (1577–80), for which he was knighted. He 'singed the King of Spain's beard' on a raid on Cadiz in 1587 and the following year helped to rout the Spanish Armada.

1 I must have the gentleman to haul and draw with the mariner, and the mariner with the gentleman ... I would know him, that would refuse to set his hand to a rope, but I know there is not any such here.
Speech, 11 August 1578, quoted in *Drake and the Tudor Navy*, vol. 1, ch. 9 (1898) by Sir Julian Corbett. Addressed to his crew off Puerto San Julian, Argentina, shortly before entering the Magellan Straits – from which he sailed the Pacific on his historic voyage around the world.

2 The advantage of time and place in all martial actions is half a victory, which being lost is irre-coverable.
Letter to ELIZABETH I, 13 April 1588, while awaiting news of the coming of the Spanish Armada, publ. in *The Life, Voyages and Exploits of Admiral Sir Francis Drake, Knight*, ch. 8 (1843) by John Barrow

3 There is plenty of time to win this game, and to thrash the Spaniards too.
Attributed, in *Dictionary of National Biography*, vol. 5. Sup-posedly said while playing bowls on Plymouth Hoe before joining battle with the Spanish Armada.

Joseph Rodman Drake
(1795–1820)
US poet

He collaborated with Fitz-Greene Halleck on The Croaker Papers, *a series of lampoons published anonymously (1819). Most of his work appeared posthumously in* The Culprit Fay and Other Poems *(1835).*

1 When Freedom, from her mountain height,
Unfurled her standard to the air,
She tore the azure robe of night,
And set the stars of glory there.
'The American Flag', st. 1 (1819), repr. in *The Culprit Fay and Other Poems* (1835)

2 Forever float that standard sheet!
Where breathes the foe but falls before us,
With Freedom's soil beneath our feet,
And Freedom's banner streaming o'er us?
'The American Flag', st. 5, ibid.

Nick Drake
(1948–74)
British singer and songwriter

His elegiac and introspective songs, recorded on three albums, were characterized by his wistful voice and nimble guitar-playing.

1 Fame is but a fruit tree
So very unsound
It can never flourish
Till its stalk is in the ground.
'Fruit Tree' (song) on the album *Five Leaves Left* (1969)

Michael Drayton
(1563–1631)
English poet

He was the first to use the Horatian ode in English, one of the various poetic forms he embraced. His works include historical narratives, satires, pastorals, sonnets and plays. Poly-Olbion (1613–22) was a celebration of England's topography, myth-ology and history.

1 But when the bowels of the earth were sought,
And men her golden entrails did espy,
This mischief then into the world was brought,
This framed the mint which coined our misery.
The Shepherd's Garland, Eclogue 8 (1593)

2 And thus began th'exordium of our woes,
The fatal dumb-show of our misery;
Here sprang the tree on which our mischief grows,
The dreary subject of world's tragedy.
Ibid. Eclogue 8

3 Let peevish worldlings prate of right and wrong;
Leave plaints and pleas to whom they do belong;
Let old men speak of chances and events,
And lawyers talk of titles and descents;
Leave fond reports to such as stories tell,
And covenants to those that buy and sell.
'Queen Katharine to Owen Tudor', publ. in *England's Heroical Epistles* (1597)

4 My Muse is rightly of the English strain,
That cannot long one fashion entertain.
Idea, 'To the Reader of These Sonnets' (1594, rev. 1619)

5 Since there's no help, come let us kiss and part,
Nay, I have done: you get no more of me,
And I am glad, yea glad with all my heart,
That thus so cleanly I myself can free.
Shake hands for ever, cancel all our vows,
And when we meet at any time again
Be it not seen in either of our brows

That we one jot of former love retain;
Now at the last gasp of Love's latest breath,
When his pulse failing, Passion speechless lies,
When Faith is kneeling by his bed of death,
And Innocence is closing up his eyes,
Now if thou wouldst, when all have given him
    over,
From death to life, thou might'st him yet recover.
Idea, sonnet 61 (1619)

6 Show me no more those snowy breasts
With azure riverets branched
Where, whilst mine eye with plenty feasts
Yet is my thirst not staunched;
O Tantalus, thy pains ne'er tell,
By me thou art prevented;
'Tis nothing to be plagued in Hell,
But thus in Heaven tormented.
'To His Coy Love', st. 2, publ. in *Poems* (1619)

7 For that fine madness still he did retain
Which rightly should possess a poet's brain.
Elegies upon Sundry Occasions, 'To Henry Reynolds, Of Poets and Poesy', ll. 109–10, publ. in *The Bataille of Agincourt* (1627). Referring to CHRISTOPHER MARLOWE.

William Drennan
(1754–1820)
Irish pamphleteer and poet

One of the leading intellectual figures in Belfast, he practised as a doctor and was a founder of the United Irishmen. His elegy 'The Wake of William Orr' (1797) commemorated the first member of the society to be executed.

1 Nor one feeling of vengeance presume to defile
The cause, or the men, of the Emerald Isle.
'Erin to her Own Tune and Words', st. 3, written 1795, publ. in *Fugitive Pieces in Verse and Prose* (1815). The first recorded use of the term 'Emerald Isle'.

Elizabeth Drew
(1887–1965)
Anglo-American author and critic

She wrote widely on literature including The Modern Novel *(1926),* Discovering Drama *(1937) and* The Literature of Gossip *(1964).*

1 The test of literature is, I suppose, whether we ourselves live more intensely for the reading of it.
The Modern Novel, 'Is There a "Feminine" Fiction?' (1926)

Thomas Drummond
(1797–1840)
Scottish engineer and government official

He worked for the Ordnance Survey from 1820, developed the 'Drummond Light' to aid surveying, and served as Under Secretary of State for Ireland from 1835.

1 Property has its duties as well as its rights.
Letter, 22 May 1838, publ. in *Life and Letters* (1889) by R. Barry O'Brien. Referring to the absentee landlords of Tipperary and elsewhere in Ireland. BENJAMIN DISRAELI also used these words in his novel *Sybil*, bk 1, ch. 11 (1845).

John Dryden
(1631–1700)
English poet, dramatist and critic

Having come to notice with Heroic Stanzas *(1659), a eulogy for* OLIVER CROMWELL, *he celebrated the Restoration with* Astraea Redux *(1660) and became the foremost literary figure in London. His range extended from his* Essay of Dramatic Poesy *(1668) to the blank-verse tragedy* All For Love *(1678) and the political satire* Absalom and Achitophel *(1681–2). See* LORD MACAULAY 9.

1 Roused by the lash of his own stubborn tail
Our lion now will foreign foes assail.
Astraea Redux, ll. 117–18 (1660)

2 By viewing nature, nature's handmaid art
Makes mighty things from small beginnings grow:
Thus fishes first to shipping did impart
Their tail the rudder and their head the prow.
Annus Mirabilis, st. 155 (1667)

3 Every age has a kind of universal genius, which inclines those that live in it to some particular studies.
An Essay of Dramatic Poesy (1668). Spoken by Crites.

4 A thing well said will be wit in all languages; and though it may lose something in the translation, yet, to him who reads it in the original, 'tis still the same.
Eugenius, ibid.

5 If by the people you understand the multitude, the *hoi polloi*, 'tis no matter what they think; they are sometimes in the right, sometimes in the wrong; their judgement is a mere lottery.
Neander, ibid.

6 He was the man who of all modern, and perhaps ancient poets, had the largest and most comprehensive soul ... He was naturally learned; he needed

not the spectacles of books to read Nature; he looked inwards, and found her there.

Neander, ibid. Referring to WILLIAM SHAKESPEARE.

7 He invades authors like a monarch; and what would be theft in other poets is only victory in him.

Neander, ibid. Referring to BEN JONSON.

8 The employment of a poet is like that of a curious gunsmith, or watchmaker: the iron or silver is not his own; but they are the least part of that which gives the value: the price lies wholly in the workmanship.

An Evening's Love, Preface (1668)

9 And he who servilely creeps after sense,
Is safe, but ne'er will reach an excellence.

Tyrannic Love, Prologue (1669)

10 Pains of love be sweeter far
Than all other pleasures are.

Ibid., Act 4, Sc. 1. Song sung by Damilcar.

11 I am as free as nature first made man,
Ere the base laws of servitude began,
When wild in woods the noble savage ran.

The Conquest of Granada, pt 1, Act 1 (1670). The words of Almanzor.

12 Thou strong seducer, Opportunity!

Ibid., pt 2, Act 4, Sc. 3. Spoken by Almahide.

13 Why should a foolish marriage vow,
Which long ago was made,
Oblige us to each other now
When passion is decayed?
We loved, and we loved, as long as we could,
Till our love was loved out in us both:
But our marriage is dead, when the pleasure is
    fled:
'Twas pleasure first made it an oath.

Marriage à la Mode, Act 1, Sc. 1 (1672). Song sung by Doralice and Beliza.

14 I am to be married within these three days; married past redemption.

Ibid., Act 1, Sc. 1. Spoken by Palamede.

15 So poetry, which is in Oxford made
An art, in London only is a trade.

Prologue to the University of Oxon ... at the Acting of The Silent Woman, ll. 28–9 (1673)

16 Death, in itself, is nothing; but we fear
To be we know not what, we know not where.

Aureng-Zebe, Act 4, Sc. 1 (1675). The words of Aureng-Zebe.

17 But she ne'er loved who durst not venture all.

Ibid., Act 5, Sc. 1. Spoken by Aureng-Zebe.

18 My love's a noble madness.

All for Love, Act 2, Sc. 1 (1678). Spoken by Cleopatra.

19 Fool that I was, upon my eagle's wings
I bore this wren, till I was tired with soaring,
And now he mounts above me.

Antony, ibid., Act 2, Sc. 1

20 Men are but children of a larger growth,
Our appetites as apt to change as theirs,
And full as craving too, and full as vain.

Dollabella, ibid., Act 4, Sc. 1. See LORD CHESTERFIELD 13.

21 Nature meant me
A wife, a silly harmless household dove,
Fond without art; and kind without deceit.

Cleopatra, ibid., Act 4, Sc. 1

22 My whole life
Has been a golden dream of love and friendship.

Antony, ibid., Act 5, Sc. 1

23 Welcome, thou kind deceiver!
Thou best of thieves; who, with an easy key,
Dost open life, and, unperceived by us,
Even steal us from ourselves.

Cleopatra, ibid., Act 5, Sc. 1

24 There is a pleasure sure,
In being mad, which none but madmen know!

The Spanish Friar, Act 2, Sc. 2 (1680). Spoken by Torrismond.

25 Dead men tell no tales.

Ibid., Act 4, Sc. 1. Dominic quotes a proverb.

26 The true end of satire is the amendment of vices by correction.

Absalom and Achitophel, pt 1, Preface (1681)

27 In pious times, ere priestcraft did begin,
Before polygamy was made a sin.

Ibid., pt 1, ll. 1–2

28 Great wits are sure to madness near allied,
And thin partitions do their bounds divide.

Ibid., pt 1, ll. 163–4

29 And all to leave what with his toil he won
To that unfeathered two-legged thing, a son.

Ibid., pt 1, ll. 169–70

30 In friendship false, implacable in hate:
Resolved to ruin or to rule the state.

Ibid., pt 1, ll. 174–5. Referring to Achitophel, who in the poem represents the statesman Anthony Ashley Cooper, Earl of Shaftesbury.

31 All empire is no more than power in trust.
Ibid., pt 1, l. 411

32 Better one suffer, than a nation grieve.
Ibid., pt 1, l. 416

33 Self-defence is Nature's eldest law.
Ibid., pt 1, l. 458

34 But far more numerous was the herd of such
Who think too little, and who talk too much.
Ibid., pt 1, ll. 533–4

35 A man so various, that he seemed to be
Not one, but all mankind's epitome.
Stiff in opinions, always in the wrong;
Was everything by starts, and nothing long:
But in the course of one revolving moon
Was chemist, fiddler, statesman and buffoon.
Ibid., pt 1, ll. 545–50. Describing Zimri, who in the poem
represents GEORGE VILLIERS, second Duke of Buckingham. A
Privy Councillor and favourite of CHARLES II, the flamboyant
Villiers had himself parodied Dryden in his comedy, *The
Rehearsal* (1671). In 1978, JAMES CALLAGHAN had quoted
these words to tease MARGARET THATCHER – then leader of
the Conservative opposition – who had trained as a chemist.

36 So over violent, or over civil
That every man with him was God or Devil.
Ibid., pt 1, ll. 557–8. Referring to Zimri.

37 Nor is the people's judgement always true:
The most may err as grossly as the few.
Ibid., pt 1, ll. 781–2

38 Never was patriot yet, but was a fool.
Ibid., pt 1, l. 968

39 Beware the fury of a patient man.
Ibid., pt 1, l. 1005

40 But 'tis the talent of our English nation
Still to be plotting some new reformation.
'The Prologue at Oxford, 1680', ll. 9–10, Prologue to NATH-
ANIEL LEE's *Sophonisba* (2nd edn, 1681)

41 The midwife laid her hand on his thick skull,
With this prophetic blessing – *be thou dull*.
Absalom and Achitophel, pt 2, ll. 476–7 (written with NAHUM
TATE, 1682). Referring to Og, who in the poem represents
THOMAS SHADWELL.

42 All human things are subject to decay,
And when fate summons, monarchs must obey.
Mac Flecknoe, ll. 1–2 (1682)

43 The rest to some faint meaning make pretence,
But Shadwell never deviates into sense.
Some beams of wit on other souls may fall,

Strike through and make a lucid interval;
But Shadwell's genuine night admits no ray,
His rising fogs prevail upon the day.
Ibid., ll. 19–24. Referring to THOMAS SHADWELL.

44 Thy genius calls thee not to purchase fame
In keen iambics, but mild anagram:
Leave writing plays, and choose for thy command
Some peaceful province in Acrostic Land.
There thou mayest wings display and altars raise,
And torture one poor word ten thousand ways.
Ibid., ll. 203–8. Referring to THOMAS SHADWELL.

45 But treason is not owned when 'tis descried;
Successful crimes alone are justified.
The Medal, ll. 207–8 (1682)

46 How can the less the greater comprehend?
Or finite reason reach infinity?
Religio Laici, ll. 39–40 (1682)

47 For bold knaves thrive without one grain of
sense,
But good men starve for want of impudence.
Constantine the Great, Epilogue, ll. 19–20 (1684)

48 Wit will shine
Through the harsh cadence of a rugged line.
To the Memory of Mr Oldham, ll. 15–16 (1684)

49 Happy the man, and happy he alone,
He who can call today his own;
He who, secure within, can say,
Tomorrow, do thy worst, for I have lived today.
Translation of Horace, *Odes*, bk 3, ode 29, ll. 65–8, publ. in
Sylvae (1685). See HORACE 44.

50 For truth has such a face and such a mien
As to be loved needs only to be seen.
The Hind and the Panther, pt 1, ll. 33–4 (1687)

51 Of all the tyrannies on humankind
The worst is that which persecutes the mind.
Let us but weigh at what offence we strike,
'Tis but because we cannot think alike.
Ibid., pt 1, ll. 239–42

52 Thus fear and interest will prevail with some,
For all have not the gift of martyrdom.
Ibid., pt 2, ll. 58–9

53 Either be wholly slaves or wholly free.
Ibid., pt 2, l. 285

54 War seldom enters but where wealth allures.
Ibid., pt 2, l. 706

55 For present joys are more to flesh and blood
Than a dull prospect of a distant good.
Ibid., pt 3, ll. 364–5

56 Jealousy, the jaundice of the soul.
Ibid., pt 3, l. 73

57 T'abhor the makers, and their laws approve,
Is to hate traitors, and the treason love.
Ibid., pt 3, ll. 706–7

58 From harmony, from heavenly harmony
This universal frame began:
From harmony to harmony
Through all the compass of the notes it ran,
The diapason closing full in Man.
A Song for St Cecilia's Day, st. 1 (1687)

59 What passion cannot music raise and quell!
Ibid., st. 2

60 The trumpet's loud clangour
Excites us to arms
With shrill notes of anger
And mortal alarms.
Ibid., st. 3

61 The soft complaining flute
In dying notes discovers
The woes of hopeless lovers.
Ibid., st. 4

62 Sharp violins proclaim
Their jealous pangs and desperation,
Fury, frantic indignation,
Depth of pains and height of passion.
Ibid., st. 5

63 So when the last and dreadful hour
This crumbling pageant shall devour,
The trumpet shall be heard on high,
The dead shall live, the living die,
And music shall untune the sky.
Ibid., 'Grand Chorus' (1687). Closing lines of poem.

64 All heiresses are beautiful.
King Arthur, Act 1, Sc. 1 (1691). Spoken by Albanat.

65 War is the trade of kings.
Arthur, ibid., Act 2, Sc. 2

66 Fairest Isle, all isles excelling,
Seat of pleasures, and of loves;
Venus here will choose her dwelling,
And forsake her Cyprian groves.
Ibid., Act 2, Sc. 5, 'Song of Venus'. Referring to England.

67 Want whets the wit, 'tis true: but wit not blest
With fortune's aid, makes beggars at the best.
Wit is not fed, but sharpened with applause,
For wealth is solid food, and wit but hungry sauce.
Love Triumphant, Act 1, Sc. 1 (1694). Spoken by Carlos.

68 Who best the gentle passions knows to move;
Ovid, the soft philosopher of love.
Ibid., Act 2, Sc. 1. Alphonso answers Victoria's question: 'But tell me what philosopher you found/To cure your pain?'

69 Happy, happy, happy pair!
None but the brave
None but the brave
None but the brave deserves the fair.
Alexander's Feast, ll. 12–15 (1697). Referring to Alexander the Great and Thais at the 'Royal Feast for Persia won'.

70 Drinking is the soldier's pleasure;
Rich the treasure,
Sweet the pleasure;
Sweet is pleasure after pain.
Ibid., ll. 57–60

71 Fallen from his high estate,
And welt'ring in his blood:
Deserted at his utmost need
By those his former bounty fed;
On the bare earth exposed he lies,
With not a friend to close his eyes.
Ibid., ll. 78–83

72 'War', he sung, 'is toil and trouble;
Honour but an empty bubble.
Never ending, still beginning.
Fighting still, and still destroying,
If the world be worth thy winning,
Think, O think it worth enjoying.'
Ibid., ll. 99–104. The song of Timotheus.

73 How blessed is he who leads a country life,
Unvexed with anxious cares, and void of strife!
Who studying peace, and shunning civil rage,
Enjoyed his youth, and now enjoys his age.
'Epistle to John Driden of Chesterton', ll. 1–4, publ. in *Fables Ancient and Modern* (1700)

74 Even victors are by victories undone.
Ibid., l. 164

75 'Tis sufficient to say according to the proverb, that here is God's plenty.
Fables Ancient and Modern, Preface (1700). Referring to GEOFFREY CHAUCER's *Canterbury Tales*. In the same preface, Dryden refers to Chaucer as 'the father of English poetry' and as 'a perpetual fountain of good sense'.

76 For while my former flames remain within,
Repentance is but want of power to sin.
Ibid., 'Palamon and Arcite', bk 3, ll. 812–13. Spoken by Arcite.

77 Since every man who lives is born to die,
And none can boast sincere felicity,
With equal mind, what happens, let us bear,
Nor joy nor grieve too much for things beyond our
   care.
Ibid., 'Palamon and Arcite', bk 3, ll. 883–6. Spoken by Egeus.

78 Like pilgrims to th'appointed place we tend;
The world's an inn, and death the journey's end.
Ibid., 'Palamon and Arcite', bk 3, ll. 887–8. Spoken by Egeus.

79 Old as I am, for ladies' love unfit,
The power of beauty I remember yet,
Which once inflamed my soul, and still inspires
   my wit.
Ibid., 'Cymon and Iphigenia', ll. 1–3

80 Then our age was in its prime,
Free from rage and free from crime,
A very merry, dancing, drinking,
Laughing, quaffing, and unthinking time.
The Secular Masque, ll. 41–4 (1700). The lines are delivered by
Janus, Chronos, Diana and Momus.

Alexander Dubček
(1921–92)
Czechoslovakian politician

*His promotion of political liberalization led to the 1968
invasion of Czechoslovakia by Warsaw Pact forces, and his
replacement as First Secretary of the Communist Party.*

1 Socialism with a human face.
Dubček's words, repeated in various forms on different
occasions, became a slogan of the 'Prague Spring' of 1968.

Al Dubin
(1891–1945)
US songwriter

*Collaborating with the composer Harry Warren during the
1930s, he wrote songs for twenty musicals, including the film
42nd Street (1933).*

1 Tiptoe through the tulips.
'Tiptoe through the Tulips' (song, 1929, with music by Joseph
Burke). The song was a hit for Tiny Tim in 1968.

W. E. B. Du Bois
(1868–1963)
US historian and civil rights leader

*William Edward Burghardt Du Bois. His writings chronicled
the history of African Americans. He was a founder of the
National Association for the Advancement of Colored People,
joined the Communist Party aged ninety-three, and died a
citizen of Ghana.*

1 An American, a Negro . . . two souls, two thoughts,
two unreconciled strivings; two warring ideals in
one dark body, whose dogged strength alone keeps
it from being torn asunder.
The Souls of Black Folk, ch. 1 (1903). 'The history of the American Negro,' continued Du Bois, 'is the history of this strife.'

2 The shadow of a mighty Negro past flits through
the tale of Ethiopia the Shadowy and of Egypt the
Sphinx. Throughout history, the powers of single
black men flash here and there like falling stars, and
die sometimes before the world has rightly gauged
their brightness.
Ibid., ch. 1

3 To be a poor man is hard, but to be a poor race in
a land of dollars is the very bottom of hardships.
Ibid., ch. 1

4 We black men seem the sole oasis of simple faith
and reverence in a dusty desert of dollars and
smartness.
Ibid., ch. 1

5 The problem of the twentieth century is the problem of the color-line – the relation of the darker to
the lighter races of men in Asia and Africa, in
America and the islands of the sea.
Ibid., ch. 2. Du Bois discussed the problem of 'the color-line'
on a number of occasions, incorporating the concept in a
speech of January 1900 at the first Pan-African Conference,
London.

6 The music of an unhappy people, of the children
of disappointment.
Of the blues, ibid., ch. 14. Blues music, wrote Du Bois, tells of
'death and suffering and unvoiced longing toward a truer
world, of misty wanderings and hidden ways'.

7 If there is anybody in this land who thoroughly
believes that the meek shall inherit the earth they
have not often let their presence be known.
The Gift of Black Folk, ch. 9 (1924)

8 Today I see more clearly than yesterday that back
of the problem of race and color lies a greater problem which both obscures and implements it: and

that is the fact that so many civilized persons are willing to live in comfort even if the price of this is poverty, ignorance and disease of the majority of their fellow men; that to maintain this privilege men have waged war until today war tends to become universal and continuous, and the excuse for this war continues largely to be color and race.

'Fifty Years After', Preface to *The Souls of Black Folk* (1953 edn)

9 One thing alone I charge you. As you live, believe in life! Always human beings will live and progress to greater, broader and fuller life. The only possible death is to lose belief in this truth simply because the great end comes slowly, because time is long.

Last message, written 26 June 1957 and read at his funeral, publ. in *Journal of Negro History* April 1964

Jean Dubuffet
(1901–85)
French sculptor and painter

He pioneered the concept of Art Brut (raw art), the antidote to museum art, derived from his graffiti and the art of children and the mentally ill, often incorporating unconventional materials.

1 Art is the most passionate orgy within man's grasp.

'Notes for the Well-Read' (1946), repr. in *Jean Dubuffet: Towards an Alternative Reality* (ed. Marc Glimcher, 1987)

2 Art should always make people laugh a little and frighten them a little. Anything but bore them. Art has no right to be boring.

Rough draft for 'Popular Lecture in Painting' (1946), repr. ibid.

3 It is not men who are great. It is man who is great. It is not wonderful to be exceptional. It is wonderful to be a man.

'Notes for the Well-Lettered', publ. in *Prospectus* (1946)

Marcel Duchamp
(1887–1968)
French artist

A precursor of conceptual art, he was a leading member of the Dada movement, famous for his 'ready-mades', everyday objects that became works of art. The urinal he entered in an exhibition (1917) and his moustachioed Mona Lisa (1919) provoked scandal.

1 I have forced myself to contradict myself in order to avoid conforming to my own taste.

Quoted in 'Marcel Duchamp: Anti-Artist' by Harriet and Sidney Janis, publ. in *View* 21 March 1945

2 I am still a victim of chess. It has all the beauty of art – and much more. It cannot be commercialized. Chess is much purer than art in its social position.

Time 10 March 1952. Duchamp had given up painting in favour of chess in the 1920s. In an address to the New York State Chess Association 30 August 1952, he said: 'I have come to the personal conclusion that while all artists are not chess players, all chess players are artists.'

3 Living is more a question of what one spends than what one makes.

Dialogues with Marcel Duchamp, ch. 4 (ed. Pierre Cabanne, 1967)

George Duffield
See HYMNS AND CAROLS 81

Carol Ann Duffy
(b. 1955)
British poet

Tackling a range of subjects in a humorous, often passionate style, she makes use of monologue to articulate character types and moral dilemmas.

1 Some nights, although we are faithless, the truth
enters our hearts, that small familiar pain;
then a man will stand stock-still, hearing his youth
in the distant Latin chanting of a train.

'Prayer', publ. in *Mean Time* (1993)

2 Whatever 'in love' means,
true love is talented.

'September 1997', publ. in the *Guardian* 6 September 1997. See CHARLES, PRINCE OF WALES 1.

3 The dead are so talented.
The living walk by the edge of a vast lake
near the wise, drowned silence of the dead.

'Eurydice', publ. in *The World's Wife* (1999)

John Foster Dulles
(1888–1959)
US politician and lawyer

As a Republican and ardent anti-communist, he championed America and NATO during the Cold War, serving as Secretary of State (1953–9) under EISENHOWER.

1 The ability to get to the verge without getting into the war is the necessary art. If you cannot master it, you inevitably get into war. If you try to run away from it, if you are scared to go to the brink, you are

lost ... We walked to the brink and we looked it in the face.

Quoted in *Life* 16 January 1956. Adlai Stevenson characterized the Dulles-Eisenhower foreign policy as 'the power of positive brinking'. See ADLAI STEVENSON 13.

Alexandre Dumas

(1802–70)

French novelist and dramatist

Known as 'Dumas père', to distinguish him from his son, he wrote numerous historical melodramas but is best known for his romantic novels The Three Musketeers *(1844) and* The Count of Monte Cristo *(1845).*

1 *Tous pour un, un pour tous.*
[All for one and one for all].
The Three Musketeers, ch. 9 and passim (1844). The Musketeers' motto.

2 *Cherchez la femme, pardieu, cherchez la femme!*
[Look for the woman!]
The Mohicans of Paris, vol. 3, ch. 10 (1854–9, written with Paul Bocage). Spoken by M. Jackal, who explains to Salvator: *'Il y a une femme dans tout ... c'est ce qui rend notre métier si difficile.'* ['There is a woman in everything ... that's what makes our profession so difficult.'] The words, implying that a mystery will be understood when the involvement of a woman can be shown, have also been attributed to revolutionary and statesman Joseph Fouché (1763–1829).

Alexandre Dumas

(1824–95)

French novelist and dramatist

'Dumas fils' is best remembered for his play Camille *(La Dame aux camélias, 1852), adapted from his own novel. Other major dramatic works include* Le Demi-monde *(1855) and* L'Affaire Clémenceau *(1864).*

1 Business? it's quite simple: it's other people's money.
La Question d'Argent, Act 2, Sc. 7 (1857). The words of Giraud.

(Dame) Daphne Du Maurier

(1907–89)

British novelist

She specialized in melodramatic romances in Cornish settings such as Jamaica Inn *(1936) and* Rebecca *(1938).*

1 Last night I dreamt I went to Manderley again.
Rebecca, ch. 1 (1938). Opening words.

Paul Laurence Dunbar

(1872–1906)

US poet and author

The first black American poet to rise to fame, he was the son of escaped slaves. His Lyrics of Lowly Life *(1896) used dialect verse, while his fiction portrayed an idealized version of the Old South.*

1 I know why the caged bird sings!
'Sympathy', st. 3, publ. in *Lyrics of the Hearthside* (1899). The line was used by MAYA ANGELOU as the title of her first volume of autobiography (1969).

William Dunbar

(c. 1460–c. 1520)

Scottish poet

After leaving the Franciscan order, he served in the foreign embassies of James IV. His court poetry, dream allegories, satires and religious verse show the strong influence of CHAUCER.

1 I that in heill wes and gladnes
Am trublit now with gret seiknes
And feblit with infirmite:
Timor mortis conturbat me.
'Lament for the Makaris', st. 1 (c. 1508). Repeated at the end of each verse, the refrain *Timor mortis conturbat me* ('Fear of death troubles me') is taken from the liturgy of the Office for the Dead.

2 Done is a battell on the dragon blak;
Our campioun Chryst confoundit hes his force:
The yettis of hell ar brokin with a crak,
The signe triumphall rasit is of the croce.
'Done is a battell on the dragon blak', st. 1 (c. 1510)

Isadora Duncan

(1878–1927)

US dancer

Born Dora Angela Duncan. She was a pioneer of modern dance, taking her inspiration from the flowing forms of classical Greek art to produce free, barefoot expression.

1 The only dance masters I could have were Jean-Jacques Rousseau, Walt Whitman and Nietzsche.
My Life, ch. 8 (1927)

2 The real American type can never be a ballet dancer. The legs are too long, the body too supple and the spirit too free for this school of affected grace and toe walking.
Ibid., ch. 30

3 Farewell, my friends. I go to glory.

Quoted in *Isadora Duncan's End*, ch. 25 (1929) by Mary Desti. Duncan was accidentally strangled when her long scarf caught in the wheel of her car moments after uttering these words (*je vais à la gloire*), which have also been rendered as 'I see glory' (*je vois la gloire*).

Ian Dunlop
(b. 1940)
British art critic

Known principally for his book The Shock of the New *(1972), he is also the author of* Degas *(1979), among other works.*

1 The Shock of the New.

Title of book (1972). The full title is *The Shock of the New: Seven Historic Exhibitions of Modern Art*.

Douglas Dunn
(b. 1942)
Scottish poet

He was influenced by PHILIP LARKIN *in his early work, which explores urban working-class culture. Later collections such as* Elegies *(1985) and* Northlight *(1988) reflect wider concerns.*

1 Film is just a reflection
Of the matchless despair of the century.
There have been twenty centuries since charity
   began.
Indignation is day-to-day stuff;
It keeps us off the streets, it keeps us watching.

'I Am a Cameraman', publ. in *Love or Nothing* (1974)

2 Politics soften everything.
Truth is known only to its victims.
All else is photographs – a documentary
The starving and the playboys perish in.
Life disguises itself with professionalism.

Ibid.

3 And I must mourn
Until Equator crawls to Capricorn
Or murder in the sun melts down
The Arctic and Antarctica.

'Reincarnations', publ. in *Elegies* (1985)

4 Snow is its own country, and it beckons
With its white finger crooked, and is calling
From the hush of its chilled bulk, its tons
And territories, its white ground falling.

'Snow Days', ibid.

5 Day by nomadic day
Our anniversaries go by,

Dates anchored in an inner sky,
To utmost ground, interior clay.

'Anniversaries', ibid.

Finley Peter Dunne
(1867–1936)
US journalist and humorist

As 'Mr Dooley', he presented a common-sense Irish-American slant on current events in newspaper sketches from 1892. He edited the Chicago Journal *1897–1900.*

1 Vice . . . is a creature of such heejous mien . . . that th' more ye see it th' bether ye like it.

Mr Dooley's Opinions, 'The Crusade Against Vice' (1901)

2 If ye live enough befure thirty ye won't care to live at all afther fifty.

Ibid., 'Casual Observations'

3 A fanatic is a man that does what he thinks th' Lord wud do if He knew th' facts iv th' case.

Ibid., 'Casual Observations'

4 Thrust ivrybody, but cut th' ca-ards.

Ibid., 'Casual Observations'. See MIGUEL DE CERVANTES 38.

5 Most vegetarians I ever see looked enough like their food to be classed as cannibals.

Ibid., 'Casual Observations'

6 Alcohol is nicissary f'r a man so that now an' thin he can have a good opinion iv himsilf, ondisturbed be th' facts.

'Mr Dooley on Alcohol', publ. in the *Chicago Tribune* 26 April 1914

7 A man's idea in a card game is war – cruel, devastating and pitiless. A lady's idea of it is a combination of larceny, embezzlement and burglary.

Mr Dooley on Making a Will, 'On the Game of Cards' (1919)

8 The mission of a modern newspaper is to comfort the afflicted and afflict the comfortable.

Attributed

J. W. Dunne
(1875–1949)
British inventor and philosopher

John William Dunne. The designer of the first British military aeroplane (1906–7), he explained his theory of the serial nature of time in An Experiment With Time *(1927).*

1 We have now arrived within introductory range of that very meek-spirited creature known to modern science as the '*Observer*'. It is a permanent obstacle

in the path of our search for external reality that we can never entirely get rid of this individual.
An Experiment with Time, ch. 3 (1927, rev. 1939)

Will Durant
(1885–1981)
US historian

Following the international success of The Story of Philosophy *(1926), he collaborated with his wife Ariel on* The Story of Civilization *(11 vols. 1935–75).*

1 Civilization is a stream with banks. The stream is sometimes filled with blood from people killing, stealing, shouting and doing the things historians usually record, while on the banks, unnoticed, people build homes, make love, raise children, sing songs, write poetry and even whittle statues. The story of civilization is the story of what happened on the banks. Historians are pessimists because they ignore the banks for the river.
Life 18 October 1963

Marguerite Duras
(1914–96)
French author and film-maker

Pseudonym of Marguerite Donnadieu. Successful as a novelist from 1950, she gained wider recognition for her screenplays, notably Hiroshima, mon amour *(1959).*

1 Journalism without a moral position is impossible. Every journalist is a moralist. It's absolutely unavoidable. A journalist is someone who looks at the world and the way it works, someone who takes a close look at things every day and reports what she sees, someone who represents the world, the event, for others. She cannot do her work without judging what she sees.
Outside: Selected Writings, Foreword (1984)

2 I believe that always, or almost always, in all childhoods and in all the lives that follow them, the mother represents madness. Our mothers always remain the strangest, craziest people we've ever met.
Practicalities, 'House and Home' (1987)

3 You have to be very fond of men! Very, very fond. You have to be very fond of them to love them. Otherwise they're simply unbearable.
Ibid., 'Men'

Paul Durcan
(b. 1944)
Irish poet

Inventive and lyrical, his poetry portrays with compassion and humour characters who are ostracized or victims of their circumstances. Collections include Jesus, Break His Fall *(1980).*

1 I have my troubles and I shall always have them
But I should rather live with you for ever
Than exchange my troubles for a changeless
  kingdom.
'The Difficulty that is Marriage', publ. in *Teresa's Bar* (1976)

2 At a ritual ceremony in a fairy ring fort
Near Bodenstown Graveyard, Co. Kildare
(Burial place of Theobald Wolfe Tone)
Margaret Thatcher joined the IRA
And the IRA joined Margaret Thatcher.
'Margaret Thatcher Joins IRA', publ. in *Sam's Cross* (1978)

3 Bring me back to the dark school – to the dark
  school of childhood:
To where tiny is tiny, and massive is massive.
'En Famille, 1979', publ. in *Jesus, Break His Fall* (1980)

4 There – but for the clutch of luck – go I.
'The Death by Heroin of Sid Vicious', publ. in *Jesus, Break His Fall* (1980). Opening line of poem, which ends: 'There – but for the clutch of luck – go we all.'

Emile Durkheim
(1858–1917)
French sociologist

A key figure in the development of sociology, he combined rigorous methodology using empirical evidence with a belief in the social causes of individual dysfunction. His important works include The Rules of Sociological Method *(1895) and* Suicide *(1897).*

1 It is too great comfort which turns a man against himself. Life is most readily renounced at the time and among the classes where it is least harsh.
Suicide, bk 3, ch. 1, sect. 1 (1897, transl. 1951)

2 There is no society known where a more or less developed criminality is not found under different forms. No people exists whose morality is not daily infringed upon. We must therefore call crime necessary and declare that it cannot be non-existent, that the fundamental conditions of social organization, as they are understood, logically imply it.
Ibid., bk 3, ch. 3, sect. 1

3 Too cheerful a morality is a loose morality; it is

appropriate only to decadent peoples and is found only among them.

Ibid., bk 3, ch. 3, sect. 1

Leo Durocher
(1906–91)
US baseball coach

Nicknamed Leo the Lip, he combined a brilliant baseball career with high living and gambling. His aggressive approach to the game attracted criticism.

1 Take a look at them. All nice guys. They'll finish last. Nice guys. Finish last.

Remark, 6 July 1946, quoted in *Nice Guys Finish Last*, pt 1 (1975). Referring to the New York Giants at a practice session.

Lawrence Durrell
(1914–91)
British author

An expatriate for most of his life, he used Mediterranean settings for his fiction and poetry, notably The Alexandria Quartet *(1957–60).* Bitter Lemons *(1957) was a depiction of Cyprus.*

1 Everyone loathes his own country and countrymen if he is any sort of artist.

Letter to HENRY MILLER, March 1948, publ. in *The Durrell-Miller Letters 1935–80* (1988)

2 Journeys, like artists, are born and not made. A thousand differing circumstances contribute to them, few of them willed or determined by the will – whatever we may think.

Bitter Lemons, 'Towards an Eastern Landfall' (1957). Opening words.

3 There are only three things to be done with a woman. You can love her, suffer for her, or turn her into literature.

Justine, pt 1 (1957). The words of Clea.

4 No one can go on being a rebel too long without turning into an autocrat.

Balthazar, pt 2, ch. 6 (1958). Pursewarden's letter to D. H. Lawrence.

5 Perhaps our only sickness is to desire a truth which we cannot bear rather than to rest content with the fictions we manufacture out of each other.

Clea, ch. 1, sect. 3 (1960). The words of Justine.

6 Music was invented to confirm human loneliness.

Clea, ibid. ch. 1, sect. 4

7 Old age is an insult. It's like being smacked.

Interview in *The Sunday Times* 20 November 1988

8 The appalling thing is the degree of charity women are capable of. You see it all the time … love lavished on absolute fools. Love's a charity ward, you know.

Interview in the *Observer* 11 November 1990

Ian Dury
(1942–2000)
British rock musician

He had numerous hits with his band the Blockheads, starting with the album New Boots and Panties *(1977), and later pursued an acting and writing career.*

1 Sex and drugs and rock and roll
Is all my brain and body need
Sex and drugs and rock and roll
Is very good indeed.

'Sex and Drugs and Rock and Roll' (song, written with Chaz Jankel) on the album *Sex and Drugs and Rock and Roll* (1976)

2 I'm from Essex, in case you couldn't tell
My given name is Dickie
I come from Billericay
And I'm doing … very well.

'Billericay Dickie' (song, written with Nugent) on the album *New Boots and Panties* (1977) by Ian Dury and the Blockheads

3 I could be the catalyst that sparks the revolution
I could be an inmate in a long-term institution
I could lean to wild extremes I could do or die
I could yawn and be withdrawn and watch them
 gallop by
What a waste.

'What a Waste' (song, 1978, written by the band) by Ian Dury and the Blockheads

4 Hit me with your rhythm stick. Hit me! Hit me!

'Hit Me with Your Rhythm Stick' (song, 1978, written with Chas Jankel) by Ian Dury and the Blockheads

5 There ain't half been some clever bastards.

'There Ain't Half Been Some Clever Bastards' (song, 1978, written with Chas Jankel) by Ian Dury and the Blockheads

6 Reasons to be cheerful.

'Reasons to be Cheerful (pt 3)' (song, written with Chaz Jankel) on the album *Do It Yourself* (1979) by Ian Dury and the Blockheads

Eleonora Duse
(1858–1924)
Italian actress

Rivalling SARAH BERNHARDT, *she toured extensively and was mistress of the poet Gabriele D'Annunzio who wrote parts for her.*

1 To save the theatre, the theatre must be destroyed, the actors and actresses must all die of the plague. They poison the air, they make art impossible. It is not drama that they play, but pieces for the theatre.
Quoted in *Studies in Seven Arts*, 'Eleonora Duse' (1906) by Arthur Symons

2 I did not use paint. I made myself up morally.
Quoted in *Le Gaulois* 27 July 1922. Duse claimed not to 'act' her parts, but to 'live' them.

Andrea Dworkin
(1946–2005)
US feminist critic and author

She called for pornography to be outlawed in Pornography: Men Possessing Women *(1981), among other works.* Scapegoat: Jews, Israel and Women's Liberation *(2000) examines the role of women in Judaism.*

1 Only when manhood is dead – and it will perish when ravaged femininity no longer sustains it – only then will we know what it is to be free.
'The Root Cause', speech at Massachusetts Institute of Technology, 26 September 1975, publ. in *Our Blood*, ch. 9 (1976). Last words of book.

2 Seduction is often difficult to distinguish from rape. In seduction, the rapist bothers to buy a bottle of wine.
'Sexual Economics: The Terrible Truth', speech, 1976, publ. in *Letters from a War-Zone* (1987)

3 No woman needs intercourse; few women escape it.
Right-Wing Women, ch. 3 (1978)

4 Marriage as an institution developed from rape as a practice. Rape, originally defined as abduction, became marriage by capture. Marriage meant the taking was to extend in time, to be not only use of but possession of, or ownership.
Pornography, ch. 1 (1981)

5 Money speaks, but it speaks with a male voice.
Ibid., ch. 1

(Sir) Edward Dyer
(1543–1607)
English poet and courtier

A friend of FULKE GREVILLE *and* PHILIP SIDNEY, *he composed melancholy verse, little of which has survived, and served on diplomatic missions to Holland and Denmark.*

1 My mind to me a kingdom is,
Such present joys therein I find,
That it excels all other bliss
That world affords or grows by kind.
Though much I want which most would have,
Yet still my mind forbids to crave.
'My mind to me a kingdom is', st. 1 (1588). Attributed. A version of the poem was set to music by William Byrd.

2 Some have too much, yet still do crave;
I have little, and seek no more.
They are but poor, though much they have.
And I am rich with little store.
They poor, I rich; they beg, I give;
They lack, I leave; they pine, I live.
Ibid., st. 5

3 Silence augmenteth grief, writing increaseth rage,
Staled are my thoughts, which loved and lost, the wonder of our age.
'Elegy on the Death of Sir Philip Sidney' (1593)

John Dyer
(1699–1757)
Welsh clergyman and poet

Ordained in 1741, he is chiefly remembered for 'Grongar Hill' (1726), describing the Towy valley in Wales. In a similar vein, he also wrote 'The Ruins of Rome' (1740) and 'The Fleece' (1757).

1 But transient is the smile of fate!
A little rule, a little sway,
A sunbeam in a winter's day,
Is all the proud and mighty have
Between the cradle and the grave.
'Grongar Hill', ll. 88–92 (1726)

Bob Dylan
(b. 1941)
US singer and songwriter

Originally Robert Zimmerman. One of the seminal influences on popular song in the 1960s, he started as a folk singer writing protest anthems. His lyrics became more abstruse and later reflected his religious convictions. For BRUCE SPRINGSTEEN, *he 'freed your mind the way Elvis freed your body'.*

1 The answer, my friend, is blowin' in the wind,
The answer is blowin' in the wind.
'Blowin' in the Wind' (song) on the album *The Freewheelin'
Bob Dylan* (1963). On the sleeve notes to the record, Dylan
wrote: 'The first way to answer the questions in the song is
by asking them. But lots of people have to first find the wind.'
Already by the end of 1964, the song had been recorded by
some sixty artists.

2 I saw ten thousand talkers whose tongues were
   all broken,
I saw guns and sharp swords in the hands of
   young children,
And it's a hard, it's a hard, it's a hard, it's a hard,
It's a hard rain's a-gonna fall.
'A Hard Rain's A-Gonna Fall' (song), ibid.

3 Come mothers and fathers
Throughout the land
And don't criticize
What you can't understand
Your sons and your daughters
Are beyond your command
Your old road is rapidly agin'.
'The Times They Are A-Changin'' (song) on the album *The
Times They Are A-Changin'* (1963)

4 The line it is drawn
The curse it is cast
The slow one now
Will later be fast
As the present now
Will later be past
The order is rapidly fadin'.
And the first one now
Will later be last
For the times they are a-changin'.
'The Times They Are A-Changin'', ibid.

5 We gazed upon the chimes of freedom flashing.
'Chimes of Freedom' (song) on the album *Another Side of Bob
Dylan* (1964)

6 Ah, but I was so much older then,
I'm younger than that now.
'My Back Pages' (song), ibid.

7 You don't need a weather man
To know which way the wind blows.
'Subterranean Homesick Blues' (song) on the album *Bringing
it all Back Home* (1965)

8 Don't follow leaders
And watch the parkin' meters.
'Subterranean Homesick Blues', ibid.

9 I ain't gonna work on Maggie's farm no more.
'Maggie's Farm' (song), ibid.

10 In the dime stores and bus stations,
People talk of situations,
Read books, repeat quotations,
Draw conclusions on the wall.
'Love Minus Zero/No Limit' (song), ibid.

11 She knows there's no success like failure
And that failure's no success at all.
'Love Minus Zero/No Limit', ibid.

12 In ceremonies of the horsemen,
Even the pawn must hold a grudge.
'Love Minus Zero/No Limit', ibid.

13 Hey! Mr Tambourine Man, play a song for me.
I'm not sleepy and there is no place I'm going to.
Hey! Mr Tambourine Man, play a song for me.
In the jingle jangle morning I'll come following
   you.
'Mr Tambourine Man' (song), ibid.

14 At times I think there are no words
But these to tell what's true
And there are no truths outside the Gates of Eden.
'Gates of Eden' (song), ibid.

15 He not busy being born
Is busy dying.
'It's Alright Ma (I'm Only Bleeding)' (song), ibid. In a 'Com-
muniqué' dated 1 May 1971, the anarchist Angry Brigade
wrote: 'If you're not busy being born you're busy buying.' (*The
Angry Brigade 1967–84: Documents and Chronology*, 1985)

16 Everything from toy guns that spark
To flesh-colored Christs that glow in the dark
It's easy to see without looking too far
That not much is really sacred.
'It's Alright Ma (I'm Only Bleeding)', ibid.

17 But even the President of the United States
Sometimes must have to stand naked.
'It's Alright Ma (I'm Only Bleeding)', ibid.

18 Although the masters make the rules
For the wise men and the fools
I got nothing, Ma, to live up to.
'It's Alright Ma (I'm Only Bleeding)', ibid.

19 Money doesn't talk, it swears.
'It's Alright Ma (I'm Only Bleeding)', ibid.

20 Strike another match, go start anew
And it's all over now, Baby Blue.
'It's All Over Now, Baby Blue' (song), ibid.

21 A song is anything that can walk by itself.
Sleeve notes, ibid.

22 How does it feel
To be without a home
Like a complete unknown
Like a rolling stone?
'Like a Rolling Stone' (song) on the album *Highway 61 Revisited* (1965)

23 Something is happening here
But you don't know what it is
Do you, Mister Jones?
'Ballad of a Thin Man' (song), ibid.

24 You know it balances on your head
Just like a mattress balances
On a bottle of wine
Your brand new leopard-skin pill-box hat.
'Leopard-Skin Pill-Box Hat' (song) on the album *Blonde on Blonde* (1966)

25 To live outside the law, you must be honest.
'Absolutely Sweet Marie' (song), ibid. A similar line is spoken in Don Siegel's film *The Line-Up* (1958).

26 She aches just like a woman
But she breaks just like a little girl.
'Just Like a Woman' (song), ibid.

27 I see my light come shining
From the west unto the east
Any day now, any day now,
I shall be released.
'I Shall Be Released' (song, recorded 1967) on the album *The Basement Tapes* (Bob Dylan and the Band, 1975)

28 If I had wings and I could fly,
I know where I would go.
But right now I'll just sit here so contentedly
And watch the river flow.
'Watching the River Flow' (song, 1971) on the album *More Greatest Hits* (1972)

29 In writing songs I've learned as much from Cézanne as I have from Woody Guthrie.
Quoted in *Dylan: Behind the Shades*, ch. 25 (1991) by Clinton Heylin

1 If we had a reliable way to label our toys good and bad, it would be easy to regulate technology wisely. But we can rarely see far enough ahead to know which road leads to damnation. Whoever concerns himself with big technology, either to push it forward or to stop it, is gambling in human lives.
Disturbing the Universe, pt 1, ch. 1 (1979)

Freeman Dyson

(b. 1923)
British-born US physicist and author

Professor of Physics at the Institute of Advanced Study, Princeton (1953–94), he came to notice for his research into quantum electrodynamics and for his work on the nuclear test ban treaty.

E

Terry Eagleton
(b. 1943)
British critic

He has written numerous books of literary criticism within a Marxist framework, including Literary Theory: an Introduction *(1983) and* The Ideology of the Aesthetic *(1990).*

1 Postmodernism is among other things a sick joke at the expense of . . . revolutionary avant-gardism.
'Capitalism, Modernism and Postmodernism', repr. in *Against the Grain*, ch. 9 (1986)

2 It is astonishing how subtle, resourceful and quick-witted men and women can be in proving themselves to be uncivilised and thick-headed.
Ideology, Introduction (1991)

Stephen T. Early
(1889–1951)
US journalist and government official

One of America's top reporters, he became, in the words of HARRY S. TRUMAN, *'Roosevelt's secretary, friend and sagacious adviser', and was involved in publicity for the New Deal.*

1 I received a card the other day from Steve Early which said, 'Don't Worry Me – I am an 8 Ulcer Man on 4 Ulcer Pay.'
Quoted by HARRY S. TRUMAN in letter, 1949, publ. in *Mr President: Personal Diaries, Private Letters, Papers and Revealing Interviews of Harry S. Truman*, pt 5 (1952) by William Hillman

Clint Eastwood
(b. 1930)
US actor and film-maker

Having established himself as the lean loner in spaghetti westerns such as The Good, the Bad and the Ugly *(1966) and crime thrillers such as* Dirty Harry *(1971), he turned to directing, receiving an Oscar for* Unforgiven *(1992).*

1 I know what you're thinking. Did he fire six shots or only five? Well, to tell you the truth, in all this excitement I've kinda lost track myself. But being this is a .44 Magnum, the most powerful handgun in the world, and would blow your head clean off –

you've got to ask yourself one question: Do I feel lucky? Well, do ya, punk?
Dirty Harry (film, 1971, screenplay by Harry and Rita Fink and Dean Riesner, directed by Don Siegel). Spoken by Harry Callahan (Clint Eastwood) to a bank-robber, at whose head Harry has his gun aimed, following a foiled heist.

2 Go ahead. Make my day.
Sudden Impact (film, 1983, screenplay by Joseph Stinson, produced and directed by Clint Eastwood). Spoken by Harry Callahan (Clint Eastwood). RONALD REAGAN, a self-confessed Eastwood fan, borrowed the words in 1985: 'I have only one thing to say to the tax increasers: Go ahead and make my day.'

Abba Eban
(1915–2002)
Israeli politician and diplomat

Originally Aubrey Solomon. He was ambassador to the United States in Washington (1950–9), won a seat in the Knesset in 1959 and was Foreign Minister 1966–74.

1 History teaches us that men and nations behave wisely once they have exhausted all other alternatives.
Speech in London, 16 December 1970, quoted in *The Times* 17 December 1970

Umberto Eco
(b. 1932)
Italian semiologist and novelist

A high-profile European intellectual and a pioneer in the science of signs, he is the author of A Theory of Semiotics *(1976) and the best-selling novels* The Name of the Rose *(1980), a postmodern medieval murder mystery, and* Foucault's Pendulum *(1988).*

1 The good of a book lies in its being read. A book is made up of signs that speak of other signs, which in their turn speak of things. Without an eye to read them, a book contains signs that produce no concepts; therefore it is dumb.
The Name of the Rose, 'Fifth Day: Vespers' (1980). Spoken by Brother William.

2 Perhaps the mission of those who love mankind is to make people laugh at the truth, *to make truth laugh*, because the only truth lies in learning to free ourselves from insane passion for the truth.
Brother William, ibid., 'Seventh Day: Night'

3 I have never doubted the truth of signs, Adso;

they are the only things man has with which to orient himself in the world.

Brother William, ibid., 'Seventh Day: Night'

4 I think of the postmodern attitude as that of a man who loves a very cultivated woman and knows he cannot say to her, 'I love you madly', because he knows that she knows (and that she knows that he knows) that these words have already been written by Barbara Cartland. Still, there is a solution. He can say, 'As Barbara Cartland would put it, I love you madly.'

Reflections on the Name of the Rose, 'Postmodernism, Irony, the Enjoyable' (1983)

(Sir) Arthur Stanley Eddington

(1882–1944)
British astronomer and physicist

He was the first to confirm EINSTEIN's *theory of relativity, while observing the stars during the solar eclipse of 1919. His books helped to popularize science, especially* The Nature of the Physical World *(1928).*

1 Let us draw an arrow arbitrarily. If as we follow the arrow we find more and more of the random element in the world, then the arrow is pointing towards the future; if the random element decreases the arrow points towards the past … I shall use the phrase 'time's arrow' to express this one-way property of time which has no analogue in space.

The Nature of the Physical World, ch. 4 (1928). 'Time's Arrow' was the title MARTIN AMIS gave to his 1991 novel in which the sequence of time is reversed.

2 I ask you to look both ways. For the road to a knowledge of the stars leads through the atom; and important knowledge of the atom has been reached through the stars.

Stars and Atoms, 'Lecture 1' (1928)

3 It cannot be denied that for a society which has to create scarcity to save its members from starvation, to whom abundance spells disaster, and to whom unlimited energy means unlimited power for war and destruction, there is an ominous cloud in the distance though at present it be no bigger than a man's hand.

New Pathways in Science, ch. 8 (1935). The last words refer to a biblical passage (1 Kings 18:44).

Mary Baker Eddy

(1821–1910)
US religious leader

She developed the theory of Christian Science, ascribing disease to mental rather than physical causes, as described in Science and Health with Key to the Scriptures *(1875), and went on to found the Church of Christ, Scientist in 1879.*

1 Chastity is the cement of civilization and progress. Without it there is no stability in society, and without it one cannot attain the Science of Life.

Science and Health, ch. 3 (1875)

2 Is civilization only a higher form of idolatry, that man should bow down to a flesh-brush, to flannels, to baths, diet, exercise, and air?

Ibid., ch. 7

3 A wicked mortal is not the idea of God. He is little else than the expression of error. To suppose that sin, lust, hatred, envy, hypocrisy, revenge, have life abiding in them, is a terrible mistake. Life and Life's idea, Truth and Truth's idea, never make men sick, sinful, or mortal.

Ibid., ch. 10

4 Error is a supposition that pleasure and pain, that intelligence, substance, life, are existent in matter. Error is neither Mind nor one of Mind's faculties. Error is the contradiction of Truth. Error is a belief without understanding. Error is unreal because untrue. It is that which seemeth to be and is not. If error were true, its truth would be error, and we should have a self-evident absurdity – namely, *erroneous truth*. Thus we should continue to lose the standard of Truth.

Ibid., ch. 14

5 Disease is an experience of the so-called mortal mind. It is fear made manifest on the body. Christian Science takes away this physical sense of discord, just as it removes a sense of moral or mental inharmony.

Ibid., ch. 14

(Sir) Anthony Eden

(1897–1977)
British politician and prime minister

First Earl of Avon. Elected a Conservative MP in 1923, he served as Foreign Secretary twice under CHURCHILL, *whom he succeeded as Prime Minister (1955–7). He resigned following criticism of his conduct in the Suez crisis. See* MALCOLM MUGGERIDGE 8.

1 It is either him or us, don't forget that.
Quoted in *Descent to Suez: Diaries 1951–56*, ch. 5, '12 March 1956' (1986) by Evelyn Shuckburgh. Referring to Colonel Nasser.

2 Everybody is always in favour of general economy and particular expenditure.
Quoted in the *Observer* 17 June 1956

3 We are in an armed conflict; that is the phrase I have used. There has been no declaration of war.
Speech to House of Commons, 1 November 1956, publ. in *Hansard*. British and French planes had bombed Egyptian airfields on the preceding day, provoking protests in Britain and abroad. Eden justified the action: 'We best avoid wars by taking even physical action to stop small ones.'

Clarissa Eden
(1920–85)
Wife of Anthony Eden

Countess of Avon. Originally Clarissa Spencer Churchill, she was the niece of WINSTON CHURCHILL, *marrying* ANTHONY EDEN *in 1952.*

1 For the past few weeks I have really felt as if the Suez Canal was flowing through my drawing room.
Speech at Gateshead, 20 November 1956, quoted in the *Gateshead Post* 23 November 1956

Marriott Edgar
(1880–1951)
Scottish poet and entertainer

He toured in the Co-Optimists show in the 1920s, and was known for his humorous narrative verse, such as The Lion and Albert *(1933), popularized in monologues by* STANLEY HOLLOWAY.

1 There's a famous seaside place called Blackpool,
That's noted for fresh air and fun,
And Mr and Mrs Ramsbottom
Went there with young Albert, their son.
The Lion and Albert (1933). Opening lines.

2 'And thank you, sir, kindly,' said she.
'What waste all our lives raising children
To feed ruddy Lions? Not me!'
Mother, ibid. Last lines.

Maria Edgeworth
(1767–1849)
Anglo-Irish author

She is known for her novels portraying Irish social life, including Castle Rackrent *(1800) and* The Absentee *(1812). Her books for and about children have a moral emphasis.*

1 We cannot judge either of the feelings or of the character of men with perfect accuracy, from their actions or appearance in public; it is from their careless conversation, their half-finished sentences, that we may hope with the greatest probability of success to discover their real characters.
Castle Rackrent, Preface (1800)

2 What a misfortune it is to be born a woman! Why seek for knowledge, which can prove only that our wretchedness is irremediable? If a ray of light break in upon us, it is but to make darkness more visible; to show us the new limits, the Gothic structure, the impenetrable barriers of our prison.
Leonora, Letter 1 (1806)

3 Well! Some people talk of morality, and some of religion, but give me a little snug property.
The Absentee, ch. 2 (1812). Spoken by Sir Terence O'Fay.

Thomas Alva Edison
(1847–1931)
US inventor

He patented over a thousand inventions, including the phonograph (1877), the carbon-filament light bulb (1879) and thermionic emission (1883), on which the electronic valve was based.

1 Genius is one per cent inspiration, ninety-nine per cent perspiration.
Remark, *c.* 1903, quoted in *Harper's Magazine* September 1932. Edison, one of the most inspired and productive inventors of his time, received only three months of formal schooling.

Jerry Edmonton
(b. 1946)
Canadian rock musician

Also known as Mars Bonfire, he was drummer with the rock band Steppenwolf in the 1960s and '70s, and occasional composer of their lyrics.

1 Born to be wild.
'Born to be Wild' (song) on the album *Steppenwolf* (1968) by Steppenwolf. The song, which became a biker's anthem, featured in the film, *Easy Rider* (1969).

Edward III

(1312–77)

King of England

His claim to the French throne through his mother Isabella led, in 1337, to the start of the Hundred Years War. He won a major victory at Crécy (1346) and by 1360 had gained control of a third of France.

1 *Honi soit qui mal y pense.*
[Evil be to him who evil thinks.]

Quoted in *Anglicae Historiae*, bk 26, ch. 19 (1546) by Polydore Vergil. Alleged remark at the falling of the Countess of Salisbury's garter, presumably when the Order of the Garter was founded in 1344. There is no contemporary evidence, but the traditional tale was current in HENRY VIII's reign.

Edward VIII

(1894–1972)

King of Great Britain and Northern Ireland

Though succeeding to the throne in 1936, he was never crowned, abdicating after eleven months in order to marry Wallis Simpson, a twice-divorced American. After the Second World War, the couple spent the rest of their lives in Paris as the Duke and Duchess of Windsor.

1 These works brought all these people here. Something should be done to get them at work again.

Quoted in the *Western Mail* 19 November 1936. Comment at the derelict Dowlais Iron and Steel Works in South Wales, 18 November 1936, where 9,000 men had recently been laid off. The remark is usually quoted: 'Something must be done.'

2 I have found it impossible to carry the heavy burden of responsibility and to discharge my duties as King as I would wish to do without the help and support of the woman I love ... I now quit altogether public affairs, and I lay down my burden.

Abdication speech, 11 December 1936, publ. in *The Times* 12 December 1936. WINSTON CHURCHILL is said to have had a hand in composing the speech, which was broadcast on radio.

3 The thing that impresses me most about America is the way parents obey their children.

Quoted in *Look* 5 March 1957

Oliver Edwards

(1711–91)

English lawyer

1 I have tried too in my time to be a philosopher;

but, I don't know how, cheerfulness was always breaking in.

Quoted in *Life of Samuel Johnson, LL.D.*, 17 April 1778 (1791) by JAMES BOSWELL

Richard Edwards

(c. 1523–66)

English composer and poet

He was Master of the Children of the Chapel Royal in 1561. His main collection of poems was The Paradise of Dainty Devices *(1576).*

1 The falling out of faithful friends, renewing is of love.

'Amantium Irae', publ. in *The Paradise of Dainty Devices* (1576). This last line of each of the poem's stanzas is an echo of an older line, from which the poem's Latin title is taken: see TERENCE 2.

Barbara Ehrenreich

(b. 1941)

US author and columnist

She is best known for her outspoken and humorous newspaper columns, mainly on issues of health, sex and class and from a feminist angle.

1 Exercise is the yuppie version of bulimia.

'Food Worship' (1985), repr. in *The Worst Years of Our Lives* (1991)

2 America is addicted to wars of distraction.

The Times 22 April 1991

John Ehrlichman

(1925–99)

Presidential assistant to Richard Nixon

As Chief Adviser on Domestic Policy under President NIXON, he attempted to block investigations into the Watergate break-in, for which he and H. R. HALDEMAN were nicknamed the 'Berlin Wall'.

1 I think we ought to let him hang there. Let him twist slowly, slowly in the wind.

Telephone conversation with John Dean, March 1973, quoted in the *Washington Post* 27 July 1973. The words refer to Patrick Gray, a nominee for director of the FBI from whom President NIXON had tacitly withdrawn his support.

2 It'll play in Peoria.

Attributed quip regarding the selling of political policy in 'middle America' (Peoria is in Illinois). Ehrlichman claimed to have originated the catch-phrase during Nixon's 1968 election campaign, though other sources suggest it was current much earlier, used in US variety shows in the 1930s.

Albert Einstein

(1879–1955)

German-born US theoretical physicist

A giant in the fields of space, time and gravitation, he was, in the words of C. P. SNOW, *'the symbol of science, the master of the 20th-century intellect'. His theory of relativity (1905) was followed by his general theory of relativity in 1915. See* ROLAND BARTHES 4.

1 E=mc₂

The usual form in which Einstein's Special Theory of Relativity is expressed. The theory first appeared in the paper, 'Does the Inertia of a Body Depend upon Its Energy Content?', publ. in *Annalen der Physik*, no. 17, September 1905, repr. in *The Principle of Relativity* (ed. Einstein, H. A. Lorentz, et al, 1923), which contained the formula: 'If a body gives off the energy L in the form of radiation its mass diminishes by L/c₂.' The theory was initially received with indifferent or negative reactions.

2 By an application of the theory of relativity to the taste of readers, today in Germany I am called a German man of science, and in England I am represented as a Swiss Jew. If I come to be regarded as a *bête noire* the descriptions will be reversed, and I shall become a Swiss Jew for the Germans and a German man of science for the English!

The Times 28 November 1919. Einstein expressed variations of this idea on different occasions.

3 God is subtle, but he is not malicious.

Quoted in *Einstein*, ch. 14 (1973) by R. W. Clark. The remark was made in April/May 1921, during Einstein's first visit to Princeton University, in response to the news that a 'nonzero aether drift' had been found at Mount Vernon observatory. The words were later carved above the fireplace of the Common Room of Fine Hall in Princeton's former Mathematical Institute. In 1946 Einstein gave a freer translation: 'God is slick, but he ain't mean.'

4 Quantum mechanics is certainly imposing. But an inner voice tells me that it is not yet the real thing. The theory says a lot, but does not really bring us any closer to the secret of the 'old one'. I, at any rate, am convinced that *He* is not playing at dice.

Letter to Max Born, 4 December 1926, publ. in *The Born-Einstein Letters* (ed. Max Born, 1971). The version usually remembered is: 'God does not play dice [with the universe].' Nearly twenty years later, Einstein wrote to Born: 'You believe in the God who plays dice, and I in complete law and order in a world which objectively exists, and which I, in a wildly speculative way, am trying to capture . . . Even the great initial success of the quantum theory does not make me believe in the fundamental dice-game, although I am well aware that our younger colleagues interpret this as a consequence of senility. No doubt the day will come when we will see whose

instinctive attitude was the correct one.' (7 September 1944) See STEPHEN HAWKING 1.

5 The whole of science is nothing more than a refinement of everyday thinking.

'Physics and Reality' (1936), repr. in *Out of My Later Years*, ch. 12, sect. 1 (1950)

6 One may say 'the eternal mystery of the world is its comprehensibility.' . . . The fact that it is comprehensible is a miracle.

Ibid.

7 Science without religion is lame, religion without science is blind.

From a scientific paper at conference in New York City, September 1940, repr. ibid., ch. 7, sect. 2, 'Science and Religion'

8 We should take care not to make the intellect our god; it has, of course, powerful muscles, but no personality.

From a broadcast for the United Jewish Appeal, 11 April 1943, ibid., ch. 50

9 The unleashed power of the atom has changed everything save our modes of thinking and we thus drift toward unparalleled catastrophe.

Telegram sent to prominent Americans, 24 May 1946, publ. in the *New York Times* 25 May 1946. Various versions of this statement exist, probably translations from the German which Einstein always preferred to use.

10 One has to divide one's time between politics and our equations. Equations are much more important to me, because politics is for the present, while . . . an equation is for eternity.

Remark at Princeton, late 1940s, quoted in *Albert Einstein*, ch. 38 (1993) by Albrecht Fösling. Einstein was then involved with the Emergency Committee of Atomic Scientists (set up to inform the public about the atomic bomb and its effects), of which he became Chairman in May 1946.

11 The most beautiful emotion we can experience is the mystical. It is the power of all true art and science. He to whom this emotion is a stranger, who can no longer wonder and stand rapt in awe, is as good as dead. To know that what is impenetrable to us really exists, manifesting itself as the highest wisdom and the most radiant beauty, which our dull faculties can comprehend only in their most primitive forms – this knowledge, this feeling, is at the center of true religiousness. In this sense, and in this sense only, I belong to the rank of devoutly religious men.

Quoted in *Einstein: His Life and Times*, ch. 12, sect. 5 (1947) by Philip Frank

12 When you are courting a nice girl an hour seems like a second. When you sit on a red-hot cinder a second seems like an hour. That's relativity.
Quoted in the *News Chronicle* 14 March 1949

13 Perfection of means and confusion of goals seem – in my opinion – to characterize our age.
Out of My Later Years, ch. 14 (1950)

14 People like us, who believe in physics, know that the distinction between past, present and future is only a stubbornly persistent illusion.
Letter, 21 March 1955, publ. in *Albert Einstein, Michele Besso: Correspondence 1903–1955*, no. 215 (1972)

15 A (Success) = X (Work) + Y (Play) + Z (Keep your mouth shut).
Quoted in *Albert Einstein: A Documentary Biography*, ch. 3 (1956) by Carl Seelig

16 As far as the laws of mathematics refer to reality, they are not certain; and as far as they are certain, they do not refer to reality.
Quoted in *The Tao of Physics*, ch. 2 (1975) by Fritjof Capra

17 Two things are infinite: the universe and human stupidity. But I'm not sure about the universe.
Attributed

Dwight D. Eisenhower
(1890–1969)
US general, politician and president

Dwight David Eisenhower. Supreme Commander of the Allied Forces leading the D-Day invasions in 1944, 'Ike' was given command over all NATO forces in Europe in 1951, and subsequently served two terms as Republican President (1953–61). The journalist Murray Kempton called him 'the great tortoise upon whose back the world sat for eight years'. See ADLAI STEVENSON 19.

1 Humility must always be the portion of any man who receives acclaim earned in the blood of his followers and the sacrifices of his friends.
Speech at Guildhall, London, 12 July 1945, publ. in *Eisenhower Speaks* (ed. Rudolph L. Treunfels, 1948)

2 Every gun that is made, every warship launched, every rocket fired, signifies, in the final sense, a theft from those who hunger and are not fed, those who are cold and are not clothed. The world in arms is not spending money alone. It is spending the sweat of its labourers, the genius of its scientists, the hopes of its children.
'The Chance for Peace', speech to the American Society of Newspaper Editors, Washington DC, 16 April 1953, publ. in *Public Papers of the Presidents of the United States* (1953)

3 You have a row of dominoes set up; you knock over the first one, and what will happen to the last one is that it will go over very quickly.
Press conference, 7 April 1954, ibid. Referring to the situation in south-east Asia following the defeat of the French by the Viet-Minh.

4 In the councils of government, we must guard against the acquisition of unwarranted influence, whether sought or unsought, by the military-industrial complex. The potential for the disastrous rise of misplaced power exists and will persist. We must never let the weight of this combination endanger our liberties or democratic processes. We should take nothing for granted.
Farewell broadcast on radio and television, 17 January 1961, quoted in the *New York Times* 18 January 1961

5 In preparing for battle I have always found that plans are useless, but planning is indispensable.
One of Eisenhower's favourite maxims, quoted by RICHARD NIXON in *Six Crises*, 'Khrushchev' (1962)

George Eliot
(1819–80)
English novelist

Pseudonym of Mary Ann Evans. She is admired for her understanding of human experience, characterization, and portrayal of provincial and rural life, in such novels as Adam Bede *(1859) and* Middlemarch *(1871–2). Lord* ACTON *said of her that no writer had 'anything like her power of manifold, but disinterested and impartially observant sympathy'.*

1 Life is too precious to be spent in this weaving and unweaving of false impressions, and it is better to live quietly under some degree of misrepresentation than to attempt to remove it by the uncertain process of letter-writing.
Letter, 8 June 1856, publ. in *The George Eliot Letters*, vol. 2 (ed. Gordon S. Haight, 1954)

2 Few women, I fear, have had such reason as I have to think the long sad years of youth were worth living for the sake of middle age.
Journal entry, 31 December 1857, publ. in *George Eliot's Life as Related in Her Letters and Journals* (ed. J. W. Cross, 1900)

3 In every parting there is an image of death.
Scenes of Clerical Life, 'Amos Barton', ch. 10 (1858)

4 Opposition may become sweet to a man when he has christened it persecution.
Ibid., 'Janet's Repentance', ch. 8. See RALPH WALDO EMERSON 6.

5 Cruelty, like every other vice, requires no motive outside itself – it only requires opportunity.
Ibid., 'Janet's Repentance', ch. 13

6 Errors look so very ugly in persons of small means – one feels they are taking quite a liberty in going astray; whereas people of fortune may naturally indulge in a few delinquencies.
Ibid., 'Janet's Repentance', ch. 25

7 Ignorance . . . is a painless evil; so, I should think, is dirt, considering the merry faces that go along with it.
Ibid., 'Mr Gilfil's Love-Story', ch. 3

8 It is generally a feminine eye that first detects the moral deficiencies hidden under the 'dear deceit' of beauty.
Adam Bede, bk 1, ch. 15 (1859)

9 Our deeds determine us, as much as we determine our deeds; and until we know what has been or will be the peculiar combination of outward with inward facts, which constitute a man's critical actions, it will be better not to think ourselves wise about his character.
Ibid., bk 4, ch. 29

10 It's them as take advantage that get advantage i' this world.
Mrs Poyser, ibid., bk 4, ch. 32

11 We hand folks over to God's mercy, and show none ourselves.
Ibid., bk 5, ch. 42

12 But the mother's yearning, that completest type of the life in another life which is the essence of real human love, feels the presence of the cherished child even in the debased, degraded man.
Ibid., bk 5, ch. 43

13 That's what a man wants in a wife, mostly; he wants to make sure o' one fool as 'ull tell him he's wise.
Mrs Poyser, ibid., bk 6, ch. 53

14 Anger and jealousy can no more bear to lose sight of their objects than love.
The Mill on the Floss, bk 1, ch. 10 (1860)

15 The dead level of provincial existence.
Philip Wakem, ibid., bk 5, ch. 3

16 If we use common words on a great occasion, they are the more striking, because they are felt at once to have a particular meaning, like old banners, or everyday clothes, hung up in a sacred place.
Maggie Tulliver, ibid., bk 6, ch. 2

17 No compliment can be eloquent, except as an expression of indifference.
Maggie Tulliver, ibid., bk 6, ch. 2. Responding to Stephen Guest's compliment on their first encounter.

18 The happiest women, like the happiest nations, have no history.
Ibid., bk 6, ch. 3. See CHARLES DE MONTESQUIEU 4.

19 I should like to know what is the proper function of women, if it is not to make reasons for husbands to stay at home, and still stronger reasons for bachelors to go out.
Stephen Guest, ibid., bk 6, ch. 6

20 Jealousy is never satisfied with anything short of an omniscience that would detect the subtlest fold of the heart.
Ibid., bk 6, ch. 10

21 More helpful than all wisdom is one draught of simple human pity that will not forsake us.
Ibid., bk 7, ch. 1

22 In the vain laughter of folly wisdom hears half its applause.
Romola, bk 1, ch. 12 (1863)

23 An ass may bray a good while before he shakes the stars down.
Bratti, ibid., bk 3, ch. 50

24 There is much pain that is quite noiseless; and vibrations that make human agonies are often a mere whisper in the roar of hurrying existence. There are glances of hatred that stab and raise no cry of murder; robberies that leave man or woman for ever beggared of peace and joy, yet kept secret by the sufferer – committed to no sound except that of low moans in the night, seen in no writing except that made on the face by the slow months of suppressed anguish and early morning tears. Many an inherited sorrow that has marred a life has been breathed into no human ear.
Felix Holt, the Radical, Introduction (1866)

25 There is no private life which has not been determined by a wider public life.
Ibid., ch. 3

26 An election is coming. Universal peace is

declared, and the foxes have a sincere interest in prolonging the lives of the poultry.
Ibid., ch. 5

27 There is hardly any mental misery worse than that of having our own serious phrases, our own rooted beliefs, caricatured by a charlatan or a hireling.
Ibid., ch. 11

28 Play not with paradoxes. That caustic which you handle in order to scorch others may happen to sear your own fingers and make them dead to the quality of things.
Mr Lyon, ibid., ch. 13. Referring to intellectual pursuits.

29 The beginning of compunction is the beginning of a new life.
Ibid., ch. 13

30 One way of getting an idea of our fellow-countrymen's miseries is to go and look at their pleasures.
Ibid., ch. 28

31 To act with doubleness towards a man whose own conduct was double, was so near an approach to virtue that it deserved to be called by no meaner name than diplomacy.
Ibid., ch. 29. On the hypocrisy and corruption present in politics at the time of the first Reform Act (1832).

32 Harold, like the rest of us, had many impressions which saved him the trouble of distinct ideas.
Ibid., ch. 47. Of Harold Transome.

33 Life is measured by the rapidity of change, the succession of influences that modify the being.
Ibid., ch. 48

34 Abroad, that large home of ruined reputations.
Ibid., Epilogue

35 We women are always in danger of living too exclusively in the affections; and though our affections are perhaps the best gifts we have, we ought also to have our share of the more independent life – some joy in things for their own sake. It is piteous to see the helplessness of some sweet women when their affections are disappointed – because all their teaching has been, that they can only delight in study of any kind for the sake of a personal love. They have never contemplated an independent delight in ideas as an experience which they could confess without being laughed at. Yet surely women

need this defence against passionate affliction even more than men.
Letter, 8 July 1870, publ. in *The George Eliot Letters*, vol. 5 (ed. Gordon S. Haight, 1956)

36 I have the conviction that excessive literary production is a social offence.
Letter, 11 September 1871, ibid., vol. 5

37 To have in general but little feeling, seems to be the only security against feeling too much on any particular occasion.
Middlemarch, bk 1, ch. 7 (1871)

38 Among all forms of mistake, prophecy is the most gratuitous.
Ibid., bk 1, ch. 10

39 Quarrel? Nonsense; we have not quarrelled. If one is not to get into a rage sometimes, what is the good of being friends?
Mary Garth to Rosamond Vincy, ibid., bk 1, ch. 12

40 Might, could, would – they are contemptible auxiliaries.
Mary Garth, ibid., bk 2, ch. 14

41 I at least have so much to do in unravelling certain human lots, and seeing how they were woven and interwoven, that all the light I can command must be concentrated on this particular web, and not dispersed over that tempting range of relevancies called the universe.
Ibid., bk 2, ch. 15

42 In the multitude of middle-aged men who go about their vocations in a daily course determined for them much in the same way as the tie of their cravats, there is always a good number who once meant to shape their own deeds and alter the world a little.
Ibid., bk 2, ch. 15

43 Our passions do not live apart in locked chambers but dress in their small wardrobe of notions, bring their provisions to a common table and mess together, feeding out of the common store according to their appetite.
Ibid., bk 2, ch. 16

44 One must be poor to know the luxury of giving!
Ibid., bk 2, ch. 17

45 Rome, the city of visible history, where the past of a whole hemisphere seems moving in funeral

procession with strange ancestral images and trophies gathered from afar.

Ibid., bk 2, ch. 20

46 We do not expect people to be deeply moved by what is not unusual. That element of tragedy which lies in the very fact of frequency, has not yet wrought itself into the coarse emotion of mankind; and perhaps our frames could hardly bear much of it.

Ibid., bk 2, ch. 20

47 If we had a keen vision and feeling of all ordinary human life, it would be like hearing the grass grow and the squirrel's heart beat, and we should die of that roar which lies on the other side of silence. As it is, the quickest of us walk about well wadded with stupidity.

Ibid., bk 2, ch. 20

48 Failure after long perseverance is much grander than never to have a striving good enough to be called a failure.

Dorothea Brooke, ibid., bk 2, ch. 22

49 To be a poet is to have a soul so quick to discern, that no shade of quality escapes it, and so quick to feel, that discernment is but a hand playing with finely-ordered variety on the chords of emotion – a soul in which knowledge passes instantaneously into feeling, and feeling flashes back as a new organ of knowledge. One may have that condition by fits only.

Will Ladislaw, ibid., bk 2, ch. 22

50 Solomon's Proverbs, I think, have omitted to say, that as the sore palate findeth grit, so an uneasy consciousness heareth innuendos.

Ibid., bk 3, ch. 31

51 What loneliness is more lonely than distrust?

Ibid., bk 5, ch. 44

52 But what we call our despair is often only the painful eagerness of unfed hope.

Ibid., bk 5, ch. 51

53 The growing good of the world is partly dependent on unhistoric acts; and that things are not so ill with you and me as they might have been, is half owing to the number who lived faithfully a hidden life, and rest in unvisited tombs.

Ibid., bk 8, 'Finale'. Closing words of book.

54 It was not that she was out of temper, but that the world was not equal to the demands of her fine organism.

Daniel Deronda bk 1, ch. 7 (1876). Referring to Gwendolen Harleth.

55 The beginning of an acquaintance whether with persons or things is to get a definite outline of our ignorance.

Ibid., bk 2, ch. 11, Epigraph

56 Gossip is a sort of smoke that comes from the dirty tobacco-pipes of those who diffuse it: it proves nothing but the bad taste of the smoker.

Ibid., bk 2, ch. 13

57 A difference of tastes in jokes is a great strain on the affections.

Ibid., bk 2, ch. 15

58 Of a truth, Knowledge is power, but it is a power reined by scruple, having a conscience of what must be and what may be; whereas Ignorance is a blind giant who, let him but wax unbound, would make it a sport to seize the pillars that hold up the long-wrought fabric of human good, and turn all the places of joy as dark as a buried Babylon.

Ibid., bk 3, ch. 21

59 There is a great deal of unmapped country within us which would have to be taken into account in an explanation of our gusts and storms.

Ibid., bk 3, ch. 24

60 Men's men: gentle or simple, they're much of a muchness.

Mrs Girdle, ibid., bk 4, ch. 31. See JOHN VANBRUGH 5.

61 Here undoubtedly lies the chief poetic energy: – in the force of imagination that pierces or exalts the solid fact, instead of floating among cloud-pictures.

Ibid., bk 4, ch. 33

62 Excellence encourages one about life generally; it shows the spiritual wealth of the world.

Daniel Deronda, ibid., bk 5, ch. 36

63 A woman's heart must be of such a size and no larger, else it must be pressed small, like Chinese feet; her happiness is to be made as cakes are, by a fixed receipt.

Ibid., bk 7, ch. 51. Deronda's mother comments on society's expectations of women.

64 No evil dooms us hopelessly except the evil we love, and desire to continue in, and make no effort to escape from.

Ibid., bk 7, ch. 57

65 Blessed is the man who, having nothing to say,
abstains from giving us wordy evidence of the fact.
Impressions of Theophrastus Such, ch. 4 (1879)

T. S. Eliot
(1888–1965)
Anglo-American poet and critic

Thomas Stearns Eliot. By the time The Waste Land *appeared (1922), he was regarded as the voice of a disillusioned post-First World War generation. His later verse plays and poetry reflect his conversion to Anglo-Catholicism.* HAROLD NICOLSON *compared him to a 'sacerdotal lawyer – dyspeptic, ascetic, eclectic'. See also* TOM PAULIN 3.

1 Let us go then, you and I,
When the evening is spread out against the sky
Like a patient etherised upon a table.
'The Love Song of J. Alfred Prufrock', publ. in *Prufrock and Other Observations* (1917). Opening lines of poem.

2 In the room the women come and go
Talking of Michelangelo.
'The Love Song of J. Alfred Prufrock', ibid.

3 And indeed there will be time
To wonder, 'Do I dare?' and, 'Do I dare?'
Time to turn back and descend the stair,
With a bald spot in the middle of my hair . . .
Do I dare
Disturb the universe?
'The Love Song of J. Alfred Prufrock', ibid.

4 Time for you and time for me,
And time yet for a hundred indecisions,
And for a hundred visions and revisions,
Before the taking of a toast and tea.
'The Love Song of J. Alfred Prufrock', ibid.

5 I have measured out my life with coffee spoons.
'The Love Song of J. Alfred Prufrock', ibid.

6 No! I am not Prince Hamlet, nor was meant to
   be:
Am an attendant lord, one that will do
To swell a progress, start a scene or two,
Advise the prince.
'The Love Song of J. Alfred Prufrock', ibid.

7 I grow old . . . I grow old . . .
I shall wear the bottoms of my trousers rolled.
'The Love Song of J. Alfred Prufrock', ibid.

8 Shall I part my hair behind? Do I dare to eat a
   peach?
I shall wear white flannel trousers, and walk upon
   the beach.

I have heard the mermaids singing, each to each.
I do not think that they will sing to me.
'The Love Song of J. Alfred Prufrock', ibid.

9 It [tradition] cannot be inherited, and if you want
it you must obtain it by great labour.
'Tradition and the Individual Talent', sect. 1 (1919), repr. in
Selected Prose of T. S. Eliot (ed. Frank Kermode, 1975)

10 Art never improves, but . . . the material of art is
never quite the same.
'Tradition and the Individual Talent', sect. 1, ibid.

11 The progress of an artist is a continual self-
sacrifice, a continual extinction of personality.
'Tradition and the Individual Talent', sect. 1, ibid.

12 Poetry is not a turning loose of emotion, but an
escape from emotion; it is not the expression of
personality, but an escape from personality. But, of
course, only those who have personality and emotions know what it means to want to escape from
these things.
'Tradition and the Individual Talent', sect. 1, ibid.

13 Uncorseted, her friendly bust
Gives promise of pneumatic bliss.
'Whispers of Immortality', publ. in *Poems* (1919). The charac-
ter described here, Grishkin, is thought to be a portrayal of
Serafima Astafieva (1876–1934), a Russian dancer with the
Diaghilev company who opened her own ballet school in
London. EZRA POUND also referred to her in his *Pisan Cantos*
77 and 79 (1945).

14 Immature poets imitate; mature poets steal.
The Sacred Wood, 'Philip Massinger' (1920)

15 Here I am, an old man in a dry month,
Being read to by a boy, waiting for rain.
'Gerontion', publ. in *Ara Vos Prec* (1920). Opening lines of
poem.

16 In the seventeenth century a dissociation of sensibility set in, from which we have never recovered;
and this dissociation, as is natural, was due to the
influence of the two most powerful poets of the
century, Milton and Dryden.
'The Metaphysical Poets' (1921), repr. in *Selected Prose of T. S.
Eliot* (ed. Frank Kermode, 1975)

17 Poets in our civilization, as it exists at present,
must be *difficult*.
Ibid.

18 April is the cruellest month, breeding
Lilacs out of the dead land, mixing

Memory and desire, stirring
Dull roots with spring rain.
The Waste Land, pt 1, 'The Burial of the Dead' (1922). Opening
lines of poem.

19 I will show you fear in a handful of dust.
Ibid. pt 1

20 Unreal City,
Under the brown fog of a winter dawn.
Ibid. pt 1. The lines are repeated in pt 3 of the poem, with
'noon' substituted for 'dawn'.

21 I had not thought death had undone so many.
Ibid. pt 1. A translation of DANTE's *Inferno*, canto 3, ll. 56–7.

22 I Tiresias, though blind, throbbing between two
   lives,
Old man with wrinkled female breasts, can see
At the violet hour, the evening hour that strives
Homeward, and brings the sailor home from sea,
The typist home at teatime, clears her breakfast,
   lights
Her stove, and lays out food in tins.
Ibid., pt 3, 'The Fire Sermon'

23 O City city, I can sometimes hear
Beside a public bar in Lower Thames Street,
The pleasant whining of a mandoline
And a clatter and a chatter from within
Where fishmen lounge at noon.
Ibid. pt 3

24 Who is the third who walks always beside you?
When I count, there are only you and I together
But when I look ahead up the white road
There is always another one walking beside you.
Ibid., pt 5, 'What the Thunder Said'

25 The awful daring of a moment's surrender
Which an age of prudence can never retract.
Ibid. pt 5

26 These fragments I have shored against my
   ruins.
Ibid. pt 5

27 We are the hollow men
We are the stuffed men
Leaning together
Headpiece filled with straw.
'The Hollow Men', sect. 1, publ. in *Poems 1909–1925* (1925).
Opening lines of poem.

28 Between the conception
And the creation
Between the emotion

And the response
Falls the Shadow.
Ibid., sect. 5

29 *This is the way the world ends*
This is the way the world ends
This is the way the world ends
Not with a bang but a whimper.
Ibid. sect. 5. Concluding lines of poem.

30 A cold coming we had of it,
Just the worst time of the year
For a journey, and such a long journey:
The ways deep and the weather sharp,
The very dead of winter.
Journey of the Magi, no. 8 of the *Ariel Poems* (1927). The lines
are inspired by 'Of the Nativity' (1622), a sermon by Lancelot
Andrewes.

31 I had seen birth and death
But had thought they were different.
Journey of the Magi, ibid.

32 The dreamcrossed twilight between birth and
   dying.
Ash-Wednesday, pt 6 (1930)

33 So far as we are human, what we do must be
either evil or good: so far as we do evil or good, we
are human: and it is better, in a paradoxical way, to
do evil than to do nothing: at least we exist.
'Baudelaire', Introduction to *The Intimate Journals of Charles
Baudelaire* (transl. CHRISTOPHER ISHERWOOD, 1930), repr.
in *Selected Prose of T. S. Eliot* (ed. Frank Kermode, 1975)

34 I gotta use words when I talk to you.
Sweeney Agonistes, 'Fragment of an Agon' (1932)

35 Where is the Life we have lost in living?
Where is the wisdom we have lost in knowledge?
Where is the knowledge we have lost in
   information?
'Choruses from "The Rock"', pt 1 (1934)

36 And the wind shall say 'Here were decent
   godless people;
Their only monument the asphalt road
And a thousand lost golf balls.'
Ibid., pt 3

37 And meanwhile we have gone on living,
Living and partly living,
Picking together the pieces,
Gathering faggots at nightfall,

Building a partial shelter,
For sleeping and eating and drinking and
    laughter.
Murder in the Cathedral, pt 1 (1935). Spoken by the Chorus of
Women of Canterbury.

38 The last temptation is the greatest treason:
To do the right deed for the wrong reason.
Thomas, ibid., pt 1

39 Time present and time past
Are both perhaps present in time future,
And time future contained in time past.
'Burnt Norton', pt 1 (1936), the first of *Four Quartets* (1943).
Opening lines.

40 Footfalls echo in the memory
Down the passage which we did not take
Towards the door we never opened
Into the rose-garden.
'Burnt Norton', pt 1, ibid.

41 Human kind
Cannot bear very much reality.
'Burnt Norton', pt 1, ibid. The words also appeared in Eliot's
Murder in the Cathedral, pt 2 (spoken by Thomas), and have
been evoked or echoed by numerous other writers; for
example GRAHAM GREENE in *Our Man in Havana* (1958),
where Hasselbacher states, 'Reality in our century is not
something to be faced', and in MARGARET DRABBLE's *Realms
of Gold* (1975): 'The human mind can bear plenty of reality
but not too much intermittent gloom.'

42 Where does one go from a world of insanity?
Somewhere on the other side of despair.
The Family Reunion, pt 2, Sc. 2 (1939). Spoken by Harry, Lord
Monchensey.

43 The Naming of Cats is a difficult matter,
It isn't just one of your holiday games;
You may think at first I'm as mad as a hatter
When I tell you, a cat must have THREE
    DIFFERENT NAMES.
'The Naming of Cats', publ. in *Old Possum's Book of Practical
Cats* (1939)

44 Jellicle Cats come out tonight
Jellicle Cats come one come all:
The Jellicle Moon is shining bright – Jellicles come
    to the Jellicle Ball.
'The Song of the Jellicles', ibid.

45 Macavity's a Mystery Cat: he's called the
    Hidden Paw –
For he's the master criminal who can defy the Law.
He's the bafflement of Scotland Yard, the Flying
    Squad's despair:

For when they reach the scene of crime –
    Macavity's not there!
'Macavity: the Mystery Cat', ibid.

46 In my beginning is my end.
'East Coker', pt 1 (1940). Opening line of the second of *Four
Quartets* (1943). See MARY, QUEEN OF SCOTS 2.

47 The dripping blood our only drink,
The bloody flesh our only food:
In spite of which we like to think
That we are sound, substantial flesh and blood –
Again, in spite of that, we call this Friday good.
Ibid., pt 4

48 Each venture
Is a new beginning, a raid on the inarticulate
With shabby equipment always deteriorating
In the general mess of imprecision of feeling.
Ibid., pt 5

49 The first condition of right thought is right sensation – the first condition of understanding a
foreign country is to smell it.
A Choice of Kipling's Verse, Introduction (1941), repr. in *On
Poetry and Poets*, pt 2, 'Rudyard Kipling' (1957)

50 I do not know much about gods; but I think
    that the river
Is a strong brown god – sullen, untamed and
    intractable.
'The Dry Salvages', pt 1 (1941), the third of *Four Quartets* (1943).
Opening lines of poem.

51 War is not a life: it is a situation,
One which may neither be ignored nor accepted.
'A Note on War Poetry' (1942), repr. in *Collected Poems 1909–
62* (1962)

52 It seems just possible that a poem might
    happen
To a very young man: but a poem is not poetry –
That is a life.
'A Note on War Poetry', ibid.

53 And what the dead had no speech for, when
    living,
They can tell you, being dead: the communication
Of the dead is tongued with fire beyond the
    language of the living.
'Little Gidding', pt 1 (1942), the fourth of *Four Quartets* (1943)

54 There are flood and drouth
Over the eyes and in the mouth,
Dead water and dead sand
Contending for the upper hand.
The parched eviscerate soil

Gapes at the vanity of toil,
Laughs without mirth.
This is the death of the earth.
'Little Gidding', pt 2, ibid.

55 For last year's words belong to last year's
language
And next year's words await another voice.
'Little Gidding', pt 2, ibid.

56 A people without history
Is not redeemed from time, for history is a pattern
Of timeless moments.
'Little Gidding', pt 5, ibid.

57 We shall not cease from exploration
And the end of all our exploring
Will be to arrive where we started
And know the place for the first time.
'Little Gidding', pt 5, ibid.

58 Culture may even be described simply as that
which makes life worth living.
Notes Towards a Definition of Culture, ch. 1 (1948)

59 The term *culture* ... includes all the character-
istic activities and interests of a people: Derby Day,
Henley Regatta, Cowes, the twelfth of August, a cup
final, the dog races, the pin table, the dart board,
Wensleydale cheese, boiled cabbage cut into sec-
tions, beetroot in vinegar, nineteenth-century
Gothic churches and the music of Elgar.
Ibid., ch. 1

60 You will find that you survive humiliation.
And that's an experience of incalculable value.
The Cocktail Party, Act 1, Sc. 1 (1950). Spoken by Unidentified
Guest (later identified as Sir Henry Harcourt-Reilly).

61 Hell is oneself,
Hell is alone, the other figures in it
Merely projections. There is nothing to escape
from
And nothing to escape to. One is always alone.
Edward, ibid., Act 1, Sc. 3

62 The years between fifty and seventy are the hardest. You are always being asked to do things, and
yet you are not decrepit enough to turn them down.
Time 23 October 1950

63 It's not wise to violate rules until you know how
to observe them.
Interview in *Writers at Work* (second series, ed. George
Plimpton, 1963)

64 It is a medium of entertainment which permits

millions of people to listen to the same joke at the
same time, and yet remain lonesome.
Of television, in the *New York Post* 22 September 1963

Elizabeth I
(1533–1603)
Queen of England

*Known as the 'Virgin Queen', she ascended to the throne in
1558. Her reign coincided with the flowering of English literature, and the growth of national consciousness. In the opinion
of* JOHN WESLEY, *she was 'as just and merciful as Nero, and
as good a Christian as Mohamet'.*

1 I am your anointed Queen. I will never be by violence constrained to do anything. I thank God I am
endued with such qualities that if I were turned out
of the Realm in my petticoat I were able to live in
any place in Christendom.
Speech to Deputation of Lords and Commons, 5 November
1566, quoted in *Elizabeth I and her Parliaments 1559–1581*, pt 3,
ch. 1 (1953), by J. E. Neale

2 I know that I have the body of a weak and feeble
woman, but I have the heart and stomach of a king,
and of a king of England too.
Speech at Tilbury, 8 August 1588, quoted in *The Tudors*, ch. 7
(1955) by Christopher Morris. Address to troops on the
approach of the Spanish Armada.

3 Though God hath raised me high, yet this I count
the glory of my crown: that I have reigned with your
loves ... And though you have had, and may have,
many mightier and wiser princes sitting in this seat;
yet you never had, nor shall have any that will love
you better.
The 'Golden Speech' to the House of Commons, 30 November
1601, publ. in *Historical Collections of the Four Last Parliaments of Queen Elizabeth* (ed. Heywood Townshend, 1680)

4 Must! Is *must* a word to be addressed to princes?
Little man, little man! thy father, if he had been
alive, durst not have used that word.
Attributed remonstrance to Sir Robert Cecil, who had urged
her to go to bed in her last illness, March 1603; both Robert
and his father William Cecil (Lord Burghley) were secretaries
of state to Elizabeth.

5 'Twas God the word that spake it,
He took the bread and brake it;
And what the word did make it;
That I believe, and take it.
Reply on being asked whether Christ was present in the Sacra-
ment, quoted in *The Marrow of Ecclesiastical History*, pt 2,
bk 1, 'The Life of Queen Elizabeth' (1675) by Samuel Clarke

6 My Lord, I had forgot the fart.

Quoted by JOHN AUBREY in *Brief Lives*, 'Edward de Vere' (ed. Andrew Clark, 1898). Remark made to Edward de Vere on his return after travelling abroad for seven years, occasioned by his embarrassment at having broken wind in the Queen's presence.

7 All my possessions for a moment of time.

Attributed last words

Elizabeth II
(b. 1926)
Queen of Great Britain and Northern Ireland

Queen since 1952, she has upheld the traditional, formal role of the monarchy while conceding a degree of modernization.

1 I declare before you all that my whole life, whether it be long or short, shall be devoted to your service and the service of our great Imperial family to which we all belong.

Speech to the Commonwealth, Cape Town, 21 April 1947, quoted in *The Times* 22 April 1947

2 My husband and I . . .

Opening words of her first Christmas Message, 1953, New Zealand. This introductory phrase became a regular feature of the Queen's speeches, though the alternative 'Prince Philip and I . . .' was introduced in the 1960s when it was apparent that the familiar formula was becoming a joke. On her 25th wedding anniversary, she joked, 'I think everybody really will concede that on this, of all days, I should begin my speech with the words "My husband and I." '

3 Like all the best families, we have our share of eccentricities, of impetuous and wayward youngsters and of family disagreements.

Quoted in the *Daily Mail* 19 October 1989

4 1992 is not a year I shall look back on with undiluted pleasure. In the words of one of my more sympathetic correspondents, it has turned out to be an Annus Horribilis.

Speech at Guildhall, 24 November 1992, quoted in *The Times* 25 November 1992. In a speech commemorating her forty years on the throne, the Queen's allusion to JOHN DRYDEN's long poem 'Annus Mirabilis' (1667) was lost on much of the nation, though the tabloid press enjoyed it (see SUN 8). Dryden had described 1666 as a 'year of marvels', whose events included the Great Fire of London. A fire had gutted some of the State Apartments in Windsor Castle a few days before the Queen's speech, while other personal disasters included the separation of the Prince and Princess of Wales amid sustained criticism of the royal family in the press.

5 Some things stay there, some things go out of the other ear, and some things don't go in at all.

Quoted in the *Guardian* 20 April 1996. On her weekly meetings with prime ministers.

Elizabeth, Queen Mother
(1900–2002)
Wife of King George VI of Great Britain and Northern Ireland

Her decision to remain in London during the Blitz earned her the lasting affection of the British public. After her husband's death she undertook extensive public duties. To her friend Cecil Beaton, she was 'everyone's favourite granny', but to Princess DIANA she was 'chief leper in the leper colony'.

1 I'm glad we've been bombed. It makes me feel I can look the East End in the face.

Quoted in *King George VI*, pt 3, ch. 6 (1958) by John Wheeler-Bennett. Said to a policeman after the bombing of Buckingham Palace by German planes. The East End bore the brunt of the destruction in London during the Second World War.

2 The children will not leave unless I do, I shall not leave unless their father does, and the King will not leave the country in any circumstances whatever.

Attributed response to the suggestion that she and Princesses Elizabeth and Margaret be evacuated to Canada during the Blitz.

Ebenezer Elliot
(1781–1849)
English pamphleteer and poet

His poetry reflected the social and political concerns of his time. He campaigned against the Corn Laws and was the author of Corn Law Rhymes *(1831), for which he is best remembered.*

1 What is a communist? One who has yearnings
For equal division of unequal earnings.
Idler, or bungler, or both, he is willing
To fork out his penny, and pocket your shilling.

'Epigram' (1831), publ. in *Poetical Works* (1840)

Jane Elliot
(1727–1805)
Scottish poet

Her literary output is confined to one poem 'The Flowers of the Forest', which she wrote for a bet. She was the last person in Edinburgh to travel by sedan chair.

1 I've heard them lilting, at the ewe milking.
Lasses a' lilting, before dawn of day;

But now they are moaning, on ilka green loaning;
The flowers of the forest are a' wede away.
'The Flowers of the Forest' (written 1756, publ. 1769). Commemorates the Scottish soldiers who fell at Flodden (1513).

Havelock Ellis
(1859–1939)
British psychologist

His major work, Studies in the Psychology of Sex *(7 vols. 1897–1928), the first encyclopaedic treatment of the subject, was deemed scandalous, a 'filthy publication', and until 1935 was only legally available in the USA to doctors. He also published popular works on sex and the arts.*

1 To be a leader of men one must turn one's back on men.
Against the Grain, Introduction (1884) by Joris Karl Huysmans

2 All civilization has from time to time become a thin crust over a volcano of revolution.
Little Essays of Love and Virtue, ch. 7 (1922)

3 A man must not swallow more beliefs than he can digest.
The Dance of Life, ch. 5 (1923)

Richard Ellmann
(1918–87)
US biographer and essayist

In the words of ANTHONY BURGESS, *he 'brought American common sense and a European sensibility' to his portraits of 19th- and 20th-century English and Irish authors, notably* YEATS, JOYCE *and* WILDE.

1 The imagination should queen it over the mind, with reason as her obsequious butler and memory as her underpaid maid-of-all-work.
'Wallace Stevens's Ice-Cream' (1957), repr. in *a long the river-run,* pt 2 (1988)

2 Criticism prevents art from forgetting, prevents it from sinking into conformity.
'The Uses of Decadence: Wilde, Yeats, Joyce', lecture at Bennington, Vermont, 28 September 1983, repr. ibid.

Ben Elton
(b. 1959)
British author and comic

He co-wrote the comedy series The Young Ones *(1982, 1984) and* Blackadder *(1986–9), and has achieved success with his novels and rock musicals.*

1 People aren't greedy any more, oh no. They're shopaholics, victims of commercialism. Victims! People don't fail any more. They experience negative success.
Popcorn, ch. 11 (1996). Spoken by Bruce Delamitri.

2 If we're going to teach the kids to speak badly let's at least have people doing it who know the rules that are being broken.
Inconceivable (1999). Spoken by Tom, Head of Youth, BBC Radio, recorded in Sam's diary entry.

3 In our sad modern world female pop stars have to be very successful indeed before it is allowable for them to perform with their clothes on.
Sam's diary entry, ibid.

Paul Éluard
(1895–1952)
French poet

He was a leading figure in the Surrealist movement and published his first verse collection in Capitale de la douleur *(1926). He joined the Communist Party in 1942 and was active in the French Resistance.*

1 *Adieu tristesse*
Bonjour tristesse
Tu es inscrite dans les lignes du plafond.
[Farewell sadness
Good-day sadness
You are inscribed in the lines of the ceiling.]
'À peine défigurée', publ. in *La Vie immédiate* (1932). *Bonjour Tristesse* was the title of FRANÇOISE SAGAN's first novel.

Ralph Waldo Emerson
(1803–82)
US essayist, poet and philosopher

With THOREAU *he is regarded as the pivotal figure in New England's Transcendentalist movement. Major works include* Nature *(1836) and* The Conduct of Life *(1860).* OLIVER WENDELL HOLMES *compared him to an 'exotic transplanted from some angelic nursery'.*

1 A sect or a party is an elegant incognito, devised to save a man from the vexation of thinking.
Journal entry, 20 June 1831, publ. in *The Journals and Miscellaneous Notebooks of Ralph Waldo Emerson,* vol. 3 (ed. Alfred R. Ferguson and William H. Gilman, 1963)

2 There is then creative reading as well as creative writing. When the mind is braced by labor and invention, the page of whatever book we read becomes luminous with manifold allusion. Every

sentence is doubly significant, and the sense of our author is as broad as the world.

'The American Scholar', sect. 2, lecture to the Phi Beta Kappa Society, Harvard University, 31 August 1837, publ. in *Nature, Addresses and Lectures* (1849)

3 The office of the scholar is to cheer, to raise, and to guide men by showing them facts amidst appearances. He plies the slow, unhonored, and unpaid task of observation . . . He is the world's eye.

'The American Scholar', sect. 3, ibid.

4 By the rude bridge that arched the flood,
Their flag to April's breeze unfurled,
Here once the embattled farmers stood,
And fired the shot heard round the world.

'Concord Hymn' (1837). Sung on 4 July 1837 at the completion of the Concord Monument, erected to commemorate the Minutemen who routed the British at Concord, 19 April 1775. This battle precipitated the American Revolution.

5 The silence that accepts merit as the most natural thing in the world is the highest applause.

Address at Divinity College, Harvard University, 15 July 1838, publ. in *Addresses and Lectures* (1849)

6 Let me never fall into the vulgar mistake of dreaming that I am persecuted whenever I am contradicted.

Journal entry, 8 November 1838, publ. in *The Journals and Miscellaneous Notebooks of Ralph Waldo Emerson.* vol. 7 (ed. A. W. Plumstead and Harrison Hayford, 1969). See GEORGE ELIOT 4.

7 Time dissipates to shining ether the solid angularity of facts.

Essays, 'History' (first series, 1841)

8 There is properly no history, only biography.

Ibid., 'History'. Thomas Carlyle similarly wrote, in his journal, 13 January 1832: 'Biography is the only true history.' See also THOMAS CARLYLE 39.

9 Nature is an endless combination and repetition of a very few laws. She hums the old well-known air through innumerable variations.

Ibid., 'History'

10 In every work of genius we recognize our own rejected thoughts: they come back to us with a certain alienated majesty.

Ibid., 'Self-Reliance'

11 Society everywhere is in conspiracy against the manhood of every one of its members . . . The virtue in most request is conformity. Self-reliance is its

aversion. It loves not realities and creators, but names and customs.

Ibid., 'Self-Reliance'

12 A foolish consistency is the hobgoblin of little minds, adored by little statesmen and philosophers and divines.

Ibid., 'Self-Reliance'

13 To be great is to be misunderstood.

Ibid., 'Self-Reliance'

14 A character is like an acrostic or Alexandrian stanza; – read it forward, backward, or across, it still spells the same thing.

Ibid., 'Self-Reliance'

15 An institution is the lengthened shadow of one man.

Ibid., 'Self-Reliance'

16 As men's prayers are a disease of the will, so are their creeds a disease of the intellect.

Ibid., 'Self-Reliance'

17 The dice of God are always loaded.

Ibid., 'Compensation'

18 Commit a crime, and the earth is made of glass.

Ibid., 'Compensation'

19 The history of persecution is a history of endeavors to cheat nature, to make water run up hill, to twist a rope of sand.

Ibid., 'Compensation'

20 The martyr cannot be dishonored. Every lash inflicted is a tongue of fame; every prison a more illustrious abode.

Ibid., 'Compensation'

21 The less a man thinks or knows about his virtues, the better we like him.

Ibid., 'Spiritual Laws'

22 Sincerity is the luxury allowed, like diadems and authority, only to the highest rank . . . Every man alone is sincere. At the entrance of a second person, hypocrisy begins.

Ibid., 'Friendship'

23 I do then with my friends as I do with my books. I would have them where I can find them, but I seldom use them.

Ibid., 'Friendship'

24 In skating over thin ice, our safety is in our speed.

Ibid., 'Prudence'

25 Heroism feels and never reasons, and therefore is always right.
Ibid., 'Heroism'

26 Nothing astonishes men so much as common sense and plain dealing.
Ibid., 'Art'

27 The only gift is a portion of thyself.
Ibid., 'Gifts'

28 Literature is the effort of man to indemnify himself for the wrongs of his condition.
'Walter Savage Landor', publ. in *The Dial*, 1841, repr. in *Complete Works*, vol. 12 (1893)

29 Sorrow makes us all children again, destroys all differences of intellect. The wisest knows nothing.
Journal entry, 30 January 1842, publ. in *The Journals and Miscellaneous Notebooks of Ralph Waldo Emerson*, vol. 8 (ed. William H. Gilpin and J. E. Parsons, 1970)

30 The sky is the daily bread of the eyes.
Journal entry, 25 May 1843, ibid.

31 An empire is an immense egotism.
'The Young American', lecture to the Mercantile Library Association, Boston, 7 February 1844, publ. in *Addresses and Lectures* (1849)

32 Men are conservatives when they are least vigorous, or when they are most luxurious. They are conservatives after dinner, or before taking their rest; when they are sick or aged. In the morning, or when their intellect or their conscience has been aroused, when they hear music, or when they read poetry, they are radicals.
'New England Reformers', lecture to the Society in Amory Hall, 3 March 1844, publ. in *Essays* (second series, 1844)

33 Language is the archives of history.
'The Poet', ibid.

34 Things are in the saddle,
and ride mankind.
'Ode' inscribed to W. H. Channing, st. 8, publ. in *Poems* (1847)

35 The frolic architecture of the snow.
'The Snowstorm', ibid. Last line of poem.

36 *Immortality*. I notice that as soon as writers broach this question they begin to quote. I hate quotation. Tell me what you know.
Journal entry, May 1849, publ. in *Emerson in His Journals* (ed. Joel Porte, 1982)

37 Great geniuses have the shortest biographies.
Representative Men, 'Plato; or, the Philosopher' (1850)

38 No man acquires property without acquiring with it a little arithmetic also.
Ibid., 'Montaigne'

39 I find the Englishman to be him of all men who stands firmest in his shoes. They have in themselves what they value in their horses, mettle and bottom.
English Traits, 'Manners' (1856)

40 If a man knew anything, he would sit in a corner and be modest; but he is such an ignorant peacock, that he goes bustling up and down, and hits on extraordinary discoveries.
Ibid., 'Cockayne'

41 Nations have lost their old omnipotence; the patriotic tie does not hold. Nations are getting obsolete, we go and live where we will.
Ibid., 'Wealth'

42 We estimate the wisdom of nations by seeing what they did with their surplus capital.
Ibid., 'Wealth'

43 The Anglican Church is marked by the grace and good sense of its forms, by the manly grace of its clergy. The gospel it preaches is, 'By taste are ye saved.' . . . It is not in ordinary a persecuting church; it is not inquisitorial, not even inquisitive, is perfectly well bred and can shut its eyes on all proper occasions. If you let it alone, it will let you alone. But its instinct is hostile to all change in politics, literature, or social arts.
Ibid., 'Religion'

44 The revelation of Thought takes men out of servitude into freedom.
The Conduct of Life, 'Fate' (1860)

45 All successful men have agreed in one thing, – they were *causationists*. They believed that things went not by luck, but by law; that there was not a weak or a cracked link in the chain that joins the first and last of things.
Ibid., 'Power'

46 The key to the age may be this, or that, or the other, as the young orators describe; the key to all ages is – Imbecility; imbecility in the vast majority of men, at all times, and, even in heroes, in all but certain eminent moments; victims of gravity, custom, and fear.
Ibid., 'Power'

47 Every man is a consumer, and ought to be a

producer ... He is by constitution expensive, and needs to be rich.
Ibid., 'Wealth'

48 Property is an intellectual production. The game requires coolness, right reasoning, promptness, and patience in the players.
Ibid., 'Wealth'

49 Art is a jealous mistress, and, if a man have a genius for painting, poetry, music, architecture or philosophy, he makes a bad husband and an ill provider.
Ibid., 'Wealth'

50 New York is a sucked orange.
Ibid., 'Culture'

51 Can we never extract the tapeworm of Europe from the brain of our countrymen?
Ibid., 'Culture'

52 Manners are the happy way of doing things; each once a stroke of genius or of love – now repeated and hardened into usage. They form at last a rich varnish, with which the routine of life is washed, and its details adorned. If they are superficial, so are the dewdrops which give such depth to the morning meadows.
Ibid., 'Behavior'

53 There is one topic peremptorily forbidden to all well-bred, to all rational mortals, namely, their distempers. If you have not slept, or if you have slept, or if you have headache, or sciatica, or leprosy, or thunder-stroke, I beseech you, by all angels, to hold your peace, and not pollute the morning.
Ibid., 'Behavior'

54 The louder he talked of his honor, the faster we counted our spoons.
Ibid., 'Worship'

55 Souls are not saved in bundles.
Ibid., 'Worship'

56 Society is a masked ball, where every one hides his real character, and reveals it by hiding.
Ibid., 'Worship'

57 Passion, though a bad regulator, is a powerful spring.
Ibid., 'Considerations by the Way'

58 There are three wants which never can be satisfied: that of the rich, who wants something more; that of the sick, who wants something different; and that of the traveler, who says, 'Anywhere but here.'
Ibid., 'Considerations by the Way'

59 The secret of ugliness consists not in irregularity, but in being uninteresting.
Ibid., 'Beauty'

60 There is no chance, and no anarchy, in the universe. All is system and gradation. Every god is there sitting in his sphere.
Ibid., 'Illusions'

61 Next to the originator of a good sentence is the first quoter of it. Many will read the book before one thinks of quoting a passage. As soon as he has done this, that line will be quoted east and west.
Journal entry, 1867, publ. in *The Journals and Miscellaneous Notebooks of Ralph Waldo Emerson*, vol. 16 (ed. Ronald Bosco and Glen Johnson, 1982). The passage later appeared in *Letters and Social Aims*, 'Quotation and Originality' (1876), in which Emerson commented, 'By necessity, by proclivity, and by delight, we all quote.'

62 Hitch your wagon to a star. Let us not fag in paltry works which serve our pot and bag alone.
Society and Solitude, 'Civilization' (1870)

63 Raphael paints wisdom; Handel sings it, Phidias carves it, Shakespeare writes it, Wren builds it, Columbus sails it, Luther preaches it, Washington arms it, Watt mechanizes it.
Ibid., 'Art'

64 We boil at different degrees.
Ibid., 'Eloquence'

65 The greatest meliorator of the world is selfish, huckstering Trade.
Ibid., 'Works and Days'

66 One definition of man is 'an intelligence served by organs'.
Ibid., 'Works and Days'. Emerson may have taken this definition from *Théorie de Pouvoir Politique et Religieux* (1796) by Louis De Bonald. EDMOND AND JULES DE GONCOURT, in *The Goncourt Journals* (1888–96), commented: 'Man is a mind betrayed, not served, by his organs' (entry, 30 July 1861).

67 Only poetry inspires poetry.
Ibid., 'Books'

68 Wisdom is like electricity. There is no permanently wise man, but men capable of wisdom, who, being put into certain company, or other favorable conditions, become wise for a short time, as glasses rubbed acquire electric power for a while.
Ibid., 'Clubs'

69 America is a country of young men.
Ibid., 'Old Age'

70 Artists must be sacrificed to their art. Like bees, they must put their lives into the sting they give.
Letters and Social Aims, 'Inspiration' (1876)

71 I have heard with admiring submission the experience of the lady who declared that 'the sense of being perfectly well dressed gives a feeling of inward tranquility which religion is powerless to bestow.'
Ibid., 'Social Aims'. The lady in question was the English writer C. F. Forbes.

72 Things said for conversation are chalk eggs. Don't *say* things. What you *are* stands over you the while, and thunders so that I cannot hear what you say to the contrary.
Ibid., 'Social Aims'

73 Sentimentalists ... adopt whatever merit is in good repute, and almost make it hateful with their praise. The warmer their expressions, the colder we feel ... Cure the drunkard, heal the insane, mollify the homicide, civilize the Pawnee, but what lessons can be devised for the debauchee of sentiment?
Ibid., 'Social Aims'

74 What is a weed? A plant whose virtues have not yet been discovered.
Fortune of the Republic (1878)

75 Glittering generalities! They are blazing ubiquities!
Attributed. Referring to the criticism by Rufus Choate of the Declaration of Independence in a letter to the Maine Whig Central Committee, 9 August 1856: 'Its constitution the glittering and sounding generalities of natural right which make up the Declaration of Independence', publ. in *The Works of Rufus Choate with a Memoir of his Life*, vol. 1 (ed. S. G. Brown, 1862).

76 If a man can write a better book, preach a better sermon, or make a better mouse-trap, than his neighbor, though he build his house in the woods, the world will make a beaten path to his door.
Attributed. Ascribed to Emerson by Sarah Yule in the anthology *Borrowings* (1889), later said by her to originate in a lecture given by Emerson in 1871. Authorship of the remark was also claimed by ELBERT HUBBARD in *A Thousand and One Epigrams* (1911).

Dick Emery

(1917–83)

British comedian

After success in the BBC radio programme Educating Archie *(1958), he displayed his skill for characterization and drag sketches in* The Dick Emery Show *(1963–71).*

1 Ooh, you are awful ... but I like you!
Catch-phrase from *The Dick Emery Show* (1963–71). Emery used the same words in the role of the ageing sex kitten Mandy in the 1950s radio show *Educating Archie*. His record, 'You Are Awful', entered the top fifty in January 1973.

Robert Emmet

(1778–1803)

Irish patriot

A member of the United Irishmen, he plotted an uprising to seize Dublin Castle and was subsequently hanged.

1 Let no man write my epitaph; for, as no man who knows my motives dares now vindicate them, let not prejudice or ignorance asperse them. Let them and me rest in obscurity and peace, and my tomb remain uninscribed, and my memory in oblivion, until other times and other men can do justice to my character.
Speech from the dock, 19 September 1803, on the eve of his execution, publ. in *The Penguin Book of Historic Speeches* (ed. Brian MacArthur, 1995)

(Sir) William Empson

(1906–84)

British poet and critic

He was Professor of English Literature at Sheffield (1953–71). The most noted of his critical works was Seven Types of Ambiguity *(1930). His* Collected Poems *were published in 1955.*

1 Seven Types of Ambiguity.
Title of book (1930)

2 Waiting for the end, boys, waiting for the end.
'Just a smack at Auden', publ. in *The Gathering Storm* (1940). First and last line of poem.

Friedrich Engels

(1820–95)

German social philosopher

With KARL MARX, *he was the architect of modern communism. As a successful businessman in Manchester, he funded Marx from 1848, and collaborated with him in the writing of* The Communist Manifesto *(1848) and other works. See* KARL MARX AND FRIEDRICH ENGELS.

1 The state is not 'abolished', it withers away.
Anti-Düring, pt 3, ch. 2 (1878)

2 People think they have taken quite an extraordinarily bold step forward when they have rid themselves of belief in hereditary monarchy and swear by the democratic republic. In reality, however, the state is nothing but a machine for the oppression of one class by another, and indeed in the democratic republic no less than in the monarchy.
Introduction (1891) to *The Civil War in France* (1871) by Karl Marx

3 By bourgeoisie is meant the class of modern capitalists, owners of the means of social production and employers of wage labour. By proletariat, the class of modern wage laborers who, having no means of production of their own, are reduced to selling their labour power in order to live.
Manifesto of the Communist Party, Footnote (1888 edn)

4 An ounce of action is worth a ton of theory.
Quoted in *The Strange Case of Victor Grayson*, ch. 2 (1975) by Reg Groves

Hans Magnus Enzensberger
(b. 1929)
German poet and critic

The best known of Germany's post-Brechtian poets, he writes in a caustic and laconic style. His publications include Poems for People Who Don't Read Poems *(1968) and the narrative* The Sinking of The Titanic *(1978).*

1 That one gets used to everything –
One gets used to that.
The usual name for it is
A learning process.
'The Force of Habit', publ. in *Gedichte 1955–70* (1971)

2 Slowly
the scab peels off. A new tobacconist,
a new address. Pariahs, horribly relieved.
Shades growing paler. These are the documents.
This is the bunch of keys. This is the scar.
'The Divorce', publ. in *Gedichte 1950–85* (1986), repr. in *Selected Poems* (1994, transl. Michael Hamburger)

3 Pleasure and terror have given way to normality, and normality, wherever time is on its side, conquers everything.
Europe, Europe, 'Epilogue: The Seacoast of Bohemia' (1989). Referring to Berlin.

Nora Ephron
(b. 1941)
US author and screenwriter

Sex, marriage and middle-class crises are her primary subject matter. Her screenplays include When Harry Met Sally *(1989) and* Sleepless in Seattle *(1993), which she also directed.*

1 I'll have what she's having.
When Harry Met Sally... (film, 1989, screenplay by Nora Ephron, directed and co-produced by Rob Reiner). Woman diner (played by Reiner's mother) to waiter, after observing Sally Albright (Meg Ryan) act out an orgasm.

Epic of Gilgamesh
(2nd millennium BC)

It tells the story of Gilgamesh, a semi-historical king of Uruk, a city in southern Mesopotamia, who sought the secret of eternal life, undergoing many trials in the process. The epic existed in an oral tradition long before it was written; the version we have today was preserved on twelve tablets from c. 2000 BC.

1 Gilgamesh was his name from the day he was
born,
two-thirds of him god but a third of him human.
Tablet 1, ll. 47–8, publ. in *The Babylonian Gilgamesh Epic*, vol. 1, ch. 11 (ed. A. R. George, 2003)

2 As for man, his days are numbered,
all that ever he did is but wind.
Tablet 2, ll. 234–5, ibid., vol. 1, ch. 11. The words of Gilgamesh to Enkidu.

3 A three-ply rope is not easily broken.
Tablet 5, l. 76, ibid., vol. 1, ch. 11. Spoken by Enkidu. Proverbial in Sumerian, Babylonian and Hebrew (see BIBLE, OLD TESTAMENT: ECCLESIASTES 13).

4 No one sees death,
no one sees the face of death,
no one hears the voice of death:
[yet] savage death is the one who hacks man
down.
Tablet 10, ll. 304–7, ibid., vol. 1, ch. 11 Spoken by Uta Napishti.

Epictetus
(c. 55–c. 135)
Greek philosopher

He was an advocate of the Stoic philosophy; his beliefs and maxims were published posthumously in Discourses *and the* Encheiridion.

1 We are not to give credit to the many, who say that none ought to be educated but the free; but

rather to the philosophers, who say that the well-educated alone are free.

Discourses, bk 2, ch. 1 (transl. Elizabeth Carter, 1758)

2 Never say of anything, 'I have lost it'; but 'I have restored it.' Is your child dead? It is restored. Is your wife dead? She is restored. Is your your estate taken away? Well: and is not that likewise restored?

Encheiridion, no. 11 (transl. Elizabeth Carter, 1758)

3 Remember that you must behave [in life] as at an entertainment. Is any thing brought round to you? Put out your hand and take your share, with moderation. Doth it pass by you? Do not stop it. Is it not yet come? Do not stretch forth your desire towards it, but wait till it reaches you. Thus [do] with regard to children, to a wife, to public posts, to riches: and you will be some time or other a worthy partner of the feasts of the gods. And if you do not so much as take the things which are set before you, but are able even to despise them, then you will not only be a partner of the gods, but of their empire also.

Ibid., no. 15

4 You are a little soul carrying around a corpse.

Epictetus – The Discourses, The Manual and Fragments, vol. 2, 'Fragments', no. 26 (ed. and transl. W. Oldfather, 1928). Also quoted by MARCUS AURELIUS in *Meditations*, bk 4, no. 41.

Desiderius Erasmus
(c. 1466–1536)
Dutch humanist

The most renowned European scholar of his day, he published his own Greek edition of the New Testament (1516), with a Latin translation which was used as the basis for the King James version. He satirized the shortcomings of the church in Colloquia Familiaria (1518).

1 In the country of the blind the one-eyed man is king.

Adages, bk 3, century 4, no. 96 (1500)

2 Jupiter, not wanting man's life to be wholly gloomy and grim, has bestowed far more passion than reason – you could reckon the ration as twenty-four to one. Moreover, he confined reason to a cramped corner of the head and left all the rest of the body to the passions.

Praise of Folly, ch. 16 (1509)

3 Now I believe I can hear the philosophers protesting that it can only be misery to live in folly, illusion, deception and ignorance, but it isn't – it's human.

Ibid., ch. 32

4 They take unbelievable pleasure in the hideous blast of the hunting horn and baying of the hounds. Dogs' dung smells sweet as cinnamon to them.

Ibid., ch. 38. Referring to hunters.

5 The entire world is my temple, and a very fine one too, if I'm not mistaken, and I'll never lack priests to serve it as long as there are men.

The Goddess of Folly, *ibid.*, ch. 47

6 It's the generally accepted privilege of theologians to stretch the heavens, that is the Scriptures, like tanners with a hide.

Ibid., ch. 64

7 It is wisdom in prosperity, when all is as thou wouldst have it, to fear and suspect the worst.

Proverbs or Adages of Erasmus, fol. 32 (ed. Richard Taverner, 1545)

Susan Ertz
(1894–1985)
British novelist

Her novels, which largely deal with family relationships, include Madame Claire *(1923),* Now We Set Out *(1935) and* Charmed Circle *(1956).*

1 Millions long for immortality who do not know what to do with themselves on a rainy Sunday afternoon.

Mrs A., in *Anger in the Sky*, ch. 5 (1943)

Robert Devereux, Earl of Essex
(1566–1601)
English soldier and courtier

He was the sometime favourite of his cousin ELIZABETH I, who, following his successful military exploits in the Netherlands, made him Master of Horse in 1587. He became a privy councillor in 1593 but lost favour with the Queen and intrigued against her, resulting in his execution.

1 I was never proud, till your Majesty sought to make me too base.

Letter to ELIZABETH I, August 1598, publ. in *The Life and Death of Robert Devereux, Earl of Essex*, ch. 12 (1937) by G. B. Harrison. After a quarrel in which the Queen had boxed his ears.

Henri Estienne
(1531–98)
French scholar and publisher

He published editions of Greek and Latin works and the Thesaurus Graecae Linguae *(1572) as well as treatises on the French language.*

1 *Si jeunesse savoit; si vieillesse pouvoit.*
[If youth but knew; if age but could.]
Les Prémices, bk 4, epigram 191 (1594)

Sir George Etherege
(1635–91)
English dramatist and diplomat

His three plays The Comical Revenge *(1664),* She Would If She Could *(1668) and* The Man of Mode *(1676) were highly popular comedies of manners in their day.*

1 When love grows diseased, the best thing we can do is to put it to a violent death; I cannot endure the torture of a lingering and consumptive passion.
The Man of Mode, Act 2, Sc. 2 (1676). Spoken by Dorimant.

2 Writing, madam, 's a mechanic part of wit! A gentleman should never go beyond a song or a *billet*.
Sir Fopling, ibid., Act 4, Sc. 1

Euclid
(*fl. c.* 300 BC)
Greek mathematician

A teacher in Alexandria, he is known for Elementa, *the standard work in geometry until the 19th century.*

1 *Quod erat demonstrandum.*
[Which was to be proved.]
Elementa, bk 1, proposition 5 and *passim*. The words are best known in the Latin translation of the Greek original, or simply as 'Q.E.D.'.

2 A line is length without breadth.
Elementa, bk 1, definition 2

Euripides
(480–406 BC)
Greek dramatist

He was the author of nineteen extant plays, including Alcestis, Medea, Electra *and* The Bacchae, *introducing to the tragic form a new realism and interest in feminine psychology.*

1 Better a serpent than a stepmother!
Alcestis, l. 310 (438 BC, transl. Gilbert Murray, 1915). Spoken by Alcestis.

2 Let mortal man keep to his own
Mortality, and not expect too much.
Herakles, ibid., ll. 799–800

3 I love the old way best, the simple way
Of poison, where we too are strong as men.
Medea, ll. 384–5 (431 BC, transl. Gilbert Murray, 1906). Spoken by Medea.

4 For the weariest road that man may wend
Is forth from the home of his father.
Corinthian women, ibid., ll. 650–1

5 Alas, a woman's bosom bears
But woman's courage, a thing born for tears.
Medea, ibid., ll. 928–9

6 Yea, I know to what bad things
I go, but louder than all thought doth cry
Anger, which maketh man's worst misery.
Medea, ibid., ll. 1078–80

7 'Twas but my tongue, 'twas not my soul that swore.
Hippolytus, l. 612 (428 BC, transl. Gilbert Murray, 1902). Spoken by Hippolytus.

8 'Tis in such gifts
As these I care for riches, to make gifts
To friends, or lead a sick man back to health
With ease and plenty. Else small aid is wealth
For daily gladness; once a man be done
With hunger, rich and poor are all as one.
Electra, ll. 426–31 (413 BC, transl. Gilbert Murray, 1902). Spoken by Peasant.

9 Lose not thy path watching a distant view.
Rhesus, l. 482 (transl. Gilbert Murray, 1913). Spoken by Hector.

10 Those whom the gods wish to destroy, they first make mad.
Attributed

Anthony H. Euwer
(1877–1955)
US author and illustrator

1 As a beauty I'm not a great star.
Others are handsomer far;
But my face – I don't mind it
Because I'm behind it;
It's the folks out in front that I jar.
Limeratomy (1917). Often quoted by WOODROW WILSON.

John Evelyn
(1620–1706)
English diarist

Chiefly remembered for his Diary, *published in 1818, he was a pioneer in forestry and gardening and a founder member of the Royal Society.*

1 A studious decliner of honours and titles.
Diary of John Evelyn, Introduction (1818). Referring to his father.

2 I saw Hamlet Prince of Denmark played, but now the old play began to disgust this refined age.
Journal entry, 26 November 1661, ibid.

Gavin Ewart
(1916–95)
British poet

His light verse is often parodic in style, as in The Pleasures of the Flesh *(1966) and* Penultimate Poems *(1989).*

1 There are sorrows in herds that are too deep for words.
'How Tragedy is Impossible', publ. in *Or Where a Young Penguin Lies Screaming* (1977). The words recall WILLIAM WORDSWORTH 93.

2 The path of true love isn't smooth,
the ruffled feathers sex can soothe
ruffle again – for couples never
spend all their lives in bed together.
'24th March 1986', publ. in *Late Pickings* (1987)

3 If men's lives are worth giving, they're also worth saving.
Who let them start the bloody thing?
That's the question, there's the sting.
'The Falklands, 1982', publ. in *Selected Poems* (1996). Closing lines of poem.

W. N. Ewer
(1885–1976)
British journalist

William Norman Ewer, nicknamed 'Trilby'. Recruited as one of 'Lansbury's Lambs', he was Foreign Correspondent on the Daily Herald *1919–64 and Overseas Service correspondent for the BBC.*

1 I gave my life for freedom – this I know:
For those who bade me fight had told me so.
'Five Souls', publ. in *Five Souls and Other Verses* (1917)

2 How odd
Of God
To choose
The Jews.
Week-End Book (1924). This caused a riposte by the American businessman Cecil Brown: 'But not so odd/As those who choose/A Jewish God/But spurn the Jews.

F

Quintus Fabius Maximus
(c. 275–203 BC)
Roman statesman and general

His strategy of caution in engaging the Carthaginian enemy after the Battle of Cannae in 216 BC caused him to be known as Fabius Cunctator (The Delayer).

1 To be turned from one's course by men's opinions, by blame, and by misrepresentation shows a man unfit to hold office.
Quoted in *Parallel Lives*, 'Fabius Maximus', sect. 5 by PLUTARCH

Robert Fabyan
(d. 1513)
English chronicler

A clothier and alderman, he was one of the first chroniclers to combine a history of London with that of England.

1 King Henry [I] being in Normandy, after some writers, fell from or with his horse, whereof he caught his death; but Ranulphe says he took a surfeit by eating of a lamprey, and thereof died.
The New Chronicles of England and France, vol. 1, ch. 229 (1516)

2 The Duke of Clarence . . . then being a prisoner in the Tower, was secretly put to death and drowned in a barrel of Malmesey wine within the said Tower.
Ibid., vol. 2, '1478'

Clifton Fadiman
(1904–99)
US essayist

Calling himself an 'odd job man', he has written widely, including literary criticism and children's books.

1 I encountered the mama of dada again . . . and as usual withdrew worsted.
Party of One (1955). Referring to GERTRUDE STEIN.

2 A cheese may disappoint. It may be dull, it may be naive, it may be oversophisticated. Yet it remains cheese, milk's leap toward immortality.
Any Number Can Play (1957)

Marianne Faithfull

(b. 1946)

British singer

She was a wistful singer of the 1960s, and the much publicized girlfriend of MICK JAGGER, *later reviving her musical career with the album* Broken English *(1979).*

1 Maybe the most you can expect from a relationship that goes bad is to come out of it with a few good songs.

Faithfull, 'Colston Hall' (1994). Referring to her relationship with MICK JAGGER.

Lord Falkland

(1610–43)

English statesman, soldier and patron

Lucius Cary, Viscount Falkland. He served as Secretary of State under CHARLES I, *and was killed fighting for the Royalists at the Battle of Newbury.*

1 When it is not necessary to change, it is necessary not to change.

'A Speech concerning Episcopacy', to House of Commons, 22 November 1641, publ. in *Discourses on the Infallibility of the Church of Rome* (1660)

Oriana Fallaci

(b. 1930)

Italian journalist and author

Renowned for her hard-nosed interviewing techniques, she has published The Useless Sex *(1960) and* Interview with History *(1976), as well as novels including* A Man *(1979).*

1 All banners, even the most noble, the most pure, are filthy with blood and shit. When you look at the glorious banners displayed in museums, in churches, venerated as relics to kneel before in the name of ideals, dreams, have no illusions: those brownish stains are not traces of rust, they are dried blood, dried shit, and more often shit than blood.

A Man, pt 5, ch. 1 (1979)

Frantz Fanon

(1925–61)

French West Indian psychiatrist, philosopher and political activist

His experiences during the Algerian revolution led him to write The Wretched of the Earth *(1961), which, urging a 'collective catharsis', became a manifesto for liberation struggles against colonial powers.*

1 Fervour is the weapon of choice of the impotent.

Black Skins White Masks, Introduction (1952, transl. 1967)

2 Colonialism is not a thinking machine, nor a body endowed with reasoning faculties. It is violence in its natural state, and it will only yield when confronted with greater violence.

The Wretched of the Earth, ch. 1 (1961)

3 Nationalism, that magnificent song that made the people rise against their oppressors, stops short, falters and dies away on the day that independence is proclaimed.

Ibid., ch. 3

Eleanor Farjeon

(1881–1965)

British children's author

She wrote plays and contributed to Punch *and the* Daily Herald, *but is best known for her numerous poems and stories written for children.*

1 Morning has broken
Like the first morning,
Blackbird has spoken
Like the first bird.

'A Morning Song (for the First Day of Spring)' (1931), publ. in *The Children's Bells* (1957). The song was a hit for CAT STEVENS in 1972.

Edward Farmer

(c. 1809–76)

English poet

1 I have no pain, dear mother, now;
But oh! I am so dry:
Just moisten poor Jim's lips once more;
And, mother, do not cry!

'The Collier's Dying Child'. See ANONYMOUS 40 for a parody of this verse.

Farouk I

(1920–65)

King of Egypt

Increasingly absorbed in his hedonistic lifestyle, the last reigning king of Egypt (1936–52) was forced to abdicate in a coup d'état. He went into exile and became a citizen of Monaco in 1959.

1 The whole world is in revolt. Soon there will be only five kings left – the King of England, the King

of Spades, the King of Clubs, the King of Hearts and the King of Diamonds.

Remark in 1948, quoted in *Life* 10 April 1950. The words were addressed to John (later Lord) Boyd-Orr, first director of the Food and Agriculture Organization, at a conference in Cairo, also quoted in Boyd-Orr's memoirs, *As I Recall*, ch. 21 (1966).

George Farquhar
(1678–1707)
Irish dramatist

He wrote spirited and witty comedies for the London stage from 1697, notably The Recruiting Officer *(1706) and* The Beaux' Stratagem *(1707). His work represented a departure from Restoration theatre and proved popular, though he died in poverty.*

1 Money is the sinews of love, as of war.

Love and a Bottle, Act 2, Sc. 1 (1698). Spoken by Roebuck.

2 Poetry is a mere drug, Sir.

Pamphlet, ibid., Act 3, Sc. 2

3 Observe this, that though a woman swear, forswear, lie, dissemble, back-bite, be proud, vain, malicious, anything, if she secures the main chance, she's still virtuous; that's a maxim.

The Constant Couple, Act 1, Sc. 2 (1699). Spoken by Lady Lurewell.

4 Grant me some wild expressions, Heavens, or I shall burst.

Lady Lurewell, ibid., Act 5, Sc. 3

5 We love the precepts for the teacher's sake.

Sir Harry Wildair, ibid., Act 5, Sc. 3

6 'Tis a strange thing, Sam, that among us people can't agree the whole week, because they go different ways upon *Sundays*.

Letter, 15 October 1700, in *Love and Business* (1701)

7 Crimes, like virtues, are their own rewards.

The Inconstant, Act 4, Sc. 2 (1702). Spoken by Oriana.

8 I could be mighty foolish, and fancy myself mighty witty; Reason still keeps its throne, but it nods a little, that's all.

The Recruiting Officer, Act 3, Sc. 2 (1706). Spoken by Plume.

9 I have fed purely upon ale; I have eat my ale, drank my ale, and I always sleep upon ale.

The Beaux' Stratagem, Act 1, Sc. 1 (1707). Spoken by the landlord Boniface.

10 There is no scandal like rags, nor any crime so shameful as poverty.

Archer, a 'gentleman of broken fortunes', ibid., Act 1, Sc. 1

11 We are the men of intrinsic value, who can strike our fortunes out of ourselves, whose worth is independent of accidents in life, or revolutions in government: we have heads to get money, and hearts to spend it.

Archer, ibid., Act 1, Sc. 1

12 I believe they talked of me, for they laughed consumedly.

Scrub, ibid., Act 3, Sc. 1

13 'Twas for the good of my country that I should be abroad. – Anything for the good of one's country – I'm a Roman for that.

Gibbet, a highwayman, ibid., Act 3, Sc. 1

David Glasgow Farragut
(1801–70)
US naval commander

As a Unionist he assisted in the capture of Vicksburg (1863) and Mobile Bay (1864), and he became the first admiral of the US navy in 1866.

1 Damn the torpedoes! Full speed ahead.

Quoted in *Great Commanders: Admiral Farragut*, ch. 10 (1892) by A. T. Mahan. Remark at the Battle of Mobile Bay, 5 August 1864.

The Fast Show

Television series on BBC 2 (1994–7), consisting of short sketches written and produced by Paul Whitehouse and Charlie Higson.

1 Does my bum look big in this?

Spoken by Arabella Weir, and the title of a book by her

2 Ooh, suit you sir!

Tailors Ken and Kenneth (Paul Whitehouse and Mark Williams)

3 Scorchio!

Weathergirl (Caroline Aherne)

William Faulkner
(1897–1962)
US novelist

His novels, including The Sound and the Fury *(1929) and* Absalom, Absalom! *(1936), are primarily narratives of 'the tragic fable of southern history' set in the fictional Mississippi county of Yoknapatawpha. 'Mr Faulkner is interested in making your mind rather than your flesh creep,' wrote* CLIFTON FADIMAN.

1 Poor man. Poor mankind.

Light in August, ch. 4 (1932). Spoken by Gail Hightower, referring to Joe Christmas, accused of murder.

2 I know that for fifty years I have not even been clay: I have been a single instant of darkness in which a horse galloped and a gun crashed.
Gail Hightower, ibid., ch. 20

3 *I don't hate it* he thought, panting in the cold air, the iron New England dark; *I don't. I don't. I don't hate it! I don't hate it!*
Absalom, Absalom!, ch. 9 (1936). Quentin on his native South, in the closing words of the novel.

4 I believe that man will not merely endure: he will prevail. He is immortal, not because he alone among creatures has an inexhaustible voice, but because he has a soul, a spirit capable of compassion and sacrifice and endurance. The poet's, the writer's, duty is to write about these things.
Nobel Prize acceptance speech in Stockholm, 10 December 1950, publ. in *The Penguin Book of Twentieth-Century Speeches* (ed. Brian MacArthur, 1999)

5 Maybe the only thing worse than having to give gratitude constantly . . . is having to accept it.
Requiem For a Nun, Act 2, Sc. 1 (1951). Spoken by Temple Drake.

6 If a writer has to rob his mother, he will not hesitate; the 'Ode on a Grecian Urn' is worth any number of old ladies.
Interview publ. in *Writers at Work* (first series, ed. Malcolm Cowley, 1958)

7 One of the saddest things is that the only thing that a man can do for eight hours a day, day after day, is work. You can't eat eight hours a day nor drink for eight hours a day nor make love for eight hours – all you can do for eight hours is work. Which is the reason why man makes himself and everybody else so miserable and unhappy.
Interview, ibid.

Guy Fawkes
(1570–1606)
English conspirator

He was executed for his part in the Gunpowder Plot which aimed to blow up the Houses of Parliament, 5 November 1605.

1 A desperate disease requires a dangerous remedy.
Remark, 6 November 1605, quoted in *The Dictionary of National Biography*, vol. 6 (1917). On the Gunpowder Plot. See also HIPPOCRATES 2.

Federico Fellini
(1920–93)
Italian film-maker

His idiosyncratic films, which he always scripted himself, include La Dolce Vita *(1960),* 8½ *(1963) and* Amarcord *(1973), all partly autobiographical. 'Although my father wanted me to become an engineer and my mother a bishop,' he stated, 'I myself am quite content to have succeeded in becoming an adjective.'*

1 Censorship is a way of admitting our own weakness and intellectual insufficiency.
  Censorship is always a political tool: certainly not an intellectual one. Criticism is an intellectual tool: it presupposes a knowledge of what one judges and opposes.
  Criticism does not destroy; it puts an object in its proper place among other objects.
  To censor is to destroy, or at least to oppose the process of reality.
'Notes on Censorship', publ. in *La Tribuna del Cinema*, no. 2, August 1958, repr. in *Fellini on Fellini* (ed. Anna Keel and Christian Strich, 1974)

2 The movie business is macabre. Grotesque. It is a combination of a football game and a brothel.
New Yorker 30 October 1965, repr. ibid., 'Miscellany II', sect. 21

3 I have invented myself entirely: a childhood, a personality, longings, dreams and memories, all in order to enable me to tell them.
L'Arc, no. 45 (1971), ibid., 'Miscellany I', sect. 10

4 Cinéma-vérité? I prefer 'cine-mendacity'. A lie is always more interesting than the truth. Lies are the soul of showmanship and I adore shows.
L'Arc, no. 45 (1971), ibid., 'Miscellany II', sect. 6

James Fenton
(b. 1949)
British poet and critic

His experience as a freelance journalist and foreign correspondent informs his poetry, which is strongly influenced by W. H. AUDEN. *His poetry collections include* The Memory of War *(1982) and* Out of Danger *(1993).*

1 It is not what they built. It is what they knocked down.
It is not the houses. It is the spaces between the houses.

It is not the streets that exist. It is the streets that
no longer exist.

'German Requiem' publ. in *The Memory of War* (1982). Opening lines.

2 I didn't exist at Creation,
I didn't exist at the Flood,
And I won't be around for Salvation
To sort out the sheep from the cud –
Or whatever the phrase is. The fact is
In soteriological terms
I'm a crude existential malpractice
And you are a diet of worms.

'God, A Poem', publ. in *Children in Exile* (1983)

3 Tienanmen
Is broad and clean
And you can't tell
Where the dead have been
And you can't tell
When they'll come again
They'll come again
To Tienanmen

'Tienanmen', publ. in *Out of Danger* (1993). The poem, dated
15 June 1989, was written in response to the savage suppression of protesters that had just taken place in Beijing's
Tienanmen Square. Fenton later revealed that he wrote it to
the tune of 'Strange Fruit' (see BILLIE HOLIDAY 1).

Edna Ferber
(1887–1968)
US author

*A prolific writer of short stories and novels that vividly evoke
America in the 1920s and '30s, she is best remembered for*
Show Boat *(1926), which became a hit on Broadway and as a
film.*

1 Roast Beef, Medium, is not only a food. It is a
philosophy.

Roast Beef, Medium, Foreword (1911)

2 I am not belittling the brave pioneer men but the
sunbonnet as well as the sombrero has helped to
settle this glorious land of ours.

Cimarron, ch. 23 (1929, filmed 1931 and 1960). Spoken by Sabra
Cravat.

3 A woman can look both moral and exciting – if
she also looks as if it was quite a struggle.

Quoted in *Reader's Digest* December 1954

4 Being an old maid is like death by drowning, a
really delightful sensation after you cease to
struggle.

Quoted in *The Algonquin Wits* (ed. Robert E. Drennan, 1968)

Ferdinand I
(1503–64)
King of Bohemia and Hungary

*He was King of Bohemia and Hungary (1526–64) and respon-
sible for the Peace of Augsburg (1555) which allowed Germany
greater autonomy over religious affairs. He was Holy Roman
Emperor 1558–64.*

1 *Fiat justitia et pereat mundus.*
[Let justice be done, though the world perish.]

Adopted as Ferdinand I's motto in the early 1530s, it has been
ascribed to Lucius Calpurnius Piso Caesoninus (d. 43 BC) in
the form, 'Let justice be done, though heaven should fall.'
[*Fiat justitia ruat coelum.*]

(Sir) Samuel Ferguson
(1810–86)
Irish poet, lawyer and antiquarian

Admired as a poet by W. B. YEATS, *he became President of the
Royal Academy in 1882.*

1 Dear thoughts are in my mind, and my soul
soars enchanted
As I hear the sweet lark sing in the clear air of the
day.

'The Lark in the Clear Air' (1850). Set to a traditional Irish air,
it was popularized as a song by John McCormack.

Ludwig Feuerbach
(1804–72)
German philosopher

His most important work The Essence of Christianity *(1841),
which suggested that Christian dogma and beliefs are illusory,
was a strong influence on* MARX *and* ENGELS.

1 If therefore my work is negative, irreligious,
atheistic, let it be remembered that atheism – at
least in the sense of this work – is the secret of
religion itself; that religion itself, not indeed on the
surface, but fundamentally, not in intention or
according to its own supposition, but in its heart, in
its essence, believes in nothing else than the truth
and divinity of human nature.

The Essence of Christianity, Preface (1843 edn)

2 The present age . . . prefers the sign to the thing
signified, the copy to the original, fancy to reality,
the appearance to the essence . . . for in these days
illusion only is *sacred, truth profane.*

Ibid., Preface

3 Man is what he eats.

Quoted in *Lehre der Nahrungsmittel: Für das Volk*, 'Advertisement' (1850) by Jacob Moleschott. See JEAN-ANTHELME BRIL-LAT-SAVARIN 1.

Eugene Field
(1850–95)
US poet and journalist

He wrote poems for children, and a popular column 'Sharps and Flats' for the Chicago Morning News *from 1883.*

1 Mr Clarke played the King all evening as though under constant fear that someone else was about to play the ace.
Denver Post *c.*1880, quoted in *The Portable Woollcott*, 'Capsule Criticism' (1946) by ALEXANDER WOOLLCOTT. Referring to actor Creston Clarke's performance as King Lear.

2 Wynken, Blynken and Nod one night
Sailed off in a wooden shoe,
Sailed on a river of crystal light,
Into a sea of dew.
'Wynken, Blynken and Nod' (1889), repr. in *Poems of Childhood* (1904)

3 No matter what conditions
Dyspeptic come to feaze,
The best of all physicians
Is apple-pie and cheese!
'Apple Pie and Cheese', publ. in *A Little Book of Western Verse* (1890)

Helen Fielding
(b. 1958)
British author

Creator of the 'Bridget Jones Diary' in the Independent *in 1995, she successfully transferred her thirty-something heroine to novel form in* Bridget Jones's Diary *(1996) and its sequel,* Bridget Jones – The Edge of Reason *(2000).*

1 You should have said 'I'm not married because I'm a *Singleton*, you smug, prematurely ageing, narrow-minded morons.'
Bridget Jones's Diary, 'Wednesday 1 February' (1996). Shazzer's advice to Bridget, who responds: 'Singletons! Hurrah for the Singletons!'

Henry Fielding
(1707–54)
English novelist and playwright

Hailed as 'the prose Homer of human nature' by BYRON, *he was the author of picaresque novels such as* Joseph Andrews *(1742), a parody of* SAMUEL RICHARDSON's Pamela *(1740), and* Tom Jones *(1749). He was also responsible for the introduction of the Bow Street Runners in 1749.*

1 Dancing begets warmth, which is the parent of wantonness. It is, Sir, the great grandfather of cuckoldom.
Love in Several Masques, Act 3, Sc. 7 (1728). Spoken by Sir Positive Trap.

2 Love and scandal are the best sweeteners of tea.
Lady Matchless, ibid., Act 4, Sc. 11

3 All nature wears one universal grin.
Tom Thumb the Great, Act 1, Sc. 1 (1730). Spoken by Doodle.

4 Oh the roast beef of England,
And old England's roast beef!
The Grub Street Opera, Act 3, Sc. 3, Air 45 (1731). 'The King's Old Courtier', sung by Susan.

5 I have found it; I have discovered the cause of all the misfortunes which befell him. A public school, Joseph, was the cause of all the calamities which he afterwards suffered. Public schools are the nurseries of all vice and immorality.
Joseph Andrews, bk 3, ch. 5 (1742). Abraham Adams, referring to his host, Wilson.

6 He in a few minutes ravished this fair creature, or at least would have ravished her, if she had not, by a timely compliance, prevented him.
Jonathan Wild, bk 3, ch. 7 (1743, rev. 1754). Referring to Fireblood's conquest of Laetitia.

7 When I mention religion, I mean the Christian religion; and not only the Christian religion, but the Protestant religion; and not only the Protestant religion, but the Church of England.
Tom Jones, bk 3, ch. 3 (1749). Spoken by Thwackum, Tom's tutor.

8 Thwackum was for doing justice, and leaving mercy to Heaven.
Ibid., bk 3, ch. 10

9 What is commonly called love, namely, the desire of satisfying a voracious appetite with a certain quantity of delicate white human flesh.
Ibid., bk 6, ch. 1

10 O! more than Gothic ignorance.
Mrs Western, ibid., bk 7, ch. 3

11 His designs were strictly honourable, as the phrase is; that is, to rob a lady of her fortune by way of marriage.
Mrs Fitzpatrick, ibid., bk 11, ch. 4. Referring to Mr Fitzpatrick.

12 The republic of letters.
Ibid., bk 14, ch. 1. See OLIVER GOLDSMITH 4.

13 It is not death, but dying, which is terrible.
Amelia, bk 3, ch. 4 (1751). The words of Booth.

14 Guilt has very quick ears to an accusation.
Booth, ibid., bk 3, ch. 11

15 One fool at least in every married couple.
Ibid., bk 9, ch. 4. Dr Harrison refers to Booth and Amelia.

16 There is not in the universe a more ridiculous, nor a more contemptible animal than a proud clergyman.
Ibid., bk 9, ch. 10

Dorothy Fields
(1904–74)
US songwriter

A prolific lyricist of such enduring songs as 'On the Sunny Side of the Street' (1930), she also wrote libretti for musicals, including Annie Get Your Gun *(1946) for* IRVING BERLIN.

1 Grab your coat, and get your hat,
Leave your worry on the doorstep,
Just direct your feet
To the sunny side of the street.
'On the Sunny Side of the Street' (song, co-written with Jimmy McHugh) in *The International Revue* (musical show, 1930)

2 You're calmer than the seals in the Arctic Ocean
At least they flap their fins to express emotion.
'A Fine Romance' (song, with music by Jerome Kern) in *Swing Time* (film, 1936)

3 So let me get right to the point.
I don't pop my cork for every guy I see.
Hey! big spender, spend a little time with me.
'Big Spender' (song, with music by Cy Coleman) in *Sweet Charity* (stage musical 1966, film 1969). The song was a hit for Shirley Bassey in 1967.

W. C. Fields
(1879–1946)
US actor

Originally William Claude Dukinfield. 'I am free of all prejudices – I hate everybody equally,' declared this red-nosed, gravel-voiced, hard drinking misogynist. He wrote many of the numerous comedies he appeared in, including My Little Chickadee *(with* MAE WEST, *1940). See also* LEO ROSTEN 1.

1 Here lies W. C. Fields. I would rather be living in Philadelphia.
Suggested epitaph, as told to *Vanity Fair* June 1925. Fields, who was born in Philadelphia, may have had in mind an anecdote about GEORGE WASHINGTON, who was reported to have uttered a similar sentiment regarding the choice of New York as federal capital in 1789. Fields' words (which were never actually used as his epitaph) are usually remembered, 'I'd rather be in Philadelphia', the form in which RONALD REAGAN quoted them when recovering in hospital from an assassination attempt in 1981.

2 And remember, dearie, never give a sucker an even break.
Professor Eustace McGargle, in *Poppy* (film, 1936, screenplay by Waldemar Young and Virginia Van Upp from play by Dorothy Donnelly, directed by A. Edward Sutherland). Fields is earlier reported to have uttered these words on stage in the musical comedy *Poppy* (1923), though they do not appear in the libretto. 'Never give a sucker an even break' became Fields' catchphrase and the title of one of his last films, made in 1941 (called *What a Man* in Britain).

3 I was in love with a beautiful blonde once, she drove me to drink. 'Tis the one thing I'm indebted to her for.
The Great Man (W. C. Fields), in *Never Give a Sucker an Even Break* (film, 1941, screenplay by John T. Neville and Prescott Chaplin based on a story by Fields, directed by Edward F. Cline)

4 Hell, I never vote *for* anybody. I always vote *against*.
Quoted in *W.C. Fields: His Follies and Fortunes*, ch. 25 (1950) by Robert Lewis Taylor. Said to Gene Fowler who wrote two books about him.

5 Fish fuck in it.
Attributed. On why he never drank water.

Anne Finch
See LADY WINCHILSEA

Ernst Fischer
(1899–1972)
Austrian editor, poet and critic

A member of the Communist Party 1934–69, he was Minister of Culture and Education in the Austrian National Assembly. The Necessity of Art (1959) and Art Against Ideology (1966) are his principal works of Marxist aesthetics.

1 As machines become more and more efficient and perfect, so it will become clear that *imperfection is the greatness of man.*
The Necessity of Art, ch. 5 (1959)

2 To provoke dreams of terror in the slumber of prosperity has become the moral duty of literature.
Art Against Ideology, ch. 1 (1966)

Michael Fish

(b. 1944)

British meteorologist

Britain's longest-serving TV weatherman (1974–2004) joined the Meteorological Office in 1962 and the London Weather Centre in 1967.

1 A woman rang to say she heard there was a hurricane on the way. Well, don't worry, there isn't.

Weather forecast on BBC TV, 15 October 1987. The 'Great Storm' which struck southern England that night claimed seventeen lives and caused approximately £300 million of damage. Winds gusted up to 110 mph, falling within the scale of hurricane force.

Carrie Fisher

(b. 1956)

US actor, author and screenwriter

Daughter of Eddie Fisher and Debbie Reynolds, she writes caustically and wittily of Hollywood in her novels. She has appeared in the films Star Wars *(as Princess Leia, 1977) and* The Blues Brothers *(1980).*

1 Who am I? I'm with him, that's who.

Surrender the Pink, ch. 7. Spoken by Dinah.

2 Look at us, we're chicks lost in the netherworld of our gender, absorbed in the world of potential purchase.

Dinah, ibid., ch. 9

H. A. L. Fisher

(1865–1940)

British historian and politician

Herbert Albert Laurens Fisher. He was Liberal MP for Hallam, Sheffield (1916–18), and the English Universities (1918–26). As President of the Board of Education, he introduced the 1918 Education Act, state scholarships to universities and the School Certificate.

1 Men wiser and more learned than I have discerned in history a plot, a rhythm, a predetermined pattern. These harmonies are concealed from me. I can see only one emergency following upon another as wave follows upon wave, only one great fact with respect to which, since it is unique, there can be no generalizations, only one safe rule for the historian: that he should recognize in the development of human destinies the play of the contingent and the unforeseen.

A History of Europe, Preface (1935)

2 Purity of race does not exist. Europe is a continent of energetic mongrels.

Ibid., ch. 1

3 Politics is the art of human happiness.

Ibid., ch. 31

Lord Fisher

(1841–1920)

British naval commander

John Arbuthnot Fisher, First Baron of Kilverstone. Appointed First Sea Lord in 1904, he was responsible for introducing Dreadnought battleships and Invincible battle cruisers in preparation for the First World War.

1 Never contradict.
Never explain.
Never apologize.

The 'secrets of a happy life', in letter to *The Times*, 5 September 1919

M. F. K. Fisher

(1908–92)

US culinary writer

Mary Frances Kennedy Fisher. One of the most highly regarded of food writers, she presented food as a metaphor for life and love in her books, which include The Gastronomical Me *(1943) and* An Alphabet for Gourmets *(1949).*

1 Once at least in the life of every human, whether he be brute or trembling daffodil, comes a moment of complete gastronomic satisfaction.

Serve It Forth, 'The Pale Yellow Glove' (1937)

2 Sharing food with another human being is an intimate act that should not be indulged in lightly.

An Alphabet for Gourmets, 'A is for Dining Alone' (1949)

3 Gastronomical perfection can be reached in these combinations: one person dining alone, usually upon a couch or a hillside; two people, of no matter what sex or age, dining in a good restaurant; six people, of no matter what sex or age, dining in a good home.

Ibid., 'From A–Z: The Perfect Dinner'

Robert Fisk

(b. 1946)

British journalist and author

Since covering events in Northern Ireland in the early 1970s, he has worked as foreign correspondent in Lebanon, and written extensively on the Israeli-Arab conflict and Iraq.

1 At best, journalists sit at the edge of history as vulcanologists might clamber to the lip of a smoking crater, trying to see over the rim, craning their necks to peer over the crumbling edge through the smoke and ash at what happens within.
Pity The Nation, Preface (1990)

2 'Terrorists' are those who use violence against the side that is using the word.
Ibid., ch. 12

3 It might be as well for the West to remember that history in the Middle East rarely rewards the just. It never favours the foreigner and it always takes its revenge upon those who see the region through their own eyes. Not once has a foreign military adventure in the Middle East achieved its end.
Quoted in the *Guardian* 14 August 1990

Edward Fitzgerald
See OMAR KHAYYÁM

F. Scott Fitzgerald
(1896–1940)
US author

Francis Scott Fitzgerald. Considered the 'white hope of American letters' by H. L. MENCKEN, *he evoked the hedonism of the Jazz Age in his short stories and the novels* The Great Gatsby *(1925) and* Tender is the Night *(1934). He was married to* ZELDA FITZGERALD. *'Sometimes I don't know whether Zelda and I are real or whether we are characters in one of my novels,' he once confessed.*

1 At eighteen our convictions are hills from which we look; at forty-five they are caves in which we hide.
Bernice Bobs Her Hair, sect. 2 (1920)

2 My idea is always to reach my generation. The wise writer . . . writes for the youth of his own generation, the critics of the next, and the schoolmasters of ever afterward.
'Self-interview' (1920), repr. in *Some Sort of Epic Grandeur*, ch. 16 (biography, 1981) by Matthew J. Bruccoli. The text was also used by Fitzgerald in 'The Author's Apology', a letter to the American Booksellers Convention, May 1920.

3 Everybody's youth is a dream, a form of chemical madness.
The Diamond as Big as the Ritz, ch. 11 (1922). Spoken by John. Kismine replies: 'How pleasant then to be insane!'

4 Personality is an unbroken series of successful gestures.
The Great Gatsby, ch. 1 (1925). Narrated by Nick Carraway.

5 Every one suspects himself of at least one of the cardinal virtues, and this is mine. I am one of the few honest people that I have ever known.
Narrator, ibid., ch. 3

6 I've been drunk for about a week now, and I thought it might sober me up to sit in a library.
Ibid., ch. 3. Spoken by an unnamed guest at one of Gatsby's parties.

7 There are only the pursued, the pursuing, the busy, and the tired.
Ibid., ch. 4

8 What'll we do with ourselves this afternoon? And the day after that, and the next thirty years?
Daisy Buchanan, ibid., ch. 7

9 Her voice is full of money.
Gatsby, of Daisy Buchanan, ibid., ch. 7. The narrator (Nick Carraway) adds: 'that was the inexhaustible charm that rose and fell in it, the jingle of it, the cymbals' song of it . . .'

10 They were careless people, Tom and Daisy – they smashed up things and creatures and then retreated back into their money or their vast carelessness, or whatever it was that kept them together, and let other people clean up the mess they had made.
Ibid., ch. 9

11 For a transitory enchanted moment man must have held his breath in the presence of this continent, compelled into an aesthetic contemplation he neither understood nor desired, face to face for the last time in history with something commensurate to his capacity for wonder.
Ibid., ch. 9

12 So we beat on, boats against the current, borne back ceaselessly into the past.
Ibid., ch. 9. Closing words of book.

13 Let me tell you about the very rich. They are different from you and me. They possess and enjoy early, and it does something to them, makes them soft where we are hard, and cynical where we are trustful, in a way that, unless you were born rich, it is very difficult to understand. They think, deep in their hearts, that they are better than we are because we had to discover the compensations and refuges of life for ourselves. Even when they enter deep into

our world or sink below us, they still think that they are better than we are. They are different.

All the Sad Young Men, 'The Rich Boy' (1926). The story's first sentence also occurs in Fitzgerald's notebooks (*The Crack-Up*, 'Notebook E,' 1945) and was taken up by Hemingway in 'The Snows of Kilimanjaro' (1936) (see ERNEST HEMINGWAY 14).

14 The early twenties when we drank wood alcohol and every day in every way grew better and better, and there was a first abortive shortening of the skirts, and girls all looked alike in sweater dresses, and people you didn't want to know said 'Yes, we have no bananas,' and it seemed only a question of a few years before the older people would step aside and let the world be run by those who saw things as they were – and it all seems rosy and romantic to us who were young then, because we will never feel quite so intensely about our surroundings any more.

'Echoes of the Jazz Age' (1931), repr. in *The Crack-Up* (ed. Edmund Wilson, 1945). 'Though the Jazz Age continued,' Fitzgerald wrote, 'it became less and less an affair of youth. The sequel was like a children's party taken over by the elders.'

15 The hangover became a part of the day as well allowed-for as the Spanish siesta.

'My Lost City' (1932), ibid.

16 One writes of scars healed, a loose parallel to the pathology of the skin, but there is no such thing in the life of an individual. There are open wounds, shrunk sometimes to the size of a pin-prick but wounds still. The marks of suffering are more comparable to the loss of a finger, or the sight of an eye. We may not miss them, either, for one minute in a year, but if we should there is nothing to be done about it.

Tender is the Night, bk 2, ch. 11 (1934)

17 The test of a first-rate intelligence is the ability to hold two opposed ideas in the mind at the same time, and still retain the ability to function.

'The Crack-Up' (1936), repr. in *The Crack-Up* (ed. Edmund Wilson, 1945). See also GEORGE ORWELL 40.

18 In a real dark night of the soul it is always three o'clock in the morning, day after day.

'Handle With Care' (1936), ibid. See SAINT JOHN OF THE CROSS 1.

19 I am not a great man, but sometimes I think the impersonal and objective quality of my talent and the sacrifices of it, in pieces, to preserve its essential value has some sort of epic grandeur.

Letter to his daughter Frances Scott Fitzgerald, spring 1940,

ibid. The words 'some sort of epic grandeur' were used by Matthew J. Bruccoli as a title for his 1981 biography of Fitzgerald.

20 There are no second acts in American lives.

The Last Tycoon, 'Hollywood, Etc.' (ed. Edmund Wilson, 1941)

21 Show me a hero and I will write you a tragedy.

The Crack-Up, 'Notebook E' (ed. Edmund Wilson, 1945)

22 No grand idea was ever born in a conference, but a lot of foolish ideas have died there.

Ibid., 'Notebook E'

23 Men get to be a mixture of the charming mannerisms of the women they have known.

Ibid., 'Notebook E'

24 Listen, little Elia: draw your chair up close to the edge of the precipice and I'll tell you a story.

Ibid., 'Notebook E'

25 All good writing is *swimming under water* and holding your breath.

Letter (undated) to his daughter Frances Scott Fitzgerald, ibid., 'Notebook E'

Zelda Fitzgerald
(1900–48)
US author

Married to F. SCOTT FITZGERALD *in 1920, she wrote a series of sketches (1928–9) which were published in* College Humor, *and a novel* Save Me the Waltz *(1932). In 1930 she suffered the first of her mental breakdowns. She died in a hospital fire.*

1 I don't want to live – I want to love first, and live incidentally.

Letter to F. SCOTT FITZGERALD, March 1919, quoted in *Zelda*, pt 1, ch. 4 (1970) by Nancy Milford

2 We grew up founding our dreams on the infinite promise of American advertising.

Save Me the Waltz, ch. 4, sect. 3 (1932). Spoken by Alabama Beggs, who continues: 'I *still* believe that one can learn to play the piano by mail and that mud will give you a perfect complexion.'

3 Ernest, don't you think Al Jolson is greater than Jesus?

Quoted by ERNEST HEMINGWAY in *A Moveable Feast*, ch. 18 (1964). Her remark anticipated John Lennon's famous claim (see JOHN LENNON 2).

Bud Flanagan
(1896–1968)
British singer and comedian

Born Reeven Weintrop. With his partner Chesney Allen he formed one of the most popular comedy duos of the 1930s and '40s, whose numbers included 'Underneath the Arches' (1932) and 'Run, Rabbit, Run' (1939). In 1929 they joined the anarchic comedy team, the Crazy Gang.

1 Underneath the Arches,
I dream my dreams away,
Underneath the Arches,
On cobble-stones I lay.

'Underneath the Arches' (song, 1932, written with Chesney Allen). According to his autobiography, *My Crazy Life*, ch. 8 (1961), Flanagan conceived what was to be Flanagan and Allen's signature tune while backstage at the Derby Hippodrome in 1926. The 'Arches' were underneath London's Charing Cross station, a gathering-place for tramps. The song was renamed 'Underneath The Bridges' in America, where it was thought 'arches' might be misconstrued as 'feet'.

Oliver Flanagan
(1920–87)
Irish politician

He joined Fine Gael in 1950 and rose to become Minister for Local Government 1975–6 and for Defence 1976–7. He strongly opposed changes in the contraceptive and divorce laws.

1 Let us hope and trust that there are sufficient proud and ignorant people left in this country to stand up to the intellectuals who are out to destroy faith and fatherland.

Quoted in the *Irish Times* 10 April 1971

2 There was no sex in Ireland until the BBC came.

Quoted in *Ireland and the Irish: Portrait of a Changing Society*, ch. 6 (1994) by John Ardagh

Michael Flanders
(1922–75)

Donald Swann
(1923–94)
British songwriters and entertainers

Between 1956 and 1967 their songwriting partnership produced such shows as At the Drop of a Hat (1956) and At the Drop of Another Hat (1963). Swann, who was confined to a wheelchair through polio, likened their collaboration to a 'cooking process', with the piano taking the place of the kitchen stove.

1 Mud, mud, glorious mud,
Nothing quite like it for cooling the blood!
So follow me, follow,
Down to the hollow
And there let us wallow
In glorious mud!

'The Hippopotamus' (song, written 1952), in *At the Drop of a Hat* (revue, 1956). The song was entirely written by Flanders who took the tune from 'Beer, Beer, Glorious Beer!', a familiar song of the time.

2 And all the world over, each nation's the same,
They've simply no notion of Playing the Game:
They argue with umpires; they cheer when they've won;
And they practise beforehand, which ruins the fun!
The English, the English, the English are best:
So up with the English, and down with the rest!

'A Song of Patriotic Prejudice' (song), in *At the Drop of Another Hat* (revue, 1965).

3 I'm a G-nu, I'm a G-nu,
The g-nicest work of g-nature at the zoo!
I'm a G-nu, how do you do?
You really ought to k-now w-ho's w-ho.

'The Gnu' (song) ibid. According to Swann's autobiography *A Life In Song* (1991), the ditty derived from the frustrations of parking in central London: Kensington Borough Council had dug up the pavement outside Flanders' studio in order to facilitate wheel-chair access for him, but the path was often blocked by a car with the number plate letters GNU.

4 That monarch of the road,
Observer of the Highway Code,
That big six-wheeler
Scarlet-painted
London Transport
Diesel-engined
Ninety-seven horse power
Omnibus!

'A Transport of Delight' (song), ibid.

5 Have Some Madeira, M'dear.

Title of song, ibid.

6 Eating people is wrong!

'The Reluctant Cannibal' (song), ibid. The words were the title of a novel (1959) by MALCOLM BRADBURY.

7 Pee! Po! Belly! Bum! Drawers!
Let's write rude words all down our street,
Stick out our tongues at the people we meet,
Let's have an intellectual treat.

'P**! P*! B****! B**! D******!' (song), from *Extiary* (1961)

Gustave Flaubert

(1821–80)

French novelist

A key figure among the French Realists, he achieved prominence for his first novel Madame Bovary *(1857) for which he was unsuccessfully prosecuted for immorality.* Trois contes *(1877) demonstrates his versatility with the short story.*

1 It is wrong to think that feeling is everything. In the arts, it is nothing without form.

Letter to Louise Colet, 12 August 1846, publ. in *The Letters of Gustave Flaubert 1830–1857* (ed. Francis Steegmuller, 1980)

2 From time to time, in the towns, I open a newspaper. Things seem to be going at a dizzy rate. We are dancing not on a volcano, but on the rotten seat of a latrine. Before very long, society is going to drown in nineteen centuries of shit, and there'll be a lot of shouting.

Letter to Louis Bouilhet, 14 November 1850, ibid.

3 What a heavy oar the pen is, and what a strong current ideas are to row in!

Letter to Louise Colet, 23 October 1851, ibid.

4 Prose was born yesterday: you have to keep that in mind. Verse is the form par excellence of ancient literatures. All possible prosodic variations have been discovered; but that is far from being the case with prose.

Letter to Louise Colet, 24 April 1852, ibid.

5 Everything one invents is true, you may be sure. Poetry is as precise as geometry.

Letter to Louise Colet, 14 August 1853, ibid.

6 Great ideas grow in the shade and on the edge of precipices, like firs.

Letter to Louise Colet, September 1853, publ. in *The Selected Letters of Gustave Flaubert* (ed. Francis Steegmuller, 1954)

7 An artist must be in his work like God in creation, invisible and all-powerful: he should be everywhere felt, but nowhere seen.

Letter to Mademoiselle Leroyer de Chantepie, 18 March 1857, ibid. See JAMES JOYCE 18.

8 Human speech is like a cracked kettle on which we tap crude rhythms for bears to dance to, while we long to make music that will melt the stars.

Madame Bovary pt 2, ch. 12 (1857)

9 Axiom: hatred of the Bourgeois is the beginning of virtue.

Letter to GEORGE SAND, 10 May 1867, publ. in *The Selected Letters of Gustave Flaubert* (ed. Francis Steegmuller, 1954)

James Elroy Flecker

(1884–1915)

English poet

His best known works are 'The Golden Journey to Samarkand' (1913) and the drama Hassan *(1922), reflecting his interests in the Orient.*

1 We who with songs beguile your pilgrimage
And swear that beauty lives though lilies die,
We poets of the proud old lineage
Who sing to find your hearts, we know not why, –
What shall we tell you? Tales, marvellous tales
Of ships and stars and isles where good men rest.

'The Golden Journey to Samarkand', Prologue, publ. in *The Golden Journey to Samarkand* (1913). Opening lines of poem.

2 For lust of knowing what should not be known,
We take the Golden Road to Samarkand.

'The Golden Journey to Samarkand', Epilogue, ibid. Spoken by a merchant. The lines also occur in *Hassan*, Act 5, Sc. 2 (1922), spoken by Ishak.

3 The dragon-green, the luminous, the dark, the
serpent-haunted sea,
The snow-besprinkled wine of earth, the
white-and-blue-flower foaming sea.

'Gates of Damascus', ibid.

4 And some to Meccah turn to pray, and I toward
thy bed, Yasmin.

'Yasmin', ibid. The line also occurs in *Hassan*, Act 1, Sc. 2 (1922), spoken by Hassan.

5 For one night or the other night
Will come the gardener in white, and gathered
flowers are dead, Yasmin.

'Yasmin', ibid. Last lines of poem.

6 A ship, an isle, a sickle moon –
With few but with how splendid stars
The mirrors of the sea are strewn
Between their silver bars!

'A Ship, an Isle, a Sickle Moon', ibid. Opening lines of poem.

7 West of these out to seas colder than the
Hebrides I must go
Where the fleet of stars is anchored and the young
Star-captains glow.

'The Dying Patriot', ibid. Last lines of poem.

8 I have seen old ships sail like swans asleep.

'The Old Ships', publ. in *The Old Ships* (1915). Opening lines of poem.

9 As from the eagle flies the dove

So friendship from the claw of love.
Hassan, Act 1, Sc. 2 (1922). Spoken by Selim.

10 It is a pity. Soft carpets make soft the sole of the foot. And they who have soft feet should ever keep them on the road of meekness.
Rafi, ibid., Act 2, Sc. 1

Ian Fleming
(1908–64)
British author

He achieved worldwide success with his spy thrillers featuring the suave agent 007, James Bond, who first appeared in Casino Royale *(1953). He referred to his books, most of which were later filmed, as 'straight pillow fantasies of the bang-bang, kiss-kiss variety'.*

1 Bond, James Bond.
Casino Royale, ch. 7 (1953). Bond's introduction of himself occurs in various similar forms in Fleming's books and in the film adaptations. James Bond was the name of an ornithologist who wrote *Field Guide to Birds of the West Indies* (1936), still considered the definitive guide.

2 A medium Vodka dry Martini – with a slice of lemon peel. Shaken and not stirred, please. I would prefer Russian or Polish vodka.
Dr. No, ch. 14 (1958). Spoken by James Bond. Bond's favourite tipple made its first appearance in *Casino Royale*, ch. 7 (1953), where it is served 'in a deep champagne goblet'. He instructs the barman: 'Three measures of Gordon's, one of vodka, half a measure of Kina Lillet. Shake it very well until it's ice-cold, then add a large slice of lemon-peel.' Fellow spy Felix Leiter calls it a 'Molotov Cocktail'. The words 'shaken and not stirred' also occur in *Diamonds are Forever* (1956).

Marjory Fleming
(1803–11)

Aged six, she was sent to Edinburgh to stay with her cousin Isa, who encouraged her to keep a journal. She died of meningitis, aged eight.

1 O lovely O most charming pug
Thy graceful air and heavenly mug.
'Sonnet', publ. in *The Complete Marjory Fleming* (ed. F. Sidgwick, 1935)

Andrew Fletcher of Saltoun
(1655–1716)
Scottish politician

A member of the Scottish parliament, he was the author of Two Discourses Concerning the Affairs of Scotland *(1698) and opposed the Act of Union of 1707.*

1 If a man were permitted to make all the ballads, he need not care who should make the laws of a nation.
An Account of a Conversation concerning a Right Regulation of Government for the Good of Mankind (1704), repr. in *Andrew Fletcher of Saltoun: Selected Political Writings and Speeches* (ed. David Daiches, 1979). In this conversation held with the Earl of Cromarty, Sir Edward Seymour and Sir Christopher Musgrave, the comment was a reply to Musgrave's statement: 'Even the poorer sort of both sexes are daily tempted to all manner of lewdness by infamous ballads sung in every corner of the streets.'

John Fletcher
(1579–1625)
English dramatist

He collaborated with FRANCIS BEAUMONT *as well as with* MASSINGER, *William Rowley and* SHAKESPEARE, *and was the author of some sixteen plays in his own right. See also* FRANCIS BEAUMONT AND JOHN FLETCHER; SHAKESPEARE: HENRY VIII *and* SHAKESPEARE: THE TWO NOBLE KINSMEN.

1 Drink today, and drown all sorrow;
You shall perhaps not do't tomorrow.
The Bloody Brother, or *Rollo, Duke of Normandy* , Act 2, Sc. 2, 'Song' (1639, written with BEN JONSON and others)

2 And he that will go to bed sober,
Falls with the leaf still in October.
 Song, ibid., Act 2, Sc. 2

3 Come landlord fill a flowing bowl until it does
 run over,
Tonight we will all merry be – tomorrow we'll get
 sober.
Song, ibid., Act 2, Sc. 2

4 Three merry boys, and three merry boys,
And three merry boys are we,
As ever did sing in a hempen string
Under the gallows tree.
Song, ibid., Act 3, Sc. 2

5 Of all the paths lead to a woman's love
Pity's the straightest.
The Knight of Malta, Act 1, Sc. 1 (written with PHILIP MASSINGER, 1647)

6 Weep no more, nor sigh, nor groan,
Sorrow calls no time that's gone;
Violets plucked, the sweetest rain
Makes not fresh nor grow again.
The Queen of Corinth, Act 3, Sc. 2 (written with PHILIP MASSINGER, 1647)

7 Hence, all you vain delights,

As short as are the nights
Wherein you spend your folly!
There's naught in this life sweet
But only melancholy;
O sweetest melancholy!

The Night's Valour, Act 3, Sc. 3 (written with THOMAS MIDDLETON, 1647). See also ROBERT BURTON 1.

Phineas Fletcher
(1582–1650)
English clergyman and poet

Ordained into the Anglican church in 1615, he is best known for his religious and scientific poem 'The Purple Island: or the Isle of Man' (1633).

1 Love's tongue is in the eyes.

Eclogue 5 ('Nicaea'), publ. in *The Purple Island: or The Isle of Man, together with Piscatory Eclogues and other Poetical Miscellanies* (1633)

2 Drop, drop, slow tears,
And bathe those beauteous feet,
Which brought from Heaven
The news and Prince of Peace.
In your deep floods
Drown all my faults and fears;
Not let His eye
See sin, but through my tears.

'Hymn', ibid.

Jean Pierre Claris de Florian
(1755–94)
French author

The writer of comedies and poetical and pastoral novels, he is best remembered for the poem 'Célestine' (1784) and his Fables *(1792).*

1 *Plaisir d'amour ne dure qu'un moment,
Chagrin d'amour dure toute la vie.*
[The pleasures of love are but a moment long
The pains of love last a lifetime through.]

'Célestine' (1784). The song was popularized by Yvonne Printemps in 1931 and JOAN BAEZ in 1968.

John Florio
(c. 1553–1625)
English author and translator

His work Second Frutes *(1591) contained six thousand Italian proverbs. He published an Italian dictionary in 1598 and a well-known translation of* MONTAIGNE *in 1603.*

1 For proverbs are the pith, the proprieties, the proofs, the purities, the elegancies, as the commonest so the commendablest phrases of a language. To use them is a grace, to understand them a good.

Second Frutes, Preface (1591)

2 To long for that which comes not. To lie a-bed and sleep not. To serve well and please not. To have a horse that goes not. To have a man obeys not. To lie in jail and hope not. To be sick and recover not. To lose one's way and know not. To wait at door and enter not, and to have a friend we trust not: are ten such spites as hell hath not.

Ibid., ch. 1. Spoken by Nolano.

3 White teeth, white hands, and neck as ivory white,
Black eyes, black brows, black hairs that hide delight:
Red lips, red cheeks, and tops of nipples red,
Long legs, long fingers, long locks of her head,
Short feet, short ears, and teeth in measure short,
Broad front, broad breast, broad hips in seemly sort,
Straight legs, straight nose and straight her pleasures place,
Full thighs, full buttocks, full her belly's space,
Thin lips, thin eyelids, and hair thin and fine,
Small mouth, small waist, small pupils of her eyes.

Ibid., ch. 8. James's notion of beauty in a woman.

4 England is the paradise of women, the purgatory of men, and the hell of horses.

Silvestro, ibid., ch. 12

5 A good husband makes a good wife.

Silvestro, ibid., ch. 12. The adage also appears in *Anatomy of Melancholy*, pt 3, sect. 3 (1621) by ROBERT BURTON.

Dario Fo
(b. 1926)
Italian playwright

His plays, usually co-written and co-produced with his wife Franca Rame, blend satire and farce with a strong left-wing slant, and have been frequently censored. His company, formed in 1957, scored an international success with Accidental Death of an Anarchist *(1970).*

1 Accidental Death of an Anarchist.

Title of play (1970). The play concerns the death of a suspect who fell, or was pushed, from the fourth-floor window of a police station during questioning.

2 We're up to our necks in shit, it's true, and that's why we walk with our heads held high.

Accidental Death of an Anarchist, Act 2. Spoken by the Madman.

3 Can't Pay? Won't Pay!

Title of play (1974, transl. 1978). The original title of *Non si paga, non si paga* was the slogan used in the play by a group of housewives in a working-class suburb of Milan protesting against supermarket prices by stealing the goods. First translated as *We Can't Pay? We Won't Pay!*, the revised English title became *Can't Pay? Won't Pay!* for its 1981 London production. See POLITICAL SLOGANS 8.

Ferdinand Foch

(1851–1929)
French general

He was Supreme Commander of the Allied Forces on the Western front in 1918 and dictated the terms of the armistice, achieving his lifelong ambition of restoring Alsace and Lorraine to France.

1 If defeat comes from moral causes, victory may come from moral causes also, and one may say: 'A battle won is a battle we will not acknowledge to be lost.'

Quoted in *Reputations*, 'Ferdinand Foch' (1928) by B. H. Liddell Hart. Foch's conclusion was reached from musing on his favourite aphorism by the French political philosopher Joseph de Maistre (1753–1821): 'A lost battle is a battle which one believes lost: in a material sense no battle can be lost.'

2 My centre is giving way, my right is in retreat; situation excellent. I shall attack.

Attributed, quoted ibid., 'Ferdinand Foch'. Allegedly a message sent to General Joffre during the Battle of the Marne 8 September 1914, the words are probably apocryphal, reflecting the grim obstinacy with which Foch was associated, indicated also by the repeated exhortation he made to his troops, even in the most hopeless conditions: *Attaquez!* According to Liddell Hart, his reckless insistence during this battle resulted in the decimation of the companies under his command, and the eventual German withdrawal astonished the exhausted French troops. Other versions of the quote include: 'My right gives way, my centre yields, everything's fine – I shall attack.'

J. Foley

(1906–70)
British songwriter

1 Old soldiers never die,
They simply fade away.

'Old Soldiers Never Die' (song, 1920). The song may have originated in or prior to the First World War.

Barbara Follett

(b. 1942)
British politician

A founder member of 'Emily's List', which promoted women's candidacy for parliamentary office (1992), she was elected Labour MP for Stevenage in 1997.

1 Lipstick is power.

Attributed in the *Observer* 25 February 1996. Follett repudiated her most quoted soundbite.

Michael Foot

(b. 1913)
British politician

A journalist and the author of literary and political biographies, he was a Labour MP 1945–92 and party leader 1980–83, stepping down after a crushing electoral defeat by MARGARET THATCHER.

1 It is not necessary that every time he [Norman Tebbit] rises he should give his famous imitation of a semi-house-trained polecat.

Speech to House of Commons, 2 March 1978, publ. in *Hansard*, col. 668

2 It's quite a change to have a Prime Minister who hasn't got any political ideas at all.

Quoted in the *Observer* 24 February 1991. Referring to JOHN MAJOR.

Samuel Foote

(1720–77)
English dramatist and actor

Called the 'English Aristophanes' he was a noted mimic and was revered and feared for his wit on and off the stage. SAMUEL JOHNSON said of him: 'Foote is quite impartial, for he tells lies of everybody.'

1 The offspring of a dunghill! Born in a cellar . . . and living in a garret; a fungus, a mushroom.

The Author, Act 2, Sc. 1 (1757). Spoken by Cadwallader.

2 What can he mean by coming among us? He is not only dull himself, but the cause of dullness in others.

Quoted in entry for 1783, in *Life of Samuel Johnson, LL.D.* (1791) by JAMES BOSWELL. Referring to 'a law-lord, who, it seems, once took a fancy to associate with the wits of London'.

3 So she went into the garden to cut a cabbage-leaf to make an apple-pie; and at the same time a great she-bear coming up the street, pops its head into the shop. 'What! no soap?' So he died, and she very

imprudently married the barber; and there were present the Picninnies, and the Joblillies, and the Garyulies, and the grand Panjandrum himself, with the little round button at top; and they all fell to playing the game of catch as catch can, till the gun powder ran out at the heels of their boots.

Quoted by Harry and Lucy's father, in *Harry and Lucy*, vol. 2 (1825) by MARIA EDGEWORTH. Given as a test of memory to the actor CHARLES MACKLIN.

Anna Ford
(b. 1943)
British broadcaster

Having presented Man Alive *and* Tomorrow's World *for the BBC (1976–8), she became an ITN newscaster and later a presenter with TV-am (1978–82).*

1 Let's face it, there are no plain women on television.

Quoted in the *Observer* 23 September 1979

Gerald Ford
(b. 1913)
US politician and president

A Republican, he was appointed Vice-President under NIXON *in 1973 and became President the following year in the wake of the Watergate scandal. The subsequent economic depression contributed to his defeat in the 1976 election. See* LYNDON B. JOHNSON 8.

1 I am a Ford, not a Lincoln.

Address on taking vice-presidential oath, 6 December 1973, quoted in *A Ford, Not a Lincoln*, ch. 2 (1975) by Richard Reeves. Ford explained: 'My addresses will never be as eloquent as Lincoln's. But I will do my best to equal his brevity and plain speaking.' Eight months later, Ford was sworn in as President. He told Congress: 'The truth is I am the people's man.' (12 August 1974)

2 Our long national nightmare is over. Our Constitution works; our great Republic is a government of laws and not of men. Here the people rule.

Speech on succeeding RICHARD NIXON as President, 9 August 1974, publ. in *Public Papers of the Presidents of the United States* (1974)

3 Truth is the glue that holds government together.

Speech, 9 August 1974, ibid. Ford used these words on various occasions.

4 There is no Soviet domination of Eastern Europe and there never will be under a Ford administration ... The United States does not concede that those countries are under the domination of the Soviet Union.

TV debate with presidential contender JIMMY CARTER, 6 October 1976, publ. in *Great Debates* (1979) by S. Kraus. When asked to explain this statement, Ford admitted: 'I was perhaps not as precise as I should have been.'

Henry Ford
(1863–1947)
US industrialist

Hailed as the 'demi-god of the machine age', he was the pioneer of mass production. In 1903 he founded the Ford Motor Company, which by 1909 had produced the famous Model T, of which 15 million were sold in the next nineteen years.

1 Any customer can have a car painted any colour that he wants so long as it's black.

My Life and Work, ch. 4 (1922) with Samuel Crowther. Remark made in 1909, referring to the Model T. He continued: 'I cannot say that anyone agreed with me.'

2 History is more or less bunk. It's tradition. We don't want tradition. We want to live in the present and the only history that is worth a tinker's damn is the history we make today.

Interview in the *Chicago Tribune* 25 May 1916. Ford had to defend his views of history during an eight-day cross-examination in the course of a libel suit he had initiated against the *Tribune*, after an editorial had described him as an 'anarchist' and 'ignorant idealist'.

3 Luck and destiny are the excuses of the world's failures.

Quoted in the *Observer* 16 March 1930

Lena Guilbert Ford
(1870–1916)
US poet

Her song 'Keep the Home Fires Burning' (1914), which she wrote while in England, was a great success during the First World War. She was killed during a German Zeppelin raid on London.

1 Keep the home fires burning,
While your hearts are yearning,
Though your lads are far away
They dream of home.
There's a silver lining
Through the dark cloud shining;
Turn the dark cloud inside out,
Till the boys come home.

'Till the Boys Come Home!' (song, 1914). Music by Ivor Novello, who is credited with the song's first line.

Richard Ford
(b. 1944)
US author

An occasional exponent of 'Dirty Realism', he is known for the novels The Sportswriter *(1986) and its sequel* Independence Day *(1995).*

1 Married life requires shared mystery even when all the facts are known.
The Sportswriter, ch. 5 (1986)

Howell Forgy
(1908–83)
US naval chaplain

1 Praise the Lord and pass the ammunition!
Quoted in the *New York Times* 1 November 1942, said during the Japanese attack on Pearl Harbor, 7 December 1941. The words have also been attributed to William Maguire, and were used as the title of a Frank Loesser song in 1942.

George Formby
(1904–61)
British entertainer and actor

Portraying himself as a gormless working-class Lancashire lad, he sang jaunty songs spiced with innuendo, accompanying himself on the ukelele. He appeared in a string of successful films in the 1930s and '40s, and was Britain's highest paid entertainer during the Second World War.

1 With my little ukelele in my hand.
'With my Little Ukelele In My Hand' (song, 1933, with music by Jack Cottrell). Formby's record company Decca withdrew the first issue of the recording after protests at the song, particularly the last verse, which tells of the birth of a baby: 'My heart did jump with joy/I could see he was a boy/For he had a ukelele in his hand.'

2 If you could see what I can see
When I'm cleaning windows!
'When I'm Cleaning Windows' (song, written by Fred E. Cliffe with music by Harry Clifford) in *Keep Your Seats, Please* (film, 1937). The record was marked NTBB ('Not to be broadcast') by the BBC, whose Controller, Lord Reith, labelled it a 'disgusting little ditty'. Particular offence was caused by the lines 'Ladies' nighties I have spied/I've often seen what goes inside/When I'm cleaning windows!'

3 I'm leaning on a lamp-post at the corner of the street,
In case a certain little lady comes by.
'Leaning on a Lamp-Post' (song, written by Noel Gay) in the film *Feather Your Nest* (1937)

4 With my little stick of Blackpool rock.

Along the Promenade I stroll
It may be sticky but I never complain
It's nice to have a nibble at it now and again.
'With My Little Stick of Blackpool Rock' (song, 1937, written by Fred E. Cliffe with music by Harry Clifford)

5 Auntie Maggie's Remedy
It's guaranteed never to fail
Now that's the stuff that will do the trick
It's sold at every chemist for one and a kick.
'Auntie Maggie's Remedy' (song, written by George Formby with music by Eddie Latta) in the film *Turned Out Nice Again!* (1941). A 'kick' was sixpence.

E. M. Forster
(1879–1970)
British novelist and essayist

Edward Morgan Forster. His fiction often describes the 'muddles' created by the English abroad, as in A Room with a View *(1908) and* A Passage to India *(1924), both later adapted as films. For* KATHERINE MANSFIELD, *however, he never got further than 'warming the teapot', while* VIRGINIA WOOLF *called him 'limp and damp and milder than the breath of a cow'. See* ANTHONY BURGESS 2.

1 It's the worst thing that can ever happen to you in all your life, and you've got to mind it . . . They'll come saying, 'Bear up – trust to time.' No, no; they're wrong. Mind it.
The Longest Journey, ch. 5 (1907). Rickie Elliot refers to death.

2 Very notable was his distinction between coarseness and vulgarity (coarseness, revealing something; vulgarity, concealing something).
Ibid., ch. 26

3 The traveller who has gone to Italy to study the tactile values of Giotto, or the corruption of the Papacy, may return remembering nothing but the blue sky and the men and women who live under it.
A Room with a View, ch. 2 (1908)

4 Railway termini . . . are our gates to the glorious and the unknown. Through them we pass out into adventure and sunshine, to them, alas! we return.
Howards End, ch. 2 (1910)

5 A funeral is not death, any more than baptism is birth or marriage union. All three are the clumsy devices, coming now too late, now too early, by which Society would register the quick motions of man.
Ibid., ch. 12

6 I believe we shall come to care about people less and less ... The more people one knows the easier it becomes to replace them. It's one of the curses of London.
Margaret Schlegel, ibid., ch.15

7 Only connect! That was the whole of her sermon. Only connect the prose and the passion, and both will be exalted, and human love will be seen at its height. Live in fragments no longer. Only connect, and the beast and the monk, robbed of the isolation that is life to either, will die.
Ibid., ch. 22. Margaret Schlegel's thoughts on the advice she would give her fiancé Henry Wilcox. 'Only connect' also appears as epigraph to the book. Goronwy Rees wrote, in *A Chapter of Accidents* (1972): 'It could be said that these two words, so seductive in their simplicity, so misleading in their ambiguity, had more influence in shaping the emotional attitudes of the English governing class between the two world wars than any other single phrase in the English language.'

8 Death destroys a man: the idea of Death saves him.
Helen Schlegel, ibid., ch. 27. The words recur in ch. 41.

9 Of all means to regeneration Remorse is surely the most wasteful. It cuts away healthy tissue with the poisoned. It is a knife that probes far deeper than the evil.
Ibid., ch. 41

10 Failure or success seem to have been allotted to men by their stars. But they retain the power of wriggling, of fighting with their star or against it, and in the whole universe the only really interesting movement is this wriggle.
'Our Diversions: The Game of Life' (1919), repr. in *Abinger Harvest*, pt 1 (1936)

11 It is not that the Englishman can't feel – it is that he is afraid to feel. He has been taught at his public school that feeling is bad form. He must not express great joy or sorrow, or even open his mouth too wide when he talks – his pipe might fall out if he did.
'Notes on the English Character' (1920), ibid.

12 The Germans are called brutal, the Spanish cruel, the Americans superficial, and so on; but we are perfide Albion, the island of hypocrites, the people who have built up an Empire with a Bible in one hand, a pistol in the other, and financial concessions in both pockets. Is the charge true? I think it is.
'Notes on the English Character', ibid. Forster defined English hypocrisy as 'unconscious deceit' and 'muddle-headedness'.

13 Mrs Moore: I don't think I understand people very well. I only know whether I like or dislike them.
Aziz: Then you are an Oriental.
A Passage to India, pt 1, ch. 2 (1924)

14 Ideas are fatal to caste.
Ibid., pt 1, ch. 7

15 The so called white races are really pinko-grey.
Mr Fielding, ibid., pt 1, ch. 7. This 'silly aside' caused scandal at Fielding's Anglo-Indian club, Forster explained, for Fielding 'did not realize that "white" has no more to do with a colour than "God Save the King" with a god, and that it is the height of impropriety to consider what it does connote'.

16 Nothing in India is identifiable, the mere asking of a question causes it to disappear or to emerge in something else.
Ibid., pt 1, ch. 8

17 Inside its cocoon of work or social obligation, the human spirit slumbers for the most part, registering the distinction between pleasure and pain, but not nearly as alert as we pretend.
Ibid., pt 2, ch. 14

18 'Boum' is the sound as far as the human alphabet can produce it ... – utterly dull. Hope, politeness, the blowing of a nose, the squeak of a boot, all produce 'boum'.
Ibid., pt 2, ch. 14. This sound of the echo in the Marabar caves, 'entirely devoid of distinction', seemed to murmur to Mrs Moore: 'Pathos, piety, courage – they exist, but are identical, and so is filth. Everything exists, nothing has value.'

19 Where there is officialism every human relationship suffers.
Ibid., pt 2, ch. 24

20 Yes – oh dear yes – the novel tells a story.
Aspects of the Novel, ch. 2 (1927)

21 Curiosity is one of the lowest of the human faculties. You will have noticed in daily life that when people are inquisitive they nearly always have bad memories and are usually stupid at bottom.
Ibid., ch. 5

22 Logic! Good gracious! What rubbish! How can I tell what I think till I see what I say?
Ibid., ch. 5. Riposte of 'that old lady in the anecdote who was accused by her nieces of being illogical'. Almost the same words also appeared in *The Art of Thought* (1926) by the political scientist Graham Wallas, this time ascribed to a 'little girl' who had been told to be sure of her meaning before she spoke.

23 *Ulysses* . . . is a dogged attempt to cover the universe with mud, an inverted Victorianism, an attempt to make crossness and dirt succeed where sweetness and light failed, a simplification of the human character in the interests of Hell.
Ibid., ch. 6. Forster also called *Ulysses* 'perhaps the most interesting literary experiment of our day'.

24 One always tends to overpraise a long book, because one has got through it.
Abinger Harvest, pt 3, 'T. E. Lawrence' (1936)

25 My law-givers are Erasmus and Montaigne, not Moses and St Paul.
'What I Believe', written 1939, publ. in *Two Cheers for Democracy* (1951)

26 Lord I disbelieve – help thou my unbelief.
'What I Believe', ibid. See BIBLE, NEW TESTAMENT: MARK 10.

27 I hate the idea of causes, and if I had to choose between betraying my country and betraying my friend, I hope I should have the guts to betray my country.
'What I Believe', ibid.

28 Two cheers for Democracy: one because it admits variety and two because it permits criticism.
'What I Believe', ibid. Forster thought two cheers were 'quite enough'; three he reserved for 'Love the Beloved Republic' (see A. C. SWINBURNE 33). KINGSLEY AMIS commented: 'Two cheers were probably as many as Forster could manage in favour of anything, from democracy to stamp-collecting.'

29 The more highly public life is organized the lower does its morality sink.
'What I Believe', ibid.

30 Tolerance is a very dull virtue. It is boring. Unlike love, it has always had a bad press. It is negative. It merely means putting up with people, being able to stand things.
'Tolerance', written 1941, ibid. The essay looked ahead to the post-war world, and the necessity to accept former enemies. 'I don't . . . regard tolerance as a great eternally established divine principle,' Forster wrote. 'It is just a makeshift, suitable for an overcrowded and overheated planet.'

31 The only books that influence us are those for which we are ready, and which have gone a little farther down our particular path than we have yet got ourselves.
'A Book that Influenced Me', written 1941, ibid.

32 The humanist has four leading characteristics – curiosity, a free mind, belief in good taste, and belief in the human race.
'Gide and George', written 1943, ibid.

33 Creative writers are always greater than the causes that they represent.
'Gide and George', ibid.

34 Art for art's sake? I should think so, and more so than ever at the present time. It is the one orderly product which our middling race has produced. It is the cry of a thousand sentinels, the echo from a thousand labyrinths, it is the lighthouse which cannot be hidden . . . it is the best evidence we can have of our dignity.
Address to PEN Club Congress, quoted in *Monitor* (ed. Huw Weldon, 1962)

Bruce Forsyth
(b. 1928)
British entertainer

Originally Bruce Forsyth-Johnson. He became a national celebrity as host of Sunday Night at the London Palladium *(1958–60) and ATV's* Bruce Forsyth Show *(1960s), and as compère of the BBC's* Generation Game *(1971–8, 1990–4).*

1 Nice to see you, to see you nice.
Catchphrase from *The Bruce Forsyth Show* (1960s)

2 Didn't he do well!
Catchphrase from the *The Generation Game* (from 1970s)

Venantius Fortunatus
(c. 530–c. 609)
Italian ecclesiastic and poet

After a period as court poet to the Merovingians, he took monastic orders and eventually became Bishop of Poitiers.

1 *Pange, lingua, gloriosi.*
Proelium certaminis.
[Sing, my tongue, the glorious battle,
Sing the ending of the fray.]
'Sing, My Tongue, the Glorious Battle' (hymn, 570, transl. J. M. Neale). The hymn was written for a procession that brought a part of the true Cross to Queen Radegunda and is sung in Holy Week.

2 The royal banners forward go [*Vexilla regis prodeunt*],
The cross shines forth in mystic glow;
Where he in flesh, our flesh Who made,
Our sentence bore, our ransom paid.
'The Royal Banners Forward Go' (hymn, 570, transl. J. M. Neale). The hymn was written for a procession that brought

a part of the true Cross to Queen Radegunda and is sung in Holy Week.

Stephen Foster
(1826–64)
US songwriter and composer

Stephen Collins Foster. His repertoire of over two hundred songs, for which he wrote both the words and the music, became seminal works in the American song tradition. These 'plantation songs' were compassionate and often written in Afro-American dialect.

1 Oh, Susanna! Oh, don't you cry for me,
I've come from Alabama, with my banjo on my
    knee.
'Oh, Susanna' (song, 1848)

2 The Camptown ladies sing this song
Doo-dah, doo-dah!
The Camptown racetrack's two miles long
Oh, de doo-dah day!
'The Camptown Races' (song, 1850)

3 Way down upon the Swanee river,
Far, far away
There's where my heart is turning ever,
There's where the old folks stay.
'Old Folks at Home' (song, 1851)

4 All the world is sad and dreary,
Everywhere I roam,
Oh! darkies how my heart grows weary,
Far from the old folks at home.
Ibid., chorus

5 All the darkies are a-weeping
Master's in the cold, cold ground.
'Massa's in the Cold, Cold Ground' (song, 1852)

6 I dream of Jeanie with the light brown hair,
Borne, like a vapor on the summer air.
'Jeanie with the Light Brown Hair' (song, 1854)

7 Some folks like to sigh,
Some folks do, some folks do;
Some folks long to die,
But that's not me nor you.
'Some Folks' (song, 1855)

8 I'm coming, I'm coming, for my head is bending
    low
I hear those gentle voices calling, 'Old Black Joe'.
'Old Black Joe' (song, 1860)

9 Beautiful dreamer, wake unto me,

Starlight and dewdrops are waiting for thee.
'Beautiful Dreamer' (song, 1862)

Michel Foucault
(1926–84)
French essayist and philosopher

Influenced both by NIETZSCHE *and by structuralist philosophy, he explored the 'principles of exclusion' by which society operates, with particular reference to the sick, the insane and the criminal. Major works include* Madness and Civilization *(1961).*

1 Freedom of conscience entails more dangers than authority and despotism.
Madness and Civilization, ch. 7 (1961)

2 Marxism exists in nineteenth-century thought as a fish exists in water; that is, it ceases to breathe anywhere else.
The Order of Things, ch. 7 (1966)

3 What is the answer to the question? The problem. How is the problem resolved? By displacing the question ... We must think problematically rather than question and answer dialectically.
'Theatrum Philosophicum' (1970), repr. in *Language, Counter-Memory, Practice*, pt 2, 'Counter-Memory: The Philosophy of Difference' (ed. Donald Bouchard and Sherry Simon, 1977)

4 In its function, the power to punish is not essentially different from that of curing or educating.
Discipline and Punish: The Birth of the Prison, pt 4, ch. 3, (1975)

5 The judges of normality are present everywhere. We are in the society of the teacher-judge, the doctor-judge, the educator-judge, the 'social worker'-judge.
Ibid., pt 4, ch. 3

6 Sexuality is a part of our behaviour. It's part of our world freedom. Sexuality is something that we ourselves create. It is our own creation, and much more than the discovery of a secret side of our desire. We have to understand that with our desires go new forms of relationships, new forms of love, new forms of creation. Sex is not a fatality; it's a possibility for creative life. It's not enough to affirm that we are gay but we must also create a gay life.
'Sex, Power and the Politics of Identity', interview October 1982, publ. in *Michel Foucault* (1989) by Didier Eribon

7 Modernity is the attitude that makes it possible to grasp the 'heroic' aspect of the present moment.
The Foucault Reader, 'What Is Enlightenment?', pt 2 (ed. Paul Rabinow, 1984)

Henry W. Fowler
(1859–1933)
English lexicographer

Henry Watson Fowler. With his brother Frank he compiled the first Concise Oxford Dictionary *(1911), but he is most associated with his* Modern English Usage *(1926), which became an essential household reference work.*

1 A writer expresses himself in words that have been used before because they give his meaning better than he can give it himself, or because they are beautiful or witty, or because he expects them to touch a chord of association in his reader, or because he wishes to show that he is learned or well read. Quotations due to the last motive are invariably ill advised; the discerning reader detects it & is contemptuous; the undiscerning is perhaps impressed, but even then is at the same time repelled, pretentious quotations being the surest road to tedium.
A Dictionary of Modern English Usage, 'Quotation' (1926). Discussing 'literary or decorative quotation'.

2 The English speaking world may be divided into (1) those who neither know nor care what a split infinitive is; (2) those who do not know, but care very much; (3) those who know and condemn; (4) those who know and approve; and (5) those who know and distinguish.
Ibid., 'Split Infinitive'. Fowler defined the first category as 'the vast majority . . . a happy folk, to be envied by most of the minority classes'.

(Sir) Norman Fowler
(b. 1938)
British politician

Elected a Conservative MP in 1970, he rose to be Minister of Employment (1987–90), special adviser to JOHN MAJOR *during the 1992 election, and Chairman of the Conservative Party (1992–4).*

1 I have a young family and for the next few years I should like to devote more time to them.
Resignation letter to the Prime Minister, publ. in the *Guardian* 4 January 1990. MARGARET THATCHER's reply was: 'I am naturally very sorry to see you go, but understand your reasons for doing so, particularly your wish to be able to spend more time with your family.' The expression 'spend more time with his family' immediately became a euphemism for getting sacked, though there was no official indication that Fowler had been dismissed.

John Fowles
(1926–2005)
British novelist

His experimental novels include The Collector *(1963),* The Magus *(1966, rev. 1977) and his pastiche of a Victorian romance,* The French Lieutenant's Woman *(1969).*

1 Duty largely consists of pretending that the trivial is critical.
The Magus, ch. 18 (1965)

2 There is only one good definition of God: the freedom that allows other freedoms to exist.
The French Lieutenant's Woman, ch. 13 (1969)

3 You do not even think of your own past as quite real; you dress it up, you gild it or blacken it, censor it, tinker with it . . . fictionalize it, in a word, and put it away on a shelf – your book, your romanced autobiography. We are all in flight from the real reality. That is the basic definition of Homo sapiens.
Ibid., ch. 13

Charles James Fox
(1749–1806)
English statesman

'A vigorous exuberancy of genius', according to HORACE WALPOLE, *he entered Parliament at the age of nineteen, formed a coalition government with his former opponent Lord North in 1783, and was the first Foreign Secretary, serving three terms in the office.*

1 How much the greatest event it is that ever happened in the world! and how much the best!
Letter, 30 July 1789, quoted in *The Life and Times of C.J. Fox*, vol. 2 (1859) by LORD JOHN RUSSELL. Referring to the fall of the Bastille. Fox's support for the French Revolution led to the rupture of his cherished friendship with EDMUND BURKE.

George Fox
(1624–91)
English preacher

Rejecting the established church, he advocated the truth of the 'inner light', and established the Friends of Truth c. 1650, later to become the Society of Friends (the Quakers).

1 I saw also that there was an ocean of darkness and death, but an infinite ocean of light and love, which flowed over the ocean of darkness.
Journal entry, 1647, publ. in *Journal* (1694)

2 Be patterns, be examples in all countries, places,

islands, nations, wherever you come, that your carriage and life may preach among all sorts of people, and to them. Then you will come to walk cheerfully over the world, answering that of God in everyone.
Journal entry, 1656, ibid.

3 Be still and cool in thy own mind and spirit from thy own thoughts, and then thou wilt feel the principle of God to turn thy mind to the Lord God.
Journal entry, 1658, ibid.

4 All bloody principles and practices, we, as to our own particulars, do utterly deny, with all outward wars and strife and fightings with outward weapons, for any end or under any pretence whatsoever. And this is our testimony to the whole world.
'A Declaration from the harmless and innocent people of God, called Quakers, against all plotters and fighters in this world' (pamphlet, 1660). The Declaration was signed by Fox and eleven others.

Janet Frame
(1924–2004)
New Zealand novelist and poet

Misdiagnosed as a schizophrenic, she spent the years 1947–54 in mental hospitals, as recounted in her autobiography (3 vols. 1982–5), filmed as An Angel at My Table *(1990). Her novels include* Owls Do Cry *(1957).*

1 For your own good is a persuasive argument that will eventually make a man agree to his own destruction.
Faces in the Water, ch. 4 (1961)

2 It would be nice to travel if you knew where you were going and where you would live at the end or do we ever know, do we ever live where we live, we're always in other places, lost, like sheep.
You Are Now Entering the Human Heart, 'The Day of the Sheep' (1983)

Anatole France
(1844–1924)
French author

Jacques Anatole François Thibault. A novelist noted for such works as Le Crime de Sylvestre Bonnard *(1881), he was roused into politics by the Dreyfus case (1896). He inveighed against church and state in such works as* The Angels' Revolt *(1914), a satire on Christian theology.*

1 The good critic is he who relates the adventures of his soul among masterpieces.
The Literary Life, Dedicatory letter (1888)

2 The law, in its majestic equality, forbids rich and poor alike to sleep under bridges, beg in the streets or steal bread.
The Red Lily, ch. 7 (1894)

3 You think you are dying for your country; you die for the industrialists.
L'Humanité 18 July 1922

Saint Francis de Sales
(1567–1622)
French ecclesiastic and devotional writer

A distinguished preacher, he was made Bishop of Geneva (1602–22) and co-founded an order of nuns. He also gave his name to the Salesian order, founded in 1859.

1 Make friends with the angels, who though invisible are always with you ... Often invoke them, constantly praise them, and make good use of their help and assistance in all your temporal and spiritual affairs.
Introduction to the Devout Life, pt 2, ch. 16 (1609)

2 There are no galley-slaves in the royal vessel of divine love – every man works his oar voluntarily!
Quoted in *The Spirit of Saint Francis de Sales*, ch. 7, sect. 3 (1952) by Bishop Jean-Pierre Camus

Saint Francis of Assisi
(c. 1181–1226)
Italian friar

After renouncing his wealth to live as a hermit and care for the needy, he founded the Franciscan Order (1209), whose rule was based on total poverty. He is often represented as the friend of birds and animals.

1 Lord, make me an instrument of Your peace!
Where there is hatred let me sow love;
Where there is injury, pardon;
Where there is doubt, faith;
Where there is despair, hope;
Where there is darkness, light;
Where there is sadness, joy.
Prayer of St Francis (attributed). This prayer for harmony was famously paraphrased by MARGARET THATCHER on the steps of 10 Downing Street, 4 May 1979, after her first election victory: 'Where there is discord, may we bring harmony. Where there is error may we bring truth. Where there is doubt may we bring faith. Where there is despair may we bring hope.' (Quoted in *One of Us*, ch. 9, 1989 by Hugo Young)

2 O divine Master, grant that I may not so much seek
To be consoled as to console;

To be understood as to understand;
To be loved as to love.
Ibid.

3 Be praised, my Lord, with all your creatures, especially master brother sun, who brings day, and you give us light by him. And he is fair and radiant with a great shining.
Canticle of All Created Things, st. 2

4 Be praised, my Lord, for sister moon and the stars, in heaven you have made them clear and precious and lovely.
Ibid., st. 3

5 Be praised, my Lord, for brother fire, by whom you illuminate the night, and he is comely and joyful and vigorous and strong.
Ibid., st. 6

6 Be praised, my Lord, for sister our mother earth, who maintains and governs us and puts forth different fruits with coloured flowers and grass.
Ibid., st. 7

7 I have sinned against my brother the ass.
Attributed dying words

Anne Frank
(1929–45)
German Jewish refugee and diarist

Her diary, an account of the years 1942–4 when she and her family were in hiding in Nazi-occupied Amsterdam, was published in 1947 by her father, the only member of the family to survive. It has since been translated into over fifty languages.

1 I want to go on living even after my death! And therefore I am grateful to God for giving me this gift, this possibility of developing myself and of writing, of expressing all that is in me.
Journal entry, 4 April 1944, publ. in *The Diary of a Young Girl* (1947)

2 I don't believe that the big men, the politicians and the capitalists alone are guilty of the war. Oh, no, the little man is just as keen, otherwise the people of the world would have risen in revolt long ago! There is an urge and rage in people to destroy, to kill, to murder, and until all mankind, without exception, undergoes a great change, wars will be waged, everything that has been built up, cultivated and grown, will be destroyed and disfigured, after which mankind will have to begin all over again.
Journal entry, 3 May 1944, ibid.

3 Is discord going to show itself while we are still fighting, is the Jew once again worth less than another? Oh, it is sad, very sad, that once more, for the umpteenth time, the old truth is confirmed: 'What *one* Christian does is his own responsibility, what *one* Jew does is thrown back at all Jews.'
Journal entry, 22 May 1944, ibid. Referring to anti-Semitism in Holland.

4 It's really a wonder that I haven't dropped all my ideals because they seem so absurd and impossible to carry out. Yet, I keep them, because in spite of everything I still believe that people are really good at heart. I simply can't build up my hopes on a foundation consisting of confusion, misery, and death. I see the world gradually being turned into a wilderness, I hear the ever-approaching thunder, which will destroy us too, I can feel the sufferings of millions and yet, if I look up into the heavens, I think that it will all come right, that this cruelty too will end, and that peace and tranquillity will return again.
Journal entry, 15 July 1944, ibid. Less than three weeks after writing this entry, Anne and the other occupants of the secret annexe in which they had been hiding were arrested by the Nazis and sent to concentration camps in Germany.

Felix Frankfurter
(1882–1965)
US academic and judge

He taught at Harvard Law School (1914–39), co-founded the American Civil Liberties Union (1920) and served as Associate Justice of the US Supreme Court (1939–62).

1 The words of the Constitution . . . are so unrestricted by their intrinsic meaning or by their history or by tradition or by prior decisions that they leave the individual Justice free, if indeed they do not compel him, to gather meaning not from reading the Constitution but from reading life.
'The Supreme Court', quoted in *Parliamentary Affairs* vol. 3, no. 1, winter 1949

Aretha Franklin
(b. 1942)
US soul singer

Known as 'Lady Soul' for her impassioned delivery, she sang gospel songs in the Detroit church of her father, C. L. Franklin, the most celebrated gospel preacher of the 1950s, before recording a series of hits in the 1960s.

1 R-E-S-P-E-C-T
Find out what it means to me.
'Respect' (song, written by Otis Redding), on the album *I Never Loved a Man the Way I Loved You* (1967). The song was a hit for Otis Redding in 1965.

Benjamin Franklin
(1706–90)
US statesman, scientist and author

Described by KEATS *as 'a philosophical Quaker full of mean and thrifty maxims', he had wide interests in the arts and sciences. His experiments with electricity led to his invention of the lightning rod. Although initially opposed to war against Britain, he helped draft the Declaration of Independence (signed in 1776), and was a signatory to the Treaty of Paris (1783).*

1   The body
             Of
        Benjamin Franklin
            Printer
    (Like the cover of an old book
       Its contents torn out
And stripped of its lettering and gilding)
      Lies here, food for worms.
    But the work shall not be lost
For it will (as he believed) appear once more
    In a new and more elegant edition
        Revised and corrected
              by
          The Author
'Epitaph on Himself', publ. in *Complete Works*, vol. 10 (ed. John Bigelow, 1888). The lines, which were composed in 1728, when Franklin was 22, were not used on his monument. In his *Autobiography*, Franklin wrote, 'I should have no objection to go over the same life from its beginning to the end: requesting only the advantage authors have, of correcting in a second edition the faults of the first.'

2 The great secret of succeeding in conversation is to admire little, to hear much; always to distrust our own reason, and sometimes that of our friends; never to pretend to wit, but to make that of others appear as much as possibly we can; to hearken to what is said and to answer to the purpose.
Miscellaneous Observations (1728), ibid., vol. 1 (1887)

3 Where there's marriage without love, there will be love without marriage.
Poor Richard's Almanack, May 1734, repr. in *The Complete Poor Richard Almanacks* (1970). Franklin published annual almanacs, 1732–57, under the pseudonym of Richard Saunders. His sayings and aphorisms were largely borrowed or adapted from previous authors.

4 Necessity never made a good bargain.
Poor Richard's Almanack, April 1735, ibid.

5 Opportunity is the great bawd.
Poor Richard's Almanack, September 1735, ibid.

6 If you would not be forgotten,
As soon as you are dead and rotten,
Either write things worthy reading,
Or do things worth the writing.
Poor Richard's Almanack, May 1738, ibid.

7 At 20 years of age, the will reigns; at 30, the wit; and at 40, the judgment.
Poor Richard's Almanack, June 1741, ibid.

8 He that lives upon hope will die fasting.
Poor Richard's Improved Almanack, Preface (1758)

9 Some punishment seems preparing for a people who are ungratefully abusing the best constitution and the best king any nation was ever blessed with.
Letter, 14 May 1768, publ. in *Complete Works*, vol. 4 (ed. John Bigelow, 1887). Written while in London during the riots following the arrest of JOHN WILKES, when 'all respect to law and government seems to be lost among the common people, who are moreover continually inflamed by seditious scribblers, to trample on authority and every thing that used to keep them in order . . .'

10 A benevolent man should allow a few faults in himself, to keep his friends in countenance.
Autobiography, ch. 6 (written 1771–90, publ. 1868)

11 The best public measures are therefore seldom adopted from previous wisdom, but forced by the occasion.
Ibid., ch. 9

12 Here Skugg
Lies snug
As a bug
In a rug.
Letter, 26 September 1772, publ. in *Papers of Benjamin Franklin*, vol. 19 (ed. W. B. Willcox, 1975). On the death of a squirrel.

13 We must indeed all hang together, or, most assuredly, we shall all hang separately.
Comment at the signing of the Declaration of Independence, 4 July 1776, quoted in *The First American: The Life and Times of Benjamin Franklin*, ch. 22 (ed. H. W. Brand, 2002). In reply to John Hancock's remark that the revolutionaries should be unanimous in their action.

14 There never was a good war or a bad peace.
Letter to Sir Joseph Banks, 27 July 1783, publ. in *Complete Works*, vol. 8 (ed. John Bigelow, 1888). Franklin wrote the

same in a letter to New England revolutionary Josiah Quincy, 11 September 1783.

15 What vast additions to the conveniences and comforts of living might mankind have acquired, if the money spent in wars had been employed in works of public utility! What an extension of agriculture, even to the tops of our mountains; what rivers rendered navigable or joined by canals; what bridges, aqueducts, new roads, and other public works, edifices, and improvements ... might have been obtained by spending those millions in doing good, which in the last war have been spent in doing mischief!
Letter to Sir Joseph Banks, 27 July 1783, ibid.

16 Our new Constitution is now established, and has an appearance that promises permanency; but in this world nothing can be said to be certain, except death and taxes.
Letter, 13 November 1789, ibid., vol. 10 (ed. John Bigelow, 1888). See also CHARLES DICKENS 69.

Michael Franti
(b. 1966)
US rapper

A six-foot-six ex-baseball player, he composed and sang with Disposable Heroes of Hiphoprisy, a band on the 'liberal' wing of 1990s rap.

1 Television, the drug of the nation,
Breeding ignorance and feeding radiation.
'Television, The Drug of the Nation' (song) on the album *Hypocrisy is the Greatest Luxury* (1992) by the Disposable Heroes of Hiphoprisy

Michael Frayn
(b. 1933)
British playwright, novelist and journalist

The satirical wit of his columns for the Manchester Guardian *and* Observer *also characterizes his many successful comedies for the stage, for example* Noises Off *(1982).*

1 It's not excellence which leads to celebrity, but celebrity which leads to excellence. One makes one's reputation, and one's reputation enables one to achieve the conditions in which one can do good work.
Towards the End of the Morning, ch. 4 (1967). Spoken by John Dyson.

2 So I want to tell you how important it is to make things. That's how man lives, by making. To be is to make. To make food, to make drink, to make shelter – yes, but also to make thought. Because to think is to make.
Make or Break, Act 1 (1980). Spoken by Horvath.

3 That's what it's all about. Doors and sardines. Getting on – getting off. Getting the sardines on – getting the sardines off. That's farce. That's the theatre. That's life.
Noises Off, Act 1 (1982). Spoken by Lloyd (the director).

(Sir) James Frazer
(1854–1941)
Scottish classicist and anthropologist

James George Frazer. His major work The Golden Bough *(1890–1915) proposed an evolutionary theory of human thought. The first chair of Anthropology was created for him at Liverpool University in 1907.*

1 The awe and dread with which the untutored savage contemplates his mother-in-law are amongst the most familiar facts of anthropology.
The Golden Bough, pt 2, ch. 2, sect. 3 (1911 edn)

Stan Freberg
(b. 1926)
US satirist

He produced parodies of early rock 'n' roll music and worked successfully in the advertising industry.

1 It's too loud, man ... It's too shrill, man, it's too piercing.
'The Banana Boat Song (Day-O)' (song, 1957). In the recording, a parody of HARRY BELAFONTE's 'Banana Boat Song', these lines were spoken by Peter Leeds, Freberg's straight man.

Frederick the Great (Frederick II)
(1712–86)
King of Prussia

Reigning 1740–86, he was renowned for his military achievements, which contributed to the doubling of Prussia's territory, and also as a patron of the arts.

1 Rogues, would you live forever?
Attributed cry, when rallying his troops at Kolin, Bohemia, 18 June 1757. See also DANIEL DALY 1.

Max Freedman

See BILL HALEY 1.

Marilyn French

(b. 1929)
US author

She is best known for her first novel The Women's Room *(1977), one of the earliest books to tackle radical feminist issues in popular fiction. Other novels include* The Bleeding Heart *(1981).*

1 I hate discussions of feminism that end up with who does the dishes, she said. So do I. But at the end, there are always the damned dishes.
The Women's Room, ch. 1, sect. 21 (1977). Spoken by Isolde.

2 Whatever they may be in public life, whatever their relations with men, in their relations with women, all men are rapists and that's all they are. They rape us with their eyes, their laws, their codes.
Valerie, ibid., ch. 5, sect. 19

Sigmund Freud

(1856–1939)
Austrian psychiatrist

He developed the basic techniques of psychoanalysis through free association and the analysis of dreams, as expounded in such volumes as The Interpretation of Dreams *(1899),* Totem and Taboo *(1913) and* The Ego and the Id *(1923). See* W. H. AUDEN 15; JOHN IRVING 1.

1 The interpretation of dreams is the royal road to a knowledge of the unconscious activities of the mind.
The Interpretation of Dreams, ch. 7 (1899)

2 The excremental is all too intimately and inseparably bound up with the sexual: the position of the genitals – *inter urinas et faeces* – remains the decisive and unchangeable factor. One might say here, varying a well-known saying of the great Napoleon: 'Anatomy is destiny.' ['*Das Anatomie ist das Schicksal.*']
On the Universal Tendency to Debasement in the Sphere of Love, sect. 3 (1912), repr. in *Complete Works, Standard Edition,* vol. 11 (ed. James Strachey and Anna Freud, 1957). NAPOLEON had said 'Politics is destiny' (as reported by GOETHE in conversation with him in 1808).

3 The act of birth is the first experience of anxiety, and thus the source and prototype of the affect of anxiety.
The Interpretation of Dreams, ch. 6, sect. E, footnote (1909 edn)

4 The psychoanalysis of individual human beings, however, teaches us with quite special insistence that the god of each of them is formed in the likeness of his father, that his personal relation to God depends on his relation to his father in the flesh and oscillates and changes along with that relation, and that at bottom God is nothing other than an exalted father.
Totem and Taboo, pt 4, sect. 6 (1913)

5 A strong egoism is a protection against disease, but in the last resort we must begin to love in order that we may not fall ill, and must fall ill if, in consequence of frustration, we cannot love.
'On Narcissism: An Introduction' (1914), repr. in *Complete Works, Standard Edition,* vol. 14 (ed. James Strachey and Anna Freud, 1954)

6 We believe that civilization has been created under the pressure of the exigencies of life at the cost of satisfaction of the instincts.
Introductory Lectures on Psychoanalysis, Lecture 1 (1915)

7 If a man has been his mother's undisputed darling he retains throughout life the triumphant feeling, the confidence in success, which not seldom brings actual success along with it.
'A Childhood Recollection from *Dichtung und Wahrheit*' (1917), repr. in *Complete Works, Standard Edition,* vol. 17 (ed. James Strachey and Anna Freud, 1955)

8 The ego is not master in its own house.
'A Difficulty in the Path of Psycho-Analysis' (1917), ibid., vol. 17. Freud's conclusion was based on his conviction that sexual instincts could not be wholly tamed, and that mental processes were unconscious and could 'only reach the ego and come under its control through incomplete and untrustworthy perceptions'.

9 I have found little that is 'good' about human beings on the whole. In my experience most of them are trash, no matter whether they publicly subscribe to this or that ethical doctrine or to none at all. That is something that you cannot say aloud, or perhaps even think.
Letter, 9 October 1918, publ. in *Psycho-Analysis and Faith: The Letters of Sigmund Freud and Oscar Pfister* (1963)

10 Incidentally, why was it that none of all the pious ever discovered psycho-analysis? Why did it have to wait for a completely godless Jew?
Letter, 9 October 1918, ibid.

11 We know less about the sexual life of little girls than of boys. But we need not feel ashamed of this

distinction; after all, the sexual life of adult women is a 'dark continent' for psychology.
The Question of Lay Analysis, pt 4 (1926). The phrase 'dark continent' was written in English.

12 A civilization which leaves so large a number of its participants unsatisfied and drives them into revolt neither has nor deserves the prospect of a lasting existence.
The Future of an Illusion, ch. 2 (1927)

13 Devout believers are safeguarded in a high degree against the risk of certain neurotic illnesses; their acceptance of the universal neurosis spares them the task of constructing a personal one.
Ibid., ch. 8

14 It is always possible to bind together a considerable number of people in love, so long as there are other people left over to receive the manifestations of their aggression.
Civilization and its Discontents, ch. 5 (1930)

15 Civilization is a process in the service of Eros, whose purpose is to combine single human individuals, and after that families, then races, peoples and nations, into one great unity, the unity of mankind. Why this has to happen, we do not know; the work of Eros is precisely this.
Ibid., ch. 6

16 The only bodily organ which is really regarded as inferior is the atrophied penis, a girl's clitoris.
New Introductory Lectures on Psychoanalysis, Lecture 31 ('The Dissection of the Psychical Personality') (1933). Freud was refuting the claims of 'Individual Psychologists' that the 'inferiority complex' can be traced back to self-perceived organic defects.

17 Where *id* was, there *ego* shall be.
Ibid., Lecture 31. The intention of psychoanalysis, Freud explained, is 'to strengthen the ego, to make it more independent of the super-ego, to widen its field of perception and enlarge its organization, so that it can appropriate fresh portions of the id ... It is a work of culture,' he added in the closing words of the lecture, 'not unlike the draining of the Zuider Zee.'

18 I do not think our successes can compete with those of Lourdes. There are so many more people who believe in the miracles of the Blessed Virgin than in the existence of the unconscious.
Ibid., Lecture 34: 'Explanations, Applications and Orientations'

19 What progress we are making. In the Middle Ages

they would have burned me. Now they are content with burning my books.
Remark in 1933, quoted in *Sigmund Freud: Life and Work*, vol. 3, pt 1, ch. 4 (1957) by Ernest Jones. Referring to the public burning of his books in Berlin by the Nazis.

20 A certain degree of neurosis is of inestimable value as a drive, especially to a psychologist.
Quoted in *Fragments of an Analysis with Freud*, ch. 3, '22 January 1935' (1954) by Joseph Wortis

21 Homosexuality is assuredly no advantage, but it is nothing to be ashamed of, no vice, no degradation; it cannot be classified as an illness; we consider it to be a variation of the sexual function, produced by a certain arrest of sexual development. Many highly respectable individuals of ancient and modern times have been homosexuals, several of the greatest men among them (Plato, Michelangelo, Leonardo da Vinci, etc.). It is a great injustice to persecute homosexuality as a crime – and a cruelty, too. If you do not believe me, read the books of Havelock Ellis.
Letter to a woman requesting treatment for her son, 9 April 1935, publ. in *The Letters of Sigmund Freud* (1961)

22 Every normal person, in fact, is only normal on the average. His ego approximates to that of the psychotic in some part or other and to a greater or lesser extent.
'Analysis Terminable and Interminable', sect. 5 (1937), repr. in *Complete Works, Standard Edition*, vol. 23 (ed. James Strachey and Anna Freud, 1964)

23 The great question that has never been answered, and which I have not yet been able to answer, despite my thirty years of research into the feminine soul, is 'What does a woman want?' ['*Was will das Weib?*']
Quoted in *Sigmund Freud: Life and Work*, vol. 2, pt 3, ch. 16 (1955) by Ernest Jones

24 Yes, America is gigantic, but a gigantic mistake.
Quoted in *Memories of a Psycho-analyst*, ch. 9 (1959) by Ernest Jones. 'America is the most grandiose experiment the world has seen,' Freud said on another occasion, 'but, I am afraid, it is not going to be a success.' (*Freud: the Man and his Cause*, pt 3, ch. 12, 1980, by Ronald W. Clark)

Nancy Friday
(b. 1937)
US author

After My Secret Garden *(1973), a study of female sexuality, she published* Men in Love *(1980) and* Women on Top *(1991), chronicles of sexual fantasies which she describes as 'the triumph of love over rage'.*

1 Women are learning that nobody gives you an orgasm, nobody makes you sexual, except yourself.
Men in Love, ch. 1 (1980)

2 For the mating game to even begin, the animal must abandon at least momentarily the search for nuts and berries to pick up the erotic scent. In the very simplest of terms, there is no time for sex in a materially greedy world.
Women on Top, pt 1, 'Report from the Erotic Interior' (1991)

3 Early twentieth-century man lived in a dizzying, swivel-headed attitude toward women's sexuality. He needed to see woman as chaste, passive, spiritual, she who was so close to heaven she could save his very soul after a murderous day of competition in the new industrial society. This was known as 'the cult of the household nun'.
Ibid., pt 2, 'A Little History'

Betty Friedan
(1921–2006)
US feminist activist and author

Her book, The Feminine Mystique *(1963) was a crucial influence on the emerging women's movement. She was a founder of the National Organization for Women (NOW) (1966) and called the first International Feminist Congress in 1973, though she later repudiated some aspects of contemporary feminism.*

1 The problem that has no name stirring in the minds of so many American women today is not a matter of loss of femininity or too much education, or the demands of domesticity. It is far more important than anyone recognizes. It is the key to these other new and old problems which have been torturing women and their husbands and children, and puzzling their doctors and educators for years. It may well be the key to our future as a nation and a culture. We can no longer ignore that voice within women that says: 'I want something more than my husband and my children and my home.'
The Feminine Mystique, ch. 1 (1963)

2 The feminine mystique has succeeded in burying millions of American women alive.
Ibid., ch. 13

3 It is easier to live through someone else than to become complete yourself.
Ibid., ch. 14

4 Make policy, not coffee.
The Second Stage, ch. 1 (1981). The slogan was adopted during the National Organization for Women's Political Caucus in 1971.

Milton Friedman
(b. 1912)
US economist

A convinced monetarist, he was adviser to President REAGAN *(1981–9) and an influence on the economic policies of the Conservative government under* MARGARET THATCHER. *See also* ANONYMOUS 92.

1 History suggests that capitalism is a necessary condition for political freedom. Clearly it is not a sufficient condition.
Capitalism and Freedom, ch. 1 (1962)

2 We are all Keynesians now.
Quoted in *Time* 31 December 1965. In a letter to the magazine's editor 4 February 1966, Friedman protested that the quote was taken out of context, since he had added 'in another [sense], nobody is any longer a Keynesian'.

3 People are out of work. Interest rates go up. Money gets tight. It's unpleasant. Only later do the good effects of an end to rising prices show up. The problem is getting through the painful cure without wanting another drink. The greatest difficulty in curtailing inflation is that, after a while, people begin to think they'd rather have the sickness than the cure.
There's No Such Thing as a Free Lunch, Introduction (1975)

4 Perfect competition is a theoretical concept like the Euclidean line, which has no width and no depth. Just as we've never seen that line there has never been truly free enterprise.
Ibid., Introduction

5 What kind of society isn't structured on greed?
Ibid., Introduction

Brian Friel
(b. 1929)
Irish playwright and author

He gained recognition with Philadelphia, Here I Come! *(1964), which, like his later plays* Translations *(1980) and* Dancing at Lughnasa *(1990), deals with his country, its customs, and emigration.*

1 People with a culture of poverty suffer much less from repression than we of the middle class suffer and indeed, if I may make the suggestion with due

qualification, they often have a hell of a lot more fun than we have.

The Freedom of the City, Act 1 (1974). Spoken by Dodds.

2 It is not the literal past, the 'facts' of history, that shape us, but images of the past embodied in language ... We must never cease renewing those images; because once we do, we fossilize.

Translations, Act 3 (1981). Spoken by Hugh.

3 The Troubles are a pigmentation in our lives here, a constant irritation that detracts from real life. But life has to do with something else as well, and it's the other things which are the more permanent and real.

Interview in *Vanity Fair* October 1991. Referring to Northern Ireland.

Max Frisch
(1911–91)
Swiss novelist and playwright

He adopted an Expressionist style in his examinations of the moral dilemmas of the mid-20th century, as in the novels Stiller *(1954) and* Homo Faber *(1957), and the plays* Andorra *(1961) and* The Fire Raisers *(1962).*

1 Technology ... the knack of so arranging the world that we don't have to experience it.

Homo Faber, 'Second Stop' (1957). Spoken by Hanna.

Erich Fromm
(1900–80)
German-born US psychologist

His books, which blend psychoanalysis with sociology and philosophy, show the influences of Marx and existentialism. His principal works are Escape from Freedom *(1941),* The Sane Society *(1955) and* The Art of Loving *(1956).*

1 Man's main task in life is to give *birth* to himself, to become what he potentially is. The most important product of his effort is his own personality.

Man for Himself, ch. 4 (1947)

2 Reason is man's instrument for arriving at the truth, intelligence is man's instrument for manipulating the world more successfully; the former is essentially human, the latter belongs to the animal part of man.

The Sane Society, ch. 3 (1955)

3 Love is often nothing but a favorable exchange between two people who get the most of what they can expect, considering their value on the personality market.

Ibid., ch. 5

4 In the nineteenth century the problem was that *God is dead*; in the twentieth century the problem is that *man is dead*. In the nineteenth century inhumanity meant cruelty; in the twentieth century it means schizoid self-alienation. The danger of the past was that men became slaves. The danger of the future is that men may become robots.

Ibid., ch. 9. Fromm was echoing a speech made by ADLAI STEVENSON at Columbia University in 1954: 'We are not in danger of becoming slaves any more, but of becoming robots.'

5 Just as modern mass production requires the standardization of commodities, so the social process requires standardization of man, and this standardization is called equality.

The Art of Loving, ch. 2 (1956)

(Sir) David Frost
(b. 1939)
British broadcaster

Having 'risen without trace', as Kitty Muggeridge famously commented to her husband MALCOLM MUGGERIDGE, *he established himself as an incisive interviewer on British and American TV. He co-founded London Weekend Television and in 1983 co-founded and presented TV-am.*

1 Hello, good evening, and welcome.

The Frost Report (TV show, 1966–7). The words were used to open each show in this and subsequent Frost series.

Robert Frost
(1874–1963)
US poet

His lyrical poetry was traditional in form and inspired by rural New England, as in the volume, New Hampshire *(1923). He won four Pulitzer prizes and came to be regarded as an unofficial US poet laureate. The critic Yvor Winters described him as a 'poet of the minor theme, the casual approach, and the discreetly eccentric attitude'.*

1 Ah, when to the heart of man
Was it ever less than a treason
To go with the drift of things
To yield with a grace to reason

And bow and accept at the end
Of a love or a season?
'Reluctance', publ. in *A Boy's Will* (1913)

2 My apple trees will never get across
And eat the cones under his pines, I tell him.
He only says, 'Good fences make good neighbors'.
'Mending Wall', publ. in *North of Boston* (1914)

3 Something there is that doesn't love a wall,
And wants it down.
'Mending Wall', ibid.

4 Before I built a wall I'd ask to know
What I was walling in or walling out,
And to whom I was like to give offence.
'Mending Wall', ibid.

5 And nothing to look backward to with pride,
And nothing to look forward to with hope.
'The Death of the Hired Man', ibid.

6 Home is the place where, when you have to go there,
They have to take you in.
Husband, ibid. Wife replies: 'I should have called it/Something you somehow haven't to deserve.'

7 The nearest friends can go
With anyone to death, comes so far short
They might as well not try to go at all.
'Home Burial', ibid.

8 Most of the change we think we see in life
Is due to truths being in and out of favor.
'The Black Cottage', ibid.

9 The best way out is always through.
'A Servant to Servants', ibid.

10 Pressed into service means pressed out of shape.
'The Self-Seeker', ibid.

11 I shall be telling this with a sigh
Somewhere ages and ages hence:
Two roads diverged in a wood, and I –
I took the one less traveled by,
And that has made all the difference.
'The Road Not Taken', publ. in *Mountain Interval* (1916)

12 I'd like to get away from earth awhile
And then come back to it and begin over.
May no fate wilfully misunderstand me
And half grant what I wish and snatch me away
Not to return. Earth's the right place for love:
I don't know where it's likely to go better.
'Birches', ibid.

13 One could do worse than be a swinger of birches.
'Birches', ibid.

14 I wonder about the trees:
Why do we wish to bear
Forever the noise of these
More than another noise
So close to our dwelling place.
'The Sound of Trees', ibid.

15 A poem . . . begins as a lump in the throat, a sense of wrong, a homesickness, a lovesickness . . . It finds the thought and the thought finds the words.
Letter to poet and anthologist Louis Untermeyer, 1 January 1916, publ. in *The Letters of Robert Frost to Louis Untermeyer* (ed. Louis Untermeyer, 1963)

16 I met a Californian who would
Talk California – a state so blessed
He said, in climate, none had ever died there
A natural death, and Vigilance Committees
Had had to organize to stock the graveyards
And vindicate the state's humanity.
'New Hampshire', publ. in *New Hampshire* (1923)

17 No wonder poets sometimes have to *seem*
So much more business-like than business men.
Their wares are so much harder to get rid of.
'New Hampshire', ibid.

18 Some say the world will end in fire,
Some say in ice.
From what I've tasted of desire
I hold with those who favor fire.
But if it had to perish twice,
I think I know enough of hate
To say that for destruction ice
Is also great
And would suffice.
'Fire and Ice', ibid.

19 My little horse must think it queer
To stop without a farmhouse near.
'Stopping by Woods on a Snowy Evening', ibid.

20 The woods are lovely, dark and deep.
But I have promises to keep,
And miles to go before I sleep,
And miles to go before I sleep.
'Stopping by Woods on a Snowy Evening', ibid. The lines were regularly quoted by JOHN F. KENNEDY to wind up speeches during his 1960 presidential campaign.

21 Tree at my window, window tree,
My sash is lowered when night comes on;

But let there never be curtain drawn
Between you and me.
'Tree at My Window', publ. in *West-Running Brook* (1928)

22 I have been one acquainted with the night.
'Acquainted with the Night', ibid. Opening line.

23 I'd as soon write free verse as play tennis with
the net down.
Quoted in *Interviews with Robert Frost* (1966) by Edward
Lathem

24 They cannot scare me with their empty spaces
Between stars – on stars where no human race is.
I have it in me so much nearer home
To scare myself with my own desert places.
'Desert Places', publ. in *A Further Range* (1936)

25 Let the cloudburst roil and toil!
The worst it can do to me
Is carry some garden soil
A little nearer to the sea.
'In Time of Cloudburst', ibid.

26 Two such as you with such a master speed
Cannot be parted nor be swept away
From one another once you are agreed
That life is only life forevermore
Together wing to wing and oar to oar.
'The Master Speed', ibid. The verse was inscribed on the grave-
stone of Frost and his wife Elinor in 1963.

27 No memory of having starred
Atones for later disregard,
Or keeps the end from being hard.
'Provide, Provide', ibid.

28 I never dared be radical when young
For fear it would make me conservative when old.
'Precaution', ibid.

29 It should be the pleasure of a poem itself to tell
it how it can. The figure a poem makes. It begins in
delight and ends in wisdom. The figure is the same
for love.
'The Figure a Poem Makes', Preface to *Collected Poems* (1939)

30 No tears in the writer, no tears in the reader.
'The Figure a Poem Makes', ibid.

31 The land was ours before we were the land's.
She was our land more than a hundred years
Before we were her people.
'The Gift Outright', publ. in *The Witness Tree* (1942). Frost
recited this poem at the inauguration of President KENNEDY,
20 January 1961.

32 Happiness Makes Up in Height What It Lacks in
Length.
Poem title, ibid.

33 And were an epitaph to be my story
I'd have a short one ready for my own.
I would have written of me on my stone:
I had a lover's quarrel with the world.
'The Lesson for Today', ibid.

34 We dance round in a ring and suppose,
But the Secret sits in the middle and knows.
'The Secret Sits', ibid.

35 Poetry is a way of taking life by the throat.
Quoted in *Robert Frost: The Trial by Existence*, ch. 18 (1960)
by Elizabeth S. Sergeant

36 Forgive, O Lord, my little jokes on Thee
And I'll forgive Thy great big one on me.
'Cluster of Faith', publ. in *In the Clearing* (1962)

37 You don't have to deserve your mother's love.
You have to deserve your father's. He's more par-
ticular . . . The father is always a Republican towards
his son, and his mother's always a Democrat.
Interview in *Writers at Work* (second series, ed. George
Plimpton, 1963)

38 Thinking isn't agreeing or disagreeing. That's
voting.
Ibid.

39 Always fall in with what you're asked to accept.
Take what is given, and make it over your way. My
aim in life has always been to hold my own with
whatever's going. Not against: with.
Vogue 14 March 1963

40 Poetry is what is lost in translation.
Quoted in *Robert Frost: a Backward Look*, ch. 1 (1964) by Louis
Untermeyer. In similar vein, SAMUEL TAYLOR COLERIDGE
wrote, in *Biographia Literaria* (1817): 'In poetry, in which every
line, every phrase, may pass the ordeal of deliberation and
deliberate choice, it is possible, and barely possible, to attain
that *ultimatum* which I have ventured to propose as the
infallible test of a blameless style; namely: its *untranslatableness* in words of the same language without injury to the
meaning.'

Christopher Fry

(1907–2005)

British playwright

Born Christopher Fry Harris. Described by John Mason Brown as 'a fellow who has wandered from one Elizabethan Age into another', he specializes in free-verse dramas that combine comedy and an underlying mysticism, as in The Lady's Not for Burning *(1948) and* Venus Observed *(1950).*

1 It is the individual man
In his individual freedom who can mature
With his warm spirit the unripe world.
The Firstborn, Act 1, Sc. 1 (1946). Spoken by Moses.

2 I travel light; as light,
That is, as a man can travel who will
Still carry his body around because
Of its sentimental value.
The Lady's Not for Burning, Act 1 (1948). Spoken by Thomas. The play's title was famously adapted: see MARGARET THATCHER 6.

3 What after all
Is a halo? It's only one more thing to keep clean.
Thomas, ibid., Act 1

4 Religion
Has made an honest woman of the supernatural,
And we won't have it kicking over the traces
    again.
Tappercoom, ibid., Act 2

5 The best
Thing we can do is to make wherever we're lost in
Look as much like home as we can.
Nicholas, ibid., Act 3

6 The moon is nothing
But a circumambulating aphrodisiac
Divinely subsidized to provoke the world
Into a rising birth-rate.
Thomas Mendip, ibid., Act 3

7 Comedy is an escape, not from truth but from despair; a narrow escape into faith.
Time 20 November 1950

8 Try thinking of love, or something.
Amor vincit insomnia.
Sleep of Prisoners (1951). Spoken by Peter, adapting the Latin proverb 'Amor vincit omnia' ('Love conquers all').

9 Coffee in England is just toasted milk.
New York Post 29 November 1962

Roger Fry

(1866–1934)

British critic and painter

A member of the Bloomsbury group, he organized the first London exhibition of Post-Impressionists (1910) and set up the Omega Workshops (1913–19) for the benefit of young artists. Brian Sewell called him 'the father of foolish criticism'.

1 Art is significant deformity.
Quoted in *Roger Fry,* ch. 8 (1940) by VIRGINIA WOOLF

Northrop Frye

(1912–91)

Canadian literary critic

He established his reputation with Fearful Symmetry *(1947) and* Anatomy of Criticism *(1957), which deal with literary archetypes. The Great Code (1982) examines the symbolism of the Bible.*

1 Popular art is normally decried as vulgar by the cultivated people of its time; then it loses favor with its original audience as a new generation grows up; then it begins to merge into the softer lighting of 'quaint', and cultivated people become interested in it, and finally it begins to take on the archaic dignity of the primitive.
Anatomy of Criticsm, 'Mythical Phase: Symbol as Archetype' (1957)

Carlos Fuentes

(b. 1928)

Mexican author and critic

Since winning recognition for his first collection of short stories, The Masked Days *(1954), he has written numerous works of fiction and criticism, including* Terra Nostra *(1975), a novel examining Latin America's cultural identity.*

1 What the United States does best is to understand itself. What it does worst is understand others.
Time 16 June 1986

2 If the Soviet Union can give up the Brezhnev Doctrine for the Sinatra Doctrine, the United States can give up the James Monroe Doctrine for the Marilyn Monroe Doctrine: Let's all go to bed wearing the perfume we like best.
Quoted in *The Times* 23 February 1990

Francis Fukuyama

(b. 1952)

US historian

His chief work, The End of History and the Last Man *(1992), was commonly cited as a description of the world in the wake of the Cold War.* State-Building *appeared in 2004.*

1 What we may be witnessing is not just the end of the Cold War but the end of history as such: that is, the end point of man's ideological evolution and the universalization of Western liberal democracy.

Independent 20 September 1989

J. William Fulbright

(1905–95)

US politician

James William Fulbright. Elected as a Democrat to Congress in 1942 and to the Senate in 1944, he established a system of exchange programmes for teachers and students between the USA and other countries (1946). He opposed McCarthyism and the Vietnam War.

1 In the long course of history, having people who understand your thought is much greater security than another submarine.

New York Times 26 June 1986. Speaking of the Fulbright scholarship programme.

R. Buckminster Fuller

(1895–1983)

US engineer and poet

Richard Buckminster Fuller. A designer and inventor who developed the geodesic dome, he became Professor of Poetry at Harvard in 1962.

1 Here is God's purpose –
for God, to me, it seems,
is a verb
not a noun,
proper or improper.

Untitled poem, written 1940, publ. in *No More Secondhand God* (1963)

2 Either war is obsolete or men are.

New Yorker 8 January 1966

3 Dare to be naïve.

Synergetics, 'Moral of the Work' (1975)

Thomas Fuller

(1608–61)

English cleric and antiquary

He was chaplain-extraordinary to Charles II and published such witty and anecdotal works as The Holy and Profane State *(1642) and* History of the Worthies of Britain *(1662).*

1 A little skill in antiquity inclines a man to Popery; but depth in that study brings him about again to our religion.

The Holy State and the Profane State, bk 2, ch. 6 ('The True Church Antiquary'), maxim 1 (1642)

2 Light, God's eldest daughter, is a principal beauty in a building.

Ibid., bk 3, ch. 7 ('Of Building'), maxim 6

3 Get the language, in part, without which key thou shalt unlock little of moment.

Ibid., bk 3, ch. 4 ('Of Travelling'), maxim 2. On travelling abroad.

4 Know most of the rooms of thy native country before thou goest over the threshold thereof.

Ibid., bk 3, ch. 4, maxim 4

5 Anger is one of the sinews of the soul; he that wants it hath a maimed mind.

Ibid., bk 3, ch. 8 ('Of Anger')

6 Memory is like a purse, – if it be over-full that it cannot shut, all will drop out of it. Take heed of a gluttonous curiosity to feed on many things, lest the greediness of the appetite of thy memory spoil the digestion thereof.

Ibid., bk 3, ch. 10 ('Of Memory'), maxim 4

7 Tombs are the clothes of the dead. A grave is but a plain suit, and a rich monument is one embroidered.

Ibid., bk 3, ch. 14 ('Of Tombs')

8 Moderation is the silken string running through the pearl-chain of all virtues.

Ibid., bk 3, ch. 20 ('Of Moderation'). Quoting Bishop Hall.

9 Deceive not thyself by over-expecting happiness in the married estate . . . Remember the nightingales which sing only some months in the spring, but commonly are silent when they have hatched their eggs, as if their mirth were turned into care for their young ones.

Ibid., bk 3, ch. 22 ('Of Marriage')

10 To smell a turf of fresh earth is wholesome for

the body; no less are thoughts of mortality cordial to the soul.
Ibid., bk 4, ch. 13 ('The Court Lady'), maxim 13

11 It is always darkest just before the day dawneth.
Pisgah-sight of Palestine, bk 2, ch. 2 (1650)

Rose Fyleman
(1877–1957)
British author for children

Although she had little time for children, she devoted a career to writing for them, as in Fairies and Chimneys *(1918).*

1 There are fairies at the bottom of our garden!
'The Fairies', publ. in *Fairies and Chimneys* (1918)

G

Clark Gable
(1901–60)
US screen actor

Hailed as 'the King of Hollywood', he starred in Mutiny on the Bounty *(1935),* Gone with the Wind *(1939) and his last film,* The Misfits *(1961).*

1 Frankly, my dear, I don't give a damn!
Gone with the Wind (film, 1939, screenplay by Sidney Howard based on the 1936 novel by Margaret Mitchell, directed by Victor Fleming and others). Rhett Butler (Clark Gable) bids farewell to Scarlett O'Hara (Vivien Leigh), responding to her lament, 'Where shall I go? What shall I do?' Because of the wish not to offend the censors, the words were spoken with the emphasis on 'give' to soften the impact of the oath; however, producer David O. Selznick was still fined $5,000. For the original version of this speech, see MARGARET MITCHELL 5.

Zsa Zsa Gabor
(b. 1919)
Hungarian-born US actor

She became a denizen of gossip columns for her wealth and numerous marriages and affairs. Her liaison with the dictator Rafael Trujillo provoked the comment, 'the most expensive courtesan since Madame de Pompadour'.

1 I never hated a man enough to give him diamonds back.
Quoted in the *Observer* 25 August 1957

2 A man in love is incomplete until he has married – then he's finished.
Quoted in *Newsweek* 28 March 1960

3 Husbands are like fires. They go out when unattended.
Ibid.

Émile Gaboriau
(c. 1835–73)
French author

Called the father of detective fiction, he created the sleuths Père Tabaret and Monsieur Lecoq, the protagonists of such novels as Widow Lerouge *(1866) and* The Mystery of Orcival *(1867).*

1 Woman submits to her fate; man makes his.
Other People's Money, pt 1, ch. 27 (1874). Spoken by Mlle. Lucienne.

Thomas Gainsborough
(1727–88)
English painter

The first great English landscape painter, he shunned the Academy in favour of experimenting with new ideas and techniques. He became a fashionable portraitist after moving to Bath in 1759, but continued to paint rural scenes set in his native Suffolk.

1 I wish you would recollect that painting and punctuality mix like oil and vinegar, and that genius and regularity are utter enemies and must be to the end of time.
Letter, 1 May 1772, publ. in *The Letters of Thomas Gainsborough* (ed. Mary Woodall, 1961). Explaining his delay in completing a commission.

2 We are all going to Heaven, and Vandyke is of the company.
Attributed last words, in *Thomas Gainsborough*, ch. 9 (1905) by William B. Boulton. Anthony Van Dyck was a seminal influence on Gainsborough's work.

Serge Gainsbourg
(1928–91)
French singer, songwriter and film-maker

Originally Lucien Ginzburg. He wrote for Johnny Hallyday and Juliette Greco, among other singers, and also recorded many of his own songs. According to his biographer, he 'acted out the country's post-war vices: alcoholism, nicotine, exhibitionism, incest, sex-mania and self-love'.

1 *Je t'aime … moi non plus.*
'Je t'aime … moi non plus' (song, 1969, sung with Jane Birkin). The erotic duet by Gainsbourg and Birkin was formally condemned by the Vatican and banned by many radio stations, even in its instrumental version, though still reached the top of the British charts. The song was originally recorded in 1967 by Brigitte Bardot but this version was not released until 1986. Gainsbourg directed a film titled *Je t'aime … moi non plus*, giving GÉRARD DEPARDIEU one of his first film roles in 1976. See also SALVADOR DALÍ 1.

Hugh Gaitskell
(1906–63)
British politician

As Labour leader (from 1955), he opposed ANTHONY EDEN's Suez policy as well as his own party's vote for unilateral disarmament (1960). For TONY BENN he was a 'divisive leader'

with 'a real civil servant's mind'. See also ANEURIN BEVAN 10.

1 I have never had a great many baths myself and I can assure those who are in the habit of having a great many baths that it does not make a great deal of difference to their health if they have fewer. And as far as appearance [goes], most of that is underneath and nobody sees it.
Speech at Hastings, 1947, quoted in *Hugh Gaitskell: A Political Biography*, ch. 6, sect. 2 (1979) by Philip M. Williams. Gaitskell, then Minister for Fuel and Power, was proposing an economy drive. The remark, which he later said was intended as a joke, elicited the rejoinder by WINSTON CHURCHILL in the House of Commons: 'When Ministers of the Crown speak like this … the Prime Minister and his friends have no need to wonder why they are getting increasingly into bad odour.'

2 There are some of us, Mr Chairman, who will fight and fight and fight again to save the Party we love.
Speech at Labour Party Conference, Scarborough, 5 October 1961, publ. in *The Penguin Book of Twentieth-Century Speeches* (ed. Brian MacArthur, 1999). Gaitskell was defending the Party's defence policy against calls for unilateral nuclear disarmament, which he believed would tear the Party asunder. The vote resulted in a defeat of the official policy, although this was overturned at the following year's Conference.

3 It does mean … the end of Britain as an independent European state … .It means the end of a thousand years of history. You may say, 'Let it end', but, my goodness, it is a decision that needs a little care and thought.
Speech at Labour Party Conference, Brighton, 3 October 1962, ibid. Referring to Britain's membership of the EEC. HAROLD MACMILLAN's Conservative government had initiated negotiations for joining the European Community, although DE GAULLE's declared intention in 1963 to veto any application by Britain made the issue a less pressing concern.

J. K. Galbraith
(1908–2006)
Canadian-born US economist

John Kenneth Galbraith. A Keynesian, he was adviser to Presidents KENNEDY and JOHNSON. His books had a popular appeal, particularly The Affluent Society *(1958) and* The Age of Uncertainty *(1977).*

1 In the usual (though certainly not in every) public decision on economic policy, the choice is between courses that are almost equally good or equally bad. It is the narrowest decisions that are most ardently debated. If the world is lucky enough to enjoy peace, it may even one day make the discovery, to the horror of doctrinaire free-enterprisers and doctrinaire planners alike, that what is called capitalism

and what is called socialism are both capable of working quite well.

'The American Economy: Its Substance and Myth', publ. in *Years of the Modern* (ed. J. W. Chase, 1949)

2 Wealth is not without its advantages and the case to the contrary, although it has often been made, has never proved widely persuasive.

The Affluent Society, ch. 1, sect. 1 (1958). Opening words of book.

3 Consumer wants can have bizarre, frivolous, or even immoral origins, and an admirable case can still be made for a society that seeks to satisfy them. But the case cannot stand if it is the process of satisfying wants that creates the wants.

Ibid., ch. 11, sect. 2

4 It is a far, far better thing to have a firm anchor in nonsense than to put out on the troubled seas of thought.

Ibid., ch. 11, sect. 4. Of the resistance of conventional wisdom to the 'economics of affluence'.

5 In a community where public services have failed to keep abreast of private consumption things are very different. Here, in an atmosphere of private opulence and public squalor, the private goods have full sway.

Ibid., ch. 18, sect. 2

6 Meetings are a great trap. Soon you find yourself trying to get agreement and then the people who disagree come to think they have a right to be persuaded. Thus they acquire power; thus meetings become a source of opposition and trouble. However, they are indispensable when you don't want to do anything.

Journal entry, 22 April 1961, publ. in *Ambassador's Journal*, ch. 5 (1969). The journal was written while Galbraith was serving as US ambassador to India 1961–3.

7 Politics is not the art of the possible. It consists in choosing between the disastrous and the unpalatable.

Letter to President Kennedy, 2 March 1962, ibid., ch. 15. Galbraith was referring to Bismarck's celebrated saying (OTTO VON BISMARCK 4).

8 By all but the pathologically romantic, it is now recognized that this is not the age of the small man.

The New Industrial State, ch. 3 (1967)

9 There are few ironclad rules of diplomacy but to one there is no exception. When an official reports

that talks were useful, it can safely be concluded that nothing was accomplished.

'The American Ambassador', publ. in *Foreign Service Journal* June 1969

10 All successful revolutions are the kicking in of a rotten door. The violence of revolutions is the violence of men who charge into a vacuum.

The Age of Uncertainty, ch. 3 (1977)

11 All of the great leaders have had one characteristic in common: it was the willingness to confront unequivocally the major anxiety of their people in their time. This, and not much else, is the essence of leadership.

Ibid., ch. 12

12 In any great organization it is far, far safer to be wrong with the majority than to be right alone.

Guardian 28 July 1989

13 There's a certain part of the contented majority who love anybody who is worth a billion dollars.

Guardian 23 May 1992. Referring to millionaire presidential candidate H. Ross Perot.

14 The Third Way is a purely political concept. The increase in numbers and power of the middle-income groups means that governments choose to meet their needs first. The Third Way is a justification of that necessity.

Interview with ROY HATTERSLEY in the *Guardian* 17 October 1998

Galilei Galileo

(1564–1642)
Italian mathematician, physicist and astronomer

The inventor of the first astronomical telescope (1609), he made great advances in interpreting the laws of physics. His theories contradicted the teachings of ARISTOTLE, and his espousal of the Copernican system of planetary motion led to his prosecution by the Inquisition in 1633.

1 Philosophy is written in this grand book, the universe, which stands continually open to our gaze. But the book cannot be understood unless one first learns to comprehend the language and read the letters in which it is composed. It is written in the language of mathematics, and its characters are triangles, circles, and other geometric figures without which it is humanly impossible to understand a single word of it.

The Assayer (1623), repr. in *Discoveries and Opinions of Galileo* (ed./transl. Stillman Drake, 1957)

2 *Eppur – si muove!*
[And yet it moves!]
Attributed. Allegedly whispered to his companion in 1633, as Galileo rose from signing a recantation – forced on him by the Inquisition in Rome – of the Copernican theory that the earth moves round the sun.

Noel Gallagher
(b. 1967)
British rock musician

He is guitarist with and main songwriter of Oasis, the Manchester band that was at the forefront of 'Britpop' in the 1990s.

1 What people have got to understand is that we are lads. We have burgled houses and nicked car stereos, and we like girls and we swear and we go to the football and take the piss.
Interview in *Melody Maker* 30 March 1996. The confession prompted an investigation by Greater Manchester police.

2 Drugs is like getting up and having a cup of tea in the morning.
Radio interview, 28 January 1997, quoted in the *Daily Telegraph* 31 January 1997

Paul Gallico
(1897–1976)
US novelist

Of his forty-odd books, best known is The Snow Goose *(1941), set in the Lincolnshire Fens.* The Poseidon Adventure *(1969) was made into one of the first big-budget disaster movies (1972).*

1 No one can be as calculatedly rude as the British, which amazes Americans, who do not understand studied insult and can only offer abuse as a substitute.
New York Times 14 January 1962. Gallico lived in England from 1936.

2 If there is any larceny in a man, golf will bring it out.
New York Times 6 March 1977

José Antonio Viera Gallo
(b. 1943)
Chilean politician

He served as Under-Secretary of Justice (1970–2) in the government of SALVADOR ALLENDE.

1 Socialism can only arrive by bicycle.
Quoted in *Energy and Equity*, Foreword (1974) by Ivan Illich

George Galloway
(b. 1954)
British politician

Chairman of the Scottish Labour Party aged 26, he was elected MP for Glasgow Hillhead in 1987. He opposed the Gulf War and military action in Afghanistan, and campaigned against sanctions on Iraq. Following his expulsion from the Labour Party in 2003, he founded a new party, Respect, for which he won a seat in 2005.

1 So, I salute your courage, your strength, your indefatigability. And I want you to know that we are with you *hatta al-nasr, hatta al-nasr, hatta al-Quds* [until victory, until victory, until Jerusalem].
Baghdad radio broadcast, 18 January 1994, quoted in *The Times* 20 January 1994. Galloway afterwards claimed that his words had been taken out of context, and he had addressed the Iraqi people in general, not specifically SADDAM HUSSEIN, as was alleged.

John Galsworthy
(1867–1933)
English novelist and playwright

The writer of numerous plays, many of them addressing social issues, he is best remembered for his chronicles of the Forsyte family (1906–28).

1 From all *I* can learn, he's got no business, no income, and no connection worth speaking of; but then, I know nothing – nobody tells me anything.
The Man of Property, pt 1, ch. 1 (1906). Spoken by James Forsyte referring to Bosinney. 'Nobody tells me anything' is the former's familiar refrain.

2 There's just one rule for politicians all over the world: Don't say in power what you say in opposition; if you do, you only have to carry out what the other fellows have found impossible.
Maid in Waiting, ch. 7 (1931). Spoken by Professor Hallorsen.

3 Religion was nearly dead because there was no longer real belief in future life; but something was struggling to take its place – service – social service – the ants' creed, the bees' creed!
Over the River, ch. 11 (1933). Sir Lawrence Mont muses on the 1930s. *Over the River* is bk 3 of *End of the Chapter*, the last instalment of the Forsyte Chronicles.

4 Everything known before it happens; and headlines twice the size of the events.
General Cherrell, ibid., ch. 27. Referring to the press.

Ray Galton and Alan Simpson

See TONY HANCOCK

Indira Gandhi

(1917–84)

Indian politician

Daughter of JAWAHARLAL NEHRU, *she was leader of the Congress Party (1966–77) and Prime Minister (1966–77, 1980–4). She stated: 'My father was a statesman, I'm a political woman. My father was a saint. I'm not.'*

1 I do not care whether I live or die. I have lived a long life and I am proud that I spent the whole of my life in the service of my people. I am only proud of this and of nothing else. I shall continue to serve until my last breath and when I die, I can say, that every drop of my blood will invigorate India and strengthen it.

Speech in Bhubaneshwar, Orissa, 30 October 1984, quoted in *Indira: The Life of Indira Nehru Gandhi*, ch. 21 (2001) by Katherine Frank. Said on the eve of her assassination by members of her Sikh bodyguard.

Mahatma Gandhi

(1869–1948)

Indian political and spiritual leader

Mohandas Karamchand Gandhi, called Mahatma ('Great soul'). As the driving force behind India's struggle for independence, he advocated non-violent civil disobedience, fasts and passive resistance, for which he came to be regarded popularly as a saint. He was assassinated by a Hindu fanatic. According to EINSTEIN, *'In our time of utter moral decadence he was the only statesman to stand for a higher human relationship in the political sphere.' See also* JAWAHARLAL NEHRU 3.

1 I claim that in losing the spinning wheel we lost our left lung. We are, therefore, suffering from galloping consumption. The restoration of the wheel arrests the progress of the fell disease.

Young India 13 October 1921

2 A policy is a temporary creed liable to be changed, but while it holds good it has got to be pursued with apostolic zeal.

Letter to the General Secretary of the Congress Party, India, 8 March 1922, publ. in *Gandhi's Letters on Indian Affairs*, 'To Co-workers' (1923)

3 Non-violence is the first article of my faith. It is the last article of my faith.

Speech at defence trial, Ahmedabad, 18 March 1922, publ. in *The Penguin Book of Twentieth-Century Speeches* (ed. Brian MacArthur, 1999). Gandhi was charged with sedition for three articles published in his newspaper *Young India*. Pleading guilty and demanding of the judge 'the highest penalty that can be inflicted upon me for what in law is a deliberate crime and what appears to me to be the highest duty of a citizen', he was sentenced to six years' imprisonment, but released after two years on grounds of ill health.

4 I have nothing new to teach the world. Truth and non-violence are as old as the hills. All I have done is to try experiments in both on as vast a scale as I could.

Harijan 28 March 1936

5 An unjust law is itself a species of violence. Arrest for its breach is more so.

Non-Violence in Peace and War, vol. 2, ch. 150 (1949)

6 Reporter: 'Mr Gandhi, what do you think of Western civilization?'

Gandhi: 'I think it would be a very good idea.'

Attributed. There is no evidence of any such exchange having taken place, although E. F. SCHUMACHER (in *Good Work*, ch. 2, 1979) mentions seeing a film of Gandhi disembarking at Southampton, England, in 1930, in which Gandhi is asked his opinion on *modern* civilization, and gives the answer as above.

Greta Garbo

(1905–90)

Swedish-born US screen actress

Originally Greta Lovisa Gustafsson. 'The only one who has ever been really mysterious,' according to Joan Crawford, she was famously reclusive, reinforcing her image as 'the Swedish Sphinx'. She starred in Anna Karenina *(1935) and* Camille *(1937), among other films, and retired in 1941.*

1 I want to be alone.

Grand Hotel (film, 1932, screenplay by William A. Drake based on *Menschen im Hotel*, the German play and novel by VICKI BAUM, directed by Edmund Goulding). Spoken by Grusinskaya (Greta Garbo). The phrase was always associated with Garbo, although she claimed never to have said it word for word: 'I only said I want to be *left* alone.' However the screenplay has her speak the words three times to the Baron (played by John Barrymore). In the film *The Single Standard* (1929), her character says: 'I am walking alone because I want to be alone.'

Jerry Garcia

(1942–95)

US rock musician

Jerome John Garcia. He was a founder member of the Grateful Dead (1966), with whom he was singer, guitarist and songwriter. Increasing drugs and alcohol problems culminated in a fatal overdose.

1 What we do is as American as lynch mobs. America has always been a complex place.
Interview in *Rolling Stone* 30 November 1989. Speaking of the Grateful Dead.

Federico García Lorca
(1898–1936)
Spanish poet and playwright

He drew on the folk and flamenco traditions of Andalusia in his poems such as Gypsy Ballads *(1928) and his trilogy of plays,* Blood Wedding *(1933),* Yerma *(1934) and* The House of Bernarda Alba *(1936). He was assassinated by fascist partisans during the Spanish Civil War.*

1 Green oh how I love you green.
Green wind. Green boughs.
'Sleepwalking Ballad', publ. in *Gypsy Ballads* (1928, transl. 1995). Opening lines of poem.

2 They ride the roads
with souls of patent leather.
Hunched and nocturnal,
they command, where they appear,
the silence of dark rubber
and fears of fine sand.
'Ballad of the Spanish Civil Guard', ibid.

3 To see you naked is to recall the earth.
'Qasida of the Recumbent Woman', written 1931–4, publ. in *The Divan of the Tamarit* (1940, transl. 1990)

4 The two elements the traveller first captures in the big city are extrahuman architecture and furious rhythm. Geometry and anguish.
'A Poet in New York', lecture in Madrid, March 1932, publ. in *Poet in New York* (1940, transl. 1988)

5 The only things that the United States has given to the world are skyscrapers, jazz, and cocktails. That is all. And in Cuba, in *our* America, they make much better cocktails.
Interview, 1933, publ. in *Obras Completas*, vol. 3 (1986)

6 I'm hurt, hurt and humiliated beyond endurance, seeing the wheat ripening, the fountains never ceasing to give water, the sheep bearing hundreds of lambs, the she-dogs, until it seems the whole country rises to show me its tender sleeping young while I feel two hammer-blows here instead of the mouth of my child.
Yerma, Act 2, Sc. 2 (1934). Spoken by Yerma.

7 At five in the afternoon.
It was exactly five in the afternoon.

A boy brought the white sheet
at five in the afternoon.
'The Goring and the Death', publ. in *Lament for Ignacio Sánchez Mejías* (1935, transl. 1995). The poem describes the death of a bullfighter.

Gabriel García Márquez
(b. 1928)
Colombian author

His most famous novel, One Hundred Years of Solitude *(1967), was one of the earliest works to be categorized as 'magical realism'. Later books include* Love in the Time of Cholera *(1985) and* Strange Pilgrims *(1992).*

1 They felt that they had been the victims of some new and showy gypsy business and they decided not to return to the movies, considering that they already had too many troubles of their own to weep over the acted-out misfortunes of imaginary beings.
One Hundred Years of Solitude (1967). Referring to the people of Macondo, who have learned from the mayor's proclamation that the movies are not real and that 'the cinema was a machine of illusion and did not merit the emotional outbursts of the audience'.

2 The only difference today between Liberals and Conservatives is that the Liberals go to mass at five o'clock and the Conservatives at eight.
Colonel Aureliano Buendía, ibid.

3 Necessity has the face of a dog.
In Evil Hour (1968). Spoken by Mina.

4 No, not rich. I am a poor man with money, which is not the same thing.
Love in the Time of Cholera (1985). Spoken by Uncle Leo XII.

5 The problem with marriage is that it ends every night after making love, and it must be rebuilt every morning before breakfast.
Dr Urbino, ibid.

6 Ultimately, literature is nothing but carpentry. With both you are working with reality, a material just as hard as wood.
Interview in *Writers at Work* (sixth series, ed. George Plimpton, 1985)

John Garfield
(1913–52)
US actor

Originally Julius Garfinkle. He was often cast as a rebel in his film roles, which frequently reflected his own experiences on the wrong side of the tracks. He was blacklisted in 1951 for failing to name friends as Communists.

1 With my brains and your looks, we could go places.
The Postman Always Rings Twice (film, 1946, screenplay by Harry Ruskin and Niven Busch adapted from James M. Cain's novel, directed by Tay Garnett). Spoken by Frank Chambers (John Garfield).

2 I wasn't strong enough to resist corruption, but I was strong enough to fight for a piece of it.
Force of Evil (film, 1948, screenplay by Abraham Polonsky and Ira Wolfert adapted from Ira Wolfert's novel, directed by Abraham Polonsky). Spoken by Joe Morse (John Garfield).

Giuseppe Garibaldi
(1807–82)
Italian patriot and soldier

A leading figure in the struggle for a free united Italy, he applied the techniques of guerrilla warfare he had learned in South America in his various campaigns on behalf of the Italian nationalist movement. His conquest of Sicily and Naples at the head of a thousand 'Redshirts' (1860) enhanced his heroic status.

1 I offer neither pay, nor quarters, nor provisions; I offer hunger, thirst, forced marches, battles and death. Let him who loves his country in his heart, and not with his lips only, follow me.
Speech to the Garibaldi legion besieged in Rome, 2 July 1849, quoted in *Garibaldi's Defence of the Roman Republic*, pt 2, ch. 11 (1907) by G. M. Trevelyan

Judy Garland
(1922–69)
US screen actor and singer

Originally Frances Gumm. She was the child star of The Wizard of Oz *(1939), and, under the direction of her husband Vincente Minnelli, the lead in* Meet Me in St Louis *(1944). Caught in a spiral of depression and drugs, she returned to the screen with* A Star Is Born *(1954).*

1 Somewhere over the rainbow
Way up high,
There's a land that I heard of
Once in a lullaby.
'Over the Rainbow' (song, written by YIP HARBURG with music by Harold Arlen), sung as Dorothy in *The Wizard of Oz* (film, 1939). The song was re-recorded by Garland on the album *The London Sessions* (1960), by which time, according to her biographer, 'the song no longer belonged to Dorothy; it belonged, forever, to Judy Garland'.

2 Toto, I've a feeling we're not in Kansas anymore ... Now I know we're not in Kansas.
The Wizard of Oz (film, 1939, screenplay by Noel Langley, Florence Ryerson and Edgar Allan Wolfe from book by L. FRANK BAUM, directed by Victor Fleming). The words, spoken by Dorothy (Judy Garland) to her dog on arriving in the Land of Oz, do not appear in L. Frank Baum's original book, *The Wonderful Wizard of Oz* (1900).

3 I was born at the age of twelve on a Metro-Goldwyn-Mayer lot.
Quoted in the *Observer* 18 February 1951

John Garner
(1868–1967)
US politician

A Democratic leader in the House of Representatives, he was chosen as Speaker in 1931 and served as Vice-President (1933–41) under FRANKLIN ROOSEVELT.

1 The vice-presidency isn't worth a pitcher of warm piss. It doesn't amount to a hill of beans.
Quoted in *Cactus Jack*, ch. 11 (1978) by O. C. Fisher. The words are commonly misquoted '... pitcher of warm spit'. In 1963 Garner declared, 'Worst damnfool mistake I ever made was letting myself be elected Vice President of the United States. Should have stuck ... as Speaker of the House ... Gave up the second most important job in Government for eight long years as Roosevelt's spare tire.'

David Garrick
(1717–79)
English actor-manager and playwright

The foremost actor and theatre manager of his time, he was closely associated with the Drury Lane Theatre, where he performed to great acclaim in both tragedies and comedies. He wrote more than twenty plays and 'entertainments' and adapted many more. See OLIVER GOLDSMITH 52.

1 Heart of oak are our ships,
Heart of oak are our men.
We always are ready;
Steady, boys, steady;
We'll fight and we'll conquer again and again.
'Heart of Oak' (song), in *Harlequin's Invasion* (1759). Set to music by William Boyce.

William Lloyd Garrison
(1805–79)
US abolitionist

One of the foremost anti-slavery campaigners of his time, he founded The Liberator *in 1831, co-founded the American*

Anti-Slavery Society in 1833, and campaigned uncompromisingly for immediate emancipation.

1 Tell a man whose house is on fire to give a moderate alarm; tell him to moderately rescue his wife from the hands of the ravisher; tell the mother to gradually extricate her babe from the fire into which it has fallen; but urge me not to use moderation in a case like the present.
The Liberator 1 January 1831. 'Salutatory address' launching his newspaper, which he edited for the next thirty-four years. Its strident, uncompromising stance in support of Garrison's anti-slavery campaign aroused savage opposition.

2 I am in earnest – I will not equivocate – I will not excuse – I will not retreat a single inch – and I will be heard!
The Liberator 1 January 1831, 'Salutatory address'

3 Our country is the world – our countrymen are all mankind.
The Liberator 15 December 1837, 'Prospectus'

(Sir) Samuel Garth
(1661–1719)
English physician and poet

A member of the Kit-Cat Club, a coterie of Whig writers and intellectuals, he is most famous for his burlesque poem, The Dispensary *(1699). As a physician, he advocated a scheme of free dispensaries for the poor.*

1 Hourly his learned impertinence affords
A barren superfluity of words.
The Dispensary, canto 2, ll. 94–5 (1699)

2 While others meanly asked whole months to slay,
I oft dispatched the patient in a day.
Ibid., canto 4, ll. 57–8

3 Some fell by laudanum, and some by steel,
And death in ambush lay in every pill.
Ibid., canto 4, ll. 62–3

4 None violated truth, invaded right;
Yet had few laws, but will and appetite.
The people's peace they studied, and protest
No politics but public interest.
Hard was their lodging, homely was their food;
For all their luxury was doing good.
Claremont, ll. 144–9 (1715). Referring to Druids.

5 For though possession be the undoubted view;
To seize, is far less pleasure than pursue.
Ibid., ll. 229–30

Marcus Garvey
(1887–1940)
Jamaican civil rights campaigner

Calling himself a 'black Napoleon', he founded the Universal Negro Improvement Association in 1914, and from New York led the first American black nationalist movement, which rejected integration and favoured resettlement in Liberia.

1 Look for me in the whirlwind or the storm, look for me all around you, for, with God's grace, I shall come and bring with me countless millions of Black slaves who have died in America and the West Indies and the millions in Africa to aid you in the fight for Liberty, Freedom and Life.
'First Message to the Negroes of the World from Atlanta Prison', 10 February 1925, publ. in *The Philosophy and Opinions of Marcus Garvey*, vol. 2 (ed. Amy Jacques Garvey, 1923, rev. 1986)

2 No race has the last word on culture and on civilization. You do not know what the black man is capable of; you do not know what he is thinking and therefore you do not know what the oppressed and suppressed Negro, by virtue of his condition and circumstance, may give to the world as a surprise.
Speech at Royal Albert Hall, London, 6 June 1928, publ. in *Marcus Garvey and the Vision of Africa*, pt 5 (ed. John Henrik Clarke, 1974)

3 Day by day we hear the cry of AFRICA FOR THE AFRICANS. This cry has become a positive, determined one. It is a cry that is raised simultaneously the world over because of the universal oppression that affects the Negro.
Quoted in *The Philosophy and Opinions of Marcus Garvey*, vol. 1, ch. 1 (ed. Amy Jacques Garvey, 1923, rev. 1986)

Elizabeth Gaskell
(1810–65)
English novelist

Her novels, for example Mary Barton *(1848) and* North and South *(1855), focused on social issues and the impact of industrialization. Her biography,* The Life of Charlotte Brontë *(1857), aroused controversy as well as acclaim.*

1 A little credulity helps one on through life very smoothly.
Cranford, ch. 11 (1853). Spoken by Miss Matty.

2 I'll not listen to reason ... Reason always means what someone else has got to say.
Miss Matty's maid, Martha, ibid., ch. 14

3 He had not an ounce of superfluous flesh on his

bones, and leanness goes a great way towards gentility.
Wives and Daughters ch. 4 (1866). Referring to Mr Gibson.

4 Madam your wife and I didn't hit it off the only time I ever saw her. I won't say she was silly, but I think one of us was silly, and it was not me.
Squire Hamley, ibid., ch. 35. Addressing Mr Gibson.

5 People may flatter themselves just as much by thinking that their faults are always present to other people's minds, as if they believe that the world is always contemplating their individual charms and virtues.
Lady Cumnor, ibid., ch. 50

6 Sometimes one likes foolish people for their folly, better than wise people for their wisdom.
Mr Gibson, ibid., ch. 54

Bill Gates
(b. 1955)
US software engineer and entrepreneur

One of the world's richest men, he is Chairman and Chief Software Architect of the Microsoft Corporation which he co-founded in 1975.

1 One thing is clear: We don't have the option of turning away from the future. No one gets to vote on whether technology is going to change our lives.
The Road Ahead, ch. 1 (1995, rev. 1996)

2 Success is a lousy teacher. It seduces smart people into thinking they can't lose.
Ibid., ch. 3

Paul Gauguin
(1848–1903)
French artist

After losing his job as a stockbroker in 1883, he devoted himself entirely to art. Rejecting naturalism in favour of flat planes, bright colours and primitive symbols, he was influenced by his experiences in the south Pacific, where he settled in 1891.

1 Life is hardly more than a fraction of a second. Such a little time to prepare oneself for eternity!!!
Undated journal entry, publ. in *Intimate Journals* (transl. Van Wyck Brooks, 1923)

2 I have always wanted a mistress who was fat, and I have never found one. To make a fool of me, they are always pregnant.
Undated journal entry, ibid.

3 We never really know what stupidity is until we have experimented on ourselves.
Undated journal entry, ibid.

4 Art requires philosophy, just as philosophy requires art. Otherwise, what would become of beauty?
Undated journal entry, ibid.

5 Life has no meaning unless one lives it with a will, at least to the limit of one's will. Virtue, good, evil are nothing but words, unless one takes them apart in order to build something with them; they do not win their true meaning until one knows how to apply them.
Undated journal entry, ibid.

6 In art one is either a plagiarist or a revolutionary.
Quoted in *The Pathos of Distance*, ch. 6 (1913) by James Huneker

John Gay
(1685–1732)
English poet and playwright

He had his greatest success with The Beggar's Opera *(1728), a satire set in London's underworld that targeted fashionable Italian opera,* ROBERT WALPOLE's *administration and contemporary social mores. His* Fables *(1727, 1738) were collections of verse tales on moral themes.*

1 Life is a jest; and all things show it.
I thought so once; but now I know it.
'My Own Epitaph', publ. in *Poems on Several Occasions* (1720). Words inscribed on Gay's monument in Westminster Abbey.

2 We only part to meet again.
Change, as ye list, ye winds: my heart shall be
The faithful compass that still points to thee.
'Sweet William's Farewell to Black-Eyed Susan', st. 4, ibid.

3 Whence is thy learning? Hath thy toil
O'er books consumed the midnight oil?
Fables, Introduction, ll. 15–16 (1727). The phrase 'midnight oil' was earlier recorded in 1635; see FRANCIS QUARLES 3.

4 An open foe may prove a curse,
But a pretended friend is worse.
Ibid., pt 1, no. 17 ('The Shepherd's Dog and the Wolf'), ll. 33–4

5 Those who in quarrels interpose,
Must often wipe a bloody nose.
Ibid., pt 1, no. 34 ('The Mastiffs'), ll. 1–2

6 Fools may our scorn, not envy, raise.
For envy is a kind of praise.
Ibid., pt 1, no. 44 ('The Hound and the Huntsman'), ll. 29–30

7 Through all the employments of life
Each neighbour abuses his brother;
Whore and rogue they call husband and wife:
All professions be-rogue one another.

The Beggar's Opera, Act 1, Sc. 1, air 1 (1728). Sung by Peachum.

8 Gamesters and highwaymen are generally very good to their whores, but they are very devils to their wives.

Peachum, ibid., Act 1, Sc. 4

9 If love the virgin's heart invade,
How, like a moth, the simple maid
Still plays about the flame!

Mrs Peachum, ibid., Act 1, Sc. 4, air 4

10 Do you think your mother and I should have lived comfortably so long together if ever we had been married? Baggage!

Peachum, ibid., Act 1, Sc. 8

11 Can you support the expense of a husband, hussy, in gaming, drinking and whoring? Have you money enough to carry on the daily quarrels of man and wife about who shall squander most?

Mrs Peachum, ibid., Act 1, Sc. 8

12 How the mother is to be pitied who hath handsome daughters! Locks, bolts, bars and lectures of morality are nothing to them; they break through them all. They have as much pleasure in cheating a father and mother, as in cheating at cards.

Mrs Peachum, ibid., Act 1, Sc. 8

13 Can love be controlled by advice?
Will Cupid our mothers obey?
Though my heart were as frozen as ice,
At his flame 'twould have melted away.
When he kissed me so closely he pressed,
'Twas so sweet that I must have complied:
So I thought it both safest and best
To marry, for fear you should chide.

Polly, ibid., Act 1, Sc. 8, air 8

14 O Polly, you might have toyed and kissed;
By keeping men off you keep them on.

Mrs Peachum, ibid., Act 1, Sc. 8, air 9

15 But money, wife, is the true fuller's earth for reputations, there is not a spot or a stain but what it can take out.

Peachum, ibid., Act 1, Sc. 9

16 A rich rogue nowadays is fit company for any gentleman; and the world, my dear, hath not such a contempt for roguery as you imagine.

Peachum, ibid., Act 1, Sc. 9

17 A fox may steal your hens, sir,
A whore your health and pence, sir,
Your daughter rob your chest, sir,
Your wife may steal your rest, sir,
A thief your goods and plate.
But this is all but picking,
With rest, pence, chest and chicken;
It ever was decreed, sir,
If lawyer's hand is fee'd, sir,
He steals your whole estate.

Peachum, ibid., Act 1, Sc. 9, air 11

18 The comfortable estate of widowhood is the only hope that keeps up a wife's spirits. Where is the woman who would scruple to be a wife, if she had it in her power to be a widow whenever she pleased?

Peachum, ibid., Act 1, Sc. 10

19 And I would love you all the day,
Every night would kiss and play,
If with me you'd fondly stray
Over the hills and far away.

Macheath and Polly, ibid., Act 1, Sc. 13, air 16

20 I must have women – there is nothing unbends the mind like them.

Macheath, ibid., Act 2, Sc. 3

21 Youth's the season made for joys;
Love is then our duty.

Macheath, ibid., Act 2, Sc. 4, air 22

22 Sure men were born to lie, and women to believe them!

Lucy, ibid., Act 2, Sc. 13

23 But his kiss was so sweet, and so closely he pressed,
That I languished and pined till I granted the rest.

Lucy, ibid., Act 3, Sc. 1, air 41

24 Lions, wolves, and vultures don't live together in herds, droves or flocks. Of all animals of prey, man is the only sociable one. Every one of us preys upon his neighbour, and yet we herd together.

Lockit, ibid., Act 3, Sc. 2

25 Of all mechanics, of all servile handycrafts-men, a gamester is the vilest. But yet, as many of the quality are of the profession, he is admitted amongst the politest company.

Matt of the Mint, ibid., Act 3, Sc. 4

26 Fill it up. I take as large draughts of liquor as I did of love. I hate a flincher in either.
Mrs Trapes, ibid., Act 3, Sc. 6

27 What then in love can woman do?
If we grow fond they shun us.
And when we fly them, they pursue:
But leave us when they've won us.
Polly and Lucy, ibid., Act 3, Sc. 8, air 49

28 Whoever heard of a man of fortune in England talk of the necessaries of life? . . . Whether we can afford it or no, we must have superfluities.
Polly, Act 1, Sc. 1 (1729). Spoken by Mrs Trapes.

29 No sir, though I was born and bred in England, I can dare to be poor, which is the only thing nowadays men are ashamed of.
Polly, ibid., Act 1, Sc. 11

30 That politician tops his part,
Who readily can lie with art.
Fables, pt 2, no. 6 ('The Squire and his Cur'), ll. 27–8 (1738)

31 Studious of elegance and ease,
Myself alone I seek to please.
Ibid., pt 2, no. 8: 'The Man, the Cat, the Dog, and the Fly', ll. 127–8

Noel Gay

See GEORGE FORMBY 3

Gloria Gaynor

(b. 1949)
US soul singer

With her powerful voice backed by disco rhythms, the 'Queen of Soul' had hits during the 1970s but lost favour with the advent of electronic dance music.

1 I never can say goodbye.
'Never Can Say Goodbye' (song, written by Clifton Davis) on the album *Never Can Say Goodbye* (1974)

2 As long as I know how to love, I know I'll stay alive,
I've got all my life to live, I've got so much love to give,
I will survive! I will survive!
'I Will Survive' (song, written by Dino Fekaris and Freddie Perren) on the album *Love Tracks* (1979). The top-selling disco hit became an enduring feminist and gay anthem and is said to be the most requested karaoke song.

(Sir) Eric Geddes

(1875–1937)
British politician

Conservative MP for Cambridge from 1917, he was Minister of Transport (1919–21) and, as Chairman of the 'Geddes Axe' committee, was responsible for devising ways of cutting government expenditure and increasing revenue.

1 The Germans, if this Government is returned, are going to pay every penny; they are going to be squeezed as a lemon is squeezed – until the pips squeak. My only doubt is not whether we can squeeze hard enough, but whether there is enough juice.
Speech at Cambridge, 10 December 1918, quoted in the *Cambridge Daily News* 11 December 1918. On German war reparations following the First World War.

(Sir) Bob Geldof

(b. 1954)
Irish rock singer

Lead singer of the Boomtown Rats (1975–86), he raised £8 million for African famine relief through the Band Aid record 'Do They Know It's Christmas?' in 1984 (re-recorded 2004), and a year later a further £48 million through Live Aid charity concerts. He has also campaigned to cancel Third World debt.

1 Most people get into bands for three very simple rock and roll reasons: to get laid, to get fame, and to get rich.
Melody Maker 27 August 1977

2 I don't like Mondays.
'I Don't Like Mondays' (song) on the album *The Fine Art of Surfacing* (1979) by the Boomtown Rats. The lyrics were inspired by the story of schoolgirl Brenda Spencer who went on a shooting spree in San Diego, California, in January 1979, giving these words as the reason. Spencer's parents attempted to have the record banned and many US radio stations refused to play it.

3 Feed the world
Let them know it's Christmas time again.
'Do They Know it's Christmas?' (song, 1984, co-written with Midge Ure). The record became the biggest-selling British single of all time.

4 Irish Americans are about as Irish as black Americans are African.
Quoted in the *Observer* 22 June 1986

Henry Geldzahler
(1935–94)
Belgian-born US curator and art critic

He has written extensively on contemporary art and was the first curator of the department of 20th-century art at New York's Metropolitan Museum of Art (1967–78).

1 The history of modern art is also the history of the progressive loss of art's audience. Art has increasingly become the concern of the artist and the bafflement of the public.
'The Art Audience and the Critic', publ. in the *Hudson Review* spring 1965

2 The thing that's extraordinary is that no art remains shocking for more than ten or twelve years. There is no shocking art that doesn't reduce itself to triviality or beauty.
Looking at Pictures (1990)

Martha Gellhorn
(1908–98)
US journalist and author

Her reportage from wars in Europe, Asia and Central America is collected in The Face of War *(1959, rev. 1967, 1986 and 1993), and she also wrote fiction. She was married to* ERNEST HEMINGWAY *1940–5.*

1 Serious, careful, honest journalism is essential, not because it is a guiding light but because it is a form of honorable behavior, involving the reporter and the reader.
The Face of War, Introduction (1959)

2 The vital interests of the state, which are always about power, have nothing to do with the vital interests of the citizens, which are private and simple and are always about a better life for themselves and their children. You do not kill for such interests, you work for them.
Ibid., Introduction (1959, rev. 1967)

3 After a lifetime of war-watching, I see war as an endemic human disease, and governments are the carriers.
Ibid., Introduction (1959, rev. 1986)

Jean Genet
(1910–86)
French playwright and novelist

Dealing chiefly with the Paris underworld, his novels, beginning with Our Lady of the Flowers *(1943), and plays, such as* The Maids *(1947), explore the nature of good and evil. His reputation was enhanced by the book* Saint Genet *(1952) by* JEAN-PAUL SARTRE.

1 To achieve harmony in bad taste is the height of elegance.
The Thief's Journal (1949, transl. 1965)

2 What we need is hatred. From it our ideas are born.
The Blacks (1958). Spoken by Bobo.

3 Are you there, Africa with the bulging chest and oblong thigh? Sulking Africa, wrought of iron, in the fire, Africa of the millions of royal slaves, deported Africa, drifting continent, are you there? Slowly you vanish, you withdraw into the past, into the tales of castaways, colonial museums, the works of scholars.
Felicity, ibid.

4 Crimes of which a people is ashamed constitute its real history. The same is true of man.
Notes for *The Screens* (1961, transl. 1973)

5 Anyone who hasn't experienced the ecstasy of betrayal knows nothing about ecstasy at all.
Prisoner of Love, pt 1 (1986)

George I
(1660–1727)
King of Great Britain and Ireland

Elector of Hanover when he assumed the British throne in 1714, he never succeeded in mastering English and maintained a distance from his subjects. He relied increasingly on his Whig ministers, ROBERT WALPOLE, *James Stanhope and Charles Townshend.*

1 I can make him a lord, but I cannot make him a gentleman.
Quoted by HORACE WALPOLE in letter, 16 July 1776, publ. in *Correspondence of Horace Walpole*, vol. 24 (ed. W. S. Lewis, 1967). The king's remark referred to William Bateman (d. 1744), MP and merchant, whom he created 1st Viscount Bateman in the Irish peerage, apparently in order to avoid making him a Knight of the Bath.

George II
(1683–1760)
King of Great Britain and Ireland

Acceding to the throne in 1727, he was a flamboyant, often frustrated ruler who resented his dependence on Whig ministers. His main interest was in military affairs, and he was the last British monarch to lead troops into battle (1743), in the War of the Austrian Succession.

1 Oh! he is mad, is he? Then I wish he would *bite* some others of my generals.

Remark, 1758, quoted in *General Wolfe*, ch. 11 (1909) by Richard Garrett. Replying to the Duke of Newcastle's assertion that Wolfe was mad.

George III
(1738–1820)
King of Great Britain and Ireland

Elector (1760–1814) and King (1814–20) of Hanover, he succeeded to the British throne in 1760. His attempt at personal government, which led indirectly to the loss of the American colonies, was curbed by the ministry of WILLIAM PITT THE YOUNGER. *He was intermittently mad from 1811.*

1 I can never suppose this country so far lost to all ideas of self-importance as to be willing to grant America independence; if that could ever be universally adopted I shall despair of this country being ever preserved from a state of inferiority and consequently falling into a very low class among the European States.

Letter to Prime Minister Lord North, 7 March 1780, publ. in *The Correspondence of King George the Third*, vol. 5 (ed. Sir John Fortescue, 1928)

2 Knavery seems to be so much the striking feature of its inhabitants that it may not in the end be an evil that they become aliens to this kingdom.

Letter, 10 November 1782, publ. in *The Correspondence of King George the Third*, vol. 6 (ed. Sir John Fortescue, 1928). Referring to Americans.

George V
(1865–1936)
King of Great Britain and Ireland

Prior to succeeding to the throne in 1910 'he did nothing at all but kill animals and stick in stamps', according to his biographer HAROLD NICOLSON. *As king, he was instrumental in the formation of the national government of 1931. 'I march with the times' was his watchword.*

1 How is the Empire?

Attributed last words, in radio broadcast, 21 January 1936. Reported to the nation the day after the king's death in a tribute by Prime Minister STANLEY BALDWIN. Other accounts deny this was the king's last utterance, although a memorandum of Lord Wigram, the king's Private Secretary, was made at 11 a.m., 20 January: 'He murmured something about the Empire, and I replied that "All is well, Sir, with the Empire"' (quoted in *Dawson of Penn*, 1950, by Francis Watson). The time of his death was given as 11.55 p.m.

2 Bugger Bognor.

Attributed deathbed remark, in *King George V*, ch. 9 (1983) by Kenneth Rose. The king apparently spoke the words on being assured by a courtier that he would soon be in Bognor. However, according to the King's Librarian, Owen Morshead, the exclamation was made much earlier, in 1929, in response to a suggestion that the town should be named Bognor Regis in commemoration of George V's convalescence there following a serious illness.

3 My father was frightened of his mother, I was frightened of my father, and I am damned well going to see to it that my children are frightened of me.

Quoted by HAROLD NICOLSON, in *Lord Derby: 'King of Lancashire'*, ch. 8 (1959) by Randolph S. Churchill.

George VI
(1895–1952)
King of Great Britain and Northern Ireland

He succeeded to the throne following the abdication of his brother EDWARD VIII *in 1936. His wartime broadcasts and his insistence on remaining in London during the Blitz won him popular support.*

1 It is not the walls that make the city, but the people who live within them. The walls of London may be battered, but the spirit of the Londoner stands resolute and undismayed.

Radio broadcast to the Empire, 23 September 1940, during the German bomber offensive

2 Abroad is bloody.

Attributed, in *A Certain World*, 'Royalty' (1970) by W. H. AUDEN. See also NANCY MITFORD 1.

Gladys George
(c. 1900–54)
US actress

Having starred in vaudeville and on Broadway, she enjoyed success in Hollywood in the films The Roaring Twenties *(1939) and* The Maltese Falcon *(1941).*

1 He used to be a big shot.

The Roaring Twenties (film, 1939, screenplay by Jerry Wald, Richard Macaulay and Robert Rossen based on a story by Mark Hellinger, directed by Raoul Walsh). Spoken by Panama Smith (Gladys George), these last words of the film refer to Eddie Bartlett (played by JAMES CAGNEY), who has been fatally shot.

Henry George

(1839–97)

US economist

His Progress and Poverty (1879) had a wide influence for its analysis of social ills, though his proposed remedy – a single tax based on income derived from uneconomic land – was not taken up.

1 Capital is a result of labor, and is used by labor to assist it in further production. Labor is the active and initial force, and labor is therefore the employer of capital.

Progress and Poverty, bk 3, ch. 1 (1879)

2 The methods by which a trade union can alone act, are necessarily destructive; its organization is necessarily tyrannical.

Ibid., bk 6, ch. 1

George, David Lloyd

See Lloyd George, David

Ira Gershwin

(1896–1983)

US lyricist

Originally Israel Gershvin. The elder brother of George Gershwin, he wrote the sophisticated lyrics to most of his brother's songs in more than twenty successful Broadway musicals. After George's death in 1937, he worked with Harold Arlen, Jerome Kern and Kurt Weill.

1 I got rhythm,
I got music,
I got my man,
Who could ask for anything more?

'I Got Rhythm' (song, with music by George Gershwin) in *Girl Crazy* (stage musical 1930, film 1932 and 1943). Originally sung by Ethel Merman, the number was performed in the 1943 film version by JUDY GARLAND, and by Gene Kelly in the film *An American in Paris* (1951).

2 Summertime and the living is easy,
Fish are jumping, and the cotton is high.

'Summertime' (song, co-written with Du Bose Heyward with music by George Gershwin) in *Porgy and Bess* (stage musical 1935, film 1959). The lyrics from this opener for *Porgy and Bess*, like those of other songs in the show, were based on an original poem in the novel *Porgy* (1926) by Du Bose Heyward. It was a hit for BILLIE HOLIDAY in 1936.

3 It ain't necessarily so,
The things that you're liable

To read in the Bible,
It ain't necessarily so.

'It Ain't Necessarily So', ibid. The song was recorded by BING CROSBY in 1938, among others, and sung by SAMMY DAVIS JR in the film adaptation.

4 A foggy day in London Town
Had me low and had me down.
I viewed the morning with alarm,
The British Museum had lost its charm.

'A Foggy Day' (song, with music by George Gershwin) in *A Damsel in Distress* (film, 1937). The number is performed in the film by Fred Astaire.

5 Holding hands at midnight
'Neath a starry sky,
Nice work if you can get it,
And you can get it if you try.

'Nice Work If You Can Get It', ibid.

6 You like potato and I like po-tah-to,
You like tomato and I like to-mah-to;
Potato, po-tah-to, tomato, to-mah-to –
Let's call the whole thing off!

'Let's Call the Whole Thing Off' (song, with music by George Gershwin) in *Shall We Dance* (film, 1937). Sung by Fred Astaire and Ginger Rogers.

Jean Paul Getty

(1892–1976)

US oil millionaire and art collector

Having expanded his father's oil business, he became one of the world's richest men. The museum he founded in California (1953) exhibited his extensive art collection.

1 If you can actually count your money, then you are not really a rich man.

Quoted in the *Observer* 3 November 1957

Edward Gibbon

(1737–94)

English historian

His magnum opus, The Decline and Fall of the Roman Empire (1776–88), is one of the most influential historical works of all time. He wrote both in French and English, served in parliament 1774–83 and lived for several years in Switzerland. His other works include an autobiography (1796).

1 The various modes of worship which prevailed in the Roman world were all considered by the people as equally true; by the philosopher as equally false; and by the magistrate as equally useful.

The Decline and Fall of the Roman Empire, vol. 1, ch. 2 (1776)

2 The principles of a free constitution are irrecoverably lost, when the legislative power is nominated by the executive.
Ibid., vol. 1, ch. 3

3 History . . . is, indeed, little more than the register of the crimes, follies and misfortunes of mankind.
Ibid., vol. 1, ch. 3. See VOLTAIRE 29.

4 Whenever the offence inspires less horror than the punishment, the rigour of penal law is obliged to give way to the common feelings of mankind.
Ibid., vol. 1, ch. 14. On Constantine's edict against rape.

5 Corruption, the most infallible symptom of constitutional liberty.
Ibid., vol. 2, ch. 21 (1781)

6 The urgent consideration of the public safety may undoubtedly authorise the violation of every positive law. How far that or any other consideration may operate to dissolve the natural obligations of humanity and justice, is a doctrine of which I still desire to remain ignorant.
Ibid., vol. 2, ch. 26

7 The courage of a soldier is found to be the cheapest and most common quality of human nature.
Ibid., vol. 2, ch. 26

8 Our sympathy is cold to the relation of distant misery.
Ibid., vol. 5, ch. 49 (1788)

9 The winds and waves are always on the side of the ablest of navigators.
Ibid., vol. 6, ch. 68 (1788)

10 All that is human must retrograde if it does not advance.
Ibid., vol. 6, ch. 71

11 Truth, naked, unblushing truth, the first virtue of all serious history, must be the sole recommendation of this personal narrative.
Memoirs of My Life, Introduction (1966 edn)

12 Style is the image of character.
Ibid., Introduction. See also quote 17.

13 It was here that I suspended my religious inquiries.
Ibid., ch. 4 (1796). Of his public readmittance to Protestantism, Christmas 1754 (aged seventeen), having adopted the Catholic faith the previous year. He now had, he wrote with some ambiguity, 'implicit belief in the tenets and mysteries which are adopted by the general consent of Catholics and Protestants'.

14 I understand by this passion the union of desire, friendship, and tenderness, which is inflamed by a single female, which prefers her to the rest of her sex, and which seeks her possession as the supreme or the sole happiness of our being.
Ibid., ch. 4. Of his youthful love for Suzanne Curchod, daughter of a pastor in Lausanne, who he claimed was the only woman in his life.

15 I sighed as a lover, I obeyed as a son.
Ibid., ch. 4, footnote. Referring to his father's insistence that Gibbon end his attachment to Suzanne Curchod.

16 I withdrew without reluctance from the noisy and expensive crowds without company, and dissipation without pleasure.
Ibid., ch. 5. Referring to London.

17 The style of an author should be the image of his mind, but the choice and command of language is the fruit of exercise.
Ibid., ch. 7

18 The author himself is the best judge of his own performance; none has so deeply meditated on the subject; none is so sincerely interested in the event.
Ibid., ch. 7

19 It has always been my practice to cast a long paragraph in a single mould, to try it by my ear, to deposit it in my memory, but to suspend the action of the pen till I had given the last polish to my work.
Ibid., ch. 7

20 The abbreviation of time and the failure of hope, will always tinge with a browner shade the evening of life.
Ibid., ch. 8

21 My English text is chaste, and all licentious passages are left in the obscurity of a learned language.
Ibid., ch. 8, note. Sometimes misquoted as 'decent obscurity', following the contemporary parody in The Anti-Jacobin Review and Magazine.

Stella Gibbons
(1902–89)
British author

She worked for much of her life as a journalist and wrote numerous novels and short stories, but is best known for her parody of rural fiction, Cold Comfort Farm (1932).

1 Something nasty in the woodshed.
Cold Comfort Farm, ch. 8 and passim (1932). This recurring motif of some unspecific secret and shameful act witnessed

in the past was a symbol of corrupting knowledge in the novel.

Wolcott Gibbs
(1902–58)
US journalist and critic

He established his reputation through his regular pieces for the New Yorker, *where he was drama critic from 1927. He also wrote short stories and the play* Season in the Sun *(1950).*

1 Backward ran sentences until reeled the mind.
'Time . . . Fortune . . . Life . . . Luce' (1936), repr. in *More in Sorrow* (1958). Satirizing the writing style of *Time* magazine.

2 He wasn't exactly hostile to facts but he was apathetic about them.
Attributed, referring to ALEXANDER WOOLLCOTT.

Kahlil Gibran
(1883–1931)
Syrian-born US poet and novelist

His writings both in Arabic and English combine romanticism with mysticism, influenced by the BIBLE, *Sufism and* WILLIAM BLAKE. *His most enduring work is* The Prophet *(1923).*

1 Love gives naught but itself and takes naught but from itself.
Love possesses not nor would it be possessed;
For love is sufficient unto love.
The Prophet, 'On Love' (1923)

2 You may give them your love but not your thoughts.
For they have their own thoughts.
You may house their bodies but not their souls,
For their souls dwell in the house of tomorrow, which you cannot visit, not even in your dreams.
Ibid., 'On Children'

3 Life is indeed darkness save when there is urge,
And all urge is blind save when there is knowledge,
And all knowledge is vain save when there is work,
And all work is empty save when there is love.
Ibid., 'On Work'

4 The lust for comfort, that stealthy thing that enters the house a guest, and then becomes a host, and then a master.
Ibid., 'On Houses'

5 Beauty is eternity gazing at itself in a mirror.
Ibid., 'On Beauty'

6 Verily the kindness that gazes upon itself in a mirror turns to stone,
And a good deed that calls itself by tender names becomes the parent to a curse.
Ibid., 'The Farewell'

7 An exaggeration is a truth that has lost its temper.
Sand and Foam (1926)

8 A little knowledge that *acts* is worth infinitely more than much knowledge that is idle.
The Voice of the Master, pt 2, ch. 8 (1960)

9 When we turn to one another for counsel we reduce the number of our enemies.
Ibid., pt 2, ch. 10

André Gide
(1869–1951)
French author

With the declared intention of 'disturbing' his readers, he founded his reputation on novels such as The Immoralist *(1902) and* Strait is the Gate *(1909). He also published literary and social criticism and helped found* La Nouvelle Revue française *(1908).*

1 Man is more interesting than men. God made *him* and not them in his image. Each one is more precious than all.
Journal entry, 1896, publ. in *Journals 1889–1949,* 'Literature and Ethics' (ed. Justin O'Brien, 1967)

2 True kindness presupposes the faculty of imagining as one's own the suffering and joys of others.
Pretexts, 'Portraits and Aphorisms' (1903)

3 No theory is good unless it permits, not rest, but the greatest work. No theory is good except on condition that one use it to go on beyond.
Journal entry 1918, publ. in *Journals 1889-1949,* 'Detached Pages' (ed. Justin O'Brien, 1967)

4 The most decisive actions of our life – I mean those that are most likely to decide the whole course of our future – are, more often than not, unconsidered.
The Counterfeiters, pt 3, ch. 16 (1925). Spoken by Hildebrant.

5 Old hands soil, it seems, whatever they caress, but they too have their beauty when they are joined in prayer. Young hands were made for caresses and the sheathing of love. It is a pity to make them join too soon.
Journal entry, 21 January 1929, publ. in *Journals 1889–1949* (ed. Justin O'Brien, 1967)

6 The sole art that suits me is that which, rising from unrest, tends toward serenity.
Journal entry, 23 November 1940, ibid.

7 *Hugo – hélas!*
[Hugo – alas!]
Quoted in *Victor Hugo*, ch. 39 (1976) by Joanna Richardson. Response on being asked who was the greatest 19th-century poet.

8 Bad literature is written with beautiful sentiments.
Letter to Francois Mauriac, 1928, attributed

Fred Gilbert
(1850–1903)

1 The Man Who Broke the Bank at Monte Carlo.
Title of song (1892). The song was popularized by Charles Coborn, and is said to refer to Joseph Jagger (1830–92), a British engineer who enjoyed success at a Monte Carlo casino after calculating the biases of its roulette wheels.

(Sir) Humphrey Gilbert
(c. 1537–83)
English soldier, navigator and explorer

The half-brother of Sir WALTER RALEGH, *he campaigned in the Netherlands and Ireland and settled Newfoundland in 1583. He drowned on the homeward journey.*

1 We are as near to heaven by sea as by land.
Quoted in *The Principal Navigations, Voyages, Traffics and Discoveries of the English Nation*, vol. 3 (1600) by Richard Hakluyt. Words shouted to his companion vessel during a storm on his last, fatal voyage back from Newfoundland, September 1583.

(Sir) W. S. Gilbert
(1836–1911)
English librettist

William Schwenck Gilbert. He began writing comic verse (the 'Bab Ballads') for magazines, but achieved much greater success with the parodic light operas he wrote from 1871 in partnership with the composer (Sir) Arthur Sullivan.

1 Down went the owners – greedy men whom hope of gain allured:
Oh, dry the starting tear, for they were heavily insured.
The 'Bab' Ballads, 'Etiquette' (1866–71)

2 'You'll soon get used to her looks,' said he, 'And a very nice girl you'll find her!

She may very well pass for forty-three
In the dusk, with a light behind her!'
Trial by Jury (1875). The judge recounts the words of a rich attorney encouraging a match with his 'elderly, ugly daughter'.

3 I am never known to quail
At the fury of a gale,
And I'm never, never sick at sea!
What, never?
No, never!
What, *never*?
Well, hardly ever!
He's hardly ever sick at sea!
Then give three cheers, and one cheer more,
For the hardy Captain of the *Pinafore*!
HMS Pinafore, Act 1 (1878). Sung by Captain Corcoran and his crew.

4 And so do his sisters, and his cousins, and his aunts!
His sisters and his cousins,
Whom he reckons up by dozens,
And his aunts!
Captain Corcoran and his crew, ibid., Act 1

5 I always voted at my party's call,
And I never thought of thinking for myself at all.
I thought so little, they rewarded me
By making me the Ruler of the Queen's Navee!
Sir Joseph Porter, ibid., Act 1

6 Things are seldom what they seem,
Skim milk masquerades as cream.
Little Buttercup (Mrs Cripps), ibid., Act 2

7 He is an Englishman!
For he himself has said it,
And it's greatly to his credit,
That he is an Englishman!
Boatswain, ibid., Act 2

8 For he might have been a Roosian,
A French, or Turk, or Proosian,
Or perhaps Ital-ian!
But in spite of all temptations
To belong to other nations,
He remains an Englishman!
Boatswain, ibid., Act 2

9 For I am a Pirate King.
And it is, it is a glorious thing
To be a Pirate King.
The Pirates of Penzance, Act 1 (1879). Sung by The Pirate King.

10 I am the very model of a modern
   Major-General,
I've information vegetable, animal, and mineral,
I know the kings of England, and I quote the fights
   historical,
From Marathon to Waterloo, in order categorical.
The Major-General, ibid., Act 1

11 I'm very good at integral and differential
   calculus,
I know the scientific names of beings
   animalculous;
In short, in matters vegetable, animal, and
   mineral,
I am the very model of a modern Major-General.
The Major-General, ibid., Act 1

12 When constabulary duty's to be done,
The policeman's lot is not a happy one.
The police chorus, ibid., Act 2

13 One moment! let me tell you who they are.
They are no members of the common throng;
They are all noblemen who have gone wrong!
Ruth, ibid., Act 2

14 No Englishman unmoved that statement hears,
Because, with all our faults, we love our House of
   Peers.
The Major-General, ibid., Act 2. Referring to the remark
quoted above.

15 Let foreigners look down with scorn
On legislators heaven-born;
We know what limpid wisdom runs
From Peers, and all their eldest sons.
Enrapt the true-born Briton hears
The wisdom of his House of Peers.
The Major-General, ibid., Act 2. The 'Hymn to the Nobility'
from which these lines are taken closed the British first-night
performance, but was omitted from subsequent productions.

16 Twenty love-sick maidens we,
Love-sick all against our will.
Twenty years hence we shall be
Twenty love-sick maidens still.
Patience, Act 1 (1881). Opening lines. Sung by the chorus of
'rapturous maidens'.

17 You must lie upon the daisies and discourse in
   novel phrases of your complicated state of mind,
The meaning doesn't matter if it's only idle chatter
   of a transcendental kind.
Bunthorne, ibid., Act 1

18 A most intense young man,
A soulful-eyed young man,
An ultra-poetical, super-aesthetical,
Out-of-the-way young man!
Bunthorne and Grosvenor, ibid., Act 2. Describing Bunthorne.

19 Francesca di Rimini, miminy, piminy,
Je-ne-sais-quoi young man!
Bunthorne, ibid., Act 2

20 Bow, bow, ye lower middle classes!
Bow, bow, ye tradesmen, bow, ye masses!
Iolanthe, Act 1 (1882). Sung by the chorus of Peers.

21 The Law is the true embodiment
Of everything that's excellent.
It has no kind of fault or flaw,
And I, my Lords, embody the Law.
Lord Chancellor, ibid., Act 1

22 Hearts just as pure and fair
May beat in Belgrave Square
As in the lowly air
Of Seven Dials.
Lord Tolloller, ibid., Act 1

23 When in that House MPs divide,
If they've a brain and cerebellum, too,
They've got to leave that brain outside,
And vote just as their leaders tell 'em to.
Private Willis, ibid., Act 2

24 When Wellington thrashed Bonaparte,
As every child can tell,
The House of Peers, throughout the war,
Did nothing in particular,
And did it very well.
Lord Mountararat, ibid., Act 2

25 On fire that glows
With heat intense
I turn the hose
Of common sense,
And out it goes
At small expense!
The Fairy Queen, ibid., Act 2

26 I love my fellow creatures – I do all the good I
   can –
Yet everybody says I'm such a disagreeable man!
Princess Ida, Act 1 (1884). Sung by King Gama.

27 I've an irritating chuckle, I've a celebrated
   sneer,
I've an entertaining snigger, I've a fascinating leer.
To everybody's prejudice I know a thing or two;

I can tell a woman's age in half a minute – and I
do.
But although I try to make myself as pleasant as I
can,
Yet everybody says I am a disagreeable man!
King Gama, ibid., Act 1

28 While Darwinian Man, though well-behaved,
At best is only a monkey shaved!
Lady Psyche, ibid., Act 2

29 I am, in point of fact, a particularly haughty and
exclusive person, of pre-Adamite ancestral descent.
You will understand this when I tell you that I can
trace my ancestry back to a protoplasmal primordial
atomic globule.
The Mikado, Act 1 (1885). Spoken by Pooh-Bah.

30 My family pride is something inconceivable. I
can't help it. I was born sneering.
Pooh-Bah, ibid., Act 1

31 As some day it may happen that a victim must
be found,
I've got a little list – I've got a little list
Of society offenders who might well be
underground,
And who never would be missed – who never
would be missed!
There's the pestilential nuisances who write for
autographs –
All people who have flabby hands and irritating
laughs –
All children who are up in dates, and floor you
with 'em flat –
All persons who in shaking hands, shake hands
with you like that –
And all third persons who on spoiling tête-à-têtes
insist –
They'd none of 'em be missed – they'd none of 'em
be missed!
Ko-Ko, ibid., Act 1

32 The idiot who praises, with enthusiastic tone,
All centuries but this, and every country but his
own.
Ko-Ko, ibid, Act 1. See also GEORGE CANNING 1, BENJAMIN
DISRAELI 52.

33 Three little maids from school are we,
Pert as a school-girl well can be,
Filled to the brim with girlish glee,
Three little maids from school!
Trio of girls, ibid., Act 1

34 To sit in solemn silence in a dull, dark dock,
In a pestilential prison, with a life-long lock,
Awaiting the sensation of a short, sharp shock,
From a cheap and chippy chopper on a big black
block!
Trio of girls, ibid., Act 1

35 Matrimonial devotion
Doesn't seem to suit her notion.
Ko-Ko, ibid., Act 2

36 My object all sublime
I shall achieve in time –
To let the punishment fit the crime –
The punishment fit the crime;
And make each prisoner pent
Unwillingly represent
A source of innocent merriment!
Of innocent merriment!
Mikado, ibid., Act 2

37 On a tree by a river a little tom-tit
Sang 'Willow, titwillow, titwillow!'
And I said to him, 'Dicky-bird, why do you sit
Singing, "Willow, titwillow, titwillow?'
Ko-Ko, ibid., Act 2

38 Are you old enough to marry, do you think?
Won't you wait until you're eighty in the shade?
There's a fascination frantic
In a ruin that's romantic;
Do you think you are sufficiently decayed?
Ko-Ko, ibid., Act 2

39 You've no idea what a poor opinion I have of
myself – and how little I deserve it.
Ruddigore, Act 1 (1887). Spoken by Sir Ruthven Murgatroyd
(disguised as Robin Oakapple).

40 This particularly rapid, unintelligible patter
Isn't generally heard, and if it is it doesn't matter!
Despard, ibid., Act 2

41 In enterprise of martial kind,
When there was any fighting,
He led his regiment from behind –
He found it less exciting.
The Gondoliers, Act 1 (1889). Sung by Duke of Plaza-Toro.

42 That celebrated,
Cultivated
Underrated
Nobleman,
The Duke of Plaza-Toro!
Duke of Plaza-Toro, ibid., Act 1

43 Life's a pudding full of plums,
Care's a canker that benumbs.
Wherefore waste our elocution
On impossible solution?
Life's a pleasant institution,
Let us take it as it comes!

Ibid., Act 1. Sung by a quintet.

44 When every one is somebodee,
Then no one's anybody!

The Gondoliers, ibid., Act 2

Terry Gilkyson

(1916–99)

US songwriter and actor

Hamilton H. Gilkyson III. Although he acted in several films in the 1950s, he became better known as songwriter for such films as Swiss Family Robinson *(1960) and* The Jungle Book *(1967).*

1 The bare necessities, the simple bare necessities
Forget about your worries and your strife.

'Bare Necessities' (song) in *The Jungle Book* (film, 1967). Sung by Phil Harris as Baloo and Bruce Reitherman as Mowgli.

Eric Gill

(1882–1940)

British sculptor, engraver, writer and typographer

A Catholic whose private life provoked calls for his work to be withdrawn, he carved the sculptures Stations of the Cross *in Westminster Cathedral (1914–18). He illustrated for the Golden Cockerell Press, and devised the first sanserif typeface, Gill Sans.*

1 That state is a state of Slavery in which a man does what he likes to do in his spare time and in his working time that which is required of him. This state can only exist when what a man likes to do is to please himself.

'Slavery and Freedom' (1918), repr. in *Art-Nonsense and Other Essays*, (1929). Opening paragraph of essay.

2 Art is skill, that is the first meaning of the word.

Art, ch. 1 (1934). In his essay 'Art and Love' (1927) Gill wrote: 'As no one would think it an adequate definition of Man to say that he is a two-legged mammal, so no one should be satisfied with the definition of Art that it is simply skill, or that it is skill in the imitation of nature.'

3 Man cannot live on the human plane, he must be either above or below it.

Autobiography, 'Conclusion' (1940)

4 Catholics are necessarily at war with this age. That we are not more conscious of the fact, that we so often endeavour to make an impossible peace with it – that is the tragedy. You cannot serve God and Mammon.

Essays, 'Idiocy or Ill-Will' (1948)

5 Man does not live by bread alone, but by science he attempts to do so. Hence the deadliness of all that is purely scientific.

Ibid., 'Art'

Penelope Gilliatt

(1932–93)

British author

She was film critic for the Observer *from 1961 and for the* New Yorker *from 1967. She published essays, short stories and novels, and wrote the screenplay for* Sunday, Bloody Sunday *(1971).*

1 Sunday, Bloody Sunday.

Title of film (1971)

Charlotte Perkins Gilman

(1860–1935)

US author and feminist

She published her first stories and poems in the 1890s, lectured widely, and edited The Forerunner *(1909–16), consisting mainly of her own writings. Her most important work was* Women and Economics *(1898).*

1 The people people choose for friends
Your common sense appall,
But the people people marry
Are the queerest folks of all.

'Queer People' (1899), repr. in *The Later Poetry of Charlotte Perkins Gilman* (ed. Denise D. Knight, 1996)

2 The labor of women in the house, certainly, enables men to produce more wealth than they otherwise could; and in this way women are economic factors in society. But so are horses.

Women and Economics, ch. 1 (1898)

3 The female of the genus homo is economically dependent on the male. He is her food supply.

Ibid., ch. 1

4 There is no female mind. The brain is not an organ of sex. As well speak of a female liver.

Ibid., ch. 8

5 Human life consists in mutual service. No grief, pain, misfortune, or 'broken heart' is excuse for cutting off one's life while any power of service remains. But when all usefulness is over, when one

is assured of an unavoidable and imminent death, it is the simplest of human rights to choose a quick and easy death in place of a slow and horrible one.
Letter, 17 August 1935, publ. in *The Living of Charlotte Perkins Gilman: an Autobiography*, ch. 21 (1935). Having been diagnosed with incurable breast cancer, Gilman 'chose chloroform over cancer', as her letter explained.

Gary Gilmore
(1941–77)
US convict

Convicted for the murder of two students, he was the first person to be executed in the USA after the reinstatement of the death penalty in 1976, a sentence which he requested in preference to life imprisonment.

1 Your Honor, I don't want to take up a lot of your time with my words. I believe I was given a fair trial and I think the sentence is proper and I am willing to accept it like a man. I don't wish to appeal . . . I desire to be executed on schedule, and I just wish to accept that with the grace and dignity of a man.
Speech to the Supreme Court, 9 November 1976, quoted in *The Executioner's Song*, bk 2, pt 1, ch. 1, sect. 7 (1979) by NORMAN MAILER. Gilmore's last words to the firing squad were 'Let's do it!'

(Sir) Ian Gilmour
(b. 1926)
British politician

A Conservative MP 1962–92, he was a cabinet minister in the HEATH *and* THATCHER *governments before being sacked in 1981.*

1 Conservatives do not worship democracy. For them majority rule is a device . . . And if it is leading to an end that is undesirable or inconsistent with itself, then there is a theoretical case for ending it.
Inside Right, pt 3, ch. 5 (1977)

Newt Gingrich
(b. 1943)
US politician

A confrontational spokesman for the Republican Party and a convinced Reaganite, he was Speaker of the House of Representatives (1994–9).

1 In every election in American history both parties have their clichés. The party that has the clichés that ring true wins.
International Herald Tribune 1 August 1988

Allen Ginsberg
(1926–97)
US poet

His Howl and Other Poems *(1956) gave the Beat generation its poetic manifesto. Outspoken on civil rights and gay liberation, he became a 'spiritual godfather' of the counterculture in the 1960s and '70s (the phrase 'flower power' reputedly came from him).*

1 Fortunately art is a community effort – a small but select community living in a spiritualized world endeavoring to interpret the wars and the solitudes of the flesh.
Journal entry, 11 July 1954, publ. in *Journals: Early Fifties Early Sixties*, 'Mexico and Return to US' (ed. Gordon Ball, 1977)

2 I saw the best minds of my generation destroyed by madness, starving hysterical naked,
dragging themselves through the negro streets at dawn looking for an angry fix,
angelheaded hipsters burning for the ancient heavenly connection to the starry dynamo in the machinery of night,
who poverty and tatters and hollow-eyed and high sat up smoking in the supernatural darkness of cold-water flats floating across the tops of cities contemplating jazz.
'Howl', publ. in *Howl and Other Poems* (1956). Opening lines of poem.

3 What thoughts I have of you tonight, Walt Whitman, for I walked down the sidestreets under the trees with a headache self-conscious looking at the full moon.
In my hungry fatigue, and shopping for images, I went into the neon fruit supermarket, dreaming of your enumerations!
'A Supermarket in California', ibid. Opening lines of poem.

4 A perfect beauty of a sunflower! a perfect excellent lovely sunflower
existence! a sweet natural eye to the new hip moon, woke up alive and excited grasping in the sunset shadow sunrise golden monthly breeze.
'Sunflower Sutra', ibid.

5 America I'm putting my queer shoulder to the wheel.
'America', ibid. Last line of poem.

6 Downtown Manhattan, clear winter noon, and I've been up all night, talking, talking, reading

the Kaddish aloud, listening to Ray Charles blues
shout blind on the phonograph

'Kaddish', sect. 1, publ. in *Kaddish and Other Poems* (1960)

7 This is the end, the redemption from Wilderness,
way for the Wonderer, House sought for All,
black handkerchief washed clean by weeping –
page beyond Psalm – Last change of mine and
Naomi – to God's perfect Darkness – Death, stay
thy phantoms!

'Kaddish', sect. 1, ibid.

8 Democracy! Bah! When I hear that word I reach
for my feather Boa!

'Subliminal', written in journal, October 1960, publ. in *Journals: Early Fifties Early Sixties*, 'New York City' (ed. Gordon Ball, 1977). See HERMANN GOERING 2.

9 What if someone gave a war and Nobody came?
Life would ring the bells of Ecstasy and Forever be
Itself again.

'Graffiti 12th Cubicle Men's Room Syracuse Airport', publ. in *The Fall of America* (1972). The words of the first line were current during the anti-war protests of the 1960s, and were adapted as the title of a 1970 film, *Suppose They Gave a War and Nobody Came?* starring Brian Keith and Tony Curtis. The original inspiration was probably a poem by Carl Sandburg: see CARL SANDBURG 7.

10 Nobody saves America by sniffing cocaine
Jiggling yr knees blankeyed in the rain
When it snows in yr nose you catch cold in yr
brain.

'Snow Blues', publ. in *Mind Breaths* (1978). The poem was written for a tour newspaper.

11 Poetry is not an expression of the party line. It's
that time of night, lying in bed, thinking what you
really think, making the private world public, that's
what the poet does.

Quoted in *Ginsberg: A Biography* by Barry Miles, ch. 17 (1989)

Nikki Giovanni

(b. 1943)
US poet

Originally Yolande Giovanni. She was prominent in the black literary movement of the late 1960s. Among her collections are Black Feeling, Black Talk *(1968) and* Cotton Candy on a Rainy Day *(1978).*

1 it's a sex object if you're pretty
and no love
or love and no sex if you're fat

'Woman Poem', publ. in *Black Judgment* (1969)

2 There're two people in the world that are not like-
able: a master and a slave.

A Dialogue (with JAMES BALDWIN, 1973). The book is a transcription of a discussion between Giovanni and Baldwin in London, 4 November 1971.

3 I think one of the nicest things that we created as
a generation was just the fact that we could say,
Hey, I don't like white people.

Ibid.

George Gipp

See RONALD REAGAN 13

Jean Giraudoux

(1882–1944)
French author and diplomat

He combined a career in the diplomatic service (1910–40) with a writing vocation. Many of his novels and plays are retellings of biblical stories and Greek myths.

1 I tell you, sir, the only safeguard of order and
discipline in the modern world is a standardized
worker with interchangeable parts. That would
solve the entire problem of management.

The Madwoman of Chaillot, Act 1 (1945). Spoken by The President.

George Gissing

(1857–1903)
English novelist, critic and essayist

Drawn from his own straitened circumstances, his naturalistic novels, for example New Grub Street *(1891), were concerned with poverty and literary struggle. The critic G. W. Stonier called him 'the English Gorki, with butterfly collar'.*

1 I know every book of mine by its *scent*, and I
have but to put my nose between the pages to be
reminded of all sorts of things.

The Private Papers of Henry Ryecroft, 'Spring', sect. 12 (1903). Narrated by Ryecroft.

2 One might define art as: an expression, satisfying
and abiding, of the zest of life.

Ryecroft, ibid., 'Spring', sect. 20

3 I have always regarded as a fact of infinite pathos
the ability men have to subdue themselves to the
conditions of life. Contentment so often means resignation.

Ryecroft, ibid., 'Autumn', sect. 7

Edna Gladney

(1886–1961)

US philanthropist

She made a career of rescuing illegitimate children and raising them in her private orphanage in Texas. She was instrumental in passing a law to eliminate from public record whether or not orphans are born illegitimately.

1 There are no illegitimate children, there are only illegitimate parents.

Quoted in *Kiss Hollywood Goodbye*, ch.18 (1974) by ANITA LOOS. MGM paid Gladney a large sum for this widely quoted line which was to form the basis of the 1941 film *Blossoms in the Dust*, based on Gladney's orphanage and starring Greer Garson (screenplay by Loos, directed and produced by Mervyn LeRoy). It is not clear whether Gladney originated the words, however. The lawyer Léon Yankwich was supposed to have made a similar remark in June 1928, during a hearing at the State District Court, Southern District of California, and he was apparently quoting the journalist O. O. McIntyre. The words have also been ascribed to Bernadette McAliskey in 1971.

W. E. Gladstone

(1809–98)

English statesman

William Ewart Gladstone. The dominant personality in the Liberal Party 1868–94, he served four terms as Prime Minister. He championed free trade, electoral reform, educational expansion and greater accessibility for army commissions and the Civil Service, but failed in his attempt to introduce Home Rule for Ireland. He was passionately disliked by Queen VICTORIA. See also BENJAMIN DISRAELI 54.

1 A war more unjust in its origin, a war more calculated in its progress to cover this country with permanent disgrace, I do not know, and I have not read of.

Speech to House of Commons, 8 April 1840, publ. in *Hansard*, vol. 53, col. 818. On the First Opium War with China.

2 Ireland, Ireland! that cloud in the west, that coming storm, the minister of God's retribution upon cruel and inveterate and but half-atoned injustice!

Letter to his wife, 12 October 1845, publ. in *Gladstone to His Wife*, ch. 3 (ed. Arthur Tilney Bassett, 1936)

3 This is the negation of God erected into a system of government.

Two Letters to the Earl of Aberdeen on the State Persecution of the Neapolitan Government (pamphlet, 1851). Gladstone had visited Naples in October 1850, where he was appalled by the conditions that he found in the prisons.

4 You cannot fight against the future. Time is on our side.

Speech on the Reform Bill, House of Commons, 27 April 1866, publ. in *Gladstone's Speeches*, pt 2 (ed. Arthur Tilney Bassett, 1916). Gladstone was defeated in his attempt to introduce the bill, but in 1867 an amended version was guided through parliament under his successor as Chancellor, DISRAELI.

5 Swimming for his life, a man does not see much of the country through which the river winds, and I probably know little of these years through which I busily work and live, beyond this, how sin and frailty deface them, and how mercy crowns them.

Journal entry, 31 December 1868, publ. in *The Gladstone Diaries*, vol. 6 (ed. M. R. D. Foot and H. C. G. Matthew, 1978)

6 We have been borne down in a torrent of gin and beer.

Letter to his brother, 6 February 1874, quoted in *Life of William Ewart Gladstone*, vol. 2, bk 6, ch. 14 (1903) by John Morley. On the defeat of the Liberal Party in the 1874 general election, in which alcohol duties played a significant part.

7 Liberalism is trust of the people tempered by prudence; Conservatism is distrust of the people tempered by fear.

Speech at Plumstead, 1878. Attributed.

8 There is no broad political idea which has entered less into the formation of the political system of this country than the love of equality.

Quoted in *Mixed Essays*, 'Equality' (1879) by MATTHEW ARNOLD

9 Remember the rights of the savage, as we call him. Remember that the happiness of his humble home, remember that the sanctity of life in the hill villages of Afghanistan among the winter snows, is as inviolable in the eye of Almighty God as can be your own.

'Second Midlothian Speech', Dalkeith, Scotland, 26 November 1879, publ. in *Political Speeches in Scotland*, vol. 1 (1879)

10 The foreign policy of England should always be inspired by the love of freedom. There should be a sympathy with freedom, a desire to give it scope, founded not upon visionary ideas, but upon the long experience of many generations within the shores of this happy isle, that in freedom you lay the firmest foundations both of loyalty and order, the firmest foundations for the development of individual character, and the best provision for the development of the nation at large.

'Third Midlothian Speech', West Calder, Scotland, 27 November 1879, ibid., vol. 1

11 We live in the age of sham. We live in the age of sham diamonds, and sham silver, and sham flour, and sham sugar, and sham butter ... We have had a great deal of sham glory, and sham courage, and sham strength. I say, let us get rid of all these shams, and fall back upon realities.
Speech at West Calder, Scotland, 2 April 1880, ibid., vol. 2 (1880)

12 We cannot reckon upon the aristocracy. We cannot reckon upon what is called the landed interest. We cannot reckon upon the clergy of the Established Church in England or in Scotland ... We cannot reckon on the wealth of the country, nor upon the rank of the country ... We must set them down among our most determined foes.
'Eighteenth Midlothian Speech', East Calder, Scotland, 2 April 1880, ibid., vol. 2

13 The downfall of Beaconsfieldism is like the vanishing of some vast magnificent castle in an Italian romance.
Letter to the Duke of Argyll, 12 April 1880, quoted in *Life of William Ewart Gladstone*, vol. 2, bk 7, ch. 8 (1903) by John Morley. On the defeat of the Conservative Party, led by DISRAELI (Lord Beaconsfield), at the 1880 general election.

14 If Germany becomes a colonising power, all I can say is 'God speed her.' She becomes our ally and partner in the execution of the great purpose of Providence for the benefit of mankind.
Speech to House of Commons, 12 March 1885, publ. in *Hansard*, vol. 295, col. 979

15 All the world over, I will back the masses against the classes.
Speech in Liverpool, 28 June 1886, publ. in *The Speeches and Public Addresses of the Right Hon. W. E. Gladstone*, vol. 9 (ed. A. W. Hutton and H. J. Cohen, 1894)

16 What that Sicilian mule was to me, I have been to the Queen.
Memorandum, 20 March 1894, publ. in *The Gladstone Diaries*, vol. 13 (ed. H. C. G. Matthew, 1994). Gladstone was recalling having ridden from Palermo to Messina by mule on a Sicilian holiday in the autumn of 1838. 'I had been on [the] back of the beast for many scores of hours; it had done me no wrong; it had rendered me much valuable service,' he wrote. 'Yet it was in vain to argue. There was the fact staring me in the face, I could not get up the smallest shred of feeling for the brute, I could neither love it nor like it.'

Ellen Glasgow
(1874–1945)
US novelist

Her unsentimental fiction describes the social divisions and hypocrisies of Virginia and the plight of women in the American South. 'Southern romance is dead,' Carl van Doren stated. 'Ellen Glasgow has murdered it.'

1 I haven't much opinion of words ... They're apt to set fire to a dry tongue, that's what I say.
The Deliverance, bk 2, ch. 4 (1904). Spoken by Sam Murray.

2 Women like to sit down with trouble as if it were knitting.
The Sheltered Life, pt 3, sect. 3 (1932). Spoken by Jenny Blair.

3 I have observed with wonder so many intellectual and literary fashions that I have come at last to rely positively upon one conviction alone. No idea is so antiquated that it was not once modern. No idea is so modern that it will not some day be antiquated ... To seize the flying thought before it escapes us is our only touch with reality.
'Empty American Novels', address to the Modern Language Association (1936), repr. in the *New York Times* 1 January 1937

George Glass
(1910–84)
US film executive

Sometimes known as Georges Glass, he worked extensively as a film producer in Europe and Hollywood in a career spanning more than thirty years.

1 An actor is a kind of guy who if you ain't talking about him ain't listening.
Quoted in *Brando*, ch. 8 (1973) by Bob Thomas. The quote is frequently ascribed to MARLON BRANDO, who may have heard it from Glass. The actor Michael Wilding is similarly quoted as saying, 'You can pick out actors by the glazed look that comes into their eyes when the conversation wanders away from themselves.'

William Henry, Duke of Gloucester
(1743–1805)

The brother of GEORGE III, he was estranged from the king following his clandestine marriage to Countess Waldegrave.

1 Another damned, thick, square book! Always scribble, scribble, scribble! Eh! Mr Gibbon?
Quoted in *Personal and Literary Memorials* (1829) by Henry Digby Beste. Addressed to EDWARD GIBBON, who had pre-

sented the Duke with the second volume of *Decline and Fall of the Roman Empire*. The words have also been attributed to GEORGE III and the Duke of Cumberland.

John A. Glover-Kind
(d. 1918)

1 I Do Like To Be Beside the Seaside.
Title of song (1909)

Jean-Luc Godard
(b. 1930)
French film-maker and author

His first feature film À Bout de souffle (Breathless, *1960) established him as a leader of the* nouvelle vague *movement in cinema. In subsequent films he made use of free improvisation and anti-narration, adopting an increasingly political stance.*

1 I don't know if I'm free because I'm unhappy or unhappy because I'm free.
Breathless (film, 1960, written and directed by Jean-Luc Godard). Spoken by Patricia Franchini (Jean Seberg).

2 Photography is truth ... and the cinema is the truth twenty-four times a second.
Le Petit soldat (film, 1960, written and directed by Jean-Luc Godard). Spoken by Bruno Forestier (Michel Subor).

3 When I hear the word culture, I take out my chequebook.
Le Mépris (film, 1963, adapted by Jean-Luc Godard from *A Ghost at Noon* by Alberto Moravia, directed by Jean-Luc Godard). Spoken by Jeremy Prokosh (Jack Palance), a film producer. See HERMANN GOERING 2.

4 More and more I see the human predicament as a dialogue between lovers.
Alphaville (film, 1965, written and directed by Jean-Luc Godard). Spoken by Natasha von Braun (Anna Karina).

5 To me style is just the outside of content, and content the inside of style, like the outside and the inside of the human body – both go together, they can't be separated.
Quoted in *Godard*, Introduction (1967) by Richard Roud

6 Every film should have a beginning, a middle and an end – but not necessarily in that order.
Quoted in *Close Up* (1972) by Len Deighton. In *Time* magazine 14 September 1981, the words are quoted as an exchange between Godard and French film-maker Georges Franju.

7 All you need for a movie is a gun and a girl.
Quoted by John Boorman in journal entry, 15 July 1991, publ. in *Projections* (ed. John Boorman and Walter Donohue, 1992)

Alfred Godley
(1856–1925)
British scholar

Deemed 'an almost perfect writer of elegant Latin', he wrote humorous and satirical prose and verse as well as works on classical authors.

1 What is this that roareth thus?
Can it be a Motor Bus?
Yes, the smell and hideous hum
Indicat Motorem Bum ...
Domine, defende nos
Contra hos Motores Bos!
'The Motor Bus' (1914), publ. in *Reliquiae*, vol. 1 (1926)

William Godwin
(1756–1836)
English author and political theorist

Born into a family of Dissenters, he became an atheist and an exponent of an anarchistic society free of coercion. He set out his ideas in An Enquiry concerning the Principles of Political Justice *(1793). He was married to* MARY WOLLSTONECRAFT.

1 Government must always depend upon the opinion of the governed. Let the most oppressed people under heaven once change their mode of thinking, and they are free.
'An Account of the Seminary ... at Epsom in Surrey' (1783), repr. in *Political and Philosophical Writings of William Godwin* (ed. M. Philp, 1993)

2 Government is very limited in its powers of making men either virtuous or happy; it is only in the infancy of society that it can do anything considerable; in its maturity it can only direct a few of our outward actions. But our moral dispositions and character depend very much, perhaps entirely, upon education.
'An Account of the Seminary ... at Epsom in Surrey' (1783), ibid.

3 Society is nothing more than an aggregation of individuals.
An Enquiry concerning the Principles of Political Justice, bk 2, ch. 8 (1793). See MARGARET THATCHER 15.

4 If government be founded in the consent of the people, it can have no power over any individual by whom that consent is refused.
Ibid., bk 3, ch. 2

5 Refer them to reading, to conversation, to

meditation; but teach them neither creeds nor catechisms, either moral or political.

Ibid., bk 6, ch. 8

6 The project of a national education ought uniformly to be discouraged, on account of its obvious alliance with national government. This is an alliance of a more formidable nature than the old and much contested alliance of church and state.

Ibid., bk 6, ch. 8

7 The assassin cannot help the murder he commits any more than the dagger.

Ibid., bk 7, ch. 1. The assassin, Godwin wrote, 'is propelled to act by necessary causes and irresistible motives'.

8 Our animal wants have long since been defined, and are stated to consist of food, clothing and shelter. If justice have any meaning, nothing can be more iniquitous, than for one man to possess superfluities, while there is a human being in existence that is not adequately supplied with these.

Ibid., bk 8, ch. 1

Joseph Goebbels
(1897–1945)
German Nazi leader

HITLER's *Minister of Propaganda from 1933, he was given extensive powers in government in 1943. Committed to Hitler to the last, he killed his six children and, with his wife, committed suicide.*

1 We enter parliament in order to supply ourselves, in the arsenal of democracy, with its own weapons ... If democracy is so stupid as to give us free tickets and salaries for this bear's work, that is its affair ... We do not come as friends, nor even as neutrals. We come as enemies. As the wolf bursts into the flock, so we come.

Der Angriff 30 April 1928

2 We can do without butter, but, despite all our love of peace, not without arms. One cannot shoot with butter, but with guns.

Speech in Berlin, 17 January 1936, quoted in *Allgemeine Zeitung* 18 January 1936. The origin of the 'guns or butter' quote is elusive. In the summer of 1936, in a radio broadcast on the Four Year Plan, HERMANN GOERING announced, 'Guns will make us powerful; butter will only make us fat.'

Hermann Goering
(1893–1946)
German Nazi leader

Having joined the Nazi government in 1933, he was responsible for founding the Gestapo, establishing concentration camps and building up the Luftwaffe. In 1940 he became Marshal of the Reich but was dismissed in 1945. He committed suicide after being sentenced at Nuremberg.

1 I herewith commission you to carry out all preparations with regard to ... a total solution of the Jewish question in those territories of Europe which are under German influence ... I furthermore charge you to submit to me as soon as possible a draft showing the ... measures already taken for the execution of the intended final solution of the Jewish question.

Military directive to Reinhard Heydrich, 31 July 1941, quoted in *The Rise and Fall of the Third Reich*, ch. 27 (1960) by William L. Shirer. According to Shirer, the German word *Endloesung* was erroneously rendered 'desired solution' at Goering's trial at Nuremberg, thus allowing the judge to accept Goering's insistence that he had never used the terms 'total' or 'final solution'. 'The first time I learned of these terrible exterminations was right here at Nuremberg,' Goering declared. Heydrich, Deputy Chief of the Gestapo, has also been associated with the phrase.

2 Whenever I hear the word culture, I reach for my revolver.

Attributed. Whether or not Goering ever uttered these words, the first recorded reference to them is in the play *Schlageter* (1933) by Hanns Johst (1890–1978), Nazi playwright and President of the Reich Chamber of Literature. The line is spoken by a stormtrooper in Act 1, Sc. 1: 'When I hear the word culture, I cock my Browning.' Many variations have been coined (see ALLEN GINSBERG 8, JEAN-LUC GODARD 3).

Johann Wolfgang von Goethe
(1749–1832)
German author, poet and dramatist

The greatest figure of the German Romantic movement, he came to prominence with the drama Götz von Berlichingen *(1773), a product of* Sturm und Drang, *and his epistolary novel* The Sorrows of Young Werther *(1774). Other key works include* Wilhelm Meister's Apprenticeship *(1795–6), a novel of character-development, and the dramatic poem* Faust *(1808, 1832). After 1775, he lived in the city of Weimar, where he was Chief Minister for ten years.*

1 Where there is much light there is also a strong shadow.

Götz von Berlichingen, Act 1, Sc. 3 (1773). Spoken by Götz.

2 One lives but once in this world.
Clavigo, Act 1, Sc. 1 (1774). Spoken by Carlos.

3 The world is for thousands a freak show; the images flicker past and vanish; the impressions remain flat and unconnected in the soul. Thus they are easily led by the opinions of others, are content to let their impressions be shuffled and rearranged and evaluated differently.
Aus Goethes Brieftasche, 'Third Pilgrimage to Erwin's Grave' (*From Goethe's Briefcase*, 1776)

4 Who ne'er his bread in sorrow ate,
Who ne'er the mournful midnight hours
Weeping upon his bed has sate,
He knows you not, ye Heavenly Powers.
Wilhelm Meister's Apprenticeship, bk 2, ch. 13 (1796). Translated by LONGFELLOW as epigraph to *Hyperion*.

5 Know'st thou the land where the lemon-trees do bloom,
[*Kennst du das Land, wo die Zitronen blühn?*]
And oranges like gold in leafy gloom;
A gentle wind from deep blue heaven blows,
The myrtle thick, and high the laurel grows?
Ibid., bk 3, ch. 1 (transl. THOMAS CARLYLE, 1824)

6 None but the lonely heart
Knows what I suffer!
Mignon's song, ibid., bk 4, ch. 11

7 One ought every day at least to hear a little song, read a good poem, see a fine picture, and, if it were possible, to speak a few reasonable words.
Ibid., bk 5, ch. 1 (transl. THOMAS CARLYLE, 1824). Spoken by Serlo.

8 Sighing within my soul for Greece again.
Iphigenia in Tauris, Act 1, Sc. 1 (1787). Spoken by Iphigenia.

9 A man becomes immortalized by battle,
If he should fall his praise is told in song.
Ibid., Act 5, Sc. 6, ll. 43–4. Spoken by Iphigenia.

10 A talent forms itself in solitude,
A character amid the stream of life.
Torquato Tasso, Act 1, Sc. 2, ll. 304–5 (1790). Spoken by Leonore.

11 Within a single moment love will grant
What effort barely gains in length of time.
Torquato Tasso, ibid., Act 2, Sc. 3, ll. 1271–2

12 He who is firm in will moulds the world to himself.
Hermann and Dorothea, pt 9, l. 304 (1797)

13 The spirits I summoned up
I now can't rid myself of.
The Sorcerer's Apprentice, st. 13 (1797)

14 No two men see the world exactly alike, and different temperaments will apply in different ways a principle that they both acknowledge. The same man will, indeed, often see and judge the same things differently on different occasions: early convictions must give way to more mature ones. Nevertheless, may not the opinions that a man holds and expresses withstand all trials, if he only remains true to himself and others?
Propyläen, Introduction (1798)

15 He who has a task to perform must know how to take sides, or he is quite unworthy of it.
Ibid., Introduction

16 One of the most striking signs of the decay of art is when we see its separate forms jumbled together.
Ibid., Introduction

17 The true, prescriptive artist strives after artistic truth; the lawless artist, following blind instinct, after an appearance of naturalness. The one leads to the highest peaks of art, the other to its lowest depths.
Ibid., Introduction

18 Who wants to understand the poem
Must go to the land of poetry;
Who wishes to understand the poet
Must go to the poet's land.
Divan of East and West, motto (1819)

19 One must *be* something in order to *do* something.
Quoted in *Conversations with Goethe*, entry for 20 October 1828 (1836) by Johann Peter Eckermann

20 Man is by all his senses and efforts directed to externals – to the world around him ... It is only when he feels joy or sorrow that he knows anything about himself, and only by joy or sorrow is he instructed what to seek and what to shun. Altogether, man is a darkened being; he knows not whence he comes, nor whither he goes; he knows little of the world , and least of himself.
Quoted ibid., entry 10 April 1829

21 Age childish makes, they say, but 'tis not true;
We're only genuine children still, in Age's season.
Faust, 'Prelude at the Theatre', ll. 182–3 (1808, transl. Bayard Taylor, 1870–1). Spoken by Merry Andrew.

22 While Man's desires and aspirations stir,
He cannot choose but err.
The Lord, ibid., Pt 1, 'Prologue in Heaven', ll. 77–8. Also translated as: 'Man errs as long as he strives.'

23 I'm Magister – yea, Doctor – hight,
And straight or cross-wise, wrong or right,
These ten years long, with many woes,
I've led my scholars by the nose.
Faust, ibid., Pt 1, Sc. 1 ('Night'), ll. 7–10

24 Two souls, alas! reside within my breast,
And each withdraws from and repels its brother.
Faust, ibid., Pt 1, Sc. 2 ('Before The City Gate'), ll. 302–3 (transl. Bayard Taylor)

25 I am the spirit that denies.
Mephistopheles, ibid., Pt 1, Sc. 3 ('The Study'), l. 152

26 My worthy friend, grey are all theories,
And green alone life's golden tree.
Mephistopheles, ibid., Pt 1, Sc. 4 ('The Study'), ll. 511–12. See HEGEL 2.

27 Culture, which smooth the whole world licks,
Also unto the Devil sticks.
Mephistopheles, ibid., Pt 1, Sc. 6 ('Witches' Kitchen'), ll. 160–1

28 Meine Ruh' ist hin,
Mein Herz ist schwer.
Ich finde sie nimmer
Und nimmermehr.
[My peace is gone,
My heart is sore:
I never shall find it,
Ah, nevermore!]
Margaret, ibid., Pt 1, Sc. 15 ('Margaret's Room'), ll. 1–4

29 Upon the creatures we have made,
We are, ourselves, at last, dependent.
Mephistopheles, ibid., Pt 2, Act 2, Sc. 2 ('Laboratory'), ll. 187–8 (1832)

30 Power and estate to win, inspires my thought!
The deed is everything, the glory naught.
Faust, ibid., Pt 2, Act 4, Sc. 1 ('High Mountains'), ll. 150–1

31 Das Ewig-Weibliche zieht uns hinan.
[The Woman-Soul leadeth us
Upward and on!]
Chorus Mysticus, ibid., Pt. 2, Act 5, Sc. 7 ('Mountain-Gorges, Forest, Rock, Desert'), ll. 267–8. Last words of play. 'Woman-soul' (Ewig-weibliche) is also translated 'Eternal Feminine'.

32 Mehr Licht!
[More light!]
Last words, quoted in The Life and Works of Goethe, ch. 8 (1855) by George Henry Lewes. According to some sources, Goethe's last words were: 'Open the second shutter, so that more light can come in.'

Oliver St John Gogarty
(1878–1957)
Irish physician, author and poet

A practising surgeon and a senator in the Irish Free State 1922–39, he published several volumes of verse and memoirs. JAMES JOYCE portrayed him as Buck Mulligan in Ulysses.

1 [His] spiritual life has been exaggerated by a chronic attack of mental gallstones.
Speech to Seanad Eireann, the Irish Senate, January 1923, quoted in Oliver St John Gogarty: A Poet and His Times, ch. 17 (1964) by Ulick O'Connor. Referring to lawyer and politician Lord Carson.

2 Politics is the chloroform of the Irish people or, rather, the hashish.
As I Was Going Down Sackville Street, ch. 1 (1937)

Nikolai Vasilyevich Gogol
(1809–52)
Russian author and dramatist

His short stories and novellas, including the picaresque Dead Souls (1842), were a key influence on the Russian realist novel. His fame as a dramatist rests on The Inspector General (1836), a satire on provincial life.

1 It is no use to blame the looking glass if your face is awry.
The Inspector General, Epigraph (1836)

2 Public opinion does not admit that lofty rapturous laughter is worthy to stand beside lofty lyrical emotion and that there is all the difference in the world between it and the antics of a clown at a fair.
Dead Souls, pt 1, ch. 7 (1842, transl. David Magarshack, 1961)

Isaac Goldberg
(1887–1938)
US critic

The literary editor of American Freeman (1923–32), he was instrumental in introducing the modern literature of Latin America to English-speaking readers.

1 Diplomacy is to do and say
The nastiest things in the nicest way.
The Reflex October 1927

(Sir) William Golding

(1911–93)

British author

He achieved success with his first novel Lord of the Flies *(1954), whose themes of human fallibility and the potential of evil recurred in such later works as* The Spire *(1964) and* Rites of Passage *(1980).*

1 Sleep is when all the unsorted stuff comes flying out as from a dustbin upset in a high wind.

Pincher Martin, ch. 6 (1956)

2 Marx, Darwin and Freud are the three most crashing bores of the Western world. The simplistic popularization of their ideas has thrust our world into a mental straitjacket from which we can only escape by the most anarchic violence.

'Belief and Creativity', lecture given in Hamburg, Germany, April 1980, publ. in *A Moving Target* (1982)

3 Childhood is a disease – a sickness that you grow out of.

Quoted in the *Guardian* 22 June 1990

Emma Goldman

(1869–1940)

Lithuanian-born US anarchist

Imprisoned for inciting unemployed workers to riot in 1893 and for opposing conscription during the First World War, she was deported from the USA in 1919 and subsequently lived in Russia and France. She wrote numerous political articles and an autobiography, Living My Life *(1931).*

1 The history of progress is written in the blood of men and women who have dared to espouse an unpopular cause, as, for instance, the black man's right to his body, or woman's right to her soul.

'What I Believe' (1908), repr. in *Red Emma Speaks* (ed. Alix Kates Shulman, 1972)

2 Anarchism is the only philosophy which brings to man the consciousness of himself; which maintains that God, the State, and society are non-existent, that their promises are null and void, since they can be fulfilled only through man's subordination. Anarchism is therefore the teacher of the unity of life; not merely in nature, but in man.

Anarchism and Other Essays, 'Anarchism: What It Really Stands For' (1910)

3 Crime is naught but misdirected energy.

Ibid., 'Anarchism: What It Really Stands For'

4 Poor human nature, what horrible crimes have been committed in thy name!

Ibid., 'Anarchism: What It Really Stands For'

5 Merely external emancipation has made of the modern woman an artificial being . . . Now, woman is confronted with the necessity of emancipating herself from emancipation, if she really desires to be free.

Ibid., 'The Tragedy of Women's Emancipation'

6 There is no hope even that woman, with her right to vote, will ever purify politics.

Ibid., 'The Tragedy of Women's Emancipation'

7 Love, the strongest and deepest element in all life, the harbinger of hope, of joy, of ecstasy; love, the defier of all laws, of all conventions; love, the freest, the most powerful moulder of human destiny; how can such an all-compelling force be synonymous with that poor little State and Church-begotten weed, marriage?

Ibid., 'Marriage and Love' (1910)

8 To the indefinite, uncertain mind of the American radical the most contradictory ideas and methods are possible. The result is a sad chaos in the radical movement, a sort of intellectual hash, which has neither taste nor character.

'Syndicalism: Its Theory and Practice' (1913), repr. in *Red Emma Speaks* (ed. Alix Kates Shulman, 1972)

9 It is safe to say that no other superstition is so detrimental to growth, so enervating and paralyzing to the minds and hearts of the people, as the superstition of Morality.

'Victims of Morality' (1913), ibid.

10 The individual whose vision encompasses the whole world often feels nowhere so hedged in and out of touch with his surroundings as in his native land.

'The Individual, Society and the State' (1940), ibid.

11 If there's no dancing, count me out.

Attributed. Referring to the Russian Revolution.

William Goldman

(b. 1931)

US screenwriter and novelist

He won Academy Awards for his screenplays of Butch Cassidy and the Sundance Kid *(1970) and* All the President's Men *(1983). He has also adapted his own novels for the screen, including* Marathon Man *in 1976.*

1 As far as the filmmaking process is concerned, stars are essentially worthless – and absolutely essential.
Adventures in the Screen Trade, ch. 1 (1983)

2 Studio executives are intelligent, brutally overworked men and women who share one thing in common with baseball managers: They wake up every morning of the world with the knowledge that sooner or later they're going to get fired.
Ibid., ch. 1

Carlo Goldoni

(1707–93)

Italian dramatist

Based in Venice and later in Paris, he revolutionized the conventions of commedia dell'arte *in such works as* Women's Gossip *and* The Liar *(both 1750–1). He wrote in Italian, Venetian dialect and French.*

1 The world is a beautiful book, but of little use to him who cannot read it.
La Pamela, Act 1, Sc. 14 (1750). Spoken by Lord Arthur.

Oliver Goldsmith

(1728–74)

Anglo-Irish author, poet and playwright

A founder-member of SAMUEL JOHNSON's *Literary Club, he was reviled for his vanity and social ineptitude and admired for his generosity and writerly skills. His works include* The Vicar of Wakefield *(1766), a novel;* The Deserted Village *(1770), a poem, and* She Stoops to Conquer *(1773), a play. According to* DAVID GARRICK, *he 'wrote like an angel, but talked like poor Poll'. See also* SAMUEL JOHNSON 131.

1 It was then that taste was united to genius.
'An Account of the Augustan Age in England' (1759), publ. in *Collected Works of Oliver Goldsmith*, vol. 1 (ed. Arthur Friedman, 1966). Referring to the reign of Queen Anne (1702–14) 'or some years before that period', which Goldsmith held to be the English 'Augustan Age'.

2 The doctors found, when she was dead –
Her last disorder mortal.
'Elegy on Mrs Mary Blaize', st. 6 (1759), ibid., vol. 1

3 As writers become more numerous, it is natural for readers to become more indolent; whence must necessarily arise a desire of attaining knowledge with the greatest possible ease.
'Upon Unfortunate Merit' (1759), ibid., vol. 1

4 You must know, sir, that the republic of letters is at present divided into three classes. One writer, for instance, excels at a plan or a title-page; another works away the body of the book; and a third is a dab at an index.
The Bee, no. 1, 6 October 1759, ibid., vol. 1. Quoting his publisher. See also HENRY FIELDING 12.

5 I esteem . . . the traveller who instructs the heart, but despise him who only indulges the imagination: a man who leaves home to mend himself and others is a philosopher; but he who goes from country to country, guided by the blind impulse of curiosity, is only a vagabond.
The Citizen of the World, Letter 7 (1762)

6 I have known a German prince with more titles than subjects, and a Spanish nobleman with more names than shirts.
Ibid., Letter 120

7 Where'er I roam, whatever realms to see,
My heart untravelled fondly turns to thee.
The Traveller, ll. 7–8 (1764)

8 And learn the luxury of doing good.
Ibid., l. 22

9 Honour sinks where commerce long prevails.
Ibid., l. 92

10 Where the broad ocean leans against the land.
Ibid., l. 284. Describing Holland.

11 Pride in their port, defiance in their eye,
I see the lords of humankind pass by.
Ibid., ll. 327–8. Referring to the British.

12 That independence Britons prize too high
Keeps man from man, and breaks the social tie.
Ibid., ll. 339–40

13 For just experience tells, in every soil,
That those that think must govern those that toil.
Ibid., ll. 371–2

14 Each wanton judge new penal statutes draw,
Laws grind the poor, and rich men rule the law.
Ibid., ll. 385–6

15 I . . . chose my wife as she did her wedding-gown, not for a fine glossy surface, but such qualities as would wear well.
The Vicar of Wakefield, ch. 1 (1766). Spoken by the narrator (Dr Charles Primrose).

16 We had no revolutions to fear, nor fatigues to undergo; all our adventures were by the fireside,

and all our migrations from the blue bed to the brown.

Narrator (Dr Charles Primrose), ibid., ch. 1

17 When any one of our relations was found to be a person of a very bad character, a troublesome guest, or one we desired to get rid of, upon his leaving my house I ever took care to lend him a riding-coat, or a pair of boots, or sometimes a horse of small value, and I always had the satisfaction of finding he never came back to return them.

Narrator (Dr Charles Primrose), ibid., ch. 1

18 The jests of the rich are ever successful.

Narrator (Dr Charles Primrose), ibid., ch. 7

19 It seemed to me pretty plain, that they had more of love than matrimony in them.

Narrator (Dr Charles Primrose), ibid., ch. 16. Of the 'fine sentiments' expressed by Squire Thornhill, regarding Olivia.

20 The man recovered of the bite,
The dog it was that died.

'An Elegy on the Death of a Mad Dog', ibid., ch. 17. Closing
lines of song sung by Bill.

21 When lovely woman stoops to folly,
And finds too late that men betray,
What charm can soothe her melancholy,
What art can wash her guilt away?

Ibid., ch. 24. Song sung by Olivia.

22 I can't say whether we had more wit among us now than usual, but I am certain we had more laugh-ing, which answered the end as well.

Narrator (Dr Charles Primrose), ibid. ch. 32

23 This same philosophy is a good horse in the stable, but an arrant jade on a journey.

The Good-Natured Man, Act 1 (1768). Spoken by Jarvis.

24 There are some faults so nearly allied to excel-lence that we can scarce weed out the vice without eradicating the virtue.

Sir William Honeywood, ibid., Act 1

25 Life at the greatest and best is but a froward child, that must be humoured and coaxed a little till it falls asleep, and then all the care is over.

Croaker, ibid., Act 1

26 Friendship is a disinterested commerce between equals; love, an abject intercourse between tyrants and slaves.

Mr Honeywood, ibid., Act 1

27 Don't let us make imaginary evils, when you know we have so many real ones to encounter.

Leontine, ibid., Act 1

28 Leontine: An only son, sir, might expect more indulgence.
Croaker: An only father, sir, might expect more obedience.

Ibid., Act 1

29 You, that are going to be married, think things can never be done too fast: but we that are old, and know what we are about, must elope methodically, madam.

Jarvis to Olivia, ibid., Act 4

30 There is no arguing with Johnson; for when his pistol misses fire, he knocks you down with the butt end of it.

Quoted by JAMES BOSWELL in *Life of Samuel Johnson, LL.D.*,
26 October 1769 (1791). The remark was apparently inspired
by 'the witty words of one of Cibber's comedies'.

31 Sweet Auburn! loveliest village of the plain.

The Deserted Village, l. 1 (1770)

32 Ill fares the land, to hastening ills a prey,
Where wealth accumulates, and men decay.

Ibid., ll. 51–2

33 Princes and lords may flourish, or may fade;
A breath can make them, as a breath has made;
But a bold peasantry, their country's pride,
When once destroyed, can never be supplied.

Ibid., ll. 53–6

34 The loud laugh that spoke the vacant mind.

Ibid., l. 122

35 Truth from his lips prevailed with double sway,
And fools, who came to scoff, remained to pray.

Ibid., ll. 179–80. Referring to the village preacher.

36 There, in his noisy mansion, skilled to rule,
The village master taught his little school.

Ibid., ll. 195–6

37 Well had the boding tremblers learned to trace
The day's disasters in his morning face.

Ibid., ll. 199–200. Referring to the village schoolmaster.

38 And still they gazed, and still the wonder grew,
That one small head could carry all he knew.

Ibid., ll. 215–16

39 Where village statesmen talked with looks profound,

And news much older than their ale went round.
Ibid., ll. 223–4

40 To me more dear, congenial to my heart,
One native charm, than all the gloss of art.
Ibid., ll. 253–4

41 In all the silent manliness of grief.
Ibid., l. 384

42 E'en now the devastation is begun
And half the business of destruction done;
E'en now, methinks, as pondering here I stand,
I see the rural virtues leave the land.
Ibid., ll. 395–8

43 Thou source of all my bliss, and all my woe,
That found'st me poor at first, and keep'st me so.
Ibid., ll. 413–14. Of 'sweet Poetry'.

44 I love everything that's old: old friends, old times, old manners, old books, old wine; and, I believe, Dorothy, you'll own I have been pretty fond of an old wife.
She Stoops to Conquer, Act 1, Sc. 1 (1773). Spoken by Hardcastle.

45 The very pink of perfection.
Miss Neville, ibid., Act 1, Sc. 1

46 Let schoolmasters puzzle their brain,
With grammar, and nonsense, and learning;
Good liquor, I stoutly maintain,
Gives genius a better discerning.
Ibid., Act 1, Sc. 2. Song sung by Tony Lumpkin.

47 I'll be with you in the squeezing of a lemon.
Tony Lumpkin, ibid., Act 1, Sc. 2

48 Girls like to be played with, and rumpled a little too, sometimes.
Hardcastle, ibid., Act 5, Sc. 1

49 As I take my shoes from the shoemaker, and my coat from the tailor, so I take my religion from the priest.
Quoted by JAMES BOSWELL in Life of Samuel Johnson, LL.D., 9 April 1773 (1791)

50 If you were to make little fishes talk, they would talk like whales.
Remark to SAMUEL JOHNSON, quoted by JAMES BOSWELL, ibid., 27 April 1773

51 Though equal to all things, for all things unfit,
Too nice for a statesman, too proud for a wit.
Retaliation, ll. 37–8 (1774). Referring to EDMUND BURKE.

52 He cast off his friends as a huntsman his pack,

For he knew when he pleased he could whistle them back.
Ibid., ll. 107–8. Referring to DAVID GARRICK.

53 When they talked of their Raphaels, Correggios, and stuff,
He shifted his trumpet, and only took snuff.
Ibid., ll. 37–8. Referring to JOSHUA REYNOLDS, who suffered from deafness.

Barry Goldwater
(1909–98)
US politician

As a Republican Senator (1953–64, 1969–87), he held an extreme anti-Communist stance. He was defeated as presidential candidate in the 1964 election, and in 1969 chaired the Armed Services Commission.

1 I would remind you that extremism in the defense of liberty is no vice! And let me remind you also that moderation in the pursuit of justice is no virtue!
Speech accepting presidential nomination at Republican National Convention, San Francisco, 16 July 1964, quoted in the *New York Times* 17 July 1964. Goldwater later attributed these words to CICERO. LYNDON B. JOHNSON, as Democratic nominee for the presidency, replied in a speech in New York, 31 October 1964: 'Extremism in the pursuit of the Presidency is an unpardonable vice. Moderation in the affairs of the nation is the highest virtue.' Johnson won a sweeping victory against Goldwater in the presidential election three days later.

Samuel Goldwyn
(1882–1974)
Polish-born US film producer

Originally Samuel Goldfish. As head of one of Hollywood's mightiest film studios, he had the knack of assembling creative teams. He was notorious for his malapropisms, although some of the most famous are apocryphal. See also G. B. SHAW 79.

1 Gentlemen, include me out!
Attributed in *The Goldwyn Touch*, ch. 10 (1986) by Michael Freedland. The remark is supposed to have been made in October 1933, on resigning from the Motion Picture Producers and Distributors of America over a labour dispute, but Goldwyn himself denied ever having used the words, claiming instead to have said, 'Gentlemen, I'm withdrawing from the association.'

2 That is the kind of ad I like. Facts, facts, facts.
Quoted in *Goldwyn: the Man Behind the Myth*, ch. 16 (1976) by Arthur Marx. Goldwyn was referring to an advertisement for the film *We Live Again* (1934), which described it: 'The greatest motion picture in all history, by the world's most

outstanding writer. The directorial genius of Mamoulian, the beauty of Anna Sten and the producing genius of Goldwyn have combined to make the greatest entertainment in the world.' The film flopped.

3 A verbal contract isn't worth the paper it is written on.

Attributed in *The Great Goldwyn*, ch. 1 (1937) by Alva Johnston. Goldwyn's actual words were said to be: 'His verbal contract is worth more than the paper it's written on,' referring to movie executive Joseph M. Schenck, who was regarded as completely trustworthy. This popular version is probably one of the many 'Goldwynisms' cooked up by Goldwyn's own staff.

4 That's the way with these directors, they're always biting the hand that lays the golden egg.
Ibid., ch. 1

5 I had a monumental idea this morning, but I didn't like it.
Ibid., ch. 1

6 [Too caustic?] To hell with the cost. If it's a good picture, we'll make it.
Quoted ibid., ch. 1. To a director who was asked his opinion of a script.

7 God makes stars. I just produce them.
Quoted in the *Daily Express* 16 May 1939

8 Any man who goes to a psychiatrist should have his head examined.
Quoted in *Moguls*, ch. 3 (1969) by Norman Zierold

9 I don't think anybody should write his autobiography until after he's dead.
Quoted in *Goldwyn: the Man Behind the Myth*, Prologue (1976) by Arthur Marx

10 Pictures are for entertainment, messages should be delivered by Western Union.
Quoted ibid., ch. 15

11 I read part of it all the way through.
Quoted ibid., ch. 27

(Sir) E. H. Gombrich
(1909–2001)
Austrian-born British art critic and historian

Ernst Hans Joseph Gombrich. He emigrated to England in 1936 to work at the Warburg Institute, University of London. Publications include The Story of Art *(1950) and* Art and Illusion *(1960).*

1 There really is no such thing as Art. There are only artists.
The Story of Art, Introduction (1950). Opening words.

Ivan Goncharov
(1812–91)
Russian novelist

Employed in the civil service, he was acclaimed for his first novel, A Common Story *(1847), but is best known for* Oblomov *(1859), a satirical portrait of the Russian landed gentry.*

1 The trouble is that no devastating or redeeming fires have ever burnt in my life . . . My life began by flickering out.
Oblomov, pt 2, ch. 4 (1859, transl. 1954). Spoken by Oblomov.

Edmond de Goncourt
(1822–96)
Jules de Goncourt
(1830–70)
French authors and journalists

They collaborated on a series of historical and artistic studies and on a journal that provides a vivid picture of social and literary life in contemporary Paris. Edmond founded the Académie Goncourt (opened 1903), responsible for awarding France's most prestigious literary prize. See also RALPH WALDO EMERSON 66.

1 The newspaper is the natural enemy of the book, as the whore is of the decent woman.
Journal entry, July 1858, publ. in *The Goncourt Journals* (1888–96), repr. in *Pages from the Goncourt Journal* (ed. Robert Baldick, 1962)

2 There have been many definitions of beauty in art. What is it? Beauty is what the untrained eyes consider abominable.
Journal entry, 17 February 1859, ibid.

3 As a general truth, it is safe to say that any picture that produces a moral impression is a bad picture.
Journal entry, 7 December 1860, ibid.

4 The facts: nothing matters but the facts: worship of the facts leads to everything, to happiness first of all and then to wealth.
Journal entry, 30 July 1861, ibid.

5 Debauchery is perhaps an act of despair in the face of infinity.
Journal entry, 30 July 1861, ibid.

6 A book is never a masterpiece: it becomes one. Genius is the talent of a dead man.
Journal entry, 23 July 1864, ibid.

7 The reason for the sadness of this modern age and

the men who live in it is that it looks for the truth in everything and finds it.
Journal entry, 23 October 1864, ibid.

8 Sickness sensitizes man for observation, like a photographic plate.
Journal entry, 27 March 1865, ibid.

9 There are only two great currents in the history of mankind: the baseness which makes conservatives and the envy which makes revolutionaries.
Journal entry, 12 July 1867, ibid.

10 The English are crooked as a nation and honest as individuals. The contrary is true of the French, who are honest as a nation and crooked as individuals.
Journal entry, 29 October 1868, ibid.

Lord Goodman
(1913–95)
British lawyer and public figure

Arnold Goodman. Chairman of the Arts Council of Great Britain (1965–72) and Director of the Royal Opera House (1972–83), he was adviser to three prime ministers, and honoured by both HAROLD WILSON *and* EDWARD HEATH.

1 That is one of the great advantages of the arts: they are a consolation for loneliness.
Interview in *Singular Encounters*, 'Lord Goodman' (1990) by Naim Attallah

Paul Goodman
(1911–72)
US author, poet and critic

His prolific output championed the cause of the individual against institutions, as in Growing Up Absurd *(1960) and* The Individual and Culture *(1969).*

1 When the Devil quotes Scriptures, it's not, really, to deceive, but simply that the masses are so ignorant of theology that somebody has to teach them the elementary texts before he can seduce them.
Five Years, 'Spring and Summer 1956', sect. 6 (1966)

Mikhail Gorbachev
(b. 1931)
Russian political leader

General Secretary of the Soviet Communist Party (1985–91) and President of the USSR (1990–1), he introduced perestroika, *and* glasnost, *which transformed the Soviet Union and led to its demise in 1991. See* MARGARET THATCHER 13.

1 The essence of perestroika lies in the fact that *it unites socialism with democracy* . . . We want more socialism and, therefore, more democracy.
Perestroika, pt 1, ch. 1 (1987)

2 I am a Communist, a convinced Communist! For some that may be a fantasy. But to me it is my main goal.
Speech at Second National Congress of People's Deputies, Moscow, December 1989, quoted in the *New York Times* 26 December 1989. A week earlier, however, *Newsweek* had quoted Gorbachev as confiding to MARGARET THATCHER, 'I don't even know if I'm a Communist any more.' Both statements are discussed in *Gorbachev*, pt 6, 'Sakharov's Warning' (1991) by Gail Sheehy.

3 The market came with the dawn of civilization and it is not an invention of capitalism . . . If it leads to improving the well-being of the people there is no contradiction with socialism.
Quoted in the *Guardian* 21 June 1990

Nadine Gordimer
(b. 1923)
South African author

Apartheid and its destructive effects, both on the privileged and the oppressed, are the main themes of her writing. Her publications include the autobiographical The Lying Days *(1953) and* The Conservationist *(1974).*

1 If people would forget about utopia! When rationalism destroyed heaven and decided to set it up here on earth, that most terrible of all goals entered human ambition. It was clear there'd be no end to what people would be made to suffer for it.
Burger's Daughter, pt 2 (1979). Spoken by Bernard.

2 There is no moral authority like that of sacrifice.
'The Essential Gesture', lecture at University of Michigan, 12 October 1984, publ. in *The Essential Gesture* (ed. Stephen Clingman, 1988)

3 Censorship is never over for those who have experienced it. It is a brand on the imagination that affects the individual who has suffered it, forever.
'Censorship and its Aftermath', address at International Writer's Day conference, London, June 1990, publ. in *Index on Censorship* August 1990

Adam Lindsay Gordon
(1833–70)
Australian poet

A sometime jockey, journalist and politician, he wrote verse on the themes of outdoor and sporting life. He shot himself on the day his last collection, Bush Ballads and Galloping Rhymes, *was published.*

1 Life is mostly froth and bubble,
Two things stand like stone,
Kindness in another's trouble,
Courage in your own.
Ye Wearie Wayfarer, 'Fytte 8' (1866)

Mack Gordon
(1904–59)
Polish-born US songwriter

Originally Morris Gittler. He teamed up with Harry Revel to create numbers for Hollywood films in the 1930s, and with Harry Warren to produce such songs as 'Chattanooga Choo-Choo' (1941) and 'Kalamazoo' (1942), both hits for Glenn Miller.

1 Pardon me boy,
Is that the Chattanooga Choo-Choo?
Track twenty-nine,
Boy you can give me a shine.
'Chattanooga Choo-Choo' (song, written 1934, with music by Harry Warren) in *Sun Valley Serenade* (musical show and film, 1941). Sung by Dorothy Dandridge in the film, the number was recorded by Glenn Miller and his Orchestra, for whom it sold a million and became the first record to be awarded a gold disc.

(Sir) David Gore-Booth
(b. 1943)
British diplomat

He was Ambassador to Saudi Arabia (1993) and British High Commissioner to India (1996–8).

1 Diplomacy is made up of equal parts of protocol, vitriol and alcohol.
Attributed

Maxim Gorky
(1868–1936)
Russian author

Pseudonym of Alexei Maximovich Peshkov. A lifelong revolutionary, he described his impoverished background in three volumes of autobiography (1913–23). Other major works include the play The Lower Depths *(1902).*

1 The proletarian state must bring up thousands of excellent 'mechanics of culture', 'engineers of the soul'.
Speech at the Writers' Congress, 1934. The phrase 'engineers of the soul' may have been borrowed from STALIN, who is quoted using the words in an address to writers at Gorky's house, October 1932. See also J. F. KENNEDY 20.

Teresa Gorman
(b. 1931)
British politician

A Conservative MP 1987–2001, she has been outspoken on women's issues and against Britain's membership of the EU.

1 The Conservative Establishment has always treated women as nannies, grannies and fannies.
Quoted in the *Guardian* 27 December 1998

Stuart Gorrell
(1902–63)
US songwriter

A schoolfriend of and collaborator with Hoagy Carmichael, he was later an editor at the Miami Herald.

1 Georgia, Georgia, no peace I find,
Just an old sweet song keeps Georgia on my mind.
'Georgia on my Mind' (song, 1930, with music by Hoagy Carmichael). The song was first sung by Hoagy Carmichael, was a hit for Mildred Bailey (1932), Ray Charles (1960) and Willie Nelson (1978), and has been adopted as the state song of Georgia.

Stephen Jay Gould
(1941–2002)
US palaeontologist and author

His award-winning books, including Hens' Teeth and Horses' Toes *(1983),* Wonderful Life *(1989) and* Eight Little Piggies *(1993), propose the theory of 'punctuated equilibrium' – evolution in stops and starts – and argue against biological determinism.*

1 *Homo Sapiens* . . . a tiny twig on an improbable branch of a contingent limb on a fortunate tree.
Wonderful Life: The Burgess Shale and the Nature of History, ch. 4 (1989)

2 Science is an integral part of culture. It's not this foreign thing, done by an arcane priesthood. It's one of the glories of the human intellectual tradition.
Independent 24 January 1990

3 We think that we are reading nature by applying rules of logic and laws of matter to our observations. But we are often telling stories – in the good sense, but stories nonetheless.
Bully for Brontosaurus, ch. 5 (1991)

4 Knowledge and wonder are the dyad of our worthy lives as intellectual beings.
Ibid., ch. 35

5 Progress in knowledge is not a tower to heaven

built of bricks from the bottom up, but a product of impasse and breakthrough, yielding a bizarre and circuitous structure that ultimately rises nonetheless.
Eight Little Piggies, pt 3, essay 9 (1993)

6 The real tragedy of human existence is not that we are nasty by nature, but that a cruel structural asymmetry grants to rare events of meanness such power to shape our history.
Ibid., pt 5, essay 19

Rémy de Gourmont
(1858–1915)
French author and critic

Associated with the Symbolist movement in France, he wrote numerous essays on a range of subjects as well as poetry and fiction. As an influential critic, he evaluated works according to strictly aesthetic criteria.

1 Man, in spite of his tendency towards mendacity, has a great respect for what he calls the truth. Truth is his staff in his voyage through life; commonplaces are the bread in his bag and the wine in his jug.
'The Dissociation of Ideas' (1899), repr. in *Selected Writings* (ed./transl. Glen S. Burne, 1966)

2 If the secret of being a bore is to tell all, the secret of pleasing is to say just enough to be – not understood, but divined.
The Culture of Ideas, 'On Style and Writing', sect. 6 (*La Culture des idées*, 1900)

3 We live less and less, and we learn more and more. Sensibility is surrendering to intelligence.
The Velvet Way, 'The Value of Education' (*Le Chemin de velours*, 1902)

4 The human mind is so complex and things are so tangled up with each other that, to explain a blade of straw, one would have to take to pieces an entire universe ... A definition is a sack of flour compressed into a thimble.
Ibid., 'Glory and the Idea of Immortality', sect. 1

5 Aesthetic emotion puts man in a state favourable to the reception of erotic emotion ... Art is the accomplice of love. Take love away and there is no longer art.
Ibid., 'Success and the Idea of Beauty', sect. 2

6 Each man must grant himself the emotions that he needs and the morality that suits him.
Ibid., 'Success and the Idea of Beauty', sect. 3

7 Science is the only truth and it is the great lie. It knows nothing, and people think it knows everything. It is misrepresented. People think that science is electricity, automobilism, and dirigible balloons. It is something very different. It is life devouring itself. It is the sensibility transformed into intelligence. It is the need to know stifling the need to live. It is the genius of knowledge vivisecting the vital genius.
Philosophical Promenades, 'Art and Science' (*Promenades philosophiques*, 1905–9)

8 The whole effort of a sincere man is to erect his personal impressions into laws.
Quoted in *Countries of the Mind*, 'A Critical Credo' (1922) by John Middleton Murry. Referring to criticism. Murry called this statement 'the motto of a true criticism, conscious of its limitations and its strengths'.

Francisco José de Goya y Lucientes
(1746–1828)
Spanish painter

His output ranged from tapestry designs to royal portraits and scenes of war. His Caprichos (1797–8) were a series of eighty etchings, satirical and grotesque in form.

1 The dream of reason produces monsters. Imagination deserted by reason creates impossible, useless thoughts. United with reason, imagination is the mother of all art and the source of all its beauty.
Caprichos, no. 43, caption (1799). Often quoted, 'The sleep of reason ...'

Baltasar Gracián
(1601–58)
Spanish author and philosopher

A member of the Jesuit order from the age of eighteen, he was the leading exponent of 'conceptism', a literary style that expressed witty ideas using elaborate verbal devices, best exemplified in his Agudeza y arte de ingenio (1642–8).

1 Allow yourself some forgivable sin. Some such carelessness is often the greatest recommendation of talent.
The Art of Worldly Wisdom, no. 83 (1647, transl. 1892)

2 There is always time to add a word, never to withdraw one. Talk as if you were making your will: the fewer words the less litigation.
Ibid., no. 160

3 Do not explain too much. Most people do not

esteem what they understand and venerate what they do not see.

Ibid., no. 253

4 At twenty a man is a peacock, at thirty a lion, at forty a camel, at fifty a serpent, at sixty a dog, at seventy an ape, at eighty nothing at all.

Ibid., no. 276

Lew Grade
(1906–98)
Ukrainian-born British film and TV entrepreneur

Baron Grade of Elstree, born Louis Winogradsky. Once a champion tap-dancer, he became a theatrical agent in 1943, Managing Director of ATV (1962–76) and a film producer.

1 All my shows are great. Some of them are bad. But they are all great.

Quoted in the *Observer* 14 September 1975

2 It would have been cheaper to lower the Atlantic.

Attributed comment on his film *Raise the Titanic* (1980), which cost $40 million to make but took only $7 million at the box office.

Graffiti

1 Clapton is God.

London, late 1960s, referring to guitarist Eric Clapton.

2 Dead twat.

On the statue of WINSTON CHURCHILL in Parliament Square, London, daubed by 'anti-capitalist' rioters, 1 May 2000

3 God made us Catholics but the armalite made us equal.

Belfast, 1970s

4 If voting changed anything, they'd abolish it.

1980s. The words were taken as the title of a book by KEN LIVINGSTONE in 1987.

5 *L'imagination prend le pouvoir.*
[Imagination has seized power.]

Paris, 1968, quoted in *Paris '68*, ch. 2 (1988) by Marc Rohan

6 It doesn't matter who you vote for, the government always gets in.

London, 1970s

7 Kilroy was here.

First World War, left by US servicemen, particularly Air Transport Command. The words may have originated with a shipyard inspector in Massachusetts, who left his name on goods he had passed.

8 Liberté! Fraternité! Sexualité!

Paris Métro, 1980s

9 One non-revolutionary weekend is infinitely more bloody than a month of permanent revolution.

School of Oriental Languages, London, 1968, publ. in *Leaving the 20th Century: The Incomplete Work of the Situationist International* (ed./transl. Christopher Gray, 1974)

10 They came, they saw, they did a little shopping.

Berlin wall, following the influx of thousands of East Berliners into West Berlin after the lifting of travel restrictions, reported in *Newsweek* 4 December 1989

11 A woman needs a man like a fish needs a bicycle.

1970s. See also GLORA STEINEM 7.

12 Workers of the world forgive me.

On the bust of KARL MARX in Bucharest, reported in *The Times* 4 May 1990

Harry Graham
(1874–1936)
British playwright and poet

A prolific playwright, journalist and author, he is best remembered for his poetry collections Ruthless Rhymes for Heartless Homes *(1899 and 1930)*

1 Billy, in one of his nice new sashes,
Fell in the fire and was burnt to ashes;
Now, although the room grows chilly,
I haven't the heart to poke poor Billy.

'Tender-Heartedness', publ. in *Ruthless Rhymes for Heartless Homes* (1899)

2 Weep not for little Leonie,
Abducted by a French Marquis!
Though loss of honour was a wrench,
Just think how it's improved her French.

'Compensation', publ. in *More Ruthless Rhymes for Heartless Homes* (1930)

Martha Graham
(1894–1991)
US dancer and choreographer

Starting her own School of Contemporary Dance in 1927, she became America's leading exponent of Expressionist dance. Her most famous works include Appalachian Spring *(1944) and* Clytemnestra *(1958).*

1 Nothing is more revealing than movement.

'The American Dance', publ. in *Modern Dance* (ed. Virginia Stewart, 1935)

2 We look at the dance to impart the sensation of

living in an affirmation of life, to energize the spectator into keener awareness of the vigor, the mystery, the humor, the variety, and the wonder of life. This is the function of the American dance.
'The American Dance', ibid.

3 No artist is ahead of his time. He *is* his time; it is just that others are behind the times.
Quoted in the *Observer* 8 July 1979

Philip L. Graham
(1915–63)
US newspaper publisher

Known as a talented fixer, he took control of the Washington Post *in 1946, turning it into a leading newspaper of the day.*

1 News is the first rough draft of history.
Attributed. The aphorism has also been ascribed to *Washington Post* editor Ben C. Bradlee, but Bradlee himself, in an interview in *Vanity Fair* September 1991, credited it to Graham, formerly his boss at the *Post*.

Gloria Grahame
(1924–81)
US screen actor

Originally Gloria Hallward. A blonde leading lady, she found her niche in film noir playing morally ambiguous women. Her films include In a Lonely Place *(1950) and* The Bad and the Beautiful *(1952).*

1 I was born when you kissed me. I died when you left me. I lived a few weeks while you loved me.
In *A Lonely Place* (film, 1950, screenplay by Andrew Solt adapted from novel by Dorothy B. Hughes, directed by Nicholas Ray). Laurel Gray (Gloria Grahame) quotes the unfinished script of screenwriter Dixon Steele (HUMPHREY BOGART) in the film's closing scene.

2 We're all sisters under the mink.
The *Big Heat* (film, 1953, screenplay by Sidney Boehm from novel by William P. McGivern, directed by Fritz Lang). Spoken by Debby Marsh (Gloria Grahame).

Kenneth Grahame
(1859–1932)
British author

An employee of the Bank of England, he published stories, sketches and essays, but is best known for his rural children's tale, The Wind in the Willows *(1908), dramatized by* A. A. MILNE *as* Toad of Toad Hall *(1930).*

1 There is *nothing* – absolutely nothing – half so much worth doing as simply messing about in boats.
The Wind in the Willows, ch. 1 (1908). Spoken by Rat, who continues, 'In or out of 'em, it doesn't matter. Nothing seems really to matter, that's the charm of it. Whether you get away, or whether you don't; whether you arrive at your destination or whether you reach somewhere else, or whether you never get anywhere at all, you're always busy, and you never do anything in particular; and when you've done it there's always something else to do, and you can do it if you like, but you'd much better not.'

2 The poetry of motion! The *real* way to travel! The *only* way to travel! Here today – in next week tomorrow! Villages skipped, towns and cities jumped – always somebody else's horizon! O bliss! O poop-poop! O my! O my!
Toad, ibid., ch. 2. On riding in a motor car.

3 The clever men at Oxford
Know all that there is to be knowed.
But they none of them know one half as much
As intelligent Mr Toad!
Toad, ibid., ch. 10

4 Well, well, perhaps I am a bit of a talker. A popular fellow such as I am – my friends get round me – we chaff, we sparkle, we tell witty stories – and somehow my tongue gets wagging. I have the gift of conversation. I've been told I ought to have a *salon*, whatever that may be.
Toad, ibid., ch. 11

Antonio Gramsci
(1891–1937)
Italian political theorist

Having established the Italian Communist Party in 1921, he became its leader in 1924, but was arrested when MUSSOLINI *banned the party in 1926. He spent the rest of his life in prison, where he wrote thirty notebooks published posthumously as* Letters from Prison *(1947).*

1 I give culture this meaning: exercise of thought, acquisition of general ideas, habit of connecting causes and effects . . . I believe that it means thinking well, whatever one thinks, and therefore acting well, whatever one does.
'Philanthropy, Good Will and Organization' (1917), repr. in *Antonio Gramsci: Selections from Cultural Writings* (ed. David Forgacs and Geoffrey Nowell-Smyth, 1985)

2 The abolition of the class struggle does not mean the abolition of the need to struggle as a principle of development.
'The Problem of the School' (1920), ibid.

3 I'm a pessimist because of intelligence, but an optimist because of will.
Letter, 19 December 1929, publ. in *Gramsci: Letters from Prison* (1947, transl. 1993)

4 A given socio-historical moment is never homogeneous; on the contrary, it is rich in contradictions.
'Art and the Struggle for a New Civilization', written 1929–35, publ. in *Antonio Gramsci: Selections from Cultural Writings* (1985)

5 If you think about it seriously, all the questions about the soul and the immortality of the soul and paradise and hell are at bottom only a way of seeing this very simple fact: that every action of ours is passed on to others according to its value, of good or evil, it passes from father to son, from one generation to the next, in a perpetual movement.
Letter to his mother, 15 June 1931, publ. in *Gramsci: Letters from Prison* (1947, transl. 1993)

6 That the religiosity of the Italians is very superficial is undeniable, as is the fact that it is of a strictly political nature, one of international hegemony.
'Humanism and Renaissance [iii]', publ. in *Antonio Gramsci: Selections from Cultural Writings* (1985)

Grandmaster Flash
(b. 1958)
US rap singer

Originally Joseph Saddler. A top DJ of the 1970s and one of the pioneers of hip-hop, he worked with the rap and break-dancing team, the Furious Five.

1 It's like a jungle sometimes,
It makes me wonder
How I keep from going under.
'The Message' (song, 1982, written by Sylvia Robinson and Duke Bootee) on the album *Greatest Messages* (1984) by Grandmaster Flash and the Furious Five

Bernie Grant
(1944–2000)
British politician

Branded 'the high priest of race conflict' by Douglas Hurd, he was one of the first three black MPs in the House of Commons when elected Labour MP for Tottenham in 1987.

1 The police were to blame for what happened on Sunday night and what they got was a bloody good hiding.
Press statement outside Tottenham Town Hall, 8 October 1985, quoted in *The Times* 9 October 1985. Grant was speaking in the wake of the Broadwater Farm riots in north London, during which PC Keith Blakelock was murdered.

Cary Grant
(1904–86)
British-born US actor

Originally Archibald Alexander Leach. For over three decades he was a debonair leading man ranging from light comedic roles as in Bringing Up Baby *(1938) to parts in* HITCHCOCK *thrillers, including* Notorious *(1946) and* North by Northwest *(1959).*

1 Old Cary Grant fine. How you?
Attributed telegram, quoted in *Cary Grant* (1983) by Richard Schickel. Supposedly in response to a cable sent by a journalist to Grant's press agent: 'How old Cary Grant?'

Ulysses S. Grant
(1822–85)
US general and president

Born Hiram Ulysses Grant, later Ulysses Simpson Grant. The commander of the Unionist forces during the last years of the Civil War, he served two terms as US President 1869–77 as a Republican. His administration was characterized by scandal and corruption.

1 Let us have peace.
Letter, 29 May 1868, accepting presidential nomination, quoted in *The Life and Campaigns of General U. S. Grant*, ch. 29 (1869) by P. C. Headley. This last line of the letter was adopted as the Republican slogan in the subsequent electoral campaign, which Grant won.

2 I know no method to secure the repeal of bad or obnoxious laws so effective as their stringent execution.
Inaugural address, 4 March 1869, ibid, ch. 29

3 Let no guilty man escape, if it can be avoided . . . No personal considerations should stand in the way of performing a duty.
Endorsement to letter, July 1875, quoted in *Ulysses S. Grant*, ch. 11 (1970) by John A. Carpenter. Referring to the scandal surrounding the so-called Whisky Ring, a group of distillers found to have defrauded the US government. In fact most of the government officials implicated did escape, including Grant's private secretary Orville Babcock; the President may have had a hand in Babcock's acquittal.

4 I know only two tunes; one of them is 'Yankee Doodle', and the other isn't.
Attributed

George Granville
(c. 1667–1735)
English poet and dramatist

Lord Lansdown. MP for Fowey in Cornwall from 1702, he attracted royal favour and in 1713 was appointed Treasurer of the Household. His plays include Heroic Love *(1698) and* The Jew of Venice *(1701).*

1 There is no vulture like despair.
Peleus and Thetis (1701). Spoken by Peleus to Prometheus, who is chained to a rock on Mount Caucasus, with a vulture gnawing his breast.

Günter Grass
(b. 1927)
German novelist

Often cast in the role of the 'conscience of his generation', he caused controversy with his first novel The Tin Drum *(1959) for its depiction of Germany under the Nazis.*

1 Even bad books are books and therefore sacred.
The Tin Drum, bk 1, 'Rasputin and the Alphabet' (1959). The words of the narrator (Oskar Matzerath).

2 Art is uncompromising and life is full of compromises.
Quoted by ARTHUR MILLER, in *Writers at Work* (third series, 1967)

3 Melancholy has ceased to be an individual phenomenon, an exception. It has become the class privilege of the wage earner, a mass state of mind that finds its cause wherever life is governed by production quotas.
From the Diary of a Snail, 'On Stasis in Progress' (1972)

4 Art is so wonderfully irrational, exuberantly pointless, but necessary all the same. Pointless and yet necessary, that's hard for a puritan to understand.
Interview in the *New Statesman and Society* 22 June 1990

John Woodcock Graves
(1795–1886)
English miller

Remembered for his hunting song 'John Peel', he often accompanied John Peel, a farmer and hunter, on hunts around Caldbeck, in Cumberland,. He emigrated to Tasmania in 1834.

1 D'ye ken John Peel with his coat so grey?
D'ye ken John Peel at the break of the day?
D'ye ken John Peel when he's far far away

With his hounds and his horn in the morning?
'John Peel' (song), written c. 1825, publ. in *Songs and Ballads of Cumberland* (ed. Sidney Gilpin, 1865–6). Often sung 'coat so gay'. It is thought that Gilpin (pen-name of George Coward) revised Graves' original words.

2 'Twas the sound of his horn called me from my bed,
And the cry of his hounds has me oft-times led;
For Peel's view-hollo would waken the dead,
Or a fox from his lair in the morning.
'John Peel', ibid.

Robert Graves
(1895–1985)
British poet and author

*Though his output included autobiography (*Goodbye to All That, *1929), historical novels (*I, Claudius, *1934), studies of mythology (*The Greek Myths, *1955) and literary criticism, he regarded himself primarily as a poet, and was Professor of Poetry at Oxford 1961–6.*

1 Children are dumb to say how hot the day is,
How hot the scent is of the summer rose,
How dreadful the black wastes of evening sky,
How dreadful the tall soldiers drumming by.
'The Cool Web', publ. in *Poems* (1927)

2 There's a cool web of language winds us in,
Retreat from too much joy or too much fear.
'The Cool Web', ibid.

3 Goodbye to All That.
Title of autobiography (1929)

4 Down, wanton, down! Have you no shame
That at the whisper of Love's name,
Or Beauty's, presto! up you raise
Your angry head and stand at gaze?
'Down, Wanton, Down!', publ. in *Poems 1930–1933* (1933)

5 To evoke posterity
Is to weep on your own grave,
Ventriloquizing for the unborn.
'To Evoke Posterity', publ. in *Collected Poems* (1938)

6 To be a poet is a condition rather than a profession.
'The Cost of Letters', reply to questionnaire in *Horizon* September 1946

7 The reason why the hairs stand on end, the eyes water, the throat is constricted, the skin crawls and a shiver runs down the spine when one writes or reads a true poem is that a true poem is necessarily an invocation of the White Goddess, or Muse, the

Mother of All Living, the ancient power of fright and lust – the female spider or the queen bee whose embrace is death.

The White Goddess, ch. 1 (1948)

8 Counting the beats,
Counting the slow heart beats,
The bleeding to death of time in slow heart beats,
Wakeful they lie.

'Counting the Beats', publ. in *Poems and Satires* (1951)

9 Why have such scores of lovely girls
Married impossible men?
Simple sacrifice may be ruled out,
And missionary endeavour, nine times out of ten.

'A Slice of Wedding Cake', publ. in *Steps* (1958)

10 Love, the sole Goddess fit for swearing by,
Concedes us graciously the little lie:
The white lie, the half lie, the lie corrective
Without which love's exchange might prove defective,
Confirming hazardous relationships
By kindly *maquillage* of Truth's pale lips.

'Friday Night', publ. in *5 Pens in Hand* (1958)

11 A difficult achievement for true lovers
Is to lie mute, without embrace or kiss,
Without a rustle or a smothered sigh,
Basking each in the other's glory.

'The Starred Coverlet', publ. in *More Poems* (1961)

12 A well-chosen anthology is a complete dispensary of medicine for the more common mental disorders, and may be used as much for prevention as cure.

On English Poetry, sect. 29 ('The Use of Poetry') (1962)

13 Nine-tenths of English poetic literature is the result either of vulgar careerism or of a poet trying to keep his hand in. Most poets are dead by their late twenties.

Quoted in the *Observer* 11 November 1962

14 If there's no money in poetry, neither is there poetry in money.

Speech at London School of Economics, 6 December 1963, publ. in *Mammon and the Black Goddess*, 'Mammon' (1965)

15 Perfect reliance on the impossible
By strict avoidance of all such conjecture
As underlies the so-called possible:
That is true love's adventure.

'To Put It Simply', publ. in *Poems 1968–70* (1970)

16 Are not all centuries, like men,

Born hopeful too and gay,
And good for seventy years, but then
Hope slowly seeps away?

'The Imminent Seventies', ibid.

17 Poets are guardians
Of a shadowy island
With granges and forest
Warmed by the Moon.

'The Title of Poet', publ. in *Poems 1970–1972* (1972)

Alasdair Gray

(b. 1934)
Scottish novelist

His picaresque narratives have a strong Scottish setting, for example Lanark *(1981),* The Fall of Kelvin Walker *(1985) and* Poor Things *(1992).*

1 Glasgow, the sort of industrial city where most people live nowadays but nobody imagines living.

Lanark, bk 3, ch. 11 (1981). Spoken by the Oracle.

2 Everyone sees life through their job. To the doctor the world is a hospital, to the broker it is a stock exchange, to the lawyer a vast criminal court, to the soldier a barracks and area of manoeuvre, to the farmer soil and bad weather, to truck-drivers a road system, to dustmen a midden, to prostitutes a brothel, to mothers an inescapable nursery, to children a school, to film stars a looking-glass, to undertakers a morgue, and to myself a security installation powered by the sun and only crackable by death.

1982, Janine, ch. 4 (1984)

John Gray

(b. 1951)
US psychotherapist and author

He is best known for Men Are from Mars, Women Are from Venus *(1992), which, like his other books, discusses gender differences and strategies for greater understanding between the sexes.*

1 Men mistakenly expect women to think, communicate, and react the way men do; women mistakenly expect men to feel, communicate and respond the way women do. We have forgotten that men and women are supposed to be different. As a result our relationships are filled with unnecessary friction and conflict. Clearly recognizing and respecting these differences dramatically reduces confusion when dealing with the opposite sex.

When you remember that men are from Mars and women are from Venus, everything can be explained.
Men Are from Mars, Women Are from Venus, ch. 1 (1992)

2 One of the big challenges for men is correctly to interpret and support a woman when she is talking about her feelings. The biggest challenge for women is correctly to interpret and support a man when he isn't talking.
Ibid., ch. 5, 'When Martians Don't Talk'

Simon Gray
(b. 1936)
British playwright

His wry and comedic plays, which take as their milieu the worlds of academia and publishing, include Wise Child *(1967),* Melon *(1987) and* Cell Mates *(1995). He has also written for television.*

1 Everybody in Los Angeles lives miles away, not from anywhere, because there isn't actually an anywhere to live away from, but from each other.
How's That for Telling 'Em, Fat Lady?, ch. 2 (1988)

2 Faith is . . . a matter of believing what's impossible to believe. Do you, um, see? Otherwise it's not faith. It's certainty.
Hidden Laughter, Act 1, Sc. 1 (1990). Spoken by Ronnie.

3 People should worry about each other. Because worry is just love in its worst form. But it's still love.
Louise, ibid., Act 1, Sc. 2

Thomas Gray
(1716–71)
English poet

His first poems appeared anonymously in 1747–8. Such works as 'Elegy Written in a Country Churchyard' (1751), said to be the most quoted poem in the English language, are now seen as precursors of English Romanticism. According to DICKENS, *'No man ever walked down to posterity with so small a book under his arm.' See also* SAMUEL JOHNSON 89.

1 Ye distant spires, ye antique towers,
That crown the watery glade.
'Ode on a Distant Prospect of Eton College', st. 1 (written 1742, publ. 1747), repr. in *The Complete Poems of Thomas Gray* (ed. H. W. Starr and J. R. Hendrickson, 1966). Opening lines. Gray was himself a pupil at Eton.

2 Some bold adventurers disdain
The limits of their little reign
And unknown regions dare descry:

Still as they run they look behind,
They hear a voice in every wind,
And snatch a fearful joy.
'Ode on a Distant Prospect of Eton College', st. 4, ibid.

3 Alas! regardless of their doom,
The little victims play!
No sense have they of ills to come
Nor care beyond today.
'Ode on a Distant Prospect of Eton College', st. 6, ibid.

4 To each his sufferings: all are men,
Condemned alike to groan;
The tender for another's pain,
Th' unfeeling for his own.
'Ode on a Distant Prospect of Eton College', st. 10, ibid.

5 Thought would destroy their paradise.
'Ode on a Distant Prospect of Eton College', st. 10, ibid.

6 Where ignorance is bliss,
'Tis folly to be wise.
'Ode on a Distant Prospect of Eton College', st. 10, ibid. Last lines of poem.

7 A favourite has no friend!
'Ode on the Death of a Favourite Cat', st. 6 (1748), ibid.

8 The curfew tolls the knell of parting day,
The lowing herd wind slowly o'er the lea,
The ploughman homeward plods his weary way,
And leaves the world to darkness and to me.
Now fades the glimmering landscape on the sight,
And all the air a solemn stillness holds,
Save where the beetle wheels his droning flight,
And drowsy tinklings lull the distant folds.
'Elegy Written in a Country Churchyard', sts 1–2 (1751), ibid.

9 Beneath those rugged elms, that yew-tree's shade,
Where heaves the turf in many a mouldering heap,
Each in his narrow cell for ever laid,
The rude forefathers of the hamlet sleep.
'Elegy Written in a Country Churchyard', st. 4, ibid.

10 The breezy call of incense-breathing Morn.
'Elegy Written in a Country Churchyard', st. 5, ibid.

11 Let not ambition mock their useful toil,
Their homely joys, and destiny obscure;
Nor grandeur hear with a disdainful smile,
The short and simple annals of the poor.
'Elegy Written in a Country Churchyard', st. 8, ibid.

12 The boast of heraldry, the pomp of power,
And all that beauty, all that wealth e'er gave,

Awaits alike th' inevitable hour.
The paths of glory lead but to the grave.
'Elegy Written in a Country Churchyard', st. 9, ibid.

13 Full many a gem of purest ray serene,
The dark unfathomed caves of ocean bear:
Full many a flower is born to blush unseen,
And waste its sweetness on the desert air.
'Elegy Written in a Country Churchyard', st. 14, ibid.

14 Some village-Hampden, that with dauntless
 breast
The little tyrant of his fields withstood;
Some mute inglorious Milton here may rest,
Some Cromwell guiltless of his country's blood.
'Elegy Written in a Country Churchyard', st. 15, ibid.

15 Far from the madding crowd's ignoble strife,
Their sober wishes never learned to stray;
Along the cool sequestered vale of life
They kept the noiseless tenor of their way.
'Elegy Written in a Country Churchyard', st. 19, ibid. 'Madding'
is used to mean 'becoming mad' or 'acting madly' rather than
'maddening'. See THOMAS HARDY 3.

16 Mindful of th' unhonoured dead.
'Elegy Written in a Country Churchyard', st. 24, ibid.

17 Here rests his head upon the lap of Earth
A youth to fortune and to fame unknown.
Fair Science frowned not on his humble birth,
And Melancholy marked him for her own.
'Elegy Written in a Country Churchyard', 'The Epitaph', st. 1,
ibid.

18 O'er her warm cheek and rising bosom move
The bloom of young desire and purple light of
 love.
The Progress of Poesy, pt 1, sect. 3, ll. 16–17 (written 1754, publ.
1757)

19 Far from the sun and summer-gale,
In thy green lap was Nature's darling laid.
Ibid., pt 3, sect. 1, ll. 1–2. Referring to SHAKESPEARE.

20 He passed the flaming bounds of place and
 time:
The living throne, the sapphire-blaze,
Where angels tremble, while they gaze,
He saw; but blasted with excess of light,
Closed his eyes in endless night.
Ibid., pt 3, sect. 2, ll. 4–8. Referring to MILTON.

21 Thoughts that breathe, and words that burn.
Ibid., pt 3, sect. 3, l. 4

22 In gallant trim the gilded vessel goes;
Youth on the prow, and Pleasure at the helm.
The Bard, pt 2, sect. 2, ll. 11–12 (1757)

23 Too poor for a bribe, and too proud to
 importune,
He had not the method of making a fortune.
'Sketch of his Own Character' (written 1761, publ. 1775) , repr.
in The Complete Poems of Thomas Gray (ed. H. W. Starr and
J. R. Hendrickson, 1966)

24 I shall be but a shrimp of an author.
Letter to HORACE WALPOLE, 25 February 1768, publ. in Gray:
Poetry and Prose (ed. J. Crofts, 1926)

25 Any fool may write a most valuable book by
chance, if he will only tell us what he heard and saw,
with veracity.
Letter to HORACE WALPOLE, 25 February 1768, ibid.

Horace Greeley
(1811–72)
US newspaper editor

*The outstanding editor of his day, he founded the New York
Tribune in 1841, which he edited until his death. He was a
candidate in the 1872 presidential election, but lost to ULYSSES
S. GRANT.*

1 Go West, young man, and grow up with the
country.
Attributed. The original wording was from an article by J. B. L.
Soule (or Soulé) in Indiana's Terre Haute Express in 1851.
Although Greeley reprinted Soule's article in the New York
Tribune, with the correct attribution, the words became
associated with Greeley.

Hannah Green
(b. 1932)
US author

*Originally Joanne Greenberg. She is mainly known for her
autobiographical novel* I Never Promised You a Rose Garden
(1964), the story of a fight against schizophrenia.

1 I Never Promised You a Rose Garden.
Title of novel (1964, filmed 1977). A song with this title written
by Joe South was the only hit for country singer Lynn Anderson (1971).

Henry Green
(1905–73)
British novelist

*Originally Henry Vincent Yorke. While working as an engineer,
he wrote impressionistic novels that relied on dialogue rather*

than plot, for example Blindness *(1926),* Living *(1929) and* Loving *(1945).*

1 Prose is not to be read aloud but to oneself at night, and it is not quick as poetry, but rather a gathering web of insinuations which go further than names however shared can ever go. Prose should be a long intimacy between strangers with no direct appeal to what both may have known. It should slowly appeal to feelings unexpressed, it should in the end draw tears out of the stone.
Pack My Bag: a Self Portrait (1940)

2 The very deaf, as I am, hear the most astounding things all round them, which have not, in fact, been said. This enlivens my replies until, through mis-hearing, a new level of communication is reached.
Interview in *Writers at Work* (second series, ed. George Plimpton, 1963)

Matthew Green
(1696–1737)
English poet

Employed in the Custom House, he is remembered for his poem The Spleen *(1737), on boredom, depression and the remedies for them.*

1 To cure the mind's wrong bias, spleen,
Some recommend the bowling-green,
Some, hilly walks; all, exercise;
Fling but a stone, the giant dies.
Laugh and be well.
The Spleen, ll. 89–93 (1737)

2 By happy alchemy of mind
They turn to pleasure all they find.
Ibid., ll. 610–11

3 Avarice, sphincter of the heart.
Ibid., l. 697

Peter Greenaway
(b. 1942)
British film-maker

His films are characterized by an intellectual obliqueness that some have found alienating. His first major success, The Draughtsman's Contract *(1982) was followed by, among others,* The Pillow-Book *(1996).*

1 The Cook, The Thief, His Wife and Her Lover.
Title of film (1989, written and directed by Peter Greenaway)

Graham Greene
(1904–91)
British author

His long writing career encompassed journalism and fiction. His novels were mainly either comedies, thrillers or 'Catholic novels' such as The Heart of the Matter *(1948), dealing with issues of faith and failure.* EVELYN WAUGH *once advised him not to give up writing about God as it would be like 'P. G. Wodehouse dropping Jeeves halfway through the Wooster series'. See also* T. S. ELIOT 41.

1 There is always one moment in childhood when the door opens and lets the future in.
The Power and the Glory, pt 1, ch. 1 (1940)

2 Against the beautiful and the clever and the suc-cessful, one can wage a pitiless war, but not against the unattractive: then the millstone weighs on the breast.
The Heart of the Matter, bk 1, pt 1, ch. 2, sect. 2 (1948)

3 People talk about the courage of condemned men walking to the place of execution: sometimes it needs as much courage to walk with any kind of bearing towards another person's habitual misery.
Ibid., bk 1, pt 1, ch. 2, sect. 3

4 The truth has never been of any real value to any human being – it is a symbol for mathematicians and philosophers to pursue. In human relations kindness and lies are worth a thousand truths.
Scobie, ibid., bk 1, pt 1, ch. 2, sect. 4

5 He felt the loyalty we feel to unhappiness – the sense that that is where we really belong.
Ibid., bk 2, pt 2, ch. 1, sect. 1. Referring to Harris.

6 His hilarity was like a scream from a crevasse.
Ibid., bk 3, pt 1, ch. 1, sect. 1. Of Major Scobie.

7 Death's at the bottom of everything, Martins. Leave death to the professionals.
The Third Man (film, 1950, screenplay by Graham Greene, directed by Carol Reed). Spoken by Major Calloway (Trevor Howard). *The Third Man* was first written as a preliminary draft for the film's screenplay, and later published as a novella (in which these lines do not appear). See also ORSON WELLES 2.

8 The world doesn't make any heroes anymore.
Major Calloway, ibid.

9 Innocence always calls mutely for protection when we would be so much wiser to guard ourselves against it: innocence is like a dumb leper who has lost his bell, wandering the world, meaning no harm.
The Quiet American, pt 1, ch. 3, sect. 3 (1955). Later in the book,

the narrator describes Pyle – the idealistic 'quiet American' of the title – in similar terms: 'What's the good? He'll always be innocent, you can't blame the innocent, they are always guiltless. All you can do is control them or eliminate them. Innocence is a kind of insanity.' (pt. 3, ch. 2, sect. 1)

10 Those who marry God can become domesticated too – it's just as hum-drum a marriage as all the others. The word 'Love' means a formal touch of the lips as in the ceremony of the Mass, and 'Ave Maria' like 'dearest' is a phrase to open a letter.
A Burnt-Out Case, pt 1, ch. 1, sect. 2 (1961)

11 Cynicism is cheap – you can buy it at any Mono-prix store – it's built into all poor-quality goods.
The Comedians, pt 1, ch. 1, sect. 3 (1966)

12 However great a man's fear of life, suicide remains the courageous act, the clear-headed act of a mathematician. The suicide has judged by the laws of chance – so many odds against one that to live will be more miserable than to die. His sense of mathematics is greater than his sense of survival.
Dr Magiot, ibid., ch. 4, sect. 1

13 We mustn't complain too much of being com-edians – it's an honourable profession. If only we could be good ones the world might gain at least a sense of style. We have failed – that's all. We are bad comedians, we aren't bad men.
The ambassador, ibid., ch. 5, sect. 2

14 Communism, my friend, is more than Marxism, just as Catholicism ... is more than the Roman Curia. There is a *mystique* as well as a *politique* ... Catholics and Communists have committed great crimes, but at least they have not stood aside, like an established society, and been indifferent. I would rather have blood on my hands than water like Pilate.
Dr Magiot, ibid., pt 3, ch. 4, sect. 4

15 If you have abandoned one faith, do not abandon all faith. There is always an alternative to the faith we lose. Or is it the same faith under another mask?
Dr Magiot, ibid., pt 3, ch. 4, sect. 4

16 God ... created a number of possibilities in case some of his prototypes failed – that is the meaning of evolution.
Travels With My Aunt, pt 2, ch. 7 (1969). Spoken by Mr Visconti.

17 Morality comes with the sad wisdom of age, when the sense of curiosity has withered.
A Sort of Life, ch. 7, sect. 1 (1971)

18 A petty reason perhaps why novelists more and more try to keep a distance from journalists is that novelists are trying to write the truth and journal-ists are trying to write fiction.
Letter to 'Atticus' (Stephen Pile), in the *Sunday Times* 18 January 1981, repr. in *Yours, Etc: Letters to the Press, 1945–1989* (1989)

19 Success is more dangerous than failure, the ripples break over a wider coastline.
Quoted in the *Independent* 4 April 1991. Recalled at Greene's death by critic Miriam Allot.

Robert Greene
(c. 1558–92)
English author and playwright

Prominent among the so-called 'university wits', he vividly evoked dissolute London life in his many pamphlets. His popu-lar plays include Friar Bacon and Friar Bungay *(c. 1591). He was said to have died from 'a fatal banquet of Rhenish wine and pickled herring'.*

1 Why, thinks King Henry's son that Margaret's love
Hangs in the uncertain balance of proud time,
That death shall make a discord of our thoughts?
Friar Bacon and Friar Bungay, Sc. 8 (written c. 1591, publ. 1594). Spoken by Margaret.

2 Ah! what is love! It is a pretty thing,
As sweet unto a shepherd as a king.
'The Shepherd's Wife's Song' (1590), repr. in *The Oxford Book of Sixteenth Century Verse* (ed. E. K. Chambers, 1932)

3 If country loves such sweet desires do gain,
What lady would not love a shepherd swain?
Ibid.

4 There is an upstart crow, beautified with our feathers, that with his tiger's heart wrapped in a player's hide supposes he is as well able to bombast out a blank verse as the best of you, and, being an absolute *Johannes factotum*, is in his own conceit the only Shake-scene in a country.
Greene's Groatsworth of Wit, Bought with a Million of Repent-ance (1592, repr. 1966, ed. G. B. Harrison). The last of Greene's pamphlets, containing the first known literary reference to SHAKESPEARE. The words 'tiger's heart wrapped in a player's hide' are themselves a parody of Shakespeare (see SHAKE-SPEARE: HENRY VI PT 3 1). Some scholars believe the pam-phlet to have been written in part or entirely by the playwright Henry Chettle, posing as Greene.

Germaine Greer

(b. 1939)

Australian author and critic

Her book The Female Eunuch *(1970) was a seminal influence on a generation of feminists. Subsequent works include* Sex and Destiny *(1984) and* The Whole Woman *(1999).*

1 If you think you are emancipated, you might consider the idea of tasting your menstrual blood – if it makes you sick, you've a long way to go, baby.

The Female Eunuch, 'The Wicked Womb' (1970)

2 Freud is the father of psychoanalysis. It had no mother.

Ibid., 'The Psychological Sell'

3 Even crushed against his brother in the Tube the average Englishman pretends desperately that he is alone.

Ibid., 'Womanpower'

4 Every time a woman makes herself laugh at her husband's often-told jokes she betrays him. The man who looks at his woman and says 'What would I do without you?' is already destroyed.

Ibid., 'Egotism'

5 Women have very little idea of how much men hate them.

Ibid., 'Loathing and Disgust'

6 Women's liberation, if it abolishes the patriarchal family, will abolish a necessary substructure of the authoritarian state, and once that withers away Marx will have come true willy-nilly, so let's get on with it.

Ibid., 'Revolution'

7 The surest guide to the correctness of the path that women take is *joy in the struggle*. Revolution is the festival of the oppressed.

Ibid., 'Revolution'

8 The tragedy of machismo is that a man is never quite man enough.

'My Mailer Problem' (1971), repr. in *The Madwoman's Underclothes* (1986)

9 The compelled mother loves her child as the caged bird sings. The song does not justify the cage nor the love the enforcement.

'Abortion' (1972), ibid.

10 We in the West do not refrain from childbirth because we are concerned about the population explosion or because we feel we cannot afford children, but because we do not like children.

Sex and Destiny, ch. 1 (1984)

11 The most threatened group in human societies as in animal societies is the unmated male: the unmated male is more likely to wind up in prison or in an asylum or dead than his mated counterpart. He is less likely to be promoted at work and he is considered a poor credit risk.

Ibid., ch. 2

12 Human beings have an inalienable right to invent themselves; when that right is pre-empted it is called brain-washing.

The Times 1 February 1986

13 English culture is basically homosexual in the sense that the men only really care about other men.

Daily Mail 18 April 1988

14 Libraries are reservoirs of strength, grace and wit, reminders of order, calm and continuity, lakes of mental energy, neither warm nor cold, light nor dark. The pleasure they give is steady, unorgastic, reliable, deep and long-lasting. In any library in the world, I am at home, unselfconscious, still and absorbed.

Daddy, We Hardly Knew You, 'Still in Melbourne, January 1987' (1989)

15 Orgasmism is a Western neurosis, but I say once you've had one, you've had them all.

Interview in *A Little Light Friction*, 'Germaine Greer' (1989) by Val Hennessy

16 An enema under the influence of Ecstasy would probably feel much like this.

Independent on Sunday 3 June 1990. Referring to D. H. LAWRENCE's description of the female orgasm in *Lady Chatterley's Lover*.

17 The misery of the middle-aged woman is a grey and hopeless thing, born of having nothing to live for, of disappointment and resentment at having been gypped by consumer society, and surviving merely to be the butt of its unthinking scorn.

The Change: Women, Ageing and the Menopause, Introduction (1991)

18 The climacteric marks the end of apologizing. The chrysalis of conditioning has once for all to break and the female woman finally to emerge.

Ibid., ch. 17

19 Reality television is not the end of civilisation as we know it, it *is* civilisation as we know it.
Quoted in the *Guardian* 8 January 2005. Greer appeared on the reality TV show Celebrity Big Brother in January 2005.

Hubert Gregg
(1914–2004)
British songwriter and entertainer

A versatile performer, he also wrote plays and composed the music and lyrics for numerous revues.

1 Maybe it's because I'm a Londoner
That I love London so,
Maybe it's because I'm a Londoner
That I think of her wherever I go.
I get a funny feeling inside of me
Just walking up and down.
Maybe it's because I'm a Londoner
That I love London Town.
'Maybe It's Because I'm a Londoner' (song, 1947). The song was recorded by BILLY COTTON and his band in 1949.

Gregory I
(c. 540–604)
Italian pope

Known as St Gregory the Great. Pope from 590, he transformed the papacy into a temporal power, promoting monasticism and establishing rules for clergy. He was also a notable theologian.

1 There are nine orders of angels, to wit, angels, archangels, virtues, powers, principalities, dominations, thrones, cherubim and seraphim.
Homilies, no. 34 (c. 600)

2 *Non Angli sed Angeli.*
[Not Angles, but angels.]
Attributed. Probably an oral rendition of words that appear in Bede's *History of the English Church and People*, bk 2, sect. 1 (completed 731, transl. 1955), in which Gregory – before he was Pope – was presented with some slaves in the market-place in Rome, with 'fair complexions, fine-cut features and beautiful hair'. 'What is the name of this race?' 'They are called Angles,' he was told. 'That is appropriate,' he said, 'for they have angelic faces, and it is right that they should become joint-heirs with the angels in heaven.' The encounter, according to Bede, inspired Gregory when Pope to send missionaries to England.

Gregory VII
(c. 1020–85)
Italian pope

Originally Hildebrand, also known as St Gregory VII. His period as Pope (from 1073) was dominated by his struggle with the Holy Roman Emperor Henry IV, originating in Gregory's decree in 1075 that prohibited lay investiture of the clergy.

1 I have loved justice and hated iniquity: therefore I die in exile.
Quoted in *The Life and Pontificate of Gregory VII*, vol. 2, bk 3, ch. 20 (1840) by J. W. Bowden. Attributed last words in Salerno, where he had taken refuge after being ousted from Rome by Henry IV.

(Lady) Augusta Gregory
(1859–1932)
Irish playwright and theatre director

Following her husband's death in 1892, she devoted herself to literature. She directed the Abbey Theatre, for which she wrote numerous short plays, and chronicled the Irish Literary Renaissance in her books and journals.

1 Well, there's no one at all, they do be saying, but is deserving of some punishment from the very minute of his birth.
Shanwalla, Act 2 (1915). Spoken by O'Malley.

Dr John Gregory
(1724–73)
Scottish physician

He was Professor of Medicine at Aberdeen and Edinburgh. A Father's Legacy to his Daughters was written after the early death of his wife.

1 A fine woman shews her charms to most advantage when she seems most to conceal them. The finest bosom in nature is not so fine as what imagination forms.
A Father's Legacy to his Daughters, 'Amusements' (1774)

Joyce Grenfell
(1910–79)
British entertainer and author

The daughter of one of the American Langhorne sisters (one of whom was NANCY ASTOR), she appeared in revue until the early 1950s, when she presented her own one-woman shows, most famously Joyce Grenfell Requests the Pleasure *(from 1954).*

1 George – don't do that.
Catch-phrase in various sketches in the 1950s, and the title of the collection, *George – Don't Do That* (1977)

2 Stately as a galleon, I sail across the floor,
Doing the military two-step, as in the days of yore.
'Stately as a Galleon' (song), publ. in *Stately as a Galleon* (1978)

3 So gay the band,
So giddy the sight,
Full evening dress is a must,
But the zest goes out of a beautiful waltz
When you dance it bust to bust.
'Stately as a Galleon', ibid.

4 Progress everywhere today does seem to come so *very* heavily disguised as Chaos.
'English Lit.', ibid.

Fulke Greville
(1554–1628)
English poet, playwright and politician

Lord Brooke. A courtier and diplomat, he rose to high office and wrote sonnets, dramas and a valuable biography of his close friend PHILIP SIDNEY. *He died at the hands of a disgruntled servant.*

1 Oh, wearisome condition of humanity,
Born under one law, to another bound.
Mustapha, Act 5, Sc. 4 (1609). Spoken by Chorus Sacerdotum (the chorus of priests).

2 The mind of man is this world's true dimension,
And knowledge is the measure of the mind;
And as the mind in her vast comprehension
Contains more worlds than all the world can find,
So knowledge doth itself far more extend
Than all the minds of men can comprehend.
'A Treaty of Human Learning', st 1, publ. in *Certain Learned and Elegant Workes of the Right Honourable Fulke Lord Brooke* (1633)

Clifford Grey
(1887–1941)
British songwriter

Originally Percival Davis. A prolific lyricist and librettist for the London and New York stages, he provided songs for a string of shows including The Bing Boys are Here *(1916) and* Mr Cinders *(1929).*

1 If you were the only girl in the world
And I were the only boy.
'If You Were the Only Girl in the World' (song, with music by Nat Ayer) in the musical show *The Bing Boys Are Here* (1916).

The song was first performed by George Robey and Violet Lorraine, popularized in America by Rudy Vallee in the film *The Vagabond Lover* (1929), and later featured in the film *By the Light of the Silvery Moon* (1953), sung by Gordon McCrae and Doris Day.

Lord Grey
(1862–1933)
British statesman

Sir Edward Grey, First Viscount of Falloden. As Foreign Secretary (1905–16), he was responsible for the Russian entente of 1907 and sided with France in the Agadir incident in 1911.

1 The lamps are going out all over Europe; we shall not see them lit again in our lifetime.
Remark, 3 August 1914, quoted in *Twenty-Five Years*, vol. 2, ch. 18 (1925). The words were spoken on the eve of Britain's declaration of war against Germany.

D. W. Griffith
(1874–1948)
US film-maker

David Wark Griffith. He originated many of the conventions of present-day cinematic technique. His masterpiece was The Birth of a Nation *(1915), an epic of the Civil War. See* WOODROW WILSON 1.

1 We do not fear censorship for we have no wish to offend with improprieties or obscenities, but we do demand, as a right, the liberty to show the dark side of wrong, that we may illuminate the bright side of virtue – the same liberty that is conceded to the art of the written word, that art to which we owe the Bible and the works of Shakespeare.
'A Plea for the Art of the Motion Picture', released as Prologue to *The Birth of a Nation* (film, 1915)

2 Viewed as a drama, the war is somewhat disappointing.
Attributed remark in 1918

Mervyn Griffith-Jones
(1909–79)
British lawyer

He was one of the British Prosecuting Counsel at the Nuremberg trials (1945–6) and a member of the standing committee on Criminal Law Revision (1958).

1 Would you approve of your young sons, young daughters – because girls can read as well as boys – reading this book? Is it a book that you would have lying around in your own house? Is it a book that

you would even wish your wife or your servants to read?

Opening address to jury during the prosecution of Penguin Books Ltd., 20 October 1961, publ. in *The Trial of Lady Chatterley* (ed. C. H. Rolph, 1961). Griffith-Jones was senior prosecuting counsel in the case brought against Penguin for publishing an unexpurgated edition of D. H. LAWRENCE's *Lady Chatterley's Lover*. Rolph noted the 'visible – and risible – effect on the jury' of these remarks, and surmised that this 'may well have been the first nail in the prosecution's coffin'.

Angelina Grimké
(1805–79)
US abolitionist and feminist

With her sister, Sarah, she joined the Quakers and became one of the first women to campaign against slavery and in favour of women's rights.

1 The doctrine of blind obedience and unqualified submission to any human power, whether civil or ecclesiastical, is the doctrine of despotism, and ought to have no place 'mong Republicans and Christians.

'An Appeal to the Christian Women of the South', publ. in the *Anti-Slavery Examiner* September 1836

2 Thou art blind to the danger of marrying a woman who feels and acts out the principle of equal rights.

Letter, February 1838, publ. in *Letters of Theodore Dwight Weld, Angelina Grimké Weld, and Sarah Grimké, 1822–1844*, vol. 2 (ed. Gilbert H. Barnes and Dwight L. Dumond, 1934). Addressed to the abolitionist Theodore Dwight Weld, Angelina's future husband.

Georg Groddeck
(1866–1934)
German psychoanalyst

Regarded as one of the founding fathers of psychosomatic medicine, he opened the sanatorium Marienhöhe in 1900 and ran it until his death. His books were burnt by the Nazis.

1 Disease is a vital expression of the human organism.

The Book of the It, 'Letter 31' (1923)

Matt Groening
(b. 1954)
US cartoonist

In 1987 he created The Simpsons *as a filler on* The Tracy Ullman Show *for the Fox TV network. A thirteen-episode series of half-hour slots premiered in January 1990 and the cartoon was subsequently syndicated worldwide.*

1 Eat my shorts!

The Simpsons (TV cartoon, from 1987). Spoken by Bart Simpson.

2 D'oh!

Homer Simpson's habitual expression of exasperation, ibid.

Andrei Gromyko
(1909–89)
Soviet statesman and diplomat

He was Soviet Ambassador to the USA from 1943 and to the UN 1946–9, during which time he exercised his right of veto no fewer than twenty-five times. He was later Foreign Minister 1957–85 and President of the USSR 1985–8.

1 Greece is a sort of American vassal; the Netherlands is the country of American bases that grow like tulip bulbs; Cuba is the main sugar plantation of the American monopolies; Turkey is prepared to kow-tow before any United States pro-consul and Canada is the boring second fiddle in the American symphony.

New York Herald Tribune 30 June 1953

Walter Gropius
(1883–1969)
German architect

An early pioneer of the International Style, he was a co-founder and Director (1919–28) of the Bauhaus School of Design, and Professor of Architecture at Harvard (1938–52). His declared aim was to bridge 'the gap between the rigid mentality of the businessman and technologist and the imagination of the creative artist'.

1 Together let us desire, conceive, and create the new structure of the future, which will embrace architecture and sculpture and painting in one unity and which will one day rise toward heaven from the hands of a million workers like the crystal symbol of a new faith.

'The Bauhaus Proclamation', April 1919, repr. in *The Bauhaus*, ch. 2 (1962) by Hans Wingler

George Grosz
(1893–1959)
German-born US artist

A member of the Berlin Dadaists after the First World War, he savagely satirized German social mores, militarism and Nazism in his drawings. His work has been described as 'the most definitive catalogue of man's depravity in all history'.

1 The bourgeoisie and the petty bourgeoisie have armed themselves against the rising proletariat with, among other things, 'culture'. It's an old ploy of the bourgeoisie. They keep a standing 'art' to defend their collapsing culture.
'The Art Scab' (1920, written with John Heartfield), repr. in *Art Is In Danger* (transl. 1987)

2 The cult of individuality and personality, which promotes painters and poets only to promote itself, is really a business. The greater the 'genius' of the personage, the greater the profit.
'Instead of a Biography' (1920), ibid.

John Guare
(b. 1938)
US playwright

Describing himself in one of his own plays as 'the world's oldest living promising young playwright', he wrote black comedies about modern America, such as The House of Blue Leaves *(1972) and* Bosoms of Neglect *(1979).*

1 Avoiding humiliation is the core of tragedy and comedy.
Independent 17 October 1988

2 Everybody on this planet is separated by only six other people. Six degrees of separation. Between us and everybody else on this planet . . . It's a profound thought . . . How every person is a new door, opening up into other worlds.
Six Degrees of Separation (1990, filmed 1993). Spoken by Ouisa Kittredge. The theory that any person can be connected to any other person through a chain of acquaintances not exceeding five intermediaries was first proposed in 1929 by the Hungarian writer Frigyes Karinthy in a short story called 'Chains'. In 1967 the theory was tested by Stanley Milgram, a US sociologist, and the results were published in *Psychology Today*, inspiring the phrase 'six degrees of separation', later popularized by Guare's play.

3 We live in a world where amnesia is the most wished-for state. When did history become a bad word?
International Herald Tribune 13 June 1990

Bob Guccione
(b. 1930)
US publisher

Chiefly identified with the soft-porn magazine Penthouse, *which he founded in 1965, he has also published a range of other magazines including* Omni *and the* Saturday Review.

1 If I were asked for a one-line answer to the question 'What makes a woman good in bed?' I would say, 'A man who is good in bed.'
Interview in *Speaking Frankly* (1978) by Wendy Leigh

Philip Guedalla
(1889–1944)
British author

A writer with a taste for the epigram, he believed that historical works should be entertaining as well as conscientious. His books include Palmerston *(1926),* The Hundred Days *(1934) and* The Hundred Years *(1936).*

1 History repeats itself. Historians repeat each other.
Supers and Supermen, 'Some Historians' (1920)

2 The work of Henry James has always seemed divisible by a simple dynastic arrangement into three reigns: James I, James II, and the Old Pretender.
Ibid., 'Some Critics'

3 Any stigma, as the old saying is, will serve to beat a dogma.
Masters and Men, 'Ministers of State' (1923)

4 Biography is a very definite region bounded on the north by history, on the south by fiction, on the east by obituary, and on the west by tedium.
Quoted in the *Observer* 3 March 1929

'Che' Guevara
(1928–67)
Argentinian revolutionary leader

Ernesto Guevara de la Serna. The most iconized figure of the 20th century, he was second in command to FIDEL CASTRO *during the Cuban revolution of 1959, and subsequently held government posts under him. He was captured and executed while campaigning in Bolivia.*

1 When asked whether or not we are Marxists, our position is the same as that of a physicist or a biologist who is asked if he is a 'Newtonian', or if he is a 'Pasteurian'.
'We Are Practical Revolutionaries' (1960), repr. in *Venceremos! The Speeches and Writings of Ernesto Che Guevara* (ed. John Gerassi, 1968)

2 Many will call me an adventurer, and I am, but of a different kind – one who risks his skin in order to prove his convictions.
Letter, 1965, ibid. From his last letter to his parents before leaving Cuba to set up guerrilla forces in Bolivia.

3 Let me say, with the risk of appearing ridiculous, that the true revolutionary is guided by strong feel-

ings of love. It is impossible to think of an authentic revolutionary without this quality.

'Socialism and Man in Cuba' (1967), publ. in *Che Guevara on Revolution* (ed. Jay Mallin, 1969)

4 The revolution is made by man, but man must forge his revolutionary spirit from day to day.

'Socialism and Man in Cuba', ibid.

Hervé Guibert

(1955–91)

French author and photographer

A photo critic for Le Monde *and editor and photographer for* L'Autre Journal, *he also wrote novels, for example* Les Aveugles *(1985). He died from AIDS.*

1 AIDS was . . . an illness in stages, a very long flight of steps that led assuredly to death, but whose every step represented a unique apprenticeship. It was a disease that gave death time to live and its victims time to die, time to discover time, and in the end to discover life.

To the Friend Who Did Not Save My Life, ch. 61 (1991)

Texas Guinan

(1884–1933)

US actor

Originally Mary Louise Cecilia Guinan. With the catch-phrase 'Hello, sucker!' she was a celebrated nightclub hostess of speak-easies in the 1920s, and as such the subject of repeated raids by Prohibition agents.

1 Fifty million Frenchmen can't be wrong.

Catch-phrase in the 1920s. This was already a popular saying among US soldiers during the First World War, and possibly dates from earlier. It was the title of a song recorded by SOPHIE TUCKER in 1927, of COLE PORTER's first Broadway hit (1929), and of a 1931 film.

Nubar Gulbenkian

(1896–1972)

British oil tycoon and socialite

Son of Calouste Gulbenkian, who established the Gulbenkian Foundation, he worked for his father and was commercial attaché to the Iranian Embassy (1926–51 and 1956–65).

1 The best number for a dinner party is two – myself and a dam' good head waiter.

Daily Telegraph 14 January 1965

Thom Gunn

(1929–2004)

British poet

Initially regarded as a Movement poet, he developed a freer style after his move to California in 1954. He wrote on his homosexuality in The Passages of Joy *(1982) and on the AIDS epidemic in* The Man with Night Sweats *(1992).*

1 I prod, you react. Thus to and fro
We turn, to see ourselves perform the same
Comical acts inside the tragic game.

'Carnal Knowledge', publ. in *Fighting Terms* (1954)

2 No plausible nostalgia, no brown shame,
I had when treating with my enemies.
And always when a living impulse came
I acted, and my action made me wise.
And I regretted nothing.

'Incident on a Journey', ibid.

3 On motorcycles, up the road, they come:
Small, black, as flies hanging in heat, the Boys,
Until the distance throws them forth, their hum
Bulges to thunder held by calf and thigh.
In goggles, donned impersonality,
In gleaming jackets trophied with the dust,
They strap in doubt – by hiding it, robust –
And almost hear a meaning in their noise.

'On the Move', publ. in *The Sense of Movement* (1957)

4 Distorting hackneyed words in hackneyed songs
He turns revolt into a style, prolongs
The impulse to a habit of the time.

'Elvis Presley', ibid. See GEORGE MELLY 1.

5 My thoughts are crowded with death
and it draws so oddly on the sexual
that I am confused
confused to be attracted
by, in effect, my own annihilation.

'In Time Of Plague', publ. in *The Man with Night Sweats* (1992)

George Gurdjieff

(c. 1877–1949)

Greek-Armenian religious teacher and mystic

Originally George S. Georgiades. He founded the first of his Institutes for the Harmonious Development of Man in Moscow (1912) where he propounded a system of raising consciousness called the Fourth Way. His ideas were transmitted by his disciple Ouspensky.

1 A man can only attain knowledge with the help of those who possess it. This must be understood from

the very beginning. *One must learn from him who knows.*
Quoted in *In Search of the Miraculous*, ch. 2 (1949) by P. D. Ouspensky

2 A considerable percentage of the people we meet on the street are people who are empty inside, that is, they are actually *already dead*. It is fortunate for us that we do not see and do not know it. If we knew what a number of people are actually dead and what a number of these dead people govern our lives, we should go mad with horror.
Quoted ibid., ch. 8

3 A man may be born, but in order to be born he must first die, and in order to die he must first awake.
Quoted ibid., ch. 11. Gurdjieff explained: 'If a man dies without having been awakened he cannot be born. If a man is born without having died he may become an "immortal thing". Thus the fact that he has not "died" prevents a man from being "born"; the fact of his not having awakened prevents him from "dying"; and should he be born without having died he is prevented from "being".'

4 A man will renounce any pleasures you like but he will not give up his suffering.
Quoted ibid., ch. 13

5 Every ceremony or rite has a value if it is performed without alteration. A ceremony is a book in which a great deal is written. Anyone who understands can read it. One rite often contains more than a hundred books.
Quoted ibid., ch. 15

6 A 'sin' is something which is not necessary.
Quoted ibid., ch. 17

Dorothy Frances Gurney
(1858–1932)
English poet

She was the author of religious poetry, of which 'God's Garden' (1913) is the best known. She also wrote hymns.

1 The kiss of the sun for pardon,
The song of the birds for mirth,
One is nearer God's Heart in a garden
Than anywhere else on earth.
'God's Garden', publ. in *Poems* (1913)

Ivor Gurney
(1890–1937)
British poet and composer

The poems in Severn and Somme *(1917) and* War's Embers *(1919) were written in hospital after being gassed at the Battle of Passchendaele. From 1922 he was in a mental hospital. Many of his poems and songs dealt with his native Gloucestershire.*

1 There are strange hells within the minds war made
Not so often, not so humiliatingly afraid
As one would have expected – the racket and fear guns made.
'Strange Hells' (1919–22), publ. in *Collected Poems* (1982)

2 Fierce indignation is best understood by those
Who have time or no fear, or a hope in its real good.
One loses it with a filed soul or in sentimental mood.
'Sonnet – September 1922', ibid.

3 And more than he,
I paid the prices of life
Standing where Rome immortal heard October's strife,
A war poet whose right of honour cuts falsehood like a knife.
'Poem for End' (1922–5), ibid.

4 Only, who thought of England as two thousand years
Must keep of today's life the proper anger and fears:
England that was paid for by building and ploughing and tears.
'Poem for End', ibid.

Arlo Guthrie
(b. 1947)
US singer and songwriter

Son of WOODY GUTHRIE, *he became known for his song 'Alice's Restaurant' (1967), from which a film was made (1969). He later opened the Guthrie Center in Housatonic, Massachusetts.*

1 You can get anything you want at Alice's Restaurant.
'Alice's Restaurant Massacree' (song) on the album *Alice's Restaurant* (1967)

2 Coming into Los Angeles, bringing in a couple of keys,

Don't touch my bags, if you please, Mister
Customs Man.

'Coming into Los Angeles' (song) on the album *Running Down
the Road* (1969)

Woody Guthrie
(1912–67)
US singer and songwriter

*Woodrow Wilson Guthrie. He travelled the road during the
Depression, gathering many of the 'Dust Bowl ballads' that
he would later perform on radio. He composed more than a
thousand songs, often directed against social injustice and
poverty.*

1 This machine kills fascists.

Written on his guitar, 1940s

2 This land is your land, this land is my land,
From California to the New York Island.
From the redwood forest to the Gulf Stream waters
This land was made for you and me.

'This Land Is Your Land' (song, 1956). The song is said to have
been written in response to the patriotic hymn, 'God Bless
America' (see IRVING BERLIN 1). In *Tarantula* (1970), BOB
DYLAN wrote: 'This land is your land and this land is my land
– sure, but the world is run by those that never listen to
music anyway.'

Nell Gwyn
(1650–87)
English actress

*Born Eleanor Gwyn. An orange-seller in the Drury Lane
Theatre, she rose to be one of London's leading actresses. She
was mistress of Charles II from around 1669. See CHARLES II 2.*

1 Be still, friends. I am the Protestant whore.

Remark, 1681, quoted in *Nell Gwyn*, ch. 8 (2000) by Derek
Parker. Addressed to angry crowds in London who believed
her to be the king's unpopular Catholic mistress, Louise de
Kérouaille, the Duchess of Portsmouth.

2 Sir John Germaine ... was put down with the
elegant remark that she 'would not lay the dog
where the deer had lain.'

Rejection of a suitor, *c.* 1685, ibid., ch. 9

H

Hadrian
(76–138)
Roman emperor

*Called by SCHILLER 'the Empire's first servant', he consolidated
Roman frontiers, including initiating the building of Hadrian's
Wall in Britain, and was a patron of the arts and architecture.*

1 *Animula vagula blandula,*
Hospes comesque corporis,
Quae nunc abibis in loca
Pallidula rigida nudula,
Nec ut soles dabis iocos!
['Dear little fleeting pleasing soul, the guest and
comrade of my body, into what regions must you
go now – pale little, cold little, naked little soul,
without your old power of jesting.']

'To His Soul', publ. in *The Penguin Book of Latin Verse* (ed.
Frederick Brittain, 1962)

(Sir) H. Rider Haggard
(1856–1925)
English author

*Henry Rider Haggard. He travelled widely in South Africa
before writing adventure novels such as* King Solomon's Mines
(1885) and She *(1887).*

1 She who must be obeyed.

She, ch. 6 and passim (1887). In JOHN MORTIMER's 'Rumpole'
series, the barrister Rumpole habitually uses the tag 'She Who
Must Be Obeyed' to refer to his domineering wife.

Merle Haggard
(b. 1937)
US country musician

*After his release from San Quentin prison, he topped the
country charts twenty-three times, with songs mostly about
hard drinking and hard living, and on blue-collar themes.*

1 I'm proud to be an Okie from Muskogee
A place where even squares can have a ball.

'Okie From Muskogee' (song, 1969, written with Phil Ochs).
Though a tongue-in-cheek homage to provincial American
values, this song and its follow-up 'The Fighting Side of Me'
(1970) won Haggard a new right-wing audience, and a reputation for being President NIXON's favourite country singer.

William Hague
(b. 1961)
British politician

Already known for his address to the Conservative Party Conference at the age of sixteen, he became a Conservative MP in 1989 and was Leader of the Opposition 1997–2001.

1 If all we had needed to govern the country was someone who repeated everything we'd said before, we could have bought a parrot.
Speech at Conservative Party Conference, Blackpool, 7 October 1999, quoted in the *Guardian* 8 October 1999

Samuel Hahnemann
(1755–1843)
German physician and founder of homeopathy

He developed a system of 'like cures like' after observing that medicine given to the healthy produced symptoms similar to the illness it was meant to cure. His main work, the Organon of Medicine, *was published in 1810.*

1 The orthodox school has witnessed for centuries that nature itself has never once cured any existing disease with another *dissimilar* one, however intense.
Organon of Medicine, sect. 39 (sixth edn, written 1842, publ. 1921, transl. 1983)

2 One might say, for example, that a patient has a *kind* of St Vitus's dance; a *kind* of dropsy; a *kind* of nerve fever; a *kind* of ague. One would *never* say, however (to end once and for all the confusion of these names), 'He *has* St Vitus's dance,' 'He *has* nerve fever,' 'He *has* dropsy,' 'He *has* ague,' since there simply are not any fixed, unchanging diseases to be known by such names.
Ibid., sect. 81

Lord Hailsham
(1907–2001)
British politician

Quintin Hogg, Viscount Hailsham of St Marylebone. Following his father into parliament in 1938, he was Chairman of the Conservative Party 1957–9 and served two terms as Lord Chancellor (1970–4 and 1979–87). Judge Pickles called him a 'quixotic dictator'.

1 Being Conservative is only another way of being British.
Remark in 1967, quoted by John Barnes in 'Ideology and Factions' publ. in *Conservative Century*, pt 2 (ed. Anthony Seldon and Stuart Ball, 1994)

J. B. S. Haldane
(1892–1964)
British-born Indian scientist

John Burdon Sanderson Haldane. He specialized in population genetics as related to evolution theory, while based at University College, London (1937–57) and at Orissa, India, where he emigrated in 1957. His books helped to popularize general scientific issues.

1 My own suspicion is that the Universe is not only queerer than we suppose, but queerer than we *can* suppose.
Possible Worlds and Other Essays, 'Possible Worlds' (1927)

2 In fact, words are well adapted for description and the arousing of emotion, but for many kinds of precise thought other symbols are much better.
The Inequality of Man, 'God-Makers' (1932)

3 I wish I had the voice of Homer
To sing of rectal carcinoma.
'Cancer's a Funny Thing', publ. in the *New Statesman* 21 February 1964. Opening lines of a poem describing Haldane's cancer. 'The main functions of my rhyme,' Haldane wrote, 'were to induce cancer patients to be operated on early and to be cheerful about it.'

4 I'd lay down my life for two brothers or eight cousins.
Attributed, in the *New Scientist* 8 August 1974

H. R. Haldeman
(1926–93)
US White House official

Harry Robbins Haldeman. He was nicknamed the 'Iron Chancellor' while White House Chief of Staff under President NIXON *(1969–73). His involvement in the Watergate cover-up led to an eighteen-month prison sentence.*

1 Once the toothpaste is out of the tube, it is awfully hard to get it back in.
Remark to John Dean, 8 April 1973, publ. in *Hearings Before the Select Committee on Presidential Campaign Activities of US Senate: Watergate and Related Activities*, vol. 4 (1973). Referring to the exposure of the White House's involvement in the bugging of the Watergate building.

Nathan Hale
(1755–76)
US revolutionary soldier

He was commissioned a captain in 1776 and was hanged shortly after by the British as a spy, without a trial. His statue stands at the CIA headquarters in Langley, Virginia.

1 I only regret that I have but one life to lose for my country.

Speech, 22 September 1776, quoted in *Nathan Hale, 1776*, ch. 7 (1914) by Henry Phelps Johnston. Spoken before his execution. See JOSEPH ADDISON 20.

Alex Haley
(1921–92)
US author

He is best known for Roots: The Saga of an American Family *(1976, televised 1977), which, in fictional form, tracked seven generations of an African-American family.*

1 It is rightly said that when a griot dies, it is as if a library has burned to the ground. The griots symbolize how all human ancestry goes back to some place, and some time, where there was no writing. Then, the memories and the mouths of ancient elders was the only way that early histories of mankind got passed along . . . for all of us today to know who we are.

Roots, 'Acknowledgements' (1976). Referring to the transmitters of oral history in West African villages.

Bill Haley
(1925–81)
US rock musician

His composition 'Crazy Man Crazy' (1953), recorded with the Comets, was considered the first 'rock and roll' record to enter Billboard's *pop chart.*

1 One-two-three o'clock, four o'clock rock!
Five-six-seven o'clock, eight o'clock rock!
Nine-ten-eleven o'clock, twelve o'clock rock!
We're gonna rock around the clock tonight!

'Rock Around the Clock' (song, 1954, written by Max Freedman and 'Jimmy De Knight', pseudonym of Haley's publisher James Myers) by Bill Haley and His Comets. The song was a minor hit in 1952 for Sunny Dae, but became the biggest hit of the rock 'n' roll era for Haley when his recording was adopted as the title music to the film *Blackboard Jungle* (1955), selling more than 25 million copies. The 1956 film *Rock Around the Clock* featured this and Haley's other hits, and caused riots in cinemas when the song was played.

2 Shake, rattle and roll.

'Shake, Rattle and Roll' (song, 1954, written by Charles Calhoun). Originally a hit for 'blues-shouter' Big Joe Turner; it was the first hit for Haley and the Comets.

3 See you later, alligator,
After 'while, crocodile;

Can't you see you're in my way, now,
Don't you know you cramp my style?

'See You Later Alligator' (song, 1956, written by Charles Calhoun). The record was Haley's last US top-ten hit.

Thomas C. Haliburton
(1796–1865)
Canadian jurist and humorist

Thomas Chandler Haliburton. A judge of the Supreme Court in Canada, he retired to England and became a Conservative MP. He is best known for the creation of the character Sam Slick.

1 Feller citizens, this country is goin' to the dogs hand over hand.

The Clockmaker, or, The Sayings and Doings of Samuel Slick of Slickville, no. 21 ('Gulling a Bluenose') (1837). Spoken by Sam Slick.

2 Punctuality is the soul of business.

Sam Slick's Wise Saws, ch. 3 (1853)

Lord Halifax
See George Savile

Edward F. Wood, Lord Halifax
(1881–1959)
British politician and diplomat

Viscount Halifax. He was Foreign Secretary (1938–40) under NEVILLE CHAMBERLAIN, *and Ambassador to the USA (1941–6).*

1 I often think how much easier the world would have been to manage if Herr Hitler and Signor Mussolini had been at Oxford.

Speech in York, 4 November 1937, attributed. Wood was at the time Chancellor of Oxford University.

(Sir) Peter Hall
(b. 1930)
British theatre, opera and film director

He established the Royal Shakespeare Company as a permanent company and was a key figure in the formation of the National Theatre.

1 The English hate the arts because they are so good at them. It's the great paradox.

Quoted in the *Observer* 7 September 1997

Radclyffe Hall
(1883–1943)
British novelist

Marguerite Radclyffe Hall. She became notorious for her novel The Well of Loneliness *(1928), banned in Britain for many years for its open treatment of lesbian love.*

1 You're neither unnatural, nor abominable, nor mad; you're as much a part of what people call nature as anyone else; only you're unexplained as yet – you've not got your niche in creation.
The Well of Loneliness, bk 2, ch. 20, sect. 3 (1928). The speech that 'Puddle' (the tutor, Miss Puddleton) resolves to make to the book's lesbian heroine, Stephen Gordon. The book was temporarily suspended in the USA, and, after a well-publicized trial, banned in Britain, where the editor of the *Sunday Express* wrote that he 'would sooner give a healthy boy or girl a dose of prussic acid than a copy of it'.

2 I am one of those whom God marked on the forehead. Like Cain, I am marked and blemished. If you come to me ... the world will abhor you, will persecute you, will call you unclean. Our love may be faithful even unto death and beyond – yet the world will call it unclean.
Stephen, ibid., ch. 37, sect. 3

Margaret Halsey
(1910–97)
US author

Calling herself a 'humorist and a moral positivist', she wrote on topics ranging from racism and neglect of children to English foibles. Her books include With Malice Toward Some *(1938) and* The Folks at Home *(1952).*

1 The boneless quality of English conversation, which, so far as I have heard it, is all form and no content. Listening to Britons dining out is like watching people play first-class tennis with imaginary balls.
With Malice Toward Some, pt 1, 'June 12' (1938)

2 Englishwomen's shoes look as if they had been made by someone who had often heard shoes described, but had never seen any.
Ibid., pt 2

William F. Halsey Jr
(1882–1959)
US naval commander

William Frederick 'Bull' Halsey. He commanded the South Pacific area in the Second World War and received the Japanese

surrender on his ship on 2 September 1945. He was promoted to the rank of admiral later that year.

1 The Third Fleet's sunken and damaged ships have been salvaged and are retiring at high speed toward the enemy.
Radio message, 14 October 1944, quoted in *Bull Halsey*, ch. 17 (1985) by E. B. Potter. Sent after Japanese claims that the US Third Fleet had been almost destroyed.

Alexander Hamilton
(1757–1804)
US statesman

He was a driving force in the ratification of the US constitution, and as Secretary to the Treasury (1789–95) restored the country's finances. He was killed in a duel by his rival Aaron Burr.

1 A national debt, if it is not excessive, will be to us a national blessing.
Letter, 30 April 1781, publ. in *The Works of Alexander Hamilton*, vol. 1 (ed. John C. Hamilton, 1850). Later, as Secretary of the Treasury (1789–95), Hamilton sponsored legislation to pay off the debt of the Continental Congress, and to charter the short-lived Bank of the United States.

Edith Hamilton
(1867–1963)
US classical scholar and translator

Headmistress of Bryn Mawr preparatory school in Baltimore (1896–1922), she wrote widely on the classics.

1 The anthropologists are busy, indeed, and ready to transport us back into the savage forest where all human things ... have their beginnings; but the seed never explains the flower.
The Greek Way, ch. 1 (1930)

2 There are few efforts more conducive to humility than that of the translator trying to communicate an incommunicable beauty. Yet, unless we do try, something unique and never surpassed will cease to exist except in the libraries of a few inquisitive book lovers.
Three Greek Plays, Introduction (1937)

Richard Hamilton
(b. 1922)
British artist

His work with the Independent Group, and particularly his collage 'Just What Is It That Makes Today's Homes So Different, So Appealing?' (1956) helped to establish Pop Art in Britain.

1 If the artist is not to lose much of his ancient purpose he may have to plunder the popular arts to recover the imagery which is his rightful inheritance.
'For the Finest Art Try – POP' (1961), repr. in *Collected Words 1953–1982* (1982)

Dag Hammarskjöld
(1905–61)
Swedish statesman

Describing himself as the 'curator of the secrets of 82 nations', he was UN Secretary-General 1953–61. He died in a plane crash in Zambia while attempting to mediate in the Congo crisis.

1 We are not permitted to choose the frame of our destiny. But what we put into it is ours.
Note, written 1950, publ. in *Markings*, 'Night is Drawing Nigh' (1964)

2 In our era, the road to holiness necessarily passes through the world of action.
Note, written 1955, ibid.

3 The UN is not just a product of do-gooders. It is harshly real. The day will come when men will see the UN and what it means clearly. Everything will be all right – you know when? When people, just people, stop thinking of the United Nations as a weird Picasso abstraction, and see it as a drawing they made themselves.
Time 27 June 1955

Oscar Hammerstein II
(1895–1960)
US songwriter

His collaborators included Jerome Kern and, for sixteen years, Richard Rodgers, with whom he produced such classic musicals as Oklahoma! *(1943) and* South Pacific *(1949).*

1 Ol' man river, dat ol' man river,
He must know sumpin', but don't say nothin'
He just keeps rollin',
He keeps on rollin' along.
'Ol' Man River' (song, with music by Jerome Kern) in the stage musical *Show Boat* (1927, filmed 1936 and 1951)

2 Darby and Joan who used to be Jack and Jill,
The folks like to be called,
What they have always been called,
'The folks who live on the hill'.
'The Folks Who Live on the Hill' (song, with music by Jerome Kern) in the film *High, Wide and Handsome* (1937)

3 The last time I saw Paris
Her heart was warm and gay,
I heard the laughter of her heart in every street café.
'The Last Time I Saw Paris' (song, with music by Jerome Kern) in the film *Lady Be Good* (1941). Hammerstein's last major collaboration with Jerome Kern was inspired by news of the German occupation of Paris, and won an Oscar. The film bears no relation to the stage musical of the same name scored by George Gershwin in 1924.

4 Oh, what a beautiful mornin',
Oh, what a beautiful day!
I got a beautiful feelin'
Ev'rything's goin' my way.
'Oh, What a Beautiful Mornin'' (song, with music by Richard Rodgers) in *Oklahoma!* (stage musical 1943, film 1955)

5 The corn is as high as an elephant's eye,
And it looks like it's climbin' clear up to the sky.
'Oh, What a Beautiful Mornin'', ibid.

6 June is bustin' out all over.
'June is Bustin' Out All Over' (song, with music by Richard Rodgers) in *Carousel* (stage musical 1945, film 1956)

7 You'll never walk alone.
'You'll Never Walk Alone', ibid. Recorded at various times by JUDY GARLAND, FRANK SINATRA and Gerry and the Pacemakers, the song has been adopted by crowds at British football matches, chiefly associated with Liverpool FC.

8 Some enchanted evening,
You may see a stranger,
You may see a stranger,
Across a crowded room.
'Some Enchanted Evening' (song, with music by Richard Rodgers) in *South Pacific* (stage musical, 1949, film, 1958)

9 There is nothin' like a dame.
'There is nothin' like a dame', ibid.

10 I'm as corny as Kansas in August,
High as a flag on the Fourth of July!
'A Wonderful Guy', ibid.

11 I'm gonna wash that man right out of my hair.
'I'm Gonna Wash That Man Right Out of My Hair', ibid.

12 The hills are alive with the sound of music.
'The Sound of Music' (song, with music by Richard Rodgers) in *The Sound of Music* (stage musical, 1959, film, 1965)

13 Climb every mountain, ford every stream
Follow every rainbow, till you find your dream!
'Climb Every Mountain', ibid.

Christopher Hampton
(b. 1946)
British playwright

He was the first resident playwright at London's Royal Court Theatre, where most of his plays have been produced. Highly regarded for his Tales from Hollywood *(1982), he scored his greatest success with his stage adaptation,* Les Liaisons Dangereuses *(1985).*

1 I have always thought of sophistication as rather a feeble substitute for decadence.
The Philanthropist, Sc. 3 (1970). Spoken by Braham.

2 Masturbation is the thinking man's television.
Braham, ibid., Sc. 3

3 I always divide people into two groups. Those who live by what they know to be a lie, and those who live by what they believe, falsely, to be the truth.
Don, ibid., Sc. 3

4 If I had to give a definition of capitalism I would say: the process whereby American girls turn into American women.
Savages, Sc. 16 (1974). Spoken by Carlos.

5 To seduce a woman famous for strict morals, religious fervour and the happiness of her marriage: what could possibly be more prestigious?
Dangerous Liaisons (film, 1988). Spoken by Valmont.

Tony Hancock
(1924–68)
British comedian

He achieved fame as the pompous and lugubrious misfit with a sardonic wit in Hancock's Half Hour, *on radio (1954–9) and television (1956–61). A decline into alcoholism ended in his suicide.*

1 It's red hot, mate. I hate to think of this sort of book getting in the wrong hands. As soon as I've finished this, I shall recommend they ban it.
'The Missing Page', broadcast 26 February 1960, in *Hancock's Half-Hour* (BBC TV series, 1956–61, written by Ray Galton and Alan Simpson)

2 I don't mind giving them a reasonable amount, but a pint . . . why that's very nearly an armful.
'The Blood Donor', broadcast 23 June 1961, ibid.

Georg Friedrich Handel
(1685–1759)
German composer

Resident in England from 1712, he composed prolifically, including operas, orchestral music, such as the Water Music *(c. 1717), and oratorios, notably the* Messiah *(1742).*

1 Whether I was in my body or out of my body as I wrote it I know not. God knows.
Attributed, referring to the 'Hallelujah Chorus' from the *Messiah* (1742)

Peter Handke
(b. 1942)
Austrian novelist, playwright and director

His first play Insulting the Audience *(1966) was an example of his anti-theatre writing, which alternately abuses and praises the audience. He has worked in collaboration with Wim Wenders.*

1 If a nation loses its storytellers, it loses its childhood.
Independent 9 June 1988

William Hanna
(1910–2001)
Joseph Barbera
(b. 1911)
US animators

They were the creators of Tom and Jerry *for MGM (1937–57) and went on to found their own company, producing cartoons such as* Yogi Bear, Huckleberry Hound *and* The Flintstones.

1 Yabba dabba do!
The Flintstones (TV cartoon, 1960–6, produced by Hanna and Barbera). Fred Flintstone's habitual gleeful cry. The character was voiced by Alan Reed.

Brian Hanrahan
(b. 1949)
British journalist

After stints as BBC Far East correspondent (1983–5) and Moscow correspondent (1986–9), he has been a diplomatic correspondent and editor.

1 I'm not allowed to say how many planes joined the raid, but I counted them all out, and I counted them all back.
BBC news report, 1 May 1982, publ. in 'I Counted Them All

Out and I Counted Them All Back', *'Air Battles'* (1982, written with Robert Fox). The broadcast from the Falkland Islands described the safe return of British Harriers to HMS *Hermes* after their first attack on the landing strip of Port Stanley.

Edmond Haraucourt

(1856–1941)
French poet

He was the author of collections of verse such as L'Âme nue (1885), verse dramas, and plays including Shylock *(1889).*

1 *Partir c'est mourir un peu,*
C'est mourir à ce qu'on aime:
On laisse un peu de soi-même
En toute heure et dans tout lieu.
[To go away is to die a little, it is to die to that which one loves: everywhere and always, one leaves behind a part of oneself.]
'Rondel de l'Adieu', publ. in *Seul* (1891)

Otto Harbach

(1873–1963)
US songwriter

A prolific lyricist and librettist, he collaborated with Sigmund Romberg, Jerome Kern and George Gershwin on such hits as the musical No, No, Nanette *(1925).*

1 When a lovely flame dies
Smoke gets in your eyes.
'Smoke Gets in your Eyes' (song, with music by Jerome Kern), in *Roberta* (musical show 1933, film 1935)

Yip Harburg

(1898–1981)
US songwriter

Born Isidore Hochberg, changed to Edgar Y. Harburg. He is identified with socially conscious and idealistic songs and was also active in civil rights movements. See also JUDY GARLAND 1.

1 Once I built a railroad,
Now it's done,
Brother, can you spare a dime?
'Brother Can You Spare a Dime?' (song, with music by Jay Gorney), in *Americana* (musical show, 1932). The line has been often rendered, 'Buddy, can you spare a dime?' Asked to update the song for the *New York Times* some fifty years later, Harburg came up with: 'Once we had depression/But with a dime/A guy wasn't out of luck./Now we've got inflation, drugs and crime./Brother can you spare a buck?'

2 Say, it's only a paper moon,
Sailing over a cardboard sea.
'It's Only a Paper Moon' (song, written with Billy Rose, music by Harold Arlen) in *The Great Magoo* (stage musical, 1932)

3 Follow the yellow brick road.
'We're Off to See the Wizard' (song, with music by Harold Arlen), in *The Wizard of Oz* (film, 1939)

4 We're off to see the Wizard
The wonderful Wizard of Oz.
'We're Off to See the Wizard', ibid.

5 I could while away the hours
Conversin' with the flowers,
Consultin' with the rain;
With the thoughts I'd be thinkin'
I could be another Lincoln
If I only had a brain . . .
'If I Only Had a Brain' (song, with music by Harold Arlen), ibid. Sung by the scarecrow.

6 Wanna cry, wanna croon.
Wanna laugh like a loon.
It's that Old Devil Moon in your eyes.
'Old Devil Moon' (song, with music by Burton Lane), in *Finian's Rainbow* (stage musical 1947, filmed 1968)

(Sir) William Harcourt

(1827–1904)
British politician

A leading figure in Liberal politics of the late 19th century, he served in all four of GLADSTONE's *governments, and, as Chancellor of the Exchequer, introduced a major reform in death duties in 1894.*

1 We are all socialists now.
Attributed, by Hubert Bland in 'The Outlook', publ. in *Fabian Essays in Socialism* (ed. GEORGE BERNARD SHAW, 1889). Remark on the passage of Lord Goschen's 1888 budget, which significantly reduced the national debt.

James Keir Hardie

(1856–1915)
Scottish politician

The co-founder and first leader of the Labour Party (1906), he remained an MP until his death.

1 From his childhood onwards this boy will be surrounded by sycophants and flatterers . . . In due course, following the precedent which has already been set, he will be sent on a tour of the world and probably rumours of a morganatic marriage alliance

will follow, and the end of it will be the country will be called upon to pay the bill.

Speech to House of Commons, 28 June 1894, publ. in *Hansard*, col. 463. Opposing a motion congratulating Queen VICTORIA on the birth of her great-grandson, the future EDWARD VIII.

Warren G. Harding
(1865–1923)
US president

Warren Gamaliel Harding. As Republican President (1921–3) he proved to be politically naïve, unprepared for the 'Teapot Dome Scandal' which exposed corruption in government. WOODROW WILSON *referred to his 'bungalow mind'.*

1 America's present need is not heroics, but healing; not nostrums, but normalcy; not revolution, but restoration.
Speech in Boston, 14 May 1920, quoted in *Rededicating America*, ch. 17 (1920) by Frederick E. Schortemeier. 'Back to normalcy' was Harding's campaign slogan in that year.

Elizabeth Hardwick
(b. 1916)
US critic and author

Known mainly for her brilliant literary and social criticism in the New York Review of Books, *which she helped to found in 1963, she also wrote novels. She was married to* ROBERT LOWELL *1949–72.*

1 The fifties – they seem to have taken place on a sunny afternoon that asked nothing of you except a drifting belief in the moment and its power to satisfy.
Bartleby in Manhattan and Other Essays, 'Domestic Manners' (1983)

Oliver Hardy
(1892–1957)
US comedian

Originally Norvell Hardy. He was the overbearing and rotund member of the comedy duo Laurel and Hardy, formed in 1926. The partnership resulted in more than 200 films, both 'silents' and 'talkies'.

1 Here's another nice mess you've gotten me into.
The Laurel-Hardy Murder Case (film, 1930). Spoken by Ollie, this is the earliest use of the famous catch-phrase which featured in various Laurel and Hardy films, always uttered by Oliver Hardy to Stan Laurel, although Laurel (1890–1965) is credited with most of the scriptwork, and directed many of the films. The words are generally misquoted as 'another fine mess', which was the title of a Laurel and Hardy short

released in 1930, but have not been traced to any dialogue in this form.

Thomas Hardy
(1840–1928)
English novelist and poet

His native Dorset, where he lived for most of his life, was the setting for his 'Wessex' novels. He later turned to poetry, which included elegies to his first wife, and an epic drama The Dynasts *(1904–8).* D. H. LAWRENCE *remarked: 'What a commonplace genius he has, or a genius for the commonplace, I don't know which.'*

1 When I set out for Lyonnesse,
A hundred miles away,
The rime was on the spray,
And starlight lit my lonesomeness
When I set out for Lyonnesse
A hundred miles away.
'When I Set Out for Lyonnesse', written 1870, publ. in *Satires of Circumstance* (1914)

2 That man's silence is wonderful to listen to.
Under the Greenwood Tree, pt 2, ch. 5 (1872). Spoken by Spinks. Some editions have the variation: 'That man's dumbness is wonderful to listen to.' The novel's title is from a song in SHAKESPEARE's *As You Like It*, Act 2, Sc. 5.

3 Far From the Madding Crowd.
Title of novel (1874). The words are from Gray's 'Elegy' (see THOMAS GRAY 15).

4 A resolution to avoid an evil is seldom framed till the evil is so far advanced as to make avoidance impossible.
Far From the Madding Crowd, ch. 18 (1874)

5 It appears that ordinary men take wives because possession is not possible without marriage, and that ordinary women accept husbands because marriage is not possible without possession.
Ibid., ch. 20

6 It is difficult for a woman to define her feelings in language which is chiefly made by men to express theirs.
Bathsheba, ibid., ch. 51

7 She was of the stuff of which great men's mothers are made. She was indispensable to high generation, hated at tea parties, feared in shops, and loved at crises.
Ibid., ch. 54. Referring to Bathsheba.

8 A lover without indiscretion is no lover at all.

Circumspection and devotion are a contradiction in terms.
The Hand of Ethelberta, ch. 20 (1875). Spoken by Ladywell.

9 Don't you go believing in sayings, Picotee: they are all made by men, for their own advantages. Women who use public proverbs as a guide through events are those who have not ingenuity enough to make private ones as each event occurs.
Ethelberta, ibid., ch. 20

10 Ethelberta breathed a sort of exclamation, not right out, but stealthily, like a parson's damn.
Ibid., ch. 26

11 The business of the poet and novelist is to show the sorriness underlying the grandest things, and the grandeur underlying the sorriest things.
Notebook entry, 19 April 1885, publ. in *The Early Life of Thomas Hardy 1840–91*, ch. 13 (1928) by Florence Hardy

12 Some folk want their luck buttered.
The Mayor of Casterbridge, ch. 13 (1886). Spoken by Mrs Cuxcom.

13 Dialect words – those terrible marks of the beast to the truly genteel.
Ibid., ch. 20

14 It is not by what is, in this life, but by what appears, that you are judged.
Henchard, ibid., ch. 25

15 That cold accretion called the world, which, so terrible in the mass, is so unformidable, even pitiable, in its units.
Tess of the D'Urbervilles, ch. 13 (1891)

16 Patience, that blending of moral courage with physical timidity.
Ibid., ch. 43

17 Once victim, always victim – that's the law!
Tess, ibid., ch. 47

18 Let him to whose ears the low-voiced best
  seems stilled by the clash of the first,
Who holds that if way to the better there be, it
  exacts a full look
at the worst,
Who feels that delight is a delicate growth
  cramped by crookedness, custom, and fear,
Get him up and be gone as one shaped awry; he
  disturbs the order
here.
'De Profundis II', written 1895–6, publ. in *Poems of the Past and Present* (1901). The poem is also known as 'In Tenebris II'.

19 What was good for God's birds was bad for God's gardener.
Jude the Obscure, pt 1, ch. 2 (1896)

20 I leant upon a coppice gate
When frost was spectre-grey,
And winter's dregs made desolate
The weakening eye of day.
'The Darkling Thrush', st. 1, publ. in *Poems of the Past and Present* (1901). Opening lines.

21 An aged thrush, frail, gaunt, and small,
In blast-beruffled plume.
Ibid., st. 3

22 So little cause for carollings
Of such ecstatic sound
Was written on terrestrial things
Afar or nigh around,
That I could think there trembled through
His happy good-night air
Some blessed hope, whereof he knew
And I was unaware.
Ibid., st. 4

23 Well: what we gain by science is, after all, sadness, as the Preacher saith. The more we know of the laws & nature of the Universe the more ghastly a business we perceive it all to be – & the non-necessity of it.
Letter, 27 February 1902, publ. in *Collected Letters*, vol. 3 (ed. Richard Little Purdy and Michael Millgate, 1982). 'The Preacher' is the alternative name for the book of Ecclesiastes; see BIBLE, OLD TESTAMENT: ECCLESIASTES 8.

24 My argument is that war makes rattling good history; but peace is poor reading.
The Dynasts, pt 1, Act 2, Sc. 5 (1904). Spoken by Spirit Sinister.

25 If all hearts were open and all desires known – as they would be if people showed their souls – how many gapings, sighings, clenched fists, knotted brows, broad grins, and red eyes should we see in the market-place!
Note, 18 August 1908, publ. in *The Later Years of Thomas Hardy 1892–1928*, ch. 10 (1930) by Florence Emily Hardy. See BOOK OF COMMON PRAYER 49.

26 Let me enjoy the earth no less
Because the all-enacting might
That fashioned forth its loveliness
Had other aims than my delight.
'Let Me Enjoy', st. 1, publ. in *Time's Laughingstocks* (1909)

27 Woman much missed, how you call to me, call
  to me,

Saying that now you are not as you were
When you had changed from the one who was all
   to me,
But as at first, when our day was fair.
'The Voice', publ. in *Satires of Circumstance*, st. 1 (1914)

28 What of the faith and fire within us
Men who march away
Ere the barn-cocks say
Night is growing grey,
To hazards whence no tears can win us;
What of the faith and fire within us
Men who march away?
'Men Who March Away', st. 1, ibid.

29 Only a man harrowing clods
In a slow silent walk
With an old horse that stumbles and nods
Half asleep as they stalk.
'In Time of "The Breaking of Nations" ', st. 1, publ. in *Moments of Vision* (1917). The title alludes to Jeremiah 51:20 'for with thee will I break in pieces the nations'.

30 Only thin smoke without flame
From the heaps of couch-grass:
Yet this will go onward the same
Though dynasties pass.
'In Time of "The Breaking of Nations" ', st. 2, ibid.

31 Yonder a maid and her wight
Come whispering by:
War's annals will cloud into the night
Ere their story die.
'In Time of "The Breaking of Nations" ', st. 3, ibid.

32 I am the family face;
Flesh perishes, I live on,
Projecting trait and trace
Through time to times anon,
And leaping from place to place
Over oblivion.
'Heredity', st. 1, ibid.

33 This is the weather the cuckoo likes,
And so do I.
'Weathers', publ. in *Late Lyrics* (1922). Opening lines of poem.

34 And rooks in families homeward go,
And so do I.
'Weathers', ibid. Last lines of poem.

35 'Peace upon earth!' was said. We sing it,
And pay a million priests to bring it.
After two thousand years of mass
We've got as far as poison-gas.
'Christmas: 1924', publ. in *Winter Words* (1928)

36 Well, World, you have kept faith with me,
Kept faith with me;
Upon the whole you have proved to be
Much as you said you were.
'He Never Expected Much', ibid. Hardy's alternative title was 'A Consideration Upon My Eighty-Sixth Birthday'.

(Sir) David Hare
(b. 1947)
British playwright

He was co-founder of the Joint Stock Theatre Company (1974) and author of numerous modern satires, including the trilogy Racing Demon *(1990),* Murmuring Judges *(1991) and* The Absence of War *(1994). See also* HOWARD BRENTON AND DAVID HARE.

1 The theatre is the best way of showing the gap between what is said and what is seen to be done, and that is why, ragged and gap-toothed as it is, it has still a far healthier potential than some poorer, abandoned arts.
'The Playwright as Historian', publ. in the *Sunday Times* 26 November 1978

2 How the right wing always appropriate good manners. Yes? They always have that. Form and decorum. A permanent excuse for not addressing themselves to what people actually say, because they can always turn their heads away if a sentence is not correctly formulated.
A Map of the World, Act 1 (1982). Spoken by Stephen.

3 England's funny. You only get the point of it eight days a year. The sun comes out and you remember. You think oh, yes, all this ... all this around us – *that's* what it's for.
Strapless, pt 5 (1989). Spoken by Anne Rice.

4 Policing's largely the fine art of getting through biros.
Murmuring Judges, Act 1, Sc. 5 (1991). Spoken by Sandra.

W. F. Hargreaves
(1846–1919)
British songwriter

1 I'm Burlington Bertie
I rise at ten thirty and saunter along like a toff,
I walk down the Strand with my gloves on my
   hand,
Then I walk down again with them off.
'Burlington Bertie from Bow' (song, 1915). The song was first performed by Ella Shields, male impersonator and Hargrea-

ves's wife. Among the artists who covered it were ELSA LANCHESTER and JULIE ANDREWS (as Gertrude Lawrence in the 1968 film *Star!*).

(Sir) John Harington
(1561–1612)
English writer and courtier

Famous for his wit and satires, he was the translator of ARIOSTO'*s* Orlando Furioso *(1591) and author of* The Metamorphosis of Ajax *(1596), which contained the earliest design for a water closet.*

1 Treason doth never prosper: what's the reason? For if it prosper, none dare call it treason.
Epigrams, bk 4, 'Of Treason' (1618)

Lord Harlech
(1918–85)
British diplomat and businessman

William David Ormsby Gore. He became Conservative MP for Oswestry in 1950, later serving as British Ambassador in Washington (1961–5). His Harlech television company won a broadcasting franchise in 1967.

1 Britain will be honoured by historians more for the way she disposed of an empire than for the way in which she acquired it.
New York Times 28 October 1962

Jean Harlow
(1911–37)
US screen actor

Originally Harlean Carpentier. The 'Blonde Bombshell' became the first sex symbol of the 'talkies', playing comedy roles in such films as Platinum Blonde *(1931) and* Bombshell *(1933). See also* MARGOT ASQUITH 5.

1 Would you be shocked if I put on something more comfortable?
Hell's Angels (film, 1930, screenplay by H. Behn, H. Estabrook and J. M. March, based on a story by Marshall Neilan and Joseph Moncure March, produced and co-directed by Howard Hughes, J. Whale, M. Nielan and L. Reed). Spoken by Helen (Jean Harlow), and usually misquoted: 'Excuse me while I slip into something more comfortable.' Harlow, aged eighteen, acted the part of an English girl who, clad in a backless velvet evening gown with beaded straps, addresses the question to Ben Lyons (Monty Rutledge).

Michael Harrington
(1928–89)
US social scientist and author

A passionate champion of the poor and dispossessed, and a member of the Catholic Worker Movement, he is principally known for his study of poverty The Other America *(1962).*

1 Clothes make the poor invisible . . . America has the best-dressed poverty the world has ever known.
The Other America, ch. 1, sect. 1 (1962)

2 Life is lived in common, but not in community.
Ibid., ch. 7, sect. 4. Of life in the slums.

Frank Harris
(1856–1931)
Irish journalist and author

Originally James Thomas Harris. He is chiefly remembered for his scandalous autobiography My Life and Loves *(5 vols. 1922–8). Other works include a biography of* GEORGE BERNARD SHAW, *who described him as a 'man of splendid visions, unreasonable expectations, fierce appetites'.*

1 All that is amiable and sweet and good in life, all that ennobles and chastens, I have won from women.
My Life and Loves, vol. 2, Foreword (1925)

2 There is a subtle compensation in everything, and the cheapening of books, the vulgarization of knowledge, has a great deal to answer for. We have forgotten how to use books, and they revenge themselves on us.
Ibid., vol. 3, ch. 1 (1926)

Joel Chandler Harris
(1848–1908)
US journalist

He was a journalist on the staff of the Atlanta Constitution *(1876–1900) and became known for his Uncle Remus stories, told in a version of southern dialect.*

1 Hongry rooster don't cackle w'en he fine a wum.
Uncle Remus: His Songs and His Sayings, 'Plantation Proverbs' (1880)

2 Watch out w'en you'er gittin all you want. Fattenin' hogs ain't in luck.
Ibid., 'Plantation Proverbs'

3 Tar-baby ain't sayin' nuthin', en Brer Fox, he lay low.
Uncle Remus and His Legends of the Old Plantation, 'The Wonderful Tar-Baby Story' (1881)

4 Bred en bawn in a brier-patch!
Ibid., 'How Mr Rabbit Was Too Sharp for Mr Fox'

5 All by my own-alone self.
Nights with Uncle Remus, ch. 36 (1883)

Robert Harris
(b. 1957)
British journalist and author

A journalist on the Observer *and* The Sunday Times, *he became a best-selling author with his fictional reworkings of history,* Fatherland *(1992),* Archangel *(1998) and* Pompeii *(2003).*

1 In Russia, the past carries razors and a pair of handcuffs.
Archangel, ch. 11 (1998). Spoken by Suvorin.

2 The great western myth ... That just because a place has a McDonalds and MTV and takes American Express it's exactly the same as everywhere else – it doesn't have a past any more, it's Year Zero.
Kelso, ibid., ch. 16

3 History is too important to be left to the historians.
Quoted in the *Observer* 25 October 1998

Rolf Harris
(b. 1930)
Australian television presenter

His career in British television, where he presented art-based and animal shows, has spanned fifty years. His hit records include 'Sun Arise' (1962 and 1997) and 'Two Little Boys' (1969 and 1970).

1 Tie me kangaroo down, sport.
'Tie Me Kangaroo Down, Sport' (song, 1960) on the album *Sun Arise* (1963)

Tony Harrison
(b. 1937)
British poet, playwright and translator

A classicist from a working-class background, he stirred controversy with his poems 'V.' (1985) and 'The Blasphemer's Banquet' (1989). His plays include Phaedra Britannica *(1975).*

1 The ones we choose to love become our anchor
   when the hawser of the blood-tie's hacked, or
      frays.
'V.' (1985)

2 The Prospero of poisons, the Faustus of the
   front,

bringing mental magic to modern armament.
Square Rounds, pt 2 (1992). The speaker represents the German chemist Fritz Haber, Nobel prizewinner and 'father' of chemical warfare.

Lorenz Hart
(1895–1943)
US songwriter

His twenty-five-year collaboration with the composer Richard Rodgers resulted in twenty-six Broadway musicals distinguished by their lyrical sophistication, notably Pal Joey *(1940).*

1 When love congeals
It soon reveals
The faint aroma of performing seals,
The double crossing of a pair of heels.
I wish I were in love again!
'I Wish I Were in Love Again' (song, with music by Richard Rodgers), in *Babes in Arms* (stage show 1937, filmed 1939). The song was a hit for SOPHIE TUCKER and Peggy Lee.

2 I get too hungry for dinner at eight.
I like the theatre, but never come late.
I never bother with people I hate.
That's why the lady is a tramp.
'The Lady is a Tramp' (song, with music by Richard Rodgers), ibid.

3 I'm wild again
Beguiled again
A simpering, whimpering child again,
Bewitched, bothered and bewildered am I.
'Bewitched, Bothered and Bewildered' (song, with music by Richard Rodgers), in *Pal Joey* (stage show 1940, filmed 1957)

Bret Harte
(1836–1902)
US poet and short story writer

Francis Bret Harte. He wrote humorous verse, and tales of the California Gold Rush, collected in The Luck of the Roaring Camp and Other Stories *(1922). He was the founder (1868) and Editor of the* Overland Monthly.

1 If, of all words of tongue and pen,
The saddest are, 'It might have been,'
More sad are these we daily see:
'It is, but hadn't ought to be!'
'Mrs Judge Jenkins', publ. in *East and West Poems* (1871)

2 Which I wish to remark,
And my language is plain,
That for ways that are dark
And for tricks that are vain,

The heathen Chinee is peculiar,
Which the same I would rise to explain.
'Plain Language from Truthful James', publ. in *Poems* (1871)

3 And he smiled a kind of sickly smile, and curled up on the floor,
And the subsequent proceedings interested him no more.
'The Society Upon the Stanislaus', st. 7, ibid.

L. P. Hartley
(1895–1972)
British author

Leslie Poles Hartley. His novels typically portray psychological relationships among the middle classes, often with a sinister slant.

1 The past is a foreign country; they do things differently there.
The Go-Between, Prologue (1953, filmed 1971). Opening sentence.

Minnie Louise Haskins
(1875–1957)
British academic, author and poet

She taught at the London School of Economics (1919–44) and published several volumes of poetry.

1 And I said to the man who stood at the gate of the year:
'Give me a light that I may tread safely into the unknown.'
And he replied:
'Go out into the darkness and put your hand into the Hand of God.
That shall be to you better than light and safer than a known way.'
'The Gate of the Year', publ. in *The Desert* (1908). The poem was made popular by GEORGE VI in his Christmas broadcast of 1939 and was read at the funeral of ELIZABETH, THE QUEEN MOTHER in 2002.

Roy Hattersley
(b. 1932)
British politician

Baron Hattersley of Sparkbrook. Elected a Labour MP in 1964, he held ministerial office in the CALLAGHAN government and was later Deputy Leader of the Labour Party (1983–92). He has also published novels, biographies and memoirs.

1 Morality and expediency coincide more than the cynics allow.
Guardian 30 September 1988

2 In politics, being ridiculous is more damaging than being extreme.
Evening Standard 9 May 1989. Hattersley himself was harshly lampooned in the television puppet satire, *Spitting Image*.

3 The proposition that Muslims are welcome in Britain if, and only if, they stop behaving like Muslims is a doctrine which is incompatible with the principles that guide a free society.
Independent 21 July 1989

Charles Haughey
(1925–2006)
Irish statesman

He was elected a Fianna Fáil MP in 1957 and dismissed from Jack Lynch's government in 1970 for allegedly importing guns for the IRA, although subsequently acquitted. He was Prime Minister 1979–81, 1982 and 1987–92.

1 Ireland is where strange tales begin and happy endings are possible.
Daily Telegraph 14 July 1988

Václav Havel
(b. 1936)
Czech playwright and president

His dissidence, expressed in his plays and his support for Charter 77, resulted in two terms of imprisonment (1979–83 and 1989). Following the Velvet Revolution of 1989, he was elected President of Czechoslovakia and was President of the independent Czech Republic 1993–2003.

1 You do not become a 'dissident' just because you decide one day to take up this most unusual career . . . It begins as an attempt to do your work well, and ends with being branded an enemy of society.
'The Power of the Powerless', sect. 14 (1978), repr. in *Living in Truth*, pt 1 (1986)

2 There are times when we must sink to the bottom of our misery to understand truth, just as we must descend to the bottom of a well to see the stars in broad daylight.
'The Power of the Powerless', sect. 16, ibid.

3 I think theatre should always be somewhat suspect.
Disturbing the Peace, ch. 2 (1986, transl. 1990)

4 Hope is definitely not the same thing as opti-

mism. It is not the conviction that something will turn out well, but the certainty that something makes sense, regardless of how it turns out.

Ibid., ch. 5

5 The cliché organizes life; it expropriates people's identity; it becomes ruler, defence lawyer, judge, and the law.

Ibid., ch. 5

6 I really do inhabit a system in which words are capable of shaking the entire structure of government, where words can prove mightier than ten military divisions.

Speech, October 1989, quoted in the *Independent* 9 December 1989. On accepting a peace prize in Germany.

7 We are finding out that what looked like a neglected house a year ago is in fact a ruin.

Quoted in the *Daily Telegraph* 3 January 1991. Referring to the state of Czechoslovakia and other ex-Soviet Bloc countries.

R. S. Hawker
(1803–75)
English clergyman and poet

Robert Stephen Hawker. Eccentric in habits and lifestyle, he was the vicar of Morwenstowe in Cornwall (1834–74) and introduced the custom of Harvest Festival.

1 And shall Trelawny live?
And shall Trelawny die?
Here's twenty thousand Cornish men
Will know the reason why!

'The Song of the Western Men' (1825). Cornwall's unofficial anthem recalls Trelawny, Bishop of Bristol, one of seven bishops imprisoned in the Tower of London by James II in 1688.

Jacquetta Hawkes
(1910–96)
British archaeologist and author

She carried out excavations in Britain, France and Palestine and was Secretary to the UK Commission for UNESCO (1943–9). She was married to J. B. PRIESTLEY.

1 The only inequalities that matter begin in the mind. It is not income levels but differences in mental equipment that keep people apart, breed feelings of inferiority.

New Statesman January 1957

Stephen Hawking
(b. 1942)
British theoretical physicist

His work on quantum mechanics, black holes and the big bang theory of the universe was partially elucidated in his surprise bestseller A Brief History of Time *(1988). He has been severely disabled by motor neurone disease since the 1960s.*

1 God not only plays dice. He also sometimes throws the dice where they cannot be seen.

Nature, vol. 257 (1975). See ALBERT EINSTEIN 4.

2 In effect, we have redefined the task of science to be the discovery of laws that will enable us to predict events up to the limits set by the uncertainty principle.

A Brief History of Time, ch. 11 (1988)

3 If we find the answer to that, it would be the ultimate triumph of human reason – for then we would know the mind of God.

Ibid., ch. 11. Closing words of book, referring to the question 'why it is that we and the universe exist'.

Nathaniel Hawthorne
(1804–64)
US author

His New England Puritan background is manifest in his fiction, such as The Scarlet Letter *(1850) and* The House of Seven Gables *(1851).* Tanglewood Tales *(1853) was written for children. See* HENRY JAMES 19.

1 In the depths of every heart, there is a tomb and a dungeon, though the lights, the music, and revelry above may cause us to forget their existence, and the buried ones, or prisoners whom they hide. But sometimes, and oftenest at midnight, those dark receptacles are flung wide open.

'The Haunted Mind' (1835), repr. in *Twice-Told Tales* (1842)

2 We sometimes congratulate ourselves at the moment of waking from a troubled dream; it may be so the moment after death.

Journal entry, 25 October 1836, publ. in *Passages from the American Notebooks* (1868)

3 Moonlight is sculpture, sunlight is painting.

Journal entry, 24 October 1838, ibid.

4 The founders of a new colony, whatever Utopia of human virtue and happiness they might originally project, have invariably recognized it among their earliest practical necessities to allot a portion of the

virgin soil as a cemetery, and another portion as the site of a prison.
The Scarlet Letter, ch. 1 (1850)

5 The scarlet letter was her passport into regions where other women dared not tread. Shame, Despair, Solitude! These had been her teachers, – stern and wild ones, – and they had made her strong, but taught her much amiss.
Ibid., ch. 18. Referring to the scarlet letter 'A' (standing for Adulteress), on Hester Prynne's gown, 'in fine red cloth, surrounded with an elaborate embroidery and fantastic flourishes of gold thread'.

6 We must not always talk in the market-place of what happens to us in the forest.
Hester Prynne, ibid., ch. 22

7 Life is made up of marble and mud.
The House of the Seven Gables, ch. 2 (1851)

8 The greatest obstacle to being heroic is the doubt whether one may not be going to prove one's self a fool; the truest heroism is to resist the doubt; and the profoundest wisdom, to know when it ought to be resisted, and when to be obeyed.
The Blithedale Romance, ch. 2 (1852)

9 A woman's chastity consists, like an onion, of a series of coats.
Journal entry, 16 March 1854, publ. in *English Notebooks* (1870)

10 Nobody has any conscience about adding to the improbabilities of a marvelous tale.
The Marble Faun, ch. 4 (1860)

11 Dr Johnson's morality was as English an article as a beefsteak.
Our Old Home, 'Lichfield and Uttoxeter' (1863)

Ian Hay
(1876–1952)
British playwright and novelist

Originally John Hay Beith. He is remembered chiefly for his novel The First Hundred Thousand *(1915), and adapted several of his own books as plays.*

1 War is hell and all that, but it has a good deal to recommend it. It wipes out all the small nuisances of peace-time.
The First Hundred Thousand, ch. 10 (1915). Spoken by Wagstaffe. Among the 'small nuisances' he listed were suffragettes, futurism, the tango, party politics and golf-maniacs.

2 What do you mean, funny? Funny-peculiar or funny ha-ha?
The Housemaster, Act 3 (1938)

Franz Joseph Haydn
(1732–1809)
Austrian composer

He was a teacher of MOZART *and* BEETHOVEN, *and Director of Music for Prince Esterházy from 1761. His output, in the classical style, included symphonies, chamber music, concertos, and oratorios such as* The Creation *(1798).*

1 My language is understood all over the world.
Quoted in *Haydn*, 'Mozart' (ed. David Wyn Jones, 2002). Reply on being advised by MOZART not to visit England because he couldn't speak the language.

Benjamin Robert Haydon
(1786–1846)
British artist

He was a painter of historical, biblical and classical subjects, but achieved greater fame for his part in the acquisition of the Elgin Marbles in 1816, and for his journals and Autobiography *(1847).*

1 Men who have reached and passed forty-five, have a look as if waiting for the secret of the other world, and as if they were perfectly sure of having found out the secret of this.
'Table Talk', publ. in *Correspondence and Table-Talk*, vol. 2 (ed. Frederic Wordsworth Haydon, 1876)

2 The explanation of the propensity of the English people to portrait painting is to be found in their relish for a fact. Let a man do the grandest things, fight the greatest battles, or be distinguished by the most brilliant personal heroism, yet the English people would prefer his portrait to a painting of the great deed. The likeness they can judge of; his existence is a fact. But the truth of the picture of his deeds they cannot judge of, for they have no imagination.
'Table Talk', ibid.

3 The only legitimate artists in England are the architects.
'Table Talk', ibid.

4 This is an age of intellectual sauces, of essence, of distillation. We have 'conclusions' without deductions, 'abridgments of history' and 'abridgments of science' without leading facts. We have 'animals' for literature, 'cabinet' encyclopaedias, 'family' lib-

raries, 'diffusion' societies, and heaven knows what else! What is all this for? Not to add knowledge to the learned, but to tell points to the ignorant, without giving them the trouble to acquire the links.
'Table Talk', ibid.

Friedrich August von Hayek
(1899–1992)
Austrian-born British economist

Called the 'father of monetarism', he was a strong critic of Keynesian theory and directly opposed to government intervention in a free market. He was Professor of Economic Science at London (1931–50).

1 Planning and competition can be combined only by planning for competition, but not by planning against competition.
The Road to Serfdom, ch. 3 (1944)

2 The system of private property is the most important guarantee of freedom, not only for those who own property, but scarcely less for those who do not.
Ibid., ch. 8

J. Milton Hayes
(1884–1940)
English actor and poet

John Milton Hayes. He wrote and performed dramatic monologues, most famously the much-parodied 'The Green Eye of the Yellow God' (1911).

1 There's a one-eyed yellow idol to the north of Khatmandu,
There's a little marble cross below the town,
There's a broken-hearted woman tends the grave of Mad Carew,
And the Yellow God forever gazes down.
'The Green Eye of the Yellow God' (1911)

Rutherford B. Hayes
(1822–93)
US president

Rutherford Birchard Hayes. A Republican, he served as President 1877–81, overseeing the end of Reconstruction.

1 He serves his party best who serves his country best.
Inaugural address, 5 March 1877, publ. in *Inaugural Addresses of the Presidents of the United States* (1974)

William Hazlitt
(1778–1830)
English essayist and critic

Controversial and epigrammatic in style, he contributed articles on literary criticism and other subjects to the Edinburgh Review *(1814–20). His essays are collected in* Table Talk *(1821–2) and* The Plain Speaker *(1826).*

1 We are the creatures of imagination, passion, and self-will, more than of reason or even of self-interest ... Even in the common transactions and daily intercourse of life, we are governed by whim, caprice, prejudice, or accident. The falling of a teacup puts us out of temper for the day; and a quarrel that commenced about the pattern of a gown may end only with our lives.
'On the Predominant Principles and Excitements in the Human Mind' (1815), repr. in *Collected Works*, vol. 11 (ed. A. R. Waller and Arnold Glover, 1904)

2 Comedy naturally wears itself out – destroys the very food on which it lives; and by constantly and successfully exposing the follies and weaknesses of mankind to ridicule, in the end leaves itself nothing worth laughing at.
The Round Table, 'On Modern Comedy' (1817)

3 The art of pleasing consists in being pleased.
Ibid., 'On Manner'

4 There is no prejudice so strong as that which arises from a fancied exemption from all prejudice.
Ibid., 'On the Tendency of Sects'

5 There is nothing good to be had in the country, or if there is, they will not let you have it.
Ibid., 'Observations on Mr Wordsworth's *Excursion*'

6 He is to the great poet, what an excellent mimic is to a great actor. There is no determinate impression left on the mind by reading his poetry ... A great mind is one that moulds the minds of others.
Lectures on the English Poets, 'On the Living Poets' (1818). Of WALTER SCOTT.

7 He talked on for ever; and you wished him to talk on for ever.
Ibid., 'On the Living Poets'. Referring to SAMUEL TAYLOR COLERIDGE, who was the first poet Hazlitt had ever known, and produced an unforgettable effect on him: 'His thoughts did not seem to come with labour and effort; but as if borne on gusts of genius, and as if the wings of his imagination lifted him off from his feet ... His mind was clothed with wings; and raised on them, he lifted philosophy to heaven.'

8 Man is the only animal that laughs and weeps;

for he is the only animal that is struck with the difference between what things are and what they ought to be.

Lectures on the English Comic Writers, Lecture 1 ('On Wit and Humour') (1819). This passage was copied and inserted in the notebooks of ADLAI STEVENSON.

9 Wit is the salt of conversation, not the food.

Ibid., Lecture 1

10 The love of liberty is the love of others; the love of power is the love of ourselves.

Political Essays, 'The Times Newspaper' (1819)

11 The most sensible people to be met with in society are men of business and of the world, who argue from what they see and know, instead of spinning cobweb distinctions of what things ought to be.

Table Talk, vol. 1, 'On the Ignorance of the Learned' (1821)

12 If we wish to know the force of human genius, we should read Shakespeare. If we wish to see the insignificance of human learning, we may study his commentators.

Ibid., vol. 1, 'On the Ignorance of the Learned'

13 There is not a more mean, stupid, dastardly, pitiful, selfish, spiteful, envious, ungrateful animal than the public. It is the greatest of cowards, for it is afraid of itself.

Ibid., vol. 1, 'On Living to One's Self'

14 The soul of a journey is liberty, perfect liberty, to think, feel, do just as one pleases.

Ibid., vol. 2, 'On Going a Journey' (1822)

15 Give me the clear blue sky over my head, and the green turf beneath my feet, a winding road before me, and a three hours' march to dinner – and then to thinking!

Ibid., vol. 2, 'On Going a Journey'

16 The English (it must be owned) are rather a foul-mouthed nation.

Ibid., vol. 2, 'On Criticism'

17 Modesty is the lowest of the virtues, and is a real confession of the deficiency it indicates. He who undervalues himself is justly undervalued by others.

Ibid., vol. 2, 'On the Knowledge of Character'

18 We find many things to which the prohibition of them constitutes the only temptation.

Characteristics: In the Manner of Rochefoucault's Maxims, no. 140 (1823)

19 To think ill of mankind and not wish ill to them, is perhaps the highest wisdom and virtue.

Ibid., no. 241

20 Every man, in his own opinion, forms an exception to the ordinary rules of morality.

Ibid., no. 305

21 To be remembered after we are dead, is but poor recompense for being treated with contempt while we are living.

Ibid., no. 429

22 The present is an age of talkers, and not of doers; and the reason is, that the world is growing old. We are so far advanced in the arts and sciences, that we live in retrospect, and dote on past achievement.

The Spirit of the Age, 'Mr Coleridge' (1825)

23 He writes as fast as they can read, and he does not write himself down . . . His worst is better than any other person's best . . . His works (taken together) are almost like a new edition of human nature. This is indeed to be an author!

Ibid., 'Sir Walter Scott'. Of WALTER SCOTT.

24 Death cancels everything but truth; and strips a man of everything but genius and virtue. It is a sort of natural canonization. It makes the meanest of us sacred – it installs the poet in his immortality, and lifts him to the skies.

Ibid., 'Lord Byron'. Referring to the death of BYRON.

25 Mr Wordsworth's genius is a pure emanation of the Spirit of the Age. Had he lived in any other period of the world, he would never have been heard of.

Ibid., 'Mr Wordsworth'

26 He indeed cloys with sweetness; he obscures with splendour; he fatigues with gaiety. We are stifled on beds of roses.

Ibid., 'Mr T. Moore – Mr Leigh Hunt'. Referring to THOMAS MOORE.

27 We are not hypocrites in our sleep.

The Plain Speaker, 'On Dreams' (1826)

28 The dupe of friendship, and the fool of love; have I not reason to hate and to despise myself? Indeed I do; and chiefly for not having hated and despised the world enough.

Ibid., 'On the Pleasure of Hating'

29 His sayings are generally like women's letters; all the pith is in the postscript.
Conversations of James Northcote (1826–7). Referring to CHARLES LAMB.

30 The least pain in our little finger gives us more concern and uneasiness than the destruction of millions of our fellow-beings.
'American Literature – Dr Channing' (1829), repr. in *Complete Works*, vol. 16 (ed. P. P. Howe, 1932)

31 When a thing ceases to be a subject of controversy, it ceases to be a subject of interest.
'The Spirit of Controversy' (1830), ibid., vol. 20

32 So have I loitered my life away, reading books, looking at pictures, going to plays, hearing, thinking, writing on what pleased me best. I have wanted only one thing to make me happy, but wanting that have wanted everything.
Literary Remains, 'My First Acquaintance with Poets' (1836)

33 Without the aid of prejudice and custom, I should not be able to find my way across the room.
Sketches and Essays, 'On Prejudice' (1839)

34 There is an unseemly exposure of the mind, as well as of the body.
Ibid., 'On Disagreeable People'. See also FRANCIS BACON 13.

35 A nickname is the heaviest stone that the devil can throw at a man. It is a bugbear to the imagination, and, though we do not believe in it, it still haunts our apprehensions.
Ibid., 'On Nicknames'

Denis Healey
(b. 1917)
British politician

Baron Healey of Riddlesden. Elected a Labour MP in 1952, he went on to become Minister of Defence (1964–70), Chancellor of the Exchequer (1974–9) and Deputy Leader (1980–3).

1 His speech was rather like being savaged by a dead sheep.
Speech to House of Commons, 14 June 1978, publ. in *Hansard*, col. 1027. Referring to a criticism of Healey's Budget proposals by Shadow Chancellor GEOFFREY HOWE. According to Healey's memoirs (*The Time of My Life*, pt 3, ch. 21, 1989), this off-the-cuff remark was inspired by WINSTON CHURCHILL's comment that an attack by Labour politician CLEMENT ATTLEE was 'like being savaged by a pet lamb'. In 1983, after being congratulated by Healey on his appointment as Foreign Secretary, Howe commented that it was 'like being nuzzled by an old ram'. Healey's rejoinder: 'It would be the end of a beautiful friendship if he accused me of necrophilia.'

2 Mrs Thatcher has added the diplomacy of Alf Garnett to the economics of Arthur Daley.
Quoted in the *Observer* 31 December 1989

Seamus Heaney
(b. 1939)
Irish poet

With its allusion to Irish tradition and myth, his lyrical poetry expresses a close relationship with the land, as in his first collection, Death of a Naturalist *(1966), and also addresses the political situation in Ireland, as in* North *(1975).* GAVIN EWART *saluted him in a poem: 'He's very popular among his mates,/ I think I'm Auden, he thinks he's Yeats.'*

1 Between my finger and my thumb
The squat pen rests.
I'll dig with it.
'Digging', publ. in *Death of a Naturalist* (1966). Closing words of poem.

2 The ground itself is kind, black butter
Melting and opening underfoot,
Missing its last definition
By millions of years.
'Bogland', publ. in *Door into the Dark* (1969)

3 Who would connive
in civilised outrage
yet understand the exact
and tribal, intimate revenge.
'Punishment', publ. in *North*, pt 1 (1975)

4 The famous
Northern reticence, the tight gag of place
And times: yes, yes. Of the 'wee six' I sing
Where to be saved you only must save face
And whatever you say, you say nothing.
'Whatever You Say Say Nothing', ibid., pt 2

5 Elderberry? It is shires dreaming wine.
'Glanmore Sonnets', publ. in *Field Work* (1979)

6 Don't be surprised
If I demur, for, be advised
My passport's green.
No glass of ours was ever raised
To toast The Queen.
'An Open Letter to Blake and Andrew' (1983). The poem is addressed to Blake Morrison and ANDREW MOTION, editors of *The Penguin Book of Contemporary British Poetry* (1982), who included him in the anthology.

7 Everywhere being nowhere,
who can prove

one place more than another?
'Birthplace', publ. in *Station Island*, pt 1 (1984)

8 We are earthworms of the earth, and all that
has gone through us is what will be our trace.
'Station Island', ibid., pt 2

9 Passive
Suffering makes the world go round.
Peace on earth, men of good will, all that
Holds good as long as the balance holds,
The scales ride steady and the angels' strain
Prolongs itself at an unearthly pitch.
'Weighing In', publ. in *Spirit Level* (1996)

10 Generations of gifted northern poets have let the
linguistic cat out of the sectarian bag, setting it free
in the great street carnival of 'protholics and cate-
stants'.
Quoted in the *Observer* 12 April 1998

(Sir) Edward Heath
(1916–2005)
British politician and prime minister

*A keen sailor and accomplished musician, he entered Parlia-
ment as a Conservative MP in 1950, and as Prime Minister
(1970–4) took Britain into the Common Market.* JONATHAN
AITKEN *called him 'a peddler of dreams from Broadstairs-les-
deux-Eglises'.*

1 When the people said 'the miners won a great
victory' or 'the Government lost that one', what did
they mean? In the country we live in, there could
not be any 'we' or 'they'. There was only 'us' – all of
us. If the Government is defeated then the country
is defeated.
Comment, February 1972, quoted in *Edward Heath*, pt 4, ch. 21
(1993) by John Campbell. Spoken after the settlement of the
miners' strike.

2 The unpleasant and unacceptable face of capitalism.
Speech to House of Commons, 15 May 1973, publ. in *Hansard*,
col. 1243. Referring to the 'Lonrho affair', in which Duncan
Sandys, a non-executive director of the company and Conservative MP, was paid £130,000 compensation via an off-
shore account during a period of deep recession. The resulting
enquiry led to legislation requiring companies to disclose
payments and MPs to register their private interests.

3 We are the trades union for the pensioners and
for children; we are the union for the disabled and
the sick; we are the union for those who live in
slums or for those who want to buy homes. We are
the union for the unemployed and the low paid. We
are the union for those in poverty and for the hard
pressed ... We are the union for the nation as a
whole.
Election campaign speech, Manchester, 20 February 1974,
quoted in *The Times* 21 February 1974. Referring to the Conservative Party.

4 We cannot live permanently by taking in each
other's washing.
Quoted in *Edward Heath*, pt 6, ch. 36 (1993) by John Campbell.
An often-repeated remark during the 1980s. Heath was concerned at the loss of Britain's manufacturing capacity, scorning the idea of a service economy.

Ben Hecht
(1894–1964)
US journalist, author and screenwriter

*He was the writer of (and uncredited collaborator in) numer-
ous screenplays, among them* The Scoundrel *(1935) and*
Notorious *(1946).*

1 Movies are one of the bad habits that corrupted
our century. Of their many sins, I offer as the worst
their effect on the intellectual side of the nation. It
is chiefly from that viewpoint I write of them – as
an eruption of trash that has lamed the American
mind and retarded Americans from becoming a cultured people.
A Child of the Century, bk 5 'What the Movies Are' (1954).
Hecht continued, 'They have slapped into the American mind
more human misinformation in one evening than the Dark
Ages could muster in a decade.'

Georg Hegel
(1770–1831)
German philosopher

*Georg Willhelm Friedrich Hegel. An idealist philosopher, he set
out his threefold system of logic, philosophy of nature and
mind in* Science of Logic *(1812–16). He also wrote on religion
and history and was a key influence on* KARL MARX.

1 What is rational is actual and what is actual is
rational.
The Philosophy of Right, Preface (1821)

2 When philosophy paints its grey on grey, then
has a shape of life grown old. By philosophy's grey
on grey it cannot be rejuvenated but only understood. The owl of Minerva spreads its wings only
with the falling of the dusk.
Ibid., Preface. See GOETHE 26.

3 An idea is always a generalization, and generaliz-

ation is a property of thinking. To generalize means to think.
Ibid., Introduction, Addition 4

4 Truth in philosophy means that concept and external reality correspond.
Ibid., Introduction, Addition 16

5 Education is the art of making man ethical.
Ibid., pt 3, Addition 97

6 The learner always begins by finding fault, but the scholar sees the positive merit in everything.
Ibid., pt 3, 'The State', Addition 160

7 As high as mind stands above nature, so high does the state stand above physical life. Man must therefore venerate the state as a secular deity ... The march of God in the world, that is what the State is.
Ibid., pt 3, 'The State', Addition 164

8 The true courage of civilized nations is readiness for sacrifice in the service of the state, so that the individual counts as only one amongst many. The important thing here is not personal mettle but aligning oneself with the universal.
Ibid., pt 3, 'The State', Addition 189

9 World history is a court of judgment.
Ibid., pt 3, 'The State', sect. 3, para. 341. See FRIEDRICH SCHILLER 5.

10 But what experience and history teach is this – that peoples and governments have never learned anything from history, or acted on principles deduced from it.
The Philosophy of History, Introduction (1837)

11 Amid the pressure of great events, a general principle gives no help.
Ibid., Introduction

12 To him who looks upon the world rationally, the world in its turn presents a rational aspect. The relation is mutual.
Ibid., Introduction

13 'No man is a hero to his valet-de-chambre,' ... I have added ... 'but not because the former is no hero, but because the latter is a valet.'
Ibid., Introduction. See also MADAME DE CORNUEL 1.

14 America is, therefore the land of the future, where, in the ages that lie before us, the burden of the world's history shall reveal itself ... It is a land

of desire for all those who are weary of the historical lumber-room of Old Europe.
Ibid., Introduction, 'Geographical Basis of History'

Martin Heidegger
(1889–1976)
German philosopher

His standing largely rests on his incomplete work Being and Time *(1927), an analysis of human existence and death. He was a key influence on* SARTRE, *though his Nazi sympathies damaged his reputation.*

1 Man acts as though *he* were the shaper and master of language, while in fact *language* remains the master of man.
'Building Dwelling Thinking', lecture, 5 August 1951, publ. in *Poetry, Language, Thought* (1971)

2 The German language 'speaks Being', while all the others merely 'speak of Being'.
Quoted in Prologue to *An Appetite for Poetry: Essays in Literary Interpretation* (1989) by Frank Kermode

Piet Hein
(1905–96)
Danish inventor and poet

Writing as Kumbel, he is known for the grook (gruk in Danish), a short aphoristic form expressing serious concerns through humour. He translated many into English.

1 The human spirit sublimates
the impulses it thwarts:
a healthy sex life mitigates
the lust for other sports.
'Hint and Suggestion', publ. in *Grooks* (1966)

2 The road to wisdom? – Well, it's plain
and simple to express:
Err
and err
and err again
but less
and less
and less.
'The Road to Wisdom', ibid.

Heinrich Heine
(1797–1856)
German poet and journalist

He is known for his lyric poetry, notably Book of Songs *(1827), much of which was set to music by Schubert and Schumann, among others. His work assumed political overtones after he moved to Paris in 1830.*

1 *Ich weiss nicht, was soll es bedeuten,*
Dass ich so traurig bin;
Ein Märchen aus alten Zeiten,
Das kommt mir nicht aus dem Sinn.
[In vain would I seek to discover
Why sad and mournful am I
My thoughts without ceasing brood over
A tale of the time gone by.]
'Die Lorelei', publ. in *Buch der Lieder* (*Book of Songs*, 1827)

2 Wherever books are burned, men also, in the end, will be burned.
Almansor, l. 245 (1823)

3 *Auf Flügeln des Gesanges.*
[On Wings of Song.]
Title of poem, publ. in *Lyrisches Intermezzo* (1823). The words were set to music by Mendelssohn in 1833.

4 In action, the English have the advantage enjoyed by free men always entitled to free discussion: of having a ready judgment on every question. We Germans, on the other hand, are always thinking. We think so much that we never form a judgment.
French Affairs, 'The English Freedom' (1832)

5 People in those old times had convictions; we moderns only have opinions. And it needs more than a mere opinion to erect a Gothic cathedral.
The French Stage, ch. 9 (1837)

6 The foolish race of mankind
Are swarming below in the night;
They shriek and rage and quarrel –
And all of them are right.
'Katharina', sect. 4, publ. in *New Poems* (1844)

7 Of course God will forgive me; that's His job.
Quoted in journal entry, 23 February 1863, in *The Goncourt Journals*, vol. 1 (1888) by EDMOND AND JULES DE GONCOURT. Heine's deathbed remark was in reply to a priest who had told him God would forgive his sins. SIGMUND FREUD commented on this: 'The force of the joke lies in its purpose. What it means to say is nothing else than: "Of course he'll forgive me. That's what he's there for, and that's the only reason I've taken him on (as one engages one's doctor or one's lawyer)." So in the dying man, as he lay there powerless, a consciousness stirred that he had created God and equipped him with power so as to make use of him when the occasion arose. What was supposed to be the created being revealed itself just before its annihilation as the creator.' (*Jokes and their Relation to the Unconscious*, 'The Purposes of Jokes', 1905)

8 Whatever tears one may shed, in the end one always blows one's nose.
Quoted in *Memoirs of a Dutiful Daughter*, bk 3 (1958) by SIMONE DE BEAUVOIR

9 No author is a man of genius to his publisher.
Attributed

Werner Heisenberg
(1901–76)
German physicist

He developed a matrix-based system of quantum mechanics, for which he won the 1932 Nobel Prize for physics.

1 An expert is someone who knows some of the worst mistakes that can be made in his subject and who manages to avoid them.
Physics and Beyond, ch. 17 (1969)

Joseph Heller
(1923–99)
US novelist

Drawing on his experience in the Second World War, he produced his bestselling satirical novel Catch-22 *(1961). Other works include the more experimental* Something Happened *(1974) and* God Knows *(1984).*

1 Death to all modifiers.
Catch-22, ch. 1 (1961). Spoken by Yossarian.

2 He had decided to live for ever or die in the attempt.
Ibid., ch. 3. Of Yossarian.

3 He was a self-made man who owed his lack of success to nobody.
Ibid., ch. 3. Referring to Colonel Cargill.

4 There's a rule saying I have to ground anyone who's crazy ... There's a catch. Catch-22. Anyone who wants to get out of combat duty isn't really crazy.
Doc Daneeka, ibid., ch. 5. The narrator explains: 'Orr was crazy and could be grounded. All he had to do was ask; and as soon as he did, he would no longer be crazy and would have to fly more missions.'

5 Some men are born mediocre, some men achieve mediocrity, and some men have mediocrity thrust upon them. With Major Major it had been all three.
Ibid., ch. 9. A reworking of lines from *Twelfth Night*: see SHAKESPEARE: TWELFTH NIGHT 25.

6 It's a wise person, I guess, who knows he's dumb, and an honest person who knows he's a liar. And

it's a dumb person, I guess, who's convinced he is wise.

Something Happened, 'The office in which I work' (1974). Narrated by Bob Slocum.

Lillian Hellman
(1905–84)
US playwright

The leading woman playwright of her generation and a left-wing activist, she dealt with political and social issues in such plays as The Children's Hour *(1934) and* The Little Foxes *(1939).* See MARY MCCARTHY 9.

1 Cynicism is an unpleasant way of saying the truth.
The Little Foxes, Act 1 (1939). Spoken by Ben.

2 It's an indulgence to sit in a room and discuss your beliefs as if they were a juicy piece of gossip.
Watch on the Rhine, Act 2 (1941). Spoken by Sara Müller.

3 I cannot and will not cut my conscience to fit this year's fashions.
Letter to John S. Wood, Chairman of the House un-American Activities Committee, 19 May 1952, quoted in the *Nation* 31 May 1952. The letter contained Hellman's refusal to testify against colleagues accused of Communist affiliations.

4 People change and forget to tell each other. Too bad – causes so many mistakes.
Toys in the Attic, Act 3 (1960). Spoken by Anna.

5 Intellectuals can tell themselves anything, sell themselves any bill of goods, which is why they were so often patsies for the ruling classes in nineteenth-century France and England, or twentieth-century Russia and America.
Journal entry, 30 April 1967, publ. in *An Unfinished Woman*, ch. 13 (memoir, 1969)

6 It is a mark of many famous people that they cannot part with their brightest hour: what worked once must always work.
Pentimento, 'Theatre' (1973). Referring to TALLULAH BANK-HEAD, who 'had been the nineteen-twenties' most daring girl, but what had been dashing, even brave, had become by 1939 shrill and tiring'.

Leona Helmsley
(b. 1920)
US businesswoman

Dubbed 'the Queen of Mean' by the tabloids, she was sentenced in 1992 to four years in prison, 750 hours of community service and $7.1 million in fines for tax evasion. In 1998 she was left a second fortune by her husband.

1 We don't pay taxes. Only the little people pay taxes.
Quoted in the *New York Times* 12 July 1989. The words were reported by Helmsley's former housekeeper during her employer's trial for tax evasion.

Héloïse
(c. 1098–1164)
French abbess

She had a child by the theologian Peter Abelard, who consequently suffered castration by her family. He joined a Benedictine monastery and she became the Abbess of the Paraclete, which Abelard had previously founded.

1 The name of wife may seem more sacred or more binding, but sweeter for me will always be the word mistress, or, if you will permit me, that of concubine or whore.
Letter to Peter Abelard, *c.* 1132, publ. in *The Letters of Abelard and Héloïse*, Letter 1 (ed. Betty Radice, 1974)

Felicia Hemans
(1793–1835)
English poet

A prolific poet, she also wrote plays and translated poems from the Welsh. Her popularity waned in the 20th century.

1 The stately homes of England,
How beautiful they stand!
Amidst their tall ancestral trees,
O'er all the pleasant land.
'The Homes of England' (1827), repr. in *Felicia Hemans: Selected Poems, Prose, and Letters* (ed. Gary Kelly, 2002). See NOEL COWARD 13, QUENTIN CRISP 6.

2 The boy stood on the burning deck
Whence all but he had fled;
The flame that lit the battle's wreck
Shone round him o'er the dead.
'Casabianca' (1829), ibid. Relating the tale of the young son of the French Commander Louis de Casabianca, who refused to leave his father's ship *L'Orient* during the Battle of the Nile in 1798, and lost his life as a result.

Ernest Hemingway
(1899–1961)
US author

Themes of honour and masculinity recur in his fiction. His novels include A Farewell to Arms *(1929),* For Whom the Bell Tolls *(1940) and* The Old Man and the Sea *(1952). He took his own life with a shotgun. 'Hemingway's words strike you, each one, as if they were pebbles fetched fresh from a brook,' wrote Ford Madox Ford.*

1 The age demanded that we dance
And jammed us into iron pants.
And in the end the age was handed
The sort of shit that it demanded.
'The Age Demanded' (1925), repr. in *Sylvia Beach and the Lost Generation*, ch. 9 (1983) by Noel Riley Fitch

2 You're an expatriate. You've lost touch with the soil. You get precious. Fake European standards have ruined you. You drink yourself to death. You become obsessed by sex. You spend all your time talking, not working. You are an expatriate, see? You hang around cafés.
The Sun Also Rises, bk 2, ch. 12 (1926, filmed 1957). Bill Gorton to Jake Barnes, who replies: 'It sounds like a swell life.'

3 In the fall the war was always there but we did not go to it any more.
Men Without Women, 'In Another Country' (1927). F. SCOTT FITZGERALD praised this as 'one of the most beautiful prose sentences I've ever read'.

4 I was always embarrassed by the words sacred, glorious and sacrifice and the expression in vain. We had heard them, sometimes standing in the rain almost out of earshot, so that only the shouted words came through, and had read them, on proclamations that were slapped up by billposters over other proclamations, now for a long time, and I had seen nothing sacred, and the things that were glorious had no glory and the sacrifices were like the stockyards at Chicago if nothing was done with the meat except to bury it.
A Farewell to Arms, ch. 27 (1929, filmed 1932 and 1957). Spoken by Frederic Henry.

5 Grace under pressure.
Interview by DOROTHY PARKER in the *New Yorker* 30 November 1929. Defining 'guts'. The words, which may have originated in the Latin motto, *Fortiter in re, suaviter in modo* ('strong in deed, gentle in manner'), were invoked by JOHN F. KENNEDY at the start of his collection of essays, *Profiles of Courage* (1956).

6 Eschew the monumental. Shun the Epic. All the guys who can paint great big pictures can paint great small ones.
Letter 5–6 January 1932, publ. in *Selected Letters* (ed. Carlos Baker, 1981)

7 About morals, I know only that what is moral is

what you feel good after and what is immoral is what you feel bad after.
Death in the Afternoon, ch. 1 (1932)

8 All our words from loose using have lost their edge.
Ibid., ch. 7

9 Bullfighting is the only art in which the artist is in danger of death and in which the degree of brilliance in the performance is left to the fighter's honor.
Ibid., ch. 9

10 Madame, all stories, if continued far enough, end in death, and he is no true-story teller who would keep that from you.
Ibid., ch. 11

11 A serious writer is not to be confounded with a solemn writer. A serious writer may be a hawk or a buzzard or even a popinjay, but a solemn writer is always a bloody owl.
Ibid., ch. 16

12 All good books are alike in that they are truer than if they had really happened and after you are finished reading one you will feel that all that happened to you and afterwards it all belongs to you; the good and the bad, the ecstasy, the remorse, and sorrow, the people and the places and how the weather was.
'Old Newsman Writes: A Letter from Cuba' (1934), repr. in *By-Line Ernest Hemingway* (ed. William White, 1967)

13 All modern American literature comes from one book by Mark Twain called *Huckleberry Finn* ... American writing comes from that. There was nothing before. There has been nothing as good since.
The Green Hills of Africa, ch. 1 (1935)

14 The rich were dull and they drank too much or they played too much backgammon. They were dull and they were repetitious. He remembered poor Julian and his romantic awe of them and how he had started a story once that began, 'The very rich are different from you and me.' And how someone had said to Julian, 'Yes, they have more money.'
'The Snows of Kilimanjaro' (1936), repr. in *The Fifth Column and the First Forty-Nine Stories* (1938). In its original publication, 'Julian' was named as F. Scott Fitzgerald, who in 1926 had opened a story 'Let me tell you about the very rich. They are different from you and me.' See F. SCOTT FITZGERALD 13.

15 But did thee feel the earth move?
For Whom the Bell Tolls, ch. 13 (1940). Robert Jordan speaking

to Maria. During their lovemaking, Jordan had 'felt the earth move out and away from under them'. The words do not appear in the 1943 film version.

16 He was just a coward and that was the worst luck any man could have.
Robert Jordan, ibid., ch. 30. Speaking of his father.

17 The world is a fine place and worth fighting for.
Robert Jordan, ibid., ch. 43

18 Cowardice, as distinguished from panic, is almost always simply a lack of ability to suspend the functioning of the imagination.
Men at War, Introduction (1942)

19 All my life I've looked at words as though I were seeing them for the first time.
Letter, 9 April 1945, publ. in *Selected Letters* (ed. Carlos Baker, 1981)

20 It wasn't by accident that the Gettysburg address was so short. The laws of prose writing are as immutable as those of flight, of mathematics, of physics.
Letter, 23 July 1945, ibid.

21 Scott took LITERATURE so solemnly. He never understood that it was just writing as well as you can and finishing what you start.
Letter to Arthur Mizener, 12 May 1950, ibid. Referring to F. SCOTT FITZGERALD. Mizener wrote a biography of Fitzgerald, and edited his essays and short stories.

22 I started out very quiet and I beat Mr Turgenev. Then I trained hard and I beat Mr de Maupassant. I've fought two draws with Mr Stendhal, and I think I had an edge in the last one. But nobody's going to get me in any ring with Mr Tolstoy unless I'm crazy or I keep getting better.
New Yorker 13 May 1950

23 Man is not made for defeat. A man can be destroyed but not defeated.
The Old Man and the Sea (1952)

24 There isn't any symbolism. The sea is the sea. The old man is an old man. The boy is a boy and the fish is a fish. The sharks are all sharks no better and no worse. All the symbolism that people say is shit. What goes beyond is what you see beyond when you know.
Letter to the critic Bernard Berenson, 13 September 1952, publ. in *Selected Letters* (ed. Carlos Baker, 1981). Referring to Hemingway's novella *The Old Man and the Sea*.

25 The most essential gift for a good writer is a built-in, shock-proof, shit detector. This is the writer's radar and all great writers have had it.
Interview in *Paris Review* (1958), repr. in *Writers at Work* (second series, ed. George Plimpton, 1963)

26 All things truly wicked start from an innocence.
A Moveable Feast, ch. 17 (1964)

27 Never confuse movement with action.
Quoted by MARLENE DIETRICH in *Papa Hemingway*, pt 1, ch. 1 (1966) by A. E. Hotchner. 'In those five words,' Dietrich commented, 'he gave me a whole philosophy.'

28 If you are lucky enough to have lived in Paris as a young man, then wherever you go for the rest of your life it stays with you, for Paris is a moveable feast.
Quoted ibid., pt 1, ch. 3. The words 'a moveable feast' were used on Hotchner's recommendation as the title of Hemingway's posthumously published Paris memoirs. This sentence appears as the book's epigraph.

29 Poor Faulkner. Does he really think big emotions come from big words? He thinks I don't know the ten-dollar words. I know them all right. But there are older and simpler and better words, and those are the ones I use.
Quoted ibid., pt 1, ch. 4. Hemingway's rebuke was made after being informed (by Hotchner) that WILLIAM FAULKNER considered Hemingway 'had no courage' and 'had never been known to use a word that might send the reader to the dictionary'. Hemingway referred to Faulkner as 'Old Corndrinking Mellifluous'.

30 To be a successful father . . . there's one absolute rule: when you have a kid, don't look at it for the first two years.
Quoted ibid., pt 2, ch. 5

Jimi Hendrix
(1942–70)
US rock musician

James Marshall Hendrix. Half-Cherokee Indian, he was the most influential rock guitarist of the 1960s, legendary for his flamboyant technique and style.

1 Hey Joe,
Where're you going with that gun in your hand?
'Hey Joe' (song, 1966, written by Billy Roberts). The song had earlier been performed by David Crosby with the Byrds, and was a US hit for LA garage band The Leaves in 1966.

2 Purple haze all in my brain,
Lately things don't seem the same,

Actin' funny, but I don't know why,
'Scuse me while I kiss the sky.
'Purple Haze' (song, 1967)

3 Blues is easy to play, but hard to feel.
Quoted in *Crosstown Traffic*, ch. 6 (1989) by Charles Shaar Murray

W. E. Henley
(1849–1903)
English poet, critic and editor

William Ernest Henley. Now largely remembered for one poem 'Invictus' (1875), he was editor of the New Review *(1898–1903) and a pioneer in the use of free verse. He was the model for* R. L. STEVENSON*'s Long John Silver in* Treasure Island.

1 In the fell clutch of circumstance,
I have not winced nor cried aloud:
Under the bludgeonings of chance
My head is bloody, but unbowed.
'Invictus: In Memoriam R. T. Hamilton Bruce', st. 2, written 1875, publ. in *Works* (1908)

2 It matters not how strait the gate,
How charged with punishments the scroll,
I am the master of my fate:
I am the captain of my soul.
'Invictus: In Memoriam R. T. Hamilton Bruce', st. 4, ibid.

3 Night with her train of stars
And her great gift of sleep.
'In Memoriam Margaritae Sororis', st. 2, written 1876, ibid.

4 Madam, Life's a piece in bloom
Death goes dogging everywhere:
She's the tenant of the room
He's the ruffian on the stair.
'To W.R.', written 1877, ibid. *The Ruffian on the Stair* is the title of a play by JOE ORTON (1963).

5 What have I done for you,
England, my England?
'Pro Rege Nostro', publ. in *For England's Sake* (1900). Opening lines of poem.

Henry II
(1133–89)
King of England

His invasion of England in 1153 established the Plantagenet dynasty on the throne. His conflict with the church was exacerbated by the murder in 1170 of the Archbishop of Canterbury, his erstwhile companion Thomas à Becket.

1 Will no one rid me of this turbulent priest?
Attributed. Referring to Thomas à Becket, Archbishop of Canterbury. Henry's outburst was said to have inspired the four knights who slew Becket in Canterbury Cathedral in December 1170.

Henry VIII
(1491–1547)
King of England

During his reign (1509–47), his efforts to divorce the first of his six wives, Catherine of Aragon, led to a break with the Roman Catholic church, the dissolution of the monasteries and the eventual establishment of Protestantism in England.

1 I see here daily that you of the Clergy preach one against another, teach one contrary to another, inveigh one against another without charity or discretion: some be too stiff in their old Mumpsimus, others be too busy and curious in their new Sumpsimus: thus all men almost be in variety and discord.
Speech to Parliament, 24 December 1545, publ. in *Chronicles of England, Scotland, and Ireland*, vol. 3 (1587, 1808 edn) by Raphael Holinshed

2 I am very sorry to know and hear how unreverently that most precious jewel, the Word of God, is disputed, rhymed, sung and jangled in every alehouse and tavern, contrary to the true meaning and doctrine of the same.
Speech to Parliament, 24 December 1545, ibid.

3 Green groweth the holly; so doth the ivy.
Though winter blasts blow never so high,
Green groweth the holly.
'The Holly' (song), publ. in *The Oxford Book of Sixteenth Century Verse* (ed. E. K. Chambers, 1932)

4 Pastime with good company
I love and shall, unto I die.
Grudge who list, but none deny!
So God be pleased, thus live will I.
For my pastance
Hunt, sing and dance,
My heart is set.
All goodly sport
For my comfort
Who shall me let?
'Pastime', st. 1 (song), ibid.

O. Henry
(1862–1910)
US short-story writer

Pseudonym of William Sydney Porter. Having served a prison term (1898–1901) for embezzlement after taking money to start the literary magazine Rolling Stones, *he had a successful career writing humorous tales of everyday life.*

1 If men knew how women pass the time when they are alone, they'd never marry.
'Memoirs of a Yellow Dog', publ. in *The Four Million* (1906)

2 A straw vote only shows which way the hot air blows.
'A Ruler of Men' (1906), repr. in *Rolling Stones* (1912). Spoken by Kansas Bill Bowers.

3 It was beautiful and simple as all truly great swindles are.
'The Octopus Marooned', publ. in *The Gentle Grafter* (1908). Spoken by Jeff Peters.

4 If ever there was an aviary overstocked with jays it is that Yaptown-on-the-Hudson.
'A Tempered Wind', ibid. Of New York, also referred to as 'Baghdad-on-the-Subway' in various of O. Henry's stories.

5 You can't appreciate home till you've left it, money till it's spent, your wife till she's joined a woman's club, nor Old Glory till you see it hanging on a broomstick on the shanty of a consul in a foreign town.
'The Fourth in Salvador', publ. in *Roads of Destiny* (1909). Spoken by Billy Casparis.

6 She plucked from my lapel the invisible strand of lint (the universal act of woman to proclaim ownership).
'A Ramble in Aphasia', publ. in *Strictly Business* (1910)

Patrick Henry
(1736–99)
US statesman

Actively opposed to British policy in the American colonies, he made the first speech in the Continental Congress (1774) and introduced the Bill of Rights as an amendment to the new Constitution. He served five terms as Governor of Virginia.

1 Caesar had his Brutus; Charles the First his Cromwell, and George the Third ... ('Treason,' cried the Speaker) ... *may profit by their example.* If *this* be treason, make the most of it.
Speech in Williamsburg, Virginia, May 1765, quoted in *Patrick Henry*, sect. 2 (1818) by William Wirt

2 I am not a Virginian, but an American.
Speech at the first Continental Congress, Philadelphia, September/October 1774, quoted in *Diary and Biography of John Adams*, vol. 2 (ed. L. H. Butterfield, 1961)

3 I know not what course others may take; but as for me, give me liberty, or give me death.
Speech in the Virginia House of Delegates, Richmond, 23 March 1775, quoted in *Patrick Henry*, pt. 4 (1818) by William Wirt

Philip Henry
(1631–96)
English cleric

Ordained into the Anglican church in 1657, he became a non-conformist. His diaries were published in 1822.

1 All this, and heaven too!
Quoted in *Life of Mr Philip Henry*, ch. 5 (1698) by Matthew Henry

Katharine Hepburn
(1909–2003)
US actress

An untypical Hollywood star for her independent, feisty spirit, she made nine films with Spencer Tracy, with whom she had a long-standing relationship. Her other films include The Philadelphia Story *(1940) and* The African Queen *(1951). See* DOROTHY PARKER 14.

1 The average Hollywood film star's ambition is to be admired by an American, courted by an Italian, married to an Englishman and have a French boyfriend.
New York Journal-American 22 February 1954

(Dame) Barbara Hepworth
(1903–75)
British sculptor

Inspired by landscape, her abstract sculptures became increasingly preoccupied by mass and space. She married the artist Ben Nicholson in 1933, living with him in Cornwall where she died in a fire at her studio.

1 Carving is unrelated masses conveying an emotion; a perfect relationship between the mind and the colour, light and weight which is the stone, made by the hand which feels. It must be so essentially sculpture that it can exist in no other way, something completely the right size but which has growth, something still and yet having movement, so very quiet and yet with a real vitality.
Unit One (ed. Herbert Read, 1934)

2 Perhaps what one wants to say is formed in child-

hood and the rest of one's life is spent in trying to say it.

Catalogue of the Barbara Hepworth Retrospective Exhibition, Whitechapel Gallery, London, 1954

3 I think the very nature of art is affirmative, and in being so it reflects the laws and the evolution of the universe – both in the power and rhythm of growth and structure as well as the infinitude of ideas which reveal themselves when one is in accord with the cosmos and the personality is then free to develop.

Barbara Hepworth: A Pictorial Biography (1970)

4 There is an inside and an outside to every form.

Ibid.

Heraclitus
(c. 535–475 BC)
Greek philosopher

Known as 'the obscure' and 'the riddler' on account of his abstruse style of oratory, he posited that the universe was composed of opposites and in a constant state of change. His writings survive in fragments.

1 This world, which is the same for all, was made neither by a god nor by man, but it ever was and is, and shall be ever-living Fire, in measures being kindled and in measures going out.

On the Universe, no. 20 (c. 480 BC)

2 God is day and night, winter and summer, war and peace, surfeit and hunger.

Ibid., no. 36

3 You cannot step twice into the same river; for other waters are ever flowing on to you.

Ibid., no. 41

4 Couples are wholes and not wholes, what agrees disagrees, the concordant is discordant. From all things one and from one all things.

Ibid., no. 49

5 The road up and the road down is one and the same.

Ibid., no. 69

6 A man's character is his fate.

Ibid., no. 121. See NOVALIS 2.

7 All things move and nothing remains still.

Quoted in Cratylus, sect. 402a by PLATO

8 All men whilst they are awake are in one common world: but each of them, when he is asleep, is in a world of his own.

Quoted in Morals, 'On Superstition', sect. 3 by PLUTARCH

(Sir) A. P. Herbert
(1890–1971)
British author and politician

Alan Patrick Herbert. A brilliant librettist for such light operas as La Vie Parisienne (1929) and Bless the Bride (1947), he also wrote poetry, plays and novels, and was an Independent MP for Oxford University 1935–50.

1 As my poor father used to say
In 1863,
Once people start on all this Art
Goodbye, moralitee!

'Lines for a Worthy Person', publ. in Ballads for Broadbrows (1930)

2 Other people's babies –
That's my life!
Mother to dozens,
And nobody's wife.

'Other People's Babies', ibid. The lyrics were used in Streamline Revue with music by Vivian Ellis (1934).

3 Holy Deadlock.

Title of novel (1934)

4 The Common Law of England has been laboriously built about a mythical figure – the figure of 'The Reasonable Man'.

Uncommon Law, no. 1 ('The Reasonable Man') (1935)

5 People must not do things for fun. We are not here for fun. There is no reference to fun in any act of Parliament.

Lord Light, ibid., no. 5 ('Is it a Free Country?')

6 The critical period in matrimony is breakfast-time.

Ibid., no. 16 ('Is Marriage Lawful?')

7 The Englishman never enjoys himself except for a noble purpose.

Mr Justice Plush, ibid., no. 31 ('Is Fox-Hunting Fun?')

8 An Act of God was defined as 'something which no reasonable man could have expected'.

Mr David, ibid., no. 49 ('Act of God')

George Herbert

(1593–1633)

English poet and clergyman

His metaphysical verse (published posthumously) is devoutly religious and characterized by simple diction, metrical inventiveness and everyday imagery. He entered the church in 1630. A selection of his poems was set to music by Ralph Vaughan Williams in Five Mystical Songs *(1911).*

1 Hearken unto a verser, who may chance
Rhyme thee to good, and make a bait of pleasure.
A verse may find him, who a sermon flies,
And turn delight into a sacrifice.
'The Church Porch', st. 1, publ. in *The Temple: Sacred Poems and Private Ejaculations* (1633)

2 Drink not the third glass, which thou canst not
    tame,
When once it is within thee.
'The Church-Porch', st. 5, ibid.

3 By all means use sometimes to be alone.
Salute thyself: see what thy soul doth wear.
Dare to look in thy chest; for 'tis thine own:
And tumble up and down what thou find'st there.
Who cannot rest till he good fellows find,
He breaks up house, turns out of doors his mind.
'The Church Porch', st. 25, ibid.

4 But who does hawk at eagles with a dove?
'The Church: The Sacrifice', st. 23, ibid.

5 Man stole the fruit, but I must climb the tree.
'The Church: The Sacrifice', st. 51, ibid.

6 I got me flowers to strew Thy way;
I got me boughs off many a tree:
But Thou wast up by break of day,
And brought'st Thy sweets along with Thee.
'The Church: Easter', st. 4, ibid.

7 Lord, with what care hast Thou begirt us round!
Parents first season us; then schoolmasters
Deliver us to laws; they send us bound
To rules of reason, holy messengers,
Pulpits and Sundays, sorrow dogging sin,
Afflictions sorted, anguish of all sizes,
Fine nets and stratagems to catch us in,
Bibles laid open, millions of surprises.
'The Church: Sin (I)', sts 1–2, ibid.

8 The sound of glory ringing in our ears:
Without, our shame; within, our consciences;
Angels and grace, eternal hopes and fears.
'The Church: Sin (I)', st. 3, ibid.

9 Yet all these fences and their whole array
One cunning bosom-sin blows quite away.
'The Church: Sin (I)', st. 4, ibid.

10 Sorrow was all my soul; I scarce believed,
Till grief did tell me roundly that I lived.
'The Church: Affliction (I)', ll. 29–30, ibid.

11 Whereas my birth and spirit rather took
The way that takes the town;
Thou didst betray me to a lingering book,
And wrap me in a gown.
'The Church: Affliction (I)', ll. 37–40, ibid.

12 I read, and sigh, and wish I were a tree;
For sure then I should grow
To fruit or shade: at least some bird would trust
Her household to me, and I should be just.
'The Church: Affliction (I)', ll. 57–60, ibid.

13 Prayer, the Church's banquet, Angels age,
God's breath in man returning to his birth,
The soul in paraphrase, heart in pilgrimage,
The Christian plummet sounding heaven and
    earth.
'The Church: Prayer (I)', st. 1, ibid.

14 Exalted manna, gladness of the best,
Heaven in ordinary, man well drest,
The Milky Way, the bird of Paradise,
Church-bells beyond the stars heard, the soul's
    blood,
The land of spices: something understood.
'The Church: Prayer (I)', ibid. Last lines of poem.

15 Let all the world in every corner sing
My God and King.
The Church with psalms must shout,
No door can keep them out:
But above all, the heart
Must bear the longest part.
'The Church: Antiphon (I)', ibid.

16 Who says that fictions only and false hair
Become a verse? Is there in truth no beauty?
Is all good structure in a winding stair?
May no lines pass, except they do their duty
Not to a true, but painted chair?
'The Church: Jordan (I)', st. 1, ibid. *The Winding Stair* was the title of a volume of verse by W. B. YEATS (1933).

17 Oh that I were an orange-tree,
That busy plant!
Then I should ever laden be,

And never want
Some fruit for Him that dressed me.
'The Church: Employment (II)', st. 5, ibid.

18 O that thou shouldst give dust a tongue
To cry to thee,
And then not hear it crying!
'The Church: Denial', ll. 16–18, ibid.

19 Sweet day, so cool, so calm, so bright,
The bridal of the earth and sky.
'The Church: Virtue', st. 1, ibid.

20 Sweet spring, full of sweet days and roses,
A box where sweets compacted lie;
My music shows ye have your closes,
And all must die.
'The Church: Virtue', st. 3, ibid.

21 Only a sweet and virtuous soul,
Like seasoned timber, never gives;
But though the whole world turn to coal,
Then chiefly lives.
'The Church: Virtue', st. 4, ibid.

22 I know the ways of pleasure, the sweet strains,
The lullings and the relishes of it.
'The Church: The Pearl', st. 3, ibid.

23 Man is all symmetry,
Full of proportions, one limb to another.
'The Church: Man', st. 3, ibid.

24 For us the winds do blow,
The earth doth rest, heaven move, and fountains
    flow.
Nothing we see, but means our good,
As our delight or as our treasure:
The whole is either our cupboard of food,
Or cabinet of pleasure.
'The Church: Man', st. 8, ibid.

25 More servants wait on Man,
Then he'll take notice of: in every path
He treads down that which doth befriend him,
When sickness makes him pale and wan.
O mighty love! Man is one world, and hath
Another to attend him.
'The Church: Man', st. 8, ibid.

26 Lord, make me coy and tender to offend:
In friendship, first I think, if that agree
Which I intend,
Unto my friend's intent and end.
I would not use a friend, as I use Thee.
'The Church: Unkindness', ibid. Opening lines.

27 I made a posy while the day ran by:
Here will I smell my remnant out, and tie
My life within this band.
But Time did beckon to the flowers, and they
By noon most cunningly did steal away,
And withered in my hand.
'The Church: Life', st. 1, ibid.

28 King of Glory, King of Peace,
I will love Thee;
And that love may never cease,
I will move Thee.
'The Church: Praise (II)', st. 1, ibid.

29 I struck the board, and cried, No more.
I will abroad. What? Shall I ever sigh and pine?
My lines and life are free; free as the road,
Loose as the wind, as large as store.
Shall I be still in suit?
'The Church: The Collar', ibid. Opening lines of poem, which describes the anguished decision that directed Herbert towards ordination as an Anglican clergyman.

30 But as I raved and grew more fierce and wild
At every word,
Methought I heard one calling, 'Child';
And I replied, 'My Lord'.
'The Church: The Collar', ibid. Last lines.

31 Come my way, my truth, my life:
Such a way as gives us breath:
Such a truth as ends all strife:
And such a life, as killeth death.
'The Church: The Call', ibid.

32 When God at first made man,
Having a glass of blessings standing by;
Let us (said he) pour on him all we can:
Let the world's riches, which dispersed lie,
Contract into a span.
'The Church: The Pulley', st. 1, ibid.

33 Let him be rich and weary, that at least,
If goodness lead him not, yet weariness
May toss him to My breast.
'The Church: The Pulley', st. 4, ibid.

34 Grief melts away
Like snow in May
As if there were no such thing.
'The Church: The Flower', st. 1, ibid.

35 Who would have thought my shrivelled heart
Could have recovered greenness?
'The Church: The Flower', st. 2, ibid.

36 And now in age I bud again,
After so many deaths I live and write;
I once more smell the dew and rain,
And relish versing: O my only Light,
It cannot be
That I am he
On whom Thy tempests fell all night.
'The Church: The Flower', st. 6, ibid.

37 The God of love my Shepherd is,
And He that doth me feed:
While He is mine, and I am His,
What can I want or need?
'The Church: The 23rd Psalm', st. 1, ibid. See BIBLE, OLD TES-
TAMENT: PSALMS 24; HYMNS AND CAROLS 48.

38 The harbingers are come. See their mark;
White is their colour, and behold my head.
'The Church: The Forerunners', st. 4, ibid.

39 Lovely enchanting language, sugar-cane,
Honey of roses.
'The Church: The Forerunners', st. 4, ibid.

40 Throw away thy rod,
Throw away thy wrath;
O my God,
Take the gentle path.
'The Church: Discipline', st. 1, ibid.

41 Love is swift of foot;
Love's a man of war,
And can shoot,
And can hit from far.
'The Church: Discipline', st. 6, ibid.

42 Teach me, my God and King,
In all things Thee to see,
And what I do in any thing
To do it as for Thee.
'The Church: The Elixir', st. 1, ibid.

43 A man that looks on glass,
On it may stay his eye;
Or if he pleaseth, through it pass,
And then the heaven espy.
'The Church: The Elixir', st. 3, ibid.

44 A servant with this clause
Makes drudgery divine:
Who sweeps a room as for Thy laws
Makes that and th' action fine.
'The Church: The Elixir', st. 5, ibid.

45 Love bade me welcome: yet my soul drew back,
Guilty of dust and sin.

But quick-eyed Love, observing me grow slack
From my first entrance in,
Drew nearer to me, sweetly questioning,
If I lacked any thing.
'The Church: Love (III)', st. 1

46 'You must sit down', says Love, 'and taste my
    meat.'
So I did sit and eat.
'The Church: Love (III)', st. 3, ibid.

47 Religion stands on tiptoe in our land,
Ready to pass to the American strand.
'The Church Militant', l. 235, ibid.

Herodotus
(c. 484–425 BC)
Greek historian

Called by CICERO *the 'father of history', he chronicled the
history of Greece and Asia Minor and was the first historian
to test and verify facts, which were then constructed into a
vivid narrative.*

1 Do you tell me to look at the queen when she has
no clothes on? No, no: 'off with her skirt, off with
her shame' – you know what they say of women.
Histories, bk 1, sect. 8. The words of Gyges, a bodyguard, to
Candaules, king of Lydia, having been ordered by the king to
gaze upon his naked wife to admire her beauty.

2 Force is always beside the point when subtlety
will serve.
Ibid., bk 3, sect. 127. Spoken by King Darius.

3 Men are at the mercy of circumstances and not
their master.
Ibid., bk 7, sect. 49. Spoken by Artabanus.

4 The worst pain a man can have is to know much
and be impotent to act.
Ibid., bk 9, sect. 16. Spoken by Attaginus.

5 Soft countries breed soft men. It is not the property of any one soil to produce fine fruits and good
soldiers too.
Ibid., bk 9, sect. 122. Spoken by King Cyrus.

Michael Herr
(b. 1940)
US journalist

He covered the Vietnam war for Esquire *in 1967, was script
consultant for the film* Apocalypse Now *(1979) and wrote the
screenplay for* Full Metal Jacket *(1987).*

1 Vietnam was what we had instead of happy childhoods.
Dispatches, 'Colleagues', sect. 3 (1977)

2 All the wrong people remember Vietnam. I think all the people who remember it should forget it, and all the people who forgot it should remember it.
Observer 15 January 1989

Robert Herrick
(1591–1674)
English poet and clergyman

He is remembered chiefly for Hesperides *(1648), a collection of poems dealing with country matters, folklore and love, much influenced by the classical poets.* ELIZABETH BARRETT BROWNING *called him 'the Ariel of poets, sucking "where the bee sucks" from the rose-heart of nature, and reproducing the fragrance idealized'.*

1 I sing of brooks, of blossoms, birds, and bowers:
Of April, May, of June, and July-flowers.
I sing of May-poles, hock-carts, wassails, wakes,
Of bride-grooms, brides, and of their bridal-cakes.
'The Arguments of his Book', st. 1, publ. in *Hesperides* (1648)

2 To get thine ends, lay bashfulness aside;
Who fears to ask, doth teach to be denied.
'No bashfulness in begging', ibid.

3 Cherry-ripe, ripe, ripe, I cry,
Full and fair ones; come and buy:
If so be, you ask me where
They do grow? I answer, there,
Where my Julia's lips do smile;
There's the land, or cherry-isle.
'Cherry-Ripe', ibid.

4 But ah! If empty dreams so please,
Love give me more such nights as these.
'The Vision to *Electra*', ibid.

5 A sweet disorder in the dress
Kindles in clothes a wantonness.
'Delight in Disorder', ibid.

6 A careless shoe-string, in whose tie
I see a wild civility:
Do more bewitch me, than when art
Is too precise in every part.
'Delight in Disorder', ibid.

7 Get up, get up for shame, the blooming morn
Upon her wings presents the god unshorn.
'Corinna's Going a-Maying', ibid. Opening lines.

8 Get up, sweet Slug-a-bed, and see
The dew bespangling herb and tree.
'Corinna's Going a-Maying', ibid., st. 1

9 So when or you or I are made
A fable, song, or fleeting shade;
All love, all liking, all delight
Lies drowned with us in endless night.
Then while time serves, and we are but
    decaying;
Come, my Corinna, come, let's go a-Maying.
'Corinna's Going a-Maying', st. 5, ibid. Last lines.

10 If smirking wine be wanting here,
There's that which drowns all care, stout beer.
'The Hock-Cart', ibid, st. l

11 Gather ye rosebuds while ye may,
Old Time is still a-flying:
And this same flower that smiles today,
Tomorrow will be dying.
'To the Virgins, to Make Much of Time', st. 1, ibid. See also PIERRE DE RONSARD 3.

12 Then be not coy, but use your time;
And while ye may, go marry:
For having lost but once your prime,
You may for ever tarry.
'To the Virgins, to Make Much of Time', st. 4, ibid.

13 What though the sea be calm? Trust to the
    shore:
Ships have been drowned, where late they danced
    before.
'Safety on the Shore', ibid.

14 Bid me to live, and I will live
Thy Protestant to be:
Or bid me love, and I will give
A loving heart to thee.
'To Anthea, Who May Command Him Anything', st. 1, ibid.

15 Bid me despair, and I'll despair,
Under that cypress tree:
Or bid me die, and I will dare
E'en death, to die for thee.
Thou art my life, my love, my heart,
The very eyes of me:
And hast command of every part,
To live and die for thee.
'To Anthea, Who May Command Him Anything', sts 5–6, ibid.

16 It is the end that crowns us, not the fight.
'The End', ibid.

17 'Tis not the food, but the content
That makes the table's merriment.
'Content, not Cates', ibid.

18 Fair daffodils, we weep to see
You haste away so soon:
As yet the early-rising sun
Has not attained his noon.
'To Daffodils', st. 1, ibid.

19 We have short time to stay, as you,
We have as short a Spring;
As quick a growth to meet decay,
As you or any thing.
'To Daffodils', st. 2, ibid.

20 Fain would I kiss my Julia's dainty leg,
Which is as white and hairless as an egg.
'Her [Julia's] Legs', ibid.

21 Her pretty feet,
Like snails, did creep
A little out, and then,
As if they started at Bo-peep,
Did soon draw in again.
'To Mistress Susanna, Southwell: Upon Her Feet', ibid.

22 Her eyes the glow-worm lend thee,
The shooting-stars attend thee;
And the elves also,
Whose little eyes glow,
Like the sparks of fire, befriend thee.
'The Night-Piece, to Julia', st. 1, ibid.

23 What is a kiss? Why this, as some approve;
The sure sweet cement, glue, and lime of love.
'A Kiss', ibid.

24 Whenas in silks my Julia goes,
Then, then (methinks) how sweetly flows
That liquefaction of her clothes.
Next, when I cast mine eyes and see
That brave vibration each way free;
O how that glittering taketh me!
'Upon Julia's Clothes', ibid.

25 Night makes no difference 'twixt the Priest and
    Clerk;
Joan as my Lady is as good i' the dark.
'No Difference i' th' Dark', ibid.

26 And yet each verse of thine
Out-did the meat, out-did the frolic wine.
'An Ode for Him [Ben Jonson]', ibid.

27 Attempt the end, and never stand to doubt;

Nothing's so hard, but search will find it out.
'Seek and Find', ibid.

28 But, for Man's fault, then was the thorn,
Without the fragrant rose-bud, born;
But ne'er the rose without the thorn.
'The Rose', publ. in *His Noble Numbers*, a subsection of *Hesperides* (1648)

Alexander Herzen
(1812–70)
Russian journalist and political thinker

He witnessed the Paris revolution of 1848, and in 1852 settled in London where he wrote political treatises. With MIKHAIL BAKUNIN, *he worked on the journal* The Bell, *which was smuggled into Russia.*

1 I am truly horrified by modern man. Such absence of feeling, such narrowness of outlook, such lack of passion and information, such feebleness of thought.
From the Other Shore, 'Epilogue 1849' (1855)

2 If nations always moved from one set of furnished rooms to another – and always into a better set – things might be easier, but the trouble is that there is no one to prepare the new rooms. The future is worse than the ocean – there is nothing there.
Ibid., ch. 3

3 Slavery is the first step towards civilization. In order to develop it is necessary that things should be much better for some and much worse for others, then those who are better off can develop at the expense of others.
Ibid., 'Consolatio'

4 Liberalism, austere in political trifles, has learned ever more artfully to unite a constant protest against the government with a constant submission to it.
Letter to IVAN TURGENEV, 1862, publ. in *My Past and Thoughts*, vol. 4, 'Ends & Beginnings' (1921, transl. Constance Garnett)

5 Modern Western thought will pass into history and be incorporated in it, will have its influence and its place, just as our body will pass into the composition of grass, of sheep, of cutlets, and of men. We do not like that kind of immortality, but what is to be done about it?
My Past and Thoughts, vol. 2, pt 5, ch. 38 (1921, transl. Constance Garnett)

6 You can no more bridle passions with logic than

you can justify them in the law courts. Passions are facts and not dogmas.

Ibid., vol. 2, pt 5, ch. 41

7 Science, which cuts its way through the muddy pond of daily life without mingling with it, casts its wealth to right and left, but the puny boatmen do not know how to fish for it.

Ibid., vol. 3, pt 8, 'Miscellaneous Pieces', sect. 1: 'Swiss Views'

Werner Herzog
(b. 1942)
German film-maker

Originally Werner Stipetic. A leading member of the New Cinema in Germany, he is associated with metaphysical films in which landscape plays a prominent role, such as Aguirre: Wrath of God *(1973).*

1 You should look straight at a film; that's the only way to see one. Film is not the art of scholars but of illiterates.

Interview in the *New York Times* 11 September 1977

2 For such an advanced civilization as ours to be without images that are adequate to it is as serious a defect as being without memory.

Ibid.

Michael Heseltine
(b. 1933)
British politician

Baron Heseltine of Thenford. Nicknamed 'Tarzan' for his out-doors image, he was a Conservative MP 1966–2001, during which time he served as Environment Secretary (1979–83), Defence Secretary (1983–6) and Deputy Prime Minister (1995–7).

1 There you have it! The final proof. Labour's brand new, shining, modernists' economic dream. But it's not Brown's – it's Balls'!

Speech to Conservative Party Conference, Bournemouth, 12 October 1994, quoted in the *Daily Telegraph* 13 October 1994. Heseltine was referring to Gordon Brown's recent speech on Labour's economic policy, specifically: 'Our new economic approach is rooted in ideas which stress the importance of macro-economics, neo-classical endogenous growth theory and the symbiotic relationships between growth and investment in people and infrastructure,' said by Heseltine to have been written by a '27-year-old choral-singing researcher named Ed Balls'.

Hesiod
(*fl. c.* 700 BC)
Greek poet

One of the earliest Greek poets, he is principally known for his didactic Works and Days, *a depiction of rural and everyday life in archaic Greece.*

1 And potter is angry with potter, and craftsman with craftsman, and beggar is jealous of beggar, and minstrel of minstrel.

Works and Days, ll. 25–6

2 Fools! They know not how much more the half is than the whole.

Ibid., l. 40

3 He does mischief to himself who does mischief to another, and evil planned harms the plotter most.

Ibid., ll. 265–6

4 If you add only a little to a little and do this often, soon that little will become great.

Ibid., ll. 361–2

Hermann Hesse
(1877–1962)
German novelist and poet

Imbued with the influences of German Romanticism, Eastern religion and Jungian psychoanalysis, his works, which include Steppenwolf *(1927) and* The Glass Bead Game *(1943), acquired a cult readership.*

1 I am fond of music I think because it is so amoral. Everything else is moral and I am after something that isn't. I have always found moralizing intolerable.

Demian, Prologue (1919). Spoken by the narrator (Sinclair).

2 One never reaches home, but wherever friendly paths intersect the whole world looks like home for a time.

Frau Eva, ibid., ch. 7

3 Every age, every culture, every custom and tradition has its own character, its own weakness and its own strength, its beauties and cruelties; it accepts certain sufferings as matters of course, puts up patiently with certain evils. Human life is reduced to real suffering, to hell, only when two ages, two cultures and religions overlap.

Steppenwolf, Preface (1927)

4 The bourgeois treasures nothing more highly than the self ... And so at the cost of intensity he achieves his own preservation and security. His

harvest is a quiet mind which he prefers to being possessed by God, as he prefers comfort to pleasure, convenience to liberty, and a pleasant temperature to that deathly inner consuming fire.
Ibid., 'Treatise on the Steppenwolf'

5 To study history means submitting to chaos and nevertheless retaining faith in order and meaning. It is a very serious task, young man, and possibly a tragic one.
The Glass Bead Game, ch. 4 (1943, transl. 1960). Spoken by Father Jacobus.

6 The call of death is a call of love. Death can be sweet if we answer it in the affirmative, if we accept it as one of the great eternal forms of life and transformation.
Letter, 1950, publ. in *Hermann Hesse: A Pictorial Biography*, 'Montagnola' (ed. Volker Michels, 1973)

Lord Hewart
(1870–1943)
British judge

Gordon, first Viscount Hewart. Liberal MP for Leicester (1913–22), Attorney General (1919–22) and Lord Chief Justice (1922–40), he was considered a brilliant advocate, less effective as a judge.

1 Justice should not only be done, but should manifestly and undoubtedly be seen to be done.
Remark in 'Rex v. Surrey Justices', 9 November 1923, publ. in *King's Bench Reports*, vol. 1 (1924). Ruling on the quashing of a conviction on technical grounds.

Robert Hewison
(b. 1943)
British cultural historian

A critic and commentator on the arts, he is the author of works such as Ruskin in Venice *(1978) and* Culture and Consensus *(1995).*

1 Individually, museums are fine institutions, dedicated to the high values of preservation, education and truth; collectively, their growth in numbers points to the imaginative death of this country.
The Heritage Industry, Introduction (1987)

2 Postmodernism is modernism with the optimism taken out.
Ibid., ch. 6

Patricia Hewitt
(b. 1948)
British politician

A Labour MP since 1997, she has held various ministerial posts since 1999, including in the departments of Trade and Industry, and Health.

1 Fifty per cent of the public don't actually know what the term fifty per cent means.
Observer 1 December 2002. On new figures revealing falling educational standards.

Du Bose Heyward
See IRA GERSHWIN 2

Thomas Heywood
(c. 1574–1641)
English playwright

Of the two hundred and twenty plays in which he had a hand, only twenty-four survive, the best known being A Woman Killed with Kindness *(1607).*

1 Within the red-leaved table of my heart.
A Woman Killed with Kindness, Act 2, Sc. 3 (1607). Spoken by Wendoll.

2 Oh God! Oh God! That it were possible
To undo things done; to call back yesterday;
That Time could turn up his swift sandy glass,
To untell the days, and to redeem these hours.
Frank, ibid., Act 4, Sc. 5

(Sir) John Richard Hicks
(1904–89)
British economist

He was Professor of Political Economy at Manchester and Oxford and is remembered for his theory of economic equilibrium, posited in such books as Value and Capital *(1939).*

1 The best of all monopoly profits is a quiet life.
Econometrica, 'The Theory of Monopoly' (1935)

George V. Higgins
(1939–99)
US novelist

George Vincent Higgins. His first-hand experiences as journalist and attorney contributed to the success of his literary thrillers, which often have Boston as a backdrop, for example The Friends of Eddie Coyle *(1972).*

1 Data is what distinguishes the dilettante from the artist.
Guardian 17 June 1988

2 Politics is a choice of enemas. You're gonna get it up the ass, no matter what you do.
Victories, ch. 7 (1991). Spoken by Ed Cobb.

Thomas Wentworth Higginson
(1823–1911)
US clergyman and writer

He campaigned for Abolition, women's and workers' rights, and was commander (1862) of the first African-American regiment. He encouraged EMILY DICKINSON *and edited her poems, and also contributed prolifically to the* Atlantic Monthly.

1 Great men are rarely isolated mountain-peaks; they are the summits of ranges.
Atlantic Essays, 'A Plea for Culture' (1871)

Benny Hill
(1925–92)
British comedian

Originally Alfred Hawthorne. He was considered the last of the visual comics, and wrote scripts and music as well as playing most of the characters in The Benny Hill Show *on television (1957–66).*

1 That's what show business is – sincere insincerity.
Quoted in the *Observer* 12 June 1977

Christopher Hill
(1912–2003)
British historian

Renowned as a Marxist historian, he has written widely on the period of the Civil War, including The English Revolution, 1640 *(1940) and* Milton and the English Revolution *(1977).*

1 Only very slowly and late have men come to realize that unless freedom is universal it is only extended privilege.
The Century of Revolution, ch. 20 (1961)

2 History has to be rewritten in every generation, because although the past does not change the present does; each generation asks new questions of the past, and finds new areas of sympathy as it re-lives different aspects of the experiences of its predecessors.
The World Turned Upside Down, Introduction (1972)

Joe Hill
(1879–1915)
US activist and songwriter

Born Joel Hägglund. He was an agitator for Industrial Workers of the World ('Wobblies') for which he composed songs of protest. He was executed for murder.

1 You will eat, bye and bye,
In that glorious land above the sky;
Work and pray, live on hay,
You'll get pie in the sky when you die.
'The Preacher and the Slave', chorus, publ. in *Songs of the Workers* (1911)

Rowland Hill
(1744–1833)
English cleric

An eloquent and eccentric preacher, he was prominent in philanthropic and evangelical movements and an early advocate of vaccination.

1 He did not see any reason why the devil should have all the good tunes.
Quoted in *The Rev. Rowland Hill*, ch. 7 (1876) by E. W. Broome

Fred Hillebrand
(1893–1963)
US actor and songwriter

As well as acting in musical-comedy shows on Broadway and in films, he wrote musical scores and such songs as 'I'll See You in C-U-B-A' (with IRVING BERLIN*).*

1 Home James, and Don't Spare the Horses.
Title of song (1934)

Lady Hillingham

1 I am happy now that Charles calls on my bedchamber less frequently than of old. As it is, I now endure but two calls a week and when I hear his steps outside my door I lie down on my bed, close my eyes, open my legs and think of England.
Attributed journal entry, quoted in *The Rise and Fall of the British Nanny*, ch. 3 (1972) by Jonathan Gathorne-Hardy. Often quoted as 'Lie back and think of England.' Other sources ascribe the words to Lady Alice Hillingdon (1857–1940), or as advice given either to Queen VICTORIA or by her to her daughter on her wedding night.

Sidney Hillman
(1887–1946)
Lithuanian-born US trade unionist

Originally Simcha Hillman. Having emigrated to the US in 1907, he became President of the Amalgamated Clothing Workers of America in 1914, a position he held until his death.

1 Politics is the science of how who gets what, when and why.
Political Primer for all Americans (1944)

Heinrich Himmler
(1900–45)
German Nazi leader

He was made head of the SS in 1929 and of the Gestapo in 1936, and was responsible for directing the extermination of the Jews. He committed suicide at the end of the Second World War.

1 *Meine Ehre heisst Treue.*
[My honour is my loyalty.]
Formulated as the watchword of the SS Nazi élite, translated by HANNAH ARENDT in *The Origins of Totalitarianism*, ch. 10 (1951). The US Government Printing Office's *Nazi Conspiracy and Aggression*, vol. 5 (1946–8) gives an alternative translation: 'My honour signifies faithfulness.'

Hippocrates
(c. 460–370 BC)
Greek physician

Recognized as the 'father of medicine', he is associated with the Hippocratic oath and credited with a body of seventy works, of which he himself probably wrote very little.

1 Life is short, the art long, opportunity fleeting, experiment treacherous, judgement difficult.
Aphorisms, sect. 1, para. 1. See GEOFFREY CHAUCER 5, SENECA 18.

2 Extreme remedies are most appropriate for extreme diseases.
Ibid., sect. 1, para. 6. See GUY FAWKES 1.

3 I swear by Apollo Physician, Aesculapius, by Health, by Panacea and by all the gods and goddesses, making them my witnesses, that I will carry out, according to my ability and judgment, this oath and this indenture.
The Hippocratic Oath

4 I swear ... to hold my teacher in this art equal to my own parents; to make him partner in my livelihood; when he is in need of money to share

mine with him; to consider his family as my own brothers, and to teach them this art, if they want to learn it, without fee or indenture.
Ibid.

5 I will use treatment to help the sick according to my ability and judgement, but never with a view to injury and wrong-doing. Neither will I administer a poison to anybody when asked to do so, nor will I suggest such a course. Similarly, I will not give to a woman a pessary to cause abortion. But I will keep pure and holy both my life and my art.
Ibid.

6 I will not use the knife, not even verily, on sufferers from stone, but I will give place to such as are craftsmen therein.
Ibid.

7 Whatsoever I shall see or hear in the course of my profession, as well as outside my profession in my intercourse with men, if it be what should not be published abroad, I will never divulge, holding such things to be holy secrets.
Ibid.

8 Time is that wherein there is opportunity, and opportunity is that wherein there is no great time.
Precepts, ch. 1

9 Healing is a matter of time, but it is sometimes also a matter of opportunity.
Ibid., ch. 1

10 Prayer indeed is good, but while calling on the gods a man should himself lend a hand.
Regimen, bk 4, sect. 27

Hirohito
(1901–89)
Emperor of Japan

Emperor from 1926, he enjoyed the longest reign of any Japanese monarch, coinciding with the country's period of expansionism (from 1931) and the Second World War. He renounced his divinity in 1946.

1 We have resolved to endure the unendurable and suffer what is unsufferable.
Statement 15 August 1945, quoted by A. J. P. TAYLOR in the *Listener* 9 September 1976. The declaration was made following the dropping of the atomic bomb on Hiroshima and was the first time a Japanese emperor had made a direct address to his people.

Damien Hirst

(b. 1965)

British artist

His often provocative installations and most famously his pickled animals raise questions of life and mortality. He won the 1995 Turner Prize with Mother and Child Divided.

1 I sometimes feel that I have nothing to say and I want to communicate this.

Independent 21 July 1992

2 The idea is more important than the object. The object can look after itself ... You can always get another shark.

Interview in *Junk Mail* (1995) by WILL SELF. Hirst was referring to one of his installations of a shark preserved in formaldehyde. Coincidentally, the day after this interview, one of his new exhibits at the Serpentine Gallery, also a preserved animal, was vandalized.

3 I think there's a handful of eye people and billions of ear people. Some people go look at it and think it's great, so they buy it, and all these other people hear that they've bought it so they buy it too.

Interview in the *Big Issue* 1–7 September 1997

(Sir) Alfred Hitchcock

(1899–1980)

British film-maker

Based in Hollywood from the 1940s, he was a master of the suspense thriller. His films include Rear Window *(1954),* Psycho *(1960) and* The Birds *(1963).*

1 Actors are cattle.

Quoted in the *Saturday Evening Post* 22 May 1943. The remark caused Carole Lombard, his star of the time, to lead a herd of oxen onto the set. He later told the press, 'I didn't say actors are cattle. What I said was, actors should be *treated* like cattle.'

2 Drama is life with the dull bits cut out.

Quoted in the *Observer* 10 July 1960. Speaking to FRANÇOIS TRUFFAUT in 1962, Hitchcock explained, 'Making a film means, first of all, to tell a story. That story can be an improbable one, but it should never be banal. It must be dramatic and human. What is drama, after all, but life with the dull bits cut out?'

3 Some films are slices of life. Mine are slices of cake.

Interview August 1962, publ. in *Hitchcock*, ch. 4 (1966, rev. 1984) by FRANÇOIS TRUFFAUT. The quote re-surfaced in *The Sunday Times* 6 March 1977 as 'For me, the cinema is not a slice of life, but a piece of cake.'

4 The invention of television can be compared to the introduction of indoor plumbing. Fundamen-tally it brought no change in the public's habits. It simply eliminated the necessity of leaving the house.

Screen Producers Guild dinner, 7 March 1965, publ. in *Hitchcock on Hitchcock*, 'After-Dinner Speech' (ed. Sidney Gottlieb, 1995)

5 One of television's greatest contributions is that it brought murder back into the home where it belongs.

Screen Producers Guild dinner, 7 March 1965, ibid.

6 Blondes are the best victims. They're like virgin snow which shows up the bloody footprints.

Sunday Times 1 September 1973

Adolf Hitler

(1889–1945)

German dictator

By 1921 he had assumed leadership of the National Socialist German Workers' Party (Nazi Party). Chancellor from 1933, he pursued fanatical anti-Semitic policies and initiated the expansionist policies that led to the Second World War. See EZRA POUND 22.

1 If today I stand here as a revolutionary, it is as a revolutionary against the Revolution.

Speech, 26 February 1924, quoted in *Hitler, a Study in Tyranny*, ch. 2, sect. 7 (1952, rev. 1962) by Alan Bullock. Hitler's statement was made while he was on trial for his part in the unsuccessful *putsch* against the Republican government in Munich, Germany, which had itself overthrown the Bavarian monarchy in 1918.

2 The broad masses of a population are more amenable to the appeal of rhetoric than to any other force.

Mein Kampf, vol. 1, ch. 3 (1925)

3 The art of leadership ... consists in consolidating the attention of the people against a single adversary and taking care that nothing will split up that attention ... The leader of genius must have the ability to make different opponents appear as if they belonged to one category.

Ibid., vol. 1, ch. 3

4 Mankind has grown strong in eternal struggles and it will only perish through eternal peace.

Ibid., vol. 1, ch. 4

5 As soon as by one's own propaganda even a glimpse of right on the other side is admitted, the cause for doubting one's own right is laid.

Ibid., vol. 1, ch. 6

6 The great mass of people . . . will more easily fall victim to a big lie than to a small one.
Ibid., vol. 1, ch. 10

7 Germany will either be a world power or will not be at all.
Ibid., vol. 2, ch. 14

8 Struggle is the father of all things . . . It is not by the principles of humanity that man lives or is able to preserve himself above the animal world, but solely by means of the most brutal struggle.
Speech at Kulmbach, 5 February 1928, quoted in *Hitler, a Study in Tyranny*, ch. 1, sect. 3 (1952, rev. 1962) by Alan Bullock

9 When an opponent declares, 'I will not come over to your side,' I calmly say, 'Your child belongs to us already . . . What are you? You will pass on. Your descendants, however, now stand in the new camp. In a short time they will know nothing else but this new community.'
Speech, 6 November 1933, quoted in *The Rise and Fall of the Third Reich*, ch. 8, 'Education in the Third Reich' (1959) by William L. Shirer

10 If it rests with Germany war will not come again. This country has a more profound impression than any other of the evil that war causes . . . In our belief Germany's present-day problems cannot be settled by war.
Interview in the *Daily Mail* 6 August 1934

11 I go the way that Providence dictates with the assurance of a sleepwalker.
Speech in Munich, 15 March 1936, quoted in *Hitler, a Study in Tyranny*, ch. 7, sect. 1 (1952, rev. 1962) by Alan Bullock. On Germany's reoccupation of the Rhineland.

12 I don't see much future for the Americans . . . Everything about the behaviour of American society reveals that it's half Judaized, and the other half negrified. How can one expect a State like that to hold together?
Remarks, 7 January 1942, recorded by Martin Bormann, publ. in *Hitler's Table Talk* (1953)

13 Churchill is the very type of a corrupt journalist. There's not a worse prostitute in politics. He himself has written that it's unimaginable what can be done in war with the help of lies. He's an utterly amoral repulsive creature. I'm convinced that he has his place of refuge ready beyond the Atlantic . . . He'll go to his friends the Yankees. As soon as this damnable winter is over, we'll remedy all that.
Ibid., 18 February 1942

14 *Brennt Paris?*
[Is Paris burning?]
Attributed inquiry by telephone to General Alfred Jodl, 25 August 1944, in Rastenburg, Germany. Hitler had ordered Paris to be destroyed rather than allow it to fall into Allied hands. The words were taken as the title of a book by Larry Collins and Dominique Lapierre (1965) and of a film with an all-star cast and screenplay contributions by GORE VIDAL and FRANCIS FORD COPPOLA (1966). In June 1940, Hitler is reported to have said to the architect Albert Speer: 'In the past I have often wondered whether we would not have to destroy Paris. But when we are finished in Berlin, Paris will only be a shadow. So why should we destroy it?'

Edward Hoagland
(b. 1932)
US author and essayist

He is best known for his writings on wild animals and nature, as in The Courage of Turtles *(1971).*

1 In order to really enjoy a dog, one doesn't merely try to train him to be semihuman. The point of it is to open oneself to the possibility of becoming partly a dog.
'Dogs and the Tug of Life' (1975), repr. in *Heart's Desire* (1988)

2 The question of whether it's God's green earth is not at centre stage, except in the sense that if so, one is reminded with some regularity that He may be dying.
Guardian 20 January 1990

Russell Hoban
(b. 1925)
US author and illustrator

His many novels include Riddley Walker *(1980), written in a post-apocalyptic language. He also writes children's books, notably the classic* The Mouse and His Child *(1969).*

1 After all, when you come right down to it, how many people speak the same language even when they speak the same language?
The Lion of Boaz-Jachin and Jachin-Boaz, ch. 27 (1973). Spoken by Boaz-Jachin.

2 Me, what's that after all? An arbitrary limitation of being bounded by the people before and after and on either side. Where they leave off, I begin, and vice versa.
Turtle Diary, ch. 11 (1975). Spoken by William G.

3 Nothing to be done really about animals. Anything you do looks foolish. The answer isn't in us.

It's almost as if we're put here on earth to show how silly they aren't.

George Fairbairn, ibid., ch. 42

4 Language is an archeological vehicle ... the language we speak is a whole palimpsest of human effort and history.

Novelists in Interview (ed. John Haffenden 1985)

Thomas Hobbes

(1588–1679)

English philosopher

His concept of the social contract was at the heart of his philosophy, as expressed in his masterpiece Leviathan *(1651). Denying the divine right of kings, he nonetheless claimed absolute monarchy to be essential to protect people from their inherent wickedness.*

1 True and false are attributes of speech not of things. And where speech is not, there is neither truth nor falsehood.

Leviathan, pt 1, ch. 4 (1651)

2 In geometry (which is the only science that it hath pleased God hitherto to bestow on mankind) men begin at settling the significations of their words; which ... they call definitions.

Ibid., pt 1, ch. 4

3 Words are wise men's counters, they do but reckon by them: but they are the money of fools.

Ibid., pt 1, ch. 4

4 The privilege of absurdity; to which no living creature is subject, but man only.

Ibid., pt 1, ch. 5

5 Science is the knowledge of consequences, and dependence of one fact upon another.

Ibid., pt 1, ch. 5

6 The secret thoughts of a man run over all things, holy, profane, clean, obscene, grave, and light, without shame or blame.

Ibid., pt 1, ch. 8

7 War consisteth not in battle only, or the act of fighting; but in a tract of time, wherein the will to contend by battle is sufficiently known.

Ibid., pt 1, ch. 13

8 No arts; no letters; no society; and which is worst of all, continual fear, and danger of violent death; and the life of man, solitary, poor, nasty, brutish, and short.

Ibid., pt 1, ch. 13. Describing the state of nature 'wherein men live without other security, than what their own strength and their own invention shall furnish them'.

9 Force and fraud are in war the two cardinal virtues.

Ibid., pt 1, ch. 13

10 The obligation of subjects to the sovereign is understood to last as long, and no longer, than the power lasteth by which he is able to protect them.

Ibid., pt 2, ch. 2

11 They that are discontented under monarchy, call it tyranny; and they that are displeased with aristocracy, call it oligarchy: so also, they which find themselves grieved under a democracy, call it anarchy, which signifies the want of government; and yet I think no man believes that want of government is any new kind of government.

Ibid., pt 2, ch. 19

12 A man's conscience and his judgement is the same thing; and as the judgement, so also the conscience, may be erroneous.

Ibid., pt 2, ch. 29

13 For it is with the mysteries of our religion, as with wholesome pills for the sick, which swallowed whole, have the virtue to cure; but chewed, are for the most part cast up again without effect.

Ibid., pt 3, ch. 32

14 Leisure is the mother of philosophy.

Ibid., pt 4, ch. 46

15 The Papacy is no other than the ghost of the deceased Roman Empire, sitting crowned upon the grave thereof.

Ibid., pt 4, ch. 47

16 The praise of ancient authors proceeds not from the reverence of the dead, but from the competition and mutual envy of the living.

Ibid., 'A Review and Conclusion'

17 Such truth as opposeth no man's profit nor pleasure is to all men welcome.

Ibid., 'A Review and Conclusion'

John Cam Hobhouse

(1786–1869)

British statesman

Lord Broughton de Gyfford. He entered the House of Commons as a radical in 1820 but became a conservative Whig after 1832. He was a close friend of BYRON, *with whom he wrote* Journey Through Albania *(1813).*

1 It is said to be hard on His Majesty's Ministers to raise objections to this proposition. For my part, I think it no more hard on His Majesty's Opposition to compel it to take this course.

Speech to House of Commons 10 April or 27 April 1826. First recorded use of the term 'His Majesty's Opposition'.

2 Near this spot are deposited the remains of one who possessed Beauty without Vanity, Strength without Insolence, Courage without Ferocity, and all the Virtues of Man without his Vices. This praise, which would be unmeaning Flattery, if inscribed over human ashes, is but a just Tribute to the Memory of BOATSWAIN, a Dog.

Quoted in *The Late Lord Byron*, ch. 10 (1961) by Doris Langley Moore. Inscription on the monument raised for LORD BYRON's dog, Boatswain, in the grounds of Newstead Abbey, Byron's seat in Nottinghamshire. The lines are commonly attributed to Byron, but a draft of a letter written by Hobhouse in 1830 shows that Byron decided to use Hobhouse's epitaph instead of his own: 'To mark a friend's remains these stones arise/I never knew but one – and here he lies.'

3 If the reviewing of books be ... 'an ungentle craft', the making of them is, for the most part, a dishonest one – and that department of literature which ought to be entrusted to those only who are distinguished for their moral qualities is, not infrequently, in the hands of authors totally devoid of good taste, good feeling, and generous sentiment. The writers of Lives have, in our time, assumed a licence not enjoyed by their more scrupulous predecessors – for they interweave the adventures of the living with the memoirs of the dead; and, pretending to portray the peculiarities which sometimes mark the man of genius, they invade the privacy and disturb the peace of his surviving associates.

Quoted ibid, ch. 11. Of the publication of John Galt's *Life of Lord Byron*, in draft for a letter dated 7 November 1830.

E. J. Hobsbawm
(b. 1917)
British historian

Eric John Hobsbawm. His acclaimed studies of European history include The Age of Revolution 1789–1848 *(1962) and* The Age of Capital 1848–75 *(1975). 'He has taken to heart Lenin's dictum "patiently explain",'* A. J. P. TAYLOR *commented.*

1 There is not much that even the most socially responsible scientists can do as individuals, or even as a group, about the social consequences of their activities.

New York Review of Books 19 November 1970

2 It seems that American patriotism measures itself against an outcast group. The right Americans are the right Americans because they're not like the wrong Americans, who are not really Americans.

Marxism Today January 1988

3 Xenophobia looks like becoming the mass ideology of the 20th-century *fin-de-siècle*. What holds humanity together today is the denial of what the human race has in common.

Lecture to the American Anthropological Association, publ. in *Anthropology Today* February 1992

4 Nations without a past are contradictions in terms. What makes a nation *is* the past, what justifies one nation against others is the past, and historians are the people who produce it.

Lecture to the American Anthropological Association, ibid.

David Hockney
(b. 1937)
British artist

Associated with the Pop Art movement in his early career, he moved to California in the 1960s, which inspired his swimming pool series. He has experimented in diverse media. ROBERT HUGHES *called him the 'Cole Porter of contemporary art'.*

1 Television is becoming a collage – there are so many channels that you move through them making a collage yourself. In that sense, everyone sees something a bit different.

Hockney On Photography, 'New York: November 1985' (ed. Wendy Brown, 1988)

2 We live in an age where the artist is forgotten. He is a researcher. I see myself that way.

Quoted in the *Observer* 9 June 1991

3 Seeing is the function of memory.

Quoted in the *Observer* 30 May 1999

Glenn Hoddle
(b. 1957)
British football player and manager

He played for teams including Tottenham Hotspur, Swindon Town and Chelsea before becoming England's manager (1996–9).

1 You and I have been physically given two hands and two legs and half decent brains. Some people have not been born like that for a reason. The karma is working from another lifetime. I have nothing to

hide about that. It is not only people with disabilities. What you sow, you have to reap.

The Times 30 January 1999. This comment, together with his reliance on the healer Eileen Drewery, caused him to lose his position as England's manager. The blind Labour minister David Blunkett commented: 'If Hoddle is right, I must have been a failed football coach in a previous incarnation.'

Ralph Hodgson

(1871–1962)
British poet

As a member of the 'Georgian' poets he composed simple verse expressing a love of nature and England. He taught in Japan 1924–38 and then moved to the USA.

1 Time, you old gypsy man,
Will you not stay,
Put up your caravan
Just for one day?

'Time, You Old Gypsy Man', st. 1, publ. in *Poems* (1917)

2 How they all pitied
Poor motherless Eve.

'Eve', st. 7, ibid.

3 I stood upon that silent hill
And stared into the sky until
My eyes were blind with stars and still
I stared into the sky.

'Song of Honour', ibid. Last lines of poem.

4 'Twould ring the bells of Heaven
The wildest peal for years,
If Parson lost his senses
And people came to theirs,
And he and they together
Knelt down with angry prayers
For tamed and shabby tigers
And dancing dogs and bears,
And wretched, blind, pit ponies,
And little hunted hares.

'Bells of Heaven', ibid.

Peter Høeg

(b. 1957)
Danish author

He established himself as one of Denmark's foremost writers with The History of Danish Dreams *(1988) and* Miss Smilla's Feeling for Snow *(1992), an international best-seller.*

1 Reading snow is like listening to music. To describe what you've read is to try to explain music in writing.

Miss Smilla's Feeling for Snow, 'The City', pt 1, ch. 7 (1992). Spoken by Smilla.

Eric Hoffer

(1902–83)
US philosopher and aphorist

A working-class, self-educated scholar and philosopher, he held a part-time job as a docker while producing collections of essays and aphorisms, for example The Passionate State of Mind *(1955).*

1 Where there is the necessary technical skill to move mountains, there is no need for the faith that moves mountains.

The Passionate State of Mind, aph. 12 (1955)

2 More! is as effective a revolutionary slogan as was ever invented by doctrinaires of discontent. The American, who cannot learn to want what he has, is a permanent revolutionary.

Ibid., aph. 22

3 When people are free to do as they please, they usually imitate each other.

Ibid., aph. 33. Hoffer added, 'A society which gives unlimited freedom to the individual, more often than not attains a disconcerting sameness. On the other hand, where communal discipline is strict but not ruthless . . . originality is likely to thrive.'

4 To have a grievance is to have a purpose in life.

Ibid., aph. 166. Hoffer added: 'It not infrequently happens that those who hunger for hope give their allegiance to him who offers them a grievance.'

5 The basic test of freedom is perhaps less in what we are free to do than in what we are free not to do. It is the freedom to refrain, withdraw and abstain which makes a totalitarian regime impossible.

Ibid., aph. 176

6 Our greatest pretenses are built up not to hide the evil and the ugly in us, but our emptiness. The hardest thing to hide is something that is not there.

Ibid., aph. 217

7 We do not really feel grateful toward those who make our dreams come true; they ruin our dreams.

Ibid., aph. 232

8 Self-esteem and self-contempt have specific odors; they can be smelled.

Ibid., aph. 246

9 Our passionate preoccupation with the sky, the

stars, and a God somewhere in outer space is a homing impulse. We are drawn back to where we came from.
New York Times 21 July 1969. Commenting on the first manned moon-landing.

10 Capitalism is at its liberating best in a noncapitalist environment. The crypto-businessman is the true revolutionary in a Communist country.
Reflections on the Human Condition, aph. 73 (1972)

11 An empty head is not really empty; it is stuffed with rubbish. Hence the difficulty of forcing anything into an empty head.
Ibid., aph. 88

12 People who bite the hand that feeds them usually lick the boot that kicks them.
Ibid., aph. 141

13 There are no chaste minds. Minds copulate wherever they meet.
Ibid., aph. 142

14 We need not only a purpose in life to give meaning to our existence but also something to give meaning to our suffering. We need as much something to suffer for as something to live for.
Ibid., aph. 153

Abbie Hoffman
(1935–89)
US political activist

Abbott Hoffman. As founder (1968) of the Youth International Party (Yippies), he received wide media coverage for his campaigns against the Vietnam War and the US political and economic establishment.

1 The first duty of a revolutionary is to get away with it.
Attributed, 1970

2 Sacred cows make the best hamburgers.
Attributed

Al Hoffman

Dick Manning
(1912–91)
US composers and songwriters

Hoffman was a composer of romantic ballads in the 1930s and of novelty songs in the 1940s and '50s. He wrote for JUDY GARLAND *and Max Bygraves. Manning, born Samuel Medoff,*

was a composer as well as a songwriter, best known for novelty songs.

1 Takes two to tango.
'Takes Two to Tango' (song, 1952). Originally sung by Pearl Bailey, it was later recorded by LOUIS ARMSTRONG, Hermione Gingold and Gilbert Harding.

Dustin Hoffman
(b. 1937)
US actor

He received accolades for his antiheroic screen roles in The Graduate *(1967) and* Midnight Cowboy *(1969), going on to win an Academy Award in* Rain Man *(1988). See* LAURENCE OLIVIER 3.

1 Mrs Robinson, you're trying to seduce me. Aren't you?
The Graduate (film, 1967, screenplay by Calder Willingham and Buck Henry based on the novel by Charles Webb, directed by Mike Nichols). Spoken by Ben Braddock (Dustin Hoffman).

August Heinrich Hoffmann
(1798–1874)
German poet and philologist

Professor of German at Breslau (now Wroclaw) 1830–42, he is best known for his Volkslieder, *patriotic and popular songs.*

1 *Deutschland, Deutschland über alles.*
[Germany above all.]
Poem title, publ. in *Das Lied der Deutschen* (1841). The poem became the German national anthem in 1922.

Heinrich Hoffmann
(1809–94)
German doctor and children's writer

He wrote books on medicine and psychiatry, and achieved international success for his cautionary tales for children, Struwwelpeter *(1845).*

1 Anything to me is sweeter
Than to see Shock-headed Peter.
'Struwwelpeter', publ. in *Struwwelpeter* (1845). The name is translated as 'Shock-headed Peter' or 'Slovenly Peter'.

2 The door flew open, in he ran,
The great, long, red-legged scissor-man.
Ibid., 'The Little Suck-a-Thumb'

3 Augustus was a chubby lad;
Fat ruddy cheeks Augustus had:
And everybody saw with joy
The plump and hearty, healthy boy.
He ate and drank as he was told,

And never let his soup get cold.
But one day, one cold winter's day,
He screamed out, 'Take the soup away!
O take the nasty soup away!
I won't have any soup today.'
Ibid., 'Augustus'

Gerard Hoffnung
(1925–59)
British humorist and musician

He first published his cartoons in the Evening Post *(1947), later drawing for* Punch *and other periodicals. In the mid-1950s he initiated the Hoffnung Music Festivals at the Festival Hall.*

1 Have you tried the famous echo in the Reading Room of the British Museum?
Speech to Oxford Union, 4 December 1958. Suggested advice to tourists.

2 Standing among savage scenery, the hotel offers stupendous revelations. There is a French widow in every bedroom, affording delightful prospects.
Ibid. Supposedly the words of a Tyrolean landlord.

James Hogg
(1770–1835)
Scottish poet

Popularly known as the Ettrick Shepherd. He was a shepherd in the service of the poet William Laidlaw and later a regular contributor to Blackwood's Magazine. *He celebrated Scottish rural life in his poems, styling himself 'King of the Mountain and Fairy School'; for* WALTER SCOTT *he was 'the honest grunter'.*

1 That undefined and mingled hum,
Voice of the desert never dumb!
'Verses to Lady Anne Scott', ll. 69–70, publ. in *Poetical Works* (1822)

2 Where the pools are bright and deep
Where the gray trout lies asleep,
Up the river and o'er the lea
That's the way for Billy and me.
'A Boy's Song', st. 1, ibid.

3 We'll o'er the water, we'll o'er the sea,
We'll o'er the water to Charlie;
Come weel, come wo, we'll gather and go,
And live or die wi' Charlie.
'O'er the Water to Charlie', in *Jacobite Relics of Scotland* (second series, 1821)

Quintin Hogg
See LORD HAILSHAM

Simon Hoggart
(b. 1946)
British journalist

After working in various capacities at Punch *and the* Observer, *he became parliamentary reporter for the* Guardian *in 1993. He chaired BBC radio's News Quiz 1996–2006.*

1 Peter Mandelson is someone who can skulk in broad daylight.
Guardian 10 July 1998

Billie Holiday
(1915–59)
US blues singer

Originally Eleanora Fagan. Known as 'Lady Day', she was distinguished for her intense emotional delivery and idiosyncratic phrasing. Her later years were blighted by drug addiction.

1 Southern trees bear a strange fruit
Blood on the leaf and blood at the root
Black bodies swingin' in the southern breeze
Strange fruit hangin' in the poplar trees.
'Strange Fruit' (song, 1939). Holiday closed her show for years with the song, which originated as an anti-lynching poem written by Lewis Allan and was set to music by Danny Mendelson and pianist Sonny White.

2 Mama may have, papa may have,
But God bless the child that's got his own!
'God Bless the Child' (song, 1941, written with Arthur Herzog Jr)

3 You can be up to your boobies in white satin, with gardenias in your hair and no sugar cane for miles, but you can still be working on a plantation.
Lady Sings the Blues, ch. 11 (written with William Dufty, 1956, rev. 1975)

4 In this country, don't forget, a habit is no damn private hell. There's no solitary confinement outside of jail. A habit is hell for those you love. And in this country it's the worst kind of hell for those who love you.
Ibid., ch. 24. Referring to her addiction to drugs. Holiday spent nearly a year in jail for narcotics offences following her first solo concert in New York, 1946.

Stanley Holloway
(1890–1982)
British actor

Famous for his monologues, he appeared in music hall and as a character actor in such films as Major Barbara *(1941) and* My Fair Lady *(1964). See* MARRIOTT EDGAR.

1 Sam, Sam, pick up tha' musket.
'Pick Up Tha' Musket' (monologue, 1929). Also known as 'Sam Small'.

2 With her head tucked underneath her arm
She walks the Bloody Tower
With her head tucked underneath her arm
At the midnight hour.
'With Her Head Tucked Underneath Her Arm' (monologue, 1934, written by R. P. Weston and Bert Lee). Referring to Anne Boleyn.

John Clellon Holmes
(1926–88)
US poet, novelist and essayist

He gave the earliest portrait of Beat culture in his novel, Go *(1952), originally titled* The Beat Generation *(published in Britain as* The Beat Boys, *1959). He later published poetry.*

1 More than mere weariness, it ['Beat'] involves the feeling of having been used, of being raw. It involves a sort of nakedness of mind, and, ultimately, of soul; a feeling of being reduced to the bedrock of consciousness. In short, it means being undramatically pushed up against the wall.
'This is the Beat Generation', publ. in the *New York Times* 16 November 1952, repr. in *Nothing More to Declare* (1967). See JACK KEROUAC 4.

2 Young Americans have immemorially been as uncritical in their surrender to the present as they are ruthless in their repudiation of the past.
'The Game of the Name' (1965), ibid.

Larry Holmes
(b. 1949)
US boxer

Known as the 'Easton Assassin', he was world heavyweight champion (1978–85), winning forty-eight out of his fifty-one contests.

1 All fighters are prostitutes and all promoters are pimps.
Quoted in the *Guardian* 24 December 1984

Richard Holmes
(b. 1945)
British biographer

He has specialized in the English Romantics, acclaimed for his biographies of SHELLEY *(1974) and* COLERIDGE *(1989, 1998).*

1 A biography is like a handshake down the years, that can become an arm-wrestle.
Remark at Waterstone's Debate, 16 October 1990, quoted in *The Sunday Times* 21 October 1990

Oliver Wendell Holmes Jr
(1841–1935)
US jurist

Nicknamed 'The Great Dissenter', he was Supreme Court Justice 1902–32, earning a reputation for the elegance of his writings and judgements on common law and equity. 'One of my old formulas is to be an enthusiast in the front part of your heart and ironical at the back,' he commented.

1 It is now the moment ... to recall what our country has done for each of us, and to ask ourselves what we can do for our country in return.
Memorial Day Address, 30 May 1884, Keene, New Hampshire, publ. in *Speeches of Oliver Wendell Holmes* (1934). See J. F. KENNEDY 8.

2 As life is action and passion, it is required of a man that he should share the passion and action of his time, at peril of being judged not to have lived.
Memorial Day Address, 30 May 1884, ibid.

3 The generation that carried on the war has been set apart by its experience. Through our great good fortune, in our youth our hearts were touched with fire. It was given to us to learn at the outset that life is a profound and passionate thing.
Memorial Day Address, 30 May 1884, ibid.

4 The most stringent protection of free speech would not protect a man in falsely shouting fire in a theater and causing a panic.
Supreme Court opinion in *Schenk v. United States, Baer v. United States* (1919)

Oliver Wendell Holmes Sr
(1809–94)
US author, poet and physician

The father of OLIVER WENDELL HOLMES JR, *he was Professor of Anatomy at Harvard (1847–82). His humorously philosophical writings were published in three volumes of* Breakfast Table Essays.

1 But hark! the air again is still,
The music all is ground,
And silence, like a poultice, comes
To heal the blows of sound.
'The Music-Grinders', st. 10 (1836), publ. in *The Poetical Works of Oliver Wendell Holmes* (ed. Eleanor M. Tilton, 1895, rev. 1975)

2 The freeman, casting with unpurchased hand
The vote that shakes the turrets of the land.
'Poetry: a Metrical Essay', ll. 83–4 (1836), ibid.

3 And when you stick on conversation's burrs,
Don't strew your pathway with those dreadful urs.
'A Rhymed Lesson' (1848), ibid.

4 All generous companies of artists, authors, philanthropists, men of science, are, or ought to be Societies of Mutual Admiration.
The Autocrat of the Breakfast-Table, ch. 1 (1858)

5 A thought is often original, though you have uttered it a hundred times.
Ibid., ch. 1

6 Little-minded people's thoughts move in such small circles that five minutes' conversation gives you an arc long enough to determine their whole curve.
Ibid., ch. 1

7 A great calamity . . . is as old as the trilobites an hour after it has happened.
Ibid., ch. 2

8 Insanity is often the logic of an accurate mind overtasked.
Ibid., ch. 2

9 Put not your trust in money, but put your money in trust.
Ibid., ch. 2

10 Sin has many tools, but a lie is the handle which fits them all.
Ibid., ch. 6

11 The axis of the earth sticks out visibly through the center of each and every town or city.
Ibid., ch. 6

12 The world's great men have not commonly been great scholars, nor its great scholars great men.
Ibid., ch. 6

13 It is the province of knowledge to speak, and it is the privilege of wisdom to listen.
The Poet at the Breakfast-Table, ch. 10 (1872)

14 The sound of a kiss is not so loud as that of a cannon, but its echo lasts a great deal longer.
Ibid., ch. 11

15 Nothing is so common-place as to wish to be remarkable.
Ibid., ch. 12

Michael Holroyd
(b. 1935)
British author

He is chiefly known for his works of biography, notably Lytton Strachey *(2 vols. 1967–8),* Augustus John *(2 vols. 1974–5) and* Bernard Shaw *(4 vols. 1988–92), which* ANTHONY BURGESS *praised as 'the crown of an astonishing period of biographical achievement'.*

1 Biographies of writers are written in collaboration with the posthumous subject of the biography. What is seen or overlooked, known and forgotten, comes to be shared between them. It is, like the process of reading itself, an 'intimacy between strangers'.
Bernard Shaw, vol. 1, ch. 1 (1988)

Miroslav Holub
(1923–98)
Czech biologist and poet

'I have a single goal but two ways to reach it,' he explained of his own dual career as immunologist and poet. Forbidden from publishing in his home country 1968–82, he became well known abroad for such verse collections as Where the Blood Flows *(1963).*

1 Here in the Lord's bosom rests
The tongues of beggars,
The lungs of generals,
The eyes of informers,
The skins of martyrs
In the absolute
Of the microscope's lenses.
'Pathology', publ. in *Day Duty* (1958)

2 The word is the first small step
to freedom
from oneself.
'Brief Reflection on the Word Pain', publ. in *On the Contrary* (1982)

3 In laughter we stretch the mouth from ear to
ear,
or at least in that direction,

we bare our teeth and in that way reveal
long-past stages in evolution
when laughter still was an expression of
triumph over a slain neighbour.
'Brief Reflection on Laughter', ibid.

4 Humankind can generally be divided into hunters
and people who cope with the consequences.
'Shedding Life', publ. in *The Dimension of the Present Moment
and Other Essays* (1990)

Lord Home

See (Sir) Alec Douglas-Home

Homer

(*c.* 8th century BC)
Greek poet

*Never historically identified, he is traditionally held to be the
author of the* Iliad, *which tells of the siege of Troy, and the*
Odyssey, *describing the subsequent wanderings of Odysseus.
Other works have also been attributed to him.*

1 Anger be now your song, immortal one,
Achilles' anger, doomed and ruinous,
that caused the Achaeans loss on bitter loss
and crowded brave souls into the undergloom,
leaving so many dead men – carrion
for dogs and birds; and the will of Zeus was done.
The Iliad, bk 1, ll. 1–6 (transl. Robert Fitzgerald, 1974). Opening
lines.

2 Then he spoke to her with wingèd words.
Ibid., bk 1, l. 201 (transl. A. T. Murray, 1924). Achilles addresses
Athene.

3 Honour the gods' will, they may honour ours.
Achilles, ibid., bk 1, l. 218 (transl. Robert Fitzgerald, 1974)

4 When Dawn spread out her fingertips of rose.
Ibid., bk 1, l. 477 and passim. Usually quoted 'rosy-fingered
dawn'. The phrase also appears in *The Odyssey*.

5 'It is no wonder
that Trojans and Achaeans under arms
should for so long have borne the pains of war
for one like this.' 'Unearthliness. A goddess the
    woman is to look at.'
Ibid., bk 3, ll. 156–8. The elders of Troy discuss Helen's beauty.

6 Words came driving on the air as thick
and fast as winter snowflakes.
Ibid., bk 3, l. 222

7 Our kind, immortals of the open sky,
will never be like yours, earth-faring man.
Apollo, ibid., bk 5, ll. 441–2

8 Very like leaves
upon this earth are the generations of men.
Glaucos, son of Hippolochus, ibid., bk 6, l. 146

9 Alien to clan and custom and hearthfire
is he who longs for war – heartbreaking war –
with his own people.
Nestor, ibid., bk 9, ll. 63–4

10 I hate
as I hate Hell's own gate that man who hides
one thought within him while he speaks
    another.
Achilles, ibid., bk 9, ll. 312–13

11 Rely on the will of Zeus
who rules all mortals and immortals. One
and only one portent is best: defend
our fatherland!
Hector, ibid., bk 12, ll. 241–3

12 The ebb and flow of cold Oceanus,
the primal source of all that lives.
Ibid., bk 16, l. 246. The words of Sleep.

13 The issue lies upon the gods' great knees.
Automedon, ibid., bk 17, l. 514. More familiarly quoted 'in the
lap of the gods'.

14 Anger that envenoms even the wise
and is far sweeter than slow-dripping honey,
clouding the hearts of men like smoke.
Achilles, ibid., bk 18, ll. 109–10

15 Grey-eyed Athena stirred them a following
    wind,
soughing from the north-west on the winedark
    sea.
Odyssey, bk 2, ll. 420–1 (transl. Robert Fitzgerald, 1962). The
phrase 'wine-dark sea' also occurs in later passages.

16 Hunger is insolent, and will be fed.
Odysseus, ibid., bk 7, l. 216 (transl. ALEXANDER POPE, 1725).
Line 300 of Pope's translation.

17 With Ossa's
mountain peak they meant to crown Olympos
and over Ossa Pelion's forest pile
for footholds up the sky.
Ibid., bk 11, ll. 315–16 (transl. Robert Fitzgerald, 1962). Odysseus
refers to peaks in Thessaly by which the giants Otus and
Ephialtes attempted to reach heaven. They were thrown back
to earth by Apollo. See HORACE 38 and VIRGIL 10.

18 You know they go in foreign guise, the gods do,
looking like strangers, turning up
in towns and settlements to keep an eye
on manners, good or bad.
Ibid., bk 17, ll. 485–7. Spoken by a member of the crowd.

19 Therefore the fame of her virtue shall never per-
ish, but the immortals shall make among men on
earth a pleasant song in honour of constant
Penelope.
Ibid., bk 24, ll. 196–8 (transl. A. T. Murray, 1924). The ghost of
Agamemnon refers to Penelope, wife of Odysseus.

Thomas Hood

(1799–1845)
English poet

*He edited literary magazines and composed a wide range of
lyrics and ballads, mostly humorous. 'The Song of the Shirt'
(1843) is a poem of social protest.*

1 They went and told the sexton, and
The sexton told the bell.
'Faithless Sally Brown', st. 17, publ. in *Whims and Oddities*
(first series, 1826)

2 O, Nelly Gray! O, Nelly Gray!
Is this your love so warm?
The love that loves a scarlet coat
Should be more uniform!
'Faithless Nelly Gray', st. 6, ibid.

3 The best of friends fall out, and so
His teeth had done some years ago.
'A True Story', st. 2, publ. in *Whims and Oddities* (second
series, 1827)

4 She stood breast high amid the corn,
Clasped by the golden light of morn,
Like the sweetheart of the sun,
Who many a glowing kiss had won.
'Ruth', st. 1, publ. in *The Plea of the Midsummer Fairies* (1827)

5 I saw old Autumn in the misty morn
Stand shadowless like Silence, listening
To silence.
'Ode: Autumn', ibid. Opening lines of poem.

6 I remember, I remember,
The house where I was born,
The little window where the sun
Came peeping in at morn.
'I Remember', st. 1, ibid.

7 Now 'tis little joy
To know I'm farther off from heaven
Than when I was a boy.
'I Remember', st. 4, ibid.

8 And then, in the fulness of joy and hope,
Seemed washing his hands with invisible soap
In imperceptible water.
'Miss Kilmansegg and her Precious Leg', 'Her Christening',
st. 10 (1840), repr. in *Complete Poetical Works* (ed. Walter
Jerrold, 1906). Referring to Sir Jacob Kilmansegg.

9 With fingers weary and worn,
With eyelids heavy and red,
A woman sat, in unwomanly rags,
Plying her needle and thread –
Stitch! stitch! stitch!
In poverty, hunger and dirt
And still with a voice of dolorous pitch
She sang the 'Song of the Shirt'.
'The Song of the Shirt', st. 1 (1843), repr. in *Complete Poetical
Works* (ed. Walter Jerrold, 1906). Opening lines. The poem was
inspired by an incident which drew public attention to the
conditions of the working poor: a widow with two young
children was charged with pawning her employer's goods;
her income as a seamstress of seven shillings a week was
considered by the court 'a good living'.

10 O men, with sisters dear!
O men, with mothers and wives!
It is not linen you're wearing out,
But human creatures' lives.
Ibid., st. 4

11 Oh, God! that bread should be so dear,
And flesh and blood so cheap!
Ibid., st. 5

12 Work – work – work,
In the dull December light,
And work – work – work,
When the weather is warm and bright –
While underneath the eaves
The brooding swallows cling
As if to show me their sunny backs
And twit me with the spring.
Ibid., st. 8

13 But evil is wrought by want of thought
As well as want of heart!
'The Lady's Dream', st. 16 (1844), ibid.

14 Take her up tenderly,
Lift her with care;

Fashioned so slenderly,
Young, and so fair!
'The Bridge of Sighs', st. 2 (1844), ibid.

15 Mad from life's history,
Glad to death's mystery,
Swift to be hurled –
Anywhere, anywhere,
Out of the world!
'The Bridge of Sighs', st. 12, ibid.

16 No sun – no moon!
No morn – no noon
No dawn – no dusk – no proper time of day.
'No', publ. in *Whimsicalities: A Periodical Gathering* (1844).
Opening lines of poem.

17 No warmth, no cheerfulness, no healthful ease,
No comfortable feel in any member –
No shade, no shine, no butterflies, no bees,
No fruits, no flowers, no leaves, no birds –
November!
'No', ibid.

18 But who would rush at a benighted man,
And give him two black eyes for being blind?
'Ode to Rae Wilson', st. 26, publ. in *Complete Poetical Works*
(ed. Walter Jerrold, 1906)

Richard Hooker
(1554–1600)
English theologian and clergyman

*He was Master of the Temple Church (1585–91) and a leading
spokesman for the emerging Anglican theology. His influential
work,* Of the Laws of Ecclesiastical Polity *(1593–7), championed
the authority of the Church of England.*

1 He that goeth about to persuade a multitude that
they are not so well governed as they ought to be,
shall never want attentive and favourable hearers.
Of the Laws of Ecclesiastical Polity, bk 1, ch. 1, sect. 1 (1593)

2 Alteration though it be from worse to better hath
in it inconveniences, and those weighty.
Ibid., bk 4, ch. 14, sect. 1. The words were quoted by SAMUEL
JOHNSON in the Preface to his *Dictionary of the English Lan-
gauge* (1755): 'Change is not made without inconvenience,
even from worse to better.'

Ellen Sturgis Hooper
(1816–41)
US poet

*A member of the New England Transcendental Club, she con-
tributed poetry to the literary magazine* The Dial.

1 I slept, and dreamed that life was beauty;
I woke, and found that life was duty.
'Beauty and Duty' (1840)

Herbert Hoover
(1874–1964)
US president

*Republican President 1929–33, he was called 'the Great
Engineer' for the public works projects initiated under his
administration, although his opposition to government intervention in the aftermath of the Depression and his repeated
assertion that 'prosperity cannot be restored by raids upon the
public treasury' caused him to lose popularity.*

1 The American system of rugged individualism.
Speech in Madison Square Garden, New York, 22 October
1928, quoted in *New Day*, 'New York City: Restored under
Republican Direction' (1928). Hoover was contrasting American values with 'a European philosophy of diametrically
opposed doctrines – doctrines of paternalism and state
socialism'.

2 The slogan of progress is changing from the full
dinner pail to the full garage.
Ibid., 'New York City: Higher Standards of Living'

3 The grass will grow in the streets of a hundred
cities, a thousand towns.
Speech, 31 October 1932, in *State Papers of Herbert Hoover*,
vol. 2 (1934). On proposals to reduce protective tariffs.

4 Older men declare war. But it is youth that must
fight and die. And it is youth who must inherit the
tribulation, the sorrow and the triumphs that are
the aftermath of war.
Speech at Republican National Convention, Chicago, 27 June
1944, publ. in *Official Report of the Proceedings of the 23rd
Republican National Convention* (1944)

J. Edgar Hoover
(1895–1972)
US director of the FBI

*John Edgar Hoover. Director of the FBI from 1924, he resisted
Communism and distrusted the civil rights movement. In the
words of* Time *magazine, 'he fashioned his career as an
improbable bureaucratic morality play peopled by bad guys
and G-men.'*

1 We of the FBI are powerless to act in cases of
oral-genital intimacy, unless it has in some way
obstructed interstate commerce.
Quoted in the *New York Times* 6 October 1980

Anthony Hope
(1863–1933)
English author and lawyer

Pseudonym of (Sir) Anthony Hope Hawkins. He gave up legal work to write full-time after the success of his 'Ruritanian' tales, The Prisoner of Zenda *(1894) and* Rupert of Hentzau *(1898).*

1 'You oughtn't to yield to temptation.'
'Well, somebody must, or the thing becomes absurd.'
The Dolly Dialogues, no. 14 (1894). Spoken by Dolly Foster and Mr Carter.

Bob Hope
(1903–2003)
British-born US comedian

Born Leslie Townes Hope. Famous for his wisecracking repartee, as in the Road to . . . *films which he made with* BING CROSBY *and Dorothy Lamour, he was a dedicated entertainer to the troops during the Second World War and the conflicts in Korea and Vietnam.*

1 Thanks for the memory
And strictly *entre nous*, darling, how are you?
And how are all the little dreams that never did
   come true?
Awfully glad I met you, cheerio, and toodle-oo
Thank you,
Thank you so much.
'Thanks for the Memory' (song, written by Leo Robin and Ralph Rainger) in *The Big Broadcast of 1938* (film, 1938). Sung as a duet with Shirley Ross, this became Hope's signature song.

2 How did you get into that dress – with a spray gun?
Road To Rio (film, 1947, screenplay by Edmund Beloin and Jack Rose, directed by Norman McLeod). Spoken by Hot Lips Barton (Bob Hope) to Lucia Maria De Andrade (Dorothy Lamour).

3 If you watch a game, it's fun. If you play it, it's recreation. If you work at it, it's golf.
Quoted in *Reader's Digest* October 1958

4 I don't generally feel anything until noon, then it's time for my nap.
International Herald Tribune 3 August 1990

Laurence Hope
(1865–1904)
Anglo-Indian poet

Pseudonym of Adela Florence Cory Nicolson. She lived most of her adult life in India and gained instant success with her first book of poetry The Garden of Kama *(1901). She took her own life following the death of her husband.*

1 Pale hands I loved beside the Shalimar,
Where are you now? Who lies beneath your spell?
'Kashmiri Song', st. 1, publ. in *The Garden of Kama* (1901). One of the *Four Indian Love Lyrics*, set to music by Amy Woodforde Finden in 1903.

2 Less than the dust beneath thy chariot wheel,
Less than the rust that never stained thy sword.
Less than the trust thou hast in me, Oh Lord,
Even less than these!
Less than the weed that grows beside thy door,
Less than the speed of hours spent far from thee,
Less than the need thou hast in life of me.
Even less am I.
'Less then the Dust', sts 1–2, ibid. One of the *Four Indian Love Lyrics*, set to music by Amy Woodforde Finden in 1903.

Gerard Manley Hopkins
(1844–89)
English poet and Jesuit priest

He became a Jesuit novice in 1868, was ordained as a priest in 1877, and was appointed Professor of Greek Literature at University College, Dublin, in 1884. His idiosyncratic poems of religion and nature, characterized by an innovative 'sprung rhythm', were not published until after his death.

1 I have desired to go
Where springs not fail,
To fields where flies no sharp and sided hail
And a few lilies blow.
'Heaven-Haven', st. 1, written 1864, publ. in *Poems* (1918)

2 Elected Silence, sing to me
And beat upon my whorlèd ear,
Pipe me to pastures still and be
The music that I care to hear.
'The Habit of Perfection', st. 1, written 1866, ibid.

3 Thou mastering me
God! Giver of breath and bread:
World's strand, sway of the sea;
Lord of living and dead;
Thou has bound bones and veins in me, fastened
   me flesh,
And after it almost unmade, what with dread,

Thy doing: and dost thou touch me afresh?
Over again I feel thy finger and find thee.
'The Wreck of the Deutschland', pt 1, st. 1, written 1876, ibid.

4 I did say yes
O at lightning and lashed rod;
Thou heardst me truer than tongue confess
Thy terror, O Christ, O God.
'The Wreck of the Deutschland', pt 1, st. 2, ibid.

5 The world is charged with the grandeur of God.
It will flame out, like shining from shook foil.
'God's Grandeur', written 1877, st. 1, ibid.

6 Generations have trod, have trod, have trod;
And all is seared with trade; bleared, smeared with
    toil;
And wears man's smudge and shares man's smell:
    the soil
Is bare now, nor can foot feel, being shod.
'God's Grandeur', st. 1, ibid.

7 Look at the stars! look, look up at the skies!
O look at all the fire-folk sitting in the air!
The bright boroughs, the circle-citadels there!
'The Starlight Night', written 1877, ibid. Opening lines of
poem.

8 Nothing is so beautiful as spring –
When weeds, in wheels, shoot long and lovely and
    lush;
Thrush's eggs look little low heavens, and thrush
Through the echoing timber does so rinse and
    wring
The ear, it strikes like lightning to hear him sing.
'Spring', st. 1, written 1877, ibid.

9 I caught this morning morning's minion,
    kingdom of daylight's dauphin, dapple-dawn-
    drawn Falcon.
'The Windhover', st. 1, written 1877, ibid. Opening lines of
poem.

10 My heart in hiding
Stirred for a bird, the achieve of, the mastery of
    the thing!
'The Windhover', st. 1, ibid.

11 Glory be to God for dappled things –
For skies of couple-colour as a brinded cow;
For rose-moles all in stipple upon trout that swim.
'Pied Beauty', written 1877, ibid. Opening lines of poem.

12 All things counter, original, spare, strange;
Whatever is fickle, freckled (who knows how?)
With swift, slow; sweet, sour; adazzle, dim;

He fathers-forth whose beauty is past change:
Praise him.
'Pied Beauty', ibid.

13 Ask of her, the mighty mother:
Her reply puts this other
Question: What is Spring? –
Growth in everything.
'The May Magnificat', written 1878, st. 4, ibid.

14 Ten or twelve, only ten or twelve
Strokes of havoc únselve
The sweet especial scene,
Rural scene, a rural scene,
Sweet especial rural scene.
'Binsey Poplars, felled 1879', st. 3, written 1879, ibid.

15 Towery city and branchy between towers;
Cuckoo-echoing, bell-swarmèd, lark-charmèd,
    rook-racked, river-rounded.
'Duns Scotus's Oxford', st. 1, written 1879. Opening lines of
poem.

16 No doubt my poetry errs on the side of oddness
... But as air, melody is what strikes me most of all
in music, and design in painting, so design, pattern,
or what I am in the habit of calling *inscape* is what
I above all aim at in poetry. Now it is the virtue of
design, pattern, or inscape to be distinctive, and it
is the vice of distinctiveness to become queer. This
vice I cannot have escaped.
Letter to ROBERT BRIDGES, 15 February 1879, publ. in *The
Correspondence of Gerard Manley Hopkins and Robert Bridges*
(ed. C. C. Abbott, 1935)

17 Felix Randal the farrier, O is he dead then? my
    duty all ended,
Who have watched his mould of man, big-boned
    and hardy-handsome
Pining, pining, till time when reason rambled in it
    and some
Fatal four disorders, fleshed there, all contended?
'Felix Randal', st. 1, written 1880, publ. in *Poems* (1918). Open-
ing lines of poem.

18 Margaret, are you grieving
Over Goldengrove unleaving?
'Spring and Fall: to a young child', written 1880. Opening
lines of poem.

19 Ah! as the heart grows older
It will come to such sights colder
By and by, not spare a sigh
Though worlds of wanwood leafmeal lie;
And yet you will weep and know why.
'Spring and Fall: to a young child', written 1880, ibid.

20 It is the blight man was born for,
It is Margaret you mourn for.
'Spring and Fall: to a young child', written 1880, ibid. Last lines of poem.

21 What would the world be, once bereft
Of wet and wildness? Let them be left,
O let them be left, wildness and wet;
Long live the weeds and the wilderness yet.
'Inversnaid', st. 4, written 1881, ibid.

22 As kingfishers catch fire, dragonflies draw
flame.
'As kingfishers catch fire', ibid. Opening line.

23 The just man justices;
Keeps grace: that keeps all his goings graces.
'As kingfishers catch fire', ibid.

24 Wild air, world-mothering air,
Nestling me everywhere,
That each eyelash or hair
Girdles; goes home betwixt
The fleeciest, frailest-fixed
Snowflake; that's fairly mixed
With, riddles, and is rife
In every least thing's life.
'The Blessed Virgin Compared to the Air We Breathe', written 1883, ll. 1–8, ibid.

25 I say that we are wound
With mercy round and round
As if with air.
'The Blessed Virgin Compared to the Air We Breathe', ll. 34–6, ibid.

26 Not, I'll not, carrion comfort, Despair, not feast
on thee;
Not untwist – lack they may be – these last strands
of man
In me or, most weary, cry *I can no more.* I can;
Can something, hope, wish day come, not choose
not to be.
'Carrion Comfort', written 1885, ibid. Opening lines of poem.

27 No worst, there is none. Pitched past pitch of
grief,
More pangs will, schooled at forepangs, wilder
wring.
Comforter, where, where is your comforting?
'No worst, there is none', written 1885, ibid. Opening line of poem.

28 O the mind, mind has mountains; cliffs of fall
Frightful, sheer, no-man-fathomed. Hold them
cheap

May who ne'er hung there.
'No worst, there is none', written 1885, ibid.

29 The fine pleasure is not to do a thing but to feel
that you could . . . If I could but get on, if I could but
produce a work I should not mind its being buried,
silenced, and going no further; but it kills me to be
time's eunuch and never to beget.
Letter to ROBERT BRIDGES, 1 September 1885, publ. in *The Correspondence of Gerard Manley Hopkins and Robert Bridges* (ed. C. C. Abbott, 1935)

30 I wake and feel the fell of dark, not day
What hours, O what black hours we have spent
This night.
'I wake and feel', ibid. Opening lines of poem.

31 I am all at once what Christ is, since he was
what I am, and
This Jack, joke, poor potsherd, patch, matchwood,
immortal diamond,
Is immortal diamond.
'That Nature is a Heraclitean Fire', written 1888, ibid. Last lines of poem.

32 Thou art indeed just, Lord, if I contend
With thee; but, sir, so what I plead is just.
Why do sinners' ways prosper? and why must
Disappointment all I endeavour end?
'Thou art indeed just, Lord', written 1889, ibid. Opening lines of poem.

33 Birds build – but not I build; no, but strain,
Time's eunuch, and not breed one work that
wakes.
Mine, O thou lord of life, send my roots rain.
'Thou art indeed just, Lord', written 1889, ibid.

Horace
(65–8 BC)
Roman poet

Quintus Horatius Flaccus. After being introduced by VIRGIL *to the patron Maecenas, he produced verse that was polished though conversational in tone, and greatly influential on 17th- and 18th-century writers. His* Odes *celebrate love, friendship, wine and the rural life. See* PETRONIUS 5.

1 How comes it, Maecenas, that no man living is
content with the lot which either his choice has
given him, or chance has thrown in his way, but
each has praise for those who follow other paths?
Satires, bk 1, no. 1, ll. 1–3 (*c.* 35 BC)

2 What is to prevent one from telling truth as he laughs?
Ibid., bk 1, no. 1, ll. 24–5

3 The story's about you.
Ibid., bk 1, no. 1, l. 69

4 There is measure in all things.
Ibid., bk 1, no. 1, l. 106

5 Beggars, actors, buffoons, and all that tribe.
Ibid., bk 1, no. 2, l. 2

6 All singers have this fault: if asked to sing among their friends they are never so inclined; if unasked, they never leave off.
Ibid., bk 1, no. 3, ll. 1–3

7 *Ab ovo*
Usque ad mala.
[From the egg-course to the fruit.]
Ibid., bk 1, no. 3, l. 6. Referring to the order of a Roman meal, from the first to the last course.

8 The limbs of a dismembered poet.
Ibid., bk 1, no. 4, l. 62. Referring to Orpheus who was torn apart by the Maenads.

9 *Ad unguem*
Factus homo.
[A man to the fingertips.]
Ibid., bk 1, no. 5, ll. 32–3. Meaning 'without flaw', in allusion to the practice of testing the seamlessness of the joints of a work of sculpture by running a fingernail over the marble surface.

10 'Tis . . . foolish to carry timber to a wood.
Ibid., bk 1, no. 10, l. 34

11 This is what I prayed for – a piece of land not so very large, where there would be a garden, and near the house a spring of ever-flowing water, and above these a bit of woodland.
Ibid., bk 2, no. 6, ll. 1–3. See JONATHAN SWIFT 22.

12 O nights and feasts divine!
Ibid., bk 2, no. 6, l. 65

13 At Rome you long for the country; in the country you extol to the stars the distant town.
Ibid., bk 2, no. 7, ll. 28–9

14 One who entertains is like a general: mishaps oft reveal his genius, smooth going hides it.
Ibid., bk 2, no. 8, l. 73

15 But if you name me among the lyric bards, I
  shall strike the stars with my exalted head.
Odes, bk 1, no. 1 (23 BC). Last lines of poem.

16 *Animae dimidium meae.*
[The half of my own soul.]
Ibid., bk 1, no. 3, l. 8. Referring to VIRGIL.

17 Pale Death beats equally at the poor man's gate and at the palaces of kings.
Ibid., bk 1, no. 4, l. 13

18 Life's brief span [*vitae summa brevis*] forbids us to enter on far-reaching hopes.
Ibid., bk 1, no. 4, l. 15

19 What slender youth, bedewed with liquid
  odours,
Courts thee on roses in some pleasant cave,
Pyrrha? For whom bind'st thou
In wreaths thy golden hair,
Plain in thy neatness [*simplex munditiis*]?
Ibid., bk 1, no. 5, ll. 1–5 (transl. JOHN MILTON, c. 1627)

20 *Nil desperandum.*
[Never despair.]
Ibid., bk 1, no. 7, l. 27. The words of Teucer to his companions on being sent into exile by his father, the King of Salamis.

21 Tomorrow, once again, we sail the vast sea.
Ibid., bk 1, no. 7, l. 32. Spoken by Teucer.

22 Cease to ask what the morrow will hold and count as gain each day that Fortune grants.
Ibid., bk 1, no. 9, l. 13

23 Do not try to find out – we're forbidden to know – what end the gods may bestow on me or you.
Ibid., bk 1, no. 11, ll. 1–2.

24 Seize the day [*Carpe diem*]: put no trust in the morrow.
Ibid., bk 1, no. 11, l. 8. See also PIERRE DE RONSARD 3, EDMUND SPENSER 16.

25 Happy, thrice happy and more, are they whom an unbroken bond unites and whose love shall know no sundering of quarrels so long as they shall live.
Ibid., bk 1, no. 13, ll. 17–20

26 *Integer vitae scelerisque purus.*
[He who is upright in his way of life and free from sin.]
Ibid., bk 1, no. 22, l. 1

27 A grudging and infrequent worshipper of the gods.
Ibid., bk 1, no. 34, l. 1

28 Now is the time for drinking [*nunc est*

bibendum], now is the time to make the earth shake with dancing.
Ibid., bk 1, no. 37, ll. 1–2. On the death of Cleopatra.

29 *Persicos odi, puer, apparatus.*
[Persian luxury, my lad, I hate.]
Ibid., bk 1, no. 38, l. 1

30 Cease your efforts to find where the last rose lingers.
Ibid., bk 1, no. 38, l. 3

31 Remember, when life's path is steep, to keep an even mind.
Ibid., bk 2, no. 3, ll. 1–2

32 Whoever cultivates the golden mean [*auream mediocritatem*] avoids the poverty of a hovel and the envy of a palace.
Ibid., bk 2, no. 10, ll. 5–6

33 *Eheu fugaces, Postume, Postume,*
Labuntur anni.
[Alas, Postumus, Postumus, the fleeting years slip by.]
Ibid., bk 2, no. 14, l. 1

34 Nothing is an unmixed blessing.
Ibid., bk 2, no. 16, ll. 27–8

35 *Odi profanum volgus et arceo.*
[I hate the common herd of men and keep them afar.]
Ibid., bk 3, no. 1, l. 1

36 *Dulce et decorum est pro patria mori.*
[It is sweet and honorable to die for one's country.]
Ibid., bk 3, no. 2, l. 13. See WILFRED OWEN 3.

37 The man who is tenacious of purpose in a rightful cause is not shaken from his firm resolve by the frenzy of his fellow citizens clamouring for what is wrong, or by the tyrant's threatening countenance.
Ibid., bk 3, no. 3, ll. 1–4

38 To pile Pelion on top of shady Olympus.
Ibid., bk 3, no. 4, l. 52. See HOMER 17 and VIRGIL 10.

39 Force without wisdom falls of its own weight.
Ibid., bk 3, no. 4, l. 65

40 Our sires' age was worse than our grandsires'. We their sons are more worthless than they: so in our turn we shall give the world a progeny yet more corrupt.
Ibid., bk 3, no. 6, ll. 46–8. Closing lines of poem.

41 Gloriously false [*splendide mendax*], a maiden famous to all time.
Ibid., bk 3, no. 11, l. 35. Referring to Hypermestra, who, unlike her forty-nine sisters, disobeyed the command of her father Danaus to murder her husband on their wedding night. *Splendide mendax* was the motto of SWIFT's hero Gulliver.

42 *O fons Bandusiae, splendidior vitro.*
[O fount Bandusian, more sparkling than glass.]
Ibid., bk 3, no. 13, l. 1

43 *Magnas inter opes inops.*
[A pauper in the midst of wealth.]
Ibid., bk 3, no. 16, l. 28

44 He will through life be master of himself and a happy man who from day to day can have said, 'I have lived: tomorrow the Father may fill the sky with black clouds or with cloudless sunshine.'
Ibid., bk 3, no. 29, ll. 41–4. See JOHN DRYDEN 49.

45 I have erected a monument more lasting than bronze.
Ibid., bk 3, no. 30, l. 1

46 I shall not wholly die.
Ibid., bk 3, no. 30, l. 6

47 I am not as I was when good Cinara was my queen.
Ibid., bk 4, no. l, l. 3. See ERNEST DOWSON 1.

48 The centuries roll back to the ancient age of gold.
Ibid., bk 4, no. 2, l. 39

49 Drown it in the depths! It comes forth fairer.
Ibid., bk 4, no. 4, l. 65

50 The snows have dispersed [*diffugere nives*], now grass returns to the fields and leaves to the trees.
Ibid., bk 4, no. 7, ll. 1–2

51 *Pulvis et umbra sumus.*
[We are but dust and shadow.]
Ibid., bk 4, no. 7, l. 16

52 Many heroes lived before Agamemnon; but all are unknown and unwept, extinguished in everlasting night, because they have no spirited chronicler.
Ibid., bk 4, no. 9, ll. 25–8

53 Mix a little foolishness with your prudence: it is sweet to let the mind unbend upon occasion.
Ibid., bk 4, no. 12, ll. 27–8

54 *Nullius addictus iurare in verba magistri.*
[In the word of no master am I bound to believe.]
Epistles, bk 1, no. 1, ll. 14–15 (22–8 BC). *Nullius in verba* is the motto of the Royal Society.

55 To flee vice is the beginning of virtue, and to have got rid of folly is the beginning of wisdom.
Ibid., bk 1, no. 1, ll. 41–2

56 Make money, money by fair means if you can, if not, by any means money.
Ibid., bk 1, no. 1, ll. 65–6

57 We are just numbers, born to consume the fruits of the earth.
Ibid., bk 1, no. 2, l. 27

58 Why do you hasten to remove anything which hurts your eye, while if something affects your soul you postpone the cure until next year?
Ibid., bk 1, no. 2, ll. 38–9

59 Well begun is half done; dare to be wise; begin.
Ibid., bk 1, no. 2, l. 40

60 Anger is a brief lunacy.
Ibid., bk 1, no. 2, l. 62

61 Think to yourself that every day is your last; the hour to which you do not look forward will come as a welcome surprise. As for me, when you want a good laugh, you will find me in a fine state, fat and sleek, a true hog of Epicurus' herd.
Ibid., bk 1, no. 4, ll. 13–16

62 You may drive out nature with a pitchfork, yet she'll be constantly running back.
Ibid., bk 1, no. 10, ll. 24–5

63 They change their clime, not their frame of mind, who rush across the sea.
Ibid., bk 1, no. 11, l. 26

64 *Concordia discors.*
[Harmony in discord.]
Ibid., bk 1, no. 12, l. 19

65 It is not everyone who can get to Corinth.
Ibid., bk 1, no. 17, l. 36. A version of a Greek proverb; Corinth was synonymous with expensive living.

66 Once a word has been allowed to escape, it cannot be recalled.
Ibid., bk 1, no. 18, l. 71

67 It is your concern when your neighbour's wall is on fire.
Ibid., bk 1, no. 18, l. 84

68 To have a great man for a friend seems pleasant to those who have never tried it; those who have, fear it.
Ibid., bk 1, no. 18, ll. 86–7

69 No poems can please for long or live that are written by water-drinkers.
Ibid., bk 1, no. 19, ll. 2–3

70 O imitators, you slavish herd.
Ibid., bk 1, no. 19, l. 19

71 Skilled or unskilled, we all scribble poems.
Ibid., bk 2, no. 1, l. 117

72 And to seek the truth in the groves of Academe.
Ibid., bk 2, no. 2, l. 45. The Academy was the school established by PLATO c. 385 BC in a park in the outskirts of Athens.

73 *Brevis esse laboro,*
Obscuro fio.
[I strive to be brief but I become obscure.]
Epistles, bk 2, no. 3, ll. 25–6. The epistle is better known as *Ars Poetica*, and is sometimes cited as bk 3 of the *Epistles*.

74 Scholars dispute, and the case is still before the courts.
Ibid., bk 2, no. 3, l. 78

75 Words a foot and a half long.
Ibid., bk 2, no. 3, l. 97

76 If you want me to weep, you must first feel grief yourself.
Ibid., bk 2, no. 3, l. 102

77 *Parturient montes, nascetur ridiculus mus.*
[The mountains will be in labour and a ridiculous mouse will be brought forth.]
Ibid., bk 2, no. 3, l. 139

78 *In medias res.*
[In the midst of things.]
Ibid., bk 2, no. 3, l. 148

79 Tiresome, complaining, a praiser of past times, when he was a boy, a castigator and censor of the young generation.
Ibid., bk 2, no. 3, l. 173. Referring to old men.

80 He gains everyone's approval who mixes the pleasant with the useful.
Ibid., bk 2, no. 3, l. 343

81 When many beauties grace a poem, I shall not take offence at a few faults.
Ibid., bk 2, no. 3, l. 351

82 Help a man against his will and you do the same as murder him.
Ibid., bk 2, no. 3, l. 467

83 Sometimes even worthy Homer nods.
Ibid., bk 2, no. 3, l. 359

84 A poem is like a picture.
Ibid., bk 2, no. 3, l. 361

Nick Hornby
(b. 1957)
British author

His fiction humorously explores themes of masculinity and relationships. His first three novels Fever Pitch *(1992),* High Fidelity *(1995) and* About a Boy *(1998) have all been filmed.*

1 The natural state of the football fan is bitter disappointment, no matter what the score.
Fever Pitch, '1968–1975: Home Début' (1992)

2 There must be many fathers around the country who have experienced the cruellest, most crushing rejection of all: their children have ended up supporting the wrong team.
Ibid., '1976–1986: My Brother'

3 You can never do the right thing by someone if you've stopped sleeping with them. You can't see a way back, or through, or round, however hard you try.
High Fidelity, ch. 25 (1995)

Janette Turner Hospital
(b. 1942)
Australian author

Her novels and short stories cross cultural and national boundaries, reflecting her own moves between Australia, Europe and America.

1 We inherit plots . . . There are only two or three in the world, five or six at most. We ride them like treadmills.
Independent 7 April 1990

A. E. Housman
(1859–1936)
British poet and classical scholar

Alfred Edward Housman. His poetic reputation grew from a single volume, A Shropshire Lad *(1896), after which he wrote little verse though he continued to write and lecture on poetry. He was appointed Professor of Latin at University College, London, in 1892 and at Cambridge in 1911.*

1 Oh who is that young sinner with the handcuffs on his wrists?
And what has he been after that they groan and shake their fists?
And wherefore is he wearing such a conscience-stricken air?
Oh they're taking him to prison for the colour of his hair.
'Additional Poems', no. 18, written 1895, publ. in *A. E. H.* (1937) by Laurence Housman. Referring to the trial and subsequent imprisonment of OSCAR WILDE.

2 Loveliest of trees, the cherry now
Is hung with bloom along the bough,
And stands about the woodland ride
Wearing white for Eastertide.
A Shropshire Lad, no. 2, st. 1 (1896)

3 And since to look at things in bloom
Fifty springs are little room,
About the woodlands I will go
To see the cherry hung with snow.
Ibid., no. 2, st. 3

4 Clay lies still, but blood's a rover;
Breath's a ware that will not keep.
Up, lad: when the journey's over
There'll be time enough to sleep.
Ibid., no. 4. Last lines of poem.

5 And naked to the hangman's noose
The morning clocks will ring
A neck God made for other use
Than strangling in a string.
Ibid., no. 9

6 When I was one-and-twenty
I heard a wise man say,
'Give crowns and pounds and guineas
But not your heart away;
Give pearls away and rubies,
But keep your fancy free.'
But I was one-and-twenty,
No use to talk to me.
Ibid., no. 13

7 In summertime on Bredon
The bells they sound so clear;
Round both the shires they ring them
In steeples far and near,
A happy noise to hear.
Here of a Sunday morning
My love and I would lie,
And see the coloured counties,
And hear the larks so high
About us in the sky.
Ibid., no. 21, sts 1–2. The lines – and other poems in *A Shropshire Lad* – were set to music by George Butterworth.

8 'Come all to church, good people,'
Oh, noisy bells, be dumb;
I hear you, I will come.

Ibid., no. 21. Last lines.

9 The lads in their hundreds to Ludlow come in
   for the fair,
There's men from the barn and the forge and the
   mill and the fold,
The lads for the girls and the lads for the liquor are
   there,
And there with the rest are the lads that will never
   be old.

Ibid., no. 23, st. 1

10 Is my team ploughing,
That I was used to drive
And hear the harness jingle
When I was man alive?

Ibid., no. 27, st. 1

11 And fire and ice within me fight
Beneath the suffocating night.

Ibid., no. 30. Last lines of poem.

12 On Wenlock Edge the wood's in trouble;
His forest fleece the Wrekin heaves;
The wind it plies the saplings double,
And thick on Severn snow the leaves.
The gale, it plies the saplings double,
It blows so hard, 'twill soon be gone:
To-day the Roman and his trouble
Are ashes under Uricon.

Ibid., no. 31, sts 1–2

13 From far, from eve and morning
And yon twelve-winded sky,
The stuff of life to knit me
Blew hither: here am I.

Ibid., no. 32, st. 1

14 Into my heart an air that kills
From yon far country blows:
What are those blue remembered hills,
What spires, what farms are those?
That is the land of lost content,
I see it shining plain,
The happy highways where I went
And cannot come again.

Ibid., no. 40. *Blue Remembered Hills* was the title of an
acclaimed television play by DENNIS POTTER (1979).

15 Think no more, lad: laugh, be jolly:
Why should men make haste to die?
Empty heads and tongues a-talking

Make the rough road easy walking,
And the feather pate of folly
Bears the falling sky.

Ibid., no. 49

16 Oh, 'tis jesting, dancing, drinking
Spins the heavy world around.
If young hearts were not so clever,
Oh, they would be young for ever:
Think no more: 'tis only thinking
Lays lads underground.

Ibid., no. 49

17 Clunton and Clunbury,
Clungunford and Clun,
Are the quietest places
Under the sun.

Ibid., Epigraph to no. 50

18 With rue my heart is laden
For golden friends I had,
For many a rose-lipped maiden
And many a lightfoot lad.

Ibid., no. 54

19 By brooks too broad for leaping
The lightfoot boys are laid;
The rose-lipped girls are sleeping
In fields where roses fade.

Ibid., no. 54

20 Say, for what were hop-yards meant,
Or why was Burton built on Trent?
Oh many a peer of England brews
Livelier liquor than the Muse,
And malt does more than Milton can
To justify God's ways to man.
Ale, man, ale's the stuff to drink
For fellows whom it hurts to think

Ibid., no. 62

21 I tell the tale that I heard told.
Mithridates, he died old.

Ibid., no. 62. Last lines of poem. Mithridates the Great (c. 135–
63 BC) made himself immune to poison by continuously
taking small quantities of venomous plants. When captured
by the Romans he was unable to poison himself, so ordered
a Gallic mercenary to kill him.

22 Pass me the can, lad; there's an end of May.

Last Poems, no. 9 (1922)

23 The troubles of our proud and angry dust
Are from eternity, and shall not fail.

Bear them we can, and if we can we must.
Shoulder the sky, my lad, and drink your ale.
Ibid., no. 9. Last lines of poem.

24 The laws of God, the laws of man,
He may keep that will and can;
Not I: let God and man decree
Laws for themselves and not for me:
And if my ways are not as theirs
Let them mind their own affairs.
Ibid., no. 12. The poem ends: 'Keep we must, if keep we can,/
These foreign laws of God and man.'

25 And how am I to face the odds
Of man's bedevilment and God's?
I, a stranger and afraid
In a world I never made.
Ibid., no. 12

26 The sumless tale of sorrow
Is all unrolled in vain:
May comes tomorrow
And Ludlow fair again.
Ibid., no. 34 ('The First of May'). Closing line of poem.

27 To think that two and two are four
And neither five nor three
The heart of man has long been sore
And long 'tis like to be.
Ibid., no. 35. Last stanza of poem.

28 These, in the day when heaven was falling,
The hour when earth's foundations fled,
Followed their mercenary calling
And took their wages and are dead.
Ibid., no. 37 ('Epitaph on an Army of Mercenaries')

29 What God abandoned, these defended,
And saved the sum of things for pay.
Ibid., no. 37

30 They say my verse is sad: no wonder:
Its narrow measure spans
Tears of eternity, and sorrow,
Not mine, but man's.
More Poems, Foreword, written 1922 (1936)

31 Because I liked you better
Than suits a man to say,
It irked you, and I promised
To throw the thought away.
Ibid., no. 31

32 The weeping Pleiads wester,
And the moon is under seas;
From bourn to bourn of midnight

Far sighs the rainy breeze.
It sighs from a lost country
To a land I have not known;
The weeping Pleiads wester
And I lie down alone.
Ibid., no. 10

33 Here dead lie we because we did not choose
To live and shame the land from which we sprung.
Life, to be sure, is nothing much to lose;
But young men think it is, and we were young.
Ibid., no. 36

34 Good-night. Ensured release
Imperishable peace,
Have these for yours,
While earth's foundations stand
And sky and sea and land
And heaven endures.
Ibid., no. 48 ('Parta Quies')

35 Experience has taught me, when I am shaving of a morning, to keep watch over my thoughts, because, if a line of poetry strays into my memory, my skin bristles so that the razor ceases to act.
'The Name and Nature of Poetry', lecture at Senate House, Cambridge, 9 May 1933, publ. in *A. E. Housman: Selected Prose* (ed. John Carter, 1961). The seat of this sensation, Housman explained, 'is the pit of the stomach'. The lecture was his first public utterance on the subject of poetry.

36 Indeed – very good. I shall – have to repeat – that – on the Golden Floor.
Last words, as reported in letter to Richard Perceval Graves, 12 May 1976, quoted in *A. E. Housman, The Scholar Poet*, ch. 12 (1979) by Richard Perceval Graves. The words were spoken to Housman's doctor, who had just recounted the response of an actor when asked what members of his profession did in their spare time: 'Well, I suppose you could say we spend half our time lying on the sands looking at the stars, and the other half lying on the stars looking at the sands!'

Michael Howard
(b. 1941)
British politician

A Conservative MP since 1983, he became Home Secretary in 1993, Shadow Chancellor (2001–3), and Leader of the Conservative Party (2003–5). See ANNE WIDDECOMBE 1.

1 The first responsibility of Government is to control the nation's borders.
Daily Telegraph 27 January 2005

(Sir) Robert Howard
(1626–98)
English playwright and politician

His Royalist sympathies led to his imprisonment during the Civil War, following which he became an MP. His most successful plays were The Committee *(1662) and* The Indian Queen *(1664), the latter co-written with* JOHN DRYDEN, *with whom he became embroiled in a famous controversy regarding the use of rhyme.*

1 D'ye think that statesmen's kindnesses proceed
From any principles but their own need?
The Vestal Virgin, Act 2 (c. 1665). Spoken by Mutius.

Geoffrey Howe
(b. 1926)
British politician

Baron Howe of Aberavon. Under MARGARET THATCHER, *he was Chancellor of the Exchequer (1979–83), Foreign Secretary (1983–9), and Deputy Prime Minister and Leader of the House of Commons (1989–90).*

1 It is rather like sending your opening batsmen to the crease only for them to find the moment that the first balls are bowled that their bats have been broken before the game by the team captain.
Resignation speech as Deputy Prime Minister to House of Commons, 13 November 1990, publ. in *Conflict of Loyalty*, Appendix 2 (1994). The speech refers to the difficulties he faced as Foreign Secretary on account of MARGARET THATCHER's anti-European stance.

Julia Ward Howe
(1819–1910)
US reformer and author

She campaigned for women's rights and the abolition of slavery, and in 1908 was the first woman to be elected to the American Academy of Arts and Letters.

1 Mine eyes have seen the glory of the coming of the Lord:
He is trampling out the vintage where the grapes of wrath are stored;
He hath loosed the fateful lightning of his terrible swift sword:
His truth is marching on.
'Battle Hymn of the Republic', publ. in the *Atlantic Monthly* (1862). Written to the tune of the anti-slavery song 'John Brown's Body'.

Kim Howells
(b. 1946)
British politician

Elected Labour MP for Pontypridd in 1992, he has occupied various ministerial positions since 1998.

1 If this is the best British artists can produce then British art is lost. It is cold, mechanical, conceptual bullshit. The attempts at contextualisation are particularly pathetic and symptomatic of a lack of conviction.
Quoted in the *Evening Standard* 31 October 2002. Written while he was Minister for Culture, Howells' note was pinned to the wall at Tate Britain after his visit to the Turner Prize exhibition.

Frankie Howerd
(1922–92)
British comedian

Originally Francis Alex Howard. A stand-up comedian from the 1940s, he is best known as the slave Lurcio in the TV series Up Pompeii *(1969–71), in which he displayed his mastery of the suggestive innuendo.*

1 I was amazed.
Catchphrase from 1940s. Other phrases associated with Howerd include 'Mock ye not!' and 'Nay, nay, and thrice nay!', adapted to 'Woe, woe, and thrice woe' as spoken by the soothsayer in the TV show, *Up Pompeii*.

Mary Howitt
(1799–1888)
English author and poet

She collaborated with her husband William in a long literary career and translated from Scandinavian literature, including HANS CHRISTIAN ANDERSEN.

1 'Will you walk into my parlour?' said a spider to a fly:
''Tis the prettiest little parlour that ever you did spy.'
'The Spider and the Fly' (1829), publ. in *Sketches of Natural History* (1834)

Edmond Hoyle
(1672–1769)
English writer on cards

He laid down the rules of whist in A Short Treatise on the Game of Whist *(1742). Subsequent editions also included descriptions of other card games and backgammon.*

1 When in doubt, win the trick.
Hoyle's Games Improved, 'Whist: Twenty-Four Short Rules for Learners' (ed. Charles Jones, 1790)

Elbert Hubbard
(1856–1915)
US author and editor

He founded the Roycroft Press in 1893, with which he published, among other works, The Philistine *magazine, which he also largely wrote. He died on the* Lusitania, *when the liner was torpedoed by the Germans.*

1 The man who, when given a letter to Garcia, quietly takes the missive, without asking any idiotic questions, and with no lurking intention of chucking it into the nearest sewer, or of doing aught else but deliver it, never gets 'laid off', nor has to go on a strike for higher wages. Civilization is one long, anxious search for just such individuals. Anything such a man asks shall be granted. He is wanted in every city, town and village – in every office, shop, store and factory. The world cries out for such; he is needed and needed badly – the man who can 'Carry a Message to Garcia'.
The Philistine March 1899. Closing sentences of article later published as a booklet, *A Message to Garcia*. In it, Hubbard extolled the unquestioning dedication demonstrated by Lieutenant A. S. Rowan, who during the Spanish-American War of 1898 was entrusted by President William McKinley to secure vital information from the Cuban revolutionary leader Calixto García y Íñigues.

2 Never explain – your friends do not need it and your enemies will not believe you anyhow.
The Motto Book (1907). See also LORD FISHER 1 and P. G. WODEHOUSE 1.

3 Art is the beautiful way of doing things. Science is the effective way of doing things. Business is the economic way of doing things.
Ibid.

4 Life is just one damned thing after another.
The Philistine December 1909. The quote has also been attributed to Frank Ward O'Malley. See also EDNA ST. VINCENT MILLAY 10.

5 One machine can do the work of fifty ordinary men. No machine can do the work of one extraordinary man.
One Thousand and One Epigrams (1911)

6 Editor: a person employed by a newspaper, whose business it is to separate the wheat from the chaff, and to see that the chaff is printed.
Roycroft Dictionary of Epigrams (1914). The epigram has also been attributed to ADLAI STEVENSON: 'An editor is someone who separates the wheat from the chaff and then prints the chaff.' (*The Stevenson Wit*, 1966)

Kin Hubbard
(1868–1930)
US humorist and journalist

Frank McKinney Hubbard. Working at the Indianapolis Sun *from 1899, he became known for caricatures of political figures, and achieved national fame for his Abe Martin character (from 1904).*

1 It's no disgrace t' be poor, but it might as well be.
Short Furrows (1911)

2 Classic music is th' kind that we keep thinkin'll turn into a tune.
Comments of Abe Martin and His Neighbors (1923)

3 Nobuddy ever fergits where he buried a hatchet.
Indianapolis News 4 January 1925, repr. in *Abe Martin's Broadcast* (1930)

4 When a fellow says, it hain't the money but the principle o' the thing, it's th' money.
Hoss Sense and Nonsense (1926)

5 Th' only way t' entertain some folks is t' listen t' 'em.
Abe Martin's Wisecracks (ed. E. V. Lucas, 1930)

6 Makin' a long stay short is a great aid t' popularity.
Ibid.

Richard Huelsenbeck
(1892–1974)
German poet and psychoanalyst

With HUGO BALL *he was the co-founder of Dadaism in 1916 and brought the movement to Berlin. In 1936 he settled in New York, where he practised as a psychoanalyst.*

1 I am firmly convinced that all art will become dadaistic in the course of time, because from Dada proceeds the perpetual urge for its renovation.
'Dada Lives', publ. in *Transition* no. 25, autumn 1936, transl. in *The Dada Painters and Poets: An Anthology* (ed. Robert Motherwell, 1951)

Arianna Huffington
(b. 1950)
Greek-born US author and columnist

Formerly Arianna Stassinopoulos. Her provocative work ranges from studies on the women's movement and spirituality to biography and politics.

1 Liberation is an evershifting horizon, a total ideology that can never fulfill its promises ... It has the therapeutic quality of providing emotionally charged rituals of solidarity in hatred – it is the amphetamine of its believers.
The Female Woman, 'The Liberated Woman? ... and Her Liberators' (1973)

Langston Hughes
(1902–67)
US poet and author

Called the 'poet laureate of Harlem', he was a major influence on the development of black literature in America. His poetry collections include The Weary Blues *(1926). His humorous sketches, 'Simple Stories', appeared in the 1950s in books, comic strips and on the stage.*

1 I've known rivers:
I've known rivers ancient in the world and older
    than the flow of human blood in human veins.
My soul has grown deep like the rivers.
'The Negro Speaks of Rivers' (1921), repr. in *The Weary Blues* (1926)

2 I got the Weary Blues
And I can't be satisfied.
'The Weary Blues', written 1922, publ. ibid. In his autobiography, Hughes claimed these lines originated in 'the first blues verse I'd ever heard'.

3 I, too, sing America.
I am the darker brother.
They send me to eat in the kitchen when company
    comes.
But I laugh,
And eat well,
And grow strong.
'I, Too' (1925), repr. in *Selected Poems* (1954)

4 I swear to the Lord
I still can't see
Why Democracy means
Everybody but me.
'The Black Man Speaks', publ. in *Jim Crow's Last Stand* (1943)

5 But softly
As the tune comes from his throat
Trouble
Mellows to a golden note.
'Trumpet Player', publ. in *Fields of Wonder* (1947)

6 Good morning, daddy!
Ain't you heard
The boogie-woogie rumble
Of a dream deferred?
'Dream Boogie', publ. in *Montage of a Dream Deferred* (1951)

7 What happens to a dream deferred?
Does it dry up
like a raisin in the sun?
Or fester like a sore –
And then run?
Does it stink like rotten meat?
Or crust and sugar over –
like a syrupy sweet?
Maybe it just sags
like a heavy load.
Or does it explode?
'Harlem', ibid.

8 It's powerful ... that one drop of Negro blood – because just *one* drop of black blood makes a man coloured. *One* drop – you are a Negro! ... Black is powerful.
Simple Takes a Wife (1953)

Robert Hughes
(b. 1938)
Australian author and critic

Senior art critic for Time *magazine since 1970, he has written on art in* The Shock of the New *(1980), on convict transports to Australia in* The Fatal Shore *(1987), and on political correctness in* Culture of Complaint *(1993).*

1 Would Australians have done anything differently if their country had not been settled as the jail of infinite space? Certainly they would. They would have remembered more of their own history.
The Fatal Shore, ch. 17 (1987)

2 The contest between education and TV – between argument and conviction by spectacle – has been won by television.
Culture of Complaint, ch. 1 (1993)

3 The self is now the sacred cow of American culture, self-esteem is sacrosanct.
Ibid., ch. 1

Ted Hughes

(1930–98)
British poet

His muscular verse is characterized by its raw nature imagery in such collections as The Hawk in the Rain *(1957) and* Crow *(1970).* Birthday Letters *(1998) chronicles his marriage to* SYLVIA PLATH. *'Among the grey-suited modern poets ... he stood out like the bloodstained survivor of a Greek tragedy,' wrote* JOHN CAREY.

1 Till, with a sudden sharp hot stink of fox
It enters the dark hole of the head.
The window is starless still; the clock ticks,
The page is printed.
'The Thought Fox', publ. in *The Hawk in the Rain* (1957)

2 I saw the horses:
Huge in the dense grey – ten together –
Megalith-still. They breathed, making no move,
With draped manes and tilted hind-hooves,
Making no sound.
I passed: not one snorted or jerked its head.
Grey silent fragments
Of a grey silent world.
'The Horses', ibid.

3 This house has been far out at sea all night,
The woods crashing through darkness, the
    booming hills,
Winds stampeding the fields under the window
Floundering black astride and blinding wet.
'Wind', ibid.

4 The future's no calamitous change
But a malingering of now,
Histories, towns, faces that no
Malice or accident much derange.
'A Woman Unconscious', ibid.

5 My feet are locked upon the rough bark.
It took the whole of Creation
To produce my foot, my each feather:
Now I hold Creation in my foot.
'Hawk Roosting', ibid.

6 Pike, three inches long, perfect
Pike in all parts, green tigering the gold.
'Pike', ibid.

7 No, the serpent did not
Seduce Eve to the apple.
All that's simply
Corruption of the facts.
Adam ate the apple.
Eve ate Adam.

The serpent ate Eve.
This is the dark intestine.
'Theology', publ. in *Wodwo*, pt 3 (1967)

8 The sea cries with its meaningless voice
Treating alike its dead and its living,
Probably bored with the appearance of heaven
After so many millions of nights without sleep,
Without purpose, without self-deception.
'Pibroch', ibid.

9 Any form of violence, any vehement form of activity, invokes the bigger energy, the elemental power circuit of the universe.
Interview in 1971, quoted in *The Sunday Times* 1 November 1998

10 Death invented the phone it looks like the altar
    of death
Do not worship the telephone
It drags its worshippers into actual graves
With a variety of devices, through a variety of
    disguised voices.
'Do Not Pick Up the Telephone', publ. in *Earth Numb* (1979)

11 The river is a god
Knee-deep among the reeds, watching men,
Or hung by the heels down at the door of a dam
It is a god, and inviolable.
And will wash itself of all deaths.
'River', publ. in *The River* (1983)

12 You were never
More than a step from Paradise.
You had instant access, your analyst told you,
To the core of your Inferno –
The pit of your hairy flower.
'Child's Park', publ. in *Birthday Letters* (1998). Addressed to SYLVIA PLATH, the poems were written over a period of twenty-five years following her suicide in 1963.

Thomas Hughes

(1822–96)
English author

A Liberal MP (1865–74) who was associated with Christian Socialism, he is remembered primarily for the novel Tom Brown's School Days *(1857), based on his experiences at Rugby School under the headmaster* THOMAS ARNOLD.

1 Life isn't all beer and skittles, but beer and skittles, or something better of the same sort, must form a good part of every Englishman's education.
Tom Brown's School Days, pt 1, ch. 2 (1857)

2 He never wants anything but what's right and

fair; only when you come to settle what's right and fair, it's everything that he wants and nothing that you want. And that's his idea of a compromise. Give me the Brown compromise when I'm on his side.
Ibid., pt 2, ch. 2. Spoken by East.

3 It's more than a game. It's an institution.
Tom Brown, ibid., pt 2, ch. 7. Referring to cricket. Arthur replies: 'Yes, the birthright of British boys old and young, as *habeas corpus* and trial by jury are of British men.'

Victor Hugo

(1802–85)

French poet, dramatist and novelist

His verse and the historical novel Notre-Dame de Paris *(The Hunchback of Notre Dame, 1831) established him as a leader of the French Romantics. He expressed his humanitarian sympathies in his numerous plays and the novel* Les Misérables *(1862). An ardent republican, he lived in exile in Guernsey 1851–70.*

1 Popularity? It's glory's small change.
Ruy Blas, Act 3, Sc. 5 (1838). Spoken by Don Salluste.

2 An invasion of armies can be resisted, but not the invasion of ideas.
The History of a Crime, Conclusion (written 1852, publ. 1877)

3 The word is the Verb, and the Verb is God.
Contemplations, bk 1, no. 8 ('Suite') (1856)

4 The three great problems of this century, the degradation of man in the proletariat, the subjection of women through hunger, the atrophy of the child by darkness.
Les Misérables, Preface (1862)

5 Do not ask the name of the person who seeks a bed for the night. He who is reluctant to give his name is the one who most needs shelter.
Bienvenu Myriel, the bishop of Digne, ibid., pt 1, bk 1, ch. 6

6 The brutalities of progress are called revolutions. When they are over we realize this: that the human race has been roughly handled, but that it has advanced.
The old revolutionary, ibid., pt 1, bk 1, ch. 10

7 The supreme happiness in life is the assurance of being loved; of being loved for oneself, even in spite of oneself.
Ibid., pt 1, bk 5, ch. 4

8 Nothing chills the heart like symmetry, for symmetry is ennui, and ennui is at the heart of grief. Despair is a yawn.
Ibid., pt 2, bk 4, ch. 1

9 The greatest blunders, like the thickest ropes, are often compounded of a multitude of strands. Take the rope apart, separate it into the small threads that compose it, and you can break them one by one. You think, 'That is all there was!' But twist them all together and you have something tremendous.
Ibid., pt 2, bk 5, ch. 10

10 We are on the side of religion as opposed to religions, and we are among those who believe in the wretched inadequacy of sermons and the sublimity of prayer.
Ibid., pt 2, bk 7, ch. 8

11 One is not idle because one is absorbed. There is both visible and invisible labour. To contemplate is to toil, to think is to do. The crossed arms work, the clasped hands act. The eyes upturned to Heaven are an act of creation.
Ibid., pt 2, bk 7, ch. 8

12 A proper distribution of amenities leads to the happiness of the individual. Proper distribution does not imply an *equal* share but an *equitable* share. Equity is the essence of equality ... Social prosperity means a happy man, a free citizen, and a great nation.
Ibid., pt 4, bk 1, ch. 4

13 There are thoughts which are prayers. There are moments when, whatever the posture of the body, the soul is on its knees.
Marius, ibid., pt 4, bk 5, ch. 4

14 Mankind is not a circle with a single centre but an ellipse with two focal points of which facts are one and ideas the other.
Ibid., pt 4, bk 7, ch. 1

15 To learn to read is to light a fire; every syllable that is spelled out is a spark.
Ibid., pt 4, bk 7, ch. 1

16 A compliment is something like a kiss through a veil.
Ibid., pt 4, bk 8, ch. 1

17 Jesus wept; Voltaire smiled [*Jésus a pleuré; Voltaire a souri*]. From that divine tear and from that

human smile is derived the grace of present civilization.

Address on the centenary of VOLTAIRE's death, 30 May 1878, publ. in *Centenaire de Voltaire* (1878)

18 There is a sacred horror about everything grand. It is easy to admire mediocrity and hills; but whatever is too lofty, a genius as well as a mountain, an assembly as well as a masterpiece, seen too near, is appalling.

Ninety-Three, pt 2, bk 3, ch. 1 (1879)

Basil Hume

(1923–99)

British ecclesiastic

A Roman Catholic Benedictine monk and Abbot of Ampleforth (1963–76), he was the first monk to occupy the office of Archbishop of Westminster (1976–99). ELIZABETH II called him 'my cardinal'.

1 If people pray, their consciousnesses become more sensitive. It is very difficult to be a praying person and then go and be beastly to your neighbour.

Quoted in *The Times* 11 April 1998

David Hume

(1711–76)

Scottish philosopher and historian

An empiricist and radical sceptic, he emphasized the primacy of direct personal observation in his writings, which included A Treatise upon Human Nature *(1739–40) and* An Enquiry Concerning Human Understanding *(1748). His* History of England *(6 vols. 1754–62) remained for many years a standard text.*

1 Reason is, and ought only to be the slave of the passions, and can never pretend to any other office than to serve and obey them.

A Treatise upon Human Nature, bk 2, pt 3, sect. 3 (1739)

2 It is not contrary to reason to prefer the destruction of the whole world to the scratching of my finger.

Ibid., bk 2, pt 3, sect. 3

3 It is, therefore, a just *political* maxim *that every man must be supposed a knave*: though at the same time, it appears somewhat strange, that a maxim should be true in *politics*, which is false in *fact*.

Essays, Moral, Political, and Literary, pt 1, 'Of the Independency of Parliament' (1742)

4 In all ages of the world, priests have been enemies to liberty.

Ibid., pt 1, 'Of the Parties of Great Britain'

5 The heart of man is made to reconcile contradictions.

Ibid., pt 1, 'Of the Parties of Great Britain'

6 Avarice, the spur of industry.

Ibid., pt 1, 'Of Civil Liberty'

7 The great end of all human industry is the attainment of happiness. For this were arts invented, sciences cultivated, laws ordained, and societies modelled, by the most profound wisdom of patriots and legislators. Even the lonely savage, who lies exposed to the inclemency of the elements and the fury of wild beasts, forgets not, for a moment, this grand object of his being.

Ibid., pt 1, 'The Stoic'

8 It cannot reasonably be doubted, but a little miss, dressed in a new gown for a dancing-school ball, receives as complete enjoyment as the greatest orator, who triumphs in the splendour of his eloquence, while he governs the passions and resolutions of a numerous assembly.

Ibid., pt 1, 'The Sceptic'

9 Beauty is no quality in things themselves. It exists merely in the mind which contemplates them; and each mind perceives a different beauty.

Ibid., pt 1, 'Of the Standard of Taste'

10 Custom, then, is the great guide of human life. It is that principle alone which renders our experience useful to us.

An Enquiry Concerning Human Understanding, sect. 5, pt 1 (1748). This statement embodied Hume's belief in political obedience arising from habit, as opposed to consent through a 'social contract'.

11 The Christian religion not only was at first attended with miracles, but even at this day cannot be believed by any reasonable person without one.

Ibid., sect. 10, pt 2

12 Money is not, properly speaking, one of the subjects of commerce; but only the instrument which men have agreed upon to facilitate the exchange of one commodity for another. It is none of the wheels of trade: it is the oil which renders the motion of the wheels more smooth and easy.

Political Discourses, pt 2 of *Essays, Moral, Political, and Literary*, 'Of Money' (1752)

13 Never literary attempt was more unfortunate

than my Treatise of Human Nature. It fell *dead-born from the press*, without reaching such distinction, as even to excite a murmur among the zealots.

My Own Life (1777). Hume added: 'But being naturally of a cheerful and sanguine temper, I very soon recovered the blow.'

Hubert H. Humphrey
(1911–78)
US politician

An eloquent speaker, he gained a liberal reputation but, as Vice-President under LYNDON B. JOHNSON *from 1964, alienated many by his support for the Vietnam War. As the Democratic presidential candidate, he narrowly lost to* NIXON *in 1968.*

1 The right to be heard does not automatically include the right to be taken seriously.

Speech to National Student Association at Madison, 23 August 1965, quoted in the *New York Times* 24 August 1965

2 Here we are, just as we ought to be, here we are, the people, here we are in a spirit of dedication, here we are the way politics ought to be in America, the politics of happiness, the politics of purpose and the politics of joy.

Speech in Washington DC, 27 April 1968, quoted in the *New York Times* 28 April 1968. 'The Politics of Joy' was Humphrey's presidential campaign slogan in 1968.

G. W. Hunt
(1829–1904)
English songwriter

1 We don't want to fight, but by Jingo if we do,
We've got the ships, we've got the men, and got the money too!

'We Don't Want to Fight' (music hall song, 1878). The song became popular when BENJAMIN DISRAELI advocated British military action against Russia; 'jingo', a term which had been used earlier by OLIVER GOLDSMITH and THOMAS HOOD (though not in a political context), was applied to Disraeli's supporters.

Leigh Hunt
(1784–1859)
English poet, critic and essayist

James Henry Leigh Hunt. Outspoken in politics, he was the Editor of the radical Examiner *(1808–22), a key member of the circle of* BYRON, KEATS *and* SHELLEY, *and defender of what was disparagingly termed the 'Cockney School of Poetry'. See also* P. B. SHELLEY 50.

1 Never lay yourself open to what is called conviction: you might as well open your waist-coat to receive a knock-down blow.

'Rules for the Conduct of Newspaper Editors', publ. in the *Examiner* 6 March 1808, repr. in *Selected Writings*, 'Of Political Controversy' (ed. David Jesson Dibley, 1990)

2 This Adonis in loveliness was a corpulent man of fifty.

Examiner 22 March 1812. repr. in *The Selected Writings of Leigh Hunt*, vol. 1 (ed. Greg Kucich and Jeffrey N. Cox, 2003). The remark, referring to the Prince Regent, caused Hunt two years' imprisonment.

3 The two divinest things this world has got,
A lovely woman in a rural spot!

The Story of Rimini, canto 3, ll. 257–8 (1816)

4 The laughing queen that caught the world's great hands.

'The Nile' (1818), repr. in *The Poetical Works of Leigh Hunt* (1844). Describing Cleopatra.

5 Poetry, in the most comprehensive application of the term, I take to be the flower of any kind of experience, rooted in truth, and issuing forth into beauty.

The Story of Rimini, Preface (1832 edn)

6 The pretension is nothing; the performance everything. A good apple is better than an insipid peach.

Ibid., Preface

7 Abou Ben Adhem (may his tribe increase!)
Awoke one night from a deep dream of peace.

'Abou Ben Adhem' (1834), repr. in *The Poetical Works of Leigh Hunt* (1844). Opening lines of poem.

8 I pray thee then,
Write me as one that loves his fellow-men.

'Abou Ben Adhem', ibid.

9 Jenny kissed me when we met,
Jumping from the chair she sat in;
Time, you thief, who love to get
Sweets into your list, put that in:
Say I'm weary, say I'm sad,
Say that health and wealth have missed me,
Say I'm growing old, but add,
Jenny kissed me.

'Rondeau' (1838), ibid.

10 Wit is the clash and reconcilement of incongruities; the meeting of extremes round a corner; the flashing of an artificial light from one object to

another, disclosing some unexpected resemblance or connection.

Wit and Humour, Selected from the English Poets, 'An Illustrative Essay on Wit and Humour' (1846)

11 His forehead was prodigious–a great piece of placid marble; and his fine eyes, in which all the activity of his mind seemed to concentrate, moved under it with a sprightly ease, as if it was pastime to them to carry all that thought.

Autobiography, ch. 16 (1850). Describing S. T. COLERIDGE.

Robert Hunter
(b. 1938)
US rock lyricist

He wrote lyrics for the Grateful Dead, and also recorded solo albums, for example Tiger Rose *(1975) and* Jack O'Roses *(1980).*

1 What a long strange trip it's been.

'Truckin'' (song) on the album *American Beauty* (1971) by the Grateful Dead. This best-known of the Grateful Dead's lyrics ('WALSTIB' to dedicated fans) has been adopted on badges and posters and as the title of books and articles evoking the 1960s. A retrospective Grateful Dead album of 1977 also had this as the title.

Herman Hupfeld
(1894–1951)
US songwriter

Among the numerous songs he contributed for stage shows and films of the 1920s and '30s, he is best remembered for 'As Time Goes By' (1931).

1 You must remember this, a kiss is still a kiss,
A sigh is just a sigh;
The fundamental things apply,
As time goes by.

'As Time Goes By' (song), in *Everybody's Welcome* (show, 1931). The song was picked up and featured in the film *Casablanca* (1943), sung by Dooley Wilson as Sam – though the extent of Wilson's active involvement has been questioned. In *Everybody's Welcome*, the song was sung by Frances Williams. See also INGRID BERGMAN 1.

Zora Neale Hurston
(1903–60)
US author and anthropologist

A leading figure of the Harlem Renaissance, she influenced generations of black women writers with her novel Their Eyes Were Watching God *(1937) and her collections of African-American folk tales. See also* YOKO ONO 1.

1 But I am not tragically colored. There is no great sorrow dammed up in my soul, nor lurking behind my eyes. I do not mind at all. I do not belong to the sobbing school of negrohood who hold that nature somehow has given them a lowdown dirty deal ... No, I do not weep at the world – I am too busy sharpening my oyster knife.

'How It Feels to Be Colored Me' (1928), repr. in *I Love Myself When I Am Laughing* (1979)

2 Ships at a distance have every man's wish on board.

Their Eyes Were Watching God, ch. 1 (1937)

Jan Hus
(c. 1370–1415)
Bohemian religious reformer

Also known as John Huss. The Dean of the Philosophy Faculty and later Rector at the University of Prague, he was embroiled in the controversy surrounding the Great Schism and was executed for his heretical views.

1 O sancta simplicitas!
[O holy simplicity!]

Attributed last words, on seeing a peasant woman add a bundle of wood to the stake where he was to die

Saddam Hussein
(b. 1937)
Iraqi president

As President and head of the armed forces of Iraq from 1979, he waged war against Iran (1980–8), suppressed Kurdish separatists and invaded Kuwait (1990). He was defeated by a coalition of forces in the 1991 Gulf War, and captured by US forces after the invasion of Iraq in 2003.

1 The great, the jewel and the mother of battles has begun.

Speech at the start of the Gulf War, 6 January 1991, quoted in the *Independent* 19 January 1991

2 Baghdad, its people and leadership, is determined to force the Mongols of our age to commit suicide at its gates.

Speech in Baghdad, 17 January 2003, quoted in the *Daily Telegraph* 18 January 2003. The speech, which marked the twelfth anniversary of the onset of the Gulf War, compared Britain and America to the Mongol hordes which destroyed Baghdad in 1258.

3 These weapons do not come in small pills that you can hide in your pocket. These are weapons of mass destruction and it is easy to work out if Iraq has them or not.

Interview with TONY BENN, Baghdad, 2 February, 2003,

quoted in the *Daily Telegraph* 5 February 2003. The interview was the first granted by Saddam Hussein to a Western figure for twelve years.

4 So now you are using the law that Saddam signed against Saddam ... Is it allowed to call a president elected by the people and charge him according to a law that was enacted under his will and the will of the people? There is some contradiction.
The Times 3 July 2004. Spoken at Saddam's first court appearance in Baghdad, 2 July 2004.

John Huston
(1906–87)
US film-maker and actor

Prolific but unpredictable, he excelled in adventure pictures and film noir. He made his debut with The Maltese Falcon *(1941) and won an Oscar for* The Treasure of the Sierra Madre *(1948).*

1 After all, crime is only a lefthanded form of human endeavour.
The Asphalt Jungle (film, 1950, written and directed by John Huston from novel by W. R. Burnett). Spoken by Emmerich (Louis Calhern).

Francis Hutcheson
(1694–1746)
Scottish philosopher

Professor of Moral Philosophy at Glasgow from 1729, and a popular preacher, he postulated a moral sense in man, and anticipated the utilitarianism of JEREMY BENTHAM *in his evaluation of actions according to their contribution to the general good.*

1 Wisdom denotes the pursuing of the best ends by the best means.
An Inquiry into the Original of Our Ideas of Beauty and Virtue, Treatise 1, sect. 5, subsect. 16 (1725)

2 That action is best which procures the greatest happiness for the greatest numbers.
Ibid., Treatise 2, sect. 3, subsect. 8. See also JEREMY BENTHAM 1.

Will Hutton
(b. 1950)
British journalist and author

An influential thinker on government and society, he was Editor-in-Chief of the Observer *(1998–9). His books analyse the economic, social and political condition of Britain.*

1 There needs to be fear and greed in the system in order to make it tick.
The State We're In, ch. 7 (1995)

Aldous Huxley
(1894–1963)
British author

His early novels of the 1920s were brilliant satires of upper class and intellectual life; but he produced his best work in the 1930s, including the dystopic Brave New World *(1932). The* Doors of Perception *(1954) recorded his experiments with psychotropic drugs in California, where he lived from 1937.*

1 Beauty for some provides escape,
Who gain a happiness in eyeing
The gorgeous buttocks of the ape
Or Autumn sunsets exquisitely dying.
'Ninth Philosopher's Song', in *Leda* (1920)

2 I can sympathise with people's pains, but not with their pleasures. There is something curiously boring about somebody else's happiness.
Limbo, 'Cynthia' (1920)

3 Most of one's life is one prolonged effort to prevent oneself thinking.
Mortal Coils, 'Green Tunnels' (1922). Spoken by Mr Topes.

4 There are few who would not rather be taken in adultery than in provincialism.
Antic Hay, ch. 10 (1923). Spoken by Mr Boldero.

5 I have discovered the most exciting, the most arduous literary form of all, the most difficult to master, the most pregnant in curious possibilities. I mean the advertisement ... It is far easier to write ten passably effective Sonnets, good enough to take in the not too inquiring critic, than one effective advertisement that will take in a few thousand of the uncritical buying public.
On the Margin, 'Advertisement' (1923)

6 I'm afraid of losing my obscurity. Genuineness only thrives in the dark. Like celery.
Those Barren Leaves, pt 1, ch. 1 (1925). Spoken by Miss Thriplow.

7 Science has 'explained' nothing; the more we know the more fantastic the world becomes and the profounder the surrounding darkness.
Along the Road, pt 2 'Views of Holland' (1925)

8 If it were not for the intellectual snobs who pay – in solid cash – the tribute which philistinism owes

to culture, the arts would perish with their starving practitioners. Let us thank heaven for hypocrisy.
Jesting Pilate, pt 1 (1926)

9 Thought is barred in this City of Dreadful Joy and conversation is unknown.
Ibid., pt 4. Of Los Angeles, where Huxley later lived.

10 Those who believe that they are exclusively in the right are generally those who achieve something.
Proper Studies, 'A Note on Dogma: Varieties of Human Type' (1927)

11 It takes two to make a murder. There are born victims, born to have their throats cut, as the cutthroats are born to be hanged.
Point Counter Point, ch. 12 (1928). Spoken by Maurice Spandrell.

12 A bad book is as much of a labour to write as a good one; it comes as sincerely from the author's soul.
Ibid., ch. 13

13 Consistency is contrary to nature, contrary to life. The only completely consistent people are the dead.
Do What You Will, 'Wordsworth in the Tropics' (1929)

14 A man may be a pessimistic determinist before lunch and an optimistic believer in the will's freedom after it.
Ibid., 'Pascal', sect. 23

15 Single-mindedness is all very well in cows or baboons; in an animal claiming to belong to the same species as Shakespeare it is simply disgraceful.
Ibid. 'Pascal', sect. 24

16 Experience is not what happens to a man; it is what a man does with what happens to him.
Texts and Pretexts, Introduction (1932)

17 So long as men worship the Caesars and Napoleons, Caesars and Napoleons will duly rise and make them miserable.
Ends and Means, ch. 8 (1937)

18 Speed, it seems to me, provides the one genuinely modern pleasure.
Music at Night and Other Essays, 'Wanted, a New Pleasure' (1949)

19 Man is an intelligence, not served by, but in servitude to his organs.
Themes and Variations, 'Variations on a Philosopher' (1950)

20 Pure Spirit, one hundred degrees proof – that's a drink that only the most hardened contemplation-guzzlers indulge in. Bodhisattvas dilute their Nirvana with equal parts of love and work.
Island, ch. 15 (1962). Spoken by Susila.

21 It's with bad sentiments that one makes good novels.
Letter, 10 July 1962, quoted in *Aldous Huxley: the Critical Heritage* (ed. Donald Watt, 1975). Huxley believed this to be the explanation for why his novel *Island* – published that year and greatly criticized – was 'so inadequate'.

22 Idealism is the noble toga that political gentlemen drape over their will to power.
Quoted in obituary, the *New York Herald Tribune* 25 November 1963

(Sir) Julian Huxley
(1887–1975)
British biologist

He was the first Director of UNESCO (1946–8), helped found the World Wildlife Fund (now called World Wide Fund for Nature) and wrote popular science books including Essays of a Biologist *(1923).*

1 God can no longer be considered controller of the universe in any but a Pickwickian sense. Operationally, God is beginning to resemble not a ruler but the last fading smile of a cosmic Cheshire cat.
Religion without Revelation, ch. 3 (1957 edn)

T. H. Huxley
(1825–95)
English scientist

Thomas Henry Huxley. The grandfather of ALDOUS HUXLEY *and* JULIAN HUXLEY, *he performed valuable work in the fields of biology, physiology, palaeontology and taxonomy. He published prolifically and became known as 'Darwin's bulldog' for his defence of evolution.*

1 Sit down before fact as a little child, be prepared to give up every preconceived notion, follow humbly wherever and to whatever abysses nature leads, or you shall learn nothing.
Letter to CHARLES KINGSLEY, 23 September 1860, publ. in *Life and Letters of Thomas Henry Huxley*, vol. 1 (1900) by Leonard Huxley

2 The chess-board is the world; the pieces are the phenomena of the universe; the rules of the game are what we call the laws of Nature. The player on the other side is hidden from us. We know that his play is always fair, just, and patient. But also we

know, to our cost, that he never overlooks a mistake, or makes the smallest allowance for ignorance.
'A Liberal Education' (1868), publ. in *Lay Sermons, Addresses, and Reviews* (1870)

3 Fact I know; and Law I know; but what is this Necessity, save an empty shadow of my own mind's throwing?
'On The Physical Basis Of Life' (1868), publ. in *Collected Essays*, vol. 1 (1893)

4 Mathematics may be compared to a mill of exquisite workmanship, which grinds your stuff to any degree of fineness; but, nevertheless, what you get out depends on what you put in; and as the grandest mill in the world will not extract wheat flour from peascods, so pages of formulae will not get a definite result out of loose data.
'Geological Reform' (1869), ibid., vol. 8 (1894)

5 The great tragedy of science – the slaying of a beautiful theory by an ugly fact.
'Biogenesis and Abiogenesis', presidential address to the British Association for the Advancement of Science, 1870, ibid., vol. 8

6 Patience and tenacity of purpose are worth more than twice their weight of cleverness.
'On Medical Education', address at University College, London, 1870, ibid., vol. 3 (1893)

7 Books are the money of Literature, but only the counters of Science.
'Universities: Actual and Ideal', rectorial address, Aberdeen, 1874, ibid., vol. 3

8 All truth, in the long run, is only common sense clarified.
'On the Study of Biology', lecture at South Kensington Museum, London, 1876, ibid., vol. 3

9 Logical consequences are the scarecrows of fools and the beacons of wise men.
Science and Culture, 'On the Hypothesis that Animals are Automata' (1881)

10 It is the customary fate of new truths, to begin as heresies, and to end as superstitions.
Ibid., 'The Coming of Age of *The Origin of Species*'

11 Irrationally held truths may be more harmful than reasoned errors.
Ibid., 'The Coming of Age of *The Origin of Species*'

12 I asserted – and I repeat – that a man has no reason to be ashamed of having an ape for his grand-father. If there were an ancestor whom I should feel shame in recalling it would rather be a man – a man

of restless and versatile intellect – who, not content with an equivocal success in his own sphere of activity, plunges into scientific questions with which he has no real acquaintance, only to obscure them by an aimless rhetoric, and distract the attention of his hearers from the real point at issue by eloquent digressions and skilled appeals to religious prejudice.
Debating evolution at Oxford, June 1860, quoted in letter publ. in *Life and Letters of Thomas Henry Huxley*, vol. 1, ch. 14 (1900) by Leonard Huxley. In reply to Samuel Wilberforce, Bishop of Oxford, who had asked whether it was through his grandfather or his grandmother that Huxley claimed his descent from a monkey.

Hymns and Carols

Entries are arranged alphabetically according to title. See also THOMAS AQUINAS 1–3; BIBLE, NEW TESTAMENT: PHILIPPIANS 3; WILLIAM BLAKE 80; BOOK OF COMMON PRAYER 9; SYDNEY CARTER 2; WILLIAM COWPER 2–6; ELEANOR FARJEON 1; PHINEAS FLETCHER 2; VENANTIUS FORTUNATUS 1, 2; GEORGE HERBERT 15, 25, 28, 42, 43, 44; JULIA WARD HOWE 1; JOHN KEBLE 1–3; MARTIN LUTHER 4; JOHN HENRY NEWMAN 15, 16; CHRISTINA ROSSETTI 15; NAHUM TATE 4.

1 Abide with me; fast falls the eventide;
The darkness deepens; Lord with me abide!
When other helpers fail, and comforts flee,
Help of the helpless, O abide with me.
Change and decay in all around I see;
O Thou who changest not, abide with me.
'Abide with me', sts 1–2 (1847), written by Henry Francis Lyte, publ. in *The Remains of H. F. Lyte MA* (1850). Also known as 'Evening'. In the BIBLE, St Luke 24:29, the words appear: 'Abide with us: for it is toward evening, and the day is far spent.'

2 Adam lay ybounden,
Bounden in a bond,
Four thousand winter
Thought he not too long.
And all was for an apple,
An apple that he took,
As clerkës finden written
In their book.
'Adam lay ybounden' (traditional, 15th century)

3 *Adeste, fideles,*
Laeti triumphantes;
Venite, venite in Bethlehem;
Natum videte regem angelorum.
Venite, adoremus Dominum.
[O come, all ye faithful,

Joyful and triumphant,
O come ye, O come ye to Bethlehem;
Come and behold him,
Born the King of angels:
O come, let us adore him Christ the Lord!]

'Adeste Fideles' ('O come all ye faithful'), st. 1 and refrain. The original Latin was written by John Francis Wade (c. 1743), publ. in *Evening Offices of the Church* (1760), transl. by Frederick Oakley (1841).

4 All for Jesus! All for Jesus!
All my days and all my hours.

'All for Jesus', st. 1, written by Mary D. James (1871) and set to music by John Stainer in *The Crucifixion* (1887)

5 All glory, laud, and honour
To Thee, Redeemer, King,
To whom the lips of children
Made sweet hosannas ring.

'All glory, laud and honour', refrain, written by Bishop Theodulph of Orleans (c. 820), transl. from the Latin by John Mason Neale in *Hymns Ancient and Modern* (1861)

6 All my hope on God is founded;
He doth still my trust renew,
Me through change and chance he guideth,
Only good and only true.
God unknown,
He alone
Calls my heart to be his own.

'All my hope on God is founded', written by Joachim Neander (1650–80), transl. from the German by ROBERT BRIDGES in *The Yattendon Hymnal* (1899)

7 All people that on earth do dwell,
Sing to the Lord with cheerful voice.
Him serve with fear, His praise forth tell;
Come ye before Him and rejoice.

'All people that on earth do dwell', st. 1, written by William Kethe, publ. in *Fourscore and Seven Psalms of David* (1561). Sung to the tune 'Old Hundredth'.

8 All things bright and beautiful,
All creatures great and small,
All things wise and wonderful,
The Lord God made them all.
Each little flower that opens,
Each little bird that sings,
He made their glowing colours,
He made their tiny wings.
The rich man in his castle,
The poor man at his gate,
God made them, high or lowly,

And ordered their estate.

'All things bright and beautiful', sts 1–3, written by Cecil Frances Alexander, publ. in *Hymns for Little Children* (1848)

9 Amazing grace! how sweet the sound
That saved a wretch like me!
I once was lost, but now am found,
Was blind, but now I see.

'Amazing grace', written by John Newton, publ. in *Olney Hymns* (1799)

10 Angels, from the realms of glory,
Wing your flight o'er all the earth.

'Angels, from the realms of glory', st. 1 (1816), written by James Montgomery, publ. in *The Christian Psalmist* (1825)

11 Art thou weary, art thou languid,
Art thou sore distressed?

'Art thou weary?' (8th century), written by St Stephen the Sabaite, transl. from the Greek by John Mason Neale in *Hymns for the Eastern Church* (1862)

12 As with gladness men of old
Did the guiding star behold,
As with joy they hailed its light,
Leading onward, beaming bright,
So, most gracious Lord, may we
Evermore be led to Thee.

'As with gladness men of old', st. 1, written by William Dix, publ. in *Hymns Ancient and Modern* (1861)

13 Before the ending of the day,
Creator of the world, we pray
That Thou with wonted love wouldst keep
Thy watch around us while we sleep.

'Before the ending of the day', st. 1, written by Ambrose of Milan (5th–6th century), transl. from the Latin by John Mason Neale in *Hymns Ancient and Modern* (1861)

14 Brightest and best of the sons of the morning,
Dawn on our darkness and lend us thine aid;
Star of the east, the horizon adorning,
Guide where our infant Redeemer is laid.

'Brightest and best of the sons of the morning', st. 1 (1811), written by Reginald Heber, repr. ibid.

15 Christians, awake! salute the happy morn,
Whereon the Saviour of the world was born.

'Christians, awake', st. 1, written by John Byrom (1746), repr. in *Hymns Ancient and Modern* (1875)

16 Christ is made the sure Foundation,
Christ the head and cornerstone,
Chosen of the Lord, and precious,
Binding all the Church in one.

'Christ is made the sure Foundation', st. 1 (7th century), transl.

from the Latin by John Mason Neale, publ. in *Mediaeval Hymns and Sequences* (1851)

17 The Church's one foundation
Is Jesus Christ, her Lord;
She is his new creation
By water and the Word.
From heaven he came and sought her
To be his holy Bride;
With his own blood he bought her
And for her life he died.

'The Church's one foundation', st. 1, written by Samuel J. Stone, publ. in *Lyra Fidelium; Twelve Hymns of the Twelve Articles of the Apostle's Creed* (1866)

18 Come down, O Love divine,
Seek Thou this soul of mine,
And visit it with Thine own ardour glowing;
O Comforter, draw near,
Within my heart appear,
And kindle it, Thy holy flame bestowing.

'Come down, O Love divine', written by Bianco di Siena (c. 1350–1434), transl. by Richard Littledale, publ. in *The People's Hymnal* (1867). Set to the tune 'Down Ampney' by Ralph Vaughan Williams.

19 Dear Lord and Father of mankind,
Forgive our foolish ways!
Re-clothe us in our rightful mind,
In purer lives thy service find,
In deeper reverence praise.

'Dear Lord and Father of mankind', st. 1, written by JOHN GREENLEAF WHITTIER, publ. as 'The Brewing of Soma', st. 12 (1872), repr. in *The Poetical Works of John Greenleaf Whittier* (ed. W. Garrett Horder, 1911)

20 Eternal Father, strong to save,
Whose arm doth bind the restless wave,
Who bidd'st the mighty ocean deep
Its own appointed limits keep;
O hear us when we cry to Thee,
For those in peril on the sea.

'Eternal Father, strong to save', st. 1, written by William Whiting, publ. in *Hymns Ancient and Modern* (1861)

21 All praise to Thee, my God, this night,
For all the blessings of the light;
Keep me, O keep me, King of Kings,
Beneath thy own almighty wings.
Teach me to live that I may dread
The grave as little as my bed.

'Evening Hymn', sts 1 and 3, written by Thomas Ken, publ. in *Manual of Prayers for the Use of the Scholars in Winchester College* (1695), and set to 'Tallis's Canon' by Thomas Tallis.

The first line was later changed to 'Glory to Thee, my God, this night'.

22 Faith of our fathers, living still,
In spite of dungeon, fire and sword;
O how our hearts beat high with joy
Whenever we hear that glorious Word!

'Faith of our fathers', st. 1, written by William Frederick Faber, publ. in *Jesus and Mary: or Catholic Hymns for Singing and Reading* (1849). The hymn's refrain 'Faith of our fathers, holy faith!/We will be true to Thee till death' was added by James G. Walton in 1874.

23 Fight the good fight with all thy might;
Christ is thy strength, and Christ thy right;
Lay hold on life, and it shall be
Thy joy and crown eternally.

'Fight the good fight', written by John S. B. Monsell, publ. in *Hymns of Love and Praise for the Church's Year* (1863)

24 The first Nowell, the angel did say
Was to certain poor shepherds in fields as they lay.

'The first Nowell', st. 1 (traditional, 17th century), publ. in *Christmas Carols, Ancient and Modern* (ed. William Sandys, 1833)

25 For all the saints who from their labours rest,
Who Thee by faith before the world confessed,
Thy name O Jesu, be for ever blest.
Alleluia!
From earth's wide bounds, from ocean's farthest coast,
Through gates of pearl streams in the countless host,
Singing to Father, Son, and Holy Ghost,
Alleluia!

'For all the saints', sts 1 and 8, written by William Walsham How, publ. in. *Hymns for Saints Days* (ed. Earl Nelson, 1864). Set to music by Ralph Vaughan Williams for *The English Hymnal* (1906)

26 Forth in thy name, O Lord, I go,
My daily labour to pursue;
Thee, only Thee, resolved to know,
In all I think or speak or do.

'Forth in thy name, O Lord, I go', st. 1, written by Charles Wesley, publ. in *Hymns and Sacred Poems* (1749)

27 From Greenland's icy mountains,
From India's coral strand,
Where Afric's sunny fountains
Roll down their golden sand.

'From Greenland's icy mountains', st. 1, written by Reginald Heber (1821), repr. in *Hymns Ancient and Modern* (1875)

28 Gentle Jesus, meek and mild,
Look upon a little child;

Pity my simplicity,
Suffer me to come to Thee.
'Gentle Jesus, meek and mild', st. 1, written by Charles Wesley, ibid.

29 Glorious things of Thee are spoken,
Zion, city of our God!
'Glorious things of Thee are spoken', st. 1, written by John Newton, publ. in *Olney Hymns* (1799). The hymn's tune was originally written by JOSEPH HAYDN, and was also used for the Austrian and German national anthems. See A. H. HOFFMANN 1.

30 God is gone up on high
With a triumphant noise.
'God is gone up', st. 1, written by Charles Wesley, publ. in *Hymns for our Lord's Resurrection* (1746). See BIBLE, OLD TESTAMENT: PSALMS 60.

31 God is working his purpose out as year succeeds
  to year;
God is working his purpose out and the time is
  drawing near;
Nearer and nearer draws the time, the time that
  shall surely be,
When the earth shall be filled with the glory of
  God as the waters cover the sea.
'God is working his purpose out', st. 1, written by Arthur Campbell Ainger (1894), repr. in *The English Hymnal* (1906)

32 God rest ye merry, gentlemen,
Let nothing you dismay.
For Jesus Christ our Saviour
Was born on Christmas Day.
O tidings of comfort and joy.
'God rest ye merry, gentlemen', st. 1 and refrain (traditional, 18th century), publ. in *Christmas Carols Ancient and Modern* (ed. William Sandys, 1833)

33 Good King Wenceslas looked out
On the feast of Stephen,
When the snow lay round about,
Deep and crisp and even.
'Good King Wenceslas', st. 1, written by John Mason Neale, publ. in *Carols for Christmas-Tide* (1853)

34 Guide me, O Thou great Redeemer,
Pilgrim through this barren land;
I am weak, but Thou art mighty;
Hold me with thy powerful hand:
Bread of heaven, bread of heaven,
Feed me now and evermore.
'Guide me, O Thou great Redeeemer', st. 1 (1745), written by William Williams, transl. from the Welsh by Peter Williams in *Hymns on Various Subjects* (1771). Sung to the tune of 'Cwm Rhondda' (1907) by John Hughes.

35 Hark! the herald-angels sing
Glory to the new born king.
Peace on earth and mercy mild,
God and sinners reconciled.
Hail, the heaven-born Prince of Peace!
Hail, the Sun of Righteousness!
'Hark the herald-angels sing', sts 1–2, publ. in *Hymns for Social Worship* (1753) by George Whitefield. The first two lines were changed by Whitefield from Charles Wesley's original 'Hymn for Christmas' (1739): 'Hark! how all the welkin rings,/Glory to the King of kings'. Set to music by Felix Mendelssohn from his cantata *Festgesang* (1840).

36 He who would valiant be
'Gainst all disaster,
Let him in constancy
Follow the Master.
There's no discouragement
Shall make him once relent
His first avowed intent
To be a pilgrim.
'He who would valiant be', st. 1, modified from John Bunyan's version by Percy Dearmer, publ. in *The English Hymnal* (1906). See JOHN BUNYAN 14–16.

37 Holy, Holy, Holy! Lord God Almighty!
Early in the morning our song shall rise to Thee:
Holy, Holy, Holy! merciful and mighty!
God in Three Persons, blessèd Trinity!
Holy, Holy, Holy! all the saints adore Thee,
Casting down their golden crowns around the
  glassy sea,
Cherubim and Seraphim falling down before
  Thee,
Which wert, and art, and evermore shalt be.
'Holy, Holy, Holy', sts 1–2, written by Reginald Heber, publ. in *Hymns Written and Adapted to the Weekly Church Service of the Year* (1827)

38 O Lord my God, when I in awesome wonder
Consider all the works Thy hand hath made,
I see the stars, I hear the mighty thunder
Thy power throughout the universe displayed.
Then sings my soul, my Saviour God to Thee,
How great Thou art, how great Thou art!
'How great Thou art', st. 1 and refrain (1885), written by the Swedish pastor Carl Boburg, transl. by Stuart K. Hine (1899)

39 How sweet the name of Jesus sounds
In a believer's ear!
It soothes his sorrows, heals his wounds,
And drives away his fear.
'How sweet the name of Jesus sounds', written by John Newton, publ. in *Olney Hymns* (1799)

40 Immortal, invisible God only wise,
In light inaccessible hid from our eyes,
Most blessèd, most glorious, the Ancient of Days,
Almighty, victorious, thy great name we praise.
'Immortal, invisible God only wise', written by Walter C.
Smith, publ. in *Hymns of Christ and the Christian Life* (1867)

41 I sing of a maiden
That is makeless;
King of all kings
To her son she ches.
He came all so still
Where his mother was,
As dew in April
That falleth on the grass.
'I sing of a maiden', sts 1–2 (traditional, 15th century), publ.
in *Songs and Carols* (ed. Thomas Wright, 1856)

42 It came upon the midnight clear,
That glorious song of old,
From Angels bending near the earth
To touch their harps of gold;
'Peace on the earth, good will to man
From Heaven's all gracious King.'
The world in solemn stillness lay
To hear the angels sing.
'It came upon the midnight clear', written by Edmund Hamilton Sears, publ. as 'That Glorious Song of Old', in the *Christian Register*, vol. 28 (1849)

43 I vow to thee, my country – all earthly things
   above –
Entire and whole and perfect, the service of my
   love,
The love that asks no question: the love that
   stands the test,
That lays upon the altar the dearest and the best:
The love that never falters, the love that pays the
   price,
The love that makes undaunted the final sacrifice.
'I Vow to Thee, My Country' (1918) by Cecil Spring-Rice. The
hymn was set to the tune of 'Thaxted', a version of 'Jupiter'
from Holst's *Planet Suite*.

44 Jesu, lover of my soul,
Let me to thy bosom fly,
While the nearer waters roll,
While the tempest still is high;
Hide me, O my Saviour, hide,
Till the storm of life is past;
Safe into the haven guide,
O receive my soul at last.
'Jesu, lover of my soul', written by Charles Wesley, publ. as
'In Temptation' in *Hymns and Sacred Poems* (1740)

45 Jesus' blood never failed me yet,
Never failed me yet,
Jesus' blood never failed me yet.
There's one thing I know
For he loves me so.
Jesus' Blood Never Failed Me Yet (1973) by Gavin Bryars. The
words, the origin of which is unknown, were sung by a
London street tramp, and looped and orchestrated by Bryars.

46 Jesus Christ is risen today, Alleluia!
Our triumphant holy day, Alleluia!
Who did once, upon the cross, Alleluia!
Suffer to redeem our loss, Alleluia!
'Jesus Christ is risen today', st. 1 (Bohemian Latin carol, 14th
century), transl. in *Lyra Davidica* (1708)

47 Jesus, good above all other,
Gentle Child of gentle Mother,
In a stable born our Brother,
Give us grace to persevere.
'Jesus, good above all other', st. 1, written by Adam of St Victor
(12th century), adapted by Percy Dearmer in *The English Hymnal* (1906)

48 The King of love my shepherd is,
Whose goodness faileth never;
I nothing lack if I am his
And he is mine for ever.
In death's dark vale I fear no ill
With Thee, dear Lord, beside me;
Thy rod and staff my comfort still,
Thy cross before to guide me.
'The King of love my shepherd is', sts 1 and 4 (1868), written
by Henry Williams Baker, publ. in *Hymns Ancient and Modern*
(1868). See BIBLE, OLD TESTAMENT: PSALMS 24, 25.

49 Lead, kindly Light, amid the encircling
   gloom,
Lead Thou me on!
The night is dark, and I am far from home –
Lead Thou me on!
Keep Thou my feet; I do not ask to see
The distant scene – one step enough for me.
'Lead, kindly Light', st. 1, written by JOHN HENRY NEWMAN,
publ. as 'The Pillar of the Cloud', in *Lyra Apostolica* (1836)

50 Lead us, Heavenly Father, lead us
O'er the world's tempestuous sea;
Guard us, guide us, keep us, feed us,
For we have no help but Thee;
Yet possessing every blessing,
If our God our Father be.
'Lead us, Heavenly Father', st. 1, written by James Edmeston,
publ. in *Sacred Lyrics, Set Two* (1821)

51 Lo! He comes with clouds descending,
Once for favoured sinners slain;
Thousand thousand Saints attending
Swell the triumph of His train.

'Lo! He comes', written by Charles Wesley, publ. in *Hymns of Intercession for all Mankind* (1758)

52 Lord Jesus, think on me,
And purge away my sin;
From earthborn passions set me free,
And make me pure within.

'Lord Jesus, think on me', written by Synesius of Cyrene (c. 375–430), transl. by Allen W. Chatfield in *Songs and Hymns of the Earliest Greek Christian Poets, Bishops and Others* (1876)

53 Lord of all hopefulness, Lord of all joy,
Whose trust, ever childlike, no cares could destroy,
Be there at our waking, and give us, we pray,
Your bliss in our hearts, Lord, at the break of the
  day.

'Lord of all hopefulness', written by Jan Struther (pseudonym of Joyce Anstruther Graham Placzek), publ. in *Songs of Praise* (1931)

54 The Lord's my Shepherd, I'll not want.
He makes me down to lie
In pastures green; he leadeth me
The quiet waters by.
My soul he doth restore again;
And me to walk doth make
Within the paths of righteousness,
E'en for his own name's sake.
Yea, though I walk in death's dark vale,
Yet will I fear no ill;
For Thou art with me; and thy rod
And staff me comfort still.

'The Lord's my shepherd', sts 1–3, publ. in the *Scottish Psalter* (1850), sung to the tune of 'Crimond' (1872) by Jessie S. Irvine. See BIBLE, OLD TESTAMENT: PSALMS 25

55 Lord, thy word abideth,
And our footsteps guideth;
Who its truth believeth
Light and joy receiveth.

'Lord, thy word abideth', written by Henry Williams Baker, publ. in *Hymns Ancient and Modern* (1861)

56 Love divine, all loves excelling,
Joy of heav'n, to earth come down,
Fix in us thy humble dwelling,
All thy faithful mercies crown.
Jesu, Thou art all compassion,
Pure unbounded love Thou art;

Visit us with thy salvation,
Enter every trembling heart.

'Love divine', st. 1, written by Charles Wesley, publ. in *Hymns for those that seek . . . Redemption* (1747)

57 Make me a channel of your peace.
Where there is hatred let me bring your love;
Where there is injury, your pardon, Lord;
And where there's doubt, true faith in you.

'Make me a channel of your peace', st. 1 (1967), repr. in *Hymns Old and New* (1996). The words are adapted from a prayer of St Francis. See FRANCIS OF ASSISI 1.

58 Awake, my soul, and with the sun
Thy daily stage of duty run;
Shake off dull sloth, and joyful rise
To pay thy morning sacrifice.

'Morning Hymn', st. 1, written by Thomas Ken, publ. in *Manual of Prayers for the Use of the Scholars in Winchester College* (1700)

59 My God, how wonderful Thou art,
Thy majesty, how bright;
How beautiful thy mercy seat
In depths of burning light!

'My God, how wonderful Thou art', written by William Frederick Faber, publ. in *Jesus and Mary: or Catholic Hymns for Singing and Reading* (1849)

60 Nearer, my God, to Thee, nearer to Thee!
E'en though it be a cross that raiseth me,
Still all my song shall be, nearer, my God, to Thee.

'Nearer My God to Thee', written by Sarah Flower Adams, publ. in *Hymns and Anthems* (ed. William Johnson Fox, 1841). Said to have been played by the orchestra as the ship *Titanic* was sinking (1912).

61 Now thank we all our God,
With heart and hands and voices,
Who wondrous things hath done,
In whom this world rejoices;
Who from our mother's arms
Hath blessed us on our way
With countless gifts of love,
And still is ours today.

'Now thank we all our God', written by Martin Rinkart (as 'Nun danket alle Gott', 1636), transl. from the German by Catherine Winkworth in *Lyra Germanica* (1858)

62 Now the day is over,
Night is drawing nigh,
Shadows of the evening
Steal across the sky.

'Now the day is over', written by Sabine Baring-Gould, publ. in *Hymns Ancient and Modern* (1868)

63 O for a thousand tongues to sing
My great Redeemer's praise.

'O for a thousand tongues to sing', written by Charles Wesley as 'For the Anniversary Day of One's Conversion' in *Hymns and Sacred Poems* (1740)

64 O brother man! fold to thy heart thy
   brother.
Where pity dwells, the peace of God is there;
To worship rightly is to love each other,
Each smile a hymn, each kindly word a prayer.

'O brother man!', written as 'Worship' by JOHN GREENLEAF WHITTIER (1848), repr. in *The Poetical Works of John Greenleaf Whittier* (ed. W. Garrett Horder, 1911)

65 O come, O come, Emmanuel,
and ransom captive Israel,
that mourns in lonely exile here
until the Son of God appear.
Rejoice! Rejoice!
Emmanuel shall come to Thee, O Israel.

'O come, O come, Emmanuel', st. 1 and refrain, transl. from the 12th-century Latin by John Mason Neale in *Mediaeval Hymns and Sequences* (1851). Neale's original first line was 'Draw nigh, draw nigh, Emmanuel'.

66 Oft in danger, oft in woe,
Onward, Christians, onward go.

'Oft in danger, oft in woe', st. 1, written by H. Kirke White (1812), publ. in the *Mitre Hymn Book* (1836)

67 O Jesus, I have promised
To serve Thee to the end;
Be Thou forever near me,
My Master and my Friend.
I shall not fear the battle
If Thou art by my side,
Nor wander from the pathway
If Thou wilt be my Guide.

'O Jesus, I have promised', st. 1, written by John Ernest Bode, publ. in *Psalms and Hymns of the Society for the Propagation of Christian Knowledge*, Appendix (1869)

68 So I'll cherish the old rugged cross,
Till my trophies at last I lay down;
I will cling to the old rugged cross
And exchange it some day for a crown.

'The Old Rugged Cross', refrain, written by George Bennard (1913), repr. in the *Baptist Hymnal* (1975)

69 O little town of Bethlehem,
How still we see Thee lie!
Above thy deep and dreamless sleep
The silent stars go by.
Yet in thy dark streets shineth
The everlasting light;

The hopes and fears of all the years
Are met in Thee to-night.

'O little town of Bethlehem' written (1868) by Phillips Brooks, publ. in *Hymns Ancient and Modern* (1875)

70 Once in royal David's city
Stood a lowly cattle-shed,
Where a mother laid her baby
In a manger for his bed:
Mary was that mother mild,
Jesus Christ her little child.

'Once in royal David's city', st. 1, written by Cecil Frances Alexander, publ. in *Hymns for Little Children* (1848)

71 Onward, Christian soldiers,
Marching as to war,
With the cross of Jesus
Going on before.

'Onward, Christian Soldiers', written by Sabine Baring Gould, publ. in *Hymns Ancient and Modern* (1868)

72 O sacred head, sore wounded,
Defiled and put to scorn;
O kingly head surrounded
With mocking crown of thorn.

'O sacred head, sore wounded', st. 1, written by Paul Gerhardt (1607–76), transl. from the German by ROBERT BRIDGES (1899), whose version started 'O sacred head, surrounded'. The words have been attributed to St Bernard of Clairvaux (1090–1153), and were incorporated into the *St Matthew Passion*, set to music (1729) by J. S. Bach.

73 O worship the Lord in the beauty of holiness!
Bow down before him, his glory proclaim;
With gold of obedience, and incense of lowliness,
Kneel and adore him: the Lord is his Name!

'O worship the Lord', st. 1, written by John S. B. Monsell, publ. in *Hymns of Love and Praise for the Church's Year* (1863)

74 Praise, my soul, the King of heaven;
To his feet thy tribute bring.
Ransomed, healed, restored, forgiven,
Who like me his praise should sing?
Praise him! Praise him!
Praise him! Praise him!
Praise the everlasting King.

'Praise, my soul, the King of heaven', written by Henry F. Lyte, publ. in *Spirit of the Psalms* (1834)

75 Rejoice, the Lord is King!
Your Lord and King adore;
Mortals, give thanks and sing,
And triumph evermore:
Lift up your heart, lift up your voice;

Rejoice, again, I say rejoice.

'Rejoice, the Lord is King!', written by Charles Wesley, publ. in *Hymns for our Lord's Resurrection* (1746)

76 Ride on, ride on, in majesty!
In lowly pomp ride on to die;
Bow thy meek head to mortal pain,
Then take, O God, thy power, and reign.

'Ride on, ride on, in majesty', st. 5, written by Henry Hart Milman (1827), repr. in *The English Hymnal* (1906)

77 Rock of Ages, cleft for me,
Let me hide myself in Thee;
Let the water and the blood,
From thy wounded side which flowed,
Be of sin the double cure;
Save from wrath and make me pure.

'Rock of Ages, cleft for me', written by Augustus Montague Toplady (1776), repr. in *Hymns Ancient and Modern* (1861). JOHN WESLEY wrote of 'Christ the Rock/Of eternal ages' in his hymn 'Praise By All to Christ is Given' (1788), while the lines 'These waters are the well of life, and lo! The Rock of Ages, there, from whence they flow,' appear in *Pilgrimage to Waterloo*, pt 2, st. 3 by ROBERT SOUTHEY.

78 I bind unto myself today
The strong Name of the Trinity,
By invocation of the same,
The Three in One, and One in Three.
Christ be with me, Christ within me,
Christ behind me, Christ before me,
Christ beside me, Christ to win me,
Christ to comfort and restore me.
Christ beneath me, Christ above me,
Christ in quiet, Christ in danger,
Christ in hearts of all that love me,
Christ in mouth of friend and stranger.

'St Patrick's Breastplate', st 1, 8, attributed to St Patrick, transl. (1889) from the Gaelic by Cecil Frances Alexander, publ. in *The English Hymnal* (1906). See SAINT PATRICK 1.

79 Shall we gather at the river,
Where bright angel feet have trod,
With its crystal tide forever
Flowing by the throne of God?
Yes, we'll gather at the river,
The beautiful, the beautiful river;
Gather with the saints at the river
That flows by the throne of God.

'Shall we gather at the river', st. 1 and refrain, written by Robert Lowry, publ. in *Happy Voices* (1865)

80 Soldiers of Christ, arise,
And put your armour on.

Soldiers of Christ, arise', st. 1, written by Charles Wesley as 'The Whole Armour of God' in *Hymns and Sacred Poems* (1749)

81 Stand up, stand up for Jesus, ye soldiers of the cross;
Lift high His royal banner, it must not suffer loss.

'Stand up, stand up for Jesus', st. 1 (1858), written by George Duffield, repr. in *The English Hymnal* (1906)

82 The strife is o'er, the battle done;
Now is the Victor's triumph won;
O let the song of praise be sung:
Alleluia!

'The strife is o'er', st. 1 (*c.* 12th century), transl. from the Latin by Francis Pott in *Hymns Ancient and Modern* (1861)

83 Tell me the old, old story
Of unseen things above,
Of Jesus and his glory,
Of Jesus and his love.

'Tell me the old, old story', written by A. Katherine Hankey, publ. in *The Story Wanted* (1866)

84 There is a green hill far away
Without a city wall,
Where the dear Lord was crucified,
Who died to save us all.

'There is a green hill far away', st. 1, written by Cecil Frances Alexander, publ. in *Hymns for Little Children* (1848)

85 Through the night of doubt and sorrow,
Onward goes the pilgrim band,
Singing songs of expectation,
Marching to the promised land.

'Through the night of doubt and sorrow', st. 1, written by Bernhardt Severin Ingemann (1826), transl. from the Danish by Sabine Baring Gould, publ. in *The People's Hymnal* (1867)

86 We plough the fields, and scatter
The good seed on the land,
But it is fed and watered
By God's almighty hand.

'We plough the fields and scatter', st. 1 (1782), written by the German poet Matthias Claudius, transl. by Jane Montgomery Campbell (1861) in *Hymns Ancient and Modern* (1868)

87 We three kings of Orient are;
Bearing gifts we traverse afar,
Field and fountain, moor and mountain,
Following yonder star.
O star of wonder, star of light,
Star with royal beauty bright,
Westward leading, still proceeding,
Guide us to thy perfect light.

'We three kings', st 1 and refrain, written by John Henry Hopkins Jr (1857), publ. in *Carols, Hymns and Songs* (1863)

88 When a knight won his spurs in the stories of
old,
He was gentle and brave he was gallant and bold.
With a shield on his hand and a lance in his hand,
For God and for valour he rode through the land.
'When a knight won his spurs', written by Jan Struther
(pseudonym of Joyce Anstruther Graham Placzek), publ. in
Songs of Praise (1931)

I

Dolores Ibárruri
(1895–1989)
Spanish politician and journalist

*Known as 'La Pasionaria' (The Passion Flower), she was the
Republic's most effective propagandist during the Spanish
Civil War. She was elected as a Communist deputy to the Cortes
in 1936 and lived in the USSR after Franco's victory, returning
to be re-elected to the Cortes at the age of eighty-one.*

1 *No pasarán!*
[They shall not pass!]
Radio broadcast from Paris, 18 July 1936, quoted in *The
Spanish Civil War*, bk 2, ch. 16 (1961, rev. 1965) by Hugh
Thomas. This rallying call for the women of Spain to defend
the Republic became a slogan in the ensuing civil war. Previous attributions for the words include Marshal Pétain
(1856–1951) during the defence of Verdun in 1916: *Ils ne pas-
seront pas.*

2 It is better to die on your feet than to live on your
knees!
Radio broadcast from Paris, 3 September 1936, quoted ibid. In
her autobiography (1966), Ibárruri stated that she had first
used the words in a previous broadcast in Spain, 18 July. They
also have an earlier attribution, to Mexican revolutionary
Emiliano Zapata (c. 1877–1919).

Henrik Ibsen
(1828–1906)
Norwegian dramatist

*Having been playwright for the National Theatre in Bergen
and director of Oslo's Norwegian Theatre, he lived in Germany
and Italy 1864–91, when he wrote most of his plays. His major
works such as* Ghosts *(1881) and* Hedda Gabler *(1890) combined character study with social realism.*

1 Ah, I fancy it is just the same with most of what
you call your 'emancipation'. You have read yourself
into a number of new ideas and opinions. You have
got a sort of smattering of recent discoveries in
various fields – discoveries that seem to overthrow
certain principles which have hitherto been held
impregnable and unassailable. But all this has only
been a matter of intellect, Miss West – superficial
acquisition. It has not passed into your blood.
Rosmersholm, Act 3 (1866). Rector Kroll, addressing REBECCA
WEST.

2 What business has science and capitalism got,

bringing all these new inventions into the works, before society has produced a generation educated up to using them!

Pillars of Society, Act 2 (1877). Spoken by Aune.

3 What in fact have I achieved, however much it may seem? Bits and pieces . . . trivialities. But here they won't tolerate anything else, or anything more. If I wanted to take one step in advance of the current views and opinions of the day, that would put paid to any power I have. Do you know what we are . . . those of us who count as pillars of society? We are society's tools, neither more nor less.

Bernick, ibid., Act 4

4 The spirit of truth and the spirit of freedom – these are the pillars of society.

Lona Hessel, ibid., Act 4

5 Our home has been nothing but a play-room. I've been your doll-wife here, just as at home I was Papa's doll-child. And the children have been my dolls in their turn. I liked it when you came and played with me, just as they liked it when I came and played with them. That's what our marriage has been, Torvald.

A Doll's House, Act 3 (1879). Spoken by Nora Helmer.

6 I almost think we're all of us Ghosts, Pastor Manders. It's not only what we have inherited from our father and mother that 'walks' in us. It's all sorts of dead ideas, and lifeless old beliefs, and so forth. They have no vitality, but they cling to us all the same, and we can't get rid of them. Whenever I take up a newspaper, I seem to see Ghosts gliding between the lines. There must be Ghosts all the country over, as thick as the sand of the sea. And then we are, one and all, so pitifully afraid of the light.

Ghosts, Act 2 (1881). Spoken by Mrs Alving.

7 The worst enemy of truth and freedom in our society is the compact majority. Yes, the damned, compact, liberal majority.

An Enemy of the People, Act 4 (1882). Spoken by Dr Stockmann.

8 I'm plotting revolution against this lie that the majority has a monopoly of the truth. What are these truths that always bring the majority rallying round? Truths so elderly they are practically senile. And when a truth is as old as that, gentlemen, you can hardly tell it from a lie.

Dr Stockmann, ibid., Act 4

9 You should never have your best trousers on when you turn out to fight for freedom and truth.

Mrs Stockmann, ibid., Act 5

10 The thing is, you see, that the strongest man in the world is the man who stands alone.

Dr Stockmann, ibid., Act 5

11 A marriage based on full confidence, based on complete and unqualified frankness on both sides; they are not keeping anything back; there's no deception underneath it all. If I might so put it, it's an agreement for the mutual forgiveness of sin.

The Wild Duck, Act 4 (1884). Hjalmar Ekdal, referring to Mrs Sörby's marriage.

12 Don't use that foreign word 'ideals'. We have that excellent native word 'lies'.

Reilling, ibid., Act 5

13 Take the life-lie away from the average man and straight away you take away his happiness.

Reilling, ibid., Act 5

Ice Cube

(b. 1969)

US rap musician

Born O'Shea Jackson. He was a founder member of the LA rap group Niggaz With Attitude (NWA), and has also starred in films, including Boyz 'n the Hood *(1991).*

1 If I'm more of an influence to your son as a rapper than you are as a father . . . you got to look at yourself as a parent.

Interview in *Rolling Stone* 4 October 1994

Ice-T

(b. 1958)

US rap musician

Born Tracey Marrow. He was hailed LA's first hip-hop artist with the release of 'The Coldest Rapper' (1983), and went on to become one of the West Coast's most outspoken 'gangsta' rappers.

1 Crime is an equal-opportunity employer. It never discriminates. Anybody can enter the field. You don't need a college education. You don't need a G.E.D. You don't have to be any special color. You don't need white people to like you. You're self-employed. As a result, criminals are very independent people.

The Ice Opinion, ch. 3 (written with Heidi Sigmund, 1994)

2 Passion makes the world go round. Love just makes it a safer place.

Ibid., ch. 4

Harold L. Ickes
(1874–1952)
US politician

Harold LeClair Ickes. A Republican turned Democrat, he was a loyal supporter of F. D. ROOSEVELT, *and was his 'hatchet man' during presidential campaigns. As head of the Public Works Administration (1933–9), he implemented New Deal projects.*

1 The trouble with Senator Long is that he is suffering from halitosis of the intellect. That's presuming Emperor Long has an intellect.

Speech, 1935, quoted in *The Politics of Upheaval*, pt 2, ch. 14, sect. 5 (1960) by ARTHUR J. SCHLESINGER JR. The remarks were a riposte to Senator Huey Long's suggestion that Ickes could go 'slap damn to hell', during an altercation over ROOSEVELT's New Deal, which Long, nicknamed 'Emperor of Louisiana', strongly opposed.

2 I am against government by crony.

Press conference, 13 February 1946, publ. in *Truman*, ch. 11 (1992) by David McCullough. Announcing his resignation from his post as Secretary of the Interior, and referring to Truman's appointment of oil man and Democratic Party fundraiser Ed Pauley as Under Secretary of the Navy.

Saint Ignatius of Loyola
(1491–1556)
Spanish theologian and founder of the Jesuits

San Ignacio de Loyola. Ordained in 1537, he won papal approval for the establishment of a new order, the Society of Jesus, or Jesuits, which he headed until his death. Much of his emphasis was on missionary work and education.

1 Teach us, good Lord, to serve Thee as Thou
   deservest:
To give and not to count the cost;
To fight and not to heed the wounds;
To toil and not to seek for rest;
To labour and not to ask for any reward
Save that of knowing that we do Thy will.

'Prayer for Generosity' (1548)

2 Let me look at the foulness and ugliness of my body. Let me see myself as an ulcerous sore running with every horrible and disgusting poison.

Spiritual Exercises, 'First Week', no. 58 (1548)

3 We should always be prepared so as never to err

to believe that what I see as white is black, if the hierarchic Church defines it thus.

Ibid., 'Rules', no. 365

Ivan Illich
(1926–2002)
Austrian-born US social and educational theorist

His works such as Deschooling Society *(1971) and* Towards a History of Need *(1978) are critiques of economic and social policy, particularly in respect of the Third World.*

1 The compulsion to do good is an innate American trait. Only North Americans seem to believe that they always should, may, and actually can choose somebody with whom to share their blessings. Ultimately this attitude leads to bombing people into the acceptance of gifts.

Celebration of Awareness, Preface to ch. 2 (1969)

2 There is no greater distance than that between a man in prayer and God.

Ibid., ch. 4

3 My friends, it is your task to surprise yourselves, and us, with the education you succeed in inventing for your children. Our hope of salvation lies in our being surprised by the Other. Let us learn always to receive further surprises.

Ibid., ch. 9

4 Man must choose whether to be rich in things or in the freedom to use them.

Deschooling Society, ch. 4 (1971)

Gary Indiana
(b. 1950)
US author

After Scar Tissue *(1987), a collection of fictional commentaries on contemporary culture, he gained wider recognition with* Horse Crazy *(1989), a novel, and* Three Month Fever *(1999), a study of Andrew Cunanan, Versace's killer.*

1 Affection is the mortal illness of lonely people.

Horse Crazy, ch. 1 (1989)

William Ralph Inge
(1860–1954)
British philosopher and ecclesiastic

As Dean of St Paul's, London (1911–34), he was known as the 'Gloomy Dean' on account of his pessimistic sermons and newspaper articles. He also wrote studies of Plotinus on whom he was an expert.

1 It takes in reality only one to make a quarrel. It is useless for the sheep to pass resolutions in favour of vegetarianism, while the wolf remains of a different opinion.
Outspoken Essays, 'Patriotism' (first series, 1919)

2 Public opinion, a vulgar, impertinent, anonymous tyrant who deliberately makes life unpleasant for anyone who is not content to be the average man.
Ibid., 'Our Present Discontents'

3 A man may build himself a throne of bayonets, but he cannot sit on it.
Lecture, St Andrews, Scotland, 1918, repr. in *The Philosophy of Plotinus*, vol. 2, lecture 22 (1923). The words were quoted by BORIS YELTSIN from a tank during the failed military coup in Russia, August 1991.

4 Every institution not only carries within it the seeds of its own dissolution, but prepares the way for its most hated rival.
'The Victorian Age', Rede Lecture, Cambridge University, 1922, publ. in *Outspoken Essays* (second series, 1922)

5 Literature flourishes best when it is half a trade and half an art.
'The Victorian Age', ibid.

6 Events in the past may be roughly divided into those which probably never happened and those which do not matter. This is what makes the trade of historian so attractive.
Assessments and Anticipations, 'Prognostications' (1929)

7 I think middle-age is the best time, if we can escape the fatty degeneration of the conscience which often sets in at about fifty.
Quoted in the *Observer* 8 June 1930

8 Worry is interest paid on trouble before it falls due.
Observer 14 February 1932

Robert G. Ingersoll
(1833–99)
US lawyer and orator

Robert Green Ingersoll. He was known as 'the great agnostic' for his unorthodox religious views. These prevented his advancement in the Republican Party, though he was in great demand as a lecturer.

1 An honest God is the noblest work of man.
The Gods, and Other Essays, 'The Gods' (1876)

2 Hope is the only universal liar who never loses his reputation for veracity.
Speech at Manhattan Liberal Club, publ. in the *Truth-Seeker* 28 February 1892

(Sir) Bernard Ingham
(b. 1932)
British government press officer

He was Chief Information Officer under TONY BENN *(1975–8) and Chief Press Secretary to* MARGARET THATCHER *(1979–90). Gruff and forthright, he was called 'the sewer rather than the sewage' by John Biffen, but was highly esteemed by Thatcher.*

1 I sometimes compare press officers to riflemen on the Somme – mowing down wave upon wave of distortion, taking out rank upon rank of supposition, deduction and gossip.
Address at Press Gallery luncheon, quoted in the *Independent* 8 February 1990

Eugène Ionesco
(1912–94)
Romanian-born French playwright

Regarding humour as his 'outlet, release and salvation', he was a prominent figure of the Theatre of the Absurd. His early one-act plays deal with self-estrangement and failure of communication, while his later full-length plays feature the semi-autobiographical character Bérenger.

1 Life is an abnormal business.
The Rhinoceros, Act 1 (1959). Spoken by Jean.

2 Banality is a symptom of non-communication. Men hide behind their clichés.
Notes and Counter Notes, pt 4, 'Further Notes, 1960' (1962)

3 All history is nothing but a succession of 'crises' – of rupture, repudiation and resistance ... When there is no 'crisis', there is stagnation, petrification and death.
Ibid., 'Have I Written Anti-Theatre?'

4 Beauty is a precious trace that eternity causes to appear to us and that it takes away from us. A manifestation of eternity, and a sign of death as well.
Present Past – Past Present, ch. 5 (1968)

5 Boredom! I've got used to that. You get used to it, or rather, you don't get used to it, but you get used to not getting used to it.
Journeys Among the Dead (1981). Spoken by Jean.

6 Shakespeare was the great one before us. His place was between God and despair.
International Herald Tribune 17 June 1988

(Sir) Muhammad Iqbal
(1877–1938)
Indian poet and philosopher

His writings, classical in style and intended for recitation, were formative on the movement which led to the creation of the separate Muslim state of Pakistan. His best known work is Secrets of the Self (1915).

1 You made the night, I made the lamp;
You made the earthen bowl, I made the goblet.
You made deserts, mountains and valleys;
I made gardens, meadows and parks.
I am one who makes a mirror out of stone,
And turns poison into sweet, delicious drink.
'A Dialogue Between God and Man: Man', publ. in *A Tulip in the Desert: A Selection of the Poetry of Muhammad Iqbal* (ed./ transl. Mustansir Mir, 2000)

John Irving
(b. 1942)
US author

He is noted for his surreal yet plausible black comedies, often with a homicidal thread, notably The World According to Garp (1978) and The Cider House Rules (1985).

1 Sigmund Freud was a novelist with a scientific background. He just didn't know he was a novelist. All those damn psychiatrists after him, they didn't know he was a novelist either.
Interview in *Writers at Work* (eighth series, ed. George Plimpton, 1988)

Washington Irving
(1783–1859)
US author

He wrote the comic A History of New York (1809) under the pseudonym Diedrich Knickerbocker, and established his reputation with The Sketch Book of Geoffrey Crayon, Gent. (1819– 20). He also wrote travel books on Spain, where he was a diplomat, and on the American West.

1 Who ever hears of fat men heading a riot, or herding together in turbulent mobs? – no – no, it is your lean, hungry men who are continually worrying society, and setting the whole community by the ears.
A History of New York, bk 3, ch. 2 (1809)

2 A tart temper never mellows with age, and a sharp tongue is the only edged tool that grows keener with constant use.
The Sketch Book of Geoffrey Crayon, Gent., 'Rip Van Winkle' (1819–20)

3 Rip, in fact, was no politician; the changes of states and empires made but little impression on him; but there was one species of despotism under which he had long groaned, and that was – petticoat government. Happily that was at an end; he had got his neck out of the yoke of matrimony, and could go in and out whenever he pleased, without dreading the tyranny of Dame Van Winkle.
Ibid., 'Rip Van Winkle'

4 A woman's whole life is a history of the affections. The heart is her world.
Ibid., 'The Broken Heart'

5 The great British Library – an immense collection of volumes of all ages and languages, many of which are now forgotten, and most of which are seldom read: one of these sequestered pools of obsolete literature to which modern authors repair, and draw buckets full of classic lore, or 'pure English, undefiled' wherewith to swell their own scanty rills of thought.
Ibid., 'The Art of Book-Making'

6 They who drink beer will think beer.
Ibid., 'Stratford-on-Avon'. The quotation has also been attributed to William Warburton, Bishop of Gloucester (1698–1779).

7 Luxury spreads its ample board before their eyes; but they are excluded from the banquet. Plenty revels over the fields; but they are starving in the midst of its abundance: the whole wilderness has blossomed into a garden; but they feel as reptiles that infest it.
Ibid., 'Traits of Indian Character'. Writing of Native Americans.

8 Whenever a man's friends begin to compliment him about looking young, he may be sure that they think he is growing old.
Bracebridge Hall, 'Bachelors' (1822)

9 There is a certain relief in change, even though it be from bad to worse; as I have found in traveling in a stage-coach, that it is often a comfort to shift one's position and be bruised in a new place.
Tales of a Traveler, Preface (1824)

10 The almighty dollar, that great object of universal devotion.
'The Creole Village' (1836), repr. in *Wolfert's Roost* (1855)

Christopher Isherwood
(1904–86)
British-born US author

His life as a teacher in Germany (1929–33) inspired the stories in Mr Norris Changes Trains *(1935) and* Goodbye to Berlin *(1939). He emigrated to the USA in 1939 with* W. H. AUDEN, *with whom he collaborated on three verse plays.*

1 I am a camera with its shutter open, quite passive, recording, not thinking.
Goodbye to Berlin, 'A Berlin Diary (Autumn 1930)' (1939). Opening sentence of story. Isherwood's collection was later to form the basis of John Van Druten's play *I Am a Camera* (1951) and the Broadway musical *Cabaret* (1966, filmed 1972).

2 California is a tragic country – like Palestine, like every Promised Land.
'Los Angeles' (1947), repr. in *Exhumations* (1966)

Kazuo Ishiguro
(b. 1954)
Japanese-born British novelist

Set in Japan or Britain, Ishiguro's novels are a melancholy reassessment of the past. The best known are An Artist of the Floating World *(1986) and* The Remains of the Day *(1989).*

1 A 'great' butler can only be, surely, one who can point to his years of service and say that he has applied his talents to serving a great gentleman – and through the latter, to serving humanity.
The Remains of the Day, 'Day Two – Afternoon' (1989). Spoken by Mr Stevens.

J

Andrew Jackson
(1767–1845)
US president

A military hero after winning victories in the War of 1812, 'Old Hickory' was elected president in 1828 and 1832. His 'Jacksonian democracy' encouraged greater popular participation in government.

1 Our Union: It must be preserved.
Toast at Jefferson Day dinner, 13 April 1830, quoted in *Andrew Jackson: Portrait of a President*, ch. 30, sect. 4 (1937) by Marquis James. The toast, which indicated Jackson's withdrawal of support for the Southern cause of nullification, was followed by another by John C. Calhoun, the Vice-President: 'The Union, next to our liberty most dear. May we all remember that it can only be preserved by respecting the rights of the States and by distributing equally the benefits and burdens of the Union.' Calhoun resigned the vice-presidency in 1832. Jackson apparently altered the wording of his toast to 'Our Federal Union' when it was given to the press, and many sources reported it in this form.

George Jackson
(1941–71)
US black activist and author

Sentenced in 1960 for armed robbery, he became a black activist in St Quentin and Soledad prisons. He was accused with three others (together known as the Soledad Brothers) of the murder of a prison guard, and was later killed in controversial circumstances.

1 If we are to be men again we must stop working for nothing, competing against each other for the little they allow us to possess, stop selling our women or allowing them to be used and handled against their will, stop letting our children be educated by the barbarian, using their language, dress, and customs, and most assuredly stop turning our cheeks.
Letter to his father from Soledad Prison, 30 March 1965, publ. in *Soledad Brother* (1970)

2 Nonviolent theory is practicable in civilized lands among civilized people, the Asians and Africans, but a look at European history shows that anything of great value that ever changed hands was taken by force of arms.
Letter to his mother from Soledad Prison, March 1967, ibid.

Helen Hunt Jackson
(1830–85)
US author and poet

Her concern for the rights of Native Americans was expressed in A Century of Dishonor *(1881) and* Ramona *(1884), the novel for which she is best known. Much of her work was published anonymously.*

1 Oh, write of me, not 'Died in bitter pains',
But 'Emigrated to another star!'
'Emigravit', publ. in *Sonnets & Lyrics* (1886). Closing lines of poem.

2 O suns and skies and clouds of June,
And flowers of June together,
Ye cannot rival for one hour
October's bright blue weather.
'October's Bright Blue Weather', st. 1, ibid.

Holbrook Jackson
(1874–1948)
British author and critic

He wrote on literary figures, particularly WILLIAM MORRIS *in whom he had a lifelong interest, in such books as* On Art and Socialism *(1947). He was also a passionate bibliophile.*

1 Pedantry is the dotage of knowledge.
Anatomy of Bibliomania, vol. 1, pt 7, 'A Cure for Pedantry' (1930)

Jesse Jackson
(b. 1941)
US clergyman and civil rights leader

A persuasive Baptist preacher and black civil rights activist, he founded the National Rainbow Coalition in 1984. The same year, and again in 1988, he was a candidate for the Democratic Party's presidential nomination, the first African-American to bid for the office.

1 I hear that melting-pot stuff a lot, and all I can say is that we haven't melted.
Playboy November 1969

2 When we're unemployed, we're called lazy; when the whites are unemployed it's called a depression.
Interview in *The Americans,* 'When Whites Are Unemployed, It's Called a Depression' (1970) by David Frost

3 The burden of being black is that you have to be superior just to be equal. But the glory of it is that, once you achieve, you have achieved, indeed.
Christian Science Monitor 26 September 1979

4 Our flag is red, white, and blue, but our nation is a rainbow – red, yellow, brown, black and white, we are *all* precious in God's sight!
Speech at Democratic National Convention, San Francisco, 17 July 1984, quoted in *Jesse: The Life and Pilgrimage of Jesse Jackson,* ch. 15 (1996) by Marshall Frady. Jackson – who also compared America to a quilt: 'many pieces, many colors, many sizes, all woven and held together by a common thread' – named his political organization the 'National Rainbow Coalition'.

5 My constituency is the desperate, the damned, the disinherited, the disrespected and the despised.
Speech at Democratic National Convention, San Francisco, 17 July 1984, quoted in *Jesse Jackson,* ch. 8 (1991) by Robert Jakoubek

Mahalia Jackson
(1911–72)
US gospel singer

In 1947, her song 'Move On Up a Little Higher' became the first gospel record to sell a million copies. She was active in the civil rights movement from 1955.

1 This musical thing has been here since America been here. This is trial and tribulation music.
Quoted in *Time* magazine 28 June 1968

Michael Jackson
(b. 1958)
US singer and dancer

The youngest member of the soul pop family group the Jackson Five, he has sold a world record 40 million copies of his album Thriller *(1982). His reclusive lifestyle and cosmetic makeover have generated much press interest.*

1 I'm not going to spend
My life being a color
Don't tell me you agree with me
When I saw you kicking dirt in my eye
But, if you're thinkin' about my baby
It don't matter if you're black or white.
'Black or White' (song) on the album *Dangerous* (1991)

(Sir) Mick Jagger
(b. 1943)

Keith Richards
(b. 1943)
British rock musicians

The Jagger–Richards partnership produced nearly all of the Rolling Stones' original material. Their r-'n'-b-driven songs

articulated the energy and sexuality of the 1960s. See also
KEITH RICHARDS.

1 I can't get no satisfaction.
'(I Can't Get No) Satisfaction' (song, 1965) on the album *Big
Hits (High Tide and Green Grass)* (1966) by the Rolling Stones

2 Get off of my cloud.
'Get Off Of My Cloud' (song, 1965), ibid.

3 She goes running for the shelter
Of a mother's little helper,
And it helps her on her way,
Gets her through her busy day.
'Mother's Little Helper' (song) on the album *Aftermath* (1966)
by the Rolling Stones

4 I shouted out, 'Who killed the Kennedys?'
When after all, it was you and me.
'Sympathy for the Devil' (song) on the album *Beggars' Ban-
quet* (1969) by the Rolling Stones

5 But what can a poor boy do
Except to sing for a rock 'n' roll band,
'Cause in sleepy London town
There's just no place for a street fighting man!
'Street Fighting Man' (song), ibid.

6 You can't always get what you want
But if you try sometimes
You just might find
You get what you need.
'You Can't Always Get What You Want' (song) on the album
Let It Bleed (1970) by the Rolling Stones

7 I know it's only rock 'n' roll but I like it.
'It's Only Rock 'n' Roll' (song) on the album *It's Only Rock 'n'
Roll* (1974) by the Rolling Stones

Lord Jakobovits
(1921–99)
British rabbi

*Emmanuel Jakobovits. As Chief Rabbi of the Commonwealth
(1967–91), he was conservative in outlook but instrumental in
mending rifts within Britain's Jewish community.*

1 Silence, indifference and inaction were Hitler's
principal allies.
Independent 5 December 1989. Referring to the prosecution
of war criminals.

2 We must pursue the peace efforts as if there were
no terrorism, and fight the terrorists as if there were
no peace efforts.
Letter to *The Times* 5 March 1996, following a spate of bomb
attacks by Hamas in Tel Aviv and Jerusalem

James I (James VI of Scotland)
(1566–1625)
King of England, Scotland and Ireland

The son of MARY, QUEEN OF SCOTS, *he ascended to the Scottish throne in 1567, and succeeded to the English throne in 1603.
He wrote several scholarly works and supported literature and
theatre, earning him the accolade, attributed both to Henri IV
of France and Duc de Sully: 'the wisest fool in Christendom'.*

1 A custom loathsome to the eye, hateful to the
nose, harmful to the brain, dangerous to the lungs,
and in the black, stinking fume thereof nearest
resembling the horrible Stygian smoke of the pit
that is bottomless.
A Counterblast to Tobacco (1604). Written shortly after
WALTER RALEGH *had introduced tobacco to England from
the New World, and published anonymously.*

2 The state of monarchy is the supremest thing
upon earth: for kings are not only God's Lieutenants
upon earth, and sit upon God's throne, but even by
God himself they are called Gods.
Address to Parliament, 21 March 1609, publ. in *The Penguin
Book of Historic Speeches* (ed. Brian MacArthur, 1995)

3 Dr Donne's verses are like the peace of God: they
pass all understanding.
Attributed. Referring to JOHN DONNE. See BIBLE, NEW TES-
TAMENT: PHILIPPIANS 9.

Alice James
(1848–92)
US diarist

The sister of HENRY JAMES *and* WILLIAM JAMES, *she was an
invalid for much of her life. Her diaries, written from 1886
after her move to England, contain astute observations on her
family and times.*

1 When will women begin to have the first glimmer
that above all other loyalties is the loyalty to Truth,
i.e., to yourself, that husband, children, friends and
country are as nothing to that?
Journal entry, 19 November 1889, publ. in *The Diary of Alice
James* (ed. Leon Edel, 1964)

2 It is an immense loss to have all robust and sustaining expletives refined away from one! At . . .
moments of trial refinement is a feeble reed to lean
upon.
Journal entry, 12 December 1889, ibid.

3 I suppose one has a greater sense of intellectual

degradation after an interview with a doctor than from any human experience.

Journal entry, 27 September 1890, ibid.

4 The difficulty about all this dying, is that you can't tell a fellow anything about it, so where does the fun come in?

Journal entry, 11 December 1891, ibid.

C. L. R. James
(1901–89)
Trinidadian journalist and author

Cyril Lionel Robert James. He came to England in 1933 to work as cricket correspondent on the Manchester Guardian. *His essentially Marxist political ideas evolved during his time in the US 1938–53. He is best known for* Beyond a Boundary *(1963), a blend of sport and politics.*

1 Cricket is first and foremost a dramatic spectacle. It belongs with the theatre, ballet, opera and the dance.

Beyond a Boundary, pt 6, ch. 16 (1963)

Clive James
(b. 1939)
Australian author, critic and broadcaster

He has published several volumes of criticism, verse and 'unreliable memoirs', and displays his wise-cracking wit in frequent TV appearances.

1 All television ever did was shrink the demand for ordinary movies. The demand for extraordinary movies increased. If any one thing is wrong with the movie industry today, it is the unrelenting effort to astonish.

'Postcard from Los Angeles 1' (1979), repr. in *Flying Visits* (1984)

2 A sceptic finds *Dallas* absurd. A cynic thinks the public doesn't.

Glued to the Box, Introduction (1983). Referring to the US soap opera that captured a world-wide market 1978–91.

3 Anyone afraid of what he thinks television does to the world is probably just afraid of the world.

Ibid., Introduction

Henry James
(1843–1916)
US author

An American transplanted to Europe, he returned frequently in his novels to the theme of the old and new worlds and the collision between them. WILLIAM FAULKNER *called him 'the nicest old lady I ever met', while for* VIRGINIA WOOLF *he was 'that courtly, worldly, sentimental old gentleman [who] can still make us afraid of the dark'. See also* SOMERSET MAUGHAM 10, H. G. WELLS 5.

1 It exhibits the effort of an essentially prosaic mind to lift itself, by a prolonged muscular strain, into poetry.

Review of WALT WHITMAN's volume of impressions of the Civil War, *Drum Taps* (1865), repr. in *Views and Reviews* (1908). James later became more appreciative of Whitman's verse.

2 The face of nature and civilization in this our country is to a certain point a very sufficient literary field. But it will yield its secrets only to a really *grasping* imagination . . . To write well and worthily of American things one need even more than elsewhere to be a *master*.

Letter to editor and critic Charles Eliot Norton, 16 January 1871, publ. in *Henry James Letters*, vol. 1 (ed. Leon Edel, 1974)

3 It's a complex fate, being an American, and one of the responsibilities it entails is fighting against a superstitious valuation of Europe.

Letter to Charles Eliot Norton, 4 February 1872, ibid.

4 Cats and monkeys, monkeys and cats – all human life is there!

'The Madonna of the Future' (1873), repr. in *The Novels and Tales of Henry James*, vol. 13 (1908). See NEWS OF THE WORLD 1.

5 It takes a great deal of history to produce a little literature.

Hawthorne, ch. 1 (1879)

6 One might enumerate the items of high civilization, as it exists in other countries, which are absent from the texture of American life, until it should become a wonder to know what was left. No state, in the European sense of the word, and indeed barely a specific national name. No sovereign, no court, no personal loyalty, no aristocracy, no church, no clergy, no army, no diplomatic service, no country gentlemen, no palaces, no castles, nor manors, nor old country-houses, nor parsonages, nor thatched cottages nor ivied ruins; no cathedrals, nor abbeys, nor little Norman churches; no great universities nor public schools – no Oxford, nor Eton, nor Harrow; no literature, no novels, no museums, no pictures, no political society, no sporting class – no Epsom nor Ascot! Some such list as that might be drawn up of the absent things in American life.

Ibid., ch. 2. 'The American knows that a good deal remains,' added James: 'what it is that remains – that is his secret, his joke, as one may say.' Nearly thirty-five years later, in a letter, 1 April 1913 to his sister-in-law, James wrote, 'Dearest Alice, I could come back to America (could be carried on a stretcher) to die – but never, never to live.'

7 Whatever question there may be of his talent, there can be none, I think, of his genius. It was a slim and crooked one, but it was eminently personal. He was unperfect, unfinished, inartistic; he was worse than provincial – he was parochial.

Ibid., ch. 4. Of HENRY DAVID THOREAU.

8 It is, I think, an indisputable fact that Americans are, as Americans, the most self-conscious people in the world, and the most addicted to the belief that the other nations of the earth are in a conspiracy to under value them.

Ibid., ch. 6

9 Under certain circumstances there are few hours in life more agreeable than the hour dedicated to the ceremony known as afternoon tea.

The Portrait of a Lady, ch. 1 (1881). Opening sentence of book.

10 An Englishman's never so natural as when he's holding his tongue.

Isabel Archer, ibid., ch. 10

11 To read between the lines was easier than to follow the text.

Ibid., ch. 13. Ralph Touchett's appraisal of Henrietta Stackpole.

12 Money's a horrid thing to follow, but a charming thing to meet.

Ibid., ch. 35. Gilbert Osmond, speaking of Isabel Archer's fortune.

13 The only obligation to which in advance we may hold a novel without incurring the accusation of being arbitrary, is that it be interesting.

Partial Portraits, 'The Art of Fiction' (1888)

14 Experience is never limited and it is never complete; it is an immense sensibility, a kind of huge spider-web, of the finest silken threads, suspended in the chamber of consciousness and catching every air-borne particle in its tissue. It is the very atmosphere of the mind.

Ibid., 'The Art of Fiction'

15 The power to guess the unseen from the seen, to trace the implications of things, to judge the whole piece by the pattern, the condition of feeling life in general so completely that you are well on your way to knowing any particular corner of it – this cluster

of gifts may almost be said to constitute experience.

Ibid., 'The Art of Fiction'

16 What is character but the determination of incident? What is incident but the illustration of character?

Ibid., 'The Art of Fiction'

17 We work in the dark – we do what we can – we give what we have. Our doubt is our passion and our passion is our task. The rest is the madness of art.

'The Middle Years' (1893), repr. in The Complete Tales of Henry James, vol. 9 (ed. Leon Edel, 1964). Spoken by Dencombe.

18 The time-honoured bread-sauce of the happy ending.

Theatricals, Prefatory Note (second series, 1894)

19 He is outside of everything, and alien everywhere. He is an aesthetic solitary. His beautiful, light imagination is the wing that on the autumn evening just brushes the dusky window.

Anthology Library of the World's Best Literature, vol. 12, Introduction (1897). Of NATHANIEL HAWTHORNE.

20 Most English talk is a quadrille in a sentry-box.

The Awkward Age, bk 5, ch. 4 (1899). Spoken by The Duchess.

21 If I were to live my life over again, I would be an American. I would steep myself in America, I would know no other land.

Remark to writer Hamlin Garland, 1899, quoted by Tony Tanner in Introduction to Hawthorne (1879)

22 I mourn the safe and motherly old middle-class queen, who held the nation warm under the fold of her big, hideous Scotch-plaid shawl and whose duration had been so extraordinarily convenient and beneficent. I felt her death much more than I should have expected; she was a sustaining symbol – and the wild waters are upon us now.

Letter to OLIVER WENDELL HOLMES JR, 20 February 1901, publ. in Letters of Henry James, vol. 4 (ed. Leon Edel, 1984). On the death of Queen VICTORIA.

23 The fatal futility of Fact.

Preface to 'The Spoils of Poynton', publ. in The Novels and Tales of Henry James, vol. 10 (1908). 'The Spoils of Poynton' was originally published in 1897.

24 To criticize is to appreciate, to appropriate, to take intellectual possession, to establish in fine a relation with the criticized thing and to make it one's own.

Preface to What Maisie Knew, publ. in The Novels and Tales of

Henry James, vol. 11 (1908). *What Maisie Knew* was originally published in 1897.

25 There are moods in which one feels the impulse to enter a tacit protest against too gross an appetite for pure aesthetics in this starving and sinning world. One turns half away, musingly, from certain beautiful useless things.
Italian Hours, 'Florentine Notes', sect. 2 (1909)

26 In art economy is always beauty.
Preface to 'The Altar of the Dead', publ. in *The Novels and Tales of Henry James*, vol. 17 (1909). 'The Altar of the Dead' was originally published in 1895.

27 The terrible fluidity of self-revelation.
Preface to *The Ambassadors*, publ. in *The Novels and Tales of Henry James*, vol. 21 (1909). *The Ambassadors* was originally published in 1903.

28 However British you may be, I am more British still.
Quoted in *Henry James at Home*, ch. 7, sect. 5 (1969) by H. Montgomery Hyde. The remark, addressed to two English friends in August 1914, was reported in a letter written to *The Times* 4 March 1916 by the poet and critic Edmund Gosse. James had lived in England since 1876 and took British citizenship in 1915 as a gesture of support for Britain's war effort.

29 It is art that *makes* life, makes interest, makes importance . . . and I know of no substitute whatever for the force and beauty of its process.
Letter to H. G. WELLS, 10 July 1915, publ. in *Henry James Letters*, vol. 4 (ed. Leon Edel, 1984). Wells replied (13 July): 'I don't clearly understand your concluding phrases . . . I can only read sense into it by assuming that you are using "art" for every conscious human activity. I use the word for a research and attainment that is technical and special.'

30 Happy you poets who can be present and *so* present by a simple flicker of your genius, and not, like the clumsier race, have to lay a train and pile up faggots that may not after prove in the least combustible!
Letter to W. B. Yeats, 25 August 1915, in private collection. This observation was later incorporated into Yeats's poem, 'In Memory of Major Robert Gregory' (see W. B. YEATS 28).

31 Tell the boys to follow, to be faithful, to take me seriously.
Last words, quoted in *Henry James at Home*, ch. 7, sect. 4 (1969) by H. Montgomery Hyde. James is said to have uttered the words in one of his last conscious moments when his mind was dwelling on his work. He died 28 February 1916.

32 So here it is at last, the distinguished thing!
Attributed, often claimed to be James's last words. However, in *A Backward Glance*, ch. 14 (1934) by EDITH WHARTON, the remark was said to have been *heard* by him when he suffered a stroke at the beginning of his last illness, around 2 December 1915. This anecdote was recounted to Wharton by James's friend Lady Prothero, though James's biographer Leon Edel described it as 'a beautiful bit of apocrypha'.

33 Summer afternoon – summer afternoon; to me those have always been the two most beautiful words in the English language.
Quoted in *A Backward Glance*, ch. 10 (1934) by EDITH WHARTON. Remark during 'one perfect afternoon we spent at Bodiam' (Bodiam Castle, Kent).

34 I hate American simplicity. I glory in the piling up of complications of every sort. If I could pronounce the name James in any different or more elaborate way I should be in favour of doing it.
Said to James's niece Peggy (Margaret Mary James), quoted by Leon Edel in his Introduction to *Letters of Henry James*, vol. 4 (1984)

Henry James Sr
(1811–82)
US philosopher and theologian

The father of ALICE JAMES, HENRY JAMES *and* WILLIAM JAMES, *he became acquainted with the writings of Swedenborg which formed the basis of his own philosophy. His writings were edited and published by William in 1885.*

1 Thomas Carlyle is incontestably dead at last, by the acknowledgment of all newspapers. I had, however, the pleasure of an intimate intercourse with him when he was an infinitely deader man than he is now.
Atlantic Monthly May 1881

P. D. James
(b. 1920)
British author

Phyllis Dorothy White, Baroness James of Holland Park. Her work in the forensic science and criminal law departments of the Home Office provided useful background for her chilling detective novels, for example Death of an Expert Witness *(1977).*

1 What the detective story is about is not murder but the restoration of order.
Interview in *The Face* December 1986

2 Great literature cannot grow from a neglected or impoverished soil. Only if we actually tend or care will it transpire that every hundred years or so we might get a *Middlemarch*.
Daily Telegraph 14 April 1988

3 Creativity in sound and vision doesn't flourish in an atmosphere of despotism, coercion and fear.

Speech to House of Lords, 3 March 1999, quoted in the *Guardian* 4 March 1999. Commenting on management practices in the BBC under John Birt. P. D. James is a former governor of the BBC.

William James
(1842–1910)
US psychologist and philosopher

Brother of ALICE JAMES *and* HENRY JAMES, *he made his name with* Principles of Psychology *(1890), and was subsequently acclaimed for his study of the psychology of religion,* The Varieties of Religious Experience *(1902). He was a leader of the Pragmatist school of philosophy.*

1 Habit is thus the enormous fly-wheel of society, its most precious conservative agent. It alone is what keeps us all within the bounds of ordinance, and saves the children of fortune from the envious uprisings of the poor.

Principles of Psychology, vol. 1, ch. 4 (1890)

2 It is well for the world that in most of us, by the age of thirty, the character has set like plaster, and will never soften again.

Ibid., vol. 1, ch. 4

3 There is no more miserable human being than one in whom nothing is habitual but indecision, and for whom the lighting of every cigar, the drinking of every cup, the time of rising and going to bed every day, and the beginning of every bit of work, are subjects of express volitional deliberation.

Ibid., vol. 1, ch. 4

4 Metaphysics means nothing but an unusually obstinate effort to think clearly.

Ibid., vol. 1, ch. 6

5
$$\text{Self-esteem} = \frac{\text{Success}}{\text{Pretensions}}$$

Ibid., vol. 1, ch. 10

6 The art of being wise is the art of knowing what to overlook.

Ibid., vol. 2, ch. 22

7 If merely 'feeling good' could decide, drunkenness would be the supremely valid human experience.

The Varieties Of Religious Experience, Lecture 1 ('Religion and Neurology') (1902)

8 For morality life is a war, and the service of the highest is a sort of cosmic patriotism which also calls for volunteers.

Ibid., Lecture 2 ('Circumscription of the Topic')

9 The world is all the richer for having a devil in it, *so long as we keep our foot upon his neck.*

Ibid., Lecture 2

10 A little cooling down of animal excitability and instinct, a little loss of animal toughness, a little irritable weakness and descent of the pain-threshold, will bring the worm at the core of all our usual springs of delight into full view, and turn us into melancholy metaphysicians.

Ibid., Lectures 6 and 7 ('The Sick Soul')

11 Smitten as we are with the vision of social righteousness, a God indifferent to everything but adulation, and full of partiality for his individual favorites, lacks an essential element of largeness.

Ibid., Lectures 14 and 15 ('The Value of Saintliness')

12 As there is no worse lie than a truth misunderstood by those who hear it, so reasonable arguments, challenges to magnanimity, and appeals to sympathy or justice, are folly when we are dealing with human crocodiles and boa-constrictors.

Ibid., Lectures 14 and 15 ('The Value of Saintliness')

13 The prevalent fear of poverty among the educated classes is the worst moral disease from which our civilization suffers.

Ibid., Lectures 14 and 15

14 The sway of alcohol over mankind is unquestionably due to its power to stimulate the mystical faculties of human nature, usually crushed to earth by the cold facts and dry criticisms of the sober hour. Sobriety diminishes, discriminates, and says no; drunkenness expands, unites, and says yes.

Ibid., Lectures 16 and 17 ('Mysticism')

15 Our normal waking consciousness, rational consciousness as we call it, is but one special type of consciousness, whilst all about it, parted from it by the filmiest of screens, there lie potential forms of consciousness entirely different.

Ibid., Lectures 16 and 17

16 Knowledge about life is one thing; effective occupation of a place in life, with its dynamic currents passing through your being, is another.

Ibid., Lecture 20 ('Conclusions')

17 The further limits of our being plunge, it seems to me, into an altogether other dimension of exist-

ence from the sensible and merely 'understandable' world. Name it the mystical region, or the supernatural region, whichever you choose. So far as our ideal impulses originate in this region (and most of them do originate in it, for we find them possessing us in a way for which we cannot articulately account), we belong to it in a more intimate sense than that in which we belong to the visible world, for we belong in the most intimate sense wherever our ideals belong.

Ibid., Lecture 20

18 The moral flabbiness born of the exclusive worship of the bitch-goddess SUCCESS. That – with the squalid cash interpretation put on the word success – is our national disease.

Letter to H. G. WELLS, 11 September 1906, publ. in *The Letters of William James*, vol. 2 (ed. Henry James, 1920)

19 Philosophy is at once the most sublime and the most trivial of human pursuits.

Pragmatism, Lecture 1 ('The Present Dilemma in Philosophy') (1907)

20 Our esteem for facts has not neutralized in us all religiousness. It is itself almost religious. Our scientific temper is devout.

Ibid., Lecture 1

21 What every genuine philosopher (every genuine man, in fact) craves most is *praise* – although the philosophers generally call it 'recognition'!

Letter to HENRI BERGSON, 13 June 1907, publ. in *The Letters of William James*, vol. 2 (ed. Henry James, 1920)

22 What a magnificent land and race is this Britain! Everything about them is of better quality than the corresponding thing in the US ... Yet I believe (or suspect) that ours is eventually the bigger destiny, if we can only succeed in living up to it.

Letter, 2 July 1908, ibid., vol. 2

23 To be a real philosopher all that is necessary is to *hate* some one else's type of thinking.

Letter, 29 January 1909, ibid., vol. 2

Elizabeth Janeway
(1913–93)
US author

A major advocate on women's issues, she is remembered as a balanced, sometimes ironic commentator on shifting gender roles. Her books include Men's World – Woman's Place *(1971).*

1 In this nadir of poetic repute, when the only verse that most people read from one year's end to the next is what appears on greetings cards, it is well for us to stop and consider our poets ... Poets are the leaven in the lump of civilization.

The Writer's Book, ch. 30 (ed. Helen Hull, 1950)

Derek Jarman
(1942–94)
British film-maker, theatre director and artist

He was experimental in his work both on stage and on screen. The first of his films, Sebastiane *(1976), had Latin dialogue, while one of his last,* Blue *(1993), showed an unchanging blue screen.*

1 Understand that sexuality is as wide as the sea. Understand that your morality is not law. Understand that we are you. Understand that if we decide to have sex whether safe, safer, or unsafe, it is our decision and you have no rights in our lovemaking.

At Your Own Risk: A Saint's Testament, '1940's' (1992)

2 All men are homosexual, some turn straight. It must be very odd to be a straight man because your sexuality is hopelessly defensive. It's like an ideal of racial purity.

Ibid., '1940's'

3 Paradise haunts gardens, and some gardens are paradises. Mine is one of them. Others are like bad children – spoilt by their parents, over-watered and covered with noxious chemicals.

Derek Jarman's Garden (text by Derek Jarman, photographs by Howard Sooley, 1995). Jarman created his own garden on an inhospitable stretch of shingle on the Kent coast, within sight of the nuclear power station at Dungeness. He incorporated driftwood, shells and sculptures made from stones and flotsam found on the beach.

Randall Jarrell
(1914–65)
US poet and critic

His often harrowing poetry was written, according to Time *magazine, in 'plain American, which dogs and cats can read'. Verse collections include* The Woman at the Washington Zoo *(1960) and* The Lost World *(1965).*

1 Six miles from earth, loosed from its dream of
    life,
I woke to black flak and the nightmare fighters.
When I died they washed me out of the turret with
    a hose.

'The Death of the Ball Turret Gunner' (1945), repr. in *Selected Poems* (1955)

2 When you begin to read a poem you are entering

a foreign country whose laws and language and life are a kind of translation of your own; but to accept it because its stews taste exactly like your old mother's hash, or to reject it because the owl-headed goddess of wisdom in its temple is fatter than the Statue of Liberty, is an equal mark of that want of imagination, that inaccessibility to experience, of which each of us who dies a natural death will die.

Poetry and the Age, 'The Obscurity of the Poet' (1953)

3 The work of art is as done as it will ever get, and all the critics in the world can't make its crust a bit browner; they may help *us*, the indigent readers, but they haven't done a thing to it. Around the throne of God, where all the angels read perfectly, there are no critics – there is no need for them.

Ibid., 'The Age of Criticism'

4 His voice not only took you into his confidence, it laid a fire for you and put your slippers by it and then went into the other room to get into something more comfortable.

Pictures from an Institution, pt 1, ch. 10 (1954). Referring to President Robbins.

5 Old faces are forbidding or beautiful for what is expressed in them; in a face that is young enough almost everything but the youth is hidden, so that it is beautiful both for what is there and what cannot yet be there.

Ibid., pt 4, ch. 4

6 It is better to entertain an idea than to take it home to live with you for the rest of your life.

Ibid., pt 4, ch. 9

7 Europeans and Americans are like men and women: they understand each other worse, and it matters less, than either of them suppose.

Ibid., pt 4, ch. 9

Alfred Jarry
(1873–1907)
French playwright and author

His plays and novels are said to have prefigured Dada, Surrealism and the Theatre of the Absurd. Ubu roi (1896), a stylized farce, was followed by less successful sequels. He also wrote short stories and poetry.

1 You're looking exceptionally ugly tonight, Madam, is it because we have company?

Ubu roi, Act 1, Sc. 2 (1896). Spoken by Père Ubu.

2 It is because the public are a mass – inert, obtuse, and passive – that they need to be shaken up from time to time so that we can tell from their bear-like grunts where they are – and also where they stand. They are pretty harmless, in spite of their numbers, because they are fighting against intelligence.

'Theatre Questions' (1897), repr. in *The Selected Works of Alfred Jarry* (ed. Roger Shattuck and Simon Watson Taylor, 1965)

3 We shall not have succeeded in demolishing everything unless we demolish the ruins as well. But the only way I can see of doing that is to use them to put up a lot of fine, well-designed buildings.

Ubu enchaîné, Epigraph (*Ubu Enchained*, 1900)

4 Blind and unwavering indiscipline at all times constitutes the real strength of all free men.

Corporal, ibid., Act 1, Sc. 2

5 God is the tangential point between zero and infinity.

Gestes et Opinions du Docteur Faustroll Pataphysicien, bk 8, ch. 41 (1911)

6 We believe . . . that the applause of silence is the only kind that counts.

'Twelve Theatrical Topics', topic 12, (1960), repr. in *The Selected Works of Alfred Jarry* (ed. Roger Shattuck and Simon Watson Taylor, 1965)

(Sir) Antony Jay
(b. 1930)
British author and journalist and

Jonathan Lynn
(b. 1943)
British screenwriter and film-maker

Jay worked as a director and producer for the BBC (1955–64), while Lynn has written and directed the films Clue *(1985) and* Nuns on the Run *(1990). Together they co-scripted the television series satirizing high politics,* Yes Minister *(1980–2) and* Yes Prime Minister *(1986–8).*

1 Jim Hacker: Don't tell me about the press. I know exactly who reads the papers. The *Daily Mirror* is read by people who think they run the country. The *Guardian* is read by people who think they ought to run the country. *The Times* is read by people who actually do run the country. The *Daily Mail* is read by the wives of the people who run the country. The *Financial Times* is read by people who own the country. The *Morning Star* is read by people who think the country ought to be run by another country. And the *Daily Telegraph* is read by people who think it is.

Sir Humphrey: Prime Minister, what about the people who read the *Sun*?

Bernard Woolley: *Sun* readers don't care who runs the country, as long as she's got big tits.

Yes Prime Minister (BBC TV series), 'A Conflict of Interest', broadcast 29 December 1987

Douglas Jay
(1907–96)
British politician

Baron Jay of Battersea. Labour MP 1945–83, he was Financial Secretary to the Cabinet 1950–1 and President of the Board of Trade 1964–7. He was dismissed from the Cabinet for his opposition to British entry to the EEC.

1 In the case of nutrition and health, just as in the case of education, the gentleman in Whitehall really does know better what is good for people than the people know themselves.

The Socialist Case, ch. 30 (1937)

(Sir) James Jeans
(1877–1946)
British astrophysicist and mathematician

His Dynamical Theory of Gases *(1904) became a standard technical text, while later works did much to popularize astronomy.*

1 From the intrinsic evidence of his creation, the Great Architect of the Universe now begins to appear as a pure mathematician.

The Mysterious Universe, ch. 5 (1930)

Thomas Jefferson
(1743–1826)
US statesman and president

The principal author of the Declaration of Independence *(1776), he was governor of Virginia (1779–81), ambassador to Paris (1785–9), Vice-President (1797–1801) and, at the head of what was to become the Democratic Party, US President (1801–09). He pursued interests in science, philosophy and architecture, and co-founded the University of Virginia.*

1 The god who gave us life, gave us liberty at the same time: the hand of force may destroy, but cannot disjoin them.

A Summary View of the Rights of British America (pamphlet, 1774) repr. in *The Papers of Thomas Jefferson*, vol. 1 (ed. Julian P. Boyd, 1950)

2 When, in the course of human events, it becomes necessary for one people to dissolve the political bands which have connected them with another, and to assume among the powers of the earth the separate and equal station to which the laws of nature and of nature's God entitle them, a decent respect to the opinions of mankind requires that they should declare the causes which impel them to the separation.

Declaration of Independence, adopted by the Second Continental Congress, 4 July 1776, ibid., vol. 1. Opening lines. Jefferson is thought to have been responsible for most if not all of the document. Other members of the committee entrusted to it were JOHN ADAMS, BENJAMIN FRANKLIN, Robert Livingstone and Roger Sherman.

3 We hold these truths to be self-evident: that all men are created equal; that they are endowed by their Creator with certain unalienable rights; that among these are life, liberty, and the pursuit of happiness; that to secure these rights, governments are instituted among men, deriving their just powers from the consent of the governed; that whenever any form of government becomes destructive of these ends, it is the right of the people to alter or to abolish it, and to institute new government, laying its foundation on such principles, and organizing its powers in such form, as to them shall seem most likely to effect their safety and happiness.

Declaration of Independence, ibid., vol. 1. Jefferson's rough draft of the document, dated June 1776, read: 'We hold these truths to be sacred and undeniable; that all men are created equal and independent, that from that equal creation they derive rights inherent and inalienable, among which are the preservation of life, and liberty, and the pursuit of happiness.'

4 All experience hath shown that mankind are more disposed to suffer while evils are sufferable, than to right themselves by abolishing the forms to which they are accustomed.

Declaration of Independence, ibid., vol. 1.

5 The whole commerce between master and slave is a perpetual exercise of the most boisterous passions, the most unremitting despotism on the one part, and degrading submissions on the other. Our children see this, and learn to imitate it.

Notes on the State of Virginia, query 18 (1785), repr. in *The Writings of Thomas Jefferson*, vol. 3 (ed. Paul L. Ford, 1894)

6 Indeed I tremble for my country when I reflect that God is just: that his justice cannot sleep forever.

Notes on the State of Virginia, query 18, ibid., vol. 3. Referring to the practice of slavery. The words are inscribed on the northeast quadrant of the Jefferson Memorial, Washington DC.

7 Whenever there are in any country uncultivated lands and unemployed poor, it is clear that the laws of property have been so far extended as to violate natural right. The earth is given as a common stock for man to labor and live on ... The small land-owners are the most precious part of a state.
Letter to JAMES MADISON, 28 October 1785, publ. in *The Papers of Thomas Jefferson*, vol. 8 (ed. Julian Boyd, 1953)

8 The art of life is the art of avoiding pain; and he is the best pilot, who steers clearest of the rocks and shoals with which it is beset.
Letter, 12 October 1786, ibid., vol. 10 (1954). Articulating his 'head', arguing against his 'heart'.

9 Friendship is but another name for an alliance with the follies and the misfortunes of others. Our own share of miseries is sufficient: why enter then as volunteers into those of another?
Letter, 12 October 1786, ibid., vol. 10. Articulating his 'head', arguing against his 'heart'.

10 I hold it that a little rebellion now and then is a good thing, and as necessary in the political world as storms in the physical ... It is a medicine necessary for the sound health of government.
Letter to JAMES MADISON, 30 January 1787, ibid., vol. 11 (1955). Referring to Daniel Shays's Rebellion of poor farmers in Massachusetts. Jefferson, writing from Paris, was the only one of the American leaders not alarmed by news of the revolt.

11 Question with boldness even the existence of a god; because, if there be one, he must more approve the homage of reason, than that of blindfolded fear.
Letter 10 August 1787, ibid., vol. 12 (1955)

12 What signify a few lives lost in a century or two? The tree of liberty must be refreshed from time to time with the blood of patriots and tyrants. It is its natural manure.
Letter, 13 November 1787, ibid., vol. 12 (1955). Referring to Daniel Shays's Rebellion.

13 There is not a crowned head in Europe whose talents or merit would entitle him to be elected a vestryman by the people of any parish in America.
Letter to GEORGE WASHINGTON, 2 May 1788, ibid., vol. 13 (1956). Written while Jefferson was living in Paris.

14 The republican is the only form of government which is not eternally at open or secret war with the rights of mankind.
Letter, 11 March 1790, ibid., vol. 16 (1961)

15 Public employment contributes neither to advantage nor happiness. It is but honorable exile from one's family and affairs.
Letter, 18 April 1790, ibid., vol. 16

16 If there be one principle more deeply rooted than any other in the mind of every American, it is that we should have nothing to do with conquest.
Letter, 28 July 1791, ibid., vol. 20 (1982)

17 No government ought to be without censors: and where the press is free, no one ever will.
Letter to GEORGE WASHINGTON, 9 September 1792, ibid., vol. 24 (1990)

18 No man will ever bring out of that office the reputation which carries him into it. The honeymoon would be as short in that case as in any other, and its moments of ecstasy would be ransomed by years of torment and hatred.
Letter, 27 December 1796, publ. in *The Writings of Thomas Jefferson*, vol. 9 (ed. Albert Ellery Bergh and Andrew A. Lipscomb, 1905). On the presidency. Jefferson was shortly to begin a four-year term as Vice-President followed by eight years as President.

19 An association of men who will not quarrel with one another is a thing which never yet existed, from the greatest confederacy of nations down to a town meeting or a vestry.
Letter, 1 June 1798, ibid., vol. 10

20 Whenever a man has cast a longing eye on [political offices], a rottenness begins in his conduct.
Letter, 21 May 1799, ibid., vol. 7 (ed. Paul L. Ford, 1896)

21 I have sworn upon the altar of God eternal hostility against every form of tyranny over the mind of man.
Letter, 23 September 1800, ibid., vol. 10 (ed. Albert Ellery Bergh and Andrew A. Lipscomb, 1905)

22 Peace, commerce, and honest friendship with all nations – entangling alliances with none.
First Inaugural Address, 4 March 1801, ibid., vol. 3

23 Freedom of religion; freedom of the press; freedom of person under the protection of the *habeas corpus*; and trial by juries impartially selected – these principles form the bright constellation which has gone before us, and guided our steps through an age of revolution and reformation.
First Inaugural Address, 4 March 1801, ibid., vol. 3

24 Agriculture, manufactures, commerce, and navigation, the four pillars of our prosperity, are then

most thriving when left most free to individual enterprise.

First Annual Message to Congress, 8 December 1801, ibid., vol. 3. Jefferson added: 'Protection from casual embarrassments, however, may sometimes be seasonably interposed.'

25 Great innovations should not be forced on slender majorities.

Letter 2 May 1808, ibid., vol. 12

26 The selfish spirit of commerce, which knows no country, and feels no passion or principle but that of gain.

Letter 15 April 1809, ibid., vol. 12

27 A strict observance of the written laws is doubtless one of the high virtues of a good citizen, but it is not the highest. The laws of necessity, of self-preservation, of saving our country when in danger, are of higher obligation.

Letter, 20 September 1810, ibid., vol. 12

28 We may consider each generation as a distinct nation, with a right, by the will of its majority, to bind themselves, but none to bind the succeeding generation, more than the inhabitants of another country.

Letter, 24 June 1813, ibid., vol. 13. Referring to the incurring of a national debt.

29 For I agree with you that there is a natural aristocracy among men. The grounds of this are virtue and talents.

Letter to JOHN ADAMS, 28 October 1813, ibid., vol. 13

30 His mind was great and powerful, without being of the very first order; his penetration strong, though not so acute as that of a Newton, Bacon, or Locke; and as far as he saw, no judgment was ever sounder. It was slow in operation, being little aided by invention or imagination, but sure in conclusion.

Letter, 2 January 1814, ibid., vol. 14. Describing GEORGE WASHINGTON.

31 Merchants have no country. The mere spot they stand on does not constitute so strong an attachment as that from which they draw their gains.

Letter, 17 March 1814, ibid., vol. 14

32 I hope our wisdom will grow with our power, and teach us, that the less we use our power the greater it will be.

Letter, 12 June 1815, ibid., vol. 14

33 I sincerely believe ... that banking establishments are more dangerous than standing armies, and that the principle of spending money to be paid by posterity, under the name of funding, is but swindling futurity on a large scale.

Letter, 28 May 1816, ibid., vol. 15. Addressed to political philosopher and senator John Taylor, whose book *An Inquiry into the Principles and Policy of the Government of the United States* (1814) had argued against the harmful effects of finance capitalism.

34 The boisterous sea of liberty is never without a wave.

Letter, 20 October 1820, ibid., vol. 15

35 Books constitute capital. A library book lasts as long as a house, for hundreds of years. It is not, then, an article of mere consumption but fairly of capital, and often in the case of professional men, setting out in life, it is their only capital.

Letter to JAMES MADISON, Sept 1821, publ. in *The Republic of Letters: The Correspondence Between Thomas Jefferson and James Madison 1776–1826*, vol. 3 (ed. James Morton Smith, 1995)

36 I have ever deemed it fundamental for the United States never to take active part in the quarrels of Europe. Their political interests are entirely distinct from ours. Their mutual jealousies, their balance of power, their complicated alliances, their forms and principles of government, are all foreign to us. They are nations of eternal war.

Letter to President JAMES MONROE, 11 June 1823, publ. in *The Writings of Thomas Jefferson*, vol. 15 (ed. Albert Ellery Bergh and Andrew A. Lipscomb, 1905). Written six months before Munroe's formulation of US foreign policy, the Monroe Doctrine, which reflected Jefferson's view.

37 I candidly confess that I have ever looked on Cuba as the most interesting addition which could ever be made to our system of States. The control which, with Florida Point, this island would give us over the Gulf of Mexico, and the countries and isthmus bordering on it, as well as all those whose waters flow into it, would fill up the measure of our political well-being.

Letter to President JAMES MONROE, 24 October 1823, ibid., vol. 15

38 When angry, count ten, before you speak; if very angry, an hundred.

Decalogue of Canons for Observation in Practical Life, no. 10, in letter to Thomas Jefferson Smith, 21 February 1825, ibid., vol. 16. See MARK TWAIN 12.

(Sir) Geoffrey Jellicoe

(1900–96)

British architect and historian

His writings, notably Landscape of Man *(1975), were influential on the development of landscapes and gardens. His designs often incorporate water and sculpture.*

1 Architecture is to make us know and remember who we are.

International Herald Tribune 6 November 1989

David Jenkins

(b. 1925)

British ecclesiastic

He was Professor of Theology at Leeds University (1979–84) before becoming Bishop of Durham (1984–94), in which capacity he caused controversy over his interpretation of basic biblical tenets.

1 I wouldn't put it past God to arrange a virgin birth if He wanted, but I very much doubt if He would.

Church Times 4 May 1984

2 No statement about God is simply, literally true. God is far more than can be measured, described, defined in ordinary language, or pinned down to any particular happening.

Guardian 24 December 1984

3 As I get older I seem to believe less and less and yet to believe what I do believe more and more.

Daily Telegraph 2 November 1988

Roy Jenkins

(1920–2003)

British politician and author

Baron Jenkins of Hillhead. Elected a Labour MP in 1948, he was Home Secretary (1965–7 and 1974–6) Chancellor of the Exchequer (1967–70), and co-founded the Social Democratic Party in 1981. He was noted for his patrician tastes; ROBERT HARRIS *called him 'the most clubbable Coriolanus British politics has ever produced'.*

1 There is nobody in politics I can remember and no case I can think of in history where a man combined such a powerful political personality with so little intelligence.

Quoted in *The Crossman Diaries*, 5 September 1969 (1979). Remark concerning JAMES CALLAGHAN, made to RICHARD CROSSMAN, who demurred: 'I think Jim Callaghan is a wonderful political personality, easily the most accomplished politician in the Labour Party.'

2 The politics of the left and centre of this country

are frozen in an out-of-date mould which is bad for the political and economic health of Britain and increasingly inhibiting for those who live within the mould. Can it be broken?

Speech to Parliamentary Press Gallery, 9 June 1980, quoted in *The Times* 10 June 1980. The Social Democratic Party, which Jenkins co-founded the following year, was said to have 'broken the mould of British politics'.

Elizabeth Jennings

(1926–2001)

British poet

Writing in traditional verse form, she explores personal themes of suffering and isolation, influenced by her Roman Catholic faith and by a period of mental illness. Her collections include The Mind Has Mountains *(1966).*

1 But every season is a kind
Of rich nostalgia. We give names –
Autumn and summer, winter, spring –
As though to unfasten from the mind
Our moods and give them outward forms.
We want the certain, solid thing.

'Song at the Beginning of Autumn', publ. in *A Way of Looking* (1955)

2 Do they know they're old,
These two who are my father and my mother
Whose fire from which I came, has now grown
   cold?

'One Flesh', publ. in *The Mind Has Mountains* (1966)

3 At last now you can be
What the old cannot recall
And the young long for in dreams,
Yet still include them all.

'Accepted', publ. in *Growing Pains* (1975)

4 I have come into the hour of a white healing.
Grief's surgery is over and I wear
The scar of my remorse and of my feeling.

'Into the Hour', publ. in *Moments of Grace* (1979)

5 Never to possess,
Therefore never lose, –
This is a creed of fire, The burning of excess,
The cold ash of loss,
Continual desire.

'Ways', publ. in *Extending the Territory* (1985)

Saint Jerome
(*c.* 345–*c.* 420)
Christian scholar

The most learned of the Fathers of the Church, he wrote numerous monastic and theological works, as well as commentaries based on Biblical texts. His translations of the Old and New Testaments into Latin came to form the basis of the Roman Catholic Vulgate.

1 Avoid like the plague a clergyman who is also a man of business, one who has risen from wealth, from obscurity to a high position.
Letters, Letter 52 (*c.* 400)

2 A clergyman soon becomes an object of contempt, if, however often he is invited to dinner, he does not refuse.
Ibid., Letter 52

3 The Roman world is falling, yet we hold our heads erect instead of bowing our necks.
Ibid., Letter 60

4 Every day we die, every day we are changed, and yet we believe ourselves to be eternal.
Ibid., Letter 60

5 Christians are not born but made.
Ibid., Letter 107

Jerome K. Jerome
(1859–1927)
British author

Jerome Klapka Jerome. He enjoyed literary success with Idle Thoughts of an Idle Fellow *(1886), a volume of light-hearted essays, and* Three Men in a Boat *(1889), the humorous tale of a boating trip on the Thames. He co-edited* The Idler *1892–7.*

1 It is impossible to enjoy idling thoroughly unless one has plenty of work to do. There is no fun in doing nothing when you have nothing to do. Wasting time is merely an occupation then, and a most exhausting one. Idleness, like kisses, to be sweet must be stolen.
Idle Thoughts of an Idle Fellow, 'On Being Idle' (1886)

2 Love is like the measles; we all have to go through it. Also like the measles, we take it only once.
Ibid., 'On Being in Love'. DOUGLAS JERROLD had earlier written: 'Love's like the measles – all the worse when it comes late in life.' (*The Wit and Opinions of Douglas Jerrold*, 'Love', 1859)

3 It is in our faults and failings, not in our virtues, that we touch each other, and find sympathy ... It is in our follies that we are one.
Ibid., 'On Vanity and Vanities'

4 The weather is like the government, always in the wrong.
Ibid., 'On the Weather'

5 Throw the lumber over, man! Let your boat of life be light, packed with only what you need – a homely home and simple pleasures, one or two friends, worth the name, someone to love and someone to love you, a cat, a dog, and a pipe or two, enough to eat and enough to wear, and a little more than enough to drink; for thirst is a dangerous thing.
Three Men in a Boat, ch. 3 (1889)

6 I like work; it fascinates me. I can sit and look at it for hours. I love to keep it by me; the idea of getting rid of it nearly breaks my heart.
Ibid., ch. 15

7 Some people are under the impression that all that is required to make a good fisherman is the ability to tell lies easily and without blushing; but this is a mistake. Mere bald fabrication is useless; the veriest tyro can manage that. It is in the circumstantial detail, the embellishing touches of probability, the general air of scrupulous – almost of pedantic – veracity, that the experienced angler is seen.
Ibid., ch. 17

8 It is always the best policy to speak the truth, unless of course you are an exceptionally good liar.
The Idler February 1892

9 I want a house that has got over all its troubles; I don't want to spend the rest of my life bringing up a young and inexperienced house.
They and I, ch. 11 (1909)

Douglas Jerrold
(1803–57)
English playwright and humorist

A contributor to Punch *when it was first published, he wrote for a variety of other journals and had success with his play* Black-Eyed Susan *(1829). He also wrote novels and essays. See* JEROME K. JEROME 2.

1 I've heard say wedlock's like wine – not to be properly judged of till the second glass.
The Wit and Opinions of Douglas Jerrold, 'Second Marriages' (1859)

2 Earth is here so kind, that just tickle her with a hoe and she laughs with a harvest.
Ibid., 'A Land of Plenty'

3 In this world, truth can wait; she's used to it.
Ibid., 'Truth'

4 Readers are of two sorts. There is a reader who carefully goes through a book; and there is a reader who as carefully lets the book go through him.
Ibid., 'Readers'

William Stanley Jevons
(1835–82)
British economist and logician

He made important contributions to economic theory, notably in his paper 'General Mathematical Theory of Political Economy' (1861) and book The Theory of Political Economy *(1871).*

1 Repeated reflection and inquiry have led me to the somewhat novel opinion, that *value depends entirely upon utility.*
The Theory of Political Economy, ch. 1 (1871)

2 All classes of society are trades unionists at heart, and differ chiefly in the boldness, ability, and secrecy with which they pursue their respective interests.
The State in Relation to Labour, Introduction (1882)

3 Value is the most invincible and impalpable of ghosts, and comes and goes unthought of while the visible and dense matter remains as it was.
Investigations in Currency and Finance, pt 2, ch. 4 (1884)

Sarah Orne Jewett
(1849–1909)
US author

Most of her fiction is set in her native Maine, including her most influential work, The Country of the Pointed Firs *(1896). She also published books for children and verse.*

1 Wrecked on the lee shore of age.
The Country of the Pointed Firs, ch. 7 (1896)

2 Tact is after all a kind of mind-reading.
Ibid., ch. 10

3 The thing that teases the mind over and over for years, and at last gets itself put down rightly on paper – whether little or great, it belongs to Literature.
Letter to WILLA CATHER, quoted in The Country of the Pointed Firs and Other Stories, Preface (1925 edn)

C. E. M. Joad
(1891–1953)
British philosopher and author

Cyril Edwin Mitchinson Joad. Author of more than forty books, he made the subject of philosophy accessible to the general reader, often incorporating his own controversial views.

1 A good soul like a good body should be as unobtrusive as possible; in so far as it functions properly, it should not be noticed for good or for ill.
The Book of Joad, ch. 2, 'Food and Women' (1932)

2 It all depends what you mean by . . .
Typical intervention when answering questions on 'The Brains Trust', BBC radio (1941–8).

Saint Joan of Arc
(c. 1412–31)
French patriot and martyr

Jeanne d'Arc. Having persuaded the future Charles VII that she had a divine mission to expel the English from northern France, she raised the siege of Orléans in 1429 and enabled his coronation at Reims. The Maid of Orléans, as she was afterwards known, was captured by Burgundians, sold to the English, and burnt as a witch.

1 If I am not, may God put me there; and if I am, may God so keep me.
Statement, 24 February 1431, quoted in The Trial of Jeanne d'Arc (ed. W. P. Barrett, 1931). On being asked if she knew she was in God's grace.

2 You say that you are my judge; I do not know if you are; but take good heed not to judge me ill, because you would put yourself in great peril.
Quoted ibid.

John XXIII
(1881–1963)
Italian pope

Angelo Giuseppe Roncalli. Elected Pope in 1958, he was responsible for convening the Second Vatican Council in 1962 by which he intended to update and reform the Church, but died after the first session. The Council was continued by Pope Paul VI.

1 Governmental authority . . . is a postulate of the moral order and derives from God. Consequently, laws and decrees passed in contravention of the moral order, and hence of the divine will, can have no binding force in conscience, since 'it is right to obey God rather than men'.
Encyclical, 11 April 1963: Pacem in Terris, pt 2, sect. 51

2 If they are to imbue civilization with right ideals and Christian principles, it is not enough for our sons to be illumined by the heavenly light of faith and to be fired with enthusiasm for a cause; they must involve themselves in the work of these institutions, and strive to influence them effectively from within. But in a culture and civilization like our own, which is so remarkable for its scientific knowledge and its technical discoveries, clearly no one can insinuate himself into public life unless he be scientifically competent, technically capable, and skilled in the practice of his own profession.

Encyclical, 11 April 1963: *Pacem in Terris*, pt 5, sect. 147–8

Saint John of the Cross
(1542–91)
Spanish mystic and poet

Juan de Yepes y Álvarez (Juan de la Cruz). With St Teresa of Ávila, he founded an ascetic order of Carmelite monks in 1568. He wrote some of his finest poetry while in prison 1577–8.

1 The Dark Night of the Soul.

Title of treatise (1578). Elaborating on the poem 'In a Dark Night' (*'En una noche oscura'*), which is usually translated as 'The Dark Night of the Soul'. See F. SCOTT FITZGERALD 18.

(Sir) Elton John
(b. 1947)
British rock musician

Originally Reginald Kenneth Dwight. A regular chart-topper from the 1970s to the 1990s, he is known for his flamboyant performances and extravagant lifestyle. Bestselling albums include Goodbye Yellow Brick Road *(1973).*

1 And it seems to me you lived your life
Like a candle in the wind.

'Candle in the Wind' (song, with lyrics by Bernie Taupin), on the album *Goodbye Yellow Brick Road* (1973). The song, which was about MARILYN MONROE, was re-released in 1997 with new words addressed to Princess DIANA (see 4 below). 'Candle in the Wind' is the title of a 1941 play by MAXWELL ANDERSON.

2 Saturday night's alright for fighting.

'Saturday Night's Alright for Fighting' (song, with lyrics by Bernie Taupin), ibid.

3 It's sad, so sad
It's a sad, sad situation
And it's getting more and more absurd
It's sad, so sad
Why can't we talk it over

Oh it seems to me
That sorry seems to be the hardest word.

'Sorry Seems to be the Hardest Word' (song, with lyrics by Bernie Taupin) on the album *Blue Moves* (1976)

4 Goodbye English rose,
May you ever grow in our hearts.

'Candle in the Wind '97' (song, 1997, with lyrics by Bernie Taupin). The 1973 song was re-written to mark the death of Princess DIANA and performed by Elton John at her funeral in Westminster Abbey.

John Paul II
(1920–2005)
Polish pope

Karol Jozef Wojtyla. The first non-Italian to be elected Pope (1978) since 1522, he travelled extensively, speaking out against married priests, birth control, abortion, genetic manipulation and capital punishment.

1 As the family goes, so goes the nation and so goes the whole world in which we live.

Quoted in the *Observer* 7 December 1986

2 The question confronting the Church today is not any longer whether the man in the street can grasp a religious message, but how to employ the communications media so as to let him have the full impact of the Gospel message.

International Herald Tribune 8 May 1989

3 The cemetery of the victims of human cruelty in our century is extended to include yet another vast cemetery, that of the unborn.

Quoted in the *Observer* 9 June 1991

4 It would be simplistic to say that Divine Providence caused the fall of Communism. In a certain sense Communism as a system fell by itself. It fell as a consequence of its own mistakes and abuses. *It proved to be a medicine more dangerous than the disease itself.* It did not bring about true social reform, yet it did become a powerful threat and challenge to the entire world. But *it fell by itself, because of its own inherent weakness.*

Crossing the Threshold of Hope, 'Was God at Work in the Fall of Communism?' (1994)

Boris Johnson
(b. 1964)
British journalist and politician

Conservative MP for Henley from 2001, he was dismissed from his posts as Shadow Minister of Arts and Party Chairman in 2004 following disparaging remarks made about the city of Liverpool in the Spectator, *which he edited 1999–2005.*

1 It is an inverted pyramid of piffle.
Mail on Sunday 7 November 2004. Denying allegations of an affair with Petronella Wyatt.

Gerald W. Johnson
(1890–1980)
US author

Gerald White Johnson. He was an authority on American history and government. His prolific writing career spanned six decades.

1 Heroes are created by popular demand, sometimes out of the scantiest materials, or none at all.
American Heroes and Hero-Worship, ch. 1 (1943)

Hiram Johnson
(1866–1945)
US politician

He helped to found the Progressive Party in 1912 but was later a reforming Republican and a staunch isolationist.

1 When war is declared, Truth is the first casualty.
Attributed speech to Senate, c. 1918. There is no evidence that Johnson ever said these words. The first recorded use is as an epigraph to a book detailing propaganda techniques in the First World War: *Falsehood in Wartime* (1928) by Arthur Ponsonby. The words may have been inspired by a passage written by Dr Johnson (see SAMUEL JOHNSON 37), and have also been ascribed, in different versions, to AESCHYLUS and WINSTON CHURCHILL.

James Weldon Johnson
(1871–1938)
US author and diplomat

He was consul in Venezuela and Nicaragua (1906–12) and prominent in the National Association for the Advancement of Colored People (1916–30). His varied literary output contributed to the Harlem Renaissance of the 1920s.

1 O black and unknown bards of long ago,
How came your lips to touch the sacred fire?
'O Black and Unknown Bards', st. 1, written c. 1907, publ. in *Fifty Years and Other Poems* (1917). Opening lines of poem.

2 I believe it to be a fact that the colored people of this country know and understand the white people better than the white people know and understand them.
The Autobiography of an Ex-Colored Man, ch. 2 (1912)

3 And God stepped out on space,
And He looked around and said,
'I'm lonely –
I'll make me a world.'
'The Creation', st. 1 (1918), repr. in *God's Trombones: Seven Negro Sermons in Verse* (1927)

4 Young man –
Young man –
Your arm's too short to box with God.
'The Prodigal Son', ibid.

5 It is from the blues that all that may be called American music derives its most distinctive character.
Black Manhattan, ch. 11 (1930)

Lady Bird Johnson
(b. 1912)
US First Lady

Claudia Alta Taylor Johnson. She owned and operated the KTBC radio and TV station in Austin, Texas, and was active in the political campaigns of her husband, LYNDON B. JOHNSON.

1 It all began so beautifully. After a drizzle in the morning, the sun came out bright and clear. We were driving into Dallas. In the lead car were President and Mrs Kennedy . . .
First journal entry, 22 November 1963, publ. in *A White House Diary* (1970)

2 The first lady is, and always has been, an unpaid public servant elected by one person, her husband.
Journal entry, 14 March 1968, ibid.

Linton Kwesi Johnson
(b. 1952)
Anglo-Jamaican poet and singer

Since the 1970s he has been the voice of dub poetry. Among his collections, written in Jamaican patois, are Dread Beat 'n' Blood *(1975, album 1978) and* Mi Revalueshanary Fren: Selected Poems *(2002).*

1 Brothers and sisters rocking,
a dread beat pulsing fire, burning.
'Dread Beat 'n' Blood' (poem, 1975), set to music and released on the album *Dread, Beat 'n' Blood* (1978) by Poet and the Roots

2 Inglan is a bitch
There's no escapin' it.
'Inglan is a Bitch' on the album *Bass Culture* (1980)

Lyndon B. Johnson
(1908–73)
US politician and president

Lyndon Baines Johnson. A Texan Democrat, he served as President (1963–9) following JOHN KENNEDY's *assassination. For* RALPH ELLISON *he was 'the greatest American president for the poor and for the Negroes', though his escalation of the Vietnam War lost him popularity. See also* BARRY GOLDWATER 1, POLITICAL SLOGANS 15.

1 Son, in politics you've got to learn that overnight chicken shit can turn to chicken salad.

Of RICHARD NIXON, quoted in *Richard Nixon: The Shaping of his Character*, ch. 25 (1983) by Fawn Brodie. Johnson, who had previously referred to Nixon as 'chicken shit', was replying to a reporter who had questioned him on his embracing Nixon on the latter's return from a vice-presidential tour of South America in May 1958, during which he had been mobbed by an angry crowd in Caracas. WALTER LIPPMANN called the tour 'a diplomatic Pearl Harbor' and the *Boston Globe* said it was 'one of the most ineptly handled episodes in this country's foreign relations'.

2 The world has narrowed to a neighborhood before it has broadened to a brotherhood.

Speech in New York City, 17 December 1963, publ. in *Public Papers of the Presidents of the United States, Lyndon B. Johnson: 1963–64*

3 This administration today, here and now, declares unconditional war on poverty in America.

State of the Union address to Congress, 8 January 1964, ibid.

4 The Great Society is a place where every child can find knowledge to enrich his mind and to enlarge his talents ... It is a place where the city of man serves not only the needs of the body and the demands of commerce but the desire for beauty and the hunger for community ... It is a place where men are more concerned with the quality of their goals than the quantity of their goods.

Speech in Ann Arbor, Michigan, 22 May 1964, ibid. The slogan 'Great Society' had been current for several years, possibly originating as the title of a book by economist Graham Wallas in 1914. As suggested by Richard N. Goodwin, Secretary General of the International Peace Corps Secretariat and occasional speechwriter, it became closely associated with Johnson's presidency, featuring in his acceptance speech at the Democratic Party National Convention, August 1964 (see Hugh Sidey's *A Very Personal Presidency*, 1968).

5 We are not about to send American boys 9 or 10,000 miles away from home to do what Asian boys ought to be doing for themselves.

Speech at Akron University, Ohio, 21 October 1964, ibid.

6 I don't want loyalty. I want *loyalty*. I want him to kiss my ass in Macy's window at high noon and tell me it smells like roses. I want his pecker in my pocket.

Quoted in *The Best and the Brightest*, ch. 20 (1972) by David Halberstam. Referring to a prospective assistant.

7 Better to have him inside the tent pissing out, than outside pissing in.

Ibid., ch. 20. Of J. EDGAR HOOVER.

8 Jerry Ford is so dumb he can't fart and chew gum at the same time.

Quoted in *A Ford, Not a Lincoln*, ch. 1 (1975) by Richard Reeves. Reeves asserts that Johnson's put-down was 'cleaned up' by 'the late President's aides and history'.

Philip Johnson
(1906–2005)
US architect

He coined the term 'International Style' in 1932, and, following the theories of MIES VAN DER ROHE, *embraced postmodernism. He was Director of Architecture and Design at New York's Museum of Modern Art 1932–54.*

1 The automobile is the greatest catastrophe in the entire history of City architecture.

'The Town and the Automobile, or the Pride of Elm Street' (1955), repr. in *Writings* (1979)

2 Architecture is the art of how to waste space.

New York Times 27 December 1964

3 All architects want to live beyond their deaths.

Quoted in the *Observer* 27 December 1987

R. W. Johnson
(b. 1916)
US journalist and newspaper executive

1 Any solution to a problem changes the problem.

Washingtonian November 1979

Samuel Johnson
(1709–84)
English author, poet and lexicographer

Dr Johnson. At the centre of London's literary society in the 18th century, he was renowned as a conversationalist and for his critical and biographical studies of English poets, his verse satire The Vanity of Human Wishes *(1749), his philosophical romance* Rasselas *(1759) and, probably his greatest achievement, his* Dictionary *(1755). His mordant humour was recorded in the biography written by his friend* JAMES BOSWELL.

On Johnson, see THOMAS CARLYLE 44, NATHANIEL HAWTHORNE 11, TOBIAS SMOLLETT 3 .

1 Here falling houses thunder on your head,
And here a female atheist talks you dead.
'London', ll. 17–18 (1738), repr. in *The Works of Samuel Johnson*, vol. 6 (ed. E. L. McAdam Jr and G. Milne, 1964). The poem is an imitation of JUVENAL's third satire.

2 This mournful truth is everywhere confessed,
Slow rises worth by poverty depressed.
'London', ll. 176–7, ibid., vol. 6. See JUVENAL 8.

3 Prepare for death, if here at night you roam,
And sign your will before you sup from home.
'London', ll. 224–5, ibid., vol. 6

4 Cruel with guilt, and daring with despair,
The midnight murderer bursts the faithless bar;
Invades the sacred hour of silent rest
And leaves, unseen, a dagger in your breast.
'London', ll. 238–41, ibid., vol. 6

5 Hard is his lot that here by fortune placed
Must watch the wild vicissitudes of taste.
'Prologue at the Opening of the Theatre in Drury Lane', ll. 47–8 (1747), ibid., vol. 6

6 The drama's laws the drama's patrons give,
For we that live to please, must please to live.
'Prologue at the Opening of the Theatre in Drury Lane', ll. 53–4, ibid., vol. 6

7 There mark what ills the scholar's life assail,
Toil, envy, want, the patron, and the jail.
'The Vanity of Human Wishes', ll. 159–60 (1749), ibid., vol. 6. In his *Life of Dr Johnson LL.D.* (1791), BOSWELL noted that the second line of Johnson's couplet had read, 'Toil, envy, want, the *garret*, and the gaol', but had changed it 'after experiencing the uneasiness which Lord Chesterfield's fallacious patronage made him feel'.

8 He left the name, at which the world grew pale,
To point a moral, or adorn a tale.
'The Vanity of Human Wishes', ll. 221–2, ibid., vol. 6. Describing Charles XII of Sweden, whose early military triumphs ended with his disastrous defeat by the Russian army in 1709.

9 Enlarge my life with multitude of days,
In health, in sickness, thus the suppliant prays;
Hides from himself his state, and shuns to know
That life protracted is protracted woe.
Time hovers o'er, impatient to destroy,
And shuts up all the passages of joy.
'The Vanity of Human Wishes', ll. 255–60, ibid., vol. 6

10 The natural flights of the human mind are not from pleasure to pleasure, but from hope to hope.
The Rambler, no. 2, 24 March 1750, repr. in *The Works of Samuel Johnson*, vol. 3 (ed. W. J. Bate and Albrecht B. Strauss, 1969)

11 That observation which is called knowledge of the world will be found much more frequently to make men cunning than good.
The Rambler, no. 4, 31 March 1750, ibid., vol. 3

12 The vanity of being known to be trusted with a secret is generally one of the chief motives to disclose it.
The Rambler, no. 13, 1 May 1750, ibid., vol. 3

13 Sorrow is a kind of rust of the soul, which every new idea contributes in its passage to scour away. It is the putrefaction of stagnant life, and is remedied by exercise and motion.
The Rambler, no. 47, 28 August 1750, ibid., vol. 3

14 Disease generally begins that equality which death completes.
The Rambler, no. 48, 1 September 1750, ibid., vol. 3

15 The conversation of the old and young ends generally with contempt or pity on either side.
The Rambler, no. 69, 13 November 1750, ibid., vol. 3

16 There are minds so impatient of inferiority that their gratitude is a species of revenge, and they return benefits, not because recompense is a pleasure, but because obligation is a pain.
The Rambler, no. 87, 15 January 1751, ibid., vol. 3

17 Curiosity is one of the most permanent and certain characteristics of a vigorous intellect.
The Rambler, no. 103, 12 March 1751, ibid., vol. 4 (1969)

18 No place affords a more striking conviction of the vanity of human hopes than a public library.
The Rambler, no. 106, 23 March 1751, ibid., vol. 4

19 Almost all absurdity of conduct arises from the imitation of those whom we cannot resemble.
The Rambler, no. 135, 2 July 1751, ibid., vol. 4

20 Just praise is only a debt, but flattery is a present.
The Rambler, no. 155, 10 September 1751, ibid., vol. 5 (1969)

21 Turn on the prudent ant thy heedful eyes,
Observe her labours, sluggard, and be wise.
'The Ant', written c. 1752, publ. 1766, repr. in *The Works of Samuel Johnson*, vol. 6 (ed. E. L. McAdam Jr and G. Milne, 1964). Opening lines, based on a passage in the Bible: see BIBLE, OLD TESTAMENT: PROVERBS 10.

22 The world will never be long without some good reason to hate the unhappy.

The Adventurer, no. 99, 16 October 1753, repr. ibid., vol. 2 (ed. W. J. Bate, John M. Bullitt and L. F. Powell, 1963)

23 Composition is, for the most part, an effort of slow diligence and steady perseverance, to which the mind is dragged by necessity or resolution, and from which the attention is every moment starting to more delightful amusements.

The Adventurer, no. 138, 2 March 1754, ibid., vol. 2

24 A fly, Sir, may sting a stately horse and make him wince; but one is but an insect, and the other is a horse still.

Quoted in *Life of Samuel Johnson, LL.D.*, 1754 note (1791) by JAMES BOSWELL. On the relative merits of two authors.

25 They teach the morals of a whore, and the manners of a dancing master.

Quoted ibid. Referring to LORD CHESTERFIELD's *Letters to His Son*. Of Chesterfield – his erratic patron – Johnson remarked: 'This man I thought had been a lord among wits; but, I find, he is only a wit among lords.'

26 Is not a patron, my lord, one who looks with unconcern on a man struggling for life in the water, and, when he has reached ground, encumbers him with help? The notice which you have been pleased to take of my labours, had it been early, had been kind; but it has been delayed till I am indifferent, and cannot enjoy it; till I am solitary, and cannot impart it; till I am known, and do not want it.

Letter to his patron LORD CHESTERFIELD, 7 February 1755, ibid. See quote 32.

27 If a man does not make new acquaintance as he advances through life, he will soon find himself left alone. A man, Sir, should keep his friendship in constant repair.

Quoted ibid., 1755 note (1791). BOSWELL records that Johnson's comment was made 'at a subsequent period of his life'.

28 Every other author may aspire to praise; the lexicographer can only hope to escape reproach, and even this negative recompense has been yet granted to very few.

Dictionary of the English Language, Preface (1755)

29 I am not yet so lost in lexicography as to forget that *words are the daughters of earth, and that things are the sons of heaven*. Language is only the instrument of science, and words are but the signs of ideas: I wish, however, that the instrument might

be less apt to decay, and that signs might be permanent, like the things which they denote.

Ibid., Preface. Johnson was paraphrasing a line from Samuel Madden's poem, 'Boulter's Monument' (1745), which Johnson had revised for publication: 'Words are men's daughters, but God's sons are things.'

30 Every quotation contributes something to the stability or enlargement of the language.

Ibid., Preface. Referring to the quotations illustrating usage in the dictionary.

31 Lexicographer. A writer of dictionaries, a harmless drudge, that busies himself in tracing the original, and detailing the signification of words.

Ibid. Under the entry for 'Dull' Johnson gave the following illustration: 'To make dictionaries is *dull* work.'

32 Patron. One who countenances, supports or protects. Commonly a wretch who supports with insolence, and is paid with flattery.

Ibid. See quote 26.

33 A hardened and shameless tea-drinker, who has, for twenty years, diluted his meals with only the infusion of this fascinating plant; whose kettle has scarcely time to cool, who with tea amuses the evening, with tea solaces the midnights, and with tea welcomes the morning.

Describing himself, in review in the *Literary Magazine*, no. 13, 15 April–15 May 1757, repr. in *The Samuel Johnson Encyclopedia*, 'Tea' (ed. Pat Rogers, 1996). BOSWELL vouched for Johnson's passion for tea in his *Life*: 'I suppose no person ever enjoyed with more relish the infusion of that fragrant leaf than Johnson.' (1756)

34 When I was as you are now, towering in the confidence of twenty-one, little did I suspect that I should be at forty-nine, what I now am.

Letter, 9 January 1758, publ. in *Life of Samuel Johnson, LL.D.* (1791) by JAMES BOSWELL

35 As peace is the end of war, so to be idle is the ultimate purpose of the busy.

'The Idler', no. 1, (1758), repr. in *The Works of Samuel Johnson*, vol. 2 (ed. W. J. Bate, John M. Bullitt and L. F. Powell, 1963). 'Perhaps man,' Johnson wrote, 'is the only being that can properly be called idle.'

36 To be idle and to be poor have always been reproaches, and therefore every man endeavours with his utmost care to hide his poverty from others, and his idleness from himself.

'The Idler', no. 17 (1758), ibid., vol. 2

37 Among the calamities of war may be justly numbered the diminution of the love of truth, by the

falsehoods which interest dictates and credulity encourages.

'The Idler', no. 30 (1758), ibid., vol. 2. See also HIRAM JOHNSON 1.

38 When speculation has done its worst, two and two still make four.

'The Idler', no. 36 (1758), ibid., vol. 2

39 Promise, large promise, is the soul of an advertisement.

'The Idler', no. 40 (1759), ibid., vol. 2

40 The trade of advertising is now so near perfection that it is not easy to propose any improvement. But as every art ought to be exercised in due subordination to the public good, I cannot but propose it as a moral question to these masters of the public ear, whether they do not sometimes play too wantonly with our passions.

'The Idler', no. 40 (1759), ibid., vol. 2

41 No man will be a sailor who has contrivance enough to get himself into a jail; for being in a ship is being in a jail, with the chance of being drowned . . . A man in a jail has more room, better food and commonly better company.

Quoted in *Life of Samuel Johnson, LL.D.*, 16 March 1759 (1791) by JAMES BOSWELL. In a later entry in the biography (10 April 1778), when told 'We find people fond of being sailors,' Johnson replied: 'I cannot account for that, any more than I can account for other strange perversions of imagination.'

42 Virtue is too often merely local.

'The Idler', no. 53 (1759), repr. in *The Works of Samuel Johnson*, vol. 2 (ed. W. J. Bate, John M. Bullitt and L. F. Powell, 1963)

43 Nothing is more hopeless than a scheme of merriment.

'The Idler', no. 58 (1759), ibid., vol. 2

44 Some desire is necessary to keep life in motion, and he whose real wants are supplied must admit those of fancy.

The History of Rasselas, ch. 8 (1759). Spoken by Imlac.

45 He must write as the interpreter of nature, and the legislator of mankind, and consider himself as presiding over the thoughts and manners of future generations; as a being superior to time and place.

Imlac, ibid., ch. 10. On the role of poets. See PERCY BYSSHE SHELLEY 91.

46 Marriage has many pains, but celibacy has no pleasures.

Nekayah, ibid., ch. 26

47 Integrity without knowledge is weak and useless,

and knowledge without integrity is dangerous and dreadful.

The astronomer, ibid., ch. 41

48 I have always considered it as treason against the great republic of human nature, to make any man's virtues the means of deceiving him.

Rasselas, ibid., ch. 46

49 I have purchased knowledge at the expense of all the common comforts of life: I have missed the endearing elegance of female friendship, and the happy commerce of domestic tenderness.

The astronomer, ibid., ch. 46

50 The world is not yet exhausted; let me see something tomorrow which I never saw before.

Nekayah, ibid., ch. 47

51 In all pointed sentences, some degree of accuracy must be sacrificed to conciseness.

'The Bravery of the English Common Soldiers' (1760), repr. in *The Works of Samuel Johnson*, vol. 10 (ed. Donald J. Greene, 1977)

52 There is, indeed, nothing that so much seduces reason from vigilance, as the thought of passing life with an amiable woman.

Letter, 21 December 1762, publ. in *Life of Samuel Johnson, LL.D.* (1791) by JAMES BOSWELL

53 Great abilities are not requisite for an historian; for in historical composition, all the greatest powers of the human mind are quiescent. He has facts ready to his hand; so there is no exercise of invention. Imagination is not required in any degree; only about as much as is used in the lowest kinds of poetry. Some penetration, accuracy, and colouring, will fit a man for the task, if he can give the application which is necessary.

Quoted ibid., 6 July 1763

54 Norway, too, has noble prospects; and Lapland is remarkable for prodigious noble wild prospects. But, Sir, let me tell you, the noblest prospect which a Scotchman ever sees is the high road that leads him to England!

Quoted ibid., 6 July 1763

55 A man ought to read just as inclination leads him; for what he reads as a task will do him little good.

Quoted ibid., 14 July 1763. However, Johnson continued: 'A young man should read five hours in a day, and so may acquire a great deal of knowledge.'

56 If he does really think that there is no distinction

between virtue and vice, why, Sir, when he leaves our houses let us count our spoons.

Quoted ibid., 14 July 1763

57 There is nothing, Sir, too little for so little a creature as man. It is by studying little things that we attain the great art of having as little misery and as much happiness as possible.

Quoted ibid., 14 July 1763. Johnson was replying to BOSWELL's fear that, should he keep a journal (as Johnson proposed), he would put into it too many little incidents.

58 Truth, Sir, is a cow which will yield such people no more milk, and so they are gone to milk the bull.

Quoted ibid., 21 July 1763. Referring to DAVID HUME 'and other sceptical innovators'.

59 A woman preaching is like a dog's walking on his hinder legs. It is not done well; but you are surprised to find it done at all.

Quoted ibid., 31 July 1763

60 He who does not mind his belly, will hardly mind anything else.

Quoted ibid., 5 August 1763. BOSWELL further described Johnson's dedication to eating: 'I never knew any man who relished good eating more than he did. When at table he was totally absorbed in the business of the moment ... To those whose sensations were delicate, this could not but be disgusting; and it was doubtless not very suitable to the character of a philosopher ... But it must be owned that Johnson, though he could be rigidly *abstemious*, was not a *temperate* man.'

61 This was a good dinner enough, to be sure: but it was not a dinner to *ask* a man to.

Quoted ibid., 5 August 1763

62 Nature has given women so much power that the law has very wisely given them little.

Letter, 18 August 1763, publ. in *The Letters of Samuel Johnson*, vol. 1, no. 157 (ed. R. W. Chapman, 1952)

63 I know not, Madam, that you have a right, upon moral principles, to make your readers suffer so much.

Quoted in *Life of Samuel Johnson, LL.D.* 1763 (1791) by JAMES BOSWELL. Addressed to Mrs Thomas Sheridan, on publication of her novel *Memoirs of Mrs Sydney Biddulph*.

64 Sir John, Sir, is a very unclubbable man.

Quoted ibid., spring 1764. Referring to eminent musicologist Sir John Hawkins. He was Johnson's literary executor and published an inaccurate *Life* (1787–9) and an edition of Johnson's works.

65 A quibble is to Shakespeare what luminous vapours are to the traveller; he follows it at all adventures, it is sure to lead him out of his way, and sure to engulf him in the mire.

The Plays of William Shakespeare, Preface (1765). A 'quibble' here refers to a pun or play on words.

66 Notes are often necessary, but they are necessary evils ... The mind is refrigerated by interruption; the thoughts are diverted from the principle subject; the reader is weary, he suspects not why; and at last throws away the book, which he has too diligently studied.

Ibid., Preface. Referring to notes in the text.

67 So far is it from being true that men are naturally equal, that no two people can be half an hour together, but one shall acquire an evident superiority over the other.

Quoted in *Life of Samuel Johnson, LL.D.*, 15 February 1766 (1791) by JAMES BOSWELL

68 Sir, that all who are happy are equally happy is not true. A peasant and a philosopher may be equally *satisfied*, but not equally *happy*. Happiness consists in the multiplicity of agreeable consciousness.

Quoted ibid., February 1766. Johnson was arguing against the proposition by DAVID HUME (in his essay 'The Sceptic') that 'a little miss, dressed in a new gown for a dancing-school ball, receives as complete enjoyment as the greatest orator, who triumphs in the splendour of his eloquence.' See also ALEXANDER POPE 138.

69 Our tastes greatly alter. The lad does not care for the child's rattle, and the old man does not care for the young man's whore.

Quoted ibid., spring 1766

70 Why, Sir, most schemes of political improvement are very laughable things.

Quoted ibid., 26 October 1769

71 It matters not how a man dies, but how he lives. The act of dying is not of importance, it lasts so short a time.

Quoted ibid., 26 October 1769

72 That fellow seems to me to possess but one idea, and that is a wrong one.

Quoted ibid., 1770. Speaking of 'a dull tiresome fellow, whom he chanced to meet'.

73 The triumph of hope over experience.

Quoted ibid., 1770. Referring to the remarriage of 'a gentleman who had been very unhappy in marriage'. In contrast, Johnson had stated on another occasion (30 September 1769): 'By taking a second wife he pays the highest compliment to the first, by shewing that she made him so happy as a married man, that he wishes to be so a second time.'

74 A decent provision for the poor is the true test of civilization.
Quoted ibid., 1770

75 Nobody can write the life of a man, but those who have eat and drunk and lived in social intercourse with him.
Quoted ibid., 31 March 1772. Johnson was referring specifically to OLIVER GOLDSMITH's *Life of Parnell*. He later reiterated and qualified this statement: 'They only who live with a man can write his life with any genuine exactness and discrimination; and few people who have lived with a man know what to remark about him.' (20 March 1776)

76 I would not give half a guinea to live under one form of government rather than another. It is of no moment to the happiness of an individual.
Quoted ibid., 31 March 1772

77 No government power can be abused long. Mankind will not bear it . . . There is a remedy in human nature against tyranny, that will keep us safe under every form of government.
Quoted ibid., 31 March 1772

78 Much may be made of a Scotchman, if he be *caught* young.
Quoted ibid., spring 1772

79 Grief is a species of idleness.
Letter to Mrs Hester Thrale (later Piozzi), 17 March 1773, publ. in *The Letters of Samuel Johnson*, vol. 1, no. 302 (ed. R. W. Chapman, 1952)

80 Read over your compositions, and wherever you meet with a passage which you think is particularly fine, strike it out.
Quoted in *Life of Samuel Johnson, LL.D.*, 30 April 1773 (1791) by JAMES BOSWELL. Quoting a college tutor. See also ARTHUR QUILLER-COUCH 1.

81 I am always sorry when any language is lost, because languages are the pedigree of nations.
Quoted in *The Journal of a Tour to the Hebrides*, 18 September 1773 (1785) by JAMES BOSWELL

82 Men know that women are an over-match for them, and therefore they choose the weakest or most ignorant. If they did not think so, they never could be afraid of women knowing as much as themselves.
Quoted ibid., 19 September 1773

83 The return of my birthday, if I remember it, fills me with thoughts which it seems to be the general care of humanity to escape.
Letter to Mrs Hester Thrale (later Piozzi), 21 September 1773, publ. in *The Letters of Samuel Johnson*, vol. 1, no. 326 (ed. R. W. Chapman, 1952). Johnson added: 'I can now look back upon threescore and four years, in which little has been done, and little has been enjoyed, a life diversified by misery, spent part in the sluggishness of penury, and part under the violence of pain, in gloomy discontent, or importunate distress.'

84 Any of us would kill a cow, rather than not have beef.
Quoted in *The Journal of a Tour to the Hebrides*, 23 September 1773 (1785) by JAMES BOSWELL

85 The happiest part of a man's life is what he passes lying awake in bed in the morning.
Quoted ibid., 24 October 1773

86 I am sorry I have not learnt to play at cards. It is very useful in life: it generates kindness, and consolidates society.
Quoted ibid., 21 November 1773. Boswell noted that Johnson's remark would be 'a valuable text for many decent old dowagers, and other good company, in various circles, to descant upon'.

87 The Irish are a fair people; they never speak well of one another.
Quoted in *Life of Samuel Johnson, LL.D.*, February 1775 (1791) by JAMES BOSWELL

88 There are few ways in which a man can be more innocently employed than in getting money.
Quoted ibid., 27 March 1775

89 Sir, he was dull in company, dull in his closet, dull everywhere. He was dull in a new way, and that made many people think him *great*.
Quoted ibid., 27 March 1775. Of THOMAS GRAY.

90 Attack is the reaction; I never think I have hit hard unless it rebounds.
Quoted ibid., 2 April 1775

91 It is wonderful when a calculation is made, how little the mind is actually employed in the discharge of any profession.
Quoted ibid., 6 April 1775

92 The greatest part of a writer's time is spent in reading, in order to write; a man will turn over half a library to make one book.
Quoted ibid., 6 April 1775

93 Patriotism is the last refuge of a scoundrel.
Quoted ibid., 7 April 1775. AMBROSE BIERCE, in his entry for 'Patriotism' in his *Devil's Dictionary* (1881–1906), wrote: 'In

Dr Johnson's famous dictionary patriotism is defined as the last resort of a scoundrel. With all due respect to an enlightened but inferior lexicographer I beg to submit that it is the first.'

94 Their learning is like bread in a besieged town: every man gets a little, but no man gets a full meal.
Quoted ibid., 11 April 1775. Referring to the Scots.

95 Knowledge is of two kinds. We know a subject ourselves, or we know where we can find information upon it.
Quoted ibid., 11 April 1775

96 Politics are now nothing more than means of rising in the world. With this sole view do men engage in politics, and their whole conduct proceeds upon it.
Quoted ibid., 11 April 1775

97 Players, Sir! I look on them as no better than creatures set upon tables and joint stools to make faces and produce laughter, like dancing dogs.
Quoted ibid., October/November 1775

98 In lapidary inscriptions a man is not upon oath.
Quoted ibid., 1775

99 At seventy-seven it is time to be in earnest.
A Journey to the Western Islands of Scotland, 'Col' (1775)

100 There is no private house in which people can enjoy themselves so well as at a capital tavern . . . No, Sir; there is nothing which has yet been contrived by man by which so much happiness is produced as by a good tavern or inn.
Quoted in *Life of Samuel Johnson, LL.D.*, 21 March 1776 (1791) by JAMES BOSWELL

101 Questioning is not the mode of the conversation among gentlemen.
Quoted ibid., 25 March 1776

102 If a madman were to come into this room with a stick in his hand, no doubt we should pity the state of his mind; but our primary consideration would be to take care of ourselves. We should knock him down first, and pity him afterwards.
Quoted ibid., 3 April 1776

103 No man but a blockhead ever wrote, except for money.
Quoted ibid., 5 April 1776

104 A man who has not been in Italy, is always conscious of an inferiority.
Quoted ibid., 11 April 1776

105 There are some sluggish men who are improved by drinking; as there are fruits that are not good until they are rotten.
Quoted ibid., 12 April 1776

106 Sir, you have but two topics, yourself and me. I am sick of both.
Quoted ibid., May 1776

107 Life admits not of delays; when pleasure can be had, it is fit to catch it: every hour takes away part of the things that please us, and perhaps part of our disposition to be pleased.
Letter to Boswell, 1 September 1777, ibid.

108 Men hate more steadily than they love.
Quoted ibid., 15 September 1777

109 If I had no duties, and no reference to futurity, I would spend my life in driving briskly in a post-chaise with a pretty woman.
Quoted ibid., 19 September 1777

110 Depend upon it, Sir, when a man knows he is to be hanged in a fortnight, it concentrates his mind wonderfully.
Quoted ibid., 19 September 1777

111 Life will not bear refinement. You must do as other people do.
Quoted ibid., 19 September 1777. Advising BOSWELL not to 'refine' in the education of his children.

112 You find no man, at all intellectual, who is willing to leave London. No, Sir, when a man is tired of London, he is tired of life; for there is in London all that life can afford.
Quoted ibid., 20 September 1777

113 In a man's letters you know, Madam, his soul lies naked, his letters are only the mirror of his breast, whatever passes within him is shown undisguised in its natural process. Nothing is inverted, nothing distorted, you see systems in their elements, you discover actions in their motives.
Letter to Mrs Hester Thrale (later Piozzi), 27 October 1777, publ. in *The Letters of Samuel Johnson*, vol. 2, no. 559 (ed. R. W. Chapman, 1952)

114 All argument is against it; but all belief is for it.
Quoted in *Life of Samuel Johnson, LL.D.*, 31 March 1778 (1791) by JAMES BOSWELL. Speaking of the existence of ghosts.

115 Every man thinks meanly of himself for not having been a soldier, or not having been at sea.
Quoted ibid., 10 April 1778

116 I am willing to love all mankind, *except an American*.

Quoted ibid., 15 April 1778. 'Sir, they are a race of convicts,' Johnson stated in 1769, 'and ought to be thankful for anything we allow them short of hanging' (quoted in *Life*, 21 March 1775).

117 As the Spanish proverb says, 'He who would bring home the wealth of the Indies, must carry the wealth of the Indies with him.' So it is in travelling; a man must carry knowledge with him, if he would bring home knowledge.

Quoted ibid., 17 April 1778

118 Lawyers know life practically. A bookish man should always have them to converse with.

Said to the lawyer OLIVER EDWARDS, quoted ibid., 17 April 1778

119 I would rather be attacked than unnoticed. For the worst thing you can do to an author is to be silent as to his works. An assault upon a town is a bad thing; but starving it is still worse.

Quoted ibid., 26 March 1779

120 Claret is the liquor for boys; port for men; but he who aspires to be a hero must drink brandy.

Quoted ibid., 7 April 1779

121 A man who exposes himself when he is intoxicated, has not the art of getting drunk.

Quoted ibid., 24 April 1779

122 Worth seeing? Yes; but not worth going to see.

Quoted ibid., 12 October 1779. In answer to BOSWELL's question, 'Is not the Giant's Causeway worth seeing?'

123 If you are idle, be not solitary; if you are solitary, be not idle.

Letter to Boswell, 27 October 1779, quoted in *Life of Samuel Johnson, LL.D.* (1791) by JAMES BOSWELL. See ROBERT BURTON 13.

124 The most heterogeneous ideas are yoked by violence together; nature and art are ransacked for illustrations, comparisons, and allusions; their learning instructs, and their subtlety surprises; but the reader commonly thinks his improvement dearly bought and, though he sometimes admires, is seldom pleased.

Lives of the English Poets, 'Cowley' (1779–81). On metaphysical poets.

125 His scorn of the great is repeated too often to be real; no man thinks much of that which he despises.

Ibid., 'Pope'. Of ALEXANDER POPE.

126 It was his peculiar happiness that he scarcely ever found a stranger whom he did not leave a friend; but it must likewise be added, that he had not often a friend long without obliging him to become a stranger.

Ibid., 'Savage'. Of the poet Richard Savage.

127 He that outlives a wife whom he has long loved, sees himself disjoined from the only mind that has the same hopes, and fears, and interest; from the only companion with whom he has shared much good and evil; and with whom he could set his mind at liberty, to retrace the past or anticipate the future. The continuity of being is lacerated; the settled course of sentiment and action is stopped; and life stands suspended and motionless.

Letter, 20 January 1780, publ. in *Life of Samuel Johnson, LL.D.* (1791) by JAMES BOSWELL

128 Nothing is more common than mutual dislike, where mutual approbation is particularly expected.

Letter to Mrs Hester Thrale (later Piozzi), 1 May 1780, ibid.

129 Depend upon it that if a man *talks* of his misfortunes there is something in them that is not disagreeable to him.

Quoted ibid., 1780

130 Every man has a right to utter what he thinks truth, and every other man has a right to knock him down for it. Martyrdom is the test.

Quoted ibid., 1780

131 No man was more foolish when he had not a pen in his hand, or more wise when he had.

Quoted ibid., 1780. Of OLIVER GOLDSMITH.

132 Mrs Montagu has dropped me. Now, Sir, there are people whom one should like very well to drop, but would not wish to be dropped by.

Quoted ibid., March 1781. Referring to Lady MARY WORTLEY MONTAGU.

133 This merriment of parsons is mighty offensive.

Quoted ibid., March 1781. Referring to 'several clergymen, who thought that they should appear to advantage by assuming the lax jollity of men of the world'.

134 Classical quotation is the *parole* of literary men all over the world.

Quoted ibid., 8 May 1781

135 The happiest conversation is that of which nothing is distinctly remembered but a general effect of pleasing impression.

Quoted ibid., 1781

136 Resolve not to be poor: whatever you have,

spend less. Poverty is a great enemy to human happiness; it certainly destroys liberty, and it makes some virtues impracticable, and others extremely difficult.

Letter to JAMES BOSWELL, 7 December 1782, ibid.

137 The black dog I hope always to resist, and in time to drive though I am deprived of almost all those that used to help me . . . When I rise my breakfast is solitary, the black dog waits to share it, from breakfast to dinner he continues barking.

Letter to Mrs Hester Thrale (later Piozzi), 28 June 1783, publ. in *The Letters of Samuel Johnson*, vol. 3, no. 857 (ed. R. W. Chapman, 1952). Johnson's 'black dog' of melancholia anticipated the 'black dogs', or depressions, of WINSTON CHURCHILL.

138 Sir, a man may be so much of everything, that he is nothing of anything.

Quoted in *Life of Samuel Johnson, LL.D.*, 1783 (1791) by JAMES BOSWELL

139 Milton, Madam, was a genius that could cut a Colossus from a rock; but could not carve heads upon cherry-stones.

Quoted ibid., 13 June 1784. Response to HANNAH MORE, who had wondered how a poet capable of writing *Paradise Lost* could have written such poor sonnets.

140 Sir, I have found you an argument; but I am not obliged to find you an understanding.

Quoted ibid., June 1784

141 No man is a hypocrite in his pleasures.

Quoted ibid., June 1784. In response to a remark by JOSHUA REYNOLDS 'that the real character of a man was found out by his amusements'.

142 Don't *attitudenise*.

Quoted ibid., June 1784. Reproach to a gesticulating man.

143 Dictionaries are like watches, the worst is better than none, and the best cannot be expected to go quite true.

Letter, 21 August 1784, ibid.

144 Sir, I look upon every day to be lost, in which I do not make a new acquaintance.

Quoted ibid., November 1784

145 I will be conquered; I will not capitulate.

Quoted ibid., November 1784. Said in his last illness.

146 There are few things that we so unwillingly give up, even in advanced age, as the supposition that we still have the power of ingratiating ourselves with the fair sex.

Quoted in 'Johnsoniana' (1785), repr. in *Johnsonian Miscel-*

lanies, vol. 2, 'Anecdotes by George Steevens' (ed. George Birkbeck Hill, 1897)

147 Solitude is dangerous to reason, without being favourable to virtue . . . Remember that the solitary mortal is certainly luxurious, probably superstitious, and possibly mad.

Quoted in *Anecdotes of the Late Samuel Johnson* (1786) by Hester Piozzi, ibid., vol. 1

148 A man seldom thinks with more earnestness of anything than he does of his dinner.

Quoted in *Anecdotes of the Late Samuel Johnson* (1786) by Hester Piozzi, ibid., vol. 1

149 It is very strange, and very melancholy, that the paucity of human pleasures should persuade us ever to call hunting one of them.

Quoted in *Anecdotes of the Late Samuel Johnson* (1786) by Hester Piozzi, ibid., vol. 1

150 Dear Bathurst was a man to my very heart's content: he hated a fool, and he hated a rogue, and he hated a whig; he was a very good hater.

Quoted in *Anecdotes of the Late Samuel Johnson* (1786) by Hester Piozzi, ibid., vol. 1

151 I would be loath to speak ill of any person who I do not know deserves it, but I am afraid he is an *attorney*.

Quoted in *Anecdotes of the Late Samuel Johnson* (1786) by Hester Piozzi, ibid., vol. 1. Also reported, in a variant version, in BOSWELL's *Life*, entry for 1770.

152 A man is in general better pleased when he has a good dinner upon his table, than when his wife talks Greek.

Quoted in *Works*, vol. 11 (ed. Sir John Hawkins, 1787–9), ibid., vol. 2, 'Apophthegms, Sentiments, Opinions'

153 I had rather see the portrait of a dog that I know, than all the allegorical paintings they can show me in the world.

Quoted in *Works*, vol. 11 (ed. Sir John Hawkins, 1787–9), ibid., vol. 2

154 Whoever thinks of going to bed before twelve o'clock is a scoundrel.

Quoted in *Works*, vol. 11 (ed. Sir John Hawkins, 1787–9), ibid., vol. 2

155 [Music] is the only sensual pleasure without vice.

Quoted in *European Magazine*, 1795, ibid., vol. 2, 'Anecdotes by William Seward'

156 Difficult do you call it, Sir? I wish it were impossible.

Quoted in *Anecdotes of Distinguished Persons* (1797) by William Seward, ibid., vol. 2, 'Anecdotes by William Seward'. Referring to a violinist's playing.

157 What is written without effort is in general read without pleasure.

Quoted in *Biographia* (1799) by William Seward, ibid. vol. 2, 'Anecdotes by William Seward'

158 Love is the wisdom of the fool and the folly of the wise.

Quoted in *Life of Samuel Foote*, vol. 2 (1805) by William Cooke, ibid., vol. 2

159 What provokes your risibility, Sir? Have I said anything that you understand? Then I ask pardon of the rest of the company.

Quoted in *Memoirs*, 'Anecdotes' (1807) by Richard Cumberland, ibid., vol. 2

160 Abstinence is as easy to me, as temperance would be difficult.

Quoted in *Memoirs of the Life and Correspondence of Mrs Hannah More*, vol. 1 (ed. William Roberts, 1834)

161 A mere literary man is a *dull* man; a man who is solely a man of business is a *selfish* man; but when literature and commerce are united, they make a *respectable* man.

Quoted by Robert Barclay, in *Life of Samuel Johnson, LL.D.*, Appendix (ed. John Wilson Croker, 1847) by JAMES BOSWELL

Hanns Johst

See HERMANN GOERING 2

Al Jolson

(1886–1950)
Russian-born US singer and entertainer

Originally Asa Yoelson. He wooed vaudeville audiences of the 1920s as a blackface comedian and singer of sentimental songs. George Burns observed that it was easy to make him happy: 'You just had to cheer him for breakfast, applaud wildly for lunch, and give him a standing ovation for dinner.'

1 California here I come.

'California Here I Come' (song, co-written by Jolson, BUDDY DE SYLVA and Joseph Mayer) in the stage musical *Bombo* (1921)

2 Wait a minute, wait a minute, you ain't heard nothing yet. Wait a minute I tell you. You ain't heard nothing yet. Do you want to hear 'Toot, Toot, Tootsie'?

The Jazz Singer (film, 1927, screenplay by Alfred A. Cohen, directed by Louis Silver). Spoken by Jakie Rabinowitz (Al Jolson), these were *the* first spoken words in the first *major* talking picture. The screenplay was based on *The Day of Atonement*, a story written and adapted for the stage by Samson Raphaelson and supposedly based on Al Jolson's own life. 'You ain't heard nothing yet' had been Jolson's slogan since 1906 and was the title of a song recorded by him in 1919, written by BUDDY DE SYLVA and GUS KAHN (Kahn also co-wrote 'Toot, Toot, Tootsie').

Chuck Jones

(1912–2002)
US animator and cartoon director

Originally Charles Jones. He worked for Warner Brothers from 1933, creating the characters Road Runner and Wile E. Coyote and directing Bugs Bunny and Daffy Duck cartoons.

1 Beep! Beep!

Looney Tunes/Merrie Melodies (Warner Brothers cartoon, 1949–66). Spoken by the Road Runner. This only line of dialogue between the Road Runner at full sprint and Wile E. Coyote was voiced by Mel Blanc. The characters were created by Chuck Jones (who directed most of the episodes) and Michael Maltese and first introduced in a Warner Brothers' *Looney Tunes* cartoon called *Fast and Furry-Ous* (1949).

John Paul Jones

(1747–92)
US naval officer

He won major naval engagements against the British during the American War of Independence, most famously off the English coast in 1779.

1 I have not yet begun to fight.

Quoted in *The Life and Character of the Chevalier John Paul Jones* (1825) by John Henry Sherburne. Response to a call to surrender by the captain of the *Serapis*, a British ship, off the east coast of England, 23 September 1779. The US flotilla went on to win the battle.

Mother Jones

(1830–1930)
Irish-born US labour activist

Mary Harris Jones. Having lost all her possessions in the great Chicago fire of 1871, she immersed herself in the union movement, touring the country and making speeches. She helped found the Industrial Workers of the World in 1905.

1 Pray for the dead and fight like hell for the living!
Speech to miners in West Virginia, quoted in *The Autobiography of Mother Jones*, ch. 6 (1925)

Steve Jones
(b. 1944)
British geneticist

Called the 'Charles Darwin of the television era', he is Professor of Genetics at London University and a noted popularizer of science. His publications include The Language of Genes *(1993) and* Almost Like A Whale *(1999).*

1 Evolution is to the social sciences as statues are to birds: a convenient platform upon which to deposit badly digested ideas.
Almost Like A Whale: The Origin of the Species Updated, 'An Historical Sketch of the Progress of Opinion on the Origin of Species' (1999). Jones had earlier used the aphorism in another context: 'Evolution is to allegory as statues are to birdshit: a convenient platform upon which to deposit badly digested ideas' (quoted in the *Guardian* 31 July 1997).

2 Evolution is, for most of the time, a race to stay in the same place.
Ibid., ch. 6

Erica Jong
(b. 1942)
US author and poet

Her first volume of poetry, Fruits and Vegetables *(1971), established her as a feminist writer, although she is best known for her first novel* Fear of Flying *(1973) and its sequel* How to Save Your Own Life *(1977), which wittily chronicled the sexual adventures of Isadora Wing.*

1 Perhaps all artists were, in a sense, housewives: tenders of the earth household.
'The Artist as Housewife: the Housewife as Artist', publ. in *The First Ms. Reader* (ed. Francine Klagsbrun, 1972)

2 Solitude is un-American ... There is simply no dignified way for a woman to live alone. Oh, she can get along financially perhaps (though not nearly as well as a man), but emotionally she is never left in peace. Her friends, her family, her fellow workers never let her forget that her husbandlessness, her childlessness – her *selfishness*, in short – is a reproach to the American way of life.
Fear of Flying, ch. 1 (1973). Narrated by Isadora Wing.

3 The zipless fuck is absolutely pure. It is free of ulterior motives. There is no power game. The man is not 'taking' and the woman is not 'giving'. No one is attempting to cuckold a husband or humiliate a wife. No one is trying to prove anything or get anything out of anyone. The zipless fuck is the purest thing there is. And it is rarer than the unicorn. And I have never had one.
Ibid., ch. 1. Jong explained, 'Zipless ... because the incident has all the swift compression of a dream and is seemingly free of all remorse and guilt.'

4 Men have always detested women's gossip because they suspect the truth: their measurements are being taken and compared ... Men can mock it, but they can't prevent it. Gossip is the opiate of the oppressed.
Ibid., ch. 6

5 Horrible as successful artists often are, there is nothing crueler or more vain than a failed artist.
Ibid., ch. 9

6 Men and women, women and men. It will never work.
Ibid., ch. 16

7 Each month
the blood sheets down
like good red rain.
'Gardener', publ. in *Half Lives* (1973)

8 Jealousy is all the fun you *think* they had ...
How To Save Your Own Life, Epigraph to 'Bennett tells all in Woodstock...' (1977)

9 In a bad marriage, friends are the invisible glue.
Ibid., 'A day in the life...'

10 Every country gets the circus it deserves. Spain gets bullfights. Italy gets the Catholic Church. America gets Hollywood.
Ibid., Epigraph to 'Take the Red-Eye...'

11 Orgasm is no proof of anything. Orgasm is proof of orgasm. Someday every woman will have orgasms – like every family has color TV – and we can all get on with the real business of life.
Ibid., 'The street where I lived...'

Ben Jonson
(c. 1572–1637)
English dramatist and poet

Shortly after his debut as an actor and playwright, he had a popular success with Every Man in His Humour *(1598), a comedy in which* SHAKESPEARE *performed. Other works include* Volpone *(1605),* The Alchemist *(1610) and* Bartholomew Fair *(1614), all comedies. He also wrote tragedies, masques and poetry. See* JOHN DRYDEN 7.

1 Well, as he brews, so he shall drink.
Every Man in His Humour, Act 2, Sc. 2 (1598). Spoken by Downright.

2 A new disease? I know not, new or old,
But it may well be called poor mortals' plague:
For, like a pestilence, it doth infect
The houses of the brain. First it begins
Solely to work upon the fantasy,
Filling her seat with such pestiferous air
As soon corrupts the judgement; and from thence
Sends like contagion to the memory:
Still each to other giving the infection.
Which as a subtle vapour spreads itself
Confusedly through every sensitive part,
Till not a thought or motion in the mind
Be free from the black poison of suspect.
Kitely, ibid., Act 2, Sc. 3

3 I do honour the very flea of his dog.
Cob, ibid., Act 4, Sc. 4

4 Art hath an enemy called ignorance.
Every Man out of His Humour, Act 1, Sc. 1 (1599). Spoken by Asper.

5 Blueness doth express trueness.
Cynthia's Revels, Act 5, Sc. 2 (1600). Spoken by Amorphus.

6 Queen and huntress, chaste and fair,
Now the sun is laid to sleep,
Seated in thy silver chair,
State in wonted manner keep:
Hesperus entreats thy light,
Goddess excellently bright.
'Hymn to Diana', ibid., Act 5, Sc. 6

7 'Tis the common disease of all your musicians that they know no mean, to be entreated, either to begin or end.
The Poetaster, Act 2, Sc. 2 (1601). Spoken by Julia.

8 Where guilt is, rage and courage both abound.
Sejanus, Act 2, l. 259 (1603). Spoken by Sejanus.

9 He threatens many that hath injured one.
Silius, ibid., Act 2, l. 476

10 Sir, calumnies are answered best with silence.
Volpone, Act 2, Sc. 2 (1605). Spoken by Sir Politic Would-be.

11 I can feel
A whimsy in my blood: I know not how,
Success hath made me wanton. I could skip
Out of my skin now like a subtle snake,
I am so limber.
Mosca, ibid., Act 3, Sc. 1

12 Almost
All the wise world is little else in nature
But parasites or sub-parasites.
Mosca, ibid., Act 3, Sc. 1

13 Come, my Celia, let us prove,
While we can, the sports of love.
Volpone, ibid., Act 3, Sc. 7. The lines also appear (with slight variations) in Jonson's *The Forest*, no. 5: 'Song to Celia' (1616).

14 Suns that set may rise again,
But if once we lose this light,
'Tis with us perpetual night.
Volpone, ibid., Act 3, Sc. 7. Probably inspired by Catullus: see CATULLUS 6.

15 Give me a look, give me a face,
That makes simplicity a grace;
Robes loosely flowing, hair as free:
Such sweet neglect more taketh me,
Than all the adulteries of art;
They strike mine eyes, but not my heart.
Epicene, or The Silent Woman, Act 1, Sc. 1 (1609). Song sung by Boy.

16 We'll therefore go withal, my girl, and live
In a free state, where we will eat our mullets,
Soused in high-country wines, sup pheasants' eggs,
And have our cockles boiled in silver shells;
Our shrimps to swim again, as when they lived,
In a rare butter made of dolphin's milk,
Whose cream does look like opals; and with these
Delicate meats set ourselves high for pleasure,
And take us down again, and then renew
Our youth and strength with drinking the elixir,
And so enjoy a perpetuity
Of life and lust!
The Alchemist, Act 4, Sc. 1 (1610). Spoken by Sir Epicure Mammon.

17 Neither do thou lust after that tawny weed, tobacco.
Bartholomew Fair, Act 2, Sc. 6 (1614). Spoken by Justice Overdo.

18 Hence it is that the lungs of the tobacconist are rotted, the liver spotted, the brain smoked like the backside of the pig-woman's booth here, and the whole body within, black as her pan you saw e'en now, without.
Justice Overdo, ibid., Act 2, Sc. 6

19 I will be more tender hereafter. I see compassion may become a justice, though it be a weakness, I confess; and nearer a vice than a virtue.
Justice Overdo, ibid., Act 4, Sc. 1

20 Rest in soft peace, and, asked, say here doth lie
Ben Jonson his best piece of poetry.
Epigrams, no. 45 ('On My First Son') (1616)

21 Tonight, grave Sir, both my poor house and I
Do equally desire your company:
Not that we think us worthy such a guest,
But that your worth will dignify our feast,
With those that come; whose grace may make that
    seem
Something, which, else, could hope for no esteem.
Ibid., no. 118 ('On Inviting a Friend to Supper')

22 Nor shall our cups make any guilty men:
But, at our parting, we will be as when
We innocently met. No simple word
That shall be uttered at our mirthful board
Shall make us sad next morning: or affright
The liberty that we'll enjoy tonight.
Ibid., no. 118. Closing lines of epigram.

23 Thou art not, Penshurst, built to envious show
Of touch or marble, nor canst boast a row
Of polished pillars, or a roof of gold;
Thou hast no lantern whereof tales are told,
Or stair, or courts; but standst an ancient pile,
And these grudged at, art reverenced the while.
The Forest, no. 2 ('To Penshurst'), ll. 1–6 (1616)

24 Then hath thy orchard fruit, thy garden
    flowers,
Fresh as the air, and new as are the hours.
The early cherry, with the later plum,
Fig, grape, and quince, each in his time doth come:
The blushing apricot and woolly peach
Hang on thy walls, that every child may reach.
Ibid., no. 2, ll. 39–45

25 Freedom doth with degree dispense.
Ibid., no. 3 ('To Sir Robert Wroth'), l. 58

26 Drink to me only with thine eyes,
And I will pledge with mine;
Or leave a kiss but in the cup,
And I'll not look for wine.
Ibid., no. 9 ('Song: To Celia'). The lines were adapted from
Epistle 24 of the Greek sophist Philostratus.

27 Donne, for not keeping of accent, deserved hanging . . . Shakespeare wanted art . . . Sharpham, Day,
Dekker, were all rogues.
Conversations with William Drummond of Hawthornden,
written 1619, publ. 1641, repr. in *Ben Jonson's Conversations
with William Drummond of Hawthornden* (ed. R. F. Patterson,
1923)

28 A pure pedantic schoolmaster, sweeping his living from the posteriors of little children.
Conversations with William Drummond, ibid.

29 Soul of the age!
The applause, delight, the wonder of our stage!
'To the Memory of My Beloved, the Author, Master William
Shakespeare', ll. 17–18, first publ. in Folio edn of SHAKE-
SPEARE's plays (1623), repr. in *The Complete Poems* (ed. George
Parfitt, 1975)

30 Thou hadst small Latin, and less Greek.
'To the Memory of My Beloved, the Author, Master William
Shakespeare', l. 31, ibid.

31 He was not of an age, but for all time!
'To the Memory of My Beloved, the Author, Master William
Shakespeare', l. 43, ibid.

32 Sweet Swan of Avon! What a sight it were
To see thee in our waters yet appear,
And make those flights upon the banks of Thames
That so did take Eliza, and our James!
'To the Memory of My Beloved, the Author, Master William
Shakespeare', ll. 71–4, ibid.

33 We are persons of quality, I assure you, and
women of fashion, and come to see and to be seen.
The Staple of News, Induction ll. 8–10 (1626). Spoken by Mirth.
See OVID 3.

34 O, for an engine, to keep back all clocks,
Or make the sun forget his motion!
The New Inn, Act 4, Sc. 3 (1629). Spoken by Lady Frampul.

35 Come, leave the loathèd stage,
And the more loathsome age,
Where pride and impudence, in faction knit,
Usurp the chair of wit:
Indicting and arraigning every day
Something they call a play.
Let their fastidious, vain
Commission of the brain
Run on and rage, sweat, censure, and condemn:
They were not made for thee, less thou for them.
'Ode To Himself', st. 1 (1632), repr. in *The Complete Poems* (ed.
George Parfitt, 1975). Written on the poor reception of his late
comedy, *The New Inn*.

36 Many might go to heaven with half the labour
they go to hell, if they would venture their industry
the right way.
Timber, or Discoveries Made upon Men and Matter, para. 27
('Deploratis facilis descensus Averni') (1641)

37 Talking is the disease of age.
Ibid., para. 46 ('Lingua Sapientis')

38 The players have often mentioned it as an honour to Shakespeare, that in his writing, whatsoever he penned, he never blotted out [a] line. My answer hath been, 'Would he had blotted a thousand.'
Ibid., para. 64 ('De Shakespeare Nostrati')

39 For I loved the man and do honour his memory, on this side idolatry, as much as any.
Ibid., para. 64

40 Wheresoever manners and fashions are corrupted, language is. It imitates the public riot.
Ibid., para. 74 ('De corruptela morum')

41 They say princes learn no art truly, but the art of horsemanship. The reason is, the brave beast is no flatterer. He will throw a prince as soon as his groom.
Ibid., para. 95 ('Illiteratus Princeps'). The aphorism is attributed to the Greek philosopher Carneades by MONTAIGNE: 'Princes' children learnt nothing aright but to manage and ride horses; forsomuch as in all other exercises every man yieldeth and giveth them the victory; but a horse, who is neither a flatterer nor a courtier, will as soon throw the child of a king as the son of a base porter.' (*Essays*, bk 3, ch. 7, 'Of the Incommodity of Greatness', 1588)

42 Though ambition itself be a vice, it is often the cause of great virtue. Give me that wit whom praise excites, glory puts on, or disgrace grieves; he is to be nourished with ambition, pricked forward with honour, checked with reprehension, and never to be suspected of sloth.
Ibid., para. 114 ('Immo serviles')

43 Language most shows a man: speak, that I may see thee.
Ibid., para. 121 ('Oratio Imago Animi')

Janis Joplin
(1943–70)
US rock singer

An impassioned blues-style singer ('I'd rather not sing than sing quiet'), she performed with the band Big Brother and the Holding Company before going solo in 1968. Her biggest hit 'Me and Bobby McGee' was released posthumously in 1971.

1 Fourteen heart attacks and he had to die in my week. In MY week.
Quoted in the *New Musical Express* 12 April 1969. Referring to former President EISENHOWER, whose death prevented Joplin appearing on the cover of *Newsweek*.

2 Oh, Lord, won't you buy me a Mercedes Benz?
My friends all drive Porsches,
I must make amends.
'Mercedes Benz' (song) on the album *Pearl* (1971)

3 On stage I make love to 25,000 people, then I go home alone.
Quoted in the *New Yorker* 14 August 1971

June Jordan
(1936–2002)
US poet and civil rights activist

She campaigned on issues of feminism and racism, and for the inclusion of black studies on university curricula. Her poetry collections include Passion *(1980).*

1 Body and soul, Black America reveals the extreme questions of contemporary life, questions of freedom and identity: *How can I be who I am?*
'Black Studies: Bringing Back The Person' (1969), repr. in *Moving Towards Home: Political Essays* (1989)

2 I am a feminist, and what that means to me is much the same as the meaning of the fact that I am Black: it means that I must undertake to love myself and to respect myself as though my very life depends upon self-love and self-respect.
'Where is the Love?', address to Black Writers' Conference, Howard University, 1978, ibid.

3 We are the wrong people of
the wrong skin in the wrong continent and what
in the hell is everybody being reasonable about
'Poem about My Rights', publ. in *Passion* (1980)

Chief Joseph
(c. 1840–1904)
Nez Percé leader

Head of his tribe from 1871, he defied a US government order to relocate to a reservation in 1877, leading his followers on a thousand-mile journey in an attempt to reach Canada. He surrendered after successfully evading his pursuers for three months.

1 If you tie a horse to a stake, do you expect he will grow fat? If you pen an Indian up on a small spot of earth, and compel him to stay there, he will not be contented, nor will he grow and prosper. I have asked some of the great white chiefs where they get their authority to say to the Indian that he shall stay in one place, while he sees white men going where they please. They can not tell me.
North American Review April 1879

2 Hear me, my chiefs! I am tired; my heart is sick and sad. From where the sun now stands I will fight no more forever.

Quoted in *Bury My Heart at Wounded Knee*, ch. 13 (1970) by Dee Brown. Speech to tribe after surrender at the battle of Bear Paw Mountains, Montana, October 1877.

Jenny Joseph
(b. 1932)
British poet

Her poetry collections include Beyond Descartes *(1983) and* Extended Similes *(1997). She has also written for children.*

1 When I am an old woman I shall wear purple
With a red hat which doesn't go, and doesn't suit me.
And I shall spend my pension on brandy and summer gloves
And satin sandals, and say we've got no money for butter.

'Warning', publ. in *Rose in the Afternoon* (1974)

2 I shall go out in my slippers in the rain
And pick the flowers in other people's gardens
And learn to spit.

'Warning', ibid.

Joseph Joubert
(1754–1824)
French essayist and moralist

In Paris from 1778, he was a member of the circle of d'Alembert, DIDEROT, *for whom he worked as secretary, and* CHATEAU-BRIAND, *who described him as 'an egoist who was only interested in other people'. He was later elected a magistrate.*

1 Imagination is the eye of the soul.

Pensées (1842), repr. in *Joubert: a Selection from his Thoughts*, ch. 2, no. 14 (transl. Katharine Lyttelton, 1898)

2 Ambition is pitiless; all merit that does not serve its ends is despicable in its eyes.

Ibid., ch. 4, no. 69

3 What in youth is passion, in old age is vice.

Ibid., ch. 6, no. 8

4 The evening of life comes bearing its own lamp.

Ibid., ch. 6, no. 13

5 The true *bon-mot* surprises him who makes it as much as those who hear it.

Ibid., ch. 7, no. 57

6 Never cut what you can unravel.

Ibid., ch. 8, no. 10

7 To teach is to learn twice.

Ibid., ch. 18, no. 18

Marcel Jouhandeau
(1888–1979)
French author

Almost entirely autobiographical, his novels usually portray inhabitants of Chaminadour, a fictionalized version of his native town, and include La Jeunesse de Théophile *(1921).*

1 To really know someone is to have loved and hated him in turn.

Défense de l'enfer, 'Erotologie' (1935)

Benjamin Jowett
(1817–93)
English scholar and essayist

Professor of Greek and Vice-Chancellor of Oxford University, he is best known for his translations of classical texts.

1 One man is as good as another until he has written a book.

Quoted in *The Life and Letters of Benjamin Jowett*, vol. 1, ch. 8 (ed. Evelyn Abbott and Lewis Campbell, 1897)

2 Nowhere probably is there more true feeling, and nowhere worse taste, than in a churchyard.

Letters of Benjamin Jowett, ch. 6 (ed. E. Abbott and L. Campbell, 1899)

James Joyce
(1882–1941)
Irish author

He revolutionized the novel with his use of experimental language and writing techniques in Ulysses *(1922) and* Finnegans Wake *(1939), both written in self-imposed exile from Ireland. He shocked many of his contemporaries (see* E. M. FORSTER 23, D. H. LAWRENCE 23, VIRGINIA WOOLF 4), *but for* SAMUEL BECKETT, *'his writing is not about something. It is the thing itself.'*

1 Poetry, even when apparently most fantastic, is always a revolt against artifice, a revolt, in a sense, against actuality.

James Clarence Mangan lecture, University College, Dublin, 15 February 1902, publ. in *Critical Writings*, sect. 8 (ed. Ellsworth Mason and Richard Ellmann, 1959)

2 There is no heresy or no philosophy which is so abhorrent to the church as a human being.

Letter, 22 November 1902, in private collection. An inaccurate text taken from a typescript of the letter is published in *Letters of James Joyce*, vol. 1 (ed. Stuart Gilbert, 1957).

3 All things are inconstant except the faith in the soul, which changes all things and fills their inconstancy with light, but though I seem to be driven out of my country as a misbeliever I have found no man yet with a faith like mine.
Letter, 22 November 1902, ibid.

4 By an epiphany he meant a sudden spiritual manifestation, whether in vulgarity of speech or of gesture or in a memorable phase of the mind itself. He believed that it was for the man of letters to recover these epiphanies with extreme care, seeing that they are the most delicate and evanescent of moments.
Stephen Hero, ch. 25 (written *c*. 1904–6, publ. 1944). Linked to its religious connotation (from the Greek, *epiphaneia*, meaning 'manifestation, appearance'), the term 'epiphany' was coined by Joyce to describe the sudden revelation of a particular moment, occasioned by an encounter, remark or coincidence, that encapsulates a truth – when 'the soul of the commonest object . . . seems to us radiant'.

5 I am damnably sick of Italy, Italian and Italians, outrageously, illogically sick . . . I hate to think that Italians ever did anything in the way of art . . . What did they do but illustrate a page or so of the New Testament! They themselves think they have a monopoly in the line. I am dead tired of their bello and bellezza.
Letter to his brother from Rome, 7 December 1906, publ. in *Letters of James Joyce*, vol. 2 (ed. Richard Ellmann, 1966)

6 No pen, no ink, no table, no room, no time, no quiet, no inclination.
Letter to his brother, 7 December 1906, written from Rome, ibid., vol. 2

7 No one who has any self-respect stays in Ireland, but flees afar as though from a country that has undergone the visitation of an angered Jove.
'Ireland, Island of Saints and Sages', lecture at Università Popolare Triestina, 27 April 1907, publ. in *Critical Writings*, sect. 35 (ed. Ellsworth Mason and Richard Ellmann, 1959)

8 I confess that I do not see what good it does to fulminate against the English tyranny while the Roman tyranny occupies the palace of the soul.
'Ireland, Island of Saints and Sages', ibid.

9 Saying that a great genius is mad, while at the same time recognizing his artistic worth, is like saying that he had rheumatism or suffered from diabetes. Madness, in fact, is a medical term that can claim no more notice from the objective critic than he grants the charge of heresy raised by the theologian, or the charge of immorality raised by the police.
William Blake lecture, ibid.

10 Love between man and man is impossible because there must not be sexual intercourse and friendship between man and woman is impossible because there must be sexual intercourse.
Dubliners, 'A Painful Case' (1914). Mr Duffy, speaking of his relationship with Mrs Sinico.

11 He gnawed the rectitude of his life; he felt that he had been outcast from life's feast.
Ibid., 'A Painful Case'. Referring to Mr Duffy.

12 Yes, the newspapers were right: snow was general all over Ireland. It was falling on every part of the dark central plain, on the treeless hills, falling softly upon the Bog of Allen and, farther westward, softly falling into the dark mutinous Shannon waves. It was falling, too, upon every part of the lonely churchyard on the hill where Michael Furey lay buried. It lay thickly drifted on the crooked crosses and headstones, on the spears of the little gate, on the barren thorns. His soul swooned slowly as he heard the snow falling faintly through the universe and faintly falling, like the descent of their last end, upon all the living and the dead.
Ibid., 'The Dead'. Closing lines of story.

13 What did that mean, to kiss? You put your face up like that to say goodnight and then his mother put her face down. That was to kiss. His mother put her lips on his cheek; her lips were soft and they wetted his cheek; and they made a tiny little noise: kiss. Why did people do that with their two faces?
A Portrait of the Artist as a Young Man, ch. 1 (1916). Spoken by Stephen Dedalus.

14 When the soul of a man is born in this country there are nets flung at it to hold it back from flight. You talk to me of nationality, language, religion. I shall try to fly by those nets.
Ibid., ch. 5. Stephen Dedalus to the young patriot Davin.

15 Do you know what Ireland is? Ireland is the old sow that eats her farrow.
Stephen Dedalus, ibid., ch. 5

16 To speak of these things and to try to understand their nature and, having understood it, to try slowly and humbly and constantly to express, to press out again, from the gross earth or what it brings forth, from sound and shape and colour which are the

prison gates of our soul, an image of the beauty we have come to understand – that is art.
Stephen Dedalus, ibid., ch. 5

17 Art is the human disposition of sensible or intelligible matter for an aesthetic end.
Stephen Dedalus, ibid., ch. 5. The definition appeared earlier in Joyce's 'Paris Notebook' dated 28 March 1903.

18 The artist, like the God of the creation, remains within or behind or beyond or above his handiwork, invisible, refined out of existence, indifferent, paring his fingernails.
Stephen Dedalus, ibid., ch. 5. See GUSTAVE FLAUBERT 7.

19 Whatever else is unsure in this stinking dunghill of a world a mother's love is not.
Cranly, ibid., ch. 5

20 I will tell you what I will do and what I will not do. I will not serve that in which I no longer believe, whether it call itself my home, my fatherland, or my church: and I will try to express myself in some mode of life or art as freely as I can and as wholly as I can, using for my defence the only arms I allow myself to use – silence, exile and cunning.
Stephen Dedalus, ibid., ch. 5

21 Welcome, O life! I go to encounter for the millionth time the reality of experience and to forge in the smithy of my soul the uncreated conscience of my race . . . Old father, old artificer, stand me now and ever in good stead.
Ibid., ch. 5. Said by Stephen departing from Ireland, in the closing lines of the book. 'Old artificer' is a reference to the mythical craftsman Daedalus, whose flight from Crete ended in the drowning of his son. Joyce's own experience on fleeing Ireland was largely of debt and penury.

22 Writing in English is the most ingenious torture ever devised for sins committed in previous lives. The English reading public explains the reason why.
Letter, 5 September 1918, publ. in *Selected Letters of James Joyce* (ed. Richard Ellmann, 1975)

23 The snotgreen sea. The scrotumtightening sea.
Ulysses, ch. 1 ('Telemachus') (1922). Spoken by Buck Mulligan.

24 It is a symbol of Irish art. The cracked lookingglass of a servant.
Stephen Dedalus, ibid., ch. 1. Referring to Buck Mulligan's purloined mirror.

25 I fear those big words which make us so unhappy.
Stephen Dedalus, ibid., ch. 2 ('Nestor')

26 History is a nightmare from which I am trying to awake.
Stephen Dedalus, ibid., ch. 2

27 A man of genius makes no mistakes. His errors are volitional and are the portals of discovery.
Stephen Dedalus, ibid. ch. 9 ('Scylla and Charybdis')

28 A nation is the same people living in the same place.
Leopold Bloom, ibid., ch. 12 ('Cyclops')

29 Greater love than this, he said, no man hath that a man lay down his wife for his friend. Go thou and do likewise. Thus, or words to that effect, said Zarathustra, sometime regius professor of French letters to the university of Oxtail nor breathed there ever that man to whom mankind was more beholden.
Stephen Dedalus, ibid., ch. 14 ('Oxen of the Sun'). In this parody of the words of Jesus (SEE BIBLE, NEW TESTAMENT: JOHN 54), Joyce refers to 'those delicate poets' FRANCIS BEAUMONT and JOHN FLETCHER, who 'had but the one doxy between them'.

30 British Beatitudes! . . . Beer, beef, business, bibles, bulldogs, battleships, buggery and bishops.
Ibid., ch. 14

31 frseeeeeeeefronnnng train somewhere whistling the strength those engines have in them like big giants and the water rolling all over and out of them all sides like the end of Loves old sweeeetsonnnng the poor men that have to be out all the night from their wives and families in those roasting engines
Ibid., ch. 18 ('Penelope'). Molly Bloom's soliloquy.

32 He kissed me under the Moorish wall and I thought well as well him as another and then I asked him with my eyes to ask again yes and then he asked me would I yes to say yes my mountain flower and first I put my arms around him yes and drew him down to me so he could feel my breasts all perfume yes and his heart was going like mad and yes I said yes I will Yes.
Ibid., ch. 18 ('Penelope'). Molly Bloom's soliloquy. Closing words of book.

33 riverrun, past Eve and Adam's, from swerve of shore to bend of bay, brings us by a commodious vicus of recirculation back to Howth Castle and Environs.
Finnegans Wake, pt 1, ch. 1 (1939). Opening words of book. The book's concluding words ('A way a lone a last a loved a long the') form the first part of this sentence, which provided a

title for a volume of essays by Joyce's biographer RICHARD ELLMANN: *a long the riverrun* (1988).

34 That ideal reader suffering from an ideal insomnia.
Ibid., pt 1, ch. 5

35 O, you were excruciated, in honour bound to the cross of your own cruelfiction!
Shaun, ibid., pt 1, ch. 7

36 Oft in the smelly night will they wallow for a clutch of the famished hand, I say, them bearded jezabelles you hired to rob you, while on your sodden straw impolitely you encored (Airish and nawboggaleesh!) those hornmade ivory dreams you reved of the Ruth you called your companionate, a beauty from the bible, of the flushpots of Euston and the hanging garments of Marylebone.
Ibid., pt 1, ch. 7

37 All moanday, tearsday, wailsday, thumpsday, frightday, shatterday till the fear of the Law.
Ibid., pt 2, ch. 2

38 Three quarks for Muster Mark!
Ibid., pt 2, ch. 4. This seabirds' chorus song is the origin of the name 'quark' given to the hypothetical particle postulated by the physicists Murray Gell-Mann and George Zweig in 1963.

39 I should tell you that honestly, on my honour of a Nearwicked, I always think in a wordworth's of that primed favourite continental poet, Daunty, Gouty and Shopkeeper, A.G., whom the generality admoyers in this that is and that this is to come.
Ibid., pt 3, ch. 3. Humphrey Chimpden Earwicker, making an incoherent speech in his defence.

40 When I hear the word 'stream' uttered with such a revolting primness, what I think of is urine and not the contemporary novel. And besides, it isn't new, it is far from the *dernier cri*. Shakespeare used it continually, much too much in my opinion, and there's *Tristam Shandy*, not to mention the *Agamemnon* ...
On 'the stream of consciousness', quoted in *Voices: A Memoir*, 'At Sylvia's' (1983) by Frederic Prokosch. Joyce was replying to the assertion by the young author and poet Prokosch that Molly Bloom's final monologue in *Ulysses* exemplified this form. 'Molly Bloom was a down-to-earth lady,' Joyce said. 'She would never have indulged in anything so refined as a stream of consciousness.'

William Joyce
(1906–46)
US-born German propagandist

Having founded the British National Socialist League in 1937, he broadcast propaganda against Britain throughout the Second World War, earning him the byname 'Lord Haw-Haw'. He was hanged for treason after his capture.

1 Germany calling! Germany calling!
Opening words of propaganda broadcasts from Hamburg, September 1939–April 1945

Jack Judge
(1878–1938)
Harry Williams
(1874–1924)
British songwriters

Judge was a fishmonger and music hall entertainer, best known for the song 'It's a Long Way to Tipperary' (1912). Williams was a musician and publican.

1 It's a long way to Tipperary,
It's a long way to go;
It's a long way to Tipperary,
To the sweetest girl I know!
Goodbye, Piccadilly,
Farewell, Leicester Square,
It's a long, long way to Tipperary,
But my heart's right there!
'It's a Long Way to Tipperary', refrain (song, 1912). Judge, the lyricist and principal composer, had never been to Ireland, though his grandparents were from County Tipperary. According to some versions, the last line of the song is 'But my heart lies there!'

Julian the Apostate
(c. 332–63)
Roman emperor

Flavius Claudius Julianus. A noted scholar and military leader, he was baptized and raised a Christian but revived pagan worship and persecuted Christians, thereby acquiring the byname 'the Apostate'.

1 *Vicisti, Galilaee.*
[You have won, Galilean.]
Attributed last words, uttered after his victory against the Persians. See A. C. SWINBURNE 13.

Julian of Norwich
(1343–c. 1416)
English anchoress

Calling herself a 'simple creature unlettered', she is considered one of the greatest English mystics for her visions of Jesus. Her meditations are recorded in Revelations of Divine Love *(c. 1393).*

1 It behoved that there should be sin; but all shall be well, and all shall be well, and all manner of thing shall be well.
Revelations of Divine Love, ch. 27, Revelation 13 (*c.* 1393). The lines were incorporated by T. S. ELIOT in *The Four Quartets*, 'Little Gidding' (1943).

Carl Jung
(1875–1961)
Swiss psychiatrist

He was a collaborator with FREUD *until his work* The Psychology of the Unconscious *(1912) instigated a rift. Jung's 'analytical psychology' emphasized the 'collective unconscious' and 'individuation', and his* Psychological Types *(1921) introduced the concept of introversion and extroversion.*

1 Where love reigns, there is no will to power; and where the will to power is paramount, love is lacking. The one is but the shadow of the other.
'On the Psychology of the Unconscious' (1912, rev. 1917, 1926 and 1943), repr. in *Collected Works*, vol. 7 (ed. HERBERT READ, Michael Fordham and Gerhard Adler, 1953)

2 Psychoanalysis cannot be considered a method of education if by education we mean the topiary art of clipping a tree into a beautiful artificial shape. But those who have a higher conception of education will prize most the method of cultivating a tree so that it fulfils to perfection its own natural conditions of growth.
'The Theory of Psychoanalysis' (1913), ibid., vol. 4 (1961)

3 So often among so-called 'primitives' one comes across spiritual personalities who immediately inspire respect, as though they were the fully matured products of an undisturbed fate.
'Marriage as a Psychological Relationship' (1925), ibid., vol. 17 (1954)

4 Nothing is more repulsive than a furtively prurient spirituality; it is just as unsavoury as gross sensuality.
'Marriage as a Psychological Relationship', ibid.

5 The wine of youth does not always clear with advancing years; sometimes it grows turbid.
'The Stages of Life' (1930), ibid., vol. 8 (1960)

6 The psychiatrist knows only too well how each of us becomes the helpless but not pitiable victim of his own sentiments. Sentimentality is the superstructure erected upon brutality.
'Ulysses: A Monologue' (1932), ibid., vol. 15 (1966)

7 If there is anything that we wish to change in the child, we should first examine it and see whether it is not something that could better be changed in ourselves.
'The Development of Personality' (1934), ibid., vol. 17 (1954)

8 Personality is the supreme realization of the innate idiosyncrasy of a living being. It is an act of high courage flung in the face of life, the absolute affirmation of all that constitutes the individual, the most successful adaptation to the universal conditions of existence coupled with the greatest possible freedom for self-determination.
'The Development of Personality', ibid., vol. 17

9 Instead of being at the mercy of wild beasts, earthquakes, landslides, and inundations, modern man is battered by the elemental forces of his own psyche. This is the World Power that vastly exceeds all other powers on earth. The Age of Enlightenment, which stripped nature and human institutions of gods, overlooked the God of Terror who dwells in the human soul.
'The Development of Personality', ibid., vol. 17

10 From the middle of life onward, only he remains vitally alive who is ready to *die with life*.
'The Soul and Death' (1934), ibid., voi. 8 (1960)

11 Neurosis is always a substitute for legitimate suffering.
'Psychology and Religion' (1938), ibid., vol. 11 (1958)

12 Our blight is ideologies – they are the long-expected Antichrist!
'Psychological Commentary on *The Tibetan Book of the Great Liberation*' (1939, rev. 1954), ibid., vol. 11 (1958)

13 Yoga in Mayfair or Fifth Avenue, or in any other place which is on the telephone, is a spiritual fake.
'Psychological Commentary on *The Tibetan Book of the Great Liberation*', ibid., vol. 11

14 Masses are always breeding grounds of psychic epidemics.
'Concerning Rebirth' (1940), ibid., vol. 9 (1959)

15 It is a fact that cannot be denied: the wickedness of others becomes our own wickedness because it kindles something evil in our own hearts.
'After the Catastrophe' (1945), ibid., vol. 10 (1964)

16 The wise man who is not heeded is counted a fool, and the fool who proclaims the general folly first and loudest passes for a prophet and Führer, and sometimes it is luckily the other way round as well, or else mankind would long since have perished of stupidity.
Mysterium Coniunctionis (1955–6), ibid., vol. 14 (1963)

17 Resistance to the organized mass can be effected only by the man who is as well organized in his individuality as the mass itself.
The Undiscovered Self, ch. 4 (1957)

18 Because the European does not know his own unconscious, he does not understand the East and projects into it everything he fears and despises in himself.
Foreword to *Beelden uit het onbewuste* (1957) by R. J. Van Helsdingen, repr. in *The Collected Works*, vol. 18 (ed. HERBERT READ, Michael Fordham and Gerhard Adler, 1977)

19 In all chaos there is a cosmos, in all disorder a secret order.
'Archetypes of the Collective Unconscious' (1935, rev. 1954), ibid., vol. 9, pt 1 (1959)

20 The images of the unconscious place a great responsibility upon a man. Failure to understand them, or a shirking of ethical responsibility, deprives him of his wholeness and imposes a painful fragmentariness on his life.
Memories, Dreams, Reflections, ch. 6 (1962)

21 A man who has not passed through the inferno of his passions has never overcome them.
Ibid., ch. 9, sect. 4

22 As far as we can discern, the sole purpose of human existence is to kindle a light in the darkness of mere being.
Ibid., ch. 11

23 Every form of addiction is bad, no matter whether the narcotic be alcohol or morphine or idealism.
Ibid., ch. 12

24 Life is – or has – meaning and meaninglessness. I cherish the anxious hope that meaning will preponderate and win the battle.
Ibid., 'Retrospect'

25 I am incapable of determining ultimate worth or worthlessness; I have no judgement about myself and my life. There is nothing I am quite sure about. I have no definite convictions – not about anything really. I only know that I was born and exist, and it seems to me that I have been carried along.
Ibid., 'Retrospect'

Junius
(*fl.* 1769–72)

Pseudonym of writer of a series of letters to the Public Advertiser. *The author of the letters, which were a sustained attack on the Tory ministries of the Duke of Grafton and Lord North, has never been identified; candidates include Sir William Francis and Lord Shelburne.*

1 Let it be impressed upon your minds, let it be instilled into your children, that the liberty of the press is the *palladium* of all the civil, political and religious rights of an Englishman.
The Letters of Junius, 'Dedication to the English Nation' (ed. Henry Sampson Woodfall, 1772)

2 There is a holy mistaken zeal in politics as well as in religion. By persuading others, we convince ourselves.
Letter to the *Public Advertiser*, 19 December 1769, repr. ibid., no. 35

3 We lament the mistakes of a good man, and do not begin to detest him until he affects to renounce his principles.
Letter to Lord Mansfield, 14 November 1770, ibid., no. 41

4 The injustice done to an individual is sometimes of service to the public. Facts are apt to alarm us more than the most dangerous principles.
Letter to Lord Mansfield, 14 November 1770, ibid., no. 41

Juvenal
(*c.* 60–*c.* 127)
Roman satiric poet

Decimus Junius Juvenalis. His sixteen satires were rhetorical, polished and highly scathing attacks on the morals and affectations of Roman society. He was mainly unrecognized during his lifetime.

1 *Difficile est saturam non scribere.*
[It is hard *not* to write satire.]
Satires, no. 1, l. 30

2 Honesty is praised and left to shiver.
Ibid., no. 1, l. 74

3 Though nature say me nay, indignation will prompt my verse.
Ibid., no. 1, l. 79

4 All the doings of mankind, their vows, their fears, their angers and their pleasures, their joys and goings to and for, shall form the motley subject of my page.
Ibid., no. 1, ll. 85–6. The lines were translated and embellished by ALEXANDER POPE as 'Whate'er men do, or say, or think, or dream,/Our motley paper seizes for its theme', and used for the epigraph of the 'Prospectus' in the first issue of RICHARD STEELE's *Tatler* magazine, 12 April 1709. Juvenal's original listed more of men's actions, and referred to a 'little book' or 'notebook' (*libellus*), rather than a newspaper.

5 A hairy body, and arms stiff with bristles, give promise of a manly soul.
Ibid., no. 2, ll. 11–12

6 No one becomes depraved in a moment.
Ibid., no. 2, l. 83

7 Of all the woes of luckless poverty none is harder to endure than this, that it exposes men to ridicule.
Ibid., no. 3, ll. 152–3

8 It is no easy matter, anywhere, for a man to rise when poverty stands in the way of his merits.
Ibid., no. 3, l. 164. The line is usually quoted according to Johnson's wording in his poem 'London', an imitation of Juvenal's third satire: see SAMUEL JOHNSON 2.

9 We all live in a state of ambitious poverty.
Ibid., no. 3, ll. 182–3

10 Nothing can be had in Rome for nothing.
Ibid., no. 3, ll. 183–4

11 It is something, in whatever spot, however remote, to have become the possessor of a single lizard.
Ibid., no. 3, ll. 230–1

12 We are now suffering the calamities of a long peace. Luxury, more deadly than any foe, has laid her hand upon us, and avenges a conquered world.
Ibid., no. 6, ll. 292–3

13 *Sed quis custodiet ipsos Custodes?*
[But who will ward the warders?]
Ibid., no. 6, ll. 347–8

14 The itch for writing and making a name holds you fast as with a noose, and becomes inveterate in your distempered brain.
Ibid., no. 7, ll. 51–2

15 *Stemmata quid faciunt?*
[What avail your pedigrees?]
Ibid., no. 8, l. 1

16 Two things only the people anxiously desire, Bread and circuses [*panem et circenses*].
Ibid., no. 10, ll. 80–1

17 You should pray for a sound mind in a sound body [*mens sana in corpore sano*]; ask for a stout heart that has no fear of death.
Ibid., no. 10, ll. 356–7

18 It is rarity that gives zest to pleasure.
Ibid., no. 11, l. 208

19 The first punishment is this: that no guilty man is acquitted at the bar of his own conscience.
Ibid., no. 13, ll. 2–3

20 For vengeance is always the delight of a little, weak, and petty mind.
Ibid., no. 13, ll. 189–90

21 You owe the greatest reverence to the young.
Ibid., no. 14, l. 47

K

Pauline Kael

(1919–2001)

US film critic

'The sanest, saltiest, most resourceful and least attitudinizing movie critic in the USA,' according to writer and producer Richard Schickel, she reviewed for the New Yorker *1968–91.*

1 The first prerogative of an artist in any medium is to make a fool of himself.
'Is There a Cure for Film Criticism?' (1962), repr. in *I Lost It At the Movies* (1965)

2 The words 'Kiss Kiss Bang Bang', which I saw on an Italian movie poster, are perhaps the briefest statement imaginable of the basic appeal of movies. This appeal is what attracts us, and ultimately what makes us despair when we begin to understand how seldom movies are more than this.
Kiss Kiss Bang Bang, 'A Note on the Title' (1968)

3 Irresponsibility is part of the pleasure of all art, it is the part the schools cannot recognize.
'Trash, Art, and the Movies' (1968), repr. in *Going Steady* (1970)

4 In the arts, the critic is the only independent source of information. The rest is advertising.
Quoted in *Newsweek* 24 December 1973

Franz Kafka

(1883–1924)

Czech author

His short stories, notably The Metamorphosis *(1915), and his novels, for example* The Trial *(1925) and* The Castle *(1926), depicted a 'Kafkaesque' world where the individual is overwhelmed by labyrinths of totalitarian bureaucracy. All were written in German. The critic Edmund Wilson called him 'denationalized, discouraged, disaffected, disabled'.*

1 Don't despair, not even over the fact that you don't despair.
Journal entry, 21 July 1913, publ. in *The Diaries of Franz Kafka: 1910–1923*, vol. 1 (ed. Max Brod, 1948)

2 As Gregor Samsa awoke one morning from uneasy dreams he found himself transformed in his bed into a gigantic insect.
The Metamorphosis, ch. 1 (1915, transl. 1933). Opening sentence.

3 A first sign of the beginning of understanding is the wish to die.
The Collected Aphorisms, no. 13 (written October 1917–February 1918), publ. in *Shorter Works*, vol. 1 (ed./transl. Malcolm Pasley, 1973)

4 In theory there is a possibility of perfect happiness: To believe in the indestructible element within one, and not to strive towards it.
Ibid., no. 68

5 A belief is like a guillotine, just as heavy, just as light.
Ibid., no. 87

6 It is not necessary that you leave the house. Remain at your table and listen. Do not even listen, only wait. Do not even wait, be wholly still and alone. The world will present itself to you for its unmasking, it can do no other, in ecstasy it will writhe at your feet.
Ibid., no. 109

7 My guiding principle is this: Guilt is never to be doubted.
In the Penal Settlement (1920), repr. in *Metamorphosis and Other Stories* (1961). Spoken by an officer.

8 Someone must have been telling lies about Joseph K., for without having done anything wrong he was arrested one fine morning.
The Trial, ch. 1 (1925, transl. 1935). Opening words.

9 You may object that it is not a trial at all; you are quite right, for it is only a trial if I recognize it as such.
Joseph K., ibid., ch. 2

10 It's often safer to be in chains than to be free.
The Advocate, ibid., ch. 8. See JEAN-JACQUES ROUSSEAU 1.

11 Human nature, essentially changeable, unstable as the dust, can endure no restraint; if it binds itself it soon begins to tear madly at its bonds, until it rends everything asunder, the wall, the bonds and its very self.
The Great Wall of China (1931, transl. 1949), repr. in *Metamorphosis and Other Stories* (1961)

Gus Kahn

(1886–1941)

US songwriter

A Tin Pan Alley writer for films and Broadway shows, he provided a number of hit songs for AL JOLSON. *Other compositions include 'Yes, Sir, That's My Baby' (1925) and 'My Baby Just Cares for Me' (1930).*

1 There's nothing surer,
The rich get rich and the poor get children.
In the meantime, in between time,
Ain't we got fun.
'Ain't We Got Fun' (song, 1921, written with Raymond B. Egan)

2 All God's chillun got rhythm.
'All God's Chillun Got Rhythm' (song, with music by Bronislaw Kaper and Walter Jurmann) in the Marx Brothers' film, *A Day at the Races* (1937). The number was sung by Ivie Andersen in the film, and subsequently recorded by Benny Bergan and his Orchestra, JUDY GARLAND and June Christy.

Immanuel Kant
(1724–1804)
German philosopher

The metaphysics of his major work, Critique of Pure Reason *(1781), laid the groundwork for the Idealism of Fichte,* HEGEL *and* SCHELLING, *and greatly influenced other branches of modern philosophy. He was a student and, from 1770, Professor of Logic and Metaphysics at Königsberg, Prussia.*

1 Intuition and concepts constitute . . . the elements of all our knowledge, so that neither concepts without an intuition in some way corresponding to them, nor intuition without concepts, can yield knowledge.
Critique of Pure Reason, 'Transcendental Doctrine of Elements', pt 2, sect. 1 (1781)

2 All the interests of my reason, speculative as well as practical, combine in the three following questions:
1. What can I know?
2. What ought I to do?
3. What may I hope?
Ibid., 'Transcendental Doctrine of Method', ch. 2, sect. 2

3 Out of timber so crooked as that from which man is made nothing entirely straight can be carved.
Idea for a General History with a Cosmopolitan Purpose, Proposition 6 (1784). Quoted as epigraph to ISAIAH BERLIN's, *Crooked Timber of Humanity* (1990).

4 I am never to act otherwise than so that I could also will that my maxim should become a universal law.
Fundamental Principles of the Metaphysics of Ethics, sect. 1 (1785)

5 Happiness is not an ideal of reason but of imagination.
Ibid., sect. 2

6 So act as to treat humanity, whether in thine own person or in that of any other, in every case as an end withal, never as means only.
Ibid., sect. 2

7 Two things fill the mind with ever new and increasing admiration and awe, the oftener and the more steadily we reflect on them: the starry heavens above and the moral law within.
Critique of Practical Reason, 'Conclusion' (1788)

Ryszard Kapuściński
(b. 1932)
Polish journalist

His books include a portrait of Haile Selassie, The Emperor *(1978), and writings on Africa, Kyrgyzstan and Poland.*

1 In Poland a man must be one thing: white or black, here or there, with us or against us – clearly, openly, without hesitations . . . We lack the liberal, democratic tradition rich in all its gradations. We have instead the tradition of struggle: the extreme situation, the final gesture.
'A Warsaw Diary', publ. in *Granta*, no. 15 (1985)

2 First you destroy those who create values. Then you destroy those who know what the values are, and who also know that those destroyed before were in fact the creators of values. But real barbarism begins when no one can any longer judge or know that what he does is barbaric.
'A Warsaw Diary', ibid.

3 The so-called new Russian man is characterized mainly by his complete exhaustion. You may find yourself wondering if he has the strength to enjoy his new-found freedom. He is like a long-distance runner who, on reaching the finishing line, is incapable even of raising his hands in a gesture of victory.
Independent on Sunday 27 October 1991

Alphonse Karr
(1808–90)
French journalist and novelist

Autobiography and romance combined in his successful novels. He was an editor of Le Figaro *and started the monthly satirical journal* Les Guêpes *in 1839. He also wrote on gardens and helped to develop the trade in cut flowers on the Riviera.*

1 If we are to abolish the death penalty, I should like to see the first step taken by my friends the murderers.
Les Guêpes 31 January 1849. An alternative source attributes

this to a voice from the hall in the French Chamber during a debate on the death penalty, when a speech proposing abolition was being tumultuously applauded.

2 *Plus ça change, plus c'est la même chose.*
[The more things change, the more they remain the same.]
Les Guêpes 31 January 1849

George S. Kaufman
(1889–1961)
US playwright and director

He was author of many 1920s and '30s Broadway hits which he often directed. He collaborated with EDNA FERBER *in* Dinner at Eight *(1932) and with Moss Hart in* You Can't Take It With You *(1936).*

1 Satire is what closes Saturday night.
Quoted in *George S. Kaufman and His Friends*, ch. 6 (1974) by Scott Meredith

(Sir) Gerald Kaufman
(b. 1930)
British politician

Elected Labour MP for Manchester in 1970, he was Under-Secretary of State in the Department of Industry (1975–9) and later Shadow Foreign Secretary (1987–92).

1 The longest suicide note in history.
Quoted in *The Time of My Life*, ch. 23 (1989) by DENIS HEALEY. Referring to the Labour Party's manifesto for the 1983 general election, 'New Hope For Britain'. 'The scale of our defeat was devastating,' Healey wrote of the results of the subsequent election.

Paul Kaufman and Mike Anthony
US songwriters

1 Poetry in Motion.
Title of song (1960). Sung by Johnny Tillotson, the teen ballad topped the charts in 1960.

Christoph Kaufmann
(1753–95)
German author and critic

He was responsible for renaming the historical drama Der Wirrwarr *by Friedrich Maximilian Klinger* Sturm und Drang, *which became the term used to characterize a German literary movement (1767–85).*

1 *Sturm und Drang.*
[Storm and stress.]
Title of play (1776). The *Sturm und Drang* movement, whose major exponents were GOETHE and SCHILLER, was distinguished for its exaltation of nature and human individualism.

Kenneth Kaunda
(b. 1924)
Zambian politician and president

He led Zambia to independence, becoming its first President (1964–91), and rallied other southern African nations in opposition to the white minority governments of South Africa and Rhodesia. He survived several coups in the 1980s, but lost the 1991 election.

1 When [the Englishman] wants a new market for his adulterated Manchester goods, he sends a missionary to teach the Natives the Gospel of Peace. The Natives kill the missionary, he flies to arms in defence of Christianity, fights for it, conquers for it, and takes the market as a reward from heaven.
Letter to missionaries, March 1952, publ. in *Zambia Shall Be Free*, ch. 16 (1962)

2 The moment you have protected an individual you have protected society.
Quoted in the *Observer* 6 May 1962

3 Some people draw a comforting distinction between 'force' and 'violence'. They define 'violence' as the improper use of 'force', and 'force' as 'violence sanctioned by the law'. I refuse to cloud the issue by such word-play ... With some exceptions, the power which establishes a state is violence; the power which maintains it is violence; the power which eventually overthrows it is violence – or if you prefer a nicer word 'force' ... Call an elephant a rabbit only if it gives you comfort to feel that you are about to be trampled to death by a rabbit.
Kaunda on Violence, pt 1, 'Living by the Sword' (1980)

4 I fear that the drama can only be brought to its climax in one of two ways – through the selective brutality of terrorism or the impartial horrors of war.
Ibid., pt 2, 'Illusion of Innocence'. Referring to the situation in South Africa.

Patrick Kavanagh
(1904–67)
Irish poet and author

Initially labelled a 'peasant poet' after the publication of his first collection Ploughman and Other Poems *(1936), he achieved wider recognition for the new realism of 'The Great Hunger' (1942), an epic poem of the Irish famine.*

1 I have what every poet hates in spite
Of all the solemn talk of contemplation.
Oh, Alexander Selkirk knew the plight
Of being king and government and nation.
A road, a mile of kingdom, I am king
Of banks and stones and every blooming thing.
'Inniskeen Road: July Evening', publ. in *Ploughman and Other Poems* (1936)

2 Clay is the word and clay is the flesh
Where the potato-gatherers like mechanized
      scarecrows move
Along the side-fall of the hill – Maguire and his
      men.
'The Great Hunger' (1942), repr. in *Soul for Sale* (1947)

3 I had a very pleasant journey, thank you
      sincerely
For giving me my madness back, or nearly.
'Come Dance with Kitty Stobling', publ. in *Come Dance with Kitty Stobling* (1960). Closing lines of poem.

4 A man is original when he speaks the truth that has always been known to all good men.
Collected Prose, 'Signposts' (1967)

Ted Kavanagh
(1892–1959)
British scriptwriter

He is best remembered for the scripts of ITMA *(1939–49), the radio series which he wrote with Tommy Handley.*

1 Cecil: After you, Claude.
Claude: No, after you, Cecil.
Catchphrase, in ITMA (BBC radio programme, 1939–49)

2 Can I do you now, sir?
Catchphrase, spoken by Mrs Mopp, ibid.

3 I don't mind if I do.
Catchphrase, spoken by Colonel Chinstrap, ibid.

4 I go – I come back.
Catchphrase, spoken by Ali Oop, ibid.

Nikos Kazantzakis
(1883–1957)
Greek author

The best known of his many novels are Zorba the Greek *(1946) and* The Last Temptation of Christ *(1959).*

1 Life is trouble. Death, no. To live – do you know what that means? To undo your belt and look for trouble.
Zorba the Greek, ch. 8 (1946). Spoken by Zorba.

Safinaz Kazem
(b. 1937)
Egyptian author and critic

A prolific author and journalist, she has been politically active since the 1960s, and spent periods in prison under Sadat's regime. She later exchanged her Marxist sympathies for a commitment to Islamist beliefs.

1 Even if we have to do without poetry or literature for the sake of Islam, it's all right. We do not consider art as a sacred thing. This is a Greek ideology.
Guardian 31 March 1989

2 For years, we ran around in short skirts and bare arms saying to them, 'Look, see, we're just like you.' Enough. It got us nowhere. We're not like them, and they shouldn't matter. We have to find a way to be ourselves.
Four Women of Egypt (documentary film, 1997)

Diane Keaton
(b. 1946)
US screen actress

Originally Diane Hall. She has appeared in The Godfather *(1972, 1974, 1990) and opposite* WOODY ALLEN *in* Annie Hall *(1977). The critic John Simon compared her acting style to a 'nervous breakdown in slow motion'.*

1 Well, la-de-da!
Annie Hall (film, 1977, screenplay by WOODY ALLEN and Marshall Brickman, directed by Woody Allen). Said by Annie (Diane Keaton).

John Keats
(1795–1821)
English poet

His sensuous lyric verse marked him as one of the foremost English Romantics. Endymion *(1818), a long mythological work, was harshly criticized, though* Lamia and Other Poems *(1820) was better received. His letters are also highly regarded for their poetic insights. He died in Rome from tuberculosis.* BYRON *considered him a 'tadpole of the Lakes', but* OSCAR WILDE *praised his 'unerring sense of beauty'. See also* LORD BYRON 111, 152, P. B. SHELLEY 69.

1 And then there crept
A little noiseless noise among the leaves,
Born of the very sigh that silence heaves.
'I stood tip-toe upon a little hill', ll. 10–12, publ. in *Poems* (1817)

2 Here are sweet peas, on tip-toe for a flight,
With wings of gentle flush o'er delicate white.
'I stood tip-toe upon a little hill', ll. 57–8, ibid.

3 How many bards gild the lapses of time!
'How many bards gild the lapses of time', ibid. Opening line of poem.

4 Yet the sweet converse of an innocent mind,
Whose words are images of thoughts refined,
Is my soul's pleasure; and it sure must be
Almost the highest bliss of human-kind,
When to thy haunts two kindred spirits flee.
'O Solitude! If I must with thee dwell', ll. 10–14, ibid.

5 Much have I travelled in the realms of gold,
And many goodly states and kingdoms seen.
'On First Looking into Chapman's Homer', ibid. Opening lines of poem.

6 Then felt I like some watcher of the skies
When a new planet swims into his ken;
Or like stout Cortez when with eagle eyes
He stared at the Pacific – and all his men
Looked at each other with a wild surmise –
Silent, upon a peak in Darien.
'On First Looking into Chapman's Homer', ll. 9–14, ibid.

7 The poetry of earth is never dead:
When all the birds are faint with the hot sun,
And hide in cooling trees, a voice will run
From hedge to hedge about the new-mown mead.
'On the Grasshopper and the Cricket', ibid. Opening lines of poem.

8 Stop and consider! life is but a day;
A fragile dew-drop on its perilous way
From a tree's summit; a poor Indian's sleep
While his boat hastens to the monstrous steep
Of Montmorenci.
'Sleep and Poetry', ll. 85–8, ibid.

9 O for ten years, that I may overwhelm
Myself in poesy; so I may do the deed
That my own soul has to itself decreed.
'Sleep and Poetry', ll. 96–8, ibid.

10 And they shall be accounted poet kings
Who simply tell the most heart-easing things.
'Sleep and Poetry', ll. 267–8, ibid.

11 It keeps eternal whisperings around
Desolate shores, and with its mighty swell
Gluts twice ten thousand caverns.
'On the Sea', in letter, 17 April 1817, publ. in *The Letters of John Keats*, vol. 1, no. 22 (ed. H. E. Rollins, 1958). Opening lines of poem.

12 A long poem is a test of invention which I take to be the polar star of poetry, as fancy is the sails, and imagination the rudder.
Letter, 8 October 1817, ibid., vol. 1, no. 38

13 I am certain of nothing but the holiness of the heart's affections, and the truth of imagination.
Letter, 22 November 1817, ibid., vol. 1, no. 43

14 O for a life of sensations rather than of thoughts!
Letter, 22 November 1817, ibid., vol. 1, no. 43

15 Negative capability, that is when man is capable of being in uncertainties, mysteries, doubts, without any irritable reaching after fact and reason.
Letter to his brothers George and Thomas Keats, 21 December 1817, ibid., vol. 1, no. 45

16 With a great poet the sense of beauty overcomes every other consideration, or rather obliterates all consideration.
Letter to his brothers, 21 December 1817, ibid., vol. 1, no. 45

17 There is not a fiercer hell than the failure in a great object.
Endymion, Preface (1818)

18 The imagination of a boy is healthy, and the mature imagination of a man is healthy; but there is a space of life between, in which the soul is in a ferment, the character undecided, the way of life uncertain, the ambition thick-sighted: thence proceeds mawkishness.
Ibid., Preface

19 A thing of beauty is a joy for ever:
Its loveliness increases; it will never
Pass into nothingness; but still will keep
A bower quiet for us, and a sleep
Full of sweet dreams, and health, and quiet
   breathing.
Ibid., bk 1, ll. 1–5

20 The grandeur of the dooms
We have imagined for the mighty dead.
Ibid., bk 1, ll. 20–1

21 Wide sea, that one continuous murmur breeds
Along the pebbled shore of memory!
Ibid., bk 2, ll. 16–17

22 'Tis the pest
Of love, that fairest joys give most unrest.
Ibid., bk 2, ll. 365–6

23 Their smiles,
Wan as primroses gathered at midnight
By chilly fingered spring.
Ibid., bk 4, ll. 969–71

24 There is nothing stable in the world – uproar's
your only music.
Letter to his brothers George and Thomas Keats, 13–
19 January 1818, publ. in *The Letters of John Keats*, vol. 1, no. 52
(ed. H. E. Rollins, 1958)

25 There's a blush for won't, and a blush for
    shan't,
And a blush for having done it:
There's a blush for thought and a blush for naught,
And a blush for just begun it.
Untitled poem, st. 2, written in letter, 31 January 1818, ibid.,
vol. 1, no. 58. The poem has subsequently been titled 'Sharing
Eve's Apple'.

26 When I have fears that I may cease to be
Before my pen has gleaned my teeming brain,
Before high-piled books, in charactery,
Hold like rich garners the full ripened grain –
When I behold upon the night's starred face,
Huge cloudy symbols of a high romance
And feel that I may never live to trace
Their shadows with the magic hand of chance;
And when I feel, fair creature of an hour,
That I shall never look upon thee more,
Never have relish in the fairy power
Of unreflecting love: then on the shore
Of the wide world I stand alone and think
Till love and fame to nothingness do sink.
Untitled sonnet, written in letter, 31 January 1818, ibid., vol. 1,
no. 58

27 For the sake of a few fine imaginative or domestic
passages, are we to be bullied into a certain philosophy engendered in the whims of an egotist?
Letter, 3 February 1818, ibid., vol. 1, no. 59. Referring to the
influence of WILLIAM WORDSWORTH.

28 We hate poetry that has a palpable design upon
us – and if we do not agree, seems to put its hand
in its breeches pocket. Poetry should be great &
unobtrusive, a thing which enters into one's soul,

and does not startle it or amaze it with itself, but
with its subject.
Letter, 3 February 1818, ibid., vol. 1, no. 59

29 It appears to me that almost any man may like
the spider spin from his own inwards his own airy
citadel.
Letter, 19 February 1818, ibid., vol. 1, no. 62

30 O fret not after knowledge – I have none,
And yet my song comes native with the warmth.
O fret not after knowledge – I have none,
And yet the Evening listens.
'What the Thrush Said', ll. 9–12, in a letter, 19 February 1818,
ibid., vol. 1, no. 62

31 Poetry should surprise by a fine excess and not
by singularity – it should strike the reader as a wording of his own highest thoughts, and appear almost
a remembrance.
Letter, 27 February 1818, ibid., vol. 1, no. 65

32 If poetry comes not as naturally as the leaves to
a tree it had better not come at all.
Letter, 27 February 1818, ibid., vol. 1, no. 65

33 Scenery is fine – but human nature is finer.
Letter, 13 March 1818, ibid., vol. 1, no. 67

34 The public . . . a thing I cannot help looking upon
as an enemy, and which I cannot address without
feelings of hostility.
Letter, 9 April 1818, ibid., vol. 1, no. 76. Keats continued: 'I
never wrote one single line of poetry with the least shadow
of public thought.'

35 I would jump down Etna for any public good –
but I hate a mawkish popularity.
Letter, 9 April 1818, ibid., vol. 1, no. 76

36 It is impossible to live in a country which is
continually under hatches . . . Rain! Rain! Rain!
Letter, 10 April 1818, ibid., vol. 1, no. 77

37 I am in that temper that if I were under water I
would scarcely kick to come to the top.
Letter, 21–25 May 1818, ibid., vol. 1, no. 83

38 Praise or blame has but a momentary effect on
the man whose love of beauty in the abstract makes
him a severe critic on his own works.
Letter, 8 October 1818, ibid., vol. 1, no. 109. In his preface to
his elegy *Adonais*, SHELLEY asserted that Keats had suffered
from the savage criticism of *Endymion* (publ. April 1818),
which, Shelley claimed, 'produced the most violent effect
on his susceptible mind' and led to Keats' last, fatal illness.
However, in the letter quoted above, Keats himself described
Endymion as 'slip-shod': 'Had I been nervous about its being

a perfect piece, & with that view asked advice, & trembled over every page, it would not have been written.'

39 In Endymion, I leaped headlong into the sea, and thereby have become better acquainted with the soundings, the quicksands, and the rocks, than if I had stayed upon the green shore, and piped a silly pipe, and took tea and comfortable advice.
Letter, 8 October 1818, ibid., vol. 1, no. 110

40 I think I shall be among the English poets after my death.
Letter to his brother and sister-in-law, George and Georgiana Keats, 14–31 October 1818, ibid., vol. 1, no. 120

41 Though the most beautiful creature were waiting for me at the end of a journey or a walk; though the carpet were of silk, the curtains of the morning clouds; the chairs and sofa stuffed with cygnet's down; the food manna, the wine beyond claret, the window opening on Winander Mere . . . my happiness would not be so fine, a[nd] my solitude is sublime.
Letter to his brother and sister-in-law, 14–31 October 1818, ibid., vol. 1, no. 120

42 The roaring of the wind is my wife and the stars through the window pane are my children. The mighty abstract idea I have of beauty in all things stifles the more divided and minute domestic happiness.
Letter to his brother and sister-in-law, 14–31 October 1818, ibid., vol. 1, no. 120. George and Georgiana Keats, recently married and settled in America, had urged the poet to think of starting a family.

43 The opinion I have of the generality of women – who appear to me as children to whom I would rather give a sugar plum than my time, forms a barrier against matrimony which I rejoice in.
Letter to his brother and sister-in-law, 14–31 October 1818, ibid., vol. 1, no. 120. Two years later (August 1820) Keats wrote: 'I am certain that I have said nothing in a spirit to displease any woman I would care to please; but still there is a tendency to class women in my books with roses and sweetmeats.'

44 Fanatics have their dreams, wherewith they weave
A paradise for a sect.
The Fall of Hyperion, canto 1 (written 1819, publ. 1856). Opening lines of poem.

45 'Are there not thousands in the world,' said I,
Encouraged by the sooth voice of the shade,
'Who love their fellows even to the death,
Who feel the giant agony of the world,

And more, like slaves to poor humanity,
Labour for mortal good?'
Ibid., canto 1, ll. 154–9

46 The poet and the dreamer are distinct,
Diverse, sheer opposite, antipodes.
The one pours out a balm upon the world,
The other vexes it.
Ibid., canto 1, ll. 199–202

47 My passions are all asleep from my having slumbered till nearly eleven and weakened the animal fibre all over me to a delightful sensation about three degrees on this side of faintness – if I had teeth of pearl and the breath of lilies I should call it languor – but as I am I must call it laziness. In this state of effeminacy the fibres of the brain are relaxed in common with the rest of the body, and to such a happy degree that pleasure has no show of enticement and pain no unbearable frown. Neither poetry, nor ambition, nor love have any alertness of countenance as they pass by me.
Letter to his brother and sister-in-law, George and Georgiana Keats, 19 March 1819, publ. in The Letters of John Keats, vol. 2, no. 159 (ed. H. E. Rollins, 1958)

48 Though a quarrel in the streets is a thing to be hated, the energies displayed in it are fine; the commonest man shows a grace in his quarrel.
Letter to his brother and sister-in-law, 19 March 1819, ibid., vol. 2, no. 159

49 Call the world if you please 'the vale of soul-making'. Then you will find out the use of the world.
Letter to his brother and sister-in-law, 21 April 1819, ibid., vol. 2, no. 159

50 Do you not see how necessary a world of pains and troubles is to school an intelligence and make it a soul?
Letter to his brother and sister-in-law, 21 April 1819, ibid., vol. 2, no. 159

51 I have met with women whom I really think would like to be married to a poem and to be given away by a novel.
Letter to his fiancée, Fanny Brawne, 8 July 1819, ibid., vol. 2, no. 174

52 I equally dislike the favour of the public with the love of a woman – they are both a cloying treacle to the wings of independence.
Letter, 23 August 1819, ibid., vol. 2, no. 183

53 Who would wish to be among the commonplace

crowd of the little famous – who are each individually lost in a throng made up of themselves?
Letter, 23 August 1819, ibid., vol. 2, no. 183

54 I will give you a definition of a proud man – he is a man who has neither vanity nor wisdom – one filled with hatreds cannot be vain – neither can he be wise.
Letter, 23 August 1819, ibid., vol. 2, no. 183. Keats condoned his own pride in the same letter: 'This pride and egotism will enable me to write finer things than anything else could – so I will indulge it.'

55 Give me books, fruit, French wine and fine weather and a little music out of doors, played by someone I do not know ... I admire lolling on a lawn by a water-lilied pond to eat white currants and see goldfish: and go to the fair in the evening if I'm good. There is not hope for that – one is sure to get into some mess before evening.
Letter to his sister Fanny Keats, 28 August 1819, ibid., vol. 2, no. 186

56 You speak of Lord Byron and me – there is this great difference between us. He describes what he sees – I describe what I imagine. Mine is the hardest task.
Letter to his brother and sister-in-law, 20 September 1819, ibid., vol. 2, no. 199

57 The only means of strengthening one's intellect is to make up one's mind about nothing – to let the mind be a thoroughfare for all thoughts. Not a select party.
Letter to his brother and sister-in-law, 24 September 1819, ibid., vol. 2, no. 199

58 I have been astonished that men could die martyrs for religion – I have shuddered at it. I shudder no more – I could be martyred for my religion – Love is my religion – I could die for that.
Letter to his fiancée Fanny Brawne, 13 October 1819, ibid., vol. 2, no. 203

59 If you still behave in dancing rooms and other societies as I have seen you – I do not want to live – if you have done so I wish this coming night may be my last. I cannot live without you, and not only you but *chaste you; virtuous you.*
Letter to his fiancée Fanny Brawne, May/June 1820, ibid., vol. 2, no. 271

60 She was a gordian shape of dazzling hue,
Vermilion-spotted, golden, green, and blue;

Striped like a zebra, freckled like a pard,
Eyed like a peacock, and all crimson barred.
'Lamia', pt 1, ll. 47–50, publ. in *Lamia, Isabella, The Eve of St. Agnes and Other Poems* (1820)

61 Love in a hut, with water and a crust,
Is – Love, forgive us! – cinders, ashes, dust;
Love in a palace is perhaps at last
More grievous torment than a hermit's fast.
'Lamia', pt 2, ll. 1–4, ibid.

62 That purple-linèd palace of sweet sin.
'Lamia', pt. 2, l. 31, ibid.

63 In pale contented sort of discontent.
'Lamia', pt. 2, l. 135, ibid.

64 Do not all charms fly
At the mere touch of cold philosophy?
There was an awful rainbow once in heaven:
We know her woof, her texture; she is given
In the dull catalogue of common things.
Philosophy will clip an angel's wings,
Conquer all mysteries by rule and line,
Empty the haunted air, and gnomèd mine –
Unweave a rainbow.
'Lamia', pt. 2, ll. 229–37, ibid. *Unweaving the Rainbow* was the title of a book by RICHARD DAWKINS (1998). See MARK TWAIN 3.

65 And she forgot the stars, the moon, and sun,
And she forgot the blue above the trees,
And she forgot the dells where waters run,
And she forgot the chilly autumn breeze;
She had no knowledge when the day was done,
And the new morn she saw not: but in peace
Hung over her sweet Basil evermore,
And moistened it with tears unto the core.
'Isabella; or The Pot of Basil', st. 53, ibid.

66 St Agnes' Eve – Ah, bitter chill it was!
The owl, for all his feathers, was a-cold;
The hare limped trembling through the frozen grass,
And silent was the flock in woolly fold.
'The Eve of St Agnes', st. 1. Opening lines of poem.

67 The sculptured dead, on each side, seem to freeze,
Emprisoned in black, purgatorial rails.
'The Eve of St Agnes', st. 2, ibid.

68 Soon, up aloft,
The silver, snarling trumpets 'gan to chide.
'The Eve of St Agnes', st. 4, ibid.

69 And soft adorings from their loves receive
Upon the honeyed middle of the night.
'The Eve of St Agnes', st. 6, ibid.

70 The music, yearning like a god in pain.
'The Eve of St Agnes', st. 7, ibid.

71 Sudden a thought came like a full-blown rose,
Flushing his brow, and in his pained heart
Made purple riot.
'The Eve of St Agnes', st. 16, ibid.

72 A poor, weak, palsy-stricken, churchyard thing.
'The Eve of St Agnes', st. 18, ibid.

73 A casement high and triple-arched there was,
All garlanded with carven imageries
Of fruits, and flowers, and bunches of knot-grass,
And diamonded with panes of quaint device,
Innumerable of stains and splendid dyes,
As are the tiger-moth's deep-damasked wings.
'The Eve of St Agnes', st. 24, ibid.

74 Full on this casement shone the wintry moon,
And threw warm gules on Madeline's fair breast.
As down she knelt for heaven's grace and boon;
Rose-bloom fell on her hands, together pressed,
And on her silver cross soft amethyst,
And on her hair a glory like a saint:
She seemed a splendid angel, newly dressed,
Save wings, for heaven.
'The Eve of St Agnes', st. 25, ibid.

75 Unclasps her warmed jewels one by one;
Loosens her fragrant bodice; by degrees
Her rich attire creeps rustling to her knees.
'The Eve of St Agnes', st. 26, ibid.

76 And still she slept an azure-lidded sleep,
In blanchèd linen, smooth, and lavendered,
While he from forth the closet brought a heap
Of candied apple, quince, and plum, and gourd;
With jellies soother than the creamy curd,
And lucent syrups, tinct with cinnamon;
Manna and dates, in argosy transferred
From Fez; and spiced dainties, every one,
From silken Samarcand to cedared Lebanon.
'The Eve of St Agnes', st. 30, ibid.

77 He played an ancient ditty, long since mute,
In Provence called, 'La belle dame sans mercy'.
'The Eve of St Agnes', st. 33, ibid.

78 And they are gone: aye, ages long ago
These lovers fled away into the storm.
'The Eve of St Agnes', st. 42, ibid.

79 The Beadsman, after thousand aves told,
For aye unsought for slept among his ashes cold.
'The Eve of St Agnes', st. 42, ibid. Last lines of poem.

80 My heart aches, and a drowsy numbness pains
My sense, as though of hemlock I had drunk,
Or emptied some dull opiate to the drains
One minute past, and Lethe-wards had sunk:
'Tis not through envy of thy happy lot,
But being too happy in thine happiness –
That thou, light-wingèd Dryad of the trees,
In some melodious plot
Of beechen green, and shadows numberless,
Singest of summer in full-throated ease.
'Ode to a Nightingale', st. 1, ibid.

81 O for a beaker full of the warm South,
Full of the true, the blushful Hippocrene,
With beaded bubbles winking at the brim,
And purple-stainèd mouth;
That I might drink, and leave the world unseen,
And with thee fade away into the forest dim.
'Ode to a Nightingale', st. 2, ibid.

82 Fade far away, dissolve, and quite forget
What thou among the leaves hast never known,
The weariness, the fever, and the fret
Here, where men sit and hear each other groan;
Where palsy shakes a few, sad, last grey hairs,
Where youth grows pale, and spectre-thin, and
    dies;
Where but to think is to be full of sorrow
And leaden-eyed despairs.
'Ode to a Nightingale', st. 3, ibid.

83 Tender is the night.
'Ode to a Nightingale', st. 4, ibid. The words were used by F.
SCOTT FITZGERALD as the title of his 1934 novel.

84 I cannot see what flowers are at my feet,
Nor what soft incense hangs upon the boughs,
But, in embalmèd darkness, guess each sweet.
'Ode to a Nightingale', st. 5, ibid.

85 Fast fading violets covered up in leaves;
And mid-May's eldest child,
The coming musk-rose, full of dewy wine,
The murmurous haunt of flies on summer eves.
'Ode to a Nightingale', st. 5, ibid.

86 Darkling I listen; and, for many a time
I have been half in love with easeful Death,
Called him soft names in many a musèd rhyme,
To take into the air my quiet breath;

Now more than ever seems it rich to die,
To cease upon the midnight with no pain.
'Ode to a Nightingale', st. 6, ibid.

87 Thou wast not born for death, immortal bird!
No hungry generations tread thee down;
The voice I hear this passing night was heard
In ancient days by emperor and clown:
Perhaps the self-same song that found a path
Through the sad heart of Ruth, when, sick for
  home,
She stood in tears amid the alien corn;
The same that oft-times hath
Charmed magic casements, opening on the foam
Of perilous seas, in faery lands forlorn.
'Ode to a Nightingale', st. 7, ibid.

88 Forlorn! the very word is like a bell
To toll me back from thee to my sole self!
Adieu! the fancy cannot cheat so well
As she is famed to do, deceiving elf.
'Ode to a Nightingale', st. 8, ibid.

89 Was it a vision, or a waking dream?
Fled is that music: – do I wake or sleep?
'Ode to a Nightingale', st. 8, ibid.

90 Thou still unravished bride of quietness,
Thou foster-child of silence and slow time.
'Ode on a Grecian Urn', st. 1, ibid. Opening lines of poem.

91 What men or gods are these? What maidens
  loth?
What mad pursuit? What struggle to escape?
What pipes and timbrels? What wild ecstasy?
'Ode on a Grecian Urn', st. 1, ibid.

92 Heard melodies are sweet, but those unheard
Are sweeter.
'Ode on a Grecian Urn', st. 2, ibid.

93 For ever wilt thou love, and she be fair!
'Ode on a Grecian Urn', st. 2, ibid.

94 For ever piping songs for ever new.
'Ode on a Grecian Urn', st. 3, ibid.

95 For ever warm and still to be enjoyed,
For ever panting, and for ever young;
All breathing human passion far above,
That leaves a heart high-sorrowful and cloyed,
A burning forehead, and a parching tongue.
'Ode on a Grecian Urn', st. 3, ibid.

96 Who are these coming to the sacrifice?
To what green altar, O mysterious priest,
Lead'st thou that heifer lowing at the skies,

And all her silken flanks with garlands dressed?
What little town by river or sea shore,
Or mountain-built with peaceful citadel,
Is emptied of this folk, this pious morn?
'Ode on a Grecian Urn', st. 4, ibid.

97 O Attic shape! Fair attitude!
'Ode on a Grecian Urn', st. 5, ibid.

98 'Beauty is truth, truth beauty', – that is all
Ye know on earth, and all ye need to know.
'Ode on a Grecian Urn', st. 5, ibid. Closing lines of poem.

99 Nor virgin-choir to make delicious moan
Upon the midnight hours.
'Ode to Psyche', st. 3, ibid.

100 A bright torch, and a casement ope at night,
To let the warm love in.
'Ode to Psyche', st. 5, ibid.

101 Ever let the fancy roam,
Pleasure never is at home.
'Fancy', ll. 1–2, ibid.

102 Souls of poets dead and gone,
What Elysium have ye known,
Happy field or mossy cavern,
Choicer than the Mermaid Tavern?
Have ye tippled drink more fine
Than mine host's Canary wine?
'Lines on the Mermaid Tavern', st. 1, ibid.

103 Season of mists and mellow fruitfulness,
Close bosom-friend of the maturing sun;
Conspiring with him how to load and bless
With fruit the vines that round the thatch-eaves
  run.
'To Autumn', st. 1, ibid.

104 Who hath not seen thee oft amid thy store?
Sometimes whoever seeks abroad may find
Thee sitting careless on a granary floor,
Thy hair soft-lifted by the winnowing wind;
Or on a half-reaped furrow sound asleep,
Drowsed with the fume of poppies, while thy hook
Spares the next swath and all its twinèd flowers.
'To Autumn', st. 2, ibid.

105 Where are the songs of Spring? Ay, where are
  they?
Think not of them, thou hast thy music too.
'To Autumn', st. 3, ibid.

106 No, no, go not to Lethe, neither twist
Wolf's-bane, tight-rooted, for its poisonous wine.
'Ode on Melancholy', st. 1, ibid.

107 But when the melancholy fit shall fall
Sudden from heaven like a weeping cloud,
That fosters the droop-headed flowers all,
And hides the green hill in an April shroud;
Then glut thy sorrow on a morning rose,
Or on the rainbow of the salt sand-wave,
Or on the wealth of globèd peonies;
Or if thy mistress some rich anger shows,
Emprison her soft hand, and let her rave,
And feed deep, deep upon her peerless eyes.
'Ode on Melancholy', st. 2, ibid.

108 She dwells with Beauty – Beauty that must
    die;
And Joy, whose hand is ever at his lips
Bidding adieu; and aching Pleasure nigh,
Turning to poison while the bee-mouth sips:
Ay, in the very temple of Delight
Veiled Melancholy has her sovran shrine,
Though seen of none save him whose strenuous
    tongue
Can burst Joy's grape against his palate fine;
His soul shall taste the sadness of her might,
And be among her cloudy trophies hung.
'Ode on Melancholy', st. 3, ibid.

109 Deep in the shady sadness of a vale
Far sunken from the healthy breath of morn,
Far from the fiery noon, and eve's one star,
Sat grey-haired Saturn, quiet as a stone.
'Hyperion: a Fragment', ibid. Opening lines of poem.

110 O how frail
To that large utterance of the early gods!
'Hyperion: a Fragment', bk 1, ll. 50–1, ibid.

111 O aching time! O moments big as years!
'Hyperion: a Fragment', bk 1, l. 64, ibid.

112 As when, upon a trancèd summer-night,
Those green-robed senators of mighty woods,
Tall oaks, branch-charmèd by the earnest stars,
Dream, and so dream all night without a stir.
'Hyperion: a Fragment', bk 1, ll. 72–5, ibid.

113 Sometimes eagle's wings,
Unseen before by gods or wondering men,
Darkened the place.
'Hyperion: a Fragment', bk 1, ll. 182–4, ibid.

114 And still they were the same bright, patient
    stars.
'Hyperion: a Fragment', bk 1, l. 353, ibid.

115 Knowledge enormous makes a god of me.
'Hyperion: a Fragment', bk 3, l. 113, ibid.

116 'If I should die,' said I to myself, 'I have left no immortal work behind me – nothing to make my friends proud of my memory – but I have loved the principle of beauty in all things, and if I had had time I would have made myself remembered.'
Letter to his fiancée Fanny Brawne, February 1820, publ. in *The Letters of John Keats*, vol. 2, no. 231 (ed. H. E. Rollins, 1958). Written while ill from tuberculosis.

117 Health is my expected heaven.
Letter to Fanny Brawne, *c.* 1 March 1820, ibid., vol. 2, no. 239

118 My imagination is a monastery and I am its monk.
Letter to P. B. SHELLEY, 16 August 1820, ibid., vol. 2, no. 285

119 Land and sea, weakness and decline are great separators, but death is the great divorcer for ever.
Letter, 30 September 1820, ibid., vol. 2, no. 302. Written shortly after embarking from England on his last journey to Italy.

120 I can scarcely bid you goodbye, even in a letter. I always made an awkward bow.
Letter, 30 November 1820, ibid., vol. 2, no. 310. Last words of the last letter sent by Keats. Two weeks earlier, desperately ill with tuberculosis, the poet had arrived in Rome, where he died 23 February 1821.

121 I shall soon be laid in the quiet grave – thank God for the quiet grave – O! I can feel the cold earth upon me – the daisies growing over me – O for this quiet – it will be my first.
Quoted by Joseph Severn in letter, 6 March 1821, publ. in *The Letters of John Keats*, vol. 2, no. 318 (ed. H. E. Rollins, 1958)

122 Here Lies One
Whose Name was writ in Water.
'Epitaph for Himself' (1821), publ. in *Life, Letters and Literary Remains of John Keats*, vol. 2 (1848). Keats's epitaph is inscribed on his grave in the English cemetery in Rome. A few days before he died, the poet stipulated that there should be no mention of his name or country on the headstone. It is reported that he had in mind lines from the play by BEAUMONT AND FLETCHER, *Philaster, or Love Lies A-Bleeding* (1609): 'All your better deeds/Shall be in water writ, but this in marble.' See also SHAKESPEARE: HENRY VIII 15 for another possible source.

John Keble
(1792–1866)
English cleric and poet

His sermon 'National Apostasy' (1833) gave inspiration for the Oxford Movement which advocated a return to High Church ideals. He was Professor of Poetry at Oxford (1831–41) and best known for his book of verse, The Christian Year *(1827).*

1 New every morning is the love
Our wakening and uprising prove;
Through sleep and darkness safely brought,
Restored to life, and power, and thought.
The Christian Year, 'Morning', st. 1 (1827)

2 The trivial round, the common task,
Would furnish all we ought to ask;
Room to deny ourselves; a road
To bring us, daily, nearer God.
Ibid., 'Morning' , st. 6

3 Blessed are the pure in heart,
For they shall see our God,
The secret of the Lord is theirs,
Their soul is Christ's abode.
Ibid., 'The Purification', st. 1

Brian Keenan
(b. 1950)
Irish teacher and author

Kidnapped while a lecturer at the American University in Beirut, he spent nearly five years (1986–90) held captive by a fundamentalist Shi'ite group, as recounted in An Evil Cradling *(1992).*

1 Hostage is a crucifying aloneness. It is a silent, screaming slide into the bowels of ultimate despair. Hostage is a man hanging by his fingernails over the edge of chaos, feeling his fingers slowly straightening. Hostage is the humiliating stripping away of every sense and fibre of body and mind and spirit that make us what we are. Hostage is a mutant creation filled with fear, self-loathing, guilt and death-wishing. But he is a man, a rare, unique and beautiful creation of which these things are no part.
News conference, Dublin, 30 August 1990, quoted in the *Independent* 31 August 1990. Referring to his four-and-a-half-year ordeal as a hostage.

Garrison Keillor
(b. 1942)
US broadcaster and author

His wry and laconic tales of Lake Wobegon, based on his memories of semi-rural Minnesota, were first heard on his live, weekly show on National Public Radio, 'A Prairie Home Companion' (from 1974).

1 It has been a quiet week in Lake Wobegon.
A Prairie Home Companion (radio show, from 1974). Opening words of each broadcast.

2 Lake Wobegon . . . where all the women are strong, all the men are good-looking, and all the children are above average.
Ibid.

3 Nothing you do for children is ever wasted. They seem not to notice us, hovering, averting our eyes, and they seldom offer thanks, but what we do for them is never wasted.
Leaving Home, 'Easter' (1987)

4 Humor, a good sense of it, is to Americans what manhood is to Spaniards and we will go to great lengths to prove it. Experiments with laboratory rats have shown that, if one psychologist in the room laughs at something a rat does, all of the other psychologists in the room will laugh equally. Nobody wants to be left holding the joke.
We Are Still Married, Introduction (1989)

5 Even in a time of elephantine vanity and greed, one never has to look far to see the campfires of gentle people.
Ibid., 'The Meaning of Life'

Helen Keller
(1880–1968)
US author and lecturer

Blind and deaf since infancy, she devoted her life to campaigning and raising funds for the deaf and blind, as related in The Story of My Life *(1902) and other books.*

1 There is no king who has not had a slave among his ancestors, and no slave who has not had a king among his.
The Story of My Life, pt 1, ch. 1 (1902)

2 Toleration is the greatest gift of the mind; it requires the same effort of the brain that it takes to balance oneself on a bicycle.
Ibid., pt 3, ch. 2

3 Science may have found a cure for most evils; but it has found no remedy for the worst of them all – the apathy of human beings.
My Religion, pt 1, ch. 6 (1927)

David Kelly
(1944–2003)
British scientist

An expert microbiologist, he was an adviser on biological warfare in Iraq 1994–99, and later Chief Scientific Officer and Senior Adviser to the Proliferation and Arms Control Secretariat of the Ministry of Defence.

1 I will probably be found dead in the woods.

Remark to UN diplomat David Broucher, in Geneva, 27 February, 2003, quoted in the *Guardian* 22 August 2003. Kelly was found dead in July 2003 in woods on Harrowdown Hill, Oxfordshire, after he had been revealed as the source for a BBC report stating that the British government had 'sexed up' intelligence documents about Iraq's weaponry.

Petra Kelly

(1947–92)

German politician

Originally Petra Lehmann. She co-founded Die Grünen (Green Party) in 1979, which entered the Bundestag in 1983 with twenty-eight seats. She died in an apparent joint suicide pact with her lover, an ex-general.

1 We, the generation that faces the next century, can add the ... solemn injunction 'If we don't do the impossible, we shall be faced with the unthinkable'.

Quoted in *Vanity Fair* January 1993

Thomas à Kempis

See under Thomas

Thomas Ken

See HYMNS AND CAROLS 21, 58

Thomas Keneally

(b. 1935)

Australian novelist

His 'faction' novels chart critical moments in history, as in Confederates *(1979). His Holocaust tale* Schindler's Ark *(1982) was filmed as* Schindler's List *(1993). He is a leading figure in the Australian Republican Movement.*

1 We have found that it *is* possible for Australians to have literary ideas about the place, that Australia is not outside the universe. In short Australia – which used to have one unifying rite, cricket – has now become pluralist. I cannot but predict it will be a disaster for Australian cricket.

Summer Days, 'The Cyclical Supremacy of Australia in World Cricket' (1981)

Florynce R. Kennedy

(1916–2000)

US lawyer and civil rights activist

Florynce Rae Kennedy. She championed the rights of African-Americans, women, the poor, homosexuals and prostitutes. In 1966 she founded the Media Workshop to combat racism in the media.

1 Niggerization is the result of oppression – and it doesn't just apply to the black people. Old people, poor people, and students can also get niggerized.

Quoted by GLORIA STEINEM, in 'The Verbal Karate of Florynce R. Kennedy, Esq.', publ. in *Ms.* March 1973

2 If men could get pregnant, abortion would be a sacrament.

Ibid.

3 There are very few jobs that actually require a penis or vagina. All other jobs should be open to everybody.

Quoted by John Brady, in 'Freelancer with No Time to Write', publ. in *Writer's Digest* February 1974

G. A. Studdert Kennedy

(1883–1929)

British cleric and poet

(Rev.) Geoffrey Anketell Studdert Kennedy. He was awarded the Military Cross for his service as chaplain in the First World War and later became chaplain to GEORGE V. *As 'Woodbine Willie', he published* Rough Rhymes of a Padre *(1918).*

1 Waste of Blood, and waste of Tears,
Waste of youth's most precious years,
Waste of ways the saints have trod,
Waste of Glory, waste of God,
War!

'Waste', publ. in *More Rough Rhymes of a Padre* (1919) by 'Woodbine Willie'

Jimmy Kennedy

(1902–84)

British songwriter

Before teaming up with Michael Carr (see below), he had hits with 'The Teddy Bears' Picnic' (1932) and 'The Isle of Capri' (1934), sung by Gracie Fields. He co-wrote 'Red Sails in the Sunset' (1935) and had success in America with 'South of the Border' (1940).

1 If you go down in the woods today
You're sure of a big surprise
If you go down in the woods today
You'd better go in disguise
For every Bear that ever there was
Will gather there for certain because,
Today's the day the Teddy Bears have their Picnic.

'Teddy Bears' Picnic' (song, 1932). The words, set to a 1904 tune by John W. Bratton, were supposed to be about THEODORE ROOSEVELT taking time off from his presidential campaigning to go bear-hunting. The song was recorded by Henry Hall in 1933, quickly becoming a children's classic.

2 In out in out shake it all about,
You do the Hokey Cokey
And you turn around,
That's what it's all about.

'Hokey Cokey' (song, 1942). The 'Cockney' lyrics were set to a traditional tune.

Jimmy Kennedy
(1902–84)
Michael Carr
(1904–68)
British songwriters

Their string of hits began in 1935 and ranged from cowboy songs to show tunes. Carr, born Maurice Cohen, later composed 'Man of Mystery' (1960) and 'Kon-Tiki' (1961) for the Shadows.

1 We're going to hang out our washing on the Siegfried Line.

'We're Going to Hang Out Our Washing on the Siegfried Line' (song, 1939). This 'Tipperary' of the Second World War was the last of the numerous hits enjoyed by the Kennedy/Carr partnership. The Siegfried Line was Germany's main belt of militarization on its western frontier in 1939.

John F. Kennedy
(1917–63)
US politician and president

John Fitzgerald Kennedy. A Democrat, he was, in 1960, the first Roman Catholic and youngest man to become President. Popular for his wit, charm and youth, he was assassinated in Dallas. Said by one senator to combine the best qualities of ELVIS PRESLEY *and* FRANKLIN D. ROOSEVELT, *he called himself 'an idealist without illusions'.*

1 I just received the following wire from my generous Daddy – 'Dear Jack, Don't buy a single vote more than is necessary. I'll be damned if I'm going to pay for a landslide.'

Speech at Gridiron Dinner, Washington DC, 15 March 1958, quoted in *The Wit of President Kennedy*, 'The Family' (1964) by Bill Adler

2 We stand today on the edge of a new frontier – the frontier of the 1960s – a frontier of unknown opportunities and perils – a frontier of unfulfilled hopes and threats ... The New Frontier of which I speak is not a set of promises – it is a set of challenges.

Acceptance speech at the Democratic Convention, Los Angeles, 15 July 1960, publ. in *The Penguin Book of Twentieth-*

Century Speeches (ed. Brian MacArthur, 1999). Theodore C. Sorensen in his biography *Kennedy* (1965) took credit for drafting the speech.

3 Do you realize the responsibility I carry? I'm the only person between Nixon and the White House.

Teasing remark to a supporter during the 1960 election campaign, quoted in *Kennedy*, pt 2, ch. 7 (1965) by Theodore C. Sorensen. In the event, NIXON won 49.6 per cent of the total vote, giving Kennedy the narrowest victory in a presidential election since 1888.

4 To those people in the huts and villages across the globe struggling to break the bonds of mass misery, we pledge our best efforts to help them help themselves, for whatever period is required – not because the Communists may be doing it, not because we seek their votes, but because it is right. If a free society cannot help the many who are poor, it cannot save the few who are rich.

Inaugural address, Washington DC, 20 January 1961, publ. in *The Penguin Book of Twentieth-Century Speeches* (ed. Brian MacArthur, 1999)

5 We dare not tempt them with weakness. For only when our arms are sufficient beyond doubt can we be certain beyond doubt that they will never be employed.

Inaugural address, Washington DC, 20 January 1961, ibid.

6 Let us never negotiate out of fear. But let us never fear to negotiate.

Inaugural address, Washington DC, 20 January 1961, ibid.

7 All this will not be finished in the first 100 days. Nor will it be finished in the first 1,000 days, nor in the life of this Administration, nor even perhaps in our lifetime on this planet. But let us begin.

Inaugural address, Washington DC, 20 January 1961, ibid. On his reform programme. Kennedy's administration lasted a little over 1,000 days.

8 And so, my fellow Americans, ask not what your country can do for you – ask what you can do for your country. My fellow citizens of the world, ask not what America will do for you, but what together we can do for the freedom of man.

Inaugural address, Washington DC, 20 January 1961, ibid. Kennedy had previously expressed the same idea in a televised campaign address, 20 September 1960. See OLIVER WENDELL HOLMES JR 1.

9 I do not think it altogether inappropriate to introduce myself to this audience. I am the man who accompanied Jacqueline Kennedy to Paris, and I have enjoyed it.

Speech at SHAPE Headquarters, Paris, 2 June 1961, publ. in

Public Papers of the Presidents of the United States: John F. Kennedy, 1961. Referring to the massive publicity generated by the Kennedys' visit to Paris – focused particularly on Jackie Kennedy.

10 Conformity is the jailer of freedom and the enemy of growth.

Address to UN General Assembly, 25 September 1961, ibid.

11 Washington is a city of Southern efficiency and Northern charm.

Remark in November 1961, quoted in *Portrait of a President* (1962) by William Manchester

12 We must use time as a tool, not as a couch.

Quoted in the *Observer* 10 December 1961

13 We test and then they test and we have to test again. And you build up until somebody uses them.

Remark in 1961, quoted in *A Thousand Days*, ch. 17 (1965) by ARTHUR M. SCHLESINGER JR

14 Those who make peaceful revolution impossible will make violent revolution inevitable.

Speech at the White House, 13 March 1962, publ. in *Public Papers of the Presidents of the United States: John F. Kennedy, 1962.* Addressing diplomats representing Latin American republics.

15 I think this is the most extraordinary collection of talent, of human knowledge, that has ever been gathered together at the White House – with the possible exception of when Thomas Jefferson dined alone.

Remark at a dinner for Nobel prize-winners, 29 April 1962, Washington DC, publ. in *Public Papers of the Presidents of the United States: John F. Kennedy, 1962*

16 If we cannot end now our differences, at least we can help make the world safe for diversity.

Commencement address, American University, Washington DC, 10 June 1963, publ. in *Public Papers of the Presidents of the United States: John F. Kennedy, 1963.* Referring to Soviet-American relations.

17 No one has been barred on account of his race from fighting or dying for America – there are no 'white' or 'colored' signs on the foxholes or grave-yards of battle.

Message to Congress, 19 June 1963, quoted in the *New York Times* 20 June 1963. Referring to the proposed civil rights bill.

18 All free men, wherever they may live, are citizens of Berlin. And therefore, as a free man, I take pride in the words 'Ich bin ein Berliner'.

Speech in West Berlin, 26 June 1963, publ. in *The Penguin Book of Twentieth-Century Speeches* (ed. Brian MacArthur, 1999). Recalling CICERO 1. Kennedy should more correctly

have said *Ich bin Berliner*; *ein Berliner* suggests a local type of doughnut.

19 When power leads man towards arrogance, poetry reminds him of his limitations. When power narrows the area of man's concern, poetry reminds him of the richness and diversity of existence. When power corrupts, poetry cleanses.

Speech at Amherst College, 26 October 1963, quoted in the *New York Times* 27 October 1963. The occasion of Kennedy's last major public address was the dedication of the Robert Frost Library at the college. Previously, in a speech at Harvard, 14 June 1956, Kennedy had said: 'If more politicians knew poetry, and more poets knew politics, I am convinced the world would be a little better place to live.'

20 In free society art is not a weapon . . . Artists are not engineers of the soul.

Speech at Amherst College, 26 October 1963, ibid. The phrase 'Engineers of human souls' had been previously used in the 1930s by JOSEF STALIN; see also MAXIM GORKY 1.

21 We in this country, in this generation, are – by destiny rather than choice – the watchmen on the walls of world freedom.

Address prepared for the Dallas luncheon on the day he was assassinated, 22 November 1963, publ. in *Public Papers of the Presidents of the United States: John F. Kennedy, 1963*

22 It was involuntary. They sank my boat.

Quoted in *A Thousand Days*, ch. 4 (1965) by ARTHUR M. SCHLESINGER JR. Answer to small boy who asked how he became a war hero.

23 Domestic policy can only defeat us; foreign policy can kill us.

Quoted in *The Imperial Presidency*, ch. 11, sect. 7 (1973) by ARTHUR M. SCHLESINGER JR

24 You never know what's hit you. A gunshot is the perfect way.

Quoted in *The Kennedys*, pt 3, ch. 3 (1984) by Peter Collier and David Horowitz. Remark when asked how he would choose to die.

25 Forgive your enemies, but never forget their names.

Attributed. The quote has also been ascribed to ROBERT F. KENNEDY.

Joseph P. Kennedy

(1888–1969)

US tycoon and diplomat

Joseph Patrick Kennedy. A self-made millionaire by the age of thirty, he was Ambassador to Britain (1937–40) and sub-sequently concentrated on grooming his sons JOHN F. KEN-NEDY, ROBERT F. KENNEDY *and Edward for political careers.*

1 When the going gets tough, the tough get going.
Quoted in *Honey Fitz*, ch. 20 (1962) by J. H. Cutler. The quotation has also been ascribed to US football coach Knute Rockne (1888–1931).

Robert F. Kennedy

(1925–68)

US politician and lawyer

Robert Francis Kennedy. He was presidential campaign manager for his brother JOHN F. KENNEDY *and as Attorney-General (1961–4) promoted the Civil Rights Act of 1964. He was assassinated while campaigning for presidential nomination. The journalist Murray Kempton called him 'the highest ranking withdrawn adolescent since Alexander Hamilton in 1794'.*

1 Every society gets the kind of criminal it deserves. What is equally true is that every community gets the kind of law enforcement it insists on.
The Pursuit of Justice, pt 3, 'Eradicating Free Enterprise in Organized Crime' (1964)

2 One-fifth of the people are against everything all the time.
Speech at University of Pennsylvania, 6 May 1964, quoted in the *Philadelphia Inquirer* 7 May 1964

Jack Kerouac

(1922–69)

US author

Born Jean Louis Kerouac. His novel On the Road *(1957) established him as the voice of the Beat generation. 'My work comprises one vast book like Proust's* Remembrance of Things Past,*' he once said, 'except that my remembrances are written on the run instead of afterwards in a sickbed.'*

1 All of life is a foreign country.
Letter, 24 June 1949, publ. in *The Beat Vision: A Primary Sourcebook* (ed. Arthur and Kit Knight, 1987)

2 But then they danced down the street like dingledodies, and I shambled after as I've been doing all my life after people who interest me, because the only people for me are the mad ones, the ones who are mad to live, mad to talk, mad to be saved, desirous of everything at the same time, the ones who never yawn or say a commonplace thing, but burn, burn, burn, like fabulous yellow roman candles exploding like spiders across the stars and in the middle you see the blue centerlight pop and everybody goes 'Awww!'
On the Road, pt 1, ch. 1 (1957). Narrated by Sal Paradise.

3 Standing in front of everybody, ragged and broken and idiotic, right under the lightbulbs, his bony mad face covered with sweat and throbbing veins, saying, 'Yes, yes, yes,' as though tremendous revelations were pouring into him all the time now, and I am convinced they were, and the others suspected as much and were frightened. He was BEAT – the root, the soul of Beatific.
Ibid., pt 3, ch. 3. Of Dean Moriarty, whose character was modelled on that of NEAL CASSADY.

4 John Clellon Holmes . . . and I were sitting around trying to think up the meaning of the Lost Generation and the subsequent Existentialism and I said, 'You know, this is really a beat generation' and he leapt up and said 'That's it, that's right!'
Interview in *Playboy* June 1959, explaining the origin of the label 'Beat Generation'. On another occasion, Kerouac ascribed the expression's origin to Herbert Huncke, a Times Square hustler he'd met a decade earlier. The term also appeared as the title of an article by Holmes and in his novel, *Go* (1952). See JOHN CLELLON HOLMES 1.

Jean Kerr

(1923–2003)

US author and playwright

In her own words, she wrote 'realistic comedy' set in an affluent suburbia, for example the play Mary, Mary *(1961). She was married to* WALTER KERR, *with whom she sometimes collaborated.*

1 As someone pointed out recently, if you can keep your head when all about you are losing theirs, it's just possible you haven't grasped the situation.
Please Don't Eat the Daisies, Introduction (1957)

2 I'm tired of all this nonsense about beauty being only skin-deep. That's deep enough. What do you want – an adorable pancreas?
The Snake Has All the Lines, 'Mirror, Mirror on the Wall' (1958)

3 Hope is the feeling you have that the feeling you have isn't permanent.
Finishing Touches, Act 3 (1973). Spoken by Felicia.

Walter Kerr

(1913–96)

US critic

Drama critic with the New York Herald Tribune (1951–66) and New York Times (1966–83), he was praised by KENNETH TYNAN *for 'vaulting over the barrier we erect between "serious" and "light" criticism'.*

1 Me no Leica.
Attributed, in *No Turn Unstoned*, ch. 5 (1982) by Diana Rigg. The words are said to be Kerr's response to *I Am A Camera*

(1951), John Van Druten's dramatization of 'Sally Bowles' from *Goodbye to Berlin* by CHRISTOPHER ISHERWOOD.

Ken Kesey
(1935–2001)
US author

His experience as an aide in a mental hospital formed the basis of his bestselling satirical novel One Flew Over the Cuckoo's Nest *(1962). He later became leader of the 'Merry Pranksters', whose exploits were recorded in* The Electric Kool-Aid Acid Test *(1968) by* TOM WOLFE.

1 I'd rather be a lightning rod than a seismograph.
Quoted in *The Electric Kool-Aid Acid Test*, ch. 1 (1968) by TOM WOLFE

2 You're either on the bus or off the bus. If you're on the bus, and you get left behind, then you'll find it again. If you're off the bus in the first place – then it won't make a damn.
Quoted ibid., ch. 6

Ellen Key
(1849–1926)
Swedish author and feminist

She wrote on a range of women's issues, most famously in The Century of the Child *(1900).*

1 Art, that great undogmatized church.
The Renaissance of Motherhood, pt 2, ch. 1 (1914)

Francis Scott Key
(1779–1843)
US lawyer

He owes his fame to 'The Star-Spangled Banner', which he wrote after witnessing the defence of Fort McHenry by American forces against the British in 1814.

1 'Tis the star-spangled banner; O long may it wave
O'er the land of the free, and the home of the brave!
'The Star-Spangled Banner', publ. in the *Baltimore Patriot* 20 September 1814. The flag flown over Fort McHenry, outside Baltimore, measured thirty by forty-two feet so that the British would 'have no trouble in seeing it from a distance'. The poem was officially adopted as the national anthem of the USA in 1931.

John Maynard Keynes
(1883–1946)
British economist

Baron Keynes of Tilton. Regarding himself as 'a voice crying in the wilderness' who 'had, therefore, to cry loudly', he was a pioneer of macroeconomics, arguing in favour of increased government spending as a cure for rising unemployment. His major works are A Treatise on Money *(1930) and* The General Theory of Employment, Interest and Money *(1936).*

1 The disruptive powers of excessive national fecundity may have played a greater part in bursting the bonds of convention than either the power of ideas or the errors of autocracy.
The Economic Consequences of the Peace, ch. 2, sect. 1 (1919)

2 Lenin was certainly right. There is no subtler, no surer means of overturning the existing basis of society than to debauch the currency. The process engages all the hidden forces of economic law on the side of destruction, and does it in a manner which not one man in a million is able to diagnose.
Ibid., ch. 6. Keynes repeated this assertion in *Essays in Persuasion*, pt 2, sect. 1 (1931): 'Lenin is said to have declared that the best way to destroy the capitalist system was to debauch the currency. By a continuing process of inflation governments can confiscate, secretly and unobserved, an important part of the wealth of their citizens.' The words attributed to LENIN have never been found in his writings.

3 *Long run* is a misleading guide to current affairs. *In the long run* we are all dead.
A Tract on Monetary Reform, ch. 3 (1923)

4 Marxian Socialism must always remain a portent to the historians of Opinion – how a doctrine so illogical and so dull can have exercised so powerful and enduring an influence over the minds of men, and, through them, the events of history.
Ibid., ch. 3

5 I think that Capitalism, wisely managed, can probably be made more efficient for attaining economic ends than any alternative system yet in sight, but that in itself it is in many ways extremely objectionable.
Ibid., ch. 5

6 A study of the history of opinion is a necessary preliminary to the emancipation of the mind. I do not know which makes a man more conservative – to know nothing but the present, or nothing but the past.
Essays in Persuasion, pt. 4, 'The End of Laissez-Faire', sect. 1 (1931)

7 The Labour Party ... is a class party, and the class is not my class ... The *class* war will find me on the side of the educated *bourgeoisie*.
Essays in Persuasion, pt 4, 'Am I a Liberal?' (1931)

8 Most men love money and security more, and creation and construction less, as they get older.
Ibid., pt 5, 'Clissold'

9 For at least another hundred years we must pretend to ourselves and to every one that fair is foul and foul is fair; for foul is useful and fair is not. Avarice and usury and precaution must be our gods for a little longer still. For only they can lead us out of the tunnel of economic necessity into daylight.
Ibid., pt 5, 'Economic Possibilities for Our Grandchildren'. Keynes argued that the 'detestable ... love of money' and other vices of greed must continue until the economy has grown enough to satisfy human wants and provide the potential for removing poverty.

10 If economists could manage to get themselves thought of as humble, competent people on a level with dentists, that would be splendid!
Ibid., pt 5, 'Economic Possibilities for Our Grandchildren'. Last words of book.

11 The decadent international but individualistic capitalism in the hands of which we found ourselves after the war is not a success. It is not intelligent. It is not beautiful. It is not just. It is not virtuous. And it doesn't deliver the goods.
'National Self-Sufficiency', sect. 3 (1933), repr. in *Collected Writings*, vol. 21 (ed. Donald Moggridge, 1982)

12 The difficulty lies, not in the new ideas, but in escaping from the old ones, which ramify, for those brought up as most of us have been, into every corner of our minds.
The General Theory of Employment, Interest and Money, Preface (1936)

13 It is better that a man should tyrannise over his bank balance than over his fellow-citizens and whilst the former is sometimes denounced as being but a means to the latter, sometimes at least it is an alternative.
Ibid., bk 6, ch. 24, sect. 1

14 The ideas of economists and political philosophers, both when they are right and when they are wrong, are more powerful than is commonly understood. Indeed the world is ruled by little else. Practical men, who believe themselves to be quite exempt from any intellectual influence, are usually the slaves of some defunct economist.
Ibid., bk 6, ch. 24, sect. 5

15 It is ideas, not vested interests, which are dangerous for good or evil.
Ibid. bk 6, ch. 24, sect. 5. Last words of book.

16 The day is not far off when the economic problem will take the back seat where it belongs, and the arena of the heart and the head will be occupied or reoccupied, by our real problems – the problems of life and of human relations, of creation and behaviour and religion.
First Annual Report of the Arts Council (1945–6)

Omar Khayyám
(c. 1048–1122)
Persian astronomer and poet

His poetry was little known in the West until the publication of The Rubáiyát of Omar Khayyám *(1859), a translation by Edward Fitzgerald of the robáiyát (quatrains) traditionally attributed to him. Its popularity contributed to the possibly erroneous perception of him as a hedonist. He was responsible for reforming the Muslim calendar.*

1 Awake! for morning in the bowl of night
Has flung the stone that puts the stars to flight:
And lo! the hunter of the east has caught
The sultan's turret in a noose of light.
The Rubáiyát of Omar Khayyám, st. 1 (transl. Edward Fitzgerald, first edn, 1859)

2 Come, fill the cup, and in the fire of spring
The winter garment of repentance fling:
The bird of time has but a little way
To fly – and lo! the bird is on the wing.
Ibid., st. 7

3 Here with a loaf of bread beneath the bough,
A flask of wine, a book of verse – and thou
Beside me singing in the wilderness –
And wilderness is paradise enow.
Ibid., st. 11

4 Oh, the brave music of a distant drum!
Ibid., st. 12

5 I sometimes think that never blows so red
The rose as where some buried Caesar bled.
That every hyacinth the garden wears
Dropped in her lap from some once lovely
    head.
Ibid., st. 18

6 Ah, my belovèd, fill the cup that clears
Today of past regrets and future fears:
Tomorrow? – Why, tomorrow I may be
Myself with yesterday's seven thousand years.
Ibid., st. 20

7 Lo! some we loved, the loveliest and best
That Time and Fate of all their vintage pressed,
Have drunk their cup a round or two before,
And one by one crept silently to rest.
Ibid., st. 21

8 Ah, make the most of what we yet may spend,
Before we too into the dust descend.
Dust into dust, and under dust, to lie,
Sans wine, sans song, sans singer, and – sans end!
Ibid., st. 23

9 Oh, come with old Khayyám, and leave the wise
To talk; one thing is certain, that life flies;
One thing is certain, and the rest is lies;
The flower that once hath blown for ever dies.
Ibid., st. 26

10 Myself when young did eagerly frequent
Doctor and saint, and heard great argument
About it and about: but evermore
Came out by the same door as in I went.
Ibid., st. 27

11 You know, my friends, how long since in my
   house
For a new marriage I did make carouse:
Divorced old barren reason from my bed,
And took the daughter of the vine to spouse.
Ibid., st. 40

12 The grape that can with logic absolute
The two-and-seventy jarring sects confute.
Ibid., st. 43

13 For in and out, above, about, below,
'Tis nothing but a magic shadow-show,
Played in a box whose candle is the sun,
Round which we phantom figures come and go.
Ibid., st. 46

14 'Tis all a chequer-board of nights and days
Where destiny with men for pieces plays:
Hither and thither moves, and mates, and slays,
And one by one back in the closet lays.
Ibid., st. 49

15 The moving finger writes; and, having writ,
Moves on: nor all thy piety nor wit

Shall lure it back to cancel half a line,
Nor all thy tears wash out a word of it.
Ibid., st. 51

16 And that inverted bowl we call the sky,
Whereunder crawling cooped we live and die,
Lift not thy hands to *it* for help – for *it*
Rolls impotently on as thou or I.
Ibid., st. 52

17 Who *is* the potter, pray, and who the pot?
Ibid., st. 60

18 Alas, that spring should vanish with the rose!
That youth's sweet-scented manuscript should
   close.
Ibid., st. 72

19 Ah, moon of my delight who know'st no wane.
Ibid., st. 74

20 And when Thyself with shining foot shall pass
Among the guests star-scattered on the grass,
And in thy joyous errand reach the spot
Where I made one – turn down an empty glass!
Ibid., st. 75

21 Each morn a thousand roses brings, you say;
Yes, but where leaves the rose of yesterday?
Ibid., st. 9 (transl. Edward Fitzgerald, fourth edn 1879)

22 Drink! for you know not whence you came nor
   why:
Drink! for you know not why you go, nor where.
Ibid., st. 74 (fourth edn, 1879)

Ayatollah Ruhollah Khomeini
(1900–89)
Iranian religious and political leader

*Originally Ruhollah Musawi. After the Iranian Revolution of
1979, he established a fundamentalist Islamic republic and
was named Iran's political and religious leader for life.*

1 I would like to inform all the intrepid Muslims in
the world that the author of the book entitled *The
Satanic Verses*, which has been compiled, printed
and published in opposition to Islam, the prophet
and the Qur'an, as well as those publishers who were
aware of its contents, have been declared *madhur el
dam* ['those whose blood must be shed']. I call on all
zealous Muslims to execute them quickly, wherever
they find them, so that no one will dare to insult

Islam again. Whoever is killed in this path will be regarded as a martyr.

Fatwa, or legal ruling, issued 14 February 1989, quoted in *A Satanic Affair*, ch. 5 (1990) by Malise Ruthven

Nikita Khrushchev
(1894–1971)
Soviet politician and premier

During his terms as First Secretary of the Communist Party (1953–64) and Premier (1958–64), he broke with Stalinist policies and laid the basis for liberalizing Soviet Communism and for the independence of European Communist parties.

1 If anyone believes that our smiles involve abandonment of the teaching of Marx, Engels and Lenin he deceives himself. Those who wait for that must wait until a shrimp learns to whistle.

Speech in Moscow, 17 September 1955, quoted in the *New York Times* 18 September 1955

2 Comrades! We must abolish the cult of the individual decisively, once and for all.

Speech to the secret session of the Twentieth Congress of the Soviet Communist Party, 25 February 1956, quoted in the *Manchester Guardian* 11 June 1956. Khrushchev used the occasion to identify STALIN as the chief exponent of the cult of the individual (also translated 'cult of the personality') by 'the glorification of his own person'. See also V. I. LENIN 9.

3 Everyone can err, but Stalin considered that he never erred, that he was always right. He never acknowledged to anyone that he made any mistake, large or small, despite the fact that he made not a few mistakes in the matter of theory and in his practical activity.

Speech to the Twentieth Congress of the Soviet Communist Party, February 1956, quoted in *Stalin*, pt 2, ch. 6 (ed. T. H. Rigby, 1966)

4 It doesn't depend on you whether or not we exist. If you don't like us, don't accept our invitations and don't invite us to come to see you. Whether you like it or not, history is on our side. We will bury you.

Speech to Western diplomats at the Kremlin, 18 November 1956, quoted in *The Times* 19 November 1956. Khrushchev later explained this remark as an idiomatic expression to mean 'we will outlive you' (i.e. Communism will triumph). On another occasion, 24 August 1963, addressing a group of Westerners in Split, Yugoslavia, he referred to his controversial statement: 'Of course we will not bury you with a shovel. Your own working class will bury you.'

5 If one cannot catch a bird of paradise, better take a wet hen.

Quoted in *Time* 6 January 1958

6 When you are skinning your customers you should leave some skin on to grow again so that you can skin them again.

Quoted in the *Observer* 28 May 1961. Advice to British businessmen.

7 They talk about who won and who lost. Human reason won. Mankind won.

Quoted in the *Observer* 11 November 1962. Referring to the Cuban missile crisis.

8 Politicians are the same all over: they promise to build a bridge even where there is no river.

Quoted in the *New York Herald-Tribune* 22 August 1963. Khrushchev used the same figure of speech at a press conference, Glen Cove, New York, October 1960.

9 He who cannot eat horsemeat need not do so. Let him eat pork. But he who cannot eat pork, let him eat horsemeat. It's simply a question of taste.

New York World-Telegram and Sun 25 August 1964

10 If we were to promise people nothing better than only revolution, they would scratch their heads and say: 'Is it not better to have good goulash?'

Quoted in the *Observer* 27 December 1964

Søren Kierkegaard
(1813–55)
Danish philosopher and theologian

One of the founders of existentialism, he resisted the prevailing Hegelian philosophy of his time and stressed the importance of individual choice and experience, which was also reflected in his attitude to organized Christianity. His works include Either/Or *(1846) and* The Sickness Unto Death *(1849).*

1 Adversity draws men together and produces beauty and harmony in life's relationships, just as the cold of winter produces ice-flowers on the window-panes, which vanish with the warmth.

Journal entry, January 1836, publ. in *The Journals of Søren Kierkegaard: A Selection*, no. 37 (ed./transl. Alexander Dru, 1938)

2 The paradox is really the *pathos* of intellectual life and just as only great souls are exposed to passions it is only the great thinker who is exposed to what I call paradoxes, which are nothing else than grandiose thoughts in embryo.

Journal entry, 1838, ibid., no. 206

3 God creates out of *nothing*, wonderful, you say: yes, to be sure, but he does what is still more wonderful: he makes saints out of sinners.

Journal entry, 1838, ibid., no. 209

4 Concepts, like individuals, have their histories and are just as incapable of withstanding the ravages of time as are individuals. But in and through all this they retain a kind of homesickness for the scenes of their childhood.
The Concept of Irony, Introduction to pt 1 (1841, transl. 1966)

5 It belongs to the imperfection of everything human that man can only attain his desire by passing through its opposite.
Journal entry, 1841, publ. in *The Journals of Søren Kierkegaard: A Selection*, no. 358 (ed./transl. Alexander Dru, 1938)

6 The more a man can forget, the greater the number of metamorphoses which his life can undergo, the more he can remember the more divine his life becomes.
Journal entry, 1842, ibid., no. 429

7 People commonly travel the world over to see rivers and mountains, new stars, garish birds, freak fish, grotesque breeds of human; they fall into an animal stupor that gapes at existence and they think they have seen something.
Fear and Trembling, 'Preamble from the Heart' (1843, transl. 1985)

8 Faith is the highest passion in a human being. Many in every generation may not come that far, but none comes further.
Ibid., Epilogue

9 What is a poet? An unhappy person who conceals profound anguish in his heart but whose lips are so formed that as sighs and cries pass over them they sound like beautiful music.
Either/Or, vol. 1, 'Diapsalmata' (1843, transl. 1987). Opening lines.

10 I feel as if I were a piece in a game of chess, when my opponent says of it: That piece cannot be moved.
Ibid., vol. 1, 'Diapsalmata'

11 Most men pursue pleasure with such breathless haste that they hurry past it.
Ibid., vol. 1, 'Diapsalmata'

12 Since boredom advances and boredom is the root of all evil, no wonder, then, that the world goes backwards, that evil spreads. This can be traced back to the very beginning of the world. The gods were bored; therefore they created human beings.
Ibid., vol. 1, 'Rotation of Crops'

13 Personality is only ripe when a man has made the truth his own.
Journal entry, 1843, publ. in *The Journals of Søren Kierkegaard: A Selection*, no. 432 (ed./transl. Alexander Dru, 1938)

14 It is perfectly true, as philosophers say, that life must be understood backwards. But they forget the other proposition, that it must be lived forwards. And if one thinks over that proposition it becomes more and more evident that life can never really be understood in time simply because at no particular moment can I find the necessary resting-place from which to understand it – backwards.
Journal entry, 1843, ibid., no. 465

15 The ethical reality of the individual is the only reality.
Concluding Unscientific Postscript, bk 2, pt 2, ch. 3 (1846, transl. 1941)

16 From my earliest childhood the arrow of sorrow was embedded in my heart. So long as it remains I am ironical – if it were withdrawn I should die.
Journal entry, 1847, publ. in *The Journals of Søren Kierkegaard: A Selection*, no. 685 (ed./transl. Alexander Dru, 1938)

17 The most terrible fight is not when there is one opinion against another, the most terrible is when two men say the same thing – and fight about the interpretation.
Journal entry, 1850, ibid., no. 1057

18 The truth is a snare: you cannot have it, without being caught. You cannot have the truth in such a way that you catch it, but only in such a way that it catches you.
The Papers of Søren Kierkegaard, vol. 11, pt 1, sect. 352 (ed. P. A. Heiberg and V. Kuhr, 1909)

Joyce Kilmer
(1886–1918)
US poet

Alfred Joyce Kilmer. He published three verse collections before his death in the First World War. 'Trees' (1914) is his most remembered poem.

1 I think that I shall never see
A poem lovely as a tree.
'Trees', publ. in *Trees and Other Poems* (1914). OGDEN NASH wrote a reply: 'I think that I shall never see/A billboard lovely as a tree./Perhaps unless the billboards fall,/I'll never see a tree at all.' ('Song of the Open Road', in *Happy Days*, 1933)

2 Poems are made by fools like me,
But only God can make a tree.
'Trees', ibid.

Francis Kilvert
(1840–79)
English clergyman and diarist

His diary, written 1870–9, records the daily life of a country clergyman in the Welsh borders.

1 If there is one thing more hateful than another it is being told what to admire and having objects pointed out to one with a stick. Of all noxious animals too the most noxious is a tourist. And of all tourists the most vulgar, illbred, offensive and loathsome is the British tourist.
Journal entry, 5 April 1870, publ. in *Selections from the Diary of the Rev. Francis Kilvert* (ed. WILLIAM PLOMER, 1944)

2 It is a fine thing to be out on the hills alone. A man can hardly be a beast or a fool alone on a great mountain.
Journal entry, 29 May 1871, ibid.

Don King
(b. 1931)
US boxing promoter

From a criminal background he became boxing's most successful promoter, numbering among his clients MUHAMMAD ALI, Sugar Ray Leonard and Mike Tyson. According to LARRY HOLMES: 'He doesn't care about black or white. He just cares about green.'

1 I'm one of the world's great survivors. I'll always survive because I've got the right combination of wit, grit and bullshit.
Quoted in *The Sunday Times* 18 December 1994

Florence King
(b. 1936)
US author

Calling herself a woman who 'rips the teats off sacred cows', she has written Southern Ladies and Gentlemen *(1975) and* When Sisterhood Was in Flower *(1978), as well as essays and erotic novels.*

1 He travels fastest who travels alone, and that goes double for she. Real feminism is spinsterhood.
Reflections in a Jaundiced Eye, 'Spinsterhood is Powerful' (1989). Referring to RUDYARD KIPLING 9.

2 The witty woman is a tragic figure in American life. Wit destroys eroticism and eroticism destroys wit, so women must choose between taking lovers and taking no prisoners.
Ibid., 'The State of the Funny Bone'

Martin Luther King Jr
(1929–68)
US clergyman and civil rights leader

Coming from a Baptist background, he was an inspiring orator and a leader of the civil rights movement of the 1950s and '60s. His campaigns included the 1955 bus boycott in Montgomery, Alabama, and the 1963 march of 200,000 demonstrators on Washington DC. He was assassinated in Memphis, Tennessee.

1 It is my hope that as the Negro plunges deeper into the quest for freedom and justice he will plunge even deeper into the philosophy of non-violence. The Negro all over the South must come to the point that he can say to his white brother: 'We will match your capacity to inflict suffering with our capacity to endure suffering. We will meet your physical force with soul force. We will not hate you, but we will not obey your evil laws. We will soon wear you down by our capacity to suffer.'
Letter, 28 October 1957, publ. in *The Papers of Martin Luther King*, vol. 4 (ed. Clayborne Carson, Susan Carson, Adrienne Clay and Kieran Taylor, 2000)

2 I want to be the white man's brother, not his brother-in-law.
New York Journal-American 10 September 1962

3 It may be true that the law cannot make a man love me, but it can keep him from lynching me, and I think that's pretty important.
Quoted in the *Wall Street Journal* 13 November 1962

4 Nothing in all the world is more dangerous than sincere ignorance and conscientious stupidity.
Strength to Love, ch. 4, sect. 3 (1963)

5 The means by which we live have outdistanced the ends for which we live. Our scientific power has outrun our spiritual power. We have guided missiles and misguided men.
Ibid., ch. 7

6 We have genuflected before the god of science only to find that it has given us the atomic bomb, producing fears and anxieties that science can never mitigate.
Ibid., ch. 13

7 Freedom is never voluntarily given by the oppressor; it must be demanded by the oppressed.

'Letter from Birmingham Jail', open letter to clergymen, 16 April 1963, publ. in *Why We Can't Wait* (1963)

8 I submit that an individual who breaks a law that conscience tells him is unjust, and who willingly accepts the penalty of imprisonment in order to arouse the conscience of the community over its injustice, is in reality expressing the highest respect for law.

'Letter from Birmingham Jail', ibid.

9 I have almost reached the regrettable conclusion that the Negro's great stumbling block in his stride toward freedom is not the White Citizen's Counciler or the Ku Klux Klanner, but the white moderate.

'Letter from Birmingham Jail', ibid.

10 Shallow understanding from people of good will is more frustrating than absolute misunderstanding from people of ill will.

'Letter from Birmingham Jail', ibid.

11 We who engage in nonviolent direct action are not the creators of tension. We merely bring to the surface the hidden tension that is already alive.

'Letter from Birmingham Jail', ibid.

12 We will have to repent in this generation not merely for the hateful words and actions of the bad people but for the appalling silence of the good people.

'Letter from Birmingham Jail', ibid.

13 The question is not whether we will be extremist but what kind of extremist will we be.

'Letter from Birmingham Jail', ibid.

14 There can be no deep disappointment where there is not deep love.

'Letter from Birmingham Jail', ibid. Speaking of the church which 'we have blemished and scarred ... through social neglect and through fear of being nonconformists'.

15 Abused and scorned though we may be, our destiny is tied up with America's destiny. Before the pilgrims landed at Plymouth, we were here. Before the pen of Jefferson etched the majestic words of the Declaration of Independence across the pages of history, we were here. For more than two centuries our forebears labored in this country without wages; they made cotton king; they built the homes of their masters while suffering gross injustice and shameful humiliation – and yet out of a bottomless vitality they continued to thrive and develop. If the inexpressible cruelties of slavery could not stop us, the opposition we now face will surely fail.

'Letter from Birmingham Jail', ibid. The first sentence of this extract recalls a speech by FREDERICK DOUGLASS in Boston, 12 February 1862: 'The destiny of the colored American ... is the destiny of America.'

16 If a man hasn't discovered something that he will die for, he isn't fit to live.

Speech in Detroit, 23 June 1963, quoted in *The Days of Martin Luther King*, ch. 4 (1971) by James Bishop

17 No, no, we are not satisfied, and we will not be satisfied until justice rolls down like waters and righteousness like a mighty stream.

'I Have a Dream', speech at civil rights march, Washington DC, 28 August 1963, publ. in *A Testament of Hope: Essential Writings* (ed. James Melvin Washington, 1986). See BIBLE, OLD TESTAMENT: AMOS 4.

18 I have a dream that one day on the red hills of Georgia the sons of former slaves and the sons of former slave owners will be able to sit down together at the table of brotherhood. I have a dream that one day even the state of Mississippi, a desert state sweltering with the heat of injustice and oppression, will be transformed into an oasis of freedom and justice. I have a dream that my four little children will one day live in a nation where they will not be judged by the color of their skin but by the content of their character. I have a dream today.

'I Have a Dream', ibid.

19 A riot is at bottom the language of the unheard.

Where Do We Go From Here?, ch. 4 (1967)

20 It doesn't matter with me now. Because I've been to the mountaintop. And I don't mind. Like anybody, I would like to live a long life. Longevity has its place. But I'm not concerned about that now. I just want to do God's will. And He's allowed me to go up to the mountain. And I've looked over, and I've seen the Promised Land ... Mine eyes have seen the glory of the coming of the Lord.

'I See the Promised Land', speech in Memphis, 3 April 1968, publ. in *A Testament of Hope: Essential Writings* (ed. James Melvin Washington, 1986). The last words are from 'Battle Hymn of the Republic' (see JULIA WARD HOWE 1). The speech was made on the day preceding King's assassination.

21 Free at last, Free at last
Thank God Almighty
I'm free at last

Epitaph on King's tomb, in South View Cemetery, Atlanta,

Georgia. The words are from the spiritual with which he often closed his speeches.

Charles Kingsley
(1819–75)
English author and clergyman

Although his social novels were influential, he is better remembered for the historical romance Westward Ho! *(1855) and the children's book* The Water Babies *(1863). He was appointed chaplain to Queen* VICTORIA *in 1873.*

1 We have used the Bible as if it was a mere special constable's handbook, an opium dose for keeping beasts of burden patient while they are being overloaded.
Letters to the Chartists, no. 2 (1848). Kingsley signed his numerous articles on the theme of Christian Socialism 'Parson Lot'. His notion of religion as 'an opium dose' recalls KARL MARX 1.

2 'O Mary, go and call the cattle home,
And call the cattle home,
And call the cattle home,
Across the sands of Dee.'
The western wind was wild and dank with foam,
And all alone went she.
'The Sands of Dee', written 1849, publ. in *Andromeda and Other Poems* (1858)

3 For men must work, and women must weep,
And there's little to earn, and many to keep,
Though the harbour bar be moaning.
'The Three Fishers', st. 1, written 1851, ibid.

4 'Tis the hard grey weather
Breeds hard English men.
'Ode to the North-East Wind', written 1854, ibid.

5 Be good, sweet maid, and let who will be clever.
'A Farewell', st. 3, written 1856, ibid.

6 When all the world is young, lad,
And all the trees are green;
And every goose a swan, lad,
And every lass a queen;
Then hey for boot and horse, lad,
And round the world away;
Young blood must have its course, lad,
And every dog his day.
'Young and Old', publ. in *The Water Babies*, ch. 2 (1863)

7 I am the ugliest fairy in the world, and I shall be till people behave themselves as they ought to do.

And then I shall grow as handsome as my sister . . .
Mrs Doasyouwouldbedoneby.
Mrs Bedonebyasyoudid, ibid., ch. 5

8 There is a great deal of human nature in man.
At Last: A Christmas in the West Indies, ch. 2 (1871). Quoting the words of 'the wise Yankee'.

9 The age of chivalry is never past, so long as there is a wrong left unredressed on earth, or a man or woman left to say, I will redress that wrong, or spend my life in the attempt.
Quoted in *Charles Kingsley: His Letters and Memories of His Life*, vol. 2, ch. 28 (ed. Frances Eliza Kingsley, 1877)

Neil Kinnock
(b. 1942)
British politician

Baron Kinnock of Bedwellty. Labelled a Welsh firebrand, he was leader of the Labour Party 1983–92, and was a European Commissioner 1995–2004. See SUN 6.

1 If Margaret Thatcher wins – I warn you not to be ordinary. I warn you not to be young. I warn you not to fall ill. I warn you not to get old.
Speech at Bridgend, 7 June 1983, publ. in *The Penguin Book of Twentieth-Century Speeches* (ed. Brian MacArthur, 1999). The eve-of-election speech made a strong impact, contributing to Kinnock's election as Labour leader four months later.

2 I would die for my country, but I could never let my country die for me.
Speech to Labour Party Conference, 30 September 1986, quoted in the *Guardian* 1 October 1986. On the issue of nuclear disarmament.

3 The enemy of idealism is zealotry.
Quoted in the *Observer* 27 December 1987

Rudyard Kipling
(1865–1936)
English author and poet

Born in India, he returned there to work as a journalist (1882–9), and he made it the setting of Kim *(1901),* Plain Tales from the Hills *(1888), and* The Jungle Book *(1894) among other prose works. His popular and skilfully crafted poetry reflected the concerns of the common man.* T. S. ELIOT *called him 'a laureate without laurels'. See also* OSCAR WILDE 29.

1 Call a truce, then, to our labours – let us feast
  with friends and neighbours,
And be merry as the custom of our caste;

For if 'faint and forced the laughter,' and if sadness
  follow after,
We are richer by one mocking Christmas past.
'Christmas in India', publ. in *Departmental Ditties* (1886). Closing lines of poem.

2 The toad beneath the harrow knows
Exactly where each tooth point goes:
The butterfly upon the road
Preaches contentment to that toad.
'Pagett, M.P.', ibid.

3 A million surplus Maggies are willing to bear the
  yoke;
And a woman is only a woman, but a good cigar is
  a smoke.
'The Betrothed', st. 25, ibid.

4 Lalun is a member of the most ancient profession
in the world.
In Black and White, 'On the City Wall' (1888)

5 The Man Who Would be King.
Title of short story, publ. in *The Phantom Rickshaw* (1888)

6 The Three in One, the One in Three? Not so!
To my own gods I go.
It may be they shall give me greater ease
Than your cold Christ and tangled trinities.
Plain Tales from the Hills, 'Lispeth', chapter heading (1888)

7 The silliest woman can manage a clever man; but
it takes a very clever woman to manage a fool!
Ibid., 'Three and – an Extra'

8 Gawd knows, an' 'E won't split on a pal.
Wee Willie Winkie, 'Drums of the Fore and Aft' (1888). Spoken
by Lew.

9 He travels the fastest who travels alone.
'The Winners', refrain ('L'Envoi' to 'The Story of the Gadsbys',
1888), repr. in *Soldiers Three* (1895)

10 Bite on the bullet, old man, and don't let them
think you are afraid.
The Light That Failed, ch. 11 (1891). Spoken by Torpenhow to
Dick.

11 Let it be clearly understood that the Russian is a
delightful person till he tucks in his shirt. As an
Oriental he is charming. It is only when he insists
on being treated as the most easterly of western
peoples instead of the most westerly of easterns that
he becomes a racial anomaly extremely difficult to
handle.
Life's Handicap, 'The Man Who Was' (1891)

12 Asia is not going to be civilized after the methods
of the West. There is too much Asia and she is too
old. You cannot reform a lady of many lovers, and
Asia has been insatiable in her flirtations aforetime.
She will never attend Sunday-school or learn to vote
save with swords for tickets.
Ibid., 'The Man Who Was'

13 For they're hangin' Danny Deever, you can hear
  the Dead March play,
The regiment's in 'ollow square – they're hangin'
  him to-day;
They've taken of his buttons off an' cut his stripes
  away,
An' they're hangin' Danny Deever in the mornin'.
'Danny Deever', st. 1, publ. in *Ballads and Barrack-Room
Ballads* (1892)

14 O it's Tommy this, an' Tommy that, an'
  'Tommy, go away';
But it's 'Thank you, Mister Atkins,' when the band
  begins to play.
'Tommy', st. 1, ibid.

15 Then it's Tommy this, an' Tommy that, an'
  'Tommy 'ow's yer soul?'
But it's 'Thin red line of 'eroes' when the drums
  begin to roll.
'Tommy', st. 3, ibid. See W. H. RUSSELL 1.

16 We aren't no thin red 'eroes, nor we aren't no
  blackguards too,
But single men in barricks, most remarkable like
  you;
And if sometimes our conduck isn't all your fancy
  paints,
Why, single men in barricks don't grow into
  plaster saints.
'Tommy', st. 4, ibid.

17 For it's Tommy this, an' Tommy that, an' 'Chuck
  him out, the brute!'
But it's 'Saviour of 'is country' when the guns
  begin to shoot.
'Tommy', st. 5, ibid.

18 So 'ere's *to* you, Fuzzy-Wuzzy, at your 'ome in
  the Soudan;
You're a pore benighted 'eathen but a first-class
  fightin' man;
An' 'ere's *to* you, Fuzzy-Wuzzy, with your 'ayrick
  'ead of 'air –
You big black boundin' beggar – for you broke a
  British square!
'Fuzzy-Wuzzy', st. 4, ibid.

19 Though I've belted you and flayed you,
By the livin' Gawd that made you,
You're a better man than I am, Gunga Din!
'Gunga Din', st. 5, ibid.

20 'Ave you 'eard o' the Widow at Windsor
With a hairy gold crown on 'er 'ead?
She 'as ships on the foam – she 'as millions at
    'ome,
An' she pays us poor beggars in red.
'The Widow at Windsor', st. 1, ibid. Referring to Queen
VICTORIA.

21 When you're wounded and left on Afghanistan's
    plains,
And the women come out to cut up what remains,
Jest roll to your rifle an' blow out your brains
An' go to your Gawd like a soldier.
'The Young British Soldier', st. 13, ibid.

22 By the old Moulmein Pagoda, lookin' eastward
    to the sea,
There's a Burma girl a-settin', and I know she
    thinks o' me;
For the wind is in the palm-trees, an' the
    temple-bells they say:
'Come you back, you British soldier; come you
    back to Mandalay!'
'Mandalay', st. 1, ibid. The poem was set to music by Oley
Speaks in 1908.

23 On the road to Mandalay,
Where the flyin'-fishes play,
An' the dawn comes up like thunder outer China
    'crost the Bay!
'Mandalay', refrain, ibid.

24 An' I seed her first a-smokin' of a whackin'
    white cheroot,
An' wastin' Christian kisses on an 'eathen idol's
    foot
'Mandalay', st. 2, ibid.

25 Ship me somewhere east of Suez, where the
    best is like the worst,
Where there aren't no Ten Commandments an' a
    man can raise a thirst.
Mandalay, st. 6, ibid.

26 We're poor little lambs who've lost our way,
Baa! Baa! Baa!
We're little black sheep who've gone astray,
Baa-aa-aa!
Gentleman-rankers out on the spree,
Damned from here to eternity,

God ha' mercy on such as we,
Baa! Yah! Bah!
'Gentleman-Rankers', refrain, ibid.

27 We have done with hope and honour, we are
    lost to love and truth,
We are dropping down the ladder rung by rung,
And the measure of our torment is the measure of
    our youth,
God help us, for we knew the worst too young!
'Gentleman-Rankers', st. 4, ibid.

28 Four things greater than all things are –
Women and horses and power and war.
'The Ballad of the King's Jest', st. 4, ibid.

29 Oh, East is East, and West is West, and never
    the twain shall meet,
Till earth and sky stand presently at God's great
    judgement seat;
But there is neither east nor west, border, nor
    breed, nor birth,
When two strong men stand face to face, tho' they
    come from the ends of the earth.
'The Ballad of East and West', ibid. Opening and closing lines.

30 And the first rude sketch that the world had
    seen was joy to his mighty heart,
Till the Devil whispered behind the leaves 'It's
    pretty, but is it Art?'
'The Conundrum of the Workshops', st. 1, ibid. Referring to
'Our father Adam', who 'sat under the tree and scratched with
a stick in the mould'.

31 And what should they know of England who
    only England know?
'The English Flag', st. 1, ibid. G. K. CHESTERTON responded to
this: 'It is a far deeper and sharper question to ask, "What can
they know of England who know only the world?"' (Heretics,
'On Mr. Rudyard Kipling and Making the World Small', 1905)

32 For the sin that ye do two by two ye must pay
    for one by one.
'Tomlinson', l. 60, ibid. Spoken by the Devil.

33 And the end of the fight is a tombstone white
    with the name of the late deceased,
And the epitaph drear: 'A fool lies here who tried
    to hustle the East.'
The Naulahka, ch. 5, heading (1892)

34 He wrapped himself in quotations – as a beggar
would enfold himself in the purple of Emperors.
Many Inventions, 'The Finest Story in the World' (1893)

35 A Man-cub is a Man-cub, and he must learn *all* the Law of the Jungle.
The Jungle Book, 'Kaa's Hunting' (1894). Spoken by Baloo.

36 We be one blood, thou and I. I take my life from thee to-night. My kill shall be thy kill if ever thou art hungry, O Kaa.
Ibid., 'Kaa's Hunting'. Spoken by Mowgli.

37 Brother, thy tail hangs down behind!
'Road Song of the Bandar-log', ibid., 'Kaa's Hunting'

38 The tumult and the shouting dies;
The Captains and the Kings depart:
Still stands Thine ancient sacrifice,
An humble and a contrite heart.
Lord God of Hosts, be with us yet,
Lest we forget – lest we forget!
'Recessional', st. 2 (1894) repr. in *The Five Nations* (1903). 'Lest we forget' was adopted as an epitaph by the War Graves Commission – for which Kipling worked – after the First World War.

39 Far-called our navies melt away –
On dune and headland sinks the fire –
Lo, all our pomp of yesterday
Is one with Nineveh, and Tyre!
'Recessional', st. 3, ibid.

40 If, drunk with sight of power, we loose
Wild tongues that have not Thee in awe –
Such boasting as the Gentiles use,
Or lesser breeds without the Law.
'Recessional', st. 4, ibid.

41 Now this is the Law of the Jungle – as old and as true as the sky;
And the Wolf that shall keep it may prosper, but the Wolf that shall break it must die.
The Second Jungle Book, 'The Law of the Jungle', st. 1 (1895)

42 Now these are the Laws of the Jungle, and many and mighty are they;
But the head and the hoof of the Law and the haunch and the hump is – Obey!
Ibid., 'The Law of the Jungle', st. 19

43 From coupler-flange to spindle-guide I see Thy Hand, O God –
Predestination in the stride o' yon connectin'-rod.
'McAndrew's Hymn', publ. in *The Seven Seas* (1896)

44 The Liner she's a lady, an' she never looks nor 'eeds –
The Man-o'-War's 'er 'usband, an' 'e gives 'er all she needs;

But, oh, the little cargo boats that sail the wet seas roun',
They're just the same as you an' me a-plyin' up and down!
'The Liner She's a Lady', st. 1, ibid.

45 There are nine and sixty ways of constructing tribal lays,
And – every – single – one – of – them – is – right!
'In the Neolithic Age', st. 5, ibid. Words of the narrator.

46 When 'Omer smote 'is bloomin' lyre,
He'd 'eard men sing by land an' sea;
An' what he thought 'e might require,
'E went an' took – the same as me!
'When 'Omer smote 'is bloomin' lyre', st. 1, ibid.

47 I've taken my fun where I've found it,
An' now I must pay for my fun,
For the more you 'ave known o' the others
The less will you settle to one.
'The Ladies', st. 7, ibid.

48 When you get to a man in the case,
They're like as a row of pins –
For the Colonel's Lady an' Judy O'Grady
Are sisters under their skins.
'The Ladies', st. 8, ibid.

49 When Earth's last picture is painted and the tubes are twisted and dried,
When the oldest colours have faded, and the youngest critic has died,
We shall rest, and, faith, we shall need it – lie down for an aeon or two,
Till the Master of All Good Workmen shall put us to work anew!
'When Earth's Last Picture is Painted', st. 1, ibid.

50 A fool there was and he made his prayer
(Even as you and I!)
To a rag and a bone and a hank of hair
(We called her the woman who did not care)
But the fool he called her his lady fair –
(Even as you and I!)
'The Vampire', st. 1 (1897), repr. in *Rudyard Kipling's Verse: Definitive Edition* (1940)

51 When you've shouted 'Rule Britannia', when you've sung 'God save the Queen',
When you've finished killing Kruger with your mouth,
Will you kindly drop a shilling in my little tambourine

For a gentleman in khaki ordered South?
'The Absent-minded Beggar', st. 1 (1899), ibid.

52 Take up the White Man's burden –
Send forth the best ye breed –
Go, bind your sons to exile
To serve your captives' need.
'The White Man's Burden', st. 1 (1899), repr. in *The Five Nations*
(1903). Addressed to the American people, on the US occupa-
tion of the Philippines at the end of the Spanish-American
War of 1898.

53 Little Friend of all the World.
Kim, ch. 1 (1901). Kim's nickname.

54 You must *not* forget the suspenders, Best
Beloved.
The Just-So Stories, 'How the Whale Got His Throat' (1902)

55 One Elephant – a new Elephant – an Elephant's
Child – who was full of 'satiable curtiosity.
Ibid., 'The Elephant's Child'

56 Then Kolokolo Bird said, with a mournful cry,
'Go to the banks of the great grey-green, greasy Limpopo River, all set about with fever-trees, and find
out.'
Ibid., 'The Elephant's Child'

57 I keep six honest serving-men
(They taught me all I knew);
Their names are What and Why and When
And How and Where and Who.
Ibid., 'The Elephant's Child'

58 Yes, weekly from Southampton,
Great steamers, white and gold,
Go rolling down to Rio
(Roll down – roll down to Rio!).
Ibid., 'The Beginning of the Armadilloes'

59 The Cat. He walked by himself, and all places
were alike to him.
Ibid., 'The Cat That Walked By Himself'

60 And he went back through the Wet Wild Woods,
waving his wild tail and walking by his wild lone.
But he never told anybody.
Ibid., 'The Cat That Walked By Himself'

61 Who hath desired the Sea? – the sight of salt
water unbounded –
The heave and the halt and the hurl and the crash
of the comber wind-hounded?
The sleek-barrelled swell before storm, grey,
foamless, enormous, and growing –

Stark calm on the lap of the Line or the crazy-eyed
hurricane blowing.
'The Sea and the Hills', st. 1, publ. in *The Five Nations* (1903)

62 God gives all men all earth to love,
But, since man's heart is small,
Ordains for each one spot shall prove
Belovèd over all.
'Sussex', st. 1, ibid.

63 Each to his choice, and I rejoice
The lot has fallen to me
In a fair ground – in a fair ground –
Yes, Sussex by the sea.
'Sussex', st. 2, ibid.

64 A Nation spoke to a Nation,
A Throne sent word to a Throne:
'Daughter am I in my mother's house,
But mistress in my own.
The gates are mine to open,
As the gates are mine to close,
And I abide by my Mother's House,'
Said our Lady of the Snows.
'Our Lady of the Snows', st. 1, ibid.

65 Then ye returned to your trinkets; then ye
contented your souls
With the flannelled fools at the wicket or the
muddied oafs at the goals.
'The Islanders', ibid.

66 Foot – foot – foot – foot – sloggin' over Africa –
(Boots – boots – boots – boots – movin' up and
down again!)
There's no discharge in the war!
'Boots', st. 1, ibid.

67 'Tisn't beauty, so to speak, nor good talk necessarily. It's just IT. Some women'll stay in a man's
memory if they once walked down a street.
Traffics and Discoveries, 'Mrs Bathurst' (1904). Spoken by Mr
Pyecroft, referring to Mrs Bathurst.

68 Of all the trees that grow so fair,
Old England to adorn,
Greater are none beneath the sun,
Than oak, and ash, and thorn.
'A Tree Song', st. 1, in *Puck of Pook's Hill*, 'Weland's Sword'
(1906)

69 What is a woman that you forsake her,
And the hearth-fire and the home-acre,
To go with the old grey Widow-maker?
'Harp Song of the Dane Women', st. 1, ibid., 'The Knights of
the Joyous Venture'

70 Cities and thrones and powers
Stand in time's eye,
Almost as long as flowers,
Which daily die?

'Cities and Thrones and Powers', st. 1, ibid., 'A Centurion of the Thirtieth'

71 Five and twenty ponies
Trotting through the dark –
Brandy for the Parson,
'Baccy for the Clerk;
Laces for a lady, letters for a spy,
And watch the wall, my darling, while the
    Gentlemen go by!

'A Smuggler's Song', st. 1, ibid., 'Hal o' the Draft'

72 There is sorrow enough in the natural way
From men and women to fill our day;
But when we are certain of sorrow in store,
Why do we always arrange for more?
Brothers and Sisters, I bid you beware
Of giving your heart to a dog to tear.

'The Power of the Dog', st. 1 (1909), repr. in *Rudyard Kipling's Verse: Definitive Edition* (1940)

73 They shut the road through the woods
Seventy years ago.
Weather and rain have undone it again,
And now you would never know
There was once a road through the woods.

'The Way Through the Woods', st. 1, publ. in *Rewards and Fairies*, 'Marklake Witches' (1910)

74 If you can keep your head when all about you
Are losing theirs and blaming it on you,
If you can trust yourself when all men doubt you,
But make allowance for their doubting you;
If you can wait and not be tired by waiting,
Or being lied about, don't deal in lies,
Or being hated, don't give way to hating,
And yet don't look too good, nor talk too wise.

'If – ', st. 1, ibid., 'Brother Square Toes'

75 If you can dream – and not make dreams your
    master;
If you can think – and not make thoughts your
    aim;
If you can meet with triumph and disaster
And treat those two imposters just the same;
If you can bear to hear the truth you've spoken
Twisted by knaves to make a trap for fools,
Or watch the things you gave your life to broken,
And stoop and build 'em up with worn-out tools.

'If – ', st. 2, ibid.

76 If you can talk with crowds and keep your
    virtue,
Or walk with kings – nor lose the common touch,
If neither foes nor loving friends can hurt you,
If all men count with you, but none too much;
If you can fill the unforgiving minute
With sixty seconds' worth of distance run,
Yours is the earth and everything that's in it,
And – which is more – you'll be a man, my son!

'If – ', st. 4, ibid.

77 For the female of the species is more deadly
    than the male.

'The Female of the Species', st. 1 (1911), repr. in *The Years Between* (1919)

78 And that is called paying the Dane-geld;
But we've proved it again and again,
That if once you have paid him the Dane-geld
You never get rid of the Dane.

'Dane-Geld', st. 4, publ. in *History of England* (1911, written with C. R. L. Fletcher)

79 England's on the anvil – hear the hammers
    ring –
Clanging from the Severn to the Tyne!
Never was a blacksmith like our Norman King –
England's being hammered, hammered,
    hammered into line!

'The Anvil', st. 1, ibid.

80 Oh, Adam was a gardener, and God who made
    him sees
That half a proper gardener's work is done upon
    his knees,
So when your work is finished, you can wash your
    hands and pray
For the glory of the garden, that it may not pass
    away!

'The Glory of the Garden', st. 8, ibid.

81 Power without responsibility – the prerogative
of the harlot throughout the ages.

Quoted in *The Kipling Journal* December 1971, repr. in *Kipling: Interviews and Recollections* (ed. Harold Orel, 1983). The remark was supposedly made *c.* 1917 in reply to press baron Max Aitken (Lord Beaverbrook), who had said to Kipling, regarding Aitken's recent acquisition of the *Daily Express*: 'What I want is power. Kiss 'em one day and kick 'em the next.' The words were borrowed (with Kipling's permission) by his cousin STANLEY BALDWIN in a speech, 17 March 1931, attacking Lord Beaverbrook and Lord Rothermere, whose newspapers he described as 'engines of propaganda'.

82 What answer from the North?
One Law, one Land, one Throne.

If England drive us forth
We shall not stand alone!
'Ulster', st. 6, publ. in *The Years Between* (1919)

83 If any question why we died,
Tell them, because our fathers lied.
'Common Form', in *The Years Between*, 'Epitaphs of the War'
(1919)

84 As it will be in the future, it was at the birth of
man –
There are only four things certain since social
progress began: –
That the dog returns to his vomit and the sow
returns to her mire,
And the burnt fool's bandaged finger goes
wabbling back to the fire.
'The Gods of the Copybook Headings', st. 9 (1919), repr. in
Rudyard Kipling's Verse: Definitive Edition (1940)

85 Their Name Liveth for Evermore.
Inscription carved over lists of the dead in the Commonwealth war cemeteries (from 1919); see BIBLE, APOCRYPHA:
ECCLESIASTICUS 65. Kipling, who had himself lost his
eighteen-year-old son in the First World War, had been invited
to devise suitable texts by the Imperial War Graves Commission.

86 Words are, of course, the most powerful drug
used by mankind.
Speech, 14 February 1923, quoted in *The Times* 15 February
1923

87 A people always ends by resembling its shadow.
Remark to ANDRÉ MAUROIS, *c.* 1930, quoted in *The Art of
Writing*, 'The Writer's Craft', sect. 2 (1960) by André Maurois.
Referring to the situation in Germany.

88 There rise her timeless capitals of empires
daily born,
Whose plinths are laid at midnight and whose
streets are packed at morn;
And here come tired youths and maids that feign
to love or sin
In tones like rusty razor blades to tunes like
smitten tin.
'Naaman's Song', publ. in *Rudyard Kipling's Verse: Definitive
Edition* (1940). Interpreted as a description of Hollywood.

89 Now I possess and am possessed of the land
where I would be,
And the curve of half Earth's generous breast shall
sooth and ravish me!
'The Prairie (Canada)', st. 5, ibid. Closing lines of poem.

90 For undemocratic reasons and for motives not
of state,

They arrive at their conclusions – largely
inarticulate.
Being void of self-expression they confide their
views to none;
But sometimes in a smoking room, one learns why
things were done.
'The Puzzler', st. 3, ibid.

91 But remember please, the Law by which we live,
We are not built to comprehend a lie,
We can neither love nor pity nor forgive.
If you make a slip in handling us you die.
'The Secret of the Machines', ibid.

Henry Kissinger
(b. 1923)
German-born US politician and diplomat

Considered the second most powerful member of the NIXON
*administration, he served as National Security Adviser (1968–
73) and as Secretary of State (1973–7). His 'shuttle diplomacy'
was crucial in Arab-Israeli peace negotiations. 'Satire died the
day they gave Henry Kissinger the Nobel Peace Prize,'* TOM
LEHRER *declared. 'There were no jokes left after that.'*

1 The conventional army loses if it does not win.
The guerrilla wins if he does not lose.
Foreign Affairs January 1969. Writing of the Vietnam War.

2 We are all the President's men.
Said in 1970, after the invasion of Cambodia, quoted in *The
Sunday Times* 4 May 1975. Kissinger's statement inspired the
title of the book by *Washington Post* reporters Carl Bernstein
and Bob Woodward, *All the President's Men* (1974, filmed 1976),
describing their investigation into the Watergate break-in.

3 Power is the great aphrodisiac.
Quoted in the *New York Times* 19 January 1971

4 We cannot always assure the future of our friends;
we have a better chance of assuring our future if we
remember who our friends are.
The White House Years, ch. 29 (1979). Referring to the changing
US policy towards the Shah of Iran.

5 The superpowers often behave like two heavily-
armed blind men feeling their way around a room,
each believing himself in mortal peril from the
other, whom he assumes to have perfect vision.
Quoted in the *Observer* 30 September 1979

6 Most foreign policies that history has marked
highly, in whatever country, have been originated
by leaders who were opposed by experts . . . It is,

after all, the responsibility of the expert to operate the familiar and that of the leader to transcend it.
Years of Upheaval, ch. 10, 'The Foreign Service' (1982)

7 Moderation is a virtue only in those who are thought to have an alternative.
Quoted in the *Observer* 24 January 1982

8 Mr Clinton does not have the strength of character to be a war criminal.
Independent 16 January 1999

Eartha Kitt
(b. 1927)
US singer and actress

She has worked in films, television and cabaret and is known for her distinctive purring voice. Her hit songs include 'C'est Si Bon' (1952) and 'Just an Old Fashioned Girl' (1958).

1 I'm just an old fashioned girl with an old
   fashioned mind,
Not sophisticated, I'm the sweet and simple kind.
I want an old fashioned house, with an old
   fashioned fence
And an old fashioned millionaire.
'Just an Old Fashioned Girl' (song, 1958)

Paul Klee
(1879–1940)
Swiss artist

He joined the Expressionist group Der Blaue Reiter (1911–12) and taught at the Bauhaus (1920–31). His paintings, such as 'Twittering Machine' (1922), suggest a childlike innocence and were hugely influential.

1 Colour possesses me. I don't have to pursue it. It will possess me always, I know it. That is the meaning of this happy hour: Colour and I are one. I am a painter.
Journal entry, written in Tunisia, 16 April 1914, publ. in *The Diaries of Paul Klee 1898–1918*, no. 926 (1957, transl. 1965)

2 One eye sees, the other feels.
Journal entry, 1914, ibid. no. 937

3 The more horrible this world . . . the more abstract our art, whereas a happy world brings forth an art of the here and now.
Journal entry, 1915, ibid. no. 951

4 Art does not reproduce the visible; rather, it makes visible.
'Creative Credo', sect. 1 (1920), repr. in *The Inward Vision* (1957)

5 An active line on a walk, moving freely without a goal. A walk for a walk's sake.
Pedagogical Sketchbook, ch. 1 (1925). On his hieroglyphic drawing style.

Joe Klein
(b. 1946)
US journalist and author

A journalist for three decades, he first denied, then confirmed his authorship of the anonymously published bestseller Primary Colors (1996), a political novel closely modelled on the rise of the Clintons to the White House.

1 We tell them [politicians] what they want to hear – and when we tell them something they *don't* want to hear, it's usually because we've calculated that's what they really want. We live an eternity of false smiles – and why? Because it's the price you pay to lead.
Primary Colors, ch. 9 (1996). Spoken by Jack Stanton.

John Knox
(1505–72)
Scottish Presbyterian leader

He fell under the influence of John Calvin while in exile and, on his return to Scotland in 1559, led a party of reform to establish the Church of Scotland.

1 The monstrous regiment of women.
The First Blast of the Trumpet Against the Monstrous Regiment of Women (pamphlet, 1558). 'Nature doth paint them further to be weak, frail, impatient, feeble and foolish,' Knox wrote, 'and experience hath declared them to be unconstant, variable, cruel, and lacking the spirit of counsel.'

2 To promote a woman to bear rule, superiority, dominion or empire, above any realm, nation, or city, is repugnant to nature; contumely to God, a thing most contrarious to his revealed will and approved ordinance, and finally it is the subversion of good order, of all equity and justice.
Ibid. Referring to the first year of ELIZABETH I's reign.

Ronald Knox
(1888–1957)
British scholar and priest

An Anglican chaplain, he converted to Roman Catholicism and became Catholic chaplain to Oxford University (1926–39). He wrote an authorized translation of the Bible (1945–9), works on religion and detective novels.

1 When suave politeness, tempering bigot zeal,
Corrected 'I believe' to 'One does feel.'
'Absolute and Abitofhell', ll. 99–100 (1913), repr. in *Essays in Satire* (1928)

2 There was once a man who said, 'God
Must think it exceedingly odd
If he finds that this tree
Continues to be
When there's no one about in the Quad.'
The Complete Limerick Book (1924) by Langford Reed. Knox's limerick was anonymously answered: 'Dear Sir, Your astonishment's odd:/I am always about in the Quad./And that's why the tree/Will continue to be,/Since observed by Yours faithfully,/God.'

3 Only man has dignity; only man, therefore, can be funny.
Essays in Satire, Introduction (1928)

4 It is stupid of modern civilization to have given up believing in the devil, when he is the only explanation of it.
Let Dons Delight, ch. 8 (1939)

5 A loud noise at one end and no sense of responsibility at the other.
Attributed, of babies. RONALD REAGAN adapted Knox's definition during his campaign for the governorship of California in 1965, when he described government as 'an alimentary canal with a big appetite at one end and no responsibility at the other'.

Ted Koehler
(1894–1973)
US songwriter

He wrote for numerous musical films and had hit songs in collaboration with Harold Arlen, Burton Lane and other composers.

1 Don't know why
There's no sun up in the sky,
Stormy weather
Since my man and I ain't together
It keeps raining all the time.
'Stormy Weather' (song, 1933, music by Harold Arlen). Originally sung by Ethel Walters in *Cotton Club Review* (musical show, 1933), the song was later performed by Lena Horne in the film *Stormy Weather* (1943) and by Connee Boswell in the film *Swing Parade* (1946).

Arthur Koestler
(1905–83)
Hungarian-born British author

A journalist and one-time member of the Communist Party, he escaped to England in 1940 where he published Darkness at Noon *(1940), a fictional account of the Stalinist purges. He also wrote on politics, parapsychology and the history of science.*

1 The ultimate truth is penultimately always a falsehood. He who will be proved right in the end appears to be wrong and harmful before it.
Darkness at Noon, 'The Second Hearing' (1940). Extract from Rubashov's diary.

2 The definition of the individual was: a multitude of one million divided by one million.
Ibid., 'The Grammatical Fiction'. On the teaching of the Party.

3 Space-ships and time machines are no escape from the human condition. Let Othello subject Desdemona to a lie-detector test; his jealousy will still blind him to the evidence. Let Oedipus triumph over gravity; he won't triumph over his fate.
'The Boredom of Fantasy', publ. in *The Trail of the Dinosaur*, pt 2 (1955)

4 If conquerors be regarded as the engine-drivers of History, then the conquerors of thought are perhaps the pointsmen who, less conspicuous to the traveller's eye, determine the direction of the journey.
The Sleepwalkers, pt 1, ch. 2, sect. 4 (1959)

5 True creativity often starts where language ends.
The Act of Creation, bk 1, pt 2, ch. 7 (1964)

6 God seems to have left the receiver off the hook, and time is running out.
The Ghost in the Machine, ch. 18 (1967)

7 Prometheus is reaching out for the stars with an empty grin on his face.
New York Times 21 July 1969. On the first manned moon-landing.

8 The most persistent sound which reverberates through man's history is the beating of war drums.
Janus: A Summing Up, 'Prologue: The New Calendar', sect. 1 (1978)

Helmut Kohl
(b. 1930)
German politician

The longest-serving post-war German leader, he became Chairman of the Christian Democratic Party in 1973, Chancellor of

West Germany in 1982 and Chancellor of a united Germany (1990–8).

1 Everybody should know that Germany will not go it alone: there will be no restless Reich.
International Herald Tribune 3 October 1990

Käthe Kollwitz
(1867–1945)
German artist

Once described as the last great German Expressionist, she articulated her radical and pacifist sympathies in her bold and powerful lithographs, etchings and woodcuts, which often depicted victims of poverty and war.

1 I am gradually approaching the period in my life when work comes first ... No longer diverted by other emotions, I work the way a cow grazes.
Journal entry, April 1910, publ. in *Diaries and Letters* (ed. Hans Kollwitz, 1955). In her entry for 1 January 1912, Kollwitz wrote: 'For the last third of life there remains only work. It alone is always stimulating, rejuvenating, exciting and satisfying.'

2 Bisexuality is almost a necessary factor in artistic production.
Journal entry, 1942, ibid.

George Konrád
(b. 1933)
Hungarian author

His novels include The Case Worker *(1969) and* The City Builder *(1977). Believing that his duty as a writer was to remain in Hungary under Communist rule, he was briefly imprisoned in 1974 for alleged subversive agitation.*

1 You take a number of small steps which you believe are right, thinking maybe tomorrow somebody will treat this as a dangerous provocation. And then you wait. If there is no reaction, you take another step: courage is only an accumulation of small steps.
Sunday Correspondent 15 April 1990. On surviving as a writer in Communist Hungary.

Koran

The Koran, the sacred book of Islam, contains the revelations of God to the prophet Muhammad, received between 610 and 632. The text of 114 suras was committed to written form between 644 and 656 and translated into Latin by 1143. The translation used here is that of Arthur J. Arberry (1955).

1 In the Name of God, the Merciful, the Compassionate.
Sura 1 ('The Opening'). Introductory words of each Sura.

2 Praise belongs to God, the Lord of all Being, the All-merciful, the All-compassionate, the Master of the Day of Doom.
Sura 1 ('The Opening'), vs 2–4

3 Thee only we serve: to Thee alone we pray for succour.
Guide us in the straight path,
the path of those whom Thou hast blessed,
not of those against whom Thou art wrathful,
nor of those who are astray.
Sura 1 ('The Opening'), vs 5–7

4 That is the Book, wherein is no doubt,
a guidance to the godfearing
who believe in the unseen.
Sura 2 ('The Cow'), vs 2–3

5 Do not confound the truth with vanity,
and do not conceal the truth wittingly.
Sura 2 ('The Cow'), v. 39

6 The Jews say, 'The Christians stand not on anything';
the Christians say, 'The Jews stand not on anything'.
Sura 2 ('The Cow'), v. 107

7 From whatsoever place thou issuest, turn thy face towards the Holy Mosque.
Sura 2 ('The Cow'), v. 145

8 It is not piety, that your turn your faces to the East and to the West.
True piety is this:
to believe in God, and the last Day,
the angels, the Book, and the Prophets,
to give of one's substance, however cherished,
to kinsmen, and orphans,
the needy, the traveller, beggars,
and to ransom the slave,
to perform the prayer, to pay the alms.
Sura 2 ('The Cow'), vs 172–3

9 Better
it is for him who volunteers good,
and that you should fast is better for you,
if you but know;
the month of Ramadan, wherein the Koran
was sent down to be a guidance
to the people, and as clear signs
of the Guidance and the Salvation.

So let those of you, who are present
At the month, fast it.
Sura 2 ('The Cow'), vs 180–1

10 And fight in the way of God with those
who fight with you, but aggress not: God loves
not the aggressors.
And slay them wherever you come upon them,
and expel them from where they expelled you;
persecution is more grievous than slaying.
But fight them not by the Holy Mosque
until they should fight you there;
then, if they fight you, slay them –
such is the recompense of unbelievers –
but if they give over, surely God is
All-forgiving, All-compassionate.
Sura 2 ('The Cow'), vs 187–9

11 God
there is no god but He, the
Living, the Everlasting.
Slumber seizes Him not, neither sleep;
to Him belongs
all that is in the heavens and the earth.
Who is there that shall intercede with Him
save by His leave?
He knows what lies before them
and what is after them,
and they comprehend not anything of His
   knowledge
save such as He wills.
Sura 2 ('The Cow'), v. 256

12 No compulsion is there in religion.
Sura 2 ('The Cow'), v. 258. Cited v. 256 in some editions.

13 Say to the unbelievers: 'You shall be
   overthrown, and mustered into Gehenna – an
   evil cradling!'
Sura 3 ('The House of Imran'), v. 10. *An Evil Cradling* is the
title of BRIAN KEENAN's account of his captivity as a hostage.

14 The true religion with God is Islam.
Sura 3 ('The House of Imran'), v. 17

15 No; Abraham in truth was not a Jew,
neither a Christian; but he was a Muslim
and one pure of faith; certainly he was never
of the idolaters.
Sura 3 ('The House of Imran'), v. 60

16 Every soul shall taste of death; you shall surely
be paid in full your wages on the Day
of Resurrection. Whosoever is removed
from the Fire and admitted to Paradise, shall

win the triumph. The present life is but the
joy of delusion.
Sura 3 ('The House of Imran'), v. 182

17 Men are the managers of the affairs of women
for that God has preferred in bounty
one of them over another, and for that
they have expended of their property.
Righteous women are therefore obedient,
guarding the secret for God's guarding.
And those you fear may be rebellious
admonish; banish them to their couches,
and beat them. If they then obey you,
look not for any way against them.
Sura 4 ('Women'), v. 38

18 Souls are very prone to avarice. If you do good
and are godfearing, surely God is aware of
the things you do.
Sura 4 ('Women'), v. 128

19 O believers, believe in God and His Messenger
and the Book He has sent down on His Messenger
and the Book which He sent down before.
Whoso disbelieves in God and His angels
and His Books, and His Messengers,
and the Last Day, has surely gone astray
into far error.
Sura 4 ('Women'), v. 135. Cited v. 136 in some editions.

20 O believers, when you stand up to pray
wash your faces, and your hands up to the
elbows, and wipe your heads, and your feet
up to the ankles.
Sura 5 ('The Table'), v. 9

21 I have no power to profit
for myself; or hurt, but as God will.
Had I knowledge of the Unseen
I would have acquired much good,
and evil would not have touched me.
I am only a warner, and a bearer of
good tidings, to a people believing.
Sura 7 ('The Battlements'), v. 188

22 When the sacred months are drawn away,
slay the idolaters wherever you find them,
and take them, and confine them, and lie in wait
for them at every place of ambush. But if they
repent, and perform the prayer, and pay the alms,
   then
let them go their way.
Sura 9 ('Repentance'), v. 5

23 Surely God wrongs not men anything, but themselves men wrong.
Sura 10 ('Jonah'), v. 45

24 Not so much as the weight of an ant in earth or heaven escapes from thy Lord, neither is aught smaller than that, or greater, but in a Manifest Book.
Sura 10 ('Jonah'), v. 63

25 God changes not what is in a people, until they change what is in themselves.
Sura 13 ('Thunder'), v. 11

26 As for evildoers, for them awaits a painful chastisement;
but for those who believe, and do deeds of righteousness, they shall be admitted to gardens underneath which rivers flow, therein dwelling forever,
by the leave of their Lord, their greeting therein: 'Peace!'
Sura 14 ('Abraham'), v. 28

27 A good word is as a good tree –
its roots are firm,
and its branches are in heaven;
it gives its produce every season
by the leave of its Lord.
Sura 14 ('Abraham'), vs 29–30

28 Glory be to Him, who carried His servant by night
from the Holy Mosque to the Further Mosque
the precincts of which We have blessed,
that We might show him some of Our signs.
He is the All-hearing, the All-seeing.
Sura 17 ('The Night Journey'), v. 1

29 And walk not in the earth exultantly; certainly thou wilt never tear the earth open, nor attain the mountains in height.
Sura 17 ('The Night Journey'), v. 39

30 And do not say, regarding anything,
'I am going to do that tomorrow,'
but only, 'If God will' [Inshallah].
Sura 18 ('The Cave'), v. 23

31 If the sea were ink
For the words of my Lord,
the sea would be spent before the Words of my Lord are spent.
Sura 18 ('The Cave') v. 109

32 We have sent it down
as an Arabic Koran, and We
have turned about in it something
of threats, that haply they may be
godfearing, or it may arouse in
them remembrance.
Sura 20 ('Ta Ha'), v. 113

33 He
named you Muslims
aforetime and in this, that the Messenger
might be a witness against you, and that
you might be witnesses against mankind.
Sura 22 ('The Pilgrimage'), v. 78

34 God is the Light of the heavens and the earth;
the likeness of His Light is as a niche
wherein is a lamp
(the lamp in a glass,
the glass as it were a glittering star)
kindled from a Blessed Tree,
an olive that is neither of the East nor of the West
whose oil wellnigh would shine, even if no fire touched it;
Light upon Light.
Sura 24 ('Light'), v. 35

35 And as for the unbelievers,
their works are as a mirage in a spacious plain
which the man athirst supposes to be water,
till, when he comes to it, he finds it is nothing;
there indeed he finds God,
and He pays him his account in full; (and God is swift
at the reckoning).
Sura 24 ('Light'), v. 39

36 Call not upon any other god with God;
there is no god but He.
All things perish, except His Face.
His is the Judgment, and unto Him you shall be returned.
Sura 28 ('The Story'), v. 88

37 Muhammad is not the father of any one
of your men, but the Messenger of God,
and the Seal of the Prophets.
Sura 33 ('The Confederates'), v. 40

38 He makes the night to enter into the day
and makes the day to enter into the night,

and He has subjected the sun and the moon, each
  of them running
to a stated term.
Sura 35 ('The Angels'), v. 13

39 And those who are slain in the way of God, He
will not send their works astray.
He will guide them, and dispose their minds
  aright,
and He will admit them to Paradise,
that He has made known to them.
Sura 47 ('Muhammad'), vs 6–7. Cited vs 4–6 in some editions.

40 Muhammad is the Messenger of God,
and those who are with him are hard
against the unbelievers, merciful
one to another. Thou seest them
bowing, prostrating, seeking bounty
from God and good pleasure. Their
mark is on their faces, the trace of
prostration. That is their likeness
in the Torah, and their likeness
in the Gospel.
Sura 48 ('Victory'), v. 29

41 As a seed that puts
forth its shoot, and strengthens it,
and it grows stout and rises straight
upon its stalk, pleasing the sowers,
that through them He may enrage
the unbelievers, God has promised
those of them who believe and do deeds
of righteousness forgiveness and
a mighty wage.
Sura 48 ('Victory'), v. 29

42 We indeed created man; and We know
what his soul whispers within him,
and We are nearer to him than the
jugular vein.
Sura 50 ('Qaf'), v. 15

43 Have you considered the water you drink?
Did you send it down from the clouds, or did We
  send it?
Did We will, We would make it bitter; so why are
  you not thankful?
Sura 56 ('The Terror'), vs 67–9. Cited vs 68–70 in some
editions.

44 He is the First and the Last, the Outward and
  the Inward;
He has knowledge of everything.
Sura 57 ('Iron'), v. 3

45 He is God,
the Creator, the Maker, the Shaper.
To Him belong the Names Most Beautiful.
All that is in the heavens and the earth magnifies
  Him;
He is the All-mighty, the All-wise.
Sura 59 ('The Mustering'), v. 25

46 Have you not regarded how God
created seven heavens one upon another,
and set the moon therein for a light
and the sun for a lamp?
And God caused you to grow out of the earth,
then He shall return you into it,
and bring you forth.
And God has laid the earth for you as a carpet,
that thereof you may thread ways, ravines.
Sura 71 ('Noah'), vs 14–19. Cited vs 15–20 in some editions.

47 Have We not made the earth as a cradle
and the mountains as pegs?
And We created you in pairs,
and We appointed your sleep for a rest;
and We appointed night for a garment,
and We appointed day for a livelihood.
And We have built above you seven strong ones,
and We appointed a blazing lamp
and have sent down out of the rain-clouds water
  cascading
that We may bring forth thereby grain and plants,
  and gardens luxuriant.
Sura 78 ('The Tiding'), vs 6–16

48 When the sun shall be darkened,
when the stars shall be thrown down,
when the mountains shall be set moving,
when the pregnant camels shall be neglected,
when the savage beasts shall be mustered,
when the seas shall be set boiling,
when the souls shall be when Hell shall be set
  blazing,
when Paradise shall be brought nigh,
then shall a soul know what it has produced.
Sura 81 ('The Darkening'), vs 1–14

49 So let man consider of what he was created;
he was created of gushing water
issuing between the loins and the breast-bones.
Sura 86 ('The Night-Star'), vs 5–7

50 Recite: In the Name of thy Lord who created,
created Man of a blood-clot.
Recite: And thy Lord is the Most Generous,

who taught by the Pen,
taught Man that he knew not.
Sura 96 ('The Blood-Clot'), vs 1–5

51 O unbelievers,
I serve not what you serve
and you are not serving what I serve,
nor am I serving what you have served,
neither are you serving what I serve.
To you your religion, and to me my religion!
Sura 109 ('The Unbelievers'), vs 1–5

Heinrich Kramer

See JACOB SPRENGER AND HEINRICH KRAMER

Larry Kramer

(b. 1935)
US playwright and novelist

He produced and scripted Ken Russell's film Women in Love
*(1969), but became better known for his writings on New York's
gay scene. His play* The Normal Heart *(1985) was an indictment
of the responses to AIDS.*

1 We're all going to go crazy, living this epidemic
every minute, while the rest of the world goes on
out there, all around us, as if nothing is happening
... We're living through war, but where they're living it's peacetime, and we're all in the same country.
The Normal Heart, Act 2, Sc. 11 (1985). Spoken by Ned.

2 The only way we'll have real pride is when we
demand recognition of a culture that isn't just
sexual.
Ned, ibid., Act 2, Sc. 13

Karl Kraus

(1874–1936)
Austrian satirist and poet

He edited his own satirical journal Die Fackel *(The Torch)
1899–1936, in which he waged a one-man war against corruption and hypocrisy. He was particularly scathing about the
liberal press and the bourgeoisie, which he also attacked in his
poetry and plays.*

1 The sound principle of a topsy-turvy lifestyle in
the framework of an upside-down world order has
stood every test.
'In Praise of a Topsy-Turvy Lifestyle' (1908), repr. in *In These
Great Times: A Karl Kraus Reader* (ed. Harry Zohn, 1976)

2 Squeeze human nature into the straitjacket of
criminal justice and crime will appear.
Morality and Criminal Justice, 'The Riehl Case' (1908)

3 An aphorism can never be the whole truth; it is
either a half-truth or a truth-and-a-half.
Die Fackel 19 January 1909, quoted in *Anti-Freud: Karl Kraus's
Criticism of Psychoanalysis and Psychiatry*, ch. 8 (1976) by
THOMAS SZASZ

4 Sexuality poorly repressed unsettles some
families; well repressed, it unsettles the whole
world.
Die Fackel 26 January 1911, ibid., ch. 8

5 Hate must make a man productive. Otherwise one
might as well love.
Pro Domo et Mundo, ch. 6 (1912)

6 In these great times which I knew when they were
this small; which will become small again, provided
they have time left for it; and which, because in the
realm of organic growth, no such transformation is
possible, we had better call fat times and, truly hard
times as well; in these times in which things are
happening that could not be imagined and in which
what can no longer be *imagined* must *happen*, for
if one could imagine it, it would not happen; in
these serious times which have died laughing at the
thought that they might become serious; which,
surprised by their own tragedy, are reaching for
diversion and, catching themselves redhanded, are
groping for words; in these loud times which boom
with the horrible symphony of actions which produce reports and of reports which cause actions: in
these times you should not expect any words of my
own from me – none but these words which barely
manage to prevent silence from being misinter-
preted.
'In These Great Times', speech in Vienna, 19 November 1914,
publ. in *In These Great Times: A Karl Kraus Reader* (ed. Harry
Zohn, 1976)

7 Culture is the tacit agreement to let the means of
subsistence disappear behind the purpose of existence. Civilization is the subordination of the latter
to the former.
'In These Great Times', ibid.

8 If the reporter has killed our imagination with his
truth, he threatens our life with his lies.
'In These Great Times', ibid.

9 The esthete stands in the same relation to beauty
as the pornographer stands to love, and the poli-
tician stands to life.
Die Fackel 5 October 1915, quoted in *Anti-Freud: Karl Kraus's
Criticism of Psychoanalysis and Psychiatry*, ch. 8 (1976) by
THOMAS SZASZ

10 My unconscious knows more about the consciousness of the psychologist than his consciousness knows about my unconscious.
Die Fackel 18 January 1917, ibid., ch. 6

11 News reports stand up as people, and people wither into editorials. Clichés walk around on two legs while men are having theirs shot off.
Prologue (1917) to *The Last Days of Mankind* (1919), repr. in *In These Great Times: A Karl Kraus Reader* (ed. Harry Zohn, 1976)

12 Only he is an artist who can make a riddle out of a solution.
Nachts, ch. 2 (1918)

Jiddu Krishnamurti
(1895–1986)
Indian mystic

As an obscure youth he was hailed as a 'world teacher' and messiah by the Theosophical Society's President, Annie Besant, but in 1929 he renounced organized religion in favour of complete spiritual freedom.

1 I maintain that Truth is a pathless land, and you cannot approach it by any path whatsoever, by any religion, by any sect.
Speech in Holland, 3 August 1929, quoted in *Krishnamurti*, ch. 2 (1931) by Lilly Heber

Kris Kristofferson
(b. 1936)
US singer, songwriter and actor

He made his name with two songs, 'Me and Bobby McGhee' (1969) and 'Help Me Make It Through the Night' (1971). He went on to record country albums and star in films.

1 Freedom's just another word for nothing left to lose.
'Me and Bobby McGhee' (song, 1969, written with Fred Foster). The song, first recorded by ROGER MILLER in 1969, was a posthumous hit for JANIS JOPLIN in 1971, and the title track of a Kristofferson album later that year.

Joseph Wood Krutch
(1893–1970)
US author and critic

He was drama critic for The Nation (1924–52) and also published essays, biographies and works on nature. 'Maybe the most I can claim,' he wrote, 'is that I know more about botany than any other New York critic, and more about the theatre than any other botanist.'

1 Cats seem to go on the principle that it never does any harm to ask for what you want.
Twelve Seasons, 'February' (1949)

2 The most serious charge which can be brought against New England is not Puritanism but February.
Ibid., 'February'

Stanley Kubrick
(1928–99)
US film-maker

Famed for his meticulous procedures and ambitious technique, he worked in a range of genres from science fiction (2001: A Space Odyssey, 1968) to youth violence (A Clockwork Orange, 1971) and horror (The Shining, 1979).

1 The great nations have always acted like gangsters, and the small nations like prostitutes.
Guardian 5 June 1963

2 Confront a man in his office with a nuclear alarm, and you have a documentary. If the news reaches him in his living room, you have a drama. If it catches him in the lavatory, the result is comedy.
Quoted in *Stanley Kubrick Directs* (1972) by Alexander Walker. Discussing comic method in his film *Dr. Strangelove* (1964).

Milan Kundera
(b. 1929)
Czech-born French author and critic

The critic Edmund White described him as 'currently the favored spokesman for the uneasy conscience of the French intellectual'. He moved to France in 1975 after being banned in his home country. His novels blend fact with fiction, philosophy and politics and include The Joke (1967) and Immortality (1991).

1 Optimism is the opium of the people.
The Joke, pt 3, ch. 3 (1967, transl. 1982). The line, written by Ludvik on a postcard, was used by the Party as incriminating evidence against him, though it was only meant as 'a joke'. See KARL MARX 1.

2 No great movement designed to change the world can bear to be laughed at or belittled. Mockery is a rust that corrodes all it touches.
Kostka, ibid., pt 6, ch. 18

3 The struggle of man against power is the struggle of memory against forgetting.
The Book of Laughter and Forgetting, pt 1, sect. 2 (1978). Spoken by Mirek.

4 Her drama was a drama not of heaviness but of

lightness. What fell to her lot was not the burden but the unbearable lightness of being.

The Unbearable Lightness of Being, pt 3, ch. 10 (1984). Referring to Sabina.

5 Mankind's true moral test, its fundamental test (which lies deeply buried from view), consists of its attitude towards those who are at its mercy: animals.

Ibid., pt 7, ch. 2

6 A novel that does not uncover a hitherto unknown segment of existence is immoral. Knowledge is the novel's only morality.

New York Review of Books 19 July 1984

7 Hate traps us by binding us too tightly to our adversary.

Immortality, pt 1, ch. 5 (1991)

8 War and culture, those are the two poles of Europe, her heaven and hell, her glory and shame, and they cannot be separated from one another. When one comes to an end, the other will end also and one cannot end without the other. The fact that no war has broken out in Europe for fifty years is connected in some mysterious way with the fact that for fifty years no new Picasso has appeared either.

Ibid., pt 1, ch. 5

9 *I think, therefore I am* is the statement of an intellectual who underrates toothaches.

Ibid., pt 4, ch. 11. See RENÉ DESCARTES 3.

10 All great novels, all true novels, are bisexual.

The Times 16 May 1991

Akira Kurosawa

(1910–98)

Japanese film-maker

He introduced Japanese cinema to the West with Rashomon *(1950), and his samurai epics such as* The Seven Samurai *(1954) were the inspiration for Hollywood and spaghetti westerns.*

1 We have survived again.

The Seven Samurai (film, 1954, screenplay by Shinobu Hashimoto, Hideo Oguni and Akira Kurosawa, directed by Akira Kurosawa). Spoken by the samurai Kanbei to Shichiroji, after they have battled to save a village from a bandit attack.

Thomas Kyd

(1558–94)

English dramatist

His revenge play The Spanish Tragedy *(c. 1589) made him the most popular dramatist of his day. He was imprisoned in 1593 on charges of atheism and heresy.*

1 Where words prevail not, violence prevails;
But gold doth more than either of them both.

The Spanish Tragedy, Act 2, Sc. 2 (*c.* 1589). Spoken by Lorenzo.

2 Oh eyes, no eyes, but fountains fraught with tears;
Oh life, no life, but lively form of death;
Oh world, no world, but mass of public wrongs,
Confused and filled with murder and misdeeds.

Hieronimo, ibid., Act 3, Sc. 2

3 For what's a play without a woman in it?

Hieronimo, ibid., Act 4, Sc. 1

L

Henry Labouchere

(1831–1912)

English journalist and politician

He had a varied career as a diplomat and journalist, entering Parliament as a Liberal in 1865, and later standing as a radical (1880–1905).

1 I do not object to Gladstone's always having the ace of trumps up his sleeve, but only to his pretence that God had put it there.

Quoted in *Dictionary of National Biography* (1912–21)

Edouard Laboulaye

(1811–83)

French scholar and author

As Professor of Comparative Legislation at the College of France, he won fame for his Political History of the United States *(3 vols., 1855–66). He entered politics in 1871.*

1 The first day a man is a guest, the second a burden, the third a pest.

Abdallah, ch. 9 (1871). Spoken by Abdallah.

Labour Party Constitution

1 To secure for the workers by hand or by brain the full fruits of their industry, and the most equitable distribution thereof that may be possible, upon the basis of the common ownership of the means of production, distribution, and exchange.

Clause 4, drafted in 1918 by SIDNEY WEBB and Arthur Henderson, and revised in 1926. There were several attempts to drop this commitment to nationalization, including by HUGH GAITSKELL after Labour's defeat in 1959, and by ROY HATTERSLEY in 1993; it was finally rescinded by New Labour in 1995.

Jean de La Bruyère

(1645–96)

French essayist and moralist

His Caractères *(1688), which first appeared as an appendage to his translation of the Greek peripatetic philosopher Theophrastus, combined moral maxims with portraits of contemporary social types. He was a librarian at the house of Condé from 1684.*

1 Everything has been said, and we have come too late, now that men have been living and thinking for seven thousand years and more.

The Characters, or the Manners of the Age, 'Of Books', aph. 1 (1688)

2 Making a book is a craft, like making a clock; it needs more than native wit to be an author.

Ibid., 'Of Books', aph. 3

3 There are certain things in which mediocrity is intolerable: poetry, music, painting, public eloquence.

Ibid., 'Of Books', aph. 7

4 A well-born man is fortunate, but so is the man about whom people no longer ask, is he well-born?

Ibid., 'Of Personal Merit', aph. 21

5 From time to time there appear on the face of the earth men of rare and consummate excellence, who dazzle us by their virtue, and whose outstanding qualities shed a stupendous light. Like those extraordinary stars of whose origins we are ignorant, and of whose fate, once they have vanished, we know even less, such men have neither forebears nor descendants: they are the whole of their race.

Ibid., 'Of Personal Merit', aph. 22

6 False greatness is unsociable and remote: conscious of its own frailty, it hides, or at least averts its face, and reveals itself only enough to create an illusion and not be recognized as the meanness that it really is. True greatness is free, kind, familiar and popular; it lets itself be touched and handled, it loses nothing by being seen at close quarters; the better one knows it, the more one admires it.

Ibid., 'Of Personal Merit', aph. 42

7 That man is good who does good to others; if he suffers on account of the good he does, he is very good; if he suffers at the hands of those to whom he has done good, then his goodness is so great that it could be enhanced only by greater sufferings; and if he should die at their hands, his virtue can go no further: it is heroic, it is perfect.

Ibid., 'Of Personal Merit', aph. 44

8 We can recognize the dawn and the decline of love by the uneasiness we feel when alone together.

Ibid., 'Of the Heart', aph. 33

9 One seeks to make the loved one entirely happy, or, if that cannot be, entirely wretched.

Ibid., 'Of the Heart', aph. 39

10 Generosity lies less in giving much than in giving at the right moment.
Ibid., 'Of the Heart', aph. 47

11 We should laugh before being happy, for fear of dying without having laughed.
Ibid., 'Of the Heart', aph. 63

12 Nothing more clearly shows how little God esteems his gift to men of wealth, money, position and other worldly goods, than the way he distributes these, and the sort of men who are most amply provided with them.
Ibid., 'Of Worldly Goods', aph. 24. See JONATHAN SWIFT 24.

13 There are only two ways of getting on in the world: either by one's own cunning efforts, or by other people's foolishness.
Ibid., 'Of Worldly Goods', aph. 52

14 The giving is the hardest part; what does it cost to add a smile?
Ibid., 'Of the Court', aph. 45

15 There are only three things that happen to a man: birth, life and death. He is unaware of birth, he suffers at death, and he forgets to live.
Ibid., 'Of Man', aph. 48

16 Lofty posts make great men greater still, and small men much smaller.
Ibid., 'Of Man', aph. 95

17 One mark of a second-rate mind is to be always telling stories.
Ibid., 'Of Opinions', aph. 52

18 Between good sense and good taste there lies the difference between a cause and its effect.
Ibid., 'Of Opinions', aph. 56

Pierre Choderlos de Laclos
(1741–1803)
French soldier and author

An artillery officer and eventually a general under NAPOLEON, *he had immediate success with his first novel,* Les Liaisons dangereuses *(1782). Written in epistolary form, it portrayed the immorality of society and the corruption of innocence.*

1 It has become necessary for me to have this woman, so as to save myself from the ridicule of being in love with her: for to what lengths will a man not be driven by thwarted desire?
Les Liaisons dangereuses, Letter 4 (1782; *Dangerous Liaisons*). Spoken by the Vicomte de Valmont.

2 Monsieur de Valmont ... early realized that to achieve influence in society no more is required than to practise the arts of adulation and ridicule with equal skill.
Madame de Volanges, ibid., Letter 32

3 A man enjoys the happiness he feels, a woman the happiness she gives ... Giving pleasure for him is only a means to success; while for her it is success itself.
Madame de Rosemonde, ibid., Letter 130

4 One is very soon bored with everything, my angel; it is a law of nature. It is not my fault.
Marquise de Merteuil, ibid., Letter 141. Recounting a letter written to an acquaintance whose favourite expression was: 'It was not my fault.'

Christian Lacroix
(b. 1951)
French fashion designer

Known for his ornate designs, he opened his own couture and ready-to-wear business in 1987.

1 Haute Couture should be fun, foolish and almost unwearable.
Quoted in the *Observer* 27 December 1987

Suzanne LaFollette
(1893–1983)
US editor and author

As a committed libertarian and feminist, she advocated economic freedom for both sexes in such works as Concerning Women *(1926). She became an ardent anti-Communist in the 1940s, and co-founded the* National Review *in 1955.*

1 There is nothing more innately human than the tendency to transmute what has become customary into what has been divinely ordained.
Concerning Women, 'The Beginnings of Emancipation' (1926)

2 Laws are felt only when the individual comes into conflict with them.
Ibid., 'The Beginnings of Emancipation'

Jean de La Fontaine
(1621–95)
French poet and fabulist

Publishing a miscellany of poems and dramatic pieces from 1657, he achieved greatest prominence as the writer of elegant fables written in free verse (1668, 1678–9 and 1694), in which animals are the protagonists. Other works include Les Amours de Psyché et de Cupidon, *a prose narrative (1669).*

1 I bend, indeed, but never break.
Fables, bk 1, no. 22 ('The Oak and the Reed') (1668). The words of the reed to the oak.

2 It is doubly sweet to deceive the deceiver.
Ibid., bk 2, no. 15 ('The Cock and the Fox'). Moral of fable.

3 In short, luck's always to blame.
Ibid., bk 5, no. 11 ('Fortune and the Boy'). Moral of fable.

4 Death never takes the wise man by surprise,
He is always ready to go.
Ibid., bk 8, no. 1 ('Death and the Dying') (1678–9). See also MONTAIGNE 2.

5 A foolish friend may cause more woe
Than could, indeed, the wisest foe.
Ibid., bk 8, no. 10 ('The Bear and the Amateur Gardener'). Moral of fable.

6 And, while he knows the universe,
Himself he does not know.
Ibid., bk 8, no. 26 ('Democritus and the People of Abdera'). Spoken by the messengers.

Jules Laforgue
(1860–87)
French poet

A Symbolist who popularized vers libre, *he also wrote short stories and art criticism. He died in poverty.*

1 *Et pour tuer le temps, en attendant la mort,*
Je fume au nez des dieux de fines cigarettes.
[And to kill time while awaiting death,
I smoke slender cigarettes thumbing my nose to the gods.]
'La Cigarette', st. 1, written 1880, publ. in *Le Sanglot de la Terre* (1901)

2 *Ah! que la vie est quotidienne . . .*
[What a day-to-day affair life is . . .]
'Complainte sur certains ennuis', st. 1, publ. in *Les Complaintes* (1885)

Jean-François de La Harpe
(1739–1803)
French critic and playwright

He wrote a number of unsuccessful plays, but was most respected as a critic of 17th-century literature and as the editor of Mercure de France.

1 We always weaken whatever we exaggerate.
Mélanie, Act 1, Sc. 1 (1778). Spoken by M. de Faublas.

2 We never forgive those who make us blush.
Mélanie, ibid., Act 3, Sc. 1

John Lahr
(b. 1941)
US author and critic

Theatre critic for the Village Voice *and the* New Yorker, *he has written biographies of* JOE ORTON, FRANK SINATRA, *and his father Bert Lahr, the actor.*

1 Society drives people crazy with lust and calls it advertising.
Guardian 2 August 1989

R. D. Laing
(1927–89)
British psychiatrist

Ronald David Laing. The leading light of the anti-psychiatry movement, he made extensive studies of schizophrenia, believing it to spring from tensions within the nuclear family.

1 Schizophrenia cannot be understood without understanding despair.
The Divided Self, pt 1, ch. 2 (1959)

2 We are all murderers and prostitutes – no matter to what culture, society, class, nation one belongs, no matter how normal, moral, or mature, one takes oneself to be.
The Politics of Experience, Introduction (1967)

3 Alienation as our present destiny is achieved only by outrageous violence perpetrated by human beings on human beings.
Ibid., Introduction

4 From the moment of birth, when the stone-age baby confronts the twentieth-century mother, the baby is subjected to these forces of violence, called love, as its mother and father have been, and their parents and their parents before them. These forces are mainly concerned with destroying most of its potentialities. This enterprise is on the whole successful.
Ibid., ch. 3

5 The experience and behaviour that gets labelled schizophrenic is a special strategy that a person invents in order to live in an unlivable situation.
Ibid., ch. 5

6 Madness need not be all breakdown. It may also be break-through. It is potential liberation and renewal as well as enslavement and existential death.
Ibid., ch. 6

Alphonse de Lamartine
(1790–1869)
French statesman, poet and author

He established his literary reputation with his verse collection,
Méditations poétiques (1820), a key work of the Romantic
movement. He went on to publish history and fiction and was a
Deputy from 1833, briefly heading the provisional government
after the 1848 revolution.

1 O time, arrest your flight! and you, propitious hours, arrest your course! Let us savour the fleeting delights of our most beautiful days!
'Le Lac', st. 6, publ. in *Méditations poétiques* (1820)

2 Utopia is a reality whose time has not yet come.
Attributed

(Lady) Caroline Lamb
(1785–1828)
English novelist

Famously eccentric, she is remembered for her affair with
LORD BYRON *1812–13. She had married William Lamb (later*
LORD MELBOURNE) *in 1805, and separated from him in 1825.*

1 Mad, bad, and dangerous to know.
Journal entry, March 1812, publ. in *Lady Caroline Lamb*, ch. 6 (1932) by Elizabeth Jenkins. Referring to BYRON, after their first meeting at a ball. Byron wrote in a letter to her in April 1812 that he considered her 'the cleverest, most agreeable, absurd, amiable, perplexing, dangerous, fascinating little being that lives now or ought to have lived 2000 years ago'.

Charles Lamb
(1775–1834)
English essayist and critic

With his sister Mary Lamb he produced a children's edition of
SHAKESPEARE's *plays (1807), while his* Specimens of English Dramatic Poets *(1808) helped to revive interest in Elizabethan drama. As 'Elia' he contributed essays to the* London Magazine *from 1820, and he also wrote poetry. See* WILLIAM HAZLITT 29.

1 I have had playmates, I have had companions,
In my days of childhood, in my joyful school days –
All, all are gone, the old familiar faces.
'The Old Familiar Faces', publ. in *Blank Verse* (1798)

2 Please to blot out *gentle hearted*, and substitute drunken dog, ragged head, seld-shaven, odd-eyed, stuttering, or any other epithet which truly and properly belongs to the gentleman in question.
Letter to SAMUEL TAYLOR COLERIDGE, 14 August 1800, publ.

in *The Letters of Charles and Mary Anne Lamb*, vol. 1 (ed. Edwin W. Marrs, 1975). Referring to lines Coleridge had inserted in his poem 'This Lime Tree Bower My Prison': 'For thee, my gentle-hearted Charles, to whom/No sound is dissonant which tells of life.' In a previous letter (6 August 1800), Lamb had written: 'For God's sake (I never was more serious) don't make me ridiculous any more by terming me gentle-hearted in print.'

3 Separate from the pleasure of your company, I don't much care if I never see another mountain in my life.
Letter to WILLIAM WORDSWORTH, 30 January 1801, ibid., vol. 1

4 I have passed all my days in London, until I have formed as many and intense local attachments as any of you mountaineers can have done with dead nature. The lighted shops of the Strand and Fleet Street, the innumerable trades, tradesmen, and customers, coaches, waggons, playhouses, all the bustle and wickedness round about Covent Garden, the very women of the town, the watchmen, drunken scenes, rattles; – life awake, if you awake, at all hours of the night, the impossibility of being dull in Fleet Street, the crowds, the very dirt & mud, the sun shining upon houses and pavements, the print shops, the old book stalls, parsons cheap'ning books, coffee houses, steams of soups from kitchens, pantomimes, London itself, a pantomime and a masquerade, – all these things work themselves into my mind and feed me without a power of satiating me. The wonder of these sights impels me into nightwalks about her crowded streets, and I often shed tears in the motley Strand from fullness of joy at so much life.
Letter to WILLIAM WORDSWORTH, 30 January 1801, ibid., vol. 1

5 The man must have a rare recipe for melancholy, who can be dull in Fleet Street.
Letter to the traveller Thomas Manning, 15 February 1802, ibid., vol. 2

6 Gone before
To that unknown and silent shore.
'Hester', st. 7, written 1803, publ. in *The Works of Charles Lamb* (1818)

7 For thy sake, Tobacco, I
Would do anything but die.
'A Farewell to Tobacco', ll. 122–3, written 1805, ibid.

8 Nothing puzzles me more than time and space;

and yet nothing troubles me less, as I never think about them.

Letter, 2 January 1810, publ. in *The Letters of Charles and Mary Anne Lamb*, vol. 3 (ed. Edwin W. Marrs, 1975)

9 I think his essentials not touched, he is very bad, but then he wonderfully picks up another day, and his face when he repeats his verses hath its ancient glory, an Archangel a little damaged.

Describing SAMUEL TAYLOR COLERIDGE, in letter to WILLIAM WORDSWORTH, 26 April 1816, ibid., vol. 3

10 The human species, according to the best theory I can form of it, is composed of two distinct races, *the men who borrow* and *the men who lend*.

Essays of Elia, 'The Two Races of Men' (1823)

11 *Borrowers of books* – those mutilators of collections, spoilers of the symmetry of shelves, and creators of odd volumes.

Ibid., 'The Two Races of Men'

12 But cards are war, in disguise of a sport.

Ibid., 'Mrs Battle's Opinions on Whist'

13 In everything that relates to *science*, I am a whole encyclopaedia behind the rest of the world.

Ibid., 'The Old and the New Schoolmaster'

14 Boys are capital fellows in their own way, among their mates; but they are unwholesome companions for grown people.

Ibid., 'The Old and the New Schoolmaster'

15 Why are we never quite at ease in the presence of a schoolmaster? Because we are conscious that he is not quite at his ease in ours. He is awkward, and out of place in the society of his equals. He comes like Gulliver from among his little people, and he cannot fit the stature of his understanding to yours.

Ibid., 'The Old and the New Schoolmaster'. Of the schoolmaster, Lamb wrote: 'He can receive no pleasure from a casual glimpse of nature, but must catch at it as an object of instruction . . . The universe – that Great Book, as it has been called – is to him, indeed, to all intents and purposes, a book out of which he is doomed to read tedious homilies to distasting schoolboys.'

16 Not many sounds in life . . . exceed in interest a knock at the door.

Ibid., 'Valentine's Day'

17 I have been trying all my life to like Scotchmen, and am obliged to desist from the experiment in despair.

Ibid., 'Imperfect Sympathies'

18 'Presents', I often say, 'endear absents.'

Ibid., 'A Dissertation Upon Roast Pig'

19 When I consider how little of a rarity children are – that every street and blind alley swarms with them, that the poorest people commonly have them in most abundance, that there are few marriages that are not blest with at least one of these bargains, how often they turn out ill, and defeat the fond hopes of their parents, taking to vicious courses, which end in poverty, disgrace, the gallows, etc. – I cannot for my life tell what cause for pride there can possibly be in having them.

Ibid., 'A Bachelor's Complaint of the Behaviour of Married People'

20 Damn the age; I will write for antiquity!

Letter, 22 January 1829, publ. in *The Letters of Charles Lamb*, vol. 3 (ed. E. V. Lucas, 1935). On the rejection of a sonnet.

21 A poor relation is the most irrelevant thing in nature, a piece of impertinent correspondency, an odious approximation, a haunting conscience, a preposterous shadow, lengthening in the noon-tide of our prosperity . . . He is known by his knock.

Last Essays of Elia, 'Poor Relations' (1833). Opening lines of essay.

22 The teller of a mirthful tale has latitude allowed him. We are content with less than absolute truth.

Ibid., 'Stage Illusion'

23 An ingenious acquaintance of my own . . . has left off reading altogether, to the great improvement of his originality.

Ibid., 'Detached Thoughts on Books and Reading'

24 Books think for me.

Ibid., 'Detached Thoughts on Books and Reading'

25 Newspapers always excite curiosity. No one ever lays one down without a feeling of disappointment.

Ibid., 'Detached Thoughts on Books and Reading'

26 How sickness enlarges the dimensions of a man's self to himself.

Ibid., 'The Convalescent'

27 A pun is not bound by the laws which limit nicer wit. It is a pistol let off at the ear; not a feather to tickle the intellect.

Ibid., 'Popular Fallacies', no. 9 ('That the Worst Puns are the Best')

28 The greatest pleasure I know, is to do a good

action by stealth, and to have it found out by accident.

'Table Talk by the Late Elia' (1834), repr. in *The Works of Charles and Mary Lamb*, vol. 1 (ed. E. V. Lucas, 1903)

(Sir) William Lamb

See LORD MELBOURNE

Lamentations of Khakheperre-seneb

(19th century BC)

Also known as The Complaints (*or* Words) *of Khakheperre-seneb, this hieroglyphic document from ancient Egypt honours King Senusret II, while lamenting the personal and social misfortunes that have befallen the speaker.*

1 Had I unknown phrases
Sayings that are strange
Novel, untried words
Free of repetition
Not transmitted sayings
Spoken by ancestors.
I wring my out body for what it holds,
Sifting through all my words;
For what has been said is just repetition,
What has been said has been said.

'The Complaints of Khakheperre-seneb', publ. in *The Unfolding of Language*, ch. 3 (2005) by Guy Deutscher

Norman Lamont

(b. 1942)

British politician

Baron Lamont of Lerwick. He was elected Conservative MP in 1972 and became Chancellor of the Exchequer in 1990. Following Britain's withdrawal from the European Exchange Rate Mechanism, he was replaced in 1993 and became a critic of Conservative policies.

1 The green shoots of economic spring are appearing once again.

Speech at Conservative Party Conference, Blackpool, 9 October 1991, quoted in *The Times* 10 October 1991. The phrase is usually remembered 'green shoots of economic recovery'.

2 We give the impression of being in office but not in power.

Resignation statement to House of Commons, 9 June 1993, publ. in *The Times* 10 June 1993. Lamont had been replaced as Chancellor of the Exchequer in a Cabinet reshuffle two weeks earlier.

Giuseppe Tomasi di Lampedusa

(1896–1957)

Sicilian author

His only novel, The Leopard *(1958), tells the nostalgic but cynical tale of an aristocratic family in Sicily at the time of Italy's unification.*

1 If we want everything to remain as it is, it will be necessary for everything to change.

The Leopard, ch. 1 (1958). Spoken by Prince Tancredi.

(Sir) Osbert Lancaster

(1908–86)

British author and cartoonist

Described by JOHN BETJEMAN *as writing 'deliciously convoluted prose', he was a satirist of mores and architecture, coining the phrase 'stockbroker Tudor'. He drew cartoons for the* Daily Express *from 1939 until his death.*

1 For self-revelation, whether it be a Tudor villa on the by-pass or a bomb-proof chalet at Berchtesgaden, there's no place like home.

Homes Sweet Homes, Preface (1939)

Elsa Lanchester

(1902–86)

British-born US actor

Originally Elizabeth Sullivan. Among her films are The Bride of Frankenstein *(1935) and* Witness for the Prosecution *(1957). She was married to the actor Charles Laughton.*

1 She looked as though butter wouldn't melt in her mouth – or anywhere else.

Attributed remark referring to actress Maureen O'Hara

Letitia Elizabeth Landon

(1802–38)

English poet and novelist

She published verse from 1821 and fiction from 1831, and was in great demand as a contributor to annuals. She died of poisoning in Africa.

1 Ah tell me not that memory
Sheds gladness o'er the past;
What is recalled by faded flowers
Save that they did not last?

'Despondency', publ. in *Complete Works* (1853)

2 Were it not better to forget
Than but remember and regret?

'Despondency', ibid.

3 Few, save the poor, feel for the poor.
'The Poor', ibid.

Walter Savage Landor
(1775–1864)
English author and poet

Though admired by ROBERT BROWNING *and* T. S. ELIOT, *his poetry was little appreciated in his time. His most enduring work is* Imaginary Conversations (1824–9), *a series of dialogues.*

1 Ah, what avails the sceptred race!
Ah, what the form divine!
'Rose Aylmer', publ. in *Simonidea* (1806), repr. in *Works* (ed. John Forster, 1846)

2 A solitude is the audience-chamber of God.
Imaginary Conversations of Literary Men and Statesmen, vol. 1, 'Lord Brooke and Sir Philip Sidney' (1824). Spoken by Lord Brooke.

3 Ternissa: O what a thing is age!
Leontion: Death without death's quiet.
Ibid., vol. 5, 'Epicurus, Leontion, and Ternissa' (1829)

4 I strove with none, for none was worth my
strife;
Nature I loved, and, next to Nature, Art.
I warmed both hands before the fire of life;
It sinks; and I am ready to depart.
'Dying Speech of an Old Philosopher', written 1849, repr. in *Last Fruit off an Old Tree* (1853). Composed on his seventy-fifth birthday.

(Sir) Edwin Landseer
(1802–73)
English painter and sculptor

Specializing in animals, often portrayed in a sentimental or symbolic style, he was responsible for 'Monarch of the Glen' (1851) and the bronze lions in London's Trafalgar Square (1867).

1 If people only knew as much about painting as I do, they would never buy my pictures.
Quoted in *Landseer the Victorian Paragon*, ch. 12 (1976) by Campbell Lennie

Andrew Lang
(1844–1912)
Scottish author and poet

His diverse output ranged from verse and fiction to collections of fairy tales and translations of HOMER.

1 They hear like ocean on a western beach
The surge and thunder of the Odyssey.
'The Odyssey' (1881), publ. in *The Poetical Works of Andrew Lang*, vol. 2 (ed. Mrs Lang, 1923)

2 He uses statistics as a drunken man uses lamp-posts – for support rather than illumination.
Quoted in *The Harvest of a Quiet Eye* (1977) by Alan L. Mackay

Julia Lang
(b. 1921)
British broadcaster

1 Are you sitting comfortably? Then I'll begin.
Listen with Mother (daily children's stories on BBC radio, 1950–82). Introductory words, sometimes spoken: '...Then we'll begin.'

Dorothea Lange
(1895–1979)
US photographer

Her photographs in An American Exodus: A Record of Human Erosion *(1939), produced in collaboration with her husband, the economist Paul Taylor, memorably documented the homeless of San Francisco and the migrant workers of the Depression.*

1 The camera is an instrument that teaches people how to see without a camera.
Quoted in the *Los Angeles Times* 13 August 1978

Susanne K. Langer
(1895–1985)
US philosopher

Susanne Knauth Langer. She wrote on aesthetics and linguistic analysis, as in Feeling and Form *(1953) and* Mind: An Essay on Human Feeling *(3 vols. 1967–82).*

1 Art is the objectification of feeling, and the subjectification of nature.
Mind: An Essay on Human Feeling, vol. 1, pt 2, ch. 4 (1967)

William Langland
(c. 1332–c. 1400)
English poet

He was the presumed author of the alliterative Middle English poem Piers Plowman *(1362–98), a religious allegory which appeared in three versions, known as the A, B and C texts. Little is known of his life.*

1 In a somer seson, whan softe was the sonne,
I shoop me into shroudes as I a sheep were,

In habite as an heremite unholy of werkes,
Went wide in this world wondres to here.
The Vision of William Concerning Piers Plowman, Prologue,
ll. 1–4 (B text, *c.* 1379, ed. A. V. C. Schmidt, 1987)

2 A faire feeld ful of folk fond I ther bitwene –
Of alle manere of men, the meene and the riche,
Werchynge and wandrynge as the world asketh.
Ibid., Prologue, ll. 17–19

3 A gloton of wordes.
Ibid., Prologue, l. 139

4 Grammer, the ground of al.
Ibid., Passus 15, l. 370

Lao-tzu

See TAO TE CHING

Lewis H. Lapham

(b. 1935)
US essayist and editor

He has been Editor of Harper's *magazine since 1975, and has commented extensively on US materialism and the world economy in such books as* The Agony of Mammon *(1999) and* 30 Satires *(2003).*

1 Under the rules of a society that cannot distinguish between profit and profiteering, between money defined as necessity and money defined as luxury, murder is occasionally obligatory and always permissible.
Money and Class in America, ch. 4 (1988)

2 If a foreign country doesn't look like a middle-class suburb of Dallas or Detroit, then obviously the natives must be dangerous as well as badly dressed.
Ibid., ch. 5, sect. 1

3 The more prosperous and settled a nation, the more readily it tends to think of war as a regrettable accident; to nations less fortunate the chance of war presents itself as a possible bountiful friend.
Harper's March 1991

Frances Moore Lappé

(b. 1944)
US ecologist and author

Her arguments for more equitable control over food production and distribution to prevent world hunger are expressed in Diet for a Small Planet *(1971) and* Food First: Beyond the Myth of Scarcity *(1977).*

1 The act of putting into your mouth what the earth has grown is perhaps your most direct interaction with the earth.
Diet for a Small Planet, pt 1 (1971)

Philip Larkin

(1922–85)
British poet

A librarian all his life (at Hull from 1955), he was preoccupied with transience and death at the cost of being, as he put it, a 'gloomy old sod'. His volumes include The Less Deceived *(1955) and* High Windows *(1974).*

1 I have just farted with the sound of an iron ruler twanging in a desk-lid and the smell of a west wind over a decaying patch of red cabbages.
Letter, 31 December 1941, publ. in *Selected Letters of Philip Larkin 1940–1985* (ed. Anthony Thwaite, 1992)

2 Poetry = heightened talking. Novel = a heightened story. Painting = a heightened seeing.
Letter, 23 May 1947, ibid.

3 I search myself for illusions like a monkey looking for fleas.
Letter, 13 July 1949, ibid.

4 I am beginning to think of the creative imagination as a fruit machine on which victories are rare and separated by much vain expense, and represent a rare alignment of mental and spiritual qualities that normally are quite at odds.
Letter, 26 February 1950, ibid.

5 I have no ideas about poetry at all. For me, a poem is the crossroads of my thoughts, my feelings, my imaginings, my wishes, & my verbal sense: normally these run parallel; often two or more cross; but only when all cross at one point do you get a poem.
Letter, 10 July 1951, ibid.

6 What are days for?
Days are where we live.
They come, they wake us
Time and time over.
'Days', written 1953, publ. in *The Whitsun Weddings* (1964)

7 A serious house on serious earth it is,
In whose blent air all our compulsions meet,
Are recognised, and robed as destinies.
'Church Going', publ. in *The Less Deceived* (1955)

8 Why should I let the toad *work*
Squat on my life?
Can't I use my wit as a pitchfork

And drive the brute off?
'Toads', ibid.

9 Home is so sad. It stays as it was left,
Shaped to the comfort of the last to go
As if to win them back.
'Home is so Sad', written 1958, publ. in *The Whitsun Weddings*
(1964)

10 The only way of getting shut of your family is to
put your neck into the noose of another one. Such
is nature's abhorrence of a vacuum.
Letter, 25 May 1958, publ. in *Selected Letters of Philip Larkin
1940–1985* (ed. Anthony Thwaite, 1992)

11 Selflessness is like waiting in a hospital
In a badly-fitting suit on a cold wet morning.
Selfishness is like listening to good jazz
With drinks for further orders and a huge fire.
'None of the books have time', written 1960, publ. in *Collected
Poems* (1988)

12 Give me your arm, old toad;
Help me down Cemetery Road.
'Toads Revisited', publ. in *The Whitsun Weddings* (1964)

13 A poem is usually a highly professional artificial
thing, a verbal device designed to reproduce a
thought or emotion indefinitely: it shd have no dead
parts, & every word should be completely unchangeable and unmoveable.
Letter, 12 March 1965, publ. in *Selected Letters* (ed. Anthony
Thwaite, 1992)

14 The trees are coming into leaf
Like something almost being said.
'The Trees', written 1967, publ. in *High Windows* (1974)

15 Sexual intercourse began
In nineteen sixty-three
(Which was rather late for me) –
Between the end of the *Chatterley* ban
And the Beatles' first LP.
'Annus Mirabilis', written 1967, ibid.

16 The hardness and the brightness and the plain
Far-reaching singleness of that wide stare
Is a reminder of the strength and pain
Of being young; that it can't come again,
But is for others undiminished somewhere.
'Sad Steps', written 1968, ibid.

17 They fuck you up, your mum and dad.
They may not mean to, but they do.
They fill you with the faults they had
And add some extra, just for you.
'This Be The Verse', written 1971, ibid. In a letter, 6 June 1982,

Larkin complained of the notoriety of this poem, which 'will
clearly be my "Lake Isle of Innisfree". I fully expect to hear it
recited by a thousand Girl Guides before I die.'

18 Man hands on misery to man.
It deepens like a coastal shelf.
Get out as early as you can,
And don't have any kids yourself.
'This Be The Verse', ibid.

19 Quarterly, is it, money reproaches me:
'Why do you let me lie here wastefully?
I am all you never had of goods and sex.
You could get them still by writing a few cheques.'
'Money', ibid.

20 Perhaps being old is having lighted rooms
Inside your head, and people in them, acting.
People you know, yet can't quite name.
'The Old Fools', ibid.

21 Deprivation is for me what daffodils were for
Wordsworth.
Interview in the *Observer* 1979, repr. in *Required Writing* (1983)

22 I see life more as an affair of solitude diversified
by company than an affair of company diversified
by solitude.
Interview in the *Observer* 1979, ibid.

23 One of the sadder things, I think,
Is how our birthdays slowly sink:
Presents and parties disappear,
The cards grow fewer year by year,
Till, when one reaches sixty-five,
How many care we're still alive?
'Dear CHARLES, My Muse, asleep or dead', written for
CHARLES CAUSLEY, 1982, publ. in *Collected Poems* (1988)

François, Duc de La Rochefoucauld
(1613–80)
French moralist

*The head of a noble family, he opposed Richelieu and Mazarin
and supported the House of Condé during the political turmoil
of 1648–53. He is best known for his witty and cynical epigrams
published in five editions (1665–78).*

1 In the misfortunes of our best friends we always
find something not altogether displeasing to us.
Réflexions, ou Sentences et Maximes Morales, no. 99 (1665 edn)

2 There are crimes which become innocent and

even glorious through their splendour, number and excess.
Ibid., no. 192

3 Our virtues are mostly our vices in disguise.
Ibid., Epigraph (1678 edn)

4 The passions are the only orators which always persuade.
Ibid., no. 8

5 If we had no faults of our own, we should not take so much pleasure in noticing those in others.
Ibid., no. 31

6 To establish oneself in the world, one does all one can to seem established there already.
Ibid., no. 56

7 There are few people who are not ashamed of their love affairs when the infatuation is over.
Ibid., no. 71

8 True love is like ghosts, which everyone talks about but few have seen.
Ibid., no. 76

9 The love of justice is, in most men, nothing more than the fear of suffering injustice.
Ibid., no. 78. A variation of this aphorism appeared in the work of LAUTRÉAMONT, in *Poésies*, ch. 2 (1870): 'Love of justice is for most men only the courage to suffer injustice.'

10 It is more shameful to distrust one's friends than to be deceived by them.
Ibid., no. 84

11 Everyone complains of his memory, none of his judgement.
Ibid., no. 89

12 The more one loves a mistress, the more one is ready to hate her.
Ibid., no. 111

13 The surest way to be deceived is to consider one-self cleverer than others.
Ibid., no. 127

14 The only good copies are those which make us see the absurdity of bad originals.
Ibid., no. 133

15 We are never so ridiculous through what we are as through what we pretend to be.
Ibid., no. 134

16 It is easier to appear worthy of a position one does not hold, than of the office which one fills.
Ibid., no. 164

17 Perfect courage is to do without witnesses what one would be capable of doing with the world looking on.
Ibid., no. 216

18 Hypocrisy is a tribute that vice pays to virtue.
Ibid., no. 218

19 Too great a hurry to discharge an obligation is a kind of ingratitude.
Ibid., no. 226

20 It's the height of folly to want to be the only wise one.
Ibid., no. 231

21 The height of cleverness is being able to conceal it.
Ibid., no. 245

22 What is called generosity is usually only the vanity of giving; we enjoy the vanity more than the thing given.
Ibid., no. 263

23 There is hardly a man clever enough to recognize the full extent of the evil he does.
Ibid., no. 269

24 Absence lessens the minor passions and increases the great ones, as the wind douses a candle and kindles a fire.
Ibid., no. 276. See COMTE DE BUSSY-RABUTIN 2.

25 In most of mankind gratitude is merely a secret hope of further favours.
Ibid., no. 298

26 We often forgive those who bore us, but we cannot forgive those whom we bore.
Ibid., no. 304

27 How is it that we remember the least triviality that happens to us, and yet not remember how often we have recounted it to the same person?
Ibid., no. 313

28 Jealousy contains more of self-love than of love.
Ibid., no. 324

29 We only confess our little faults to persuade people that we have no big ones.
Ibid., no. 327

30 We pardon to the extent that we love.
Ibid., no. 330

31 The accent of one's birthplace remains in the mind and in the heart as in one's speech.
Ibid., no. 342

32 Few people know how to be old.
Ibid., no. 423

33 Nothing so much prevents our being natural as the desire to seem so.
Ibid., no. 431

Christopher Lasch
(1932–94)
US historian

The Culture of Narcissism (1979) is the best known of his powerful indictments of the consumer society, which he blamed for eroding community values and the work ethic.

1 Today Americans are overcome not by the sense of endless possibility but by the banality of the social order they have erected against it.
The Culture of Narcissism, ch. 1, 'The Therapeutic Sensibility' (1979)

2 Every age develops its own peculiar forms of pathology, which express in exaggerated form its underlying character structure.
Ibid., ch. 2, 'Social Influences on Narcissism'

3 The job of the press is to encourage debate, not to supply the public with information.
'Journalism, Publicity, and the Lost Art of Political Argument', publ. in Harper's September 1990. According to Lasch, 'Information, usually seen as the precondition of debate, is better understood as its by-product.'

4 Knowledge is what we get when an observer, preferably a scientifically trained observer, provides us with a copy of reality that we can all recognize.
'Journalism, Publicity, and the Lost Art of Political Argument', ibid.

John Lasseter
(b. 1957)
US film-maker

Specializing in animation, he wrote and directed the first wholly computer-generated full-length feature film, Toy Story (1995), as well as A Bug's Life (1998) and Toy Story 2 (1999).

1 You are a sad, strange little man, and you have my pity. Farewell.
Toy Story (film, 1995, written by Lasseter, Peter Docter et al., directed by John Lasseter). Spoken by Buzz Lightyear (voiced by Tim Allen) to Sheriff Woody (voiced by Tom Hanks).

2 To infinity, and beyond!
Buzz Lightyear, ibid. Buzz Lightyear is a space-ranger.

Hugh Latimer
(1485–1555)
English churchman

Having converted to Protestantism c. 1525, he was Bishop of Worcester 1535–9 and won fame for his sermons in favour of the Reformation. He was arrested on MARY 1's accession, and, with fellow reformer Nicholas Ridley, burned as a heretic.

1 Be of good comfort, Master Ridley, and play the man. We shall this day light such a candle, by God's grace, in England, as (I trust) shall never be put out.
Said to Bishop Nicholas Ridley at their execution pyre in Oxford, 16 October 1555, quoted in Actes and Monuments (1570) by John Foxe

Harry Lauder
(1870–1950)
Scottish music-hall entertainer

After working as a coal miner, he became successful c. 1900 as a singer of hearty Scottish airs, including many written by himself. He had a large international audience and entertained the troops in both world wars.

1 I love a lassie, a bonnie, bonnie lassie,
She's as pure as the lily in the dell.
She's as sweet as the heather,
The bonnie bloomin' heather –
Mary, ma Scotch Bluebell.
'I Love a Lassie' (song, 1905)

2 Roamin' in the gloamin',
On the bonnie banks o' Clyde.
Roamin' in the gloamin'
Wae my lassie by my side.
'Roamin' in the Gloamin'' (song, 1911). The song's title became the title of a volume of Lauder's memoirs (1928).

3 Keep right on to the end of the road,
Keep right on to the end.
Tho' the way be long, let your heart be strong,
Keep right on round the bend.
'The End of the Road' (song, 1924)

Stan Laurel
See OLIVER HARDY 1

Comte de Lautréamont
(1846–70)
French author and poet

Pseudonym of Isidore-Lucien Ducasse. His best known work, the prose poem Les Chants de Maldoror, *was withdrawn in 1869 but, published posthumously (1890), became an influential text for the Surrealist movement. He died in obscure circumstances in Paris.*

1 Throughout my life, I have seen narrow-shouldered men, without a single exception, committing innumerable stupid acts, brutalizing their fellows and perverting souls by all means. They call the motive for their actions fame.
Les Chants de Maldoror, bk 1, ch. 5 (1869; *The Songs of Maldoror*)

2 The great universal family of men is a utopia worthy of the most mediocre logic.
Ibid., bk 1, ch. 9

3 Taste is the fundamental quality which sums up all the other qualities. It is the *nec plus ultra* of the intelligence. Through this alone is genius the supreme health and balance of all the faculties.
Poésies, ch. 1 (1870)

4 Melancholy and sadness are the start of doubt ... doubt is the beginning of despair; despair is the cruel beginning of the differing degrees of wickedness.
Ibid., ch. 1

5 Sleep is a reward for some, a punishment for others. For all, it is a sanction.
Ibid., ch. 2

Johann Kaspar Lavater
(1741–1801)
Swiss clergyman and poet

A pastor in Zürich, he was interested in the interrelation of mind and body, which led him to develop a theory of physiognomics. His poetry, published in Schweizerlieder *(Swiss Songs, 1767) and later volumes, is lyrical in style and mystical in content.*

1 You may tell a man thou art a fiend, but not your nose wants blowing; to him alone who can bear a thing of that kind, you may tell all.
Aphorisms on Man, no. 84 (1788)

2 Say not you know another entirely till you have divided an inheritance with him.
Ibid., no. 157

3 Have you ever seen a pedant with a warm heart?
Ibid., no. 260

4 If you see one cold and vehement at the same time, set him down for a fanatic.
Ibid., no. 282

5 Let none turn over books, or roam the stars in quest of God, who sees him not in man.
Ibid., no. 398

6 The public seldom forgive twice.
Ibid., no. 595

James Laver
(1899–1975)
British art critic and author

A curator at London's Victoria and Albert Museum (1922–59), he wrote on art criticism, but is chiefly known for his works on the history of fashion, such as Taste and Fashion *(1937).*

1 The same costume will be

Indecent	10 years before its time
Shameless	5 years before its time
Outré (daring)	1 year before its time
Smart	
Dowdy	1 year after its time
Hideous	10 years after its time
Ridiculous	20 years after its time
Amusing	30 years after its time
Quaint	50 years after its time
Charming	70 years after its time
Romantic	100 years after its time
Beautiful	150 years after its time.

Taste and Fashion, ch. 18 (1937)

2 The erogenous zone is always shifting, and it is the business of fashion to pursue it, without ever catching it up.
Quoted in *New Society* 2 February 1984

D. H. Lawrence
(1885–1930)
British author

David Herbert Lawrence. Although acclaimed for his novel Sons and Lovers *(1913), he was forced abroad by hostile reaction to subsequent work such as* The Rainbow *(1915), which provoked outrage for its frank treatment of sexuality. He is also remembered for his poetry. See* GERMAINE GREER 16.

1 My soul is my great asset and my great misfortune.
Letter, 13 May 1908, publ. in *The Letters of D.H. Lawrence*, vol. 1 (ed. James T. Boulton, 1979)

2 One could laugh at the world better if it didn't mix tender kindliness with its brutality.
Letter, 3 October 1910, ibid., vol. 1

3 Be a good animal, true to your animal instincts.
The White Peacock, pt 2, ch. 2 (1911). Motto of the woodkeeper Annable.

4 Tragedy is like strong acid – it dissolves away all but the very gold of truth.
Letter, 1 April 1911, publ. in *The Letters of D.H. Lawrence*, vol. 1 (ed. James T. Boulton, 1979)

5 Literature is a toil and a snare, a curse that bites deep.
Letter, 25 September 1911, ibid., vol. 1

6 Why, why, why was I born an Englishman! – my cursed, rotten-boned, pappy-hearted countrymen, *why* was I sent to *them*?
Letter to author and critic Edward Garnett, 3 July 1912, ibid., vol. 1

7 I shall always be a priest of love.
Letter, 25 December 1912, ibid., vol. 1

8 There's always the hyena of morality at the garden gate.
Letter, 17 January 1913, ibid., vol. 1

9 One sheds one's sicknesses in books – repeats and presents again one's emotions, to be master of them.
Letter, 26 October 1913, publ. in ibid., vol. 2 (ed. George J. Zytaruk and James T. Boulton, 1981)

10 Primarily I am a passionately religious man, and my novels must be written from the depth of my religious experience.
Letter to author and critic Edward Garnett, 22 April 1914, ibid., vol. 2

11 The source of all life and knowledge is in man and woman, and the source of all living is in the interchange and the meeting and mingling of these two: man-life and woman-life, man-knowledge and woman-knowledge, man-being and woman-being.
Letter, 2 June 1914, ibid., vol. 2

12 You must drop all your democracy. You must not believe in 'the people'. One class is no better than another. It must be a case of Wisdom, or Truth. Let the working classes *be* working classes. That is the truth. There must be an aristocracy of people who have wisdom, and there must be a Ruler: a Kaiser: no Presidents and democracies.
Letter to BERTRAND RUSSELL, *c.* 14 July 1915, ibid., vol. 2. 'The more I see of democracy the more I dislike it', wrote Lawrence seven years later while in Australia. 'It just brings everything

down to the mere vulgar level of wages and prices, electric light and water closets, and nothing else' (letter, 13 June 1922).

13 Not I, not I, but the wind that blows through me!
A fine wind is blowing the new direction of Time.
'Song of a Man Who has Come Through', publ. in *Look! We Have Come Through!* (1917)

14 Comes over one an absolute necessity to move. And what is more, to move in some particular direction. A double necessity then: to get on the move, and to know whither.
Sea and Sardinia, ch. 1 (1923). Opening words of book.

15 How beautiful maleness is, if it finds its right expression.
Ibid., ch. 3

16 The human being is a most curious creature. He thinks he has got one soul, and he has got dozens.
Ibid., ch. 8

17 Never trust the artist. Trust the tale. The proper function of a critic is to save the tale from the artist who created it.
Studies in Classic American Literature, ch. 1 (1923)

18 That is your trick, your bit of filthy magic: Invisibility, and the anaesthetic power
To deaden my attention in your direction.
'The Mosquito', publ. in *Birds, Beasts and Flowers* (1923)

19 A snake came to my water-trough
On a hot, hot day, and I in pyjamas for the heat,
To drink there.
'Snake', ibid. Opening lines.

20 To the Puritan, all things are impure, as somebody says.
Etruscan Places, ch. 1 (written 1927, publ. 1932). See BIBLE, NEW TESTAMENT: TITUS 2.

21 Ours is essentially a tragic age, so we refuse to take it tragically.
Lady Chatterley's Lover, ch. 1 (1928). Opening words of book.

22 John Thomas says good-night to lady Jane, a little droopingly, but with a hopeful heart.
Ibid., ch. 19. Closing words of letter from Mellors to Connie Chatterley, and last words of book. An expurgated version of the book that first appeared in 1932 was published in 1972 with the title *John Thomas and Lady Jane*.

23 My God, what a clumsy *olla putrida* James Joyce is! Nothing but old fags and cabbage-stumps of quo-

tations from the Bible and the rest, stewed in the juice of deliberate, journalistic dirty-mindedness.

Letter to Maria and ALDOUS HUXLEY, 15 August 1928, publ. in *The Letters of D.H. Lawrence*, vol. 6 (ed. James T. Boulton, Margaret H. Boulton and Gerald M. Lacy, 1991). *Olla putrida* is Latin for 'putrid pot', or incongruous mixture.

24 How beastly the bourgeois is
especially the male of the species
– presentable, eminently presentable.

'How Beastly the Bourgeois Is', publ. in *Pansies* (1929)

25 I never saw a wild thing
Sorry for itself.
A small bird will drop frozen dead
From a bough
Without ever having felt sorry for itself.

'Self-Pity', ibid.

26 When I read Shakespeare I am struck with
   wonder
That such trivial people should muse and thunder
In such lovely language.

'When I Read Shakespeare', ibid.

27 The upshot was, my picture must burn
that English artists might finally learn
when they painted a nude, to put a *cache sexe* on,
a cache sexe, a cache sexe, or else begone!

'Innocent England', publ. in NETTLES (1930). Referring to the suppression of an exhibition of Lawrence's paintings in London, on grounds of obscenity.

28 If a woman hasn't got a tiny streak of a harlot in her, she's a dry stick as a rule.

Pornography and Obscenity (1930), repr. in *Phoenix: The Posthumous Papers of D.H. Lawrence*, pt 3 (ed. E. McDonald, 1936)

29 Pornography is the attempt to insult sex, to do dirt on it.

Pornography and Obscenity, ibid. Lawrence conceded, however, that the definition of pornography varies according to the individual: 'What is pornography to one man is the laughter of genius to another.'

30 The one thing that it seems impossible to escape from, once the habit is formed, is masturbation. It goes on and on, on into old age, in spite of marriage or love affairs or anything else. And it always carries this secret feeling of futility and humiliation, futility and humiliation. And this is, perhaps, the deepest and most dangerous cancer of our civilization. Instead of being a comparatively pure and harmless vice, masturbation is certainly the most dangerous sexual vice that a society can be afflicted with, in the long run. Comparatively pure it may be – purity being what it is. But harmless!!!

Pornography and Obscenity, ibid.

31 The horse, the horse! The symbol of surging potency and power of movement, of action, in man.

Apocalypse, ch. 10 (1931)

32 And if tonight my soul may find her peace
in sleep, and sink in good oblivion,
and in the morning wake like a new-opened flower
then I have been dipped again in God, and
   new-created.

'Shadows', publ. in *Last Poems* (1932)

Frieda Lawrence
(1879–1956)
German wife of D. H. Lawrence

Married to a university professor at Nottingham, she met D. H. LAWRENCE *in 1912 and accompanied him abroad, marrying him in 1914 and settling in New Mexico after his death.*

1 Of course in war all madnesses come out in a man, that is the fault of *war* not of a *man* or a *nation*.

Letter *c.* 13 September 1914, publ. in *The Letters of D.H. Lawrence*, vol. 2 (ed. George J. Zytaruk and James T. Boulton, 1981). Frieda's brother was the celebrated pilot Manfred von Richthofen – the 'Red Baron'.

T. E. Lawrence
(1888–1935)
British soldier and scholar

Thomas Edward Lawrence. He assumed iconic status as Lawrence of Arabia after leading the Arab revolt against the Turks in the First World War, as recorded in The Seven Pillars of Wisdom *(1926). He was killed in a motorcycle accident.*

1 I loved you, so I drew these tides of men into my
   hands and wrote my will across the sky in stars
To earn you freedom, the seven-pillared worthy
   house, that your eyes might be shining for me
When we came.

The Seven Pillars of Wisdom, Dedication (1926)

2 Often I wish I had known at the beginning the weary lag that any sudden reputation brings. I should have refrained from doing even the little that I did; and now I would be left alone and able to live as I chose. To have news value is to have a tin can tied to one's tail.

Letter, 1 April 1935, publ. in *The Letters of T. E. Lawrence* (ed. Malcolm Brown, 1988). Written a few weeks before his death.

Nigella Lawson
(b. 1960)
British journalist and broadcaster

The daughter of the former Conservative Chancellor of the Exchequer Nigel Lawson, she writes for various newspapers and is famous for her cookery programmes and spin-off books.

1 Sometimes ... we want to feel not like a post-modern, post-feminist, overstretched modern woman but, rather, a domestic goddess, trailing nutmeggy fumes of baking pie in our languorous wake.
How To Be a Domestic Goddess, Preface (2000)

Irving Layton
(b. 1912)
Canadian poet

Originally Israel Lazarovitch. His verse, encompassing both satirical digs against the bourgeoisie and explicitly erotic love poetry, appears in Here and Now *(1945) and* The Swinging Flesh *(1961), among other collections.*

1 If poetry is like an orgasm, an academic can be likened to someone who studies the passion-stains on the bedsheets.
The Whole Bloody Bird, 'Obs II' (1969)

2 In Pierre Elliot Trudeau, Canada has at last produced a political leader worthy of assassination.
Ibid., 'Obs II'

3 Conscience: self-esteem with a halo.
Ibid., 'Aphs'

4 When you argue with your inferiors, you convince them of only one thing: they are as clever as you.
Ibid., 'Aphs'

5 Idealist: a cynic in the making.
Ibid., 'Aphs'

6 My neighbour
doesn't want to be loved
as much as
he wants to be envied.
Ibid., 'Aphs'

7 An aphorism
should be
like a burr:
sting,
stick,
and leave

a little soreness
afterwards.
Ibid., 'Aphs'

Emma Lazarus
(1849–87)
US poet

She published verse, fiction and translations. The Russian pogroms inspired her to champion the cause of oppressed Jews and of immigrants into the USA. 'The New Colossus' is her best remembered poem.

1 Here at our sea-washed, sunset gates shall stand
A mighty woman with a torch, whose flame
Is the imprisoned lightning, and her name
Mother of Exiles.
'The New Colossus' (1883), repr. in *The Poems of Emma Lazarus*, vol. 1 (1888). The sonnet was engraved on the pedestal of the Statue of Liberty in New York.

2 'Keep, ancient lands, your storied pomp!' cries she
With silent lips. 'Give me your tired, your poor,
Your huddled masses yearning to breathe free,
The wretched refuse of your teeming shore.
Send these, the homeless, tempest-tossed, to me;
I lift my lamp beside the golden door.'
'The New Colossus', ibid. Closing lines.

3 Still on Israel's head forlorn,
Every nation heaps its scorn.
'The World's Justice', st. 3, publ. ibid., vol. 2

Bernard Leach
(1887–1979)
British potter

As a leading figure in ceramics for more than fifty years, he aimed to combine functionality with beauty. He lived and studied in Japan before establishing his pottery in St Ives, Cornwall.

1 The pot is the man: his virtues and his vices are shown therein – no disguise is possible.
The Potter's Challenge, ch. 4 (1976)

Stephen Leacock
(1869–1944)
British-born Canadian humorist and economist

He lectured and wrote on political economics but is best known for his humorous observations of social foibles, including Literary Lapses *(1910) and* Frenzied Fiction *(1917).*

1 It takes a good deal of physical courage to ride a

horse. This, however, I have. I get it at about forty cents a flask, and take it as required.
Literary Lapses, 'Reflections on Riding' (1910)

2 Lord Ronald said nothing; he flung himself from the room, flung himself upon his horse and rode madly off in all directions.
Nonsense Novels, 'Gertrude the Governess' (1911)

3 Advertising may be described as the science of arresting the human intelligence long enough to get money from it.
The Garden of Folly, 'The Perfect Salesman' (1924)

Edward Lear
(1812–88)
English author and artist

Already established as an animal illustrator, he popularized the limerick in The Book of Nonsense *(1846) and in further volumes of 'nonsense verse'. He also wrote travel books and painted landscapes. He spent most of his later life in Italy.*

1 There was an old man with a beard,
Who said, 'It is just as I feared! –
Two owls and a hen,
Four larks and a wren,
Have all built their nests in my beard!'
The Book of Nonsense (1846)

2 'How pleasant to know Mr Lear!'
Who has written such volumes of stuff!
Some think him ill-tempered and queer,
But a few think him pleasant enough.
Nonsense Songs and Stories, Preface, st. 1 (1871)

3 He has many friends, laymen and clerical,
Old Foss is the name of his cat:
His body is perfectly spherical,
He weareth a runcible hat.
Ibid., Preface, st. 5

4 The Owl and the Pussy-Cat went to sea
In a beautiful pea-green boat.
They took some honey, and plenty of money,
Wrapped up in a five-pound note.
The Owl looked up to the stars above
And sang to a small guitar,
'Oh lovely Pussy! O Pussy, my love,
What a beautiful Pussy you are.'
'The Owl and the Pussy-Cat', st. 1, publ. ibid. Opening lines of poem.

5 Pussy said to the Owl, 'You elegant fowl!
How charmingly sweet you sing!
O let us be married! too long we have tarried:

But what shall we do for a ring?'
They sailed away for a year and a day,
To the land where the Bong-tree grows,
And there in a wood a Piggy-wig stood,
With a ring at the end of his nose.
'The Owl and the Pussy-Cat', st. 2, ibid.

6 They dined on mince, and slices of quince,
Which they ate with a runcible spoon;
And hand in hand, on the edge of the sand,
They danced by the light of the moon.
'The Owl and the Pussy-Cat', st. 3, ibid.

7 Far and few, far and few,
Are the lands where the Jumblies live;
Their heads are green, and their hands are blue,
And they went to sea in a sieve.
'The Jumblies', Refrain, ibid.

8 When awful darkness and silence reign
Over the great Gromboolian plain,
Through the long, long wintry nights.
'The Dong with a Luminous Nose', ibid. Opening lines.

9 The Dong! the Dong!
The Dong with a luminous nose!
'The Dong with a Luminous Nose', st. 3, ibid.

10 On the coast of Coromandel
Where the early pumpkins blow,
In the middle of the woods,
Lived the Yonghy-Bonghy-Bò.
Two old chairs, and half a candle, –
One old jug without a handle, –
These were all his worldly goods.
'The Courtship of the Yonghy-Bonghy-Bò', ibid. Opening lines.

11 The Pobble who has no toes
Had once as many as we;
When they said, 'Some day you may lose them all;' –
He replied, – 'Fish fiddle de-dee!'
'The Pobble Who Has No Toes', ibid. Opening lines.

12 And she said, – 'It's a fact the whole world knows,
That Pobbles are happier without their toes.'
'The Pobble Who Has No Toes', ibid. Closing lines.

13 On the top of the Crumpetty Tree
The Quangle Wangle sat,
But his face you could not see,
On account of his Beaver Hat.
'The Quangle Wangle's Hat', ibid. Opening lines.

14 Who or why, or which, or *what*,
Is the Akond of Swat?

'The Akond of Swat', ibid. Opening lines.

Timothy Leary
(1920–96)
US psychologist

He was branded by RICHARD NIXON *'the most dangerous man in America' for his advocacy of psychotropic drugs, for which he was several times imprisoned.*

1 My advice to people today is as follows: If you take the game of life seriously, if you take your nervous system seriously, if you take your sense organs seriously, if you take the energy process seriously, you must turn on, tune in, and drop out.

Lecture, 1966, publ. in *The Politics of Ecstasy*, ch. 21 (1968). Nearly thirty years later, Leary suggested a variation of this slogan: 'Tune in, turn on, boot up' (*Guardian* 2 December 1995).

2 In the information age, you don't teach philosophy as they did after feudalism. You perform it. If Aristotle were alive today he'd have a talk show.

Evening Standard 8 February 1989

William Least Heat-Moon
(b. 1939)
US author

Originally William Trogdon. Of mixed Native American descent, he writes about those parts of America 'where time and men and deeds connect', as in Blue Highways *(1983) and* River Horse *(1999).*

1 Beware thoughts that come in the night. They aren't turned properly; they come in askew, free of sense and restriction, deriving from the most remote of sources.

Blue Highways: A Journey into America, pt 1, ch. 1 (1983). Opening sentences of book.

2 Whoever the last true cowboy in America turns out to be, he's likely to be an Indian.

Ibid., pt 5, ch. 2

F. R. Leavis
(1895–1978)
British literary critic

Frank Raymond Leavis. A devotee of high standards in English literature and criticism, he founded and edited the quarterly Scrutiny *(1932–53) with his wife Q. D. Leavis. His works include* The Great Tradition *(1948) and* The Common Pursuit *(1952).*

1 The opposition to the Georgians was already at the time in question (just after the war) Sitwellism. But the Sitwells belong to the history of publicity rather than of poetry.

New Bearings in English Poetry, ch. 2 (1932). On Georgian poetry.

2 It is well to start by distinguishing the few really great – the major novelists who count in the same way as the major poets, in the sense that they not only change the possibilities of the art for practitioners and readers, but that they are significant in terms of the human awareness they promote; awareness of the possibilities of life.

The Great Tradition, ch. 1 (1948)

3 One of the supreme debts one great writer can owe another is the realization of unlikeness.

Ibid., ch. 1

4 I have, then, given my hostages. What I think and judge I have stated as responsibly and clearly as I can. Jane Austen, George Eliot, Henry James, Conrad, and D. H. Lawrence: the great tradition of the English novel is *there*.

Ibid., ch. 1

Fran Lebowitz
(b. 1951)
US journalist

Her satirical essays, tart and light-hearted in style, were collected in Metropolitan Life *(1978) and* Social Studies *(1981).*

1 All God's children are not beautiful. Most of God's children are, in fact, barely presentable.

Metropolitan Life, 'Manners' (1978)

2 There is no such thing as inner peace. There is only nervousness or death. Any attempt to prove otherwise constitutes unacceptable behavior.

Ibid., 'Manners'

3 Being a woman is of special interest only to aspiring male transsexuals. To actual women simply it is merely a good excuse not to play football.

Ibid., 'Letters'

4 Original thought is like original sin: both happened before you were born to people you could not have possibly met.

Social Studies, 'People' (1981)

5 The opposite of talking isn't listening. The opposite of talking is waiting.

Ibid., 'People'

6 Do not, on a rainy day, ask your child what he feels like doing, because I assure you that what he feels like doing, you won't feel like watching.
Ibid., 'Parental Guidance'

7 Remember that as a teenager you are at the last stage in your life when you will be happy to hear that the phone is for you.
Ibid., 'Tips for Teens'

8 Stand firm in your refusal to remain conscious during algebra. In real life, I assure you, there is no such thing as algebra.
Ibid., 'Tips for Teens'

9 To put it rather bluntly, I am not the type who wants to go back to the land; I am the type who wants to go back to the hotel.
Ibid., 'Things'

10 If you are a dog and your owner suggests that you wear a sweater . . . suggest that he wear a tail.
Ibid. 'Pointers for Pets'

John Le Carré
(b. 1931)
British novelist

Pen name of David Cornwell. Employed in the Foreign Service (1960–4), he began writing the series of complex spy thrillers with which he is most associated, featuring the self-effacing agent George Smiley.

1 The Spy Who Came in From the Cold.
Book title (1963)

2 What do you think spies are: priests, saints and martyrs? They're a squalid procession of vain fools, traitors too, yes; pansies, sadists and drunkards, people who play cowboys and Indians to brighten their rotten lives.
The Spy Who Came in From the Cold, ch. 25 (1963). Spoken by Leamas.

3 It's easy to forget what intelligence consists of: luck and speculation. Here and there a windfall, here and there a scoop.
The Looking-Glass War, pt 2, ch. 9 (1965). Spoken by Leclerc.

4 For decades to come the spy world will continue to be the collective couch where the subconscious of each nation is confessed.
Quoted in the *Observer* 19 November 1989

5 It was *man* who ended the Cold War in case you didn't notice. It wasn't weaponry, or technology, or armies or campaigns. It was just *man*. Not even

Western man either, as it happened, but our sworn enemy in the East, who went into the streets, faced the bullets and the batons and said: we've had enough. It was *their* emperor, not ours, who had the nerve to mount the rostrum and declare he had no clothes. And the ideologies trailed after these impossible events like condemned prisoners, as ideologies do when they've had their day . . . One day, history may tell us who really won.
The Secret Pilgrim, ch. 12 (1990). Spoken by Smiley.

Le Corbusier
(1887–1965)
Swiss-born French architect

Pseudonym of Charles-Édouard Jeanneret. He was a pioneer of the International Style, characterized by the use of steel and reinforced concrete, open-plan interiors and geometric forms.

1 *Une maison est une machine-à-habiter.*
[A house is a machine for living in.]
Towards a New Architecture, ch. 1, 'Eyes Which Do Not See: Airplanes' (1923, transl. 1946)

2 Our own epoch is determining, day by day, its own style. Our eyes, unhappily, are unable yet to discern it.
Ibid., ch. 1

3 A hundred times have I thought New York is a catastrophe . . . it is a beautiful catastrophe.
Quoted in the *New York Herald Tribune* 6 August 1961

Huddie 'Leadbelly' Ledbetter
(1889–1949)
US folk and blues musician

Of black and Cherokee Indian origins, he worked as a cotton-picker and labourer but spent much of his life in prison, where he was recorded by the archivists John and Alan Lomax.

1 Look a here people, listen to me,
Don't try to find no home in Washington DC
Lord, it's a bourgeois town, it's a bourgeois town.
'Bourgeois Blues' (song, *c.* 1933, written with Alan Lomax) on the album *Easy Rider* (1962). The song was recorded in Louisiana State Prison by musicologist Alan Lomax, who helped to obtain Leadbelly's release in 1934 and later launched him on the New York folk scene.

2 Let the Midnight Special
Shine her light on me.
'Midnight Special' (song, 1940, traditional). Already known as a southern prison ballad when Leadbelly recorded it, the song refers to a train running past Sugarland Prison, Texas, whose

headlight shining on an inmate supposedly indicated that he would soon be free.

Alexandre-Auguste Ledru-Rollin
(1807–74)
French lawyer and politician

A strident republican, he was a Deputy from 1839 and became Minister of the Interior in 1848. His involvement in an insurrection against Louis-Napoléon led to his exile 1849–70.

1 I'm their leader, I've got to follow them!
Attributed remark among the Paris mob at the barricades, 1848, quoted in *Histoire Contemporaine*, no. 79 (1857)

Gerald Stanley Lee
(1862–1944)
US clergyman and author

Director of the Training School for Balance and Coordination from 1926, he wrote on diverse topics, including the church, democracy and self-development.

1 Turning the other cheek is a kind of moral jiu-jitsu.
Crowds, bk 4, ch. 9 (1913)

Gypsy Rose Lee
(1914–70)
US striptease artiste

Originally Rose Louise Hovick. She was the most famous stripper of the 1930s and appeared in the Ziegfeld Follies (1936). Her autobiography (1957) was adapted for the stage musical Gypsy (1959).

1 God is love, but get it in writing.
Attributed

Harper Lee
(b. 1926)
US author

She won the Pulitzer Prize for literature for her first and only novel To Kill a Mockingbird (1960), a tale of racial injustice in the American South narrated by a six-year-old girl.

1 Until I feared I would lose it, I never loved to read. One does not love breathing.
To Kill a Mockingbird, ch. 2 (1960). Narrated by Scout.

2 The one thing that doesn't abide by majority rule is a person's conscience.
Atticus Finch, ibid., ch. 11

3 I'm no idealist to believe firmly in the integrity of our courts and in the jury system – that is no ideal to me, it is a living, working reality. Gentlemen, a court is no better than each man of you sitting before me on this jury. A court is only as sound as its jury, and a jury is only as sound as the men who make it up.
Speech to the jury by Atticus Finch, ibid., ch. 20

4 As you grow older, you'll see white men cheat black men every day of your life, but let me tell you something and don't you forget it – whenever a white man does that to a black man, no matter who he is, how rich he is, or how fine a family he comes from, that white man is trash.
Atticus Finch to his son Jem, ibid., ch. 23

Laurie Lee
(1914–97)
British author

He is chiefly remembered for Cider with Rosie (1959), an account of his childhood in the Cotswolds. As I Walked Out One Midsummer Morning (1969) describes a journey through Spain on the eve of the Spanish Civil War.

1 It is not crime that has increased but its definition. The modern city, for youth, is a police trap.
Cider with Rosie, 'First Bite at the Apple' (1959)

2 Quiet incest flourished where the roads were bad.
Ibid., 'First Bite at the Apple'

Nathaniel Lee
(c. 1653–92)
English playwright

Originally an actor, he produced his first play in 1674, and enjoyed enduring success with The Rival Queens (1677), a blank verse tragedy. He also collaborated with DRYDEN.

1 He speaks the kindest words and looks such things,
Vows with much passion, swears with so much grace,
That 'tis a kind of heaven to be deluded by him.
The Rival Queens, Act 1, Sc. 2 (1677). Spoken by Statira, of Alexander the Great.

2 'Tis beauty calls, and glory shows the way.
Alexander, ibid., Act 4, Sc. 2

3 When Greeks joined Greeks, then was the tug of war!
Clytus, ibid., Act 4, Sc. 2

4 Man: false man, smiling, destructive man.
Theodosius, Act 3, Sc. 2 (1680). Spoken by Athenais.

Robert E. Lee
(1807–70)
US general

Robert Edward Lee. As one of the principal commanders of Southern forces during the Civil War, he had a number of successes but was defeated at Gettysburg (1863) and surrendered to ULYSSES S. GRANT *in 1865.*

1 It is well that war is so terrible: we would grow too fond of it!
Attributed remark at the Battle of Fredericksburg, 13 December 1862. Said to be a comment to James Longstreet, on seeing a Unionist charge repulsed.

Henri Lefebvre
(1901–91)
French philosopher

He was artistic director of the radio broadcasting company Radiodiffusion Français 1944–9, and also wrote widely on philosophy, notably on KARL MARX.

1 The most remarkable aspect of the transition we are living through is not so much the passage from want to affluence as the passage from labour to leisure . . . Leisure contains the future, it is the new horizon.
Everyday Life in the Modern World (1962), ch. 1, 'What Should the New Society be Called?'

Ursula Le Guin
(b. 1929)
US author

Her science fiction and fantasy novels depict alternative worlds analogous to our own, as in The Left Hand of Darkness *(1969) and* The Dispossessed *(1974).*

1 When action grows unprofitable, gather information; when information grows unprofitable, sleep.
The Left Hand of Darkness, ch. 3 (1969). An 'Ekumenical' saying.

2 It is a terrible thing, this kindness that human beings do not lose. Terrible, because when we are finally naked in the dark and cold, it is all we have. We who are so rich, so full of strength, we end up with that small change. We have nothing else to give.
Narrator (Estraven), ibid., ch. 13

3 In so far as one denies what is, one is possessed by what is not, the compulsions, the fantasies, the terrors that flock to fill the void.
The Lathe of Heaven, ch. 10 (1971)

4 The children of the revolution are always ungrateful, and the revolution must be grateful that it is so.
'Reciprocity of Prose and Poetry', address in Washington DC, 1983, publ. in *Dancing at the Edge of the World* (1989)

5 If science fiction is the mythology of modern technology, then its myth is tragic.
'The Carrier Bag Theory of Fiction', ibid.

6 We are volcanoes. When we women offer our experience as our truth, as human truth, all the maps change. There are new mountains.
Bryn Mawr Commencement Address, 1986, ibid.

7 If you want your writing to be taken seriously, don't marry and have kids, and above all, don't die. But if you have to die, commit suicide. They approve of that.
'Prospects for Women in Writing', speech in Portland, Maine, September 1986, ibid.

David Lehman
(b. 1948)
US poet, editor and critic

He was book critic for Newsweek *and has published the poetry collections* Some Nerve *(1973) and* Day One *(1979), as well as a study of crime fiction,* The Perfect Murder *(1989).*

1 There is an air of last things, a brooding sense of impending annihilation, about so much deconstructive activity, in so many of its guises; it is not merely postmodernist but preapocalyptic.
Signs of the Times, ch. 1 (1991)

2 Obscurantism is the academic theorist's revenge on society for having consigned him or her to relative obscurity – a way of proclaiming one's superiority in the face of one's diminished influence.
Ibid., ch. 3

Ernest Lehman
(b. 1920)
US author and screenwriter

He turned from short stories to screenplays, including North by Northwest *(1959) and* West Side Story *(1961). He also produced and directed films in the 1960s and '70s.*

1 I allowed the soothing music and the muted

sounds of the city and the rich, sweet smell of success that permeated the room to lull my senses.
Tell Me About it Tomorrow (1950). Lehman adapted his novella as a screenplay for the film *Sweet Smell of Success* (1957).

Tom Lehrer
(b. 1928)
US humorist

A professor of mathematics at Harvard, he wrote and performed sharply satirical songs throughout the 1950s and '60s, famous for their black humour, pastiche and parody.

1 All the world seems in tune
On a spring afternoon,
When you're poisoning pigeons in the park.
'When You're Poisoning Pigeons in the Park' (song) on the album *An Evening Wasted with Tom Lehrer* (1959)

2 Even though the prospect sickens,
Brother, here we go again.
On Christmas Day you can't get sore,
Your fellow man you must adore,
There's time to rob him all the more
The other three hundred and sixty-four.
'A Christmas Carol' (song), ibid.

3 I ache for the touch of your lips, dear,
But much more for the feel of your whips, dear,
You can raise welts
Like nobody else,
As we dance to the Masochism Tango!
'The Masochism Tango' (song), ibid.

4 Life is like a sewer. What you get out of it depends on what you put into it.
Preamble to 'We Will All Go Together When We Go' (song), ibid.

5 And we'll all go together when we go,
Every Hottentot and every Eskimo,
When the air becomes uranious,
We will all go simultaneous,
Yes, we all will go together when we go.
'We Will All Go Together When We Go' (song), ibid.

Jerry Leiber
and
Mike Stoller
See ELVIS PRESLEY 1

Gottfried Wilhelm Leibniz
(1646–1716)
German scientist, mathematician and philosopher

Independently of and concurrently with ISAAC NEWTON, *he developed calculus. In his metaphysical works, he posited the existence of monads, the basic units of the universe arranged hierarchically. His accomplishments extended to optics, history and theology.*

1 *Nihil est sine ratione.*
[There is nothing without a reason.]
Studies in Physics and the Nature of Body (1671), publ. in *Leibniz: Philosophical Papers and Letters* (ed. and transl. by Leroy E. Loemker, 1969)

2 God wills the things which he understands to be the best and most harmonious and selects them, as it were, from an infinite number of all possibilities.
Letter, 1671, ibid. Leibniz's stance was satirized by Voltaire: see VOLTAIRE 13.

3 It is God who is the ultimate reason of things, and the knowledge of God is no less the beginning of science than his essence and will are the beginning of beings.
'Letter on a General Principle Useful in Explaining the Laws of Nature' (1687), ibid.

Augusta Leigh
(1783–1851)

She and her half-brother BYRON *were almost strangers when they met in 1813. After the disintegration of the poet's marriage, rumours of incest between the two circulated, which she denied.*

1 Thank God! none of my children have an atom of poetry in their composition!
Letter to BYRON's publisher John Murray, 1 January 1833, quoted in *The Late Lord Byron*, ch. 15 (1961, rev. 1976) by Doris Langley Moore

Fred W. Leigh
(1870–1924)
British songwriter

He joined the publishing firm Francis Day and Hunter c. 1900 and became literary editor there, a post he held until his death. He wrote songs performed by Marie Lloyd, among others.

1 Can't get away to marry you today,
My wife won't let me!
'Waiting at the Church' (song, 1906, with music by Henry E. Pether)

2 I always hold in having it if you fancy it,
If you fancy it that's understood!
And suppose it makes you fat? I don't worry over
    that,
'Cos a little of what you fancy does you good!
'A Little of What You Fancy Does You Good' (song, 1915, written with George Arthurs)

3 Why am I always the bridesmaid,
Never the blushing bride?
'Why Am I Always the Bridesmaid?' (song, 1917, written with CHARLES COLLINS and Lily Morris)

4 My old man said, 'Follow the van,
Don't dilly-dally on the way!'
'Don't Dilly-Dally on the Way' (song, 1919, written with CHARLES COLLINS). The song, which was also known as 'My Old Man Says "Follow the Van"' and 'The Cock-linnet Song', was popularized by Marie Lloyd.

Henry Sambrooke Leigh
(1837–83)
English author and poet

His collections of lyrics drew largely on London life. He also translated French comic opera.

1 The rapturous, wild, and ineffable pleasure
Of drinking at somebody else's expense.
'Stanzas to an Intoxicated Fly', publ. in *Carols of Cockayne* (1869)

2 If you wish to grow thinner, diminish your
    dinner,
And take to light claret instead of pale ale;
Look down with an utter contempt upon butter,
And never touch bread till it's toasted – or stale.
'A Day for Wishing', ibid.

Mike Leigh
(b. 1943)
British film-maker

His work on stage and screen is by turns mundane, poignant, funny and bleak. His best known television play is Abigail's Party *(1977); his films include* Vera Drake *(2004).*

1 Morals are a matter of taste.
Interview in *Naked and Other Screenplays* (1995)

Prue Leith
(b. 1940)
British chef, caterer and author

Regarded as the doyenne of British cookery, she has been a culinary writer and broadcaster for thirty years.

1 When you get to fifty-two food becomes more important than sex.
Guardian 11 November 1992

Curtis E. LeMay
(1906–90)
US air force officer

He directed the bombers that dropped the atom bombs on Japan in 1945 and was subsequently the first head of the USAF's elite nuclear bomber strike force (1948–57) and Air Force Chief of Staff (1961–5).

1 My solution to the problem would be to tell them [the North Vietnamese] they've got to draw in their horns and stop aggression or we're going to bomb them back into the Stone Age.
Quoted in *Mission with LeMay* (1965). The words inspired the ironic slogan 'Bombs Away with Curt LeMay!'

Vladimir Ilyich Lenin
(1870–1924)
Russian revolutionary leader

Originally Vladimir Ilyich Ulyanov. He was the leading figure in the Bolshevik revolution of 1917 and became the first head of a Soviet government. The Marxist-Leninist policies that he established came to be the basis of communist ideology.

1 Without revolutionary theory there can be no revolutionary movement.
What Is To Be Done?, sect. 1 D, (1902), repr. in *The Essentials of Lenin*, vol. 1 (ed. Marx-Engels-Lenin Institute, 1947)

2 The history of all countries shows that the working class exclusively by its own effort is able to develop only trade-union consciousness.
What Is To Be Done?, sect. 2 A, ibid.

3 Literature must become Party literature . . . Down with un-partisan litterateurs! Down with the superman of literature! Literature must become a part of the general cause of the proletariat.
'Party Organization and Party Literature' (1905), repr. in *Collected Works*, vol. 10 (ed. Andrew Rothstein, 1967)

4 Imperialism is capitalism at that stage of development at which the dominance of monopolies and finance capitalism is established; in which the

export of capital has acquired pronounced importance; in which the division of the world among the international trusts has begun, in which the division of all territories of the globe among the biggest capitalist powers has been completed.

Imperialism, the Highest Stage of Capitalism, ch. 7 (1916). The formulation has been paraphrased: 'Imperialism is the monopoly stage of capitalism.'

5 Capitalists are no more capable of self-sacrifice than a man is capable of lifting himself up by his own bootstraps.

Letters From Afar, ch. 4 (1917)

6 When one makes a Revolution, one cannot mark time; one must always go forward – or go back. He who now talks about the 'freedom of the press' goes backward, and halts our headlong course towards Socialism.

Speech at Smolny, 17 November 1917, quoted in *Ten Days That Shook the World*, ch. 11 (1919) by JOHN REED

7 If Socialism can only be realized when the intellectual development of all the people permits it, then we shall not see Socialism for at least five hundred years.

Speech at Peasants' Congress, Petrograd, 27 November 1917, ibid. ch. 12

8 Politics begin where the masses are, not where there are thousands, but where there are millions, that is where serious politics begin.

Report to Seventh Congress of the Russian Communist Party, 7 March 1918, publ. in *Selected Works*, vol. 7 (1937)

9 All our lives we fought against exalting the individual, against the elevation of the single person, and long ago we were over and done with the business of a hero, and here it comes up again: the glorification of one personality. This is not good at all. I am just like everybody else.

Remark after being shot in 1918, quoted in 'Cult of Personality' by V. D. Bonch-Bruevich, publ. in *Not By Politics Alone*, pt 2 (ed. Tamara Deutsche, 1973). See NIKITA KHRUSHCHEV 2.

10 Authority poisons everybody who takes authority on himself.

Lenin to Kropotkin in May 1919, quoted in 'Meeting with Kropotkin' by V. D. Bonch-Bruevich, ibid., pt 2

11 You cannot make a revolution in white gloves.

Lenin to Kropotkin in May 1919, quoted ibid., pt 2

12 While the State exists there can be no freedom; when there is freedom there will be no State.

The State and Revolution, ch. 5, sect. 4 (1919)

13 A good man fallen among Fabians.

Remark made to Arthur Ransome referring to GEORGE BERNARD SHAW, quoted in *Six Weeks in Russia in 1919*, 'Notes of a Conversation with Lenin' (1919) by Arthur Ransome

14 You all know that even when women have full rights, they still remain factually downtrodden because all housework is left to them. In most cases housework is the most unproductive, the most barbarous and the most arduous work a woman can do. It is exceptionally petty and does not include anything that would in any way promote the development of the woman.

'The Tasks of the Working Women's Movement in the Soviet Republic' (1919), repr. in *Collected Works*, vol. 30 (1965)

15 Communism is Soviet power plus the electrification of the whole country.

Report on the Work of the Council of People's Commissars, 22 December 1920, ibid., vol. 31 (1966). The words were used as a slogan to promote the plans of the State Committee for the Electrification of Russia.

16 It is true that liberty is precious – so precious that it must be rationed.

Attributed in *Soviet Communism: A New Civilisation?*, ch. 12, 'Where is Freedom?' (1936) by Beatrice and SIDNEY WEBB

John Lennon
(1940–80)
British rock musician

After separating from the Beatles in 1970 he pursued a solo career with such albums as Imagine *(1971) and* Double Fantasy *(1980). He was murdered by a fan outside his New York apartment. See* JOHN LENNON AND PAUL MCCARTNEY; YOKO ONO 1.

1 Will people in the cheaper seats clap your hands? All the rest of you, if you'll just rattle your jewellery.

To the audience at Royal Command Performance, London, 4 November 1963, quoted in *Shout! The True Story of the Beatles*, pt 2, 'November 1963' (1981) by Philip Norman. Lennon, here announcing the band's final number of their performance, 'Twist and Shout', had earlier warned manager Brian Epstein that he was going to ad lib if the audience proved unresponsive: 'I'll just tell 'em to rattle their fuckin' jewellery.'

2 Christianity will go. It will vanish and shrink. I needn't argue with that; I'm right and I will be proved right. We're more popular than Jesus now; I don't know which will go first – rock and roll or Christianity.

Interview in the *Evening Standard* 4 March 1966. 'Jesus was all right,' Lennon explained, 'but his disciples were thick and ordinary. It's them twisting it that ruins it for me.' His remarks provoked an angry reaction, especially in the USA, causing Lennon to explain himself at a press conference in Chicago, 11 August 1966: 'I'm not saying that we're better or greater, or comparing us with Jesus Christ as a person, or God as a thing, or whatever it is. I just said what I said, and it was wrong, or it was taken wrong. And now it's all this.' See also ZELDA FITZGERALD 3.

3 Christ, you know it ain't easy,
You know how hard it can be,
The way things are going
They're going to crucify me.
'The Ballad of John and Yoko' (song, 1969) on the album *Hey Jude* (1970) by the Beatles. The song, which was banned by some radio stations for its perceived blasphemy, is also credited to PAUL MCCARTNEY, who played piano, bass and drums on the record.

4 All we are saying is give peace a chance.
'Give Peace a Chance' (song, 1969) by the Plastic Ono Band. The song (also credited to PAUL MCCARTNEY), was originally recorded during the eight-day 'bed-in' by Lennon and YOKO ONO in an Amsterdam hotel in May 1969, with participation by ALLEN GINSBERG and TIMOTHY LEARY, among others. It became an anthem for anti-Vietnam and other peace pro-testers.

5 A working class hero is something to be
If you want to be a hero then just follow me.
'Working Class Hero' (song) on the album *John Lennon/Plastic Ono Band* (1970) by John Lennon and the Plastic Ono Band

6 God is a concept by which we measure our pain.
'God' (song), ibid.

7 You have to be a bastard to make it, and that's a fact. And the Beatles are the biggest bastards on earth.
Interview in *Lennon Remembers* (ed. Jann Wenner, 1970)

8 Imagine there's no heaven,
It's easy if you try,
No hell below us,
Above us only sky.
'Imagine' (song) on the album *Imagine* (1971)

9 Life is what happens to you while you're busy making other plans.
'Beautiful Boy' (song) on the album *Starting Over* (1980). The line has also been attributed to Betty Talmadge (divorced wife of Senator Herman Talmadge) and Thomas La Mance (unknown).

10 It's amazing how low you go to get high.
Skywriting by Word of Mouth, 'The Art of Deception is in the Eye of the Beholder' (ed. YOKO ONO, 1986)

11 'Avant-garde' is French for bullshit.
Attributed

John Lennon
(1940–80)
Paul McCartney
(b. 1942)
British rock musicians

Hailed by the critic William Mann as the most important songwriters since Schubert, they co-wrote most of the songs recorded by the Beatles, Lennon's mordant and surreal wit a foil for McCartney's pop sensibility. See also JOHN LENNON *and* PAUL MCCARTNEY.

1 She loves you, yeh, yeh, yeh.
'She Loves You' (song, 1963) on the album *The Beatles' Second Album* (US only, 1964). The song was the group's all-time top-selling UK single.

2 It's been a hard day's night,
And I've been working like a dog.
'A Hard Day's Night' (song) on the album *A Hard Day's Night* (1964) by the Beatles. The phrase 'hard day's night' originated with RINGO STARR's comment on a heavy schedule shooting the film which was later given this title. It was called a typical 'Ringoism' by JOHN LENNON, who also used the words in his book, *In His Own Write*.

3 I don't care too much for money,
Money can't buy me love.
'Can't Buy Me Love' (song), ibid.

4 She's got a ticket to ride, but she don't care.
'Ticket to Ride' (song) on the album *Help!* (1965) by the Beatles

5 Yesterday, all my troubles seemed so far away,
Now it looks as though they're here to stay.
Oh I believe in yesterday.
'Yesterday' (song), ibid. The song, wholly written by McCartney, became the most covered recording ever.

6 He's a real nowhere man
Sitting in his nowhere land
Making all his nowhere plans for nobody.
'Nowhere Man' (song) on the album *Rubber Soul* (1966) by the Beatles

7 Waits at the window,
Wearing the face that she keeps in a jar by the door.
Who is it for?
'Eleanor Rigby' (song) on the album *Revolver* (1966) by the Beatles

8 We all live in a yellow submarine.
'Yellow Submarine' (song), ibid.

9 The Magical Mystery Tour
Is coming to take you away.
'Magical Mystery Tour' (song) on TV film and US album *Magical Mystery Tour* (1967) by the Beatles

10 I get by with a little help from my friends.
'With a Little Help from my Friends' (song) on the album *Sgt. Pepper's Lonely Hearts Club Band* (1967) by the Beatles

11 I've got to admit it's getting better.
'Getting Better' (song), ibid.

12 Will you still need me,
Will you still feed me,
When I'm sixty-four?
'When I'm Sixty-four' (song), ibid.

13 I heard the news today, oh boy.
Four thousand holes in Blackburn Lancashire.
And though the holes were rather small,
They had to count them all.
'A Day in the Life' (song), ibid.

14 I'd love to turn you on.
'A Day in the Life' (song), ibid.

15 All you need is love.
'All You Need is Love' (song, 1967) on the album *Yellow Submarine* (1969) by the Beatles. The song was written specially for 'Our World', the first worldwide satellite TV broadcast, 25 July 1967, in which it was performed and transmitted live to 400 million viewers. The words were used as the title of both a book and TV documentary by Tony Palmer charting the history of popular music (1976).

16 When I hold you in my arms
And I feel my finger on your trigger
I know no one can do me no harm
Because happiness is a warm gun.
'Happiness is a Warm Gun' (song), on *The Beatles* (1968). The title was inspired by an advertising slogan for the National Rifle Association in the USA.

17 And in the end, the love you take
Is equal to the love you make.
'The End' (song), on the album *Abbey Road* (1970) by the Beatles. Lennon called these the best lines McCartney had ever written.

Annie Lennox
(b. 1954)
British singer

Born Griselda Anne Lennox. Her powerful voice helped to make the Eurythmics one of the most successful bands of the 1980s.

1 Sisters are doing it for themselves,
Standing on their own two feet,
Ringing on their own bells.
'Sisters Are Doing It For Themselves' (song, written by Dave Stewart) on the album *Be Yourself Tonight* (1985) by the Eurythmics. Sung as a duet with ARETHA FRANKLIN.

Dan Leno
(1860–1904)
English music hall entertainer

Originally George Galvin. Appearing on stage from the age of four, he became a champion clog dancer, and, from 1888, a star of the annual pantomime at the Drury Lane Theatre.

1 Ah! what is man? Wherefore does he why? Whence did he whence? Whither is he withering?
Dan Leno Hys Booke, ch. 1 (1901)

(Sir) Graham Leonard
(b. 1921)
British ecclesiastic

He argued against the proposed unification of Anglicans and Methodists in the 1970s, and as Bishop of London (1981–91) opposed the ordination of women to the priesthood. He converted to Roman Catholicism in 1994.

1 The purpose of population is not ultimately peopling earth. It is to fill heaven.
Speech to Church of England Synod, 10 February 1983, quoted in the *Observer* 13 February 1983

Leonardo da Vinci
(1452–1519)
Italian artist and scientist

His wide-ranging interests and versatility made him the archetypal Renaissance man. He was employed as a military engineer by Cesare Borgia (c. 1500), created such iconic paintings as the Mona Lisa (c. 1503) and produced volumes of notebooks devoted to his drawings and scientific studies.

1 Life well spent is long.
Leonardo da Vinci's Notebooks, vol. 1, ch. 1 (ed. and transl. Edward MacCurdy, 1938)

2 Iron rusts from disuse; stagnant water loses its purity and in cold weather becomes frozen; even so does inaction sap the vigour of the mind.
Ibid., vol. 1, ch. 2

3 The function of muscle is to pull and not to push, except in the case of the genitals and the tongue.
Ibid., vol. 1, ch. 3, 'On the Movements of the Muscles of the Mouth With Its Lateral Muscles'

4 The tears come from the heart and not the brain.
Ibid., vol. 1, ch. 3, 'How Much Blood Is the Liver Able to Give It Through the Opening of the Heart'

5 Human subtlety . . . will never devise an invention more beautiful, more simple or more direct than does Nature, because in her inventions nothing is lacking, and nothing is superfluous.
Ibid., vol. 1, ch. 3, 'The Muscles of the Tongue'

6 If you call painting 'dumb poetry', then the painter may say of the poet that his art is 'blind painting'. Consider then which is the more grievous affliction, to be blind or to be dumb.
Ibid., vol. 2, ch. 28. See SIMONIDES 1.

7 Perspective is the bridle and rudder of painting.
Ibid., vol. 2, ch. 29

Mikhail Lermontov
(1814–41)
Russian poet and novelist

A major figure in the Russian Romantic movement, he is remembered for such poetic works as 'The Angel' (1832) and The Demon *(1841), and the novel* A Hero of Our Time *(1840). Exiled in 1837 for his poem 'Death of a Poet', protesting the death of* PUSHKIN *in a duel, he was himself killed in a duel.*

1 No, I'm not Byron, it's my role
To be an undiscovered wonder,
Like him, a persecuted wand'rer,
But furnished with a Russian soul.
'No, I'm not Byron' (written 1832), repr. in *An Age Ago: A Selection of Nineteenth Century Russian Poetry* (ed. and transl. Alan Myers, 1988)

2 Beneath the azure current floweth;
Above, the golden sunlight glows.
Rebellious, the storm it wooeth,
As if the storms could give repose.
'A Sail', st. 3 (written 1832, publ. 1841), repr. in *A Book of Russian Verse* (ed. C. M. Bowra, 1943)

3 I am like a man yawning at a ball; the only reason he does not go home to bed is that his carriage has not arrived yet.
A Hero of Our Time, bk 5 ('Princess Mary') (1840). Narrated by Pechorin.

Alan Jay Lerner
(1918–86)
US songwriter

He collaborated with Frederick Loewe on such Broadway musicals as Paint Your Wagon *(1951),* My Fair Lady *(1956) and the film* Gigi *(1958). See also* MAURICE CHEVALIER 1.

1 All I want is a room somewhere,
Far away from the cold night air,
With one enormous chair –
Oh, wouldn't it be loverly?
'Wouldn't it be Loverly?' (song, with music by Frederick Loewe) in *My Fair Lady* (stage show 1956, film 1964). Sung by Eliza Doolittle.

2 The rain in Spain stays mainly in the plain.
'The Rain in Spain', ibid. A phonetic exercise devised by Henry Higgins for Eliza Doolittle.

3 In Hertford, Hereford and Hampshire,
    hurricanes hardly happen.
'The Rain in Spain', ibid.

4 I could have danced all night.
'I Could Have Danced All Night', ibid. Sung by Eliza Doolittle.

5 I'm getting married in the morning,
Ding! dong! the bells are gonna chime.
Pull out the stopper;
Let's have a whopper;
But get me to the church on time!
'Get Me to the Church on Time', ibid. Sung by Alfred Doolittle.

6 Don't let it be forgot
That once there was a spot
For one brief shining moment that was known
As Camelot.
'Camelot' (song, with music by Frederick Loewe), in *Camelot* (stage show 1960, film 1967). The song was named by JACQUELINE KENNEDY in an interview shortly after JOHN F. KENNEDY's assassination as having had particular significance for her husband's presidency: 'Camelot had suddenly become the symbol of those thousand days when people the world over saw a bright new light of hope shining from the White House. For myself, I have never been able to see a performance of *Camelot* again.' Official Kennedy biographer William Manchester called his book *One Brief Shining Moment* (1983).

Max Lerner
(1902–92)
Russian-born US journalist, author and scholar

Born Mikhail Lerner. His liberal views were aired in his articles for The Nation *(which he edited 1936–8) and in his* New York Post *columns (from 1949). He taught political science and published books on diverse subjects.*

1 A President is best judged by the enemies he makes when he has really hit his stride.
'The Education of Harry Truman' (1949), repr. in *The Unfinished Country*, pt 4 (1959)

2 There is a hate layer of opinion and emotion in America. There will be other McCarthys to come who will be hailed as its heroes.
'McCarthyism: The Smell of Decay' (1950), ibid., pt 4. The article saw the first coining of the word 'McCarthyism', as Lerner affirmed in a later column, 3 February 1954, in which he commented: 'For my own part I doubt seriously whether the word will outlast the political power of the man from whom it derives.'

3 I am neither an optimist nor pessimist, but a possibilist.
Entry in *Who's Who in America* (1992)

Alain-René Le Sage
(1668–1747)
French playwright and novelist

He wrote a number of Spanish-influenced plays but is best known for the picaresque Gil Blas *(1715–35), one of the earliest novels of manners.*

1 I wish you all manner of prosperity, with a little more taste.
Histoire de Gil Blas de Santillane bk 7, ch. 4 (1715–35; *The Adventures of Gil Blas*, transl. TOBIAS SMOLLETT, 1749). The Archbishop of Granada's dismissal of Gil Blas, who has incurred his disfavour by criticizing one of his sermons.

2 Facts are stubborn things.
Ibid., bk 10, ch. 1

Doris Lessing
(b. 1919)
British novelist

Brought up in Rhodesia, she moved to London in 1949 where she published her first novel The Grass is Singing *(1950), a study of interracial relationships in Africa. Subsequent works include* The Golden Notebook *(1962), considered a milestone of feminist literature.*

1 When old settlers say 'One has to understand the country,' what they mean is, 'You have to get used to our ideas about the native.' They are saying, in effect, 'Learn our ideas, or otherwise get out; we don't want you.'
The Grass is Singing, ch. 1 (1950)

2 It is terrible to destroy a person's picture of himself in the interests of truth or some other abstraction.
Ibid., ch. 2

3 There's only one real sin, and that is to persuade oneself that the second-best is anything but the second-best.
The Golden Notebook, 'Free Women 5' (1962). The thoughts of Anna Wulf.

4 If a fish is the movement of water embodied, given shape, then cat is a diagram and pattern of subtle air.
Particularly Cats, ch. 2 (1967)

5 What is charm then? The free giving of a grace, the spending of something given by nature in her role of spendthrift . . . something extra, superfluous, unnecessary, essentially a power thrown away.
Ibid., ch. 9

6 Space or science fiction has become a dialect for our time.
Guardian 7 November 1988

7 Political correctness is the natural continuum from the party line. What we are seeing once again is a self-appointed group of vigilantes imposing their views on others. It is a heritage of communism, but they don't seem to see this.
Sunday Times 10 May 1992

Gotthold Ephraim Lessing
(1729–81)
German dramatist and critic

A leading figure of the Enlightenment, he wrote on art, philosophy and poetry in such works as Laocöon *(1766). His plays include* Minna von Barnhelm *(1767), a comedy, and* Nathan the Wise *(1779), which argued for religious tolerance.*

1 The most deadly fruit is borne by the hatred which one grafts on an extinguished friendship.
Philotas, Act 3 (1759). Spoken by Philotas.

2 A single thankful thought towards heaven is the most perfect of all prayers.
Minna von Barnhelm, Act 2, Sc. 7 (1767; *The Soldier's Fortune*). Spoken by Minna.

3 He who doesn't lose his wits over certain things has no wits to lose.
Emilia Galotti, Act 4, Sc. 7 (1772). Spoken by Orsina, repeated by Odoardo in Act 5, Sc. 5.

Kathy Lette
(b. 1958)
Australian novelist

Her books are wisecracking tales of independent women. 'I like a female character who's got a bit of armpit stubble and occasionally goes for gold in the hypocrisy olympics,' she declared.

1 I didn't 'fall' pregnant! I was bloody well pushed.
Foetal Attraction, pt 1, 'First Stage' (1993). Spoken by Madeline Wolfe.

2 I speak as your native guide to the mysterious tribe called the English. Dress code is everything. You can be a card-carrying Nazi, you can pay gigolos to eat gnocchi out of your navel and you won't be pilloried – as long as you never, ever wear linen with tweed.
Gillian Cassells, ibid., pt 1, 'A New Taste Sensation'

Oscar Levant
(1906–72)
US pianist and composer

He wrote film scores for Hollywood in the 1920s and '30s and was a respected interpreter of Gershwin. He appeared as himself in the films Rhapsody in Blue *(1945) and* An American in Paris *(1951).*

1 Epigram: a wisecrack that played Carnegie Hall.
Coronet Magazine September 1958

2 Strip away the phony tinsel of Hollywood and you find the real tinsel underneath.
Inquisition in Eden (1965)

Charles James Lever
(1809–72)
Irish novelist

Having studied and practised medicine in Ireland, he served as British consul in Italy and wrote lively novels of Dublin and army life, for example Charles O'Malley *(1841).*

1 Och, Dublin City, there is no doubtin',
Bates every city upon the say;
'Tis there you'll see O'Connell spoutin',
An' Lady Morgan makin' tay;
For 'tis the capital of the finest nation,
Wid charmin' pisintry on a fruitful sod,
Fightin' like divils for conciliation
An' hatin' each other for the love of God.
'Dublin City' (song). Attributed to Lever. The novelist Lady Sydney Morgan, in an entry for 30 October 1826 in her *Memoirs* (vol. 2, 1862), mentions the song sung to her by a street ballad singer.

Denise Levertov
(1923–97)
British-born US poet

She came under the influence of WILLIAM CARLOS WILLIAMS *and the Black Mountain poets in the 1950s and was later active in anti-Vietnam War protests. Her collections include* Footprints *(1972).*

1 two by two in the ark of
the ache of it.
'The Ache of Marriage', publ. in *O Taste and See* (1964)

2 If woman is inconstant,
good, I am faithful to
ebb and flow, I fall
in season and now
is a time of ripening.
'Stepping Westward', publ. in *The Sorrow Dance* (1967)

Carlo Levi
(1902–75)
Italian author and painter

His first and most successful novel, Christ Stopped at Eboli *(1945), was based on his experience of internment during the Second World War as a consequence of his anti-fascist activities.*

1 Christ never came this far, nor did time, nor the individual soul, nor hope, nor the relation of cause to effect, nor reason nor history.
Christ Stopped at Eboli, ch. 1 (1945). Referring to Basilicata, in southern Italy. The book was the first to publicize the true plight of the Italian south.

Primo Levi
(1919–87)
Italian chemist and author

His survival of the concentration camp at Auschwitz was a constant theme in his books, and formed the basis for his autobiographical trilogy beginning with If This Is a Man *(1947).*

1 Consider whether this is a man,
Who labours in the mud
Who knows no peace
Who fights for a crust of bread
Who dies at a yes or a no.
'Shemà', written 1946, publ. in *Shemà: Collected Poems of Primo Levi* (1976)

2 In order for the wheel to turn, for life to be lived,

impurities are needed, and the impurities of impurities in the soil, too, as is known, if it is to be fertile. Dissension, diversity, the grain of salt and mustard are needed: Fascism does not want them, forbids them, and that's why you're not a Fascist; it wants everybody to be the same, and you are not. But immaculate virtue does not exist either, or if it exists it is detestable.
The Periodic Table, 'Zinc' (1975)

3 The future of humanity is uncertain, even in the most prosperous countries, and the quality of life deteriorates; and yet I believe that what is being discovered about the infinitely large and infinitely small is sufficient to absolve this end of the century and millennium. What a very few are acquiring in knowledge of the physical world will perhaps cause this period not to be judged as a pure return of barbarism.
Other People's Trades, 'News from The Sky' (1985)

4 To be considered stupid and to be told so is more painful than being called gluttonous, mendacious, violent, lascivious, lazy, cowardly: every weakness, every vice, has found its defenders, its rhetoric, its ennoblement and exaltation, but stupidity hasn't.
Ibid., 'The Irritable Chess-players'

5 The bond between a man and his profession is similar to that which ties him to his country; it is just as complex, often ambivalent, and in general it is understood completely only when it is broken: by exile or emigration in the case of one's country, by retirement in the case of a trade or profession.
Ibid., 'Ex-Chemist'

6 Anyone who has obeyed nature by transmitting a piece of gossip experiences the explosive relief that accompanies the satisfying of a primary need.
'About Gossip' (1986), repr. in *The Mirror Maker* (1989)

7 The aims of life are the best defence against death.
The Drowned and the Saved, ch. 6 (1988)

Bernard Levin
(1928–2004)
British journalist and critic

He wrote political commentary and criticism for numerous newspapers and magazines, and was also a radio scriptwriter and broadcaster. His books include The Way We Live Now *(1984).*

1 In every age of transition men are never so firmly bound to one way of life as when they are about to abandon it, so that fanaticism and intolerance reach their most intense forms just before tolerance and mutual acceptance come to be the natural order of things.
The Pendulum Years, ch. 4 (1970). Discussing John Profumo, 'the last victim of the old, unpermissive standards'.

2 Between them, then, Walrus and Carpenter, they divided up the Sixties.
Ibid., ch. 12. Referring to HAROLD MACMILLAN and HAROLD WILSON.

Emmanuel Levinas
(1905–95)
French philosopher

One of the foremost exponents of the work of Husserl, and an influence on SARTRE *and* DERRIDA, *he expounded his philosophy of ethics in* Existence and Existents *(1947) and* Totality and Infinity *(1961), among other works.*

1 If the 1945 victory demonstrates that in history, vice is ultimately punished and virtue recognized, we do not wish once more to bear the brunt of this demonstration.
'The Diary of Leon Brunschvicg' (1949), repr. in *Difficult Freedom*, pt 1 (1990)

2 The faith that moves mountains and conceives of a world without slaves immediately transports itself to utopia, separating the reign of God from the reign of Caesar. This reassures Caesar.
'Place and Utopia' (1950), ibid., pt 3

3 Evil is not a mystical principle that can be effaced by a ritual, it is an offence perpetrated on man by man. No one, not even God, can substitute himself for the victim.
'A Religion for Adults' (1957), ibid., pt 1

4 Monotheism has not only a horror of idols, but a nose for false prophecy. A special patience – Judaism – is required to refuse all premature messianic claims.
'Judaism and the Present' (1969), ibid., pt 5

Duc de Lévis
(1764–1830)
French soldier and wit

Gaston Pierre Marc. A supporter of constitutional monarchy, he fled to England after the fall of Louis XVI and was a government adviser after the restoration of the monarchy. He wrote Maximes et réflexions sur différents sujets *(1808) and* Souvenirs et portraits *(1813), among other works.*

1 *Noblesse oblige.*
[Nobility has its obligations.]
Maximes et réflexions, 'Sur la Noblesse' (1808)

Claude Lévi-Strauss
(b. 1908)
French anthropologist

He formulated the principles of structuralism through his studies of kinship, myth and religion, elaborating his theories in Mythologies *(4 vols. 1964–71).*

1 Being human signifies, for each one of us, belonging to a class, a society, a country, a continent and a civilization.
Tristes tropiques, ch. 38 (1955)

2 The world began without man, and it will end without him.
Ibid., ch. 40

3 Language is a form of human reason, which has its internal logic of which man knows nothing.
The Savage Mind, ch. 9 (1962)

4 The scientific mind does not so much provide *the right answers as ask the right questions.*
The Raw and the Cooked, 'Overture' (1964)

5 I therefore claim to show, not how men think in myths, but how myths operate in men's minds without their being aware of the fact.
Ibid., 'Overture'

6 Journeys, those magic caskets full of dreamlike promises, will never again yield up their treasures untarnished . . . The first thing we see as we travel around the world is our own filth, thrown into the face of mankind.
Quoted in the *Independent on Sunday* 4 August 1991

Bernard-Henri Lévy
(b. 1948)
French philosopher

As a 'New Philosopher', he came to the forefront of radical French thought in the mid-1970s. His Barbarism with a Human Face *(1977) was a denunciation of Marxism.*

1 The only successful revolution of this century is totalitarianism.
Time 12 September 1977

2 I think enthusiasm is one of the worst temptations for an intellectual. It is almost a rule that when intellectuals enthuse, they are wrong.
International Herald Tribune 21 January 1991

3 Between the barbarity of capitalism, which censures itself much of the time, and the barbarity of socialism, which does not, I guess I would choose capitalism.
Quoted in the *Independent on Sunday* 31 March 1991

Monica Lewinsky
(b. 1973)
US former White House intern

She was catapulted to fame over her sexual relationship with President CLINTON, *begun in 1995. She testified at the Senate Hearing Committee in 1998.*

1 I would just like to say that no one ever asked me to lie, and I was never promised a job for my silence. And I am sorry, I'm really sorry for everything that's happened. And I hate Linda Tripp.
Concluding her evidence to the Grand Jury, quoted in the *Daily Telegraph* 23 September 1998. Linda Tripp was a colleague at the White House who taped Lewinsky's confidences regarding her affair with President CLINTON.

C. S. Lewis
(1898–1963)
British author and scholar

Clive Staples Lewis. He published more than forty works on Christian subjects, notably the satirical Screwtape Letters *(1942). Christian allegory also runs through his classic series for children* The Chronicles of Narnia *(1950–6) and his works of science fiction.*

1 The safest road to Hell is the gradual one – the gentle slope, soft underfoot, without sudden turnings, without milestones, without signposts.
The Screwtape Letters, 'Letter 12' (1942). Spoken by Screwtape.

2 Much of the modern resistance to chastity comes from men's belief that they 'own' their bodies – those vast and perilous estates, pulsating with the energy that made the worlds, in which they find themselves without their consent and from which they are ejected at the pleasure of Another!
Ibid., 'Letter 21'

3 Courage is not simply *one* of the virtues but the form of every virtue at the testing point, which means at the point of highest reality.
Quoted in *The Unquiet Grave*, pt 3 (1944, rev. 1951) by CYRIL CONNOLLY

4 I remember summing up what I took to be our destiny, in conversation with my best friend at Chartres, by the formula, 'Term, holidays, term,

holidays, till we leave school, and then work, work, work till we die.'
Surprised by Joy, ch. 4 (1955)

5 Literary experience heals the wound, without undermining the privilege, of individuality.
An Experiment in Criticism, Epilogue (1961)

6 No one ever told me that grief felt so like fear.
A Grief Observed, pt 1 (1961). Opening words of book of mourning for Lewis's dead wife.

7 Talk to me about the truth of religion and I'll listen gladly. Talk to me about the duty of religion and I'll listen submissively. But don't come talking to me about the consolations of religion or I shall suspect that you don't understand.
Ibid., pt 2

8 There is, hidden or flaunted, a sword between the sexes till an entire marriage reconciles them.
Ibid., pt 3

9 If, as I can't help suspecting, the dead also feel the pains of separation (and this may be one of their purgatorial sufferings), then for both lovers, and for all pairs of lovers without exception, bereavement is a universal and integral part of our experience of love.
Ibid., pt 3

10 Can a mortal ask questions which God finds unanswerable? Quite easily, I should think. All nonsense questions are unanswerable.
Ibid., pt 4

Jerry Lee Lewis
(b. 1935)
US rock 'n' roll musician

His piano-pounding in 'Whole Lotta Shakin' Going On' and 'Great Balls of Fire' (both 1957) caught the public imagination, though scandals and his erratic behaviour set back his career.

1 You shake my nerves and you rattle my brain.
Too much love drives a man insane.
You broke my will, but what a thrill.
Goodness gracious, great balls of fire!
'Great Balls of Fire' (song, 1957, written by Jack Hammer and Otis Blackwell). *Great Balls of Fire!* was the title of a 1989 bio-pic.

Sinclair Lewis
(1885–1951)
US novelist

He caused a sensation with Main Street *(1920), the first of a series of novels that satirized small-town life in the Midwest. In 1930 he was the first American to be awarded the Nobel Prize for Literature.*

1 In other countries, art and literature are left to a lot of shabby bums living in attics and feeding on booze and spaghetti, but in America the successful writer or picture-painter is indistinguishable from any other decent businessman.
Babbitt, ch. 14, sect. 3 (1922). Spoken by George Follansbee Babbitt.

2 Damn the great executives, the men of measured merriment, damn the men with careful smiles, damn the men that run the shops, oh, damn their measured merriment.
Arrowsmith, ch. 25 (1925). Martin Arrowsmith.

3 Our American professors like their literature clear and cold and pure and very dead.
Speech to Swedish Academy in Stockholm, 12 December 1930, on accepting the Nobel Prize for Literature, quoted in *Literature 1901–1967* (1969) by H. Frenz

(Percy) Wyndham Lewis
(1882–1957)
British author and painter

He was a leader of the Vorticist school of abstract painting and served as a war artist in the First World War. His writings include the satires The Apes of God *(1930) and* The Revenge for Love *(1937). His reputation suffered on account of his pro-Fascist sympathies, later recanted.*

1 It is more *comfortable* for me, in the long run, to be rude than polite.
Little Review May 1917. From one of the 'Imaginary Letters' exchanged between Lewis and EZRA POUND.

2 Almost anything that can be praised or advocated has been put to some disgusting use. There is no principle, however immaculate, that has not had its compromising manipulator.
The Art of Being Ruled, 'The Family and Feminism', sect. 8 (1926)

3 A sort of war of revenge on the intellect is what, for some reason, thrives in the contemporary social atmosphere.
Ibid., 'The "Vicious" Circle', sect. 3

4 *We are the first men of a Future that has not*

materialized. We belong to a 'great age' that has not 'come off'. We moved too quickly for the world. We set too sharp a pace.

Blasting and Bombardiering, pt 5, 'The Period of "Ulysses", "Blast", "The Waste Land"' (1937)

5 I feel most at home in the United States, not because it is intrinsically a more interesting country, but because no one really belongs there any more than I do. We are all there together in its wholly excellent vacuum.

America and Cosmic Man, 'The Case Against Roots' (1948)

Liberace

(1919–87)

US entertainer

Originally Wladziu Valentino Liberace. Sporting rhinestones, gold lamé and coiffed hair, he played romantic arrangements of popular classics.

1 When the reviews are bad I tell my staff that they can join me as I cry all the way to the bank.

Liberace: An Autobiography, ch. 2. (1973). The catch-phrase 'I cried all the way to the bank' was used in Liberace's stage act from the 1950s.

Georg Christoph Lichtenberg

(1742–99)

German physicist and aphorist

Professor of Physics at Göttingen University, he became known as a satirist and for his incisive aphorisms, collected in his numerous notebooks, or Sudelbücher *('waste books').*

1 Erudition can produce foliage without bearing fruit.

Aphorisms, Notebook C, aph. 26 (written 1765–99, transl. R. J. Hollingdale)

2 Even truth needs to be clad in new garments if it is to appeal to a new age.

Ibid., Notebook C, aph. 33

3 The journalists have constructed for themselves a little wooden chapel, which they also call the Temple of Fame, in which they put up and take down portraits all day long and make such a hammering you can't hear yourself speak.

Ibid., Notebook D, aph. 20

4 Nowadays three witty turns of phrase and a lie make a writer.

Ibid., Notebook D, aph. 25

5 That man is the noblest creature may also be inferred from the fact that no other creature has yet contested this claim.

Ibid., Notebook D, aph.58

6 To do the opposite of something is also a form of imitation, namely an imitation of its opposite.

Ibid., Notebook D, aph. 96

7 Nothing can contribute more to peace of soul than the lack of any opinion whatever.

Ibid., Notebook E, aph. 11

8 A handful of soldiers is always better than a mouthful of arguments.

Ibid., Notebook E, aph. 19

9 A book is a mirror: if an ape looks into it an apostle is hardly likely to look out.

Ibid., Notebook E, aph. 49

10 A good metaphor is something even the police should keep an eye on.

Ibid., Notebook E, aph. 91

11 We say that someone occupies an official position, whereas it is the official position that occupies him.

Ibid., Notebook F, aph. 47

12 I am often of one opinion when I am lying down and of another when I am standing up.

Ibid., Notebook F, aph. 73

13 Much reading has brought upon us a learned barbarism.

Ibid., Notebook F, aph. 144

14 There are very many people who read simply to prevent themselves from thinking.

Ibid., Notebook G, aph. 29

15 We accumulate our opinions at an age when our understanding is at its weakest.

Ibid., Notebook H, aph. 4

16 The most dangerous untruths are truths slightly distorted.

Ibid., Notebook H, aph. 7

17 He who is enamoured of himself will at least have the advantage of being inconvenienced by few rivals.

Ibid., Notebook H, aph. 10

18 We cannot remember too often that when we observe nature, and especially the ordering of nature, it is always ourselves alone we are observing.

Ibid., Notebook J, aph. 65

19 The fly that does not want to be swatted is safest if it sits on the fly-swat.
Ibid., Notebook J, aph. 70

20 Boorishness, too, has its geniuses.
Ibid., Notebook J, aph. 101

21 Nothing makes one old so quickly as the ever-present thought that one is growing older.
Ibid., Notebook K, aph. 13

22 Man is to be found in reason, God in the passions.
Ibid., Notebook K, aph. 21

23 The sure conviction that we could if we wanted to is the reason so many good minds are idle.
Ibid., Notebook K, aph. 27

24 What most clearly characterizes true freedom and its true employment is its misemployment.
Ibid., Notebook L, aph. 49

Thomas Linacre
(c. 1460–1524)
English physician and scholar

He studied at Oxford and in Italy and was physician to Henry VIII. He founded the Royal College of Physicians in 1518.

1 Either this is not the Gospel, or we are not Christians.
Attributed remark, said toward the end of his life, on reading the Gospels for the first time

Abraham Lincoln
(1809–65)
US president

Born in a log cabin in Kentucky and largely self-educated, he practised law before entering politics. He won the presidential elections in 1860 and 1864 for the Republican Party, and strove to maintain the Union during the turmoil of the Civil War period. He was assassinated by JOHN WILKES BOOTH *five days after the Confederate surrender. See* JAMES RUSSELL LOWELL *14, 15.*

1 At what point then is the approach of danger to be expected? I answer, if it ever reach us, it must spring up amongst us. It cannot come from abroad. If destruction be our lot, we must ourselves be its author and finisher. As a nation of freemen, we must live through all time, or die by suicide.
'The Perpetuation of Our Political Institutions', speech, 27 January 1838, Springfield, Illinois, publ. in *Collected Works of Abraham Lincoln*, vol. 1 (ed. Roy P. Basler, 1953)

2 Let reverence for the laws be breathed by every American mother to the lisping babe that prattles on her lap – let it be taught in schools, in seminaries, and in colleges; let it be written in primers, spelling books, and in almanacs; let it be preached from the pulpit, proclaimed in legislative halls, and enforced in the courts of justice. And, in short, let it become the political religion of the nation.
'The Perpetuation of Our Political Institutions', ibid., vol. 1

3 I believe, if we take habitual drunkards as a class, their heads and their hearts will bear an advantageous comparison with those of any other class. There seems ever to have been a proneness in the brilliant and the warm-blooded to fall into this vice.
Speech to the Washington Temperance Society, ibid., vol. 1

4 If you would win a man to your cause, first convince him that you are his sincere friend. Therein is a drop of honey that catches his heart, which, say what he will, is the great high road to his reason, and which, when once gained, you will find but little trouble in convincing his judgment of the justice of your cause.
Speech to the Washington Temperance Society, Springfield, Illinois, 22 February 1842, ibid., vol. 1

5 Few can be induced to labor exclusively for posterity; and none will do it enthusiastically. Posterity has done nothing for us; and theorise on it as we may, practically we shall do very little for it, unless we are made to think we are at the same time doing something for ourselves.
Speech to the Washington Temperance Society, ibid., vol. 1

6 Military glory – that attractive rainbow that rises in showers of blood.
'The War with Mexico', speech to House of Representatives, 12 January 1848, ibid., vol. 1. Lincoln accused President Polk of pursuing war in order to divert the 'public gaze'.

7 The legitimate object of government is to do for a community of people whatever they need to have done, but cannot do at all, or cannot so well do, for themselves in their separate, and individual capacities. In all that the people can individually do as well for themselves, government ought not to interfere.
Fragment on government, 1 July 1854 [?], ibid., vol. 2

8 No man is good enough to govern another man, without that other's consent.
'The Repeal of the Missouri Compromise', speech, Peoria, Illinois, 16 October 1854, publ. ibid., vol. 2

9 Slavery is founded in the selfishness of man's

nature – opposition to it is his love of justice. These principles are an eternal antagonism; and when brought into collision so fiercely as slavery extension brings them, shocks and throes and convulsions must ceaselessly follow.

'The Repeal of the Missouri Compromise', speech, ibid., vol. 2

10 The ballot is stronger than the bullet.

Speech, Bloomington, Illinois, 29 May 1856, publ. in *The Writings of Abraham Lincoln* (ed. Arthur Brooks Lapsley, 1905). This speech to the first Republican State Convention of Illinois was reconstructed 40 years afterwards; more reliable sources exist for a variant and later form of this famous line: 'To give victory to the right, not bloody bullets, but peaceful ballots only, are necessary' (speech, *c.* 18 May 1858, publ. in *Collected Works*, vol. 2, ed. Roy P. Basler, 1953).

11 'A house divided against itself cannot stand.' I believe this government cannot endure permanently half slave and half free. I do not expect the Union to be *dissolved* – I do not expect the house to *fall* – but I *do* expect it will cease to be divided. It will become *all* one thing, or *all* the other.

'A House Divided', speech at Republican State Convention, Springfield, Illinois, 16 June 1858, publ. in *Collected Works of Abraham Lincoln*, vol. 2 (ed. Roy P. Basler, 1953). See BIBLE, NEW TESTAMENT: MARK 3.

12 As I would not be a *slave*, so I would not be a *master*. This expresses my idea of democracy.

Autograph fragment, *c.* 1 August 1858, ibid., vol. 2

13 I have no purpose to introduce political and social equality between the white and black races. There is a physical difference between the two, which, in my judgment, will probably forever forbid their living together upon the footing of perfect equality; and inasmuch as it becomes a necessity that there must be a difference, I ... am in favour of the race to which I belong having the superior position.

Speech, Ottawa, Illinois, 21 August 1858, ibid., vol. 2. The speech formed part of the celebrated debates with Stephen A. Douglas for election to the Senate.

14 What is conservatism? Is it not adherence to the old and tried, against the new and untried?

Speech, Cooper Institute, New York, 27 February 1860, ibid., vol. 3 (1953)

15 Let us have faith that right makes might, and in that faith let us to the end dare to do our duty as we understand it.

Speech, Cooper Institute, New York, 27 February 1860, ibid., vol. 3. Closing words of speech.

16 If, by the mere force of numbers, a majority should deprive a minority of any clearly written constitutional right, it might in a moral point of view justify revolution – certainly would, if such a right were a vital one.

First Inaugural Address, 4 March 1861, ibid., vol. 4 (1853)

17 Though passion may have strained, it must not break our bonds of affection. The mystic chords of memory, stretching from every battlefield and patriot grave to every living heart and hearthstone all over this broad land, will yet swell the chorus of the Union, when again touched, as surely they will be, by the better angels of our nature.

First Inaugural Address, 4 March 1861, ibid., vol. 4. Closing words of address.

18 Labor is prior to, and independent of, capital. Capital is only the fruit of labor, and could never have existed if labor had not first existed. Labor is the superior of capital, and deserves much the higher consideration.

First Annual Message to Congress, 3 December 1861, ibid., vol. 5

19 My paramount object in this struggle is to save the Union, and is not either to save or to destroy slavery. If I could save the Union without freeing any slave I would do it, and if I could save it by freeing all the slaves, I would do it; and if I could save it by freeing some and leaving others alone I would also do that.

Letter to HORACE GREELEY, 22 August 1862, ibid., vol. 5 (1853). However, Lincoln added: 'I have here stated my purpose according to my view of official duty; and I intend no modification of my oft-expressed personal wish that all men everywhere could be free.'

20 The dogmas of the quiet past are inadequate to the stormy present. The occasion is piled high with difficulty, and we must rise with the occasion. As our case is new, so we must think anew and act anew. We must disenthrall ourselves, and then we shall save our country.

Second Annual Message to Congress, 1 December 1862, ibid., vol. 5

21 In giving freedom to the slave, we assure freedom to the free – honorable alike in what we give and what we preserve. We shall nobly save, or meanly lose, the last best hope of earth.

Second Annual Message to Congress, 1 December 1862, ibid., vol. 5

22 Quarrel not at all. No man resolved to make the most of himself can spare time for personal

contention. Still less can he afford to take all the consequences, including the vitiating of his temper and the loss of self-control. Yield larger things to which you can show no more than equal right; and yield lesser ones, though clearly your own. Better give your path to a dog than be bitten by him in contesting for the right. Even killing the dog would not cure the bite.

Letter, 26 October 1863, ibid., vol. 6 (1853)

23 Fourscore and seven years ago our fathers brought forth on this continent a new nation, conceived in liberty, and dedicated to the proposition that all men are created equal.

'Gettysburg Address', 19 November 1863, ibid., vol. 7 (1853). Opening words of Lincoln's dedication of the cemetery at Gettysburg, scene of the most devastating battle of the Civil War. His brief address, which took him only about three minutes to deliver, is claimed to be the most quoted speech of all time.

24 We cannot dedicate – we cannot consecrate – we cannot hallow – this ground. The brave men, living and dead, who struggled here, have consecrated it far above our poor power to add or detract. The world will little note nor long remember what we say here, but it can never forget what they did here.

'Gettysburg Address', 19 November 1863, ibid., vol. 7

25 We here highly resolve that these dead shall not have died in vain – that this nation, under God, shall have a new birth of freedom – and that government of the people, by the people, for the people, shall not perish from the earth.

'Gettysburg Address', 19 November 1863, ibid., vol. 7. Concluding words of speech.

26 Common looking people are the best in the world: that is the reason the Lord makes so many of them.

Quoted by Lincoln's secretary John Hay in journal entry, 23 December 1863, publ. in Lincoln and the Civil War in the Diaries and Letters of John Hay (ed. Tyler Dennett, 1939). The words were apparently spoken in a dream, in reply to one who had called Lincoln 'common-looking'. An alternative version is quoted in Our Presidents, ch. 6 (1928) by James Morgan: 'The Lord prefers common-looking people. That is the reason He makes so many of them.'

27 Tell me what brand of whiskey that Grant drinks. I would like to send a barrel of it to my other generals.

Quoted in the New York Herald 26 November 1863. Attributed reply to comments about ULYSSES S. GRANT's drinking habits.

28 I claim not to have controlled events, but confess plainly that events have controlled me.

Letter, 4 April 1864, publ. in Collected Works of Abraham Lincoln, vol. 7 (ed. Roy P. Basler, 1953)

29 With malice toward none; with charity for all; with firmness in the right, as God gives us to see the right, let us strive on to finish the work we are in; to bind up the nation's wounds; to care for him who shall have borne the battle, and for his widow and his orphan – to do all which may achieve and cherish a just and lasting peace among ourselves, and with all nations.

Second Inaugural Address, 4 March 1865, publ. ibid., vol. 8 (1953). Conclusion of speech.

30 I don't like to hear cut and dried sermons. No – when I hear a man preach, I like to see him act as if he were fighting bees!

Quoted in Century Magazine December 1881

31 People who like this sort of thing will find this the sort of thing they like.

Quoted in Collections and Recollections, 'The Art of Putting Things' (1898) by G. W. E. RUSSELL. Referring to 'an unreadably sentimental book'. According to Lincoln's Own Stories (1912) by Anthony Gross, Lincoln's remark was to Robert Dale Owen, a spiritualist who had insisted on reading to Lincoln a long manuscript on spiritualism.

32 I don't know who my grandfather was; I am much more concerned to know what his grandson will be.

Quoted in Lincoln's Own Stories (1912) by Anthony Gross

33 You may fool all the people some of the time; you can even fool some of the people all the time; but you can't fool all of the people all the time.

Quoted in 'Abe' Lincoln's Yarns and Stories, '"Fooling" the People' (1904) by Alexander K. McClure. The aphorism has also been attributed to PHINEAS T. BARNUM.

34 I do not agree with those who say that slavery is dead. We are like whalers who have been long on a chase – we have at last got the harpoon into the monster, but we must now look how we steer, or, with one 'flop' of his tail, he will yet send us all into eternity!

Quoted ibid., 'Beware of the Tail'

R. M. Lindner
(1914–56)
US novelist

Robert Mitchell Lindner. His books include Rebel Without a Cause: the Hypnoanalysis of a Criminal Psychopath *(1944) and* Must You Conform? *(1956).*

1 Rebel Without a Cause.
Title of book (1944, filmed 1955). The phrase is most associated with the film's star James Dean, whose role was touted in the publicity as 'the bad boy from a good family'.

Vachel Lindsay
(1879–1931)
US poet

Inspired by the oral and troubadour traditions of poetry, he wandered America, living from his dramatic recitations of his rhythmic verse. His career declined in the 1920s and, impoverished, he committed suicide.

1 Booth died blind and still by faith he trod,
Eyes still dazzled by the ways of God.
'General William Booth Enters into Heaven', pt 2, publ. in *General William Booth Enters into Heaven and Other Poems* (1913)

2 Then I saw the Congo, creeping through the black,
Cutting through the forest with a golden track.
'The Congo', pt 1, publ. in *The Congo and Other Poems* (1914)

3 Factory windows are always broken.
Somebody's always throwing bricks,
Somebody's always heaving cinders,
Playing ugly Yahoo tricks.
'Factory Windows', st. 1, ibid.

Carl Linnaeus
(1707–78)
Swedish botanist

Carl von Linné, or Carolus Linnaeus. In Systema Naturae *(1735) and* Genera Plantarum *(1737), he presented the system of plant classification which became the basis of modern taxonomy. He also classified animals and minerals.*

1 Nature does not proceed by leaps.
Philosophia Botanica, sect. 77 (1751)

Lin Yutang
(1895–1976)
Chinese author

Having studied in Germany and the USA, he returned to China but was at odds with the government line on literature. He lived mainly in America from 1936, founded magazines and wrote about China, also writing novels and translations.

1 A good traveller is one who does not know where he is going to, and a perfect traveller does not know where he came from.
The Importance of Living, ch. 11 (1937)

Walter Lippmann
(1889–1974)
US journalist

The newspaper column was for him 'the laboratory or clinic in which I test the philosophy and keep it from becoming too abstract'. His columns were syndicated through the New York Herald Tribune *(1931–62) and the* Washington Post *(1962–7).*

1 The great social adventure of America is no longer the conquest of the wilderness but the absorption of fifty different peoples.
A Preface to Politics, ch. 6 (1913)

2 The best servants of the people, like the best valets, must whisper unpleasant truths in the master's ear. It is the court fool, not the foolish courtier, whom the king can least afford to lose.
Ibid., ch. 6

3 In making the great experiment of governing people by consent rather than by coercion, it is not sufficient that the party in power should have a majority. It is just as necessary that the party in power should never outrage the minority.
'The Indispensable Opposition' (1939), repr. in *The Essential Lippmann*, pt 6, sect. 2 (ed. Clinton Rossiter and James Lare, 1982)

4 The final test of a leader is that he leaves behind him in other men the conviction and the will to carry on.
'Roosevelt Is Gone' (1945), ibid., pt 10, sect. 5. 'The genius of a good leader,' Lippmann added, 'is to leave behind him a situation which common sense, without the grace of genius, can deal with successfully.'

5 Successful democratic politicians are insecure and intimidated men. They advance politically only as they placate, appease, bribe, seduce, bamboozle, or

otherwise manage to manipulate the demanding and threatening elements in their constituencies.
The Public Philosophy, ch. 2, sect. 4 (1955)

Little Britain

With sketches written and performed by Matt Lucas and David Walliams, the series was initially broadcast on BBC Radio 4 (2001–2), later transferring to BBC 3 (2003) and BBC 1 (2004).

1 *I'm* the only gay in the village.
Dafydd Thomas (Matt Lucas)

2 I'm a *lady*.
Transvestite, Emily Howard (David Walliams)

3 No but yeah but no.
Vicky Pollard (Matt Lucas)

4 I want that one.
Lou (Matt Lucas)

Little Richard
(b. 1932)
US rock 'n' roll musician

Originally Richard Penniman. Raised a Seventh-Day Adventist in Georgia, he had one of the most powerful voices in rock 'n' roll and a flamboyant stage presence. His run of hits ended when he turned to religion.

1 Awop-bop-a-loo-mop alop-bam-boom!
'Tutti-Frutti' (song, 1955, written with J. Lubin and Dorothy La Bostrie)

2 The Girl Can't Help It.
Title of song (1956, written by BOBBY TROUP) and film (1956)

Joan Littlewood
(1914–2002)
British theatre director

With EWAN MACCOLL she set up the Theatre Union in the 1930s and Theatre Workshop in 1945, based in London's Stratford East from 1953. Her experimental techniques were acclaimed in such productions as The Good Soldier Schweik *(1955).*

1 Oh What a Lovely War!
Title of song and stage show (1963, written with Charles Chilton and Gerry Raffles; filmed 1969)

Maxim Litvinov
(1876–1951)
Soviet diplomat

As Commissar for Foreign Affairs under STALIN *1930–9, he advocated disarmament and urged a common international front against Nazi Germany.*

1 Peace is indivisible.
Note to the Allies, 25 February 1920, quoted in *Maxim Litvinoff*, ch. 8, sect. 2 (1943) by Arthur Upham Pope. Litvinov used the phrase on a number of occasions, later remarking that this was 'my contribution to the abstract science of peace'.

Penelope Lively
(b. 1933)
British novelist

A vivid sense of the past and of place pervades her writing, both in her work for children and in her adult fiction. Titles include the novel Moontiger *(1987) and* Oleander, Jacaranda *(1994), a memoir.*

1 Wars are fought by children. Conceived by their mad demonic elders, and fought by boys.
Moontiger, ch. 8 (1987)

2 I believe that the experience of childhood is irretrievable. All that remains, for any of us, is a headful of brilliant frozen moments, already dangerously distorted by the wisdoms of maturity.
Oleander, Jacaranda, Preface (1994)

Ken Livingstone
(b. 1945)
British politician and mayor

The left-wing leader of the Greater London Council (1981–6), he was elected Labour MP for Brent East, London, in 1987, and mayor of London in 2000.

1 The problem is that many MPs never see the London that exists beyond the wine bars and brothels of Westminster.
The Times 19 February 1987

2 Politics is a marathon not a sprint.
New Statesman 10 October 1997

Livy
(59 BC–AD 17)
Roman historian

Titus Livius. Extending from the mythological foundation of Rome to 9 BC, his history of the city was intended to highlight its glorious traditions. Thirty-five of the original 142 books survive and some of the rest have been reconstructed.

1 *Vae victis.*
[Woe to the vanquished.]
Ab Urbe Condita, bk 5, ch. 48, sect. 9. Attributed to the Gallic king Brennus, on capturing Rome in 390 BC.

2 On small things often depends the course of great events.
Ibid., bk 27, ch. 9, sect. 1

3 It is safer for a criminal to go unaccused than to be acquitted.
Ibid., bk 34, ch. 4, sect. 19

4 Hot-headed and bold decisions were fair at first sight, hard to follow through, disastrous in result.
Ibid., bk 35, ch. 32, sect. 13

Llosa
See VARGAS LLOSA

David Lloyd George
(1863–1945)
British statesman

First Earl of Dwyfor. A Liberal MP from 1890, he was Chancellor of the Exchequer (1908–15) and head of the coalition government (1916–22). His measures to alleviate poverty laid the foundations of the welfare state. JOHN MAYNARD KEYNES *called him a 'half-human visitor to our age'. See also* MARGOT ASQUITH 4.

1 The landlord is a gentleman . . . who does not earn his wealth. He has a host of agents and clerks to receive for him. He does not even take the trouble to spend his wealth. He has a host of people around him to do the actual spending for him. He never sees it until he comes to enjoy it. His sole function, his chief pride, is stately consumption of wealth produced by others.
Speech at Limehouse, London, 30 July 1909, publ. in *Life of David Lloyd George*, vol. 4, Speech 7 (ed. Herbert du Parcq, 1912)

2 The question will be asked whether five hundred men, ordinary men, chosen accidentally from among the unemployed, should override the judgement – the deliberate judgement – of millions of people who are engaged in the industry which makes the wealth of this country.
Speech at Newcastle, 9 October 1909, ibid., vol. 4, Speech 8. Referring to the House of Lords.

3 A fully-equipped duke costs as much to keep up

as two Dreadnoughts; and they are just as great a terror and they last longer.
Speech at Newcastle, 9 October 1909, ibid., vol. 4, Speech 8

4 We have been living in a sheltered valley for generations. We have been too comfortable and too indulgent – many, perhaps, too selfish – and the stern hand of fate has scourged us to an elevation where we can see the great everlasting things that matter for a nation – the great peaks we had forgotten, of Honour, Duty, Patriotism, and, clad in glittering white, the great pinnacle of Sacrifice pointing like a rugged finger to Heaven.
Speech at Queen's Hall, London, 21 September 1914, quoted in *Lloyd George: From Peace to War, 1912–1916*, ch. 7 (1985) by John Grigg. The speech was reproduced as a wartime pamphlet by the Parliamentary Recruiting Committee, with the title 'Through Terror to Triumph'.

5 At eleven o'clock this morning came to an end the cruellest and most terrible war that has ever scourged mankind. I hope we may say that thus, this fateful morning, came to an end all wars.
Speech to House of Commons, 11 November 1918, publ. in *Hansard*, col. 2463. The speech was made on the day that the armistice was signed between the allied powers and Germany. *The War That Will End War* was the title of a novel by H. G. WELLS (1914).

6 What is our task? To make Britain a fit country for heroes to live in.
Speech, Wolverhampton, 24 November 1918, quoted in *Lloyd George*, ch. 12 (1975) by Peter Rowland. The words were frequently recalled in the years of low wages and unemployment that followed. They are often misquoted: '. . . a country fit for heroes'.

7 The finest eloquence is that which gets things done and the worst is that which delays them.
Speech at Paris Peace Conference, 18 January 1919, quoted in *Source Records of World War I*, vol. 7 (ed. Charles F. Horne, 1998)

8 Diplomats were invented simply to waste time.
Attributed comment on preparations for the Versailles Peace Conference, November 1918

9 He will be just like the scent on a pocket handkerchief.
Remark, 9 June 1922, quoted in *Whitehall Diary*, vol. 1 (1969) by Thomas Jones. On A. J. BALFOUR's place in history.

10 In business a refusal to face disagreeable facts leads to bankruptcy; in war it leads to defeat; in science it leads to false conclusions; in theology it is commonly believed to lead to perdition; in

politics it lands you in all these unpleasant consequences.

Speech at National Liberal Club, London, 12 May 1924, quoted in *Slings and Arrows*, 'Maxims' (1929)

John Locke
(1632–1704)
English philosopher

The founder of British empiricism, he established his reputation with his two most important works: An Essay Concerning Human Understanding *(1689), which argued for the importance of sensory experience, and* Two Treatises of Government *(1690), which embodied his theory of the social contract.*

1 New opinions are always suspected, and usually opposed, without any other reason but because they are not already common. But truth, like gold, is not the less so for being newly brought out of the mine.

An Essay Concerning Human Understanding, 'Dedicatory Epistle' (1689)

2 The senses at first let in particular ideas, and furnish the yet empty cabinet, and the mind by degrees growing familiar with some of them, they are lodged in the memory, and names got to them. Afterwards, the mind proceeding further, abstracts them, and by degrees learns the use of general names. In this manner the mind comes to be furnished with ideas and language.

Ibid., bk 1, ch. 1, sect. 15

3 Let us then suppose the mind to be, as we say, white paper, void of all characters, without any ideas: how comes it to be furnished? Whence comes it by that vast store which the busy and boundless fancy of man has painted on it with an almost endless variety? Whence has it all the materials of reason and knowledge? To this I answer, in one word, from experience. In that all our knowledge is founded; and from that it ultimately derives itself.

Ibid., bk 2, ch. 1, sect. 2

4 No man's knowledge here can go beyond his experience.

Ibid., bk 2, ch. 1, sect. 19

5 There seems to be a constant decay of all our ideas, even of those which are struck deepest.

Ibid., bk 2, ch. 10, sect. 5

6 We are utterly incapable of universal and certain knowledge.

Ibid., bk 4, ch. 3, sect. 28

7 Religion, which should most distinguish us from beasts, and ought most peculiarly to elevate us, as rational creatures, above brutes, is that wherein men often appear most irrational, and more senseless than beasts themselves.

Ibid., bk 4, ch. 18, sect. 11

8 How men, whose plentiful fortunes allow them leisure to improve their understandings, can satisfy themselves with a lazy ignorance, I cannot tell: but methinks they have a low opinion of their souls.

Ibid., bk 4, ch. 20, sect. 6

9 They who are blind will always be led by those that see, or else fall into the ditch: and he is certainly the most subjected, the most enslaved, who is so in his understanding.

Ibid., bk 4, ch. 20, sect. 6

10 Freedom of men under government is to have a standing rule to live by, common to every one of that society, and made by the legislative power erected in it; a liberty to follow my own will in all things, where the rule prescribes not; and not to be subject to the inconstant, uncertain, unknown, arbitrary will of another man.

Second Treatise of Government, ch. 4, sect. 22 (1690)

11 Men being ... by nature all free, equal, and independent, no one can be put out of this estate, and subjected to the political power of another, without his own consent.

Ibid., ch. 8, sect. 95

12 The only way by which any one divests himself of his natural liberty and puts on the bonds of civil society is by agreeing with other men to join and unite into a community.

Ibid., ch. 8, sect. 95

13 The great and chief end, therefore, of men's uniting into commonwealths, and putting themselves under government, is the preservation of their property.

Ibid., ch. 9, sect. 124. The words have been misquoted: 'Government has no other end but the preservation of property.'

14 Wherever law ends, tyranny begins.

Ibid., ch. 18, sect. 202

15 A sound mind in a sound body, is a short, but full description of a happy state in this world: he that has these two, has little more to wish for; and

he that wants either of them, will be little the better for anything else.

Some Thoughts Concerning Education, sect. 1 (1693). Opening sentence. See JUVENAL 17.

16 Good and evil, reward and punishment, are the only motives to a rational creature: these are the spur and reins whereby all mankind are set on work, and guided.

Ibid., sect. 54

17 The only fence against the world is a thorough knowledge of it.

Ibid., sect. 88

Frederick Locker-Lampson
(1821–95)
English man of letters

His slender output of light, humorous verse appeared in London Lyrics *(1857) and its subsequent revisions. He also published anthologies.*

1 But where is now the courtly troop
That once rode laughing by?
I miss the curls of Cantelupe,
The laugh of Lady Di:
They all could laugh from night to morn,
And Time has laughed them all to scorn.

'Rotten Row' (1867), publ. in *London Lyrics* (1876)

2 They eat, and drink, and scheme, and plod,
And go to church on Sunday –
And many are afraid of God –
And more of Mrs. Grundy.

'The Jester's Plea' (1868)

3 The world's as ugly, ay, as sin,
And almost as delightful.

Ibid.

Francis Lockier
(1669–1740)
English prelate

A well-travelled man of letters, he was Dean of Peterborough Cathedral from 1725.

1 The one book necessary to be understood by a divine, is the Bible; any others are to be read, chiefly, in order to understand that.

Quoted in *Anecdotes, Observations, and Characters, of Books and Men*, sect. 2 (1820) by Joseph Spence

2 In all my travels I never met with any one Scotchman but what was a man of sense: I believe every-

body of that country that has any, leaves it as fast as they can.

Quoted ibid., sect. 2

3 No one will ever shine in conversation, who thinks of saying fine things: to please, one must say many things indifferent, and many very bad.

Quoted ibid., sect. 2

Belva Lockwood
(1830–1917)
US lawyer

After obtaining a law degree (1873), she became the first woman to practise before the US Supreme Court in 1879, and was an effective advocate of equal rights for women.

1 The glory of each generation is to make its own precedents.

Quoted in *Lady for the Defense*, pt 3, ch. 13 (1975) by Mary Virginia Fox. Arguing in favour of admitting women to practise in the US Supreme Court, for which there was no precedent.

David Lodge
(b. 1935)
British author, critic and academic

His literary criticism applies structuralist and post-structuralist analysis, while his fiction mixes realism and parody, as in Changing Places *(1975),* Small World *(1984) and* Thinks . . . *(2001), all of which have academic settings.*

1 Literature is mostly about having sex and not much about having children. Life is the other way round.

The British Museum Is Falling Down, ch. 4 (1965). Spoken by Adam Appleby.

2 As to our universities . . . they are élitist where they should be egalitarian and egalitarian where they should be élitist.

Nice Work, pt 5, ch. 4 (1988). Spoken by Charles.

Henry Cabot Lodge Jr
(1902–85)
US politician and diplomat

He held a Republican seat in the Senate 1937–44 and 1947–52 and served as US ambassador to the United Nations (1953–60), South Vietnam (1963–4 and 1965–7) and West Germany (1968–9).

1 This organization is created to prevent you from

going to hell. It isn't created to take you to heaven.
New York Times 28 January 1954. Referring to the United
Nations.

Thomas Lodge
(c.1557–1625)
English author and poet

*He led an adventurous life as a pamphleteer, freebooter and
Catholic exile, and worked as a physician in London from
1612. His prose romance* Rosalynde *(1590) was the model for*
SHAKESPEARE's As You Like It.

1 Love in my bosom like a bee
Doth suck his sweet;
Now with his wings he plays with me,
Now with his feet.
Within mine eyes he makes his nest,
His bed amidst my tender breast;
My kisses are his daily feast,
And yet he robs me of my rest.
Ah, wanton, will ye?
Rosalynde, 'Rosalynde's madrigal', st. 1 (1590)

2 Love guards the roses of thy lips
And flies about them like a bee;
If I approach he forward skips,
And if I kiss he stingeth me.
'Love guards the roses of thy lips', st. 1, publ. in *Phillis* (1593)

3 Devils are not so black as they be painted.
A Margarite of America (1596). Spoken by Margarita.

Friedrich von Logau
(1604–55)
German poet and aphorist

*He developed the epigram to a fine art, directing his satire
against courtly life and the influence of foreign manners. His*
Erstes Hundert Teutscher Reimensprüche *(1638) was enlarged
in 1654, and re-titled* Sinn Gedichte *in 1759.*

1 Though the mills of God grind slowly, yet they
    grind exceeding small;
Though with patience He stands waiting, with
    exactness grinds He all.
Erstes Hundert Teutscher Reimensprüche, bk 3, pt 2, no. 24
(1638, rev. 1654; *First Hundred German Proverbs in Rhyme*).
Translated by HENRY WADSWORTH LONGFELLOW as 'Retribution' (1870). The first line is borrowed from an anonymous
classical author.

Jack London
(1876–1916)
US novelist

*John Griffith London. An adventurer and active socialist, he
wrote romantic but also harshly realistic novels and short
stories.*

1 The Call of the Wild.
Title of novel (1903). London's tale of a sledge-dog in Alaska
brought him worldwide fame.

2 I would rather be ashes than dust! I would rather
that my spark should burn out in a brilliant blaze
than it should be stifled by dry-rot. I would rather
be a superb meteor, every atom of me in magnificent glow, than a sleepy and permanent planet. The
proper function of man is to live, not to exist. I shall
not waste my days in trying to prolong them. I shall
use my time.
'London's Credo', quoted in *Jack London's Tales of Adventure*,
Introduction (ed. Irving Shepard, 1956). The words have never
been found in London's own writings, though the journalist
Ernest J. Hopkins reported in the *San Francisco Bulletin*
2 December 1916 that London had uttered a form of them a
few weeks before his death. Earlier, while visiting Australian
suffragette Vida Goldstein in Melbourne, the author had written in her Autograph Book, dated 13 January 1909: 'Seven
years ago I wrote you that I'd rather be ashes than dust. I still
subscribe to that sentiment.'

Henry Wadsworth Longfellow
(1807–82)
US poet

*A professor of modern languages at Harvard until 1854, he
created a body of American legends in his ballads and long
narrative poems* Evangeline *(1847),* The Song of Hiawatha
(1855) and The Courtship of Miles Standish *(1858). He also
published novels and travel sketches and translated* DANTE's
Divine Comedy *(1867).*

1 In this world a man must either be anvil or
hammer.
Hyperion, bk 4, ch. 7 ('The Story of Brother Bernardus') (1839).
Spoken by Berkley.

2 I heard the trailing garments of the Night
Sweep through her marble halls!
I saw her sable skirts all fringed with light
From the celestial walls!
'Hymn to the Night', st. 1, publ. in *The Voices of the Night*
(1839)

3 Life is real! Life is earnest!
And the grave is not its goal;

Dust thou art, to dust returnest,
Was not spoken of the soul.
'A Psalm of Life', st. 2, ibid.

4 Lives of great men all remind us
We can make our lives sublime,
And, departing, leave behind us
Footprints on the sands of time.
'A Psalm of Life', st. 7, ibid.

5 It was the schooner Hesperus,
That sailed the wintry sea;
And the skipper had taken his little daughter,
To bear him company.
'The Wreck of the Hesperus', st. 1, publ. in *Ballads and Other Poems* (1842)

6 'O father! I see a gleaming light,
Oh, say, what may it be?'
But the father answered never a word,
A frozen corpse was he.
'The Wreck of the Hesperus', st. 12, ibid.

7 Under a spreading chestnut tree
The village smithy stands;
The smith, a mighty man is he,
With large and sinewy hands;
And the muscles of his brawny arms
Are strong as iron bands.
'The Village Blacksmith', st. 1, ibid.

8 Each morning sees some task begin,
Each evening sees it close;
Something attempted, something done
Has earned a night's repose.
'The Village Blacksmith', st. 7, ibid.

9 Thy fate is the common fate of all,
Into each life some rain must fall.
'The Rainy Day', st. 3, ibid.

10 And so we plough along, as the fly said to the ox.
The Spanish Student, Act 3, Sc. 6 (1843). Spoken by Chispa.

11 And the night shall be filled with music,
And the cares, that infest the day,
Shall fold their tents, like the Arabs,
And as silently steal away.
'The Day is Done', st. 11, publ. in *The Belfry of Bruges and Other Poems* (1845)

12 This is the forest primeval. The murmuring
pines and the hemlocks,
Bearded with moss, and in garments green,
indistinct in the twilight,

Stand like Druids of old, with voices sad and
prophetic.
Evangeline: A Tale of Acadie (1847). Opening lines.

13 Thou, too, sail on, O Ship of State!
Sail on, O Union, strong and great!
Humanity with all its fears,
With all the hopes of future years,
Is hanging breathless on thy fate!
'The Building of the Ship', ll. 378–82, publ. in *The Seaside and the Fireside* (1849)

14 O flames that glowed! O hearts that yearned!
They were indeed too much akin,
The drift-wood fire without that burned,
The thoughts that burned and glowed within.
'The Fire of Drift-wood', st. 12, ibid. Closing lines of poem.

15 We judge ourselves by what we feel capable of doing, while others judge us by what we have already done.
Kavanagh, bk 1, ch. 1 (1849)

16 Men of genius are often dull and inert in society; as the blazing meteor, when it descends to earth, is only a stone.
Ibid., bk 1, ch. 13. One of the meditations of Mr Churchill, inscribed on his pulpit.

17 Critics are sentinels in the grand army of letters, stationed at the corners of newspapers and reviews, to challenge every new author.
Ibid., bk 1, ch. 13. One of the meditations of Mr Churchill.

18 There was a little girl
Who had a little curl
Right in the middle of her forehead,
When she was good
She was very, very good,
But when she was bad she was horrid.
'There Was a Little Girl', composed for his infant daughter, c. 1850, publ. in *Random Memories* (1922) by E. W. Longfellow

19 By the shores of Gitche Gumee,
By the shining Big-Sea-Water,
Stood the wigwam of Nokomis,
Daughter of the Moon, Nokomis.
The Song of Hiawatha, pt 3 ('Hiawatha's Childhood') (1855)

20 From the waterfall he named her,
Minnehaha, Laughing Water.
Ibid., pt 4 ('Hiawatha and Mudjekeewis')

21 Lo! in that house of misery
A lady with a lamp I see

Pass through the glimmering gloom,
And flit from room to room.

'Santa Filomena', st. 6, publ. in *Birds of Passage*, 'Flight the
First' (1858). Of FLORENCE NIGHTINGALE.

22 Were a star quenched on high,
For ages would its light,
Still travelling downward from the sky,
Shine on our mortal sight.
So when a great man dies,
For years beyond our ken,
The light he leaves behind him lies
Upon the paths of men.

'Charles Sumner', sts 8–9, publ. in *Birds of Passage*, 'Flight
the Fourth' (1858)

23 The heights by great men reached and kept
Were not attained by sudden flight,
But they, while their companions slept,
Were toiling upward in the night.

'The Ladder of Saint Augustine', st. 10, publ. in *The Courtship
of Miles Standish and Other Poems* (1858)

24 Listen, my children, and you shall hear
Of the midnight ride of Paul Revere,
On the eighteenth of April, in Seventy-five;
Hardly a man is now alive
Who remembers that famous day and year.

Tales of a Wayside Inn, pt 1, 'The Landlord's Tale: Paul Revere's
Ride', st. 1 (1863). Longfellow's ballad relates the famous 'midnight ride' made by a hero of the American Revolution to
warn of an impending British raid on Concord, Massachusetts.

25 The fate of a nation was riding that night.

Ibid., pt 1, 'The Landlord's Tale: Paul Revere's Ride', st. 8

26 Ships that pass in the night, and speak each
    other in passing,
Only a signal shown and a distant voice in the
    darkness;
So on the ocean of life we pass and speak one
    another,
Only a look and a voice; then darkness again and a
    silence.

Ibid., pt 3, 'The Theologian's Tale: Elizabeth', sect. 4

27 My own thoughts
Are my companions; my designs and labors
And aspirations are my only friends.

'The Masque of Pandora', pt 3, publ. in *The Masque of Pandora
and Other Poems* (1875). Spoken by Prometheus.

28 The love of learning, the sequestered nooks,
And all the sweet serenity of books.

'Morituri Salutamus', st. 21, ibid.

29 Age is opportunity no less
Than youth itself, though in another dress,
And as the evening twilight fades away
The sky is filled with stars, invisible by day.

'Morituri Salutamus', st. 24, ibid.

30 Not in the clamor of the crowded street,
Not in the shouts and plaudits of the throng,
But in ourselves, are triumph and defeat.

'The Poets', publ. in *A Book of Sonnets* (1876). Closing lines.

31 The holiest of all holidays are those
Kept by ourselves in silence and apart;
The secret anniversaries of the heart,
When the full river of feeling overflows.

'Holidays', ibid.

32 In the long, sleepless watches of the night,
A gentle face – the face of one long dead -
Looks at me from the wall.

'The Cross of Snow', ll. 1–3, written 1879, publ. in *Longfellow:
Poems and Other Writings* (ed. J. D. McClatchy, 2000)

33 Like a French poem is life; being only perfect in
    structure
When with the masculine rhymes mingled the
    feminine are.

'Elegiac Verse', st. 7, publ. in *In the Harbor* (1882)

34 Ah, to build, to build!
That is the noblest art of all the arts.
Painting and sculpture are but images,
Are merely shadows cast by outward things
On stone or canvas, having in themselves
No separate existence. Architecture,
Existing in itself, and not in seeming
A something it is not, surpasses them
As substance shadow.

Michael Angelo, pt 1, 'San Silvestro' (1883), repr. in *The Complete Poetical Works of Henry Wadsworth Longfellow* ('Riverside' edn, ed. Horace E. Scudder, 1886). The words of Michael
Angelo.

Longinus

(*fl.* 1st century AD)
Greek scholar

*Longinus, Dionysius Longinus and Pseudo-Longinus are the
names variously assigned to the author of* On the Sublime, *an
influential work of literary criticism probably dating from the
1st century.*

1 Sublimity is the echo of great mind.

On The Sublime, sect. 9. The words have also been translated:
'Great writing is the echo of great mind.'

Alice Roosevelt Longworth
(1884–1980)
US hostess

The daughter of THEODORE ROOSEVELT, *she played an active part in the Republican party and was famous for her scathing wit. She published magazine columns and* Crowded Hours *(1933), a memoir.*

1 Harding was not a bad man. He was just a slob.
Crowded Hours, ch. 20 (1933). Referring to President WARREN HARDING.

2 If you can't say something good about someone, sit right here by me.
Quoted in *Time* 9 December 1966. The words were apparently embroidered on a cushion.

Anita Loos
(1888–1981)
US novelist and screenwriter

In six decades she wrote 150 screenplays and scenarios as well as Broadway plays and memoirs. Her novel Gentlemen Prefer Blondes *(1925) was a witty portrait of the Roaring Twenties.*

1 Gentlemen Prefer Blondes.
Title of book (1925)

2 Leave them while you're looking good.
Gentlemen Prefer Blondes, ch. 1 (1925). Lorelei Lee's journal entry for 22 March, quoting an 'old adage' of hers.

3 I really think that American gentlemen are the best after all, because kissing your hand may make you feel very very good but a diamond and a sapphire bracelet lasts forever.
Ibid., ch. 4. Lorelei Lee's journal entry for 27 April.

4 Pleasure that isn't paid for is as insipid as everything else that's free.
Kiss Hollywood Good-by, ch. 2 (1974)

5 Show business is the best possible therapy for remorse.
Ibid., ch. 13

Lorca
See GARCÍA LORCA

Konrad Lorenz
(1903–89)
Austrian ethologist

Called the father of ethology, he contributed to the knowledge of behavioural patterns in animals, particularly in birds. His books include Man Meets Dog *(1950) and* On Aggression *(1963).*

1 It is a good morning exercise for a research scientist to discard a pet hypothesis every day before breakfast. It keeps him young.
On Aggression, ch. 2 (1963)

2 Historians will have to face the fact that natural selection determined the evolution of cultures in the same manner as it did that of species.
Ibid., ch. 13

Louis XIV
(1638–1715)
King of France

He was crowned in 1643 but did not take effective control until the death of Cardinal Mazarin in 1661. His reign was autocratic and characterized by extravagance and lavish patronage of the arts, for which he was known as the 'Sun King'.

1 *L'état c'est moi.*
[I am the state.]
Quoted in *Histoire de Paris*, vol. 6 (1834) by J. A. Dulaure. The remark, probably apocryphal, is said to have been made before the Parlement de Paris in 1655.

2 Every time I bestow a vacant office I make a hundred discontented persons and one ingrate.
Quoted in *Le Siècle de Louis XIV*, ch. 26 (1751) by VOLTAIRE. Remark made following the disgrace of the Duke of Lauzun, c. 1669.

3 The Pyrenees are no more.
Quoted ibid., ch. 26. Remark in 1700, on the accession of his grandson to the Spanish throne.

4 Has God forgotten everything I have done for him?
Attributed remark, following the defeat of the French army either at Blenheim (1704) or Malplaquet (1709)

Louis XVIII
(1755–1824)
King of France

Proclaimed king in 1795, he was only able to assume power on the expulsion of NAPOLEON *in 1814, and was finally reinstalled on the throne following Napoleon's final defeat in 1815. His liberal policies were undermined by ultra-royalist ministers after 1820.*

1 *L'exactitude est la politesse des rois.*
[Punctuality is the politeness of kings.]
Remark c. 1814, attributed in *Souvenirs de Jean Lafitte*, bk 1, ch. 3 (1844)

2 A king should die on his feet.
Alleged deathbed remark

Joe Louis
(1914–81)
US boxer

Originally Joseph Louis Borrow. 'The Brown Bomber' won sixty-seven out of seventy professional fights, and was World Heavy-weight Champion 1937–49.

1 He can run. But he can't hide.
Quoted in *Louis: My Life Story* (1947). The threat was addressed to Billy Conn, his opponent in a World Championship match, 19 June 1946, which Louis won.

Richard Lovelace
(1618–58)
English poet

A dashing 'Cavalier poet', he was gaoled in 1642 for petitioning for the restoration of royal rule, which occasioned his famous lines, 'To Althea, from Prison'. During a second gaol term, he prepared his collection Lucasta *(1649).*

1 Tell me not, sweet, I am unkind,
That from the nunnery
Of thy chaste breast, and quiet mind,
To war and arms I fly.
True; a new mistress now I chase,
The first foe in the field;
And with a stronger faith embrace
A sword, a horse, a shield.
'To Lucasta, Going to the Wars', sts 1–2, publ. in *Lucasta* (1649)

2 I could not love thee, dear, so much,
Loved I not honour more.
'To Lucasta, Going to the Wars', st. 3, ibid.

3 When love with unconfinèd wings
Hovers within my gates.
'To Althea, from Prison', st. 1, ibid. Opening lines of poem.

4 Stone walls do not a prison make,
Nor iron bars a cage;
Minds innocent and quiet take
That for an hermitage;
If I have freedom in my love,
And in my soul am free;
Angels alone, that soar above,
Enjoy such liberty.
'To Althea, from Prison', st. 4, ibid.

5 Forbear, thou great good husband, little ant;
A little respite from thy flood of sweat!
'The Ant', st. 1, ibid. Opening lines.

(Sir) Bernard Lovell
(b. 1913)
British astronomer

A pioneer in the study of radio astronomy, he founded Jodrell Bank Experimental Station (now Nuffield Radio Astronomy Laboratories) and was its Director 1951–81.

1 The pursuit of the good and evil are now linked in astronomy as in almost all science ... The fate of human civilization will depend on whether the rockets of the future carry the astronomer's telescope or a hydrogen bomb.
'Fourth Reith Lecture', publ. in *The Individual and the Universe* (1959)

James Lovell
(b. 1928)
US astronaut

Crew member of the Gemini 7 (1965), Gemini 12 (1966) and Apollo 8 (1968) space missions, and commander of the unsuccessful Apollo 13 moon mission (1970), he was Deputy Director of the Johnson Space Center in Houston, Texas, 1971–3.

1 Houston, we've had a problem.
Radio transmission from Apollo 13, 14 April 1970, quoted in *The Times* 15 April 1970. The message was given following an explosion in the service module which led to the abandonment of the moon landing, although the crew was able to return safely to earth three days later. The words have also been ascribed to another crew member, John Swigert, and are often misquoted 'Houston, we've got a problem', the title of a TV movie in 1974.

William Lovett
(1800–77)
English Chartist leader

A vocal advocate of electoral reform, he helped found the London Workingmen's Association, which drafted the People's Charter in 1838. Later marginalized from Chartism, he concentrated on working-class education.

1 So long as the people of any country place their hopes of political salvation *in leadership of any description*, so long will disappointment attend them.
Public letter to Daniel O'Connell, 1843, quoted in *Life and Struggles of William Lovett*, ch. 16 (autobiography, 1876)

Amy Lowell

(1874–1925)

US poet

After her first collection, A Dome of Many-Colored Glass *(1912), she became the leader of the Imagist movement in America, writing what she called 'polyphonic prose' and 'unrhymed cadence'. Other works include* What's O'Clock *(1925).*

1 Time! Joyless emblem of the greed
Of millions, robber of the best
Which earth can give, the vulgar creed
Has seared upon the night its flaming ruthless
   screed.
'New York at Night', st. 2, publ. in *A Dome of Many-Colored Glass* (1912)

2 For books are more than books, they are the life
The very heart and core of ages past,
The reason why men lived and worked and died,
The essence and quintessence of their lives.
'The Boston Athenaeum', ibid.

3 All books are either dreams or swords,
You can cut, or you can drug, with words.
'Sword Blades and Poppy Seed', publ. in *Sword Blades and Poppy Seed* (1914)

4 For the man who should loose me is dead,
Fighting with the Duke in Flanders,
In a pattern called a war.
Christ! What are patterns for?
'Patterns', publ. in *Men, Women and Ghosts* (1916)

5 Moon!
Moon!
I am prone before you.
Pity me,
And drench me in loneliness.
'On a Certain Critic' (1919), repr. in *Complete Poetical Works* (1955)

6 A man must be sacrificed now and again
To provide for the next generation of men.
'A Critical Fable', st. 2 (1922), ibid.

James Russell Lowell

(1819–91)

US man of letters

While Professor of Modern Languages at Harvard, he edited the Atlantic Monthly *and the* North American Review. *His verse is variously satirical, as in* The Biglow Papers *(1848 and 1867), and critical, as in* A Fable for Critics *(1848). He served as US ambassador to Britain 1880–5.*

1 It is mediocrity which makes laws and sets man-traps and spring-guns in the realm of free song, saying thus far shalt thou go and no further.
'Elizabethan Dramatists, Omitting Shakespeare: John Webster' (1843), repr. in *Early Prose Writings of James Russell Lowell* (1902)

2 No man is born into the world, whose work
Is not born with him; there is always work,
And tools to work withal, for those who will:
And blessèd are the horny hands of toil!
'A Glance Behind the Curtain', ll. 201–4 (1843), repr. in *The Complete Poetical Works of James Russell Lowell* (ed. Horace A. Scudder, 1896)

3 Truth forever on the scaffold, Wrong forever on
   the throne.
'The Present Crisis', st. 8 (1844), ibid.

4 Ez fer war, I call it murder –
There you hev it plain an' flat;
I don't want to go no furder
Than my Testament fer that;
God hez sed so plump and fairly,
It's ez long ez it is broad,
An' you've gut to git up airly
Ef you want to take in God.
The Biglow Papers, no. 1 ('A Letter'), st. 5 (first series, 1848)

5 Though a weed is no more than a flower in
   disguise,
Which is seen through at once, if love gives a man
   eyes.
A Fable for Critics, ll. 97–8 (1848)

6 A reading machine, always wound up and going,
He mastered whatever was not worth the knowing.
Ibid., ll. 164–5. Of a reviewer.

7 There comes Poe, with his raven, like Barnaby
   Rudge,
Three-fifths of him genius, and two-fifths sheer
   fudge.
Who talks like a book of iambs and pentameters,
In a way to make people of common sense damn
   metres,
Who has written some things quite the best of
   their kind,
But the heart somehow seems all squeezed out by
   the mind.
Ibid., 'Poe and Longfellow', ll. 1216–21

8 Books are the bees which carry the quickening pollen from one to another mind.
'Nationality in Literature', a review of LONGFELLOW's *Kavanagh*, publ. in *North American Review* July 1849

9 Before Man made us citizens, great Nature made us men.

'On the Capture of Fugitive Slaves near Washington', st. 6 (1854), repr. in *The Complete Poetical Works of James Russell Lowell* (ed. Horace A. Scudder, 1896)

10 They talk about their Pilgrim blood,
Their birthright high and holy!
A mountain-stream that ends in mud
Methinks is melancholy.

'An Interview with Miles Standish', st. 11 (1858), repr. in *The Complete Poetical Works of James Russell Lowell* (ed. Horace A. Scudder, 1896)

11 There is nothing so desperately monotonous as the sea, and I no longer wonder at the cruelty of pirates.

Fireside Travels, 'At Sea' (1864)

12 What a sense of security in an old book which Time has criticized for us!

'Library of Old Authors' (1864), repr. in *Literary Essays*, vol. 1 (1890)

13 Some day the soft Ideal that we wooed
Confronts us fiercely, foe-beset, pursued,
And cries reproachful: 'Was it then my praise,
And not myself was loved? Prove now thy truth;
I claim of thee the promise of thy youth.'

'Commemoration Ode', or 'Ode Recited at the Harvard Commemoration', st. 5 (1865), repr. in *The Complete Poetical Works of James Russell Lowell* (ed. Horace A. Scudder, 1896)

14 Such was he, our Martyr-Chief,
Whom late the nation he had led,
With ashes on her head,
Wept with the passion of an angry grief.

'Commemoration Ode', st. 6, ibid. Referring to ABRAHAM LINCOLN.

15 Our children shall behold his fame,
The kindly-earnest, brave, forseeing man,
Sagacious, patient, dreading praise, not blame,
New birth of our new soil, the first American.

'Commemoration Ode', st. 6, ibid. Referring to ABRAHAM LINCOLN.

16 Democ'acy gives every man
The right to be his own oppressor.

The Biglow Papers, no. 7 ('Latest Views of Mr. Biglow'), st. 13 (second series, 1867)

17 Every man feels instinctively that all the beautiful sentiments in the world weigh less than a single lovely action.

'Rousseau and the Sentimentalists' (1867), repr. in *Among My Books* (first series, 1870). The words also occur in Lowell's essay, 'New England Two Centuries Ago'.

18 The mind can weave itself warmly in the cocoon of its own thoughts, and dwell a hermit anywhere.

'On a Certain Condescension in Foreigners' (1869), repr. in *My Study Windows* (1871)

19 We are worth nothing except so far as we have disinfected ourselves of Anglicism.

'On a Certain Condescension in Foreigners', ibid.

20 I have always been of the mind that in a democracy manners are the only effective weapons against the bowie-knife.

Letter, 4 March 1873, publ. in *Letters of James Russell Lowell*, vol. 2 (ed. Charles Eliot Norton, 1894)

21 Sorrow, the great idealizer.

Among My Books, 'Spenser' (second series, 1876)

22 There is no good in arguing with the inevitable. The only argument available with an east wind is to put on your overcoat.

'Democracy', address, Birmingham, England, 6 October 1884, publ. in *Democracy and Other Addresses* (1887)

23 Compromise makes a good umbrella but a poor roof.

'Democracy', ibid.

24 What men prize most is a privilege, even if it be that of chief mourner at a funeral.

'Democracy', ibid.

25 As life runs on, the road grows strange
With faces new – and near the end
The milestones into headstones change,
'Neath every one a friend.

'Sixty-Eighth Birthday', publ. in *Heartsease and Rue*, pt 5 (1888)

Robert Lowell
(1917–77)
US poet

His early collections reflected the conflict between his religious leanings and his Boston ancestry. Life Studies (1959), which dealt with episodes from his personal life, indicated a new ironic style, developed in such later volumes as The Old Glory (1965).

1 I saw the spiders marching through the air,
Swimming from tree to tree that mildewed day
In latter August when the hay
Came creaking to the barn.

'Mr Edwards and the Spider', publ. in *Poems 1938–1949* (1950)

2 This is death.
To die and know it. This is the Black Widow, death.
'Mr Edwards and the Spider', ibid.

3 These are the tranquilized *Fifties*,
and I am forty. Ought I to regret my seedtime?
'Memories of West Street and Lepke', publ. in *Life Studies*
(1959)

4 I was a fire-breathing Catholic C.O.,
and made my manic statement,
telling off the state and president, and then
sat waiting sentence in the bull pen
beside a Negro boy with curlicues
of marijuana in his hair.
'Memories of West Street and Lepke', ibid. Lowell was an
ardent convert to Roman Catholicism in the 1940s.

5 At forty-five,
What next, what next?
I meet my father,
my age, still alive.
'Middle Age', publ. in *For The Union Dead* (1964)

6 Their monument sticks like a fishbone
in the city's throat.
'For The Union Dead', st. 8, ibid.

7 The Aquarium is gone. Everywhere,
giant finned cars nose forward like fish;
a savage servility
slides by on grease.
'For The Union Dead', st. 17, ibid. Closing lines.

8 If we see light at the end of the tunnel,
It's the light of the oncoming train.
'Since 1939', publ. in *Day by Day* (1977)

9 Folly comes from something –
the present, yes,
we are in it,
it's the infection
of things gone.
'We Took Our Paradise', ibid.

Malcolm Lowry
(1909–57)
British novelist

His best-known novel, Under the Volcano *(1947), which narrates the last day of a British consul in Mexico, drew on his
own experience as a nomadic alcoholic.*

1 How alike are the groans of love to those of the
dying.
Under the Volcano, ch. 12 (1947). Words of the narrator.

St Ignatius of Loyola
See Ignatius

Lucan
(39–65)
Roman poet

Marcus Annaeus Lucanus. His one extant poetical work,
Bellum Civile *(The Civil War), also known as* Pharsalia *from
its vivid description of that battle, chronicled the struggle
between* JULIUS CAESAR *and Pompey. Implicated in Piso's
conspiracy to assassinate Nero, he committed suicide.*

1 The mere shadow of a mighty name he stood.
The Civil War, bk 1, l. 135 (1st century AD). Referring to Pompey.

2 Caesar . . . thought nothing done while anything
remained to do.
Ibid., bk 2, l. 657

3 Has he any dwelling-place save earth and sea, the
air of heaven and virtuous hearts? Why seek we
further for deities? All that we see is God; every
motion we make is God also.
Ibid., bk 9, ll. 578–80

E. V. Lucas
(1868–1938)
British journalist and essayist

*Edward Verrall Lucas. He was a prolific writer of novels, travel
books, and essays in the style of* CHARLES LAMB, *on whom he
was an authority. His essay collections include* Adventures
and Misgivings *(1938).*

1 I have noticed that the people who are late are
often so much jollier than the people who have to
wait for them.
365 Days and One More, 'October 3' (1926). 'I am a believer in
punctuality,' Lucas wrote in 1932, 'though it makes me very
lonely.'

2 There can be no defence like elaborate courtesy.
Reading, Writing and Remembering, ch. 8 (1932)

George Lucas
(b. 1944)
US film-maker

Called by STEVEN SPIELBERG *'Walt Disney's version of a mad
scientist', he co-wrote and directed* American Graffiti *(1973)
and wrote and directed* Star Wars *(1977), also contributing to
the latter's various sequels.*

1 Star Wars.
Title of film (1977, written and directed by George Lucas). The

Strategic Defense Initiative, a missile system based in space, was immediately nicknamed the Star Wars defence on its announcement by President REAGAN in 1983.

2 May the Force be with you!
Ben 'Obi-wan' Kenobi (Alec Guinness), ibid.

3 The Empire Strikes Back.
Title of film (1980, screenplay by Leigh Brackett and Laurence Kasdan from original story by George Lucas, directed by Irvin Kershner)

Clare Boothe Luce
(1903–87)
US playwright, politician and diplomat

Born Clare Boothe. Author of the Broadway hits The Women *(1936) and* Kiss the Boys Goodbye *(1938), she was elected in 1942 to the House of Representatives as a Republican, and was US ambassador to Italy 1953–7.*

1 Lying increases the creative faculties, expands the ego, lessens the friction of social contacts ... It is only in lies, wholeheartedly and bravely told, that human nature attains through words and speech the forbearance, the nobility, the romance, the idealism, that – being what it is – it falls so short of in fact and in deed.
Vanity Fair October 1930

2 A man has only one escape from his old self: to see a different self – in the mirror of some woman's eyes.
The Women, Act 1, Sc. 3 (1936). Spoken by Mrs Morehead.

3 Much of what Mr Wallace calls his global thinking is, no matter how you slice it, still 'globaloney'. Mr Wallace's warp of sense and his woof of nonsense is very tricky cloth out of which to cut the pattern of a post-war world.
Speech to Congress, 9 February 1943, publ. in *Congressional Record*, vol. 89. Referring to Vice-President Henry Wallace's views on foreign policy, in Boothe Luce's maiden speech in the House, in which she first coined the term *globaloney*.

4 Communism is the opiate of the intellectuals [with] no cure except as a guillotine might be called a cure for dandruff.
Newsweek 24 January 1955. See KARL MARX 1.

5 But if God had wanted us to think just with our wombs, why did He give us a brain?
Slam the Door Softly (1970). Spoken by Nora.

Lucretius
(c. 99–c. 55 BC)
Roman poet and philosopher

Titus Lucretius Carus. Based on the theories of Epicurus, according to which all matter is made up of combinations of atoms, his interpretation of the laws of the universe was expressed in the long poem De Rerum Natura *(On the Nature of Things). Little is known of his life.*

1 So potent was superstition in persuading to evil deeds.
De Rerum Natura, bk 1, l. 101. Referring to Agamemnon's sacrifice of his daughter Iphigenia.

2 Nothing can be created from nothing.
Ibid., bk 1, l. 155

3 Pleasant it is, when on a great sea the winds trouble the waters, to gaze from shore upon another's great tribulation; not because any man's troubles are a delectable joy, but because to perceive you are free yourself is pleasant.
Ibid., bk 2, ll. 1–4. See FRANCIS BACON 5.

4 Life is one long struggle in the dark.
Ibid., bk 2, l. 54

5 Therefore death is nothing to us, it matters not one jot, since the nature of the mind is understood to be mortal.
Ibid., bk 3, ll. 830–1

6 Why not, like a banqueter fed full of life, withdraw with contentment and rest in peace, you fool?
Ibid., bk 3, ll. 938–9

7 From the very fountain of enchantment rises a drop of bitterness to torment even in the flowers.
Ibid., bk 4, ll. 1133–4

Karl Lueger
(1844–1910)
Austrian politician

He was elected to the Austrian Reichsrat in 1885 and four years later helped found the Christian Social Party. Serving as mayor of Vienna from 1897, he modernized the city but promoted anti-semitic and racist policies.

1 *I* determine who is a Jew.
Quoted in *Hitler, a Study in Tyranny*, ch. 1, sect. 4 (1962) by Alan Bullock. The statement has also been attributed to HERMANN GOERING.

John Lukacs

(b. 1924)

Hungarian-born US historian

Known as a 'philosopher historian', he has published Decline and Rise of Europe *(1965) and* Outgrowing Democracy: A History of the United States in the Twentieth Century *(1984), among other works.*

1 All the isms are wasms – except one, the most powerful ism of this century, indeed, of the entire democratic age, which is nationalism.

'The Stirrings of History', publ. in *Harper's* August 1990

Martin Luther

(1483–1546)

German religious leader

An Augustinian friar, he came to notice for his criticism of the sale of indulgences. His ninety-five theses posted in Wittenberg (1517) marked the start of the Protestant Reformation. Excommunicated in 1521, he translated the Bible into German and endorsed the Augsburg Confession (1530), the basis of Lutheranism.

1 I cannot and will not recant anything, for to go against conscience is neither right nor safe. Here I stand, I can do no other, so help me God. Amen.

Attributed speech at the Diet of Worms, Germany, 18 April 1521. Luther was summoned to Worms by the Holy Roman Emperor CHARLES V in an attempt to effect a conciliation between Luther and the established Church. The words, 'Here I stand, I can do no other' – apparently added in Luther's handwriting to the first printed version of the speech – were later inscribed on the monument to Luther at Worms: *Hier steh' ich, ich kann nicht anders.*

2 If he have faith, the believer cannot be restrained. He betrays himself. He breaks out. He confesses and teaches this gospel to the people at the risk of life itself.

Preface to his translation of the New Testament (1522)

3 Anyone who can be proved to be a seditious person is an outlaw before God and the emperor; and whoever is the first to put him to death does right and well ... Therefore let everyone who can, smite, slay and stab, secretly or openly, remembering that nothing can be more poisonous, hurtful, or devilish than a rebel.

Against the Robbing and Murdering Hordes of Peasants, pamphlet, May 1525, repr. in *Werke*, vol. 4 (ed. Karin Bornkamm and Gerhard Ebeling, 1982). Luther's opposition to the Peasants' Revolt in Germany lost much popular support for the Reformation.

4 A safe stronghold our God is still,
A trusty shield and weapon.

'Eine Feste Burg ist unser Gott' (1529; 'A safe stronghold our God is still', transl. THOMAS CARLYLE), ibid., vol. 5

5 Peace is more important than all justice; and peace was not made for the sake of justice, but justice for the sake of peace.

On Marriage (1530)

6 For, where God built a church, there the Devil would also build a chapel ... Thus is the Devil ever God's ape.

Table-Talk, sect. 67 (1569). See THOMAS BECON 1, DANIEL DEFOE 4.

7 The Devil begat darkness; darkness begat ignorance; ignorance begat error and his brethren; error begat free-will and presumption; free-will begat works; works begat forgetfulness of God; forgetfulness begat transgression; transgression begat superstition; superstition begat satisfaction; satisfaction begat the mass-offering; the mass-offering begat the priest; the priest begat unbelief; unbelief begat hypocrisy; hypocrisy begat traffic in offerings for gain; traffic in offerings for gain begat Purgatory; Purgatory begat the annual solemn vigils; the annual vigils begat church-livings; church-livings begat avarice; avarice begat swelling superfluity; swelling superfluity begat fullness; fullness begat rage; rage begat licence; licence begat empire and domination; domination begat pomp; pomp begat ambition; ambition begat simony; simony begat the Pope and his brethren, about the time of the Babylonish captivity.

Ibid., sect. 500

8 The reproduction of mankind is a great marvel and mystery. Had God consulted me in the matter, I should have advised him to continue the generation of the species by fashioning them of clay.

Ibid., sect. 572. See THOMAS BROWNE 14.

Witold Lutoslawski

(1913–94)

Polish composer and conductor

A prolific composer and a conductor of his own pieces, he is best known for his orchestral work, which developed from traditional pieces to aleatory and improvisational compositions.

1 One can create a masterpiece by using any means of expression, no matter how absurd, just as one

can make a beautiful gesture lying at the edge, or even the bottom, of a precipice.

Conversations with Witold Lutoslawski, ch. 9 (ed. Tadeusz Kaczynski, 1972, transl. 1984)

2 People whose sensibility is destroyed by music in trains, airports, lifts, cannot concentrate on a Beethoven quartet.

Independent on Sunday 13 January 1991

Rosa Luxemburg
(1870–1919)
Polish-born German revolutionary

She moved to Germany in 1898, where she helped set up the Spartacus League in 1916, the precursor of the German Communist Party. She was murdered after helping to organize an uprising in Berlin.

1 Freedom is always and exclusively freedom for the one who thinks differently.

Prison notes, 1918, publ. in *The Russian Revolution*, ch. 6 (1922, transl. 1961)

2 Without general elections, without unrestricted freedom of press and assembly, without a free struggle of opinion, life dies out in every public institution, becomes a mere semblance of life, in which only the bureaucracy remains as the active element. Public life gradually falls asleep, a few dozen party leaders of inexhaustible energy and boundless experience direct and rule ... Such conditions must inevitably cause a brutalization of public life: attempted assassinations, shootings of hostages, etc.

Prison notes, 1918, ibid.

John Lydgate
(c. 1370–c. 1450)
English cleric and poet

Ordained a priest in 1397, he wrote prolifically but unevenly. He is best known for his translations from the French and Latin, for example The Troy Book *and* The Siege of Thebes.

1 Sithe off oure language he was the lodesterre.

The Fall of Princes, Prologue, l. 252 (written 1431–9). Referring to GEOFFREY CHAUCER.

John Lydon
(b. 1957)
British rock musician

As Johnny Rotten, he was singer with the band the SEX PISTOLS, *whose punk anthems included 'Anarchy in the UK' (1976). He later formed Public Image Limited.*

1 Sex is two minutes of squelching.

Quoted in *Vox* March 1994

John Lyly
(1554–1606)
English author

The elaborate, high-flown style of his prose romances Euphues: the Anatomy of Wit *(1579) and* Euphues and his England *(1580) gave rise to a fashion for 'euphuism' in the late 16th century. His plays helped establish prose as a form for comic dialogue. See also* F. W. BOURDILLON 1.

1 The sun shineth upon the dunghill, and is not corrupted.

Euphues: The Anatomy of Wit (1579, ed. Edward Arber, 1868)

2 Go to bed with the lamb, and rise with the lark: late watching in the night breedeth unquiet: and long sleeping in the day, ungodliness.

Euphues and His England (1580, ed. Edward Arber, 1868)

3 A rose is sweeter in the bud than full-blown. Young twigs are sooner bent than old trees. White snow sooner melted than hard ice: which proveth that the younger she is, the sooner she is to be wooed, and the fairer she is, the likelier to be won.

Ibid.

4 A clear conscience is a sure card.

Euphues: The Anatomy of Wit, 'To My Very Good Friends the Gentlemen Scholars of Oxford' (1581 edn)

David Lynch
(b. 1946)
US film-maker

His first film, Eraserhead *(1977), established him as a film-maker of dark originality. The TV series* Twin Peaks *(1990–1) gave him mainstream success.*

1 Damned fine cup of coffee!

Twin Peaks (TV series, 1990–1, written and created by David Lynch and Mark Frost). Spoken by Agent Dale Cooper (Kyle MacLachlan), 'Damned fine cheesecake!' and 'Damned fine pie!' are other frequent remarks associated with Agent Cooper.

Russell Lynes

(1910–91)

US editor and critic

Most of his journalistic career was devoted to Harper's *magazine, of which he became Assistant Editor in 1944. His books include* Snobs *(1950) and* The Tastemakers *(1954), both critiques of social pretension in America.*

1 It is always well to accept your own shortcomings with candor but to regard those of your friends with polite incredulity.

Vogue 1 September 1952

2 The art of acceptance is the art of making someone who has just done you a small favor wish that he might have done you a greater one.

Reader's Digest December 1954

3 A lady is nothing very specific. One man's lady is another man's woman; sometimes, one man's lady is another man's wife. Definitions overlap but they almost never coincide.

'Is There a Lady in the House?', publ. in *Look* 22 July 1958

(Dame) Vera Lynn

(b. 1917)

British singer

She became 'the Forces' Sweetheart' during the Second World War, catching the mood of the moment with her optimistic and patriotic songs. She broadcast her own radio show Sincerely Yours *1941–7.*

1 There'll be bluebirds over
The white cliffs of Dover,
Tomorrow, just you wait and see.
There'll be love and laughter
And peace ever after
Tomorrow when the world is free.

'The White Cliffs of Dover' (song, 1941, written by Nat Burton, with music by Walter Kent)

2 We'll meet again
Don't know where, don't know when,
But I know we'll meet again
Some sunny day.

'We'll Meet Again' (song, 1941, written by ROSS PARKER AND HUGH CHARLES)

Jean François Lyotard

(1924–98)

French philosopher

He abandoned his position as a Marxist in the 1950s and '60s to become a leading theorist of postmodernism. His publications include The Postmodern Condition *(1979).*

1 A work can become modern only if it is first postmodern. Postmodernism thus understood is not modernism at its end but in the nascent state, and this state is constant.

'Answering the Question: What is Postmodernism?' (1982), repr. in *The Postmodern Condition: A Report on Knowledge* (1986 edn)

Henry Francis Lyte

See HYMNS AND CAROLS 1, 74

Lord Lytton

See EDWARD BULWER-LYTTON

M

Douglas MacArthur
(1880–1964)
US general

He was Supreme Commander of the South West Pacific Area in the Second World War, and led UN forces during the Korean War (1950–1), but was dismissed when he advocated extending the war against China. EISENHOWER *remarked, 'I studied dramatics under him for twelve years.'*

1 I came through and I shall return.
Statement in Adelaide, Australia, 20 March 1942, quoted in the *New York Times* 21 March 1942. The pledge was made on disembarking from the Philippines, which he had been ordered to evacuate following an unsuccessful defence of the Bataan peninsula. MacArthur subsequently pursued a brilliant 'leap-frogging' strategy which enabled him to return to the Philippines in October 1944. His men celebrated his victory with the song, 'By the grace of God and a few Marines/ MacArthur returned to the Philippines.'

2 Like the old soldier of the ballad, I now close my military career and just fade away, an old soldier who tried to do his duty as God gave him the light to see that duty. Goodbye.
Speech to Congress, 19 April 1951, publ. in *Congressional Record* vol. 97. Referring to his dismissal as commander of UN forces in Korea, for dissenting from the Truman administration's conduct of the war. TRUMAN called the speech 'nothing but a bunch of damn bullshit' (in Merle Miller's *Plain Speaking: Conversations with Harry S. Truman*, 1973). The 'ballad' referred to by MacArthur was a barrack-room song (see J. FOLEY 1).

Rose Macaulay
(1881–1958)
British author and essayist

She was a writer of humorous and urbane novels, for example Potterism *(1920),* The World My Wilderness *(1950) and* The Towers of Trebizond *(1956). She also published travel books and journalism.*

1 Cranks live by theory, not by pure desire. They want votes, peace, nuts, liberty, and spinning-looms not because they love these things, as a child loves jam, but because they think they ought to have them. That is one element which makes the crank.
A Casual Commentary, 'Cranks' (1925)

2 'Take my camel, dear,' said my aunt Dot, as she climbed down from this animal on her return from High Mass.
The Towers of Trebizond, ch. 1 (1956). Opening words.

Thomas, Lord Macaulay
(1800–59)
English historian and politician

Thomas Babington, 1st Baron Macaulay. He became a Whig MP in 1830 and was Secretary of War 1839–41. His popular Lays of Ancient Rome *appeared in 1842, but his major work was the* History of England from the Accession of James II *(5 vols. 1848–61).* THOMAS CARLYLE *commented that he was 'well for a while, but one wouldn't' live under Niagara'. See also* LORD MELBOURNE 2.

1 The dust and silence of the upper shelf.
'Milton' (1825), repr. in *Critical and Historical Essays*, vol. 1 (1843)

2 As civilization advances, poetry almost necessarily declines.
'Milton', ibid., vol. 1

3 Perhaps no person can be a poet, or can even enjoy poetry, without a certain unsoundness of mind.
'Milton', ibid., vol. 1

4 Logicians may reason about abstractions. But the great mass of men must have images. The strong tendency of the multitude in all ages and nations to idolatry can be explained on no other principle.
'Milton', ibid., vol. 1

5 There is only one cure for the evils which newly acquired freedom produces, and that cure is freedom.
'Milton', ibid., vol. 1

6 Many politicians of our time are in the habit of laying it down as a self-evident proposition that no people ought to be free till they are fit to use their freedom. The maxim is worthy of the fool in the old story who resolved not to go into the water until he had learnt to swim. If men are to wait for liberty till they become wise and good in slavery, they may indeed wait forever.
'Milton', ibid., vol. 1

7 Nothing is so useless as a general maxim.
'Machiavelli' (1827), ibid., vol. 1

8 The English Bible – a book which, if everything else in our language should perish, would alone

suffice to show the whole extent of its beauty and power.
'John Dryden' (1828), publ. in *Miscellaneous Writings of Lord Macaulay*, vol. 1 (ed. T. F. Ellis, 1860)

9 His imagination resembled the wings of an ostrich. It enabled him to run, though not to soar.
'John Dryden', ibid., vol. 1. Referring to DRYDEN.

10 This province of literature is a debatable land. It lies on the confines of two distinct territories. It is under the jurisdiction of two hostile powers; and, like other districts similarly situated, it is ill defined, ill cultivated, and ill regulated. Instead of being equally shared between its two rulers, the Reason and the Imagination, it falls alternately under the sole and absolute dominion of each. It is sometimes fiction. It is sometimes theory.
'History' (1828), ibid., vol. 1

11 History, it has been said, is philosophy teaching by examples. Unhappily, what the philosophy gains in soundness and depth the examples generally lose in vividness.
'History' (1828), ibid., vol. 1

12 Knowledge advances by steps, and not by leaps.
'History' (1828), ibid., vol. 1

13 A ... church is ... disaffected when it is persecuted, quiet when it is tolerated, and actively loyal when it is favoured and cherished.
'Hallam' (1828), repr. in *Critical and Historical Essays*, vol. 1 (1843)

14 The gallery in which the reporters sit has become a fourth estate of the realm.
'Hallam', ibid., vol. 1

15 Turn where we may, within, around, the voice of great events is proclaiming to us, Reform, that you may preserve!
Speech to House of Commons, 2 March 1831, publ. in *Complete Writings of Lord Macaulay*, vol. 17 (1900). Referring to the First Reform Bill debate.

16 We know no spectacle so ridiculous as the British public in one of its periodical fits of morality.
'Byron' (1831), publ. in *Critical and Historical Essays*, vol. 1 (1843)

17 From the poetry of Lord Byron they drew a system of ethics, compounded of misanthropy and voluptuousness, a system in which the two great commandments were, to hate your neighbour, and to love your neighbour's wife.
'Byron', ibid., vol. 1. Referring to BYRON 'enthusiasts'.

Macaulay added: 'A few more years will destroy whatever yet remains of that magical potency which once belonged to the name of Byron.'

18 Boswell was one of the smallest men that ever lived ... a man of the meanest and feeblest intellect ... He was the laughing-stock of the whole of that brilliant society which has owed to him the greater part of its fame. He was always laying himself at the feet of some eminent man, and begging to be spit upon and trampled upon ... Servile and impertinent, shallow and pedantic, a bigot and a sot, bloated with family pride, and eternally blustering about the dignity of a born gentleman, yet stooping to be a talebearer, an eavesdropper, a common butt in the taverns of London.
'Samuel Johnson' (1831), ibid., vol. 1

19 In the foreground is that strange figure which is as familiar to us as the figures among whom we have been brought up, the gigantic body, the huge massy face, seamed with the scars of disease, the brown coat, the black worsted stockings, the grey wig with the scorched foretop, the dirty hands, the nails bitten and pared to the quick.
'Samuel Johnson', ibid., vol. 1

20 He knew that the essence of war is violence, and that moderation in war is imbecility.
'John Hampden' (1831), ibid., vol. 1. Referring to the Parliamentarian John Hampden.

21 The reluctant obedience of distant provinces generally costs more than it [the territory] is worth. Empires which branch out widely are often more flourishing for a little timely pruning.
'War of the Succession in Spain' (1833), ibid., vol. 1

22 The highest intellects, like the tops of mountains, are the first to catch and to reflect the dawn.
'Sir James Mackintosh' (1835), ibid., vol. 2

23 The history of England is emphatically the history of progress.
'Sir James Mackintosh', ibid, vol. 2

24 An acre in Middlesex is better than a principality in Utopia.
'Lord Bacon' (1837), ibid., vol. 2

25 He had a wonderful talent for packing thought close, and rendering it portable.
'Lord Bacon' (1837), ibid., vol. 2. Referring to FRANCIS BACON.

26 Every schoolboy knows who imprisoned Montezuma, and who strangled Atahualpa.
'Lord Clive' (1840), ibid., vol. 2

27 She may still exist in undiminished vigour when some traveller from New Zealand shall, in the midst of a vast solitude, take his stand on a broken arch of London Bridge to sketch the ruins of St Paul's.
'Von Ranke' (1840), ibid., vol. 2. Referring to the Catholic Church.

28 She thoroughly understands what no other Church has ever understood, how to deal with enthusiasts.
'Von Ranke', ibid., vol. 2. Referring to the Catholic Church.

29 The Chief Justice was rich, quiet and infamous.
'On Warren Hastings' (1841), ibid., vol. 3

30 Lars Porsena of Clusium
By the Nine Gods he swore
That the great house of Tarquin
Should suffer wrongs no more.
'Horatius', st. 1, publ. in *Lays of Ancient Rome* (1842). Opening lines of poem.

31 Then out spake brave Horatius,
The Captain of the Gate:
'To every man upon this earth
Death cometh soon or late.
And how can man die better
Than facing fearful odds,
For the ashes of his fathers,
And the temples of his gods?'
'Horatius', st. 27, ibid.

32 Now who will stand on either hand,
And keep the bridge with me?
'Horatius', st. 29, ibid. The words of Horatius.

33 Was none who would be foremost
To lead such dire attack:
But those behind cried 'Forward!'
And those before cried 'Back!'
'Horatius', st. 50, ibid.

34 And even the ranks of Tuscany
Could scarce forbear to cheer.
'Horatius', st. 60, ibid.

35 With weeping and with laughter
Still is the story told,
How well Horatius kept the bridge
In the brave days of old.
'Horatius', st. 70, ibid.

36 He was a rake among scholars, and a scholar among rakes.
'The Life and Writings of Addison', publ. in *Critical and Historical Essays*, vol. 3 (1843). Referring to RICHARD STEELE.

37 Persecution produced its natural effect on them. It found them a sect; it made them a faction.
History of England, vol. 1, ch. 1 (1849). Referring to the Puritans and Calvinists.

38 The Puritan hated bearbaiting, not because it gave pain to the bear, but because it gave pleasure to the spectators.
Ibid., vol. 1, ch. 2

39 There were gentlemen and there were seamen in the navy of Charles the Second. But the seamen were not gentlemen; and the gentlemen were not seamen.
Ibid., vol. 1, ch. 3

40 In every age the vilest specimens of human nature are to be found among demagogues.
Ibid., vol. 1, ch. 5

Joseph McCarthy
(1908–57)
US politician

A Republican senator, he made unproven allegations of infiltration of the State Department by Communists in 1950. The ensuing investigations ended in 1954 when he was censured by the Senate for unbecoming conduct. HARRY S. TRUMAN *called him 'a pathological character assassin'. See also* ED MURROW 1.

1 McCarthyism is Americanism with its sleeves rolled.
Speech in Wisconsin, 1952, quoted in *Senator Joe McCarthy*, ch. 1 (1973) by Richard Rovere

Mary McCarthy
(1912–89)
US author and critic

She was a contributor to the Partisan Review, *among other publications, and the writer of such satirical novels as* The Groves of Academe *(1952) and* The Group *(1963).*

1 The American character looks always as if it had just had a rather bad haircut, which gives it, in our eyes at any rate, a greater humanity than the European, which even among its beggars has an all too professional air.
'America the Beautiful: the Humanist in the Bathtub' (1947), repr. in *On the Contrary* (1961)

2 The happy ending is our national belief.
'America the Beautiful: the Humanist in the Bathtub', ibid.

3 The immense popularity of American movies

abroad demonstrates that Europe is the unfinished negative of which America is the proof.

'America the Beautiful: the Humanist in the Bathtub', ibid.

4 Liberty, as it is conceived by current opinion, has nothing inherent about it; it is a sort of gift or trust bestowed on the individual by the state pending *good behavior.*

'The Contagion of Ideas', speech, 1952, ibid.

5 Every age has a keyhole to which its eye is pasted.

'My Confession' (1953), ibid.

6 There are no new truths, but only truths that have not been recognized by those who have perceived them without noticing. A truth is something that everybody can be shown to know and to have known, as people say, all along.

'The Vita Activa' (1958), ibid.

7 The labor of keeping house is labor in its most naked state, for labor is toil that never finishes, toil that has to be begun again the moment it is completed, toil that is destroyed and consumed by the life process.

'The Vita Activa' (1958), ibid.

8 In violence we forget who we are.

On the Contrary, pt 3, 'Characters in Fiction' (1961)

9 Every word she [Lillian Hellman] writes is a lie, including 'and' and 'the'.

Interview on *Dick Cavett Show*, January 1980, quoted in the *New York Times* 16 February 1980. McCarthy was quoting herself referring to LILLIAN HELLMAN in the 1930s. McCarthy's remark resulted in a row and prolonged law-suit which probably contributed to the wasting illness that eventually killed her.

(Sir) Paul McCartney
(b. 1942)
British rock musician

Labelled as the gentler, more melodic half of the Lennon/McCartney partnership, he was bass guitarist with the Beatles and went on to form the band Wings. He later co-wrote (with Colin Davis) the classical 'Liverpool Oratorio' (1991) and co-founded the Liverpool Institute of Performing Arts (1996). See also JOHN LENNON AND PAUL MCCARTNEY.

1 I didn't leave The Beatles. The Beatles have left The Beatles but no one wants to be the one to say the party's over.

Said in 1970, quoted in *The Beatles . . . After the Break-up*, 'You Say Goodbye and I Say Hello . . .' (1991) by David Bennahum

2 It's a drag.

Response to reporters asking him to comment on JOHN LENNON's death, 9 December 1980, quoted in *Paul McCartney: Many Years From Now*, ch. 14, 'How Do You Sleep?' (1997) by Barry Miles. 'It looked so callous in print,' he later explained. 'You can't take the print back and say, "Look, let me just rub that print in shit and pee over it and then cry over it for three years, then you'll see what I meant when I said that word" . . . What I meant was "Fuck off! Don't invade my privacy." '

3 What's wrong with sentimental? Sentimental means you *love*, you *care*, you *like* stuff. The thing is, we're *frightened* to be sentimental.

Interview in *Smash Hits* 24 November 1983

4 Ballads and babies. That's what happened to me.

Time 8 June 1992. Said shortly before his fiftieth birthday.

Ewan MacColl
(1915–89)
British folk singer and songwriter

Originally James Miller. After forming the influential Theatre Workshop with JOAN LITTLEWOOD *in 1945, he became a leading figure in the folk revival of the 1950s and '60s. With his wife Peggy Seeger he devised the innovatory Radio Ballads series for the BBC (1958–65).*

1 I found my love by the gasworks crofts
Dreamed a dream by the old canal
Kissed my girl by the factory wall
Dirty old town, dirty old town.

'Dirty Old Town' (song, 1950). MacColl wrote the song (which refers to Salford) to facilitate a scene change in his play *Landscape with Chimneys*. It was later revived by the Spinners and the Pogues.

Frank McCourt
(b. 1931)
US author

Of Irish parentage, he was a teacher and lecturer in New York before his first book Angela's Ashes *(1996) became an international bestseller. This bleak memoir of his Irish childhood was followed by a sequel* 'Tis *in 1999.*

1 When I look back on my childhood I wonder how I survived at all. It was, of course, a miserable childhood: the happy childhood is hardly worth your while. Worse than the ordinary miserable childhood is the miserable Irish childhood, and worse yet is the miserable Irish Catholic childhood.

Angela's Ashes, ch. 1 (1996)

John McCrae

(1872–1918)

Canadian poet and doctor

He fought in the Boer War and served with the medical corps in the First World War. His most famous poem 'In Flanders Fields' was written during the battle of Ypres, spring 1915.

1 In Flanders fields the poppies blow
Between the crosses, row on row,
That mark our place; and in the sky
The larks, still bravely singing, fly
Scarce heard amid the guns below.
'In Flanders Fields', st. 1 (1915), repr. in *In Flanders Fields and other Poems* (1919)

2 To you from failing hands we throw
The torch; be yours to hold it high.
If ye break faith with us who die
We shall not sleep, though poppies grow
In Flanders fields.
'In Flanders Fields', st. 1, ibid.

Carson McCullers

(1917–67)

US author

Described as 'Southern Gothic' in style, her fiction focuses on the misfits and outcasts of society, as in her first novel The Heart Is a Lonely Hunter *(1940) and her novella* The Ballad of the Sad Café *(1951). She was confined to a wheelchair from the age of twenty-nine.*

1 All men are lonely. But sometimes it seems to me that we Americans are the loneliest of all. Our hunger for foreign places and new ways has been with us almost like a national disease. Our literature is stamped with a quality of longing and unrest, and our writers have been great wanderers.
'Look Homeward, Americans' (1940), repr. in *The Mortgaged Heart* (ed. Margarita G. Smith, 1972)

2 There's nothing that makes you so aware of the improvisation of human existence as a song unfinished. Or an old address book.
'The Sojourner', publ. in *The Ballad of the Sad Café* (1951). Spoken by Ferris.

Hugh MacDiarmid

(1892–1978)

Scottish poet and critic

Originally Christopher Murray Grieve. With its use of Scots dialect and colloquialisms, his major work A Drunk Man Looks at the Thistle *(1926) established him as the leading figure of the 'Scottish Renaissance'. He was an ardent Marxist, and co-founder of the Scottish Nationalist Party (1928).*

1 I'll ha'e nae hauf-way hoose, but aye be whaur
Extremes meet – it's the only way I ken
To dodge the curst conceit o' bein' richt
That damns the vast majority o' men.
A Drunk Man Looks at the Thistle, ll. 141–4 (1926)

2 What happens to us
Is irrelevant to the world's geology
But what happens to the world's geology
Is not irrelevant to us.
We must reconcile ourselves to the stones,
Not the stones to us.
'On a Raised Beach', publ. in *Stony Limits and Other Poems* (1934)

3 The rose of all the world is not for me.
I want for my part
Only the little white rose of Scotland
That smells sharp and sweet – and breaks the
  heart.
'The Little White Rose', ibid.

4 Auden, MacNeice, Day Lewis, I have read them
  all,
Hoping against hope to hear the authentic call.
. . .
And I know the explanation I must pass is this
– You cannot light a match on a crumbling wall.
'British Leftish Poetry, 1930–1940', from poem sequence *Impavidi Progrediamur* (c. 1940–60), publ. in *Collected Poems* (1962)

5 Man does not cease to interest me
When he ceases to be miserable.
Quite the contrary!
That it is important to aid him
In the beginning goes without saying,
Like a plant it is essential
To water at first,
But this is in order to get it to flower
And I *am concerned with the blossom*.
'Reflections in a Slum', *Impavidi Progrediamur*, ibid. Concluding lines of poem.

Country Joe McDonald

(b. 1942)

US singer and songwriter

Performing politically inspired songs from c. 1960, he formed Country Joe and the Fish in 1965, a band combining protest with West Coast psychedelic rock.

1 And it's one, two, three what are we fightin' for?
Don't ask me I don't give a damn, next stop is
    Vietnam!
And it's five, six, seven, open up the pearly gates,
There ain't no time to wonder why,
Whoopee! – we're all going to die.
'I-Feel-Like-I'm-Fixin'-to-Die-Rag' (song, 1965) on the album
I-Feel-Like-I'm-Fixin'-to-Die-Rag (1968) by Country Joe and the
Fish. The song became a feature of the anti-war rallies and
festivals at which Country Joe appeared.

John McEnroe

(b. 1959)
US tennis player

*Known as an unorthodox and temperamental player, he has
won three Wimbledon and four US Open singles titles.*

1 Man, you cannot be serious!
Quoted in *Serious*, ch. 6 (2002). Retort to umpire's warning at
Wimbledon, July 1981. McEnroe smashed his racquet when
he doubted the validity of line calls. He continued: 'You guys
are the absolute pits of the world!'

Ian McEwan

(b. 1948)
British author

His early work, beginning with the stories First Love, Last
Rites *(1975), is often erotic and macabre in style. Later novels,
including* Amsterdam *(1998),* Atonement *(2001) and* Saturday
(2005), describe the disruption of ordinary lives.

1 One has to have the courage of one's pessimism.
Interview in the *Guardian* 26 May 1983

2 It is not the first duty of the novelist to provide
blueprints for insurrection, or uplifting tales of successful resistance for the benefit of the opposition.
The naming of what is there is what is important.
A Move Abroad, Preface (1989). On writing novels.

3 This is our mammalian conflict – what to give to
the others, and what to keep for yourself. Treading
that line, keeping the others in check, and being
kept in check by them, is what we call morality.
Enduring Love, ch. 1 (1997)

4 Mostly, we are good when it makes sense. A good
society is one that makes sense of being good.
Ibid., ch. 1

5 There is only love, and then oblivion. Love was all
they had to set against the hatred of their murderers.
Guardian 15 September 2001. On the last calls to loved
ones made by people in the World Trade Center before it
collapsed.

Bobby McFerrin

(b. 1950)
US singer and musician

*A versatile singer with a four-octave range, and adept in classi-
cal, jazz and pop traditions, he had a worldwide hit with* Don't
Worry, Be Happy *(1988).*

1 Don't worry, be happy.
'Don't Worry, Be Happy' (song) on the album *Simple Pleasures*
(1988)

Phyllis McGinley

(1905–78)
US poet and author

*A wry essayist and deftly humorous versifier, she was praised
by* W. H. AUDEN *among others. Her poetry collections include*
A Pocketful of Wry *(1940) and* Times Three *(1960).*

1 A Mother's hardest to forgive.
Life is the fruit she longs to hand you,
Ripe on a plate. And while you live,
Relentlessly she understands you.
'The Adversary', publ. in *A Certain Age* (1960)

2 The knowingness of little girls
Is hidden underneath their curls.
'What Every Woman Knows', publ. in *Times Three* (1960)

3 For little boys are rancorous
When robbed of any myth,
And spiteful and cantankerous
To all their kin and kith.
But little girls can draw conclusions
And profit from their lost illusions.
'What Every Woman Knows', ibid.

William McGonagall

(c. 1825–1902)
Scottish poet

*Hailed as the 'world's best bad poet' he deluded himself that
his doggerel was of note. He toured widely giving readings
and became a cult figure in his lifetime.*

1 Beautiful Railway Bridge of the Silv'ry Tay!
Alas, I am very sorry to say
That ninety lives have been taken away
On the last Sabbath day of 1879,
Which will be remembered for a very long time.
'The Tay Bridge Disaster', publ. in *Poetic Gems* (1878)

Patrick McGoohan
(b. 1928)
US-born British actor

He has appeared in numerous adventure films, but is best known for his TV roles as secret agent John Drake in Danger Man *(1960–7) and as Number Six in the cult series* The Prisoner *(1967–8).*

1 I am not a number – I am a free man!
The Prisoner (TV series, 1967–8, created by Patrick McGoohan, George Markstein and David Tomblin). Preamble to each episode, spoken by Number Six (Patrick McGoohan). Number Six (who is never named) states during one episode: 'I will not be pushed, stamped, filed, indexed, briefed, debriefed, or numbered. My life is my own.'

Roger McGough
(b. 1937)
British poet

With Brian Patten and Adrian Henri, he made his name as one of the 'Liverpool Poets'. He also writes for children and presents Poetry Please *on BBC Radio 4.*

1 Let me die a youngman's death
Not a free from sin tiptoe in
Candle wax & waning death
Not a curtains drawn by angels borne
'What a nice way to go' death
'Let Me Die a Youngman's Death', publ. in *The Mersey Sound* (1967)

2 Teach me, o Lord, to be permissive
the 'sixties way to save the soul
three leers for sexual freedom
let the good times rock'nroll.
'My little plastic mac', publ. in *Watchwords* (1969)

3 May your poems run away from home
    and live between the lines.
May they break and enter, assault and batter,
    and loiter in the mind with intent.
'The most unforgettable character I've ever met gives advice to the young poet', publ. in *Gig* (1973)

Roger McGuinn
(b. 1942)
US rock musician

Born Jim McGuinn. In 1964 he founded the folk-rock West Coast group the Byrds, whose album Sweetheart of the Rodeo *(1968) set the pattern for country rock.*

1 Eight miles high,
And when you touch down

You'll find that
It's stranger than known.
'Eight Miles High' (song, written by Roger McGuinn, Gene Clark and David Crosby) on the album *Fifth Dimension* (1966) by the Byrds.

Barry McGuire
(b. 1937)
US singer and songwriter

The lead vocalist with the New Christy Minstrels, he had an international solo hit with the protest song 'Eve of Destruction' (1965). He later became a religious singer as a born-again Christian.

1 And you tell me
Over and over and over again my friend
That you don't believe we're on the eve of
    destruction.
'Eve of Destruction' (song, written by P. F. Sloan) on the album *Eve of Destruction* (1965). The song was countered soon afterwards by the conservative 'Dawn of Correction' by the Spokesmen (1965).

Niccolò Machiavelli
(1469–1527)
Italian political philosopher and statesman

Exiled from public life by the Medicis in 1513 on charges of conspiracy, he devoted himself to writing. His best-known work is The Prince *(Il Principe), a treatise of statecraft which advocated that ends justify the means.*

1 One change always leaves a toothing-stone for the next.
The Prince, ch. 2. (written 1513, publ. 1532). A 'toothing-stone' refers to a projection at the end of a wall for further building. Commonly quoted 'One change always leaves the way open for others.'

2 There is no avoiding war; it can only be postponed to the advantage of others.
Ibid., ch. 3

3 Governments set up overnight, like everything in nature whose growth is forced, lack strong roots and ramifications. So they are destroyed in the first bad spell.
Ibid., ch. 7

4 It should be noted that when he seizes a state the new ruler ought to determine all the injuries that he will need to inflict. He should inflict them once and for all, and not have to renew them every day.
Ibid., ch. 8. 'Whoever acts otherwise,' Machiavelli added, 'either through timidity or bad advice, is always forced to

have the knife ready in his hand ... Violence should be inflicted once and for all; people will then forget what it tastes like and so be less resentful.'

5 Benefits should be conferred gradually; and in that way they will taste better.
Ibid., ch. 8

6 The main foundations of every state, new states as well as ancient or composite ones, are good laws and good arms ... You cannot have good laws without good arms, and where there are good arms, good laws inevitably follow.
Ibid., ch. 12

7 The fact is that a man who wants to act virtuously in every way necessarily comes to grief among so many who are not virtuous.
Ibid., ch. 15

8 Because it is difficult to combine them, it is far better to be feared than loved if you cannot be both.
Ibid., ch. 17

9 One can make this generalization about men: they are ungrateful, fickle, liars, and deceivers, they shun danger and are greedy for profit; while you treat them well, they are yours.
Ibid., ch. 17

10 Men sooner forget the death of their father than the loss of their patrimony.
Ibid., ch. 17

11 As a prince is forced to know how to act like a beast, he should learn from the fox and the lion; because the lion is defenceless against traps and a fox is defenceless against wolves. Therefore one must be a fox in order to recognize traps, and a lion to frighten off wolves.
Ibid., ch. 18

12 There are three kinds of intelligence: one kind understands things for itself, the other appreciates what others can understand, the third understands neither for itself nor through others. This first kind is excellent, the second good, and the third kind useless.
Ibid., ch. 22

13 The only way to safeguard yourself against flatterers is by letting people understand that you are not offended by the truth; but if everyone can speak the truth to you then you lose respect.
Ibid., ch. 23

Colin MacInnes
(1914–76)
British author and critic

According to GEORGE MELLY *he was 'the first adult to recognize the significance of pop'. He is most remembered for his 'London' trilogy,* City of Spades *(1957),* Absolute Beginners *(1959) and* Mr Love and Justice *(1960).*

1 In England, pop art and fine art stand resolutely back to back.
'Pop Songs and Teenagers' (1958), repr. in *England, Half English* (1961)

2 Today, age is needy and, as its powers decline, so does its income; but full-blooded youth has wealth as well as vigour. In this decade, we witness the second Children's Crusade, armed with strength and beauty, against all 'squares', all adult nay-sayers.
'Pop Songs and Teenagers', ibid.

William McKinley
(1843–1901)
US president

Elected to the presidency in 1896 on a Republican, strongly protectionist ticket, he became associated with US territorial expansion by his decision to embark on the Spanish-American War (1898). He was assassinated shortly after his re-election in 1900.

1 The mission of the United States is one of benevolent assimilation substituting the mild sway of justice and right for arbitrary rule.
Letter, 21 December 1898, publ. in *In the Days of McKinley*, ch.15 (1959) by Margaret Leech. Addressed to General Elwell S. Otis, commander of the US troops then occupying the Philippines, the letter anticipated formal annexation of the country.

(Sir) James Mackintosh
(1765–1832)
Scottish author, lawyer and politician

He wrote works of history and philosophy, including Vindiciae Gallicae *(1791) in reply to* EDMUND BURKE's Reflections on the French Revolution *(1789). He later served as a judge in Bombay (1806–12) and became an MP.*

1 The Commons, faithful to their system, remained in a wise and masterly inactivity.
Vindiciae Gallicae, ch. 1 (1791). The phrase 'wise and masterly inactivity' is also associated with US statesman John Caldwell Calhoun (1782–1850).

Charles Macklin
(*c.* 1699–1797)
Irish actor and playwright

He played at the Drury Lane Theatre (1733–48) and at Covent Garden until 1789. He made his reputation in the role of Shylock and as the protagonists in his own comedies Love à la Mode *(1759) and* The Man of the World *(1781).*

1 The law is a sort of hocus-pocus science, that smiles in yer face while it picks yer pocket: and the glorious uncertainty of it is of more use to the professors than the justice of it.
Love à la Mode, Act 2, Sc. 1 (1759). Spoken by Sir Archy MacSarcasm (originally played by Macklin).

Don McLean
(b. 1945)
US singer and songwriter

Appointed 'Hudson River Troubadour' by the New York State Council on the Arts, he toured schools and small communities around the eastern USA 1968–70. His song 'American Pie' became an unexpected radio hit, as did 'Vincent' (both 1971).

1 Bye bye, Miss American Pie,
Drove my Chevy to the levee but the levee was
dry,
And the good old boys were drinking whiskey and
rye
Singing 'This'll be the day that I die.'
'American Pie', refrain (song) on the album *American Pie* (1971)

2 And the three men I admire the most,
The Father, Son and Holy Ghost,
They caught the last train for the coast
The day the music died.
'American Pie', ibid. On the deaths of rock 'n' rollers Buddy Holly, the Big Bopper and Richie Valens in a plane crash while on tour, 2 February 1959.

Archibald MacLeish
(1892–1982)
US poet and government official

After publishing the narrative poem Conquistador *(1932), he turned to writing political verse plays, including* Air Raid *(1938). He had a parallel career as an academic and public official, and helped draft the* UNESCO CONSTITUTION.

1 A poem should not mean
But be.
'Ars Poetica', publ. in *Streets in the Moon* (1926)

2 America is promises to
Take!
America is promises to
Us
To take them
Brutally
With love but
Take them.
'America Was Promises', publ. in *America Was Promises* (1939)

3 To see the earth as we now see it, small and beautiful in that eternal silence where it floats, is to see ourselves as riders on the earth together, brothers on that bright loveliness in the unending night – brothers who *see* now they are truly brothers.
'Riders on Earth Together, Brothers in Eternal Cold' (1968), repr. in *Riders on Earth* (1978) as 'Bubble of Blue Air'. Referring to the first pictures of the earth from the moon.

4 Poets . . . are literal-minded men who will squeeze a word till it hurts.
'Apologia' (1972), repr. ibid. as 'Art and Law'

5 We are as great as our belief in human liberty – no greater. And our belief in human liberty is only ours when it is larger than ourselves.
'Now Let Us Address the Main Question: Bicentennial of What?' (1976), repr. ibid. as 'The Ghost'

Marshall McLuhan
(1911–80)
Canadian communications theorist

He wrote epigrammatically on the effects of mass media on contemporary society in The Gutenberg Galaxy *(1962) and* Understanding Media *(1964), concluding that 'all media work us over completely'.*

1 Today it is not the classroom nor the classics which are the repositories of models of eloquence, but the ad agencies.
The Mechanical Bride, 'Plain Talk' (1951)

2 For tribal man space was the uncontrollable mystery. For technological man it is time that occupies the same role.
Ibid., 'Magic that Changes Mood'

3 The new electronic interdependence recreates the world in the image of a global village.
The Gutenberg Galaxy, 'Chapter Gloss' (1962). GUY DEBORD commented on this famous phrase: 'The Sage of Toronto . . . spent several decades marvelling at the numerous freedoms created by a 'global village' instantly and effortlessly accessible to all. Villages, unlike towns, have always been ruled by conformism, isolation, petty surveillance, boredom and

repetitive malicious gossip about the same families. Which is a precise enough description of the global spectacle's present vulgarity.'

4 A point of view can be a dangerous luxury when substituted for insight and understanding.
Ibid., 'Typographic Man Can Express but is Helpless to Read the Configuration of Print Technology'

5 The medium is the message. This is merely to say that the personal and social consequences of any medium – that is, of any extension of ourselves – result from the new scale that is introduced into our affairs by each extension of ourselves, or by any new technology.
Understanding Media, ch. 1 (1964)

6 Money: The poor man's credit card.
Ibid., title of ch. 14

7 The car has become the carapace, the protective and aggressive shell, of urban and suburban man.
Ibid., ch. 22

8 Diaper backward spells repaid. Think about it.
Remark at American Booksellers Association luncheon, Washington DC, June 1969, quoted in the *Vancouver Sun* 7 June 1969

9 Television brought the brutality of war into the comfort of the living room. Vietnam was lost in the living rooms of America – not on the battlefields of Vietnam.
Quoted in the *Montreal Gazette* 16 May 1975

Harold Macmillan
(1894–1986)
British politician and prime minister

Lord Stockton. He was elected Conservative MP in 1926 and was Prime Minister 1957–63. Nicknamed 'Supermac' by the cartoonist Vicky, he was intellectual and aristocratic in style, and famously imperturbable. See ANEURIN BEVAN 13.

1 Forever poised between a cliché and an indiscretion.
Newsweek 30 April 1956. On the role of the Foreign Secretary.

2 Let us be frank about it: most of our people have never had it so good.
Speech in Bedford, 20 July 1957, quoted in *The Times* 22 July 1957. The slogan was already current in the USA at the end of the Second World War.

3 I thought the best thing to do was to settle up these little local difficulties, and then turn to the wider vision of the Commonwealth.
Statement at London airport, 7 January 1958, quoted in *The*

Times 8 January 1958. The remark, made when Macmillan was preparing to leave on a Commonwealth tour, referred to the resignation of the Chancellor of the Exchequer Peter Thorneycroft and treasury ministers ENOCH POWELL and Nigel Birch in protest against public spending increases. His words furthered Macmillan's reputation for 'unflappability'.

4 At home you always have to be a politician. When you're abroad you almost feel yourself a statesman.
Speech in Melbourne, 17 February 1958, quoted in *Look* 15 April 1958. Remark made during the first visit to Australia by a British prime minister.

5 We have seen the awakening of national consciousness in peoples who have for centuries lived in dependence upon some other power . . . The wind of change is blowing through the continent, and, whether we like it or not, this growth of national consciousness is a political fact.
Speech to South African Parliament, Cape Town, 3 February 1960, publ. in *The Penguin Book of Twentieth-Century Speeches* (ed. Brian MacArthur, 1999)

6 Power? It's like a dead sea fruit. When you achieve it, there's nothing there.
Quoted in *The New Anatomy of Britain*, ch. 37 (1971) by Anthony Sampson

7 If you don't believe in God, all you have to believe in is decency . . . Decency is very good. Better decent than indecent. But I don't think it's enough.
Quoted in *Macmillan*, vol. 2, ch. 19 (1989) by Alistair Horne. Said to William F. Buckley Jr on *Firing Line* (TV show) recorded 20 November 1980.

8 Memorial services are the cocktail parties of the geriatric set.
Quoted ibid., ch. 20

9 It is the duty of Her Majesty's Government neither to flap nor to falter.
Attributed

Louis MacNeice
(1907–63)
British poet

Associated with the left-wing poets of the 1930s, he combined lyricism and colloquial speech patterns in such collections as Autumn Journal (1938) and Solstices (1961). He also worked as a radio producer and wrote innovative documentaries and dramas for the BBC.

1 Down the road someone is practising scales,
The notes like little fishes vanish with a wink of
    tails,

Man's heart expands to tinker with his car
For this is Sunday morning, Fate's great bazaar.
'Sunday Morning', st. 1, publ. in *Poems* (1933)

2 World is crazier and more of it than we think,
Incorrigibly plural. I peel and portion
A tangerine and spit the pips and feel
The drunkenness of things being various.
'Snow', st. 2, publ. in *Poems* (1935). The Belfast poet Michael
Longley has commented that the line 'The drunkenness of
things being various' could be the motto for the whole of
MacNeice's life and work.

3 The sunlight on the garden
Hardens and grows cold,
We cannot cage the minute
Within its net of gold,
When all is told
We cannot beg for pardon.
'Sunlight on the Garden', publ. in *The Earth Compels* (1938)

4 It's no go the merrygoround, it's no go the
rickshaw,
All we want is a limousine and a ticket for the
peepshow.
'Bagpipe Music', ibid., st. 1

5 It's no go the Government grants, it's no go the
elections,
Sit on your arse for fifty years and hang your hat
on a pension.
'Bagpipe Music', ibid., st. 9

6 The glass is falling hour by hour, the glass will
fall for ever,
But if you break the bloody glass you won't hold
up the weather.
'Bagpipe Music', ibid., st. 10

7 Time was away and somewhere else
There were two glasses and two chairs
And two people with the one pulse
(Somebody stopped the moving stairs):
Time was away and somewhere else.
'Meeting Point', st. 1, publ. in *Autumn Journal* (1939)

8 Some on commission, some for the love of
learning,
Some because they have nothing better to do
Or because they hope these walls of books will
deaden
The drumming of the demon in their ears.
'The British Museum Reading Room', publ. in *Plant and Phantom* (1941)

Geoffrey Madan
(1895–1947)
English bibliophile

Known as a connoisseur and wit, he mixed with the literati of his day, moving between London, Oxford, Cambridge and country houses.

1 The dust of exploded beliefs may make a fine sunset.
Geoffrey Madan's Notebooks, 'Twelve Reflections' (1934) (ed. J. Gere and John Sparrow, 1981)

2 An anthology for the forgotten sayings of great men, and the great sayings of forgotten men.
Ibid., 'Extracts and Summaries'

3 It is dangerous to be right for the wrong reasons: but fatal to be wrong for the right ones.
Ibid., 'Extracts and Summaries'

4 Alive, in the sense that he can't legally be buried.
Ibid., 'Extracts and Summaries'

5 *The Times* obituary department: emotion anticipated in tranquillity.
Ibid., 'Extracts and Summaries'. See WILLIAM WORDSWORTH 30.

James Madison
(1751–1836)
US statesman

A leading Jeffersonian, he played a central role in the drafting of the US Constitution (1787) and, as a member of the new House of Representatives, sponsored the first ten amendments to it. His two terms as President (1809–17) coincided with the 1812 war with Britain.

1 As long as the reason of man continues fallible, and he is at liberty to exercise it, different opinions will be formed. As long as the connection subsists between his reason and his self-love, his opinions and his passions will have a reciprocal influence on each other; and the former will be objects to which the latter will attach themselves. The diversity in the faculties of men, from which the rights of property originate, is not less an insuperable obstacle to a uniformity of interests. The protection of these faculties is the first object of government.
The Federalist Papers, no. 10 (1787), repr. in *The Federalist* (ed. Benjamin F. Wright, 1961)

2 The proposed Constitution ... is, in strictness, neither a national nor a federal constitution; but a composition of both. In its foundation it is federal,

not national; in the sources from which the ordinary powers of the government are drawn, it is partly federal and partly national; in the operation of these powers, it is national, not federal; in the extent of them, again, it is federal, not national; and, finally, in the authoritative mode of introducing amendments, it is neither wholly federal nor wholly national.

The Federalist Papers, no. 39 (1788), ibid.

3 The accumulation of all powers, legislative, executive, and judiciary, in the same hands, whether of one, a few, or many, and whether hereditary, self-appointed, or elective, may justly be pronounced the very definition of tyranny.

The Federalist Papers, no. 47 (1788), ibid.

4 But what is government itself, but the greatest of all reflections on human nature? If men were angels, no government would be necessary. If angels were to govern men, neither external nor internal controls on government would be necessary.

The Federalist Papers, no. 51 (1788), ibid.

5 War contains so much folly, as well as wickedness, that much is to be hoped from the progress of reason; and if any thing is to be hoped, every thing ought to be tried.

'Universal Peace', publ. in the *National Gazette* 2 February 1792, repr. in *The Writings of James Madison*, vol. 6 (ed. Gaillard Hunt, 1906). Inscribed in Madison Memorial Hall, Library of Congress.

Madonna

(b. 1959)

US singer and actor

Madonna Louise Ciccone. She made the first of many dance-driven albums in 1983, since when she has become an icon of female independence and sexuality. She has also starred in films, for example Evita *(1996).*

1 You know that we are living in a material world
And I am a material girl.

'Material Girl' (song, written by Peter Brown and Robert Rans) on the album *Like a Virgin* (1984)

2 Like a virgin
Touched for the very first time
Like a virgin
When your heart beats
Next to mine.

'Like a Virgin' (song, written by Billy Steinberg and Tom Kelly), ibid.

3 Express yourself
So you can respect yourself

'Express Yourself' (song, written by Madonna and Stephen Bray) on the album *Like a Prayer* (1989)

4 I always thought of losing my virginity as a career move.

Quoted in *Madonna Unauthorized*, Epilogue (1991) by Christopher Andersen

Maurice Maeterlinck

(1862–1949)

Belgian poet, playwright and essayist

He established himself as a leading member of the Symbolist movement with the prose dramas La Princesse Maleine *(1889), and* Pelléas et Mélisande *(1892), on which Debussy's opera was based.* L'Oiseau bleu *(1908) enjoyed great popularity.*

1 They believe that nothing will happen because they have closed their doors.

Intérieur (1894; *Interior*). Spoken by the old man, who is looking in on a family who have yet to discover that one of their number has died.

2 Silence is the element in which great things fashion themselves.

Le Trésor des humbles, 'Silence' (1896; *The Treasure of the Humble*)

3 There are no dead.

L'Oiseau bleu, Act 5, Sc. 2 (1909; *The Blue Bird*). Spoken by the fairy.

John Gillespie Magee

(1922–41)

US pilot

He died while serving with the Royal Canadian Air Force on a bombing mission over Germany, leaving as a legacy the poem 'High Flight'.

1 Oh! I have slipped the surly bonds of earth,
And danced the skies on laughter-silvered wings.

'High Flight', written 1941, publ. in *More Poems from the Forces* (ed. K. Rhys, 1943). Opening lines of sonnet, made famous when quoted by RONALD REAGAN following the Challenger space shuttle disaster in 1986.

2 And while with silent lifting mind I've trod
The high, untrespassed sanctity of space,
Put out my hand and touched the face of God.

Ibid. Last lines.

Magna Carta
(1215)

The 'Great Charter' of liberties was a response by English barons to what they saw as the intrusive powers of the crown. It was signed by King John at Runnymede, by the River Thames, and reissued with amendments in later years.

1 No free man shall be seized or imprisoned, or stripped of his rights or possessions, or outlawed or exiled, or deprived of his standing in any other way, nor will we proceed with force against him, or send others to do so, except by the lawful judgement of his equals or by the law of the land.
Clause 39

2 To no one will we sell, to no one deny or delay right or justice.
Clause 40

(Sir) Magnus Magnusson
(b. 1929)
British author and broadcaster

He is known for his popular television documentaries and books on archaeology, and for chairing the inquisitorial TV quiz programme Mastermind *(1972–97).*

1 I've started, so I'll finish.
Mastermind quiz series (BBC, 1972–97). Also the title of a book (1997). Magnusson's words after his final show were: 'I've started, now I've finished.'

René Magritte
(1898–1967)
Belgian Surrealist painter

Joining the Paris Surrealists in 1927, he became a leading practitioner and theorist of Surrealism. He is probably best known for his images of figures in bowler hats, as in the painting Threatened Assassin *(1927).*

1 To be a surrealist ... means barring from your mind all remembrance of what you have seen, and being always on the lookout for what has never been.
Time 21 April 1947

2 The mind loves the unknown. It loves images whose meaning is unknown, since the meaning of the mind itself is unknown.
Quoted in *Magritte*, ch. 1 (1970) by Suzi Gablik

3 The present reeks of mediocrity and the atom bomb.
Quoted ibid., ch. 5

Norman Mailer
(b. 1923)
US author

He won immediate fame with The Naked and the Dead *(1948), a war novel that was primarily a critique of American society.* Armies of the Night *(1968) and* Executioner's Song *(1979) were examples of his 'new journalism'.* GORE VIDAL *remarked: 'He is now what he wanted to be: the patron saint of bad journalism.'*

1 For jazz is orgasm, it is the music of orgasm, good orgasm and bad, and so it spoke across a nation ... It was indeed a communication by art because it said, 'I feel this, and now you do too'.
'The White Negro', sect. 2 (1957), repr. in *Advertisements for Myself* (1959)

2 Hip is the sophistication of the wise primitive in a giant jungle.
Ibid., sect. 3

3 The White Protestant's ultimate sympathy must be with science, factology, and committee rather than with sex, birth, heat, flesh, creation, the sweet and the funky; they must vote, manipulate, control, and direct, these Protestants who are the center of power in our land, they must go for what they believe is reason when it is only the Square logic of the past.
Advertisements for Myself, pt 5, 'Advertisement for "Games and Ends"' (1959)

4 A modern democracy is a tyranny whose borders are undefined; one discovers how far one can go only by traveling in a straight line until one is stopped.
The Presidential Papers, Preface (1963)

5 Ultimately a hero is a man who would argue with the gods, and so awakens devils to contest his vision. The more a man can achieve, the more he may be certain that the devil will inhabit a part of his creation.
Ibid., Preface

6 Sentimentality is the emotional promiscuity of those who have no sentiment.
Cannibals and Christians, 'My Hope for America' (1966)

7 The horror of the Twentieth Century was the size of each new event, and the paucity of its reverberation.
A Fire on the Moon, pt 1, ch. 1 (1970)

8 So we think of Marilyn who was every man's love affair with America. Marilyn Monroe who was

blonde and beautiful and had a sweet little rinky-dink of a voice and all the cleanliness of all the clean American backyards.

Marilyn, ch. 1 (1973)

9 There is nothing safe about sex. There never will be.

International Herald Tribune 24 January 1992

Joseph de Maistre
(1753–1821)
French diplomat and philosopher

Following the French Revolution he was a powerful spokesman of the neo-Catholics and conservatives, and lived mostly in exile, including a period in Russia as Sardinian ambassador at St Petersburg (1803–17). His works include Du Pape *(1819) and* Les Soirées de Saint-Pétersbourg *(1821).*

1 A constitution that is made for all nations is made for none.

Considérations sur la France, ch. 6 (1796; *Considerations on France*)

2 Every country has the government it deserves.

Letter, 15 August 1811, publ. in *Lettres et opuscules inédits*, vol. 1, no. 53 (1851). See THOMAS CARLYLE 51.

3 Man in general, if reduced to himself, is too wicked to be free.

Quatre chapitres inédits sur la Russie, ch. 1 (written 1811–12, publ. 1859; *Four Chapters on Russia*)

4 There is no philosophy without the art of ignoring objections.

Les Soirées de Saint-Pétersbourg, 'Fifth Dialogue' (1821; *St Petersburg Dialogues*). Spoken by The Count.

5 The whole earth, perpetually steeped in blood, is nothing but an immense altar on which every living thing must be sacrificed without end, without restraint, without respite until the consummation of the world, the extinction of evil, the death of death.

Ibid., 'Seventh Dialogue'. Spoken by the Senator.

6 War is thus divine in itself, since it is a law of the world. War is divine in the mysterious glory that surrounds it and in the no less inexplicable attraction that draws us to it.

The Senator, ibid., 'Seventh Dialogue'

7 It is one of man's curious idiosyncrasies to create difficulties for the pleasure of resolving them.

De la Souveraineté du peuple, bk 1, ch. 2 (1884; *Study on Sovereignty*)

(Sir) John Major
(b. 1943)
British politician and prime minister

Succeeding MARGARET THATCHER *as Conservative Prime Minister in 1990, he won the 1992 general election but, dogged by criticism over the economy and European policy, suffered the greatest ever Tory election defeat in 1997. He retired from parliament in 2000. See* MICHAEL FOOT 2.

1 The harsh truth is that if the policy isn't hurting, it isn't working. I know there is a difficult period ahead but the important thing is that we cannot and must not fudge the determination to stop inflation in its tracks.

Speech at Northampton, 27 October 1989, quoted in *The Times* 28 October 1989. This was Major's first speech as Chancellor of the Exchequer after the resignation of Nigel Lawson.

2 I want to see us build a country that is at ease with itself, a country that is confident, and a country that is prepared and willing to make the changes necessary to provide a better quality of life for all our citizens. I don't promise you that it will be easy, and I don't promise you that it will be quick, but I believe it is an immensely worthwhile job. Now, if you will forgive me, because it will be neither easy nor quick, I will go into Number 10 straight away and make a start right now.

Speech outside No. 10 Downing Street, 28 November 1990, quoted in *John Major*, ch. 1 (1991) by Nesta Wyn Ellis. Major had won the Conservative Party leadership election, thereby becoming Prime Minister.

3 Society needs to condemn a little more and understand a little less.

Interview in the *Mail on Sunday* 21 February 1993. On the killing of James Bulger.

4 Fifty years on from now, Britain will still be the country of long shadows on county grounds, warm beer, invincible green suburbs, dog lovers and – as George Orwell said – old maids bicycling to Holy Communion through the morning mist.

Speech to Conservative Group for Europe, Intercontinental Hotel, London, 22 April 1993, quoted in the *Daily Telegraph* 23 April 1993. See GEORGE ORWELL 12.

5 It is time to get back to basics: to self-discipline and respect for the law, to consideration for others, to accepting responsibility for yourself and your family, and not shuffling it off on the state.

Speech to Conservative Party Conference, Blackpool, 8 October 1993, quoted in *The Times* 9 October 1993

Malcolm X

(1925–65)

US black civil rights activist

Born Malcolm Little, changed to Malcolm X and later to El-Hajj Malik El-Shabazz. He converted to Islam and joined the Black Muslims (Nation of Islam) while in prison for burglary (1946–53). His founding of the Organization of Afro-American Unity in 1964 caused a rift with Black Muslims which led to his assassination.

1 If you're born in America with a black skin, you're born in prison, and the masses of black people in America today are beginning to regard our plight or predicament in this society as one of a prison inmate.

Interview in June 1963, publ. in *Malcolm X: The Man and His Times*, pt 3, 'Malcolm X Talks with Kenneth B. Clark' (ed. John Henrik Clarke, 1969)

2 There is nothing in our book, the Koran, that teaches us to suffer peacefully. Our religion teaches us to be intelligent. Be peaceful, be courteous, obey the law, respect everyone; but if someone puts his hand on you, send him to the cemetery. That's a good religion.

'Message to the Grass Roots', speech in Detroit, November 1963, publ. in *Malcolm X Speaks*, ch. 1 (1965). See also ALICE WALKER 11.

3 Sitting at the table doesn't make you a diner, unless you eat some of what's on that plate. Being here in America doesn't make you an American. Being born here in America doesn't make you an American.

'The Ballot or the Bullet', speech in Cleveland, Ohio, 3 April 1964, ibid., ch. 3

4 We have formed an organization known as the Organization of Afro-American Unity ... To fight whoever gets in our way, to bring about the complete independence of people of African descent here in the Western hemisphere, and first here in the United States, and bring about the freedom of these people by any means necessary. That's our motto. We want freedom by any means necessary. We want justice by any means necessary. We want equality by any means necessary.

Speech at OAAU Founding Rally, Audubon Ballroom, New York, 28 June 1964, publ. in *Malcolm X By Any Means Necessary* (ed. George Breitman, 1970). The words 'by any means necessary' became a rallying call among radical movements in the 1960s.

5 The common goal of 22 million Afro-Americans is respect as *human beings*, the God-given right to be a *human being*. Our common goal is to obtain the *human rights* that America has been denying us. We can never get civil rights in America until our *human rights* are first restored. We will never be recognized as citizens there until we are first recognized as *humans*.

'Racism: the Cancer that is Destroying America', publ. in the *Egyptian Gazette* 25 August 1964

6 You can't separate peace from freedom because no one can be at peace unless he has his freedom.

'Prospects for Freedom in 1965', speech in New York, 7 January 1965, publ. in *Malcolm X Speaks*, ch. 12 (1965)

John Malkovich

(b. 1953)

US actor

He was co-founder of the Steppenwolf Theatre Company in Chicago (1976), making his cinematic debut in Places in the Heart (1984). In 1999 he played himself in Being John Malkovich.

1 Where women are concerned, the rule is never to go out with anyone better dressed than you.

Interview in the *Independent on Sunday* 5 April 1992

François de Malherbe

(1555–1628)

French poet

The official poet of Henri IV and Louis XIII, he advocated technical precision and simplicity of verse.

1 And the fruits will outdo what the flowers have promised.

'Prière pour Henri le Grand allant en Limosin', st. 14 (1605), repr. in *Malherbe* (ed. R. G. Maber, 1983)

Stéphane Mallarmé

(1842–98)

French poet

A leading Symbolist, he wrote evocative, often obscure poetry, using unusual syntax and typography. His most influential works include the poem 'L'Après-midi d'un faune' ('The Afternoon of a Faun', 1876), which inspired Debussy, and his translations of EDGAR ALLAN POE.

1 There is only beauty – and it has only one perfect expression – Poetry. All the rest is a lie – except for

those who live by the body, love, and, that love of the mind, friendship.
Letter, 14 May 1867, quoted in *Mallarmé*, ch. 1 (1969) by Frederic Chase St Aubyn

2 Alas, the flesh is weary, and I've read all the books.
'Brise Marine', st. 1, publ. in *Poésies* (1887, transl. 1977)

3 Will lovely, lively, virginal today
Shatter for us with a swing's drunken blow
This hard, forgotten lake haunted in snow
By the sheer ice of flocks not flown away!
'Plusieurs Sonnets', no. 2, ibid.

4 Every soul is a melody which needs renewing.
'Crise de vers', publ. in *Variations sur un sujet* (1895)

5 A Throw of the Dice Will Never Abolish Chance.
Title of poem, 'Un Coup de dés jamais n'abolira le hasard' (1897), repr. in *Oeuvres Complètes* (ed. Henri Mondor and G. Jean-Aubry, 1945). Gordan Millan wrote a biography of Mallarmé entitled *A Throw of the Dice* (1994).

George Leigh Mallory
(1886–1924)
British mountaineer

Assistant Master at Charterhouse School, Surrey (1910–15), he lost his life during his third attempt to climb Everest after previous ventures in 1921 and 1922.

1 Because it's there.
Interview in the *New York Times* 18 March 1923. On being asked why he wanted to climb Mount Everest.

(Sir) Thomas Malory
(c. 1430–71)
English author

His major work, La Morte d'Arthur *(1485), printed by William Caxton, was the first account in prose of the Arthurian legends, drawing on French sources. His exact identity is uncertain, but he was probably a knight of Newbold Revell in Warwickshire, who spent long periods in prison.*

1 Whoso pulleth out this sword of this stone and anvil is rightwise King born of all England.
Le Morte d'Arthur, bk 1, ch. 5 (1485)

2 For like as herbs and trees bringen forth fruit and flourish in May, in likewise every lusty heart that is in any manner a lover, springeth and flourisheth in lusty deeds.
Ibid., bk 18, ch. 25

3 Queen Guenever, for whom I make here a little mention, that while she lived she was a true lover, and therefore she had a good end.
Ibid., bk 18, ch. 25

4 Such a fellowship of good knights shall never be together in no company.
Ibid., bk 20, ch. 9

5 Leave this opinion or I shall curse you with book and bell and candle.
Ibid., bk 21, ch. 1. Said by 'the noble clerk' referring to the ceremony of excommunication. The phrase is commonly spoken, 'bell, book and candle'.

6 But many men say that there is written upon his tomb this verse: *Hic iacet Arthurus, rex quondam rexque futurus.*
Ibid., bk 21, ch. 7. *The Once and Future King* was the title given by T. H. White to his novel based on the Arthurian myths, from the English translation of the Latin: 'Here lies Arthur, the once and future king'. See T. H. WHITE 1.

7 Thou were never matched of earthly knight's hand. And thou were the courteoust knight that ever bare shield. And thou were the truest friend to thy lover that ever bestrad horse. And thou were the truest lover of a sinful man that ever loved woman. And thou were the kindest man that ever struck with sword. And thou were the goodliest person that ever came among press of knights. And thou was the meekest man and the gentlest that ever ate in hall among ladies. And thou were the sternest knight to thy mortal foe that ever put spear in the rest.
Ibid., bk 21, ch. 13. Sir Ector's eulogy for Sir Launcelot.

André Malraux
(1901–76)
French man of letters and statesman

Best known for such novels as La Condition Humaine *(Man's Fate, 1933) and* L'Espoir *(Man's Hope (1937), he fought in Indochina, Spain and France and was France's first Minister of Cultural Affairs (1959–69).*

1 There are not fifty ways of fighting, there's only one, and that's to win. Neither revolution nor war consists in doing what one pleases.
Man's Hope, pt 2, sect. 2, ch. 12 (1937)

2 All art is a revolt against man's fate.
The Voices of Silence, pt 4, ch. 7 (1951)

3 The human mind invents its Puss-in-boots and its coaches that change into pumpkins at dawn because

neither the believer nor the atheist is completely satisfied with appearances.

Anti-Memoirs, Preface (1967)

4 The genius of Christianity is to have proclaimed that the path to the deepest mystery is the path of love.

Ibid., 'Anti-Memoirs', sect. 6

5 Hell is not horror; hell is being degraded to the point of death, whether death comes or passes by: the appalling abjection of the victim, the mysterious abjection of the executioner. Satan is the Degrader.

Ibid., 'The Human Condition', sect. 2. Referring to the concentration camps in Nazi Germany. A few lines further, Malraux states: 'The attempt to force human beings to despise themselves. That is what I call hell.'

Thomas Robert Malthus
(1766–1834)
English economist and sociologist

His theory that population growth would outstrip food supply, as described in his Essay on the Principle of Population *(1798), was highly influential. His later writings focused more closely on economics.*

1 Population, when unchecked, increases in a geometrical ratio. Subsistence increases only in an arithmetical ratio. A slight acquaintance with numbers will show the immensity of the first power in comparison of the second.

An Essay on the Principle of Population, ch. 1 (1798)

2 The passion between the sexes has appeared in every age to be so nearly the same, that it may always be considered, in algebraic language as a given quantity.

Ibid., ch. 7

David Mamet
(b. 1947)
US playwright

His breakthrough play was American Buffalo *(1975), and he subsequently won the Pulitzer Prize for* Glengarry Glen Ross *(1984). He has also written screenplays and essays.*

1 We respond to a drama to that extent to which it corresponds to our dreamlife.

Writing in Restaurants, 'A National Dream-Life' (1986)

2 The poker player learns that sometimes both science and common sense are wrong; that the bumblebee *can* fly; that, perhaps, one should never trust an expert; that there are more things in heaven and earth than are dreamt of by those with an academic bent.

Ibid., 'Things I Have Learned Playing Poker on the Hill'

3 A good film script should be able to do completely without dialogue.

Independent 11 November 1988

4 I can envision no device more capable of spreading ignorance and illiteracy than the computer. It is, I think, like the atom bomb, a naturally evolved engine of destruction, a sign, like the Tower of Babel, that civilization has run its course.

Jafsie and John Henry, 'Why Don't You Write With a Computer?' (1999)

Nelson Mandela
(b. 1918)
South African political leader

The international symbol of the anti-apartheid movement, he spent the years 1964–90 in prison for his role in the banned African National Congress. On his release he was elected President of the ANC and South Africa's first black President (1994–9).

1 For my own part I have made my choice. I will not leave South Africa, nor will I surrender. Only through hardship, sacrifice and militant action can freedom be won. The struggle is my life. I will continue fighting for freedom until the end of my days.

Press statement, 26 June 1961, repr. in *The Struggle Is My Life*, pt 2, 'The Struggle Is My Life' (1978)

2 Whatever he himself may say in his defence, the white man's moral standards in this country must be judged by the extent to which he has condemned the vast majority of its inhabitants to serfdom and inferiority.

Defence statement at trial in Pretoria, 15 October–7 November 1962, ibid., pt 2, 'Black Man in a White Court'

3 The whole life of any thinking African in this country drives him continuously to a conflict between his conscience on the one hand and the law on the other.

Address to court after closure of prosecution case, ibid., pt 2, 'Black Man in a White Court'

4 Only free men can negotiate. Prisoners cannot enter into contracts.

Statement from prison, 10 February 1985, quoted in *Higher than Hope*, ch. 30 (1988) by Fatima Meer. Refusing the terms set for his release by South African President P. W. Botha. The statement was read by Zindzi Mandela, Nelson's daughter, at a United Democratic Front rally at the Jabulani Stadium, Soweto.

5 To be father of a nation is a great honour, but to be the father of a family is a greater joy.
Long Walk to Freedom, ch. 109 (1994)

6 True reconciliation does not consist in merely forgetting the past. It does not rest with black forgiveness, sensitivity to white fears, and tolerance of an unjust status quo, on one hand, and white gratitude and appreciation underlined by a tenacious clinging to exclusive privilege, on the other.
Speech, 8 January 1996, publ. on ANC website, www.anc.org.za

Winnie Mandela
(b. 1934)
South African political leader

Nomzano Zaniewe Winifred Mandela. For many years, she campaigned for the release of her husband NELSON MANDELA and for the African National Congress. Charged with kidnapping (1991) and fraud (2002), she separated from and divorced him in 1996.

1 Together, hand in hand, with that stick of matches, with our necklace, we shall liberate this country.
Speech in black townships, quoted in the *Guardian* 15 April 1986

Osip Mandelstam
(1891–1938)
Russian poet

Associated with the Acmeist movement, he published the collections Kamen *(1913) and* Tristia *(1922). He was harshly criticized by the Bolsheviks and in 1934 was arrested and exiled for a poem denouncing STALIN. He died en route to a forced labour camp.*

1 I have studied the science of good-byes,
the bare-headed laments of night.
'Tristia', st. 1, publ. in *Tristia* (1922), repr. in *Selected Poems* (1973)

2 O indigence at the root of our lives,
how poor is the language of happiness!
Everything's happened before and will happen
    again,
but still the moment of each meeting is sweet.
'Tristia', st. 3, ibid.

3 No matter how you stars want to shine,
First apply on the dotted line,

We're sure to renew your permission
For shining or writing or extinction.
Untitled poem, written 1930, publ. in *Osip Mandelstam: 50 poems* (1977)

4 Poetry, you put storms to good use.
'To the German Language', written 1932, publ. in *Selected Poems* (1973)

5 But whenever there's a snatch of talk
it turns to the Kremlin mountaineer,
the ten thick worms his fingers,
his words like measures of weight,
the huge laughing cockroaches on his top lip
the glitter of his boot-rims.
'The Stalin Epigram', written 1933, ibid. Referring to JOSEF STALIN. The private circulation of the poem led to Mandelstam's first arrest in 1934.

6 A quotation is not an excerpt. A quotation is a cicada. Its natural state is that of unceasing sound. Having once seized hold of the air, it will not let it go.
'Conversation About Dante', sect. 2, written 1933–4, publ. in *The Complete Critical Prose and Letters* (ed. Jane Gary Harris et al., 1979)

Bernard de Mandeville
(1670–1733)
Dutch-born English author and physician

Settling in London in the 1690s to practise medicine, he composed the verse satire The Grumbling Hive *(1705), revised with prose commentaries as* The Fable of the Bees *in 1714 and 1723.*

1 We seldom call anybody lazy, but such as we reckon inferior to us, and of whom we expect some service.
The Fable of the Bees, 'Remark (V)' (1714, rev. 1723)

2 No habit or quality is more easily acquired than hypocrisy, nor anything sooner learned than to deny the sentiments of our hearts and the principle we act from.
Ibid., 'An Essay on Charity and Charity-Schools'

Thomas Mann
(1875–1955)
German-born US author and critic

His most celebrated works include Buddenbrooks *(1901),* Tonio Kröger *(1902),* Death in Venice *(1912) and* The Magic Mountain *(1924). Much of his fiction examines the role of the artist in society. A supporter of the Weimar Republic, he fled Nazi Germany and in 1940 became an American citizen.*

1 Solitude gives birth to the original in us, to beauty unfamiliar and perilous – to poetry. But also, it gives birth to the opposite: to the perverse, the illicit, the absurd.

Death in Venice (1912)

2 A man lives not only his personal life, as an individual, but also, consciously or unconsciously, the life of his epoch and his contemporaries.

The Magic Mountain, ch. 2, 'At Tienappels" (1924)

3 Time has no divisions to mark its passage, there is never a thunderstorm or blare of trumpets to announce the beginning of a new month or year. Even when a new century begins it is only we mortals who ring bells and fire off pistols.

Ibid., ch. 5, 'Whims of Mercurius'

4 Opinions cannot survive if one has no chance to fight for them.

Ibid., ch. 6, 'Of The City of God'

5 A man's dying is more the survivors' affair than his own.

Ibid., ch. 6, 'A Soldier, And Brave'

6 An art whose medium is language will always show a high degree of critical creativeness, for speech is itself a critique of life: it names, it characterizes, it passes judgment, in that it creates.

'Lessing speech', Prussian Academy of Art, Berlin, 22 January 1929, publ. in *Essays of Three Decades* (1942)

7 Unhappy German nation, how do you like the Messianic rôle allotted to you, not by God, nor by destiny, but by a handful of perverted and bloody-minded men?

'This War' (1939), repr. in *Order of the Day* (1942)

8 It is a strange fact that freedom and equality, the two basic ideas of democracy, are to some extent contradictory. Logically considered, freedom and equality are mutually exclusive, just as society and the individual are mutually exclusive.

'The War and the Future', speech 1940, publ. in *Order of the Day* (1942)

9 I have always been an admirer, I regard the gift of admiration as indispensable if one is to amount to something; I don't know where I would be without it.

Letter, 1950, quoted in *Thomas Mann and His Family*, 'Thomas Mann – The Birth of Criticism' (1987) by Marcel Reich-Ranicki

10 Every reasonable human being should be a moderate Socialist.

New York Times 18 June 1950, quoted in *Thomas Mann: A Critical Study*, ch. 2 (1971) by R. J. Hollingdale

Katherine Mansfield

(1888–1923)

New Zealand-born British author

Her stories, collected in Bliss *(1919) and* The Garden Party *(1920) among other titles, are noted for their psychological realism. She also wrote poetry, posthumously edited and published by her husband* JOHN MIDDLETON MURRY. VIRGINIA WOOLF *wrote of her: 'Her mind is a very thin soil, laid an inch or two upon very barren rock.'*

1 Now it is Loneliness who comes at night
Instead of Sleep, to sit beside my bed.
Like a tired child I lie and wait her tread,
I watch her softly blowing out the light.

'Loneliness' (1910), repr. in *Poems* (1924)

2 To work – to work! It is such infinite delight to know that we still have the best things to do.

Letter to BERTRAND RUSSELL, 7 December 1916, publ. in *Collected Letters*, vol. 1 (ed. Vincent O'Sullivan and Margaret Scott, 1984)

3 It's a terrible thing to be alone – yes it is – it is – but don't lower your mask until you have another mask prepared beneath – as terrible as you like – but a *mask*.

Letter to JOHN MIDDLETON MURRY, July 1917, ibid. Referring to Murry's current writing which she found 'indecent' for his tendency to 'abase' himself, during a period when he was most influenced by the style of D. H. LAWRENCE.

4 Everything in life that we really accept undergoes a change. So suffering must become Love. That is the mystery.

Journal entry, 19 December 1920, publ. in *The Journal of Katherine Mansfield* (1927)

Mao Zedong

(1893–1976)

Chinese leader

One of the founders of the Chinese Communist Party in 1921, he became its leader in 1943 and Chairman of the People's Republic of China in 1949. His 'Thoughts' became doctrine in China and were cited by radicals everywhere. His name is also associated with the oppression of the Cultural Revolution (1966–9).

1 A revolution is not a dinner party, or writing an essay, or painting a picture, or doing embroidery;

it cannot be so refined, so leisurely and gentle, so temperate, kind, courteous, restrained and magnanimous. A revolution is an insurrection, an act of violence by which one class overthrows another.
Report, March 1927, publ. in *Selected Works*, vol. 1 (1954)

2 Politics is war without bloodshed while war is politics with bloodshed.
'On Protracted War', lecture, May 1938, ibid., vol. 2 (1954)

3 Our attitude towards ourselves should be 'to be insatiable in learning' and towards others 'to be tireless in teaching'.
'The Role of the Chinese Communist Party in the National War' (1938), ibid., vol. 2

4 Every Communist must grasp the truth, 'Political power grows out of the barrel of a gun'.
'Problems of War and Strategy', speech, 6 November 1938, ibid., vol. 2. JEAN GENET commented: 'Power may be at the end of a gun, but sometimes it's also at the end of the shadow or the image of a gun.'

5 War can only be abolished through war, and in order to get rid of the gun it is necessary to take up the gun.
'Problems of War and Strategy', speech, 6 November 1938, ibid., vol. 2

6 So long as a person who has made mistakes does not hide his sickness for fear of treatment or persist in his mistakes until he is beyond cure, so long as he honestly and sincerely wishes to be cured and to mend his ways, we should welcome him and cure his sickness so that he can become a good comrade. We can never succeed if we just let ourselves go and lash out at him. In treating an ideological or a political malady, one must never be rough and rash but must adopt the approach of 'curing the sickness to save the patient', which is the only correct and effective method.
'Rectify the Party's Style of Work', 1 February 1942, ibid. vol. 3 (1954)

7 Take the ideas of the masses (scattered and unsystematic ideas) and concentrate them (through study turn them into concentrated and systematic ideas), then go to the masses and propagate and explain these ideas until the masses embrace them as their own, hold fast to them and translate them into action, and test the correctness of these ideas in such action. Then once again concentrate ideas from the masses and once again go to the masses so that the ideas are persevered in and carried through. And so on, over and over again in an endless spiral, with the ideas becoming more correct, more vital and richer each time. Such is the Marxist theory of knowledge.
'Some Questions Concerning Methods of Leadership', 1 June 1943, ibid., vol. 3

8 The people, and the people alone, are the motive force in the making of world history.
'On Coalition Government', 24 April 1945, ibid., vol. 3

9 All reactionaries are paper tigers. In appearance, the reactionaries are terrifying, but in reality they are not so powerful. From a long-term point of view, it is not the reactionaries but the people who are really powerful.
'Talk with the American correspondent Anne Louise Strong', August 1946, ibid. vol. 4 (1956). Mao returned to this theme in a later speech in Moscow, 18 November 1957: 'Was not Hitler a paper tiger? Was Hitler not overthrown? ... US imperialism has not yet been overthrown and it has the atomic bomb. I believe it also will be overthrown. It, too, is a paper tiger.'

10 Communism is not love. Communism is a hammer which we use to crush the enemy.
Quoted in *Time* 18 December 1950

11 Letting a hundred flowers blossom and a hundred schools of thought contend is the policy for promoting the progress of the arts and the sciences and a flourishing socialist culture in our land.
'On the Correct Handling of Contradictions Among the People', speech in Beijing, 27 February 1957, quoted in *Quotations from Chairman Mao Tse-Tung*, ch. 32 (1966)

12 Apart from their other characteristics, the outstanding thing about China's 600 million people is that they are 'poor and blank'. This may seem a bad thing, but in reality it is a good thing. Poverty gives rise to the desire for change, the desire for action and the desire for revolution. On a blank sheet of paper free from any mark, the freshest and most beautiful characters can be written, the freshest and most beautiful pictures can be painted.
'Introducing a Co-operative', 15 April 1958, ibid., ch. 3

Diego Maradona
(b. 1960)
Argentinian footballer

A brilliant and controversial striker, he became the world's most expensive footballer on joining Barcelona for £5 million in 1982. He played a key role in Argentina's victory in the 1986 World Cup, but his career was later marred by cocaine use.

1 The goal was scored a little bit by the hand of God, a little by the head of Maradona.
Quoted in the *Observer* 29 June 1986. Referring to the goal bounced off his fist, thereby ousting England from the World Cup finals in Mexico.

Greil Marcus
(b. 1945)
US rock journalist

A contributor of articles and reviews to the New York Times, Village Voice *and* Rolling Stone, *where he was Associate Editor (1969–70) and Book Editor (1975–80), he wrote the classic* Mystery Train: Images of America in Rock 'n' Roll Music *(1975).*

1 We make the oldest stories new when we succeed, and we are trapped by the old stories when we fail.
Mystery Train, Prologue (1975)

2 Rock 'n' roll is a combination of good ideas dried up by fads, terrible junk, hideous failings in taste and judgment, gullibility and manipulation, moments of unbelievable clarity and invention, pleasure, fun, vulgarity, excess, novelty and utter enervation.
Ibid., 'Randy Newman: Pop'

3 It is a sure sign that a culture has reached a dead end when it is no longer intrigued by its myths.
Ibid., 'Elvis: Presliad: Fanfare'

Herbert Marcuse
(1898–1979)
German-born US political philosopher

The blend of psychoanalytic theory and libertarian left-wing thought in such works as Eros and Civilization *(1955) and* One-Dimensional Man *(1964) was a major influence on young intellectuals in the 1960s.*

1 Self-determination, the autonomy of the individual, asserts itself in the right to race his automobile, to handle his power tools, to buy a gun, to communicate to mass audiences his opinion, no matter how ignorant, how aggressive, it may be.
An Essay on Liberation, ch. 1 (1969)

William Learned Marcy
(1786–1857)
US politician

A Democrat, he was Governor of New York (1833–8), Secretary of War (1845–9) and Secretary of State (1853–7).

1 The politicians of the United States . . . see nothing wrong in the rule, that to the victor belong the spoils of the enemy.
Speech to the Senate, 25 January 1832, publ. in *Register of Debates in Congress*, vol. 8 (1833)

Marguerite of Angoulême
(1492–1549)
French author and Queen of Navarre

The sister of Francis I, she married Henry II of Navarre in 1527. She was a noted patron of reformers, artists and writers, and herself wrote, among other works, the Heptaméron *(1558), seventy-two stories modelled on* BOCCACCIO's Decameron.

1 One unhappy person seeks out another.
Heptaméron, pt 21 (1558)

2 Love is not a flame that one holds in the hand.
Ibid., pt 47

Marie-Antoinette
(1755–93)
French queen

She was married to the Dauphin (1770), later Louis XVI (from 1774). Her extravagant behaviour, support of Austria and opposition to reform eventually led to her imprisonment and execution.

1 Let them eat cake.
Attributed, on hearing that the Parisians had no bread. Usually quoted in French as *'S'ils n'ont pas de pain, qu'on leur donne de la brioche'* ['If they don't have any bread, then give them cake.']

Tommaso Marinetti
(1876–1944)
Italian playwright

The ideological founder of the Futurist movement, he extolled violence and glorified war in his writings, later joining the Italian Fascist party in 1919. Among his works are The Bleeding Mummy *(1904) and* Mafarka the Futurist *(1910).*

1 The world's magnificence has been enriched by a new beauty; the beauty of speed.
'The Founding and Manifesto of Futurism', sect. 4 (1909), repr. in *Marinetti: Selected Writings* (ed. R. W. Flint, 1972)

2 Except in struggle there is no more beauty. No work without an aggressive character can be a masterpiece. Poetry must be conceived as a violent attack on unknown forces, to reduce and prostrate before man.
'The Founding and Manifesto of Futurism', sect. 7, ibid.

3 We will glorify war – the world's only hygiene –

militarism, patriotism, the destructive gesture of freedom-bringers, beautiful ideas worth dying for, and scorn for woman.

'The Founding and Manifesto of Futurism', sect. 9, ibid.

4 The past is necessarily inferior to the future. That is how we wish it to be.

'We Abjure our Symbolist Masters, the Last Lovers of the Moon', publ. in *War, the World's Only Hygiene* (1915), ibid.

Jacques Maritain
(1882–1973)
French philosopher

As a neo-Thomist philosopher and Catholic theologian, he drew controversy for his liberal and left-wing interpretation of Roman Catholic doctrine. Published works include The Degrees of Knowledge *(1932) and* Scholasticism in Politics *(1940).*

1 I don't see America as a mainland, but as a sea, a big ocean. Sometimes a storm arises, a formidable current develops, and it seems it will engulf everything. Wait a moment, another current will appear and bring the first one to naught.

Reflections on America, ch. 4 (1948)

2 Gratitude is the most exquisite form of courtesy.
Ibid., ch.17

Edwin Markham
(1852–1940)
US poet

His most famous poem 'The Man with the Hoe' (1899) was the product of his mystic beliefs and his interest in the difficulties of the working poor.

1 Bowed by the weight of centuries he leans
Upon his hoe and gazes on the ground,
The emptiness of ages in his face,
And on his back the burden of the world.

'The Man with the Hoe', st. 1, publ. in *The Man with the Hoe and Other Poems* (1899)

Leo Marks
(1920–2001)
British author

He worked as a cryptographer and headed the Special Operations Executive during the Second World War, after which he became a playwright and screenwriter.

1 The life that I have
Is all that I have
And the life that I have

Is yours.
The love that I have
Of the life that I have
Is yours and yours and yours.

'The Life That I Have', written 1943, publ. in *Between Silk and Cyanide*, ch. 65 (memoir, 1998). The poem, which was given to Violette Szabo as a cipher for a mission in France during the Second World War, was made famous in the film *Carve Her Name With Pride* (1958), spoken by Violette Szabo (played by Virginia McKenna).

Bob Marley
(1945–81)
Jamaican reggae musician

He made his first record in 1961, but it was not until the albums Catch a Fire *(1972) and* Natty Dread *(1975), recorded with the Wailers, that he achieved international success. His songs drew heavily on his Rastafarian beliefs.*

1 Get up, stand up,
Stand up for your rights.
Get up, stand up,
Don't give up the fight.

'Get Up, Stand Up' (song, written with Peter Tosh) on the album *Burnin'* (1973) by the Wailers

2 I shot the sheriff
But I didn't shoot no deputy.

'I Shot the Sheriff' (song, written with Peter Tosh), ibid.

3 Them belly full but we 'ungry
A hungry mob is a angry mob.

'Them Belly Full' (song, written by Legon Cogil and Carlton Barrett) on the album *Natty Dread* (1975) by Bob Marley and the Wailers

4 Until the philosophy which holds one race superior and another inferior is finally and permanently discredited and abandoned, everywhere is war ... and until there are no longer first-class and second-class citizens of any nation, until the colour of a man's skin is of no more significance than the colour of his eyes, me seh war. And until the basic human rights are equally guaranteed to all without regard to race, there is war. And until that day, the dream of lasting peace, world citizenship, rule of international morality, will remain but a fleeting illusion to be pursued, but never attained ... now everywhere is war.

'War' (song) on the album *Rastaman Vibration* (1976) by Bob Marley and the Wailers. The words of the song are based on a speech given to the United Nations by the Ethiopian emperor Haile Selassie in 1968.

5 Emancipate yourselves from mental slavery.
None but ourselves can free our minds.
'Redemption Song' (song) on the album *Uprising* (1980) by
Bob Marley and the Wailers

Christopher Marlowe
(1564–93)
English dramatist and poet

A master of blank verse, he had success with his plays Tamburlaine the Great *(1587) and* The Tragical History of Dr Faustus
(c. 1592), and may have contributed to some of SHAKE-
SPEARE's *early plays. He was killed during a brawl in a tavern.
According to* SWINBURNE, *he was 'the first English poet whose
powers can be called sublime'. See also* MICHAEL DRAYTON 7.

1 Come live with me, and be my love,
And we will all the pleasures prove.
That valleys, groves, hills, and fields,
Woods or steepy mountain yields.
'The Passionate Shepherd to his Love', st. 1 (*c.* 1589), publ. in
England's Helicon (1600). A close version of the poem appears
in *The Passionate Pilgrim*, an anthology of 1599, together with
a quatrain, 'Love's Answer'. See also JOHN DONNE 20 and
WALTER RALEGH 5; another variation was written by ROBERT
HERRICK.

2 By shallow rivers, to whose falls,
Melodious birds sing madrigals.
'The Passionate Shepherd to his Love', st. 2, ibid. The lines
also appear in SHAKESPEARE's *The Merry Wives of Windsor*,
sung by Evans in Act 3, Sc. 1.

3 And I will make thee beds of roses
And a thousand fragrant posies.
'The Passionate Shepherd to his Love', st. 3, ibid.

4 I count religion but a childish toy,
And hold there is no sin but ignorance.
The Jew of Malta, Prologue (written *c.* 1589, publ. 1633). Spoken
by Machiavel. The second line sometimes appears as 'no sin
but innocence'.

5 Thus methinks should men of judgement frame
Their means of traffic from the vulgar trade,
And, as their wealth increaseth, so enclose
Infinite riches in a little room.
Barabas, ibid., Act 1, Sc. 1

6 I will teach [thee] that shall stick by thee.
First, be thou void of these affections:
Compassion, love, vain hope, and heartless fear;
Be moved at nothing, see thou pity none,
But to thyself smile when Christians moan.
Barabas, ibid., Act 2, Sc. 3

7 As for myself, I walk abroad o' nights
And kill sick people groaning under walls:
Sometimes I go about and poison wells.
Barabas, ibid., Act 2, Sc. 3

8 Friar Barnadine: Thou hast committed –
Barabas: Fornication? But that was in another
country,
And besides, the wench is dead.
Ibid., Act 4, Sc. 1

9 Our swords shall play the orators for us.
Tamburlaine the Great, pt 1, Act 1, Sc. 2 (written 1587, publ.
1590). Spoken by Techelles.

10 Accursed be he that first invented war.
Ibid., pt 1, Act 2, Sc. 4. Spoken by Mycetes, King of Persia.

11 Is it not passing brave to be a King,
And ride in triumph through Persepolis?
Tamburlaine, ibid., pt 1, Act 2, Sc. 5

12 Nature that framed us of four elements,
Warring within our breasts for regiment,
Doth teach us all to have aspiring minds.
Tamburlaine, ibid., pt 1, Act 2, Sc. 7

13 The ripest fruit of all,
That perfect bliss and sole felicity,
The sweet fruition of an earthly crown.
Tamburlaine, ibid., pt 1, Act 2, Sc. 7

14 My men, like satyrs grazing on the lawns,
Shall with their goat feet dance an antic hay.
Edward II, Act 1, Sc. 1 (1593). Spoken by Piers Gaveston. 'Antic
hay' refers to a playful dance.

15 What are kings, when regiment is gone,
But perfect shadows in a sunshine day?
King Edward, ibid., Act 5, Sc. 1

16 All places are alike,
And every earth is fit for burial.
King Edward, ibid., Act 5, Sc. 1

17 Where both deliberate, the love is slight:
Who ever loved, that loved not at first sight?
Hero and Leander, 'First Sestiad', ll. 175–6 (1598). The words
are recalled in SHAKESPEARE's play *As You Like It*, Act 3, Sc. 5,
ll. 175–6, which appeared a year after Marlowe's poem: 'Dead
shepherd, now I find thy saw of might:/ "Who ever loved that
loved not at first sight?"'

18 I'll have them fly to India for gold,
Ransack the ocean for the Orient pearl.
The Tragical History of Dr Faustus Act 1, Sc. 3 (written *c.* 1592,
publ. 1604, rev. 1616). Spoken by Mephostophilis.

19 Why, this is hell, nor am I out of it.
Mephostophilis, ibid., Act 1, Sc. 3. In reply to Faust's question: 'How comes it then that thou art out of hell?'

20 Hell hath no limits, nor is circumscribed
In one self place. But where we are is hell,
And where hell is, there must we ever be.
And, to be short, when all the world dissolves
And every creature shall be purified,
All places shall be hell that is not heaven.
Mephostophilis, ibid., Act 1, Sc. 5

21 Was this the face that launched a thousand
ships,
And burnt the topless towers of Ilium?
Faustus, ibid., Act 5, Sc. 1. Referring to Helen of Troy, conjured up by Faustus.

22 Sweet Helen, make me immortal with a kiss.
Faustus, ibid., Act 5, Sc. 1. Referring to Helen of Troy.

23 Oh thou art fairer than the evening's air,
Clad in the beauty of a thousand stars.
Faustus, ibid., Act 5, Sc. 1. Referring to Helen of Troy.

24 *O lente, lente currite noctis equi*:
The stars move still, time runs, the clock will
strike,
The devil will come, and Faustus must be damned.
O I'll leap up to my God: who pulls me down?
See, see, where Christ's blood streams in the
firmament.
One drop would save my soul, half a drop, ah my
Christ!
Faustus, ibid., Act 5, Sc. 2. The Latin is translated as: 'Run slowly, slowly, horses of the night.'

25 You stars that reigned at my nativity,
Whose influence hath allotted death and hell.
Faustus, ibid., Act 5, Sc. 2

26 O soul, be changed into little water drops,
And fall into the ocean, ne'er be found.
Faustus, ibid., Act 5, Sc. 2

27 I'll burn my books.
Faustus, ibid., Act 5, Sc. 2

28 Cut is the branch that might have grown full
straight,
And burnèd is Apollo's laurel-bough,
That sometime grew within this learned man.
Faustus is gone: regard his hellish fall,
Whose fiendful fortune may exhort the wise
Only to wonder at unlawful things,

Whose deepness doth entice such forward wits
To practise more than heavenly power permits.
Faustus, ibid., Act 5, Sc. 3. Closing lines of play.

Márquez
See García Márquez

Don Marquis
(1878–1937)
US humorist and journalist

Known for his poems, essays and humorous writings, he was the creator in 1927 of archy and mehitabel, a cat and a literary-minded cockroach who debate life's complexities in light verse.

1 A fierce unrest seethes at the core
Of all existing things:
It was the eager wish to soar
That gave the gods their wings.
'Unrest', publ. in *Dreams and Dust* (1915)

2 my youth i shall never forget
but there s nothing i really regret
wotthehell wotthehell
there s a dance in the old dame yet
toujours gai toujours gai
'the song of mehitabel', publ. in *archy and mehitabel* (1927)

3 persian pussy from over the sea
demure and lazy and smug and fat
none of your ribbons and bells for me
ours is the zest of the alley cat
'mehitabel s extensive past', ibid.

4 procrastination is the
art of keeping
up with yesterday
'certain maxims of archy', ibid.

5 an optimist is a guy
who has never had
much experience
'certain maxims of archy', ibid.

6 did you ever
notice that when
a politician
does get an idea
he usually
gets it all wrong
'mehitabel again', publ. in *archys life of mehitabel* (1933)

7 now and then
there is a person born
who is so unlucky

that he runs into accidents
which started out to happen
to somebody else

'archy says', ibid.

8 Bores bore each other too; but it never seems to teach them anything.

Quoted in *A Little Book of Aphorisms* (1947) by Frederic B. Wilcox

9 The art of newspaper paragraphing is to stroke a platitude until it purrs like an epigram.

Ibid. ADLAI STEVENSON adapted this epigram when he quipped: 'The Republicans stroke platitudes until they purr like epigrams' (quoted in *The Fine Art of Political Wit*, ch. 1, 1964 by Leon Harris).

10 Middle age is the time when a man is always thinking that in a week or two he will feel as good as ever.

Ibid.

11 A demagogue is a person with whom we disagree as to which gang should mismanage the country.

Ibid.

12 Writing a book of poetry is like dropping a rose petal down the Grand Canyon and waiting for the echo.

Quoted in *O Rare Don Marquis*, ch. 6 (1962) by E. Anthony. This aphorism emerged as the distillation of what had been a long piece on the futility of writing poetry for Don Marquis's 'Sun Dial' column, which he rejected on the grounds of it being too much a plaint, publishing instead this one sentence.

13 Poetry is what Milton saw when he went blind.

Ibid., ch. 11. 'That line would have pleased Milton himself,' observed the poet Louis Untermeyer.

14 By the time a bartender knows what drink a man will have before he orders, there is little else about him worth knowing.

Ibid., ch. 11. FRANKLIN P. ADAMS cited this aphorism to illustrate Marquis's gift for 'telling a whole story in a sentence'.

Anthony Marriott
(b. 1931)
Alistair Foot
British playwrights

They collaborated on a number of plays, including Uproar in the House *(1967) and* No Sex Please – We're British *(1971), a long-running West End farce.*

1 No Sex Please – We're British.

Title of play (1971)

George C. Marshall
(1880–1959)
US general and politician

Chief of Staff of the US Army during the Second World War, he later served as Democratic Secretary of State (1947–9) and Secretary of Defense (1950–1). The Marshall Plan proposed by him in 1947 underpinned post-war reconstruction in Western Europe.

1 Our policy is directed not against any country or doctrine but against hunger, poverty, desperation and chaos. Its purpose should be the revival of a working economy in the world so as to permit the emergence of political and social conditions in which free institutions can exist.

Speech at Harvard University, 5 June 1947, publ. in *A Decade of American Foreign Policy: Basic Documents* (1950). Announcing the European Recovery Program for recovery in post-war Europe, later known as the Marshall Plan.

Thomas R. Marshall
(1854–1925)
US politician

A Democratic Governor of Indiana (1909–13), he served two terms as Vice-President under WOODROW WILSON *(1913–21).*

1 What this country needs is a really good 5-cent cigar.

Quoted in the *New York Tribune* 4 January 1920

Yann Martel
(b. 1963)
Canadian author

After publishing The Facts Behind the Helsinki Roccamatios *(1993), a collection of short stories, and the novel* Self *(1996), he won acclaim for his second novel* Life of Pi *(2001).*

1 It is not atheists who get stuck in my craw, but agnostics. Doubt is useful for a while. We must all pass through the garden of Gethsemane. If Christ played with doubt, so must we. If Christ spent an anguished night in prayer, if He burst out from the Cross, 'My God, my God, why have you forsaken me?' then surely we are also permitted doubt. But we must move on. To choose doubt as a philosophy of life is akin to choosing immobility as a means of transportation.

Life of Pi, pt 1, ch. 7 (2001). Narrated by Pi.

José Martí
(1853–95)
Cuban poet, essayist and patriot

Jose Julián Martí y Pérez. His poetry and essays established him as an original modernist writer, and voiced his zeal for Cuban independence. He co-founded the Cuban Revolutionary Party in New York and was killed during the final Cuban insurrection against Spain.

1 Let those who desire a secure homeland conquer it. Let those who do not conquer it live under the whip and in exile, watched over like wild animals, cast from one country to another, concealing the death of their souls with a beggar's smile from the scorn of free men.
Obras Completas, vol. 3, 'April 1894' (1963)

2 It is my duty to prevent, through the independence of Cuba, the USA from spreading over the West Indies and falling with added weight upon other lands of Our America. All I have done up to now and shall do hereafter is to that end ... I know the Monster, because I have lived in its lair – and my weapon is only the slingshot of David.
Letter, 18 May 1895, publ. ibid., vol. 4, 'May 1895'. This was Martí's last letter; he was killed in an ambush the following day.

Martial
(c. 40–c. 103)
Roman poet

Marcus Valerius Martialis. Born in Spain, he settled in Rome in 64, where he earned a living by his vivid portrayals of Roman society in witty, sometimes bawdy epigrams.

1 My page is wanton, but my life is virtuous.
Epigrams, bk 1, no. 4

2 Believe me, the wise man does not say 'I shall live'. Tomorrow's life is too late. Live today.
Ibid., bk 1, no. 15

3 I like you not, Sabidius, and I can't tell why. All I can tell is this: I like you not.
Ibid., bk 1, no. 32. See THOMAS BROWN 1.

4 Better that the blemish, perhaps a trifling one, be frankly shown. Trouble concealed is believed to be greater than it is.
Ibid., bk 3, no. 42

5 I could do without your face and neck and hands and legs and breasts and buttocks and hips and (not to be at the trouble of going through particulars) I could do without you, Chloe, in your entirety.
Ibid., bk 3, no. 53

6 So how does the virtuous girl behave? She doesn't do it. She doesn't say no.
Ibid., bk 4, no. 71

7 We feel our good days slip away and leave us; they are wasted and put to our account.
Ibid., bk 5, no. 20

8 Be not heavy upon her, earth; she was not heavy upon you.
Ibid., bk 5, no. 34. Referring to the death of a little girl of six, and parodied in an epitaph penned for JOHN VANBRUGH: 'Lie heavy on him, earth! for he/Laid many heavy loads on thee.'

9 Life is not being alive, but being well.
Ibid., bk 6, no. 70

10 You are difficult and easy, pleasant and sour; and I can't live with you nor yet without you.
Ibid., bk 12, no. 46

11 *Rus in urbe.*
[The country in the town.]
Ibid., bk 12, no. 57

Strother Martin
(1919–80)
US screen actor

He played character parts on television and in numerous films from the 1950s, such as the westerns True Grit *and* Butch Cassidy and the Sundance Kid *(both 1969).*

1 What we've got here is a failure to communicate.
Cool Hand Luke (film, 1967, screenplay and original novel by Donn Pearce, directed by Stuart Rosenberg). Spoken by the Camp Commandant (Strother Martin). The words appeared as the film's publicity tag-line.

Harriet Martineau
(1802–76)
English author and journalist

Her popular works on religion, politics and economics attracted a wide readership. She expressed her feminist and anti-slavery views in Society in America *(1837) and in numerous articles. Her* Autobiographical Memoir *(1877) includes sketches of her literary contemporaries.*

1 If a test of civilisation be sought, none can be so

sure as the condition of that half of society over which the other half has power.
Society in America, pt 3, ch. 2 (1837)

2 Religion is a temper, not a pursuit.
Ibid., pt 3, ch. 2

3 The sum and substance of female education in America, as in England, is training women to consider marriage as the sole object in life, and to pretend that they do not think so.
Ibid., pt 3, ch. 2

4 Laws and customs may be creative of vice; and should be therefore perpetually under process of observation and correction: but laws and customs cannot be creative of virtue: they may encourage and help to preserve it; but they cannot originate it.
Ibid., pt 3, ch. 2, sect. 1

5 Readers are plentiful: thinkers are rare.
Ibid., pt 3, ch. 2, sect. 2. Referring to American ladies.

Andrew Marvell
(1621–78)
English poet

A leading wit and satirist of his time, he is most admired for his metaphysical verse, notably 'To His Coy Mistress', and pastoral poems such as 'The Garden'. His 'Horatian Ode' to OLIVER CROMWELL *(1650) expressed his qualified support for the Parliamentary cause. He was a Member of Parliament from 1659.*

1 He nothing common did, or mean,
Upon the memorable scene:
But with his keener eye
The axe's edge did try:
Nor called the gods with vulgar spite
To vindicate his helpless right,
But bowed his comely head,
Down, as upon a bed.
'An Horatian Ode upon Cromwell's Return from Ireland', ll. 57–64, written 1650, publ. in *Miscellaneous Poems* (1681). Referring to CHARLES I at his execution.

2 So much one man can do,
That does both act and know.
'An Horatian Ode upon Cromwell's Return from Ireland', ll. 75–6, ibid.

3 Had we but world enough, and time,
This coyness, lady, were no crime.
'To His Coy Mistress', ll. 1–2, written *c.* 1650, ibid.

4 But at my back I always hear
Time's wingèd chariot hurrying near:

And yonder all before us lie
Deserts of vast eternity.
'To His Coy Mistress', ll. 21–4, ibid.

5 Thy beauty shall no more be found;
Nor, in thy marble vault, shall sound
My echoing song; then worms shall try
That long preserved virginity:
And your quaint honour turn to dust;
And into ashes all my lust.
'To His Coy Mistress', ll. 25–30, ibid.

6 The grave's a fine and private place,
But none I think do there embrace.
'To His Coy Mistress', ll. 31–2, ibid.

7 Let us roll all our strength, and all
Our sweetness, up into one ball:
And tear our pleasures with rough strife,
Thorough the iron gates of life.
Thus, though we cannot make our sun
Stand still, yet we will make him run.
'To His Coy Mistress', ll. 41–6, ibid. Closing lines.

8 My love is of a birth as rare
As 'tis for object strange and high:
It was begotten by despair
Upon impossibility.
'The Definition of Love', st. 1, written 1651–2, ibid.

9 While all flowers and all trees do close
To weave the garlands of repose.
'The Garden', st. 1, written 1651–2, ibid.

10 Society is all but rude,
To this delicious solitude.
'The Garden', st. 2, ibid.

11 What wondrous life in this I lead!
Ripe apples drop about my head;
The luscious clusters of the vine
Upon my mouth do crush their wine;
The nectarine, and curious peach,
Into my hands themselves do reach;
Stumbling on melons, as I pass,
Ensnared with flowers, I fall on grass.
'The Garden', st. 5, ibid.

12 The mind, that ocean where each kind
Does straight its own resemblance find;
Yet it creates, transcending these,
Far other worlds, and other seas.
'The Garden', st. 6, ibid.

13 Annihilating all that's made
To a green thought in a green shade.
'The Garden', st. 6, ibid.

14 Two Paradises 'twere in one,
To live in Paradise alone.
'The Garden', st. 8, ibid.

15 So the soul, that drop, that ray
Of the clear fountain of eternal day,
Could it within the human flower be seen,
Remembering still its former height,
Shuns the sweet leaves and blossoms green;
And, recollecting its own light,
Does, in its pure and circling thoughts, express
The greater heaven in an heaven less.
'On a Drop of Dew', ll. 19–26, written 1651–2, ibid.

16 So of translators they are authors grown,
For ill translators make the book their own.
Others do strive with words and forced phrase
To add such lustre, and so many rays,
That but to make the vessel shining, they
Much of the precious metal rub away.
He is translation's thief that addeth more,
As much as he that taketh from the store
Of the first author.
'To His Worthy Friend Doctor Witty', st. 5, written 1651–2, ibid.

17 'Tis not, what once it was, the world;
But a rude heap together hurled;
All negligently overthrown,
Gulfs, deserts, precipices, stone.
'Upon Appleton House', st. 96, written 1651–2, ibid.

18 Where the remote Bermudas ride
In th' ocean's bosom unespied.
'Bermudas', ll. 1–2, written c. 1653, ibid.

19 The wanton troopers riding by
Have shot my fawn and it will die.
Ungentle men! They cannot thrive
To kill thee. Thou ne'er didst alive
Them any harm: alas, nor could
Thy death yet do them any good.
'The Nymph Complaining for the Death of her Fawn', ll. 1–6, ibid.

20 Self-preservation, nature's first great law,
All the creatures, except man, doth awe.
'Hodge's Vision', publ. in *A Collection of Poems on Affairs of State* (1689). The poem is attributed to Marvell, but may have been the work of a contemporary.

Holt Marvell
See ERIC MASCHWITZ

Groucho Marx
(1895–1977)
US comic actor

Originally Julius Marx. The most garrulous of the Marx Brothers, he was famous for his cigar, sloping walk and caustic asides. In the opinion of S. J. PERELMAN, *'The man was a major comedian, which is to say that he had the compassion of an icicle, the effrontery of a carnival shill and the generosity of a pawnbroker.'*

1 I hope all your teeth have cavities, and don't forget; abscess makes the heart grow fonder.
The Cocoanuts (film, 1929, screenplay by Morrie Ryskind based on the play by GEORGE KAUFMAN and IRVING BERLIN, directed by Robert Florey and Joseph Santley). Spoken by Hammer (Groucho Marx).

2 One morning I shot an elephant in my pajamas. How he got into my pajamas I'll never know.
Animal Crackers (film, 1930, screenplay by Morrie Ryskind based on a musical by Morrie Ryskind and GEORGE KAUFMAN, directed by Victor Heerman). Spoken by Capt Jeffrey Spaulding (Groucho Marx).

3 That's what I always say. Love flies out the door when money comes innuendo.
Monkey Business (film, 1931, screenplay by Arthur Sheekman based on a story by S. J. PERELMAN, W. B. Johnstone and Roland Pertwee, directed by Norman McLeod). The words of Groucho as himself.

4 Oh, why can't we break away from all this, just you and I, and lodge with my fleas in the hills? I mean, flee to my lodge in the hills.
Ibid.

5 Oh, I realize it's a penny here and a penny there, but look at me: I've worked myself up from nothing to a state of extreme poverty.
Ibid.

6 Remember, you're fighting for this woman's honor, which is probably more than she ever did.
Duck Soup (film, 1933, screenplay by Bert Kalmar, Arthur Sheekman, Nat Perrin and Harry Ruby, directed by Leo McCarey). Referring to Mrs Teasdale (Margaret Dumont). Spoken by Rufus T. Firefly (Groucho Marx).

7 Either he's dead or my watch has stopped.
A Day at the Races (film, 1937, screenplay by Robert Pirosh, George Seaton and George Oppenheimer, directed by Sam Wood). Spoken by Dr Hackenbush (Groucho Marx).

8 Emily, I've a little confession to make. I really am a horse doctor. But marry me, and I'll never look at another horse.
Ibid. Dr Hackenbush proposes to Mrs Upjohn (Margaret Dumont).

9 Please accept my resignation. I don't want to belong to any club that will accept me as a member.
Groucho And Me, ch. 26 (1959)

10 From the moment I picked your book up until I laid it down I was convulsed with laughter. Someday I intend reading it.
Quoted in *Life* 9 February 1962. Referring to *Dawn Ginsbergh's Revenge* by S. J. PERELMAN.

11 I never forget a face, but in your case I'll be glad to make an exception.
Quoted in *People I Have Loved, Known or Admired*, 'Groucho', sect. 2 (1970) by LEO ROSTEN

12 I find television very educational. Every time someone switches it on I go into another room and read a good book.
Quoted in *Halliwell's Filmgoer's Companion* (1984)

13 I've been around so long I can remember Doris Day before she was a virgin.
Attributed in *Halliwell's Who's Who in the Movies* (ed. John Walker, 1999)

Harpo Marx
(1888–1964)
US comic actor

Originally Adolph Marx. The silent member of the Marx Brothers, he took his stage-name from the harp he played. His main props were a red wig and an oversized coat holding bizarre bric-a-brac.

1 Join the Army and See the Navy.
Duck Soup (film, 1933, screenplay by Bert Kalmar, Arthur Sheekman, Nat Perrin and Harry Ruby, directed by Leo McCarey). Sign paraded by Brownie (Harpo Marx).

Karl Marx
(1818–83)
German political theorist and social philosopher

Hugely influential in the fields of history, sociology and economics, he developed the theory of dialectical materialism to explain historical and economic cycles. With FRIEDRICH ENGELS, *he established the basis of Marxism in* The German Ideology *(1846) and* The Communist Manifesto *(1848). His monumental work,* Capital *(1867–94), was completed after his death from his notes by Engels.*

1 Religion is the sigh of the oppressed creature, the heart of a heartless world, just as it is the spirit of spiritless conditions. It is the *opium* of the people.
A Contribution to the Critique of Hegel's Philosophy of Right, Preface (1844), repr. in *Karl Marx and Friedrich Engels: Collected Works*, vol. 3 (ed. Jack Cohen, *et al.*, 1975). The formulation has been paraphrased many times, including by Edmund Wilson in *Letters on Literature and Politics* (1977), 'Marxism is the opium of the intellectuals,' and the psychiatrist THOMAS SZASZ in *The Second Sin* (1973), 'In the United States today, opiates are the religion of the people.' See also CHARLES KINGSLEY 1 and MILAN KUNDERA 1.

2 The philosophers have only *interpreted* the world in various ways; the point is to *change* it.
Theses on Feuerbach, no. 11, written 1845, publ. 1888, ibid., vol. 5 (1976). The observation also appeared in *The German Ideology* (written 1845–6), written with FRIEDRICH ENGELS, and was inscribed as an epitaph on Marx's tomb in Highgate Cemetery, London.

3 We should not say that one man's hour is worth another man's hour, but rather that one man during an hour is worth just as much as another man during an hour. Time is everything, man is nothing: he is at the most time's carcass.
The Poverty of Philosophy, ch. 1, sect. 2 (1847), ibid., vol. 9

4 Machines were, it may be said, the weapon employed by the capitalists to quell the revolt of specialized labour.
The Poverty of Philosophy, ch. 2, sect. 5, ibid., vol. 9

5 As for myself, I do not claim to have discovered either the existence of classes in modern society or the struggle between them. Long before me, bourgeois historians had described the historical development of this struggle between the classes, as had bourgeois economists their economic anatomy. My own contribution was 1. to show that the existence of classes is merely bound up with certain historical phases in the development of production; 2. that the class struggle necessarily leads to the dictatorship of the proletariat; 3. that this dictatorship itself constitutes no more than a transition to the abolition of all classes and to a classless society.
Letter, 5 March 1852, ibid., vol. 39 (1983)

6 Hegel remarks somewhere that all facts and personages of great importance in world history occur, as it were, twice. He forgot to add: the first time as tragedy, the second as farce.
The Eighteenth Brumaire of Louis Bonaparte, pt 1 (1852), repr. in *Selected Works*, vol. 2 (1942). This opening sentence is usually misquoted: 'History repeats itself, first as tragedy, second

as farce.' Numerous variations on the theme have been offered, including: 'History repeats itself. Historians repeat each other', ascribed to 'Quintilian or Max Beerbohm' by PHILIP GUEDALLA in *Supers and Supermen*, 'Some Historians' (1920), and the anonymous quip, 'Every time history repeats itself the price goes up.'

7 Men make their own history, but they do not make it just as they please; they do not make it under circumstances chosen by themselves, but under circumstances directly encountered, given and transmitted from the past. The tradition of all the dead generations weighs like a nightmare on the brain of the living.
The Eighteenth Brumaire of Louis Bonaparte, pt 1, ibid., vol. 2

8 The human being is in the most literal sense a political animal, not merely a gregarious animal, but an animal which can individuate itself only in the midst of society.
Grundrisse, Notebook M, sect. 1, written 1857–8, publ. in *Karl Marx and Friedrich Engels: Collected Works*, vol. 28 (1986). See ARISTOTLE 15.

9 Society does not consist of individuals but expresses the sum of interrelations, the relations within which these individuals stand.
Grundrisse, Notebook 2, ibid., vol. 29 (1987). See MARGARET THATCHER 15.

10 The country that is more developed industrially only shows, to the less developed, the image of its own future.
Das Kapital, vol. 1, Preface (1867; *Capital*)

11 A commodity appears at first sight an extremely obvious, trivial thing. But its analysis brings out that it is a very strange thing, abounding in metaphysical subtleties and theological niceties.
Ibid., vol. 1, ch. 1

12 All social rules and all relations between individuals are eroded by a cash economy, avarice drags Pluto himself out of the bowels of the earth.
Ibid., vol. 1, ch. 3

13 While the miser is merely a capitalist gone mad, the capitalist is a rational miser.
Ibid., vol. 1, ch. 4

14 Capital is dead labour, which, vampire-like, lives only by sucking living labour, and lives the more, the more labour it sucks.
Ibid., vol. 1, ch. 10

15 Labour in a white skin cannot emancipate itself where it is branded in a black skin.
Ibid., vol. 1, ch. 10

16 On a level plain, simple mounds look like hills; and the insipid flatness of our present bourgeoisie is to be measured by the altitude of its 'great intellects'.
Ibid., vol. 1, ch. 16

17 The English have all the *material* necessary for the social revolution. What they lack is the *spirit of generalization* and *revolutionary ardour*.
'Confidential Communication on Bakunin', circular letter, 1 January 1870, publ. in *Karl Marx and Friedrich Engels: Collected Works*, vol. 21 (1985)

18 In a higher phase of communist society . . . only then can the narrow horizon of bourgeois right be crossed in its entirety and society inscribe on its banners: from each according to his ability, to each according to his needs!
Critique of the Gotha Programme, sect. 1, written 1875, publ. 1891, repr. ibid., vol. 24 (1989). The concluding phrase is believed to be quoting either the journalist Louis Blanc or Morelly, writer of *Code de la Nature* (1755).

19 All I know is that I am not a Marxist.
Quoted by FRIEDRICH ENGELS in letter, 5 August 1890, publ. in *Correspondence of Marx and Engels, 1846–95* (ed. V. Adoratsky, 1936). Engels had earlier quoted the same remark in French ('*Ce qu'il y a de certain, c'est que moi je ne suis pas Marxiste*') in a letter 2–3 November 1882, recalling Marx's words to his son-in-law, French socialist Paul Lafargue, when he rejected the French 'Marxists' of the late 1870s.

Karl Marx
(1818–83)
Friedrich Engels
(1820–95)
German political theorists and social philosophers

Collaborators from 1844, they established the fundamental principles of Communist doctrine in their works, which were written mainly in England. See also FRIEDRICH ENGELS *and* KARL MARX.

1 History does nothing; it does not possess immense riches, it does not fight battles. It is men, real, living, who do all this . . . History is nothing but the activity of men in pursuit of their ends.
The Holy Family (1845)

2 We know only a single science, the science of history. One can look at history from two sides and divide it into the history of nature and the history

of men. The two sides are, however, inseparable; the history of nature and the history of men are dependent on each other so long as men exist.

The German Ideology, vol. 1, pt 1, sect. 1, footnote, written 1845–6, publ. in *Karl Marx and Friedrich Engels: Collected Works*, vol. 5 (ed. Jack Cohen, et al, 1976). The note was crossed out in the finished version of the work.

3 In communist society, where nobody has one exclusive sphere of activity but each can become accomplished in any branch he wishes, society regulates the general production and thus makes it possible for me to do one thing today and another tomorrow, to hunt in the morning, fish in the afternoon, rear cattle in the evening, criticize after dinner, just as I have a mind, without ever becoming hunter, fisherman, shepherd or critic.

The German Ideology, vol. 1, pt 2, sect. 4, ibid., vol. 5. Marx later abandoned this attempt to reconcile the conflicting doctrines of the abolition of the division of labour and the necessity of highly developed forms of production.

4 The ideas of the ruling class are in every epoch the ruling ideas, i.e. the class which is the ruling *material* force of society, is at the same time its ruling *intellectual* force.

The German Ideology, ibid., vol. 1, pt 3, sect. 1, ibid., vol. 5. The dictum was reiterated in *The Communist Manifesto*, pt 2 (1848).

5 Philosophy stands in the same relation to the study of the actual world as masturbation to sexual love.

The German Ideology, pt 2, ibid.

6 A spectre is haunting Europe – the spectre of Communism.

The Communist Manifesto, pt 1 (1848). Opening sentence.

7 The history of all hitherto existing society is the history of class struggles.

Ibid., pt 1

8 The bourgeoisie ... has been the first to show what man's activity can bring about. It has accomplished wonders far surpassing Egyptian pyramids, Roman aqueducts and Gothic cathedrals ... The bourgeoisie ... draws all, even the most barbarian nations into civilization ... It has created enormous cities ... and has thus rescued a considerable part of the population from the idiocy of rural life ... The bourgeoisie, during its rule of scarce one hundred years, has created more massive and more colossal

productive forces than have all preceding generations together.

Ibid., pt 1

9 The theory of the Communists may be summed up in the single sentence: Abolition of private property.

Ibid., pt 2

10 Let the ruling classes tremble at a communist revolution. The proletarians have nothing to lose but their chains. They have a world to win. Working-men of all countries, unite!

Ibid., pt 4. These closing words are commonly rendered: 'Workers of the world unite, you have nothing to lose but your chains!'

Mary I (Mary Tudor)
(1516–58)
Queen of England

The daughter of HENRY VIII *and Catharine of Aragon, she was a fervent Catholic who, following her accession in 1553, reversed the pro-Reformation policies of her predecessors. Her persecution of Protestants led to her becoming known as 'Bloody Mary' during her own lifetime.*

1 When I am dead and opened, you shall find 'Calais' lying in my heart.

Quoted in *Chronicles of England, Scotland, and Ireland*, vol. 4 (1587, 1808 edn) by Raphael Holinshed. The French capture of Calais in 1558, a town that had been held by England since 1346 and was its last toehold on the European mainland, contributed to Mary's unpopularity among her subjects. See ROBERT BROWNING 40.

Mary, Queen of Scots
(1542–87)
Queen of Scotland

Mary Stuart, or Stewart. Succeeding to the Scottish throne when just six days old, she was raised in France where she married the Dauphin, later Francis II (1558). She returned to Scotland in 1561, but was deposed (1567) and subsequently imprisoned by ELIZABETH I *from 1568 until her execution.*

1 No more tears now; I will think upon revenge.

Remark after hearing of the murder of her favourite David Riccio, 9 March 1566, quoted in *Mary Queen of Scots*, ch. 14 (1969) by Antonia Fraser. Most of the conspirators were eventually killed, including Mary's husband Lord Darnley in 1567.

2 *En ma fin est mon commencement.*

[In my end is my beginning.]

Motto embroidered (probably by her) while in captivity at Tutbury, Staffordshire, 1569, ibid., ch. 21. See T. S. ELIOT 46.

Eric Maschwitz
(1901–69)
British songwriter and author

One of the most prominent and prolific writers for musical theatre from the 1930s to the mid-1950s, he wrote operettas, screenplays and novels. He worked at the BBC from 1926.

1 Oh, how the ghost of you clings –
These foolish things remind me of you.

'These Foolish Things Remind Me of You' (song, 1936, with music by Jack Strachey and Harry Link). Written under his pseudonym, Holt Marvell.

2 A Nightingale Sang in Berkeley Square.

Title of song, with music by Manning Sherwin, in *New Faces* (musical revue, 1940)

John Masefield
(1878–1967)
British poet and playwright

After working as a sailor and a journalist, he gained fame with the poetry collections Salt-Water Ballads *(1902). His long narrative poems include* The Everlasting Mercy *(1911), and he also wrote plays and novels. He was Poet Laureate from 1930.*

1 I must down to the seas again, to the lonely sea and the sky,
And all I ask is a tall ship and a star to steer her by,
And the wheel's kick and the wind's song and the white sail's shaking,
And a grey mist on the sea's face and a grey dawn breaking.

'Sea Fever', st. 1, publ. in *Salt-Water Ballads* (1902). The line appears as 'I must go down to the sea again . . .' in some collections, and in John Ireland's musical setting of the poem, though apparently not in Masefield's drafts, nor in the first published version.

2 I must down to the seas again for the call of the running tide
Is a wild call and a clear call that may not be denied.

'Sea Fever', st. 2, ibid.

3 I must down to the seas again, to the vagrant gypsy life,
To the gull's way and the whale's way where the wind's like a whetted knife;
And all I ask is a merry yarn from a laughing fellow-rover,

And quiet sleep and a sweet dream when the long trick's over.

'Sea Fever', st. 3, ibid.

4 Dirty British coaster with a salt-caked smoke stack,
Butting through the Channel in the mad March days,
With a cargo of Tyne coal,
Road-rails, pig lead,
Firewood, ironware, and cheap tin trays.

'Cargoes', st. 3, publ. in *Ballads* (1903)

5 Commonplace people dislike tragedy because they dare not suffer and cannot exult.

The Tragedy of Nan, Preface (1908)

6 But to see him, the town's disgrace,
With God's commandments broke in's face.

The Everlasting Mercy, ll. 1247–8 (1911)

Philip Massinger
(1583–1640)
English dramatist

Associated from 1613 with the King's Men, the leading theatre company of the day, he was a prolific writer of histories, satirical comedies and tragedies, either on his own, as in A New Way to Pay Old Debts *(c. 1622), or in collaboration with* THOMAS DEKKER, JOHN FLETCHER *and others.*

1 Patience, the beggar's virtue,
Shall find no harbour here.

A New Way To Pay Old Debts, Act 5, Sc. 1 (c. 1622). Spoken by Sir Giles Overreach, 'a cruel extortioner'.

2 He that would govern others, first should be
The master of himself.

The Bondman, Act 1, Sc. 3 (1623). Spoken by Timoleon.

3 And what, in a mean man, I should call folly,
Is in your majesty remarkable wisdom.

The Picture, Act 1, Sc. 2 (1630). Spoken by Eubulus, adviser to the King Ladislaus of Hungary.

4 Death has a thousand doors to let out life,
I shall find one . . . From a loathed life,
I'll not an hour outlive.

A Very Woman, Act 5, Sc. 4 (1634). Spoken by Almera. This image of death was a common one, also used by Massinger in *The Custom of the Country* (co-written with JOHN FLETCHER); see also SENECA 19 and JOHN WEBSTER 21.

Edgar Lee Masters
(1868–1950)
US poet and novelist

The publication of Spoon River Anthology *(1915), a volume of free verse epitaphs in which the occupants of a small-town cemetery narrate their lives, placed him in the vanguard of Chicago's literary renaissance.*

1 Where are Elmer, Herman, Bert, Tom and
   Charley,
The weak of will, the strong of arm, the clown, the
   boozer, the fighter?
All, all, are sleeping on the hill.
'The Hill', publ. in *Spoon River Anthology* (1915)

Cotton Mather
(1663–1728)
Congregational minister and author

Ordained in 1685, he became one of the most celebrated of New England's Puritan ministers. He wrote more than four hundred books, most notably Magnalia Christi Americana *(1702), an ecclesiastical history of America.*

1 I write the wonders of the Christian religion, flying from the depravations of Europe, to the American strand; and, assisted by the Holy Author of that religion, I do with all conscience of truth, required therein by Him, who is the Truth itself, report the wonderful displays of His infinite power, wisdom, goodness, and faithfulness, wherewith His Divine Providence hath irradiated an Indian Wilderness.
Magnalia Christi Americana, 'A General Introduction' (1702). Opening sentence.

Henri Matisse
(1869–1954)
French artist

A leading post-impressionist and Fauvist painter, his work was characterized by sinuous lines and flamboyant colour, as in Portrait of Madame Matisse *(1905) and* The Dance *(1910). He studied and worked in Paris, living in the French Riviera from the 1920s.*

1 You study, you learn, but you guard the original naïveté. It has to be within you, as desire for drink is within the drunkard or love is within the lover.
Quoted in *Time* 26 June 1950

2 There is nothing more difficult for a truly creative painter than to paint a rose, because before he can do so he has first to forget all the roses that were ever painted.
Comment recalled in obituaries, 5 November 1954

W. Somerset Maugham
(1874–1965)
British author

William Somerset Maugham. He first achieved success as a playwright in 1907, and went on to write essays and short stories, but was most successful as a novelist. His most popular works include Of Human Bondage *(1915),* Cakes and Ale *(1930) and* The Razor's Edge *(1944).*

1 Anyone can tell the truth, but only very few of us can make epigrams.
Entry, 1896, in *A Writer's Notebook* (1949). 'In the nineties, however,' Maugham added, 'we all tried to.'

2 Few misfortunes can befall a boy which bring worse consequences than to have a really affectionate mother.
Entry, 1896, ibid.

3 I can imagine no more comfortable frame of mind for the conduct of life than a humorous resignation.
Entry, 1902, ibid.

4 Like all weak men he laid an exaggerated stress on not changing one's mind.
Of Human Bondage, ch. 39 (1915). Referring to the Vicar of Blackstable.

5 Money is like a sixth sense without which you cannot make a complete use of the other five.
Monsieur Foinet, ibid., ch. 51

6 Impropriety is the soul of wit.
The Moon and Sixpence, ch. 4 (1919). See WILLIAM SHAKESPEARE: HAMLET 58.

7 It is not true that suffering ennobles the character; happiness does that sometimes, but suffering, for the most part, makes men petty and vindictive.
Ibid., ch. 17. Maugham used almost identical words to describe the suffering he witnessed as a medical student, in *The Summing Up*, ch. 19 (1938).

8 The ideal has many names, and beauty is but one of them.
Cakes and Ale, ch. 11 (1930)

9 From the earliest times the old have rubbed it into the young that they are wiser than they, and before the young had discovered what nonsense this was they were old too, and it profited them to carry on the imposture.
Ashenden, ibid., ch. 11

10 Poor Henry, he's spending eternity wandering round and round a stately park and the fence is just too high for him to peep over and they're having tea just too far away for him to hear what the countess is saying.

Ibid., ch. 11. Edward Driffield referring to HENRY JAMES, who, he said, 'had turned his back on one of the great events of the world's history, the rise of the United States, in order to report tittle-tattle at tea parties in English country houses'. In a notebook entry in 1937, Maugham wrote of James: 'He did not live, he observed life from a window, and too often was inclined to content himself with no more than what his friends told him they saw when *they* looked out of a window.'

11 Every production of an artist should be the expression of an adventure of his soul.

The Summing Up, ch. 48 (1938)

12 The common idea that success spoils people by making them vain, egotistic, and self-complacent is erroneous; on the contrary, it makes them, for the most part, humble, tolerant, and kind. Failure makes people cruel and bitter.

Ibid., ch. 48

13 There is no explanation for evil. It must be looked upon as a necessary part of the order of the universe. To ignore it is childish, to bewail it senseless.

Ibid., ch. 73

14 Sentimentality is only sentiment that rubs you up the wrong way.

Entry, 1941, in *A Writer's Notebook* (1949)

15 I made up my mind long ago that life was too short to do anything for myself that I could pay others to do for me.

Entry, 1941, ibid.

16 I am told that today rather more than 60 per cent of the men who go to university go on a Government grant. This is a new class that has entered upon the scene. It is the white-collar proletariat ... They do not go to university to acquire culture but to get a job, and when they have got one, scamp it. They have no manners and are woefully unable to deal with any social predicament. Their idea of a celebration is to go to a public house and drink six beers. They are mean, malicious and envious ... They are scum.

Sunday Times 25 December 1955. Referring to the generation of 'Angry Young Men' as portrayed in KINGSLEY AMIS's 1954 novel *Lucky Jim*. These people, Maugham continued, 'will in due course leave the university. Some will doubtless sink back, perhaps with relief, into the modest social class from which they emerged; some will take to drink, some to crime

and go to prison ... A few will go into Parliament, become Cabinet Ministers and rule the country. I look upon myself as fortunate that I shall not live to see it.'

17 The crown of literature is poetry. It is its end and aim. It is the sublimest activity of the human mind. It is the achievement of beauty and delicacy. The writer of prose can only step aside when the poet passes.

Saturday Review 20 July 1957

Guy de Maupassant
(1850–93)
French author

He made his name with his short stories, publishing some three hundred between 1880 and 1890. He also wrote novels and travel sketches.

1 Great artists are those who impose their particular illusion on humanity.

Pierre et Jean, Preface (1888)

Armistead Maupin
(b. 1944)
US journalist and author

He is best known for the six-novel sequence Tales of the City *(1978–90), a sympathetic portrait of gay life in San Francisco.* The Night Listener *was published in 2000.*

1 Too much of a good thing is wonderful.

More Tales of the City, 'The Road to Ruin' (1980). Motto inscribed on a brass plaque outside the Pinus club.

2 I think a lot of gay people who are not dealing with their homosexuality get into right-wing politics.

Guardian 22 April 1988

André Maurois
(1885–1967)
French author and critic

Born Émile Salomon Wilhelm Herzog. A prominent man of letters for fifty years, he wrote such novels as The Thought Reading Machine *(1938) as well as histories, essays and fictionalized biographies, for example* Ariel *(1923), a life of* SHELLEY.

1 Self-pity comes so naturally to all of us, that the most solid happiness can be shaken by the compassion of a fool.

Ariel, ch. 16 (1923)

2 A successful marriage is an edifice that must be rebuilt every day.
The Art of Living, 'The Art of Marriage' (1940)

3 Growing old is no more than a bad habit which a busy man has no time to form.
Ibid., 'The Art of Growing Old'. 'The true evil,' Maurois wrote, 'is not the weakening of the body, but the indifference of the soul.'

4 Style [is] the hallmark of a temperament stamped on the material in hand.
The Art of Writing, 'The Writer's Craft', sect. 2 (1960)

5 A great biography should, like the close of a great drama, leave behind it a feeling of serenity. We collect into a small bunch the flowers, the few flowers, which brought sweetness into a life, and present it as an offering to an accomplished destiny.
Ibid., 'The Writer's Craft', sect. 5

Robert Maxwell
(1923–91)
Czech-born British publisher

Originally Jan Ludvik Hoch. He had worldwide business interests and in Britain was Chairman of the Mirror Group from 1984. Following his mysterious death at sea, it emerged that he had siphoned money from employee pension funds to offset business losses.

1 It's the editors who interfere in the publisher's prerogative, not the other way round.
Said in July 1985, quoted in *Maxwell: The Outsider*, ch. 13 (1988, rev. 1991) by Tom Bower. Referring to his relations with Mirror Group Newspapers.

2 Ordinary people may not understand the meaning of democracy but they've a passionate regard for fair play.
Quoted in *Maxwell*, ch. 1 (1988) by Joe Haines

3 When I fire someone it is like a thunderclap. My primary duty is to hire and fire editors. I treat them like a Field Marshal.
Independent 13 May 1990

4 When I pass a belt, I can't resist hitting below it.
International Herald Tribune 18 March 1991

Vladimir Mayakovsky
(1893–1930)
Russian poet and dramatist

A founder of the Russian Futurist movement, he embraced the Bolshevik cause with 'Ode to Revolution' (1918), and with his play 150,000,000 (1920). Five years after he took his own life,

STALIN *declared that 'indifference to his memory and works is a crime'.*

1 No grey hair in my soul
no doddering tenderness.
I rock the world with the thunder of my voice,
strolling, looking good –
twenty-two.
'The Cloud in Trousers', Prologue, st. 2 (1915), repr. in *Russian Poetry: the Modern Period* (ed. John Glad and Daniel Weissbort, 1978)

2 Or if you prefer,
as the sky changes tone,
I'll be absolutely tender,
not a man, but a cloud in trousers.
'The Cloud in Trousers', Prologue, st. 6, ibid.

3 Too slow the wagon of years,
The oxen of days – too glum.
Our god is the god of speed,
Our heart – our battle drum.
'Our March', written 1917, publ. in *Selected Verse*, vol. 1 (1985)

4 Comrade life,
let us
march faster,
March
faster through what's left
of the five-year plan.
'At the top of my voice', st. 3, written 1929–30, repr. in *Twentieth-Century Russian Poetry* (ed. Albert C. Todd and Max Hayward, 1993)

5 My verse
has brought me
no roubles to spare:
no craftsmen have made
mahogany chairs for my house.
'At the top of my voice', st. 4, ibid.

6 The ship of love has foundered on life's reef.
You and I are even. And why should we list
our mutual grievances, our hurts, our griefs?
See how still the world has grown.
Unfinished poem in letter, written 12 April 1930, ibid. Mayakovsky's last poem was found in his papers after his suicide.

Curtis Mayfield
(b. 1942)
US singer and songwriter

After eleven years leading the gospel-influenced soul group the Impressions, he had solo hits with 'Move On Up' (1970) and his soundtrack to the film Superfly *(1972).*

1 People get ready
There's a train a-coming
You don't need no baggage
You just get on board.
'People Get Ready' (song, 1964) by the Impressions

Giuseppe Mazzini
(1805–72)
Italian nationalist

A leading figure in Italy's Risorgimento, he founded the revolutionary society Young Italy (1832) and participated in the political ferment of 1848 and in the Roman Republic of 1849. He remained a republican throughout his life.

1 The republic . . . means association, a new philosophy of life, a divine ideal that shall move the world, the only means of regeneration vouchsafed to the human race.
Faith and the Future, sect. 1 (1835), repr. in *Essays by Joseph Mazzini* (ed. Bolton King, 1894)

2 The theory of *rights* enables us to rise and overthrow obstacles, but not to found a strong and lasting accord between all the elements which compose the nation.
The Duties of Man, ch. 1 (1844–58, transl. 1907)

3 Without country you have neither name, token, voice, nor rights, no admission as brothers into the fellowship of the peoples. You are the bastards of humanity. Soldiers without a banner, Israelites among the nations, you will find neither faith nor protection; none will be sureties for you. Do not beguile yourselves with the hope of emancipation from unjust social conditions if you do not first conquer a country for yourselves.
Ibid., ch. 5

4 A country is not a mere territory; the particular territory is only its foundation. The country is the idea which rises upon that foundation; it is the sentiment of love, the sense of fellowship which binds together all the sons of that territory.
Ibid., ch. 5

5 God has given you your country as cradle, and humanity as mother; you cannot rightly love your brethren of the cradle if you love not the common mother.
'Address to the Memory of the Martyrs of Cosenza', speech, 25 July 1848, Milan, publ. in *Life and Writings of Joseph Mazzini*, vol. 5 (1891)

Margaret Mead
(1901–78)
US anthropologist

Described by JACOB BRONOWSKI *as 'splendidly sensible', she popularized anthropology, notably with the classic* Coming of Age in Samoa *(1928). She was outspoken on women's rights and environment issues.*

1 As the traveler who has once been from home is wiser than he who has never left his own doorstep, so a knowledge of one other culture should sharpen our ability to scrutinize more steadily, to appreciate more lovingly, our own.
Coming of Age in Samoa, Introduction (1928)

2 A society which is clamoring for choice, which is filled with many articulate groups, each urging its own brand of salvation, its own variety of economic philosophy, will give each new generation no peace until all have chosen or gone under, unable to bear the conditions of choice. The stress is in our civilization.
Ibid., ch. 14

3 I was brought up to believe that the only thing worth doing was to add to the sum of accurate information in the world.
New York Times 9 August 1964

4 The mind is not sex-typed.
Blackberry Winter, ch. 5 (1972)

(Sir) Peter Medawar
(1915–87)
British immunologist

He shared a Nobel Prize in 1960 for his work on immunology, and was Director of the Institute for Medical Research 1962–75. His publications include general essays on science, collected in The Art of the Soluble *(1967) and* The Limits of Science *(1985).*

1 If politics is the art of the possible, research is surely the art of the soluble. Both are immensely practical-minded affairs.
The Art of the Soluble, 'The Act of Creation' (1967). See OTTO VON BISMARCK 4.

2 Considered in its entirety, psychoanalysis won't do. It's an end product, moreover, like a dinosaur or a zeppelin; no better theory can ever be erected on its ruins, which will remain for ever one of the

saddest and strangest of all landmarks in the history of twentieth-century thought.

The Hope of Progress, 'Further Comments on Psychoanalysis' (1972)

3 Today the world changes so quickly that in growing up we take leave not just of youth but of the world we were young in ... Fear and resentment of what is new is really a lament for the memories of our childhood.

Pluto's Republic, 'On "The Effecting of All Things Possible"' (1982)

Golda Meir
(1898–1978)
Ukrainian-born Israeli politician and prime minister

Originally Goldie Myerson. After emigrating to the USA in 1906, she moved to Palestine in 1921 where she was prominent in the Labour Movement. She held government posts following the creation of the state of Israel and was Prime Minister 1966–74.

1 There was no such thing as a Palestinian people ... it is not as though there was a Palestinian people and we came and threw them out and took their country away from them. They did not exist.

Sunday Times 15 June 1969

2 We have always said that in our war with the Arabs we had a secret weapon – no alternative.

Life 3 October 1969

3 To be or not to be is not a question of compromise. Either you be or you don't be.

Quoted in the *New York Times* 12 December 1974. On the future of Israel.

4 Pessimism is a luxury that a Jew can never allow himself.

Quoted in the *Observer* 29 December 1974

Lord Melbourne
(1779–1848)
English statesman

William Lamb, second Viscount Melbourne. Serving as Prime Minister 1834 and 1835–41, he was a conciliatory, old-fashioned Whig who rejected radical reform. He was the husband of CAROLINE LAMB *and the confidant of the young Queen* VICTORIA.

1 It is not much matter which we say, but mind, we must all say the same.

Remark at a Cabinet meeting, March 1841, quoted in *The*

English Constitution, ch. 1 (1867) by WALTER BAGEHOT. Discussing whether to lower the price of corn.

2 I wish I was as cocksure of anything as Tom Macaulay is of everything.

Quoted by Melbourne's nephew, Earl Cowper in *Lord Melbourne's Papers*, Preface (ed. Lloyd Charles Sanders, 1889). Referring to THOMAS, LORD MACAULAY.

3 Things have come to a pretty pass when religion is allowed to invade the sphere of private life!

Quoted in *Collections and Recollections*, ch. 6 (1898) by G. W. E. RUSSELL. After hearing 'a rousing Evangelical sermon about sin and its consequences'.

4 Nobody ever did anything very foolish except from some strong principle.

Quoted in *The Young Melbourne*, ch. 9 (1939) by David Cecil

5 Once is orthodox, twice is puritanical.

Reply to the Archbishop of York's invitation to attend evening service, quoted ibid., ch. 9. Melbourne is attributed with the remark: 'While I cannot be regarded as a pillar, I must be regarded as a buttress of the Church, because I support it from the outside' (also attributed to WINSTON CHURCHILL).

6 Neither man nor woman can be worth anything until they have discovered that they are fools. This is the first step towards becoming either estimable or agreeable; and until it be taken there is no hope.

Quoted ibid., ch. 9

7 The whole duty of government is to prevent crime and to preserve contracts.

Quoted in *Lord M*, ch. 3 (1954) by David Cecil

8 That is no use at all. What I want is men who will support me when I am in the wrong.

Quoted ibid., ch. 4. Reply to a politician's pledge: 'I will support you as long as you are in the right.'

9 If it was not absolutely necessary, it was the foolishest thing ever done.

Comment on the Reform Bill of 1832, quoted ibid., ch. 4

10 My esoteric doctrine, is that if you entertain any doubt, it is safest to take the unpopular side in the first instance. Transit from the unpopular, is easy ... but from the popular to the unpopular is so steep and rugged that it is impossible to maintain it.

Quoted ibid., ch. 4

David Mellor
(b. 1949)
British politician

Elected Conservative MP for Putney in 1979, he was Minister for the Arts in 1990 and Chief Secretary to the Treasury 1990–

2. *Revelations about an extra-marital affair forced him to resign from his position as Secretary of State for National Heritage in 1992.*

1 The popular press is drinking in the last chance saloon.

Interview on Channel 4, 21 December 1989. The comment was sparked by intrusive press coverage of the recent Hillsborough disaster. 'What is of interest to the public is not always in the public interest,' Mellor added.

George Melly
(b. 1926)
British jazz musician, critic and author

He has sung blues and jazz with John Chilton's Feetwarmers since the 1970s, worked as a television and film reviewer and published memoirs and books of social history.

1 The pop manner has become respectable, pop matter is suspect. In the mass media too the revolt has turned into a style.

Revolt into Style, 'Film, TV, Radio, Theatre: All My Hating'. The phrase 'revolt into style' is borrowed from lines by Thom Gunn: see THOM GUNN 4.

2 Surely nothing could be that funny.

Quoted in the *Independent on Sunday* 1 January 1995. On being told by MICK JAGGER that his wrinkles were laughter lines.

Herman Melville
(1819–91)
US author and poet

The novel Redburn *(1849) and his greatest work, the whaling epic* Moby-Dick *(1851), were inspired by his experiences at sea. He worked in the New York customs office 1866–85 and died in obscurity.* Billy Budd *(1924) was the basis of an opera by* BENJAMIN BRITTEN *(1951).*

1 Let America first praise mediocrity even, in her children, before she praises ... the best excellence in the children of any other land.

'Hawthorne and His Mosses', publ. in *Literary World* 17 and 24 August 1850, repr. in *Moby-Dick* (ed. Harrison Hayford and Hershel Parker, 1967)

2 Call me Ishmael.

Moby-Dick, ch. 1 (1851). Opening words of book, spoken by the narrator (Ishmael). In the Old Testament, Ishmael was the son of Abraham and Abraham's hand-maiden, Hagar, who was banished with his mother into the desert (see BIBLE, OLD TESTAMENT: GENESIS 43). The poet and critic CHARLES OLSON took these words as the title of his influential study of Melville (1947).

3 A whaleship was my Yale College and my Harvard.

Ibid., ch. 24

4 In truth, a mature man who uses hair-oil, unless medicinally, that man has probably got a quoggy spot in him somewhere. As a general rule, he can't amount to much in his totality.

Ibid., ch. 25

5 Old age is always wakeful; as if, the longer linked with life, the less man has to do with aught that looks like death.

Ibid., ch. 29

6 Oh, horrible vulturism of earth! from which not the mightiest whale is free.

Ibid., ch. 69

7 Give me a condor's quill! Give me Vesuvius' crater for an inkstand!

Narrator (Ishmael), ibid., ch. 104

8 For whatever is truly wondrous and fearful in man, never yet was put into words or books.

Ibid., ch. 110

9 Our souls are like those orphans whose unwedded mothers die in bearing them: the secret of our paternity lies in their grave, and we must there to learn it.

Ibid., ch. 114

10 Ha, ha, my ship! thou mightest well be taken now for the sea-chariot of the sun. Ho, ho! all ye nations before my prow, I bring the sun to ye! Yoke on the further billows ... I drive the sea!

Captain Ahab, ibid., ch. 124

11 When I think of this life I have led; the desolation of solitude it has been; the masoned, walled-town of a Captain's exclusiveness, which admits but small entrance to any sympathy from the green country without – oh, weariness! heaviness! Guinea-coast slavery of solitary command!

Captain Ahab, ibid., ch. 132

12 Let me look into a human eye; it is better than to gaze into sea or sky; better than to gaze upon God.

Captain Ahab, ibid., ch. 132

13 He says NO! in thunder; but the Devil himself cannot make him say *yes*.

Referring to NATHANIEL HAWTHORNE, in letter to Hawthorne, 16 April 1851, publ. in *The Letters of Herman Melville* (ed. Merrell R. Davis and William H. Gilman, 1960). Melville added, 'For all men who say *yes*, lie; and all men who say *no*,

– why, they are in the happy condition of judicious, unencumbered travelers in Europe; they cross the frontiers into Eternity with nothing but a carpet bag.'

14 Why, ever since Adam, who has got to the meaning of this great allegory – the world? Then we pygmies must be content to have our paper allegories but ill comprehended.
Letter to NATHANIEL HAWTHORNE, 17 November 1851, ibid.

15 Of all the preposterous assumptions of humanity over humanity, nothing exceeds most of the criticisms made on the habits of the poor by the well-housed, well-warmed, and well-fed.
'Poor Man's Pudding and Rich Man's Crumbs' (1854), repr. in *Selected Writings of Herman Melville* (1952)

16 Yea and Nay –
Each hath his say;
But God He keeps the middle way.
'The Conflict of Convictions', publ. in *Battle-Pieces and Aspects of the War* (1866)

Menander
(*c. 342–c. 291 BC*)
Greek dramatist

He was considered the greatest exponent of Athenian New Comedy. Of the hundred and five plays he is claimed to have written, only Dyskolos *(The Bad-tempered Man) has survived in its entirety, along with fragments and Latin adaptations.*

1 The man dies young on whom the gods bestow their love.
The Double Deceiver, publ. in *Menander: the Principal Fragments*, 'Fragments from Identified Plays', Fragment 125 (transl. F. G. Allinson, 1951)

2 The truth, sometimes not sought for, comes forth to the light.
The Girl Who Gets Flogged, ibid., Fragment 433

3 We live, not as we wish to, but as we can.
The Lady of Andros, ibid., Fragment 610

4 *Deus ex machina.*
[The god from the machine.]
The Woman Possessed with a Divinity, ibid., Fragment 227

5 A woman who is chaste ought not to dye her hair yellow.
Menander: The Principal Fragments, 'Unidentified Minor Fragments', Fragment no. 610 (transl. F. G. Allinson, 1951)

6 Whenever you talk much but do not learn, you will be in the position of having imparted your store of knowledge without learning mine.
Ibid., Fragment no. 685

Mencius (Meng-tzu or Mengzi)
(*c. 372–c. 289 BC*)
Chinese philosopher

Widely known by the Latinized form of his name, he was a key interpreter of Confucianism, emphasizing the duties of rulers to provide for their subjects and the innate goodness of humanity.

1 The Way lies close at hand, yet men seek for it afar.
Mencius, bk 4, pt A, v. 12

2 We should speak of the shortcomings of others only when their shortcomings are likely to have disastrous consequences.
Ibid., bk 4, pt B, v. 9

3 The great man is he who never loses his child-like touch.
Ibid., bk 4, pt B, v. 12

4 Man's nature is inherently good, just as it is the nature of water to flow downwards. As there is no water that flows upwards, so there are no men whose natures inherently are bad.
Ibid., bk 6, pt A, v. 2

5 Humanity is the mind of man. Justice, the path he follows.
Ibid., bk 6, pt A, v. 11

6 Seek and we find; let go and we lose.
Ibid., bk 7, pt A, v. 13

H. L. Mencken
(1880–1956)
US journalist

Henry Louis Mencken. Known as 'the sage of Baltimore' for his lifelong association with the Baltimore Sun, he used his columns to lambast hypocrisy and provincialism in middle-class America. WALTER LIPPMANN called him 'the most powerful personal influence on this whole generation of educated people'.

1 Democracy is the theory that the common people know what they want, and deserve to get it good and hard.
Little Book in C Major (1916)

2 Conscience: the inner voice which warns us that someone may be looking.
Ibid.

3 Time is a great legalizer, even in the field of morals.
A Book of Prefaces, ch. 4, sect. 6 (1917)

4 Philadelphia has always been one of the most Pecksniffian of American cities, and thus probably leads the world.

The American Language, note (1919). Referring to the replacement of 'a virgin' by 'a young girl' in the city's public ledger describing characters in a play in 1916. Seth Pecksniff is a hypocritically benevolent architect in *Martin Chuzzlewit* (1843) by CHARLES DICKENS.

5 All successful newspapers are ceaselessly querulous and bellicose. They never defend anyone or anything if they can help it; if the job is forced upon them, they tackle it by denouncing someone or something else.

Prejudices, ch. 13 (first series, 1919)

6 Every man sees in his relatives, and especially in his cousins, a series of grotesque caricatures of himself.

Smart Set August 1919, repr. in *Prejudices*, 'The Relative' (third series, 1922)

7 Puritanism: The haunting fear that someone, somewhere, may be happy.

A Book of Burlesques, 'Sententiae' (1920)

8 An idealist is one who, on noticing that a rose smells better than a cabbage, concludes that it will also make better soup.

Ibid., 'Sententiae'

9 Adultery is the application of democracy to love.

Ibid., 'Sententiae'

10 It is the dull man who is always sure, and the sure man who is always dull.

Prejudices, ch. 1 (second series, 1920)

11 To sum up:
1. The cosmos is a gigantic fly-wheel making 10,000 revolutions a minute.
2. Man is a sick fly taking a dizzy ride on it.
3. Religion is the theory that the wheel was designed and set spinning to give him the ride.

Smart Set December 1920, repr. in *A Mencken Chrestomathy*, pt 1, 'Coda' (1949)

12 Injustice is relatively easy to bear; what stings is justice.

Prejudices, ch. 3 (third series, 1922)

13 Faith may be defined briefly as an illogical belief in the occurrence of the improbable ... A man full of faith is simply one who has lost (or never had) the capacity for clear and realistic thought. He is not a mere ass: he is actually ill.

Ibid., ch. 14

14 No one in this world, so far as I know ... has ever lost money by underestimating the intelligence of the great masses of the plain people.

Chicago Tribune 19 September 1926

15 It is the place where all the aspirations of the Western World meet to form one vast master aspiration, as powerful as the suction of a steam dredge. It is the icing on the pie called Christian civilization.

Prejudices, ch. 9 (sixth series, 1927). Referring to New York.

16 If Los Angeles is not the one authentic rectum of civilization, then I am no anatomist. Any time you want to go out again and burn it down, count me in.

Letter to F. SCOTT FITZGERALD and ZELDA FITZGERALD, 15 March 1927, on their return from working in Hollywood, quoted in *Invented Lives* (1984) by James R. Mellon

17 Whenever you hear a man speak of his love for his country, it is a sign that he expects to be paid for it.

A Mencken Chrestomathy, 'Sententiae: The Mind of Man' (1949)

18 Self-respect – The secure feeling that no one, as yet, is suspicious.

Ibid., 'Sententiae: The Mind of Man'

19 When women kiss it always reminds one of prize-fighters shaking hands.

Ibid., 'Sententiae: Masculum et Feminam Creavit Eos'

20 Whenever a husband and wife begin to discuss their marriage they are giving evidence at a coroner's inquest.

Ibid., 'Sententiae: Masculum et Feminam Creavit Eos'

21 Husbands never become good; they merely become proficient.

Ibid., 'Sententiae: Masculum et Feminam Creavit Eos'

22 Archbishop – A Christian ecclesiastic of a rank superior to that attained by Christ.

Ibid., 'Sententiae: Arcana Coelestia'

23 Theology – An effort to explain the unknowable by putting it into terms of the not worth knowing.

Ibid., 'Sententiae: Arcana Coelestia'

24 A society made up of individuals who were all capable of original thought would probably be unendurable.

Minority Report: H. L. Mencken's Notebooks, no. 13 (1956)

25 It is now quite lawful for a Catholic woman to avoid pregnancy by a resort to mathematics, though

she is still forbidden to resort to physics and chemistry.
Ibid., no. 62

26 There are people who read too much: bibliobibuli. I know some who are constantly drunk on books, as other men are drunk on whiskey or religion. They wander through this most diverting and stimulating of worlds in a haze, seeing nothing and hearing nothing.
Ibid., no. 71

27 The chief contribution of Protestantism to human thought is its massive proof that God is a bore.
Ibid., no. 309

(Sir) Robert Menzies
(1894–1978)
Australian politician and prime minister

Leader of the Australian Liberal Party, he was Australia's longest serving prime minister, occupying the post 1939–1941 and 1949–66.

1 Men of genius are not to be analyzed by commonplace rules. The rest of us who have been or are leaders, more commonplace in our quality, will do well to remember two things. One is *never to forget posterity when devising a policy*. The other is *never to think of posterity when making a speech*.
The Measure of The Years, ch. 1 (1970)

2 A Prime Minister exercises his greatest public influence by creating a public impression of himself, hoping all the time that the people will be generous rather than just.
Quoted in *Australian Politics. A Third Reader*, ch. 60 (1973) by Henry Mayer and Helen Nelson

Johnny Mercer
(1909–76)
US songwriter

A highly prolific lyricist, he collaborated with Harold Arlen on the musicals St Louis Woman *(1946) and* Saratoga *(1959), and also recorded his own compositions, such as 'Baby It's Cold Outside' (1949). He founded Capitol Records in 1942.*

1 That old black magic.
Title of song (with music by Harold Arlen) in *Star Spangled Rhythm* (film, 1943). First sung by Johnny Johnston, the song was later associated with singer Billy Daniels.

2 You've got to ac-cent-tchu-ate the positive
Elim-my-nate the negative

Latch on to the affirmative
Don't mess with Mister In-between.
'Ac-cent-tchu-ate the Positive' (song, with music by Harold Arlen) in the musical film *Here Come the Waves* (1944). The song was originally sung by BING CROSBY, and was also recorded by Mercer himself.

3 We're after the same rainbow's end
Waiting round the bend
My Huckleberry friend
Moon River and me.
'Moon River' (song, with music by Henry Mancini) in the film *Breakfast at Tiffany's* (1961)

George Meredith
(1828–1909)
English novelist and poet

Called by G. K. CHESTERTON *'a sort of daintily dressed Walt Whitman', he established his reputation with his novels, notably* The Ordeal of Richard Feverel *(1859) and* The Egoist *(1879). His verse collection,* Modern Love *(1862), describes the disillusionment of marriage.*

1 I expect that Woman will be the last thing civilised by Man.
The Ordeal of Richard Feverel, ch. 1 (1859). Quoting the 'Pilgrim's Scrip'.

2 Who rises from prayer a better man, his prayer is answered.
Ibid., ch. 12. Quoting the 'Pilgrim's Scrip'.

3 Sentimentalists are they who seek to enjoy without incurring the Immense Debtorship for a thing done.
Ibid., ch. 24. Sir Austin Feverel, quoting the 'Pilgrim's Scrip'. Speaking of sentimentalism, Sir Austin continued: 'It is a happy pastime and an important science to the timid, the idle, and the heartless; but a damning one to them who have anything to forfeit.' JAMES JOYCE, for whom Meredith was an early influence, quoted this aphorism in *Ulysses* (1922).

4 Kissing don't last: cookery do!
Mrs Berry, ibid., ch. 28

5 Not till the fire is dying in the grate,
Look we for any kinship with the stars.
Oh, wisdom never comes when it is gold,
And the great price we paid for it full worth:
We have it only when we are half earth.
Little avails that coinage to the old!
Modern Love, Sonnet 4 (1862)

6 A kiss is but a kiss now! and no wave
Of a great flood that whirls me to the sea.

But, as you will! we'll sit contentedly,
And eat our pot of honey on the grave.
Ibid., Sonnet 29

7 That rarest gift
To Beauty, Common Sense!
Ibid., Sonnet 32

8 Passions spin the plot:
We are betrayed by what is false within.
Ibid., Sonnet 43

9 Ah, what a dusty answer gets the soul
When hot for certainties in this our life!
Ibid., Sonnet 50

10 Cynicism is intellectual dandyism without the
coxcomb's feathers.
The Egoist, ch. 7 (1879). Spoken by Clara Middleton, quoting
Mr Whitford. She adds: 'It seems to me that cynics are only
happy in making the world as barren to others as they have
made it for themselves.'

11 Enter these enchanted woods,
You who dare.
'The Woods of Westermain', publ. in *Poems and Lyrics of the
Joy of Earth* (1883)

12 A witty woman is a treasure; a witty beauty is a
power.
Diana of the Crossways, ch. 1 (1885)

13 'Tis Ireland gives England her soldiers, her generals too.
Ibid., ch. 2

Owen Meredith
(1831–91)
English poet and diplomat

*Pseudonym of Edward Robert Bulwer, Earl of Lytton, son of
EDWARD BULWER-LYTTON. He was Viceroy of India (1876–
80) and Ambassador to Paris from 1887 until his death. His
earlier verse was published under his pseudonym.*

1 We may live without poetry, music and art;
We may live without conscience, and live without
heart;
We may live without friends; we may live without
books;
But civilized man cannot live without cooks.
Lucile, pt 1, canto 2, st. 19 (1860)

2 Genius does what it must, and Talent does what
it can.
'Last Words of a Sensitive Second-Rate Poet' (1868)

Robert King Merton
(1910–2003)
US sociologist

*He was Professor of Sociology at Columbia University 1941–79
and a pivotal figure in the study of bureaucracy, the mass
media and science and society. His major works include* Social
Theory and Social Structure *(1949).*

1 The self-fulfilling prophecy is, in the beginning,
a *false* definition of the situation evoking a new
behavior which makes the originally false conception come *true*. The specious validity of the self-
fulfilling prophecy perpetuates a reign of error.
Social Theory and Social Structure, pt 2, ch. 13 (1949). First
recorded use of the term 'self-fulfilling prophecy'.

Prince Metternich
(1773–1859)
Austrian statesman

*Klemens, Fürst von Metternich. An astute diplomat, he was
Foreign Minister 1809–48, playing a major part in the Congress of Vienna (1814–15). He strove to maintain the balance
of power in Europe but, identified with the reactionary party,
was forced to resign following the revolutions of 1848.*

1 Any plan conceived in moderation must fail when
the circumstances are set in extremes.
Letter 2 December 1822, attributed

2 When Paris sneezes, Europe catches cold.
Attributed, 1830

3 The word 'Italy' is a geographical expression.
Letter, 12 April 1847, publ. in *Metternich's Surviving Papers*,
vol. 7 (ed. Richard Metternich-Winneburg, 1883). The words
have also been attributed to Metternich in a letter to LORD
PALMERSTON, 6 August 1847, and later in a letter dated
19 November 1849.

4 Error has never approached my spirit.
Remark to François Guizot in the summer of 1848, quoted in
Mémoires, vol. 4 (1858–67) by François Guizot

5 Having seen what was done in the name of fraternity, if I had a brother, I would call him cousin.
Quoted in *The Price of Revolution*, ch. 1 (1951) by Denis Brogan

6 I have long experience of the world's affairs and
I have always observed that no matter is so easily
settled as that which appears to present insuperable
difficulties.
Quoted in *Metternich*, pt 1, sect. 3 (1975) by Andrew Milne

Alice Meynell

(1847–1922)

English poet, journalist and essayist

With her husband Wilfrid Meynell, she wrote for and edited several periodicals. Her poetry, first published in Preludes *(1875), had a popular appeal, and her numerous essays were collected in such volumes as* The Rhythm of Life *(1893).*

1 Spirit of place! It is for this we travel, to surprise its subtlety; and where it is a strong and dominant angel, that place, seen once, abides entire in the memory with all its own accidents, its habits, its breath, its name.

The Spirit of Place and Other Essays, 'The Spirit of Place' (1899)

2 If there is a look of human eyes that tells of perpetual loneliness, so there is also the familiar look that is the sign of perpetual crowds.

Ibid., 'Solitude'

Princess Michael of Kent

(b. 1945)

Marie-Christine, Baroness von Reibnitz. Married to Prince Michael of Kent (cousin of ELIZABETH II*), she lectures widely and writes on historical themes.*

1 The English take the breeding of their horses and dogs more seriously than they do their children. God forbid that the wrong drop of blood should get into their labrador. But their children marry everywhere.

Interview with the German newspaper, *Welt am Sonntag*, quoted in the *Guardian* 17 February 2005. See WILLIAM PENN 4.

Michelangelo Buonarroti

(1475–1564)

Italian sculptor, painter and poet

Apprenticed to Ghirlandaio in Florence (1488), he learned the elements of fresco painting and developed his life-long interest in sculpture. His talent attracted the patronage of the Medici family in Florence and the popes in Rome, for whom he painted the ceiling of the Sistine chapel (1508–12). He was also an architect and an accomplished writer of sonnets.

1 The marble not yet carved can hold the form
Of every thought the greatest artist has,
And no conception can yet come to pass
Unless the hand obeys the intellect.

'Non ha l'ottimo artista alcun concetto' (written 1538–40), publ. in *The Sonnets of Michelangelo*, no. 165 (transl. ELIZABETH JENNINGS, 1961)

2 No one who follows others can ever get in front of them, and those who can't do good work on their own account can hardly make good use of what others have done.

Quoted in *Lives of the Most Excellent Sculptors, Painters and Architects*, 'The Life of Michelangelo Buonarroti' (1550, rev. 1568, transl. George Bull) by Giorgio Vasari

3 The greater danger for most of us lies not in setting our aim too high and falling short, but in setting our aim too low, and achieving our mark.

Attributed

Thomas Middleton

(c. 1580–1627)

English dramatist

In 1620 he was appointed chronologer for the City of London, for which he wrote ceremonial pageants and masques. He is remembered for The Revenger's Tragedy *(1607),* The Changeling *(1622, written with William Rowley) and* Women Beware Women *(1620–7).*

1 The better the day, the better the deed.

Michaelmas Term, Act 3, Sc. 1 (written 1604, publ. 1607). Spoken by a country wench.

2 Have you summoned your wits from woolgathering?

The Family of Love, Act 5, Sc. 3 (1608). Spoken by Gerardine.

3 Anything for a Quiet Life.

Title of play (written with JOHN WEBSTER, *c.* 1621, publ. 1662)

4 He was my nearest and dearest enemy.

Anything for a Quiet Life, Act 5, Sc. 1. Spoken by Old Franklin, referring to his son. See WILLIAM SHAKESPEARE: HENRY IV PART 1 35.

Ludwig Mies Van Der Rohe

(1886–1969)

German-born US architect

Originally Ludwig Mies. He was Director of the Bauhaus (1930–3) before moving to America, where he became the leading figure of the International Style and pioneer of the glass and steel skyscraper.

1 Less is more.

Quoted in the *New York Herald Tribune* 28 June 1959. Among the many rejoinders to it, ROBERT VENTURI stated, 'Less is a bore' (*Complexity and Contradiction in Architecture*, 1966), and FRANK LLOYD WRIGHT wrote, 'Less is only more where more is no good' (*The Future of Architecture*, 1953). See also ROBERT BROWNING 35.

George Mikes

(1912–87)

Hungarian-born British humorist

Settling in Britain in 1938, he recorded his observations on his adopted country in a series of satirical books including How to Be an Alien *(1946) and* As Others See You *(1961).*

1 On the Continent people have good food; in England people have good table manners.

How to Be an Alien: A Handbook for Beginners and More Advanced Pupils, *ch. 1, sect. 1 (1946)*

2 Continental people have sex lives; the English have hot-water bottles.

Ibid., ch. 1, sect. 6. Thirty years later, Mikes referred to this notorious pronouncement: 'Things *have* progressed. Not on the continent, where people still have sex lives; but they have progressed here because the English now have electric blankets' (*How To Be Decadent*, 1977).

3 An Englishman, even if he is alone, forms an orderly queue of one.

Ibid., ch. 1, sect. 14. Mikes expanded on this in *How To Be Decadent* (1977): 'In shops the English stand in queues; in government offices they sit in queues; in churches they kneel in queues; at sale times, they lie in queues all night.'

John Stuart Mill

(1806–73)

English philosopher and economist

A leading liberal intellectual, he was an early advocate of Benthamite utilitarianism and a Radical MP 1865–8. His major works are A System of Logic *(1843),* On Liberty *(1859) and* The Subjection of Women *(1869).* GLADSTONE *called him the 'saint of rationalism'.*

1 All that makes existence valuable to any one depends on the enforcement of restraints upon the actions of other people.

On Liberty, *ch. 1 (1859)*

2 The sole end for which mankind are warranted, individually or collectively in interfering with the liberty of action of any of their number, is self-protection.

Ibid., ch. 1

3 If all mankind minus one, were of one opinion, and only one person were of the contrary opinion, mankind would be no more justified in silencing that one person, than he, if he had the power, would be justified in silencing mankind.

Ibid., ch. 2

4 We can never be sure that the opinion we are endeavouring to stifle is a false opinion; and even if we were sure, stifling it would be an evil still.

Ibid., ch. 2

5 A party of order or stability, and a party of progress or reform, are both necessary elements of a healthy state of political life.

Ibid., ch. 2

6 The general tendency of things throughout the world is to render mediocrity the ascendant power among mankind.

Ibid., ch. 3

7 Eccentricity has always abounded when and where strength of character has abounded; and the amount of eccentricity in a society has generally been proportional to the amount of genius, mental vigour, and moral courage which it contained. That so few now dare to be eccentric, marks the chief danger of the time.

Ibid., ch. 3

8 The despotism of custom is everywhere the standing hindrance to human advancement.

Ibid., ch. 3

9 The individual is not accountable to society for his actions, in so far as these concern the interests of no person but himself.

Ibid., ch. 5

10 That the whole or any large part of the education of the people should be in State hands, I go as far as anyone in deprecating . . . A general State education is a mere contrivance for moulding people to be exactly like one another.

Ibid., ch. 5

11 The worth of a State, in the long run, is the worth of the individuals composing it . . . a State which dwarfs its men, in order that they may be more docile instruments in its hands even for beneficial purposes – will find that with small men no great thing can really be accomplished.

Ibid., ch. 5

12 War is an ugly thing, but not the ugliest of things: the decayed and degraded state of moral and patriotic feeling which thinks nothing *worth* a war, is worse.

Dissertations and Discussions, *vol. 3, 'The Contest in America' (1867)*

13 A man who has nothing which he is willing to fight for, nothing which he cares more about than

he does about his personal safety, is a miserable creature who has no chance of being free, unless made and kept so by the exertions of better men than himself.

Ibid., 'The Contest in America'

14 No slave is a slave to the same lengths, and in so full a sense of the word, as a wife is.

The Subjection of Women, ch. 2 (1869)

15 Marriage is the only actual bondage known to our law. There remain no legal slaves, except the mistress of every house.

Ibid., ch. 4

16 Ask yourself whether you are happy, and you cease to be so.

Autobiography, ch. 5 (1873)

Edna St Vincent Millay
(1892–1950)
US poet

The foremost American woman poet of the 1920s and a skilful sonneteer, she epitomized the free spirit of the Jazz Age in such volumes as A Few Figs from Thistles *(1920) and* The Harp-Weaver and Other Poems *(1923).*

1 God, I can push the grass apart
And lay my finger on Thy heart.

'Renascence', publ. in *Renascence and Other Poems* (1917)

2 The soul can split the sky in two,
And let the face of God shine through.

'Renascence', ibid.

3 My candle burns at both ends;
It will not last the night;
But ah, my foes, and oh, my friends –
It gives a lovely light.

'First Fig', publ. in *A Few Figs From Thistles* (1920)

4 Safe upon the solid rock the ugly houses stand:
Come and see my shining palaces built upon the sand!

'Second Fig', ibid.

5 Death devours all lovely things;
Lesbia with her sparrow
Shares the darkness – presently
Every bed is narrow.

'Passer Mortuus Est', publ. in *Second April* (1921). See CATULLUS 3.

6 After all, my erstwhile dear,
My no longer cherished,

Need we say it was not love,
Now that love is perished?

'Passer Mortuus Est', ibid.

7 I know I am but summer to your heart,
And not the full four seasons of the year.

'I Know I Am But Summer to Your Heart', publ. in *The Harp-Weaver and Other Poems* (1923)

8 Euclid alone
Has looked on Beauty bare. Fortunate they
Who, though once only and then but far away,
Have heard her massive sandal set on stone.

'Euclid Alone Has Looked on Beauty Bare', ibid.

9 Love is not all: it is not meat nor drink
Nor slumber nor a roof against rain;
Nor yet a floating spar to men that sink.

'Love Is Not All', publ. in *Fatal Interview* (1931)

10 It is not true that life is one damn thing after another – it is one damn thing over and over.

Letter, 24 October 1930, publ. in *Letters of Edna St Vincent Millay* (ed. Allan Ross Macdougall, 1952). See ELBERT HUBBARD 4.

11 Childhood is the kingdom where nobody dies. Nobody that matters, that is.

'Childhood is the Kingdom Where Nobody Dies', publ. in *Wine From These Grapes* (1934)

12 Set the foot down with distrust on the crust of the world – it is thin.

'The Underground System', publ. in *Huntsman, What Quarry?* (1939)

Alice Duer Miller
(1874–1942)
US author and poet

Her short stories and novellas appeared in the collection Summer Holiday *(1941), and her most famous poem is* The White Cliffs *(1940). She was active in the women's suffrage movement.*

1 They make other nations seem pale and flighty,
But they do think England is God almighty,
And you must remind them now and then
That other countries breed other men.

The White Cliffs (1940). Part of a long narrative poem extolling Britain's resistance during the Second World War.

2 I am American bred,
I have seen much to hate here – much to forgive,
But in a world where England is finished and dead,
I do not wish to live.

Ibid. Closing lines of poem.

Arthur Miller

(1915–2005)
US playwright

He established himself as a master dramatist with his plays
Death of a Salesman *(1949) and* The Crucible *(1953), which
took the Salem witch trials of 1692 as an allegory for the
McCarthyism of which Miller had personal experience in the
1950s. His marriage (1956–61) to* MARILYN MONROE *was the
inspiration for his screenplay for* The Misfits *(1960), in which
she starred.*

1 He's liked, but he's not well liked.
Death of a Salesman, Act 1 (1949). Spoken by Biff, referring to
his schoolfriend Bernard.

2 A small man can be just as exhausted as a great
man.
Linda, ibid., Act 1. Referring to her husband Willy Loman.

3 I don't say he's a great man. Willy Loman never
made a lot of money. His name was never in the
paper. He's not the finest character that ever lived.
But he's a human being, and a terrible thing is happening to him. So attention must be paid.
Linda, ibid., Act 1

4 For a salesman, there is no rock bottom to the
life. He don't put a bolt to a nut, he don't tell you
the law or give you medicine. He's a man way out
there in the blue, riding on a smile and a shoeshine.
And when they start not smiling back – that's an
earthquake. And then you get yourself a couple of
spots on your hat, and you're finished. Nobody dast
blame this man. A salesman is got to dream, boy. It
comes with the territory.
Charley, ibid., 'Requiem'

5 A good newspaper, I suppose, is a nation talking
to itself.
Quoted in the *Observer* 26 November 1961

6 A suicide kills two people, Maggie. That's what it's
for.
After the Fall, Act 2 (1964). Spoken by Quentin.

7 The concentration camp is the final expression of
human separateness and its ultimate consequence.
It is organized abandonment.
Interview publ. in *Writers at Work* (third series, ed. George
Plimpton, 1967). Miller regarded this concept as under-
pinning his 1964 play *After the Fall*, which included a concentration camp in its staging.

8 In the theater, while you recognized that you were
looking at a house, it was a house in quotation

marks. On screen, the quotation marks tend to be
blotted out by the camera.
New York Times 15 September 1985. On a television production of *Death of a Salesman*.

9 Without alienation, there can be no politics.
Interview in *Marxism Today* January 1988

10 I love her too, but our neuroses just don't match.
The Ride Down Mount Morgan, Act 1 (1991). Spoken by Lyman,
of his wife.

11 Maybe all one can do is hope to end up with the
right regrets.
Tom, ibid., Act 1

Henry Miller

(1891–1980)
US author

*While in Paris (1930–9) he wrote the books for which he is best
known:* Tropic of Cancer *(1934),* Black Spring *(1936) and* Tropic
of Capricorn *(1938), banned in the UK and USA until the 1960s.
The author Gerald Brenan remarked: 'Miller is not really a
writer but a non-stop talker to whom someone has given a
typewriter.' See also* EZRA POUND 18.

1 It is true I swim in a perpetual sea of sex but the
actual excursions are fairly limited.
Letter, 1 February 1932, publ. in *Letters to Anaïs Nin*, pt 1 (1965)

2 Every man with a bellyful of the classics is an
enemy to the human race.
Tropic of Cancer (1934)

3 Confusion is a word we have invented for an order
which is not understood.
Tropic of Capricorn, 'On the Ovarian Trolley: An Interlude'
(1939)

4 What holds the world together, as I have learned
from bitter experience, is sexual intercourse.
Ibid.

5 The aim of life is to live, and to live means to be
aware, joyously, drunkenly, serenely, divinely
aware.
The Wisdom of the Heart, 'Creative Death' (1941)

6 In expanding the field of knowledge, we but
increase the horizon of ignorance.
Ibid., 'The Wisdom of the Heart'

7 The American ideal is youth – handsome, empty
youth.
Ibid., 'Raimu'. In America, Miller explained, 'youth means
simply athleticism, disrespect, gangsterism, or sickly
idealism.'

8 Life, as it is called, is for most of us one long postponement.
Ibid., 'The Enormous Womb'

9 Sex is one of the nine reasons for reincarnation. The other eight are unimportant.
Sexus, ch. 21 (1949)

10 Obscenity is a cleansing process, whereas pornography only adds to the murk.
Interview, 1961, publ. in *Writers at Work* (second series, ed. George Plimpton, 1963). Miller is quoted as saying: 'I am for obscenity and against pornography.'

11 Whenever a taboo is broken, something good happens, something vitalizing.
Interview, ibid.

Jonathan Miller
(b. 1934)
British doctor, humorist and director

Combining careers in medical research and the arts, he came to notice in the Beyond the Fringe *revues (1961–4), and subsequently as an innovative director of Shakespeare and opera.*

1 Attitudes to museums have changed. If it had Marilyn Monroe's knickers or Laurence Olivier's jockstrap they would flock to it.
Daily Telegraph 7 June 1989. On the low attendances at his recently opened Theatre Museum.

2 There are no élitist people there are only élitist ideas.
Interview in the *Guardian* 12 September 1998

Roger Miller
(1936–92)
US country singer and songwriter

His self-penned songs 'Dang Me' (1964) and 'King of the Road' (1965) were million-sellers, notching up eight Grammy awards between them. Later hits included 'Little Green Apples' (1968).

1 I'm a man of means by no means
King of the road.
'King of the Road' (song, 1965)

2 England swings like a pendulum do
Bobbies on bicycles two by two
Westminster Abbey, the tower of Big Ben,
The rosy red cheeks of the little children.
'England Swings' (song, 1965)

Kate Millett
(b. 1934)
US feminist author

Her first book, Sexual Politics *(1970), was an indictment of the patriarchal value systems which she perceived in politics and literature. She was active in civil rights movements in the 1970s.*

1 However muted its present appearance may be, sexual dominion obtains nevertheless as perhaps the most pervasive ideology of our culture and provides its most fundamental concept of power.
Sexual Politics, ch. 2 (1970)

2 Because of our social circumstances, male and female are really two cultures and their life experiences are utterly different.
Ibid., ch. 2, sect. 2

3 To be a rebel is not to be a revolutionary. It is more often but a way of spinning one's wheels deeper in the sand.
Ibid., ch. 8, sect. 2

Spike Milligan
(1918–2002)
British comedian and humorous writer

Born Terence Alan Milligan. He wrote and performed in The Goon Show *for BBC radio (1951–60), which* JOHN LENNON *called 'a conspiracy against reality, a coup d'état of the mind'. He was the author of many humorous books of autobiography, fiction and verse.*

1 You silly twisted boy!
The Goon Show (BBC radio comedy series, 1951–60, written by Spike Milligan). Favourite expression of Lance Brigadier Grytpype-Thynne (Peter Sellers).

2 Ying tong iddle I po.
Ibid. Spoken by Ned Seagoon (Harry Secombe). The words were set to music and released as 'The Ying Tong Song' in 1956.

3 I'm a hero wid coward's legs, I'm a hero from the waist up.
Puckoon, ch. 2 (1963)

4 Money couldn't buy friends, but you got a better class of enemy.
Mrs Doonan, ibid., ch. 6

5 Contraceptives should be used on every conceivable occasion.
Camden Theatre, London, 30 April 1972, publ. in *The Last Goon Show of Them All* (1972)

C. Wright Mills

(1916–62)
US sociologist

Charles Wright Mills. Influenced by KARL MARX *and* MAX
WEBER *in his critique of the American establishment, he contributed to the popular understanding of sociology with such
books as* The Power Elite *(1956).*

1 By the power elite, we refer to those political, economic, and military circles which as an intricate set of
overlapping cliques share decisions having at least
national consequences. In so far as national events
are decided, the power elite are those who decide
them.
The Power Elite, ch. 1 (1956)

2 Power is not of a man. Wealth does not center in
the person of the wealthy. Celebrity is not inherent
in any personality. To be celebrated, to be wealthy,
to have power requires access to major institutions.
Ibid., ch. 1

A. A. Milne

(1882–1958)
British author

*Alan Alexander Milne. Although well known during the 1920s
as a writer of light comedies, he is now remembered for his
classic children's stories and poems written for his son, Christopher Robin. His play* Toad of Toad Hall *(1929) is based on*
KENNETH GRAHAME'*s* Wind in the Willows.

1 They're changing guard at Buckingham Palace –
Christopher Robin went down with Alice.
Alice is marrying one of the guard.
'A soldier's life is terrible hard,'
Says Alice.
'Buckingham Palace', publ. in *When We Were Very Young*
(1924)

2 James James
Morrison Morrison
Wetherby George Dupree
Took great care of his Mother,
Though he was only three.
James James
Said to his Mother,
'Mother,' he said, said he;
'You must never go down to the end of the town, if
   you don't go down with me.'
'Disobedience', ibid.

3 Nobody,
My darling

Could call me
A fussy man – BUT
I do like a little bit of butter to my bread!
'The King's Breakfast', ibid.

4 A bear, however hard he tries,
Grows tubby without exercise.
'Teddy Bear', ibid.

5 Little Boy kneels at the foot of the bed,
Droops on the little hands little gold head.
Hush! Hush! Whisper who dares!
Christopher Robin is saying his prayers.
'Vespers', ibid.

6 Isn't it funny
How a bear likes honey?
Buzz! Buzz! Buzz!
I wonder why he does?
Winnie-the-Pooh, ch. 1 (1926). Spoken by Winnie-the-Pooh.

7 How sweet to be a Cloud
Floating in the Blue!
Winnie-the-Pooh, ibid., ch. 1

8 I am a Bear of Very Little Brain, and long words
Bother me.
Ibid., ch. 4

9 Pathetic. That's what it is. Pathetic.
Eeyore, ibid., ch. 6

10 Now then, Pooh, time for a little something.
Piglet, ibid., ch. 6

11 My spelling is Wobbly. It's good spelling but it
Wobbles, and the letters get in the wrong places.
Winnie-the-Pooh, ibid., ch. 6

12 He respects Owl, because you can't help respecting anybody who can spell TUESDAY, even if he
doesn't spell it right; but spelling isn't everything.
There are days when spelling Tuesday simply
doesn't count.
The House at Pooh Corner, ch. 5 (1928). Spoken by Rabbit,
referring to Christopher Robin.

Czeslaw Milosz

(1911–2004)
Lithuanian-born Polish poet

*During the 1930s he established himself as Poland's leading
avant-garde poet but subsequently spent thirty-five years in
exile in France and America. His collections include* Bells in
Winter *(1978).*

1 Grow your tree of falsehood from a small grain
   of truth.

Do not follow those who lie in contempt of reality.
Let your lie be even more logical than the truth
   itself,
So the weary travellers may find repose.
'Child of Europe', sect. 4, publ. in *Selected Poems* (1973)

2 Blessed be jubilation.
Vintages and harvests.
Even if not everyone
Is granted serenity.
'A Poem for the End of the Century', publ. in *Provinces* (1991)

John Milton
(1608–74)
English poet

Apart from a period as a student at Cambridge and a year spent in Italy (1638–9), he lived mostly in London. His early works include 'Il Penseroso' (c. 1631) and the masque Comus *(1634). He expressed his Puritan sympathies in a series of pamphlets, while* Areopagitica *(1644) argued in favour of freedom of expression. His greatest work,* Paradise Lost *(1667, rev. 1674), relates the expulsion of Adam and Eve from Eden.* Paradise Regained *and the verse drama* Samson Agonistes *(both 1671) were also based on biblical subjects. See* JOHN AUBREY 3; THOMAS GRAY 20; SAMUEL JOHNSON 139; WILLIAM WORDSWORTH 61.

1 This is the month, and this the happy morn,
Wherein the son of heaven's eternal king,
Of wedded maid and virgin mother born,
Our great redemption from above did bring.
'On the Morning of Christ's Nativity', st. 1, written 1629, publ. in *Poems* (1645)

2 It was the winter wild,
While the heaven-born child
All meanly wrapped in the rude manger lies.
'On the Morning of Christ's Nativity', 'The Hymn', st. 1, ibid.

3 Ring out, ye crystal spheres,
Once bless our human ears
(If ye have power to touch our senses so),
And let your silver chime
Move in melodious time.
'On the Morning of Christ's Nativity', 'The Hymn', st. 13, ibid.

4 Time will run back and fetch the age of gold.
'On the Morning of Christ's Nativity', 'The Hymn', st. 14, ibid.

5 The oracles are dumb.
'On the Morning of Christ's Nativity', 'The Hymn', st. 19, ibid.

6 What needs my Shakespeare for his honoured
   bones,
The labour of an age in pilèd stones,

Or that his hallowed relics should be hid
Under a star-ypointing pyramid?
Dear son of memory, great heir of fame,
What need'st thou such weak witness of thy
   name?
'On Shakespeare', ll. 1–6 (1630), repr. ibid.

7 Now the bright morning star, day's harbinger,
Comes dancing from the east, and leads with her
The flowery May, who from her green lap throws
The yellow cowslip and the pale primrose.
Hail, bounteous May, that dost inspire
Mirth and youth and warm desire!
Woods and groves are of thy dressing,
Hill and dale doth boast thy blessing.
Thus we salute thee with our early song,
And welcome thee, and wish thee long.
'Song: On May Morning', written c. 1630, publ. ibid.

8 Thy liquid notes that close the eye of day.
Sonnet 1 ('To the Nightingale'), written c. 1630, ibid.

9 How soon hath Time, the subtle thief of
   youth,
Stolen on his wing my three-and-twentieth
   year!
Sonnet 7 ('How soon hath time'), written 1632, ibid. The sonnet is also known as 'On His Having Arrived at the Age of Twenty-three'.

10 Such sweet compulsion doth in music lie,
To lull the daughters of Necessity.
'Arcades', ll. 68–9 (c. 1633), ibid.

11 Hence, loathèd Melancholy,
Of Cerberus and blackest Midnight born,
In Stygian cave forlorn
'Mongst horrid shapes, and shrieks, and sights
   unholy.
'L'Allegro', ll. 1–4, written c. 1631, ibid.

12 So buxom, blithe, and debonair.
'L'Allegro', l. 24, ibid.

13 Haste thee, Nymph, and bring with thee
Jest and youthful jollity,
Quips and cranks, and wanton wiles,
Nods and becks and wreathèd smiles.
'L'Allegro', ll. 25–8, ibid.

14 Sport that wrinkled Care derides,
And Laughter holding both his sides.
Come, and trip it as ye go
On the light fantastic toe,

And in thy right hand lead with thee,
The mountain nymph, sweet Liberty.
'L'Allegro', ll. 31–6, ibid.

15 While the cock with lively din
Scatters the rear of darkness thin,
And to the stack or the barn door,
Stoutly struts his dames before;
Oft listening how the hounds and horn
Cheerly rouse the slumbering morn.
'L'Allegro', ll. 49–54, ibid.

16 And every shepherd tells his tale
Under the hawthorn in the dale.
'L'Allegro', ll. 67–8, ibid.

17 And young and old come forth to play
On a sunshine holiday,
Till the livelong daylight fail:
Then to the spicy nut-brown ale.
'L'Allegro', ll. 97–100, ibid.

18 Towered cities please us then,
And the busy hum of men.
'L'Allegro', ll. 117–18, ibid.

19 Such sights as youthful poets dream
On summer eves by haunted stream.
Then to the well-trod stage anon,
If Jonson's learnèd sock be on,
Or sweetest Shakespeare, Fancy's child,
Warble his native wood-notes wild.
'L'Allegro', ll. 129–34, ibid.

20 Hence, vain deluding joys,
The brood of Folly without father bred.
'Il Penseroso', ll. 1–2, written c. 1631, ibid.

21 Hail, divinest Melancholy,
Whose saintly visage is too bright
To hit the sense of human sight.
'Il Penseroso', ll. 12–14, ibid.

22 Come, pensive nun, devout and pure,
Sober, steadfast, and demure,
All in a robe of darkest grain,
Flowing with majestic train.
'Il Penseroso', ll. 31–4, ibid.

23 Sweet bird, that shunn'st the noise of folly,
Most musical, most melancholy!
'Il Penseroso', ll. 61–2, ibid.

24 And missing thee, I walk unseen
On the dry smooth-shaven green,
To behold the wandering moon,
Riding near her highest noon,

Like one that had been led astray
Through the heaven's wide pathless way;
And oft, as if her head she bowed,
Stooping through a fleecy cloud.
'Il Penseroso', ll. 65–72, ibid.

25 Where glowing embers through the room
Teach light to counterfeit a gloom,
Far from all resort of mirth,
Save the cricket on the hearth.
'Il Penseroso', ll. 79–82, ibid.

26 Or bid the soul of Orpheus sing
Such notes as, warbled to the string,
Drew iron tears down Pluto's cheek
And made hell grant what love did seek.
'Il Penseroso', ll. 105–8, ibid.

27 But let my due feet never fail
To walk the studious cloister's pale,
And love the high embowèd roof,
With antique pillars' massy proof,
And storied windows richly dight,
Casting a dim religious light.
There let the pealing organ blow
To the full-voiced quire below,
In service high, and anthems clear,
As may with sweetness, through mine ear,
Dissolve me into ecstasies,
And bring all heaven before mine eyes.
'Il Penseroso', ll. 155–66, ibid.

28 Where the bright seraphim in burning row
Their loud uplifted angel-trumpets blow.
'At a Solemn Music', ll. 10–11, written c. 1633, ibid.

29 Before the starry threshold of Jove's Court
My mansion is, where those immortal shapes
Of bright aerial spirits live insphered
In regions mild of calm and serene air,
Above the smoke and stir of this dim spot
Which men call earth.
Comus, ll. 1–6 (performed 1634, publ. 1637). Spoken by Attendant Spirit.

30 Yet some there be that by due steps aspire
To lay their just hands on that golden key
That opes the palace of eternity.
Attendant Spirit, ibid., ll. 12–14

31 An old and haughty nation proud in arms.
Attendant Spirit, ibid., l. 33. Referring to the tract of Wales and the Welsh borders ruled by the Earl of Bridgewater, in whose castle at Ludlow Milton's masque was first performed in 1634.

32 Bacchus, that first from out the purple grape
Crushed the sweet poison of misusèd wine.
Attendant Spirit, ibid., ll. 46–7

33 What hath night to do with sleep?
Attendant Spirit, ibid., l. 122

34 Was I deceived, or did a sable cloud
Turn forth her silver lining on the night?
The Lady, ibid., ll. 221–2

35 Sweet Echo, sweetest nymph that liv'st unseen
Within thy airy shell
By slow Meander's margent green,
And in the violet-embroidered vale.
Song, ibid., ll. 230–3

36 But he that hides a dark soul and foul thoughts
Benighted walks under the mid-day sun;
Himself is his own dungeon.
Elder Brother, ibid., ll. 383–5

37 'Tis chastity, my brother, chastity.
She that has that is clad in complete steel,
And like a quivered nymph with arrows keen
May trace huge forests and unharboured heaths,
Infamous hills and sandy perilous wilds,
Where, through the sacred rays of chastity,
No savage fierce, bandit, or mountaineer
Will dare to soil her virgin purity.
Elder Brother, ibid., ll. 420–7

38 How charming is divine philosophy!
Not harsh and crabbèd, as dull fools suppose,
But musical as is Apollo's lute,
And a perpetual feast of nectared sweets,
Where no crude surfeit reigns.
Second Brother, ibid., ll. 476–80

39 And filled the air with barbarous dissonance.
Attendant Spirit, ibid., l. 550

40 That power
Which erring men call chance.
Elder Brother, ibid., ll. 587–8

41 Beauty is Nature's brag, and must be shown
In courts, at feasts, and high solemnities
Where most may wonder at the workmanship;
It is for homely features to keep home,
They had their name thence; coarse complexions
And cheeks of sorry grain will serve to ply
The sampler, and to tease the housewife's wool.
What need a vermeil-tinctured lip for that,
Love-darting eyes, or tresses like the morn?
Comus, ibid., ll. 745–53

42 Sabrina fair,
Listen where thou art sitting
Under the glassy, cool, translucent wave,
In twisted braids of lilies knitting
The loose train of thy amber-dropping hair.
Song, ibid., ll. 859–63

43 Yet once more, O ye laurels, and once more,
Ye myrtles brown, with ivy never sere,
I come to pluck your berries harsh and crude,
And with forced fingers rude
Shatter your leaves before the mellowing year.
'Lycidas', ll. 1–5 (1638), repr. in Poems (1645)

44 For Lycidas is dead, dead ere his prime,
Young Lycidas, and hath not left his peer.
Who would not sing for Lycidas? He knew
Himself to sing, and build the lofty rhyme.
'Lycidas', ll. 8–11, ibid. The elegy was written for Edward King,
a graduate of Milton's college at Cambridge, who had died in
a shipwreck.

45 Alas! what boots it with uncessant care
To tend the homely slighted shepherd's trade,
And strictly meditate the thankless Muse?
'Lycidas', ll. 64–6, ibid.

46 Fame is the spur that the clear spirit doth raise
(That last infirmity of noble mind).
'Lycidas', ll. 70–1, ibid.

47 But the fair guerdon when we hope to find,
And think to burst out into sudden blaze,
Comes the blind Fury with th' abhorrèd shears,
And slits the thin-spun life.
'Lycidas', ll. 73–6, ibid.

48 Fame is no plant that grows on mortal soil.
'Lycidas', l. 78, ibid. The words of Phoebus.

49 Last came, and last did go,
The pilot of the Galilean lake;
Two massy keys he bore of metals twain
(The golden opes, the iron shuts amain).
'Lycidas', ll. 108–11, ibid. Referring to St Peter.

50 Bring the rathe primrose that forsaken dies,
The tufted crow-toe, and pale jessamine,
The white pink, and the pansy freaked with jet,
The glowing violet,
The musk-rose, and the well-attired woodbine,
With cowslips wan that hang the pensive head,
And every flower that sad embroidery wears.
Bid amaranthus all his beauty shed,
And daffadillies fill their cups with tears,

To strew the laureate hearse where Lycid lies.
'Lycidas', ll. 142–51, ibid.

51 Look homeward, angel, now, and melt with ruth.
'Lycidas', l. 163, ibid. *Look Homeward, Angel* is the title of an autobiographical novel by THOMAS WOLFE (1929).

52 So sinks the day-star in the ocean bed.
'Lycidas', l. 168, ibid.

53 At last he rose, and twitched his mantle blue: Tomorrow to fresh woods, and pastures new.
'Lycidas', ll. 192–3, ibid. Concluding lines of poem.

54 I began this far to assent ... to an inward prompting ... that by labour and intent study (which I take to be my portion in this life), joined with the strong propensity of nature, I might perhaps leave something so written to aftertimes, as they should not willingly let it die.
The Reason of Church Government, bk 2, Introduction (pamphlet, 1642), repr. in *The Complete Prose Works of John Milton*, vol. 1 (ed. Don M. Wolfe, 1953)

55 Beholding the bright countenance of truth in the quiet and still air of delightful studies.
The Reason of Church Government, bk 2, Introduction, ibid., vol. 1

56 For Truth is as impossible to be soiled by any outward touch, as the sunbeam. Though this ill hap wait on her nativity, that she never comes into the world but like a bastard, to the ignominy of him that brought her forth: till Time the midwife rather then the mother of Truth, have washed and salted the Infant, [and] declared her legitimate.
The Doctrine and Discipline of Divorce, 'To the Parliament of England' (pamphlet, 1643, rev. 1644), ibid., vol. 2 (ed. Ernest Sirluck, 1959)

57 Let not England forget her precedence of teaching nations how to live.
The Doctrine and Discipline of Divorce, 'To the Parliament of England', ibid., vol. 2

58 Men of most renowned virtue have sometimes by transgressing, most truly kept the law.
Tetrachordon (pamphlet, March 1644), ibid., vol. 2

59 Some allured to the trade of law, grounding their purposes not on the prudent and heavenly contemplation of justice and equity which was never taught them, but on the promising and pleasing thoughts of litigious terms, fat contentions, and flowing fees.
Of Education (pamphlet, June 1644), ibid., vol. 2

60 When complaints are freely heard, deeply considered and speedily reformed, then is the utmost bound of civil liberty attained that wise men look for.
Areopagitica: a Speech for the Liberty of Unlicensed Printing to the Parliament of England (pamphlet, November 1644), ibid., vol. 2

61 For books are not absolutely dead things, but do contain a potency of life in them to be as active as that soul was whose progeny they are; nay, they do preserve as in a vial the purest efficacy and extraction of that living intellect that bred them. I know they are as lively, and as vigorously productive, as those fabulous dragon's teeth; and being sown up and down, may chance to spring up armed men.
Areopagitica, ibid., vol. 2

62 As good almost kill a man as kill a good book; who kills a man kills a reasonable creature, God's image; but he who destroys a good book, kills reason itself, kills the image of God, as it were in the eye.
Areopagitica, ibid., vol. 2

63 A good book is the precious life-blood of a master spirit, embalmed and treasured up on purpose to a life beyond life.
Areopagitica, ibid., vol. 2

64 What wisdom can there be to choose, what continence to forbear without the knowledge of evil? He that can apprehend and consider vice with all her baits and seeming pleasures, and yet abstain, and yet distinguish, and yet prefer that which is truly better, he is the true wayfaring Christian.
Areopagitica, ibid., vol. 2

65 I cannot praise a fugitive and cloistered virtue, unexercised and unbreathed, that never sallies out and sees her adversary, but slinks out of the race where that immortal garland is to be run for, not without dust and heat.
Areopagitica, ibid., vol. 2

66 A man may be a heretic in the truth; and if he believe things only because his pastor says so, or the assembly so determines, without knowing other reason, though his belief be true, yet the very truth he holds becomes his heresy.
Areopagitica, ibid., vol. 2

67 Lords and Commoners of England, consider what nation it is whereof ye are, and whereof ye are the governors; a nation not slow and dull, but of a quick, ingenious and piercing spirit, acute to invent, subtle and sinewy to discourse, not beneath the reach of

any point the highest that human capacity can soar to.

Areopagitica, ibid., vol. 2

68 Behold now this vast city; a city of refuge, the mansion house of liberty, encompassed and surrounded with his protection; the shop of war hath not there more anvils and hammers waking, to fashion out the plates and instruments of armed justice in defence of beleaguered truth, than there be pens and hands there, sitting by their studious lamps, musing, searching, revolving new notions and ideas.

Areopagitica, ibid., vol. 2. Describing London.

69 Where there is much desire to learn, there of necessity will be much arguing, much writing, many opinions; for opinion in good men is but knowledge in the making. Under these fantastic terrors of sect and schism, we wrong the earnest and zealous thirst after knowledge and understanding which God hath stirred up in this city.

Areopagitica, ibid., vol. 2

70 Methinks I see in my mind a noble and puissant nation rousing herself like a strong man after sleep, and shaking her invincible locks. Methinks I see her as an eagle mewing her mighty youth, and kindling her undazzled eyes at the full midday beam.

Areopagitica, ibid., vol. 2

71 Give me the liberty to know, to utter, and to argue freely according to conscience, above all liberties.

Areopagitica, ibid., vol. 2

72 New Presbyter is but old Priest writ large.

'On the New Forcers of Conscience under the Long Parliament', written c. 1646, publ. in *Poems* (1673). Milton strongly disagreed with the more rigid and intolerant strands of the Presbyterian system, which was adopted in England by parliamentary ordinances during 1646.

73 For what can war but endless war still breed,
Till truth and right from violence be freed?

Sonnet 15 ('On the Lord General Fairfax at the Siege of Colchester'), written 1648, publ. in *Poetical Works* (ed. Douglas Bush, 1966)

74 None can love freedom heartily, but good men; the rest love not freedom, but licence.

The Tenure of Kings and Magistrates (pamphlet, February 1649), repr. in *The Complete Prose Works of Milton*, vol. 3 (ed. Merrit Y. Hughes, 1962)

75 No man who knows aught, can be so stupid to deny that all men naturally were born free.

The Tenure of Kings and Magistrates, ibid., vol. 3. See JEAN-JACQUES ROUSSEAU 1.

76 Cromwell, our chief of men.

Sonnet 16 ('To the Lord General Cromwell'), written 1652, publ. in *Poetical Works* (ed. Douglas Bush, 1966). Opening words.

77 Peace hath her victories
No less renowned than war.

Sonnet 16, ibid.

78 When I consider how my light is spent,
Ere half my days, in this dark world and wide,
And that one talent which is death to hide
Lodged with me useless.

Sonnet 19 ('When I Consider How My Light is Spent'), written c. 1652, publ. in *Poems* (1673). Also known as 'On His Blindness'. Milton became completely blind in the winter of 1651–2.

79 They also serve who only stand and wait.

Sonnet 19, ibid.

80 Methought I saw my late espousèd saint
Brought to me like Alcestis from the grave.

Sonnet 23 ('Methought I saw my late espousèd saint'), written 1658, ibid. Also known as 'On His Deceased Wife'.

81 But oh as to embrace me she inclined
I waked, she fled, and day brought back my night.

Sonnet 23, ibid. Last lines of sonnet.

82 Rhyme being no necessary adjunct or true ornament of poem or good verse, in longer works especially, but the invention of a barbarous age, to set off wretched matter and lame metre.

Paradise Lost, 'The Verse' (1667, rev. 1674). Milton complained, in this preface added in 1668, of 'the troublesome and modern bondage of rhyming'.

83 Of man's first disobedience, and the fruit
Of that forbidden tree, whose mortal taste
Brought death into the world, and all our woe,
With loss of Eden, till one greater Man
Restore us, and regain the blissful seat,
Sing, heavenly Muse.

Ibid., bk. 1, ll. 1–2

84 What in me is dark
Illumine, what is low raise and support;
That to the height of this great argument
I may assert eternal providence,
And justify the ways of God to men.

Ibid., bk 1, ll. 22–6. See ALEXANDER POPE 115

85 Th' infernal serpent; he it was whose guile,
Stirred up with envy and revenge, deceived
The mother of mankind.
Ibid., bk 1, ll. 34–6

86 Yet from those flames
No light, but rather darkness visible
Served only to discover sights of woe,
Regions of sorrow, doleful shades.
Ibid., bk 1, ll. 62–5

87 What though the field be lost?
All is not lost; the unconquerable will,
And study of revenge, immortal hate,
And courage never to submit or yield:
And what is else not to be overcome?
Ibid., bk 1, ll. 105–9. Spoken by Satan.

88 To do aught good never will be our task,
But ever to do ill our sole delight.
Satan, ibid., bk 1, ll. 159–60

89 And out of good still to find means of evil.
Satan, ibid., bk 1, l. 165

90 And re-assembling our afflicted powers,
Consult how we may henceforth most offend.
Satan, ibid., bk 1, ll. 186–7

91 What reinforcement we may gain from hope;
If not, what resolution from despair.
Satan, ibid., bk 1, ll. 190–1

92 The mind is its own place, and in itself
Can make a heaven of hell, a hell of heaven.
Satan, ibid., bk 1, ll. 254–5

93 Better to reign in hell than serve in heaven.
Satan, ibid., bk 1, l. 263

94 Thick as autumnal leaves that strew the brooks
In Vallombrosa.
Ibid., bk 1, ll. 302–3. Vallombrosa lies in Tuscany (ancient Etruria).

95 For spirits when they please
Can either sex assume, or both; so soft
And uncompounded is their essence pure.
Ibid., bk 1, ll. 423–5

96 And when night
Darkens the streets, then wander forth the sons
Of Belial, flown with insolence and wine.
Ibid., bk 1, ll. 500–2

97 His face
Deep scars of thunder had entrenched, and care
Sat on his faded cheek, but under brows

Of dauntless courage, and considerate pride
Waiting revenge.
Ibid., bk 1, ll. 600–4. Referring to Satan.

98 Who overcomes
By force hath overcome but half his foe.
Ibid., bk 1, ll. 648–9

99 Mammon, the least erected spirit that fell
From heaven, for even in heaven his looks and
  thoughts
Were always downward bent, admiring more
The riches of heaven's pavement, trodden gold,
Than aught divine or holy else enjoyed
In vision beatific.
Ibid., bk 1, ll. 679–84

100 Let none admire
That riches grow in hell; that soil may best
Deserve the precious bane.
Ibid., bk 1, ll. 690–2

101 Nor aught availed him now
To have built in heaven high towers; nor did he
  scape
By all his engines, but was headlong sent
With his industrious crew to build in hell.
Ibid., bk 1, ll. 748–51. Referring to the architect Mulciber, the builder of Pandemonium, 'high capital/Of Satan and his peers'.

102 High on a throne of royal state, which far
Outshone the wealth of Ormuz and of Ind,
Or where the gorgeous East with richest hand
Showers on her kings barbaric pearl and gold,
Satan exalted sat, by merit raised
To that bad eminence; and from despair
Thus high uplifted beyond hope.
Ibid., bk 2, ll. 1–7

103 For none sure will claim in hell
Precedence, none whose portion is so small
Of present pain that with ambitious mind
Will covet more.
Satan, ibid., bk 2, ll. 32–5

104 Rather than be less
Cared not to be at all.
Ibid., bk 2, ll. 47–8. Referring to Moloch, 'the strongest and the fiercest spirit'.

105 My sentence is for open war.
Ibid., bk 2, l. 51. Moloch's advice at the 'Stygian council', convened by Satan to decide whether to launch a battle to recover heaven.

106 But all was false and hollow, though his
tongue
Dropped manna, and could make the worse appear
The better reason, to perplex and dash
Maturest counsels.
Ibid., bk 2, ll. 112–15. Referring to Belial.

107 The never-ending flight
Of future days.
Belial, ibid., bk 2, ll. 221–2

108 Thus Belial with words clothed in reason's
garb,
Counselled ignoble ease, and peaceful sloth,
Not peace.
Ibid., bk 2, ll. 226–8

109 With grave
Aspect he rose, and in his rising seemed
A pillar of state; deep on his front engraven
Deliberation sat and public care;
And princely counsel in his face yet shone,
Majestic though in ruin.
Ibid., bk 2, ll. 300–5. Beelzebub prepares to speak.

110 This would surpass
Common revenge.
Ibid., bk 2, ll. 370–1. Beelzebub speaks of the plan to 'Seduce
[humanity] to our party'.

111 To sit in darkness here
Hatching vain empires.
Beelzebub, ibid., bk 2, ll. 377–8

112 Long is the way
And hard, that out of hell leads up to light.
Satan, ibid., bk 2, ll. 432–3

113 Others apart sat on a hill retired,
In thoughts more elevate, and reasoned high
Of providence, foreknowledge, will and fate,
Fixed fate, free will, foreknowledge absolute,
And found no end, in wandering mazes lost.
Of good and evil much they argued then,
Of happiness and final misery,
Passion and apathy, and glory and shame,
Vain wisdom all, and false philosophy.
Ibid., bk 2, ll. 557–65. Referring to the 'rangèd powers' of hell,
having dispersed after the assembly.

114 Far off from these a slow and silent stream,
Lethe, the river of oblivion, rolls
Her watery labyrinth, whereof who drinks
Forthwith his former state and being forgets,
Forgets both joy and grief, pleasure and pain.
Ibid., bk 2, ll. 582–6

115 Whence and what art thou, execrable shape?
Ibid., bk 2, l. 681. Satan addresses his son, Death.

116 A race of upstart creatures.
Satan, ibid., bk 2, l. 834. Referring to the human race.

117 Hot, cold, moist and dry, four champions
fierce,
Strive here for mastery.
Ibid., bk 2, ll. 898–9. The four elements of fire, earth, water
and air.

118 Chaos umpire sits,
And by decision more embroils the fray
By which he reigns; next him high arbiter
Chance governs all.
Ibid., bk 2, ll. 907–10

119 With ruin upon ruin, rout on rout,
Confusion worse confounded.
Ibid., bk 2, ll. 995–6

120 And fast by hanging in a golden chain
This pendent world.
Ibid., bk 2, ll. 1051–2

121 Hail, holy Light, offspring of heaven first-born,
Or of th' eternal co-eternal beam
May I express thee unblamed? since God is light,
And never but in unapproachèd light
Dwelt from eternity, dwelt then in thee,
Bright effluence of bright essence increate.
Ibid., bk 3, ll. 1–6

122 I made him just and right,
Sufficient to have stood, though free to fall.
Such I created all th' ethereal powers
And spirits, both them who stood and them who
failed;
Freely they stood who stood, and fell who fell.
Ibid., bk 3, ll. 98–102. The lines, in which God speaks of Satan
and his other heavenly creations, encapsulate Milton's view
in the poem of free will.

123 Into a limbo large and broad, since called
The Paradise of Fools, to few unknown.
Ibid., bk 3, ll. 495–6

124 The pure marble air.
Ibid., bk 3, l. 564

125 For neither man nor angel can discern
Hypocrisy, the only evil that walks
Invisible, except to God alone.
Ibid., bk 3, ll. 682–4

126 This new world, at whose sight all the stars
Hide their diminished heads.
Ibid., bk 4, ll. 34–5

127 Me miserable! which way shall I fly
Infinite wrath, and infinite despair?
Which way I fly is hell; myself am hell;
And in the lowest deep a lower deep
Still threatening to devour me opens wide,
To which the hell I suffer seems a heaven.
Satan, ibid., bk 4, ll. 73–8

128 For never can true reconcilement grow
Where wounds of deadly hate have pierced so
   deep.
Satan, ibid., bk 4, ll. 98–9

129 So farewell hope, and with hope farewell fear,
Farewell remorse! All good to me is lost;
Evil, be thou my good.
Satan, ibid., bk 4, ll. 108–10

130 A heaven on earth, for blissful Paradise
Of God the garden was.
Ibid., bk 4, ll. 208–9

131 Out of the fertile ground he caused to grow
All trees of noblest kind for sight, smell, taste;
And all amid them stood the Tree of Life,
High eminent, blooming ambrosial fruit
Of vegetable gold.
Ibid., bk 4, ll. 216–20. God's creation of Eden.

132 Groves whose rich trees wept odorous gums
   and balm,
Others whose fruit burnished with golden rind
Hung amiable, Hesperian fables true,
If true, here only.
Ibid., bk 4, ll. 248–51. Describing Eden.

133 Flowers of all hue, and without thorn the rose.
Ibid., bk 4, l. 256. Describing Eden.

134 Two of far nobler shape erect and tall,
God-like erect, with native honour clad
In naked majesty seemed lords of all,
And worthy seemed, for in their looks divine
The image of their glorious maker shone.
Ibid., bk 4, ll. 288–92. Of Adam and Eve.

135 Though both
Not equal, as their sex not equal seemed;
For contemplation he and valour formed,
For softness she and sweet attractive grace;
He for God only, she for God in him.

His fair large front and eye sublime declared
Absolute rule.
Ibid., bk 4, ll. 295–301. Of Adam and Eve.

136 Hyacinthine locks
Round from his parted forelock manly hung
Clustering, but not beneath his shoulders broad:
She as a veil down to the slender waist
Her unadornèd golden tresses wore
Dishevelled, but in wanton ringlets waved
As the vine curls her tendrils.
Ibid., bk 4, ll. 301–7. Of Adam and Eve.

137 Yielded with coy submission, modest pride,
And sweet reluctant amorous delay.
Ibid., bk 4, ll. 310–11. Of Eve.

138 So hand in hand they passed, the loveliest pair
That ever since in love's embraces met,
Adam the goodliest man of men since born
His sons, the fairest of her daughters Eve.
Ibid., bk 4, ll. 321–4

139 These two
Imparadised in one another's arms,
The happier Eden, shall enjoy their fill
Of bliss on bliss.
Ibid., bk 4, ll. 505–8. Satan observes Adam and Eve.

140 Now came still evening on, and twilight grey
Had in her sober livery all things clad.
Ibid., bk 4, ll. 598–9

141 God is thy law, thou mine; to know no more
Is woman's happiest knowledge and her praise.
Ibid., bk 4, ll. 637–8. Eve's words to Adam were quoted by
LYDIA M. CHILD in a letter, January 1843, with her comment:
'May Milton be forgiven' (Letters from New York, vol. 1, 1843).

142 With thee conversing I forget all time.
Eve to Adam, ibid., bk 4, l. 639

143 Hail wedded love, mysterious law, true source
Of human offspring, sole propriety
In Paradise of all things common else.
Ibid., bk 4, ll. 750–2

144 Not to know me argues yourselves unknown.
Ibid., bk 4, l. 830. Satan addresses 'two fair angels'.

145 But wherefore thou alone? Wherefore with
   thee
Came not all hell broke loose?
Ibid., bk 4, ll. 917–18. Gabriel questions Satan.

146 Now morn her rosy steps in th' eastern clime
Advancing, sowed the earth with orient pearl.
Ibid., bk 5, ll. 1–2

147 Awake,
My fairest, my espoused, my latest found,
Heaven's last best gift, my ever new delight.
Ibid., bk 5, ll. 17–19. Adam rouses Eve from her sleep.

148 Here, happy creature, fair angelic Eve,
Partake thou also; happy though thou art,
Happier thou mayest be, worthier canst not be;
Taste this, and be henceforth among the gods
Thyself a goddess.
Ibid., bk 5, ll. 74–8. Satan tempts Eve, in her dream.

149 Best image of myself and dearer half.
Adam to Eve, ibid., bk 5, l. 95

150 Nor jealousy
Was understood, the injured lover's hell.
Ibid., bk 5, ll. 449–50

151 Freely we serve,
Because we freely love, as in our will
To love or not; in this we stand or fall.
The angel Raphael, ibid., bk 5, ll. 538–40

152 Though what if earth
Be but the shadow of heaven, and things therein
Each to other like, more than on earth is thought?
The angel Raphael, ibid., bk 5, ll. 574–6

153 They eat, they drink, and in communion sweet
Quaff immortality and joy.
Ibid., bk 5, ll. 637–8. The angels' banquet.

154 Servant of God, well done, well hast thou
    fought
The better fight, who single hast maintained
Against revolted multitudes the cause
Of truth, in word mightier than they in arms.
Ibid., bk 6, ll. 29–32. God greets the seraph Abdiel.

155 Headlong themselves they threw
Down from the verge of heaven, eternal wrath
Burnt after them to the bottomless pit.
Ibid., bk 6, ll. 864–6. Satan's armies plunge to hell.

156 And in his hand
He took the golden compasses, prepared
In God's eternal store, to circumscribe
This universe, and all created things.
One foot he centred, and the other turned
Round through the vast profundity obscure,
And said, 'Thus far extend, thus far thy bounds,
This be thy just circumference, O world!'
Ibid., bk 7, ll. 224–31. The Messiah's creation of the earth.

157 There Leviathan
Hugest of living creatures, on the deep

Stretched like a promontory sleeps or swims,
And seems a moving land, and at his gills
Draws in, and at his trunk spouts out a sea.
Ibid., bk 7, ll. 412–16. See also BIBLE, OLD TESTAMENT: JOB 47.

158 The planets in their stations listening stood,
While the bright pomp ascended jubilant.
'Open, ye everlasting gates,' they sung,
'Open, ye heavens, your living doors; let in
The great Creator from his work returned
Magnificent, his six days' work, a world.'
Ibid., bk 7, ll. 563–8

159 From man or angel the great architect
Did wisely to conceal, and not divulge
His secrets to be scanned by them who ought
Rather admire; or if they list to try
Conjecture, he his fabric of the heavens
Hath left to their disputes, perhaps to move
His laughter at their quaint opinions wide
Hereafter, when they come to model heaven
And calculate the stars, how they will wield
The mighty frame, how build, unbuild, contrive
To save appearances, how gird the sphere
With centric and eccentric scribbled o'er,
Cycle and epicycle, orb in orb.
Ibid., bk 8, ll. 72–84. The angel Raphael explains God's conceal-
ment of knowledge.

160 Heaven is for thee too high
To know what passes there; be lowly wise:
Think only what concerns thee and thy being;
Dream not of other worlds, what creatures there
Live, in what state, condition or degree,
Contented that thus far hath been revealed
Not of earth only but of highest heaven.
Ibid., bk 8, ll. 172–8. Raphael's answer to Adam's enquiries
'concerning celestial motions'.

161 In solitude
What happiness? Who can enjoy alone
Or all enjoying, what contentment find?
Ibid., bk 8, ll. 364–6. Adam laments of life without a com-
panion, to which God responds: 'What call'st thou solitude?
Is not the earth/With various living creatures, and the air/
Replenished, and all these at thy command/To come and play
before thee?' Adam's plea is finally granted by the creation
of Eve.

162 Among unequals what society
Can sort, what harmony or true delight?
Adam, ibid., bk 8, ll. 383–4

163 When I approach
Her loveliness, so absolute she seems

And in herself complete, so well to know
Her own, that what she wills to do or say
Seems wisest, virtuousest, discreetest, best;
All higher knowledge in her presence falls
Degraded.

Ibid., bk 8, ll. 546–52. Adam tells of Eve's effect on him.

164 Oft-times nothing profits more
Than self esteem, grounded on just and right
Well managed.

Raphael, ibid., bk 8, ll. 571–3

165 Love refines
The thoughts, and heart enlarges, hath his seat
In reason, and is judicious, is the scale
By which to heavenly love thou mayest ascend,
Not sunk in carnal pleasure.

Raphael, ibid., bk 8, ll. 589–93

166 Those graceful acts,
Those thousand decencies, that daily flow
From all her words and actions, mixed with love
And sweet compliance, which declare unfeigned
Union of mind, or in us both one soul.

Adam, ibid., bk 8, ll. 600–4. Describing Eve.

167 Thus the orb he roamed
With narrow search, and with inspection deep
Considered every creature, which of all
Most opportune might serve his wiles, and found
The serpent subtlest beast of all the field.

Ibid., bk 9, ll. 82–6. Satan searches for a 'fit vessel . . . in whom/
To enter'. See BIBLE, OLD TESTAMENT: GENESIS 16.

168 The more I see
Pleasures about me, so much more I feel
Torment within me, as from the hateful siege
Of contraries; all good to me becomes
Bane.

Satan, ibid., bk 9, ll. 119–23

169 For nothing lovelier can be found
In woman, than to study household good,
And good works in her husband to promote.

Adam, ibid., bk 9, ll. 232–4. Addressing Eve.

170 As one who long in populous city pent.

Ibid., bk 9, ll. 445–9

171 Her rash hand in evil hour
Forth reaching to the fruit, she plucked, she eat.
Earth felt the wound, and Nature from her seat
Sighing through all her works gave signs of woe
That all was lost.

Ibid., bk 9, ll. 780–4. Eve takes the forbidden fruit. The phrase
'in evil hour' is repeated in l. 1067.

172 O fairest of creation, last and best
Of all God's works, creature in whom excelled
Whatever can to sight or thought be formed,
Holy, divine, good, amiable, or sweet!

Ibid., bk 9, ll. 896–9. Adam extols Eve.

173 I feel
The link of nature draw me: flesh of flesh,
Bone of my bone thou art, and from thy state
Mine shall never be parted, bliss or woe.

Adam, ibid., bk 9, ll. 913–16. Addressing Eve, shortly before he
partakes of 'the fair enticing fruit'.

174 For what thou art is mine;
Our state cannot be severed; we are one,
One flesh; to lose thee were to lose myself.

Adam, ibid., bk 9, ll. 957–9. Addressing Eve, after she has
confessed her sin.

175 Thus they in mutual accusation spent
The fruitless hours, but neither self-condemning,
And of their vain contest appeared no end.

Ibid., bk 9, ll. 1187–9. Of Adam and Eve.

176 Yet I shall temper so
Justice with mercy.

Ibid., bk 10, ll. 77–8. The Son of God declares how he shall
judge Adam and Eve.

177 So having said, a while he stood, expecting
Their universal shout and high applause
To fill his ear; when contrary, he hears,
On all sides, from innumerable tongues
A dismal universal hiss, the sound
Of public scorn.

Ibid., bk 10, ll. 504–9. Satan ends his address to 'the Stygian
throng'.

178 How gladly would I meet
Mortality, my sentence, and be earth
Insensible! how glad would lay me down,
As in my mother's lap! There I should rest
And sleep secure.

Adam, ibid., bk 10, ll. 775–9

179 O why did God,
Creator wise, that peopled highest heaven
With spirits masculine, create at last
This novelty on earth, this fair defect
Of nature, and not fill the world at once
With men as angels without feminine,
Or find some other way to generate
Mankind?

Adam, ibid., bk 10, ll. 888–95

180 Demoniac frenzy, moping melancholy
And moon-struck madness.
Ibid., bk 11, ll. 485–6. Describing the vision of human ailments.

181 Nor love thy life, nor hate; but what thou liv'st
Live well, how long or short permit to heaven.
Ibid., bk 11, ll. 553–4. The advice of the angel Michael.

182 A bevy of fair women, richly gay
In gems and wanton dress; to the harp they sung
Soft amorous ditties, and in dance came on.
Ibid., bk 11, ll. 582–4

183 The evening star,
Love's harbinger.
Ibid., bk 11, ll. 588–9

184 Only add
Deeds to thy knowledge answerable, add faith,
Add virtue, patience, temperance, add love,
By name to come called charity, the soul
Of all the rest: then wilt thou not be loath
To leave this Paradise, but shalt possess
A paradise within thee, happier far.
Ibid., bk 12, ll. 581–7. Michael's advice to Adam.

185 They looking back, all the eastern side beheld
Of Paradise, so late their happy seat,
Waved over by that flaming brand, the gate
With dreadful faces thronged and fiery arms.
Some natural tears they dropped, but wiped them
    soon;
The world was all before them, where to choose
Their place of rest, and Providence their guide:
They hand in hand, with wandering steps and
    slow,
Through Eden took their solitary way.
Ibid., bk 12, ll. 641–9. Adam and Eve depart from Paradise in the closing lines of the work.

186 Most men admire
Virtue who follow not her lore.
Paradise Regained, bk 1, ll. 482–3 (1671). The words of Satan.

187 And what the people but a herd confused,
A miscellaneous rabble, who extol
Things vulgar, and well weighed, scarce worth the
    praise?
They praise and they admire they know not what,
And know not whom, but as one leads the other;
And what delight to be by such extolled,
To live upon their tongues and be their talk,
Of whom to be dispraised were no small praise?
Christ, *ibid.*, bk 3, ll. 49–56

188 The childhood shows the man,
As morning shows the day.
Satan, *ibid.*, bk 4, ll. 220–1

189 Athens, the eye of Greece, mother of arts
And eloquence, native to famous wits.
Satan, *ibid.*, bk 4, ll. 240–1

190 See there the olive grove of Academe,
Plato's retirement, where the Attic bird
Trills her thick-warbled notes the summer long.
Satan, *ibid.*, bk 4, ll. 244–6. Describing Athens.

191 The first and wisest of them all professed
To know this only, that he nothing knew.
Ibid., bk 4, ll. 293–4. Christ refers to SOCRATES 11.

192 Who reads
Incessantly, and to his reading brings not
A spirit and judgement equal or superior
(And what he brings, what needs he elsewhere
    seek?)
Uncertain and unsettled still remains,
Deep versed in books and shallow in himself.
Christ, *ibid.*, bk 4, ll. 322–7

193 Ask for this great deliverer now, and find him
Eyeless in Gaza at the mill with slaves,
Himself in bonds under Philistian yoke.
Samson Agonistes, ll. 40–2 (1671). Samson describes his predicament. ALDOUS HUXLEY's novel *Eyeless in Gaza* (1936) tells the story of a man who discovers he has been spiritually blind.

194 O impotence of mind, in body strong!
But what is strength without a double share
Of wisdom? Vast, unwieldy, burdensome,
Proudly secure, yet liable to fall
By weakest subtleties.
Samson, *ibid.*, ll. 52–6

195 O loss of sight, of thee I most complain!
Blind among enemies, O worse than chains,
Dungeon, or beggary, or decrepit age!
Light, the prime work of God, to me is extinct,
And all her various objects of delight
Annulled, which might in part my grief have
    eased.
Inferior to the vilest now become
Of man or worm; the vilest here excel me,
They creep, yet see; I, dark in light, exposed
To daily fraud, contempt, abuse and wrong,
Within doors, or without, still as a fool,

In power of others, never in my own;
Scarce half I seem to live, dead more than half.
Samson, ibid., ll. 67–79

196 O dark, dark, dark, amid the blaze of noon,
Irrecoverably dark, total eclipse
Without all hope of day!
Samson, ibid., ll. 80–2

197 Exiled from light,
As in the land of darkness, yet in light,
To live a life half dead, a living death,
And buried.
Samson, ibid., ll. 98–101

198 Just are the ways of God,
And justifiable to men;
Unless there be who think not God at all.
Chorus, ibid., ll. 293–5

199 If weakness may excuse,
What murtherer, what traitor, parricide,
Incestuous, sacrilegious, but may plead it?
All wickedness is weakness: that plea therefore
With God or man will gain thee no remission.
Samson to Dalila, ibid., ll. 831–5

200 Yet beauty, though injurious, hath strange
  power,
After offence returning, to regain
Love once possessed.
Chorus, ibid., ll. 1003–5

201 Love-quarrels oft in pleasing concord end.
Samson, ibid., l. 1008

202 He all their ammunition
And feats of war defeats,
With plain heroic magnitude of mind
And celestial vigour armed.
Chorus, of Samson, ibid., ll. 1277–80

203 Lords are lordliest in their wine.
Samson, ibid., l. 1418

204 His servants he, with new acquist
Of true experience from this great event,
With peace and consolation hath dismissed,
And calm of mind, all passion spent.
Chorus, ibid., ll. 1755–8. Closing lines of work.

205 They who have put out the people's eyes,
reproach them of their blindness.
Attributed

206 To be blind is not miserable; not to be able to
bear blindness, that is miserable.
Attributed

Liza Minnelli
(b. 1946)
US screen actor and singer

The daughter of JUDY GARLAND *and director Vincente Minnelli, she inherited her mother's powerful and vibrant singing voice. Her most famous roles were in the films* Cabaret *(1972) and* New York, New York *(1977).*

1 Money makes the world go round
The world go round
The world go round,
Money makes the world go round
That clinking clanking sound!
'Money' (song, written by Fred Ebb and John Kander) in *Cabaret* (musical play by Joe Masterhoff, 1966, filmed 1972). The words are sung by Sally Bowles (Liza Minnelli) and the Master of Ceremonies (Joel Grey).

Octave Mirbeau
(1850–1917)
French journalist and author

An advocate of anarchism from 1885, he savagely satirized clericalism and militarism in his novels and plays. His prolific output included some 1,200 articles and short stories, and he was a founding member of the Académie Goncourt in 1903.

1 The greatest danger of bombs is in the explosion of stupidity that they provoke.
'Pour Jean Grave', publ. in *Le Journal* 19 February 1894. Mirbeau was referring to a bombing campaign which Jean Grave had allegedly incited by his inflammatory anarchist pamphlets, for which he was to face trial.

2 The universe appears to me like an immense, inexorable torture-garden ... Passions, greed, hatred, and lies; law, social institutions, justice, love, glory, heroism, and religion: these are its monstrous flowers and its hideous instruments of eternal human suffering.
The Torture Garden, ch. 9 ('The Garden') (1899)

3 When one tears away the veils and shows them naked, people's souls give off such a pungent smell of decay.
The Diary of a Chambermaid, '14 September' (1900)

Yukio Mishima
(1925–70)
Japanese author

Pseudonym of Kimitake Hiraoka. Considered the most important Japanese novelist of modern times, he also wrote poetry and versions of Noh and Kabuki plays. The Sea of Fertility tetralogy (1965–71) evokes, in his own words, 'the old beautiful tradition of Japan, which is disappearing very quickly day by day'.

1 The sound of the rain is like the voices of tens of thousands of monks reading sutras.
Ai No Kawaki ch. 4 (1950; *Thirst for Love*, transl. 1969)

2 From the moment that a man no longer responds in the slightest to the motives that regulate the material world, that world appears to be at complete repose.
Death in Midsummer and Other Stories, 'The Priest of Shiga Temple and His Love' (1966)

3 Literary art takes its materials from life, but although life is thus the mother of literature, it is also her bitter enemy; although life is inherent in the author himself, it is also the eternal antithesis of art.
Mishima on Hagakure, '*Hagakure* and I' (1977)

4 If we value so highly the dignity of life, how can we not also value the dignity of death? No death may be called futile.
Ibid., 'How to Read *Hagakure*'. Following an attempt to rally support for the overthrow of the Japanese Constitution, Mishima committed *seppuku*, a ritual Samurai suicide.

The Missal

The Missal contains the liturgy of the Roman Catholic mass and prayers for feasts and seasons for use throughout the year. It was first printed in Latin in 1474 and in English in 1973. Much of the wording in English is found in the BOOK OF COMMON PRAYER.

1 *In Nomine Patris, et Filii, et Spiritus Sancti.*
[In the Name of the Father, and of the Son, and of the Holy Ghost.]
Ordinary of the Mass

2 *Introibo ad altare Dei.*
[I will go in unto the altar of God.]
Ibid.

3 *Gloria Patri, et Filio, et Spiritui Sancto. Sicut erat in principio, et nunc, et semper, et in saecula saeculorum.*
[Glory be to the Father, and to the Son, and to the Holy Ghost. As it was in the beginning, is now, and ever shall be, world without end.]
Ibid., 'The Doxology'

4 *Mea culpa, mea maxima culpa.*
[Through my fault, my most grievous fault.]
Ibid., 'Confession' or 'Confiteor'

5 *Dominus vobiscum.*
Et cum spiritu tuo.
[The Lord be with you.
And with thy spirit.]
Ibid.

6 *Kyrie eleison . . . Christe eleison.*
[Lord, have mercy upon us . . . Christ, have mercy upon us.]
Ibid., 'Kyrie Eleison'

7 *Gloria in excelsis Deo, et in terra pax hominibus bonae voluntatis. Laudamus te, benedicimus te, adoramus te, glorificamus te.*
[Glory be to God on high, and on earth peace to men of good will. We praise thee, we bless thee, we adore thee, we give Thee thanks for Thy great glory.]
Ibid., 'Gloria'

8 *Oremus.*
[Let us pray.]
Ibid.

9 *Deo gratias.*
[Thanks be to God.]
Ibid.

10 *Credo in unum Deum, Patrem omnipotentem, factorem coeli et terrae, visibilium omnium et invisibilium.*
[I believe in one God, the Father almighty, maker of heaven and earth, and of all things visible and invisible.]
Ibid., 'The Nicene Creed'

11 *Deum de Deo, lumen de lumine, Deum verum de Deo vero.*
[God of God, light of light; true God of true God.]
Ibid., 'The Nicene Creed'

12 *Et incarnatus est de Spiritu Sancto, ex Maria Virgine; ET HOMO FACTUS EST.*
[And became incarnate by the Holy Ghost, of the Virgin Mary; AND WAS MADE MAN.]
Ibid., 'The Nicene Creed'

13 *Sursum corda.*
[Lift up your hearts.]
Ibid.

14 *Dignum et justum est.*
[It is meet and just.]
Ibid.

15 *Sanctus, sanctus, sanctus, Dominus Deus Sabaoth. Pleni sunt coeli et terra gloria tua. Hosanna in excelsis. Benedictus qui venit in nomine Domini.*

[Holy, holy, holy, Lord God of Hosts. Heaven and earth are full of thy glory. Hosanna in the highest. Blessed is he that cometh in the name of the Lord.]
Ibid., 'Sanctus'

16 *HOC EST CORPUS MEUM.*
[For this is my body.]
Ibid., 'Consecration'

17 *HOC EST CALIX SANGUINIS MEI.*
[For this is the chalice of my blood.]
Ibid., 'Consecration'

18 *Pater noster, qui es in coelis, sanctificetur nomen tuum; adveniat regnum tuum; fiat voluntas tua sicut in coelo, et in terra.*
[Our Father, who art in heaven, hallowed be Thy name; Thy kingdom come; Thy will be done on earth, as it is in heaven.]
Ibid., 'Pater Noster'. See BIBLE, NEW TESTAMENT: MATTHEW 38.

19 *Sed libera nos a malo.*
[But deliver us from evil.]
Ibid. See BIBLE, NEW TESTAMENT: MATTHEW 38.

20 *Pax Domini sit semper vobiscum.*
[The peace of the Lord be always with you.]
Ibid.

21 *Agnus Dei, qui tollis peccata mundi, miserere nobis.*
Agnus Dei, qui tollis peccata mundi, dona nobis pacem.
[Lamb of God, who takest away the sins of the world, have mercy on us.
Lamb of God, who takest away the sins of the world, grant us peace.]
Ibid., 'Agnus Dei'

22 *Domine, non sum dignus ut intres sub tectum meum; sed tantum dic verbo, et sanabitur anima mea.*
[Lord, I am not worthy that Thou shouldst enter under my roof; say but the word, and my soul shall be healed.]
Ibid.

23 *Ite missa est.*
[Go, you are dismissed.]
Ibid. Also known as 'Go, the Mass is ended.'

24 *Requiem aeternam dona eis, Domine: et lux perpetua luceat eis.*

[Grant them eternal rest, O Lord; and let perpetual light shine on them.]
Order of Mass for the Dead

25 *Dies irae, dies illa,*
Solvet saeclum in favilla,
Teste David cum Sibylla.
[Day of wrath, day of mourning,
earth in smouldering ashes lying,
so spake David and the Sibyl.]
Ibid., 'Sequentia', st. 1. Commonly known as the Dies Irae, it is generally ascribed to Thomas of Celano (c. 1190–1260).

26 *Tuba mirum spargens sonum*
Per sepulcra regionum,
Coget omnes ante thronum.
Mors stupebit et natura,
Cum resurget creatura
Iudicanti responsura.
[The trumpet, sending its wondrous sound
through the tombs in every land,
shall bring all before the throne.
Death shall stun and nature quake
when all creatures rise again
to answer to the Judge.]
Order of Mass for the Dead, 'Sequentia', sts 3–4

27 *Judex ergo cum sedebit,*
quidquid latet apparebit:
nil inultum remanebit.
[Therefore, when the Judge shall be seated
nothing shall be held hidden any longer,
no wrong shall remain unpunished.]
Order of Mass for the Dead, 'Sequentia', st. 6

28 *Requiescant in pace.*
[May they rest in peace.]
Ibid.

Mistinguett
(1874–1956)
French dancer and singer

Originally Jeanne Marie Bourgeois. A popular and vivacious music hall artiste, she performed at the Folies-Bergère with her partner MAURICE CHEVALIER, and at the Moulin Rouge.

1 A kiss can be a comma, a question mark or an exclamation point. That's basic spelling that every woman ought to know.
Theatre Arts December 1955

Adrian Mitchell

(b. 1932)

British poet

He was a key figure of the underground and performance poetry of the 1960s, who described himself: 'My brain socialist/ My heart anarchist/My eyes pacifist/My blood revolutionary.' His collections include Out Loud *(1968).*

1 Most people ignore most poetry
because
most poetry ignores most people.
Poems, Epigraph (1964)

2 I was run over by the truth one day.
Ever since the accident I've walked this way
So stick my legs in plaster
Tell me lies about Vietnam.
'To Whom it May Concern', publ. in *Out Loud* (1968). Opening lines of poem.

Elma Mitchell

(1919–2000)

British poet

Elizabeth Manuel Mitchell. Her collections include The Human Cage *(1979) and* Furnished Room *(1983).*

1 Women reminded him of lilies and roses.
Me they remind rather of blood and soap,
Armed with a warm rag, assaulting noses,
Ears, neck, mouth and all the secret places.
'Thoughts After Ruskin', publ. in *The Poor Man in the Flesh* (1976)

Joni Mitchell

(b. 1943)

Canadian-born US singer and songwriter

Originally Roberta Joan Anderson. She set the pattern for musical introspection in the late 1960s and '70s with her folk-based albums such as Blue *(1971). Later recordings, for example* Mingus *(1979), mixed jazz and rock.*

1 We are stardust,
We are golden,
And we got to get ourselves
Back to the garden.
'Woodstock' (song, 1969) on the album *Ladies of the Canyon* (1970). The song was a hit for Matthews Southern Comfort.

2 They paved paradise
And put up a parking lot.
'Big Yellow Taxi' (song), ibid.

3 All the people at this party, they've got a lot of style,
They've got stamps of many countries, they've got passport smiles.
'People's Parties' (song) on the album *Court and Spark* (1974)

4 There are things to confess that enrich the world, and things that need not be said.
Independent 13 May 1988

Juliet Mitchell

(b. 1940)

New Zealand-born British author

An editor with New Left Review, *she wrote her early books such as* Woman's Estate *(1971) from a Marxist feminist persepective. Other works include* Psychoanalysis and Feminism *(1974).*

1 A fixed image of the future is in the worst sense ahistorical.
'Women – The Longest Revolution', publ. in *New Left Review* November-December 1966

2 In not wishing to act like 'men', there is no need for us to act like 'women'. The rise of the oppressed should not be a glorification of oppressed characteristics.
Woman's Estate, ch. 10 (1971)

Margaret Mitchell

(1900–49)

US novelist

Over a period of ten years she wrote her first and only novel Gone With the Wind *(1936), a romantic drama set in the American Civil War and memorably filmed in 1939. It was, she said, 'basically just a simple yarn of fairly simple people'.*

1 Land is the only thing in the world that amounts to anything, for 'tis the only thing in this world that lasts . . .'Tis the only thing worth working for, worth fighting for – worth dying for.
Gone With the Wind, vol. 1, pt 1, ch. 2 (1936). Spoken by Gerald O'Hara.

2 What most people don't seem to realize is that there is just as much money to be made out of the wreckage of a civilization as from the upbuilding of one.
Rhett Butler, ibid., vol. 1, pt 2, ch. 9

3 Southerners can never resist a losing cause.
Rhett Butler, ibid., vol. 2, pt 4, ch. 34

4 Death and taxes and childbirth! There's never any convenient time for any of them!
Scarlett O'Hara, ibid., vol. 2, pt 4, ch. 38

5 I was never one to patiently pick up broken fragments and glue them together again and tell myself that the mended whole was as good as new. What is broken is broken – and I'd rather remember it as it was at its best than mend it and see the broken places as long as I lived . . . I wish I could care what you do or where you go, but I can't. My dear, I don't give a damn.
Ibid. vol. 2, pt 5, ch. 63. Rhett Butler's farewell to Scarlett O'Hara. See CLARK GABLE 1 for the film version of this speech.

6 After all, tomorrow is another day.
Ibid. , vol. 2, pt 5, ch. 63. Closing words of book and film, spoken by Scarlett O'Hara.

Maria Mitchell
(1818–89)
US astronomer

The first woman to be elected to the American Academy of Arts and Sciences after her discovery of a comet in 1847, she was Professor of Astronomy at Vassar College from 1865.

1 Every formula which expresses a law of nature is a hymn of praise to God.
Written in 1866, inscribed on her memorial bust in the Bronx Hall of Fame

Warren Mitchell
(b. 1926)
British actor

Originally Warren Misell. Best known as the foul-mouthed bigot Alf Garnett in the TV sitcom Till Death Us Do Part *(1965–75), he is also noted for his theatre performances, including in the part of Willy Loman in* Death of a Salesman *(1979).*

1 Comedy comes from conflict, from hatred.
The Times 31 December 1990

Nancy Mitford
(1904–73)
British author

The eldest of the six aristocratic Mitford sisters, she wrote the autobiographical novels The Pursuit of Love *(1945) and* Love in a Cold Climate *(1949). Her sister Jessica described her as having the 'aspect of an elegant pirate's moll'. See* ALAN S. C. ROSS.

1 Uncle Matthew's four years in France and Italy between 1914 and 1918 had given him no great opinion of foreigners. 'Frogs,' he would say, 'are slightly better than Huns or Wops, but abroad is unutterably bloody and foreigners are fiends.'
The Pursuit of Love, ch. 15 (1945). See also GEORGE VI 2.

2 Ancestry has never counted much in England. The English lord knows himself to be such a very genuine article that, when looking for a wife, he can rise above such baubles as seize quartiers. Kind hearts, in his view, are more than coronets, and large tracts of town property more than Norman blood.
Noblesse Oblige, 'The English Aristocracy' (1956)

Wilson Mizner
(1876–1933)
US dramatist and wit

Before becoming a playwright, he was a hustler for a medicine show, a professional cardsharp, a boxing manager and a gold prospector. His most successful plays were co-written, including The Only Law *(1909, with G. Bronson Howard).*

1 Be nice to people on your way up because you'll meet them on your way down.
Quoted in *The Legendary Mizners*, ch. 4 (1953) by Alva Johnson. Also attributed to the comic Jimmy Durante.

2 A trip through a sewer in a glass-bottomed boat.
Ibid., ch. 4. Mizner's description of Hollywood was reworked in a speech by James J. Walker, Mayor of New York, in 1928: 'A reformer is a guy who rides through a sewer in a glass-bottomed boat.'

3 If you steal from one author, it's plagiarism; if you steal from many, it's research.
Ibid., ch. 4

4 Working for Warner Brothers is like fucking a porcupine: it's a hundred pricks against one.
Quoted in *Bring on the Empty Horses*, 'Degrees of Friendliness' (1975) by David Niven

Molière
(1622–73)
French dramatist

Pen name of Jean Baptiste Poquelin. One of the founders of the Illustre Théâtre *in 1643, he wrote, directed and acted in numerous plays that steered French drama away from its reliance on classical themes. His broad farces and satiric comedies often provoked official censure, and included* Tartuffe *(1664),* Le Misanthrope *(1666) and* Le Malade imaginaire *(1673). For* VOLTAIRE, *he was 'the painter of France'.*

1 One dies only once, and it's for such a long time!
Le Dépit amoureux, Act 5, Sc. 3 (performed 1656; *The Amorous Quarrel*). Spoken by Mascarille.

2 People of quality know everything without ever having learned anything.

Les Précieuses ridicules, Sc. 9 (performed 1659; *The Affected Young Ladies*). Spoken by Mascarille.

3 I always write a good first line, but I have trouble in writing the others.

Mascarille, ibid., Sc. 11

4 It's an odd job, making decent people laugh.

La Critique de l'école des femmes, Sc. 6 (performed 1663; *The Critique of the School for Wives*). Spoken by Dorante.

5 It's true Heaven forbids some pleasures, but a compromise can usually be found.

Le Tartuffe, Act 4, Sc. 5 (performed 1664; *Tartuffe*). Spoken by Tartuffe.

6 It is the public scandal that offends; to sin in secret is no sin at all.

Tartuffe, ibid., Act 4, Sc. 5

7 There's nothing quite like tobacco: it's the passion of decent folk, and whoever lives without tobacco doesn't deserve to live.

Don Juan, Act 1, Sc. 1 (performed 1665). Spoken by Sganarelle.

8 Of all follies there is none greater than wanting to make the world a better place.

Le Misanthrope, Act 1, Sc. 1 (1666; *The Misanthropist*). Spoken by Philinte.

9 It disturbs me no more to find men base, unjust, or selfish than to see apes mischievous, wolves savage, or the vulture ravenous for its prey.

Philinte, ibid., Act 1, Sc. 1

10 He's a wonderful talker, who has the art of telling you nothing in a great harangue.

Célimène, of Damon, ibid., Act 2, Sc. 5

11 The more we love our friends, the less we flatter them; it is by excusing nothing that pure love shows itself.

Alceste, ibid., Act 2, Sc. 5

12 You've asked for it, George Dandin, you've asked for it.

George Dandin, Act 1, Sc. 7 (performed 1668). Spoken by Dandin.

13 Assassination's the fastest way.

Le Sicilien, Sc. 13 (1668; *The Sicilian*). Spoken by Don Pedro.

14 One should eat to live and not live to eat.

L'Avare, Act 3, Sc. 1 (1669; *The Miser*). Valère quotes 'an ancient philosopher' (Socrates).

15 Here they hang a man first, and try him afterwards.

Monsieur de Pourceaugnac, Act 3, Sc. 2 (performed 1669). Spoken by Sbrigani, referring to the custom in Paris.

16 All that is not prose is verse; and all that is not verse is prose.

Le Bourgeois gentilhomme, Act 2, Sc. 4 (1670; *The Would-be Gentleman*). Spoken by the Philosopher. The play's title has also been translated *The Prodigious Snob*.

17 Good Heavens! For more than forty years I have been speaking prose without knowing it.

M. Jourdain, ibid., Act 2, Sc. 4

18 Grammar, which even rules over kings.

Les Femmes savantes, Act 2, Sc. 6 (1672; *The Blue-Stockings*). Spoken by Philaminte. The play's title has also been translated *The Learned Ladies*.

19 A learned fool is more foolish than an ignorant fool.

Clitandre, ibid., Act 4, Sc. 3

20 Books agree ill with matrimony.

Martine, ibid., Act 5, Sc. 3

21 He must have killed a lot of men to have made so much money.

Le Malade imaginaire, Act 1, Sc. 5 (1673; *The Imaginary Invalid*). Spoken by Toinette, referring to M. Purgon, the doctor.

22 Ah, there are no longer any children!

Argan, ibid., Act 2, Sc. 8

23 Nearly all men die of their remedies, and not of their illnesses.

Béralde, ibid., Act 3, Sc. 3

Walter Mondale
(b. 1928)
US politician and vice-president

A Democratic senator 1964–76, he was JIMMY CARTER's *Vice-President (1977–81). He won the Democratic presidential nomination in 1984, but was heavily defeated by* RONALD REAGAN.

1 Where's the beef?

Campaign slogan for 1984 Democratic presidential nomination. Originally an advertising slogan for Wendy's Hamburgers, the words were taken up by Mondale's campaign team after a televised debate 11 March 1984, in which the candidate told rival Gary Hart, 'When I hear your new ideas I'm reminded of that ad, *Where's the beef?*'

Le Monde

1 *Nous sommes tous Américains.*
[We are all Americans.]
Headline, 13 September 2001. Expressing French sympathy and solidarity with the United States in the wake of '9/11'.

Claude Monet
(1840–1926)
French painter

One of the key figures of Impressionism, he favoured outdoor painting, especially landscapes, and repeatedly treated such subjects as the water-lilies in his garden at Giverny.

1 Colour is my day-long obsession, joy and torment.
Remark to GEORGES CLEMENCEAU, quoted by him in *Claude Monet: Les Nymphéas*, ch. 2 (1926)

James Monroe
(1758–1831)
US president

Having been Governor of Virginia and a diplomat, he was elected US President in 1816 and 1820. His administration, which coincided with the so-called 'Era of Good Feeling', was characterized by the expansion and consolidation of US frontiers.

1 The occasion has been judged proper for asserting, as a principle in which the rights and interests of the United States are involved, that the American continents, by the free and independent condition which they have assumed and maintain, are henceforth not to be considered as subjects for future colonization by any European powers.
Seventh Annual Message to Congress, 2 December 1823, publ. in *American Historical Documents* (1910). 'The Monroe Doctrine', as it later came to be known, was formulated with the help of John Quincy Adams and formed the basis of US foreign policy in the ambit of central and South America. THEODORE ROOSEVELT's corollary in 1904 that disturbances in Latin America might compel US intervention to pre-empt European involvement was invoked by presidents Taft and Wilson to justify operations in the Caribbean.

2 In the wars of the European powers, in matters relating to themselves, we have never taken any part, nor does it comport with our policy so to do.
Seventh Annual Message to Congress, 2 December 1823, ibid.

3 We owe it, therefore, to candor and to the amicable relations existing between the United States and those powers, to declare that we should consider any attempt on their part to extend their system to any portion of this hemisphere as dangerous to our peace and safety. With the existing colonies or dependencies of any European power we have not interfered, and shall not interfere. But with the governments who have declared their independence, and maintained it, and whose independence we have, on great consideration and on just principles, acknowledged, we could not view any interposition for the purpose of oppressing them, or controlling in any other manner their destiny, by any European power in any other light than as the manifestation of an unfriendly disposition towards the United States.
Seventh Annual Message to Congress, 2 December 1823, ibid.

Marilyn Monroe
(1926–62)
US screen actor

Originally Norma Jean Mortenson or Baker. Described by LAURENCE OLIVIER *(with whom she acted) as a 'professional amateur', she was the supreme 1950s sex icon and the archetypal 'dumb blonde' in the comedies* Gentlemen Prefer Blondes *(1953) and* Some Like It Hot *(1959). See* NORMAN MAILER 8, BILLY WILDER 1.

1 Does this boat go to Europe, France?
Gentlemen Prefer Blondes (film, 1953, screenplay by Charles Lederer based on novel by Anita Loos, directed by Howard Hawkes). Spoken by Lorelei Lee (Marilyn Monroe). The words do not appear in the 1925 novel by ANITA LOOS.

2 Diamonds are a girl's best friend.
'Diamonds Are a Girl's Best Friend' (song, written by Leo Robin with music by Jule Styne), ibid. The song first appeared in the 1949 stage show of *Gentlemen Prefer Blondes*.

3 I always get the fuzzy end of the lollipop.
Some Like It Hot (film, 1959, screenplay by Billy Wilder and I. A. L. Diamond, directed by BILLY WILDER). Spoken by Sugar Kane (Marilyn Monroe).

4 Fame will go by and, so long, I've had you, fame. If it goes by, I've always known it was fickle. So at least it's something I experienced, but that's not where I live.
Life 3 August 1962. Conclusion of taped conversation, published on the day that Monroe died.

5 Hollywood's a place where they'll pay you a thousand dollars for a kiss, and fifty cents for your soul. I know, because I turned down the first offer often enough and held out for the fifty cents.
Quoted in *Marilyn Monroe In Her Own Words*, 'Acting' (1990)

6 Husbands are chiefly good as lovers when they are betraying their wives.

Ibid., 'Weddings & Divorces'

Lady Mary Wortley Montagu
(1689–1762)
English author and poet

She wrote essays, verse and drama, but became best known for her highly descriptive letters, published posthumously. She is also rememberred for having introduced smallpox inoculation to England from Turkey, where her husband was ambassador. See also SAMUEL JOHNSON 132.

1 Nature is seldom in the wrong, custom always.

Letter, 8 August 1709, publ. in *Selected Letters* (ed. Robert Halsband, 1970)

2 Take back the beauty and wit you bestow upon me; leave me my own mediocrity of agreeableness and genius, but leave me also my sincerity, my constancy, and my plain dealing; 'tis all I have to recommend me to the esteem either of others or myself.

Letter, 21 August 1709, ibid.

3 I know a love may be revived which absence, inconstancy, or even infidelity has extinguished, but there is no returning from a *dégoût* given by satiety.

Letter to her future husband, Wortley Montagu, 25 April 1710, ibid.

4 There is nothing can pay one for that invaluable ignorance which is the companion of youth, those sanguine groundless hopes, and that lively vanity which makes all the happiness of life.

Letter to her husband, *c.* 6 December 1712, ibid.

5 Let this sure Maxim be my Virtue's Guide,
In part to blame she is, who has been tried;
Too near he has approached, who is denied.

'Written ... in a Glass Window' (*c.* 1713), publ. in *Essays and Poems* (ed. Robert Halsband and Isobel Grundy, 1977). The lines, also known as 'The Lady's Resolve', were supposed to have been written on a window soon after her marriage.

6 'Tis a sort of duty to be rich, that it may be in one's power to do good, riches being another word for power.

Letter to her husband, *c.* 24 September 1714, publ. in *Selected Letters* (ed. Robert Halsband 1970)

7 A man that is ashamed of passions that are natural and reasonable is generally proud of those that are shameful and silly.

Letter to her husband, *c.* 24 November 1714, ibid.

8 We travellers are in very hard circumstances. If we say nothing but what has been said before us, we are dull and have observed nothing. If we tell anything new, we are laughed at as fabulous and romantic.

Letter to her sister, 10 March 1718, ibid.

9 But the fruit that can fall without shaking,
Indeed is too mellow for me.

'Answered by Me, Mary Wortley Montagu', written 1733, st. 3, publ. in *Essays and Poems* (ed. Robert Halsband and Isobel Grundy, 1977)

10 Be plain in dress, and sober in your diet;
In short, my deary, kiss me and be quiet.

Untitled poem, written 1733, ibid. The lines were written in response to Lord Lyttelton's poem 'Advice to a Lady' (1733), and have subsequently become known as: 'A Summary of Lord Lyttelton's Advice'.

11 Satire should, like a polished razor keen,
Wound with a touch that's scarcely felt or seen.

'Verses Addressed to the Imitator of the First Satire of the Second Book of Horace', ll. 25–6, written 1733, ibid.

12 Though she does not pique herself upon fidelity to any one man (which is but a narrow way of thinking), she boasts that she has always been true to her nation, and, notwithstanding foreign attacks, has always reserved her charms for the use of her own countrymen.

Letter, January 1739, publ. in *Selected Letters* (ed. Robert Halsband 1970). Writing of Lady Vane, who had deserted her husband in Paris and later published *Memoirs of a Lady of Quality* (1751).

13 I see nothing that marks man's unreason so positively as war. Indeed, what folly to kill one another for interests often imaginary, and always for the pleasure of persons who do not think themselves even obliged to those who sacrifice themselves for them!

Letter, 12 July 1744, ibid.

14 The universal inclination of humankind is to be led by the ears, and I am sometimes apt to imagine that they are given to men as they are to pitchers, purposely that they may be carried about by them.

Letter to her daughter Lady Bute, 1 March 1752, ibid.

15 The use of knowledge in our sex (beside the amusement of solitude) is to moderate the passions and learn to be contented with a small expense,

which are the certain effects of a studious life and, it may be, preferable even to that fame which men have engrossed to themselves and will not suffer us to share.
Letter to her daughter, 28 January 1753, ibid.

16 Whoever will cultivate their own mind will find full employment. Every virtue does not only require great care in the planting, but as much daily solicitude in cherishing as exotic fruits and flowers; the vices and passions (which I am afraid are the natural product of the soil) demand perpetual weeding. Add to this the search after knowledge ... and the longest life is too short.
Letter to her daughter, 6 March 1753, ibid.

17 Nature has not placed us in an inferior rank to men, no more than the females of other animals, where we see no distinction of capacity, though I am persuaded if there was a commonwealth of rational horses (as Doctor Swift has supposed) it would be an established maxim amongst them that a mare could not be taught to pace.
Letter to her daughter, 6 March 1753, ibid.

C. E. Montague
(1867–1928)
British author and journalist

Charles Edward Montague. A journalist with the Manchester Guardian *from 1898, he wrote numerous books including* Disenchantment *(1922), which recounts his experience of the First World War, and the novel* Rough Justice *(1926).*

1 There is no limit to what a man can do so long as he does not care a straw who gets the credit for it.
Disenchantment, ch. 15, sect. 3 (1922)

2 A lie will easily get you out of a scrape, and yet, strangely and beautifully, rapture possesses you when you have taken the scrape and left out the lie.
Ibid., ch. 15, sect. 4

3 War hath no fury like a non-combatant.
Ibid., ch. 16

Michel de Montaigne
(1533–92)
French essayist

Considered the creator of the essay as a literary form, he published two volumes of Essais *in 1580, and a third in 1588. The essays were popularized in England by* JOHN FLORIO's *translation of 1603. Montaigne served as a magistrate and was Mayor of Bordeaux 1581–5.*

1 If my fortune had been to have lived among those nations which yet are said to live under the sweet liberty of nature's first and uncorrupted laws, I assure thee, I would most willingly have portrayed myself fully and naked. Thus, gentle reader, myself am the groundwork of my book.
Essays, bk 1, 'To the Reader' (1580, transl. JOHN FLORIO, 1603)

2 *Il faut être toujours botté et prêt à partir.*
[A man should ever, as much as in him lieth, be ready booted to take his journey.]
Ibid., bk 1, ch. 19 ('That to Philosophise is to Learn How to Die'). Referring to the imminence of death. See JEAN DE LA FONTAINE 4.

3 Let death seize upon me whilst I am setting my cabbages, careless of her dart, but more of my unperfect garden.
Ibid., bk 1, ch. 19. See RABELAIS 9.

4 The profit of life consists not in the space, but rather in the use. Some man hath lived long, that hath a short life, Follow it whilst you have time. It consists not in number of years, but in your will.
Ibid., bk 1, ch. 19

5 For truly it is to be noted, that children's plays are not sports, and should be deemed as their most serious actions.
Ibid., bk 1, ch. 22 ('Of Custom')

6 If a man urge me to tell wherefore I loved him, I feel it cannot be expressed but by answering: Because it was he, because it was myself.
Ibid., bk 1, ch. 27 ('Of Friendship'). Referring to Étienne de la Boétie (1530–63), a humanist scholar and Montaigne's great friend and mentor.

7 The greatest thing of the world is for a man to know how to be his own.
Ibid., bk 1, ch. 38 ('Of Solitariness')

8 *Mon métier et mon art c'est vivre.*
[My art and profession is to live.]
Ibid., bk 2, ch. 6 ('Of Exercise or Practice')

9 Virtue rejects facility to be her companion ... She requires a craggy, rough and thorny way.
Ibid., bk 2, ch. 11 ('Of Cruelty')

10 When I am playing with my cat, who knows whether she have more sport in dallying with me than I have in gaming with her?
Ibid., bk 2, ch. 12 ('An Apology of Raimond Sebond')

11 This concept is more certainly conceived by an interrogation: What can I tell? [*Que sais-je?*]

Ibid., bk 2, ch. 12 ('An Apology of Raimond Sebond'). Discussing the stance of sceptics, more familiarly translated 'What do I know?'

12 Oh senseless man, who cannot possibly make a worm, and yet will make Gods by dozens.

Ibid., bk 2, ch. 12

13 The senses are the beginning and end of human knowledge.

Ibid., bk 2, ch. 12

14 Those which have compared our life unto a dream, have happily had more reason so to do than they were aware. When we dream, our soul liveth, worketh and exerciseth all her faculties, even and as much as when it waketh ... We wake sleeping, and sleep waking.

Ibid., bk 2, ch. 12. See also EDGAR ALLAN POE 1 and PEDRO CALDERÓN 1.

15 We endeavour more that men should speak of us, than how and what they speak, and it sufficeth us that our name run in men's mouths, in what manner soever. It seemeth that to be known is in some sort to have life and continuance in other men's keeping.

Ibid., bk 2, ch. 16 ('Of Glory')

16 I will follow the best side to the fire, but not into it, if I can choose.

Ibid., bk 3, ch. 1 ('Of Profit and Honesty') (1588)

17 Every man beareth the whole stamp of human condition.

Ibid., bk 3, ch. 2 ('Of Repenting')

18 I speak truth, not my belly-full, but as much as I dare; and I dare the more the more I grow into years.

Ibid., bk 3, ch. 2

19 Wisdom hath her excesses, and no less need of moderation than folly.

Ibid., bk 3, ch. 5 ('Upon Some Verses of Virgil')

20 We cannot do without it [marriage], and yet we disgrace and vilify the same. It may be compared to a cage, the birds without despair to get in, and those within despair to get out.

Ibid., bk 3, ch. 5. See JOHN WEBSTER 4.

21 After mature deliberation of counsel, the good Queen to establish a rule and imitable example unto all posterity, for the moderation and required modesty in a lawful marriage, ordained the number of

six times a day as a lawful, necessary and competent limit.

Ibid., bk 3, ch. 5. The Queen of Aragon's 'sentence' on 'matrimonial intercourse'.

22 Even from their infancy we frame them [girls] to the sports of love: their instruction, behaviour, attire, grace, learning and all their words aimeth only at love, respects only affection. Their nurses and their keepers imprint no other thing in them, than the loveliness of love.

Ibid., bk 3, ch. 5

23 Women's policy hath a mystical proceeding, we must be content to leave it to them.

Ibid., bk 3, ch. 5

24 Nature should have been pleased to have made this age miserable, without making it also ridiculous.

Ibid., bk 3, ch. 5. Referring to the age of the 'eleventh *lustre*', or fifty-five – Montaigne's own age.

25 I love her so tenderly that even her spots, her blemishes and her warts are desire unto me. I am no perfect Frenchman, but by this great-matchless city, great in people, great in the felicity of her situation; but above all, great and incomparable in variety and diversity of commodities. The glory of France, and one of the noblest and chief ornaments of the world.

Ibid., bk 3, ch. 9 ('Of Vanity'). Writing of Paris.

26 With me no pleasure is fully delightsome without communication, and no delight absolute except imparted. I do not so much as apprehend one rare conceipt, or conceive one excellent good thought in my mind, but me thinks I am much grieved and grievously perplexed to have produced the same alone and that I have no sympathizing companion to impart it unto.

Ibid., bk 3, ch. 9

27 By some might be said of me that here I have but gathered a nosegay of strange flowers, and have put nothing of mine unto it but the thread to bind them.

Ibid., bk 3, ch. 12 ('Of Physiognomy'). Referring to Montaigne's own essays, which are permeated with classical quotations.

28 There's more ado to interpret interpretations than to interpret things, and more books upon books than upon any other subject. We do but inter-

gloss ourselves. All swarmeth with commentaries; of authors there is great penury.
Ibid., bk 3, ch. 13 ('Of Experience')

29 Let nature work; let her have her will; she knoweth what she hath to do, and understands herself better then we do.
Ibid., bk 3, ch. 13

Eugenio Montale
(1896–1981)
Italian poet

Director of the Italian Scientific-Literary Cabinet 1929–38, he was literary and music editor of the Milan newspaper Corriere della Sera *from 1947. His poems focus on the 'pain of living'.*

1 To make one, too many lives are needed.
'Summer', publ. in *Le Occasioni* (1939)

2 All religions of the only God
are one: just the cooks and the cooking vary.
'The Death of God', publ. in *Satura* (1962). Opening words of poem.

3 Words
are everyone's property and in vain
do they hide in dictionaries,
for there's always a rogue
who digs up the rarest
and most stinking truffles.
'Words', ibid.

4 Youth is the vilest of all illusions.
'Sorapis, 40 Years Ago', publ. in *Diario del '71 e del '72* (1973)

Charles de Montesquieu
(1689–1755)
French lawyer and political philosopher

Charles Louis de Secondat, Baron de La Brède et de Montesquieu. He is most famed for The Spirit of Laws *(1748), a study of law and politics that strongly influenced the USA and other constitutions.* Persian Letters *(1721) was an imaginary correspondence consisting of satirical observations on French society.*

1 There should be weeping at a man's birth, not at his death.
Persian Letters, no. 40 (1721)

2 If triangles had a god, they would give him three sides.
Ibid., no. 59

3 Useless laws weaken the necessary ones.
De l'Esprit des lois, vol. 29, ch. 16 (1748, *The Spirit of Laws*)

4 Happy the people whose annals are blank in history-books!
Quoted in *The History of Friedrich II of Prussia, Called Frederick the Great,* bk 16, ch. 1 (1858–65) by THOMAS CARLYLE

Maria Montessori
(1870–1952)
Italian educationist

The first woman in Italy to gain a medical degree (1894), she gave her name to a system of education for children aged from three to six, which emphasizes freedom of expression and self-direction.

1 Discipline must come through liberty ... We do not consider an individual disciplined only when he has been rendered as artificially silent as a mute and as immovable as a paralytic. He is an individual annihilated, not disciplined.
The Montessori Method, ch. 5 (1912)

2 The task of the educator lies in seeing that the child does not confound *good* with *immobility*, and *evil* with *activity*.
Ibid., ch. 5

3 If help and salvation are to come, they can only come from the children, for the children are the makers of men.
The Absorbent Mind, ch. 1 (1949)

Viscount Montgomery
(1887–1976)
British soldier

Bernard Montgomery, First Viscount Montgomery of Alamein. As commander of the Eighth Army, 'Monty' defeated Rommel at the battle of El Alamein (1942) and played a key role in the invasion of Italy the following year. See WINSTON CHURCHILL 57.

1 Rule 1, on page 1 of the book of war, is: 'Do not march on Moscow'. Various people have tried it, Napoleon and Hitler, and it is no good ... Rule 2 of war ... is: 'Do not go fighting with your land armies in China'.
Speech to House of Lords, 30 May 1962, publ. in *Hansard* (Lords), col. 227

2 Far from helping these unnatural practices along, surely our task is to build a bulwark which will defy evil influences which are seeking to undermine the very foundations of our national character – defy them; do not help them. I have heard some say ... that such practices are allowed in France and in

other NATO countries. We are not French, and we are not other nationals. We are British, thank God!

Speech to House of Lords, 26 May 1965, debating the Sexual Offences Bill, ibid., col. 648. On homosexual practices.

Percy Montrose

US songwriter

1 Oh, my darling, oh my darling, oh my darling
   Clementine,
You are lost and gone for ever, dreadful sorry,
   Clementine!

'Clementine'. Attributed to Montrose (about whom nothing is known), the California mining song was published in 1884, though the words are also credited to H. S. Thompson in 1863.

Monty Python's Flying Circus

The surreal BBC TV comedy series (1969–74) was written and performed by Graham Chapman (1941–89), JOHN CLEESE, *Terry Gilliam (b. 1940), Eric Idle (b. 1943), Terry Jones (b. 1942) and Michael Palin (b. 1943), and spawned several films.*

1 And now for something completely different.

Spoken by John Cleese, as newsreader. The catch-phrase came to be used by various characters as a link between sketches.

2 Nudge, nudge, wink, wink, say no more, know what I mean . . .

Eric Idle, in first series, episode 3, first broadcast 19 October 1969

3 This parrot is no more! It has ceased to be! It's expired and gone to meet its maker! This is a late parrot! It's a stiff! . . . THIS IS AN EX-PARROT!

John Cleese, ibid., episode 8, first broadcast 7 December 1969

4 I'm a lumberjack
And I'm OK,
I sleep all night
And I work all day.

I cut down trees, I skip and jump,
I like to press wild flowers.
I put on women's clothing
And hang around in bars.

'The Lumberjack Song', ibid., episode 9, first broadcast 14 December 1969

5 Nobody expects the Spanish Inquisition!

Michael Palin, in second series, episode 2, first broadcast 22 September 1970

6 One minute I'm a leper with a trade, next minute my livelihood's gone. Not so much as a by-your-leave. You're cured, mate. Bloody do-gooder!

Monty Python's Life of Brian (film, 1979, written by John Cleese, Graham Chapman, Terry Gilliam, Eric Idle, Terry Jones and Michael Palin, directed by Terry Jones). Spoken by a beggar (Michael Palin), on being cured by Jesus.

7 Apart from the sanitation, the medicine, education, wine, public order, irrigation, roads, the fresh water system and public health, what have the Romans ever done for us?

The leader of the People's Front of Judea (John Cleese), ibid. A voice pipes up, 'Brought peace?'

8 When you're chewing on life's gristle
Don't grumble, give a whistle
And this'll help turn things out for the best . . .
And . . . always look on the bright side of life.

Mr Frisbee III (Eric Idle), ibid. On being crucified.

Clayton Moore

(1914–99)
US screen actor

Originally Jack Carlton Moore. He played small roles in Hollywood throughout the 1940s, and in 1949 was assigned the role of the Lone Ranger when the radio hit was transferred to television. He remained in the part until the series ended in 1957.

1 Hi-yo, Silver, away!

The Lone Ranger (TV series, 1949–57, created by Fran Striker and George Trendle). Spoken by the Lone Ranger (Clayton Moore), the Masked Man on his 'fiery horse with the speed of light'. The words were heard at the beginning of each episode of the show, which ran for sixteen years on radio before making its TV debut with Moore.

Clement C. Moore

(1779–1863)
US scholar

Professor of Oriental Greek and Oriental Literature at New York's General Theological Seminary, he compiled a Hebrew dictionary but is now remembered for the ballad, 'A Visit from St Nicholas', attributed to him.

1 'Twas the night before Christmas, when all
   through the house
Not a creature was stirring, not even a mouse;
The stockings were hung by the chimney with
   care,
In hopes that St Nicholas soon would be there.

'A Visit from St Nicholas', st. 1. The work was said to have been written by Moore for his daughters in 1822 and copied by a house guest who published it anonymously in 1823. It finally appeared in Moore's *Poems* (1844). However, Moore's authorship of it has recently been questioned, and it has been ascribed instead to Major Henry Livingston Jr (1748–1828), a surveyor, Justice of the Peace and poet who published most of his work anonymously.

Edward Moore
(1712–57)
English playwright

His reputation rests primarily on his prose tragedy The Gamester *(1753). He also wrote two sentimental comedies,* The Foundling *(1748) and* Gil Blas *(1751), and composed verse fables.*

1 Now, in my opinion, a woman has no business with Power – Power admits no equal, and dismisses friendship for flattery. Besides, it keeps the men at a distance, and that is not always what we wish.
The Foundling, Act 1, Sc. 2 (1748). Spoken by Fidelia.

2 I am rich beyond the dreams of avarice.
The Gamester, Act 2, Sc. 7 (1753). Spoken by Mrs Beverley.

George Moore
(1852–1933)
Irish author and critic

A co-founder of Dublin's Literary Theatre, from which the Abbey Theatre developed, he wrote plays including The Strike at Arlington *(1893) and* The Bending of the Bough *(1900), and naturalistic fiction, notably* Esther Waters *(1894). He also wrote verse, autobiography and works of criticism.*

1 The lot of critics is to be remembered by what they failed to understand.
Impressions and Opinions, 'Balzac' (1891)

2 Our contention is . . . that acting is therefore the lowest of the arts, if it be an art at all.
Ibid., 'Mummer-Worship'

3 There are no new ideals, and the old ideals will suffice when you understand them.
The Bending of the Bough, Act 3 (1900). Spoken by Jasper Dean.

4 The difficulty in life is the choice, and all the wonder of life is in the choice.
Jasper Dean, ibid. Act 4

5 It would seem to me that a cause is lost when it becomes respectable.
Arabella Dean, ibid. Act 4

6 My one claim to originality among Irishmen is that I have never made a speech.
Ave, ch. 4 (1911)

7 A man travels the world over in search of what he needs and returns home to find it.
The Brook Kerith, ch. 11 (1916). Spoken by Jesus.

Jo Moore
(b. 1963)
British government adviser

She was appointed adviser to Stephen Byers at the Department of Trade and Industry in 2000, and resigned in controversial circumstances in 2002.

1 It is now a very good day to get out anything we want to bury.
E-mail to members of her department, sent thirty minutes after the attack on the World Trade Center in New York, 11 September 2001, quoted in the *Guardian* 9 October 2001. Often misquoted as: 'A good day to bury bad news'.

Marianne Moore
(1887–1972)
US poet

T. S. ELIOT *praised the 'swift dissolving image' of her verse, which is characterized by its individual metrical style and her sharp wit. Her publications include* Observations *(1924) and* Nevertheless *(1944). She edited* The Dial *1925–9.*

1 nor till the poets among us can be
'literalists of
the imagination' – above
insolence and triviality and can present
for inspection, 'imaginary gardens with real toads
   in them,' shall we have
it.
'Poetry' (1919), repr. in *Selected Poems* (1935)

2 with its baby rivers and little towns, each with
   its abbey or its cathedral,
with voices – one voice perhaps, echoing through
   the transept – the
criterion of suitability and convenience.
'England' (1920), ibid.

3 My father used to say,
'Superior people never make long visits,
have to be shown Longfellow's grave
or the glass flowers at Harvard.'
'Silence' (1924), ibid.

4 The deepest feeling always shows itself in
   silence;
not in silence, but restraint.
'Silence', ibid.

5 Poetry, that is to say the poetic, is a primal necessity.
'Comment' (1926), repr. in *Complete Prose* (1987)

6 When one cannot appraise out of one's own experience, the temptation to blunder is minimized, but even when one can, appraisal seems chiefly useful as appraisal of the appraiser.
'Comment' (1928), ibid.

7 The catnip that art is, or *ignis fatuus*, or drop on the cactus, does seem worth the martyrdom of pursuit.
Letter to WILLIAM CARLOS WILLIAMS, 26 January 1934, publ. in *The Selected Letters of Marianne Moore*, 'The Poet in Brooklyn: 1930–1934' (ed. Bonnie Costello, 1998)

8 A place as kind as it is green,
the greenest place I've never seen.
Every name is a tune.
'Spenser's Ireland', publ. in *What Are Years* (1941)

9 The Irish say your trouble is their
trouble and your
joy their joy? I wish
I could believe it;
I am troubled, I'm dissatisfied, I'm Irish.
'Spenser's Ireland', ibid. Closing lines of poem.

10 O to be a dragon
a symbol of the power of Heaven – of silkworm
size or immense; at times invisible.
Felicitous phenomenon!
'O To Be a Dragon', publ. in *O To Be a Dragon* (1959)

11 Camels are snobbish
and sheep, unintelligent;
water buffaloes, neurasthenic –
even murderous.
Reindeer seem over-serious.
'The Arctic Ox (Or Goat)', ibid.

12 I see no reason for calling my work poetry except that there is no other category in which to put it.
Quoted in the *New York Mirror* 31 May 1959. On accepting the National Book Award for poetry.

Michael Moore
(b. 1954)
US author, film-maker and political activist

Regarded as a fearless political commentator, he has made the documentary films Bowling for Columbine *(2002) and* Fahrenheit 9/11 *(2004), and is the author of* Stupid White Men *(2002).*

1 The bad guys are just a bunch of silly, stupid white men. And there's a helluva lot more of us than there are of them. Use your power. You deserve better.
Stupid White Men, ch. 12 (2002). Closing words of book.

2 We live in fictitious times. We live in a time with fictitious election results that elect fictitious presidents. We live in a time where we have a man sending us to war for fictitious reasons. We are against this war, Mr Bush. Shame on you, shame on you.
Speech at Academy Awards, 23 March 2003, accepting an Oscar for Best Documentary Feature for his anti-gun film *Bowling for Columbine*, quoted in *The Times* 24 March 2003

Thomas Moore
(1779–1852)
Irish poet

One of the most popular poets of the Romantic movement, he is best remembered for his collection of folk songs and poems set to music, Irish Melodies *(1807–35), and the long narrative* Lalla Rookh *(1817). He also wrote a history of Ireland and a biography of his close friend* BYRON. *See* WILLIAM HAZLITT 26.

1 Oh! breathe not his name, let it sleep in the
shade,
Where cold and unhonoured his relics are laid.
'Oh! breathe not his name', st. 1, publ. in *Irish Melodies* (1807–35)

2 The harp that once through Tara's halls
The soul of music shed,
Now hangs as mute on Tara's walls,
As if that soul were fled.
'The harp that once through Tara's halls', st. 1, ibid.

3 Believe me, if all those endearing young charms,
Which I gaze on so fondly today,
Were to change by tomorrow, and fleet in my
arms,
Like fairy-gifts fading away,
Thou wouldst still be adored, as this moment thou
art.
Let thy loveliness fade as it will.
And around the dear ruin each wish of my heart
Would entwine itself verdantly still.
'Believe me, if all those endearing young charms', st. 1, ibid.

4 Oh! blame not the bard, if he fly to the bowers,
Where pleasure lies carelessly smiling at fame;
He was born for much more, and in happier hours
His soul might have burned with a holier flame.
'Oh! blame not the bard', st. 1, ibid.

5 No, there's nothing half so sweet in life
As love's young dream.
'Love's Young Dream', st. 1, ibid.

6 'Tis the last rose of summer,
Left blooming alone;
All her lovely companions
Are faded and gone.
''Tis the last rose of summer', st. 1, ibid.

7 You may break, you may shatter the vase, if you
will,
But the scent of the roses will hang round it still.
'Farewell! – but whenever you welcome the hour', st. 3, ibid.
Closing lines of poem.

8 The time I've lost in wooing,
In watching and pursuing
The light, that lies
In woman's eyes,
Has been my heart's undoing.
'The time I've lost in wooing', st. 1, ibid.

9 My only books
Were woman's looks
And folly's all they've taught me.
'The time I've lost in wooing', st. 1, ibid.

10 Oft, in the stilly night,
Ere Slumber's chain has bound me,
Fond Memory brings the light
Of other days around me.
'Oft, in the stilly night', st. 1, publ. in National Airs (1815)

11 Every season hath its pleasures;
Spring may boast her flowery prime,
Yet the vineyard's ruby treasures
Brighten Autumn's soberer time.
So life's year begins and closes;
Days though shortening still can shine;
What though youth gave love and roses,
Age still leaves us friends and wine.
'Spring and Autumn', st. 1, ibid.

12 It is only to the happy that tears are a luxury.
Lalla Rookh, 'The Fire-Worshippers', pt 2, Prologue (1817)

13 Like Dead Sea fruits that tempt the eye,
But turn to ashes on the lips!
Ibid., 'The Fire-Worshippers', pt 2, ll. 484–5

14 'Come, come,' said Tom's father, 'at your time
of life,
There's no longer excuse for thus playing the
rake –

It is time you should think, boy, of taking a wife.'
'Why, so it is, father – whose wife shall I take?'
'A Joke Versified', publ. in Poetical Works (1841)

15 Heaven grant him now some noble nook,
For, rest his soul! he'd rather be
Genteelly damned beside a duke,
Than saved in vulgar company.
'Epitaph on a Tuft-Hunter', st. 5, ibid.

Alberto Moravia
(1907–90)
Italian author

Originally Alberto Pincherle. He explored themes of middle-class decadence, alienation and loveless sexuality in such works as The Time of Indifference *(1929) and* The Woman of Rome *(1947).*

1 Although not all men possess the same intellectual capacity and the same knowledge, they all, even the most wretched, have their own moral world in its entirety.
The Woman of Rome, Preface (1947)

Hannah More
(1745–1833)
English author and reformer

Having written for the London stage, she became increasingly assertive of traditional Christian values, working to improve education among the poor and establish local societies for women. Her writings include religious tracts and a novel, Coelebs in Search of a Wife *(1808).*

1 Going to the opera, like getting drunk, is a sin that carries its own punishment with it.
Letter to her sister, 1775, publ. in The Letters of Hannah More (ed. R. Brimley Johnson, 1925)

2 How much it is to be regretted that the British ladies should ever sit down contented to polish, when they are able to reform; to entertain, when they might instruct; and to dazzle for an hour, when they are candidates for eternity!
Essays on Various Subjects ... for Young Ladies, 'On Dissipation' (1777)

3 Small habits, well pursued betimes,
May reach the dignity of crimes.
Florio, pt 1, ll. 77–8 (1786), repr. in Poetical Works (1854)

4 The wretch who digs the mine for bread,
Or ploughs that others may be fed,

Feels less fatigue than that decreed
To him who cannot think, or read.
Florio, pt 1, ll. 89–92, ibid.

5 He liked those literary cooks
Who skim the cream of others' books;
And ruin half an author's graces
By plucking bon-mots from their places.
Florio, pt 1, ll. 123–6, ibid.

6 Here sober duchesses are seen,
Chaste wits, and critics void of spleen;
Physicians, fraught with real science,
And Whigs and Tories in alliance;
Poets, fulfilling Christian duties,
Just lawyers, reasonable beauties.
The Bas Bleu: or, Conversation, ll. 202–7 (1787), ibid. Referring
to the assemblies of 'Blue Stockings', described by More as
'small societies ... composed of persons distinguished, in
general, for their rank, talents, or respectable character, who
met frequently at Mrs Vesey's and at a few other houses, for
the sole purpose of conversation.'

7 Hail, Conversation, soothing power,
Sweet goddess of the social hour!
The Bas Bleu: or, Conversation, ll. 254–5, ibid.

8 If none behold, ah! wherefore fair?
Ah! wherefore wise, if none must hear?
Our intellectual ore must shine,
Not slumber idly in the mine.
Let education's moral mint
The noblest images imprint.
The Bas Bleu: or, Conversation, ll. 286–91, ibid.

9 In taste, in learning, wit, or science,
Still kindred souls demand alliance;
Each in the other joys to find
The image answering to his mind.
But sparks electric only strike
On souls electrical alike;
The flash of intellect expires,
Unless it meet congenial fires.
The Bas Bleu: or, Conversation, ll. 358–65, ibid.

10 'Tis more than wit, 'tis moral beauty,
'Tis pleasure rising out of duty.
Nor vainly think the time you waste,
When temper triumphs over taste.
The Bas Bleu: or, Conversation, ll. 438–41, ibid. Closing lines
of poem.

11 My plan of instruction is extremely simple and
limited. They learn, on weekdays, such coarse works
as may fit them for servants. I allow of no writing
for the poor. My object is not to make fanatics, but
to train up the lower classes in habits of industry
and piety.
Letter to the Bishop of Bath and Wells, 1801, publ. in *The
Letters of Hannah More* (ed. R. Brimley Johnson, 1925)

12 For you'll ne'er mend your fortunes, nor help
the just cause,
By breaking of windows, or breaking of laws.
'An Address to the Meeting in Spa Fields' (1817), publ. in
Life of Hannah More, Appendix, no. 7 (1838) by Henry
Thompson

(Sir) Thomas More
(1478–1535)
English statesman and author

Already known as a humanist scholar and the author of Utopia
(1516), he served as Lord Chancellor (1529–32) under
HENRY VIII, *but fell out of royal favour for his opposition to
the Act of Succession. He was executed and in 1935 canonized.
His friend* ERASMUS *described him as* omnium horarum
homo, *later rendered as 'a man for all seasons'.*

1 As he is a foolish physician that cannot cure his
patient's disease unless he cast him in another sickness, so he that cannot amend the lives of his subjects but by taking from them the wealth and
commodity of life, he must needs grant that he
knoweth not the feat how to govern men.
Utopia, bk 1 (1516)

2 Where possessions be private, where money beareth all the stroke, it is hard and almost impossible
that there the weal-public may justly be governed
and prosperously flourish.
Ibid., bk 1. Spoken by Raphael Hythloday.

3 For this is one of the ancientest laws among them;
that no man shall be blamed for reasoning in the
maintenance of his own religion.
Ibid., bk 2, 'Of the Religions in Utopia'

4 I pray you, Sir, see me safe up, and for my coming
down let me shift for myself.
Quoted in *Sir Thomas More*, ch. 13 (1953) by Leslie Paul. Spoken
to an officer on mounting the scaffold.

5 Thou wilt do me this day greater benefit than ever
any mortal man can be able to give me; pluck up
thy spirit man, and be not afraid to do thy office;
my neck is very short; take heed therefore that thou
strike not awry, for saving of thine honesty.
Ibid., ch. 13. Spoken to his executioner.

Thomas Morell

(1703–84)

English librettist

A classical scholar, he wrote libretti for oratorios by HANDEL.

1 See, the conquering hero comes!
Sound the trumpets, beat the drums!
Libretto in Handel's oratorios *Judas Maccabeus*, 'A Chorus of Youths' (1747) and *Joshua*, pt 3 (1748)

Christopher Morley

(1890–1957)

US novelist, journalist and poet

Best known for his novel Kitty Foyle *(1939), he also published poetry and essay collections.*

1 Life is a foreign language: all men mispronounce it.
Thunder on the Left, ch. 14 (1925)

John, Lord Morley

(1838–1923)

English statesman and biographer

Viscount Morley of Blackburn. Having edited the Fortnightly Review *and the* Pall Mall Gazette*, he entered politics as a Liberal in 1883 and held high office under* GLADSTONE. *He published numerous biographies, including works on Gladstone,* VOLTAIRE *and* OLIVER CROMWELL.

1 They act as if they supposed that to be very sanguine about the general improvement of mankind is a virtue that relieves them from taking trouble about any improvement in particular.
On Compromise, ch. 5 (1874)

2 You have not converted a man because you have silenced him.
Ibid., ch. 5

3 Literature, the most seductive, the most deceiving, the most dangerous of professions.
Life of Burke, ch. 1 (1879)

4 They are the guiding oracles which man has found out for himself in that great business of ours, of learning how to be, to do, to do without, and to depart.
'Address on Aphorisms', Edinburgh, 1887, publ. in *Studies in Literature*, 'Aphorisms' (1890)

5 The next great task of science is to create a religion for mankind.
Quoted in *The Harvest of a Quiet Eye* (1977) by Alan L. Mackay

Robert Morley

(1908–92)

British actor and humorist

He remained a committed stage actor while also pursuing a screen career from 1938, appearing in such films as Oscar Wilde *(1960).*

1 The British tourist is always happy abroad as long as the natives are waiters.
Quoted in the *Observer* 20 April 1958

2 The French are a logical people, which is one reason the English dislike them so intensely. The other is that they own France, a country which we have always judged to be much too good for them.
A Musing Morley, 'France and the French' (1974)

Desmond Morris

(b. 1928)

British zoologist

He was presenter of television's Zoo Time *and keeper of mammals for the Zoological Society before his bestsellers* The Naked Ape *(1967) and* The Human Zoo *(1969) made him a household name.*

1 We never stop investigating. We are never satisfied that we know enough to get by. Every question we answer leads on to another question. This has become the greatest survival trick of our species.
The Naked Ape, ch. 4 (1967)

2 The city is not a concrete jungle, it is a human zoo.
The Human Zoo, Introduction (1969)

Estelle Morris

(b. 1952)

British politician

Baroness Morris of Yardley. Having worked as a teacher, she was elected to a Labour seat in 1992 and served as Education Minister 2001–2 and as Minister for the Arts 2003–5.

1 I've learned what I'm good at and also what I'm less good at. I'm good at dealing with the issues and in communicating to the teaching profession. I am less good at strategic management of a huge department and I am not good at dealing with the modern media. All this has meant that with some of the recent situations I have been involved in, I have not felt I have been as effective as I should be.
Letter to TONY BLAIR, 23 October 2002, publ. in the *Guardian*

24 October 2002. Resigning as Secretary of State for Education and Skills.

William Morris
(1834–96)
English artist, author, printer and reformer

A champion of the Arts and Crafts movement, he sought to revive the traditions of medieval art, notably in the fields of decoration, design and stained glass. He formed the Socialist League in 1884 and expressed his dissatisfaction with industrialism in such books as News From Nowhere *(1891).*

1 Had she come all the way for this,
To part at last without a kiss?
Yea, had she borne the dirt and rain
That her own eyes might see him slain
Beside the haystack in the floods?
'The Haystack in the Floods', ll. 1–5, publ. in *The Defence of Guenevere and Other Poems* (1858)

2 Everything made by man's hands has a form, which must be either beautiful or ugly; beautiful if it is in accord with Nature, and helps her; ugly if it is discordant with Nature, and thwarts her; it cannot be indifferent.
'The Decorative Arts: Their Relation to Modern Life and Progress', lecture, 4 December 1877, publ. in *Hopes and Fears for Art* (1882) as 'The Lesser Arts'. Morris's first public lecture was delivered before the Trades' Guild of Learning.

3 To give people pleasure in the things they must perforce *use*, that is one great office of decoration; to give people pleasure in the things they must perforce *make*, that is the other use of it.
'The Decorative Arts', ibid.

4 What is an artist but a workman who is determined that, whatever else happens, his work shall be excellent?
'The Decorative Arts', ibid.

5 Nothing can be a work of art which is not useful.
'The Decorative Arts', ibid.

6 I do not want art for a few, any more than education for a few, or freedom for a few.
'The Decorative Arts', ibid.

7 If you want a golden rule that will fit everything, this is it: Have nothing in your houses that you do not know to be useful or believe to be beautiful.
'The Beauty of Life', lecture to the Birmingham Society of Arts and School of Design, 19 February 1880, ibid.

8 Simplicity of life, even the barest, is not a misery, but the very foundation of refinement; a sanded floor and whitewashed walls and the green trees, and flowery meads, and living waters outside; or a grimy palace amid the same with a regiment of housemaids always working to smear the dirt together so that it may be unnoticed; which, think you, is the most refined, the most fit for a gentleman of those two dwellings?
'The Prospects of Architecture in Civilisation', lecture at the London Institution, 10 March 1880, ibid.

9 I love art, and I love history, but it is living art and living history that I love . . . It is in the interest of living art and living history that I oppose so-called restoration. What history can there be in a building bedaubed with ornament, which cannot at the best be anything but a hopeless and lifeless imitation of the hope and vigour of the earlier world?
'The History of Pattern-Designing', lecture at the Kensington Vestry Hall, London, 1882, repr. in *The Collected Works of William Morris*, vol. 22 (ed. May Morris, 1914)

10 So long as the system of competition in the production and exchange of the means of life goes on, the degradation of the arts will go on; and if that system is to last for ever, then art is doomed, and will surely die; that is to say, civilization will die.
'Art Under Plutocracy', lecture to Russell Club, University Hall, Oxford, 1883, ibid., vol. 23 (ed. May Morris, 1914)

11 Art is man's expression of his joy in labour.
'Art under Plutocracy', ibid., vol. 23. Morris adds: 'If those are not Professor Ruskin's words they embody at least his teaching on this subject.'

12 A man at work, making something which he feels will exist because he is working at it and wills it, is exercising the energies of his mind and soul as well as of his body. Memory and imagination help him as he works. Not only his own thoughts, but the thoughts of the men of past ages guide his hands; and, as part of the human race, he creates. If we work thus we shall be men, and our days will be happy and eventful.
'Useful Work *versus* Useless Toil', lecture to Hampstead Liberal Club, 16 January 1884, publ. in *Signs of Change* (1888)

13 Nothing should be made by man's labour which is not worth making; or which must be made by labour degrading to the makers.
'Art and Socialism', lecture to the Leicester Secular Society, 23 January 1884, publ. in *The Collected Works of William Morris*, vol. 22 (ed. May Morris, 1914)

14 Of rich men it telleth, and strange is the story

How they have, and they hanker, and grip far and
wide;
And they live and they die, and the earth and its
glory
Has been but a burden they scarce might abide.
The Pilgrims of Hope, 'The Message of the March Wind' (1885)

15 I pondered all these things, and how men fight
and lose the battle, and the thing that they fought
for comes about in spite of their defeat, and when
it comes turns out not to be what they meant, and
other men have to fight for what they meant under
another name.
A Dream of John Ball, ch. 4 (1888)

16 The reward of labour is *life*. Is that not enough?
News From Nowhere, ch. 15 (1891). Spoken by Hammond.

Jim Morrison
(1943–71)
US rock musician

*Styling himself the Lizard King, he was the singer and main
inspiration of the Doors, a Los Angeles rock group formed in
1966. Increasingly erratic and in thrall to drugs, he died in
mysterious circumstances in Paris.*

1 Come on baby light my fire.
'Light My Fire' (song, written by the Doors) on the album *The
Doors* (1967) by the Doors

2 This is the end,
Beautiful friend.
This is the end,
My only friend, the end.
It hurts to set you free
But you'll never follow me.
'The End' (song, written by the Doors), ibid. The song featured
in FRANCIS FORD COPPOLA's film *Apocalypse Now* (1979).

3 'Father?'
'Yes, son?'
'I want to kill you.'
'Mother, I want to . . .'
'The End', ibid.

4 We want the world and we want it now!
'When the Music's Over' (song, written by the Doors) on the
album *Strange Days* (1967) by the Doors

5 I am the Lizard King
I can do anything.
'The Celebration of the Lizard' (poem and song) on the album
Waiting For the Sun (1968) by the Doors

6 They got the guns but we got the numbers.
'Five to One' (song, written by the Doors), ibid.

7 I'm interested in anything about revolt, disorder,
chaos, especially activity that appears to have no
meaning. It seems to me to be the road toward
freedom.
Quoted in *Time* 24 January 1968

Toni Morrison
(b. 1931)
US novelist and editor

*Chloe Anthony Morrison. Her novels use the history and cul-
ture of African-Americans as the basis for explorations of emotions and relationships, and include* Beloved *(1987). In 1993
she was the first African-American to win the Nobel Prize for
Literature.*

1 Grab this land! Take it, hold it, my brothers, make
it, my brothers, shake it, squeeze it, turn it, twist it,
beat it, kick it, kiss it, whip it, stomp it, dig it, plow
it, seed it, reap it, rent it, buy it, sell it, own it, build
it, multiply it, and pass it on – can you hear me?
Pass it on!
Song of Solomon, pt 1, ch. 10 (1977). Spoken by Macon Dead.

2 An innocent man is a sin before God. Inhuman
and therefore untrustworthy. No man should live
without absorbing the sins of his kind, the foul air
of his innocence, even if it did wilt rows of angel
trumpets and cause them to fall from their vines.
Tar Baby, ch. 8 (1981)

3 In this country American means white. Everybody
else has to hyphenate.
Guardian 29 January 1992

Van Morrison
(b. 1945)
Northern Irish rock musician

Originally George Ivan Morrison. He formed the R'n'B band
Them *in 1963.* Astral Weeks *(1968) and* Moondance *(1970) were
the first of a long series of solo albums.*

1 Music is spiritual. The music business is not.
The Times 6 July 1990

Morrissey
(b. 1959)
British rock musician

*Stephen Patrick Morrissey. He was singer with the Smiths, an
influential Manchester band which split in 1987, and subsequently released solo recordings.*

1 I was happy in the haze of a drunken hour
But heaven knows I'm miserable now.
'Heaven Knows I'm Miserable Now' (song, 1984, written with Johnny Marr) on the album *Hatful of Hollow* (1985) by the Smiths

2 Hang the deejay.
'Panic' (song, 1986, written with Johnny Marr) on the album *The World Won't Listen* (1987) by the Smiths

Dwight Morrow
(1873–1931)
US lawyer, financier and diplomat

After working as a lawyer, he entered business and held various government posts after 1918. He was Ambassador to Mexico in 1927 and was elected Senator in 1930.

1 Any party which takes credit for the rain must not be surprised if its opponents blame it for the drought.
Campaign speech, October 1930, attributed

2 We judge ourselves by our motives and others by their actions.
Attributed, in entry in ADLAI STEVENSON's notebooks, quoted in *The Fine Art of Political Wit*, ch. 10 (1964) by Leon Harris

John Mortimer
(b. 1923)
British barrister and author

He is best known for his novels featuring the amiable and eccentric lawyer Rumpole and adapted for television as Rumpole of the Bailey (1978–80). He has also written translations, screenplays and plays, including A Voyage Round My Father *(1970).*

1 The shelf life of the modern hardback writer is somewhere between the milk and the yoghurt.
Quoted in *The Sunday Times* 27 December 1987

2 When you get to my age life seems little more than one long march to and from the lavatory.
Summer's Lease, pt 2, ch. 3 (1988). Spoken by Haverford Downs.

3 The freedom to make a fortune on the Stock Exchange has been made to sound more alluring than freedom of speech.
Quoted in the *Independent* 29 October 1988

4 Farce is tragedy played at a thousand revolutions per minute.
The Times 9 September 1992

5 At Harrow, you could have any boy for a box of Cadbury's milk chocolate.
Quoted in *The Sunday Times* 27 September 1998. Referring to his schooldays at Harrow.

6 The main aim of education should be to send children out into the world with a reasonably sized anthology in their heads so that, while seated on the lavatory, waiting in doctors' surgeries, on stationary trains or watching interviews with politicians, they may have something interesting to think about.
Quoted in *The Times* 30 December 2000

7 Champagne socialist.
Attributed description of himself, as a Labour-supporting member of the upper-middle classes

Thomas Morton
(1764–1838)
English playwright

He wrote a series of popular comedies for the Theatre Royal in Covent Garden, including Speed the Plough *(1798) and* The School of Reform *(1805).*

1 Approbation from Sir Hubert Stanley is praise indeed.
A Cure for the Heartache, Act 5, Sc. 2 (1797). Spoken by Young Rapid.

2 Always ding, dinging Dame Grundy into my ears – what will Mrs Grundy zay? What will Mrs Grundy think?
Speed the Plough, Act 1, Sc. 1 (1798). Farmer Ashfield remonstrates over his wife's constant anxiety concerning the opinions of their neighbour, who never appears on stage. The name Mrs Grundy has passed into literature: see FREDERICK LOCKER-LAMPSON 2.

(Sir) Oswald Mosley
(1896–1980)
British fascist leader

He was successively a Conservative, Independent and Labour MP (1918–31) before founding the British Union of Fascists ('the Blackshirts') in 1932. Interned during the Second World War, he founded the right-wing Union Movement in 1948.

1 Great men of action ... never mind on occasion being ridiculous; in a sense it is part of their job, and at times they all are. A prophet or an achiever must never mind an occasional absurdity, it is an occupational risk.
My Life, ch. 12 (1968)

2 I am not, and never have been, a man of the right.

My position was on the left and is now in the centre of politics.

Letter to *The Times* 26 April 1968

Robert Motherwell

(1915–91)

US artist and critic

He was a key member of the New York Abstract Expressionists in the 1940s, producing massive painted images and collages, such as Elegies to the Spanish Republic *(1949–76). He wrote prolifically on modern art.*

1 The public history of modern art is the story of conventional people not knowing what they are dealing with.

The Dada Painters and Poets: An Anthology, Preface (ed. Robert Motherwell, 1951)

Andrew Motion

(b. 1952)

British poet and biographer

His reflective verse shows the influence of KEATS, EDWARD THOMAS *and* PHILIP LARKIN, *all of whom have been subjects of critical studies and biographies by him. He became Poet Laureate in 1999.*

1 I admit that I also yearn to leave my mark on
  society,
and not see machines or people trample it
  foolishly.
On the one hand it's only shit; on the other, shit's
  shit,
and what we desire in the world is less, not more,
  of it.

'It is an Offence', publ. in *Love in a Life* (1991)

2 For a million years one life simply turns into the
  next –
The spider hangs between driftwood and sea holly,
the sparrow hawk balances exactly over a shrew,
the hare sits bolt upright and urgent, all ears:
there is no reason why any of this should change.

'Salt Water', publ. in *Salt Water* (1997)

3 Beside the river, swerving under ground,
your future tracked you, snapping at your heels:
Diana, breathless, hunted by your own quick
  hounds.

'Mythology', publ. in *News That Stays News* (ed. Simon Rae, 1999)

4 The fact of the matter is that it is a difficult time

in our history for white, straight, middle-aged, middle-class males.

Quoted in the *Daily Telegraph* 20 May 1999. Said on his appointment as Poet Laureate.

John Lothrop Motley

(1814–77)

US historian

Having published two novels, he produced his most famous work, The Rise of the Dutch Republic *(1856), followed by further works on Holland. He also served as a diplomat.*

1 As long as he lived, he was the guiding-star of a whole brave nation, and when he died the little children cried in the streets.

The Rise of the Dutch Republic, pt 6, ch. 7 (1856). Referring to William of Orange (WILLIAM III). See W. H. AUDEN 13.

2 Give us the luxuries of life, and we will dispense with its necessaries.

Quoted in *The Autocrat of the Breakfast-Table*, ch. 6 (1858) by OLIVER WENDELL HOLMES SR

Wolfgang Amadeus Mozart

(1756–91)

Austrian composer

One of the greatest composers of all time, he was a child prodigy in his native Salzburg, writing his first pieces aged five. He mastered the symphonic form, Italian opera buffa, string quartets and piano concertos. In Vienna from 1781, he became court composer to Joseph II but died in poverty.

1 One must not make oneself cheap here – that is a cardinal point – or else one is done. Whoever is *most impertinent* has the best chance.

Letter to his father, 5 September 1781, publ. in *The Letters of Mozart and His Family*, vol. 3 (ed. Emily Anderson, 1938). Complaining of the coarse linen shirts that Mozart was forced to wear in Vienna.

2 Melody is the very essence of music. When I think of a good melodist I think of a fine race horse. A contrapuntist is only a post-horse.

Remark to Michael Kelly, *c.* 1786, publ. in *Reminiscences* (1826) by Michael Kelly. In answer to the Irish tenor's question whether he should study counterpoint.

3 As death, when we come to consider it closely, is the true goal of our existence, I have formed during the last few years such close relations with this best and truest friend of mankind that his image is not only no longer terrifying to me, but is indeed very soothing and consoling! And I thank my God for graciously granting me the opportunity . . . of learn-

ing that death is the *key* which unlocks the door to our true happiness.

Letter to his father, 4 April 1787, publ. in *The Letters of Mozart and His Family*, vol. 3 (ed. Emily Anderson, 1938)

Malcolm Muggeridge
(1903–90)
British journalist and broadcaster

He worked for various newspapers and was Editor of Punch *1953–7. His views were iconoclastic and informed by his Christian beliefs, which earned him the nickname 'Saint Mug'.* KENNETH TYNAN *compared him to a 'garden gnome expelled from Eden . . . come to rest as a gargoyle brooding over a derelict cathedral'.*

1 Good taste and humour are a contradiction in terms, like a chaste whore.

Time 14 September 1953. Defending his editorship of *Punch*.

2 There's nothing in this world more instinctively abhorrent to me than finding myself in agreement with my fellow-humans.

Any Questions?, BBC radio broadcast, 29 April 1955, publ. in *Muggeridge Through the Microphone*, 'Mini-Mania' (1967)

3 This horror of pain is a rather low instinct and . . . if I think of human beings I've known and of my own life, such as it is, I can't recall any case of pain which didn't, on the whole, enrich life.

Meeting Point, BBC1 television broadcast, 11 August 1963, ibid., 'The Problem of Pain'

4 There is something ridiculous and even quite indecent in an individual *claiming* to be happy. Still more a people or a nation making such a claim . . . This lamentable phrase 'the pursuit of happiness' is responsible for a good part of the ills and miseries of the modern world.

Woman's Hour, BBC radio broadcast, 5 October 1965, ibid., 'Happiness'

5 Sex is the mysticism of materialism and the only possible religion in a materialistic society.

Television broadcast, BBC1, 21 October 1965, ibid., 'The American Way of Sex'

6 Television was not invented to make human beings vacuous, but is an emanation of their vacuity.

Tread Softly For You Tread on My Jokes, 'I Like Dwight' (1966)

7 In our time man has not written one word, thought one thought, put two notes or two bricks together, splashed colour on to canvas or concrete

into space, in a manner which will be of any conceivable *imaginative* interest to posterity.

Ibid., 'I Like Dwight'

8 As has been truly said in his days as an active politician, he was not only a bore; he bored for England.

Ibid., 'Boring for England'. Referring to ANTHONY EDEN.

9 It has been said that when human beings stop believing in God they believe in nothing. The truth is much worse: they believe in anything.

Woman's Hour, BBC radio broadcast, 23 March 1966, publ. in *Muggeridge Through the Microphone*, 'An Eighth Deadly Sin' (1967)

10 The trouble with kingdoms of heaven on earth is that they're liable to come to pass, and then their fraudulence is apparent for all to see. We need a kingdom of heaven in Heaven, if only because it can't be realised.

Jesus Rediscovered, 'Me and Myself' (1979)

11 Civilisation – a heap of rubble scavenged by scrawny English Lit vultures.

Quoted in *New Society* 6 October 1983

Edwin Muir
(1887–1959)
British poet

Brought up on the island of Orkney, he later lived in Prague where he published translations of FRANZ KAFKA. *His poetry collections, including* The Voyage *(1946) and* The Labyrinth *(1949), combine myth and dreams.*

1 Late in the summer the strange horses came.
We heard a distant tapping on the road,
A deepening drumming; it stopped, went on again
And at the corner changed to hollow thunder.
We saw the heads
Like a wild wave charging and were afraid.

'The Horses', publ. in *One Foot in Eden* (1956)

Frank Muir
(1920–98)
British humorist

With Denis Norden he formed a successful comedy-writing team responsible for such series as Take It From Here *(1947–58). He appeared regularly on radio and television, for example on the panel game* My Word.

1 Wit is a weapon. Jokes are a masculine way of

inflicting superiority. But humour is the pursuit of a gentle grin, usually in solitude.

Daily Mail 26 April 1990

2 The thinking man's crumpet.

Attributed description of Joan Bakewell

Ethel Watts Mumford

(1878–1940)

US novelist and humorist

She wrote poetry, plays and novels, including Out of the Ashes *(1913).*

1 God gives us our relatives – thank God we can choose our friends.

The Cynic's Calendar (1903, written with Addison Mizner and Oliver Herford)

2 In the midst of life we are in debt.

The Altogether New Cynic's Calendar (1907, written with Addison Mizner and Oliver Herford). See BOOK OF COMMON PRAYER 89.

Lewis Mumford

(1895–1990)

US social philosopher

His books Technics and Civilization *(1934) and* Myth and Machine *(1967, 1970) analysed the impact of technology on society, while* The Culture of Cities *(1938) and* The City in History *(1961) were celebrated studies of urbanism.*

1 Every generation revolts against its fathers and makes friends with its grandfathers.

The Brown Decades, ch. 1 (1931)

2 The clock, not the steam-engine, is the key-machine of the modern industrial age.

Technics and Civilization, ch. 1, sect. 2 (1934)

3 War is the supreme drama of a completely mechanized society.

Ibid., ch. 6, sect. 11

4 Today, the notion of progress in a single line without goal or limit seems perhaps the most parochial notion of a very parochial century.

Ibid., ch. 8, sect. 12

5 However far modern science and technics have fallen short of their inherent possibilities, they have taught mankind at least one lesson: Nothing is impossible.

Ibid., ch. 8, sect. 13

6 The city is a fact in nature, like a cave, a run of

mackerel or an ant-heap. But it is also a conscious work of art, and it holds within its communal framework many simpler and more personal forms of art. Mind *takes form* in the city; and in turn, urban forms condition mind.

The Culture of Cities, Introduction (1938)

7 By his very success in inventing labor-saving devices, modern man has manufactured an abyss of boredom that only the privileged classes in earlier civilizations have ever fathomed.

The Conduct of Life, 'The Challenge of Renewal' (1951)

8 Every new baby is a blind desperate vote for survival: people who find themselves unable to register an effective political protest against extermination do so by a biological act.

The City in History, ch. 18 (1961)

(Dame) Iris Murdoch

(1919–99)

British novelist and philosopher

A fellow in philosophy at Oxford (1948–63), she wove intricate plots around the emotions and relationships of her characters in such novels as The Bell *(1958),* The Sea, the Sea *(1978) and* The Green Knight *(1993).*

1 One doesn't have to get anywhere in a marriage. It's not a public conveyance.

A Severed Head, ch. 3 (1961). Spoken by Martin Lynch-Gibbon.

2 You cannot have both truth and what you call civilisation.

Honor Klein, ibid., ch. 9

3 Falling out of love is chiefly a matter of *forgetting* how charming someone is.

Anderson Palmer, ibid., ch. 24

4 Being good is just a matter of temperament in the end.

The Nice and the Good, ch. 14 (1968). Spoken by Kate Gray.

5 No love is entirely without worth, even when the frivolous calls to the frivolous and the base to the base.

Narrator, ibid., ch. 39

6 Writing is like getting married. One should never commit oneself until one is amazed at one's luck.

The Black Prince, 'Bradley Pearson's Foreword' (1972). The narrator is here discussing his own literary output: three short books in forty years.

7 A good man often appears *gauche* simply because he does not take advantage of the myriad mean

little chances of making himself look stylish. Preferring truth to form, he is not constantly at work upon the façade of his appearance.
Bradley Pearson, ibid., pt 1

8 Bereavement is a darkness impenetrable to the imagination of the unbereaved.
The Sacred and Profane Love Machine (1974). Spoken by Montague Small.

9 The priesthood is a marriage. People often start by falling in love, and they go on for years without realizing that that love must change into some other love which is so unlike it that it can hardly be recognised as love at all.
Henry and Cato, pt 2, 'The Great Teacher' (1976). Spoken by Brendan Craddock.

10 Human affairs are not serious, but they have to be taken seriously.
Brendan Craddock, ibid., pt 2, 'The Great Teacher'

11 Art is the final cunning of the human soul which would rather do anything than face the gods.
Acastos: Two Platonic Dialogues, 'Art and Eros: A Dialogue about Art' (first performed on stage 1980, publ. 1986). Spoken by Plato.

12 In philosophy if you aren't moving at a snail's pace you aren't moving at all.
Socrates, ibid., 'Above the Gods: A Dialogue about Religion'

13 He ... was a sociologist; he had got into an intellectual muddle early on in life and never managed to get out.
The Philosopher's Pupil, 'The Events in Our Town' (1983). Referring to Whit Meynell.

14 As for truth – well, it's like brown – it's not in the spectrum ... Truth is *sui generis*.
Rozanov, ibid., 'The Events in Our Town'

15 All art is a struggle to be, in a particular sort of way, virtuous.
Novelists in Interview (ed. John Haffenden, 1985)

16 Philosophy! Empty thinking by ignorant conceited men who think they can digest without eating!
The Book and the Brotherhood, pt 1, 'Midsummer' (1987). Spoken by Levquist.

17 Perhaps misguided moral passion is better than confused indifference.
Jenkin Riderhood, ibid., pt 2, 'Midwinter'

18 We shall be better prepared for the future if we see how terrible, how *doomed* the present is.
David Crimond, ibid.

19 I daresay anything can be made holy by being sincerely worshipped.
The Message to the Planet, pt 5 (1989). Spoken by Maisie Tether.

20 Perhaps when distant people on other planets pick up some wave-length of ours all they hear is a continuous scream.
Alfred Ludens, ibid., pt 6

21 A bad review is even less important than whether it is raining in Patagonia.
The Times 6 July 1989

Rupert Murdoch
(b. 1931)
Australian-born US media tycoon

His newspaper empire in Britain ranges from the Sun *to* The Times, *while in America, he acquired the* New York Post *and* Twentieth-Century Fox *film studios. In 1989 he set up the satellite network* Sky Television *(now BSkyB).*

1 William Shakespeare wrote for the masses. If he were alive today, he'd probably be the chief scriptwriter on *All in the Family* or *Dallas*.
Quoted in the *Sunday Express* 30 December 1984

2 Much of what passes for quality on British television is no more than a reflection of the narrow élite which controls it and has always thought that its tastes were synonymous with quality.
Address to the Edinburgh Television Festival, 25 August 1989, quoted in the *Guardian* 1 January 1990

3 Modernization is Americanization. It is the American way of organizing society that is prevailing in the world.
'The Wriston Lecture', Manhattan Institute, New York, 9 November 1989, quoted in *Rupert Murdoch: Ringmaster of the Information Circus*, ch. 14 (1992) by William Shawcross

Arthur Murphy
(1727–1805)
Irish-born English playwright

He contributed to and edited various London periodicals, acted, translated and worked as a barrister, but is best remembered for such unsentimental comedies as Three Weeks After Marriage *(1776).*

1 The people of England are never so happy as when you tell them they are ruined.
The Upholsterer, Act 2, Sc. 1 (1858). Spoken by Pamphlet (a political writer).

Fred Murray
US songwriter

1 I'm Henery the Eighth, I am!
Title of song (1911)

Les Murray
(b. 1938)
Australian poet

His rural upbringing gave him a close acquaintance with the Australian landscape which he celebrates in his verse. His collections include Translations from the Natural World *(1992).*

1 Axe-fall, echo and silence. It will be centuries
before many men are truly at home in this
   country,
and yet, there have always been some, in each
   generation,
there have always been some who could live in the
   presence of silence.
'Noonday Axeman', publ. in *The Ilex Tree* (1965)

2 Men must have legends, else they will die of
   strangeness.
'Noonday Axeman', ibid.

3 Nothing's said till it's dreamed out in words
and nothing's true that figures in words only.
'Poetry and Religion', publ. in *The Daylight Moon* (1987)

4 Then, strung out and spotty, you wriggle and
   sigh
and kiss all the fellows and make them all die.
'Midnight Lake', publ. in *Dog Fox Field* (1991)

5 Australians are like most who won't read this
   poem
or any, since literature turned on them
and bodiless jargons without reverie
scorn their loves as illusion and biology,
compared with bloody History, the opposite of
   home.
'A Brief History', publ. in *Subhuman Redneck Poems* (1996)

6 Sex is a Nazi. The students all knew
this at your school. To it, everyone's subhuman
for parts of their lives. Some are all their lives.
You'll be one of those if these things worry you.
'Rock Music', ibid.

7 For the truth, we are silent. For the flattering
   dream,
in massed farting reassurance, we spasm and
   scream.
'Rock Music', ibid.

Ed Murrow
(1908–65)
US newscaster

An esteemed figure in American broadcasting, he reported on wartime Britain for CBS and produced and presented the current affairs shows See It Now *(1951–8) and* Person to Person *(1953–60).*

1 No one can terrorize a whole nation, unless we are all his accomplices.
Of JOSEPH MCCARTHY, in 'See It Now', CBS television broadcast, 7 March 1954. Murrow's exposé of McCarthy in 1954 contributed to the latter's downfall.

2 He mobilized the English language and sent it into battle to steady his fellow countrymen and hearten those Europeans upon whom the long dark night of tyranny had descended.
Of WINSTON CHURCHILL, in TV broadcast to mark Churchill's eightieth birthday, 30 November 1954, publ. in *In Search of Light* (1967)

John Middleton Murry
(1889–1957)
British critic and editor

Founder and editor of the journal The Adelphi *(1923–48), he was married to* KATHERINE MANSFIELD, *and edited her poems, stories and correspondence. He published her biography in 1933.*

1 If the Nazis have really been guilty of the unspeakable crimes circumstantially imputed to them, then – let us make no mistake – pacifism is faced with a situation with which it cannot cope. The conventional pacifist conception of a reasonable or generous peace is irrelevant to this reality.
Peace News 22 September 1944. Murry became a radical Christian and a prominent pacifist, editing *Peace News* 1940–46.

Alfred de Musset
(1810–57)
French poet and playwright

He was prominent among the French Romantics, especially for such poetry as Contes d'Espagne et d'Italie *(1830) and 'Les Nuits' (1835–7), which traced his stormy affair with* GEORGE SAND. *His plays include* La Nuit vénitienne *(1830).*

1 Great artists have no country.
Lorenzaccio, Act 1, Sc. 5 (1834). Spoken by the Goldsmith.

2 I do not believe, O Christ! in your holy word
I have come too late into a world too old.
'Rolla', pt 1, st. 3, publ. in *Poésies Complètes* (1840)

3 The most despairing songs are the loveliest of all,
I know immortal ones composed only of tears.
'La Nuit de mai', st. 9, ibid. The words of the Muse.

Benito Mussolini
(1883–1945)
Italian dictator

He helped found the Italian fascist movement in 1919, and by 1925 had established himself as dictator, or 'Duce', of Italy. He annexed Abyssinia (1936) and entered the Second World War on HITLER's *side. He was killed while attempting to flee Italy. See* EZRA POUND 17.

1 I could have transformed this grey hall into an armed camp of Blackshirts, a bivouac for corpses. I could have nailed up the doors of Parliament.
Speech, 16 November 1922, quoted in *Benito Mussolini*, pt 1, ch. 4 (1962, rev. 1965 and 1975) by Christopher Hibbert. First speech to the Italian Chamber of Deputies after becoming Prime Minister.

2 If I go forward, follow me. If I retreat, kill me. If I die, avenge me.
Speech to party officials and government workers following an attempt on his life, 7 April 1926, quoted in *Mussolini*, ch. 10 (2002) by R. J. B. Bosworth. See also NGO DINH DIEM 1.

3 Fascism, the more it considers and observes the future and the development of humanity, quite apart from political considerations of the moment, believes neither in the possibility nor the utility of perpetual peace.
'The Political and Social Doctrine of Fascism', publ. in *Enciclopedia Italiana* (1932)

4 War alone brings up to their highest tension all human energies and imposes the stamp of nobility upon the peoples who have the courage to make it.
'The Political and Social Doctrine of Fascism', ibid.

5 It is humiliating to remain with our hands folded while others write history. It matters little who wins. To make a people great it is necessary to send them to battle even if you have to kick them in the pants. That is what I shall do.
Quoted in journal entry by GALEAZZO CIANO, 11 April 1940, publ. in *Diary 1939–1943* (1946) by Galeazzo Ciano. Said to Count Ciano, Mussolini's son-in-law and Minister for Foreign

Affairs. Italy entered the Second World War on 10 June 1940.

Mike Myers
(b. 1964)
Canadian comic actor and screenwriter

Coming to notice on NBC's Saturday Night Live *(1989–94), he adapted his 'Wayne's World' sketch into two successful films and subsequently starred in a sequence of films as the spoof spy Austin Powers.*

1 No way dude.
Wayne's World (film, 1992, screenplay by Mike Myers, Bonnie Turner and Terry Turner, directed by Penelope Spheeris). Spoken by Wayne Campbell (Mike Myers). The oft-repeated line was featured regularly on 'Saturday Night Live'.

2 Shall we shag now, or shall we shag later?
Austin Powers: International Man of Mystery (film, 1997, screenplay by Mike Myers, directed by Jay Roach). Spoken by Austin Powers (Mike Myers).

N

Vladimir Nabokov
(1899–1977)
Russian-born US novelist and poet

He gained instant notoriety for Lolita *(1955), a showcase for his wit and erudition. Other novels include* Pnin *(1957) and* Pale Fire *(1962). 'He writes prose the only way it should be written,'* JOHN UPDIKE *commented, ' – that is ecstatically.'*

1 Lolita, light of my life, fire of my loins. My sin, my soul. Lo-lee-ta: the tip of the tongue taking a trip of three steps down the palate to tap, at three, on the teeth. Lo. Lee. Ta.
Lolita, pt 1, ch. 1 (1955). Opening lines of book, narrated by Humbert Humbert.

2 You can always count on a murderer for a fancy prose style.
Humbert Humbert, ibid., pt 1, ch. 1

3 My very photogenic mother died in a freak accident (picnic, lightning) when I was three, and, save for a pocket of warmth in the darkest past, nothing of her subsists within the hollows and dells of memory.
Humbert Humbert, ibid., pt 1, ch. 2

4 Between the age limits of nine and fourteen there occur maidens who, to certain bewitched travelers, twice or many times older than they, reveal their true nature which is not human, but nymphic (that is, demoniac); and these chosen creatures I propose to designate as 'nymphets'.
Humbert Humbert, ibid., pt 1, ch. 5. This passage was cut in the 1962 film directed by STANLEY KUBRICK.

5 The tiny madman in his padded cell.
Humbert Humbert, ibid., pt 1, ch. 11. Describing an embryo.

6 The cradle rocks above an abyss, and common sense tells us that our existence is but a brief crack of light between two eternities of darkness.
Speak, Memory, ch. 1, sect. 1 (1955, rev. 1966). Opening words of Nabokov's autobiography.

7 Imagination, the supreme delight of the immortal and the immature, should be limited. In order to enjoy life, we should not enjoy it too much.
Ibid., ch. 1, sect. 1

8 A novelist is, like all mortals, more fully at home on the surface of the present than in the ooze of the past.
Strong Opinions, ch. 20 (1973)

(Sir) V. S. Naipaul
(b. 1932)
Trinidad-born British author

Vidiadhar Surajprasad Naipaul. Describing himself as 'content to be a colonial, without a past, without ancestors', he explores themes of alienation and faith in such books as A House for Mr Biswas *(1961) and* Among the Believers *(1981).*

1 I'm the kind of writer that people think other people are reading.
Radio Times 24–30 March 1979

2 To read a newspaper for the first time is like coming into a film that has been on for an hour. Newspapers are like serials. To understand them you have to take knowledge to them; the knowledge that serves best is the knowledge provided by the newspaper itself.
The Enigma of Arrival, 'The Journey' (1987). On reading the New York Times for the first time.

3 My writing is like fine wine; the more you read, the more you get from it. Reading it once is like taking a dog to the theatre.
Quoted in The Times 20 October 2001

John Napier
(1550–1617)
Scottish mathematician

He was the inventor of logarithms (1614) and 'Napier's bones', an early mechanical device for calculating multiplication and division.

1 Multiplication is vexation,
Division is as bad;
The rule of three doth puzzle me,
And practice drives me mad.
'A Description of the Admirable Table of Logarithmes...', written 1570, publ. 1618

Napoleon I
(1769–1821)
French general and emperor

Napoléon Buonaparte, later Bonaparte. Having launched on an army career, he became commander of the army in Italy in 1796 and was made First Consul of France after the coup of 18 Brumaire, 1799. He instituted legal and administrative reforms while pursuing an expansionist policy abroad, proclaiming himself Emperor in 1804. He was finally defeated at Waterloo (1815) and exiled.

1 Do you suppose I mean to found a republic? What an idea! A republic of thirty millions of people! With our morals, our vices! how is such a thing possible? The nation wants a chief, a chief covered with glory, not theories of government, phrases, ideological essays, that the French do not understand.
Said in May 1797, following his invasion of Italy, quoted in *A Short History of Napoleon the First*, ch. 2, sect. 2 (1886) by John Robert Seeley

2 Soldiers, forty centuries look down upon you.
Speech to his troops in Egypt, 21 July 1798, quoted in *Bonaparte in Egypt*, ch. 3 (1964) by J. Christopher Herold . Referring to the pyramids, before the Battle of the Pyramids, in which the Mamelukes were heavily defeated.

3 The Channel is a ditch which needs but a pinch of courage to cross.
Letter, 16 November 1803, quoted in *Napoleon Bonaparte: His Rise and Fall*, ch. 9 (1963) by J. M. Thompson

4 For the Pope's purposes, I am Charlemagne. Like Charlemagne, I join the crown of France with the crown of the Lombards. My empire, like Charlemagne's, marches with the East.
Quoted in *Napoleon Bonaparte*, ch. 10, sect. 4 (1952) by J. M. Thompson

5 There is only one step from the sublime to the ridiculous.
Remark to Polish ambassador Abbé De Pradt, December 1812, quoted in *Histoire de l'Ambassade dans le Grand-duché de Varsovie en 1812* (1815 edn) by D. G. De Pradt. Referring to Napoleon's retreat by sledge after the failure of his Russian campaign. THOMAS PAINE had earlier observed: 'One step above the sublime, makes the ridiculous; and one step above the ridiculous, makes the sublime again.' (*The Age of Reason*, pt 2, 1795)

6 France has more need of me than I have need of France.
Speech, 1813 or 1814, attributed

7 As to moral courage, I have rarely met with two o'clock in the morning courage; I mean instantaneous courage.
Remark, December 1815, quoted in *Mémorial de Sainte-Hélène*, vol. 1, pt 2 (1823) by E. A. de Las Cases

8 England is a nation of shopkeepers.
Remark made while in exile on St Helena, quoted in *Napoleon in Exile*, vol. 2 (1822) by Barry E. O'Meara. It is thought that Napoleon heard the phrase from Bernard de Vieuzac Barère, who may have adopted it from Adam Smith (see ADAM SMITH 8).

9 You must not fight too often with one enemy, or you will teach him all your art of war.
Quoted in *Representative Men*, 'Uses of Great Men' (1850) by RALPH WALDO EMERSON

10 I made all my generals out of mud.
Quoted ibid., 'Napoleon'

11 When soldiers have been baptized in the fire of a battle-field, they have all one rank in my eyes.
Quoted ibid., 'Napoleon'

12 There are two levers for moving men – interest and fear.
Quoted ibid., 'Napoleon'

13 The men who have changed the universe have never succeeded by capturing the leaders, but always by moving the masses.
Quoted in *Napoleon*, ch. 10 (1912) by H. A. L. Fisher

14 Aristocracy always exists. Destroy it in the nobility, it removes itself immediately to the rich and powerful houses of the middle class. Destroy it in these, it survives and takes refuge with the leaders of the workshops and the people.
Maxim, ibid., Appendix 1

15 Cleverness is not wanted in war. What is wanted is accuracy, character and simplicity.
Maxim, ibid., Appendix 1

16 In government, never retrace your steps.
Maxim, ibid., Appendix 1

17 An army marches on its stomach.
Attributed. The saying is also attributed to FREDERICK THE GREAT.

18 Circumstances! I make circumstances!
Attributed

19 I want from now on to live like a justice of the peace.
Attributed, on arrival in exile on the island of St Helena

20 Not tonight, Josephine.
Attributed remark to the Empress Joséphine

21 *On s'engage et puis on voit.*
[You engage in battle and see what happens.]
Attributed

22 A revolution is an opinion backed by bayonets.
Attributed

23 Soldiers win battles and generals get the credit.
Attributed. Possibly linked to an Italian proverb: 'It is the blood of the soldier that makes the general great.'

Napoleon III
(1808–73)
French emperor

Also known as Louis-Napoléon. The nephew of NAPOLEON I, *he was President (1850–2) and then Emperor (1852–70) of France. After two decades of stable but authoritarian rule, he was defeated in the Franco-Prussian war and died in exile.*

1 The Empress is Legitimist, my cousin is Republican, Morny is Orleanist, I am a Socialist; the only Bonapartist is Persigny, and he is mad.
Attributed, late 1850s. Conversational remark referring to the leading figures of the Second Empire.

Ogden Nash
(1902–71)
US poet

A frequent contributor to the New Yorker, *he caused both scandal and amusement with his puns, parodies and clever rhymes, published in numerous collections.*

1 Candy
Is dandy
But liquor
Is quicker.
'Reflections on Ice-Breaking', publ. in *Hard Lines* (1931)

2 The cow is of the bovine ilk;
One end is moo, the other, milk.
'The Cow', publ. in *Free Wheeling* (1931)

3 Man is a victim of dope
In the incurable form of hope.
'Good-by, Old Year, You Oaf or Why Don't They Pay the Bonus?', publ. in *The Primrose Path* (1935)

4 Every New Year is the direct descendant, isn't it, of a long line of proven criminals?
'Good-by, Old Year, You Oaf or Why Don't They Pay the Bonus?', ibid.

5 Here is a pen and here is a pencil,
Here's a typewriter, here's a stencil,
Here is a list of today's appointments,
And all the flies in all the ointments,
The daily woes that a man endures –
Take them, George, they're yours!
'Let George Do It, If You Can Find Him', ibid.

6 The most exciting happiness is the happiness generated by forces beyond your control.
'The Anatomy of Happiness', publ. in *I'm a Stranger Here Myself* (1938)

7 I think remorse ought to stop biting the consciences that feed it.
'A Clean Conscience Never Relaxes', ibid.

8 Every Englishman is convinced of one thing, viz.:
That to be an Englishman is to belong to the most exclusive club there is.
'England Expects', ibid.

9 How easy for those who do not bulge
To not overindulge!
'A Necessary Dirge', ibid.

10 Whether elected or appointed
He considers himself the Lord's anointed,
And indeed the ointment lingers on him
So thick you can't get your fingers on him.
'The Politician', ibid.

11 I have a bone to pick with Fate.
Come here and tell me, girlie,
Do you think my mind is maturing late,
Or simply rotted early?
'Lines on Facing Forty', publ. in *Good Intentions* (1942)

12 The further through life I drift
The more obvious it becomes that I am lacking in thrift.
'A Penny Saved is Impossible from Good Intentions', ibid.

13 Your hair may be brushed, but your mind's untidy,
You've had about seven hours' sleep since Friday,
No wonder you feel that lost sensation;
You're sunk from a riot of relaxation.
'We'll All Feel Better By Wednesday', publ. in *Versus* (1949)

14 A door is what a dog is perpetually on the wrong side of.
'A Dog's Best Friend is his Illiteracy', publ. in *The Private Dining Room* (1953)

15 Good wine needs no bush,
And perhaps products that people really want need no hard-sell or soft-sell TV push.
Why not?
Look at pot.
'Most Doctors Recommend or Yours For Fast Fast Fast Relief', publ. in *The Old Dog Barks Backwards* (1972)

Paul Nash
(1889–1946)
British artist

He was the official war artist of both world wars and remembered above all for the Cubist-influenced 'The Menin Road' (1918), and 'Totes Meer' ('Dead Sea', 1940–1).

1 I am no longer an artist, interested and curious. I am a messenger who will bring back word from the men who are fighting to those who want the war to go on for ever. Feeble, inarticulate, will be my message, but it will have a bitter truth, and may it burn their lousy souls.
Letter to his wife, 13 November 1917, publ. in *Outline: An Autobiography and Other Writings* (1949)

Thomas Nashe
(1567–1601)
English satirist and pamphleteer

Also known as Thomas Nash. He wrote anti-Puritan pamphlets in the Marprelate controversy and engaged in literary disputes of the day. Summer's Last Will and Testament (1592), a masque, contains some of his most memorable writing, while The Unfortunate Traveller (1594) has picaresque elements.

1 Adieu, farewell earth's bliss,
This world uncertain is;
Fond are life's lustful joys,
Death proves them all but toys,
None from his darts can fly:
I am sick, I must die.
Lord, have mercy on us!
'Adieu, farewell earth's bliss', st. 1, written 1592, publ. in *Summer's Last Will and Testament*, st. 3 (1600). The song, sung by Summer in the text, is also known as 'In Time of Pestilence' or 'In Time of Plague'.

2 Beauty is but a flower
Which wrinkles will devour;
Brightness falls from the air,
Queens have died young and fair,
Dust hath closed Helen's eye.
I am sick, I must die.
Lord, have mercy on us!
'Adieu, farewell earth's bliss', st. 3, ibid.

3 Cold doth increase, the sickness will not cease,
And here we lie, God knows, with little ease.
From winter, plague and pestilence, good Lord,
    deliver us!
'Autumn', st. 1, ibid.

George Jean Nathan
(1882–1958)
US editor and critic

Said to be the highest paid drama critic ever, he co-edited the magazine Smart Set *with* H. L. MENCKEN, *and in 1924 founded with Mencken the* American Mercury. *He also wrote plays.*

1 The aim of great drama is not to make men happy with themselves as they are, but with themselves as they might, yet alas cannot, be.
The Critic and the Drama, ch. 2, sect. 1 (1922)

2 In the words of a friend of mine, I drink to make other people interesting.
The Autobiography of an Attitude, 'On Alcohol' (1925). The joke is usually ascribed to Nathan himself.

3 To speak of morals in art is to speak of legislature in sex. Art is the sex of the imagination.
American Mercury July 1926

4 All criticism, after all, is a criticism of the critic himself before it is one of the criticized.
Art of the Night, 'Advice to a Young Critic', no. 18 (1928)

5 The test of a real comedian is whether you laugh at him before he opens his mouth.
American Mercury September 1929

Terry Nation
(1930–97)
British scriptwriter

He began as a stand-up comedian but made his reputation as the creator of science fiction adventures on TV, notably the BBC series Dr Who *(from 1963).*

1 We will obey! . . . Exterminate! Exterminate!
Doctor Who (BBC television serial, from 1963). Spoken by the Daleks. Appearing in some eighty episodes of *Dr Who*, the Daleks were originally voiced by Peter Hawkins, who also voiced the Flowerpot Men, and David Graham, who also voiced the chauffeur Parker in *Thunderbirds*.

Myron 'Grim' Natwick
(1890–1990)
US animator

He started as an animator at William Randolph Hearst's International Film Studio in New York in 1916, and subsequently worked at Fleischer Studios and Walt Disney Studios, where he was responsible for animating Snow White *(1937).*

1 Boop-boop-a-doop.
Talkartoons (cartoon series), created by Grim Natwick in 1930 for the Fleischer Studios. Catchphrase of Betty Boop, who

starred in her own show 1932–9, and was dropped following a wave of puritanical attacks, mostly by women's clubs. The character was said to have been modelled on the actress Helen Kane, who later sued the studio for $250,000 and lost.

Martina Navratilova
(b. 1956)
Czech-born US tennis player

The dominant woman player of the 1980s, she won a record nine Wimbledon singles titles before retiring from competitive singles tennis in 1994.

1 I'm not just involved in tennis but commited. Do you know the difference between involvement and commitment? Think of ham and eggs. The chicken is involved. The pig is committed.
Quoted in the *International Herald Tribune* 3 September 1982

John Mason Neale
See HYMNS AND CAROLS 5, 11, 13, 16, 33, 65

Jawaharlal Nehru
(1889–1964)
Indian statesman

Known as 'Pandit' ('Teacher') Nehru, he led the socialist wing of the Indian National Congress. Despite spending eighteen years in prison, he was instrumental in achieving Indian independence in 1947, and served as the country's first prime minister until his death. He was the father of INDIRA GANDHI.

1 The British Government in India is like a tooth that is decaying but is still strongly embedded. It is painful, but it cannot be easily pulled out.
Towards Freedom (1935)

2 Long years ago we made a tryst with destiny, and now the time comes when we shall redeem our pledge, not wholly or in full measure, but very substantially. At the stroke of the midnight hour, while the world sleeps, India will awake to life and freedom.
Speech to Indian Assembly, 14 August 1947, publ. in *The Penguin Book of Twentieth-Century Speeches* (ed. Brian MacArthur, 1999). Spoken on the eve of independence.

3 Friends and comrades, the light has gone out of our lives and there is darkness everywhere. I do not know what to tell you and how to say it. Our beloved leader, Bapu as we called him, the father of the nation, is no more.
Broadcast on All-India Radio, 30 January 1948, ibid. Following the assassination of GANDHI by a Hindu fanatic, an event which provoked nationwide rioting.

4 I shall be the last Englishman to rule in India.
Quoted in *A Life in Our Times*, ch. 26 (1981) by J. K. GALBRAITH. Nehru spent the years 1905–12 in England: at Harrow School and Trinity College, Cambridge, and at the Inner Temple, London, where he qualified as a barrister.

Horatio, Lord Nelson
(1758–1805)
British admiral

Viscount Nelson of the Nile. A national hero, he joined the navy in 1770, and lost his right eye and right arm in the wars against France. He achieved his greatest glory at the Battle of the Nile (1798) and at the Battle of Trafalgar (1805), where he was mortally wounded.

1 Before this time tomorrow I shall have gained a peerage, or Westminster Abbey.
Said before the Battle of the Nile in 1798, quoted in *Life of Nelson*, ch. 5 (1813) by ROBERT SOUTHEY. In the event, Nelson inflicted a significant defeat on the French fleet as a result of which he became Baron Nelson of the Nile, and the king of Naples conferred on him the title of Duke of Bronte.

2 I have only one eye, I have a right to be blind sometimes – I really do not see the signal!
Said at the Battle of Copenhagen, 2 April 1801, ibid., ch. 7. In response to a signal to disengage by Admiral Hyde Parker. Nelson persevered to victory shortly after.

3 England expects every man 'to do his duty!'
Signal to the fleet at 11.35am, the morning of the Battle of Trafalgar, 21 October 1805, ibid., ch. 9. The original instruction for the signal, before being amended, is variously reported to have begun 'Nelson expects' or 'England confides'.

4 Kiss me, Hardy.
Spoken to the Captain of the *Victory* as Nelson lay mortally wounded at the Battle of Trafalgar, 21 October 1805, ibid., ch. 9

5 Thank God I have done my duty.
Nelson's final words, ibid., ch. 9. As heard by the ship's chaplain.

Howard Nemerov
(1920–91)
US poet, novelist and critic

Best known for his poetry, which takes in nature and philosophical issues, he also wrote novels and works of criticism. JOYCE CAROL OATES *called him unclassifiable, being a 'romantic, realist, comedian, satirist, relentless and indefatigable brooder upon the most ancient mysteries'.*

1 And I speak to you now with the land's voice, It is the cold, wild land that says to you

A knowledge glimmers in the sleep of things:
The old hills hunch before the north wind blows.
'A Spell before Winter', publ. in *The Next Room of the Dream*
(1962)

2 I've never read a political poem that's accomplished anything. Poetry makes things happen, but rarely what the poet wants.
International Herald Tribune 14 October 1988

Nero
(37–68)
Roman emperor

Born Lucius Domitius Ahenobarbus, and later known as Nero Claudius Caesar. Emperor from AD 54, he was renowned for his debauched excesses and for his persecution of the Christians. Faced with a general revolt, he committed suicide.

1 What an artist dies with me!
Said shortly before taking his own life, quoted in *Lives of the Caesars*, 'Nero', sect. 49, by Suetonius. Claiming to be a connoisseur of the arts, Nero wrote verse and performed publicly as an actor and singer.

Pablo Neruda
(1904–73)
Chilean poet and diplomat

Pseudonym of Ricardo Neftalí Reyes. He was already known for his poetry before serving as a diplomat and Senator (1927–48). His major work, Canto General (1950), was a hymn to Latin America. GARCIA LORCA *called him 'a poet closer to death than to philosophy, closer to pain than to insight, closer to blood than to ink'.*

1 If you should ask me where I've been all this
time
I have to say 'Things happen'.
'No Hay Olvido (Sonata)' ('There is No Forgetting: Sonata'),
publ. in *Residencia en la Tierra (1925–1935)* (1935)

2 The dark of a day gone by
Grown fat on our grieving blood.
'No Hay Olvido (Sonata)', ibid.

3 Night, snow, and sand make up the form
of my thin country,
all silence lies in its long line,
all foam flows from its marine beard,
all coal covers it with mysterious kisses.
Gold burns in its fingers like an ember
and silver illuminates like a green moon
its thickened shadow of a sullen planet.
'Descubridores de Chile' ('Discoverers of Chile'), publ. in *Canto General* (1950)

4 No one can claim the name of Pedro,
nobody is Rosa or Maria,
all of us are dust or sand,
all of us are rain under rain.
They have spoken to me of Venezuelas,
of Chiles and Paraguays;
I have no idea what they are saying.
I know only the skin of the earth
and I know it has no name.
'Demasiados nombres' ('Too Many Names'), publ. in *Estravagario* (1958)

5 The word
was born in the blood,
grew in the dark body, beating,
And flew through the lips and the mouth.
'La Palabra' ('The Word'), publ. in *Plenos Poderes* (1962)

6 And it was at that age ... Poetry arrived
in search of me. I don't know, I don't know where
it came from, from winter or a river.
I don't know how or when,
no, they were not voices, they were not
words, nor silence,
but from the street I was summoned,
from the branches of night,
abruptly from the others,
among violent fires
or returning alone,
there I was without a face
and it touched me.
'La Poesia' ('Poetry'), publ. in *Memorial de Isla Negra* (1964)

7 Using language like clothes or the skin on your body, with its sleeves, its patches, its transpirations, and its blood and sweat stains, that's what shows a writer's mettle. This is style.
Memoirs, ch. 11 (1974)

8 The human crowd has been the lesson of my life. I can come to it with the born timidity of the poet, with the fear of the timid, but once I am in its midst, I feel transfigured. I am part of the essential majority, I am one more leaf on the great human tree.
Ibid., ch. 11

Gérard de Nerval
(1808–55)
French author and poet

Pseudonym of Gérard Labrunie. His writings, which include the travelogue Voyage en Orient *(1851), fiction, poetry and translations, prefigured symbolism and surrealism. Afflicted wth periodic insanity, he committed suicide.*

1 Every flower is a soul blossoming in Nature.
'Vers Dorés' (1845), repr. in *Selected Writings* (ed./transl. Geoffrey Wagner, 1958)

2 I am the darkly shaded, the bereaved, the inconsolate,
The prince of Aquitaine, with the blasted tower.
'El Desdichado', publ. in *Les Chimères* (1854). T. S. ELIOT quotes the original French of this sonnet in *The Waste Land*, pt 5 (1922): 'Le Prince d'Aquitaine à la tour abolie.'

3 The tree of knowledge is not the tree of life! And yet can we cast out of our spirits all the good or evil poured into them by so many learned generations? Ignorance cannot be learned.
Aurélia, pt 2, ch. 1 (1855). See LORD BYRON 69.

4 It has been rightly said that nothing is unimportant, nothing powerless in the universe; a single atom can dissolve everything, and save everything! What terror! There lies the eternal distinction between good and evil.
Ibid., pt 2, ch. 6

(Sir) Henry Newbolt
(1862–1938)
British poet

He was known for his patriotic and nautical ballads, such as the rousing 'Drake's Drum' and 'The Fighting Téméraire'. He worked for the War Propaganda Bureau during the First World War and wrote on naval history.

1 Take my drum to England, hang et by the shore,
Strike et when your powder's runnin' low;
If the Dons sight Devon, I'll quit the port o' Heaven,
An' drum them up the Channel as we drummed them long ago.
'Drake's Drum', publ. in *Admirals All and Other Verses* (1897). The poem was set to music by Charles Stanford.

2 There'll be many grim and gory,
There'll be few to tell the story,
But we'll all be one in glory
With the Fighting Téméraire.
'The Fighting Téméraire', st. 4 (1897), ibid.

3 When Mehtab Singh rode from the gate
His chin was on his breast:
The captains said, 'When the strong command Obedience is best.'
'A Ballad of John Nicholson', ibid. Closing lines.

4 There's a breathless hush in the Close to-night –
Ten to make and the match to win –
A bumping pitch and a blinding light,
An hour to play and the last man in.
And it's not for the sake of a ribboned coat,
Or the selfish hope of a season's fame,
But his Captain's hand on his shoulder smote –
'Play up! play up! and play the game!'
'Vitaï Lampada', st. 1 (1897), ibid.

5 To set the cause above renown,
To love the game beyond the prize,
To honour, while you strike him down,
The foe that comes with fearless eyes;
To count the life of battle good,
And dear the land that gave you birth,
And dearer yet the brotherhood
That binds the brave of all the earth.
'Clifton Chapel', st. 2, publ. in *The Island Race* (1898)

6 'Qui procul hinc,' the legend's writ –
The frontier-grave is far away –
'Qui ante diem periit:
Sed miles, sed pro patria.'
'Clifton Chapel', st. 4, ibid.

John Henry Newman
(1801–90)
English churchman and theologian

As an Anglican cleric, he called for the revival of Catholic practices in Tracts for the Times *(1833–41), which gave rise to the Tractarian Movement, later called the Oxford Movement. He converted to Catholicism in 1845 and was made a cardinal in 1879.* Apologia pro Vita Sua *(1864) was his spiritual autobiography. See* HYMNS AND CAROLS 49.

1 It is as absurd to argue men, as to torture them, into believing.
'The Usurpation of Reason', sermon at Oxford, 11 December 1831, publ. in *Oxford University Sermons* (1843)

2 When men understand what each other mean, they see, for the most part, that controversy is either superfluous or hopeless.
'Faith and Reason, Contrasted as Habits of Mind', sermon at Oxford, Epiphany, 1839, ibid.

3 It is often said that second thoughts are best; so they are in matters of judgement, but not in matters of conscience.
'Obedience without Love, as Instanced in the Character of Balaam', publ. in *Parochial and Plain Sermons*, vol. 4, Sermon 2 (1839)

4 We must make up our minds to be ignorant of much, if we would know anything.
'Secular Knowledge not the Antecedent of Moral Improvement' (1841), repr. in *Discussions and Arguments*, pt 4 (1872)

5 For myself, certainly I think that that style which, whatever be its origin, is called Gothic, is endowed with a profound and a commanding beauty, such as no other style possesses with which we are acquainted, and which probably the Church will not see surpassed till it attain to the Celestial City. No other architecture, now used for sacred purposes, seems to be the growth of an idea, whereas the Gothic style is as harmonious and as intellectual as it is graceful.
The Idea of a University, pt 1, Discourse 4 ('Bearing of Other Knowledge on Theology'), sect. 7 (1852). Newman had earlier written in a letter to Henry Wilberforce from Milan, 24 September 1846: 'However my reason may go with Gothic, my heart has ever gone with Grecian.'

6 A university is, according to the usual designation, an *Alma Mater*, knowing her children one by one, not a foundry, or a mint, or a treadmill.
Ibid., pt 1, Discourse 6 ('Knowledge Viewed in Relation to Learning'), sect. 8

7 It is almost a definition of a gentleman to say he is one who never inflicts pain.
Ibid., pt 1, Discourse 8 ('Knowledge Viewed in Relation to Religious Duty'), sect. 10

8 England, surely, is the paradise of little men, and the purgatory of great ones.
'The Reverse of the Picture', written spring 1855, publ. in *Discussions and Arguments*, pt 5, Letter 6 (1872)

9 I do hereby profess *ex animo*, with an absolute internal assent and consent, that Protestantism is the dreariest of possible religions; that the thought of the Anglican service makes me shiver, and the thought of the Thirty-nine Articles makes me shudder. Return to the Church of England! No! 'The net is broken, and we are delivered.' I should be a consummate fool (to use a mild term), if in my old age I left 'the land flowing with milk and honey' for the city of confusion and the house of bondage.
Letter to the editor of the *Globe* newspaper, 1862, quoted in *Cardinal Newman*, ch. 5 (1907) by Wilfrid Meynell. Newman's denial of a rumour that he was about to leave the Birmingham Oratory and rejoin the Church of England.

10 From the age of fifteen, dogma has been the fundamental principle of my religion: I know no other religion; I cannot enter into the idea of any other sort of religion; religion, as a mere sentiment, is to me a dream and a mockery.
Apologia pro Vita Sua, 'History of my Religious Opinions from 1833–1839' (1864)

11 This is what the Church is said to want, not party men, but sensible, temperate, sober, well-judging persons, to guide it through the channel of no-meaning, between the Scylla and Charybdis of Aye and No.
Ibid., 'History of my Religious Opinions from 1839–1841'

12 Ten thousand difficulties do not make one doubt.
Ibid., 'Position of my Mind since 1845'

13 The all-corroding, all-dissolving scepticism of the intellect in religious enquiries.
Ibid., 'Position of my Mind since 1845'

14 You discharge your olive-branch as if from a catapult.
A Letter Addressed to the Rev. E. B. Pusey, D.D. on Occasion of his Eirenicon, 'Introductory Remarks', publ. as *Certain Difficulties Felt by Anglicans in Catholic Teaching*, vol. 2 (1865)

15 Firmly I believe and truly
God is Three, and God is One;
And I next acknowledge duly
Manhood taken by the Son.
'Firmly I believe and truly' (hymn), publ. in *The Dream of Gerontius* (1866)

16 Praise to the Holiest in the height,
And in the depth be praise;
In all His words most wonderful,
Most sure in all His ways.
'Praise to the Holiest in the height' (hymn), ibid.

17 Abuse is as great a mistake in controversy as panegyric in biography.
Letter, 1866, quoted in *The Life of John Henry Cardinal Newman*, ch. 23 (1912) by Wilfrid Ward

News of the World

1 All human life is there.
Slogan from the 1950s. See HENRY JAMES 4.

(Sir) Isaac Newton
(1642–1727)
English mathematician and physicist

An eccentric but highly gifted pioneer in the fields of light, mechanics and mathematics, he established the three laws of motion, discovered the law of universal gravitation and developed calculus. His most important works were Philosophiae Naturalis Principia Mathematica (1686–7) and Opticks (1704). He was also drawn to the study of alchemy. See WIL-LIAM WORDSWORTH 16.

1 Amicus Plato – amicus Aristoteles, magis amica veritas.
[Plato is my friend – Aristotle is my friend, but my greatest friend is truth.]
Questiones quaedam Philosophicae ('Certain Philosophical Questions'), pt 3, epigraph, written c. 1664, publ. in Certain Philosophical Questions: Newton's Trinity Notebook (ed. J. E. McGuire and Martin Tamny, 1983)

2 If I have seen further it is by standing on the shoulders of giants.
Letter to Robert Hooke, 5 February 1676, publ. in Isaac Newton's Papers and Letters on Natural Philosophy (ed. I. Bernard Cohen, 1978)

3 The errors are not in the art but in the artificers.
Principia Mathematica, Preface (1687, transl. Andrew Motte, 1729)

4 Every body continues in its state of rest, or of uniform motion in a right line, unless it is compelled to change that state by forces impressed upon it.
Ibid., 'Laws of Motion: 1'

5 The alteration of motion is ever proportional to the motive force impressed; and is made in the direction of the right line in which that force is impressed.
Ibid., 'Laws of Motion: 2'

6 To every action there is always opposed an equal reaction: or, the mutual actions of two bodies upon each other are always equal, and directed to contrary parts.
Ibid., 'Laws of Motion: 3'

7 I frame no hypotheses [Hypotheses non fingo]; for whatever is not deduced from the phenomena is to be called an hypothesis, and hypotheses, whether metaphysical or physical, whether of occult qualities or mechanical, have no place in experimental philosophy.
Ibid., 'General Scholium'

8 To us it is enough that gravity does really exist, and act according to the laws which we have explained, and abundantly serves to account for all the motions of the celestial bodies, and of our sea.
Ibid., 'General Scholium'

9 I seem to have been only like a boy playing on the seashore, and diverting myself in now and then finding a smoother pebble or a prettier shell than ordinary, whilst the great ocean of truth lay all undiscovered before me.
Quoted in Memoirs of the Life, Writings, and Discoveries of Sir Isaac Newton, vol. 2, ch. 27 (1855) by David Brewster

John Newton
See HYMNS AND CAROLS 9, 29, 39

New York Times

1 All the news that's fit to print.
Motto, devised by publisher Adolph S. Ochs (1878–1935) and appearing on the newspaper's front page since 10 February 1897

Ngo Dinh Diem
(1901–63)
Vietnamese politician

Having ousted Emperor Bao Dai in 1955, he established himself as President of the newly declared Republic of Vietnam (South Vietnam). He was assassinated in a military coup.

1 Follow me if I advance! Kill me if I retreat! Revenge me if I die!
Quoted in Time 8 November 1963. On becoming President of Vietnam in 1955. See also MUSSOLINI 2.

(Sir) Harold Nicolson
(1886–1968)
British diplomat, journalist and author

He held various diplomatic posts until 1929, when he took up journalism. His publications include biographies and critical studies, but he is best remembered for his Diaries and Letters (1967–8).

1 We shall have to walk and live a Woolworth life hereafter.
Journal entry, 4 June 1941, publ. in Diaries and Letters 1939–45 (ed. Nigel Nicolson, 1967). On post-war Britain.

2 God how I loathe these communists! My hatred for Mussolini was just a passing dislike, my fear of Hitler but a momentary apprehension, compared to my deep and burning detestation of the Marxists.
Letter to his wife, VITA SACKVILLE-WEST, 25 September 1947, publ. in Diaries and Letters 1945–62 (ed. Nigel Nicolson, 1968)

3 It is some relief to reflect that to be a good diarist one must have a little snouty sneaky mind.
Journal entry, 9 November 1947, ibid. Writing of SAMUEL PEPYS.

Reinhold Niebuhr

(1892–1971)

US theologian and historian

He was a Lutheran pastor before becoming an influential teacher at the Union Theological Seminary, New York (1928–60). He worked to obtain social justice from within the Socialist Party and subsequently the Democratic Party.

1 Life is a battle between faith and reason in which each feeds upon the other, drawing sustenance from it and destroying it.

Entry, 1928, in *Leaves from the Notebook of a Tamed Cynic* (1930)

2 Man's capacity for justice makes democracy possible, but man's inclination to injustice makes democracy necessary.

The Children of Light and the Children of Darkness, Foreword (1944)

3 O God, give us serenity to accept what cannot be changed, courage to change what should be changed, and wisdom to distinguish the one from the other.

'Serenity Prayer', ascribed to Niebuhr in *Courage to Change* (1961) by June Bingham. The prayer, which exists in varying forms, has been used by Alcoholics Anonymous since the 1940s. 'It may have been spooking around for years, even centuries, but I don't think so,' Niebuhr stated. 'I honestly do believe that I wrote it myself.' However, claims have been made of previous versions from both 14th-century England and 18th-century Germany.

Martin Niemöller

(1892–1984)

German Protestant pastor and theologian

Released from a Nazi concentration camp, he was responsible for the 'Stuttgart Confession of Guilt' (1945), an apology for not opposing HITLER *more forcefully. He was President of the World Council of Churches 1961–8.*

1 When Hitler attacked the Jews ... I was not a Jew, therefore, I was not concerned. And when Hitler attacked the Catholics, I was not a Catholic, and therefore, I was not concerned. And when Hitler attacked the unions and the industrialists, I was not a member of the unions and I was not concerned. Then, Hitler attacked me and the Protestant church – and there was nobody left to be concerned.

Attributed. The original passage has never been traced.

Friedrich Nietzsche

(1844–1900)

German philosopher

His rejection of Christianity and his conception of a 'will to power' and of a 'superman' who might transcend the nihilism of life greatly influenced 20th-century thought. Mentally ill during the last eleven years of his life, he was nursed by his sister who later edited and distorted his works to reflect her own proto-Nazi sympathies. Also Sprach Zarathustra *(1883–5) was his acknowledged masterpiece.*

1 Man is no longer an artist, he has become a work of art.

The Birth of Tragedy, ch. 1 (1872)

2 The exuberant fertility of the universal will.

Ibid., ch. 17

3 Art is not merely an imitation of the reality of nature, but in truth a metaphysical supplement to the reality of nature, placed alongside thereof for its conquest.

Ibid., ch. 24

4 Existence really is an imperfect tense that never becomes a present.

The Use and Abuse of History, sect. 1 (1874)

5 We often contradict an opinion for no other reason than that we do not like the tone in which it is expressed.

Human, All Too Human, aph. 303 (1878)

6 Arrogance on the part of the meritorious is even more offensive to us than the arrogance of those without merit: for merit itself is offensive.

Ibid., aph. 332

7 Women are quite able to make friends with a man; but to preserve such a friendship – that no doubt requires the assistance of a slight physical antipathy.

Ibid., aph. 390

8 An idealist is incorrigible: if he is ejected from his Heaven he makes an ideal out of Hell.

Assorted Opinions and Maxims, pt 1, no. 23 (1879; later publ. as first supplement to *Human, All Too Human*, 1886 edn)

9 The philosopher believes that the value of his philosophy lies in the whole, in the building: posterity discovers it in the bricks with which he built and which are then often used again for better building: in the fact, that is to say, that that building

can be destroyed and *nonetheless* possess value as material.
Ibid., aph. 201

10 So long as you are praised think only that you are not yet on your own path but on that of another.
Ibid., aph. 340

11 It says nothing against the ripeness of a spirit that it has a few worms.
Ibid., aph. 353

12 We would not let ourselves be burned to death for our opinions: we are not sure enough of them for that. But perhaps for the right to have our opinions and to change them.
The Wanderer and His Shadow, aph. 333 (1880)

13 God is dead: but considering the state the species Man is in, there will perhaps be caves, for ages yet, in which his shadow will be shown.
The Gay Science, aph. 108 (1882). Nietzsche repeated his famous statement 'God is dead' in several other works.

14 Let us beware of saying there are laws in nature. There are only necessities: there is no one to command, no one to obey, no one to transgress.
Ibid., aph. 109 (1887 edn)

15 I fear animals regard man as a creature of their own kind which has in a highly dangerous fashion lost its healthy animal reason – as the mad animal, as the laughing animal, as the weeping animal, as the unhappy animal.
Ibid., aph. 224 (1887 edn)

16 The secret of realizing the greatest fruitfulness and the greatest enjoyment of existence is: to *live dangerously!* Build your cities on the slopes of Vesuvius! Send your ships out into uncharted seas! Live in conflict with your equals and with yourselves! Be robbers and ravagers as long as you cannot be rulers and owners, you men of knowledge! The time will soon be past when you could be content to live concealed in the woods like timid deer!
Ibid., aph. 283

17 *I teach you the Superman* [*Übermenschen*]. Man is something that should be overcome.
Thus Spoke Zarathustra, pt 1, 'Zarathustra's Prologue', sect. 3 (1883–5)

18 Not when truth is dirty, but when it is shallow, does the enlightened man dislike to wade into its waters.
Ibid., pt 1, 'Of Chastity'

19 Mistrust all in whom the urge to punish is strong!
Ibid., pt 2, 'Of the Tarantulas'

20 No one *lies* so much as the indignant man.
Beyond Good and Evil, pt 2 ('The Free Spirit'), aph. 26 (1886)

21 Madness is something rare in individuals – but in groups, parties, peoples, ages it is the rule.
Ibid., pt 4 ('Maxims and Interludes'), aph. 156

22 The thought of suicide is a powerful solace: by means of it one gets through many a bad night.
Ibid., pt 4, aph. 157

23 At the ground of all these noble races, the beast of prey, the splendid, *blond beast*, lustfully roving in search of spoils and victory, cannot be mistaken.
The Genealogy of Morals, 'First Essay', aph. 11 (1887)

24 *All* sciences now must do the preparatory work for the future task of the philosopher: understanding this task to be, that the philosopher has to solve the *problem of value*, that he has to determine the *rank-sequence of values*.
Ibid., 'First Essay', sect. 17, note

25 Only the day after tomorrow belongs to me. Some are born posthumously.
The Anti-Christ, Foreword (written 1888, publ. 1895)

26 What is good? – All that heightens the feeling of power, the will to power, power itself in man.
Ibid., aph. 2

27 Fanatics are picturesque, mankind would rather see gestures than listen to *reasons*.
Ibid., aph. 54

28 Wherever there are walls I shall inscribe this eternal accusation against Christianity upon them . . . I call Christianity the one great curse, the one great intrinsic depravity, the one great instinct for revenge for which no expedient is sufficiently poisonous, secret, subterranean, petty – I call it the one immortal blemish of mankind.
Ibid., aph. 62. 'In reality there has been only one Christian, and he died on the Cross,' Nietzsche wrote.

29 The man of knowledge must be able not only to love his enemies but also to hate his friends.
Ecce Homo, Foreword (written 1888, publ. 1908)

30 I believe only in French culture and consider everything in Europe that calls itself 'culture' a misunderstanding, not to speak of German culture.
Ibid., 'Why I Am So Clever', sect 3

31 As an *artist* one has no home in Europe except in Paris.
Ibid., 'Why I Am So Clever', sect. 5

32 Religions are affairs of the rabble, I have need of washing my hands after contact with religious people.
Ibid., 'Why I Am a Destiny', sect. 1

33 I fear we are not getting rid of God because we still believe in grammar.
Twilight of the Idols, '"Reason" in Philosophy', aph. 5 (1889)

34 The two great European narcotics, alcohol and Christianity.
Ibid., 'What the Germans Lack', aph. 2

35 How much dreary heaviness, lameness, dampness, sloppiness, how much *beer* there is in the German intellect!
Ibid., 'What the Germans Lack', aph. 2. Nietzsche had earlier written: 'Everything ponderous, viscous, and pompously clumsy, all long-winded and wearying species of style are developed in profuse variety among Germans.' (*Beyond Good and Evil*, ch. 2, aph. 28, 1886)

36 For art to exist, for any sort of aesthetic activity or perception to exist, a certain physiological precondition is indispensable: *intoxication*.
Ibid., 'Expeditions of an Untimely Man', aph. 8

37 The English are the nation of consummate cant.
Ibid., 'Expeditions of an Untimely Man', aph. 12

38 The literary woman, unsatisfied, agitated, desolate in heart and entrails, listening every minute with painful curiosity to the imperative which whispers from the depths of her organism '*aut liberi aut libri*'.
Ibid., 'Expeditions of an Untimely Man', aph. 27. The Latin phrase '*aut liberi aut libri*' means 'either children or books'.

39 How is freedom measured, in individuals as in nations? By the resistance which has to be overcome, by the effort it costs to stay *aloft*.
Ibid., 'Expeditions of an Untimely Man', aph. 38

40 The aphorism, the apophthegm, in which I am the first master among Germans, are the forms of 'eternity'; my ambition is to say in ten sentences what everyone else says in a book – what everyone else *does not* say in a book.
Ibid., 'Expeditions of an Untimely Man', aph. 51

Florence Nightingale
(1820–1910)
English nurse

'The Lady with the Lamp' became famous for her nursing work during the Crimean War (1854–6). In England, she strove to improve medical conditions in the army and in 1860 founded a nurses' school at St Thomas's Hospital, London. She was an invalid for the last fifty years of her life. See H. W. LONGFELLOW 21.

1 What the horrors of war are, no one can imagine. They are not wounds and blood and fever, spotted and low, or dysentery, chronic and acute, cold and heat and famine. They are intoxication, drunken brutality, demoralisation and disorder on the part of the inferior . . . jealousies, meanness, indifference, selfish brutality on the part of the superior.
Letter to her family from Balaklava, 5 May 1855, publ. in *Ever Yours, Florence Nightingale: Selected Letters*, ch. 2 (ed. Martha Vicinus and Bea Nergaard, 1989)

2 There is not an official who would not burn me like Joan of Arc if he could, but they know the War Office cannot turn me out because the country is with me – that is my position.
Letter from the Crimea, November 1855, quoted in *Florence Nightingale*, ch. 10 (1951, rev. 1955) by Cecil Woodham-Smith

3 No *man*, not even a doctor, ever gives any other definition of what a nurse should be than this – 'devoted and obedient'. This definition would do just as well for a porter. It might even do for a horse. It would not do for a policeman.
Notes on Nursing (1860)

4 Instead of wishing to see more doctors made by women joining what there are, I wish to see as few doctors, either male or female, as possible. For, mark you, the women have made no improvement – they have only tried to be 'men' and they have only succeeded in being third-rate men.
Letter to JOHN STUART MILL, 12 September 1860, publ. in *Ever Yours, Florence Nightingale: Selected Letters*, ch. 3 (ed. Martha Vicinus and Bea Nergaard, 1989)

5 Women have no sympathy . . . and my experience of women is almost as large as Europe.
Letter, 13 December 1861, ibid., ch. 3. Rejecting the argument that women had been more sympathetic to her work than men.

6 It may seem a strange principle to enunciate as the very first requirement in a hospital that it should do the sick no harm.
Notes on Hospitals, Preface (1863 edn)

7 The martyr sacrifices *her*self (*him*self in a few instances) entirely in vain. Or rather not in vain; for she (or he) makes the selfish more selfish, the lazy more lazy, the narrow narrower.
Letter to BENJAMIN JOWETT, c. 1867, publ. in *Ever Yours, Florence Nightingale: Selected Letters*, ch. 4 (ed. Martha Vicinus and Bea Nergaard, 1989)

8 Too kind, too kind.
Quoted in *Florence Nightingale*, ch. 24 (1951, rev. 1955) by Cecil Woodham-Smith. On being presented with the Order of Merit, November 1907. She was the first woman to receive this award.

Anaïs Nin
(1903–77)
French-born US novelist and diarist

She was known principally for her journals (7 vols. 1966–80), a chronicle of avant-garde society in Paris and New York. Her novels include House of Incest *(1936).*

1 Woman does not forget she needs the fecundator, she does not forget that everything that is born of her is planted in her.
Journal entry, August 1937, publ. in *The Diary of Anaïs Nin*, vol. 2 (1967)

2 Electric flesh-arrows ... traversing the body. A rainbow of colour strikes the eyelids. A foam of music falls over the ears. It is the gong of the orgasm.
Journal entry, October 1937, ibid.

Richard Nixon
(1913–92)
US politician and president

As Republican President (1969–74) he oversaw American withdrawal from Vietnam and the resumption of diplomatic relations with China. In 1974, in the wake of the Watergate scandal, he became the first and only US president to resign. See ANONYMOUS 23, JOHN F. KENNEDY 3, ADLAI STEVENSON 9, HUNTER S. THOMPSON 1.

1 A public man must never forget that he loses his usefulness when he as an individual, rather than his policy, becomes the issue.
Life 8 June 1959. The remark appeared in a tribute to JOHN FOSTER DULLES on his death. Dulles, Nixon wrote, recognized this 'fundamental truth'.

2 As I leave you I want you to know – just think how much you're going to be missing. You won't have Nixon to kick around any more because, gentlemen, this is my last press conference.
Press conference, 5 November 1962, quoted in the *New York Times* 8 November 1962. Following defeat in the California gubernatorial election.

3 The Cold War isn't thawing; it is burning with a deadly heat. Communism isn't sleeping; it is, as always, plotting, scheming, working, fighting.
'Cuba, Castro and John F. Kennedy', publ. in *Reader's Digest* November 1964

4 Let us begin by committing ourselves to the truth, to see it like it is and tell it like it is, to find the truth, to speak the truth and to live the truth.
Speech accepting the Republican presidential nomination, 8 August 1968, Miami, quoted in the *New York Times* 9 August 1968

5 This is the greatest week in the history of the world since the Creation, because as a result of what happened in this week, the world is bigger, infinitely.
Remarks on USS *Hornet*, 24 July 1969, welcoming back the crew of Apollo 11 four days after the first manned moon-landing, quoted in *Nixon: The Triumph of a Politician*, vol. 2, ch. 13 (1989) by Stephen Ambrose. A few days later, Ambrose relates, the evangelist Billy Graham mentioned three greater days: Christ's birth, Christ's death, and Christ's resurrection. Nixon's scribbled response was: 'Tell Billy RN referred to a *week* not *a day*.'

6 To you, the great silent majority of my fellow Americans – I ask for your support.
Television address, 3 November 1969, publ. in *Public Papers of the Presidents of the United States, 1969*. Defending his decision to keep US troops in Vietnam. An administration official later clarified Nixon's concept of 'silent majority': a 'large and normally undemonstrative cross section of the country that until last night refrained from articulating its opinions on the war' (quoted in the *New York Times* 5 November 1969). In his *Memoirs*, Nixon commented: 'Very few speeches actually influence the course of history. The November 3 speech was one of them.'

7 Let us understand: North Vietnam cannot defeat or humiliate the United States. Only Americans can do that.
Television address, 3 November 1969, ibid.

8 There can be no whitewash at the White House.
Television address, 30 April 1973, quoted in the *New York Times* 1 May 1973. Referring to the Watergate revelations, after agents of Nixon's re-election committee were arrested in the Democratic Party headquarters in July 1972 after attempting to tap telephones there; Nixon denied all knowledge of the break-in.

9 I welcome this kind of examination because people have got to know whether or not their President is a crook. Well, I'm not a crook.

Press conference, 17 November 1973, quoted in the *New York Times* 18 November 1973

10 Defeat doesn't finish a man – quit does. A man is not finished when he's defeated. He's finished when he quits.

Note written with reference to Edward Kennedy and the Chappaquiddick Bridge incident, July 1969, quoted in *Before the Fall*, pt 3, ch. 4 (1975) by William Safire

11 When the President does it, that means that it is not illegal.

TV interview with DAVID FROST, 20 May 1977, publ. in *I Gave Them a Sword*, ch. 8 (1978) by David Frost

12 Castro couldn't even go to the bathroom unless the Soviet Union put the nickel in the toilet.

Remark to interviewer September 1980, quoted in *Exile: The Unquiet Oblivion of Richard M. Nixon*, ch. 17 (1984) by Robert Sam Anson

13 No event in American history is more misunderstood than the Vietnam War. It was misreported then, and it is misremembered now.

'No More Vietnams', publ. in the *New York Times* 28 March 1985

14 Finishing second in the Olympics gets you silver. Finishing second in politics gets you oblivion.

Quoted in *The Sunday Times* 13 November 1988. On the defeat of Michael Dukakis by GEORGE BUSH in the presidential election.

15 I played by the rules of politics as I found them.

The Times 26 March 1990

Kwame Nkrumah
(1909–72)
Ghanaian president

Leader of the Gold Coast's struggle for independence, he served as Prime Minister of Ghana, as it was re-named, 1957–60. As President (1960–6), he maintained an authoritarian regime until his overthrow.

1 The best way of learning to be an independent sovereign state is to be an independent sovereign state.

Speech to Legislative Assembly, Accra, 18 May 1956, quoted in *Axioms of Kwame Nkrumah* (1967)

2 Revolutions are brought about by men, by men who think as men of action and act as men of thought.

Consciencism, ch. 2 (1964)

Roden Noel
(1834–94)
English poet

One of the foremost among the lesser Victorian poets, he wrote prolifically, most notably A Little Child's Monument *(1881), commemorating his son, who died aged five.*

1 What if men take to following where He leads, Weary of mumbling Athanasian creeds?

'The Red Flag', publ. in *The Red Flag* (1872)

(Sir) Sidney Nolan
(1917–92)
Australian artist

He painted subjects taken from his travels, from mythology, and from the Australian outback, most famously the 'Ned Kelly' series (1946).

1 When the critics come around it's always too late.

Quoted in the *Daily Telegraph* 15 September 1992

Peggy Noonan
(b. 1950)
US author and presidential speechwriter

She was special assistant and speechwriter to RONALD REAGAN *and* GEORGE BUSH, *recording her experiences in her memoir* What I Saw at the Revolution *(1990). See also* GEORGE BUSH 3, 5.

1 A speech is poetry: cadence, rhythm, imagery, sweep! A speech reminds us that words, like children, have the power to make dance the dullest beanbag of a heart.

What I Saw at the Revolution, ch. 5 (1990)

2 The battle for the mind of Ronald Reagan was like the trench warfare of World War I: Never have so many fought so hard for such barren terrain.

Ibid., ch. 14

3 Beware the politically obsessed. They are often bright and interesting, but they have something missing in their natures; there is a hole, an empty place, and they use politics to fill it up.

Ibid., 'Another Epilogue'

Christopher North

See John Wilson

Charles Eliot Norton

(1827–1908)

US scholar and editor

Professor of Art History at Harvard University, he co-edited the North American Review *and co-founded the* Nation *(1865). His publications include a notable translation of* DANTE.

1 The voice of protest, of warning, of appeal is never more needed than when the clamor of fife and drum, echoed by the press and too often by the pulpit, is bidding all men fall in and keep step and obey in silence the tyrannous word of command. Then, more than ever, it is the duty of the good citizen not to be silent, and spite of obloquy, misrepresentation and abuse, to insist on being heard, and with sober counsel to maintain the everlasting validity of the principles of the moral law.

'True Patriotism', address delivered at Men's Club of the Prospect Street Congregational Church, Cambridge, Massachusetts, 7 June 1898, publ. in *Letters of Charles Eliot Norton* (ed. Sara Norton and M. A. DeWolfe, 1913)

Novalis

(1772–1801)

German poet and novelist

Pseudonym of Friedrich von Hardenberg. A key influence on German Romanticism, he expressed his mystical belief in the unity of nature in his verse. His prose poems Hymns to the Night *(1800) expressed a yearning for death, while his unfinished novel* Heinrich von Ofterdingen *(1802) introduced the symbol of the blue flower, later taken to represent all Romanticism.*

1 Love is the final end of the world's history, the Amen of the universe.

Thoughts on Religion, pt 1, from *Fragments* (1799–1800), publ. in *Hymns and Thoughts on Religion* (ed./transl. W. Hastie, 1888)

2 I often feel, and ever more deeply I realize, that fate and character are the same conception.

Heinrich von Ofterdingen, bk 2 (1802), repr. in *Gesammelte Werke* (ed. Carl Seelig, 1945). Spoken by Heinrich. Often quoted as 'character is destiny', as in *The Mill on the Floss*, bk 6, ch. 6 (1860) by GEORGE ELIOT, who describes it as 'one of [Novalis's] questionable aphorisms'. See also HERACLITUS 6.

3 A God-intoxicated man.

Attributed, referring to SPINOZA

Ivor Novello

See LENA GUILBERT FORD 1

Nursery rhymes

The obscure roots of nursery rhymes in the oral tradition mean that few can be accurately dated. In England, many were first published in chapbooks, pamphlets and booklets from the 16th century. The first major collections were made in the 18th and 19th centuries. The following list of the most quoted nursery rhymes is arranged alphabetically according to title or the name they are best known by.

1 As I was going to St Ives,
I met a man with seven wives.

'As I was going to St Ives' (17th–18th century)

2 Baa, baa, black sheep,
Have you any wool?
Yes sir, yes sir,
Three bags full;
One for the master,
One for the dame,
And one for the little boy
That lives down the lane.

'Baa, baa, black sheep' (17th–18th century)

3 Bye, baby bunting,
Daddy's gone a-hunting.

'Bye, baby bunting' (18th century)

4 Diddle, diddle, dumpling, my son John,
Went to bed with his trousers on;
One shoe off, and one shoe on,
Diddle, diddle, dumpling, my son John!

'Diddle, diddle, dumpling' (18th century)

5 Ding dong bell
Pussy's in the well.
Who put her in?
Little Johnny Flynn.
Who pulled her out?
Little Tommy Stout.

'Ding dong bell' (from 16th century). An alternative version has: 'Who put her in?/Little Johnny Green.' The words 'Ding dong bell' occur in SHAKESPEARE's works.

6 Doctor Foster
Went to Gloucester
In a shower of rain.
He stepped in a puddle
Right up to his middle
And never went there again!

'Doctor Foster'. The origins of this rhyme are said to date

back to the 13th century and to refer to Edward I falling from his horse while on a visit to Gloucester.

7 Fee, fi, fo, fum,
I smell the blood of an Englishman.
Be he alive or be he dead
I'll grind his bones to make my bread.
'Fee, fi, fo, fum' (15th century). See WILLIAM SHAKESPEARE: KING LEAR 37.

8 For want of a nail the shoe was lost.
For want of a shoe the horse was lost.
For want of a horse the rider was lost.
For want of a rider the battle was lost.
For want of a battle the kingdom was lost.
And all for the want of a horseshoe nail.
'For want of a nail' (14th century)

9 Georgie Porgie pudding and pie,
Kissed the girls and made them cry;
When the boys came out to play,
Georgie Porgie ran away.
'Georgie Porgie' (17th century). Said to refer to the courtier George Villiers, 1st Duke of Buckingham (1592–1628).

10 Goosey Goosey Gander, whither shall I wander,
Upstairs, downstairs and in my lady's chamber;
There I met an old man who wouldn't say his
    prayers,
I took him by the left leg and threw him down the
    stairs.
'Goosey Goosey Gander'(16th century). Thought to be a reference to Catholics who sought refuge in 'priest's holes' during the years of religious persecution.

11 The Grand old Duke of York he had ten
    thousand men
He marched them up to the top of the hill
And he marched them down again.
When they were up, they were up;
And when they were down, they were down;
And when they were only halfway up
They were neither up nor down.
'The Grand old Duke of York' (15th century). The words are reputed to refer to Richard, Duke of York (1411–60), a claimant to the English throne during the Wars of the Roses; at the Battle of Wakefield, having marched his troops to his hilltop castle, he inexplicably abandoned his defensive position to battle against the Lancastrians and was defeated and killed.

12 Hark, hark, the dogs do bark,
The beggars are coming to town,
Some in rags and some in jags
And one in a velvet gown.
'Hark, hark, the dogs do bark'. According to various versions, the lines may originate in the 13th century, when wandering

minstrels concealed secret messages of dissent in their songs, or the period of the Dissolution of the Monasteries, when monks went begging in the streets, or the seventeenth century, referring to William of Orange and his Dutch followers.

13 Hey diddle diddle, the cat and the fiddle,
The cow jumped over the moon.
The little dog laughed to see such fun
And the dish ran away with the spoon!
'Hey diddle diddle' (18th century)

14 Hickory dickory dock
The mouse ran up the clock
The clock struck one
The mouse ran down
Hickory dickory dock.
'Hickory dickory dock' (18th century)

15 Humpty Dumpty sat on a wall,
Humpty Dumpty had a great fall.
All the King's horses, And all the King's men
Couldn't put Humpty together again!
'Humpty Dumpty' (17th century). Said to refer to a large cannon that collapsed from a wall during the siege of Colchester in 1648.

16 Jack and Jill went up the hill to fetch a pail of
    water;
Jack fell down and broke his crown,
And Jill came tumbling after.
'Jack and Jill' (18th century). Claimed to refer to Louis XVI and MARIE ANTOINETTE, both guillotined in the French Revolution.

17 Jack Sprat could eat no fat
His wife could eat no lean
And so betwixt the two of them
They licked the platter clean.
'Jack Sprat' (17th century)

18 Ladybird, ladybird, fly away home,
Your house is on fire and your children are gone.
'Ladybird, ladybird' (18th century). 'Ladybug' in the USA.

19 The lion and the unicorn were fighting for the
    crown
The lion beat the unicorn all around the town.
Some gave them white bread, and some gave them
    brown;
Some gave them plum cake and drummed them
    out of town.
'The Lion and the Unicorn' (17th century). Thought to refer to the coats of arms of England and Scotland, featuring lions and unicorns respectively.

20 Little Bo-peep has lost her sheep
And doesn't know where to find them.

Leave them alone and they'll come home,
Bringing their tails behind them.
'Little Bo-peep' (18th–19th century)

21 Little Jack Horner sat in the corner
Eating his Christmas pie,
He put in his thumb and pulled out a plum
And said, What a good boy am I!
'Little Jack Horner' (from 16th century)

22 Little Miss Muffet sat on a tuffet
Eating her curds and whey,
Along came a spider,
Who sat down beside her
And frightened Miss Muffet away.
'Little Miss Muffet' (16th century). Said to be written by
Thomas Muffet (or Moufet) (1553–1604), a renowned ento-
mologist, describing his step-daughter's encounter with an
escaped specimen spider.

23 London Bridge is falling down,
My fair lady.
'London Bridge is falling down' (16th century). An early ver-
sion is 'London Bridge is broken down.'

24 Mary had a little lamb,
Its fleece was white as snow;
And everywhere that Mary went
The lamb was sure to go.
'Mary's Little Lamb', written by Sarah Hale, publ. in *Poems
for Our Children* (1830). The words were recorded by THOMAS
EDISON on his tin-foil phonograph in 1877, the first successful
sound recording.

25 Mary, Mary, quite contrary,
How does your garden grow?
With silver bells and cockle shells
And pretty maids all in a row.
'Mary Mary, quite contrary' (16th century). Thought to refer
to MARY I ('Bloody Mary'). The 'garden' has been interpreted
as the country's cemeteries swelling with the number of Protestant martyrs under her reign; the 'silver bells and cockle
shells' may have been instruments of torture and the
'Maiden' a form of guillotine; alternatively, the cockle shells
were her crucifixes, and the pretty maids her rosary.

26 Old King Cole was a merry old soul,
And a merry old soul was he;
He called for his pipe and he called for his bowl
And he called for his fiddlers three.
'Old King Cole'. The rhyme may allude to any of three Celtic
kings, all called Cole, or Coel, though the earliest known publi-
cation date is 1708–9.

27 Old Mother Hubbard
Went to the cupboard
To fetch her poor doggie a bone,

But when she got there
The cupboard was bare
And so the poor dog had none.
'Old Mother Hubbard' (from 16th century)

28 Oranges and lemons, say the bells of
St Clement's;
You owe me five farthings, say the bells of
St Martin's;
When will you pay me? say the bells of Old Bailey;
When I grow rich, say the bells of Shoreditch;
When will that be? say the bells of Stepney;
I do not know, say the great bells of Bow;
Here comes a candle to light you to bed,
And here comes a chopper to chop off your head!
'Oranges and lemons' (18th century)

29 Pease pudding hot, pease pudding cold,
Pease pudding in the pot nine days old.
Some like it hot, some like it cold,
Some like it in the pot nine days old.
'Pease pudding hot' (18th century)

30 Polly put the kettle on,
We'll all have tea.
. . .
Sukey take it off again,
They've all gone away.
'Polly put the kettle on' (19th century)

31 Half a pound of tuppenny rice,
Half a pound of treacle.
That's the way the money goes,
Pop! goes the weasel.
'Pop goes the weasel' (19th century). Attributed to W. R. Mand-
ale or Charles Twiggs, both songwriters, with the second line
'In and out the Eagle'. 'Pop! goes the weasel' is said to refer
to pawning ('pop') a suit or coat ('weasel').

32 Pussycat pussycat, where have you been?
I've been to London to visit the Queen.
'Pussycat, pussycat' (from 16th century)

33 The Queen of Hearts she made some tarts
All on a summer's day;
The Knave of Hearts he stole the tarts
And took them clean away.
'The Queen of Hearts' (18th century)

34 Ride a cock-horse to Banbury Cross
To see a fine lady upon a white horse;
With rings on her fingers and bells on her toes,
She shall have music wherever she goes.
'Ride a cock horse' (16th century). Said originally to refer to
ELIZABETH I, who travelled to Banbury to see a stone cross
erected there.

35 Ring-a-ring o' roses,
A pocket full of posies –
A-tishoo! A-tishoo!
We all fall down!

'Ring-a-ring o' roses' (17th century). Associated with the Great Plague of London, 1665, whose symptoms included rosy-red rashes on the skin.

36 Rock-a-bye baby on the tree top,
When the wind blows the cradle will rock,
When the bough breaks the cradle will fall,
And down will come baby, cradle and all.

'Rock-a-bye baby' (17th century). Possibly deriving from America, where Native Americans would suspend cradles from the branches of a tree. The first line is also sung 'Hush-a-bye baby'.

37 Rub-a-dub-dub,
Three men in a tub
And how do you think they got there?
The butcher, the baker, the candlestick-maker,
They all jumped out of a rotten potato
'Twas enough to make a man stare.

'Rub-a-dub-dub' (18th century)

38 Round and round the garden
Like a teddy bear.

'Round and round the garden' (20th century)

39 See-saw, Margery Daw,
Johnny shall have a new master;
He shall earn but a penny a day
Because he can't work any faster.

'See-saw, Margery Daw' (18th century). Some sources give 'Jacky shall have' instead of 'He shall earn'.

40 Sing a song of sixpence, a pocket full of rye,
Four and twenty blackbirds baked in a pie.
When the pie was opened the birds began to sing,
Wasn't that a dainty dish to set before the king?
The king was in his counting house counting out
    his money,
The queen was in the parlour eating bread and
    honey,
The maid was in the garden hanging out the
    clothes,
When down came a blackbird and pecked off her
    nose!

'Sing a song of sixpence' (18th century)

41 Twinkle, twinkle, little star,
How I wonder what you are!
Up above the world so high,

Like a diamond in the sky!

'The Star', st. 1, written by ANN AND JANE TAYLOR, publ. in *Rhymes for the Nursery* (1806). See LEWIS CARROLL 12.

42 There was a crooked man and he walked a
    crooked mile,
He found a crooked sixpence upon a crooked stile;
He bought a crooked cat, which caught a crooked
    mouse,
And they all lived together in a little crooked
    house.

'There was a crooked man' (17th century). Reputed to refer to the Scottish general Alexander Leslie, who signed the Solemn League and Covenant in 1643 to secure religious and political freedom for Scotland; according to this interpretation, the 'crooked stile' was the border between England and Scotland, and 'the little crooked house' signifies the agreement that the English and Scots had at last reached.

43 There was an old woman who lived in a shoe,
She had so many children she didn't know what to
    do!
So she gave them some broth without any bread,
And she whipped them all soundly and sent them
    to bed!

'There was an old woman who lived in a shoe' (18th century). Thought to refer either to Queen Caroline, wife of GEORGE II, who had eight children, or to George himself, whose enthusiasm for white powdered wigs led to his being nick-named 'the old woman'.

44 This is the farmer sowing his corn
That kept the cock that crowed in the morn
That waked the priest all shaven and shorn
That married the man all tattered and torn
That kissed the maiden all forlorn
That milked the cow with the crumpled horn
That tossed the dog that worried the cat
That killed the rat that ate the malt
That lay in the house that Jack built!

'This is the house that Jack built' (from 16th century)

45 This little piggy went to market,
This little piggy stayed at home,
This little piggy had roast beef,
This little piggy had none.
And this little piggy went
'Wee wee wee' all the way home.

'This little piggy' (17th–18th century)

46 Three blind mice, three blind mice,
See how they run, see how they run,
They all ran after the farmer's wife,
Who cut off their tails with a carving knife,
Did you ever see such a thing in your life,

As three blind mice?

'Three blind mice' (16th century). Said to refer to MARY I, wife of Philip II; the 'three blind mice' were supposedly three Protestant nobles convicted of plotting against the Queen and burnt at the stake.

47 Tom, Tom, the piper's son,
Stole a pig and away he run,
The pig was eat and Tom was beat,
And Tom went roaring down the street.

'Tom, Tom, the piper's son' (18th century)

48 Three geese in a flock;
One flew east, and one flew west,
And one flew over the cuckoo's nest.

'Vintery, mintery, cutery, corn', variant of American 'Mother Goose' rhyme publ. 1814. *One Flew Over the Cuckoo's Nest* was the title of a 1962 novel by KEN KESEY (filmed 1975).

49 What are little boys made of?
Frogs and snails, and puppy dogs' tails –
That's what little boys are made of!
What are little girls made of?
Sugar and spice and all things nice –
That's what little girls are made of!

'What are little boys made of?' (18th–19th century). Some versions have 'Snips and snails, and puppy dogs' tails'.

50 What is your fortune, my pretty maid?
My face is my fortune, Sir, she said.

'Where are you going to my pretty maid?' (18th century)

51 Who killed Cock Robin? I, said the Sparrow,
With my bow and arrow, I killed Cock Robin.
Who saw him die? I, said the Fly,
With my little eye, I saw him die.
Who caught his blood? I, said the Fish,
With my little dish, I caught his blood.
Who'll make the shroud? I, said the Beetle,
With my thread and needle, I'll make the shroud.

'Who killed Cock Robin?', publ. 1744, but possibly much older, referring to Robin Hood

Bill Nye
(1850–96)
US humorist

Pen-name of Edgar Wilson Nye. His articles and tales appeared in the Laramie Boomerang, *which he co-founded in Wyoming in 1881, and were later published in collections.*

1 I have been told that Wagner's music is better than it sounds.

Quoted in *Autobiography*, vol. 1, 'About General Sickles (16–17th January 1906)' (written from 1870, publ. 1924) by MARK TWAIN.

O

Ann Oakley
(b. 1944)
British sociologist and author

Her non-fiction work examines the roles of housewives and mothers, as in Woman's Work *(1974). Her best known novel is* The Men's Room *(1988).*

1 Housework is work directly opposed to the possibility of human self-actualization.

Woman's Work: The Housewife, Past and Present, ch. 9 (1974)

Joyce Carol Oates
(b. 1938)
US author

Using a range of genres from Gothic horror fiction to social commentary, she exposes the violence and decay in American life. Her novels include Them *(1969) and* Blonde *(2000), based on the life of* MARILYN MONROE.

1 The worst cynicism: a belief in luck.

Do What You Will, pt 2, ch. 15 (1970)

2 I used to think getting old was about vanity – but actually it's about losing people you love. Getting wrinkles is trivial.

Interview in the *Guardian* 18 August 1989

Lawrence Oates
(1880–1912)
English soldier and explorer

Having entered the army in 1898, he joined ROBERT F. SCOTT*'s Antarctic expedition in 1910. He was one of the party of five selected to reach the South Pole, all of whom perished on the return journey. His body was never found.*

1 I am just going outside and may be some time.

Quoted in the diary of ROBERT F. SCOTT, 16–17 March 1912, publ. in *Scott's Last Expedition*, vol. 1, ch. 20 (ed. L. Huxley, 1913). Last words, before walking out into an Antarctic blizzard. Scott recorded: 'We knew it was the act of a brave man and an English gentleman.'

Conor Cruise O'Brien
(b. 1917)
Irish historian, diplomat and journalist

He published a powerful eyewitness account of the Congo crisis, To Katanga and Back *(1962), held a seat in the Irish parliament (1969–77) and is a regular commentator on international affairs.*

1 Irishness is not primarily a question of birth or blood or language; it is the condition of being involved in the Irish situation, and usually of being mauled by it.
'Irishness', publ. in the *New Statesman* 17 January 1959, written as Donat O'Donnell

2 Nothing does more to activate Christian divisions than talk about Christian unity.
The Times 3 October 1989

Edna O'Brien
(b. 1932)
Irish author

Her novels, some of which were banned in Ireland for their treatment of sex, typically narrate attempts to escape repressive situations, and include The Country Girls *(1960) and* A Pagan Place *(1970).*

1 After the rich, the most obnoxious people in the world are those who serve the rich.
August Is a Wicked Month, ch. 8 (1965). Spoken by Ellen.

2 In every question and every remark tossed back and forth between lovers who have not played out the last fugue, there is one question and it is this: 'Is there someone new?'
Lantern Slides, 'Long Distance' (1990)

Flann O'Brien
(1911–66)
Irish author

Pseudonym of Brian O'Nolan. Influenced by JAMES JOYCE, *he published the experimental* At Swim-Two-Birds *(1939) and* The Poor Mouth *(1941), originally written in Gaelic. As Myles na Gopaleen, he wrote a lively column for the* Irish Times *from 1940.*

1 When money's tight and is hard to get
And your horse has also ran,
When all you have is a heap of debt –
A PINT OF PLAIN IS YOUR ONLY MAN.
At Swim-Two-Birds, ch. 1 (1939)

2 The gross and net result of it is that people who spent most of their natural lives riding iron bicycles over the rocky roadsteads of this parish get their personalities mixed up with the personalities of their bicycle as a result of the interchanging of the atoms of each of them and you would be surprised at the number of people in these parts who nearly are half people and half bicycles.
The Third Policeman, ch. 6 (written 1940, publ. 1967). The Sergeant explains the effects of the 'Atomic Theory'.

Richard O'Brien
(b. 1942)
British actor and screenwriter

Originally Richard Timothy Smith. He was the creator of the cult Rocky Horror Show *(1973, filmed as* The Rocky Horror Picture Show *1975), which he called 'a mix of sex, rock 'n' roll and gothic horror'. He later hosted* The Crystal Maze *for Channel 4 TV (1990–3).*

1 Give yourself over to absolute pleasure.
The Rocky Horror Picture Show (film, 1975, screenplay by Jim Sharman and Richard O'Brien, based on Richard O'Brien's stage musical, directed by Jim Sharman). Spoken by Dr Frank N. Furter (Tim Curry).

2 Don't dream it. Be it.
Dr Frank N. Furter, ibid.

Sean O'Casey
(1880–1964)
Irish playwright

Originally John Casey. He is best remembered for his early realist works documenting recent Irish history, notably Juno and the Paycock *(1924) and* The Plough and the Stars *(1926). He settled in England after* The Silver Tassie *(1929) was rejected by Dublin's Abbey Theatre.*

1 You cannot put a rope around the neck of an idea; you cannot put an idea up against a barrack-square wall and riddle it with bullets; you cannot confine it in the strongest prison cell that your slaves could ever build.
The Story of Thomas Ashe, ch. 4 (1917)

2 Th' whole worl's in a state o' chassis!
Juno and the Paycock, Act 1 and *passim* (1924). Spoken by Jack Boyle, who repeats the expression in the last line of the play. In Act 2, he says: 'The whole counthry's in a state o' chassis.'

3 As far as I can see, the Polis as Polis, in this city, is Null an' Void!
Mrs Madigan, ibid., Act 3. Referring to Dublin during the Irish Civil War in 1922.

4 There's no reason to bring religion into it. I think we ought to have as great a regard for religion as we can, so as to keep it out of as many things as possible.

The Plough and the Stars, Act 1 (1926). Spoken by Fluther Good.

5 It's my rule never to lose me temper till it would be dethrimental to keep it.

Fluther Good, ibid., Act 1

William of Occam

(c. 1285–c. 1348)

English philosopher

Also known as William of Ockham. He studied logic as a Franciscan friar, and came to reject the Aristotelian belief in universal truths, proposing instead a version of nominalism. His views led him into conflict with university authorities and the church.

1 Entities are not to be multiplied beyond necessity.

Occam's Razor (or Ockham's Razor). William of Occam was said to have repeated this cornerstone of nominalism in various forms on numerous occasions, for example applying it to refute the entities posited by scholastic philosophers to interpret reality. The words cannot be found in Occam's writings in this form, though variations include 'Plurality should not be assumed without necessity', in *Quodlibeta*, no. 5, question 1, article 2 (c. 1320). However, this 'Law of Economy' or 'Law of Parsimony' had been expressed earlier by other theologians and philosophers. The axiom is commonly rendered: 'Do not do with more what can be done with less.'

Adolph S. Ochs

See NEW YORK TIMES 1

Flannery O'Connor

(1925–64)

US author

Raised a devout Roman Catholic in the Protestant fundamentalist South, she took as her main theme the nature of evil. Her 'Southern Gothic' novels and short stories, often peopled by the marginalized and the violent, include Wise Blood *(1952).*

1 I preach there are all kinds of truth, your truth and somebody else's. But behind all of them there is only one truth and that is that there's no truth.

Wise Blood, ch. 10 (1952). Spoken by the preacher Hazel Motes.

2 I have found that anything that comes out of the South is going to be called grotesque by the Northern reader, unless it *is* grotesque, in which case it is going to be called realistic.

'Some Aspects of The Grotesque in Southern Fiction', lecture in Macon, Georgia, autumn 1960 (1965), repr. in *Mystery and Manners*, pt 2 (ed. Sally and Robert Fitzgerald, 1972)

3 While the South is hardly Christ-centered, it is most certainly Christ-haunted.

'Some Aspects of The Grotesque in Southern Fiction', ibid., pt 2

4 I have found, in short, from reading my own writing, that my subject in fiction is the action of grace in territory held largely by the devil.

'On Her Own Work', ibid., pt 3

Theodore O'Hara

(1820–67)

US soldier and poet

Having volunteered and served as an officer in the Mexican War (1846), he wrote the poem for which he is best known, 'The Bivouac of the Dead'. He later fought in the Civil War.

1 On fame's eternal camping ground
Their silent tents are spread,
And glory guards, with solemn round,
The bivouac of the dead.

'The Bivouac of the Dead', st. 1 (1847), repr. in *The Yale Book of American Verse* (ed. Thomas Lounsbury, 1912). Written in memory of Kentucky troops killed in the Mexican War, 1847, later often quoted to commemorate the Civil War dead.

2 Sons of the dark and bloody ground.

Ibid., st. 9. Referring to the state of Kentucky.

Georgia O'Keeffe

(1887–1986)

US artist

First exhibited in 1916 by the photographer Alfred Stieglitz, whom she later married, she took inspiration from the desert landscape of New Mexico for her abstract and figurative art, as in 'Black Iris' (1926).

1 I am trying with all my skill to do a painting that is all of women, as well as all of me.

Debate reported in the *New York World* 16 March 1930, quoted in *Portrait of an Artist*, ch. 9 (1986) by Laurie Lisle

2 When you take a flower in your hand and really look at it, it's your world for the moment. I want to give that world to someone else. Most people in the city rush around so, they have no time to look at a flower. I want them to see it whether they want to or not.

New York Post 16 May 1946, ibid., ch. 6. Flowers were a favourite subject of O'Keeffe's.

3 I hate flowers – I paint them because they're cheaper than models and they don't move.
Quoted in the *New York Herald Tribune* 18 April 1954, ibid., ch. 6. Responding to the remark, 'How perfect to meet you with flowers in your hands!'

John O'Keeffe
(1747–1833)
Irish playwright

He wrote his first play, The Gallant, *aged fifteen, acted in Dublin and settled in London c. 1780. Of his sixty-odd plays and comic operas,* Wild Oats *(1791) had the most enduring success.*

1 Amo, amas, I love a lass,
As a cedar tall and slender;
Sweet cowslip's grace
Is her nominative case,
And she's of the feminine gender.
The Agreeable Surprise, Act 2, Sc. 2 (1781). Song.

Ben Okri
(b. 1959)
Nigerian author

The New York Times *likened his work to 'a continent dreamed up, in tandem, by Hieronymus Bosch and Jorge Luis Borges'. His novels include* The Famished Road *(1991). An African Elegy (1992) is a poetry collection.*

1 Many people have walked out of life because they stopped seeing it. Many have fallen into the abyss because they were looking for solid ground, for certainties. Happy are those who are still, and to whom things come.
The Famished Road, bk 4, ch. 13 (1991)

John Oldham
(1653–83)
English poet

After graduating from Oxford University, he taught, translated JUVENAL *and composed verse. His work was published posthumously.*

1 And all your future lies beneath your hat.
'A Satire, Addressed to a Friend, that is about to leave the University, and come abroad in the world', l. 26, publ. in *Poems and Translations* (1684)

William Oldys
(1696–1761)
English antiquary and editor

He edited WALTER RALEGH's History of the World *(1736), and later collaborated with* SAMUEL JOHNSON *on a catalogue of the Harleian Library and an anthology,* The Harleian Miscellany *(1744–6). He also wrote verse modelled on the Greek Anacreon.*

1 Busy, curious, thirsty fly,
Gently drink, and drink as I;
Freely welcome to my cup,
Could'st thou sip, and sip it up;
Make the most of life you may,
Life is short and wears away.
'The Fly', publ. in *The Scarborough Miscellany* (1732). The second line has also been quoted: 'Drink with me, and drink as I.'

2 Just alike, both mine and thine,
Hasten quick to their decline;
Thine's a summer, mine's no more,
Though repeated to threescore;
Threescore summers when they're gone,
Will appear as short as one.
'The Fly', ibid.

Margaret Oliphant
(1828–97)
Scottish author

Her prolific literary output included fiction, history and biography. She is best known for Chronicles of Carlingford *(1863–76), a sequence of novels set, like much of her work, in Scotland.*

1 The first thing which I can record concerning myself is, that I was born ... These are wonderful words. This life, to which neither time nor eternity can bring diminution – this everlasting living soul, *began*. My mind loses itself in these depths.
Memoirs and Resolutions of Adam Graeme, of Mossgray, vol. 1, bk 1, ch. 1 (1852)

2 For everybody knows that it requires very little to satisfy the gentlemen, if a woman will only give her mind to it.
Miss Marjoribanks, ch. 13 (fourth of *Chronicles of Carlingford*, 1866)

3 Temptations come, as a general rule, when they are sought.
Miss Marjoribanks, ibid., ch. 47

4 It has been my fate in a long life of production to be credited chiefly with the equivocal virtue of

industry, a quality so excellent in morals, so little satisfactory in art.

The Heir Presumptive and the Heir Apparent, Preface (1892)

(Sir) Laurence Olivier
(1907–89)
British actor and director

Baron Olivier of Brighton. Regarded by many as the greatest actor of his generation, he played all the major Shakespearian roles on the stage and in film. He was the first director of the National Theatre (1963–73).

1 This is the tragedy of a man who could not make up his mind.
Hamlet (film, 1948, screenplay by Alan Dent, directed by Laurence Olivier). Spoken introduction, written by Alan Dent.

2 Shakespeare – the nearest thing in incarnation to the eye of God.
Kenneth Harris Talking To, 'Sir Laurence Olivier' (1971)

3 Why don't you try acting, dear boy – it's so much easier.
Attributed advice to DUSTIN HOFFMAN, his co-star in the film *Marathon Man* (1976), who stayed awake for days on end in order to 'inhabit' his role

4 Acting is a masochistic form of exhibitionism. It is not quite the occupation of an adult.
Time 3 July 1978

Charles Olson
(1910–70)
US poet and critic

Spokesman of the Black Mountain poets, he argued that poetry should depend on the rhythms of breathing rather than rhyme and metre in his influential essay 'Projective Verse' (1950). He is also known for a study of HERMAN MELVILLE, Call Me Ishmael (1947), and The Maximus Poems (1953–70).

1 I take SPACE to be the central fact to man born in America ... I spell it large because it comes large here. Large and without mercy.
Call Me Ishmael, sect. 1 (1947)

2 Get on with it, keep moving, keep in, speed, the nerves, their speed, the perceptions, theirs, the acts, the split second acts, the whole business, keep it moving as fast as you can, citizen ... So there we are, fast, there's the dogma.
'Projective Verse' (1950), publ. in *Selected Writings of Charles Olson* (ed. Robert Creeley, 1951)

Frank Ward O'Malley
See ELBERT HUBBARD 4

Michael Ondaatje
(b. 1943)
Sri Lankan-born Canadian novelist and poet

He has published numerous volumes of verse, including The Cinnamon Peeler *(1990), but he is best known for his novels, notably* The English Patient *(1992).*

1 The past is still, for us, a place that is not safely settled.
The Faber Book of Contemporary Canadian Short Stories, Introduction (1990)

Eugene O'Neill
(1888–1953)
US playwright

The first American dramatist to win the Nobel Prize for Literature (1936), he also won a total of four Pulitzer Prizes, including one for the autobiographical Long Day's Journey into Night *(1956), generally considered his finest work. 'O'Neill gave birth to the American theatre and died for it,' according to* TENNESSEE WILLIAMS.

1 Life is for each man a solitary cell whose walls are mirrors.
Lazarus Laughed, Act 2, Sc. 1 (1927). Spoken by Lazarus.

2 When men make gods, there is no God!
Lazarus, ibid., Act 2, Sc. 2

3 Man's loneliness is but his fear of life.
Lazarus, ibid., Act 3, Sc. 2

4 The old – like children – talk to themselves, for they have reached that hopeless wisdom of experience which knows that though one were to cry it in the streets to multitudes, or whisper it in the kiss to one's beloved, the only ears that can ever hear one's secrets are one's own!
Tiberius, ibid., Act 4, Sc. 1

5 Life is perhaps most wisely regarded as a bad dream between two awakenings, and every day is a life in miniature.
Marco Millions, Act 2, Sc. 2 (1928). Spoken by Chu-Yin.

6 The only living life is in the past and future – the present is an interlude – strange interlude in which we call on past and future to bear witness we are living.
Strange Interlude, pt 2, Act 8 (1928). Spoken by Nina.

7 The sea hates a coward!
Mourning Becomes Electra, pt 2, Act 4 (1931). Spoken by Bryant.

8 The lie of a pipe dream is what gives life to the whole misbegotten mad lot of us, drunk or sober.
The Iceman Cometh, Act 1 (1946). Spoken by Larry. 'It is a play about pipe dreams,' O'Neill remarked about this work. 'And the philosophy is that there is always one dream left, one final dream, no matter how low you have fallen, down there at the bottom of the bottle. I know, because I saw it.'

9 None of us can help the things life has done to us. They're done before you realize it, and once they're done they make you do other things until at last everything comes between you and what you'd like to be, and you've lost your true self forever.
Long Day's Journey into Night, Act 2, Sc. 1 (1956). Spoken by Mary.

10 I knew it. I knew it. Born in a hotel room – and God damn it – died in a hotel room.
Attributed, shortly before his death in the Shelton Hotel, Boston, 27 November 1953

11 We fought so long against small things that we became small ourselves.
Quoted by VÁCLAV HAVEL in *Disturbing the Peace*, ch. 3 (1986)

Yoko Ono
(b. 1933)
Japanese-born US artist

Yoko Ono Lennon. As painter, sculptor and performance artist, she was a prominent member of New York's neo-Dadaist Fluxus group in the 1960s. She campaigned for peace alongside her husband JOHN LENNON.

1 Woman is the nigger of the world.
Interview in *Nova* 1968, quoted in *The Lennon Tapes* (1981). The words were the basis of the eponymously titled song by JOHN LENNON on the album *Some Time in New York City* (1972), and recall those of ZORA NEALE HURSTON: 'De nigger woman is de mule uh de world so fur as Ah can see.' (*Their Eyes Were Watching God*, ch. 2, 1937)

2 The odds of not meeting in this life are so great that every meeting is like a miracle. It's a wonder that we don't make love to every single person we meet.
Feeling the Space, sleevenotes (album, 1973)

J. Robert Oppenheimer
(1904–67)
US physicist

Julius Robert Oppenheimer. In 1943 he became Director at the Los Alamos laboratory, overseeing the Manhattan Project to develop the atomic bomb. Horrified at the bomb's destructive power, he resigned in 1945, later arguing unsuccessfully for joint US-Soviet control of atomic energy.

1 In some sort of crude sense, which no vulgarity, no humor, no overstatement can quite extinguish, the physicists have known sin; and this is a knowledge which they cannot lose.
'Physics in the Contemporary World', lecture at Massachusetts Institute of Technology, 25 November 1947 (1948), repr. in *Open Mind*, ch. 5 (1955). Oppenheimer's remark became notorious after it was quoted in *Time* magazine 23 February and 8 November 1948.

2 When you see something that is technically sweet, you go ahead and do it and you argue about what to do about it only after you have had your technical success. That is the way it was with the atomic bomb.
In the Matter of J. Robert Oppenheimer: USAEC Transcript of Hearing Before Personnel Security Board (1954). Statement during hearings investigating allegations of former communist associations, in connection with Oppenheimer's involvement in the Los Alamos project to develop the atomic bomb.

Susie Orbach
(b. 1946)
British psychotherapist and author

Her work is directed to understanding eating disorders, which she discusses in her books, most famously Fat is a Feminist Issue *(1978).*

1 Fat is a social disease, and fat is a feminist issue.
Fat is a Feminist Issue, Introduction (1978). 'Fat,' Orbach wrote, 'is a way of saying "no" to powerlessness and self-denial.'

Baroness Orczy
(1865–1947)
Hungarian-born British author and playwright

Her most successful work, The Scarlet Pimpernel *(1905), narrated the adventures of Sir Percy Blakeney during the French Revolution. It was followed by several sequels, and she also wrote detective fiction.*

1 We seek him here, we seek him there,
Those Frenchies seek him everywhere.
Is he in heaven? – Is he in hell?
That demmed, elusive Pimpernel.
The Scarlet Pimpernel, ch. 12 (1905). Sir Percy's 'bon mot', enthusiastically received at a ball.

2 An apology? Bah! Disgusting! Cowardly! Beneath

the dignity of any gentleman, however wrong he might be.

I Will Repay, Prologue no. 1 (1906)

John Boyle O'Reilly

(1844–90)

Irish poet, author and editor

While serving as a soldier, he was court-martialled for his involvement in the Fenian movement and transported to Australia. Escaping in 1869, he became editor of The Pilot, *a Boston newspaper, and its co-proprietor from 1876.*

1 The organized charity, scrimped and iced,
In the name of a cautious, statistical Christ.

'In Bohemia', st. 5, publ. in *In Bohemia* (1886)

(Sir) Tony O'Reilly

(b. 1936)

Irish entrepreneur

After a career as a rugby international, he went into business and was Chairman (1987–2000) of the Heinz International Corporation and subsequently Executive Chairman of Independent News and Media.

1 Truly great brands are far more than just labels for products; they are symbols that encapsulate the desires of consumers; they are standards held aloft under which the masses congregate.

Speech to British Council of Shopping Centres, 1990, quoted in 'Brand Leader' by Fintan O'Toole, publ. in *Granta* no. 53, spring 1996

Leoluca Orlando

(b. 1947)

Sicilian politician

Mayor of Palermo 1985–2001, he was expelled from the Christian Democrat Party in 1990 and formed his own party, La Rete ('Network'), dedicated to eradicating Mafia influence and reinvigorating the city.

1 In Italy it is not important who you are but whom you belong to.

Quoted in the *International Herald Tribune* 25 April 1991

P. J. O'Rourke

(b. 1947)

US journalist

Patrick John O'Rourke. He is notorious for his acidic sketches of public affairs from a humorous right-wing perspective, collected in Holidays in Hell *(1988) and* The Enemies List *(1996),*

among other titles. Time *magazine called him 'an acerbic master of gonzo journalism'.*

1 Name me, if you can, a better feeling than the one you get when you've half a bottle of Chivas in the bag with a gram of coke up your nose and a teenage lovely pulling off her tube top in the next seat over while you're doing a hundred miles an hour in a suburban side street.

Republican Party Reptile, 'How to Drive Fast On Drugs While Getting Your Wing Wang Squeezed and Not Spill Your Drink' (1987)

2 Western civilization not only provides a bit of life, a pinch of liberty and the occasional pursuance of happiness, it's also the only thing that's ever tried to. Our civilization is the first in history to show even the slightest concern for average, undistinguished, none-too-commendable people like us.

Holidays in Hell, Introduction (1988)

3 In the end we beat them with Levi 501 jeans. Seventy-two years of Communist indoctrination and propaganda was drowned out by a three-ounce Sony Walkman. A huge totalitarian system ... has been brought to its knees because nobody wants to wear Bulgarian shoes ... Now they're lunch, and we're number one on the planet.

Give War A Chance, 'The Death of Communism' (1992)

4 We spend all day broadcasting on the radio and TV telling people back home what's happening here. And we learn what's happening here by spending all day monitoring the radio and TV broadcasts from back home.

Ibid., 'Gulf Diary'. On reporting the Gulf War.

5 Whatever it is that the government does, sensible Americans would prefer that the government do it to somebody else. This is the idea behind foreign policy.

Parliament of Whores, 'Very Foreign Policy' (1991)

6 Every government is a parliament of whores. The trouble is, in a democracy the whores are us.

Ibid., 'At Home In the Parliament of Whores'

José Ortega y Gasset

(1883–1955)

Spanish essayist and philosopher

He played a significant part in introducing Spanish readers to modernist fiction. His major work, The Revolt of the Masses *(1930), denounced the anti-intellectualism and intolerance of both left and right in the years preceding the Spanish Civil War.*

1 I am I plus my surroundings and if I do not preserve the latter, I do not preserve myself.
Meditations on Quixote, 'To the Reader' (1914)

2 I do not deny that there may be other well-founded causes for the hatred which various classes feel toward politicians, but the *main one seems to me that politicians are symbols of the fact that every class must take every other class into account.*
Invertebrate Spain, ch. 2, 'Direct Action' (1921)

3 Poetry has become the higher algebra of metaphors.
The Dehumanization of Art, 'More About the Dehumanization of Art' (1925)

4 The characteristic of the hour is that the commonplace mind, knowing itself to be commonplace, has the assurance to proclaim the rights of the commonplace and to impose them wherever it will.
The Revolt of the Masses, ch. 1 (1930)

5 Civilization is nothing else than the attempt to reduce force to being the *ultima ratio*.
Ibid., ch. 8

6 Liberalism – it is well to recall this today – is the supreme form of generosity; it is the right which the majority concedes to minorities and hence it is *the noblest cry* that has ever resounded in this planet. It announces the determination to share existence with the enemy; more than that, with an enemy which is weak.
Ibid., ch. 8

7 We have need of history in its entirety, not to fall back into it, but to see if we can escape from it.
Ibid., ch. 10

8 A revolution does not last more than fifteen years, the period which coincides with the flourishing of a generation.
Ibid., ch. 10

9 Youth does not require reasons for living, it only needs pretexts.
Ibid., ch. 14, sect. 3

10 Biography is: a system in which the contradictions of a human life are unified.
'In Search of Goethe from Within' (1949), repr. in *The Dehumanization of Art and Other Essays* (1968)

11 Poetry is adolescence fermented, and thus preserved.
'In Search of Goethe from Within', ibid.

Joe Orton
(1933–67)
British playwright

Originally John Kingsley. The hallmarks of his farces, such as Entertaining Mr Sloane *(1964) and* Loot *(1966), are black humour, bad taste and cutting dialogue. He was murdered by his lover, Kenneth Halliwell, who then took his own life.*

1 I always say to myself that the theatre is the Temple of Dionysus, and not Apollo. You do the Dionysus thing on your typewriter, and then you allow a little Apollo in, just a little to shape and guide it along certain lines you may want to go along. But you can't allow Apollo in completely.
Interview on BBC Radio, 28 July 1964, quoted in *Prick Up Your Ears: the Biography of Joe Orton*, ch. 1 (1978) by JOHN LAHR

2 Every luxury was lavished on you – atheism, breast-feeding, circumcision.
Loot, Act 1 (performed 1966, publ. 1967). Spoken by Hal to Dennis.

3 Reading isn't an occupation we encourage among police officers. We try to keep the paper work down to a minimum.
Truscott, ibid., *Act 2*

4 You were born with your legs apart. They'll send you to the grave in a Y-shaped coffin.
What the Butler Saw, Act 1 (1969). Spoken by Dr Prentice to his wife.

5 In an age of declining faith, sir, surely it's enough for the young to hold spiritual convictions. It's an act of pedantry to ask that they should be the right ones.
Notes for dialogue in *What the Butler Saw*, quoted in *Prick Up Your Ears: the Biography of Joe Orton*, ch. 6 (1978) by JOHN LAHR

George Orwell
(1903–50)
British author and essayist

Pseudonym of Eric Blair. After working as an Imperial Police officer in Burma, he lived in Europe, often performing menial jobs. His exploits in the Spanish Civil War were described in Homage to Catalonia *(1938), while* Animal Farm *(1945) and* Nineteen Eighty-Four *(1949) expressed his disillusionment with socialism.* CYRIL CONNOLLY *remarked: 'He could not blow his nose without moralizing on conditions in the hand-kerchief industry.'*

1 He was an embittered atheist (the sort of atheist who does not so much disbelieve in God as personally dislike Him).

Down and Out in Paris and London, ch. 30 (1933). Referring to Bozo, a London 'screever' or pavement artist.

2 As with the Christian religion, the worst advertisement for Socialism is its adherents.

The Road to Wigan Pier, ch. 11 (1937)

3 The high-water mark, so to speak, of Socialist literature is W.H. Auden, a sort of gutless Kipling, and the even feebler poets who are associated with him.

Ibid., ch. 11. In his essay 'Inside the Whale' (1940), Orwell wrote: 'Some years ago I described Auden as "a sort of gutless Kipling". As criticism this was quite unworthy, indeed it was merely a spiteful remark, but it is a fact that in Auden's work, especially his earlier work, an atmosphere of uplift – something rather like Kipling's *If* or Newbolt's *Play up, Play up, and Play the Game!* – never seems to be very far away.'

4 We of the sinking middle class ... may sink without further struggles into the working class where we belong, and probably when we get there it will not be so dreadful as we feared, for, after all, we have nothing to lose but our aitches.

Ibid., ch. 13

5 And then England – southern England, probably the sleekest landscape in the world. It is difficult when you pass that way ... to believe that anything is really happening anywhere. Earthquakes in Japan, famines in China, revolutions in Mexico? Don't worry, the milk will be on the doorstep tomorrow morning, the *New Statesman* will come out on Friday ... And then the huge peaceful wilderness of outer London, the barges on the miry river, the familiar streets, the posters telling of cricket matches and Royal weddings, the men in bowler hats, the pigeons in Trafalgar Square, the red buses, the blue policemen – all sleeping the deep, deep sleep of England, from which I sometimes fear that we shall never wake till we are jerked out of it by the roar of bombs.

Homage to Catalonia, ch. 14 (1938). Closing words of book, describing Orwell's return from Spain.

6 I'm fat, but I'm thin inside. Has it ever struck you that there's a thin man inside every fat man, just as they say there's a statue inside every block of stone?

Coming Up For Air, pt 1, ch. 3 (1939). See also KINGSLEY AMIS 4, CYRIL CONNOLLY 18.

7 Of course there is much more in *Ulysses* than this ['commonplaceness of material'], because Joyce is a kind of poet and also an elephantine pedant, but his real achievement has been to get the familiar on to paper.

Inside the Whale and Other Essays, 'Inside the Whale', sect. 1 (1940)

8 The 'Communism' of the English intellectual is something explicable enough. It is the patriotism of the deracinated.

Ibid., 'Inside the Whale', sect. 2

9 Good novels are not written by orthodoxy-sniffers, nor by people who are conscience-stricken about their own orthodoxy. Good novels are written by people who are *not frightened.*

Ibid., 'Inside the Whale', sect. 2

10 Progress is not an illusion, it happens, but it is slow and invariably disappointing.

Ibid., 'Charles Dickens', sect. 1

11 Most revolutionaries are potential Tories, because they imagine that everything can be put right by altering the *shape* of society; once that change is effected, as it sometimes is, they see no need for any other.

Ibid., 'Charles Dickens', sect. 6

12 The clatter of clogs in the Lancashire mill towns, the to-and-fro of the lorries on the Great North Road, the queues outside the Labour Exchanges, the rattle of pin-tables in the Soho pubs, the old maids biking to Holy Communion through the mists of the autumn mornings – all these are not only fragments, but *characteristic* fragments, of the English scene. How can one make a pattern out of this muddle?

The Lion and the Unicorn, pt 1, 'England Your England', sect. 1 (1941). John Major nostalgically evoked this passage: see JOHN MAJOR 4.

13 England ... resembles a family, a rather stuffy Victorian family, with not many black sheep in it but with all its cupboards bursting with skeletons. It has rich relations who have to be kowtowed to and poor relations who are horribly sat upon, and there is a deep conspiracy of silence about the source of the family income. It is a family in which the young are generally thwarted and most of the power is in the hands of irresponsible uncles and bed-ridden aunts. Still, it is a family. It has its private language and its common memories, and at the approach of an enemy it closes its ranks. A family

with the wrong members in control – that, perhaps, is as near as one can come to describing England in a phrase.

Ibid., pt 1, 'England Your England', sect. 3

14 Probably the battle of Waterloo *was* won on the playing-fields of Eton, but the opening battles of all subsequent wars have been lost there.

Ibid., pt 1, 'England Your England', sect. 4. See DUKE OF WELLINGTON 6.

15 Whatever is funny is subversive, every joke is ultimately a custard pie, and the reason why so large a proportion of jokes centre round obscenity is simply that all societies, as the price of survival, have to insist on a fairly high standard of sexual morality. A dirty joke is not, of course, a serious attack upon morality, but it is a sort of mental rebellion, a momentary wish that things were otherwise.

'The Art of Donald McGill' (1941), repr. in *The Collected Essays, Journalism and Letters of George Orwell*, vol. 2 (ed. Sonia Orwell and Ian Angus, 1968)

16 To a surprising extent the war-lords in shining armour, the apostles of the martial virtues, tend not to die fighting when the time comes. History is full of ignominious getaways by the great and famous.

'Who Are the War Criminals?' (1943), ibid., vol. 2

17 Autobiography is only to be trusted when it reveals something disgraceful. A man who gives a good account of himself is probably lying, since any life when viewed from the inside is simply a series of defeats.

'Benefit of Clergy: Some Notes on Salvador Dali' (1944), ibid., vol. 3. The essay was suppressed by the publishers of *The Saturday Book* and appeared in *Dickens, Dali and Others* (ed. George Orwell, 1946).

18 As a rule they will refuse even to sample a foreign dish, they regard such things as garlic and olive oil with disgust, life is unliveable to them unless they have tea and puddings.

'The English People: England at First Glance' (written 1944, publ. 1947), ibid., vol. 3. On the English attitude to food.

19 To write or even speak English is not a science but an art. There are no reliable words ... Whoever writes English is involved in a struggle that never lets up even for a sentence. He is struggling against vagueness, against obscurity, against the lure of the decorative adjective, against the encroachment of Latin and Greek, and, above all, against the worn-out

phrases and dead metaphors with which the language is cluttered up.

'The English People: The English Language', ibid., vol. 3. Consequently, Orwell explained, 'the peculiarities of the English language make it almost impossible for anyone who has left school at fourteen to learn a foreign language after he has grown up.'

20 Language ought to be the joint creation of poets and manual workers.

'The English People: The English Language', ibid., vol. 3

21 The English are probably more capable than most peoples of making revolutionary change without bloodshed. In England, if anywhere, it would be possible to abolish poverty without destroying liberty.

'The English People: The English Language', ibid., vol. 3

22 For all I know, by the time this book is published my view of the Soviet régime may be the generally accepted one. But what use would that be in itself? To exchange one orthodoxy for another is not necessarily an advance. The enemy is the gramophone mind, whether or not one agrees with the record that is being played at the moment.

'The Freedom of the Press', proposed preface to *Animal Farm* (written 1945, publ. 1972), repr. in *Animal Farm* fiftieth anniversary edn (1995)

23 If liberty means anything at all it means the right to tell people what they do not want to hear. The common people still vaguely subscribe to that doctrine and act on it. In our country – it is not the same in all countries: it was not so in republican France, and it is not so in the USA today – it is the liberals who fear liberty and the intellectuals who want to do dirt on the intellect.

'The Freedom of the Press', ibid.

24 Four legs good, two legs bad.

Animal Farm, ch. 3 (1945). By the end of the story, the animals' revolutionary maxim has become: 'Four legs good, two legs *better*' (ch. 10).

25 All animals are equal but some animals are more equal than others.

Ibid., ch. 10. The animals' commandment as it appeared at the end of the story, originally 'All animals are equal'.

26 To walk through the ruined cities of Germany is to feel an actual doubt about the continuity of civilization.

Observer 8 April 1945

27 Serious sport has nothing to do with fair play. It is bound up with hatred, jealousy, boastfulness, and

disregard of all the rules and sadistic pleasure in witnessing violence: in other words it is war minus the shooting.

'Sporting Spirit' (1945), repr. in *The Collected Essays, Journalism and Letters of George Orwell*, vol. 4 (ed. Sonia Orwell and Ian Angus, 1968)

28 He is a man of thirty-five, but looks fifty. He is bald, has varicose veins and wears spectacles, or would wear them if his only pair were not chronically lost. If things are normal with him, he will be suffering from malnutrition, but if he has recently had a lucky streak, he will be suffering from a hangover. At present it is half past eleven in the morning, and according to his schedule he should have started work two hours ago; but even if he had made any serious effort to start he would have been frustrated by the almost continuous ringing of the telephone bell, the yells of the baby, the rattle of an electric drill out in the street, and the heavy boots of his creditors clumping up the stairs. The most recent interruption was the arrival of the second post, which brought him two circulars and an income tax demand printed in red. Needless to say this person is a writer.

'Confessions of a Book Reviewer' (1946), ibid., vol. 4

29 In our time, political speech and writing are largely the defence of the indefensible.

'Politics and the English Language' (1946), ibid., vol. 4

30 The great enemy of clear language is insincerity. When there is a gap between one's real and one's declared aims, one turns as it were instinctively to long words and exhausted idioms, like a cuttlefish squirting out ink.

'Politics and the English Language', ibid., vol. 4

31 The Catholic and the Communist are alike in assuming that an opponent cannot be both honest and intelligent.

'The Prevention of Literature' (1946), ibid., vol. 4

32 The quickest way of ending a war is to lose it.

'Second Thoughts on James Burnham' (1946), ibid., vol. 4. The essay is reprinted in *Collected Essays* with the title 'James Burnham and the Managerial Revolution'.

33 No one can look back on his schooldays and say with truth that they were altogether unhappy.

'Such, Such were the Joys', sect. 3 (written 1947, publ. 1952), ibid., vol. 4. Orwell himself attended Eton.

34 It was a bright, cold day in April and the clocks were striking thirteen.

Nineteen Eighty-Four, pt 1, ch. 1 (1949). Opening words of book.

35 BIG BROTHER IS WATCHING YOU.

Caption to 'Ingsoc' poster, ibid., pt 1, ch. 1. The poster is described as 'one of those pictures which are so contrived that the eyes follow you about when you move'.

36 War is peace. Freedom is slavery. Ignorance is strength.

Ingsoc party slogan, ibid., pt 1, ch. 1

37 Who controls the past controls the future: who controls the present controls the past.

Ingsoc party slogan, ibid., pt 1, ch. 3

38 Don't you see that the whole aim of Newspeak is to narrow the range of thought? In the end we shall make thoughtcrime literally impossible, because there will be no words in which to express it.

Symes, ibid., pt 1, ch. 5

39 Freedom is the freedom to say that two plus two make four. If that is granted, all else follows.

Ibid., pt 2, ch. 7. Winston Smith's diary.

40 *Doublethink* means the power of holding two contradictory beliefs in one's mind simultaneously, and accepting both of them.

Ibid., pt 2, ch. 9. Extract from Goldstein's book. See F. SCOTT FITZGERALD 17.

41 Power is not a means, it is an end. One does not establish a dictatorship in order to safeguard a revolution; one makes the revolution in order to establish the dictatorship.

O'Brien, ibid., pt 3, ch. 3

42 If you want a vision of the future, imagine a boot stamping on a human face – forever.

O'Brien, ibid., pt 3, ch. 3

43 One cannot really be a Catholic and grown-up.

Manuscript Notebook (1949), repr. in *The Collected Essays, Journalism and Letters of George Orwell*, vol. 4 (ed. Sonia Orwell and Ian Angus, 1968)

44 At 50, everyone has the face he deserves.

Last entry in Orwell's notebook, 17 April 1949, ibid. ALBERT CAMUS, in *The Fall* (1956), expressed much the same notion: 'After a certain age every man is responsible for his face.'

45 Saints should always be judged guilty until they are proved innocent.

'Reflections on Gandhi', publ. in *Shooting an Elephant* (1950). Orwell expressed scepticism of all forms of sainthood: 'It is probable,' he wrote, 'that some who achieve or aspire to sainthood have never felt much temptation to be human beings.'

John Osborne

(1929–94)
British playwright

His character Jimmy Porter in Look Back in Anger *(1956) became the mouthpiece of a generation of 'angry young men'. The critic Milton Shulman wrote that the play 'aims at being a despairing cry but achieves only the stature of a self-pitying snivel', but for others it resonated strongly and revitalized British theatre.* The Entertainer *(1957) was equally successful.*

1 Look Back in Anger.
Title of play (1956)

2 Why do I do this every Sunday? Even the book reviews seem to be the same as last week's. Different books – same reviews.
Look Back in Anger, Act 1 (1956). Opening words of play, spoken by Jimmy Porter.

3 Oh heavens, how I long for a little ordinary human enthusiasm. Just enthusiasm – that's all. I want to hear a warm, thrilling voice cry out Hallelujah! Hallelujah! I'm alive!
Jimmy Porter, ibid., Act 1

4 Anyone who's never watched somebody die is suffering from a pretty bad case of virginity.
Jimmy Porter, ibid., Act 2, Sc. 1

5 The whole point of a sacrifice is that you give up something you never really wanted in the first place . . . People are doing it around you all the time. They give up their careers, say – or their beliefs – or sex.
Jimmy Porter, ibid., Act 3, Sc. 1

6 There aren't any good, brave causes left. If the big bang does come, and we all get killed off, it won't be in aid of the old-fashioned grand design. It'll just be for the Brave New-nothing-very-much-thank-you. About as pointless and inglorious as stepping in front of a bus. No, there's nothing left for it, me boy, but to let yourself be butchered by the women.
Jimmy Porter, ibid., Act 3, Sc. 1

7 It's no good trying to fool yourself about love. You can't fall into it like a soft job, without dirtying up your hands. It takes muscle and guts. And if you can't bear the thought of messing up your nice, clean soul, you'd better give up the whole idea of life, and become a saint. Because you'll never make it as a human being. It's either this world or the next.
Jimmy Porter, ibid., Act 3, Sc. 2

8 What are we hoping to get out of it, what's it all in aid of – is it really just for the sake of a gloved hand waving at you from a golden coach?
The Entertainer, no. 10 (1957). Spoken by Jean.

9 Here we are, we're alone in the universe, there's no God, it just seems that it all began by something as simple as sunlight striking on a piece of rock. And here we are. We've only got ourselves. Somehow, we've just got to make a go of it. *We've only got ourselves.*
Jean, ibid., no. 12

10 It's easy to answer the ultimate questions – it saves you bothering with the immediate ones.
Epitaph for George Dillon, Act 2 (1958, written with Anthony Creighton). Spoken by George.

11 Damn you England. You're rotting now, and quite soon you'll disappear. My hate will outrun you yet, if only for a few seconds. I wish it could be eternal.
Letter to *Tribune* 18 August 1961, repr. in *Almost a Gentleman*, ch. 22 (autobiography, 1991)

12 Inside every playwright there is a Falstaff, gathering like a boil to be lanced by his liege employers – fashion and caprice.
Almost a Gentleman, ch. 18 (autobiography, 1991)

(Sir) William Osler

(1849–1919)
Canadian physician

He was renowned as a medical historian and teacher, and was Regius Professor of Medicine at Oxford from 1905. His Principles and Practice of Medicine *(1892), which codified clinical practice, became a standard textbook.*

1 To talk of diseases is a sort of Arabian Nights' entertainment.
Nurse and Patient (1897), repr. in *Aphorisms from His Bedside Teachings and Writings*, no. 275 (ed. William Bennett Bean, 1950)

2 The greater the ignorance the greater the dogmatism.
'Chauvinism in Medicine', publ. in *Montreal Medical Journal* September 1902, ibid., no. 173

3 The natural man has only two primal passions, to get and to beget.
Science and Immortality, ch. 2 (1904)

4 The teacher's life should have three periods, study until twenty-five, investigation until forty, profession until sixty, at which age I would have him retired on a double allowance.
Farewell address at Johns Hopkins Medical School,

22 February 1905, publ. in *Aphorisms from His Bedside Teachings and Writings*, no. 354 (ed. William Bennett Bean, 1950)

5 My second fixed idea is the uselessness of man above sixty years of age, and the incalculable benefit it would be in commercial, political, and in professional life if, as a matter of course, men stopped work at this age.

Farewell address at Johns Hopkins Medical School, 22 February 1905, ibid., no. 356. Osler's remarks were the source of a fierce attack by the press, for their alleged view of people as mere productive machines.

6 What is the student but a lover courting a fickle mistress who ever eludes his grasp?

Aequanamitas, 'The Student Life', sect. 1 (1906)

7 No bubble is so iridescent or floats longer than that blown by the successful teacher.

Address in Glasgow, 4 October 1911, quoted in *Life of Sir William Osler*, vol. 2, ch. 31 (1925) by Harvey Cushing

8 Failure to examine the throat is a glaring sin of omission, especially in children. One finger in the throat and one in the rectum makes a good diagnostician.

Quoted in *Aphorisms from His Bedside Teachings and Writings*, no. 205 (ed. William Bennett Bean, 1950)

Haley Joel Osment
(b. 1988)
US screen actor

He acted in advertisements from an early age, and earned an Oscar nomination for his performance in The Sixth Sense *(1999). He later starred in* Artifical Intelligence: AI *(2001).*

1 I see dead people.

The Sixth Sense (film, 1999, written and directed by M. Night Shyamalan). Spoken by Cole Sear (Haley Joel Osment).

John Louis O'Sullivan
(1813–95)
US editor

After practising law, he turned to journalism, editing the United States Magazine and Democratic Review *1841–46 and co-founding the* New York Morning News *in 1844. He was arrested for his involvement in the movement to annex Cuba to the USA and later lived in Europe until 1879.*

1 The fulfilment of our manifest destiny [is] to overspread the continent allotted by Providence for the free development of our yearly multiplying millions.

US Magazine and Democratic Review July–August 1845, edi-

torial. O'Sullivan vociferously supported the US annexation of Texas, Cuba and the Oregon Territory. The doctrine of 'manifest destiny' was first taken up by the Democrats and was revived as a Republican policy in the 1890s.

2 A torchlight procession marching down your throat.

Attributed, in *Collections and Recollections*, ch. 19 (1898) by G. W. E. RUSSELL. Referring to whisky. It is not clear that the O'Sullivan quoted is John Louis O'Sullivan.

James Otis
(1725–83)
US lawyer and statesman

A leader of the radical wing of the anti-colonialists, he served in the Massachusetts legislature from 1761. He became insane after an altercation with a crown officer in 1769. See also ANONYMOUS 96.

1 Taxation without representation is tyranny.

'Arguments on the Illegality of the Writs of Assistance', speech to Superior Court of Massachusetts, February 1761. No contemporary evidence exists for Otis's exact words, though he is known to have used a similar expression in his *Rights of the Colonies* (1764). See POLITICAL SLOGANS 28.

Thomas Otway
(1652–85)
English dramatist and poet

Having failed as an actor, he had success with his tragedy Alcibiades *(1675), and later with* The Orphan *(1680) and* Venice Preserved *(1682). He also translated and wrote poetry. He died destitute.*

1 Happy a while in Paradise they lay;
But quickly woman longed to go astray:
Some foolish new adventure needs must prove,
And the first devil she saw, she changed her love:
To his temptations, lewdly she inclined
Her soul, and, for an apple, damned mankind.

The Orphan, Act 3, Sc. 1 (1680). Spoken by Castalio.

2 Let us embrace, and from this very moment vow an eternal misery together.

Polydore to Monimia, ibid., Act 4, Sc. 2

3 Honest men
Are the soft easy cushions on which knaves
Repose and fatten.

Venice Preserved, Act 1, Sc. 1 (1682). Spoken by Pierre.

4 Shining through tears, like April suns in showers,
That labour to o'ercome the cloud that loads 'em.

Pierre, of Belvidera, ibid., Act 1, Sc. 1

5 No praying, it spoils business.
Pierre, ibid., Act 2, Sc. 2

Ouida
(1839–1908)
English novelist

Pseudonym of Marie Louise de la Ramée. A prolific and popular writer, she specialized in sentimental romances, such as Under Two Flags *(1867), and stories for children, for example* A Dog of Flanders *(1872). See also* MADAME ROLAND 2.

1 Petty laws breed great crimes.
'Pipistrello' (1880), repr. in *Pipistrello and Other Stories* (1884)

2 Take hope from the heart of man, and you make him a beast of prey.
A Village Commune, ch. 20 (1881)

3 To vice, innocence must always seem only a superior kind of chicanery.
Bébée, or Two Little Wooden Shoes, ch. 13 (1896)

4 Sport inevitably creates deadness of feeling. No one could take pleasure in it who was sensitive to suffering; and therefore its pursuit by women is much more to be regretted than its pursuit by men, because women pursue much more violently and recklessly what they pursue at all.
Critical Studies, 'The Quality of Mercy' (1900)

5 In a few generations more, there will probably be no room at all allowed for animals on the earth: no need of them, no toleration of them. An immense agony will have then ceased, but with it there will also have passed away the last smile of the world's youth.
Ibid., 'The Quality of Mercy'

Ovid
(43 BC–AD 17)
Roman poet

Publius Ovidius Naso. His verse was noted for its supreme technical accomplishment, notably in Ars Amatoria, *on the subject of love, and* Metamorphoses, *a collection of mythological stories.* Fasti *was an account of the Roman year and its festivals, while* Tristia *dwelt on the pangs of exile, written following his banishment to the Black Sea for unknown reasons in AD 8.*

1 Run softly, steeds of night!
Amores, bk 1, no. 13, l. 40 (from 20 BC)

2 Away from me, far away, ye austere fair!
Ibid., bk 2, no. 1, l. 3

3 They come to see; they come that they themselves may be seen.
Ars Amatoria, bk 1, l. 99 (1 BC; *The Art of Love*)

4 By night are blemishes hid, and every fault is forgiven: that hour makes any woman fair.
Ibid., bk 1, ll. 249–50

5 It is expedient there should be gods, and as it is expedient, let us deem that gods exist.
Ibid., bk 1, ll. 637–8. See VOLTAIRE 30.

6 Skill makes love unending.
Ibid., bk 3, l. 42

7 Perhaps too my name will be joined to theirs.
Ibid., bk 3, l. 339. Referring to the names of the great poets.

8 Chaos, a rough, unordered mass of things.
Metamorphoses, bk 1, l. 7 (c. AD 8)

9 *Medio tutissimus ibis.*
[In the middle is the safest path.]
Ibid., bk 2, l. 137

10 But behold, the hero's helper, Pallas, gliding down through the high air, stands beside him, and she bids him plough the earth and plant therein the dragon's teeth, destined to grow into a nation. He obeys and, having opened up the furrows with his deep-sunk plough, he sows in the ground the teeth as he is bid, a man-producing seed.
Ibid., bk 3, ll. 101–5

11 The very abundance of my riches beggars me.
Ibid., bk 3, l. 466

12 I see better and approve it, but I follow the worse.
Ibid., bk 7, l. 20. See BIBLE, NEW TESTAMENT: ROMANS 17.

13 All things are changing; nothing dies ... All things are in a state of flux, and everything is brought into being with a changing nature. Time itself flows on in constant motion, just like a river. For neither the river nor the swift hour can stop its course.
Ibid., bk 15, ll. 165–81. Spoken by Pythagoras.

14 *Tempus edax rerum.*
[O Time, thou great devourer.]
Ibid., bk 15, l. 234

15 And now my work is done, which neither the wrath of Jove, nor fire, nor sword, nor the gnawing tooth of time shall ever be able to undo.
Ibid., bk 15, ll. 871–2

16 By what sweet charm I know not the native land draws all men nor allows them to forget her.
Epistulae Ex Ponto, bk 1, no. 3, l. 35 (from AD 9; *Letters From the Black Sea*)

17 Note too that a faithful study of the liberal arts humanizes character and permits it not to be cruel.
Ibid., bk 2, no. 9, l. 47

18 Even though I lack the strength, yet the will is praiseworthy.
Ibid., bk 3, no. 4, l. 79. See BIBLE, NEW TESTAMENT: MATTHEW 163.

19 Poetry comes fine-spun from a mind at peace.
Tristia, bk 1, no. 1, l. 39 (from AD 9)

20 *Vergilium vidi tantum.*
[Virgil I only saw.]
Ibid., bk 4, no. 10, l. 51

Wilfred Owen
(1893–1918)
British poet

He received the Military Cross as an infantry officer in the First World War, although he was traumatized by the experience of trench warfare. SIEGFRIED SASSOON encouraged him to write and, after Owen's death in action a week before the Armistice, published his poems. YEATS characterized him as 'all blood, dirt and sucked sugar stick'.

1 What passing-bells for these who die as cattle?
Only the monstrous anger of the guns.
'Anthem for Doomed Youth', written 1917, publ. in *The Poems of Wilfred Owen* (ed. Edmund Blunden, 1931)

2 Red lips are not so red
As the stained stones kissed by the English dead.
'Greater Love', written 1917, ibid. Opening lines of poem.

3 If you could hear, at every jolt, the blood
Come gargling from the froth-corrupted lungs,
Bitter as the cud
Of vile, incurable sores on innocent tongues, –
My friend, you would not tell with such high zest
To children ardent for some desperate glory,
The old Lie: Dulce et decorum est
Pro patria mori.
'Dulce et Decorum Est', written 1918, ibid. See HORACE 36.

4 Was it for this the clay grew tall?
O what made fatuous sunbeams toil
To break earth's sleep at all?
'Futility', written 1918, ibid.

5 Courage was mine, and I had mystery,

Wisdom was mine, and I had mastery.
'Strange Meeting', written 1918, ibid.

6 I am the enemy you killed, my friend.
I knew you in this dark; for so you frowned
Yesterday through me as you jabbed and killed.
I parried; but my hands were loath and cold.
Let us sleep now . . .
'Strange Meeting', ibid. Closing lines of poem, of which variant versions exist.

7 Above all I am not concerned with Poetry.
My subject is War, and the pity of War.
The Poetry is in the pity.
Draft preface, written 1918, ibid. The lines were the motto for BENJAMIN BRITTEN's *War Requiem* (1962), which combined Owen's poems with the Latin Mass for the Dead.

8 All a poet can do to-day is warn. That is why the true Poets must be truthful.
Draft preface, ibid.

Cynthia Ozick
(b. 1928)
US author

Her work, deeply rooted in Jewish culture and folklore, has been praised by A. Alvarez for its 'crooked flights of imagination'. Her novels include The Messiah of Stockholm *(1987). She is also an accomplished essayist and writer of short stories.*

1 People who mistake facts for ideas are incomplete thinkers; they are gossips.
'We are the Crazy Lady and Other Feisty Feminist Fables' (1972), repr. in *The First Ms. Reader* (ed. Francine Klagsbrun, 1972)

2 The usefulness of madmen is famous: they demonstrate society's logic flagrantly carried out down to its last scrimshaw scrap.
'The Hole/Birth Catalog' (1972), ibid.

P

Vance Packard
(1914–96)
US author and journalist

Described as 'a blend of amateur sociologist and crusading journalist', he addresses anxieties raised by rapid social change. His most influential work, The Hidden Persuaders *(1957), is a study of the inroads of consumer advertising.*

1 The professional persuaders . . . see us as bundles of day-dreams, misty hidden yearnings, guilt complexes, irrational emotional blockages. We are image lovers given to impulsive and compulsive acts. We annoy them with our seemingly senseless quirks, but we please them with our growing docility in responding to their manipulation of symbols that stir us to action.
The Hidden Persuaders, ch. 1 (1957)

Camille Paglia
(b. 1947)
US author and critic

In Sexual Personae *(1990) and subsequent books, she berates orthodox feminist theory for downplaying the role of eroticism. Her fast-talking, contentious style has alienated many. 'I'm an egomaniac,' she admitted. 'I have no rivals . . . I was born with the killer instinct.'*

1 Men know they are sexual exiles. They wander the earth seeking satisfaction, craving and despising, never content. There is nothing in that anguished motion for women to envy.
Sexual Personae, ch. 1 (1990)

2 Male urination really *is* a kind of accomplishment, an arc of transcendence. A woman merely waters the ground she stands on.
Ibid., ch. 1

3 If civilization had been left in female hands we would still be living in grass huts.
Ibid., ch. 1

4 Out with stereotypes, feminism proclaims. But stereotypes are the west's stunning sexual personae, the vehicles of art's assault against nature. The moment there is imagination, there is myth.
Ibid., ch. 1

5 Popular culture is the new Babylon, into which so much art and intellect now flow. It is our imperial sex theater, supreme temple of the western eye. We live in the age of idols. The pagan past, never dead, flames again in our mystic hierarchies of stardom.
Ibid., ch. 4

6 There is no female Mozart because there is no female Jack the Ripper.
International Herald Tribune 26 April 1991

7 We need a new kind of feminism, one that stresses personal responsibility and is open to art and sex in all their dark, unconsoling mysteries.
Sex, Art, and American Culture, Introduction (1992)

8 Gay men may seek sex without emotion; lesbians often end up in emotion without sex.
Ibid., 'Homosexuality at the Fin de Siècle' (1992)

Marcel Pagnol
(1895–1974)
French dramatist and film director

His plays and films are rooted in his upbringing in Marseille and rural Provence, for example Manon des Sources *(film, 1953). He founded* Cahiers du film *in 1931.*

1 One has to look out for engineers – they begin with sewing machines and end up with the atomic bomb.
Critique des critiques, ch. 3 (1949)

Thomas Paine
(1737–1809)
English-born political theorist and author

Emigrating to Philadelphia in 1774, he became involved in the movement for American independence. His radical ideas, published in Common Sense *(1776), found a wide readership. He subsequently lived in France, where his* Rights of Man *(1791–2) was written in defence of the Revolution, and he was elected to a seat in the National Convention. He died in poverty in New York.*

1 Society in every state is a blessing, but government, even in its best state, is but a necessary evil; in its worst state, an intolerable one. Government, like dress, is the badge of lost innocence; the palaces of kings are built upon the ruins of the bowers of paradise.
Common Sense, ch. 1 (1776)

2 Though we have been wise enough to shut and lock a door against absolute monarchy, we at the

same time have been foolish enough to put the crown in possession of the key.
Ibid., ch. 1

3 Freedom hath been hunted round the globe. Asia and Africa have long expelled her. Europe regards her like a stranger, and England hath given her warning to depart. O! receive the fugitive, and prepare in time an asylum for mankind.
Ibid., ch. 3

4 Suspicion is the companion of mean souls, and the bane of all good society.
Ibid., ch. 4

5 When we are planning for posterity, we ought to remember that virtue is not hereditary.
Ibid., ch. 4

6 These are the times that try men's souls. The summer soldier and the sunshine patriot will, in this crisis, shrink from the service of his country; but he that stands it NOW deserves the love and thanks of man and woman.
The American Crisis, no. 1, Introduction (pamphlet, 1776), repr. in The Writings of Thomas Paine, vol. 1 (ed. Moncure D. Conway, 1894). GEORGE WASHINGTON ordered this paper to be read to his troops on the eve of the Battle of Trenton, New Jersey, 26 December 1776.

7 What we obtain too cheap we esteem too lightly; it is dearness only that gives everything its value.
The American Crisis, no. 1, ibid.

8 Character is much easier kept than recovered.
Ibid., no. 13 (1783)

9 Our citizenship in the United States is our national character. Our citizenship in any particular state is only our local distinction. By the latter we are known at home, by the former to the world. Our great title is AMERICANS – our inferior one varies with the place.
Ibid., no. 13

10 He is not affected by the reality of distress touching his heart, but by the showy resemblance of it striking his imagination. He pities the plumage, but forgets the dying bird.
The Rights of Man, pt 1 (1791). Referring to his political adversary EDMUND BURKE and his essay Reflections on the Revolution in France (1790)

11 To establish any mode to abolish war, however advantageous it might be to nations, would be to take from such government the most lucrative of its branches.
Ibid., pt 1, 'Conclusion'

12 All hereditary government is in its nature tyranny. An heritable crown, or an heritable throne, or by what other fanciful name such things may be called, have no other significant explanation than that mankind are heritable property. To inherit a government is to inherit the people, as if they were flocks and herds.
The Rights of Man, pt 2, ch. 3 (1792)

13 My country is the world, and my religion is to do good.
Ibid., pt 2, ch. 5

14 Every religion is good that teaches man to be good; and I know of none that instructs him to be bad.
Ibid., pt 2, ch. 5. See P. B. SHELLEY 4.

15 The final event to himself has been that as he rose like a rocket, he fell like the stick.
'Letter to the Addressers on the Late Proclamation' (pamphlet, 1792), repr. in The Writings of Thomas Paine, vol. 3 (ed. Moncure D. Conway, 1895). Referring to EDMUND BURKE.

16 A thing moderately good is not so good as it ought to be. Moderation in temper is always a virtue; but moderation in principle is always a vice.
'Letter to the Addressers on the Late Proclamation', ibid., vol. 3

17 I believe in the equality of man; and I believe that religious duties consist in doing justice, loving mercy, and endeavouring to make our fellow-creatures happy.
The Age of Reason, pt 1, ch. 1 (1794)

18 It is necessary to the happiness of man that he be mentally faithful to himself. Infidelity does not consist in believing, or in disbelieving; it consists in professing to believe what he does not believe.
Ibid., pt 1, ch. 1

Ian Paisley
(b. 1926)
Northern Irish politician

Founder in 1951 of the Free Presbyterian Church of Ulster, he is leader of the Democratic Unionist Party, and has been an MP in Westminster since 1970. He is known for his anti-nationalist political stance and fundamentalist religious beliefs.

1 I would rather be British than just.
Quoted in Ulster, ch. 3 (1972) by The Sunday Times Insight Team. The remark was addressed to Bernadette Devlin.

2 I would be quite happy to see the Devil's butter-milk banned from society.
Quoted in the *Irish Times* 14 March 1998. Referring to draught Guinness.

William Paley
(1743–1805)
English theologian

He spent most of his life as a cleric and was the author of numerous text books, of which Natural Theology, or Evidences of the Existence and Attributes of the Deity Collected from the Appearances of Nature *(1802) was the most popular.*

1 Who can refute a sneer?
Principles of Moral and Political Philosophy, vol. 2, bk 5, ch. 9 (1785)

2 Suppose I had found a watch upon the ground, and it should be enquired how the watch happened to be in that place ... the inference, we think, is inevitable; that the watch must have had a maker, that there must have existed, at some time and at some place or other, an artificer or artificers, who formed it for the purpose which we find it actually to answer; who comprehended its construction, and designed its use.
Natural Theology, ch. 1 (1802)

Lord Palmerston
(1784–1865)
English politician and prime minister

Henry John Temple, 3rd Viscount Palmerston. Nicknamed 'Firebrand Palmerston' for his robust defence of British interests, he served three terms as a Whig Foreign Secretary. He later served as Prime Minister 1855–8 and 1859–65.

1 What is merit? The opinion one man entertains of another.
Quoted in 'Shooting Niagara: And After?', sect. 8 (1867) by THOMAS CARLYLE, repr. in *Critical and Miscellaneous Essays*, vol. 5 (1899)

2 We have no eternal allies and we have no perpetual enemies. Our interests are eternal and perpetual, and those interests it is our duty to follow.
Speech in House of Commons, 1 March 1848, in *Hansard*, vol. 97, col. 122

3 Die, my dear doctor! That's the last thing I shall do!
Attributed last words

Emmeline Pankhurst
(1858–1928)
English suffragette

Supported by her daughters Christabel and Sylvia Pankhurst, she founded the Women's Social and Political Union in 1903. Their campaign to obtain the vote for women led to her arrest and imprisonment on several occasions.

1 The argument of the broken window pane is the most valuable argument in modern politics.
Votes for Women February 1912

2 There is something that governments care for far more than human life, and that is the security of property, and so it is through property that we shall strike the enemy ... Be militant each in your own way ... I incite this meeting to rebellion.
Speech at the Albert Hall, London, 17 October 1912, quoted in *My Own Story*, bk 3, ch. 3 (1914)

3 We never went to prison in order to be martyrs. We went there in order that we might obtain the rights of citizenship. We were willing to break laws that we might force men to give us the right to make laws.
Ibid., bk 2, ch. 8

Charlie Parker
(1920–55)
US jazz musician

Nicknamed 'Bird' or 'Yardbird', he was a master alto sax player, composer and bandleader, who, with trumpeter Dizzy Gillespie, helped to create the bebop style of jazz with such recordings as 'Ornithology' (1944–7).

1 Music is your own experience, your own thoughts, your wisdom. If you don't live it, it won't come out of your horn. They teach you there's a boundary line to music. But, man, there's no boundary line to art.
Quoted in *Hear Me Talkin' to Ya*, 'Coda' (ed. Nat Shapiro and Nat Hentoff, 1955)

Dorothy Parker
(1893–1967)
US humorous writer

Described by ALEXANDER WOOLLCOTT *as 'a blend of Little Nell and Macbeth', she became drama critic at* Vanity Fair *in 1917, moving to* Life *soon after with* ROBERT BENCHLEY *and Robert Sherwood. All three became key figures of the Algonquin literary circle in the 1920s. Her popular writings include* Enough Rope *(poetry, 1926) and* Here Lies *(short stories, 1939).*

1 Brevity is the soul of lingerie.

Caption publ. in *Vogue*, 1916, quoted in *While Rome Burns*, 'Our Mrs Parker' (1934) by ALEXANDER WOOLLCOTT. See WILLIAM SHAKESPEARE: HAMLET 58.

2 Where's the man could ease a heart
Like a satin gown?

'The Satin Dress', publ. in *Enough Rope* (1926)

3 Oh, life is a glorious cycle of song,
A medley of extemporanea;
And love is a thing that can never go wrong;
And I am Marie of Roumania.

'Comment', ibid.

4 Four be the things I'd been better without:
Love, curiosity, freckles, and doubt.

'Inventory', ibid.

5 Razors pain you;
Rivers are damp;
Acids stain you;
And drugs cause cramp.
Guns aren't lawful;
Nooses give;
Gas smells awful;
You might as well live.

'Résumé', ibid.

6 Scratch a lover, and find a foe.

'Ballade of a Great Weariness', ibid.

7 Why is it no one ever sent me yet
One perfect limousine, do you suppose?
Ah no, it's always just my luck to get
One perfect rose.

'One Perfect Rose', ibid.

8 Men seldom make passes
At girls who wear glasses.

'News Item', ibid.

9 If, with the literate, I am
Impelled to try an epigram,
I never seek to take the credit;
We all assume that Oscar said it.

'A Pig's-Eye View of Literature', publ. in *Sunset Gun* (1928)

10 Tonstant Weader fwowed up.

New Yorker 20 October 1928, repr. in *The Collected Dorothy Parker*, pt 2 (1973). Closing words of review of *The House at Pooh Corner*, by A. A. MILNE, in Parker's 'Constant Reader' column.

11 Drink, and dance and laugh and lie,
Love the reeling midnight through,

For tomorrow we shall die!
(But, alas, we never do.)

'The Flaw in Paganism', publ. in *Death and Taxes* (1931)

12 How do they know?

Remark on hearing the announcement that CALVIN COOLIDGE had died (1933), quoted in *Writers at Work* (first series, ed. Malcolm Cowley, 1958)

13 *The House Beautiful* is the play lousy.

New Yorker, 1933, ibid. Review of *The House Beautiful* by Channing Pollock.

14 She runs the gamut of emotions from A to B.

Theatre review of *The Lake* (1933), quoted in obituary, *Publishers Weekly* 19 June 1967. Referring to KATHARINE HEPBURN.

15 Excuse my dust.

Suggested epitaph, quoted in *While Rome Burns*, 'Our Mrs Parker' (1934) by ALEXANDER WOOLLCOTT

16 That woman speaks eighteen languages and can't say No in any of them.

Quoted ibid. Of a departing guest.

17 Good work, Mary. We all knew you had it in you.

Quoted ibid. Telegram to a friend (Mrs Robert Sherwood) who had become a mother after a prolonged pregnancy.

18 Sorrow is tranquility remembered in emotion.

'Sentiment', publ. in *Here Lies* (1939). Adapting WILLIAM WORDSWORTH 30.

19 There's a helluva distance between wisecracking and wit. Wit has truth in it; wisecracking is simply calisthenics with words.

Interview in *Writers at Work* (first series, ed. Malcolm Cowley, 1958)

20 Hollywood money isn't money. It's congealed snow, melts in your hand, and there you are.

Ibid.

21 Enjoyed it! One more drink and I'd have been under the host.

Quoted in *The Algonquin Wits* (ed. Robert E. Drennan, 1968). On being asked whether she had enjoyed a party.

22 You can lead a horticulture, but you can't make her think.

Quoted in *You Might As Well Live*, pt 1, ch. 5 (1970) by John Keats. Reply when challenged to make a sentence using the word 'horticulture'.

23 It serves me right for putting all my eggs in one bastard.

Ibid., pt 2, ch. 3. On her abortion.

Lord Parker
(1900–72)
British judge

Hubert Lister, Baron Parker of Waddington. He was made a Lord Justice of Appeal in 1954 and was Lord Chief Justice of England 1958–71.

1 A judge is not supposed to know anything about the facts of life until they have been presented in evidence and explained to him at least three times.
Observer 12 March 1961

Ross Parker
(1914–74)
Hugh Charles
(1907–95)
British songwriters

The two collaborated on songs throughout the Second World War. Hugh Charles also worked with Noel Gay, among others, and later concentrated on theatre productions. See also VERA LYNN 2.

1 There'll always be an England
While there's a country lane,
Wherever there's a cottage small
Beside a field of grain.
'There'll Always Be an England' (song, 1939). Originally performed by BILLY COTTON and his Orchestra.

(Sir) Henry Parkes
(1815–96)
English-born Australian statesman

He emigrated to Sidney in 1839, served in parliament from 1854 and was five times Premier of New South Wales.

1 I have been disappointed in all my expectations of Australia, except as to its wickedness; for it is far more wicked than I have conceived it possible for any place to be, or than it is possible for me to describe to you in England.
Letter, 1 May 1840, publ. in *An Emigrant's Home Letters* (ed. Annie T. Parkes, 1896). The letter was written a year after Parkes arrived as an immigrant in Australia.

C. Northcote Parkinson
(1909–93)
British historian and political scientist

Cyril Northcote Parkinson. He wrote a number of historical, political and economic works, but is best known for Parkin-

son's Law *(1957), a tongue-in-cheek look at businesses and bureaucracies.*

1 Work expands so as to fill the time available for its completion. General recognition of this fact is shown in the proverbial phrase 'It is the busiest man who has time to spare'.
Parkinson's Law or The Pursuit of Progress, 'Parkinson's Law or the Rising Pyramid' (1957). Opening words of book.

2 A committee is organic rather than mechanical in its nature: it is not a structure but a plant. It takes root and grows, it flowers, wilts, and dies, scattering the seed from which other committees will bloom in their turn.
Ibid., 'Directors and Councils'

3 The Law of Triviality … briefly stated, it means that the time spent on any item of the agenda will be in inverse proportion to the sum involved.
Ibid., 'High Finance or the Point of Vanishing Interest'

4 The man who is denied the opportunity of taking decisions of importance begins to regard as important the decisions he is allowed to take.
Ibid., 'Pension Point or the Age of Retirement'

5 Expenditure rises to meet income.
The Law and the Profits, ch. 1 (1960). Opening sentence of book.

6 Expansion means complexity, and complexity decay.
In-laws and Outlaws, 'The Third Law' (1962)

Michael Parkinson
(b. 1935)
British journalist and broadcaster

Renowned for his smooth style and professional composure, he hosted the television chat show Parkinson *(1971–82 and from 1998), and was co-founder and presenter of* TV-am *(1983–4). He has also written widely on sport.*

1 The kind of show I do consists of two consenting adults performing unnatural acts in public.
Sunday Times 27 December 1987. On his new chat show, *One to One*, on Yorkshire TV 1987–8.

Norman Parkinson
(1913–90)
British fashion photographer

Originally Ronald William Parkinson Smith. For fifty years he was one of Britain's most famous fashion and portrait photographers, noted for his official portraits of the royal family.

1 I could never bear to be buried with people to whom I had not been introduced.
Quoted in obituary in the *Guardian* 16 February 1990

Charles Parnell
(1846–91)
Irish politician

He became an MP in 1875 and was elected President of the Irish National Land League (1879). From 1886 he supported GLADSTONE's *Home Rule bill. He was forced to retire from politics in 1890 following the exposure of his adulterous affair with Kitty O'Shea.*

1 No man has a right to fix the boundary of the march of a nation; no man has a right to say to his country, 'Thus far shalt thou go and no further.'
Speech in Cork, 21 January 1885, quoted in *The Times* 22 January 1885

2 My policy is not a policy of conciliation, but a policy of retaliation.
Attributed remark, 1877, referring to his parliamentary tactics in the House of Commons

Matthew Parris
(b. 1949)
British politician and journalist

Since his parliamentary career as a Conservative MP (1979–86), he has been presenter of LWT's Weekend World *(1986–8), parliamentary sketch-writer for* The Times *and columnist for the* Spectator.

1 Being an MP feeds your vanity and starves your self-respect.
The Times 9 February 1994

2 Since the dawn of man every politician has been torn between a wish to say something memorable, and a terror of saying something which is remembered.
Introduction to *Read My Lips* (1996) by Matthew Parris and Phil Mason

Elsie Clews Parsons
(1875–1941)
US anthropologist and feminist critic

Dubbed 'the Left's favourite anthropologist', she was the first woman president of the American Anthropological Association (1940–1). Her writings include Fear and Conventionality *(1914).*

1 Some day there may be a 'masculism' movement to allow men to act 'like women'.
The Journal of a Feminist, April 1914 (1994). Narrated by Cynthia.

Talcott Parsons
(1902–79)
US sociologist

His principal works, The Structure of Social Action *(1937) and* The Social System *(1951), proposed a functionalist view of society that prevailed in US sociology until the 1960s.*

1 Science is intimately integrated with the whole social structure and cultural tradition. They mutually support one other – only in certain types of society can science flourish, and conversely without a continuous and healthy development and application of science such a society cannot function properly.
The Social System, ch. 8 (1951)

Tony Parsons
(b. 1955)
British journalist and novelist

A 'street-wise' writer on popular culture, he was, at the age of eighteen, a leader writer on the New Musical Express *and one of the first champions of punk. His successful novels include* Man and Boy *(1999) and* One for My Baby *(2001).*

1 The trouble with the working class today is that they are such peasants. Something has died in them – a sense of grace, all feelings of community, their intelligence, decency and wit. Socialism is finished here because it is no longer possible to feel sentimental about the workers.
Dispatches from the Front Line of Popular Culture, 'The Tattooed Jungle' (1994)

2 Begging defaces the city, degrades the spirit. It dehumanises you as well as them; it brutalises us all. You learn to walk past these people, you have to, and it makes it easier to turn away from the truly needy. These professional leeches … harden your heart, put callouses on your soul. They make every cry for help seem like junk mail.
'Ibid., 'Street Trash'

3 Pornography is many things to many men. But it is never adult. Pornography exists in a state of perpetual adolescence … Planet porn is Disneyland for habitual monkey-spankers.
GQ January 2000

Frances Partridge

(1900–2004)

British translator and author

She was for years at the centre of the Bloomsbury literary set, whose exploits she portrayed in her memoirs Love in Bloomsbury *(1981) and* A Bloomsbury Album *(1987). She was a literary translator for much of her life.*

1 It is a purely relative matter where one draws the plimsoll-line of condemnation, and . . . if you find the whole of humanity falls below it you have simply made a mistake and drawn it too high. And are probably below it yourself.

Journal entry, 3 September 1959, publ. in *Julia,* ch. 17 (1983)

Blaise Pascal

(1623–62)

French scientist and philosopher

A child prodigy, he invented a calculating machine (1647), followed by the barometer and hydraulic press. After entering a Jansenist convent he wrote Lettres Provinciales *(1656–7) and* Pensées *(1670), classics of devotional thought.*

1 I have only made this [letter] longer because I have not had the time to make it shorter.

Lettres Provinciales, no. 16 (1657; *Provincial Letters*)

2 Men despise religion. They hate it and are afraid it may be true.

Pensées (1670), no. 12 (transl. A. J. Krailsheimer, 1966); no. 187 (transl. L. Brunschvicg, 1909)

3 *Vanity of science.* Knowledge of physical science will not console me for ignorance of morality in time of affliction, but knowledge of morality will always console me for ignorance of physical science.

Ibid., no. 23 (Brunschvicg, no. 67)

4 Habit is a second nature that destroys the first. But what is nature? Why is habit not natural? I am very much afraid that nature itself is only a first habit, just as habit is a second nature.

Ibid., no. 126 (Brunschvicg, no. 93)

5 I have often said that the sole cause of a man's unhappiness is that he does not know how to stay quietly in his room.

Ibid., no. 136 (Brunschvicg, no. 139)

6 *On mourra seul.*
[We shall die alone.]

Ibid., no. 151 (Brunschvicg, no. 211)

7 We run heedlessly into the abyss after putting something in front of us to stop us seeing it.

Ibid., no. 166 (Brunschvicg, no. 183)

8 For, after all, what is man in nature? A nothing compared to the infinite, a whole compared to the nothing, a middle point between all and nothing.

Ibid., no. 199 (Brunschvicg, no. 72)

9 Man is only a reed, the weakest in nature; but he is a thinking reed.

Ibid., no. 200 (Brunschvicg, no. 347)

10 The eternal silence of these infinite spaces fills me with dread.

Ibid., no. 201 (Brunschvicg, no. 206)

11 It is superstitious to put one's hopes in formalities, but arrogant to refuse to submit to them.

Ibid., no. 364 (Brunschvicg, no. 249)

12 Had Cleopatra's nose been shorter, the whole face of the world would have changed.

Ibid., no. 413 (Brunschvicg, no. 162)

13 'Either God is or he is not.' But to which view shall we be inclined? . . . Let us weigh the gain and the loss involved in calling heads that God exists. Let us assess the two cases; if you win, you win everything, if you lose, you lose nothing. Do not hesitate then; wager that he does exist.

Ibid., no. 418 (Brunschvicg, no. 233). Known as 'Pascal's wager'.

14 *Le coeur a ses raisons que la raison ne connaît point.*
[The heart has its reasons of which reason knows nothing.]

Ibid., no. 423 (Brunschvicg, no. 277)

15 It is the heart which perceives God and not the reason. That is what faith is: God perceived by the heart, not by the reason.

Ibid., no. 424 (Brunschvicg, no. 278)

16 The more intelligent one is, the more men of originality one finds. Ordinary people find no difference between men.

Ibid., no. 510 (Brunschvicg, no. 7)

17 To have no time for philosophy is to be a true philosopher.

Ibid., no. 513 (Brunschvicg, no. 4)

18 We like security: we like the pope to be infallible in matters of faith, and grave doctors to be so in moral questions so that we can feel reassured.

Ibid., no. 516 (Brunschvicg, no. 880)

19 *Le* moi *est haïssable.*
[The *self* is hateful.]
Ibid., no. 597 (Brunschvicg, no. 455)

20 Man is obviously made for thinking. Therein lies all his dignity and his merit; and his whole duty is to think as he ought.
Ibid., no. 620 (Brunschvicg, no. 146)

21 When we see a natural style we are quite amazed and delighted, because we expected to see an author and find a man.
Ibid., no. 675 (Brunschvicg, no. 29)

22 I maintain that, if everyone knew what others said about him, there would not be four friends in the world.
Ibid., no. 792 (Brunschvicg, no. 101)

23 Men never do evil so fully and cheerfully as when we do it out of conscience.
Ibid., no. 813 (Brunschvicg, no. 895)

24 The last thing one discovers in composing a work is what to put first.
Ibid. no. 976 (Brunschvicg, no. 19)

25 FIRE.
God of Abraham, God of Isaac, God of Jacob,
not of the philosophers or of the learned.
Certainty. Certainty. Feeling. Joy. Peace.
The 'Memorial', publ. in *Neither Angel nor Beast; the Life and Work of Blaise Pascal*, pt 1, ch. 4 (1986) by Francis X. J. Coleman. Writing found stitched to Pascal's coat after his death.

Boris Pasternak
(1890–1960)
Russian poet, novelist and translator

He began his literary career as a poet and author of short fiction. His reputation in the West was established with his only novel Dr Zhivago (1957), an epic of the Russian Revolution and its aftermath that was banned in the Soviet Union.

1 We live in days to come, I tell them firmly,
And share one lot in common now. If crippled,
No matter! Stay. We are in fact run over
By the New Man in the wagon of his Plan.
'When I Grow Weary', publ. in *Second Birth* (1932)

2 Yet the order of the acts is planned
And the end of the way inescapable.
I am alone; all drowns in the Pharisees' hypocrisy.
To live your life is not as simple as to cross a field.
'Hamlet', st. 4 (1954), repr. in *Dr Zhivago*, 'Zhivago's Poems' (1957). The last line is a Russian proverb.

3 Snow swept over the earth,
Swept it from end to end.
The candle on the table burned,
The candle burned.
'Winter Night' (1954), ibid.

4 My soul, you are a mourner
Of all where I survive.
You are a mausoleum
Of those tortured alive.
'My Soul' (1957), repr. in *Modern Russian Poetry* (ed. Vladimir Markov and Merrill Sparks, 1966)

5 What is history? Its beginning is that of the centuries of systematic work devoted to the solution of the enigma of death, so that death itself may eventually be overcome. That is why people write symphonies, and why they discover mathematical infinity and electromagnetic waves.
Doctor Zhivago, pt 1, ch. 1, sect. 5 (1957). Spoken by Nikolay Nikolayevich.

6 Man is born to live, not to prepare for life. Life itself – the gift of life – is such a breathtakingly serious thing!
Zhivago, ibid., pt 2, ch. 9, sect. 14

7 No deep and strong feeling, such as we may come across here and there in the world, is unmixed with compassion. The more we love, the more the object of our love seems to us to be a victim.
Ibid., pt 2, ch. 12, sect. 7

8 Most people experience love, without noticing that there is anything remarkable about it.
Ibid., pt 2, ch. 13, sect. 10

9 I don't like people who have never fallen or stumbled. Their virtue is lifeless and it isn't of much value. Life hasn't revealed its beauty to them.
Zhivago, ibid., pt 2, ch. 13, sect. 12

10 Everything established, settled, everything to do with home and order and the common round, has crumbled into dust and been swept away in the general upheaval and reorganization of the whole of society. The whole human way of life has been destroyed and ruined. All that's left is the bare, shivering human soul, stripped to the last shred, the naked force of the human psyche for which nothing has changed because it was always cold and shivering and reaching out to its nearest neighbour, as cold and lonely as itself.
Lara, ibid., pt 2, ch. 13, sect. 13. Describing life in communist Russia.

11 It is no longer possible for lyric poetry to express the immensity of our experience. Life has grown too cumbersome, too complicated. We have acquired values which are best expressed in prose.
Interview in *Writers at Work* (second series, ed. George Plimpton, 1963)

Louis Pasteur
(1822–95)
French chemist

A pioneer in biochemistry, he proved that fermentation and disease were caused by micro-organisms and introduced pasteurization. He was the first to use vaccine against rabies, anthrax and chicken cholera.

1 There does not exist a category of science to which one can give the name applied science. There are science and the applications of science, bound together as the fruit of the tree which bears it.
'Pourquoi la France n'a pas trouvé d'hommes supérieurs au moment du péril', publ. in *Revue Scientifique* (1871)

2 The universe is asymmetric and I am persuaded that life, as it is known to us, is a direct result of the asymmetry of the universe or of its indirect consequences. The universe is asymmetric.
Comptes rendus de l'Académie des Sciences 1 June 1874, repr. in *Works*, vol. 1

Walter Pater
(1839–94)
English essayist and critic

His Studies in the History of the Renaissance *(1873) and his doctrine of 'art for art's sake' had a profound influence on the development of the Aesthetic Movement.*

1 She is older than the rocks among which she sits; like the vampire, she has been dead many times, and learned the secrets of the grave.
Studies in the History of the Renaissance, 'Leonardo da Vinci' (1873). Referring to the Mona Lisa.

2 All art constantly aspires towards the condition of music.
Ibid., 'The School of Giorgione'

3 Not the fruit of experience, but experience itself, is the end.
Ibid., 'Conclusion'

4 To burn always with this hard, gemlike flame, to maintain this ecstasy, is success in life.
Ibid., 'Conclusion'. Referring to 'the focus where the greatest number of vital forces unite in their purest energy'.

Andrew Barton 'Banjo' Paterson
(1864–1941)
Australian poet and journalist

He contributed to the Sydney Bulletin *under the name of 'The Banjo'. His verse collection* The Man from Snowy River *(1895) secured his reputation as Australia's pre-eminent folk poet, while his poem 'Waltzing Matilda' has become the unofficial national anthem of Australia.*

1 Oh, there once was a swagman camped in a Billabong,
Under the shade of a Coolabah tree;
And he sang as he looked at his old billy boiling,
'Who'll come a-waltzing Matilda with me?'
'Waltzing Matilda' (song), written 1895, publ. in *Saltbush Bill, J.P., and Other Verses* (1917)

Coventry Patmore
(1823–96)
English poet

His major work The Angel in the House *(1854–62) dealt with married love. After the death of his first wife in 1862, he converted to Catholicism and wrote on mystical and religious topics.*

1 'I saw you take his kiss!' ''Tis true.'
'O, modesty!' ''Twas strictly kept:
He thought me asleep; at least I knew
He thought I thought he thought I slept.'
'The Kiss', publ. in *The Angel in the House*, bk 2, 'The Espousal', canto 8 (1856)

2 A woman is a foreign land,
Of which, though there he settle young,
A man will ne'er quite understand
The customs, politics, and tongue.
'The Foreign Land', ibid., bk 2, 'The Espousal', canto 9

Alan Paton
(1903–88)
South African author

He is best known for his first novel Cry, the Beloved Country *(1948) which brought international attention to the issue of apartheid. He was a founder of the Liberal Party of South Africa (1953) and remained its president until 1968.*

1 Cry, the Beloved Country.
Title of novel (1948)

2 I have one great fear in my heart, that one day

when they are turned to loving, they will find we are turned to hating.

Cry, the Beloved Country, bk 1, ch. 7 (1948). Spoken by Msimangu.

Saint Patrick

(5th century)

Patron saint and Apostle of Ireland

Of Romano-British parentage, he experienced a religious conversion while a slave in Ireland. After escaping to Gaul, he was ordained and returned to Ireland (c. 432), where he is credited with the legend of the shamrock as a symbol of the Trinity and with driving snakes from Ireland.

1 Christ ever with me, Christ before me, Christ behind me,
Christ within me, Christ beneath me, Christ above me,
Christ to my right side, Christ to my left side,
Christ in his breadth, Christ in his length, Christ in depth,
Christ in the heart of every man who thinks of me,
Christ in the mouth of every man who speaks to me,
Christ in every eye that sees me,
Christ in every ear that hears me.

'St Patrick's Breastplate', attributed. See HYMNS AND CAROLS 78

Tom Paulin

(b. 1949)

Brtish poet

Although born in Leeds, he is known as an Ulster poet, whose vision of a non-sectarian Ireland is expressed in such works as A State of Justice *(1977) and* The Liberty Tree *(1983).*

1 I live in the half-light
of a strange
shivering translation
where the kingdom of letters
is like the postal system
of a frozen state
and your last question
slips through like code.

'What Kind of Formation are B Specials?', publ. in *The Liberty Tree* (1983)

2 Maybe the true taste of it
is knowing the limits of your own fraudulence

'Middle Age', publ. in *Walking a Line* (1994)

3 His work seems endlessly subtle and intelligent, many of his cadences are perfect, but there is a malignity in it which is terrifying. It's so firm and so quiet, because like a true politician Eliot never apologizes and he never explains.

Of T. S. ELIOT, in 'T. S. Eliot and Anti-Semitism' (review of Anthony Julius, *T. S. Eliot, Anti-Semitism and Literary Form*, 1996), repr. in *Writing to the Moment* (1996). 'I can think of no other modern writer whose prejudices have been treated with such tolerance,' wrote Paulin of Eliot.

Cesare Pavese

(1908–50)

Italian poet, novelist and translator

His translations helped to popularize modern English and American literature in Italy. His novels include The Moon and the Bonfires *(1950) and* The House on the Hill *(1961). Regarded by some as an anti-Fascist hero, he considered himself a coward and grew disillusioned with politics.*

1 Living is like working out a long addition sum, and if you make a mistake in the first two totals you will never find the right answer. It means involving oneself in a complicated chain of circumstances.

Journal entry, 5 May 1936, publ. in *This Business of Living: Diary 1935–1950* (1952, transl. 1961)

2 Perfect behaviour is born of complete indifference.

Journal entry, 21 February 1940, ibid.

3 Artists are the monks of the bourgeois state.

Journal entry, 25 July 1940, ibid.

4 At great periods you have always felt, deep within you, the temptation to commit suicide. *You gave yourself to it*, breached your own defences. You were a child. The idea of suicide was a protest against life; by dying, you would escape this longing for death.

Journal entry, 1 January 1950, ibid. Suicide was a continuing theme in Pavese's diaries. 'No one ever lacks a good reason for suicide,' he wrote in 1938. He took his own life in a Turin hotel, shortly after being awarded the Strega Prize.

5 I have knocked about the world enough to know that one lot of flesh and blood is as good as another. But that's why you get tired and try to put down roots. To find somewhere where you belong so that you are worth more than the usual round of the seasons and last a bit longer.

The Moon and the Bonfires, ch. 1 (1950). Spoken by the narrator (Anguilla).

6 When they're dealing with the dead, priests are always right.

Ibid., ch. 12

Jeremy Paxman
(b. 1950)
British television presenter and journalist

Famous for his probing and abrasive style on BBC2's News-night, he once asked MICHAEL HOWARD *the same question thirteen times in succession. He has also authored reflections on British society, for example* The English *(1998).*

1 The BBC is rather like a cross between the Church of England and the Post Office.
Friends in High Places, ch. 4 (1990)

2 It's very difficult to remain calm when you're listening to someone talk complete bollocks.
Quoted in the *Observer* 6 April 1997

Cynthia Payne
(b. 1934)
British housewife and hostess

Revelations about her suburban 'vicarage tea-parties with sex thrown in' led to a court case and prison sentence in 1980, and formed the basis of the film Personal Services *(1987).*

1 To me it's just like having a cup of tea. After two abortions I am not particularly interested in sex, but I know it makes other people happy.
The Times 4 February 1987. Remark after being acquitted of running a brothel in Streatham, South London.

John Howard Payne
(1791–1852)
US playwright, actor and songwriter

He wrote over fifty plays, but is remembered only for the song 'Home Sweet Home' (1823). He also played on the London stage.

1 Mid pleasures and palaces though we may roam,
Be it ever so humble, there's no place like home;
A charm from the skies seems to hallow us there,
Which, seek through the world, is ne'er met with
    elsewhere.
Home, home, sweet, sweet home!
There's no place like home! there's no place like
    home!
'Home, Sweet Home' (song), from the operetta *Clari or The Maid of Milan* (1823)

Octavio Paz
(1914–98)
Mexican poet and essayist

Among his poetry collections are Eagle or Sun? *(1951) and* Salamandra *(1962), which includes the long poem 'Sal'. His most important prose work is* The Labyrinth of Solitude *(1950), an analysis of Mexican culture and history. He served as a diplomat 1945–68.*

1 Man, even man debased by the neocapitalism and pseudosocialism of our time, is a marvellous being because he sometimes *speaks*. Language is the mark, the sign, not of his fall but of his original innocence. Through the Word we may regain the lost kingdom and recover powers we possessed in the far-distant past.
Alternating Current, 'André Breton or the Quest of the Beginning' (1967)

2 Art is an invention of aesthetics, which in turn is an invention of philosophers ... What we call art is a game.
Ibid., 'André Breton or the Quest of the Beginning'

3 To read a poem is to hear it with our eyes; to hear it is to see it with our ears.
Ibid., 'Recapitulations'

4 Social criticism begins with grammar and the re-establishing of meanings.
The Other Mexico: Critique of the Pyramid, 'Development and Other Mirages' (1972)

5 Wisdom lies neither in fixity nor in change, but in the dialectic between the two.
The Times 8 June 1989

Thomas Love Peacock
(1785–1866)
English author

He is known for his prose satires, such as Headlong Hall *(1816) and* Nightmare Abbey *(1818), which he himself called 'comic romances', relying on witty dialogue rather than character or plot.*

1 Better vexation than stagnation: marriage may often be a stormy lake, but celibacy is almost always a muddy horsepond.
Melincourt, ch. 7 (1817). Spoken by Sir Telegraph Paxarett.

2 The waste of plenty is the resource of scarcity.
Ibid., ch. 24

3 The mountain sheep are sweeter,
But the valley sheep are fatter;
We therefore deemed it meeter
To carry off the latter.
The Misfortunes of Elphin, 'The War-song of Dinas Vawr' (1829)

4 Respectable means rich, and decent means poor. I should die if I heard my family called decent.
Crotchet Castle, ch. 3 (1831). Spoken by Lady Clarinda.

5 Ancient sculpture is the true school of modesty. But where the Greeks had modesty, we have cant; where they had poetry, we have cant; where they had patriotism, we have cant; where they had anything that exalts, delights, or adorns humanity, we have nothing but cant, cant, cant.
Mr Crotchet, ibid., ch. 7

6 A book that furnishes no quotations is, *me judice*, no book – it is a plaything.
Dr Folliot, ibid., ch. 9

Mervyn Peake
(1911–68)
British author and illustrator

His fantasy trilogy, Titus Groan *(1946),* Gormenghast *(1950), and* Titus Alone *(1959), became a cult classic. He also wrote verse and illustrated. His ambition, he declared, was to 'create arabesques, abstracts, of thrilling colour, worlds on their own, landscapes and roofscapes and skyscapes peopled with hierophants and lords'.*

1 They resemble rubber, your ladyship, ha, ha, ha. Just a core of india-rubber, with an elastic centre. Oh yes, they are. Very, very much so. Resilience is no word for it – oh dear me, no. Every ounce, a bounce, ha, ha, ha! Every ounce, a bounce.
Titus Groan, 'Titus is Christened' (1946). Doctor Prunesquallor describing babies to the Countess of Groan.

2 There is a kind of laughter that sickens the soul. Laughter when it is out of control: when it screams and stamps its feet, and sets the bells jangling in the next town. Laughter in all its ignorance and cruelty. Laughter with the seed of Satan in it.
Sometime, Never, 'Boy in Darkness' (1956)

3 Each day I live in a glass room
Unless I break it with the thrusting
Of my senses and pass through
The splintered walls to the great landscape.
'Each Day I Live in a Glass Room', publ. in *A Reverie of Bone* (1967)

Norman Vincent Peale
(1898–1993)
US clergyman and author

He helped establish the American Foundation of Religion and Psychiatry next to the church where he was a minister in New York (1932–84), publishing his insights in his bestselling books, notably The Power of Positive Thinking *(1952).*

1 The Power of Positive Thinking.
Title of book (1952)

2 One of the greatest tragedies of the average person is the tendency to spend our whole lives perfecting our faults.
The Power of Positive Thinking, ch. 15 (1952)

Patrick Henry Pearse
(1879–1916)
Irish nationalist leader

He joined the Irish Republican Brotherhood in 1915 and was appointed Commander-in-Chief of the 1916 Easter Rising, when he was proclaimed President of a provisional Irish government. He was shot after the failure of the Rising.

1 Life springs from death and from the graves of patriot men and women spring living nations. The Defenders of this Realm have worked well in secret and in the open. They think that they have pacified Ireland. They think that they have pacified half of us and intimidated the other half. They think that they have foreseen everything, think that they have provided against everything; but the fools, the fools, the fools! – they have left us our Fenian dead, and while Ireland holds these graves, Ireland unfree shall never be at peace.
Graveside oration, 1 August 1915, quoted in *Patrick Pearse: The Triumph of Failure*, 'Politics' (1977) by Ruth Dudley Edwards. The last part of this speech was incorporated into SEAN O'CASEY's *The Plough and the Stars*, Act 2 (1926)

Hesketh Pearson
(1887–1964)
British biographer

Having been a successful actor and theatre director, he turned to biography in 1931. His subjects included GILBERT AND SULLIVAN *(1935),* GEORGE BERNARD SHAW *(1942) and* BENJAMIN DISRAELI *(1951).*

1 Misquotation is, in fact, the pride and privilege of the learned. A widely-read man never quotes accurately, for the rather obvious reason that he has read too widely.
Common Misquotations, Introduction (1934). 'Misquotations,' Pearson wrote, 'are the only quotations that are never misquoted.'

William Penn

(1644–1718)

English religious leader

A Quaker from 1666, he was imprisoned four times for his preaching and pamphleteering. He travelled in Holland and Germany, and in 1682 founded Pennsylvania as a haven of religious toleration.

1 No pain, no palm; no thorns, no throne; no gall, no glory; no cross, no crown.
No Cross, No Crown (pamphlet, 1669)

2 They have a right to censure that have a heart to help.
Some Fruits of Solitude, pt 1, no. 46 (1693)

3 It is a reproach to religion and government to suffer so much poverty and excess.
Ibid., pt 1, no. 52

4 Men are generally more careful of the breed of their horses and dogs than of their children.
Ibid., pt 1, no. 85. See PRINCESS MICHAEL 1.

5 Truth often suffers more by the heat of its defenders than from the arguments of its opposers.
Ibid., pt 2, no. 142

6 Have a care therefore where there is more sail than ballast.
Ibid., pt 3, no. 260

7 Let the people think they govern and they will be governed.
Ibid., pt 4, no. 337

8 *Method* goes far to prevent trouble in business: for it makes the task easy, hinders confusion, saves abundance of time, and instructs those that have business depending, both what to do and what to hope.
Ibid., pt 4, no. 403

9 Much reading is an oppression of the mind, and extinguishes the natural candle, which is the reason of so many senseless scholars in the world.
Advice to His Children (1699)

Samuel Pepys

(1633–1703)

English diarist

His Diary (1660–9), written in code and not deciphered until 1825, presents a vivid picture of contemporary life. He became Secretary to the Admiralty in 1672 but lost his post in 1679 through alleged complicity in the Popish Plot. He was reinstated in 1684, when he also became President of the Royal Society.

1 And so to bed.
Journal entry, 20 April 1660 and *passim*, publ. in *The Diary of Samuel Pepys* (ed. Robert Latham and William Matthews, 1977–83)

2 I went out to Charing Cross to see Major-General Harrison hanged, drawn and quartered – which was done there – he looking as cheerful as any man could do in that condition.
Journal entry, 13 October 1660, ibid. Thomas Harrison was one of the regicides responsible for the execution of CHARLES I. It was said that Harrison met his death with courage, making a final speech on the scaffold: 'God hath covered my head many times in the day of battle. By God I have leapt over a wall, by God I have run through a troop, and by God I will go through this death, and he will make it easy.'

3 A good honest and painful sermon.
Journal entry, 17 March 1661, ibid.

4 But Lord! to see the absurd nature of Englishmen, that cannot forbear laughing and jeering at everything that looks strange.
Journal entry, 27 November 1662, ibid.

5 My wife . . . poor wretch.
Journal entry, 18 September 1662 and *passim*, ibid.

6 Find myself £43 worse than I was the last month . . . chiefly arisen from my layings-out in clothes for myself and wife; viz., for her, about £12, and for myself, £55 or thereabouts.
Journal entry, 31 October 1663

7 I saw a dead corpse in a coffin lie in the close unburied – and watch is constantly kept there, night and day, to keep the people in – the plague making us cruel as dogs to one another.
Journal entry, 4 September 1665, ibid.

8 Strange to see how a good dinner and feasting reconciles everybody.
Journal entry, 9 November 1665, ibid.

9 Saw a wedding in the church . . . Strange, to see what delight we married people have to see these poor fools decoyed into our condition, every man and wife gazing and smiling at them.
Journal entry, 25 December 1665, ibid.

10 God forgive me, I do still see that my nature is not to be quite conquered, but will esteem pleasure above all things; though, yet in the middle of it, it hath reluctancy after my business, which is neglected by my following my pleasure. However,

music and women I cannot but give way to, whatever my business is.
Journal entry, 9 March 1666, ibid.

11 The truth is, I do indulge myself a little the more in pleasure, knowing that this is the proper age of my life to do it; and, out of my observation that most men that do thrive in the world do forget to take pleasure during the time that they are getting their estate but reserve that till they have got one, and then it is too late for them to enjoy it with any pleasure.
Journal entry, 10 March 1666, ibid.

12 A most horrid malicious bloody flame . . . It made me weep to see it.
Journal entry, 2 September 1666, ibid. Referring to the Great Fire of London.

13 But it is pretty to see what money will do.
Journal entry, 21 March 1667, ibid.

14 I find my wife hath something in her gizzard, that only waits an opportunity of being provoked to bring up; but I will not, for my content-sake, give it.
Journal entry, 17 June 1668, ibid.

15 And so I betake myself to that course, which is almost as much as to see myself go into my grave – for which, and all the discomforts that will accompany my being blind, the good God prepare me!
Journal entry, 31 May 1669, ibid.

S. J. Perelman
(1904–79)
US humorist

Sidney Joseph Perelman. Describing himself as 'button cute, rapier keen, wafer-thin and pauper-poor', he contributed regular articles to the New Yorker. *His Hollywood screenplays included* Monkey Business *(1931) and* Horse Feathers *(1932) for the Marx Brothers.*

1 There is nothing like a good, painstaking survey full of decimal points and guarded generalizations to put a glaze like a Sung vase on your eyeball.
Keep It Crisp (1946)

2 English life, while very pleasant, is rather bland. I expected kindness and gentility and I found it, but there is such a thing as too much couth.
Quoted in the *Observer* 24 September 1971

Shimon Peres
(b. 1923)
Polish-born Israeli politician and prime minister

Originally Shimon Perski. In 1994, he shared the Nobel Peace Prize with Itzhak Rabin and YASSER ARAFAT *for helping to bring about the Israel-PLO peace accord. He was Labour Prime Minister 1984–6 and 1995–6 and Deputy Prime Minister 2001–3.*

1 Television has made dictatorship impossible, but democracy unbearable.
Quoted in the *Financial Times* 31 January 1995

Gabriel Péri
(d. 1942)
French Communist deputy

1 I will soon be going out to shape all the singing tomorrows.
Letter written shortly before his execution by the Germans, July 1942, quoted in the *New York Times* 11 April 1943

Pericles
(c. 495–429 BC)
Athenian statesman

The pre-eminent Athenian statesman and apologist for democracy, he presided over the Golden Age of Athens and commissioned the building of the Parthenon in 447 BC. He built up Athenian sea-power as a bulwark against Sparta in the Peloponnesian War (431–404 BC).

1 Our love of what is beautiful does not lead to extravagance; our love of the things of the mind does not make us soft.
Funeral oration, Athens, 430 BC, quoted in *History of the Peloponnesian War*, bk 2, sect. 40 by THUCYDIDES (transl. Rex Warner)

2 They won praises that never grow old, the most splendid of sepulchres – not the sepulchre in which their bodies are laid, but where their glory remains eternal in men's minds . . . For famous men have the whole earth as their memorial.
Ibid., bk 2, sect. 43

3 Happiness depends on being free, and freedom depends on being courageous.
Ibid., bk 2, sect. 43

Anthony Perkins

(1932–92)

US screen actor

He specialized in roles as a troubled young man before achieving international fame as Norman Bates in the film Psycho *(1960). Later films include* Catch-22 *(1970).*

1 A boy's best friend is his mother.

Psycho (film, 1960, screenplay by Joseph Stefano based on novel by Robert Bloch, directed by ALFRED HITCHCOCK). Spoken by Norman Bates (Anthony Perkins).

2 We all go a little mad sometimes.

Norman Bates (Anthony Perkins), ibid.

Carl Perkins

(1932–98)

US country and rock musician

His hit 'Blue Suede Shoes' (1956), a blend of black beat and country, became the anthem of rockabilly music. His songs were recorded by The Beatles, and he enjoyed periodic revivals of interest.

1 It's one for the money,
Two for the show,
Three to get ready,
Now go, cat, go!
But don't you step on my Blue Suede Shoes.
You can do anything but lay off my Blue Suede
  Shoes.

'Blue Suede Shoes' (song, 1956). A million-seller, Perkins' recording was eclipsed by the cover released shortly afterwards by ELVIS PRESLEY.

Eva Perón

(1919–52)

Argentinian politician

An actress before marrying JUAN PERÓN *(1945), 'Evita', as she was popularly known, became his chief adviser when he was elected President in 1946. She founded the Peronista Feminist Party in 1949 and undertook considerable work for the poor, among whom she was idolized. See also* TIM RICE 1.

1 Almsgiving tends to perpetuate poverty; aid does away with it once and for all. Almsgiving leaves a man just where he was before. Aid restores him to society as an individual worthy of all respect and not as a man with a grievance. Almsgiving is the generosity of the rich; social aid levels up social inequalities. Charity separates the rich from the poor; aid raises the needy and sets him on the same level with the rich.

'My Labour in the Field of Social Aid', speech to the American Congress of Industrial Medicine, 5 December 1949

2 Never abandon the poor – they are the only ones who know how to be loyal.

Quoted in *Evita: An Intimate Portrait of Eva Perón* (1997) by Tomás de Elia and Juan Pablo Queiroz. Spoken to JUAN PERÓN, 25 July 1952, the day before her death.

3 I will come again, and I will be millions.

Evita: The Real Lives of Eva Perón, Epilogue (1996) by Nicholas Fraser and Marysa Navarro

Juan Perón

(1895–1974)

Argentinian politician

Elected President in 1946, he won the support of the masses through a programme of social reforms known as 'justicialismo'. He was overthrown and went into exile in 1955, returning to power in 1973.

1 I never killed anybody. Nobody died with his shoes on.

Quoted in *Eva Perón*, Epilogue (1978) by John Barnes

Jimmy Perry

(b. 1923)

British scriptwriter

With David Croft he was the scriptwriter and producer of over eighty episodes of the comedy series Dad's Army *for BBC television (1968–77).*

1 Who do you think you are kidding, Mister Hitler? If you think we're on the run?

'Who do you think you are kidding, Mister Hitler' (theme song of *Dad's Army*, BBC television, 1968–77), written with Derek Taverner and sung by BUD FLANAGAN

2 It Ain't 'Alf 'Ot, Mum!

Title of comedy series on BBC television (1976–81, written by Jimmy Perry and David Croft)

Persius

(34–62)

Roman satirist

Aulus Persius Flaccus. Influenced by Stoicism, he was the author of six satires, all published posthumously.

1 The belly is the teacher of art and the liberal bestower of wit.

Satires, Prologue, l. 10

2 Is your knowledge
Nothing unless another person knows you know?
Satires, no. 1, l. 27

3 Nothing can be born of nothing,
nothing can be resolved into nothing.
Satires, no. 3, l. 83

4 Why, like the hindmost chariot wheels art
   cursed
Still to be near but ne'er to reach the first.
Satires, no. 5, l. 71 (transl. JOHN DRYDEN, 1693). One of the
mottoes of the *Spectator*.

Laurence J. Peter
(1919–90)
US-Canadian author

Laurence Johnston Peter. His book The Peter Principle *(1969)
argues that people are promoted to positions for which they
are incompetent. He also published sequels and anthologies
of quotations.*

1 In a hierarchy every employee tends to rise to his
level of incompetence.
The 'Peter Principle', in *The Peter Principle*, ch. 1 (1969, written
with Raymond Hull). Liz Filkin proposed the 'Paula Principle':
'Women stay below their level of competence, because they
hold back from promotion' (quoted in the *Observer*
19 October 1986).

Petrarch
(1304–74)
Italian poet

*Francesco Petrarca. One of the foremost scholars of his age, he
perfected the sonnet form in his* Canzoniere, *inspired by an
unrequited love. He promoted the spread of humanist ideas
and he was made Poet Laureate in Rome in 1341.*

1 Shame is the fruit of my vanities,
and remorse, and the clearest knowledge
of how the world's delight is a brief dream.
Canzoniere, no. 1

2 My Italy, though words cannot heal
the mortal wounds
so dense, I see on your lovely flesh.
Ibid., no. 128

3 I find no peace, and yet I make no war:
and fear, and hope: and burn, and I am ice:
and fly above the sky, and fall to earth,
and clutch at nothing, and embrace the world.
Ibid., no. 134

Petronius
(1st century AD)
Roman satirist

In the words of TACITUS *he was the 'arbiter of taste' (*arbiter
elegantiae*) at Nero's court. He is remembered for the*
Satyricon, *which lampooned the licentiousness of Roman
society. He committed suicide when accused of conspiring
against* NERO.

1 A great dog on a chain was painted on the wall,
and over him was written in large letters 'BEWARE
OF THE DOG' [*CAVE CANEM*].
Satyricon, sect. 29

2 How we bladders of wind strut about. We are
meaner than flies; flies have their virtues, we are
nothing but bubbles.
Ibid., sect. 42

3 *Abiit ad plures.*
[He has gone over to the majority.]
Ibid., sect. 42

4 Like master, like man.
Ibid., sect. 58

5 *Horatii curiosa felicitas.*
[The studied felicity of Horace.]
Ibid., sect. 118

Phaedrus
(1st century AD)
Latin fabulist

*Born in Thrace or Macedonia, he came to Rome as a slave. He
is most famous for translating* AESOP'S FABLES *into Latin,
and he also authored his own fables.*

1 Endure this evil, lest a worse come upon you.
Fables, bk 1, no. 2

2 Things are not always what they seem.
Ibid., bk 4, no. 2

3 A nation rushing hastily too and fro, busily
employed in idleness.
Ibid., bk 5, no. 2

4 What wilt thou do to thyself, who hast added
insult to injury?
Ibid., bk 5, no. 3

Kim Philby
(1912–88)
British intelligence officer and Soviet spy

Harold Adrian Russell Philby. Recruited by the Soviets before being employed by British intelligence in 1940, he was dismissed from the service in 1955 for his Communist sympathies. He defected to the USSR in 1963 and took Russian citizenship.

1 To betray, you must first belong. I never belonged.
Sunday Times 17 December 1967

Philip, Duke of Edinburgh
(b. 1921)

The Greek-born Philip Mountbatten adopted British nationality in 1947, marrying the future ELIZABETH II *the same year. Notorious for his insensitive remarks, he has set up the Duke of Edinburgh Award Scheme for training young people.*

1 Dentopedalogy is the science of opening your mouth and putting your foot in it. I've been practising it for years.
Address to General Dental Council, quoted in *Time* 21 November 1960

2 If you stay here much longer you'll all be slitty-eyed.
Quoted in *The Times* 17 October 1986. Remark to British students in China.

3 When a man opens the car door for his wife, it's either a new car or a new wife.
Today 2 March 1988

4 I don't think a prostitute is more moral than a wife, but they are doing the same thing.
Speech, 6 December 1988, quoted in the *Daily Mail* 7 December 1988. Prince Philip was dismissing claims that those who sell slaughtered meat have greater moral authority than those who participate in blood sports.

Ambrose Philips
(1674–1749)
English poet and politician

A member of ADDISON's *circle, he was praised for* The Distressed Mother *(1702) and satirized by* ALEXANDER POPE *for his Pastorals. He was MP for Armagh in 1727.*

1 The flowers anew, returning seasons bring!
But beauty faded has no second spring.
The First Pastoral, 'Lobbin', ll. 55–6 (1709)

Wendell Phillips
(1811–84)
US abolitionist and orator

In 1865 he became leader of the Anti-Slavery Society, and he later campaigned for women's rights, temperance and universal suffrage.

1 We live under a government of men and morning newspapers.
'The Press', speech to Massachusetts Anti-Slavery Society, 28 January 1852, quoted in *Prophet of Liberty*, ch. 22 (1958) by Oscar Sherwin

Edith Piaf
(1918–63)
French singer

Originally Edith Giovanna Gassion. Helped to a mainstream career by MAURICE CHEVALIER, *she was known for her powerful voice and waif-like appearance, to which she owed her name Piaf (Parisian slang for 'little sparrow'). Her funeral brought Paris traffic to a standstill.*

1 When he takes me in his arms
He speaks to me in a low voice
I see *la vie en rose*.
'La Vie en rose' (song, 1946, written by Louiguy, Piaf and Mal Davis)

2 *Non! Rien de rien* . . .
Non, je ne regrette rien!
[No, I regret nothing . . .]
'Non, je ne regrette rien' (song, 1961, written by Charles Dumont and Michael Vaucaire)

Francis Picabia
(1878–1953)
French painter and poet

He was linked to all the principal art movements of the early 20th century, and, with MARCEL DUCHAMP *and* MAN RAY *introduced Dadaism to New York. He edited the anti-art magazine variously titled 291, 391, 491 and 591.*

1 Wherever art appears, life disappears.
'L'Humour poétique' (1951), publ. in *Écrits*, vol. 2 (ed. Olivier Revault d'Allones and Dominique Bouissou, 1978)

2 Nature is unfair? So much the better, inequality is the only bearable thing, the monotony of equality can only lead us to boredom.
'L'Humour poétique', ibid., vol. 2

Pablo Picasso

(1881–1973)

Spanish artist

Associated with Cubism, of which his Les Demoiselles d'Avignon *(1906–7) is generally considered the first major example, he explored many other areas of painting and sculpture, incorporating harlequins, minotaurs and African imagery in his work.* Guernica *(1937), showing the bombing of a Basque town during the Spanish Civil War, achieved iconic status.*

1 We all know that Art is not truth. Art is a lie that makes us realize truth, at least the truth that is given us to understand. The artist must know the manner whereby to convince others of the truthfulness of his lies.

'Picasso Speaks' (1923), repr. in *Picasso: Fifty Years of His Art* (1946) by Alfred H. Barr Jr

2 Everything is a miracle. It is a miracle that one does not dissolve in one's bath like a lump of sugar.

Quoted in *Opium* (1929) by JEAN COCTEAU

3 Art is not the application of a canon of beauty but what the instinct and the brain can conceive beyond any canon. When we love a woman we don't start measuring her limbs.

'Conversation avec Picasso' (1935), repr. in *Picasso: Fifty Years of His Art* (1946) by Alfred H. Barr Jr

4 To finish a work? To finish a picture? What nonsense! To finish it means to be through with it, to kill it, to rid it of its soul, to give it its final blow . . . the *coup de grâce* for the painter as well as for the picture.

Quoted in *Picasso: portraits et souvenirs*, ch. 7 (1946) by Jaime Sabartés

5 The genius of Einstein leads to Hiroshima.

Remark to Françoise Gilot in 1946, quoted in *Life with Picasso*, pt 2 (1964) by Françoise Gilot and Carlton Lake

6 Now at least we know everything that painting isn't.

Said in Rome 1949, quoted in *Scritti di Picasso* (1964) by Mario De Micheli. On whether figurative painting was still possible after the advances made by photography and cinema, reported by artist Renato Guttuso in his journals.

7 Painting is a blind man's profession. He paints not what he sees, but what he feels, what he tells himself about what he has seen.

Quoted in *Journals*, pt 1, 'War and Peace' (1956) by JEAN COCTEAU

8 Art is never chaste. It ought to be forbidden to ignorant innocents, never allowed into contact with those not sufficiently prepared. Yes, art is dangerous. Where it is chaste, it is not art.

Quoted in *Pablo Picasso*, ch. 11 (1957) by Antonina Vallentin

9 If all the ways I have been along were marked on a map and joined up with a line, it might represent a minotaur.

Official catalogue of the Musée d'Antibes (Musée Picasso), quoted in *Picasso in Antibes* (1960) by Dor de la Souchère

10 Today, as you know, I am famous and very rich. But when I am alone with myself, I haven't the courage to consider myself an artist, in the great and ancient sense of that word . . . I am only a public entertainer, who understands his age.

Le Spectacle du monde November 1962, repr. in *The Trousered Ape*, ch. 2 (1971) by Duncan Williams

11 God is really only another artist. He invented the giraffe, the elephant, and the cat. He has no real style. He just keeps on trying other things.

Quoted in *Life with Picasso*, pt 1 (1964) by Françoise Gilot and Carlton Lake

12 Is there anything more dangerous than sympathetic understanding?

Quoted in *Picasso Says . . .*, 'Solitude' (1966) by Hélène Parmelin

Pindar

(518–438 BC)

Greek poet

The leading lyric poet of ancient Greece, he is most celebrated for the Epinikia *(Triumphal Odes), four books which celebrated victories at the Olympian and other games.*

1 Best of all things is water; but gold, like a
   gleaming fire,
by night outshines all pride of wealth beside.

Olympian Odes, no. 1, ll. 1–2

2 Days to come are the wisest witnesses.

Ibid., no. 1, l. 34

3 There are many sharp shafts in the quiver under
   my arm.
They speak to the understanding; for most men,
   they need interpreters.
The wise man knows many things by nature: the
   vulgar are taught.
They will say anything. They clatter vainly like
   crows
against the divine bird of Zeus.

Ibid., no. 2, ll. 83–8

4 Men's prosperity will not walk far
safe, when it fares under its own deep weight.
I will be small in small things, great among great.
Pythian Odes, no. 3, ll. 105–7

5 We are things of a day. What are we? What are
we not? The dream of a shadow
is man, no more. But when the brightness comes,
and God gives it,
there is a shining of light on men, and their life is
sweet.
Ibid., no. 8, ll. 95–7

6 Not every sheer truth
is the better for showing her face. Silence also
many times is the wisest thing for a man to have
in his mind.
Nemean Odes, no. 5, ll. 17–19

7 O bright and violet-crowned and famed in song,
bulwark of Greece, famous Athens, divine city!
Fragment 76

8 Whatever is beautiful is beautiful by necessity.
Attributed

(Sir) Arthur Wing Pinero
(1855–1934)
British playwright

*A writer of comedies and farces, he is better known for his
plays that deal with social issues, notably* The Second Mrs
Tanqueray *(1893).*

1 I've heard you say that from forty till fifty a man
is at heart either a stoic or a satyr.
The Second Mrs Tanqueray, Act 1 (1893). Spoken by Aubrey
Tanqueray to Cayley Drummle.

Harold Pinter
(b. 1930)
British playwright and actor

*When asked what his plays were about, he once answered, 'the
weasel under the cocktail cabinet'. Early works include* The
Birthday Party *(1957),* The Caretaker *(1960) and* The Homecoming *(1965), while later plays are more explicitly political,
for example* Mountain Language *(1988).*

1 If only I could get down to Sidcup! I've been waiting for the weather to break. He's got my papers,
this man I left them with, it's got it all down there,
I could prove everything.
The Caretaker, Act 1 (1960). Spoken by Davies.

2 The earth's about five million years old, at least.
Who can afford to live in the past?
The Homecoming, Act 2, Sc. 1 (1965). Spoken by Max.

3 Apart from the known and the unknown, what
else is there?
Lenny, ibid., Act 2, Sc. 1

4 I tend to believe that cricket is the greatest thing
that God ever created on earth.
'Pinter on Pinter', in the *Observer* 5 October 1980

5 I hate despair. I find it intolerable. The stink of it
gets up my nose. It's a blemish. Despair, old fruit, is
a cancer. It should be castrated. Indeed I've often
found that that works. Chop the balls off and despair
goes out the window.
One for the Road (1985). Spoken by Nicholas.

6 It comes easily for the English people to mock.
It's a very odd situation indeed in England; you try
to address real facts of life that surround you and
are treated with great hostility.
Various Voices, 'Writing, Politics and *Ashes to Ashes*' (1998).
On the public response to his political involvement.

Luigi Pirandello
(1867–1936)
Italian playwright

His novel The Late Mattia Pascal *(1903) and the plays* Six
Characters in Search of an Author *(1921) and* Henry IV *(1922)
share the themes of tragic alienation and the illusion of personality. He established his own theatre, the Teatro d'Arte, in
1925.*

1 But you must play your part, just as I am playing
mine. It's all in the game . . . Each of us must play
his part through to the end.
The Rules of the Game Act 2 (1919, transl. 1959). Spoken by
Leone.

2 Six Characters in Search of an Author.
Title of play (1921)

3 Whoever has the luck to be born a character can
laugh even at death. Because a character will never
die! A man will die, a writer, the instrument of creation: but what he has created will never die!
Six Characters in Search of an Author, Act 1 (1921). Spoken by
The Father.

4 Each of us, face to face with other men, is clothed
with some sort of dignity, but we know only too
well all the unspeakable things that go on in the
heart.
The Father, ibid., Act 1

5 You know what it means to be with a madman? To be with someone who shakes the foundations, the logic of the whole structure of everything you've built in and around yourselves.
Henry IV, Act 2 (1922). Spoken by Henry IV.

Robert M. Pirsig
(b. 1928)
US author

He had a cult hit with Zen and the Art of Motorcycle Mainten-ance *(1974), an account of a motorcycle journey across America narrated as both a physical expedition and a psychological quest, which he subtitled 'An Inquiry into Values'.*

1 Zen and the Art of Motorcycle Maintenance.
Title of book (1974)

2 The Buddha, the Godhead, resides quite as comfortably in the circuits of a digital computer or the gears of a cycle transmission as he does at the top of a mountain or in the petals of a flower.
Zen and the Art of Motorcycle Maintenance, pt 1, ch. 1 (1974)

3 A motorcycle functions entirely in accordance with the laws of reason, and a study of the art of motorcycle maintenance is really a miniature study of the art of rationality itself.
Ibid., pt 2, ch. 8

4 One thing about pioneers that you don't hear mentioned is that they are invariably, by their nature, mess-makers.
Ibid., pt 3, ch. 21

5 Traditional scientific method has always been at the very *best*, 20–20 hindsight. It's good for seeing where you've been. It's good for testing the truth of what you think you know, but it can't tell you where you *ought* to go.
Ibid., pt 3, ch. 24

Walter B. Pitkin
(1878–1953)
US author

His numerous works of popular psychology include The Psy-chology of Happiness *(1929) and* Let's Get What We Want *(1935).*

1 Life Begins at Forty.
Title of book (1932)

William Pitt ('the Elder')
(1708–78)
English statesman

First Earl of Chatham. He became Secretary of State in 1756 and led coalition governments in 1757–61 and 1766–8. His strategy of war against France secured Britain's status as an imperial power. He was called 'the Great Commoner' for his insistence on constitutional rights.

1 The atrocious crime of being a young man ... I shall neither attempt to palliate nor deny, but con-tent myself with wishing that I may be one of those whose follies may cease with their youth, and not of that number who are ignorant in spite of experience.
Speech to the House of Commons, 10 March 1741, publ. in *Hansard*, vol. 12, col. 115. The wording of Pitt's speech, which was in response to an attack on his youth by HORACE WAL-POLE, was mainly the work of SAMUEL JOHNSON.

2 The poorest man may in his cottage bid defiance to all the forces of the Crown. It may be frail – its roof may shake – the wind may blow through it – the storm may enter – the rain may enter – but the King of England cannot enter! – all his force dares not cross the threshold of the ruined tenement!
Speech to the House of Commons, March 1763, quoted in *Historical Sketches of Statesmen who Flourished in the Time of George III*, vol. 1 (1839) by Henry Peter Brougham

3 I cannot give them my confidence; pardon me, gentlemen, confidence is a plant of slow growth in an aged bosom: youth is the season of credulity.
Speech to House of Commons, 14 January 1766, publ. in *Han-sard*, vol. 16, col. 97. Attacking the Rockingham ministry.

4 Unlimited power is apt to corrupt the minds of those who possess it; and this I know, my lords, where law ends, tyranny begins!
Speech to House of Lords, 9 January 1770, publ. in *Hansard*, vol. 16, col. 665. Closing words of speech.

5 There is something behind the throne greater than the King himself.
Speech to House of Lords, 2 March 1770, publ. in *Hansard*, vol. 16, col. 843. Referring to 'the secret influence of the Earl of Bute' over GEORGE III.

6 The little I know of it has not served to raise my opinion of what is vulgarly called the monied interest; I mean, that blood-sucker, that muck-worm, which calls itself the friend of government.
Speech to House of Lords, 22 November 1770, publ. in *Han-sard*, vol. 16, col. 1106

7 If I were an American, as I am an Englishman,

while a foreign troop was landed in my country, I would never lay down my arms – never – never – never.

Speech to House of Lords, 18 November 1777, publ. in *Hansard*, vol. 19, col. 363

William Pitt ('the Younger')
(1759–1806)
English statesman

The son of 'Pitt the Elder', he became the country's youngest ever prime minister aged 24. During his two terms of office (1783–1801 and 1804–6), he opposed corruption and extended the power of parliament. For EDMUND BURKE *he was 'not merely the chip of the old block, but the old block itself', while* WILLIAM COBBETT *called him the 'great snorting bawler'.*

1 Necessity is the plea for every infringement of human freedom. It is the argument of tyrants; it is the creed of slaves.

Speech to House of Commons, 18 November 1783, publ. in *Hansard*, vol. 23, col. 1209. Referring to the East India Bill.

2 Europe is not to be saved by any single man. England has saved herself by her exertions, and will, as I trust, save Europe by her example.

Speech at the Lord Mayor's banquet, Guildhall, London, 9 November 1805, publ. in *The War Speeches of William Pitt the Younger*, 'The War: Third Phase (1803–1806)', sect. 6 (ed. R. Coupland, 1915). Pitt's reply to the toast as 'Saviour of Europe' was his last speech.

3 Roll up that map; it will not be wanted these ten years.

Quoted in *Life of the Rt. Hon. William Pitt*, vol. 4, ch. 43 (1862) by Earl Stanhope. Referring to a map of Europe, upon hearing of NAPOLEON's victory at Austerlitz, December 1805.

4 I think that I could eat one of Bellamy's veal pies.

Attributed last words

Pius IX
(1792–1878)
Italian pope

Giovanni Maria Mastai-Ferrati. An anti-modernist, he decreed the dogma of the Immaculate Conception (1854) and convoked the First Vatican Council (1869–70) which defined the dogma of papal infallibility. He was beatified in 2000.

1 It is an error to believe that the Roman Pontiff can and ought to reconcile himself to, and agree with, progress, liberalism, and contemporary civilization.

Syllabus of Errors (1864)

Pius XI
(1857–1939)
Italian pope

Ambrogio Damiano Achille Ratti. Pope from 1922, he was responsible for signing the Lateran Treaty (1929) with MUSSO-LINI, *a concordat that established the independence of the Vatican State.*

1 Whether considered as a doctrine, or as an historical fact, or as a movement, socialism, if it really remains socialism, cannot be brought into harmony with the dogmas of the Catholic church . . . Religious socialism, Christian socialism, are expressions implying a contradiction in terms.

Quadragesimo Anno (encyclical, 1931)

Pius XII
(1876–1958)
Italian pope

Eugenio Pacelli. He was made Pope in 1939 and is remembered for his conservative approach to doctrine and politics. He maintained diplomatic relations with both Allied and Axis governments, but failed to speak out against Nazi atrocities.

1 The Church welcomes technological progress and receives it with love, for it is an indubitable fact that technological progress comes from God and, therefore, can and must lead to Him.

Christmas message, 1953, publ. in *The Harvest of a Quiet Eye* (ed. Alan L. Mackay, 1977)

Max Planck
(1858–1947)
German physicist

Professor at Berlin (1892–1926), he broke with classical physics when he proposed his revolutionary quantum theory (1900), one of the main foundations of 20th-century physics.

1 A new scientific truth does not triumph by convincing its opponents and making them see the light, but rather because its opponents eventually die, and a new generation grows up that is familiar with it.

Scientific Autobiography and Other Papers, 'Scientific Autobiography' (1948)

Sylvia Plath
(1932–63)
US poet

Her best-known works are the partly autobiographical novel The Bell Jar *(1963) and* Ariel *(1965), a collection of her late poems. Her suicide, a year after separating from her husband* TED HUGHES, *was the culmination of a series of attempts on her own life.*

1 How frail the human heart must be –
a mirrored pool of thought . . .
'I Thought I Could Not Be Hurt', quoted in Introduction to *Letters Home: Correspondence 1950–1963* (1975) by Aurelia Schober Plath. Plath's first poem, written at the age of fourteen.

2 Overnight, very
Whitely, discreetly,
Very quietly
Our toes, our noses
Take hold on the loam,
Acquire the air.
'Mushrooms', publ. in *The Colossus* (1960)

3 Widow. The word consumes itself . . .
'Widow', written 1961, publ. in *Crossing the Water* (1971)

4 Is there no way out of the mind?
'Apprehensions', written 1962, ibid.

5 If neurotic is wanting two mutually exclusive things at one and the same time, then I'm neurotic as hell. I'll be flying back and forth between one mutually exclusive thing and another for the rest of my days.
The Bell Jar, ch. 8 (1963). Spoken by the narrator (Esther Greenwood).

6 Love set you going like a fat gold watch.
The midwife slapped your footsoles, and your bald
  cry
Took its place among the elements.
'Morning Song', publ. in *Ariel* (1965)

7 A living doll, everywhere you look.
It can sew, it can cook,
It can talk, talk, talk.
It works, there is nothing wrong with it.
You have a hole, it's a poultice.
You have an eye, it's an image.
My boy, it's your last resort.
Will you marry it, marry it, marry it.
'The Applicant', ibid.

8 Dying
Is an art, like everything else.
I do it exceptionally well.

I do it so it feels like hell.
I do it so it feels real.
I guess you could say I've a call.
'Lady Lazarus', sts 15–16, ibid.

9 Out of the ash
I rise with my red hair
And I eat men like air.
'Lady Lazarus', st. 28, ibid. Final stanza of poem.

10 I have always been scared of you,
With your Luftwaffe, your gobbledygoo.
And your neat moustache
And your Aryan eye, bright blue.
Panzer-man, panzer-man, O You –
'Daddy', st. 9, ibid.

11 Every woman adores a Fascist,
The boot in the face, the brute
Brute heart of a brute like you.
'Daddy', st. 10, ibid.

12 Perfection is terrible, it cannot have children.
'The Munich Mannequins', ibid.

13 Kindness glides about my house.
Dame Kindness, she is so nice!
The blue and red jewels of her rings smoke
In the windows, the mirrors
Are filling with smiles.
'Kindness', ibid.

14 The woman is perfected.
Her dead
Body wears the smile of accomplishment.
'Edge', ibid. Opening lines of Plath's last poem, written a week before her suicide.

Plato

(*c.* 427–347 BC)
Greek philosopher

A disciple of SOCRATES *and the teacher of* ARISTOTLE, *he founded and presided over the Academy at Athens, where philosophical and scientific ideas were discussed. Such works as* The Republic *and* Symposium *had a far-reaching influence on Western thought and Christian theology. Many of his writings took the form of dialogues; those relating to Socrates are quoted under* SOCRATES.

1 You cannot conceive the many without the one.
Parmenides, sect. 166

2 He who is of a calm and happy nature will hardly feel the pressure of age, but to him who is of an opposite disposition youth and age are equally a burden.
The Republic, bk 1, sect. 329d (transl. BENJAMIN JOWETT, 1871). Spoken by Cephalus.

3 Justice is nothing else than the interest of the stronger.

Thrasymachus, ibid., bk 1, sect. 338c

4 Everything that deceives may be said to enchant.

Adeimantus, ibid., bk 3, sect. 413c

5 Astronomy compels the soul to look upwards, and leads us from this world to another.

Glaucon, ibid., bk 7, sect. 529a. In the dialogue, Socrates disagrees: 'Those that elevate astronomy into philosophy treat it in such a way as to make us look downwards and not upwards.'

6 The true order of going, or being led by another, to the things of love, is to begin from the beauties of earth and mount upwards for the sake of that other beauty, using these as steps only, and from one going on to two, and from two to all fair forms, and from fair forms to fair practices, and from fair practices to fair notions, until from fair notions he arrives at the notion of absolute beauty, and at last knows what the essence of beauty is.

Symposium, sect. 211

Plautus
(254–184 BC)
Roman playwright

Titus Maccius Plautus. His plays were modelled on New Greek Comedy and exerted a strong influence on the drama of the Renaissance. His comic themes included the lure of money, family discord and mistaken identity, often expressed in slapstick humour using vernacular idioms.

1 Manliness [*virtus*] is the best prize; manliness in truth precedes all things; by it are protected and kept freedom, safety, life, property and parents, fatherland and children.

Amphitruo, Act 2, Sc. 2. Spoken by Alcmena.

2 He ties a bag in front at night to avoid losing breath . . . He grudges to part with his washing water . . . He wouldn't give you hunger, if you asked for it . . . He treasures the parings of his nails.

Aulularia (The Pot of Gold), Act 2, Sc. 3. Strobilus, speaking of Euclio, the miser.

3 Slander-mongers and those who listen to slander, if I had my way, would all be strung up, the talkers by the tongue, the listeners by the ears.

Pseudolus, Act 1, Sc. 5. Spoken by Callipho.

4 Consider the little mouse, how sagacious an animal it is which never entrusts its life to one hole only.

Truculentus, Act 4, Sc. 4, l. 15. Spoken by Phronesium.

5 Nothing is there more friendly to a man than a friend in need.

Epidicus, Act 3, Sc. 43, l. 44. A proverbial expression quoted by Periphanes, usually remembered 'A friend in need is a friend indeed.'

6 No guest is so welcome in a friend's house that he will not become a nuisance after three days.

Miles Gloriosus, Act 3, Sc. 1, l. 144. Spoken by Pleusicles.

7 No man is wise enough by himself.

Ibid., Act 3, Sc. 3, l. 885. Spoken by Periplectomenus

Pliny the Elder
(c. 23–79)
Roman scholar

Gaius Plinius Secundus. His only surviving work, the Natural History *(AD 77), was an encyclopaedia in thirty-seven volumes which remained a standard text book throughout the Middle Ages. He was killed while observing the eruption of Vesuvius.*

1 When collating authorities I have found that the most professedly reliable and modern writers have copied the old authors word for word, without acknowledgement.

Historia Naturalis (Natural History), Preface

2 The only certainty is that nothing is certain; and nothing more miserable and yet more arrogant than man.

Ibid., bk 2, sect. 7

3 *Bruta fulmina et vana.*
[Thunderbolts that strike blindly and in vain.]

Ibid., bk 2, sect 113

4 Man is the only one that knows nothing, that can learn nothing without being taught. He can neither speak nor walk nor eat, and in short he can do nothing at the prompting of nature only, but weep.

Ibid., bk 7, sect. 4

5 *Semper aliquid novi Africam adferre.*
[There is always something new out of Africa.]

Ibid., bk. 8, sect. 42. Citing a Greek proverb. The words are often quoted: 'Ex Africa semper aliquid novi.' See ISAK DINESEN 2.

6 The master's eye is the best fertilizer.

Ibid., bk 18, sect. 24

7 The best course is to profit by the folly of other people.
Ibid., bk 18, sect. 31

8 With a grain of salt.
Ibid., bk 23, sect. 8. Pliny himself, in his writings, appeared to make no distinction between the true and the wildly fantastic.

9 Why is it that we entertain the belief that for every purpose odd numbers are the most effectual?
Ibid., bk 28, sect. 23

Pliny the Younger
(c. 61–112)
Roman administrator and writer

Gaius Plinius Caecilius Secundus. He was adopted by his uncle, PLINY THE ELDER, *and became consul in AD 100. He is best remembered for his letters illustrating everyday life in the Roman empire.*

1 You say that you have nothing to write about. Well you can at least write about *that* – or else simply the phrase our elders used to start a letter with: 'If you are well, well and good; I am well.' That will do for me – it is all that matters.
Letter to Fabius Justus, in *Letters*, bk 1, no. 11

2 This expression of ours 'Father of a family [*pater-familias*]'.
Letter to Valerius Paulinus, ibid., bk 5, no. 19

3 That indolent but agreeable condition of doing nothing.
Letter to Ursus, ibid., bk 8, no. 9

William Plomer
(1903–73)
South African author and poet

His first novel Turbott Wolfe *(1925) dealt with racism. In 1929 he settled in London where he published both light and serious verse and wrote librettos for* BENJAMIN BRITTEN. STEPHEN SPENDER *described his work as 'wind-blown, sun-saturated, sparkling'.*

1 On a sofa upholstered in panther skin
Mona did researches in original sin.
'Mews Flat Mona', st. 6, publ. in *Collected Poems* (1960)

2 Peristalsis calls for roughage,
Haulms and fibres, husks and grit,
Nature's way to open bowels,
Maybe – let them practise it.
'The Flying Bum: 1944', st. 5, ibid.

3 The dead are non-living
the hungry are non-fed:
don't think because you're non-unconscious
that you're alive – you're non-dead.
'Bureaucratic Negatives', st. 3, ibid.

Plutarch
(46–120)
Greek essayist and biographer

He is best known for Parallel Lives *which recorded and illustrated with anecdotes the lives of twenty-three Greeks and twenty-three Romans. The work was a source for* SHAKESPEARE's *Roman plays. His* Moralia *are a collection of sixty treatises on various subjects.*

1 It is, indeed, a desirable thing to be well-descended; but the glory belongs to our ancestors.
Morals, 'The Education of Children' (c. AD 100). Plutarch's authorship of this essay has been questioned.

2 For to err in opinion, though it be not the part of wise men, is at least human.
Ibid., 'Against Colotes', sect 31. The words were already proverbial in Plutarch's time.

3 A Roman divorced from his wife, being highly blamed by his friends, who demanded, 'Was she not chaste? Was she not fair? Was she not fruitful?' holding out his shoe, asked them whether it was not new and well made. 'Yet', added he, 'none of you can tell where it pinches me.'
Parallel Lives, 'Aemilius Paulus', ch. 5, sect. 1–2

4 Not Philip, but Philip's gold, took the cities of Greece.
Ibid., 'Aemilius Paulus', ch. 12, sect. 6. Greek saying referring to Philip II of Macedon.

Edgar Allan Poe
(1809–45)
US poet, critic and short-story writer

He broke new ground with his tales of the grotesque and macabre, and is credited with the first detective story in English literature, The Murders in the Rue Morgue *(1841). His poem 'The Raven' (1845) brought him immediate fame, but his journalistic career was uneven. According to* PAUL VALÉRY: *'Poe is the only impeccable writer. He was never mistaken.' See also* JAMES RUSSELL LOWELL 7.

1 All that we see or seem
Is but a dream within a dream.
'A Dream Within a Dream', written 1829, publ. in *The Collected Works of Edgar Allan Poe*, vol. 6 (ed. Thomas Ollive Mabbott, 1969)

2 Whose wreathèd friezes intertwine
The viol, the violet, and the vine.
'The City in the Sea', st. 2 (1831), repr. in *The Raven and Other Poems* (1845)

3 Helen, thy beauty is to me
Like those Nicean barks of yore,
That gently, o'er a perfumed sea,
The weary, way-worn wanderer bore
To his own native shore.
On desperate seas long wont to roam,
Thy hyacinth hair, thy classic face,
Thy Naiad airs have brought me home
To the glory that was Greece,
And the grandeur that was Rome.
'To Helen', sts 1–2 (1831), ibid.

4 During the whole of a dull, dark, and soundless day in the autumn of the year, when the clouds hung oppressively low in the heavens, I had been passing alone, on horseback, through a singularly dreary tract of country; and at length found myself, as the shades of the evening drew on, within view of the melancholy House of Usher.
'The Fall of the House of Usher', publ. in *Tales of the Grotesque and Arabesque* (1840). Opening lines of story.

5 As the strong man exults in his physical ability, delighting in such exercises as call his muscles into action, so glories the analyst in that moral activity which *disentangles*.
'The Murders in the Rue Morgue' (1841), repr. in *The Prose Romances of Edgar A. Poe* (1843). Referring to detective work.

6 There is something in the unselfish and self-sacrificing love of a brute which goes directly to the heart of him who has had frequent occasion to test the paltry friendship and gossamer fidelity of mere *Man*.
'The Black Cat', publ. in *Tales* (1845)

7 Once upon a midnight dreary, while I pondered, weak and weary,
Over many a quaint and curious volume of forgotten lore –
While I nodded, nearly napping, suddenly there came a tapping,
As of some one gently rapping, rapping at my chamber door.
'The Raven', st. 1, publ. in *The Raven and Other Poems* (1845)

8 Eagerly I wished the morrow; – vainly had I sought to borrow
From my books surcease of sorrow – sorrow for the lost Lenore –
For the rare and radiant maiden whom the angels name Lenore –
Nameless *here* for evermore.
'The Raven', st. 2, ibid.

9 'Ghastly, grim and ancient Raven wandering from the Nightly shore –
Tell me what thy lordly name is on the night's Plutonian shore!'
Quoth the Raven, 'Nevermore'.
'The Raven', st. 8, ibid.

10 Take thy beak from out my heart, and take thy form from off my door!
Quoth the Raven, 'Nevermore'.
'The Raven', st. 17, ibid.

11 And this maiden she lived with no other thought
Than to love and be loved by me.
'Annabel Lee', st. 1, publ. in *The Works of the Late Edgar Allan Poe*, vol. 2 (ed. R. W. Griswold, J. R. LOWELL and N. P. Willis, 1850). The poem is addressed to Poe's cousin, Virginia Clemm, whom he married when she was thirteen.

12 *I* was a child and *she* was a child,
In this kingdom by the sea,
But we loved with a love which was more than love –
I and my Annabel Lee.
'Annabel Lee', st. 2, ibid.

13 And so, all the night-tide, I lie down by the side
Of my darling – my darling – my life and my bride,
In her sepulchre there by the sea –
In her tomb by the side of the sea.
'Annabel Lee', st. 6, ibid.

14 That man is not truly brave who is afraid either to seem or to be, when it suits him, a coward.
'Marginalia' (1846), repr. in *Essays and Reviews* (1984)

15 Mournful and never-ending remembrance.
'The Philosophy of Composition' (1846), ibid. Explanation of the meaning of the symbolic bird in Poe's poem *The Raven*. The phrase was used as the title of Kenneth Silverman's study of Poe (1992).

16 The skies were ashen and sober;
The leaves they were crispèd and sere –
The leaves they were withering and sere;
It was night in the lonesome October
Of my most immemorial year.
'Ulalume', st. 1, publ. in *The Works of the Late Edgar Allan Poe*, vol. 2 (ed. R. W. Griswold, J. R. LOWELL and N. P. Willis, 1850)

17 To be *thoroughly* conversant with a Man's heart,

is to take our final lesson in the iron-clasped volume of despair.
'Marginalia' (1849), repr. in *Essays and Reviews* (1984)

18 The nose of a mob is its imagination. By this, at any time, it can be quietly led.
'Marginalia' (1849), ibid.

19 Keeping time, time, time,
In a sort of Runic rhyme,
To the tintinnabulation that so musically wells
From the bells, bells, bells, bells.
'The Bells', st. 1, publ. in *The Works of the Late Edgar Allan Poe*, vol. 2 (ed. R. W. Griswold, J. R. LOWELL and N. P. Willis, 1850)

20 Thank Heaven! the crisis –
The danger, is past,
And the lingering illness
Is over at last –
And the fever called 'Living'
Is conquered at last.
'For Annie', st. 1, ibid.

Political slogans

See also STOKELY CARMICHAEL 1; JESSE COLLINGS 1; JOHN LENNON 4; MALCOLM X 4.

1 America, love it or leave it.
Slogan (1960s). The slogan was applied in America to hippies and peace activists who refused involvement in the Vietnam war.

2 Ban the bomb.
US anti-nuclear slogan, from 1953, adopted in Britain by the Campaign for Nuclear Disarmament

3 A bayonet is a weapon with a worker at each end.
British pacifist slogan, 1940s

4 Better to break the law than break the poor.
Slogan of the British anti-Poll Tax campaign, late 1980s, thought to have been coined by members of Militant Tendency

5 Better red than dead.
Slogan of the Campaign for Nuclear Disarmament, late 1950s

6 Black is beautiful.
Slogan of the Black Power movement, 1960s

7 Burn, baby, burn!
Slogan linked to the race riots in Watts, Los Angeles, August 1965

8 Can't pay, won't pay.
Slogan by anti-Poll Tax protesters in the 1990s. See DARIO FO 3.

9 Coal not dole.
Slogan, early 1990s, protesting plans of the Conservative government to close British coal mines

10 *Ein Reich, ein Volk, ein Führer.*
[One realm, one people, one leader.]
Nazi Party slogan, early 1930s

11 Every mother a willing mother. Every child a wanted child.
Abortion rights slogan, early 1970s

12 Fight for your right to party.
Slogan of the Advance Party, formed to resist the provisions of the Criminal Justice Act of 1994 banning open-air raves. Possibly taken from the title of a song by the Beastie Boys in 1987.

13 Freedom to drive or freedom to breathe.
Anti-roads slogan from early 1990s

14 Hell no, we won't go.
Chant of US draft resisters refusing to serve in the Vietnam War

15 Hey, hey, LBJ, how many kids did you kill today?
Anti-Vietnam slogan, opposing LYNDON B. JOHNSON's continuation of the war

16 If not us, who? If not now, when?
Slogan by Czech university students in Prague, November 1989

17 It takes up to 40 dumb animals to make a fur coat but only one to wear it.
Slogan of anti-fur trade group Lynx, mid-1980s. The words appeared on a banner in DAVID BAILEY's celebrated video in support of the group.

18 It's morning again in America.
Presidential campaign slogan for RONALD REAGAN

19 It's the economy, stupid.
Democratic Party slogan, 1992. Originating from a sign put up at BILL CLINTON's headquarters by political strategist James Carville in Little Rock, Arkansas, during the presidential election campaign.

20 Keep your rosaries out of our ovaries.
Women's Action Committee against anti-abortionists, 1992

21 *Kraft durch Freude*
[Strength through joy.]
German Labour Front slogan from 1933, credited to Robert Ley (1890–1945), German Nazi and head of the Labour Front 1933–45

22 Land. Bread. Peace.
Revolutionary slogan of 1917 calling for land reform, access to food, and Russian withdrawal from the First World War. Taken up and promoted by the Bolsheviks.

23 Let Nicaragua Live.

Slogan opposing the REAGAN administration's campaign against Nicaragua's Sandinista government, mid-1980s

24 *Liberté! Égalité! Fraternité!*
[Freedom! Equality! Brotherhood!]

Motto of the French Revolution, 1789

25 Make love not war.

Hippy slogan of the 1960s

26 Make poverty history.

Slogan adopted by charities for alleviating poverty in the developing world, 2004

27 No compromise in defence of the earth.

Slogan of the international direct action movement, Earth First, 1990s

28 No taxation without representation.

Watchword of the American Revolution, 1776. See JAMES OTIS 1.

29 Not in my name.

Pacifist slogan in the USA and Britain, 2002–3, protesting against war against Iraq

30 *El pueblo unido*
Jamás será vencido.
[The people united
Will never be defeated.]

Chanted on demonstrations against US intervention in Central America, 1980s. Also used in the Seattle protests against the World Trade Organization, in November 1999.

31 Power to the people.

Slogan of the Black Panther movement, c. 1968. Also the title of a song by JOHN LENNON (1971).

32 Resistance as global as capital.

Slogan of 'anti-capitalist' protesters, from late 1990s. Directed against policies of the World Trade Organisation and the International Monetary Fund.

33 Save the whale.

Greenpeace slogan from 1970s

34 Think globally, act locally.

Friends of the Earth slogan, mid-1980s

35 *Tiocfaidh Ar La.*
[Our day will come.]

IRA slogan, 1920s

36 Today he plays jazz; tomorrow he betrays his country.

Stalinist propaganda slogan in the Soviet Union, 1920s

37 Ulster says no.

Unionist slogan opposing the Anglo-Irish Agreement of 15 November 1985

38 War will cease when men refuse to fight. What are *you* going to do about it?

Pacifist slogan, c. 1936. In May 1940, the Peace Pledge Union was prosecuted under Defence Regulation 39a for a poster with these words. The editor, Canon Stuart Morris, told the court that the poster was 'two-year-old stock' and 'inappropriate at the present time' as activists were anxious 'not to be thought to be obstructing the war effort'. The slogan is often quoted: 'Wars will cease . . .'

39 We shall not be moved.

Title of labour and civil rights song, 1930s, adapted from an earlier gospel hymn

40 Who governs Britain?

Conservative slogan for 1974 general election. In the wake of the industrial disputes which had undermined the government of EDWARD HEATH and which had precipitated the election, the Conservative Party made the struggle with the unions the central issue of their electoral campaign.

41 With an armalite in one hand and a ballot box in the other.

Phrase to characterize IRA policy, coined in 1981 by IRA and Sinn Fein member Danny Morrison (b. 1953)

Jackson Pollock
(1912–56)
US artist

Paul Jackson Pollock. He was a leading Abstract Expressionist, earning the nickname 'Jack the Dripper' for his use of dripped or poured paint to achieve his 'action paintings'.

1 I *can* control the flow of paint: there is no accident, just as there is no beginning and no end.

Narrative to 1951 film made by Hans Nemuth and Paul Falkenberg, repr. in *Jackson Pollock* (1960) by Bryan Robertson

Madame de Pompadour
(1721–64)
Mistress of Louis XV of France

Jeanne Antoinette Poisson, Marquise de Pompadour. The lifelong confidante of Louis XV, and his mistress from 1745, she maintained influence at court, was a notable patron of the arts and founded the Sèvres porcelain factory.

1 *Après nous le déluge.*
[After us, the flood.]

Remark to Louis XV, 5 November 1757, quoted in *Mémoires de Madame du Hausset* (1824). Supposedly uttered after the defeat of the French army by FREDERICK THE GREAT at the Battle of Rossbach, the phrase has also been attributed to Louis XV, but in any case may already have been current as a proverb.

Georges Pompidou
(1911–74)
French president

Holding government posts since 1946, he was Gaullist Prime Minister 1962–8 and President 1969–74.

1 There are three roads to ruin; women, gambling and technicians. The most pleasant is with women, the quickest is with gambling, but the surest is with technicians.
Quoted in the *Sunday Telegraph* 26 May 1968

Alexander Pope
(1688–1744)
English poet

Called the 'Wicked Wasp of Twickenham' for his caustic wit, he embodied the spirit of English Neo-classicism and was considered the literary dictator of the age. His verse, typically in heroic couplets, is epigrammatic and didactic in style, and often savagely satirical. 'I have a dark suspicion that a modern poet might manufacture an admirable lyric out of almost every line of Pope,' wrote G. K. CHESTERTON. *See also* SAMUEL JOHNSON 123.

1 Happy the man, whose wish and care
A few paternal acres bound,
Content to breathe his native air,
In his own ground.
'Ode on Solitude', st. 1, written *c.* 1709, publ. in *Poems on Several Occasions* (1717). Opening lines of poem.

2 Thus let me live, unseen, unknown;
Thus unlamented let me die;
Steal from the world, and not a stone
Tell where I lie.
'Ode on Solitude', st. 5, ibid. Concluding lines.

3 Let sinful bachelors their woes deplore,
Full well they merit all they feel, and more:
Unawed by precepts, human or divine,
Like birds and beasts, promiscuously they join.
'January and May', ll. 29–32, publ. in *Poetical Miscellanies* (1709). A version of CHAUCER's *The Merchant's Tale*, written aged sixteen or seventeen.

4 There goes a saying, and 'twas shrewdly said,
Old fish at table, but young flesh in bed.
'January and May', ll. 101–2, ibid.

5 To church the parties went,
At once with carnal and devout intent.
'January and May', ll. 319–20, ibid.

6 Where'er you walk, cool gales shall fan the glade,
Trees, where you sit, shall crowd into a shade:

Where'er you tread, the blushing flowers shall rise,
And all things flourish where you turn your eyes.
'Summer: The Second Pastoral', ll. 73–6, ibid. The lines have been set to music by Handel in his opera *Semele* (1744).

7 Histories are more full of examples of the fidelity of dogs than of friends.
Letter, 19 October 1709, publ. in *The Correspondence of Alexander Pope*, vol. 1 (ed. George Sherburn, 1956)

8 Some are bewildered in the maze of schools,
And some made coxcombs nature meant but fools.
An Essay on Criticism, ll. 26–7 (1711)

9 One science only will one genius fit;
So vast is art, so narrow human wit.
Ibid., ll. 60–1

10 First follow nature, and your judgement frame
By her just standard, which is still the same:
Unerring nature, still divinely bright,
One clear, unchanged, and universal light,
Life, force and beauty must to all impart,
At once the source, and end, and test of art.
Ibid., ll. 68–73.

11 Learn hence for ancient rules a just esteem;
To copy nature is to copy them.
Ibid., ll. 139–40

12 Those oft are stratagems which errors seem,
Nor is it Homer nods, but we that dream.
Ibid., ll. 179–80. See HORACE 83

13 A little learning is a dangerous thing;
Drink deep, or taste not the Pierian spring:
There shallow draughts intoxicate the brain,
And drinking largely sobers us again.
Ibid., ll. 215–18. Pieria was the fabled birth-place of the Muses.

14 Hills peep o'er hills, and Alps on Alps arise!
Ibid., l. 232

15 True wit is nature to advantage dressed,
What oft was thought, but ne'er so well expressed.
Ibid., ll. 297–8

16 Words are like leaves; and where they most abound,
Much fruit of sense beneath is rarely found.
Ibid., ll. 309–10

17 Expression is the dress of thought.
Ibid., l. 318

18 As some to church repair,
Not for the doctrine, but the music there.
Ibid., l. 342

19 Then, at the last and only couplet fraught
With some unmeaning thing they call a thought,
A needless Alexandrine ends the song,
That, like a wounded snake, drags its slow length
    along.
Ibid., ll. 354–7

20 True ease in writing comes from art, not
    chance,
As those move easiest who have learned to dance.
'Tis not enough no harshness gives offence,
The sound must seem an echo to the sense.
Ibid., ll. 362–5

21 At every trifle scorn to take offence,
That always shows great pride, or little sense.
Ibid., ll. 386–7

22 Yet let not each gay turn thy rapture move,
For fools admire, but men of sense approve.
Ibid., ll. 390–1

23 Some judge of authors' names, not works, and
    then
Nor praise nor blame the writings, but the men.
Ibid., ll. 412–13

24 What woeful stuff this madrigal would be,
In some starved hackney sonneteer, or me?
But let a lord once own the happy lines,
How the wit brightens! how the style refines!
Ibid., ll. 418–21

25 So much they scorn the crowd, that if the throng
By chance go right, they purposely go wrong.
Ibid., ll. 426–7

26 Some praise at morning what they blame at
    night;
But always think the last opinion right.
Ibid., ll. 430–1

27 We think our fathers fools, so wise we grow;
Our wiser sons, no doubt will think us so.
Ibid., ll. 438–9

28 Fondly we think we honour merit then,
When we but praise ourselves in other men.
Ibid., ll. 454–5

29 Good nature and good sense must ever join;
To err is human, to forgive, divine.
Ibid., ll. 524–5

30 All seems infected that th'infected spy,
As all looks yellow to the jaundiced eye.
Ibid., ll. 558–9

31 Fools rush in where angels fear to tread.
Ibid., l. 625

32 Vital spark of heavenly flame!
Quit, oh quit this mortal frame:
Trembling, hoping, lingering, flying,
Oh the pain, the bliss of dying!
'The Dying Christian to his Soul', publ. in Ode on St Cecilia's
Day MDCCVIII and Other Pieces for Music (1713)

33 To wake the soul by tender strokes of art,
To raise the genius, and to mend the heart;
To make mankind, in conscious virtue bold,
Live o'er each scene, and be what they behold:
For this the Tragic Muse first trod the stage.
'Prologue to Addison's Tragedy of Cato', ll. 1–5 (1713), repr. in
Poetical Works (ed. Herbert Davis, 1966)

34 They dream in courtship, but in wedlock wake.
'The Wife of Bath', l. 103 (1713), ibid.

35 Here hills and vales, the woodland and the
    plain,
Here earth and water seem to strive again,
Not chaos-like together crushed and bruised,
But, as the world, harmoniously confused:
Where order in variety we see,
And where, though all things differ, all agree.
'Windsor Forest', ll. 11–16 (1713), ibid.

36 What dire offence from amorous causes
    springs,
What mighty contests rise from trivial things.
The Rape of the Lock, canto 1, l. 1 (1714)

37 With varying vanities, from every part,
They shift the moving toyshop of their heart.
Ibid., canto 1, ll. 99–100

38 If to her share some female errors fall,
Look on her face, and you'll forget 'em all.
Ibid., canto 2, ll. 17–18

39 Fair tresses man's imperial race ensnare,
And beauty draws us with a single hair.
Ibid., canto 2, ll. 27–8

40 He saw, he wished, and to the prize aspired.
Resolved to win, he meditates the way,
By force to ravish, or by fraud betray;
For when success a lover's toil attends,
Few ask if fraud or force attained his ends.
Ibid., canto 2, ll. 30–4

41 Smooth flow the waves, and the zephyrs gently
    play,

Belinda smiled, and all the world was gay.
Ibid., canto 2, ll. 51–2

42 Here thou, great Anna! whom three realms obey,
Dost sometimes counsel take – and sometimes tea.
Ibid., canto 3, ll. 7–8

43 At every word a reputation dies.
Ibid., canto 3, l. 16

44 Let spades be trumps! She said, and trumps they were.
Ibid., canto 3, l. 46

45 The hungry judges soon the sentence sign,
And wretches hang that jurymen may dine.
Ibid., canto 3, ll. 21–2

46 Coffee, (which makes the politician wise,
And see through all things with his half-shut eyes).
Ibid., canto 3, ll. 117–18

47 But when to mischief mortals bend their will,
How soon they find fit instruments of ill.
Ibid., canto 3, ll. 125–6

48 Not louder shrieks to pitying heaven are cast,
When husbands or when lapdogs breathe their last.
Ibid., canto 3, ll. 157–8

49 Beauties in vain their pretty eyes may roll;
Charms strike the sight, but merit wins the soul.
Ibid., canto 5, ll. 33–4

50 Dear, damned, distracting town, farewell!
Thy fools no more I'll tease:
This year in peace, ye critics, dwell,
Ye harlots, sleep at ease!
'A Farewell to London', st. 1 (1715), repr. in *Poetical Works* (ed. Herbert Davis, 1966)

51 Luxurious lobster-nights, farewell
For sober, studious days.
'A Farewell to London', st. 12, ibid.

52 Achilles' wrath, to Greece the direful spring
Of woes unnumbered, heavenly goddess, sing!
The Iliad, bk 1, ll. 1–2 (translation, 1715). See HOMER 1.

53 Unruly murmurs or ill-timed applause
Wrong the best speaker or the justest cause.
Ibid., bk 2, ll. 86–7

54 She went, to plain-work, and to purling brooks,
Old-fashioned halls, dull aunts, and croaking rooks:
She went from opera, park, assembly, play,

To morning-walks, and prayers three hours a day;
To pass her time 'twixt reading and Bohea,
To muse, and spill her solitary tea,
Or o'er cold coffee trifle with the spoon,
Court the slow clock, and dine exact at noon.
'Epistle to Miss Blount, on her leaving the Town, after the Coronation', ll. 10–18 (1717), repr. in *Poetical Works* (ed. Herbert Davis, 1966)

55 Oh happy state! when souls each other draw,
When love is liberty, and nature, law:
All then is full, possessing, and possessed,
No craving void left aching in the breast.
'Eloisa to Abelard', ll. 91–4, ibid.

56 Of all affliction taught a lover yet,
'Tis sure the hardest science to forget!
'Eloisa to Abelard', ll. 189–90, ibid.

57 How shall I lose the sin, yet keep the sense,
And love th'offender, yet detest th'offence?
'Eloisa to Abelard', ll. 191–2, ibid.

58 How happy is the blameless Vestal's lot?
The world forgetting, by the world forgot.
'Eloisa to Abelard', ll. 207–8, ibid.

59 What beckoning ghost, along the moonlight shade
Invites my step, and points to yonder glade?
'Elegy to the Memory of an Unfortunate Lady', ll. 1–2, ibid.

60 Is it, in heaven, a crime to love too well?
To bear too tender, or too firm a heart,
To act a lover's or a Roman's part?
Is there no bright reversion in the sky,
For those who greatly think, or bravely die?
'Elegy to the Memory of an Unfortunate Lady', ll. 6–10, ibid.

61 Ambition first sprung from your blest abodes;
The glorious fault of angels and of gods.
'Elegy to the Memory of an Unfortunate Lady', ll. 13–14, ibid.

62 How loved, how honoured once, avails thee not,
To whom related, or by whom begot;
A heap of dust alone remains of thee;
'Tis all thou art, and all the proud shall be!
'Elegy to the Memory of an Unfortunate Lady', ll. 71–4, ibid.

63 Let me tell you I am better acquainted with you for a long absence, as men are with themselves for a long affliction: absence does but hold off a friend, to make one see him the truer.
Letter to JONATHAN SWIFT, 14 December 1725, publ. in *The Correspondence of Alexander Pope*, vol. 2 (ed. George Sherburn, 1956)

64 Party is the madness of many for the gain of a few.

'Thoughts on Various Subjects', publ. in *Miscellanies*, vol. 2, (1727), repr. in *The Prose Works of Alexander Pope*, vol. 2 (ed. Rosemary Cowler, 1986). Pope had previously written, in a letter, 27 August 1714: 'I find myself . . . hoping a total end of all the unhappy divisions of mankind by party-spirit, which at best is but the madness of many for the gain of a few.' (*Correspondence of Alexander Pope*, vol. 1 (ed. George Sherburn, 1956).)

65 To endeavour to work upon the vulgar with fine sense, is like attempting to hew blocks with a razor.

'Thoughts on Various Subjects', ibid.

66 Some people will never learn anything; for this reason, because they understand everything too soon.

'Thoughts on Various Subjects', ibid.

67 There are some solitary wretches, who seem to have left the rest of mankind only as Eve left Adam, to meet the devil in private.

'Thoughts on Various Subjects', ibid.

68 It is with narrow-souled people as with narrow-necked bottles: the less they have in them, the more noise they make in pouring it out.

'Thoughts on Various Subjects', ibid.

69 The most positive men are the most credulous.

'Thoughts on Various Subjects', ibid.

70 I have many years ago magnified in my own mind, and repeated to you, a ninth Beatitude, added to the eight in the Scripture: *Blessed is he who expects nothing, for he shall never be disappointed*.

Letter to JOHN GAY, 16 October 1727, publ. in *The Correspondence of Alexander Pope*, vol. 2 (ed. George Sherburn, 1956)

71 The Mighty Mother, and her Son who brings
The Smithfield muses to the ear of kings.

The Dunciad, bk 1 (1728, rev. 1743). Opening lines of poem. In the original version of 1728, the first line is: 'Books and the man I sing, the first who brings . . .' (see VIRGIL 17).

72 Poetic Justice, with her lifted scale,
Where, in nice balance, truth with gold she weighs,
And solid pudding against empty praise.

Ibid., bk 1, ll. 52–4

73 A brain of feathers, and a heart of lead.

Ibid., bk 2, l. 44

74 Peeled, patched and piebald, linsey-wolsey brothers,

Grave mummers! sleeveless some and shirtless others.
That once was Britain – happy!

Ibid., bk 3, ll. 115–17

75 Proceed, great days! 'till Learning fly the shore,
'Till Birch shall blush with noble blood no more,
'Till Thames see Eton's sons for ever play,
'Till Westminster's whole year be holiday,
'Till Isis' elders reel, their pupils' sport,
And Alma mater lie dissolved in port!

Ibid., bk 3, ll. 333–8

76 A wit with dunces, and a dunce with wits.

Ibid., bk 4, l. 90

77 Leave not a foot of verse, a foot of stone,
A page, a grave, that they can call their own;
But spread, my sons, your glory thin or thick,
On passive paper, or on solid brick.

Ibid., bk 4, ll. 127–30

78 Whate'er the talents, or howe'er designed,
We hang one jingling padlock on the mind.

Ibid., bk 4, ll. 161–2

79 The Right Divine of Kings to govern wrong.

Ibid., bk 4, l. 187

80 For thee we dim the eyes, and stuff the head
With all such reading as was never read:
For thee explain a thing till all men doubt it,
And write about it, Goddess, and about it.

Ibid., bk 4, ll. 249–52

81 With the same cement, ever sure to bind,
We bring to one dead level every mind.
Then take him to develop, if you can,
And hew the block off, and get out the man.

Ibid., bk 4, ll. 267–70

82 Isles of fragrance, lily-silvered vales.

Ibid., bk 4, l. 303

83 She marked thee there,
Stretched on the rack of a too easy chair,
And heard thy everlasting yawn confess
The pains and penalties of idleness.

Ibid., bk 4, ll. 343–6

84 See skulking Truth to her old cavern fled,
Mountains of casuistry heaped o'er her head!
Philosophy, that leaned on Heaven before,
Shrinks to her second cause, and is no more.
Physic of Metaphysic begs defence,
And Metaphysic calls for aid on Sense!

Ibid., bk 4, ll. 641–6

85 Religion blushing veils her sacred fires,
And unawares Morality expires.
Ibid., bk 4, ll. 649–50

86 Lo! thy dread empire, Chaos! is restored;
Light dies before thy uncreating word:
Thy hand, great Anarch! lets the curtain fall;
And universal darkness buries all.
Ibid., bk 4, ll. 653–6. Closing lines of poem.

87 Nature and nature's laws lay hid in night;
God said *Let Newton be!* and all was light.
'Epitaph Intended for Sir Isaac Newton in Westminster Abbey'
(1730), repr. in *Poetical Works* (ed. Herbert Davis, 1966). The
author J. C. (Sir John) Squire (1884–1958) coined the following
epigram in answer to Pope's: 'It did not last: the Devil, howling "Ho!/ Let Einstein be!" restored the status quo.'

88 'Tis from high life high characters are drawn;
A saint in crape is twice a saint in lawn.
Epistles to Several Persons (also known as *Moral Essays*, 1731–
5), Epistle 1 ('To Sir Richard Temple, Lord Cobham'), ll. 135–6

89 'Tis education forms the common mind,
Just as the twig is bent, the tree's inclined.
Ibid., Epistle 1, ll. 149–50, ibid.

90 Search then the ruling passion: There, alone,
The wild are constant, and the cunning known;
The fool consistent, and the false sincere.
Ibid., Epistle 1, ll. 174–6, ibid.

91 Old politicians chew on wisdom past,
And totter on in business to the last.
Ibid., Epistle 1, ll. 228–9

92 Nothing so true as what you once let fall,
'Most women have no characters at all.'
Epistle 2 ('To a Lady'), ll. 1–2, ibid.

93 Chaste to her husband, frank to all beside,
A teeming mistress, but a barren bride.
Epistle 2, ll. 71–2, ibid.

94 Virtue she finds too painful an endeavour,
Content to dwell in decencies for ever.
Epistle 2, ll. 163–4, ibid.

95 She, while her lover pants upon her breast,
Can mark the figures on an Indian chest.
Epistle 2, ll. 167–8, ibid.

96 In men, we various ruling passions find;
In women, two almost divide the kind;
Those, only fixed, they first or last obey,
The love of pleasure, and the love of sway.
Epistle 2, ll. 207–10, ibid.

97 Men, some to business, some to pleasure take;
But every woman is at heart a rake:
Men, some to quiet, some to public strife;
But every lady would be queen for life.
Epistle 2, ll. 215–18, ibid.

98 Still round and round the ghosts of Beauty
glide,
And haunt the places where their honour
died.
See how the world its veterans rewards!
A youth of frolics, an old age of cards.
Epistle 2, ll. 241–4, ibid.

99 She, who ne'er answers till a husband
cools,
Or, if she rules him, never shows she rules;
Charms by accepting, by submitting sways,
Yet has her humour most, when she obeys.
Epistle 2, ll. 261–4, ibid.

100 And mistress of herself, though china fall.
Epistle 2, l. 268, ibid.

101 Woman's at best a contradiction still.
Epistle 2, l. 270, ibid.

102 Who shall decide, when doctors disagree,
And soundest casuists doubt, like you and me?
Epistle 3 ('To Lord Bathurst'), ll. 1–2, ibid.

103 Blest paper-credit! last and best supply!
That lends corruption lighter wings to fly!
Epistle 3, ll. 39–40, ibid.

104 But thousands die without or this or that,
Die, and endow a college, or a cat:
To some, indeed, Heav'n grants the happier fate,
T'enrich a bastard, or a son they hate.
Epistle 3, ll. 95–8, ibid.

105 The ruling passion, be it what it will,
The ruling passion conquers reason still.
Epistle 3, ll. 153–4, ibid.

106 Consult the genius of the place in all.
Epistle 4 ('To the Earl of Burlington'), l. 57, ibid. See VIRGIL 45.

107 To rest, the cushion and soft Dean invite,
Who never mentions Hell to ears polite.
Epistle 4, ll. 149–50, ibid.

108 Another age shall see the golden ear
Imbrown the slope, and nod on the parterre,
Deep harvests bury all his pride has planned,
And laughing Ceres reassume the land.
Epistle 4, ll. 173–6, ibid.

109 'Tis use alone that sanctifies expense,
And splendour borrows all her rays from sense.
Epistle 4, ll. 179–80, ibid.

110 You too proceed! make falling arts your care,
Erect new wonders, and the old repair;
Jones and Palladio to themselves restore,
And be whate'er Vitruvius was before.
Epistle 4, ll. 191–4, ibid.

111 You beat your pate, and fancy wit will come:
Knock as you please, there's nobody at home.
'Another Epigram', publ. in *Miscellanies* vol. 3 (1732)

112 Sir, I admit your general rule,
That every poet is a fool,
But you yourself may serve to show it,
That every fool is not a poet.
'Epigram from the French', ibid.

113 Good God! how often are we to die before we go
quite off this stage? In every friend we lose a part
of ourselves, and the best part.
Letter to JONATHAN SWIFT, 5 December 1732, publ. in *The
Correspondence of Alexander Pope*, vol. 3 (ed. George Sherburn, 1956). Written the day after the death of playwright
JOHN GAY.

114 Awake, my St John! leave all meaner things
To low ambition, and the pride of kings.
Let us (since Life can little more supply
Than just to look about us and to die)
Expatiate free o'er all this scene of man;
A mighty maze! but not without a plan.
An Essay on Man, Epistle 1, ll. 1–6 (1733). Addressing HENRY
ST JOHN, VISCOUNT BOLINGBROKE.

115 Eye nature's walks, shoot folly as it flies,
And catch the manners living as they rise;
Laugh where we must, be candid where we can;
But vindicate the ways of God to man.
Ibid., Epistle 1, ll. 13–16. See JOHN MILTON 84.

116 Observe how system into system runs,
What other planets circle other suns.
Ibid., Epistle 1, ll. 25–6

117 Pleased to the last, he crops the flowery food,
And licks the hand just raised to shed his blood.
Ibid., Epistle 1, ll. 83–4. Referring to a lamb about to be
slaughtered.

118 Who sees with equal eye, as God of all,
A hero perish, or a sparrow fall,
Atoms or systems into ruin hurled,
And now a bubble burst, and now a world.
Ibid., Epistle 1, ll. 87–90

119 Hope springs eternal in the human breast:
Man never is, but always to be blest.
Ibid., Epistle 1, ll. 95–6

120 Lo! the poor Indian, whose untutored mind
Sees God in clouds, or hears him in the wind;
His soul proud science never taught to stray
Far as the solar walk, or milky way;
Yet simple nature to his hope has given,
Behind the cloud-topped hill, an humbler heaven.
Ibid., Epistle 1, ll. 99–104

121 Pride still is aiming at the blest abodes,
Men would be angels, angels would be gods.
Ibid., Epistle 1, ll. 125–6

122 Why has not man a microscopic eye?
For this plain reason, man is not a fly.
Ibid., Epistle 1, ll. 193–4

123 Die of a rose in aromatic pain.
Ibid., Epistle 1, l. 200. See LADY WINCHILSEA 1.

124 The spider's touch, how exquisitely fine!
Feels at each thread, and lives along the line.
Ibid., Epistle 1, ll. 217–18

125 All are but parts of one stupendous whole,
Whose body, nature is, and God the soul.
Ibid., Epistle 1, ll. 267–8

126 All nature is but art, unknown to thee;
All chance, direction, which thou canst not see;
All discord, harmony, not understood;
All partial evil, universal good:
And, spite of pride, in erring reason's spite,
One truth is clear, 'Whatever is, is right.'
Ibid., Epistle 1, ll. 289–94

127 Know then thyself, presume not to God to
scan;
The proper study of mankind is man.
Placed on this isthmus of a middle state,
A being darkly wise, and rudely great.
With too much knowledge for the sceptic side,
With too much weakness for the stoic's pride,
He hangs between; in doubt to act, or rest,
In doubt to deem himself a god, or beast;
In doubt his mind or body to prefer,
Born but to die, and reasoning but to err;
Alike in ignorance, his reason such,
Whether he thinks too little, or too much.
Ibid., Epistle 2, ll. 1–12. See PIERRE CHARRON 1.

128 Created half to rise, and half to fall;
Great lord of all things, yet a prey to all;

Sole judge of truth, in endless error hurled;
The glory, jest, and riddle of the world!
Ibid., Epistle 2, ll. 15–18

129 Go, teach Eternal Wisdom how to rule –
Then drop into thyself, and be a fool!
Ibid., Epistle 2, ll. 29–30

130 Fixed like a plant on his peculiar spot,
To draw nutrition, propagate, and rot.
Ibid., Epistle 2, ll. 63–4

131 Vice is a monster of so frightful mien,
As, to be hated, needs but to be seen;
Yet seen too oft, familiar with her face,
We first endure, then pity, then embrace.
Ibid., Epistle 2, ll. 217–20

132 The learned is happy nature to explore,
The fool is happy that he knows no more.
Ibid., Epistle 2, ll. 263–4

133 Behold the child, by nature's kindly law,
Pleased with a rattle, tickled with a straw:
Some livelier plaything gives his youth delight,
A little louder, but as empty quite:
Scarfs, garters, gold, amuse his riper stage;
And beads and prayer books are the toys of age:
Pleased with this bauble still, as that before;
'Till tired he sleeps, and life's poor play is o'er!
Ibid., Epistle 2, ll. 275–82

134 Learn from the birds what food the thickets
  yield;
Learn from the beasts the physic of the field;
The arts of building from the bee receive;
Learn of the mole to plough, the worm to weave.
Ibid., Epistle 3, ll. 173–6

135 For forms of government let fools contest;
Whate'er is best administered is best.
Ibid., Epistle 3, ll. 303–4

136 Thus God and nature linked the general frame,
And bade self-love and social be the same.
Ibid., Epistle 3, ll. 317–18. Last words of epistle.

137 Oh happiness! our being's end and aim!
Good, pleasure, ease, content! whate'er thy name:
That something still which prompts th'eternal
  sigh,
For which we bear to live, or dare to die.
Ibid., Epistle 4, ll. 1–4 (1734)

138 Order is heaven's first law; and this confessed,
Some are, and must be, greater than the rest,

More rich, more wise; but who infers from
  hence
That such are happier, shocks all common
  sense.
  . . .
Condition, circumstance, is not the thing;
Bliss is the same in subject or in king.
Ibid., Epistle 4, ll. 49–58. See SAMUEL JOHNSON 68.

139 A wit's a feather, and a chief a rod;
An honest man's the noblest work of God.
Ibid., Epistle 4, ll. 247–8

140 Say, shall my little bark attendant sail,
Pursue the triumph and partake the gale?
Ibid., Epistle 4, ll. 385–6

141 All our knowledge is ourselves to know.
Ibid., Epistle 4, l. 398. Last line of poem.

142 Shut, shut the door, good John! fatigued I said,
Tie up the knocker, say I'm sick, I'm dead,
The dog-star rages!
'Epistle to Dr Arbuthnot, Prologue to the Satires', ll. 1–3, publ.
in *Imitations of Horace* (1733–8)

143 Why did I write? what sin to me unknown
Dipped me in ink, my parents', or my own?
'Epistle to Dr Arbuthnot', ll. 125–6, ibid.

144 As yet a child, nor yet a fool to fame,
I lisped in numbers, for the numbers came.
'Epistle to Dr Arbuthnot', ll. 127–8, ibid.

145 This long disease, my life.
'Epistle to Dr Arbuthnot', l. 132, ibid.

146 Did some more sober critic come abroad?
If wrong, I smiled; if right, I kissed the rod.
'Epistle to Dr Arbuthnot', ll. 157–8, ibid.

147 Pretty! in amber to observe the forms
Of hairs, or straws, or dirt, or grubs, or worms!
The things, we know, are neither rich nor rare,
But wonder how the devil they got there?
'Epistle to Dr Arbuthnot', ll. 169–172, ibid.

148 And he, whose fustian's so sublimely bad,
It is not poetry, but prose run mad.
'Epistle to Dr Arbuthnot', ll. 187–8, ibid.

149 Damn with faint praise, assent with civil leer,
And without sneering, teach the rest to sneer;
Willing to wound, and yet afraid to strike,
Just hint a fault, and hesitate dislike.
'Epistle to Dr Arbuthnot', ll. 201–4, ibid. Referring to JOSEPH
ADDISON.

150 Like Cato, give his little senate laws,
And sit attentive to his own applause.
'Epistle to Dr Arbuthnot', ll. 209–10, ibid. Referring to JOSEPH
ADDISON.

151 Who breaks a butterfly upon a wheel?
'Epistle to Dr Arbuthnot', l. 308, ibid. Referring to the politician and wit Lord Hervey. The line achieved notoriety when
it was used to head the London *Times* leader of 1 July 1967,
commenting on the arrest of MICK JAGGER and KEITH
RICHARDS on drugs charges – an article which was thought
to have contributed to their acquittal.

152 And he himself one vile antithesis.
'Epistle to Dr Arbuthnot', l. 325, ibid. Referring to Lord Hervey.

153 A cherub's face, a reptile all the rest.
'Epistle to Dr Arbuthnot', l. 331, ibid. Referring to Lord Hervey.

154 Wit that can creep, and pride that licks the
   dust.
'Epistle to Dr Arbuthnot', l. 333, ibid.

155 Unlearned, he knew no schoolman's subtle art,
No language, but the language of the heart.
'Epistle to Dr Arbuthnot', ll. 398–9, ibid. Referring to his
father.

156 For I, who hold sage Homer's rule the best,
Welcome the coming, speed the going guest.
'The Second Satire of the Second Book of Horace Imitated',
ll. 159–60, ibid. A similar phrase, 'Speed the parting guest',
appears in Pope's translation of the Odyssey, bk 15, l. 84
(1725–6).

157 Not to go back, is somewhat to advance,
And men must walk at least before they dance.
'The First Epistle of the First Book of Horace Imitated', ll. 53–4,
ibid.

158 Get place and wealth, if possible, with grace;
If not, by any means get wealth and place.
'The First Epistle of the First Book of Horace Imitated',
ll. 103–4, ibid. See HORACE 56.

159 The people's voice is odd,
It is, and it is not, the voice of God.
'The First Epistle of the Second Book of Horace Imitated',
ll. 89–90, ibid.

160 But those who cannot write, and those who
   can,
All rhyme, and scrawl, and scribble, to a man.
'The First Epistle of the Second Book of Horace Imitated',
ll. 187–8, ibid.

161 Learn to live well, or fairly make your will;
You've played, and loved, and eat, and drunk your
   fill:

Walk sober off; before a sprightlier age
Comes tittering on, and shoves you from the stage:
Leave such to trifle with more grace and ease,
Whom folly pleases, and whose follies please.
'The Second Epistle of the Second Book of Horace Imitated',
ll. 322–7, ibid. Last lines of poem.

162 The worst of madmen is a saint run mad.
'The Sixth Epistle of the First Book of Horace Imitated', l. 27,
ibid.

163 I've often wished that I had clear
For life, six hundred pounds a year,
A handsome house to lodge a friend,
A river at my garden's end,
A terrace walk, and half a rood
Of land set out to plant a wood.
'The Sixth Satire of the Second Book of Horace', ll. 1–6, ibid

164 I am his Highness' dog at Kew;
Pray tell me, sir, whose dog are you?
'Epigram Engraved on the Collar of a Dog which I Gave to His
Royal Highness' (1738), repr. in *Poems of Alexander Pope*, vol. 6
(ed. John Butt, 1954). Dedicated to Frederick, Prince of Wales.

165 Teach me to feel another's woe;
To hide the fault I see;
That mercy I to others show,
That mercy show to me.
'The Universal Prayer', ll. 37–40 (1738), repr. in *Poetical Works*
(ed. Herbert Davis, 1966)

166 Cibber! write all thy verses upon glasses,
The only way to save 'em from our arses.
'Epigrams Occasioned by Cibber's Verses in Praise of Nash',
no. 2, publ. in *Minor Poems* (ed. Norman Ault and John Butt,
1954). Referring to COLLEY CIBBER.

(Sir) Karl Popper
(1902–94)
Austrian-born British philosopher

His first and major book The Logic of Scientific Discovery
*(1934) posits the doctrine that true scientific theories must pass
the test of 'falsifiability'. Later works criticized* PLATO, HEGEL
and MARX. *He was a professor at the London School of Economics 1949–69.*

1 We may become the makers of our own fate when
we have ceased to pose as its prophets.
The Open Society and its Enemies, Introduction (1945)

2 All science is cosmology, I believe, and for me the
interest of philosophy, no less than that of science,

lies solely in the contributions which it has made to it.

Preface (1959) to *The Logic of Scientific Discovery* (1934)

3 For this, indeed, is the true source of our ignorance – the fact that our knowledge can only be finite, while our ignorance must necessarily be infinite.

Lecture to British Academy, 20 January 1960, publ. in *Proceedings of the British Academy*, vol. 4 (1960)

4 Science may be described as the art of systematic over-simplification.

Quoted in the *Observer* 1 August 1982

Cole Porter

(1893–1964)

US composer and lyricist

The epitome of suave sophistication, he was unequalled for his deft and witty wordplay set to perfectly adapted melodies. His hit musical shows include Anything Goes *(1934) and* Kiss Me Kate *(1948).*

1 If you want to buy my wares
Follow me and climb the stairs . . .
Love for sale.

'Love For Sale' (song) in *The New Yorkers* (stage musical, 1930)

2 Night and day, you are the one,
Only you beneath the moon and under the sun.

'Night and Day' (song) in *The Gay Divorce* (stage musical, 1932, filmed as *The Gay Divorcee*, 1934). Originally sung by Fred Astaire.

3 Oh, give me land, lots of land
Under starry skies above
Don't fence me in.

'Don't Fence Me In' (song, 1934). The song was a hit for BING CROSBY with the Andrews Sisters and revived in *Hollywood Canteen* (film musical, 1944).

4 I've got you under my skin.

'I've Got You Under My Skin' (song, 1934), in *Born to Dance* (film musical, 1936)

5 In olden days a glimpse of stocking
Was looked on as something shocking
But now, God knows,
Anything goes.

'Anything Goes' (song) in *Anything Goes* (stage musical 1934, film 1956). Sung by Ethel Merman in the musical and by Mitzi Gaynor in the film version.

6 Good authors, too, who once knew better words
Now only use four-letter words

Writing prose . . .
Anything goes.

'Anything Goes', ibid.

7 At words poetic, I'm so pathetic
That I always have found it best
Instead of getting 'em off my chest,
To let 'em rest unexpressed.

'You're the Top' (song), ibid. Sung by William Gaxton and Ethel Merman in the original show, the song was recorded by Porter himself and later covered by Ella Fitzgerald and Buddy Greco, among others. The lyrics were adapted by P. G. WODEHOUSE for the 1935 London show.

8 You're the Nile,
You're the Tower of Pisa,
You're the smile
On the Mona Lisa . . .
But if, baby, I'm the bottom,
You're the top!

'You're the Top', ibid.

9 I get no kick from champagne.
Mere alcohol doesn't thrill me at all,
So tell me why should it be true
That I get a kick out of you.

'I Get a Kick Out of You' (song), ibid.

10 Miss Otis regrets (she's unable to lunch today).

'Miss Otis Regrets' (song) in *Hi Diddle Diddle* (stage musical, 1934)

11 There's no love song finer,
But how strange the change from major to minor
Every time we say goodbye.

'Ev'ry Time We Say Goodbye' (song) in *Seven Lively Arts* (stage musical, 1944). The song was a hit for Benny Goodman (1945) and recorded by Ella Fitzgerald (1956), in a version described by her biographer Stuart Nicholson as 'a "We'll Meet Again" for the Cold War generation'.

12 He may have hair upon his chest
But, sister, so has Lassie.

'I Hate Men' (song) in *Kiss Me Kate* (stage musical 1948, filmed 1953)

13 I love Paris in the springtime.

'I Love Paris' (song) in *Can-Can* (stage musical, 1953, film 1960)

14 Birds do it, bees do it,
Even educated fleas do it.
Let's do it, let's fall in love.

'Let's Do It' (song, 1954). The song was first featured in a 1928 show, *Paris*, without this verse.

15 Who wants to be a millionaire?

'Who wants to be a millionaire' (song) in *High Society* (film musical, 1956)

Katherine Anne Porter

(1890–1980)
US author

Her first short story collection, Flowering Judas, *appeared in 1928. Her best known work,* Ship of Fools *(1962), stirred controversy for its allegorical depiction of inter-war Germany.*

1 They had both noticed that a life of dissipation sometimes gave to a face the look of gaunt suffering spirituality that a life of asceticism was supposed to give and quite often did not.
Ship of Fools, pt 3 (1962). Referring to Herr Freytag and Mrs Treadwell.

Peter Porter

(b. 1929)
Australian poet

Living outside Australia since 1951, he has won acclaim for such collections as Preaching to the Converted *(1972) and* English Subtitles *(1981).* CLIVE JAMES *once quipped that Porter's poems are 'so freighted with learned references that I can't even tell if I don't know what they mean'.*

1 The channels of our lives are blocked,
The hand is stopped upon the clock,
No one can say why hearts will break
And marriages are all opaque:
A map of loss, some posted cards,
The living house reduced to shards,
The abstract hell of memory,
The pointlessness of poetry.
'An Exequy', publ. in *The Cost of Seriousness* (1978)

2 Nobody feels well after his fortieth birthday
But the convalescence is touched by glory.
'Returning', publ. in *English Subtitles* (1981)

Beilby Porteus

(1731–1809)
English clergyman and author

A leading Abolitionist and supporter of evangelical reformers, he helped establish the system of Sunday Schools and published sermons and tracts. He was Bishop of London 1787–1809.

1 One murder made a villain,
Millions a hero.
Death, ll. 154–5 (1759). The remark was revived in CHARLIE CHAPLIN's 1947 film *Monsieur Verdoux.* See JEAN ROSTAND 1.

2 War its thousands slays, Peace, its ten thousands.
Ibid., l. 178. See BIBLE, OLD TESTAMENT: 1 SAMUEL 17 .

Beatrix Potter

(1866–1943)
English author

She is known for her children's stories of animals, beginning with The Tale of Peter Rabbit *(1900), which were illustrated with her own watercolours.*

1 Now my dears, you may go into the fields or down the lane, but don't go into Mr McGregor's garden: your Father had an accident there; he was put in a pie by Mrs McGregor.
The Tale of Peter Rabbit (1900). Spoken by Mrs Rabbit to Flopsy, Mopsy, Cotton-tail and Peter.

2 I am worn to a ravelling . . . I am undone and worn to a thread-paper, for I have NO MORE TWIST.
The Tailor of Gloucester (1903). Spoken by the tailor.

Dennis Potter

(1935–94)
British dramatist and screenwriter

The writer of controversial and innovative plays for the BBC for nearly thirty years, he often evoked memories of his own youth in his work, as in Pennies from Heaven *(1978),* Blue Remembered Hills *(1979) and* The Singing Detective *(1986).*

1 To be a candidate is to submit to a personally humiliating experience, in which the set smile freezes on your face like a grin on a corpse. Dead ideas. Dead thoughts. Dead slogans. All of them sicked up on your doorstep. No wonder people are disgusted by this gruesome charade.
Vote Vote Vote For Nigel Barton, Sc. 24 (BBC play, broadcast 15 December 1965). Nigel Barton addresses the council.

2 The patch of blue sky. The gold of the, of the bleed'n dawn, or – the light in somebody's eyes – Pennies From Heaven, that's what it is. And we can't see 'em, clinking and clinking, all around, all over the place . . . just bend down and pick 'em up.
Pennies From Heaven, episode 2 (BBC television series, 1978). Spoken by Arthur.

3 The trouble with words is that you never know whose mouths they've been in.
Guardian 15 February 1993

4 Religion to me has always been the wound, not the bandage.
Interview with Melvyn Bragg, Channel 4, 5 April 1994

5 I think we should always look back on our own past with a sort of tender contempt. As long as the tenderness is there but also please let some of the

contempt be there, because we know what we're like, we know how we hustle and bustle and shove and push, and you sometimes use grand words to cloak it.
Ibid.

6 Cheap songs, so-called, actually do have something of the Psalms of David about them. They do say the world is other than it is. They do illuminate. This is why people say, 'Listen, they're playing our song'. It's not because that particular song actually expresses the depth of the feelings that they felt when they met each other and heard it. It is that somehow it re-evokes it, but with a different coating of irony and self-knowledge.
Ibid.

Eugène Pottier
(1816–87)
French poet and communard

He was an agitator during the Revolution of 1848 and a member of the Commune in 1871, when he wrote his best-known work, the 'Internationale'.

1 *Debout! les damnés de la terre!*
Debout! les forçats de la faim!
[Arise, you wretched of the earth
Arise, you prisoners of starvation.]
'L'Internationale' (1871). Set to a marching tune of Pierre Deygeter (1888), these words have been sung by socialists and communists throughout the world in various versions.

2 *C'est la lutte finale*
Groupons-nous, et demain
L'Internationale
Sera le genre humain.
['Tis the final conflict, let each stand in his place. The International shall be the human race.]
Ibid., refrain

Ezra Pound
(1885–1972)
US poet and critic

A founder of the Imagist movement while in London (1908–20), he settled in Italy in 1925, from where he broadcast Fascist propaganda during the Second World War. He was confined to a mental hospital 1945–58. His main works are the Cantos *(written 1917–70), and he also translated widely. See* GERTRUDE STEIN 4.

1 'Tis the white stag, Fame, we're a-hunting,
Bid the world's hounds come to horn!
'The White Stag', publ. in *Personae* (1909)

2 Humanity is the rich effluvium, it is the waste and the manure and the soil, and from it grows the tree of the arts.
Poetry October 1914. Objecting to words by Walt Whitman used as the motto on the cover of the magazine *Poetry*. See WALT WHITMAN 38.

3 The Image is more than an idea. It is a vortex or cluster of fused ideas and is endowed with energy.
'Affirmations – As for Imagisme' (1915), repr. in *Selected Prose 1909–1965*, pt 7 (ed. William Cookson, 1973)

4 If a patron buys from an artist who needs money (needs money to buy tools, time, food), the patron then makes himself equal to the artist; he is building art into the world; he creates.
Letter, 8 March 1915, publ. in *The Letters of Ezra Pound 1907–1941* (ed. D. D. Paige, 1951). Pound was urging US collector John Quinn to support the new renaissance of the arts that Pound believed was imminent.

5 The leaves fall early this autumn, in wind.
The paired butterflies are already yellow with
    August
Over the grass in the West garden;
They hurt me. I grow older.
If you are coming down through the narrows of
    the river Kiang,
Please let me know beforehand,
And I will come out to meet you
As far as Cho-fu-sa.
'The River Merchant's Wife: A Letter', publ. in *Lustra* (1916). Translated from the Chinese poet Li Po, or Rihaku (701–62).

6 The apparition of these faces in the crowd;
Petals on a wet, black bough.
'In a Station of the Metro', ibid.

7 Winter is icummen in,
Lhude sing Goddamm,
Raineth drop and staineth slop,
And how the wind doth ramm!
Sing: Goddamm.
'Ancient Music', publ. in *Lustra* (1917 edn). Pound's pastiche of the medieval song 'Sumer is icumen in' (see ANONYMOUS 90) was originally dropped from the 1916 edition of *Lustra*, having been considered offensive.

8 A man of genius has a right to any mode of expression.
Letter to the painter J. B. Yeats (father of W. B. YEATS), 4 February 1918, quoted in *A Serious Character*, pt 2, ch. 10 (1988) by Humphrey Carpenter

9 For three years, out of key with his time,
He strove to resuscitate the dead art

Of poetry; to maintain 'the sublime'
In the old sense. Wrong from the start –
No, hardly, but seeing he had been born
In a half-savage country, out of date;
Bent resolutely on wringing lilies from the acorns;
Capaneus; trout for factitious bait.

'E. P. Ode pour l'élection de son sépulcre', pt 1, publ. in *Hugh Selwyn Mauberley* (1920)

10 The age demanded an image
Of its accelerated grimace,
Something for the modern stage,
Not, at any rate, an Attic grace;
Not, not certainly, the obscure reveries
Of the inward gaze;
Better mendacities
Than the classics in paraphrase!

'E. P. Ode pour l'élection de son sépulcre', pt 2, ibid.

11 Some quick to arm,
some for adventure,
some from fear of weakness,
some from fear of censure,
some for love of slaughter, in imagination,
learning later ...
some in fear learning love of slaughter;
Died some, pro patria, non 'dulce' non 'et décor'
walked eye-deep in hell
believing in old men's lies, the unbelieving
came home, home to a lie.

'E. P. Ode pour l'élection de son sépulcre', pt 4. See HORACE 36 and WILFRED OWEN 3.

12 There died a myriad,
And of the best, among them,
For an old bitch gone in the teeth,
For a botched civilization.

'E. P. Ode pour l'élection de son sépulcre', pt 5, ibid.

13 The curse of me & my nation is that we always think things can be bettered by immediate action of some sort, *any* sort rather than no sort.

Letter to JAMES JOYCE, 7–8 June 1920, publ. in *Pound/Joyce: The Letters of Ezra Pound to James Joyce* (ed. Forrest Read, 1968)

14 Great literature is simply language charged with meaning to the utmost possible degree.

How to Read, pt 2 (1931)

15 The author's conviction on this day of New Year is that music begins to atrophy when it departs too far from the dance; that poetry begins to atrophy when it gets too far from music; but this must not be taken as implying that all good music is dance music or all poetry lyric. Bach and Mozart are never too far from physical movement.

ABC of Reading, 'Warning' (1934)

16 Literature is news that STAYS news.

Ibid., ch. 2

17 AS A MIND, who the hell else is there left for me to take an interest IN??

Letter, 28 August 1934, quoted in *A Serious Character*, pt 3, ch. 13 (1988) by Humphrey Carpenter. Referring to MUSSO-LINI. Interviewed in May 1945, Pound described Mussolini as 'a very human, imperfect character who lost his head', and in the opening lines of canto 74 (first of his *Pisan Cantos*, written in 1948 while he was awaiting trial for treason), he spoke of 'the enormous tragedy of the dream in the peasant's bent shoulders'.

18 Here is a dirty book worth reading ... a bawdy which will be very useful to put Wyndham and JJ into their proper cubby holes; cause Miller is sore and without kinks.

Letter, 1 December 1934, quoted by Karl Shapiro in 'The Great-est Living Author', preface to *Tropic of Cancer* (1960 edn) by Henry Miller. Referring to HENRY MILLER's *Tropic of Cancer*, which was first published in Paris in 1934, but suppressed in the USA and Britain. 'Wyndham' was WYNDHAM LEWIS, 'JJ' JAMES JOYCE.

19 Man is an over-complicated organism. If he is doomed to extinction he will die out for want of simplicity.

Guide to Kulchur, pt 3, sect. 5, ch. 19 (1938)

20 In our time, the curse is monetary illiteracy, just as inability to read plain print was the curse of earlier centuries.

Ibid. pt 4, sect. 8, ch. 31

21 Mass ought to be in Latin, unless you cd. do it in Greek or Chinese. In fact, *any* abracadabra that no bloody member of the public or half-educated ape of a clargimint cd. think he understood.

Letter, 7 March 1940, publ. in *The Letters of Ezra Pound 1907–1941* (ed. D. D. Paige, 1951)

22 Adolf Hitler was a Jeanne d'Arc, a saint. He was a martyr. Like many martyrs, he held extreme views.

Interview in the *Philadelphia Record* and *Chicago Sun* 9 May 1945

23 I guess the definition of a lunatic is a man sur-rounded by them.

Quoted in *Charles Olson and Ezra Pound*, 'Canto 3, January 24 1946' (1975) by Catherine Seelye. Said to CHARLES OLSON in 1945, when Olson visited Pound in St Elizabeth's Hospital, Washington, the institution for the criminally insane in which Pound was detained pending a judgement on his war-time broadcasts from Rome.

24 With one day's reading a man may have the key in his hands.
Pisan Cantos, canto 74 (1948)

25 As a lone ant from a broken ant-hill
from the wreckage of Europe, ego scriptor.
Ibid., canto 76

26 WOT IZZA COMIN'?
'I'll tell you wot izza comin'
Sochy-lism is a-comin''
Ibid., canto 77

27 The ant's a centaur in his dragon world.
Pull down thy vanity, it is not man
Made courage, or made order, or made grace,
Pull down thy vanity, I say pull down.
Learn of the green world what can be thy place
In scaled invention or true artistry,
Pull down thy vanity,
Paquin pull down!
The green casque has outdone your elegance.
Ibid., canto 81

28 There once was a brainy baboon
Who always breathed down a bassoon,
For he said, 'It appears
That in billions of years
I shall certainly hit on a tune.'
Letter, 21 July 1949, quoted in *A Serious Character*, pt 2, ch. 16 (1988) by Humphrey Carpenter. Pound himself took up the bassoon for a few months in 1921.

29 Technique is the test of sincerity. If a thing isn't worth getting the technique to say, it is of inferior value.
Interview in *Writers at Work* (second series, ed. George Plimpton, 1963)

30 No verse is *libre* for the man who wants to do a good job.
Ibid.

31 There is natural ignorance and there is artificial ignorance. I should say at the present moment the artificial ignorance is about eighty-five per cent.
Ibid.

32 If the individual, or heretic, gets hold of some essential truth, or sees some error in the system being practised, he commits so many marginal errors himself that he is worn out before he can establish his point.
Ibid. Pound was obliquely referring to his own 'heresy' which resulted in his incarceration in a US mental institution.

33 Somebody said that I am the last American living the tragedy of Europe.
Ibid.

34 The worst mistake I made was that stupid, sub-urban prejudice of anti-Semitism.
In conversation with ALLEN GINSBERG in June 1968, quoted in *A Serious Character*, pt 5, ch. 5 (1988) by Humphrey Carpenter

Anthony Powell
(1905–2000)
British novelist

He is best known for his novel sequence A Dance to the Music of Time *(12 vols. 1951–75), in which he surveys and satirizes the upper middle classes over a period of fifty years.*

1 A Dance to the Music of Time.
Title of novel sequence (1951–75)

2 Parents ... are sometimes a bit of a disappointment to their children. They don't fulfil the promise of their early years.
A Buyer's Market, ch. 2 (1952, second book of *A Dance to the Music of Time*). Spoken by Stringham.

3 Self-love seems so often unrequited.
The Acceptance World, ch. 1 (1955, third book of *A Dance to the Music of Time*). Narrated by Nicholas Jenkins.

4 Growing old's like being increasingly penalized for a crime you haven't committed.
Temporary Kings, ch. 1 (1973, eleventh book of *A Dance to the Music of Time*). Spoken by Dick Umfraville.

Colin Powell
(b. 1937)
US general and politician

A professional soldier for thirty-five years, he became Chairman of the Joint Chiefs of Staff (1989–93) and Secretary of State under GEORGE W. BUSH *2001–4.*

1 A great tragedy has struck our country. It will not affect the nature of our society.
Press conference in Lima, quoted in *The Times* 12 September 2001. Referring to the terrorist attacks on the World Trade Center and the Pentagon, 11 September 2001.

Enoch Powell
(1912–98)
British politician

A classical scholar, austere intellectual and devotee of High Toryism, he became a Conservative MP in 1950 and was Minister of Health (1960–3). His outspoken views on immigration caused him to lose his position in the shadow cabinet in 1968, and he resigned from the Conservative Party in 1974 to serve as an Ulster Unionist MP.

1 History is littered with the wars which everybody knew would never happen.
Speech to Conservative Party Conference, Scarborough, 19 October 1967, quoted in *The Times* 20 October 1967

2 Those whom the gods wish to destroy, they first make mad. We must be mad, literally mad, as a nation to be permitting the annual inflow of some fifty thousand dependants, who are for the most part the material of the future growth of the immigrant-descended population. It is like watching a nation busily engaged in heaping up its own funeral pyre.
Speech to West Midlands Conservatives, Birmingham, 20 April 1968, publ. in *The Penguin Book of Twentieth-Century Speeches* (ed. Brian MacArthur, 1999). Powell was dropped from EDWARD HEATH's shadow cabinet the day after making this notorious warning about the consequences of immigration into Britain from Commonwealth countries. See EURIPIDES 10.

3 As I look ahead, I am filled with foreboding. Like the Roman, I seem to see 'the River Tiber foaming with much blood'.
Speech, 20 April 1968, ibid. Quoting the Sybil's prophesy. See VIRGIL 38. The phrase 'rivers of blood' had been used previously in different contexts by THOMAS JEFFERSON and WINSTON CHURCHILL, among others.

4 I do not keep a diary. Never have. To write a diary every day is like returning to one's own vomit.
Sunday Times 6 November 1977

5 All political lives, unless they are cut off in midstream at a happy juncture, end in failure, because that is the nature of politics and of human affairs.
Joseph Chamberlain, Epilogue (1977)

6 No battle is worth fighting except the last one.
Quoted in the *Observer* 2 January 1983

7 Command and obedience, Establishment and deference, they're two sides of the same coin. The Establishment is unacknowledged power. It is *the power that need not speak its name.*
Quoted in *Friends in High Places*, Introduction (1990) by JEREMY PAXMAN.

8 In politics there are no friendships, there are only allegiances.
Attributed

Vince Powell
and
Harry Driver
British TV comedy scriptwriters

Among the numerous series co-scripted by the pair are Bless this House, Love Thy Neighbour *and, their greatest success,* Never Mind the Quality, Feel the Width *(1967–71).*

1 Never Mind the Quality, Feel the Width.
Title of comedy series on ITV (1967–71). The series began as a single play for ABC TV's *Armchair Theatre*.

John Cowper Powys
(1872–1963)
British author and critic

A prolific writer of poetry, essays and fiction, he is best known for his novels A Glastonbury Romance *(1932),* Weymouth Sands *(1934) and* Maiden Castle *(1936), all drawing on themes from his West Country childhood.*

1 The strongest of all psychic forces in the world is unsatisfied desire.
A Glastonbury Romance, vol. 1, ch. 4 (1932)

2 If you give up *possession*, if you give up trying to possess what attracts you, a lovely, thrilling happiness flows through you and you feel you're in touch with the secret of everything. There are only two mortal sins in the world; one of these is to be cruel and the other is *to possess*, and they are both destructive of happiness.
Sam Dekker, ibid. ch. 7

Elvis Presley
(1935–77)
US singer

He was the first white singer to introduce overt sexuality into his rock'n'roll performances. In the 1960s he concentrated mainly on films. 'Everything starts and ends with him,' said BRUCE SPRINGSTEEN. *'He wrote the book.' See also* THOM GUNN 4.

1 You ain't nothin' but a hound dog,
Cryin' all the time.

'Hound Dog' (song, 1952, written by Jerry Leiber and Mike Stoller). The song was the Leiber/Stoller partnership's first hit when recorded by Big Mama Thornton in 1952, though Presley's 1956 recording was a much bigger success.

2 Now since my baby left me
I've found a new place to dwell
Down at the end of Lonely Street
At Heartbreak Hotel.

'Heartbreak Hotel' (song, 1956, written by Mae Boren Axton, Tommy Durden and Elvis Presley). Presley's first no. 1 hit is mainly credited to Mae Boren Axton, mother of HOYT AXTON.

Jacques Prévert
(1900–77)
French poet, critic and screenwriter

Influenced by Surrealism, he became popular in the 1920s with humorous 'song poems' about Paris street life. His verse collections include Paroles *(1946) and* Imaginaires *(1970). He was also an eminent film critic and wrote the screenplay for* Les Enfants du Paradis *(1944).*

1 Our Father which art in heaven
Stay there
And we will stay on earth
Which is sometimes so pretty.

'Pater Noster', publ. in *Paroles* (1946, rev. 1949, transl. Lawrence Ferlinghetti, 1958). Opening lines of poem.

2 An orange on the table
Your dress on the rug
And you in my bed
Sweet present of the present
Cool of night
Warmth of my life.

'Alicante', ibid.

3 Man
You beheld the saddest and dreariest of all the
    flowers of the earth
And as with other flowers you gave it a name
You called it Thought.

'Flowers and Wreaths', ibid.

4 When truth is no longer free, freedom is no longer real: the truths of the police are the truths of today.

'Intermède', publ. in *Spectacle* (1951)

Gerald Priestland
(1927–91)
British broadcaster

He was religious correspondent for BBC TV and radio, and the author of America *(1968) and* Dilemmas of Journalism *(1979), among other writings.*

1 Journalists belong in the gutter because that is where the ruling classes throw their guilty secrets.

Radio London, 19 May 1988

J. B. Priestley
(1894–1984)
British author and playwright

John Boynton Priestley. Cambridge-educated, with strong Yorkshire roots, he published numerous works of literary criticism before having success with his humorous novel The Good Companions *(1929) and the plays* Time and the Conways *(1937) and* An Inspector Calls *(1947).*

1 This is the age, among other things, of chocolate.

English Journey, ch. 4, sect. 3

2 Men are much better than their ordinary life allows them to be.

Ibid., ch. 6, sect. 3. Referring to the contrast between the comradeship of soldiers in war and 'the civilian life to which they returned, a condition of things in which they found their manhood stunted, their generous impulses baffled, their double instinct for leadership and loyalty completely checked'.

3 The Theatre is no place to think in. You can think much better quietly at home. An intelligent book will make more people think than the most exquisite production of the finest play. But what the dramatist can do . . . is to make his audience feel.

Two Time Plays, Introduction (1937)

4 Our trouble is that we drink too much tea. I see in this the slow revenge of the Orient, which has diverted the Yellow River down our throats.

Quoted in the *Observer* 15 May 1949

5 Already we Viewers, when not viewing, have begun to whisper to one another that the more we elaborate our means of communication, the less we communicate.

Thoughts in the Wilderness, 'Televiewing' (1957)

6 I can't help feeling wary when I hear anything said about the masses. First you take their faces

from 'em, calling them the masses, and then you accuse 'em of not having any faces.

Saturn Over the Water, ch. 5 (1961). Narrated by Henry Sulgrave.

J. A. Primo de Rivera

(1903–36)

Spanish politician

José Antonio Primo de Rivera. Son of the military dictator who ruled Spain 1923–30, he founded the Spanish Fascist Party, Falange Española, in 1933. He was executed by the Republicans at the start of the Civil War.

1 Fascism is a European inquietude. It is a way of knowing everything – history, the State, the achievement of the proletarianization of public life, a new way of knowing the phenomena of our epoch.

Quoted in *The Spanish Civil War*, bk 1, ch. 8 (1961) by Hugh Thomas

2 We, who have already borne on the road to Paradise the lives of the best among us, want a difficult, erect, implacable Paradise; a Paradise where one can never rest and which has, beside the threshold of the gates, angels with swords.

Quoted in *Falange*, ch. 7 (1962) by Stanley Payne

Matthew Prior

(1664–1721)

English poet and diplomat

An accomplished epigrammatist, he is best known for his miscellaneous verse collected in Poems on Several Occasions *(1709). He participated in the brokering of the Treaty of Ryswick (1697) and the Peace of Utrecht (1713), known as 'Matt's peace'.*

1 They never taste who always drink;
They always talk who never think.

'Upon this Passage in Scaligerana', written 1697 [?], publ. in *The Literary Works of Matthew Prior* (ed. H. B. Wright and M. K. Spears, 1959)

2 Forbear to mention what thou canst not praise.

'Carmen Seculare', st. 8, written 1699, publ. in *Poems on Various Occasions* (1718)

3 Be to her virtues very kind;
Be to her faults a little blind;
Let all her ways be unconfined;
And clap your padlock – on her mind.

'An English Padlock', ibid. Last lines of poem.

4 He ranged his tropes, and preached up patience;
Backed his opinion with quotations.

'Paulo Purganti and his Wife', ll. 138–9, ibid.

5 Cured yesterday of my disease,
I died last night of my physician.

'The Remedy Worse than the Disease', written 1714, publ. in *The Literary Works of Matthew Prior* (ed. H. B. Wright and M. K. Spears, 1959)

6 Venus, take my votive glass;
Since I am not what I was,
What from this day I shall be,
Venus, let me never see.

'The Lady who Offers her Looking-Glass to Venus', publ. in *Poems on Various Occasions* (1718)

7 To John I owed great obligation;
But John, unhappily, thought fit
To publish it to all the nation:
Sure John and I are more than quit.

'Epigram – Another', ibid.

8 No, no; for my virginity,
When I lose that, says Rose, I'll die:
Behind the elms last night, cried Dick,
Rose, were you not extremely sick?

'A True Maid', ibid.

9 And 'tis remarkable that they
Talk most who have the least to say.

'Alma', canto 2, l. 345–6, ibid.

(Sir) V. S. Pritchett

(1900–97)

British author and critic

Victor Sawdon Pritchett. The 'wise, foxy and kindly grandfather of present English letters' was literary critic at the New Statesman *for twenty years. His criticism, short stories, novels and volumes of autobiography are all highly regarded.*

1 The principle of procrastinated rape is said to be the ruling one in all the great bestsellers.

The Living Novel, 'Clarissa' (1946)

2 The detective novel is the art-for-art's-sake of our yawning Philistinism, the classic example of a specialized form of art removed from contact with the life it pretends to build on.

Books in General, 'The Roots of Detection' (1953)

3 It is often said that in Ireland there is an excess of genius unsustained by talent; but there is talent in the tongues.

Midnight Oil, ch. 6 (second volume of autobiography, 1971)

4 Life – how curious is that habit that makes us think it is not here, but elsewhere.

Ibid., ch. 6 See RIMBAUD 19.

5 How extraordinary it is that one feels most guilt about the sins one is unable to commit.

Ibid., ch. 10

Adelaide Ann Procter
(1825–64)
English poet

Highly popular in her day, she contributed poems to various periodicals and published such collections as Legends and Lyrics *(1858 and 1861). She also performed philanthropic works.*

1 Seated one day at the organ,
I was weary and ill at ease,
And my fingers wandered idly
Over the noisy keys.

'A Lost Chord', st. 1, publ. in *The Poems of Adelaide A. Procter* (1858). The poem was later set to music by Sir Arthur Sullivan.

2 I have sought, but I seek it vainly,
That one lost chord divine.

'A Lost Chord', st. 6, ibid.

3 It may be that Death's bright angel
Will speak in that chord again,
It may be that only in Heaven
I shall hear that grand Amen.

'A Lost Chord', st. 7, ibid.

Propertius
(c. 48 BC–c. AD 15)
Roman poet

A member of the poetic circle supported by Maecenas, and a close friend of OVID, *he wrote four books of elegies inspired by the love of his mistress Cynthia.*

1 The seaman's story is of tempest, the ploughman's of his team of bulls; the soldier tells his wounds, the shepherd his tale of sheep.

Elegies, bk 2, no. 1, ll. 43–4

2 Let each man pass his days in that wherein his skill is greatest.

Elegies, bk 2, no. 1, l. 46

3 What though strength fails? Boldness is certain to win praise. In mighty enterprises, it is enough to have had the determination.

Ibid., bk 2, no. 10, ll. 5–6

Pierre-Joseph Proudhon
(1809–65)
French political theorist

His work, notably What is Property? *(1840), argued against violent revolution in favour of a gradual evolution of society into anarchy.*

1 *La propriété, c'est le vol.*
[Property is theft.]

What is Property?, ch. 1 (1840)

Marcel Proust
(1871–1922)
French novelist

After his mother's death in 1905 he became a recluse, exploring in fictional form the psychology of human memory. His novel sequence À la recherche du temps perdu *(1913–27, translated* Remembrance of Things Past *and* In Search of Lost Time) *was influenced by Bergson's observations on time. 'After Proust, there are certain things that simply cannot be done again,'* FRANÇOISE SAGAN *declared. 'He marks off for you the boundaries of your talent.'*

1 Your soul . . . is a dark forest. But the trees are of a particular species, they are genealogical trees.

Pleasures and Regrets, 'Fragments From Italian Comedy', no. 7, sect. 4 (1896, transl. 1948)

2 A fashionable milieu is one in which everybody's opinion is made up of the opinion of all the others. Has everybody a different opinion? Then it is a literary milieu.

Ibid., 'Fragments From Italian Comedy', no. 10

3 The most benighted and the most deplorable prejudices have had their moment of novelty when fashion lent them its fragile grace.

Ibid., 'Regrets, Reveries, Changing Skies', no. 5

4 Let us be grateful to people who make us happy; they are the charming gardeners who make our souls blossom.

Ibid., 'Regrets, Reveries, Changing Skies', no. 12

5 For a long time I used to go to bed early.

Swann's Way, 'Overture' (vol. 1 of *Remembrance of Things Past*, 1913, transl. C. K. Scott Moncrieff, 1922, rev. Terence Kilmartin, 1981). Opening sentence of book.

6 And suddenly the memory revealed itself. The taste was that of the little piece of madeleine which on Sunday mornings at Combray . . . my aunt Léonie used to give me, dipping it first in her own cup of tea or tisane.

Ibid., 'Overture'

7 People who, not being in love themselves, feel that a clever man ought to be unhappy only about such persons as are worth his while; which is rather like being astonished that anyone should condescend to die of cholera at the bidding of so insignificant a creature as the common bacillus.
Ibid., 'Swann in Love'

8 One becomes moral as soon as one is unhappy.
Within a Budding Grove, 'Madame Swann at Home' (vol. 1 of *Remembrance of Things Past* (1919, transl. C. K. Scott Moncrieff, rev. Terence Kilmartin, 1981)

9 The charms of the passing stranger are generally in direct ratio to the swiftness of our passage.
Ibid., 'Place-Names: The Place'

10 If a little day-dreaming is dangerous, the cure for it is not to dream less but to dream more, to dream all the time.
Ibid., 'Place-Names: The Place'. Spoken by Elstir.

11 The features of our face are hardly more than gestures which force of habit made permanent. Nature, like the destruction of Pompeii, like the metamorphosis of a nymph, has arrested us in an accustomed movement.
Ibid., 'Place-Names: The Place'

12 For one disorder that doctors cure with medicaments (as I am assured they do occasionally succeed in doing) they produce a dozen others in healthy subjects by inoculating them with that pathogenic agent a thousand times more virulent than all the microbes in the world, the idea that one is ill.
The Guermantes Way, ch. 1 (vol. 2 of *Remembrance of Things Past*, 1922, transl. C. K. Scott Moncrieff, rev. Terence Kilmartin, 1981). Spoken by Dr du Boulbon.

13 Everything we think of as great has come to us from neurotics. It is they and they alone who found religions and create great works of art.
Dr du Boulbon, ibid., ch. 1

14 We may, indeed, say that the hour of death is uncertain, but when we say this we think of that hour as situated in a vague and remote expanse of time; it does not occur to us that it can have any connexion with the day that has already dawned and can mean that death – or its first assault and partial possession of us, after which it will never leave hold of us again – may occur this very afternoon, so far from uncertain, this afternoon whose

time-table, hour by hour, has been settled in advance.
Ibid., ch. 1

15 A change in the weather is sufficient to create the world and ourselves anew.
Ibid., ch. 2

16 Illness is the most heeded of doctors: to kindness and wisdom we make promises only; pain we obey.
Cities of the Plain, pt 2, ch. 1 (vol. 2 of *Remembrance of Things Past*, 1922, transl. C. K. Scott Moncrieff, rev. Terence Kilmartin, 1981)

17 The regularity of a habit is generally in proportion to its absurdity.
The Captive (vol. 3 of *Remembrance of Things Past*, 1923, transl. C. K. Scott Moncrieff, rev. Terence Kilmartin, 1981)

18 No banishment, indeed, to the South Pole, or to the summit of Mont Blanc, can separate us so entirely from our fellow creatures as a prolonged sojourn in the seclusion of an inner vice.
The Captive, ibid.

19 That translucent alabaster of our memories.
The Captive, ibid.

20 When two people part it is the one who is not in love who makes the tender speeches.
The Captive, ibid.

21 We find a little of everything in our memory; it is a sort of pharmacy, a sort of chemical laboratory, in which our groping hand may come to rest, now on sedative drug, now on a dangerous poison.
The Captive, ibid.

22 The human plagiarism which is most difficult to avoid, for individuals . . . is self-plagiarism.
The Fugitive (vol. 3 of *Remembrance of Things Past*, 1925, transl. C. K. Scott Moncrieff, rev. Terence Kilmartin, 1981)

23 Let us leave pretty women to men with no imagination.
The Fugitive, ibid. The line originally appeared in Proust's early novel *Jean Santeuil* (1899).

24 The true paradises are paradises we have lost.
Time Regained (vol. 3 of *Remembrance of Things Past*, 1927, transl. Andreas Mayor, rev. Terence Kilmartin, 1981)

25 A work in which there are theories is like an object which still has its price-tag on it.
Time Regained, ibid.

26 I understood that all these materials for a work of literature were simply my past life; I understood that they had come to me, in frivolous pleasures, in

indolence, in tenderness, in unhappiness, and that I had stored them up without divining the purpose for which they were destined or even their continued existence any more than a seed does when it forms within itself a reserve of all the nutritious substances from which it will feed a plant.
Time Regained, ibid.

27 If unhappiness develops the forces of the mind, happiness alone is salutary to the body.
Time Regained, ibid.

28 As for happiness, that is really useful to us in one way only, by making unhappiness possible.
Time Regained, ibid.

William Prynne
(1600–69)
English Puritan pamphleteer

He was imprisoned, had his ears severed and was branded following the publication of Histriomastix *(1632), an attack on the theatre which was said to slander Queen Henrietta Maria. He helped bring about Laud's execution, but opposed the regicides and supported the Restoration.*

1 It hath evermore been the notorious badge of prostituted strumpets and the lewdest harlots, to ramble abroad to plays, to playhouses; whither no honest, chaste or sober girls or women, but only branded whores and infamous adulteresses, did usually resort in ancient times.
Histriomastix (1632)

Publilius Syrus
(1st century BC)
Roman writer of mimes

A former slave, he became one of the leading mimeographers of his age. His Sententiae *are aphorisms collected or originated by him.*

1 A good reputation is more valuable than money.
Sententiae, no. 108

2 Pain forces even the innocent to lie.
Ibid., no. 171

3 The weeping of an heir is laughter in disguise.
Ibid., no. 221. MONTAIGNE, in his *Essays*, bk. 1 ch. 37, attributes this aphorism to the 2nd-century Roman grammarian Aulus Gellius.

4 A fair exterior is a silent recommendation.
Ibid., no. 267

5 A cock has great influence on his own dunghill.
Ibid., no. 357

6 It is a bad plan that admits of no modification.
Ibid., no. 469

7 It is not every question that deserves an answer.
Ibid., no. 581

8 Speech is the mirror of the soul.
Ibid., no. 1073

Alexander Pushkin
(1799–1837)
Russian poet

From an early age he was an acclaimed master in diverse poetic genres. He worked in government, was exiled twice (1820 and 1824) and was finally killed in a duel. His greatest work was Eugene Onegin *(1831), a novel in verse that was a seminal influence in Russian literature. In* GORKY's *words, he was 'the beginning of beginnings'.*

1 There yet remains but one concluding tale,
And then this chronicle of mine is ended –
Fulfilled, the duty God ordained to me,
A sinner. Not without purpose did the Lord
Put me to witness much for many years
And educate me in the love of books.
One day some indefatigable monk
Will find my conscientious, unsigned work;
Like me, he will light up his ikon-lamp
And, shaking from the scroll the age-old dust,
He will transcribe these tales in all their truth.
Boris Godunov, prologue, sect. 5, ll. 18–28 (1825, transl. Philip L. Barbour, 1953). The words of Father Pimen.

2 Heaven's gift is habit, let us bless
That substitute for happiness.
Eugene Onegin, ch. 2, st. 31 (1833, transl. Oliver Elton, 1943)

3 Sad that our finest aspirations,
Our freshest dreams and meditations,
In swift succession should decay,
Like autumn leaves that rot away.
Ibid., ch. 8, st. 10

4 'Tis time, my friend, 'tis time!
For rest the heart is aching;
Days follow days in flight, and everyday is taking
Fragments of being, while together you and I
Make plans to live. Look, all is dust, and we shall die.
'It's time, my dear', ll. 1–5 (1834, transl. C. M. Bowra, 1943)

Israel Putnam
(1718–90)
US general

Appointed a general at the outbreak of the American Revolution, he distinguished himself at the Battle of Bunker Hill (1775), though his subsequent performance failed to match expectations.

1 Men, you are all marksmen – don't one of you fire until you see the whites of their eyes.
Command at Battle of Bunker Hill, 17 June 1775, quoted in *The History of the Siege of Boston*, ch. 5 (1849) by Richard Frothingham. In the first major engagement of the War of Independence (actually at Breed's Hill, Mass.), the militiamen defending Boston waited until the attackers were within 15–20 paces before firing a volley, following which the fallen bodies lay 'as thick as sheep in a fold'. The words are also attributed to William Prescott (1726–95) at Bunker Hill, Prince Charles of Prussia (18th century) at Jagerndorf, and FREDERICK THE GREAT of Prussia at Prague.

Mario Puzo
(1920–99)
US novelist

His novel of the Sicilian Mafia in New York, The Godfather (1969), brought him great success. He also co-scripted the films drawn from the book (1972, 1974 and 1990).

1 He's a businessman . . . I'll make him an offer he can't refuse.
The Godfather, bk 1, ch. 1 (1969). Spoken by Don Vito Corleone. The line also appears in FRANCIS FORD COPPOLA's film adaptation, written in collaboration with Puzo (1972).

2 A lawyer with his briefcase can steal more than a hundred men with guns.
Ibid., bk 1, ch. 1. A favourite saying of the Don, dropped from the screenplay.

John Pym
(1584–1643)
English Parliamentarian leader

The leader of the House of Commons in the period immediately before the Civil War, he played a major part in drafting the Grand Remonstrance (1641). In 1642 he imposed the first excise duties.

1 A Parliament is that to the Commonwealth which the soul is to the body, which is only able to apprehend and understand the symptoms of all such diseases, which threaten the body politic. It behoves us therefore to keep the facility of that soul from distemper.
Speech to House of Commons, 17 April 1640, publ. in *Historical Collections*, vol. 3 (1721) by John Rushworth

Thomas Pynchon
(b. 1937)
US novelist

Experimental, esoteric and crammed with mathematical and scientific information, his novels include his first book V (1963) and his magnum opus Gravity's Rainbow (1973), a darkly farcical anti-war satire.

1 If there is something comforting – religious, if you want – about paranoia, there is still also anti-paranoia, where nothing is connected to anything, a condition not many of us can bear for long.
Gravity's Rainbow, pt 3 (1973)

2 There's nothing so loathsome as a sentimental surrealist.
ibid. pt 4

Pyrrhus
(c. 318–272 BC)
King of Epirus

As an ally of the Tarentum, he invaded Italy in 280, and won two victories against the Romans, though sustaining heavy losses. He returned to Greece after a subsequent defeat at Beneventum (275 BC).

1 One more such victory and we are lost.
Quoted in *Parallel Lives*, 'Pyrrhus', ch. 2, sect. 9 by PLUTARCH. Referring to his costly defeat of the Roman army at Asculum, 279 BC. The scale of his losses gave rise to the term 'Pyrrhic victory'.

Pythagoras
(c. 580–c. 500 BC)
Greek mathematician and philosopher

The study of numbers dominated his scholarly inquiries, which ranged from geometry to metaphysics. He applied his philosophical principles in the city of Kroton, Southern Italy.

1 Reason is immortal, all else mortal.
Quoted in *Lives of Eminent Philosophers*, bk 8, sect. 30 by Diogenes Laertius

Q

Mary Quant
(b. 1934)
British fashion designer

Having opened one of London's first boutiques, Bazaar, in Chelsea (1955), she became a prime mover in 1960s fashion. Her 'mod' and affordable designs included the mini-skirt, which she is credited with inventing.

1 Having money is rather like being a blond. It is more fun but not vital.
Quoted in the *Observer* 2 November 1986

Francis Quarles
(1592–1644)
English poet

Much of his religious verse was destroyed during the Civil War, when he was identified with the Royalist cause. Emblems *(1635) was the most notable of 'emblem books', consisting of symbolic pictures with commentaries, and* Enchiridion *(1640), a collection of aphorisms, was also popular.*

1 The way to bliss lies not on beds of down,
And he that hath no cross deserves no crown.
Esther, sect. 9, Meditation 9 (1621). WILLIAM PENN took the title of his pamphlet *No Cross, No Crown* (1669) from these lines.

2 My soul, sit thou a patient looker-on;
Judge not the play before the play is done:
Her plot hath many changes; every day
Speaks a new scene; the last act crowns the play.
Emblems, bk 1, no. 15 ('Respice Finem') (1635)

3 We spend our midday sweat, our midnight oil;
We tire the night in thought, the day in toil.
Ibid., bk 2, no. 2

4 This bubble's man; hope, fear, false joy and trouble,
Are those four winds which daily toss this bubble.
Hieroglyphics of the Life of Man, Epigraph (1638)

5 Thus lifeless, lightless, worthless first began
That glorious, that presumptuous thing, called man.
Ibid., no. 1

6 They be
The secret springs
That make our minutes flee
On wheels more swift than eagles' wings:
Our life's a clock, and every gasp of breath
Breathes forth a warning grief, till Time shall strike a death.
Ibid., no. 9, st. 6

Dan Quayle
(b. 1947)
US politician and Vice-president

As Vice-President under GEORGE BUSH *(1989–93), he was mocked for his gaffes; for* P. J. O'ROURKE *he was a 'twink'. See also* LLOYD BENTSEN 1.

1 You do the policy, I'll do the politics.
Remark to aide, quoted in the *International Herald Tribune* 13 January 1992

(Sir) Arthur Quiller-Couch
(1863–1944)
British author, poet and critic

Professor of English Literature at Cambridge from 1912, he wrote essays and verse, and edited anthologies of poetry and prose. He was also known for his novels set in his native Cornwall, published under the pen-name Q.

1 If you require a practical rule of me, I will present you with this: Whenever you feel an impulse to perpetrate a piece of exceptionally fine writing, obey it – wholeheartedly – and delete it before sending your manuscript to press. *Murder Your Darlings*.
'On Style', lecture at Cambridge University, 28 January 1914, publ. in *On the Art of Writing*, Lecture 12 (1916). See also SAMUEL JOHNSON 60.

Edgar Quinet
(1803–75)
French poet, historian and politician

His stance against the influence of religion led to his dismissal from his professorship in Paris in 1846. As a supporter of the 1848 revolution, he was exiled 1851–70, and he subsequently served as a Deputy in the National Assembly. His writings include The Religious Revolution in the Nineteenth Century *(1857).*

1 Today as in the time of Pliny and Columella, the hyacinth flourishes in Wales, the periwinkle in Illyria, the daisy on the ruins of Numantia; while around them cities have changed their masters and their names, collided and smashed, disappeared into nothingness, their peaceful generations have

crossed down the ages as fresh and smiling as on the days of battle.

Introduction to his translation of Johann Herder's *Philosophy of Human History* (1825), repr. in *Complete Works*, vol. 2 (1857)

2 It is certain that if you would have the whole secret of a people, you must enter into the intimacy of their religion.

'The Roman Church and History – Vico', lecture, 15 May 1844, publ. in *Ultramontanism, or The Roman Church and Modern Society* (1845)

3 Universal orthodoxy is enriched by every new discovery of truth: what at first appeared universal, by wishing to stand still, sooner or later becomes a sect.

'The Roman Church and History – Vico', ibid.

Quintilian
(c. 35–c. 95)
Roman rhetorician and teacher

Marcus Fabius Quintilianus. Born in Spain, he lived in Rome, where he taught in the household of the Emperor Domitian. His major work, Istitutio Oratoria, *a wide-ranging survey of rhetoric, oratory and education, had considerable influence.*

1 A liar needs a good memory.

Istitutio Oratoria, bk 4, ch. 2, sect. 91. See ALGERNON SIDNEY 1.

2 For it is feeling and force of imagination that make us eloquent.

Ibid., bk 10, ch. 7, sect. 15

R

François Rabelais
(c. 1494–c. 1553)
French satirist

After a period as a Franciscan monk and a practising physician, he wrote satires on French religious and legal institutions in five books (1534–64), collectively known as Gargantua and Pantagruel. *These were later a strong influence on* BALZAC, SWIFT *and* VOLTAIRE, *among other writers.*

1 To laugh is proper to man.

Gargantua and Pantagruel, bk 1, Prologue, 'Rabelais to the Reader' (1534, transl. Sir Thomas Urquhart and Peter Motteux, 1653). Quoting Angeston.

2 I drink for the thirst to come.

Ibid., bk 1, ch. 5

3 Appetite comes with eating . . . but the thirst goes away with drinking.

Ibid., bk 1, ch. 5. Quoting Angeston.

4 *Natura abhorret vacuum.*
[Nature abhors a vacuum.]

Ibid., bk 1, ch. 5. Quoting a Latin maxim.

5 By robbing Peter he paid Paul, he kept the moon from the wolves, and hoped to catch larks if ever the heavens should fall.

Ibid., bk 1, ch. 11

6 Nature cannot endure a sudden change, without great violence.

Ibid., bk 1, ch. 23

7 In all their rule and strictest tie of their order there was but this one clause to be observed, Do What Thou Wilt; because men that are free, well-born, well-bred, and conversant in honest companies, have naturally an instinct and spur that prompteth them unto virtuous actions, and withdraws them from vice, which is called honour.

Ibid., bk 1, ch. 57. Rules of monastic life, laid down by Gargantua.

8 Knowledge without conscience is but the ruin of the soul.

Ibid., bk 2, ch. 8. Letter from Gargantua to Pantagruel.

9 O twice and thrice happy those that plant cabbages! O destinies, why did you not spin me for a cabbage-planter? O how few are there to whom

Jupiter hath been so favourable as to predestinate them to plant cabbages! They have always one foot on the ground, and the other not far from it. Dispute who will of felicity and *summum bonum*, for my part whosoever plants cabbages is now, by my decree, proclaimed most happy.

Ibid, bk 4, ch. 18 (1548, transl. Peter Motteux, 1708). Spoken by Panurge. See MONTAIGNE 3.

10 Do not believe what I tell you here, any more than if it were some tale of a tub.

Ibid., bk 4, ch. 38. See JOHN WEBSTER 5.

11 Whose cockloft is unfurnished.

Ibid., bk 5, Author's Prologue (1564, transl. Peter Motteux, 1708)

12 Speak the truth and shame the devil.

Ibid., bk 5, Author's Prologue

13 Like hearts of oak.

Ibid., bk 5, Author's Prologue

14 Ignorance is the mother of all evils.

Ibid., bk 5, ch. 7

Jean Racine
(1639–99)
French dramatist

Regarded as the foremost tragedian of his time, he was the author of Andromaque *(1667),* Britannicus *(1669) and* Phèdre *(1677). His plays derive their themes from Greek and Roman literature and are governed by the unities of time, place and action.*

1 I loved him too much not to hate him at all.

Andromaque, act 2, sc. 1 (1667). Spoken by Hermione.

2 Silent anguish is the more dangerous.

Cléone, ibid., act 3, sc. 3

3 It's no longer a warmth hidden in my veins: it's Venus entire and whole fastening on her prey.

Phèdre, act 1, sc. 3 (1677). Spoken by Phèdre.

4 Crime like virtue has its degrees; and timid innocence was never known to blossom suddenly into extreme licence.

Hippolytus, ibid., act 4, sc. 2

5 Without money honour is merely a disease.

Les Plaideurs, act 1, sc. 1 (1668; *The Pleaders*). Spoken by Petit Jean.

James Rado
(b. 1939)
Gerome Ragni
(b. 1942)
US songwriters

They are known principally as lyricists for the first rock musical Hair *(1967), which prompted the reaction by Brendan Gill of the* New Yorker: *'One can't not consent to this merry mind-blowing exercise in holy gibberish.'*

1 This is the dawning of the age of Aquarius.

'Aquarius' (song, with music by Galt MacDermot) in *Hair* (stage musical 1967, filmed 1979)

Thomas Rainborowe
(d. 1648)
English soldier

Name also spelled Rainborow, Rainborough or Rainsborough. A naval commander and subsequently a colonel in the Parliamentarian army and an MP, he was a prominent Leveller, advocating greater democracy and toleration.

1 The poorest he that is in England hath a life to live, as the greatest he.

Speech in the army debates, 29 October 1647, publ. in *The Penguin Book of Historic Speeches* (ed. Brian MacArthur, 1995). Debating Leveller proposals with army officers at St Mary's Church, Putney.

Craig Raine
(b. 1944)
British poet and critic

He is chief exponent of what JAMES FENTON *named the 'Martian' school, which treats familiar objects from an alien perspective, as in* A Martian Sends a Postcard Home *(1979). He wrote the libretto for the opera* The Electrification of the Soviet Union *(1986).*

1 But time is tied to the wrist
or kept in a box, ticking with impatience.

'A Martian Sends a Postcard Home', publ. in *A Martian Sends a Postcard Home* (1979)

2 The mind is a museum
to be looted at night.

'The Grey Boy', publ. in *Rich* (1984)

Kathleen Raine

(1908–2003)
British poet

Her meditative and lyrical work, much of it inspired by the natural world, includes Stone and Flower *(1943) and* The Hollow Hill *(1965). She was an authority on* WILLIAM BLAKE *and in 1981 founded the journal* Temenos.

1 Unwise we feel, but wise we know
Living in time is but to seem –
Like green leaves on a tree we grow,
But each must fall and fade alone.
'Seen in a Glass', publ. in *Living in Time* (1946)

2 The ghosts are hungry, the ghosts are divine,
but the pigs eat the meal, and the priests drink the
 wine.
'Maternal Grief', publ. in *Stone and Flower* (1943). Closing lines of poem.

3 Love mourns its dead
Not by number, but, one by one, each by name.
'Statistical Grief', publ. in *The Oracle in the Heart (Poems 1975–1978)* (1980)

4 I couldn't claim that I have never felt the urge to explore evil, but when you descend into hell you have to be very careful.
The Times 18 April 1992

(Sir) Walter Ralegh

(1552–1618)
English author, soldier and explorer

He was a favourite of ELIZABETH I *and organized three expeditions to America. Imprisoned in 1603 by* JAMES I, *he was released in 1616 to search for gold in South America. When the attempt proved unsuccessful, he was executed on the original charges of conspiracy.*

1 A maze wherein affection finds no end,
A ranging cloud that runs before the wind,
A substance like the shadow of the sun,
A goal of grief for which the wisest run.
'Farewell false love', st. 3 (1588), repr. in *The Poems of Sir Walter Ralegh* (ed. Agnes M. Latham, 1951)

2 As you came from the holy land
Of Walsinghame,
Met you not with my true love
By the way as you came?
'As you came from the holy land', st. 1, written 1593, publ. 1628, repr. ibid.

3 But true love is a durable fire,
In the mind ever burning,

Never sick, never old, never dead,
From itself never turning.
'As you came from the Holy Land', st. 11. Closing lines of poem.

4 Our passions are most like to floods and
 streams,
The shallow murmur, but the deep are dumb.
'Sir Walter Ralegh to the Queen', st. 1, written *c.* 1599, publ. 1655, ibid. Opening lines of poem.

5 If all the world and love were young,
And truth in every shepherd's tongue,
These pretty pleasures might me move
To live with thee, and be thy love.
'The Nymph's Reply to the Passionate Shepherd', st. 1 (1600), ibid. Written in response to CHRISTOPHER MARLOWE 1. See also JOHN DONNE 20.

6 Desire attained is not desire,
But as the cinders of the fire.
'A Poesie to Prove that Affection is not Love' (1602), ibid.

7 Give me my scallop-shell of quiet,
My staff of faith to walk upon,
My scrip of joy, immortal diet,
My bottle of salvation,
My gown of glory, hope's true gage,
And thus I'll take my pilgrimage.
'The Passionate Man's Pilgrimage' (1604), ibid. The poem was written while awaiting execution on charges of treason against JAMES I. The scallop-shell was the symbol worn by pilgrims.

8 Go, Soul, the body's guest,
Upon a thankless arrant:
Fear not to touch the best;
The truth shall be thy warrant:
Go, since I needs must die,
And give the world the lie.
'The Lie', st. 1 (1608), ibid.

9 Tell zeal it wants devotion;
Tell love it is but lust;
Tell time it metes but motion;
Tell flesh it is but dust:
And wish them not reply,
For thou must give the lie.
'The Lie', st. 6, ibid.

10 What is our life? a play of passion,
Our mirth the music of division,
Our mothers wombs the tiring-houses be,
When we are dressed for this short comedy,
Heaven the judicious sharp spectator is,
That sits and marks still who doth act amiss,

Our graves that hide us from the searching sun,
Are like drawn curtains when the play is done,
Thus march we playing to our latest rest,
Only we die in earnest, that's no jest.

'On the Life of Man', st. 1 (1612), ibid.

11 [History] hath triumphed over time, which besides it, nothing but eternity hath triumphed over.

The History of the World, Preface (1614)

12 Whosoever, in writing a modern history, shall follow truth too near the heels, it may haply strike out his teeth.

Ibid., Preface. Ralegh's *History* was banned by JAMES I soon after its publication, precisely because, it was alleged, he followed too closely the 'heels of truth'. According to biographer Robert Lacey in *Sir Walter Ralegh*, ch. 41 (1973), Ralegh 'took every opportunity he could in his book to pour scorn on famous sodomites, and James took the point'.

13 O eloquent, just, and mighty Death! whom none could advise, thou hast persuaded; what none hath dared, thou hast done; and whom all the world hath flattered, thou only hath cast out of the world and despised. Thou hast drawn together all the far-stretched greatness, all the pride, cruelty, and ambition of man, and covered it all over with these two narrow words, *Hic jacet* [Here lies].

Ibid., bk 5, pt 1, ch. 6, sect. 12

14 Even such is Time which takes in trust
Our youth, our joys, and all we have,
And pays us but with age and dust,
Who in the dark and silent grave
When we have wandered all our ways
Shuts up the story of our days.
And from which earth and grave and dust,
The Lord shall raise me up, I trust.

'Even Such is Time' (1618), ibid. Written the night before his death, this version of the last stanza of one of Ralegh's earlier poems was found in the flyleaf of his Bible in the Abbey Gatehouse at Westminster.

15 There is nothing exempt from the peril of mutation; the earth, heavens, and whole world is thereunto subject.

The Cabinet Council, ch. 24, repr. in *The Works of Sir Walter Raleigh*, vol. 1 (1751)

16 All histories do shew, and wise politicians do hold it necessary that, for the well-governing of every Commonweal, it behoveth man to presuppose that all men are evil, and will declare themselves so to be when occasion is offered.

The Cabinet Council, ch. 25, ibid., vol. 1

17 War begets quiet, quiet idleness, idleness disorder, disorder ruin; likewise ruin order, order virtue, virtue glory, and good fortune.

The Cabinet Council, ch. 25, ibid., vol. 1

18 But it is hard to know them from friends, they are so obsequious and full of protestations; for a wolf resembles a dog, so doth a flatterer a friend.

Instructions to His Son and to Posterity, ch. 3 (1632), ibid., vol. 2

19 Be advised what thou dost discourse of, and what thou maintainest whether touching religion, state, or vanity; for if thou err in the first, thou shalt be accounted profane; if in the second, dangerous; if in the third, indiscreet and foolish.

Instructions to His Son and to Posterity ch. 4, ibid., vol. 2

20 Fain would I climb, yet fear I to fall.

Quoted in *History of the Worthies of England* (1662) by THOMAS FULLER. Line scratched with a diamond ring on a window-pane, to which ELIZABETH I replied, using the same method, 'If thy heart fail thee, climb not at all.' Some versions of the quote give 'fail' for 'fall'.

(Sir) Walter Raleigh
(1861–1922)
British scholar and critic

His confessed aim in writing was 'to explain people', as in his studies of WILLIAM BLAKE *and* SAMUEL JOHNSON. *His lighter pieces were collected in* Laughter from a Cloud *(1923).*

1 I wish I loved the Human Race;
I wish I loved its silly face;
I wish I liked the way it walks;
I wish I liked the way it talks;
And when I'm introduced to one
I wish I thought *What Jolly Fun!*

'Wishes of an Elderly Man', publ. in *Laughter from a Cloud* (1923)

Ayn Rand
(1905–82)
Russian-born US author

Originally Alissa Rosenbaum. She is remembered for two novels, The Fountainhead *(1943) and* Atlas Shrugged *(1957), which advocate the primacy of human reason.*

1 Civilization is the progress toward a society of privacy. The savage's whole existence is public,

ruled by the laws of his tribe. Civilization is the process of setting man free from men.
The Fountainhead (1943)

Jeannette Rankin
(1880–1973)
US suffragist and politician

She was the first woman to be elected to Congress, serving two terms (1917–19 and 1941–3). A Republican and a pacifist, she campaigned vigorously for women's rights and in 1941 was the only member to vote against war with Japan.

1 The individual woman is required ... a thousand times a day to choose either to accept her appointed role and thereby rescue her good disposition out of the wreckage of her self-respect, or else follow an independent line of behavior and rescue her self-respect out of the wreckage of her good disposition.
Quoted in *Jeannette Rankin: First Lady in Congress*, ch. 3 (1974) by Hannah Josephson

2 You can no more win a war than you can win an earthquake.
Quoted ibid., ch. 8

John Crowe Ransom
(1888–1974)
US poet and critic

He was a founder of the Kenyon Review and established New Criticism with his book of that name (1941) which laid greater emphasis on examination of the text itself, rather than its context.

1 Here lies a lady of beauty and high degree.
Of chills and fever she died, of fever and chills,
The delight of her husband, her aunt, an infant of
  three,
And of medicos marvelling sweetly on her ills.
'Here Lies a Lady', st. 1, publ. in *Chills and Fever* (1924)

2 Two evils, monstrous either one apart,
Possessed me, and were long and loath at going:
A cry of Absence, Absence, in the heart,
And in the wood the furious winter blowing.
'Winter Remembered', ibid.

3 God have mercy on the sinner
Who must write with no dinner,
No gravy and no grub,
No pewter and no pub,
No belly and no bowels,
Only consonants and vowels.
'Survey of Literature', publ. in *Selected Poems* (1945)

Frederic Raphael
(b. 1931)
British author and critic

A writer of novels and plays which explore contemporary social issues, he is best known for The Graduate Wife (1962) and The Glittering Prizes (1976).

1 City of perspiring dreams.
Glittering Prizes, ch. 3 (1976). Referring to Cambridge. See MATTHEW ARNOLD 42.

Gerald Ratner
(b. 1949)
British businessman

He was Chief Executive of the Ratners Group 1986–92, resigning after his remarks about the poor quality of Ratners products received widespread publicity.

1 People say how can you sell this for such a low price. I say because it is total crap ... We even sell a pair of earrings for under £1, which is cheaper than a prawn sandwich from Marks & Spencers. But I have to say the earrings probably won't last as long.
Speech to the Institute of Directors, Albert Hall, 23 April 1991, quoted in *The Times*, 24 April 1991

(Sir) Terence Rattigan
(1911–77)
British playwright

The comedy French Without Tears (1936) was the first of numerous West End successes. His more serious plays include The Winslow Boy (1946), The Deep Blue Sea (1952) and Separate Tables (1954).

1 It is easy to do justice – very hard to do right. Unfortunately while the appeal of justice is intellectual, the appeal of right appears for some odd reason to induce tears in court.
The Winslow Boy, act 4 (1946). Spoken by Sir Robert Morton.

2 The headmaster said you ruled them with a rod of iron. He called you the Himmler of the lower fifth.
The Browning Version (1948). Spoken by Peter Gilbert to Andrew Crocker-Harris.

Irina Ratushinskaya
(b. 1954)
Russian poet

She spent a term in a labour camp (1982–6) as a result of campaigning for human rights. Her poems are collected in

No, I'm Not Afraid *(1986)* and Grey is the Colour of Hope *(1988)*. *'For a poet,'* she said, *'it is more important to keep in touch with God than politicians.'*

1 In order to understand birds
You have to be a convict.
And if you share your bread –
It means your time is done.
'The Sparrows of Butyrki', publ. in *No, I'm Not Afraid* (1986)

Man Ray
(1890–1976)
US painter and photographer

Originally Emanuel Rabinovitch. He co-founded a Dadaist group in New York, before settling in Paris. Taking up photography to finance his painting, he also made Surrealist films.

1 I paint what cannot be photographed, that which comes from the imagination or from dreams, or from an unconscious drive. I photograph the things that I do not wish to paint, the things which already have an existence.
Interview, publ. in *Caméra*, repr. in *Man Ray: Photographer* (ed. Philippe Sers, 1981). Man Ray repeated this remark in slightly different forms on various occasions.

2 An original is a creation
motivated by desire.
Any reproduction of an original
is motivated by necessity . . .
It is marvelous that we are
the only species that creates
gratuitous forms.
To create is divine, to reproduce
is human.
'Originals Graphic Multiples', publ. in *Man Ray*, ch. 24 (1988) by Neil Baldwin

Sam Rayburn
(1882–1961)
US legislator and politician

Describing himself as 'without prefix, without suffix, and without apology', he was a Democrat in the House of Representatives 1913–61 and an architect of FRANKLIN ROOSEVELT*'s New Deal.*

1 If you want to get along, go along.
Quoted in *Forge of Democracy*, ch. 6 (1963) by Neil MacNeil. Rayburn's forty-eight years in Congress was the longest term on record, which together with his political influence earned him the sobriquet 'Mr Democrat'.

(Sir) Herbert Read
(1893–1968)
British critic and poet

He was the leading interpreter of modern British art from the 1930s, as in Art and Society *(1936) and* The Meaning of Art *(1955). His poetry, inspired by his war experiences, was published in* The Naked Warriors *(1919).*

1 I saw him stab
And stab again
A well-killed Boche.
This is the happy warrior,
This is he . . .
'The Happy Warrior', publ. in *The Naked Warriors*, 'The Scene of War' (1919)

2 But one thing we learned: there is no glory in the deed
Until the soldier wears a badge of tarnished braid.
'To a Conscript of 1940', st. 7, publ. in *Thirty Five Poems* (1940)

3 Art is . . . pattern informed by sensibility.
The Meaning of Art, ch. 1 (1955)

Piers Paul Read
(b. 1941)
British author

Praised by MALCOLM BRADBURY *as 'a densely social novelist who knows that public and private worlds intersect at every point', he had success with* A Married Man *(1979) and* On the Third Day *(1990).*

1 Sins become more subtle as you grow older: you commit sins of despair rather than lust.
Daily Telegraph 3 October 1990

W. Winwood Reade
(1838–75)
English traveller and author

He wandered in Africa and was the Times *correspondent in the Ashanti War (1873). Having had little success as a novelist, he wrote travel books and his most popular work,* The Martyrdom of Man *(1872), a free-thinking history of civilization.*

1 Artistic genius is an expansion of monkey imitativeness.
The Martyrdom of Man, ch. 3 (1872)

2 We live between two worlds; we soar in the atmosphere; we creep upon the soil; we have the aspirations of creators and the propensities of quadrupeds. There can be but one explanation of this fact. We are passing from the animal into a

higher form, and the drama of this planet is in its second act.

Ibid., ch. 3

Peter Reading

(b. 1946)

British poet

Called by TOM PAULIN *'the unofficial laureate of a decaying England', he writes of the degradation of contemporary life in uncompromising language. His collections include* Ukulele Music *(1985) and* Eschatological *(1996).*

1 Nothing can ever be done;
things are intractably thus;
all know the bite of grief, all will be brought to destiny's issue;
those who have precognition suffer
sorrow beforehand;
bodies are bankrupt, the main Expedition has left us behind it.

Untitled poem, publ. in *Perduta Gente* (1989). Concluding lines.

Nancy Reagan

(b. 1923)

US screen actress and First Lady

Known as Nancy Davis before her marriage to RONALD REAGAN *in 1952, she appeared in* The Next Voice You Hear *(1950),* Donovan's Brain *(1953) and, opposite her husband,* Hellcats of the Navy *(1957).*

1 A woman is like a teabag – only in hot water do you realize how strong she is.

Quoted in the *Observer* 29 March 1981. The quote has also been ascribed to ELEANOR ROOSEVELT, as cited by HILLARY CLINTON.

2 I see the first lady as another means to keep a president from becoming isolated.

International Herald Tribune 26 May 1988

3 Just say no.

Slogan for campaign to persuade people not to take illegal drugs, 1980s

Ronald Reagan

(1911–2004)

US screen actor, politician and president

The 'Great Communicator' signed a Hollywood contract in 1937 and appeared in some fifty films. As President of the Screen Actors' Guild (1947–52), he was politically a liberal Democrat but switched to the Republican Party in 1962. He
was elected Governor of California in 1966 and was US President 1980–9. See also JACK DEMPSEY 1, RONALD KNOX 5, *and* GORE VIDAL 7.

1 Randy – where's the rest of me?

Kings Row (film, 1942, screenplay by Casey Robinson, based on the novel by Henry Bellamann, directed by Sam Wood). The words of Drake McHugh (Ronald Reagan) to Randy Monaghan (Ann Sheridan). McHugh is a war veteran who wakes to find his legs amputated by a malicious doctor. The line provided Reagan with a title for his 1965 autobiography, *Where's the Rest of Me?*

2 We are at war with the most dangerous enemy that has ever faced mankind in his long climb from the swamp to the stars, and it has been said if we lose that war, and in so doing lose this way of freedom of ours, history will record with the greatest astonishment that those who had the most to lose did the least to prevent its happening.

'A Time for Choosing', television address, 27 October 1964, publ. in *Speaking My Mind* (1989). Referring to the Vietnam War.

3 Government does not solve problems; it subsidizes them.

Speech, 11 December 1972, publ. in *Speaking My Mind*, 'The Wit and Wisdom of Ronald Reagan' (1989)

4 Inflation is as violent as a mugger, as frightening as an armed robber and as deadly as a hit man.

Speech at Republican Party fund-raising dinner, quoted in the *Los Angeles Times* 20 October 1978

5 Of the four wars in my lifetime, none came about because the US was too strong.

Quoted in the *Observer* 29 June 1980

6 There is nothing better for the inside of a man than the outside of a horse.

Remark 13 August 1987, North Platte, Nebraska, quoted in *Time* 28 December 1987. Said to be one of Reagan's favourite expressions, uttered on various occasions, and probably not original.

7 So, in your discussions of the nuclear freeze proposals, I urge you to beware the temptation of pride – the temptation of blithely declaring yourselves above it all and label both sides equally at fault, to ignore the facts of history and the aggressive impulses of an evil empire, to simply call the arms race a giant misunderstanding and thereby remove yourself from the struggle between right and wrong, good and evil.

Speech at Annual Convention of the National Association of Evangelicals, Orlando, Florida, 8 March 1983, publ. in *Speaking My Mind* (1989). In the same speech, Reagan declared, speaking of those who live in 'totalitarian darkness': 'Let us be aware that while they preach the supremacy of the state, declare its omnipotence over individual man, and predict its eventual domination of all peoples of the earth – they are the focus of evil in the modern world.'

8 My fellow Americans, I am pleased to tell you I just signed legislation which outlaws Russia forever. The bombing begins in five minutes.

Microphone test for radio broadcast, 11 August 1984, quoted in the *New York Times* 13 August 1984

9 They [Nicaraguan Contras] are our brothers, these freedom fighters ... They are the moral equal of our Founding Fathers and the brave men and women of the French Resistance. We cannot turn away from them, for the struggle here is not right versus left; it is right versus wrong.

Speech to Conservative Political Action Conference, Washington DC, 1 March 1985, publ. in *Speaking My Mind* (1989)

10 Freedom-loving people around the world must say: I am a Berliner. I am a Jew in a world still threatened by anti-Semitism. I am an Afghan, and I am a prisoner of the gulag. I am a refugee in a crowded boat foundering off the coast of Vietnam. I am Laotian, a Cambodian, a Cuban, and a Miskito Indian in Nicaragua. I, too, am a potential victim of totalitarianism.

Speech at Bitburg, West Germany, 27 May 1985, ibid.

11 After seeing *Rambo* last night I know what to do next time this happens.

Following the hijack of an aeroplane carrying US passengers in 1985, quoted in *City Limits* 16 December 1987. *Rambo* star Sylvester Stallone was quoted in the *Sunday Express* 17 July 1988 as saying, 'When President Reagan stood up and said: "Having seen *Rambo* I know what to do with Libya", it was the kiss of death. He made Rambo a Republican.'

12 No one can kill Americans and brag about it. No one.

Quoted in the *Observer* 27 April 1986, after the US attack on Libya, 15 April 1986. The attack followed the bombing of a discotheque in West Berlin, at which two American servicemen were killed and 200 injured.

13 Would you go out there and win one for the Gipper?

Speech in San Diego, 7 November 1988, publ. in *Speaking My Mind* (1989). One of Reagan's favourite sayings, this is associated with the football star George Gipp (1895–1931), whom he played in the 1940 film *Knute Rockne – All-American*.

14 Information is the oxygen of the modern age. It

seeps through the walls topped by barbed wire, it wafts across the electrified borders.

Quoted in the *Guardian* 14 June 1989

Red Cloud
(1822–1909)
Native American chief

A principal chief of the Oglala Teton Dakota (Sioux), he led the opposition of the Sioux and Cheyenne against US development of the Bozeman Trail (1865–67) in Montana, which resulted in the Second Treaty of Fort Laramie (1868).

1 You have heard the sound of the white soldier's axe upon the Little Piney. His presence here is ... an insult to the spirits of our ancestors. Are we then to give up their sacred graves to be plowed for corn? Dakotas, I am for war.

Speech at council at Fort Laramie, Wyoming (1866), publ. in *Indian Heroes and Great Chieftains* (1918) by Charles A. Eastman

Helen Reddy
(b. 1942)
Australian-born US singer and songwriter

Her song 'I am Woman' (1972) became an anthem for the women's liberation movement of the 1970s. Later hits included 'Angie Baby' (1974).

1 Yes, I am wise, but it's wisdom born of pain
Yes, I've paid the price, but look how much I've gained
If I have to, I can do anything
I am strong, I am invincible, I am woman.

'I am Woman' (song), on the album *I Am Woman* (1972).

Henry Reed
(1914–86)
British poet and playwright

He established his reputation as a poet with A Map of Verona *(1946) and later went on to write a series of witty radio plays including* The Private Life of Hilda Tablet *(1954).*

1 Today we have naming of parts. Yesterday,
We had daily cleaning. And tomorrow morning,
We shall have what to do after firing. But today,
Today we have naming of parts. Japonica

Glistens like coral in all of the neighbouring
   gardens,
And today we have naming of parts.

'Lessons of the War: 1. Naming of Parts', publ. in *A Map of
Verona* (1946). First stanza of poem.

2 They call it easing the Spring: it is perfectly easy
If you have any strength in your thumb: like the
   bolt,
And the breech, and the cocking-piece, and the
   point of balance,
Which in our case we have not got.

'Lessons of the War: 1. Naming of Parts', ibid. Last stanza of
poem.

3 And the various holds and rolls and throws and
   breakfalls
Somehow or other I always seemed to put
In the wrong place. And as for war, my wars
Were global from the start.

'Lessons of the War: 3. Unarmed Combat', st. 6, ibid.

4 As we get older we do not get any younger.
Seasons return, and today I am fifty-five,
And this time last year I was fifty-four,
And this time next year I shall be sixty-two.

'Chard Whitlow (Mr Eliot's Sunday Evening Postscript)', ibid.

5 Gland: I would say it's somehow redolent, and full
of vitality.
Hilda: Well, I would say it's got about as much life
in it as a potted shrimp.
Gland: Well, I think we're probably both trying to
say the same thing in different words.

The Primal Scene, as it were (1958 radio play), publ. in *Hilda
Tablet and Others* (1971)

John Reed
(1887–1920)
US journalist and author

He was the author of Insurgent Mexico *(1914) and* Ten Days
That Shook the World *(1919). After helping to found the Communist Labor Party in the US, he worked in the Soviet propaganda bureau and was buried in the Kremlin.*

1 Ten Days that Shook the World.

Book title (1919). Reed's pioneering work of reportage was an
eye-witness account of the October Revolution as it unfolded
in St Petersburg.

2 In the relations of a weak Government and a rebellious people there comes a time when every act of

the authorities exasperates the masses, and every
refusal to act excites their contempt.

Ten Days That Shook the World, ch. 3 (1919)

Lou Reed
(b. 1944)
US rock musician

*His often dark and sombre songs defined the sound of the
Velvet Underground, the proto-punk New York art band which
he co-founded in 1965. See also* NELSON ALGREN 1.

1 I'm waiting for my man
Twenty-six dollars in my hand.

'I'm Waiting for the Man' (song) on the album *The Velvet
Underground and Nico* (1967) by the Velvet Underground and
Nico

2 I don't know just where I'm going
But I'm gonna try for the kingdom if I can
'Cause it makes me feel like I'm a man
When I put a spike into my vein
And I'll tell ya, things aren't quite the same.

'Heroin' (song), ibid.

3 You're so vicious.

'Vicious' (song) on the album *Transformer* (1972)

4 It's such a perfect day
I'm glad I spent it with you
Oh such a perfect day
You just keep me hanging on.

'Perfect Day' (song), ibid. The song was a million-seller when
released as a single recorded by various artists for charity in
1997.

William Rees-Mogg
(b. 1928)
British journalist and public figure

Baron Rees-Mogg of Hinton Blewitt. After editing The Times
*(1967–81), he was Chairman of the Arts Council (1982–9) and
first head of the Broadcasting Standards Council (1988–93).*

1 As long as Archer remained the candidate the dor-
mant Ethics and Integrity Committee was as much
a sign of virtue as an unread Bible in a brothel.

The Times 22 November 1999. JEFFREY ARCHER was forced
to withdraw from the London mayoral election following
the revelation that he lied in a previous libel case in 1986.
WILLIAM HAGUE had earlier endorsed Archer as 'a candidate
of probity and integrity'.

Martha Reeves

(b. 1941)

US singer

A secretary to Tamla Motown A&R executive William 'Mickey' Stevenson, she had hits with the Vandellas, including 'Heatwave' (1963), 'Dancing in the Street' (1964) and 'Nowhere to Run' (1965).

1 Calling out around the world
Are you ready for a brand new beat?
Summer's here and the time is right
For dancing in the street.
'Dancing in the Street' (song, 1964, written by William 'Mickey' Stevenson and Marvin Gaye) on the album *Dance Party* (1965) by Martha and the Vandellas

Wilhelm Reich

(1897–1957)

Austrian-born US psychoanalyst and biophysicist

His principal work was The Function of the Orgasm *(1927). He emigrated to the USA in 1939, where he founded the Orgone Institute, was prosecuted for fraudulent practices and died in gaol.*

1 The pleasure of living and the pleasure of the orgasm are identical. Extreme orgasm anxiety forms the basis of the general fear of life.
The Function of the Orgasm, ch. 5, sect. 4 (1927, transl. 1942)

Jamie Reid

(b. 1947)

British artist

He came to notice in the 1970s for his contributions to the iconography of punk, such as his depiction of the Queen pierced with a safety pin.

1 Please wash your hands before leaving the 20th century.
Title of multi-media exhibition, 1970s, quoted in *The Incomplete Works of Jamie Reid*, 'Death' (1987) by Jamie Reid and Jon Savage

Jimmy Reid

(b. 1932)

British trade union official

A Communist shop steward, he was prominent in industrial disputes in the early 1970s, notably at the Upper Clyde Shipyard.

1 A rat race is for rats. We're not rats. We're human beings. Reject the insidious pressures in society that would blunt your critical faculties to all that is happening around you, that would caution silence in the face of injustice lest you jeopardize your chances of promotion and self-advancement. This is how it starts and, before you know where you are, you're a fully paid-up member of the rat pack. The price is too high.
Rectorial address, Glasgow University, April 1972, quoted in *Writings on the Wall*, pt 1 (ed. TONY BENN, 1984)

Keith Reid

(b. 1946)

British songwriter

He was lyricist with the progressive rock group Procol Harum on all their major hits, including 'A Whiter Shade of Pale', 'Homburg' (both 1967) and 'A Salty Dog' (1969).

1 Her face at first just ghostly
Turned a whiter shade of pale.
'A Whiter Shade of Pale' (song, 1967, with music by Gary Brooker)

Thomas Reid

(1710–96)

Scottish philosopher

A Presbyterian pastor, he was a leading proponent of the 'common sense' school of philosophy, which argued against the scepticism of DAVID HUME.

1 There is no greater impediment to the advancement of knowledge than the ambiguity of words.
Essays on the Intellectual Powers of Man, Essay 1 ('Explication of Words') (1785). Opening words of essay.

Theodor Reik

(1888–1969)

US psychologist

Although a lifelong friend of FREUD, *he differed from him in his belief that neuroses developed from a weakness in the ego. His books include* Myth and Guilt *(1957) and* The Need To Be Loved *(1963).*

1 In our civilization, men are afraid that they will not be men enough and women are afraid that they may be considered only women.
Esquire December 1958

Ad Reinhardt

(1913–67)

US artist

Adolf Reinhardt. He joined the avant-garde American Abstract Artists association in 1937. His later minimal, monochrome style was typified in his series of 'Black Paintings' (from the late 1950s).

1 Art is art-as-art and everything else is everything else. Art-as-art is nothing but art. Art is not what is not art.
'Art-as-Art', publ. in *Art International*, December 1962, repr. in *The Selected Writings of Ad Reinhardt*, ch. 2 (ed. Barbara Rose, 1975)

2 Art is too serious to be taken seriously.
Quoted in *Ad Reinhardt*, pt 1 (1981) by Lucy R. Lippard

Erich Maria Remarque
(1898–1970)
German-born US novelist

Drafted into the German army at the age of eighteen, he described his wartime experiences in his major work All Quiet on the Western Front *(1929). He emigrated to the USA in 1939, and was naturalized in 1947.*

1 All Quiet on the Western Front.
English title of novel, *Im Westen nichts Neues* (1929), which describes the daily routine of soldiers fighting in the trenches in the First World War.

Ernest Renan
(1823–92)
French author, critic and scholar

Having trained for the priesthood, he left the Church in 1845 and devoted himself to scholarship in diverse fields. He was particularly interested in the origins of religions, and caused controversy with his Vie de Jésus *(1863) for its perceived atheism.*

1 Let us pardon him his hope of a vain apocalypse, and of a second coming in great triumph upon the clouds of heaven. Perhaps these were the errors of others rather than his own; and if it be true that he himself shared the general illusion, what matters it, since his dream rendered him strong against death, and sustained him in a struggle to which he might otherwise have been unequal?
Vie de Jésus, ch. 17 (1863; *Life of Jesus*)

2 As a rule, all heroism is due to a lack of reflection, and thus it is necessary to maintain a mass of imbeciles. If they once understand themselves the ruling men will be lost.
Caliban, act 2, sc. 1 (1878). Spoken by Orlando.

3 He whom God has touched will always be a being

apart: he is, whatever he may do, a stranger among men; he is marked by a sign.
L'Avenir de la Science, ch. 23 (1890; *The Future of Science*)

4 I can die when I wish to: that is my elixir of life.
Quoted in *Ernest Renan: a Critical Biography*, 'The Republic' (1964) by H. W. Wardman

Jules Renard
(1864–1910)
French novelist and playwright

He is remembered chiefly for Poil de carotte *(1894, transl. Carrots, 1946), an ironical account of his loveless childhood, which was an enduring influence on his writings.*

1 *Les bourgeois, ce sont les autres.*
[The bourgeois are other people.]
Journal entry, 28 January 1890, publ. in *Journal 1877–1910* (1925–7)

2 To succeed you must add water to your wine, until there is no more wine.
Journal entry, 3 July 1894, ibid.

3 If I am no longer young, I would very much like to know at what hour of which day my youth left me.
Journal entry, April 1898, ibid.

4 Do not ask me to be good; just ask me to act as though I were.
Journal entry, April 1898, ibid.

5 We don't understand life any better at forty than at twenty, but we know it and admit it.
Journal entry, 12 February 1907, ibid.

Agnes Repplier
(1858–1950)
US author and social critic

A humorous and popular speaker and essayist on diverse subjects, she published such works as Books and Men *(1888) and* Points of Fiction *(1920).*

1 Anyone, however, who has had dealings with dates knows that they are worse than elusive, they are perverse. Events do not happen at the right time, nor in their proper sequence. That sense of harmony with place and season which is so strong in the historian – if he be a readable historian – is lamentably lacking in history, which takes no pains to verify his most convincing statements.
To Think of Tea!, ch. 1 (1932)

2 It has been well said that tea is suggestive of a

thousand wants, from which spring the decencies and luxuries of civilization.
Ibid., ch. 2

3 Humor brings insight and tolerance. Irony brings a deeper and less friendly understanding.
In Pursuit of Laughter, ch. 9 (1936)

James Reston
(1909–95)
Scottish-born US journalist

He was associated with the New York Times *for fifty years. For* ALISTAIR COOKE *he was 'the most agile filcher of confidential agreements, the most alert, the most probing, the most knowledgeable – the best – of all Washington correspondents.'*

1 All politics . . . are based on the indifference of the majority.
New York Times 12 June 1968

David Reuben
(b. 1933)
US psychiatrist

GORE VIDAL *called him a 'relentlessly cheery, often genuinely funny writer . . . a moralist, expressing the hang-ups of today's middle-aged, middle-class American Jews'.*

1 Everything You Always Wanted To Know About Sex, But Were Afraid To Ask.
Title of book (1969). Reuben's manual became America's number-one nonfiction bestseller, giving the title to WOODY ALLEN's satirical film released in 1972.

Kenneth Rexroth
(1905–82)
US poet, critic and translator

Known as the 'Godfather of the Beats', he covered diverse themes and poetic techniques in his collections The Phoenix and the Tortoise *(1944),* The Signature of All Things *(1950) and* The Morning Star *(1979).*

1 Into the gap between technology and environment, a black and fearsome chasm, man pours himself.
'The Mirror of Magic' (1948), repr. in *With Eye and Ear* (1970)

2 Inside, the hideous British
Necrophilia and the rancid
Stink of the Church of England.
'The Dragon and the Unicorn', pt 1, publ. in *Collected Longer Poems* (1968). Referring to Salisbury Cathedral.

(Sir) Joshua Reynolds
(1723–92)
English artist and critic

A noted portraitist, he was the first President of the Royal Academy (1768) and helped direct British painting from an anecdotal to a grander style. His annual Discourses Delivered at the Royal Academy *(1769–91) had a wide influence. See* HORACE WALPOLE 16.

1 Few have been taught to any purpose who have not been their own teachers.
Lecture to the Royal Academy, 11 December 1769, publ. in *Discourses on Art*, no. 2 (ed. R. Wark, 1975)

2 If you have great talents, industry will improve them: if you have but moderate abilities, industry will supply their deficiency. Nothing is denied to well directed labour: nothing is to be obtained without it.
Lecture to the Royal Academy, 11 December 1769, ibid., no. 2

3 A mere copier of nature can never produce anything great.
Lecture to the Royal Academy, 14 December 1770, ibid., no. 3

4 I should desire that the last words which I should pronounce in this Academy, and from this place, might be the name of – Michael Angelo.
Lecture to the Royal Academy, 10 December 1790, ibid., no. 15. These were indeed Reynolds' last words in the Academy: he died fourteen months later.

Malvina Reynolds
(1900–78)
US songwriter

Married to a labour organizer, she wrote numerous children's and topical songs, sometimes in collaboration with WOODY GUTHRIE *and* PETE SEEGER. *She later wrote for television's* Sesame Street.

1 Little boxes on the hillside,
Little boxes made of ticky tacky;
Little boxes on the hillside
Little boxes all the same.
There's a green one, and a pink one,
And a blue one, and a yellow one
And they're all made out of ticky tacky,
and they all look just the same.
'Little Boxes' (song, 1962). The song was made famous by PETE SEEGER, whose first hit it was after years of being blacklisted.

Cecil Rhodes

(1853–1902)

British imperialist and business magnate

In Africa from 1870, he formed the De Beers Consolidated Mines Company (1888), extended British territory to Bechuanaland (Botswana) and, through the British South Africa Company, developed Rhodesia. He was Prime Minister of Cape Colony (1890–6), resigning after the Jameson raid.

1 So little done, so much to do.
Said on the day of his death, quoted in *Life of Rhodes*, vol. 2, ch. 39 (1910) by Lewis Michell. See LORD TENNYSON 108.

2 Remember that you are an Englishman and have consequently won first prize in the lottery of life.
Attributed

Jean Rhys

(c. 1890–1979)

British author

Pen-name of Ella Gwendoline Rees Williams. Her best known novel, Wide Sargasso Sea *(1966), developed the story of Rochester's mad wife in* CHARLOTTE BRONTË*'s* Jane Eyre.

1 The perpetual hunger to be beautiful and that thirst to be loved which is the real curse of Eve.
'Illusion', publ. in *The Left Bank* (1927)

2 The feeling of Sunday is the same everywhere, heavy, melancholy, standing still. Like when they say, 'As it was in the beginning, is now, and ever shall be, world without end.'
Voyage in the Dark, pt 1, ch. 4 (1934). Narrated by Anna Morgan.

Ruggiero Ricci

(b. 1918)

US violinist

Noted for his command of the 19th-century bravura repertoire, he toured widely in America and Europe, and in 1971 introduced Paganini's rediscovered Concerto No. 4.

1 A specialist is someone who does everything else worse.
Daily Telegraph 25 May 1990

Condoleezza Rice

(b. 1954)

US politician

A staunch Republican, she became the first female National Security Adviser (2001) and Secretary of State (2005) under President GEORGE W. BUSH.

1 Punish France, ignore Germany and forgive Russia.
Washington Post 13 April 2003. Referring to America's post-Iraq War policy.

Grantland Rice

(1880–1954)

US sports writer

The first American sportswriter, he is associated with the 'gee-whiz' school of writing. He worked for the New York Tribune *(1919–30) and also published prose and poetry on other topics.*

1 For when the One Great Scorer comes to mark
  against your name,
He writes – not that you won or lost – but how you
  played the Game.
'Alumnus Football', publ. in *Only the Brave* (1941)

2 All wars are planned by old men
In council rooms apart.
'The Two Sides of War', publ. in *The Final Answer* (1955)

(Sir) Tim Rice

(b. 1944)

British songwriter

His collaborations with composer Andrew Lloyd Webber include Jesus Christ Superstar *(1971) and* Evita *(1978). He was also the lyricist for* Chess *(1984) and* The Lion King *(1994).*

1 Don't Cry For Me Argentina.
Title of song (1976, music by Andrew Lloyd Webber) in *Evita* (stage musical, 1978). The song was a hit for Julie Covington in 1976 and 1978, and for MADONNA in 1996.

Mandy Rice-Davies

(b. 1944)

British model and club hostess

In 1963 she gave evidence in the trial of Christine Keeler, following the Profumo scandal.

1 He would, wouldn't he?
Remark in court, 29 June 1963, quoted in the *Guardian* 1 July 1963. In response to the statement that Lord Astor, one of her alleged clients, had denied having had sex with her.

Adrienne Rich

(b. 1929)

US poet and author

She addresses feminist themes in both her poetry, such as Snapshots of a Daughter-in-Law *(1963) and* The Will to Change

(1971), and her prose writings, which include Of Woman Born (1976) and the essays Blood, Bread, and Poetry (1986).

1 We who were loved will never
unlive that crippling fever.
'After a Sentence in "Malte Laurids Brigge"', publ. in *Snapshots of a Daughter-in-Law* (1963)

2 The mind's passion is all for singling out.
Obscurity has another tale to tell.
'Focus', publ. in *Necessities of Life* (1966)

3 I came to explore the wreck.
'Diving into the Wreck', st. 6, publ. in *Diving into the Wreck* (1973)

4 Now, again, poetry
violent, arcane, common,
hewn of the commonest living substance
into archway, portal, frame
I grasp for you, your bloodstained splinters, your
ancient and stubborn poise
– as the earth trembles –
burning out from the grain
'The Fact of a Doorframe', publ. in *The Fact of a Doorframe* (1974)

5 No one lives in this room
without confronting the whiteness of the wall
behind the poems, planks of books,
photographs of dead heroines.
Without contemplating last and late
the true nature of poetry. The drive
to connect. The dream of a common language.
'Origins and History of Consciousness', publ. in *The Dream of a Common Language* (1978)

6 They can rule the world while they can persuade
us
our pain belongs in some order.
Is death by famine worse than death by suicide,
than a life of famine and suicide . . . ?
'Hunger', ibid.

7 How we dwelt in two worlds
the daughters and the mothers
in the kingdom of the sons.
'Sibling Mysteries', ibid.

8 The connections between and among women are
the most feared, the most problematic, and the most
potentially transforming force on the planet.
'Disloyal To Civilization: Feminism, Racism, Gynophobia' (1979), repr. in *On Lies, Secrets, and Silence* (1979)

Frank Rich

(b. 1949)
US critic

He has been a New York Times columnist since 1980 and has written widely on culture and politics. His publications include Ghost Light: A Memoir *(2000).*

1 Yesterday's 'Revolution' can always be tomorrow's Nike commercial.
Quoted in the *New York Times Magazine* 16 November 2002

(Sir) Cliff Richard

(b. 1940)
British singer

Originally Harry Webb. Backed by the Shadows he was promoted as Britain's answer to ELVIS PRESLEY. *'Move It' (1958) was the first of a series of hits, and he also appeared in such family films as* Summer Holiday *(1963).*

1 The young ones
Darling we're the young ones
And the young ones should never be afraid.
'The Young Ones' (song, written by Sid Tepper and Roy Bennett) on the album *The Young Ones* (1961) by Cliff Richard and the Shadows. The song featured in the film of the same name (1962), and the title was used for the TV comedy *The Young Ones* (1982–4).

2 He said, 'Son, you are a bachelor boy
And that's the way to stay.
Son, you'll be a bachelor boy
Until your dying day.'
'Bachelor Boy' (song, written by Bruce Welch and Cliff Richard, 1962) by Cliff Richard and the Shadows

3 We're all going on a summer holiday,
No more worries for a week or two.
'Summer Holiday' (song, written by Bruce Welch and Brian Bennett) on the album *Summer Holiday* by Cliff Richard and the Shadows and in the eponymous film (both 1963)

Ann Richards

(b. 1933)
US state official

After becoming Texas State Treasurer, she served as Democrat Governor of Texas (1991–5).

1 Poor George, he can't help it. He was born with a silver foot in his mouth.
Keynote speech at Democratic Convention, quoted in the *Independent* 20 July 1988. Referring to GEORGE BUSH.

Keith Richards
(b. 1943)
British rock musician

Originally Keith Richard. The lean rhythm guitarist of the Rolling Stones, and an iconic symbol of rock 'n' roll debauchery, he has co-written (with MICK JAGGER*) most of the band's material.*

1 Music for the neck downwards.
Of rock 'n' roll, quoted in *Sound Effects: Youth, Leisure and the Politics of Rock*, ch. 7 (1979) by Simon Frith

Samuel Richardson
(1689–1761)
English novelist

His first major work, Pamela *(1740), was written in the form of letters and journals, and helped establish the epistolary novel. His masterpiece,* Clarissa *(7 vols. 1747–8), is the longest novel written in English.*

1 Mine is the most plotting heart in the world.
Clarissa, vol. 4, Letter 5 ('Mr Lovelace in Continuation') (1747)

2 Love, upon occasion, will draw an elephant through a key-hole.
Ibid., vol. 8, Letter 58 ('Mr Lovelace to John Belford, Esq.') (1748)

3 Instruction without entertainment . . . would have but few readers. Instruction, Madam, is the pill: amusement is the gilding.
Letter to Lady Echlin, 22 September 1755, publ. in *Selected Letters of Samuel Richardson* (ed. John Carroll, 1964)

Cardinal Richelieu
(1585–1642)
French statesman

Armand Jean du Plessis. Chief Minister to Louis XIII from 1624, he led France to a dominant position in Europe by destroying the power of the Huguenots and allying with the Swedish king against the Habsburgs in the Thirty Years War.

1 To know how to dissimulate is the knowledge of kings.
Testament Politique, 'Maxims' (1641)

2 Secrecy is the first essential in affairs of the State.
Ibid., 'Maxims'

3 Give me six lines written by the most honourable of men, and I will find an excuse in them to hang him.
Attributed

Hans Richter
(1843–1916)
Hungarian conductor

One of the finest conductors of his era, he was known for his performances of Beethoven and Wagner. He held a long connection with the Vienna Opera and initiated the Richter concerts in London.

1 Your damned nonsense can I stand twice or once, but sometimes always, by God, never.
Quoted in *The Fine Art of Political Wit*, ch. 12 (1964) by Leon Harris. Supposedly spoken to the second flute in the Covent Garden orchestra.

Johann Paul Richter
(1763–1825)
German novelist

His lively satirical novels published under the name Jean Paul established his reputation, notably Titan *(1800–3). The Introduction to Aesthetics (1804) made him one of the earliest theorists of the novel.*

1 The greatest hatred, like the greatest virtue and the worst dogs, is silent.
Hesperus, ch. 12 (1795)

Laura Riding
(1901–91)
US poet and author

Originally Laura Reichenthal. Associated with the Fugitives, a group of Southern writers, she used unconventional rhythms and concrete imagery in her verse. With ROBERT GRAVES*, she established the Seizin Press (1927–38) and the journal* Epilogue *(1935–8).*

1 The next world is
As near to this
As time is similar
To truth familiar.
'From Later to Earlier', publ. in *The Poems of LR* (1938). Last lines of poem.

2 Art, whose honesty must work through artifice, cannot avoid cheating truth.
Selected Poems: In Five Sets, Preface (1975)

Anne Ridler
(1912–2001)
British poet

Her work, appearing in such collections as The Nine Bright Shiners *(1943) and* A Matter of Life and Death *(1959), evokes everyday life in a metaphysical frame.*

1 And when our baby stirs and struggles to be
born
It compels humility: what we began
Is now its own.
'For a Child Expected', publ. in *The Nine Bright Shiners* (1943)

2 Nothing is lost.
We are too sad to know that, or too blind;
Only in visited moments do we understand:
It is not that the dead return –
They are about us always, though unguessed.
'Nothing is Lost', publ. in *A Matter of Life and Death* (1959)

3 In every generation
The young acquire an image of their elders
Tranquil, assured, with every day mapped out
From punctual meals to reading by the fire.
Threescore and ten is not like that at all
We find on getting there.
'Threescore and Ten', publ. in *New and Selected Poems* (1988)

4 Immortality
Is not mere repetition:
It is a blue flash,
A kingfisher vision
It is a new-feathered
And procreant love,
Seen where the halcyon
Nests on the waves.
'The Halcyons', ibid.

Rainer Maria Rilke
(1875–1926)
Austro-German poet

His two major works, Duino Elegies *and* Sonnets to Orpheus *(both 1923), are characterized by innovative and subtle imagery. He travelled widely in Europe and Russia, living in Paris and Switzerland.*

1 The great renewal of the world will perhaps consist in this, that man and maid, freed of all false feelings and reluctances, will seek each other not as opposites, but as brother and sister, as neighbours, and will come together as *human* beings.
Letter, 16 July 1903, publ. in *Letters to a Young Poet* (1934, rev. 1954)

2 Surely all art is the result of one's having been in danger, of having gone through an experience all the way to the end, where no one can go any further.
Letter to his wife, 24 June 1907, publ. in *Rilke's Letters on Cézanne* (1952, transl. 1985)

3 He reproduced himself with so much humble objectivity, with the unquestioning, matter of fact interest of a dog who sees himself in a mirror and thinks: there's another dog.
Letter, 23 October 1907, ibid. Referring to Cézanne.

4 For beauty is nothing but
the beginning of terror, that we are still able to
bear,
and we revere it so, because it calmly disdains
to destroy us. Every Angel is terror.
Duino Elegies, no. 1 (1923, transl. 2001)

5 Aren't lovers
always arriving at boundaries, each of the other,
who promised distance, hunting, and home?
Ibid., no. 2

6 See, we don't love like flowers, in a
single year: when we love, an ancient
sap rises in our arms.
Ibid., no. 3

7 Who has turned us round like this, so that,
whatever we do, we always have the aspect
of one who leaves? Just as they
will turn, stop, linger, for one last time,
on the last hill, that shows them all their valley –
so we live, and are always taking leave.
Ibid., no. 8

Arthur Rimbaud
(1854–91)
French poet

His hallucinatory, dreamlike verse prefigured Symbolism and was all written by the age of twenty, after which he travelled extensively in Europe and Africa. His major works include the long poem 'The Drunken Boat' (1871) and A Season in Hell *(1873), a confessional prose poem in nine fragments.*

1 The Sun, the hearth of affection and life, pours burning love on the delighted earth.
'Soleil et chair' ('Sun and Flesh'), sect. 1, written 1870, publ. in *Collected Poems* (ed. Oliver Bernard, 1962)

2 And again: No more gods! no more gods! Man is King, Man is God! – But the great Faith is Love!
'Soleil et chair', sect. 1, ibid.

3 When you are seventeen you aren't really serious.
'Roman' ('Romance'), sects. 1 and 4, written 1870, ibid.

4 *JE est un autre.*
[*I* is someone else.]
Letter, 13 May 1871, ibid.

5 The poet makes himself a *seer* by a long,

prodigious, and rational *disordering* of *all the senses*. Every form of love, of suffering, of madness; he searches himself, he consumes all the poisons in him, and keeps only their quintessences.
Letter, 15 May 1871, ibid.

6 I danced like a cork on the billows.
'Le Bâteau ivre', st. 4, written 1871 ('The Drunken Boat', transl. SAMUEL BECKETT, 1976), ibid.

7 Sweeter than the flesh of sour apples to children, the green water penetrated my pinewood hull.
'Le Bâteau ivre', st. 5, ibid.

8 I bathed in the Poem of the Sea, star-infused and churned into milk, devouring the green azures.
'Le Bâteau ivre', st. 6, ibid.

9 I have seen the low-hanging sun speckled with mystic horrors lighting up long violet coagulations like the performers in antique dramas.
'Le Bâteau ivre', st. 9, ibid.

10 I long for Europe with its age-old parapets.
'Le Bâteau ivre', st. 21, ibid.

11 But, truly, I have wept too much! The dawns are heartbreaking. Every moon is atrocious and every sun bitter.
'Le Bâteau ivre', st. 23, ibid.

12 Idle youth, enslaved to everything, by being too sensitive I have wasted my life.
'Chanson de la plus haute tour' ('Song of the Highest Tower'), written 1872, ibid.

13 Once, if I remember correctly [*Jadis, si je me souviens bien*], my life was a feast at which all hearts opened and all wines flowed.
Une Saison en enfer (1873; *A Season in Hell*). Opening lines.

14 One evening I sat Beauty on my knees – And I found her bitter – And I reviled her.
Ibid. See SALVADOR DALI 4.

15 Only divine love bestows the keys of knowledge.
Ibid., 'Mauvais sang' ('Bad Blood')

16 Life is the farce which everyone has to perform.
Ibid., 'Mauvais sang'

17 I believe that I am in hell, therefore I am there.
Ibid., 'Nuit de l'enfer' ('Night in Hell')

18 I am the slave of my baptism. Parents, you have caused my misfortune, and you have caused your own.
Ibid., 'Nuit de l'enfer'

19 What a life! True life is elsewhere. We are not in the world.
Ibid., 'Délires 1' ('Ravings 1'). The words 'Life is elsewhere' were used by MILAN KUNDERA as the title of his novel (1973) in which he cites André Breton's Surrealist Manifesto (see ANDRÉ BRETON 2) and the adoption of the words as a slogan by students in Paris, May 1968.

20 I invented the colours of the vowels! – *A* black, *E* white, *I* red, *O* blue, *U* green – I made rules for the form and movement of each consonant, and, with instinctive rhythms, I flattered myself that I had created a poetic language accessible, some day, to all the senses. I reserved translation rights.
Ibid., 'Délires 2: Alchimie du verbe' ('Ravings 2: Alchemy of the Word'). Rimbaud had previously expressed the notion of the vowels possessing particular colours in his poem 'Voyelles' (1871).

21 I saw that all beings are fated to happiness: action is not life, but a way of wasting some force, an enervation. Morality is the weakness of the brain.
Ibid., 'Délires 2: Alchimie du Verbe'

22 Eternity. It is the sea mingled with the sun.
Ibid., 'Délires 2: Faim' ('Ravings 2: Hunger')

23 *Il faut être absolument moderne.*
[One must be absolutely modern.]
Ibid., 'Adieu' ('Farewell')

Paul Robeson
(1898–1976)
US singer and actor

He was famous for both his acting and singing prowess, as in Othello *in London (1930) and* Show Boat *(1927), in which he sang 'Ol' Man River' (see* OSCAR HAMMERSTEIN II 1*). His left-wing sympathies caused him to be ostracized and to leave America 1958–63.*

1 Songs of liberation – who can lock them up? The spirit of freedom – who can jail it? A people's unity – what lash can beat it down? Civil rights – what doubletalk can satisfy our needs?
'A Lesson from Our South African Brothers and Sisters', publ. in *Freedom* September 1952

Maximilien Robespierre
(1758–94)
French revolutionary leader

Called the 'Incorruptible', he became the leader of the radical Jacobins in the National Assembly where he called for the execution of Louis XVI. He dominated the Committee of Public Safety during the Reign of Terror (1793–4) until, having lost support, he was arrested and guillotined. See THOMAS CARLYLE 32.

1 Every institution which does not assume that the people are good, and the magistrate corruptible, is vicious.

Déclaration des droits de l'homme, article 31, 24 April 1793, publ. in Robespierre *(ed. George Rudé, 1967). The articles are differently numbered in other collections.*

2 If the basis of popular government in time of peace is virtue, its basis in a time of revolution is both virtue and intimidation – virtue, without which intimidation is disastrous, and intimidation, without which virtue is powerless.

Report to the Convention, 5 February 1794, quoted in The French Revolution, *ch. 25 (1943) by J. M. Thompson*

3 Pity is treason.

Speech to the National Convention, Paris, 26 February 1794, attributed

4 Death is the beginning of immortality.

Speech, 26 July 1794, publ. in The Penguin Book of Historic Speeches *(ed. Brian MacArthur, 1995). Robespierre's last public speech. He was arrested and guillotined, with twenty-one of his supporters, two days later.*

Leo Robin

See MARILYN MONROE 2

Anne Robinson

(b. 1944)
British TV presenter and journalist

Called 'as cuddly as a cornered ferret' by Lynn Barber, she presented the BBC TV programme Points of View *(1988–94), and in 2000 became the acerbic host of the show* The Weakest Link.

1 You are the weakest link. Goodbye.

Catchphrase used when expelling contestants on The Weakest Link *(BBC1 game show, from 2000)*

Bruce Robinson

(b. 1946)
British film-maker

He wrote the screenplay for The Killing Fields *(1984), then wrote and directed* Withnail and I *(1987) and* How to Get Ahead in Advertising *(1989), both of which attracted a cult following.*

1 I don't advise a haircut, man. All hairdressers are in the employment of the government. Hairs are your aerials. They pick up signals from the cosmos, and transmit them directly into the brain. This is the reason bald-headed men are uptight.

Withnail and I *(film, 1987, written and directed by Bruce Robinson). Spoken by Danny (Ralph Brown).*

2 Flowers are essentially tarts. Prostitutes for the bees.

Monty (Richard Griffiths), ibid.

3 We've gone on holiday by mistake.

Withnail (Richard E. Grant), ibid.

4 As a youth I used to weep in butchers' shops.

Monty (Richard Griffiths), ibid.

5 We want the finest wines available to humanity. And we want them *here*, and we want them *now*.

Withnail, ibid.

6 The joint I am about to roll requires a craftsman and can utilise up to twelve skins. It's called a Camberwell carrot ... I invented it in Camberwell and it's shaped like a carrot.

Danny (Ralph Brown), ibid.

Edward G. Robinson

(1893–1973)
Romanian-born US actor

Originally Emmanuel Goldenberg. A prolific stage performer, he gained stardom with his screen portrayal of the vicious gangster Rico in Little Caesar *(1930), which led on to similar roles in films such as* Key Largo *(1948). 'Some people have youth,' he once said, 'some have beauty – I have menace.'*

1 Mother of Mercy, is this the end of Rico?

Little Caesar *(film, 1931, screenplay by Francis E. Faragoh and Robert W. Lee based on novel by W. R. Burnett, directed by Mervyn LeRoy). Dying words of Rico Bandello (Edward G. Robinson), having been gunned down by the police.*

Edwin Arlington Robinson

(1869–1935)
US poet

His early work described the residents of a small New England town. Later publications include the narrative works The Man Who Died Twice *(1924) and* Tristram *(1927). He was the first person to receive a Pulitzer Prize for poetry, for his* Collected Poems *(1921).*

1 Miniver Cheevy, born too late,
Scratched his head and kept on thinking;
Miniver coughed and called it fate,
And kept on drinking.

'Miniver Cheevy', publ. in The Town Down the River *(1910)*

2 I shall have more to say when I am dead.
'John Brown', publ. in *The Three Taverns* (1920). Last line of poem.

Mary Robinson
(b. 1944)
Irish politician and president

As an Irish Senator (1969–89), she campaigned for reform of the laws on contraception, abortion and homosexuality. She was Ireland's first woman president 1990–7, and subsequently UN Commissioner on Human Rights.

1 Instead of rocking the cradle, they rocked the system.
Referring to Irish women, in speech on becoming President, quoted in *The Times* 10 November 1990. See WILLIAM ROSS WALLACE 1.

John Wilmot, Lord Rochester
(1647–80)
English poet and courtier

Famously dissolute, he is regarded as one of the first Augustans, writing sexually explicit love poems and verse satires, of which A Satire Against Mankind *(1680) is the best known.* HORACE WALPOLE *commented that his poems 'have much more obscenity than wit, more wit than poetry, more poetry than politeness'.*

1 Restless, he rolls about from whore to whore,
A merry monarch, scandalous and poor.
'I' the Isle of Britain', ll. 14–15 (1673), repr. in *Collected Works* (ed. J. Hayward, 1926). Of CHARLES II.

2 Tell me no more of constancy,
That frivolous pretence,
Of cold age, narrow jealousy,
Disease, and want of sense.
'Against Constancy', st. 1 (1676), ibid.

3 Love, the most generous passion of the mind,
The softest refuge innocence can find,
The safe director of unguided youth,
Fraught with kind wishes, and secured by truth,
That cordial drop heaven in our cup has thrown
To make the nauseous draught of life go down.
'A Letter Fancied from Artemisia in the Town to Chloe in the Country', ll. 40–5 (1679), ibid.

4 Were I, who to my cost already am
One of those strange, prodigious creatures, man,
A spirit free to choose, for my own share,
What case of flesh and blood I pleased to wear,
I'd be a dog, a monkey or a bear,

Or anything but that vain animal
Who is so proud of being rational.
A Satire Against Mankind, ll. 1–7 (1679), ibid.

5 Stumbling from thought to thought, falls headlong down
Into doubt's boundless sea, where, like to drown,
Books bear him up a while, and make him try
To swim with bladders of philosophy.
A Satire Against Mankind, ll. 18–21, ibid.

6 Then Old Age, and Experience, hand in hand,
Lead him to death, and make him understand,
After a search so painful, and so long,
That all his life he has been in the wrong:
Huddled in dirt the reasoning engine lies,
Who was so proud, so witty and so wise.
A Satire Against Mankind, l. 25–30, ibid.

7 Our sphere of action is life's happiness,
And he that thinks beyond thinks like an ass.
A Satire Against Mankind, ll. 96–7, ibid.

8 For all men would be cowards if they durst.
A Satire Against Mankind, l. 158, ibid.

9 French truth, Dutch prowess, British policy,
Hibernian learning, Scotch civility,
Spaniards' dispatch, Danes' wit, are mainly seen in thee.
'Upon Nothing', st. 16 (1679), ibid.

10 'Is there then no more?'
She cries. 'All this to love and rapture's due;
Must we not pay a debt to pleasure too?'
'The Imperfect Enjoyment', ll. 22–4 (1680), ibid.

11 Thou treacherous, base deserter of my flame,
False to my passion, fatal to my fame,
Through what mistaken magic dost thou prove
So true to lewdness, so untrue to love?
'The Imperfect Enjoyment', ll. 46–9, ibid.

12 All my past life is mine no more,
The flying hours are gone,
Like transitory dreams given o'er,
Whose images are kept in store
By memory alone.
'Love and Life', st. 1 (1680), ibid.

13 Such natural freedoms are but just:
There's something generous in mere lust.
'A Ramble in St James's Park', ll. 97–8 (1680), ibid.

14 Here lies our Sovereign Lord, the King
Whose word no man relies on:

He never said a foolish thing
Nor ever did a wise one.

'The King's Epitaph', ibid. Written on the door of CHARLES II's bedchamber; on seeing it, the king is said to have replied, 'This is very true: for my words are my own, and my actions are my ministers'.'

Knute Rockne

See JOSEPH P. KENNEDY 1

Gene Roddenberry

(1921–91)
US TV producer and writer

A police officer in Los Angeles, he wrote TV scripts in his spare time for the crime serial Dragnet, *before writing full-time for shows including* Dr Kildare. *He is best known as creator of the science fiction* Star Trek *series (1966–9 and 1987–94).*

1 Space – the final frontier. These are the voyages of the starship *Enterprise*. Its five-year mission: to explore strange new worlds, to seek out new life and new civilizations, to boldly go where no man has gone before.

Star Trek (TV series 1966–9, created and produced by Gene Roddenberry). This preamble to each episode includes what is probably the most famous split infinitive ever recorded.

2 It's life, Jim, but not life as we know it.

Star Trek: The Motion Picture (film, 1979, written by Gene Roddenberry, Alan Dean Foster and Harry Livingston, directed by Robert Wise). The words of Spock (Leonard Nimoy) to Kirk (William Shatner) and often misquoted 'It's life, Jim, but not as we know it', as in 'Star Trekkin'', a UK no. 1 hit by The Firm in 1987.

3 Beam me up, Scotty.

Attributed to Captain James T. Kirk (William Shatner), ibid. These words were never actually spoken in the TV series: the nearest is 'Beam us up, Mr Scott,' said by Captain Kirk to his chief engineer.

Anita Roddick

(b. 1943)
British businesswoman

With her husband she opened the first Body Shop in Brighton in 1976, since when it has grown into an international retailer of beauty products adhering to ethical and ecological principles. She was Chief Executive of the company 1994–8.

1 I think that business practices would improve immeasurably if they were guided by 'feminine' principles – qualities like love and care and intuition.

Body and Soul, ch. 1 (1991)

Richard Rodriguez

(b. 1944)
US author and essayist

Raised in California but with his roots in Mexico, he describes his writing as a 'marriage of journalism and literature'. His publications include a trilogy of memoirs and social observations, concluding with Brown: the Last Discovery of America *(2002).*

1 In tragic cultures, the old have something to teach the young. And they are believed.

Frontiers, 'Night and Day' (1990)

2 In America, the Indian is relegated to the obligatory first chapter – the Once Great Nation chapter – after which the Indian is cleared away as easily as brush, using a very sharp rhetorical tool called an 'alas'.

'Mixed Blood', publ. in *Harper's Magazine* November 1991

Theodore Roethke

(1908–63)
US poet

Influenced by YEATS, *his poems are characterized by ironic lyricism and an empathy for landscape and nature, as in* The Lost Son and Other Poems *(1948) and* The Waking *(1953).*

1 My secrets cry aloud.
I have no need for tongue.
My heart keeps open house,
My doors are widely swung.

'Open House', publ. in *Open House* (1941). Opening lines of poem.

2 I have known the inexorable sadness of pencils,
Neat in their boxes, dolor of pad and paper-weight,
All the misery of manilla folders and mucilage,
Desolation in immaculate public places.

'Dolor', publ. in *The Lost Son and Other Poems* (1948)

3 A lively understandable spirit
Once entertained you.
It will come again.
Be still.
Wait.

'The Lost Son', sect. 5, publ. in *Praise to the End* (1951)

4 I wake to sleep, and take my waking slow.
I feel my fate in what I cannot fear.
I learn by going where I have to go.
'The Waking', publ. in *The Waking: Poems, 1933–1953* (1953)

5 I knew a woman, lovely in her bones,
When small birds sighed, she would sigh back at
them;
Ah, when she moved, she moved more ways than
one:
The shapes a bright container can contain!
'I Knew a Woman', publ. in *Words for the Wind* (1958)

6 I long for the imperishable quiet at the heart of
form.
'The Longing', publ. in *The Far Field*, pt 1 (1964)

7 All finite things reveal infinitude.
'The Far Field', sect. 4, ibid., pt 1

8 In a dark time, the eye begins to see.
'In a Dark Time', st. 1, ibid., pt 4

9 What's the worst portion in this mortal life?
A pensive mistress and a yelping wife.
'The Marrow', st. 1, ibid., pt 4

10 Lord, hear me out, and hear me out this day:
From me to Thee's a long and terrible way.
'The Marrow', st. 3, ibid., pt 4

Ginger Rogers
(1911–95)
US screen actress

Originally Virginia Katherine McMath. She appeared in more than seventy films, in ten of them as the dancing partner of Fred Astaire, for example The Gay Divorcee *(1934) and* Shall We Dance *(1937). As* KATHARINE HEPBURN *remarked, 'He gives her class and she gives him sex.'*

1 Cigarette me, big boy.
Young Man of Manhattan (film, 1930, screenplay by Robert Presnell based on a story by Katherine Brush, directed by Monta Bell). Playing her first screen role as Puff Randolph.

(Sir) Richard Rogers
(b. 1933)
British architect

Baron Rogers of Riverside. His notable buildings include the Pompidou Centre, Paris (with Renzo Piano, 1979), and the Lloyds (1985) and Reuters (1992) buildings in London.

1 Form follows profit is the aesthetic principle of
our times.
The Times 13 February 1991

Will Rogers
(1879–1935)
US humorist

Wisecracking and homespun philosophy were his hallmarks in the Ziegfeld Follies (1916–25). He later became a national institution for his aphoristic columns in the New York Times (from 1922), radio broadcasts and films.

1 Everything is funny as long as it is happening to
somebody else.
The Illiterate Digest, 'Warning to Jokers: Lay Off the Prince' (1924)

2 The United States never lost a war or won a conference.
Wit and Wisdom (ed. Jack Lait, 1936). Remark following the Versailles Peace Conference, at which President WOODROW WILSON spurned all suggestions that the US should take territory or payment as a result of participating in the First World War.

3 Communism to me is one-third practice and two-
thirds explanation.
Ibid.

4 There's only one thing that can kill the movies,
and that's education.
The Autobiography of Will Rogers, ch. 6 (1949)

5 You can't say that civilization don't advance . . .
for in every war they kill you a new way.
Ibid., ch. 14

6 I don't know jokes; I just watch the government
and report the facts.
Quoted in 'A Rogers Thesaurus', in the *Saturday Review* 25 August 1962

Ernst Röhm
(1887–1934)
German Nazi leader

An early supporter of HITLER, *he was the leader of the Nazi 'Brownshirts' but was executed, along with 100 others, on the Night of the Long Knives, for his alleged part in the plot to assassinate Hitler.*

1 All revolutions devour their own children.
Remark to Hans Frank, 30 June 1933, recorded by Frank in his memoirs (1955), quoted in *The Face of the Third Reich*, 'Ernst Röhm and the Lost Generation' (1963, transl. 1970) by Joachim C. Fest. A similar remark has been earlier credited to PIERRE VERGNIAUD.

Madame Roland

(1754–93)

French revolutionary

Vicomtesse Jeanne Manon Philipon Roland de la Platière. A leading member of the Girondist faction, she was arrested at the outbreak of the Jacobin insurrection and executed for treason.

1 O liberty! O liberty! What crimes are committed in thy name!

Remark at the guillotine, 8 November 1793, quoted in *Histoire des Girondins*, bk 51, ch. 8 (1847) by Alphonse de Lamartine. The words were apparently addressed to a huge statue of Liberty erected nearby.

2 The more I see of men, the more I like dogs.

Attributed. The remark has also been attributed to OUIDA, Madame de Sévigné and MADAME DE STAËL.

Pierre de Ronsard

(1524–85)

French poet

Acknowledged as a master of the Alexandrine form, he was a leader of the Pléiade *group of poets, which aimed to raise the status of literary French.*

1 See, Mignonne, hath not the rose
That this morning did unclose
Her purple mantle to the light,
Lost, before the day be dead,
The glory of her raiment red,
Her colour, bright as yours is bright?

'À Cassandre', publ. in *Odes*, bk 1, no. 17 (1555, transl. ANDREW LANG)

2 When you are old, at evening candlelit,
Beside the fire bending to your wool,
Read out my verse and murmur, 'Ronsard writ
This praise for me when I was beautiful.'

Sonnets pour Hélène, bk 2, no. 42, ll. 1–4 (1578). See W. B. YEATS 11.

3 Live now, believe me, wait not till tomorrow;
Gather the roses of life today

[*Cueillez dès aujourd'hui les roses de la vie.*]

Ibid., bk 2, no. 42, ll. 13–14. See ROBERT HERRICK 11, HORACE 24, EDMUND SPENSER 16.

Mickey Rooney

(b. 1920)

US actor and entertainer

Originally Joe Yule. Described by critic James Agee as 'a rope-haired, kazoo-voiced kid with a comic strip face', he became

known for his juvenile roles, for example Boys Town *(1938) and* National Velvet *(1944).*

1 Women liked me because I made them laugh. And what is an orgasm, except laughter of the loins?

Life is Too Short, ch. 32 (1991). Rooney was married eight times, first to Ava Gardner.

Eleanor Roosevelt

(1884–1962)

US diplomat and First Lady

After her marriage to FRANKLIN D. ROOSEVELT *in 1905, she became a public figure in her own right and a champion of liberal causes. She stood in for her husband during his illness and after his death was delegate to the UN Assembly (1946–52). See* ADLAI STEVENSON 17.

1 No one can make you feel inferior without your consent.

This Is My Story (1937)

Franklin D. Roosevelt

(1882–1945)

US politician and president

Franklin Delano Roosevelt. A Democrat, he rose to become the only US president to win four elections (1933–45). He countered the Depression with the New Deal economic programme, and was the first president to broadcast over the radio, using his 'Fireside Chats' to explain issues and policies. He was disabled by polio in 1921.

1 These unhappy times call for the building of plans that . . . build from the bottom up and not from the top down, that put their faith once more in the forgotten man at the bottom of the economic pyramid.

Radio broadcast, 7 April 1932, publ. in *Public Papers and Addresses of Franklin D. Roosevelt*, vol. 1 (1938)

2 I pledge you, I pledge myself, to a new deal for the American people.

Acceptance speech at Democratic National Convention, Chicago, 2 July 1932, ibid. At the height of the economic crisis, the 'New Deal' became the slogan of Roosevelt's successful campaign for the presidency.

3 Let me assert my firm belief that the only thing we have to fear is fear itself – nameless, unreasoning, unjustified terror which paralyzes needed efforts to convert retreat into advance.

Inaugural address, 4 March 1933, publ. in *The Penguin Book of Twentieth-Century Speeches* (ed. Brian MacArthur, 1999). Roosevelt had used the expression 'the only thing we have to fear is fear itself' on previous occasions, and it has numerous earlier attributions, including the BIBLE, WINSTON CHUR-CHILL (in his wartime broadcasts), MONTAIGNE, H. D. THOREAU and the DUKE OF WELLINGTON.

4 In the field of world policy I would dedicate this nation to the policy of the good neighbor.

Inaugural address, 4 March 1933, ibid.

5 I see one-third of a nation ill-housed, ill-clad, ill-nourished.

Second inaugural address, 20 January 1937, publ. in *Public Papers and Addresses of Franklin D. Roosevelt*, vol. 6 (1941)

6 War is a contagion.

Speech in Chicago, 5 October 1937, quoted in *The Wit and Wisdom of Franklin D. Roosevelt*, 'War' (ed. Maxwell Meyersohn, 1950)

7 A radical is a man with both feet firmly planted in the air. A conservative is a man with two perfectly good legs, who, however, has never learned to walk forward. A reactionary is a somnambulist walking backwards. A liberal is a man who uses his legs and his hands at the behest ... of his head.

Radio broadcast, 26 October 1939, publ. in *Public Papers and Addresses of Franklin D. Roosevelt*, vol. 8 (1941)

8 And while I am talking to you mothers and fathers, I give you one more assurance. I have said this before, but I shall say it again and again and again: Your boys are not going to be sent into any foreign wars.

Speech in Boston, 30 October 1940, ibid., vol. 9. Roosevelt made the speech while campaigning for his third term as president. He declared war against Japan just over a year later (see below).

9 We have the men – the skill – the wealth – and above all, the will ... We must be the great arsenal of democracy.

'Fireside Chat', radio broadcast, 29 December 1940, publ. in *The Penguin Book of Twentieth-Century Speeches* (ed. Brian MacArthur, 1999)

10 We look forward to a world founded upon four essential human freedoms. The first is freedom of speech and expression – everywhere in the world. The second is freedom of every person to worship God in his own way – everywhere in the world. The third is freedom from want ... everywhere in the world. The fourth is freedom from fear ... anywhere in the world.

Annual Message to Congress, Washington DC, 6 January 1941, ibid.

11 Yesterday, December 7, 1941 – a date which will live in infamy – the United States of America was suddenly and deliberately attacked by naval and air forces of the Empire of Japan.

Address to Congress, 8 December 1941, publ. in *Public Papers and Addresses of Franklin D. Roosevelt*, vol. 10 (1950). The attack on Pearl Harbor precipitated an immediate declaration of war on Japan by both the US and Britain.

12 Books can not be killed by fire. People die, but books never die. No man and no force can abolish memory ... In this war, we know, books are weapons. And it is a part of your dedication always to make them weapons for man's freedom.

'Message to the Booksellers of America', 6 May 1942, publ. in *Publisher's Weekly* 9 May 1942

13 More than an end to war, we want an end to the beginnings of all wars.

Speech prepared for Jefferson Day broadcast, 13 April 1945, publ. in *Public Papers and Addresses of Franklin D. Roosevelt*, vol. 13 (1950). Roosevelt died suddenly the day before the speech was due to be made.

Theodore Roosevelt

(1858–1919)

US politician and president

A Republican, he was the youngest US president (1901–9) to date, remembered for his Square Deal programme of social reform and regulation of business monopolies. He unsuccessfully stood for president in the 1912 election as head of the newly formed Progressive (Bull Moose) Party.

1 I wish to preach, not the doctrine of ignoble ease, but the doctrine of the strenuous life.

Speech in Chicago, 10 April 1899, publ. in *The Penguin Book of Twentieth-Century Speeches* (ed. Brian MacArthur, 1992). Roosevelt devoted much of his life to 'strenuous' pursuits, building up a slender frame by vigorous exercise, and enduring extreme conditions as rancher and soldier.

2 Speak softly and carry a big stick.

Quoting a favourite adage, in speech at Minnesota State Fair, 2 September 1901, publ. in *The Works of Theodore Roosevelt*, vol. 13. Referring to military preparation and the Monroe Doctrine.

3 I am as strong as a bull moose and you can use me to the limit.

Letter to Mark Hanna, 27 June 1900, publ. in *The Works of Theodore Roosevelt*, vol. 23 (Memorial edn, 1926). 'Bull Moose' subsequently became the sobriquet of the Progressive Party.

4 The first requisite of a good citizen in this republic of ours is that he shall be able and willing to pull his weight.

Speech at New York City, 11 November 1902, publ. in *Addresses and Presidential Messages* (1904)

5 A man who is good enough to shed his blood for his country is good enough to be given a square deal afterwards. More than that no man is entitled to, and less than that no man shall have.
Speech at Springfield, Illinois, 4 June 1903, ibid.

6 The men with the muck-rakes are often indispensable to the well-being of society; but only if they know when to stop raking the muck.
Speech, Washington DC, 14 April 1906, publ. in *The Penguin Book of Twentieth-Century Speeches* (ed. Brian MacArthur, 1992). The 'Man with the Muck-rake' is a character in JOHN BUNYAN's *Pilgrim's Progress*.

7 The things that will destroy America are prosperity-at-any-price, peace-at-any-price, safety-first instead of duty-first, the love of soft living, and the get-rich-quick theory of life.
Letter, 10 January 1917, publ. in *The Letters of Theodore Roosevelt*, vol. 8 (ed. Elting E. Morison, 1954)

8 There is no room in this country for hyphenated Americanism ... The one absolutely certain way of bringing this nation to ruin, of preventing all possibility of its continuing to be a nation at all, would be to permit it to become a tangle of squabbling nationalities.
Speech in New York, 12 October 1915, publ. in *The Works of Theodore Roosevelt*, vol. 20 (Memorial edn, 1926)

9 One of our defects as a nation is a tendency to use what have been called 'weasel words'. When a weasel sucks eggs the meat is sucked out of the egg. If you use a 'weasel word' after another there is nothing left of the other.
Speech in St Louis, Missouri, 31 May 1916, ibid., vol. 24 (1926). Referring to WOODROW WILSON's proposal for 'universal voluntary military training'.

10 There can be no fifty-fifty Americanism in this country. There is room here for only 100% Americanism, only for those who are Americans and nothing else.
Speech at State Republican Party Convention, Saratoga, New York, 19 July 1918, publ. in *Roosevelt Policy*, vol. 3 (1919). Roosevelt had earlier drawn attention to 'hyphenated Americans' in a speech, 12 October 1915: 'Americanism is a matter of the spirit and the soul. Our allegiance must be purely to the United States.'

11 A man who has never gone to school may steal from a freight car; but if he has a university education, he may steal the whole railroad.
Attributed

12 The most successful politician is he who says what everybody is thinking most often and in the loudest voice.
Attributed

Lord Rosebery
(1847–1929)
English politician and prime minister

Archibald Philip Primrose, 5th Earl of Rosebery. After holding posts as Secretary of Foreign Affairs he succeeded GLADSTONE *as Liberal Prime Minister (1894–5).*

1 It is beginning to be hinted that we are a nation of amateurs.
Glasgow University Rectorial Address, 16 November 1900, publ. in *The Times* 17 November 1900

2 I must plough my furrow alone.
Speech at City Liberal Club luncheon, 19 July 1901, publ. in *Rosebery*, ch. 12 (1963) by Robert Rhodes James

Richard Dean Rosen
(b. 1949)
US journalist and critic

He published his first book, 'a premature memoir', while still an undergraduate, and later worked as an editor and critic.

1 It's apparent that we can't proceed any further without a name for this institutionalized garrulousness, this psychological patter, this need to catalogue the ego's condition. Let's call it psychobabble, this spirit which now tyrannizes conversation in the seventies.
Psychobabble: Fast Talk and Quick Cure in the Era of Feeling, 'Psychobabble' (1977). Rosen invented the word 'psychobabble' to describe the idiom that emerged in the Bay area of San Francisco in the 1970s. The jargon of 'psychobabble', he explained, 'is now spoken by magazine editors, management consultants, sandal makers, tool and die workers, chiefs of state, Ph.D.s in clinical psychology, and just about everyone else'. It consists of 'a set of repetitive verbal formalities that kills off the very spontaneity, candor, and understanding it pretends to promote. It's an idiom that reduces psychological insight to a collection of standardized observations, that provides a frozen lexicon to deal with an infinite variety of problems.'

2 Confession, alas, is the new handshake.
Ibid., 'Psychobabble'

Harold Rosenberg

(1906–78)

US art critic and author

In 1952 he coined the phrase 'action painting' to describe the work of a group of American Abstract Expressionists including WILLEM DE KOONING *and* JACKSON POLLOCK. *He discussed his theories in* The Anxious Object *(1964). From 1966 he was art critic of the* New Yorker.

1 Revolution in art lies not in the will to destroy but in the revelation of what has already been destroyed. Art kills only the dead.
The Tradition of the New, ch. 6 (1960)

2 Kitsch is the daily art of our time, as the vase or the hymn was for earlier generations.
Ibid., ch. 18

3 What better way to prove that you understand a subject than to make money out of it?
'The Cultural Situation Today', Introduction to *Discovering the Present* (1973)

4 Art is the laboratory for making new men.
Discovering the Present, ch. 24 (1973)

Isaac Rosenberg

(1890–1918)

British poet

Before being killed in France in the First World War, he published two volumes of poetry, Night and Day *(1912) and* Youth *(1915).*

1 The darkness crumbles away –
It is the same old druid Time as ever.
'Break of Day in the Trenches', written 1916, publ. in *Poems* (1922). Opening lines of poem.

2 Droll rat, they would shoot you if they knew
Your cosmopolitan sympathies.
'Break of Day in the Trenches', ibid.

3 Death could drop from the dark
As easily as song.
'Returning, We Hear the Larks', written 1917, ibid.

Alan S. C. Ross

(1907–80)

British linguistics scholar

Alan Strode Campbell Ross. Author of numerous studies of German and Scandinavian etymology, he is popularly remembered for coining the expressions 'U' and 'non-U' to denote upper-class and non-upper-class linguistic usage, in a lightly satirical essay in 1954.

1 There are, it is true, still a few minor points of life which may serve to demarcate the upper class, but they are only minor ones ... When drunk, gentlemen often become amorous or maudlin or vomit in public, but they never become truculent.
'U and Non-U: An Essay in Sociological Linguistics' (1954), repr. in *Noblesse Oblige* (1956) by NANCY MITFORD

2 It must be remembered that, in these matters, U-speakers have ears to hear, so that one single pronunciation, word, or phrase will suffice to brand an apparent U-speaker as originally non-U (for U-speakers themselves never make 'mistakes').
'U and Non-U: An Essay in Sociological Linguistics', ibid.

Christina Rossetti

(1830–94)

English poet and lyricist

The sister of DANTE GABRIEL ROSSETTI, *and a High Anglican, she wrote technically accomplished religious and love poetry, as well as works for children.* Goblin Market and Other Poems *(1862) was her most famous collection.*

1 When I am dead, my dearest,
Sing no sad songs for me;
Plant thou no roses at my head,
Nor shady cypress tree:
Be the green grass above me
With showers and dewdrops wet;
And if thou wilt, remember,
And if thou wilt, forget.
'Song' ('When I am dead'), st. 1, written 1848, publ. in *Goblin Market and Other Poems* (1862)

2 Oh roses for the flush of youth,
And laurel for the perfect prime;
But pluck an ivy branch for me
Grown old before my time.
'Song' ('Oh roses for the flush of youth'), written 1849, ibid.

3 Remember me when I am gone away,
Gone far away into the silent land.
'Remember', written 1849, ibid.

4 Better by far you should forget and smile
Than that you should remember and be sad.
'Remember', ibid.

5 She gave up beauty in her tender youth,
Gave all her hope and joy and pleasant ways;
She covered up her eyes lest they should gaze
On vanity, and chose the bitter truth.
'A Portrait', written 1850, publ. in *The Prince's Progress and Other Poems* (1866)

6 My heart is like a singing bird
Whose nest is in a watered shoot.
'A Birthday', st. 1, written 1857, publ. in *Goblin Market and Other Poems* (1862)

7 Because the birthday of my life
Is come, my love is come to me.
'A Birthday', st. 2, ibid.

8 Does the road wind up-hill all the way?
Yes, to the very end.
Will the day's journey take the whole long day?
From morn to night, my friend.
'Up-Hill', st. 1, written 1858, ibid.

9 For there is no friend like a sister
In calm or stormy weather;
To cheer one on the tedious way,
To fetch one if one goes astray,
To lift one if one totters down,
To strengthen whilst one stands.
'Goblin Market', ll. 562–7, written 1859, ibid. Last lines of poem.

10 Rise above
Quibbles and shuffling off and on:
Here's friendship for you if you like; but love,
No, thank you, John.
" 'No, Thank You' ", st. 8, written 1860, ibid.

11 And all the winds go sighing
For sweet things dying.
'A Dirge', written 1865, publ. in *Poems* (1875)

12 One day in the country
Is worth a month in town.
'Summer', st. 4, publ. in *The Prince's Progress and Other Poems* (1866)

13 Hope is like a harebell trembling from its birth.
'Hope Is Like a Harebell', publ. in *Sing Song* (1872)

14 Who has seen the wind?
Neither you nor I:
But when the trees bow down their heads,
The wind is passing by.
'Who has seen the wind?', st. 2, ibid.

15 In the bleak mid-winter
Frosty wind made moan,
Earth stood hard as iron,
Water like a stone;
Snow had fallen, snow on snow,
Snow on snow,
In the bleak mid-winter,
Long ago.
'A Christmas Carol', publ. in *Poems* (1875)

Dante Gabriel Rossetti
(1828–82)
English painter and poet

A founding member of the Pre-Raphaelite Brotherhood (1848), he took scenes from DANTE *as subjects for his paintings. His idealized images of women include* Beata Beatrix *(c. 1863) and* The Blessed Damozel *(1871–9). He was the brother of* CHRISTINA ROSSETTI.

1 The blessed damozel leaned out
From the gold bar of Heaven;
Her eyes were deeper than the depth
Of waters stilled at even;
She had three lilies in her hand,
And the stars in her hair were seven.
'The Blessed Damozel', st. 1 (1850), repr. in *Poems* (1870)

2 As low as where this earth
Spins like a fretful midge.
'The Blessed Damozel', st. 6, ibid.

3 And the souls mounting up to God
Went by her like thin flames.
'The Blessed Damozel', st. 7, ibid.

4 I have been here before,
But when or how I cannot tell:
I know the grass beyond the door,
The sweet keen smell,
The sighing sound, the lights around the shore.
'Sudden Light', written 1854, publ. in *Poems* (1870)

5 A sonnet is a moment's monument,
Memorial from the soul's eternity
To one dead deathless hour.
The House of Life, Introduction (1881)

6 'Tis visible silence, still as the hour-glass.
Ibid., pt 1, 'Silent Noon'

7 Give honour unto Luke Evangelist;
For he it was (the aged legends say)
Who first taught Art to fold her hands and pray.
Ibid., pt 2, 'Old and New Art'

8 Look in my face; my name is Might-have-been;
I am also called No-more, Too-late, Farewell.
Ibid., pt 2, 'A Superscription'

9 Sleepless with cold commemorative eyes.
Ibid., pt 2, 'A Superscription'

10 When vain desire at last and vain regret
Go hand in hand to death, and all is vain,
What shall assuage the unforgotten pain
And teach the unforgetful to forget?
Ibid., pt 2 , 'The One Hope'

Edmond Rostand

(1868–1918)

French poet and playwright

He is best known for his colourful poetic and romantic drama Cyrano de Bergerac *(1897). His reputation declined with* Chantecler *(1910) which was poorly received by contemporaries.*

1 'Tis well known, a big nose is indicative
Of a soul affable, and kind, and courteous,
Liberal, brave.
Cyrano de Bergerac, act 1, sc. 4 (1897). Spoken by Cyrano.

2 I recoil, overcome with the glory of my rosy hue and the knowledge that I, a mere cock, have made the sun rise.
Chantecler, act 2, sc. 3 (1910). Spoken by Chantecler.

Jean Rostand

(1894–1977)

French biologist and author

Alongside his books for the scientific community, he wrote popular works for a wider audience, such as Life and Its Problems *(1939) and* A Biologist's View *(1954). He was known for his astute insights into the social and psychological context of scientific research. He was the son of* EDMOND ROSTAND.

1 Kill a man, one is a murderer; kill a million, a conqueror; kill them all, a God.
Pensées d'un biologiste (1939; *A Biologist's Thoughts*), repr. in *The Substance of Man*, ch. 5 (1962)

2 To be adult is to be alone.
Ibid., ch. 6

3 I still understand a few words in life, but I no longer think they make a sentence.
Ibid., ch. 6

4 To reflect is to disturb one's thoughts.
Ibid., ch. 10

5 Hatred, for the man who is not engaged in it, is a little like the odour of garlic for one who hasn't eaten any.
Ibid., ch. 10

6 To love an idea is to love it a little more than one should.
Carnets d'un biologiste (1959; *A Biologist's Notebook*), ibid.

7 God, that dumping ground of our dreams.
Carnets d'un biologiste, ibid.

Leo Rosten

(1908–97)

US author

He is best known for his humorous sketches about a new immigrant in the US, The Education of H*y*m*a*n K*a*p*l*a*n *(1937) and its sequels, and for* The Joys of Yiddish *(1968).*

1 Anybody who hates dogs and babies can't be all bad.
Speech in honour of W. C. FIELDS, at Masquers' Club Dinner, Hollywood, 16 February 1939, quoted in the *Saturday Review* 12 June 1976. Often erroneously ascribed to Fields, with the words: 'Anyone who hates children and dogs can't be all bad.'

Philip Roth

(b. 1933)

US novelist

An irreverent satirist, he portrays a love-hate relationship with his ancestral Jewish faith in his books, which blend autobiography with fiction and include Portnoy's Complaint *(1969),* Zuckerman Unbound *(1981) and* American Pastoral *(1997).*

1 A Jewish man with parents alive is a fifteen-year-old boy, and will remain a fifteen-year-old boy until *they die*!
Portnoy's Complaint, 'Cunt Crazy' (1969)

2 My God! The English language is a *form of communication*! Conversation isn't just crossfire where you shoot and get shot at! Where you've got to duck for your life and aim to kill! Words aren't only bombs and bullets – no, they're little gifts, containing *meanings*!
Ibid., 'The Most Prevalent Form of Degradation in Erotic Life'

3 All I can tell you with certainty is that I, for one, have no self, and that I am unwilling or unable to perpetrate upon myself the joke of a self . . . What I have instead is a variety of impersonations I can do, and not only of myself – a troupe of players that I have internalised, a permanent company of actors that I can call upon when a self is required . . . I am a theater and nothing more than a theater.
The Counterlife, ch. 5 (1986). Zuckerman writing to Maria.

4 Obviously the facts are never just coming at you but are incorporated by an imagination that is formed by your previous experience. Memories of the past are not memories of facts but memories of your imaginings of the facts.
The Facts, opening letter to Zuckerman (1988)

5 Family indivisibility, the first commandment.
Ibid., Prologue

6 I cannot and do not live in the world of discretion, not as a writer, anyway. I would prefer to, I assure you – it would make life easier. But discretion is, unfortunately, not for novelists.
Deception (1990). Spoken by Philip to his wife.

Mark Rothko
(1903–70)
Latvian-born US painter

Originally Marcus Rothkovich. From 1938 he experimented with 'automatism' and produced increasingly abstract paintings. From 1958 to 1966 he worked on a series of fourteen immense canvases which were placed in a nondenominational chapel in Houston, Texas, renamed the Rothko Chapel after his death by suicide.

1 Both the sense of community and of security depend on the familiar. Freed of them, transcendental experience becomes possible.
'The Romantics Were Prompted' (1947–8), repr. in *Theories of Modern Art*, ch. 9 (1968) by Herschel B. Chipp

2 Pictures must be miraculous: the instant one is completed, the intimacy between the creation and the creator is ended. He is an outsider. The picture must be for him, as for anyone experiencing it later, a revelation, an unexpected and unprecedented resolution of an eternally familiar need.
'The Romantics Were Prompted', ibid.

Jean-Jacques Rousseau
(1712–78)
Swiss-born French philosopher, political theorist and novelist

He drew controversy with his Discourses on the Origins of Inequality *(1754) and* The Social Contract *(1762), works that postulated the notion of the 'noble savage' corrupted by civilized society. His novel* Émile *(1762) proposed a radical new system of education, while his posthumous* Confessions *(1782) was a prototype of modern autobiography.*

1 Man is born free, and everywhere he is in chains.
Du Contrat Social, ch. 1 (1762; *The Social Contract*). Opening sentence of work. See JOHN MILTON 75.

2 Childhood is the sleep of reason.
Émile; or, On Education, bk 2 (1762)

3 We are born, so to speak, twice over; born into existence, and born into life; born a human being, and born a man.
Ibid., bk 4

4 Whenever the last trumpet shall sound, I will present myself before the sovereign Judge with this book in my hand, and loudly proclaim, 'Thus have I acted; these were my thoughts; such was I. With equal freedom and veracity have I related what was laudable or wicked, I have concealed no crimes, added no virtues.'
The Confessions of Jean-Jacques Rousseau, bk 1, Foreword (written 1766–70, publ. 1781)

5 It is too difficult to think nobly when we think for a livelihood.
Ibid., bk 9 (publ. 1788)

Martin Joseph Routh
(1755–1854)
English classicist

President of Magdalen College, Cambridge, from 1791, he took holy orders in 1810 and edited early ecclesiastical and classical texts.

1 You will find it a very good practice always to verify your references, sir!
Essay in *Quarterly Review* July 1878, quoted in *Lives of Twelve Good Men*, vol. 1, 'Memoir of Dr Routh' (1888) by John William Burgon

Joseph Roux
(1834–86)
French priest and author

A village priest, he was the author of Chanson Limousina *(1889), which contributed to a literary revival in Limousin.*

1 Say nothing good of yourself, you will be distrusted; say nothing bad of yourself, you will be taken at your word.
Meditations of a Parish Priest, no. 22 (1886)

2 Poetry is truth in its Sunday clothes.
Ibid., pt 1, no. 76

3 Experience comprises illusions lost, rather than wisdom gained.
Ibid., pt 4, no. 28

Helen Rowland
(1875–1950)
US journalist

Her humorous observations on the subject of marriage and the single life were published in Reflections of a Bachelor Girl *(1903),* The Sayings of Mrs Solomon *(1920) and* A Guide to Men *(1922).*

1 A husband is what is left of a lover, after the nerve has been extracted.
A Guide to Men, Prelude (1922)

2 Somehow, a bachelor never quite gets over the idea that he is a thing of beauty and a boy for ever!
Ibid., 'Bachelors'. See JOHN KEATS 19.

3 A fool and her money are soon courted.
Ibid., 'First Interlude'

4 A widow is a fascinating being with the flavor of maturity, the spice of experience, the piquancy of novelty, the tang of practised coquetry, and the halo of one man's approval.
Ibid., 'Widows'

Richard Rowland
(1880–1947)
US film producer

He was joint founder (1916) of the Metro Pictures Corporation.

1 The lunatics have taken charge of the asylum.
Comment in 1920, quoted in *A Million and One Nights*, vol. 2, ch. 79 (1926) by Terry Ramsaye. On the formation of *United Artists* film production company by CHARLIE CHAPLIN, Douglas Fairbanks, D. W. GRIFFITH and Mary Pickford.

J. K. Rowling
(b. 1966)
British author

Joanne Kathleen Rowling. The international success of her first book, the fantasy Harry Potter and the Philosopher's Stone *(1997), revolutionized the children's book industry. This and its equally popular sequels have been filmed.*

1 There are all kinds of courage. It takes a great deal of bravery to stand up to our enemies, but just as much to stand up to our friends.
Harry Potter and the Philosopher's Stone, ch. 17 (1997). Spoken by Albus Dumbledore.

2 It is our choices, Harry, that show what we truly are, far more than our abilities.
Harry Potter and the Chamber of Secrets, ch. 18 (1998). Spoken by Albus Dumbledore.

A. L. Rowse
(1903–97)
British historian and critic

Alfred Leslie Rowse. A fellow of All Souls College, Oxford, he was known for his studies of 16th-century England, as well as for biographies, memoirs and general works such as The Use of History *(1946).*

1 In an imperfect world, it seems to me that, of all human institutions, the university of Oxford, and in it the college of All Souls, come nearest to perfection.
The Saturday Book, 'All Souls' (1945)

Arundhati Roy
(b. 1961)
Indian novelist

Her upbringing in the minority Syrian Christian community in the state of Kerala forms the setting for her award-winning novel The God of Small Things *(1997). Her outspoken support of environmental causes and her political protests have made her a controversial figure in India.*

1 It is curious how sometimes the memory of death lurks on for so much longer than the memory of life that it purloined.
The God of Small Things, ch. 1 (1997)

2 If there is a nuclear war, our foes will not be China or America or even each other. Our foe will be the earth herself. The very elements – the sky, the air, the land, the wind and water – will all turn against us. Their wrath will be terrible.
'The End of Imagination' publ. in *The Cost of Living* (1999)

3 What we need to search for and find, what we need to hone and perfect into a magnificent, shining thing, is a new kind of politics. Not the politics of governance, but the politics of resistance. The politics of opposition. The politics of forcing accountability. The politics of slowing things down. The politics of joining hands across the world and preventing certain destruction. In the present circumstances, I'd say that the only thing worth globalizing is dissent. It's India's best export.
Power Politics, ch. 1 (2001)

Richard Rumbold
(1622–85)
English soldier and conspirator

Implicated in the Rye House Plot of 1683 to assassinate CHARLES II, *he was captured and executed.*

1 I never will believe that Providence has sent a few men into the world, ready booted and spurred to ride, and millions ready saddled and bridled to be ridden.
Speech on the scaffold, Edinburgh, 1685, quoted in *History of England*, vol. 1, ch. 5 (1849) by LORD MACAULAY

Donald Rumsfeld
(b. 1932)
US politician and business executive

He was elected a Republican congressman in 1962, has held various posts in the private business sector and became the youngest US Secretary for Defense (1974–5), taking up the office again in 2001 and 2005.

1 If you are not criticized, you may not be doing much.
Rumsfeld's Rules, ch. 2 (1974)

2 As we know, there are known knowns; there are things we know we know. We also know there are known unknowns; that is to say we know there are some things we do not know. But there are also unknown unknowns – the ones we don't know we don't know.
News briefing, 12 February 2002, quoted on Defense Department website, www.defenselink.mil. In reply to the question: 'Is there any evidence to indicate that Iraq has attempted to or is willing to supply terrorists with weapons of mass destruction?' Rumsfeld added: 'I could have said that the absence of evidence is not evidence of absence, or vice versa.' His words were published in *Pieces of Intelligence: The Existential Poetry of Donald H. Rumsfeld* (ed. Hart Seely, 2003).

3 You are thinking of Europe as Germany and France. I don't. I think that's old Europe . . . If you look at the entire NATO Europe today, the center of gravity is shifting to the east. And there are a lot of new members.
Washington Post 24 January 2003

Robert Runcie
(1921–2000)
British ecclesiastic

Baron Runcie of Cuddesden. Decorated in the Second World War, he was ordained in 1951. While Archbishop of Canterbury 1980–91, he criticized the THATCHER *government's 'pharisaical attitudes' to the poor.*

1 Those who dare to interpret God's will must never claim Him as an asset for one nation or group rather than another. War springs from the love and loyalty which should be offered to God being applied to some God substitute, one of the most dangerous being nationalism.
Sermon at the Falkland Islands Thanksgiving Service, St Paul's Cathedral, London, 26 July 1982, publ. in *The Times* 27 July 1982. Runcie refused to treat the commemorative service at the end of the Falklands War as a victory celebration, instead urging reconciliation.

Damon Runyon
(1884–1946)
US author

Previously a war correspondent and a sports reporter, he wrote lively tales of New York street-life, published in Guys and Dolls *(1931, stage musical 1950),* Blue Plate Special *(1934) and* Take it Easy *(1939).*

1 My boy . . . always try to rub up against money, for if you rub up against money long enough, some of it may rub off on you.
'A Very Honorable Guy', publ. in *Guys and Dolls* (1931). Spoken by Feet Samuels.

2 I long ago come to the conclusion that all life is six to five against.
'A Nice Price', publ. in *Money from Home* (1935). Spoken by Sam the Gonoph.

Salman Rushdie
(b. 1947)
Indian-born British author

He has imaginatively depicted both Western and Indian society in such works as Midnight's Children *(1981). Publication of* The Satanic Verses *(1988) led to a death sentence for blasphemy issued by Iran's* AYATOLLAH KHOMEINI *and a life in hiding, from which he has gradually re-entered public life.*

1 Sometimes legends make reality, and become more useful than the facts.
Midnight's Children, bk 1, 'Hit-the-spittoon' (1981)

2 To explain why we become attached to our birthplaces we pretend that we are trees and speak of roots. Look under your feet. You will not find gnarled growths sprouting through the soles. Roots, I sometimes think, are a conservative myth, designed to keep us in our places.
Shame, ch. 5 (1983)

3 Between shame and shamelessness lies the axis upon which we turn; meteorological conditions at both these poles are of the most extreme, ferocious type. Shamelessness, shame: the roots of violence.
Ibid., ch. 7

4 Such is the miraculous nature of the future of exiles: what is first uttered in the impotence of an overheated apartment becomes the fate of nations.
The Satanic Verses, 'Ayesha' (1988). Referring to the Imam, exiled in London.

5 Where there is no belief, there is no blasphemy.
Ibid., 'Return to Jahilia'. Spoken by the narrator.

6 If Woody Allen were a Muslim, he'd be dead by now.

Quoted in the *Independent* 18 February 1989. Of the death threats by Muslim extremists following the publication of *The Satanic Verses*.

7 The idea of the sacred is quite simply one of the most conservative notions in any culture, because it seeks to turn other ideas – uncertainty, progress, change – into crimes.

'Is Nothing Sacred?', Herbert Read Memorial Lecture, ICA, London, 6 February 1990, publ. in *Imaginary Homelands*, pt 12 (1991). In the wake of Khomeini's fatwa, the lecture was read by HAROLD PINTER.

8 Free speech is the whole thing, the whole ball game. Free speech is life itself.

Interview in the *Guardian* 8 November 1990

9 Civilisation is the sleight of hand that conceals our natures from ourselves.

The Moor's Last Sigh, ch. 18

10 As human knowledge has grown, it has also become plain that every religious story ever told about how we got here is quite simply wrong. This, finally, is what all religions have in common. They didn't get it right. There was no celestial churning, no maker's dance, no vomiting of galaxies, no snake or kangaroo ancestors, no Valhalla, no Olympus, no six-day conjuring trick followed by a day of rest. Wrong, wrong, wrong.

'Imagine No Heaven', publ. in *Step Across This Line* (2002)

11 The Islamic world today is being held prisoner, not by Western but by Islamic captors, who are fighting to keep closed a world that a badly outnumbered few are trying to open.

New York Times 27 November 2002

Dean Rusk
(1909–94)
US politician

A Democrat, he held a succession of foreign affairs posts in HARRY S. TRUMAN*'s administration (1947–51), and was Secretary of State under* JOHN F. KENNEDY *and* LYNDON B. JOHNSON. *A vehement anti-communist, he was instrumental in escalating the Vietnam War.*

1 One of the best ways to persuade others is with your ears – by listening to them.

Reader's Digest July 1961

2 We're eyeball to eyeball, and I think the other fellow just blinked.

Remark 24 October 1962, quoted in the *Saturday Evening Post* 8 December 1962. Referring to the Cuban missile crisis, in which Rusk played a key role.

John Ruskin
(1819–1900)
English art critic and author

Through his books The Seven Lamps of Architecture *(1849) and* The Stones of Venice *(3 vols. 1851–3), he became a major influence on public taste and the leading social and art critic of his day. He championed J. M. W. Turner in* Modern Painters *(1843–60) and the Gothic Revival in architecture.*

1 An architect should live as little in cities as a painter. Send him to our hills, and let him study there what nature understands by a buttress, and what by a dome.

The Seven Lamps of Architecture, ch. 3 ('The Lamp of Power'), sect. 24 (1849)

2 I believe the right question to ask, respecting all ornament, is simply this: Was it done with enjoyment – was the carver happy while he was about it?

Ibid., ch. 5 ('The Lamp of Life'), sect. 24

3 When we build, let us think that we build for ever.

Ibid., ch. 6 ('The Lamp of Memory'), sect. 10

4 In order that people may be happy in their work, these three things are needed: They must be fit for it: They must not do too much of it: and they must have a sense of success in it.

Pre-Raphaelitism (pamphlet, 1851)

5 You were made for enjoyment, and the world was filled with things which you will enjoy, unless you are too proud to be pleased by them, or too grasping to care for what you cannot turn to other account than mere delight.

The Stones of Venice, vol. 1, ch. 2, sect. 17 (1851)

6 Remember that the most beautiful things in the world are the most useless; peacocks and lilies for instance.

Ibid., vol. 1, ch. 2, sect. 17

7 Men are more evanescent than pictures, yet one sorrows for lost friends, and pictures *are* my friends. I have none others. I am never long enough with men to attach myself to them; and whatever feelings of attachment I have are to material things.

Letter to his father, 28 January 1852, quoted in *Ruskin Today*, sect. 36 (ed. Kenneth Clark, 1964)

8 No person who is not a great sculptor or painter can be an architect. If he is not a sculptor or painter, he can only be a builder.

Lectures on Architecture and Painting, no. 61 (1853)

9 The purest and most thoughtful minds are those which love colour the most.

The Stones of Venice, vol. 2, ch. 5, sect. 30 (1853)

10 The great cry that rises from all our manufacturing cities, louder than their furnace blast, is all in very deed for this – that we manufacture everything there except men.

Ibid., vol. 2, ch. 6, sect. 16

11 No architecture is so haughty as that which is simple.

Ibid., vol. 2, ch. 6, sect. 78

12 The higher a man stands, the more the word 'vulgar' becomes unintelligible to him.

Modern Painters vol. 3, pt 4, ch. 7, sect. 9 (1856)

13 All violent feelings . . . produce in us a falseness in all our impressions of external things, which I would generally characterize as the 'Pathetic Fallacy'.

Ibid., vol. 3, pt 4, ch. 12

14 The greatest thing a human soul ever does in this world is to *see* something, and tell what it *saw* in a plain way. Hundreds of people can talk for one who can think, but thousands can think for one who can see. To see clearly is poetry, prophecy, and religion – all in one.

Ibid., vol. 3, pt 4, ch. 16

15 Mountains are the beginning and the end of all natural scenery.

Ibid., vol. 4, pt 5, ch. 20

16 Fine art is that in which the hand, the head, and the heart of man go together.

The Two Paths, Lecture 2 (1859)

17 There is no wealth but life.

Unto This Last, Essay 4 ('Ad Valorem') (1862)

18 All books are divisible into two classes, the books of the hour, and the books of all time.

Sesame and Lilies, 'Of Kings' Treasuries', sect. 1 (1865)

19 Be sure that you go to the author to get at *his* meaning, not to find yours.

Ibid., 'Of Kings' Treasuries', sect. 1

20 How long most people would look at the best book before they would give the price of a large turbot for it!

Ibid., 'Of Kings' Treasuries', sect. 2

21 You may chisel a boy into shape, as you would a rock, or hammer him into it, if he be of a better kind, as you would a piece of bronze. But you cannot hammer a girl into anything. She grows as a flower does.

Ibid., 'Of Queens' Gardens', sect. 2

22 The distinguishing sign of slavery is to have a price, and to be bought for it.

The Crown of Wild Olive, Lecture 3 ('War') (1866)

23 It does not matter what the whip is; it is none the less a whip, because you have cut thongs for it out of your own souls.

Ibid., Lecture 3 ('War')

24 Life without industry is guilt, and industry without art is brutality.

Lectures on Art, Lecture 3 ('The Relation of Art to Morals'), sect. 95 (1870)

25 Of all the things that oppress me, this sense of the evil working of nature herself – my disgust at her barbarity – clumsiness – darkness – bitter mockery of herself – is the most desolating.

Letter, 3 April 1871, quoted in *Ruskin Today*, sect. 115 (ed. Kenneth Clark, 1964)

26 Every increased possession loads us with a new weariness.

The Eagle's Nest, ch. 5 (1872)

27 I have seen, and heard, much of Cockney impudence before now; but never expected to hear a coxcomb ask two hundred guineas for flinging a pot of paint in the public's face.

Letter, 18 June 1877, publ. in *Fors Clavigera*, vol. 7 (1877). Referring to J. M.WHISTLER's *Nocturne in Black and Gold: The Falling Rocket*. OSCAR WILDE commented that the painting was 'worth looking at for about as long as one looks at a real rocket, that is, for somewhat less than a quarter of a minute'. Whistler took more seriously Ruskin's remarks, which he made the subject of a law-suit, which he won, being awarded costs of a farthing. See J. M. WHISTLER 2.

28 Men don't and can't live by exchanging articles , but by producing them. They don't live by trade, but by work. Give up that foolish and vain title of Trades Unions; and take that of Labourers' Unions.

Open letter to the Trades Unions of England, 31 August 1880, ibid., vol. 8 (1884)

29 In health of mind and body, men should see

with their own eyes, hear and speak without trumpets, walk on their feet, not on wheels, and work and war with their arms, not with engine-beams, nor rifles warranted to kill twenty men at a shot before you can see them.

Praeterita, vol. 2, ch. 10, sect. 200 (1899)

30 Sunshine is delicious, rain is refreshing, wind braces us up, snow is exhilarating; there is really no such thing as bad weather, only different kinds of good weather.

Attributed

31 There is hardly anything in the world that someone cannot make a little worse and sell a little cheaper, and the people who consider price alone are that person's lawful prey.

Attributed

Bertrand Russell
(1872–1970)
British philosopher and mathematician

Earl Russell of Kingston. Influential both as a thinker and a liberal activist, he first came to notice with Principia Mathematica *(1910–13), co-authored with his former tutor* A. N. WHITEHEAD. *Later publications include* A History of Western Philosophy *(1945) and his* Autobiography *(1967–9). A lifelong pacifist, he was gaoled for his stand against conscription in the First World War and again, aged almost ninety, as an anti-nuclear campaigner.*

1 Mathematics may be defined as the subject in which we never know what we are talking about, nor whether what we are saying is true.

'Recent Work in the Philosophy of Mathematics' (1901), repr. in *Mysticism and Logic*, ch. 5 (1918). In a letter of March 1912 to Lady Ottoline Morrell, Russell wrote: 'I like mathematics because it is not human and has nothing particular to do with this planet or with the whole accidental universe – because, like Spinoza's God, it won't love us in return.'

2 Mathematics, rightly viewed, possesses not only truth, but supreme beauty – a beauty cold and austere, like that of sculpture, without appeal to any part of our weaker nature, without the gorgeous trappings of painting or music, yet sublimely pure, and capable of a stern perfection such as only the greatest art can show.

'The Study of Mathematics' (1907), repr. ibid., ch. 4

3 A hallucination is a fact, not an error; what is erroneous is a judgment based upon it.

'On the Nature of Acquaintance: Neutral Monism' (1914), repr. in *Logic and Knowledge* (1956)

4 And all this madness, all this rage, all this flaming death of our civilization and our hopes, has been brought about because a set of official gentlemen, living luxurious lives, mostly stupid, and all without imagination or heart, have chosen that it should occur rather than that any one of them should suffer some infinitesimal rebuff to his country's pride.

Letter to the *Nation*, 16 August 1914, repr. in *The Autobiography of Bertrand Russell*, vol. 2, ch. 1 (1968). The letter was written 12 August 1914, eight days after the declaration of war.

5 Organic life, we are told, has developed gradually from the protozoon to the philosopher, and this development, we are assured, is indubitably an advance. Unfortunately it is the philosopher, not the protozoon, who gives us this assurance.

Herbert Spencer lecture, Oxford, 1914, repr. in *Mysticism and Logic*, ch. 6 (1918)

6 It is clear that thought is not free if the profession of certain opinions makes it impossible to earn a living. It is clear also that thought is not free if all the arguments on one side of a controversy are perpetually presented as attractively as possible, while the arguments on the other side can only be discovered by diligent search.

Moncure Conway Lecture, 1922, publ. in *Sceptical Essays*, 'Free Thought and Official Propaganda' (1928)

7 Machines are worshipped because they are beautiful and valued because they confer power; they are hated because they are hideous and loathed because they impose slavery.

Sceptical Essays, 'Machines and the Emotions' (1928)

8 It is obvious that 'obscenity' is not a term capable of exact legal definition; in the practice of the Courts, it means 'anything that shocks the magistrate'.

Ibid., 'The Recrudescence of Puritanism'

9 Advocates of capitalism are very apt to appeal to the sacred principles of liberty, which are all embodied in one maxim: *The fortunate must not be restrained in the exercise of tyranny over the unfortunate.*

Ibid., 'Freedom in Society'

10 The fundamental defect of fathers, in our competitive society, is that they want their children to be a credit to them.

Ibid., 'Freedom versus Authority in Education'

11 Marriage is for women the commonest mode of livelihood, and the total amount of undesired sex

endured by women is probably greater in marriage than in prostitution.

Marriage and Morals, 'Prostitution' (1929)

12 Men who are unhappy, like men who sleep badly, are always proud of the fact.

The Conquest of Happiness, ch. 1 (1930)

13 Boredom is . . . a vital problem for the moralist, since at least half the sins of mankind are caused by the fear of it.

Ibid., ch. 4

14 To be able to fill leisure intelligently is the last product of civilization.

Ibid., ch. 14. At present, Russell added, 'very few people have reached this level.'

15 The fundamental concept in social science is Power, in the same sense in which Energy is the fundamental concept in physics.

Power, ch. 1 (1938)

16 To acquire immunity to eloquence is of the utmost importance to the citizens of a democracy.

Ibid., ch. 18, sect. 4

17 Religions, which condemn the pleasures of sense, drive men to seek the pleasures of power. Throughout history power has been the vice of the ascetic.

New York Herald-Tribune Magazine 6 May 1938

18 The essence of the Liberal outlook lies not in *what* opinions are held, but in *how* they are held: instead of being held dogmatically, they are held tentatively, and with a consciousness that new evidence may at any moment lead to their abandonment.

Unpopular Essays, 'Philosophy and Politics' (1950)

19 Admiration of the proletariat, like that of dams, power stations, and aeroplanes, is part of the ideology of the machine age.

Ibid., 'The Superior Virtue of the Oppressed'

20 Man is a credulous animal, and must believe *something*; in the absence of good grounds for belief, he will be satisfied with bad ones.

Ibid., 'An Outline of Intellectual Rubbish'

21 For my part I distrust *all* generalizations about women, favourable and unfavourable, masculine and feminine, ancient and modern; all alike, I should say, result from paucity of experience.

Ibid., 'An Outline of Intellectual Rubbish'

22 We used to think that Hitler was wicked when he wanted to kill all the Jews, but Kennedy and Macmillan and others both in the East and in the West pursue policies which will probably lead to killing not only all the Jews but all the rest of us too. They are much more wicked than Hitler and this idea of weapons of mass extermination is utterly and absolutely horrible and it is a thing which no man with one spark of humanity can tolerate and I will not pretend to obey a government which is organising the massacre of the whole of mankind. I will do anything I can to oppose such Governments in any non-violent way that seems likely to be fruitful, and I should exhort all of you to feel the same way. We cannot obey these murderers. They are wicked and abominable. They are the wickedest people that ever lived in the history of man and it is our duty to do what we can.

Extempore comment added to speech at a disarmament conference, Birmingham, 15 April 1961, publ. in *The Autobiography of Bertrand Russell*, vol. 3, ch. 3 (1967). The closing words of this speech made headlines in the press in the following days.

23 Three passions, simple but overwhelmingly strong, have governed my life: the longing for love, the search for knowledge, and unbearable pity for the suffering of mankind.

The Autobiography of Bertrand Russell, vol. 1, Prologue: 'What I Have Lived For' (1967). Opening words.

24 I had supposed until that time that it was quite common for parents to love their children, but the war persuaded me that it is a rare exception. I had supposed that most people liked money better than almost anything else, but I discovered that they liked destruction even better. I had supposed that intellectuals frequently loved truth, but I found here again that not ten per cent of them prefer truth to popularity.

Ibid., vol. 2, ch. 1. Referring to the First World War.

Dora Russell

(1894–1986)

British author and activist

Founder of the Workers' Birth Control Group (1924), she helped establish the National Council for Civil Liberties (now Liberty), and with her former husband BERTRAND RUSSELL *was a leading member of CND in the 1950s.*

1 We want better reasons for having children than not knowing how to prevent them.

Hypatia, ch. 4 (1925)

G. W. E. Russell

See Æ

Lord John Russell

(1792–1878)

British politician and prime minister

He entered the House of Commons as a Whig in 1813, supported Catholic emancipation in 1829 and helped to draft the Reform Bill of 1832. He was Prime Minister 1846–52 and 1865–6.

1 If peace cannot be maintained with honour, it is no longer peace.

Speech at Greenock, Scotland, 19 September 1853, quoted in *The Times* 21 September 1853. Of the growing crisis in the Crimea, which erupted into war the following year. See also NEVILLE CHAMBERLAIN 2, BENJAMIN DISRAELI 53.

2 Among the defects of the Bill, which were numerous, one provision was conspicuous by its presence and another by its absence.

Speech in London, April 1859, quoted in *The Times* 9 April 1859

(Sir) William Howard Russell

(1820–1907)

Irish-born British journalist

Associated with The Times *from 1843, he was highly regarded as a war reporter. His despatches from the Crimean War (published 1856) led to criticism of the British Army.*

1 Gathering speed at every stride, they dashed on towards that thin red streak tipped with a line of steel.

The Times 14 November 1854, repr. in *William Russell: Special Correspondent of* The Times (ed. Roger Hudson, 1995). Of the Russian cavalry charging the Highland Brigade at Balaklava, during the Crimean War. In Russell's later account, *The British Expedition to the Crimea* (1858), he wrote that the Russians 'dashed on towards that thin red line tipped with steel' – the more familiar form in which the words are quoted. See RUDYARD KIPLING 15.

(Sir) Ernest Rutherford

(1871–1937)

New Zealand physicist

Baron Rutherford of Nelson. His pioneering research in nuclear physics led him to discover alpha, beta and gamma rays, and to posit a nuclear theory of the atom (1911).

1 All science is either physics or stamp collecting.

Quoted in *Rutherford at Manchester* (1962) by J. B. Birks

Gilbert Ryle

(1900–76)

British philosopher

Known for his work in linguistic philosophy at Oxford, he was author of The Concept of Mind *(1949),* Dilemmas *(1954) and* On Thinking *(1979), among other writings.*

1 A myth is, of course, not a fairy story. It is the presentation of facts belonging to one category in the idioms appropriate to another. To explode a myth is accordingly not to deny the facts but to re-allocate them.

The Concept of Mind, Introduction (1949)

S

Rafael Sabatini
(1875–1950)
British author

He achieved international success with Scaramouche *(1921), set in the French Revolution. His other historical novels include* The Sea Hawk *(1915) and* Captain Blood *(1922).*

1 He was born with a gift of laughter and a sense that the world was mad. And that was all his patrimony.
Scaramouche, bk 1, ch. 1 (1921). These opening words which describe the book's hero, André-Louis Moreau, are inscribed on the gate of the Hall of Graduate Studies, Yale University.

Leopold von Sacher-Masoch
(1836–95)
Austrian novelist

His writings on the pleasures of being subjugated and beaten led the psychiatrist Krafft-Ebing to coin the term 'masochism' for this form of gratification. His most famous work is Venus in Furs *(1870).*

1 I have repeatedly told you that suffering has a peculiar attraction for me. Nothing can intensify my passion more than tyranny, cruelty, and especially the faithlessness of a beautiful woman. And I cannot imagine this woman, this strange ideal derived from an aesthetics of ugliness, this soul of Nero in the body of a Phryne, except in furs.
Venus in Furs (1870). Spoken by Severin.

2 The moral of the tale is this: whoever allows himself to be whipped, deserves to be whipped.
Severin, ibid.

Jonathan Sacks
(b. 1948)
British Chief Rabbi

He has been rabbi of Golders Green (1978–82) and Marble Arch (1983–90) synagogues. His books include The Persistence of Faith *(1991) and* The Politics of Hope *(1997).*

1 Modernity is the transition from fate to choice.
'The Persistence of Faith', 1990 Reith Lecture, publ. in *The Persistence of Faith*, ch. 1 (1991)

2 We no longer talk of virtues but of values, and values are tapes we play on the Walkman of the mind: any tune we choose so long as it does not disturb others.
Ibid., ch. 2, 'The Eclipse of Morality'

Oliver Sacks
(b. 1933)
British neurologist

He has found a wide readership for his accounts of unusual neurological conditions, Awakenings *(1973) and* The Man Who Mistook His Wife for a Hat *(1985).*

1 The Man Who Mistook His Wife for a Hat.
Title of book (1985)

(Lady) Margaret Sackville
(1882–1963)
British poet

She was said to have dictated her first poem aged six, and following her 'discovery' by Wilfred Scawen Blunt went on to publish a total of twenty-one volumes of verse, including The Pageant of War *(1916).*

1 When all is said and done, monotony may after all be the best condition for creation.
The Works of Susan Ferrier, vol. 1, Introduction (1929)

Vita Sackville-West
(1892–1962)
British author, poet and gardener

Victoria Mary Sackville-West. A prolific writer of poetry, fiction, history and biography, she was the wife of HAROLD NICOLSON *and a close friend of* VIRGINIA WOOLF. *She travelled widely before settling at Sissinghurst Castle, whose gardens she made famous.*

1 Women ought to have freedom the same as men when they are young. It is a rotten and ridiculous system at present; it's simply cheating one of one's youth. It was alright for Victorians. But this generation is discarding, and the next one will have discarded, the chrysalis. Women, like men, ought to have their youth so glutted with freedom that they hate the very idea of freedom.
Letter to her husband HAROLD NICOLSON, 1 June 1919, quoted in *Portrait of a Marriage*, pt 4 (1973) by Nigel Nicolson

2 Travel is the most private of pleasures. There is no greater bore than the travel bore. We do not in the least want to hear what he has seen in Hong-Kong.
Passenger to Teheran, ch. 1 (1926)

Sade

See DE SADE

Françoise Sagan

(1935–2004)

French novelist

Originally Françoise Quoirez. She became an overnight phenomenon with her first book, Bonjour Tristesse *(1954), written aged eighteen. In a similar vein,* A Certain Smile *(1956) addressed the emotions and disillusions of adolescence.*

1 Jazz music is an intensified insouciance.
A Certain Smile, pt 1, ch. 7 (1956). Spoken by Dominique.

2 Of course the illusion of art is to make one believe that great literature is very close to life, but exactly the opposite is true. Life is amorphous, literature is formal.
Interview in *Writers at Work* (first series, ed. Malcolm Cowley, 1958)

3 To jealousy, nothing is more frightful than laughter.
La Chamade, ch. 9 (1965). Spoken by Lucile.

Edward Said

(1935–2003)

Palestinian-born US social and literary critic

A critic of US foreign policy, he has written forcefully on Middle Eastern issues in such works as Orientalism *(1978),* Culture and Imperialism *(1993) and* Reflections on Exile and Other Essays *(2000).*

1 Taking the late eighteenth century as a very roughly defined starting point Orientalism can be discussed and analyzed as the corporate institution for dealing with the Orient – dealing with it by making statements about it, authorizing views of it, describing it, by teaching it, settling it, ruling over it: in short, Orientalism as a Western style for dominating, restructuring, and having authority over the Orient.
Orientalism, Introduction (1978)

2 Culture is a sort of theatre where various political and ideological causes engage one another. Far from being a placid realm of Apollonian gentility, culture can even be a battleground on which causes expose themselves to the light of day and contend with one another.
Culture and Imperialism, Introduction (1993)

3 There are far too many politicized people on earth today for any nation readily to accept the finality of America's historical mission to lead the world.
Ibid., ch. 4, sect. 1

4 Truly this has been the age of Ayatollahs, in which a phalanx of guardians (Khomeni, the Pope, Margaret Thatcher) simplify and protect one or another creed, essence, primordial faith. One fundamentalism invidiously attacks the others in the name of sanity, freedom, and goodness.
Ibid., ch. 4, sect. 3

5 Power, after all, is not just military strength. It is the social power that comes from democracy, the cultural power that comes from freedom of expression and research, the personal power that entitles every Arab citizen to feel that he or she is in fact a citizen, and not just a sheep in some great shepherd's flock.
'A Powerless People', publ. in the *Guardian* 25 April 1996. Discussing Arab 'powerlessness'.

Antoine de Saint-Exupéry

(1900–44)

French aviator and author

He recounted his adventurous life as a pilot in Wind, Sand and Stars *(1939), and also wrote the novel* Night Flight *(1931) and the allegory* The Little Prince *(1943). He disappeared while on a wartime reconnaissance mission.*

1 Only the unknown frightens men. But once a man has faced the unknown, that terror becomes the known.
Wind, Sand and Stars, ch. 2, sect. 2 (1939; *Terre des hommes*)

2 The machine does not isolate man from the great problems of nature but plunges him more deeply into them.
Ibid., ch. 3

3 Transport of the mails, transport of the human voice, transport of flickering pictures – in this century as in others our highest accomplishments still have the single aim of bringing men together.
Ibid., ch. 3

4 The aeroplane has unveiled for us the true face of the earth.
Ibid., ch. 5

5 Love does not consist in gazing at each other but in looking together in the same direction.
Ibid., ch. 8

6 Night, the beloved. Night, when words fade and

things come alive. When the destructive analysis of day is done, and all that is truly important becomes whole and sound again. When man reassembles his fragmentary self and grows with the calm of a tree.
Flight to Arras, ch. 1 (1942)

7 If France is to be judged, judge her not by the effects of her defeat but by her readiness to sacrifice herself.
Ibid., ch. 15

8 Grown-ups never understand anything for themselves, and it is tiresome for children to be always and forever explaining things to them.
The Little Prince, ch. 1 (1943)

9 It is only with the heart that one can see rightly; what is essential is invisible to the eye.
Ibid., ch. 21

Yves Saint Laurent
(b. 1936)
French fashion designer

Having worked with CHRISTIAN DIOR *from 1954, he established his own house in 1962, created 'power dressing', and launched the Rive Gauche chain of boutiques in 1966 to retail his ready-to-wear clothes.*

1 Fashions fade, style is eternal.
Andy Warhol's Interview 13 April 1975

2 We must never confuse elegance with snobbery.
Interview in *Ritz* no. 85, 1984

3 A good model can advance fashion by ten years.
Ibid.

Saki
(1870–1916)
British author and journalist

Pseudonym of Hector Hugh Munro. He worked as a journalist from 1896, and had success with his idiosyncratic short stories and novels satirizing the upper echelons of Edwardian society. He was killed on the Western Front, having volunteered for service aged forty-four.

1 Hors d'oeuvres have always a pathetic interest for me; they remind me of one's childhood that one goes through wondering what the next course is going to be like – and during the rest of the menu one wishes one had eaten more of the hors d'oeuvres.
Reginald, 'Reginald at the Carlton' (1904). Spoken by Reginald.

2 Scandal is merely the compassionate allowance which the gay make to the humdrum. Think how many blameless lives are brightened by the blazing indiscretions of other people.
Reginald, ibid., 'Reginald at the Carlton'

3 But, good gracious, you've got to educate him first. You can't expect a boy to be vicious till he's been to a good school.
Reginald in Russia, 'The Baker's Dozen' (1910). Spoken by Major Richard Dumbarton.

4 You needn't tell me that a man who doesn't love oysters and asparagus and good wines has got a soul, or a stomach either. He's simply got the instinct for being unhappy highly developed.
The Chronicles of Clovis, 'The Match-Maker' (1911). Spoken by Clovis.

5 No one has ever said it, but how painfully true it is that the poor have us always with them.
The Unbearable Bassington, ch. 7 (1912). Spoken by Lady Caroline. See BIBLE, NEW TESTAMENT: MATTHEW 153.

6 A buzz of recognition came from the front rows of the pit, together with a craning of necks on the part of those in less favoured seats. It heralded the arrival of Sherard Blaw, the dramatist who had discovered himself, and who had given so ungrudgingly of his discovery to the world.
Ibid., ch. 13. A satire of GEORGE BERNARD SHAW. Lady Caroline, in the audience, comments: 'They say the poor man is haunted by the fear that he will die during a general election, and that his obituary notices will be seriously curtailed by the space taken up by the election results. The curse of our party system, from his point of view, is that it takes up so much room in the press.'

7 He spends his life explaining from his pulpit that the glory of Christianity consists in the fact that though it is not true it has been found necessary to invent it.
Ibid., ch.13. The Archdeacon, speaking of De la Poulett.

8 We all know that Prime Ministers are wedded to the truth, but like other wedded couples they sometimes live apart.
Lady Caroline, ibid., ch. 13

9 Children with Hyacinth's temperament don't know better as they grow older; they merely know more.
The Toys of Peace, 'Hyacinth' (1919). Spoken by Mrs Panstreppon.

10 A little inaccuracy sometimes saves tons of explanation.

The Square Egg, 'Clovis on the Alleged Romance of Business' (1924)

J. D. Salinger
(b. 1919)
US author

Jerome David Salinger. Called 'the greatest mind ever to stay in prep school' by NORMAN MAILER, *he is known for his only novel* The Catcher in the Rye *(1951), which quickly became a classic text of adolescent rebellion. His other publications are short stories.*

1 If you really want to hear about it, the first thing you'll probably want to know is where I was born, and what my lousy childhood was like, and how my parents were occupied and all before they had me, and all that David Copperfield kind of crap, but I don't feel like going into it.

Catcher in the Rye, ch. 1 (1951). Opening lines of book, narrated by Holden Caulfield.

2 What I like best is a book that's at least funny once in a while . . . What really knocks me out is a book that, when you're all done reading it, you wish the author that wrote it was a terrific friend of yours and you could call him up on the phone whenever you felt like it. That doesn't happen much, though.

Ibid., ch. 3

3 I don't know about bores. Maybe you shouldn't feel too sorry if you see some swell girl getting married to them. They don't hurt anybody most of them, and maybe they're all terrific whistlers or something. Who the hell knows? Not me.

Ibid., ch. 17

4 I don't even like *old* cars. I mean they don't even interest me. I'd rather have a goddam horse. A horse is at least *human*, for God's sake.

Ibid., ch. 17

5 I keep picturing all these little kids playing some game in this big field of rye and all . . . If they're running and they don't look where they're going I have to come out from somewhere and *catch* them. That's all I'd do all day. I'd just be the catcher in the rye and all. I know it's crazy, but that's the only thing I'd really like to be.

Ibid., ch. 22

Lord Salisbury
(1830–1903)
English statesman

Robert Cecil, 3rd Marquess of Salisbury. A Conservative MP from 1853, he became Foreign Secretary in 1878 and served three terms as Prime Minister, often combining the post with the office of Foreign Secretary. He was a skilful, sometimes brutal politician, described by DISRAELI *as 'a great master of jibes and sneers'.*

1 English policy is to float lazily downstream, occasionally putting out a diplomatic boathook to avoid collisions.

Letter to Lord Lytton, 9 March 1877, quoted in *Life of Robert, Marquis of Salisbury*, vol. 2, ch. 5 (1921) by Lady Gwendolen Cecil

2 You never should trust experts. If you believe the doctors, nothing is wholesome: if you believe the theologians, nothing is innocent: if you believe the soldiers, nothing is safe. They all require to have their strong wine diluted by a very large admixture of insipid common sense.

Letter to Lord Lytton, 15 June 1877, ibid., vol. 2, ch. 4

3 We are part of the community of Europe and we must do our duty as such.

Speech at Caernarvon, 10 April 1888, quoted in *Salisbury, 1830–1903: Portrait of a Statesman*, ch. 20, sect. 1 (1953) by A. L. Kennedy

4 A journal produced by office-boys for office-boys.

Quoted in *Northcliffe: an Intimate Biography*, ch. 4 (1930) by H. Hamilton Fyfe. Referring to the *Daily Mail*.

5 [A politician is] no higher in the scale of things than a policeman, whose utility would be gone if the workers of mischief disappeared.

Quoted in *Lord Salisbury*, 'Conclusion' (1975) by Robert Taylor

6 The federated action of Europe, if we can maintain it . . . is our sole hope of escaping from the constant terror and calamity of war, the constant pressure of the burdens of an armed peace, which weigh down the spirits and darken the prospect of every nation in this part of the world. The Federation of Europe is the only hope we have.

Speech at Caernarvon, 10 April 1888, quoted in *Salisbury, 1830–1903: Portrait of a Statesman*, ch. 26, sect. 5 (1953) by A. L. Kennedy

Sallust

(*c.* 86–*c.* 34 BC)
Roman historian and politician

Gaius Sallustius Crispus. His principal works, Bellum Catilinae *and* Bellum Jugurthinum, *deal with intrigue, corruption and political rivalry in Rome. He fought with* JULIUS CAESAR *in the civil war and was rewarded with official positions, retiring from public life c.* 45 BC.

1 He preferred to be good rather than to seem good.
Bellum Catilinae, ch. 54 (43–42 BC; *War with Catiline*). Referring to CATO THE ELDER.

2 For their country, their children, their altars, and their hearths.
Ibid., ch. 59

3 A city for sale and doomed to speedy destruction if it finds a purchaser.
Bellum Jugurthinum, ch. 35 (41–40 BC; *War with Jugurtha*). Jugurtha speaking of Rome.

4 *Punica fide.*
[With Punic faith.]
Ibid., ch. 108. Referring to Carthaginian treachery.

Anthony Sampson

(1926–2004)
British journalist and author

He edited Drum *in South Africa 1951–5 and later worked on the* Observer *in Britain. His many publications include* Anatomy of Britain *(1962), his analysis of British society which was updated in subsequent editions.*

1 Once you touch the trappings of monarchy, like opening an Egyptian tomb, the inside is liable to crumble.
Anatomy of Britain Today, ch. 2 (1965)

2 In America journalism is apt to be regarded as an extension of history: in Britain, as an extension of conversation.
Ibid., ch. 9

3 Members rise from CMG (known sometimes in Whitehall as 'Call Me God') to KCMG ('Kindly Call Me God') to GCMG ('God Calls Me God').
Ibid., ch. 18. The joke has appeared in various forms, notably in the TV political comedy *Yes Minister*, written by ANTONY JAY AND JONATHAN LYNN.

George Sand

(1804–76)
French novelist

Pseudonym of Amandine-Aurore-Lucie Dupin, Baronne Dudevant. She left her husband in 1831 to make her living as a writer in Paris. Her work ranged from erotic fiction to tales of rustic life. She was also famous for her male attire and for her liaisons with Chopin and ALFRED DE MUSSET.

1 The trade of authorship is a violent, and indestructible obsession.
Letter, 4 March 1831, publ. in *The Letters of George Sand* (ed./ transl. Veronica Lucas, 1930)

2 Art is not a study of positive reality, it is the seeking for ideal truth.
La Mare au diable, ch. 1 (1846; *The Haunted Pool*, also transl. *The Enchanted Lake*)

3 He who draws noble delights from the sentiments of poetry is a true poet, though he has never written a line in all his life.
Ibid., ch. 2

4 I see upon their noble brows the seal of the Lord, for they were born kings of the earth far more truly than those who possess it only from having bought it.
Ibid., ch. 2. Speaking of peasants.

5 Faith is an excitement and an enthusiasm: it is a condition of intellectual magnificence to which we must cling as to a treasure, and not squander on our way through life in the small coin of empty words, or in exact and priggish argument.
Letter, 25 May 1866, publ. in *Correspondance de George Sand,* vol. 19, no. 12666 (ed. Georges Lubin, 1985)

6 One approaches the journey's end. But the end is a goal, not a catastrophe.
Journal entry, September 1868, publ. in *The Intimate Journal of George Sand* (ed./transl. Marie Jenny Howe, 1929). Closing words of Sand's journal.

Carl Sandburg

(1878–1967)
US poet and author

In the words of Louis Untermeyer: 'The great mid-West, that vast region of steel mills and slaughterhouses, of cornfields and prairies, of crowded cities and empty skies, spoke through Carl Sandburg.' His reputation was established with his first volumes of poetry, Chicago Poems *(1916) and* Cornhuskers *(1918). He also wrote prose works.*

1 Hog Butcher for the World,
Tool Maker, Stacker of Wheat,
Player with Railroads and the Nation's Freight
   Handler;
Stormy, husky, brawling,
City of the Big Shoulders.
'Chicago', publ. in *Chicago Poems* (1916)

2 The fog comes
on little cat feet.
It sits looking
over harbour and city
on silent haunches
and then moves on.
'Fog', ibid.

3 I tell you the past is a bucket of ashes.
'Prairie', publ. in *Cornhuskers* (1918)

4 Pile the bodies high at Austerlitz and Waterloo.
Shovel them under and let me work –
I am the grass; I cover all.
'Grass', ibid.

5 Poetry is the opening and closing of a door, leaving those who look through to guess about what is seen during a moment.
'Poetry Considered', publ. in the *Atlantic Monthly* March 1923

6 The sea speaks a language polite people never
   repeat.
It is a colossal scavenger slang and has no respect.
Is it a terrible thing to be lonely?
'Two Nocturns', publ. in *Good Morning, America* (1928)

7 The girl held still and studied.
'Do you know ... I know something?'
'Yes, what is it you know?'
'Sometime they'll give a war and nobody will
   come.'
The People, Yes, sect. 23 (1936). Referring to a girl watching a military parade. The words were popularized during the anti-war protests of the 1960s and were adapted for the film *Suppose They Gave a War and Nobody Came?* (1970). See ALLEN GINSBERG 9.

8 The greatest cunning is to have none at all.
Ibid., sect. 94

9 In the darkness with a great bundle of grief the people march. In the night, and overhead a shovel of stars for keeps, the people march:
   'Where to? What next?'
Ibid., sect. 107. Closing lines of book.

10 A baby is God's opinion that life should go on.
Remembrance Rock, ch. 2 (1948)

11 Slang is a language that rolls up its sleeves, spits on its hands and goes to work.
New York Times 13 February 1959

George Sanders
(1906–72)
British actor

He played cads, crooks and bounders for more than thirty years in Hollywood, and had slightly more demanding parts in the films Rebecca *(1940) and* All About Eve *(1950). 'I was beastly but never coarse,' he commented. 'A high-class sort of heel.'*

1 Miss Caswell is an actress, a graduate of the Copacabana school of dramatic arts.
All About Eve (film, 1950, written and directed by Joseph L. Mankiewicz). Addison De Witt (George Sanders) introduces his protégée Miss Caswell (MARILYN MONROE) to Margo Channing (BETTE DAVIS). Sanders won an Oscar for his part as the venomous drama critic.

2 Dear World, I am leaving because I am bored. I feel I have lived long enough. I am leaving you with your worries in this sweet cesspool. Good luck.
Suicide note, publ. in *George Sanders: An Exhausted Life*, ch. 20 (1991) by Richard Vanderbeets

Margaret Sanger
(1883–1966)
US leader of birth control movement

Having been imprisoned for setting up a birth-control clinic in 1916, she founded the American Birth Control League in 1921, serving as its President until 1928. Her writings include What Every Mother Should Know *(1917).*

1 A mutual and satisfied sexual act is of great benefit to the average woman, the magnetism of it is health giving. When it is not desired on the part of the woman and she gives no response, it should not take place. The submission of her body without love or desire is degrading to the woman's finer sensibility, all the marriage certificates on earth to the contrary notwithstanding.
Family Limitation, 'Coitus Interruptus' (1914)

2 No woman can call herself free who does not own and control her body. No woman can call herself free until she can choose consciously whether she will or will not be a mother.
Parade 1 December 1963

George Santayana
(1863–1952)
Spanish-American philosopher, poet and novelist

Born Jorge de Santayana. His reputation rests mainly on his work as a materialist sceptic philosopher. His publications include The Sense of Beauty *(1896) and* Realms of Being *(1927–40), as well as poetry and fiction. He resigned his Harvard professorship in 1912 and settled in Europe.*

1 Fanaticism consists in redoubling your effort when you have forgotten your aim.
The Life of Reason, vol. 1 (*Reason in Common Sense*), Introduction (1905)

2 Happiness is the only sanction of life; where happiness fails, existence remains a mad and lamentable experiment.
Ibid., vol. 1, ch. 10

3 Those who cannot remember the past are condemned to repeat it.
Ibid., vol. 1, ch. 12. William L. Shirer made these words the epigraph for his *Rise and Fall of the Third Reich* (1959)

4 It takes patience to appreciate domestic bliss; volatile spirits prefer unhappiness.
Ibid., vol. 2 (*Reason in Society*), ch. 2 (1905)

5 To knock a thing down, especially if it is cocked at an arrogant angle, is a deep delight to the blood.
Ibid., vol. 2, ch. 3

6 When men and women agree, it is only in their conclusions; their reasons are always different.
Ibid., vol. 2, ch. 6

7 A soul is but the last bubble of a long fermentation in the world.
Ibid., vol. 3 (*Reason in Religion*), ch. 10 (1905)

8 Perhaps the only true dignity of man is his capacity to despise himself.
Spinoza's Ethics, Introduction (1910)

9 Oxford, the paradise of dead philosophies.
Egotism in German Philosophy (1916). Santayana lived in Oxford during the First World War.

10 He carries his English weather in his heart wherever he goes, and it becomes a cool spot in the desert, and a steady and sane oracle amongst all the delirium of mankind.
Soliloquies in England, 'The British Character' (1922). On the Englishman.

11 There is no cure for birth and death save to enjoy the interval.
Ibid., 'War Shrines'

12 Scepticism is the chastity of the intellect, and it is shameful to surrender it too soon or to the first comer; there is nobility in preserving it coolly and proudly through a long youth, until at last, in the ripeness of instinct and discretion, it can be safely exchanged for fidelity and happiness.
Scepticism and Animal Faith, ch. 9 (1923)

13 The young man who has not wept is a savage, and the old man who will not laugh is a fool.
Dialogues in Limbo, ch. 3 (1925)

Sappho
(7th–6th century BC)
Greek poet

Beyond her birth on the island of Lesbos, little is known of her life. The few surviving fragments of her love lyrics have had a widespread influence. Of the various metres she used, one, the Sapphic, is named after her.

1 Throned in bright colours, deathless Aphrodite,
Zeus' most subtle daughter, now I pray you,
Do not thus violate my soul with sorrow,
And pain, O Goddess!
'To Venus Aphrodite, Goddess of Love', publ. in *Sappho of Lesbos* (ed./transl. Beram Saklatvala, 1968); no. 1 in *Lyra Graeca* (ed. J. M. Edmonds, 1922)

2 Of air are the words I speak, and yet they are fair and lovely!
Fragment, ibid.; no. 1a in *Lyra Graeca*

3 Ah, in my mind he shares the high gods' fortune,
And is their equal, who may come beside you,
And sit with you, and to your voice so lovely
Attend and listen!
And he may hear your laughter, love-awaking,
Which makes my heart beat swiftly in my bosom.
But when I see you, Brachea, O my voice
Fails me and falters!
'To the Girl Brachea', ibid.; no. 2 in *Lyra Graeca*

4 I desire neither the bees nor yet the honey.
'The Flowers of Love', ibid.; no. 106 in *Lyra Graeca*

5 But now the moon at last has set
With the Pleiades; and midnight
Comes, and swiftly time is going;
Alone upon my bed I lie.
'Waiting for Love', ibid.; no. 111 in *Lyra Graeca*

John Singer Sargent

(1856–1925)

US artist

Brought up in Italy and based for most of his life in London, he specialized in society portraits for which he was in great demand. He also painted impressionistic watercolour landscapes.

1 I *hate* to paint portraits! I hope never to paint another portrait in my life ... Portraiture may be all right for a man in his youth, but after forty I believe that manual dexterity deserts one, and, besides, the colour-sense is less acute. Youth can better stand the exactions of a personal kind that are inseparable from portraiture. I have had enough of it.

Quoted in 'My Recollections of John Sargent', by Walter Tittle, publ. in the *Illustrated London News*, vol. 166, no. 724 (1925), repr. in *John Singer Sargent*, ch. 6 (1970) by Richard Ormond. Sargent frequently inveighed against what he called 'paughtraights' and 'mugs' though these were the basis of his reputation. The remark, 'Every time I paint a portrait I lose a friend' has been attributed to him. He gave up portraiture in 1910.

Jean-Paul Sartre

(1905–80)

French philosopher and author

The leading exponent of existentialism, he co-founded with SIMONE DE BEAUVOIR *the journal* Les Temps modernes *in 1946. As well as his philosophical writings, his works include the novels* Nausea *(1938) and* Roads to Freedom *(1945–9) and the plays* The Flies *(1943) and* No Exit *(1944). See* CHARLES DE GAULLE 13.

1 I am condemned to be free.

Being and Nothingness, pt 4, ch. 1, sect. 1 (1943, transl. 1956)

2 Existence precedes and commands essence.

Ibid., pt 4, ch. 1, sect. 1. Sartre ascribed the notion to HEIDEGGER, although the latter specifically repudiated Sartre's reading of his maxim.

3 Man is a useless passion.

Ibid., pt 4, ch. 2, sect. 2

4 All human actions are equivalent ... and ... all are on principle doomed to failure.

Ibid., 'Conclusion', sect. 2

5 Human life begins on the far side of despair.

Les Mouches, Act 3, Sc. 2 (1943; *The Flies*). Spoken by Orestes.

6 *L'enfer, c'est les autres.*
[Hell is other people.]

Huis clos, Sc. 5 (1944; *No Exit*). Spoken by Garcin.

7 One is still what one is going to cease to be and already what one is going to become. One lives one's death, one dies one's life.

Saint Genet: Actor and Martyr, bk 2, 'The Melodious Child Dead in Me ...' (1952, transl. 1963)

8 The French bourgeois doesn't dislike shit, provided it is served up to him at the right time.

Ibid., bk 2, 'To Succeed in Being All, Strive to be Nothing in Anything'

9 Fascism is not defined by the number of its victims, but by the way it kills them.

Libération 22 June 1953. Referring to the execution of Julius and Ethel Rosenberg.

10 Communism I like, but Communist intellectuals are savages.

Quoted in the *Observer* 25 March 1956

11 I hate victims who respect their executioners.

The Condemned of Altona, Act 1, Sc. 1 (1960). Spoken by Leni.

12 She [my grandmother] believed in nothing; only her scepticism kept her from being an atheist.

Les Mots, 'Lire' (1964; *Words*)

13 I confused things with their names: that is belief.

Ibid., 'Écrire'

14 One does not *adopt* an idea, one slips into it.

Notebooks for an Ethics, Notebook 1 (1983)

Siegfried Sassoon

(1886–1967)

British poet and author

Remembered chiefly for his powerful anti-war poems published in Counter-Attack *(1918) and other collections, he also wrote a semi-fictionalized autobiography,* The Complete Memoirs of George Sherston *(3 vols. 1928–36).*

1 Soldiers are citizens of death's grey land,
Drawing no dividend from time's tomorrows.

'Dreamers', publ. in *Counter-Attack and Other Poems* (1918)

2 Soldiers are sworn to action; they must win
Some flaming, fatal climax with their lives.
Soldiers are dreamers; when the guns begin
They think of firelit homes, clean beds and wives.

'Dreamers', ibid.

3 'Good-morning; good morning!' the General said
When we met him last week on our way to the
   line.
Now the soldiers he smiled at are most of 'em
   dead,
And we're cursing his staff for incompetent swine.
'He's a cheery old card,' grunted Harry to Jack
As they slogged up to Arras with rifle and pack.
But he did for them both by his plan of attack.
'The General', ibid. The lines recall the Irish anti-recruiting
song 'Arthur McBride'.

4 But the past is just the same, – and War's a
   bloody game . . .
Have you forgotten yet? . . .
Look down, and swear by the slain of the War that
   you'll never forget.
'Aftermath', publ. in *The War Poems of Siegfried Sassoon* (1919)

5 Everyone suddenly burst out singing;
And I was filled with such delight
As prisoned birds must find in freedom.
'Everyone Sang', ibid.

6 The song was wordless; the singing will never be
   done.
'Everyone Sang', ibid.

7 In me the tiger sniffs the rose.
The Heart's Journey, no. 7 (1928)

8 Who will remember, passing through this Gate,
The unheroic Dead who fed the guns?
Who shall absolve the foulness of their fate, –
Those doomed, conscripted, unvictorious ones?
'On Passing the New Menin Gate', ibid., no. 21

9 Here was the world's worst wound. And here
   with pride
'Their name liveth for ever' the Gateway claims.
Was ever an immolation so belied
As these intolerably nameless names?
'On Passing the New Menin Gate', ibid., no. 21

Bernard-Joseph Saurin
(1706–81)
French playwright

A friend of MONTESQUIEU, VOLTAIRE *and other luminaries
of the day, he was first published late in life and went on to
write some of the classic works of the Comédie Française. He
also practised as a lawyer.*

1 Valour is common but great souls are rare.
Spartacus, Act 3, Sc. 1 (1760). Spoken by Spartacus.

2 The law often allows what honour forbids.
Blanche et Guiscard, Act 5, Sc. 6 (1763). Spoken by Blanche.

3 Nothing is sacred to a gamester.
Béverlei, Act 1, Sc. 1 (1768). Spoken by Henriette.

Saussure
See DE SAUSSURE

George Savile, Lord Halifax
(1633–95)
English statesman and essayist

*He entered politics in 1660 and rose to become a member of
the Privy Council. A contentious figure, he was dismissed by
James II in 1685. His political tracts and essays include* The
Character of a Trimmer *(1688), an argument in favour of the
middle path, for which he became known as 'The Trimmer'.*

1 To the question, What shall we do to be saved in
this world? there is no answer but this, Look to your
moat.
A Rough Draft of a New Model at Sea (1694), repr. in *Complete
Works* (ed. WALTER RALEIGH, 1912)

2 The best party is but a kind of conspiracy against
the rest of the nation.
Political, Moral and Miscellaneous Thoughts and Reflections,
'Of Parties' (1750)

3 When the people contend for their liberty they
seldom get anything by their victory but new
masters.
Ibid., 'Of Prerogative, Power and Liberty'

4 Men are not hanged for stealing horses, but that
horses may not be stolen.
Ibid., 'Of Punishment'

5 Most men's anger against religion is as if two men
should quarrel for a lady they neither of them care
for.
Complete Works, 'Religion' (ed. WALTER RALEIGH, 1912)

6 Popularity is a crime from the moment it is
sought; it is only a virtue where men have it
whether they will or no.
Ibid., 'Of Ambition'

7 The vanity of teaching often tempteth a man to
forget he is a blockhead.
Ibid., 'Of Vanity'

8 They who are of opinion that money will do
everything, may very well be suspected to do everything for money.
Ibid., 'Of Money'

9 An old man concludeth from his knowing mankind, that they know him too, and that maketh him very wary.
Ibid., 'Miscellaneous Thoughts and Reflections'

10 He that leaveth nothing to chance will do few things ill, but he will do very few things.
Ibid., 'Miscellaneous Thoughts and Reflections'

11 Education is what remains when we have forgotten all that we have been taught.
Attributed

Dorothy L. Sayers
(1893–1957)
British author and translator

Dorothy Leigh Sayers. She is best known for her popular detective novels featuring the elegant and erudite Lord Peter Wimsey. The Man Born to Be King *(1941–2) was a controversial sequence of radio plays about the life of Christ.*

1 Lawyers enjoy a little mystery, you know. Why, if everybody came forward and told the truth, the whole truth, and nothing but the truth straight out, we should all retire to the workhouse.
Clouds of Witness, ch. 3 (1926). Spoken by Sir Impey Biggs. for the book's title, see BIBLE, NEW TESTAMENT: HEBREWS 7.

2 She always says, my lord, that facts are like cows. If you look them in the face hard enough they generally run away.
Bunter, ibid., ch. 4

3 Death seems to provide the minds of the Anglo-Saxon race with a greater fund of amusement than any other single subject.
The Third Omnibus of Crime, Introduction (1935)

Alexei Sayle
(b. 1952)
British comedian, actor and author

He performed in the Comedy Store in the late 1970s and gained a television audience in The Young Ones *(1982) and* Alexei Sayle's Stuff *(1988). He also writes fiction.*

1 'Ullo John Got a New Motor?
Title of song (1984)

Simon Schama
(b. 1945)
British historian

His evocative descriptions and racy narrative style, both on the page and in his television programmes, have drawn a wide audience. His acclaimed books include Citizens: A Chronicle of the French Revolution *(1989).*

1 Historians are left forever chasing shadows, painfully aware of their inability ever to reconstruct a dead world in its completeness however thorough or revealing their documentation . . . We are doomed to be forever hailing someone who has just gone around the corner and out of earshot.
Dead Certainties, 'Afterword' (1991)

2 Landscapes are culture before they are nature; constructs of the imagination projected onto wood and water and rock.
Landscape and Memory, ch. 1, sect. 3 (1995)

3 So instead of listening to cowboy pieties . . . we turn to those who . . . understand, especially when they hear the word 'revenge' thundered out by talk-show warriors, that the best, the only revenge, when you're fighting a cult that fetishises death, is life.
Guardian 14 September 2001. Referring to the responses to '9/11'.

Felix E. Schelling
(1858–1935)
US academic

A specialist in English Renaissance literature, he published, among other works, English Literature During the Lifetime of Shakespeare *(1910) and* A History of English Drama *(1914).*

1 True education makes for inequality; the inequality of individuality, the inequality of success, the glorious inequality of talent, of genius; for inequality, not mediocrity, individual superiority, not standardization, is the measure of the progress of the world.
Pedagogically Speaking, ch. 8 (1929)

Friedrich von Schelling
(1775–1854)
German philosopher

Influenced by the works of Fichte and KANT, *he was a leading figure in the development of Idealist philosophy. His* System of Transcendental Idealism *(1800) argued for the key role of art in generating self-awareness.*

1 Architecture in general is frozen music.
Philosophie der Kunst (1809; The Philosophy of Art), repr. in Werke, vol. 3 (1916)

Elsa Schiaparelli

(1890–1973)

Italian-born French fashion designer

She opened her Paris salon in 1928 and quickly became famed for her striking use of bright colours, shoulder pads and flamboyant hats.

1 Fashion is born by small facts, trends, or even politics, never by trying to make little pleats and furbelows, by trinkets, by clothes easy to copy, or by the shortening or lengthening of a skirt.
Shocking Life, ch. 9 (1954)

Friedrich Schiller

(1759–1805)

German dramatist, poet and historian

Following the success of The Robbers *(1781), his first play, and* Don Carlos *(1787), he settled in Weimar where he became close to* GOETHE. *Later successes included* Wallenstein *(1798–9) and* Mary Stuart *(1800). As a poet, he wrote ballads, reflective pieces and long didactic poems, for example* The Artists *(1789). He also translated* RACINE *and* SHAKESPEARE *and wrote important historical works and treatises on aesthetics.*

1 External forms are but the trappings of the man. My heaven and my hell is within.
The Robbers, Act 4, Sc. 5 (1781). Spoken by Brutus.

2 Art is the right hand of nature. The latter only gave us being, but the former made us men.
Fiesco, Act 2, Sc. 17 (1783). Spoken by Fiesco.

3 *Alles zu retten, muss alles gewagt werden.*
[To save all we must risk all.]
Fiesco, ibid., Act 4, Sc. 6

4 *Freude, schöner Götterfunken,*
Tochter aus Elysium,
Wir betreten feuertrunken,
Himmlische, dein Heiligtum.
Deine Zauber binden wieder,
Was der Mode Schwert geteilt
Bettler werden Fuerstenbrueder
Wo dein sanfter Fluegel weilt.
[Joy, thou shining spark of God,
Daughter of Elysium,
With fiery rapture, goddess,
We approach thy shrine.
Your magic reunites
What custom's sword has parted;
Beggars become princes' brothers
Under your protective wing.]
'An die Freude', ll. 1–8 ('Ode to Joy', 1785). The lines were given

musical settings by Schubert (1815), BEETHOVEN (in the final movement of his Ninth Symphony, 1824) and Tchaikovsky (1865). In Beethoven's version, which was adopted as the European anthem in 1972, ll. 5–7 were altered to: *'Deine Zauber binden wieder,/Was die Mode streng geteilt,/Alle Menschen werden Brüder.'* ['Your magic reunites/That which stern custom has parted;/All humans will become brothers.']

5 *Die Weltgeschichte ist das Weltgericht.*
[The history of the world is the world's court of justice.]
'Resignation', st. 17, publ. in *Thalia* (1786). See GEORG HEGEL 9.

6 Eternity gives nothing back of what one leaves out of the minutes.
Ibid., st. 18. Last lines of poem.

7 I am called
The richest monarch in the Christian world;
The sun in my dominions never sets.
Don Carlos, Act 1, Sc. 6 (1787). Spoken by Philip II.

8 Utility is the great idol of the age, to which all powers must do service and all talents swear allegiance.
On the Aesthetic Education of Man, 'Second Letter' (1795)

9 They would need to be already wise, in order to love wisdom.
Ibid., 'Eighth Letter'

10 No doubt the artist is the child of his time; but woe to him if he is also its disciple, or even its favourite.
Ibid., 'Ninth Letter'

11 Man only plays when in the full meaning of the word he is a man, and *he is only completely a man when he plays.*
Ibid., 'Fifteenth Letter'

12 Hunger and love are what moves the world.
'Die Weltweisen', st. 6 (1795; 'The Philosophers'), repr. in *Werke*, vol. 1 (1992)

13 Posterity weaves no garlands for imitators.
Wallenstein's Camp, Prologue (1798)

14 The hat is the pride of man; for he who cannot keep his hat on before kings and emperors is no free man.
The Piccolomini, Act 4, Sc. 5 (1799, transl. S. T. COLERIDGE). Spoken by Kellermeister (the Master of the Cellar).

15 Time consecrates;
And what is grey with age becomes religion.
The Death of Wallenstein, Act 1, Sc. 4 (1799, transl. S. T. COLERIDGE). Spoken by Wallenstein.

16 Against stupidity the very gods
Themselves contend in vain.
The Maid of Orleans, Act 3, Sc. 6 (1801). Spoken by Talbot.
NIETZSCHE wrote, in *The Anti-Christ*, aph. 48 (1895): 'Against
boredom the gods themselves fight in vain.'

17 *Der Starke ist am mächtigsten allein.*
[The strong man is strongest when alone.]
Wilhelm Tell, Act 1, Sc. 3 (1804). Spoken by Tell.

18 No cause has he to say his doom is harsh,
Who's made the master of his destiny.
Gessler, ibid., Act 3, Sc. 3

19 *Das Universum ist ein Gedanke Gottes.*
[The universe is one of God's thoughts.]
Philosophische Briefe, Letter 4 ('Theosophy of Julius') (1786;
Philosophical Letters)

Friedrich von Schlegel
(1772–1829)
German philosopher, author and critic

*While at the University of Jena, he published, with his brother,
the* Athenaeum *(1798–1800), which became the principal
organ of the German Romantics. His lectures and writings on
history, literature and linguistics were highly acclaimed.*

1 We should demand genius from everybody, without, however, expecting it.
Athenaeum 1797, quoted in *Dialogue on Poetry and Literary
Aphorisms*, 'Selected Aphorisms from *The Athenaeum*', aph.
16 (1968)

2 Good drama must be drastic.
Athenaeum 1798, ibid., aph. 42

3 Every uneducated person is a caricature of
himself.
Athenaeum 1798, ibid., aph. 63. Elsewhere, Schlegel wrote:
'Innocence is the only thing which can ennoble lack of education.' (Ibid., aph. 31)

Arthur M. Schlesinger Jr
(b. 1917)
US historian

Arthur Meier Schlesinger. He was adviser to presidents KEN-
NEDY *and* JOHNSON, *but quit in opposition to the Vietnam
War. His works include* The Age of Jackson *(1945) and* A Thou-
sand Days: John F. Kennedy in the White House *(1965).*

1 Science and Technology revolutionize our lives,
but memory, tradition and myth frame our
response. Expelled from individual consciousness
by the rush of change, history finds its revenge by
stamping the collective unconscious with habits,

values, expectations, dreams. The dialectic between
past and future will continue to form our lives.
'The Challenge of Change', publ. in the *New York Times Magazine* 27 July 1986

2 Only a cad tells the truth about his love affairs.
Sunday Times Review 27 September 1998. Referring to BILL
CLINTON's affair with MONICA LEWINSKY.

Artur Schnabel
(1882–1951)
German-born US pianist

*Making his concert début at the age of eight, he became an
international celebrity, specializing in Beethoven, Mozart and
Schubert. He also composed extensively for the piano. Fleeing
the Nazis, he settled in the USA in 1939.*

1 Applause is a receipt, not a bill.
Quoted in *The Musical Life*, 'Ovation and Triumph' (1958) by
Irving Kolodin. Explaining why he did not render applause
the tribute of encores.

2 The notes I handle no better than many pianists.
But the pauses between the notes – ah, that is where
the art resides.
Quoted in the *Chicago Daily News* 11 June 1958

Arthur Schopenhauer
(1788–1860)
German philosopher

His most important work, The World as Will and Idea *(1819),
expounds his notion of the primacy of the will and the conflicts
associated with it. Opposed to the Idealist philosophers then
in favour, he lived his last years as a recluse, though his ideas
came to influence later writers, philosophers and composers.*

1 The fundament upon which all our knowledge
and learning rests is the inexplicable.
Parerga and Paralipomena, vol. 2, ch. 1, sect. 1 (1851)

2 All the cruelty and torment of which the world is
full is in fact merely the necessary result of the
totality of the forms under which the will to live is
objectified.
Ibid., vol. 2, ch. 14, sect. 164

3 *Hatred* is an affair of the heart; *contempt* that of
the head.
Ibid., vol. 2, ch. 24, sect. 324

4 Every parting gives a foretaste of death, every
reunion a hint of the resurrection.
Ibid., vol. 2, ch. 26, sect. 310

Olive Schreiner
(1855–1920)
South African author

Self-educated, she worked as a governess while writing The Story of an African Farm *(1883), a semi-autobiographical tale of a girl growing up in the veld. The novel, published pseudonymously as Ralph Iron, brought her immediate success. She later expressed her support for women's rights in* Woman and Labour *(1911).*

1 The troubles of the young are soon over; they leave no external mark. If you wound the tree in its youth the bark will quickly cover the gash; but when the tree is very old, peeling the bark off, and looking carefully, you will see the scar there still.
The Story of an African Farm, pt 1, ch. 13 (1883)

2 Everything has two sides – the outside that is ridiculous, and the inside that is solemn.
Lyndall, ibid., pt 2, ch. 4

3 There was never a great man who had not a great mother.
Lyndall, ibid., pt 2, ch. 4

4 If Nature here wishes to make a mountain, she runs a range for five hundred miles; if a plain, she levels eighty; if a rock, she tilts five thousand feet of strata on end; our skies are higher and more intensely blue; our waves larger than others; our rivers fiercer. There is nothing measured, small nor petty in South Africa.
Thoughts on South Africa, ch. 1 (1892)

Charles Schulz
(1922–2000)
US cartoonist

A freelancer for the Saturday Evening Post, *he created the characters Charlie Brown, Snoopy and others for his* Li'l Folks *cartoon strip. The strip was bought by United Features in 1950 and, renamed* Peanuts, *gained an international readership.*

1 Big sisters are the crab grass in the lawn of life.
Peanuts (strip cartoon, 1952). Spoken by Linus.

E. F. Schumacher
(1911–77)
German-born British economist

Ernst Friedrich Schumacher. A consultant on the 1942 Beveridge Report, he advised government on energy policy in the 1950s. He founded the Intermediate Technology Development Group in 1966, and set out his theories in the best-selling Small is Beautiful *(1973).*

1 Small is Beautiful. A Study of Economics as if People Mattered.
Title of book (1973)

2 Call a thing immoral or ugly, soul-destroying or a degradation of man, a peril to the peace of the world or to the well-being of future generations; as long as you have not shown it to be 'uneconomic' you have not really questioned its right to exist, grow, and prosper.
Ibid., pt 1, ch. 3

3 I have no doubt that it is possible to give a new direction to technological development, a direction that shall lead it back to the real needs of man, and that also means: *to the actual size of man*. Man is small, and, therefore, small is beautiful. To go for giantism is to go for self-destruction.
Ibid., pt 2, ch. 10

Joseph Schumpeter
(1883–1950)
Moravian-born US economist

He attributed economic growth to the activity of a few creative entrepreneurs in The Theory of Economic Development *(1912). Other works include* Business Cycles *(1939) and the influential* Capitalism, Socialism and Democracy *(1942).*

1 For the duration of its collective life, or the time during which its identity may be assumed, each class resembles a hotel or an omnibus, always full, but always of different people.
Social Classes, ch. 3, no. 7 (1927)

2 Marxism is essentially a product of the bourgeois mind.
Capitalism, Socialism and Democracy, ch. 1 (1942)

3 Economic progress, in capitalist society, means turmoil.
Ibid., ch. 3

4 The evolution of the capitalist style of life could be easily – and perhaps most tellingly – described in terms of the genesis of the modern Lounge Suit.
Ibid., ch. 11

5 Capitalism inevitably and by virtue of the very logic of its civilization creates, educates and subsidizes a vested interest in social unrest.
Ibid., ch. 13, sect. 2

6 Bureaucracy is not an obstacle to democracy but an inevitable complement to it.
Ibid., ch. 18

7 Democracy is a political *method*, that is to say, a certain type of institutional arrangement for arriving at political – legislative and administrative – decisions and hence incapable of being an end in itself.
Ibid., ch. 20, sect. 3

Carl Schurz
(1829–1906)
German-born politician and journalist

Fleeing Europe for America in 1852, he was Republican Senator for Missouri (1868–75) and Secretary of the Interior (1877–81). In politics and as a journalist he campaigned against corruption, enjoying a reputation for courage and integrity.

1 My country, right or wrong; if right, to be kept right; and if wrong, to be set right.
Speech to the US Senate, 29 February 1872, quoted in *Carl Schurz: a Biography*, ch. 11 (1982) by Hans L. Trefousse. In reply to a senator who had expressed the sentiment 'My country, right or wrong'. Schurz returned to this theme in a speech before the Anti-Imperialistic Conference, Chicago, 17 October 1899, when he again denounced 'that deceptive cry of mock patriotism: "Our country, right or wrong!"' See also STEPHEN DECATUR 1, G. K. CHESTERTON 2.

Delmore Schwartz
(1913–66)
US poet, short story writer and critic

Noted for his portrayals of alienation and the search for identity, he combined verse and prose in such collections as In Dreams Begin Responsibilities (1938). He was an editor with the Partisan Review *1942–55. See also* W. B. YEATS 24.

1 Time is the school in which we learn,
Time is the fire in which we burn.
'For Rhoda', publ. in *In Dreams Begin Responsibilities* (1938)

2 That inescapable animal walks with me.
Has followed me since the black womb held,
Moves where I move, distorting my gesture,
A caricature, a swollen shadow.
'The Heavy Bear Who Goes With Me', st. 3, publ. in *In Dreams Begin Responsibilities* (1938)

3 Even a paranoid can have enemies.
Attributed. The remark has also been credited to WOODY ALLEN and HENRY KISSINGER, among others.

Arnold Schwarzenegger
(b. 1947)
Austrian-born US screen actor and politician

As 'the Austrian Oak', he was five times Mr Universe, and seven times Mr Olympia. He established his acting career with the films Conan the Barbarian *(1982) and* The Terminator *(1984). He was elected Governor of California in 2003.*

1 I'll be back.
The Terminator (film, 1984, written and directed by James Cameron). Spoken by The Terminator (Arnold Schwarzenegger). The words 'I'll be back' were uttered in six other films starring Schwarzenegger.

2 Hasta la vista, baby.
Terminator 2: Judgment Day (film, 1991, written, directed and produced by James Cameron). Spoken by The Terminator (Arnold Schwarzenegger).

Albert Schweitzer
(1875–1965)
German theologian, missionary and musician

In 1913, in a spirit 'not of benevolence but of atonement', he founded the leprosy hospital at Lamberéné in French-occupied Equatorial Africa, where he spent the rest of his life. His books include a study of J. S. Bach and studies of theology and philosophy.

1 Pessimism is depreciated will-to-live.
The Philosophy of Civilization, vol. 2 ('Civilization and Ethics'), ch. 2 (1923)

2 True ethics begin where the use of language ceases.
Ibid., vol. 2, ch. 21

3 The African is my brother – but he is my younger brother by several centuries.
Quoted in the *Observer* 23 October 1955

Scipio Africanus
(c. 236–c. 183 BC)
Roman general and politician

Publius Cornelius Scipio Africanus. Called 'Major' or 'the Elder' to distinguish him from his namesake (c. 185–129 BC), he won fame for his victory over the Carthaginians in the Second Punic War (202 BC).

1 Never less idle than when wholly idle, nor less alone than when wholly alone.
Quoted in *De Officiis*, bk 3, sect. 1 (45 BC; *On Duties*) by CICERO

Martin Scorsese
(b. 1942)
US film-maker

Described by critic David Thomson as a 'devotee of intelligence, visual beauty, and verbal style', he returns frequently in his work to the themes of masculinity and alienation. His films include Mean Streets *(1973),* Raging Bull *(1980) and* Goodfellas *(1990).*

1 You don't make up for your sins in church. You do it on the streets. You do it at home. The rest is bullshit and you know it.

Mean Streets *(film, 1973, screenplay by Martin Scorsese and Mardik Martin, directed by Martin Scorsese). Voiceover.*

C. P. Scott
(1846–1932)
British author and journalist

Charles Prestwich Scott. He became Editor of the Manchester Guardian *aged twenty-five, a position he held for fifty-nine years, the longest editorship of a national newspaper anywhere. He was a Liberal MP 1895–1906.*

1 A newspaper is of necessity something of a monopoly, and its first duty is to shun the temptations of monopoly. Its primary office is the gathering of news. At the peril of its soul it must see that the supply is not tainted. Neither in what it gives, nor in what it does not give, nor in the mode of presentation, must the unclouded face of truth suffer wrong. Comment is free, but facts are sacred.

Manchester Guardian *5 May 1921. Editorial marking the paper's first hundred years.* TOM STOPPARD *in* Night and Day *(1978) adapted the aphorism: 'Comment is free, but facts are on expenses.'*

Paul Scott
(1920–78)
British author

He wrote chiefly about India and Malaya, and is best known for The Raj Quartet *(1966–75), a chronicle of life among the British and Anglo-Indians in the last years of the Raj.*

1 Ah, well, the truth is always one thing, but in a way it's the other thing, the gossip, that counts. It shows where people's hearts lie.

The Day of the Scorpion, *bk 1, pt 3, ch. 3 (second volume of* The Raj Quartet, *1968). Spoken by Count Bronowsky.*

Robert Falcon Scott
(1868–1912)
British naval officer and explorer

He discovered Edward VII Peninsula and surveyed the coast of Victoria Land on his first Antarctic expedition (1901–4). On his second (1910–12), he was beaten to the South Pole by Roald Amundsen and died with all his party on the journey back to his ship.

1 It seems a pity, but I do not think I can write more . . . For God's sake look after our people.

Last journal entry, 29 March 1912, publ. in Scott's Last Expedition, *vol. 1, ch. 20 (ed. Leonard Huxley, 1913)*

2 Make the boy interested in natural history if you can; it is better than games.

Last letter to his wife, ibid., vol. 1, ch. 20. Scott's son, Peter Scott, became an eminent wildlife artist and ornithologist, and the founder of the Wildfowl Trust at Slimbridge.

3 What lots and lots I could tell you of this journey. How much better has it been than lounging in too great comfort at home. What tales you would have for the boy. But what a price to pay.

Last letter to his wife, ibid., vol. 1, ch. 20

4 Had we lived I should have had a tale to tell of the hardihood, endurance and courage of my companions which would have stirred the heart of every Englishman. These rough notes and our dead bodies must tell the tale.

'Message to the Public', written in his journal shortly before his death, ibid, vol. 1, ch. 20

(Sir) Walter Scott
(1771–1832)
Scottish novelist and poet

Inspired by Scottish history and legend, the 'Wizard of the North' enjoyed great popularity and the respect of his literary contemporaries. He turned from writing long narrative poems, for example Marmion *(1808), to romantic novels such as* The Bride of Lammermoor *(1818) and* Ivanhoe *(1819). His prodigious output also included translation, biography, literary criticism and journalism. See* WILLIAM HAZLITT 6, 23.

1 If thou would'st view fair Melrose aright,
Go visit it by the pale moonlight;
For the gay beams of lightsome day
Gild, but to flout, the ruins grey.

The Lay of the Last Minstrel, *canto 2, st. 1 (1805)*

2 For ne'er
Was flattery lost on poet's ear:

A simple race! they waste their toil
For the vain tribute of a smile.
Ibid., canto 4, Conclusion

3 It is the secret sympathy,
The silver link, the silken tie,
Which heart to heart, and mind to mind,
In body and in soul can bind.
Ibid., canto 5, st. 13

4 Breathes there the man, with soul so dead,
Who never to himself hath said,
This is my own, my native land!
Whose heart hath ne'er within him burned,
As home his footsteps he hath turned
From wandering on a foreign strand!
Ibid., canto 6, st. 1

5 O Caledonia! stern and wild,
Meet nurse for a poetic child!
Land of brown heath and shaggy wood,
Land of the mountain and the flood,
Land of my sires! what mortal hand
Can e'er untie the filial band
That knits me to thy rugged strand!
Ibid., canto 6, st. 2

6 And come he slow, or come he fast,
It is but Death who comes at last.
Marmion, canto 2, st. 30 (1808)

7 O, young Lochinvar is come out of the west,
Through all the wide Border his steed was the best.
Ibid., canto 5, st. 12 ('Lochinvar', st. 1)

8 So faithful in love, and so dauntless in war,
There never was knight like the young Lochinvar.
Ibid., canto 5, st. 12 ('Lochinvar', st. 1)

9 Heap on more wood! the wind is chill;
But let it whistle as it will,
We'll keep our Christmas merry still.
Each age has deemed the new-born year
The fittest time for festal cheer.
Ibid., canto 6, Introduction, st. 1

10 'Twas Christmas broached the mightiest ale;
'Twas Christmas told the merriest tale;
A Christmas gambol oft could cheer
The poor man's heart through half the year.
Ibid., canto 6, Introduction, st. 3

11 O, what a tangled web we weave,
When first we practise to deceive!
Ibid., canto 6, st. 17. The lines have spawned various responses, including: 'But when we've practised quite a while/How

vastly we improve our style' (J. R. Pope, in 'A Word of Encouragement'), and 'And when the practice is perfected/We're just the boys to get elected' (A. R. D. Fairburn, in 'Political Jotting').

12 O Woman! in our hours of ease,
Uncertain, coy, and hard to please,
And variable as the shade
By the light quivering aspen made;
When pain and anguish wring the brow,
A ministering angel thou!
Ibid., canto 6, st. 30

13 Tradition, legend, tune, and song,
Shall many an age that wail prolong:
Still from the sire the son shall hear
Of the stern strife, and carnage drear,
Of Flodden's fatal field,
Where shivered was fair Scotland's spear,
And broken was her shield!
Ibid., canto 6, st. 34

14 Hail to the Chief who in triumph advances!
The Lady of the Lake, canto 2, st. 19 ('The Boat Song', st. 1) (1810)

15 Like the dew on the mountain,
Like the foam on the river,
Like the bubble on the fountain,
Thou art gone, and forever!
Ibid., canto 3, st. 16 ('Coronach', st. 3)

16 Rhyme, which is a handcuff to an inferior poet, he who is master of his art wears as a bracelet.
The Works of Jonathan Swift, DD, vol. 1, 'Memoir: Conclusion' (1814)

17 A lawyer without history or literature is a mechanic, a mere working mason; if he possesses some knowledge of these, he may venture to call himself an architect.
Guy Mannering, ch. 37 (1815). Spoken by Pleydell.

18 Look not thou on beauty's charming,
Sit thou still when kings are arming,
Taste not when the wine-cup glistens,
Speak not when the people listens,
Stop thine ear against the singer,
From the red gold keep thy finger,
Vacant heart, and hand, and eye,
Easy live and quiet die.
The Bride of Lammermoor, ch. 3 (1819). Lucy Ashton's song.

19 We must rouse the lion from his lair.
The Talisman, ch. 6 (1825). Quoted in chapter heading from an 'old play'.

20 If you keep a thing seven years you are sure to find a use for it at last.

Woodstock, ch. 28 (1826). Spoken by Charles II, quoting a saying by 'my canny subjects of Scotland'.

21 There is a vulgar incredulity, which, in historical matters as well as in those of religion, finds it easier to doubt than to examine.

The Fair Maid of Perth, Introduction (1828). Spoken by Mrs Baliol.

22 Your connection with any newspaper would be a disgrace and a degradation. I would rather sell gin to poor people and poison them that way.

Letter to J. G. Lockhart, 1829, publ. in *Letters of Sir Walter Scott*, vol. 11 (ed. H. J. C. Grierson, 1936). Expressing approval of his friend's refusal to involve himself in partisan journalism on behalf of a group of aristocratic Tories.

23 So let each cavalier who loves honour and me,
Come follow the bonnet of Bonny Dundee.
Come fill up my cup, come fill up my can,
Come saddle your horses, and call up your men;
Come open the West Port, and let me gang free,
And it's room for the bonnets of Bonny Dundee!

'Bonny Dundee' (song), in *The Doom of Devorgoil*, Act 2, Sc. 2 (1830). A version of the song appeared earlier in Scott's *Rob Roy* (1817).

(Sir) William Scott

See Lord Stowell

Gil Scott-Heron

(b. 1949)
US musician and author

A novelist and poet, he set his work to music and composed political songs, as on the album Free Will *(1972). He later turned to rap.*

1 The revolution will not be televised, will not be
   televised,
Will not be televised, will not be televised,
The revolution will be no rerun, brother,
The revolution will be live.

'The Revolution Will Not Be Televised' (song, written with Brian Jackson) on the album *Pieces of a Man* (1971)

2 What's the word?
Tell me brother, have you heard
from Johannesburg?

'Johannesburg' (song) on the album *From South Africa to South California* (1976)

George Seaton

(1911–79)
US screenwriter and director

Pseudonym of George Stenius. The original voice of the Lone Ranger on radio (1933), he contributed to the screenplays of Marx Brothers films. His biggest successes were The Song of Bernadette *(1943),* Miracle On 34th Street *(1947) and* The Country Girl *(1954), which he also directed.*

1 To those who believe in God, no explanation is necessary. To those who do not believe in God, no explanation is possible.

The Song of Bernadette, Prologue (film, 1943, screenplay by George Seaton based on novel by Franz Werfel, directed by Henry King). The words are credited in the film to a 15th-century monk.

Seattle

(c. 1787–1866)
Native American leader

Also known as Seathl. As chief of the Suquamish and allied Indian tribes, he was converted to Roman Catholicism by French settlers. In 1855, he avoided war by signing the Port Elliot Treaty, according to which his people agreed to live on reservations. The town of Seattle was named after him.

1 It matters little where we pass the remnant of our days. They are not many. The Indian's night promises to be dark.

Speech, 12 January 1855, publ. in *The Penguin Book of Historic Speeches* (ed. Brian MacArthur, 1995). The speech, addressed to Isaac I. Stevens, Governor of Washington Territory and Superintendent of Indian Affairs, announced Seattle's agreement to abide by the Port Elliot Treaty. The authenticity of the speech, which was first recorded in the *Seattle Sunday Star* 29 October 1887, has been questioned.

2 Men come and go like the waves of the sea ... It is the order of Nature. Even the white man, whose God walked and talked with him as friend to friend, is not exempt from the common destiny. We may be brothers, after all.

Speech, 12 January 1855, ibid.

3 When the last Red Man shall have perished from the earth and his memory among the white men shall have become a myth, these shores will swarm with the invisible dead of my tribe; and when your children's children shall think themselves alone in the fields, the store, the shop, upon the highway, or in the silence of the pathless woods, they will not be alone. In all the earth there is no place dedicated to solitude. At night, when the streets of your cities

and villages will be silent and you think them deserted, they will throng with the returning hosts that once filled and still love this beautiful land. The white man will never be alone. Let him be just and deal kindly with my people, for the dead are not powerless.
Speech, 12 January 1855, ibid.

(Sir) Charles Sedley
(c. 1639–1701)
English playwright and poet

After a dissolute life in London, he became MP for Romney and a patron of the arts. His plays include The Mulberry Garden *(1668) and* Bellamira *(1687), but he is most renowned for his lyrics and verse translations.*

1 Phyllis is my only joy,
Faithless as the winds or seas;
Sometimes coming, sometimes coy,
Yet she never fails to please.
'Song', st. 1, publ. in *Works* (1702)

Alan Seeger
(1888–1916)
US poet

On the outbreak of the First World War, he joined the French Foreign Legion and was killed in the Somme offensive. His popular poems 'I Have a Rendezvous with Death' and 'Ode in Memory of the American Volunteers' were published in Poems *(1916).*

1 I have a rendezvous with Death
At some disputed barricade.
'I Have a Rendezvous with Death', publ. in *Poems* (1916)

2 And I to my pledged word am true,
I shall not fail that rendezvous.
'I Have a Rendezvous with Death', ibid.

Pete Seeger
(b. 1919)
US folk singer and songwriter

A Communist Party member until 1951, he co-founded the Almanac Singers (1940–1), a campaigning folk band which included WOODY GUTHRIE, *and the Weavers (1948–58).*

1 If I had a hammer, I'd hammer in the morning, I'd hammer in the evening all over this land.
'The Hammer Song' (song, 1949, written by Pete Seeger and Lee Hays). The song was a hit for Peter, Paul and Mary in 1962 as 'If I Had a Hammer', becoming a staple at protests in the 1960s.

2 Where have all the flowers gone?
'Where Have All the Flowers Gone?' (song, c. 1956). The song, which was covered by the Kingston Trio as well as Peter, Paul and Mary in 1962, was inspired by a passage in the novel *And Quiet Flows the Don* (1934) by Mikhail Sholokhov, quoting a Ukrainian folk song: 'Where are the flowers, the girls have plucked them./Where are the girls, they've all taken husbands./Where are the men, they're all in the army.'

(Sir) J. R. Seeley
(1834–95)
English classicist and historian

John Robert Seeley. Professor of Latin at University College, London, and subsequently Professor of Modern History at Cambridge, he published a controversial life of Jesus, Ecce Homo *(1865), and works on the growth of the British Empire.*

1 We seem, as it were, to have conquered and peopled half the world in a fit of absence of mind.
The Expansion of England, Lecture 1 (1883)

Erich Segal
(b. 1937)
US author

A Yale professor who has published scholarly works on Greco-Roman comedy, he has also written screenplays, notably for the film Love Story *(1970).*

1 Love means never having to say you're sorry.
Love Story (film, 1970, screenplay by Erich Segal, directed by Arthur Hiller). Spoken by Jenny Cavilleri (Ali MacGraw), the words appeared in Segal's novelization of the film as 'Love means not ever having to say you're sorry' (ch. 13). The line was used as a publicity slogan for the film and spawned numerous variations.

E. C. Segar
(1894–1938)
US cartoonist

Elzie Crisler Segar. He began The Thimble Theatre *comic strip for the New York* Evening Journal *in 1919, featuring the Oyl Family, later joined by Popeye the sailor.*

1 I yam what I yam.
Catch-phrase of Popeye from 1929. Originally created for the *Thimble Theatre* syndicated cartoon strip, Popeye's character subsequently featured in films for the Fleischer Studio's *Talkartoon* series from 1933, opposite Betty Boop. After Segar's death, the strip was drawn by different animators in various TV cartoons.

2 I likes to eat my spinach.
Popeye's catch-phrase, ibid.

John Selden
(1584–1654)
English antiquarian, lawyer and politician

A member of parliament from 1623, he published books on law, antiquities and Eastern religion. His History of Tithes *(1618) was suppressed for its criticisms of the clergy, while* Table Talk *was a popular compilation of his sayings (1689).*

1 A glorious Church is like a magnificent feast; there is all the variety that may be, but every one chooses out a dish or two that he likes, and lets the rest alone: how glorious soever the Church is, every one chooses out of it his own religion, by which he governs himself, and lets the rest alone.
Table Talk, 'Church' (ed. Richard Milward, 1689)

2 To preach long, loud, and Damnation, is the way to be cried up. We love a man that damns us, and we run after him again to save us.
Ibid., 'Damnation'

3 Humility is a virtue all preach, none practise, and yet everybody is content to hear. The master thinks it good doctrine for his servant, the laity for the clergy, and the clergy for the laity.
Ibid., 'Humility'

4 A king is a thing men have made for their own sakes, for quietness' sake. Just as in a family one man is appointed to buy the meat.
Ibid., 'King'

5 Of all actions of a man's life, his marriage does least concern other people, yet of all actions of our life 'tis most meddled with by other people.
Ibid., 'Marriage'

6 Pleasures are all alike simply considered in themselves: he that hunts, or he that governs the commonwealth, they both please themselves alike, only we commend that, whereby we ourselves receive some benefit.
Ibid., 'Pleasure'

7 They that govern most, make least noise.
Ibid., 'Power'

8 Syllables govern the world.
Ibid., 'Power'

9 Prayer should be short, without giving God Almighty reasons why he should grant this, or that; he knows best what is good for us.
Ibid., 'Prayer'

10 'Tis not seasonable to call a man traitor, that has an army at his heels.
Ibid., 'Traitor'

11 Wise men say nothing in dangerous times.
Ibid., 'Wisdom'

Will Self
(b. 1961)
British author

Known for his dark humour, he has drawn on his own experience of heroin for his short stories The Quantity Theory of Insanity *(1991) and his novel* My Idea of Fun *(1994). Later titles include* How the Dead Live *(2000).*

1 *Wake up.* The avant-garde is dead. It's been marketed.
Interview in *The Idler* November/December 1993

2 Some people are born slack – others have slacking thrust upon them.
Junk Mail, 'Slack Attack' (1995)

W. C. Sellar
(1898–1951)
R. J. Yeatman
(1897–1968)
British authors

Walter Carruthers Sellar, a schoolteacher, and Robert Julian Yeatman, a copywriter and advertising manager, collaborated on 1066 and All That *(1930), a classic compendium of cod-history and schoolroom howlers.*

1 History is not what you thought. *It is what you can remember.* All other history defeats itself.
1066 and All That, 'Compulsory Preface' (1930)

2 The Roman Conquest was, however, a Good Thing, since the Britons were only natives at the time.
Ibid., ch. 1, 'Culture Among the Ancient Britons'

3 We come at last to the Central Period of British History ... consisting in the *utterly memorable Struggle between the Cavaliers (Wrong but Womantic) and the Roundheads (Right but Repulsive).*
Ibid., ch. 35, 'Charles I and the Civil War'

4 King Edward's new policy of peace was very successful and culminated in the Great War to End War. This pacific and inevitable struggle was undertaken in the reign of His Good and memorable Majesty King George V and it was the cause of nowadays and the end of History.
Ibid., ch. 61, 'The Great War'

5 Do not on any account attempt to write on both sides of the paper at once.

Ibid., 'Test Paper V'. Closing words of book.

Seneca

(c. 4 BC–AD 65)

Roman playwright, philosopher and statesman

Lucius Annaeus Seneca, also known as Seneca the Younger. Born in Spain, he was tutor to NERO *who made him a consul in 57. He was the author of a study of physics and of essays expressing his Stoic beliefs, while his tragedies were a major influence on Renaissance drama. After being implicated in Piso's conspiracy he was ordered to commit suicide.*

1 *Tanta stultitia mortalium est.*
[What fools these mortals be.]

Epistulae Morales ad Lucilium (*Moral Epistles*), Epistle 1, sect. 3. See WILLIAM SHAKESPEARE: MIDSUMMER NIGHT'S DREAM 28.

2 Most men ebb and flow in wretchedness between the fear of death and the hardship of life; they are unwilling to live, and yet they do not know how to die. [*Vivere nolunt, mori nesciunt.*]

Ibid., Epistle 4, sect. 5

3 *Ad supervacua sudatur.*
[It is the superfluous things for which men sweat.]

Ibid., Epistle 4, sect. 11

4 Whatever is well said by another, is mine.

Ibid., Epistle 16, sect. 7

5 The final hour when we cease to exist does not itself bring death; it merely of itself completes the death-process. We reach death at that moment, but we have been a long time on the way.

Ibid, Epistle 24, sect. 20

6 Nothing becomes so offensive so quickly as grief. When fresh it finds someone to console it, but when it becomes chronic, it is ridiculed, and rightly.

Ibid., Epistle 63, sect. 13

7 Just as I shall select my ship when I am about to go on a voyage, or my house when I propose to take a residence, so I shall choose my death when I am about to depart from life.

Ibid., Epistle 70, sect. 11

8 Drunkenness is nothing but voluntary madness.

Ibid., Epistle 83, sect. 18

9 Believe me, that was a happy age, before the days of architects, before the days of builders.

Ibid., Epistle 90, sect. 9

10 It makes a great deal of difference whether one wills not to sin or has not the knowledge to sin.

Ibid., Epistle 90, sect. 46

11 Remember that pain has this most excellent quality: if prolonged it cannot be severe, and if severe it cannot be prolonged.

Ibid., Epistle 94, sect. 7

12 We often want one thing and pray for another, not telling the truth even to the gods.

Ibid., Epistle 95, sect. 2

13 The display of grief makes more demands than grief itself. How few men are sad in their own company.

Ibid., Epistle 99, sect. 16

14 A large part of mankind is angry not with the sins, but with the sinners.

Epistulae Morales (*Moral Essays*), 'De Ira' ('On Anger'), bk 2, sect. 28

15 Those whom they have injured they also hate.

Ibid, 'De Ira', bk 2, sect. 33. See TACITUS 5.

16 Disaster is virtue's opportunity.

Ibid., 'De Providentia' ('Of Providence'), sect. 4

17 The evil which assails us is not in the localities we inhabit but in ourselves. We lack strength to endure the least task, being incapable of suffering pain, powerless to enjoy pleasure, impatient with everything. How many invoke death when, after having tried every sort of change, they find themselves reverting to the same sensations, unable to discover any new experience.

Ibid., 'De Tranquillitate Animi' ('On Tranquillity of Mind'), sect. 2, subsect. 15

18 *Vitam brevem esse, longam artem.*
[Life is short, art is long.]

Ibid., 'De Brevitate Vitae', sect. 1. Usually known as 'Ars longa vita brevis'. See GEOFFREY CHAUCER 5, HIPPOCRATES 1.

19 Anyone can stop a man's life, but no one his death: a thousand doors open on to it.

Phoenissae, ll. 152–3. Spoken by Oedipus. See PHILIP MASSINGER 4, JOHN WEBSTER 21.

20 Small sorrows speak; great ones are silent.

Phaedra, l. 607. Spoken by Phaedra. The play is also known as *Hippolytus*.

21 What difference does it make how much you

have? What you do not have amounts to much more.

Attributed in *Noctes Atticae*, bk 12, ch. 2, sect. 13 (2nd century AD) by Aulus Gellius

Rod Serling
(1924–75)
US scriptwriter and television producer

Edwin Rodman Serling. He was the creator and host of the science fiction TV series The Twilight Zone *(1959–64) and the author of more than 200 plays for television. He also wrote screenplays, co-scripting* The Planet of the Apes *(1968).*

1 There is a fifth dimension beyond those known to man. It is a dimension vast as space and timeless as infinity. It is the middle ground between light and shadow, between the pit of his fears and the summit of his knowledge. This is the dimension of imagination. It is an area called the Twilight Zone.

The Twilight Zone, Preamble (TV series, created, written and narrated by Rod Serling, 1959–64)

Robert W. Service
(1874–1958)
English-born Canadian poet

Robert William Service. He emigrated to Canada in 1897 where his spirited ballads about frontier life were popular. He later wrote verse based on his experiences in the First World War, as well as novels and two volumes of autobiography.

1 This is the Law of the Yukon, that only the
  strong shall thrive;
That surely the weak shall perish, and only the fit
  survive.

'The Law of the Yukon', st. 1, publ. in *Songs of a Sourdough* (1907). The volume was later published as *The Spell of the Yukon* (1915)

2 Back of the bar, in a solo game, sat Dangerous
  Dan McGrew,
And watching his luck was his light-o'-love, the
  lady that's known as Lou.

'The Shooting of Dan McGrew', st. 1, ibid.

3 Now a promise made is a debt unpaid, and the
  trail has its own stern code.

'The Cremation of Sam McGee', st. 8, ibid.

4 God! and is it time to go?
Ah! the clock is always slow;
It is later than you think.

'It is Later Than You Think', st. 7, publ. in *Ballads of a Bohemian* (1921)

Anna Sewell
(1820–78)
English author

She wrote Black Beauty *(1877), her only novel, after becoming an invalid. Narrated by a horse brought low by maltreatment, it quickly became one of the most famous animal stories of all time.*

1 Though I am an old horse, and have seen and heard a great deal, I never yet could make out why men are so fond of this sport; they often hurt themselves, often spoil good horses, and tear up the fields, and all for a hare, or a fox, or a stag, that they could get more easily some other way; but we are only horses, and don't know.

Black Beauty, ch. 2 (1877). Spoken by Duchess (Black Beauty's mother).

2 We have no right to distress any of God's creatures without a very good reason; we call them dumb animals, and so they are, for they cannot tell us how they feel, but they do not suffer less because they have no words.

Ibid., ch. 46. A lady remonstrates with Jakes on his use of the check-rein. *Black Beauty* is said to have been instrumental in abolishing the cruel practice of using the check-rein, a harness designed to keep a horse's head raised.

The Sex Pistols
British punk band

Formed in 1975 under the guidance of Malcolm McLaren, the group comprised Johnny Rotten (see JOHN LYDON*), Steve Jones, Glen Matlock, Paul Cook and later Sid Vicious. They released a string of controversial, anthemic singles and an album before splitting.*

1 I am an Anti-Christ
I am an anarchist
Don't know what I want but I know how to get it
I wanna destroy the passer-by
'Cos I wanna be anarchy!

'Anarchy in the U.K.' (song, 1976, written by Johnny Rotten, Steve Jones, Glen Matlock and Paul Cook)

2 When there's no future
How can there be sin
We're the flowers in the dustbin
We're the poison in your human machine
We're the future
Your future
God Save the Queen.

'God Save the Queen/No Future' (song, 1977, written by

Johnny Rotten, Steve Jones, Glen Matlock and Paul Cook). The song was released to coincide with the twenty-fifth anniversary celebrations of Queen ELIZABETH II's accession.

3 We're pretty . . . pretty vacant
And we don't care.
'Pretty Vacant' (song, 1977, written by Johnny Rotten, Steve Jones, Glen Matlock and Paul Cook)

Anne Sexton
(1928–74)
US poet

Her verse, collected in Bedlam and Back *(1960) and* Live or Die *(1966) among other titles, is confessional in style and drew criticism for its candour. Afflicted by emotional breakdowns and depression, she committed suicide.*

1 Everyone has left me
except my muse,
that good nurse.
She stays in my hand,
a mild white mouse.
'Flee on Your Donkey', publ. in *Live or Die* (1966). The title quotes from RIMBAUD's *Fêtes de la faim* (1872).

2 But suicides have a special language.
Like carpenters they want to know *which tools.*
They never ask *why build.*
'Wanting to Die', ibid.

3 The sea is mother-death and she is a mighty female, the one who wins, the one who sucks us all up.
Entry, 19 November 1971, in 'A Small Journal', publ. in *The Poet's Story* (ed. Howard Moss, 1974)

4 It doesn't matter who my father was; it matters who I remember he was.
Entry, 1 January 1972, ibid.

5 God owns heaven
but He craves the earth.
'The Earth', publ. in *The Awful Rowing Toward God* (1975). In his essay 'A Visionary' (1891), W. B. YEATS recalls G. W. E. RUSSELL (referred to as 'X–') meeting an old peasant who 'dumb to most men, poured out his cares for him . . . Once he burst out with, "God possesses the heavens – God possesses the heavens – but He covets the world".'

6 My faith
is a great weight
hung on a small wire,
as doth the spider
hang her baby on a thin web.
'Small Wire', ibid.

7 My ideas are a curse.
They spring from a radical discontent
With the awful order of things.
'February 3rd', publ. in *Scorpio, Bad Spider, Die: the Horoscope Poems* (1978)

Thomas Shadwell
(c. 1642–92)
English playwright and poet

His most successful works were satirical comedies, for example Epsom Wells *(1676) and* Bury Fair *(1689), and he also wrote opera and a blank-verse tragedy,* The Libertine *(1675). He was lampooned by Dryden (see* JOHN DRYDEN 41, 43, 44*) and in 1689 succeeded him as Poet Laureate.*

1 Words may be false and full of art,
Sighs are the natural language of the heart.
Psyche, Act 5 (1675). Spoken by Cupid.

2 Ladies are your finger watches, that go just as you set them.
A True Widow, Act 1, Sc. 1 (1679). Spoken by Bellamour.

3 And wit's the noblest frailty of the mind.
Young Maggot, ibid., Act 1, Sc. 1. In DRYDEN's play, *The Indian Emperor*, Act 2, Sc. 2 (1665), appears the line: 'And love's the noblest frailty of the mind.'

William Shakespeare
(1564–1616)
English dramatist and poet

Commonly recognized as the greatest figure in English literature, he had left Stratford-upon-Avon by 1589 for London, where he worked as an actor and playwright. His blank verse comedies, histories and tragedies brought him fame and financial security, and he retired to Stratford c. 1610. After his death, his plays were frequently adapted and cut, and it was only following the critical reassessment of COLERIDGE *and* HAZLITT *that the original texts were restored. His sonnets and long narrative poems are also highly regarded. The works below are arranged chronologically according to the dates in which they are thought to have been composed or first performed. See* JANE AUSTEN 18, LORD BYRON 48, SAMUEL TAYLOR COLERIDGE 58, JOHN DRYDEN 6, THOMAS GRAY 19, ROBERT GREENE 4, BEN JONSON 29–32, D. H. LAWRENCE 26, JOHN MILTON 6.

Henry VI Pt 1

(c. 1591)

1 Comets, importing change of times and states,
Brandish your crystal tresses in the sky.
Bedford, Act 1, Sc. 1, ll. 2–3

2 And I have heard it said unbidden guests
Are often welcomest when they are gone.
Bedford, Act 2, Sc. 2, ll. 55–6

3 I have perhaps some shallow spirit of
judgement;
But in these nice sharp quillets of the law,
Good faith, I am no wiser than a daw.
Warwick, Act 2, Sc. 4, ll. 16–18

4 Choked with ambition of the meaner sort.
Richard Plantagenet, Act 2, Sc. 5, l. 123

5 Defer no time; delays have dangerous ends.
Regnier, Act 3, Sc. 2, l. 33

6 She's beautiful, and therefore to be wooed;
She is a woman, therefore to be won.
Suffolk, of Margaret of Anjou, Act 5, Sc. 3, ll. 78–9. See TITUS
ANDRONICUS 2.

7 I am a soldier and unapt to weep
Or to exclaim on fortune's fickleness.
Regnier, Act 3, Sc. 2, l. 33–4

8 For what is wedlock forcèd but a hell,
An age of discord and continual strife?
Whereas the contrary bringeth bliss
And is a pattern of celestial peace.
Suffolk, Act 5, Sc. 5, ll. 62–5

Henry VI Pt 2

(c. 1591)

1 Put forth thy hand, reach at the glorious gold.
Duchess of Gloucester, Act 1, Sc. 2, l. 11. Urging her husband,
the Duke of Gloucester, to seize the throne.

2 Could I come near your beauty with my nails,
I could set my ten commandments on your face.
Duchess of Gloucester, Act 1, Sc. 3, ll. 139–40. To Queen Margaret, who has boxed the Duchess's ears.

3 What stronger breastplate than a heart
untainted!
Thrice is he armed that hath his quarrel just;
And he but naked, though locked up in steel,
Whose conscience with injustice is corrupted.
King Henry, Act 3, Sc. 2, ll. 232–5

4 The gaudy, blabbing, and remorseful day
Is crept into the bosom of the sea.
Lieutenant, Act 4, Sc. 1, ll. 1–2

5 Well, I say it was never merry world in England
since gentlemen came up.
John Holland, Act 4, Sc. 2, ll. 7–9

6 The first thing we do, let's kill all the lawyers.
Dick the butcher, Act 4, Sc. 2, l. 72

7 And Adam was a gardener.
Jack Cade, Act 4, Sc. 2, l. 126

8 And more than that, he can speak French; and
therefore he is a traitor.
Jack Cade, Act 4, Sc. 2, ll. 156–8. Explaining his reasons why
Lord Say should die.

9 Thou hast most traitorously corrupted the youth of the realm in erecting a grammar school.
Jack Cade, Act 4, Sc. 7, ll. 29–30

10 Away with him! Away with him! He speaks Latin.
Jack Cade, of Lord Say, Act 4, Sc. 7, l. 53

Henry VI Pt 3
(c. 1591)

1 O tiger's heart wrapped in a woman's hide!
York, of Queen Margaret, Act 1, Sc. 4, l. 137. See ROBERT GREENE 4.

2 Thou setter-up and plucker-down of kings.
Edward, praying to God, Act 2, Sc. 3, l. 37. The words recall the Bible (*Daniel* 2:21). The Earl of Warwick ('the Kingmaker') is described in similar terms in Act 3, Sc. 3, l. 157 and Act 5, Sc. 1, l. 26.

3 This battle fares like to the morning's war,
When dying clouds contend with growing light.
King Henry, Act 2, Sc. 5, ll. 1–2

4 Would I were dead, if God's good will were so!
For what is in this world but grief and woe?
O God! Methinks it were a happy life,
To be no better than a homely swain;
To sit upon a hill, as I do now;
To carve out dials quaintly, point by point,
Thereby to see the minutes how they run:
How many makes the hour full complete,
How many hours brings about the day,
How many days will finish up the year,
How many years a mortal man may live.
King Henry, Act 2, Sc. 5, ll. 19–29

5 Why, love forswore me in my mother's womb;
And, for I should not deal in her soft laws,
She did corrupt frail nature with some bribe
To shrink mine arm up like a withered shrub;
To make an envious mountain on my back,
Where sits deformity to mock my body;
To shape my legs of an unequal size;
To disproportion me in every part.
Richard, Duke of Gloucester, Act 3, Sc. 2, ll. 153–60

6 Why, I can smile, and murder whiles I smile,
And cry 'Content!' to that which grieves my heart,
And wet my cheeks with artificial tears,
And frame my face to all occasions.
Richard, Duke of Gloucester, Act 3, Sc. 2, ll. 182–5

7 Suspicion always haunts the guilty mind;
The thief doth fear each bush an officer.
Richard, Duke of Gloucester, Act 5, Sc. 6, ll. 11–12

8 Thy mother felt more than a mother's pain,
And yet brought forth less than a mother's hope,
To wit, an indigested and deformèd lump,
Not like the fruit of such a goodly tree.
Teeth hadst thou in thy head when thou wast born,
To signify thou camest to bite the world.
King Henry to Richard, Duke of Gloucester, Act 5, Sc. 6, ll. 49–54

The Taming of the Shrew
(c. 1591)

1 No profit grows where is no pleasure ta'en.
In brief, sir, study what you most affect.
Tranio, advising Lucentio, Act 1, Sc. 1, ll. 39–40

2 There's small choice in rotten apples.
Hortensio, Act 1, Sc. 1, ll. 132–3

3 Such wind as scatters young men through the world
To seek their fortunes farther than at home,
Where small experience grows.
Petruchio, Act 1, Sc. 2, ll. 49–51. In answer to Hortensio's question: 'What happy gale/Blows you to Padua here from old Verona?'

4 We will have rings, and things, and fine array,
And kiss me, Kate, we will be married o' Sunday.
Petruchio, Act 2, Sc. 1, ll. 316–17. The words 'Kiss me, Kate', which recur twice in Act 5, are the title of a stage musical based on Shakespeare's play by COLE PORTER (1948).

5 He took the bride about the neck,
And kissed her lips with such a clamorous smack
That at the parting all the church did echo.
Gremio, Act 3, Sc. 2, ll. 176–8. Describing the wedding of Petruchio and Katherina.

6 This is a way to kill a wife with kindness,
And thus I'll curb her mad and headstrong humour.
He that knows better how to tame a shrew,
Now let him speak – 'tis charity to show.
Petruchio, Act 4, Sc. 1, ll. 194–7. Of his plans to 'tame' his wife, Katherina.

7 For 'tis the mind that makes the body rich,
And as the sun breaks through the darkest clouds,
So honour peereth in the meanest habit.
Petruchio, Act 4, Sc. 3, ll. 168–70

8 He that is giddy thinks the world turns round.
The Widow, Act 5, Sc. 2, l. 20

9 A woman moved is like a fountain troubled,
Muddy, ill-seeming, thick, bereft of beauty.
Katherina, Act 5, Sc. 2, ll. 141–2

10 Such duty as the subject owes the prince,
Even such a woman oweth to her husband.
And when she is froward, peevish, sullen, sour,
And not obedient to his honest will,
What is she but a foul contending rebel
And graceless traitor to her loving lord?
Katherina, Act 5, Sc. 2, ll. 154–9

Richard III
(c. 1592)

1 Now is the winter of our discontent
Made glorious summer by this sun of York,
And all the clouds that loured upon our house
In the deep bosom of the ocean buried.
Richard, Duke of Gloucester, Act 1, Sc. 1, ll. 1–4. The play opens with Richard's brother, formerly the Duke of York, now installed on the throne as Edward IV.

2 Grim-visaged war hath smoothed his wrinkled front,
And now, instead of mounting barbèd steeds
To fright the souls of fearful adversaries,
He capers nimbly in a lady's chamber
To the lascivious pleasing of a lute.
Richard, Duke of Gloucester, Act 1, Sc. 1, ll. 9–13

3 Not shaped for sportive tricks
Nor made to court an amorous looking-glass.
Richard, Duke of Gloucester, Act 1, Sc. 1, ll. 14–15. Describing himself.

4 No beast so fierce but knows some touch of pity.
Lady Anne, Act 1, Sc. 2, l. 71

5 Was ever woman in this humour wooed?
Was ever woman in this humour won?
Richard, Duke of Gloucester, of Lady Anne, Act 1, Sc. 1, ll. 227–8

6 And thus I clothe my naked villainy
With odd old ends stolen forth of Holy Writ,
And seem a saint, when most I play the devil.
Richard, Duke of Gloucester, Act 1, Sc. 3, ll. 335–7

7 O Lord! Methought what pain it was to drown!
What dreadful noise of waters in mine ears!
What sights of ugly death within mine eyes!
Methoughts I saw a thousand fearful wracks;
A thousand men that fishes gnawed upon;

Wedges of gold, great anchors, heaps of pearl,
Inestimable stones, unvalued jewels,
All scattered in the bottom of the sea.
Some lay in dead men's skulls, and in the holes
Where eyes did once inhabit, there were crept,
As 'twere in scorn of eyes, reflecting gems,
That wooed the slimy bottom of the deep
And mocked the dead bones that lay scattered by.
Clarence, Act 1, Sc. 4, ll. 21–33. Relating a dream, which prefigures his death by drowning in a butt of Malmsey wine.

8 Unto the kingdom of perpetual night.
Clarence, Act 1, Sc. 4, l. 47

9 You cloudy princes and heart-sorrowing peers.
Buckingham, Act 2, Sc. 2, l. 112

10 So wise so young, they say, do never live long.
Richard, Duke of Gloucester, Act 3, Sc. 1, l. 79. Referring to Prince Edward, who is dead by Act 4 Sc. 3.

11 Talk'st thou me of 'ifs'? Thou art a traitor.
Off with his head!
Richard, Duke of Gloucester, to Hastings, Act 3, Sc. 4, ll. 75–6. Queen Margaret also used the words 'Off with his head' at the end of Act 1 of Henry VI pt 3. See also COLLEY CIBBER 5.

12 Thou art all ice; thy kindness freezes.
Richard, Duke of Gloucester, to Buckingham, Act 4, Sc. 2, l. 22

13 I am not in the giving vein today.
Richard, Duke of Gloucester, Act 4, Sc. 2, ll. 115–16

14 Cancel his bond of life, dear God, I pray,
That I may live and say, 'The dog is dead.'
Queen Margaret, of Richard, now king, Act 4, Sc. 4, ll. 77–8

15 Thou cam'st on earth to make the earth my hell.
A grievous burden was thy birth to me;
Tetchy and wayward was thy infancy;
Thy schooldays frightful, desperate, wild, and furious;
Thy prime of manhood daring, bold, and venturous;
Thy age confirmed, proud, subtle, sly, and bloody,
More mild, but yet more harmful – kind in hatred.
What comfortable hour canst thou name
That ever graced me with thy company?
Duchess of York to her son, Richard, Act 4, Sc. 4, ll. 167–75

16 Bloody thou art, bloody will be thy end;
Shame serves thy life and doth thy death attend.
Duchess of York to her son, Richard, Act 4, Sc. 4, ll. 195–6

17 Besides, the King's name is a tower of strength,
Which they upon the adverse faction want.
King Richard, Act 5, Sc. 3, ll. 12–13

18 My conscience hath a thousand several
   tongues,
And every tongue brings in a several tale,
And every tale condemns me for a villain.
King Richard, Act 5, Sc. 3, ll. 194–6

19 Conscience is but a word that cowards use,
Devised at first to keep the strong in awe.
King Richard, Act 5, Sc. 3, ll. 310–11

20 A horse! A horse! My kingdom for a horse!
King Richard, Act 5, Sc. 4, l. 7 and 13. Richard's last words at
the Battle of Bosworth.

Titus Andronicus
(c. 1592)

1 Sweet mercy is nobility's true badge.
Tamora, Act 1, Sc. 1, l. 122

2 She is a woman, therefore may be wooed;
She is a woman, therefore may be won;
She is Lavinia, therefore must be loved.
Demetrius, Act 2, Sc. 1, ll. 82–4. With his brother Chiron, he
subsequently rapes and mutilates Lavinia. See SHAKE-
SPEARE: HENRY VI PT 1 6.

3 What fool hath added water to the sea,
Or brought a faggot to bright-burning Troy?
Titus, Act 3, Sc. 1, ll. 68–9

4 Come, and take choice of all my library,
And so beguile thy sorrow.
Titus, to his daughter Lavinia, Act 4, Sc. 1, ll. 34–5

5 What, what, ye sanguine shallow-hearted boys,
Ye white-limed walls, ye alehouse painted signs!
Coal-black is better than another hue,
In that it scorns to bear another hue.
Aaron, Act 4, Sc. 2, ll. 96–9

6 Ah, why should wrath be mute and fury dumb?
I am no baby, I, that with base prayers
I should repent the evils I have done.
Ten thousand worse than ever yet I did
Would I perform if I might have my will.
If one good deed in all my life I did
I do repent it from my very soul.
Aaron, Act 5, Sc. 3, ll. 183–9. His closing speech in the play.

The Two Gentlemen of Verona
(c. 1592)

1 Home-keeping youth have ever homely wits.
Valentine, Act 1, Sc. 1, l. 2

2 I have no other but a woman's reason:
I think him so, because I think him so.
Lucetta, Act 1, Sc. 2, ll. 23–4. Referring to her high opinion of
Proteus.

3 O, how this spring of love resembleth
The uncertain glory of an April day,
Which now shows all the beauty of the sun,
And by and by a cloud takes all away.
Proteus, Act 2, Sc. 1, ll. 84–7

4 Much is the force of heaven-bred poesy.
The Duke of Milan, Act 3, Sc. 2, l. 72

5 Write till your ink be dry, and with your tears
Moist it again, and frame some feeling line
That may discover such integrity.
Proteus, advising Thurio, Act 3, Sc. 2, ll. 75–7

6 Who is Silvia? What is she,
That all our swains commend her?
Holy, fair, and wise is she;
The heaven such grace did lend her,
That she might admirèd be.
Proteus, singing, Act 4, Sc. 2, ll. 38–42. The words of the song
were set to music by Schubert, among others.

7 Then to Silvia let us sing
That Silvia is excelling;
She excels each mortal thing
Upon the dull earth dwelling.
To her let us garlands bring.
Proteus, singing, Act 4, Sc. 2, ll. 48–52

8 Black men are pearls in beauteous ladies' eyes.
Proteus, quoting a saying, Act 5, Sc. 2, l. 12

Venus and Adonis
(1593)

1 Love is a spirit all compact of fire,
Not gross to sink, but light, and will aspire.
ll. 149–50

2 Graze on my lips, and if those hills be dry,
Stray lower, where the pleasant fountains lie.
ll. 233–4

3 O! what a war of looks was then between them.
l. 355

4 For he being dead, with him is beauty slain,
And, beauty dead, black chaos comes again.
ll. 1019–20

5 The grass stoops not, she treads on it so light.
l. 1028

The Rape of Lucrece
(1594)

1 Beauty itself doth of itself persuade
The eyes of men without an orator.
ll. 29–30

2 Who buys a minute's mirth to wail a week?
Or sells eternity to get a toy?
For one sweet grape who will the vine destroy?
Or what fond beggar, but to touch the crown,
Would with the sceptre straight be strucken down?
ll. 213–17

3 O comfort-killing night, image of hell,
Dim register and notary of shame,
Black stage for tragedies and murders fell,
Vast sin-concealing chaos, nurse of blame!
ll. 764–7

4 Time's glory is to calm contending kings,
To unmask falsehood and bring truth to light,
To stamp the seal of time in aged things,
To wake the morn and sentinel the night,
To wrong the wronger till he render right,
To ruinate proud buildings with thy hours,
And smear with dust their glittering golden
    towers.
ll. 939–45

5 For greatest scandal waits on greatest state.
l. 1006

6 And now this pale swan in her watery nest
Begins the sad dirge of her certain ending.
ll. 1611–12

The Comedy of Errors
(c. 1594)

1 They say this town is full of cozenage,
As nimble jugglers that deceive the eye,
Dark-working sorcerers that change the mind,
Soul-killing witches that deform the body,
Disguisèd cheaters, prating mountebanks,
And many suchlike liberties of sin.
Antipholus of Syracuse, Act 1, Sc. 2, ll. 97–102. Describing
Ephesus.

2 They say every why hath a wherefore.
Dromio of Syracuse, Act 1, Sc. 2, ll. 44–5. See SAMUEL BUTLER
(1612–80) 4.

3 Be not thy tongue thy own shame's orator.
Luciana, Act 3, Sc. 2, l. 10

4 A wolf, nay, worse, a fellow all in buff;
A backfriend, a shoulder-clapper.
Dromio of Syracuse, Act 1, Sc. 2, ll. 44–5

5 The venom clamours of a jealous woman
Poisons more deadly than a mad dog's tooth.
Aemilia, Act 5, Sc. 1, ll. 69–70

A Midsummer Night's Dream
(c. 1594)

1 For aye to be in shady cloister mewed,
To live a barren sister all your life,
Chanting faint hymns to the cold fruitless moon.
Theseus, Act 1, Sc. 1, ll. 71–3

2 But earthlier happy is the rose distilled
Than that which, withering on the virgin thorn,
Grows, lives, and dies in single blessedness.
Theseus, Act 1, Sc. 1, ll. 76–8

3 The course of true love never did run smooth.
Lysander, Act 1, Sc. 1, l. 134

4 So quick bright things come to confusion.
Lysander, Act 1, Sc. 1, l. 149

5 Things base and vile, holding no quantity,
Love can transpose to form and dignity.
Love looks not with the eyes, but with the mind,
And therefore is winged Cupid painted blind.
Helena, Act 1, Sc. 1, ll. 232–5

6 Marry, our play is *The most lamentable comedy,
and most cruel death of Pyramus and Thisbe.*
Quince, Act 1, Sc. 2, ll. 11–12

7 Masters, spread yourselves.
Bottom, instructing the 'mechanicals', Act 1, Sc. 2, l. 15

8 Nay, faith, let me not play a woman – I have a
beard coming.
Flute, Act 1, Sc. 2, ll. 43–4. On hearing he is to play Thisbe.

9 I will roar you as gently as any sucking dove. I
will roar you an 'twere any nightingale.
Bottom, Act 1, Sc. 2, ll. 76–8

10 Over hill, over dale,
Thorough bush, thorough briar,
Over park, over pale,

Thorough flood, thorough fire –
I do wander everywhere
Swifter than the moon's sphere.
Fairy, Act 2, Sc. 1, ll. 2–7

11 And I serve the Fairy Queen,
To dew her orbs upon the green.
The cowslips tall her pensioners be;
In their gold coats spots you see –
Those be rubies, fairy favours;
In those freckles live their savours.
I must go seek some dewdrops here,
And hang a pearl in every cowslip's ear.
Fairy, Act 2, Sc. 1, ll. 8–15

12 I am that merry wanderer of the night.
I jest to Oberon, and make him smile
When I a fat and bean-fed horse beguile,
Neighing in likeness of a filly foal;
And sometime lurk I in a gossip's bowl
In very likeness of a roasted crab;
And when she drinks, against her lips I bob,
And on her withered dewlap pour the ale.
Puck (Robin Goodfellow), Act 2, Sc. 1, ll. 43–50

13 Ill met by moonlight, proud Titania!
Oberon, Act 2, Sc. 1, l. 60

14 I have forsworn his bed and company.
Titania, referring to Oberon, Act 2, Sc. 1, l. 62

15 These are the forgeries of jealousy.
Titania, Act 2, Sc. 1, l. 81

16 But with thy brawls thou hast disturbed our
sport.
Titania to Oberon, Act 2, Sc. 1, l. 87

17 Therefore the moon, the governess of floods,
Pale in her anger, washes all the air,
That rheumatic diseases do abound;
And thorough this distemperature we see
The seasons alter; hoary-headed frosts
Fall in the fresh lap of the crimson rose,
And on old Hiems' thin and icy crown
An odorous chaplet of sweet summer buds
Is as in mockery set. The spring, the summer,
The childing autumn, angry winter change
Their wonted liveries, and the mazèd world,
By their increase now knows not which is which.
And this same progeny of evils comes
From our debate, from our dissension.
We are their parents and original.
Titania to Oberon, Act 2, Sc. 1, ll. 103–17. On the disruption
resulting from their quarrel.

18 Thou rememberest
Since once I sat upon a promontory
And heard a mermaid on a dolphin's back
Uttering such dulcet and harmonious breath,
That the rude sea grew civil at her song,
And certain stars shot madly from their spheres
To hear the sea-maid's music?
Oberon to Puck, Act 2, Sc. 1, ll. 148–54

19 I'll put a girdle round about the earth
In forty minutes!
Puck, Act 2, Sc. 1, ll. 175–6. Boasting of how quickly he can
fetch the love charm ordered by Oberon.

20 Fie, Demetrius,
Your wrongs do set a scandal on my sex.
We cannot fight for love, as men may do;
We should be wooed, and were not made to woo.
Helena, Act 2, Sc. 1, ll. 239–42

21 I know a bank where the wild thyme blows,
Where oxlips and the nodding violet grows,
Quite overcanopied with luscious woodbine,
With sweet muskroses and with eglantine.
There sleeps Titania some time of the night,
Lulled in these flowers with dances and delight.
And there the snake throws her enamelled skin,
Weed wide enough to wrap a fairy in.
Oberon, Act 2, Sc. 1, ll. 249–56

22 You spotted snakes with double tongue,
Thorny hedgehogs, be not seen.
Newts and blindworms, do no wrong,
Come not near our Fairy Queen.
The fairies' lullaby, Act 2, Sc. 2, ll. 9–12

23 To bring in – God shield us – a lion among ladies
is a most dreadful thing; for there is not a more
fearful wildfowl than your lion living.
Bottom, Act 3, Sc. 1, ll. 27–30

24 Bless thee, Bottom! Bless thee! Thou art
translated!
Quince, Act 3, Sc. 1, l. 112. On seeing Bottom with an ass's head.

25 What angel wakes me from my flowery bed?
Titania, woken by Bottom's singing, Act 3, Sc. 1, l. 122

26 I pray thee, gentle mortal, sing again!
Mine ear is much enamoured of thy note.
So is mine eye enthrallèd to thy shape,
And thy fair virtue's force perforce doth move me
On the first view to say, to swear, I love thee.
Titania to Bottom, Act 3, Sc. 1, ll. 130–4

27 To say the truth, reason and love keep little company together nowadays.
Bottom, Act 3, Sc. 1, ll. 136–7

28 Shall we their fond pageants see?
Lord, what fools these mortals be!
Puck, Act 3, Sc. 2, ll. 114–15. Referring to the antics of the Athenians under the influence of magic potions. See SENECA 1.

29 So we grew together,
Like to a double cherry, seeming parted
But yet an union in partition,
Two lovely berries moulded on one stem;
So with two seeming bodies but one heart.
Helena, Act 3, Sc. 2, ll. 208–12. Referring to her friendship with Hermia.

30 How low am I, thou painted maypole? Speak!
How low am I? – I am not yet so low
But that my nails can reach unto thine eyes.
Hermia to Helena, Act 3, Sc. 2, ll. 295–8

31 Get you gone, you dwarf,
You minimus of hindering knot-grass made,
You bead, you acorn.
Lysander to Hermia (his former lover), Act 3, Sc. 2, ll. 327–9

32 Jack shall have Jill;
Nought shall go ill.
The man shall have his mare again, and all shall be well.
Puck, Act 3, Sc. 2, ll. 461–3

33 Methinks I have a great desire to a bottle of hay.
Good hay, sweet hay hath no fellow.
Bottom, Act 4, Sc. 1, ll. 32–3

34 My Oberon, what visions have I seen!
Methought I was enamoured of an ass.
Titania, Act 4, Sc. 1, ll. 75–6

35 I have had a most rare vision. I have had a dream past the wit of man to say what dream it was. Man is but an ass if he go about to expound this dream.
Bottom, Act 4, Sc. 1, ll. 203–5

36 The eye of man hath not heard, the ear of man hath not seen, man's hand is not able to taste, his tongue to conceive, nor his heart to report what my dream was!
Bottom, Act 4, Sc. 1, ll. 208–13. See BIBLE, NEW TESTAMENT: 1 CORINTHIANS 4.

37 Lovers and madmen have such seething brains,

Such shaping fantasies, that apprehend
More than cool reason ever comprehends.
Theseus, Act 5, Sc. 1, ll. 4–6

38 The lunatic, the lover, and the poet
Are of imagination all compact.
One sees more devils than vast hell can hold.
That is the madman. The lover, all as frantic,
Sees Helen's beauty in a brow of Egypt.
The poet's eye, in a fine frenzy rolling,
Doth glance from heaven to earth, from earth to
   heaven.
And as imagination bodies forth
The forms of things unknown, the poet's pen
Turns them to shapes, and gives to airy nothing
A local habitation and a name.
Theseus, Act 5, Sc. 1, ll. 7–17

39 Or in the night, imagining some fear,
How easy is a bush supposed a bear?
Theseus, Act 5, Sc. 1, ll. 21–2

40 To show our simple skill,
That is the true beginning of our end.
Quince, Act 5, Sc. 1, ll. 110–11. Prologue to *Pyramus and Thisbe*.

41 Whereat with blade – with bloody, blameful
   blade –
He bravely broached his boiling bloody breast.
Quince, Act 5, Sc. 1, ll. 145–6. Second prologue to *Pyramus and Thisbe*, describing the death of Pyramus.

42 All that I have to say is to tell you that the lantern is the moon, I the man i' th' moon, this thorn bush my thorn bush, and this dog my dog.
Starveling as Moonshine, Act 5, Sc. 1, ll. 250–2

43 The iron tongue of midnight hath told twelve.
Lovers, to bed; 'tis almost fairy time.
Theseus, Act 5, Sc. 1, ll. 353–4

44 Not a mouse
Shall disturb this hallowed house:
I am sent with broom before,
To sweep the dust behind the door.
Puck, Act 5, Sc. 1, ll. 377–80. Puck is traditionally associated with house-cleaning at midnight.

45 If we shadows have offended,
Think but this, and all is mended:
That you have but slumbered here
While these visions did appear.
And this weak and idle theme,
No more yielding but a dream.
Puck's epilogue, Act 5, Sc. 1, ll. 413–18

Richard II
(1595)

1 The purest treasure mortal times afford
Is spotless reputation. That away,
Men are but gilded loam, or painted clay.
Mowbray, Act 1, Sc. 1, ll. 177–9

2 We were not born to sue, but to command.
King Richard, Act 1, Sc. 1, l. 196

3 That which in mean men we entitle patience
Is pale cold cowardice in noble breasts.
Duchess of Gloucester, Act 1, Sc. 2, ll. 33–4

4 The language I have learnt these forty years,
My native English, now I must forego,
And now my tongue's use is to me no more
Than an unstringèd viol or a harp.
Mowbray, Act 1, Sc. 3, ll. 159–62

5 How long a time lies in one little word!
Bolingbroke, Act 1, Sc. 3, l. 213

6 Things sweet to taste prove in digestion sour.
John of Gaunt, Act 1, Sc. 3, l. 236

7 Must I not serve a long apprenticehood
To foreign passages, and in the end,
Having my freedom, boast of nothing else
But that I was a journeyman to grief?
Bolingbroke, Act 1, Sc. 3, ll. 271–4

8 There is no virtue like necessity.
John of Gaunt, Act 1, Sc. 3, l. 278

9 O, who can hold a fire in his hand
By thinking on the frosty Caucasus,
Or cloy the hungry edge of appetite
By bare imagination of a feast,
Or wallow naked in December snow
By thinking on fantastic summer's heat?
O no, the apprehension of the good
Gives but the greater feeling to the worse.
Fell sorrow's tooth doth never rankle more
Than when he bites, but lanceth not the sore.
Bolingbroke, Act 1, Sc. 3, ll. 294–303

10 Where'er I wander, boast of this I can:
Though banished, yet a trueborn Englishman!
Bolingbroke, Act 1, Sc. 3, ll. 308–9

11 Report of fashions in proud Italy,
Whose manners still our tardy-apish nation
Limps after in base imitation.
Duke of York, Act 2, Sc. 1, ll. 21–3

12 This royal throne of kings, this sceptred isle,
This earth of majesty, this seat of Mars,
This other Eden – demi-paradise –
This fortress built by nature for herself
Against infection and the hand of war,
This happy breed of men, this little world,
This precious stone set in the silver sea,
Which serves it in the office of a wall,
Or as a moat defensive to a house
Against the envy of less happier lands.
John of Gaunt, Act 2, Sc. 1, ll. 40–9

13 This blessèd plot, this earth, this realm, this
    England,
This nurse, this teeming womb of royal kings,
Feared by their breed, and famous by their birth.
John of Gaunt, Act 2, Sc. 1, ll. 50–52

14 This land of such dear souls, this dear dear land,
Dear for her reputation through the world,
Is now leased out – I die pronouncing it –
Like to a tenement or pelting farm.
John of Gaunt, Act 2, Sc. 1, ll. 57–60

15 England, bound in with the triumphant sea
Whose rocky shore beats back the envious siege
Of watery Neptune, is now bound in with shame,
With inky blots and rotten parchment bonds.
That England that was wont to conquer others
Hath made a shameful conquest of itself.
John of Gaunt, Act 2, Sc. 1, ll. 61–6

16 I count myself in nothing else so happy
As in a soul remembering my good friends.
Bolingbroke, Act 2, Sc. 3, ll. 46–7

17 The caterpillars of the commonwealth,
Which I have sworn to weed and pluck away.
Bolingbroke, Act 2, Sc. 3, ll. 165–6. Referring to King Richard's
counsellors.

18 Eating the bitter bread of banishment.
Bolingbroke, Act 3, Sc. 1, l. 21

19 Not all the water in the rough rude sea
Can wash the balm off from an anointed king.
The breath of worldly men cannot depose
The deputy elected by the Lord.
King Richard, Act 3, Sc. 2, ll. 54–7

20 O, call back yesterday – bid time return.
Salisbury, Act 3, Sc. 2, l. 69

21 Cry woe, destruction, ruin and decay:
The worst is death, and death will have his day.
King Richard, Act 3, Sc. 2, ll. 102–3

22 Of comfort no man speak.
Let's talk of graves, of worms, and epitaphs;
Make dust our paper, and with rainy eyes
Write sorrow on the bosom of the earth.
Let's choose executors and talk of wills.
King Richard, Act 3, Sc. 2, ll. 144–8

23 Let us sit upon the ground
And tell sad stories of the death of kings –
How some have been deposed, some slain in war,
Some haunted by the ghosts they have deposed,
Some poisoned by their wives, some sleeping
    killed,
All murdered. For within the hollow crown
That rounds the mortal temples of a king
Keeps death his court.
King Richard, Act 3, Sc. 2, ll. 155–62

24 Cover your heads, and mock not flesh and
    blood
With solemn reverence. Throw away respect,
Tradition, form and, ceremonious duty;
For you have but mistook me all this while.
I live with bread, like you; feel want,
Taste grief, need friends. Subjected thus,
How can you say to me I am a king?
King Richard, Act 3, Sc. 2, ll. 171–7

25 What must the King do now? Must he
    submit?
The King shall do it. Must he be deposed?
The King shall be contented. Must he lose
The name of king? A God's name, let it go.
I'll give my jewels for a set of beads,
My gorgeous palace for a hermitage,
My gay apparel for an almsman's gown,
My figured goblets for a dish of wood,
My sceptre for a palmer's walking-staff,
My subjects for a pair of carvèd saints,
And my large kingdom for a little grave,
A little, little grave, an obscure grave.
King Richard, Act 3, Sc. 3, ll. 143–54

26 God save the King! Will no man say Amen?
Am I both priest and clerk? Well then, Amen.
God save the King, although I be not he;
And yet Amen if Heaven do think him me.
King Richard, Act 4, Sc. 1, ll. 172–5

27 The shadow of your sorrow hath destroyed
The shadow of your face.
Bolingbroke, to King Richard, Act 4, Sc. 1, ll. 291–2

28 How sour sweet music is
When time is broke, and no proportion kept.
So is it in the music of men's lives.
King Richard, Act 5, Sc. 5, ll. 42–4

29 I wasted time, and now doth time waste me;
For now hath time made me his numbering clock.
King Richard, Act 5, Sc. 5, ll. 49–50

30 Mount, mount, my soul. Thy seat is up on high,
Whilst my gross flesh sinks downward here to die.
King Richard, Act 5, Sc. 5, ll. 111–12. Dying words.

Love's Labour's Lost
(c. 1595)

1 When, spite of cormorant devouring Time,
Th'endeavour of this present breath may buy
That honour which shall bate his scythe's keen
    edge,
And make us heirs of all eternity.
Ferdinand, King of Navarre, Act 1, Sc. 1, ll. 4–7

2 O, these are barren tasks, too hard to keep,
Not to see ladies, study, fast, not sleep.
Berowne, Act 1, Sc. 1, ll. 47–8

3 Light seeking light doth light of light beguile;
So, ere you find where light in darkness lies,
Your light grows dark by losing of your eyes.
Berowne, Act 1, Sc. 1, ll. 77–9

4 Study is like the heaven's glorious sun,
That will not be deep-searched with saucy looks.
Small have continual plodders ever won,
Save base authority from others' books.
These earthly godfathers of heaven's lights,
That give a name to every fixèd star,
Have no more profit of their shining nights,
Than those that walk and wot not what they are.
Berowne, Act 1, Sc. 1, ll. 84–91

5 At Christmas I no more desire a rose
Than wish a snow in May's new-fangled shows,
But like of each thing that in season grows.
Berowne, Act 1, Sc. 1, ll. 105–7

6 The world was very guilty of such a ballad some
three ages since, but I think now 'tis not to be found;
or, if it were, it would neither serve for the writing
nor the tune.
Mote, Act 1, Sc. 2, ll. 106–9

7 Assist me, some extemporal god of rhyme, for I

am sure I shall turn sonnet. Devise, wit; write, pen;
for I am for whole volumes in folio.
Don Armado, Act 1, Sc. 2, ll. 176–8

8 Good Lord Boyet, my beauty, though but mean,
Needs not the painted flourish of your praise.
Beauty is bought by judgement of the eye,
Not uttered by base sale of chapmen's tongues.
The Princess of France, Act 2, Sc. 1, ll. 13–16

9 Warble, child; make passionate my sense of
hearing.
Don Armado, Act 3, Sc. 1, ll. 1–2. Requesting a song from his
page Mote.

10 This wimpled, whining, purblind, wayward
   boy,
This Signor Junior, giant-dwarf, Dan Cupid;
Regent of love-rhymes, lord of folded arms,
The'nointed sovereign of sighs and groans,
Liege of all loiterers and malcontents,
Dread prince of plackets, king of codpieces.
Berowne, of Cupid, Act 3, Sc. 1, ll. 176–81

11 Sir, he hath never fed of the dainties that are bred
in a book. He hath not eat paper, as it were; he hath
not drunk ink. His intellect is not replenished. He is
only an animal, only sensible in the duller parts.
Nathaniel, of the constable Dull, Act 4, Sc. 2, ll. 24–7

12 Never durst poet touch a pen to write
Until his ink were tempered with Love's sighs.
O, then his lines would ravish savage ears
And plant in tyrants mild humility.
Berowne, Act 4, Sc. 3, ll. 322–5

13 From women's eyes this doctrine I derive:
They sparkle still the right Promethean fire;
They are the books, the arts, the academes,
That show, contain, and nourish all the world.
Berowne, Act 4, Sc. 3, ll. 326–9

14 They have been at a great feast of languages and
stolen the scraps.
Mote, Act 5, Sc. 1, ll. 36–7. Of Holofernes, Nathaniel and
Armado.

15 In the posteriors of this day, which the rude multitude call the afternoon.
Don Armado, Act 5, Sc. 1, ll. 83–5. Holofernes comments: 'The
posterior of the day . . . is liable, congruent and measurable
for the afternoon. The word is well culled, choice, sweet, and
apt, I do assure you, sir.'

16 Taffeta phrases, silken phrases precise,
Three-piled hyperboles, spruce affection,
Figures pedantical – these summer flies

Have blown me full of maggot ostentation.
I do forswear them.
Berowne, Act 5, Sc. 2, ll. 406–10

17 Honest plain words best pierce the ear of grief.
Berowne, Act 5, Sc. 2, l. 748

18 The words of Mercury are harsh after the songs
of Apollo. You that way; we this way.
Don Armado, Act 5, Sc. 2, ll. 919–20. Closing words of play.

Romeo and Juliet
(c. 1595)

1 A pair of star-crossed lovers.
Chorus, Prologue, l. 6

2 The fearful passage of their death-marked
   love,
And the continuance of their parents' rage,
Which, but their children's end, naught could
   remove,
Is now the two hours' traffic of our stage.
Chorus, Prologue, ll. 9–12

3 Do you bite your thumb at us, sir?
Abram, Act 1, Sc. 1, l. 43. The Montague retainer addresses
Sampson, of the Capulet household.

4 Here's much to-do with hate, but more with
   love.
Why then, O brawling love, O loving hate,
O anything, of nothing first create!
Romeo, Act 1, Sc. 1, ll. 175–7

5 Love is a smoke made with the fume of sighs;
Being purged, a fire sparkling in lovers' eyes;
Being vexed, a sea nourished with lovers' tears.
What is it else? A madness most discreet,
A choking gall and a preserving sweet.
Romeo, Act 1, Sc. 1, ll. 190–4

6 For I am proverbed with a grandsire phrase.
Romeo, Act 1, Sc. 4, l. 37

7 In delay
We waste our lights in vain, like lamps by day.
Mercutio, Act 1, Sc. 4, ll. 44–5

8 I see Queen Mab hath been with you.
She is the fairies' midwife, and she comes
In shape no bigger than an agate stone
On the forefinger of an alderman,
Drawn with a team of little atomies
Over men's noses as they lie asleep.
Mercutio to Romeo, Act 1, Sc. 4, ll. 53–8

9 For you and I are past our dancing days.
Capulet, to a kinsman, Act 1, Sc. 5, l. 32

10 O, she doth teach the torches to burn bright!
It seems she hangs upon the cheek of night
As a rich jewel in an Ethiop's ear –
Beauty too rich for use, for earth too dear!
Romeo, on first seeing Juliet, Act 1, Sc. 5, ll. 44–7

11 My only love, sprung from my only hate!
Too early seen unknown, and known too late!
Prodigious birth of love it is to me
That I must love a loathèd enemy.
Juliet, Act 1, Sc. 5, ll. 138–41

12 He jests at scars that never felt a wound.
Romeo, Act 2, Sc. 2, l. 1. Spoken of Mercutio, who has mocked
Romeo's love-lorn state.

13 But, soft! What light through yonder window
 breaks?
It is the East, and Juliet is the sun!
Romeo, Act 2, Sc. 2, ll. 2–3. On glimpsing Juliet, in 'the balcony
scene'.

14 O Romeo, Romeo! – wherefore art thou Romeo?
Deny thy father and refuse thy name.
Or, if thou wilt not, be but sworn my love,
And I'll no longer be a Capulet.
Juliet, Act 2, Sc. 2, ll. 33–6

15 What's in a name? That which we call a rose
By any other word would smell as sweet.
Juliet, Act 2, Sc. 2, ll. 43–4. The text in the First Quarto and
other editions has 'By any other name', the form in which
the quote has become proverbial.

16 For stony limits cannot hold love out.
Romeo, Act 2, Sc. 2, l. 67

17 Dost thou love me? I know thou wilt say 'Ay'.
And I will take thy word. Yet, if thou swearest,
Thou mayst prove false. At lovers' perjuries,
They say, Jove laughs.
Juliet, Act 2, Sc. 2, ll. 90–3

18 O, swear not by the moon, th'inconstant moon,
That monthly changes in her circled orb,
Lest that thy love prove likewise variable.
Juliet, Act 2, Sc. 2, ll. 109–11

19 This bud of love, by summer's ripening breath,
May prove a beauteous flower when next we meet.
Juliet, Act 2, Sc. 2, ll. 121–2

20 How silver-sweet sound lovers' tongues by
 night,

Like softest music to attending ears!
Romeo, Act 2, Sc. 2, ll. 165–6

21 Parting is such sweet sorrow
That I shall say goodnight till it be morrow.
Juliet, Act 2, Sc. 2, ll. 184–5

22 Care keeps his watch in every old man's eye,
And where care lodges, sleep will never lie.
Friar Laurence, Act 2, Sc. 3, ll. 31–2

23 Young men's love then lies
Not truly in their hearts, but in their eyes.
Friar Laurence, Act 2, Sc. 3, ll. 63–4

24 O flesh, flesh, how art thou fishified!
Mercutio, Act 2, Sc. 4, ll. 37–8

25 I am the very pink of courtesy.
Mercutio, Act 2, Sc. 4, l. 56

26 These violent delights have violent ends
And in their triumph die.
Friar Laurence, Act 2, Sc. 6, ll. 9–10

27 'Tis not so deep as a well, nor so wide as a church-
door. But 'tis enough. 'Twill serve. Ask for me
tomorrow, and you shall find me a grave man.
Mercutio, Act 3, Sc. 1, ll. 96–8. Of the wound he has received.

28 A plague a'both your houses!
They have made worms' meat of me.
Mercutio, Act 3, Sc. 1, ll. 106–7. Mercutio utters the oath three
times after being mortally wounded during an altercation
with the Capulets.

29 O, I am fortune's fool!
Romeo, Act 3, Sc. 1, l. 136

30 I will be deaf to pleading and excuses.
Nor tears nor prayers shall purchase out abuses.
Prince Escalus, Act 3, Sc. 1, ll. 192–3. Referring to Romeo's
crime.

31 Mercy but murders, pardoning those that kill.
Prince Escalus, Act 3, Sc. 1, l. 197

32 Come, civil night,
Thou sober-suited matron, all in black,
And learn me how to lose a winning match,
Played for a pair of stainless maidenhoods.
Juliet, Act 3, Sc. 2, ll. 10–13

33 He was not born to shame.
Upon his brow shame is ashamed to sit.
For 'tis a throne where honour may be crowned
Sole monarch of the universal earth.
Juliet, of Romeo, Act 3, Sc. 2, ll. 91–4

34 Affliction is enamoured of thy parts,
And thou art wedded to calamity.
Friar Laurence to Romeo, Act 3, Sc. 3, ll. 2–3

35 Adversity's sweet milk, philosophy.
Friar Laurence, Act 3, Sc. 3, l. 56. Romeo rejects the comfort of philosophy: 'Hang up philosophy! . . . It helps not, it prevails not.'

36 Look, love, what envious streaks
Do lace the severing clouds in yonder East.
Night's candles are burnt out, and the jocund day
Stands tiptoe on the misty mountain tops.
Romeo, Act 3, Sc. 5, ll. 7–10

37 'Tis an ill cook that cannot lick his own fingers.
Servingman, Act 4, Sc. 2, ll. 6–7

38 Death lies on her like an untimely frost
Upon the sweetest flower of all the field.
Capulet, of Juliet, Act 4, Sc. 5, ll. 28–9

39 O mischief, thou art swift
To enter in the thoughts of desperate men.
Romeo, Act 5, Sc. 1, ll. 35–6

40 Tempt not a desperate man.
Romeo, Act 5, Sc. 3, l. 59

41 Death, that hath sucked the honey of thy
 breath,
Hath had no power yet upon thy beauty.
Thou art not conquered. Beauty's ensign yet
Is crimson in thy lips and in thy cheeks,
And death's pale flag is not advancèd there.
Romeo, addressing the lifeless form of Juliet, Act 5, Sc. 3, ll. 92–6

42 Come, bitter conduct, come, unsavoury guide!
Thou desperate pilot, now at once run on
The dashing rocks thy seasick weary bark!
Here's to my love! O true Apothecary!
Thy drugs are quick. Thus with a kiss I die.
Romeo's dying words, Act 5, Sc. 3, ll. 116–20

Henry IV Pt 1
(c. 1596)

1 So shaken as we are, so wan with care.
King Henry, Act 1, Sc. 1, l. 1

2 What a devil hast thou to do with the time of the day? Unless hours were cups of sack and minutes capons, and clocks the tongues of bawds, and dials the signs of leaping-houses, and the blessed sun himself a fair hot wench in flame-coloured taffeta,

I see no reason why thou shouldst be so superfluous to demand the time of the day.
Prince Hal, Act 1, Sc. 2, ll. 6–11

3 Let us be Diana's foresters, gentlemen of the shade, minions of the moon.
Falstaff, Act 1, Sc. 2, ll. 25–6

4 How now, how now, mad wag? What, in thy quips and thy quiddities?
Falstaff to Hal, Act 1, Sc. 2, ll. 44–5

5 Shall there be gallows standing in England when thou art King?
Falstaff to Hal, Act 1, Sc. 2, ll. 58–9

6 Thou hast the most unsavoury similes, and art indeed the most comparative, rascalliest sweet young prince.
Falstaff to Hal, Act 1, Sc. 2, ll. 79–81

7 'Tis my vocation, Hal; 'tis no sin for a man to labour in his vocation.
Falstaff to Hal, Act 1, Sc. 2, ll. 104–5. Referring to his stealing.

8 Well then, once in my days I'll be a madcap.
Prince Hal, Act 1, Sc. 2, ll. 140–1

9 I know you all, and will awhile uphold
The unyoked humour of your idleness.
Prince Hal, Act 1, Sc. 2, ll. 193–4

10 If all the year were playing holidays,
To sport would be as tedious as to work.
Prince Hal, Act 1, Sc. 2, ll. 202–3

11 O, the blood more stirs
To rouse a lion than to start a hare!
Falstaff, Act 1, Sc. 3, ll. 195–6

12 By heaven, methinks it were an easy leap
To pluck bright honour from the pale-faced moon,
Or dive into the bottom of the deep,
Where fathom-line could never touch the ground,
And pluck up drownèd honour by the locks.
Hotspur, Act 1, Sc. 3, ll. 199–203

13 I know a trick worth two of that.
First Carrier, Act 2, Sc. 1, ll. 37–8

14 I am bewitched with the rogue's company. If the rascal have not given me medicines to make me love him, I'll be hanged.
Falstaff of Prince Hal, Act 2, Sc. 2, ll. 16–18

15 Could thou and I rob the thieves, and go merrily to London, it would be argument for a week, laughter for a month, and a good jest for ever.
Prince Hal, Act 2, Sc. 2, ll. 92–4

16 Out of this nettle, danger, we pluck this flower, safety.
Hotspur, Act 2, Sc. 3, ll. 10–11

17 This is no world
To play with mammets, and to tilt with lips.
We must have bloody noses, and cracked crowns.
Hotpsur, Act 2, Sc. 3, ll. 94–6

18 I have sounded the very bass string of humility.
Prince Hal, Act 2, Sc. 4, ll. 5–6

19 I am not yet of Percy's mind, the Hotspur of the north, he that kills me some six or seven dozen of Scots at a breakfast, washes his hands, and says to his wife, 'Fie upon this quiet life! I want work.'
Prince Hal, Act 2, Sc. 4, ll. 100–3

20 If I fought not with fifty of them I am a bunch of radish.
Falstaff, exaggerating his encounter with 'villains', Act 2, Sc. 4, ll. 180–1

21 Mark now how a plain tale shall put you down.
Prince Hal, Act 2, Sc. 4, ll. 249–50

22 What doth gravity out of his bed at midnight?
Falstaff, Act 2, Sc. 4, l. 287. Referring to the king's messenger.

23 You may buy land now as cheap as stinking mackerel.
Falstaff, Act 2, Sc. 4, ll. 352–3

24 If sack and sugar be a fault, God help the wicked! If to be old and merry be a sin, then many an old host that I know is damned. If to be fat be to be hated, then Pharaoh's lean kine are to be loved.
Falstaff (in the role of Hal), Act 2, Sc. 4, ll. 456–9

25 For sweet Jack Falstaff, kind Jack Falstaff, true Jack Falstaff, valiant Jack Falstaff – and therefore more valiant, being as he is old Jack Falstaff – banish not him thy Harry's company, banish not him thy Harry's company. Banish plump Jack, and banish all the world.
Falstaff (in the role of Hal), Act 2, Sc. 4, ll. 461–5

26 Diseasèd nature oftentimes breaks forth
In strange eruptions.
Hotspur, Act 3, Sc. 1, ll. 24–5

27 These signs have marked me extraordinary,
And all the courses of my life do show
I am not in the roll of common men.
Glendower, Act 3, Sc. 1, ll. 38–40

28 Tell truth, and shame the devil.
Hotspur, Act 3, Sc. 1, l. 55

29 I had rather be a kitten, and cry 'mew'
Than one of these same metre ballad-mongers.
I had rather hear a brazen canstick turned,
Or a dry wheel grate on the axle-tree,
And that would set my teeth nothing on edge,
Nothing so much as mincing poetry.
'Tis like the forced gait of a shuffling nag.
Hotspur, Act 3, Sc. 1, ll. 123–9

30 Such a deal of skimble-skamble stuff.
Hotspur, Act 3, Sc. 1, l. 148

31 O, he is as tedious
As a tired horse, a railing wife,
Worse than a smoky house. I had rather live
With cheese and garlic in a windmill, far,
Than feed on cates and have him talk to me
In any summer house in Christendom.
Hotspur, Act 3, Sc. 1, ll. 153–8. Referring to Glendower.

32 Swear me, Kate, like a lady as thou art,
A good mouth-filling oath.
Hotspur, Act 3, Sc. 1, ll. 247–8. Speaking to his wife (Lady Percy).

33 Could such inordinate and low desires,
Such poor, such bare, such lewd, such mean
    attempts,
Such barren pleasures, rude society,
As thou art matched withal, and grafted to,
Accompany the greatness of thy blood
And hold their level with thy princely heart?
King Henry to Prince Hal, Act 3, Sc. 2, ll. 12–17

34 He was but as the cuckoo is in June,
Heard, not regarded.
King Henry, Act 3, Sc. 2, ll. 75–6. Referring to Richard II.

35 My nearest and dearest enemy.
King Henry, Act 3, Sc. 2, l. 123. Referring to Prince Hal.

36 Company, villainous company, hath been the spoil of me.
Falstaff, Act 3, Sc. 3, ll. 9–10

37 I never see thy face but I think upon hell-fire.
Falstaff to Bardolph, Act 3, Sc. 3, l. 31

38 Thou seest I have more flesh than another man, and therefore more frailty.
Falstaff, Act 3, Sc. 3, ll. 164–6

39 Doomsday is near. Die all, die merrily.
Hotspur, Act 4, Sc. 1, l. 134

40 Greatness knows itself.
Hotspur, Act 4, Sc. 3, l. 74

41 For nothing can seem foul to those that win.
King Henry, Act 5, Sc. 1, l. 8

42 For mine own part I could be well content
To entertain the lag-end of my life
With quiet hours.
Worcester, Act 5, Sc. 1, ll. 23–5

43 Rebellion lay in his way, and he found it.
Falstaff, of Worcester, Act 5, Sc. 1, l. 28

44 Thou owest God a death.
Prince Hal, to Falstaff, Act 5, Sc. 1, l. 126. See SHAKESPEARE:
HENRY IV PT 2 22.

45 Honour pricks me on. Yea, but how if honour
prick me off when I come on, how then? Can honour
set to a leg? No. Or an arm? No. Or take away the
grief of a wound? No. Honour hath no skill in surgery then? No. What is honour? A word. What is in
that word honour? What is that honour? Air. A trim
reckoning! Who hath it? He that died a' Wednesday.
Doth he feel it? No. Doth he hear it? No. 'Tis insensible, then? Yea, to the dead. But will it not live with
the living? No. Why? Detraction will not suffer it.
Therefore I'll none of it. Honour is a mere scutcheon
– and so ends my catechism.
Falstaff, Act 5, Sc. 1, ll. 129–40

46 Two stars keep not their motion in one sphere.
Prince Hal, Act 5, Sc. 4, l. 64

47 And time, that takes survey of all the world,
Must have a stop.
Hotspur, Act 5, Sc. 4, ll. 81–2. Dying words.

48 Thy ignominy sleep with thee in the grave,
But not remembered in thy epitaph.
Prince Hal, Act 5, Sc. 4, ll. 99–100. Referring to the slain
Hotspur.

49 The better part of valour is discretion.
Falstaff, Act 5, Sc. 4, ll. 118–19

50 Lord, Lord, how this world is given to lying!
Falstaff, Act 5, Sc. 4, ll. 144–5. See HENRY IV PT 2 23.

King John

(c. 1596)

1 And if his name be George, I'll call him Peter;
For new-made honour doth forget men's names.
The Bastard, Act 1, Sc. 1, ll. 186–7. On his elevation to the
knighthood.

2 Sweet, sweet, sweet poison for the age's tooth.
The Bastard, Act 1, Sc. 1, l. 213

3 That smooth-faced gentleman, tickling
commodity;
Commodity, the bias of the world.
The Bastard, Act 2, Sc. 1, ll. 573–4

4 Well, whiles I am a beggar, I will rail
And say there is no sin but to be rich;
And being rich, my virtue then shall be
To say there is no vice but beggary.
The Bastard, Act 2, Sc. 1, ll. 593–6

5 Old Time the clock-setter, that bald sexton Time.
The Bastard, Act 3, Sc. 1, l. 324

6 Bell, book, and candle shall not drive me back
When gold and silver becks me to come on.
The Bastard, Act 3, Sc. 3, ll. 12–13

7 Death! Death, O amiable, lovely death!
Thou odoriferous stench! Sound rottenness!
Arise forth from the couch of lasting night,
Thou hate and terror to prosperity,
And I will kiss thy detestable bones.
Constance, Act 3, Sc. 4, ll. 25–9

8 Grief fills the room up of my absent child,
Lies in his bed, walks up and down with me,
Puts on his pretty looks, repeats his words,
Remembers me of all his gracious parts,
Stuffs out his vacant garments with his form.
Constance, Act 3, Sc. 4, ll. 93–7. On her separation from her
son Arthur, taken prisoner by John.

9 There's nothing in this world can make me joy.
Life is as tedious as a twice-told tale,
Vexing the dull ear of a drowsy man.
Lewis the Dauphin, Act 3, Sc. 4, ll. 107–9

10 To gild refinèd gold, to paint the lily,
To throw a perfume on the violet,
To smooth the ice, or add another hue
Unto the rainbow, or with taper-light
To seek the beauteous eye of heaven to garnish,
Is wasteful and ridiculous excess.
Salisbury, Act 4, Sc. 2, ll. 11–16

11 When workmen strive to do better than well,
They do confound their skill in covetousness.
Pembroke, Act 4, Sc. 2, ll. 28–9

12 And oftentimes excusing of a fault
Doth make the fault the worser by th'excuse.
Pembroke, Act 4, Sc. 2, ll. 30–1

13 How oft the sight of means to do ill deeds
Make deeds ill done!
King John, Act 4, Sc. 2, ll. 219–20

14 Now my soul hath elbow-room.
King John, Act 5, Sc. 7, l. 28

15 I am a scribbled form, drawn with a pen
Upon a parchment, and against this fire
Do I shrink up.
King John, dying from fever, Act 5, Sc. 7, ll. 32–4

16 I do not ask you much –
I beg cold comfort; and you are so strait
And so ingrateful you deny me that.
King John, Act 5, Sc. 7, ll. 41–3. The words of the dying king to
his son, Prince Henry, and the English nobles. The phrase
'cold comfort' was already current.

17 Naught shall make us rue
If England to itself do rest but true!
The Bastard, Act 5, Sc. 7, ll. 117–18. Concluding lines of play.

The Merchant of Venice
(c. 1597)

1 I thank my fortune for it
My ventures are not in one bottom trusted,
Nor to one place; nor is my whole estate
Upon the fortune of this present year.
Antonio, Act 1, Sc. 1, ll. 41–4

2 Nature hath framed strange fellows in her time:
Some that will evermore peep through their eyes
And laugh like parrots at a bagpiper,
And other of such vinegar aspect
That they'll not show their teeth in way of smile
Though Nestor swear the jest be laughable.
Solanio, Act 1, Sc. 1, ll. 51–6

3 You have too much respect upon the world;
They lose it that do buy it with much care.
Gratiano, to Antonio, Act 1, Sc. 1, ll. 74–5

4 There are a sort of men whose visages
Do cream and mantle like a standing pond,
And do a wilful stillness entertain
With purpose to be dressed in an opinion
Of wisdom, gravity, profound conceit,
As who should say, 'I am Sir Oracle,
And when I ope my lips, let no dog bark.'
Gratiano, Act 1, Sc. 1, ll. 88–94

5 But fish not with this melancholy bait
For this fool gudgeon, this opinion.
Gratiano, Act 1, Sc. 1, ll. 101–2

6 Gratiano speaks an infinite deal of nothing, more
than any man in all Venice. His reasons are as two
grains of wheat hid in two bushels of chaff: you

shall seek all day ere you find them, and when you
have them they are not worth the search.
Bassanio, Act 1, Sc. 1, ll. 114–18

7 For aught I see, they are as sick that surfeit with
too much as they that starve with nothing.
Nerissa, Act 1, Sc. 2, ll. 5–6

8 If to do were as easy as to know what were good
to do, chapels had been churches, and poor men's
cottages princes' palaces.
Portia, Act 1, Sc. 2, ll. 12–14

9 The brain may devise laws for the blood, but a
hot temper leaps o'er a cold decree.
Portia, Act 1, Sc. 2, ll. 12–14

10 God made him and therefore let him pass for a
man.
Portia, Act 1, Sc. 2, ll. 53–4. Referring to Monsieur Le Bon, a
'princely suitor'.

11 I am glad this parcel of wooers are so reasonable,
for there is not one among them but I dote on
his very absence, and I pray God grant them a fair
departure.
Portia, Act 1, Sc. 2, ll. 102–5

12 Ships are but boards, sailors but men; there be
land rats and water rats, water thieves and land
thieves, I mean pirates; and then there is the peril
of waters, winds, and rocks.
Shylock, Act 1, Sc. 3, ll. 21–4

13 I will buy with you, sell with you, talk with you,
walk with you, and so following; but I will not eat
with you, drink with you, nor pray with you.
Shylock, Act 1, Sc. 3, ll. 33–5. Declining an invitation to dine
with Bassanio and Antonio.

14 The devil can cite Scripture for his purpose.
Antonio, Act 1, Sc. 3, l. 95

15 Still have I borne it with a patient shrug,
For sufferance is the badge of all our tribe.
You call me misbeliever, cut-throat dog,
And spit upon my Jewish gaberdine,
And all for use of that which is mine own.
Shylock, Act 1, Sc. 3, ll. 106–10

16 Mislike me not for my complexion,
The shadowed livery of the burnished sun,
To whom I am a neighbour and near bred.
The Prince of Morocco, Act 2, Sc. 1, ll. 1–3

17 The boy was the very staff of my age, my very
prop.
Gobbo, of his son Launcelot, Act 2, Sc. 2, ll. 60–1

18 It is a wise father that knows his own child.
Launcelot, Act 2, Sc. 2, ll. 70–1

19 The vile squealing of the wry-necked fife.
Shylock, Act 2, Sc. 5, l. 29

20 But stop my house's ears, I mean my
   casements;
Let not the sound of shallow foppery enter
My sober house.
Shylock, Act 2, Sc. 5, ll. 33–5

21 What, must I hold a candle to my shames?
Jessica, Act 2, Sc. 6, l. 41

22 A golden mind stoops not to shows of dross.
Morocco, Act 2, Sc. 7, l. 20

23 I will not choose what many men desire,
Because I will not jump with common spirits
And rank me with the barbarous multitudes.
Arragon, Act 2, Sc. 9, ll. 31–3

24 Some there be that shadows kiss;
Such have but a shadow's bliss.
Arragon, Act 2, Sc. 9, ll. 66–7. Reading the contents of Portia's
silver casket.

25 Let him look to his bond.
Shylock, Act 3, Sc. 1, l. 43. The words are uttered three times
in the speech, referring to Antonio's pledge of a 'pound of
flesh' for failing to repay his debt on time.

26 He hath disgraced me and hindered me half a
million, laughed at my losses, mocked at my gains,
scorned my nation, thwarted my bargains, cooled
my friends, heated mine enemies, and what's his
reason? I am a Jew.
Shylock, of Antonio, Act 3, Sc. 1, ll. 49–53

27 Hath not a Jew eyes? Hath not a Jew hands,
organs, dimensions, senses, affections, passions?
Fed with the same food, hurt with the same
weapons, subject to the same diseases, healed by
the same means, warmed and cooled by the same
winter and summer as a Christian is? If you prick
us, do we not bleed? If you tickle us, do we not
laugh? If you poison us, do we not die? And if you
wrong us, shall we not revenge?
Shylock, Act 3, Sc. 1, ll. 53–61

28 The villainy you teach me I will execute, and it
shall go hard but I will better the instruction.
Shylock, Act 3, Sc. 1, ll. 65–6

29 The world is still deceived with ornament.
In law, what plea so tainted and corrupt,
But being seasoned with a gracious voice,
Obscures the show of evil? In religion,
What damnèd error but some sober brow
Will bless it and approve it with a text,
Hiding the grossness with fair ornament?
There is no vice so simple but assumes
Some mark of virtue on his outward parts.
Bassanio, Act 3, Sc. 2, ll. 74–82

30 The full sum of me
Is sum of something, which to term in gross,
Is an unlessoned girl, unschooled, unpractisèd,
Happy in this, she is not yet so old
But she may learn; happier than this,
She is not bred so dull but she can learn.
Portia, Act 3, Sc. 2, ll. 157–62

31 How every fool can play upon the word! I think
the best grace of wit will shortly turn into silence,
and discourse grow commendable in none only but
parrots.
Lorenzo, Act 3, Sc. 5, ll. 40–2

32 Some men there are love not a gaping pig,
Some that are mad if they behold a cat,
And others, when the bagpipe sings i'th'nose,
Cannot contain their urine.
Shylock, Act 4, Sc. 1, ll. 47–50. Explaining his behaviour toward
Antonio, which he ascribes to natural antipathy.

33 I never knew so young a body with so old a head.
Bellario's letter, Act 4, Sc. 1, ll. 161–2. Referring to Balthasar,
who is actually Portia in disguise.

34 The quality of mercy is not strained,
It droppeth as the gentle rain from heaven
Upon the place beneath. It is twice blest,
It blesseth him that gives and him that takes.
'Tis mightiest in the mightiest, it becomes
The thronèd monarch better than his crown.
Portia (as Balthasar), Act 4, Sc. 1, ll. 181–6

35 Though justice be thy plea, consider this:
That in the course of justice none of us
Should see salvation. We do pray for mercy,
And that same prayer doth teach us all to render
The deeds of mercy.
Portia (as Balthasar), Act 4, Sc. 1, ll. 195–9

36 Wrest once the law to your authority,
To do a great right, do a little wrong.
Bassanio to Portia (as Balthasar), Act 4, Sc. 1, ll. 212–13

37 Nay, take my life and all! Pardon not that!
You take my house when you do take the prop
That doth sustain my house. You take my life

When you do take the means whereby I live.
Shylock to Portia (as Balthasar), Act 4, Sc. 1, ll. 371–4

38 Look how the floor of heaven
Is thick inlaid with patens of bright gold.
There's not the smallest orb which thou beholdest
But in this motion like an angel sings,
Still quiring to the young-eyed cherubins;
Such harmony is in immortal souls,
But whilst this muddy vesture of decay
Doth grossly close it in, we cannot hear it.
Lorenzo, Act 5, Sc. 1, ll. 58–65

39 The man that hath no music in himself,
Nor is not moved with concord of sweet sounds,
Is fit for treasons, stratagems, and spoils,
The motions of his spirit are dull as night,
And his affections dark as Erebus.
Let no such man be trusted.
Lorenzo, Act 5, Sc. 1, ll. 83–8

40 How far that little candle throws his beams!
So shines a good deed in a naughty world.
Portia, Act 5, Sc. 1, ll. 90–1

41 The crow doth sing as sweetly as the lark
When neither is attended, and I think
The nightingale, if she should sing by day
When every goose is cackling, would be thought
No better a musician than the wren.
How many things by season seasoned are
To their right praise and true perfection!
Portia, Act 5, Sc. 1, ll. 102–8

42 These blessèd candles of the night.
Bassanio, of the stars, Act 5, Sc. 1, l. 220

The Merry Wives of Windsor
(c. 1597)

1 I will make a Star-Chamber matter of it.
Justice Shallow, Act 1, Sc. 1, ll. 1–2. Of Falstaff's trespass and poaching.

2 Thou art the Mars of malcontents.
Pistol, to Nym, Act 1, Sc. 3, l. 95

3 Here will be an old abusing of God's patience and the King's English.
Mistress Quickly, Act 1, Sc. 4, ll. 4–5. Of the outcome of Doctor Caius discovering a stranger in his house.

4 I will find you twenty lascivious turtles ere one chaste man.
Mistress Page, Act 2, Sc. 1, ll. 75–6

5 I love not the humour of bread and cheese.
Nym, Act 2, Sc. 1, ll. 126–7

6 Look where my ranting host of the Garter comes. There is either liquor in his pate or money in his purse when he looks so merrily.
Page, of the landlord of the Garter Inn, Act 2, Sc. 1, ll. 177–9

7 Why then, the world's mine oyster,
Which I with sword will open.
Pistol, Act 2, Sc. 2, ll. 2–3

8 O, what a world of vile ill-favoured faults
Looks handsome in three hundred pounds a year!
Anne Page, Act 3, Sc. 4, ll. 32–3

9 If I be served such another trick, I'll have my brains ta'en out and buttered, and give them to a dog for a new-year's gift.
Falstaff, Act 3, Sc. 5, ll. 6–8. On being dropped into the Thames.

10 The rankest compound of villainous smell that ever offended nostril.
Falstaff, Act 3, Sc. 5, ll. 83–5. Referring to the 'foul clothes' in which he hid.

11 Wives may be merry, and yet honest too.
Mistress Page, Act 4, Sc. 2, l. 99

12 He shall die a flea's death.
Mistress Ford, Act 4, Sc. 2, ll. 141–2

13 They say there is divinity in odd numbers, either in nativity, chance, or death.
Falstaff, Act 5, Sc. 1, ll. 3–4

14 But stay – I smell a man of middle earth.
Evans, as a satyr, Act 5, Sc. 5, l. 80

15 Heavens defend me from that Welsh fairy, lest he transform me to a piece of cheese.
Falstaff, of Evans (disguised as a satyr), Act 5, Sc. 5, ll. 81–2. The Welsh were supposed to be great eaters of cheese.

Henry IV Pt 2
(c. 1598)

1 Rumour is a pipe
Blown by surmises, jealousies, conjectures,
And of so easy and so plain a stop
That the blunt monster with uncounted heads,
The still-discordant wavering multitude,
Can play upon it.
Rumour, Induction, ll. 15–20. According to the Folio stage direction, the figure of Rumour appears 'painted full of tongues'.

2 The times are wild; contention, like a horse
Full of high feeding, madly hath broke loose

And bears down all before him.
Northumberland, Act 1, Sc. 1, ll. 9–11

3 Yet the first bringer of unwelcome news
Hath but a losing office, and his tongue
Sounds ever after as a sullen bell
Remembered tolling a departing friend.
Northumberland, Act 1, Sc. 1, ll. 100–3

4 I am not only witty in myself, but the cause that
wit is in other men.
Falstaff, Act 1, Sc. 2, ll. 9–10

5 Your lordship, though not clean past your youth,
have yet some smack of age in you, some relish of
the saltness of time.
Falstaff, to the Lord Chief Justice, Act 1, Sc. 2, ll. 96–8

6 It is the disease of not listening, the malady of
not marking, that I am troubled withal.
Falstaff, Act 1, Sc. 2, ll. 122–3

7 Do you set down your name in the scroll of youth,
that are written down old with all the characters of
age? Have you not a moist eye, a dry hand, a yellow
cheek, a white beard, a decreasing leg, an increasing
belly? Is not your voice broken, your wind short,
your chin double, your wit single, and every part
about you blasted with antiquity? And will you yet
call yourself young?
Lord Chief Justice to Falstaff, Act 1, Sc. 2, ll. 180–7

8 It was alway yet the trick of our English nation, if
they have a good thing, to make it too common.
Falstaff, Act 1, Sc. 2, ll. 216–17

9 I were better to be eaten to death with a rust than
to be scoured to nothing with perpetual motion.
Falstaff, Act 1, Sc. 2, ll. 220–2

10 I can get no remedy against this consumption of
the purse; borrowing only lingers and lingers it out,
but the disease is incurable.
Falstaff, Act 1, Sc. 2, ll. 238–40

11 When we mean to build,
We first survey the plot, then draw the model,
And when we see the figure of the house,
Then must we rate the cost of the erection,
Which if we find outweighs ability,
What do we then but draw anew the model
In fewer offices, or at least desist
To build at all?
Lord Bardolph, Act 1, Sc. 3, ll. 41–8

12 O thoughts of men accursed!
Past and to come seems best; things present,
    worst.
Archbishop of York, Act 1, Sc. 3, ll. 107–8

13 Away, you scullion! You rampallian! You fustil-
arian! I'll tickle your catastrophe!
Page to Hostess (Mistress Quickly), Act 2, Sc. 1, ll. 57–8

14 He hath eaten me out of house and home; he
hath put all my substance into that fat belly of his.
Hostess (Mistress Quickly), Act 2, Sc. 1, ll. 72–3. Referring to
Falstaff.

15 He was indeed the glass
Wherein the noble youth did dress themselves.
Lady Percy, Act 2, Sc. 3, ll. 21–2. Referring to her dead husband,
Hotspur.

16 Is it not strange that desire should so many years
outlive performance?
Poins, Act 2, Sc. 4, ll. 255–6

17   O sleep, O gentle sleep,
Nature's soft nurse, how have I frighted thee,
That thou no more wilt weigh my eye-lids down
And steep my senses in forgetfulness?
King Henry, Act 3, Sc. 1, ll. 5–8

18 Uneasy lies the head that wears a crown.
King Henry, Act 3, Sc. 1, l. 31

19 O God, that one might read the book of fate,
And see the revolution of the times
Make mountains level, and the continent,
Weary of solid firmness, melt itself
Into the sea.
King Henry, Act 3, Sc. 1, ll. 45–9

20 There is a history in all men's lives.
Warwick, Act 3, Sc. 1, l. 76

21 We have heard the chimes at midnight, Master
Shallow.
Falstaff, Act 3, Sc. 2, ll. 209–10. Referring to the youthful antics
of Falstaff and Justice Shallow. *Chimes at Midnight* is the
title of ORSON WELLES's 1966 film based on Shakespeare's
portrayal of Falstaff, with Welles himself in the central role.

22 A man can die but once; we owe God a death. I'll
ne'er bear a base mind. An't be my destiny, so; an't
be not, so. No man's too good to serve's prince; and,
let it go which way it will, he that dies this year is
quit for the next.
Feeble, Act 3, Sc. 2, ll. 228–32. On being pressed into military
service. See HENRY IV PT 1 44.

23 Lord, Lord, how subject we old men are to this vice of lying!

Falstaff, Act 3, Sc. 2, ll. 292–3. See HENRY IV PT 1 50.

24 Skill in the weapon is nothing without sack, for that sets it a-work, and learning a mere hoard of gold kept by a devil, till sack commences it and sets it in act and use.

Falstaff, Act 4, Sc. 3, ll. 111–14

25 Thy wish was father, Harry, to that thought.

King Henry, Act 4, Sc. 5, l. 93. In answer to Prince Hal's remark: 'I never thought to hear you speak again.'

26 Now, neighbour confines, purge you of your scum!
Have you a ruffian that will swear, drink, dance,
Revel the night, rob, murder, and commit
The oldest sins the newest kind of ways?

King Henry, Act 4, Sc. 5, ll. 124–7

27 A foutre for the world and worldlings base!
I speak of Africa and golden joys.

Pistol, Act 5, Sc. 3, ll. 99–100

28 I know thee not, old man. Fall to thy prayers.
How ill white hairs becomes a fool and jester.

King Henry V to Falstaff, Act 5, Sc. 5, ll. 50–1

29 Presume not that I am the thing I was.

King Henry V to Falstaff, Act 5, Sc. 5, l. 59

Much Ado About Nothing
(c. 1598)

1 He is a very valiant trencher-man, he hath an excellent stomach.

Beatrice, of Benedick, Act 1, Sc. 1, ll. 47–8

2 There's a skirmish of wit between them.

Leonato, of Beatrice and Benedick, Act 1, Sc. 1, ll. 58–9

3 He wears his faith but as the fashion of his hat; it ever changes with the next block.

Beatrice, of Benedick, Act 1, Sc. 1, ll. 69–71

4 Messenger: I see, lady, the gentleman is not in your books.
Beatrice: No; an he were, I would burn my study.

Of Benedick, Act 1, Sc. 1, ll. 72–3

5 Thou wast ever an obstinate heretic in the despite of beauty.

Don Pedro, to Benedick, Act 1, Sc. 1, ll. 116–17

6 Lord, I could not endure a husband with a beard on his face! I had rather lie in the woollen.

Beatrice, Act 2, Sc. 1, ll. 26–7

7 Friendship is constant in all other things
Save in the office and affairs of love.

Claudio, Act 2, Sc. 1, ll. 160–1

8 Let every eye negotiate for itself,
And trust no agent.

Claudio, Act 2, Sc. 1, ll. 163–4

9 I was born to speak all mirth and no matter.

Beatrice, Act 2, Sc. 1, ll. 304–5

10 Is it not strange that sheep's guts should hale souls out of men's bodies?

Benedick, Act 2, Sc. 3, ll. 56–8

11 Sigh no more, ladies, sigh no more,
Men were deceivers ever,
One foot in sea and one on shore,
To one thing constant never

Balthasar's song, Act 2, Sc. 3, ll. 60–3

12 Sits the wind in that corner?

Benedick, Act 2, Sc. 3, ll. 99–100

13 A man loves the meat in his youth that he cannot endure in his age.

Benedick, Act 2, Sc. 3, ll. 231–2

14 The world must be peopled. When I said I would die a bachelor, I did not think I should live till I were married.

Benedick, Act 2, Sc. 3, ll. 234–6

15 From the crown of his head to the sole of his foot, he is all mirth; he hath twice or thrice cut Cupid's bow-string and the little hangman dare not shoot at him. He hath a heart as sound as a bell and his tongue is the clapper, for what his heart thinks, his tongue speaks.

Don Pedro, of Benedick, Act 3, Sc. 2, ll. 8–13

16 Everyone can master a grief but he that has it.

Benedick, Act 3, Sc. 2, ll. 26–7

17 Are you good men and true?

Dogberry, to the Watchmen, Act 3, Sc. 3, l. 1

18 You are thought here to be the most senseless and fit man for the constable of the watch; therefore bear you the lantern.

Dogberry, to the Second Watchman, Act 3, Sc. 3, ll. 21–4

19 When rich villains have need of poor ones, poor ones may make what price they will.

Borachio, Act 3, Sc. 3, ll. 110–12

20 Comparisons are odorous.

Dogberry, Act 3, Sc. 5, l. 15. The saying 'Comparisons are odious' was already well known by the 15th century, and later appeared in the works of JOHN DONNE, CHRISTOPHER MARLOWE and CERVANTES.

21 A good old man, sir, he will be talking; as they say, 'When the age is in, the wit is out.'
Dogberry, Act 3, Sc. 5, ll. 32–3

22 O, what men dare do! What men may do! What men daily do, not knowing what they do!
Claudio, Act 4, Sc. 1, ll. 17–18

23 Manhood is melted into curtsies, valour into compliment, and men are only turned into tongue, and trim ones too.
Beatrice, Act 4, Sc. 1, ll. 313–15

24 Patch grief with proverbs.
Leonato, Act 5, Sc. 1, l. 17

25 For there was never yet philosopher
That could endure the toothache patiently.
Leonato, Act 5, Sc. 1, ll. 35–6

26 I was not born under a rhyming planet.
Benedick, Act 5, Sc. 2, ll. 39–40

Henry V
(1599)

1 O for a Muse of fire, that would ascend
The brightest heaven of invention,
A kingdom for a stage, princes to act,
And monarchs to behold the swelling scene!
Prologue, Chorus, ll. 1–4

2 Can this cockpit hold
The vasty fields of France? Or may we cram
Within this wooden O the very casques
That did affright the air at Agincourt?
Prologue, Chorus, ll. 11–14

3 Consideration like an angel came
And whipped th'offending Adam out of him.
Canterbury, Act 1, Sc. 1, ll. 28–9. Referring to the change that Henry underwent on becoming king.

4 When he speaks,
The air, a chartered libertine, is still,
And the mute wonder lurketh in men's ears
To steal his sweet and honeyed sentences.
Canterbury, of King Henry, Act 1, Sc. 1, ll. 47–50

5 Therefore doth heaven divide
The state of man in divers functions,
Setting endeavour in continual motion;
To which is fixed as an aim or butt
Obedience.
Canterbury, Act 1, Sc. 2, ll. 183–7

6 For so work the honey-bees,
Creatures that by a rule in nature teach
The act of order to a peopled kingdom.
They have a king, and officers of sorts,
Where some, like magistrates, correct at home;
Others, like merchants, venture trade abroad;
Others, like soldiers, armèd in their stings,
Make boot upon the summer's velvet buds;
Which pillage they with merry march bring home
To the tent-royal of their emperor;
Who, busied in his majesty, surveys
The singing masons building roofs of gold,
The civil citizens kneading up the honey,
The poor mechanic porters crowding in
Their heavy burdens at his narrow gate,
The sad-eyed justice, with his surly hum,
Delivering o'er to executors pale
The lazy yawning drone.
Canterbury, Act 1, Sc. 2, ll. 187–204

7 Now all the youth of England are on fire,
And silken dalliance in the wardrobe lies.
Act 2, Chorus, ll. 1–2

8 O England! model to thy inward greatness,
Like little body with a mighty heart,
What mightst thou do, that honour would thee do,
Were all thy children kind and natural!
Act 2, Chorus, ll. 16–19

9 Nay, sure, he's not in hell: he's in Arthur's bosom, if ever man went to Arthur's bosom.
Hostess (Mistress Quickly), of the dead Falstaff, Act 2, Sc. 3, ll. 9–10

10 After I saw him fumble with the sheets, and play with flowers, and smile upon his fingers' ends, I knew there was but one way; for his nose was as sharp as a pen, and 'a babbled of green fields.
Hostess (Mistress Quickly), Act 2, Sc. 3, ll. 13–17. Describing the death of Falstaff. The 1733 alteration of the Folio edition's 'table of green fields' to 'babbled of green fields' is one of the most famous of Shakespeare emendations.

11 Trust none;
For oaths are straws, men's faiths are wafer-cakes,
And Holdfast is the only dog, my duck.
Pistol to Hostess (Mistress Quickly), Act 2, Sc. 3, ll. 47–9

12 A vain, giddy, shallow, humorous youth.
Dauphin, of King Henry, Act 2, Sc. 4, l. 28

13 Once more unto the breach, dear friends, once more,
Or close the wall up with our English dead!

In peace there's nothing so becomes a man
As modest stillness and humility:
But when the blast of war blows in our ears,
Then imitate the action of the tiger;
Stiffen the sinews, conjure up the blood,
Disguise fair nature with hard-favoured rage;
Then lend the eye a terrible aspect.

King Henry, Act 3, Sc. 1, ll. 1–9. Address to the troops at the siege of Harfleur.

14 The game's afoot!
Follow your spirit, and upon this charge
Cry, 'God for Harry, England, and Saint George!'

King Henry, Act 3, Sc. 1, ll. 32–4

15 He hath a killing tongue, and a quiet sword.

Boy, of Pistol, Act 3, Sc. 2, l. 34

16 Is not their climate foggy, raw, and dull,
On whom, as in despite, the sun looks pale,
Killing their fruit with frowns?

Constable, of the English, Act 3, Sc. 5, ll. 16–18

17 Give them great meals of beef, and iron and steel;
they will eat like wolves, and fight like devils.

Constable, of the English, Act 3, Sc. 7, ll. 145–7

18 Now entertain conjecture of a time
When creeping murmur and the poring dark
Fills the wide vessel of the universe.

Act 4, Chorus, ll. 1–3

19 Who will behold
The royal Captain of this ruined band
Walking from watch to watch, from tent to tent.

Act 4, Chorus, ll. 28–30

20 A little touch of Harry in the night.

Act 4, Chorus, l. 47

21 The King's a bawcock, and a heart of gold,
A lad of life, an imp of fame;
Of parents good, of fist most valiant.
I kiss his dirty shoe, and from heartstring
I love the lovely bully.

Pistol, Act 4, Sc. 1, ll. 44–8

22 The King is but a man as I am. The violet smells to him as it doth to me; the element shows to him as it doth to me; all his senses have but human conditions. His ceremonies laid by, in his nakedness he appears but a man; and though his affections are higher mounted than ours, yet when they stoop, they stoop with the like wing.

King Henry (in disguise), Act 4, Sc. 1, ll. 99–105

23 Every subject's duty is the King's, but every subject's soul is his own.

King Henry (in disguise), Act 4, Sc. 1, ll. 171–2

24 What infinite heart's ease
Must kings neglect that private men enjoy!
And what have kings that privates have not too,
Save ceremony, save general ceremony?
And what art thou, thou idol ceremony?
What kind of god art thou, that suffer'st more
Of mortal griefs than do thy worshippers?
What are thy rents? What are thy comings-in?
O ceremony, show me but thy worth!

King Henry, Act 4, Sc. 1, ll. 229–37

25 O that we now had here
But one ten thousand of those men in England
That do no work today!

Westmorland, Act 4, Sc. 3, ll. 16–18

26 If we are marked to die, we are enough
To do our country loss; and if to live,
The fewer men, the greater share of honour.

King Henry, Act 4, Sc. 3, ll. 20–2

27 But if it be a sin to covet honour,
I am the most offending soul alive.

King Henry, Act 4, Sc. 3, ll. 28–9

28 This day is called the Feast of Crispian:
He that outlives this day, and comes safe home,
Will stand a-tiptoe when this day is named,
And rouse him at the name of Crispian.

King Henry, Act 4, Sc. 3, ll. 40–3

29 We few, we happy few, we band of brothers:
For he today that sheds his blood with me
Shall be my brother; be he ne'er so vile,
This day shall gentle his condition;
And gentlemen in England now abed
Shall think themselves accursed they were not
  here,
And hold their manhoods cheap whiles any speaks
That fought with us upon Saint Crispin's day.

King Henry, Act 4, Sc. 3, ll. 60–7. Before the battle of Agincourt.

30 By this leek, I will most horribly revenge – I eat and eat, I swear.

Pistol, Act 5, Sc. 1, ll. 44–5. On being forced to eat a leek by the Welsh Fluellen.

As You Like It
(c. 1599)

1 They say many young gentlemen flock to him every day, and fleet the time carelessly, as they did in the golden world.
Charles, Act 1, Sc. 1, ll. 110–12. Referring to the banished Duke (Duke Senior) in the Forest of Arden.

2 Those that she makes fair she scarce makes honest, and those that she makes honest she makes very ill-favouredly.
Celia, Act 1, Sc. 2, ll. 36–8. Referring to 'the good housewife Fortune'. 'Honest' here means 'chaste'.

3 For always the dullness of the fool is the whetstone of the wits.
Celia, Act 1, Sc. 2, ll. 52–3. Possibly a punning reference to *The Whetstone of Witte*, a famous treatise on algebra by Robert Recorde published in 1557.

4 Hereafter, in a better world than this,
I shall desire more love and knowledge of you.
Le Beau to Orlando, Act 1, Sc. 2, ll. 273–4

5 O, how full of briars is this working-day world!
Rosalind, Act 1, Sc. 3, ll. 11–12

6 Hath not old custom made this life more sweet
Than that of painted pomp? Are not these woods
More free from peril than the envious court?
Here feel we not the penalty of Adam,
The seasons' difference, as the icy fang
And churlish chiding of the winter's wind,
Which when it bites and blows upon my body,
Even till I shrink with cold, I smile and say
'This is no flattery; these are counsellors
That feelingly persuade me what I am'?
Duke Senior, Act 2, Sc. 1, ll. 2–11

7 Sweet are the uses of adversity,
Which, like the toad, ugly and venomous,
Wears yet a precious jewel in his head.
Duke Senior, Act 2, Sc. 1, ll. 12–14

8 And this our life, exempt from public haunt,
Finds tongues in trees, books in the running brooks,
Sermons in stones, and good in everything.
Duke Senior, Act 2, Sc. 1, ll. 15–17

9 Though I look old, yet I am strong and lusty,
For in my youth I never did apply
Hot and rebellious liquors in my blood,
Nor did not with unbashful forehead woo
The means of weakness and debility;

Therefore my age is as a lusty winter,
Frosty, but kindly.
Adam, Act 2, Sc. 3, ll. 47–53

10 O good old man, how well in thee appears
The constant service of the antique world,
When service sweat for duty, not for meed!
Thou art not for the fashion of these times,
Where none will sweat but for promotion.
Orlando praising Adam, Act 2, Sc. 3, ll. 56–60

11 Ay, now am I in Arden, the more fool I. When I was at home I was in a better place, but travellers must be content.
Touchstone, Act 2, Sc. 4, ll. 13–15

12 We that are true lovers run into strange capers.
Touchstone, Act 2, Sc. 4, ll. 49–50

13 I can suck melancholy out of a song, as a weasel sucks eggs.
Jaques, Act 2, Sc. 5, ll. 11–12

14 Who doth ambition shun,
And loves to live i' th' sun,
Seeking the food he eats,
And pleased with what he gets:
Come hither, come hither, come hither.
Here shall he see
No enemy
But winter and rough weather.
Song, Act 2, Sc. 5, ll. 35–42

15 'Tis but an hour ago since it was nine,
And after one hour more 'twill be eleven.
And so from hour to hour we ripe, and ripe,
And then from hour to hour we rot, and rot,
And thereby hangs a tale.
The 'motley fool' Touchstone, reported by Jaques, Act 2, Sc. 7, ll. 24–8

16 My lungs began to crow like Chanticleer,
That fools should be so deep-contemplative;
And I did laugh, sans intermission,
An hour by his dial. O noble fool!
A worthy fool: motley's the only wear!
Jaques, Act 2, Sc. 7, ll. 30–4. Motley garments were the traditional dress of professional jesters, probably quartered in primary colours, or else woven from different coloured threads.

17 True is it that we have seen better days.
Duke Senior, Act 2, Sc. 7, l. 121

18 All the world's a stage,
And all the men and women merely players;
They have their exits and their entrances,

And one man in his time plays many parts,
His Acts being seven ages. At first the infant,
Mewling and puking in the nurse's arms;
Then the whining schoolboy, with his satchel
And shining morning face, creeping like snail
Unwillingly to school; and then the lover,
Sighing like furnace, with a woeful ballad
Made to his mistress' eyebrow; then, a soldier,
Full of strange oaths, and bearded like the pard,
Jealous in honour, sudden and quick in quarrel,
Seeking the bubble reputation
Even in the cannon's mouth; and then, the
   justice,
In fair round belly, with good capon lined,
With eyes severe, and beard of formal cut,
Full of wise saws and modern instances,
And so he plays his part; the sixth age shifts
Into the lean and slippered pantaloon,
With spectacles on nose and pouch on side,
His youthful hose, well saved, a world too wide
For his shrunk shank, and his big manly voice,
Turning again toward childish treble, pipes
And whistles in his sound; last Scene of all,
That ends this strange eventful history,
Is second childishness, and mere oblivion,
Sans teeth, sans eyes, sans taste, sans everything.
Jaques, Act 2, Sc. 7, ll. 140–67

19 Blow, blow, thou winter wind.
Thou art not so unkind
As man's ingratitude.
Song sung by Amiens, Act 2, Sc. 7, ll. 175–7

20 Sir, I am a true labourer: I earn that I eat, get
that I wear, owe no man hate, envy no man's happiness, glad of other men's good, content with my
harm; and the greatest of my pride is to see my
ewes graze and my lambs suck.
Corin, Act 3, Sc. 2, ll. 69–73

21 Let us make an honourable retreat, though not
with bag and baggage, yet with scrip and scrippage.
Touchstone, Act 3, Sc. 2, ll. 156–8

22 O wonderful, wonderful, and most wonderful
wonderful, and yet again wonderful, and after that
out of all whooping!
Celia, Act 3, Sc. 2, ll. 185–7

23 Do you not know I am a woman? When I think,
I must speak. Sweet, say on.
Rosalind, Act 3, Sc. 2, ll. 242–3

24 I do desire we may be better strangers.
Orlando to Jaques, Act 3, Sc. 2, l. 251

25 There's no clock in the forest.
Orlando, Act 3, Sc. 2, ll. 292–3

26 Time travels in divers paces with divers persons.
I'll tell you who Time ambles withal, who Time trots
withal, who Time gallops withal and who he stands
still withal.
Rosalind (disguised as Ganymede), Act 3, Sc. 2, ll. 299–302

27 Praised be the gods for thy foulness; sluttishness
may come hereafter. But be it as it may be, I will
marry thee.
Touchstone, Act 3, Sc. 3, ll. 36–8. In response to Audrey's
remark: 'I am not a slut, though I thank the gods I am foul.'

28 I pray you, do not fall in love with me,
For I am falser than vows made in wine.
Rosalind (disguised as Ganymede) to Phebe, Act 3, Sc. 5, ll. 72–3

29 A traveller! By my faith, you have great reason
to be sad.
Rosalind (disguised as Ganymede) to Jaques, Act 4, Sc. 1, ll. 19–
20

30 I had rather have a fool to make me merry than
experience to make me sad.
Rosalind (disguised as Ganymede), Act 4, Sc. 1, ll. 24–6

31 Farewell, Monsieur Traveller. Look you lisp and
wear strange suits; disable all the benefits of your
own country; be out of love with your nativity, and
almost chide God for making you that countenance
you are; or I will scarce think you have swam in a
gondola.
Rosalind (disguised as Ganymede) to the departing Jaques,
Act 4, Sc. 1, ll. 29–34

32 Come, woo me, woo me: for now I am in a holiday
humour, and like enough to consent.
Rosalind to Orlando, Act 4, Sc. 1, ll. 61–2

33 Men have died from time to time and worms
have eaten them, but not for love.
Rosalind, Act 4, Sc. 1, ll. 96–8

34 No sooner met but they looked; no sooner looked
but they loved; no sooner loved but they sighed;
no sooner sighed but they asked one another the
reason; no sooner knew the reason but they sought
the remedy: and in these degrees have they
made a pair of stairs to marriage which they will

climb incontinent or else be incontinent before marriage.

Rosalind, disguised as Ganymede, Act 5, Sc. 2, ll. 31–8. Referring to Oliver and Celia.

35 O, how bitter a thing it is to look into happiness through another man's eyes!

Orlando, Act 5, Sc. 2, ll. 41–2

36 It is to be all made of fantasy,
All made of passion, and all made of wishes;
All adoration, duty and observance,
All humbleness, all patience, and impatience,
All purity, all trial, all observance.

Silvius, describing love, Act 5, Sc. 2, ll. 89–93

37 A poor virgin, sir, an ill-favoured thing, sir, but mine own.

Touchstone to Duke Senior, Act 5, Sc. 4, ll. 56–7. Referring to Audrey. Usually quoted 'A poor thing . . . but mine own.'

38 I will name you the degrees. The first, the Retort Courteous; the second, the Quip Modest; the third, the Reply Churlish; the fourth, the Reproof Valiant; the fifth, the Countercheck Quarrelsome; the sixth, the Lie with Circumstance; the seventh, the Lie Direct.

Touchstone, listing the degrees of lying, Act 5, Sc. 4, ll. 88–93

39 Your 'If' is the only peace-maker; much virtue in 'If'.

Touchstone, Act 5, Sc. 4, ll. 99–100

40 He uses his folly like a stalking-horse, and under the presentation of that he shoots his wit.

Duke Senior, Act 5, Sc. 4, ll. 103–4. Referring to Touchstone.

Julius Caesar
(c. 1599)

1 Beware the ides of March.

Soothsayer, Act 1, Sc. 2, l. 18. The warning is repeated in l. 23, and rejected by Caesar ('He is a dreamer. Let us leave him'). According to the Julian calendar, the ides were the 15th day in March, May, July and October.

2 Set honour in one eye, and death i'th'other,
And I will look on both indifferently.

Brutus, Act 1, Sc. 2, ll. 86–7

3 Honour is the subject of my story.

Cassius, Act 1, Sc. 2, l. 92

4 Why, man, he doth bestride the narrow world
Like a Colossus, and we petty men
Walk under his huge legs, and peep about
To find ourselves dishonourable graves.

Men at some time are masters of their fates;
The fault, dear Brutus, is not in our stars,
But in ourselves, that we are underlings.

Cassius, of Caesar, Act 1, Sc. 2, ll. 134–40

5 Upon what meat doth this our Caesar feed,
That he is grown so great?

Cassius, Act 1, Sc. 2, ll. 148–9

6 Let me have men about me that are fat,
Sleek-headed men, and such as sleep a-nights.
Yond Cassius has a lean and hungry look;
He thinks too much; such men are dangerous.

Caesar, Act 1, Sc. 2, ll. 191–4

7 He reads much,
He is a great observer, and he looks
Quite through the deeds of men. He loves no plays,
As thou dost, Antony; he hears no music;
Seldom he smiles, and smiles in such a sort
As if he mocked himself, and scorned his spirit
That could be moved to smile at anything.

Caesar, of Cassius, Act 1, Sc. 2, ll. 200–6

8 Those that understood him smiled at one another, and shook their heads; but for mine own part, it was Greek to me.

Casca, of Cicero, Act 1, Sc. 2, ll. 279–81

9 Cassius from bondage will deliver Cassius.
Therein, ye gods, you make the weak most strong;
Therein, ye gods, you tyrants do defeat.
Nor stony tower, nor walls of beaten brass,
Nor airless dungeon, nor strong links of iron,
Can be retentive to the strength of spirit;
But life, being weary of these worldly bars,
Never lacks power to dismiss itself.
If I know this, know all the world besides,
That part of tyranny that I do bear
I can shake off at leisure.

Cassius, Act 1, Sc. 3, ll. 90–100

10 It is the bright day that brings forth the adder,
And that craves wary walking.

Brutus, Act 2, Sc. 1, ll. 14–15

11 Th'abuse of greatness is when it disjoins
Remorse from power.

Brutus, Act 2, Sc. 1, ll. 18–19

12 Between the acting of a dreadful thing
And the first motion, all the interim is
Like a phantasma or a hideous dream.

Brutus, Act 2, Sc. 1, ll. 63–5

13 O conspiracy,
Sham'st thou to show thy dangerous brow by
    night,
When evils are most free? O then, by day
Where wilt thou find a cavern dark enough
To mask thy monstrous visage?
Brutus, Act 2, Sc. 1, ll. 77–81

14 Let us be sacrificers, but not butchers, Caius.

    . . .

Let's kill him boldly, but not wrathfully;
Let's carve him as a dish fit for the gods,
Not hew him as a carcass fit for hounds.
Brutus, Act 2, Sc. 1, ll. 166 and 172–4. Discussing the assassina-
tion of Caesar.

15 Enjoy the honey-heavy dew of slumber;
Thou hast no figures nor no fantasies,
Which busy care draws in the brains of men.
Brutus, Act 2, Sc. 1, ll. 230–2. To the boy Lucius, asleep.

16 What, is Brutus sick?
And will he steal out of his wholesome bed
To dare the vile contagion of the night?
Portia, Act 2, Sc. 1, ll. 263–5

17 Am I your self
But, as it were, in sort or limitation,
To keep with you at meals, comfort your bed,
And talk to you sometimes? Dwell I but in the
    suburbs
Of your good pleasure?
Portia, Act 2, Sc. 1, ll. 282–6. To her husband, Brutus.

18 When beggars die, there are no comets seen;
The heavens themselves blaze forth the death of
    princes.
Calphurnia, Act 2, Sc. 2, ll. 30–1

19 Cowards die many times before their deaths;
The valiant never taste of death but once.
Caesar, Act 2, Sc. 2, ll. 32–3

20 But I am constant as the northern star,
Of whose true-fixed and resting quality
There is no fellow in the firmament.
Caesar, Act 3, Sc. 1, ll. 60–2

21 *Et tu, Brute?* – Then fall Caesar!
Caesar, Act 3, Sc. 1, l. 77. Dying words. Brutus was among
the conspirators who stabbed Caesar. In his biography *Julius
Caesar*, Suetonius ascribes to Caesar an utterance in Greek
from which this phrase could be derived. The words had
occurred in previous dramas of the period.

22 Ambition's debt is paid.
Brutus, Act 3, Sc. 1, l. 83. On the assassination of Caesar.

23 How many ages hence
Shall this our lofty scene be acted over,
In states unborn, and accents yet unknown!
Cassius, Act 3, Sc. 1, ll. 111–13. On the assassination of Caesar.

24 O mighty Caesar! Dost thou lie so low?
Are all thy conquests, glories, triumphs, spoils
Shrunk to this little measure?
Antony, Act 3, Sc. 1, ll. 148–50. On seeing Caesar's corpse.

25 The choice and master spirits of this age.
Antony, Act 3, Sc. 1, l. 163. Referring to Caesar's killers.

26 And Caesar's spirit, ranging for revenge,
With Ate by his side, come hot from hell,
Shall in these confines with a monarch's voice
Cry havoc and let slip the dogs of war,
That this foul deed shall smell above the earth
With carrion men, groaning for burial.
Antony, Act 3, Sc. 1, ll. 270–5. Prophesying the turmoil follow-
ing Caesar's assassination. Ate was, according to Hesiod, the
daughter of Strife, cast out of Olympus by Zeus.

27 Not that I loved Caesar less, but that I loved Rome
more.
Brutus, Act 3, Sc. 2, ll. 21–2. Justifying his part in Caesar's
assassination.

28 As he was valiant, I honour him; but, as he was
ambitious, I slew him.
Brutus, of Caesar, Act 3, Sc. 2, ll. 25–6

29 Friends, Romans, countrymen, lend me your
ears;
I come to bury Caesar, not to praise him.
The evil that men do lives after them,
The good is oft interrèd with their bones.
Antony, Act 3, Sc. 2, ll. 74–7. Delivering Caesar's funeral
oration.

30 For Brutus is an honourable man;
So are they all, all honourable men.
Antony, Act 3, Sc. 2, ll. 83–4. The words 'Brutus is an honour-
able man' are repeated throughout the funeral oration.

31 When that the poor hath cried, Caesar hath
wept;
Ambition should be made of sterner stuff.
Antony, Act 3, Sc. 2, ll. 92–3

32 O judgement! thou art fled to brutish beasts,
And men have lost their reason.
Antony, Act 3, Sc. 2, ll. 105–6

33 If you have tears, prepare to shed them now.
Antony, Act 3, Sc. 2, l. 170. To the plebeians, in Caesar's funeral
oration.

34 This was the most unkindest cut of all.
Antony, Act 3, Sc. 2, l. 184. Of Brutus's stabbing of Caesar.

35 I come not, friends, to steal away your hearts;
I am no orator, as Brutus is,
But, as you know me all, a plain, blunt man,
That love my friend.
Antony, Act 3, Sc. 2, ll. 217–20

36 For I have neither wit, nor words, nor worth,
Action, nor utterance, nor the power of speech,
To stir men's blood; I only speak right on.
I tell you that which you yourselves do know.
Antony, Act 3, Sc. 2, ll. 222–5

37 Here was a Caesar! When comes such another?
Antony, Act 3, Sc. 2, l. 253

38 Now let it work. Mischief, thou art afoot,
Take thou what course thou wilt.
Antony, Act 3, Sc. 2, ll. 262–3

39 When love begins to sicken and decay,
It useth an enforcèd ceremony.
Brutus, Act 4, Sc. 2, ll. 20–1

40 Let me tell you, Cassius, you yourself
Are much condemned to have an itching palm.
Brutus, Act 4, Sc. 3, ll. 9–10

41 I had rather be a dog, and bay the moon,
Than such a Roman.
Brutus, Act 4, Sc. 3, ll. 27–8. Warning against involvement in bribery.

42 Good reasons must of force give place to better.
Brutus, Act 4, Sc. 3, l. 201

43 There is a tide in the affairs of men,
Which, taken at the flood, leads on to fortune;
Omitted, all the voyage of their life
Is bound in shallows and in miseries.
Brutus, Act 4, Sc. 2, ll. 216–19. BYRON adapted this passage in Don Juan, canto 6, st. 2 (1823): 'There is a tide in the affairs of women,/Which, taken at the flood, leads – God knows where.'

44 The deep of night is crept upon our talk,
And nature must obey necessity,
Which we will niggard with a little rest.
Brutus, Act 4, Sc. 2, ll. 224–6

45 But for your words, they rob the Hybla bees,
And leave them honeyless.
Cassius, to Antony, Act 5, Sc. 1, ll. 34–5

46 If we do meet again, why, we shall smile;
If not, why then this parting was well made.
Brutus, Act 5, Sc. 1, ll. 117–18. Bidding farewell to Cassius before battle.

47 O Julius Caesar, thou art mighty yet!
Thy spirit walks abroad, and turns our swords
In our own proper entrails.
Brutus, Act 5, Sc. 3, ll. 94–6

48 This was the noblest Roman of them all.
Antony, of Brutus, Act 5, Sc. 5, l. 68

49 His life was gentle, and the elements
So mixed in him, that nature might stand up
And say to all the world, 'This was a man!'
Antony, of Brutus, Act 5, Sc. 5, ll. 73–5

Hamlet
(c. 1600)

1 For this relief much thanks. 'Tis bitter cold,
And I am sick at heart.
Francisco, Act 1, Sc. 1, ll. 8–9

2 Not a mouse stirring.
Francisco, Act 1, Sc. 1, l. 10

3 This bodes some strange eruption to our state.
Horatio, Act 1, Sc. 1, l. 69

4 In the most high and palmy state of Rome,
A little ere the mightiest Julius fell,
The graves stood tenantless and the sheeted dead
Did squeak and gibber in the Roman streets.
Horatio, Act 1, Sc. 1, ll. 113–16

5 And then it started, like a guilty thing
Upon a fearful summons.
Horatio, of the ghost, Act 1, Sc. 1, ll. 149–50

6 It faded on the crowing of the cock.
Some say that ever 'gainst that season comes
Wherein our Saviour's birth is celebrated,
This bird of dawning singeth all night long.
And then, they say, no spirit dares stir abroad;
The nights are wholesome; then no planets strike;
No fairy takes; nor witch hath power to charm.
So hallowed and so gracious is the time.
Marcellus, of the ghost, Act 1, Sc. 1, ll. 158–65

7 The morn, in russet mantle clad
Walks o'er the dew of yon high eastward hill.
Horatio, Act 1, Sc. 1, ll. 167–8

8 Our sometime sister, now our queen.
Claudius, of Gertrude, Act 1, Sc. 2, l. 8

9 The head is not more native to the heart,
The hand more instrumental to the mouth,
Than is the throne of Denmark to thy father.
Claudius, to Laertes, Act 1, Sc. 2, ll. 47–9. Referring to Polonius.

10 A little more than kin, and less than kind!
Hamlet, Act 1, Sc. 2, l. 65

11 Do not for ever with thy vailèd lids
Seek for thy noble father in the dust.
Thou knowest 'tis common. All that lives must
    die,
Passing through nature to eternity.
Gertrude, to Hamlet, Act 1, Sc. 2, ll. 70–3

12 'Seems', madam? Nay, it is. I know not 'seems'.
Hamlet, to Gertrude, Act 1, Sc. 2, l. 76

13 But I have that within which passes show –
These but the trappings and the suits of woe.
Hamlet, Act 1, Sc. 2, ll. 85–6

14 To persever
In obstinate condolement is a course
Of impious stubbornness. 'Tis unmanly grief.
Claudius, Act 1, Sc. 2, ll. 92–4

15 O that this too too sullied flesh would melt,
Thaw, and resolve itself into a dew;
Or that the Everlasting had not fixed
His canon 'gainst self-slaughter.
Hamlet, Act 1, Sc. 2, ll. 129–32. Usually quoted 'solid flesh' in
l. 129, following the text of the first Folio edition.

16 O God, God,
How weary, stale, flat, and unprofitable
Seem to me all the uses of this world!
Fie on't, ah, fie, 'tis an unweeded garden
That grows to seed. Things rank and gross in
    nature
Possess it merely.
Hamlet, Act 1, Sc. 2, ll. 132–7

17 So excellent a king, that was to this
Hyperion to a satyr; so loving to my mother
That he might not beteem the winds of heaven
Visit her face too roughly. Heaven and earth,
Must I remember? Why, she would hang on him
As if increase of appetite had grown
By what it fed on.
Hamlet, of his father, Act 1, Sc. 2, ll. 139–45

18 Frailty, thy name is woman.
Hamlet, Act 1, Sc. 2, l. 146

19 A beast that wants discourse of reason
Would have mourned longer.
Hamlet, Act 1, Sc. 2, ll. 150–1. Of his mother's recovery from
her husband's death, after she had mourned him 'Like Niobe,
all tears'.

20 It is not, nor it cannot come to good.
But break, my heart, for I must hold my tongue.
Hamlet, Act 1, Sc. 2, ll. 158–9

21 A truant disposition, good my lord.
Horatio, Act 1, Sc. 2, l. 169

22 We'll teach you to drink deep ere you depart.
Hamlet to Horatio, Act 1, Sc. 2, l. 175

23 The funeral baked meats
Did coldly furnish forth the marriage tables.
Horatio, Act 1, Sc. 2, ll. 180–1

24 Hamlet: My father – methinks I see my
    father.
Horatio: Where, my lord?
Hamlet: In my mind's eye, Horatio.
Act 1, Sc. 2, ll. 184–5

25 'A was a man. Take him for all in all,
I shall not look upon his like again.
Hamlet, Act 1, Sc. 2, ll. 187–8

26 Distilled
Almost to jelly with the act of fear.
Horatio, Act 1, Sc. 2, ll. 204–5

27 My father's spirit! In arms! All is not well.
I doubt some foul play. Would the night were
    come!
Till then sit still, my soul. Foul deeds will rise,
Though all the earth o'erwhelm them, to men's
    eyes.
Hamlet, Act 1, Sc. 2, ll. 255–8

28 I shall the effect of this good lesson keep
As watchman to my heart.
Ophelia, Act 1, Sc. 3, ll. 45–6. Of the lengthy advice given to
her by her brother Laertes.

29 Do not, as some ungracious pastors do,
Show me the steep and thorny way to heaven
Whiles like a puffed and reckless libertine
Himself the primrose path of dalliance treads
And recks not his own rede.
Ophelia, Act 1, Sc. 3, ll. 47–51. See SHAKESPEARE:
MACBETH 43.

30 Give thy thoughts no tongue,
Nor any unproportioned thought his act.
Be thou familiar, but by no means vulgar.
Polonius, Act 1, Sc. 3, ll. 59–61. Giving advice to his son Laertes,
departing for France.

31 Those friends thou hast, and their adoption
    tried,
Grapple them unto thy soul with hoops of steel.

But do not dull thy palm with entertainment
Of each new-hatched, unfledged courage.
Polonius to Laertes, Act 1, Sc. 3, ll. 62–5

32 Give every man thine ear but few thy voice.
Take each man's censure, but reserve thy
    judgement.
Polonius to Laertes, Act 1, Sc. 3, ll. 68–9

33 Costly thy habit as thy purse can buy,
But not expressed in fancy; rich, not gaudy;
For the apparel oft proclaims the man.
Polonius to Laertes, Act 1, Sc. 3, ll. 70–2

34 Neither a borrower nor a lender be,
For loan oft loses both itself and friend,
And borrowing dulleth edge of husbandry.
Polonius to Laertes, Act 1, Sc. 3, ll. 75–7

35 This above all: to thine own self be true,
And it must follow, as the night the day,
Thou canst not then be false to any man.
Polonius to Laertes, Act 1, Sc. 3, ll. 78–80

36 'Tis in my memory locked,
And you yourself shall keep the key of it.
Ophelia, Act 1, Sc. 3, ll. 85–6

37 Pooh! You speak like a green girl,
Unsifted in such perilous circumstance.
Polonius to Ophelia, Act 1, Sc. 3, ll. 101–2

38 Ay, springes to catch woodcocks.
Polonius, Act 1, Sc. 3, l. 115. Of Hamlet's vows to Ophelia. See
also SHAKESPEARE: HAMLET 158.

39 But to my mind, though I am native here
And to the manner born, it is a custom
More honoured in the breach than the observance.
Hamlet, Act 1, Sc. 4, ll. 14–16. Referring to the custom of
fanfares accompanying the king's toast-making.

40 Angels and ministers of grace defend us!
Be thou a spirit of health or goblin damned,
Bring with thee airs from heaven or blasts from
    hell.
Hamlet, on seeing the ghost, Act 1, Sc. 4, ll. 39–41

41 I do not set my life at a pin's fee.
And for my soul, what can it do to that,
Being a thing immortal as itself?
Hamlet, Act 1, Sc. 4, ll. 65–7

42 Unhand me, gentlemen.
By heaven, I'll make a ghost of him that lets me!
Hamlet, Act 1, Sc. 4, ll. 84–5

43 Something is rotten in the state of Denmark.
Marcellus, Act 1, Sc. 4, l. 90

44 I am thy father's spirit,
Doomed for a certain term to walk the night,
And for the day confined to fast in fires,
Till the foul crimes done in my days of nature
Are burnt and purged away.
Ghost, Act 1, Sc. 5, ll. 9–13

45 But that I am forbid
To tell the secrets of my prison house,
I could a tale unfold whose lightest word
Would harrow up thy soul, freeze thy young blood,
Make thy two eyes like stars start from their
    spheres,
Thy knotted and combined locks to part,
And each particular hair to stand on end
Like quills upon the fretful porpentine.
Ghost, Act 1, Sc. 5, ll. 13–20

46 Revenge his foul and most unnatural murder.
Ghost, Act 1, Sc. 5, l. 25

47 Murder most foul, as in the best it is,
But this most foul, strange, and unnatural.
Ghost, Act 1, Sc. 5, ll. 27–8

48 O my prophetic soul!
Hamlet, Act 1, Sc. 5, l. 40

49 But soft, methinks I scent the morning air.
Ghost, Act 1, Sc. 5, l. 58

50 Thus was I sleeping by a brother's hand
Of life, of crown, of queen at once dispatched,
Cut off even in the blossoms of my sin,
Unhouseled, disappointed, unaneled,
No reckoning made, but sent to my account
With all my imperfections on my head.
O, horrible! O, horrible! Most horrible!
Ghost, Act 1, Sc. 5, ll. 74–80

51 Taint not thy mind, nor let thy soul contrive
Against thy mother aught. Leave her to heaven
And to those thorns that in her bosom lodge
To prick and sting her.
Ghost, Act 1, Sc. 5, ll. 85–8

52 O most pernicious woman!
O villain, villain, smiling, damnèd villain!
My tables – meet it is I set it down
That one may smile, and smile, and be a villain.
Hamlet, Act 1, Sc. 5, ll. 105–8

53 These are but wild and whirling words.
Horatio, Act 1, Sc. 5, l. 133

54 There are more things in heaven and earth, Horatio,
Than are dreamt of in your philosophy.
Hamlet, Act 1, Sc. 5, ll. 166–7

55 To put an antic disposition on.
Hamlet, Act 1, Sc. 5, l. 172

56 Rest, rest, perturbèd spirit!
Hamlet, to the Ghost, Act 1, Sc. 5, l. 182

57 The time is out of joint. O, cursèd spite,
That ever I was born to set it right!
Hamlet, Act 1, Sc. 5, ll. 188–9

58 Brevity is the soul of wit,
And tediousness the limbs and outward flourishes.
Polonius, Act 2, Sc. 2, ll. 90–1

59 I will be brief. Your noble son is mad.
Mad call I it. For, to define true madness,
What is't but to be nothing else but mad?
Polonius, to Gertrude, Act 2, Sc. 2, ll. 92–4

60 More matter, with less art.
Gertrude, Act 2, Sc. 2, l. 95

61 Doubt thou the stars are fire.
Doubt that the sun doth move.
Doubt truth to be a liar.
But never doubt I love.
Polonius, Act 2, Sc. 2, ll. 115–18. Reading a letter from Hamlet to Ophelia.

62 Words, words, words.
Hamlet, Act 2, Sc. 2, l. 193. In response to Polonius's question: 'What do you read, my lord?'

63 Though this be madness, yet there is method in't.
Polonius, Act 2, Sc. 2, ll. 205–6

64 There is nothing either good or bad but thinking makes it so.
Hamlet, Act 2, Sc. 2, ll. 248–9

65 O God, I could be bounded in a nutshell and count myself a king of infinite space, were it not that I have bad dreams.
Hamlet, Act 2, Sc. 2, ll. 253–5

66 I have of late – but wherefore I know not – lost all my mirth, forgone all custom of exercises. And indeed it goes so heavily with my disposition that this goodly frame the earth seems to me a sterile promontory. This most excellent canopy, the air, look you, this brave o'erhanging firmament, this majestical roof fretted with golden fire – why, it appeareth nothing to me but a foul and pestilent congregation of vapours.
Hamlet, Act 2, Sc. 2, ll. 295–303

67 What a piece of work is a man, how noble in reason, how infinite in faculties, in form and moving how express and admirable, in action how like an angel, in apprehension how like a god: the beauty of the world, the paragon of animals!
Hamlet, Act 2, Sc. 2, ll. 303–7

68 And yet, to me, what is this quintessence of dust? Man delights not me – nor woman neither.
Hamlet, Act 2, Sc. 2, ll. 307–9

69 There is something in this more than natural, if philosophy could find it out.
Hamlet, Act 2, Sc. 2, ll. 365–7

70 I am but mad north-north-west. When the wind is southerly, I know a hawk from a handsaw.
Hamlet, Act 2, Sc. 2, ll. 377–8

71 They say an old man is twice a child.
Rosencrantz, Act 2, Sc. 2, l. 384

72 The play, I remember, pleased not the million.
Hamlet, Act 2, Sc. 2, ll. 434–5

73 Good my lord, will you see the players well bestowed? Do you hear? Let them be well used, for they are the abstract and brief chronicles of the time. After your death you were better have a bad epitaph than their ill report while you live.
Hamlet to Polonius, Act 2, Sc. 2, ll. 520–4. Referring to the actors.

74 Use every man after his desert, and who should 'scape whipping? Use them after your own honour and dignity.
Hamlet, Act 2, Sc. 2, ll. 527–8

75 O, what a rogue and peasant slave am I!
Hamlet, Act 2, Sc. 2, l. 547

76 For Hecuba!
What's Hecuba to him, or he to her,
That he should weep for her?
Hamlet, Act 2, Sc. 2, ll. 555–7. Of the acting abilities of the players.

77 He would drown the stage with tears
And cleave the general ear with horrid speech,
Make mad the guilty and appal the free,
Confound the ignorant, and amaze indeed
The very faculties of eyes and ears.
Hamlet, Act 2, Sc. 2, ll. 559–63

78 Yet I,
A dull and muddy-mettled rascal.
Hamlet, Act 2, Sc. 2, ll. 563–4

79 But I am pigeon-livered and lack gall
To make oppression bitter.
Hamlet, Act 2, Sc. 2, ll. 574–5

80 Bloody, bawdy villain!
Remorseless, treacherous, lecherous, kindless
villain!
O, vengeance!
Hamlet, of Claudius, Act 2, Sc. 2, ll. 577–9

81 For murder, though it have no tongue, will
speak
With most miraculous organ.
Hamlet, Act 2, Sc. 2, ll. 591–2

82 The play's the thing
Wherein I'll catch the conscience of the King.
Hamlet, Act 2, Sc. 2, ll. 602–3

83 'Tis too much proved, that with devotion's
visage
And pious action we do sugar o'er
The devil himself.
Polonius, Act 3, Sc. 1, ll. 47–9

84 To be, or not to be – that is the question;
Whether 'tis nobler in the mind to suffer
The slings and arrows of outrageous fortune
Or to take arms against a sea of troubles
And by opposing end them.
Hamlet, Act 3, Sc. 1, ll. 56–60

85 The heartache and the thousand natural shocks
That flesh is heir to.
Hamlet, Act 3, Sc. 1, ll. 62–3

86 To sleep – perchance to dream.
Hamlet, Act 3, Sc. 1, l. 65

87 For in that sleep of death what dreams may
come
When we have shuffled off this mortal coil
Must give us pause.
Hamlet, Act 3, Sc. 1, ll. 66–8

88 For who would bear the whips and scorns of
time,
Th'oppressor's wrong, the proud man's contumely,
The pangs of despised love, the law's delay,
The insolence of office, and the spurns
That patient merit of th'unworthy takes,
When he himself might his quietus make

With a bare bodkin?
Hamlet, Act 3, Sc. 1, ll. 70–6

89 The dread of something after death,
The undiscovered country, from whose bourn
No traveller returns.
Hamlet, Act 3, Sc. 1, ll. 78–80

90 Thus conscience does make cowards of us all;
And thus the native hue of resolution
Is sicklied o'er with the pale cast of thought,
And enterprises of great pitch and moment
With this regard their currents turn awry
And lose the name of action.
Hamlet, Act 3, Sc. 1, ll. 83–8

91 Nymph, in thy orisons
Be all my sins remembered.
Hamlet, to Ophelia, Act 3, Sc. 1, ll. 89–90

92 To the noble mind
Rich gifts wax poor when givers prove unkind.
Ophelia, Act 3, Sc. 1, ll. 100–1

93 If you be honest and fair, your honesty should
admit no discourse to your beauty.
Hamlet, to Ophelia, Act 3, Sc. 1, ll. 107–8

94 Get thee to a nunnery. Why wouldst thou be a
breeder of sinners?
Hamlet, to Ophelia, Act 3, Sc. 1, ll. 121–2

95 Be thou as chaste as ice, as pure as snow, thou
shalt not escape calumny.
Hamlet, to Ophelia, Act 3, Sc. 1, ll. 136–7

96 If thou wilt needs marry, marry a fool. For wise
men know well enough what monsters you make of
them.
Hamlet, to Ophelia, Act 3, Sc. 1, ll. 138–40

97 God hath given you one face, and you make
yourselves another.
Hamlet, Act 3, Sc. 1, ll. 144–5

98 I say we will have no more marriage. Those that
are married already – all but one – shall live. The
rest shall keep as they are.
Hamlet, Act 3, Sc. 1, ll. 148–50

99 O, what a noble mind is here o'erthrown!
Ophelia, Act 3, Sc. 1, l. 151. Referring to Hamlet's bizarre
behaviour.

100 O, woe is me
T'have seen what I have seen, see what I see!
Ophelia, Act 3, Sc. 1, ll. 161–2

101 Madness in great ones must not unwatched go.
Claudius, Act 3, Sc. 1, l. 189

102 Speak the speech, I pray you, as I pronounced it to you, trippingly on the tongue. But if you mouth it as many of our players do, I had as lief the town crier spoke my lines. Nor do not saw the air too much with your hand, thus. But use all gently. For in the very torrent, tempest, and, as I may say, whirlwind of your passion, you must acquire and beget a temperance that may give it smoothness.
Hamlet, instructing the players, Act 3, Sc. 2, ll. 1–8

103 O, it offends me to the soul to hear a robustious periwig-pated fellow tear a passion to tatters, to very rags, to split the ears of the groundlings, who for the most part are capable of nothing but inexplicable dumb shows and noise. I would have such a fellow whipped for o'erdoing Termagant. It out-Herods Herod. Pray you avoid it.
Hamlet, instructing the players, Act 3, Sc. 2, ll. 8–14

104 Let your own discretion be your tutor. Suit the action to the word, the word to the action, with this special observance, that you o'erstep not the modesty of nature.
Hamlet, instructing the players, Act 3, Sc. 2, ll. 16–19

105 Though it make the unskilful laugh, cannot but make the judicious grieve.
Hamlet, Act 3, Sc. 2, ll. 25–6

106 Give me that man
That is not passion's slave, and I will wear him
In my heart's core, ay, in my heart of heart.
Hamlet, Act 3, Sc. 2, ll. 81–3

107 Here's metal more attractive.
Hamlet, of Ophelia, Act 3, Sc. 2, l. 119

108 Die two months ago, and not forgotten yet? Then there's hope a great man's memory may outlive his life half a year.
Hamlet, of his father, Act 3, Sc. 2, ll. 139–41

109 Ophelia: 'Tis brief, my lord.
Hamlet: As woman's love.
Act 3, Sc. 2, ll. 162–3

110 That's wormwood.
Hamlet, Act 3, Sc. 2, l. 191

111 The lady doth protest too much, methinks.
Queen Gertrude, Act 3, Sc. 2, l. 240. Referring to the Player Queen in the play-within-a-play.

112 Hamlet: They do but jest, poison in jest. No offence i' th'world.

Claudius: What do you call the play?
Hamlet: *The Mousetrap*.
Act 3, Sc. 2, ll. 244–7. *The Mousetrap* is the title of AGATHA CHRISTIE's's whodunnit which became the longest-running production in London's West End.

113 What, frighted with false fire?
Hamlet, of Claudius, Act 3, Sc. 2, l. 275

114 'Tis now the very witching time of night,
When churchyards yawn, and hell itself breathes out
Contagion to this world. Now could I drink hot blood
And do such bitter business as the day
Would quake to look on.
Hamlet, Act 3, Sc. 2, ll. 395–9

115 I will speak daggers to her, but use none.
My tongue and soul in this be hypocrites.
Hamlet, of his mother, Gertrude, Act 3, Sc. 2, ll. 403–4

116 O, my offence is rank. It smells to heaven.
It hath the primal eldest curse upon't,
A brother's murder.
Claudius, Act 3, Sc. 3, ll. 36–8

117 Bow, stubborn knees.
Claudius, Act 3, Sc. 3, l. 70

118 My words fly up, my thoughts remain below.
Words without thoughts never to heaven go.
Claudius, Act 3, Sc. 3, ll. 97–8

119 How now? A rat? Dead for a ducat, dead!
Hamlet, on killing Polonius, Act 3, Sc. 4, l. 25

120 A bloody deed – almost as bad, good mother,
As kill a king and marry with his brother.
Hamlet, Act 3, Sc. 4, ll. 29–30. Referring to his 'rash and bloody deed' of killing Polonius.

121 Thou wretched, rash, intruding fool, farewell!
I took thee for thy better.
Hamlet, Act 3, Sc. 4, ll. 32–3. Addressing the dead Polonius.

122 Speak no more.
Thou turnest mine eyes into my very soul.
Gertrude, to Hamlet, Act 3, Sc. 4, ll. 89–90

123 Nay, but to live
In the rank sweat of an enseamèd bed,
Stewed in corruption, honeying and making love
Over the nasty sty.
Hamlet, Act 3, Sc. 4, ll. 92–5

124 A king of shreds and patches.
Hamlet, of Claudius, Act 3, Sc. 4, l. 103

125 Assume a virtue, if you have it not.

Hamlet, to Gertrude, Act 3, Sc. 4, l. 161

126 I must be cruel only to be kind.

Hamlet, Act 3, Sc. 4, l. 179

127 For 'tis the sport to have the enginer
Hoist with his own petar.

Hamlet, Act 3, Sc. 4, ll. 207–8. Referring to the untrustworthiness of Rosencrantz and Guildenstern. A 'petar' or 'petard' was an explosive device used by engineers. The lines do not appear in the 1623 Folio edition.

128 Indeed, this counsellor
Is now most still, most secret, and most grave,
Who was in life a foolish prating knave.

Hamlet, of the dead Polonius, Act 3, Sc. 4, ll. 214–16

129 He's loved of the distracted multitude,
Who like not in their judgement but their eyes.

Claudius, of Hamlet, Act 4, Sc. 3, ll. 4–5

130 Diseases desperate grown
By desperate appliance are relieved,
Or not at all.

Claudius, Act 4, Sc. 3, ll. 9–10

131 We go to gain a little patch of ground
That hath in it no profit but the name.

Captain, Act 4, Sc. 4, ll. 18–19

132 What is a man,
If his chief good and market of his time
Be but to sleep and feed? A beast, no more.
Sure He that made us with such large discourse,
Looking before and after, gave us not
That capability and godlike reason
To fust in us unused.

Hamlet, Act 4, Sc. 4, ll. 33–9

133 Rightly to be great
Is not to stir without great argument,
But greatly to find quarrel in a straw
When honour's at the stake.

Hamlet, Act 4, Sc. 4, ll. 53–6

134 He is dead and gone, lady.
He is dead and gone.
At his head a grass-green turf,
At his heels a stone.

Ophelia's song, Act 4, Sc. 5, ll. 29–32

135 We know what we are, but know not what we may be.

Ophelia, Act 4, Sc. 5, ll. 43–4

136 Come, my coach! Good night, ladies, good night.
Sweet ladies, good night, good night.

Ophelia, Act 4, Sc. 5, ll. 71–3. The words were used at the end of *The Waste Land*, pt 2 (1922) by T. S. ELIOT.

137 When sorrows come, they come not single spies,
But in battalions.

Claudius, Act 4, Sc. 5, ll. 79–80

138 O heat, dry up my brains! Tears seven times salt
Burn out the sense and virtue of mine eye!

Laertes, Act 4, Sc. 5, ll. 156–7

139 There's rosemary, that's for remembrance. Pray you love, remember. And there is pansies, that's for thoughts.

Ophelia, Act 4, Sc. 5, ll. 176–8

140 There's fennel for you, and columbines. There's rue for you, and here's some for me. We may call it herb of grace o' Sundays. O, you must wear your rue with a difference. There's a daisy. I would give you some violets, but they withered all when my father died. They say 'a made a good end.

Ophelia, Act 4, Sc. 5, ll. 181–6

141 And where th'offence is, let the great axe fall.

Claudius, Act 4, Sc. 5, l. 218

142 Down her weedy trophies and herself
Fell in the weeping brook. Her clothes spread wide,
And mermaid-like awhile they bore her up;
Which time she chanted snatches of old tunes,
As one incapable of her own distress,
Or like a creature native and indued
Unto that element. But long it could not be
Till that her garments, heavy with their drink,
Pulled the poor wretch from her melodious lay
To muddy death.

Gertrude, Act 4, Sc. 7, ll. 174–83. Describing Ophelia's death by drowning.

143 Too much of water hast thou, poor Ophelia,
And therefore I forbid my tears. But yet
It is our trick. Nature her custom holds,
Let shame say what it will.

Laertes, Act 4, Sc. 7, ll. 185–8

144 There is no ancient gentlemen but gardeners, ditchers, and grave-makers. They hold up Adam's profession.

First Clown, Act 5, Sc. 1, ll. 29–31

145 Cudgel thy brains no more about it, for your dull ass will not mend his pace with beating.
First Clown, Act 5, Sc. 1, ll. 56–7

146 Where be his quiddities now, his quillets, his cases, his tenures, and his tricks?
Hamlet, Act 5, Sc. 1, ll. 97–8. Of a lawyer's skull.

147 Alas, poor Yorick! I knew him, Horatio. A fellow of infinite jest, of most excellent fancy . . . Where be your gibes now? Your gambols, your songs, your flashes of merriment that were wont to set the table on a roar?
Hamlet, Act 5, Sc. 1, ll. 181–8. Said of Hamlet's father's jester, whose skull has just been dug up.

148 Imperious Caesar, dead and turned to clay, Might stop a hole to keep the wind away.
Hamlet, Act 5, Sc. 1, ll. 209–10

149 Lay her i'th'earth,
And from her fair and unpolluted flesh
May violets spring! I tell thee, churlish priest,
A ministering angel shall my sister be
When thou liest howling.
Laertes, of Ophelia, Act 5, Sc. 1, ll. 234–8

150 Sweets to the sweet! Farewell.
I hoped thou shouldst have been my Hamlet's wife.
I thought thy bride-bed to have decked, sweet maid,
And not have strewed thy grave.
Gertrude, Act 5, Sc. 1, ll. 239–42. Scattering flowers on Ophelia's grave.

151 Though I am not splenitive and rash,
Yet have I in me something dangerous.
Hamlet, Act 5, Sc. 1, ll. 257–8

152 I loved Ophelia. Forty thousand brothers
Could not with all their quantity of love
Make up my sum.
Hamlet, Act 5, Sc. 1, ll. 265–7

153 Let Hercules himself do what he may,
The cat will mew, and dog will have his day.
Hamlet, Act 5, Sc. 1, ll. 287–8

154 There's a divinity that shapes our ends,
Rough-hew them how we will.
Hamlet, Act 5, Sc. 2, ll. 10–11

155 It did me yeoman's service.
Hamlet, Act 5, Sc. 2, l. 36. Of his ability 'to write fair'.

156 We defy augury. There is special providence in the fall of a sparrow. If it be now, 'tis not to come.

If it be not to come, it will be now. If it be not now, yet it will come. The readiness is all.
Hamlet, Act 5, Sc. 2, ll. 213–16

157 A hit, a very palpable hit.
Osrick, Act 5, Sc. 2, l. 275. Judging that Hamlet has struck Laertes, his opponent in a duel.

158 Why, as a woodcock to mine own springe, Osrick.
I am justly killed with mine own treachery.
Laertes, Act 5, Sc. 2, ll. 300–1. See also HAMLET 38.

159 This fell sergeant, Death,
Is strict in his arrest.
Hamlet, Act 5, Sc. 2, ll. 330–1

160 Report me and my cause aright.
Hamlet, Act 5, Sc. 2, l. 333

161 O God, Horatio, what a wounded name,
Things standing thus unknown, shall I leave behind me!
If thou didst ever hold me in thy heart,
Absent thee from felicity awhile,
And in this harsh world draw thy breath in pain,
To tell my story.
Hamlet, Act 5, Sc. 2, ll. 338–43

162 The rest is silence.
Hamlet, Act 5, Sc. 2, l. 352. Dying words.

163 Now cracks a noble heart. Good night, sweet Prince,
And flights of angels sing thee to thy rest!
Horatio, Act 5, Sc. 2, ll. 353–4. Of the dead Hamlet.

164 Rosencrantz and Guildenstern are dead.
Ambassador, Act 5, Sc. 2, l. 365. The words, reporting the success of Hamlet's plan, are the title of a play by TOM STOPPARD (1966).

165 For he was likely, had he been put on,
To have proved most royal.
Fortinbras, Act 5, Sc. 2, ll. 391–2. Closing speech of play, referring to Hamlet.

Twelfth Night
(c. 1601)

1 If music be the food of love, play on,
Give me excess of it that, surfeiting,
The appetite may sicken, and so die.
Orsino, Act 1, Sc. 1, ll. 1–3. Opening lines of play. See also ANTONY AND CLEOPATRA 18.

2 Enough, no more!
'Tis not so sweet now as it was before.
Orsino, Act 1, Sc. 1, ll. 7–8

3 O, when mine eyes did see Olivia first,
Methought she purged the air of pestilence.
Orsino, Act 1, Sc. 1, ll. 20–1

4 And what should I do in Illyria?
My brother, he is in Elysium.
Viola, Act 1, Sc. 2, ll. 3–4

5 You must confine yourself within the modest limits of order.
Maria, to Sir Toby Belch, Act 1, Sc. 3, ll. 7–8

6 Methinks sometimes I have no more wit than a Christian or an ordinary man has; but I am a great eater of beef, and I believe that does harm to my wit.
Sir Andrew Aguecheek, Act 1, Sc. 3, ll. 80–3. Reflecting a popular medical belief.

7 I would I had bestowed that time in the tongues that I have in fencing, dancing, and bear-baiting. O, had I but followed the arts!
Sir Andrew Aguecheek, Act 1, Sc. 3, ll. 88–91

8 Many a good hanging prevents a bad marriage.
Feste, Act 1, Sc. 5, l. 18

9 Not yet old enough for a man, nor young enough for a boy; as a squash is before 'tis a peascod, or a codling when 'tis almost an apple. 'Tis with him in standing water between boy and man. He is very well-favoured, and he speaks very shrewishly. One would think his mother's milk were scarce out of him.
Malvolio, Act 1, Sc. 5, ll. 151–6. Describing Cesario (Viola in disguise).

10 The rudeness that hath appeared in me have I learned from my entertainment.
Viola, disguised as Cesario, Act 1, Sc. 5, ll. 206–7

11 'Tis beauty truly blent, whose red and white
Nature's own sweet and cunning hand laid on.
Lady, you are the cruellest she alive,
If you will lead these graces to the grave,
And leave the world no copy.
Viola, Act 1, Sc. 5, ll. 228–32. Describing Olivia's face.

12 Make me a willow cabin at your gate,
And call upon my soul within the house;
Write loyal cantons of contemnèd love
And sing them loud even in the dead of night;
Hallow your name to the reverberate hills

And make the babbling gossip of the air
Cry out 'Olivia!' O, you should not rest
Between the elements of air and earth,
But you should pity me.
Viola, Act 1, Sc. 5, ll. 257–65. On how she would respond to being rejected in love.

13 Thou'rt a scholar. Let us therefore eat and drink.
Sir Toby Belch, to Sir Andrew Aguecheek, Act 2, Sc. 3, ll. 12–13

14 O mistress mine! Where are you roaming?
O, stay and hear: your true love's coming,
That can sing both high and low.
Trip no further, pretty sweeting;
Journeys end in lovers meeting,
Every wise man's son doth know.
Feste's song, Act 2, Sc. 3, ll. 37–42

15 Present mirth hath present laughter,
What's to come is still unsure.
Feste's song, Act 2, Sc. 3, ll. 46–7. The lines gave NOËL COWARD the title for his play Present Laughter.

16 Then come kiss me, sweet and twenty,
Youth's a stuff will not endure.
Feste's song, Act 2, Sc. 3, ll. 49–50

17 He does well enough if he be disposed, and so do I too. He does it with a better grace, but I do it more natural.
Sir Andrew Aguecheek, Act 2, Sc. 3, ll. 80–2. Referring to Sir Toby Belch's 'admirable fooling'.

18 Dost thou think, because thou art virtuous, there shall be no more cakes and ale?
Sir Toby Belch, Act 2, Sc. 3, ll. 111–12. Speaking to the puritanical Malvolio. Cakes and Ale was the title of a novel by W. SOMERSET MAUGHAM (1930).

19 I was adored once too.
Sir Andrew Aguecheek, Act 2, Sc. 3, l. 174

20 Then let thy love be younger than thyself,
Or thy affection cannot hold the bent.
Orsino to Viola (disguised as Cesario), Act 2, Sc. 4, ll. 36–7

21 The spinsters, and the knitters in the sun,
And the free maids that weave their thread with bones.
Orsino, Act 2, Sc. 4, ll. 44–5

22 Come away, come away, death,
And in sad cypress let me be laid.
Fie away, fie away, breath!
I am slain by a fair cruel maid.
Feste's song, Act 2, Sc. 4, ll. 50–3

23 She never told her love,
But let concealment, like a worm i'the bud,
Feed on her damask cheek.

Viola (disguised as Cesario), Act 2, Sc. 4, ll. 109–11. Voicing her love to Orsino, under the pretence of describing her sister's love

24 Here comes the trout that must be caught with tickling.

Maria, of Malvolio, Act 2, Sc. 5, ll. 31–2

25 Be not afraid of greatness. Some are born great, some achieve greatness, and some have greatness thrust upon 'em.

Malvolio, Act 2, Sc. 5, ll. 140–2. Reading out Maria's letter, supposed to be from Olivia.

26 The Lady Olivia has no folly. She will keep no fool, sir, till she be married, and fools are as like husbands as pilchers are to herrings; the husband's the bigger. I am indeed not her fool, but her corrupter of words.

Feste, Act 3, Sc. 1, ll. 31–5

27 This fellow is wise enough to play the fool;
And to do that well craves a kind of wit.

Viola of Feste, Act 2, Sc. 5, ll. 58–9

28 O world, how apt the poor are to be proud!

Olivia, Act 3, Sc. 1, l. 124

29 O, what a deal of scorn looks beautiful
In the contempt and anger of his lip!

Olivia, of Cesario (Viola), Act 3, Sc. 1, ll. 142–3

30 Love sought, is good; but given unsought, is
    better.

Olivia, Act 3, Sc. 1, l. 153

31 I have dogged him like his murderer.

Maria, of Malvolio, Act 3, Sc. 2, ll. 72–3

32 Why, this is very midsummer madness.

Olivia, Act 3, Sc. 4, l. 56. Referring to Malvolio's unusual behaviour.

33 Go, hang yourselves all. You are idle shallow, things; I am not of your element.

Malvolio, Act 3, Sc. 4, ll. 122–3. Addressing Sir Toby, Fabian and Maria.

34 More matter for a May morning!

Fabian, Act 3, Sc. 4, l. 141

35 Swear horrible; for it comes to pass oft that a terrible oath, with a swaggering accent sharply twanged off, gives manhood more approbation than ever proof itself would have earned him.

Sir Toby Belch, Act 3, Sc. 4, ll. 175–9

36 I hate ingratitude more in a man
Than lying, vainness, babbling drunkenness,
Or any taint of vice whose strong corruption
Inhabits our frail blood.

Viola, Act 3, Sc. 4, ll. 345–8

37 In nature, there's no blemish but the mind;
None can be called deformed, but the unkind.

Antonio, Act 3, Sc. 4, ll. 358–9

38 Endeavour thyself to sleep and leave thy vain bibble-babble.

Feste, to Malvolio, Act 4, Sc. 2, ll. 96–7

39 And thus the whirligig of time brings in his revenges.

Feste, Act 5, Sc. 1, ll. 373–4

40 When that I was and a little tiny boy,
With hey-ho, the wind and the rain;
A foolish thing was but a toy,
For the rain it raineth every day.

Feste, Act 5, Sc. 1, ll. 386–9. A shorter version of this song, which closes the play, is in *King Lear* (see KING LEAR 30). 'The Rain it Raineth Every Day' was the title of a painting by Norman Garstin (1889).

Troilus and Cressida
(c. 1602)

1 Helen must needs be fair,
When with your blood you daily paint her thus.

Troilus, Act 1, Sc. 1, ll. 92–3. Of the conflicting armies in the Trojan War.

2 Women are angels, wooing;
Things won are done; joy's soul lies in the doing.
That she beloved knows naught that knows not
    this:
Men prize the thing ungained more than it is.

Cressida, Act 1, Sc. 2, ll. 286–9

3 O, when degree is shaked,
Which is the ladder to all high designs,
The enterprise is sick. How could communities,
Degrees in schools, and brotherhoods in cities,
Peaceful commerce from dividable shores,
The primogenitive and due of birth,
Prerogative of age, crowns, sceptres, laurels,
But by degree, stand in authentic place?
Take but degree away, untune that string,
And hark what discord follows!

Ulysses, Act 1, Sc. 3, ll. 101–10

4 And appetite, an universal wolf,
So doubly seconded with will and power,

Must make perforce an universal prey,
And last eat up himself.

Ulysses, Act 1, Sc. 3, ll. 121–4

5 'Tis mad idolatry
To make the service greater than the god.

Hector, Act 2, Sc. 1, ll. 57–8

6 All the argument is a whore and a cuckold; a good quarrel to draw emulous factions and bleed to death upon.

Thersites, Act 2, Sc. 3, ll. 71–3. Of the Trojan War.

7 I stalk about her door,
Like a strange soul upon the Stygian banks
Staying for waftage.

Troilus, Act 3, Sc. 2, ll. 7–9. Of his infatuation for Cressida.

8 This is the monstruosity in love, lady, that the will is infinite, and the execution confined; that the desire is boundless, and the act a slave to limit.

Troilus, Act 3, Sc. 2, ll. 79–81

9 To be wise and love
Exceeds man's might – that dwells with gods above.

Cressida, Act 3, Sc. 2, ll. 154–5

10 Time hath, my lord, a wallet at his back,
Wherein he puts alms for oblivion,
A great-sized monster of ingratitudes.

Ulysses, Act 3, Sc. 3, ll. 145–7

11 Perseverance, dear my lord,
Keeps honour bright.

Ulysses, Act 3, Sc. 3, ll. 150–1

12 One touch of nature makes the whole world kin.

Ulysses, Act 3, Sc. 3, l. 175

13 Fie, fie upon her!
There's language in her eye, her cheek, her lip,
Nay, her foot speaks; her wanton spirits look out
At every joint and motive of her body.
O, these encounterers, so glib of tongue,
That give accosting welcome ere it comes,
And wide unclasp the tables of their thoughts
To every tickling reader! Set them down
For sluttish spoils of opportunity
And daughters of the game.

Ulysses, of Cressida, Act 4, Sc. 5, ll. 54–63

14 The end crowns all;
And that old common arbitrator, Time,
Will one day end it.

Hector, Act 4, Sc. 5, ll. 224–6

15 To such as boasting show their scars
A mock is due.

Troilus, Act 4, Sc. 5, ll. 290–1

16 Lechery, lechery, still wars and lechery; nothing else holds fashion!

Thersites, Act 5, Sc. 2, ll. 197–8

17 O world, world, world! Thus is the poor agent despised! O traitors and bawds, how earnestly are you set a-work, and how ill requited! Why should our endeavour be so desired, and the performance so loathed?

Pandarus, Act 5, Sc. 10, ll. 36–40

Othello

(c. 1603)

1 Horribly stuffed with epithets of war.

Iago, of Othello, Act 1, Sc. 1, l. 14

2 'Tis the curse of service:
Preferment goes by letter and affection,
And not by old gradation, where each second
Stood heir to th'first.

Iago, Act 1, Sc. 1, ll. 35–8

3 In following him, I follow but myself.

Iago, of Othello, Act 1, Sc. 1, l. 59

4 For when my outward action doth demonstrate
The native act and figure of my heart
In compliment extern, 'tis not long after,
But I will wear my heart upon my sleeve
For daws to peck at – I am not what I am.

Iago, Act 1, Sc. 1, ll. 62–6

5 Even now, now, very now, an old black ram
Is tupping your white ewe.

Iago to Brabantio, Act 1, Sc. 1, ll. 89–90. Of Othello and Desdemona.

6 Your daughter and the Moor are now making the beast with two backs.

Iago to Brabantio, Act 1, Sc. 1, ll. 116–18. Of Othello and Desdemona.

7 Keep up your bright swords, for the dew will rust them.

Othello, Act 1, Sc. 2, l. 59

8 So opposite to marriage that she shunned
The wealthy curlèd darlings of our nation.
Brabantio, of his daughter, Desdemona, Act 1, Sc. 2, ll. 67–8

9 Rude am I in my speech
And little blessed with the soft phrase of peace.
Othello, Act 1, Sc. 3, ll. 81–2

10 I will a round unvarnished tale deliver
Of my whole course of love.
Othello, Act 1, Sc. 3, ll. 90–1

11 A maiden never bold;
Of spirit so still and quiet that her motion
Blushed at herself.
Brabantio, of his daughter Desdemona, Act 1, Sc. 3, ll. 94–6

12 And of the Cannibals that each other eat,
The Anthropophagi, and men whose heads
Do grow beneath their shoulders.
Othello, Act 1, Sc. 3, ll. 142–4. Of the tales of his travels that he has recounted.

13 My story being done,
She gave me for my pains a world of sighs:
She swore, in faith 'twas strange, 'twas passing strange,
'Twas pitiful, 'twas wondrous pitiful;
She wished she had not heard it, yet she wished
That heaven had made her such a man.
Othello, of Desdemona, Act 1, Sc. 3, ll. 157–62

14 I do perceive here a divided duty.
Desdemona, Act 1, Sc. 3, l. 179

15 The robbed that smiles steals something from the thief;
He robs himself that spends a bootless grief.
Duke of Venice, Act 1, Sc. 3, ll. 206–7

16 Since I could distinguish betwixt a benefit and an injury, I never found a man that knew how to love himself.
Iago, Act 1, Sc. 3, ll. 309–11

17 'Tis in ourselves that we are thus, or thus. Our bodies are our gardens, to the which our wills are gardeners.
Iago, Act 1, Sc. 3, ll. 316–18

18 There are many events in the womb of time, which will be delivered.
Iago, Act 1, Sc. 3, ll. 364–5

19 You are pictures out of doors, bells in your parlours, wild-cats in your kitchens, saints in your injuries, devils being offended, players in your housewifery, and housewives in your beds.
Iago, Act 2, Sc. 1, ll. 108–11

20 Do not put me to't,
For I am nothing if not critical.
Iago, Act 2, Sc. 1, ll. 117–18

21 To suckle fools, and chronicle small beer.
Iago, Act 2, Sc. 1, l. 157. Describing the role of a 'deserving woman'. Desdemona calls this a 'most lame and impotent conclusion'.

22 If it were now to die,
'Twere now to be most happy; for, I fear
My soul hath her content so absolute
That not another comfort like to this
Succeeds in unknown fate.
Othello, Act 2, Sc. 1, ll. 183–7. On being reunited with Desdemona.

23 A slipper and subtle knave, a finder out of occasions; that has an eye can stamp and counterfeit advantages, though true advantage never present itself.
Iago, of Cassio, Act 2, Sc. 1, ll. 235–7

24 I have very poor and unhappy brains for drinking. I could well wish courtesy would invent some other custom of entertainment.
Cassio, Act 2, Sc. 3, ll. 30–2. Refusing a drink with Iago.

25 I learned it in England, where indeed they are most potent in potting. Your Dane, your German, and your swag-bellied Hollander – drink, ho! – are nothing to your English.
Iago, Act 2, Sc. 3, ll. 71–4. According to Iago, the Englishman 'drinks you with facility your Dane dead drunk; he sweats not to overthrow your Almain; he gives your Hollander a vomit, ere the next pottle can be filled'.

26 'Tis the soldier's life
To have their balmy slumbers waked with strife.
Othello, Act 2, Sc. 3, ll. 250–1

27 Reputation, reputation, reputation! O, I have lost my reputation! I have lost the immortal part of myself, and what remains is bestial.
Cassio, Act 2, Sc. 3, ll. 255–8

28 Drunk! And speak parrot! And squabble! Swagger! Swear! And discourse fustian with one's own shadow? O, thou invisible spirit of wine, if thou hast no name to be known by, let us call thee devil.
Cassio, Act 2, Sc. 3, ll. 272–5

29 O God, that men should put an enemy in their mouths to steal away their brains! That we should

with joy, pleasance, revel and applause transform
ourselves into beasts!
Cassio, Act 2, Sc. 3, ll. 281–4

30 How poor are they that have not patience!
What wound did ever heal but by degrees?
Iago, Act 2, Sc. 3, ll. 359–60

31 O, thereby hangs a tail.
Clown, Act 3, Sc. 1, l. 8. See AS YOU LIKE IT 15.

32 Men should be what they seem.
Iago, Act 3, Sc. 3, l. 125

33 Good name in man and woman, dear my lord,
Is the immediate jewel of their souls.
Who steals my purse steals trash; 'tis something,
    nothing;
'Twas mine, 'tis his, and has been slave to
    thousands:
But he that filches from me my good name
Robs me of that which not enriches him
And makes me poor indeed.
Iago, Act 3, Sc. 3, ll. 154–60

34 O, beware, my lord, of jealousy!
It is the green-eyed monster, which doth mock
The meat it feeds on.
Iago, Act 3, Sc. 3, ll. 163–5

35 O, curse of marriage!
That we can call these delicate creatures ours
And not their appetites! I had rather be a toad,
And live upon the vapour of a dungeon
Than keep a corner in the thing I love
For others' uses.
Othello, Act 3, Sc. 3, ll. 265–70

36 Trifles light as air
Are to the jealous confirmations strong
As proofs of holy writ.
Iago, Act 3, Sc. 3, ll. 319–21

37 Not poppy, nor mandragora,
Nor all the drowsy syrups of the world,
Shall ever medicine thee to that sweet sleep
Which thou owed'st yesterday.
Iago, Act 3, Sc. 3, ll. 327–30

38 He that is robbed, not wanting what is stolen,
Let him not know't, and he's not robbed at all.
Othello, Act 3, Sc. 3, ll. 339–40

39 I had been happy if the general camp,
Pioners and all, had tasted her sweet body,
So I had nothing known.
Othello, of Desdemona, Act 3, Sc. 3, ll. 342–4

40 O, now, for ever
Farewell the tranquil mind! Farewell content!
Farewell the plumèd troop, and the big wars
That make ambition virtue – O, farewell!
Farewell the neighing steed, and the shrill trump,
The spirit-stirring drum, th'ear-piercing fife,
The royal banner and all quality,
Pride, pomp and circumstance of glorious war!
And, O you mortal engines, whose rude throats
Th'immortal Jove's dread clamours counterfeit,
Farewell! Othello's occupation's gone.
Othello, Act 3, Sc. 3, ll. 344–54

41 But this denoted a foregone conclusion.
Othello, Act 3, Sc. 3, l. 425

42 But jealous souls will not be answered so;
They are not ever jealous for the cause,
But jealous for they're jealous. It is a monster
Begot upon itself, born on itself.
Emilia, Act 3, Sc. 4, ll. 155–8

43 But yet the pity of it, Iago! O, Iago, the pity of it,
Iago!
Othello, Act 4, Sc. 1, ll. 194–5

44 O, well-painted passion!
Othello, of Desdemona, Act 4, Sc. 1, l. 259

45 Is this the nature
Whom passion could not shake? Whose solid
    virtue
The shot of accident nor dart of chance,
Could neither graze nor pierce?
Lodovico, of Othello, Act 4, Sc. 1, ll. 266–9

46 Had it pleased heaven
To try me with affliction, had they rained
All kinds of sores and shames on my bare head.
Steeped me in poverty to the very lips,
Given to captivity me and my utmost hopes,
I should have found in some place of my soul
A drop of patience. But, alas, to make me
A fixèd figure for the time of scorn
To point his slow unmoving finger at!
Othello, Act 4, Sc. 2, ll. 46–54

47 Turn thy complexion there,
Patience, thou young and rose-lipped cherubin,
Ay, there look grim as hell!
Othello, Act 4, Sc. 2, ll. 61–3

48 Unkindness may do much,
And his unkindness may defeat my life,
But never taint my love.
Desdemona, Act 4, Sc. 2, ll. 158–60

49 But I do think it is their husbands' faults
If wives do fall. Say that they slack their duties,
And pour our treasures into foreign laps;
Or else break out in peevish jealousies,
Throwing restraint upon us; or say they strike us,
Or scant our former having in despite –
Why, we have galls, and though we have some
    grace,
Yet have we some revenge. Let husbands know
Their wives have sense like them: they see and
    smell
And have their palates both for sweet and sour
As husbands have. What is it that they do
When they change us for others? Is it sport?
I think it is. And doth affection breed it?
I think it doth. Is't frailty that thus errs?
It is so too. And have not we affections,
Desires for sport, and frailty, as men have?
Then let them use us well: else let them know
The ills we do, their ills instruct us so.
Emilia, Act 4, Sc. 3, ll. 85–102

50 He hath a daily beauty in his life
That makes me ugly.
Iago, of Cassio, Act 5, Sc. 1, ll. 19–20

51 She was false as water.
Othello, of Desdemona, Act 5, Sc. 2, l. 135

52 I will play the swan
And die in music.
Emilia, Act 5, Sc. 2, ll. 245–6. Swans were supposed to sing before dying.

53 An honourable murderer, if you will:
For naught did I in hate, but all in honour.
Othello, Act 5, Sc. 2, ll. 291–2

54 Speak of me as I am: nothing extenuate,
Nor set down aught in malice. Then must you
    speak
Of one that loved not wisely, but too well;
Of one, not easily jealous but, being wrought,
Perplexed in the extreme; of one whose hand
Like the base Indian threw a pearl away
Richer than all his tribe; of one whose subdued
    eyes,
Albeit unusèd to the melting mood,
Drop tears as fast as the Arabian trees
Their med'cinal gum.
Othello, Act 5, Sc. 2, ll. 338–47. Spoken to his arresting officers.

Measure for Measure
(c. 1604)

1 Our natures do pursue,
Like rats that ravin down their proper bane,
A thirsty evil, and when we drink we die.
Claudio, Act 1, Sc. 2, ll. 127–9

2 Liberty plucks justice by the nose;
The baby beats the nurse, and quite athwart
Goes all decorum.
The Duke, Act 1, Sc. 3, ll. 29–31

3 I hold you as a thing enskied and sainted,
By your renouncement an immortal spirit
And to be talked with in sincerity,
As with a saint.
Lucio, to Isabella, Act 1, Sc. 4, ll. 34–7

4 A man whose blood
Is very snow-broth, one who never feels
The wanton stings and motions of the sense,
But doth rebate and blunt his natural edge
With profits of the mind, study, and fast.
Lucio, of Angelo, Act 1, Sc. 4, ll. 57–61

5 Our doubts are traitors
And make us lose the good we oft might win,
By fearing to attempt.
Lucio, Act 1, Sc. 4, ll. 77–9

6 We must not make a scarecrow of the law,
Setting it up to fear the birds of prey,
And let it keep one shape, till custom make it
Their perch and not their terror.
Angelo, Act 2, Sc. 1, ll. 1–4

7 The jury, passing on the prisoner's life
May in the sworn twelve have a thief or two
Guiltier than him they try.
Angelo, Act 2, Sc. 1, ll. 19–21

8 Some rise by sin, and some by virtue fall.
Escalus, Act 2, Sc. 1, l. 38

9 Condemn the fault, and not the actor of it?
Angelo, Act 2, Sc. 2, l. 37

10 The law hath not been dead, though it hath
    slept.
Angelo, Act 2, Sc. 2, l. 90

11 O, 'tis excellent
To have a giant's strength, but it is tyrannous
To use it like a giant.
Isabella, Act 2, Sc. 2, ll. 107–9

12 Man, proud man,
Dressed in a little brief authority,
Most ignorant of what he's most assured,
His glassy essence, like an angry ape
Plays such fantastic tricks before high heaven,
As make the angels weep.
Isabella, Act 2, Sc. 2, ll. 117–22

13 That in the captain's but a choleric word
Which in the soldier is flat blasphemy.
Isabella, Act 2, Sc. 2, ll. 130–1

14 O cunning enemy that, to catch a saint,
With saints dost bait thy hook.
Angelo, Act 2, Sc. 2, ll. 180–1

15 The miserable have no other medicine
But only hope.
Claudio, Act 3, Sc. 1, ll. 2–3

16 If I must die,
I will encounter darkness as a bride,
And hug it in mine arms.
Claudio, Act 3, Sc. 1, ll. 86–8

17 Ay, but to die, and go we know not where,
To lie in cold obstruction and to rot;
This sensible warm motion to become
A kneaded clod; and the delighted spirit
To bathe in fiery floods, or to reside
In thrilling region of thick-ribbèd ice,
To be imprisoned in the viewless winds
And blown with restless violence round about
The pendent world; or to be worse than worst
Of those that lawless and incertain thought
Imagine howling, 'tis too horrible.
The weariest and most loathèd worldly life
That age, ache, penury, and imprisonment
Can lay on nature is a paradise
To what we fear of death.
Claudio, Act 3, Sc. 1, ll. 121–35

18 There, at the moated grange, resides this dejected
Mariana.
The Duke, Act 3, Sc. 1, ll. 265–6. Of Angelo's fomer fiancée.
'Mariana in the moated grange' was the epigraph to TENNY-
SON's poem 'Mariana' (1830).

19 Music oft hath such a charm
To make bad good, and good provoke to harm.
The Duke, Act 4, Sc. 1, ll. 14–15

20 The old fantastical Duke of dark corners.
Lucio, Act 4, Sc. 3, ll. 155–6

21 Let the devil
Be sometime honoured for his burning throne.
The Duke, Act 5, Sc. 1, ll. 290–1

22 Haste still pays haste, and leisure answers
leisure,
Like doth quit like, and Measure still for Measure.
The Duke, Act 5, Sc. 1, ll. 407–8

23 They say best men are moulded out of faults,
And, for the most, become much more the better
For being a little bad. So may my husband.
Mariana, of Angelo, Act 5, Sc. 1, ll. 436–8

24 Marrying a punk, my lord, is pressing to death,
whipping, and hanging.
Lucio, to the Duke, Act 5, Sc. 1, ll. 519–20. 'Punk' here means
'whore'.

All's Well That Ends Well
(c. 1605)

1 Love all, trust a few,
Do wrong to none. Be able for thine enemy
Rather in power than use, and keep thy friend
Under thy own life's key. Be checked for silence,
But never taxed for speech.
The Countess, Act 1, Sc. 1, ll. 62–6

2 'Twere all one
That I should love a bright particular star
And think to wed it, he is so above me.
Helena, Act 1, Sc. 1, ll. 84–6

3 The hind that would be mated by the lion
Must die for love.
Helena, Act 1, Sc. 1, ll. 90–1

4 Your virginity, your old virginity, is like one of
our French withered pears: it looks ill, it eats drily.
Parolles, Act 1, Sc. 1, ll. 157–9

5 Our remedies oft in ourselves do lie,
Which we ascribe to heaven.
Helena, Act 1, Sc. 1, ll. 212–13

6 The soul of this man is his clothes. Trust him not
in matter of heavy consequence.
Lafew, Act 2, Sc. 5, ll. 43–5. Referring to Parolles.

7 All's well that ends well; still the fine's the
crown.
Whate'er the course, the end is the renown.
Helena, Act 4, Sc. 4, ll. 35–6

8 Th'inaudible and noiseless foot of time.
King of France, Act 5, Sc. 3, l. 41

Timon of Athens

(c. 1605)

1 A thousand moral paintings I can show
That shall demonstrate these quick blows of
    Fortune's
More pregnantly than words.

Painter, Act 1, Sc. 1, ll. 93–5

2 'Tis not enough to help the feeble up,
But to support him after.

Timon, Act 1, Sc. 1, ll. 111–12

3 The strain of man's bred out
Into baboon and monkey.

Apemantus, Act 1, Sc. 1, ll. 254–5

4 Ceremony was but devised at first
To set a gloss on faint deeds, hollow welcomes,
Recanting goodness, sorry ere 'tis shown;
But where there is true friendship there needs
    none.

Timon, Act 1, Sc. 2, ll. 14–17

5 Here's that which is too weak to be a sinner,
Honest water, which ne'er left man i'th'mire.

Apemantus, Act 1, Sc. 2, ll. 57–8

6 Men shut their doors against a setting sun.

Apemantus, Act 1, Sc. 2, l. 142

7 What a coil's here,
Serving of becks and jutting-out of bums!

Apemantus, Act 1, Sc. 2, ll. 235–6

8 The fault's bloody.
'Tis necessary he should die;
Nothing emboldens sin so much as mercy.

First Senator, Act 3, Sc. 5, ll. 1–3. Of one of Timon's soldiers,
sentenced to death for manslaughter.

9 Let's yet be fellows. Let's shake our heads, and
    say,
As 'twere a knell unto our master's fortunes,
'We have seen better days'.

Flavius, Act 4, Sc. 2, ll. 25–7. Timon's steward bids farewell to
the servants.

10 O the fierce wretchedness that glory brings us!
Who would not wish to be from wealth exempt,
Since riches point to misery and contempt?

Flavius, Act 4, Sc. 2, ll. 30–2

11 I am Misanthropos, and hate mankind.

Timon, Act 4, Sc. 3, l. 54

12 The sun's a thief, and with his great attraction
Robs the vast sea. The moon's an arrant thief,
And her pale fire she snatches from the sun.
The sea's a thief, whose liquid surge resolves
The moon into salt tears. The earth's a thief,
That feeds and breeds by a composture stolen
From general excrement. Each thing's a thief.

Timon, Act 4, Sc. 3, ll. 338–44

13 Lips, let four words go by and language end:
What is amiss, plague and infection mend!
Graves only be men's works, and death their gain!
Sun, hide thy beams! Timon hath done his reign.

Timon, Act 5, Sc. 1, ll. 218–21. His final words in the play.
Timon is the only tragic hero in Shakespeare to walk off stage,
rather than being carried off.

King Lear

(1606)

1 Nothing will come of nothing. Speak again.

Lear, Act 1, Sc. 1, l. 90. Responding to Cordelia, and echoing
the Latin proverb: 'Ex nihilo nihil fit.'

2 I love your majesty
According to my bond; nor more nor less.

Cordelia to Lear, Act 1, Sc. 1, ll. 92–3

3 Lear: So young, and so untender?
Cordelia: So young, my lord, and true.

Act 1, Sc. 1, ll. 106–7

4 Come not between the dragon and his wrath.

Lear, Act 1, Sc. 1, l. 122. Addressed to Kent, attempting to
restrain Lear.

5 I want that glib and oily art,
To speak and purpose not.

Cordelia, Act 1, Sc. 1, ll. 224–5

6 It is no vicious blot, murder or foulness,
No unchaste action or dishonoured step
That hath deprived me of your grace and favour,
But even for want of that for which I am richer:
A still-soliciting eye and such a tongue
That I am glad I have not.

Cordelia, Act 1, Sc. 1, ll. 227–32

7 Fairest Cordelia, that art most rich, being poor;
Most choice, forsaken, and most loved, despised.

King of France, Act 1, Sc. 1, ll. 250–1

8 Time shall unfold what plighted cunning hides;
Who cover faults, at last with shame derides.

Cordelia, Act 1, Sc. 1, ll. 280–1

9 'Tis the infirmity of his age. Yet he hath ever but
slenderly known himself.

Gonerill, Act 1, Sc. 1, ll. 292–3

10 Thou, Nature, art my goddess; to thy law
My services are bound.
Edmund, Act 1, Sc. 2, ll. 1–2

11 I grow. I prosper.
Now gods stand up for bastards!
Edmund, Act 1, Sc. 2, ll. 1–2

12 This is the excellent foppery of the world, that
when we are sick in fortune – often the surfeits of
our own behaviour – we make guilty of our disasters
the sun, the moon, and stars, as if we were villains
on necessity, fools by heavenly compulsion, knaves,
thieves, and treachers by spherical predominance,
drunkards, liars, and adulterers by an enforced
obedience of planetary influence; and all that we
are evil in by a divine thrusting on. An admirable
evasion of whoremaster man, to lay his goatish disposition to the charge of a star.
Edmund, Act 1, Sc. 2, ll. 118–28

13 Edgar – [Enter Edgar] pat he comes like the catastrophe of the old comedy. My cue is villainous melancholy, with a sigh like Tom o'Bedlam.
Edmund, Act 1, Sc. 2, ll. 132–5

14 Ingratitude, thou marble-hearted fiend,
More hideous when thou showest thee in a child
Than the sea-monster!
Lear, Act 1, Sc. 2, ll. 256–8

15 Hear, Nature, hear! Dear goddess, hear!
Suspend thy purpose if thou didst intend
To make this creature fruitful.
Into her womb convey sterility,
Dry up in her the organs of increase,
And from her derogate body never spring
A babe to honour her.
Lear, cursing Gonerill, Act 1, Sc. 2, ll. 272–8

16 How sharper than a serpent's tooth it is
To have a thankless child!
Lear, Act 1, Sc. 4, ll. 285–6

17 Striving to better, oft we mar what's well.
Albany, Act 1, Sc. 4, l. 343

18 O, let me not be mad, not mad, sweet heaven!
Keep me in temper; I would not be mad!
Lear, Act 1, Sc. 5, ll. 43–4

19 Thou whoreson zed, thou unnecessary letter!
Kent, to the 'villainous' messenger Oswald, Act 2, Sc. 2, l. 62

20 Down, thou climbing sorrow!
Thy element's below.
Lear, Act 2, Sc. 4, ll. 55–6

21 O sir, you are old.
Nature in you stands on the very verge
Of his confine. You should be ruled and led
By some discretion that discerns your state
Better than you yourself.
Regan to Lear, Act 2, Sc. 4, ll. 141–5

22 I will not trouble thee, my child. Farewell.
We'll no more meet, no more see one another.
But yet thou art my flesh, my blood, my
    daughter –
Or rather a disease that's in my flesh,
Which I must needs call mine. Thou art a boil,
A plague-sore, or embossed carbuncle,
In my corrupted blood.
Lear to Gonerill, Act 2, Sc. 4, ll. 214–20

23 Touch me with noble anger,
And let not women's weapons, water drops,
Stain my man's cheeks.
Lear, Act 2, Sc. 4, ll. 271–3

24 I have full cause of weeping; but this heart
Shall break into a hundred thousand flaws
Or ere I'll weep.
Lear, Act 2, Sc. 4, ll. 279–81

25 Blow, winds, and crack your cheeks! Rage! Blow!
You cataracts and hurricanoes, spout
Till you have drenched our steeples, drowned the
    cocks!
You sulphurous and thought-executing fires,
Vaunt-curriers of oak-cleaving thunderbolts,
Singe my white head! And thou all-shaking
    thunder,
Strike flat the thick rotundity o' the world,
Crack Nature's moulds, all germens spill at once
That makes ingrateful man!
Lear, Act 3, Sc. 2, ll. 1–9

26 Here I stand, your slave,
A poor, infirm, weak, and despised old man.
Lear, Act 3, Sc. 2, ll. 19–20

27 There was never yet fair woman but she made
mouths in a glass.
Fool, Act 3, Sc. 2, ll. 35–6

28 I am a man
More sinned against than sinning.
Lear, Act 3, Sc. 2, ll. 59–60

29 The art of our necessities is strange
And can make vile things precious.
Lear, Act 3, Sc. 2, ll. 70–1

30 He that has and a little tiny wit,
With heigh-ho, the wind and the rain,
Must make content with his fortunes fit,
Though the rain it raineth every day.
Fool, Act 3, Sc. 2, ll. 74–7. See also TWELFTH NIGHT 40.

31 O, that way madness lies; let me shun that;
No more of that!
Lear, Act 3, Sc. 4, ll. 21–2

32 Poor naked wretches, whereso'er you are,
That bide the pelting of this pitiless storm,
How shall your houseless heads and unfed sides,
Your looped and windowed raggedness, defend
    you
From seasons such as these? O, I have ta'en
Too little care of this! Take physic, pomp;
Expose thyself to feel what wretches feel,
That thou mayst shake the superflux to them
And show the heavens more just.
Lear, Act 3, Sc. 4, ll. 28–36

33 Wine loved I deeply, dice dearly, and in woman
out-paramoured the Turk – false of heart, light of
ear, bloody of hand; hog in sloth, fox in stealth, wolf
in greediness, dog in madness, lion in prey.
Edgar, disguised as Poor Tom, Act 3, Sc. 4, ll. 87–90

34 Let not the creaking of shoes nor the rustling of
silks betray thy poor heart to woman. Keep thy foot
out of brothels, thy hand out of plackets, thy pen
from lenders' books, and defy the foul fiend.
Edgar, disguised as Poor Tom, Act 3, Sc. 4, ll. 91–4

35 The prince of darkness is a gentleman.
Edgar, disguised as Poor Tom, Act 3, Sc. 4, l. 136

36 Poor Tom's a-cold.
Edgar, disguised as Poor Tom, Act 3, Sc. 4, l. 140

37 Child Roland to the dark tower came;
His word was still 'Fie, foh, and fum,
I smell the blood of a British man.'
Edgar, disguised as Poor Tom, Act 3, Sc. 4, ll. 176–8. 'Childe
Roland to the Dark Tower came' is the title and last line of
a poem by ROBERT BROWNING (1855). See also NURSERY
RHYMES 7.

38 He's mad that trusts in the tameness of a wolf, a
horse's health, a boy's love, or a whore's oath.
Fool, Act 3, Sc. 6, ll. 18–19

39 Out, vile jelly!
Where is thy lustre now?
Cornwall, on gouging out Gloucester's eyes, Act 3, Sc. 7, ll. 82–3

40 And worse I may be yet. The worst is not,

So long as we can say 'This is the worst.'
Edgar, Act 4, Sc. 1, ll. 27–8

41 As flies to wanton boys are we to the gods;
They kill us for their sport.
Gloucester, Act 4, Sc. 1, ll. 36–7

42 'Tis the times' plague when madmen lead the
    blind.
Gloucester, Act 4, Sc. 1, l. 46

43 Wisdom and goodness to the vile seem vile;
Filths savour but themselves. What have you
    done,
Tigers not daughters, what have you performed?
Albany, Act 4, Sc. 2, ll. 38–40. Referring to Gonerill and Regan.

44 It is the stars,
The stars above us govern our conditions.
Kent, Act 4, Sc. 3, ll. 32–3

45 Here's the place. Stand still! How fearful
And dizzy 'tis to cast one's eyes so low!
The crows and choughs that wing the midway air
Show scarce so gross as beetles. Halfway down
Hangs one that gathers sampire – dreadful trade!
Methinks he seems no bigger than his head.
The fishermen that walk upon the beach
Appear like mice, and yon tall anchoring bark
Diminished to her cock; her cock, a buoy
Almost too small for sight. The murmuring surge
That on th'unnumbered idle pebble chafes
Cannot be heard so high. I'll look no more,
Lest my brain turn, and the deficient sight
Topple down headlong.
Edgar, Act 4, Sc. 6, ll. 11–24. Describing to his blind father,
Gloucester, the imagined view from a cliff at Dover.

46 Ay, every inch a king:
When I do stare, see how the subject quakes.
Lear, Act 4, Sc. 6, ll. 107–8

47 Adultery?
Thou shalt not die. Die for adultery?
No. The wren goes to't, and the small gilded fly
Does lecher in my sight.
Let copulation thrive.
Lear, Act 4, Sc. 6, ll. 110–14

48 Give me an ounce of civet; good apothecary,
sweeten my imagination.
Lear, Act 4, Sc. 6, ll. 130–1. An alternative reading is: 'Give me
an ounce of civet, good apothecary, to sweeten my
imagination.'

49 O ruined piece of nature! This great world
Shall so wear out to naught.
Gloucester, of Lear, Act 4, Sc. 6, ll. 135–6

50 Thorough tattered clothes great vices do
   appear;
Robes and furred gowns hide all. Plate sins with
   gold,
And the strong lance of justice hurtless breaks;
Arm it in rags, a pigmy's straw does pierce it.
Lear, Act 4, Sc. 6, ll. 165–8. The Quarto text has 'small vices
do appear', corrected in the Folio edition.

51 Get thee glass eyes,
And, like a scurvy politician, seem
To see the things thou dost not.
Lear, Act 4, Sc. 6, ll. 171–3

52 When we are born we cry that we are come
To this great stage of fools.
Lear, Act 4, Sc. 6, ll. 183–4

53 And when I have stolen upon these sons-in-law,
Then, kill, kill, kill, kill, kill, kill!
Lear, Act 4, Sc. 6, ll. 187–8

54 Thou art a soul in bliss; but I am bound
Upon a wheel of fire, that mine own tears
Do scald like molten lead.
Lear to Cordelia, Act 4, Sc. 7, ll. 46–8

55 Pray do not mock me.
I am a very foolish fond old man,
Four score and upward, not an hour more nor less,
And, to deal plainly,
I fear I am not in my perfect mind.
Lear to Cordelia, Act 4, Sc. 7, ll. 59–63

56 Men must endure
Their going hence even as their coming hither;
Ripeness is all.
Edgar, Act 5, Sc. 2, ll. 9–11. Addressed to his father Gloucester,
who wishes only for death.

57 We are not the first
Who with best meaning have incurred the worst.
Cordelia to Lear, Act 5, Sc. 3, ll. 3–4

58 Come, let's away to prison.
We two alone will sing like birds i'the cage;
When thou dost ask me blessing I'll kneel down
And ask of thee forgiveness; so we'll live,
And pray, and sing, and tell old tales, and laugh
At gilded butterflies, and hear poor rogues
Talk of court news; and we'll talk with them too –
Who loses and who wins, who's in, who's out –

And take upon's the mystery of things
As if we were God's spies.
Lear to Cordelia, Act 5, Sc. 3, ll. 8–17

59 Upon such sacrifices, my Cordelia,
The gods themselves throw incense.
Lear to Cordelia, Act 5, Sc. 3, ll. 20–1

60 The gods are just, and of our pleasant vices
Make instruments to plague us.
Edgar, Act 5, Sc. 3, ll. 168–9

61 The wheel is come full circle.
Edmund, Act 5, Sc. 3, l. 172

62 Her voice was ever soft,
Gentle and low – an excellent thing in woman.
Lear of Cordelia, Act 5, Sc. 3, ll. 270–1

63 And my poor fool is hanged! No, no, no life!
Why should a dog, a horse, a rat, have life,
And thou no breath at all? Thou'lt come no more;
Never, never, never, never, never.
Lear of Cordelia, Act 5, Sc. 3, ll. 303–6

64 Vex not his ghost. O, let him pass. He hates
   him
That would upon the rack of this tough world
Stretch him out longer.
Kent, on Lear's death, Act 5, Sc. 3, ll. 311–13

65 The weight of this sad time we must obey;
Speak what we feel, not what we ought to say.
The oldest hath borne most; we that are young
Shall never see so much nor live so long.
Edgar, Act 5, Sc. 3, ll. 321–4. Closing lines of play.

Antony and Cleopatra
(c. 1606)

1 You shall see in him
The triple pillar of the world transformed
Into a strumpet's fool.
Philo, of Antony, Act 1, Sc. 1, ll. 11–13

2 There's beggary in the love that can be reckoned.
Philo, of Antony, Act 1, Sc. 1, l. 15

3 Let Rome in Tiber melt, and the wide arch
Of the ranged empire fall! Here is my space.
Kingdoms are clay.
Antony, Act 1, Sc. 1, ll. 33–5

4 In Nature's infinite book of secrecy
A little I can read.
Soothsayer, Act 1, Sc. 2, ll. 10–11

5 I love long life better than figs.
Charmian, Act 1, Sc. 2, l. 33

6 The nature of bad news infects the teller.
Messenger, Act 1, Sc. 2, l. 96

7 Eternity was in our lips and eyes,
Bliss in our brows' bent.
Cleopatra, Act 1, Sc. 3, ll. 35–6

8 O, my oblivion is a very Antony,
And I am all forgotten.
Cleopatra, Act 1, Sc. 3, ll. 90–1

9 Give me to drink mandragora . . .
That I might sleep out this great gap of time
My Antony is away.
Cleopatra, Act 1, Sc. 5, ll. 4–6

10 O happy horse, to bear the weight of Antony!
Do bravely, horse, for wot'st thou whom thou
    mov'st?
The demi-Atlas of this earth, the arm
And burgonet of men.
Cleopatra, Act 1, Sc. 5, ll. 21–4

11 Where's my serpent of old Nile?
Cleopatra, Act 1, Sc. 5, l. 25. Imagining Antony's words.

12 My salad days,
When I was green in judgement, cold in blood.
Cleopatra, Act 1, Sc. 5, ll. 73–4. Of her former love for Julius
Caesar.

13 I do not much dislike the matter, but
The manner of his speech.
Octavius Caesar, of Enobarbus, Act 2, Sc. 2, ll. 116–17

14 The barge she sat in, like a burnished throne,
Burned on the water. The poop was beaten gold;
Purple the sails, and so perfumèd that
The winds were lovesick with them. The oars were
    silver,
Which to the tune of flutes kept stroke and made
The water which they beat to follow faster,
As amorous of their strokes. For her own person,
It beggared all description.
Enobarbus, Act 2, Sc. 2, ll. 196–203. Describing Cleopatra's
arrival at her first meeting with Antony. T. S. ELIOT wrote a
pastiche of this passage in The Waste Land, 'A Game of Chess'.

15 He ploughed her, and she cropped.
Agrippa, of Julius Caesar and Cleopatra, Act 2, Sc. 2, l. 233

16 Age cannot wither her, nor custom stale
Her infinite variety. Other women cloy

The appetites they feed, but she makes hungry
Where most she satisfies.
Enobarbus, of Cleopatra, Act 2, Sc. 2, ll. 240–3

17 I will to Egypt:
And though I make this marriage for my peace,
I'th'East my pleasure lies.
Antony, Act 2, Sc. 3, ll. 39–41

18 Give me some music – music, moody food
Of us that trade in love.
Cleopatra, Act 2, Sc. 5, ll. 1–2. See also TWELFTH NIGHT 1

19 I will praise any man that will praise me.
Enobarbus, Act 2, Sc. 6, l. 88

20 He will to his Egyptian dish again.
Enobarbus, of Antony, Act 2, Sc. 6, l. 124

21 We have kissed away
Kingdoms and provinces.
Scarus, Act 3, Sc. 10, ll. 7–8. Referring to Antony's defeat at
Actium.

22 He wears the rose
Of youth upon him; from which the world should
    note
Something particular.
Antony, of Octavius Caesar, Act 3, Sc. 13, ll. 20–2

23 Sir, sir, thou art so leaky
That we must leave thee to thy sinking, for
Thy dearest quit thee.
Enobarbus, Act 3, Sc. 13, ll. 64–6. Referring to Antony.

24 I found you as a morsel cold upon
Dead Caesar's trencher.
Antony, Act 3, Sc. 13, ll. 16–17. To Cleopatra, referring to her
liaison with Julius Caesar.

25 Come,
Let's have one other gaudy night. Call to me
All my sad captains. Fill our bowls once more.
Let's mock the midnight bell.
Antony, Act 3, Sc. 13, ll. 181–4. THOM GUNN took the phrase
'my sad captains' as the title of a poem and volume of verse
(1961).

26 When valour preys on reason,
It eats the sword it fights with.
Enobarbus, Act 3, Sc. 13, ll. 198–9

27 To business that we love we rise betime
And go to't with delight.
Antony, Act 4, Sc. 4, ll. 20–1

28 O infinite virtue, com'st thou smiling from
The world's great snare uncaught?
Cleopatra, Act 4, Sc. 8, ll. 17–18. Addressed to Antony, who has
been victorious in battle.

29 But I will be
A bridegroom in my death, and run into't
As to a lover's bed.
Antony, Act 4, Sc. 14, ll. 99–101

30 None but Antony
Should conquer Antony.
Cleopatra, Act 4, Sc. 15, ll. 16–17

31 I am dying, Egypt, dying.
Antony, Act 4, Sc. 15, l. 18

32 The crown o'th'earth doth melt. My Lord!
O, withered is the garland of the war,
The soldier's pole is fall'n; young boys and girls
Are level now with men. The odds is gone,
And there is nothing left remarkable
Beneath the visiting moon.
Cleopatra, on the death of Antony, Act 4, Sc. 15, ll. 63–8

33 Then is it sin
To rush into the secret house of death
Ere death dare come to us?
Cleopatra, Act 4, Sc. 15, ll. 79–81

34 We'll bury him; and then, what's brave,
what's noble,
Let's do't after the high Roman fashion,
And make death proud to take us.
Cleopatra, of Antony, Act 4, Sc. 15, ll. 85–7

35 'Tis paltry to be Caesar;
Not being Fortune, he's but Fortune's knave,
A minister of her will. And it is great
To do that thing that ends all other deeds,
Which shackles accidents and bolts up change;
Which sleeps, and never palates more the dung,
The beggar's nurse and Caesar's.
Cleopatra, contemplating suicide, Act 5, Sc. 2, ll. 2–8

36 His legs bestrid the ocean; his reared arm
Crested the world; his voice was propertied
As all the tunèd spheres, and that to friends;
But when he meant to quail and shake the orb,
He was as rattling thunder. For his bounty,
There was no winter in't; an Antony it was
That grew the more by reaping. His delights
Were dolphin-like; they showed his back above
The element they lived in. In his livery
Walked crowns and crownets; realms and islands
were

As plates dropped from his pocket.
Cleopatra's 'dream' of Antony, Act 5, Sc. 2, ll. 82–92. Numerous
editions (but not the Folio) give 'autumn' for 'Antony' in l. 87.

37 He words me, girls, he words me, that I should
not
Be noble to myself.
Cleopatra, Act 5, Sc. 2, ll. 191–2. On Octavius Caesar's attempts
at persuasion.

38 Finish, good lady; the bright day is done,
And we are for the dark.
Iras, to Cleopatra, Act 5, Sc. 2, ll. 193–4

39 The quick comedians
Extemporally will stage us, and present
Our Alexandrian revels. Antony
Shall be brought drunken forth, and I shall see
Some squeaking Cleopatra boy my greatness
I'th'posture of a whore.
Cleopatra, Act 5, Sc. 2, ll. 26–31. Imagining how she will be
presented in Rome.

40 I have nothing
Of woman in me. Now from head to foot
I am marble-constant; now the fleeting moon
No planet is of mine.
Cleopatra, Act 5, Sc. 2, ll. 238–41

41 I wish you all joy of the worm.
Clown to Cleopatra, Act 5, Sc. 2, l. 259. Referring to the asp he
has brought, referred to as the 'pretty worm of Nilus'.

42 Give me my robe; put on my crown; I have
Immortal longings in me.
Cleopatra, Act 5, Sc. 2, ll. 279–80

43 Husband, I come.
Cleopatra, Act 5, Sc. 2, l. 286

44 I am fire and air; my other elements
I give to baser life.
Cleopatra, Act 5, Sc. 2, l. 288–9

45 Dost thou not see my baby at my breast,
That sucks the nurse asleep?
Cleopatra, of the asp, Act 5, Sc. 2, ll. 308–9

46 Now boast thee, death, in thy possession lies
A lass unparalleled.
Charmian, of Cleopatra, Act 5, Sc. 2, ll. 314–15

Macbeth
(c. 1606)

1 First Witch: When shall we three meet again?
In thunder, lightning, or in rain?
Second Witch: When the hurly-burly's done,

When the battle's lost and won.
Act 1, Sc. 1, ll. 1–4

2 Fair is foul, and foul is fair,
Hover through the fog and filthy air.
Three Witches, Act 1, Sc. 1, ll. 9–10

3 But in a sieve I'll thither sail
And like a rat without a tail
I'll do, I'll do, and I'll do.
First Witch, Act 1, Sc. 3, ll. 8–10

4 The Weird Sisters, hand in hand,
Posters of the sea and land,
Thus do go, about, about;
Thrice to thine, and thrice to mine,
And thrice again, to make up nine.
Peace! the charm's wound up.
Three Witches, Act 1, Sc. 3, ll. 31–6

5 So foul and fair a day I have not seen.
Macbeth, Act 1, Sc. 3, l. 37

6 What are these,
So withered and so wild in their attire,
That look not like the inhabitants o'the earth,
And yet are on't?
Banquo, Act 1, Sc. 3, ll. 38–41. Referring to the Three Witches.

7 All hail, Macbeth! Hail to thee, Thane of Cawdor!
Second Witch, Act 1, Sc. 3, l. 48

8 If you can look into the seeds of time
And say which grain will grow and which will not,
Speak then to me, who neither beg nor fear
Your favours nor your hate.
Banquo, Act 1, Sc. 3, ll. 57–60

9 Say from whence
You owe this strange intelligence; or why
Upon this blasted heath you stop our way
With such prophetic greeting?
Macbeth to the Witches, Act 1, Sc. 3, ll. 74–7

10 Were such things here as we do speak about?
Or have we eaten on the insane root
That takes the reason prisoner?
Banquo, Act 1, Sc. 3, ll. 82–4

11 Why do you dress me
In borrowed robes?
Macbeth, Act 1, Sc. 3, ll. 107–8

12 Oftentimes, to win us to our harm,
The instruments of darkness tell us truths;
Win us with honest trifles, to betray's
In deepest consequence.
Banquo, Act 1, Sc. 3, ll. 122–5

13 Present fears
Are less than horrible imaginings.
Macbeth, Act 1, Sc. 3, ll. 136–7

14 Come what come may,
Time and the hour runs through the roughest day.
Macbeth, Act 1, Sc. 3, ll. 146–7

15 Nothing in his life
Became him like the leaving it. He died
As one that had been studied in his death
To throw away the dearest thing he owed
As 'twere a careless trifle.
Malcolm, Act 1, Sc. 4, ll. 8–12. Referring to the Thane of Cawdor.

16 There's no art
To find the mind's construction in the face.
Duncan, Act 1, Sc. 4, ll. 12–13

17 Yet do I fear thy nature:
It is too full o'the milk of human-kindness.
Lady Macbeth, of Macbeth, Act 1, Sc. 5, ll. 14–15

18 Thou wouldst be great,
Art not without ambition, but without
The illness should attend it.
Lady Macbeth, of Macbeth, Act 1, Sc. 5, ll. 16–18

19 Come, you spirits
That tend on mortal thoughts, unsex me here
And fill me from the crown to the toe top-full
Of direst cruelty. Make thick my blood;
Stop up the access and passage to remorse,
That no compunctious visitings of nature
Shake my fell purpose, nor keep peace between
The effect and it. Come to my woman's breasts
And take my milk for gall, you murdering
    ministers,
Wherever, in your sightless substances,
You wait on nature's mischief.
Lady Macbeth, Act 1, Sc. 5, ll. 38–48

20 Your face, my thane, is as a book where men
May read strange matters.
Lady Macbeth to Macbeth, Act 1, Sc. 5, ll. 60–1

21 If it were done when 'tis done, then 'twere well
It were done quickly. If the assassination
Could trammel up the consequence, and catch
With his surcease success – that but this blow
Might be the be-all and the end-all! – here,
But here, upon this bank and shoal of time,
We'd jump the life to come.
Macbeth, Act 1, Sc. 7, ll. 1–7. Meditating on his plan to murder
Duncan.

22 We but teach
Bloody instructions, which, being taught, return
To plague the inventor.
Macbeth, Act 1, Sc. 7, ll. 8–10

23 This even-handed justice
Commends the ingredience of our poisoned
    chalice
To our own lips.
Macbeth, Act 1, Sc. 7, ll. 10–12

24 This Duncan
Hath borne his faculties so meek, hath been
So clear in his great office, that his virtues
Will plead like angels, trumpet-tongued against
The deep damnation of his taking-off.
Macbeth, Act 1, Sc. 7, ll. 16–20

25 I have no spur
To prick the sides of my intent but only
Vaulting ambition which o'erleaps itself
And falls on the other.
Macbeth, Act 1, Sc. 7, ll. 25–8

26 I have bought
Golden opinions from all sorts of people.
Macbeth, Act 1, Sc. 7, ll. 32–3

27 I dare do all that may become a man;
Who dares do more is none.
Macbeth, Act 1, Sc. 7, ll. 46–7

28 I have given suck, and know
How tender 'tis to love the babe that milks me;
I would, while it was smiling in my face
Have plucked my nipple from his boneless gums
And dashed the brains out, had I so sworn as you
Have done to this.
Lady Macbeth, Act 1, Sc. 7, ll. 54–9

29 But screw your courage to the sticking place,
And we'll not fail.
Lady Macbeth to Macbeth, Act 1, Sc. 7, ll. 60–1

30 Bring forth men-children only!
For thy undaunted mettle should compose
Nothing but males.
Macbeth to Lady Macbeth, Act 1, Sc. 7, ll. 72–4

31 Mock the time with fairest show:
False face must hide what the false heart doth
    know.
Macbeth, Act 1, Sc. 7, ll. 81–2

32 Is this a dagger which I see before me,
The handle toward my hand? Come, let me clutch
    thee –

I have thee not and yet I see thee still!
Art thou not, fatal vision, sensible
To feeling as to sight? Or art thou but
A dagger of the mind, a false creation,
Proceeding from the heat-oppressèd brain?
Macbeth, Act 2, Sc. 1, ll. 33–9

33 Now o'er the one half-world
Nature seems dead, and wicked dreams abuse
The curtained sleep. Witchcraft celebrates
Pale Hecat's offerings; and withered Murder,
Alarumed by his sentinel the wolf,
Whose howl's his watch, thus with his stealthy
    pace,
With Tarquin's ravishing strides, towards his
    design
Moves like a ghost.
Macbeth, Act 2, Sc. 1, ll. 49–56

34 I go, and it is done; the bell invites me.
Hear it not, Duncan, for it is a knell
That summons thee to heaven or to hell.
Macbeth, Act 2, Sc. 1, ll. 62–4

35 The attempt and not the deed
Confounds us.
Lady Macbeth, Act 2, Sc. 2, ll. 10–11

36 Had he not resembled
My father as he slept, I had done't.
Lady Macbeth, Act 2, Sc. 2, ll. 12–13. Of the murder of Duncan.

37 I had most need of blessing, and 'Amen'
Stuck in my throat.
Macbeth, Act 2, Sc. 2, ll. 32–3

38 Methought I heard a voice cry, 'Sleep no more!
Macbeth does murder sleep – the innocent sleep,
Sleep that knits up the ravelled sleave of care,
The death of each day's life, sore labour's bath,
Balm of hurt minds, great nature's second course,
Chief nourisher in life's feast.'
Macbeth, Act 2, Sc. 2, ll. 35–40

39 Glamis hath murdered sleep, and therefore
    Cawdor
Shall sleep no more, Macbeth shall sleep no more.
Macbeth, Act 2, Sc. 2, ll. 42–3. Reporting the words of a voice
he has heard.

40 The sleeping and the dead
Are but as pictures. 'Tis the eye of childhood
That fears a painted devil.
Lady Macbeth, Act 2, Sc. 2, ll. 53–5

41 Will all great Neptune's ocean wash this blood

Clean from my hand? No, this my hand will rather
The multitudinous seas incarnadine,
Making the green one red.
Macbeth, Act 2, Sc. 2, ll. 60–3

42 A little water clears us of this deed.
Lady Macbeth, Act 2, Sc. 2, l. 67

43 The primrose way to the everlasting bonfire.
Porter, Act 2, Sc. 3, l. 18. See SHAKESPEARE: HAMLET 29.

44 Drink, sir, is a great provoker of three things
... nose-painting, sleep, and urine. Lechery, sir, it
provokes and unprovokes: it provokes the desire
but it takes away the performance.
Porter, Act 2, Sc. 3, ll. 23–8

45 The night has been unruly.
Lennox, Act 2, Sc. 3, l. 51

46 O horror, horror, horror!
Tongue nor heart cannot conceive nor name thee!
Macduff, Act 2, Sc. 3, ll. 60–1. On finding Duncan murdered.

47 Confusion now hath made his masterpiece;
Most sacrilegious murder hath broke ope
The Lord's anointed temple and stole thence
The life o'the building.
Macduff, Act 2, Sc. 3, ll. 63–6

48 Awake!
Shake off this downy sleep, death's counterfeit.
Macduff, Act 2, Sc. 3, ll. 72–3

49 Had I but died an hour before this chance
I had lived a blessed time; for, from this instant
There's nothing serious in mortality.
All is but toys, renown and grace is dead,
The wine of life is drawn, and the mere lees
Is left this vault to brag of.
Macbeth, Act 2, Sc. 3, ll. 88–93

50 Who can be wise, amazed, temperate and
    furious,
Loyal and neutral, in a moment? No man.
Macbeth, Act 2, Sc. 3, ll. 105–6

51 Where we are
There's daggers in men's smiles. The nea'er in
    blood
The nearer bloody.
Donalbain, Act 2, Sc. 3, ll. 136–8

52 I must become a borrower of the night
For a dark hour or twain.
Banquo, Act 3, Sc. 1, ll. 26–7

53 To be thus is nothing;
But to be safely thus!
Macbeth, Act 3, Sc. 1, ll. 47–8

54 In the catalogue ye go for men,
As hounds and greyhounds, mongrels, spaniels,
    curs,
Shoughs, water-rugs, and demi-wolves are clept
All by the name of dogs.
Macbeth, to the two Murderers, Act 3, Sc. 1, ll. 91–4

55 I am one, my liege,
Whom the vile blows and buffets of the world
Hath so incensed that I am reckless what I do
To spite the world.
Second Murderer, Act 3, Sc. 1, ll. 107–10

56 Leave no rubs nor botches in the work.
Macbeth, to the Murderers, Act 3, Sc. 1, l. 133

57 Naught's had, all's spent,
Where our desire is got without content.
Lady Macbeth, Act 3, Sc. 2, ll. 4–5

58 Things without all remedy
Should be without regard; what's done is done.
Lady Macbeth, Act 3, Sc. 2, ll. 11–12

59 We have scorched the snake, not killed it.
Macbeth, Act 3, Sc. 2, l. 13. Often quoted 'scotched the snake',
following some editions.

60 Duncan is in his grave;
After life's fitful fever he sleeps well;
Treason has done his worst. Nor steel, nor poison,
Malice domestic, foreign levy, nothing
Can touch him further.
Macbeth, Act 3, Sc. 2, ll. 22–6

61 Come, seeling night,
Scarf up the tender eye of pitiful day,
And with thy bloody and invisible hand
Cancel and tear to pieces that great bond
Which keeps me pale. Light thickens
And the crow makes wing to the rooky wood;
Good things of day begin to droop and drowse,
While night's black agents to their preys do rouse.
Macbeth, Act 3, Sc. 2, ll. 46–53

62 The west yet glimmers with some streaks of
    day.
Now spurs the lated traveller apace
To gain the timely inn.
First Murderer, Act 3, Sc. 3, ll. 5–7

63 Then comes my fit again. I had else been
    perfect,

Whole as the marble, founded as the rock,
As broad and general as the casing air;
But now I am cabined, cribbed, confined, bound in
To saucy doubts and fears.

Macbeth, Act 3, Sc. 4, ll. 20–4. On learning of Fleance's escape.

64 Thou canst not say I did it; never shake
Thy gory locks at me.

Macbeth to Banquo's ghost, Act 3, Sc. 4, ll. 49–50

65 This is the very painting of your fear.
This is the air-drawn dagger which you said
Led you to Duncan.

Lady Macbeth to Macbeth, Act 3, Sc. 4, ll. 60–2

66 The times has been
That, when the brains were out, the man would
    die,
And there an end. But now they rise again
With twenty mortal murders on their crowns,
And push us from our stools.

Macbeth, Act 3, Sc. 4, ll. 77–81

67 What man dare, I dare.
Approach thou like the rugged Russian bear,
The armed rhinoceros, or the Hyrcan tiger,
Take any shape but that, and my firm nerves
Shall never tremble. Or be alive again,
And dare me to the desert with thy sword:
If trembling I inhabit then, protest me
The baby of a girl. Hence, horrible shadow!
Unreal mockery, hence!

Macbeth, Act 3, Sc. 4, ll. 98–106. Addressing Banquo's ghost.

68 It will have blood, they say; blood will have
    blood.
Stones have been known to move and trees to
    speak.

Macbeth, Act 3, Sc. 4, ll. 121–2

69 I am in blood
Stepped in so far, that, should I wade no more,
Returning were as tedious as go o'er.

Macbeth, Act 3, Sc. 4, ll. 135–7

70 My strange and self-abuse
Is the initiate fear that wants hard use.
We are yet but young in deed.

Macbeth, Act 3, Sc. 4, ll. 141–3

71 Double, double, toil and trouble;
Fire burn, and cauldron bubble.

The Three Witches, Act 4, Sc. 1, ll. 10–11. The incantation is
uttered three times in the scene.

72 Fillet of a fenny snake
In the cauldron boil and bake;
Eye of newt, and toe of frog,
Wool of bat, and tongue of dog,
Adder's fork, and blind-worm's sting,
Lizard's leg and howlet's wing,
For a charm of powerful trouble,
Like a hell-broth, boil and bubble.

Second Witch, Act 4, Sc. 1, ll. 12–19

73 By the pricking of my thumbs,
Something wicked this way comes.
Open, locks, whoever knocks!

Second Witch, Act 4, Sc. 1, ll. 44–6

74 Macbeth: How now, you secret, black, and
    midnight hags!
What is't you do?
The Witches: A deed without a name.

Act 4, Sc. 1, ll. 47–8

75 Be bloody, bold, and resolute; laugh to scorn
The power of man; for none of woman born
Shall harm Macbeth.

Second Apparition, Act 4, Sc. 1, ll. 78–80

76 That I may tell pale-hearted fear it lies,
And sleep in spite of thunder.

Macbeth, Act 4, Sc. 1, ll. 84–5

77 Macbeth shall never vanquished be, until
Great Birnam Wood to high Dunsinane Hill
Shall come against him.

Third Apparition, Act 4, Sc. 1, ll. 91–3

78 When our actions do not,
Our fears do make us traitors.

Lady Macduff, Act 4, Sc. 2, ll. 3–4

79 He loves us not.
He wants the natural touch.

Lady Macduff, of Macduff, Act 4, Sc. 2, ll. 8–9

80 I am in this earthly world, where to do harm
Is often laudable, to do good sometime
Accounted dangerous folly.

Lady Macduff, Act 4, Sc. 2, ll. 75–7

81 Angels are bright still though the brightest fell.

Malcolm, Act 4, Sc. 3, l. 22

82 Ne'er pull your hat upon your brows.
Give sorrow words: the grief that does not speak
Whispers the o'er-fraught heart and bids it break.

Malcolm to Macduff, Act 4, Sc. 3, ll. 208–10

83 All my pretty ones? Did you say all?
O hell-kite! All? What, all my pretty chickens

And their dam, at one fell swoop?

Macduff, Act 4, Sc. 3, ll. 216–18. On receiving the news that his family has been 'savagely slaughtered'.

84 Malcolm: Dispute it like a man.
Macduff: I shall do so;
But I must also feel it as a man.

Act 4, Sc. 3, ll. 219–20

85 Out, damned spot! Out, I say!

Lady Macbeth, Act 5, Sc. 1, l. 34. On apparently seeing blood of the murdered Duncan staining her hands.

86 Fie, my lord, fie! A soldier and afeard?

Lady Macbeth, Act 5, Sc. 1, ll. 35–6

87 Yet who would have thought the old man to have had so much blood in him?

Lady Macbeth, Act 5, Sc. 1, ll. 38–9. Of the murdered Duncan

88 Here's the smell of the blood still. All the perfumes of Arabia will not sweeten this little hand.

Lady Macbeth, Act 5, Sc. 1, ll. 48–9

89 What's done cannot be undone.

Lady Macbeth, Act 5, Sc. 1, ll. 63–4

90 More needs she the divine than the physician.

The Doctor, of Lady Macbeth, Act 5, Sc. 1, l. 70

91 Now does he feel his title
Hang loose about him like a giant's robe
Upon a dwarfish thief.

Angus, of Macbeth, Act 5, Sc. 2, ll. 20–2

92 I have lived long enough: my way of life
Is fallen into the sere, the yellow leaf;
And that which should accompany old age,
As honour, love, obedience, troops of friends,
I must not look to have.

Macbeth, Act 5, Sc. 3, ll. 22–6

93 Canst thou not minister to a mind diseased,
Pluck from the memory a rooted sorrow,
Raze out the written troubles of the brain,
And with some sweet oblivious antidote
Cleanse the stuffed bosom of that perilous stuff
Which weighs upon the heart?

Macbeth, Act 5, Sc. 3, ll. 40–5. The Doctor replies: 'Therein the patient/Must minister to himself.'

94 Throw physic to the dogs! I'll none of it.

Macbeth, Act 5, Sc. 3, l. 47

95 I have supped full with horrors.

Macbeth, Act 5, Sc. 5, l. 13

96 Tomorrow, and tomorrow, and tomorrow,
Creeps in this petty pace from day to day

To the last syllable of recorded time.

Macbeth, Act 5, Sc. 5, ll. 19–21

97 And all our yesterdays have lighted fools
The way to dusty death.

Macbeth, Act 5, Sc. 5, ll. 22–3

98 Out, out, brief candle!
Life's but a walking shadow, a poor player
That struts and frets his hour upon the stage
And then is heard no more. It is a tale
Told by an idiot, full of sound and fury,
Signifying nothing.

Macbeth, Act 5, Sc. 5, ll. 23–8. The last words proposed by Hector Berlioz for his own epitaph.

99 I bear a charmèd life which must not yield
To one of woman born.

Macbeth, Act 5, Sc. 6, ll. 51–2

100 Macduff was from his mother's womb
Untimely ripped.

Macduff, Act 5, Sc. 6, ll. 54–5. Referring to a birth by Caesarean section, showing Macbeth his delusion in invoking the Witches' promise.

101 The snares of watchful tyranny.

Malcolm, Act 5, Sc. 6, l. 106

Coriolanus
(c. 1608)

1 He's a very dog to the commonalty.

First Citizen, of Caius Marius (later Coriolanus), Act 1, Sc. 1, ll. 26–7

2 You may as well
Strike at the heaven with your staves as lift them
Against the Roman state.

Menenius, Act 1, Sc. 1, ll. 65–7. Addressing the mutinous citizens.

3 What's the matter, you dissentious rogues,
That rubbing the poor itch of your opinion
Make yourselves scabs?

Caius Marius (later Coriolanus), Act 1, Sc. 1, ll. 162–4. Addressing the mutinous citizens.

4 You would be another Penelope. Yet they say all the yarn she spun in Ulysses' absence did but fill Ithaca full of moths.

Valeria, Act 1, Sc. 3, ll. 83–5. Addressed to Virgilia, wife of Coriolanus.

5 Faith, there hath been many great men that have flattered the people, who ne'er loved them; and

there be many that they have loved, they know not wherefore.
Second Officer, Act 2, Sc. 2, ll. 7–10

6 What is the city but the people?
Sicinius, Act 3, Sc. 1, l. 198

7 Despising
For you the city, thus I turn my back.
There is a world elsewhere.
Coriolanus, Act 3, Sc. 3, ll. 133–5. On being banished from Rome.

8 The beast
With many heads butts me away.
Coriolanus, Act 4, Sc. 1, ll. 1–2. Referring to his banishment from Rome.

9 Let me have war, say I. It exceeds peace as far as day does night. It's spritely walking, audible, and full of vent. Peace is a very apoplexy, lethargy; mulled, deaf, sleepy, insensible; a getter of more bastard children than war's a destroyer of men.
First Servingman, Act 4, Sc. 5, ll. 228–32

10 O, a kiss
Long as my exile, sweet as my revenge!
Coriolanus, Act 5, Sc. 3, ll. 44–5

11 The tartness of his face sours ripe grapes.
Menenius, of Coriolanus, Act 5, Sc. 4, ll. 17–18

12 He wants nothing of a god but eternity and a heaven to throne in.
Menenius, of Coriolanus, Act 5, Sc. 4, ll. 23–4

Pericles
(c. 1608)

1 See where she comes, apparelled like the spring.
Pericles, of Antiochus's daughter, Act 1, Sc. 1, l. 13

2 Few love to hear the sins they love to act.
Pericles, Act 1, Sc. 1, l. 93

3 But thou knowest this,
'Tis time to fear when tyrants seem to kiss.
Pericles, Act 1, Sc. 2, ll. 78–9

4 Thou that beget'st him that did thee beget.
Pericles, to his daughter Marina, Act 5, Sc. 1, l. 196

Sonnets
(publ. 1609)

1 From fairest creatures we desire increase,
That thereby beauty's rose might never die.
Sonnet 1

2 When forty winters shall besiege thy brow,
And dig deep trenches in thy beauty's field.
Sonnet 2

3 Thou art thy mother's glass and she in thee
Calls back the lovely April of her prime;
So thou through windows of thine age shalt see,
Despite of wrinkles, this thy golden time.
Sonnet 3

4 Shall I compare thee to a summer's day?
Thou art more lovely and more temperate.
Rough winds do shake the darling buds of May,
And summer's lease hath all too short a date.
Sonnet 18

5 But thy eternal summer shall not fade.
Sonnet 18

6 O, let my books be then the eloquence
And dumb presagers of my speaking breast.
Sonnet 23

7 When in disgrace with Fortune and men's eyes,
I all alone beweep my outcast state,
And trouble deaf heaven with my bootless cries,
And look upon myself, and curse my fate.
Sonnet 29

8 When to the sessions of sweet silent thought
I summon up remembrance of things past,
I sigh the lack of many a thing I sought,
And with old woes new wail my dear time's waste.
Sonnet 30

9 For precious friends hid in death's dateless night.
Sonnet 30

10 Full many a glorious morning have I seen
Flatter the mountain tops with sovereign eye,
Kissing with golden face the meadows green,
Gilding pale streams with heavenly alchemy.
Sonnet 33

11 No more be grieved at that which thou hast done:
Roses have thorns, and silver fountains mud:
Clouds and eclipses stain both moon and sun,
And loathsome canker lives in sweetest bud;
All men make faults.
Sonnet 35

12 Be thou the tenth Muse, ten times more in worth
Than those old nine which rhymers invoke.
Sonnet 38

13 Against that time when thou shalt strangely
      pass,
And scarcely greet me with that sun, thine eye.
Sonnet 49

14 Not marble nor the gilded monuments
Of princes shall outlive this powerful rhyme.
Sonnet 55

15 Like as the waves make towards the pebbled
      shore,
So do our minutes hasten to their end.
Sonnet 60

16 When I have seen the hungry ocean gain
Advantage on the kingdom of the shore.
Sonnet 64

17 Art made tongue-tied by authority.
Sonnet 66

18 Thus is his cheek the map of days outworn.
Sonnet 68

19 No longer mourn for me when I am dead
Than you shall hear the surly sullen bell
Give warning to the world that I am fled
From this vile world with vilest worms to dwell.
Sonnet 71

20 Thou by thy dial's shady stealth mayst know
Time's thievish progress to eternity.
Sonnet 77

21 You still shall live – such virtue hath my pen –
Where breath most breathes, even in the mouths
      of men.
Sonnet 81

22 Farewell, thou art too dear for my possessing,
And like enough thou know'st thy estimate.
Sonnet 87

23 Thus have I had thee as a dream doth flatter,
In sleep a king, but waking no such matter.
Sonnet 87

24 They that have power to hurt and will do
      none,
That do not do the thing they most do show,
Who, moving others, are themselves as stone,
Unmovèd, cold, and to temptation slow.
Sonnet 94

25 They are the lords and owners of their faces,
Others but stewards of their excellence.
Sonnet 94

26 For sweetest things turn sourest by their deeds;
Lilies that fester smell far worse than weeds.
Sonnet 94

27 How like a winter hath my absence been
From thee, the pleasure of the fleeting year!
What freezings have I felt, what dark days seen –
What old December's bareness everywhere!
Sonnet 97

28 The teeming autumn, big with rich increase,
Bearing the wanton burden of the prime,
Like widowed wombs after their lords' decease.
Sonnet 97

29 To me, fair friend, you never can be old,
For as you were when first your eye I eyed,
Such seems your beauty still.
Sonnet 104

30 In the chronicle of wasted time.
Sonnet 106

31 For we, which now behold these present days,
Have eyes to wonder, but lack tongues to praise.
Sonnet 106

32 Not mine own fears, nor the prophetic soul
Of the wide world dreaming on things to come.
Sonnet 107

33 O, never say that I was false of heart,
Though absence seemed my flame to qualify.
As easy might I from myself depart
As from my soul which in thy breast doth lie.
That is my home of love; if I have ranged,
Like him that travels I return again.
Sonnet 109

34 My nature is subdued
To what it works in, like the dyer's hand.
Sonnet 111

35 Let me not to the marriage of true minds
Admit impediments; love is not love
Which alters when it alteration finds,
Or bends with the remover to remove.
O no, it is an ever-fixèd mark
That looks on tempests and is never shaken;
It is the star to every wandering bark,
Whose worth's unknown, although his height be
      taken.
Sonnet 116

36 Love's not Time's fool, though rosy lips and
      cheeks
Within his bending sickle's compass come;

Love alters not with his brief hours and weeks,
But bears it out even to the edge of doom.
If this be error and upon me proved,
I never writ, nor no man ever loved.
Sonnet 116

37 Th'expense of spirit in a waste of shame
Is lust in action, and, till action, lust
Is perjured, murd'rous, bloody, full of blame,
Savage, extreme, rude, cruel, not to trust,
Enjoyed no sooner but despisèd straight.
Sonnet 129

38 My mistress' eyes are nothing like the sun;
Coral is far more red than her lips' red;
If snow be white, why then her breasts are dun;
If hairs be wires, black wires grow on her head.
Sonnet 130

39 When my love swears that she is made of truth
I do believe her, though I know she lies.
Sonnet 138

40 For I have sworn thee fair, and thought thee
  bright,
Who art as black as hell, as dark as night.
Sonnet 147

41 Love is too young to know what conscience is.
Sonnet 151

Cymbeline
(c. 1610)

1 As I told you always, her beauty and her brain go
not together: she's a good sign, but I have seen small
reflection of her wit.
First Lord, Act 1, Sc. 2, ll. 29–31. Attempting to mollify Cloten
after Imogen's rejection of him.

2 All of her that is out of door most rich!
If she be furnished with a mind so rare,
She is alone th'Arabian bird, and I
Have lost the wager. Boldness be my friend;
Arm me audacity from head to foot,
Or, like the Parthian, I shall flying fight;
Rather, directly fly.
Jachimo, Act 1, Sc. 6, ll. 15–21. On first meeting Imogen, whom
he intends to seduce, following a wager.

3 When a gentleman is disposed to swear it is not
for any standers-by to curtail his oaths.
Cloten, Act 2, Sc. 1, ll. 10–11

4 Hark, hark, the lark at heaven's gate sings,
And Phoebus 'gins arise,

His steeds to water at those springs
On chaliced flowers that lies;
And winking Mary-buds begin to ope their golden
  eyes;
With every thing that pretty is, my lady sweet
  arise:
Arise, arise!
Song, Act 2, Sc. 3, ll. 19–25

5 The thanks I give
Is telling you that I am poor of thanks,
And scarce can spare them.
Imogen to Cloten, Act 2, Sc. 3, ll. 85–7

6 I thought her
As chaste as unsunned snow.
Posthumus of Imogen, Act 2, Sc. 4, ll. 164–5

7 O for a horse with wings!
Imogen, Act 3, Sc. 2, l. 47

8 How hard it is to hide the sparks of nature!
Belarius, Act 3, Sc. 3, l. 79

9 Slander,
Whose edge is sharper than the sword, whose
  tongue
Outvenoms all the worms of Nile, whose breath
Rides on the posting winds and doth belie
All corners of the world. Kings, queens, and states,
Maids, matrons, nay, the secrets of the grave
This viperous slander enters.
Pisanio, Act 3, Sc. 4, ll. 31–7

10 Our stomachs
Will make what's homely savoury. Weariness
Can snore upon the flint when resty sloth
Finds the down pillow hard.
Belarius, Act 3, Sc. 6, ll. 32–5

11 Fear no more the heat o'th'sun,
Nor the furious winter's rages.
Thou thy worldly task hast done,
Home art gone and ta'en thy wages.
Golden lads and girls all must,
As chimney-sweepers, come to dust.
Guiderius, Act 4, Sc. 2, ll. 258–63. 'Fidele's Dirge' is sung as a
duet with Arviragus over the supposedly dead body of Fidele
(the disguised Imogen).

12 Fortune brings in some boats that are not
  steered.
Pisanio, Act 4, Sc. 3. l. 46

The Winter's Tale
(c. 1610)

1 Nine changes of the watery star hath been
The shepherd's note.
Polixenes, Act 1, Sc. 2, ll. 1–2. Describing the nine months he
has been away from his kingdom.

2 We were, fair Queen,
Two lads that thought there was no more behind
But such a day tomorrow as today,
And to be boy eternal.

. . .

We were as twinned lambs that did frisk i'th'sun,
And bleat the one at th'other: what we changed
Was innocence for innocence: we knew not
The doctrine of ill-doing, nor dreamed
That any did.
Polixenes, Act 1, Sc. 2, ll. 62–71. Describing to Hermione his
long friendship with her husband, Leontes.

3 But to be paddling palms and pinching fingers,
As now they are, and making practised smiles
As in a looking-glass.
Leontes, Act 1, Sc. 2, ll. 115–17. Of the apparent intimacy
between Polixenes and Hermione.

4 Is whispering nothing?
Is leaning cheek to cheek? Is meeting noses?
Kissing with inside lip? Stopping the career
Of laughter with a sigh? – a note infallible
Of breaking honesty. Horsing foot on foot?
Skulking in corners? Wishing clocks more swift?
Hours minutes? Noon midnight? And all eyes
Blind with the pin and web but theirs, theirs only,
That would unseen be wicked? – is this nothing?
Why, then the world and all that's in't is nothing;
The covering sky is nothing; Bohemia nothing;
My wife is nothing; nor nothing have these
    nothings,
If this be nothing.
Leontes, Act 1, Sc. 2, ll. 284–96

5 A sad tale's best for winter. I have one
Of sprites and goblins.
Mamillius, Act 2, Sc. 1, ll. 25–6

6 It is an heretic that makes the fire,
Not she which burns in't.
Paulina, Act 2, Sc. 3, ll. 114–15

7 I am a feather for each wind that blows.
Leontes, Act 2, Sc. 3, l. 153

8 Thou art perfect, then, our ship hath touched
    upon
The deserts of Bohemia?
Antigonus, Act 3, Sc. 3, ll. 1–2. As was pointed out by BEN
JONSON and LAURENCE STERNE, Bohemia has no coasts.

9 Exit, pursued by a bear.
Stage direction, Act 3, Sc. 3, l. 57. This most famous of all stage
directions, accompanying the sudden exit of Antigonus, has
led some critics to ask whether the bear was real, introduced
as a theatrical coup. Most stage directions in Shakespeare's
plays were additions by later editors.

10 I would there were no age between ten and three-
and-twenty, or that youth would sleep out the rest:
for there is nothing in the between but getting
wenches with child, wronging the ancientry, stealing, fighting.
Shepherd, Act 3, Sc. 3, ll. 58–62

11 When daffodils begin to peer,
With heigh, the doxy over the dale,
Why, then comes in the sweet o' the year,
For the red blood reigns in the winter's pale.
Autolycus (singing), Act 4, Sc. 3, ll. 1–4

12 My father named me Autolycus, who, being, as I
am, littered under Mercury, was likewise a snap-
per-up of unconsidered trifles.
Autolycus, Act 4, Sc. 3, ll. 24–6. In mythology, Autolycus was
the son of Mercury (god of thieves); here, Autolycus was born
when the planet Mercury was in the ascendant.

13 For the life to come, I sleep out the thought of it.
Autolycus, Act 4, Sc. 3, ll. 29–30

14 Daffodils,
That come before the swallow dares, and take
The winds of March with beauty.
Perdita, Act 4, Sc. 3, ll. 118–20

15 Good sooth, she is
The queen of curds and cream.
Camillo, of Perdita, Act 4, Sc. 4, ll. 160–1

16 The selfsame sun that shines upon his court
Hides not his visage from our cottage, but
Looks on alike.
Perdita, Act 4, Sc. 4, ll. 441–3

17 Prosperity's the very bond of love,
Whose fresh complexion and whose heart together
Affliction alters.
Camillo, Act 4, Sc. 4, ll. 570–2

18 Though I am not naturally honest, I am so sometimes by chance.
Autolycus, Act 4, Sc. 4, ll. 707–8

19 Let me have no lying: it becomes none but tradesmen.
Autolycus, Act 4, Sc. 4, ll. 717–18

20 Stars, stars,
And all eyes else dead coals!
Leontes, Act 5, Sc. 1, ll. 67–8. Remembering Hermione's eyes.

The Tempest
(1611)

1 What cares these roarers for the name of king?
Boatswain, Act 1, Sc. 1, ll. 16–17

2 I have great comfort from this fellow: methinks he hath no drowning mark upon him; his complexion is perfect gallows.
Gonzalo, Act 1, Sc. 1, ll. 28–30. Referring to the Boatswain.

3 Now would I give a thousand furlongs of sea for an acre of barren ground, long heath, brown furze, anything. The wills above be done, but I would fain die a dry death.
Gonzalo, Act 1, Sc. 1, ll. 61–4. Referring to the Boatswain.

4 What seest thou else
In the dark backward and abysm of time?
Prospero to Miranda, Act 1, Sc. 2, ll. 49–50

5 Your tale, sir, would cure deafness.
Miranda to Prospero, Act 1, Sc. 2, l. 106

6 My library
Was dukedom large enough.
Prospero, Act 1, Sc. 2, ll. 109–10

7 A freckled whelp, hag-born – not honoured with
A human shape.
Prospero, of Caliban, Act 1, Sc. 2, ll. 283–4

8 You taught me language, and my profit on't
Is, I know how to curse. The red plague rid you
For learning me your language!
Caliban to Miranda, Act 1, Sc. 2, ll. 363–5

9 Full fathom five thy father lies,
Of his bones are coral made;
Those are pearls that were his eyes:
Nothing of him that doth fade,
But doth suffer a sea-change
Into something rich and strange.
Ariel's song, Act 1, Sc. 2, ll. 397–402. The last three lines are inscribed above SHELLEY's ashes in the Protestant Cemetery in Rome.

10 The fringèd curtains of thine eye advance,
And say what thou seest yond.
Prospero to Miranda, Act 1, Sc. 2, ll. 409–10

11 He receives comfort like cold porridge.
Sebastian, of Alonso, Act 2, Sc. 1, ll. 10–11

12 Look, he's winding up the watch of his wit. By and by it will strike.
Sebastian, Act 2, Sc. 1, ll. 14–15. Referring to Gonzalo's attempts to comfort Alonso.

13 Thou dost snore distinctly.
There's meaning in thy snores.
Sebastian to Antonio, Act 2, Sc. 1, ll. 221–2

14 A very ancient and fishlike smell.
Trinculo, Act 2, Sc. 2, ll. 25–6

15 Misery acquaints a man with strange bed-fellows.
Trinculo, Act 2, Sc. 2, l. 39

16 My man-monster hath drowned his tongue in sack.
Stephano, Act 3, Sc. 2, ll. 11–12

17 He that dies pays all debts.
Stephano, Act 3, Sc. 2, l. 132. Adopting a proverbial saying.

18 Be not afeard; the isle is full of noises,
Sounds, and sweet airs, that give delight and hurt
     not.
Sometimes a thousand twangling instruments
Will hum about mine ears; and sometime voices
That, if I then had waked after long sleep,
Will make me sleep again: and then, in dreaming,
The clouds methought would open, and show
     riches
Ready to drop upon me, that when I waked
I cried to dream again.
Caliban, Act 3, Sc. 2, ll. 136–44

19 We are such stuff
As dreams are made on; and our little life
Is rounded with a sleep.
Prospero, Act 4, Sc. 1, ll. 156–8

20 I told you, sir, they were red-hot with drinking.
So full of valour that they smote the air
For breathing in their faces, beat the ground
For kissing of their feet.
Ariel, Act 4, Sc. 1, ll. 171–4. Reporting to Prospero of the drunken state in which he left Trinculo, Stephano and Caliban.

21 I do begin to have bloody thoughts.
Stephano, Act 4, Sc. 1, ll. 220–1

22 We shall lose our time,
And all be turned to barnacles, or to apes
With foreheads villainous low.
Caliban, Act 4, Sc. 1, ll. 247–9

23 The rarer action is
In virtue than in vengeance
Prospero, Act 5, Sc. 1, ll. 27–8

24 Graves at my command
Have waked their sleepers, oped, and let 'em forth
By my so potent art. But this rough magic
I here abjure.
Prospero, Act 5, Sc. 1, ll. 48–51

25 Where the bee sucks, there suck I,
In a cowslip's bell I lie;
There I couch when owls do cry.
On the bat's back I do fly
After summer merrily.
Merrily, merrily shall I live now,
Under the blossom that hangs on the bough.
Ariel's song, Act 5, Sc. 1, ll. 88–94

26 O, wonder!
How many goodly creatures are there here!
How beauteous mankind is! O brave new world,
That has such people in't!
Miranda, Act 5, Sc. 1, ll. 181–4. Prospero replies: ''Tis new to
thee.' *Brave New World* was the title of ALDOUS HUXLEY's
dystopian novel (1932).

27 Let us not burden our remembrances with
A heaviness that's gone.
Prospero, Act 5, Sc. 1, ll. 199–200

Henry VIII
(originally *All is True*, 1613, probably
written with JOHN FLETCHER)

1 No man's pie is freed
From his ambitious finger.
Buckingham, of Wolsey, Act 1, Sc. 1, ll. 52–3

2 Be advised:
Heat not a furnace for your foe so hot
That it do singe yourself.
Norfolk to Buckingham, Act 1, Sc. 1, ll. 139–41

3 Go with me like good angels to my end,
And as the long divorce of steel falls on me
Make of your prayers one sweet sacrifice,
And lift my soul to heaven.
Buckingham, Act 1, Sc. 1, ll. 175–8. Requesting his friends to
accompany him to his execution.

4 I swear again, I would not be a queen
For all the world.
Anne Bullen (Boleyn), Act 2, Sc. 3, ll. 45–6. She is crowned in
Act 4.

5 You have many enemies that know not
Why they are so, but, like to village curs,
Bark when their fellows do.
King Henry to Wolsey, Act 2, Sc. 4, ll. 158–60

6 They should be good men, their affairs as
righteous:
But all hoods make not monks.
Queen Katherine, Act 3, Sc. 1, ll. 22–3. Referring to Cardinals
Wolsey and Campeius.

7 Ye have angels' faces, but heaven knows your
hearts.
Queen Katherine, Act 3, Sc. 1, l. 145. Referring to Cardinals
Wolsey and Campeius.

8 I have touched the highest point of all my
greatness,
And from that full meridian of my glory
I haste now to my setting. I shall fall
Like a bright exhalation in the evening,
And no man see me more.
Wolsey, Act 3, Sc. 2, ll. 223–7

9 Farewell, a long farewell, to all my greatness!
This is the state of man: today he puts forth
The tender leaves of hopes, tomorrow blossoms,
And bears his blushing honours thick upon him.
The third day comes a frost, a killing frost,
And when he thinks, good easy man, full surely
His greatness is a-ripening, nips his root,
And then he falls, as I do.
Wolsey, Act 3, Sc. 2, ll. 351–8

10 O, how wretched
Is that poor man that hangs on princes' favours!
There is betwixt that smile we would aspire to,
That sweet aspect of princes, and their ruin,
More pangs and fears than wars or women have;
And when he falls, he falls like Lucifer,
Never to hope again.
Wolsey, Act 3, Sc. 2, ll. 366–72

11 I know myself now, and I feel within me
A peace above all earthly dignities,
A still and quiet conscience.
Wolsey, Act 3, Sc. 2, ll. 378–80

12 Love thyself last, cherish those hearts that hate
thee;
Corruption wins not more than honesty.
Still in thy right hand carry gentle peace
To silence envious tongues. Be just, and fear not.
Let all the ends thou aim'st at be thy country's,

Thy God's, and truth's. Then if thou fall'st, O
   Cromwell,
Thou fall'st a blessèd martyr.
Wolsey's advice to Thomas Cromwell, Act 3, Sc. 2, ll. 443–9

13 Had I but served my God with half the zeal
I served my King, He would not in mine age
Have left me naked to mine enemies.
Wolsey, Act 3, Sc. 2, ll. 455–7. See THOMAS WOLSEY 1.

14 He was a man
Of an unbounded stomach, ever ranking
Himself with princes.
Katherine, of the dead Wolsey, Act 4, Sc. 2, ll. 33–5

15 Men's evil manners live in brass, their virtues
We write in water.
Griffith, Act 4, Sc. 2, ll. 45–6. See JOHN KEATS 122.

16 He was a scholar, and a ripe and good one,
Exceeding wise, fair-spoken, and persuading;
Lofty and sour to them that loved him not,
But, to those men that sought him, sweet as
   summer.
Griffith, of the dead Wolsey, Act 4, Sc. 2, ll. 33–5

17 To dance attendance on their lordships'
   pleasures.
King Henry, Act 5, Sc. 2, l. 30

18 Men so noble,
However faulty, yet should find respect
For what they have been. 'Tis a cruelty
To load a falling man.
Cromwell, Act 5, Sc. 3, ll. 74–7. Rebuking Gardiner for his
treatment of Cranmer.

19 There's a trim rabble let in: are all these
Your faithful friends o'th'suburbs?
Lord Chamberlain, Act 5, Sc. 4, ll. 70–1. Referring to the crowds
gathered to see the christening of the future Queen Elizabeth.

20 Some come to take their ease,
And sleep an act or two.
Epilogue, ll. 2–3. Referring to theatre-goers.

The Two Noble Kinsmen
(c. 1614)

1 This world's a city full of straying streets,
And death's the market place, where each one
   meets.
Third Queen, Act 1, Sc. 5, ll. 15–16

Epitaph

1 Good friend for Jesus' sake forbear
To dig the dust enclosed here
Blessed be the man that spares these stones
And cursed be he that moves my bones.
On Shakespeare's tomb at Holy Trinity Church, Stratford-
upon-Avon. Critics have disputed whether Shakespeare wrote
his own epitaph.

Bill Shankly
(1913–81)
British footballer and manager

*He played for Preston North End and Scotland in the 1930s,
and went on to be one of the most successful and respected
football managers. He managed Liverpool FC (1959–74), the
team with which he is most associated.*

1 Some people think football is a matter of life and
death. I don't like that attitude. I can assure them it
is much more serious than that.
Interview on Granada chat-show, quoted in *The Sunday Times*
4 October 1981

George Bernard Shaw
(1856–1950)
Irish dramatist and critic

*He was a music and drama critic before launching his career
as a playwright. His prodigious output combined fierce wit
with a passion for social reform, for example* Mrs Warren's
Profession *(1894) and* Pygmalion *(1913). He also wrote novels
and essays. See also* JAMES AGATE 2, MRS PATRICK
CAMPBELL 1, V. I. LENIN 13, BERT LESTON TAYLOR 2, W. B.
YEATS 41.

1 The fickleness of the women I love is only equalled
by the infernal constancy of the women who love
me.
The Philanderer, Act 2 (written 1893, performed 1905). Spoken
by Charteris.

2 People are always blaming their circumstances
for what they are. I don't believe in circumstances.
The people who get on in this world are the people
who get up and look for the circumstances they
want, and, if they can't find them, make them.
Mrs Warren's Profession, Act 2 (written 1894, performed 1905).
Spoken by Vivie Warren.

3 We have no more right to consume happiness
without producing it than to consume wealth without producing it.
Candida, Act 1 (1895). Spoken by Morell.

4 It is easy – terribly easy – to shake a man's faith in himself. To take advantage of that to break a man's spirit is devil's work.

Morell, ibid., Act 1

5 Man can climb to the highest summits; but he cannot dwell there long.

Morell, ibid., Act 3

6 I'm only a beer teetotaller, not a champagne teetotaller.

Proserpine, ibid., Act 3

7 There is nothing so bad or so good that you will not find an Englishman doing it; but you will never find an Englishman in the wrong. He does everything on principle. He fights you on patriotic principles; he robs you on business principles; he enslaves you on imperial principles; he bullies you on manly principles; he supports his king on loyal principles and cuts off his king's head on republican principles. His watchword is always Duty; and he never forgets that the nation which lets its duty get on the opposite side to its interest is lost.

The Man of Destiny (1895). Spoken by Napoleon.

8 The worst sin towards our fellow creatures is not to hate them, but to be indifferent to them; that's the essence of inhumanity.

The Devil's Disciple, Act 2 (1897). Spoken by Anderson.

9 He is a barbarian, and thinks that the customs of his tribe and island are the laws of nature.

Caesar and Cleopatra, Act 2 (1898). Spoken by Caesar, of his secretary Britannus, 'an islander from the western end of the world, a day's voyage from Gaul'.

10 When a stupid man is doing something he is ashamed of, he always declares that it is his duty.

Apollodorus, ibid., Act 3

11 A man of great common sense and good taste – meaning thereby a man without originality or moral courage.

Ibid., Notes, 'Julius Caesar'

12 Whenever you wish to do anything against the law, Cicely, always consult a good solicitor first.

Captain Brassbound's Conversion, Act 1 (1899). Spoken by Sir Howard.

13 Nothing makes a man so selfish as work.

Brassbound, ibid., Act 3

14 The more I see of the moneyed classes, the more I understand the guillotine.

Letter, 25 September 1899, publ. in *Collected Letters*, vol. 2 (ed. Dan Laurence, 1972)

15 English decency is a rather dirty thing. It is responsible for more indecency than anything else in the world. It is a string of taboos.

Unpublished letter to *The Times*, c. 1900, quoted in *Bernard Shaw*, vol. 1, ch. 7, sect. 1 (1988) by Michael Holroyd

16 It seems impossible to root out of an Englishman's mind the notion that vice is delightful, and that abstention from it is privation.

Preface (1902) to *Mrs Warren's Profession*

17 This is the true joy in life, the being used for a purpose recognized by yourself as a mighty one; the being thoroughly worn out before you are thrown on the scrap heap; the being a force of Nature instead of a feverish selfish little clod of ailments and grievances complaining that the world will not devote itself to making you happy.

Man and Superman, Epistle Dedicatory (1903)

18 The more things a man is ashamed of, the more respectable he is.

Tanner, ibid., Act 1

19 The true artist will let his wife starve, his children go barefoot, his mother drudge for his living at seventy, sooner than work at anything but his art.

Tanner, ibid., Act 1

20 There is no love sincerer than the love of food.

Tanner, ibid., Act 1

21 Hell is full of musical amateurs: music is the brandy of the damned.

Don Juan, ibid., Act 3

22 Englishmen never will be slaves: they are free to do whatever the Government and public opinion allow them to do.

The Devil, ibid., Act 3

23 An Englishman thinks he is moral when he is only uncomfortable.

The Devil, ibid., Act 3

24 A broken heart is a very pleasant complaint for a man in London if he has a comfortable income.

Ann, ibid., Act 4

25 Revolutions have never lightened the burden of tyranny: they have only shifted it to another shoulder.

Ibid., 'The Revolutionist's Handbook', Preface

26 Englishmen hate Liberty and Equality too much to understand them. But every Englishman loves and desires a pedigree.
Ibid., 'The Revolutionist's Handbook', sect. 10

27 The art of government is the organization of idolatry.
Ibid., 'Maxims for Revolutionists: Idolatry'

28 Vulgarity in a king flatters the majority of the nation.
Ibid., 'Maxims for Revolutionists: Royalty'

29 Democracy substitutes election by the incompetent many for appointment by the corrupt few.
Ibid., 'Maxims for Revolutionists: Democracy'

30 He who can, does. He who cannot, teaches.
Ibid., 'Maxims for Revolutionists: Education'

31 Marriage is popular because it combines the maximum of temptation with the maximum of opportunity.
Ibid., 'Maxims for Revolutionists: Marriage'

32 Man is the only animal which esteems itself rich in proportion to the number and voracity of its parasites.
Ibid., 'Maxims for Revolutionists: Servants'

33 Ladies and gentleman are permitted to have friends in the kennel, but not in the kitchen.
Ibid., 'Maxims for Revolutionists: Servants'

34 If you strike a child, take care that you strike it in anger, even at the risk of maiming it for life. A blow in cold blood neither can nor should be forgiven.
Ibid., 'Maxims for Revolutionists: How to Beat Children'

35 The reasonable man adapts himself to the world; the unreasonable one persists in trying to adapt the world to himself. Therefore, all progress depends on the unreasonable man.
Ibid., 'Maxims for Revolutionists: Reason'

36 Life levels all men: death reveals the eminent.
Ibid., 'Maxims for Revolutionists: Fame'

37 Every man over forty is a scoundrel.
Ibid., 'Maxims for Revolutionists: Stray Sayings'

38 Self-sacrifice enables us to sacrifice other people without blushing.
Ibid., 'Maxims for Revolutionists: Self-Sacrifice'

39 What really flatters a man is that you think him worth flattering.
John Bull's Other Island, Act 4 (1904). Spoken by Broadbent.

40 My religion? Well, my dear, I am a Millionaire. That is my religion.
Major Barbara, Act 2 (1905). Spoken by Andrew Undershaft.

41 He never does a proper thing without giving an improper reason for it.
Lady Britomart of Undershaft, ibid., Act 3

42 He knows nothing; and he thinks he knows everything. That points clearly to a political career.
Undershaft, of his son Stephen, ibid., Act 3

43 The seven deadly sins . . . Food, clothing, firing, rent, taxes, respectability and children. Nothing can lift those seven millstones from Man's neck but money; and the spirit cannot soar until the millstones are lifted.
Undershaft, ibid., Act 3

44 All professions are conspiracies against the laity.
The Doctor's Dilemma, Act 1 (1906). Spoken by Sir Patrick Cullen.

45 Life does not cease to be funny when people die any more than it ceases to be serious when people laugh.
Ridgeon, ibid., Act 5

46 There is no subject on which more dangerous nonsense is talked and thought than marriage.
Getting Married, Preface (1908). Opening words.

47 How can you dare teach a man to read until you've taught him everything else first?
Misalliance (1910). Spoken by Lord Summerhays.

48 Nothing is worth doing unless the consequences may be serious.
Hypatia, ibid.

49 Suppose the world were only one of God's jokes, would you work any the less to make it a good joke instead of a bad one?
Letter to LEO TOLSTOY, 14 February 1910, publ. in Collected Letters, vol. 2 (ed. Dan Laurence, 1972). Tolstoy had criticized Shaw for his facetious tone in Arms and the Man, saying that one 'should not speak jestingly of such a subject as the purpose of human life, the causes of its perversion, and the evil that fills the life of humanity today'.

50 A life spent in making mistakes is not only more honorable but more useful than a life spent doing nothing.
Preface (1911) to The Doctor's Dilemma, 'The Technical Problem'

51 Of all the anti-social vested interests the worst is the vested interest in ill health.
Preface, ibid., 'The Latest Theories'

52 Assassination is the extreme form of censorship.
Preface (1911) to *The Shewing-Up of Blanco Posnet*, 'The Rejected Statement', pt 1, 'The Limits to Toleration'

53 As long as I have a want, I have a reason for living. Satisfaction is death.
Overruled (1912). Spoken by Gregory Lunn.

54 I don't want to talk grammar. I want to talk like a lady.
Pygmalion, Act 2 (1913). Spoken by Liza Doolittle.

55 I'm one of the undeserving poor: that's what I am. Think of what that means to a man. It means that he's up agen middle class morality all the time. If there's anything going, and I put in for a bit of it, it's always the same story: 'You're undeserving; so you can't have it.'
Alfred Doolittle, ibid., Act 2. He continues: 'What is middle class morality? Just an excuse for never giving me anything.'

56 Gin was mother's milk to her.
Liza Doolittle, of her aunt, ibid., Act 3

57 We are a nation of governesses.
New Statesman 12 April 1913

58 The secret of being miserable is to have leisure to bother about whether you are happy or not. The cure for it is occupation.
Parents and Children, 'Children's Happiness' (1914)

59 A perpetual holiday is a good working definition of hell.
Ibid., 'Children's Happiness'

60 It is impossible for an Englishman to open his mouth without making some other Englishman hate or despise him.
Preface (1916) to *Pygmalion*

61 All great truths begin as blasphemies.
Annajanska, the Bolshevik Princess (1917). Spoken by the Grand Duchess.

62 It is a curious sensation: the sort of pain that goes mercifully beyond our powers of feeling. When your heart is broken, your boats are burned: nothing matters any more. It is the end of happiness and the beginning of peace.
Heartbreak House, Act 2 (1919). Spoken by Ellie.

63 Old men are dangerous: it doesn't matter to them what is going to happen to the world.
Captain Shotover, ibid., Act 2. Ellie responds: 'I should have

thought nothing else mattered to old men. They can't be very interested in what is going to happen to themselves.'

64 Never waste jealousy on a real man: it is the imaginary man that supplants us all in the long run.
Hector Hushabye, ibid.

65 Go anywhere in England where there are natural, wholesome, contented, and really nice English people; and what do you always find? That the stables are the real centre of the household . . . There are only two classes in good society in England: the equestrian classes and the neurotic classes.
Lady Utterword, ibid., Act 3

66 You see things; and you say 'Why?' But I dream things that never were; and I say 'Why not?'
Back to Methusaleh, 'In the Beginning', Act 1 (1920). These words (spoken by the Serpent) are often associated with ROBERT F. KENNEDY, after they were quoted by him in an address to the Irish Parliament in Dublin, June 1963, and attributed to him by Edward Kennedy at Robert's funeral service in 1968.

67 Life is too short for men to take it seriously.
Franklyn, ibid., 'The Gospel of the Brothers Barnabas'

68 Life is a disease; and the only difference between one man and another is the stage of the disease at which he lives. You are always at the crisis: I am always in the convalescent stage. I enjoy convalescence. It is the part that makes illness worth while.
Lubin, ibid. Addressing his political rival Burge.

69 A nap, my friend, is a brief period of sleep which overtakes superannuated persons when they endeavour to entertain unwelcome visitors or to listen to scientific lectures.
The Elderly Gentleman, ibid., 'Tragedy of an Elderly Gentleman', Act 1

70 In Ireland they try to make a cat cleanly by rubbing its nose in its own filth. Mr Joyce has tried the same treatment on the human subject. I hope it may prove successful.
Of *Ulysses*, in letter to JAMES JOYCE's publisher Sylvia Beach, 10 October 1921, publ. in *Letters of James Joyce*, vol. 3 (ed. RICHARD ELLMAN, 1966). Shaw refused the invitation to purchase a copy of the book, calling it a 'revolting record of a disgusting phase of civilization; but it is a truthful one'. In *The Table Talk of GBS* (1924), Shaw is quoted: 'I could not write the words Mr Joyce used: my prudish hand would refuse to form the letters.'

71 It is difficult, if not impossible, for most people

to think otherwise than in the fashion of their own period.
Saint Joan, Preface (1924)

72 We want a few mad people now. See where the sane ones have landed us!
Poulengey, ibid., Sc. 1

73 A miracle is an event which creates faith. That is the purpose and nature of miracles ... Frauds deceive. An event which creates faith does not deceive: therefore it is not a fraud, but a miracle.
The Archbishop, ibid., Sc. 2

74 What Englishman will give his mind to politics as long as he can afford to keep a motor car?
The Apple Cart, Act 1 (1929). Spoken by Balbus.

75 A king is not allowed the luxury of a good character. Our country has produced millions of blameless greengrocers, but not one blameless monarch.
King Magnus, ibid., Act 1

76 The national anthem belongs to the eighteenth century. In it you find us ordering God about to do our political dirty work.
The Adventures of the Black Girl in Her Search for God (1932). Spoken by a member of the Caravan of the Curious.

77 When Satan makes impure verses, Allah sends a divine tune to cleanse them.
The Arab, ibid.

78 Newspapers are unable, seemingly, to discriminate between a bicycle accident and the collapse of civilisation.
Preface (1934) to Too True to be Good

79 The trouble, Mr Goldwyn, is that you are only interested in art and I am only interested in money.
Quoted in *The Great Goldwyn*, ch. 3 (1937) by Alva Johnson. Addressed to SAMUEL GOLDWYN, according to publicity chief HOWARD DIETZ, during talks to engage Shaw as a writer for Hollywood. The words, released in a press statement, are probably an approximation of the original dialogue.

80 A man of my spiritual intensity does not eat corpses.
Quoted in *Bernard Shaw: His Life and Personality*, ch. 9 (1942) by Hesketh Pearson. Shaw, Pearson reported, believed vegetarians had radically different experiences from meat-eaters: 'The odd thing about being a vegetarian is, not that the things that happen to other people don't happen to me – they all do – but that they happen differently: pain is different, pleasure different, fever different, cold different, even love different.'

81 The ideal love-affair is one conducted by post.

My correspondence with Ellen Terry was a wholly satisfactory love-affair. I could have met her at any time; but I did not wish to complicate such a delightful intercourse. She got tired of five husbands; but she never got tired of me.
Quoted ibid., ch. 15

82 In literature the ambition of the novice is to acquire the literary language: the struggle of the adept is to get rid of it.
Quoted ibid., ch. 16

83 A government which robs Peter to pay Paul can always depend on the support of Paul.
Everybody's Political What's What, ch. 30 (1944)

84 [Dancing is] a perpendicular expression of a horizontal desire.
Attributed in the *New Statesman* 23 March 1962

85 Lord Northcliffe: The trouble with you, Shaw, is that you look as if you were the famine in the land.
   Shaw: The trouble with you, Northcliffe, is that you look as if you were the cause of it.
Attributed

86 Shaw: Would you sleep with me for £1,000?
Lady: I would consider the proposal.
Shaw: Would you sleep with me for £1?
Lady: What do you think I am?
Shaw: Madam, we have established what you are.
   We are simply haggling over the price.
Attributed

Henry Wheeler Shaw
See Josh Billings

(Sir) Hartley Shawcross
(1902–2003)
British lawyer

Baron Shawcross of Friston. Attorney-General 1945–51, he was chief British prosecutor at the Nuremberg Trials (1945–6) and led the prosecution of the Klaus Fuchs 'atomic spy' case (1950).

1 You cannot do justice to the dead. When we talk about doing justice to the dead we are talking about retribution for the harm done to them. But retribution and justice are two different things.
Quoted in the *Daily Telegraph* 1 May 1991. Discussing the War Crimes Bill and the prosecution of ex-Nazis living in Britain.

(Sir) Martin Archer Shee

(1769–1850)

Irish artist

A pupil of JOSHUA REYNOLDS, *he became a fashionable portrait painter and was President of the Royal Academy from 1830. He also wrote verse, fiction and for the theatre.*

1 Dug from the tomb of taste-refining time,
Each form is exquisite, each block sublime.
Or good, or bad, – disfigured, or depraved, –
All art, is at its resurrection saved;
All crowned with glory in the critic's heaven,
Each merit magnified, each fault forgiven.

Rhymes on Art, or the Remonstrance of a Painter, pt 2, ll. 340–5 (1805)

2 Give me the critic bred in Nature's school,
Who neither talks by rote, nor thinks by rule;
Who feeling's honest dictates still obeys,
And dares, without a precedent, to praise.

Ibid., pt 2, ll. 490–3

Hellen Shelley

(1799–1885)

Sister of Percy Bysshe Shelley

1 After Shelley, Byron and Scott, you know, one cannot care about other poets.

Remark at dinner with WILLIAM ALLINGHAM, quoted by Allingham in journal entry, 29 October 1864, publ. in *Diaries of William Allingham*, ch. 6 (1907)

Mary Wollstonecraft Shelley

(1797–1851)

English novelist

The daughter of WILLIAM GODWIN *and* MARY WOLLSTONE-CRAFT, *she married* PERCY BYSSHE SHELLEY *in 1816 and shared his wandering life in Europe. Her best-known work,* Frankenstein *(1818), originated as a horror story related to Shelley and* BYRON *while in Switzerland. Other romances, also in the Gothic tradition, include* Valperga *(1823) and* The Last Man *(1826).*

1 I beheld the wretch – the miserable monster whom I had created.

Frankenstein, or the Modern Prometheus, ch. 5 (1818). Frankenstein narrates being woken by his creation, the monster.

2 Everywhere I see bliss, from which I alone am irrevocably excluded. I was benevolent and good; misery made me a fiend.

Frankenstein's monster, ibid., ch. 5

3 Life is obstinate and clings closest where it is most hated.

Ibid., ch. 23

Percy Bysshe Shelley

(1792–1822)

English poet

Born into a wealthy family, he was a lifelong opponent of social injustice and political oppression, and a poet of visionary intensity. He was expelled from Oxford for his pamphlet The Necessity of Atheism *(1811), and eventually settled in Italy (1818) where he died while sailing. Early poems such as* Queen Mab *(1813) reflected his political ideals. Later work included 'Peter Bell the Third' (1819), a satire on* WORDSWORTH, *and* Prometheus Unbound *(1820), a lyric drama. See* MATTHEW ARNOLD 61.

1 I think that the leaf of a tree, the meanest insect on which we trample, are in themselves arguments more conclusive than any which can be adduced that some vast intellect animates Infinity.

Letter, 3 January 1811, publ. in *The Letters of Percy Bysshe Shelley*, vol. 1 (ed. Frederick L. Jones, 1964)

2 Here I swear that never will I forgive Christianity! It is the only point on which I allow myself to encourage revenge ... Oh, how I wish I *were* the Antichrist, that it were *mine* to crush the Demon; to hurl him to his native Hell never to rise again – I expect to gratify some of this insatiable feeling in poetry.

Letter, 3 January 1811, ibid.

3 Yes, *marriage* is hateful, detestable. A kind of ineffable, sickening disgust seizes my mind when I think of this most despotic, most unrequited fetter which prejudice has forged to confine its energies.

Letter, 2 May 1811, ibid., vol. 1. In another letter to the same correspondent (Thomas Jefferson Hogg), 8 October 1811, Shelley justified his own marriage on the grounds that, until considerable improvement of morals had been brought about, it was advisable to maintain the institution of matrimony.

4 All religions are good which make men good.

An Address to the Irish People (1812), publ. in *Shelley's Prose* (ed. David L. Clark, 1954). See THOMAS PAINE 14.

5 Government is an evil; it is only the thoughtlessness and vices of men that make it a necessary evil. When all men are good and wise, government will of itself decay.

An Address to the Irish People, ibid.

6 How wonderful is Death,
Death and his brother Sleep!
Queen Mab, canto 1, ll. 1–2 (1813)

7 Power, like a desolating pestilence,
Pollutes whate'er it touches; and obedience,
Bane of all genius, virtue, freedom, truth,
Makes slaves of men, and, of the human frame,
A mechanized automaton.
Ibid., canto 3, ll. 176–80

8 War is the statesman's game, the priest's delight,
The lawyer's jest, the hired assassin's trade.
Ibid., canto 4, ll. 168–9

9 Commerce has set the mark of selfishness,
The signet of its all-enslaving power,
Upon a shining ore, and called it gold:
Before whose image bow the vulgar great,
The vainly rich, the miserable proud,
The mob of peasants, nobles, priests, and kings,
And with blind feelings reverence the power
That grinds them to the dust of misery.
Ibid., canto 5, ll. 53–60

10 All things are sold: the very light of Heaven
Is venal; earth's unsparing gifts of love,
The smallest and most despicable things
That lurk in the abysses of the deep,
All objects of our life, even life itself,
And the poor pittance which the laws allow
Of liberty, the fellowship of man,
Those duties which his heart of human love
Should urge him to perform instinctively,
Are bought and sold as in a public mart
Of undisguising selfishness, that sets
On each its price, the stamp-mark of her reign.
Ibid., canto 5, ll. 177–88

11 Not even the intercourse of the sexes is exempt
from the despotism of positive institution. Law pretends even to govern the indisciplinable wanderings
of passion, to put fetters on the clearest deductions
of reason, and, by appeals to the will, to subdue
the involuntary affections of our nature. Love is
inevitably consequent upon the perception of loveliness. Love withers under constraint: its very
essence is liberty: it is compatible neither with
obedience, jealousy, nor fear: it is there most pure,
perfect, and unlimited, where its votaries live in
confidence, equality, and unreserve.
Ibid., Note: 'Even Love is Sold'

12 Love is free; to promise for ever to love the same

woman is not less absurd than to promise to believe
the same creed; such a vow in both cases excludes
us from all inquiry.
Ibid., Note: 'Even Love is Sold'

13 Chastity is a monkish and evangelical superstition, a greater foe to natural temperance even
than unintellectual sensuality.
Ibid., Note: 'Even Love is Sold'

14 Prostitution is the legitimate offspring of marriage and its accompanying errors.
Ibid., Note: 'Even Love is Sold'

15 Let the advocate of animal food force himself to
. . . tear a living lamb with his teeth, and plunging his
head into its vitals slake his thirst with the steaming
blood; when fresh from the deed of horror, let him
revert to the irresistible instincts of nature that
would rise in judgement against it, and say, 'Nature
formed me for such work as this.' Then, and then
only, would he be consistent.
Ibid., Note: 'A Vindication of Natural Diet'. The title was added
when the essay was published separately as a pamphlet.
Shelley became a vegetarian in 1812.

16 Man's yesterday may ne'er be like his morrow;
Nought may endure but Mutability.
'Mutability', st. 4, written 1814, publ. in *Poetical Works* (ed.
Thomas Hutchinson, 1905)

17 What is love? Ask him who lives, what is life? Ask
him who adores, what is God?
'On Love', written c. 1815, publ. in *Shelley's Prose* (ed. David L.
Clark, 1954). Opening words of essay.

18 If we reason, we would be understood; if we
imagine, we would that the airy children of our
brain were born anew within another's; if we feel,
we would that another's nerves should vibrate to
our own, that the beams of their eyes should kindle
at once and mix and melt into our own, that lips of
motionless ice should not reply to lips quivering
and burning with the heart's best blood. This is Love.
'On Love', ibid.

19 The awful shadow of some unseen Power
Floats though unseen among us, – visiting
This various world with as inconstant wing
As summer winds that creep from flower to flower.
'Hymn to Intellectual Beauty, st. 1, written 1816, publ. in *Poeti-
cal Works* (ed. Thomas Hutchinson, 1905). Opening lines,
referring to the 'Spirit of Beauty'.

20 While yet a boy I sought for ghosts, and sped
Through many a listening chamber, cave, and ruin,

And starlight wood, with fearful steps pursuing
Hopes of high talk with the departed dead.
'Hymn to Intellectual Beauty', st. 5, ibid.

21 There is a harmony
In autumn, and a lustre in its sky,
Which through the summer is not heard or
    seen,
As if it could not be, as if it had not been!
'Hymn to Intellectual Beauty', st. 7, ibid.

22 Lord Byron is an exceedingly interesting person,
and as such is it not to be regretted that he is a slave
to the vilest and most vulgar prejudices, and as mad
as the winds?
Letter to THOMAS LOVE PEACOCK, 17 July 1816, publ. in *The
Letters of Percy Bysshe Shelley*, vol. 1 (ed. Frederick L. Jones,
1964)

23 I met a traveller from an antique land
Who said: Two vast and trunkless legs of stone
Stand in the desert. Near them, on the sand,
Half sunk, a shattered visage lies, whose frown,
And wrinkled lip, and sneer of cold command,
Tell that its sculptor well those passions read
Which yet survive, stamped on these lifeless
    things,
The hand that mocked them, and the heart that
    fed:
And on the pedestal these words appear:
'My name is Ozymandias, king of kings:
Look on my works, ye Mighty, and despair!'
'Ozymandias', ll. 1–11, written 1817, publ. in *Poetical Works* (ed.
Thomas Hutchinson, 1905). The poem was probably written
in competition with Horace Smith, whose sonnet is extant,
but does not name Ozymandias.

24 Alas! I have nor hope nor health,
Nor peace within nor calm around,
Nor that content surpassing wealth
The sage in meditation found.
'Stanzas Written in Dejection, near Naples', st. 3, written 1818,
ibid.

25 I love all waste
And solitary places; where we taste
The pleasure of believing what we see
Is boundless, as we wish our souls to be.
'Julian and Maddalo', ll. 14–17, written 1818–19, ibid.

26 Concerning God, freewill and destiny:
Of all that earth has been or yet may be,
All that vain men imagine or believe,

Or hope can paint or suffering may achieve,
We descanted.
'Julian and Maddalo', ll. 42–6, ibid. The poem recreates a night
spent in discussion with BYRON in Venice, August 1818.

27 Thou Paradise of exiles, Italy!
'Julian and Maddalo', l. 57, ibid.

28 It is our will
That thus enchains us to permitted ill –
We might be otherwise – we might be all
We dream of happy, high, majestical.
Where is the love, beauty, and truth we seek
But in our mind?
'Julian and Maddalo', ll. 170–5, ibid.

29 But *me* – whose heart a stranger's tear might
    wear
As water-drops the sandy fountain-stone,
Who loved and pitied all things, and could
    moan
For woes which others hear not, and could see
The absent with the glance of phantasy,
And with the poor and trampled sit and weep,
Following the captive to his dungeon deep;
Me – who am as a nerve o'er which do creep
The else unfelt oppressions of this earth.
'Julian and Maddalo', ll. 442–50, ibid. Spoken by Count
Maddalo.

30 Most wretched men
Are cradled into poetry by wrong,
They learn in suffering what they teach in song.
'Julian and Maddalo', ll. 544–6, ibid.

31 Chameleons feed on light and air:
Poets' food is love and fame.
'An Exhortation', st. 1, written 1819, ibid.

32 All things by a law divine
In one spirit meet and mingle.
Why not I with thine?
'Love's Philosophy', st. 1 (1819), ibid.

33 I met Murder on the way –
He had a mask like Castlereagh –
Very smooth he looked, yet grim;
Seven bloodhounds followed him.
'The Mask of Anarchy', st. 2, written 1819, ibid. In common
with other critics of the Tory administration of the day,
Shelley despised above all Robert Stewart, Viscount Castle-
reagh, though there is nothing to suggest that the latter had
any specific role in the Peterloo Massacre in August 1819,
when troops fired on a Reform meeting in Manchester –
the event that stirred Shelley to write this poem. See LORD
BYRON 132.

34 For one by one, and two by two,
He tossed them human hearts to chew.
'The Mask of Anarchy', st. 3, ibid.

35 O wild West Wind, thou breath of Autumn's
    being,
Thou, from whose unseen presence the leaves
    dead
Are driven, like ghosts from an enchanter fleeing,
Yellow, and black, and pale, and hectic red,
Pestilence-stricken multitudes.
'Ode to the West Wind', ll. 1–5, written 1819, ibid.

36 Wild Spirit, which art moving everywhere;
Destroyer and preserver; hear, oh, hear!
'Ode to the West Wind', ll. 13–14, ibid.

37 Thou dirge
Of the dying year, to which this closing night
Will be the dome of a vast sepulchre,
Vaulted with all thy congregated might
Of vapours, from whose solid atmosphere
Black rain, and fire, and hail will burst: oh, hear!
'Ode to the West Wind', ll. 23–8, ibid.

38 Oh, lift me as a wave, a leaf, a cloud!
I fall upon the thorns of life! I bleed!
'Ode to the West Wind', ll. 53–4, ibid.

39 Make me thy lyre, even as the forest is:
What if my leaves are falling like its own!
The tumult of thy mighty harmonies
Will take from both a deep, autumnal tone,
Sweet though in sadness. Be thou, Spirit fierce,
My spirit! Be thou me, impetuous one!
'Ode to the West Wind', ll. 57–62, ibid.

40 Drive my dead thoughts over the universe
Like withered leaves to quicken a new birth!
And, by the incantation of this verse,
Scatter, as from an unextinguished hearth
Ashes and sparks, my words among mankind!
Be through my lips to unawakened earth
The trumpet of a prophecy!
'Ode to the West Wind', ll. 63–9, ibid.

41 O, Wind,
If Winter comes, can Spring be far behind?
'Ode to the West Wind', ll. 69–70, ibid. Closing lines of poem.

42 Hell is a city much like London –
A populous and a smoky city.
'Peter Bell the Third', pt 3 ('Hell'), st. 1, written 1819, ibid.

43 And this is Hell – and in this smother
All are damnable and damned;

Each one damning, damns the other;
They are damned by one another.
By none other are they damned.
'Peter Bell the Third', pt 3, st. 15, ibid.

44 Men of England, wherefore plough
For the lords who lay ye low?
Wherefore weave with toil and care
The rich robes your tyrants wear?
'Song to the Men of England', st. 1, written 1819, ibid.

45 The seed ye sow, another reaps;
The wealth ye find, another keeps;
The robes ye weave, another wears;
The arms ye forge, another bears.
'Song to the Men of England', st. 5, ibid.

46 An old, mad, blind, despised, and dying king,
Princes, the dregs of their dull race, who flow
Through public scorn, mud from a muddy spring,
Rulers who neither see, nor feel, nor know,
But leech-like to their fainting country cling.
'Sonnet: England in 1819', ll. 1–5, written 1819, ibid. Of GEORGE
III.

47 That orbèd maiden with white fire laden,
Whom mortals call the Moon,
Glides glimmering o'er my fleece-like floor,
By the midnight breezes strewn.
'The Cloud', ll. 45–8, written 1820, ibid.

48 You are now
In London, that great sea, whose ebb and flow
At once is deaf and loud, and on the shore
Vomits its wrecks, and still howls on for more.
Yet in its depth what treasures!
'Letter to Maria Gisborne', ll. 192–6, written 1820, ibid.

49 You will see Coleridge – he who sits obscure
In the exceeding lustre and the pure
Intense irradiation of a mind,
Which, with its own internal lightning blind,
Flags wearily through darkness and despair –
A cloud-encircled meteor of the air,
A hooded eagle among blinking owls.
'Letter to Maria Gisborne', ll. 202–8, ibid.

50 You will see Hunt – one of those happy souls
Which are the salt of the earth, and without whom
This world would smell like what it is – a tomb.
'Letter to Maria Gisborne', ll. 209–11, ibid. Of LEIGH HUNT.

51 Have you not heard
When a man marries, dies, or turns Hindoo,
His best friends hear no more of him?
'Letter to Maria Gisborne', ll. 235–7, ibid.

52 The good want power, but to weep barren tears.
The powerful goodness want: worse need for them.
The wise want love; and those who love want
   wisdom;
And all best things are thus confused to ill.
Prometheus Unbound, Act 1, ll. 625–8 (1820), ibid.

53 Peace is in the grave.
The grave hides all things beautiful and good:
I am a God and cannot find it there.
Prometheus Unbound, Act 1, ll. 638–40, ibid. Spoken by Prometheus.

54 The dust of creeds outworn.
Prometheus Unbound, Act 1, l. 697, ibid.

55 To be
Omnipotent but friendless is to reign.
Prometheus Unbound, Act 2, Sc. 4, ll. 47–8, ibid.

56 He gave man speech, and speech created
   thought,
Which is the measure of the universe.
Prometheus Unbound, Act 2, Sc. 4, ll. 72–3, ibid.

57 Death is the veil which those who live call
   life:
They sleep, and it is lifted.
Prometheus Unbound, Act 3, Sc. 3, ll. 113–14, ibid.

58 The loathsome mask has fallen, the man
   remains
Sceptreless, free, uncircumscribed, but man
Equal, unclassed, tribeless, and nationless,
Exempt from awe, worship, degree, the king
Over himself.
Prometheus Unbound, Act 3, Sc. 4, ll. 193–7, ibid.

59 Familiar acts are beautiful through love.
Prometheus Unbound, Act 4, l. 403, ibid.

60 Man, who wert once a despot and a slave;
A dupe and a deceiver; a decay;
A traveller from the cradle to the grave
Through the dim night of this immortal day.
Prometheus Unbound, Act 4, ll. 549–52, ibid.

61 To suffer woes which Hope thinks infinite;
To forgive wrongs darker than death or night;
To defy Power, which seems omnipotent;
To love, and bear; to hope till Hope creates
From its own wreck the thing it contemplates;
Neither to change, nor falter, nor repent;
This, like thy glory, Titan, is to be

Good, great and joyous, beautiful and free;
This is alone Life, Joy, Empire, and Victory!
Prometheus Unbound, Act 4, ll. 570–8, ibid. Closing lines of
work.

62 Art thou pale for weariness
Of climbing heaven and gazing on the earth,
Wandering companionless
Among the stars that have a different birth?
'To the Moon', ll. 1–4, written 1820, ibid.

63 Hail to thee, blithe Spirit!
Bird thou never wert,
That from Heaven, or near it,
Pourest thy full heart
In profuse strains of unpremeditated art.
'To a Skylark', st. 1, written 1820, ibid. Opening lines.

64 And singing still dost soar, and soaring ever
   singest.
'To a Skylark', st. 2, ibid.

65 Thou art unseen, but yet I hear thy shrill
   delight.
'To a Skylark', st. 4, ibid.

66 We look before and after,
And pine for what is not:
Our sincerest laughter
With some pain is fraught;
Our sweetest songs are those that tell of saddest
   thought.
'To a Skylark', st. 18, ibid.

67 Teach me half the gladness
That thy brain must know,
Such harmonious madness
From my lips would flow
The world should listen then – as I am listening
   now.
'To a Skylark', st. 21, ibid. Closing lines.

68 A lovely lady garmented in light
From her own beauty – deep her eyes, as are
Two openings of unfathomable night.
'The Witch of Atlas', st. 5, written 1820, ibid.

69 I weep for Adonais – he is dead!
O, weep for Adonais! though our tears
Thaw not the frost which binds so dear a head!
'Adonais', st. 1, written 1821, ibid. Opening lines of elegy written for JOHN KEATS.

70 The quick Dreams,
The passion-wingèd Ministers of thought.
'Adonais', st. 9, ibid.

71 Lost Angel of a ruined Paradise!
'Adonais', st. 10, ibid.

72 Ah, woe is me! Winter is come and gone,
But grief returns with the revolving year.
'Adonais', st. 18, ibid.

73 Alas! that all we loved of him should be,
But for our grief, as if it had not been,
And grief itself be mortal!
'Adonais', st. 21, ibid.

74 But the pure spirit shall flow
Back to the burning fountain whence it came,
A portion of the Eternal.
'Adonais', st. 38, ibid.

75 Peace, peace! he is not dead, he doth not sleep –
He hath awakened from the dream of life –
'Tis we, who lost in stormy visions, keep
With phantoms an unprofitable strife.
'Adonais', st. 39, ibid.

76 *We* decay
Like corpses in a charnel; fear and grief
Convulse us and consume us day by day,
And cold hopes swarm like worms within our
     living clay.
'Adonais', st. 39, ibid.

77 He has outsoared the shadow of our night;
Envy and calumny and hate and pain,
And that unrest which men miscall delight,
Can touch him not and torture not again;
From the contagion of the world's slow stain
He is secure, and now can never mourn
A heart grown cold, a head grown grey in vain.
'Adonais', st. 40, ibid.

78 He lives, he wakes – 'tis Death is dead, not he.
'Adonais', st. 41, ibid.

79 He is made one with Nature: there is heard
His voice in all her music, from the moan
Of thunder, to the song of night's sweet bird;
He is a presence to be felt and known
In darkness and in light.
'Adonais', st. 42, ibid.

80 He is a portion of the loveliness
Which once he made more lovely.
'Adonais', st. 43, ibid.

81 The One remains, the many change and pass;
Heaven's light forever shines, Earth's shadows fly;

Life, like a dome of many-coloured glass,
Stains the white radiance of Eternity.
'Adonais', st. 52, ibid.

82 I am borne darkly, fearfully, afar;
Whilst, burning through the inmost veil of
     Heaven,
The soul of Adonais, like a star,
Beacons from the abode where the Eternal are.
'Adonais', st. 55, ibid. Closing lines of poem.

83 Hence the vanity of translation; it were as wise
to cast a violet into a crucible that you might discover the formal principle of its colour and odour,
as seek to transfuse from one language into another
the creations of a poet. The plant must spring again
from its seed, or it will bear no flower – and this is
the burthen of the curse of Babel.
A Defence of Poetry, written 1821, publ. in *Shelley's Prose* (ed.
David L. Clark, 1954)

84 A story of particular facts is a mirror which
obscures and distorts that which should be beautiful; poetry is a mirror which makes beautiful that
which it distorts.
A Defence of Poetry, ibid.

85 Every epoch, under names more or less specious,
has deified its peculiar errors.
A Defence of Poetry, ibid.

86 Poetry lifts the veil from the hidden beauty of
the world, and makes familiar objects be as if they
were not familiar.
A Defence of Poetry, ibid.

87 A man, to be greatly good, must imagine
intensely and comprehensively; he must put himself in the place of another and of many others; the
pains and pleasures of his species must become his
own. The great instrument of moral good is the
imagination.
A Defence of Poetry, ibid.

88 Poetry is a sword of lightning, ever unsheathed,
which consumes the scabbard that would contain
it.
A Defence of Poetry, ibid.

89 Tragedy delights by affording a shadow of the
pleasure which exists in pain. The pleasure that is
in sorrow is sweeter than the pleasure of pleasure
itself.
A Defence of Poetry, ibid.

90 Poetry is the record of the best and happiest moments of the happiest and best minds.
A Defence of Poetry, ibid.

91 Poets are the hierophants of an unapprehended inspiration; the mirrors of the gigantic shadows which futurity casts upon the present; the words which express what they understand not; the trumpets which sing to battle and feel not what they inspire; the influence which is moved not, but moves. Poets are the unacknowledged legislators of the world.
A Defence of Poetry, ibid. Closing words of essay. See SAMUEL JOHNSON 45.

92 January gray is here,
Like a sexton by her grave;
February bears the bier,
March with grief doth howl and rave,
And April weeps – but, O ye hours!
Follow with May's fairest flowers.
'Dirge for the Year', st. 4, written 1821, publ. in *Poetical Works* (ed. Thomas Hutchinson, 1905)

93 I never was attached to that great sect,
Whose doctrine is, that each one should select
Out of the crowd a mistress or a friend,
And all the rest, though fair and wise, commend
To cold oblivion, though it is in the code
Of modern morals.
'Epipsychidion', ll. 149–54, written 1821, ibid.

94 With one chained friend, perhaps a jealous foe,
The dreariest and the longest journey go.
'Epipsychidion', ll. 158–9, ibid.

95 Narrow
The heart that loves, the brain that contemplates,
The life that wears, the spirit that creates
One object, and one form, and builds thereby
A sepulchre for its eternity.
'Epipsychidion', ll. 169–73, ibid.

96 The world's great age begins anew,
The golden years return,
The earth doth like a snake renew
Her winter weeds outworn:
Heaven smiles, and faiths and empires gleam,
Like wrecks of a dissolving dream.
Hellas, ll. 1060–5, written 1821, ibid.

97 Rarely, rarely, comest thou,
Spirit of Delight!
'Song' ('Rarely, rarely, comest thou'), written 1821, ibid.

98 Man who man would be,
Must rule the empire of himself; in it
Must be supreme, establishing his throne
On vanquished will, quelling the anarchy
Of hopes and fears, being himself alone.
'Sonnet: Political Greatness', written 1821, ibid.

99 Music, when soft voices die,
Vibrates in the memory –
Odours, when sweet violets sicken,
Live within the sense they quicken.
'To – ' ('Music, when soft voices die'), written 1821, ibid.

100 I can give not what men call love,
But wilt thou accept not
The worship the heart lifts above
And the Heavens reject not, –
The desire of the moth for the star,
Of the night for the morrow,
The devotion to something afar
From the sphere of our sorrow?
'To – ' ('One word is too often profaned'), st. 2, written 1821, ibid.

101 When the lamp is shattered
The light in the dust lies dead –
When the cloud is scattered
The rainbow's glory is shed.
When the lute is broken,
Sweet tones are remembered not;
When the lips have spoken,
Loved accents are soon forgot.
'Lines: When the Lamp is Shattered', st. 1, written 1822, ibid.

102 Away, away, from men and towns,
To the wild wood and the downs –
To the silent wilderness
Where the soul need not repress
Its music lest it should not find
An echo in another's mind.
'To Jane: the Invitation', ll. 21–6, written 1822, ibid.

103 I leave this notice on my door
For each accustomed visitor:
'I am gone into the fields
To take what this sweet hour yields;
Reflection, you may come tomorrow,
Sit by the fireside with Sorrow.
You with the unpaid bill, Despair,
You, tiresome verse-reciter, Care,
I will pay you in the grave,
Death will listen to your stave.'
'To Jane: the Invitation', ll. 29–38, ibid.

Gilbert Shelton
(b. 1940)
US cartoonist

His creations, the Fabulous Furry Freak Brothers, made their first appearance in The LA Free Press *in 1967, and subsequently featured in* The Fabulous Furry Freak Brothers, *the most popular underground comic, and constantly in print.*

1 We have plenty of grass, and as we all know, dope will get you through times of no money better than money will get you through times of no dope.
'The Freaks Pull a Heist' (1971), publ. in *The Fabulous Furry Freak Brothers* (strip cartoon, from 1968). Originally spoken by Freewheelin' Franklin, the line became a motto for the Freak Brothers and their following.

William Shenstone
(1714–63)
British poet and landscape gardener

His poetic output was derided by SAMUEL JOHNSON, *but 'The School-mistress' was praised by* THOMAS GRAY. *The garden he created at his Shropshire estate was a showpiece of the picturesque style.*

1 Whoe'er has travelled life's dull round,
Where'er his stages may have been,
May sigh to think he still has found
The warmest welcome, at an inn.
'Written at an Inn at Henley', st. 5 (1758) repr. in *Works in Verse and Prose*, vol. 1 (1764)

2 The world may be divided into people that read, people that write, people that think, and fox-hunters.
'On Writing and Books', sect. 3, ibid., vol. 2 (1764)

3 There is nothing more universally commendable than a fine day; the reason is, that people can commend it without envy.
'Of Men and Manners', sect. 34, ibid., vol. 2

Philip Henry Sheridan
(1831–88)
US general

A cavalry officer, he fought with distinction for the Unionists during the Civil War and ended his career as General of the US Army.

1 The only good Indians I ever saw were dead.
Attributed remark at Fort Cobb, Indian Territory, January 1869. Later denied by Sheridan.

Richard Brinsley Sheridan
(1751–1816)
Irish dramatist

The popularity of his comedies of manners, for instance The Rivals *(1775) and* School for Scandal *(1777), made him the most successful playwright of his day. After 1776, he wrote all his dramatic works for the Drury Lane Theatre, in which he owned a share. He became an MP in 1780. See* LORD BYRON 67.

1 I ne'er could any lustre see
In eyes that would not look on me.
The Duenna, Act 1, Sc. 2 (1775). Air sung by Don Antonio.

2 Conscience has no more to do with gallantry than it has with politics.
Isaac Mendoza, ibid., Act 2, Sc. 4

3 Here, my dear Lucy, hide these books. Quick, quick. Fling *Peregrine Pickle* under the toilet – throw *Roderick Random* into the closet – put *The Innocent Adultery* into *The Whole Duty of Man* – thrust *Lord Aimworth* under the sofa – cram *Ovid* behind the bolster – there – put *The Man of Feeling* into your pocket – so, so, now lay *Mrs Chapone* in sight, and leave *Fordyce's Sermons* open on the table ... Fling me *Lord Chesterfield's Letters*. – Now for 'em.
The Rivals, Act 1, Sc. 2 (1775). Lydia Languish rearranges her books before a visit.

4 Illiterate him, I say, quite from your memory ... There is nothing on earth so easy as to *forget,* if a person chooses to set about it. I'm sure I have as much forgot your poor, dear uncle, as if he had never existed – and I thought it my duty to do so.
Mrs Malaprop, ibid., Act 1, Sc. 2. The character's 'ingeniously misapplied' words and expressions which fill the play have given rise to the word 'malapropism'. Her name is from the French, *mal à propos*, or 'inappropriate'.

5 'Tis safest in matrimony to begin with a little aversion.
Mrs Malaprop, ibid., Act 1, Sc. 2

6 Madam, a circulating library in a town is as an evergreen tree of diabolical knowledge! It blossoms through the year! And depend on it ... that they who are so fond of handling the leaves will long for the fruit at last.
Sir Anthony Absolute, ibid., Act 1, Sc. 2

7 I would by no means wish a daughter of mine to be a progeny of learning; I don't think so much learning becomes a young woman; for instance, I would never let her meddle with Greek, or Hebrew, or Algebra, or Simony, or Fluxions, or Paradoxes, or

such inflammatory branches of learning – neither would it be necessary for her to handle any of your mathematical, astronomical, diabolical instruments. But . . . I would send her, at nine years old, to a boarding-school, in order to learn a little ingenuity and artifice. Then, sir, she should have a supercilious knowledge in accounts; and as she grew up, I would have her instructed in geometry, that she might know something of the contagious countries; but above all . . . she should be mistress of orthodoxy, that she might not mis-spell, and mis-pronounce words so shamefully as girls usually do; and likewise that she might reprehend the true meaning of what she is saying. This . . . is what I would have a woman know; and I don't think there is a superstitious article in it.
Mrs Malaprop, ibid., Act 1, Sc. 2

8 When delicate and feeling souls are separated, there is not a feature in the sky, not a movement of the elements, not an aspiration of the breeze, but hints some cause for a lover's apprehension!
Faulkland, ibid., Act 2, Sc. 1

9 Ay, ay, the best terms will grow obsolete. Damns have had their day.
Acres, ibid., Act 2, Sc. 1

10 Modesty . . . is a quality in a lover more praised by the women than liked.
Sir Lucius O'Trigger, ibid., Act 2, Sc. 2

11 Nay, but, Jack, such eyes! such eyes so innocently wild! so bashfully irresolute! Not a glance but speaks and kindles some thought of love! Then, Jack, her cheeks, Jack! so deeply blushing at the insinuations of her tell-tale eyes! Then, Jack, her lips! O Jack, lips smiling at their own discretion; and if not smiling, more sweetly pouting; more lovely in sullenness! . . . Then, Jack, her neck! O Jack! Jack!
Sir Anthony Absolute, ibid., Act 3, Sc. 1. Describing Lydia Languish to his son, whom he wants her to marry.

12 He is the very pineapple of politeness!
Mrs Malaprop, ibid., Act 3, Sc. 3. Referring to Captain Absolute.

13 Sure if I reprehend anything in this world, it is the use of my oracular tongue, and a nice derangement of epitaphs!
Mrs Malaprop, ibid., Act 3, Sc. 3

14 She's as headstrong as an allegory on the banks of the Nile.
Mrs Malaprop, ibid., Act 3, Sc. 3. Describing her niece, Lydia.

15 Our ancestors are very good kind of folks; but

they are the last people I should choose to have a visiting acquaintance with.
David, ibid., Act 4, Sc. 1

16 You are not like Cerberus, three gentlemen at once, are you?
Mrs Malaprop, ibid., Act 4, Sc. 2. Addressing Captain Absolute.

17 The quarrel is a very pretty quarrel as it stands, we should only spoil it by trying to explain it.
Sir Lucius Trigger, ibid., Act 4, Sc. 3

18 My valour is certainly going – it is sneaking off! I feel it oozing out as it were at the palms of my hands!
Acres, ibid., Act 5, Sc. 2

19 There's no possibility of being witty without a little ill-nature: the malice of a good thing is the barb that makes it stick.
The School for Scandal, Act 1, Sc. 1 (1777). Spoken by Lady Sneerwell.

20 I think you will like them, when you shall see them on a beautiful quarto page, where a neat rivulet of text shall meander through a meadow of margin.
Sir Benjamin Backbite, ibid., Act 1, Sc. 1. Of his love elegies.

21 Mercy on me! here is the whole set! a character dead at every word, I suppose.
Sir Peter Teazle, ibid., Act 2, Sc. 2. On entering Lady Sneerwell's salon.

22 No person should be permitted to kill characters and run down reputations, but qualified old maids and disappointed widows.
Sir Peter Teazle, ibid., Act 2, Sc. 2

23 Here's to the maiden of bashful fifteen;
Here's to the widow of fifty;
Here's to the flaunting extravagant queen,
And here's to the housewife that's thrifty.
Let the toast pass,
Drink to the lass,
I'll warrant she'll prove an excuse for the glass.
Song, sung by Sir Harry Bumper, ibid., Act 3, Sc. 3

24 An unforgiving eye, and a damned disinheriting countenance!
Careless, ibid., Act 4, Sc. 1. Describing a portrait.

25 The *newspapers*! Sir, they are the most villainous – licentious – abominable – infernal – Not that I ever read them – No – I make it a rule never to look into a newspaper.
The Critic, Act 1, Sc. 1 (1779). Spoken by Sir Fretful Plagiary.

26 For if there is anything to one's praise, it is foolish vanity to be gratified at it, and if it is abuse – why one is always sure to hear of it from one damned good-natured friend or another!
Sir Fretful Plagiary, ibid., Act 1, Sc. 1. On not reading his reviews.

27 I am, sir, a practitioner in panegyric, or to speak more plainly – a professor of the art of puffing, at your service – or anybody else's.
Puff, ibid., Act 1, Sc. 2

28 An oyster may be crossed in love!
Tilburina, ibid., Act 3, Sc. 1. A line from the play-within-a-play *The Spanish Armada*.

29 The Right Honourable gentleman is indebted to his memory for his jests, and to his imagination for his facts.
Reply to Mr Dundas in the House of Commons, quoted in *Memoirs of the Life of . . . Richard Brinsley Sheridan*, vol. 2, ch. 21 (1825) by THOMAS MOORE

Sidney Sherman
(1805–73)
US general

He led Houston's Second Regiment of the Texas Volunteers at the Battle of San Jacinto (1836), after which he rose to the rank of Major General of the Militia. He was later Commandant of Galveston.

1 Remember the Alamo!
Attributed battle cry at San Jacinto, 21 April 1836, evoking the massacre of 183 Texan volunteers by a Mexican army at the Alamo in March 1835

William Tecumseh Sherman
(1820–91)
US general

Regarded as one of the ablest generals in the Civil War, he was victorious in the Vicksburg and Chattanooga campaigns (1863), and commanded the army that captured and burned Atlanta (1864), pursuing a scorched earth policy. He was General of the US army 1869–84.

1 Grant stood by me when I was crazy, and I stood by him when he was drunk, and now we stand by each other.
Attributed, c. 1870. On his loyalty to ULYSSES S. GRANT, then US president.

2 There is many a boy here today who looks on war as all glory, but, boys, it is all hell.
Speech at Columbus, Ohio, 11 August 1880, quoted in *Fighting Prophet* (1932) by Lloyd Lewis Sherman. 'War is hell' was an assertion frequently repeated by Sherman, while maintaining his belief in 'total war'.

3 I will not accept if nominated, and will not serve if elected.
Telegram to Republican National Convention, 5 June 1884, quoted in *Memoirs*, ch. 27 (fourth edn, 1891). On being urged to stand as Republican candidate in the 1884 US presidential election.

Carol Shields
(1935–2003)
US-born Canadian author

Coming to notice with The Republic of Love *(1992), she won wide acclaim for* The Stone Diaries *(1993), a chronicle of the life of an 'ordinary' Canadian woman.* Larry's Party *(1996) is written from a male perspective.*

1 Canada is a country where nothing seems ever to happen. A country always dressed in its Sunday go-to-meeting clothes. A country you wouldn't ask to dance a second waltz. Clean. Christian. Dull. Quiescent. But growing. Yes, it must be admitted, the Dominion is growing.
The Stone Diaries, ch. 3 (1993)

James Shirley
(1596–1666)
English dramatist

After converting to Catholicism, he lost his post as a schoolteacher and earned his livelihood from his plays. From 1625, he produced a succession of cleverly plotted tragedies, including The Traitor *(1631), and comedies, such as* The Lady of Pleasure *(1635). He died as a result of the Great Fire of London.*

1 How little room
Do we take up in death, that, living know
No bounds?
The Wedding, Act 4, Sc. 4 (performed 1626)

2 The glories of our blood and state
Are shadows, not substantial things;
There is no armour against fate;
Death lays his icy hand on kings.
The Contention of Ajax and Ulysses, Act 1, Sc. 3 (c. 1640, publ. 1659). Calchas' hymn at the funeral of Ajax.

3 The garlands wither on your brow;
Then boast no more your mighty deeds!
Ibid., Act 1, Sc. 3. Calchas' hymn at the funeral of Ajax.

Clare Short
(b. 1946)
British politician

An outspoken Labour MP for Birmingham Ladywood since 1983, she was Secretary of State for International Development 1997–2003, resigning after the invasion of Iraq.

1 Political correctness is a concept invented by hard-rightwing forces to defend their right to be racist, to treat women in a degrading way and to be truly vile about gay people. They invent this idea of people who are politically correct, with a rigid, monstrous attitude to life so they can attack them. But we have all had to learn to modify our language. That's all part of being a decent human being.
Interview in the *Guardian* 18 February 1995

2 It will be golden elephants next.
Quoted in the *Observer* 24 August 1997. Referring to calls to increase aid to Montserrat following the eruption there.

Algernon Sidney
(1622–83)
English soldier and politician

He was a cavalry officer for the Parliamentarians during the Civil War and went into exile at the Restoration. Allowed to return in 1677, he became implicated in the Rye House Plot and was executed. See also ANONYMOUS 96.

1 Liars ought to have good memories.
Discourses Concerning Government, ch. 2, sect. 15 (1698). See QUINTILIAN 1.

2 'Tis not necessary to light a candle to the sun.
Ibid., ch. 2, sect. 23

(Sir) Philip Sidney
(1554–86)
English author, poet and soldier

A courtier and an MP from 1581, he was considered the archetypal Renaissance man. His writings include the prose romance Arcadia *(1590), the sonnet sequence* Astrophel and Stella *(1591) and* Apology for Poetry *(1595), an early work of literary criticism. He was appointed Governor of Flushing, in the Netherlands, in 1585 and died from wounds received in a skirmish.*

1 Leave me, O Love which reachest but to dust,
And thou, my mind, aspire to higher things;
Grow rich in that which never taketh rust;
Whatever fades, but fading pleasure brings.
Certain Sonnets, Sonnet 32 (written *c.* 1577–81, publ. 1598). The

sonnet is also known as *Splendidis longum valedico nugis* ('I bid farewell to brilliant trifles').

2 The poet . . . goeth hand in hand with nature, not enclosed within the narrow warrant of her gifts, but freely ranging only within the zodiac of his own wit. Nature never set forth the earth in so rich tapestry as diverse poets have done, neither with pleasant rivers, fruitful trees, sweet smelling flowers, nor whatsoever else may make the too much loved earth more lovely. Her world is brazen, the poets only deliver a golden.
An Apology for Poetry, 'The Functions of Poetry . . .' (also called *The Defence of Poetry*, written 1579–80, publ. 1595, ed. J. Churton Collins, 1907)

3 Poetry therefore is an art of imitation . . . that is to say, a representing, counterfeiting, or figuring forth: to speak metaphorically, a speaking picture: with this end, to teach and delight.
Ibid., 'Poetry an Art of Imitation . . .'

4 With a tale forsooth he cometh unto you, with a tale which holdeth children from play, and old men from the chimney corner.
Ibid., 'The Attractive Form . . .' Referring to poets.

5 Admitted into the company of the paper-blurrers.
Ibid., 'Or to Men . . . Not Born Poets'

6 My true love hath my heart and I have his,
By just exchange one for the other given;
I hold his dear, and mine he cannot miss,
There never was a better bargain driven.
Old Arcadia, bk 3 (written *c.* 1580, publ. 1926)

7 Thus, with child to speak, and helpless in my throes,
Biting my truant pen, beating myself for spite:
Fool! said my muse to me, look in thy heart, and write.
Astrophel and Stella, Sonnet 1 (written *c.* 1582, publ. 1591)

8 With how sad steps, O Moon, thou climb'st the skies;
How silently, and with how wan a face.
Ibid., Sonnet 31

9 Come sleep, O sleep, the certain knot of peace,
The baiting-place of wit, the balm of woe,
The poor man's wealth, the prisoner's release,
Th'indifferent judge between the high and low.
Ibid., Sonnet 39

10 I am no pick-purse of another's wit.
Ibid., Sonnet 74

11 Stella, think not that I by verse seek fame,
Who seek, who hope, who love, who live, but thee;
Thine eyes my pride, thy lips my history:
If thou praise not, all other praise is shame.
Ibid., Sonnet 90

12 Nightingales seldom sing, the pie still
   chattereth:
The wood cries most, before it throughly kindled
   be,
Deadly wounds inward bleed, each slight sore
   mattereth.
Hardly they heard, which by good hunters singled
   be:
Shallow brooks murmur most, deep silent slide
   away,
Nor true love loves those loves with others
   mingled be.
The Countess of Pembroke's Arcadia ('New Arcadia'), bk 1, 'First
Eclogues' (1590)

13 Thy necessity is yet greater than mine.
Quoted in *Life of Sir Philip Sidney*, ch. 12 (1652) by FULKE
GREVILLE. Offering his water to a dying soldier, at the battle
of Zutphen, 22 September 1586, where Sidney himself was
wounded, dying three weeks later.

Jerry Siegel
(1914–96)
US cartoonist and

Joe Shuster
(1914–92)
Canadian-born US cartoonist

*Schoolmates Siegel and Shuster devised a prototype of Super-
man, Man of Steel, in a fanzine in 1933 and the hero was taken
up by Action Comics in 1938, later appearing on radio and TV
and in films. Siegel wrote Superman's adventures until 1948
and 1959–65, Shuster drew them until 1947.*

1 Is it a bird? Is it a plane? No, it's SUPERMAN!
Superman (cartoon, from 1933). Voices in the crowd, sometimes rendered as 'It's a bird . . . It's a plane . . .'

2 Faster than a speeding bullet! More powerful than
a locomotive! Able to leap tall buildings at a single
bound! . . . Strange visitor from another planet, who
came to earth with powers and abilities far beyond
those of mortal men. Superman! Who can change
the course of mighty rivers, bend steel with his bare
hands, and who . . . fights a never ending battle for
truth, justice and the American way!
Superman (radio adaptation, from 1940). Voiceover at the
start of each radio (and later TV) broadcast.

Emmanuel-Joseph Sieyès
(1748–1836)
French political theorist and revolutionary

*A member of the National Assembly 1789–93, he later con-
spired with NAPOLEON Bonaparte and others to bring about
the coup of 18 Brumaire, which installed him as one of the
provisional consuls (1799). His influence subsequently declined
and he lived in exile 1815–30.*

1 J'ai vécu.
[I survived.]
On how he had passed the Reign of Terror, quoted in *Notice
historique sur la vie et travaux de M. le Comte de Sièyes* (1836)
by F. A. M. Mignet

Alan Sillitoe
(b. 1928)
British author

*A factory worker who left school aged fourteen, he had
immediate success with his first book Saturday Night and
Sunday Morning (1958), which like later works portrayed
Northern working-class culture.*

1 The Loneliness of the Long-Distance Runner.
Title of novel (1959)

2 What I want is a good time; the rest is all propa-
ganda.
Opening narration of *Saturday Night and Sunday Morning*
(film, 1960, screenplay by Alan Sillitoe, directed by Karel
Reisz). Spoken by Arthur Seaton (played by Albert Finney).
The words do not appear in Sillitoe's original novel.

Georges Simenon
(1903–85)
French crimewriter

*The author of over 500 novels, he made his name with the
Maigret detective series (from 1931), known worldwide through
film and television adaptations. 'I have no imagination,' he
stated, 'I take everything from life.'*

1 Writing is not a profession, but a vocation of
unhappiness.
Interview in *Writers at Work* (first series, ed. Malcolm Cowley,
1958)

Paul Simon

(b. 1941)

US singer and songwriter

He wrote most of the material performed with Art Garfunkel as Simon and Garfunkel. His solo recordings (from 1971) have explored music from around the world, for example Graceland *(1986).*

1 Hello darkness, my old friend,
I've come to talk with you again.

'The Sound of Silence' (song) on the album *Wednesday Morning 3 a.m.* (1964) by Simon and Garfunkel

2 People talking without speaking,
People hearing without listening,
People writing songs that voices never shared
No one dared disturb the sound of silence.

'The Sound of Silence', ibid.

3 And here's to you, Mrs Robinson
Jesus loves you more than you will know.
God bless you please, Mrs Robinson
Heaven holds a place for those who pray.

'Mrs Robinson' (song) in the film *The Graduate* (1967), released on the soundtrack and, in a different version, on the album *Bookends* (1968) by Simon and Garfunkel

4 They've all gone to look for America.

'America' (song) on the album *Bookends* (1968) by Simon and Garfunkel

5 When times get rough,
And friends just can't be found
Like a bridge over troubled water
I will lay me down.

'Bridge Over Troubled Water' (song) on the album *Bridge Over Troubled Water* (1970) by Simon and Garfunkel

6 One man's ceiling is another man's floor.

'One Man's Ceiling is Another Man's Floor' (song) on the album *There Goes Rhymin' Simon* (1973)

7 Still crazy after all these years.

'Still Crazy After All These Years' (song) on the album *Still Crazy After All These Years* (1975)

8 There must be fifty ways to leave your lover.

'Fifty Ways to Leave Your Lover' (song), ibid.

9 You just slip out the back, Jack
Make a new plan, Stan
You don't need to be coy, Roy
Just get yourself free
Hop on the bus, Gus
You don't need to discuss much

Just drop off the key, Lee
And get yourself free.

'Fifty Ways to Leave Your Lover' (song), ibid.

10 The Mississippi Delta was shining
Like a National guitar.

'Graceland' (song) on the album *Graceland* (1986)

11 Improvisation is too good to leave to chance.

International Herald Tribune 12 October 1990

Nina Simone

(1933–2003)

US singer and musician

Originally Eunice Kathleen Waymon. Her career in jazz and soul music spanned four decades, starting with the double release of 'I Loves You Porgy' and 'My Baby Just Cares for Me' in 1959. In the 1960s she was the 'poet laureate of the civil rights movement'.

1 Alabama's got me so upset
Tennessee made me lose my rest
And everybody knows about Mississippi –
    Goddam.

'Mississippi – Goddam' (song) on the album *Nina Simone in Concert* (1964). Inspired by the murder of Medgar Evers, NAACP field officer in Mississippi.

2 To be young, gifted and black
Is where it's at!

'Young, Gifted and Black' (song, 1969, written by Weldon J. Irvine Jr) on the album *Black Gold* (1970)

Simonides of Ceos

(c. 556–468 BC)

Greek poet

A rival of PINDAR *at the court at Syracuse, he was renowned for his epigrammatic verse and his epitaphs. He is said to have originated the epinician ode for victors of the Olympic Games.*

1 Simonides ... calls painting silent poetry and poetry painting that speaks; for the actions which painters depict as they are being performed, words describe after they are done.

Morals, 'The Glory of Athens', sect. 3 (c. AD 100) by PLUTARCH. Elsewhere Plutarch records this as an 'oft-repeated saying'. See also LEONARDO DA VINCI 6.

2 Go, tell the Spartans, thou who passest by,
That here obedient to their laws we lie.

Epitaph for the fallen Greeks at Thermopylae (480 BC), attributed

Tom Simpson
(1937–67)
British cyclist

The first Briton to make a mark on European cycling, he won several trophies during the 1960s and died in the 1967 Tour de France.

1 Put me back on my bike.
Attributed last words, addressed to spectators after collapsing on Mont Ventoux during the Tour de France. However, in *Put Me Back on My Bike*, ch. 2 (2002) by William Fotheringham, his final words are quoted: 'On, on, on.'

George Robert Sims
(1847–1922)
English playwright and journalist

He began writing theatre reviews, then plays, starting with Lights of London (1895). He also wrote and lectured on social issues.

1 It is Christmas Day in the Workhouse.
'In the Workhouse – Christmas Day' (1879), repr. in *The Dagonet and Other Poems* (1903). Opening line.

Frank Sinatra
(1915–98)
US singer and actor

He first had success as a singer in the 1940s but his career peaked in the 1950s with his role in From Here to Eternity *(film, 1953) and the albums* Songs for Swinging Lovers *(1956) and* Come Fly With Me *(1959). The singer and politician Sonny Bono commented: 'Frank walks like America. Cocksure.'*

1 Fly me to the moon,
And let me play among the stars,
Let me see what life is like
On Jupiter and Mars.
'Fly Me to the Moon' (song, written and composed by Bart Howard) on the album *It Might As Well Be Swing* (1964)

2 Strangers in the night, exchanging glances
Wond'ring in the night, what were the chances
We'd be sharing love before the night was through.
'Strangers in the Night' (song, written by Charles Singleton and Eddie Snyder with music by Bert Kaempfert) on the album *Strangers in the Night* (1966)

3 And now the end is near
And so I face the final curtain,
I'll state my case of which I'm certain.
I've lived a life that's full, I traveled each and every
   highway,

And more, much more than this. I did it my way.
'My Way' (song, 1969, written by Claude François, Jacques Revaux and Paul Anka) on the album *My Way* (1969). The Canadian songwriter Paul Anka adapted the song from a French original, 'Comme d'habitude', for Sinatra, whose signature tune it became.

4 Ol' Blue Eyes is Back.
Title of album (1973). Reversing a decision made in 1970 to retire.

5 The most brutal, ugly, desperate, vicious form of expression it has been my misfortune to hear.
Quoted in *Sound Effects: Youth, Leisure and the Politics of Rock*, ch. 5 (1979) by Simon Frith. On rock 'n' roll.

Nancy Sinatra
(b. 1940)
US singer

The daughter of FRANK SINATRA, *she had six hits 1966–7 under the tutelage of Lee Hazlewood, including a duet with her father, 'Somethin' Stupid' (1967).*

1 These boots are made for walkin'
And that's just what they'll do
One of these days these boots are going to walk all
   over you.
'These Boots are Made for Walkin'' (song, 1966, written by Lee Hazlewood)

Upton Sinclair
(1878–1968)
US novelist and social reformer

Regarding his writing as a conduit for his political beliefs, he published more than eighty titles, of which the best known is The Jungle *(1906), a novel about immigrant workers in the Chicago meat industry.*

1 I aimed at the public's heart, and by accident I hit it in the stomach.
Cosmopolitan October 1906. Referring to his novel *The Jungle* (1906).

2 It is up to you to prove that human beings do not have to be prowling wolves or sly lynxes, but can be rational, just, and kindly members of a commonwealth.
I, Governor of California and How I Ended Poverty in California (Democratic Party campaign pamphlet, 1934)

Peter Singer
(b. 1946)
Australian philosopher

A utilitarian, he has been denounced for his views on the value of human and animal life, as expressed in Animal Liberation *(1975), in which he attacked 'speciesism', and* Practical Ethics *(1979).*

1 The tyranny of human over nonhuman animals ... has caused and today is still causing an amount of pain and suffering that can only be compared with that which resulted from the centuries of tyranny by white humans over black humans. The struggle against this tyranny is a struggle as important as any of the moral and social issues that have been fought over in recent years.
Animal Liberation: Towards an End to Man's Inhumanity, Preface (1975)

2 If possessing a higher degree of intelligence does not entitle one human to use another for his own ends, how can it entitle humans to exploit non-humans for the same purpose?
Ibid., ch. 1

3 The belief that human life, and only human life, is sacrosanct is a form of speciesism.
Ibid., ch. 1

4 Killing them [infants], therefore, cannot be equated with killing normal human beings, or any other self-conscious beings. No infant – disabled or not – has as strong a claim to life as beings capable of seeing themselves as distinct entities, existing over time.
Practical Ethics, ch. 7 (1979)

5 The difficult issue is not whether the end can ever justify the means, but which means are justified by which ends.
Ibid., ch. 11

(Dame) Edith Sitwell
(1887–1964)
British poet and critic

Her eccentric appearance, which she herself called 'the ordinary carried to a high degree of pictorial perfection', was made famous by the photographs of Cecil Beaton, for whom she possessed 'the mad moonstruck ethereality of a ghost'. Her experimental poetry was inspired by dance and jazz rhythms, for example in Façade *(1923). See* F. R. LEAVIS 1.

1 Jane, Jane,
Tall as a crane,
The morning light creaks down again.
'Aubade', publ. in *Façade* (1923). Sitwell originally recited the poems in this collection through a microphone to the accompaniment of music by William Walton.

2 Daisy and Lily,
Lazy and silly,
Walk by the shore of the wan grassy sea –
Talking once more 'neath a swan-bosomed tree.
'Valse', ibid. The poem was later titled 'Waltz'.

3 Still falls the Rain–
Dark as the world of man, black as our loss –
Blind as the nineteen hundred and forty nails
Upon the Cross.
'The Raids, 1940. Night and Dawn', publ. in *Street Songs* (1942). Opening lines of poem later set to music by BENJAMIN BRITTEN.

4 Rhythm is one of the principal translators between dream and reality. Rhythm might be described as, to the world of sound, what light is to the world of sight. It shapes and gives new meaning. Rhythm was described by Schopenhauer as melody deprived of its pitch.
The Canticle of the Rose, 'Some Notes on My Own Poetry' (1949)

5 Eccentricity is *not*, as dull people would have us believe, a form of madness. It is often a kind of innocent pride, and the man of genius and the aristocrat are frequently regarded as eccentrics because genius and aristocrat are entirely unafraid of and uninfluenced by the opinions and vagaries of the crowd.
Taken Care Of, ch. 15 (1965)

6 Vulgarity is, in reality, nothing but a modern, chic, pert descendant of the goddess Dullness.
Ibid., ch. 19

John Skelton
(c. 1460–1529)
English poet and satirist

In 1489 he was appointed court poet to Henry VII, and later tutored HENRY VIII. *His poetic skill is evident in* The Garland of Laurel *(1523). His short, unmetered lines were labelled 'Skeltonics'.*

1 The sovereign'st thing that any man may have
Is little to say, and much to hear and see.
The Bowge of Court, ll. 211–12 (1499)

2 Far may be sought
Erst than ye can find

So courteous, so kind,
As Merry Margaret, the midsummer flower,
Gentle as falcon, or hawk of the tower.
'To Mistress Margaret Hussey', publ. in *The Garland of Laurel*
(1523)

Robert Skidelsky
(b. 1939)
British historian

Baron Skidelsky of Tilton. His books include The World After
Communism *(1994) and a biography of* JOHN MAYNARD
KEYNES *(3 vols. 1983–2000).*

1 Historians are pessimistic by nature, because the
only future they can imagine is the past.
Remark at Cheltenham Festival of Literature, 6–15 October
1995, quoted in the *Daily Telegraph* 21 October 1995

B. F. Skinner
(1904–90)
US psychologist

*Burrhus Frederic Skinner. The founder of Behaviourism, he
applied the theory of 'conditioned response' in animal experiments to human behaviour. His publications include* The
Behavior of Organisms *(1938) and* Science and Human
Behavior *(1974).*

1 Education is what survives when what has been
learned has been forgotten.
New Scientist 21 May 1964

2 The real question is not whether machines think
but whether men do.
Contingencies of Reinforcement, ch. 9 (1969)

Grace Slick
(b. 1939)
US rock musician

*Starting out with the San Francisco band the Great Society,
she joined Jefferson Airplane as lead singer and songwriter in
1966, recording with them such successful albums as* Surrealistic Pillow *(1967) and* Volunteers *(1969).*

1 One pill makes you larger
And one pill makes you small.
And the ones that mother gives you
Don't do anything at all.
Go ask Alice
When she's ten feet tall.
'White Rabbit' (song) on the album *Surrealistic Pillow* (1967)
by Jefferson Airplane

2 Remember what the dormouse said:
'Feed your head.'
'White Rabbit', ibid. In an interview in 1977, Slick explained:
"'Feed your head" doesn't mean take every ... drug that
comes along, "Feed your head" means read ... listen and
read' (quoted in *Shaman Woman, Mainline Lady*, ed. Cynthia
Palmer and Michael Horowitz, 1982).

Joe Slovo
(1926–95)
Lithuanian-born South African activist

*Although he was in exile for twenty-seven years, he was one
of the leading figures in the African National Congress, and
after 1990 a key negotiator between the nationalist parties
and the government. He was Minister of Housing under* NEL-
SON MANDELA *(1994–5).*

1 There are only two sorts of people in life you can
trust – good Christians and good Communists.
Independent 4 November 1988

Christopher Smart
1722–71
English poet

*As a consequence of his religious mania, he was confined three
times in an asylum, where he wrote* Jubilate Agno *and* The
Song to David *(1763). His vivid imagery gained him the recognition of* SAMUEL JOHNSON, DAVID GARRICK *and* OLIVER
GOLDSMITH.

1 Rejoice in God, o ye Tongues; give glory to the
Lord and the Lamb.
Jubilate Agno, Fragment A, written *c.* 1758–63, first publ. 1939,
repr. in *Christopher Smart: Selected Poems* (ed. Karina Wil-
liamson and Marcus Walsh, 1990). Opening line. BENJAMIN
BRITTEN set excerpts of the poem to music in *Rejoice in the
Lamb* (1943).

2 For in my nature I quested for beauty, but God,
God hath sent me to sea for pearls.
Jubilate Agno, Fragment B, l. 31, ibid.

3 For Charity is cold in the multitude of
possessions, and the rich are covetous of their
crumbs.
Jubilate Agno, Fragment B, l. 154, ibid.

4 For there is a sound reasoning upon all flowers.
For elegant phrases are nothing but flowers.
For flowers are peculiarly the poetry of Christ.
Jubilate Agno, Fragment B, ll. 504–6, ibid.

5 For the mouse is a creature of great personal
valour.
Jubilate Agno, Fragment B, l. 637, ibid.

6 For I will consider my Cat Jeoffry.
For he is the servant of the Living God duly and
daily serving him.
For at the first glance of the glory of God in the
East he worships in his way.
For this is done by wreathing his body seven times
round with elegant quickness.
Jubilate Agno, Fragment B, ll. 695–8, ibid.

7 Let Ross, house of Ross rejoice with the Great
Flabber Dabber Flat Clapping Fish with hands.
Jubilate Agno, Fragment D, l. 11, ibid.

8 For ADORATION seasons change,
And order, truth, and beauty range,
Adjust, attract, and fill:
The grass the polyanthus cheques;
And polished porphyry reflects,
By the descending rill.
A Song to David, st. 52 (1763), ibid.

9 Strong against tide, th' enormous whale
Emerges as he goes.
A Song to David, st. 76 (1763), ibid.

10 But stronger still, in earth and air,
And in the sea, the man of prayer;
And far beneath the tide;
And in the seat to faith assigned,
Where ask is have, where seek is find,
Where knock is open wide.
A Song to David, st. 77 (1763), ibid.

11 Glorious the northern lights astream;
Glorious the song, when God's the theme;
Glorious the thunder's roar;
Glorious hosanna from the den;
Glorious the catholic amen;
Glorious the martyr's gore.
A Song to David, st. 85 (1763), ibid.

12 Lo, through her works gay nature grieves
How brief she is and frail,
As ever o'er the falling leaves
Autumnal winds prevail.
Yet still the philosophic mind
Consolatory food can find,
And hope her anchorage maintain:
We never are deserted quite;
'Tis by succession of delight
That love supports his reign.
'On a Bed of Guernsey Lilies', st. 2 (1764), ibid.

Elizabeth Smart
(1913–86)
Canadian novelist and poet

Her major work, By Grand Central Station I Sat Down and
Wept *(1945), was inspired by her affair with poet George Barker,
narrated in highly charged language.* The Assumption of the
Rogues and the Rascals *(1977) dealt with her experiences in
England.*

1 Vanity is a vital aid to nature: completely and
absolutely necessary to life. It is one of nature's
ways to bind you to the earth.
Journal entry, 25 June 1933, publ. in *Necessary Secrets*, pt 1,
ch. 2 (ed. Alice Van Wart, 1991)

2 By Grand Central Station I Sat Down and Wept.
Title of book (1945)

Slogans
See ADVERTISING SLOGANS, POLITICAL SLOGANS

Samuel Smiles
(1812–1904)
Scottish author and social reformer

*A surgeon, newspaper editor and entrepreneur in Leeds, he
wrote a number of improving works that enjoyed a wide
readership, notably* Self-Help *(1859).*

1 The spirit of self-help is the root of all genuine
growth in the individual; and, exhibited in the lives
of many, it constitutes the true source of national
vigour and strength.
Self-Help, ch. 1 (1859)

2 We often discover what *will* do, by finding out
what will not do; and probably he who never made
a mistake never made a discovery.
Ibid., ch. 11

Adam Smith
(1723–90)
Scottish social philosopher and political economist

*Professor of Logic (1751–2) and of Moral Philosophy (1752–64)
at Glasgow University, he was acclaimed for his first book,* The
Theory of Moral Sentiments *(1759). His major work was* The
Wealth of Nations *(1776), the first systematic study of political
economy, in which he analysed the effects of market forces and
proposed a balance between free trade, law and government.*

1 The propensity to truck, barter and exchange one

thing for another . . . is common to all men, and to be found in no other race of animals.

An Inquiry into the Nature and Causes of the Wealth of Nations, bk 1, ch. 2 (1776)

2 It is not from the benevolence of the butcher, the brewer, or the baker, that we expect our dinner, but from their regard to their own interest. We address ourselves, not to their humanity but to their self-love, and never talk to them of our necessities but of their advantages.

Ibid., bk 1, ch. 2

3 The real price of everything, what everything really costs to the man who wants to acquire it, is the toil and trouble of acquiring it.

Ibid., bk 1, ch. 5

4 No society can surely be flourishing and happy, of which the far greater part of the members are poor and miserable. It is but equity, besides, that they who feed, clothe, and lodge the whole body of the people, should have such a share of the produce of their own labour as to be themselves tolerably well fed, clothed, and lodged.

Ibid., bk 1, ch. 8

5 People of the same trade seldom meet together, even for merriment and diversion, but the conversation ends in a conspiracy against the public, or in some contrivance to raise prices.

Ibid., bk 1, ch. 10

6 With the greater part of rich people, the chief enjoyment of riches consists in the parade of riches, which in their eye is never so complete as when they appear to possess those decisive marks of opulence which nobody can possess but themselves.

Ibid., bk 1, ch. 11, sect. 2

7 Every individual necessarily labours to render the annual revenue of the society as great as he can. He generally, indeed, neither intends to promote the public interest, nor knows how much he is promoting it. By preferring the support of domestic to that of foreign industry, he intends only his own security; and by directing that industry in such a manner as its produce may be of the greatest value, he intends only his own gain, and he is in this, as in many other cases, led by an invisible hand to promote an end which was no part of his intention. Nor is it always the worse for the society that it was no part of it. By pursuing his own interest he frequently promotes that of the society more effectually than when he really intends to promote it. I have never known much good done by those who affected to trade for the public good.

Ibid., bk 4, ch. 2. Smith had previously made reference to the 'invisible hand' in *The Theory of Moral Sentiments* (1759).

8 To found a great empire for the sole purpose of raising up a people of customers, may at first sight appear a project fit only for a nation of shopkeepers. It is, however, a project altogether unfit for a nation of shopkeepers, but extremely fit for a nation that is governed by shopkeepers.

Ibid., bk 4, ch. 7. A similar notion was earlier expressed by the economist Josiah Tucker in *Four Tracts on Political and Commercial Subjects* (1766), though Adam Smith's wording was probably the source for its wider dissemination, and the origin of Napoleon's more famous utterance: see NAPOLEON 8.

9 Consumption is the sole end and purpose of all production; and the interest of the producer ought to be attended to only so far as it may be necessary for promoting that of the consumer. The maxim is so perfectly self evident that it would be absurd to attempt to prove it. But in the mercantile system the interest of the consumer is almost constantly sacrificed to that of the producer; and it seems to consider production, and not consumption, as the ultimate end and object of all industry and commerce.

Ibid., bk 4, ch. 8

10 All systems either of preference or of restraint, therefore, being thus completely taken away, the obvious and simple system of natural liberty establishes itself of its own accord. Every man, as long as he does not violate the laws of justice, is left perfectly free to pursue his own interest his own way, and to bring both his industry and capital into competition with those of any other man, or order of men. The sovereign is completely discharged from a duty, in the attempting to perform which he must always be exposed to innumerable delusions, and for the proper performance of which no human wisdom or knowledge could ever be sufficient; the duty of superintending the industry of private people, and of directing it towards the employments most suitable to the interest of the society.

Ibid., bk 4, ch. 9

11 Science is the great antidote to the poison of enthusiasm and superstition.

Ibid., bk 5, ch. 1, sect. 3, article 3

12 There is no art which one government sooner learns of another than that of draining money from the pockets of the people.
Ibid., bk 5, ch. 2

13 The machines that are first invented to perform any particular movement are always the most complex, and succeeding artists generally discover that, with fewer wheels, with fewer principles of motion, than had originally been employed, the same effects may be more easily produced. The first systems, in the same manner, are always the most complex.
Essays on Philosophical Subjects, 'The Principles which Lead and Direct Philosophical Inquiries', sect. 4 (1795). Referring to philosophical systems.

Alexander Smith
(1830–67)
Scottish poet

A designer of lace patterns by trade, he was labelled a prime exponent of the 'Spasmodic' school of poetry after an early work of his, 'A Life-Drama' (1853), was lampooned for its linguistic extravagance by W. E. AYTOUN. *Later works include* Edwin of Deira *(1861) and collections of essays.*

1 If you wish to preserve your secret, wrap it up in frankness.
Dreamthorp, 'On the Writing of Essays' (1863)

2 We are never happy; we can only remember that we were so once.
Ibid., 'On Death and the Fear of Dying'

3 A man's real possession is his memory. In nothing else is he rich, in nothing else is he poor.
Ibid., 'On Death and the Fear of Dying'

4 To be occasionally quoted is the only fame I care for.
Ibid., 'Men of Letters'

5 I would rather be remembered by a song than by a victory.
Ibid., 'Men of Letters'

6 We do not love a man for his respectability, his prudence and foresight in business, his capacity for living within his income, or his balance at his banker's. The things that really move liking in human beings are the gnarled nodosities of character, vagrant humours, freaks of generosity, some little unextinguishable spark of the aboriginal savage, some sweet savour of the old Adam.
Ibid., 'On Vagabonds'

Alfred E. Smith
(1873–1944)
US politician

Alfred Emanuel Smith, known as Al Smith. He was four times Democratic Governor of New York (1918–26) and in 1928 the first Roman Catholic to run for the presidency, losing to HERBERT HOOVER.

1 All the ills of democracy can be cured by more democracy.
Speech in Albany, 27 June 1933, quoted in the *New York Times* 28 June 1933

2 No sane local official who has hung up an empty stocking over the municipal fireplace, is going to shoot Santa Claus just before a hard Christmas.
New Outlook December 1933. The phrase 'Nobody shoots at Santa Claus' was used repeatedly by Smith in campaign speeches in 1936, attacking FRANKLIN D. ROOSEVELT and the allegedly spendthrift policies of the New Deal.

(Sir) Cyril Smith
(b. 1928)
British politician

Conspicuous for his twenty-seven-stone figure, he was the Liberal (1972–88) and Liberal Democrat (1988–92) MP for Rochdale.

1 This place is the longest running farce in the West End.
Remark, July 1973, quoted in *Big Cyril*, ch. 8 (1977). On the House of Commons.

Delia Smith
(b. 1941)
British cookery writer and broadcaster

She is a household name in Britain for her clear, simple recipes, published in several bestselling collections.

1 A hen's egg is, quite simply, a work of art, a masterpiece of design and construction with, it has to be said, brilliant packaging!
How to Cook, bk 1, ch. 1 (1998)

2 If you sometimes feel depressed or let down, if you're suffering from the pressures of life, or simply having a plain old grey day, my advice is to roast a chicken.
How to Cook, bk 2, ch. 4 (1999)

F. E. Smith
(1872–1930)
British lawyer and politician

Frederick Edwin Smith, First Earl of Birkenhead. A renowned speaker and wit, he was a Conservative MP from 1906, Attorney-General (1915–19), Lord Chancellor (1919–22) and Secretary of State for India (1924–8). MARGOT ASQUITH *thought him 'very clever, but his brains go to his head'.*

1 The world continues to offer glittering prizes to those who have stout hearts and sharp swords.
Rectorial Address, Glasgow University, 7 November 1923, publ. in *The Times* 8 November 1923. The words provided the title of FREDERIC RAPHAEL's novel about Cambridge graduates, *The Glittering Prizes* (1976). Smith's whole life has been portrayed as a quest for 'glittering prizes'.

Iain Duncan Smith
(b. 1954)
British politician

Elected Conservative MP for Chingford in 1992, 'IDS' was appointed Shadow Defence Secretary in 1999 and was leader of the Conservative Party 2001–3.

1 Those who do not know me yet will come to understand this: When I say a thing, I mean it. When I set myself a task, I do it. When I settle on a course, I stick to it. Do not underestimate the determination of a quiet man.
Speech to Conservative Party Conference, Bournemouth, 10 October 2002, quoted in the *Daily Telegraph* 11 October 2002. The original 'quiet man' was JOHN WAYNE, who starred in John Ford's film *The Quiet Man* (1952) as an Irish ex-boxer who returns to his native land in search of a peaceful life.

2 I'm a great believer in free speech, but as a right, not a continuous obligation.
Quoted in the *Guardian* 16 November 2002

Ian Smith
(b. 1919)
Rhodesian politician and prime minister

He founded the Rhodesian Front (later Republican Front) in 1962, became Prime Minister of a white minority government in 1964 and unilaterally declared Rhodesian independence in 1965. He remained active in the Republican Front until 1987.

1 We have the happiest Africans in the world.
Quoted in the *Observer* 20 November 1971

2 Let me say again, I don't believe in black majority rule in Rhodesia – not in a thousand years. I believe in blacks and whites working together.
Speech, broadcast 20 March 1976, quoted in the *Sunday Times* 21 March 1976. Smith finally conceded majority rule in 1979.

Liz Smith
(b. 1923)
US columnist

She is famous for her gossip columns, which have appeared in the New York Daily News *(later* New York Newsday) *since 1976, among numerous other magazines and newspapers.*

1 Gossip is news running ahead of itself in a red satin dress.
American Way, syndicated column, 3 September 1985

2 Most good gossip columnists have a touch of Savonarola in them.
International Herald Tribune 4 April 1991

Logan Pearsall Smith
(1865–1946)
US-born British essayist and aphorist

A lexicographer, bibliographer and essayist, he is chiefly remembered for his collections of aphorisms, Afterthoughts *(1931) and* All Trivia *(1933, rev. 1945).*

1 How awful to reflect that what people say of us is true!
Afterthoughts, 'Life and Human Nature' (1931)

2 There are few sorrows, however poignant, in which a good income is of no avail.
Ibid., 'Life and Human Nature'

3 There is more felicity on the far side of baldness than young men can possibly imagine.
Ibid., 'Age and Death'

4 What music is more enchanting than the voices of young people, when you can't hear what they say?
Ibid., 'Age and Death'

5 There are people who are beautiful in dilapidation, like old houses that were hideous when new.
Ibid., 'Age and Death'

6 The denunciation of the young is a necessary part of the hygiene of older people, and greatly assists the circulation of their blood.
Ibid., 'Age and Death'

7 The mere process of growing old together will

make the slightest acquaintance seem like bosom friends.

Ibid., 'Age and Death'

8 I cannot forgive my friends for dying; I do not find these vanishing acts of theirs at all amusing.

Ibid., 'Age and Death'

9 Those who set out to serve both God and Mammon soon discover that there is no God.

Ibid., 'Other People'

10 Most people sell their souls, and live with a good conscience on the proceeds.

Ibid., 'Other People'

11 The test of a vocation is the love of the drudgery it involves.

Ibid., 'Art and Letters'

12 A best-seller is the gilded tomb of a mediocre talent.

Ibid., 'Art and Letters'. See also CYRIL CONNOLLY 2.

13 The notion of making money by popular work, and then retiring to do good work, is the most familiar of all the devil's traps for artists.

Ibid., 'Art and Letters'

14 People say that life is the thing, but I prefer reading.

Ibid., 'Myself'

15 What I like in a good author isn't what he says, but what he whispers.

All Trivia, 'Art and Letters' (1933)

16 There is one thing that matters – to set a chime of words tinkling in the minds of a few fastidious people.

Quoted by CYRIL CONNOLLY in obituary, the New Statesman 9 March 1946. In answer to the question, two weeks before his death, whether he had discovered any meaning in life.

Patti Smith

(b. 1946)

US rock musician and poet

She wrote avant-garde poetry, co-wrote the play Cowboy Mouth *with Sam Shepard (1971), and sang.* Horses *(1975), by the Patti Smith Group, was one of the key albums of US punk.*

1 Jesus died for somebody's sins but not mine.

Preamble to 'Gloria' (song, written by VAN MORRISON) on the album *Horses* (1975)

Samuel Francis Smith

(1808–95)

US journalist and clergyman

He taught languages and edited various Christian publications, including all those of the Baptist Missionary Union from 1854. He also wrote hymns.

1 My country, 'tis of thee,
Sweet land of liberty,
Of thee I sing:
Land where my fathers died,
Land of the pilgrims' pride,
From every mountainside
Let freedom ring.

'America', st. 1 (song, 1832). Regarded as the great national hymn of the United States, and its semi-official national anthem. It was set to the same tune as that of the British national anthem, possibly German in origin.

Stevie Smith

(1902–71)

British poet and novelist

Originally Florence Margaret Smith. She first came to notice with her Novel on Yellow Paper *(1936), but became better known for her unconventional verse, which she illustrated herself. Her collections include* Mother, What Is Man? *(1942) and* Not Waving But Drowning *(1957). 'She looks at the world with a mental squint,' remarked* SEAMUS HEANEY, *'there is a discouraging wobble in the mirror she holds up to nature.'*

1 A Good Time Was Had By All.

Title of collection of verse (1937). Given as the original source of this expression in *A Dictionary of Catch Phrases* by Eric Partridge (ed. Paul Beale, 1985).

2 This Englishwoman is so refined
She has no bosom and no behind.

'This Englishwoman', publ. in *A Good Time Was Had By All* (1937)

3 I'm sorry to say my dear wife is a dreamer,
And as she dreams she gets paler and leaner.
'Then be off to your Dream, with his fly-away hat,
I'll stay with the girls who are happy and fat.'

'BE OFF!', publ. in *Mother, What is Man?* (1942)

4 Fourteen-year-old, why must you giggle and dote,
Fourteen-year-old, why are you such a goat?
I'm fourteen years old, that is the reason,
I giggle and dote in season.

'The Conventionalist', ibid.

5 I may be smelly, and I may be old,
Rough in my pebbles, reedy in my pools,
But where my fish float by I bless their swimming
And I like people to bathe in me, especially
    women.
'The River God', publ. in *Harold's Leap* (1950)

6 Oh, no no no, it was too cold always
(Still the dead one lay moaning)
I was much too far out all my life
And not waving but drowning.
'Not Waving But Drowning', publ. in *Not Waving But Drowning* (1957)

7 Marred pleasure's best, shadow makes the sun
    strong.
'The Queen and the Young Princess', ibid.

8 Why does my Muse only speak when she is
    unhappy?
She does not, I only listen when I am unhappy
When I am happy I live and despise writing
For my Muse this cannot but be dispiriting.
'My Muse', publ. in *Selected Poems* (1962)

9 Oh these illegitimate babies!
Oh girls, girls,
Silly little valuable things,
You should have said, No, I am valuable,
And again, It is because I am valuable
I say, No.
'Valuable', publ. in *The Frog Prince and Other Poems* (1966)

Sydney Smith
(1771–1845)
English clergyman and author

A co-founder of the Edinburgh Review *in 1802, he expressed his liberal sympathies in numerous articles and pamphlets. Peter Plymley's Letters (1807–8) argued in favour of Catholic emancipation. He was a popular preacher and was appointed a canon of St Paul's Cathedral in 1831.*

1 The moment the very name of Ireland is mentioned, the English seem to bid adieu to common feeling, common prudence, and common sense, and to act with the barbarity of tyrants and the fatuity of idiots.
The Letters of Peter Plymley, no. 2 (1807–8)

2 I look upon Switzerland as an inferior sort of Scotland.
Letter to Lord Holland, 1815, publ. in *Memoir*, vol. 2, no. 112 (1855) by Lady Holland

3 It is safest to be moderately base – to be flexible in shame, and to be always ready for what is generous, good and just, when anything is to be gained by virtue.
'Catholics', publ. in the *Edinburgh Review* (1827), repr. in *Works* (1851)

4 I have no relish for the country; it is a kind of healthy grave.
Letter, 1838, publ. in *Memoir*, vol. 2, no. 405 (1855) by Lady Holland

5 Correspondences are like small-clothes before the invention of suspenders; it is impossible to keep them up.
Letter, 31 January 1841, ibid., vol. 2, no. 443

6 It is a bore, I admit, to be past seventy, for you are left for execution, and are daily expecting the death-warrant; but . . . it is not anything very capital we quit. We are, at the close of life, only hurried away from stomach-aches, pains in the joints, from sleepless nights and unamusing days, from weakness, ugliness, and nervous tremors; but we shall all meet again in another planet, cured of all our defects.
Letter, 13 September 1842, ibid., vol. 2, no. 482

7 Bishop Berkeley destroyed this world in one volume octavo; and nothing remained, after his time, but mind; which experienced a similar fate from the hand of Mr Hume in 1737.
Sketches of Moral Philosophy, Introduction (1850)

8 Among the smaller duties of life I hardly know any one more important than that of not praising where praise is not due.
Ibid., Lecture 9

9 If you choose to represent the various parts in life by holes upon a table, of different shapes, some circular, some triangular, some square, some oblong, and the persons acting these parts by bits of wood of similar shapes, we shall generally find that the triangular person has got into the square hole, the oblong into the triangular, and a square person has squeezed himself into the round hole. The officer and the office, the doer and the thing done, seldom fit so exactly that we can say they were almost made for each other.
Ibid., Lecture 9. Thought to be the origin of the expression 'square peg in a round hole'.

10 It requires a surgical operation to get a joke well into a Scotch understanding. Their only idea of wit, or rather that inferior variety of the electric talent

which prevails occasionally in the North, and which, under the name of WUT, is so infinitely distressing to people of good taste, is laughing immoderately at stated intervals.

Quoted in *Memoir*, vol. 1, ch. 2 (1855) by Lady Holland

11 That garret of the earth – that knuckle-end of England – that land of Calvin, oat-cakes, and sulphur.

Ibid., vol. 1, ch. 2. Referring to Scotland.

12 Avoid shame but do not seek glory – nothing so expensive as glory.

Ibid., vol. 1, ch. 4

13 Great men hallow a whole people, and lift up all who live in their time.

Ibid., vol. 1, ch. 7

14 Madam, I have been looking for a person who disliked gravy all my life; let us swear eternal friendship.

Ibid., vol. 1, ch. 9

15 How can a bishop marry? How can he flirt? The most he can say is 'I will see you in the vestry after service.'

Ibid., vol. 1, ch. 9

16 I have, alas, only one illusion left, and that is the Archbishop of Canterbury.

Ibid., vol. 1, ch. 9

17 Ah, you flavour everything; you are the vanille of society.

Ibid., vol. 1, ch. 9

18 As the French say, there are three sexes – men, women, and clergymen.

Ibid., vol. 1, ch. 9

19 Daniel Webster struck me much like a steam-engine in trousers.

Ibid., vol. 1, ch. 9

20 Heat, ma'am! It was so dreadful here, that I found there was nothing left for it but to take off my flesh and sit in my bones.

Ibid., vol. 1, ch. 9

21 Marriage . . . resembles a pair of shears, so joined that they cannot be separated; often moving in opposite directions, yet always punishing anyone who comes between them.

Ibid., vol. 1, ch. 11

22 His enemies might perhaps have said before . . . that he talked rather too much; but now he has occasional flashes of silence, that make his conversation perfectly delightful.

Ibid., vol. 1, ch. 11. Referring to THOMAS MACAULAY, whom Smith called 'a book in breeches'.

23 Oh, don't tell me of facts – I never believe facts: you know Canning said nothing was so fallacious as facts, except figures.

Ibid., vol. 1, ch. 11

24 Thank God for tea! What would the world do without tea? How did it exist?

Ibid., vol. 1, ch. 11

25 [He] deserves to be preached to death by wild curates.

Ibid., vol. 1, ch. 11. Referring to a Dean.

26 I never read a book before reviewing it; it prejudices a man so.

Quoted in *The Smith of Smiths*, ch. 3 (1934) by HESKETH PEARSON

27 My idea of heaven is eating *paté de foie gras* to the sound of trumpets.

Ibid., ch. 10

28 What a pity it is that we have no amusements in England but vice and religion!

Ibid., ch. 10

29 What two ideas are more inseparable than beer and Britannia?

Ibid., ch. 11

Zadie Smith

(b. 1975)
British author

Her bestselling debut novel White Teeth *(2000), written while she was still an undergraduate, was, in her own words, 'the literary equivalent of a hyperactive ginger-haired, tap-dancing 10-year-old'.* The Autograph Man *was published in 2002.*

1 You must live life with the full knowledge that your actions will *remain*. We are creatures of consequence . . . Our children will be born of our actions. *Our accidents will become their destinies.*

White Teeth, ch. 5 (2000). Spoken by Samad.

2 The English are the only people who want to teach you and steal from you at the same time.

Alsana, ibid., ch. 13

3 Cold, wet, miserable, terrible food, dreadful newspapers – who would want to stay? . . . But you have made a devil's pact . . . it drags you in and suddenly you are unsuitable to return, your children are

unrecognizable, you belong nowhere ... And then you begin to give up the very *idea* of belonging.
Samad, ibid., ch. 15

Tobias Smollett
(1721–71)
Scottish novelist and surgeon

He served as a ship's surgeon before devoting himself to literature. His greatest successes were the picaresque and satirical novels The Adventures of Roderick Random *(1748),* The Adventures of Peregrine Pickle *(1751) and* The Expedition of Humphry Clinker *(1771). He also wrote plays, poetry and travel books, and edited journals.*

1 Mourn, hapless Caledonia, mourn
Thy banished peace, thy laurels torn.
'The Tears of Scotland' (1746), repr. in *The Works of Tobias Smollett* (ed. George Saintsbury, 1895)

2 The capital is become an overgrown monster; which like a dropsical head, will in time leave the body and extremities without nourishment and support.
The Expedition of Humphry Clinker, vol. 1, letter from Matthew Bramble, 29 May (1771)

3 That great Cham of literature, Samuel Johnson.
Letter to JOHN WILKES, 16 March 1759, publ. in *The Letters of Tobias Smollett* (ed. Lewis M. Knapp, 1970) . Meaning, 'the great monarch' or 'the great dictator'.

(Dame) Ethel Smyth
(1858–1944)
British composer and feminist

Considered the first significant British woman composer, she is known for her operas, such as The Wreckers *(1906), as well as for songs and choral pieces. 'The March of the Women' (1911) became the anthem for the suffragette movement, of which she was an active supporter.*

1 The habit some writers indulge in of perpetual quotation is one it behoves lovers of good literature to protest against, for it is an insidious habit which in the end must cloud the stream of thought, or at least check spontaneity. If it be true that *le style c'est l'homme*, what is likely to happen if *l'homme* is for ever eking out his own personality with that of some other individual?
Streaks of Life, 'The Quotation-Fiend' (1924)

C. P. Snow
(1905–80)
British novelist, scientist and government administrator

Charles Percy Snow, Baron Snow of Leicester. Trained as a scientist, he began writing detective fiction and went on to produce the novel sequence Strangers and Brothers *(1940–70). He was a scientific adviser to the government during the Second World War, and subsequently a Civil Service Commissioner.*

1 The official world, the corridors of power, the dilemmas of conscience and egotism – she disliked them all.
Homecomings, ch. 22 (1956). Snow later published a novel titled *Corridors of Power* (1963).

2 It was through living among these groups ... that I got occupied with the problem of what, long before I put it on paper, I christened to myself as the 'two cultures'. For constantly I felt I was moving among two groups – comparable in intelligence, identical in race, not grossly different in social origin, earning about the same incomes, who had almost ceased to communicate at all, who in intellectual, moral and psychological climate had so little in common that instead of going from Burlington House or South Kensington to Chelsea, one might have crossed an ocean.
'The Two Cultures and the Scientific Revolution', Rede Lecture (1959). The lecture gave rise to a bitter attack by F. R. LEAVIS, among others, and the 'Two Cultures' controversy. Snow had previously published an article called 'The Two Cultures' in the *New Statesman* 6 October 1956.

3 Literary intellectuals at one pole – at the other scientists, and as the most representative, the physical scientists. Between the two a gulf of mutual incomprehension – sometimes (particularly among the young) hostility and dislike, but most of all lack of understanding. They have a curious distorted image of each other. Their attitudes are so different that, even on the level of emotion, they can't find much common ground.
Ibid.

Socrates
(469–399 BC)
Greek philosopher

One of the founders of Western philosophy, he taught that knowledge, elicited through a dialectical process, would lead to virtue and good ethical conduct. His life and teachings are known mainly through his disciple PLATO, *who recorded his dialogues in such works as* The Republic *and* Phaedo. *Accused of corrupting youths, he was sentenced to death and took his own life by drinking hemlock.*

1 What do the slanderers say? They shall be my prosecutors, and I will sum up their words in an affidavit. 'Socrates is an evil-doer, a meddler who searches into things under the earth and in heaven, and makes the worse appear the better cause, and he teaches the aforesaid doctrines to others.'
Quoted in *Apology*, sect. 19b by PLATO (transl. BENJAMIN JOWETT, 1871, rev. 1953). Speech to the court, while on trial on charges of impiety and corruption of youth.

2 I am at least wiser than this fellow – for he knows nothing, and thinks that he knows; I neither know nor think that I know.
Ibid., sect. 21d. Referring to a man with a 'reputation of wisdom'.

3 Socrates is a doer of evil, inasmuch as he corrupts the youth, and does not receive the gods whom the state receives, but has a new religion of his own. Such is the charge.
Ibid., sect. 24b

4 For the fear of death is indeed the pretence of wisdom, and not real wisdom, being a pretence of knowing the unknown; and no one knows whether death, of which men are afraid because they apprehend it to be the greatest evil, may not be the greatest good.
Ibid., sect. 29a

5 I tell you that virtue is not given by money, but that from virtue come money and every other good of man, public as well as private.
Ibid., sect. 30b

6 I showed, not in words only, but in deed, that . . . I care not a straw for death, and that my great and only care is lest I should do an unrighteous or unholy thing.
Ibid., sect. 32d

7 The unexamined life is no life for a human being.
Ibid., sect. 38a. Explaining why it would be impossible for him to go into exile and keep his opinions to himself. Usually quoted: 'The unexamined life is not worth living' (known as the Socratic dictum).

8 The hour of departure has arrived, and we go our ways – I to die and you to live. Which is the better, only God knows.
Ibid., sect. 42a. Last words of his speech to the court on being sentenced to death.

9 I only wish . . . that the many could do the greatest evil; for then they would also be able to do the greatest good.
Quoted in *Crito*, sect. 44d by PLATO

10 How many things I can do without!
Quoted in *Lives of the Philosophers*, bk 2, sect. 25 by Diogenes Laertius. Said to be his response when seeing a quantity of goods on sale.

11 I know nothing except the fact of my ignorance.
Quoted ibid., bk 2, sect. 32. See JOHN MILTON 191.

12 The true votary of philosophy is likely to be misunderstood by other men; they do not perceive that of his own accord he is always engaged in the pursuit of dying and death.
Quoted in *Phaedo*, sect. 64a by PLATO (transl. BENJAMIN JOWETT, 1871, rev. 1953)

13 All wars are occasioned by the love of money, and money has to be acquired for the sake of the body and in slavish ministration to it.
Ibid., sect. 66c

14 If we would have pure knowledge of anything we must be quit of the body – the soul by herself must behold things by themselves: and then we shall attain that which we desire, and of which we say that we are lovers – wisdom; not while we live, but . . . only after death.
Ibid., sect. 66d–e

15 I was afraid that my soul might be blinded altogether if I looked at things with my eyes or tried to apprehend them by the help of particular senses.
Ibid., sect. 99e

16 False words are not only evil in themselves, but they infect the soul with evil.
Ibid., sect. 115e

17 The makers of fortunes have a second love of money as a creation of their own, resembling the affection of authors for their own poems, or of parents for their children, besides that natural love of it for the sake of use and profit which is common to them and all men. And hence they are very bad company, for they insist on measuring the value of things in terms of wealth.
Quoted in *The Republic*, bk 1, sect. 330c by PLATO (transl. BENJAMIN JOWETT, 1871, rev. 1953)

18 No physician, in so far as he is a physician, considers his own good in what he prescribes, but the good of his patient; for the true physician is also a

ruler having the human body as a subject, and is not a mere money-maker.
Ibid., bk 1, sect. 342d

19 It is most important that the tales which the young first hear should be models of virtuous thoughts.
Ibid., bk 2 sect. 378e

20 If anyone at all is to have the privilege of lying, the rulers of the state should be the persons; and they, in their dealings either with enemies or with their own citizens, may be allowed to lie for the public good. But nobody else should meddle with anything of the kind.
Ibid., bk 3, sect. 389b

21 Wealth ... and poverty; the one is the parent of luxury and indolence, and the other of meanness and viciousness, and both of a revolutionary spirit.
Ibid., bk 4, sect. 422a

22 For any musical innovation is to be shunned, as likely to bring danger to the whole state ... When modes of music change, the fundamental laws of the state always change with them.
Ibid., bk 4, sect. 424c. Socrates continues: 'Our guardians must lay the foundations of their fortress in music.'

23 The direction in which education starts a man will determine his future life.
Ibid., bk 4, sect. 425b

24 Behold! human beings housed in an underground cave ... Like ourselves ... do you think they have seen anything of themselves, and of one another, except the shadows which the fire throws on the opposite side wall of the cave.
Ibid., bk 7, sect. 514a–15a

25 A freeman ought not to acquire knowledge of any kind like a slave ... Knowledge which is acquired under compulsion obtains no hold on the mind ... Let early education be a sort of amusement; you will then also be better able to find out the natural bent.
Ibid., bk 7, sect. 536e

26 These ... characteristics are proper to democracy, which will be, it seems to me, a charming form of government, full of variety and disorder, and dispensing a sort of equality to equals and unequals alike.
Ibid., bk 8, sect. 558c

27 He lives from day to day indulging the appetite of the hour; and sometimes he is lapped in drink and strains of the flute; then he becomes a water-drinker, and tries to get thin; then he takes a turn at gymnastics; sometimes idling and neglecting everything, then once more living the life of a philosopher.
Ibid., bk 8, sect. 561c. Describing the life of a youth in a democracy.

28 The people have always some champion whom they are wont to set over them and nurse them into greatness ... Whenever tyranny appears, the protectorship of the people is the root from which it all springs.
Ibid., bk 8, sect. 565c–d

29 There are three arts which are concerned with all things: one which uses, another which makes, a third which imitates them.
Ibid., bk 10, sect. 601d

30 Virtue is free, and as a man honours or dishonours her he will have more or less of her; the responsibility is with the chooser – God is not responsible.
Ibid., bk 10, sect. 617e. Socrates is quoting the Interpreter.

Steven Soderbergh
(b. 1963)
US film-maker

Since his quirky debut, sex, lies, and videotape *(1989), he has explored a variety of genres with varying success, for example* King of the Hill *(1993),* Out of Sight *(1998) and* Solaris *(2002).*

1 Lying is like alcoholism. You are always recovering.
sex, lies, and videotape (film, 1989, written and directed by Steven Soderbergh). Spoken by Graham Dalton (James Spader).

Valerie Solanas
(1936–88)
US feminist

An actor in ANDY WARHOL's *film* I, a Man *(1967), she achieved notoriety for shooting Warhol in 1968, and was judged schizophrenic in the ensuing trial (when she was defended by* FLORYNCE R. KENNEDY). *Her intended victim had been Maurice Girodias, whose Olympia Press later published her extremist* SCUM Manifesto *(1968).*

1 Life in this society being, at best, an utter bore and no aspect of society being at all relevant to women, there remains to civic-minded, responsible, thrill-

seeking females only to overthrow the government, eliminate the money system, institute complete automation and destroy the male sex.

The SCUM Manifesto (1968), repr. in *Sisterhood is Powerful* (ed. Robin Morgan, 1970). The acronym *SCUM* stood for 'Society for Cutting Up Men'.

2 To call a man an animal is to flatter him; he's a machine, a walking dildo.

The SCUM Manifesto, ibid.

3 I consider that a moral act. And I consider it immoral that I missed. I should have done target practice.

Interview in *Village Voice* 1 August 1977. Of her shooting of ANDY WARHOL.

Solon

(*c.* 640–*c.* 558 BC)
Athenian statesman and poet

His social, political and legal reforms helped to reduce poverty and injustice in Athens. He travelled widely and wrote poetry, and was counted among the 'Seven Wise Men' by later generations. See also ANONYMOUS 51.

1 Let no man be called happy before his death. Until then, he is only fortunate.

Attributed, in answer to CROESUS, who had asked him who was the happiest man Solon had encountered on his travels, expecting him to name Croesus himself. Croesus dismissed Solon, only to remember his words when sentenced to death following his disastrous invasion of Persia (though the sentence was rescinded when the Persian king, Cyrus, heard the tale). The story is related by HERODOTUS in *The Histories*, bk 1, sect. 32, though it has no historical basis: Solon died before he could have met Croesus.

Alexander Solzhenitsyn

(b. 1918)
Russian novelist

The political nature of his writing led to his persecution, imprisonment and exile (1974–94). His books include One Day in the Life of Ivan Denisovich *(1962) and* The Gulag Archipelago *(1973). 'I belong to the Russian convict world no less ... than I do to Russian literature,' he stated. 'I got my education there, and it will last forever.'*

1 Here, lads, we live by the law of the *taiga*. But even here people manage to live. D'you know who are the ones the camps finish off? Those who lick other men's left-overs, those who set store by the doctors, and those who peach on their mates.

One Day in the Life of Ivan Denisovich (1962). Spoken by Kuziomin.

2 Literature that is not the breath of contemporary society, that dares not transmit the pains and fears of that society, that does not warn in time against threatening moral and social dangers – such literature does not deserve the name of literature; it is only a façade. Such literature loses the confidence of its own people, and its published works are used as wastepaper instead of being read.

Open letter to the Fourth Soviet Writers' Congress, 16 May 1967, repr. in *Solzhenitsyn: A Documentary Record*, 'The Struggle Intensifies' (ed. Leopold Labedz, 1970, rev. 1974)

3 One should never direct people towards happiness, because happiness too is an idol of the marketplace. One should direct them towards mutual affection. A beast gnawing at its prey can be happy too, but only human beings can feel affection for each other, and this is the highest achievement they can aspire to.

Cancer Ward, pt 2, ch. 10 (1968). Spoken by Shulubin.

4 You only have power over people so long as you don't take *everything* away from them. But when you've robbed a man of *everything* he's no longer in your power – he's free again.

The First Circle, ch. 17 (1968). Spoken by Bobynin.

5 For a country to have a great writer ... is like having another government. That's why no régime has ever loved great writers, only minor ones.

Innokenty, ibid., ch. 57

6 Violence finds its only refuge in falsehood, falsehood its only support in violence. Any man who has once acclaimed violence as his METHOD must inexorably choose falsehood as his PRINCIPLE.

Nobel Prize lecture, 1970, publ. in *Solzhenitsyn: A Documentary Record*, 'The Struggle Continues' (ed. Leopold Labedz, 1970, rev. 1974)

7 There are many ways of killing a poet.

'Asphyxiation', written 1971, publ. in *The Oak and the Calf*, 'Second Supplement' (1980). Solzhenitsyn repeated these words on numerous occasions.

8 Woe to that nation whose literature is cut short by the intrusion of force. This is not merely interference with freedom of the press but the sealing up of a nation's heart, the excision of its memory.

Time 25 February 1974

9 For us in Russia, communism is a dead dog, while, for many people in the West, it is still a living lion.

Radio broadcast on BBC Russian service, publ. in the *Listener* 15 February 1979

10 The clock of communism has stopped striking. But its concrete building has not yet come crashing down. For that reason, instead of freeing ourselves, we must try to save ourselves from being crushed by its rubble.

'How We Must Rebuild Russia', publ. in *Komsomolskaya Pravda* 18 September 1990. Opening sentence of essay.

William Somerville

(1675–1742)
English poet

He published Occasional Poems *in 1727, but was better known for his works extolling outdoor pursuits, particularly the long poem,* The Chase *(1735), on hunting.* SAMUEL JOHNSON *said of him: 'He writes very well for a gentleman.'*

1 Let all the learned say what they can,
'Tis ready money makes the man.

'Ready Money', publ. in *Occasional Poems* (1727)

2 My hoarse-sounding horn
Invites thee to the chase, the sport of kings;
Image of war, without its guilt.

The Chase, bk 1, ll. 13–15 (1735). See R. S. SURTEES 2.

Anastasio Somoza

(1925–80)
Nicaraguan dictator

Anastasio Somoza Debayle. His presidency from 1967 was associated with repression and corruption. He was toppled by the Sandinistas in 1979 and assassinated a year later.

1 Indeed, you won the elections, but I won the count.

Quoted in the *Guardian* 17 June 1977. Addressed to an opponent who accused him of rigging the election. See also TOM STOPPARD 7.

Stephen Sondheim

(b. 1930)
US songwriter and composer

Rated one of the greatest Broadway wordsmiths, he provided the lyrics to LEONARD BERNSTEIN'*s* West Side Story *(1957) and wrote both words and music for such shows as* A Little Night Music *(1973) and* Sunday in the Park with George *(1984).*

1 I like to be in America!
OK by me in America!
Everything free in America,
For a small fee in America!

'America' (song, with music by Leonard Bernstein) in *West Side Story* (stage musical 1957, film 1961)

2 Everything's gonna be bright lights and lollipops!
Everything's coming up roses for me and for you!

'Everything's Coming Up Roses' (song, with music by Jule Styne) in *Gypsy* (stage musical, 1959)

3 The concerts you enjoy together
Neighbors you annoy together
Children you destroy together
That make marriage a joy.

'The Little Things You Do Together' (song) in *Company* (stage musical, 1970)

4 A toast to that invincible bunch
The dinosaurs surviving the crunch
Let's hear it for the ladies who lunch.

'The Ladies Who Lunch' (song), ibid. Performed by Elaine Stritch in the original production.

5 Every day a little death
On the lips and in the eyes,
In the murmurs, in the pauses,
In the gestures, in the sighs.
Every day a little dies.

'Every Day a Little Death' (song) in *A Little Night Music* (stage musical 1973, filmed 1977).

6 But where are the clowns ?
Quick, send in the clowns.
Don't bother, they're here.

'Send in the Clowns' (song), ibid. The song was a hit for Judy Collins in 1975, and performed by Elizabeth Taylor in the film version. In circus or vaudeville, the words are the traditional desperate summons for some distraction for the audience when something goes badly wrong.

Susan Sontag

(1933–2004)
US author and critic

Called 'a foraging pluralist' by ELIZABETH HARDWICK *and 'probably the most intelligent woman in America' by* JONATHAN MILLER, *she wrote incisively on culture and society in such works as* Against Interpretation *(1966) and* Illness as a Metaphor *(1979).*

1 Interpretation is the revenge of the intellect upon art. Even more. It is the revenge of the intellect upon the world. To interpret is to impoverish, to deplete the world – in order to set up a shadow world of 'meanings'.

Against Interpretation, 'Against Interpretation', sect. 4 (1966)

2 Art is seduction, not rape.

Ibid., 'On Style'

3 Intelligence . . . is really a kind of taste: taste in ideas.
Ibid., 'Notes on "Camp"'

4 What is most beautiful in virile men is something feminine; what is most beautiful in feminine women is something masculine.
Ibid., 'Notes on "Camp"', Note 9

5 As the dandy is the nineteenth century's surrogate for the aristocrat in matters of culture, so Camp is the modern dandyism. Camp is the answer to the problem: how to be a dandy in the age of mass culture.
Ibid., 'Notes on "Camp"', Note 45

6 Jews and homosexuals are the outstanding creative minorities in contemporary urban culture. Creative, that is in the truest sense: they are creators of sensibilities. The two pioneering forces of modern sensibility are Jewish moral seriousness and homosexual aestheticism and irony.
Ibid., 'Notes on "Camp"', Note 51

7 What pornography is really about, ultimately, isn't sex but death.
Styles of Radical Will, 'The Pornographic Imagination', sect. 4 (1969)

8 The truth is that Mozart, Pascal, Boolean algebra, Shakespeare, parliamentary government, baroque churches, Newton, the emancipation of women, Kant, Marx, and Balanchine ballets don't redeem what this particular civilization has wrought upon the world. The white race *is* the cancer of human history.
Ibid., 'What's Happening in America'

9 Now there is a master scenario available to everyone. The color is black, the material is leather, the seduction is beauty, the justification is honesty, the aim is ecstasy, the fantasy is death.
Under the Sign of Saturn, 'Fascinating Fascism' (1980). Discussing Nazi symbolism in sado-masochism.

10 The taste for quotations (and for the juxtaposition of incongruous quotations) is a Surrealist taste.
On Photography, 'Melancholy Objects' (1977)

11 Illness is the night-side of life, a more onerous citizenship. Everyone who is born holds dual citizenship, in the kingdom of the well and in the kingdom of the sick. Although we all prefer to use only the good passport, sooner or later each of us is obliged, at least for a spell, to identify ourselves as citizens of that other place.
Illness As Metaphor, Preface (1978). Opening words.

12 Any important disease whose causality is murky, and for which treatment is ineffectual, tends to be awash in significance.
Ibid., ch. 8

13 Victims suggest innocence. And innocence, by the inexorable logic that governs all relational terms, suggests guilt.
AIDS and Its Metaphors, ch. 1 (1989)

14 Societies need to have one illness which becomes identified with evil, and attaches blame to its 'victims'.
Ibid., ch. 1

Sophocles
(c. 496–406 BC)
Greek dramatist

A rival to his contemporaries AESCHYLUS *and* EURIPIDES, *he broke new ground in the staging of his plays, of which only seven out of 123 survive in their entirety. With strong characterization and skilful structure, such tragedies as* Antigone *and* Oedipus the King *greatly influenced Renaissance drama.*

1 Wonders are many, and none is more wonderful than man.
Antigone, l. 333 (c. 441 BC, transl. R. C. Jebb). Spoken by the Chorus.

2 The gods implant reason in men, the highest of all things that we call our own.
Haemon, ibid., ll. 684–5

3 Love, unconquered in the fight, Love, who makest havoc of wealth, who keepest thy vigil on the soft cheek of a maiden; thou roamest over the sea, and among the homes of dwellers in the wilds; no immortal can escape thee, nor any among men whose life is for a day; and he to whom thou hast come is mad.
Chorus, ibid., ll. 781–9

4 Of all human ills
Greatest is fortune's wayward tyranny.
Ajax, ll. 486–7 (c. 440 BC, transl. R. C. Trevelyan). Spoken by Tecmessa.

5 So now I find that ancient proverb true,
Foes' gifts are no gifts: profit bring they none.
Ajax, ibid., ll. 664–5

6 Sleep, that masters all,
Binds life awhile, yet loosens soon the bond.
Ajax, ibid., ll. 675–6

7 Men of ill judgment oft ignore the good
That lies within their hands, till they have lost it.
Tecmessa, ibid., ll. 964–5

8 All his desire
He now has won, that death for which he longed.
Why then should they deride him? 'Tis the gods
Must answer for his death, not these men, no.
Tecmessa, ibid., ll. 967–80. Speaking of the death of Ajax, and the attitude of the Greek leaders.

9 This wedlock with thy mother fear not thou.
How oft it chances that in dreams a man
Has wed his mother! He who least regards
Such brain-sick fantasies lives most at ease.
Oedipus the King, ll. 977–80 (c. 429 BC, transl. F. Storr). Spoken by Jocasta to Oedipus.

10 Stranger on foreign soil,
Beware, poor wanderer:
Hate whatsoever we have learned to hate,
And what we love, revere.
Oedipus at Colonus, ll. 184–7 (c. 406 BC, transl. E. F. Watling). Spoken by the Chorus.

11 Say what you will, the greatest boon is not to be;
But, life begun, soonest to end is best,
And to that bourne from which our way began
Swiftly return.
Chorus, ibid., ll. 1224–7

12 In particular I may mention Sophocles the poet, who was once asked in my presence, 'How do you feel about love, Sophocles? are you still capable of it?' to which he replied, 'Hush! if you please: to my great delight I have escaped from it, and feel as if I had escaped from a frantic and savage master.'
The Republic, bk 1, sect. 329, by PLATO

Robert Southey

(1774–1843)
English poet, journalist and author

A friend of COLERIDGE *and* WORDSWORTH, *he became known for his lyrics and ballads and was Poet Laureate from 1813. He also wrote histories and biographies, including* Life of Nelson *(1813). He abandoned his early radical views and contributed to the Tory* Quarterly Review *from 1809.*

1 It was a summer evening,
Old Kaspar's work was done,

And he before his cottage door
Was sitting in the sun,
And by him sported on the green
His little grandchild Wilhelmine.
'The Battle of Blenheim', st. 1 (1798), repr. in *Minor Poems* (1815). Opening lines.

2 But what they fought each other for,
I could not well make out;
But everybody said, quoth he,
That 'twas a famous victory.
'The Battle of Blenheim', st. 6, ibid.

3 For many thousand bodies here
Lay rotting in the sun;
But things like that, you know, must be
After a famous victory.
'The Battle of Blenheim', st. 9, ibid.

4 And everybody praised the Duke,
Who this great fight did win.
But what good came of it at last?
Quoth little Peterkin.
Why that I cannot tell, said he,
But 'twas a famous victory.
'The Battle of Blenheim', st. 11, ibid. Closing lines.

5 You are old, Father William, the young man cried,
The few locks which are left you are grey;
You are hale, Father William, a hearty old man,
Now tell me the reason, I pray.
'The Old Man's Comforts', st. 1 (1799), ibid. This poem is less well known than its parody: see LEWIS CARROLL 8.

6 Till the vessel strikes with a shivering shock –
'O Christ! it is the Inchcape Rock!'
'The Inchcape Rock', st. 15 (1803), ibid.

7 My name is Death: the last best friend am I.
The Lay of the Laureate: Carmen Nuptiale, st. 87 (1816)

8 My days among the dead are past;
Around me I behold,
Where'er these casual eyes are cast,
The mighty minds of old;
My never-failing friends are they,
With whom I converse day by day.
'My Days among the Dead are Past', st. 1 (1818), publ. in *Poetical Works*, vol. 2 (1837)

9 Our professors of the arts babblative and scribblative.
Colloquies on the Progress and Prospects of Society, no. 10, sect. 2 (1829)

10 The march of intellect is proceeding at quick

time; and if its progress be not accompanied by a corresponding improvement in morals and religion, the faster it proceeds, with the more violence will you be hurried down the road to ruin.
Ibid., no. 14

Robert Southwell
(c. 1561–95)
English poet and Catholic martyr

A Jesuit, he was ordained priest in 1585, and was arrested in 1592, tortured and executed. His devotional lyrics and prose works are noted for their directness and striking imagery.

1 As I in hoary winter's night stood shivering in
  the snow,
Surprised I was with sudden heat which made my
  heart to glow;
And lifting up a fearful eye to view what fire was
  near,
A pretty Babe all burning bright did in the air
  appear.
'The Burning Babe', publ. in *St Peter's Complaint and Other Poems* (1595). Opening lines.

2 Behold a silly tender Babe
In freezing winter night
In homely manger trembling lies,
Alas, a piteous sight!
'New Prince, New Pomp', st. 1, ibid.

3 The lopped tree in time may grow again,
Most naked plants renew both fruit and flower;
The sorriest wight may find release of pain,
The driest soil suck in some moistening shower.
Times go by turns, and chances change by course,
From foul to fair, from better hap to worse.
'Times Go By Turns', st. 1, ibid.

(Dame) Muriel Spark
(1918–2006)
British author and poet

She chiefly published poetry and short stories, but is best known for her novels, notably The Prime of Miss Jean Brodie *(1961), which she herself described as 'more progressive than I realized'. Other titles include* The Girls of Slender Means *(1963) and* The Driver's Seat *(1970).*

1 Being over seventy is like being engaged in a war. All our friends are going or gone and we survive amongst the dead and the dying as on a battlefield.
Memento Mori, ch. 4 (1959). Spoken by Miss Taylor.

2 Without an ever-present sense of death life is insipid. You might as well live on the whites of eggs.
Henry Mortimer, ibid., ch. 11

3 I am putting old heads on your young shoulders; all my pupils are the crème de la crème.
The Prime of Miss Jean Brodie, ch. 1 (1961). Spoken by Miss Brodie.

4 Give me a girl at an impressionable age, and she is mine for life!
Miss Brodie, ibid., ch. 1. The words echo a Jesuit maxim: see ANONYMOUS 28.

5 One's prime is elusive. You little girls, when you grow up, must be on the alert to recognize your prime at whatever time of your life it may occur. You must then live it to the full.
Miss Brodie, ibid., ch. 1

6 Art and religion first; then philosophy; lastly science. That is the order of the great subjects of life, that's their order of importance.
Miss Brodie, ibid., ch. 2

7 To me education is a leading out of what is already there in the pupil's soul. To Miss Mackay it is a putting in of something that is not there, and that is not what I call education, I call it intrusion.
Miss Brodie, ibid., ch. 2

8 If you're going to do a thing, you should do it thoroughly. If you're going to be a Christian, you may as well be a Catholic.
Independent 2 August 1989

Charles Spencer
(b. 1964)
British journalist and businessman

Earl Spencer, Viscount Althorp. He was NBC correspondent and presenter (1987–91 and 1993–6) and a reporter for Granada Television (1991–3). Following the death of his sister Princess DIANA, *he was outspoken against the press and the royal family.*

1 I . . . always believed the press would kill her in the end. But not even I could believe they would take such a direct hand in her death as seems to be the case.
Speech to press outside his home in Cape Town, 31 August 1997, publ. in *The Times* 1 September 1997. On the death of Princess DIANA.

2 It would appear that every proprietor and every editor of every publication that had paid for intrusive and exploitative photographs of her, encouraging greedy and ruthless individuals to risk

everything in pursuit of Diana's image, has blood on his hands today.
Ibid.

3 It is a point to remember that, of all the ironies about Diana, perhaps the greatest was this: a girl given the name of the ancient goddess was, in the end, the most hunted person of the modern age.
Funeral oration at Westminster Abbey, 6 September 1997, quoted in the *Observer* 7 September 1997

Herbert Spencer
(1820–1903)
English philosopher

In his first book, Social Statics *(1851), and subsequent works, he argued in favour of social and political laissez-faire and for individualism as the primary engine of society and ethics. His theory of evolution predated and had much in common with* DARWIN*'s, and he sought to extend it in the various volumes of* The Synthetic Philosophy *(1855–96).*

1 Progress, therefore, is not an accident, but a necessity . . . It is a part of nature.
Social Statics, pt 1, ch. 2, sect. 4 (1851)

2 Hero-worship is strongest where there is least regard for human freedom.
Ibid., pt 4, ch. 30, sect. 6

3 No one can be perfectly free till all are free; no one can be perfectly moral till all are moral; no one can be perfectly happy till all are happy.
Ibid., pt 4, ch. 30, sect. 16

4 People are beginning to see that the first requisite to success in life is to be a good animal.
Education, ch. 2 (1861)

5 Science is organized knowledge.
Ibid., ch. 2

6 The preservation of health is a *duty*. Few seem conscious that there is such a thing as physical morality.
Ibid., ch. 4

7 The more specific idea of evolution now reached is – a change from an indefinite, incoherent homogeneity to a definite, coherent heterogeneity, accompanying the dissipation of motion and integration of matter.
First Principles, vol. 1, pt 2, ch. 16, para. 138 (1862)

8 A living thing is distinguished from a dead thing by the multiplicity of the changes at any moment taking place in it.
Principles of Biology, pt 1, ch. 4 (1865)

9 It cannot but happen . . . that those will survive whose functions happen to be most nearly in equilibrium with the modified aggregate of external forces . . . this survival of the fittest implies multiplication of the fittest.
Ibid., pt 3, ch. 12. In the fifth edition of his *Origin of Species* (1869), CHARLES DARWIN added a note to his definition of the term 'natural selection' in ch. 3: 'The expression often used by Mr Herbert Spencer of the Survival of the Fittest is more accurate, and is sometimes equally convenient.'

10 The Republican form of government is the highest form of government; but because of this it requires the highest type of human nature – a type nowhere at present existing.
Essays, vol. 3, 'The Americans' (1891)

11 The ultimate result of shielding men from the effects of folly, is to fill the world with fools.
Ibid., vol. 3, 'State Tamperings with Money and Banks'

(Sir) Stephen Spender
(1909–95)
British poet

Described by Robert Craft as 'the least insular writer of his generation', he co-founded with CYRIL CONNOLLY *the magazine* Horizon, *of which he was editor 1939–41. He later co-edited* Encounter *1953–67. His poetry collections include* Poems from Spain *(1939) and* The Edge of Darkness *(1949). See* W. H. AUDEN 52.

1 My parents kept me from children who were rough
And who threw words like stones and who wore torn clothes.
'My parents kept me from children who were rough', publ. in *Poems*, no. 12 (1933)

2 I think continually of those who were truly great.
Who, from the womb, remembered the soul's history
Through corridors of light where the hours are suns,
Endless and singing.
'I Think Continually', st. 1, ibid., no. 23

3 The names of those who in their lives fought for life,
Who wore at their hearts the fire's centre.

Born of the sun they travelled a short while
  toward the sun
And left the vivid air signed with their honour.
'I Think Continually', st. 3, ibid., no. 23

4 After the first powerful plain manifesto
The black statement of pistons, without more fuss
But gliding like a queen, she leaves the station.
'The Express', ll. 1–3, ibid., no. 26

5 Steaming through metal landscape on her lines,
She plunges new eras of white happiness,
Where speed throws up strange shapes, broad
  curves
And parallels clean like the steel of guns.
'The Express', ll. 17–20, ibid., no. 26. Spender later amended
the last line to read '... like trajectories from guns'.

6 Now over these small hills they have built the
  concrete
That trails black wire:
Pylons, those pillars
Bare like nude, giant girls that have no secret.
'The Pylons', ibid., no. 28. The poem provided the label 'Pylon
Poets' for the 1930s poets who wrote about the modern indus-
trialized landscape, including Spender, W. H. AUDEN and C.
DAY LEWIS.

7 Finally, they cease to hate: for although hate
Bursts from the air and whips the earth like hail
Or pours it up in fountains to marvel at,
And although hundreds fell, who can connect
The inexhaustible anger of the guns
With the dumb patience of these tormented
  animals?
'Two Armies', publ. in *The Still Centre* (1939)

8 The guns spell money's ultimate reason
In letters of lead on the spring hillside.
'Ultima Ratio Regum', publ. in *Poems for Spain* (ed. Stephen
Spender and John Lehmann, 1939)

Oswald Spengler
(1880–1936)
German historian

His reputation rests on his major work The Decline of the
West *(2 vols. 1918–22), which argues, through what he termed
a 'morphological method', a cyclical theory of human development in accordance with 'historical destiny'.*

1 In place of a world, there is a *city*, a *point*, in which
the whole life of broad regions is collecting while
the rest dries up. In place of a type-true people, born
of and grown on the soil, there is a new sort of

nomad, cohering unstably in fluid masses, the
parasitical city dweller, traditionless, utterly matter-
of-fact, religionless, clever, unfruitful, deeply contemptuous of the countryman and especially that
highest form of countryman, the country
gentleman.
The Decline of the West, vol. 1, ch. 1, sect. 12 (1918)

2 The last man of the world-city no longer *wants* to
live – he may cling to life as an individual, but as a
type, as an aggregate, no, for it is a characteristic of
this collective existence that it eliminates the terror
of death.
Ibid., vol. 2, ch. 4, sect. 5 (1922)

Edmund Spenser
(c. 1522–99)
English poet

*His verse is renowned for its rich imagery and his use of what
came to be known as the 'Spenserian stanza', adapted from
the Italian ottava rima. Six books survive of his best-known
work,* The Faerie Queene *(1590–6), an allegorical epic, archaic
in style. Other works include* The Shepherd's Calendar *(1579)
and* Astrophel *(1586), an elegy on the death of his friend
PHILIP SIDNEY.*

1 So now they have made our English tongue a gallimaufry or hodgepodge of all other speeches.
The Shepherd's Calendar, 'Letter to Gabriel Harvey' (1579)

2 To be wise and eke to love,
Is granted scarce to God above.
Ibid., 'March: Willy's Emblem'

3 And he that strives to touch the stars,
Oft stumbles at a straw.
Ibid., 'July', ll. 99–100

4 The general end therefore of all the book is to
fashion a gentleman or noble person in virtuous
and gentle discipline.
The Faerie Queene, Prefatory Letter to Sir Walter Ralegh (1590)

5 Fierce wars and faithful loves shall moralize my
song.
Ibid., 'Introduction'

6 A gentle knight was pricking on the plain.
Ibid., bk 1, canto 1, st. 1. Opening line.

7 But on his breast a bloody cross he bore,
The dear remembrance of his dying Lord.
Ibid., bk 1, canto 1, st. 2

8 A bold bad man, that dared to call by name
Great Gorgon, Prince of darkness and dead night.
Ibid., bk 1, canto 1, st. 37

9 Her angel's face
As the great eye of heaven shinèd bright,
And made a sunshine in the shady place;
Did never mortal eye behold such heavenly grace.
Ibid., bk 1, canto 3, st. 4

10 The noble heart, that harbours virtuous
    thought,
And is with child of glorious great intent,
Can never rest, until it forth have brought
Th' eternal brood of glory excellent.
Ibid., bk 1, canto 5, st. 1

11 A cruel crafty crocodile,
Which in false grief hiding his harmful guile,
Doth weep full sore, and sheddeth tender tears.
Ibid., bk 1, canto 5, st. 18

12 But who can turn the stream of destiny,
Or break the chain of strong necessity?
Ibid., bk 1, canto 5, st. 25

13 Ay me, how many perils do enfold
The righteous man, to make him daily fall.
Ibid., bk 1, canto 8, st. 1

14 Sleep after toil, port after stormy seas,
Ease after war, death after life does greatly please.
Ibid., bk 1, canto 9, st. 40. The words are inscribed on JOSEPH
CONRAD's tombstone.

15 And all for love, and nothing for reward.
Ibid., bk 2, canto 8, st. 2

16 Gather therefore the rose, whilst yet is prime,
For soon comes age, that will her pride deflower:
Gather the rose of love, whilst yet is time,
Whilst loving thou mayst lovèd be with equal
    crime.
Ibid., bk 2, canto 12, st. 75. See also ROBERT HERRICK 11,
PIERRE DE RONSARD 3.

17 And painful pleasure turns to pleasing pain.
Ibid., bk 3, canto 10, st. 60

18 And as she looked about, she did behold,
How over that same door was likewise writ,
Be bold, be bold, and everywhere Be bold,
That much she mused, yet could not construe it
By any riddling skill, or common wit.
At last she spied at that room's upper end,
Another iron door, on which was writ
Be not too bold; whereto though she did bend

Her earnest mind, yet wist not what it might
    intend.
Ibid., bk 3, canto 11, st. 54

19 But when I plead, she bids me play my part,
And when I weep, she says tears are but water:
And when I sigh, she says I know the art,
And when I wail she turns herself to laughter.
So do I weep and wail and plead in vain,
Whiles she as steel and flint doth still remain.
Amoretti, Sonnet 18 (1591)

20 The merry cuckoo, messenger of Spring,
His trumpet shrill hath thrice already sounded.
Ibid., Sonnet 19

21 I hate the day, because it lendeth light
To see all things, and not my love to see.
Daphnaida, ll. 407–8 (1591)

22 Of such deep learning little had he need,
Ne yet of Latin, ne of Greek that breed
Doubts 'mongst divines, and difference of texts,
From whence arise diversity of sects,
And hateful heresies.
Prosopopoia, or Mother Hubberd's Tale, ll. 385–9 (1591)

23 Hark how the cheerful birds do chant their lays
And carol of love's praise.
The merry lark her matins sings aloft,
The thrush replies, the mavis descant plays,
The ouzel shrills, the ruddock warbles soft,
So goodly all agree with sweet consent,
To this day's merriment.
Epithalamion, ll. 78–84 (1595)

24 Her goodly eyes like sapphires shining bright,
Her forehead ivory white,
Her cheeks like apples which the sun hath rudded,
Her lips like cherries charming men to bite,
Her breast like to a bowl of cream uncrudded,
Her paps like lilies budded,
Her snowy neck like to a marble tower,
And all her body like a palace fair.
Ibid., ll. 171–8

25 Open the temple gates unto my love,
Open them wide that she may enter in.
Ibid., ll. 204–5

26 Pour out the wine without restraint or stay,
Pour not by cups, but by the belly full,
Pour out to all that will,
And sprinkle all the posts and walls with wine,
That they may sweat, and drunken be withal.
Ibid., ll. 250–4

27 Ah! when will this long weary day have end,
And lend me leave to come unto my love?
How slowly do the hours their numbers spend!
How slowly does sad Time his feathers move!
Ibid., ll. 278–81

28 Dan Chaucer, well of English undefiled,
On Fame's eternal beadroll worthy to be filed.
The Faerie Queene, bk 4, canto 2, st. 32 (1596)

29 For all that nature by her mother wit
Could frame in earth.
Ibid., bk 4, canto 10, st. 21

30 Ill can he rule the great, that cannot reach the
small.
Ibid., bk 5, canto 2, st. 43

31 O sacred hunger of ambitious minds.
Ibid., bk 5, canto 12, st. 1

32 The gentle mind by gentle deeds is known.
For a man by nothing is so well bewrayed,
As by his manners.
Ibid., bk 6, canto 3, st. 1

33 For of the soul the body form doth take;
For soul is form, and doth the body make.
'Hymn in Honour of Beauty', ll. 132–3, publ. in *Four Hymns*
(1596)

34 Sweet Thames run softly, till I end my song.
Prothalamion, refrain (1596). The line recurs in T. S. ELIOT's
The Waste Land (1922).

35 With that, I saw two swans of goodly hue
Come softly swimming down along the Lee.
Ibid., ll. 37–8

36 What man that sees the ever-whirling wheel
Of change, the which all mortal things doth sway,
But that thereby doth find, and plainly feel,
How Mutability in them doth play
Her cruel sports, to many men's decay?
The Faerie Queene, bk 7 ('The Mutability Cantos'), canto 6, st. 1
(1609)

37 For all that moveth doth in change delight.
Ibid., bk 7, canto 8, st. 2

The Spice Girls
British pop group

*Britain's most successful female vocal group shot to fame in
1996 with their hit 'Wannabe'. The group consisted of Melanie
Chisholm ('Mel C', or 'Sporty Spice'), Emma Bunton ('Baby
Spice'), Victoria Adams (later Beckham, 'Posh Spice'), Geri Halli-*

well ('Ginger Spice') and Melanie Brown ('Mel B', or 'Scary
Spice').

1 I'll tell you what I want what I really really want
(So tell me what you want, what you really really
want)
If you wanna be my lover
Gotta get with my friends
Make it last forever
Friendship never ends!
'Wannabe' (song, written by Matthew Rowbottom and
Richard Stannard) on the album *Spice* (1996)

Steven Spielberg
(b. 1947)
US film-maker

*The most commercially successful director to date, he has
made a series of blockbuster films including* Jaws *(1975)*, E. T.
(1982) and Jurassic Park *(1993). J. G.* BALLARD *hailed him as
'the Puccini of the cinema, a little too sweet for some tastes,
but what melodies, what orchestrations, what cathedrals of
emotion'.*

1 Close Encounters of the Third Kind.
Title of film (written and directed by Steven Spielberg, 1977)

Benedict Spinoza
(1632–77)
Dutch philosopher

*Originally Baruch Spinoza. Born into an Iberian Jewish family
settled in Amsterdam, he was a lens-grinder by trade. His
pantheistic, rationalist view of the world is laid out in
Tractatus Theologico-Politicus (1670), his only work published
during his lifetime, and in his main work* Ethics *(1677). See
NOVALIS 3.*

1 God I understand to be a being absolutely infinite,
that is, a substance consisting of infinite attributes,
each of which expresses eternal and infinite essence.
Ethica, pt 1, Definition 6 (1677; *Ethics*, transl. Andrew Boyle)

2 Nothing exists from whose nature some effect
does not follow.
Ibid., pt 1, Proposition 36

3 Truth is its own standard.
Ibid., pt 2, Proposition 43, Note

4 Love is nothing else than pleasure accompanied
by the idea of an external cause; and hate, pain
accompanied by the idea of an external cause.
Ibid., pt 3, Proposition 13, Note

5 The definition that man is a social animal must
be very apparent; and in truth things are so ordered

that from the common society of men far more conveniences arise than the contrary.
Ibid., pt 4, Proposition 35, Note

6 Fear cannot be without hope nor hope without fear.
Ibid., pt 3, Definition 13, Explanation

7 In truth, avarice, ambition, lust, etc., are nothing but species of madness, although they are not enumerated among diseases.
Ibid., pt 4, Proposition 44, Note

8 We feel and know that we are eternal.
Ibid., pt 5, Proposition 23, Note

9 The more we understand individual things, the more we understand God.
Ibid., pt 5, Proposition 24

10 For the things which ... are esteemed as the greatest good of all ... can be reduced to these three headings: to wit, Riches, Fame, and Pleasure. With these three the mind is so engrossed that it cannot scarcely think of any other good.
Tractatus de Intellectus Emendatione, pt 1, sect. 3 (1677; Treatise on the Correction of the Understanding, transl. Andrew Boyle)

11 I have laboured carefully, not to mock, lament, or execrate, but to understand human actions.
Tractatus Politicus, ch. 1, sect. 4 (1677; Political Treatise, transl. A. H. Gosset)

12 Men are not born fit for citizenship, but must be made so.
Ibid., ch. 5, sect. 2

13 The fields, and the whole soil, and, if it can be managed, the houses should be public property, that is, the property of him who holds the right of the commonwealth: and let him let them at a yearly rent to the citizens, whether townsmen or countrymen, and with this exception let them all be free or exempt from every kind of taxation in time of peace.
Ibid., ch. 6, sect. 12

Benjamin Spock
(1903–98)
US paediatrician and author

His seminal work The Common Sense Book of Baby and Child Care *(1946) advocated a more relaxed and sympathetic attitude to child-rearing. He later rebutted criticism of being responsible for a permissive new generation.*

1 I think that more of our children would grow up happier and more stable if they were acquiring a conviction, all through childhood, that the most important thing that human beings can do is serve humanity in some function and to live by their ideals.
Baby and Child Care, 'The Parents' Part', sect. 11 (1946, rev. 1968)

2 Man can build a magnificent reality in adulthood out of what was only an illusion in early childhood – his loving, joyous, trusting, ingenuous, unrealistic over-idealization of his two parents.
Ibid., 'The Parents' Part', sect. 13

3 A child loves his play, not because it's easy, but because it's hard.
Ibid., 'Managing Young Children', sect. 457

4 I was proud of the youths who opposed the war in Vietnam because they were my babies.
The Times 2 May 1988

William Archibald Spooner
(1844–1930)
English clergyman and scholar

He became notorious for his verbal slips during his long association with New College, Oxford, where he was Dean (1876–89) and Warden (1903–24). Numerous 'Spoonerisms', in which the initial letters of words are transposed, have been wrongly attributed to him.

1 Kinkering Congs Their Titles Take.
Attributed, announcing a hymn. Said to be the only one of his 'Spoonerisms' that, aged 86, he could remember having uttered.

2 Sir, you have deliberately tasted two whole worms; you have hissed all my mystery lectures and been caught fighting a liar in the quad; you will leave by the next town drain.
Attributed, reprimanding a student. One of many 'Spoonerisms' now considered apocryphal.

Jacob Sprenger
and
Heinrich Kramer
(15th century)
German Dominican monks and theologians

Sprenger, Dean of the University of Cologne, and Kramer, Professor of Theology at the University of Salzburg and inquisitor in the Tirol region, were in 1484 authorized by Pope Innocent VIII to extirpate witchcraft in Germany. Their codifi-

cation of the Church's policies on witchcraft, the Malleus Maleficarum *(c. 1486), remained in use for 300 years.*

1 For when girls have been corrupted, and have been
scorned by their lovers after they have immodestly
copulated with them in the hope and promise of
marriage with them, and have found themselves
disappointed in all their hopes and everywhere
despised, they turn to the help and protection of
devils; either for the sake of vengeance by bewitching those lovers or the wives they have married, or
for the sake of giving themselves up to every sort
of lechery. Alas! experience tells us that there is no
number to such girls, and consequently the witches
that spring from this class are innumerable.
Malleus Maleficarum, pt 2, ch. 1 (c. 1486; The Hammer of
Witches, *transl. Montague Summers)*

Cecil Spring-Rice

See HYMNS AND CAROLS 43

Jerry Springer

(b. 1944)

US television host

*He served as Mayor of Cincinnati until the day his personal
cheque was found in a Kentucky brothel. His confessional* Jerry
Springer Show, *with which he boasts he is 'proud to set a new
low', has been seen globally since its inception in 1991.*

1 My show is the stupidest show on TV. If you are
watching it, get a life. I would not watch my show.
My show is a circus. That's all it is.
Independent on Sunday 7 March 1999

Bruce Springsteen

(b. 1949)

US rock musician

*Nicknamed 'The Boss', he became an icon of blue-collar rock
'n' roll and subsequently an international star with his albums*
Born to Run *(1975) and* Born in the USA *(1984). He has the
ability 'to make his music bleed', according to* GREIL MARCUS.

1 In the day we sweat it out in the streets of a
  runaway American dream
At night we ride through mansions of glory in
  suicide machines.
'Born to Run' (song) on the album *Born to Run* (1975) by Bruce
Springsteen and the E Street Band

2 Baby this town rips the bones from your back,
It's a death trap, it's a suicide rap,

We gotta get out while we're young
'Cause tramps like us baby we were born to run.
'Born to Run', ibid.

3 Born in the USA.
Title of song and album (1984) by Bruce Springsteen and the
E Street Band

Madame de Staël

(1766–1817)

Swiss-French author and wit

*Born Anne Louise Germaine Necker. Her Parisian salon was a
cultural and political centre until her opposition to* NAPOLEON
forced her into exile in 1803. Her major work, Germany *(1813),
helped to diffuse the ideas of German Romanticism. She also
wrote novels and memoirs. See* MADAME ROLAND 2, CHARLES
DE TALLEYRAND 4.

1 A man must know how to fly in the face of
opinion; a woman to submit to it.
Delphine, Epigraph (1802)

2 *Tout comprendre rend très indulgent.*
[To understand everything makes one very indul-
gent.]
Corinne, bk 18, ch. 5 (1807). Probably the origin of the dictum,
'Tout comprendre [or *savoir*], *c'est tout pardonner.'*

3 Wit lies in recognising the resemblance among
things which differ and the difference between
things which are alike.
De l'Allemagne, pt 3, ch. 8 (1813; *Germany*)

4 The desire of the man is for the woman, but the
desire of the woman is for the desire of the man.
Attributed. See also S. T. COLERIDGE 66.

Josef Stalin

(1879–1953)

Soviet leader

*Originally Josef Vissarionovich Dzhugashvili. Having suc-
ceeded to power after* LENIN*'s death in 1924, he went on to
establish the USSR as a modern industrial state at the cost of
millions of deaths.* TROTSKY *called him 'Our party's most
outstanding mediocrity'. See also* MAXIM GORKY 1; NIKITA
KHRUSHCHEV 2, 3; OSIP MANDELSTAM 5; LEON TROTSKY
4, 12; YEVGENY YEVTUSHENKO 5.

1 He who wants to lead a movement, and at the
same time keep in touch with the masses, must
wage a war on two fronts – against those who lag
behind and against those who rush on ahead.
Pravda 2 March 1930, quoted in *Hitler and Stalin: Parallel
Lives*, ch. 8, sect. 2 (1998) by Alan Bullock

2 The Pope! How many divisions has *he* got?
Said 13 May 1935, quoted in *The Second World War*, vol. 1 ('The Gathering Storm'), ch. 8 (1948) by WINSTON CHURCHILL. Addressed to French Foreign Minister Pierre Laval in reply to a suggestion that the Soviet Union should encourage Catholicism in order to propitiate the Pope.

3 Gratitude . . . is a sickness suffered by dogs.
Quoted in *Stalin's Secret War*, ch. 2 (1981) by Nikolai Tolstoy

4 Cadres determine everything.
One of his favourite watchwords, quoted in *Hitler and Stalin: Parallel Lives*, ch. 4, sect. 3 (1998) by Alan Bullock

5 A single death is a tragedy, a million deaths is a statistic.
Attributed

Konstantin Stanislavsky
(1863–1938)
Russian theatrical director, actor and theorist

He is known for his pioneering approach to acting in which actors aim, through minute study, to 'become' the characters they play. Co-founder in 1897 of the Moscow Art Theatre, he directed the first productions of CHEKHOV.

1 In the creative process there is the father, the author of the play; the mother, the actor pregnant with the part; and the child, the role to be born.
An Actor Prepares, ch. 16 (1936)

2 Talent is nothing but a prolonged period of attention and a shortened period of mental assimilation.
The Art of the Stage, ch. 22 (1950)

(Sir) Henry Morton Stanley
(1841–1904)
British journalist and explorer

Having emigrated to America in 1859, he joined the New York Herald *in 1867 and travelled in Africa as a correspondent. He explored the Congo River and Lake Tanganyika and founded the Congo Free State. He later settled in England, where he was an MP 1895–1900.*

1 Dr Livingstone, I presume?
Quoted in *How I Found Livingstone*, ch. 11 (1872). Greeting to the missing explorer and missionary, Dr David Livingstone, at Ujiji, Lake Tanganyika, 10 November 1871. Stanley had been dispatched to find Livingstone by the *New York Herald*, a task he accomplished after an eight-month voyage. In SHERIDAN's play, *School for Scandal*, one character (Sir Oliver Surface) greets another with the line, 'Mr Stanley, I presume?' (Act 5, Sc. 1)

Vivian Stanshall
(1943–95)
British musician and entertainer

A full-time English eccentric, he was a member of the Bonzo Dog Doo-Dah Band in the 1960s and later created the bufferish Sir Henry at Rawlinson End on radio, record and film.

1 Cool Britannia
Britannia take a trip
Britons ever ever ever will be hip.
'Cool Britannia' (song) on album *Gorilla* (1967) by the Bonzo Dog Doo-Dah Band. Thought to be the first use of 'Cool Britannia' subsequently used on a *Newsweek* cover and associated with Britain during TONY BLAIR's first term as prime minister.

Elizabeth Cady Stanton
(1815–1902)
US campaigner for women's rights

After helping to organize the first women's rights convention in Seneca Falls, New York (1848), she launched the women's suffrage movement and co-edited, with SUSAN B. ANTHONY, the feminist periodical Revolution *(1868). She later co-wrote a history of the women's suffrage movement.*

1 We hold these truths to be self-evident: that all men and women are created equal.
'Declaration of Sentiments and Resolutions', adopted at the first women's rights convention, Seneca Falls, New York, 19–20 July 1848, publ. in *The History of Woman Suffrage*, vol. 1 (ed. Matilda Joslyn Gage and Elizabeth Cady Stanton, 1881). See THOMAS JEFFERSON 3.

2 Marriage, as we now have it, is opposed to all God's laws. It is by no means an equal partnership. The silent partner loses everything.
Letter to Lucy Stone, National Convention, Cooper Institute, New York, 1856, ibid., vol. 1

3 Of all kinds of aristocracy, that of sex is the most odious and unnatural . . . subjugating everywhere moral power to brute power.
Written 1869, quoted in *Voices from Women's Liberation*, pt 2 ('Observations') (ed. Leslie B. Tanner, 1970)

4 And thus it ever is: so long as woman labors to second man's endeavors and exalt his sex above her own her virtues pass unquestioned; but when she dares to demand rights and privileges for herself, her motives, manners, dress, personal appearance, and character are subjects for ridicule and detraction.
Eighty Years and More: Reminiscences 1815–1897, ch. 15 (1898)

(Dame) Freya Stark

(1893–1993)

British travel writer

She spent most of her adult life travelling in the Middle East, and during the Second World War worked for the British Ministry of Information in Aden, Egypt and Iraq. Her books include Valley of the Assassins *(1934) and* West is East *(1945).*

1 It is not our stupidity, but the fact that we prove it possible to live by non-intellectual standards, which makes us disliked.
Perseus in the Wind, ch. 4 (1948). Referring to the British.

2 The thwarting of the instinct to love is the root of all sorrow and not sex only but divinity itself is insulted when it is repressed. To disapprove, to condemn – the human soul shrivels under barren righteousness.
Traveller's Prelude, ch. 10 (1950)

Edwin Starr

(1942–2003)

US soul singer

A soul-shouter in the style of James Brown, he is best known for his song 'War' and the albums Soulmaster *(1968) and* War & Peace *(1970).*

1 War . . .
What is it good for?
Absolutely nothing.
'War' (song, 1970, written by Norman Whitfield and Barrett Strong) on the album *War & Peace* (1970)

Ringo Starr

(b. 1940)

British rock musician

Originally Richard Starkey. Drummer and occasional singer with the Beatles, he subsequently had hits as a solo artist and acted in films.

1 It was just like Butlins.
Quoted in *The Beatles Illustrated Lyrics*, vol. 1 (ed. Alan Aldridge, 1969). On India, after returning from meditating at Rishikesh.

(Sir) David Steel

(b. 1938)

British politician

Lord Steel of Aikwood. The youngest MP in Parliament when first elected in 1965, he led the Liberal Party 1976–88, forging the alliance with the Social Democratic Party *(1983) that led to the merger of the two parties in 1989.*

1 I have the good fortune to be the first Liberal leader for over half a century who is able to say to you at the end of our annual assembly: go back to your constituencies and prepare for government.
Speech at Liberal Party Assembly, Llandudno, 18 September 1981, quoted in *The Times* 19 September 1981. In the subsequent general election of 1983, the Liberals won only twenty-three seats.

(Sir) Richard Steele

(1672–1729)

English dramatist, essayist and editor

He achieved most renown through his journalistic enterprises: the Tatler, *which he founded in 1709, and the* Spectator, *co-founded with* JOSEPH ADDISON *in 1711. His polished essays appeared in these and other publications. His most successful play was* The Conscious Lovers *(1722), a comedy. He briefly served as an MP and was appointed patentee of the Theatre Royal, Drury Lane. See* LORD MACAULAY *36.*

1 A little in drink, but at all times your faithful husband.
Midnight letter to his wife, 27 September 1708, publ. in *The Correspondence of Sir Richard Steele* (ed. R. Blanchard, 1941)

2 It is to be noted that when any part of this paper appears dull there is a design in it.
The Tatler, no. 38, 7 July 1709, repr. in *The Tatler*, vol. 1 (ed. G. A. Aitken, 1898)

3 To behold her is an immediate check to loose behaviour; to love her is a liberal education.
The Tatler, no. 49, 2 August 1709, ibid. Referring to 'Aspasia', the name given to Lady Elizabeth Hastings in the pages of *Tatler*. In edition no. 42 of the magazine (16 July 1709), she is described by WILLIAM CONGREVE as 'a female philosopher, who does not only live up to the resignation of the most retired lives of the ancient sages, but also to the schemes and plans which they thought beautiful, though inimitable. This lady is the most exact economist, without appearing busy; the most strictly virtuous, without tasting the praise of it; and shuns applause with as much industry, as others do reproach.'

4 Reading is to the mind what exercise is to the body.
The Tatler, no. 147, 18 March 1710, ibid.

5 They shift coffee-houses and chocolate-houses from hour to hour, to get over the insupportable labour of doing nothing.
The Spectator, no. 54, 2 May 1711, repr. in *The Spectator* (ed. D. F. Bond, 1965). Referring to 'loungers . . . satisfied with being

merely part of the number of mankind, without distinguishing themselves from amongst them.'

6 The inquisitive are the funnels of conversation; they do not take in anything for their own use, but merely to pass it to another.
The Spectator, no. 228, 21 November 1711, ibid.

7 The married state, with and without the affection suitable to it, is the completest image of heaven and hell we are capable of receiving in this life.
The Spectator, no. 479, 9 September 1712, ibid.

Lincoln Steffens
(1866–1936)
US author and editor

One of the chief 'muckraker' journalists of his time, he set out to expose corruption in business and politics as a reporter on the New York Evening Post *(1892–8) and Editor of* McClure's, American, *and* Everybody's *magazines (1902–11).*

1 We Americans can't seem to get it that you can't commit rape a little.
Quoted in *Lincoln Steffens*, ch. 11, sect. 3 (1974) by Justin Kaplan. Referring to US intervention in Mexico in 1914.

2 I have been over into the future, and it works.
Autobiography, ch. 18 (1931). Remark on his return from the Soviet Union in 1919, addressed to BERNARD BARUCH.

Gertrude Stein
(1874–1946)
US author

An experimental writer described by CLIFTON FADIMAN *as 'a past master in making nothing happen very slowly', she is famous for her obscure, repetitive word-play in works such as* Three Lives *(1909) and* Tender Buttons *(1914). The Autobiography of Alice B. Toklas (1933) is Stein's own fictionalized autobiography. See* CLIFTON FADIMAN 1.

1 Rose is a rose is a rose is a rose.
'Sacred Emily', written 1913, publ. in *Geography and Plays* (1922). Thought to refer to the artist Sir Francis Rose, one of whose paintings was hung in Stein's Paris drawing-room

2 All of you young people who served in the war. You are a lost generation . . . You have no respect for anything. You drink yourselves to death.
Remark to ERNEST HEMINGWAY, quoted as the epigraph to Hemingway's novel *The Sun Also Rises* (1926), which describes the lives of expatriates in Paris in the 1920s. The words are also quoted in his memoir of his own time in Paris, *A Moveable Feast*, ch. 3 (1964). In Stein's *Everybody's Autobiography*, ch. 2 (1937), she recalls that the expression 'lost generation' originated with a hotel-keeper in conversation with her.

3 Pigeons on the grass alas.
Pigeons on the grass alas.
Short longer grass short longer longer shorter yellow grass. Pigeons large pigeons on the shorter longer yellow grass alas pigeons on the grass.
Four Saints in Three Acts, Act 3, Sc. 2 (1929), publ. in *Operas and Plays* (1932)

4 He was a village explainer, excellent if you were a village, but if you were not, not.
The Autobiography of Alice B. Toklas, ch. 7 (1933). Referring to EZRA POUND, whom Stein 'liked . . . but did not find amusing'.

5 Hemingway, remarks are not literature.
Ibid., ch. 7. Referring to the inclusion by ERNEST HEMINGWAY of a comment he had made about E. E. CUMMINGS's autobiographical novel *The Enormous Room* ('the greatest book he had ever read') in a manuscript of short stories shown to Stein.

6 The unreal is natural, so natural that it makes of unreality the most natural of anything natural. That is what America does, and that is what America is.
'I Came and Here I Am' (1936), repr. in *How Writing Is Written* (ed. Robert Bartlett Haas, 1974)

7 In the United States there is more space where nobody is than where anybody is. That is what makes America what it is.
The Geographical History of America (1936)

8 It is funny the two things most men are proudest of is the thing that any man can do and doing does in the same way, that is being drunk and being the father of their son.
Everybody's Autobiography, ch. 2 (1937)

9 It takes a lot of time to be a genius, you have to sit around so much doing nothing, really doing nothing.
Ibid., ch. 2

10 The minute you or anybody else knows what you are you are not it, you are what you or anybody else knows you are and as everything in living is made up of finding out what you are it is extraordinarily difficult really not to know what you are and yet to be that thing.
Ibid., ch. 3

11 Counting is the religion of this generation it is its hope and its salvation.
Ibid., ch. 3

12 There is no there there.

Ibid., ch. 4. Referring to Oakland, California, where Stein spent her childhood.

13 Just before she died she asked, 'What *is* the answer?' No answer came. She laughed and said, 'In that case, what is the question?' Then she died.

Quoted in *Gertrude Stein, A Biography of Her Work*, ch. 6 (1951) by Donald Sutherland. The biography concludes: 'Those were her last words, but they say what she had always been saying.'

14 Nature is commonplace. Imitation is more interesting.

Quoted in *My Autobiography*, ch. 20 (1964) by CHARLIE CHAPLIN

15 In France one must adapt oneself to the fragrance of a urinal.

Quoted in *Voices: A Memoir*, 'Style' (1983) by Frederic Prokosch

John Steinbeck
(1902–68)
US novelist

He first came to notice with Tortilla Flat *(1935), a humorous portrait of California farmers. Subsequent novels were bleaker in tone, including* In Dubious Battle *(1936),* Of Mice and Men *(1937) and* The Grapes of Wrath *(1939), all dealing with agricultural and migrant workers.*

1 Man, unlike anything organic or inorganic in the universe, grows beyond his work, walks up the stairs of his concepts, emerges ahead of his accomplishments.

The Grapes of Wrath, ch. 14 (1939)

2 Fear the time when Manself will not suffer and die for a concept, for this one quality is the foundation of Manself, and this one quality is man, distinctive in the universe.

Ibid., ch. 14

3 We could love that tractor then as we have loved this land when it was ours. But this tractor does two things – it turns the land and turns us off the land. There is little difference between this tractor and a tank. The people are driven, intimidated, hurt by both. We must think about this.

Ibid., ch. 14

4 Wherever they's a fight so hungry people can eat, I'll be there. Wherever they's a cop beatin' up a guy, I'll be there ... I'll be in the way guys yell when they're mad an' – I'll be in the way kids laugh when they're hungry an' they know supper's ready. An'

when our folks eat the stuff they raise an' live in the houses they build – why, I'll be there.

Tom Joad, ibid., ch. 28. Farewell speech to his mother, in which he articulates union-organizer Jim Casy's belief that human beings make up 'one big soul ever'body's a part of'.

5 A journey is like marriage. The certain way to be wrong is to think you control it.

Travels With Charley: in Search of America, pt 1 (1961)

6 This monster of a land, this mightiest of nations, this spawn of the future, turns out to be the macrocosm of microcosm me.

Ibid., pt 3

7 Time is the only critic without ambition.

'On Critics', publ. in *Writers at Work* (fourth series, ed. George Plimpton, 1977)

Gloria Steinem
(b. 1934)
US feminist author and editor

She co-founded the Women's Action Alliance in 1970 and the National Women's Political Caucus in 1971, and was founding editor of the feminist magazine Ms. *(1981–7). Her books include* Revolution from Within *(1992).*

1 No man can call himself liberal, or radical, or even a conservative advocate of fair play, if his work depends in any way on the unpaid or underpaid labor of women at home, or in the office.

New York Times 26 August 1971

2 Pornography is about dominance. Erotica is about mutuality.

'Erotica vs. Pornography', adapted from articles in *Ms.* August 1977 and November 1978, repr. in *Outrageous Acts and Everyday Rebellions* (1983)

3 If men could menstruate ... clearly, menstruation would become an enviable, boast-worthy, masculine event: Men would brag about how long and how much ... Sanitary supplies would be federally funded and free. Of course, some men would still pay for the prestige of such commercial brands as Paul Newman Tampons, Muhammed Ali's Rope-a-Dope Pads, John Wayne Maxi Pads, and Joe Namath Jock Shields – 'For Those Light Bachelor Days'.

'If Men Could Menstruate', publ. in *Ms.* October 1978, ibid.

4 Power can be taken, but not given. The process of the taking is empowerment in itself.

'Far From the Opposite Shore', adapted from articles in *Ms.* July 1978 and July/August 1982, repr. in *Outrageous Acts and Everyday Rebellions* (1983)

5 The authority of any governing institution must stop at its citizen's skin.

'Night Thoughts of a Media-Watcher', publ. in *Ms.* November 1981

6 We are becoming the men we wanted to marry.

Ms. July/August 1982

7 A woman without a man is like a fish without a bicycle.

Attributed. Usually ascribed to Steinem, though the words were current as graffiti in the 1970s (see GRAFFITI 11).

George Steiner
(b. 1929)
French-born US critic and novelist

A leading figure in the study of comparative literature and of language, he is known both for his critical studies, such as The Death of Tragedy *(1960), and for his fiction, for example* The Portage to San Cristobal of A.H. *(1981).*

1 We know that a man can read Goethe or Rilke in the evening, that he can play Bach and Schubert, and go to his day's work at Auschwitz in the morning.

Language and Silence, Preface (1967)

2 Language can only deal meaningfully with a special, restricted segment of reality. The rest, and it is presumably the much larger part, is silence.

Ibid., 'The Retreat from the Word'

3 To shoot a man because one disagrees with his interpretation of Darwin or Hegel is a sinister tribute to the supremacy of ideas in human affairs – but a tribute nevertheless.

Ibid., 'Marxism and the Literary Critic'

4 The immense majority of human biographies are a gray transit between domestic spasm and oblivion.

In Bluebeard's Castle, ch. 3 (1971)

5 The age of the book is almost gone.

Daily Mail 27 June 1988

6 There is something terribly wrong with a culture inebriated by noise and gregariousness.

Daily Telegraph 23 May 1989

7 We Jews walk closer to our children than other men . . . because to have children is possibly to condemn them.

Interview in the *Guardian* 6 January 1996

Stendhal
(1783–1842)
French author

Pseudonym of Henri Beyle. Having fought in NAPOLEON's *army, he lived for many years in Italy writing under his pen name. His masterpieces are* The Red and the Black *(1830) and* The Charterhouse of Parma *(1839), both novels of melodramatic narratives and realistic settings. He also wrote studies of art and music, and autobiographical works.*

1 I think no woman I have had ever gave me so sweet a moment, or at so light a price, as the moment I owe to a newly heard musical phrase.

Letter, 29 October 1808, publ. in *Correspondance*, vol. 1 (ed. Henri Martineau, 1962)

2 In love, unlike most other passions, the recollection of what you have had and lost is always better than what you can hope for in the future.

De l'Amour, ch. 1 (1822; *On Love*)

3 A wise woman never yields by appointment. It should always be an unforeseen happiness.

Ibid., ch. 60

4 Beauty is only the promise of happiness.

Ibid., ch. 17, footnote

5 One can acquire everything in solitude except character.

Ibid., 'Various Fragments', sect. 1

6 It is better to have a prosaic husband and to take a romantic lover.

Ibid., 'Various Fragments', sect. 10

7 Intelligence and genius lose twenty-five per cent of their value on landing in England.

Le Rouge et le noir, pt 2, ch. 7 (1830; *Scarlet and Black*, or, *The Red and the Black*). Spoken by Julien Sorel.

8 Why, my good sir, a novel is a mirror journeying down the high road. Sometimes it reflects to your view the azure blue of heaven, sometimes the mire in the puddles on the road below.

Ibid., pt 2, ch. 19

9 Politics are like a stone tied to the neck of literature which, in less than six months, will drown it. Politics in the middle of things that concern the imagination are like a pistol-shot in the middle of a concert. The noise is ear-splitting and yet lacks point.

Ibid., pt 2, ch. 22

10 The only excuse for God is that he doesn't exist.

Attributed

James Stephens

(1882–1950)

Irish poet and author

He published a collection of poems and a novel before having success with The Crock of Gold *(1912), a meandering prose fantasy that blended folk legend and myth. He was active in the nationalist cause.*

1 Women are stronger than men – they do not die of wisdom.
They are better than men because they do not seek wisdom.
They are wiser than men because they know less and understand more.
The Crock of Gold, bk 1, ch. 2 (1912). The words of the Grey Woman of Dun Gortin.

2 Finality is death. Perfection is finality. Nothing is perfect. There are lumps in it.
The Philosopher, ibid., bk 1, ch. 4

3 I hear a sudden cry of pain!
There is a rabbit in a snare;
Now I hear the cry again,
But I cannot tell from where.
'The Snare', st. 1, publ. in *Songs from the City* (1915)

4 Little one! Oh, little one!
I am searching everywhere.
'The Snare', st. 4, ibid.

5 The vice of English fiction is not that it is romantic or sentimental, but that it is ill-informed. It has never grown up. It is written on the playing grounds of Eton. It is eternally a boy's tale, and the authors of it are naturally ashamed and anonymous.
Letter, March 1924 (1925), repr. in *Letters of James Stephens* (ed. Richard J. Finneran, 1974)

6 A woman is a branchy tree
And man a singing wind;
And from her branches carelessly
He takes what he can find.
'A Woman is a Branchy Tree', publ. in *Collected Poems* (1926)

Laurence Sterne

(1713–68)

Anglo-Irish author

Having taken holy orders, he settled in a vicarage in Yorkshire in 1738. His experimental novel, Life and Opinions of Tristram Shandy *(1759–67), with its narrative and structural innovations, influenced 20th-century fiction. A second, equally radical novel,* A Sentimental Journey through France and Italy *(1768), was based on his travels abroad.*

1 I wish either my father or my mother, or indeed both of them, as they were in duty both equally bound to it, had minded what they were about when they begot me.
The Life and Opinions of Tristram Shandy, Gentleman, vol. 1, ch. 1 (1759–67). Opening words of book.

2 Pray my dear, quoth my mother, 'have you not forgot to wind up the clock?' 'Good G–!' cried my father, making an exclamation, but taking care to moderate his voice at the same time, 'Did ever woman, since the creation of the world, interrupt a man with such a silly question?'
Ibid., vol. 1, ch. 1. Events occurring at the conception of Tristram Shandy, on account of which, according to his father, 'My Tristram's misfortunes began nine months before ever he came into the world.'

3 So long as a man rides his Hobby-Horse peaceably and quietly along the King's highway, and neither compels you or me to get up behind him, pray, Sir, what have either you or I to do with it?
Ibid., vol. 1, ch. 7

4 'Tis no extravagant arithmetic to say, that for every ten jokes, thou hast got an hundred enemies; and till thou hast gone on, and raised a swarm of wasps about thine ears, and art half stung to death by them, thou wilt never be convinced it is so.
Ibid., vol. 1, ch. 12

5 'Tis known by the name of perseverance in a good cause, and of obstinacy in a bad one.
Ibid., vol. 1, ch. 17

6 Digressions, incontestably, are the sunshine; they are the life, the soul of reading; take them out of this book for instance, you might as well take the book along with them.
Ibid., vol. 1, ch. 22

7 The history of a soldier's wound beguiles the pain of it.
Ibid., vol. 1, ch. 25

8 Writing, when properly managed (as you may be sure I think mine is) is but a different name for conversation.
Ibid., vol. 2, ch. 11

9 Go, poor devil, get thee gone, why should I hurt thee? This world surely is wide enough to hold both thee and me.
Ibid., vol. 2, ch. 12. Spoken by Uncle Toby to a fly.

10 'Tis only a description, honest man, quoth Slop,

there's not a word of truth in it. That's another story, replied my father.

Ibid., vol. 2, ch. 17

11 Whenever a man talks loudly against religion, always suspect that it is not his reason, but his passions, which have got the better of his creed. A bad life and a good belief are disagreeable and troublesome neighbours, and where they separate, depend upon it, 'tis for no other cause but quietness' sake.

Trim, reading a sermon, ibid., vol. 2, ch. 17

12 Trust that man in nothing, who has not a conscience in everything.

Trim's sermon, ibid., vol. 2, ch. 17

13 It is the nature of an hypothesis, when once a man has conceived it, that it assimilates everything to itself, as proper nourishment, and from the first moment of your begetting it, it generally grows the stronger by everything you see, hear, read, or understand. This is of great use.

Ibid., vol. 2, ch. 19

14 The *corregiescity* of Corregio.

Ibid., vol. 3, ch. 12

15 Of all the cants which are canted in this canting world – though the cant of hypocrites may be the worst – the cant of criticism is the most tormenting!

Ibid., vol. 3, ch. 12

16 I am convinced, Yorick, that there is a North-west passage to the intellectual world.

Tristram's father, ibid., vol. 5, ch. 42

17 The Accusing Spirit, which flew up to heaven's chancery with the oath, blushed as he gave it in; and the Recording Angel, as he wrote it down, dropped a tear upon the word, and blotted it out for ever.

Ibid., vol. 6, ch. 8

18 A man should know something of his own country too, before he goes abroad.

Ibid., vol. 7, ch. 2

19 Ho! 'tis the time of salads.

Ibid., vol. 7, ch. 17

20 Nothing is so perfectly amusement as a total change of ideas.

Ibid., vol. 9, 'A Dedication'

21 All womankind, from the highest to the lowest . . . love jokes; the difficulty is to know how they choose to have them cut; and there is no knowing that, but by trying, as we do with our artillery in the field, by raising or letting down their breeches, till we hit the mark.

Trim, ibid., vol. 9, ch. 8

22 L–d! said my mother, what is all this story about?
A Cock and a Bull, said Yorick – And one of the best of its kind, I ever heard.

Ibid., vol. 9, ch. 33. Final words of book.

23 This sad vicissitude of things.

Sermons, vol. 1, no. 16 (1760)

24 They order, said I, this matter better in France.

A Sentimental Journey through France and Italy (1768). Opening words of book.

25 A large volume of adventures may be grasped within this little span of life, by him who interests his heart in everything.

Ibid., 'In the Street – Calais'

26 I pity the man who can travel from Dan to Beersheba, and cry, 'Tis all barren.

Ibid., 'In the Street – Calais'

27 Hail, ye small sweet courtesies of life, for smooth do ye make the road of it!

Ibid., 'The Pulse. Paris'

28 There are worse occupations in this world than feeling a woman's pulse.

Ibid., 'The Pulse. Paris'

29 God tempers the wind to the shorn lamb.

Maria, ibid., 'Maria'. Quoting a French proverb, first recorded by HENRI ESTIENNE (*Les Premices*, 1594).

30 We do not love people so much for the good they have done us, as for the good we have done them.

Quoted in *War and Peace*, bk 1, ch. 28 (1865–9) by LEO TOLSTOY

Cat Stevens

(b. 1948)
British singer and songwriter

Born Stephen Demetre Georgiou. His hit records include 'Matthew and Son' (1967) and 'Moonshadow' (1971). He changed his name to Yusuf Islam on converting to the Islamic faith in 1978.

1 The first cut is the deepest.

'The First Cut is the Deepest' (song) on the album *New Masters* (1967). The song was popularized by P. P. Arnold and Rod Stewart.

Wallace Stevens

(1879–1955)
US poet

He worked most of his life in law and insurance while estab-
lishing a reputation as a poet. His verse, published in Harmonium *(1923) and* The Auroras of Autumn *(1950) among*
other collections, explores the transformative power of the
poetic imagination.

1 The day of the sun is like the day of a king. It is a
promenade in the morning, a sitting on the throne
at noon, a pageant in the evening.

Journal entry, 20 April 1920, publ. in *Souvenirs and Proph-*
ecies: the Young Wallace Stevens, ch. 6 (ed. Holly Stevens,
1966)

2 Poetry is the supreme fiction, madame.
Take the moral law and make a nave of it
And from the nave build haunted heaven.

'A High-Toned Old Christian Woman', publ. in *Harmonium*
(1923)

3 The only emperor is the emperor of ice-cream.

'The Emperor of Ice-Cream', ibid.

4 I do not know which to prefer,
The beauty of inflections
Or the beauty of innuendoes,
The blackbird whistling
Or just after.

'Thirteen Ways of Looking at a Blackbird', ibid.

5 Civilization must be destroyed. The hairy saints
Of the North have earned this crumb by their
    complaints.

'New England Verses': 'Land of Pine and Marble', ibid. (1931
edn)

6 Everything is complicated; if that were not so, life
and poetry and everything else would be a bore.

Letter, 19 December 1935, publ. in *Letters of Wallace Stevens*
(ed. Holly Stevens, 1967)

7 Union of the weakest develops strength
Not wisdom. Can all men, together, avenge
One of the leaves that have fallen in autumn?
But the wise man avenges by building his city in
    snow.

'Like Decorations in a Nigger Cemetery', sect. 50, publ. in
Ideas of Order (1936)

8 They said, 'You have a blue guitar,
You do not play things as they are.'
The man replied, 'Things as they are

Are changed upon the blue guitar.'

'The Man with the Blue Guitar', publ. in *The Man with the*
Blue Guitar (1937)

9 It is the unknown that excites the ardor of
scholars, who, in the known alone, would shrivel up
with boredom.

'The Irrational Element in Poetry', lecture (*c.* 1937), publ. in
Opus Posthumous (1957)

10 The squirming facts exceed the squamous
    mind,
If one may say so.

'Connoisseur of Chaos', publ. in *Parts of a World* (1942)

11 The reason can give nothing at all
Like the response to desire.

'Dezembrum', ibid.

12 We have been a little insane about the truth. We
have had an obsession.

'The Noble Rider and the Sound of Words', lecture, 1942, repr.
in *The Necessary Angel* (1951)

13 The philosopher proves that the philosopher
exists. The poet merely enjoys existence.

'The Figure of the Youth as Virile Poet', lecture, August 1943,
ibid.

14 The greatest poverty is not to live
In a physical world, to feel that one's desire
Is too difficult to tell from despair.

'Esthètique du mal', sect. 15, publ. in *Transport to Summer*
(1947)

15 The whole race is a poet that writes down
The eccentric propositions of its fate.

'Men Made Out of Words', ibid.

16 What our eyes behold may well be the text of life
but one's meditations on the text and the disclos-
ures of these meditations are no less a part of the
structure of reality.

The Necessary Angel, 'Three Academic Pieces', no. 1 (1951)

17 To regard the imagination as metaphysics is to
think of it as part of life, and to think of it as part
of life is to realize the extent of artifice. We live in
the mind.

Ibid., 'Imagination as Value'

18 If poetry should address itself to the same needs
and aspirations, the same hopes and fears, to which
the Bible addresses itself, it might rival it in distribution.

Ibid., 'Imagination as Value'

19 Thought is an infection. In the case of certain thoughts, it becomes an epidemic.
Opus Posthumous, 'Adagia' (ed. Samuel French Morse, 1957)

20 As life grows more terrible, its literature grows more terrible.
Ibid., 'Adagia'

21 Intolerance respecting other people's religion is toleration itself in comparison with intolerance respecting other people's art.
Ibid., 'Adagia'

22 Perhaps it is of more value to infuriate philosophers than to go along with them.
Ibid., 'Adagia'

23 One cannot spend one's time in being modern when there are so many more important things to be.
Ibid., 'Adagia'

24 Most modern reproducers of life, even including the camera, really repudiate it. We gulp down evil, choke at good.
Ibid., 'Adagia'

25 A poem need not have a meaning and like most things in nature often does not have.
Ibid., 'Adagia'

26 One's ignorance is one's chief asset.
Ibid., 'Adagia'

27 The imagination is man's power over nature.
Ibid., 'Adagia'

28 Style is not something applied. It is something that permeates. It is of the nature of that in which it is found, whether the poem, the manner of a god, the bearing of a man. It is not a dress.
Ibid., 'Two or Three Ideas'

Adlai Stevenson
(1900–65)
US politician

He helped establish the United Nations in the 1940s, and while US ambassador there (1960–5) famously persuaded delegates of the presence of Soviet missiles in Cuba with the aid of aerial photos. He stood unsuccessfully as Democratic presidential candidate against EISENHOWER *in 1952 and 1956. See also* ELBERT HUBBARD 6.

1 Let's face it. Let's talk sense to the American people. Let's tell them the truth, that there are no gains without pains, that we are now on the eve of great decisions, not easy decisions.
Acceptance speech at Democratic National Convention, Chicago, 26 July 1952, publ. in *Speeches* (1953)

2 What do we mean by patriotism in the context of our times? I venture to suggest that what we mean is a sense of national responsibility . . . a patriotism which is not short, frenzied outbursts of emotion, but the tranquil and steady dedication of a lifetime.
'The Nature of Patriotism', speech to American Legion Convention, New York, 27 August 1952, ibid.

3 The sound of tireless voices is the price we pay for the right to hear the music of our own opinions. But there is also, it seems to me, a moment at which democracy must prove its capacity to act. Every man has a right to be heard; but no man has the right to strangle democracy with a single set of vocal cords.
Speech in New York, 28 August 1952, publ. in *The Papers of Adlai E. Stevenson*, vol. 4 (1974). See also quote 16.

4 A hungry man is not a free man.
'Farm Policy', speech at Kasson, Minnesota, 6 September 1952, publ. in *The Speeches of Adlai Stevenson* (1952)

5 I have been thinking that I would make a proposition to my Republican friends. That if they will stop telling lies about Democrats, we will stop telling the truth about them.
Campaign speech, 10 September 1952, Fresno, California, quoted in *Adlai Stevenson of Illinois*, ch. 8 (1976) by John Bartlow Martin. The remark has been earlier attributed to Republican Chauncey Depew (senator 1899–1911), though with the party names reversed.

6 There is no evil in the atom; only in men's souls.
'The Atomic Future', speech at Hartford, Connecticut, 18 September 1952, publ. in *Speeches* (1953)

7 In America any boy may become President, and I suppose it's just one of the risks he takes!
Speech in Indianapolis, 26 September 1952, publ. in *Major Campaign Speeches of Adlai E. Stevenson: 1952* (1953)

8 Nothing so dates a man as to decry the younger generation.
Speech at University of Wisconsin, Madison, 8 October 1952, publ. in *Speeches* (1953)

9 The Republican Vice Presidential Candidate . . . asks you to place him a heartbeat from the Presidency.
Speech in Cleveland, Ohio, 23 October 1952, ibid. Referring to RICHARD NIXON. Nixon became Vice-President under EISENHOWER in the November election, and was re-elected 1956. This is thought to be the first use of the phrase 'heart-

beat from the presidency' to describe the position of Vice-President.

10 The Republican Party makes even its young men seem old; the Democratic Party makes even its old men seem young.

Quoted in *Richard Nixon: A Political and Personal Portrait*, ch. 7 (1959) by Earl Mazo. Comparing RICHARD NIXON to the septuagenarian Democratic Vice-President Alben Barkley, during the 1952 presidential race.

11 A funny thing happened to me on the way to the White House.

Speech in Washington DC, 13 December 1952, quoted in *Portrait: Adlai E. Stevenson*, ch. 1 (1965) by Alden Whitman. Said after his landslide defeat in the presidential election against EISENHOWER.

12 We cannot be any stronger in our foreign policy – for all the bombs and guns we may heap up in our arsenals – than we are in the spirit which rules inside the country. Foreign policy, like a river, cannot rise above its source.

Speech in New Orleans, 4 December 1954, publ. in *What I Think* (1956)

13 We hear the Secretary of State [John Foster Dulles] boasting of his brinkmanship – the art of bringing us to the edge of the abyss.

Speech at Hartford, Connecticut, 25 February 1956, quoted in the *New York Times* 26 February 1956. See also JOHN FOSTER DULLES 1

14 Freedom is not an ideal, it is not even a protection, if it means nothing more than freedom to stagnate, to live without dreams, to have no greater aim than a second car and another television set.

'Putting First Things First', publ. in *Foreign Affairs* January 1960

15 With the supermarket as our temple and the singing commercial as our litany, are we likely to fire the world with an irresistible vision of America's exalted purpose and inspiring way of life?

Wall Street Journal 1 June 1960

16 The first principle of a free society is an untrammeled flow of words in an open forum.

New York Times 19 January 1962

17 She would rather light a candle than curse the darkness, and her glow has warmed the world.

Quoted in the *New York Times* 8 November 1962. Comment on learning of the death of ELEANOR ROOSEVELT, echoing the motto of the Christopher Society: 'It is better to light one candle than curse the darkness.'

18 A politician is a statesman who approaches every question with an open mouth.

Quoted in *The Fine Art of Political Wit*, ch. 10 (1964) by Leon Harris

19 The General has dedicated himself so many times, he must feel like the cornerstone of a public building.

Referring to President EISENHOWER, ibid., ch. 10

Robert Louis Stevenson

(1850–94)

Scottish novelist, essayist and poet

Beset by ill health for most of his life, he travelled widely, and his early works were drawn from his wanderings in Europe. His adventure tales, Treasure Island *(1883) and* Kidnapped *(1886), and the thriller* Dr Jekyll and Mr Hyde *(1886) brought him fame and wealth.* A Child's Garden of Verses *(1885) also had enduring appeal. He settled in Samoa in 1889.*

1 Mankind was never so happily inspired as when it made a cathedral.

An Inland Voyage, 'Noyons Cathedral' (1878)

2 It is the mark of a good action that it appears inevitable in retrospect.

'Reflections and Remarks on Human Life' sect. 4 (1878), repr. in *Works of Robert Louis Stevenson*, vol. 15 (ed. Edmund Gosse, 1907)

3 For my part, I travel not to go anywhere, but to go. I travel for travel's sake. The great affair is to move; to feel the needs and hitches of our life more nearly; to come down off this feather-bed of civilisation, and find the globe granite underfoot and strewn with cutting flints.

Travels with a Donkey, 'Cheylard and Luc' (1879)

4 Night is a dead monotonous period under a roof; but in the open world it passes lightly, with its stars and dews and perfumes, and the hours are marked by changes in the face of Nature. What seems a kind of temporal death to people choked between walls and curtains, is only a light and living slumber to the man who sleeps afield.

Ibid., 'A Night Among the Pines'

5 There is a fellowship more quiet even than solitude, and which, rightly understood, is solitude made perfect.

Ibid., 'A Night Among the Pines'

6 In marriage, a man becomes slack and selfish, and undergoes a fatty degeneration of his moral being.

Virginibus Puerisque, 'Virginibus Puerisque', sect. 1 (1881)

7 Even if we take matrimony at its lowest, even if we regard it as no more than a sort of friendship recognised by the police.
Ibid., 'Virginibus Puerisque', sect. 1

8 You could read Kant by yourself, if you wanted; but you must share a joke with someone else.
Ibid., 'Virginibus Puerisque', sect. 1

9 Marriage is like life in this – that it is a field of battle, and not a bed of roses.
Ibid., 'Virginibus Puerisque', sect. 1

10 Once you are married, there is nothing for you, not even suicide, but to be good.
Ibid., 'Virginibus Puerisque', sect. 2

11 Man is a creature who lives not upon bread alone, but principally by catchwords; and the little rift between the sexes is astonishingly widened by simply teaching one set of catchwords to the girls and another to the boys.
Ibid., 'Virginibus Puerisque', sect. 2

12 The cruellest lies are often told in silence. A man may have sat in a room for hours and not opened his mouth, and yet come out of that room a disloyal friend or a vile calumniator.
Ibid., 'Virginibus Puerisque', sect. 4

13 Most of our pocket wisdom is conceived for the use of mediocre people, to discourage them from ambitious attempts, and generally console them in their mediocrity.
Ibid., 'Crabbed Age and Youth'

14 Old and young, we are all on our last cruise.
Ibid., 'Crabbed Age and Youth'

15 Some people swallow the universe like a pill; they travel on through the world, like smiling images pushed from behind. For God's sake give me the young man who has brains enough to make a fool of himself!
Ibid., 'Crabbed Age and Youth'

16 Books are good enough in their own way, but they are a mighty bloodless substitute for life.
Ibid., 'An Apology for Idlers'

17 A faculty for idleness implies a catholic appetite and a strong sense of personal identity.
Ibid., 'An Apology for Idlers'

18 Perpetual devotion to what a man calls his business is only to be sustained by neglect of many other things.
Ibid., 'An Apology for Idlers'

19 There is no duty we so much underrate as the duty of being happy.
Ibid., 'An Apology for Idlers'

20 He sows hurry and reaps indigestion.
Ibid., 'An Apology for Idlers'. Of 'industrious fellows'.

21 We are so fond of life that we have no leisure to entertain the terror of death. It is a honeymoon with us all through, and none of the longest. Small blame to us if we give our whole hearts to this glowing bride of ours, to the appetites, to honour, to the hungry curiosity of the mind, to the pleasure of the eyes in nature, and the pride of our own nimble bodies.
Ibid., 'Aes Triplex'

22 To travel hopefully is a better thing than to arrive.
Ibid., 'El Dorado'

23 I regard you with an indifference closely bordering on aversion.
'Story of the House With the Green Blinds', publ. in *New Arabian Nights*, 'The Rajah's Diamond' (1882). Spoken by Mr. Vandeleur to Francis Scrymgeour.

24 Fifteen men on the dead man's chest –
Yo-ho-ho, and a bottle of rum!
Drink and the devil had done for the rest –
Yo-ho-ho, and a bottle of rum!
Treasure Island, pt 1, ch. 1 (1883). Billy Bones's 'eternal song'.

25 Doctors is all swabs.
Billy Bones, ibid., pt 1, ch. 3

26 Ah! Black Dog. *He's* a bad un; but there's worse that put him on.
Billy Bones, ibid., pt 1, ch. 3

27 But you won't peach unless they get the black spot on me, or unless you see that Black Dog again or a seafaring man with one leg, Jim – him above all.
Billy Bones to Jim Hawkins, ibid., pt 1, ch. 3. The 'black spot', Bones explains, is a 'summons'.

28 Pieces of eight! pieces of eight! pieces of eight!
Long John Silver's parrot (Cap'n Flint), ibid., pt 1, ch. 10. A piece of eight was the old Spanish silver peso of eight reals – marked with an '8' – current in the eighteenth and nineteenth centuries.

29 In winter I get up at night
And dress by yellow candle-light.

In summer quite the other way,
I have to go to bed by day.
'Bed in Summer', st. 1, publ. in *A Child's Garden of Verses*
(1885)

30 A child should always say what's true
And speak when he is spoken to,
And behave mannerly at table;
At least as far as he is able.
'Whole Duty of Children', ibid.

31 To where the roads on either hand
Lead onward into fairy land,
Where all the children dine at five,
And all the playthings come alive.
'Foreign Lands', st. 5, ibid.

32 Whenever the moon and stars are set,
Whenever the wind is high,
All night long in the dark and wet,
A man goes riding by.
Late in the night when the fires are out,
Why does he gallop and gallop about?
'Windy Nights', st. 1, ibid.

33 I was the giant great and still
That sits upon the pillow-hill,
And sees before him, dale and plain,
The pleasant land of counterpane.
'The Land of Counterpane', st. 4, ibid.

34 From breakfast on through all the day
At home among my friends I stay,
But every night I go abroad
Afar into the land of Nod.
'Foreign Lands', st. 5, ibid.

35 I have a little shadow that goes in and out with
    me,
And what can be the use of him is more than I can
    see.
He is very, very like me from the heels up to the
    head;
And I see him jump before me, when I jump into
    my bed.
'My Shadow', st. 1, ibid.

36 Must we to bed indeed? Well then,
Let us arise and go like men,
And face with an undaunted tread
The long black passage up to bed.
'North-West Passage. Good-Night', st. 3, ibid.

37 He does not hear, he will not look,
Nor yet be lured out of this book.
For, long ago, the truth to say,

He has grown up and gone away,
And it is but a child of air
That lingers in the garden there.
'To Any Reader', ibid., 'Envoys'

38 Am I no a bonny fighter?
Kidnapped, ch. 10 (1886). Spoken by Alan Breck.

39 The Strange Case of Dr Jekyll and Mr Hyde.
Title of novel (1886)

40 The obscurest epoch is today.
'The Day After Tomorrow' (1887), repr. in *Works of Robert
Louis Stevenson*, vol. 15 (ed. Edmund Gosse, 1907)

41 I have thus played the sedulous ape to Hazlitt,
to Lamb, to Wordsworth, to Sir Thomas Browne, to
Defoe, to Hawthorne, to Montaigne, to Baudelaire
and to Obermann.
Memories and Portraits, ch. 4 (1887)

42 Each has his own tree of ancestors, but at the top
of all sits Probably Arboreal.
Ibid., ch. 6

43 Marriage is one long conversation, chequered by
disputes.
Ibid., ch. 11

44 Let first the onion flourish there,
Rose among roots, the maiden-fair,
Wine-scented and poetic soul
Of the capacious salad bowl.
'To a Gardener', publ. in *Underwoods*, bk 1 (1887)

45 Under the wide and starry sky,
Dig the grave and let me lie.
Glad did I live and gladly die,
And I laid me down with a will.
This be the verse you grave for me:
Here he lies where he longed to be;
Home is the sailor, home from sea.
And the hunter home from the hill.
'Requiem', ibid., bk 1. The lines are inscribed on Stevenson's
gravestone on Mount Vaea, Samoa.

46 Everyone lives by selling something, whatever
be his right to it.
Across the Plains, 'Beggars', sect. 3 (1892)

47 If your morals make you dreary, depend upon it
they are wrong. I do not say 'give them up', for they
may be all you have; but conceal them like a vice,
lest they should spoil the lives of better and simpler
people.
Ibid., 'A Christmas Sermon', sect. 2

48 Here lies one who meant well, tried a little, failed

much: – surely that may be his epitaph, of which he need not be ashamed.

Ibid., 'A Christmas Sermon', sect. 4

49 I have been so long waiting for death, I have unwrapped my thoughts from about life so long, that I have not a filament left to hold by; I have done my fiddling so long under Vesuvius, that I have almost forgotten to play, and can only wait for the eruption, and think it long of coming. Literally, no man has more wholly outlived life than I. And still it's good fun.

Letter, September 1894, publ. in *The Letters of Robert Louis Stevenson to His Family and Friends*, vol. 2 (ed. Sidney Colvin, 1899). Stevenson died in December of that year.

50 If you are going to make a book end badly, it must end badly from the beginning.

Letter to J. M. BARRIE, 1 November 1894, ibid., vol. 2

51 Wealth I ask not, hope nor love,
Nor a friend to know me;
All I ask, the heaven above
And the road below me.

'The Vagabond', st. 4, publ. in *Songs of Travel* (1896)

52 I will make you brooches and toys for your
   delight
Of bird-song at morning and star-shine at night.

'I will make you brooches and toys for your delight', st. 1, ibid.

53 In the highlands, in the country places,
Where the old plain men have rosy faces,
And the young fair maidens
Quiet eyes.

'In the highlands, in the country places', st. 1, ibid.

54 Trusty, dusky, vivid, true,
With eyes of gold and bramble-dew,
Steel-true and blade-straight
The great artificer
Made my mate.

'My Wife', st. 1, ibid. The lines 'Steel true/Blade straight' are inscribed on the gravestone of ARTHUR CONAN DOYLE, in Minstead, Hampshire.

55 To be wholly devoted to some intellectual exercise is to have succeeded in life; and perhaps only in law and the higher mathematics may this devotion be maintained, suffice to itself without reaction, and find continual rewards without excitement.

Weir of Hermiston, ch. 2 (1896)

56 So long as we love we serve: so long as we are loved by others, I would almost say that we are

indispensable; and no man is useless while he has a friend.

Lay Morals, ch. 4 (1911)

Stephen Stills
(b. 1945)
US rock musician

He wrote many of the songs recorded by the LA folk-rock band Buffalo Springfield, of which he was a founder member (1966–8). He later performed with Crosby, Stills and Nash, made solo albums and formed the band Manassas.

1 You better stop, hey,
What's that sound?
Everybody look what's goin' down.

'For What it's Worth' (song, 1967) on the album *Retrospective* (1969) by Buffalo Springfield. The song, written after the 1967 riots in Los Angeles, became a protest anthem against police brutality.

2 If you can't be with the one you love,
Love the one you're with.

'Love the One You're With' (song) on the album *Stephen Stills* (1970). The lyrics of the song, which was also a hit for the Isley Brothers, recall the 1947 song by YIP HARBURG, 'When I'm Not Near the Girl I Love': 'When I'm not near the girl I love,/I love the girl I'm near.'

Sting
(b. 1951)
British rock musician

Born Gordon Sumner. The singer, bassist and principal song-writer with the Police until 1986, he has had a successful solo career while campaigning for Amnesty International and the Brazilian rain forest.

1 Music has ceased to belong to the young . . . The rock rebel is defunct. He's meaningless.

Interview in *Smash Hits* 19 August 1982

2 If You Love Somebody Set Them Free.

Title of song on the album *The Dream of the Blue Turtles* (1985)

3 Celebrity is good for kick-starting ideas, but often celebrity is a lead weight around your neck. It's like you pointing at the moon, but people are looking at your finger.

Interview in *Mojo* February 1995

Karlheinz Stockhausen
(b. 1928)
German composer

He was a member of the Paris-based 'Musique Concrète' group and in 1953 helped found the electronic music studio at Cologne, Westdeutscher Rundfunk, becoming its director (1963–77). His work combines electronic and orchestral sounds, as in Kontakte (1960) and his operatic cycle Licht, begun in 1977.

1 The whole planning looked like Lucifer's greatest work of art.

Quoted in *Bild* 18 September 2001, referring to the terrorist attacks of '9/11'. In the resulting furore, Stockhausen insisted that his remarks, made at a press conference for the Hamburg Festival of New Music, 17 September 2001, had been 'ripped out of context'. The composer had been asked whether Lucifer, who appears in his work *Licht*, is a historical figure, and had replied that Lucifer had been present at the attack on the World Trade Center. He later explained: 'Of course I used the designation "work of art" to mean the work of destruction personified in Lucifer. In the context of my other comments this was unequivocal.'

Bram Stoker
(1847–1912)
Irish author

He was drama critic of Dublin's Evening Mail *while working as a civil servant. Settling in London, he became manager to the actor Henry Irving, about whom he published a book of reminiscences.* Dracula *(1897) was the most famous of his works of fiction.*

1 I am Dracula. And I bid you welcome.

Dracula, ch. 2 (1897). Spoken by Count Dracula. The line is best remembered as uttered by Bela Lugosi in the film adaptation *Dracula* (1931).

2 There is reason that all things are as they are, and did you see with my eyes and know with my knowledge, you would perhaps better understand.

Count Dracula, ibid., ch. 2

Mike Stoller
See ELVIS PRESLEY 1

Matt Stone
(b. 1971)
Trey Parker
(b. 1972)
US animators

South Park, *the controversial cartoon series created by Stone and Parker (full name Donald McKay Parker), and featuring the eight-year-olds Kyle, Stan, Kenny and Cartman, became a global hit from its debut in 1997.*

1 Oh my God, they've killed Kenny!

South Park (cartoon series, from 1997, written by Matt Stone and Trey Parker). The exclamation, or a variation of it, is made by one of the characters towards the end of most episodes.

Robert Stone
(b. 1937)
US novelist

He is best known for Dog Soldiers *(1974) and for his fictionalized study of US imperialism* A Flag for Sunrise *(1981).*

1 Life is a means of extracting fiction.

Interview in *Writers at Work* (eighth series, ed. George Plimpton, 1988)

Marie Carmichael Stopes
(1880–1958)
British scientist and pioneer of birth control

She published more than seventy books in her lifetime, including the controversial and influential Married Love *(1918), which advocated birth control. She founded the first British birth control clinic in London in 1921.*

1 An impersonal and scientific knowledge of the structure of our bodies is the surest safeguard against prurient curiosity and lascivious gloating.

Married Love, ch. 5 (1918)

(Sir) Tom Stoppard
(b. 1937)
Czech-born British playwright

Born Thomas Straussler. His work aspires to be, he has said, 'a perfect marriage between the play of ideas and farce'. He came to prominence with Rosencrantz and Guildenstern are Dead *(1966), followed by* The Real Inspector Hound *(1968),* Jumpers *(1972) and* Travesties *(1974). He has also written fiction and screenplays.*

1 My problem is that I am not frightfully interested

in anything, except myself. And of all forms of fiction autobiography is the most gratuitous.
Lord Malquist and Mr Moon, pt 2, ch. 3 (1966). Spoken by Lord Malquist.

2 Let it be said of me that I was born appalled, lived disaffected, and died in the height of fashion.
Lord Malquist, ibid., pt 6, ch. 2

3 We do on stage things that are supposed to happen off. Which is a kind of integrity, if you look on every exit as being an entrance somewhere else.
Rosencrantz and Guildenstern are Dead, Act 1 (1966). Spoken by Player.

4 Eternity is a terrible thought. I mean, where's it going to end?
Rosencrantz, ibid., Act 2

5 The bad end unhappily, the good unluckily. That is what tragedy means.
Player, ibid., Act 2. See also OSCAR WILDE 103.

6 Life is a gamble at terrible odds – if it was a bet, you wouldn't take it.
Player, ibid., Act 3

7 It's not the voting that's democracy, it's the counting.
Jumpers, Act 1 (1972). Spoken by Dotty. See also ANASTASIO SOMOZA 1.

8 It's better to be quotable than honest.
Quoted in the *Guardian* 21 March 1973

9 War is capitalism with the gloves off and many who go to war know it but they go to war because they don't want to be a hero.
Travesties, Act 1 (1974). Spoken by Tzara.

10 I'm with you on the free press. It's the newspapers I can't stand.
Night and Day, Act 1 (1978). Spoken by Ruth.

11 I don't think I can be expected to take seriously any game which takes less than three days to reach its conclusion.
Quoted in the *Guardian* 24 December 1984. On baseball. Stoppard is known to be a dedicated cricket fan.

Anthony Storr
(1920–2001)
British psychiatrist

His insights into the role of psychology in everyday life are contained in such works as The Art of Psychotherapy *(1980) and* Churchill's Black Dog *(1988).*

1 Self-realization is not an anti-social principle; it is firmly based on the fact that men need each other in order to be themselves.
The Integrity of the Personality, ch. 2 (1960)

Harriet Beecher Stowe
(1811–96)
US author

She wrote prolifically from 1834, and had international success with her first novel, Uncle Tom's Cabin *(1852). Of this anti-slavery tale of the South, she commented: 'God wrote it. I merely did His dictation.' She was the sister of* HENRY WARD BEECHER.

1 I 'spect I grow'd. Don't think nobody never made me.
Uncle Tom's Cabin, ch. 20 (1852). Spoken by Topsy, a slave, in answer to the question: 'Do you know who made you?'

2 Whipping and abuse are like laudanum: you have to double the dose as the sensibilities decline.
St. Clare, ibid., ch. 20

Lord Stowell
(1745–1836)
English lawyer

Sir William Scott. Having taken up law in 1780, he became a distinguished judge and was MP for Oxford 1801–21. He was a close friend of SAMUEL JOHNSON.

1 A dinner lubricates business.
Quoted in *Life of Samuel Johnson, LL.D.*, 1781, by JAMES BOSWELL, as note publ. in *Works of Samuel Johnson*, vol. 8 (1835)

2 A precedent embalms a principle.
Quoted by BENJAMIN DISRAELI in speech to House of Commons, 22 February 1848, publ. in *Hansard*, col. 1066. The axiom is often erroneously ascribed to Disraeli.

Strabo
(c. 63 BC–c. AD 24)
Greek geographer and historian

He travelled widely in Europe, Africa and Asia, living several years in Italy. Almost all his work has perished, though the seventeen books of his Geography *survive, and provide valuable information on the ancient world.*

1 The poets were not alone in sanctioning myths, for long before the poets the states and the law-makers had sanctioned them as a useful expedient ... They needed to control the people by super-

stitious fears, and these cannot be aroused without myths and marvels.

Geographia, bk 1, sect. 2, subsect. 8

Lytton Strachey
(1880–1932)
British biographer and historian

A member of the Bloomsbury group of writers and artists, he was the author of Eminent Victorians *(1918), described by* CYRIL CONNOLLY *as 'the work of a great anarch'.* T. E. LAWRENCE *remembered him as 'an outraged wet mackerel of a man', while* EDITH SITWELL *judged him to have been 'cut out of very thin cardboard'.*

1 The history of the Victorian Age will never be written: we know too much about it.

Eminent Victorians, Preface (1918). Opening words. Strachey's preface has been described by his biographer MICHAEL HOLROYD as 'a manifesto for modern biographers'.

2 Ignorance is the first requisite of the historian – ignorance, which simplifies and clarifies, which selects and omits, with a placid perfection unattainable by the highest art.

Ibid., Preface

3 Human beings are too important to be treated as mere symptoms of the past. They have a value which is independent of any temporal processes – which is eternal, and must be felt for its own sake.

Ibid., Preface

4 Discretion is not the better part of biography.

Quoted in *Lytton Strachey*, vol. 1, Preface (1967) by MICHAEL HOLROYD

5 If this is dying, then I don't think much of it.

Last words, ibid., vol. 2, pt 2, ch. 6 (1968)

Igor Stravinsky
(1882–1971)
Russian-born US composer

A seminal figure in 20th-century music, he composed ballets, operas, religious pieces and works for piano and orchestra. The Firebird *(1910),* Petrushka *(1911) and* The Rite of Spring *(1913) were all written for* DIAGHILEV *ballets. 'We have a duty towards music,' he asserted, 'namely to invent it.'*

1 Academism results when the reasons for the rule change, but not the rule.

Conversations with Igor Stravinsky (1958) by Igor Stravinsky and Robert Craft

2 My music is best understood by children and animals.

Quoted in the *Observer* 8 October 1961

J. August Strindberg
(1849–1912)
Swedish dramatist, author and poet

Johan August Strindberg. Despite a tumultuous private life he produced around seventy plays as well as stories, histories and verse. The naturalism and psychological elements of his plays had a significant impact on European drama. His chief works include Miss Julie *(1888),* A Dream Play *(1902) and* The Ghost Sonata *(1907).*

1 That is the thankless position of the father in the family – the provider for all, and the enemy of all.

The Son of a Servant, vol. 1 (autobiography, 1886)

2 Family ... the home of all social evil, a charitable institution for comfortable women, an anchorage for house-fathers, and a hell for children.

Ibid., vol. 1

3 Friendship can only exist between persons with similar interests and points of view. Man and woman by the conventions of society are born with different interests and different points of view.

Ibid., vol. 1

4 A man with a so-called character is often a simple piece of mechanism; he has often only one point of view for the extremely complicated relationships of life.

Ibid., vol. 1

5 I dream, therefore I exist.

Le Plaidoyer d'un fou, pt 1, ch. 7 (written 1887–8, first publ. 1893, repr. 1912 as *The Confession of a Fool*). Also translated as *A Madman's Defence* and *A Madman's Manifesto*.

6 Why is it so painful to watch a person sink? Because there is something unnatural in it, for nature demands personal progress, evolution, and every backward step means wasted energy.

Ibid., pt 2, ch. 5

7 I always disliked dogs, those protectors of cowards who lack the courage to fight an assailant themselves.

Ibid., pt 3, ch. 1

8 Happiness consumes itself like a flame. It cannot burn for ever, it must go out, and the presentiment of its end destroys it at its very peak.

A Dream Play (written 1901, performed 1907). Spoken by the Husband.

Joe Strummer
(1952–2002)
Mick Jones
(b. 1955)
British rock musicians

The two wrote some of the greatest anthems of the punk era for their band the Clash. Jones later recorded with Big Audio Dynamite; Strummer (born John Graham Mellor) went on to form the Mescaleros.

1 No Elvis, Beatles or the Rolling Stones
In 1977
'1977' (song, 1977) by the Clash

2 White riot! I wanna riot!
White riot! a riot of my own.
'White Riot' (song) on the album *The Clash* (1977) by the Clash

3 Career opportunities, the ones that never knock,
Every job they offer you is to keep you out the
    dock.
'Career Opportunities' (song), ibid.

Jan Struther
See HYMNS AND CAROLS 53, 88

Mary Stuart
See MARY, QUEEN OF SCOTS

G. A. Studdert Kennedy
See KENNEDY, G. A. STUDDERT

(Sir) John Suckling
(1609–42)
English poet and playwright

A 'Cavalier poet', he was known for his wit, easy poetic style and extravagance, which included a love of gaming. He wrote lyrics, ballads and satires, and also had success with his tragedy Aglaura (1637). Implicated in a plot to free the Earl of Strafford (1641), he died a fugitive in France.

1 Why so pale and wan, fond lover?
Prithee, why so pale?
Will, when looking well can't move her,
Looking ill prevail?
Prithee, why so pale?
Aglaura, Act 4, Sc. 1, 'Song', st. 1 (1637)

2 If of herself she will not love,
Nothing can make her:
The devil take her.
Ibid., Act 4, Sc. 1, 'Song', st. 3

3 Her feet beneath her petticoat,
Like little mice, stole in and out,
As if they feared the light.
'A Ballad upon a Wedding', st. 8, publ. in *Fragmenta Aurea* (1646)

4 Love is the fart
Of every heart;
It pains a man when 'tis kept close;
And others doth offend, when 'tis let loose.
'Love's Offence', ibid.

Louis Henry Sullivan
(1856–1924)
US architect

His skyscrapers, innovative ornamentation and architectural theories led him to be known as the father of modernism. His partnership with Dankmar Adler 1881–95 produced more than a hundred buildings, including the Chicago Stock Exchange and the Wainwright Building, St Louis.

1 Whether it be the sweeping eagle in his flight, or the open apple-blossom, the toiling work-horse, the blithe swan, the branching oak, the winding stream at its base, the drifting clouds, over all the coursing sun, *form ever follows function*, and this is the law. Where function does not change form does not change.
'The Tall Office Building Artistically Considered' (1896), repr. in *Louis Sullivan: The Public Papers* (ed. Robert Twombly, 1988)

Arthur Hays Sulzberger
(1891–1968)
US newspaper proprietor

Publisher of the New York Times from 1935, he was also Chairman of the Board (1957–61). He expanded the sales of 'the good grey Times', as he called it, and wrote letters to the paper signed A. Aitchess (A.H.S.).

1 We [journalists] tell the public which way the cat is jumping. The public will take care of the cat.
Quoted in *Time* 8 May 1950

Edith Summerskill
(1901–80)
British politician

Baroness Summerskill of Kenwood. A Labour MP (1938–55) and Chairman of the Party (1954–5), she was responsible for administering food rationing in ATTLEE's *government. She campaigned for hygiene in food, good health care and women's rights.*

1 Nagging is the repetition of unpalatable truths.
Speech to the Married Women's Association, House of Commons, 14 July 1960, quoted in *The Times* 15 July 1960

Charles Sumner
(1811–74)
US politician

As Senator for Massachusetts (1851–74), he was a persistent abolitionist, and opposed the Reconstruction policies of President Andrew Johnson in favour of greater equality for blacks in the southern states.

1 Where Slavery is, there Liberty cannot be; and where Liberty is, there Slavery cannot be.
Slavery and the Rebellion are One and Inseparable (pamphlet, 1864). Originally a speech at Cooper Institute, New York, 5 November 1864.

The Sun

See ANTONY JAY AND JONATHAN LYNN 1.

1 Crisis? What crisis?
Headline, 11 January 1979. On James Callaghan's blithe denial of 'mounting chaos' in the economy. See JAMES CALLAGHAN 1.

2 Stick it up your junta!
Headline, 20 April 1982. Referring to a boycott of Argentine corned beef during the Falklands conflict.

3 GOTCHA!
Headline, 4 May 1982. On the sinking of the Argentinian cruiser *General Belgrano*. The headline appeared in the first edition only; subsequent editions were toned down, with the replacement: 'Did 1200 Argies drown?'

4 Freddie Starr ate my hamster.
Headline, 13 March 1986

5 Up yours, Delors.
Headline, 1 November 1990. On Jacques Delors, President of the European Commission, seen to be attempting to increase EU powers at the expense of British sovereignty.

6 If Kinnock wins today, will the last person to leave Britain please turn out the lights.
Headline, 9 April 1992. On election day, in which NEIL KINNOCK was the Labour challenger to JOHN MAJOR.

7 It was the Sun wot won it.
Headline, 10 April 1992. Following the unexpected Conservative victory in the general election, maintaining JOHN MAJOR in power and giving the Conservatives their fourth successive term in office.

8 One's bum year.
Headline, 25 November 1992. Reporting the Queen's speech of the preceding day, in which she had referred to her '*annus horribilis*'. See ELIZABETH II 4.

9 Is THIS the most dangerous man in Britain?
Headline, 24 June 1998. Of Prime Minister TONY BLAIR, suspected of favouring Britain's membership of the Single European Currency.

Sun Tzu (Sunzi)
(6th–5th century BC)
Chinese general

In the service of the Wu state from c. 512 BC, *he is traditionally held to be the author of* The Art of War, *a manual of military science whose emphasis on intelligence, flexibility and political will in devising strategy had an enduring influence. The work may have been written in a later period, however.*

1 Hence to fight and conquer in all your battles is not supreme excellence; supreme excellence consists in breaking the enemy's resistance without fighting.
The Art of War, ch. 3, axiom 2 (transl. Lionel Giles, ed. James Clavell, 1981)

2 If you know the enemy and know yourself, you need not fear the result of a hundred battles. If you know yourself but not the enemy, for every victory gained you will also suffer a defeat. If you know neither the enemy nor yourself, you will succumb in every battle.
Ibid., ch. 3, axiom 18

3 The quality of decision is like the well-timed swoop of a falcon which enables it to strike and destroy its victim.
Ibid., ch. 5, axiom 13

4 Simulated disorder postulates perfect discipline; simulated fear postulates courage; simulated weakness postulates strength.
Ibid., ch. 5, axiom 17

5 That general is skilful in attack whose opponent

does not know what to defend; and he is skilful in defence whose opponent does not know what to attack.

Ibid., ch. 6, axiom 8

R. S. Surtees
(1803–64)
English journalist and novelist

Robert Smith Surtees. Country sports formed the main subject matter of his humorous tales. His character Jorrocks, a Cockney grocer passionately interested in fox-hunting, first appeared in the New Sporting Magazine, *which he co-founded in 1831.*

1 I confess that I'm a martyr to it – a perfect wictim – no one knows wot I suffer from my ardour. If ever I'm wisited with the last infirmity of noble minds, it will be caused by my ingovernable passion for the chase. The sight of a saddle makes me sweat. An 'ound makes me perfectly wild. A red coat throws me into a scarlet fever. Never throughout life have I had a good night's rest before an 'unting morning.

Jorrocks's Jaunts and Jollities, ch. 5 (1838). Spoken by Mr Jorrocks.

2 I am a sportsman all over, and to the back-bone. 'Unting is all that's worth living for – all time is lost wot is not spent in 'unting – it is like the hair we breathe – if we have it not we die – it's the sport of kings, the image of war without its guilt, and only five-and-twenty per cent of its danger.

Handley Cross, ch. 7 (1843). Letter written by Mr Jorrocks. See WILLIAM SOMERVILLE 2.

3 It ar'nt that I loves the fox less, but that I loves the 'ound more.

Mr Jorrocks, ibid., ch. 18

4 Crack! crack! crack! go the whips; 'ounds, 'osses, and men, are in a glorious state of excitement! Full o' beans and benevolence!

Mr Jorrocks, ibid., ch. 32

5 Three things I never lends – my 'oss, my wife, and my name.

Hillingdon Hall, ch. 33 (1845). Spoken by Mr Jorrocks.

6 More people are flattered into virtue than bullied out of vice.

The Analysis of the Hunting Field, ch. 1 (1846)

7 Women never look so well as when one comes in wet and dirty from hunting.

Mr Sponge's Sporting Tour, ch. 21 (1853). Spoken by Sponge.

8 There is no secret so close as that between a rider and his horse.

Ibid., ch. 31

9 The only infallible rule we know is, that the man who is always talking about being a gentleman never is one.

Ask Mamma, ch. 1 (1858)

Gloria Swanson
(1897–1983)
US screen actress

Born Gloria Svensson. The highest paid star of the silent era, she appeared as a leading sophisticate in the films of CECIL B. DE MILLE. Sadie Thompson *(1928) was made by her own production company, and* Sunset Boulevard *revived her career in 1950.*

1 I *am* big. It's the pictures that got small.

Sunset Boulevard (film, 1950, screenplay by Billy Wilder, Charles Brackett and D. M. Marsham Jr, directed by BILLY WILDER). Riposte by Norma Desmond (Gloria Swanson) to Joe Gillis (William Holden), who exclaimed: 'You're Norma Desmond! You used to be in silent pictures. Used to be big.'

2 You see, this is my life. It always will be! There's nothing else. Just us, and the cameras, and those wonderful people out there in the dark. All right, Mr De Mille. I'm ready for my closeup.

Ibid. Last lines of film.

3 When I die, my epitaph should read: *She Paid the Bills.* That's the story of my private life.

Quoted in the *Saturday Evening Post* 22 July 1950

Graham Swift
(b. 1949)
British author

His novels and short stories concern ordinary characters at critical points of their lives, and explore themes of memory, history and landscape. His most notable works are Waterland *(1983),* Last Orders *(1996) and* The Light of Day *(2003).*

1 Life is one tenth Here and Now, nine-tenths a history lesson. For most of the time the Here and Now is neither now nor here.

Waterland, ch. 8 (1983)

2 People die when curiosity goes. People have to find out, people have to know. How can there be any true revolution till we know what we are made of?

Ibid., ch. 27

3 It's the best thing that's ever been invented. If it

hadn't been invented we'd've had to invent it. And it aint just a seat on wheels. It's a workmate. It's a mate. It won't ask no questions, it won't tell no lies. It's somewhere you can be and be who you are. If you aint got no place to call your own, you're okay in a motor.

Last Orders, 'Vince' (1996). Ray, referring to the car.

4 Crying's like pissing. You don't want to get caught short.

Narrator (Ray), ibid., 'Rochester'

Jonathan Swift
(1667–1745)
Anglo-Irish satirist

Ordained an Anglican cleric in 1694, he was made prebendary (1699) and dean (1713) of St Patrick's Cathedral, Dublin. Moving away from his Whig roots, he became the Tories' chief pamphleteer and edited The Examiner *1710–11. His* Journal to Stella *(1710–13) described life in London, while* The Tale of a Tub *(1704) and* Gulliver's Travels *(1726) were allegorical works combining outlandish humour with vehement satire. See* W. B. YEATS 55.

1 Satire is a sort of glass, wherein beholders do generally discover everybody's face but their own; which is the chief reason for that kind of reception it meets in the world, and that so very few are offended with it.

The Battle of the Books, Preface (written 1697, publ. 1704)

2 In these books is wonderfully instilled and preserved the spirit of each warrior while he is alive; and after his death his soul transmigrates thither to inform them. This, at least, is the more common opinion; but I believe it is with libraries as with other cemeteries, where some philosophers affirm that a certain spirit, which they call *Brutum Hominis*, hovers over the monument, till the body is corrupted and turns to dust or to worms, but then vanishes or dissolves; so, we may say, a restless spirit haunts over every book, till dust or worms have seized upon it.

Ibid., Preface

3 Whatever we have got has been by infinite labour, and search, and ranging through every corner of nature; the difference is that instead of dirt and poison, we have rather chosen to fill our hives with honey and wax, thus furnishing mankind with the two noblest of things, which are sweetness and light.

Aesop, ibid. Arguing on behalf of the Ancients, Aesop likens

them to a bee, as opposed to the spider which stands for the Moderns. See MATTHEW ARNOLD 51.

4 Books, like men their authors, have no more than one way of coming into the world, but there are ten thousand to go out of it and return no more.

A Tale of a Tub, 'Epistle Dedicatory' (1704)

5 Where I am not understood, it shall be concluded that something very useful and profound is couched underneath.

Ibid., 'Author's Preface'

6 Satire, being levelled at all, is never resented for an offence by any.

Ibid., 'Author's Preface'

7 Books, the children of the brain.

Ibid., sect. 1

8 We have just enough religion to make us *hate*, but not enough to make us *love* one another.

'Thoughts on Various Subjects', written 1706, publ. in *Miscellanies in Prose and Verse* (1711), repr. in *Jonathan Swift: A Critical Edition of the Major Works*, 'Apothegms and Maxims' (ed. Angus Ross and David Woolley, 1984)

9 When a true genius appears in the world, you may know him by this sign, that the dunces are all in confederacy against him.

'Thoughts on Various Subjects', ibid.

10 There are but three ways for a man to revenge himself of a censorious world. To despise it; to return the like; or to endeavour to live so as to avoid it. The first of these is usually pretended; the last is almost impossible; the universal practice is for the second.

'Thoughts on Various Subjects', ibid.

11 Ambition often puts men upon doing the meanest offices; so climbing is performed in the same posture with creeping.

'Thoughts on Various Subjects', ibid.

12 Censure is the tax a man pays to the public for being eminent.

'Thoughts on Various Subjects', ibid.

13 Complaint is the largest tribute heaven receives; and the sincerest part of our devotion.

'Thoughts on Various Subjects', ibid.

14 Every man desires to live long; but no man would be old.

'Thoughts on Various Subjects', ibid.

15 Laws are like cobwebs, which may catch small flies, but let wasps and hornets break through.
'A Critical Essay upon the Faculties of the Mind', written 1709, publ. in *Miscellanies in Prose and Verse by Pope, Swift and Gay*, vol. 1 (ed. Jonathan Swift, 1727), repr. in *The Works of Jonathan Swift*, DD, vol. 9 (ed. Sir Walter Scott, 1814)

16 There is nothing in this world constant, but inconstancy.
'A Critical Essay upon the Faculties of the Mind', ibid.

17 We are so fond of one another, because our ailments are the same.
Letter, 1 February 1711, in *Journal to Stella* (1766–8), repr. in *Journal to Stella*, vol. 1 (ed. Harold Williams, 1948)

18 I love good creditable acquaintance: I love to be the worst of the company: I am not of those that say, For want of company, welcome trumpery.
Letter, 17 May 1711, publ. in *Journal to Stella*, ibid.

19 He showed me his bill of fare to tempt me to dine with him; Poh, said I, I value not your bill of fare, give me your bill of company.
Letter, 2 September 1711, publ. in *Journal to Stella*, ibid.

20 I dined with him, and we were to do more business after dinner. But after dinner is after dinner – an old saying and a true, Much drinking, little thinking.
Letter, 26 February 1712, publ. in *Journal to Stella*, ibid.

21 It is the folly of too many to mistake the echo of a London coffee-house for the voice of the kingdom.
The Conduct of the Allies (pamphlet, 1711), repr. in *Jonathan Swift: A Critical Edition of the Major Works* (ed. Angus Ross and David Woolley, 1984)

22 I often wished that I had clear,
For life, six hundred pounds a-year,
A handsome house to lodge a friend,
A river at my garden's end,
A terrace walk, and half a rood
Of land, set out to plant a wood.
Imitation of Horace, *Satires*, bk 2, no. 6, ll. 1–6, written 1714, publ. in *Miscellanies in Prose and Verse* (1727), repr. in *Jonathan Swift: the Complete Poems* (ed. Pat Rogers, 1983). See HORACE 11.

23 Proper words in proper places, make the true definition of a style.
Letter to a Young Gentleman lately entered into Holy Orders, 9 January 1720, ibid., repr. in *The Prose Works of Jonathan Swift*, vol. 9 (ed. Herbert Davis, 1957)

24 If Heaven had looked upon riches to be a valu-able thing, it would not have given them to such a scoundrel.
Letter, 12 August 1720, publ. in *The Correspondence of Jonathan Swift*, vol. 2 (ed. Harold Williams, 1963). See JEAN DE LA BRUYÈRE 12.

25 Once kick the world, and the world and you will live together at a reasonably good understanding.
Letter of Advice to a Young Poet, 1 December 1720 (1721), repr. in *The Prose Works of Jonathan Swift*, vol. 9 (ed. Herbert Davis, 1957)

26 How haughtily he lifts his nose,
To tell what every schoolboy knows.
'The Journal', ll. 81–2 (1721), repr. in *Poems* (1735)

27 Your notions of friendship are new to me; I believe every man is born with his quantum, and he cannot give to one without robbing another. I very well know to whom I would give the first place in my friendship, but they are not in the way, I am condemned to another scene, and therefore I distribute it in pennyworths to those about me, and who displease me least, and should do the same to my fellow prisoners if I were condemned to a jail.
Letter to ALEXANDER POPE, 20 September 1723, publ. in *The Correspondence of Jonathan Swift*, vol. 2 (ed. Harold Williams, 1963). Pope had previously written to Swift: 'My friendships are increased by new ones, yet no part of the warmth I felt for the old is diminished.'

28 In church your grandsire cut his throat;
To do the job too long he tarried:
He should have had my hearty vote,
To cut his throat before he married.
'Verses on the Upright Judge', written 1724, publ. in *Poems* (1735)

29 Principally I hate and detest that animal called man; although I heartily love John, Peter, Thomas, and so forth.
Letter to ALEXANDER POPE, 29 September 1725, publ. in *The Correspondence of Jonathan Swift*, vol. 3 (ed. Harold Williams, 1963)

30 I cannot but conclude the bulk of your natives to be the most pernicious race of little, odious vermin that nature ever suffered to crawl upon the surface of the earth.
Gulliver's Travels, 'A Voyage to Brobdingnag', ch. 6 (1726). The King of Brobdingnag addressing Gulliver.

31 And he gave it for his opinion, that whoever could make two ears of corn, or two blades of grass, to grow upon a spot of ground where only one grew before, would deserve better of mankind, and do

more essential service to his country, than the whole race of politicians put together.

Ibid., 'A Voyage to Brobdingnag', ch. 7. Referring to the King of Brobdingnag. The physicist Henry Augustus Rowland (1848–1901) is quoted in *The Politics of Pure Science* (1967) by D. S. Greenberg: 'He who makes two blades of grass grow where one grew before is the benefactor of mankind, but he who obscurely worked to find the laws of such growth is the intellectual superior as well as the greater benefactor of mankind.'

32 He had been eight years upon a project for extracting sunbeams out of cucumbers, which were to be put into vials hermetically sealed, and let out to warm the air in raw, inclement summers.

Ibid., 'A Voyage to Laputa', ch. 5. Of a scientist at the grand academy of Lagado.

33 In the school of political projectors, I was but ill entertained, the professors appearing, in my judgment, wholly out of their senses; which is a scene that never fails to make me melancholy. These unhappy people were proposing schemes for persuading monarchs to choose favourites upon the score of their wisdom, capacity, and virtue; of teaching ministers to consult the public good; of rewarding merit, great abilities, and eminent services, of instructing princes to know their true interest, by placing it on the same foundation with that of their people; of choosing for employment persons qualified to exercise them; with many other wild impossible chimeras, that never entered before into the heart of man to conceive; and confirmed in me the old observation, that there is nothing so extravagant and irrational which some philosophers have not maintained for truth.

Ibid., 'A Voyage to Laputa', ch. 6

34 He replied that I must needs be mistaken, or that I *said the thing which was not*. (For they have no word in their language to express lying or falsehood.)

Ibid., 'A Voyage to the Country of the Houyhnhnms', ch. 3

35 Poor nations are hungry, and rich nations are proud; and pride and hunger will ever be at variance.

Ibid., 'A Voyage to the Country of the Houyhnhnms', ch. 5. On reasons for going to war.

36 I said there was a society of men among us, bred up from their youth in the art of proving by words multiplied for the purpose, that white is black, and black is white, according as they are paid. To this society all the rest of the people are as slaves.

Ibid., 'A Voyage to the Country of the Houyhnhnms', ch. 5. Describing the lawyers of his native land.

37 It is a maxim among these lawyers, that whatever hath been done before, may legally be done again: and therefore they take special care to record all the decisions formerly made against common justice and the general reason of mankind.

Ibid., 'A Voyage to the Country of the Houyhnhnms', ch. 5.

38 I have been assured by a very knowing American of my acquaintance in London, that a young healthy child, well nursed, is at a year old, a most delicious, nourishing, and wholesome food, whether *stewed, roasted, baked,* or *boiled*; and I make no doubt that it will equally serve in a *fricassee*, or a *ragout*.

A Modest Proposal for Preventing the Children of Ireland from Being a Burden to their Parents or the Country (pamphlet, 1729), repr. in *The Prose Works of Jonathan Swift*, vol. 12 (ed. Herbert Davis, 1957)

39 Nor do they trust their tongue alone,
But speak a language of their own;
Can read a nod, a shrug, a look,
Far better than a printed book;
Convey a libel in a frown,
And wink a reputation down.

'The Journal of a Modern Lady', ll. 188–93 (1729), repr. in *Poems* (1735)

40 But you think ... that it is time for me to have done with the world, and so I would if I could get into a better before I was called into the best, and not die here in a rage, like a poisoned rat in a hole.

Letter to VISCOUNT BOLINGBROKE, 21 March 1729, publ. in *The Correspondence of Jonathan Swift*, vol. 3 (ed. Harold Williams, 1963)

41 In all distresses of our friends,
We first consult our private ends;
While nature, kindly bent to ease us,
Points out some circumstance to please us.

'Verses on the Death of Dr Swift', ll. 7–10 (written 1731, publ. 1739), repr. in *Jonathan Swift: The Complete Poems* (ed. Pat Rogers, 1983). Inspired by a maxim of La Rochefoucauld: see LA ROCHEFOUCAULD 1.

42 What poet would not grieve to see
His brethren write as well as he?
But rather than they should excel,
He'd wish his rivals all in Hell.

'Verses on the Death of Dr Swift', ll. 31–4, ibid.

43 Faith! he must make his stories shorter
Or change his comrades once a quarter.
'Verses on the Death of Dr Swift', ll. 95–6, ibid.

44 Yet, malice never was his aim;
He lashed the vice but spared the name;
No individual could resent,
Where thousands equally were meant.
His satire points at no defect,
But what all mortals may correct;
For he abhorred that senseless tribe,
Who call it humour when they jibe.
'Verses on the Death of Dr Swift', ll. 463–70, ibid.

45 All human race would fain be wits.
And millions miss, for one that hits.
'On Poetry: A Rhapsody', ll. 1–2 (1733), repr. in *Poems* (1735)

46 Then rising with Aurora's light,
The Muse invoked, sit down to write;
Blot out, correct, insert, refine,
Enlarge, diminish, interline.
'On Poetry: A Rhapsody', ll. 85–8, ibid.

47 Hobbes clearly proves, that every creature
Lives in a state of war by nature.
'On Poetry: A Rhapsody', ll. 335–6, ibid.

48 So, naturalists observe, a flea
Hath smaller fleas that on him prey;
And these have smaller still to bite 'em,
And so proceed *ad infinitum*.
Thus every poet, in his kind,
Is bit by him that comes behind.
'On Poetry: A Rhapsody', ll. 353–8, ibid.

49 O Grub Street! how do I bemoan thee,
Whose graceless children scorn to own thee!
Their filial piety forgot,
Deny their country like a Scot;
Though by their idiom and grimace,
They soon betray their native place.
Yet *thou* hast greater cause to be
Ashamed of them, than they of thee.
'On Poetry: A Rhapsody', ll. 373–80, ibid. SAMUEL JOHNSON, in his *Dictionary* (1755), defined 'Grub Street': 'Originally the name of a street in Moorfields in London, much inhabited by writers of small histories, dictionaries, and temporary poems, whence any mean production is called *grubstreet*.'

50 A footman may swear; but he cannot swear like a lord. He can swear as often: but can he swear with equal delicacy, propriety, and judgment?
Polite Conversation, Introduction (1738), repr. in *The Prose Works of Jonathan Swift*, vol. 4 (ed. Herbert Davis, 1957)

51 She wears her clothes, as if they were thrown on her with a pitchfork.
Lady Smart, ibid., Dialogue 1

52 He was a bold man that first eat an oyster.
Colonel Atwit, ibid., Dialogue 2

53 Better belly burst than good liquor be lost.
Neverout, ibid., Dialogue 2. Quoting a proverb first collected in James Howell's *Paroimiographia* (1659).

54 The best doctors in the world are Doctor Diet, Doctor Quiet, and Doctor Merryman.
Lord Smart, ibid., Dialogue 2. Repeating an adage first recorded by the physician William Bullein in *Government of Health*, Folio 50 (1558).

55 May you live all the days of your life.
The Colonel, ibid., Dialogue 2

56 The want of belief is a defect that ought to be concealed when it cannot be overcome.
Thoughts on Religion (1765), repr. in *The Prose Works of Jonathan Swift*, vol. 9 (ed. Herbert Davis, 1957)

57 I never saw, heard, nor read, that the clergy were beloved in any nation where Christianity was the religion of the country. Nothing can render them popular but some degree of persecution.
Thoughts on Religion, ibid.

58 It is impossible that anything so natural, so necessary, and so universal as death, should ever have been designed by Providence as an evil to mankind.
Thoughts on Religion, ibid.

59 *Ubi saeva indignatio ulterius cor lacerare nequit.* [Where fierce indignation can no longer tear his heart.]
Epitaph, publ. in *Jonathan Swift: A Critical Edition of the Major Works* (ed. Angus Ross and David Woolley, 1984). Composed by Swift in his will, the words were inscribed on his tomb in St Patrick's Cathedral, Dublin, where Swift had served as Dean for thirty years.

60 Good God! what a genius I had when I wrote that book!
Quoted in *The Works of Jonathan Swift, DD*, vol. 1 ('Memoir'), sect. 2 (ed. WALTER SCOTT, 1814). Speaking of his allegory, *The Tale of a Tub* (1704).

Algernon Charles Swinburne
(1837–1909)
English poet and critic

Emerging from the Pre-Raphaelite circle, he first had success with Atalanta in Calydon *(1865), a verse drama in classical*

Greek form. His defiance of Victorian values was expressed in Poems and Ballads (1866), which flouted conventional attitudes towards politics and religion but revealed his mastery of all poetic styles.

1 When the hounds of spring are on winter's
   traces,
The mother of months in meadow or plain
Fills the shadows and windy places
With lisp of leaves and ripples of rain.
Atalanta in Calydon, chorus, 'When the hounds of spring',
st. 1 (1865)

2 For winter's rains and ruins are over,
And all the seasons of snows and sins;
The days dividing lover and lover,
The light that loses, the night that wins;
And time remembered is grief forgotten,
And frosts are slain and flowers begotten,
And in green underwood and cover
Blossom by blossom the spring begins.
Ibid., chorus, 'When the hounds of spring', st. 4

3 Before the beginning of years
There came to the making of man
Time, with a gift of tears,
Grief, with a glass that ran;
Pleasure, with pain for leaven;
Summer, with flowers that fell;
Remembrance fallen from heaven,
And madness risen from hell;
Strength without hands to smite,
Love that endures for a breath,
Night, the shadow of light,
And life, the shadow of death.
Ibid., chorus, 'Before the beginning of years', st. 1

4 But from sharp words and wits men pluck no
   fruit,
And gathering thorns they shake the tree at root;
For words divide and rend;
But silence is most noble till the end.
Ibid., chorus, 'Who hath given man speech?'

5 Ah yet would God this flesh of mine might be
Where air might wash and long leaves cover me,
Where tides of grass break into foam of flowers,
Or where the wind's feet shine along the sea.
'Laus Veneris', st. 14, publ. in *Poems and Ballads* (first series,
1866)

6 There will no man do for your sake, I think,
What I would have done for the least word said.

I had wrung life dry for your lips to drink,
Broken it up for your daily bread.
'The Triumph of Time', st. 12, ibid.

7 I will go back to the great sweet mother,
Mother and lover of men, the sea.
I will go down to her, I and no other,
Close with her, kiss her and mix her with me.
'The Triumph of Time', st. 33, ibid.

8 I shall sleep, and move with the moving ships,
Change as the winds change, veer in the tide;
My lips will feast on the foam of thy lips,
I shall rise with thy rising, with thee subside.
'The Triumph of Time', st. 35, ibid.

9 Swallow, my sister, O sister swallow,
How can thine heart be full of the spring?
A thousand summers are over and dead.
What hast thou found in the spring to follow?
What hast thou found in thine heart to sing?
What wilt thou do when the summer is shed?
'Itylus', st. 1, ibid.

10 O sister, sister, thy first-begotten!
The hands that cling and the feet that follow,
The voice of the child's blood crying yet
Who hath remembered me? who hath forgotten?
Thou hast forgotten, O summer swallow,
But the world shall end when I forget.
'Itylus', st. 10, ibid.

11 I have lived long enough, having seen one thing,
   that love hath an end.
'Hymn to Proserpine', l. 1, ibid.

12 Yea, is not even Apollo, with hair and
   harpstring of gold,
A bitter God to follow, a beautiful God to behold?
'Hymn to Proserpine', ll. 7–8, ibid.

13 Thou hast conquered, O pale Galilean; the world
   has grown grey from thy breath;
We have drunken of things Lethean, and fed on
   the fullness of death.
'Hymn to Proserpine', ll. 35–6, ibid. Swinburne also used the
words 'Thou hast conquered, Galilean' in his poem 'The Last
Oracle'. See JULIAN THE APOSTATE 1.

14 Though the feet of thine high priests tread
   where thy lords and our forefathers trod,
Though these that were Gods are dead, and thou
   being dead art a God,
Though before thee the throned Cytherean be
   fallen, and hidden her head,

Yet thy kingdom shall pass, Galilean, thy dead
   shall go down to thee dead.
'Hymn to Proserpine', ll. 71–4, ibid.

15 So long I endure, no longer; and laugh not
   again, neither weep.
For there is no God found stronger than death;
   and death is a sleep.
'Hymn to Proserpine', ll. 109–10, ibid.

16 If love were what the rose is,
And I were like the leaf,
Our lives would grow together
In sad or singing weather,
Blown fields or flowerful closes,
Green pleasure or grey grief.
'A Match', st. 1, ibid.

17 Princes, and ye whom pleasure quickeneth,
Heed well this rhyme before your pleasure tire;
For life is sweet, but after life is death.
This is the end of every man's desire.
'A Ballad of Burdens' ('L'Envoy'), ibid.

18 We shift and bedeck and bedrape us,
Thou art noble and nude and antique.
'Dolores', st. 7, ibid.

19 Could you hurt me, sweet lips, though I hurt
   you?
Men touch them, and change in a trice
The lilies and languors of virtue
For the raptures and roses of vice.
'Dolores', st. 9, ibid.

20 There are sins it may be to discover,
There are deeds it may be to delight.
What new work wilt thou find for thy lover,
What new passions for daytime or night?
'Dolores', st. 10, ibid.

21 Ah beautiful passionate body
That never has ached with a heart!
'Dolores', st. 11, ibid.

22 The delight that consumes the desire,
The desire that outruns the delight.
'Dolores', st. 14, ibid.

23 O my sister, my spouse, and my mother,
Our Lady of Pain.
'Dolores', st. 19, ibid.

24 For the crown of our life as it closes
Is darkness, the fruit thereof dust;

No thorns go as deep as a rose's,
And love is more cruel than lust.
'Dolores', st. 20, ibid.

25 Time turns the old days to derision,
Our loves into corpses or wives;
And marriage and death and division
Make barren our lives.
'Dolores', st. 20, ibid.

26 Here, where the world is quiet;
Here, where all trouble seems
Dead winds' and spent waves' riot
In doubtful dreams of dreams.
'The Garden of Proserpine', st. 1, ibid.

27 I am tired of tears and laughter,
And men that laugh and weep;
Of what may come hereafter
For men that sow to reap:
I am weary of days and hours,
Blown buds of barren flowers,
Desires and dreams and powers
And everything but sleep.
'The Garden of Proserpine', st. 2, ibid.

28 Pale, beyond porch and portal,
Crowned with calm leaves, she stands
Who gathers all things mortal
With cold immortal hands.
'The Garden of Proserpine', st. 7, ibid.

29 We are not sure of sorrow,
And joy was never sure;
To-day will die to-morrow;
Time stoops to no man's lure.
'The Garden of Proserpine', st. 10, ibid.

30 From too much love of living,
From hope and fear set free,
We thank with brief thanksgiving
Whatever gods may be
That no life lives for ever;
That dead men rise up never;
That even the weariest river
Winds somewhere safe to sea.
'The Garden of Proserpine', st. 11, ibid.

31 Ah that such sweet things should be
   fleet,
Such fleet things sweet!
'Félise', st. 22, ibid.

32 And the best and the worst of this is
That neither is most to blame,

If you have forgotten my kisses
And I have forgotten your name.
'An Interlude', st. 14, ibid.

33 Even love, the beloved Republic, that feeds
upon freedom and lives.
'Hertha', st. 38, publ. in *Songs before Sunrise* (1871)

34 Glory to Man in the highest! for Man is the
master of things.
'Hymn of Man', ibid. Last line of poem.

35 Villon, our sad bad glad mad brother's name.
'A Ballad of François Villon', refrain, publ. in *Poems and
Ballads* (second series, 1878)

36 Body and spirit are twins: God only knows
which is which:
The soul squats down in the flesh, like a tinker
drunk in a ditch.
'The Higher Pantheism in a Nutshell', ll. 13–14, publ. in *The
Heptalogia* (1880)

37 God, whom we see not, is: and God, who is not,
we see:
Fiddle, we know, is diddle: and diddle, we take it, is
dee.
'The Higher Pantheism in a Nutshell', ll. 25–6, ibid.

38 Where might is, the right is:
Long purses make strong swords.
Let weakness learn meekness:
God save the House of Lords!
'A Word for the Country', st. 1, publ. in *A Midsummer Holiday
and Other Poems* (1884)

39 Not with dreams, but with blood and with iron,
Shall a nation be moulded to last.
'A Word for the Country', st. 13, ibid.

James Joseph Sylvester
(1814–97)
English mathematician and poet

An algebraist, he founded the American Journal of Mathematics *(1878) and with Arthur Cayley he devised invariant
theory. He is recognized for his work on matrices, determinants
and the theory of numbers, and published* Laws of Verse *in
1870.*

1 Mathematics is not a book confined within a cover
and bound between brazen clasps, whose contents
it needs only patience to ransack; it is not a mine,
whose treasures may take long to reduce into possession, but which fill only a limited number of
veins and lodes; it is not a soil, whose fertility can
be exhausted by the yield of successive harvests; it

is not a continent or an ocean, whose area can be
mapped out and its contour defined: it is limitless
as that space which it finds too narrow for its aspirations; its possibilities are as infinite as the worlds
which are forever crowding in and multiplying
upon the astronomer's gaze.
Commemoration Day Address at Johns Hopkins University,
27 February 1877 (publ. 1877)

Quintus Aurelius Symmachus
(c. 345–c. 402)
Roman statesman

*He served as senator and was Proconsul of Africa (373), Prefect
of Rome (384) and consul (391). He eloquently defended the
pagan religion against the growing influence of Christianity.*

1 And so we ask for peace for the gods of our fathers,
for the gods of our native land. It is reasonable
that whatever each of us worships is really to be
considered one and the same. We gaze up at the
same stars, the sky covers us all, the same universe
compasses us. What does it matter what practical
systems we adopt in our search for the truth? Not
by one avenue only can we arrive at so tremendous
a secret.
Letter to the Christian Emperor Valentinian II, written 384,
publ. in *Roman Letters: History from a Personal Point of View*,
ch. 10 (1991) by Finley Hooper and Matthew Schwartz. The
plea for the continuation of pagan ceremonies was defeated,
largely due to the opposition of St Ambrose.

John Millington Synge
(1871–1909)
Irish dramatist

His tragedies depicted the gritty reality of rural life, as in Riders
to the Storm *(1904). With* W. B. YEATS *and* LADY GREGORY, *he
co-founded the Abbey Theatre, where his comedy* The Playboy
of the Western World *(1907) and other works of the Irish
Renaissance were performed.*

1 In the middle classes the gifted son of a family is
always the poorest – usually a writer or artist with
no sense for speculation – and in a family of peasants, where the average comfort is just over penury,
the gifted son sinks also, and is soon a tramp on the
roadside.
'The Vagrants of Wicklow', written 1901–2, publ. in *Collected
Works of J. M. Synge*, vol. 2 (ed. Robin Skelton, 1982)

2 The grief of the keen ... seems to contain the
whole passionate rage that lurks somewhere in
every native of the island. In this cry of pain the

inner consciousness of the people seems to lay itself bare for an instant, and to reveal the mood of beings who feel their isolation in the face of a universe that wars on them with winds and seas.

The Aran Islands, pt 1 (1907). Of the burial of an inhabitant of Inishmaan, one of the Aran Islands off Ireland's western coast.

3 In a good play every speech should be as fully flavoured as a nut or apple.

The Playboy of the Western World, Introduction (1907)

4 Oh my grief, I've lost him surely. I've lost the only Playboy of the Western World.

Ibid., Act 3. Spoken by Pegeen Mike, in the closing words of the play.

Thomas Szasz
(b. 1920)
Hungarian-born US psychiatrist

His arguments that mental illness does not exist, that psychiatry is 'neither a science nor a healing art' and that psychiatrists act as social police are set out in The Myth of Mental Illness *(1961) and* The Manufacture of Madness *(1971).*

1 In the past, men created witches; now they create mental patients.

The Manufacture of Madness, Introduction (1971). 'Institutional psychiatry is a continuation of the Inquisition,' Szasz wrote. 'All that has really changed is the vocabulary and the social style.'

2 Permissiveness is the principle of treating children as if they were adults; and the tactic of making sure they never reach that stage.

The Second Sin, 'Social Relations' (1973)

3 A child becomes an adult when he realizes that he has a right not only to be right but also to be wrong.

Ibid., 'Childhood'

4 A teacher should have maximal authority, and minimal power.

Ibid., 'Education'

5 Happiness is an imaginary condition, formerly often attributed by the living to the dead, now usually attributed by adults to children, and by children to adults.

Ibid., 'Emotions'

6 The proverb warns that 'You should not bite the hand that feeds you.' But maybe you should, if it prevents you from feeding yourself.

Ibid., 'Control and Self-control'

7 The stupid neither forgive nor forget; the naïve forgive and forget; the wise forgive but do not forget.

Ibid., 'Personal Conduct'

8 Adulthood is the ever-shrinking period between childhood and old age. It is the apparent aim of modern industrial societies to reduce this period to a minimum.

Ibid., 'Social Relations'

9 Narcissist: psychoanalytic term for the person who loves himself more than his analyst; considered to be the manifestation of a dire mental disease whose successful treatment depends on the patient learning to love the analyst more and himself less.

Ibid., 'Psychoanalysis'

10 If you talk to God, you are praying; if God talks to you, you have schizophrenia. If the dead talk to you, you are a spiritualist; if God talks to you, you are a schizophrenic.

Ibid., 'Schizophrenia'

11 There is no psychology; there is only biography and autobiography.

Ibid., 'Psychology'

T

Tacitus
(c. 55–c. 120)
Roman historian

Cornelius Tacitus. His main works on the history of the Roman Empire only partially survive: the Annals *cover the years 14–68 and the* Histories *the years 69–96. He married the daughter of Agricola, the conqueror of Britain.*

1 Noble character is best appreciated in those ages in which it can most readily develop.
Agricola, sect. 1

2 Who the first inhabitants of Britain were, whether natives or immigrants, remains obscure; one must remember we are dealing with barbarians.
Ibid., sect. 11

3 We have enjoyed the impressiveness of the unknown. But today the boundary of Britain is exposed.
Ibid., sect. 30. Spoken by the British chief Calgacus.

4 Robbery, butchery, rapine, the liars call empire; they create a desolation and call it peace.
Ibid., sect. 30. Spoken by Calgacus.

5 It is a sin peculiar to man to hate his victim.
Ibid., sect. 42. See SENECA 15.

6 Even war is preferable to a shameful peace.
Annals, bk 3, ch. 44

7 The arbiter of taste.
Ibid., bk 15, ch. 18. Referring to the satirist PETRONIUS.

8 A shocking crime was committed on the unscrupulous initiative of few individuals, with the blessing of more, and amid the passive acquiescence of all.
The Histories, bk 1, sect. 28. Referring to the assassination of Emperor Galba.

9 No one would have doubted his ability to reign had he never been emperor.
Ibid., bk 1, sect. 49. Of Emperor Galba.

10 The principal office of history I take to be this: to prevent virtuous actions from being forgotten, and that evil words and deeds should fear an infamous reputation with posterity.
Ibid., bk 3, sect. 6

11 Valour is of no service, chance rules all, and the bravest often fall by the hands of cowards.
Ibid., bk 4, sect. 29

12 *Experientia docuit.*
[Experience teaches.]
Ibid., bk 5, sect. 6. Literally 'Experience has taught'.

William Taft
(1857–1930)
US politician and president

As Republican President (1909–13), he initially continued the policies of his mentor THEODORE ROOSEVELT, *but his conservatism soon alienated the progressives in the party. The Republican vote was split in the 1912 election, which both men lost to* WOODROW WILSON.

1 Next to the right of liberty, the right of property is the most important individual right guaranteed by the Constitution and the one which, united with that of personal liberty, has contributed more to the growth of civilization than any other institution established by the human race.
Popular Government, ch. 3 (1913)

2 Socialism proposes no adequate substitute for the motive of enlightened selfishness that to-day is at the basis of all human labor and effort, enterprise and new activity.
Ibid., ch. 3

Charles Maurice de Talleyrand
(1754–1838)
French statesman

Prince of Benevento from 1806. He was instrumental in bringing NAPOLEON *to power and was Foreign Minister 1799–1807. He later led the anti-Napoleonic faction and became Foreign Minister again under* LOUIS XVIII.

1 *Voilà le commencement de la fin.*
[It is the beginning of the end.]
Quoted in M. de Talleyrand, ch. 3 (1870) by Charles-Augustin Sainte-Beuve. Referring to Napoleon's Pyrrhic victory at Borodino, 1812. See WINSTON CHURCHILL 32.

2 They have learnt nothing and forgotten nothing.
Attributed, referring to the Bourbons at the restoration of LOUIS XVIII in spring 1814

3 Whoever has not lived in the years around 1789 does not know what pleasure life can give.
Quoted in *Mémoires*, vol. 1, ch. 6 (1858) by François Guizot

4 She is such a good friend that she would throw

all her acquaintances into the water for the pleasure of fishing them out again.

Quoted in *Talleyrand*, ch. 3 (1932) by Duff Cooper. Remark made to NAPOLEON referring to MADAME DE STAËL.

Tao Te Ching (Daode jing)
(6th century BC)

Chinese philosophic book. The primary Taoist text, it is traditionally ascribed to the sage Lao-tzu (Laozi), said to have lived in about the 6th century BC, but it was probably in fact the work of many different people and compiled c. 300 BC.

1 The Way that can be spoken of
Is not the constant way;
The name that can be named
Is not the constant name.
The nameless was the beginning of heaven and
    earth;
The named was the mother of the myriad
    creatures.
Tao Te Ching, ch. 1 (transl. D. C. Lau, 1963)

2 Heaven and earth are ruthless, and treat the
    myriad creatures as straw dogs;
the sage is ruthless, and treats the people as straw
    dogs.
Ibid., ch. 5

3 The best of all rulers is but a shadowy presence
    to his subjects.
Next comes the ruler they love and praise;
Next comes one they fear;
Next comes one with whom they take liberties.
When there is not enough faith, there is lack of
    good faith.
Hesitant, he does not utter words lightly.
When his task is accomplished and his work done
The people all say 'It happened to us naturally.'
Ibid., ch. 17

4 Exterminate learning and there will no longer be
    worries.
Exterminate the sage, discard the wise,
And the people will benefit a hundredfold;
Exterminate benevolence, discard rectitude,
And the people will again be filial;
Exterminate ingenuity, discard profit,
And there will be no more thieves and bandits.
Ibid., ch. 19

5 Exhibit the unadorned and embrace the
    uncarved block,

Have little thought of self and as few desires as
    possible.
Ibid., ch. 19

6 He who tip-toes cannot stand; he who strides
    cannot walk.
Ibid., ch. 24

7 He who knows others is clever;
He who knows himself has discernment.
Ibid., ch. 33

8 Turning back is how the way moves;
Weakness is the means the way employs.
The myriad creatures in the world are born from
Something, and Something from Nothing.
Ibid., ch. 40

9 Without stirring abroad,
One can know the whole world;
Without looking out of the window
One can see the way of heaven.
The further one goes
The less one knows.
Ibid., ch. 47

10 One who knows does not speak; one who
    speaks does not know.
Ibid., ch. 56

11 Let your wheels move only along old ruts.
This is known as mysterious sameness.
Ibid., ch. 56

12 The better known the laws and edicts
The more thieves and robbers there are.
Ibid., ch. 57

13 A tree that can fill the span of a man's arms
Grows from a downy tip;
A terrace nine storeys high
Rises from hodfuls of earth;
A journey of a thousand miles
Starts from beneath one's feet.
Ibid., ch. 64

14 To know yet to think that one does not know is
    best;
Not to know yet to think that one knows will lead
    to difficulty.
Ibid., ch. 71

15 The net of heaven is cast wide.
Though the mesh is not fine, yet nothing ever slips
    through.
Ibid., ch. 73

16 In the world there is nothing more submissive and weak than water.
Yet for attacking that which is hard and strong nothing can surpass it.
Ibid., ch. 78

17 Truthful words are not beautiful;
Beautiful words are not truthful.
Good words are not persuasive;
Persuasive words are not good.
Ibid., ch. 81

18 The sage does not hoard.
Having bestowed all he has on others, he has yet more;
Having given all he has to others, he is richer still.
Ibid., ch. 81

Quentin Tarantino
(b. 1963)
US film-maker

After a brief acting career, he made his debut as a director with Reservoir Dogs *(1992), controversial for its violence and savage humour. Other films include* Pulp Fiction *(1994), and he has also written screenplays.*

1 Let's go to work.
Reservoir Dogs (film, 1992, written and directed by Quentin Tarantino). Spoken by Joe Cabot (Lawrence Tierney) and featured in the film's publicity.

2 I'm gonna git medieval on your ass.
Pulp Fiction (film, 1994), written and directed by Quentin Tarantino. Spoken by Marsellus Wallace (Ving Rhames) to Zed as he prepares to sodomize him.

3 Zed's dead, baby, Zed's dead.
Butch Coolidge (Bruce Willis), ibid.

4 Great artists steal, they don't do homages.
Interview in *Empire* November 1994

Booth Tarkington
(1869–1946)
US novelist and playwright

He was a prolific and popular writer on childhood and adolescence as in Penrod *(1914),* Seventeen *(1917) and numerous plays, but received most plaudits for such novels as* The Magnificent Ambersons *(1918).*

1 There are two things that will be believed of any man whatsoever, and one of them is that he has taken to drink.
Penrod, ch. 10 (1914)

Andrey Tarkovsky
(1932–86)
Russian film-maker

His films combine an epic style and spirituality, most notably in Andrei Rublev *(1966), which was initially banned in the USSR, the science fiction* Solaris *(1972), and* The Sacrifice *(1986), made two years after he had defected to Italy.*

1 Of course life has no point. If it had man would not be free, he'd become a slave to that point and his life would be governed by completely new criteria: the criteria of slavery.
Journal entry, 5 September 1970, publ. in *Time Within Time: The Diaries 1970–1986* (1989)

2 A person fulfils his duty to society in the name of an idea, always doing violence to someone or something.
Journal entry, 22 January 1981, ibid.

Nahum Tate
(1652–1715)
English poet and playwright

Poet Laureate from 1692, he wrote popular adaptations of SHAKESPEARE, JOHN FLETCHER *and* JOHN WEBSTER, *and co-wrote a metrical version of the psalms (1696).*

1 When I am laid in earth my wrongs create.
No trouble in thy breast,
Remember me, but ah! forget my fate.
Dido and Aeneas, Act 3 (opera, 1689). Known as 'Dido's Lament'. The music was composed by Henry Purcell.

2 Through all the changing scenes of life,
In trouble and in joy,
The praises of my God shall still
My heart and tongue employ.
New Version of the Psalms, Psalm 34 (1696, written with Nicholas Brady)

3 As pants the hart for cooling streams
When heated in the chase.
Ibid., Psalm 42. See BIBLE, OLD TESTAMENT: PSALMS 53.

4 While shepherds watched their flocks by night,
All seated on the ground,
The angel of the Lord came down,
And glory shone around.
Psalter, 'While Shepherds Watched' (1702)

A. J. Taylor
(1906–90)
British historian

Alan John Percivale Taylor. Likened to THOMAS MACAULAY *for his breadth and accessibility, he was an authority on the Habsburg monarchy and* BISMARCK. *His major works include* The Struggle for Mastery in Europe, 1848–1918 *(1954) and* The Origins of the Second World War *(1961).*

1 There is nothing more agreeable in life than to make peace with the Establishment – and nothing more corrupting.
New Statesman 29 August 1953

2 The crusade against Communism was even more imaginary than the spectre of Communism.
The Origins of the Second World War, ch. 2 (1961)

3 Human blunders ... usually do more to shape history than human wickedness.
Ibid., ch. 10

4 The First World War had begun – imposed on the statesmen of Europe by railway timetables. It was an unexpected climax to the railway age.
The First World War, ch. 1 (1963)

5 Perfect soldier, perfect gentleman ... never gave offence to anyone not even the enemy.
Letter, 16 March 1973, publ. in *Letters to Eva* (ed. Eva Haraszti Taylor, 1991). Of Field Marshal Alexander.

6 In my opinion, most of the great men of the past were only there for the beer – the wealth, prestige and grandeur that went with the power.
Quoted in *Voices 1870–1914*, Introduction (1984) by Peter Vansittart. See ADVERTISING SLOGANS 13.

Ann Taylor
(1782–1866)

Jane Taylor
(1783–1824)
English children's authors

Together they wrote pious and cautionary verse and hymns for children. See NURSERY RHYMES 41.

1 Who ran to help me when I fell,
And would some pretty story tell,
Or kiss the place to make it well?
My mother.
'My Mother', st. 6, publ. in *Original Poems for Infant Minds* (1804)

2 So, while their bodies moulder here
Their souls with God himself shall dwell, –
But always recollect, my dear,
That wicked people go to hell.
'About Dying', attributed

Bayard Taylor
(1825–75)
US poet, journalist and translator

Known in his day for his lively travel narratives, he is now principally remembered for his translation of GOETHE's Faust *(1870–1).*

1 Till the sun grows cold,
And the stars are old,
And the leaves of the Judgment Book unfold.
'Bedouin Song', refrain, written 1853, publ. in *The Poetical Works of Bayard Taylor* (1907)

Bert Leston Taylor
(1866–1921)
US humorist and columnist

From 1900 he worked for the Chicago Tribune, *where his column 'A Line-o'-Type or Two' appeared for twenty years. His books include* A Line-O-Verse Or Two *(1911) and* The So-Called Human Race *(1922).*

1 A bore is a man who, when you ask him how he is, tells you.
The So-Called Human Race (1922)

2 All we can get out of a Shaw play is two hours and a half of mental exhilaration. We are, inscrutably, denied the pleasure of wondering what Shaw means, or whether he is sincere.
ibid.

(Sir) Henry Taylor
(1800–86)
English author

He wrote poetry and articles, but was famous for the play Philip von Artevelde *(1834) and* The Statesman *(1836), which contained maxims and practical advice from his career in the Civil Service.*

1 Shy and unready men are great betrayers of secrets; for there are few wants more urgent for the moment than the want of something to say.
The Statesman, ch. 18 (1836)

2 The hope, and not the fact, of advancement, is the spur to industry.
Ibid., ch. 23

Jeremy Taylor
(1613–67)
English churchman and devotional writer

Called the 'Shakespeare and Spenser of the pulpit', he was held the leading Anglican devotional writer of his times. His works include Holy Living *(1650) and* Holy Dying *(1651) and* Twenty-five Sermons *(1653). He was Bishop of Down and Connor from 1660.*

1 Every schoolboy knows it.
The Real Presence in the Blessed Sacrament, sect. 5 (1654). What 'every schoolboy knows' is that 'This thing . . . that can be understood and not expressed, may take a neuter gender.'

2 God hath prepared . . . a little coronet or special reward (extraordinary and beside the great crown of all faithful souls) for those who have not defiled themselves with women.
The Rule and Exercises of Holy Living, ch. 2, sect. 3 (1650)

3 Curiosity is the direct incontinency of the spirit.
Ibid., ch. 2, sect. 5

4 As our life is very short, so it is very miserable, and therefore it is well it is short.
The Rule and Exercises of Holy Dying, ch. 1, sect. 4 (1651)

5 Habits are the daughters of action, but then they nurse their mother, and produce daughters after her image, but far more beautiful and prosperous.
Twenty-Five Sermons Preached at Golden Grove, Sermon 14 ('Of Lukewarmness and Zeal') (1651)

6 The union of hands and hearts.
Ibid., Sermon 17 ('The Marriage Ring', pt 1)

7 A celibate, like the fly in the heart of an apple, dwells in a perpetual sweetness, but sits alone, and is confined and dies in singularity.
Ibid., Sermon 17

8 He that loves not his wife and children feeds a lionness at home, and broods a nest of sorrows.
Ibid., Sermon 18 ('The Marriage Ring', pt 2)

Norman Tebbit
(b. 1931)
British politician

Baron Tebbit of Chingford. A loyal Thatcherite, labelled 'the Chingford skinhead' for his confrontational style. he held various Cabinet posts and was Party Chairman 1985–7. He was the architect of anti-trade union and privatization legislation. See MICHAEL FOOT 1.

1 He didn't riot. He got on his bike and looked for work.
Speech to Conservative Party Conference, Blackpool, 15 October 1981, quoted in the *Daily Telegraph* 16 October 1981. Tebbit's speech, which contrasted his unemployed father's self-help approach during the Depression with the attitude of rioters in Britain, was given a rousing ovation by the conference but drew criticism elsewhere in the country at a time when unemployment stood at three million.

2 The word 'conservative' is used by the BBC as a portmanteau word of abuse for anyone whose views differ from the insufferable, smug, sanctimonious, naive, guilt-ridden, wet, pink orthodoxy of that sunset home of the third-rate minds of that third-rate decade, the nineteen-sixties.
Quoted in the *Independent* 24 February 1990. In his memoirs, Tebbit lambasted the BBC for its coverage of the Falklands War: 'For me the British Broadcasting Corporation might better called itself the Stateless Persons Broadcasting Corporation for it certainly did not reflect the mood of the British people who finance it' (ch. 8).

3 The cricket test – which side do they cheer for? . . . Are you still looking back to where you came from or where are you?
Quoted in the *Daily Telegraph* 20 April 1990

4 Parliament must not be told a direct untruth, but it's quite possible to allow them to mislead themselves.
Quoted in the *Observer* 17 March 1991

Alfred Lord Tennyson
(1809–92)
English poet

First Baron Tennyson of Aldworth and Freshwater. The major poet of Victorian Britain, he reflected the changing religious and scientific attitudes of the times. The rich imagery and metrical variety of epic verse, such as In Memoriam *(1850) and* Idylls of the King *(1859–72), brought him great popularity.* GERARD MANLEY HOPKINS *called his poetry 'chryselephantine'.*

1 Airy, fairy Lilian.
'Lilian', publ. in *Poems, Chiefly Lyrical* (1830)

2 Weeded and worn the ancient thatch
Upon the lonely moated grange.
She only said, 'My life is dreary,
He cometh not,' she said;

She said, 'I am aweary, aweary,
I would that I were dead!'
'Mariana', st. 1, ibid.

3 Vex not thou the poet's mind
With thy shallow wit:
Vex not thou the poet's mind;
For thou canst not fathom it.
'The Poet's Mind', ll. 1–4, ibid.

4 Below the thunders of the upper deep;
Far, far beneath in the abysmal sea,
His ancient, dreamless, uninvaded sleep
The Kraken sleepeth.
'The Kraken', ll. 1–4, ibid.

5 Love lieth deep: Love dwells not in lip-depths.
'The Lover's Tale', l. 456, written 1832, publ. 1879, repr. in *The Poems of Tennyson*, vol. 1 (ed. Christopher Ricks, 1969)

6 On either side the river lie
Long fields of barley and of rye,
That clothe the wold and meet the sky;
And through the field the road runs by
To many-towered Camelot.
'The Lady of Shalott', pt 1, st. 1, publ. in *Poems* (1832, rev. 1842)

7 Willows whiten, aspens quiver,
Little breezes dusk and shiver.
'The Lady of Shalott', pt 1, st. 2, ibid.

8 Only reapers, reaping early
In among the bearded barley,
Hear a song that echoes cheerly
From the river winding clearly,
Down to towered Camelot.
'The Lady of Shalott', pt 1, st. 4, ibid.

9 Or when the moon was overhead,
Came two young lovers lately wed;
'I am half sick of shadows,' said
The Lady of Shalott.
'The Lady of Shalott', pt 2, st. 4, ibid.

10 A bow-shot from her bower-eaves,
He rode between the barley-sheaves,
The sun came dazzling through the leaves,
And flamed upon the brazen greaves
Of bold Sir Lancelot.
A red-cross knight for ever kneeled
To a lady in his shield,
That sparkled on the yellow field,
Beside remote Shalott.
'The Lady of Shalott', pt 3, st. 1, ibid.

11 All in the blue unclouded weather
Thick-jewelled shone the saddle-leather,
The helmet and the helmet-feather
Burned like one burning flame together,
As he rode down to Camelot.
'The Lady of Shalott', pt 3, st. 3, ll. 91–5, ibid.

12 'Tirra lirra,' by the river
Sang Sir Lancelot.
'The Lady of Shalott', pt 3, st. 4, ibid.

13 She left the web, she left the loom,
She made three paces through the room,
She saw the water-lily bloom,
She saw the helmet and the plume,
She looked down to Camelot.
Out flew the web and floated wide;
The mirror cracked from side to side;
'The curse is come upon me,' cried
The Lady of Shalott.
'The Lady of Shalott', pt 3, st. 5, ibid. The Lady of Shalott defies the injunction not to gaze upon the world unless through a mirror, as Lancelot passes.

14 But Lancelot mused a little space:
He said 'She has a lovely face;
God in his mercy lend her grace,
The Lady of Shalott.'
'The Lady of Shalott', pt 4, st. 6, ibid. Last lines of the poem.

15 Dead sounds at night come from the inmost
hills,
Like footsteps upon wool.
'Oenone', ll. 245–6, ibid.

16 I built my soul a lordly pleasure-house,
Wherein at ease for aye to dwell.
'The Palace of Art', ibid. Opening lines of poem.

17 You must wake and call me early, call me early,
mother dear;
Tomorrow 'ill be the happiest time of all the glad
New-year;
Of all the glad New-year, mother, the maddest
merriest day;
For I'm to be Queen o' the May, mother, I'm to be
Queen o' the May.
'The May Queen', st. 1, ibid.

18 In the afternoon they came unto a land
In which it seemed always afternoon.
'The Lotos-Eaters', st. 1, ibid.

19 Music that gentlier on the spirit lies,
Than tired eyelids upon tired eyes.
'The Lotos-Eaters', Choric Song, st. 1, ibid.

20 Death is the end of life; ah, why
Should life all labour be?
'The Lotos-Eaters', Choric Song, st. 4, ibid.

21 Let us alone. Time driveth onward fast,
And in a little while our lips are dumb.
Let us alone. What is it that will last?
All things are taken from us, and become
Portions and parcels of the dreadful Past.
'The Lotos-Eaters', Choric Song, st. 4, ibid.

22 Surely, surely, slumber is more sweet than toil,
    the shore
Than labour in the deep mid-ocean, wind and
    wave and oar;
Oh rest ye, brother mariners, we will not wander
    more.
'The Lotos-Eaters', Choric Song, st. 8, ibid.

23 A daughter of the gods, divinely tall,
And most divinely fair.
'A Dream of Fair Women', ll. 87–8, ibid.

24 Howe'er it be, it seems to me,
'Tis only noble to be good.
Kind hearts are more than coronets,
And simple faith than Norman blood.
'Lady Clara Vere de Vere', st. 7, publ. in *Poems* (1842). *Kind
Hearts and Coronets* was an Ealing Studios film of 1949.

25 Half light, half shade,
She stood, a sight to make an old man young.
'The Gardener's Daughter', ll. 139–40, written 1833–4, ibid.

26 It little profits that an idle king,
By this still hearth, among these barren crags,
Matched with an agèd wife, I mete and dole
Unequal laws unto a savage race.
'Ulysses', ll. 1–4, ibid.

27 I cannot rest from travel. I will drink
Life to the lees.
'Ulysses', ll. 6–7, ibid.

28 Much have I seen and known; cities of men
And manners, climates, councils, governments,
Myself not least, but honoured of them all;
And drunk delight of battle with my peers,
Far on the ringing plains of windy Troy.
I am a part of all that I have met;
Yet all experience is an arch wherethrough
Gleams that untravelled world, whose margin
    fades
For ever and for ever when I move.
'Ulysses', ll. 13–21, ibid.

29 How dull it is to pause, to make an end,
To rust unburnished, not to shine in use!
As though to breathe were life.
'Ulysses', ll. 22–4, ibid.

30 This grey spirit yearning in desire
To follow knowledge like a sinking star,
Beyond the utmost bound of human thought.
'Ulysses', ll. 30–2, ibid.

31 This is my son, mine own Telemachus.
'Ulysses', l. 33, ibid.

32 Death closes all: but something ere the end,
Some work of noble note, may yet be done,
Not unbecoming men that strove with gods.
'Ulysses', ll. 51–3, ibid.

33 The deep
Moans round with many voices. Come, my friends,
'Tis not too late to seek a newer world.
Push off, and sitting well in order smite
The sounding furrows; for my purpose holds
To sail beyond the sunset, and the baths
Of all the western stars, until I die.
It may be that the gulfs will wash us down:
It may be we shall touch the Happy Isles,
And see the great Achilles.
'Ulysses', ll. 55–64, ibid.

34 One equal temper of heroic hearts,
Made weak by time and fate, but strong in will
To strive, to seek, to find, and not to yield.
'Ulysses', ll. 68–70, ibid.

35 In the spring a livelier iris changes on the
    burnished dove;
In the spring a young man's fancy lightly turns to
    thoughts of love.
'Locksley Hall', ll. 19–20, ibid.

36 He will hold thee, when his passion shall have
    spent its novel force,
Something better than his dog, a little dearer than
    his horse.
'Locksley Hall', ll. 49–50, ibid.

37 This is truth the poet sings,
That a sorrow's crown of sorrow is remembering
    happier things.
'Locksley Hall', ll. 75–6, ibid. See also BOETHIUS 1, DANTE 11.

38 With a little hoard of maxims preaching down
    a daughter's heart.
'Locksley Hall', l. 94, ibid.

39 But the jingling of the guinea helps the hurt
   that Honour feels.
'Locksley Hall', l. 105, ibid.

40 For I dipped into the future, far as human eye
   could see,
Saw the vision of the world, and all the wonder
   that would be;
Saw the heavens fill with commerce, argosies of
   magic sails,
Pilots of the purple twilight, dropping down with
   costly bales;
Heard the heavens fill with shouting, and there
   rained a ghastly dew
From the nations' airy navies grappling in the
   central blue.
'Locksley Hall', ll. 119–24, ibid.

41 Till the war-drum throbbed no longer, and the
   battle-flags were furled
In the Parliament of man, the Federation of the
   world.
'Locksley Hall', ll. 127–8, ibid.

42 Science moves, but slowly slowly, creeping on
   from point to point.
'Locksley Hall', l. 134, ibid.

43 Yet I doubt not through the ages one increasing
   purpose runs,
And the thoughts of men are widened with the
   process of the suns.
'Locksley Hall', ll. 137–8, ibid.

44 Knowledge comes, but wisdom lingers, and I
   linger on the shore,
And the individual withers, and the world is more
   and more.
Knowledge comes, but wisdom lingers, and he
   bears a laden breast,
Full of sad experience, moving toward the stillness
   of his rest.
'Locksley Hall', ll. 141–4, ibid.

45 I will take some savage woman, she shall rear
   my dusky race.
'Locksley Hall', l. 168, ibid.

46 I the heir of all the ages, in the foremost files of
   time.
'Locksley Hall', l. 178, ibid.

47 Let the great world spin for ever down the
   ringing grooves of change.
'Locksley Hall', l. 182, ibid.

48 Better fifty years of Europe than a cycle of
   Cathay.
'Locksley Hall', l. 184, ibid.

49 A still small voice spake unto me,
'Thou art so full of misery,
Were it not better not to be?'
'The Two Voices', ll. 1–3, ibid.

50 Then to the still small voice I said;
'Let me not cast in endless shade
What is so wonderfully made.'
'The Two Voices', ll. 4–6, ibid.

51 I know that age to age succeeds,
Blowing a noise of tongues and deeds,
A dust of systems and of creeds.
'The Two Voices', ll. 205–7, ibid.

52 No life that breathes with human breath
Has ever truly longed for death.
'The Two Voices', ll. 395–6, ibid.

53 My strength is as the strength of ten,
Because my heart is pure.
'Sir Galahad', st. 1, ibid.

54 I grow in worth, and wit, and sense,
Unboding critic-pen,
Or that eternal want of pence,
Which vexes public men.
'Will Waterproof's Lyrical Monologue', st. 6, ibid.

55 And others' follies teach us not,
Nor much their wisdom teaches;
And most, of sterling worth, is what
Our own experience preaches.
'Will Waterproof's Lyrical Monologue', st. 22, ibid.

56 Every moment dies a man,
Every moment one is born.
'The Vision of Sin', sect. 4, ibid.

57 A little grain of conscience made him sour.
'The Vision of Sin', sect. 5, ibid.

58 Break, break, break,
On thy cold grey stones, O Sea!
And I would that my tongue could utter
The thoughts that arise in me.
'Break, Break, Break', st. 1, ibid.

59 And the stately ships go on
To their haven under the hill;
But O for the touch of a vanished hand,
And the sound of a voice that is still!
'Break, Break, Break', st. 3, ibid.

60 But the tender grace of a day that is dead
Will never come back to me.
'Break, Break, Break', st. 4, ibid.

61 And the nightingale thought, 'I have sung many
   songs,
But never a one so gay,
For he sings of what the world will be
When the years have died away.'
'The Poet's Song', st. 2, ibid.

62 Shall eagles not be eagles? wrens be wrens?
If all the world were falcons, what of that?
The wonder of the eagle were the less,
But he not less the eagle.
'The Golden Year', ll. 37–40, publ. in *Poems* (1846)

63 But we grow old. Ah! When shall all men's good
Be each man's rule, and universal peace
Lie like a shaft of light across the land,
And like a lane of beams athwart the sea
Through all the circle of the golden year?
'The Golden Year', ll. 47–51, ibid.

64 And blessings on the falling out
That all the more endears,
When we fall out with those we love
And kiss again with tears!
'The Princess', pt 2, song, ll. 6–9, publ. in *The Princess: A Medley* (1847, rev. 1850)

65 This barren verbiage current among men,
Light coin, the tinsel clink of compliment.
'The Princess', pt 2, ll. 40–1, ibid.

66 And quoted odes, and jewels five-words-long
That on the stretched forefinger of all Time
Sparkle for ever.
'The Princess', pt 2, ll. 355–7, ibid.

67 Sweet and low, sweet and low,
Wind of the western sea,
Low, low, breathe and blow,
Wind of the western sea!
Over the rolling waters go,
Come from the dying moon, and blow,
Blow him again to me;
While my little one, while my pretty one, sleeps.
'The Princess', pt 3, song, ll. 1–8, ibid.

68 The splendour falls on castle walls
And snowy summits old in story:
The long light shakes across the lakes,
And the wild cataract leaps in glory.

Blow, bugle, blow, set the wild echoes flying,
Blow, bugle; answer, echoes, dying, dying, dying.
'The Princess', pt 4, song, ll. 1–6, ibid.

69 O sweet and far from cliff and scar
The horns of Elfland faintly blowing!
'The Princess', pt 4, song, ll. 9–10, ibid.

70 Tears, idle tears, I know not what they mean,
Tears from the depth of some divine despair
Rise in the heart, and gather to the eyes,
In looking on the happy autumn-fields,
And thinking of the days that are no more.
'The Princess', pt 4, song, ll. 21–5, ibid.

71 Dear as remembered kisses after death,
And sweet as those by hopeless fancy feigned
On lips that are for others; deep as love,
Deep as first love, and wild with all regret;
O Death in Life, the days that are no more.
'The Princess', pt 4, song, ll. 36–40, ibid.

72 O Swallow, Swallow, flying, flying South,
Fly to her, and fall upon her gilded eaves,
And tell her, tell her, what I tell to thee.
'The Princess', pt 4, song, ll. 75–7, ibid.

73 Man is the hunter; woman is his game:
The sleek and shining creatures of the chase,
We hunt them for the beauty of their skins;
They love us for it, and we ride them down.
'The Princess', pt 5, ll. 147–50, ibid.

74 Home they brought her warrior dead.
She nor swooned, nor uttered cry:
All her maidens, watching said,
'She must weep or she will die.'
'The Princess', pt 6, song, ll. 1–4, ibid.

75 Ask me no more: what answer should I give?
I love not hollow cheek or faded eye:
Yet, O my friend, I will not have thee die!
Ask me no more, lest I should bid thee live.
'The Princess', pt 7, song, ll. 6–9, ibid.

76 Now sleeps the crimson petal, now the white;
Nor waves the cypress in the palace walk;
Nor winks the gold fin in the porphyry font:
The fire-fly wakens: waken thou with me.
'The Princess', pt 7, song, ll. 161–4, ibid.

77 Now droops the milkwhite peacock like a ghost,
And like a ghost she glimmers on to me.
Now lies the Earth all Danaë to the stars,
And all thy heart lies open unto me.
'The Princess', pt 7, song, ll. 165–8, ibid.

78 Now folds the lily all her sweetness up,
And slips into the bosom of the lake:
So fold thyself, my dearest, thou, and slip
Into my bosom and be lost in me.
'The Princess', pt 7, song, ll. 171–4, ibid.

79 For Love is of the valley, come thou down
And find him; by the happy threshold, he,
Or hand in hand with Plenty in the maize,
Or red with spirted purple of the vats,
Or foxlike in the vine; nor cares to walk
With Death and Morning on the silver horns.
'The Princess', pt 7, song, ll. 184–9 , ibid.

80 Sweet is every sound,
Sweeter thy voice, but every sound is sweet;
Myriads of rivulets hurrying through the lawn,
The moan of doves in immemorial elms,
And murmuring of innumerable bees.
'The Princess', pt 7, song, ll. 203–7, ibid.

81 God bless the narrow sea which keeps her off,
And keeps our Britain, whole within herself,
A nation yet, the rulers and the ruled –
Some sense of duty, something of a faith,
Some reverence for the laws ourselves have made.
Some patient force to change them when we will,
Some civic manhood firm against the crowd.
'The Princess', Conclusion, ll. 51–7, ibid.

82 Thou madest man, he knows not why,
He thinks he was not made to die;
And thou hast made him: thou art just.
In Memoriam A. H. H., Prologue, st 3 (1850)

83 Our little systems have their day;
They have their day and cease to be:
They are but broken lights of thee,
And thou, O Lord, art more than they.
Ibid., Prologue, st 5

84 Let knowledge grow from more to more,
But more of reverence in us dwell;
That mind and soul, according well,
May make one music as before.
Ibid., Prologue, st 7

85 I held it truth, with him who sings
To one clear harp in divers tones,
Men may rise on stepping-stones
Of their dead selves to higher things.
Ibid., canto 1, st 1

86 But who shall so forecast the years
And find in loss a gain to match?

Or reach a hand through time to catch
The far-off interest of tears?
Ibid., canto 1, st. 2

87 I sometimes hold it half a sin
To put in words the grief I feel;
For words, like Nature, half reveal
And half conceal the soul within.
Ibid., canto 5, st. 1

88 But, for the unquiet heart and brain,
A use in measured language lies;
The sad mechanic exercise,
Like dull narcotics, numbing pain.
Ibid., canto 5, st. 2

89 Never morning wore
To evening, but some heart did break.
Ibid., canto 6, st. 2

90 The last red leaf is whirled away,
The rooks are blown about the skies.
Ibid., canto 15, st. 1

91 And from his ashes may be made
The violet of his native land.
Ibid., canto 18, st. 1

92 A time to sicken and to swoon,
When Science reaches forth her arms
To feel from world to world, and charms
Her secret from the latest moon.
Ibid., canto 21, st. 5

93 And Thought leapt out to wed with Thought
Ere Thought could wed itself with Speech.
Ibid., canto 23, st. 4

94 I envy not in any moods
The captive void of noble rage,
The linnet born within the cage,
That never knew the summer woods.
Ibid., canto 27, st. 1

95 'Tis better to have loved and lost
Than never to have loved at all.
Ibid., canto 27, st. 4. The words were already proverbial, and
have been variously adapted: see JAMES THURBER 5.

96 Her eyes are homes of silent prayer.
Ibid., canto 32, st. 1

97 How fares it with the happy dead?
Ibid., canto 44, st. 1

98 Be near me when my light is low,
When the blood creeps, and the nerves prick

And tingle; and the heart is sick,
And all the wheels of Being slow.
Ibid., canto 50, st. 1

99 And Time, a maniac scattering dust,
And Life, a Fury slinging flame.
Ibid., canto 50, st. 2

100 Hold thou the good: define it well:
For fear divine Philosophy
Should push beyond her mark, and be
Procuress to the Lords of Hell.
Ibid., canto 53, st. 4

101 Oh yet we trust that somehow good
Will be the final goal of ill.
Ibid., canto 54, st. 1

102 Behold, we know not anything;
I can but trust that good shall fall
At last – far off – at last, to all,
And every winter change to spring.
Ibid., canto 54, st. 4

103 So runs my dream: but what am I?
An infant crying in the night:
An infant crying for the light:
And with no language but a cry.
Ibid., canto 54, st. 5

104 So careful of the type she seems,
So careless of the single life.
Ibid., canto 55, st. 2

105 The great world's altar-stairs
That slope through darkness up to God.
Ibid., canto 55, st. 4

106 Nature, red in tooth and claw.
Ibid., canto 56, st. 4

107 O Sorrow, wilt Thou live with me
No casual mistress, but a wife.
Ibid., canto 59, st. 1

108 So many worlds, so much to do,
So little done, such things to be.
Ibid., canto 73, st. 1. See CECIL RHODES 1.

109 Death has made
His darkness beautiful with thee.
Ibid., canto 74, st. 3

110 God's finger touched him, and he slept.
Ibid., canto 85, st. 5

111 Fresh from brawling courts
And dusty purlieus of the law.
Ibid., canto 89, st. 3

112 There lives more faith in honest doubt,
Believe me, than in half the creeds.
Ibid., canto 96, st. 3

113 He seems so near and yet so far.
Ibid., canto 97, st. 6

114 Ring out, wild bells, to the wild sky,
The flying cloud, the frosty light:
The year is dying in the night;
Ring out, wild bells, and let him die.
Ring out the old, ring in the new,
Ring, happy bells, across the snow:
The year is going, let him go;
Ring out the false, ring in the true.
Ibid., canto 106, sts 1–2

115 Ring out old shapes of foul disease;
Ring out the narrowing lust of gold;
Ring out the thousand wars of old,
Ring in the thousand years of peace.
Ring in the valiant man and free,
The larger heart, the kindlier hand;
Ring out the darkness of the land;
Ring in the Christ that is to be.
Ibid., canto 106, sts 7–8

116 Wearing all that weight
Of learning lightly like a flower.
Ibid., Epilogue, st. 10

117 One God, one law, one element,
And one far-off divine event,
To which the whole creation moves.
Ibid., Epilogue, st. 36. Final stanza of poem.

118 He clasps the crag with crooked hands;
Close to the sun in lonely lands,
Ringed with the azure world, he stands.

The wrinkled sea beneath him crawls;
He watches from his mountain walls,
And like a thunderbolt he falls.
'The Eagle', publ. in *Poems* (1851)

119 That man's the true Conservative
Who lops the mouldered branch away.
'Hands All Round', ll. 7–8 (1852), repr. in *The Poems of Tennyson*, vol. 2 (ed. Christopher Ricks, 1969). The poem was revised in 1882, when the lines were set to music by Tennyson's wife Emily to celebrate Queen VICTORIA's birthday.

120 Gigantic daughter of the West,
We drink to thee across the flood,

We know thee most, we love thee best,
For art thou not of British blood?
'Hands All Round', ll. 37–40, ibid.

121 Faultily faultless, icily regular, splendidly null,
Dead perfection, no more.
'Maud', pt 1, sect. 2, publ. in *Maud, and Other Poems* (1855)

122 And most of all would I flee from the cruel
  madness of love,
The honey of poison-flowers and all the
  measureless ill.
'Maud', pt 1, sect. 4, st. 10, ibid.

123 That oiled and curled Assyrian bull,
Smelling of musk and of insolence.
'Maud', pt 1, sect. 6, st. 6, ibid.

124 Ah God, for a man with heart, head, hand,
Like some of the simple great ones gone
For ever and ever by,
One still strong man in a blatant land,
Whatever they call him, what care I,
Aristocrat, democrat, autocrat – one
Who can rule and dare not lie.
'Maud', pt 1, sect. 10, st. 5, ibid.

125 Gorgonised me from head to foot,
With a stony British stare.
'Maud', pt 1, sect. 13, st. 2, ibid.

126 Come into the garden, Maud,
For the black bat, night, has flown,
Come into the garden, Maud,
I am here at the gate alone;
And the woodbine spices are wafted abroad,
And the musk of the rose is blown.
'Maud', pt 1, sect. 22, st. 1, ibid.

127 For a breeze of morning moves,
And the planet of Love is on high,
Beginning to faint in the light that she loves
On a bed of daffodil sky.
'Maud', pt 1, sect. 22, st. 2, ibid.

128 All night has the casement jessamine stirred
To the dancers dancing in tune;
Till a silence fell with the waking bird,
And a hush with the setting moon.
'Maud', pt 1, sect. 22, st. 3, ibid.

129 There has fallen a splendid tear
From the passion-flower at the gate.
She is coming, my dove, my dear;
She is coming, my life, my fate;
The red rose cries, 'She is near, she is near;'

And the white rose weeps, 'She is late;'
The larkspur listens, 'I hear, I hear;'
And the lily whispers, 'I wait.'
'Maud', pt 1, sect. 22, st. 10, ibid.

130 She is coming, my own, my sweet;
Were it ever so airy a tread,
My heart would hear her and beat,
Were it earth in an earthy bed;
My dust would hear her and beat;
Had I lain for a century dead;
Would start and tremble under her feet,
And blossom in purple and red.
'Maud', pt 1, sect. 22, st. 11, ibid.

131 Ah Christ, that it were possible
For one short hour to see
The souls we loved, that they might tell us
What and where they be.
'Maud', pt 2, sect. 4, st. 3, ibid.

132 But the churchmen fain would kill their
  church,
As the churches have killed their Christ.
'Maud', pt 2, sect. 5, st. 2, ibid.

133 My life has crept so long on a broken wing
Through cells of madness, haunts of horror and
  fear,
That I come to be grateful at last for a little thing.
'Maud', pt 3, sect. 6, st. 1, ibid.

134 The blood-red blossom of war with a heart of
  fire.
'Maud', pt 3, sect. 6, st. 4, ibid.

135 I come from haunts of coot and hern,
I make a sudden sally
And sparkle out among the fern,
To bicker down a valley.
'The Brook', ll. 23–6, ibid.

136 For men may come and men may go,
But I go on for ever.
'The Brook', ll. 33–4, ibid.

137 The last great Englishman is low.
'Ode on the Death of the Duke of Wellington', st. 3, ibid.

138 O iron nerve to true occasion true,
O fallen at length that tower of strength
Which stood four-square to all the winds that
  blew!
'Ode on the Death of the Duke of Wellington', st. 4, ibid.

139 Not once or twice in our rough island story
The path of duty was the way to glory.
'Ode on the Death of the Duke of Wellington', st. 8, ibid.

140 Half a league, half a league,
Half a league onward,
All in the valley of death
Rode the six hundred.
'The Charge of the Light Brigade', st. 1, ibid. Referring to the charge of the Light Brigade at Balaklava, Crimea, 25 October 1854.

141 'Forward, the Light Brigade!'
Was there a man dismayed?
Not though the soldier knew
Some one had blundered.
'The Charge of the Light Brigade', st. 2, ibid.

142 Theirs not to make reply,
Theirs not to reason why,
Theirs but to do and die.
'The Charge of the Light Brigade', st. 2, ibid.

143 Into the valley of death
Rode the six hundred.
'The Charge of the Light Brigade', st. 2, ibid.

144 Cannon to right of them,
Cannon to left of them,
Cannon in front of them
Volleyed and thundered.
'The Charge of the Light Brigade', st. 3, ibid.

145 Into the jaws of death,
Into the mouth of hell
Rode the six hundred.
'The Charge of the Light Brigade', st. 3, ibid.

146 Wearing the white flower of a blameless life,
Before a thousand peering littlenesses,
In that fierce light which beats upon a throne,
And blackens every blot.
Idylls of the King, Dedication, ll. 24–7 (1859–85). Dedicated and referring to Albert, the Prince Consort.

147 Man's word is God in Man.
Ibid., 'The Coming of Arthur', l. 132

148 Clothed in white samite, mystic and wonderful.
Ibid, 'The Coming of Arthur', l. 284

149 From the great deep to the great deep he goes.
Ibid, 'The Coming of Arthur', l. 410

150 Live pure, speak true, right wrong, follow the King –
Else, wherefore born?
Ibid., 'Gareth and Lynette', ll. 117–18

151 The city is built
To music, therefore never built at all,
And therefore built for ever.
Ibid., 'Gareth and Lynette', ll. 272–4

152 Our hoard is little, but our hearts are great.
Ibid. 'The Marriage of Geraint', l. 352

153 For man is man and master of his fate.
Ibid., 'The Marriage of Geraint', l. 355

154 Full seldom doth a man repent, or use
Both grace and will to pick the vicious quitch
Of blood and custom wholly out of him,
And make all clean, and plant himself afresh.
Ibid., 'Geraint and Enid', ll. 901–4. ('Quitch' is couch grass.)

155 It is the little rift within the lute,
That by and by will make the music mute,
And ever widening slowly silence all.
Ibid., 'Merlin and Vivien', ll. 388–90. Vivien quoting Lancelot.

156 Man dreams of fame while woman wakes to love.
Ibid., 'Merlin and Vivien', l. 458

157 Where blind and naked Ignorance
Delivers brawling judgements, unashamed,
On all things all day long.
Ibid., 'Merlin and Vivien', ll. 662–4

158 Elaine the fair, Elaine the loveable,
Elaine, the lily maid of Astolat.
Ibid., 'Lancelot and Elaine', ll. 1–2

159 He is all fault who hath no fault at all:
For who loves me must have a touch of earth.
Ibid., 'Lancelot and Elaine', ll. 131–2. Spoken by Guinevere.

160 In me there dwells
No greatness, save it be some far-off touch
Of greatness to know well I am not great.
Ibid., 'Lancelot and Elaine', ll. 447–9. Spoken by Lancelot.

161 I know not if I know what true love is,
But if I know, then, if I love not him,
I know there is none other I can love.
Ibid., 'Lancelot and Elaine', ll. 672–4. Spoken by Elaine.

162 The Queen, who sat
With lips severely placid, felt the knot

Climb in her throat, and with her feet unseen
Crushed the wild passion out against the floor.
Ibid., 'Lancelot and Elaine', ll. 734–7

163 The shackles of an old love straitened him,
His honour rooted in dishonour stood,
And faith unfaithful kept him falsely true.
Ibid., 'Lancelot and Elaine', ll. 870–2. Referring to Lancelot.

164 He makes no friend who never made a foe.
Ibid., 'Lancelot and Elaine', l. 1082. Spoken by Elaine.

165 I will be deafer than the blue-eyed cat,
And thrice as blind as any noonday owl,
To holy virgins in their ecstasies,
Henceforward.
Ibid., 'The Holy Grail', ll. 862–4. Spoken by Gawain.

166 The woods are hushed, their music is no
more:
The leaf is dead, the yearning past away:
New leaf, new life – the days of frost are o'er;
New life, new love, to suit the newer day:
New loves are sweet as those that went before:
Free love – free field – we love but while we may.
Ibid., 'The Last Tournament', ll. 276–81

167 The greater man, the greater courtesy.
Ibid., 'The Last Tournament', l. 628

168 For manners are not idle, but the fruit
Of loyal nature and of noble mind.
Ibid., 'Guinevere', ll. 333–4. Spoken by Guinevere.

169 To reverence the King, as if he were
Their conscience, and their conscience as their
King,
To break the heathen and uphold the Christ,
To ride abroad redressing human wrongs,
To speak no slander, no, nor listen to it,
To honour his own word as if his God's.
Ibid., 'Guinevere', ll. 465–70. Spoken by King Arthur.

170 To love one maiden only, cleave to her,
And worship her by years of noble deeds,
Until they won her; for indeed I knew
Of no more subtle master under heaven
Than is the maiden passion for a maid,
Not only to keep down the base in man,
But teach high thought, and amiable words
And courtliness, and the desire of fame,
And love of truth, and all that makes a man.
Ibid., 'Guinevere', ll. 472–80. Spoken by King Arthur.

171 The days will grow to weeks, the weeks to
months,
The months will add themselves and make the
years,
The years will roll into the centuries,
An mine will ever be a name of scorn.
Ibid., 'Guinevere', ll. 619–22. Spoken by Guinevere.

172 It was my duty to have loved the highest:
It surely was my profit had I known:
It would have been my pleasure had I seen.
We needs must love the highest when we see it,
Not Lancelot, nor another.
Ibid., 'Guinevere', ll. 652–6. Spoken by Guinevere.

173 I found Him in the shining of the stars,
I marked Him in the flowering of His fields,
But in His ways with men I find Him not.
Ibid., 'The Passing of Arthur', ll. 9–11. The words of Arthur.

174 So all day long the noise of battle rolled
Among the mountains by the winter sea.
Ibid. 'The Passing of Arthur', ll. 170–1

175 Authority forgets a dying king.
Ibid. 'The Passing of Arthur', l. 289

176 And the days darken round me, and the years,
Among new men, strange faces, other minds.
Ibid. 'The Passing of Arthur', ll. 405–6. Spoken by Sir Bedivere.

177 The old order changeth, yielding place to new,
And God fulfils himself in many ways,
Lest one good custom should corrupt the world.
Ibid., 'The Passing of Arthur', ll. 408–10. Spoken by King
Arthur.

178 More things are wrought by prayer
Than this world dreams of.
Ibid. 'The Passing of Arthur', ll. 415–16

179 Forgive! How many will say, 'forgive', and find
A sort of absolution in the sound
To hate a little longer!
'Sea Dreams', ll. 60–2, publ. in *Enoch Arden and Other Poems*
(1864)

180 The worst is yet to come.
'Sea Dreams', l. 301, ibid.

181 That a lie which is all a lie may be met and
fought with outright,
But a lie which is part a truth is a harder matter to
fight.
'The Grandmother', st. 8, ibid.

182 The woods decay, the woods decay and fall,
The vapours weep their burthen to the ground,

Man comes and tills the field and lies beneath,
And after many a summer dies the swan.
Me only cruel immortality
Consumes: I wither slowly in thine arms,
Here at the quiet limit of the world.
'Tithonus', ll. 1–7, ibid.

183 Doänt thou marry for munny, but goä wheer
munny is!
'Northern Farmer: New Style', st. 5, publ. in *The Holy Grail
and Other Poems* (1869)

184 Flower in the crannied wall,
I pluck you out of the crannies,
I hold you here, root and all, in my hand,
Little flower – but *if* I could understand
What you are, root and all, and all in all,
I should know what God and man is.
'Flower in the Crannied Wall', ibid.

185 At Flores in the Azores Sir Richard Grenville
lay,
And a pinnace, like a fluttered bird, came flying
from far away:
'Spanish ships of war at sea! we have sighted
fifty-three!'
Then sware Lord Thomas Howard: ''Fore God I am
no coward;
But I cannot meet them here, for my ships are out
of gear,
And the half my men are sick. I must fly, but
follow quick.
We are six ships of the line; can we fight with
fifty-three?'
'Revenge', st. 1, publ. in *Ballads and Other Poems* (1880)

186 And Sir Richard said again: 'We be all good
English men.
Let us bang these dogs of Seville, the children of
the devil,
For I never turned my back upon Don or devil yet.'
'Revenge', st. 4, ibid.

187 And they praised him to his face with their
courtly foreign grace;
But he rose upon their decks, and he cried:
'I have fought for Queen and Faith like a valiant
man and true;
I have only done my duty as a man is bound to do:
With a joyful spirit I Sir Richard Grenville die!'
And he fell upon their decks, and he died.
'Revenge', st. 13, ibid.

188 All the charm of all the Muses often flowering
in a lonely word.
'To Virgil', st. 3, publ. in *Tiresias, and Other Poems* (1885)

189 Once more the Heavenly Power
Makes all things new,
And domes the red-plowed hills
With loving blue;
The blackbirds have their wills,
The throstles too.
'Early Spring', st. 1, ibid.

190 Truth for truth, and good for good! The Good,
the True, the Pure, the Just –
Take the charm 'For ever' from them, and they
crumble into dust.
'Locksley Hall Sixty Years After', ll. 71–2, publ. in *Locksley Hall
Sixty Years After* (1886)

191 Half the marvels of my morning, triumphs
over time and space
Staled by frequence, shrunk by usage into
commonest commonplace!
'Locksley Hall Sixty Years After', ll. 75–6, ibid.

192 Hope the best, but hold the Present fatal
daughter of the Past,
Shape your heart to front the hour, but dream not
that the hour will last.
'Locksley Hall Sixty Years After', ll. 105–6, ibid.

193 Is there evil but on earth? or pain in every
peopled sphere?
Well, be grateful for the sounding watchword
'Evolution' here.
'Locksley Hall Sixty Years After', ll. 197–8, ibid.

194 Evolution ever climbing after some ideal good
And Reversion ever dragging Evolution in the
mud.
'Locksley Hall Sixty Years After', ll. 199–200, ibid.

195 Science grows and Beauty dwindles.
'Locksley Hall Sixty Years After', l. 246, ibid.

196 Launch your vessel,
And crowd your canvas,
And, ere it vanishes
Over the margin,
After it, follow it,
Follow The Gleam.
'Merlin and the Gleam', st. 9, publ. in *Demeter and Other
Poems* (1889). Last lines of poem.

197 Sunset and evening star,
And one clear call for me!

And may there be no moaning of the bar,
When I put out to sea.

'Crossing the Bar', st. 1, ibid. Tennyson's last poem describes a crossing made from Lymington to the Isle of Wight, where he lived; the poet requested his publisher to include this poem at the end of each section of his works. SEAN O'CASEY titled his memoirs *Sunset and Evening Star* (1939–56).

198 Twilight and evening bell,
And after that the dark!
And may there be no sadness of farewell,
When I embark;
For though from out our bourne of time and place
The flood may bear me far,
I hope to see my pilot face to face
When I have crossed the bar.

'Crossing the Bar', sts 3–4, ibid.

199 A louse in the locks of literature.

Quoted in *Life and Letters of Sir Edmund Gosse*, ch. 14 (1931) by Evan Charteris. Referring to critic J. Churton Collins.

Terence

(c. 190–159 BC)
Roman dramatist

His six surviving comedies are based on Greek New Comedy, using the same characters though conferring 'greater realism' on his characters. The plays were influential on Renaissance and Restoration comedy.

1 *Hinc illae lacrimae.*
[Hence these tears.]

Andria (*The Woman of Andros*), Act 1, Sc. 1, l. 126. Spoken by Simo. The phrase in Latin became proverbial for 'That's the explanation of it'.

2 Lovers' quarrels are love's renewal.

Ibid., Act 3, Sc. 3, l. 555. Spoken by Chremes. See RICHARD EDWARDS 1.

3 In the end nothing is said now which has not been said before.

Eunuchus (*The Eunuch*), Prologue, l. 41

4 *Homo sum; humani nil a me alienum puto.*
[I am human and consider that nothing human is alien to me.]

Heauton Timorumenos (*The Self-Tormentor*), Act 1, Sc. 1, l. 76. Spoken by Chremes.

5 How unfair all fathers are in their judgement of the young!

Ibid., Act 1, Sc. 2, l. 213. Spoken by Clitipho.

6 Nothing is so difficult but that it may be found out by seeking.

Ibid., Act 4, Sc. 2, l. 675. Spoken by Syrus.

7 *Fortis fortuna adiuvat.*
[Fortune favours the brave.]

Phormio, Act 1, Sc. 3, l. 203. Spoken by Geta. See also VIRGIL 48.

8 *Quot homines tot sententiae: suus cuique mos.*
[So many men, so many opinions; everyone his own way.]

Phormio, Act 2, Sc. 4, l. 454. Spoken by Hegio.

Mother Teresa

(1910–97)
Albanian-born Roman Catholic missionary

Born Agnes Gonxha Bojaxhin. In India since 1928, and an Indian citizen since 1949, she devoted her life to alleviating the plight of Calcutta's slum-dwellers. She founded the Congregation of the Missionaries of Charity in 1950, which extended worldwide by the time of her death.

1 The biggest disease today is not leprosy or tuberculosis, but rather the feeling of being unwanted.

Quoted in the *Observer* 3 October 1971

2 Our life of poverty is as necessary as the work itself. Only in heaven will we see how much we owe to the poor for helping us to love God better because of them.

A Gift for God, 'Carriers of Christ's Love' (1975)

3 We ourselves feel that what we are doing is just a drop in the ocean. But if that drop was not in the ocean, I think the ocean would be less because of that missing drop. I do not agree with the big way of doing things.

Ibid., 'Carriers of Christ's Love'

4 I try to give to the poor people for love what the rich could get for money. No, I wouldn't touch a leper for a thousand pounds; yet I willingly cure him for the love of God.

Ibid., 'Riches'

5 Many people mistake our work for our vocation. Our vocation is the love of Jesus.

From documentary film *Mother Teresa*, quoted in the *New York Times* 28 November 1986

Tertullian

(c. 160–c. 225)

Latin church father

A theologian, moralist and polemicist, he wrote against heathens, Jews and heretics and was the first to use ecclesiastical Latin. He left orthodox Christianity (c. 207) to become head of the Montanist sect.

1 O evidence of a naturally Christian soul.
Apologeticus, ch. 17, sect. 6

2 Look how they love one another.
Ibid., ch. 39, sect. 7. Ironically referring to antagonistic Christian sects.

3 The blood of Christians is the seed.
Ibid., ch. 50, sect. 13. More commonly quoted: 'The blood of martyrs is the seed of the Church.'

4 *Certum quia impossibile est.*
[It is certain because it is impossible.]
De Carne Christi, ch. 5, sect. 4. The words are also quoted *Credo quia impossibile*, and are also ascribed to SAINT AUGUSTINE.

William Makepeace Thackeray

(1811–63)

English author

He was the author of satirical and moralistic tales of upper middle-class life, the best known of which being Vanity Fair, *published in serial form (1847–8), followed by* Pendennis *(1848–50) and* The Newcomes *(1853–5). A contemporary reviewer stated: 'He dissects his victims with a smile.' In 1860 he became the first editor of the* Cornhill Magazine.

1 This I set down as a positive truth. A woman with fair opportunities and without a positive hump, may marry whom she likes.
Vanity Fair, ch. 4 (1847–8)

2 Whenever he met a great man he grovelled before him, and my-lorded him as only a free-born Briton can do.
Ibid., ch. 13. Referring to Mr Osborne.

3 If a man's character is to be abused, say what you will, there's nobody like a relation to do the business.
Ibid., ch. 19

4 Them's my sentiments.
Ibid., ch. 19. Spoken by Fred Bullock.

5 Nothing like blood, sir, in hosses, dawgs, and men.
Ibid., ch. 35. Spoken by James Crawley.

6 How to live well on nothing a year.
Ibid., title of ch. 36

7 Ah! *Vanitas vanitatum!* Which of us is happy in this world? Which of us has his desire? Or having it, is satisfied?
Ibid., ch. 67. See BIBLE: THE VULGATE 7.

8 Come children, let us shut up the box and the puppets, for our play is played out.
Ibid., ch. 67. Closing words of book.

9 He who meanly admires mean things is a Snob.
The Book of Snobs, ch. 2 (1848)

10 It is best to love wisely, no doubt: but to love foolishly is better than not to be able to love at all.
Pendennis, ch. 6 (1848–50)

11 Yes, I am a fatal man, Madame Fribsbi. To inspire hopeless passion is my destiny.
Ibid., ch. 23

12 Remember, it is as easy to marry a rich woman as a poor woman.
Ibid., ch. 28

13 'Tis not the dying for a faith that's so hard, Master Harry – every man of every nation has done that – 'tis the living up to it that is difficult.
Henry Esmond, bk 1, ch. 6 (1852)

14 Charlotte, having seen his body
Borne before her on a shutter,
Like a well-conducted person,
Went on cutting bread and butter.
'Sorrows of Werther', publ. in *Ballads* (1855)

15 There is no good . . . in living in a society where you are merely the equal of everybody else . . . The true pleasure of life is to live with your inferiors.
The Newcomes, bk 1, ch. 9 (1853–5)

16 What money is better bestowed than that of a schoolboy's tip? How the kindness is recalled by the recipient in after days! It blesses him that gives and him that takes.
Ibid., bk 1, ch. 16

17 It is to the middle-class we must look for the safety of England.
The Four Georges, 'George the Third' (1860)

18 Kindnesses are easily forgotten; but injuries! – what worthy man does not keep *those* in mind?
Lovel the Widower, ch. 1 (1860)

19 Despair is perfectly compatible with a good dinner, I promise you.
Ibid., ch. 6

Margaret Thatcher
(b. 1925)
British politician and prime minister

Baroness Thatcher of Kesteven. Called 'the best man in England' by RONALD REAGAN, *she became Conservative Party leader in 1975 and Britain's first woman prime minister in 1979. She was eventually forced out of office in 1990 on the issue of Europe. See* JULIAN CRITCHLEY 2, NORMAN FOWLER 1, DENIS HEALEY 2, NEIL KINNOCK 1.

1 No woman in my time will be Prime Minister or Chancellor or Foreign Secretary – not the top jobs. Anyway I wouldn't want to be Prime Minister. You have to give yourself 100%.

Interview in the *Sunday Telegraph* 26 October 1969. Mrs Thatcher was then Shadow Education Spokesman.

2 In politics if you want anything said, ask a man. If you want anything done, ask a woman.

People 15 September 1975

3 Ladies and gentlemen, I stand before you tonight in my red chiffon evening gown, my face softly made up, my fair hair gently waved . . . the Iron Lady of the Western World! Me? A cold war warrior? Well, yes – if that is how they wish to interpret my defence of values and freedoms fundamental to our way of life.

Speech at Finchley, 31 January 1976, quoted in the *Sunday Times* 1 February 1976. A week earlier, an article in the Soviet newspaper *Red Star* had branded Thatcher an 'Iron Lady'.

4 No one would remember the Good Samaritan if he'd only had good intentions – he had money as well.

Television interview, 6 January 1980, quoted in *The Times* 12 January 1980

5 We have to get our production and our earnings into balance. There's no easy popularity in what we are proposing, but it is fundamentally sound. Yet I believe people accept there is no real alternative.

Speech at Conservative Women's Conference, 21 May 1980, quoted in the *Daily Telegraph* 22 May 1980. Thatcher's repetition of the formula 'There is no alternative' led to her being given the acronym 'Tina'.

6 To those waiting with bated breath for that favourite media catch-phrase, the U-turn, I have only this to say. You turn, if you want; the lady's not for turning.

Speech to the Conservative Party Conference, Brighton, 10 October 1980, publ. in *The Times* 11 October 1980. On her determination to persist in monetarist policies. The punning

reference is to the play by CHRISTOPHER FRY, *The Lady's Not for Burning* (1948).

7 Just rejoice at that news and congratulate our forces and the marines.

Quoted in *The Times* 26 April 1982. Said to journalists on the recapture of South Georgia during the Falklands conflict, 25 April 1982, and usually remembered as 'Rejoice, rejoice . . .'

8 When you've spent half your political life dealing with humdrum issues like the environment, it's exciting to have a real crisis on your hands.

Speech to Scottish Conservative Party Conference, 14 May 1982, quoted in *One of Us*, ch. 13 (1989) by Hugo Young. Referring to the Falklands campaign.

9 We have to see that the spirit of the South Atlantic – the real spirit of Britain – is kindled not only by war but can now be fired by peace. We have the first prerequisite. We know we can do it – we haven't lost the ability. That is the Falklands Factor. We have proved ourselves to ourselves. It is a lesson we must not now forget.

Speech to Conservative women, Cheltenham, 3 July 1982, publ. in *The Penguin Book of Twentieth-Century Speeches* (ed. Brian MacArthur, 1999). The 'Falklands Factor' was widely seen as crucial in securing the Conservative Party's election win in 1983.

10 I am extraordinarily patient provided I get my own way in the end.

Quoted in the *Observer* 2 January 1983

11 It was then that the iron entered my soul.

On her time in EDWARD HEATH's cabinet, quoted in the *Observer* 27 March 1983. Thatcher and Heath were to become irreconcilable political opponents. See BIBLE, OLD TESTAMENT: PSALMS 110.

12 I was asked whether I was trying to restore Victorian values. I said straight out I was. And I am.

Speech to British Jewish Community, 21 July 1983, quoted in *Thatcher's Reign*, 'Let Our Children Grow Tall – The Family' (1984) by Melanie McFadyean and Margaret Renn. Referring to interview by Brian Walden on 'Weekend World' 17 January 1983, when she stated that Victorian values 'were the values when our country became great . . . As our people prospered, so they used their independence and initiative to prosper others, not compulsion by the state.'

13 We can do business together.

Quoted in *The Times* 18 December 1984. Of MIKHAIL GORBACHEV, after a meeting at which he had declared Soviet willingness to discuss nuclear arms reductions. Gorbachev became First Secretary of the Soviet Communist Party three months later.

14 We must try to find ways to starve the terrorist

and the hijacker of the oxygen of publicity on which they depend.

Speech to American Bar Association, London, 15 July 1985, quoted in *The Times* 16 July 1985

15 There is no such thing as society: there are individual men and women, and there are families. And no government can do anything except through people, and people must look after themselves first. It is our duty to look after ourselves and then, also, to look after our neighbours.

Interview in *Woman's Own* 31 October 1987. See WILLIAM GODWIN 3, KARL MARX 9.

16 We have not successfully rolled back the frontiers of the State in Britain only to see them reimposed at a European level, with a European super-State exercising a new dominance from Brussels.

'The Bruges Speech', 20 September 1988, publ. in *The Penguin Book of Twentieth-Century Speeches* (ed. Brian MacArthur, 1999). The speech was drafted by Sir Charles Powell, Thatcher's adviser on foreign affairs.

17 We have become a grandmother.

Quoted in *The Times* 4 March 1989

18 I think perhaps we manage our revolutions much more quietly in this country.

Daily Telegaph 12 July 1989. Said in the wake of the bicentenary celebrations of the French revolution in Paris.

19 If it is once again one against forty-eight, then I am very sorry for the forty-eight.

Quoted in the *Daily Telegraph* 25 October 1989. Referring to the pending 1989 Commonwealth Conference.

20 I am in favour of agreement but against consensus.

Quoted in *One of Us*, ch. 18 (1989) by Hugo Young. On one occasion Thatcher had the word 'consensus' removed from a Commonwealth conference communiqué in favour of 'agreement'. 'To me, consensus seems to be the process of abandoning all beliefs, principles, values and policies,' she explained. 'So it is something in which no one believes and to which no one objects.'

21 Every Prime Minister needs a Willie.

Quoted in the *Guardian* 7 August 1990. Remark at farewell dinner for William Whitelaw.

22 The President of the Commission, M. Delors, said at this conference the other day that he wanted the European Parliament to be the democratic body of the Community, he wanted the Commission to be the Executive, and he wanted the Council of Ministers to be the Senate. No. No. No.

Speech to House of Commons, 30 October 1990, publ. in *Hansard*. Referring to talks at the EU summit in Rome.

23 I seem to smell the stench of appeasement in the air.

Quoted in the *Independent* 31 October 1990. Referring to the Gulf crisis.

24 I shan't be pulling the levers there but I shall be a very good back-seat driver.

Quoted in the *Independent* 27 November 1990. On the appointment of JOHN MAJOR as the next prime minister.

25 Home is where you come to when you have nothing better to do.

Interview in *Vanity Fair* June 1991

26 The lesson of the century has been that the people feel far more comfortable and more stable with a nation state. It is the nation state which is the unit of loyalty. Ours is the United Kingdom.

Sunday Telegraph 13 December 1992

27 In my lifetime Europe has been the source of our problems, not the source of our solutions. It's America and Britain that saved the world.

Interview in *Saga Magazine* September 1998. Thatcher repeated the assertion at the following year's Conservative Party Conference: 'In my lifetime all our problems have come from mainland Europe, and the solutions have come from the English-speaking nations of the world.' (*The Times* 9 October 1999)

28 Is he one of us?

Attributed, referring to candidates for office. The words gave Hugo Young the title for his biography of Thatcher, *One of Us* (1989).

Themistocles
(c. 528–c. 462 BC)
Athenian general and statesman

Encouraging the development of Piraeus as a port (493 BC) and building up the Athenian fleet (483 BC), he defeated the Persians at the Battle of Salamis (480 BC). He was later ostracized and served in Asia Minor as Governor of Magnesia.

1 The wooden wall is your ships.

Quoted in *Parallel Lives*, 'Themistocles', sect. 10 by PLUTARCH. Interpretation of the Second Delphic oracle to the Athenians in 480, before the Battle of Salamis, which, according to HERODOTUS in *Histories*, bk 7, sect. 141, stated: 'That the wooden wall shall not fall, but help you and your children.'

2 The Athenians govern the Greeks; I govern the

Athenians; you, my wife, govern me; your son governs you.

Ibid., 'Themistocles', sect. 18. Alleging that his son was the most powerful man in Greece.

3 I have with me two gods, Persuasion and Compulsion.

Ibid., 'Themistocles', sect. 21. On demanding tribute from the people of Andros. HERODOTUS tells the story in his *Histories*, bk 8: 'He had put it to them that they would be unable to avoid paying, because the Athenians had the support of two powerful deities, one called Persuasion and the other Compulsion, and the Andrians replied that Athens was lucky to have two such useful gods, who were obviously responsible for her wealth and greatness; unfortunately, however, they themselves, in their small and inadequate land, had two utterly useless deities, who refused to leave the island . . . and their names were Poverty and Inability. With the support of these, no money would be forthcoming.'

Paul Theroux
(b. 1941)
US author

He has written extensively of the expatriate experience, as in his novels Jungle Lovers *(1971) and* The Mosquito Coast *(1981), and of railway journeys, notably* The Great Railway Bazaar *(1975).*

1 I have seldom heard a train go by and not wished I was on it. Those whistles sing bewitchment: railways are irresistible bazaars, snaking along perfectly level no matter what the landscape, improving your mood with speed, and never upsetting your drink.

The Great Railway Bazaar, ch. 1 (1975)

2 Extensive traveling induces a feeling of encapsulation, and travel, so broadening at first, contracts the mind.

Ibid., ch. 21

3 The man who is tired of London is tired of looking for a parking space.

Interview in the *Daily Telegraph* 30 November 1998. See SAMUEL JOHNSON 112. Theroux made a similar observation in *The Kingdom by the Sea*, ch. 1 (1983).

Thomas à Kempis
(c. 1380–1471)
German monk and theologian

Born Thomas Hemerken (or Haemmerlein) at Kempen (Kempis), near Düsseldorf, he entered an Augustinian monastery in the Netherlands, where he was ordained c. 1413. De Imitatione Christi, *a work emphasizing the spiritual life, has*

traditionally been attributed to him, though there is no proof of his authorship.

1 Meek knowing of thyself is more acceptable to God than deep inquiry after knowing.

De Imitatione Christi, pt 1, ch. 3 (written c. 1441, publ. 1471; *The Imitation of Christ*)

2 *O quam cito transit gloria mundi.*
[O Lord how soon passeth the glory of this world.]

Ibid., pt 1, ch. 3. See also ANONYMOUS 87.

3 Ask not who said this, but take heed what is said.

Ibid., pt 1, ch. 5

4 For man purposeth and God disposeth.

Ibid., pt 1, ch. 19. Usually quoted: 'Man proposes, but God disposes.'

5 No man commandeth safely but he that hath learned to obey.

Ibid., pt 1, ch. 20

6 This day a man is and tomorrow he appeareth not . . . And when man is out of sight soon he passeth out of mind.

Ibid., pt 1, ch. 23

7 Would God we had lived well in this world one day.

Ibid., pt 1, ch. 23

8 If it be dreadful to die peradventure it is more perilous to live long: blissful is he that hath the hour of his death ever before his eyes and that every day disposeth himself to die.

Ibid., pt 1, ch. 23

9 If thou bear the cross gladly, it shall bear thee.

Ibid., pt 2, ch. 12

10 Love feeleth no burden, it accounteth no labour, it desireth more than it may attain, it complaineth never of impossibility, for it deemeth itself mighty to all things, and all things be lawful to it.

Ibid., pt 3, ch. 6

11 Love is swift, pure, holy, jocund, merry, strong, patient, true, prudent, long-abiding, manly and never seeking himself.

Ibid., pt 3, ch. 6

12 Of two evils the less is ever to be chosen.

Ibid., pt 3, ch. 13

13 Study, son, rather to do the will of another than thine own. Choose evermore rather to have less than more. Seek ever the lower place and to be under all. Desire ever to pray that the will of God be all and

wholly done. Lo, such a man entereth into the coasts of peace and quiet.

Ibid., pt 3, ch. 25

Dylan Thomas

(1914–53)

Welsh poet

He published 18 Poems *in 1934 and gained further recognition with* Deaths and Entrances *(1946). He narrated his 'play for voices',* Under Milk Wood, *on radio in New York shortly before his death from alcohol poisoning. 'I am in the path of Blake,' he declared, 'but so far behind that only the wings of his heels are in sight.'*

1 Never be lucid, never state,
If you would be regarded great,
The simplest thought or sentiment
(For thought, we know, is decadent).

'A Letter to My Aunt Discussing the Correct Approach to Modern Poetry', written 1933, publ. in *The Poems* (ed. Daniel Jones, 1971)

2 The force that through the green fuse drives the
  flower
Drives my green age; that blasts the roots of trees
Is my destroyer.

'The force that through the green fuse drives the flower', publ. in *18 Poems* (1934)

3 Light breaks where no sun shines;
Where no sea runs, the waters of the heart
Push in their tides.

'Light breaks where no sun shines', ibid.

4 The hand that signed the treaty bred a fever,
And famine grew, and locusts came;
Great is the hand that holds dominion over
Man by a scribbled name.

'The hand that signed the paper felled a city', publ. in *25 Poems* (1936)

5 Though lovers be lost love shall not;
And death shall have no dominion.

'And death shall have no dominion', ibid. See BIBLE, NEW TESTAMENT: ROMANS 15. An earlier version of the poem was published in the *New English Weekly* 18 May 1933, the first of Thomas's poems to be accepted by a London literary magazine.

6 I know we're not saints or virgins or lunatics; we know all the lust and lavatory jokes, and most of the dirty people; we can catch buses and count our change and cross the roads and talk real sentences. But our innocence goes awfully deep, and our discreditable secret is that we don't know anything at all, and our horrid inner secret is that we don't care that we don't.

Letter to Caitlin Macnamara, later his wife, end of 1936, publ. in *The Collected Letters of Dylan Thomas* (ed. Paul Ferris, 1985)

7 The hunchback in the park
A solitary mister
Propped between trees and water.

'The hunchback in the park', publ. in *New Poems 1942* (1942)

8 A poet writing a poem is at peace with everything except words, which are eternal actions; only in the lulls between the warring work on words can he be at war with men.

Letter, 30 July 1945, publ. in *The Collected Letters of Dylan Thomas* (ed. Paul Ferris, 1985)

9 Deep with the first dead lies London's daughter,
Robed in the long friends,
The grains beyond age, the dark veins of her
  mother,
Secret by the unmourning water
Of the riding Thames.
After the first death, there is no other.

'A Refusal to Mourn the Death, by Fire, of a Child in London', publ. in *Deaths and Entrances* (1946)

10 In my craft or sullen art
Exercised in the still night
When only the moon rages
And the lovers lie abed
With all their griefs in their arms,
I labour by singing light.

'In my craft or sullen art', ibid.

11 Now as I was young and easy under the apple
  boughs
About the lilting house and happy as the grass was
  green.

'Fern Hill', ibid. Opening lines of poem.

12 Time held me green and dying
Though I sang in my chains like the sea.

'Fern Hill', st. 6, ibid. Closing lines.

13 Do not go gentle into that good night,
Old age should burn and rage at close of day;
Rage, rage, against the dying of the light.

'Do not go gentle into that good night', publ. in *Collected Poems* (1952)

14 The land of my fathers. My fathers can have it.

Referring to Wales, in *Adam* December 1953. 'Land of my Fathers' is the Welsh national anthem.

15 To begin at the beginning: It is spring, moonless night in the small town, starless and bible-black, the

cobblestreets silent and the hunched courters'-and-rabbits' wood limping invisible down to the sloe-black, slow, black, crowblack, fishingboat-bobbing sea.
Under Milk Wood (1954). Opening words.

16 I must put my pyjamas in the drawer marked pyjamas.
Mr Ogmore, ibid.

17 And before you let the sun in, mind it wipes its shoes.
Mrs Ogmore-Pritchard, ibid. The same character utters an almost identical line in an untitled poem in *Quite Early One Morning* (1954), which includes earlier versions of *Under Milk Wood*.

18 Oh, I'm a martyr to music.
Mrs Organ Morgan, ibid.

19 You just wait. I'll sin till I blow up!
Mae Rose Cottage, ibid.

20 We are not wholly bad or good
Who live our lives under Milk Wood.
First Voice, ibid.

21 I've had eighteen straight whiskies. I think that's the record.
Quoted in *Dylan Thomas in America*, ch. 8 (1956) by John Malcolm Brinnin. On the day after he spoke these words in a New York hotel, Thomas fell into a coma from which he never recovered.

22 [An alcoholic is] a man you don't like who drinks as much as you do.
Quoted in *The Life of Dylan Thomas*, ch. 6 (1965) by Constantine Fitzgibbon

Edward Thomas
(1878–1917)
British poet and author

Originally Edward Eastaway. He was encouraged by ROBERT FROST *to write poetry in 1914. Most of his verse appeared in* Poems *(1917) and in* Last Poems *(1918), published after his death at the battle of Arras.*

1 The past is the only dead thing that smells sweet.
'Early One Morning', publ. in *Poems* (1917)

2 The steam hissed. Someone cleared his throat.
No one left and no one came
On the bare platform. What I saw
Was Adlestrop – only the name.
'Adlestrop', ibid.

3 There's none less free than who
Does nothing and has nothing else to do,
Being free only for what is not to his mind,
And nothing is to his mind.
'Liberty', ibid.

4 I have come to the borders of sleep,
The unfathomable deep
Forest where all must lose
Their way, however straight,
Or winding, soon or late;
They cannot choose.
'Lights Out', ibid.

5 As for myself,
Where first I met the bitter scent is lost.
I, too, often shrivel the grey shreds,
Sniff them and think and sniff again and try
Once more to think what it is I am remembering,
Always in vain. I cannot like the scent,
Yet I would gather up others more sweet,
With no meaning, than this bitter one.
'Old Man', publ. in *Last Poems* (1918)

6 This is no case of petty right or wrong
That politicians or philosophers
Can judge. I hate not Germans, nor grow hot
With love of Englishmen, to please newspapers.
Beside my hate for one fat patriot
My hatred of the Kaiser is love true.
'This is no case of petty right or wrong', ibid. Opening lines of poem.

Lewis Thomas
(1913–93)
US physician and educator

He found a wide readership for his reflections on biology and medicine, published in The Lives of a Cell *(1974),* The Medusa and the Snail *(1979) and* The Fragile Species *(1992).*

1 We are built to make mistakes, coded for error.
The Medusa and the Snail, 'To Err is Human' (1979)

2 If you want to use a cliché you must take full responsibility for it yourself and not try to job it off on anon., or on society.
Ibid.,'Notes on Punctuation'

3 Music is the effort we make to explain to ourselves how our brains work. We listen to Bach transfixed because this is listening to a human mind.
Ibid., 'On Thinking About Thinking'

R. S. Thomas
(1913–2000)
Welsh poet and clergyman

Ronald Stuart Thomas. A committed Welsh nationalist, he was ordained an Anglican vicar in 1936. His poems describe the Welsh landscape and those who dwell there, as in The Stones of the Field *(1946) and* Song at the Year's Turning *(1955).*

1 There is no present in Wales,
And no future;
There is only the past,
Brittle with relics,
Wind-bitten towers and castles
With sham ghosts;
Mouldering quarries and mines;
And an impotent people,
Sick with inbreeding,
Worrying the carcase of an old song.
'Welsh Landscape', publ. in *An Acre of Land* (1952). Closing lines of poem.

2 There is always the thin pane of glass set up
    between us
And our desires.
We stare and stare and stare, until the night comes
And the glass is superfluous.
'The Minister', publ. in *Song at the Year's Turning* (1955)

3 Stay, then, village, for round you spins
On slow axis a world as vast
And meaningful as any posed
By great Plato's solitary mind.
'The Village', ibid.

4 But what to do? Doctors in verse
Being scarce now, most poets
Are their own patients, compelled to treat
Themselves first, their complaint being
Peculiar always.
'The Cure', publ. in *Poetry for Supper* (1958). Opening lines of poem.

5 It was the mind's weight
Kept me bent, as I grew tall.
'Sorry', publ. in *The Bread of Truth* (1963)

6 I never thought other than
That God is that great absence
In our lives, the empty silence
Within, the place where we go
Seeking, not in hope to
Arrive or find.
'Via Negativa', publ. in *H'm* (1972)

Francis Thompson
(1859–1907)
English poet

Associated with the aesthetic movement of the 1890s, he used mystical and religious imagery, as in his most famous poem 'The Hound of Heaven' (1893). He was rescued from poverty by Wilfrid and ALICE MEYNELL.

1 I fled Him, down the nights and down the days;
I fled Him, down the arches of the years;
I fled Him, down the labyrinthine ways
Of my own mind; and in the mist of tears
I hid from Him, and under running laughter.
'The Hound of Heaven', ll. 1–5, publ. in *Poems* (1893)

2 But with unhurrying chase,
And unperturbèd pace,
Deliberate speed, majestic instancy,
They beat – and a Voice beat
More instant than the Feet –
'All things betray thee, who betrayest Me.'
'The Hound of Heaven', ll. 10–15, ibid.

3 I said to dawn: Be sudden – to eve: Be soon.
'The Hound of Heaven', l. 30, ibid.

4 My days have crackled and gone up in smoke.
'The Hound of Heaven', l. 122, ibid.

5 There is no expeditious road
To pack and label men for God,
And save them by the barrel-load.
Some may perchance, with strange surprise,
Have blundered into Paradise.
'A Judgement in Heaven', Epilogue, ll. 22–6, ibid.

6 The fairest things have fleetest end,
Their scent survives their close:
But the rose's scent is bitterness
To him that loved the rose!
'Daisy', st. 10, ibid.

7 Nothing begins, and nothing ends,
That is not paid with moan:
For we are born in others' pain,
And perish in our own.
'Daisy', st. 15, ibid.

8 Look for me in the nurseries of Heaven.
'To My Godchild Francis M.W.M.', ibid. Last line of poem. The words were inscribed by ERIC GILL on Thompson's tombstone in Kensal Green, London.

9 Summer set lip to earth's bosom bare,
And left the flushed print in a poppy there.
'The Poppy', ibid. Opening lines of poem.

10 All things by immortal power,
Near or far,
Hiddenly
To each other linkèd are,
That thou canst not stir a flower
Without troubling of a star.
'The Mistress of Vision', st. 21, publ. in *New Poems* (1897)

11 O world invisible, we view thee,
O world intangible, we touch thee,
O world unknowable, we know thee,
Inapprehensible, we clutch thee!
'In No Strange Land', st. 1, publ. in *Collected Works of Francis Thompson*, vol. 2 (ed. Wilfrid Meynell, 1913). The poem is also known as 'The Kingdom of God'.

12 The angels keep their ancient places;
Turn but a stone, and start a wing:
'Tis ye, 'tis your estrangèd faces,
That miss the many-splendoured thing.
'In No Strange Land', st. 4, ibid.

13 But (when so sad thou canst not sadder)
Cry; – and upon thy so sore loss
Shall shine the traffic of Jacob's ladder
Pitched betwixt Heaven and Charing Cross.
'In No Strange Land', st. 5, ibid.

14 And lo, Christ walking on the water
Not of Gennesareth, but Thames!
'In No Strange Land', st. 6, ibid.

Hunter S. Thompson
(1939–2005)
US journalist

Hunter Stockton Thompson. A 'New Journalist' of the 1960s, he invented the 'gonzo' genre of reporting, offering highly subjective accounts of the world with himself as protagonist. His books, including Fear and Loathing in Las Vegas *(1972), were searing but witty indictments of American society.*

1 Richard Nixon has never been one of my favourite people, anyway. For years I've regarded his very existence as a monument to all the rancid genes and broken chromosomes that corrupt the possibilities of the American Dream; he was a foul caricature of himself, a man with no soul, no inner convictions, with the integrity of a hyena and the style of a poison toad.
'Presenting: the Richard Nixon Doll (Overhauled 1968 Model)', publ. in *Pageant* July 1968, repr. in *The Great Shark Hunt*, pt. 2 (1979)

2 Fear and Loathing in Las Vegas.
Book title (1972). The core of the book, whose title was frequently adapted for other publications by Thompson, originally appeared in articles in *Rolling Stone* in November 1971 under his pseudonym Raoul Duke.

3 *Gonzo* journalism . . . is a style of 'reporting' based on William Faulkner's idea that the best fiction is far more *true* than any kind of journalism – and the best journalists have always known this . . . True *gonzo* reporting needs the talents of a master journalist, the eye of an artist/photographer and the heavy balls of an actor. Because the writer *must* be a participant in the scene, while he's writing it – or at least taping it, or even sketching it. Or all three.
The Great Shark Hunt, 'Jacket Copy for Fear and Loathing in Las Vegas' (1979)

James Thomson
(1700–48)
Scottish poet

The most esteemed poet of the first half of the 18th century after ALEXANDER POPE, *he is regarded as a precursor of Romanticism in his treatment of nature and use of sensuous imagery. Among his best known poems are* The Seasons *(1746) and* The Castle of Indolence *(1748).*

1 I know no subject more elevating, more amazing, more ready to the poetical enthusiasm, the philosophical reflection, and the moral sentiment than the works of nature. Where can we meet such variety, such beauty, such magnificence?
The Seasons, Preface (1746)

2 Delightful task! to rear the tender thought,
To teach the young idea how to shoot.
Ibid., 'Spring', ll. 1152–3

3 An elegant sufficiency, content,
Retirement, rural quiet, friendship, books.
Ibid., 'Spring', ll. 1161–2

4 Ships, dim-discovered, dropping from the clouds.
Ibid., 'Summer', l. 946

5 Sighed and looked unutterable things.
Ibid., 'Summer', l. 1188

6 For loveliness
Needs not the foreign aid of ornament,
But is when unadorned adorned the most.
Ibid., 'Autumn', ll. 204–6

7 The pale descending year, yet pleasing still,
A gentler mood inspires; for now the leaf

Incessant rustles from the mournful grove,
Oft startling such as studious, walk below,
And slowly circles through the waving air.
Ibid., 'Autumn', ll. 988–92

8 See, Winter comes to rule the varied year,
Sullen and sad.
Ibid., 'Winter', l. 1

9 Welcome, kindred glooms!
Congenial horrors, hail!
Ibid., 'Winter', ll. 5–6

10 A little, round, fat, oily man of God.
Castle of Indolence, canto 1, st. 69 (1748)

11 Ah! what avail the largest gifts of Heaven,
When drooping health and spirits go amiss?
How tasteless then whatever can be given!
Health is the vital principle of bliss,
And exercise of health.
Ibid., canto 2, st. 57, ibid.

James Thomson
(1834–82)
Scottish poet

His personal despair and the philosophical pessimism of the late Victorian age is encapsulated in his most famous poem 'The City of Dreadful Night' (1874).

1 The City of Dreadful Night.
Title of poem (1874), repr. in *The City of Dreadful Night, and Other Poems* (1880)

2 The City is of Night; perchance of Death,
But certainly of Night.
'The City of Dreadful Night', pt 1, st. 1, ibid.

Henry David Thoreau
(1817–62)
US philosopher, author and naturalist

With RALPH WALDO EMERSON, *he was a pivotal figure of the Transcendentalist movement. His chief work was* Walden *(1854) which he wrote after two years spent in a log cabin at Walden Pond, Massachusetts. His acute observations were kept in the journal he kept from 1837. See* HENRY JAMES 7.

1 Make the most of your regrets; never smother your sorrow, but tend and cherish it till it come to have a separate and integral interest. To regret deeply is to live afresh.
Journal entry, 13 November 1839, publ. in *Journals* (1906)

2 I have been breaking silence these twenty-three years and have hardly made a rent in it.
Journal entry, 9 February 1841, ibid.

3 Being is the great explainer.
Journal entry, 26 February 1841, ibid.

4 We are not what we are, nor do we treat or esteem each other for such, but for what we are capable of being.
Letter to Mrs Lucy Brown, 2 March 1842, publ. in *The Correspondence of Henry David Thoreau* (1958). Lucy Brown was the sister-in-law of RALPH WALDO EMERSON.

5 We cannot well do without our sins; they are the highway of our virtue.
Journal entry, 22 March 1842, publ. in *Journals* (1906)

6 The really efficient laborer will be found not to crowd his day with work, but will saunter to his task surrounded by a wide halo of ease and leisure.
Journal entry, 31 March 1842, ibid. The thought also found its way into Thoreau's *A Week on the Concord and Merrimack Rivers*, 'Sunday' (1849).

7 I was born upon thy bank, river,
My blood flows in thy stream,
And thou meanderest forever
At the bottom of my dream.
Journal entry, 1842, ibid.

8 The stars are the apexes of what triangles!
Journal entry, 5 October 1847, ibid. Thoreau was thinking of RALPH WALDO EMERSON, who had just set out on his second voyage to England: 'I just looked up at a fine twinkling star and thought that a voyager whom I know, now many days' sail from this coast, might possibly be looking up at that same star with me.'

9 Methinks my own soul must be a bright invisible green.
A Week on the Concord and Merrimack Rivers, 'Wednesday' (1849)

10 It takes two to speak the truth – one to speak and another to hear.
Ibid., 'Wednesday'

11 Go where we will on the *surface* of things, men have been there before us.
Ibid., 'Thursday'

12 The frontiers are not east or west, north or south, but wherever a man *fronts* an act.
Ibid., 'Thursday'

13 I heartily accept the motto, 'That government is best which governs least'; and I should like to see it acted up to more rapidly and systematically. Carried

out, it finally amounts to this, which also I believe – 'That government is best which governs not at all'.
On the Duty of Civil Disobedience (1849). Opening lines of essay.

14 I think that we should be men first, and subjects afterward. It is not desirable to cultivate a respect for the law, so much as for the right.
Ibid.

15 After the first blush of sin comes its indifference.
Ibid.

16 I came into this world, not chiefly to make this a good place to live in, but to live in it, be it good or bad.
Ibid.

17 There will never be a really free and enlightened State until the State comes to recognize the individual as a higher and independent power, from which all its own power and authority are derived, and treats him accordingly. I please myself with imagining a State at last which can afford to be just to all men, and to treat the individual with respect as a neighbor; which even would not think it inconsistent with its own repose if a few were to live aloof from it, not meddling with it, nor embraced by it, who fulfilled all the duties of neighbors and fellow men. A State which bore this kind of fruit, and suffered it to drop off as fast as it ripened, would prepare the way for a still more perfect and glorious State, which I have also imagined, but not yet anywhere seen.
Ibid. Closing lines of essay. Referring to Thoreau's refusal to pay a poll tax, for which he went to jail for one night in July 1846. The essay was often quoted by GANDHI in his campaign of passive resistance. Later, Thoreau wrote, 'I was never molested by any person but those who represented the State.' (*Walden*, ch. 8, 'The Village', 1854)

18 What does education often do? It makes a straight-cut ditch of a free, meandering brook.
Journal entry October/November 1850, publ. in *Journals* (1906)

19 The bluebird carries the sky on his back.
Journal entry, 3 April 1852, ibid.

20 The youth gets together his materials to build a bridge to the moon, or, perchance, a palace or temple on the earth, and, at length, the middle-aged man concludes to build a woodshed with them.
Journal entry, 14 July 1852, ibid.

21 What men call social virtues, good fellowship, is commonly but the virtue of pigs in a litter, which lie close together to keep each other warm.
Journal entry, 23 October 1852, ibid.

22 I should not talk so much about myself if there were anybody else whom I knew as well.
Walden, ch. 1 ('Economy') (1854)

23 I have traveled a good deal in Concord.
Ibid., ch. 1. Born in Concord, Massachusetts, Thoreau spent most of his life there and in the surrounding area.

24 Public opinion is a weak tyrant compared with our own private opinion. What a man thinks of himself, that it is which determines, or rather indicates, his fate.
Ibid., ch. 1

25 As if you could kill time without injuring eternity.
Ibid., ch. 1

26 The mass of men lead lives of quiet desperation.
Ibid., ch. 1. Thoreau commented: 'What is called resignation is confirmed desperation.'

27 I say, beware of all enterprises that require new clothes, and not rather a new wearer of clothes.
Ibid., ch. 1

28 We worship not the Graces, nor the Parcae, but Fashion. She spins and weaves and cuts with full authority. The head monkey at Paris puts on a traveler's cap, and all the monkeys in America do the same.
Ibid., ch. 1

29 Our inventions are wont to be pretty toys, which distract our attention from serious things. They are but improved means to an unimproved end.
Ibid., ch. 1

30 As for doing good, that is one of the professions which are full. Moreover, I have tried it fairly, and ... am satisfied that it does not agree with my constitution.
Ibid., ch. 1. Thoreau added, 'If I knew for a certainty that a man was coming to my house with the conscious design of doing me good, I should run for my life.'

31 There is no odor so bad as that which arises from goodness tainted.
Ibid., ch. 1

32 A man is rich in proportion to the number of things which he can afford to let alone.
Ibid., ch. 2 ('Where I Lived, and What I Lived For')

33 I went to the woods because I wished to live

deliberately, to front only the essential facts of life, and see if I could not learn what it had to teach, and not, when I came to die, discover that I had not lived . . . I wanted to live deep and suck out all the marrow of life, to live so sturdily and Spartan-like as to put to rout all that was not life, to cut a broad swath and shave close, to drive life into a corner, and reduce it to its lowest terms.
Ibid., ch. 2

34 Simplicity, simplicity, simplicity! I say, let your affairs be as two or three, and not a hundred or a thousand; instead of a million count half a dozen, and keep your accounts on your thumb-nail.
Ibid., ch. 2

35 To a philosopher all *news*, as it is called, is gossip, and they who edit it and read it are old women over their tea.
Ibid., ch. 2

36 To read well, that is, to read true books in a true spirit, is a noble exercise, and one that will task the reader more than any other exercise which the customs of the day esteem. It requires a training such as the athletes underwent, the steady intention almost of the whole life to this object. Books must be read as deliberately and reservedly as they were written.
Ibid., ch. 3

37 I never found the companion that was so companionable as solitude.
Ibid., ch. 5 ('Solitude')

38 I had three chairs in my house; one for solitude, two for friendship, three for society.
Ibid., ch. 6 ('Visitors')

39 I was determined to know beans.
Ibid., ch. 7 ('The Bean-Field')

40 Wherever a man goes, men will pursue him and paw him with their dirty institutions, and, if they can, constrain him to belong to their desperate odd-fellow society.
Ibid., ch. 8 ('The Village')

41 A lake is the landscape's most beautiful and expressive feature. It is earth's eye; looking into which the beholder measures the depth of his own nature.
Ibid., ch. 9 ('The Ponds')

42 Give me the poverty that enjoys true wealth.
Ibid., ch. 9

43 I have no doubt that it is a part of the destiny of the human race, in its gradual improvement, to leave off eating animals, as surely as the savage tribes have left off eating each other when they came in contact with the more civilized.
Ibid., ch. 11 ('Higher Laws'). Thoreau believed that 'every man who has ever been earnest to preserve his higher or poetic faculties in the best condition has been particularly inclined to abstain from animal food, and from much food of any kind.'

44 Of all ebriosity, who does not prefer to be intoxicated by the air he breathes?
Ibid., ch. 11

45 Our whole life is startlingly moral. There is never an instant's truce between virtue and vice.
Ibid., ch. 11

46 Heaven is under our feet as well as over our heads.
Ibid., ch. 16 ('The Pond in Winter')

47 The universe is wider than our views of it.
Ibid., ch. 18 ('Conclusion')

48 Nay, be a Columbus to whole new continents and worlds within you, opening new channels, not of trade, but of thought. Every man is the lord of a realm beside which the earthly empire of the Czar is but a petty state, a hummock left by the ice.
Ibid., ch. 18

49 Yet some can be patriotic who have no *self-respect*, and sacrifice the greater to the less. They love the soil which makes their graves, but have no sympathy with the spirit which may still animate their clay. Patriotism is a maggot in their heads.
Ibid., ch. 18

50 It is not worth the while to go round the world to count the cats in Zanzibar.
Ibid., ch. 18

51 If you have built castles in the air, your work need not be lost; that is where they should be. Now put the foundations under them.
Ibid., ch. 18

52 If a man does not keep pace with his companions, perhaps it is because he hears a different drummer. Let him step to the music which he hears, however measured or far away.
Ibid., ch. 18

53 The government of the world I live in was not

framed, like that of Britain, in after-dinner conversations over the wine.

Ibid., ch. 18

54 The light which puts out our eyes is darkness to us. Only that day dawns to which we are awake. There is more day to dawn. The sun is but a morning star.

Ibid., ch. 18. Closing lines of *Walden*.

55 Any fool can make a rule
And every fool will mind it.

Journal entry, 3 February 1860, ibid.

56 In wildness is the preservation of the world.

'Walking', publ. in *Atlantic Monthly* June 1862

57 I am not aware that we ever quarreled.

Quoted in *Walden and Other Writings*, Introduction (ed. Joseph Wood Krutch, 1962). Remark made shortly before his death, on being asked (by 'a pious relative') whether he had made his peace with God.

58 Oh, one world at a time!

Quoted in *A Thoreau Profile*, ch. 25 (1962) by Milton Meltzer and Walter Harding. Reply made when near death, in answer to Parker Pillsbury's remark: 'You seem so near the brink of the dark river, that I almost wonder how the opposite shore may appear to you.' BROOKS ATKINSON, in *Walden and Other Writings of Thoreau*, claimed Thoreau's words were addressed to his closest friend William Ellery Channing.

Jeremy Thorpe
(b. 1929)
British politician

He served as Liberal MP for North Devon (1959–79) and was a popular leader of the Party (1967–76). Forced to resign by a scandal in which he was acquitted of charges of conspiracy to murder a male lover, he lost his seat at the next general election.

1 Greater love hath no man than this, that he lay down his friends for his life.

Remark, 1962, quoted in *The General Election of 1964*, ch. 1 (1965) by D. E. Butler and Anthony King. Following a Cabinet 'reorganization' in which many members of the Cabinet were sacked by HAROLD MACMILLAN. See BIBLE, NEW TESTAMENT: JOHN 54.

Colin Thubron
(b. 1919)
British travel writer

He has based such books as Among the Russians *(1983) and* Behind the Wall *(1987) on his travels in Asia. His novels include* Falling *(1989) and* Turning Back the Sun *(1991).*

1 If a man would be happy for a week (ran a saying), he could take a wife; if he planned happiness for a month, he must kill a pig; but if he desired happiness for ever, he should plant a garden.

Behind the Wall: a Journey Through China, ch. 4, 'To the Nineflower Mountain' (1987)

Thucydides
(c. 460–c. 400 BC)
Athenian historian

During his exile from Athens he wrote the History of the Peloponnesian War *in eight volumes, which covers the struggle between Athens and Sparta in the 5th century BC.*

1 It may well be that my history will seem less easy to read because of the absence in it of a romantic element. It will be enough for me, however, if these words of mine are judged useful by those who want to understand clearly the events which happened in the past and which (human nature being what it is) will, at some time or other and in much the same ways, be repeated in the future. My work is not a piece of writing designed to meet the taste of an immediate public, but was done to last for ever.

History of the Peloponnesian War, bk 1, sect. 22 (transl. Rex Warner)

2 History is philosophy teaching by examples.

Quoted by historian Dionysius of Halicarnassus, in *Ars Rhetorica*, ch. 11, sect. 2

James Thurber
(1894–1961)
US humorist and illustrator

He was Managing Editor of the New Yorker *1927–33, to which he contributed wry sketches, cartoons and stories until his death. His short story 'The Secret Life of Walter Mitty' (1932) prompted Larry Adler to comment: 'Freud discovered the Id, and Thurber named it Walter Mitty.'*

1 It's a naïve domestic Burgundy without any breeding, but I think you'll be amused by its presumption.

Cartoon caption, in the *New Yorker* 27 March 1937, repr. in *The Thurber Carnival*, pt 9 (1945). Spoken by a pleased-looking host, to the consternation of his guests at dinner.

2 Well, if I called the wrong number, why did you answer the phone?

Woman on phone, in cartoon caption, in the *New Yorker* 5 June 1937, ibid.

3 Early to rise and early to bed makes a male healthy and wealthy and dead.

Fables for our Time, 'The Shrike and the Chipmunks' (1940)

4 You might as well fall flat on your face as lean over too far backward.
Ibid., 'The Bear who Let it Alone'

5 It is better to have loafed and lost than never to have loafed at all.
Ibid., 'The Courtship of Arthur and Al'. See LORD TENNY-SON 95.

6 Discussion in America means dissent.
'The Duchess and the Bugs' (c. 1953), repr. in *Lanterns and Lances* (1961)

7 With sixty staring me in the face, I have developed inflammation of the sentence structure and definite hardening of the paragraphs.
Quoted in the *New York Post* 30 June 1955

8 When all things are equal, translucence in writing is more effective than transparency, just as glow is more revealing than glare.
Ibid.

9 Humor is emotional chaos remembered in tranquility.
New York Post 29 February 1960. An earlier version of Thurber's quip was attributed to him by Max Eastman in *Enjoyment of Laughter* (1936): 'Humor is a kind of emotional chaos told about calmly and quietly in retrospect. There is always a laugh in the utterly familiar.' See WILLIAM WORDSWORTH 30.

Paul Tillich
(1886–1965)
German-born US theologian

An influential Protestant thinker, he formulated a theology that incorporated existentialist themes, as set out in his major work Systematic Theology *(3 vols. 1951–63). Expelled by the Nazis, he fled to the USA in 1933.*

1 Religion is the state of being grasped by an ultimate concern, a concern which qualifies all other concerns as preliminary and which itself contains the answer to the question of a meaning of our life.
Christianity and the Encounter of the World Religions, ch. 1 (1963)

Alexis de Tocqueville
(1805–59)
French social philosopher

His fame rests on Democracy in America *(1835–40), a penetrating analysis of US society and institutions written after a nine-month tour. A liberal egalitarian, he entered politics in 1839 and after the revolution of 1848 was briefly Foreign Minister.*

1 As one digs deeper into the national character of the Americans, one sees that they have sought the value of everything in this world only in the answer to this single question: how much money will it bring in?
Letter, 9 June 1831, publ. in *Selected Letters on Politics and Society* (ed. Roger Boesche, 1985)

2 In America the majority raises formidable barriers around the liberty of opinion; within these barriers an author may write what he pleases, but woe to him if he goes beyond them.
Democracy in America, vol. 1, ch. 15 (1835)

3 I know of no country in which there is so little independence of mind and real freedom of discussion as in America.
Ibid., vol. 1, ch. 15

4 The whole life of an American is passed like a game of chance, a revolutionary crisis, or a battle.
Ibid., vol. 1, ch. 18

5 There are at the present time two great nations in the world ... I allude to the Russians and the Americans ... Their starting-point is different and their courses are not the same; yet each of them seems marked out by the will of Heaven to sway the destinies of half the globe.
Ibid., vol. 1, ch. 18

6 The main business of religions is to purify, control, and restrain that excessive and exclusive taste for well-being which men acquire in times of equality.
Ibid., vol. 2, pt 1, ch. 5 (1840)

7 The genius of democracies is seen not only in the great number of new words introduced but even more in the new ideas they express.
Ibid., vol. 2, pt 1, ch. 16

8 Nothing is quite so wretchedly corrupt as an aristocracy which has lost its power but kept its wealth and which still has endless leisure to devote to nothing but banal enjoyments. All its great thoughts and passionate energy are things of the past, and nothing but a host of petty, gnawing vices now cling to it like worms to a corpse.
Ibid., vol. 2, pt 3, ch. 11

9 If anyone asks me what I think the chief cause of the extraordinary prosperity and growing power of this nation, I should answer that it is due to the superiority of their women.
Ibid., vol. 2, pt 3, ch. 12

10 Trade is the natural enemy of all violent passions. Trade loves moderation, delights in compromise, and is most careful to avoid anger. It is patient, supple, and insinuating, only resorting to extreme measures in cases of absolute necessity. Trade makes men independent of one another and gives them a high idea of their personal importance: it leads them to want to manage their own affairs and teaches them to succeed therein. Hence it makes them inclined to liberty but disinclined to revolution.

Ibid., vol. 2, pt 3, ch. 21

11 In no other country in the world is the love of property keener or more alert than in the United States, and nowhere else does the majority display less inclination toward doctrines which in any way threaten the way property is owned.

Ibid., vol. 2, pt 3, ch. 21

12 If there ever are great revolutions there, they will be caused by the presence of the blacks upon American soil. That is to say, it will not be the equality of social conditions but rather their inequality which may give rise to it.

Ibid., vol. 2, pt 3, ch. 21

13 Two things in America are astonishing: the changeableness of most human behaviour and the strange stability of certain principles. Men are constantly on the move, but the spirit of humanity seems almost unmoved.

Ibid., vol. 2, pt 3, ch. 21

14 I cannot help fearing that men may reach a point where they look on every new theory as a danger, every innovation as a toilsome trouble, every social advance as a first step toward revolution, and that they may absolutely refuse to move at all for fear of being carried off their feet. The prospect really does frighten me that they may finally become so engrossed in a cowardly love of immediate pleasures that their interest in their own future and in that of their descendants may vanish, and that they will prefer tamely to follow the course of their destiny rather than make a sudden energetic effort necessary to set things right.

Ibid., vol. 2, pt 3, ch. 21

15 There are two things which will always be very difficult for a democratic nation: to start a war and to end it.

Ibid., vol. 2, pt 3, ch. 22. Tocqueville added: 'All those who seek to destroy the freedom of the democratic nations must know that war is the surest and shortest means to accomplish this. That is the very first axiom of their science.'

16 What is most important for democracy is not that great fortunes should not exist, but that great fortunes should not remain in the same hands. In that way there are rich men, but they do not form a class.

Ibid., vol. 2, Appendix 5, 'Democracy'

17 Grant me thirty years of equal division of inheritances and a free press, and I will provide you with a republic.

Ibid., vol. 2, Appendix 5, 'About Virtue in Republics'

Alvin Toffler
(b. 1928)
US author

As a 'futurologist', he has written of the advent of information technology as the 'Third Wave' of civilization, after agriculture and the industrial revolution. His books include Future Shock *(1970) and* Powershift *(1990).*

1 Future shock is the dizzying disorientation brought on by the premature arrival of the future. It may well be the most important disease of tomorrow.

Future Shock, pt 1, ch. 1, 'The Unprepared Visitor' (1970)

J. R. R. Tolkien
(1892–1973)
British novelist and scholar

John Ronal Reuel Tolkien. An Oxford professor and leading philologist, he was author of numerous academic publications, but is best remembered for his fantasies The Hobbit *(1937) and* The Lord of the Rings *(1954–5).*

1 Curse it! Curse it! Curse it! Curse the Baggins! It's gone! What has it got in its pocketses? Oh we guess, we guess, my precious. He's found it, yes he must have. My birthday-present.

The Hobbit, ch. 5 (1937). Gollum is referring to the ring which he has guessed Bilbo Baggins has in his pocket, in a game of riddles played for Bilbo's life.

2 One Ring to rule them all, One Ring to find them
One Ring to bring them all and in the darkness
   bind them.

The Lord of the Rings, pt 1 (*The Fellowship of the Ring*), Epigraph (1954)

3 The Road goes ever on and on
Down from the door where it began

Now far ahead the Road has gone,
And I must follow, if I can,
Pursuing it with eager feet,
Until it joins some larger way
Where many paths and errands meet.
And whither then? I cannot say.

Bilbo Baggins, ibid., bk 1, ch. 1. The rhyme recurs with variations elsewhere in the work, and a version appears at the end of *The Hobbit*.

4 Faithless is he that says farewell when the road darkens.

The dwarf Gimli, ibid., bk 2, ch. 3

5 The realm of Sauron is ended! The Ring-bearer has fulfilled his Quest.

Gandalf , ibid., pt 3 (*The Return of the King*), bk 6, ch. 4 (1955). Describing the outcome of the struggle between Frodo and Gollum on the edge of the Cracks of Doom, as Gollum topples into the abyss, taking the Ring with him to destruction.

Leo Tolstoy
(1828–1910)
Russian novelist and philosopher

Born into an aristocratic family, he became one of the greatest writers of realist fiction, notably War and Peace *(1865–9).* MATTHEW ARNOLD *commented that* Anna Karenina *(1875–7) should not be taken as a work of art but 'a piece of life'. He was also known for his moral and religious writings.*

1 The hero of my tale – whom I love with all the power of my soul, whom I have tried to portray in all his beauty, who has been, is, and will be beautiful – is Truth.

Sevastopol in May, ch. 16 (1855, transl. Louise and Aylmer Maude)

2 Man lives consciously for himself, but is an unconscious instrument in the attainment of the historic, universal, aims of humanity.

War and Peace, bk 9, ch. 1 (1865–9, transl. Louise and Aylmer Maude)

3 In historic events, the so-called great men are labels giving names to events, and like labels they have but the smallest connection with the event itself. Every act of theirs, which appears to them an act of their own will, is in an historical sense involuntary and is related to the whole course of history and predestined from eternity.

Ibid., bk 9, ch. 1

4 A Frenchman is self-assured because he regards himself personally both in mind and body as irre-sistibly attractive to men and women. An Englishman is self-assured as being a citizen of the best-organized state in the world and always knows what he should do and knows that all he does as an Englishman is undoubtedly correct. An Italian is self-assured because he is excitable and easily forgets himself and other people. A Russian is self-assured just because he knows nothing and does not want to know anything, since he does not believe that anything can be known. The German's self-assurance is worst of all, stronger and more repulsive than any other, because he imagines that he knows the truth – science – which he himself has invented but which is for him the absolute truth.

Ibid., bk 9, ch. 10

5 The best generals I have known were . . . stupid or absent-minded men . . . Not only does a good army commander not need any special qualities, on the contrary he needs the absence of the highest and best human attributes – love, poetry, tenderness, and philosophic inquiring doubt. He should be limited, firmly convinced that what he is doing is very important (otherwise he will not have sufficient patience), and only then will he be a brave leader. God forbid that he should be humane, should love, or pity, or think of what is just and unjust.

Prince Andrew, ibid., bk 9, ch. 11

6 Our body is a machine for living. It is organised for that, it is its nature. Let life go on in it unhindered and let it defend itself, it will do more than if you paralyse it by encumbering it with remedies.

Ibid., bk 10, ch. 29

7 All happy families resemble one another, each unhappy family is unhappy in its own way.

Anna Karenina, pt 1, ch. 1 (1875–7, transl. Louise and Aylmer Maude). Opening words of book.

8 Pretence about anything sometimes deceives the wisest and shrewdest man, but, however cunningly it is hidden, a child of the meanest capacity feels it and is repelled by it.

Ibid., pt 3, ch. 9

9 There are no conditions of life to which a man cannot accustom himself, especially if he sees that every one around him lives in the same way.

Ibid., pt 7, ch. 13

10 To say that a work of art is good, but incomprehensible to the majority of men, is the same as

saying of some kind of food that it is very good but that most people can't eat it.

What Then Must We Do?, ch. 10 (1886, transl. Aylmer Maude)

11 I sit on a man's back, choking him and making him carry me, and yet assure myself and others that I am very sorry for him and wish to ease his lot by all possible means – except by getting off his back.

Ibid., ch. 16

12 The chief difference between words and deeds is that words are always intended for men for their approbation, but deeds can be done only for God.

Letter, 23 February 1903, publ. in *Tolstoy's Letters*, vol. 2 (ed. R. F. Christian, 1978)

13 But the peasants – how do the *peasants* die?

Attributed last words, quoted in *A Certain World*, 'Words, Last' (1970) by W. H. AUDEN

Lily Tomlin
(b. 1939)
US comedian

She came to notice on the cast of the TV show Rowan and Martin's Laugh-in *(1969–72) and acted in numerous films, among them* Nashville *(1975) and* Tea with Mussolini *(1999). She is also known for her one-woman stage shows.*

1 The Fifties was the most sexually frustrated decade ever: ten years of foreplay. And the Sixties, well, the Sixties was like coitus interruptus. The only thing we didn't pull out of was Vietnam.

Appearing Nightly (Broadway show, 1977), recorded on *Lily Tomlin on Stage*, 'Glenna – A Child of the Sixties' (album, 1977, material written by Lily Tomlin and Jane Wagner)

Augustus Montague Toplady
See HYMNS AND CAROLS 77

Michael Torke
(b. 1961)
US composer

Regarded as a rhythmic and melodic minimalist, he is one of the most widely choreographed contemporary composers, whose works include Brick Symphony *(1997).*

1 Why waste money on psychotherapy when you can listen to the B Minor Mass?

Independent 21 September 1990

Sue Townsend
(b. 1946)
British author

She is best known for her satirical works The Secret Diary of Adrian Mole aged 13¾ *(1982), its sequels, and the novels* The Queen and I *(1992) and* Number 10 *(2002).*

1 Marriage is nothing like being in prison! Women are let out every day to go to the shops and stuff, and quite a lot go to work.

Journal entry, 2 March, in *The Secret Diary of Adrian Mole aged 13¾* (1982)

Pete Townshend
(b. 1945)
British rock musician

He was the guitarist and chief songwriter of the leading 'mod' band the Who. His guitar-smashing antics on stage epitomized the group's nihilistic image. He composed the 'rock opera', Tommy, *in 1969.*

1 People try to put us down
(Talkin' 'bout my generation)
Just because we get around
(Talkin' 'bout my generation)
Things they do look awful c-c-cold
(Talkin' 'bout my generation)
Hope I die before I get old.

'My Generation' (song) on the album *My Generation* (1965) by the Who

2 I was born with a plastic spoon in my mouth.

'Substitute', ibid.

A. J. Toynbee
(1889–1975)
British historian

Arnold Joseph Toynbee. One of a family of distinguished historians, he was Director and Research Professor of the Royal Institute of International Affairs (1925–55) and a prolific author. His magnum opus is A Study of History *(12 vols. 1934–61).*

1 Civilization is a movement and not a condition, a voyage and not a harbour.

Reader's Digest October 1958

2 We human beings do have some genuine freedom of choice and therefore some effective control over our own destinies. I am not a determinist. But I also believe that the decisive choice is seldom the latest choice in the series. More often than not, it will turn

out to be some choice made relatively far back in the past.

'Some Great "If's" of History', publ. in the *New York Times* 5 March 1961

Polly Toynbee
(b. 1946)
British journalist

Granddaughter of A. J. TOYNBEE, *she has been writer and editor for various newspapers including the* Observer, *the* Guardian *and the* Independent.

1 Feminism is the most revolutionary idea there has ever been. Equality for women demands a change in the human psyche more profound than anything Marx dreamed of. It means valuing parenthood as much as we value banking.

Guardian 19 January 1987

Thomas Traherne
(1636–74)
English clergyman, poet and mystic

A metaphysical poet, he exalted the untutored wisdom of children as well as commonplace objects as vehicles of mystic revelation. The greater part of his poetry was undiscovered until 1896.

1 An empty book is like an infant's soul, in which anything may be written. It is capable of all things, but containeth nothing. I have a mind to fill this with profitable wonders.

Centuries of Meditation, 'First Century', no. 1, written *c*. 1672, publ. 1908. Opening words.

2 I will not by the noise of bloody wars and the dethroning of kings advance you to glory: but by the gentle ways of peace and love.

Ibid., 'First Century', no. 4

3 You never enjoy the world aright, till the sea itself floweth in your veins, till you are clothed with the heavens and crowned with the stars: and perceive yourself to be the sole heir of the whole world.

Ibid., 'First Century', no. 29

4 Certainly Adam in Paradise had not more sweet and curious apprehensions of the world, than I when I was a child.

Ibid., 'Third Century', no. 1

5 All appeared new, and strange at first, inexpressibly rare and delightful and beautiful. I was a little stranger, which at my entrance into the world was saluted and surrounded with innumerable joys. My knowledge was divine.

Ibid., 'Third Century', no. 2

6 The corn was orient and immortal wheat, which never should be reaped, nor was ever sown. I thought it had stood from everlasting to everlasting. The green trees when I saw them first . . . transported and ravished me, their sweetness and unusual beauty made my heart to leap, and almost mad with ecstasy, they were such strange and wonderful things.

Ibid., 'Third Century', no. 3. Referring to Traherne's first impressions of the world.

7 O what venerable and reverend creatures did the aged seem! Immortal cherubims! And young men glittering and sparkling angels, and maids strange seraphic pieces of life and beauty! Boys and girls tumbling in the street, and playing, were moving jewels. I knew not that they were born or should die; but all things abided eternally as they were in their proper places.

Ibid., 'Third Century', no. 3

8 So that with much ado I was corrupted, and made to learn the dirty devices of this world. Which now I unlearn, and become, as it were, a little child again that I may enter into the Kingdom of God.

Ibid., 'Third Century', no. 3

9 More company increases happiness, but does not lighten or diminish misery.

Ibid., 'Fourth Century', no. 14

10 A little grit in the eye destroyeth the sight of the very heavens, and a little malice or envy a world of joys. One wry principle in the mind is of infinite consequence.

Ibid., 'Fourth Century', no. 17

11 To think the world therefore a general Bedlam, or place of madmen, and oneself a physician, is the most necessary point of present wisdom: an important imagination, and the way to happiness.

Ibid., 'Fourth Century', no. 20

12 Had we not loved ourselves at all, we could never have been obliged to love anything. So that self-love is the basis of all love.

Ibid., 'Fourth Century', no. 55

13 The soul is made for action, and cannot rest till it be employed. Idleness is its rust. Unless it will up and think and taste and see, all is in vain.

Ibid., 'Fourth Century', no. 95

Merle Travis
(1917–83)
US country singer and songwriter

As well known for his guitar-playing and compositions, which were widely covered, as for his own recordings, he had a series of country hits from the 1940s.

1 Sixteen tons, what do you get?
Another day older and deeper in debt.
Say brother, don't you call me 'cause I can't go
I owe my soul to the company store.
'Sixteen Tons' on the album *Folk Songs of the Hills* (1947). The song is better known in its later recording by 'Tennessee' Ernie Ford (1955).

(Sir) Herbert Beerbohm Tree
(1853–1917)
English actor-manager

An acclaimed character actor, he built His Majesty's Theatre (1897) and founded the Royal Academy of Dramatic Art (RADA) in 1904. He was half brother to MAX BEERBOHM.

1 Cynicism is the humour of hatred.
Quoted in *Beerbohm-Tree*, ch. 12 (1956) by HESKETH PEARSON

2 Every man is a potential genius until he does something.
Ibid., ch. 12

3 People are too apt to treat God as if he were a minor royalty.
Ibid., ch. 12

George Macaulay Trevelyan
(1876–1962)
British historian

He authored studies of GARIBALDI (1907–11) before embarking on the social histories of England for which he is best known. He was Professor of Modern History at Cambridge 1927–51.

1 Socrates gave no diplomas or degrees, and would have subjected any disciple who demanded one to a disconcerting catechism on the nature of true knowledge.
History of England, bk 2, ch. 4 (1926)

2 Social history might be defined negatively as the history of a people with the politics left out.
English Social History, Introduction (1942)

3 Disinterested intellectual curiosity is the life blood of real civilisation.
Ibid., Introduction

4 In those days, before it became scientific, cricket was the best game in the world to watch, with its rapid sequence of amusing incidents, each ball a potential crisis! Squire, farmer, blacksmith, and labourer, with their women and children came to see the fun, were at ease together and happy all the summer afternoon. If the French *noblesse* had been capable of playing cricket with their peasants, their chateaux would never have been burnt.
Ibid., ch. 8. Referring to England in the 18th century.

5 Education . . . has produced a vast population able to read but unable to distinguish what is worth reading, an easy prey to sensations and cheap appeals.
Ibid., ch. 18

Calvin Trillin
(b. 1935)
US journalist and author

A debunker of pomposity, he was a commentator on regional stories across the USA, and he wrote as a roving gourmand in Alice, Let's Eat (1978) and Third Helpings (1983).

1 As far as I'm concerned, 'whom' is a word that was invented to make everyone sound like a butler.
'Whom Says So?', publ. in the *Nation* 8 June 1985

Lionel Trilling
(1905–75)
US critic

His critical works, which include The Liberal Imagination (1950) and Sincerity and Authenticity (1972), upheld the moral dimension of culture in the liberal tradition of MATTHEW ARNOLD, on whom he wrote a standard text (1939).

1 Probably it is impossible for humor to be ever a revolutionary weapon. Candide can do little more than generate irony.
Notebook entry *c.* 1931–2, publ. in *Partisan Review 50th Anniversary Edition* (ed. William Philips, 1985)

2 We are all ill: but even a universal sickness implies an idea of health.
'Art and Neurosis' (1945), repr. in *The Liberal Imagination* (1950)

David Trimble
(b. 1944)
Northern Irish politician

MP for Upper Bann (1990–2005), he was leader of the Ulster Unionist Party (1995–2005) and was a key figure in the Good Friday agreement in 1998. He was elected First Minister of the Northern Ireland Assembly in 1998.

1 We have never said that because someone has a past, they can't have a future.
Quoted in the *Guardian* 3 July 1998. Acceptance speech on election as First Minister of the Northern Ireland Assembly, Stormont, referring to the particpation of Sinn Féin and other groups in the new Assembly.

Anthony Trollope
(1815–82)
English novelist

A prolific writer, he was the author of the six 'Barsetshire' novels (1855–67), describing the life of West Country clergy, and the Palliser series of political novels (1864–80). He stated that 'a novel should give a picture of common life enlivened by humour and sweetened by pathos'. He also worked for thirty-three years in the postal service and introduced the pillar box.

1 The tenth Muse, who now governs the periodical press.
The Warden, ch. 14 (1855)

2 I know no life that must be so delicious as that of a writer for newspapers, or a leading member of the opposition – to thunder forth accusations against men in power; to show up the worst side of everything that is produced; to pick holes in every coat; to be indignant, sarcastic, jocose, moral, or supercilious; to damn with faint praise, or crush with open calumny! What can be so easy as this when the critic has to be responsible for nothing?
Barchester Towers, ch. 21 (1857). Spoken by Mr Arabin.

3 There is no road to wealth so easy and respectable as that of matrimony; that is, of course, provided that the aspirant declines the slow course of honest work.
Doctor Thorne, ch. 18 (1858)

4 For the most of us, if we do not talk of ourselves, or at any rate of the individual circles of which we are the centres, we can talk of nothing. I cannot hold with those who wish to put down the insignificant chatter of the world.
Framley Parsonage, ch. 10 (1860)

5 We cannot bring ourselves to believe it possible that a foreigner should in any respect be wiser than ourselves. If any such point out to us our follies, we at once claim those follies as the special evidences of our wisdom.
Orley Farm, ch. 18 (1862). Spoken by Felix Graham.

6 It may almost be a question whether such wisdom as many of us have in our mature years has not come from the dying out of the power of temptation, rather than as the results of thought and resolution.
The Small House at Allington, ch. 14 (1864)

7 With many women I doubt whether there be any more effectual way of touching their hearts than ill-using them and then confessing it. If you wish to get the sweetest fragrance from the herb at your feet, tread on it and bruise it.
Miss Mackenzie, ch. 10 (1865)

8 She understood how much louder a cock can crow in its own farmyard than elsewhere.
The Last Chronicle of Barset, vol. 1, ch. 17 (1867). Referring to Mrs Proudie.

9 It's dogged as does it. It ain't thinking about it.
Ibid., vol. 1, ch. 61. Spoken by Giles Hoggett.

10 She knew how to allure by denying, and to make the gift rich by delaying it.
Phineas Finn, ch. 57 (1869). Referring to Madame Max Goesler.

11 What man thinks of changing himself so as to suit his wife? And yet men expect that women shall put on altogether new characters when they are married, and girls think that they can do so.
Phineas Redux, ch. 3 (1874). Lady Chiltern addressing Phineas Finn.

12 It is the necessary nature of a political party in this country to avoid, as long as it can be avoided, the consideration of any question which involves a great change ... The best carriage horses are those which can most steadily hold back against the coach as it trundles down the hill.
Ibid., ch. 4

13 As to that leisure evening of life, I must say that I do not want it. I can conceive of no contentment of which toil is not to be the immediate parent.
Letter, 8 June 1876, publ. in *The Letters of Anthony Trollope*, vol. 2 (ed. N. John Hall, 1983)

14 I hold that gentleman to be the best-dressed whose dress no one observes.
Thackeray, ch. 9 (1879)

15 He must have known me if he had seen me as he was wont to see me, for he was in the habit of flogging me constantly. Perhaps he did not recognise me by my face.
Autobiography, ch. 1 (1883)

16 Satire, though it may exaggerate the vice it lashes, is not justified in creating it in order that it may be lashed.
Ibid., ch. 5

17 Three hours a day will produce as much as a man ought to write.
Ibid., ch. 15

18 The spirit which produces the satire is honest enough but the very desire which moves the satirist to do his work energetically makes him dishonest.
Ibid., ch. 20

Leon Trotsky
(1879–1940)
Russian revolutionary

Originally Lev Davidovich Bronstein. Until the death of LENIN *he was the second most powerful man in the Soviet Union, responsible for modernizing the Red Army as Commissar for Military Affairs (1918–24). However, alienated from* STALIN, *he was exiled in 1929 and eventually assassinated in Mexico.*

1 The Federated Republic of Europe – the United States of Europe – that is what must be. National autonomy no longer suffices. Economic evolution demands the abolition of national frontiers. If Europe is to remain split into national groups, then Imperialism will recommence its work. Only a Federated Republic of Europe can give peace to the world.
Conversation at Smolny, 30 October 1917, quoted in *Ten Days That Shook the World*, ch. 3 (1926) by JOHN REED

2 The literary 'fellow travellers' of the Revolution.
Literature and Revolution, ch. 2 (1923). By 'fellow travellers' (*paputchiki*), a term originally used by the 'old Socialists', Trotsky referred to writers who sympathized with the Bolshevik Revolution but had no 'revolutionary past' and to whom 'the Communist ideal is foreign'. It later came to be used to mean any uncommitted sympathizers of a cause. The phrase appeared in English in an article by MAX LERNER, 'Mr Roosevelt and his Fellow-Travelers' (1936).

3 Ideas that enter the mind under fire remain there securely and for ever.
My Life, ch. 35 (1930)

4 It was the supreme expression of the mediocrity

of the apparatus that Stalin himself rose to his position.
Ibid., ch. 40

5 Where force is necessary, there it must be applied boldly, decisively and completely. But one must know the limitations of force; one must know when to blend force with a manoeuvre, a blow with an agreement.
What Next?, ch. 14 (1932)

6 Revolutions are always verbose.
History of the Russian Revolution, vol. 2, ch. 12 (1933). Referring to the initial stages of the Russian Revolution.

7 There is a limit to the application of democratic methods. You can inquire of all the passengers as to what type of car they like to ride in, but it is impossible to question them as to whether to apply the brakes when the train is at full speed and accident threatens.
Ibid., vol. 3, ch. 6

8 You are pitiful isolated individuals; you are bankrupts; your role is played out. Go where you belong from now on – into the dustbin of history!
Ibid., vol. 3, ch. 10. Referring to the Mensheviks, who participated in Kerensky's provisional government in 1917, were overthrown by the Bolsheviks and suppressed.

9 The historic ascent of humanity, taken as a whole, may be summarized as a succession of victories of consciousness over blind forces – in nature, in society, in man himself.
Ibid., vol. 3, 'Conclusions'

10 England is nothing but the last ward of the European madhouse, and quite possibly it will prove to be the ward for particularly violent cases.
Journal entry, 11 April 1935, publ. in *Diary in Exile* (1959)

11 Old age is the most unexpected of all things that happen to a man.
Journal entry, 8 May 1935, ibid.

12 Under all conditions well-organized violence seems to him [Stalin] the shortest distance between two points.
Stalin, ch. 3 (1947)

Bobby Troup
(1918–99)
US songwriter

He wrote songs for his wife, the singer and actress Julie London, as well as for FRANK SINATRA, LITTLE RICHARD, *and Tommy*

Dorsey, whom he played in The Gene Krupa Story *(film, 1959).*
See also LITTLE RICHARD 2.

1 If you ever plan to motor west,
Travel my way, take the highway that's the best –
Get your kicks on Route 66.
'Route 66' (song, 1946). The song was a hit for the Nat Cole Trio and was widely covered.

François Truffaut
(1932–84)
French film-maker

He was a pioneer of New Wave cinema, gaining an international reputation with The Four Hundred Blows *(1959),* Jules and Jim *(1961) and* Day for Night *(1973). 'I make films that I would like to have seen when I was a young man,' he stated.*

1 I've always had the impression that real militants are like cleaning women, doing a thankless, daily but necessary job.
Letter to JEAN-LUC GODARD, May–June 1973, publ. in *Letters* (1988)

Harry S. Truman
(1884–1972)
US politician and president

As Democratic President 1945–52, he issued the order to drop the atom bomb on Japan, initiated the Marshall Plan for European aid and helped found NATO. His 'Truman Doctrine', which promised US support for those threatened by the Soviets, exacerbated the Cold War.

1 The human animal cannot be trusted for anything *good* except en masse. The combined thought and action of the whole people of any race, creed or nationality, will always point in the right direction.
Memorandum, 22 May 1945, publ. in *Mr President*, pt 3 (1952) by William Hillman

2 There is nothing new in the world except the history you do not know.
Quoted ibid., pt 2, ch. 1

3 Study men, not historians.
Letter, 19 July 1950, publ. in *Off the Record* (ed. Robert H. Ferrell, 1980)

4 A politician is a man who understands government and it takes a politician to run a government. A statesman is a politician who's been dead ten or fifteen years.
Speech to Reciprocity Club, Washington DC, 11 April 1958, quoted in the *New York World-Telegram and Sun* 12 April 1958

5 It's a recession when your neighbor loses his job: it's a depression when you lose yours.
Quoted in the *Observer* 13 April 1958

6 If you can't stand the heat, get out of the kitchen.
Favourite saying of Truman's, quoted in *Mr Citizen*, ch. 15 (1960)

7 The buck stops here.
Motto on Truman's desk at the White House, quoted in *The Man from Missouri* (1962) by Alfred Steinberg

8 When you get to be President, there are all those things, the honors, the twenty-one gun salutes, all those things. You have to remember it isn't for you. It's for the Presidency.
Plain Speaking: Conversations with Harry S. Truman, ch. 15 (1973) by Merle Miller

Dalton Trumbo
(1905–76)
US screenwriter and author

A member of the Hollywood Ten who refused to testify before the House Un-American Activities Committee, he served a year in prison and was blacklisted 1947–60. He wrote the screenplays for Kitty Foyle *(1940) and* Roman Holiday *(1953, as Ian McKellan Hunter).*

1 Nothing is bigger than life. There's nothing noble in death. What's noble about lying in the ground and rotting? What's noble about never seeing the sunshine again? What's noble about having your arms and legs blown off? What's noble about being an idiot? What's noble about being blind and deaf and dumb? What's noble about being dead?
Johnny Got His Gun, bk 1, ch. 10 (1939). Spoken by Joe Bonham.

Donald Trump
(b. 1946)
US businessman

A high-profile property tycoon, he is the owner of real estate, an airline and casinos.

1 Deals are my art form. Other people paint beautifully on canvas or write wonderful poetry. I like making deals, preferably big deals. That's how I get my kicks.
Trump: The Art of the Deal, ch. 1 (1987, written with Tony Schwartz)

Marina Tsvetaeva
(1892–1941)
Russian poet

She is best known for The Encampment of Swans *(1917–22), written in praise of counter-revolutionaries,* Craft *(1923) and* After Russia *(1928). She left Russia in 1922, but returned in 1939 when her husband was shot and her daughter arrested. She later committed suicide.*

1 Freedom! A wanton slut on a profligate's breast!
'Verses about Sonechka' (1917), repr. in *The Heritage of Russian Verse* (ed. Dimitri Obolensky, 1965)

2 Love is a stepmother, and no mother.
Then expect no justice and mercy from her.
'Two Songs: 2' (1920), repr. in *Twentieth-Century Russian Poetry* (ed. Albert C. Todd, Max Hayward and Daniel Weissbort, 1993)

3 My desk, most loyal friend
thank you. You've been with me on
every road I've taken.
My scar and my protection.
'Desk', written 1933–5, publ. in *Selected Poems* (1971, transl. Elaine Feinstein)

4 It crawls, the underground snake,
crawls, with its load of people.
And each one has his
newspaper, his skin
disease; a twitch of chewing;
newspaper *caries*.
Masticator of gum,
readers of newspapers.
'Readers of Newspapers', written 1935, ibid.

5 A deception that elevates us is dearer than a host of low truths.
Pushkin and Pugachev (1937), repr. in *A Captive Spirit: Selected Prose* (ed. and transl. J. Marin King, 1980)

Barbara Tuchman
(1912–89)
US historian

Her bestselling books, which combine a literary and narrative approach, include The Guns of August *(1962), and* Stilwell and the American Experience in China: 1911–1945 *(1970).*

1 Dead battles, like dead generals, hold the military mind in their dead grip.
The Guns of August, ch. 2 (1962)

2 No more distressing moment can ever face a British government than that which requires it to come to a hard, fast and specific decision.
Ibid., ch. 9

3 Diplomacy means all the wicked devices of the Old World, spheres of influence, balances of power, secret treaties, triple alliances, and, during the interwar period, appeasement of Fascism.
'If Mao Had Come to Washington in 1945', publ. in *Foreign Affairs* October 1972. Referring to 'the deep-seated American distrust . . . of diplomacy and diplomats'.

Sophie Tucker
(1884–1966)
Russian-born US singer

Originally Sophie Abuza. With a career spanning more than sixty years, she appeared in vaudeville, burlesque, nightclubs and music halls, and became known as 'the last of the red-hot mamas' for her blues and jazz singing style.

1 I've been rich and I've been poor. Believe me, honey, rich is better.
Some of These Days (1945). The words were later said by GLORIA GRAHAME in *The Big Heat* (film, 1953).

2 From birth to 18 a girl needs good parents. From 18 to 35, she needs good looks. From 35 to 55, good personality. From 55 on, she needs good cash. I'm saving my money.
Remark, 1953, quoted in *Sophie*, 'When They Get Too Wild For Everyone Else' (1978) by Michael Freedland

Martin Tupper
(1810–89)
British author

His moralizing series of Proverbial Philosophy *(1838–67) went through fifty editions. He could turn his hand to any subject, though his work was criticized for its perceived pretentiousness.*

1 A good book is the best of friends, the same today and for ever.
Proverbial Philosophy, 'Of Reading' (first series, 1838)

Ivan Turgenev
(1818–83)
Russian author

From the 1850s he spent much of his time in western Europe. After the play A Month in the Country *(1850) he wrote realistic novels, such as* Fathers and Sons *(1862), which addressed the social and political concerns of the Russian intelligentsia and peasantry.*

1 However much you knock at nature's door, she will never answer you in comprehensible words.
On the Eve, ch. 1 (1860). Spoken by Shubin.

2 Nature is not a temple, but a workshop, and man's the workman in it.
Fathers and Sons, ch. 9 (1862). Spoken by Bazarov.

3 I share no one's ideas. I have my own.
Ibid., ch. 13

4 Your sort, the nobility, can never go farther than noble resignation or noble indignation, but those things are trifles.
Bazarov, ibid., ch. 26

5 Whatever a man prays for, he prays for a miracle. Every prayer reduces itself to this: Great God, grant that twice two be not four.
'Prayer', publ. in *Poems in Prose* (1881)

Walter James Redfern Turner
(1889–1946)
Australian-born British author and critic

A prolific author, he was associated with the Georgian poets. The Hunter and other Poems (1916) was the first of his sixteen volumes of poetry. He was also a music and theatre critic, and a newspaper editor.

1 When I was but thirteen or so
I went into a golden land,
Chimborazo, Cotopaxi
Took me by the hand.
'Romance', publ. in *Georgian Poetry 1916–17* (ed. Edward Marsh, 1917)

Thomas Tusser
(c. 1520–c. 1580)
English writer on agriculture

Written in verse, the advice in such works as Good Husbandry *(1557) for farmers and* Good Housewifery *(1570) for housewives achieved great popularity.*

1 Fear God, and offend not the prince, nor his laws,
And keep thyself out of the magistrate's claws.
One Hundred Points of Good Husbandry, ch. 10 ('Good Husbandry Lessons') (1557, rev. 1573)

2 At Christmas play, and make good cheer,
For Christmas comes but once a year.
Ibid., ch. 12 ('The Farmer's Daily Diet')

3 14. Two first seven years for a rod they do whine,
28. Two next as a pearl in the world they do shine.
42. Two next trim beauty beginneth to swerve,

56. Two next matrons or drudges they serve.
70. Two next doth crave a staff for a stay,
84. Two next a bier to fetch them away.
One Hundred Points of Good Houswifery, 'The Description of a Woman's Age' (1570)

Desmond Tutu
(b. 1931)
South African churchman

The first black bishop of Johannesburg (1985–6) and Archbishop of Cape Town (1986–96), he campaigned for a democratic, non-racial South Africa, advocating economic sanctions but deploring the use of violence. He was Chairman of the Truth and Reconciliation Commission 1996–2003.

1 Be nice to the whites, they need you to rediscover their humanity.
Quoted in the *New York Times* 19 October 1984

2 I am a leader by default, only because nature does not allow a vacuum.
Christian Science Monitor 20 December 1984

3 Having looked the past in the eye, having asked for forgiveness and having made amends, let us shut the door on the past – not in order to forget it but in order not to allow it to imprison us.
Report of South Africa's Truth and Reconciliation Committee, Foreword, quoted in the *Daily Telegraph* 30 October 1998

Mark Twain
(1835–1910)
US author

Pseudonym of Samuel Clemens. He worked as a pilot on the Mississippi before turning to journalism and fiction, creating some of the great archetypes of American fiction in such works as The Adventures of Tom Sawyer *(1876) and* The Adventures of Huckleberry Finn *(1884). His versatile wit extended to travel narratives and satires, and he lectured widely.*

1 Lump the whole thing! Say that the Creator made Italy from designs by Michael Angelo!
The Innocents Abroad, ch. 27 (1869). Spoken by Dan. Twain's surfeit of and exasperation with Michelangelo during his visit to Rome was eloquently expressed: 'I used to worship the mighty genius of Michael Angelo . . . But I do not want Michael Angelo for breakfast – for luncheon – for dinner – for tea – for supper – for between meals . . . Here – here it is frightful. He designed St Peter's; he designed the Pope . . . the eternal bore designed the Eternal City, and unless all men and books do lie, he painted everything in it!'

2 There comes a time in every rightly constructed

boy's life when he has a raging desire to go some-where and dig for hidden treasure.
The Adventures of Tom Sawyer, ch. 26 (1876)

3 We have not the reverent feeling for the rainbow that a savage has, because we know how it is made. We have lost as much as we gained by prying into that matter.
A Tramp Abroad, ch. 43 (1879). See JOHN KEATS 64.

4 You perceive I generalize with intrepidity from single instances. It is the tourist's custom.
Notebook entry, February–September 1879, publ. in *Mark Twain's Notebooks and Journals,* vol. 2, 'Notebook 18' (ed. Frederick Anderson, 1975)

5 War talk by men who have been in a war is always interesting; whereas moon talk by a poet who has not been in the moon is likely to be dull.
Life on the Mississippi, ch. 45 (1883)

6 Persons attempting to find a motive in this narrative will be prosecuted; persons attempting to find a moral in it will be banished; persons attempting to find a plot in it will be shot.
The Adventures of Huckleberry Finn, 'Notice – By Order of the Author' (1884)

7 What, then, is the true gospel of consistency? Change. Who is the really consistent man? The man who changes. Since change is the law of his being, he cannot be consistent if he stick in a rut.
'Consistency', paper read in Hartford, Connecticut in 1884, publ. 1923, repr. in *Complete Essays* (ed. Charles Neider, 1963)

8 Loyalty to petrified opinions never yet broke a chain or freed a human soul in this world – and never will.
Paper read at Hartford, Connecticut, 1884, ibid. The first part of the statement is inscribed beneath Twain's bust in the Hall of Fame, New York University.

9 Whenever the literary German dives into a sentence, that is the last you are going to see of him till he emerges on the other side of his Atlantic with his verb in his mouth.
A Connecticut Yankee in King Arthur's Court, ch. 22 (1889). Twain's bewilderment with the German language was a recurring subject: it is 'the language which enables a man to travel all day in one sentence without changing cars'.

10 Whoever has lived long enough to find out what life is, knows how deep a debt of gratitude we owe to Adam, the first great benefactor of our race. He brought death into the world.
Pudd'nhead Wilson, ch. 3 (1894)

11 Training is everything. The peach was once a bitter almond; cauliflower is nothing but cabbage with a college education.
Ibid., ch. 5

12 When angry, count four; when very angry, swear.
Ibid., ch. 10. See THOMAS JEFFERSON 38.

13 Nothing so needs reforming as other people's habits.
Ibid., ch. 15

14 Put all your eggs in the one basket and – WATCH THAT BASKET.
Ibid., ch. 15

15 If you pick up a starving dog and make him prosperous, he will not bite you. This is the principal difference between a dog and a man.
Ibid., ch. 16

16 Few things are harder to put up with than the annoyance of a good example.
Ibid., ch. 19

17 I have found out that there ain't no surer way to find out whether you like people or hate them than to travel with them.
Tom Sawyer Abroad, ch. 11 (1894)

18 Be good and you will be lonesome.
Following the Equator, Frontispiece (1897). Caption for author's photograph.

19 Truth is the most valuable thing we have. Let us economize it.
Ibid., ch. 7. See SIR ROBERT ARMSTRONG 1.

20 We should be careful to get out of an experience only the wisdom that is in it – and stop there; lest we be like the cat that sits down on a hot stove-lid. She will never sit down on a hot stove-lid again – and that is well; but also she will never sit down on a cold one any more.
Ibid., ch. 11

21 Grief can take care of itself, but to get the full value of a joy you must have somebody to divide it with.
Ibid., ch. 12

22 Truth *is* stranger than fiction, but it is because fiction is obliged to stick to possibilities; truth isn't.
Ibid., ch. 15

23 Pity is for the living, envy is for the dead.
Ibid., ch. 19

24 It is by the goodness of God that in our country

we have those three unspeakably precious things: freedom of speech, freedom of conscience, and the prudence never to practice either of them.

Ibid., ch. 20

25 Classic – a book which people praise and don't read.

Ibid., ch. 25

26 Man is the only animal that blushes. Or needs to.

Ibid., ch. 27

27 There are several good protections against temptations but the surest is cowardice.

Ibid., ch. 36. The epigram also appears as an entry, 1898, in Twain's *Notebook*, ch. 31 (ed. Albert Bigelow Paine, 1935)

28 By trying we can easily learn to endure adversity. Another man's, I mean.

Ibid., ch. 39

29 It takes your enemy and your friend, working together, to hurt you to the heart: the one to slander you and the other to get the news to you.

Ibid., ch. 45

30 The very ink in which history is written is merely fluid prejudice.

Ibid., ch. 69

31 Everybody talks about the weather, but nobody does anything about it.

Attributed in *Hartford Courant* (Connecticut) 27 August 1897, quoted in an editorial by Charles D. Warner, though his actual words were, 'A well-known US writer once said that while everyone talked about the weather, nobody seemed to do anything about it.' The remark is generally ascribed to Twain, with whom Warner collaborated on the novel, *The Gilded Age* (1873).

32 Always do right – this will gratify some and astonish the rest.

Message, 16 February 1901, to the Young People's Society, New York City. President TRUMAN is reported to have had this remark framed behind his desk in the Oval Office.

33 The report of my death was an exaggeration.

New York Journal 2 June 1897. More commonly quoted 'Reports of my death have been greatly exaggerated.'

34 Humor must not professedly teach and it must not professedly preach, but it must do both if it would live forever.

Autobiography, ch. 55 (ed. Charles Neider, 1959). 'By forever', Twain added, 'I mean thirty years. With all its preaching it is not likely to outlive so long a term as that.'

35 We never become really and genuinely our entire and honest selves until we are dead – and not then until we have been dead years and years. People ought to start dead and then they would be honest so much earlier.

Ibid., ch. 55

36 Golf is a good walk spoiled.

Attributed in *Greatly Exaggerated*, 'Golf' (ed. Alex Ayres, 1988)

Henry Twells
(1823–1900)
English clergyman and poet

After periods as a headmaster and an Anglican clergyman, he was made Canon of Peterborough Cathedral (1884). He produced numerous books of poetry and was also a writer of hymns.

1 When as a child I laughed and wept,
Time crept.
When as a youth I waxed more bold,
Time *strolled*.
When I became a full-grown man,
Time RAN.
When older still I daily grew,
Time FLEW.
Soon I shall find, in passing on,
Time *gone*.
O Christ! wilt Thou have saved me then?
Amen.

'Time's Paces', quoted in *The Harvest of a Quiet Eye* (ed. Alan L. Mackay, 1977). The poem is attached to the front of the clock-case in the north transept of Chester Cathedral.

Kenneth Tynan
(1927–80)
British critic

Drama critic of the Observer *(1954–63) and literary manager of London's National Theatre (1963–9), he championed the work of* JOHN OSBORNE, *vigorously opposed censorship and authored the notoriously risqué revue* Oh! Calcutta! *(1969). For* GEORGE STEINER, *he was 'an anti-intellectual to the tip of his brilliant, histrionic fingers'.*

1 A neurosis is a secret you don't know you're keeping.

Journal entry, 9 July 1961, publ. in *The Life of Kenneth Tynan*, ch. 18 (1987) by Kathleen Tynan

2 Satire is protest, couched in wit, against the notion that there is anything more important than the fact that all men must die.

Observer 29 April 1962, ibid.

3 A good drama critic is one who perceives what is happening in the theatre of his time. A great drama critic also perceives what is not happening.
Tynan Right and Left, Foreword (1967)

Tristan Tzara
(1896–1963)
Romanian-born French Dadaist

Originally Sami Rosenstock. After launching the Dada movement in Zurich in 1916 he moved to Paris where he took part in the movement's 'happenings'. He published Vingt-cinq poèmes *(1918) and later more conventional lyrical poetry such as* Mouchoir de nuages *(1925).*

1 DADA doubts everything. Dada is an armadillo. Everything is Dada, too. Beware of Dada. Antidadaism is a disease: selfkleptomania, man's normal condition, is DADA. But the real dadas are against DADA.
'Dada Manifesto on Feeble Love and Bitter Love', sect. 7, publ. in *La Vie des lettres* no. 4, 1921, repr. in *The Dada Painters and Poets* (ed. Robert Motherwell, 1951)

2 Death should be a long, beautiful voyage
and limitless vacations of the flesh.
'La Mort de Guillaume Apollinaire', publ. in *De nos oiseaux* (1923)

U

Harlan K. Ullman
(b. 1940)
US consultant

James P. Wade
US politician

After twenty years as a naval pilot, Ullman became a senior associate at the Center for Strategic and International Studies and a columnist for the Washington Times. *Wade was formerly Under-secretary for Defense.*

1 The basis for Rapid Dominance rests in the ability to affect the will, perception, and understanding of the adversary through imposing sufficient Shock and Awe to achieve the necessary political, strategic and operational goals of the conflict or crisis that led to the use of force.
Shock and Awe, ch. 2 (1996). During the 2003 war in Iraq, Ullman conceded: 'The phrase, as used by the Pentagon now, has not been helpful. It has created a Doomsday approach . . . The British have a much better phrase for it: effects-based operations.'

Miguel de Unamuno
(1864–1936)
Spanish author, poet and philosopher

An influential member of the 'Generación del 98', who sought to regenerate Spanish culture, he explored themes of faith, intellect and existence in his fiction and poetry. His major philosophical works were The Tragic Sense of Life *(1913) and* The Agony of Christianity *(1924).*

1 Cure yourself of the affliction of caring how you appear to others. Concern yourself only with how you appear before God, concern yourself only with the idea that God may have of you.
The Life of Don Quixote and Sancho, 'The Sepulchre of Don Quixote' (1905)

2 Life is doubt,
And faith without doubt is nothing but death.
'Salmo II', publ. in *Poesias* (1907)

3 Science is a cemetery of dead ideas.
The Tragic Sense of Life, ch. 5 (1913)

4 For it is the suffering flesh, it is suffering, it is death, that lovers perpetuate upon the earth. Love is at once the brother, son, and father of death,

which is its sister, mother, and daughter. And thus it is that in the depth of love there is a depth of eternal despair, out of which springs hope and consolation.
Ibid., ch. 7

5 We need God, not in order to understand the *why*, but in order to feel and sustain the ultimate *wherefore*, to give a meaning to the universe.
Ibid., ch. 7

6 There is no true love save in suffering, and in this world we have to choose either love, which is suffering, or happiness ... Man is the more man – that is, the more divine – the greater his capacity for suffering, or rather, for anguish.
Ibid., ch. 9

7 To fall into a habit is to begin to cease to be.
Ibid., ch. 9

8 The sceptic does not mean him who doubts, but him who investigates or researches, as opposed to him who asserts and thinks that he has found.
Essays and Soliloquies, 'My Religion' (1924)

UNESCO constitution

1 Since wars begin in the minds of men, it is in the minds of men that the defences of peace must be constructed.
Preamble to constitution (1945). The wording is said to have been drafted by both CLEMENT ATTLEE and ARCHIBALD MACLEISH, who was then Chairman of the US delegation to the London conference responsible for drawing up the constitution.

United States Constitution

1 A well-regulated militia, being necessary to the security of a free State, the right of the people to keep and bear arms shall not be infringed.
Second Amendment (ratified 1791). The clause was already contained in the Virginia Declaration of Rights (1776), the Vermont Constitution (1777) and the Articles of Confederation (1781).

Universal Declaration of Human Rights

1 All human beings are born free and equal in dignity and rights. They are endowed with reason and conscience and should act towards one another in a spirit of brotherhood.
Article 1 (1948, based on a draft by René Cassin)

John Updike
(b. 1932)
US author and critic

His many novels of middle-class alienation and adultery include Couples *(1968) and the sequences following the fortunes of car salesman 'Rabbit' Angstrom and the novelist Henry Bech.*

1 School is where you go between when your parents can't take you and industry can't take you.
The Centaur, ch. 4 (1963). Spoken by George Caldwell.

2 A healthy male adult bore consumes each year one and a half times his own weight in other people's patience.
Assorted Prose, 'Confessions of a Wild Bore' (1965)

3 If men do not keep on speaking terms with children, they cease to be men, and become merely machines for eating and for earning money.
Ibid. 'A Foreword for Younger Readers'

4 Sex is like money; only too much is enough.
Couples, ch. 5 (1968). Spoken by Piet Hanema.

5 The first breath of adultery is the freest; after it, constraints aping marriage develop.
Ibid., ch. 5

6 Confusion is just a local view of things working out in general.
Rabbit Redux (1971). Narrated by Harry 'Rabbit' Angstrom.

7 To be President of the United States, sir, is to act as advocate for a blind, venomous, and ungrateful client; still, one must make the best of the case, for the purposes of Providence.
Buchanan Dying, Act 2 (1974). Spoken by President James Polk.

8 I think 'taste' is a social concept and not an artistic one. I'm willing to show good taste, if I can, in somebody else's living room, but our reading life is too short for a writer to be in any way polite. Since his words enter into another's brain in silence and intimacy, he should be as honest and explicit as we are with ourselves.
Interview in the New York Times Book Review 10 April 1977, repr. in Hugging the Shore, Appendix (1983)

9 I would rather have as my patron a host of anonymous citizens digging into their own pockets for the price of a book or a magazine than a small body

of enlightened and responsible men administering public funds. I would rather chance my personal vision of truth striking home here and there in the chaos of publication that exists than attempt to filter it through a few sets of official, honorably public-spirited scruples.

Testimony given before the House of Representatives Committee on Education and Labor, 30 January 1978, Boston, publ. in ibid.

10 That a marriage ends is less than ideal; but all things end under heaven, and if temporality is held to be invalidating, then nothing real succeeds.

Too Far To Go, Foreword (1979)

11 America is a vast conspiracy to make you happy.

Problems, 'How to Love America and Leave it at the Same Time' (1980)

12 We must lighten ourselves to survive. We must not cling. Safety lies in lessening, in becoming random and thin enough for the new to enter.

The Witches of Eastwick, pt 1 (1984, filmed 1987). Referring to the 'natural principle of divestment'.

13 It [the literary interview] rots a writer's brain, it cretinizes you. You say the same thing again and again, and when you do that happily you're well on the way to being a cretin. Or a politician.

Interview by MARTIN AMIS in the *Observer* 30 August 1987, repr. in *Visiting Mrs Nabokov*, 'John Updike' (1993) by Martin Amis

14 Peace is not something we are entitled to but an illusory respite we earn. On both the personal and national level, islands of truce created by balances of terror and potential violence are the best we can hope for.

Self-Consciousness, ch. 2 (1989)

15 Religion enables us to ignore nothingness and get on with the jobs of life.

Ibid., ch. 6

16 Celebrity is a mask that eats into the face. As soon as one is aware of being 'somebody,' to be watched and listened to with extra interest, input ceases, and the performer goes blind and deaf in his overanimation. One can either see or be seen.

Ibid., ch. 6

17 Now that I am sixty, I see why the idea of elder wisdom has passed from currency.

New Yorker November 1992

18 Life robs us of ourselves, piece by small piece. What is eventually left is someone else.

Brazil, ch. 23 (1994)

(Sir) Peter Ustinov

(1921–2004)

British actor, director and author

Esteemed as a raconteur and broadcaster, he had success with his play Romanoff and Juliet *(1956). Later plays include* Halfway Up the Tree *(1967) and* Beethoven's Tenth *(1983). He also acted in numerous plays and films.*

1 Laughter would be bereaved if snobbery died.

Quoted in the *Observer* 13 March 1955

2 A diplomat these days is nothing but a head-waiter who's allowed to sit down occasionally.

Romanoff and Juliet, Act 1 (1956). Spoken by the General, played by Ustinov in the first production of the play.

3 If Botticelli were alive today he'd be working for *Vogue*.

Quoted in the *Observer* 21 October 1962

4 To refuse awards . . . is another way of accepting them with more noise than is normal.

Quoted in *Marlon Brando*, ch. 13 (1974, rev. 1989) by David Shipman. Of the refusal of Oscars by MARLON BRANDO and George C. Scott.

5 What is a more irrefutable proof of madness than an inability to have a doubt?

Dear Me, ch. 1 (1977)

6 I do not believe that friends are necessarily the people you like best, they are merely the people who got there first.

Ibid., ch. 5

7 Sex is a conversation carried out by other means. If you get on well out of bed, half the problems of bed are solved.

Interview in *Speaking Frankly* (1978) by Wendy Leigh

8 Unfortunately, the balance of nature decrees that a super-abundance of dreams is paid for by a growing potential for nightmares.

Independent 25 February 1989. Referring to the USA.

9 The truth is really an ambition which is beyond us.

International Herald Tribune 12 March 1990

V

Paul Valéry
(1871–1945)
French poet and essayist

After abandoning poetry for almost twenty years in favour of scientific studies, he established himself as one of France's leading poets of the time with The Young Fate *(1917) and* Enchantments *(1922), which included the major work 'The Graveyard by the Sea'.*

1 Science means simply the aggregate of all the recipes that are always successful. All the rest is literature.
Moralités (1932). See PAUL VERLAINE 5.

2 An intelligent woman is a woman with whom one can be as stupid as one wants.
Mauvaises Pensées et Autres (1941)

3 God created man and, finding him not sufficiently alone, gave him a companion to make him feel his solitude more keenly.
Tel Quel 1, 'Moralités' (1941)

4 Politics is the art of preventing people from taking part in affairs which properly concern them.
Tel Quel 2, 'Rhumbs' (1943)

(Sir) John Vanbrugh
(1664–1726)
English architect and playwright

His plays mark a development from Restoration drama and include The Relapse *(1696) and* The Provoked Wife *(1697). He was also one of the chief architects of English Baroque, the designer of Blenheim Palace and Castle Howard. According to* VOLTAIRE, *'he is as sprightly in his writings as he is heavy in his buildings.'*

1 When once a woman has given you her heart, you can never get rid of the rest of her body.
The Relapse; or, Virtue in Danger, Act 3, Sc. 1 (1696). Spoken by Lord Foppington.

2 You may build castles in the air, and fume, and fret, and grow thin and lean, and pale and ugly, if you please. But I tell you, no man worth having is true to his wife, or can be true to his wife, or ever was, or will be so.
Berinthia, ibid., Act 3, Sc. 2

3 Belinda: Ay, but you know we must return good for evil.
Lady Brute: That may be a mistake in the translation.
The Provoked Wife, Act 1, Sc. 1 (1697)

4 Lady Brute: 'Tis a hard fate I should not be believed.
Sir John: 'Tis a damned atheistical age, wife.
Ibid., Act 5, Sc. 2

5 Much of a muchness.
The Provoked Husband, Act 1, Sc. 1 (1728). Spoken by John Moody.

William H. Vanderbilt
(1821–85)
US industrialist

William Henry Vanderbilt. The wealthiest man of his time, he was a railway magnate and involved in a number of philanthropic causes.

1 The public be damned!
Reply to a newspaper reporter, 2 October 1882, quoted in *American Railroads*, ch. 5 (1961, repr. 1997) by John F. Stover. On whether the New York Central Railroad should be run as a public trust.

Laurens van der Post
(1906–96)
South African writer and philosopher

Described by author Jan Morris as 'a mystic, disguised as a novelist and man of action', he became a mentor to PRINCE CHARLES. *He wrote on ecology from a holistic viewpoint in* The Lost World of the Kalahari *(1958) and* The Heart of the Hunter *(1961).*

1 We suffer from a hubris of the mind. We have abolished superstition of the heart only to install a superstition of the intellect in its place.
The Heart of the Hunter (1961)

2 What is most threatening and destructive in human society today is the human being who is split in his own nucleus: it is the fission in the modern soul which makes nuclear fission so dangerous – he is a split atom. He has got to heal himself, make himself whole.
A Walk with a White Bushman (1986)

3 Somehow we should learn to know that our problems are our most precious possessions. They are

the raw materials of our salvation: no problem, no redemption.

Ibid.

4 I feel that Buddhism is a religion of the high mountains. It is a religion of altitude. Christianity is a religion of serving creation in the here and now; it is very much of the earth, where man does his ploughing and sowing, his begetting and his suffering, seeking to find the great in the small, infinity in a grain of sand.

Ibid. See WILLIAM BLAKE 69.

Raoul Vaneigem

(b. 1934)

Belgian philosopher

Associated with the Situationists, he challenged what he considered the puritanism of the traditional Left with his conception of playfully subversive activism. His book The Revolution of Everyday Life *(1967) was a major influence on the New Left of the 1960s.*

1 There are more truths in twenty-four hours of a man's life than in all the philosophies.

The Revolution of Everyday Life, ch. 1, sect. 1 (1967)

2 People who talk about revolution and class struggle without referring explicitly to everyday life, without understanding what is subversive about love and what is positive in the refusal of constraints, such people have a corpse in their mouth.

Ibid., ch. 1, sect. 4. The last words were graffitied onto walls in Paris during the 1968 revolt.

3 Never before has a civilization reached such a degree of contempt for life; never before has a generation, drowned in mortification, felt such a rage to live.

Ibid., ch. 5

4 Work to survive, survive by consuming, survive to consume: the hellish cycle is complete.

Ibid., ch. 7, sect. 2

Vincent Van Gogh

(1853–90)

Dutch painter

Settling in Paris in 1886, he was influenced by the work of the Impressionists, GAUGUIN *and others. He later moved to Provence where he suffered fits of insanity. In one of these, he severed part of his own ear, and he eventually committed*

suicide. Among his best known works are his paintings of sunflowers and A Starry Night *(1889).*

1 It is not the language of painters but the language of nature which one should listen to . . . The feeling for the things themselves, for reality, is more important than the feeling for pictures.

Letter to his brother Theo, 21 July 1882, publ. in *The Complete Letters of Vincent Van Gogh*, vol. 1 (ed. J. van Gogh-Bonger, 1958)

2 An artist needn't be a clergyman or a churchwarden, but he certainly must have a warm heart for his fellow men.

Letter to his brother, November 1882, ibid., vol. 1

3 There is no blue without yellow and without orange.

Letter, June 1888, ibid., vol. 3

4 Painting and fucking a lot are not compatible; it weakens the brain.

Letter, June 1888, ibid., vol. 3

5 Those Dutchmen had hardly any imagination or fantasy, but their good taste and their scientific knowledge of composition were enormous.

Letter, July 1888, ibid., vol. 3. Referring to Rembrandt and other Dutch painters.

6 A good picture is equivalent to a good deed.

Letter, 1890, ibid., vol. 3

Nicholas Van Hoogstraten

(b. 1945)

British businessman

An outspoken property tycoon, he was named Britain's youngest millionaire at the age of twenty-three. In 2002 he was given a ten-year prison sentence for the manslaughter of a former business associate, but was acquitted the following year.

1 The ramblers are just a bunch of the dirty mac brigade. The great unwashed. Would you have a lot of Herberts in your garden?

Quoted in the *Independent on Sunday* 6 December 1998. Referring to protesters demanding access to footpaths on his Uckfield estate. After being taken to court by the Ramblers Association, he was obliged to allow right of way in 2000.

Bartolomeo Vanzetti

(1888–1927)

Italian-born US political activist

Having emigrated to the United States in 1908, he was together with Nicola Sacco convicted of murder in 1921. Despite an international outcry alleging that the two were being pros-

ecuted for their anarchist beliefs, the death sentences were carried out.

1 My conviction is that I have suffered for things that I am guilty of. I am suffering because I am a radical, and indeed I am a radical; I have suffered because I was an Italian, and indeed I am an Italian; I have suffered more for my family and for my beloved than for myself; but I am so convinced to be right that if you would execute me two times, and if I could be reborn two other times, I would live again to do what I have done already.

Last speech to court, Dedham, Massachusetts, 19 April 1927, publ. in *The Penguin Book of Twentieth-Century Speeches* (ed. Brian MacArthur, 1999)

Mario Vargas Llosa
(b. 1936)
Peruvian novelist

His fiction frequently describes hypocrisy and corruption in domestic politics, and his first novel, The Time of the Hero *(1962), was publicly burned. Later titles include* Conversation in the Cathedral *(1969) and* Aunt Julia and the Scriptwriter *(1977). He stood unsuccessfully for president in Peru in 1990.*

1 Since it is impossible to know what's really happening, we Peruvians lie, invent, dream and take refuge in illusion. Because of these strange circumstances, Peruvian life, a life in which so few actually do read, has become literary.

The Real Life of Alejandro Mayta, ch. 9 (1984). Spoken by the narrator.

2 There is an incompatibility between literary creation and political activity.

International Herald Tribune 1 April 1988

3 Eroticism has its own moral justification because it says that pleasure is enough for me; it is a statement of the individual's sovereignty.

International Herald Tribune 23 October 1990

4 Prosperity or egalitarianism – you have to choose. I favour freedom – you never achieve real equality anyway: you simply sacrifice prosperity for an illusion.

Independent on Sunday 5 May 1991

Variety

1 Wall St. lays an egg.

Headline, 30 October 1929. Referring to the Wall Street crash.

2 Sticks nix hick pix.

Headline, 17 July 1935. On the poor reception of films with rural themes in the country. Attributed to Abel Green.

3 Egghead marries hourglass.

Headline, July 1956. On the marriage on 29 June of ARTHUR MILLER and MARILYN MONROE.

Henry Vaughan
(1622–95)
Welsh poet

Signing himself 'the Silurist', after the ancient people that inhabited South Wales, he was the last of the metaphysical poets. He is most remembered for his collection of religious verse Silex Scintillans *(1650–5), which showed the influence of* GEORGE HERBERT.

1 Happy those early days! when I
Shined in my angel-infancy.
Before I understood this place
Appointed for my second race,
Or taught my soul to fancy aught
But a white, celestial thought.

Silex Scintillans, pt 1, 'The Retreat', ll. 1–6 (1650)

2 But felt through all this fleshly dress
Bright shoots of everlastingness.

Ibid., pt 1, 'The Retreat', ll. 19–20

3 Some men a forward motion love,
But I by backward steps would move,
And when this dust falls to the urn,
In that state I came, return.

Ibid., pt 1, 'The Retreat', ll. 29–32

4 My soul, there is a country
Far beyond the stars,
Where stands a wingèd sentry
All skilful in the wars;
There above noise, and danger
Sweet Peace sits crowned with smiles,
And One born in a manger
Commands the beauteous files.

Ibid., pt 1, 'Peace', ll. 1–8

5 I saw Eternity the other night
Like a great ring of pure and endless light,
All calm, as it was bright,
And round beneath it, Time in hours, days, years,
Driven by the spheres
Like a vast shadow moved, in which the world
And all her train were hurled.

Ibid., pt 1, 'The World', st. 1. Opening lines.

6 Man hath still either toys, or care:
He hath no root, nor to one place is tied,
But ever restless and irregular
About this earth doth run and ride.
He knows he hath a home, but scarce knows where,
He says it is so far
That he has quite forgot how to go there.
Ibid., pt 1, 'Man', st. 3

7 Man is the shuttle, to whose winding quest
And passage through these looms
God ordered motion, but ordained no rest.
Ibid., pt 1, 'Man', st. 4

8 They are all gone into the world of light,
And I alone sit lingering here.
Ibid., pt 2, 'They are all gone', st. 1 (1655)

9 I see them walking in an air of glory,
Whose light doth trample on my days:
My days, which are at best but dull and hoary,
Mere glimmering and decays.
Ibid., pt 2, 'They are all gone', st. 3

10 Dear, beauteous death! the jewel of the just,
Shining nowhere, but in the dark;
What mysteries do lie beyond thy dust,
Could man outlook that mark!
Ibid., pt 2, 'They are all gone', st. 5

11 And yet, as angels in some brighter dreams
Call to the soul, when man doth sleep;
So some strange thoughts transcend our wonted
    themes,
And into glory peep.
Ibid., pt 2, 'They are all gone', st. 7

12 Dear night! this world's defeat;
The stop to busy fools; care's check and curb;
The day of spirits; my soul's calm retreat
Which none disturb!
Ibid., pt 2, 'The Night', st. 5

13 So stick up ivy and the bays,
And then restore the heathen ways,
Green will remind you of the spring,
Though this great day denies the thing,
And mortifies the earth, and all,
But your wild revels, and loose hall.
'The True Christmas', ll. 1–6, publ. in *Pious Thoughts and Ejaculations* (1678)

Luc de Vauvenargues
(1715–47)
French moralist

Luc de Clapiers, Marquis de Vauvenargues. After retiring from the army, he turned to writing and produced Refléxions et Maximes *(1746), which* VOLTAIRE *considered one of the best books in the French language.*

1 Our failings sometimes bind us to one another as closely as could virtue itself.
Refléxions et Maximes, no. 176 (1746)

2 The art of pleasing is the art of deceiving.
Ibid., no. 329

3 Lazy people are always anxious to be doing something.
Ibid., no. 458

4 The things we know best are the things we haven't been taught.
Ibid., no. 479

Thorstein Veblen
(1857–1929)
US economist and social scientist

He gained his reputation with his first book The Theory of the Leisure Class *(1899) which applied an evolutionary approach to contemporary economic life.*

1 Conspicuous consumption of valuable goods is a means of reputability to the gentleman of leisure.
The Theory of the Leisure Class, ch. 4 (1899)

Vegetius
(4th century)
Roman military strategist

Flavius Vegetius Renatus. Though little regarded in its time, his work Epitoma Rei Militaris *was studied in the middle ages and remained influential into the 18th century.*

1 *Qui desiderat pacem, praeparet bellum.*
[Let him who desires peace prepare for war.]
Epitoma Rei Militaris, bk 3, prologue. See GEORGE WASHINGTON 5.

Robert Venturi
(b. 1925)
US architect

From the 1960s he led the postmodern revolt against the functionalism of modernist architecture. His works express a pref-

erence for an architecture that is complex, contradictory and rich in symbolism. See also MIES VAN DER ROHE 1.

1 In iconographic terms, the cathedral is a decorated shed.
Learning from Las Vegas, pt 2 (1972, rev. 1977) by Robert Venturi, Denise Scott Brown and Stephen Izenour

Pierre Vergniaud
(1753–93)
French revolutionary leader

As leader of the Girondist faction, he was one of the greatest orators of the French Revolution. He opposed the Montagnard faction and ROBESPIERRE, *and was guillotined after the arrest of the Girondists.*

1 Citizens, you are about to exercise a great act of justice . . . When justice has spoken, humanity ought to be listened to in its turn.
Speech to the National Assembly, 17 January 1793, quoted in *Pierre Vergniaud: Voice of the French Revolution*, ch. 14 (1950) by Claude G. Bowers. Announcing the death sentence on Louis XVI, as voted by a majority of deputies in the National Convention, including (reluctantly) Vergniaud himself. Four days later the king was guillotined.

Paul Verlaine
(1844–96)
French poet

An early leader of the Symbolists, he had a tempestuous relationship with ARTHUR RIMBAUD, *which ended with his attempt to kill the younger poet and a two-year prison sentence. His work, published in such collections as* Poèmes saturniens *(1866) and* Sagesse *(1881), was marked by lyricism and innovation.*

1 The long sobs
Of the violins
Of autumn
Pierce my heart
With monotonous languor.
'Chanson d'automne', publ. in *Poèmes saturniens* (1866)

2 There is weeping in my heart
Like the rain falling on the city.
'Ariettes oubliées', no. 3, publ. in *Romances sans paroles* (1874)

3 Music above all, and for this
Choose the irregular.
'L'Art poétique', written 1874, publ. in *Jadis et naguère* (1884). Opening lines of poem.

4 Take eloquence and wring its neck.
'L'Art poétique', ibid., st. 6

5 All the rest is mere fine writing.
'L'Art poétique', ibid. Last line of poem. See PAUL VALÉRY 1.

Hendrik Verwoerd
(1901–66)
South African politician and prime minister

As Minister for Native Affairs (1950–8) and as Prime Minister (1958–66), he was responsible for much of the apartheid legislation. In 1961 he withdrew South Africa from the Commonwealth and declared a republic. He was assassinated in the House of Assembly in Cape Town.

1 Is not our role to stand for the one thing which means our own salvation here but with which it will also be possible to save the world, and with which Europe will be able to save itself, namely the preservation of the white man and his state?
Speech, 1964, quoted in *The Oxford History of South Africa*, vol. 2, ch. 10 (ed. M. Wilson and L. Thompson, 1971)

Vespasian
(9–79)
Roman emperor

Titus Flavius Vespasianus. Emperor 69–79, he was founder of the Flavian dynasty. He restored governmental and financial order, rebuilt the Capitol and initiated the Colosseum (30).

1 Dear me! I must be turning into a god.
Quoted in *Lives of the Caesars*, 'Vespasian', sect. 23, by Suetonius (transl. ROBERT GRAVES). Dying words.

Giambattista Vico
(1688–1744)
Italian philosopher and historian

He is regarded as the precursor of cultural anthropology. His landmark work, La scienza nuova *(1725), was later to influence* KARL MARX *and* UMBERTO ECO.

1 Common sense is judgment without reflection, shared by an entire class, an entire nation, or the entire human race.
La scienza nuova, bk 1, para. 142 (1725; *The New Science*)

2 Uniform ideas originating among entire peoples unknown to each other must have a common ground of truth.
Ibid., bk 1, para. 144

3 The nature of peoples is first crude, then severe, then benign, then delicate, finally dissolute.
Ibid., bk 1, para. 242

4 Metaphysics abstracts the mind from the senses, and the poetic faculty must submerge the whole mind in the senses. Metaphysics soars up to universals, and the poetic faculty must plunge deep into particulars.

Ibid., bk 3, ch. 4, para. 821

Queen Victoria

(1819–1901)

Queen of Great Britain and Ireland

She was Queen from 1837 and, at DISRAELI*'s instigation, Empress of India from 1876. She retired from public life and went into seclusion after the death of her husband Albert in 1861, but regained popular goodwill with the Golden and Diamond jubilees of her reign. She was 'the greatest of English-women', in the opinion of* JOSEPH CHAMBERLAIN. *See also* HENRY JAMES 22.

1 I will be good.

Remark, 1830, on being shown the line of succession, quoted in *Queen Victoria: Her Life and Times*, vol. 1, ch. 3 (1972) by Cecil Woodham-Smith. Victoria later recalled: 'I cried much on learning it [how close she was to inheriting the throne] and ever deplored this contingency.'

2 We women are not *made* for governing – and if we are good women, we must *dislike* these masculine occupations; but there are times which force one to take *interest* in them *mal gré, bon gré*, and I do, of course, *intensely*.

Letter to Leopold I, King of the Belgians, 3 February 1852, publ. in *Letters of Queen Victoria*, vol. 2, ch. 21 (ed. A. C. Benson and Viscount Esher, 1907)

3 I positively think that ladies who are always *enceinte* quite disgusting; it is more like a rabbit or guinea-pig than anything else and really it is not very nice.

Letter to her daughter Princess Frederick William, 15 June 1859, publ. in *Queen Victoria in Her Letters and Journals* (ed. Christopher Hibbert, 1984)

4 When I think of a merry, happy, free young girl – and look at the ailing, aching state a young wife generally is doomed to – which you can't deny is the penalty of marriage.

Letter to her daughter Princess Frederick William, 16 May 1860, ibid.

5 The poor fatherless baby of eight months is now the utterly broken-hearted and crushed widow of forty-two! My *life* as a *happy* one is *ended*! the world is gone for *me*! If I *must live* on (and I will do nothing to make me worse than I am), it is henceforth for our poor fatherless children – for my unhappy country,

which has lost *all* in losing him – and in *only* doing what I know and *feel* he would wish, for he *is* near me – his spirit will guide and inspire me!

Letter to Leopold I, King of the Belgians, 20 December 1861, publ. in *Letters of Queen Victoria*, vol. 3, ch. 30 (ed. A. C. Benson and Viscount Esher, 1907). Of the death of Albert, the Prince Consort. Victoria's three-year seclusion and long mourning earned her the sobriquet 'The Widow of Windsor' (see RUDYARD KIPLING 20).

6 I would venture to warn against too great intimacy with artists as it is very seductive and a little dangerous.

Letter to her daughter Crown Princess of Prussia, 21 May 1878, publ. in *Queen Victoria in Her Letters and Journals* (ed. Christopher Hibbert, 1984)

7 He speaks to Me as if I was a public meeting.

Quoted in *Collections and Recollections*, ch. 14 (1898) by G. W. E. Russell. Attributed comment on W. E. GLADSTONE. 'No image except that of a flood can convey the notion of Mr Gladstone's table-talk,' Russell observed. Earlier, ALEXIS DE TOCQUEVILLE wrote: 'An American cannot converse, but he can discuss, and his talk falls into a dissertation. He speaks to you as if he was addressing a meeting' (*Democracy in America*, vol. 1, ch. 14, 1835).

8 We are not interested in the possibilities of defeat; they do not exist.

Letter to A. J. BALFOUR, December 1899, quoted in *Life of Robert, Marquis of Salisbury*, vol. 3, ch. 6 (1931) by Lady Gwendolen Cecil. Comment made during the 'Black Week' of the Boer War.

9 We are not amused.

Quoted by Caroline Holland in journal entry, 2 January 1900, publ. in *Notebooks of a Spinster Lady*, ch. 21 (1919). Rebuke addressed to the equerry Hon. Alexander Yorke, who had apparently ventured a scandalous joke. She later denied having made the remark.

Gore Vidal

(b. 1925)

US novelist and critic

An urbane and sardonic social commentator, he caused scandal for his treatment of homosexuality and transsexuality in such novels as Myra Breckinridge *(1968),* Julian *(1964),* Burr *(1973) and* Lincoln *(1984) fictionally explore the lives of historical figures.* FREDERIC RAPHAEL *called him 'a tribune who has little use for the plebs but no deference towards the patricians'.*

1 Sex is. There is nothing more to be done about it. Sex builds no roads, writes no novels and sex

certainly gives no meaning to anything in life but itself.
'Norman Mailer's Self-Advertisements' (1960), repr. in *Collected Essays 1952–1972* (1974)

2 It is the spirit of the age to believe that any fact, no matter how suspect, is superior to any imaginative exercise, no matter how true.
'French Letters: Theories of the New Novel' (1967), ibid.

3 There is something about a bureaucrat that does not like a poem.
Sex, Death and Money, Preface (1968)

4 I'm all for bringing back the birch, but only between consenting adults.
Television interview with DAVID FROST, quoted in *The Sunday Times* 16 September 1973

5 Whenever a friend succeeds, a little something in me dies.
Television interview, ibid.

6 A narcissist is someone better looking than you are.
New York Times 12 March 1981

7 A triumph of the embalmer's art.
Quoted in the *Observer* 26 April 1981. Of RONALD REAGAN.

8 There is no such thing as a homosexual or a heterosexual person. There are only homo- or heterosexual acts. Most people are a mixture of impulses if not practises.
Armageddon? Essays 1983–1987, 'Tennessee Williams: Someone to Laugh at the Squares With', sect. 1 (1987). Vidal has reiterated this remark on various occasions.

9 Everything changes except the avant-garde.
Attributed

10 He will lie even when it is inconvenient, the sign of a true artist.
Attributed

11 It is not enough to succeed. Others must fail.
Attributed

King Vidor
(1895–1982)
US film-maker

A key figure of Hollywood's silent era, he established a reputation for his films emphasizing social issues, notably The Big Parade *(1925) and* The Crowd *(1928).*

1 Marriage isn't a word – it's a *sentence*!
The Crowd, caption (silent film, 1928)

Alfred de Vigny
(1797–1863)
French poet and playwright

Les Destinées (1864) earned him a reputation as a melancholy philosopher-poet. His historical drama Chatterton *(1835) is considered one of the best Romantic dramas.*

1 I love the sound of the horn, at night, in the depth of the woods.
'Le cor' ('The Horn'), publ. in *Poèmes antiques et modernes* (1826)

2 *Seul le silence est grand; tout le reste est faiblesse.*
[Silence alone is great; all else is weakness.]
'Le mort du loup' ('The Death of the Wolf'), sect. 3, written 1843, publ. in *Les Destinées* (1864)

François Villon
(1431–c. 1465)
French poet

A lyric poet, he is best known for the poem Le Testament *(c. 1461). He was a member of the criminal organization The Brotherhood of the Coquille and spent much of his time in prison. A death sentence in 1463 was commuted to banishment, after which nothing more is known of him.*

1 *Mais où sont les neiges d'antan?*
[But where are the snows of yester-year?]
'Ballade des dames du temps jadis', st. 4, publ. in *Le Grand testament* (1461). Translated by DANTE GABRIEL ROSSETTI as 'Ballade of ladies of bygone days'.

2 *En cette foi je veux vivre et mourir.*
[In this faith I wish to live and die.]
'Ballade pour prier Notre Dame', ibid.

3 *De nôtre mal personne ne s'en rie;*
Mais priez Dieu que tous nous veuille absoudre!
[Let no one laugh at our misfortune:
But pray that God absolve us all!]
'Ballade des pendus' ('Ballad of the Hanged'), st. 1, also known as 'L'Épitaphe Villon'

Virgil
(70–19 BC)
Roman poet

Publius Vergilius Maro. His fame as one of the greatest Roman poets is founded on his pastoral poems, Eclogues *(37 BC);* Georgics *(29 BC), a treatise on farming, and the* Aeneid *(from c. 30 BC), an epic poem of Roman history and aspirations modelled on* HOMER. *See* HORACE 16.

1 A god has brought us this peace.
Eclogues, no. 1, l. 6 (37 BC). Spoken by Meliboeus.

2 There's a snake lurking in the grass.
Ibid., no. 3, l. 93. Spoken by Damoetus.

3 Now I know what love is.
Ibid., no. 8, l. 43. Spoken by Damon.

4 *Non omnia possumus omnes.*
[We can't all do everything.]
Ibid., no. 8, l. 63

5 Your descendants shall gather your fruits.
Ibid., no. 9, l. 50. Spoken by Lycidas.

6 Time bears away all things.
Ibid., no. 9, l. 51. Spoken by Moeris.

7 Love conquers everything [*Amor vincit omnia*]: let us, too, yield to love.
Ibid., no. 10, l. 69. Spoken by Gallus.

8 *Ultima Thule.*
[Furthermost Thule.]
Georgics, bk 1, l. 30 (29 BC). The phrase is used to denote a far-off land: Thule was said to be six days' travel north of England – possibly Iceland.

9 *Audacibus annue coeptis.*
[Look with favour on a bold enterprise.]
Ibid., bk 1, l. 40. The words 'annuit coeptis' were inscribed on the reverse side of the Great Seal of the United States of America in 1782.

10 Thrice they tried to pile Ossa on Pelion, yes, and roll up leafy Olympus upon Ossa; thrice the Father of Heaven split the mountains apart with his thunderbolt.
Ibid., bk 1, ll. 281–3. See HOMER 17 and HORACE 38.

11 O farmers excessively fortunate, if only they recognised their blessings!
Ibid., bk 2, l. 458

12 Happy the man who has been able to know the reasons for things.
Ibid., bk 2, l. 490. Thought to refer to the poet and philosopher LUCRETIUS.

13 All the best days of life slip away from us poor mortals first.
Ibid., bk 3, l. 66

14 Old age grows cold to love.
Ibid., bk 3, l. 97

15 *Fugit irreparabile tempus.*
[Time is flying, never to return.]
Ibid., bk 3, l. 284. Usually quoted *tempus fugit.*

16 All aglow is the work.
Ibid., bk 4, l. 169. Virgil compares bees to the Vulcan's workmen, the Cyclopes.

17 *Arma virumque cano.*
[Arms, and the man I sing.]
Aeneid, bk 1, l. 1 (19 BC). Opening line of the Aeneid, translated by JOHN DRYDEN, 1697, from which GEORGE BERNARD SHAW took the title of his satire (1894).

18 Can heavenly minds yield to such rage?
Ibid., bk 1, l. 11

19 So vast was the struggle to found the race of Rome.
Ibid., bk 1, l. 33

20 Fury provides arms.
Ibid., bk 1, l. 150

21 O you who have borne even heavier things, God will grant an end to these too.
Ibid., bk 1, ll. 199–200. Aeneas addresses his men on the difficulties of the journey to Latium.

22 Perhaps one day even this will be pleasant to remember.
Aeneas, ibid., bk 1, l. 203. Referring to the adversities endured by his men.

23 *Dux femina facti.*
[The leader of the enterprise, a woman.]
Ibid., bk 1, l. 364. Of Dido, Queen of Carthage.

24 *Sunt lacrimae rerum et mentem mortalia tangunt.*
[There are tears shed for things and mortality touches the heart.]
Aeneas, ibid., bk 1, ll. 461–2

25 If the divine powers take note of the dutiful in any way, if there is any justice anywhere and a mind recognizing in itself what is right, may the gods bring you your earned rewards.
Aeneas to Dido, ibid., bk 1, l. 603

26 I have known sorrow and learned to aid the wretched.
Aeneas to Dido, ibid., bk 1, l. 630

27 Unspeakable, O Queen, is the sorrow you bid me renew.
Aeneas, ibid., bk 2, l. 3

28 Do not trust the horse, Trojans. Whatever it is, I fear the Greeks even when they bear gifts.
Ibid., bk 2, ll. 48–9. Laocoön refers to the horse, containing soldiers, which the Greeks have left outside the walls of Troy as a ploy.

29 From a single crime know the nation.
Ibid., bk 2, l. 65

30 We have been Trojans; Troy has been.
Panthus, ibid., bk 2, l. 325

31 There is but one safety to the vanquished – to expect none.
Aeneas, ibid., bk 2, l. 354

32 The gods thought otherwise.
Ibid., bk 2, l. 428

33 To what do you not drive human hearts, cursed craving for gold.
Aeneas, ibid., bk 3, ll. 56–7

34 Rumour flies.
Ibid., bk 3, l. 121

35 I feel again a spark of that ancient flame.
Dido, ibid., bk 4, l. 23

36 Deep in her breast lives the silent wound.
Ibid., bk 4, l. 67. Referring to Dido, deserted by Aeneas.

37 *Varium et mutabile semper
Femina.*
[A woman is always a fickle, unstable thing.]
Ibid., bk 4, ll. 569–70. Spoken by Mercury in a vision to Aeneas.

38 *Bella, horrida bella,
Et Thybrim multo spumantem sanguine cerno.*
[I see wars, horrible wars, and the Tiber foaming with much blood.]
The Sibyl of Cumae prophesying to Aeneas, ibid., bk 6, ll. 86–7. See ENOCH POWELL 3.

39 The gates of Hell are open night and day;
Smooth the descent, and easy is the way:
But, to return, and view the cheerful skies;
In this, the task and mighty labour lies.
The Sibyl of Cumae, ibid., bk 6, ll. 126–9 (transl. JOHN DRYDEN, 1697)

40 *Procul, o procul este, profani.*
[Far hence be souls profane.]
Sibyl of Cumae, ibid., bk 6, l. 258 (transl. JOHN DRYDEN)

41 That happy place, the green groves of the dwelling of the blest.
Ibid., bk 6, ll. 638–9 . Referring to the Elysian Fields, a stop on Aeneas's journey to the Underworld.

42 The spirit within nourishes, and the mind, diffused through all its members, sways the mass and mingles with the whole frame.
Ibid., bk 6, ll. 726–7

43 Each of us suffers his own fate in the after-life.
Ibid., bk 6, l. 743. Anchises addresses his son Aeneas in the Underworld.

44 Be it your concern, Roman, to rule the nations under law (this is your proper skill) and establish the way of peace; to spare the conquered and put down the mighty from their seat.
Ibid., bk 6, ll. 851–4. Anchises describes to Aeneas the task of the Romans.

45 *Geniumque loci.*
[Spirit of the place.]
Ibid., bk 7, l. 136. The origin of the phrase '*genius loci*'. See ALEXANDER POPE 106.

46 If I cannot prevail upon heaven, I shall move hell.
Ibid., bk 7, l. 312. Spoken by Juno on realizing that she will be unable to prevent Aeneas from gaining Latium.

47 Blessings on your young courage, boy; that's the way to the stars.
Ibid., bk 9, l. 641. Apollo addresses Iulus, son of Aeneas.

48 Fortune favours the brave.
Ibid., bk 10, l. 284. Spoken by Turnus, King of the Rutulians, who fought against and was killed by Aeneas. The words were in common usage; see TERENCE 7.

49 *E pluribus unus.*
[From many, one.]
Moretum, l. 104. See ANONYMOUS 19.

50 Mantua brought me life, Calabria death; now Naples holds me: I sang of flocks and farms and heroes.
Supposed epitaph on his (now vanished) tomb near Naples, according to a commentary on Virgil attributed to Suetonius by Aelius Donatus

Stephen Vizinczey

(b. 1933)
Hungarian novelist and critic

After participating in the 1956 Hungarian uprising he fled to Canada. His best-selling novel In Praise of Older Women *(1965) was followed by his essay collections,* The Rules of Chaos *(1968) and* Truth and Lies in Literature *(1986).*

1 Consistency is a virtue for trains: what we want from a philosopher is insights, whether he comes by them consistently or not.
Book review (1974), repr. in *Truth and Lies in Literature*, 'Good Faith and Bad' (1986)

2 We now have a whole culture based on the

assumption that people know nothing and so anything can be said to them.

Book review in the *Observer* 24 June 1990

V. N. Volosinov
(1905–60)
Russian linguist

Valentin Nikolaevic Volosinov. Associated with Mikhail Bakhtin and his school of criticism which sought to strip away preconceptions about literature, he was author of Marxism and the Philosophy of Language *(1929), among other works.*

1 Everything ideological possesses *meaning*: it represents, depicts, or stands for something lying outside itself. In other words, it is a *sign. Without signs there is no ideology.*

Marxism and the Philosophy of Language, ch. 1 (1929)

Voltaire
(1694–1778)
French philosopher, dramatist and author

Born François-Marie Arouet. A key figure of the Enlightenment, he caused controversy through his lampoons and satires, which led to periods of imprisonment. Exiled in England 1726–9, he extolled the political institutions he found there and the virtue of religious toleration in such works as Lettres philosophiques *(1733). Other writings include* Candide *(1759), a novel, and* Dictionnaire philosophique *(1768). He lived in Switzerland from 1755.*

1 To the living we owe respect, but to the dead we owe only the truth.

'Première Lettre sur Oedipe' (1719), repr. in *Oeuvres Complètes*, vol. 1 (ed. Theodore Besterman, 1968)

2 What parish priest would not like to be Pope?

Letters on England, Letter 5 ('On the Anglican Religion') (1731)

3 If there were only one religion in England there would be danger of despotism, if there were two, they would cut each other's throats, but there are thirty, and they live in peace and happiness.

Ibid., Letter 6 ('On the Presbyterians')

4 Time, which alone makes the reputation of men, ends by making their defects respectable.

Ibid., Letter 18 ('On Tragedy')

5 Woe to the makers of literal translations, who by rendering every word weaken the meaning! It is indeed by so doing that we can say the letter kills and the spirit gives life.

Ibid., Letter 18. Earlier in the essay, Voltaire prefaced a translated extract from SHAKESPEARE ('To be or not to be . . .')

with the words: 'Have pity on the copy for the sake of the original, and always bear in mind when you see a translation that you are only looking at a feeble print of a great picture.'

6 Governments need to have both shepherds and butchers.

'The Piccini Notebooks' (*c.* 1735–50), repr. in *Oeuvres Complètes*, vol. 82 (ed. Theodore Besterman, 1968)

7 God is not on the side of the big battalions, but on the side of those who shoot best.

'The Piccini Notebooks', ibid., vol. 82. See JEAN ANOUILH 8, ROGER DE BUSSY-RABUTIN 3.

8 The superfluous, a very necessary thing.

Le Mondain, l. 22 (1736), ibid., vol. 16 (ed. Nicholas Cronk, 2003)

9 History should be written as philosophy.

Letter, 31 October 1738, publ. in *Oeuvres Complètes*, vol. 89 (ed. Theodore Besterman, 1969)

10 The secret of being a bore is to tell everything.

Sept discours en vers sur l'homme, 'De la nature de l'homme' (1738)

11 The husband who decides to surprise his wife is often very much surprised himself.

La Femme Qui a Raison, Act 2, Sc. 2 (1749). Spoken by M. Gripon.

12 This agglomeration which was called and which still calls itself the Holy Roman Empire was neither holy, nor Roman, nor an empire.

Essai sur l'histoire générale et sur les moeurs et l'esprit des nations, ch. 70 (1756)

13 In this best of all possible worlds . . . all is for the best.

Candide, ch. 1 (1759). Spoken by Pangloss. Later in ch. 6, Candide muses: 'If this is the best of all possible worlds, what are the others like?'

14 If we do not find anything very pleasant, at least we shall find something new.

Ibid., ch. 17. Spoken by Cacambo, on journeying downriver into unknown country.

15 In this country it's a good thing to kill an admiral now and then to encourage the others [*pour encourager les autres.*]

Ibid., ch. 23. Reported as the words of English bystanders at the execution of Admiral John Byng, 14 March 1757. Byng had failed to relieve the island of Minorca, when it was besieged by the French.

16 We must cultivate our own garden . . . When man was put in the garden of Eden he was put there so

that he should work, which proves that man was not born to rest.

Ibid., ch. 30. Spoken by Candide and Pangloss, exchanging the fruits of their experience, in a passage said to encapsulate Voltaire's philosophy of common sense as against the complacency of 'optimism'.

17 Let us work without theorizing, 'tis the only way to make life endurable.

Martin, ibid., ch. 30

18 In the case of news, we should always wait for the sacrament of confirmation.

Letter, 28 August 1760, publ. in *Oeuvres Complètes*, vol. 106 (ed. Theodore Besterman, 1976)

19 The embarrassment of riches.

Le Droit du Seigneur, Act 2, Sc. 6 (1762). Spoken by de Gernance.

20 Common sense is not so common.

Philosophical Dictionary, 'Common Sense' (1764)

21 In general, the art of government consists in taking as much money as possible from one part of the citizens to give to the other.

Ibid., 'Money'

22 The best is the enemy of the good.

Ibid., 'Dramatic Art' (1770 edn). Quoting an Italian proverb.

23 Men who are occupied in the restoration of health to other men, by the joint exertion of skill and humanity, are above all the great of the earth. They even partake of divinity, since to preserve and renew is almost as noble as to create.

Ibid., 'Physicians'

24 One merit of poetry few persons will deny: it says more and in fewer words than prose.

Ibid., 'Poets'

25 They use thought only to justify their injustices, and speech only to disguise their thoughts.

Dialogues, Dialogue 15 ('Le Chapon et la Poularde') (1765). Spoken by Le Chapon, describing the ways of men. The words echo a 1676 sermon by Robert South (1634–1716), an English theologian and preacher.

26 It is amusing that a virtue is made of the vice of chastity; and it's a pretty odd sort of chastity at that, which leads men straight into the sin of Onan, and girls to the waning of their colour.

Letter, 28 March 1766, publ. in *Oeuvres Complètes*, vol. 114 (ed. Theodore Besterman, 1973)

27 When the masses get involved in reasoning, everything is lost.

Letter, 1 April 1766, ibid.

28 I have only ever made one prayer to God, a very short one: 'O Lord, make my enemies ridiculous.' And God granted it.

Letter, 16 May 1767, ibid., vol. 116

29 Indeed, history is nothing more than a tableau of crimes and misfortunes.

L'Ingénu, ch. 10 (1767; *The Pupil of Nature*). See EDWARD GIBBON 3.

30 If God did not exist, it would be necessary to invent him.

Épîtres, no. 96 ('À l'auteur du livre des trois imposteurs') (1770). See OVID 5.

31 The composition of a tragedy requires *testicles*.

Quoted by LORD BYRON in letter to publisher John Murray, 2 April 1817, publ. in *Byron's Letters and Journals*, vol. 5 (ed. Leslie A. Marchand, 1976). In reply to the question 'why no woman has ever written a tolerable tragedy'.

32 I disapprove of what you say, but I will defend to the death your right to say it.

Paraphrase of Voltaire's sentiments in his 'Essay on Tolerance' (1763), quoted in *The Friends of Voltaire* (1907) by S. G. Tallentyre. In February 1770, Voltaire wrote to M. le Riche: 'Monsieur l'Abbé, I detest what you write, but I would give my life to make it possible for you to continue to write.'

33 They are like their own beer: froth on the top, dregs at the bottom, the middle excellent.

Attributed, referring to the English

Kurt Vonnegut

(b. 1922)
US novelist

He blends science fiction and fantasy with social comment in his novels, such as his first, Piano Player *(1952), and* Breakfast of Champions *(1973). His best known,* Slaughterhouse Five *(1969), draws on his experience as a prisoner of war in Germany during and after the fire-bombing of Dresden.*

1 Only in superstition is there hope. If you want to become a friend of civilization, then become an enemy of the truth and a fanatic for harmless balderdash.

Wampeters, Foma and Granfallons, 'When I Was Twenty-One' (1974)

2 I was taught that the human brain was the crowning glory of evolution so far, but I think it's a very poor scheme for survival.

Quoted in the *Observer* 27 December 1987

Andrei Voznesensky
(b. 1933)
Russian poet

His experimental verse, known for its use of metaphor, 'the engine of form' as he put it, has been published in Parabola *(1960),* Heart of Achilles *(1966) and* Nostalgia for the Present *(1978), among other collections.*

1 I am Goya
of the bare field, by the enemy's beak gouged
till the craters of my eyes gape
I am grief

I am the tongue
of war, the embers of cities
on the snows of the year 1941
I am hunger
'I am Goya' (1960, transl. Stanley Kunitz), repr. in *Antiworlds and the Fifth Ace* (ed. Patricia Blake and Max Hayward, 1966)

2 Along a parabola life like a rocket flies,
Mainly in darkness, now and then on a rainbow.
'Parabolic Ballad' (1960, transl. W. H. AUDEN), ibid. Opening lines of poem.

3 The urge to kill, like the urge to beget,
Is blind and sinister. Its craving is set
Today on the flesh of a hare: tomorrow it can
Howl the same way for the flesh of a man.
'Hunting a Hare' (1964, transl. W. H. AUDEN), ibid.

W

Terry Waite
(b. 1939)
British ecclesiastic and negotiator

As special envoy of the Archbishop of Canterbury, ROBERT RUNCIE, *he negotiated for the release of British and US hostages held in Beirut, but was himself taken hostage (1987–91).*

1 Freeing hostages is like putting up a stage set, which you do with the captors, agreeing on each piece as you slowly put it together; then you leave an exit through which both the captor and the captive can walk with sincerity and dignity.
Television broadcast, ABC TV, 3 November 1986. On his work in Lebanon to negotiate the release of hostages, eleven weeks before his own abduction.

Derek Walcott
(b. 1930)
West Indian poet and playwright

Born in St Lucia, he has spent most of his life in Trinidad, where he founded (1959) and for twenty-five years ran the Trinidad Theatre Workshop. He is best known for his verse collections such as The Fortunate Traveller *(1981) and the epic* Omeros *(1990).*

1 I who have cursed
The drunken officer of British rule, how choose
Between this Africa and the English tongue I love?
Betray them both, or give back what they give?
'A Far Cry From Africa', publ. in *In a Green Night* (1962)

2 The peace of white horses,
The pastures of ports,
The litany of islands,
The rosary of archipelagoes.
'A Sea-Chantey', ibid.

3 Irascibility, muse of middle age.
'The Estranging Sea', ch. 18, sect. 3, publ. in *Another Life* (1973)

4 Adam had an idea.
He and the snake would share
the loss of Eden for a profit.
So both made the New World. And it looked good.
'New World', publ. in *Sea Grapes* (1976)

5 I try to forget what happiness was,
and when that don't work, I study the stars.
'The Schooner *Flight*', sect. 11, publ. in *The Star-Apple Kingdom*
(1980)

6 *I going to bite them young ladies, partner,*
like a hot dog or a hamburger
and if you thin, don't be in a fright
is only fat women I going to bite.
'The Spoiler's Return', publ. in *The Fortunate Traveller*, pt 2
(1981)

7 Famine sighs like a scythe
across the field of statistics and the desert
is a moving mouth. In the hold of this earth
10,000,000 shoreless souls are drifting.
Somalia: 765,000, their skeletons will go under the
     tidal sand.
'The Fortunate Traveller', sect. 1, ibid., pt 3

8 To curse your birthplace is the final evil.
'Poem 29', sect. 1, publ. in *Midsummer* (1984)

9 I come from a place that likes grandeur; it likes
large gestures; it is not inhibited by flourish; it is a
rhetorical society; it is a society of physical performance; it is a society of style.
Interview in *Writers at Work* (eighth series, ed. George
Plimpton, 1988)

10 The English language is nobody's special property. It is the property of the imagination: it is the
property of the language itself.
Ibid.

11 Poetry, which is perfection's sweat but which
must seem as fresh as the raindrops on a statue's
brow, combines the natural and the marmoreal; it
conjugates both tenses simultaneously: the past
and the present, if the past is the sculpture and the
present the beads of dew or rain on the forehead of
the past.
Nobel Lecture, 1992, publ. in *The Antilles, Fragments of Epic
Memory* (1993)

12 Break a vase, and the love that reassembles the
fragments is stronger than that love which took its
symmetry for granted when it was whole.
'Dissolving the Sigh of History', publ. in the *Guardian*
16 December 1992

George Wald
(1906–97)
US biochemist

*After research work in Berlin, he was based at Harvard (1932–
77), where he worked on the biochemistry of vision. He shared
the 1967 Nobel Prize for Physiology or Medicine with Ragnar
Granit and Haldan Hartline.*

1 We are the products of editing, rather than of
authorship.
'The Origin of Optical Activity', publ. in *Annals of the New
York Academy of Sciences*, vol. 69 (1957)

2 It would be a poor thing to be an atom in a universe without physicists, and physicists are made of
atoms. A physicist is an atom's way of knowing
about atoms.
The Fitness of the Environment, Foreword (1959) by L. J.
Henderson

Lech Walesa
(b. 1943)
Polish trade union leader and president

*In 1980 he founded the 'free trade union' Solidarity at the
Gdansk shipyards, winning economic and political concessions
from the government. He led Solidarity to victory in the 1989
election and served as Poland's President 1990–5.*

1 You have riches and freedom here but I feel no
sense of faith or direction. You have so many computers, why don't you use them in the search for
love?
Quoted in the *Daily Telegraph* 14 December 1988. Said in Paris
on his first visit outside the Soviet Bloc.

2 The supply of words in the world market is plentiful but the demand is falling. Let deeds follow words
now.
Newsweek 27 November 1989

Alice Walker
(b. 1944)
US author and critic

Her novels include The Third Life of Grange Copeland *(1970)
and* The Color Purple *(1982), which focuses on the racial and
sexual oppression of black women. She has also published
verse and essays, and an indictment of female circumcision,*
Possessing the Secret of Joy *(1992).*

1 It seems our fate to be incorrect ... and in our
incorrectness stand.
Interviews with Black Writers (ed. John O'Brien, 1973)

2 Oh those Africans!
Everywhere you look
they're bleeding
and crying
Crying and bleeding
on some of the whitest necks
in your town.

'The Diamonds on Liz's Bosom', publ. in *Horses Make a Landscape Beautiful* (1979)

3 The trouble with our people is as soon as they got out of slavery they didn't want to give the white man nothing else. But the fact is, you got to give 'em something. Either your money, your land, your woman or your ass.

The Color Purple (1982). Spoken by Pa.

4 She say, Celie, tell the truth, have you ever found God in church? I never did. I just found a bunch of folks hoping for him to show. Any God I ever felt in church I brought in with me. And I think all the other folks did too. They come to church to *share* God, not find God.

Shug, ibid.

5 I think it pisses God off if you walk by the color purple in a field somewhere and don't notice it.

Shug, ibid.

6 Womanist is to feminist as purple is to lavender.

In Search of Our Mothers' Gardens, Epigraph (1983)

7 It is healthier, in any case, to write for the adults one's children will become than for the children one's 'mature' critics often are.

Ibid., 'A Writer Because of, Not in Spite of, Her Children'

8 The original 'crime' of 'niggers' and lesbians is that they prefer themselves.

Ibid., 'Breaking Chains and Encouraging Life'

9 The good news may be that Nature is phasing out the white man, but the bad news is that's who She thinks we all are.

'Nuclear Madness: What You Can Do', ibid.

10 Anybody can observe the Sabbath, but making it holy surely takes the rest of the week.

Ibid., 'To the Editors of *Ms.* Magazine'

11 If Malcolm X had been a black woman his last message to the world would have been entirely different. The brotherhood of Moslem men – all colors – may exist ... but part of the glue that holds it together is the thorough suppression of women.

Ibid., 'To the Editors of *Ms.* Magazine'

12 Writing saved me from the sin and inconvenience of violence.

'*One* Child of One's Own' (1979), ibid.

13 There are those who believe Black people possess the secret of joy and that it is this that will sustain them through any spiritual or moral or physical devastation.

Possessing the Secret of Joy, Epigraph (1992)

George Wallace

(1919–98)

US politician

As Governor of the state of Alabama (1963–7), he attempted to block desegregation in schools. He was shot and paralysed while running for nomination as the Democratic Party presidential candidate in 1972.

1 Segregation now, segregation tomorrow and segregation forever!

Inaugural address as Governor of Alabama, January 1963, publ. in the *Birmingham World* 19 January 1963. Wallace's speechwriter, Asa Carter (1926–79), was a Ku Klux Klansman who went on to have literary success under the name of Forrest Carter, with, for example, *Gone to Texas*, filmed by CLINT EASTWOOD as *The Outlaw Josey Wales* (1976).

Henry Wallace

(1888–1965)

US politician

As Vice-President (1941–5) under FRANKLIN ROOSEVELT, he formulated and administered the New Deal legislation, especially with regard to farming.

1 The century on which we are entering – the century which will come out of this war – can be and must be the century of the common man.

Speech in New York, 8 May 1942, publ. in *Vital Speeches*, vol. 8 (1942)

William Ross Wallace

(1810–91)

US poet

By profession a lawyer, he contributed to periodicals, and after the Civil War was the author of patriotic songs.

1 The hand that rocks the cradle
Is the hand that rules the world.

'The Hand that Rocks the Cradle', publ. in *Meditations in America, and Other Poems* (1851). See MARY ROBINSON 1.

Edmund Waller

(1606–87)

English poet

Elected to Parliament aged 16, he had an active political life, and suffered banishment 1643–52 for his involvement in a Royalist plot. Polished heroic couplets were addressed to both OLIVER CROMWELL *and* CHARLES II.

1 Go, lovely rose!
Tell her that wastes her time and me,
That now she knows,
When I resemble her to thee,
How sweet and fair she seems to be.
'Go, lovely rose', st. 1, publ. in *Poems* (1645)

2 Poets that lasting marble seek
Must carve in Latin or in Greek.
We write in sand, our language grows,
And like the tide, our work o'erflows.
'On English Verse', st. 4, ibid.

3 That which her slender waist confined
Shall now my joyful temples bind;
No monarch but would give his crown
His arms might do what this has done.
'On a Girdle', st. 1, ibid.

4 So all we know of what they do above,
Is that they happy are, and that they love.
'Upon the Death of My Lady Rich', ll. 75–6, ibid.

5 Illustrious acts high raptures do infuse,
And every conqueror creates a muse.
'Panegyric to My Lord Protector', st. 46 (1655), repr. in *Poems* (1664)

6 The Muse's friend, tea does our fancy aid,
Repress those vapours which the head invade,
And keeps that palace of the soul serene.
'Of Tea, Commended by Her Majesty', publ. in *Poems* (1664)

7 The yielding marble of her snowy breast.
'On a Lady Passing through a Crowd of People', l. 12, ibid.

8 The fear of hell, or aiming to be blessed,
Savours too much of private interest.
'Of Divine Love', canto 2, publ. in *Divine Poems* (1685)

9 The soul's dark cottage, battered and decayed
Lets in new light through chinks that time has
   made;
Stronger by weakness, wiser men become,
As they draw near to their eternal home.

Leaving the old, both worlds at once they view,
That stand upon the threshold of the new.
'Of the Last Verses in the Book', st. 3, ibid.

Horace Walpole

(1717–97)

English author

Lord Orford. His correspondence of three thousand letters documents the mores of his age. He was an MP 1741–68, though played little active role in politics. His novel, The Castle of Otranto (1765) is regarded as the earliest Gothic romance, while the remodelling of his estate at Strawberry Hill, Twicken-ham (1754–94), set the taste for the Gothic revival in architecture.

1 Our supreme governors, the mob.
Letter, 7 September 1743, publ. in *Correspondence*, vol. 18 (ed. W. S. Lewis, 1955)

2 It is a little plaything-house that I got out of Mrs Chenevix's shop, and is the prettiest bauble you ever saw. It is set in enamelled meadows, with filigree hedges.
Letter, 8 June, 1747, ibid., vol. 37 (1974). Of Strawberry Hill, sublet to him by Mrs Chenevix who owned a famous toyshop in London. He later purchased the property.

3 The Methodists love your big sinners, as proper subjects to work upon.
Letter, 3 May 1749, ibid., vol. 20 (1960)

4 Every drop of ink in my pen ran cold.
Letter, 30 July 1752, ibid, vol. 9 (1941)

5 One of the greatest geniuses that ever existed, Shakespeare, undoubtedly wanted taste.
Letter, 9 August 1764, ibid., vol. 40 (1980)

6 What has one to do, when one grows tired of the world, as we both do, but to draw nearer and nearer, and gently waste the remains of life with friends with whom one began it?
Letter, 21 November 1765, ibid., vol. 10 (1941)

7 It is charming to totter into vogue.
Letter, 2 December 1765, ibid., vol. 30 (1961)

8 The best sun we have is made of Newcastle coal, and I am determined never to reckon upon any other.
Letter, 15 June 1768, ibid., vol. 10 (1941)

9 It was easier to conquer it than to know what to do with it.
Letter, 27 March 1772, ibid., vol. 23 (1967). Referring to the East.

10 The way to ensure summer in England is to have it framed and glazed in a comfortable room.
Letter, 28 May 1774, ibid., vol. 1 (1937)

11 The next Augustan age will dawn on the other side of the Atlantic. There will, perhaps, be a Thucydides at Boston, a Xenophon at New York, and, in time, a Virgil at Mexico, and a Newton at Peru. At last, some curious traveller from Lima will visit England and give a description of the ruins of St Paul's, like the editions of Balbec and Palmyra.
Letter, 24 November 1774, ibid., vol. 24 (1967)

12 The world is a comedy to those that think, a tragedy to those who feel.
Letter, 16 August 1776, ibid., vol. 32 (1965). A favourite aphorism of Walpole.

13 When will the world know that peace and propagation are the two most delightful things in it?
Letter, 7 July 1778, ibid., vol. 24 (1967)

14 He leapt the fence, and saw that all nature was a garden.
The History of the Modern Taste in Gardening, publ. 1780. Referring to the landscape gardener William Kent.

15 Prognostics do not always prove prophecies – at least the wisest prophets make sure of the event first.
Letter, 19 February 1785, ibid., vol. 36 (1973)

16 All his own geese are swans, as the swans of others are geese.
Letter, 1 December 1786, ibid., vol. 33 (1965). Of JOSHUA REYNOLDS.

(Sir) Robert Walpole
(1676–1745)
English statesman

Earl of Orford. A prominent Whig, he is traditionally regarded as the first British prime minister (1721–42), his premiership coinciding with a period of stability and prosperity. He was the father of HORACE WALPOLE.

1 My Lord Bath, you and I are now two as insignificant men as any in England.
Remark to Pulteney, Earl of Bath, February 1742, quoted in *Political and Literary Anecdotes* (1819) by William King. On their elevation to the House of Lords.

William Walsh
(1662–1708)
English poet

His Letters and Poems, Amorous and Gallant *(written 1692) were designed to portray the 'faithful image of an amorous heart'. He is principally remembered as the friend and correspondent of* ALEXANDER POPE.

1 A lover forsaken
A new love may get,
But a neck when once broken
Can never be set.
'The Despairing Lover', ll. 18–21, written 1692, publ. 1716, repr. in *Letters and Poems, Amorous and Gallant* (1736)

2 In love alone we hate to find
Companions of our woe.
'Rivals', st. 1, publ. in *Works in Prose and Verse* (1736)

2 I can endure my own despair,
But not another's hope.
'Rivals', st. 2, ibid.

Izaak Walton
(1593–1683)
English author

The Compleat Angler (1653), his discourse on fishing, interspersed with folklore, meditations and anecdotes, achieved a lasting success. He was a close friend of JOHN DONNE *and* BEN JONSON, *and wrote biographies of literary and ecclesiastical figures of the day, known as Walton's Lives.*

1 But God, who is able to prevail, wrestled with him, as the Angel did with Jacob, and marked him; marked him for his own.
Life and Death of Dr Donne (1640). Referring to JOHN DONNE.

2 Angling may be said to be so like the mathematics, that it can never be fully learnt.
The Compleat Angler, 'Epistle to the Reader' (1653)

3 As no man is born an artist, so no man is born an angler.
Ibid., 'Epistle to the Reader'

4 I am, sir, a brother of the angle.
Ibid., pt 1, ch. 1. Spoken by Piscator.

5 Sir Henry Wotton . . . was also a most dear lover, and a frequent practiser of the art of angling; of which he would say, 'it was an employment for his idle time, which was then not idly spent . . . a rest to his mind, a cheerer of his spirits, a diverter of sadness, a calmer of unquiet thoughts, a moderator of passions, a procurer of contentedness; and that

it begat habits of peace and patience in those that professed and practised it.'
Piscator, ibid., pt 1, ch. 1

6 You will find angling to be like the virtue of humility, which has a calmness of spirit and a world of other blessings attending upon it.
Piscator, ibid., pt 1, ch. 2

7 Good company and good discourse are the very sinews of virtue.
Piscator, ibid., pt 1, ch. 2

8 An excellent angler, and now with God.
Piscator, ibid., pt 1, ch. 4. Of Sir George Hastings.

9 I love such mirth as does not make friends ashamed to look upon one another next morning.
Piscator, ibid., pt 1, ch. 5

10 No man can lose what he never had.
Piscator, ibid., pt 1, ch. 5

11 We may say of angling, as Dr Boteler said of strawberries, 'Doubtless God could have made a better berry, but doubtless God never did'; and so, if I might be judge, God never did make a more calm, quiet, innocent recreation than angling.
Piscator, ibid., pt 1, ch. 5. See WILLIAM BUTLER 1.

12 This dish of meat is too good for any but anglers, or very honest men.
Piscator, ibid., pt 1, ch. 8

13 Look to your health; and if you have it, praise God, and value it next to a good conscience; for health is the second blessing that we mortals are capable of; a blessing that money cannot buy.
Piscator, ibid., pt 1, ch. 21

14 Let the blessing of St Peter's Master be ... upon all that are lovers of virtue; and dare trust in His providence; and be quiet; and go a-angling.
Piscator, ibid., pt 1, ch. 21

15 The great secretary of nature and all learning, Sir Francis Bacon.
Life of Mr George Herbert (1670)

Artemus Ward
(1834–67)
US journalist

Pseudonym of Charles Farrar Browne. As a humorist and debunker, he wrote misspelled, ungrammatical and pun-laden letters to the Plain Dealer, Vanity Fair *and* Punch. *His deadpan lecturing brought him greater fame.*

1 Mister Ward, don't yur blud bile at the thawt that three million and a half of your culled brethren air a clanking their chains in the South? – Sez I, not a bile! Let 'em clank!
Artemus Ward: His Book, 'Oberlin' (1862)

2 The female woman is one of the greatest institooshuns of which this land can boste.
Ibid., 'Woman's Rights'

3 Let's have the Union restored as it was, if we can; but if we can't, *I'm in favor of the Union as it wasn't.*
Artemus Ward: His Travels, 'In Canada' (1865)

4 It is a pity that Chawcer, who had geneyus, was so unedicated. He's the wuss speller I know of.
Artemus Ward in London, ch. 4 (1867)

5 I can't sing. As a singist I am not a success. I am saddest when I sing. So are those who hear me. They are sadder even than I am.
Artemus Ward's Lecture, 'Proscenium' (ed. T. W. Robertson and E. P. Hingston, 1869)

6 He is dreadfully married. He's the most married man I ever saw in my life.
Ibid., 'Brigham Young's Palace'. Referring to the Mormon Brigham Young.

7 Why is this thus? What is the reason of this thusness?
Ibid., 'Heber C. Kimball's Harem'

(Dame) Barbara Ward
(1914–81)
British economist and journalist

Baroness Jackson of Lodsworth. She and her husband, UN official Robert Jackson, worked as advisers on development planning in India and Pakistan. Her popular writings on conservation and ecology include Spaceship Earth *(1966) and* Only One Earth *(1972, written with René Dubos).*

1 We cannot cheat on DNA. We cannot get round photosynthesis. We cannot say I am not going to give a damn about phytoplankton. All these tiny mechanisms provide the preconditions of our planetary life. To say we do not care is to say in the most literal sense that 'we choose death'.
'Only One Earth', publ. in Who Speaks for Earth? (ed. Maurice F. Strong, 1973)

Andy Warhol
(c. 1928–87)
US artist and film-maker

Originally Andrew Warhola. A leading figure in 1960s Pop Art, he specialized in depicting popular icons and mass-produced commodities. GORE VIDAL *called him 'a genius with the IQ of a moron', while for* EDMUND WHITE *he was 'the man whose heart is as warm as a hanky soaked in ethyl chloride'.*

1 If you want to know all about Andy Warhol, just look at the surface: of my paintings and films and me, and there I am. There's nothing behind it.
'Warhol in his Own Words' (1967), repr. in *Andy Warhol: A Retrospective* (1986)

2 In the future everybody will be world famous for fifteen minutes.
Andy Warhol (exhibition catalogue, 1968). Ten years later, in *Andy Warhol's Exposures*, 'Studio 54' (1979), he wrote, 'I'm bored with that line. I never use it any more. My new line is, "In fifteen minutes everybody will be famous."'

3 Fantasy love is much better than reality love. Never doing it is very exciting. The most exciting attractions are between two opposites that never meet.
From A to B and Back Again, ch. 3 (1975)

4 Being good in business is the most fascinating kind of art . . . Making money is art and working is art and good business is the best art.
Ibid., ch. 6

5 I suppose I have a really loose interpretation of 'work', because I think that just being alive is so much work at something you don't always want to do. Being born is like being kidnapped. And then sold into slavery. People are working every minute. The machinery is always going. Even when you sleep.
Ibid., ch. 6

6 Since people are going to be living longer and getting older, they'll just have to learn how to be babies longer.
ibid. ch. 7

7 Isn't life a series of images that change as they repeat themselves?
Quoted in *Warhol*, 'Too Much Work 1980–84' (1989) by Victor Bokris

Charles Dudley Warner
(1829–1900)
US editor and essayist

He came to prominence with My Summer in a Garden *(1871), co-authored* The Gilded Age *with* MARK TWAIN *(1873) and wrote numerous travel essays.*

1 Mud-pies gratify one of our first and best instincts. So long as we are dirty, we are pure.
My Summer in a Garden, 'Preliminary' (1871)

2 What a man needs in gardening is a cast-iron back, with a hinge in it.
Ibid., 'Third Week'

3 Politics makes strange bed-fellows.
Ibid., 'Fifteenth Week'. See WILLIAM SHAKESPEARE: THE TEMPEST 15.

4 It is fortunate that each generation does not comprehend its own ignorance. We are thus enabled to call our ancestors barbarous.
Backlog Studies, 'Second Study' (1873)

Jack Warner
(1895–1981)
British actor

He appeared in such films as The Captive Heart *(1946) and* The Blue Lamp *(1950), in which he played PC Dixon, a role extended into the TV series* Dixon of Dock Green.

1 Evenin' all.
Dixon of Dock Green (BBC TV series, 1955–76, created by Ted Willis). Spoken by Sergeant George Dixon (Jack Warner). Each episode of the series started and ended with these words.

Sylvia Townsend Warner
(1893–1978)
British author and poet

Highly regarded for her wit and elegance of style, she was the author of short fiction, poetry and novels, such as Lolly Willowes *(1926) and* The Flint Anchor *(1954).*

1 There are some women . . . in whom conscience is so strongly developed that it leaves little room for anything else. Love is scarcely felt before duty rushes to encase it, anger impossible because one must always be calm and see both sides, pity evaporates in expedients, even grief is felt as a sort of bruised sense of injury, a resentment that one should have grief forced upon one when one has always acted for the best.
Autumn River, 'Total Loss' (1966)

2 When other helpers fail and comforts flee, when the senses decay and the mind moves in a narrower and narrower circle, when the grasshopper is a burden and the postman brings no letters, and even the Royal Family is no longer quite what it was, an obituary column stands fast.

Ibid., 'Their Quiet Lives'

Charles Marquis Warren

(1917–90)

US screenwriter, director and producer

He is best known for writing and directing westerns during the 1950s and '60s, helping to shape the popular stereotype of the Wild West in the TV series Gunsmoke, The Virginian *and* Rawhide *as well as numerous films.*

1 Head 'em up, move 'em out, rope 'em in, head 'em off, pull 'em down, move 'em on.

Preamble to *Rawhide* (TV series, 1959–66, created by Charles Marquis Warren). The series, which ran for 217 episodes and included CLINT EASTWOOD among its stars, was based on the 1866 diary of drover and pioneer cowboy George Duffield.

Earl Warren

(1891–1974)

US politician and judge

As Chief Justice (1953–69), he promoted civil liberties and achieved the prohibition of segregation in schools (1954). He also headed the commission of enquiry into the assassination of President JOHN F. KENNEDY *(1964).*

1 We conclude that in the field of public education the doctrine of 'separate but equal' has no place.

Brown v. Board of Education of Topeka (1954)

Robert Penn Warren

(1905–89)

US poet and novelist

A leading exponent of the New Criticism, he won three Pulitzer Prizes for the poetry collections Promises *(1957) and* Now and Then: Poems 1976–78 *(1978) and the novel* All the King's Men *(1946). He became the first US Poet Laureate in 1986.*

1 Storytelling and copulation are the two chief forms of amusement in the South. They're inexpensive and easy to procure.

Newsweek 25 August 1980

Booker T. Washington

(1856–1915)

US academic and reformer

An emancipated slave, he was the first president of the Tuskegee Normal and Industrial Institute (Tuskegee University) which trained black teachers. His support for segregation was severely criticized by W. E. B. DUBOIS *and other black leaders.*

1 No race can prosper till it learns there is as much dignity in tilling a field as in writing a poem.

Atlanta Exposition Address, 18 September 1895, publ. in *Up From Slavery*, ch. 14 (1901)

2 You can't hold a man down without staying down with him.

Attributed

George Washington

(1732–99)

US general and president

He was Commander-in-Chief of the colonial armies in the War of Independence (1775–83), presided over the convention that drew up the American Constitution (1787) and was subsequently the first President of the USA (1789–97). He is known as the father of his country. See LORD BYRON 44, THOMAS JEFFERSON 30.

1 I can't tell a lie, Pa; you know I can't tell a lie. I did cut it with my hatchet.

Quoted in *Life of George Washington*, ch. 2 (1810) by M. L. Weems. Remark after cutting down a cherry-tree as a boy.

2 When we assumed the soldier, we did not lay aside the citizen.

Address to the New York legislature, 26 June 1775

3 The time is now near at hand which must probably determine whether Americans are to be freemen or slaves; whether they are to have any property they can call their own; whether their houses and farms are to be pillaged and destroyed, and they consigned to a state of wretchedness from which no human efforts will probably deliver them. The fate of unborn millions will now depend, under God, on the courage and conduct of this army – Our cruel and unrelenting enemy leaves us no choice but a brave resistance, or the most abject submission; that is all we can expect – We have therefore to resolve to conquer or die.

General orders, 2 July 1776, publ. in *The Writings of George Washington*, vol. 5 (ed. John C. Fitzpatrick, 1932)

4 Few men have virtue to withstand the highest bidder.
Letter, 17 August 1779, quoted in *Maxims of Washington*, 'Virtue and Vice' (ed. John F. Schroeder, 1942)

5 To be prepared for war is one of the most effectual means of preserving peace.
First Annual Address to both Houses of Congress, 8 January 1790, repr. in *The Writings of George Washington*, vol. 30 (ed. John C. Fitzpatrick, 1939). See VEGETIUS 1.

6 Let me ... warn you in the most solemn manner against the baneful effects of the spirit of party.
Farewell Address, 17 September 1796, ibid., vol. 35 (1940). On retiring from public life.

7 The nation which indulges toward another an habitual hatred or an habitual fondness is in some degree a slave. It is a slave to its animosity or to its affection, either of which is sufficient to lead it astray from its duty and its interest.
Farewell Address, 17 September 1796, ibid., vol. 35

8 Europe has a set of primary interests, which to us have none, or a very remote relation. Hence she must be engaged in frequent controversies, the causes of which are essentially foreign to our concerns. Hence, therefore, it must be unwise in us to implicate ourselves, by artificial ties, in the ordinary vicissitudes of her politics, or the ordinary combinations and collisions of her friendships or enmities.
Farewell Address, 17 September 1796, ibid., vol. 35. Europe was at this time embroiled in the Napoleonic Wars.

9 'Tis our true policy to steer clear of permanent alliances with any portion of the foreign world.
Farewell Address 17 September 1796, ibid., vol. 35

10 There can be no greater error than to expect, or calculate, upon real favors from nation to nation. It is an illusion which experience must cure, which a just pride ought to discard.
Farewell Address, 17 September 1796, ibid., vol. 35

Keith Waterhouse
(b. 1929)
British author

His whimsical novel Billy Liar *(1959) drew on his Yorkshire working-class background. He co-wrote the screenplays for* Whistle Down the Wind *(1961) and* A Kind of Loving *(1962), and later had success with the stage show* Jeffrey Bernard is Unwell *(1989).*

1 Lying in bed, I abandoned the facts again and was back in Ambrosia.
Billy Liar, ch. 1 (1959). Narrated by Billy Fisher. Opening sentence of book.

2 Jeffrey Bernard is Unwell.
Title of stage adaptation of Jeffrey Bernard's *Spectator* columns (1989). Referring to the *Spectator's* customary notice of the non-appearance of the column written by Bernard (1932–97), whose notoriously dissolute lifestyle frequently resulted in missed editorial deadlines. The show, starring Peter O'Toole, ran in London's West End in 1989 and 1999.

(Sir) William Watson
(1858–1935)
British poet

He was a prolific writer of lyrical and political verse, which showed the influence of MATTHEW ARNOLD *and* LORD TENNYSON.

1 His friends he loved. His direst earthly foes –
Cats – I believe he did but feign to hate.
My hand will miss the insinuated nose,
Mine eyes the tail that wagged contempt at Fate.
'An Epitaph' (1884), repr. in *Collected Poems* (1906). Dedicated to his dog.

2 April, April,
Laugh thy girlish laughter;
Then, the moment after,
Weep thy girlish tears!
'April' (1885), ibid.

3 Pain with the thousand teeth.
The Dream of Man, st. 2 (1892). The line was later modified to 'That thing of a thousand talons, fierce Pain that none may assuage.'

4 We hold our hate too choice a thing
For light and careless lavishing.
'Hate', st. 2, publ. in *New Poems* (1909)

5 The thirst to know and understand –
A large and liberal discontent.
'The Things That Are More Excellent', st. 8, publ. in *The Poems of William Watson* (1936)

Alan Watts
(1915–73)
British-born US philosopher and author

He was ordained an Episcopalian priest in 1944 and became known as a lecturer and broadcaster on comparative philosophy and religion. Such works as The Spirit of Zen *(1936) and* The Meaning of Happiness *(1953) labelled him 'the brain and Buddha of American Zen'.*

1 Zen . . . does not confuse spirituality with thinking about God while one is peeling potatoes. Zen spirituality is just to peel the potatoes.
The Way of Zen, pt 2, ch. 2 (1957)

2 Trying to define yourself is like trying to bite your own teeth.
Life 21 April 1961

Isaac Watts
(1674–1748)
English hymn-writer

Regarded as the father of English and children's hymnody, he wrote over six hundred hymns as well as poetry and theological discourses.

1 Let dogs delight to bark and bite,
For God hath made them so.
Divine Songs for Children, no. 16 ('Against Quarrelling and Fighting'), st. 1 (1715)

2 But, children, you should never let
Such angry passions rise:
Your little hands were never made
To tear each other's eyes.
Ibid., no. 16, st. 2

3 Birds in their little nests agree
And 'tis a shameful sight,
When children of one family
Fall out, and chide, and fight.
Ibid., no. 17 ('Love between Brothers and Sisters'), st. 2

4 How doth the little busy bee
Improve each shining hour,
And gather honey all the day
From every opening flower!
Ibid., no. 20 ('Against Idleness and Mischief'), st. 1. See LEWIS CARROLL 4 for a parody of this verse.

5 For Satan finds some mischief still
For idle hands to do.
Ibid., no. 20, st. 3. The saying is proverbial, with variations traced back as early as SAINT JEROME.

6 Let me be dressed fine as I will,
Flies, worms, and flowers, exceed me still.
Ibid., no. 22 ('Against Pride in Clothes'), st. 4

7 Hush, my dear! Lie still, and slumber!
Holy angels guard thy bed!
Heavenly blessings, without number,
Gently falling on thy head.
Ibid., no. 35 ('A Cradle Hymn'), st. 1

8 'Tis the voice of the sluggard; I heard him complain,
'You have waked me too soon, I must slumber again.'
As the door on its hinges, so he on his bed,
Turns his sides and his shoulders and his heavy head.
Ibid., no. 39 ('The Sluggard'), st. 1. LEWIS CARROLL parodied these lines in 'The Lobster Quadrille', in *Alice's Adventures in Wonderland*, ch. 10 (1865): ''Tis the voice of the Lobster: I heard him declare "You have baked me too brown, I must sugar my hair." '

Evelyn Waugh
(1903–66)
British novelist

After his social satires, Decline and Fall *(1928) and* Scoop *(1938), he adopted a more serious, elegiac style in* Brideshead Revisited *(1945). He regarded his conversion to Catholicism in 1928 as the most important event of his life, once commenting: 'You don't know how much nastier I would be if I hadn't become a Catholic.'*

1 I expect you'll be becoming a schoolmaster, sir. That's what most of the gentlemen does, sir, that gets sent down for indecent behaviour.
Decline and Fall, 'Prelude' (1928). Spoken by the porter.

2 We schoolmasters must temper discretion with deceit.
Dr Fagan, ibid., pt 1, ch. 2

3 That's the public-school system all over. They may kick you out, but they never let you down.
Captain Grimes, ibid., pt 1, ch. 3. Paul Pennyfeather, to whom these words are addressed, had been given a letter of recommendation by his housemaster after being expelled from school.

4 We can trace almost all the disasters of English history to the influence of Wales.
Dr Fagan, ibid., pt 1, ch. 8

5 I came to the conclusion many years ago that almost all crime is due to the repressed desire for aesthetic expression.
Prison Governor Sir Wilfred Lucas-Dockery, ibid., pt 3, ch. 1. Spoken to Paul Pennyfeather, who has just been informed that he is to be put to work in the Arts and Crafts Workshop.

6 Anyone who has been to an English public school will always feel comparatively at home in prison. It

is the people brought up in the gay intimacy of the slums . . . who find prison so soul-destroying.
Prison Governor Sir Wilfred Lucas-Dockery, ibid. pt 3, ch. 4. See JONATHAN AITKEN 2.

7 If we can't stamp out literature in the country, we can at least stop its being brought in from outside.
Vile Bodies, ch. 2 (1930). Spoken by a customs officer at Dover.

8 All this fuss about sleeping together. For physical pleasure I'd sooner go to my dentist any day.
Nina Blount, ibid., ch. 6. Spoken to her fiancé Adam Fenwick-Symes.

9 *Feather-footed through the plashy fen passes the questing vole.*
William Boot's 'Lush Places' column, in *Scoop*, bk 1, ch. 1, sect. 4 (1938). Considered an example of 'good style' by the staff of *The Beast*.

10 News is what a chap who doesn't care much about anything wants to read. And it's only news until he's read it. After that it's dead.
Corker, ibid., bk 1, ch. 5, sect. 1

11 You should ask me whether I have any message for the British public. I have. It is this: *Might must find a way.* Not '*Force*', remember; other nations use 'force'; we Britons alone use 'Might'.
Mr Baldwin, ibid., bk 2, ch. 5, sect. 1

12 It is a curious thing that every creed promises a paradise which will be absolutely uninhabitable for anyone of civilised taste.
Put Out More Flags, ch. 1, sect. 7 (1942). Spoken by Ambrose.

13 Charm is the great English blight. It does not exist outside these damp islands. It spots and kills anything it touches. It kills love; it kills art; I greatly fear, my dear Charles, it has killed you.
Brideshead Revisited, bk. 3, ch. 2 (1945). Anthony Blanche addressing Charles Ryder.

14 His courtesy was somewhat extravagant. He would write and thank people who wrote to thank him for wedding presents and when he encountered anyone as punctilious as himself the correspondence ended only with death.
Life 8 April 1946

15 They are a very decent generous lot of people out here and *they don't expect you to listen* . . . It's the secret of social ease in this country. They talk entirely for their own pleasure. Nothing they say is designed to be heard.
The Loved One (1948). Sir Francis Hinsley, describing Californians.

16 You never find an Englishman among the underdogs – except in England, of course.
Sir Ambrose Abercrombie, ibid.

17 That impersonal insensitive friendliness which takes the place of ceremony in that land of waifs and strays.
Sir Ambrose Abercrombie, ibid. Referring to Aimée Thanatogenos, an American.

18 In the dying world I come from quotation is a national vice. It used to be the classics, now it's lyric verse.
Dennis Barlow, ibid.

19 Impotence and sodomy are socially O.K. but birth control is flagrantly middle-class.
'An Open Letter . . . On a Very Serious Subject', publ. in *Encounter*, repr. in *Noblesse Oblige*, pt 3 (ed. NANCY MITFORD, 1956)

20 We are American at puberty. We die French.
Journal entry, 18 July 1961, publ. in *The Diaries of Evelyn Waugh* (ed. Michael Davie, 1976)

21 Punctuality is the virtue of the bored.
Journal entry, 26 March 1962, ibid.

22 Manners are especially the need of the plain. The pretty can get away with anything.
Quoted in the *Observer* 15 April 1962

23 It was announced that the trouble was not 'malignant.' . . . It was a typical triumph of modern science to find the only part of Randolph that was not malignant and remove it.
Journal entry, March 1964, publ. in *The Diaries of Evelyn Waugh* (ed. Michael Davie, 1976). Referring to Randolph Churchill, son of WINSTON CHURCHILL and an erstwhile friend of Waugh's.

John Wayne
(1907–79)
US screen actor

Orginally Marion Michael Morrison. Known as 'The Duke', he played a succession of manly roles in westerns and war films, including Red River *(1948) and* True Grit *(1969). 'I play John Wayne in every picture regardless of the character,' he once remarked, 'and I've been doing all right, haven't I?'*

1 A man oughta do what he thinks is right.
Hondo (film, 1953, screenplay by James Edward Grant, directed by John Farrow). Spoken by Hondo Lane (John Wayne).

2 Out here, due process is a bullet.
The Green Berets (film, 1968, screenplay by James Lee Barrett,

directed by John Wayne and Ray Kellogg). Spoken by Colonel Mike Kirby (John Wayne).

Frederick Weatherly
(1848–1929)
English songwriter and author

He was a lawyer, poet and author of fantasy and children's books, but is best remembered for the song 'Danny Boy' (1913).

1 Oh Danny boy, the pipes, the pipes are calling,
From glen to glen and down the mountainside,
The summer's gone and all the leaves are falling,
'Tis you, 'tis you must go and I must bide.
'Danny Boy' (song, 1913). Set to the tune of the Londonderry Air.

2 Roses are flowering in Picardy,
But there's never a rose like you.
'Roses of Picardy' (song, 1916)

Mary Webb
(1881–1927)
British author

Her romantic fiction set in the Shropshire countryside became popular after her novel Precious Bane *(1924) was praised by* STANLEY BALDWIN. *Her melodramatic style was satirized by* STELLA GIBBONS *in* Cold Comfort Farm *(1932).*

1 Saddle your dreams afore you ride 'em.
Precious Bane, bk 1, ch. 6 title (1924)

Sidney Webb
(1859–1947)
British socialist

Baron Passfield. Founder of the Fabian Society (1884) and of the London School of Economics (1895), he was instrumental in drafting the LABOUR PARTY CONSTITUTION, *entering parliament as a Labour MP in 1922. With his wife Beatrice he founded the* New Statesman *(1913).*

1 Let me insist on what our opponents habitually ignore, and indeed, what they seem intellectually incapable of understanding, namely the inevitable gradualness of our scheme of change.
Speech to Labour Party Conference, London, 26 June 1923, publ. in *The Labour Party on the Threshold* (Fabian Tract no. 207, 1923). Referring to the programme of the Labour Party, then in opposition.

2 Marriage is the waste-paper basket of the emotions.
Quoted in *Autobiography*, vol. 1, ch. 4 (1967) by BERTRAND RUSSELL. This was a habitual saying, according to his wife

Beatrice Webb, though Russell denied ever hearing it. The Webbs were, he wrote, 'the most completely married couple that I have ever known. They were, however, very averse from any romantic view of love or marriage. Marriage was a social institution designed to fit instinct into a legal framework.'

Max Weber
(1864–1920)
German sociologist

He is regarded as the founder of modern sociology, and wrote the key works The Protestant Ethic and the Spirit of Capitalism *(1904) and* Economy and Society *(1922).*

1 The experience of the irrationality of the world has been the driving force of all religious revolution.
'Politics as a Vocation' (1919), repr. in *Essays in Sociology* (ed. H. H. Gerth and C. WRIGHT MILLS, 1946)

2 Only he has the calling for politics who is sure that he will not crumble when the world from his point of view is too stupid or base for what he wants to offer. Only he who in the face of all this can say 'In spite of all!' has the calling for politics.
'Politics as a Vocation', ibid. Last words of essay.

3 Only by strict specialization can the scientific worker become fully conscious, for once and perhaps never again in his lifetime, that he has achieved something that will endure. A really definitive and good accomplishment is today always a specialized accomplishment.
'Science as a Vocation' (1919), ibid.

4 The fate of our times is characterized by rationalization and intellectualization and, above all, by the 'disenchantment of the world'. Precisely the ultimate and most sublime values have retreated from public life either into the transcendental realm of mystic life or into the brotherliness of direct and personal human relations. It is not accidental that our greatest art is intimate and not monumental.
'Science as a Vocation', ibid.

Daniel Webster
(1782–1852)
US statesman and lawyer

A notable orator, he served as a Congressman and Senator, before becoming Secretary of State (1841–3 and 1850–2). He supported free trade and negotiated the Webster-Ashburton treaty with Great Britain (1842). SYDNEY SMITH *said that Webster struck him 'like a steam engine in trousers'. See also* THOMAS CARLYLE 2.

1 The past, at least, is secure.
Second Speech to the Senate on Foote's Resolution, 26 January 1830, publ. in *The Writings and Speeches of Daniel Webster*, vol. 6 (ed. J. W. McIntyre, 1903)

2 The people's government, made for the people, made by the people, and answerable to the people.
Second Speech to the Senate on Foote's Resolution, 26 January 1830, ibid., vol. 6

3 Everywhere, spread all over in characters of living light, blazing on all its ample folds, as they float over the sea and over the land, and in every wind under the whole heavens, that other sentiment, dear to every true American heart – Liberty *and* Union, now and forever, one and inseparable.
Second Speech to the Senate on Foote's Resolution, 26 January 1830, ibid., vol. 6

4 A fearful concatenation of circumstances.
'Argument on the Murder of Captain White', speech at Salem, Massachusetts, 6 April 1830, ibid., vol. 11

5 There is no refuge from confession but suicide, and suicide is confession.
'Argument on the Murder of Captain White', speech at Salem, Massachusetts, 6 April 1830, ibid., vol. 11

6 On this question of principle, while actual suffering was yet afar off, they [the Colonies] raised their flag against a power, to which, for purposes of foreign conquest and subjugation, Rome, in the height of her glory, is not to be compared; a power which has dotted over the surface of the whole globe with her possessions and military posts, whose morning drum-beat, following the sun, and keeping company with the hours, circles the earth with one continuous and unbroken strain of the martial airs of England.
Speech on the President's Protest to the Senate, 7 May 1834, publ. in ibid., vol. 7

7 Whatever government is not a government of laws, is a despotism, let it be called what it may.
Speech at a reception in Bangor, Maine, 25 August 1835, ibid., vol. 2

8 When *tillage* begins, other arts follow. The farmers, therefore, are the founders of human civilization.
Speech, 'Remarks on the Agriculture of England', at Boston, 13 January 1840, ibid.

9 I was born an American; I will live an American; I shall die an American.
Speech on the Compromise Bill to the Senate, 17 July 1850, ibid, vol. 10

John Webster
(1580–1625)
English dramatist

He collaborated with other dramatists, including THOMAS DEKKER, *but is most famous for* The White Devil *(1612) and* The Duchess of Malfi *(1613). Unpopular in his own day, he was later championed by* CHARLES LAMB.

1 Is not old wine wholesomest, old pippins toothsomest, old wood burn brightest, old linen wash whitest? Old soldiers, sweetheart, are surest, and old lovers are soundest.
Westward Ho!, Act 2, Sc. 2 (written with THOMAS DEKKER, performed 1604). Spoken by Mistress Birdlime, a procuress.

2 I saw him even now going the way of all flesh, that is to say towards the kitchen.
Mistress Birdlime, ibid., Act 2, Sc. 2. See BIBLE, OLD TESTAMENT: JOSHUA 4.

3 Fortune's a right whore.
If she give ought, she deals it in small parcels,
That she may take away all at one swoop.
The White Devil, Act 1, Sc. 1, ll. 4–6 (1612). Spoken by Lodovico.

4 'Tis just like a summer bird cage in a garden; the birds that are without despair to get in, and the birds that are within despair, and are in a consumption, for fear they shall never get out.
Flamineo, ibid., Act 1, Sc. 2, ll. 41–3. Referring to seduction. See MONTAIGNE 20.

5 A mere tale of a tub, my words are idle.
Francisco de Medicis, ibid., Act 2, Sc. 1, l. 96. A 'tale of a tub', meaning a cock-and-bull story, was the title of SWIFT's satire of the Church (1704). See RABELAIS 10.

6 For your names
Of 'whore' and 'murderess', they proceed from you,
As if a man should spit against the wind,
The filth returns in 's face.
Vittoria Corombona, ibid., Act 3, Sc. 2, ll. 152–5

7 Cowardly dogs bark loudest.
Brachiano, ibid., Act 3, Sc. 2, l. 169

8 A rape! a rape! . . .
Yes, you have ravished justice;
Forced her to do your pleasure.
Vittoria Corombona, ibid., Act 3, Sc. 2, ll. 284–6

9 I have heard grief named the eldest child of sin.
Giovanni, ibid., Act 5, Sc. 4, l. 19

10 Call for the robin-red-breast and the wren,
Since o'er shady groves they hover,

And with leaves and flowers do cover
The friendless bodies of unburied men.
Cornelia, ibid., Act 5, Sc. 4, ll. 89–92

11 But keep the wolf far thence, that's foe to men,
For with his nails he'll dig them up again.
Cornelia, ibid., Act 5, Sc. 4, ll. 97–8

12 We think caged birds sing, when indeed they
cry.
Flamineo, ibid., Act 5, Sc. 4, l. 117

13 And of all axioms this shall win the prize –
'Tis better to be fortunate than wise.
Flamineo, ibid., Act 5, Sc. 6, ll. 182–3

14 There's nothing of so infinite vexation
As man's own thoughts.
Flamineo, ibid., Act 5, Sc. 6, ll. 206–7

15 Prosperity doth bewitch men, seeming clear;
But seas do laugh, show white, when rocks are
near.
Flamineo, ibid., Act 5, Sc. 6, ll. 250–1

16 That curious engine, your white hand.
The Duchess of Malfi, Act 3, Sc. 2, l. 336 (performed *c.* 1613,
publ. 1623). Spoken by Bosola.

17 A politician is the devil's quilted anvil;
He fashions all sins on him, and the blows
Are never heard.
Bosola, ibid., Act 3, Sc. 2, ll. 371–3

18 What's this flesh? a little crudded milk, fantasti-
cal puff-paste.
Ibid., Act 4, Sc. 2, ll. 124–5. Bosola addresses the Duchess of
Malfi. 'Crudded' or 'cruded' means curdled.

19 I am the Duchess of Malfi still.
Duchess of Malfi, ibid., Act 4, Sc. 2, l. 139

20 Glories, like glow-worms, afar off shine
bright,
But looked to near, have neither heat nor light.
Bosola, ibid., Act 4, Sc. 2, ll. 141–2

21 I know death hath ten thousand several doors
For men to take their exits.
The Duchess, ibid., Act 4, Sc. 2, ll. 225–6. See PHILIP
MASSINGER 4, SENECA 19 and JONATHAN SWIFT 4.

22 Heaven-gates are not so highly arched
As princes' palaces: they that enter there
Must go upon their knees.
The Duchess, ibid., Act 4, Sc. 2, ll. 239–41

23 Other sins only speak; murder shrieks out:
The element of water moistens the earth,
But blood flies upwards, and bedews the heavens.
Bosola, ibid., Act 4, Sc. 2, ll. 278–80

24 Cover her face. Mine eyes dazzle: she died
young.
Ferdinand, ibid., Act 4, Sc. 2, l. 281. Referring to the strangled
duchess, his twin. Bosola replies, 'I think not so: her infelicity/
Seemed to have years too many.'

25 Eagles commonly fly alone. They are crows, daws,
and starlings that flock together.
Ferdinand, ibid., Act 5, Sc. 2, ll. 31–2

26 When I go to hell, I mean to carry a bribe: for
look you, good gifts evermore make way for the
worst persons.
Ferdinand, ibid., Act 5, Sc. 2, ll. 40–2

27 I do love these ancient ruins.
We never tread upon them, but we set
Our foot upon some reverend history.
Antonio, ibid., Act 5, Sc. 3, ll. 10–12

28 We are merely the stars' tennis-balls, struck and
bandied
Which way please them.
Bosola, ibid., Act 5, Sc. 4, ll. 63–4

29 Vain the ambition of kings,
Who seek by trophies and dead things,
To leave a living name behind,
And weave but nets to catch the wind.
The Devil's Law-Case, Act 5, Sc. 4, ll. 143–6 (1623). Romelio's
song.

Josiah Wedgwood
(1730–95)
English potter

*He established pottery factories in Staffordshire in the 1760s
and is known for his jasper ware, inspired by neo-classical
designs and embossed with cameos. He was a philanthropist
and sympathetic with America's struggle for independence
and the abolitionist cause.*

1 Am I not a man and a brother?
Legend on jasper ware, above a cameo of a chained African
slave (1787). The words and image were adopted by the Society
for the Abolition of the Slave Trade (later the Anti-Slavery
Society), which was actively supported by Wedgwood and
other Quakers.

Simone Weil

(1909–43)

French philosopher and mystic

Passionately concerned with religious matters, social equality and pacifism, she interspersed teaching philosophy with manual work, and died from pleurisy after restricting herself to the same diet as those in Nazi labour camps. Her works include Gravity and Grace *(1947) and* Waiting on God *(1950).*

1 What a country calls its vital economic interests are not the things which enable its citizens to live, but the things which enable it to make war. Petrol is more likely than wheat to be a cause of international conflict.

'The Power of Words' (1937), repr. in *Selected Essays* (ed. Richard Rees, 1962)

2 It is not the cause for which men took up arms that makes a victory more just or less, it is the order that is established when arms have been laid down.

'The Great Beast: Conclusion' (1939–40), ibid.

3 I would suggest that barbarism be considered as a permanent and universal human characteristic which becomes more or less pronounced according to the play of circumstances.

'Hitler and Roman Foreign Policy', publ. in *Nouveaux Cahiers* 1 January 1940

4 When a contradiction is impossible to resolve except by a lie, then we know that it is really a door.

New York Notebook, written 1942 (1950), repr. in *First and Last Notebooks*, pt 3 (ed. Richard Rees, 1970)

5 Real genius is nothing else but the supernatural virtue of humility in the domain of thought.

'Human Personality' (1943), repr. in *Selected Essays* (ed. Richard Rees, 1962)

6 It is only the impossible that is possible for God. He has given over the possible to the mechanics of matter and the autonomy of his creatures.

'A War of Religions' (1943), publ. in ibid.

7 A test of what is real is that it is hard and rough. Joys are found in it, not pleasure. What is pleasant belongs to dreams.

Gravity and Grace, 'Illusions' (1947)

8 Purity is the power to contemplate defilement.

Ibid., 'Attention and Will'

9 A work of art has an author and yet, when it is perfect, it has something which is essentially anonymous about it.

Ibid., 'Beauty'

10 Those who are unhappy have no need for anything in this world but people capable of giving them their attention.

Ibid., 'Reflections on the Right Use of School Studies'

11 In the Church, considered as a social organism, the mysteries inevitably degenerate into beliefs.

Quoted in *Simone Weil: Utopian Pessimist*, ch. 9 (1989) by David McLellan

Steven Weinberg

(b. 1933)

US theoretical physicist

From 1967 he developed a model of particle interaction potentially capable of providing a universal theory of nature. His publications include Dreams of a Final Theory *(1993) and* The Quantum Theory of Fields *(1995–6).*

1 The more the universe seems comprehensible, the more it also seems pointless.

The First Three Minutes, ch. 8 (1977)

2 The effort to understand the universe is one of the very few things that lifts human life a little above the level of farce, and gives it some of the grace of tragedy.

Ibid., ch. 8. Closing sentence of book.

Fay Weldon

(b. 1931)

British novelist

She writes with astute irony of women in adversity. Among her many novels are The Life and Loves of a She-Devil *(1983) and* The Hearts and Lives of Men *(1987). She has also written numerous plays, scripts and television adaptations See also* ADVERTISING SLOGANS 9.

1 We shelter children for a time; we live side by side with men; and that is all. We owe them nothing, and are owed nothing. I think we owe our friends more, especially our female friends.

Praxis, ch. 19 (1978). Narrated by Praxis Duveen.

2 You end up as you deserve. In old age you must put up with the face, the friends, the health, and the children you have earned.

Praxis Duveen, ibid., ch. 21

3 Writers were never meant to be professionals. Writing is not a profession, it is an activity, an essen-

tially amateur occupation. It is what you do when you are not living. It is something you do with your hands, like knitting.

Letters to Alice, Letter 5 (1984)

4 That to be good is to be happy is not something particularly evident in any of our experiences of real life, yet how badly we want it, and need it, to be true.

Ibid., Letter 5. On JANE AUSTEN's promise, 'If you are good . . . you will be happy.'

5 The Life and Loves of a She-Devil.

Title of novel (1984)

6 Your generation does too much sharing. To share grief is to double grief, not halve it.

Wicked Women, 'A Good Sound Marriage' (1995). Spoken by Christabel.

7 Experts are never in real danger. Everyone needs them. The chambermaid always survives the palace revolution. Someone has to make the beds.

Defoe Desmond, ibid., 'The End of the Line'

8 Rape isn't actually the worst thing that can happen to a woman if you're safe and alive and unmarked after the event.

Independent on Sunday 5 July 1998

9 Even God has become female. God is no longer the bearded patriarch in the sky. He has had a sex change and turned into Mother Nature.

Quoted in *The Times* 29 August 1998. On the feminization of society.

Orson Welles
(1915–85)
US film-maker and actor

'A bravura personality' according to KENNETH TYNAN, *he founded the Mercury Theatre in 1937 and went on to make what many consider the greatest film ever made,* Citizen Kane *(1941), in which he was producer, director, screenwriter and leading actor. Later works were praised by critics but commercial failures.*

1 Ladies and gentlemen, I have a grave announcement to make. Incredible as it may seem, strange beings who landed in New Jersey tonight are the vanguard of an invading army from Mars.

CBS radio broadcast, Hallowe'en, 1938, from a reading of *The War of the Worlds* (1898) by H. G. WELLS. According to later reports, despite clear warnings that the broadcast was science fiction, listeners jammed switchboards and roads as they abandoned their homes in large numbers, with some people claiming they had actually seen the Martians.

2 In Italy for thirty years under the Borgias they had warfare, terror, murder, bloodshed – they produced Michelangelo, Leonardo da Vinci and the Renaissance. In Switzerland they had brotherly love, five hundred years of democracy and peace, and what did they produce? The cuckoo clock!

The Third Man, (film, 1949, screenplay by GRAHAM GREENE, directed by Carol Reed). Spoken by Harry Lime. Welles starred in the film and contributed the speech to Greene's screenplay; he later claimed that his words were based on a fragment of an old Hungarian play.

3 The essential is to excite the spectators. If that means playing *Hamlet* on a flying trapeze or in an aquarium, you do it.

Les Nouvelles littéraires, 1953, quoted in *Citizen Welles*, ch. 16 (1989) by Frank Brady

4 The biggest electric train set any boy ever had!

Quoted in *The Fabulous Orson Welles*, ch. 7 (1956) by Peter Noble. Referring to RKO studios.

5 I hate television. I hate it as much as peanuts. But I can't stop eating peanuts.

New York Herald Tribune 12 October 1956

6 When you are down and out something always turns up – and it is usually the noses of your friends.

New York Times 1 April 1962

7 A good artist should be isolated. If he isn't isolated, something is wrong.

Interview in *Hollywood Voices* (ed. Andrew Sarris, 1971)

Duke of Wellington
(1769–1852)
English general and prime minister

Arthur Wellesley. Already acclaimed for his victories in the Peninsular War (1808–14), he became a national hero after defeating NAPOLEON *at the Battle of Waterloo (1815). As Tory Prime Minister 1828–30, he supported Catholic emancipation and opposed parliamentary reform. William IV said he was 'the only subject I shake hands with'. See also* LORD TENNYSON 137.

1 I don't know what effect these men will have upon the enemy, but, by God, they terrify me.

Attributed dispatch, 29 August 1810. Speaking of his generals, though commonly thought to refer to the rank-and-file soldiers. A similar remark is attributed to Prime Minister Lord North.

2 We have in the service the scum of the earth as common soldiers.

Dispatch to Lord Bathurst, War Minister, from Vitoria, Spain,

2 July 1813, quoted in *Wellington: The Years of the Sword*, pt 2, ch. 16 (1969) by Elizabeth Longford

3 Hard pounding this, gentlemen; let's see who will pound longest.
Remark to his officers at the Battle of Waterloo, 18 June 1815, ibid., pt 3, ch. 23

4 Publish and be damned!
Ibid., pt 2, ch. 10. Referring to a threat to blackmail him by the publication of his love letters to his mistress Harriette Wilson, December 1824. Wellington's words were, according to legend, written in flaming red ink.

5 I never saw so many shocking bad hats in my life.
On seeing the first Reformed Parliament in 1832, quoted in *Words on Wellington* (1889) by Sir William Fraser

6 The Battle of Waterloo was won on the playing fields of Eton.
Attributed in *Words on Wellington* (1889) by Sir William Fraser. In *De L'Avenir politique de L'Angleterre*, ch. 10 (1856) by C. F. R. Montalembert, Wellington's words were recorded as: 'It is here that the battle of Waterloo was won' while visiting his former school 'during his declining years'. See GEORGE ORWELL 14.

7 Next to a battle lost, the greatest misery is a battle gained.
Quoted in *The Diary of Frances, Lady Shelley 1787–1817*, vol. 1, ch. 9 (ed. Richard Edgcumbe, 1912). Said on various occasions.

H. G. Wells
(1866–1946)
British author

Herbert George Wells. He was a pioneer of science fiction with such works as The Time Machine *(1895) and* The War of the Worlds *(1898), and the author of comic novels, including* Kipps *(1905) and* The History of Mr Polly *(1910). He also wrote on history, science and socialism. His lover* REBECCA WEST *described him as 'the old maid among novelists'. See* HENRY JAMES 29.

1 The Social Contract is nothing more or less than a vast conspiracy of human beings to lie to and humbug themselves and one another for the general Good. Lies are the mortar that bind the savage individual man into the social masonry.
Love and Mr Lewisham, ch. 23 (1900). Spoken by Chaffery.

2 Cycle tracks will abound in Utopia.
A Modern Utopia, ch. 2, sect. 3 (1905)

3 Moral indignation is jealousy with a halo. It is the peculiar snare of the perplexed orthodox.
The Wife of Sir Isaac Harman, ch. 9, sect. 2 (1914)

4 Nothing could have been more obvious to the people of the early twentieth century than the rapidity with which war was becoming impossible. And as certainly they did not see it. They did not see it until the atomic bombs burst in their fumbling hands.
The World Set Free: A Story of Mankind, ch. 2, sect. 5 (1914). In his fantasy, Wells predicted an age of atomic energy starting with a war commencing in 1956.

5 It is leviathan retrieving pebbles. It is a magnificent but painful hippopotamus resolved at any cost, even at the cost of its dignity, upon picking up a pea which has got into a corner of its den.
Boon, ch. 4 (1915). Spoken by George Boon, referring to HENRY JAMES.

6 Beauty isn't a special inserted sort of thing. It is just life, pure life, life nascent, running clear and strong.
Quoted by REBECCA WEST in book review in the *Daily News* 14 August 1915, repr. in *The History of Mr Wells*, ch. 5 (1995) by MICHAEL FOOT

7 He was inordinately proud of England and he abused her incessantly.
Mr Britling Sees it Through, bk 1, ch. 2, sect. 2 (1916). Referring to Mr Britling.

8 We English are everlasting children in an everlasting nursery.
Ibid., ch. 2, sect. 5

9 Human history becomes more and more a race between education and catastrophe.
The Outline of History, vol. 2, ch. 41 (1920)

10 In England we have come to rely upon a comfortable time-lag of fifty years or a century intervening between the perception that something ought to be done and a serious attempt to do it.
The Work, Wealth and Happiness of Mankind, ch. 2 (1931)

11 The Shape of Things to Come.
Title of novel (1933)

Irvine Welsh
(b. 1958)
Scottish author

His novel Trainspotting *(1993) accorded him cult status for its unsentimental portrayal of the subculture of heroin addicts. The* Acid House *(1994) and* Ecstasy *(1996) are collections of short stories inspired by dance culture.*

1 Take yir best orgasm, multiply the feeling by twenty, and you're still fuckin miles off the pace. Ma dry, cracking bones are soothed and liquefied by

ma beautiful heroine's tender caresses. The earth moved, and it's still moving.

Trainspotting, 'Kicking' (1993). Narrated by Renton.

2 Ah don't hate the English. They're just wankers. We are colonised by wankers. We can't even pick a decent, healthy culture to be colonised by. No. We're ruled by effete arseholes. What does that make us?

Renton, ibid., 'Relapsing'

3 Choose us. Choose life. Choose mortgage payments; choose washing machines; choose cars; choose sitting oan a couch watching mind-numbing and spirit-crushing game shows, stuffing fuckin junk food intae yir mooth. Choose rotting away, pishing and shiteing yersel in a home, a total fuckin embarrassment tae the selfish, fucked-up brats ye've produced. Choose life.

Well, ah choose no tae choose life.

Renton, ibid., 'Blowing It: Searching for the Inner Man'

4 You can't afford a conscience in this life, that has become a luxury for the rich and a social ball and chain for the rest of us.

Filth, 'At Home with the Blades' (1998). Spoken by Robertson.

Eudora Welty
(1909–2001)
US author

Her upbringing in the Mississippi delta coloured her fiction, which includes A Curtain of Green *(1941), a short story collection, and the novels* The Ponder Heart *(1954) and* The Optimist's Daughter *(1972).*

1 The excursion is the same when you go looking for your sorrow as when you go looking for your joy.

The Wide Net, 'The Wide Net' (1943)

2 I am a writer who came of a sheltered life. A sheltered life can be a daring life as well. For all serious daring starts from within.

One Writer's Beginnings, 'Finding a Voice' (1984)

Arnold Wesker
(b. 1932)
British playwright

He once claimed his role to be that of a 'propagandist, direct or indirect, for world socialism'. His plays include Roots *(1959),* Chips with Everything *(1962) and* Caritas *(1981).*

1 Chips with every damn thing. You breed babies and you eat chips with everything.

Chips with Everything, Act 1, Sc. 2 (1962). Spoken by Pip.

Charles Wesley
See HYMNS AND CAROLS 26, 28, 30, 35, 44, 51, 56, 63, 75, 80

John Wesley
(1703–91)
English evangelist and founder of Methodism

Ordained in 1728, he began preaching out of doors in 1739, when Anglican churches refused to admit him, and travelled throughout Britain and to Georgia, USA. His numerous congregations consisted mainly of the 'plain people'. The Methodists formally separated from the Church of England in 1791. He was brother of the hymn-writer Charles Wesley.

1 The Gospel of Christ knows of no religion but social; no holiness but social holiness.

Hymns and Sacred Poems, Preface (1739) by Charles Wesley

2 I look upon the world as my parish.

Journal entry, 11 June 1739, publ. in *Journal*, vol. 2 (ed. Nehemiah Curnock, 1910)

3 I design plain truth for plain people.

Sermons on Several Occasions, Preface (1746)

4 Having, first, gained all you can, and, secondly saved all you can, then 'give all you can'.

Ibid., Sermon 50 ('On Money')

5 If you desire to be a faithful and a wise steward . . . first, provide things needful for yourself, food to eat, raiment to put on, whatever nature moderately requires for preserving the body in health and strength. Secondly, provide these for your wife, your children, your servants, or any others who pertain to your household. If when this is done there be an overplus left, then 'do good to them that are of the household of faith.' If there be an overplus still, 'as you have the opportunity, do good to all men.'

Ibid., Sermon 50 ('On Money')

6 My ground is the Bible. Yea, I am a Bible-bigot. I follow it in all things, both great and small.

Journal entry 5 June 1766, publ. in *The Journal of John Wesley*, vol. 5 (ed. Nehemiah Curnock, 1910)

7 That execrable sum of all villainies commonly called a Slave Trade.

Journal entry, 12 February 1772, ibid., vol. 5

8 I let you loose, George, on the great continent of

America. Publish your message in the open face of the sun, and do all the good you can.

Letter, March 1773, publ. in *Letters*, vol. 6 (ed. John Telford, 1931) to the preacher George Shadford.

9 Though I am always in haste, I am never in a hurry.

Letter, 10 December 1777, ibid., vol. 6

10 Slovenliness is no part of religion; that neither this, nor any text of Scripture, condemns neatness of apparel. Certainly this is a duty, not a sin. 'Cleanliness is, indeed, next to godliness.'

Sermons on Several Occasions, no. 88 ('On Dress') (1788). The maxim may be derived from the Talmud.

11 Those that desire to write or say anything to me have no time to lose; for time has shaken me by the hand and death is not far behind.

Letter, 1 February 1791, publ. in *Letters*, vol. 8 (ed. John Telford, 1931)

12 Do all the good you can,
By all the means you can,
In all the ways you can,
In all the places you can,
To all the people you can,
As long as ever you can.

'Rules of Conduct', attributed

Mae West
(1892–1980)
US screen actor

She wrote and produced a play, Sex *(1926), for which she spent a week in prison for 'corrupting the morals of youth'. She later applied her vampish persona to the screen in a series of films including* I'm No Angel *(1933). Mistress of the double entendre, she claimed to have written all her own lines.*

1 Goodness had nothing to do with it, dearie.

Night After Night (film, 1932, screenplay by Vincent Laurence, directed by Archie Mayo). Maudie Triplett's response to checkroom girl's exclamation: 'Goodness, what beautiful diamonds!' *Goodness Had Nothing To Do With It* was the title of West's autobiography (1960).

2 Is that a gun in your pocket, or are you just glad to see me?

She Done Him Wrong (film, 1933, screenplay by Harvey Thew and John Bright based on Mae West's play *Diamond Lil*, directed by Lowell Sherman). Spoken by Lady Lou (Mae West).

3 Am I making myself clear, boys?

Lady Lou, ibid.

4 Why don't you come up sometime 'n see me? I'm home every evening . . . come on up, I'll tell your fortune.

Lady Lou, ibid.

5 I've been things and seen places.

Lady Lou, ibid.

6 It's not the men in my life, but the life in my men.

I'm No Angel (film, 1933, screenplay by Mae West and Harlan Thompson, directed by Wesley Ruggles). Spoken by Tira (Mae West), rephrasing a reporter's remarks.

7 Beulah, peel me a grape.

Tira, ibid.

8 When I'm good, I'm very, very good, but when I'm bad, I'm better.

Tira, ibid.

9 When choosing between two evils, I always like to pick the one I never tried before.

Klondike Annie (film, 1936, screenplay by Mae West, directed by Raoul Walsh). Spoken by Frisco Doll (Mae West).

10 I always say, keep a diary and some day it'll keep you.

Every Day's a Holiday (film, 1937, screenplay by Mae West, directed by A. Edward Sutherland). Spoken by Peaches O'Day (Mae West).

11 Too much of a good thing can be wonderful.

Goodness Had Nothing To Do With It, ch. 21 (1960)

12 I used to be Snow White – but I drifted.

Attributed

13 A hard man's good to find.

Attributed. Sometimes quoted with the added '. . . but you'll mostly find him asleep'.

(Dame) Rebecca West
(1892–1983)
British author

Original name Cicily Isabel Fairfield. An ardent feminist, she was the author of psychological novels, for instance The Thinking Reed *(1936), but is best known for her reports of the Nuremberg trials and for her study of the Balkans,* Black Lamb and Grey Falcon *(1942).*

1 There is no such thing as conversation. It is an illusion. There are intersecting monologues, that is all.

The Harsh Voice, 'There Is No Conversation' (1935)

2 It is queer how it is always one's virtues and not one's vices that precipitate one into disaster.

Ibid., 'There Is No Conversation'

3 All good biography, as all good fiction, comes

down to the study of original sin, of our inherent disposition to choose death when we ought to choose life.

Time and Tide (1941)

4 There is no wider gulf in the universe than yawns between those on the hither and thither side of vital experience.

Black Lamb and Grey Falcon, vol. 1, 'Serbia' (1942)

5 All men should have a drop of treason in their veins, if nations are not to go soft like so many sleepy pears.

The Meaning of Treason, pt 4, 'Conclusion' (1949)

6 Any authentic work of art must start an argument between the artist and his audience.

The Court and the Castle, pt 1, ch. 1 (1957)

7 Motherhood is the strangest thing, it can be like being one's own Trojan horse.

Letter, 20 August 1959, quoted in *Rebecca West: A Life*, pt 5, ch. 8 (1987) by Victoria Glendinning

8 He is every other inch a gentleman.

Quoted ibid., pt 3, ch. 5. Referring to novelist Michael Arlen. ALEXANDER WOOLLCOTT is also credited with this remark about Arlen in *Wit's End* (ed. Robert E. Drennan, 1968).

9 People call me a feminist whenever I express sentiments that differentiate me from a doormat or a prostitute.

Attributed

Vivienne Westwood

(b. 1941)

British fashion designer

From selling punk fashions in the 1970s, she helped create the New Romantic look of the 1980s and later showed a long-standing interest in 'innerwear as outerwear'.

1 It is elegance that is potent and subversive. Elegance in a world of vulgarity.

Quoted in *Fashion and Perversity*, pt 1 (1996) by Fred Vermorel

2 The English aristocracy is now only the middle class with knobs on.

Guardian 22 February 1997

Edith Wharton

(1862–1937)

US author

Encouraged by HENRY JAMES, *she established her reputation as a novelist of manners with* The House of Mirth *(1905). Much*

of her work satirized her own aristocratic class in Europe and America.

1 I despair of the Republic! Such dreariness, such whining callow women, such utter absence of the amenities, such crass food, crass manners, crass landscape! . . . What a horror it is for a whole nation to be developing without a sense of beauty, and eating bananas for breakfast.

Letter, 19 August 1904, publ. in *The Letters of Edith Wharton* (ed. R. W. B. Leavis and Nancy Lewis, 1988)

2 Mrs Ballinger is one of the ladies who pursue Culture in bands, as though it were dangerous to meet it alone.

Xingu and Other Stories, 'Xingu' (1916)

3 When people ask for time, it's always for time to say no. Yes has one more letter in it, but it doesn't take half as long to say.

The Children, ch. 25 (1928). Spoken by Judith.

4 Almost everybody in the neighborhood had 'troubles', frankly localized and specified; but only the chosen had 'complications'. To have them was in itself a distinction, though it was also, in most cases, a death warrant. People struggled on for years with 'troubles', but they almost always succumbed to 'complications'.

Ethan Frome, ch. 7 (1911)

5 There's no such thing as old age; there is only sorrow.

A Backward Glance, 'A First Word' (1934)

6 The real marriage of true minds is for any two people to possess a sense of humour or irony pitched in exactly the same key, so that their joint glances at any subject cross like interarching searchlights.

Ibid., ch. 8. Referring to her friendship with HENRY JAMES. Wharton added: 'in that sense Henry James was perhaps the most intimate friend I ever had.'

Richard Whately

(1787–1863)

English theologian and philosopher

His Elements of Logic *(1826) became a standard reference book. Appointed Archbishop of Dublin in 1831, he devised a non-sectarian system of religious instruction for children.*

1 Happiness is no laughing matter.

Apophthegms (1854)

2 It is folly to expect men to do all that they may reasonably be expected to do.

Ibid.

James McNeill Whistler
(1834–1903)
US artist

Based in London from 1859, he caused controversy by his paint-
ings which were studies in muted colour and tone, such as
'Arrangement in Grey and Black, No. 1: The Artist's Mother'
(1872) and the depictions of nocturnal London. OSCAR WILDE
called him a 'miniature Mephistopheles, mocking the major-
ity'. See also OSCAR WILDE 7.

1 I maintain that two and two would continue to make four, in spite of the whine of the amateur for three, or the cry of the critic for five.

Whistler v. Ruskin: Art and Art Critics (pamphlet, 1878)

2 No, I ask it for the knowledge of a lifetime.

Quoted in *Whistler Stories* (1913) by D. C. Seitz. Answer given during Whistler's lawsuit against John Ruskin, 15 November 1878, to the question from Ruskin's counsel: 'The labour of two days ... is that for which you ask two hundred guineas?' See JOHN RUSKIN 27.

3 To say of a picture, as is often said in its praise, that it shows great and earnest labour, is to say that it is incomplete and unfit for view.

The Gentle Art of Making Enemies, 'Propositions No. 2' (1890)

4 The masterpiece should appear as the flower to the painter – perfect in its bud as in its bloom – with no reason to explain its presence – no mission to fulfill – a joy to the artist – a delusion to the phil-anthropist – a puzzle to the botanist – an accident of sentiment and alliteration to the literary man.

Ibid., 'Propositions No. 2'

5 Yes, madam, Nature is creeping up.

Quoted in *Whistler Stories* (1913) by D. C. Seitz. Remark to a lady who said a landscape view reminded her of his work.

6 You should not say it is not good. You should say you do not like it; and then, you know, you're perfectly safe.

Ibid.

7 I'm lonesome. They are all dying. I have hardly a warm personal enemy left.

Ibid.

E. B. White
(1899–1985)
US author and editor

Elwyn Brooks White. He began a long association with the New
Yorker *in 1925, writing its 'Talk of the Town' column. His books*
include Is Sex Necessary? *(1929), co-authored with* JAMES
THURBER, *and his children's classic* Charlotte's Web *(1952).*

1 I say it's spinach, and I say the hell with it.

Cartoon caption, in the *New Yorker* 8 December 1928. Little girl in reply to her mother's remark, 'It's broccoli, dear.' (Drawing by Carl Rose.)

2 Democracy is the recurrent suspicion that more than half of the people are right more than half of the time.

New Yorker 3 July 1944

3 One of the most time-consuming things is to have an enemy.

'A Report in January' (1958), publ. in *Essays of E. B. White* (1977)

4 The terror of the atom age is not the violence of the new power but the speed of man's adjustment to it – the speed of his acceptance.

The Second Tree From the Corner, 'Notes on Our Time' (1954)

5 Commuter – one who spends his life
In riding to and from his wife;
A man who shaves and takes a train,
And then rides back to shave again.

'The Commuter', publ. in *Poems and Sketches* (1982)

Edmund White
(b. 1940)
US author

He is best known for his essays and criticism, and for the
novel A Boy's Own Story *(1982), which describes an adolescent*
coming to terms with his homosexuality.

1 In the lifelong romance each man has with him-self, he should know which vows he's sworn.

'The Gay Philosopher', written 1969, publ. in *The Burning Library* (1994)

2 All men want quick, uncomplicated sexual adven-ture (as well as sustained romantic passion); in a world of all men, that desire is granted.

'Sexual Culture' (1983), repr. ibid.

3 The AIDS epidemic has rolled back a big rotting log and revealed all the squirming life underneath it, since it involves, all at once, the main themes of our existence: sex, death, power, money, love, hate,

disease and panic. No American phenomenon has been so compelling since the Vietnam War.

States of Desire: Travels in Gay America (1986 edn) 'Afterword – AIDS: An American Epidemic'

T. H. White
(1906–64)
British author

Terence Hanbury White. Writing mostly for children, he is best known for The Once and Future King *(1939–58), based on Arthurian legend. His other works are a similar mix of medievalism, fantasy and science fiction.*

1 The Once and Future King.
Title of novel (1939–58). See THOMAS MALORY 6.

Alfred North Whitehead
(1861–1947)
British philosopher

He established his reputation with his work on mathematical logic, collaborating with his former pupil BERTRAND RUSSELL *on* Principia Mathematica *(1910–13). His metaphysical theory was published in* Process and Reality *(1929), and he also wrote numerous popular works.*

1 Civilization advances by extending the number of important operations which we can perform without thinking about them.
Introduction to Mathematics, ch. 5 (1911)

2 Uneducated clever women, who have seen much of the world, are in middle life so much the most cultured part of the community. They have been saved from this horrible burden of inert ideas.
The Organisation of Thought, 'The Aims of Education' (1917)

3 Every philosophy is tinged with the colouring of some secret imaginative background, which never emerges explicitly into its train of reasoning.
Science and the Modern World, ch. 1 (1926)

4 The safest general characterization of the European philosophical tradition is that it consists of a series of footnotes to Plato.
Process and Reality, pt 2, ch. 1, sect. 1 (1929)

5 Life is an offensive, directed against the repetitious mechanism of the Universe.
Adventures of Ideas, pt 1, ch. 5 (1933)

6 It is more important that a proposition be interesting than that it be true. This statement is almost a tautology. For the energy of operation of a proposition in an occasion of experience is its interest, and is its importance. But of course a true proposition is more apt to be interesting than a false one.
Ibid., pt 4, ch. 16

7 There are no whole truths; all truths are half-truths. It is trying to treat them as whole truths that plays the devil.
Dialogues of Alfred North Whitehead, Prologue (ed. Lucien Price, 1954)

8 The vitality of thought is an adventure. *Ideas won't keep.* Something must be done about them. When the idea is new, its custodians have fervour, live for it, and, if need be, die for it.
Ibid., '28 April 1938'

9 What is morality in any given time or place? It is what the majority then and there happen to like, and immorality is what they dislike.
Ibid., '30 August 1941'

10 Art is the imposing of a pattern on experience, and our aesthetic enjoyment is recognition of the pattern.
Ibid., '10 June 1943'

11 The English never abolish anything. They put it in cold storage.
Ibid., '19 January 1945'

Katharine Whitehorn
(b. 1926)
British journalist

She was a columnist (1960–96) and Assistant Editor (1980–8) at the Observer. *In 1997 she became agony aunt for* Saga *magazine.*

1 Hats divide generally into three classes: offensive hats, defensive hats, and shrapnel.
Shouts and Murmurs, 'Hats' (1963)

2 I wouldn't say when you've seen one Western you've seen the lot; but when you've seen the lot you get the feeling you've seen one.
Sunday Best, 'Decoding the West' (1976)

Gough Whitlam
(b. 1916)
Australian politician and prime minister

Elected the first Australian Labor prime minister for twenty-three years in 1972, he was dismissed by the Governor General in controversial circumstances in 1975, retiring from politics in 1977.

1 The punters know that the horse named Morality rarely gets past the post, whereas the nag named Self-Interest always runs a good race.

Daily Telegraph 19 October 1989

Walt Whitman
(1819–92)
US poet

His Leaves of Grass, *first published in 1855 and revised and expanded until his death, was radical in form and content. In it he celebrates democracy, universality, the cyclical nature of life and the supremacy of the self. He lived and worked mainly in New York and Washington.* D. H. LAWRENCE *complained of 'all his privacy leaking out in a sort of dribble, oozing into the universe'. See also* HENRY JAMES 1.

1 The United States themselves are essentially the greatest poem.

Leaves of Grass, Preface (1855)

2 The art of art, the glory of expression and the sunshine of the light of letters, is simplicity.

Ibid., Preface

3 As soon as histories are properly told there is no more need of romances.

Ibid., Preface

4 The proof of a poet is that his country absorbs him as affectionately as he has absorbed it.

Ibid. Closing words of preface.

5 And I will show that nothing can happen more beautiful than death.

'Starting From Paumanok', sect. 12, publ. in *Leaves of Grass* (1855, rev. 1856–92)

6 I celebrate myself, and sing myself.

'Song of Myself', sect. 1, ibid. Opening line of poem.

7 The beautiful uncut hair of graves.

'Song of Myself', sect. 6, ibid.

8 Have you heard that it was good to gain the day?
I also say it is good to fall, battles are lost in the same spirit in which they are won.

'Song of Myself', sect. 18

9 I am he that walks with the tender and growing night,
I call to the earth and sea half-held by the night.
Press close bare-bosomed night – press close magnetic nourishing night!

Night of south winds! night of the large few stars!
Still nodding night! mad naked summer night.

'Song of Myself', sect. 21, ibid.

10 Walt Whitman, a kosmos, of Manhattan the son,
Turbulent, fleshy, sensual, eating, drinking and breeding,
No sentimentalist, no stander above men and women or apart from them,
No more modest than immodest.

'Song of Myself', sect. 24, ibid.

11 Logic and sermons never convince,
The damp of the night drives deeper into my soul.

'Song of Myself', sect. 30, ibid.

12 I believe a leaf of grass is no less than the journey-work of the stars.

'Song of Myself', sect. 31, ibid.

13 And the running blackberry would adorn the parlors of heaven.

'Song of Myself', sect. 31, ibid.

14 I think I could turn and live with animals, they are so placid and self-contained,
I stand and look at them long and long.
They do not sweat and whine about their condition,
They do not lie awake in the dark and weep for their sins,
They do not make me sick discussing their duty to God,
Not one is dissatisfied, not one is demented with the mania of owning things.
Not one kneels to another, nor to his kind that lived thousands of years ago,
Not one is respectable or unhappy over the whole earth.

'Song of Myself', sect. 32, ibid.

15 Behold, I do not give lectures or a little charity,
When I give I give myself.

'Song of Myself', sect. 40, ibid.

16 I heard what was said of the universe,
Heard it and heard it of several thousand years;
It is middling well as far as it goes – but is that all?

'Song of Myself', sect. 41, ibid.

17 And whoever walks a furlong without sympathy walks to his own funeral dressed in his shroud.

'Song of Myself', sect. 48, ibid.

18 And there is no object so soft but it makes a
   hub for the wheeled universe.
'Song of Myself', sect. 48, ibid.

19 In the faces of men and women I see God, and
   in my own face in the glass,
I find letters from God dropped in the street, and
   every one is signed by God's name.
And I leave them where they are, for I know that
   wheresoe'er I go,
Others will punctually come for ever and ever.
'Song of Myself', sect. 48, ibid.

20 There is that in me – I do not know what it is –
   but I know it is in me.
   . . .
I do not know it – it is without name – it is a word
   unsaid,
It is not in any dictionary, utterance, symbol.
   . . .
Do you see O my brothers and sisters?
It is not chaos or death – it is form, union, plan – it
   is eternal life – it is Happiness.
'Song of Myself', sect. 50

21 Do I contradict myself?
Very well then I contradict myself,
(I am large, I contain multitudes).
'Song of Myself', sect. 51, ibid.

22 I sound my barbaric yawp over the roofs of the
   world.
'Song of Myself', sect. 52, ibid.

23 I sing the body electric.
'I Sing the Body Electric', ibid. Opening line of poem.

24 Sex contains all, bodies, souls,
Meanings, proofs, purities, delicacies, results,
   promulgations,
Songs, commands, health, pride, the maternal
   mystery, the seminal milk,
All hopes, benefactions, bestowals, all the passions,
   loves, beauties, delights of the earth,
All the governments, judges, gods, followed
   persons of the earth,
These are contained in sex as parts of itself and
   justifications of itself.
'A Woman Waits for Me', ibid.

25 Afoot and light-hearted I take to the open road,
Healthy, free, the world before me,
The long brown path before me leading wherever I
   choose.
'Song of the Open Road', sect. 1, ibid. Opening lines of poem.

26 Henceforth I ask not good-fortune, I myself am
   good-fortune,
Henceforth I whimper no more, postpone no
   more, need nothing,
Done with indoor complaints, libraries, querulous
   criticisms,
Strong and content I travel the open road.
'Song of the Open Road', sect. 1

27 O public road, I say back I am not afraid to
   leave you, yet I love you,
You express me better than I can express myself,
You shall be more to me than my poem.
'Song of the Open Road', sect. 4

28 Why are there trees I never walk under but
   large and melodious thoughts descend upon
   me?
'Song of the Open Road', sect. 7

29 Old age, calm, expanded, broad with the
   haughty breadth of the universe,
Old age, flowing free with the delicious near-by
   freedom of death.
'Song of the Open Road', sect. 12

30 Camerado, I give you my hand!
I give you my love more precious than money,
I give you myself before preaching or law;
Will you give me yourself?
'Song of the Open Road', sect. 15

31 A great city is that which has the greatest man
   or woman;
If it be a few ragged huts, it is still the greatest city
   in the whole world.
'Song of the Broad Axe', sect. 4, ibid.

32 Come my tan-faced children,
Follow well in order, get your weapons ready,
Have you your pistols? have you your sharp-edged
   axes?
Pioneers! O pioneers!
'Pioneers! O Pioneers!', st. 1, ibid. Opening lines.

33 When I, sitting, heard the astronomer, where he
   lectured with much applause in the lecture
   room,
How soon, unaccountable, I became tired and sick;
Till rising and gliding out, I wandered off by
   myself,
In the mystical moist night-air, and from time to
   time
Looked up in perfect silence at the stars.
'When I heard the learn'd astronomer', ibid.

34 *Come lovely and soothing death,*
Undulate round the world, serenely arriving,
  arriving,
In the day, in the night, to all, to each,
Sooner or later delicate death.
'When lilacs last in the dooryard bloom'd', sect. 14

35 O Captain! my Captain! our fearful trip is done,
The ship has weathered every rack, the prize we
  sought is won,
The port is near, the bells I hear, the people all
  exulting.
'O Captain! My Captain!', st. 1, ibid. (1867). The poem was
written to commemorate the death of ABRAHAM LINCOLN.

36 Exult O shores, and ring O bells!
But I with mournful tread,
Walk the deck my Captain lies,
Fallen cold and dead.
'O Captain! My Captain!', st. 3, ibid. Closing lines of poem.

37 Camerado, this is no book,
Who touches this touches a man.
'So Long!', ibid.

38 To have great poets, there must be great audiences too.
Notes Left Over, 'Ventures on an Old Theme' (1881). This motto
was printed on the front of *Poetry* magazine (Chicago, 1913),
provoking the vitriolic disapproval of Ezra Pound, who, in
1914, wrote in the pages of the magazine: 'The artist is not
dependent on the multitude of his listeners ... This rabble,
this multitude – does *not* create the great artist. They are
aimless and drifting without him.' See EZRA POUND 2.

39 So here I sit in the early candle-light of old age –
I and my book – casting backward glances over our
traveled road.
November Boughs, 'A Backward Glance O'er Traveled Roads'
(1888)

John Greenleaf Whittier
(1807–92)
US poet

He became the voice of rural New England through his numer-
ous ballads and poems, notably 'The Barefoot Boy' (1856) and
'Snowbound' (1866). A spokesman for the abolitionist cause,
he was, according to ROBERT PENN WARREN, *'a sort of minor*
saint in outmoded Quaker dress'. See also HYMNS AND
CAROLS 19, 64.

1 When faith is lost, when honor dies,
The man is dead!
'Ichabod', st. 8 (1850), repr. in *The Poetical Works of John*
Greenleaf Whittier (ed. W. Garrett Horder, 1911)

2 Of all that Orient lands can vaunt
Of marvels with our own competing,
The strangest is the Haschish plant,
And what will follow on its eating.
'The Haschish', st. 1 (1854), ibid.

3 For of all sad words of tongue or pen,
The saddest are these: 'It might have been!'
'Maud Muller', ll. 105–6 (1854), ibid.

4 Oh, for boyhood's painless play,
Sleep that wakes in laughing day,
Health that mocks the doctor's rules,
Knowledge never learned of schools.
'The Barefoot Boy', ll. 19–22 (1855), ibid.

5 The age is dull and mean. Men creep,
Not walk.
'For Righteousness' Sake', st. 1 (1855), ibid.

6 The dreariest spot in all the land
To Death they set apart;
With scanty grace from Nature's hand,
And none from that of Art.
'The Old Burying-Ground', st. 2 (1858), ibid.

7 Give fools their gold, and knaves their power;
Let fortune's bubbles rise and fall;
Who sows a field, or trains a flower,
Or plants a tree, is more than all.
'A Song of Harvest', st. 6 (1858), ibid.

8 'Shoot, if you must, this old gray head,
But spare your country's flag,' she said.
'Barbara Frietchie', st. 18 (1863), ibid. Spoken by Barbara Fri-
etchie.

9 O Time and Change! – with hair as gray
As was my sire's that winter day,
How strange it seems, with so much gone
Of life and love, to still live on!
'Snow-Bound', ll. 179–182 (1866), ibid.

10 Before me, even as behind,
God is and all is well.
'My Birthday', st. 2 (1871), ibid.

Robert Whittington
(c. 1480–c. 1530)
English grammarian

After writing grammars and elementary Latin school books,
he turned his attention to English translations of Latin works.

1 More is a man of angel's wit and singular learning;
I know not his fellow. For where is the man of that
gentleness, lowliness, and affability? And as time

requireth, a man of marvellous mirth and pastimes, and sometime of as sad gravity, as who say: a man for all seasons.

Vulgaria, pt. 2, 'De constructione nominum' (1521). Referring to THOMAS MORE. ERASMUS had earlier described More as *omnium horarum hominem* ('a man of all hours') in *Praise of Folly*, Preface (1509).

Anne Widdecombe
(b. 1947)
British politician

An outspoken Conservative MP since 1987, she was a junior minister in the Home Office (1995–7) and became Shadow Home Secretary in 1999, the same year she converted to Roman Catholicism.

1 He has something of the night in him.

Quoted in *The Sunday Times* 11 May 1997. Referring to MICHAEL HOWARD, whose candidature in the Conservative Party leadership election was said to have been seriously damaged by Widdecombe's remark.

Norbert Wiener
(1894–1964)
US mathematician and educator, founder of cybernetics

He taught at the Massachusetts Institute of Technology (1919–60), where he became interested in the 'science of control and communication in the animal and machine'. He coined the word 'cybernetics' to describe this process in his book Cybernetics *(1948).*

1 The idea that information can be stored in a changing world without an overwhelming depreciation of its value is false. It is scarcely less false than the more plausible claim that after a war we may take our existing weapons, fill their barrels with cylinder oil, and coat their outsides with sprayed rubber film, and let them statically await the next emergency.

The Human Use of Human Beings, ch. 7 (1950)

Elie Wiesel
(b. 1928)
Romanian-born US author

A survivor of Auschwitz, he drew on his traumatic personal experiences in his writings, including three novels Night *(1958),* Dawn *(1961) and* The Accident *(1961). He has worked as a journalist in Israel and the United States.*

1 The opposite of love is not hate, it's indifference. The opposite of art is not ugliness, it's indifference.

The opposite of faith is not heresy, it's indifference. And the opposite of life is not death, it's indifference.

US News and World Report 27 October 1986

2 When you see the abyss, and we have looked into it, then what? There isn't much room at the edge – one person, another, not many. If you are there, others cannot be there. If you are there, you become a protective wall. What happens? You become part of the abyss.

Interview in *Writers at Work* (eighth series, ed. George Plimpton, 1988)

3 I marvel at the resilience of the Jewish people. Their best characteristic is their desire to remember. No other people has such an obsession with memory.

Daily Mail 15 July 1988. Wiesel's 'major preoccupation', he said on a previous occasion, is 'the kingdom of memory. I want to protect and enrich that kingdom, glorify that kingdom and serve it.'

4 It is true that not all the victims were Jews. But all the Jews were victims.

Address at fiftieth anniversary of liberation of Auschwitz, 27 January 1995, publ. in *The Penguin Book of Twentieth-Century Speeches* (ed. Brian MacArthur, 1999)

Richard Wilbur
(b. 1921)
US poet and translator

His poems deal with everyday experience in simple and refined language. In the words of THEODORE ROETHKE *he has 'not a graceful mind . . . but a mind of grace, an altogether different and higher thing'. He is also a noted translator, specializing in 17th-century French dramas.*

1 The eyes open to a cry of pulleys,
And spirited from sleep, the astounded soul
Hangs for a moment bodiless and simple
As false dawn.
Outside the open window
The morning air is all awash with angels.

'Love Calls Us to the Things of This World', st. 1, publ. in *Things of This World* (1956)

2 Mind in its purest play is like some bat
That beats about in caverns all alone,
Contriving by a kind of senseless wit
Not to conclude against a wall of stone.

'Mind', st. 1, ibid.

3 Ask us, prophet, how we shall call
Our natures forth when that live tongue is all
Dispelled, that glass obscured or broken.
'Advice to a Prophet', st. 7, publ. in *Advice to a Prophet and
Other Poems* (1961)

4 Love is the greatest mercy,
A volley of the sun
That lashes all with shade,
That the first day be mended.
'Someone Talking to Himself', st. 3, ibid.

5 What can I do but move
From folly to defeat
And call that sorrow sweet
That teaches us to see
The final face of love
In what we cannot be?
'Someone Talking to Himself', st. 3, ibid.

6 All that we do
Is touched with ocean, yet we remain
On the shore of what we know.
'For Dudley', publ. in *New Poems and Translations* (1969)

7 What you hope for
Is that at some point of the pointless journey,
Indoors or out, and when you least expect it,
Right in the middle of your stride, like that,
So neatly that you never feel a thing,
The kind assassin Sleep will draw a bead
And blow your brains out.
'Walking to Sleep', ll. 93–100, ibid.

Ella Wheeler Wilcox
(1855–1919)
US poet

*She wrote over thirty volumes of platitudinous and sentimen-
tal verse. Her collection* Poems of Passion *(1883) was at first
rejected for publication on grounds of immorality.*

1 Laugh, and the world laughs with you;
Weep, and you weep alone;
For the sad old earth must borrow its mirth,
But has trouble enough of its own.
'Solitude', st. 1, publ. in *Poems of Passion* (1883)

2 So many gods, so many creeds,
So many paths that wind and wind,
While just the art of being kind
Is all the sad world needs.
'The World's Need', publ. in *Poems of Power* (1903)

3 One ship drives east and another drives west
With the self-same winds that blow;

'Tis the set of the sails
And not the gales
That tells them the way to go.
'The Winds of Fate', publ. in *Poems of Optimism* (1915)

Oscar Wilde
(1854–1900)
Anglo-Irish playwright and poet

*Oscar Fingal O'Flahertie Wills Wilde. Based in London from
the early 1880s, he established a reputation as a flamboyant
aesthete, achieving great popularity for his epigrammatic wit
and sharp observation in a series of comedies of manners
and in his only novel* The Picture of Dorian Gray *(1890). His
homosexual relationship with* LORD ALFRED DOUGLAS *led
to a notorious trial and his imprisonment 1895–7. See* JOHN
BETJEMAN 4, DOROTHY PARKER 9.

1 I have nothing to declare except my genius.
Attributed remark at the New York Customs, 3 January 1882,
publ. in *Oscar Wilde*, ch. 6 (1987) by RICHARD ELLMANN. No
contemporary evidence for the remark exists.

2 Popularity is the crown of laurel which the world
puts on bad art. Whatever is popular is wrong.
Lecture to students of the Royal Academy, London, 30 June
1883, repr. in *Aristotle at Afternoon Tea: The Rare Oscar Wilde*
(1991) by John Wyse Jackson

3 We have really everything in common with
America nowadays, except, of course, language.
The Canterville Ghost, ch. 1 (1887). These or similar words are
often attributed to GEORGE BERNARD SHAW, though they
have not been found in his published writings. BERTRAND
RUSSELL made a similar point in *Saturday Evening Post* 3 June
1944: 'It is a misfortune for Anglo-American friendship that
the two countries are supposed to have a common language.'

4 We Irish are too poetical to be poets; we are a
nation of brilliant failures, but we are the greatest
talkers since the Greeks.
Remark to W. B. YEATS, Christmas 1888, quoted in *Oscar
Wilde*, ch. 11 (1987) by RICHARD ELLMANN.

5 I like to do all the talking myself. It saves time,
and prevents arguments.
The Happy Prince and Other Tales, 'The Remarkable Rocket'
(1888). Spoken by the Frog.

6 A thing is not necessarily true because a man dies
for it.
The Portrait of Mr W. H., ch. 1, publ. in *Blackwood's Edinburgh
Magazine* July 1889, repr. in *Complete Works of Oscar Wilde*
(ed. J. B. Foreman, 1966). Spoken by Erskine.

7 Mr Whistler always spelt art, and we believe still spells it, with a capital 'I'.

'The New President' (1889), repr. in *Aristotle at Afternoon Tea: The Rare Oscar Wilde* (1991) by John Wyse Jackson

8 Charity creates a multitude of sins.

'The Soul of Man Under Socialism' (1891), repr. in *Complete Works of Oscar Wilde* (ed. J. B. Foreman, 1966). See BIBLE, NEW TESTAMENT: 1 PETER 10.

9 Disobedience, in the eyes of any one who has read history, is man's original virtue. It is through disobedience that progress has been made, through disobedience and through rebellion.

'The Soul of Man Under Socialism', ibid.

10 Democracy means simply the bludgeoning of the people by the people for the people.

'The Soul of Man Under Socialism', ibid.

11 A map of the world that does not include Utopia is not worth even glancing at, for it leaves out the one country at which Humanity is always landing.

'The Soul of Man Under Socialism', ibid.

12 In America the President reigns for four years, and Journalism governs for ever and ever.

'The Soul of Man Under Socialism', ibid.

13 The past is of no importance. The present is of no importance. It is with the future that we have to deal. For the past is what man should not have been. The present is what man ought not to be. The future is what artists are.

'The Soul of Man Under Socialism', ibid.

14 Pleasure is Nature's test, her sign of approval. When man is happy, he is in harmony with himself and his environment.

'The Soul of Man Under Socialism', ibid.

15 Thinking is the most unhealthy thing in the world, and people die of it just as they die of any other disease. Fortunately, in England at any rate, thought is not catching. Our splendid physique as a people is entirely due to our national stupidity.

'The Decay of Lying', publ. in *Intentions* (1891). Spoken by Vivian.

16 The more one analyses people, the more all reasons for analysis disappear. Sooner or later one comes to that dreadful universal thing called human nature.

Vivian, 'The Decay of Lying', ibid.

17 Wordsworth went to the Lakes, but he was never a lake poet. He found in stones the sermons he had already hidden there.

Vivian, 'The Decay of Lying', ibid. See also SHAKESPEARE: AS YOU LIKE IT 8.

18 Literature always anticipates life. It does not copy it, but moulds it to its purpose. The nineteenth century, as we know it, is largely an invention of Balzac.

Vivian, 'The Decay of Lying', ibid.

19 In fact, the whole of Japan is a pure invention. There is no such country, there are no such people . . . The Japanese people are . . . simply a mode of style, an exquisite fancy of art.

Vivian, 'The Decay of Lying', ibid.

20 Man can believe the impossible, but man can never believe the improbable.

Vivian, 'The Decay of Lying', ibid.

21 I seem to have heard that observation before . . . It has all the vitality of error and all the tediousness of an old friend.

Intentions, 'The Critic as Artist', pt 1 (1891). Spoken by Gilbert.

22 Education is an admirable thing, but it is well to remember from time to time that nothing that is worth knowing can be taught.

Gilbert, ibid., 'The Critic as Artist', pt 1

23 Whatever, in fact, is modern in our life we owe to the Greeks. Whatever is an anachronism is due to mediaevalism.

Gilbert, ibid., 'The Critic as Artist', pt 1

24 Anybody can make history. Only a great man can write it.

Gilbert, ibid., 'The Critic as Artist', pt 1

25 It is well for his peace that the saint goes to his martyrdom. He is spared the sight of the horror of his harvest.

Gilbert, ibid., 'The Critic as Artist', pt 1

26 Conversation should touch everything, but should concentrate itself on nothing.

Gilbert, ibid., 'The Critic as Artist', pt 2

27 Man is least himself when he talks in his own person. Give him a mask, and he will tell you the truth.

Gilbert, ibid., 'The Critic as Artist', pt 2

28 Mere colour, unspoiled by meaning, and unallied with definite form, can speak to the soul in a thousand different ways.

Gilbert, ibid., 'The Critic as Artist', pt 2

29 From the point of view of literature Mr Kipling is a genius who drops his aspirates. From the point of view of life, he is a reporter who knows vulgarity better than any one has ever known it.
Gilbert, ibid., 'The Critic as Artist', pt 2

30 There is no sin except stupidity.
Gilbert, ibid., 'The Critic as Artist', pt 2

31 As long as war is regarded as wicked, it will always have its fascination. When it is looked upon as vulgar, it will cease to be popular.
Gilbert, ibid., 'The Critic as Artist', pt 2

32 A Truth in art is that whose contradictory is also true.
Ibid., 'The Truth of Masks'

33 The world is a stage, but the play is badly cast.
Lord Arthur Savile's Crime, ch. 1 (1891)

34 There is no such thing as a moral or immoral book. Books are well written, or badly written. That is all.
The Picture of Dorian Gray, Preface (1891)

35 All art is quite useless.
Ibid., Preface

36 There is only one thing in the world worse than being talked about, and that is not being talked about.
Lord Henry, ibid., ch. 1

37 Laughter is not at all a bad beginning for a friendship, and it is far the best ending for one.
Lord Henry, ibid., ch. 1

38 I like persons better than principles, and I like persons with no principles better than anything else in the world.
Lord Henry, ibid., ch. 1

39 I choose my friends for their good looks, my acquaintances for their good characters, and my enemies for their intellects. A man cannot be too careful in the choice of his enemies.
Lord Henry, ibid., ch. 1

40 The mind of the thoroughly well-informed man is a dreadful thing. It is like a bric-à-brac shop, all monsters and dust, with everything priced above its proper value.
Lord Henry, ibid., ch. 1

41 Those who are faithful know only the trivial side of love: it is the faithless who know love's tragedies.
Lord Henry, ibid., ch. 1

42 It is only shallow people who do not judge by appearances. The true mystery of the world is the visible, not the invisible.
Lord Henry, ibid., ch. 1

43 The only way to get rid of a temptation is to yield to it.
Lord Henry, ibid., ch. 2

44 The only difference between a caprice and a life-long passion is that the caprice lasts a little longer.
Lord Henry, ibid., ch. 2

45 Philanthropic people lose all sense of humanity. It is their distinguishing characteristic.
Lord Henry, ibid., ch. 3

46 The way of paradoxes is the way of truth. To test Reality we must see it on the tight-rope. When the Verities become acrobats we can judge them.
Mr Erskine, ibid., ch. 3

47 The advantage of the emotions is that they lead us astray.
Lord Henry, ibid., ch. 3

48 He was always late on principle, his principle being that punctuality is the thief of time.
Ibid., ch. 4. Of Lord Henry. See EDWARD YOUNG 8.

49 Men marry because they are tired; women, because they are curious; both are disappointed.
Lord Henry, ibid., ch. 4

50 There is always something infinitely mean about other people's tragedies.
Lord Henry, ibid., ch. 4

51 The basis of optimism is sheer terror.
Lord Henry, ibid., ch. 6

52 When we are happy we are always good, but when we are good we are not always happy.
Lord Henry, ibid., ch. 6

53 A cigarette is the perfect type of a perfect pleasure. It is exquisite, and it leaves one unsatisfied. What more can one want?
Lord Henry, ibid., ch. 6

54 We live in an age when unnecessary things are our only necessities.
Ibid., ch. 8

55 It is the confession, not the priest, that gives us absolution.
Ibid., ch. 8

56 One can always be kind to people about whom one cares nothing.
Lord Henry, ibid., ch. 8

57 It is better to be beautiful than to be good. But ... it is better to be good than to be ugly.
Lord Henry, ibid., ch. 17

58 Names are everything ... The man who could call a spade a spade should be compelled to use one. It is the only thing he is fit for.
Lord Henry, ibid., ch. 17

59 Scepticism is the beginning of Faith.
Dorian Gray, ibid., ch. 17

60 We can have in life but one great experience at best, and the secret of life is to reproduce that experience as often as possible.
Lord Henry, ibid., ch. 17

61 There is no such thing as an omen. Destiny does not send us heralds. She is too wise or too cruel for that.
Lord Henry, ibid., ch. 17

62 Anybody can be good in the country. There are no temptations there.
Lord Henry, ibid., ch. 19

63 Death and vulgarity are the only two facts in the nineteenth century that one cannot explain away.
Lord Henry, ibid., ch. 19

64 Murder is always a mistake. One should never do anything that one cannot talk about after dinner.
Lord Henry, ibid., ch. 19

65 His work was that curious mixture of bad painting and good intentions that always entitles a man to be called a representative British artist.
Lord Henry, ibid., ch. 19. Of Basil Hallward.

66 If you pretend to be good, the world takes you very seriously. If you pretend to be bad, it doesn't. Such is the astounding stupidity of optimism.
Lady Windermere's Fan, Act 1 (1892). Spoken by Lord Darlington.

67 It is absurd to divide people into good and bad. People are either charming or tedious.
Lord Darlington, ibid., Act 1

68 I can resist everything except temptation.
Lord Darlington, ibid., Act 1

69 She is absolutely inadmissible into society.

Many a woman has a past, but I am told that she has at least a dozen, and that they all fit.
The Duchess of Berwick, ibid. Referring to Mrs Erlynne.

70 Crying is the refuge of plain women but the ruin of pretty ones.
Duchess of Berwick, ibid.

71 Between men and women there is no friendship possible. There is passion, enmity, worship, love, but no friendship.
Lord Darlington, ibid., Act 2

72 Nothing looks so like innocence as an indiscretion.
Cecil Graham, ibid., Act 2

73 A man who moralises is usually a hypocrite, and a woman who moralises is invariably plain.
Cecil Graham, ibid., Act 3

74 Gossip is charming! History is merely gossip. But scandal is gossip made tedious by morality.
Cecil Graham, ibid., Act 3

75 We are all in the gutter, but some of us are looking at the stars.
Lord Darlington, ibid., Act 3. Wilde's aphorism recalls one by ALEXANDER SMITH: 'A man gazing on the stars is proverbially at the mercy of the puddles in the road.' (*Dreamthorp*, 'Men of Letters', 1863)

76 In this world there are two tragedies. One is not getting what one wants, and the other is getting it. The last is much the worst.
Dumby, ibid., Act 3. GEORGE BERNARD SHAW expressed a similar idea in *Man and Superman*, Act 4 (1903): 'There are two tragedies in life. One is to lose your heart's desire. The other is to gain it.'

77 Cecil Graham: What is a cynic?
Lord Darlington: A man who knows the price of everything and the value of nothing.
Ibid., Act 3. The same notion was expressed in *The Picture of Dorian Gray*, ch. 4 (1891): 'Nowadays people know the price of everything and the value of nothing.'

78 Experience is the name every one gives to their mistakes.
Dumby, ibid., Act 3. The words also appear in *The Picture of Dorian Gray*, ch. 4 (1891).

79 The youth of America is their oldest tradition. It has been going on now for three hundred years.
A Woman of No Importance, Act 1 (1893). Spoken by Lord Illingworth.

80 One knows so well the popular idea of health.

The English country gentleman galloping after a fox – the unspeakable in full pursuit of the uneatable.

Lord Illingworth, ibid., Act 1

81 Twenty years of romance make a woman look like a ruin, but twenty years of marriage make her something like a public building.

Lord Illingworth, ibid., Act 1

82 One can survive anything these days, except death, and live down anything except a good reputation.

Lord Illingworth, ibid., Act 1. Similar sentiments appeared in Wilde's *The Picture of Dorian Gray*, ch. 19 (1891).

83 I adore simple pleasures. They are the last refuge of the complex.

Lord Illingworth, ibid., Act 1

84 Life, Lady Stutfield, is simply a *mauvais quart d'heure* made up of exquisite moments.

Mrs Allonby, ibid., Act 2

85 Lord Illingworth: All women become like their
    mothers. That is their tragedy.

Mrs Allonby: No man does. That is his.

Ibid., Act 2. This aphorism was also spoken by Algernon in *The Importance of Being Earnest*, Act 1.

86 Discontent is the first step in the progress of a man or a nation.

Lord Illingworth, ibid., Act 2

87 Children begin by loving their parents. After a time they judge them. Rarely, if ever, do they forgive them.

Lord Illingworth, ibid., Act 2. Wilde had used almost the same words in *The Picture of Dorian Gray*, ch. 5 (1891).

88 The worst form of tyranny the world has ever known . . . the tyranny of the weak over the strong. It is the only tyranny that lasts.

Lord Illingworth, ibid., Act 3. Referring to the 'tyranny' of women.

89 The only difference between the saint and the sinner is that every saint has a past, and every sinner has a future.

Lord Illingworth, ibid., Act 3

90 Moderation is a fatal thing . . . Nothing succeeds like excess.

Lord Illingworth, ibid., Act 3

91 Religions die when they are proved to be true. Science is the record of dead religions.

'Phrases and Philosophies for the Use of the Young', publ. in *Chameleon* December 1894, repr. in *Complete Works of Oscar Wilde* (ed. J. B. Foreman, 1966)

92 One should either be a work of art, or wear a work of art.

'Phrases and Philosophies for the Use of the Young', ibid.

93 The Love that dare not speak its name in this century is such a great affection of an elder for a younger man as there was between David and Jonathan, such as Plato made the very basis of his philosophy, and such as you find in the sonnets of Michelangelo and Shakespeare. It is that deep, spiritual affection that is as pure as it is perfect . . . It is in this century misunderstood . . . and on account of it I am placed where I am now.

Statement made during Wilde's first trial for 'indecent acts', *Regina v. Wilde and Taylor* 30 April 1895, quoted in *Oscar Wilde*, ch. 6 (1976) by H. Montgomery Hyde. See LORD ALFRED DOUGLAS 1.

94 Morality is simply the attitude we adopt towards people we personally dislike.

An Ideal Husband, Act 2 (1895). Spoken by Mrs Cheveley.

95 Really, if the lower orders don't set us a good example, what on earth is the use of them? They seem, as a class, to have absolutely no sense of moral responsibility.

The Importance of Being Earnest, Act 1 (1895). Spoken by Algernon.

96 The truth is rarely pure and never simple. Modern life would be very tedious if it were either, and modern literature a complete impossibility!

Algernon, ibid., Act 1

97 I have invented an invaluable permanent invalid called Bunbury, in order that I may be able to go down into the country whenever I choose.

Algernon, ibid., Act 1

98 Pray don't talk to me about the weather . . . Whenever people talk to me about the weather, I always feel quite certain that they mean something else.

Gwendolen, ibid., Act 1

99 I do not approve of anything that tampers with natural ignorance. Ignorance is like a delicate exotic fruit; touch it and the bloom is gone. The whole theory of modern education is radically unsound. Fortunately in England, at any rate, education produces no effect whatsoever.

Lady Bracknell, ibid., Act 1

100 To lose one parent may be regarded as a misfortune . . . to lose both seems like carelessness.
Lady Bracknell, ibid., Act 1

101 A handbag?
Lady Bracknell, ibid., Act 1. Echoing Jack's response on being asked where, as an abandoned baby, he had been found.

102 Relations are simply a tedious pack of people, who haven't got the remotest knowledge of how to live, nor the smallest instinct about when to die.
Algernon, ibid., Act 1

103 The good ended happily, and the bad unhappily. That is what Fiction means.
Miss Prism, ibid., Act 2. Speaking of her own novel. See TOM STOPPARD 5.

104 I never travel without my diary. One should always have something sensational to read in the train.
Gwendolen, ibid., Act 3

105 It is very vulgar to talk about one's business. Only people like stockbrokers do that, and then merely at dinner parties.
Algernon, ibid., Act 3

106 Never speak disrespectfully of Society, Algernon. Only people who can't get into it do that.
Lady Bracknell, ibid., Act 4

107 Thirty-five is a very attractive age. London society is full of women of the highest birth who have, of their own free choice, remained thirty-five for years.
Lady Bracknell, ibid., Act 4

108 No woman should ever be quite accurate about her age. It looks so calculating.
Lady Bracknell, ibid., Act 4

109 I never saw a man who looked
With such a wistful eye
Upon that little tent of blue
Which prisoners call the sky.
The Ballad of Reading Gaol, pt 1, st. 3 (1898). In 1895, Wilde was tried for 'indecent acts' and sentenced to two years' hard labour in Reading Gaol.

110 Yet each man kills the thing he loves,
By each let this be heard,
Some do it with a bitter look,
Some with a flattering word.
The coward does it with a kiss,
The brave man with a sword!
Ibid., pt 1, st. 7. The lines are often interpreted as referring

to Lord ALFRED DOUGLAS, whom Wilde reproached for his behaviour towards him during and after his trial.

111 It is sweet to dance to violins
When Love and Life are fair:
To dance to flutes, to dance to lutes
Is delicate and rare:
But it is not sweet with nimble feet
To dance upon the air!
Ibid., pt 2, st. 9

112 And the wild regrets, and the bloody sweats,
None knew so well as I:
For he who lives more lives than one
More deaths than one must die.
Ibid., pt 3, st. 37

113 For his mourners will be outcast men,
And outcasts always mourn.
Ibid., pt 4, st. 23. The words are inscribed on Wilde's tomb in Père Lachaise cemetery, Paris.

114 I know not whether laws be right
Or whether laws be wrong;
All that we know who live in gaol
Is that the wall is strong;
And that each day is like a year,
A year whose days are long.
Ibid., pt 5, st. 1

115 How else but through a broken heart
May Lord Christ enter in?
Ibid., pt 5, st. 14

116 Where there is sorrow there is holy ground.
De Profundis (1905)

117 A man's very highest moment is, I have no doubt at all, when he kneels in the dust, and beats his breast, and tells all the sins of his life.
De Profundis (1905). Wilde's letter of reminiscence and confession was written to LORD ALFRED DOUGLAS while in prison.

118 What is said of a man is nothing. The point is, who says it.
De Profundis (1905)

119 I put all my genius into my life; I put only my talent into my works.
Quoted in Oscar Wilde 'In Memoriam' (1910) by ANDRÉ GIDE, also in Gide's journal entry, 29 June 1913, publ. in Journals 1889–1949 (1951)

120 I don't like Switzerland; it has produced nothing but theologians and waiters.
Remark during his exile in Europe, quoted in Oscar Wilde, ch. 9 (1976), by H. Montgomery Hyde

121 Work is the curse of the drinking classes.
Quoted in *Life of Oscar Wilde*, ch. 12 (1946) by Hesketh Pearson

122 A man's face is his autobiography. A woman's face is her work of fiction.
Quoted in *Oscar Wilde*, ch. 9 (1976) by H. Montgomery Hyde

123 Either that wallpaper goes, or I do.
Attributed. Last words as he lay dying in a drab Paris hotel room, recorded in variant forms in *Life of Oscar Wilde* (1906) by R. H. Sherard, and *Oscar Wilde* (1988) by RICHARD ELLMANN.

Billy Wilder
(1906–2002)
US film-maker

Originally Samuel Wilder. Working in Hollywood from 1934, he enjoyed a long association with co-writers Charles Brackett and later I. A. L. Diamond on films such as Double Indemnity *(1944),* Sunset Boulevard *(1950) and* The Seven Year Itch *(1955).*

1 Look at that! Look how she moves! That's just like jell-O on springs. She must have some sort of built-in motor or something, huh? I tell you it's a whole different sex.
Some Like It Hot (film, 1959, screenplay by Billy Wilder and I. A. L. Diamond, directed and produced by Billy Wilder). Spoken by Jerry/Daphne (Jack Lemmon) to Joe/Josephine (Tony Curtis), the first time they set eyes on Sugar Kane (MARILYN MONROE).

2 Well, nobody's perfect.
Ibid. Spoken by Osgood E. Fielding III (Joe E. Brown) who utters these closing words of the film on discovering that his bride-to-be (Jack Lemmon) is a man.

3 Hindsight is always twenty-twenty.
Quoted in *Wit and Wisdom of the Moviemakers* (ed. John Robert Columbo, 1979) ch. 7

Thornton Wilder
(1897–1975)
US novelist and playwright

His work dealt primarily with 'those things which repeat and repeat and repeat in the lives of millions', as he once described it. He won Pulitzer prizes for his novel The Bridge of San Luis Rey *(1927) and the plays* Our Town *(1938) and* The Skin of Our Teeth *(1942).*

1 I've never forgotten for long at a time that living is struggle. I know that every good and excellent thing in the world stands moment by moment on the razor-edge of danger and must be fought for – whether it's a field, or a home, or a country.
The Skin of Our Teeth, Act 3 (1942). Spoken by Antrobus.

2 Literature is the orchestration of platitudes.
Time 12 January 1953

3 Marriage is a bribe to make a housekeeper think she's a householder.
The Matchmaker, Act 1 (1954). Spoken by Vendergelder. The play was adapted from a previous work, *The Merchant of Yonkers* (1939), and was later the basis for the Broadway musical *Hello Dolly!* (1963).

4 Never support two weaknesses at the same time. It's your combination sinners – your lecherous liars and your miserly drunkards – who dishonor the vices and bring them into bad repute.
Malachi, ibid., Act 3

5 A dramatist is one who believes that the pure event, an action involving human beings, is more arresting than any comment that can be made upon it.
Interview in *Writers at Work* (first series, ed. Malcolm Cowley, 1958)

John Wilkes
(1725–97)
English politician

He established the North Briton *(1762), which attacked* GEORGE III *and the government, and was elected Lord Mayor of London in 1774. Repeatedly expelled from Parliament, he campaigned for parliamentary reform and was seen as a champion of liberty.*

1 Earl of Sandwich: 'Pon my soul, Wilkes, I don't know whether you'll die upon the gallows or of the pox.
Wilkes: That depends, my Lord, whether I first embrace your Lordship's principles, or your Lordship's mistresses.
Quoted in *The Four Georges* (1935) by Sir Charles Petrie

Emma Hart Willard
(1787–1870)
US academic

She was a pioneer in women's education, establishing the influential Troy Female Seminary in 1821 which offered teacher education for women. She also published text books and a volume of verse.

1 And calm and peaceful shall I sleep,
Rocked in the cradle of the deep.
'The Cradle of the Deep', publ. in *The Fulfilment of a Promise* (1831)

William III (William of Orange)

(1650–1702)

King of Great Britain and Ireland

Stadtholder of the United Provinces of the Netherlands (1672–1702), he ascended the English throne in 1688 following the 'Glorious Revolution', reigning jointly with his wife Mary II. He has been called 'the first English king who was a good European'. See JOHN LOTHROP MOTLEY 1.

1 'Do you not see your country is lost?' asked the Duke of Buckingham. 'There is one way never to see it lost' replied William, 'and that is to die in the last ditch.'

History of My Own Time (1838 edn) by Bishop Gilbert Burnet

2 Every bullet has its billet.

Quoted by JOHN WESLEY in journal entry, 6 June 1765, publ. in *Journal* (1827)

Hank Williams

(1923–53)

US country musician

Performing at southern honky-tonks in his teens, he made his first recordings in 1946 and rose to become country music's biggest star. He died of an alcohol-related heart disease.

1 Your Cheatin' Heart.

Title of song (1953), film biopic (1964) and biography by Chet Flippo (1981). Recorded on Williams' last session in Nashville, the song posthumously topped both *Billboard* and *Cashbox* country charts for months and was much covered.

Shirley Williams

(b. 1930)

British politician

Baroness Williams of Crosby. Daughter of VERA BRITTAIN, *she became the first elected MP of the new Social Democratic Party in 1981, and its President 1982–3. She was Leader of the Liberal Democrats in the House of Lords 2001–4.*

1 The Catholic Church has never really come to terms with women. What I object to is being treated either as Madonnas or Mary Magdalenes.

Observer 22 March 1981

Tennessee Williams

(1911–83)

US playwright

His background of genteel poverty in the deep South is relayed in most of his plays, not least in his first success The Glass Menagerie *(1944). He won Pulitzer Prizes for* A Streetcar Named Desire *(1947) and* Cat on a Hot Tin Roof *(1955).*

1 In memory everything seems to happen to music.

The Glass Menagerie, Sc. 1 (1944). Spoken by Tom.

2 Time is the longest distance between two places.

Tom, ibid. Sc. 7

3 I have always depended on the kindness of strangers.

A Streetcar Named Desire, Sc. 11 (1947). The final words of Blanche DuBois.

4 Time rushes toward us with its hospital tray of infinitely varied narcotics, even while it is preparing us for its inevitably fatal operation.

The Rose Tattoo, 'The Timeless World of a Play' (1951)

5 You said 'They're harmless dreamers and they're loved by the people.' – 'What,' I asked you, 'is harmless about a dreamer, and what,' I asked you, 'is harmless about the love of the people? – Revolution only needs good dreamers who remember their dreams.'

Camino Real (1953), block 2. Spoken by Gutman to the Generalissimo.

6 The most dangerous word in any human tongue is the word for brother. It's inflammatory.

Gutman, ibid., block 2

7 We have to distrust each other. It is our only defence against betrayal.

Marguerite Gautier, ibid., block 10

8 We're all of us guinea pigs in the laboratory of God. Humanity is just a work in progress.

The Gipsy, ibid., block 12

9 Mendacity is a system that we live in. Liquor is one way out an' death's the other.

Cat on a Hot Tin Roof, Act 2 (1955). Spoken by Brick.

10 We're all of us sentenced to solitary confinement inside our own skins, for life!

Orpheus Descending, Act 2, Sc. 1 (1957). Spoken by Val Xavier.

11 We all live in a house on fire, no fire department to call; no way out, just the upstairs window to look out of while the fire burns the house down with us trapped, locked in it.

The Milk Train Doesn't Stop Here Anymore, Sc. 6 (1963). Spoken by Chris.

William Carlos Williams

(1883–1963)

US poet

He is known for celebrating the everyday in his verse, often in unconventional rhythm and metre. His major work Paterson

(1946–58) was based on themes of the eponymous city in New Jersey. His final verse collection Pictures from Breughel (1962) won a Pulitzer Prize.

1 The pure products of America
go crazy –
mountain folk from Kentucky
or the ribbed north end of
Jersey
with its isolate lakes and
valleys, its deaf-mutes, thieves.
'To Elsie', publ. in Spring and All (1923)

2 so much depends
upon
a red wheel
barrow
glazed with rain
water
beside the white
chickens
'The Red Wheelbarrow', ibid.

3 It's the anarchy of poverty
delights me.
'The Poor', publ. in Recent Verse (1938)

4 Say it! No ideas but in things.
Paterson, bk 1, 'The Delineaments of the Giants', sect. 1 (1946, rev. 1963). Williams' poetic dictum – to present the subject concretely, without literary artifice – was influential on the Beat writers, notably ALLEN GINSBERG.

5 It is difficult
to get the news from poems
yet men die miserably every day
for lack
of what is found there.
'Asphodel, That Greeny Flower', publ. in Journey to Love (1955)

Roy Williamson
(1937–90)
Scottish folk musician

He was a founding member of the Corrie Folk Trio, which formed in the 1960s and continued as a duo, the Corries, with Ronnie Brown until 1990.

1 O Flower of Scotland,
When will we see
Your like again,
That fought and died for,
Your wee bit hill and glen,
And stood against him,
Proud Edward's Army,

And sent him homeward,
Tae think again.
'Flower of Scotland' (song, 1968) on the album The Corries in Concert (1969) by the Corries. The song has come to be regarded as Scotland's unofficial national anthem.

Wendell L. Willkie
(1892–1944)
US lawyer and politician

He ran as Republican candidate for the presidency in 1940 but was narrowly defeated by F. D. ROOSEVELT. Committed to international cooperation and civil rights, he published One World (1943), based on his travels.

1 Freedom is an indivisible word. If we want to enjoy it, and fight for it, we must be prepared to extend it to everyone, whether they are rich or poor, whether they agree with us or not, no matter what their race or the color of their skin.
One World, ch. 13 (1943)

2 The constitution does not provide for first and second class citizens.
An American Programme, ch. 2 (1944)

John Wilmot
See EARL OF ROCHESTER

(Sir) Angus Wilson
(1931–91)
British author

On the staff of the British Museum Library until 1955, he had success with his stories satirizing the middle class, and the novels Hemlock and After (1952) and Anglo-Saxon Attitudes (1956).

1 Once a Catholic always a Catholic.
The Wrong Set, 'Significant Experience' (1949). Spoken by Jeremy.

Charles E. Wilson
(1890–1961)
US industrialist and politician

He was President of General Motors 1941–53 and served as Secretary of Defense under EISENHOWER 1953–7.

1 For years I thought what was good for our country was good for General Motors and vice versa. The difference did not exist. Our company is too big. It goes with the welfare of the country.
Statement to US Senate committee, 15 January 1953, quoted in the New York Times 24 February 1953. The words – usually

quoted 'What's good for the country is good for General Motors, and *vice versa*' – were pounced upon by the Democrats on the committee, who were in a majority, to question his true loyalties.

Harold Wilson
(1916–95)
British politician and prime minister

Baron Wilson of Rivaulx. He delighted in his 'common touch', expressed in his fondness for HP sauce, Gannex raincoats and pipe-smoking. He was Labour Prime Minister 1964–70 and 1974–6, introducing economic sanctions against Rhodesia in 1965 and renegotiating Britain's terms of entry into the EEC in 1974.

1 All the little gnomes of Zurich.
Speech to House of Commons, 12 November 1956, publ. in Hansard col. 578. Describing international financiers who, Wilson claimed, exerted excessive influence over the British economy.

2 This Party is a moral crusade or it is nothing.
Speech to Labour Party Conference, 1 October 1962, quoted in *The Times* 2 October 1962. The words were recalled by TONY BLAIR on Wilson's death.

3 If I had the choice between smoked salmon and tinned salmon, I'd have it tinned. With vinegar.
Quoted in the *Observer* 11 November 1962

4 We are redefining and we are restating our Socialism in terms of the scientific revolution. But that revolution cannot become a reality unless we are prepared to make far-reaching changes in economic and social attitudes which permeate our whole system of society. The Britain that is going to be forged in the white heat of this revolution will be no place for restrictive practices or for outdated methods on either side of industry.
Speech to Labour Party Conference in Scarborough, 1 October 1963, publ. in *The Penguin Book of Twentieth-Century Speeches* (ed. Brian MacArthur, 1999). In his first conference speech as party leader, Wilson attempted to associate Labour with what became known as the 'white heat of the technological revolution', in contrast to the perceived old-fashioned ideas of ALEC DOUGLAS-HOME's Conservative Party.

5 A week is a long time in politics.
Attributed, *c.* 1964. Wilson was unable to remember when or even if he had uttered this aphorism always associated with him. The words were probably said off the record to lobby correspondents.

6 From now the pound abroad is worth fourteen per cent or so less in terms of other currencies. It does not mean, of course, that the pound here in Britain, in your pocket or purse, or in your bank, has been devalued.
Broadcast, 19 November 1967, BBC TV, quoted in *The Times* 20 November 1967

7 One man's wage rise is another man's price increase.
Speech at Blackburn, 8 January 1970, quoted in the *Observer* 11 January 1970

John Wilson
(1785–1854)
Scottish author and critic

A member of the editorial staff at Blackwood's Magazine from 1817, he contributed a large number of the 'Noctes Ambrosianae' papers, using the pseudonym Christopher North.

1 His Majesty's dominions, on which the sun never sets.
'Noctes Ambrosianae', no. 42, publ. in *Blackwood's Magazine* April 1829

2 Such accidents will happen in the best-regulated families.
'Noctes Ambrosianae', no. 67, ibid., August 1834. See CHARLES DICKENS 71.

Woodrow Wilson
(1856–1924)
US politician and president

Thomas Woodrow Wilson. As Democratic president (1913–21), he reluctantly entered the First World War in 1917, contributed to the armistice with his 'Fourteen Points' plan and championed the League of Nations. 'In Wilson, the whole of mankind breaks camp, sets out from home and wrestles with the universe and its gods,' commented William Bolitho.

1 It is like writing history with lightning and my only regret is that it is all so terribly true.
Attributed remark at the White House, 18 February 1915, quoted in *The Image*, ch. 4 (1962) by DANIEL J. BOORSTIN. On seeing D. W. GRIFFITH's film, *The Birth of a Nation*.

2 No nation is fit to sit in judgement upon any other nation.
Speech in New York, 20 April 1915, publ. in *Selected Addresses* (1918)

3 We have stood apart, studiously neutral.
Speech to Congress, 7 December 1915, publ. in the *New York Times* 8 December 1915

4 Once lead this people into war and they will forget there ever was such a thing as tolerance.
Quoted in *Mr Wilson's War*, pt 3, ch. 12 (1917) by JOHN DOS PASSOS

5 It must be a peace without victory . . . Only a peace between equals can last.
Address to the Senate, 22 January 1917, publ. in *The Messages and Papers of Woodrow Wilson*, vol. 1 (ed. Albert Shaw, 1924)

6 A little group of wilful men reflecting no opinion but their own have rendered the great Government of the United States helpless and contemptible.
Statement, 4 March 1917, quoted in the *New York Times* 5 March 1917. Referring to a successful filibuster against Wilson's bill to arm US merchant ships against German submarine attacks.

7 The world must be made safe for democracy. Its peace must be planted upon the tested foundations of political liberty.
Speech to Congress, 2 April 1917, publ. in *Selected Addresses* (1918). Proposing a state of war against Germany, which was almost unanimously voted four days later. A year earlier, Wilson had run his re-election campaign on the boast of having 'kept us out of war', having pursued a policy of remaining 'studiously neutral'. See also THOMAS WOLFE 2.

8 Armed neutrality is ineffectual enough at best.
Speech to Congress, 2 April 1917, ibid.

9 Sometimes people call me an idealist. Well, that is the way I know I am an American . . . . America is the only idealistic nation in the world.
Speech at Sioux Falls, North Dakota, 8 September 1919, publ. in *The Messages and Papers of Woodrow Wilson*, vol. 2 (ed. Albert Shaw, 1924)

Anne Finch, Lady Winchilsea
(1660–1720)
English poet

She came to prominence with her poem 'The Spleen' (1701). Her subjects include nature, the rights of women and the restrictions of wives.

1 Now the jonquil o'ercomes the feeble brain;
We faint beneath the aromatic pain.
'The Spleen', ll. 40–1 (1701), repr. in *Miscellany Poems, on Several Occasions* (1713). See ALEXANDER POPE 123.

2 Alas! a woman that attempts the pen,
Such an intruder on the rights of men,
Such a presumptuous creature is esteemed,
The fault can by no virtue be redeemed.
They tell us we mistake our sex and way;

Good breeding, fashion, dancing, dressing, play,
Are the accomplishments we should desire;
To write, or read, or think, or to enquire
Would cloud our beauty, and exhaust our time;
And interrupt the conquests of our prime.
'The Introduction', ll. 9–18, ibid.

3 How are we fallen, fallen by mistaken rules?
And education's, more than nature's fools,
Debarred from all improvements of the mind,
And to be dull, expected and designed.
'The Introduction', ll. 51–4, ibid.

4 Love (if such a thing there be)
Is all despair, or ecstasy.
Poetry's the feverish fit,
Th' o'erflowing of unbounded wit.
'Enquiry after Peace', ll. 38–41, ibid.

Jeanette Winterson
(b. 1959)
British author

She came to notice with her first novel, the autobiographical Oranges Are Not the Only Fruit *(1985), in which she recounts her self-fulfilment as a lesbian. This was followed by* Written on the Body *(1992),* Art and Lies *(1994), and* The Powerbook *(2000) among others.*

1 Oranges Are Not the Only Fruit.
Title of novel (1985)

2 Why is it that the most unoriginal thing we can say to one another is still the thing we long to hear? 'I love you' is always a quotation. You did not say it first and neither did I, yet when you say it and when I say it we speak like savages who have found three words and worship them.
Written on the Body (1992)

3 There's no such thing as autobiography there's only art and lies.
Art and Lies, 'Sappho' (1994)

Ludwig Wittgenstein
(1889–1951)
Austrian-born British philosopher

He studied mathematics and logic under BERTRAND RUSSELL *at Cambridge and wrote his seminal work on logical positivism,* Tractatus Logico-Philosophicus *(1921), in an Italian prison camp. His* Philosophical Investigations *(1953) discusses the uses and inherent logic of language.*

1 Logic takes care of itself; all we have to do is to look and see how it does it.

Entry, 13 October 1914, publ. in *Notebooks 1914–1916* (ed. G. E. M. Anscombe, 1961). Also in *Tractatus Logico-Philosophicus*, sect. 5:473 (1921)

2 The logic of the world is prior to all truth and falsehood.

Entry, 18 October 1914, ibid. Reformulated in *Tractatus Logico-Philosophicus*, sect. 5:552 (1921): 'Logic is *prior* to every experience – that something *is so*.'

3 Don't get involved in partial problems, but always take flight to where there is a free view over the whole *single* great problem, even if this view is still not a clear one.

Entry, 1 November 1914, ibid.

4 It is one of the chief skills of the philosopher not to occupy himself with questions which do not concern him.

Entry, 1 May 1915, ibid.

5 Language is a part of our organism and no less complicated than it.

Entry, 14 May 1915, ibid. Also in *Tractatus Logico-Philosophicus*, sect. 4:002 (1921): 'Everyday language is a part of the human organism and is no less complicated than it.'

6 The philosophical I is not the human being, not the human body or the human soul with the psychological properties, but the metaphysical subject, the boundary (not a part) of the world.

Entry, 2 September 1915, ibid. Also in *Tractatus Logico-Philosophicus*, sect. 5:641 (1921).

7 I am my world. (The microcosm).

Tractatus Logico-Philosophicus, sect. 5:63

8 Death is not an event in life: we do not live to experience death. If we take eternity to mean not infinite temporal duration but timelessness, then eternal life belongs to those who live in the present.

Ibid., sect. 6:4311

9 Whereof one cannot speak, thereof one must be silent.

Ibid., sect. 7. Wittgenstein had elaborated in the book's Preface: 'What can be said at all can be said clearly, and what we cannot talk about we must pass over in silence.' KARL POPPER, in his *Conjectures and Refutations* (1963), reported Franz Urbach's rejoinder to this: 'But it is only here that speaking becomes worthwhile.'

10 You get tragedy where the tree, instead of bending, breaks.

Journal entry, 1929, publ. in *Culture and Value* (ed. G. H. von Wright with Heikki Nyman, 1980)

11 Philosophy is like trying to open a safe with a combination lock: each little adjustment of the dials seems to achieve nothing, only when everything is in place does the door open.

Conversation in 1930, publ. in *Personal Recollections*, ch. 6 (ed. Rush Rhees, 1981)

12 The face is the soul of the body.

Journal entry, 1932–4, publ. in *Culture and Value* (ed. G. H. von Wright with Heikki Nyman, 1980)

13 Never stay up on the barren heights of cleverness, but come down into the green valleys of silliness.

Journal entry, 1948, publ. in ibid.

14 Philosophy is a battle against the bewitchment of our intelligence by means of language.

Philosophical Investigations, pt 1, sect. 109 (1953). Wittgenstein argued that most philosophical problems arose from the systematic misuse of language, and could be solved by a new critical method of linguistic analysis.

15 The real discovery is the one which enables me to stop doing philosophy when I want to. – The one that gives philosophy peace, so that it is no longer tormented by questions which bring *itself* into question.

Ibid., pt 1, sect. 133

16 If you do know that *here is one hand*, we'll grant you all the rest.

On Certainty, sect. 1 (ed. G. E. M. Anscombe and G. H. von Wright, 1969). Opening sentence of response to a lecture by the philosopher G. E. Moore which countered Hegelianism on the grounds of common sense. Moore had famously declared, as he raised his hand: 'I *know* this is a hand.'

P. G. Wodehouse

(1881–1975)
British novelist

Pelham Grenville Wodehouse. Called 'English literature's performing flea' by SEAN O'CASEY, *he was the author of bestselling humorous fiction centring on the upper classes. After internment by the Germans in the Second World War, he made a series of radio broadcasts from Berlin which led to accusations of Nazi collusion. He subsequently lived in America, taking US citizenship in 1955.*

1 It is a good rule in life never to apologize. The right sort of people do not want apologies, and the wrong sort take a mean advantage of them.

The Man Upstairs, 'The Man Upstairs' (1914)

2 'What ho!' I said.
'What ho!' said Motty.
'What ho! What ho!'

'What ho! What ho! What ho!'
After that it seemed rather difficult to go on with the conversation.
My Man Jeeves, 'Jeeves and the Unbidden Guest' (1919)

3 In this matter of shimmering into rooms the chappie is rummy to a degree ... He moves from point to point with as little uproar as a jellyfish.
Bertie Wooster of Jeeves, ibid., 'Jeeves and the Hard-Boiled Egg'

4 What a queer thing Life is! So unlike anything else, don't you know, if you see what I mean.
Ibid., 'Rallying Round Old George'

5 Chumps always make the best husbands. When you marry, Sally, grab a chump. Tap his forehead first, and if it rings solid, don't hesitate. All the unhappy marriages come from the husbands having brains. What good are brains to a man? They only unsettle him.
The Adventures of Sally, ch. 10 (1920). Spoken by Miss Winch.

6 Few things draw two men together more surely than a mutual inability to master golf, coupled with an intense and ever-increasing love for the game.
The Clicking of Cuthbert, ch. 2 (1922)

7 Women have to learn to bear anecdotes from men they love. It is the curse of Eve.
Ibid. ch. 5

8 Alf Todd ... has about as much chance as a one-armed blind man in a dark room trying to shove a pound of melted butter into a wild cat's left ear with a red-hot needle.
Ukridge, ch. 5 (1924). Spoken by Ukridge.

9 Jeeves coughed one soft, low, gentle cough like a sheep with a blade of grass stuck in its throat.
The Inimitable Jeeves, ch. 13 (1923)

10 [He] was a tubby little chap who looked as if he had been poured into his clothes and had forgotten to say 'When!'
Very Good, Jeeves!, 'Jeeves and the Impending Doom' (1930)

11 Into the face of the young man who sat on the terrace of the Hotel Magnifique at Cannes there had crept a look of furtive shame, the shifty, hangdog look which announces that an Englishman is about to talk French.
The Luck of the Bodkins, ch. 1 (1935). Opening words.

12 There is only one cure for grey hair. It was invented by a Frenchman. It is called the guillotine.
The Old Reliable, ch. 1 (1951)

13 You can't stick lighted matches between the toes of an English butler. He would raise his eyebrows and freeze you with a glance. You'd feel as if he had caught you using the wrong fork.
Bill, ibid., ch. 17

14 Ice formed on the butler's upper slopes.
Pigs Have Wings, ch. 5 (1952)

15 Has anybody ever seen a dramatic critic in the daytime? Of course not. They come out after dark, up to no good.
Quoted in the *New York Mirror* 27 May 1955

16 She's one of those soppy girls, riddled from head to foot with whimsy. She holds the view that the stars are God's daisy chain, that rabbits are gnomes in attendance on the Fairy Queen, and that every time a fairy blows its wee nose a baby is born, which, as we know, is not the case. She's a drooper.
Stiff Upper Lip, Jeeves, ch. 2 (1963). Spoken by Bertie Wooster.

17 Marriage is not a process for prolonging the life of love. It merely mummifies the corpse.
Company for Henry, ch. 5, sect. 2 (1967). Spoken by Mr Ferris.

(Sir) Terry Wogan
(b. 1938)
Irish broadcster and writer

Associated with the BBC since 1965, he is known for his cosily irreverent humour in his radio shows and for hosting the annual Eurovision Song Contest *on television.*

1 Television contracts the imagination and radio expands it.
Quoted in the *Observer* 30 December 1984

Naomi Wolf
(b. 1962)
US feminist

Her critique of the stereotypes imposed on women The Beauty Myth *(1990) inspired* FAY WELDON *to hail her as an 'early heroine of Woman's World, Nineties Style'.*

1 'Beauty' is a currency system like the gold standard. Like any economy, it is determined by politics, and in the modern age in the West it is the last, best belief system that keeps male dominance intact.
The Beauty Myth, 'The Beauty Myth' (1990)

2 To ask women to become unnaturally thin is to ask them to relinquish their sexuality.
Ibid., 'Hunger'

Charles Wolfe

(1791–1823)
Irish poet

He was ordained a Church of Ireland priest in 1817 and drew praise for his poem 'The Burial of Sir John Moore at Corunna' (1817).

1 Not a drum was heard, not a funeral note,
As his corse to the rampart we hurried.
'The Burial of Sir John Moore at Corunna', st. 1 (1817), repr. in *The Burial of Sir John Moore, and Other Poems* (1909). Moore, at the head of a small army, was killed at Corunna (Coruña), Spain, in January 1809.

2 We buried him darkly at dead of night,
The sods with our bayonets turning.
'The Burial of Sir John Moore at Corunna', st. 3, ibid.

3 We carved not a line, and we raised not a stone –
But we left him alone with his glory.
'The Burial of Sir John Moore at Corunna', st. 8, ibid.

Humbert Wolfe

(1885–1940)
British poet

His writings include London Sonnets *(1919),* Lampoons *(1925) and* Requiem *(1927) as well as studies of Tennyson, Shelley and George Moore.*

1 You cannot hope
to bribe or twist
(thank God!) the
British journalist.
But, seeing what
the man will do
unbribed, there's
no occasion to.
The Uncelestial City, bk 1, 'Over the Fire' (1930)

Thomas Wolfe

(1900–38)
US author

His small output includes Look Homeward, Angel *(1929), its sequel* Of Time and the River *(1935) and the semi-autobiographical* The Web and The Rock *(1939), published posthumously.*

1 Which of us has not remained forever prison-pent? Which of us is not forever a stranger and alone?
Look Homeward, Angel, Foreword (1929)

2 Making the world safe for hypocrisy.
Luke, ibid., pt 3, ch. 36. Referring to the naval base at Norfolk, Virginia. See WOODROW WILSON 7 on making the world 'safe for democracy'.

3 If a man has a talent and cannot use it, he has failed. If he has a talent and uses only half of it, he has partly failed. If he has a talent and learns somehow to use the whole of it, he has gloriously succeeded, and won a satisfaction and a triumph few men ever know.
The Web and the Rock, ch. 29 (1939)

Tom Wolfe

(b. 1931)
US author and journalist

He was a major figure in the New Journalism with his portrait of 1960s counter-culture, The Electric Kool-Aid Acid Test *(1968), and such essays as 'Radical Chic and Mau-Mauing the Flak-Catchers' (1970). His biggest success was his fable of New York in the 1980s,* The Bonfire of the Vanities *(1987).*

1 The Electric Kool-Aid Acid Test.
Title of book (1968)

2 Radical Chic, after all, is only radical in Style; in its heart it is part of Society and its traditions – Politics, like Rock, Pop, and Camp, has its uses.
Radical Chic and Mau-Mauing the Flak-Catchers (1970)

3 We are now in the Me Decade – seeing the upward roll of . . . the third great religious wave in American history.
Mauve Gloves and Madmen, Clutter and Vine, 'The Me Decade and the Third Great Awakening' (1976)

4 The idea was to prove at every foot of the way up that you were one of the elected and anointed ones who had *the right stuff* and could move higher and higher and even – ultimately, God willing, one day – that you might be able to join that special few at the very top, that elite who had the capacity to bring tears to men's eyes, the very Brotherhood of the Right Stuff itself.
The Right Stuff, ch. 2 (1979). Of pilots and astronauts on the NASA training programme.

5 Bonfire of the Vanities.
Title of novel (1987)

6 A liberal is a conservative who has been arrested.
Ibid., ch. 24

Mary Wollstonecraft

(1759–1797)

English feminist and writer

She was a member of the radical circle of 'English Jacobins'. Her best-known work A Vindication of the Rights of Woman *(1792) argues for equality of rights for women. She married* WILLIAM GODWIN *in 1797 and died after giving birth to their daughter* MARY SHELLEY. HORACE WALPOLE *described her as a 'philosophizing serpent . . . that hyena in petticoats'.*

1 Independence I have long considered as the grand blessing of life, the basis of every virtue; and independence I will ever secure by contracting my wants, though I were to live on a barren heath.

A Vindication of the Rights of Woman, Dedication (1792)

2 If the abstract rights of man will bear discussion and explanation, those of women, by a parity of reasoning, will not shrink from the same test: though a different opinion prevails in this country.

Ibid., Dedication

3 Children, I grant, should be innocent; but when the epithet is applied to men, or women, it is but a civil term for weakness.

Ibid., ch. 2

4 Gentleness, docility, and a spaniel-like affection are . . . consistently recommended as the cardinal virtues of the sex . . . . She was created to be the toy of man, his rattle, and it must jingle in his ears whenever, dismissing reason, he chooses to be amused.

Ibid., ch. 2

5 Till women are more rationally educated, the progress in human virtue and improvement in knowledge must receive continual checks.

Ibid., ch. 3

6 Taught from infancy that beauty is woman's sceptre, the mind shapes itself to the body, and roaming round its gilt cage, only seeks to adorn its prison.

Ibid., ch. 3

7 A king is always a king – and a woman always a woman: his authority and her sex ever stand between them and rational converse.

Ibid., ch. 4

8 It would be an endless task to trace the variety of meannesses, cares, and sorrows, into which women are plunged by the prevailing opinion, that they were created rather to feel than reason, and that all the power they obtain, must be obtained by their charms and weakness.

Ibid., ch. 4

9 When a man seduces a woman, it should, I think, be termed a left-handed marriage.

Ibid., ch. 4

10 A slavish bondage to parents cramps every faculty of the mind.

Ibid., ch. 11

Thomas Wolsey

(c. 1475–1530)

English prelate and statesman

He was Archbishop of York (1514–30), Cardinal (1515–30) and Lord Chancellor (1515–29). Having failed to obtain a papal dispensation for the annulment of HENRY VIII's *marriage to Catherine of Aragon, he was arrested for treason, but died before his trial.*

1 If I had served God as diligently as I have done the king, He would not have given me over in my grey hairs. Howbeit, this is the just reward that I must receive for my worldly diligence and [the] pains that I have had to do the king's service, only to satisfy his vain pleasure, not regarding my godly duty.

Quoted in *Life of Cardinal Wolsey* (1558) by George Cavendish. See WILLIAM SHAKESPEARE: HENRY VIII 13

Kenneth Wolstenholme

(1920–2002)

British sports commentator

Having joined the BBC in 1946, he became the channel's leading football commentator during the 1950s and '60s, notably for Match of the Day.

1 They think it's all over – it is now.

BBC television broadcast from Wembley, 30 July 1966. Commentary in closing seconds of World Cup Final, at which England beat West Germany 4–2 in extra time.

Thomas Woodrooffe

(1899–1978)

British naval officer

After holding office as a naval commander in the Second World War he became a commentator for the BBC and published naval novels.

1 At the present moment, the whole Fleet's lit up. When I say 'lit up', I mean lit up by fairy lamps.

Radio commentary of Spithead Review, 20 May 1937, quoted in *History of Broadcasting in the UK*, vol. 2, pt 2, ch. 2 (1965) by Asa Briggs. Britain's first live outside broadcast, conducted when Woodrooffe was evidently drunk (or 'lit up').

Virginia Woolf
(1882–1941)
British novelist

A central figure of the Bloomsbury Group, she founded the Hogarth Press in 1917 with her husband Leonard Woolf. Her ground-breaking writings include To the Lighthouse *(1927),* Orlando *(1928) and* The Waves *(1931). Afflicted with mental illness all her life, she committed suicide.* EDITH SITWELL *considered her 'a beautiful little knitter'.*

1 The eyes of others our prisons; their thoughts our cages.
Monday or Tuesday, 'An Unwritten Novel' (1921)

2 One likes people much better when they're battered down by a prodigious siege of misfortune than when they triumph.
Journal entry, 13 August 1921, publ. in *The Diary of Virginia Woolf*, vol. 1 (ed. Anne O. Bell, 1978)

3 It's not catastrophes, murders, deaths, diseases, that age and kill us; it's the way people look and laugh, and run up the steps of omnibuses.
Jacob's Room, ch. 9 (1922)

4 Never did I read such tosh. As for the first two chapters we will let them pass, but the 3rd 4th 5th 6th – merely the scratching of pimples on the body of the bootboy at Claridges.
Letter to LYTTON STRACHEY, 24 August 1922, publ. in *Letters*, vol. 2 (ed. Nigel Nicolson, 1976). Referring to *Ulysses* by JAMES JOYCE.

5 In or about December, 1910 human nature changed . . . All human relations have shifted – those between masters and servants, husbands and wives, parents and children. And when human relations change there is at the same time a change in religion, conduct, politics, and literature.
'Mr Bennett and Mrs Brown' (1924), repr. in *The Captain's Deathbed* (1950)

6 Humour is the first of the gifts to perish in a foreign tongue.
The Common Reader, 'On Not Knowing Greek' (first series, 1925)

7 The word-coining genius, as if thought plunged into a sea of words and came up dripping.
Ibid., 'Notes on an Elizabethan Play'. Referring to Elizabethan drama.

8 Once conform, once do what other people do

because they do it, and a lethargy steals over all the finer nerves and faculties of the soul. She becomes all outer show and inward emptiness; dull, callous, and indifferent.
Ibid., 'Montaigne'

9 Life is not a series of gig lamps symmetrically arranged; life is a luminous halo, a semi-transparent envelope surrounding us from the beginning of consciousness to the end.
Ibid., 'Modern Fiction'

10 *Middlemarch*, the magnificent book which with all its imperfections is one of the few English novels for grown-up people.
Ibid., 'George Eliot'

11 Those comfortably padded lunatic asylums which are known, euphemistically, as the stately homes of England.
Ibid., 'Lady Dorothy Nevill'

12 We are nauseated by the sight of trivial personalities decomposing in the eternity of print.
Ibid., 'The Modern Essay'. Referring to inferior essayists.

13 A good essay must have this permanent quality about it; it must draw its curtain round us, but it must be a curtain that shuts us in not out.
Ibid., 'The Modern Essay'

14 Really I don't like human nature unless all candied over with art.
Journal entry, 13 May 1926, publ. in *The Diary of Virginia Woolf*, vol. 3 (ed. Anne O. Bell, 1980)

15 For love . . . has two faces; one white, the other black; two bodies; one smooth, the other hairy. It has two hands, two feet, two tails, two, indeed, of every member and each one is the exact opposite of the other. Yet, so strictly are they joined together that you cannot separate them.
Orlando, ch. 2 (1928)

16 Every secret of a writer's soul, every experience of his life, every quality of his mind is written large in his works.
Ibid., ch. 4

17 Where the Mind is biggest, the Heart, the Senses, Magnanimity, Charity, Tolerance, Kindliness, and the rest of them scarcely have room to breathe.
Ibid., ch. 4

18 The first duty of a lecturer – to hand you after an hour's discourse a nugget of pure truth to wrap up

between the pages of your notebooks and keep on the mantlepiece for ever.

A Room of One's Own, ch. 1 (1929). The book was originally a paper read to women students at Cambridge University.

19 A woman must have money and a room of her own if she is to write fiction.

Ibid., ch. 1

20 One cannot think well, love well, sleep well, if one has not dined well.

Ibid., ch. 1

21 Women have served all these centuries as looking-glasses possessing the magic and delicious power of reflecting the figure of man at twice its natural size.

Ibid., ch. 2

22 Fiction is like a spider's web, attached ever so lightly perhaps, but still attached to life at all four corners. Often the attachment is scarcely perceptible.

Ibid., ch. 3

23 Publicity in women is detestable. Anonymity runs in their blood. The desire to be veiled still possesses them. They are not even now as concerned about the health of their fame as men are, and, speaking generally, will pass a tombstone or a signpost without feeling an irresistible desire to cut their names on it.

Ibid., ch. 3

24 Who shall measure the heat and violence of the poet's heart when caught and tangled in a woman's body?

Ibid., ch. 3

25 On the outskirts of every agony sits some observant fellow who points.

The Waves (1931). Spoken by Bernard.

26 Things have dropped from me. I have outlived certain desires; I have lost friends, some by death . . . others through sheer inability to cross the street.

Bernard, ibid.

27 Against you I will fling myself, unvanquished and unyielding, O Death!

Bernard, ibid. Final words of the novel, chosen by Leonard Woolf as Virginia's epitaph at her burial-place and former home, Monk's House, Rodmell, Sussex.

28 One has to secrete a jelly in which to slip quota-

tions down people's throats – and one always secretes too much jelly.

Letter, 4 July 1938, publ. in *Letters*, vol. 6 (ed. Nigel Nicolson, 1980)

29 There can be no two opinions as to what a highbrow is. He is the man or woman of thoroughbred intelligence who rides his mind at a gallop across country in pursuit of an idea.

The Death of the Moth, 'Middlebrow' (1942)

Alexander Woollcott
(1887–1943)
US columnist and critic

Described by Life *magazine as 'testy as a wasp and much more poisonous', he was a New York theatre critic and a broadcaster in his show* Town Crier *(1929–42).*

1 All the things I really like to do are either immoral, illegal, or fattening.

The Knock at the Stage Door (1933)

Elizabeth Wordsworth
(1840–1932)
English academic and author

A champion of women's education, she was the first Principal of Lady Margaret Hall, Oxford (1879) and founded St Hugh's College, Oxford in 1886. She was the great niece of WILLIAM WORDSWORTH.

1 If all the good people were clever,
And all clever people were good,
The world would be nicer than ever
We thought that it possibly could.
But somehow, 'tis seldom or never
The two hit it off as they should;
The good are so harsh to the clever,
The clever so rude to the good!

'The Good and the Clever', publ. in *St Christopher and Other Poems* (1890)

William Wordsworth
(1770–1850)
English poet

He grew up and lived most of his life in the Lake District, where he was the central figure of the 'Lake Poets'. His poetic reputation was established with the publication of Lyrical Ballads *(1798), a collaboration with* SAMUEL TAYLOR COLERIDGE *and a key work of English Romanticism. His early radicalism gave way to a more conservative outlook as he grew older, but he retained a lifelong devotion to nature. Later works include* The Excursion *(1814), part of a never-completed autobiographical work,* The Recluse. *See* ROBERT BROWN-ING 12; LORD BYRON 8, 9; WILLIAM HAZLITT 25; JOHN KEATS 27; OSCAR WILDE 17.

1 A simple child, dear brother Jim,
That lightly draws its breath,
And feels its life in every limb,
What should it know of death?
'We are Seven', st. 1, publ. in *Lyrical Ballads* (1798). The words 'dear brother Jim' were omitted in later versions.

2 If this belief from heaven be sent,
If such be Nature's holy plan,
Have I not reason to lament
What man has made of man.
'Lines Written in Early Spring', st. 6, ibid.

3 Come forth into the light of things,
Let Nature be your teacher.
'The Tables Turned', st. 4, ibid.

4 One impulse from a vernal wood
May teach you more of man,
Of moral evil and of good,
Than all the sages can.
'The Tables Turned', st. 6, ibid.

5 That best portion of a good man's life;
His little, nameless, unremembered acts
Of kindness and of love.
'Lines Written a Few Miles Above Tintern Abbey', ll. 34–6, ibid.

6 That blessed mood
In which the burthen of the mystery,
In which the heavy and the weary weight
Of all this unintelligible world
Is lightened.
'Lines Written a Few Miles Above Tintern Abbey', ll. 38–42, ibid.

7 With an eye made quiet by the power
Of harmony, and the deep power of joy,
We see into the life of things.
'Lines Written a Few Miles Above Tintern Abbey', ll. 48–50, ibid.

8 For I have learned
To look on nature, not as in the hour
Of thoughtless youth, but hearing oftentimes
The still, sad music of humanity,
Nor harsh nor grating, though of ample power
To chasten and subdue.
'Lines Written a Few Miles Above Tintern Abbey', ll. 89–94, ibid.

9 I have felt
A presence that disturbs me with the joy
Of elevated thoughts; a sense sublime
Of something far more deeply interfused,
Whose dwelling is the light of setting suns,
And the round ocean and the living air,
And the blue sky, and in the mind of man.
'Lines Written a Few Miles Above Tintern Abbey', ll. 94–100, ibid.

10 Neither evil tongues,
Rash judgements, nor the sneers of selfish men,
Nor greetings where no kindness is, nor all
The dreary intercourse of daily life,
Shall e'er prevail against us.
'Lines Written a Few Miles Above Tintern Abbey', ll. 129–33, ibid.

11 Escaped
From the vast city, where I long had pined
A discontented sojourner; now free,
Free as a bird to settle where I will.
The Prelude, bk 1, ll. 6–9 (written 1799–1805, publ. 1850)

12 Make one long bathing of a summer's day.
Ibid., bk 1, l. 290

13 Fair seed-time had my soul, and I grew up
Fostered alike by beauty and by fear.
Ibid., bk 1, ll. 301–2

14 Dust as we are, the immortal spirit grows
Like harmony in music; there is a dark
Inscrutable workmanship that reconciles
Discordant elements, makes them cling together
In one society.
Ibid., bk 1, ll. 340–4

15 And I was taught to feel, perhaps too much,
The self-sufficing power of solitude.
Ibid., bk 2, ll. 76–7

16 Where the statue stood
Of Newton with his prism, and silent face:
The marble index of a mind for ever
Voyaging through strange seas of thought, alone.
Ibid., bk 3, ll. 60–3. Referring to the statue of ISAAC NEWTON at Trinity College, Cambridge University.

17 A day
Spent in a round of strenuous idleness.
Ibid., bk. 4, ll. 376–7

18 But Europe at that time was thrilled with joy,
France standing on the top of golden hours,
And human nature seeming born again.
Ibid., bk 6, ll. 339–41

19 We were brothers all
In honour, as in one community,
Scholars and gentlemen.
Ibid., bk 9, ll. 227–9

20 Bliss was it in that dawn to be alive,
But to be young was very heaven!
Ibid., bk 11, ll. 108–9. The lines also appeared in 'The French
Revolution as it Appeared to Enthusiasts' (1809).

21 Not in Utopia, subterranean fields,
Or some secreted island, Heaven knows where!
But in the very world, which is the world
Of all of us, the place where in the end
We find our happiness, or not at all!
Ibid., bk. 11, ll. 140–4

22 There is
One great society alone on earth,
The noble living, and the noble dead.
Ibid., bk. 11, ll. 393–5

23 I shook the habit off
Entirely and for ever, and again
In Nature's presence stood, as now I stand,
A sensitive being, a *creative* soul.
Ibid., bk. 12, ll. 204–7

24 Imagination, which in truth,
Is but another name for absolute power
And clearest insight, amplitude of mind,
And Reason, in her most exalted mood.
Ibid., bk. 14, ll. 190–3

25 Happier of happy though I be, like them
I cannot take possession of the sky,
Mount with a thoughtless impulse, and wheel
    there,
One of a mighty multitude whose way
And motion is a harmony and dance
Magnificent.
'Home at Grasmere', ll. 287–92, written 1800, publ. as *The
Recluse* (1888)

26 Is there not
An art, a music, and a stream of words
That shalt be life, the acknowledged voice of life?
'Home at Grasmere', ll. 620–2, ibid.

27 The human mind is capable of excitement without the application of gross and violent stimulants;
and he must have a very faint perception of its
beauty and dignity who does not know this.
Lyrical Ballads, Preface (second edn, 1800)

28 A multitude of causes unknown to former times

are now acting with a combined force to blunt the
discriminating powers of the mind, and unfitting it
for all voluntary exertion to reduce it to a state of
almost savage torpor.
Ibid., Preface. Among the causes Wordsworth perceived were
'the great national events which are daily taking place, and
the increasing accumulation of men in cities, where the uniformity of their occupations produces a craving for extraordinary incident which the rapid communication of intelligence
hourly gratifies'.

29 Poetry is the breath and finer spirit of all knowledge; it is the impassioned expression which is in
the countenance of all Science.
Ibid., Preface

30 Poetry is the spontaneous overflow of powerful
feelings: it takes its origin from emotion recollected
in tranquillity.
Ibid., Preface. This sentiment, which is a central tenet in
Wordsworth's criticism, has parallels in SCHILLER's *Über Bür-
gers Gedichte* as well as COLERIDGE's *Notebooks*, in which he
speaks of 'recalling passion in tranquillity'.

31 She dwelt among the untrodden ways
Beside the springs of Dove,
A maid whom there were none to praise
And very few to love.
'Song' ('She dwelt among the untrodden ways'), st. 1, ibid.,
vol. 2

32 A violet by a mossy stone
Half hidden from the eye!
– Fair as a star, when only one
Is shining in the sky.
'Song', st. 2, ibid., vol. 2

33 She lived unknown, and few could know
When Lucy ceased to be;
But she is in her grave, and, oh,
The difference to me!
'Song', st. 3, ibid. vol. 2

34 A slumber did my spirit seal;
I had no human fears:
She seemed a thing that could not feel
The touch of earthly years.
'A slumber did my spirit seal', st. 1, ibid., vol. 2

35 No motion has she now, no force;
She neither hears nor sees;
Rolled round in earth's diurnal course,
With rocks, and stones, and trees.
'A slumber did my spirit seal', st. 2, ibid., vol. 2

36 Physician art thou? – one, all eyes,
Philosopher! – a fingering slave,

One that would peep and botanize
Upon his mother's grave?
'A Poet's Epitaph', st. 5, ibid., vol. 2

37 A reasoning, self-sufficing thing,
An intellectual All-in-all!
'A Poet's Epitaph', st. 8, ibid., vol. 2

38 In common things that round us lie
Some random truths he can impart,
The harvest of a quiet eye
That broods and sleeps on his own heart.
'A Poet's Epitaph', st. 13, ibid., vol. 2

39 She was a phantom of delight
When first she gleamed upon my sight;
A lovely apparition, sent
To be a moment's ornament.
'She was a phantom of delight', st. 1, publ. in *Poems in Two Volumes*, vol. 1 (1807)

40 And now I see with eye serene
The very pulse of the machine;
A being breathing thoughtful breath;
A traveller betwixt life and death.
'She was a phantom of delight', st. 3, ibid., vol. 1

41 A perfect woman; nobly planned,
To warn, to comfort, and command;
And yet a spirit still, and bright
With something of an angel light.
'She was a phantom of delight', st. 3, ibid., vol. 1

42 Who is the happy warrior? Who is he
Whom every man in arms should wish to be?
'Character of the Happy Warrior', ll. 1–2, ibid., vol. 1

43 My apprehensions come in crowds;
I dread the rustling of the grass;
The very shadows of the clouds
Have power to shake me as they pass:
I question things and do not find
One that will answer to my mind;
And all the world appears unkind.
'The Affliction of Margaret – ', st. 10, ibid., vol. 1

44 I travelled among unknown men,
In lands beyond the sea;
Nor, England! did I know till then
What love I bore to thee.
'I Travelled Among Unknown Men', st. 1, ibid., vol. 1

45 Stern daughter of the voice of God!
O Duty! if that name thou love

Who art a light to guide, a rod
To check the erring, and reprove.
'Ode to Duty', st. 1, ibid., vol. 1

46 Me this unchartered freedom tires;
I feel the weight of chance desires:
My hopes no more must change their name,
I long for a repose which ever is the same.
'Ode to Duty', st. 5, ibid., vol. 1

47 I thought of Chatterton, the marvellous
      boy,
The sleepless soul that perished in its pride;
Of him who walked in glory and in joy
Behind his plough, upon the mountain side:
By our own spirits are we deified.
'Resolution and Independence', st. 7, ibid., vol. 1

48 We poets in our youth begin in gladness;
But thereof comes in the end despondency and
      madness.
'Resolution and Independence', st. 7, ibid., vol. 1

49 Choice words, and measured phrase; above the
      reach
Of ordinary men; a stately speech!
'Resolution and Independence', st. 15, ibid., vol. 1

50 Nuns fret not at their convent's narrow room;
And hermits are contented with their cells.
'Nuns fret not', ll. 1–2, ibid., vol. 1

51 Earth has not anything to show more fair:
Dull would he be of soul who could pass by
A sight so touching in its majesty.
'Composed Upon Westminster Bridge', ll. 1–3, ibid., vol. 1

52 This city now doth, like a garment, wear
The beauty of the morning; silent, bare,
Ships, towers, domes, theatres and temples lie
Open unto the fields, and to the sky;
All bright and glittering in the smokeless air.
'Composed Upon Westminster Bridge', ll. 4–8, ibid., vol. 1

53 Ne'er saw I, never felt, a calm so deep!
The river glideth at its own sweet will:
Dear God! the very houses seem asleep;
And all that mighty heart is lying still!
'Composed Upon Westminster Bridge', ll. 11–14, ibid., vol. 1

54 The world is too much with us; late and soon,
Getting and spending, we lay waste our powers.
Sonnet 18 ('The world is too much with us'), ll. 1–2, ibid., vol. 1

55 Great God! I'd rather be
A pagan suckled in a creed outworn;
So might I, standing on this pleasant lea,

Have glimpses that would make me less forlorn;
Have sight of Proteus rising from the sea;
Or hear old Triton blow his wreathèd horn.

Sonnet 18, ll. 9–14, ibid., vol. 1

56 It is a beauteous evening, calm and free;
The holy time is quiet as a nun
Breathless with adoration.

Sonnet 19 ('It is a beauteous evening'), ll. 1–3, ibid., vol. 1

57 Once did she hold the gorgeous East in fee,
And was the safeguard of the West.

'On the Extinction of the Venetian Repbublic', ll. 1–2, ibid.,
vol. 1

58 There's not a breathing of the common wind
That will forget thee; thou hast great allies;
Thy friends are exultations, agonies,
And love, and man's unconquerable mind.

'To Toussaint L'Ouverture', ll. 11–14, ibid., vol. 1

59 Plain living and high thinking are no more:
The homely beauty of the good old cause
Is gone; our peace, our fearful innocence,
And pure religion breathing household laws.

'Written in London', ll. 11–14, ibid., vol. 1

60 Milton! thou should'st be living at this hour:
England hath need of thee.

'London, 1802', ll. 1–2, ibid., vol. 1

61 Thy soul was like a star and dwelt apart:
Thou hadst a voice whose sound was like the sea;
Pure as the naked heavens, majestic, free,
So didst thou travel on life's common way,
In cheerful godliness.

'London, 1802', ll. 9–13, ibid., vol. 1. Of JOHN MILTON.

62 We must be free or die, who speak the tongue
That Shakespeare spake: the faith and morals hold
Which Milton held.

Sonnet 16 ('It is not to be thought of'), ll. 11–13, ibid., vol. 1

63 The good old rule
Sufficeth them, the simple plan,
That they should take who have the power,
And they should keep who can.

'Rob Roy's Grave', st. 9, ibid., vol. 2

64 Behold her, single in the field,
Yon solitary Highland lass!

'The Solitary Reaper', st. 1, ibid., vol. 2

65 Will no one tell me what she sings?
Perhaps the plaintive numbers flow
For old, unhappy, far-off things,

And battles long ago.

'The Solitary Reaper', st. 3, ibid., vol. 2

66 The music in my heart I bore,
Long after it was heard no more.

'The Solitary Reaper', st. 4, ibid., vol. 2

67 My heart leaps up when I behold
A rainbow in the sky:
So was it when my life began;
So is it now I am a man;
So be it when I shall grow old,
Or let me die!
The child is father of the man;
And I could wish my days to be
Bound each to each by natural piety.

'My heart leaps up when I behold', ibid., vol. 2

68 I wandered lonely as a cloud
That floats on high o'er vales and hills,
When all at once I saw a crowd,
A host of golden daffodils;
Beside the lake, beneath the trees,
Fluttering and dancing in the breeze.

'I wandered lonely as a cloud', st. 1 (revised 1815), ibid., vol. 2.
Wordsworth's original version had: 'A host of dancing daffodils;/Along the lake, beneath the trees,/Ten thousand dancing in the breeze.'

69 Continous as the stars that shine
And twinkle on the Milky Way.

'I wandered lonely as a cloud', st. 2, ibid., vol. 2

70 Ten thousand saw I at a glance,
Tossing their heads in sprightly dance.

'I wandered lonely as a cloud', st. 2, ibid., vol. 2

71 A poet could not but be gay,
In such a jocund company:
I gazed – and gazed – but little thought
What wealth the show to me had brought.

'I wandered lonely as a cloud', st. 3, ibid., vol. 2

72 For oft, when on my couch I lie
In vacant or in pensive mood,
They flash upon that inward eye
Which is the bliss of solitude;
And then my heart with pleasure fills,
And dances with the daffodils.

'I wandered lonely as a cloud', st. 4, ibid., vol. 2

73 O blithe new-comer! I have heard,
I hear thee and rejoice:
O Cuckoo! Shall I call thee bird,
Or but a wandering voice?

'To the Cuckoo', st. 1, ibid., vol. 2

74 But an old age, alive and bright,
And lovely as a Lapland night,
Shall lead thee to thy grave.
'To a Young Lady', st. 3, ibid., vol. 2

75 Thou unassuming common-place
Of Nature, with that homely face.
'To the Daisy', st. 1, ibid., vol. 2

76 The silence that is in the starry sky,
The sleep that is among the lonely hills.
'Song at the Feast of Brougham Castle', ll. 167–8, ibid., vol. 2

77 Ah! then, if mine had been the painter's hand,
To express what then I saw; and add the gleam,
The light that never was, on sea or land,
The consecration, and the poet's dream.
'Elegiac Stanzas, Suggested by a Picture of Peele Castle in a
Storm', st. 4, ibid., vol. 2

78 There was a time when meadow, grove, and
  stream,
The earth, and every common sight,
To me did seem
Apparelled in celestial light,
The glory and the freshness of a dream.
It is not now as it hath been of yore;
Turn wheresoe'er I may,
By night or day,
The things which I have seen I now can see no
  more.
'Ode. Intimations of Immortality from Recollections of Early
Childhood', st. 1, ibid., vol. 2

79 The rainbow comes and goes,
And lovely is the rose,
The moon doth with delight
Look round her when the heavens are bare;
Waters on a starry night
Are beautiful and fair;
The sunshine is a glorious birth;
But yet I know, where'er I go,
That there hath passed away a glory from the earth.
'Ode. Intimations of Immortality from Recollections of Early
Childhood', st. 2, ibid., vol. 2

80 A timely utterance gave that thought relief,
And I again am strong.
The cataracts blow their trumpets from the steep,
No more shall grief of mine the season wrong;
I hear the echoes through the mountains throng,
The winds come to me from the fields of sleep.
'Ode. Intimations of Immortality from Recollections of Early
Childhood', st. 3, ibid., vol. 2

81 Whither is fled the visionary gleam?
Where is it now, the glory and the dream?
'Ode. Intimations of Immortality from Recollections of Early
Childhood', st. 4, ibid., vol. 2

82 Our birth is but a sleep and a forgetting;
The soul that rises with us, our life's star,
Hath had elsewhere its setting,
And cometh from afar:
Not in entire forgetfulness,
And not in utter nakedness,
But trailing clouds of glory do we come
From God, who is our home.
'Ode. Intimations of Immortality from Recollections of Early
Childhood', st. 5, ibid., vol. 2

83 Heaven lies about us in our infancy!
Shades of the prison-house begin to close
Upon the growing boy.
'Ode. Intimations of Immortality from Recollections of Early
Childhood', st. 5, ibid., vol. 2. AMBROSE BIERCE made a riposte
to this in The Devil's Dictionary (1881–1906): 'Heaven lies
about us in our infancy . . . and the world begins lying about
us pretty soon afterward.'

84 The youth, who daily farther from the East
Must travel, still is Nature's priest,
And by the vision splendid
Is on his way attended;
At length the man perceives it die away,
And fade into the light of common day.
'Ode. Intimations of Immortality from Recollections of Early
Childhood', st. 5, ibid., vol. 2

85 As if his whole vocation
Were endless imitation.
'Ode. Intimations of Immortality from Recollections of Early
Childhood', st. 7, ibid., vol. 2

86 Thou eye among the blind,
That, deaf and silent, read'st the eternal deep,
Haunted for ever by the eternal mind.
'Ode. Intimations of Immortality from Recollections of Early
Childhood', st. 8, ibid., vol. 2

87 Full soon thy soul shall have her earthly
  freight,
And custom lie upon thee with a weight,
Heavy as frost, and deep almost as life!
'Ode. Intimations of Immortality from Recollections of Early
Childhood', st. 8, ibid., vol. 2

88 O joy! that in our embers
Is something that doth live,
That nature yet remembers
What was so fugitive!

The thought of our past years in me doth
  breed
Perpetual benedictions.

'Ode. Intimations of Immortality from Recollections of Early
Childhood', st. 9, ibid., vol. 2

89 Not for these I raise
The song of thanks and praise;
But for those obstinate questionings
Of sense and outward things,
Fallings from us, vanishings;
Blank misgivings of a creature
Moving about in worlds not realised,
High instincts, before which our mortal nature
Did tremble like a guilty thing surprised.

'Ode. Intimations of Immortality from Recollections of Early
Childhood', st. 9, ibid., vol. 2

90 Our noisy years seem moments in the
  being
Of the eternal silence: truths that wake,
To perish never.

'Ode. Intimations of Immortality from Recollections of Early
Childhood', st. 9, ibid., vol. 2

91 Hence, in a season of calm weather,
Though inland far we be,
Our souls have sight of that immortal sea
Which brought us hither,
Can in a moment travel thither,
And see the children sport upon the shore,
And hear the mighty waters rolling evermore.

'Ode. Intimations of Immortality from Recollections of Early
Childhood', st. 9, ibid., vol. 2

92 What though the radiance which was once so
  bright
Be now for ever taken from my sight,
Though nothing can bring back the hour
Of splendour in the grass, of glory in the flower;
We will grieve not, rather find
Strength in what remains behind.

'Ode. Intimations of Immortality from Recollections of Early
Childhood', st. 10, ibid.

93 To me the meanest flower that blows can give
Thoughts that do often lie too deep for tears.

'Ode. Intimations of Immortality from Recollections of Early
Childhood', st. 11, ibid., vol. 2. Closing lines of poem.

94 On man, on nature, and on human life,
Musing in solitude.

The Excursion, Preface, ll. 1–2 (1814)

95 Not Chaos, not
The darkest pit of lowest Erebus,

Nor aught of blinder vacancy, scooped out
By help of dreams – can breed such fear and awe
As fall upon us often when we look
Into our minds, into the mind of man –
My haunt, and the main region of my song.

Ibid., Preface, ll. 35–41. A version of these lines had first
appeared in 'Home at Grasmere', ll. 984–9 (1800), beginning:
'The darkest pit/Of the profoundest hell, chaos, night.'

96 Strongest minds
Are often those of whom the noisy world
Hears least.

Ibid., bk 1, ll. 91–3

97 The good die first
And they whose hearts are dry as summer dust
Burn to the socket.

Ibid., bk 1, ll. 500–2

98 Society became my glittering bride,
And airy hopes my children.

Ibid., bk 3, ll. 735–6

99 For by superior energies; more strict
Affiance in each other; faith more firm
In their unhallowed principles, the bad
Have fairly earned a victory o'er the weak,
The vacillating, inconsistent good.

Ibid., bk 4, ll. 305–9

100 Lost in a gloom of uninspired research.

Ibid., bk 4, l. 626

101 Mark the babe
Not long accustomed to this breathing world;
One that hath barely learned to shape a smile,
Though yet irrational of soul, to grasp
With tiny finger – to let fall a tear;
And, as the heavy cloud of sleep dissolves,
To stretch his limbs, bemocking, as might seem,
The outward functions of intelligent man.

Ibid., bk 5, ll. 261–8

102 Spires whose 'silent finger points to heaven'.

Ibid., bk 6, l. 19. The phrase is borrowed from S. T. COLERIDGE.

103 A man he seems of cheerful yesterdays
And confident tomorrows.

Ibid., bk 7, ll. 557–8

104 The gods approve
The depth, and not the tumult, of the soul.

'Laodamia', ll. 74–5, publ. in *Poems* (1815)

105 Of all that is most beauteous – imaged there
In happier beauty; more pellucid streams,

An ampler ether, a diviner air,
And fields invested with purpureal gleams.
'Laodamia', ll. 103–6, ibid.

106 Surprised by joy – impatient as the wind
I wished to share the transport – Oh! with whom
But thee, long buried in the silent tomb.
'Surprised by joy', ibid.

107 Still glides the stream, and shall forever glide;
The form remains, the function never dies.
Sonnet 34 ('Afterthought'), ll. 5–6, publ. in *The River Duddon* (1820)

108 Enough, if something from our hands have
  power
To live, and act, and serve the future hour;
And if, as toward the silent tomb we go,
Through love, through hope, and faith's
  transcendent dower,
We feel that we are greater than we know.
Sonnet 34, ll. 10–14 ('Afterthought'), ibid.

109 Give all thou canst; high Heaven rejects the
  lore
Of nicely-calculated less or more.
Sonnet 43, ll. 6–7 ('Inside of King's College Chapel, Cambridge'), publ. in *Ecclesiastical Sonnets* (1822). Also known as 'Tax not the royal saint'.

110 Ethereal minstrel! pilgrim of the sky!
Dost thou despise the earth where cares abound?
'To a Skylark', st. 1, publ. in *Poems* (1827). Opening lines of poem.

111 Type of the wise who soar, but never roam;
True to the kindred points of heaven and home!
'To a Skylark', st. 2, ibid.

112 Scorn not the sonnet; critic, you have frowned,
Mindless of its just honours; with this key
Shakespeare unlocked his heart.
'Scorn not the sonnet', ll. 1–3, ibid.

Henry Wotton
(1568–1639)
English poet and diplomat

He served terms as Ambassador at Venice and other diplomatic missions (1604–24), and was Provost of Eton (1624–39). His small output of poems was published in Reliquiae Wottonianae *(1651).*

1 An ambassador is an honest man sent to lie abroad
for the good of his country.
Written in the album of Christopher Fleckmore c. 1612, quoted in IZAAK WALTON's *Life of Sir Henry Wotton*, publ. in

Reliquiae Wottonianae (1651). Wotton wrote the remark while in Germany, en route to Venice where he was serving as JAMES I's envoy. However, he spoiled his pun by writing it in Latin, thus reducing 'to lie' (*ad mentiendum*) to one meaning only – and thereby ruining his career.

2 You meaner beauties of the night,
That poorly satisfy our eyes
More by your number than your light;
You common people of the skies,
What are you when the sun shall rise?
'On His Mistress, the Queen of Bohemia', st. 1 (1624), repr. in *Reliquiae Wottonianae* (1651)

3 He first deceased; she for a little tried
To live without him, liked it not, and died.
'Death of Sir Albertus Moreton's Wife', publ. ibid.

4 Love lodged in a woman's breast
Is but a guest.
'O faithless world', ibid. The poem is also known as 'A Woman's Heart'.

5 Lord of himself, though not of lands;
And having nothing, yet hath all.
'The Character of a Happy Life', st. 6, ibid.

Frank Lloyd Wright
(1869–1959)
US architect

He specialized in geometric forms utilizing modern engineering technology. Among his best-known buildings are the Imperial Hotel in Tokyo (1920, now demolished) and the Guggenheim Museum, New York (1959).

1 The physician can bury his mistakes, but the architect can only advise his client to plant vines – so they should go as far as possible from home to build their first buildings.
New York Times Magazine 4 October 1953

2 All fine architectural values are human values, else not valuable.
The Living City, pt 3, 'Recapitulation' (1958)

Allie Wrubel
(1905–73)
US composer and musician

Active from the 1920s to the '50s, he wrote both music and lyrics, contributing to many films and collaborating with MORT DIXON.

1 Zip a dee doo dah,
Zip a dee ay,

My, oh my, what a wonderful day.
'Zip A Dee Doo Dah' (song, with music by Ray Gilbert), in *Song of the South* (film musical, 1946)

Wuer Kaixi
Chinese student leader

Prominent during the student demonstrations in Tiananmen Square (1989), he headed the Autonomous Student Association, and later escaped to France.

1 A black sun has appeared in the sky of my motherland.
Quoted in the *Independent* 29 June 1989. On the massacre in Tiananmen Square, Beijing, 3 June.

Thomas Wyatt
(1503–42)
English poet

He held official positions under HENRY VIII. *He is generally regarded as the founder of the English school of lyric poetry, and through his translations of* PETRARCH *introduced the sonnet form to England. His poems were published posthumously.*

1 Go trouble younger hearts
And in me claim no more authority.
With idle youth go use thy property
And thereon spend thy many brittle darts:
For hitherto though I have lost all my time,
Me lusteth no longer rotten boughs to climb.
'Farewell, Love' (1557), repr. in *Sir Thomas Wyatt: the Complete Poems* (ed. R. A. Rebholz, 1978)

2 My lute, awake! Perform the last
Labour that thou and I shall waste,
And end that I have now begun;
For when this song is said and past,
My lute, be still, for I have done.
'My lute, awake!' (1557), ibid.

3 They flee from me, that sometime did me seek
With naked foot, stalking in my chamber.
I have seen them gentle, tame, and meek,
That now are wild and do not remember
That sometime they put themselves in danger
To take bread at my hand.
'They flee from me' (1557), ibid.

4 Throughout the world, if it were sought,
Fair words enough a man shall find.
They be good cheap; they cost right naught;
Their substance is but only wind.
But well to say and so to mean –

That sweet accord is seldom seen.
'Throughout the world' (1557), ibid.

William Wycherley
(1640–1716)
English dramatist

He is noted for the mordant wit, crude satire and comic realism of his plays, such as The Country Wife *(1675) and* The Plain Dealer *(1677). In the words of* WILLIAM CONGREVE: *'Since the Plain-Dealer's scenes of manly rage,/Not one has dared to lash this crying age.'*

1 Women of quality are so civil, you can hardly distinguish love from good breeding.
The Country Wife, Act 1 (performed c. 1673). Spoken by Horner.

2 Women serve but to keep a man from better company . . . Good fellowship and friendship are lasting, rational and manly pleasures.
Horner, ibid., Act 1

3 A mistress should be like a little country retreat near the town, not to dwell in constantly, but only for a night and away, to taste the town the better when a man returns.
Dorilant, ibid., Act 1

4 I will have only those glorious, manly pleasures of being very drunk and very slovenly.
Horner, ibid., Act 1

5 He's a fool that marries, but he's a greater that does not marry a fool; what is wit in a wife good for, but to make a man a cuckold?
Pinchwife, ibid., Act 1

6 Go, go to your business, I say, pleasure, whilst I go to my pleasure, business.
Sir Jaspar Fidget, ibid., Act 2

7 Marrying to increase love is like gaming to become rich; alas, you only lose what little stock you had before.
Lucy, ibid., Act 4

8 I have heard people eat most heartily of another man's meat, that is, what they do not pay for.
Lady Fidget, ibid. Act 5

9 First, you who scribble, yet hate all that write,
And keep each other company in spite,
As rivals in your common mistress, fame,
And with faint praises one another damn.
The Plain Dealer, Prologue (performed 1674)

10 Counterfeit honour will not be current with me:

I weigh the man, not his title; 'tis not the king's stamp can make the metal better or heavier.
Manly, ibid., Act 1

Tammy Wynette
(1942–98)
US country singer

Originally Virginia Wynette Pugh. From 1966, her partnership with producer Billy Sherrill, co-writer of her hit 'Stand By Your Man', made her country music's most successful female singer.

1 Our D-I-V-O-R-C-E becomes final today
Me and Little Joe will be going away
I love you both and this will be pure H-E double L for me.
Oh, I wish that we could stop this D-I-V-O-R-C-E.
'D-I-V-O-R-C-E' (song, 1968, written with Bobby Braddock and Curly Putman)

2 Sometimes it's hard to be a woman
Giving all your love to just one man.
'Stand by Your Man' (song, 1968, written with Billy Sherrill)

3 Stand by your man.
Give him two arms to cling to
And something warm to come to.
Ibid.

X

Xenophon
(*c.* 431–*c.* 354 BC)
Greek historian and military commander

He is called the first journalist for his personal experiences and views of history, as in Anabasis, an account of his campaign with Cyrus, and Hellenica, a history of Greece. He also wrote on the life and teachings of SOCRATES.

1 The sea! The sea!
Anabasis, bk 4, ch. 7, sect. 24. Taken by IRIS MURDOCH as the title of a novel (1978).

Augustin, Marquis de Ximénèz
(1726–1817)
French poet

He wrote polemics against ROUSSEAU. His verse and tragedies were collected in Oeuvres (1772).

1 Let us attack in her own waters perfidious Albion!
'L'Ère des Français' (October 1793), repr. in *Poésies révolutionnaires et contre-révolutionnaires*, vol. 1 (1821). The words became a recruiting slogan during the Napoleonic wars. See JACQUES-BÉNIGNE BOSSUET 1.

Y

W. B. Yeats

(1865–1939)

Irish poet and playwright

William Butler Yeats. At the forefront of Ireland's cultural and literary revival, he was the author of plays written for Dublin's Abbey Theatre, which he helped to found in 1904. His poems, steeped in symbolism and mysticism, include the collections The Wild Swans at Coole *(1919) and* The Tower *(1928). He was a senator of the Irish Free State (1922–8). See also* W. H. AUDEN *16, 18.*

1 The woods of Arcady are dead,
And over is their antique joy;
Of old the world on dreaming fed;
Grey Truth is now her painted toy.
'The Song of the Happy Shepherd', publ. in *The Wanderings of Oisin and Other Poems* (1889)

2 Down by the salley gardens my love and I did
    meet;
She passed the salley gardens with little
    snow-white feet.
She bid me take love easy, as the leaves grow on
    the tree;
But I, being young and foolish, with her would not
    agree.
'Down by the Salley Gardens', ibid.

3 She bid me take love easy, as the grass grows on
    the weirs;
But I was young and foolish, and now am full of
    tears.
'Down by the Salley Gardens', ibid.

4 Words are always getting conventionalized to some secondary meaning. It is one of the works of poetry to take the truants in custody and bring them back to their right senses.
Letter, 3 February 1889, publ. in *Collected Letters*, vol. 1 (ed. John Kelly, 1986). 'Poets are the policemen of language,' Yeats added, 'they are always arresting those old reprobates the words.'

5 The years like great black oxen tread the world,
And God the herdsman goads them on behind,
And I am broken by their passing feet.
The Countess Cathleen, Sc. 5 (1892). Spoken by Oona, in the last lines of the play.

6 Red Rose, proud Rose, sad Rose of all my days!
Come near me, while I sing the ancient ways.
'To the Rose upon the Rood of Time', st. 1, publ. in *The Countess Cathleen, and Various Legends and Lyrics* (1892)

7 I will arise and go now, and go to Innisfree,
And a small cabin build there, of clay and wattles
    made;
Nine bean rows will I have there, a hive for the
    honey bee,
And live alone in the bee-loud glade.
'The Lake Isle of Innisfree', st. 1, ibid., publ. in *The Countess Cathleen, and Various Legends and Lyrics* (1892)

8 And I shall have some peace there, for peace
    comes dropping slow,
Dropping from the veils of the morning to where
    the cricket sings;
There midnight's all a glimmer, and noon a purple
    glow,
And evening full of the linnet's wings.
'The Lake Isle of Innisfree', st. 2, ibid.

9 A pity beyond all telling,
Is hid in the heart of love.
'Pity of Love', ibid.

10 The brawling of a sparrow in the eaves,
The brilliant moon and all the milky sky,
And all that famous harmony of leaves,
Had blotted out man's image and his cry.
'The Sorrow of Love', st. 1, ibid.

11 When you are old and grey and full of sleep,
And nodding by the fire, take down this book,
And slowly read, and dream of the soft look
Your eyes had once, and of their shadows deep.
'When You Are Old', st. 1, ibid. See PIERRE DE RONSARD 2.

12 How many loved your moments of glad grace,
And loved your beauty with love false or true,
But one man loved the pilgrim soul in you,
And loved the sorrows of your changing face.
'When You Are Old', st. 2, ibid.

13 The Land of Faery
Where nobody gets old and godly and grave,
Where nobody gets old and crafty and wise,
Where nobody gets old and bitter of tongue.
The Land of Heart's Desire, ll. 48–51 (1894). Spoken by Mary Bruin.

14 Land of Heart's Desire,
Where beauty has no ebb, decay no flood,
But joy is wisdom, time an endless song.
Faery child, ibid., ll. 373–5

15 And pluck till time and times are done
The silver apples of the moon,
The golden apples of the sun.
'The Song of Wandering Aengus', st. 3, publ. in *The Wind Among the Reeds* (1899)

16 Had I the heavens' embroidered cloths,
Enwrought with golden and silver light,
The blue and the dim and the dark cloths
Of night and light and the half light,
I would spread the cloths under your feet:
But I, being poor, have only my dreams;
I have spread my dreams under your feet;
Tread softly because you tread on my dreams.
'He Wishes for the Cloths of Heaven', ibid.

17 Never give all the heart, for love
Will hardly seem worth thinking of
To passionate women if it seem
Certain, and they never dream
That it fades out from kiss to kiss;
For everything that's lovely is
But a brief, dreamy, kind delight.
'Never Give All the Heart', publ. in *In the Seven Woods* (1904)

18 A line will take us hours maybe;
Yet if it does not seem a moment's thought,
Our stitching and unstitching has been naught.
'Adam's Curse', st. 1, ibid.

19 For to articulate sweet sounds together
Is to work harder than all these, and yet
Be thought an idler by the noisy set
Of bankers, schoolmasters, and clergymen
The martyrs call the world.
'Adam's Curse', st. 1, ibid.

20 To be born woman is to know –
Although they do not speak of it at school –
Women must labour to be beautiful.
'Adam's Curse', st. 2, ibid. Observation by a 'beautiful mild woman', representing Kathleen Pilcher, sister of Irish freedom fighter Maud Gonne.

21 The fascination of what's difficult
Has dried the sap out of my veins, and rent
Spontaneous joy and natural content
Out of my heart.
'The Fascination of What's Difficult', publ. in *The Green Helmet and Other Poems* (1910)

22 Wine comes in at the mouth
And love comes in at the eye;
That's all we shall know for truth

Before we grow old and die.
'A Drinking Song', ibid.

23 All things can tempt me from this craft of verse:
One time it was a woman's face, or worse –
The seeming needs of my fool-driven land.
'All Things Can Tempt Me', ibid.

24 In dreams begins responsibility.
Responsibilities, Epigraph (1914). The words were the title of a short story (1937) and a collection (1938) by DELMORE SCHWARTZ.

25 Romantic Ireland's dead and gone,
It's with O'Leary in the grave.
'September 1913', refrain, ibid.

26 I made my song a coat
Covered with embroideries
Out of old mythologies
From heel to throat;
But the fools caught it,
Wore it in the world's eye
As though they'd wrought it.
Song, let them take it
For there's more enterprise
In walking naked.
'A Coat', ibid.

27 Unwearied still, lover by lover,
They paddle in the cold
Companionable streams or climb the air;
Their hearts have not grown old.
'The Wild Swans at Coole', st. 4, publ. in *The Wild Swans at Coole* (1919)

28 Some burn damp faggots, others may consume
The entire combustible world in one small room
As though dried straw, and if we turn about
The bare chimney is gone black out
Because the work had finished in that flare.
'In Memory of Major Robert Gregory', st. 11. See HENRY JAMES 30.

29 I know that I shall meet my fate
Somewhere among the clouds above;
Those that I fight I do not hate,
Those that I guard I do not love.
'An Irish Airman Foresees His Death', ll. 1–4, ibid.

30 My country is Kiltartan Cross;
My countrymen Kiltartan's poor.
'An Irish Airman Foresees His Death', ll. 5–6, ibid.

31 I balanced all, brought all to mind,
The years to come seemed waste of breath,

A waste of breath the years behind
In balance with this life, this death.
'An Irish Airman Foresees His Death', ll. 13–16, ibid.

32 All shuffle there; all cough in ink;
All wear the carpet with their shoes;
All think what other people think;
All know the man their neighbour knows.
Lord, what would they say
Did their Catullus walk that way?
'The Scholars', st. 2, ibid.

33 I think it better that in times like these
A poet's mouth be silent, for in truth
We have no gift to set a statesman right.
'On Being Asked for a War Poem', ibid.

34 I have met them at close of day
Coming with vivid faces
From counter or desk among grey
Eighteenth-century houses.
I have passed with a nod of the head
Or polite meaningless words.
'Easter, 1916', ll. 1–6, publ. in *Michael Robartes and the Dancer* (1921)

35 Too long a sacrifice
Can make a stone of the heart.
O when may it suffice?
'Easter, 1916', ll. 57–9, ibid.

36 I write it out in a verse –
MacDonagh and MacBride
And Connolly and Pearse
Now and in time to be,
Wherever green is worn,
Are changed, changed utterly:
A terrible beauty is born.
'Easter, 1916', ll. 74–80, ibid. Closing lines. The names are of leaders of the Easter Rising who were executed by the British.

37 Things fall apart; the centre cannot hold;
Mere anarchy is loosed upon the world,
The blood-dimmed tide is loosed, and everywhere
The ceremony of innocence is drowned;
The best lack all conviction, while the worst
Are full of passionate intensity.
'The Second Coming', ibid.

38 Now I know
That twenty centuries of stony sleep
Were vexed to nightmare by a rocking cradle,
And what rough beast, its hour come round at last,
Slouches towards Bethlehem to be born?
'The Second Coming', ibid. Closing lines of poem.

39 If there's no hatred in a mind
Assault and battery of the wind
Can never tear the linnet from the leaf.
'A Prayer for My Daughter', st. 7, ibid.

40 An intellectual hatred is the worst.
'A Prayer for My Daughter', st. 8, ibid.

41 I agree about Shaw – he is haunted by the mystery he flouts. He is an atheist who trembles in the haunted corridor.
Letter to George Russell (Æ), 1 July 1921, publ. in *The Letters of W. B. Yeats* (ed. Allan Wade, 1954). Yeats expressed ambiguous views of GEORGE BERNARD SHAW in his *Autobiography* (1938): 'We all hated him with the left side of our heads, while admiring him immensely with the right side.'

42 We make out of the quarrel with others, rhetoric, but of the quarrel with ourselves, poetry.
'Anima Hominis', sect. 5, publ. in *Essays* (1924)

43 After Stéphane Mallarmé, after Paul Verlaine, after Gustave Moreau, after Puvis de Chavannes, after our own verse, after all our subtle colour and nervous rhythm, after the faint mixed tints of Conder, what more is possible? After us the Savage God.
Autobiographies, 'The Trembling of the Veil', bk 4, sect. 20 (1926). A. Alvarez took from these lines the title of his study on suicide, *The Savage God* (1971).

44 Englishmen are babes in philosophy and so prefer faction-fighting to the labour of its unfamiliar thought.
Letter, 24 March 1927, publ. in *The Letters of W. B. Yeats* (ed. Allan Wade, 1954)

45 That is no country for old men. The young
In one another's arms, birds in the trees
– Those dying generations – at their song,
The salmon-falls, the mackerel-crowded seas,
Fish, flesh or fowl, commend all summer long
Whatever is begotten born and dies.
Caught in that sensual music all neglect
Monuments of unageing intellect.
'Sailing to Byzantium', st. 1, publ. in *The Tower* (1928)

46 An aged man is but a paltry thing,
A tattered coat upon a stick, unless
Soul clap its hands and sing, and louder sing
For every tatter in its mortal dress.
'Sailing to Byzantium', st. 2, ibid.

47 What shall I do with this absurdity –
O heart, O troubled heart – this caricature,

Decrepit age that has been tied to me
As to a dog's tail?
'The Tower', pt 1, ibid. Opening lines.

48 Much did I rage when young,
Being by the world oppressed,
But now with flattering tongue
It speeds the parting guest.
'Youth and Age', ibid. See ALEXANDER POPE 156.

49 A shudder in the loins engenders there
The broken wall, the burning roof and tower
And Agamemnon dead.
'Leda and the Swan', st. 3, ibid.

50 Never to have lived is best, ancient writers say;
Never to have drawn the breath of life, never to
    have looked into the eye of day;
The second best's a gay goodnight and quickly
    turn away.
'From *Oedipus at Colonus*', st. 4, ibid. See SOPHOCLES.

51 A woman can be proud and stiff
When on love intent;
But love has pitched his mansion in
The place of excrement;
For nothing can be sole or whole
That has not been rent.
'Crazy Jane Talks with the Bishop', sect. 6, publ. in *Words for
Music Perhaps* (1932)

52 The innocent and the beautiful
Have no enemy but time.
'In Memory of Eva Gore-Booth and Con Markiewicz', ll. 24–5,
publ. in *The Winding Stair and Other Poems* (1933)

53 Nor dread nor hope attend
A dying animal;
A man awaits his end
Dreading and hoping all.
'Death', ibid. Opening lines of poem.

54 We were the last romantics – chose for theme
Traditional sanctity and loveliness.
'Coole Park and Ballylee', st. 6, ibid.

55 Swift has sailed into his rest;
Savage indignation there
Cannot lacerate his breast.
Imitate him if you dare,
World-besotted traveller; he
Served human liberty.
'Swift's Epitaph', ibid.

56 The intellect of man is forced to choose
Perfection of the life, or of the work,

And if it take the second must refuse
A heavenly mansion, raging in the dark.
'The Choice', ll. 1–4, ibid.

57 The unpurged images of day recede;
The Emperor's drunken soldiery are abed.
'Byzantium', st. 1, ibid.

58 Out of Ireland have we come,
Great hatred, little room,
Maimed us at the start.
I carry from my mother's womb
A fanatic heart.
'Remorse for Intemperate Speech', st. 3, ibid.

59 The ghost of Roger Casement
Is beating on the door.
'The Ghost of Roger Casement', refrain, publ. in *New Poems*
(1938)

60 You that would judge me, do not judge
    alone
This book or that, come to this hallowed place
Where my friends' portraits hang and look
    thereon;
Ireland's history in their lineaments trace;
Think where man's glory most begins and ends
And say my glory was I had such friends.
'The Municipal Gallery Re-visited', st. 7, ibid.

61 Irish poets, learn your trade,
Sing whatever is well made,
Scorn the sort now growing up
All out of shape from toe to top.
'Under Ben Bulben', sect. 5, publ. in *Last Poems* (1939)

62 Cast your mind on other days
That we in coming days may be
Still the indomitable Irishry.
'Under Ben Bulben', sect. 5, ibid.

63 Under bare Ben Bulben's head
In Drumcliff churchyard Yeats is laid.
An ancestor was rector there
Long years ago, a church stands near,
By the road an ancient cross.
No marble, no conventional phrase;
On limestone quarried near the spot
By his command these words are cut:
Cast a cold eye
On life, on death.
Horseman pass by!
'Under Ben Bulben', sect. 6. The last three lines are inscribed
on Yeats's gravestone at Drumcliff, north of Sligo.

64 Like a long-legged fly upon the stream
His mind moves upon silence.
'Long-Legged Fly', refrain, ibid.

65 Now that my ladder's gone,
I must lie down where all the ladders start,
In the foul rag and bone shop of the heart.
'The Circus Animals' Desertion', sect. 3, ibid.

66 Man can embody truth but he cannot know it.
Letter, 4 January 1939, publ. in *The Letters of W. B. Yeats* (ed. Allan Wade, 1954). Written three weeks before his death.

67 You know what the Englishman's idea of compromise is? He says, Some people say there is a God. Some people say there is no God. The truth probably lies somewhere between these two statements.
Quoted by Wilfred Whitten in *John O'London's Weekly* 24 June 1949

68 Accursed who brings to light of day
The writings I have cast away.
'Untitled', publ. in *The Variorum Edition of the Poems of W. B. Yeats*, 'Poems Not Included in the Definitive Edition' (ed. Peter Allt and Russell K. Alspach, 1957)

Jack Yellen
(1892–1991)
Polish-born US lyricist

His songs were used in Broadway revues of the 1920s and musical films. He also co-wrote songs for SOPHIE TUCKER.

1 Happy days are here again!
The skies above are clear again.
Let us sing a song of cheer again,
Happy days are here again!
'Happy Days Are Here Again' (song, 1929, with music by Milton Ager)

Boris Yeltsin
(b. 1931)
Russian politician and president

He was elected President of the Russian Federation in 1991 and supported GORBACHEV *after the attempted coup two months later. Re-elected in 1996, he resigned in 1999 after criticism over his handling of the Chechnya conflict and recurring ill health. See also* W. R. INGE 3.

1 Let's not talk about Communism. Communism was just an idea, just pie in the sky.
Remark during a visit to the United States, quoted in the *Independent* 13 September 1989

2 Oh, where is the poet or bard who will compose

an ode to Russian rumours? Thanks to the chronic shortage of truthful (or even false) information, our people live on rumours.
Against the Grain, ch. 9 (1990)

Sergei Yesenin
(1895–1925)
Russian poet

Calling himself the 'last poet of wooden Russia', he was the leading figure of the Russian Imagist group of poets. He was briefly married to ISADORA DUNCAN *(1922–3), and hanged himself after writing a suicide note in his own blood.*

1 Have you seen it
Through the steppeland roaring
In misty lakeland rain
With its iron nostril snoring
On iron paws – the train?
'The Colt and the Train', sect. 3, publ. in *Prayers for the Dead* (1920, transl. Peter Tempest)

Yevgeny Yevtushenko
(b. 1933)
Russian poet

A spokesman for the post-Stalinist generation and for greater artistic freedom, he aroused controversy with the poems 'Babii Yar' (1961) and 'Stalin's Heirs' (1962). His later works include Love Poems *(1977) and the novel* Wild Berries *(1982).*

1 Great twentieth century: sputnik century:
what an angst is in you, what wide perplexity!
You are a good century and a century of the pit,
cannibal century to the ideas you beget,
century of the angry young men's target.
'The Angries' (1959), repr. in *Collected Translations* (1996) by Edwin Morgan

2 Give me a mystery – just a plain and simple one – a mystery which is diffidence and silence, a slim little, barefoot mystery: give me a mystery – just one!
'Mysteries', st. 10 (1960), repr. in *The Heritage of Russian Verse* (ed. Dimitri Obolensky, 1965)

3 In my blood there is no Jewish blood.
In their callous rage,
All anti-Semites must hate me now as a Jew.
For that reason
I am a true Russian.
'Babii Yar' (1961), repr. in *The Poetry of Yevgeny Yevtushenko 1953 to 1965* (1966, transl. George Reavey). Last lines of poem describing the massacre of 96,000 Jews in the Ukraine by the Nazis. The poem, which caused controversy by implying that

the Soviet régime was antisemitic, was used by Shostokovich as the centrepoint of his Thirteenth Symphony.

4 In any man who dies there dies with him
his first snow and kiss and fight . . .
Not people die but worlds die in them.
'People', publ. in *Selected Poems* (1962, transl. Robin Milner-Gulland and Peter Levi)

5 No, Stalin did not die.
He thinks that death can be fixed.
We removed
him
from the mausoleum.
But how do we remove Stalin
from Stalin's heirs?
'Stalin's Heirs', ibid.

Andrew Young
(b. 1932)
US politician and diplomat

A close associate of MARTIN LUTHER KING, *he was elected to Congress as a Democrat (1973–7) and was subsequently US representative to the United Nations (1977–9).*

1 Once the Xerox copier was invented, diplomacy died.
Playboy July 1977

2 Moral power is probably best when it is not used. The less you use it the more you have.
Observer 8 September 1979

Edward Young
(1683–1765)
English poet and playwright

He is now remembered for his long monologue Night Thoughts *(1742–5). Of his plays,* The Revenge *(1721) is considered his best.*

1 Life is the desert, life the solitude,
Death joins us to the great majority.
The Revenge, Act 4, Sc. 1 (1721). Spoken by Don Alonzo. See PETRONIUS 3.

2 Some, for renown, on scraps of learning dote,
And think they grow immortal as they quote.
The Love of Fame: The Universal Passion, satire 1, ll. 89–90 (1725–8)

3 None think the great unhappy, but the great.
Ibid., satire 1, l. 238

4 Be wise with speed;
A fool at forty is a fool indeed.
Ibid., satire 2, l. 281

5 Tired nature's sweet restorer, balmy sleep!
The Complaint, or Night-Thoughts on Life, Death and Immortality, 'Night 1', ll. 1 (1742–5)

6 The bell strikes one. We take no note of time
But from its loss.
Ibid., 'Night 1', ll. 55–6

7 Be wise today; 'tis madness to defer.
Ibid., 'Night 1', l. 390

8 Procrastination is the thief of time.
Ibid., 'Night 1', l. 393. See OSCAR WILDE 48.

9 At thirty a man suspects himself a fool;
Knows it at forty, and reforms his plan;
At fifty chides his infamous delay,
Pushes his prudent purpose to resolve;
In all the magnanimity of thought
Resolves; and re-resolves; then dies the same.
Ibid., 'Night 1', ll. 417–22

10 All men think all men mortal, but themselves.
Ibid., 'Night 1', l. 424

11 A God all mercy is a God unjust.
Ibid., 'Night 4', l. 233

12 By night an atheist half believes a God.
Ibid., 'Night 5', l. 176

13 Our birth is nothing but our death begun.
Ibid., 'Night 5', l. 718

14 To know ourselves diseased, is half our cure.
Ibid., 'Night 9', l. 38

15 Devotion! daughter of astronomy!
An undevout astronomer is mad.
Ibid., 'Night 9', ll. 769–70

16 The course of Nature is the art of God.
Ibid., 'Night 9', l. 1267

17 Illustrious examples *engross, prejudice,* and *intimidate.* They *engross* our attention, and so prevent a due inspection of ourselves; they *prejudice* our judgment in favour of their abilities, and so lessen the sense of our own; and they *intimidate* us with the splendour of their renown, and thus under diffidence bury our strength. Nature's impossibilities, and those of diffidence, lie wide asunder.
Conjectures on Original Composition (1759)

Neil Young

(b. 1945)

Canadian rock musician

A maverick in rock since the 1960s, he played with Buffalo Springfield, Crosby, Stills and Nash, and subsequently with his 'house-band' Crazy Horse.

1 My my, hey hey
Rock and roll is here to stay
It's better to burn out
Than to fade away
My my, hey hey.

'My My, Hey Hey (Out of the Blue)' (song, written with Jeff Blackburn) on the album *Rust Never Sleeps* (1979). The words were quoted by KURT COBAIN in his suicide note.

Marguerite Yourcenar

(1903–87)

French novelist

Originally Marguerite de Crayencour. She is known for her historical novels and for the long prose poem Fires *(1939). In 1980 she became the first woman to be elected to the Académie Française.*

1 Men who care passionately for women attach themselves at least as much to the temple and to the accessories of the cult as to their goddess herself.

Memoirs of Hadrian, 'Varius Multiplex Multi Formis' (1941, transl. 1954)

Z

Israel Zangwill

(1864–1926)

British playwright and novelist

He made his reputation with the novel Children of the Ghetto *(1892), which, as with his other work such as* Dreamers of the Ghetto *(1898) and the play* The Melting Pot *(1914), deals with Jewish life. An early Zionist, he was the founder of the International Jewish Territorial Organization (1905).*

1 Scratch the Christian and you find the pagan – spoiled.

Children of the Ghetto, bk 2, ch. 6 (1892)

2 America is God's Crucible, the great Melting-Pot where all the races of Europe are melting and re-forming!

The Melting Pot, act 1 (1908). Spoken by David Quixano. With this play, Zangwill introduced the term 'melting-pot' into the language.

Frank Zappa

(1940–93)

US rock musician

Known for his eclectic influences and caustically ironic style, he used a variety of genres to satirize the modern era. Freak Out *(1966) was the first of more than fifty albums he recorded, many with his band The Mothers of Invention.*

1 Most rock journalism is people who can't write, interviewing people who can't talk, for people who can't read.

Chicago Tribune 18 January 1978

2 Music, in performance, is a type of sculpture. The air in the performance is sculpted into something.

The Real Frank Zappa Book, ch. 8 (1989, written with Peter Occhiogrosso)

3 No change in musical style will survive unless it is accompanied by a change in clothing style. Rock is to dress up to.

Ibid., ch. 9

Franco Zeffirelli
(b. 1923)
Italian theatre, opera and film director

He is noted for innovative stage productions and for the visual richness of his films, which include The Taming of the Shrew *(1966) and* Romeo and Juliet *(1968).*

1 Theatre people often have a very simplistic view of politics and tend to express very black and white patriotic sentiments but perhaps that is because we know the value of illusion, how it can help strengthen the weak, and stimulate the weary.
Zeffirelli – The Autobiography of Franco Zeffirelli, ch. 12 (1986)

Fred Zinnemann
(1907–97)
Austrian-born US film-maker

After directing shorts, he scored a success with High Noon *in 1952 and went on to win Academy Awards for* From Here to Eternity *(1953) and* A Man for All Seasons *(1966).*

1 Dialogue is a necessary evil.
Interview in the *Independent on Sunday* 31 May 1992

Emile Zola
(1840–1902)
French novelist

A pioneer of naturalism, he published a series of twenty novels known as Les Rougon-Macquart, *including* Germinal *(1885),* La Terre *(1887) and* La Bête humaine *(1890). He was sentenced to prison for libel for his open letter (1898) in defence of Alfred Dreyfus, but fled to England, where he remained until being granted amnesty.*

1 Truth is on the march, and nothing can stop it.
Le Figaro 25 November 1897. Referring to the Dreyfus affair.

2 *J'accuse.*
[I accuse.]
Open letter referring to the Dreyfus affair, publ. in *L'Aurore* 13 January 1898

Index

ace
a. of trumps up his
sleeve LABOUCHERE [1]
about to play the a. FIELD [1]
ache
in the ark of/the a. of it LEVERTOV [1]
achieve
a. of, the mastery of the
thing HOPKINS [10]
Achilles
A.' wrath POPE [52]
acquaintance
A. ... well enough to borrow
from BIERCE [3]
beginning of an a. ELIOT, G. [55]
make a new a. JOHNSON, S. [144]
acre
a. of barren ground SHAKESPEARE:
TEMPEST [3]
acres
few paternal a. bound POPE [1]
Three a. and a cow COLLINGS [1]
act
A. of God was defined HERBERT,
A. P. [8]
both a. and know MARVELL [2]
every a. ... stays with
mankind ARENDT [6]
If one does not a. CHIANG KAI-
SHEK [1]
sleep an a. or two SHAKESPEARE:
HENRY VIII [20]
acting
A. is ... a neurotic impulse BRANDO [3]
A. is ... exhibitionism OLIVIER [4]
a. is ... the lowest of the arts MOORE,
G. [2]
A. ... quintessential social
lubricant BRANDO [4]
Between the a. SHAKESPEARE: JULIUS
CAESAR [12]
so delightful as good a. BYRON,
LORD [50]
Why don't you try a. OLIVIER [3]
action
A. is but coarsened thought AMIEL [1]
a. made me wise GUNN [1]
bettered by immediate a. POUND [13]
born to a. COOLEY [4]
confuse movement with
a. HEMINGWAY [27]
human beings ... must have
a. BRONTË, C. [6]
ounce of a. ENGELS [4]
Perform every a. AURELIUS [2]
public a. ... is wrong CORNFORD,
F. M. [1]
single lovely a. LOWELL, J. R. [17]
Suit the a. to the word SHAKESPEARE:
HAMLET [104]
To every a. there is ...
reaction NEWTON [6]

actions
children will be born of our a. SMITH,
Z. [1]
design of people's a. AURELIUS [19]
laboured ... to understand human
a. SPINOZA [11]
most decisive a. of our life GIDE [4]
actor
a. is a kind of guy GLASS [1]
essential of a great a. CHAPLIN [2]
actors
A. are cattle HITCHCOCK [1]
actress
for an a. to be a
success BARRYMORE [1]
acts
Those graceful a. MILTON [166]
Adam
A. had an idea WALCOTT [4]
A. lay ybounden HYMNS & CAROLS [2]
A. the goodliest man MILTON [138]
A. was a gardener KIPLING [80]
He lets the A. ... /Perform the Acts of
God AUDEN [33]
old A. ... may be so buried BOOK OF
COMMON PRAYER [69]
savour of the old A. SMITH,
ALEXANDER [6]
When A. delved and Eve span BALL,
J. [1]
whipped th'offending A. out of
him SHAKESPEARE: HENRY V [3]
adder
bright day ... brings forth the
a. SHAKESPEARE: JULIUS CAESAR [10]
addiction
Every form of a. is bad JUNG [23]
addictive
All sin tends to be a. AUDEN [49]
additions
What vast a. FRANKLIN, B. [15]
adeste
A., fideles HYMNS & CAROLS [3]
adieu
a., kind friends ANONYMOUS [1]
Adlestrop
A. – only the name THOMAS, E. [2]
admiral
good thing to kill an a. VOLTAIRE
[15]
admiration
A. is a ... short-lived
passion ADDISON [8]
A. ... polite recognition BIERCE [4]
Societies of Mutual A. HOLMES SR [4]
admire
secret of happiness is to a. BRADLEY,
F. H. [5]
admirer
I have always been an a. MANN, T. [9]
adolescence
petrified a. BEVAN [8]

Adonais
I weep for A. SHELLEY, P. B. [69]
soul of A., like a star SHELLEY, P. B. [82]
Adonis
A. in loveliness HUNT, L. [2]
adoration
For A. seasons change SMART, C. [8]
adore
Man is made to a. DISRAELI [18]
adored
I was a. once SHAKESPEARE: TWELFTH
NIGHT [19]
adulation
a. is not displeasing BYRON, LORD [35]
adult
To be a. is to be alone ROSTAND, J. [2]
adulterous
way of an a. woman BIBLE, OLD
TESTAMENT: PROVERBS [98]
would be a. BENCHLEY [1]
adultery
a. ... in his heart BIBLE, NEW
TESTAMENT: MATTHEW [28]
A. is the application of
democracy MENCKEN [9]
commit a. CARY [1]
committed a. in my heart CARTER,
J. [1]
Die for a. SHAKESPEARE: KING
LEAR [47]
Do not a. commit CLOUGH [4]
first breath of a. UPDIKE [5]
woman was taken in a. BIBLE, NEW
TESTAMENT: JOHN [30]
adulthood
A. is the ever-shrinking
period SZASZ [8]
a. itself was not an advance BAKER,
N. [2]
adults
distinction between children and
a. BARTHELME [1]
advancement
hope ... of a., is the spur TAYLOR,
H. [2]
advantage
a. of time and place DRAKE, F. [2]
them as take a. ELIOT, G. [10]
when to forgo an a. DISRAELI [56]
adventurer
Many will call me an a. GUEVARA [2]
adventures
a. may be grasped STERNE [25]
a. were by the
fireside GOLDSMITH [16]
adversitee
For of fortunes sharp a. CHAUCER [11]
adversity
a. doth best discover virtue BACON,
F. [12]
A. draws men
together KIERKEGAARD [1]

A. is sometimes hard upon a
man CARLYLE, T. [45]
bread of a. BIBLE, OLD TESTAMENT:
ISAIAH [41]
faint in the day of a. BIBLE, OLD
TESTAMENT: PROVERBS [72]
furnace of a. BIBLE, APOCRYPHA:
ECCLESIASTICUS [3]
learn to endure a. TWAIN [28]
Sweet are the uses of a. SHAKESPEARE:
AS YOU LIKE IT [7]

advertisement
effective a. ... will take in HUXLEY,
A. [5]

advertisements
We read a. ... to discover BOORSTIN [2]

advertising
a. agency is 85 per cent ALLEN, F. [2]
A. ... arresting the human
intelligence LEACOCK [3]
a. is now so near
perfection JOHNSON, S. [40]
infinite promise of American
a. FITZGERALD, Z. [2]

advice
Never trust the a. of a man in
difficulties AESOP'S FABLES [2]
will not take our a. BILLINGS [2]

advised
a. what thou dost
discourse RALEGH [19]

advises
my old girl that a. DICKENS [76]

aerials
Hairs are your a. ROBINSON, B. [1]

aeroplane
a. has unveiled SAINT-EXUPÉRY [4]

aesthetic
a. principle of our times ROGERS,
R. [1]

aesthetics
a. is the mother of ethics BRODSKY [2]
too gross ... for pure a. JAMES, H. [25]

afeard
soldier and a. SHAKESPEARE:
MACBETH [86]

affectation
a. ... in dress implies CHESTERFIELD [17]

affection
A. is the mortal illness INDIANA [1]
Set your a. on things above BIBLE,
NEW TESTAMENT: COLOSSIANS [4]
With a. beaming in one
eye DICKENS [48]

affections
history of the a. IRVING, W. [4]
living ... in the a. ELIOT, G. [35]
vile a. BIBLE, NEW TESTAMENT:
ROMANS [5]

affliction
pleased heaven/To try me with
a. SHAKESPEARE: OTHELLO [46]

Whensoever any a. assails
me DONNE [43]

affronts
Young men soon give ...
a. ADDISON [18]

afraid
be horribly a. BIBLE, OLD TESTAMENT:
JEREMIAH [1]
be not a. BIBLE, NEW TESTAMENT:
MATTHEW [105]

Africa
A. and her prodigies BROWNE [4]
A. FOR THE AFRICANS GARVEY [3]
A. is a scar BLAIR, T. [9]
A. ... is more than a glamorous
fact ANGELOU [6]
A. with the bulging chest GENET [3]
choose/Between this A. WALCOTT [1]
does A. know a song DINESEN [2]
ex A. semper aliquid novi PLINY THE
ELDER [5]
something new out of A. PLINY THE
ELDER [5]
speak of A. and golden
joys SHAKESPEARE: HENRY IV PT 2 [27]

African
A. is my brother SCHWEITZER [3]
whole life of any thinking
A. MANDELA, N. [3]

Africans
happiest A. in the world SMITH,
IAN [1]
Oh those A. WALKER [2]

Afro-Americans
goal of 22 million A. MALCOLM X [5]

after
a. you, Claude KAVANAGH, T. [1]

afternoon
always a. TENNYSON [18]
At five in the a. GARCÍA LORCA [7]

Afton
Flow gently, sweet A. BURNS [39]

against
not with me is a. me BIBLE, NEW
TESTAMENT: MATTHEW [88]
One-fifth ... are a.
everything KENNEDY, R. F. [2]

Agamemnon
A. dead YEATS [49]

age
a. ... al wole envenyme CHAUCER [34]
A. ... best in four things BACON, F. [55]
A. cannot wither her SHAKESPEARE:
ANTONY & CLEOPATRA [16]
A. ... compound for the
vices BIERCE [5]
a. demanded that we
dance HEMINGWAY [1]
a. is in, the wit is out SHAKESPEARE:
MUCH ADO [21]
A. is opportunity LONGFELLOW [29]
A. shall not weary BINYON [1]

A. still leaves us friends MOORE, T. [11]
a. succeeds to age TENNYSON [51]
a. worse than our
grandsires' HORACE [40]
accurate about her a. WILDE [108]
Cast me not off in ... old a. BIBLE, OLD
TESTAMENT: PSALMS [81]
feel the pressure of a. PLATO [2]
good old a. BIBLE, OLD TESTAMENT:
1 CHRONICLES [3]
good old a. BIBLE, OLD TESTAMENT:
GENESIS [42]
lady of a 'certain a.' BYRON, LORD [143]
lee shore of a. JEWETT [1]
Men of a. object too much BACON,
F. [33]
My a. is as a lusty
winter SHAKESPEARE: AS YOU LIKE
IT [9]
no a. between ten SHAKESPEARE:
WINTER'S TALE [10]
not of an a. JONSON [31]
now in a. I bud again HERBERT, G. [36]
tell a woman's a. GILBERT, W. S. [27]
Today, a. is needy MACINNES [2]
What's a man's a. BROWNING, R. [19]
When a., disease, or sorrows
CLOUGH [8]

aged
a. man is but a paltry
thing YEATS [46]

agent
Thus is the poor a.
despised SHAKESPEARE: TROILUS &
CRESSIDA [17]
trust no a. SHAKESPEARE: MUCH
ADO [8]

ages
How many a. hence SHAKESPEARE:
JULIUS CAESAR [23]

Agnes
Saint A.' Eve – Ah, bitter
chill KEATS [66]

agnosticism
all that a. means DARROW,
CLARENCE [1]

agnus
A. *Dei* MISSAL [21]

agony
giant a. of the world KEATS [45]
I like a look of A. DICKINSON, E. [5]
On the outskirts of every
a. WOOLF [25]

agree
all things differ, all a. POPE [35]
When men and women
a. SANTAYANA [6]

agreeable
a. person is a person who
agrees DISRAELI [46]
not want people to be very
a. AUSTEN [2]

agreement
in a. with my fellow-
humans MUGGERIDGE [2]

a-hunting
We daren't go a. ALLINGHAM [1]

aid
physical a. to their moral
consolations BURKE, E. [59]

AIDS
A. epidemic has rolled back WHITE,
E. [3]
A. pandemic is ... own-goal PRINCESS
ANNE [1]
A. was ... an illness in
stages GUIBERT [1]

ailments
our a. are the same SWIFT, J. [17]

aim
setting our a. too
low MICHELANGELO [3]

aime
Je t'a. ... moi non plus GAINSBOURG [1]

air
a., a chartered libertine SHAKESPEARE:
HENRY V [4]
Acquire the a. PLATH [2]
intoxicated by the a. THOREAU [44]
world-mothering a. HOPKINS [24]

airy
A., fairy Lilian TENNYSON [1]

aitches
nothing to lose but our a. ORWELL
[4]

Akond
A. of Swat LEAR [16]

Aladdin
money *is* A.'s lamp BYRON, LORD [155]

Alamein
Before A. we never had a
victory CHURCHILL, W. [48]

Alamo
Remember the A. SHERMAN, S. [1]

alarm
little a. now and then BURNEY [6]

alarmed
So much a. BYRON, LORD [75]

albatross
A./About my neck was
hung COLERIDGE, S. T. [23]
At length did cross an A. COLERIDGE,
S. T. [17]
I shot the A. COLERIDGE, S. T. [18]

Albert
take a message to A. DISRAELI [62]

Albion
perfidious A. XIMÉNÈZ [1]

alcohol
A. is like love CHANDLER [12]
A. is nicissary f'r a man DUNNE,
F. P. [6]
sway of a. over mankind JAMES,
W. [14]

taken more out of a. CHURCHILL,
W. [58]

ale
fed purely upon a. FARQUHAR [9]
spicy nut-brown a. MILTON [17]

Alexandrine
needless A. ends the song POPE [19]

algebra
clock doth strike, by a. BUTLER, S.
(1612–80) [3]
no such thing as a. LEBOWITZ [8]

Alice
A. moving under skies CARROLL [46]
A.'s Restaurant GUTHRIE, A. [1]

alienation
A. as our present destiny LAING [3]
escape the a. of present
day BARTHES [8]
Without a. ... can be no
politics MILLER, A. [9]

alike
everyone should be ... a. BALDWIN,
J. [1]

alive
Officiously to keep a. CLOUGH [3]

Al Jolson
A. is greater than Jesus FITZGERALD,
Z. [3]

all
a. things to all men BIBLE, NEW
TESTAMENT: 1 CORINTHIANS [22]

allegiances
two simultaneous a. BAUDELAIRE [9]

allegorical
all the a. paintings JOHNSON, S. [153]

allegory
a. on the banks of the Nile SHERIDAN,
R. B. [14]
this great a. – the world MELVILLE [14]

alliance
A. ... union of two thieves BIERCE [6]

alliances
entangling a. JEFFERSON [22]
steer clear of permanent
a. WASHINGTON, G. [9]

allies
thou hast great a. WORDSWORTH,
W. [58]

alligator
See you later, a. HALEY, B. [3]

alliteration
apt A.'s artful aid CHURCHILL,
CHARLES [4]

allone
A., withouten any
compaignye CHAUCER [28]

All Souls
college of A. ... perfection ROWSE [1]

allure
a. by denying TROLLOPE [10]

Alma mater
A. lie dissolved in port POPE [75]

alms
a. may be in secret BIBLE, NEW
TESTAMENT: MATTHEW [36]

alone
A., alone COLERIDGE, S. T. [27]
a. in races, even ... in
genders ANGELOU [10]
A. on a wide wide sea COLERIDGE,
S. T. [35]
A. upon my bed I lie SAPPHO [5]
fresh appetite for being a. BYRON,
LORD [39]
mortal millions live *a.* ARNOLD, M. [14]
Show me a man who lives
a. BUKOWSKI [2]
strongest man ... stands
alone IBSEN [10]
use sometimes to be a. HERBERT,
G. [3]
want to be a. GARBO [1]

alpha
I am A. and Omega BIBLE, NEW
TESTAMENT: REVELATION [1, 57]

alphabet
even the whole a. CERVANTES [20]

altar
a. of stone BIBLE, OLD TESTAMENT:
EXODUS [26]
earth ... is ... an immense
a. MAISTRE [5]
go unto the a. of God MISSAL [2]

altare
Introibo ad a. Dei MISSAL [2]

altar-stairs
great world's a. TENNYSON [105]

alteration
A. hath in it
inconveniences HOOKER [2]

alternative
there is no real a. THATCHER [5]

am
I a. that I am BIBLE, OLD TESTAMENT:
EXODUS [7]
I a. what I am BIBLE, NEW TESTAMENT:
1 CORINTHIANS [36]
infinite I A. COLERIDGE, S. T. [55]

amateurs
nation of a. ROSEBERY [1]

amazed
I was a. HOWERD [1]

ambassador
A. is an honest man WOTTON [1]
a. is not simply an
agent BAGEHOT [17]

ambassadors
a. for Christ BIBLE, NEW TESTAMENT:
2 CORINTHIANS [8]

amber
Pretty! in a. to observe POPE [147]

ambiguity
impediment ... a. of words REID, T. [1]
Seven Types of A. EMPSON [1]

I wish I *were* the A. SHELLEY, P. B. [2]
I am an A. SEX PISTOLS [1]

antidote
some sweet oblivious
a. SHAKESPEARE: MACBETH [93]

anti-paranoia
a., where nothing is
connected PYNCHON [1]

antipathy
assistance of ... physical
a. NIETZSCHE [7]

antiquity
blasted with a. SHAKESPEARE:
HENRY IV PT 2 [7]
write for a. LAMB, CHARLES [20]

anti-Semitism
suburban prejudice of a. POUND
[34]

antithesis
one vile a. POPE [152]

antithetical
What an a. mind BYRON, LORD [40]

Antony
None but A./Should
conquer SHAKESPEARE: ANTONY &
CLEOPATRA [30]

anvil
either be a. or
hammer LONGFELLOW [1]
England's on the a. KIPLING [79]

anything
A. goes PORTER, C. [6]

apartheid
closed the book on a. DE KLERK [1]

apathy
a. of human beings KELLER [3]

ape
having an a. for a
grandfather HUXLEY, T. [12]
played the sedulous a. STEVENSON,
R. L. [41]

aphorism
a. can never be the whole KRAUS [3]
A. should be/like a burr LAYTON [7]

aphorisms
knowledge consists of a. COLERIDGE,
S. T. [77]

apocalypse
hope of a vain a. RENAN [1]

Apollo
A., with hair and
harpstring SWINBURNE [12]
swear by A.
Physician HIPPOCRATES [3]
young A. CORNFORD, FRANCES [2]

apologize
good rule in life never to
a. WODEHOUSE [1]

apology
a.? ... Disgusting ORCZY [2]
stiff a. is a second
insult CHESTERTON [48]

apothecary
O true A. SHAKESPEARE: ROMEO &
JULIET [42]

appalled
I was born a. STOPPARD [2]

apparel
a. oft proclaims the
man SHAKESPEARE: HAMLET [33]

apparelled
a. like the spring SHAKESPEARE:
PERICLES [1]

appearance
façade of his a. MURDOCH, I. [7]

appearances
A. often are deceiving AESOP'S
FABLES [7]
satisfied with a. MALRAUX [3]

appears
by what a., that you are
judged HARDY, T. [14]

appeasement
stench of a. in the air THATCHER [23]

appetite
a., an universal wolf SHAKESPEARE:
TROILUS & CRESSIDA [4]
A. comes with eating RABELAIS [3]

appetites
Subdue your a. DICKENS [25]

applause
A. is a receipt, not a bill SCHNABEL [1]
A. is the spur COLTON [4]
attentive to his own a. POPE [150]
ill-timed a. POPE [53]
O, popular a. COWPER [35]

apple
a. of an eye BOOK OF COMMON
PRAYER [97]
a. of his eye BIBLE, OLD TESTAMENT:
DEUTERONOMY [17]
for an a., damned
mankind OTWAY [1]
good a. is better HUNT, L. [6]
never eat a windfall a. CARTER, A.
[2]
there vor me the a. tree BARNES,
W. [1]
Where the a. reddens BROWNING,
R. [22]

apple pie
a. and cheese FIELD [3]

apples
silver a. of the moon YEATS [15]
small choice in rotten
a. SHAKESPEARE: TAMING OF THE
SHREW [2]
Sweeter than ... sour a. RIMBAUD [7]

appointed
a. time to man BIBLE, OLD TESTAMENT:
JOB [15]

appoints
Man a., and God
disappoints CERVANTES [48]

appraisal
a. seems chiefly useful MOORE,
MARIANNE [6]

apprehension
cause for a lover's a. SHERIDAN,
R. B. [8]

apprehensions
My a. come in crowds WORDSWORTH,
W. [43]

appropriate
relationship ... was not a. CLINTON,
B. [2]

approve
men of sense a. POPE [22]
When the near a. CONFUCIUS [27]

apricot
blushing a. and woolly
peach JONSON [24]

April
A. is the cruellest month ELIOT,
T. S. [18]
A.,/Laugh thy girlish
laughter WATSON [2]
uncertain glory of an A.
day SHAKESPEARE: TWO
GENTLEMEN [3]

aquarium
A. is gone LOWELL, R. [7]

Aquarius
age of A. RADO/RAGNI [1]

Aquitaine
prince of A. NERVAL [2]

Arabian
She is alone th'A. bird SHAKESPEARE:
CYMBELINE [2]

Arabs
call the A. Oriental Italians CARLYLE,
T. [41]
in our war with the A. MEIR [2]

arbiter
a. of taste TACITUS [7]

arboreal
top of all sits Probably A. STEVENSON,
R. L. [42]

Arcadia
Et in A. ego ANONYMOUS [20]

Arcady
woods of A. are dead YEATS [1]

archaeologist
a. is the best husband CHRISTIE [5]

archangel
A. a little damaged LAMB, CHARLES [9]

archbishop
A. – A Christian
ecclesiastic MENCKEN [22]

Archbishop of Canterbury
one illusion ... the A. SMITH,
SYDNEY [16]

Archer
As long as A. remained REES-MOGG [1]

arches
Underneath the A. FLANAGAN, B. [1]

archewyves
Ye a., stondeth at
defense CHAUCER [38]

archipelagoes
rosary of a. WALCOTT [2]

architect
a. ... can only advise WRIGHT [1]
a. ... Send him to our hills RUSKIN [1]
A. ... who drafts a plan BIERCE [8]
Great A. of the Universe JEANS [1]
No person ... can be an a. RUSKIN [8]

architectonic
imbued with the a. spirit GROPIUS [1]

architects
a. ... get their ideas BAYLEY [1]
a. want to live JOHNSON, P. [3]
before the days of a. SENECA [9]
only legitimate artists ... are the
a. HAYDON [3]

architectural
a. values are human WRIGHT [2]

architecture
A. ... is frozen music SCHELLING,
FRIEDRICH [1]
A. is ... how to waste space JOHNSON,
P. [2]
A. is to make us know JELLICOE [1]
extrahuman a. and furious
rhythm GARCÍA LORCA [4]
it's modern a. BANKS-SMITH [1]
No a. is so haughty RUSKIN [11]

ardua
Per a. ad astra ANONYMOUS [76]

Argentina
Don't cry for me A. RICE, T. [1]

argue
a. men ... into believing NEWMAN [1]
a. with your inferiors LAYTON [4]

argument
a. for a week SHAKESPEARE: HENRY IV
PT 1 [15]
a. is a whore SHAKESPEARE: TROILUS &
CRESSIDA [6]
a. ... with an east wind LOWELL, J. R. [22]

arguments
A. are like fire-arms BUTLER, S. (1835–
1902) [17]

aristocracy
A. always exists NAPOLEON I [14]
a. ... of sex is the most
odious STANTON [3]
cannot reckon upon the
a. GLADSTONE [12]
English a. is ... middle
class WESTWOOD [2]
natural a. among men JEFFERSON [29]
so ... corrupt as an a. TOCQUEVILLE [8]
true a. DINESEN [3]

arm
bent a. for a pillow CONFUCIUS [21]

arma
A. virumque cano VIRGIL [17]

Armageddon
place called ... A. BIBLE, NEW
TESTAMENT: REVELATION [41]

armalite
a. in one hand POLITICAL SLOGANS [41]
a. made us equal GRAFFITI [3]

armament
mental magic to modern
a. HARRISON [2]

armed
Thrice ... a. that hath SHAKESPEARE:
HENRY VI PT 2 [3]

armful
very nearly an a. HANCOCK [2]

armour
put on the a. of light BIBLE, NEW
TESTAMENT: ROMANS [39]
whole a. of God BIBLE, NEW
TESTAMENT: EPHESIANS [15, 17]

arms
A., and the man I sing VIRGIL [17]
a. are sufficient beyond
doubt KENNEDY, J. F. [5]
never would lay down my a. PITT THE
ELDER [7]
one needs long a. BERNHARDT [1]
right ... to keep and bear a. UNITED
STATES CONSTITUTION [1]
world in a. is not spending
money EISENHOWER [2]

army
a. marches on its
stomach NAPOLEON I [17]
Join the A. and See MARX, H. [1]

aromatic
faint beneath the a.
pain WINCHILSEA [1]

a-roving
go no more a. BYRON, LORD [70]

arrested
he was a. one fine morning KAFKA [8]

arrows
a. ... in the hand of a mighty BIBLE,
OLD TESTAMENT: PSALMS [131]

'Arry
Know what I mean, 'A. BRUNO, F. [1]

ars
A. gratia artis DIETZ [1]
A. longa vita brevis SENECA [18]

arsenal
great a. of democracy ROOSEVELT,
F. D. [9]

art
a. appears, life disappears PICABIA [1]
a. as a sacred thing KAZEM [1]
A. ... cannot avoid cheating
truth RIDING [2]
a. constantly aspires PATER [2]
A. disturbs: science
reassures BRAQUE [4]
A. does not reproduce the
visible KLEE [4]

A. for art's sake CAO YU [1]
A. for art's sake CONSTANT [1]
A. ... great undogmatized church KEY,
E. [1]
A. has ... become the
concern GELDZAHLER [1]
a. has never contributed CATHER [9]
A. has no right to be
boring DUBUFFET [2]
A. hath an enemy called
ignorance JONSON [4]
a. is a community effort GINSBERG [1]
a. is affirmative HEPWORTH [3]
a. is a flock of sheep CHURCHILL,
W. [49]
A. is a jealous mistress EMERSON [49]
A. is an invention PAZ [2]
A. is a revolt MALRAUX [2]
a. is a struggle MURDOCH, I. [15]
a. is ... having been in
danger RILKE [2]
A. is ... joy in labour MORRIS, W. [11]
A. is never chaste PICASSO [8]
A. is not ... a canon of
beauty PICASSO [2]
A. is not ... an imitation NIETZSCHE [3]
A. is not truth PICASSO [1]
A. is not what is not REINHARDT [1]
A. is ... pattern READ, H. [3]
A. is science made clear COCTEAU [1]
A. is seduction SONTAG [1]
A. is significant deformity FRY, R. [1]
A. is skill GILL [2]
A. is so wonderfully
irrational GRASS [4]
A. is the accomplice of
love GOURMONT [5]
A. is the beautiful way HUBBARD,
E. [3]
A. is the final cunning MURDOCH,
I. [11]
A. is the human disposition JOYCE,
J. [17]
A. is the imposing of a
pattern WHITEHEAD [10]
A. is the laboratory ROSENBERG, H. [4]
A. ... is the lighthouse FORSTER [34]
A. is the most passionate
orgy DUBUFFET [1]
A. is the objectification LANGER [1]
A. is the right hand SCHILLER [2]
A. ... is the seeking for ideal SAND [2]
A. is the sex NATHAN [3]
A. is too serious REINHARDT [2]
A. is uncompromising GRASS [2]
A. kills only the dead ROSENBERG,
H. [1]
A. made tongue-tied SHAKESPEARE:
SONNETS [17]
a. must start an argument WEST,
R. [6]
A. never improves ELIOT, T. S. [10]

A. requires philosophy GAUGUIN [4]
A. ... should simplify CATHER [5]
A.'s life BROWNING, E. B. [22]
A. ... springs from
  necessity CASSADY [1]
a. that makes life JAMES, H. [29]
A. ... the zest of life GISSING [2]
A. was given for that BROWNING,
  R. [24]
A.! Who understands
  it BEETHOVEN [1]
All a. is quite useless WILDE [35]
candied over with a. WOOLF [14]
catnip that a. is MOORE, MARIANNE [7]
either be a work of a. WILDE [92]
first mistake of A. BANGS [1]
For a. to exist NIETZSCHE [36]
glory and good of A. BROWNING,
  R. [59]
keep a standing 'a.' GROSZ [1]
living a. ... that I love MORRIS, W. [9]
more abstract our a. KLEE [1]
nature's handmaid a. DRYDEN [2]
no a. remains
  shocking GELDZAHLER [2]
pretty, but is it A. KIPLING [30]
public history of modern
  a. MOTHERWELL [1]
rest is the madness of a. JAMES,
  H. [17]
say that a work of a. is
  good TOLSTOY [10]
signs of the decay of a. GOETHE [16]
sole a. that suits me GIDE [6]
So vast is a. POPE [9]
speak of these things ... is a. JOYCE,
  J. [16]
tragedy that we call modern
  a. DALÍ [9]
work of a. has an author WEIL [9]
work of a. has two
  faces BARENBOIM [1]
Arthur
he's in A.'s bosom SHAKESPEARE:
  HENRY V [9]
article
snuffed out by an a. BYRON,
  LORD [152]
artificial
all things are a. BROWNE [5]
artist
a. ... becomes historical DE
  KOONING [1]
a. ... dies blind CAMUS [21]
a. is a man of action CONRAD [15]
a. is extremely lucky BERRYMAN [4]
a. is forgotten HOCKNEY [2]
a. is not ... Jupiter's
  guest BEETHOVEN [2]
a. is the child of his
  time SCHILLER [10]
a., like the God JOYCE, J. [18]

a. must be ... like God FLAUBERT [7]
a. needn't be a clergyman VAN
  GOGH [2]
a. will let his wife starve SHAW [19]
crueler than a failed a. JONG [5]
first prerogative of an a. KAEL [1]
good a. should be isolated WELLES [7]
Man is no longer an a. NIETZSCHE [1]
Never trust the a. LAWRENCE, D. H. [17]
No a. is ahead of his time GRAHAM,
  M. [3]
no longer an a. NASH, P. [1]
Only he is an a. KRAUS [12]
progress of an a. ELIOT, T. S. [11]
true, prescriptive a.
  strives GOETHE [17]
What an a. dies with me NERO [1]
What is an a. but a workman MORRIS,
  W. [4]
artistic
A. genius is an expansion READE [1]
a. temperament CHESTERTON [6]
artists
A. are not engineers KENNEDY,
  J. F. [20]
A. are the monks PAVESE [3]
a. ... impose their particular
  illusion MAUPASSANT [1]
A. must be sacrificed EMERSON [70]
all a. were ... housewives JONG [1]
At moments we are all a. BENNETT,
  ARNOLD [1]
Great a. have no country MUSSET [1]
intimacy with a. VICTORIA [6]
There are only a. GOMBRICH [1]
arts
a. ... are a consolation GOODMAN,
  LORD [1]
a. in America BEECHAM [1]
a. would perish HUXLEY, A. [8]
Degrade first the a. BLAKE [87]
had I but followed the
  a. SHAKESPEARE: TWELFTH NIGHT [7]
interested in the a. AYCKBOURN [3]
plunder the popular a. HAMILTON,
  R. [1]
study of the liberal a. OVID [17]
three a. ... concerned with
  all SOCRATES [29]
asceticism
principle of a. BENTHAM [2]
ashamed
a. of their love affairs LA
  ROCHEFOUCAULD [7]
more things a man is a. of SHAW [18]
ashes
a. taken to
  Australia ANONYMOUS [44]
a. to ashes BOOK OF COMMON
  PRAYER [90]
past is a bucket of a. SANDBURG [3]
rather be a. than dust LONDON [2]

slept among his a. cold KEATS [79]
Asia
too much A. KIPLING [12]
ask
A., and it shall be given BIBLE, NEW
  TESTAMENT: MATTHEW [51]
A., and ye shall receive BIBLE, NEW
  TESTAMENT: JOHN [58]
A. me no more TENNYSON [75]
A. not who said this THOMAS À
  KEMPIS [3]
If you have to a. ARMSTRONG, L. [3]
Who fears to a. HERRICK [2]
asked
You've a. for it MOLIÈRE [12]
asleep
a., is in a world of his
  own HERACLITUS [8]
concerning them which are a. BIBLE,
  NEW TESTAMENT: 1 THESSALONIANS [3]
asparagus
only necessary to mention
  A. DICKENS [82]
asperges
a. me BIBLE, VULGATE [1]
aspirations
Sad that our finest a. PUSHKIN [3]
aspired
What I a. to be BROWNING, R. [44]
aspiring
teach us all to have a.
  minds MARLOWE [12]
ass
a. may bray ELIOT, G. [23]
enamoured of an a. SHAKESPEARE:
  MIDSUMMER NIGHT'S DREAM [34]
git medieval on your
  a. TARANTINO [2]
got to go out and kick a. ANGELOU [9]
my brother the a. ST FRANCIS OF
  ASSISI [7]
assassin
a. cannot help the
  murder GODWIN [7]
assassination
A. ... extreme form of
  censorship SHAW [52]
A. has never changed DISRAELI [39]
A.'s the fastest way MOLIÈRE [13]
assent
A. – and you are sane DICKINSON,
  E. [16]
assimilation
benevolent a. MCKINLEY [1]
Assyrian
oiled and curled A.
  bull TENNYSON [123]
astonish
A. me DIAGHILEV [1]
astronomer
undevout a. is mad YOUNG, E. [15]
When I ... heard the a. WHITMAN [33]

banjo
  b. on my knee FOSTER, S. [1]
bank
  cry all the way to the b. LIBERACE [1]
  What's breaking into a b. BRECHT [6]
banking
  b. establishments are ...
  dangerous JEFFERSON [33]
banks
  b. and braes BURNS [37]
banner
  b. over me was love BIBLE, OLD
  TESTAMENT: SONG OF SOLOMON [6]
  fight under his b. BOOK OF COMMON
  PRAYER [70]
banners
  All b. ... are filthy FALLACI [1]
  royal b. forward go FORTUNATUS [2]
banqueter
  b. fed full of life LUCRETIUS [6]
baptism
  slave of my b. RIMBAUD [18]
baptize
  b. you with the water BIBLE, NEW
  TESTAMENT: MATTHEW [11]
baptized
  I have need to be b. BIBLE, NEW
  TESTAMENT: MATTHEW [12]
Bapu
  B. ... is no more NEHRU [3]
bar
  crossed the b. TENNYSON [198]
  no moaning of the b. TENNYSON [197]
Barabbas
  B. was a publisher CAMPBELL, T. [10]
  B. was a robber BIBLE, NEW
  TESTAMENT: JOHN [62]
  crowd will always save B. COCTEAU [5]
barbarian
  He is a b. SHAW [9]
barbarians
  b. are due here today CAVAFY [2]
  B,. Philistines and Populace ARNOLD,
  M. [50]
  dealing with b. TACITUS [2]
  without the b. CAVAFY [3]
barbarism
  b. begins KAPUŚCIŃSKI [2]
  b. ... universal human
  characteristic WEIL [3]
barbarous
  rank me with the b.
  multitudes SHAKESPEARE: MERCHANT
  OF VENICE [23]
Barcelona
  He's from B. CLEESE [3]
bard
  blame not the b. MOORE, T. [4]
  Hear the voice of the B. BLAKE [49]
bards
  black and unknown b. JOHNSON,
  J. W. [1]

bargains
  Here's the rule for b. DICKENS [49]
barge
  b. ... like a burnished
  throne SHAKESPEARE: ANTONY &
  CLEOPATRA [14]
bark
  little b. attendant sail POPE [140]
Barkis
  B. is willin' DICKENS [65]
barren
  b. tasks, too hard to
  keep SHAKESPEARE: LOVE'S LABOUR'S
  LOST [2]
  Such b. pleasures SHAKESPEARE:
  HENRY IV PT 1 [33]
  'Tis all b. STERNE [26]
barricks
  single men in b. KIPLING [16]
bartender
  b. knows what drink MARQUIS [14]
base
  find men b., unjust, or
  selfish MOLIÈRE [9]
  greatness to be truly b. ANOUILH [4]
  safest to be moderately b. SMITH,
  SYDNEY [3]
baseball
  thing about b. DELILLO [6]
basics
  back to b. MAJOR [5]
Basil
  Hung over her sweet B. KEATS [65]
basket
  WATCH THAT B. TWAIN [14]
bass
  b. string of humility SHAKESPEARE:
  HENRY IV PT 1 [18]
bastard
  b.! He doesn't exist BECKETT [14]
bastards
  ancient families ... princes'
  b. BURTON [8]
  clever b. DURY [5]
  gods stand up for b. SHAKESPEARE:
  KING LEAR [11]
bat
  mind is like a b. WILBUR [2]
  Twinkle, twinkle, little b. CARROLL
  [12]
Bath
  who can ever be tired of
  B. AUSTEN [33]
bathing
  long b. of a summer's
  day WORDSWORTH, W. [12]
baths
  never had a great many
  b. GAITSKELL [1]
batsman
  sending your ... b. to the
  crease HOWE, G. [1]

battalions
  not single spies,/But in
  b. SHAKESPEARE: HAMLET [137]
  side of the big b. VOLTAIRE [7]
battell
  Done is a b. on the dragon DUNBAR,
  W. [2]
battle
  b. won FOCH [1]
  engage in b. and see NAPOLEON I [21]
  midst of the b. BIBLE, OLD TESTAMENT:
  2 SAMUEL [4]
  necessary to send them to
  b. MUSSOLINI [5]
  News of b. AYTOUN [1]
  Next to a b. lost WELLINGTON [7]
  No b. is worth fighting POWELL, E. [6]
  noise of b. rolled TENNYSON [174]
  Sing ... the glorious b. FORTUNATUS [1]
  There must be a b. BRADDON [2]
battles
  b. long ago WORDSWORTH, W. [65]
  Dead b. ... hold the
  military TUCHMAN [1]
  mother of b. HUSSEIN [1]
bauble
  prettiest b. you ever saw WALPOLE,
  H. [2]
  Take away that shining
  b. CROMWELL [5]
bay
  spreading ... like a green b. BIBLE, OLD
  TESTAMENT: PSALMS [47]
bayonet
  b. is a weapon POLITICAL SLOGANS [3]
BBC
  B. is ... like a cross PAXMAN [1]
be
  b., or not to be SHAKESPEARE:
  HAMLET [84]
  Cared not to b. at all MILTON [104]
  preferable to b. than not to
  be CIORAN [5]
Beaconsfieldism
  downfall of B. GLADSTONE [13]
beaker
  b. full of the warm South KEATS [81]
beam
  B. me up RODDENBERRY [3]
beamish
  my b. boy CARROLL [28]
beans
  amount to a hill o' b. BOGART [4]
  B. Meanz Heinz ADVERTISING
  SLOGANS [22]
  determined to know b. THOREAU [39]
  Full o' b. and
  benevolence SURTEES [4]
bear
  B. of Very Little Brain MILNE [8]
  bush supposed a b. SHAKESPEARE:
  MIDSUMMER NIGHT'S DREAM [39]

Exit, pursued by a b. SHAKESPEARE:
WINTER'S TALE [9]
With equal mind ... let us
b. DRYDEN [77]
beard
I have a b. coming SHAKESPEARE:
MIDSUMMER NIGHT'S DREAM [8]
not endure a husband with a
b. SHAKESPEARE: MUCH ADO [6]
old man with a b. LEAR [1]
beards
until your b. be grown BIBLE, OLD
TESTAMENT: 2 SAMUEL [7]
beast
b. on my back DOUGLAS, K. [5]
b./With many heads butts
me SHAKESPEARE: CORIOLANUS [8]
b. with two backs SHAKESPEARE:
OTHELLO [6]
every b. of the forest BIBLE, OLD
TESTAMENT: PSALMS [61]
like unto the b. BIBLE, NEW
TESTAMENT: REVELATION [32]
mark ... of the b. BIBLE, NEW
TESTAMENT: REVELATION [33]
number of the b. BIBLE, NEW
TESTAMENT: REVELATION [34]
what rough b. YEATS [38]
beastie
Wee ... tim'rous b. BURNS [17]
beasts
ask now the b. BIBLE, OLD TESTAMENT:
JOB [22]
four b. full of eyes BIBLE, NEW
TESTAMENT: REVELATION [13]
beat
b. generation KEROUAC [4]
dread b. pulsing fire JOHNSON, L. K. [1]
He was B. KEROUAC [3]
I b. people up ALI [4]
beaten
I was b. up by Quakers ALLEN, W. [4]
Beatles
B. are the biggest
bastards LENNON [7]
I didn't leave The B. MCCARTNEY [2]
beats
Counting the slow heart b. GRAVES,
R. [8]
beatus
B. vir BIBLE, VULGATE [4]
beauteous
love all b. things BRIDGES [3]
beauties
meaner b. of the night WOTTON [2]
beautiful
Against the b. ... wage a
pitiless GREENE, G. [2]
All things bright and b. HYMNS &
CAROLS [8]
b. and noble BAUDELAIRE [30]
b. by necessity PINDAR [8]

love of what is b. PERICLES [1]
most b. woman in the
room CHURCHILL, J. [1]
perception of the b. BYRON,
LORD [100]
see, not feel, how b. COLERIDGE,
S. T. [42]
to me/The entirely b. AUDEN [22]
beauty
All forms of b. BAUDELAIRE [3]
As a b. I'm not a great star EUWER [1]
as many kinds of b. BAUDELAIRE [2]
b. and her brain go not SHAKESPEARE:
CYMBELINE [1]
b. being only skin-deep KERR, J. [2]
b. calls and glory shows the way LEE,
N. [2]
B. ... doth of itself
persuade SHAKESPEARE: RAPE OF
LUCRECE [1]
b. faded PHILIPS [1]
B. for some provides escape HUXLEY,
A. [1]
b. ... hath strange
power MILTON [200]
B. in distress is ... most
affecting BURKE, E. [2]
b. in the arts is eternal DELACROIX [5]
B. is a currency system WOLF, N. [1]
B. is a matter of size ARISTOTLE [11]
B. is bought by
judgement SHAKESPEARE: LOVE'S
LABOUR'S LOST [8]
B. is but a flower NASHE [2]
B. is desired BATAILLE [3]
B. is eternity GIBRAN [5]
B. ... is just life WELLS [6]
B. is ... mysterious DOSTOYEVSKY [6]
B. is Nature's brag MILTON [41]
B. is no quality in things HUME,
D. [9]
B. is only the promise STENDHAL [4]
b. is ... terror RILKE [4]
B. is truth KEATS [98]
B. is what the untrained
eyes GONCOURT [2]
b. is woman's
sceptre WOLLSTONECRAFT [6]
B. ... manifestation of
eternity IONESCO [4]
b. ... obliterates all KEATS [16]
B. of a thousand stars MARLOWE [23]
B.'s ensign yet/Is
crimson SHAKESPEARE: ROMEO &
JULIET [41]
b. that killed the beast ARMSTRONG,
R. (1890–1973) [1]
B. too rich for use SHAKESPEARE:
ROMEO & JULIET [10]
daily b. in his life SHAKESPEARE:
OTHELLO [50]
'dear deceit' of b. ELIOT, G. [8]

essence of b. PLATO [6]
gave up b. ROSSETTI, C. [5]
Give unto them b. for ashes BIBLE,
OLD TESTAMENT: ISAIAH [84]
I have loved the principle of
b. KEATS [116]
If you get simple b. BROWNING,
R. [23]
learnt to love you late,
B. ST AUGUSTINE [4]
looked on B. bare MILLAY [8]
love of b. in the abstract KEATS [38]
power of b. I remember
yet DRYDEN [79]
sat B. on my knees RIMBAUD [14]
She dwells with B. KEATS [108]
She walks in b. BYRON, LORD [52]
Take back the b. and
wit MONTAGU [2]
terrible b. is born YEATS [36]
thing of b. and a boy ROWLAND, H.
[2]
thing of b. is a joy for ever KEATS [19]
'Tis b. truly blent SHAKESPEARE:
TWELFTH NIGHT [11]
with him is b. slain SHAKESPEARE:
VENUS AND ADONIS [4]
without a sense of b. WHARTON [1]
bed
And so to b. PEPYS [1]
b. is now as public as CARTER, A. [4]
forsworn his b. and
company SHAKESPEARE: MIDSUMMER
NIGHT'S DREAM [14]
good in b. GUCCIONE [1]
go to b. early PROUST [5]
I toward thy b., Yasmin FLECKER [4]
long black passage up to
b. STEVENSON, R. L. [36]
lying awake in b. JOHNSON, S. [85]
My b. shall comfort me BIBLE, OLD
TESTAMENT: JOB [20]
rising from b. ... a pain BOSWELL [3]
seeks a b. for the night HUGO [5]
This b. thy centre is DONNE [7]
bedevilment
man's b. and God's HOUSMAN [25]
Bedlam
think the world ... a general
B. TRAHERNE [11]
bee
b. is little BIBLE, APOCRYPHA:
ECCLESIASTICUS [24]
busy b./Improve each shining
hour WATTS, I. [4]
Oh, for a B.'s experience DICKINSON,
E. [28]
Where the b. sucks SHAKESPEARE:
TEMPEST [25]
beef
I am a great eater of b. SHAKESPEARE:
TWELFTH NIGHT [6]

rather than not have b. JOHNSON,
s. [84]
Roast B. ... is a philosophy FERBER [1]
roast b. of England FIELDING,
HENRY [4]
Where's the b. MONDALE [1]

beehive
not good for the b. AURELIUS [13]

beep
B.! Beep JONES, C. [1]

beer
b. and Britannia SMITH, SYDNEY [29]
b. and skittles HUGHES, THOMAS [1]
b. ... in the German
intellect NIETZSCHE [35]
drowns all care, stout b. HERRICK
[10]
only here for the b. ADVERTISING
SLOGANS [13]
They are like their own
b. VOLTAIRE [33]
They who drink b. will think IRVING,
W. [6]

Beer-sheba
from Dan even to B. BIBLE, OLD
TESTAMENT: 1 KINGS [2]

bees
act as if he were fighting
b. LINCOLN [30]
murmuring of innumerable
b. TENNYSON [80]
neither the b. nor yet the
honey. SAPPHO [4]

Beethoven
Roll over, B. BERRY [1]

beetle-browed
terrible, b. ... individual CARLYLE, T.
[2]

before
been here b. ROSSETTI, D. G. [4]

beget
get and to b. OSLER [3]
Thou that b.'st him SHAKESPEARE:
PERICLES [4]

beggared
b. all description SHAKESPEARE:
ANTONY & CLEOPATRA [14]

beggarly
b. elements BIBLE, NEW TESTAMENT:
GALATIANS [3]

beggars
When b. die SHAKESPEARE: JULIUS
CAESAR [18]

beggary
There's b. in the love SHAKESPEARE:
ANTONY & CLEOPATRA [2]

begging
B. defaces the city PARSONS, TONY [2]

begin
B. at the beginning CARROLL [21]

beginner
b. all his life COLLINGWOOD [2]

beginning
In the b. BIBLE, OLD TESTAMENT:
GENESIS [1]
no b. and no end POLLOCK [1]

begot
minded ... when they b. STERNE [1]

begun
Well b. is half done HORACE [59]

behaviour
on their best b. BENNETT, ALAN [5]
Perfect b. is born PAVESE [2]

Behaviourism
Of course, B. 'works' AUDEN [48]

behemoth
Behold now b. BIBLE, OLD TESTAMENT:
JOB [46]

behold
B. the Man BIBLE, VULGATE [13]

being
B. is a fiction DOWELL [1]
B. is the great explainer THOREAU [3]
German language 'speaks
B.' HEIDEGGER [2]
unbearable lightness of
b. KUNDERA [4]

Belial
sons/Of B., flown with
insolence MILTON [96]
thou man of B. BIBLE, OLD
TESTAMENT: 2 SAMUEL [11]

belief
all b. is for it JOHNSON, S. [114]
b. is like a guillotine KAFKA [5]
want of b. is a defect SWIFT, J. [56]
Where there is no b. RUSHDIE [5]

beliefs
discuss your b. HELLMAN [2]
dust of exploded b. MADAN [1]
not swallow more b. ELLIS [3]

believe
human beings ... b. in
anything MUGGERIDGE [9]
I b. in God BOOK OF COMMON
PRAYER [15]
I b. in one God MISSAL [10]
If you'll b. in me CARROLL [42]
I will not b. BIBLE, NEW TESTAMENT:
JOHN [73]
rather b. all the fables BACON, F.
[21]
seem to b. less JENKINS, D. [3]

believed
not seen, and yet have b. BIBLE, NEW
TESTAMENT: JOHN [76]

believers
Devout b. are safeguarded FREUD [13]

believeth
possible to him that b. BIBLE, NEW
TESTAMENT: MARK [9]

believing
b., ye shall receive BIBLE, NEW
TESTAMENT: MATTHEW [129]

Be not faithless, but b. BIBLE, NEW
TESTAMENT: JOHN [74]

bell
B., book, and candle SHAKESPEARE:
KING JOHN [6]
Ding dong b. NURSERY RHYMES [5]
for whom the b. tolls DONNE [55]
heart as sound as a b. SHAKESPEARE:
MUCH ADO [15]

bells
b. of hell ANONYMOUS [66]
Oh, noisy b., be dumb HOUSMAN [8]
Ring out, wild b. TENNYSON [114]
ring the b. of Heaven HODGSON [4]

belly
b. ... has no ears CATO THE ELDER [1]
b. is the teacher of art PERSIUS [1]
Better b. burst SWIFT, J. [53]
does not mind his b. JOHNSON,
s. [60]
Whose God is their b. BIBLE, NEW
TESTAMENT: PHILIPPIANS [7]

belonging
give up ... b. SMITH, Z. [3]

belongs
Man b. wherever he wants BRAUN [1]

beloved
My b. is mine BIBLE, OLD TESTAMENT:
SONG OF SOLOMON [10]
This is my b. BIBLE, OLD TESTAMENT:
SONG OF SOLOMON [21]

Belshazzar
B. ... made a great feast BIBLE, OLD
TESTAMENT: DANIEL [6]

belt
He could not see a b. ASQUITH, M. [4]
When I pass a b. MAXWELL [4]

bely
O wombe! O b. CHAUCER [43]

bend
b. ... but never break LA FONTAINE [1]

benedicite
B., omnia opera BIBLE, VULGATE [8]

benedictions
Perpetual b. WORDSWORTH, W. [88]

benefits
B. should be conferred
gradually MACHIAVELLI [5]

benevolence
b. of mankind does most
good BAGEHOT [34]
b. of the butcher SMITH, ADAM [2]

bent
mind's weight/Kept me b. THOMAS,
R.S. [5]

bereavement
B. is a darkness MURDOCH, I. [8]
b. is ... part of our experience LEWIS,
C. S. [9]

Berkeley
B. said 'there was no matter' BYRON,
LORD [150]

birthplace
curse your b. is ... evil WALCOTT [8]
birthright
sold his b. BIBLE, OLD TESTAMENT:
GENESIS [50]
bisexuality
[b.] ... doubles your chances ALLEN,
W. [11]
B. is ... a necessary
factor KOLLWITZ [2]
bishop
How can a b. marry SMITH,
SYDNEY [15]
bisy
Nowher so b. CHAUCER [20]
bitch
b. gone in the teeth POUND [12]
bitches
Come on you sons of b. DALY, D. [1]
bite
b. the hand that fed them BURKE,
E. [58]
b. the hand that feeds
them HOFFER [12]
I wish he would b. GEORGE II [1]
bitter
b. scent is lost THOMAS, E. [5]
my belly was b. BIBLE, NEW
TESTAMENT: REVELATION [29]
bitterness
b. of my soul BIBLE, OLD TESTAMENT:
ISAIAH [50]
bivouac
b. of the dead O'HARA [1]
black
b. as hell ... dark as
night SHAKESPEARE: SONNETS [40]
b., as if bereaved of light BLAKE [14]
B. is beautiful POLITICAL SLOGANS
[6]
B. is powerful HUGHES, L. [8]
B. men are pearls SHAKESPEARE: TWO
GENTLEMEN [8]
born in America with a b.
skin MALCOLM X [1]
burden of being b. JACKSON, J. [3]
don't matter if you're b. or
white JACKSON, MICHAEL [1]
embrace a b. woman CLEAVER [2]
get the b. spot on me STEVENSON,
R. L. [27]
I am b., but comely BIBLE, OLD
TESTAMENT: SONG OF SOLOMON [3]
I'm b. and I'm proud BROWN,
JAMES [3]
so long as it's b. FORD, H. [1]
young, gifted and b. SIMONE [2]
Black Dog
B... *He's* a bad un STEVENSON, R. L.
[26]
Black Power
We want B. CARMICHAEL [1]

blackberry
running b. would
adorn WHITMAN [13]
blackbird
Bye bye b. DIXON [1]
blackbirds
b. have their wills TENNYSON [189]
blackleg
False and dirty b. CONNELL [3]
Blackpool
famous seaside place called
B. EDGAR [1]
little stick of B. rock FORMBY [4]
blacks
revolutions ... caused by ...
b. TOCQUEVILLE [12]
Blackshirts
armed camp of B. MUSSOLINI [1]
bladders
we b. of wind PETRONIUS [2]
blameless
white flower of a b.
life TENNYSON [146]
blank
poor and b. MAO ZEDONG [12]
blasphemies
All great truths begin as b. SHAW [61]
blasphemy
b. ... shall not be forgiven BIBLE, NEW
TESTAMENT: MATTHEW [89]
in the soldier is flat b. SHAKESPEARE:
MEASURE FOR MEASURE [13]
bleed
I b. SHELLEY, P. B. [38]
If you prick us, do we not
b. SHAKESPEARE: MERCHANT OF
VENICE [27]
blemishes
b. are hid OVID [4]
bless
B. the Lord BIBLE, VULGATE [8]
except thou b. me BIBLE, OLD
TESTAMENT: GENESIS [53]
Lord b. thee BIBLE, OLD TESTAMENT:
NUMBERS [3]
blessed
B. are they BIBLE, NEW TESTAMENT:
MATTHEW [22]
b. art thou among women BIBLE,
NEW TESTAMENT: LUKE [1]
B. be he that cometh BIBLE, OLD
TESTAMENT: PSALMS [122]
B. is the man BIBLE, VULGATE [4]
b. them unaware COLERIDGE, S. T.
[29]
He whom thou blessest is b. BIBLE,
OLD TESTAMENT: NUMBERS [4]
Judge none b. BIBLE, APOCRYPHA:
ECCLESIASTICUS [26]
blessing
Nothing is an unmixed
b. HORACE [34]

blest
dwelling of the b. VIRGIL [41]
blethers
stringing b. up in rhyme BURNS [14]
blight
b. man was born for HOPKINS [20]
blind
accompany my being b. PEPYS [15]
b. lead the blind BIBLE, NEW
TESTAMENT: MATTHEW [109]
country of the b. ERASMUS [1]
eyes of the b. shall be opened BIBLE,
OLD TESTAMENT: ISAIAH [47]
I was b., now I see BIBLE, NEW
TESTAMENT: JOHN [38]
To be b. is not
miserable MILTON [206]
two black eyes for being b. HOOD [18]
blindness
reproach them of their
b. MILTON [205]
bliss
B. is the same POPE [138]
B. was it ... to be alive WORDSWORTH,
W. [20]
Everywhere I see b. SHELLEY, M. W. [2]
no *right* to b. ARNOLD, M. [6]
blithe
b. Spirit SHELLEY, P. B. [63]
block
hew the b. off POPE [81]
blockhead
No man but a b. JOHNSON, S. [103]
blockheads
Let b. read CHESTERFIELD [30]
blonde
It was a b. CHANDLER [3]
splendid, *b. beast* NIETZSCHE [23]
blondes
B. are the best victims HITCHCOCK
[6]
Gentlemen Prefer B. LOOS [1]
blood
b. of Christians is the
seed TERTULLIAN [3]
b. on his hands today SPENCER, C. [2]
b. sheets down JONG [7]
b., toil, tears and sweat CHURCHILL,
W. [19]
b. will have blood SHAKESPEARE:
MACBETH [68]
cleansed of the b. BIBLE, OLD
TESTAMENT: NUMBERS [11]
His b. be on us BIBLE, NEW
TESTAMENT: MATTHEW [169]
in b./Stepped in so far SHAKESPEARE:
MACBETH [69]
Let there be b. BYRON, LORD [144]
my b. will invigorate India GANDHI,
I. [1]
Neptune's ocean wash this
b. SHAKESPEARE: MACBETH [41]

book

age of the b. is almost
gone STEINER [5]

Any fool may write a ... b. GRAY,
T. [25]

B. ... guidance to the
godfearing KORAN [4]

b. is a mirror LICHTENBERG [9]

b. is made up of signs ECO [1]

b. is the precious life-
blood MILTON [63]

b.'s a book BYRON, LORD [5]

b. that you would even wish your
wife GRIFFITH-JONES [1]

b. without pictures CARROLL [2]

bad b. is as much of a labour HUXLEY,
A. [12]

Camerado, this is no b. WHITMAN
[37]

damned, thick, square
b. GLOUCESTER [1]

do not throw this b. about BELLOC [1]

empty b. is like an infant's
soul TRAHERNE [1]

give your b. a fashionable
air CERVANTES [2]

good b. ... opened with
expectation ALCOTT, A. B. [2]

good b. is the best of
friends TUPPER [1]

I'll never write another b. ARCHER [3]

kill a good b. MILTON [62]

Making a b. is a craft LA BRUYÈRE [2]

moment I picked your b. MARX,
G. [10]

moral or immoral b. WILDE [34]

myself am the groundwork of my
b. MONTAIGNE [1]

no Frigate like a B. DICKINSON, E. [33]

overpraise a long b. FORSTER [24]

reading or non-reading a b. BYRON,
LORD [108]

security in an old b. LOWELL, J. R. [12]

until he has written a b. JOWETT [1]

What I like best is a b. SALINGER [2]

bookish

Contemplative and b.
men DONNE [44]

books

All good b. are alike HEMINGWAY [12]

b. and harlots BENJAMIN [5]

B. and marriage go ill MOLIÈRE [20]

b. are divisible into two
classes RUSKIN [18]

b. are either dreams LOWELL, A. [3]

B. are fatal DISRAELI [45]

b. are more than books LOWELL, A. [2]

b. are not ... dead things MILTON [61]

B. are the bees LOWELL, J. R. [8]

B. are the money of
Literature HUXLEY, T. [7]

B., books, books BROWNING, E. B. [15]

B. ... bloodless substitute for
life STEVENSON, R. L. [16]

B. cannot be killed by fire ROOSEVELT,
F. D. [12]

B. constitute capital JEFFERSON [35]

B. ... have no more than one
way SWIFT, J. [4]

B. that have become classics ALDRICH,
T. B. [1]

b. that influence us FORSTER [31]

B., the children of the brain SWIFT,
J. [7]

B. think for me LAMB, CHARLES [24]

content with burning my
b. FREUD [19]

Deep versed in b. and
shallow MILTON [192]

Even bad b. are books GRASS [1]

forgotten how to use b. HARRIS, F. [2]

gentleman is not in your
b. SHAKESPEARE: MUCH ADO [4]

hide these b. SHERIDAN, R. B. [3]

let my b. be ... the
eloquence SHAKESPEARE:
SONNETS [6]

making many b. BIBLE, OLD
TESTAMENT: ECCLESIASTES [43]

making of b. HOBHOUSE [3]

only b./Were woman's looks MOORE,
T. [9]

sheds one's sicknesses in
b. LAWRENCE, D. H. [9]

Some b. are ... forgotten AUDEN [36]

Some b. are to be tasted BACON,
F. [37]

sweet serenity of b. LONGFELLOW [28]

walls of b. will deaden/The
drumming MACNEICE [8]

boop

B.-boop-a-doop NATWICK [1]

boorishness

B. ... has its
geniuses LICHTENBERG [20]

boot

B., saddle, to horse, and
away BROWNING, R. [7]

booted

ready b. and spurred to
ride RUMBOLD [1]

ready b. to take his
journey MONTAIGNE [2]

Booth

B. died blind LINDSAY [1]

boot-lace

hang from a b. DOYLE, A. C. [19]

boots

b. are made for walkin' SINATRA,
N. [1]

blaming on his b. the
fault BECKETT [3]

bordels

country without b. DIETRICH [4]

borders

control the nation's b. HOWARD,
M. [1]

bore

b. is a man who ... tells you TAYLOR,
BERT L. [1]

B. ... person who talks BIERCE [10]

forgive those whom we b. LA
ROCHEFOUCAULD [26]

healthy male adult b.
consumes UPDIKE [2]

travel b. SACKVILLE-WEST [2]

secret of being a b. VOLTAIRE [10]

bored

art of being b. CHAMFORT [7]

b. for England MUGGERIDGE [8]

b. with everything LACLOS [4]

I am heavy b. BERRYMAN [2]

boredom

B. is ... a vital problem RUSSELL, B. [13]

B. is ... counter-
revolutionary DEBORD [1]

b. is the dream bird BENJAMIN [10]

b. is the root of all
evil KIERKEGAARD [12]

B.! I've got used to that IONESCO [5]

Is b. anything less BERGER [2]

manufactured an abyss of
b. MUMFORD, L. [7]

bores

B. bore each other MARQUIS [8]

B. have succeeded to
dragons DISRAELI [4]

I don't know about b. SALINGER [3]

so many intensified b. DICKENS [43]

two mighty tribes, the B. and
Bored BYRON, LORD [160]

born

b., ... twice over ROUSSEAU [3]

b. when you kissed me GRAHAME,
G. [1]

Except a man be b. again BIBLE, NEW
TESTAMENT: JOHN [15]

good ... if he had not been b. BIBLE,
NEW TESTAMENT: MATTHEW [158]

He not busy being b. DYLAN [15]

I was b. ... are wonderful
words OLIPHANT [1]

man may be b. GURDJIEFF [3]

borrow

men who b. ... men who lend LAMB,
CHARLES [10]

borrowed

dress me/In b. robes SHAKESPEARE:
MACBETH [11]

borrower

b. is servant BIBLE, OLD TESTAMENT:
PROVERBS [65]

b. of the night SHAKESPEARE:
MACBETH [52]

Neither a b. nor a
lender SHAKESPEARE: HAMLET [34]

borrowers
B. of books LAMB, CHARLES [11]
borrowing
banqueting upon b. BIBLE,
APOCRYPHA: ECCLESIASTICUS [36]
bosom
finest b. in nature GREGORY, J. [1]
not a b. to repose upon DICKENS
[80]
woman's b. bears EURIPIDES [5]
bosom-sin
One cunning b. HERBERT, G. [9]
Boston
B. man is the east wind APPLETON [2]
God made B. on a wet
Sunday CHANDLER [11]
botanize
b./Upon his mother's
grave WORDSWORTH, W. [36]
botch
b. of Egypt BIBLE, OLD TESTAMENT:
DEUTERONOMY [11]
Botticelli
if B. were alive today USTINOV [3]
bottomless
key of the b. pit BIBLE, NEW
TESTAMENT: REVELATION [27]
boum
Hope, politeness ... produce
'b.' FORSTER [18]
bounce
Every ounce, a b. PEAKE [1]
bourgeois
b. always bounces up CONNOLLY,
C. [4]
b. are other people RENARD [1]
b., ce sont les autres RENARD [1]
hatred of the B. is ...
virtue FLAUBERT [9]
How beastly the b. is LAWRENCE,
D. H. [24]
it's a b. town LEDBETTER [1]
Like the dog, stands the b. BLOK [3]
You must shock the
B. BAUDELAIRE [34]
bourgeoisie
b. ... has been the first MARX/
ENGELS [8]
By b. is meant ... modern
capitalists ENGELS [3]
bow
b. cannot always stand
bent CERVANTES [23]
B., bow, ye lower middle
classes GILBERT, W. S. [20]
made an awkward b. KEATS [120]
set my b. in the cloud BIBLE, OLD
TESTAMENT: GENESIS [38]
bowels
b. of Christ CROMWELL [4]
b. of compassion BIBLE, NEW
TESTAMENT: 1 JOHN [4]

b. were moved for him BIBLE, OLD
TESTAMENT: SONG OF SOLOMON [20]
Nature's way to open b. PLOMER [2]
when the b. of the earth were
sought DRAYTON [1]
bowl
love in a golden b. BLAKE [15]
box
B. about AUBREY [4]
boxes
Little b. REYNOLDS, M. [1]
boxing
B. is just show business BRUNO, F. [2]
boy
b. stood on the burning
deck HEMANS [2]
to be b. eternal SHAKESPEARE:
WINTER'S TALE [2]
boyhood
B. is a most
complex CHESTERTON [46]
Oh, for b.'s painless play WHITTIER
[4]
boys
b. are not going to be
sent ROOSEVELT, F. D. [8]
B. are ... unwholesome
companions LAMB, CHARLES [14]
For little b. are rancorous MCGINLEY,
P. [3]
Tell the b. to follow JAMES, H. [31]
two sorts of b. DICKENS [21]
Bradshaw
vocabulary of 'B.' DOYLE, A. C. [28]
brain
b. ... is like a little empty attic DOYLE,
A. C. [2]
B. – is wider than the Sky DICKINSON,
E. [18]
b. ... poor scheme for
survival VONNEGUT [2]
b. the size of a planet ADAMS, D. [5]
If I only had a b. HARBURG [5]
brains
b. ta'en out and
buttered SHAKESPEARE: MERRY
WIVES [9]
dry up my b. SHAKESPEARE:
HAMLET [138]
nightly racking of the b., CHURCHILL,
CHARLES [10]
when the b. were out SHAKESPEARE:
MACBETH [66]
branch
Cut is the b. MARLOWE [28]
brands
great b. are far more than
labels O'REILLY, T. [1]
brandy
B. for the Parson KIPLING [71]
hero must drink b. JOHNSON, S.
[120]

brass
become as sounding b. BIBLE, NEW
TESTAMENT: 1 CORINTHIANS [29]
Men's evil manners live in
b. SHAKESPEARE: HENRY VIII [15]
brave
b. new world SHAKESPEARE:
TEMPEST [26]
Fortune favours the b. VIRGIL [48]
How sleep the b. COLLINS, WILLIAM
[1]
None but the b. DRYDEN [69]
braver
I have done one b. thing DONNE [4]
brawling
b. woman in a wide house BIBLE, OLD
TESTAMENT: PROVERBS [62]
O b. love, O loving hate SHAKESPEARE:
ROMEO & JULIET [4]
brawls
with thy b. thou hast
disturbed SHAKESPEARE:
MIDSUMMER NIGHT'S DREAM [16]
Bray
Vicar of B., sir ANONYMOUS [3]
breach
More honoured in the
b. SHAKESPEARE: HAMLET [39]
Once more unto the b. SHAKESPEARE:
HENRY V [13]
bread
b. and games JUVENAL [16]
b. of affliction BIBLE, OLD TESTAMENT:
1 KINGS [17]
b. of life BIBLE, NEW TESTAMENT:
JOHN [26]
Cast thy b. upon BIBLE, OLD
TESTAMENT: ECCLESIASTES [36]
live by b. alone BIBLE, NEW
TESTAMENT: MATTHEW [16]
Man does not live by b. alone GILL
[5]
Man doth not live by b. only BIBLE,
OLD TESTAMENT: DEUTERONOMY [5]
ne'er his b. in sorrow ate GOETHE [4]
our daily b. BIBLE, NEW TESTAMENT:
MATTHEW [38]
taste/of others' b. DANTE [28]
that b. should be so dear HOOD [11]
took b. and brake it ELIZABETH I [5]
break
B., break, break TENNYSON [58]
breakfast
b. test ARNIM [1]
breaking
b. of windows, or breaking of
laws MORE, H. [12]
breast
boiling bloody b. SHAKESPEARE:
MIDSUMMER NIGHT'S DREAM [41]
Love ... in a woman's b. WOTTON [4]
pants upon her b. POPE [95]

brutish
nasty, b., and short HOBBES [8]
bubble
No b. is so iridescent OSLER [7]
toss his b. QUARLES [4]
buck
b. stops here TRUMAN [7]
day they pass the b. AYRES [1]
buckets
dropping b. into empty
wells COWPER [38]
Buckingham
so much for B. CIBBER [5]
Buckingham Palace
changing guard at B. MILNE [1]
bud
b. of love SHAKESPEARE: ROMEO &
JULIET [19]
Buddha
B. the Godhead, resides PIRSIG [2]
Buddhism
B. is a religion of ... mountains VAN
DER POST [4]
buffers
Most of them are b. CLARK, A. [1]
buffoon
chemist, fiddler, statesman and
b. DRYDEN [35]
bugle
Blow, b., blow TENNYSON [68]
build
b. for ever RUSKIN [3]
to b. ... is the noblest
art LONGFELLOW [34]
When we mean to b. SHAKESPEARE:
HENRY IV PT 2 [11]
building
b. decayeth BIBLE, OLD TESTAMENT:
ECCLESIASTES [33]
buildings
We shape our b. CHURCHILL, W. [39]
built
city is b./To music TENNYSON [151]
bull
Taking the b. by both
horns ASHFORD [6]
they are gone to milk the
b. JOHNSON, S. [58]
bullet
b. with my name
on ANONYMOUS [47]
bite on the b. KIPLING [10]
due process is a b. WAYNE [2]
Every b. has its billet WILLIAM III
[2]
Faster than a speeding b. SIEGEL &
SHUSTER [2]
bullfighting
B. is the only art HEMINGWAY [9]
bullocks
whose talk is of b. BIBLE, APOCRYPHA:
ECCLESIASTICUS [61]

bullshit
cold, mechanical, conceptual
b. HOWELLS [1]
wit, grit and b. KING, D. [1]
bully
love the lovely b. SHAKESPEARE:
HENRY V [21]
bulrushes
ark of b. BIBLE, OLD TESTAMENT:
EXODUS [1]
bum
does my b. look big FAST SHOW [1]
One's B. Year SUN [8]
touch my b. CERVANTES [41]
bumpy
going to be a b. night DAVIS, B. [3]
bums
jutting-out of b. SHAKESPEARE:
TIMON [7]
Bunbury
permanent invalid called
B. WILDE [97]
bunting
Bye, baby b. NURSERY RHYMES [3]
burden
b. and heat of the day BIBLE, NEW
TESTAMENT: MATTHEW [125]
b. of the world MARKHAM [1]
b. of them is intolerable BOOK OF
COMMON PRAYER [57]
every man shall bear his own
b. BIBLE, NEW TESTAMENT:
GALATIANS [8]
bureaucracy
B. is not an obstacle SCHUMPETER [6]
b. is sure to think BAGEHOT [18]
bureaucrat
b. that does not like a poem VIDAL
[3]
burgled
b. houses and nicked GALLAGHER [1]
Burgundy
naïve domestic B. THURBER [1]
burial
every earth is fit for b. MARLOWE
[16]
buried
b. him darkly WOLFE, C. [2]
can't legally be b. MADAN [4]
knowledge of our b. life ARNOLD,
M. [19]
never bear to be b. PARKINSON, N. [1]
burn
B., baby, burn POLITICAL SLOGANS [7]
better to b. out YOUNG, N. [1]
I'll b. my books MARLOWE [27]
my paintings must b. LAWRENCE,
D. H. [27]
burned
clothes not be b. BIBLE, OLD
TESTAMENT: PROVERBS [13]
Wherever books are b. HEINE [2]

burnt
b. offering BIBLE, OLD TESTAMENT:
GENESIS [48]
delight in b. offerings BIBLE, OLD
TESTAMENT: 1 SAMUEL [9]
bury
anything we want to b. MOORE, J. [1]
b. Caesar, not to praise
him SHAKESPEARE: JULIUS
CAESAR [29]
disposed to b. for
nothing DICKENS [54]
we will b. you KHRUSHCHEV [4]
bus
Can it be a Motor B. GODLEY [1]
either on the b. or off the
bus KESEY [2]
he missed the b. CHAMBERLAIN, N.
[4]
bush
b. was not consumed BIBLE, OLD
TESTAMENT: EXODUS [4]
bushel
put it under a b. BIBLE, NEW
TESTAMENT: MATTHEW [25]
business
about my Father's b. BIBLE, NEW
TESTAMENT: LUKE [13]
B. carried on as usual CHURCHILL,
W. [6]
b. ... guided by 'feminine' RODDICK [1]
chief b. of the American
people COOLIDGE [3]
do b. together THATCHER [13]
few people do b. well
CHESTERFIELD [18]
good b. is the best art WARHOL [4]
If everybody minded their own
b. CARROLL [10]
man I can do b. with ADAMS, G. [1]
Perpetual devotion to ... his
b. STEVENSON, R. L. [18]
To b. that we love SHAKESPEARE:
ANTONY & CLEOPATRA [27]
vulgar to talk about one's
b. WILDE [105]
your b. ... pleasure WYCHERLEY [6]
Buss
Miss B. and Miss
Beale ANONYMOUS [58]
bust
dance it b. to bust GRENFELL [3]
Uncorseted, her friendly b. ELIOT,
T. S. [13]
butcher
b., the baker NURSERY RHYMES [37]
butchered
B. to make a Roman holiday BYRON,
LORD [86]
butchers
used to weep in b.' shops ROBINSON,
B. [4]

butler
b.'s upper slopes WODEHOUSE [14]
'great' b. ISHIGURO [1]
toes of an English b. WODEHOUSE [13]

Butlins
just like B. STARR, R. [1]

butter
B. and honey shall he eat BIBLE, OLD
TESTAMENT: ISAIAH [19]
b. wouldn't melt LANCHESTER [1]
cutting bread and b. THACKERAY
[14]
ground itself is kind, black
b. HEANEY [2]
little bit of b. to my bread MILNE [3]
men of b. ALVA [1]
One cannot shoot with
b. GOEBBELS [2]
smoother than b. BIBLE, OLD
TESTAMENT: PSALMS [68]
tell Stork from b. ADVERTISING
SLOGANS [5]

butterfly
breaks a b. upon a wheel POPE [151]
Float like a b. ALI [3]

buxom
b., blithe, and debonair MILTON [12]

Byron
B. is dead CARLYLE, J. W. [2]
B. is ... mad as the winds SHELLEY,
P. B. [22]
poetry of Lord B. MACAULAY,
LORD [17]

cabbages
setting my c. MONTAIGNE [3]
thrice happy those that plant
c. RABELAIS [9]

cabined
I am c., cribbed,
confined SHAKESPEARE: MACBETH [63]

cabinet
furnish the yet empty c. LOCKE [2]

Cabots
C. talk only to God BOSSIDY [1]

cackles
c., groans and dies CLARE [1]

cad
Only a c. tells the truth SCHLESINGER
JR [2]

cadence
harsh c. of a rugged line DRYDEN [48]

cadres
C. determine everything STALIN [4]

Caesar
C. had his Brutus HENRY, PATRICK [1]
C.'s wife must be above CAESAR, J. [3]
Here was a C. SHAKESPEARE: JULIUS
CAESAR [37]
I appeal unto C. BIBLE, NEW
TESTAMENT: ACTS [40]
Imperious C., dead SHAKESPEARE:
HAMLET [148]

Render ... unto C. BIBLE, NEW
TESTAMENT: MATTHEW [131]
'Tis paltry to be C. SHAKESPEARE:
ANTONY & CLEOPATRA [35]
unto C. shalt thou go BIBLE, NEW
TESTAMENT: ACTS [41]

Caesars
So long as men worship the
C. HUXLEY, A. [17]

caff
ace c. ADVERTISING SLOGANS [3]

cage
may be compared to a
c. MONTAIGNE [20]

caged
c. birds ... cry WEBSTER, J. [12]
why the c. bird sings DUNBAR, P. L.
[1]

Cain
C. was a tiller BIBLE, OLD TESTAMENT:
GENESIS [25]
mark upon C. BIBLE, OLD TESTAMENT:
GENESIS [28]
we are the sons of C. BURGESS, A. [3]

cake
Let them eat c. MARIE-ANTOINETTE [1]

cakes
no more c. and ale SHAKESPEARE:
TWELFTH NIGHT [18]

Calais
'C.' lying in my heart MARY I [1]

calamity
c. ... is as old as the trilobites HOLMES
SR [7]
in the power of no c. BROWNE [10]
thou art wedded to c. SHAKESPEARE:
ROMEO & JULIET [34]

calculus
integral and differential c. GILBERT,
W. S. [11]

Caledonia
C.! stern and wild SCOTT, W. [5]
Mourn, hapless C. SMOLLETT [1]

calf
Bring hither the fatted c. BIBLE, NEW
TESTAMENT: LUKE [46]

California
C. – a state so blessed FROST, R. [16]
C. here I come JOLSON [1]
C. is a fine place ALLEN, F. [1]
C. is a place in which DIDION [2]
C. is a tragic country ISHERWOOD [2]

calix
Hoc est c. sanguinis mei MISSAL [17]

call
wild c. and a clear call MASEFIELD [2]

calumnies
c. ... answered best with
silence JONSON [10]

calumny
thou shalt not escape
c. SHAKESPEARE: HAMLET [95]

Calvary
place, which is called C. BIBLE, NEW
TESTAMENT: LUKE [70]

Cambridge
C. people rarely smile BROOKE [4]
Ye fields of C. COWLEY, A. [5]

came
Tell them I c. DE LA MARE [5]

camel
c. is a horse ANONYMOUS [9]
easier for a c. BIBLE, NEW TESTAMENT:
MATTHEW [122]
Take my c. MACAULAY, R. [2]

Camelot
many-towered C. TENNYSON [6]
spot ... known as C. LERNER, A. J. [6]

camels
C. are snobbish MOORE,
MARIANNE [11]

camera
c. ... teaches people how to
see LANGE [1]
camera relieves us BERGER [6]
I am a c. ISHERWOOD [1]
virtue of the c. ATKINSON [2]

camerado
C., I give you my hand WHITMAN [30]

campaign
c. in poetry CUOMO [1]

Campbells
C. are comin' ANONYMOUS [10]

campfires
c. of gentle people KEILLOR [5]

Camptown
C. ladies sing this song FOSTER, S. [2]

can
Pass me the c., lad HOUSMAN [22]

Canaan
C. ... an everlasting possession BIBLE,
OLD TESTAMENT: GENESIS [45]

Canada
C. is a country where
nothing SHIELDS [1]
C. is not really a place DAVIES,
ROBERTSON [3]

Canadian
C. cultural nationalism ATWOOD [2]

candidate
To be a c. is to submit POTTER, D. [1]

Candide
C. can do little more TRILLING [1]

candle
book and bell and c. MALORY [5]
c. burned PASTERNAK [3]
c. burns at both ends MILLAY [3]
hold a c. to my shames SHAKESPEARE:
MERCHANT OF VENICE [21]
light a c. to the sun SIDNEY, A. [2]
Like a c. in the wind JOHN [1]
Out, out, brief c. SHAKESPEARE:
MACBETH [98]
we shall ... light such a c. LATIMER [1]

candle-light
Colours seen by c. BROWNING,
E. B. [7]

candles
blessèd c. of the night SHAKESPEARE:
MERCHANT OF VENICE [42]
Night's c. are burnt out SHAKESPEARE:
ROMEO & JULIET [36]

candlesticks
seven golden c. BIBLE, NEW
TESTAMENT: REVELATION [3]

candy
C./Is dandy NASH, O. [1]

canem
CAVE C. PETRONIUS [1]

canker
c. lives in sweetest bud SHAKESPEARE:
SONNETS [11]
c. that devours everything
else BAUDELAIRE [5]

cannon
C. to the right of
them TENNYSON [144]

cant
nothing but c. PEACOCK [5]

cantate
C. Domino BIBLE, VULGATE [2]

cants
c. ... canted in this canting
world STERNE [15]

capability
Negative c. KEATS [15]

capable
c. of being THOREAU [4]

capital
C. is a result of labor GEORGE, H. [1]
c. is become an overgrown
monster SMOLLETT [2]
C. is dead labour MARX, K. [14]
earned ... political c. BUSH, G. W. [8]

capitalism
c. ... doesn't deliver the
goods KEYNES [11]
C. ... extremely
objectionable KEYNES [5]
C. ... in a noncapitalist HOFFER [10]
c. is a necessary
condition FRIEDMAN [1]
C. ... subsidizes ... social
unrest SCHUMPETER [5]
definition of c. HAMPTON [4]
gets anything out of c. DOS PASSOS [1]
I would choose c. LÉVY [3]
unacceptable face of c. HEATH [2]

capitalist
c. is a rational miser MARX, K. [13]

capitalists
C. are no more capable LENIN [5]

capitulate
I will not c. JOHNSON, S. [145]

caprice
c. lasts a little longer WILDE [44]

captain
C. lies,/Fallen cold and
dead WHITMAN [36]
c. of my soul HENLEY [2]
O C.! my Captain WHITMAN [35]
plain, russet-coated c. CROMWELL [2]
royal C. of this ruined
band SHAKESPEARE: HENRY V [19]
walled-town of a C.'s
exclusiveness MELVILLE [11]

captains
C. and the Kings depart KIPLING [38]
C. of industry CARLYLE, T. [50]

captive
c. void of noble rage TENNYSON [94]

captivity
lead thy c. captive BIBLE, OLD
TESTAMENT: JUDGES [5]
Turn again our c. BIBLE, OLD
TESTAMENT: PSALMS [129]

car
afford to keep a motor c. SHAW [74]
c. has become the
carapace MCLUHAN [7]
c. ... is on the way out BALLARD [3]
new c. or a new wife PHILIP, DUKE OF
EDINBURGH [3]

caravan
join/The innumerable c. BRYANT [1]

carborundum
Nil c. illegitimi ANONYMOUS [62]

carbuncle
monstrous c. CHARLES, PRINCE OF
WALES [2]

carcase
Wheresoever the c. is BIBLE, NEW
TESTAMENT: MATTHEW [141]

carcinoma
To sing of rectal c. HALDANE [3]

card
man's idea in a c. game DUNNE,
F. P. [7]

cards
c. are war LAMB, CHARLES [12]
dividing a pack of c. ADDISON [4]
Never play c. with ... Doc ALGREN [2]
nothing but a pack of c. CARROLL [22]
not learnt to play at c. JOHNSON,
S. [86]

care
Begone, dull C. ANONYMOUS [7]
c. about people less FORSTER [6]
C. keeps his watch SHAKESPEARE:
ROMEO & JULIET [22]
c./Sat on his faded cheek MILTON [97]
with what c. hast Thou
begirt HERBERT, G. [7]

career
C. opportunities STRUMMER/JONES [3]

careers
People don't choose their c. DOS
PASSOS [2]

careless
c. of the single life TENNYSON
[104]
c. people FITZGERALD, F. S. [10]
C. talk costs lives ANONYMOUS [11]

cares
put c. away CATULLUS [9]

caricature
most perfect c. BEERBOHM [7]

caricatured
c. by a charlatan ELIOT, G. [27]

Carlyle
C.'s digestion had been
stronger CARLYLE, J. W. [5]
good of God to let C. BUTLER, S.
(1835–1902) [3]
Thomas C. is incontestably
dead JAMES SR, H. [1]

carnal
with c. and devout intent POPE [5]

carpe
C. diem HORACE [24]

carpenter
Is not this the c.'s son BIBLE, NEW
TESTAMENT: MATTHEW [100]

carpet
laid the earth ... as a c. KORAN [46]

carriage
c. has not arrived LERMONTOV [3]

carrot
called the Camberwell c. ROBINSON,
B. [6]

cars
c. ... equivalent of ...
cathedrals BARTHES [5]

Carthage
C. must be destroyed CATO THE
ELDER [3]
I went to C. ST AUGUSTINE [1]

carve
c. him as a dish SHAKESPEARE: JULIUS
CAESAR [14]

carver
was the c. happy RUSKIN [2]

carving
C. is unrelated masses HEPWORTH [1]

Cary Grant
Old C. fine GRANT, C. [1]

casbah
Come with me to the C. BOYER [1]

case
c. is concluded ST AUGUSTINE [9]
c. is still before the
courts HORACE [74]

cash
eroded by a c. economy MARX, K.
[12]

cash-payment
C. is not the sole nexus CARLYLE,
T. [47]
C. never ... paid one man CARLYLE,
T. [48]

chains
nothing to lose but their c. MARX/
ENGELS [10]
safer to be in c. KAFKA [10]
chairs
three c. in my house THOREAU [38]
chalice
c. of my blood MISSAL [17]
cham
great C. of literature SMOLLETT [3]
champions
four c. fierce MILTON [117]
chance
c. will bring us through ARNOLD,
M. [9]
erring men call c. MILTON [40]
leaveth nothing to c. SAVILE [10]
no c., and no anarchy EMERSON [60]
Chancery
Keep out of C. DICKENS [73]
change
all that moveth ... in c.
delight SPENSER [37]
avoid ... a great c. TROLLOPE [12]
C. begets change DICKENS [52]
c., continuing change ASIMOV [3]
c. is gonna come COOKE, S. [2]
c. ... leaves a toothing-
stone MACHIAVELLI [1]
c. what is in themselves KORAN [25]
certain relief in c. IRVING, W. [9]
measured by the rapidity of c. ELIOT,
G. [33]
necessary for everything to
c. LAMPEDUSA [1]
People c. and forget HELLMAN [4]
Plus ça c. KARR [2]
ringing grooves of c. TENNYSON
[47]
very wisest ... do not
c. CONFUCIUS [36]
Women want men to c. CONRAN [3]
When it is not necessary to
c. FALKLAND [1]
without the means of some c. BURKE,
E. [35]
changed
c. several times since
then CARROLL [6]
changes
c. except the avant-garde VIDAL [9]
Today the world c. so
quickly MEDAWAR [3]
wearied by the c. BOOK OF COMMON
PRAYER [99]
changing
All things are c. OVID [13]
not c. one's mind MAUGHAM [4]
Channel
C. is a ditch NAPOLEON I [3]
channel
Make me a c. HYMNS & CAROLS [57]

chaos
C., a rough, unordered mass OVID [8]
C. often breeds life ADAMS, H. B. [4]
C. umpire sits MILTON [118]
dread empire, C. POPE [86]
In all c. there is a cosmos JUNG [19]
mounting c. CALLAGHAN [1]
Not C., not/The darkest
pit WORDSWORTH, W. [95]
chapels
c. had been churches SHAKESPEARE:
MERCHANT OF VENICE [8]
chapter
finds us in the second c. DOYLE,
A. C. [27]
one c. is not torn out DONNE [53]
character
apparent resemblances of
c. CHAMFORT [11]
c. amid the stream of
life GOETHE [10]
c. dead at every word SHERIDAN,
R. B. [21]
c. has set like plaster JAMES, W. [2]
'c.' is a misleading concept BARNES,
J. [8]
c. is like an acrostic EMERSON [14]
C. is much easier kept PAINE [8]
c. is often a simple
piece STRINDBERG [4]
c. will never die PIRANDELLO [3]
emerges a formidable c. ANGELOU [4]
index of a man's c. CONNOLLY, C. [19]
man's c. is his fate HERACLITUS [6]
What is c. JAMES, H. [16]
characters
Six C. in Search of an
Author PIRANDELLO [2]
Charing Cross
between Heaven and C. THOMPSON,
F. [13]
chariot
swing low, sweet c. ANONYMOUS [90]
chariots
Some trust in c. BIBLE, OLD
TESTAMENT: PSALMS [20]
charities
cold c. of man to man CRABBE [1]
charity
C. begins at home DICKENS [56]
C. creates a multitude of
sins WILDE [8]
C. is cold in the multitude SMART,
C. [3]
C. never faileth BIBLE, NEW
TESTAMENT: 1 CORINTHIANS [30]
c. shall cover the multitude BIBLE,
NEW TESTAMENT: 1 PETER [10]
greatest of these is c. BIBLE, NEW
TESTAMENT: 1 CORINTHIANS [33]
have not c. BIBLE, NEW TESTAMENT:
1 CORINTHIANS [29]

in all things, c. ANONYMOUS [45]
Charlemagne
I am C. NAPOLEON I [4]
Charlie
C. don't surf COPPOLA [2]
live or die wi' C. HOGG [3]
charm
C. is the great English
blight WAUGH [13]
One native c. GOLDSMITH [40]
What is c. LESSING, D. [5]
You know what c. is CAMUS [14]
charmed
I bear a c. life SHAKESPEARE:
MACBETH [99]
charmer
Who will pity a c. BIBLE, APOCRYPHA:
ECCLESIASTICUS [28]
charming
All c. people have something to
conceal CONNOLLY, C. [10]
charms
c. of the passing stranger PROUST [9]
c. of women COWLEY, H. [1]
endearing young c. MOORE, T. [3]
reserved her c. for ...
countrymen MONTAGU [12]
chartered
each c. street BLAKE [57]
chase
ingovernable passion for the
c. SURTEES [1]
chassis
state o' c. O'CASEY [2]
chaste
c. as unsunned snow SHAKESPEARE:
CYMBELINE [6]
c. you; virtuous you KEATS [59]
What ... does a c. girl do MARTIAL [6]
chasteneth
whom the Lord loveth he c. BIBLE,
NEW TESTAMENT: HEBREWS [8]
chastisement
awaits a painful c. KORAN [26]
chastity
C. is a monkish ...
superstition SHELLEY, P. B. [13]
C. is the cement of
civilization EDDY [1]
c., my brother MILTON [37]
Give me c. and
continency ST AUGUSTINE [2]
modern resistance to c. LEWIS, C. S. [2]
virtue is made ... of c. VOLTAIRE [26]
woman's c. ... like an
onion HAWTHORNE [9]
chateaux
c. would never have been
burnt TREVELYAN [4]
Chattanooga
Is that the C. Choo-choo GORDON,
M. [1]

chills
Of c. and fever she died RANSOM [1]

Chimborazo
C. ... /Took me by the
hand TURNER [1]

chime
c. of words tinkling SMITH, LOGAN
P. [16]

chimes
c. at midnight SHAKESPEARE: HENRY IV
PT 2 [21]

china
though c. fall POPE [100]

Chinee
heathen C. is peculiar HARTE [2]

chintzy
c. cheeriness BETJEMAN [1]

chivalry
age of c. is gone BURKE, E. [37]

chocolate
age ... of c. PRIESTLEY [1]

choice
conditions of c. MEAD [2]
difficulty in life is the c. MOORE,
G. [4]
genuine freedom of c. TOYNBEE,
A.J. [2]

choices
c. ... show what we ... are ROWLING [2]

choose
c. no tae choose life WELSH [3]
c. whether to be rich ILLICH [4]

chopper
c. to chop off your head NURSERY
RHYMES [28]

chord
feel for the common c. BROWNING,
R. [42]
one lost c. divine PROCTER [2]

chosen
few are c. BIBLE, NEW TESTAMENT:
MATTHEW [130]
I have c. you BIBLE, NEW TESTAMENT:
JOHN [55]

Christ
be with C.; which is far better BIBLE,
NEW TESTAMENT: PHILIPPIANS [2]
C. before me ST PATRICK [1]
C. never came this far LEVI, C. [1]
cautious, statistical C. O'REILLY, J.B. [1]
Thou art the C. BIBLE, NEW
TESTAMENT: MATTHEW [112]
to live is C. BIBLE, NEW TESTAMENT:
PHILIPPIANS [1]
Why did you kill C. BRUCE [1]

Christabel
Shield sweet C. COLERIDGE, S. T. [38]

Christian
C. ideal has not been
tried CHESTERTON [24]
C. religion ... attended with
miracles HUME, D. [11]

exterminating every C. DIDEROT [22]
naturally C. soul TERTULLIAN [1]
object will be ... to form C.
men ARNOLD, T. [1]
persuadest me to be a C. BIBLE, NEW
TESTAMENT: ACTS [44]
Scratch the C. ZANGWILL [1]
talk about C. unity O'BRIEN, C. C. [2]
two things about the C.
religion ARNOLD, M. [59]

Christianity
C. the one great curse NIETZSCHE [28]
C. will go LENNON [2]
genius of C. MALRAUX [4]
glory of C. consists SAKI [7]
loving C. better than
truth COLERIDGE, S. T. [78]

Christians
C. are not born but
made ST JEROME [5]
C. stand not on anything KORAN [6]
call themselves C. BOOK OF COMMON
PRAYER [40]
smile when C. moan MARLOWE [6]

Christmas
C. broached the mightiest ale SCOTT,
W. [10]
C. comes but once TUSSER [2]
C. Day in the Workhouse SIMS [1]
C. is coming ANONYMOUS [12]
dreaming of a white C. BERLIN,
IRVING [6]
Ghost of C. Past DICKENS [46]
mocking C. past KIPLING [1]
night before C. MOORE, C. C. [1]
On C. Day you can't get
sore LEHRER [2]
We'll keep our C. merry SCOTT, W. [9]

chronicler
no spirited c. HORACE [52]

chumps
C. ... make the best
husbands WODEHOUSE [5]

church
all the c. did echo SHAKESPEARE:
TAMING OF THE SHREW [5]
C. for his mother ST CYPRIAN [2]
c. he ... did not attend AMIS, K. [5]
C. is disaffected MACAULAY, LORD [13]
C. is like a magnificent
feast SELDEN [1]
C. of blurred edges CAREY, G. [1]
C. welcomes technological PIUS XII [1]
not the c. in a village BUTLER, S.
(1835–1902) [26]
some to c. repair POPE [18]
where God built a c. LUTHER [6]
wheresoever God buildeth a
c. BECON [1]

Church of England
Alas the C. DEFOE [11]
C. is the Tory Party DISRAELI [63]

Stink of the C. REXROTH [2]

churches
still they stand, the c. BETJEMAN [16]

Churchill
C. is ... a corrupt journalist HITLER [13]

churchmen
c. fain would kill TENNYSON [132]

churchyard
palsy-stricken, c. thing KEATS [72]
worse taste, than in a c. JOWETT [2]

Cibber
C.! write all thy verses POPE [166]

cigar
good c. is a smoke KIPLING [3]
post-prandial c. BUCHANAN, R. [3]
really good 5-cent c. MARSHALL, T. [1]

cigarette
c. is ... a perfect pleasure WILDE [53]
C. me, big boy ROGERS, G. [1]

cigarettes
smoke slender c. LAFORGUE [1]

Cinara
when C. was my queen HORACE [47]

cinema
c. gives us a substitute
world BAZIN [1]
c. is the truth GODARD [2]

cinéma-vérité
C.? I prefer 'cine-
mendacity' FELLINI [4]

circle
nature of God is a
c. ANONYMOUS [62]

circles
Do not disturb my c. ARCHIMEDES [3]

circumcised
C. the eighth day BIBLE, NEW
TESTAMENT: PHILIPPIANS [5]
Every man child ... shall be c. BIBLE,
OLD TESTAMENT: GENESIS [46]

circumference
This be thy just c. MILTON [156]

circumstances
c. are what render BURKE, E. [31]
fearful concatenation of c. WEBSTER,
D. [4]
I don't believe in c. SHAW [2]
I make c. NAPOLEON I [18]
Men are at the mercy of
c. HERODOTUS [3]

circus
gets the c. it deserves JONG [10]

citadel
his own airy c. KEATS [29]

cities
C. and thrones and
powers KIPLING [70]
C. are ...
distinguished BAUDRILLARD [1]
Towered c. please us MILTON [18]
Two c. have been
formed ST AUGUSTINE [7]

cloudy c. ... chilly women BYRON,
LORD [78]

climb
Fain would I c. RALEGH [20]

climbing
c. is performed in the same
position SWIFT, J. [11]

clime
change their c. HORACE [63]

Clinton
C. does not have the ...
character KISSINGER [8]

clock
c. ... is the key-machine MUMFORD,
L. [2]
forgot to wind up the c. STERNE [2]
no c. can measure BLAKE [24]
no c. in the forest SHAKESPEARE: AS
YOU LIKE IT [25]

Clootie
Auld Hornie, Satan, Nick, or
C. BURNS [11]

close
moving peacefully towards its
c. DAWSON, LORD [1]

closer
Come c., boys CHILDERS [3]

close-up
I'm ready for my c. SWANSON [2]

clothes
C. make the poor
invisible HARRINGTON [1]
casts off his worn-out c. BHAGAVAD-
GITA [2]
emperor's new c. ANDERSEN [1]
enterprises that require new
c. THOREAU [27]
poured into his c. WODEHOUSE [10]
soul of this man is his
c. SHAKESPEARE: ALL'S WELL [6]
wears her c., as if SWIFT, J. [51]

clothing
Strength and honour are her c. BIBLE,
OLD TESTAMENT: PROVERBS [101]

cloths
heavens' embroidered c. YEATS [16]

cloud
Get off of my c. JAGGER/RICHARDS
[2]
How sweet to be a C. MILNE [7]

cloudburst
Let the c. roil and toil FROST, R. [25]

cloud-cuckoo-land
What about 'C.' ARISTOPHANES [4]

clouds
c. contend with growing
light SHAKESPEARE: HENRY VI PT 3 [3]
comes with c. descending HYMNS &
CAROLS [51]
cometh with c. BIBLE, NEW
TESTAMENT: REVELATION [1]
prince of the c. BAUDELAIRE [18]

cloudy
c. princes SHAKESPEARE:
RICHARD III [9]

clover
four leaf c. DIXON [2]

clown
one thing only – and that is a
c. CHAPLIN [4]

clowns
Send in the c. SONDHEIM [6]

club
don't want to belong to any c. MARX,
G. [9]

Clunton
C. and Clunbury HOUSMAN [17]

CMG
C. ... ('Call Me God') SAMPSON [3]

coal
C. not dole POLITICAL SLOGANS [9]
shortage of c. and fish BEVAN [6]

coal-black
C. is better than another
hue SHAKESPEARE: TITUS
ANDRONICUS [5]

coalition
atmosphere of a C. ASQUITH, H.
[4]

coalitions
England does not love
c. DISRAELI [36]

coals
c. of fire BIBLE, OLD TESTAMENT:
PROVERBS [76]

coaster
Dirty British c. MASEFIELD [4]

coat
c. of many colours BIBLE, OLD
TESTAMENT: GENESIS [54]
I made my song a c. YEATS [26]

Cobbleigh
Uncle Tom C. and
all ANONYMOUS [94]

cocaine
C. habit-forming BANKHEAD [4]
saves America by sniffing
c. GINSBERG [10]

cock
before the c. crow BIBLE, NEW
TESTAMENT: MATTHEW [160]
C. and a Bull STERNE [22]
c. can crow TROLLOPE [8]
c. has great influence PUBLILIUS
SYRUS [5]
c. with lively din MILTON [15]
immediately the c. crew BIBLE, NEW
TESTAMENT: MATTHEW [167]
mere c., have made the sun
rise ROSTAND, E. [2]

Cock Robin
Who killed C. NURSERY RHYMES [51]

cockloft
c. is unfurnished RABELAIS [11]

cocktail
c. is a pleasant drink ADE [3]

cocktails
skyscrapers, jazz, and c. GARCÍA
LORCA [5]

cocoa
C. is a cad and a
coward CHESTERTON [31]

coffee
C. in England is just toasted
milk FRY, C. [9]
C. ... makes the politician
wise POPE [46]
Damned fine cup of c. LYNCH [1]
measured out my life with c.
spoons ELIOT, T. S. [5]

coffee-house
echo of a London c. SWIFT, J. [21]

cogito
C., ergo sum DESCARTES [3]

coil
shuffled off this mortal
c. SHAKESPEARE: HAMLET [87]

coincidences
don't care much for c. BARNES, J. [2]

coition
trivial and vulgar way of
c. BROWNE [14]

coitum
Post c. omne animal ANONYMOUS [80]

Coke
Things go better with C. ADVERTISING
SLOGANS [30]

cold
leapt ... past the common c. AYRES [4]

Cold War
C. isn't thawing NIXON [3]
in the midst of a c. BARUCH [1]
man who ended the C. LE CARRÉ [5]

Cole
Old King C. NURSERY RHYMES [26]

Coleridge
C. – he who sits obscure SHELLEY,
P. B. [49]
C., too, has lately taken wing BYRON,
LORD [89]

collision
wish to avoid foreign c. CLAY [1]

colonialism
C. is not a thinking
machine FANON [2]

colonization
future c. by any European
powers MONROE, J. [1]

colony
founders of a new c. HAWTHORNE [4]

color-line
problem of the c. DU BOIS [5]

colour
c. ... can speak to the soul WILDE [28]
C. is my day-long
obsession MONET [1]

C. possesses me KLEE [1]

judged by the c. of their skin KING, M. L. [18]

which love c. the most RUSKIN [9]

colours

All c. will agree in the dark BACON, F. [7]

come

c. without warning DAVIS, T. [2]

comedian

test of a real c. NATHAN [5]

comedians

quick c./... will stage us SHAKESPEARE: ANTONY & CLEOPATRA [39]

We are bad c. GREENE, G. [13]

comedies

c. are ended by a marriage BYRON, LORD [113]

comedy

All I need to make a c. CHAPLIN [1]

C. comes from conflict MITCHELL, W. [1]

C. is an escape FRY, C. [7]

C. is tragedy CARTER, A. [9]

C. naturally wears itself out HAZLITT [2]

result is c. KUBRICK [2]

comest

Whence c. thou BIBLE, OLD TESTAMENT: JOB [2]

comets

C., importing change SHAKESPEARE: HENRY VI PT 1 [1]

comfort

beg cold c. SHAKESPEARE: KING JOHN [16]

c. me with apples BIBLE, OLD TESTAMENT: SONG OF SOLOMON [7]

C. must not be expected BYRON, LORD [10]

c. ... turns a man against DURKHEIM [1]

c. ye my people BIBLE, OLD TESTAMENT: ISAIAH [51]

lust for c. GIBRAN [4]

mutual society, help, and c. BOOK OF COMMON PRAYER [79]

Of c. no man speak SHAKESPEARE: RICHARD II [22]

receives c. like cold porridge SHAKESPEARE: TEMPEST [11]

comfortable

Hear what c. words BOOK OF COMMON PRAYER [58]

put on something more c. HARLOW [1]

comforter

C. ... where is your comforting HOPKINS [27]

comforters

Miserable c. BIBLE, OLD TESTAMENT: JOB [28]

coming

c., my own, my sweet TENNYSON [130]

cold c. we had of it ELIOT, T. S. [30]

command

c. me to do what you will ST AUGUSTINE [5]

dainty thing to c. CERVANTES [43]

commandeth

No man c. safely THOMAS À KEMPIS [5]

commandments

God's c. broke in's face MASEFIELD [6]

On these two c. BIBLE, NEW TESTAMENT: MATTHEW [133]

ten c. on your face SHAKESPEARE: HENRY VI PT 2 [2]

commands

I gave c. BROWNING, R. [9]

comment

I couldn't possibly c. DAVIES, A. [2]

commerce

C. has set the mark SHELLEY, P. B. [9]

selfish spirit of c. JEFFERSON [26]

committee

C. – a group of men ALLEN, F. [5]

c. is organic PARKINSON, C. N. [2]

commodity

c. appears ... obvious MARX, K. [11]

tickling c. SHAKESPEARE: KING JOHN [3]

common

C. looking people are the best LINCOLN [26]

had all things c. BIBLE, NEW TESTAMENT: ACTS [5]

Life is lived in c. HARRINGTON [2]

make it too c. SHAKESPEARE: HENRY IV PT 2 [8]

never live like c. people COCKER [1]

not in the roll of c. men SHAKESPEARE: HENRY IV PT 1 [27]

common sense

astonishes ... so much as c. EMERSON [26]

C. is judgment without VICO [1]

C. is not so common VOLTAIRE [20]

I turn the hose/Of c. GILBERT, W. S. [25]

man of great c. ... meaning thereby SHAW [11]

rarest gift/... C. MEREDITH, G. [7]

commonplace

c. crowd of the little famous KEATS [53]

C. people dislike tragedy MASEFIELD [5]

commonest c. TENNYSON [191]

Men are seldom more c. BUTLER, S. (1835–1902) [22]

rights of the c. ORTEGA Y GASSET [4]

unassuming c./Of Nature WORDSWORTH, W. [75]

communicate

do good and to c. BIBLE, NEW TESTAMENT: HEBREWS [15]

failure to c. MARTIN [1]

communication

no pleasure ... without c. MONTAIGNE [26]

communications

Evil c. corrupt BIBLE, NEW TESTAMENT: 1 CORINTHIANS [40]

communism

c. is a dead dog SOLZHENITSYN [9]

C. is a hammer MAO ZEDONG [10]

C. ... is more than Marxism GREENE, G. [14]

C. ... is one-third practice ROGERS, W. [3]

C. is Soviet power LENIN [15]

C. is the opiate LUCE [4]

'C.' of the English intellectual ORWELL [8]

C. was ... pie in the sky YELTSIN [1]

clock of c. has stopped SOLZHENITSYN [10]

crusade against C. TAYLOR, A. J. P. [2]

fall of C. JOHN PAUL II [4]

Russian C. is the ... child of Karl Marx ATTLEE [2]

spectre of c. MARX/ENGELS [6]

communist

C. intellectuals are savages SARTRE [10]

I am a C. GORBACHEV [2]

one cannot be a C. DJILAS [2]

What is a c. ELLIOT, E. [1]

community

unite into a c. LOCKE [12]

commuter

C. – one who spends his life WHITE, E. B. [5]

company

Do equally desire your c. JONSON [21]

give me your bill of c. SWIFT, J. [19]

love to be the worst of the c. SWIFT, J. [18]

More c. increases happiness TRAHERNE [9]

My idea of good c. AUSTEN [36]

Take the tone of the c. CHESTERFIELD [5]

Tell me thy c. CERVANTES [39]

villainous c. SHAKESPEARE: HENRY IV PT 1 [36]

comparisons

C. are odorous SHAKESPEARE: MUCH ADO [20]

compasses

As stiff twin c. are two DONNE [24]

compassion

C. has no place BERGER [11]

contradictory
c. is also true WILDE [32]

contraries
hateful siege/Of c. MILTON [168]
we behold ... from c. BRUNO, G. [2]
white and black are not
c. AQUINAS [4]
Without c. is no
progression BLAKE [16]

contrary
Mary, Mary, quite c. NURSERY
RHYMES [25]

contrive
head to c. CLARENDON [1]

controversy
c. is ... superfluous or
hopeless NEWMAN [2]
ceases to be a subject of
c. HAZLITT [31]

conventionality
C. is not morality BRONTË, C. [4]

conversation
boneless quality of English c. HALSEY,
M. [1]
c. of the old and young JOHNSON,
S. [15]
C. should touch
everything WILDE [26]
Hail, C., soothing power MORE, H. [7]
happiest c. JOHNSON, S. [135]
No one will ever shine in
c. LOCKIER [3]
no such thing as c. WEST, R. [1]
nothing so dangerous ... as
c. CHRISTIE [4]
secret of succeeding in c. FRANKLIN,
B. [2]
Sex is a c. USTINOV [7]
stick on c.'s burrs HOLMES SR [3]
Things said for c. EMERSON [72]

converse
sweet c. of an innocent
mind KEATS [4]

conversing
With thee c. MILTON [142]

converted
You have not c. a man MORLEY, J. [2]

conviction
Never lay yourself open to ... c. HUNT,
L. [1]

convictions
I have no definite c. JUNG [25]
our c. are hills FITZGERALD, F. S. [1]

convinces
credit goes to the man who
c. DARWIN, F. [1]

cook
C., The Thief, His Wife GREENAWAY [1]
ill c. that cannot lick SHAKESPEARE:
ROMEO & JULIET [37]
indispensable quality in a c. BRILLAT-
SAVARIN [3]

cookery
Not on morality, but on c. CARLYLE,
T. [21]

cooks
civilized man cannot live without
c. MEREDITH, O. [1]

cool
C. as a mountain stream ADVERTISING
SLOGANS [6]

coots
haunts of c. and hern TENNYSON [135]

Copacabana
graduate of the C. school SANDERS [1]

copied
writers have c. the old authors PLINY
THE ELDER [1]

copier
mere c. of nature REYNOLDS, J. [3]

copies
only good c. LA ROCHEFOUCAULD [14]

copulation
Let c. thrive SHAKESPEARE: KING
LEAR [47]

Corinth
not everyone ... can get to
C. HORACE [65]

cork
Lighter than a c. RIMBAUD [6]

cormorant
c. devouring Time SHAKESPEARE:
LOVE'S LABOUR'S LOST [1]

corn
c. is as high HAMMERSTEIN II [5]
c. was orient and immortal
wheat TRAHERNE [6]
make two ears of c. ... to grow SWIFT,
J. [31]

corner
not done in a c. BIBLE, NEW
TESTAMENT: ACTS [43]

Cornish
twenty thousand C. men HAWKER [1]

corny
c. as Kansas in
August HAMMERSTEIN II [10]

coronets
Kind hearts are more than
c. TENNYSON [24]

corporation
C. ... device for obtaining BIERCE [15]

corpse
c. in their mouth VANEIGEM [2]
frozen c. was he LONGFELLOW [6]
good-looking c. DEREK [1]
make a lovely c. DICKENS [55]

corpses
does not eat c. SHAW [80]

corpus
Hoc est c. meum MISSAL [16]

correcteth
Lord loveth he c. BIBLE, OLD
TESTAMENT: PROVERBS [4]

Corregio
corregiescity of C. STERNE [14]

correspondences
C. are like smallclothes SMITH,
SYDNEY [5]

corridors
c. of power SNOW [1]

corrupt
Among a people generally c. BURKE,
E. [25]

corrupted
manners and fashions c. JONSON
[40]
when girls have been c. SPRENGER/
KRAMER [1]

corrupter
c. of words SHAKESPEARE: TWELFTH
NIGHT [26]

corruptible
I go from a c. ... Crown CHARLES I [3]

corruption
C., the most infallible GIBBON [5]
sown in c. BIBLE, NEW TESTAMENT:
1 CORINTHIANS [42]
Stewed in c. SHAKESPEARE:
HAMLET [123]
strong enough to resist
c. GARFIELD [2]

corrupts
c. the youth SOCRATES [3]

cosmopolitan
C. critics DISRAELI [52]

cosmos
c. is a gigantic fly-
wheel MENCKEN [11]

cost
That which c. little CERVANTES [19]

costume
same c. will be LAVER [1]

cough
c. like a sheep WODEHOUSE [9]
I never let them c. BARRYMORE [2]
Keep a c. by them CHURCHILL,
CHARLES [5]

coughs
C. and sneezes ANONYMOUS [14]

counsel
c. of the ungodly BIBLE, OLD
TESTAMENT: PSALMS [1]
darkeneth c. BIBLE, OLD TESTAMENT:
JOB [40]
took sweet c. together BIBLE, OLD
TESTAMENT: PSALMS [67]
turn to one another for c. GIBRAN
[9]

counsellors
multitude of c. BIBLE, OLD TESTAMENT:
PROVERBS [22]

count
but I won the c. SOMOZA [1]

counted
c. them all out HANRAHAN [1]

countenance
light of thy c. BIBLE, OLD TESTAMENT:
PSALMS [4]
counter
things c., original, spare HOPKINS [12]
counterpane
pleasant land of c. STEVENSON,
R. L. [33]
counting
C. is the religion STEIN [11]
country
Anybody can be good in the
c. WILDE [62]
blessed is he who leads a c.
life DRYDEN [73]
c. in the town MARTIAL [11]
c. is not a mere territory MAZZINI [4]
c. is the world PAINE [13]
c. ... kind of healthy grave SMITH,
SYDNEY [4]
c. that is at ease with itself MAJOR [2]
Cry, the Beloved C. PATON [1]
die for one's c. HORACE [36]
everyday story of c. folk ARCHERS [1]
Everyone loathes his own
c. DURRELL [1]
For their c., their children SALLUST
[2]
God made the c. COWPER [32]
good of my c. FARQUHAR [13]
He likes the c. COWPER [24]
I loathe the c. CONGREVE [20]
I vow to thee my c. HYMNS &
CAROLS [43]
know ... his own c. STERNE [18]
living in the c. COLETTE [1]
long for the c. HORACE [13]
love of c. is the best
preventive BORROW [1]
My c., right or wrong SCHURZ [1]
My c., 'tis of thee SMITH, SAMUEL F. [1]
My soul, there is a c. VAUGHAN [4]
nothing good ... in the c. HAZLITT [5]
One day in the c. ROSSETTI, C. [12]
Our c. is the world GARRISON [3]
our c. ought to be lovely BURKE,
E. [39]
our c., right or wrong DECATUR [1]
speak of his love for his
c. MENCKEN [17]
what we can do for our c. HOLMES
JR [1]
what your c. can do KENNEDY, J. F. [8]
Without c. you have neither
name MAZZINI [3]
Your c. needs you ANONYMOUS [103]
courage
all kinds of c. ROWLING [1]
Be of good c. BIBLE, OLD TESTAMENT:
ISAIAH [60]
Be strong and of a good c. BIBLE, OLD
TESTAMENT: DEUTERONOMY [15]

C. is not simply LEWIS, C. S. [3]
c. is ... small steps KONRÁD [1]
c. is to do without witnesses LA
ROCHEFOUCAULD [17]
C. was mine, and I had
mystery OWEN [5]
French c. proceeds from
vanity BYRON, LORD [110]
screw your c. to the sticking-
place SHAKESPEARE: MACBETH [29]
There is danger in c. COMPTON-
BURNETT [3]
two o'clock in the morning
c. NAPOLEON I [7]
court
c. is only as sound as its jury LEE,
H. [3]
courteous
c. is not scorned CONFUCIUS [37]
courtesies
small sweet c. of life STERNE [27]
courtesy
greater man, the greater
c. TENNYSON [167]
his c. was somewhat
extravagant WAUGH [14]
very pink of c. SHAKESPEARE: ROMEO
& JULIET [25]
courts
C. and camps are the only
places CHESTERFIELD [4]
day in thy c. BIBLE, OLD TESTAMENT:
PSALMS [90]
courtship
C. to marriage CONGREVE [6]
dream in c. POPE [34]
cousins
his sisters, and his c. GILBERT, W. S.
[4]
couture
Haute C. should be fun LACROIX [1]
covenant
c. between me and thee BIBLE, OLD
TESTAMENT: GENESIS [45]
covers
c. ... are too far apart BIERCE [35]
covet
inclined to believe what they
c. BYRON, LORD [34]
Thou shalt not c. BIBLE, OLD
TESTAMENT: EXODUS [25]
Thou shalt not c. CLOUGH [5]
cow
c. jumped over the moon NURSERY
RHYMES [13]
I wrote the 'Purple C.' BURGESS, G. [2]
never saw a Purple C. BURGESS, G. [1]
work the way a c. grazes KOLLWITZ [1]
coward
He was just a c. HEMINGWAY [16]
No c. soul is mine BRONTË, E. [4]
seem or to be ... a c. POE [14]

cowardice
C. ... distinguished from
panic HEMINGWAY [18]
guilty of Noel C. DE VRIES [2]
cowardly
C. dogs bark loudest WEBSTER, J. [7]
cowards
all men would be c. ROCHESTER [8]
C. die many times SHAKESPEARE:
JULIUS CAESAR [19]
fall by the hands of c. TACITUS [11]
cowboy
last true c. in America LEAST HEAT-
MOON [2]
cows
C. are my passion DICKENS [63]
facts are like c. SAYERS [2]
cowslip
C. and shad-blow CRANE, H. [1]
coy
make me c. and tender HERBERT,
G. [26]
cozenage
this town is full of c. SHAKESPEARE:
COMEDY OF ERRORS [1]
cradle
c. of the common man WALLACE,
W. R. [1]
c. rocks above an abyss NABOKOV [6]
from the c. to the grave SHELLEY,
P. B. [60]
Instead of rocking the c. ROBINSON,
M. [1]
cradling
Gehenna – an evil c. KORAN [13]
craft
In my c. or sullen art THOMAS, D. [10]
crag
clasps the c. TENNYSON [118]
crane
Jane, Jane,/Tall as a c. SITWELL [1]
cranks
C. live by theory MACAULAY, R. [1]
crap
total c. RATNER [1]
crash
car c. harnesses ...
eroticism BALLARD [1]
crazy
Still c. after all these years SIMON [7]
cream
Skim milk masquerades as
c. GILBERT, W. S. [6]
created
by him were all things c. BIBLE, NEW
TESTAMENT: COLOSSIANS [1]
consider of what he was
c. KORAN [49]
Thou hast c. all things BIBLE, NEW
TESTAMENT: REVELATION [15]
creation
About the lords o' the c. BURNS [4]

before embarking upon
C. ALFONSO X [1]

I hold C. in my foot HUGHES, TED [5]

creative
c. imagination as a fruit
machine LARKIN [4]

In the c. process STANISLAVSKY [1]

sensitive being, a c.
soul WORDSWORTH, W. [23]

creativity
C. doesn't flourish JAMES, P. D. [3]

c. ... starts where
language KOESTLER [5]

Creator
Remember now thy C. BIBLE, OLD
TESTAMENT: ECCLESIASTES [40]

creature
c. more than the Creator BIBLE, NEW
TESTAMENT: ROMANS [4]

every c. of God is good BIBLE, NEW
TESTAMENT: 1 TIMOTHY [6]

creatures
Upon the c. we have
made GOETHE [29]

credit
Blest paper-c. POPE [103]

credo
C. in unum Deum MISSAL [10]

credulity
little c. helps GASKELL [1]

credulous
Man is a c. animal RUSSELL, B. [20]

creed
His c. no parson ever knew DOYLE,
F. [1]

Sapping a solemn c. BYRON,
LORD [60]

creeds
dust of c. outworn SHELLEY, P. B.
[54]

half-believers of our casual
c. ARNOLD, M. [29]

strewn with c. and
institutions BAGEHOT [32]

teach them neither c. GODWIN [5]

Vain are the thousand c. BRONTË,
E. [5]

creep
C. into thy narrow bed ARNOLD,
M. [48]

make your flesh c. DICKENS [8]

Men c./Not walk WHITTIER [5]

crème
c. de la crème SPARK [3]

Cretians
C. are alway liars BIBLE, NEW
TESTAMENT: TITUS [1]

cricket
C. is ... a dramatic spectacle JAMES,
C. L. R. [1]

c. is the greatest thing PINTER [4]

c. test TEBBIT [3]

far more than a game, this
c. CARDUS [1]

remembrance of English
c. ANONYMOUS [44]

cried
when he c. the little children
died AUDEN [13]

crime
C. ... has its degrees RACINE [4]

C. is an equal-opportunity ICE-T [1]

c. is due to the repressed
desire WAUGH [5]

C. is naught but
misdirected GOLDMAN, E. [3]

c. is only a lefthanded
form HUSTON [1]

C. is terribly revealing CHRISTIE [3]

Commit a c. EMERSON [18]

From a single c. know the
nation VIRGIL [29]

not c. that has increased LEE, L. [1]

original 'c.' of 'niggers' WALKER
[8]

shocking c. was
committed TACITUS [8]

Tough on c. BLAIR, T. [1]

We must ... call c.
necessary DURKHEIM [2]

crimes
c. ... and misfortunes of
mankind GIBBON [3]

C. ... are their own
rewards FARQUHAR [7]

C. of which a people is
ashamed GENET [4]

c. which become innocent LA
ROCHEFOUCAULD [2]

May reach the dignity of c. MORE,
H. [3]

criminal
Every society gets the ... c. KENNEDY,
R. F. [1]

most dangerous c. CHESTERTON [17]

crises
history is nothing
but ...'c.' IONESCO [3]

Criseÿda
C. gan al his chere
aspien CHAUCER [10]

crisis
C.? What crisis SUN [1]

exciting to have a real
c. THATCHER [8]

Crispian
day is called the Feast of
C. SHAKESPEARE: HENRY V [28]

critic
c. bred in Nature's school SHEE [2]

c. is a bundle of biases BALLIET [2]

c. is the only independent KAEL [4]

drama c. in the
daytime WODEHOUSE [15]

good c. . . . relates the
adventures FRANCE [1]

good drama c. perceives TYNAN [7]

critical
c. method DE MAN [1]

nothing if not c. SHAKESPEARE:
OTHELLO [20]

criticism
c. of the critic NATHAN [4]

C. prevents art from
forgetting ELLMANN [2]

C. should be a casual
conversation AUDEN [29]

c. should be partial BAUDELAIRE [1]

C., that fine flower CONRAD [26]

criticize
c. is to appreciate JAMES, H. [24]

don't c./What you can't
understand DYLAN [3]

criticized
If you are not c. RUMSFELD [1]

criticizes
What the public c. COCTEAU [4]

critics
Around the throne of God ... no
c. JARRELL [3]

c. all are ready made BYRON, LORD [6]

C. are sentinels LONGFELLOW [17]

children one's 'mature' c. WALKER [7]

lot of c. MOORE, G. [1]

When the c. come around NOLAN [1]

crocodile
cruel crafty c. SPENSER [11]

How doth the little c. CARROLL [4]

Cromwell
C., our chief of men MILTON [76]

crony
against government by c. ICKES [2]

ancient, trusty, drouthy c. BURNS [42]

crook
I'm not a c. NIXON [9]

crooked
c. cannot be made straight BIBLE, OLD
TESTAMENT: ECCLESIASTES [7]

There was a c. man NURSERY
RHYMES [42]

cross
Bear the c. gladly THOMAS À
KEMPIS [9]

c. of gold BRYAN [3]

cherish the old rugged c. HYMNS &
CAROLS [68]

hath no c. deserves no
crown QUARLES [1]

no c., no crown. PENN [1]

on his breast a bloody c. SPENSER [7]

crossed
What I have c. out DE MILLE [1]

crosses
clinging to their c. CHESTERTON [35]

crow
upstart c. GREENE, R. [4]

crowd
apparition of these faces in the
c. POUND [6]
c. has a silver lining BARNUM [1]
c. is not company BACON, F. [27]
human c. has been the
lesson NERUDA [8]
So much they scorn the c. POPE
[25]

crowds
C. without company GIBBON [16]
sign of perpetual c. MEYNELL [2]

crown
broke his c. NURSERY RHYMES [16]
c. of our life as it
closes SWINBURNE [24]
head that wears a c. SHAKESPEARE:
HENRY IV PT 2 [18]
sweet fruition of an earthly
c. MARLOWE [13]

crucified
When They C. My
Lord ANONYMOUS [99]

crucify
c. him BIBLE, NEW TESTAMENT:
JOHN [64]
They're going to c. me LENNON [3]

cruel
c. only to be kind SHAKESPEARE:
HAMLET [126]

cruelty
C. has a human heart BLAKE [63]
C. is ... the energy in a man DE
SADE [5]
c. ... necessary
result SCHOPENHAUER [2]
C. ... requires no motive ELIOT, G. [5]
C. ... the worst kind of
sin CHESTERTON [10]
Theatre of c. ARTAUD [2]

cruise
all on our last c. STEVENSON, R. L.
[14]

crumbs
c. ... from the rich man's table BIBLE,
NEW TESTAMENT: LUKE [52]
dogs eat of the c. BIBLE, NEW
TESTAMENT: MATTHEW [110]

crumpet
thinking man's c. MUIR, F. [2]

crusade
Party is a moral c. WILSON, H. [2]
this c., this war on terrorism BUSH,
G. W. [3]

crust
munch a c. of brown
bread CERVANTES [6]

cry
c. away DICKENS [22]

crying
C. is the refuge WILDE [70]
C.'s like pissing SWIFT, G. [4]

Cuba
C. ... the most interesting
addition JEFFERSON [37]

cubit
add one c. BIBLE, NEW TESTAMENT:
MATTHEW [44]

cuckoo
as the c. is in June SHAKESPEARE:
HENRY IV PT 1 [34]
C.! Shall I call thee
bird WORDSWORTH, W. [73]
flew over the c.'s nest NURSERY
RHYMES [48]
hear the pleasant c. DAVIES, W. H. [2]
merry c., messenger of
Spring SPENSER [20]

cuckoo clock
what did they produce? The
c. WELLES [2]

cucumbers
as cold as c. BEAUMONT AND
FLETCHER [1]
extracting sunbeams out of c. SWIFT,
J. [32]
garden of c. BIBLE, OLD TESTAMENT:
ISAIAH [2]

cudgel
C. thy brains no more SHAKESPEARE:
HAMLET [145]

culpa
Mea c. MISSAL [4]

cult
What is a c. ALTMAN [1]

culture
bastard form of mass c. BARTHES [9]
c. has reached a dead end MARCUS
[3]
C. is ... as important CONFUCIUS [25]
C. is a sort of theatre SAID [2]
C. is only true when ...
critical ADORNO [3]
C. is the tacit agreement KRAUS [7]
c. ... means thinking well GRAMSCI [1]
C. ... the best that has been
known ARNOLD, M. [56]
C. ... which makes life worth
living ELIOT, T. S. [58]
C., which smooth the whole
world GOETHE [27]
knowledge of one other c. MEAD [1]
pursue C. in bands WHARTON [2]
term c. ... includes ELIOT, T. S. [59]
Whenever I hear the word
C. GOERING [2]
When I hear the word c. GODARD [3]

cultures
two c. SNOW [2]

cunning
greatest c. is to have
none SANDBURG [8]
weak in courage is strong in
c. BLAKE [34]

cup
c. runneth over BIBLE, OLD
TESTAMENT: PSALMS [26]
drunk their c. a round KHAYYÁM [7]
fill the c. that clears KHAYYÁM [6]
let this c. pass from me BIBLE, NEW
TESTAMENT: MATTHEW [161]
life's enchanted c. BYRON, LORD [55]

cupboard
c. was bare NURSERY RHYMES [27]

Cupid
giant-dwarf, Dan C. SHAKESPEARE:
LOVE'S LABOUR'S LOST [10]

cups
Nor shall our c. make any
guilty JONSON [22]
when they are in their c. BIBLE,
APOCRYPHA: 1 ESDRAS [3]

curates
abundant shower of c. BRONTË, C.
[14]

curds
queen of c. and cream SHAKESPEARE:
WINTER'S TALE [15]

curfew
c. tolls the knell of parting day GRAY,
T. [8]

curiosities
c. would be quite forgot AUBREY [1]

curiosity
C. is ... incontinency TAYLOR, J. [3]
C. is one of the lowest ...
faculties FORSTER [21]
C. is one of the most
permanent JOHNSON, S. [17]
intellectual c. is the life
blood TREVELYAN [3]
People die when c. goes SWIFT, G. [2]

curious
c. in unnecessary matters BIBLE,
APOCRYPHA: ECCLESIASTICUS [7]

curiouser
C. and curiouser CARROLL [3]

currency
debauch the c. KEYNES [2]

current
Beneath the azure c.
floweth LERMONTOV [2]

curse
c. God, and die BIBLE, OLD TESTAMENT:
JOB [7]
c. in a dead man's eye COLERIDGE,
S. T. [28]
C. not the king BIBLE, OLD TESTAMENT:
ECCLESIASTES [35]
leave my son a c. CARNEGIE, A. [6]

curseth
c. his father BIBLE, OLD TESTAMENT:
EXODUS [28]

curtain
iron c. has descended CHURCHILL,
W. [41]

new terrors of d. ARBUTHNOT [1]

No d. may be called
futile MISHIMA [4]

No one's d. comes to pass BROCH [1]

not d., but dying FIELDING,
HENRY [13]

not in mere d. that men
die BROWNING, E. B. [18]

nothing ... more beautiful than
d. WHITMAN [5]

nothing noble in d. TRUMBO [1]

O d., how bitter BIBLE, APOCRYPHA:
ECCLESIASTICUS [62]

O D. in Life TENNYSON [71]

O D., where is thy sting-a-
ling-a-ling ANONYMOUS [65]

One lives one's d. SARTRE [7]

only a gamble with d. DELILLO [7]

owe God a d. SHAKESPEARE: HENRY IV
PT 2 [22]

Pale D. beats equally HORACE [17]

Prepare for d. JOHNSON, S. [3]

preparing themselves for ...
d. SOCRATES [12]

punish Christian men with d. BOOK
OF COMMON PRAYER [94]

rendezvous with D. SEEGER, A. [1]

report of my d. ... an
exaggeration TWAIN [33]

savage d. ... hacks man down EPIC OF
GILGAMESH [4]

secret house of d. SHAKESPEARE:
ANTONY & CLEOPATRA [33]

shadow of d. BIBLE, NEW TESTAMENT:
LUKE [6]

shall never see d. BIBLE, NEW
TESTAMENT: JOHN [36]

sharpness of d. BOOK OF COMMON
PRAYER [11]

single d. is a tragedy STALIN [5]

so universal as d. SWIFT, J. [58]

sudden d. BOOK OF COMMON
PRAYER [36]

swallow up d. in victory BIBLE, OLD
TESTAMENT: ISAIAH [34]

thou owest God a d. SHAKESPEARE:
HENRY IV PT 1 [44]

Thou shalt die the d. BIBLE,
APOCRYPHA: ECCLESIASTICUS [33]

'tis D. is dead, not he SHELLEY,
P. B. [78]

truly longed for d. TENNYSON [52]

valley of the shadow of d. BIBLE, OLD
TESTAMENT: PSALMS [25]

vasty hall of d. ARNOLD, M. [25]

death penalty
abolish the d. KARR [1]

deaths
More d. than one must
die WILDE [112]

debatable
d. land MACAULAY, LORD [10]

debauchery
D. is perhaps an act of
despair GONCOURT [5]

Deborah
I D. arose BIBLE, OLD TESTAMENT:
JUDGES [4]

debt
In ... life we are in d. MUMFORD,
E.W. [2]

debtor
d. ... to the Greeks BIBLE, NEW
TESTAMENT: ROMANS [2]

decay
d. through over-
civilization CONNOLLY, C. [17]
human things are subject to
d. DRYDEN [42]
Thy d. ... /impregnate with
divinity BYRON, LORD [81]
We d./Like corpses SHELLEY, P. B.
[76]

decayed
you are sufficiently d. GILBERT,
W. S. [38]

deceitfulness
d. of riches BIBLE, NEW TESTAMENT:
MATTHEW [97]

deceive
sweet to d. the deceiver LA
FONTAINE [2]
When first we practise to d. SCOTT,
W. [11]

deceived
surest way to be d. LA
ROCHEFOUCAULD [13]

deceiver
I'm a gay d. COLMAN [3]
Welcome, thou kind d. DRYDEN [23]

deceivers
Men were d. ever SHAKESPEARE:
MUCH ADO [11]

deceives
Everything that d. PLATO [4]

Decembers
fifteen wild D. BRONTË, E. [1]

decency
English d. is a rather dirty
thing SHAW [15]
want of d. DILLON [2]

decent
Better d. than
indecent MACMILLAN [7]
d. means poor PEACOCK [4]

decently
things be done d. BIBLE, NEW
TESTAMENT: 1 CORINTHIANS [35]

deception
d. that elevates us TSVETAEVA [5]

decision
d. is like the ... swoop SUN TZU [3]
hard, fast and specific
d. TUCHMAN [2]

decisions
bold d. were fair at first LIVY [4]
great d., not easy
decisions STEVENSON, A. [1]
opportunity of taking d. PARKINSON,
C. N. [4]
record all the d. formerly
made SWIFT, J. [37]

deconstruction
America *is* d. DERRIDA [3]

decoration
great office of d. MORRIS, W. [3]

decorum
Let them cant about d. BURNS [3]
Limping D. lingers far behind BYRON,
LORD [3]

dedicate
We cannot d. ... this
ground LINCOLN [24]

deed
d. is everything GOETHE [30]
d. without a name SHAKESPEARE:
MACBETH [74]
great just D. BROWNING, E. B. [30]
If one good d. ... I did/I do
repent SHAKESPEARE: TITUS
ANDRONICUS [6]
prompt in d. CONFUCIUS [16]

deeds
looks/Quite through the
d. SHAKESPEARE: JULIUS CAESAR [7]
our d. determine us ELIOT, G. [9]
sight of means to do ill
d. SHAKESPEARE: KING JOHN [13]
thing that ends all other
d. SHAKESPEARE: ANTONY &
CLEOPATRA [35]

deejay
Hang the d. MORRISSEY [2]

deep
After that it gets d. COPE [2]
commit his body to the d. BOOK OF
COMMON PRAYER [91]
D. calleth unto deep BIBLE, OLD
TESTAMENT: PSALMS [55]
From the great d. TENNYSON [149]
Rocked in the cradle of the
d. WILLARD [1]

deer
where the d. had lain GWYN [2]

defeat
D. doesn't finish a man NIXON [10]
Man is not made for
d. HEMINGWAY [23]
possibilities of d. VICTORIA [8]

defects
making their d.
respectable VOLTAIRE [4]

defence
d. of England BALDWIN, S. [4]
Never make a d. or
apology CHARLES I [1]

no d. like elaborate courtesy LUCAS,
  E. V. [2]
defend
  d. the bad DAY LEWIS [6]
  d. to the death your right to
    say VOLTAIRE [32]
define
  Trying to d. yourself WATTS, A. [2]
definition
  d. is a sack of flour GOURMONT [4]
dégoût
  no returning from a d. MONTAGU [3]
degree
  Freedom doth with d.
    dispense JONSON [25]
  Take but d. away SHAKESPEARE:
    TROILUS & CRESSIDA [3]
degrees
  name you the d. SHAKESPEARE: AS
    YOU LIKE IT [38]
delapidation
  beautiful in d. SMITH, LOGAN P. [5]
delay
  D. always breeds
    danger CERVANTES [17]
  In d./We waste our
    lights SHAKESPEARE: ROMEO &
    JULIET [7]
  sweet reluctant amorous
    d. MILTON [137]
delays
  d. have dangerous
    ends SHAKESPEARE: HENRY VI PT 1 [5]
  Life admits not of d. JOHNSON,
    S. [107]
delectable
  D. Mountains BUNYAN [10]
delenda
  D. est Carthago CATO THE ELDER [3]
deliberates
  woman that d. is lost ADDISON [19]
deliberation
  D. ... act of examining one's
    bread BIERCE [17]
delight
  d. in it is better CONFUCIUS [19]
  d. that consumes the
    desire SWINBURNE [22]
  my ever new d. MILTON [147]
  Some are born to sweet d. BLAKE [77]
  Spirit of D. SHELLEY, P. B. [97]
delights
  king of intimate d. COWPER [42]
  violent d. have violent
    ends SHAKESPEARE: ROMEO &
    JULIET [26]
Delors
  Up Yours, D. SUN [5]
deluded
  heaven to be d. LEE, N. [1]
déluge
  Après nous le d. POMPADOUR [1]

demagogue
  d. is a person with
    whom MARQUIS [11]
  d. is usually sly COOPER, J. F. [3]
  Whatever else a d.
    requires ARISTOPHANES [1]
demands
  d. that a gentleman
    makes CONFUCIUS [32]
democracies
  genius of d. TOCQUEVILLE [7]
  tendency of d. COOPER, J. F. [1]
democracy
  All the ills of d. SMITH, ALFRED E. [1]
  D.! Bah GINSBERG [8]
  d. ... charming form of
    government SOCRATES [26]
  D. ... election by the
    incompetent SHAW [29]
  D. gives every man LOWELL, J. R. [16]
  D. ... government by
    discussion ATTLEE [3]
  D. ... government by the
    uneducated CHESTERTON [42]
  D. is a political
    method SCHUMPETER [7]
  D. is the theory MENCKEN [1]
  d. is the worst ...
    Government CHURCHILL, W. [42]
  D. means/Everybody but
    me HUGHES, L. [4]
  D. means ... the
    bludgeoning WILDE [10]
  d. never lasts long ADAMS, J. [7]
  D./What will you bring us
    to ARISTOPHANES [5]
  If d. is so stupid GOEBBELS [1]
  justice makes d. possible NIEBUHR
    [2]
  little less d. to save ATKINSON [1]
  modern d. is a tyranny MAILER [4]
  not the voting that's d. STOPPARD [7]
  two basic ideas of d. MANN, T. [8]
  Two cheers for D. FORSTER [28]
  understand the meaning of
    d. MAXWELL [2]
  world must be made safe for
    d. WILSON, W. [7]
  worst thing I can say about
    d. BEVAN [2]
democratic
  application of d.
    methods TROTSKY [7]
  swear by the d. republic ENGELS [2]
Democratic Party
  D. is like a mule DONNELLY [1]
demon-lover
  wailing for her d. COLERIDGE, S. T. [5]
demonstrandum
  Quod erat d. EUCLID [1]
denies
  spirit that d. GOETHE [25]

dentist
  sooner go to my d. WAUGH [8]
dentopedalogy
  D. is the science PHILIP, DUKE OF
    EDINBURGH [1]
deny
  d. me thrice BIBLE, NEW TESTAMENT:
    MATTHEW [160]
  wants to d. *something* CARROLL [44]
departure
  hour of d. has arrived SOCRATES [8]
depends
  all d. what you mean JOAD [2]
depressed
  feeling very d. ADAMS, D. [3]
deprivation
  D. is for me what
    daffodils LARKIN [21]
depths
  Drown it in the d. HORACE [49]
  Out of the d. BIBLE, OLD TESTAMENT:
    PSALMS [134]
  Out of the d. BIBLE, VULGATE [6]
derangement
  d. of the *Volition* COLERIDGE, S. T. [52]
desert
  d. shall rejoice BIBLE, OLD TESTAMENT:
    ISAIAH [46]
  d. wild/Become a garden
    mild BLAKE [2]
deserter
  d. of my flame ROCHESTER [11]
design
  interior d. is a travesty BAYLEY [3]
designs
  d. were strictly honourable FIELDING,
    HENRY [11]
desire
  antidote to d. CONGREVE [24]
  d. accomplished is sweet BIBLE, OLD
    TESTAMENT: PROVERBS [30]
  D. attained is not desire RALEGH [6]
  d. gratified BLAKE [44]
  D. is a witch DAY LEWIS [1]
  d. is got without
    content SHAKESPEARE: MACBETH [57]
  d. of the woman STAËL [4]
  d. ... outlive
    performance SHAKESPEARE: HENRY IV
    PT 2 [16]
  d. shall fail BIBLE, OLD TESTAMENT:
    ECCLESIASTES [41]
  Drink ... provokes the
    d. SHAKESPEARE: MACBETH [44]
  given him his heart's d. BIBLE, OLD
    TESTAMENT: PSALMS [21]
  Land of Heart's D. YEATS [14]
  lineaments of gratified d. BLAKE [46]
  Man is a creation of d. BACHELARD [1]
  man's d. is for the
    woman COLERIDGE, S. T. [66]
  moment of d. BLAKE [48]

response to d. STEVENS, W. [11]
Some d. is necessary JOHNSON, S. [44]
unsatisfied d. POWYS [1]

desired
what I d. no longer
overstepped CONFUCIUS [3]

desires
d. but acts not BLAKE [20]

desk
My d., most loyal
friend TSVETAEVA [3]

despair
carrion comfort, D. HOPKINS [26]
D. ... compatible with a good
dinner THACKERAY [19]
d. is the cruel
beginning LAUTRÉAMONT [4]
Don't d. KAFKA [1]
Giant D. BUNYAN [9]
I hate d. PINTER [5]
Intellectual d. results BATAILLE [1]
iron-clasped volume of d. POE [17]
Never d. HORACE [20]
on the far side of d. SARTRE [5]
One path leads to d. ALLEN [25]
There is no vulture like
d. GRANVILLE [1]
what resolution from d. MILTON [91]
what we call our d. ELIOT, G. [52]

desperandum
Nil d. HORACE [20]

desperate
My constituency is the d. JACKSON,
J. [5]

desperation
lives of quiet d. THOREAU [26]

despised
d. and rejected of men BIBLE, OLD
TESTAMENT: ISAIAH [72]

despises
no man thinks much of that which
he d. JOHNSON, S. [125]

despond
name of the slough was
D. BUNYAN [4]

despondency
in the end d. and
madness WORDSWORTH, W. [48]

despotism
d. ... is indispensable BAGEHOT [29]
D. accomplishes great things
BALZAC [2]

destined
appears I am d. for
something CLIVE [1]

destiny
cry of men in face of their
d. CAMUS [2]
D. ... tyrant's authority for
crime BIERCE [18]
frame of our d. HAMMARSKJÖLD [1]
master of his d. SCHILLER [18]

walking with d. CHURCHILL, W. [45]
What do I know of man's
d. BECKETT [18]
who can turn the stream of
d. SPENSER [12]

destroy
I am not come to d. BIBLE, NEW
TESTAMENT: MATTHEW [26]
man determined to d./
himself CUMMINGS, E. E. [9]
necessary to d. the
town ANONYMOUS [46]
urge ... in people to d. FRANK [2]

destruction
d. is also a creative
passion BAKUNIN [1]
d. of the whole world HUME, D. [2]
eve of d. MCGUIRE [1]
If d. be our lot LINCOLN [1]

detection
D. is ... an exact science DOYLE,
A. C. [8]

detective
always tell a d. on TV CHANDLER [13]
believes that he is a born
d. BUCHAN [1]
d. ... is in a state of grace AUDEN [31]
d. novel is the art-for-art's-
sake PRITCHETT [2]
d. story is about ... order JAMES,
P. D. [1]

determination
enough to have ... d. PROPERTIUS [3]

deum
D. de deo MISSAL [11]

deus
D. ex machina MENANDER [4]

Deutschland
D., über alles HOFFMANN, A. H. [1]

developed
country that is more d. MARX, K. [10]

deviations
D. from common rules BURNEY [3]

devices
dirty d. of this world TRAHERNE [8]

devil
D. always builds a chapel DEFOE [4]
d. and all his works BOOK OF
COMMON PRAYER [68]
d., as a roaring lion BIBLE, NEW
TESTAMENT: 1 PETER [11]
D. begat darkness LUTHER [7]
D. did grin COLERIDGE, S. T. [81]
D. ever God's ape LUTHER [6]
D., having nothing else to
do BELLOC [13]
D.'s buttermilk PAISLEY [2]
d.'s party without
knowing BLAKE [18]
d. take her SUCKLING [2]
d. take the hin'most BUTLER, S. (1612–
80) [11]

d. will no longer have
them ARNOULD [1]
envy of the d. BIBLE, APOCRYPHA:
WISDOM OF SOLOMON [4]
every man with him was God or
D. DRYDEN [36]
given up believing in the d. KNOX,
R. [4]
If the D. doesn't
exist DOSTOYEVSKY [8]
Let the d./Be ...
honoured SHAKESPEARE: MEASURE
FOR MEASURE [21]
old serpent, which is the D. BIBLE,
NEW TESTAMENT: REVELATION [45]
Resist the d. BIBLE, NEW TESTAMENT:
JAMES [13]
richer for having a d. JAMES, W.
[9]
sugar o'er/The d. SHAKESPEARE:
HAMLET [83]
When the D. quotes
Scriptures GOODMAN, P. [1]
your father the d. BIBLE, NEW
TESTAMENT: JOHN [35]

devils
D. are not so black LODGE, T. [3]

devocioun
Farewell my bok and my
d. CHAUCER [14]

devoted
d. and obedient NIGHTINGALE [3]

devotion
at my d. BROWNE [1]

dew
continual d. of thy blessing BOOK OF
COMMON PRAYER [23]
my head is filled with d. BIBLE, OLD
TESTAMENT: SONG OF SOLOMON [19]
wet with the d. of heaven BIBLE, OLD
TESTAMENT: DANIEL [5]

dialect
D. words – those terrible
marks HARDY, T. [13]

dialogue
D. is a necessary evil ZINNEMANN [1]

diamond
d. ... lasts forever LOOS [3]
immortal d. HOPKINS [31]
like a rough d. DEFOE [3]

diamonds
D. are a girl's best friend MONROE [2]

Diana
Age of D. has not ended BURCHILL [4]
D. ... hunted by your own MOTION [3]
Great is D. BIBLE, NEW TESTAMENT:
ACTS [31]

diaper
D. backward spells
repaid MCLUHAN [8]

diarist
to be a good d. NICOLSON [3]

what's d. is done SHAKESPEARE: MACBETH [58]

ye have d. it unto me BIBLE, NEW TESTAMENT: MATTHEW [151]

Dong
D. with a luminous nose LEAR [11]

Don Juan
'D.,' ... sublime of *that there* BYRON, LORD [107]

Donne
D.'s verses ... pass all understanding JAMES I [3]

doom
Master of the Day of D. KORAN [2]

dooms
grandeur of the d. KEATS [20]

Doomsday
D. is near. Die all SHAKESPEARE: HENRY IV PT 1 [39]

door
Came out by the same d. KHAYYÁM [10]
d. is what a dog NASH, O. [14]
hardly close the d. CLARK, A. [4]
I am the d. BIBLE, NEW TESTAMENT: JOHN [39]

doors
closed their d. MAETERLINCK [1]
d. of perception BLAKE [38]

dope
d. will get you through times SHELTON [1]

Doris Day
D. before she was a virgin MARX, G. [13]

dormouse
summer of a d. BYRON, LORD [38]

double
D. double, toil and trouble SHAKESPEARE: MACBETH [71]

double-bed
peace of the d. CAMPBELL, MRS P. [2]

doubleness
act with d. ELIOT, G. [31]

doublethink
D. means the power ORWELL [40]

doubt
d. as a philosophy of life MARTEL [1]
D. thou the stars are fire SHAKESPEARE: HAMLET [61]
easier to d. than to examine SCOTT, W. [21]
Let us never, never d. BELLOC [2]
Life is d. UNAMUNO [2]
more faith in honest d. TENNYSON [112]
night of d. and sorrow HYMNS & CAROLS [85]
wherefore didst thou d. BIBLE, NEW TESTAMENT: MATTHEW [106]

doubting
D. Castle BUNYAN [9]

doubts
d. are traitors SHAKESPEARE: MEASURE FOR MEASURE [5]

dove
descending like a d. BIBLE, NEW TESTAMENT: MATTHEW [13]
wings like a d. BIBLE, OLD TESTAMENT: PSALMS [66]

Dover
white cliffs of D. LYNN [1]

down
can't hold a man d. WASHINGTON, B. T. [2]
D. and away below ARNOLD, M. [2]

downhearted
Are we d. ANONYMOUS [4]

downsitting
Thou knowest my d. BIBLE, OLD TESTAMENT: PSALMS [141]

Dr Johnson
D.'s morality HAWTHORNE [11]

Dracula
I am D. ... welcome STOKER [1]

drag
It's a d. MCCARTNEY [2]

dragon
between the d. and his wrath SHAKESPEARE: KING LEAR [4]
great d. was cast out BIBLE, NEW TESTAMENT: REVELATION [31]
O to be a d. MOORE, MARIANNE [10]

dragons
brother to d. BIBLE, OLD TESTAMENT: JOB [37]
d. in their ... palaces BIBLE, OLD TESTAMENT: ISAIAH [27]
habitation of d. BIBLE, OLD TESTAMENT: ISAIAH [45]
ye d., and all deeps BIBLE, OLD TESTAMENT: PSALMS [149]

drain
next town d. SPOONER [2]

draining
d. money from the pockets SMITH, ADAM [12]

drama
aim of great d. NATHAN [1]
D. is life HITCHCOCK [2]
Good d. must be drastic SCHLEGEL [2]
We respond to a d. MAMET [1]

drawing
back to the old d. board ARNO [1]

dream
awakened from the d. of life SHELLEY, P. B. [75]
d. of a shadow/is man PINDAR [5]
d. the impossible dream DARION [1]
d. things that never were SHAW [66]
d. within a dream POE [1]
Don't d. it O'BRIEN, R. [2]
falls into a d. CONRAD [5]

glory and the freshness of a d. WORDSWORTH, W. [78]
golden d. of love DRYDEN [22]
I d., therefore I exist STRINDBERG [5]
I have a d. KING, M. L. [18]
love's young d. MOORE, T. [5]
sleep – perchance to d. SHAKESPEARE: HAMLET [86]
waking from a troubled d. HAWTHORNE [2]
What happens to a d. deferred HUGHES, L. [7]

dreamer
Beautiful d. FOSTER, S. [9]
d. cometh BIBLE, OLD TESTAMENT: GENESIS [55]
my dear wife is a d. SMITH, STEVIE [3]

dreamers
filthy d. BIBLE, NEW TESTAMENT: JUDE [1]
Revolution only needs good d. WILLIAMS, T. [5]

dreams
armored cars of d. BISHOP [1]
as we see it in our d. CHEKHOV [5]
Come to me in my d. ARNOLD, M. [12]
d., a little personal eternity BORGES [9]
dreamer of d. BIBLE, OLD TESTAMENT: DEUTERONOMY [7]
If empty d. so please HERRICK [4]
In d. begins responsibility YEATS [24]
interpretation of d. FREUD [1]
old men shall dream d. BIBLE, OLD TESTAMENT: JOEL [5]
ruin our d. HOFFER [7]
Saddle your d. WEBB, M. [1]
such stuff/As d. are made SHAKESPEARE: TEMPEST [19]
super-abundance of d. USTINOV [8]
tread on my d. YEATS [16]
Whoso regardeth d. BIBLE, APOCRYPHA: ECCLESIASTICUS [55]

dreariest
d. spot in all the land WHITTIER [6]

dress
D. code is everything LETTE [2]
How did you get into that d. HOPE, B. [2]

dressed
being perfectly well d. EMERSON [71]
better d. than you MALKOVICH [1]
good temper when he's well d. DICKENS [47]

drift-wood
d. fire without that burned LONGFELLOW [14]

drink
d. for the thirst to come RABELAIS [2]
D.! for you know not KHAYYÁM [22]
D. not the third glass HERBERT, G. [2]

d. to make other people interesting NATHAN [2]

D. to me only JONSON [26]

D. today, and drown all sorrow FLETCHER, J. [1]

five reasons we should d. ALDRICH, H. [1]

follow strong d. BIBLE, OLD TESTAMENT: ISAIAH [12]

Give strong d. BIBLE, OLD TESTAMENT: PROVERBS [99]

I needed a d. CHANDLER [5]

Leeze me on d. BURNS [10]

Let's d. to our sons COWARD [9]

One d. is too many for me BEHAN [6]

she drove me to d. FIELDS, W. C. [3]

taken to d. TARKINGTON [1]

teach you to d. deep SHAKESPEARE: HAMLET [22]

drinking

d. at somebody else's expense LEIGH, H. S. [1]

D. is the soldier's pleasure DRYDEN [70]

D. when we are not thirsty BEAUMARCHAIS [3]

Much d., little thinking SWIFT, J. [20]

Now is the time for d. HORACE [28]

poor and unhappy brains for d. SHAKESPEARE: OTHELLO [24]

red-hot with d. SHAKESPEARE: TEMPEST [20]

sluggish men ... are improved by d. JOHNSON, S. [105]

drinks

man you don't like who d. THOMAS, D. [22]

driving

d. of Jehu BIBLE, OLD TESTAMENT: 2 KINGS [8]

like d. a car at night DOCTOROW [2]

dronke

O d. man CHAUCER [44]

drooper

She's a d. WODEHOUSE [16]

drop

turn on, tune in, and d. out LEARY [1]

dropped

not wish to be d. by JOHNSON, S. [132]

dropping

continual d. BIBLE, OLD TESTAMENT: PROVERBS [87]

drown

what pain it was to d. SHAKESPEARE: RICHARD III [7]

drowning

not waving but d. SMITH, STEVIE [6]

drudgery

love of the d. SMITH, LOGAN P. [11]

Makes d. divine HERBERT, G. [44]

drugs

D. is like ... a cup of tea GALLAGHER [2]

D. is/your own tattoos ARMITAGE [2]

drum

music of a distant d. KHAYYÁM [4]

Not a d. was heard WOLFE, C. [1]

Take my d. to England NEWBOLT [1]

drum-beat

morning d. ... circles the earth WEBSTER, D. [6]

drummer

hears a different d. THOREAU [52]

drums

beating of war d. KOESTLER [8]

drunk

art of getting d. JOHNSON, S. [121]

d. for about a week FITZGERALD, F. S. [6]

Gloriously d. COWPER [43]

Man ... must get d. BYRON, LORD [98]

pleasures of being very d. WYCHERLEY [4]

drunkard

d. ... shall come to poverty BIBLE, OLD TESTAMENT: PROVERBS [69]

drunkards

take habitual d. as a class LINCOLN [3]

drunken

d., but not with wine BIBLE, OLD TESTAMENT: ISAIAH [39]

hour to be d. BAUDELAIRE [24]

drunkenness

d. ... valid human experience JAMES, W. [7]

D. is ... voluntary madness SENECA [8]

d. of things being various MACNEICE [2]

duchess

That's my last D. BROWNING, R. [8]

duchesses

Here sober d. are seen MORE, H. [6]

duck

forgot to d. DEMPSEY [1]

dude

No way d. MYERS [1]

duke

D. of dark corners SHAKESPEARE: MEASURE FOR MEASURE [20]

fully equipped d. LLOYD GEORGE [3]

Genteelly damned beside a d. MOORE, T. [15]

dulce

D. et decorum est OWEN [3]

dull

appears d. there is a design STEELE [2]

be thou d. DRYDEN [41]

d., expected and designed WINCHILSEA [3]

d. in a new way JOHNSON, S. [89]

d. man who is always sure MENCKEN [10]

great danger of being d. CONGREVE [3]

ought to be d. sometimes ADDISON [6]

venerably d. CHURCHILL, CHARLES [1]

dullard

d.'s envy of brilliant men BEERBOHM [8]

dullness

cause of d. in others FOOTE [2]

d. of the fool SHAKESPEARE: AS YOU LIKE IT [3]

Prudent d. CHURCHILL, CHARLES [2]

dumb

D. as a drum DICKENS [12]

wise person ... knows he's d. HELLER [6]

dump

What a d. DAVIS, B. [2]

dunce

d. that has been sent to roam COWPER [16]

d. with wits POPE [76]

laughter from a d. BYRON, LORD [172]

Dundee

room for the bonnets of Bonny D. SCOTT, W. [23]

dupe

man is his own easiest dupe DEMOSTHENES [1]

dusky

rear my d. race TENNYSON [45]

dust

d. shalt thou eat BIBLE, OLD TESTAMENT: GENESIS [22]

d. thou art BIBLE, OLD TESTAMENT: GENESIS [24]

d. to dust BOOK OF COMMON PRAYER [90]

each day brings its petty d. ARNOLD, M. [13]

Excuse my d. PARKER, D. [15]

fear in a handful of d. ELIOT, T. S. [19]

give d. a tongue HERBERT, G. [18]

heap of d. alone remains POPE [62]

into the d. descend KHAYYÁM [8]

Less than the d. HOPE, L. [2]

lick the d. BIBLE, OLD TESTAMENT: PSALMS [82]

Love which reacheth but to d. SIDNEY, P. [1]

shake off the d. of your feet BIBLE, NEW TESTAMENT: MATTHEW [73]

sweep the d. behind the door SHAKESPEARE: MIDSUMMER NIGHT'S DREAM [44]

We are but d. and shadow HORACE [51]

What a d. do I raise AESOP'S FABLES [1]

what is this quintessence of d. SHAKESPEARE: HAMLET [68]

dustbin

d. of history TROTSKY [8]

Dutch

fault of the D. CANNING [5]

elope
must e. methodically GOLDSMITH [29]

eloquence
e. and wring its neck VERLAINE [4]
finest e. ... gets things done LLOYD
GEORGE [7]
immunity to e. RUSSELL, B. [16]
repositories of models of
e. MCLUHAN [1]

eloquent
feeling ... that makes us
e. QUINTILIAN [2]

Elysian
dead, but in the E. fields DISRAELI [58]

Elysium
My brother ... is in E. SHAKESPEARE:
TWELFTH NIGHT [4]

emancipation
e. has made of the modern
woman GOLDMAN, E. [5]

embalmer
triumph of the e.'s art VIDAL [7]

embers
glowing e. through the
room MILTON [25]

embraces
E. are cominglings BLAKE [85]

Emerald Isle
defile/The cause ... of the
E. DRENNAN [1]

emigration
E. ... is the quintessential
experience BERGER [8]

eminence
E. without merit CHAMFORT [3]

Emmanuel
call his name E. BIBLE, NEW
TESTAMENT: MATTHEW [2]
O come, E. HYMNS & CAROLS [65]

emotion
e. recollected in
tranquillity WORDSWORTH, W. [30]

emotional
learn to put your e.
luggage DRABBLE [3]

emotions
e. ... lead us astray WILDE [47]
gamut of e. PARKER, D. [14]
grant himself the e. GOURMONT [6]

emperor
E. ... struck by a
cannonball CHARLES V [1]
e. has nothing on ANDERSEN [2]
had he never been e. TACITUS [9]

empire
aggressive impulses of an evil
e. REAGAN, R. [7]
Britain has lost an E. ACHESON [1]
e. is an immense
egotism EMERSON [31]
e. is no more than power in
trust DRYDEN [31]

E. Strikes Back LUCAS, G. [3]
foundation of e. is art BLAKE [88]
great e. and little minds BURKE,
E. [23]
How is the E. GEORGE V [1]
rule the e. of himself SHELLEY,
P. B. [98]

empires
day of E. has come CHAMBERLAIN,
J. [1]
e. of the mind CHURCHILL, W. [38]
E. which branch out
widely MACAULAY, LORD [21]
Hatching vain e. MILTON [111]

employment:
adventure of full e. BEVERIDGE [2]

empty
e. head is not really
empty HOFFER [11]

enamoured
He who is e. of
himself LICHTENBERG [17]

enceinte
always e. quite
disgusting VICTORIA [3]

encounters
Close E. of the Third
Kind SPIELBERG [1]

encyclopaedia
I am a whole e. behind LAMB,
CHARLES [13]

end
And now the e. is near SINATRA, F. [3]
began to draw to our e. BIBLE,
APOCRYPHA: WISDOM OF SOLOMON [9]
beginning of the e. TALLEYRAND [1]
Better is the e. BIBLE, OLD TESTAMENT:
ECCLESIASTES [20]
bow and accept at the e. FROST, R. [1]
e. badly from the
beginning STEVENSON, R. L. [50]
e. is a goal SAND [6]
e. of all things is at hand BIBLE, NEW
TESTAMENT: 1 PETER [9]
e. of the beginning CHURCHILL,
W. [32]
e. of things is coming DE LA
MARE [10]
e. that crowns us HERRICK [16]
God will grant an e. VIRGIL [21]
In my beginning is my e. ELIOT,
T. S. [46]
In my e. is my beginning MARY
QUEEN OF SCOTS [2]
make me to know mine e. BIBLE, OLD
TESTAMENT: PSALMS [49]
man awaits his e. YEATS [53]
This is the e. MORRISON, J. [2]
true beginning of our
e. SHAKESPEARE: MIDSUMMER
NIGHT'S DREAM [40]
Waiting for the e., boys EMPSON [2]

what e. the gods may
bestow HORACE [23]
You e. up as you deserve WELDON [2]

ending
Before the e. of the day HYMNS &
CAROLS [13]
bread-sauce of the happy e. JAMES,
H. [18]
happy e. is our national
belief MCCARTHY, M. [2]

endow
e. a college, or a cat POPE [104]

ends
means are justified by which
e. SINGER [5]

endurance
men who learn e. DICKENS [39]

endure
resolved to e. the
unendurable HIROHITO [1]

Endymion
In E., I leaped headlong KEATS [39]

enema
e. under the influence of
Ecstasy GREER [16]

enemies
careful in the choice of his
e. WILDE [39]
Lord, make my e.
ridiculous VOLTAIRE [28]
Love your e. BIBLE, NEW TESTAMENT:
MATTHEW [33]
many e. that know not/
Why SHAKESPEARE: HENRY VIII [5]
Separate thyself from thine e. BIBLE,
APOCRYPHA: ECCLESIASTICUS [14]
wise learn ... from their
e. ARISTOPHANES [3]

enemy
e. in their mouths SHAKESPEARE:
OTHELLO [29]
e. is inside DORFMAN [1]
every man his greatest
e. BROWNE [13]
fight too often with one
e. NAPOLEON I [9]
hardly a warm personal e.
left WHISTLER [7]
I am the e. you killed OWEN [6]
know the e. SUN TZU [2]
man ... the e. of other men BORGES [1]
most dangerous e. REAGAN, R. [2]
most time-consuming things is ... an
e. WHITE, E. B. [3]
my nearest and dearest
e. MIDDLETON [4]
My nearest and dearest
e. SHAKESPEARE: HENRY IV PT 1 [35]
Never trust thine e. BIBLE,
APOCRYPHA: ECCLESIASTICUS [27]
O mine e. BIBLE, OLD TESTAMENT:
1 KINGS [15]

folly
feather pate of f. HOUSMAN [15]
fool returneth to his f. BIBLE, OLD
TESTAMENT: PROVERBS [80]
likes foolish people for their
f. GASKELL [6]
lovely woman stoops to
f. GOLDSMITH [21]
misery to live in f. ERASMUS [3]
profit by the f. of others PLINY THE
ELDER [7]
uses his f. like a stalking-
horse SHAKESPEARE: AS YOU LIKE
IT [40]

fond
haven't much time to be f. COLLINS,
WILKIE [3]

food
F. is the first thing BRECHT [3]
From f. ... are born BHAGAVAD-
GITA [7]
no love sincerer than ... f. SHAW [20]
not the f., but the
content HERRICK [17]
Sharing f. FISHER, M. F. K. [2]

fool
Answer a f. BIBLE, OLD TESTAMENT:
PROVERBS [79]
bigger f. to admire him BOILEAU-
DESPRÉAUX [4]
brains enough to make a f. of
himself STEVENSON, R. L. [15]
calls himself a f. DOSTOYEVSKY [4]
drop into thyself, and be a
f. POPE [129]
every f. is not a poet POPE [112]
f. all of the people ADAMS, F. P. [3]
f. all of the people LINCOLN [33]
f. and her money are soon
courted ROWLAND, H. [3]
f. at forty YOUNG, E. [4]
f. ... is counted wise BIBLE, OLD
TESTAMENT: PROVERBS [48]
f. must now and then be
right COWPER [19]
f. shall not enter into
Heaven BLAKE [93]
f. uttereth all his mind BIBLE, OLD
TESTAMENT: PROVERBS [94]
f. who proclaims the general
folly JUNG [16]
f. would persist in his
folly BLAKE [26]
If I am a f. BYRON, LORD [33]
I have played the f. BIBLE, OLD
TESTAMENT: 1 SAMUEL [18]
knowledgeable f. is a greater
fool MOLIÈRE [19]
man suspects himself a f. YOUNG.
E. [9]
One f. ... in every married
couple FIELDING, HENRY [15]

rash, intruding f. SHAKESPEARE:
HAMLET [121]
rather have a f. SHAKESPEARE: AS YOU
LIKE IT [30]
white hairs becomes a
f. SHAKESPEARE: HENRY IV PT 2 [28]
wise enough to play the
f. SHAKESPEARE: TWELFTH NIGHT [27]

foolish
f. things remind me MASCHWITZ [1]
God hath chosen the f. things BIBLE,
NEW TESTAMENT: 1 CORINTHIANS [3]
never said a f. thing ROCHESTER [14]

foolishest
f. thing ever done MELBOURNE [9]

fools
discourse of f. is irksome BIBLE,
APOCRYPHA: ECCLESIASTICUS [43]
discovered that they are
f. MELBOURNE [6]
F. rush in POPE [31]
fill the world with f. SPENCER, H. [11]
I am two f. DONNE [9]
suffer f. gladly BIBLE, NEW
TESTAMENT: 2 CORINTHIANS [13]
What f. these mortals be SENECA [1]
what f. these mortals
be SHAKESPEARE: MIDSUMMER
NIGHT'S DREAM [28]
wise, they became f. BIBLE, NEW
TESTAMENT: ROMANS [3]

foot
silver f. in his mouth RICHARDS, A. [1]

football
f. is a matter of life and
death SHANKLY [1]
F. is brutal DELILLO [1]

footfalls
F. echo in the memory ELIOT,
T. S. [40]

footman
f. may swear SWIFT, J. [50]

footnotes
F. are the finer-suckered
surfaces BAKER, N. [3]

footprints
F. on the sands of
time LONGFELLOW [4]

footstool
make thine enemies thy f. BIBLE, OLD
TESTAMENT: PSALMS [115]

foppery
sound of shallow f. SHAKESPEARE:
MERCHANT OF VENICE [20]

force
blend f. with a
manoeuvre TROTSKY [5]
F. is always beside the
point HERODOTUS [2]
f. that through the green
fuse THOMAS, D. [2]
F. without wisdom HORACE [39]

F., and fraud HOBBES [9]
May the F. be with you LUCAS, G. [2]
Who overcomes/By f. MILTON [98]

Ford
I am a F., not a Lincoln FORD, G. [1]

forefathers
rude f. of the hamlet sleep GRAY,
T. [9]

forehead
his f. was prodigious HUNT, L. [11]

foreheads
f. villainous low SHAKESPEARE:
TEMPEST [22]

foreign
f. country ... like middle-class
suburb LAPHAM [2]
f. policies KISSINGER [6]
understanding a f. country ELIOT,
T. S. [49]

foreigner
f. should be ... wiser TROLLOPE [5]

foreign policy
F. ... cannot rise STEVENSON, A. [12]
idea behind f. O'ROURKE [5]

forest
f. primeval LONGFELLOW [12]

foretell
ability to f. CHURCHILL, W. [59]

forget
better by far you should f. ROSSETTI,
C. [4]
do not thou f. me ASTLEY [1]
f. all too soon DIDION [4]
hardest science to f. POPE [56]
How long wilt thou f. me BIBLE, OLD
TESTAMENT: PSALMS [8]
lest we f. KIPLING [38]
more a man can f. KIERKEGAARD [6]
swear ... that you'll never
f. SASSOON [4]
Were it not better to f. LANDON [2]
will I not f. thee BIBLE, OLD
TESTAMENT: ISAIAH [67]
world shall end when I
f. SWINBURNE [10]

forgive
F. your enemies KENNEDY, J. F. [25]
Father, f. them BIBLE, NEW
TESTAMENT: LUKE [71]
God will f. me HEINE [7]
How many will say,
'f.' TENNYSON [179]
stupid neither f. nor forget SZASZ [7]
We all like to f. BUTLER, S. (1835–
1902) [28]
We never f. LA HARPE [2]

forgives
Man f. women anything ANTRIM [5]

forgot
she f. the stars, the moon KEATS [65]

forgotten
f. even by God BROWNING, R. [3]

order ... this matter better in F. STERNE [24]

wield the sword of F. DE GAULLE [3]

frank
F. and explicit DISRAELI [30]

Franklin
body/Of Benjamin F. FRANKLIN, B. [1]
F.'s quiet memory BYRON, LORD [139]

fraud
f. or force attained his ends POPE [40]

fraudulence
limits of your own f. PAULIN [2]

freaks
quality of legend about f. ARBUS [1]

freak show
world is ... a f. GOETHE [3]

freckled
f. whelp, hag-born SHAKESPEARE: TEMPEST [7]

free
best things in life are f. DE SYLVA/ BROWN [1]
condemned to be f. SARTRE [1]
f. at last KING, M. L. [21]
f. only when all ... are equally free BAKUNIN [5]
f. our minds MARLEY [5]
human beings are born f. UNIVERSAL DECLARATION [1]
I don't know if I'm f. GODARD [1]
If you love somebody set them f. STING [2]
I was f. born BIBLE, NEW TESTAMENT: ACTS [35]
Man is born f. ROUSSEAU [1]
men naturally were born f. MILTON [75]
must be f. or die WORDSWORTH, W. [62]
none less f. THOMAS, E. [3]
No one can be ... f. till all are SPENCER, H. [3]
Who would be f. themselves BYRON, LORD [20]

freedom
apprenticeship for f. BARAKA [2]
basic test of f. HOFFER [5]
But what is F. COLERIDGE, H. [1]
cause of f. versus tyranny ARENDT [7]
characterizes true f. LICHTENBERG [24]
chimes of f. flashing DYLAN [5]
cure is f. MACAULAY, LORD [5]
Every general increase of f. COOLEY [5]
F.! A wanton slut TSVETAEVA [1]
F., from her mountain height DRAKE, J. R. [1]
F. has a thousand charms COWPER [12]
F. hath been hunted PAINE [3]
F. is ... indivisible WILLKIE [1]

F. is a gift from heaven DIDEROT [3]
F. is always ... freedom LUXEMBURG [1]
F. is never voluntarily given KING, M. L. [7]
f. is no more than a *sensation* CIORAN [6]
F. is not an ideal STEVENSON, A. [14]
F. is the by-product BEVAN [1]
F. is the freedom to say ORWELL [39]
F. itself was attacked this morning BUSH, G. W. [2]
F., morality, and the human dignity BAKUNIN [7]
F. of men under government LOCKE [10]
f. of speech, freedom of conscience TWAIN [24]
f. ... only extended privilege HILL, C. [1]
F.'s banner streaming DRAKE, J. R. [2]
F.'s just another word KRISTOFFERSON [1]
F. to drive POLITICAL SLOGANS [13]
F.! yet thy banner, torn BYRON, LORD [83]
How is f. measured NIETZSCHE [39]
I gave my life for f. EWER [1]
love not f., but licence MILTON [74]
progress of f. COBDEN [3]
sympathy with f. GLADSTONE [10]

freedom fighters
our brothers, these f. REAGAN, R. [9]

freedoms
four essential human f. ROOSEVELT, F. D. [10]

freely
F. we serve MILTON [151]
f. ye have received BIBLE, NEW TESTAMENT: MATTHEW [72]

freeman
Americans are to be f. or slaves WASHINGTON, G. [3]

freer
f. subjects of a greater power DANTE [22]

free speech
f. ... continuous obligation SMITH, I. D. [2]
F. is the whole thing RUSHDIE [8]

free verse
I'd as soon write f. FROST, R. [23]

French
Englishman is about to talk F. WODEHOUSE [11]
F. are a logical people MORLEY, R. [2]
F. truth, Dutch prowess ROCHESTER [9]
he can speak F. SHAKESPEARE: HENRY VI PT 2 [8]
I believe only in F. culture NIETZSCHE [30]

Like a F. poem is life LONGFELLOW [33]
Speak in F. CARROLL [31]
We are not F. MONTGOMERY [2]
we talk F. BOUTROS-GHALI [1]

Frenchmen
Fifty million F. can't be wrong GUINAN [1]

fressh
as f. as is the month of May CHAUCER [17]

fret
F. not thyself BIBLE, OLD TESTAMENT: PSALMS [44]

Freud
F. is the father of psychoanalysis GREER [2]
Sigmund F. was a novelist IRVING, J. [1]
trouble with F. DODD [1]

freude
F., schöner Götterfunken SCHILLER [4]

Friday
more faithful ... servant than F. DEFOE [14]
we call this F. good ELIOT, T. S. [47]

friend
f. in need PLAUTUS [5]
F. of All the World KIPLING [53]
f. that sticketh closer BIBLE, OLD TESTAMENT: PROVERBS [53]
faithful f. is a strong defence BIBLE, APOCRYPHA: ECCLESIASTICUS [15]
faithful f. is the medicine BIBLE, APOCRYPHA: ECCLESIASTICUS [16]
foolish f. may cause more woe LA FONTAINE [5]
Forsake not an old f. BIBLE, APOCRYPHA: ECCLESIASTICUS [21]
great man for a f. HORACE [68]
hollow f. is but a hellish foe BRETON, N. [2]
If thou wouldest get a f. BIBLE, APOCRYPHA: ECCLESIASTICUS [13]
makes no f. TENNYSON [164]
mine own familiar f. BIBLE, OLD TESTAMENT: PSALMS [52]
One f. in a lifetime is much ADAMS, H. B. [6]
pretended f. is worse GAY, J. [4]
such a good f. TALLEYRAND [4]
To find a f. DOUGLAS, N. [5]
Trust ye not in a f. BIBLE, OLD TESTAMENT: MICAH [3]
useless while he has a f. STEVENSON, R. L. [56]
Whenever a f. succeeds VIDAL [5]

friendless
F. ... Having no favors to bestow BIERCE [25]

friendliness
impersonal insensitive f. WAUGH [17]

Galilee
Ye men of G. BIBLE, NEW TESTAMENT: ACTS [2]

gallantry
What men call g. BYRON, LORD [91]

galleon
Stately as a g. GRENFELL [2]

galley-slaves
no g. in the royal vessel ST FRANCIS DE SALES [2]

gallimaufry
English tongue a g. SPENSER [1]

gallop
Why does he g. and gallop STEVENSON, R. L. [32]

galloped
we g. all three BROWNING, R. [11]

gallows
complexion is perfect g. SHAKESPEARE: TEMPEST [2]
g. or the pox WILKES [1]
Shall there be g. SHAKESPEARE: HENRY IV PT 1 [5]

gallstones
chronic attack of mental g. GOGARTY [1]

game
g. which takes less than three STOPPARD [11]
How you played the g. RICE, G. [1]
play up! and play the g. NEWBOLT [4]
time to win this g. DRAKE, F. [3]

games
dread of g. BETJEMAN [17]

gamester
g. is the vilest GAY, J. [25]
Nothing is sacred to a g. SAURIN [3]

gamesters
G. and highwaymen GAY, J. [8]

gammon
world of g. and spinnage DICKENS [70]

Gandhi
G., a seditious ... lawyer CHURCHILL, W. [13]

gangsterism
g. is a very important avenue DOCTOROW [3]

gapes
g. at existence KIERKEGAARD [7]

garbage
chosen the g. disposal unit DEBORD [5]
they don't throw their g. away ALLEN, W. [20]

Garcia
Carry a Message to G. HUBBARD, E. [1]

garden
cultivate our own g. VOLTAIRE [16]
Don't go into Mr McGregor's g. POTTER, B. [1]

g. inclosed is my sister BIBLE, OLD TESTAMENT: SONG OF SOLOMON [17]
g. in her face CAMPION [5]
glory of the g. KIPLING [80]
God ... first planted a g. BACON, F. [35]
God the first g. made COWLEY, A. [12]
he should plant a g. THUBRON [1]
nearer God's Heart in a g. GURNEY, D. F. [1]
Round and round the g. NURSERY RHYMES [38]
she went into the g. FOOTE [3]
Show me your g. AUSTIN [1]
unweeded g./... grows to seed SHAKESPEARE: HAMLET [16]

gardener
Adam was a g. SHAKESPEARE: HENRY VI PT 2 [7]
bad for God's g. HARDY, T. [19]

gardeners
charming g. who make our souls PROUST [4]
no ancient gentlemen but g. SHAKESPEARE: HAMLET [144]

gardens
admitted/to g. KORAN [26]
Our bodies are our g. SHAKESPEARE: OTHELLO [17]
Paradise haunts g. JARMAN [3]

garlands
g. wither on your brow SHIRLEY [3]
weave the g. of repose MARVELL [9]

garleek
loved he g., oynons CHAUCER [23]

garment
grasp the hem of his g. BISMARCK [8]

Garnett
diplomacy of Alf G. HEALEY [2]

gastronomic
complete g. satisfaction FISHER, M. F. K. [1]
g. pimp BEVAN [17]

gastronomical
G. perfection can be reached FISHER, M. F. K. [3]

gate
leant upon a coppice g. HARDY, T. [20]
stood at the g. of the year HASKINS [1]

gates
twelve g. BIBLE, NEW TESTAMENT: REVELATION [52]

Gath
Tell it not in G. BIBLE, OLD TESTAMENT: 2 SAMUEL [2]

gathered
g. together in my name BIBLE, NEW TESTAMENT: MATTHEW [118]

gaudeamus
G. igitur ANONYMOUS [27]

gaudy
g., blabbing, and remorseful day SHAKESPEARE: HENRY VI PT 2 [4]
one other g. night SHAKESPEARE: ANTONY & CLEOPATRA [25]

Gaul
G. is divided into three parts CAESAR, J. [1]

gay
condition that is now called g. BALDWIN, J. [11]
g. people ... into right-wing politics MAUPIN [2]
only g. in the village LITTLE BRITAIN [1]
poet could not be g. WORDSWORTH, W. [71]

geese
G. are swans ARNOLD, M. [49]
g. are swans WALPOLE, H. [16]

genealogical
trees are ... g. PROUST [1]

genealogies
endless g. BIBLE, NEW TESTAMENT: 1 TIMOTHY [1]

general
best service a retired g. can perform BRADLEY, O. [3]
G. has dedicated himself STEVENSON, A. [19]

generalities
Glittering g. EMERSON [75]

generalization
idea is always a g. HEGEL [3]

generalizations
g. about women RUSSELL, B. [21]

generalize
g. ... from single instances TWAIN [4]
To g. is to be an idiot BLAKE [89]

General Motors
good for G. WILSON, C. E. [1]

generals
best g. I have known TOLSTOY [5]

General Strike
G. has taught the working classes BALFOUR [2]

generation
each g. ... a distinct nation JEFFERSON [28]
Every g. revolts MUMFORD, L. [1]
g. drowned in mortification VANEIGEM [3]
speak ill of our g. BECKETT [6]
stubborn and rebellious g. BIBLE, OLD TESTAMENT: PSALMS [85]
Talkin' 'bout my g. TOWNSHEND [1]

generosity
g. is ... only the vanity LA ROCHEFOUCAULD [22]
G. lies less in giving much LA BRUYÈRE [10]

impact of the G. message JOHN
PAUL II [2]
preach the g. to every creature BIBLE,
NEW TESTAMENT: MARK [16]

gossip
G. is a sort of smoke ELIOT, G. [56]
G. is news running ahead of
itself SMITH, LIZ [1]
G. is the opiate of the
oppressed JONG [4]
g., that counts SCOTT, P. [1]
transmitting a piece of g. LEVI, P. [6]

got
What've ya g. BRANDO [1]

gotcha
G. SUN [3]

Gothic
principle of the G.
architecture COLERIDGE, S. T. [75]
style which ... is called
G. NEWMAN [5]

govern
good enough to g.
another LINCOLN [8]
He that would g.
others MASSINGER [2]
knoweth not ... how to g. men MORE,
T. [1]
Let the people think they g. PENN
[7]
They that g. most SELDEN [7]

governed
godly and quietly g. BOOK OF
COMMON PRAYER [55]

governesses
nation of g. SHAW [57]

governing
women are not made for
g. VICTORIA [2]

government
all hereditary g. PAINE [12]
art of g. consists in
taking VOLTAIRE [21]
country has the g. it
deserves MAISTRE [2]
despise g. BIBLE, NEW TESTAMENT:
2 PETER [3]
divine right of g. DISRAELI [41]
drollery called a representative
g. DISRAELI [32]
duty of g. is to prevent
crime MELBOURNE [7]
forms of g. let fools
contest POPE [135]
g. always gets in GRAFFITI [6]
G. does not solve problems REAGAN,
R. [3]
G. is an evil SHELLEY, P. B. [5]
G. ... is but a necessary evil PAINE [1]
g. is not a government of
laws WEBSTER, D. [7]
G. is the great fiction BASTIAT [1]

g. is the ... symbol of its
people CARLYLE, T. [51]
G. is very limited GODWIN [2]
G. must always depend GODWIN [1]
g. of laws, and not of men. ADAMS,
J. [3]
g. of ... morning
newspapers PHILLIPS [1]
g. ... was not framed THOREAU [53]
g. ... which governs not at
all THOREAU [13]
Good g. ... outcome of private
virtue CHAPMAN, J. [3]
happiness ... is the end of g. ADAMS,
J. [4]
If g. be founded in the
consent GODWIN [4]
If the G. is defeated HEATH [1]
In g., never retrace NAPOLEON I
[16]
just watch the g. ROGERS, W. [6]
legitimate object of g. LINCOLN [7]
one form of g. JOHNSON, S. [76]
out of thy mother's belly without
g. CERVANTES [26]
prepare for g. STEEL [1]
safe under every form of g. JOHNSON,
S. [77]
stand up for your G. CACCIA [1]
unjust as a feeble g. BURKE, E. [48]
want of g. HOBBES [11]

governments
detestation of all existing g. BYRON,
LORD [45]
G. need ... shepherds and
butchers VOLTAIRE [6]
G. set up overnight MACHIAVELLI [3]

governs
Who g. Britain POLITICAL
SLOGANS [40]

gown
Like a satin g. PARKER, D. [2]
wrap me in a g. HERBERT, G. [11]

Goya
I am G./of the bare
field VOZNESENSKY [1]

grace
Amazing g. HYMNS & CAROLS [9]
g. and favour BIBLE, OLD TESTAMENT:
ESTHER [1]
g. of our Lord Jesus BIBLE, NEW
TESTAMENT: REVELATION [59]
G. under pressure HEMINGWAY [5]
He does it with a better
g. SHAKESPEARE: TWELFTH NIGHT [17]
lend her g. TENNYSON [14]
means of g. BOOK OF COMMON
PRAYER [42]

graces
an' half-mile g. BURNS [1]

gradualness
inevitability of g. WEBB, S. [1]

grammar
G. ... can govern even
Kings MOLIÈRE [18]
g., the ground of al LANGLAND [4]
we still believe in g. NIETZSCHE [33]

grammar school
corrupted the youth ... in erecting a
g. SHAKESPEARE: HENRY VI PT 2 [9]
destroy every ... g. CROSLAND [1]

gramophone
enemy is the g. mind ORWELL [22]

grand
g. style arises in poetry ARNOLD,
M. [38]
horror about everything g. HUGO [18]
What is g. is ... obscure BLAKE [64]

Grand Central Station
By G. I sat down SMART, E. [2]

grandeur
charged with the g. of
God HOPKINS [5]
place that likes g. WALCOTT [9]
some sort of epic g. FITZGERALD,
F. S. [19]

grandfather
I don't know who my g.
was LINCOLN [32]

grandmother
We have become a g. THATCHER [17]

grape
g. that can with logic KHAYYÁM [12]
peel me a g. WEST, M. [7]

grapes
eaten sour g. BIBLE, OLD TESTAMENT:
EZEKIEL [4]

grapeshot
whiff of g. CARLYLE, T. [30]

grasp
G. the subject CATO THE ELDER [4]

grass
causeth the g. to grow BIBLE, OLD
TESTAMENT: PSALMS [107]
days are as g. BIBLE, OLD TESTAMENT:
PSALMS [106]
g.; I cover all SANDBURG [4]
g. stoops not SHAKESPEARE: VENUS
AND ADONIS [5]
g. will grow in the streets HOOVER,
H. [3]
g. withereth BIBLE, NEW TESTAMENT:
1 PETER [2]
leaf of g. is no less WHITMAN [12]

gratias
Deo g. MISSAL [9]

gratitude
G. ... exquisite form of
courtesy MARITAIN [2]
g. is ... a secret hope LA
ROCHEFOUCAULD [25]
G. ... is a sickness STALIN [3]
g. is a species of revenge JOHNSON,
S. [16]

worse than having to give
g. FAULKNER [5]

grave
g.'s a fine and private
place MARVELL [6]
g., where is thy victory BIBLE, NEW
TESTAMENT: 1 CORINTHIANS [46]
laid in the quiet g. KEATS [121]
Peace is in the g. SHELLEY, P. B. [53]

graves
uncut hair of g. WHITMAN [7]

graveyards
no bone to pick with g. BECKETT [19]

gravity
g. really does exist NEWTON [8]
What doth g. out of his
bed SHAKESPEARE: HENRY IV PT 1
[22]

gravy
disliked g. all my life SMITH,
SYDNEY [14]

great
g. man need not be morally
good BERLIN, ISAIAH [2]
G. men are not always wise BIBLE,
OLD TESTAMENT: JOB [38]
G. men are ... the summits of
ranges HIGGINSON [1]
G. men hallow a whole people SMITH,
SYDNEY [13]
g. men ... have flattered SHAKESPEARE:
CORIOLANUS [5]
g. must submit to ... prudence BURKE,
E. [57]
How g. Thou art HYMNS &
CAROLS [38]
I don't say he's a g. man MILLER, A. [3]
Ill can he rule the g. SPENSER [30]
most of the g. men of the
past TAYLOR, A. J. P. [6]
None think the g. unhappy YOUNG,
E. [3]
not men who are g. DUBUFFET [3]
Some are born g. SHAKESPEARE:
TWELFTH NIGHT [25]
Those who aim at g.
deeds CRASSUS [1]
those who were truly g. SPENDER [2]
Thou wouldst be g. SHAKESPEARE:
MACBETH [18]

greater
g. than we know WORDSWORTH,
W. [108]

greatest
how much the g. event FOX, C. J. [1]
I am the g. ALI [1]

greatness
abuse of g. SHAKESPEARE: JULIUS
CAESAR [11]
farewell, to all my g. SHAKESPEARE:
HENRY VIII [9]
first element of g. ASQUITH, M. [2]

G. knows itself SHAKESPEARE:
HENRY IV PT 1 [40]
In me ... /No g. TENNYSON [160]
True g. is free LA BRUYÈRE [6]

Greece
G. is a ... vassal GROMYKO [1]
G. might still be free BYRON,
LORD [119]
glory that was G. POE [3]
Isles of G. BYRON, LORD [118]
Sighing ... for G. again GOETHE [8]

greed
G. is all right BOESKY [1]
not enough for everyone's
g. BUCHMAN [2]
structured on g. FRIEDMAN [5]

greedy
People aren't g. any more ELTON [1]
sexy g. *is* the late eighties CHURCHILL,
CARYL [2]

Greek
Every G. ... has two Greeks DE
BERNIÈRES [4]
it was G. to me SHAKESPEARE: JULIUS
CAESAR [8]
neither G. nor Jew BIBLE, NEW
TESTAMENT: COLOSSIANS [5]
wife talks G. JOHNSON, S. [152]

Greeks
G. ... when they bear gifts VIRGIL
[28]
G. had a word for it AKINS [1]
we owe to the G. WILDE [23]
When G. joined Greeks LEE, N. [3]

green
as kind as it is g. MOORE,
MARIANNE [8]
do these things in a g. tree BIBLE,
NEW TESTAMENT: LUKE [69]
G. Things upon the Earth BOOK OF
COMMON PRAYER [13]
g. thought in a green
shade MARVELL [13]
how I love you g. GARCÍA LORCA [1]
My passport's g. HEANEY [6]
speak like a g. girl SHAKESPEARE:
HAMLET [37]
wearin' o' the g. ANONYMOUS [68]

green-eyed
'G. Monster' causes much
woe ANTRIM [7]

Greenland
From G.'s icy mountains HYMNS &
CAROLS [27]

Greensleeves
G. was all my joy ANONYMOUS [2]

Grenadiers
British G. ANONYMOUS [88]

grey
cure for g. hair ...
guillotine WODEHOUSE [12]
g. are all theories GOETHE [26]

given me over in my g.
hairs WOLSEY [1]
No g. hair in my soul MAYAKOVSKY [1]

grief
pierce the ear of g. SHAKESPEARE:
LOVE'S LABOUR'S LOST [17]
display of g. makes more
demands SENECA [13]
Everyone can master a
g. SHAKESPEARE: MUCH ADO [16]
G. can take care of itself TWAIN [21]
g. ... eldest child of sin WEBSTER, J.
[9]
g. felt so like fear LEWIS, C. S. [6]
G. fills the room up SHAKESPEARE:
KING JOHN [8]
G. is a species of idleness JOHNSON,
S. [79]
G. is the agony DISRAELI [1]
g. itself be mortal SHELLEY, P. B. [73]
G. melts away/Like snow HERBERT,
G. [34]
g. returns with the revolving
year SHELLEY, P. B. [72]
goal of g. RALEGH [1]
hopeless g. is passionless BROWNING,
E. B. [4]
journeyman to g. SHAKESPEARE:
RICHARD II [7]
Nothing becomes so offensive ... as
g. SENECA [6]
Patch g. with proverbs SHAKESPEARE:
MUCH ADO [24]
Silence augmenteth g. DYER, E. [3]
share g. is to double
grief WELDON [6]
silent manliness of g. GOLDSMITH [41]
unmanly g. SHAKESPEARE:
HAMLET [14]

grievance
To have a g. is to have a
purpose HOFFER [4]

grin
nature wears one universal
g. FIELDING, HENRY [3]

grind
bastards g. you
down ANONYMOUS [62]
g. in the prison house BIBLE, OLD
TESTAMENT: JUDGES [14]
g. the faces of the poor BIBLE, OLD
TESTAMENT: ISAIAH [7]

griot
when a g. dies HALEY, A. [1]

gristle
people who are still ... in the
g. BURKE, E. [16]

grit
little g. in the eye TRAHERNE [10]

groaneth
whole creation g. BIBLE, NEW
TESTAMENT: ROMANS [21]

Gromboolian
 great G. plain LEAR [10]
grotesque
 South is ... called g. O'CONNOR, F. [2]
ground
 dark and bloody g. O'HARA [2]
 g. opens up and envelops
 me BARAKA [1]
groups
 divide people into two
 g. HAMPTON [3]
grow'd
 I 'spect I g. STOWE [1]
grown-ups
 G. never understand SAINT-
 EXUPÉRY [8]
Grub Street
 G.! how do I bemoan thee SWIFT,
 J. [49]
grudges
 g. to part with his washing
 water PLAUTUS [2]
Grundy
 more of Mrs. G. LOCKER-LAMPSON
 [2]
 what will Mrs G. zay MORTON, T. [2]
guards
 G. die but do not
 surrender CAMBRONNE [1]
Guenever
 Queen G. ... was a true
 lover MALORY [3]
guerrilla
 g. wins if he does not
 lose KISSINGER [1]
guess
 I never g. DOYLE, A. C. [10]
guest
 first day a man is a g. LABOULAYE [1]
 g. that tarrieth BIBLE, APOCRYPHA:
 WISDOM OF SOLOMON [10]
 No g. is so welcome PLAUTUS [6]
 speed the going g. POPE [156]
 troublesome g. GOLDSMITH [17]
guests
 unbidden g./Are often
 welcomest SHAKESPEARE: HENRY VI
 PT 1 [2]
guid
 ye wha are sae g. yoursel BURNS [26]
guide
 G. me, O Thou great
 Redeemer HYMNS & CAROLS [34]
guillotine
 more I understand the g. SHAW [14]
guilt
 G. has very quick ears FIELDING,
 HENRY [14]
 G. is never to be doubted KAFKA [7]
 most g. about the sins PRITCHETT [5]
 Where g. is, rage and
 courage JONSON [8]

guilty
 g. man wishes only DE BERNIÈRES [1]
 Let no g. man escape GRANT, U. [3]
 no g. man is acquitted JUVENAL [19]
 started, like a g. thing SHAKESPEARE:
 HAMLET [5]
 ten g. persons escape BLACKSTONE [3]
guinea
 jingling of the g. TENNYSON [39]
Guinness
 G. is good for you ADVERTISING
 SLOGANS [10]
guitar
 shining/Like a national g. SIMON
 [10]
 You have a blue g. STEVENS, W. [8]
gulf
 there is a great g. fixed BIBLE, NEW
 TESTAMENT: LUKE [54]
gun
 Austrian g. BLOK [2]
 g. in your pocket WEST, M. [2]
 happiness is a warm g. LENNON/
 MCCARTNEY [16]
 man with the spray g. CARSON, R. [2]
Gunga Din
 better man than I am, G. KIPLING [19]
gunpowder
 G., treason and plot ANONYMOUS
 [78]
guns
 any smoking g. BLIX [1]
 g. spell money's ...
 reason SPENDER [8]
 inexhaustible anger of the
 g. SPENDER [7]
gunshot
 g. is the perfect way KENNEDY,
 J. F. [24]
Gus
 Hop on the bus, G. SIMON [9]
gutter
 We are all in the g. WILDE [75]
gypsies
 wraggle-taggle g. ANONYMOUS [84]
gypsy
 new and showy g. business GARCÍA
 MÁRQUEZ [1]
habit
 fall into a h. UNAMUNO [7]
 H. is ... the enormous fly-
 wheel JAMES, W. [1]
 H. is a second nature PASCAL [4]
 h. is no damn private
 hell HOLIDAY [4]
 H. with him was all the test of
 truth CRABBE [6]
 Heaven's gift is h. PUSHKIN [2]
 peereth in the meanest
 h. SHAKESPEARE: TAMING OF THE
 SHREW [7]
 regularity of a h. PROUST [17]

habits
 H. are the daughters of
 action TAYLOR, J. [5]
 reforming as other people's
 h. TWAIN [13]
had
 all knew you h. it in you PARKER,
 D. [17]
hags
 black, and midnight h. SHAKESPEARE:
 MACBETH [74]
hail
 h. and farewell CATULLUS [18]
hair
 colour of his h. HOUSMAN [1]
 We lose our h. BECKETT [12]
 woman have long h. BIBLE, NEW
 TESTAMENT: 1 CORINTHIANS [27]
hair-oil
 man who uses h. MELVILLE [4]
hairs
 h. of your head BIBLE, NEW
 TESTAMENT: MATTHEW [77]
hairy
 Esau ... is a h. man BIBLE, OLD
 TESTAMENT: GENESIS [51]
 h. body, and arms stiff JUVENAL [5]
half
 dearer h. MILTON [149]
 h. of my own soul HORACE [16]
 how much more the h. is HESIOD [2]
halfway house
 ha'e no h. MACDIARMID [1]
hallowed
 So h. ... is the time SHAKESPEARE:
 HAMLET [6]
hallucination
 h. is a fact RUSSELL, B. [3]
hallucinogenic
 I am h. DALÍ [7]
halo
 What after all/Is a h. FRY, C. [3]
halters
 ill talking of h. CERVANTES [16]
ham
 Give me a h. sandwich CARROLL
 [40]
Hamlet
 H. on a flying trapeze WELLES [3]
 I am not Prince H. ELIOT, T. S. [6]
 saw H. played EVELYN [2]
hammer
 If I had a h. SEEGER, P. [1]
hammer-blows
 I feel two h. here GARCÍA LORCA [6]
hamster
 Freddie Starr ate my h. SUN [4]
hand
 curious engine, your white
 h. WEBSTER, J. [16]
 gloved h. waving OSBORNE [8]
 h. of God MARADONA [1]

some h. did break TENNYSON [89]
through a broken h. WILDE [115]
trusteth in his own h. BIBLE, OLD
TESTAMENT: PROVERBS [92]
unspeakable things ... in the
h. PIRANDELLO [4]
wear my h. upon my
sleeve SHAKESPEARE: OTHELLO [4]
When your h. is broken SHAW [62]
woman's h. must be of such a
size ELIOT, G. [63]

heartbeat
h. from the Presidency STEVENSON,
A. [9]

heartbreak
H. Hotel PRESLEY [2]

heart-easing
most h. things KEATS [10]

heartily
whatsoever ye do, do it h. BIBLE, NEW
TESTAMENT: COLOSSIANS [7]

hearts
Go trouble younger h. WYATT [1]
H. just as pure and fair GILBERT,
W. S. [22]
If all h. were open HARDY, T. [25]
Lift up your h. BOOK OF COMMON
PRAYER [59]
Lift up your h. MISSAL [13]
live in h. we leave behind CAMPBELL,
T. [8]
make clean our h. BOOK OF COMMON
PRAYER [17]
men with Splendid H. BROOKE [3]
Neither have they h. to stay BUTLER,
S. (1612–80) [18]
our h. are great TENNYSON [152]
tossed them human h. to
chew SHELLEY, P. B. [34]

heat
I want the h. AMIS, M. [5]
If you can't stand the h. TRUMAN
[6]
white h. of the technological
revolution WILSON, H. [4]

Heathcliff
I *am* Heathcliff BRONTË, E. [7]

heathen
restore the h. ways VAUGHAN [13]
Why do the h. rage BIBLE, OLD
TESTAMENT: PSALMS [2]

heaven
airs from h. or blasts SHAKESPEARE:
HAMLET [40]
and h. too HENRY, PHILIP [1]
as the h. is high BIBLE, OLD
TESTAMENT: PSALMS [105]
distant from h. alike BURTON [9]
farther off from h. HOOD [7]
floor of h./Is thick
inlaid SHAKESPEARE: MERCHANT OF
VENICE [38]

go to h. with half the
labour JONSON [36]
H. ... where the
donkey ANONYMOUS [33]
h. and my hell is within SCHILLER [1]
H. is so far of the Mind DICKINSON,
E. [13]
H. is under our feet THOREAU [46]
H. lies about us WORDSWORTH,
W. [83]
h. on earth MILTON [130]
kingdom of h. is at hand BIBLE, NEW
TESTAMENT: MATTHEW [6]
kingdoms of h. on
earth MUGGERIDGE [10]
man is as h. made
him CERVANTES [25]
own by-way to h. DEFOE [9]
starry h. above KANT [7]
summons thee to h. SHAKESPEARE:
MACBETH [34]

heaven-gates
H. are not so highly WEBSTER, J. [22]

heavens
create new h. BIBLE, OLD TESTAMENT:
ISAIAH [88]
h. declare the glory of God BIBLE, OLD
TESTAMENT: PSALMS [15]

heavenward
born to fly h. DANTE [21]

heavy
Be not h. upon her, earth MARTIAL
[8]

Hebraism
H. and Hellenism ARNOLD, M. [55]

Hecuba
What's H. to him SHAKESPEARE:
HAMLET [76]

hedge
leaping over the h. CERVANTES [10]

heights
h. by great men
reached LONGFELLOW [23]

heill
I that in h. wes DUNBAR, W. [1]

heir
h. of all the ages TENNYSON [46]
h. to the throne BENNETT, ALAN [8]
weeping of an h. is
laughter PUBLILIUS SYRUS [3]

heiresses
All h. are beautiful DRYDEN [64]

heirs
h. of all eternity SHAKESPEARE: LOVE'S
LABOUR'S LOST [1]
h. of God BIBLE, NEW TESTAMENT:
ROMANS [20]
h. through hope BOOK OF COMMON
PRAYER [65]

Helen
H. must needs be fair SHAKESPEARE:
TROILUS & CRESSIDA [1]

Helicon
watered our houses in H. CHAPMAN,
G. [5]

hell
all h. broke loose MILTON [145]
believe that I am in h. RIMBAUD [17]
Better to reign in h. MILTON [93]
build in h. MILTON [101]
fear of h. or aiming to be
blessed WALLER [8]
gates of H. are open VIRGIL [39]
H. hath no limits MARLOWE [20]
H. is full of musical
amateurs SHAW [21]
H. is not horror MALRAUX [5]
H. is not to love BERNANOS [3]
H. is oneself ELIOT, T. S. [61]
H. is other people SARTRE [6]
I shall move h. VIRGIL [46]
Let me go to h. BECKETT [15]
myself am h. MILTON [127]
never mentions H. POPE [107]
prevent you from going to h. LODGE
JR [1]
safest road to H. LEWIS, C. S. [1]
starless air of H. DANTE [5]
suffers his own H. VIRGIL [43]
this is h. MARLOWE [19]
view to crowding h. DE SADE [10]
wicked people go to h. TAYLOR, ANNE/
JANE [2]

hello
H., good evening FROST, D. [1]

hells
strange h. within the minds GURNEY,
I. [1]

help
H. a man against his will HORACE [82]
h. cometh from the Lord BIBLE, OLD
TESTAMENT: PSALMS [125]
I will make him an h. meet BIBLE,
OLD TESTAMENT: GENESIS [10]
little h. from my friends LENNON/
MCCARTNEY [10]

helper
Lord is my h. BIBLE, NEW TESTAMENT:
HEBREWS [12]
mother's little h. JAGGER/
RICHARDS [3]

hem
h. of his garment BIBLE, NEW
TESTAMENT: MATTHEW [107]

hemisphere
any portion of this h. MONROE, J. [3]

hen
better take a wet h KHRUSHCHEV [5]
h. ... an egg's way BUTLER, S. (1835–
1902) [2]

Henery
H. the Eighth, I am MURRAY, F. [1]

Henry James
work of H. ... divisible GUEDALLA [2]

H. is ... no advantage FREUD [21]

honest
few h. men are better CROMWELL [1]
h. man's the noblest work POPE [139]
H. men/Are the soft easy
cushions OTWAY [3]
not naturally h. SHAKESPEARE:
WINTER'S TALE [18]

honesty
H. is praised JUVENAL [2]
h. should admit no
discourse SHAKESPEARE: HAMLET
[93]

honey
bear likes h. MILNE [6]
h. still for tea BROOKE [6]
Pedigree of H. DICKINSON, E. [38]

honey-bees
For so work the h. SHAKESPEARE:
HENRY V [6]

honeycomb
Pleasant words are as an h. BIBLE,
OLD TESTAMENT: PROVERBS [42]

honi
H. soit qui mal y pense EDWARD III [1]

honour
delighteth to h. BIBLE, OLD
TESTAMENT: ESTHER [3]
fighting for this woman's h. MARX,
G. [6]
greater share of h. SHAKESPEARE:
HENRY V [26]
H. is the subject SHAKESPEARE: JULIUS
CAESAR [3]
h. of a family DE BERNIÈRES [2]
H. pricks me on SHAKESPEARE:
HENRY IV PT 1 [45]
H. sinks where
commerce GOLDSMITH [9]
if it be a sin to covet h. SHAKESPEARE:
HENRY V [27]
leave not a stain in thine h. BIBLE,
APOCRYPHA: ECCLESIASTICUS [54]
loss of h. was a wrench GRAHAM,
H. [2]
louder he talked of his
h. EMERSON [54]
Loved I not h. more LOVELACE [2]
My h. is my loyalty HIMMLER [1]
new-made h. doth
forget SHAKESPEARE: KING JOHN [1]
pluck bright h. SHAKESPEARE:
HENRY IV PT 1 [12]
Set h. in one eye SHAKESPEARE: JULIUS
CAESAR [2]

honourable
Brutus is an h. man SHAKESPEARE:
JULIUS CAESAR [30]

honours
decliner of h. EVELYN [1]

Honours List
Examine the H. BENNETT, ARNOLD [6]

hoods
all h. make not monks SHAKESPEARE:
HENRY VIII [6]

hoof
Whatsoever parteth the h. BIBLE, OLD
TESTAMENT: LEVITICUS [1]

hoops
h. of steel SHAKESPEARE: HAMLET [31]

hope
Abandon every h. DANTE [4]
against h. believed in hope BIBLE,
NEW TESTAMENT: ROMANS [12]
All my h. on God HYMNS &
CAROLS [6]
H. deferred BIBLE, OLD TESTAMENT:
PROVERBS [28]
H. is a long leash COPE [6]
H. is the feeling you have KERR, J. [3]
H. is the only universal
liar INGERSOLL [2]
H. is the thing with
feathers DICKINSON, E. [6]
H. ... not the same thing HAVEL [4]
H. springs eternal POPE [119]
h. to the end BIBLE, NEW TESTAMENT:
1 PETER [1]
He that lives upon h. FRANKLIN, B.
[8]
incurable form of h. NASH, O. [3]
not another's h. WALSH [3]
nursing the unconquerable
h. ARNOLD, M. [32]
some blessed h. HARDY, T. [22]
Take h. from the heart of
man OUIDA [2]
triumph of h. over
experience JOHNSON, S. [73]
ye prisoners of h. BIBLE, OLD
TESTAMENT: ZECHARIAH [6]

hopefulness
Lord of all h. HYMNS & CAROLS [53]

hopeless
inspire h. passion THACKERAY [11]

hopes
If h. were dupes CLOUGH [7]

hoping
power of h. CHESTERTON [7]

Horace
studied felicity of H. PETRONIUS [5]

horn
hideous blast of the hunting
h. ERASMUS [4]
sound of the h., at night VIGNY [1]

horny
h. hands of toil LOWELL, J. R. [2]

horror
h., horror, horror SHAKESPEARE:
MACBETH [46]
The h. CONRAD [9]

horrors
supped full with h. SHAKESPEARE:
MACBETH [95]

hors d'oeuvres
H. have always a pathetic
interest SAKI [1]

horse
Be ye not as the h. BIBLE, OLD
TESTAMENT: PSALMS [40]
between a rider and his
h. SURTEES [8]
courage to ride a h. LEACOCK [1]
flung himself upon his h. LEACOCK [2]
h. is at least *human* SALINGER [4]
h. ... symbol of surging
potency LAWRENCE, D. H. [31]
little h. must think it queer FROST,
R. [19]
My kingdom for a h. SHAKESPEARE:
RICHARD III [20]
O happy h. SHAKESPEARE: ANTONY &
CLEOPATRA [10]
outside of a h. REAGAN, R. [6]
tie a h. to a stake JOSEPH, CHIEF [1]

horseman
H. pass by YEATS [63]

horsemanship
art of h. JONSON [41]

horsemeat
let him eat h. KHRUSHCHEV [9]

horses
don't spare the h. HILLEBRAND, F. [1]
fed h. in the morning BIBLE, OLD
TESTAMENT: JEREMIAH [2]
frighten the h. CAMPBELL, MRS P. [3]
I saw the h. HUGHES, TED [2]
so are h. GILMAN [2]
strange h. came MUIR, E. [1]
value in their h. EMERSON [39]

horticulture
lead a h. PARKER, D. [22]

hospital
first requirement in a
H. NIGHTINGALE [6]
social comfort, in a h. BROWNING,
E. B. [19]

host
I see ... the heavenly h. BLAKE [95]
I'd have been under the h. PARKER,
D. [21]
Lo! the sacred H. we hail AQUINAS [2]

hostage
H. is a crucifying
aloneness KEENAN [1]

hostages
Freeing h. is like WAITE [1]

hot
Some like it h. NURSERY RHYMES [29]

hotel
died in a h. room O'NEILL [10]
events ... in a big h. BAUM, V. [1]
wants to go back to the
h. LEBOWITZ [9]

hound
ain't nothin' but a h. dog PRESLEY [1]

hounds
h. of spring SWINBURNE [1]
hour
front the h. TENNYSON [192]
h. is not yet come BIBLE, NEW
TESTAMENT: JOHN [12]
I also had my h. CHESTERTON [1]
know not what h. BIBLE, NEW
TESTAMENT: MATTHEW [145]
matched us with His h. BROOKE [13]
This was their finest h. CHURCHILL,
W. [22]
watch with me one h. BIBLE, NEW
TESTAMENT: MATTHEW [162]
hours
golden h. slip by BARRIE [18]
Unless h. were cups of
sack SHAKESPEARE: HENRY IV PT 1 [2]
housbands
H. at chirche dore she hadde
fyve CHAUCER [21]
house
h. is a machine for living in LE
CORBUSIER [1]
H. is Not a Home ADLER, P. [1]
h. shelters day-
dreaming BACHELARD [2]
h. that Jack built NURSERY
RHYMES [44]
handsome h. to lodge a friend SWIFT,
J. [22]
join h. to house BIBLE, OLD
TESTAMENT: ISAIAH [11]
Lord build the h. BIBLE, OLD
TESTAMENT: PSALMS [130]
Peace be to this h. BOOK OF COMMON
PRAYER [87]
return no more to his h. BIBLE, OLD
TESTAMENT: JOB [18]
serious h. on serious earth LARKIN [7]
Set thine h. in order BIBLE, OLD
TESTAMENT: 2 KINGS [11]
young and inexperienced
h. JEROME [9]
household
study h. good MILTON [169]
housekeepers
form good h. BYRON, LORD [161]
housekeeping
H. ain't no joke ALCOTT, L. M. [1]
House of Commons
recommend a man to ... the
H. BURKE, E. [7]
House of Lords
cure for admiring the
H. BAGEHOT [16]
God save the H. SWINBURNE [38]
H. is the ... Outer Mongolia BENN [1]
houses
H. are built to live in BACON, F. [34]
Have nothing in your h. MORRIS,
W. [7]

very h. seem asleep WORDSWORTH,
W. [53]
housewife
economics of a h. CHIRAC [1]
housewives
h. in your beds SHAKESPEARE:
OTHELLO [19]
housework
h. is the most
unproductive LENIN [14]
H. is work directly
opposed OAKLEY [1]
no need to do any h. CRISP [4]
Houston
H., we've had a problem LOVELL, J. [1]
hubris
suffer from a h. of the mind VAN DER
POST [1]
Huckleberry Finn
book ... called H. HEMINGWAY [13]
Hugo
H. – hélas GIDE [7]
H. was a madman COCTEAU [9]
hum
undefined and mingled h. HOGG [1]
human
all must love the h. form BLAKE
[6]
Being h. signifies LÉVI-STRAUSS [1]
H. affairs are not serious MURDOCH,
I. [10]
h. condition is such that
pain ARENDT [3]
h. predicament ... a
dialogue GODARD [4]
I am h. TERENCE [4]
love for h. abilities BELLOW [10]
people are only h. COMPTON-
BURNETT [1]
stamp of h.
condition MONTAIGNE [17]
To step aside is h. BURNS [28]
unravelling certain h. lots ELIOT,
G. [41]
human being
so abhorrent to the church as a
h. JOYCE, J. [2]
human beings
h. do not have to be ...
wolves SINCLAIR [2]
H. ... have a value STRACHEY [3]
humaneness
h. is nothing but a weakness DE
SADE [8]
humani
h. nil a me alienum TERENCE [4]
humanist
h. has four leading
characteristics FORSTER [32]
humanities
h. ... nursery games of
humankind BELLOW [2]

humanity
H. is just a work in
progress WILLIAMS, T. [8]
H. is the mind of man MENCIUS [5]
H. is the rich effluvium POUND [2]
historic ascent of h. TROTSKY [9]
serve h. in some function SPOCK [1]
still, sad music of h. WORDSWORTH,
W. [8]
treat h. ... as an end KANT [6]
humankind
H. can generally be
divided HOLUB [4]
human nature
December 1910 h. changed WOOLF [5]
great deal of h. in man KINGSLEY [8]
great republic of h. JOHNSON, S. [48]
H. ... can endure no
restraint KAFKA [11]
not h. we should accuse DIDEROT [7]
Poor h. GOLDMAN, E. [4]
truth and divinity of
h. FEUERBACH [1]
universal thing called h. WILDE [16]
human race
I wish I loved the H. RALEIGH [1]
humble
H. people ... don't get very far ALI [2]
never had a h. opinion BAEZ [2]
humbug
Bah! H. DICKENS [45]
humiliated
you will always be h. AUDEN [52]
humiliation
Avoiding h. GUARE [1]
H. ... beginning of
sanctification DONNE [59]
Valley of H. BUNYAN [5]
you survive h. ELIOT, T. S. [60]
humility
appearance of h. AUSTEN [9]
H. is a virtue all preach SELDEN [3]
H. must always be the
portion EISENHOWER [1]
humor
H. ... is to Americans KEILLOR [4]
humour
H. brings insight REPPLIER [3]
h. is based upon
destruction BRUCE [2]
H. is consistent with
pathos COLERIDGE, S. T. [62]
H. is emotional chaos THURBER [9]
H. is the first of the gifts to
perish WOOLF [6]
H. must not professedly
teach TWAIN [34]
h. of bread and cheese SHAKESPEARE:
MERRY WIVES [5]
own up to a lack of h. COLBY [1]
Humphrey Davy
Sir H./Abominated gravy BENTLEY [1]

difficulty lies not in the new
i. KEYNES [12]
Great i. grow in the
shade FLAUBERT [6]
Hang i. CONRAD [3]
I. ... are dangerous for good or
evil KEYNES [15]
i. must be as broad as Nature DOYLE,
A. C. [5]
i. of the ruling class MARX/ENGELS
[4]
I. that enter the mind under
fire TROTSKY [3]
I. won't keep WHITEHEAD [8]
My i. are a curse SEXTON [7]
No i. but in things WILLIAMS, W. C. [4]
share no one's i. TURGENEV [3]
total change of i. STERNE [20]
Uniform i. ... have a common
ground VICO [2]
ideologies
Our blight is i. JUNG [12]
ides
Beware the i. of March SHAKESPEARE:
JULIUS CAESAR [1]
I. of March have come CAESAR, J. [4]
idiot
i. who praises GILBERT, W. S. [32]
idle
If you are i., be not solitary JOHNSON,
S. [123]
Never less i. than when wholly SCIPIO
AFRICANUS [1]
Not only i., but tattlers also BIBLE,
NEW TESTAMENT: 1 TIMOTHY [10]
To be i. and to be poor JOHNSON,
S. [36]
to be i. is the ultimate
purpose JOHNSON, S. [35]
idleness
busily employed in i. PHAEDRUS [3]
i. implies a catholic
appetite STEVENSON, R. L. [17]
I. is an appendix to
nobility BURTON [5]
I. is its rust TRAHERNE [13]
I. [is] only a coarse name CONNOLLY,
C. [3]
pains and penalties of i. POPE [83]
round of strenuous i. WORDSWORTH,
W. [17]
unyoked humour of your
i. SHAKESPEARE: HENRY IV PT 1 [9]
idler
Be thought an i. YEATS [19]
For the perfect i. BAUDELAIRE [27]
idling
impossible to enjoy i. JEROME [1]
idol
one-eyed yellow i. HAYES, J. M. [1]
idolaters
slay the i. KORAN [22]

idolatry
on this side i. JONSON [39]
organization of i. SHAW [27]
idols
keep yourselves from i. BIBLE, NEW
TESTAMENT: 1 JOHN [9]
pollutions of i. BIBLE, NEW
TESTAMENT: ACTS [21]
if
'I.' is the only peace-
maker SHAKESPEARE: AS YOU LIKE
IT [39]
I. you can keep your
head KIPLING [74]
ignis fatuus
Better an i. DICKINSON, E. [35]
ignominy
Thy i. sleep with thee SHAKESPEARE:
HENRY IV PT 1 [48]
ignorance
blind and naked I. TENNYSON [157]
comprehend its own i. WARNER,
C. D. [4]
Don't die of
ignorance ANONYMOUS [18]
greater the i. ... greater the
dogmatism OSLER [2]
I. is a blind giant ELIOT, G. [58]
I. is an evil weed BEVERIDGE [3]
I. ... is a painless evil ELIOT, G. [7]
I. is like a delicate exotic
fruit WILDE [99]
I. is not innocence BROWNING, R. [60]
i. is one's chief asset STEVENS, W. [26]
I. is the first requisite STRACHEY [2]
I. is the mother of all
evils RABELAIS [14]
I. is the mother of devotion COLE [1]
i. must ... be infinite POPPER [3]
increase the horizon of i. MILLER,
H. [6]
invaluable i. MONTAGU [4]
know nothing except ... my
i. SOCRATES [11]
more dangerous than sincere i. KING,
M. L. [4]
more than Gothic i. FIELDING,
HENRY [10]
natural i. and ... artificial POUND [31]
understand a writer's i. COLERIDGE,
S. T. [54]
Where i. is bliss GRAY, T. [6]
ignorant
Be not i. of any thing BIBLE,
APOCRYPHA: ECCLESIASTICUS [11]
i. armies clash by night ARNOLD,
M. [47]
i. of much, if we would
know NEWMAN [4]
proud and i. people FLANAGAN, O. [1]
Ilium
topless towers of I. MARLOWE [21]

ill
i. our sole delight MILTON [88]
think i. of mankind HAZLITT [19]
We are all i. TRILLING [2]
illegitimate
Oh these i. babies SMITH, STEVIE [9]
ill-housed
one-third of a nation i. ROOSEVELT,
F. D. [5]
illiterate
I. him ... from your
memory SHERIDAN, R. B. [4]
illness
I. is the most heeded of
doctors PROUST [16]
I. is the night-side of life SONTAG [11]
Societies need to have one
i. SONTAG [14]
illusion
know the value of I. ZEFFIRELLI [1]
illusions
I search myself for i. LARKIN [3]
image
created man in his own i. BIBLE, OLD
TESTAMENT: GENESIS [4]
images
life a series of i. WARHOL [7]
long absorption in i. BALL, H. [2]
mass of men must have i. MACAULAY,
LORD [5]
to be without i. HERZOG [2]
imagination
I./... absolute power WORDSWORTH,
W. [24]
I. has seized power GRAFFITI [5]
i. is a monastery KEATS [118]
i. is man's power STEVENS, W. [27]
I. is the eye JOUBERT [2]
i. is the wing JAMES, H. [19]
I., not invention CONRAD [29]
i. of man's heart BIBLE, OLD
TESTAMENT: GENESIS [34]
i. should queen it ELLMANN [1]
I., the supreme delight NABOKOV [7]
indebted ... to his i. SHERIDAN,
R. B. [29]
instrument of ... good is the
i. SHELLEY, P. B. [87]
nose of a mob is its i. POE [18]
of i. all compact SHAKESPEARE:
MIDSUMMER NIGHT'S DREAM [38]
regard the i. as metaphysics STEVENS,
W. [17]
shaping spirit of I. COLERIDGE,
S. T. [47]
Where there is no i. DOYLE, A. C. [6]
imaginations
i. which people have COOLEY [1]
men are ruled by their i. BAGEHOT [9]
imagine
describe what I i. KEATS [56]
I. there's no heaven LENNON [8]

imbecility
key to all ages is – I. EMERSON [46]
IMF
I. is not a charity CHURCHILL, CARYL [1]
imitate
i. what one wants to
create BRAQUE [1]
Those who do not want to i. DALÍ
[8]
usually i. each other HOFFER [3]
imitation
I. is more interesting STEIN [14]
vocation/Were endless
i. WORDSWORTH, W. [85]
imitators
i., you slavish herd HORACE [70]
Immanuel
call his name I. BIBLE, OLD
TESTAMENT: ISAIAH [18]
immemorial
most i. year POE [16]
immoral
i., illegal, or fattening WOOLLCOTT
[1]
immortal
deep down ... we are i. BORGES [2]
i. ... because he has a
soul FAULKNER [4]
I. invisible, God only wise HYMNS &
CAROLS [40]
I have/I. longings SHAKESPEARE:
ANTONY & CLEOPATRA [42]
immortality
achieve i. through my work ALLEN,
W. [6]
I./Is not mere repetition RIDLER [4]
mankind's faith in its own
i. DOSTOYEVSKY [5]
Millions long for i. ERTZ [1]
Quaff i.and joy MILTON [153]
immortalized
i. by battle GOETHE [9]
immortals
i. of the open sky HOMER [7]
immovable
political will ... the i. object BLAIR,
T. [6]
imparadised
I. in one another's arms MILTON
[139]
impartial
I decline utterly to be i. CHURCHILL,
W. [9]
impartiality
What people call i. CHESTERTON [13]
imperfection
i. is the greatness of man FISCHER [1]
imperfections
all my i. on my head SHAKESPEARE:
HAMLET [50]
imperialism
I. is capitalism LENIN [4]

imperially
Learn to think I. CHAMBERLAIN, J. [3]
impertinent
most i. has the best
chance MOZART [1]
important
three most i. things BUTLER, S. (1835–
1902) [31]
impossibility
likely i. is always
preferable ARISTOTLE [14]
impossible
eliminated the i. DOYLE, A. C. [14]
i. ... is possible for God WEIL [6]
i. takes a little
longer ANONYMOUS [16]
If we don't do the i. KELLY, P. [1]
Nothing is i. MUMFORD, L. [5]
One *can't* believe i.
things CARROLL [38]
Perfect reliance on the i. GRAVES,
R. [15]
wish it were i. JOHNSON, S. [156]
imposters
treat those two i. KIPLING [75]
impotence
I. and sodomy are socially
O.K. WAUGH [19]
i. of mind MILTON [194]
impotent
i. people THOMAS, R. S. [1]
impressionable
girl at an i. age SPARK [4]
impressions
erect his personal i. GOURMONT [8]
Harold ... had many i. ELIOT, G.
[32]
weaving ... of false i. ELIOT, G. [1]
imprison
Take me to you, i. me DONNE [48]
improbable
man can never believe the
i. WILDE [20]
impropriety
I. is the soul of wit MAUGHAM [6]
improvement
general i. of mankind MORLEY, J.
[1]
I. makes straight roads BLAKE [36]
schemes of political i. JOHNSON,
S. [70]
improvisation
I. is too good to leave SIMON [11]
impudence
good men starve for want of
i. DRYDEN [47]
impurities
i. are needed LEVI, P. [2]
inaccuracy
I hate i. BUTLER, S. (1835–1902) [24]
i. sometimes saves tons of
explanation SAKI [10]

inaction
i. sap the vigour LEONARDO DA
VINCI [2]
inactivity
wise and masterly i. MACKINTOSH
[1]
inaudible
I. as dreams COLERIDGE, S. T. [12]
incense
soft i. hangs upon the
boughs KEATS [84]
incensed
so i. that I am reckless SHAKESPEARE:
MACBETH [55]
incense-smoke
stupefying i. BROWNING, R. [18]
incest
except i. and folk-
dancing ANONYMOUS [102]
quiet i. flourished LEE, L. [2]
Inchcape
I. Rock SOUTHEY [6]
include
i. me out GOLDWYN [1]
income
Annual i. twenty
pounds DICKENS [67]
desire ... to live beyond its i. BUTLER,
S. (1835–1902) [11]
incommunicable
burden of the i. DE QUINCEY [8]
incompatibility
I. ... In matrimony BIERCE [28]
incompetence
rise to his level of i. PETER [1]
incomplete
haunting curse, the I. BROWNING,
R. [57]
incomprehensibles
There are not three i. BOOK OF
COMMON PRAYER [29]
inconstancy
in Nature were i. COWLEY, A. [2]
inconvenience
adventure is only an
i. CHESTERTON [9]
incorrect
our fate to be i. WALKER [1]
incorruptible
seagreen I. CARLYLE, T. [32]
increase
God gave the i. BIBLE, NEW
TESTAMENT: 1 CORINTHIANS [5]
incredulity
first step towards philosophy is
i. DIDEROT [25]
indecision
nothing is habitual but i. JAMES,
W. [3]
indecisions
time yet for a hundred i. ELIOT,
T. S. [4]

indefatigability
salute ... your i. GALLOWAY [1]
independence
I. ... the grand
blessing WOLLSTONECRAFT [1]
i. Britons prize too
high GOLDSMITH [12]
so little i. of mind TOCQUEVILLE [3]
independent
Be i. CHAMFORT [13]
learning to be an i. sovereign
state NKRUMAH [1]
India
I. is an abstraction CHURCHILL, W. [14]
I. will awake to life NEHRU [2]
nothing in I. is
identifiable FORSTER [16]
Indian
I. is relegated RODRIGUEZ [2]
I.'s night promises to be
dark SEATTLE [1]
Lo! The poor I. POPE [120]
Indians
I. are you BALDWIN, J. [6]
only good I. ... were dead SHERIDAN,
P. H. [1]
indictment
i. against a whole people BURKE,
E. [19]
indifference
i. ... bordering on
aversion STEVENSON, R. L. [23]
i. ... half infidelity BURKE, E. [55]
opposite of love ... is i. WIESEL [1]
indifferent
i. am I BHAGAVAD-GITA [12]
worst sin ... to be i. SHAW [8]
indignatio
Ubi saeva i. ulterius SWIFT, J. [59]
indignation
fierce i. can no longer tear SWIFT,
J. [59]
Fierce i. is best understood GURNEY,
I. [2]
Moral i. is jealousy WELLS [3]
indiscipline
Blind and unwavering i. JARRY [4]
indiscretion
so like innocence as an i. WILDE
[72]
individual
abolish the cult of the
i. KHRUSHCHEV [2]
definition of the i. KOESTLER [2]
ethical reality of the
i. KIERKEGAARD [15]
i. has become the highest
form BERGMAN, INGMAR [1]
i. is not accountable MILL [9]
It is the i. man FRY, C. [1]
recognize the i. as a
higher THOREAU [17]

sacred I. ... has no
significance DEVOTO [1]
individualism
American system of rugged
i. HOOVER, H. [1]
individuality
cult of i. GROSZ [2]
expressing a new i. BROWNING,
E. B. [3]
individuals
society made up of i. MENCKEN [24]
indolence
i. as a sort of *suicide* CHESTERFIELD
[35]
indulge
i. myself a little the more PEPYS [11]
indulgence
son ... might expect more
i. GOLDSMITH [28]
industry
equivocal virtue of i. OLIPHANT [4]
i. without art is brutality RUSKIN
[24]
inelegance
continual state of i. AUSTEN [1]
inequalities
only i. that matter HAWKES [1]
inequality
i. ... is the measure SCHELLING, FELIX
E. [1]
i. is the only bearable
thing PICABIA [2]
no ... i. between the different
stations DIDEROT [12]
inevitable
good action ... appears i. STEVENSON,
R. L. [2]
inexactitude
terminological i. CHURCHILL, W. [3]
inexplicable
fundament ... is the
i. SCHOPENHAUER [1]
infamous
rich, quiet and i. MACAULAY,
LORD [29]
infamy
date which will live in i. ROOSEVELT,
F. D. [11]
infant
i. crying in the night TENNYSON
[103]
No i. ... has as strong a
claim SINGER [4]
Sooner murder an i. BLAKE [37]
inferior
No one can make you feel
i. ROOSEVELT, E. [1]
inferiority
i. of their best friends
CHESTERFIELD [29]
inferiors
live with your i. THACKERAY [15]

infidelity
I. does not consist PAINE [18]
infinite
come from the I. CHILD [2]
man's longing for the
i. BAUDELAIRE [22]
infinitive
care what a split i. is FOWLER,
H. W. [2]
when I split an i. CHANDLER [9]
infinitude
finite things reveal i. ROETHKE [7]
infinity
To i., and beyond LASSETER [2]
infirmity
'Tis the i. of his age SHAKESPEARE:
KING LEAR [9]
inflation
greatest difficulty in curtailing
i. FRIEDMAN [3]
I. is as violent as a mugger REAGAN,
R. [4]
influence
achieve i. in society LACLOS [2]
Anxiety of I. BLOOM, H. [1]
i. the strong characters ASQUITH,
M. [1]
information
add to the sum of accurate
i. MEAD [3]
gather i. LE GUIN [1]
i. can be stored WIENER [2]
I. can tell us
everything BAUDRILLARD [8]
I. is the oxygen REAGAN, R. [14]
Inglan
I. is a bitch JOHNSON, L. K. [2]
ingratiating
still have the power of i. JOHNSON,
S. [146]
ingratitude
hate i. more in a man SHAKESPEARE:
TWELFTH NIGHT [36]
I., thou marble-hearted
fiend SHAKESPEARE: KING LEAR [14]
inhale
didn't i. CLINTON, B. [1]
inheritance
divided an i. LAVATER [2]
inhumanity
Man's i. to Man BURNS [21]
iniquity
shapen in i. BIBLE, OLD TESTAMENT:
PSALMS [63]
injuries
determine all the i. MACHIAVELLI
[4]
i. ... not keep those in
mind THACKERAY [18]
injury
i. is much sooner forgotten
CHESTERFIELD [3]

intentions
City of Magnificent I. DICKENS [41]

intercourse
dreary i. of daily life WORDSWORTH, W. [10]
holds the world together ... sexual i. MILLER, H. [4]
No woman needs i. DWORKIN [3]
Sexual i. began LARKIN [15]
Sexual i. is kicking death BUKOWSKI [6]

interests
i. are eternal and perpetual PALMERSTON [2]
vital i. of citizens GELLHORN [2]

interfere
right by force to i. COBDEN [2]

interjection
life is but an i. BYRON, LORD [170]

interpret
more ado to i. interpretations MONTAIGNE [28]

interpretation
fight about the i. KIERKEGAARD [17]
I. is the revenge SONTAG [1]

interview
literary i. won't tell you AMIS, M. [6]
strange and fatal i. DONNE [32]

intestine
This is the dark i. HUGHES, TED [7]

intimacies
I. between women BOWEN, ELIZABETH [2]

intimacy
not time ... to determine i. AUSTEN [4]

intolerance
I. respecting other people's religion STEVENS, W. [21]

intoxication
best of life is but i. BYRON, LORD [98]

intuition
absolute can only be given in an i. BERGSON [3]
I. and concepts constitute KANT [1]

invasion
i. of armies HUGO [2]

invent
right to i. themselves GREER [12]

invented
I have i. myself FELLINI [3]

invention
I. flags CONGREVE [25]
i. is but the talent of a liar BYRON, LORD [72]

inventions
bringing all these new i. IBSEN [2]
i. are ... pretty toys THOREAU [29]
patent age of new i. BYRON, LORD [92]
sought out many i. BIBLE, OLD TESTAMENT: ECCLESIASTES [25]

inventor
return/To plague the i. SHAKESPEARE: MACBETH [22]

investigating
We never stop i. MORRIS, D. [1]

invisible
led by an i. hand SMITH, ADAM [7]
what is essential is i. SAINT-EXUPÉRY [9]

invited
If thou be i. of a mighty man BIBLE, APOCRYPHA: ECCLESIASTICUS [31]

ira
Ça i. ANONYMOUS [8]

irascibility
I., muse of middle age WALCOTT [3]

Ireland
I. gives England her soldiers MEREDITH, G. [13]
I. ... is nothing to me CONNOLLY, J. [3]
I. is the old sow JOYCE, J. [15]
I. is where strange tales begin HAUGHEY [1]
I.! that cloud GLADSTONE [2]
in I. there is an excess PRITCHETT [3]
Mad I. hurt you into poetry AUDEN [16]
No one ... stays in I. JOYCE, J. [7]
no sex in I. FLANAGAN, O. [2]
Romantic I.'s dead YEATS [25]
very name of I. is mentioned SMITH, SYDNEY [1]

Irish
I. Americans are about as Irish GELDOF [4]
I. are the niggers of Europe DOYLE, R. [1]
I. ... never speak well JOHNSON, S. [87]
I'm dissatisfied, I'm I. MOORE, MARIANNE [9]
symbol of I. art JOYCE, J. [24]
We I. ... are the greatest talkers WILDE [4]

Irishmen
originality among I. MOORE, G. [6]

Irishness
I. is not ... question of birth O'BRIEN, C. C. [1]

Irish question
That is the I. DISRAELI [11]

Irishry
indomitable I. YEATS [62]

iron
Any old i. COLLINS, C. [1]
i. and blood BISMARCK [1]
i. entered into his soul BIBLE, OLD TESTAMENT: PSALMS [110]
i. entered my soul THATCHER [11]
I. sharpeneth iron BIBLE, OLD TESTAMENT: PROVERBS [88]
i. tears down Pluto's cheek MILTON [26]

laid in i. BIBLE, OLD TESTAMENT: PSALMS [110]

Iron Lady
I. of the Western World THATCHER [3]

irrationality
experience of the i. of the world WEBER [1]

irresolute
resolved to be i. CHURCHILL, W. [15]

irresponsibility
I. is part of the pleasure KAEL [3]

is
meaning of the word 'i.' CLINTON, B. [3]

Ishmael
Call me I. MELVILLE [2]

Ishmaelites
because they were I. BIBLE, OLD TESTAMENT: JUDGES [8]

Islam
true religion with God is I. KORAN [14]
we must absorb I. BUNTING [4]

Islamic
I. world ... held prisoner RUSHDIE [11]

island
No man is an i. DONNE [55]
our rough i. story TENNYSON [139]
snug little I. DIBDIN [1]

islander
narrow prejudices of an I. BYRON, LORD [14]

isle
Fairest I., all isles excelling DRYDEN [66]
I. of fragrance POPE [82]
this sceptred i. SHAKESPEARE: RICHARD II [12]

Israel
I. is the Lord's portion BIBLE, APOCRYPHA: ECCLESIASTICUS [35]
I. scattered upon the hills BIBLE, OLD TESTAMENT: 1 KINGS [16]
I.'s head forlorn LAZARUS [3]
In I. ... to be a realist BEN GURION [1]
Redeem I. BIBLE, OLD TESTAMENT: PSALMS [31]
ruler in I. BIBLE, OLD TESTAMENT: MICAH [1]

it
It's just I. KIPLING [67]

Italia
I. ... hast/The fatal gift BYRON, LORD [80]

Italians
I. ... act without thinking DE BERNIÈRES [3]
religiosity of the I. GRAMSCI [6]

Italy
after seeing I. BURNEY [4]
damnably sick of I. JOYCE, J. [5]
gone to I. to study FORSTER [3]

appearance BIBLE, NEW TESTAMENT: JOHN [28]

J. not, that ye be not judged BIBLE, NEW TESTAMENT: MATTHEW [48]

j. us by what we have ... done LONGFELLOW [15]

take good heed not to j. me ill JOAN OF ARC [2]

when the J. shall be seated MISSAL [27]

judgement
j.! thou art fled to brutish beasts SHAKESPEARE: JULIUS CAESAR [32]

let j. run down as waters BIBLE, OLD TESTAMENT: AMOS [4]

looked for j. BIBLE, OLD TESTAMENT: ISAIAH [10]

you fear more to deliver j. BRUNO, G. [5]

Nor is the people's j. always true DRYDEN [37]

judges
J. don't age BAGNOLD [1]

j. of normality FOUCAULT [5]

judgest
wherein thou j. another BIBLE, NEW TESTAMENT: ROMANS [6]

judgment book
leaves of the J. unfold TAYLOR, BAYARD [1]

judgments
j. of the other mind COOLEY [3]

Judy O'Grady
Colonel's Lady an' J. KIPLING [48]

jugular
nearer to him than the/j. KORAN [42]

Julius Caesar
J., thou art mighty yet SHAKESPEARE: JULIUS CAESAR [47]

Jumblies
lands where the J. live LEAR [9]

June
J. is bustin' out HAMMERSTEIN II [6]

jungle
Laws of the J. KIPLING [42]

like a j. sometimes GRANDMASTER FLASH [1]

junk
J. is the ideal product BURROUGHS, W. [3]

junky
j. runs on junk time BURROUGHS, W. [1]

junta
Stick it up your j. SUN [2]

jury
j., passing on the prisoner's life SHAKESPEARE: MEASURE FOR MEASURE [7]

just
J. are the ways of God MILTON [198]

j. upright man BIBLE, OLD TESTAMENT: JOB [21]

path of the j. BIBLE, OLD TESTAMENT: PROVERBS [7]

spirits of j. men BIBLE, NEW TESTAMENT: HEBREWS [9]

justice
cannot do j. to the dead SHAWCROSS [1]

deny or delay right or j. MAGNA CARTA [2]

easy to do j. RATTIGAN [1]

even-handed j. SHAKESPEARE: MACBETH [23]

in the course of j. SHAKESPEARE: MERCHANT OF VENICE [35]

J. consists in doing no injury CICERO [14]

J. is nothing else PLATO [3]

j. rolls down like waters KING, M. L. [17]

J. should ... be seen HEWART [1]

Let j. be done FERDINAND I [1]

Let judges secretly despair of j. COHEN [1]

live like a j. of the peace NAPOLEON I [19]

love of j. is ... the fear LA ROCHEFOUCAULD [9]

price of j. BENNETT, ARNOLD [10]

straitjacket of criminal j. KRAUS [2]

what stings is j. MENCKEN [12]

When j. has spoken VERGNIAUD [1]

Where j. is denied DOUGLASS [4]

you have ravished j. WEBSTER, J. [8]

justices
just man j. HOPKINS [23]

justification
carry its j. in every line CONRAD [1]

justifieth
God that j. BIBLE, NEW TESTAMENT: ROMANS [24]

justify
j. the ways of God MILTON [84]

justly
to do j., and to love mercy BIBLE, OLD TESTAMENT: MICAH [2]

Kaiser
hatred of the K. is love true THOMAS, E. [6]

kangaroo
Tie me k. down HARRIS, ROLF [1]

Kansas
not in K. anymore GARLAND [2]

Kant
read K. by yourself STEVENSON, R. L. [8]

karma
k. is working HODDLE [1]

Kaspar
Old K.'s work was done SOUTHEY [1]

keen
grief of the k. SYNGE [2]

Kennedy
President and Mrs K. JOHNSON, LADY B. [1]

Kennedys
Who killed the K. JAGGER/RICHARDS [4]

kennel
friends in the k. ... not in the kitchen SHAW [33]

Kenny
they've killed K. STONE/PARKER [1]

Kensal Green
by way of K. CHESTERTON [33]

Kent
everybody knows K. DICKENS [6]

Kerouac
K. opened a million coffee bars BURROUGHS, W. [8]

kettle
how agree the k. and the ... pot BIBLE, APOCRYPHA: ECCLESIASTICUS [30]

Polly put the k. on NURSERY RHYMES [30]

Kew
Highness' dog at K. POPE [164]

keyhole
Every age has a k. MCCARTHY, M. [5]

Keynesians
We are all K. now FRIEDMAN [2]

keys
k. of the kingdom BIBLE, NEW TESTAMENT: MATTHEW [114]

khaki
gentleman in k. ordered South KIPLING [51]

kick
I get a k. out of you PORTER, C. [9]

kidding
Who do you think you are k. PERRY [1]

kill
gift designed to k. DOUGLAS, K. [2]

how many kids did you k. POLITICAL SLOGANS [15]

K. a man, one is a murderer ROSTAND, J. [1]

k. sick people MARLOWE [7]

k. yourself *too late* CIORAN [8]

Then k., kill, kill SHAKESPEARE: KING LEAR [53]

Thou shalt not k. BIBLE, OLD TESTAMENT: EXODUS [25]

Thou shalt not k. CLOUGH [3]

urge to k., like the urge to beget VOZNESENSKY [3]

killed
everyone can be k. COPPOLA [1]

must have k. a lot of men MOLIÈRE [21]

kills
man k. the thing he loves WILDE [110]

Kilroy
K. was here GRAFFITI [7]

Kiltartan
My country is K. Cross YEATS [30]

kin
little more than k. SHAKESPEARE: HAMLET [10]

kind
art of being k. WILCOX [2]
k. to people about whom one cares nothing WILDE [56]
Too k. NIGHTINGALE [8]

kinder
k., gentler nation BUSH, G. [4]

kindness
Dame K. glides about my house PLATH [13]
k. that gazes upon itself GIBRAN [6]
kill a wife with k. SHAKESPEARE: TAMING OF THE SHREW [6]
man that has done a k. AURELIUS [10]
No act of k. ... is ever wasted AESOP'S FABLES [8]
terrible thing, this k. LE GUIN [2]
True k. presupposes GIDE [2]
unremembered acts/Of k. WORDSWORTH, W. [5]
When k. has left people CATHER [6]

king
balm ... from an anointed k. SHAKESPEARE: RICHARD II [19]
despised, and dying k. SHELLEY, P. B. [46]
every inch a k. SHAKESPEARE: KING LEAR [46]
Every subject's duty is the K.'s SHAKESPEARE: HENRY V [23]
God save the k. BIBLE, OLD TESTAMENT: 1 SAMUEL [6]
God save the k. CAREY, H. [2]
heart and stomach of a k. ELIZABETH I [2]
How can you say ... I am a k. SHAKESPEARE: RICHARD II [24]
k. by your own fireside CERVANTES [1]
K. cometh unto thee BIBLE, OLD TESTAMENT: ZECHARIAH [5]
k. for a night DE NIRO [3]
k. is always a king WOLLSTONECRAFT [7]
k. is a thing men have made SELDEN [4]
K. is but a man SHAKESPEARE: HENRY V [22]
K. OF KINGS BIBLE, NEW TESTAMENT: REVELATION [44]
k. of shreds and patches SHAKESPEARE: HAMLET [124]
k. should die on his feet LOUIS XVIII [2]
k. to morrow shall die BIBLE, APOCRYPHA: ECCLESIASTICUS [23]

kill a k. and marry SHAKESPEARE: HAMLET [120]
Man Who Would be K. KIPLING [5]
no k. who has not had a slave KELLER [1]
once and future k. MALORY [6]
Once and Future K. WHITE, T. H. [1]
passing brave to be a K. MARLOWE [11]
So excellent a k. SHAKESPEARE: HAMLET [17]
What must the K. do SHAKESPEARE: RICHARD II [25]

kingdoms
all the k. of the world BIBLE, NEW TESTAMENT: MATTHEW [18]
shewed ... all the k. BIBLE, NEW TESTAMENT: LUKE [16]

kingfishers
As k. catch fire HOPKINS [22]

kings
heart of k. is unsearchable BIBLE, OLD TESTAMENT: PROVERBS [73]
k. and counsellors BIBLE, OLD TESTAMENT: JOB [9]
k. in golden suits CHEEVER [3]
Many k. have sat down BIBLE, APOCRYPHA: ECCLESIASTICUS [25]
only five k. left FAROUK [1]
sad stories of the death of k. SHAKESPEARE: RICHARD II [23]
We three k. HYMNS & CAROLS [87]
What are k., when regiment MARLOWE [15]

King's English
abusing of ... the K. SHAKESPEARE: MERRY WIVES [3]

king-times
k. are fast finishing BYRON, LORD [126]

Kipling
Auden, a sort of gutless K. ORWELL [3]
K. is a genius who drops WILDE [29]

kiss
But his k. was so sweet GAY, J. [23]
come let us k. and part DRAYTON [5]
euthanasia of a k. DE LA MARE [12]
I saw you take his k. PATMORE [5]
k. all the fellows MURRAY, L. [4]
k. can be a comma MISTINGUETT [1]
k. is but a kiss now MEREDITH, G. [6]
k. is still a kiss HUPFELD [1]
K. Kiss KAEL [2]
k./Long as my exile SHAKESPEARE: CORIOLANUS [10]
k. me and me quiet MONTAGU [10]
k. me, Kate SHAKESPEARE: TAMING OF THE SHREW [4]
last lamenting k. DONNE [28]
make me immortal with a k. MARLOWE [22]

Salute ... with an holy k. BIBLE, NEW TESTAMENT: ROMANS [44]
sound of a k. is not so loud HOLMES SR [14]
What did that mean, to k. JOYCE, J. [13]
When women k. MENCKEN [19]

kissed
and k. him BIBLE, NEW TESTAMENT: MATTHEW [165]
k. away/Kingdoms SHAKESPEARE: ANTONY & CLEOPATRA [21]
K. the girls NURSERY RHYMES [9]

kisses
k. of an enemy BIBLE, OLD TESTAMENT: PROVERBS [85]
thousand k. CATULLUS [7]

kissing
K. don't last MEREDITH, G. [4]
k., kind-hearted gentleman COWPER [31]
when the k. had to stop BROWNING, R. [25]

Kitchener
K. is a great poster ASQUITH, E. [1]

kitsch
K. is the daily art ROSENBERG, H. [2]

kitten
I had rather be a k. SHAKESPEARE: HENRY IV PT 1 [29]

knack
we've lost the k. DAY LEWIS [5]

knave
every man must be supposed a k. HUME, D. [3]
in life a foolish prating k. SHAKESPEARE: HAMLET [128]

knavery
K. seems to be ... the striking feature GEORGE III [2]

knee
every k. should bow BIBLE, NEW TESTAMENT: PHILIPPIANS [3]

knees
Bow, stubborn k. SHAKESPEARE: HAMLET [117]

knife
I will not use the k. HIPPOCRATES [6]
sharpening my oyster k. HURSTON [1]

knight
gentle k. was pricking SPENSER [6]
never matched of earthly k.'s hand MALORY [7]
When a k. won his spurs HYMNS & CAROLS [88]

knights
fellowship of good k. MALORY [4]

knitters
k. in the sun SHAKESPEARE: TWELFTH NIGHT [21]

knock
k. a thing ... is a deep
delight SANTAYANA [5]
k. at the door. LAMB, CHARLES [16]
k. him down first JOHNSON, S. [102]
stand at the door, and k. BIBLE, NEW
TESTAMENT: REVELATION [12]

knocked
what they k. down FENTON [1]

know
All men ... desire to k. ARISTOTLE [1]
How do they k. PARKER, D. [12]
I k. not the man BIBLE, NEW
TESTAMENT: MATTHEW [167]
k. much and be
impotent HERODOTUS [4]
k. not what ... know not
where DRYDEN [16]
k. not what they do BIBLE, NEW
TESTAMENT: LUKE [71]
k. someone is to have
loved JOUHANDEAU [1]
k. ... that he nothing
knew MILTON [191]
K. then thyself POPE [127]
K. thyself ANONYMOUS [51]
k. what we are SHAKESPEARE:
HAMLET [135]
merely k. more SAKI [9]
Not many people k. that CAINE [1]
not to k. what you are STEIN [10]
not young enough to k.
everything BARRIE [2]
think that one does not k. TAO TE
CHING [14]
To k. all is not to forgive all CRISP [3]
When you k. a thing CONFUCIUS [8]

knowable
We delight in one k. thing BRUNO,
G. [4]

knowe
kan hymselven k. CHAUCER [47]

knowest
k. I love thee BIBLE, NEW TESTAMENT:
JOHN [78]

knowing
Meek k. of thyself THOMAS À
KEMPIS [1]

knowingness
k. of little girls MCGINLEY, P. [2]

knowledge
all k. to be my province BACON, F.
[1]
ask it for the k. of a
lifetime WHISTLER [2]
Can k. have no bound DENHAM [1]
For k. itself is power BACON, F. [2]
incapable of universal and certain
k. LOCKE [6]
Is your k./Nothing PERSIUS [2]
K. ... acquired under
compulsion SOCRATES [25]

K. advances by steps MACAULAY,
LORD [12]
K. and wonder GOULD [4]
K., a rude unprofitable
mass COWPER [45]
K. divorced from life BELLOW [9]
K. enormous KEATS [115]
k. increaseth sorrow BIBLE, OLD
TESTAMENT: ECCLESIASTES [8]
K. is a polite word for
dead CUMMINGS, E. E. [12]
k. is bought in the market CLOUGH [1]
K. is of two kinds JOHNSON, S. [95]
k. is ourselves to know POPE [141]
K. is what we get LASCH [4]
k. of the physical world LEVI, P. [3]
k. of the world JOHNSON, S. [11]
K. puffeth up BIBLE, NEW TESTAMENT:
1 CORINTHIANS [18]
k. shall be increased BIBLE, OLD
TESTAMENT: DANIEL [14]
k. that *acts* GIBRAN [8]
K. without conscience RABELAIS [8]
love of Christ, which passeth
k. BIBLE, NEW TESTAMENT:
EPHESIANS [3]
man must carry k. with
him JOHNSON, S. [117]
province of k. to speak HOLMES
SR [13]
Such k. is too wonderful BIBLE, OLD
TESTAMENT: PSALMS [142]
three ... means of acquiring
k. DIDEROT [4]
use of k. in our sex MONTAGU [15]

known
hast thou not k. me, Philip BIBLE,
NEW TESTAMENT: JOHN [51]
Have ye not k. BIBLE, OLD TESTAMENT:
ISAIAH [58]
to be k. is ... to have
life MONTAIGNE [15]

knowns
there are known k. RUMSFELD [2]

knows
further one goes/... less one k. TAO TE
CHING [9]
He who k. himself TAO TE CHING [7]
Man ... k. nothing PLINY THE ELDER
[4]
one who k. does not speak TAO TE
CHING [10]

knuckle-end
k. of England SMITH, SYDNEY [11]

knyght
verray parfit, gentil k. CHAUCER [16]

Kool-Aid
Electric K. Acid Test WOLFE, TOM [1]

Koran
Arabic K. KORAN [32]
nothing in our book, the
K. MALCOLM X [2]

kraft
K. durch Freude POLITICAL
SLOGANS [21]

Kraken
K. sleepeth TENNYSON [4]

Kremlin
turns to the K.
mountaineer MANDELSTAM [5]

Kurtz
Mistah K. – he dead CONRAD [10]

kyrie
K. eleison MISSAL [6]

labels
flamboyant l. BEVAN [13]
great men are l. TOLSTOY [3]

laboring
interests of the l. man BAER [1]

labour
Honest l. bears a lovely
face DEKKER [1]
In all l. there is profit BIBLE, OLD
TESTAMENT: PROVERBS [34]
insupportable l. of doing
nothing STEELE [5]
L. in a white skin MARX, K. [15]
L. is prior to ... capital LINCOLN [18]
L. isn't working ADVERTISING
SLOGANS [18]
l. night and day BUNYAN [16]
l. of keeping house MCCARTHY, M. [7]
Nothing ... made by man's l. MORRIS,
W. [13]
reward of l. is *life* MORRIS, W. [16]

Labour Party
L. ... is a class party KEYNES [7]

labourer
I am a true l. SHAKESPEARE: AS YOU
LIKE IT [20]
l. is worthy of his hire BIBLE, NEW
TESTAMENT: LUKE [26]

labourers
l. are few BIBLE, NEW TESTAMENT:
MATTHEW [70]

lacrimae
Hinc illae l. TERENCE [1]
l. rerum VIRGIL [24]

ladder
behold a l. to heaven BIBLE, OLD
TESTAMENT: GENESIS [52]

la-de-da
Well, l. KEATON [1]

ladies
L. are your finger
watches SHADWELL [2]
when he has l. to please AUSTEN [23]

lads
l. that will never be old HOUSMAN [9]

lady
I'm a l. LITTLE BRITAIN [2]
I want to talk like a l. SHAW [54]
l. is nothing very specific LYNES [3]
l. of Christ's College AUBREY [3]

L., and the world laughs WILCOX [1]
l. at the world better LAWRENCE, D. H. [2]
l. before being happy LA BRUYÈRE [11]
l. that spoke the vacant mind GOLDSMITH [34]
making decent people l. MOLIÈRE [4]
nothing more silly than a silly l. CATULLUS [10]
To l. is proper to man RABELAIS [1]
unextinguishable l. in heaven BROWNE [20]
We are not here to l. DE GAULLE [14]

laughed
day on which one has not l. CHAMFORT [4]
heartily and wholly l. CARLYLE, T. [14]
they l. consumedly FARQUHAR [12]
Time has l. them all to scorn LOCKER-LAMPSON [1]

laughing
L., quaffing, and unthinking time DRYDEN [80]
we had more l. GOLDSMITH [22]

laughs
seven l. a minute DODD [2]

laughter
born with a gift of l. SABATINI [1]
distinguished ... by the faculty of l. ADDISON [15]
in l. the heart is sorrowful BIBLE, OLD TESTAMENT: PROVERBS [32]
In l. we stretch the mouth HOLUB [3]
l. and the love of friends BELLOC [6]
L. is not ... a bad beginning WILDE [37]
l., It is mad BIBLE, OLD TESTAMENT: ECCLESIASTES [9]
l. of the fool BIBLE, OLD TESTAMENT: ECCLESIASTES [19]
l. that sickens the soul PEAKE [2]
L. would be bereaved USTINOV [1]
lofty rapturous l. GOGOL [2]
Present mirth hath present l. SHAKESPEARE: TWELFTH NIGHT [15]
so illiberal ... as audible l. CHESTERFIELD [10]

laurels
once more, O ye l. MILTON [43]

lava
l. of the imagination BYRON, LORD [36]

lavatory
long march to and from the l. MORTIMER [2]

law
Better to break the l. POLITICAL SLOGANS [4]
individual who breaks a l. KING, M. L. [8]
l. cannot make a man love me KING, M. L. [3]

l. hath not been dead SHAKESPEARE: MEASURE FOR MEASURE [10]
l., in its majestic equality FRANCE [2]
l. is a ass DICKENS [23]
l. is a causeway BOLT [3]
l. is a ... hocus-pocus science MACKLIN [1]
l. is good BIBLE, NEW TESTAMENT: 1 TIMOTHY [2]
L. is the true embodiment GILBERT, W. S. [21]
l. of nature and of nations BURKE, E. [53]
l. often allows SAURIN [2]
l. ... reminds one of those outskirts BAGEHOT [24]
l. ... the perfection of reason COKE [2]
l. unto themselves BIBLE, NEW TESTAMENT: ROMANS [8]
l. was made for one thing BRECHT [5]
one great principle of the English l. DICKENS [78]
One l. for the lion and ox BLAKE [41]
One L., one Land, one Throne KIPLING [82]
outside the l., you must be honest DYLAN [25]
sharp quillets of the l. SHAKESPEARE: HENRY VI PT 1 [3]
where no l. is BIBLE, NEW TESTAMENT: ROMANS [11]
Wherever l. ends LOCKE [14]
Who to himself is l. CHAPMAN, G. [3]
windward of the l. CHURCHILL, CHARLES [6]

lawful
All things are l. BIBLE, NEW TESTAMENT: 1 CORINTHIANS [25]

law-givers
My l. are Erasmus FORSTER [25]

laws
bad or obnoxious l. GRANT, U. [2]
good l. and good arms MACHIAVELLI [6]
L. are felt LAFOLLETTE [2]
L. are like cobwebs SWIFT, J. [15]
L. are silent CICERO [7]
l. ... cannot be creative MARTINEAU [4]
L. grind the poor GOLDSMITH [14]
L. ... lean on one another BURKE, E. [5]
l. of God, the laws of man HOUSMAN [24]
l. of necessity JEFFERSON [27]
Petty l. breed great crimes OUIDA [1]
right to make l. PANKHURST [3]
unequal l. unto a savage race TENNYSON [26]
Useless l. weaken the necessary ones MONTESQUIEU [3]
whether l. be right WILDE [114]

lawyer
If l.'s hand is fee'd GAY, J. [17]

l. with his briefcase PUZO [2]
l. without history SCOTT, W. [17]

lawyers
L. enjoy a little mystery SAYERS [1]
L. know life practically JOHNSON, S. [118]
let's kill all the l. SHAKESPEARE: HENRY VI PT 2 [6]
no good l. DICKENS [32]
They become l. ALLEN, W. [8]
Woe unto you, l. BIBLE, NEW TESTAMENT: LUKE [35]

Lazarus
L., ... laid at his gate BIBLE, NEW TESTAMENT: LUKE [52]

laziness
L. ... Unwarranted repose of manner BIERCE [29]
languor ... I must call it l. KEATS [47]

lazy
L. people are always anxious VAUVENARGUES [3]
seldom call anybody l. MANDEVILLE [1]

lead
Hour of L. DICKINSON, E. [12]
L. us, Heavenly Father HYMNS & CAROLS [50]

leader
final test of a l. LIPPMANN [4]
I am a l. by default TUTU [2]
I'm their l. LEDRU-ROLLIN [1]
l. for the Labour Party BEVAN [10]
l. in talent and truth BYRON, LORD [31]
one people, one l. POLITICAL SLOGANS [10]
political l. must keep looking BARUCH [3]
To be a l. of men ELLIS [1]

leaders
Don't follow l. DYLAN [8]
l. have had one characteristic GALBRAITH [11]

leadership
art of l. is saying no BLAIR, T. [2]
l. consists in consolidating HITLER [3]
l. of any description LOVETT [1]

league
Half a l. TENNYSON [140]

Leah
I am called L. DANTE [25]

leak
good l. will do BELL, T. [2]

leaky
thou art so l. SHAKESPEARE: ANTONY & CLEOPATRA [23]

leanness
l. goes ... towards gentility GASKELL [3]

leaping
l., and praising God BIBLE, NEW TESTAMENT: ACTS [7]

l. has crept ... on a broken wing TENNYSON [133]

l. has no meaning GAUGUIN [5]

l. has no point TARKOVSKY [1]

l. hovers like a star BYRON, LORD [171]

L. ... imitates bad television ALLEN, W. [28]

L. is a battle NIEBUHR [1]

l. is a disease SHAW [68]

l. is a dream CALDERÓN DE LA BARCA [1]

l. is ... a dream and a fear CONRAD [24]

L. is a foreign country KEROUAC [1]

L. is a foreign language MORLEY, C. [1]

L. is ... a fraction of a second GAUGUIN [1]

L. is a gamble STOPPARD [6]

L. is a means of extracting fiction STONE, R. [1]

L. is an abnormal business IONESCO [1]

L. is an offensive WHITEHEAD [5]

L. is ... being well MARTIAL [9]

L. is but a campaign AURELIUS [4]

l. is but a day KEATS [8]

L. ... is but a froward child GOLDSMITH [25]

L. is but a sort of exhalation AURELIUS [12]

L. ... is but the shadow BROWNE [21]

L. is divided up into the horrible ALLEN, W. [21]

L. is filigree work CÉLINE [3]

L. is ... getting tired BUTLER, S. (1835–1902) [9]

L. is infinitely stranger DOYLE, A. C. [17]

L. is just one damned thing HUBBARD, E. [4]

L. is like a sewer LEHRER [4]

L. is like playing a violin BUTLER, S. (1835–1902) [4]

L. is made up of marble HAWTHORNE [7]

L. is mostly froth GORDON, A.L. [1]

L. ... is not here PRITCHETT [4]

L. is one long struggle LUCRETIUS [4]

L. is – or has – meaning JUNG [24]

L. is real! Life is earnest LONGFELLOW [3]

L. is short HIPPOCRATES [1]

L. is short SENECA [18]

l. is statistical improbability DAWKINS [4]

l. is sweet SWINBURNE [17]

L. is the art of drawing BUTLER, S. (1835–1902) [10]

L. is too short SHAW [67]

L. is too short to be little DISRAELI [20]

L. is trouble KAZANTZAKIS [1]

l. is very short TAYLOR, J. [4]

L. is what happens to you LENNON [9]

l., Jim RODDENBERRY [2]

L., Joy, Empire, and Victory SHELLEY, P. B. [61]

L. loves the liver of it ANGELOU [7]

l. must be understood backwards KIERKEGAARD [14]

l. of his ... contemporaries MANN, T. [2]

L. ... one damn thing over and over MILLAY [10]

L. robs us of ourselves UPDIKE [18]

l.'s a clock QUARLES [6]

L.'s a pudding full of plums GILBERT, W. S. [43]

L.'s brief span HORACE [18]

l.'s fitful fever SHAKESPEARE: MACBETH [60]

l. simply turns into the next MOTION [2]

L. ... tedious as a twice-told tale SHAKESPEARE: KING JOHN [9]

l. that I have MARKS, L. [1]

l. ... the eternal antithesis of art MISHIMA [3]

l. was a feast RIMBAUD [13]

L. was a funny thing CRISP [5]

L. was too short MAUGHAM [15]

L. well spent is long LEONARDO DA VINCI [1]

lay down my l. for two brothers HALDANE [4]

laying down l. itself DAY, DOROTHY [1]

lived a l./ ... with no blame DANTE [6]

loosed from its dream of l. JARRELL [1]

More A Way Of L. ANONYMOUS [63]

never know what l. means BROWNING, R. [58]

Nobody can write the l. of a man JOHNSON, S. [75]

Nor love thy l., nor hate MILTON [181]

one l. to lose for my country HALE [1]

one l. within us and abroad COLERIDGE, S. T. [3]

plunge both hands into l. ANOUILH [3]

profit of l. consists MONTAIGNE [4]

queer thing L. is WODEHOUSE [4]

ready to die with l. JUNG [10]

see into the l. of things WORDSWORTH, W. [7]

stuff of l. to knit me HOUSMAN [13]

things l. has done to us O'NEILL [9]

this sweet l. DANTE [29]

True l. is elsewhere RIMBAUD [19]

understand l. any better at forty RENARD [5]

We are so fond of l. STEVENSON, R. L. [21]

well-written l. is ... rare CARLYLE, T. [4]

when l.'s sweet fable ends CRASHAW [4]

Where is the L. we have lost ELIOT, T. S. [35]

You can't control l. ALLEN, W. [26]

lifeless

l., lightless, worthless QUARLES [5]

life-lie

Take the l. away IBSEN [13]

life-sentence

l. in the dungeon of self CONNOLLY, C. [20]

lift

L. up your heads BIBLE, OLD TESTAMENT: PSALMS [29]

light

burning and a shining l. BIBLE, NEW TESTAMENT: JOHN [23]

certain Slant of l. DICKINSON, E. [7]

dim religious l. MILTON [27]

fade into the l. of common day WORDSWORTH, W. [84]

God is the L. of the heavens KORAN [34]

God's first creature ... l. BACON, F. [57]

gone into the world of l. VAUGHAN [8]

Hail, holy L. MILTON [121]

how my l. is spent MILTON [78]

I am the l. of the world BIBLE, NEW TESTAMENT: JOHN [33]

l. between truth DANTE [19]

L. breaks where no sun THOMAS, D. [3]

l. given to him ... in misery BIBLE, OLD TESTAMENT: JOB [11]

L., God's eldest daughter FULLER, T. [2]

l. he leaves behind him LONGFELLOW [22]

l. of the oncoming train LOWELL, R. [8]

L. seeking light SHAKESPEARE: LOVE'S LABOUR'S LOST [3]

l. so shine before men BIBLE, NEW TESTAMENT: MATTHEW [25]

l. that never was WORDSWORTH, W. [77]

Lead, kindly L. HYMNS & CAROLS [49]

Let there be l. BIBLE, OLD TESTAMENT: GENESIS [1]

Lord is my l. BIBLE, OLD TESTAMENT: PSALMS [32]

More l. GOETHE [32]

out of hell leads up to l. MILTON [112]

seen a great l. BIBLE, OLD TESTAMENT: ISAIAH [20]

thousand points of l. BUSH, G. [5]

thy l. is come BIBLE, OLD TESTAMENT: ISAIAH [82]

true L., which lighteth BIBLE, NEW
TESTAMENT: JOHN [5]
Walk while ye have the l. BIBLE, NEW
TESTAMENT: JOHN [45]
What l. through yonder
window SHAKESPEARE: ROMEO &
JULIET [13]
Ye are the l. of the world BIBLE, NEW
TESTAMENT: MATTHEW [24]

lightning
Bring in the bottled l. DICKENS [29]
like writing history with l. WILSON,
W. [1]
rather be a l. rod KESEY [1]

like
I l. you not, Sabidius MARTIAL [3]
nothing says we have to l. DE
VRIES [5]
People who l. this sort of
thing LINCOLN [31]

liked
Because I l. you better HOUSMAN [31]
I'm so universally l. DE VRIES [4]
l., but he's not well liked MILLER,
A. [1]

likewise
Go, and do thou l. BIBLE, NEW
TESTAMENT: LUKE [32]

lilies
Consider the l. BIBLE, NEW
TESTAMENT: MATTHEW [45]
L. that fester SHAKESPEARE:
SONNETS [26]

lily
l. of the valleys BIBLE, OLD
TESTAMENT: SONG OF SOLOMON [5]
Now folds the l. TENNYSON [78]

limit
no l. to what a man can
do MONTAGUE [1]
No one who cannot l.
himself BOILEAU-DESPRÉAUX [2]

limitation
Art consists of l. CHESTERTON [21]

Limpopo
greasy L. River KIPLING [56]

Linda Tripp
I hate L. LEWINSKY [1]

line
An active l. on a walk KLEE [5]
draw a l. without blurring
it CHURCHILL, W. [43]
l. is length without
breadth EUCLID [2]
thin red l. RUSSELL, W. H. [1]
write a good first l. MOLIÈRE [3]

linea
nulla dies sine l. APELLES [1]

linen
not l. you're wearing out HOOD [10]

liner
L. she's a lady KIPLING [44]

lines
Give me six l. RICHELIEU [3]
l. are fallen unto me BIBLE, OLD
TESTAMENT: PSALMS [12]
read between the l. JAMES, H. [11]

linguistic
l. system is a series DE SAUSSURE [2]

link
weakest l. ROBINSON, A. [1]

linnet
l. born within a cage TENNYSON [94]
tear the l. from the leaf YEATS [39]

lion
Be not as a l. BIBLE, APOCRYPHA:
ECCLESIASTICUS [8]
blood more stirs/To rouse a
l. SHAKESPEARE: HENRY IV PT 1 [11]
bold as a l. BIBLE, OLD TESTAMENT:
PROVERBS [89]
l. and the unicorn NURSERY
RHYMES [19]
l. now will foreign foes
assail DRYDEN [1]
l. shall eat straw BIBLE, OLD
TESTAMENT: ISAIAH [25]
more fearful wildfowl than your
l. SHAKESPEARE: MIDSUMMER NIGHT'S
DREAM [23]
nation ... that had the l.'s
heart CHURCHILL, W. [54]
out of the mouth of the l. BIBLE, NEW
TESTAMENT: 2 TIMOTHY [8]
rouse the l. from his lair SCOTT,
W. [19]

lions
den of l. BIBLE, OLD TESTAMENT:
DANIEL [11]
feed ruddy L. EDGAR [2]

lips
l. ... like a thread of scarlet BIBLE, OLD
TESTAMENT: SONG OF SOLOMON [13]
l. of a strange woman BIBLE, OLD
TESTAMENT: PROVERBS [8]
l. say 'God be pitiful' BROWNING,
E. B. [9]
Read my l. BUSH, G. [3]
Red l. are not so red OWEN [2]

lipstick
L. is power FOLLETT [1]

liquefaction
l. of her clothes HERRICK [24]

liquid
l. notes that close the eye MILTON [8]

liquidity
Purpose in L. BROOKE [9]

liquor
Good l., I stoutly
maintain GOLDSMITH [46]
l. in his pate SHAKESPEARE: MERRY
WIVES [6]

list
I've got a little l. GILBERT, W. S. [31]

listen
don't expect you to l. WAUGH [15]

listening
disease of not l. SHAKESPEARE:
HENRY IV PT 2 [6]
L. is its own reward COPLAND [3]

lit
whole Fleet's l. up WOODROOFFE [1]

literary
acquire the l. language SHAW [82]
excessive l. production ELIOT, G. [36]
incompatibility between l.
creation VARGAS LLOSA [2]
L. experience heals the wound LEWIS,
C. S. [5]
l. intellectuals at one pole SNOW [3]
l. woman, unsatisfied NIETZSCHE [38]
l. works cannot be taken
over BRECHT [10]
not draw well with l. men BYRON,
LORD [131]

literature
Bad l. is written with
beautiful GIDE [8]
belongs to L. JEWETT [3]
can't stamp out l. WAUGH [7]
history to produce ... l. JAMES, H. [5]
l. cannot grow JAMES, P. D. [2]
l. flourishes best INGE [5]
l. grows more terrible STEVENS,
W. [20]
L. is a toil and a snare LAWRENCE,
D. H. [5]
L. ... is condemned DE MAN [2]
l. is cut short SOLZHENITSYN [8]
l. is my mistress CHEKHOV [1]
L. ... is only a façade SOLZHENITSYN [2]
l. is formal SAGAN [2]
L. is mostly about having sex LODGE,
D. [1]
L. is not exhaustible BORGES [6]
l. is nothing but carpentry GARCÍA
MÁRQUEZ [6]
L. is the art of writing CONNOLLY,
C. [6]
L. is the effort EMERSON [28]
L. is the orchestration WILDER, T. [2]
L. is *without proofs* BARTHES [11]
L. must become Party
literature LENIN [3]
L.'s ... a good card BENNETT,
ARNOLD [8]
l. seeks to communicate power DE
QUINCEY [5]
L., the most seductive MORLEY, J. [3]
materials for a work of l. PROUST [26]
moral duty of l. FISCHER [2]
national l. cannot rise
above CONNOLLY, J. [1]
Scott took L. so
solemnly HEMINGWAY [21]
test of l. DREW [1]

when l. and commerce are
united JOHNSON, S. [161]
litigious
l. terms, fat contentions MILTON [59]
little
add only a l. to a little HESIOD [4]
L. one! Oh, little one STEPHENS [4]
l. things are ... most
important DOYLE, A. C. [18]
offend one of these l. ones BIBLE,
NEW TESTAMENT: MATTHEW [117]
studying l. things JOHNSON, S. [57]
littleness
No sadder proof ... of his own
l. CARLYLE, T. [37]
liturgy
l. is best treated BENNETT, ALAN [3]
live
art and profession is to
l. MONTAIGNE [8]
Bid me to l. HERRICK [14]
can't l. with you nor ...
without MARTIAL [10]
Come l. with me DONNE [20]
Come l. with me MARLOWE [1]
easier to l. through someone
else FRIEDAN [3]
For in him we l. BIBLE, NEW
TESTAMENT: ACTS [29]
l. for the few BERNHARDT [2]
l. ... good or bad THOREAU [16]
l., not as we wish MENANDER [3]
L. pure, speak true TENNYSON [150]
L. today MARTIAL [2]
l. with thee and be thy
love RALEGH [5]
l. your life is not as
simple PASTERNAK [2]
Learn to l. well POPE [161]
Man is born to l. PASTERNAK [6]
May you l. all the days SWIFT, J. [55]
nothing ... to l. up to DYLAN [18]
shall he l. again BIBLE, OLD
TESTAMENT: JOB [27]
tell me how you l. CARROLL [43]
would you l. forever FREDERICK THE
GREAT [1]
lived
I have l. HORACE [44]
lives
If men's l. are worth giving EWART [3]
l. from day to day SOCRATES [27]
many l. are needed MONTALE [1]
One l. but once GOETHE [2]
Our l. don't really belong to
us AUSTER [2]
liveth
none of us l. to himself BIBLE, NEW
TESTAMENT: ROMANS [43]
living
as you go on l. with
someone BARNES, J. [6]

fever called 'L.' POE [20]
fight like hell for the l. JONES, M. [1]
I want to go on l. FRANK [1]
L. and partly living ELIOT, T. S. [37]
L. is ... a long addition sum
PAVESE [1]
L. is a sickness CHAMFORT [6]
L. is more ... what one
spends DUCHAMP [3]
l. thing is distinguished SPENCER,
H. [8]
land of the l. BIBLE, OLD TESTAMENT:
PSALMS [34]
long habit of l. BROWNE [27]
To the l. we owe respect VOLTAIRE [1]
Livingstone
Dr L., I presume STANLEY [1]
lizard
I am the L. King MORRISON, J. [5]
possessor of a single l. JUVENAL [11]
Lizzie Bordern
L. took an axe ANONYMOUS [55]
loafed
better to have l. and lost THURBER [5]
loaves
five l., and the two fishes BIBLE, NEW
TESTAMENT: MATTHEW [103]
lobster
l. salad and Champagne BYRON,
LORD [26]
lobster-nights
Luxurious l., farewell POPE [51]
Lochinvar
knight like the young L. SCOTT, W. [8]
L. is come out of the west SCOTT,
W. [7]
loci
geniumque l. VIRGIL [45]
locks
Hyacinthine l. MILTON [136]
never shake/Thy gory
l. SHAKESPEARE: MACBETH [64]
locust
years that the l. hath eaten BIBLE,
OLD TESTAMENT: JOEL [4]
locusts
l. and wild honey BIBLE, NEW
TESTAMENT: MATTHEW [8]
lodesterre
he was the l. LYDGATE [1]
lodge
flee to my l. in the hills MARX, G. [4]
lodgings
take l. in a head BUTLER, S. (1612–
80) [6]
logic
L. is like the sword BUTLER, S. (1835–
1902) [25]
l. of the world is
prior WITTGENSTEIN [2]
L. takes care of
itself WITTGENSTEIN [1]

L.! ... What rubbish FORSTER [22]
That's l. CARROLL [32]
loins
Gird up now thy l. BIBLE, OLD
TESTAMENT: JOB [40]
girded up his l. BIBLE, OLD
TESTAMENT: 1 KINGS [13]
Let your l. be girded BIBLE, NEW
TESTAMENT: LUKE [38]
Lolita
L., light of my life NABOKOV [1]
lolling
l. on a lawn KEATS [55]
London
Hell is a city much like L. SHELLEY,
P. B. [42]
in L. it is always a sickly
season AUSTEN [22]
L. Bridge is falling down NURSERY
RHYMES [23]
L. is a modern Babylon DISRAELI [34]
L. particular. ... A fog DICKENS [72]
L., that great cesspool DOYLE, A. C. [1]
L., that great sea SHELLEY, P. B. [48]
live and die in L. DICKENS [1]
man who is tired of L. THEROUX [3]
tired of L. ... tired of life JOHNSON,
S. [112]
vilest alleys of L. DOYLE, A. C. [23]
Londoner
because I'm a L. GREGG [1]
spirit of the L. GEORGE VI [1]
lone
walking by his wild l. KIPLING [60]
loneliness
depths of his own l. BERNANOS [4]
l. is but his fear of life O'NEILL [3]
L. of the Long-distance
Runner SILLITOE [1]
L. who comes at night MANSFIELD [1]
long
Lord, how l. BIBLE, OLD TESTAMENT:
ISAIAH [17]
longer
made this l. PASCAL [1]
lookers on
God and angels to be l. BACON, F. [45]
looking
Here's l. at you BOGART [2]
looking glass
no use to blame the l. GOGOL [1]
looking-glasses
Women have served ... as
l. WOOLF [21]
looks
war of l. ... between
them SHAKESPEARE: VENUS AND
ADONIS [3]
loore
But Cristes l. CHAUCER [22]
loquacity
ignorant l. CICERO [6]

We that are true l. SHAKESPEARE: AS YOU LIKE IT [12]

loves
new l. are sweet TENNYSON [166]
She l. you LENNON/MCCARTNEY [1]
Whoso l./Believes the impossible BROWNING, E. B. [25]

love-sick
Twenty l. maidens we GILBERT, W. S. [16]

low
when my light is l. TENNYSON [98]

lower class
While there is a l. DEBS [2]

lower classes
train up the l. MORE, H. [11]

lower orders
l. don't set us a good example WILDE [95]

lowly
be l. wise MILTON [160]

loyalty
L. to petrified opinions TWAIN [8]

lucid
he has l. intervals CERVANTES [32]
Never be l. THOMAS, D. [1]

Lucifer
fallen from heaven, O L. BIBLE, OLD TESTAMENT: ISAIAH [28]
L's greatest work of art STOCKHAUSEN [1]

luck
but for the clutch of l. DURCAN [4]
l.'s always to blame LA FONTAINE [3]
want their l. buttered HARDY, T. [12]
worst cynicism: a belief in l. OATES, J. C. [1]

lucky
Do I feel l. EASTWOOD [1]

lucre
greedy of filthy l. BIBLE, NEW TESTAMENT: 1 TIMOTHY [5]

Lucy
When L. ceased to be WORDSWORTH, W. [33]

Luftwaffe
give this much to the L. CHARLES, PRINCE OF WALES [4]

Luke
honour unto L. Evangelist ROSSETTI, D. G. [7]

lukewarm
because thou art l. BIBLE, NEW TESTAMENT: REVELATION [11]

lukewarmness
L. I account a sin COWLEY, A. [1]

lumberjack
I'm a l./And I'm OK MONTY PYTHON'S FLYING CIRCUS [4]

lump
indigested and deformèd l. SHAKESPEARE: HENRY VI PT 3 [8]

lumps
There are l. in it STEPHENS [2]

lunatic
definition of a l. POUND [23]
l. is the man who CHESTERTON [8]

lunatic asylums
comfortably padded l. WOOLF [11]

lunatics
l. have taken charge ROWLAND, R. [1]

lunch
free l. ANONYMOUS [91]
L. is for wimps DOUGLAS, M. [1]
ladies who l. SONDHEIM [4]
pessimistic determinist before l. HUXLEY, A. [14]

lust
l. in action SHAKESPEARE: SONNETS [37]
Society drives people crazy with l. LAHR [1]
something generous in mere l. ROCHESTER [13]

lustre
ne'er could any l. see SHERIDAN, R. B. [1]

lusts
abstain from fleshly l. BIBLE, NEW TESTAMENT: 1 PETER [4]

lusty
flourisheth in l. deeds MALORY [2]

lute
My l., awake WYATT [2]

luxuries
Give us the l. of life MOTLEY [2]

luxury
all their l. was doing good GARTH [4]
daily unconscious l. BAGEHOT [5]
Every l. was lavished on you ORTON [2]
l. of doing good GOLDSMITH [8]
L., more deadly than any foe JUVENAL [12]
to get used to l. CHAPLIN [3]

Lycidas
L. is ... dead ere his prime MILTON [44]

lyf
l. so short CHAUCER [5]

lying
l ... becomes none SHAKESPEARE: WINTER'S TALE [19]
l. down after a long day's work CHILDERS [2]
L. increases the creative faculties LUCE [1]
L. is like alcoholism SODERBERGH [1]
no word ... to express l. SWIFT, J. [34]
privilege of l. SOCRATES [20]
smallest amount of l. BUTLER, S. (1835–1902) [7]
subject ... to this vice of l. SHAKESPEARE: HENRY IV PT 2 [23]

world is given to l. SHAKESPEARE: HENRY IV PT 1 [50]

Lyonnesse
When I set out for L. HARDY, T. [1]

lyre
Make me thy l. SHELLEY, P. B. [39]

macaroni
called it M. ANONYMOUS [102]

Macaulay
cocksure ... as Tom M. MELBOURNE [2]

Macavity
M.'s not there ELIOT, T. S. [45]

Machiavel
much beholden to M. BACON, F. [46]

machine
cog in The M. that governs us CHAPMAN, J. [2]
living in the m. age ALLEN, F. [3]
m. can do the work of fifty HUBBARD, E. [5]
m. does not isolate man SAINT-EXUPÉRY [2]
m. kills fascists GUTHRIE, W. [1]

machinery
never be enslaved by m. CAPEK [1]

machines
M. are worshipped RUSSELL, B. [7]
M. were ... the weapon MARX, K. [4]
not whether m. think SKINNER [2]

machismo
tragedy of m. GREER [9]

mackerel
as cheap as stinking m. SHAKESPEARE: HENRY IV PT 1 [23]

mad
I am but m. north-north-west SHAKESPEARE: HAMLET [70]
let me not be m. SHAKESPEARE: KING LEAR [18]
M. about the boy COWARD [11]
M., bad, and dangerous LAMB, CAROLINE [1]
m. to live KEROUAC [2]
pleasure sure,/In being m. DRYDEN [24]
they first make m. EURIPIDES [10]
want a few m. people now SHAW [72]
We all are born m. BECKETT [10]
We all go a little m. PERKINS, A. [2]

madcap
once ... I'll be a m. SHAKESPEARE: HENRY IV PT 1 [8]

madder
m. music and ... stronger wine DOWSON [2]

madding
Far From the M. Crowd HARDY, T. [3]
m. crowd's ignoble strife GRAY, T. [15]

made
All things were m. by him BIBLE, NEW TESTAMENT: JOHN [2]

m. is the noblest
creature LICHTENBERG [5]
M. is the only animal that
laughs HAZLITT [8]
M. is the shuttle VAUGHAN [7]
M. lives consciously for
himself TOLSTOY [2]
M. meets man ARNOLD, M. [39]
m.'s a man BURNS [53]
M. that is born of a woman BIBLE,
OLD TESTAMENT: JOB [25]
M. that is born of woman BOOK OF
COMMON PRAYER [88]
people arose as one m. BIBLE, OLD
TESTAMENT: JUDGES [16]
Perfect God, and perfect M. BOOK OF
COMMON PRAYER [31]
piece of work is a m. SHAKESPEARE:
HAMLET [67]
source ... is in m. and
woman LAWRENCE, D. H. [11]
study of m. is just
beginning CANETTI [3]
This was a m. SHAKESPEARE: JULIUS
CAESAR [49]
Thou art the m. BIBLE, OLD
TESTAMENT: 2 SAMUEL [9]
Thou madest m. TENNYSON [82]
what is m. in nature PASCAL [8]
When God at first made m. HERBERT,
G. [32]
you'll be a m., my son KIPLING [76]
manacles
mind-forg'd m. BLAKE [58]
man-cub
m. is a man-cub KIPLING [35]
Mandalay
come you back to M. KIPLING [22]
On the road to M. KIPLING [23]
Mandarin
christen this style the M. CONNOLLY,
C. [5]
Mandelson
M. ... can skulk in broad
daylight HOGGART [1]
Manderley
went to M. again DU MAURIER [1]
mandoline
pleasant whining of a m. ELIOT,
T. S. [23]
mandragora
Give me to drink m. SHAKESPEARE:
ANTONY & CLEOPATRA [9]
Mandy
I'm M., fly me ADVERTISING
SLOGANS [12]
manger
wrapped in the rude m. MILTON [2]
Manhattan
Downtown M. GINSBERG [6]
manhood
Only when m. is dead DWORKIN [1]

manifest destiny
m. to overspread the
continent O'SULLIVAN [1]
manifold
m. are thy works BIBLE, OLD
TESTAMENT: PSALMS [109]
mankind
fly from, need not be to hate,
m. BYRON, LORD [57]
I hate m. ANONYMOUS [41]
m. are everywhere despicable BYRON,
LORD [13]
M. has grown strong HITLER [4]
M. is ... an ellipse HUGO [14]
m. is divisible BEERBOHM [11]
manliness
M. is the best prize PLAUTUS [1]
manna
tongue/Dropped m. MILTON [106]
manner
dislike ... /The m. of his
speech SHAKESPEARE: ANTONY &
CLEOPATRA [13]
m. is.../The substitute for
genius COWPER [13]
to the m. born SHAKESPEARE:
HAMLET [39]
mannerisms
mixture of the charming
m. FITZGERALD, F. S. [23]
manners
appropriate good m. HARE [2]
don't like my m. CHANDLER [1]
M. are love in a cool
climate CRISP [11]
m. are not idle TENNYSON [168]
M. are the happy way EMERSON
[52]
M. are the hypocrisy of a
nation BALZAC [4]
M. are ... the need of the
plain WAUGH [22]
m. are the only effective
weapons LOWELL, J. R. [20]
M. must adorn knowledge
CHESTERFIELD [12]
m. of various peoples DESCARTES [1]
manself
M. will not suffer and
die STEINBECK [2]
mansions
lasting m. of the dead CRABBE [3]
many m. BIBLE, NEW TESTAMENT:
JOHN [49]
mantle
took the m. of Elijah BIBLE, OLD
TESTAMENT: 2 KINGS [2]
manufacture
m. everything ... except
men RUSKIN [10]
many
conceive the m. PLATO [1]

many-splendoured
miss the m. thing THOMPSON, F.
[12]
map
Roll up that m. PITT THE YOUNGER [3]
mar
oft we m. what's well SHAKESPEARE:
KING LEAR [17]
marble
dwelt in m. halls BUNN [1]
m. not yet carved MICHELANGELO [1]
m. of her snowy breast WALLER [7]
pure m. air MILTON [124]
march
Men who m. away HARDY, T. [28]
On they m. with sovereign
tread BLOK [4]
Margaret
M., are you grieving HOPKINS [18]
Merry M./This midsummer
flower SKELTON [2]
Maria
Ave M., gratia plena ANONYMOUS [6]
mariage
wo that is in m. CHAUCER [33]
Mariana
resides this dejected
M. SHAKESPEARE: MEASURE FOR
MEASURE [18]
Marilyn
M. ... every man's love
affair MAILER [8]
mariner
bright-eyed M. COLERIDGE, S. T. [15]
I fear thee, ancient M. COLERIDGE,
S. T. [26]
It is an ancient M. COLERIDGE,
S. T. [14]
mariners
Ye m. of England CAMPBELL, T. [6]
mark
ever-fixèd m. SHAKESPEARE:
SONNETS [35]
I press toward the m. BIBLE, NEW
TESTAMENT: PHILIPPIANS [6]
marked
one of those whom God m. HALL,
R. [2]
market
buy in the cheapest m. COBDEN [1]
m. came with ...
civilization GORBACHEV [3]
Market Harborough
Am in M. CHESTERTON [50]
market-place
talk in the m. HAWTHORNE [6]
marriage
discuss their m. MENCKEN [20]
doesn't have to get anywhere in a
m. MURDOCH, I. [1]
if m. be such a blessed
state ASTELL [6]

his m. endureth for ever BIBLE, OLD
TESTAMENT: 1 CHRONICLES [1]
his m. endureth for ever BIBLE, OLD
TESTAMENT: PSALMS [137]
M. and truth are met together BIBLE,
OLD TESTAMENT: PSALMS [91]
M. but murders SHAKESPEARE: ROMEO
& JULIET [31]
M. has a human heart BLAKE [5]
m. is nobility's true
badge SHAKESPEARE: TITUS
ANDRONICUS [1]
m. I to others show POPE [165]
M., Pity, Peace, and Love BLAKE [4]
quality of m. is not
strained SHAKESPEARE: MERCHANT OF
VENICE [34]
temper so/Justice with
m. MILTON [176]
wound/With m. round HOPKINS [25]
merde
M. CAMBRONNE [2]
merit
m. itself is offensive NIETZSCHE [6]
m. wins the soul POPE [49]
What is m. PALMERSTON [1]
merits
do not recognize his
m. CONFUCIUS [1]
not weighing our m. BOOK OF
COMMON PRAYER [64]
mermaid
Choicer than the M.
Tavern KEATS [102]
m. on a dolphin's back SHAKESPEARE:
MIDSUMMER NIGHT'S DREAM [18]
What things ... /Done at the
M. BEAUMONT [1]
mermaids
heard the m. singing ELIOT, T. S. [8]
merriment
scheme of m. JOHNSON, S. [43]
merry
eat, drink, and be m. BIBLE, NEW
TESTAMENT: LUKE [36]
m. heart doeth good BIBLE, OLD
TESTAMENT: PROVERBS [47]
m. heart maketh a cheerful BIBLE,
OLD TESTAMENT: PROVERBS [37]
merrygoround
It's no go the m. MACNEICE [4]
mess
another nice m. HARDY, O. [1]
messenger
I will send my m. BIBLE, OLD
TESTAMENT: MALACHI [2]
met
m. them at close of day YEATS [34]
metal
Here's m. more
attractive SHAKESPEARE:
HAMLET [107]

metaphor
good m. is
something LICHTENBERG [10]
metaphors
history of a few m. BORGES [4]
metaphysic
as high/As m. wit can fly BUTLER, S.
(1612–80) [5]
metaphysicians
melancholy m. JAMES, W. [10]
metaphysics
cheating on my m. final ALLEN,
W. [19]
M. abstracts the mind VICO [4]
M. ... an unusually obstinate
effort JAMES, W. [4]
M. is the finding of bad
reasons BRADLEY, F. H. [1]
meter
use a parking m. DIANA, PRINCESS OF
WALES [1]
method
M. goes far to prevent
trouble PENN [8]
Methodists
M. love your big sinners WALPOLE,
H. [3]
Methuselah
all the days of M. BIBLE, OLD
TESTAMENT: GENESIS [30]
Metro-Goldwyn-Mayer
born ... on a M. lot GARLAND [3]
Mexico
Poor M., so far from God DIAZ [1]
mice
o' m. and men BURNS [19]
Three blind m. NURSERY RHYMES [46]
Michael
M. and his angels fought BIBLE, NEW
TESTAMENT: REVELATION [31]
Michael Angelo
made Italy from designs by
M. TWAIN [1]
Michael Caine
My name is M. CAINE [2]
Michelangelo
last words ... M. REYNOLDS, J. [4]
Talking of M. ELIOT, T. S. [2]
microscope
absolute/Of the m.'s lenses HOLUB [1]
microscopes
M. are prudent DICKINSON, E. [4]
middle
in politics the m. way is
none ADAMS, J. [5]
m. ... had the fewest
disasters DEFOE [13]
m. is the safest OVID [9]
stay in the m. of the road BEVAN [9]
middle age
dead center of m. ADAMS. F. P. [1]
for the sake of m. ELIOT, G. [2]

m. is the best time INGE [7]
M. is the time when MARQUIS [10]
most barbarous is the m. BYRON,
LORD [153]
middle-aged
misery of the m. woman GREER
[17]
multitude of m. men ELIOT, G. [42]
middle class
best political community is ... the
m. ARISTOTLE [20]
to the m. we must
look THACKERAY [17]
middle earth
I smell a man of m. SHAKESPEARE:
MERRY WIVES [14]
Middle East
history in the M. rarely
rewards FISK [3]
middleman
m. ... bamboozles one
party DISRAELI [25]
Middlemarch
M. ... for grown-up people WOOLF [10]
Middlesex
acre in M. is better MACAULAY,
LORD [24]
Midlands
I am living in the M. BELLOC [7]
midnight
came upon the m. clear HYMNS &
CAROLS [42]
cease upon the m. KEATS [86]
iron tongue of m. SHAKESPEARE:
MIDSUMMER NIGHT'S DREAM [43]
M. Special LEDBETTER [2]
'Tis the year's m. DONNE [18]
midst
In the m. of things HORACE [78]
midsummer
very m. madness SHAKESPEARE:
TWELFTH NIGHT [32]
mid-winter
In the bleak m. ROSSETTI, C. [15]
might
Britons alone use 'M.' WAUGH [11]
It m. have been HARTE [1]
It m. have been WHITTIER [3]
mighty
how are the m. fallen BIBLE, OLD
TESTAMENT: 2 SAMUEL [1]
put down the m. BIBLE, NEW
TESTAMENT: LUKE [4]
mile
go a m. BIBLE, NEW TESTAMENT:
MATTHEW [32]
milestones
m. into headstones change LOWELL,
J. R. [25]
m. on the Dover road DICKENS [81]
milieu
fashionable m. is one PROUST [2]

militant
Christ's Church M. BOOK OF COMMON PRAYER [53]

militants
m. are like cleaning women TRUFFAUT [1]

military-industrial
m. complex EISENHOWER [4]

milk
flowing with m. and honey BIBLE, OLD TESTAMENT: EXODUS [6]
m. of human-kindness SHAKESPEARE: MACBETH [17]
mother's m. ... scarce out of him SHAKESPEARE: TWELFTH NIGHT [9]
putting m. into babies CHURCHILL, W. [37]

Milk Wood
Who live ... under M. THOMAS, D. [20]

million
down to my last hundred m. ARCHER [4]

millionaire
M. ... is my religion SHAW [40]
old fashioned m. KITT [1]
Who wants to be a m. PORTER, C. [15]

millions
I will be m. PERÓN, E. [3]
What m. died CAMPBELL, T. [2]

mills
m. of God grind slowly LOGAU [1]

Milton
M. ... could cut a Colossus JOHNSON, S. [139]
M.! thou should'st be living WORDSWORTH, W. [60]
Some mute inglorious M. GRAY, T. [14]

Milton Keynes
all cities were like M. ADVERTISING SLOGANS [35]

miminy
m., piminy GILBERT, W. S. [19]

mind
AS A M. POUND [17]
could not change his state of m. ARIOSTO [2]
could not make up his m. OLIVIER [1]
cultivate their own m. MONTAGU [16]
great m. ... moulds the minds HAZLITT [6]
how little the m. is ... employed JOHNSON, S. [91]
I don't m. if I do KAVANAGH, T. [3]
If we keep an open m. BARNEY [2]
In my m.'s eye SHAKESPEARE: HAMLET [24]
Is there no way out of the m. PLATH [4]
keep an even m. HORACE [31]

look/Into ... the m. of man WORDSWORTH, W. [95]
love ... /But in our m. SHELLEY, P. B. [28]
m. and soul.../make one music TENNYSON [84]
m. be a thoroughfare KEATS [57]
m. can make/Substance BYRON, LORD [65]
m. can weave itself LOWELL, J. R. [18]
m. has mountains HOPKINS [28]
m. is a museum RAINE, C. [2]
m. is its own place MILTON [92]
m. is not a hermit's cell COOLEY [2]
M. it FORSTER [1]
m. of man is ... true dimension GREVILLE [2]
m.'s construction in the face SHAKESPEARE: MACBETH [16]
m., that ocean MARVELL [12]
m. was great and powerful JEFFERSON [30]
man's m. that hath this earth BRIDGES [5]
march of the human m. BURKE, E. [20]
Measure your m.'s height BROWNING, R. [2]
my m. is not a bed AGATE [3]
My m. to me a kingdom is DYER, E. [1]
natural flights of the human m. JOHNSON, S. [10]
never m. COBAIN [1]
no blemish but the m. SHAKESPEARE: TWELFTH NIGHT [37]
noble m. is here o'erthrown SHAKESPEARE: HAMLET [99]
nothing remained ... but m. SMITH, SYDNEY [7]
plain heroic magnitude of m. MILTON [202]
ready to speak your m. BLAKE [30]
senses deform, the m. forms BRAQUE [3]
sound m. in a sound body JUVENAL [17]
What impresses men is not m. BAGEHOT [22]
what rules the m. COLLINS, WILKIE [2]
Where the M. is biggest WOOLF [17]
worst ... persecutes the m. DRYDEN [51]

minds
best m. of my generation GINSBERG [2]
good m. are idle LICHTENBERG [23]
M. are never to be sold COWPER [49]
M. copulate wherever they meet HOFFER [13]

m. remain wretchedly unaligned BAINBRIDGE [1]
marriage of true m. SHAKESPEARE: SONNETS [35]
Stongest m./Are often those WORDSWORTH, W. [96]

Minerva
owl of M. HEGEL [2]

mingle
In one spirit meet and m. SHELLEY, P. B. [32]

minion
morning's m. HOPKINS [9]

minister
m. to a mind diseased SHAKESPEARE: MACBETH [93]
Yes, M.! No, Minister CROSSMAN [1]

ministers
passion-wingèd M. of thought SHELLEY, P. B. [70]

Miniver
M. coughed ROBINSON, E. A. [1]

Minnehaha
M., Laughing Water LONGFELLOW [20]

minority
never outrage the m. LIPPMANN [3]

minotaur
might represent a m. PICASSO [9]

minute
cannot cage the m. MACNEICE [3]

minutes
Give me five m. more CAHN [1]
m. hasten to their end SHAKESPEARE: SONNETS [15]
take care of the m. CHESTERFIELD [6]

miracle
Everything is a m. PICASSO [2]
m. is an event which creates faith SHAW [73]
M. me no miracles CERVANTES [24]

miracles
m. of the Blessed Virgin FREUD [18]

Miranda
remember an Inn, M. BELLOC [15]

mirror
little m. of himself CARLYLE, T. [5]
m. cracked from side to side TENNYSON [13]
m. of some woman's eyes LUCE [2]

mirth
all m. and no matter SHAKESPEARE: MUCH ADO [9]
house of m. BIBLE, OLD TESTAMENT: ECCLESIASTES [18]
I love such m. WALTON [9]
M. is like a flash of lightning ADDISON [10]

Misanthropos
I am M. SHAKESPEARE: TIMON [11]

mischief
M., thou art afoot SHAKESPEARE: JULIUS CAESAR [38]

m., thou art swift SHAKESPEARE:
ROMEO & JULIET [39]
when to m. mortals bend POPE [47]

miser
To the eyes of a m. BLAKE [66]

miserable
ceases to be m. MACDIARMID [5]
Heaven knows I'm m. MORRISSEY [1]
m. have no other
medicine SHAKESPEARE: MEASURE
FOR MEASURE [15]
made this age m. MONTAIGNE [24]
secret of being m. SHAW [58]

miseries
fellow-countrymen's m. ELIOT, G. [30]

misery
another person's habitual m. GREENE,
G. [3]
M. acquaints a man SHAKESPEARE:
TEMPEST [15]
M. generates hate BRONTË, C. [15]
Man hands on m. to man LARKIN [18]
poor *suffer* m. BILLINGS [3]
relation of distant m. GIBBON [8]
sink to the bottom of our
m. HAVEL [2]
so full of m. TENNYSON [49]
vow eternal m. together OTWAY [2]
Who finds himself, loses his
m. ARNOLD, M. [17]

misfortune
prodigious siege of m. WOOLF [2]
unhappiest aspect of m. BOETHIUS [1]

misfortunes
if a man *talks* of his m. JOHNSON,
S. [129]
m. of our best friends LA
ROCHEFOUCAULD [1]

misquotation
M. ... the pride and
privilege PEARSON [1]

misquote
enough of learning to m. BYRON,
LORD [7]

miss
little m. dressed in a new
gown HUME, D. [8]
millions m., for one that hits SWIFT,
J. [45]

missa
Ite m. est MISSAL [23]

missiles
guided m. and misguided men KING,
M. L. [5]

mission
on a m. from God AYKROYD [1]

Mississippi
everybody knows about
M. SIMONE [1]

mistake
m. shall not be
repeated ANONYMOUS [82]

never made a m. SMILES [2]

mistakes
built to make m. THOMAS, L. [1]
lament the m. of a good
man JUNIUS [3]
m. ... not only more
honorable SHAW [50]
person who has made m. MAO
ZEDONG [6]

mistress
m. ... like a little country
retreat WYCHERLEY [3]
m. never ... can be a friend BYRON,
LORD [32]
more one loves a m. LA
ROCHEFOUCAULD [12]
teeming m., but a barren
bride POPE [93]

misunderstanding
world ... goes round by
m. BAUDELAIRE [14]

misunderstood
To be great is to be m. EMERSON [13]

mites
threw in two m. BIBLE, NEW
TESTAMENT: MARK [14]

Mithridates
M., he died old HOUSMAN [21]

Moab
M. is my washpot BIBLE, OLD
TESTAMENT: PSALMS [72]

moan
make delicious m. KEATS [99]

moanday
All m., tearsday, wailsday JOYCE,
J. [37]

moat
Look to your m. SAVILE [1]

mob
m. ... speaks the sentiments BYRON,
LORD [24]
supreme governors, the m. WALPOLE,
H. [1]

mock
m. on BIBLE, OLD TESTAMENT: JOB [33]

mocked
God is not m. BIBLE, NEW TESTAMENT:
GALATIANS [9]

mockers
assembly of the m. BIBLE, OLD
TESTAMENT: JEREMIAH [15]

mockery
M. is a rust that
corrodes KUNDERA [2]

model
good m. can advance fashion SAINT
LAURENT [3]
M. Two mobile eyes BRESSON [1]

moderation
astonished at my own m. CLIVE [2]
m. in principle PAINE [16]
M. is a virtue KISSINGER [7]

M. is the silken string FULLER, T. [8]
urge me not to use m. GARRISON [1]

modern
Don't bother about being m. DALÍ [3]
horrified by m. man HERZEN [1]
One must be absolutely
m. RIMBAUD [23]
spend one's time in being
m. STEVENS, W. [23]

moderne
faut être absolument
m. RIMBAUD [23]

modernity
M. is ... one half of
art BAUDELAIRE [28]
M. is the transition from fate to
choice SACKS, J. [1]
M. ... makes it possible FOUCAULT [7]

moderns
Speak of the m. without
contempt CHESTERFIELD [7]

modest
m. little man CHURCHILL, W. [51]

modesty
just wore/Enough for m. BUCHANAN,
R. [2]
M. is ... more praised SHERIDAN,
R. B. [10]
M. is the lowest of the
virtues HAZLITT [17]
M. is the only sure bait
CHESTERFIELD [27]
M., 'tis a virtue not often
found CERVANTES [31]

modifiers
Death to all m. HELLER [1]

molestation
Child m. is a touchy subject ALLEN,
W. [27]

moment
Every m. dies a man TENNYSON [56]

monarch
every ... m. was insane BAGEHOT
[19]
invades authors like a m. DRYDEN
[7]
m. of all I survey COWPER [27]
merry m. ROCHESTER [1]
not one blameless m. SHAW [75]

monarchy
lock a door against absolute
M. PAINE [2]
m. is a strong
government BAGEHOT [8]
touch the trappings of
m. SAMPSON [1]

Monday
M.'s child ANONYMOUS [59]

Mondays
I don't like M. GELDOF [2]

monetary
curse is m. illiteracy POUND [20]

nudity
N. is a form of dress BERGER [3]

number
I am not a n. MCGOOHAN [1]
if I called a wrong n. THURBER [2]
Nouns of n. COBBETT [2]

numbered
As for man, his days are n. EPIC OF
GILGAMESH [2]

numbers
lisped in n. POPE [144]
We are just n. HORACE [57]
we got the n. MORRISON, J. [6]

numbness
drowsy n. pains KEATS [80]

nun
cult of the household n. FRIDAY [3]

nunnery
from the n./Of thy chaste
breast LOVELACE [1]
Get thee to a n. SHAKESPEARE:
HAMLET [94]

nuns
N. fret not WORDSWORTH, W. [50]

nurse
always keep a-hold of N. BELLOC [3]

nurseries
n. of Heaven THOMPSON, F. [8]

nymph
Haste thee, N. MILTON [13]

nymphets
propose to designate as
'n.' NABOKOV [4]

O
cram/Within this wooden
O SHAKESPEARE: HENRY V [2]

oak
hearts of o. RABELAIS [13]
o., and ash, and thorn KIPLING
[68]

oaks
last not three o. BROWNE [29]
Tall o., branch-charmèd KEATS [112]

oath
good mouth-filling o. SHAKESPEARE:
HENRY IV PT 1 [32]
not the o. that makes us
believe AESCHYLUS [6]

obedience
doctrine of blind o. GRIMKÉ [1]
O. is best NEWBOLT [3]

obedient
o. to their laws we lie SIMONIDES [2]

obey
o. God rather than
men JOHN XXIII [1]
Wilt thou o. him BOOK OF COMMON
PRAYER [82]

obeyed
She who must be o. HAGGARD, H. R. [1]

obituary
Times o. department MADAN [5]

o. column stands fast WARNER,
S. T. [2]

objection
technical o. is the first
refuge BROUN [3]

objections
art of ignoring o. MAISTRE [4]

objects
Inanimate o. are classified BAKER,
R. [1]

oblations
Bring no more vain o. BIBLE, OLD
TESTAMENT: ISAIAH [3]

obligation
hurry to discharge an o. LA
ROCHEFOUCAULD [19]

oblivion
Lethe, the river of o. MILTON [114]
o. is a very Antony SHAKESPEARE:
ANTONY & CLEOPATRA [8]

obnoxious
o. to each carping
tongue BRADSTREET [1]

obscenity
'o.' ... shocks the magistrate RUSSELL,
B. [8]
O. is a cleansing process MILLER,
H. [10]

obscurantism
O. is the academic theorist's
revenge LEHMAN, D. [2]

obscure
poor and o. ... as you are BRONTË,
C. [10]

obscurity
O. has another tale to tell RICH, A. [2]
o. of a learned language GIBBON [21]

obsequies
solemnized their o. BROWNE [24]

observer
creature known ... as the 'O.' DUNNE,
J. W. [1]
o. of human nature DICKENS [5]

obsolescence
suffering from galloping o. BENN [2]

obstinacy
O. in a bad cause BROWNE [6]

obstinate
Life is o. SHELLEY, M. W. [3]

ocean
All.../Is touched with o. WILBUR [6]
drain the o. into mill-ponds CARLYLE,
T. [9]
drop in the o. TERESA [3]
hungry o. gain/
Advantage SHAKESPEARE:
SONNETS [16]
infinite o. of light FOX, G. [1]
o. leans against the
land GOLDSMITH [10]

Oceanus
O./the primal source HOMER [12]

October
O.'s bright blue weather JACKSON,
H. H. [2]

odd
divinity in o. numbers SHAKESPEARE:
MERRY WIVES [13]
o. numbers are the most
effectual PLINY THE ELDER [9]

odi
O. et amo CATULLUS [17]

Odyssey
surge and thunder of the O. LANG,
A. [1]

offence
o. inspires less horror GIBBON [4]
pleasure of giving o. BAUDELAIRE [6]
What dire o. POPE [36]
where th'o. is SHAKESPEARE:
HAMLET [141]

offences
Remember not, Lord, our o. BOOK OF
COMMON PRAYER [33]

offend
Consult how we may ... most
o. MILTON [90]

offender
love th' o. POPE [57]

offenders
miserable o. BOOK OF COMMON
PRAYER [6]

offer
o. he can't refuse PUZO [1]

office
bestow a vacant o. LOUIS XIV [2]
in o. but not in power LAMONT [2]
mind not being in o. CONFUCIUS [11]
unfit to hold o. FABIUS MAXIMUS [1]

office-boys
journal produced by o. SALISBURY [4]

official
occupies an o.
position LICHTENBERG [11]

officialism
Where there is o. FORSTER [19]

offscouring
o. of all things BIBLE, NEW
TESTAMENT: 1 CORINTHIANS [10]

offspring
we are also his o. BIBLE, NEW
TESTAMENT: ACTS [29]

oil
consumed the midnight o. GAY, J. [3]
our midnight o. QUARLES [3]

ointment
thy name is as o. BIBLE, OLD
TESTAMENT: SONG OF SOLOMON [2]

Okie
O. from Muskogee HAGGARD, M. [1]

old
being o. is having lighted
rooms LARKIN [20]
dance in the o. dame yet MARQUIS [2]

P. ... a disappointment POWELL, A. [2]
p. obey their children EDWARD VIII [3]
slavish bondage to
p. WOLLSTONECRAFT [10]

Paris
art's philosophy,/In P. BROWNING,
E. B. [26]
I love P. in the springtime PORTER,
C. [13]
Is P. burning HITLER [14]
last time I saw P. HAMMERSTEIN II [3]
no home ... except in
P. NIETZSCHE [31]
P.: a city of pleasures CHAMFORT [18]
P. is a moveable
feast HEMINGWAY [28]
When P. sneezes METTERNICH [2]

park
wandering round ... a stately
p. MAUGHAM [10]

parking
put up a p. lot MITCHELL, JONI [2]

parliament
P. is not a *congress* BURKE, E. [13]
P. is ... to the Commonwealth PYM [1]
P. must not be told TEBBIT [4]

parlour
walk into my p. HOWITT [1]

parochial
worse than provincial – he was
p. JAMES, H. [7]

parody
most common form of p. BROWN,
C. [2]

parrot
p. is no more MONTY PYTHON'S
FLYING CIRCUS [3]
we could have bought a p. HAGUE [1]

parsimony
Mere p. is not economy BURKE, E. [61]

parson
p. knows enough COWPER [47]

parsons
merriment of p. JOHNSON, S. [133]

part
Each of us must play his
p. PIRANDELLO [1]
Mary hath chosen that good p. BIBLE,
NEW TESTAMENT: LUKE [33]
only p. to meet again GAY, J. [2]
p. at last without a kiss MORRIS,
W. [1]
take my own p. BORROW [5]
When two people p. PROUST [20]

particulars
minute p. BLAKE [83]

parties
Like other p. of the kind BYRON,
LORD [53]
little p. begin BAGEHOT [20]
Things must be done by
p. DISRAELI [26]

We give lovely p. COWARD [8]

parting
Every p. gives a
foretaste SCHOPENHAUER [4]
In every p. ... an image of
death ELIOT, G. [3]
P. is all we know of
heaven DICKINSON, E. [41]
P. is such sweet sorrow SHAKESPEARE:
ROMEO & JULIET [21]
p. of the way BIBLE, OLD TESTAMENT:
EZEKIEL [5]

partir
P. c'est mourir HARAUCOURT [1]

partners
Mr Morgan buys his p. CARNEGIE,
A. [5]

partnership
p. demands that we give CRISP [9]

partridge
As the p. sitteth on eggs BIBLE, OLD
TESTAMENT: JEREMIAH [17]

parts
naming of p. REED, H. [1]
refreshes the p. ADVERTISING
SLOGANS [11]

party
All the people at this p. MITCHELL,
JONI [3]
baneful ... spirit of p. WASHINGTON,
G. [6]
Last night, *p.* BYRON, LORD [47]
p. is but a kind of
conspiracy SAVILE [2]
p. of order or stability MILL [5]
p.'s over COMDEN/GREEN [2]
right to p. POLITICAL SLOGANS [12]
save the P. we love GAITSKELL [2]
serves his p. best HAYES, R. B. [1]
there is no P. line DJILAS [1]

party-spirit
p. ... madness of many POPE [64]

pasarán
No p. IBARRURI [1]

pass
I will p. over you BIBLE, OLD
TESTAMENT: EXODUS [17]
look and p. them by DANTE [7]
They shal not p. IBÁRRURI [1]
thou shalt strangely p. SHAKESPEARE:
SONNETS [13]

passer
P. mortuus est CATULLUS [3]

passing-bells
What p. for these OWEN [1]

passion
all p. spent MILTON [204]
crushed the wild p.
out TENNYSON [162]
Eternal p.!/eternal pain ARNOLD,
M. [24]
image of p. BARTHES [2]

Man is a useless p. SARTRE [3]
man/That is not p.'s
slave SHAKESPEARE: HAMLET [106]
misguided moral p. MURDOCH, I. [17]
more p. than reason ERASMUS [2]
O, well-painted p. SHAKESPEARE:
OTHELLO [44]
One p. doth expel another CHAPMAN,
G. [1]
p. between the sexes MALTHUS [2]
p. for happiness DIDEROT [19]
P. makes the world go ICE-T [2]
P., though a bad
regulator EMERSON [57]
ruling p. POPE [105]
Search then the ruling p. POPE [90]
When p. is mutual BAINBRIDGE [2]

passions
ashamed of p. that are
natural MONTAGU [7]
declaim against the p. DE SADE [9]
inferno of his p. JUNG [21]
men of like p. BIBLE, NEW TESTAMENT:
ACTS [20]
out of high p. comes BYRON,
LORD [125]
P. are facts and not
dogmas HERZEN [6]
p. are most like to floods RALEGH [4]
p. are the only orators LA
ROCHEFOUCAULD [4]
p. do not live apart ELIOT, G. [43]
P. spin the plot MEREDITH, G. [8]
people don't have durable
p. BELLOW [12]
Three p. ... have governed RUSSELL,
B. [23]

passive
make oneself p. DE BEAUVOIR [3]

passover
Lord's p. BIBLE, OLD TESTAMENT:
EXODUS [15]

past
afford to live in the p. PINTER [2]
because someone has a p. TRIMBLE [1]
belongs to the p. CONFUCIUS [9]
borne back ... into the p. FITZGERALD,
F. S. [12]
cannot remember the
p. SANTAYANA [3]
controls the p. controls the
future ORWELL [37]
events in the p. INGE [6]
look back on our own p. POTTER,
D. [5]
looked the past in the eye TUTU [3]
Many a woman has a p. WILDE [69]
not the literal p. FRIEL [2]
P. and to come seems
best SHAKESPEARE: HENRY IV PT 2 [12]
p. is a foreign country HARTLEY [1]
p. is a great darkness ATWOOD [4]

war is preferable to a shameful
  p. TACITUS [6]
when there is no p. BIBLE, OLD
  TESTAMENT: JEREMIAH [6]
who desires p. VEGETIUS [1]
win the p. CLEMENCEAU [3]

peacock
At twenty a man is a p. GRACIÁN
  [4]
man ... is such an ignorant
  p. EMERSON [40]
Who said, 'P. Pie' DE LA MARE [7]

pearl
as a p. in the world TUSSER [3]
p. of great price BIBLE, NEW
  TESTAMENT: MATTHEW [99]
Ransack the ocean for the Orient
  p. MARLOWE [18]

pearls
p. before swine BIBLE, NEW
  TESTAMENT: MATTHEW [50]
sent me to sea for p. SMART, C. [2]

peasantry
bold p., their country's
  pride GOLDSMITH [33]

peasants
how do the p. die TOLSTOY [13]

pebble
finding a smoother p. NEWTON [9]

pecker
p. in my pocket JOHNSON, L. B. [6]

pedant
Joyce is ... an elephantine
  p. ORWELL [7]
p. with a warm heart LAVATER [3]

pedantry
P. is the dotage of
  knowledge JACKSON, H. [1]

pedestal
place my wife under a p. ALLEN,
  W. [2]
You put us on a p. BARNES, J. [9]

pedestrians
two classes of p. DEWAR [1]

pedigrees
What avail your p. JUVENAL [15]

peer
impudence and money makes a
  p. DEFOE [7]

peerage
gained a p., or Westminster
  Abbey NELSON [1]

peers
we love our House of P. GILBERT,
  W. S. [14]
wisdom of his House of P. GILBERT,
  W. S. [15]

pelican
p. of the wilderness BIBLE, OLD
  TESTAMENT: PSALMS [104]

Pelion
pile P. on ... Olympus HORACE [38]

pen
foolish when he had not a
  p. JOHNSON, S. [131]
Here is a p. NASH, O. [5]
less brilliant p. than
  mine BEERBOHM [3]
No p., no ink, no table JOYCE, J. [6]
p. has gleaned my teeming
  brain KEATS [26]
p. is mightier than the
  sword BULWER-LYTTON [2]
squat p. rests HEANEY [1]
What a heavy oar the p.
  is FLAUBERT [3]

penance
man hath p. done COLERIDGE, S. T.
  [31]

pence
eternal want of p. TENNYSON [54]

pencils
inexorable sadness of p. ROETHKE [2]

pendent
This p. world MILTON [120]

Penelope
constant P. HOMER [19]

penis
atrophied p., a girl's
  clitoris FREUD [16]
require a p. or vagina KENNEDY,
  F. R. [3]

pennies
P. from heaven BURKE, J. [1]
P. From Heaven POTTER, D. [2]

pens
Let other p. dwell on
  guilt AUSTEN [19]

pension
hang your hat on a p. MACNEICE [5]

people
action of the whole p. TRUMAN [1]
All p. that on earth HYMNS &
  CAROLS [7]
by the p. you understand DRYDEN
  [5]
government of the p., by the
  people LINCOLN [25]
Let my p. go ANONYMOUS [30]
Let my p. go BIBLE, OLD TESTAMENT:
  EXODUS [10]
look after our p. SCOTT, R. F. [1]
P. are ... charming or
  tedious WILDE [67]
p. are good ... magistrate
  corruptible ROBESPIERRE [1]
p. are the motive force MAO
  ZEDONG [8]
P. get ready MAYFIELD [1]
p. people marry GILMAN [1]
p.'s government WEBSTER, D. [2]
thy p. shall be my people BIBLE, OLD
  TESTAMENT: RUTH [1]
true quality of p. AURELIUS [7]

peopled
world must be p. SHAKESPEARE: MUCH
  ADO [14]

peoples
absorption of fifty different
  p. LIPPMANN [1]

Peoria
It'll play in P. EHRLICHMAN [2]

perceive
To p. means to
  immobilize BERGSON [1]

per cent
Fifty p. of the public HEWITT [1]

perestroika
essence of p. GORBACHEV [1]

perfect
Be ye therefore p. BIBLE, NEW
  TESTAMENT: MATTHEW [35]
made p. in a short time BIBLE,
  APOCRYPHA: WISDOM OF SOLOMON [8]
Mark the p. man BIBLE, OLD
  TESTAMENT: PSALMS [48]
nobody's p. WILDER, B. [2]
p. day REED, L. [4]

perfected
woman is p. PLATH [14]

perfection
Dead p., no more TENNYSON [121]
P. is terrible PLATH [12]
P. of the life YEATS [56]
top of p. not to know CONGREVE [1]

perfick
P. BATES, H. E. [1]

perfide
p. Angleterre BOSSUET [1]

perfidy
usual formalities of p. CHURCHILL,
  W. [28]

perform
p. the same/Comical acts GUNN [1]
people p. well in a crisis BENNETT,
  ALAN [4]

performance
only p. that makes it CAMMELL [2]

performer
ultimate sin of any p. BANGS [2]

perfumes
p. of Arabia will not
  sweeten SHAKESPEARE: MACBETH
  [88]

perhaps
grand P. BROWNING, R. [30]

peril
those in p. on the sea HYMNS &
  CAROLS [20]

perils
defend us from all p. BOOK OF
  COMMON PRAYER [26]
many p. do enfold SPENSER [13]

perish
Let the day p. BIBLE, OLD TESTAMENT:
  JOB [8]

fall into the hand of the p. BIBLE, APOCRYPHA: ECCLESIASTICUS [58]

Honour a p. BIBLE, APOCRYPHA: ECCLESIASTICUS [56]

Luke, the beloved p. BIBLE, NEW TESTAMENT: COLOSSIANS [9]

need not a p. BIBLE, NEW TESTAMENT: MATTHEW [65]

P., heal thyself BIBLE, NEW TESTAMENT: LUKE [17]

true p. is also a ruler SOCRATES [18]

physicist
p. is an atom's way WALD [2]

physicists
p. have known sin OPPENHEIMER, J. R. [1]

physics
People ... who believe in p. EINSTEIN [14]

piano
don't shoot the p. player ANONYMOUS [77]

Picardy
Roses are flowering in P. WEATHERLY [2]

Picasso
P. is a Communist DALÍ [1]

pick-purse
p. of another's wit SIDNEY, P. [10]

Pickwickian
word in its P. sense DICKENS [3]

picture
destroy a person's p. LESSING, D. [2]

good p. is equivalent to a good deed VAN GOGH [6]

If it's a good p. GOLDWYN [6]

p. ... shows great and earnest labour WHISTLER [3]

p. that produces a moral impression GONCOURT [3]

pictures
P. are for entertainment GOLDWYN [10]

p. *are* my friends RUSKIN [7]

P. must be miraculous ROTHKO [2]

pie
p. in the sky HILL, J. [1]

piety
True p. is this KORAN [8]

piffle
pyramid of p. JOHNSON, B. [1]

these things are as p. ASHFORD [5]

pig
love not a gaping p. SHAKESPEARE: MERCHANT OF VENICE [32]

peasant becomes fond of his p. BERGER [4]

Stole a p. and away he run NURSERY RHYMES [47]

pigeon-livered
I am p. SHAKESPEARE: HAMLET [79]

pigeons
P. on the grass alas STEIN [3]

poisoning p. in the park LEHRER [1]

piggy
little p. went to market NURSERY RHYMES [45]

pigs
virtue of p. in a litter THOREAU [21]

pike
P., three inches long HUGHES, TED [6]

pile
standst an ancient p. JONSON [23]

pilgrim
loved the p. soul YEATS [12]

Onward goes the p. band HYMNS & CAROLS [85]

talk about their P. blood LOWELL, J. R. [10]

To be a p. BUNYAN [14]

To be a p. HYMNS & CAROLS [36]

pilgrimages
longen folk to goon on p. CHAUCER [15]

pilgrims
Like p. to th'appointed place DRYDEN [78]

pilgrymes
p., passynge to and fro CHAUCER [29]

pill
death in ambush lay in every p. GARTH [3]

One p. makes you larger SLICK [1]

pillar
p. of fire BIBLE, OLD TESTAMENT: EXODUS [21]

p. of state MILTON [109]

triple p. of the world SHAKESPEARE: ANTONY & CLEOPATRA [1]

pillars
hewn out her seven p. BIBLE, OLD TESTAMENT: PROVERBS [17]

these are the p. of society IBSEN [4]

pilot
p. of the Galilean lake MILTON [49]

Pimpernel
demmed, elusive P. ORCZY [1]

pimples
scratching of p. WOOLF [4]

pin
my life in a p.'s fee SHAKESPEARE: HAMLET [41]

pineapple
very p. of politeness SHERIDAN, R. B. [12]

pink
very p. of perfection GOLDSMITH [45]

pinko-grey
white races are really p. FORSTER [15]

pioneers
p. ... are ... mess-makers PIRSIG [4]

P.! O Pioneers WHITMAN [32]

pious
he was rather p. ASHFORD [4]

pipe
p., with solemn interposing puff COWPER [21]

three-p. problem DOYLE, A. C. [16]

pipe dream
lie of a p. O'NEILL [8]

piped
We have p. unto you BIBLE, NEW TESTAMENT: MATTHEW [84]

piper
P., pipe that song again BLAKE [1]

pippin
Right as a Ribstone P. BELLOC [10]

pips
until the p. squeak GEDDES [1]

pirate
To be a P. King GILBERT, W. S. [9]

piss
pitcher of warm p. GARNER [1]

pisse
make a contenaunce to p. CHAUCER [50]

pissing
inside the tent p. out JOHNSON, L. B. [7]

pistol
when his p. misses fire GOLDSMITH [30]

pistols
take a pair of p. DISRAELI [6]

pistons
black statement of p. SPENDER [4]

pit
cast him into a p. BIBLE, OLD TESTAMENT: GENESIS [56]

He that diggeth a p. BIBLE, OLD TESTAMENT: ECCLESIASTES [32]

to the bottomless p. MILTON [155]

Whoso diggeth a p. BIBLE, OLD TESTAMENT: PROVERBS [83]

pitch
He that toucheth p. BIBLE, APOCRYPHA: ECCLESIASTICUS [29]

pities
p. the plumage PAINE [10]

pity
knows some touch of p. SHAKESPEARE: RICHARD III [4]

let p. ... be the motive CERVANTES [44]

p. beyond all telling YEATS [9]

P. is for the living TWAIN [23]

P. is treason ROBESPIERRE [3]

p. of it, Iago SHAKESPEARE: OTHELLO [43]

P.'s the straightest FLETCHER, J. [5]

P. would be no more BLAKE [60]

Poetry is in the p. OWEN [7]

simple human p. ELIOT, G. [21]

place
not love a p. the less AUSTEN [37]

p. for everything BEETON [2]

rising unto p. is laborious BACON, F. [16]

Spirit of p. ... for this we travel MEYNELL [1]

spirit of the p. VIRGIL [45]

places
all p. were alike to him KIPLING [59]

we could go p. GARFIELD [1]

plagiarism
human p. ... difficult to avoid PROUST [22]

P. is necessary DEBORD [4]

steal from one author, it's p. MIZNER [3]

plague
p. a'both your houses SHAKESPEARE: ROMEO & JULIET [28]

p. making us cruel as dogs PEPYS [7]

plain
p. truth for plain people WESLEY, J. [3]

PINT OF P. IS YOUR ONLY MAN O'BRIEN, F. [1]

plain-work
She went to p. POPE [54]

plaisir
P. d'amour FLORIAN [1]

plan
Any p. conceived in moderation METTERNICH [1]

p. that admits of no modification PUBLILIUS SYRUS [6]

good old rule/... the simple p. WORDSWORTH, W. [63]

planetary
obedience of p. influence SHAKESPEARE: KING LEAR [12]

planets
other p. circle other suns POPE [116]

planning
P. and competition HAYEK [1]

p. is indispensable EISENHOWER [5]

plantation
still be working on a p. HOLIDAY [3]

platitude
p. is simply a truth repeated BALDWIN, S. [1]

Plato
rather be wrong with P. CICERO [15]

series of footnotes to P. WHITEHEAD [4]

play
child loves his p. SPOCK [3]

life ... a p. of passion RALEGH [10]

Life's poor p. is o'er POPE [133]

p. is badly cast WILDE [33]

p. is played out THACKERAY [8]

p. lousy PARKER, D. [13]

p. ... pleased not the million SHAKESPEARE: HAMLET [72]

p.'s the thing SHAKESPEARE: HAMLET [82]

p. without a woman KYD [3]

playboy
P. of the Western World SYNGE [4]

player
poor p./That struts and frets SHAKESPEARE: MACBETH [98]

players
P. ... no better than creatures JOHNSON, S. [97]

seldom listen to the p. BURNEY [2]

plays
children's p. are not sports MONTAIGNE [5]

completely a man when he p. SCHILLER [11]

strumpets ... ramble abroad to p. PRYNNE [1]

playwright
Inside every p. ... a Falstaff OSBORNE [12]

Plaza-Toro
Duke of P. GILBERT, W. S. [42]

plead
when I p., she bids me play SPENSER [19]

pleasant
mixes the p. with the useful HORACE [80]

p. in their lives BIBLE, OLD TESTAMENT: 2 SAMUEL [3]

pleasantness
ways of p. BIBLE, OLD TESTAMENT: PROVERBS [5]

please
never fails to p. SEDLEY [1]

we that live to p. JOHNSON, S. [6]

pleased
He makes people p. CHESTERFIELD [25]

pleasing
art of p. HAZLITT [3]

art of p. is ... deceiving VAUVENARGUES [2]

pleasure
A fool bolts p. ANTRIM [1]

cabinet of p. HERBERT, G. [24]

esteem p. above all things PEPYS [10]

Give yourself ... to absolute p. O'BRIEN, R. [1]

know the ways of p. HERBERT, G. [22]

Marred p.'s best SMITH, STEVIE [7]

no sterner moralist than p. BYRON, LORD [116]

only sensual p. without vice JOHNSON, S. [155]

P. at the helm GRAY, T. [22]

p. ... is become my business BURNEY [5]

p. is momentary CHESTERFIELD [41]

P. is Nature's test WILDE [14]

P. that isn't paid for LOOS [4]

p. turns to pleasing pain SPENSER [17]

pay a debt to p. ROCHESTER [10]

pursue p. with such breathless KIERKEGAARD [11]

sacrificing everything to p. DE SADE [3]

turn to p. all they find GREEN, M. [2]

pleasure-dome
p. with caves of ice COLERIDGE, S. T. [7]

pleasure-house
I built ... a lordly p. TENNYSON [16]

pleasures
cannot understand the p. AUSTEN [21]

cowardly love of immediate p. TOCQUEVILLE [14]

Heaven forbids some p. MOLIÈRE [5]

P. are all alike SELDEN [6]

p. are like poppies spread BURNS [44]

seek the p. of love DAVIES, ROBERTSON [2]

Pleiads
weeping P. wester HOUSMAN [32]

plenty
here is God's p. DRYDEN [75]

plots
good supply of tragic p. COPE [5]

We inherit p. HOSPITAL [1]

plotting
most p. heart in the world RICHARDSON [1]

plough
Men of England, wherefore p. SHELLEY, P. B. [44]

put his hand to the p. BIBLE, NEW TESTAMENT: LUKE [24]

so we p. along LONGFELLOW [10]

We p. the fields HYMNS & CAROLS [86]

ploughed
p. her, and she cropped SHAKESPEARE: ANTONY & CLEOPATRA [15]

ploughing
Is my team p. HOUSMAN [10]

plowers
p. plowed upon my back BIBLE, OLD TESTAMENT: PSALMS [133]

plures
Abiit ad p. PETRONIUS [3]

Pobble
P. who has no toes LEAR [13]

Poe
P., with his raven LOWELL, J. R. [7]

poem
beauties grace a p. HORACE [81]

figure a p. makes FROST, R. [29]

long p. is a test of invention KEATS [12]

p. ... begins as a lump FROST, R. [15]

p. is like a picture HORACE [84]

p. is that species of composition COLERIDGE, S. T. [57]

P., the Church's banquet HERBERT,
G. [13]
rises from p. a better man MEREDITH,
G. [2]
stronger still.../the man of p. SMART,
C. [10]

prayers
always in my p. BIBLE, NEW
TESTAMENT: ROMANS [1]
Christopher Robin is saying his
p. MILNE [5]
hear our p. BOOK OF COMMON
PRAYER [73]
men's p. are a disease EMERSON [16]
most perfect of all p. LESSING, G.E. [2]

prayeth
p. best, who loveth best COLERIDGE,
S. T. [36]

praying
No p., it spoils business OTWAY [5]

preached
p. as never sure to preach
again BAXTER [1]
p. to death by wild curates SMITH,
SYDNEY [25]

preaches
practised what he p. CONFUCIUS [6]

preaching
foolishness of p. BIBLE, NEW
TESTAMENT: 1 CORINTHIANS [2]
p. of the cross BIBLE, NEW TESTAMENT:
1 CORINTHIANS [4]
woman p. JOHNSON, S. [59]

preapocalyptic
not ... postmodernist but p. LEHMAN,
D. [1]

precedence
none sure will claim in hell/
P. MILTON [103]

precedent
p. embalms a principle STOWELL [2]

precedents
each generation ... its own
p. LOCKWOOD [1]

precept
p. must be upon precept BIBLE, OLD
TESTAMENT: ISAIAH [37]

precepts
love the p. FARQUHAR [5]

precious
we guess, my p. TOLKIEN [1]

predestination
P. in the stride KIPLING [43]

preferment
knocking at p.'s door ARNOLD, M. [28]
P. goes by letter SHAKESPEARE:
OTHELLO [2]

pregnancy
lawful ... to avoid p. MENCKEN [25]

pregnant
I didn't 'fall' p. LETTE [1]
If men could get p. KENNEDY, F. R. [2]

prejudice
exemption from all p. HAZLITT [4]
ink ... is merely fluid p. TWAIN [30]
P. ... vagrant opinion BIERCE [33]
Without the aid of p. and
custom HAZLITT [33]

prejudices
P. ... are most difficult BRONTË, C. [11]
p. are our mistresses
CHESTERFIELD [33]
p. have had their ...
novelty PROUST [3]

prepare
P. ye the way of the Lord BIBLE, OLD
TESTAMENT: ISAIAH [52]

prepared
BE P. BADEN-POWELL [1]

Presbyter
New P. is but old Priest MILTON [72]

presence
p. that disturbs WORDSWORTH, W. [9]

present
p. contains nothing
more BERGSON [4]
p. ... infection of things gone LOWELL,
R. [9]
p. is an interlude O'NEILL [6]
To appreciate p.
conditions BUNTING [1]

presents
P. ... endear absents LAMB,
CHARLES [18]

preserve
p. thy going out BIBLE, OLD
TESTAMENT: PSALMS [126]
P. us ... while waking BOOK OF
COMMON PRAYER [98]

presidency
it's for the P. TRUMAN [8]

president
all the P.'s men KISSINGER [2]
anybody could become P. DARROW,
CLARENCE [2]
any boy may become P. STEVENSON,
A. [7]
do not choose to run for
P. COOLIDGE [5]
P. is best judged LERNER, M. [1]
rather be right than be P. CLAY [3]
reasons to shoot at the P. DELILLO [4]
To be P. of the United
States UPDIKE [7]
well-shod p. walks ARMITAGE [3]
When the P. does it NIXON [11]

presidential
Under a P. government BAGEHOT [7]

presidents
P. start out to run a crusade COOKE,
A. [2]

press
job of the p. LASCH [3]
p. and politicians BRENTON/HARE [1]

p. ... is an excellent servant COOPER,
J. F. [4]
p. will bounce back BAKER, J. [1]
p. would kill her SPENCER, C. [1]
talks about 'freedom of the
p.' LENIN [6]
very hirelings of the p. COBBETT [1]

press officers
compare p. to riflemen INGHAM [1]

presume
P. not that I am the
thing SHAKESPEARE: HENRY IV
PT 2 [29]

pretence
P. ... deceives the wisest TOLSTOY [8]

pretences
greatest p. are built up HOFFER [6]

pretentious
P.? *Moi* CLEESE [2]

pretty
leave p. women to men PROUST [23]

preys
Every one of us p. GAY, J. [24]

price
real p. ... is the toil SMITH, ADAM [3]

pricks
hundred p. against one MIZNER [4]
kick against the p. BIBLE, NEW
TESTAMENT: ACTS [14]

pride
It is my p. CHATTERTON [2]
look backward to with p. FROST, R. [5]
once engage people's p.
CHESTERFIELD [1]
only way we'll have real
p. KRAMER [2]
p. and hunger ... at variance SWIFT,
J. [35]
P. goeth before ... a fall BIBLE, OLD
TESTAMENT: PROVERBS [41]
P. is hateful BIBLE, APOCRYPHA:
ECCLESIASTICUS [22]
rebuff to his country's p. RUSSELL,
B. [4]

priest
always be a p. of love LAWRENCE,
D. H. [7]
Like people, like p. BIBLE, OLD
TESTAMENT: HOSEA [1]
Revilest thou God's high p. BIBLE,
NEW TESTAMENT: ACTS [37]

priesthood
p. is a marriage MURDOCH, I. [9]
royal p. BIBLE, NEW TESTAMENT:
1 PETER [3]

priests
p. are always right PAVESE [6]
p. have been enemies HUME, D. [4]

prime
One's p. is elusive SPARK [5]

prime minister
No woman ... will be P. THATCHER [1]

quite a change to have a P. FOOT [2]
P. exercises ... public
influence MENZIES [2]
Unknown P. ASQUITH, H. [3]

prime ministers
P. are wedded to the truth SAKI [8]

primitives
among so-called 'p.' JUNG [3]

primrose
Bring the rathe p. MILTON [50]
p. path of dalliance SHAKESPEARE:
HAMLET [29]
p. way to the
everlasting SHAKESPEARE:
MACBETH [43]

prince
Good night, sweet P. SHAKESPEARE:
HAMLET [163]
Who made thee a p. BIBLE, OLD
TESTAMENT: EXODUS [2]

princes
hangs on p.' favours SHAKESPEARE:
HENRY VIII [10]
Put not your trust in p. BIBLE, OLD
TESTAMENT: PSALMS [147]

princess
People's P. BLAIR, T. [4]

principalities
nor p. nor powers BIBLE, NEW
TESTAMENT: ROMANS [25]

principle
general p. gives no help HEGEL [11]
no p., however immaculate LEWIS,
W. [2]
some strong p. MELBOURNE [4]

principles
all bloody p. and practices FOX, G.
[4]
easier to fight for one's p. ADLER,
A. [2]
like persons with no p.
better WILDE [38]
religious and moral p. ARNOLD, T. [2]

print
decomposing in the eternity of
p. WOOLF [12]
John, p. it BUNYAN [2]

printing
invented the art of p. CARLYLE, T.
[15]

prison
impenetrable barriers of our
p. EDGEWORTH [2]
let's away to p. SHAKESPEARE: KING
LEAR [58]
walls do not a p. make LOVELACE [4]
We are all conceived in close
p. DONNE [51]

private
p. goods have full sway GALBRAITH [5]
p. life which has not been
determined ELIOT, G. [25]

privilege
p. I claim for my own
sex AUSTEN [38]
What men prize most is a p. LOWELL,
J. R. [24]

prize
one receiveth the p. BIBLE, NEW
TESTAMENT: 1 CORINTHIANS [23]

prizes
offer glittering p. SMITH, F. E. [1]

problem
p. that has no name FRIEDAN [1]
solution to a p. JOHNSON, R. W. [1]
they can't see the p. CHESTERTON [45]

problems
involved in partial
p. WITTGENSTEIN [3]
p. are ... precious possessions VAN
DER POST [3]
three great p. of this
century HUGO [4]
two p. in my life DOUGLAS-HOME [2]
two p. of our country CARTER, J. [2]

procrastination
P. is the thief YOUNG, E. [8]
p. is the/art of keeping/
up MARQUIS [4]

procreation
ordained for the p. of children BOOK
OF COMMON PRAYER [77]
symbols of p. CYRANO DE
BERGERAC [2]

procul
P., o procul este VIRGIL [40]

procuress
P. to the Lords of
Hell TENNYSON [100]

profanation
'Twere p. of our joys DONNE [22]

profane
Far hence be souls p. VIRGIL [40]

profanum
Odi p. volgus HORACE [35]

profession
man and his p. LEVI, P. [5]
member of the most ancient
p. KIPLING [4]

professionals
Leave death to the p. GREENE, G. [7]

professions
All p. be-rogue one another GAY, J. [7]
p. are conspiracies SHAW [44]

professors
p. like their literature LEWIS, S. [3]

profit
No p. grows where is no
pleasure SHAKESPEARE: TAMING OF
THE SHREW [1]

profundis
De p. BIBLE, VULGATE [6]

progeny
p. of learning SHERIDAN, R. B. [7]

prognostics
P. do not always prove WALPOLE,
H. [15]

progress
All p. is experimental CHAPMAN, J. [1]
notion of p. in a single
line MUMFORD, L. [4]
P. everywhere today GRENFELL [4]
P. in knowledge GOULD [5]
P. is a comfortable
disease CUMMINGS, E. E. [7]
P. ... is not an accident SPENCER, H. [1]
P. is not an illusion ORWELL [10]
P. is the injustice CIORAN [9]
p. is written in the blood GOLDMAN,
E. [1]
P., man's distinctive
mark BROWNING, R. [46]
P. would not have been the
rarity BAGEHOT [30]
same each time with p. BENN [9]
slogan of p. is changing HOOVER,
H. [2]

prohibition
p. ... the only temptation HAZLITT [18]

proletariat
Admiration of the p. RUSSELL, B. [19]
dictatorship of the p. MARX, K. [5]
white-collar p. MAUGHAM [16]

prologue
long p. ... short in the story BIBLE,
APOCRYPHA: 2 MACCABEES [1]

Prometheus
new P. of new men BYRON, LORD
[101]
P. is reaching out KOESTLER [7]

promiscuous
doesn't suit women to be
p. COWARD [5]

promise
P. ... is the soul JOHNSON, S. [39]
p. made is a debt unpaid SERVICE [3]

promised
Jesus, I have p. HYMNS & CAROLS [67]

promised land
I've seen the P. KING, M. L. [20]
may never reach the
P. CALLAGHAN [3]

promises
p. to keep FROST, R. [20]

promising
gods ... first call p. CONNOLLY, C. [8]

promotion
none will sweat but for
p. SHAKESPEARE: AS YOU LIKE IT [10]

pronounce
p. that they be man and wife BOOK
OF COMMON PRAYER [86]

propaganda
As soon as by one's own p. HITLER [5]
P. is that art of lying CORNFORD,
F. M. [2]

more highly p. is
organized FORSTER [29]
P. is a situation of power BURKE,
E. [9]
public opinion
P. is a weak tyrant THOREAU [24]
p. is the worst of all CHAMFORT [5]
P. ... makes life unpleasant INGE [2]
substitute p. for law COOPER, J. F. [2]
public school
been to an English p. WAUGH [6]
p. system all over WAUGH [3]
public schools
P. ... nurseries of all vice FIELDING,
HENRY [5]
publish
P. and be damned WELLINGTON [4]
puddin'
Great chieftain o' the p.'-
race BURNS [29]
puddings
unless they have tea and
p. ORWELL [18]
puddy tat
I tawt I taw a p. CLAMPETT [1]
puff-paste
flesh ... fantastical p. WEBSTER, J. [18]
pug
most charming p. FLEMING, M. [1]
pulse
feeling a woman's p. STERNE [28]
pulvis
P. et umbra sumus HORACE [51]
pun
good p. may be
admitted BOSWELL [4]
p. is ... a pistol LAMB, CHARLES [27]
so vile a p. DENNIS [1]
punctuality
P. is the politeness of
kings LOUIS XVIII [1]
P. is the soul of
business HALIBURTON [2]
p. is the thief of time WILDE [48]
P. is the virtue of the
bored WAUGH [21]
Punic
With P. faith SALLUST [4]
punish
P. France, ignore Germany RICE, C. [1]
power to p. FOUCAULT [4]
urge to p. is strong NIETZSCHE [19]
punishment
All p. is mischief BENTHAM [3]
deserving of some p. GREGORY, A. [1]
let the p. fit the crime GILBERT,
W. S. [36]
p. is greater BIBLE, OLD TESTAMENT:
GENESIS [27]
punk
Marrying a p. SHAKESPEARE: MEASURE
FOR MEASURE [24]

P. ... just another English
spectacle BURCHILL [2]
puppy
p. dogs' tails NURSERY RHYMES [49]
purchase
world of potential p. FISHER, C. [2]
pure
led a p. life CATULLUS [16]
p. as the driven slush BANKHEAD [2]
Unto the p. all things are pure BIBLE,
NEW TESTAMENT: TITUS [2]
purgatorie
in erthe I was his p. CHAUCER [35]
Puritan
P. hated bearbaiting MACAULAY,
LORD [38]
p. ... pours righteous
indignation CHESTERTON [41]
To the P., all things are
impure LAWRENCE, D. H. [20]
puritanical
Once is orthodox, twice is
p. MELBOURNE [5]
Puritanism
P.: the haunting fear MENCKEN [7]
puriter
vitam p. egi CATULLUS [16]
purity
P. is ... to contemplate
defilement WEIL [8]
purlieus
dusty p. of the law TENNYSON [111]
purple
I shall wear p. JOSEPH, J. [1]
made p. riot KEATS [71]
P. haze all in my brain HENDRIX [2]
walk by the color p. WALKER [5]
purpose
true joy ... being used for a
p. SHAW [17]
purse
consumption of the p. SHAKESPEARE:
HENRY IV PT 2 [10]
pursued
only the p., the pursuing FITZGERALD,
F. S. [7]
pusher
God damn the p. AXTON [1]
puss-gentleman
fine p. that's all perfume COWPER
[23]
pussy
persian p. from over the
sea MARQUIS [3]
pyjamas
in the drawer marked p. THOMAS,
D. [16]
pylons
P., those pillars SPENDER [6]
pyramid
bottom of the economic
p. ROOSEVELT, F. D. [1]

Pyramus
death of P. and Thisbe SHAKESPEARE:
MIDSUMMER NIGHT'S DREAM [6]
pyre
heaping up its own funeral
p. POWELL, E. [2]
Pyrenees
P. are no more LOUIS XIV [3]
quadrille
q. in a sentry-box JAMES, H. [20]
quadruped
hairy q., ... probably
arboreal DARWIN, C. [5]
qualities
endowed with the three rare
q. BEHN [5]
quality
Never mind the q. POWELL/DRIVER [1]
People of q. know
everything MOLIÈRE [2]
We are persons of q. JONSON [33]
Women of q. are so
civil WYCHERLEY [1]
Quangle Wangle
Q. sat LEAR [15]
quantum
every man is born with his q. SWIFT,
J. [27]
quarks
Three q. for Muster Mark JOYCE,
J. [38]
quarrel
association of men who will not
q. JEFFERSON [19]
grace in his q. KEATS [48]
lover's q. with the world FROST,
R. [33]
out of the q. with others YEATS [42]
q. ... between people CHAMBERLAIN,
N. [1]
Q. not at all LINCOLN [22]
takes ... one to make a q. INGE [1]
quarreled
not aware that we ever
q. THOREAU [57]
quarrels
Love-q. oft in ... concord
end MILTON [201]
Lovers' q. are love's
renewal TERENCE [2]
q. of Europe JEFFERSON [36]
Those who in q. interpose GAY, J. [5]
Quebec
Long live Free Q. DE GAULLE [10]
Vive le Q. libre DE GAULLE [10]
queen
been to London to visit the
Q. NURSERY RHYMES [32]
ev'ry lady would be q. POPE [97]
home life of our own dear
Q. ANONYMOUS [37]
I am your anointed Q. ELIZABETH I [1]

laughing q. HUNT, L. [4]

motherly old middle-class q. JAMES, H. [22]

not be a q./For all the world SHAKESPEARE: HENRY VIII [4]

q. of people's hearts DIANA, PRINCESS OF WALES [3]

Queen Mab
Q. hath been with you SHAKESPEARE: ROMEO & JULIET [8]

queer
q. shoulder to the wheel GINSBERG [5]

question
not every q. that deserves PUBLILIUS SYRUS [7]

what is the q. STEIN [13]

questioning
Q. is not the mode JOHNSON, S. [101]

questions
easy to answer the ultimate q. OSBORNE [10]

I have answered three q. CARROLL [9]

nonsense q. are unanswerable LEWIS, C. S. [10]

quibble
q. is to Shakespeare JOHNSON, S. [65]

quick
q. and the dead BOOK OF COMMON PRAYER [15]

quickly
I come q. BIBLE, NEW TESTAMENT: REVELATION [55]

That thou doest, do q. BIBLE, NEW TESTAMENT: JOHN [46]

quiddities
thy quips and thy q. SHAKESPEARE: HENRY IV PT 1 [4]

Where be his q. now SHAKESPEARE: HAMLET [146]

quiet
All Q. on the Western Front REMARQUE [1]

Anything for a Q. Life MIDDLETON [3]

determination of a q. man SMITH, I. D. [1]

Fie upon this q. life SHAKESPEARE: HENRY IV PT 1 [19]

long for the imperishable q. ROETHKE [6]

serve thee with a q. mind BOOK OF COMMON PRAYER [46]

quietness
unravished bride of q. KEATS [90]

quill
lay down my q. BEHN [7]

quires
In Q. and Places BOOK OF COMMON PRAYER [20]

quit
q. altogether public affairs EDWARD VIII [2]

q. yourselves like men BIBLE, OLD TESTAMENT: 1 SAMUEL [3]

quitch
vicious q./Of blood TENNYSON [154]

Quixote
all too true tale/Of Q. BYRON, LORD [157]

quotable
better to be q. STOPPARD [8]

quotation
apt in q. is a ... gift DAVIES, ROBERTSON [1]

Classical q. is the *parole* JOHNSON, S. [134]

Every q. contributes JOHNSON, S. [30]

habit ... of perpetual q. SMYTH [1]

I hate q. EMERSON [36]

q. is a national vice WAUGH [18]

q. is not an excerpt MANDELSTAM [6]

q. marks ... blotted out MILLER, A. [8]

wisdom ... preserved by q. D'ISRAELI [1]

quotations
Backed his opinion with q. PRIOR [4]

book that furnishes no q. PEACOCK [6]

He wrapped himself in q. KIPLING [34]

pretentious q. FOWLER, H. W. [1]

Q. ... are like wayside robbers BENJAMIN [7]

Q. are useful DEBORD [6]

read books of q. CHURCHILL, W. [10]

Read books, repeat q. DYLAN [10]

slip q. down people's throats WOOLF [28]

taste for q. ... is a Surrealist SONTAG [10]

quote
grow immortal as they q. YOUNG, E. [2]

q. wisely and well ALCOTT, A. B. [3]

quoted
To be ... q. is the only fame SMITH, ALEXANDER [4]

rabbit
r. in a snare STEPHENS [3]

Run, r., run BUTLER, R. [2]

race
No r. has the last word GARVEY [2]

r. is not to the swift BIBLE, OLD TESTAMENT: ECCLESIASTES [30]

r. to which I belong LINCOLN [13]

whole r. is a poet STEVENS, W. [15]

Rachel
R. weeping for her children BIBLE, NEW TESTAMENT: MATTHEW [5]

racism
R. is an *ism* BENEDICT [2]

rack
r. of this tough world SHAKESPEARE: KING LEAR [64]

radical
I never dared be r. FROST, R. [28]

r. is a man with both feet ROOSEVELT, F. D. [7]

r.'s role DOCTOROW [4]

uncertain mind of the American r. GOLDMAN, E. [8]

radish
I am a bunch of r. SHAKESPEARE: HENRY IV PT 1 [20]

rag
r. and a bone KIPLING [50]

rage
heavenly minds yield to such r. VIRGIL [18]

Much did I r. when young YEATS [48]

not to get into a r. ELIOT, G. [39]

r., against the dying THOMAS, D. [13]

R. is the only quality BRESLIN [1]

rags
r. of time DONNE [6]

railroad
steal the whole r. ROOSEVELT, T. [11]

railway
climax to r. age TAYLOR, A. J. P. [4]

railways
r. are irresistible bazaars THEROUX [1]

raiment
man clothed in soft r. BIBLE, NEW TESTAMENT: MATTHEW [82]

rain
abundance of r. BIBLE, OLD TESTAMENT: 1 KINGS [12]

hard r.'s a-gonna fall DYLAN [2]

Hath the r. a father BIBLE, OLD TESTAMENT: JOB [43]

r. in Spain LERNER, A. J. [2]

r. it raineth every day SHAKESPEARE: KING LEAR [30]

r. it raineth every day SHAKESPEARE: TWELFTH NIGHT [40]

R.! Rain! Rain KEATS [36]

some r. must fall LONGFELLOW [9]

sound of the r. is like the voices MISHIMA [1]

Still falls the R. SITWELL [3]

takes credit for the r. MORROW [1]

rainbow
behold/A r. In the sky WORDSWORTH, W. [67]

God gave Noah the r. ANONYMOUS [31]

our nation is a r. JACKSON, J. [4]

reverent feeling for the r. TWAIN [3]

Somewhere over the r. GARLAND [1]

Unweave a r. KEATS [64]

raindrops
R. keep falling on my head DAVID [1]

rake
r. among scholars MACAULAY, LORD [36]

ram
black r./Is tupping SHAKESPEARE:
OTHELLO [5]

Ramadan
month of R. KORAN [9]

ramblers
r. are ... dirty mac brigade VAN
HOOGSTRATEN [1]

Rambo
After seeing R. last night REAGAN,
R. [11]

random
famous r. event ARENDT [12]

ranged
if I have r. SHAKESPEARE:
SONNETS [33]

rank
all one r. NAPOLEON I [11]
my offence is r. SHAKESPEARE:
HAMLET [116]
R. is a great beautifier BULWER-
LYTTON [1]

rape
principle of procrastinated
r. PRITCHETT [1]
R. isn't ... the worst thing WELDON [8]
you can't commit r. a
little STEFFENS [1]

raped
it is like being r. DIANA, PRINCESS OF
WALES [2]

rapists
all men are r. FRENCH [2]

rapper
influence to your son as a r. ICE
CUBE [1]

rapping
r. at my chamber door POE [7]

rarity
r. that gives zest JUVENAL [18]

rascal
dull and muddy-mettled
r. SHAKESPEARE: HAMLET [78]

rash
You look rarther r. ASHFORD [3]

rashes
Green grow the r. BURNS [31]

rat
Anyone can r. CHURCHILL, W. [8]
dirty, double-crossing r. CAGNEY [1]
Droll r., they would shoot
you ROSENBERG, I. [2]
like a poisoned r. in a hole SWIFT,
J. [40]

rat race
r. is for rats REID, JIMMY [1]

rational
make life more r. AYER [5]
so proud of being r. ROCHESTER [4]
What is r. is actual HEGEL [1]

rationalization
times ... characterized by r. WEBER [4]

rationally
looks upon the world r. HEGEL [12]

rattle
toy of man, his
r. WOLLSTONECRAFT [4]

raven
ghastly, grim and ancient r. POE [9]

ravens
r. brought him bread BIBLE, OLD
TESTAMENT: 1 KINGS [9]

ravished
r. this fair creature FIELDING,
HENRY [6]

razor
no r. come upon his head BIBLE, OLD
TESTAMENT: NUMBERS [2]
R. pain you PARKER, D. [5]

reach
man's r. should exceed his
grasp BROWNING, R. [36]

reactionaries
thank God for the r. COLLINGWOOD [1]

read
conventional good r. BRADBURY,
M. [4]
dare teach a man to r. SHAW [47]
He had r. much AUBREY [2]
I never loved to r. LEE, H. [1]
never r. a book before
reviewing SMITH, SYDNEY [26]
r. just as inclination leads JOHNSON,
S. [55]
R. not to contradict BACON, F. [36]
r. part of it all the way GOLDWYN [11]
r. ... to prevent
themselves LICHTENBERG [14]
Take it and r. ST AUGUSTINE [3]
To learn to r. is to light a
fire HUGO [15]
To r. well ... is a noble
exercise THOREAU [36]
who cannot think or r. MORE, H. [4]

reader
ideal r. suffering JOYCE, J. [34]
R., I married him BRONTË, C. [13]

readers
make your r. suffer JOHNSON, S. [63]
R. are of two sorts JERROLD [4]
R are plentiful MARTINEAU [5]
R. ... divided into four
classes COLERIDGE, S. T. [51]
r. to become more
indolent GOLDSMITH [3]
your everlasting r. COBBETT [5]

reading
creative r. EMERSON [2]
I prefer r. SMITH, LOGAN P. [14]
left off r. altogether LAMB,
CHARLES [23]
Much r. is an oppression PENN [9]
r. has brought ...
barbarism LICHTENBERG [13]

R. is not a duty BIRRELL [2]
R. isn't an occupation ORTON [3]
R. is to the mind STEELE [4]
r. machine, always wound
up LOWELL, J. R. [6]
R. maketh a full man BACON, F. [38]
r. of novels COLERIDGE, S. T. [49]
what is worth r. TREVELYAN [5]
With one day's r. POUND [24]

Reagan
battle for the mind of Ronald
R. NOONAN [2]

real
definition of the r. BAUDRILLARD [2]
r. is hard and rough WEIL [7]

reality
accidental encounter with
r. DANEY [1]
Cannot bear very much r. ELIOT,
T. S. [41]
R. ... doesn't go away DICK [1]
R. television is not the end GREER [19]

realm
Every man is the lord of a
r. THOREAU [49]

reapers
Only r., reaping early TENNYSON [8]

reason
All the interests of my r. KANT [2]
capability and god-like
r. SHAKESPEARE: HAMLET [132]
gods implant r. in men SOPHOCLES [2]
if it be against r. COKE [1]
Man is to be found in
r. LICHTENBERG [22]
nothing without a r. LEIBNIZ [1]
not r. that besieged
Troy DISRAELI [19]
R. always means what
someone GASKELL [2]
r. and love keep little
company SHAKESPEARE: MIDSUMMER
NIGHT'S DREAM [27]
R. is a whore CIORAN [1]
R. is immortal PYTHAGORAS [1]
R. is man's instrument FROMM [2]
R. is our soul's left hand DONNE
[40]
R. is ... the slave HUME, D. [1]
R. still keeps a throne FARQUHAR [8]

reasonable
figure of 'The R. Man' HERBERT,
A. P. [4]

reasoning
masses get involved in
r. VOLTAIRE [27]

reasons
Good r. must ... give
place SHAKESPEARE: JULIUS
CAESAR [42]
never convinced of your
r. CAMUS [15]

rebel
more poisonous ... than a
r. LUTHER [3]
No one can go on being a
r. DURRELL [4]
r. is not ... a revolutionary MILLETT
[3]
R. Without a Cause LINDER [1]
what is a r. CAMUS [9]

rebellion
incite this meeting to
r. PANKHURST [2]
little r. ... is a good
thing JEFFERSON [10]
R. lay in his way SHAKESPEARE:
HENRY IV PT 1 [43]
R. to tyrants is
obedience BRADSHAW [1]

recession
r. when your neighbor loses his
job TRUMAN [5]

reckoning
God is swift/at the r. KORAN [35]

recognition
philosophers ... call it 'r.' JAMES,
W. [21]

reconcilement
never can true r. grow MILTON [128]

reconciliation
true r. does not consist MANDELA,
N. [6]

rectum
finger ... in the r. OSLER [8]

red
Better r. than dead POLITICAL
SLOGANS [5]
keep the r. flag flying CONNELL [2]
right turn on a r. light ALLEN, W.
[17]

redeemed
r. his people BIBLE, NEW TESTAMENT:
LUKE [5]

redeemer
my r. liveth BIBLE, OLD TESTAMENT:
JOB [31]

redemption
destined, for the world's
r. AQUINAS [1]

reed
bruised r. shall he not break BIBLE,
OLD TESTAMENT: ISAIAH [61]
Man is only a r. PASCAL [9]
r. shaken with the wind BIBLE, NEW
TESTAMENT: MATTHEW [82]
trustest upon ... this bruised r. BIBLE,
OLD TESTAMENT: 2 KINGS [10]
trusteth in ... this broken r. BIBLE, OLD
TESTAMENT: ISAIAH [49]

reeling
R. and Writhing CARROLL [16]

references
verify your r., sir ROUTH [1]

refinement
Life will not bear r. JOHNSON, S. [111]

reflect
To r. is to disturb ROSTAND, J. [4]

reflection
r. as on the surface CHARLES, PRINCE
OF WALES [3]
R., you may come tomorrow SHELLEY,
P. B. [103]

reform
Every r. ... will itself need
reforming COLERIDGE, S. T. [53]
R., that you may preserve MACAULAY,
LORD [15]
To r. a world CARLYLE, T. [12]

refuge
God is our r. BIBLE, OLD TESTAMENT:
PSALMS [58]
surest r. ... amongst cows and
sheep DE QUINCEY [7]
thou art my strong r. BIBLE, OLD
TESTAMENT: PSALMS [80]

refugee
r. in a crowded boat REAGAN, R. [10]

refusal
great r. DANTE [8]

refuses
man ... r. to be what he is CAMUS [8]

régime
eat-and-let-eat r. ACHEBE [1]

regiment
led his r. from behind GILBERT,
W. S. [41]
monstrous r. of women KNOX, J. [1]

regret
Accept life, and ... accept r. AMIEL [4]
r. deeply is to live afresh THOREAU [1]

regrets
end up with the right r. MILLER,
A. [11]

regrette
je ne r. rien PIAF [2]

reich
Ein R., ein Volk POLITICAL
SLOGANS [10]
no restless R. KOHL [1]
R. is made BISMARCK [7]

reign
lazy, long, lascivious r. DEFOE [6]

rejoice
again I say, R. BIBLE, NEW TESTAMENT:
PHILIPPIANS [8]
Just r. at that news THATCHER [7]
R., again, I say rejoice HYMNS &
CAROLS [75]
R., O young man BIBLE, OLD
TESTAMENT: ECCLESIASTES [39]
R. with them that do rejoice BIBLE,
NEW TESTAMENT: ROMANS [31]

relation
poor r. is the most irrelevant LAMB,
CHARLES [21]

relations
great men have their poor
r. DICKENS [77]
R. are ... a tedious pack WILDE [102]

relationship
r. ... is like a shark ALLEN, W. [22]
successful r. CRISP [13]
This means a special r. CHURCHILL,
W. [40]

relatives
Every man sees in his r. MENCKEN
[6]

relativity
That's r. EINSTEIN [12]

relaxation
sunk from a riot of r. NASH, O. [13]

released
I shall be r. DYLAN [27]

religion
consolations of r. LEWIS, C. S. [7]
count r. but a childish
toy MARLOWE [4]
enough r. to make us *hate* SWIFT,
J. [8]
enter into the intimacy of their
r. QUINET [2]
Every r. is good PAINE [14]
In matters of r. and
matrimony CHESTERFIELD [37]
Men despise r. PASCAL [2]
Most men's anger against
r. SAVILE [5]
my r. from the priest GOLDSMITH [49]
mysteries of our r. HOBBES [13]
no reason to bring r. O'CASEY [4]
old-time r. ANONYMOUS [29]
one r. in England VOLTAIRE [3]
One r. is as true BURTON [11]
political r. of the nation LINCOLN [2]
r. as opposed to religions HUGO [10]
R. enables us to ignore UPDIKE [15]
R. ... has always been the
wound POTTER, D. [4]
R./Has made an honest woman FRY,
C. [4]
r. is allowed to invade MELBOURNE [3]
R. is a temper MARTINEAU [2]
R. is civilisation DISRAELI [47]
R. is ... subject of
conversation CHESTERFIELD [39]
R. is the state of being
grasped TILLICH [1]
r. is whatever BARRIE [13]
r. ... must consist of ideas COLERIDGE,
S. T. [73]
R. stands on tiptoe HERBERT, G. [47]
R.! what treasure untold COWPER [29]
R., which should most distinguish
us LOCKE [7]
reasoning in ... his own r. MORE, T. [3]
talks loudly against r. STERNE [11]
true meaning of r. ARNOLD, M. [57]

When I mention r. FIELDING,
HENRY [7]

religions
All r. are good SHELLEY, P. B. [4]
All r. of the only God MONTALE [2]
main business of r. TOCQUEVILLE [6]
R. die when they are
proved WILDE [91]
sixty different r. CARACCIOLO [1]

religious
contact with r. people NIETZSCHE [32]
every r. story … is …
wrong RUSHDIE [10]
I am a passionately r.
man LAWRENCE, D. H. [10]
suspended my r.
inquiries GIBBON [13]

remarkable
nothing left r. SHAKESPEARE: ANTONY
& CLEOPATRA [32]
wish to be r. HOLMES SR [15]

remarks
r. are not literature STEIN [5]

remedies
Extreme r. HIPPOCRATES [2]
men die of their r. MOLIÈRE [23]
r. oft in ourselves do
lie SHAKESPEARE: ALL'S WELL [5]

remedy
Auntie Maggie's R. FORMBY [5]
r. for all things but
death CERVANTES [30]

remember
I r.,/The house HOOD [6]
R. me, but ah! forget TATE [1]
R. me when I am gone ROSSETTI, C. [3]
r. me when thou comest BIBLE, NEW
TESTAMENT: LUKE [73]
We will r. them BINYON [1]
will be pleasant to r. VIRGIL [22]

remembered
r. after we are dead HAZLITT [21]
terror of … something which is
r. PARRIS [2]

remembrance
Mournful and never-ending
r. POE [15]
r. of things past SHAKESPEARE:
SONNETS [8]

remembrances
not burden our r. SHAKESPEARE:
TEMPEST [27]

remission
without … blood is no r. BIBLE, NEW
TESTAMENT: HEBREWS [3]

remorse
R. – is Memory DICKINSON, E. [25]
R. is … the most wasteful FORSTER [9]
r. ought to stop biting NASH, O. [7]
R., the fatal egg COWPER [15]

rendezvous
shall not fail that r. SEEGER, A. [2]

renewal
great r. of the world RILKE [1]

renouncement
R.: the heroism of
mediocrity BARNEY [1]

renown
set the cause above r. NEWBOLT [5]

repartee
man renowned for r. COWPER [9]

repeateth
r. a matter BIBLE, OLD TESTAMENT:
PROVERBS [46]

repent
r. at leisure CONGREVE [5]

repentance
R. is but want of power DRYDEN [76]

repetitions
use not vain r. BIBLE, NEW
TESTAMENT: MATTHEW [37]

reply
Theirs not to make r. TENNYSON [142]

report
good r. maketh the bones fat BIBLE,
OLD TESTAMENT: PROVERBS [40]
R. me and my cause
aright SHAKESPEARE: HAMLET [160]
Who hath believed our r. BIBLE, OLD
TESTAMENT: ISAIAH [71]

reporter
r. … threatens our life KRAUS [8]

reporters
gallery in which the r. sit MACAULAY,
LORD [14]

repose
earned a night's r. LONGFELLOW [8]
r. which ever is the
same WORDSWORTH, W. [46]

representative
Your r. owes you BURKE, E. [12]

reproach
no defence against r. ADDISON [5]

reproducers
Most modern r. of life STEVENS,
W. [24]

reproduction
r. of mankind is a …
marvel LUTHER [8]

reptile
r. all the rest POPE [153]

reptiles
feel as r. that infest IRVING, W. [7]
r. of the mind BLAKE [39]

republic
mean to found a r. NAPOLEON I [1]
provide you with a
r. TOCQUEVILLE [17]
r. … means association MAZZINI [1]

republican
R. form of government SPENCER,
H. [10]
r. is the only form of
government JEFFERSON [14]

We all have the r.
spirit BAUDELAIRE [33]

Republican Party
R. makes even its young STEVENSON,
A. [10]

reputation
at every word a r. dies POPE [43]
good r. is more valuable PUBLILIUS
SYRUS [1]
I have lost my r. SHAKESPEARE:
OTHELLO [27]
live down … a good r. WILDE [82]
One makes one's r. FRAYN [1]
purest treasure … /Is spotless
r. SHAKESPEARE: RICHARD II [1]
r. which carries him JEFFERSON [18]
wink a r. down SWIFT, J. [39]

reputations
murdered r. of the
week CONGREVE [15]

requiem
R. aeternam dona eis MISSAL [24]

requiescant
R. in pace MISSAL [28]

research
gloom of uninspired
r. WORDSWORTH, W. [100]
goal of all r. … is truth DEUTSCH [1]
r. is … the art of the
soluble MEDAWAR [1]

reserve
There is safety in r. AUSTEN [25]

resignation
humorous r. MAUGHAM [3]
noble r. or …
indignation TURGENEV [4]

resist
respect … those who r. me DE
GAULLE [11]

resistance
breaking the enemy's r. SUN TZU [1]
R. as global as capital POLITICAL
SLOGANS [32]

resources
How many inner r. BARNEY [5]

respect
lasting r. in society DALÍ [6]
R./Find out what it means FRANKLIN,
A. [1]
r. or natural love CONRAD [20]
too much r. upon the
world SHAKESPEARE: MERCHANT OF
VENICE [3]

respecter
no r. of persons BIBLE, NEW
TESTAMENT: ACTS [18]

responds
moment that a man no longer
r. MISHIMA [2]

rest
Grant them eternal r. MISSAL [24]
May they r. in peace MISSAL [28]

rock

built his house upon a r. BIBLE, NEW TESTAMENT: MATTHEW [57]

Lord is my r. BIBLE, OLD TESTAMENT: PSALMS [13]

r. ... higher than I BIBLE, OLD TESTAMENT: PSALMS [73]

R. a bye baby NURSERY RHYMES [36]

r. around the clock HALEY, B. [1]

R. is to dress up to ZAPPA [3]

R. of Ages HYMNS & CAROLS [77]

r. rebel is defunct STING [1]

upon this r. I will build BIBLE, NEW TESTAMENT: MATTHEW [113]

rock 'n' roll

hail, hail r. BERRY [2]

only r. JAGGER/RICHARDS [6]

R. is a combination MARCUS [2]

sing for a r. band JAGGER/ RICHARDS [5]

rocket

rose like a r. PAINE [15]

rod

kissed the r. POPE [146]

r. of correction BIBLE, OLD TESTAMENT: PROVERBS [66]

r. of iron BIBLE, NEW TESTAMENT: REVELATION [9]

spareth his r. BIBLE, OLD TESTAMENT: PROVERBS [31]

Take thy r. BIBLE, OLD TESTAMENT: EXODUS [12]

Throw away thy r. HERBERT, G. [40]

roe

be thou like to a r. BIBLE, OLD TESTAMENT: SONG OF SOLOMON [30]

Roger Casement

ghost of R./Is beating YEATS [59]

rogue

r. and peasant slave am I SHAKESPEARE: HAMLET [75]

rich r. ... is fit company GAY, J. [16]

rogues

Such a parcel of r. BURNS [38]

Roland

Child R. to the dark tower SHAKESPEARE: KING LEAR [37]

rolling

Like a r. stone DYLAN [22]

r. English road CHESTERTON [32]

Roman

after the high R. fashion SHAKESPEARE: ANTONY & CLEOPATRA [34]

R. Conquest was ... a Good Thing SELLAR/YEATMAN [2]

R. tyranny occupies the palace JOYCE, J. [1]

R. world is falling ST JEROME [3]

romance

Twenty years of r. WILDE [81]

Where's the r. gone AYCKBOURN [2]

romances

no more need of r. WHITMAN [3]

R. I ne'er read BYRON, LORD [163]

Romans

what have the R. ever done MONTY PYTHON'S FLYING CIRCUS [7]

romantics

We were the last r. YEATS [54]

Rome

Everyone ... comes round by R. BROWNING, R. [52]

grandeur that was R. POE [3]

Happy R. CICERO [4]

high and palmy state of R. SHAKESPEARE: HAMLET [4]

I found R. built of bricks AUGUSTUS [3]

keep R. Rome CORSO [2]

Let R. in Tiber melt SHAKESPEARE: ANTONY & CLEOPATRA [3]

loved R. more SHAKESPEARE: JULIUS CAESAR [27]

Nothing can be had in R. JUVENAL [10]

R.! my country BYRON, LORD [82]

R., the city of visible history ELIOT, G. [45]

struggle to found the race of R. VIRGIL [19]

Romeo

wherefore art thou R. SHAKESPEARE: ROMEO & JULIET [14]

Romish

countries professing the R. religion COLERIDGE, S. T. [71]

rooks

r. are blown about the skies TENNYSON [90]

r. in families homeward go HARDY, T. [34]

room

large upper r. furnished BIBLE, NEW TESTAMENT: LUKE [65]

r. of her own WOOLF [19]

Roosian

he might have been a R. GILBERT, W. S. [8]

rooster

Hongry r. don't cackle HARRIS, J. C. [1]

root

Each new man strikes r. ARNOLD, M. [8]

roots

R. ... are a conservative myth RUSHDIE [2]

send my r. rain HOPKINS [33]

try to put down r. PAVESE [5]

rope

three-ply r. is not easily broken EPIC OF GILGAMESH [3]

rosaries

Keep your r. out POLITICAL SLOGANS [20]

rose

Gather the r. of love SPENSER [16]

Go, lovely r. WALLER [1]

Goodbye English r. JOHN [4]

happy is the r. distilled SHAKESPEARE: MIDSUMMER NIGHT'S DREAM [2]

hath not the r. RONSARD [1]

last r. of summer MOORE, T. [6]

la vie en r. PIAF [1]

lovely is the r. WORDSWORTH, W. [79]

my luve's like a red, red r. BURNS [49]

never blows so red/The r. KHAYYÁM [5]

never promised you a r. garden GREEN, HANNAH [1]

O R., thou art sick BLAKE [52]

One perfect r. PARKER, D. [7]

paint a r. MATISSE [2]

r./By any other word SHAKESPEARE: ROMEO & JULIET [15]

r. in spring AURELIUS [9]

R. is a rose STEIN [2]

r. is sweeter in the bud LYLY [3]

r. of yesterday KHAYYÁM [21]

Red R., proud Rose YEATS [6]

Roves back the r. DE LA MARE [3]

wears the r./Of youth SHAKESPEARE: ANTONY & CLEOPATRA [22]

where the last r. lingers HORACE [30]

without thorn the r. MILTON [133]

rosebuds

crown ourselves with r. BIBLE, APOCRYPHA: WISDOM OF SOLOMON [3]

Gather ye r. while ye may HERRICK [11]

rose-lipped

r. girls are sleeping HOUSMAN [19]

rosemary

r. ... for remembrance SHAKESPEARE: HAMLET [139]

Rosemounde

Suffyseth me to love you, R. CHAUCER [7]

Rosencrantz

R. and Guildenstern are dead SHAKESPEARE: HAMLET [164]

roses

Everything's coming up r. SONDHEIM [2]

Gather the r. of life RONSARD [3]

make thee beds of r. MARLOWE [3]

r. for the flush of youth ROSSETTI, C. [2]

r. in December BARRIE [15]

r., roses, all the way BROWNING, R. [27]

scent of the r. MOORE, T. [7]

stifled on beds of r. HAZLITT [26]

s. and mournful am I HEINE [1]

s. bad glad mad brother's
name SWINBURNE [35]

s., strange little man LASSETER [1]

Saddam

law that S. signed HUSSEIN [4]

sadder

s. and a wiser man COLERIDGE,
S. T. [37]

saddle

Things are in the s. EMERSON [34]

sadists

As repressed s. CONNOLLY, C. [7]

safe

s. to go back ADVERTISING
SLOGANS [17]

see me s. up MORE, T. [4]

safety

cares more about ... personal
S. MILL [13]

consideration of the public
s. GIBBON [6]

one s. to the vanquished VIRGIL [31]

s. lies in lessening UPDIKE [12]

said

Everything has been s. LA BRUYÈRE [1]

nothing ... has not been s. TERENCE [3]

Whatever is well s. ... is
mine SENECA [4]

what has been s. KHAKHEPERRE-
SENEB [1]

What is s. of a man WILDE [118]

sail

A s.! a sail COLERIDGE, S. T. [24]

more s. than ballast PENN [6]

Tomorrow ... we s. the vast
sea HORACE [21]

sails

set of the s. WILCOX [3]

saint

late espousèd s. MILTON [80]

neither s.- nor sophist-led ARNOLD,
M. [5]

s. goes to his martyrdom WILDE
[25]

s. in crape POPE [88]

s. run mad POPE [162]

seem a s. ... play the
devil SHAKESPEARE: RICHARD III [6]

saintliness

S. is also a temptation ANOUILH [9]

saints

death of his s. BIBLE, OLD TESTAMENT:
PSALMS [120]

For all the s. HYMNS & CAROLS [25]

hairy s./Of the North STEVENS, W.
[5]

Let the s. be joyful BIBLE, OLD
TESTAMENT: PSALMS [150]

s. out of sinners KIERKEGAARD [3]

S. should always be judged
guilty ORWELL [45]

With s. dost bait thy
hook SHAKESPEARE: MEASURE FOR
MEASURE [14]

sais

Que s.-je MONTAIGNE [11]

salad

My s. days SHAKESPEARE: ANTONY &
CLEOPATRA [12]

salads

'tis the time of s. STERNE [19]

salesman

s. is got to dream MILLER, A. [4]

salley

Down by the s. gardens YEATS [2]

Sally

none like pretty S. CAREY, H. [1]

salmon

smoked s. and tinned WILSON, H.
[3]

salmonella

infected with s. CURRY [1]

saloon

drinking in the last chance
S. MELLOR [1]

salt

eat a peck of s. CERVANTES [9]

pillar of s. BIBLE, OLD TESTAMENT:
GENESIS [47]

s. of the earth BIBLE, NEW TESTAMENT:
MATTHEW [23]

With a grain of s. PLINY THE ELDER [8]

saltness

s. of time SHAKESPEARE: HENRY IV
PT 2 [5]

salus

S. populi suprema lex CICERO [10]

salvation

all things necessary to s. BOOK OF
COMMON PRAYER [93]

no s. outside the
Church ST CYPRIAN [1]

Work out your own s. BIBLE, NEW
TESTAMENT: PHILIPPIANS [4]

Sam

Play it S. BERGMAN, INGRID [1]

Samaritan

remember the Good S. THATCHER [4]

S. ... had compassion BIBLE, NEW
TESTAMENT: LUKE [31]

Samarkand

take the Golden Road to
S. FLECKER [2]

same

we must all say the s. MELBOURNE [1]

sameness

mysterious s. TAO TE CHING [11]

samite

Clothed in white s. TENNYSON [148]

San Francisco

I left my heart in S. BENNETT, T. [1]

sanctus

S., sanctus MISSAL [15]

sand

built his house upon the s. BIBLE,
NEW TESTAMENT: MATTHEW [58]

number the s. of the sea BIBLE,
APOCRYPHA: ECCLESIASTICUS [1]

S. in the sandwiches BETJEMAN [7]

Such quantities of s. CARROLL [33]

world in a grain of s. BLAKE [69]

sands

Here are s., ignoble
things BEAUMONT [2]

Riddle of the S. CHILDERS [1]

sanity

never return to s. BELL, G [4]

S. ... the great virtue ARNOLD, M. [34]

sans-culotte

good S. Jesus DESMOULINS [2]

Santa Claus

going to shoot S. SMITH, ALFRED E. [2]

sap

ancient s./rises in our arms RILKE [6]

sarcasm

S. ... language of the Devil CARLYLE,
T. [19]

S.: the last refuge DOSTOYEVSKY [1]

sardines

Doors and s. ... That's the
theatre FRAYN [3]

Life ... is ... opening a tin of
s. BENNETT, ALAN [1]

Satan

beheld S. as lightning BIBLE, NEW
TESTAMENT: LUKE [27]

Get thee behind me, S. BIBLE, NEW
TESTAMENT: MATTHEW [115]

Get thee hence, S. BIBLE, NEW
TESTAMENT: MATTHEW [19]

S. exalted sat MILTON [102]

S. finds ... mischief WATTS, I. [5]

S. makes impure verses SHAW [77]

S. trembles when he sees COWPER [4]

Satanic

book entitled The S.
Verses KHOMEINI [1]

dark S. mills BLAKE [80]

satire

hard not to write s. JUVENAL [1]

let s. be my song BYRON, LORD [4]

s., ever moral BOILEAU-DESPRÉAUX [7]

S. is a sort of glass SWIFT, J. [1]

S. ... is never resented SWIFT, J. [6]

S. is protest TYNAN [1]

S. is tragedy plus time BRUCE [3]

S. is what closes KAUFMAN,
GEORGE [1]

S. should ... /Wound with a
touch MONTAGU [11]

S., though it may
exaggerate TROLLOPE [16]

spirit which produces the
s. TROLLOPE [18]

true end of s. DRYDEN [26]

satirist
no s. could breathe this
air DICKENS [51]
s. is a humorist BROWN, C. [3]

satisfaction
can't get no s. JAGGER/RICHARDS [1]
S. is death SHAW [53]

Saturday
S. night's alright JOHN [2]

Saturn
S., quiet as a stone KEATS [109]

sauce
no s. ... like hunger CERVANTES [27]

Saul
Is S. ... among the prophets BIBLE,
OLD TESTAMENT: 1 SAMUEL [5]
whose name was S. BIBLE, NEW
TESTAMENT: ACTS [10]

saunter
s. to his task THOREAU [6]

savage
Remember the rights of the
S. GLADSTONE [9]
wild in woods the noble
s. DRYDEN [11]

Savanarola
touch of S. SMITH, LIZ [2]

save
died to s. their
country CHESTERTON [39]
himself he cannot s. BIBLE, NEW
TESTAMENT: MATTHEW [170]
If thou be Christ, s. thyself BIBLE,
NEW TESTAMENT: LUKE [72]
To s. all we must risk all SCHILLER [3]

saved
To get a man soundly s. BOOTH,
W. [2]
we are not s. BIBLE, OLD TESTAMENT:
JEREMIAH [8]
What must I do to be s. BIBLE, NEW
TESTAMENT: ACTS [22]

saving
You begin s. the world BUKOWSKI [3]

saviour
S. of 'is country KIPLING [17]

say
having nothing to s. ELIOT, G. [65]
little to s., and much to
hear SKELTON [1]
S. on BIBLE, OLD TESTAMENT:
1 KINGS [1]
what people s. of us SMITH, LOGAN
P. [1]
When you have nothing to
s. COLTON [2]

sayings
Don't you go believing in s. HARDY,
T. [9]
s. are ... like women's
letters HAZLITT [29]
forgotten s. of great men MADAN [2]

scales
fell from his eyes ... s. BIBLE, NEW
TESTAMENT: ACTS [16]

scallop-shell
s. of quiet RALEGH [7]

scandal
greatest s. waits on greatest
state SHAKESPEARE: RAPE OF
LUCRECE [5]
In the case of s. CHESTERFIELD [16]
Retired to their tea and
s. CONGREVE [8]
S. ... compassionate
allowance SAKI [2]
S. is an importunate
wasp CHAMFORT [14]
s. is gossip made tedious WILDE
[74]

scapegoat
let him go for a s. BIBLE, OLD
TESTAMENT: LEVITICUS [3]

scar
see the s. there still SCHREINER [1]
This is the s. ENZENSBERGER [2]

scare
They cannot s. me FROST, R. [24]

scarecrow
make a s. of the law SHAKESPEARE:
MEASURE FOR MEASURE [6]

scarlet
s. letter was her
passport HAWTHORNE [5]
sins be as s. BIBLE, OLD TESTAMENT:
ISAIAH [4]

scars
boasting show their s. SHAKESPEARE:
TROILUS & CRESSIDA [15]
jests at s. SHAKESPEARE: ROMEO &
JULIET [12]

scenario
s. available to everyone SONTAG [9]

scenery
S. is fine KEATS [33]

scent
like the s. on a ... handkerchief LLOYD
GEORGE [9]
man has his distinctive ...
s. AUDEN [41]
s. survives their close THOMPSON,
F. [6]

sceptic
s. does not mean him who
doubts UNAMUNO [8]

scepticism
all-dissolving s. NEWMAN [13]
S. ... defeats itself BERLIN, ISAIAH [5]
S. ... is not intellectual CARLYLE, T.
[43]
S. is the beginning of
Faith WILDE [59]
S. is the chastity SANTAYANA [12]
s. kept her from being SARTRE [12]

sceptre
S. shall rise out of Israel BIBLE, OLD
TESTAMENT: NUMBERS [9]

sceptred
this s. isle SHAKESPEARE:
RICHARD II [12]
what avails the s. race LANDOR [1]

sceptreless
S., free SHELLEY, P. B. [58]

schemes
best laid s. BURNS [19]

schizophrenia
God talks ... you have s. SZASZ [10]
S. cannot be understood LAING [1]

schizophrenic
behaviour that gets labelled
s. LAING [5]

scholar
office of the s. is to
cheer EMERSON [3]
s., and a ripe and good
one SHAKESPEARE: HENRY VIII [16]
Thou'rt a s. SHAKESPEARE: TWELFTH
NIGHT [13]
what ills the s.'s life assail JOHNSON,
S. [7]

scholars
great men have not ... been great
s. HOLMES SR [12]
led my s. by the nose GOETHE [23]
S. and gentlemen WORDSWORTH,
W. [19]

scholarship
Pure s. ... is entirely
useless ALDINGTON [2]

school
Dogs bark/S.'s out DAVIES, W. H. [3]
go to s. in a summer morn BLAKE
[13]
s. is not a factory CARR, J. L. [1]
S. is where you go UPDIKE [1]

schoolboy
Every s. knows it TAYLOR, J. [1]
tell what every s. knows SWIFT, J. [26]
whining s. SHAKESPEARE: AS YOU LIKE
IT [18]

schooldays
look back on his s. ORWELL [33]

schoolmaster
presence of a s. LAMB, CHARLES [15]
pure pedantic s. JONSON [28]
s. is abroad BROUGHAM [2]
s. should have an
atmosphere BAGEHOT [2]
you'll be becoming a s. WAUGH [1]

schoolmasters
s. must temper discretion WAUGH [2]

schoolrooms
Better build s. for 'the boy' COOK,
E. [1]

schools
bewildered in the maze of s. POPE [8]

science

All s. is cosmology POPPER [2]
essence of s. BRONOWSKI [5]
genuflected before ... s. KING, M. L. [6]
great tragedy of s. HUXLEY, T. [5]
In s., we must be interested CURIE [1]
next great task of s. MORLEY, J. [5]
No s. is immune to ...
 politics BRONOWSKI [4]
O Star-eyed S. CAMPBELL, T. [3]
redefined the task of s. HAWKING [2]
s. and the applications of PASTEUR [1]
S. ... expression for our
 ignorance BUTLER, S. (1835–1902) [27]
S. grows and Beauty
 dwindles TENNYSON [195]
S. has 'explained' nothing HUXLEY, A. [7]
S. has nothing to be
 ashamed BRONOWSKI [3]
s. has succeeded BRONOWSKI [1]
S. is a cemetery of dead
 ideas UNAMUNO [3]
S. is an integral part GOULD [2]
S. is intimately integrated PARSONS, TALCOTT [1]
S. is organized knowledge SPENCER, H. [5]
s. is ... stamp
 collecting RUTHERFORD [1]
S. is the great antidote SMITH, ADAM [11]
S. ... is the great lie GOURMONT [7]
S. is the knowledge HOBBES [5]
S. knows only one
 commandment BRECHT [13]
s. leads only to the
 insoluble DISRAELI [42]
S. may be described POPPER [4]
S. moves, but slowly TENNYSON [42]
S. reaches forth her
 arms TENNYSON [92]
S., which cuts its way HERZEN [1]
s. will not console me PASCAL [3]
S. without religion is
 lame EINSTEIN [7]
true s. and study of man CHARRON [1]
whole of s. is nothing
 more EINSTEIN [5]

science fiction

Everything is becoming
 s. BALLARD [2]
If s. is the mythology LE GUIN [5]
S. is no more written ALDISS [1]
s. has become a dialect LESSING, D. [6]
s. writers ... do not know DICK [2]
S. writers foresee the
 inevitable ASIMOV [2]

sciences

One aim of the physical
 s. BRONOWSKI [6]

scientific

new s. truth does not
 triumph PLANCK [1]
s. mind does not ... provide LÉVI-STRAUSS [4]
s. temper is devout JAMES, W. [20]
Traditional s. method PIRSIG [5]

scientist

exercise for a research s. LORENZ [1]

scientists

in the company of s. AUDEN [40]
socially responsible s. HOBSBAWM [1]

scissor-man

long, red-legged s. HOFFMANN, H. [2]

scoff

fools, who came to s. GOLDSMITH [35]

scorchio

S. FAST SHOW [3]

scorn

deal of s. looks
 beautiful SHAKESPEARE: TWELFTH NIGHT [29]
ever be a name of s. TENNYSON [171]
sound/Of public s. MILTON [177]

scorned

woman s. CONGREVE [14]

scorpions

chastise you with s. BIBLE, OLD TESTAMENT: 1 KINGS [7]

Scotch

guid, auld S. Drink BURNS [6]
joke ... into a S. understanding SMITH, SYDNEY [10]
S. are hard BARRIE [10]

Scotchman

Much may be made of a S. JOHNSON, S. [78]
one S. but what was a
 man LOCKIER [2]

Scotchmen

trying ... to like S. LAMB, CHARLES [17]

Scotia

old S.'s grandeur springs BURNS [16]

Scotland

Flower of S. WILLIAMSON [1]
little white rose of S. MACDIARMID [3]
S., my auld, respected
 mither BURNS [7]

Scotsman

grandest moral attribute of a
 S. BARRIE [11]
S. on the make BARRIE [9]

scream

all they hear is a continuous
 s. MURDOCH, I. [20]

scribble

All rhyme, and scrawl, and
 s. POPE [160]

scribbled

I am a s. form SHAKESPEARE: KING JOHN [15]

scribbler

Nothing ... so despicable as a
 s. BYRON, LORD [15]

scribes

Beware of the s. BIBLE, NEW TESTAMENT: MARK [13]

scrip

nor s., nor shoes BIBLE, NEW TESTAMENT: LUKE [25]

script

good film s. should be
 able MAMET [3]

scripture

devil can cite S. SHAKESPEARE: MERCHANT OF VENICE [14]
s. is given by inspiration BIBLE, NEW TESTAMENT: 2 TIMOTHY [4]

scriptures

Search the s. BIBLE, NEW TESTAMENT: JOHN [24]

scrofulous

Figure him ... with his s.
 diseases CARLYLE, T. [44]

Scrooge

hand at the grindstone,
 S. DICKENS [44]

scrunch

s. or be scrunched DICKENS [91]

sculpture

Moonlight is s. HAWTHORNE [3]
What s. is to a block of
 marble ADDISON [7]

scum

s. of the earth WELLINGTON [2]
wash all this s. off the streets DE NIRO [1]

scutcheon

blot in thy s. CERVANTES [42]

Scylla

S. and Charybdis of Aye and
 No NEWMAN [11]

sea

bathed in the Poem of the
 S. RIMBAUD [8]
From s. to shining sea BATES, K. L. [1]
I drive the s. MELVILLE [10]
If the s. were ink KORAN [31]
immortal s./Which brought
 us WORDSWORTH, W. [91]
Into that silent s. COLERIDGE, S. T. [19]
life at s. CONRAD [2]
monotonous as the s. LOWELL, J. R. [11]
Mother and lover of men, the
 s. SWINBURNE [7]
near to heaven by s. GILBERT, H. [1]
ourselves we find in the
 s. CUMMINGS, E. E. [13]
s. cries with its meaningless
 voice HUGHES, TED [8]

s. has never been
friendly CONRAD [16]
s. hates a coward O'NEILL [7]
s. is calm tonight ARNOLD, M. [45]
s. is his, and he made it BIBLE, OLD
TESTAMENT: PSALMS [99]
s. is mother-death SEXTON [3]
s. is the sea HEMINGWAY [24]
s. lies all about us CARSON, R. [1]
s. speaks a language SANDBURG [6]
salt, estranging s. ARNOLD, M. [15]
serpent-haunted s. FLECKER [3]
snotgreen s. JOYCE, J. [23]
The s. XENOPHON [1]
who hath desired the S. KIPLING [61]
Wide s., that one continuous
murmur KEATS [21]

sea-change
suffer a s. SHAKESPEARE: TEMPEST [9]
seagull
happy and free as a s. CHEKHOV [7]
seagulls
s. follow the trawler CANTONA [1]
seal
s. upon thine heart BIBLE, OLD
TESTAMENT: SONG OF SOLOMON [28]
seventh s. BIBLE, NEW TESTAMENT:
REVELATION [25]
seals
book ... sealed with seven s. BIBLE,
NEW TESTAMENT: REVELATION [16]
calmer than the s. FIELDS, D. [2]
seamen
gentlemen and there were
s. MACAULAY, LORD [39]
search
s. will find it out HERRICK [27]
seas
I must down to the s. MASEFIELD [1]
s. do laugh, show white WEBSTER,
J. [15]
Till a' the s. gang dry BURNS [50]
seaside
beside the s. GLOVER-KIND [1]
season
Be instant in s. BIBLE, NEW
TESTAMENT: 2 TIMOTHY [5]
each thing that in s.
grows SHAKESPEARE: LOVE'S LABOUR'S
LOST [5]
every s. is a/... nostalgia JENNINGS [1]
have a convenient s. BIBLE, NEW
TESTAMENT: ACTS [39]
many things by s. seasoned
are SHAKESPEARE: MERCHANT OF
VENICE [41]
S. of mists KEATS [103]
To every thing there is a s. BIBLE, OLD
TESTAMENT: ECCLESIASTES [11]
seasons
know the times or the s. BIBLE, NEW
TESTAMENT: ACTS [1]

man for all s. WHITTINGTON [1]
we see/The s. alter SHAKESPEARE:
MIDSUMMER NIGHT'S DREAM [17]
second
Finishing s. in politics NIXON [14]
s. thoughts are best NEWMAN [3]
second-best
s. is anything but LESSING, D. [3]
secrecy
habit of s. BACON, F. [13]
S. is the first essential RICHELIEU [2]
secret
Every s. of a writer's soul WOOLF
[16]
Every thing s. degenerates ACTON [1]
His mind of man, a s.
makes DICKINSON, E. [39]
If you wish to preserve your
s. SMITH, ALEXANDER [1]
nothing is s. BIBLE, NEW TESTAMENT:
LUKE [23]
profound s. and
mystery DICKENS [86]
S. sits in the middle FROST, R. [34]
s. things belong unto the Lord BIBLE,
OLD TESTAMENT: DEUTERONOMY [13]
s. thoughts of a man HOBBES [6]
so tremendous a s. SYMMACHUS [1]
trusted with a s. JOHNSON, S. [12]
secrets
Men with s. tend to be
drawn DELILLO [3]
My s. cry aloud ROETHKE [1]
never divulge ... holy
s. HIPPOCRATES [7]
None are so fond of s. COLTON [1]
S. with girls CRABBE [7]
sect
attached to that great s. SHELLEY,
P. B. [93]
s. ... is an elegant
incognito EMERSON [1]
sectarian
cat out of the s. bag HEANEY [10]
security
We like s. PASCAL [18]
seduce
s. a woman famous for strict
morals HAMPTON [5]
trying to s. me HOFFMAN, D. [1]
seduction
S. is ... difficult to
distinguish DWORKIN [2]
see
come up ...'n s. me WEST, M. [4]
not worth going to s. JOHNSON,
S. [122]
now can s. no more WORDSWORTH,
W. [78]
s. clearly is poetry RUSKIN [14]
To s. oursels as others see BURNS
[23]

seed
As a s. that puts/forth its
shoot KORAN [41]
s. never explains the
flower HAMILTON, E. [1]
s. ye sow, another reaps SHELLEY,
P. B. [45]
sow thy s. BIBLE, OLD TESTAMENT:
ECCLESIASTES [38]
seeds
look into the s. of time SHAKESPEARE:
MACBETH [8]
seed-time
Fair s. had my soul WORDSWORTH,
W. [13]
s. and harvest BIBLE, OLD TESTAMENT:
GENESIS [35]
seeing
S. is the function of
memory HOCKNEY [3]
seek
S. and we find MENCIUS [6]
seekest
s. thou great things BIBLE, OLD
TESTAMENT: JEREMIAH [20]
seeking
found out by s. TERENCE [6]
seem
Men should be what they
s. SHAKESPEARE: OTHELLO [32]
not always what they s. PHAEDRUS
[2]
seems
I know not 's.' SHAKESPEARE:
HAMLET [12]
seen
come to see ... may be s. OVID [3]
s. what I have seen SHAKESPEARE:
HAMLET [100]
segregation
S. now ... forever WALLACE, G. [1]
seize
S. the day HORACE [24]
to s., is far less pleasure GARTH [5]
seized
No free man shall be s. MAGNA
CARTA [1]
selection
natural s. determined the
evolution LORENZ [2]
self
s. is hateful PASCAL [19]
s. is now the sacred cow HUGHES,
R. [3]
self-consumer
I am the s. of my woes CLARE [2]
self-deception
s. remains the most
difficult DIDION [1]
self-defence
S. is Nature's eldest law DRYDEN
[33]

self-destruction
When the beginnings of s.
enter CHEEVER [1]
self-determination
s. ... asserts itself MARCUSE [1]
self-esteem
S. and self-contempt HOFFER [8]
S. = Success/Pretensions JAMES,
W. [5]
self-help
s. is the root SMILES [1]
self-interest
S. always runs a good
race WHITLAM [1]
self-interests
guided only by their s. CARLYLE, T.
[8]
selfishness
enlightened s. ... basis TAFT [2]
S. is like listening LARKIN [11]
self-love
s. and social be the same POPE [136]
s. is the basis of all
love TRAHERNE [12]
S. ... so often unrequited POWELL,
A. [3]
self-made
He is a s. man BRIGHT [5]
He was a s. man HELLER [3]
self-pity
S. comes so naturally MAUROIS [1]
self-poisoner
s. by cocaine and tobacco DOYLE,
A. C. [20]
self-preservation
S., nature's first great
law MARVELL [20]
self-realization
S. is not ... anti-social STORR [1]
self-respect
S. – The secure feeling MENCKEN [18]
self-revelation
terrible fluidity of s. JAMES, H. [27]
self-sacrifice
S. enables us to sacrifice SHAW [38]
selling
Everyone lives by s. STEVENSON,
R. L. [46]
semenza
Considerate la vostra s. DANTE [14]
send
Here am I; s. me BIBLE, OLD
TESTAMENT: ISAIAH [16]
sensation
great object in life is S. BYRON,
LORD [28]
sensational
something s. to read WILDE [104]
sensations
O for a life of s. KEATS [14]
sense
creeps after s. DRYDEN [9]

general s. of what was ...
said THUCYDIDES [1]
Make s. who may BECKETT [23]
Take care of the s. CARROLL [15]
senseless
most s. and fit man SHAKESPEARE:
MUCH ADO [18]
senses
In all the s. BHAGAVAD-GITA [8]
s. are the beginning MONTAIGNE
[13]
sensibility
dissociation of s. ELIOT, T. S. [16]
sensible
most s. people to be met
with HAZLITT [11]
sentence
s. is for open war MILTON [105]
sentences
Backward ran s. GIBBS [1]
say in ten s. NIETZSCHE [40]
sententiae
Quot homines tot s. TERENCE [9]
sentiment
as healthy to enjoy
s. CHESTERTON [40]
sentimental
What's wrong with s. MCCARTNEY [3]
sentimentalists
S. ... adopt whatever
merit EMERSON [73]
S. ... seek to enjoy MEREDITH, G. [3]
sentimentality
no place for s. BURROUGHS, W. [9]
S. is ... erected upon
brutality JUNG [6]
S. is only sentiment MAUGHAM [14]
S. is the emotional
promiscuity MAILER [6]
sentiments
Them's my s. THACKERAY [4]
separate
's. but equal' has no place WARREN,
E. [1]
separation
Six degrees of s. GUARE [2]
solid and lasting peace ... a
s. CHESTERFIELD [36]
September
When you reach S. ANDERSON, M. [1]
sepulchre
s. for its eternity SHELLEY, P. B. [95]
stone taken away from the s. BIBLE,
NEW TESTAMENT: JOHN [70]
sepulchres
like unto whited s. BIBLE, NEW
TESTAMENT: MATTHEW [136]
sera
Que s. sera DAY, DORIS [1]
seraphim
bright s. in burning row MILTON
[28]

sere
fallen into the s. SHAKESPEARE:
MACBETH [92]
serenity
God, give us s. to accept NIEBUHR
[3]
serious
You cannot be s. MCENROE [1]
sermon
honest and painful s. PEPYS [3]
sermons
found in stones the s. WILDE [17]
S. and soda-water BYRON, LORD [97]
S. in stones SHAKESPEARE: AS YOU LIKE
IT [8]
serpent
infernal s. MILTON [85]
s. ate Eve HUGHES, TED [7]
s. beguiled me BIBLE, OLD TESTAMENT:
GENESIS [21]
s. subtlest beast of all MILTON [167]
s. was more subtil BIBLE, OLD
TESTAMENT: GENESIS [16]
Where's my s. of Old
Nile SHAKESPEARE: ANTONY &
CLEOPATRA [11]
serpents
be ye ... wise as s. BIBLE, NEW
TESTAMENT: MATTHEW [74]
servant
good and faithful s. BIBLE, NEW
TESTAMENT: MATTHEW [147]
lettest thou thy s. depart BIBLE, NEW
TESTAMENT: LUKE [12]
s. unto all BIBLE, NEW TESTAMENT:
1 CORINTHIANS [21]
thy s. heareth BIBLE, OLD TESTAMENT:
1 SAMUEL [2]
servants
best s. of the people LIPPMANN [2]
s. as good as
themselves CERVANTES [40]
serve
I s. not what you serve KORAN [51]
s. Thee as Thou
deservest ST IGNATIUS [1]
They also s. MILTON [79]
served
Had I but s. my God SHAKESPEARE:
HENRY VIII [13]
serveth
he that s. BIBLE, NEW TESTAMENT:
LUKE [66]
service
devoted to your s. ELIZABETH II [1]
Pressed into s. FROST, R. [10]
s. greater than the god SHAKESPEARE:
TROILUS & CRESSIDA [5]
s. is perfect freedom BOOK OF
COMMON PRAYER [18]
s. ranks the same with
God BROWNING, R. [6]

I am a s. and unapt to
weep SHAKESPEARE: HENRY VI PT 1 [7]
not having been a s. JOHNSON, S. [115]
old s. of the ballad MACARTHUR [2]
Perfect s., perfect gentleman TAYLOR,
A. J. P. [5]
s.'s life/To have their balmy
slumbers SHAKESPEARE: OTHELLO [26]
s. wears a badge READ, H. [2]
When we assumed the
s. WASHINGTON, G. [2]
soldiers
handful of s. is …
better LICHTENBERG [8]
Old s. never die FOLEY [1]
Onward, Christian s. HYMNS &
CAROLS [71]
S. are citizens SASSOON [1]
S. are sworn to action SASSOON [2]
S. of Christ, arise HYMNS &
CAROLS [80]
S. win battles NAPOLEON I [23]
soldiery
drunken s. are abed YEATS [57]
rapacious and licentious s. BURKE,
E. [28]
solicitor
always consult a good s. SHAW [12]
solitary
Be not s., be not idle BURTON [13]
Life is … a s. cell O'NEILL [1]
s. men know the full joys CATHER [9]
s. wretches … meet the
devil POPE [67]
sentenced to s.
confinement WILLIAMS, T. [10]
Yon s. Highland lass WORDSWORTH,
W. [64]
solitude
companion … so companionable as
s. THOREAU [37]
delicious s. MARVELL [10]
everything in s. except
character STENDHAL [5]
feel his s. more keenly VALÉRY [3]
In s. … we are *least* alone BYRON,
LORD [59]
In s./What happiness MILTON [161]
life more as an affair of s. LARKIN [22]
Musing in s. WORDSWORTH, W. [94]
Oh, s.! where are the
charms COWPER [28]
S. gives birth to the original MANN,
T. [1]
S. is dangerous to reason JOHNSON,
S. [147]
s. is sublime KEATS [41]
S. is the audience-
chamber LANDOR [2]
S. is un-American JONG [2]
self-sufficing power of
s. WORDSWORTH, W. [15]

Whosoever is delighted in
s. ARISTOTLE [16]
Solomon
greater than S. is here BIBLE, NEW
TESTAMENT: MATTHEW [94]
S. in all his glory BIBLE, NEW
TESTAMENT: MATTHEW [45]
S. loved many strange BIBLE, OLD
TESTAMENT: 1 KINGS [5]
wisdom of S. BIBLE, OLD TESTAMENT:
1 KINGS [4]
solstice
door of the s. still wide CARTER, A. [1]
solution
final s. BERLIN, ISAIAH [4]
you're part of the s. CLEAVER [3]
somebodee
When every one is s. GILBERT,
W. S. [44]
somebody
How dreary – to be – S. DICKINSON,
E. [9]
somer
In a s. seson LANGLAND [1]
something
be s. … to *do* something GOETHE
[19]
S. from Nothing TAO TE CHING [8]
S. should be done EDWARD VIII [1]
time for a little s. MILNE [10]
son
Behold thy s. BIBLE, NEW TESTAMENT:
JOHN [67]
good s. does not
wander CONFUCIUS [13]
I obeyed as a s. GIBBON [15]
one like the S. of man came BIBLE,
OLD TESTAMENT: DANIEL [13]
s. dishonoureth the father BIBLE, OLD
TESTAMENT: MICAH [4]
s. will run away BAUDELAIRE [7]
This is my beloved S. BIBLE, NEW
TESTAMENT: MATTHEW [14]
two-legged thing, a s. DRYDEN [29]
wise s. maketh a glad father BIBLE,
OLD TESTAMENT: PROVERBS [19]
song
best of all trades to make
s. BELLOC [5]
hear a little s. GOETHE [7]
On wings of s. HEINE [3]
remembered by a s. SMITH,
ALEXANDER [5]
s. is anything that can
walk DYLAN [21]
s. of songs BIBLE, OLD TESTAMENT:
SONG OF SOLOMON [1]
s. was wordless SASSOON [6]
sing unto the Lord a new s. BIBLE,
OLD TESTAMENT: PSALMS [102]
songs
cheap s. … illuminate POTTER, D. [6]

despairing s. are the
loveliest MUSSET [3]
few good s. FAITHFULL [1]
For ever piping s. KEATS [94]
sonnet
s. is a moment's
monument ROSSETTI, D. G. [5]
Scorn not the s. WORDSWORTH,
W. [112]
sonneteer
starved hackney s. POPE [24]
sons
in the kingdom of the s. RICH, A. [7]
sooner
No s. looked but they
loved SHAKESPEARE: AS YOU LIKE
IT [34]
soot
in s. I sleep BLAKE [7]
sophistication
s. as rather a feeble
substitute HAMPTON [1]
sore
heart of man has long been
s. HOUSMAN [27]
sorriness
s. underlying the grandest
things HARDY, T. [11]
sorrow
arrow of s. was
embedded KIERKEGAARD [16]
Down, thou climbing s. SHAKESPEARE:
KING LEAR [20]
Give s. words SHAKESPEARE:
MACBETH [82]
glut thy s. on a … rose KEATS [107]
I have known s. VIRGIL [26]
Nought but vast S. DE LA MARE [8]
s. and sighing shall flee BIBLE, OLD
TESTAMENT: ISAIAH [48]
S. is a kind of rust JOHNSON, S. [13]
S. is better BIBLE, OLD TESTAMENT:
ECCLESIASTES [18]
S. is knowledge BYRON, LORD [69]
S. is tranquility remembered PARKER,
D. [18]
s. like unto my sorrow BIBLE, OLD
TESTAMENT: LAMENTATIONS [2]
S. makes us all
children EMERSON [29]
s.'s crown of sorrow TENNYSON [37]
S., the great idealizer LOWELL, J. R.
[21]
S. was all my soul HERBERT, G. [10]
S., wilt Thou live with
me TENNYSON [107]
sumless tale of s. HOUSMAN [26]
Unspeakable … is the s. VIRGIL [27]
violate my soul with s. SAPPHO [1]
We are not sure of s. SWINBURNE
[29]
Where there is s. WILDE [116]

sorrows
few s. ... in which a good income SMITH, LOGAN P. [2]
s. in herds EWART [1]
small s. speak SENECA [20]
sorry
s. for itself LAWRENCE, D. H. [25]
s. seems to be the hardest JOHN [3]
sorted
s. out for E's & wizz COCKER [2]
sorts
all s. and conditions of men BOOK OF COMMON PRAYER [39]
soul
adventure of his s. MAUGHAM [11]
bare, shivering human s. PASTERNAK [10]
channel to the s. BELLOW [8]
Dear little s. HADRIAN [1]
depth ... of the s. WORDSWORTH, W. [104]
from the s. itself COLERIDGE, S. T. [45]
gambled on my s. BAUDELAIRE [25]
good s. like a good body JOAD [1]
he that hides a dark s. MILTON [36]
if I have a s. ANONYMOUS [67]
little s. carrying ... a corpse EPICTETUS [4]
lose his own s. BIBLE, NEW TESTAMENT: MARK [8]
man became a living s. BIBLE, OLD TESTAMENT: GENESIS [7]
most comprehensive s. DRYDEN [6]
Mount, mount, my s. SHAKESPEARE: RICHARD II [30]
My s. has wings DELACROIX [3]
My s., sit thou a patient QUARLES [2]
My s. thirsteth for thee BIBLE, OLD TESTAMENT: PSALMS [74]
My s., you are a mourner PASTERNAK [4]
Now my s. hath elbow-room SHAKESPEARE: KING JOHN [14]
One certainly has a s. BYRON, LORD [73]
parts of the s. CHAMFORT [8]
Poor intricated s. DONNE [57]
s. be changed into ... water drops MARLOWE [26]
s. ... bright invisible green THOREAU [9]
s. can split the sky MILLAY [2]
s. is a melody MALLARMÉ [4]
s. is but the last bubble SANTAYANA [7]
s. is form SPENSER [33]
s. is my great asset LAWRENCE, D. H. [1]
s. is on its knees HUGO [13]
s. might be blinded SOCRATES [15]
s. of a man is born in this country JOYCE, J. [14]
s. of the age JONSON [29]
s.'s dark cottage WALLER [9]
s. shall be required of thee BIBLE, NEW TESTAMENT: LUKE [37]
s. shall have her earthly freight WORDSWORTH, W. [87]
s., that drop, that ray MARVELL [15]
S. unto itself DICKINSON, E. [21]
sells his s. BAUDELAIRE [23]
single s. ... in two bodies ARISTOTLE [23]
sweet and virtuous s. HERBERT, G. [21]
Their s. is Christ's abode KEBLE [3]
thinks he has got one s. LAWRENCE, D. H. [16]
turnest mine eyes into my very s. SHAKESPEARE: HAMLET [122]
What is beyond the s. is he BHAGAVAD-GITA [10]
whom my s. loveth BIBLE, OLD TESTAMENT: SONG OF SOLOMON [11]
yields oneself ... to one's s. DELACROIX [1]
soul-making
vale of s. KEATS [49]
souls
American, a Negro ... two s. DU BOIS [1]
good morrow to our waking s. DONNE [2]
great s. are rare SAURIN [1]
low opinion of their s. LOCKE [8]
Most people sell their s. SMITH, LOGAN P. [10]
people's s. ... smell of decay MIRBEAU [3]
pure lovers' s. descend DONNE [25]
s. are like those orphans MELVILLE [9]
s. are not saved EMERSON [55]
s. mounting up to God ROSSETTI, D. G. [3]
see/The s. we loved TENNYSON [131]
Two s. ... reside within GOETHE [24]
Unquiet s. ARNOLD, M. [37]
soun
S. ys noght but eyr ybroken CHAUCER [1]
sound
s. mind in a sound body LOCKE [15]
What's that s. STILLS [1]
soundbites
not a time for s. BLAIR, T. [5]
sounds
sympathy with s. COWPER [44]
soup
Beautiful S. CARROLL [19]
south
S. is avenged BOOTH, J. W. [1]
While the S. is ... Christ-haunted O'CONNOR, F. [3]

South Africa
nothing measured ... in S. SCHREINER [4]
Southerner
S. has the speech patterns BRYSON [2]
Southerners
S. ... never resist a losing MITCHELL, MARGARET [3]
souviens
si je me s. bien RIMBAUD [13]
sovereign
obligation of subjects to the s. HOBBES [10]
S. has ... three rights BAGEHOT [15]
sovereignties
two s. to whom I owe allegiance CLAY [2]
sovereignty
s. be not necessary ASTELL [4]
Soviet
no S. domination FORD, G. [4]
Soviet Union
If the S. can give up FUENTES [2]
sower
s. went forth to sow BIBLE, NEW TESTAMENT: MATTHEW [95]
soweth
whatsoever a man s. BIBLE, NEW TESTAMENT: GALATIANS [9]
space
artifact designed for s. travel BURROUGHS, W. [7]
king of infinite s. SHAKESPEARE: HAMLET [65]
more s. where nobody is STEIN [7]
S. to be the central fact OLSON [1]
s. was the uncontrollable mystery MCLUHAN [2]
space-ships
S. ... are no escape KOESTLER [3]
spake
Never man s. like this man BIBLE, NEW TESTAMENT: JOHN [29]
Spanish
speak S. to God CHARLES V [2]
Spanish Inquisition
Nobody expects the S. MONTY PYTHON'S FLYING CIRCUS [5]
spare
s. the beechen tree CAMPBELL, T. [5]
spark
s. ... in a grain of wheat BRYAN [4]
sparks
as the s. fly upward BIBLE, OLD TESTAMENT: JOB [13]
like s. among the stubble BIBLE, APOCRYPHA: WISDOM OF SOLOMON [6]
sparrow
brawling of a s. YEATS [10]
s. alone upon the house BIBLE, OLD TESTAMENT: PSALMS [104]

starter
Few thought he was even a
s. ATTLEE [1]

state
Man must ... venerate the s. HEGEL [7]
Our s. cannot be
severed MILTON [174]
reinforcement of the ... s. CAMUS [10]
S. ... most flagrant
negation BAKUNIN [2]
s. ... withers away ENGELS [1]
s. exists for ... a good
life ARISTOTLE [19]
s. is a state of Slavery GILL [1]
sail on, O Ship of S. LONGFELLOW [13]
While the S. exists LENIN [12]
worth of a S. MILL [11]

statesman
constitutional s. BAGEHOT [3]
first requirement of a s. ACHESON [2]
s. is a politician ... dead TRUMAN [4]
three great ends ... a s. COLERIDGE,
S. T. [70]
Too nice for a s. GOLDSMITH [51]

statesmen
s.'s kindnesses proceed HOWARD,
R. [1]

stations
know our proper s. DICKENS [61]

statisticians
Thou shalt not sit/With s. AUDEN
[28]

statistics
lies, damned lies and s. DISRAELI [59]
uses s. as a drunken man LANG, A. [2]

statue
ask why I have no s. CATO THE
ELDER [2]

staves
Strike at the heaven with your
s. SHAKESPEARE: CORIOLANUS [2]

stay
Makin' a long s. short HUBBARD
[6]

S. T.C.
one thought in prayer for
S. COLERIDGE, S. T. [83]

steal
Great artists s. TARANTINO [4]
Thou shalt not s. BIBLE, OLD
TESTAMENT: EXODUS [25]

stealth
do a good action by s. LAMB,
CHARLES [28]

steam-engine
s. in trousers. SMITH, SYDNEY [19]

steaming
S. through metal
landscape SPENDER [5]

steel
long divorce of s. SHAKESPEARE:
HENRY VIII [3]

pangs of dust and s. CRANE, H. [4]
S.-true and blade-straight STEVENSON,
R. L. [54]

Stein
I don't like the family
S. ANONYMOUS [39]

stelle
uscimmo a riveder le s. DANTE [16]

stench
s. in the nostrils DE FOREST [1]

stenches
counted two and seventy
s. COLERIDGE, S. T. [82]

step
One more s. along the world CARTER,
S. [2]
one small s. for a man ARMSTRONG,
N. [2]

stepmother
Better a serpent than a
s. EURIPIDES [1]

steppeland
Through the s. roaring YESENIN [1]

stepping-stones
Men may rise on s. TENNYSON [85]

stereotypes
Out with s., feminism
proclaims PAGLIA [4]

sterility
Into her womb convey
s. SHAKESPEARE: KING LEAR [15]

sterres
in the s. ... /Is writen CHAUCER [32]

stewards
s. of the mysteries BIBLE, NEW
TESTAMENT: 1 CORINTHIANS [8]

stick
carry a big s. ROOSEVELT, T. [2]

sticks
S. nix hick pix VARIETY [2]

stiffnecked
s. people BIBLE, OLD TESTAMENT:
EXODUS [31]

stiffness
too much s. in refusing BOOK OF
COMMON PRAYER [1]

stigma
s. ... to beat a dogma GUEDALLA [3]

still
be s. and cool FOX, G. [3]
be wholly s. and alone KAFKA [6]
Happy are those who are s. OKRI [1]

still-soliciting
s. eye and such a
tongue SHAKESPEARE: KING LEAR
[6]

stimulants
without ... gross and violent
s. WORDSWORTH, W. [27]

stir
S. up, we beseech thee BOOK OF
COMMON PRAYER [48]

stirrup
Betwixt the s. and the
ground CAMDEN [1]
one foot ... in the s. CERVANTES
[54]

stitching
s. and unstitching has been
naught YEATS [18]

St Ives
As I was going to S. NURSERY
RHYMES [1]

St James's
ladies of S. DOBSON [2]

Stock Exchange
make a fortune on the
S. MORTIMER [3]

stocking
glimpse of s. PORTER, C. [5]

stomach
healthy s. is nothing BUTLER, S.
(1835–1902) [15]
little wine for thy s.'s sake BIBLE,
NEW TESTAMENT: 1 TIMOTHY [11]
unbounded s. SHAKESPEARE:
HENRY VIII [14]

stone
Fling but a s. GREEN, M. [1]
s. which the builders refused BIBLE,
OLD TESTAMENT: PSALMS [121]
turned to s. inside DANTE [15]
will he give him a s. BIBLE, NEW
TESTAMENT: MATTHEW [52]

stones
five smooth s. BIBLE, OLD TESTAMENT:
1 SAMUEL [15]
reconcile ourselves to the
s. MACDIARMID [2]
S. have been known to
move SHAKESPEARE: MACBETH [68]
s. of the field BIBLE, OLD TESTAMENT:
JOB [14]
s. would ... cry out BIBLE, NEW
TESTAMENT: LUKE [61]

stony
Some fell upon s. places BIBLE, NEW
TESTAMENT: MATTHEW [95]

store
seen thee oft amid thy s. KEATS [104]

stories
all s. ... end in death HEMINGWAY [10]
always telling s. LA BRUYÈRE [17]
make his s. shorter SWIFT, J. [43]
make the oldest s. new MARCUS [1]
only two or three human
s. CATHER [2]

storm
infernal s., eternal in its
rage DANTE [10]
s. is over BRIDGES [4]

stormy
O s. peple CHAUCER [37]
S. weather KOEHLER [1]

suburbs
faithful friends o'th's. SHAKESPEARE: HENRY VIII [19]
s. are incubators of apathy CONNOLLY, C. [14]
s./Of your good pleasure SHAKESPEARE: JULIUS CAESAR [17]

succeed
not enough to s. VIDAL [11]

success
A (S.) = X (Work) EINSTEIN [15]
bitch-goddess S. JAMES, W. [18]
idea that s. spoils people MAUGHAM [12]
not in mortals to command s. ADDISON [17]
penalty of s. ASTOR [2]
S. is a lousy teacher GATES [2]
S. is counted sweetest DICKINSON, E. [1]
S. is more dangerous GREENE, G. [19]
sweet smell of s. LEHMAN, E. [1]

successful
S. crimes ... are justified DRYDEN [45]

suck
I have given s. SHAKESPEARE: MACBETH [28]

sucker
never give a s. FIELDS, W. C. [2]
s. born every minute. BARNUM [2]

suckle
s. fools, and chronicle SHAKESPEARE: OTHELLO [21]

sucks
s. the nurse asleep SHAKESPEARE: ANTONY & CLEOPATRA [45]

sue
not born to s. SHAKESPEARE: RICHARD II [2]

Suez
S. ... flowing through EDEN, C. [1]
somewhere east of S. KIPLING [25]

suffer
Better one s. DRYDEN [32]
can they s. BENTHAM [4]
Mankind are ... disposed to s. JEFFERSON [4]
need ... something to s. for HOFFER [14]
Nobody can tell what I s. AUSTEN [10]
They say that men s. COPE [4]

sufferance
s. is the badge SHAKESPEARE: MERCHANT OF VENICE [15]

suffered
s. for things that I am guilty of VANZETTI [1]

sufferer
The best of men/ ... was a s. DEKKER [3]

suffering
About s. they were never wrong AUDEN [23]
Is s. so very serious COLETTE [2]
marks of s. FITZGERALD, F. S. [16]
no true love save in s. UNAMUNO [6]
reduced to real s. HESSE [3]
s. ennobles the character MAUGHAM [7]
s. has a peculiar attraction SACHER-MASOCH [1]
S. makes the world go round HEANEY [9]
s. must become Love MANSFIELD [4]
will not give up his s. GURDJIEFF [4]

sufferings
To each his s. GRAY, T. [4]

sufficiency
elegant s. THOMSON, J. (1700–48) [3]

sufficient
S. unto the day BIBLE, NEW TESTAMENT: MATTHEW [47]

suffrage
least hope in 'Universal S.' CARLYLE, T. [55]
S. is the pivotal right ANTHONY [3]

sugar
S. and spice NURSERY RHYMES [49]
spoonful of s. ANDREWS [1]

suicide
If I commit s. ARTAUD [1]
If you must commit s. BORROW [3]
longest s. note in history KAUFMAN, GERALD [1]
no refuge ... but s. WEBSTER, D. [5]
s. is a powerful solace NIETZSCHE [22]
s. is not worth the trouble BENJAMIN [9]
s. kills two people MILLER, A. [6]
s. remains the courageous act GREENE, G. [12]
temptation to commit s. PAVESE [4]

suicides
s. have a special language SEXTON [2]

suit
s. you sir FAST SHOW [2]

suitability
criterion of s. and convenience MOORE, MARIANNE [2]

Sumatra
giant rat of S. DOYLE, A. C. [35]

sumer
S. is icumen in ANONYMOUS [89]

summer
but s. to your heart MILLAY [7]
compare thee to a s.'s day SHAKESPEARE: SONNETS [4]
ensure s. in England WALPOLE. H. [10]
eternal s. shall not fade SHAKESPEARE: SONNETS [5]
invincible s. CAMUS [12]
s. afternoon JAMES, H. [33]

S. has set in COLERIDGE, S. T. [80]
s. hath his joys CAMPION [3]
s. in full-throated ease KEATS [80]

summers
Threescore s. when they're gone OLDYS [2]

summertime
no cure for the s. blues COCHRAN [1]
S. and the living is easy GERSHWIN [2]

summits
climb to the highest s. SHAW [5]

sun
before you let the s. in THOMAS, D. [17]
black s. has appeared WUER KAIXI [1]
Busy old fool, unruly S. DONNE [5]
cannot make our s./Stand still MARVELL [7]
day of the s. STEVENS, W. [1]
eyes are nothing like the s. SHAKESPEARE: SONNETS [38]
Had tired the s. CALLIMACHUS [1]
Had tired the s. CORY [1]
her s. is gone down BIBLE, OLD TESTAMENT: JEREMIAH [13]
low-hanging s. speckled RIMBAUD [9]
maketh his s. to rise BIBLE, NEW TESTAMENT: MATTHEW [34]
master brother s. ST FRANCIS OF ASSISI [3]
No s. – no moon HOOD [16]
on which the s. never sets WILSON, J. [1]
place in the s. BÜLOW [1]
s. also ariseth BIBLE, OLD TESTAMENT: ECCLESIASTES [2]
s. be darkened BIBLE, NEW TESTAMENT: MATTHEW [142]
s. descending in the west BLAKE [9]
s. has got its hat on BUTLER, R. [1]
s. in my dominions never sets SCHILLER [7]
s. is but a morning star THOREAU [54]
s. shall be darkened KORAN [48]
s. shall not smite thee BIBLE, OLD TESTAMENT: PSALMS [125]
s. shineth upon the dunghill LYLY [1]
s. that shines upon his court SHAKESPEARE: WINTER'S TALE [16]
S., the hearth of affection RIMBAUD [1]
s. went round the earth ARNOLD, T. [3]
S. wot won it SUN [7]
see the s. the other way BISHOP [4]
stand out of my s. DIOGENES [6]

sunbonnet
s. as well as the sombrero FERBER [2]

sunburnt
s. by the glare of life BROWNING, E. B. [21]

like to do all the t. myself WILDE [5]
opposite of t. isn't
listening LEBOWITZ [5]
T. is the disease of age JONSON [37]

talking-machine
redtape t. CARLYLE, T. [52]

tambourine
T. Man DYLAN [13]

tangere
Noli me t. BIBLE, VULGATE [14]

tango
Takes two to t. HOFFMAN AND
MANNING [1]

tar-baby
T. ain't sayin' nuthin' HARRIS, J. C. [3]

tarry
You may for ever t. HERRICK [12]

tartness
t. of his face sours SHAKESPEARE:
CORIOLANUS [11]

tarts
Knave of Hearts he stole the
t. NURSERY RHYMES [33]

Tarzan
Me T., you Jane BURROUGHS, E. R. [1]

task
common t. KEBLE [2]
He who has a t. to
perform GOETHE [15]

taste
Between friends differences in
t. AUDEN [42]
Between good sense and good t. LA
BRUYÈRE [18]
Ghastly Good T. BETJEMAN [3]
Good t. and humour MUGGERIDGE [1]
Good t. is better than bad BENNETT,
ARNOLD [11]
harmony in bad t. GENET [1]
never t. who always drink PRIOR [1]
O t. and see BIBLE, OLD TESTAMENT:
PSALMS [42]
T. is a merciless betrayer BAYLEY [2]
't.' is a social concept UPDIKE [8]
T. is the fundamental
quality LAUTRÉAMONT [3]
t. was united to genius GOLDSMITH
[1]
Things sweet to t. SHAKESPEARE:
RICHARD II [6]
wild vicissitudes of t. JOHNSON, S. [5]

taste-refining
tomb of t. time SHEE [1]

taught
nothing ... can be t. WILDE [22]
things we haven't been
t. VAUVENARGUES [4]

tavern
good t. or inn JOHNSON, S. [100]
t. for his friends DOUGLAS, N. [3]

tax
To t. and to please BURKE, E. [11]

taxation
no t. without
representation POLITICAL
SLOGANS [28]
T. without representation OTIS [1]

taxed
all the world should be t. BIBLE, NEW
TESTAMENT: LUKE [7]

taxes
death and t. FRANKLIN, B. [16]
I like the t. BYRON, LORD [77]
Only the little people pay
t. HELMSLEY [1]
people overlaid with t. BACON, F. [30]
true as t. DICKENS [69]

Tay
Bridge of the Silv'ry
T. MCGONAGALL [1]

tea
best sweeteners of t. FIELDING,
HENRY [2]
ceremony known as afternoon
t. JAMES, H. [9]
like having a cup of t. PAYNE, C. [1]
no Latin word for T. BELLOC [4]
sometimes counsel ... sometimes
t. POPE [42]
T. ... beverage of the intellectual DE
QUINCEY [4]
t. does our fancy aid WALLER [6]
t. for two CAESAR, I. [1]
T. ... is a gentleman CHESTERTON [31]
t. is suggestive of a thousand
wants REPPLIER [2]
T.! Thou soft, thou sober,
sage CIBBER [6]
Thank God for t. SMITH, SYDNEY [24]
we drink too much t. PRIESTLEY [4]

teabag
woman is like a t. REAGAN, N. [1]

teach
t. is to learn twice JOUBERT [7]
T. me thy way BIBLE, OLD TESTAMENT:
PSALMS [33]
T. me, my God and King HERBERT,
G. [42]
t. to talk unjustly ARISTOPHANES [2]

teacher
fit to be a t. CONFUCIUS [5]
t. affects eternity ADAMS, H. B. [5]
t. ... equal to my own
parents HIPPOCRATES [4]
t. should be sparing of his
smile COWPER [18]
t. should have maximal
authority SZASZ [4]
t.'s life should have three
periods OSLER [4]
true t. defends his pupils ALCOTT,
A. B. [1]
whip the t. DIOGENES [4]
You are my t. DANTE [2]

teachers
have not been their own t. REYNOLDS,
J. [1]
t. ... are taught to learn BRECHT [11]

teaches
He who cannot, t. SHAW [30]

teaching
It is by t. that we teach
ourselves AMIEL [3]
T. is not a lost art BARZUN [2]
vanity of t. often tempteth SAVILE [7]

tea-drinker
hardened and shameless t. JOHNSON,
S. [33]

team
supporting the wrong t. HORNBY [2]

tear
drying up a single t. BYRON,
LORD [145]
fallen a splendid t. TENNYSON [129]
t. each other's eyes WATTS, I. [2]
t. is an intellectual thing BLAKE [68]
unanswerable t. BYRON, LORD [43]

tears
drop, slow t. FLETCHER, P. [1]
explanation of his t. TERENCE [1]
far-off interest of t. TENNYSON [86]
If you have t., ... shed
them SHAKESPEARE: JULIUS
CAESAR [33]
No more t. now MARY QUEEN OF
SCOTS [1]
No t. in the writer FROST, R. [30]
Nor t. nor prayers shall
purchase SHAKESPEARE: ROMEO &
JULIET [30]
t. are a luxury MOORE, T. [12]
t. come from the heart LEONARDO DA
VINCI [4]
t. of the world are ...
constant BECKETT [5]
t. shed for things VIRGIL [24]
T., idle tears TENNYSON [70]
wipe away all t. BIBLE, NEW
TESTAMENT: REVELATION [50]

technically
something that is t.
sweet OPPENHEIMER, J. R. [2]

Technik
Vorsprung durch T. ADVERTISING
SLOGANS [32]

technique
T. is communication BERNSTEIN [1]
T. is the test of sincerity POUND [29]

technology
Progress through t. ADVERTISING
SLOGANS [32]
Science and t. multiply BALLARD [4]
T. ... the knack of so arranging the
world FRISCH [1]
T. is making gestures
precise ADORNO [1]

theologians
privilege of t. ERASMUS [6]
theology
supreme tyranny of t. BAKUNIN
[6]
T. – An effort to
explain MENCKEN [23]
theories
work in which there are
t. PROUST [25]
theorize
capital mistake to t. DOYLE, A. C.
[15]
theorizing
work without t. VOLTAIRE [17]
theory
No t. is good GIDE [3]
t. can be said to be true AYER [4]
there
Because it's t. MALLORY [1]
I'll be t. STEINBECK [4]
There is no t. there STEIN [12]
Theseus
let off T. lightly DANTE [12]
thief
Each thing's a t. SHAKESPEARE:
TIMON [12]
I come as a t. BIBLE, NEW TESTAMENT:
REVELATION [40]
t. in the night BIBLE, NEW TESTAMENT:
1 THESSALONIANS [4]
thieves
den of t. BIBLE, NEW TESTAMENT:
MATTHEW [128]
fell among t. BIBLE, NEW TESTAMENT:
LUKE [29]
thimbles
They sought it with t. CARROLL [50]
thin
ask women to become ... t. WOLF,
N. [2]
thine
all that I have is t. BIBLE, NEW
TESTAMENT: LUKE [48]
things
been t. and seen places WEST, M. [5]
this solicitude for t. BOWEN,
ELIZABETH [3]
think
I t., therefore I am DESCARTES [3]
Lord Jesus, t. on me HYMNS &
CAROLS [52]
T. in the morning BLAKE [31]
t. otherwise than in the
fashion SHAW [71]
t. too little ... talk too
much DRYDEN [34]
those that t. must
govern GOLDSMITH [13]
to t. is to make FRAYN [2]
When I t., I must speak SHAKESPEARE:
AS YOU LIKE IT [23]

thinker
t. who has thought
thoroughly CHESTERTON [14]
thinking
effort to prevent oneself t. HUXLEY,
A. [3]
lateral t. DE BONO [1]
Man is obviously made for
t. PASCAL [20]
only t./Lays lads
underground HOUSMAN [16]
Power of Positive T. PEALE [1]
T. is the most unhealthy
thing WILDE [15]
T. isn't agreeing or
disagreeing FROST, R. [38]
t. makes it so SHAKESPEARE:
HAMLET [64]
then to t. HAZLITT [15]
thinks
live the way one t. BOURGET [1]
thinner
If you wish to grow t. LEIGH, H.S. [2]
Third Way
T. is a purely political
concept GALBRAITH [14]
Third World
T is not a reality ARENDT [13]
thirst
I t. BIBLE, NEW TESTAMENT: JOHN
[68]
thirteen
clocks were striking t. ORWELL [34]
thirty
I am past t. ARNOLD, M. [33]
live enough befure t. DUNNE, F. P. [2]
next t. years FITZGERALD, F. S. [8]
t. as the barrier BYRON, LORD [167]
thirty-five
T. is a very attractive age WILDE [107]
thorn
Instead of the t. BIBLE, OLD
TESTAMENT: ISAIAH [78]
ne'er the rose without the
t. HERRICK [28]
t. in the flesh BIBLE, NEW TESTAMENT:
2 CORINTHIANS [15]
thorns
t. in your sides BIBLE, OLD TESTAMENT:
JUDGES [1]
t. that in her bosom
lodge SHAKESPEARE: HAMLET [51]
thorny
steep and t. way to
heaven SHAKESPEARE: HAMLET [29]
thought
Modern Western t. HERZEN [5]
One t. fills immensity BLAKE [29]
revelation of T. EMERSON [44]
slumbering t. BYRON, LORD [66]
splendour of a sudden t. BROWNING,
R. [45]

strange seas of t. WORDSWORTH,
W. [16]
T. is an infection STEVENS, W. [19]
t. is not free RUSSELL, B. [6]
t. is often original HOLMES SR [5]
T. leapt out to wed TENNYSON [93]
T. once awakened CARLYLE, T. [38]
t.,/... the measure of the
universe SHELLEY, P. B. [56]
t. ... to justify their
injustices VOLTAIRE [25]
T. would destroy their paradise GRAY,
T. [5]
talent for packing t. close MACAULAY,
LORD [25]
utmost bound of human
t. TENNYSON [30]
You called it T. PRÉVERT [3]
thoughtcrime
make t. literally
impossible ORWELL [38]
thoughts
begin to have bloody t. SHAKESPEARE:
TEMPEST [21]
Give thy t. no tongue SHAKESPEARE:
HAMLET [30]
in a shroud/Of thoughts BYRON,
LORD [62]
Little-minded people's t. HOLMES
SR [6]
My own t./Are my
companions LONGFELLOW [27]
ought to control our t. DARWIN, C. [4]
so infinite vexation/as ... t. WEBSTER,
J. [14]
T. ... too deep for tears WORDSWORTH,
W. [93]
t. are not your thoughts BIBLE, OLD
TESTAMENT: ISAIAH [77]
t. of men are widened TENNYSON
[43]
T. that breathe GRAY, T. [21]
True t. ... do not
understand ADORNO [2]
thousand
end of a t. years of
history GAITSKELL [3]
little one shall become a t. BIBLE, OLD
TESTAMENT: ISAIAH [83]
one ten t. of those men SHAKESPEARE:
HENRY V [25]
t. moral paintings I can
show SHAKESPEARE: TIMON [1]
t. years in thy sight BIBLE, OLD
TESTAMENT: PSALMS [92]
went out there for a t. a
week ALGREN [3]
Would he had blotted a
t. JONSON [38]
thousands
Saul hath slain his t. BIBLE, OLD
TESTAMENT: 1 SAMUEL [17]

V. is as American as cherry
pie BROWN, H. R. [1]
V. ... refuge in
falsehood SOLZHENITSYN [6]
well-organized v. TROTSKY [12]

violet
v. by a mossy stone WORDSWORTH,
W. [32]
v. of his native land TENNYSON [91]

violins
Sharp v. proclaim DRYDEN [62]
sobs/Of the v. VERLAINE [1]

viper
v. thoughts COLERIDGE, S. T. [48]

vipers
generation of v. BIBLE, NEW
TESTAMENT: MATTHEW [9]

Virgil
V. I only saw OVID [20]

virgin
arrange a v. birth JENKINS, D. [1]
Like a v. MADONNA [2]
love the v.'s heart invade GAY, J. [9]
v. who is a whore DAHLBERG [3]

Virginia Woolf
Who's Afraid of V. ALBEE [2]

Virginian
not a V., but an American HENRY,
PATRICK [2]

virginity
long preserved v. MARVELL [5]
losing my v. as a career
move MADONNA [4]
v. ... like one of our
French SHAKESPEARE: ALL'S WELL [4]

virgins
amount of v. ... today is
stupendous CARTLAND [1]
ten v. BIBLE, NEW TESTAMENT:
MATTHEW [146]

virile
beautiful in v. men SONTAG [4]

virtue
Assume a virtue SHAKESPEARE:
HAMLET [125]
flattered into v. SURTEES [6]
fugitive and cloistered v. MILTON [65]
loss of v. ... is
irretrievable AUSTEN [11]
Man may aspire to v. CHAMFORT [15]
Most men admire/V. MILTON [186]
Most v. is a demand BARNEY [4]
no ... ready way to v. BROWNE [11]
produce ... a disposition to
v. ARISTOTLE [7]
rarer action is/In v. SHAKESPEARE:
TEMPEST [23]
sinews of v. WALTON [7]
v. had gone out of him BIBLE, NEW
TESTAMENT: MARK [5]
V. is free SOCRATES [30]
V. is ... merely local JOHNSON, S. [42]

v. is not given by
money SOCRATES [5]
v. is not hereditary PAINE [5]
V. is the truest
nobility CERVANTES [21]
V. rejects facility MONTAIGNE [9]
V. she finds too painful POPE
[94]
v., without which
intimidation ROBESPIERRE [2]

virtues
at least one of the cardinal
v. FITZGERALD, F. S. [5]
have done with v. DE SADE [4]
knows about his v. EMERSON [21]
none of the moral v.
arises ARISTOTLE [8]
Our v. are mostly our vices LA
ROCHEFOUCAULD [3]

virtuous
As v. men pass mildly
away DONNE [21]
she's still v. FARQUHAR [3]
Who can find a v. woman BIBLE, OLD
TESTAMENT: PROVERBS [100]

virtuously
act v. in every way MACHIAVELLI [7]

visible
all things v. and invisible BOOK OF
COMMON PRAYER [51]
mystery of the world is the
v. WILDE [42]

vision
every v. faileth BIBLE, OLD TESTAMENT:
EZEKIEL [2]
fake ... the inner v. DAVIES,
ROBERTSON [4]
most rare v. SHAKESPEARE:
MIDSUMMER NIGHT'S DREAM [35]
v. of Christ that thou dost
see BLAKE [96]
v. thing BUSH, G. [1]
Was it a v. KEATS [89]
Where there is no v. BIBLE, OLD
TESTAMENT: PROVERBS [95]
Write the v. BIBLE, OLD TESTAMENT:
HABAKKUK [1]

visionary
Whither is fled the v.
gleam WORDSWORTH, W. [81]

visions
I have multiplied v. BIBLE, OLD
TESTAMENT: HOSEA [6]

visits
never make long v. MOORE,
MARIANNE [3]

vista
Hasta la v. SCHWARZENEGGER [2]

vita
dolce v. DANTE [29]

vitae
v. summa brevis HORACE [18]

vitality
derive our v. from ...
madness CIORAN [3]

vitam
V. brevem esse SENECA [18]

Vitruvius
be whate'er V. was before POPE
[110]

vivamus
V., mea Lesbia CATULLUS [6]

vocation
labour in his v. SHAKESPEARE:
HENRY IV PT 1 [7]
Our v. is the love of Jesus TERESA [5]
walk worthy of the v. BIBLE, NEW
TESTAMENT: EPHESIANS [5]

vogue
totter into v. WALPOLE, H. [7]

voice
hear a v. in every wind GRAY, T. [2]
people's v. is odd POPE [159]
sound of a v. that is
still TENNYSON [59]
still small v. BIBLE, OLD TESTAMENT:
1 KINGS [14]
v. not only took you JARRELL [4]
v. of many waters BIBLE, NEW
TESTAMENT: REVELATION [35]
v. that commands the
story CALVINO [1]

voices
sound of tireless v. is the
price STEVENSON, A. [3]

volcanoes
factions are v. burnt out BURKE,
E. [52]
range of exhausted v. DISRAELI [49]
We are v. LE GUIN [6]

vole
passes the questing v. WAUGH [9]

Voltaire
Jesus wept; V. smiled HUGO [17]
One does not arrest V. DE GAULLE [13]

voluntary
v. part of a man BAGEHOT [6]

voluptuary
true v. will never abandon BYRON,
LORD [41]

vomit
As a dog returneth to his v. BIBLE,
OLD TESTAMENT: PROVERBS [80]
dog is turned to his own v. BIBLE,
NEW TESTAMENT: 2 PETER [4]
dog returns to his v. KIPLING [84]

vortex
v. or cluster of fused ideas POUND [3]

vote
Don't buy a single v. more KENNEDY,
J. F. [1]
I always v. against FIELDS, W. C. [4]
v. just as their leaders GILBERT,
W. S. [23]

W. is the statesman's game SHELLEY, P. B. [8]

W. is the supreme drama MUMFORD, L. [3]

W. is the trade of kings DRYDEN [65]

W. is thus divine in itself MAISTRE [6]

W. ... is toil and trouble DRYDEN [72]

W. is too important CLEMENCEAU [1]

W. makes ... good history HARDY, T. [24]

w. more unjust in its origin GLADSTONE [1]

W.'s a brain-spattering ... art BYRON, LORD [147]

W. seldom enters DRYDEN [54]

W. talk by men TWAIN [5]

w. tends to become universal DU BOIS [8]

w., the blood-swollen god CRANE, S. [1]

W. ... the continuation of policy CLAUSEWITZ [1]

w. – the world's only hygiene MARINETTI [3]

w. to be just AQUINAS [5]

W. was always there HEMINGWAY [3]

W. ... /What is it good for STARR, E. [1]

W. will cease POLITICAL SLOGANS [38]

w. will not come again HITLER [10]

welcomed the w. ASQUITH, M. [3]

well that w. is so terrible LEE, R. E. [1]

what can w. but endless war MILTON [73]

What if someone gave a W. GINSBERG [9]

wrong w., at the wrong place BRADLEY, O. [2]

warble
W., child; make passionate SHAKESPEARE: LOVE'S LABOUR'S LOST [9]

ward
who will w. the warders JUVENAL [13]

warm
w. and still to be enjoyed KEATS [95]

warn
All a poet can do to-day is w. OWEN [8]

warner
I am only a w. KORAN [21]

warrior
This is the happy w. READ, H. [1]
Who is the happy w. WORDSWORTH, W. [42]

wars
end all w. LLOYD GEORGE [5]
end to the beginnings of all w. ROOSEVELT, F. D. [13]
four w. in my lifetime REAGAN, R. [5]
History is littered with the w. POWELL, E. [1]

thou shalt have w. BIBLE, OLD TESTAMENT: 2 CHRONICLES [1]

w. and rumours of wars BIBLE, NEW TESTAMENT: MATTHEW [139]

w. are occasioned by SOCRATES [13]

w. are planned by old men RICE, G. [2]

w./were global REED, H. [3]

warts
pimples, w., and everything CROMWELL [8]

wash
W. me throughly BIBLE, OLD TESTAMENT: PSALMS [62]
w. that man HAMMERSTEIN II [11]

washed
w. his hands BIBLE, NEW TESTAMENT: MATTHEW [168]

washing
taking in each other's w. HEATH [4]
w. his hands with invisible soap HOOD [8]

Washington
Bequeathed the name of W. BYRON, LORD [44]
W. is a city KENNEDY, J. F. [11]
W.'s a watchword BYRON, LORD [140]

wasps
Smoking out a w. nest CHURCHILL, W. [7]

waste
I love all w. SHELLEY, P. B. [25]
To what purpose is this w. BIBLE, NEW TESTAMENT: MATTHEW [152]
W. of Blood, and waste of Tears KENNEDY, G. A. S. [1]
w. of plenty PEACOCK [2]
What a w. DURY [3]

wasted
chronicle of w. time SHAKESPEARE: SONNETS [30]

watch
like a fat gold w. PLATH [6]
my w. has stopped MARX, G. [7]
w. must have had a maker PALEY [2]
W. ye therefore BIBLE, NEW TESTAMENT: MARK [15]

watcher
w. of the skies KEATS [6]

watches
people looking at their w. BIRKETT [1]

watching
you won't feel like w. LEBOWITZ [6]

watchmaker
blind w. DAWKINS [3]

watchman
W., what of the night BIBLE, OLD TESTAMENT: ISAIAH [30]

watchmen
w. on the walls of the world KENNEDY, J. F. [21]

water
added w. to the sea SHAKESPEARE: TITUS ANDRONICUS [3]

as w. spilt on the ground BIBLE, OLD TESTAMENT: 2 SAMUEL [10]

Christ walking on the w. THOMPSON, F. [14]

drinketh of this w. BIBLE, NEW TESTAMENT: JOHN [20]

From a drop of w. DOYLE, A. C. [4]

Have you considered the w. KORAN [43]

Honest w., which ne'er left SHAKESPEARE: TIMON [5]

Name was writ in W. KEATS [122]

nature of w. to flow downwards MENCIUS [4]

not born of w. BIBLE, NEW TESTAMENT: JOHN [16]

nothing more submissive ... than w. TAO TE CHING [16]

plunge your hands in w. AUDEN [12]

poured out like w. BIBLE, OLD TESTAMENT: PSALMS [23]

safe to go back in the w. ANONYMOUS [50]

sweet w. and bitter BIBLE, NEW TESTAMENT: JAMES [11]

w. clears us of this deed SHAKESPEARE: MACBETH [42]

w. is wide ANONYMOUS [96]

w. of life BIBLE, NEW TESTAMENT: REVELATION [53]

W., water, everywhere COLERIDGE, S. T. [21]

wetter w., slimier slime BROOKE [10]

women's weapons, w. drops SHAKESPEARE: KING LEAR [23]

water-closet
w. doormat DICKENS [42]

Waterloo
W. sunset DAVIES, RAY [2]
W. was won on the playing fields WELLINGTON [6]

water-man
great-grandfather was but a w. BUNYAN [8]

waters
As the w. fail from the sea BIBLE, OLD TESTAMENT: JOB [26]

cold w. to a thirsty soul BIBLE, OLD TESTAMENT: PROVERBS [77]

come ye to the w. BIBLE, OLD TESTAMENT: ISAIAH [76]

Once more upon the w. BYRON, LORD [54]

Stolen w. are sweet BIBLE, OLD TESTAMENT: PROVERBS [18]

w. cover the sea BIBLE, OLD TESTAMENT: ISAIAH [25]

w. were a wall BIBLE, OLD TESTAMENT: EXODUS [22]

watery
Nine changes of the w.
star SHAKESPEARE: WINTER'S TALE [1]

Watson
Good old W. DOYLE, A. C. [34]

wavereth
he that w. BIBLE, NEW TESTAMENT:
JAMES [2]

waves
proud w. be stayed BIBLE, OLD
TESTAMENT: JOB [42]

way
best w. out is ... through FROST, R. [9]
Come my W., my Truth HERBERT,
G. [31]
I am the w. BIBLE, NEW TESTAMENT:
JOHN [50]
This is the w. BIBLE, OLD TESTAMENT:
ISAIAH [42]
W. lies close at hand MENCIUS [1]
W. that can be spoken of TAO TE
CHING [1]

weak
support the w. BIBLE, NEW
TESTAMENT: ACTS [33]
w. have one weapon BIDAULT [1]
when I am w., then am I
strong BIBLE, NEW TESTAMENT:
2 CORINTHIANS [17]

weakness
All wickedness is w. MILTON [199]

weaknesses
Never support two w. WILDER, T. [4]

wealth
by any means get w. POPE [158]
duty of the man of w. CARNEGIE,
A. [2]
how little God esteems ... w. LA
BRUYÈRE [12]
no w. but life RUSKIN [17]
w. accumulates ... men
decay GOLDSMITH [32]
w. is ... not the good we are
seeking ARISTOTLE [5]
W. is not without its
advantages GALBRAITH [2]
W. is the parent of
luxury SOCRATES [21]
W. maketh many friends BIBLE, OLD
TESTAMENT: PROVERBS [54]
w. should be found
everywhere BURKE, E. [26]

weapon
other hand held a w. BIBLE, OLD
TESTAMENT: NEHEMIAH [1]

weapons
lawful ... to wear w. BOOK OF
COMMON PRAYER [95]
W. are like money AMIS, M. [4]
w. of mass destruction HUSSEIN [3]
w. of war perished BIBLE, OLD
TESTAMENT: 2 SAMUEL [6]

weariness
Art thou pale for w. SHELLEY, P. B. [62]
W./Can snore upon the
flint SHAKESPEARE: CYMBELINE [10]

wearisome
w. condition of
humanity GREVILLE [1]

weary
Art thou w. HYMNS & CAROLS [11]
be w. in well doing BIBLE, NEW
TESTAMENT: GALATIANS [10]
Let him be rich and w. HERBERT,
G. [33]

weasel
w. words ROOSEVELT, T. [9]

weather
change in the w. is
sufficient PROUST [15]
don't talk ... about the w. WILDE [98]
Everybody talks about the
w. TWAIN [31]
hard grey w. KINGSLEY [4]
no such thing as bad w. RUSKIN [30]
w. is like the government JEROME [4]
w. the cuckoo likes HARDY, T. [33]
won't hold up the w. MACNEICE [6]

weather-beaten
Never w. sail CAMPION [2]

weatherman
don't need a w. DYLAN [7]

web
tangled w. we weave SCOTT, W. [11]

Webb
Captain W. from
Dawley BETJEMAN [6]

wedded
Hail w. love, mysterious
law MILTON [143]

wedding
w. is a funeral which
masquerades BURCHILL [5]

wedlock
w.'s like wine JERROLD [1]
w.'s the devil BYRON, LORD [2]
what is w. forcèd but a
hell SHAKESPEARE: HENRY VI PT 1 [8]

weed
Pernicious w. COWPER [22]
w. is no more than a flower LOWELL,
J. R. [5]
w. that grows in every soil BURKE,
E. [22]
What is a w. EMERSON [74]

weeds
W. and nettles ... have
thriven CROMWELL [7]
w. and tares of mine own
brain BROWNE [8]

week
greatest w. in ... history NIXON [5]
w. is a long time in politics WILSON,
H. [5]

weep
if you want me to w. HORACE [76]
W. bitterly BIBLE, APOCRYPHA:
ECCLESIASTICUS [59]
w. for yourselves BIBLE, NEW
TESTAMENT: LUKE [68]
W. no more FLETCHER, J. [6]
w. or she will die TENNYSON [74]

weepest
Woman, why w. thou BIBLE, NEW
TESTAMENT: JOHN [71]

weeping
I have full cause of w. SHAKESPEARE:
KING LEAR [24]
w. in my heart VERLAINE [2]

weeps
Nature ... w. from
gladness DISRAELI [21]

weighed
w. in the balances BIBLE, OLD
TESTAMENT: DANIEL [9]

weight
w. of days is terrible CAMUS [18]
w. of this sad time SHAKESPEARE:
KING LEAR [65]
willing to pull his w. ROOSEVELT, T. [4]

weird
W. Sisters, hand in
hand SHAKESPEARE: MACBETH [4]
when a man is ... good, he is
w. ANTRIM [2]

welfare
w. his true aim ARNOLD, M. [7]

well
all shall be w. JULIAN OF NORWICH [1]
All's w. that ends well SHAKESPEARE:
ALL'S WELL [7]
Didn't he do w. FORSYTH [2]
not so deep as a w. SHAKESPEARE:
ROMEO & JULIET [27]

well-born
w. man is fortunate LA BRUYÈRE [4]

well-educated
w. alone are free EPICTETUS [1]

well-housed
w., well-warmed MELVILLE [15]

Wellington
Proud W., with eagle beak BYRON,
LORD [141]

wells
w. of salvation BIBLE, OLD TESTAMENT:
ISAIAH [26]

Welsh
defend me from that W.
fairy SHAKESPEARE: MERRY WIVES [15]

Weltgeschichte
W. ist das Weltgericht SCHILLER [5]

Wenceslas
Good King W. HYMNS & CAROLS [33]

wens
greatest persons are but great
w. DONNE [42]

w. and women ... have
infatuated BURTON [6]
W. comes in at the mouth YEATS [22]
W. is a mocker BIBLE, OLD TESTAMENT:
PROVERBS [57]
W. is as good as life BIBLE,
APOCRYPHA: ECCLESIASTICUS [52]
W. is the strongest BIBLE, APOCRYPHA:
1 ESDRAS [1]
When the w. is in BECON [2]

wine-dark
w. sea HOMER [15]

winepress
I have trodden the w. BIBLE, OLD
TESTAMENT: ISAIAH [85]
w. of ... God BIBLE, NEW TESTAMENT:
REVELATION [44]

wines
finest w. available to
humanity ROBINSON, B. [5]

wing
w. and a pray'r ADAMSON [1]

wingèd
w. words HOMER [2]

wings
healing in his w. BIBLE, OLD
TESTAMENT: MALACHI [3]
O for a horse with w. SHAKESPEARE:
CYMBELINE [7]
under the shadow of thy w. BIBLE,
OLD TESTAMENT: PSALMS [43]
w. of the morning BIBLE, OLD
TESTAMENT: PSALMS [143]

winning
most w. woman I ever knew DOYLE,
A. C. [12]

winnow
W. not with every wind BIBLE,
APOCRYPHA: ECCLESIASTICUS [9]

wins
almost w. BROUN [1]

winter
English w. – ending in July BYRON,
LORD [159]
From w., plague and
pestilence NASHE [3]
If W. comes, can Spring be
far SHELLEY, P. B. [41]
In w. I get up at night STEVENSON,
R. L. [29]
sad tale's best for w. SHAKESPEARE:
WINTER'S TALE [5]
w. change to spring TENNYSON [102]
W. comes to rule THOMSON, J. (1700–
48) [8]
W. is icummen in POUND [7]
w. of our discontent SHAKESPEARE:
RICHARD III [1]
w.'s rains and ruins SWINBURNE [2]

winters
When forty w. shall
besiege SHAKESPEARE: SONNETS [2]

wipe
w. away all tears BIBLE, NEW
TESTAMENT: REVELATION [24]

wisdom
all the knowledge and
w. CUDWORTH [1]
beginning of w. BIBLE, OLD
TESTAMENT: PSALMS [116]
dwelleth with w. BIBLE, APOCRYPHA:
WISDOM OF SOLOMON [12]
Is in your majesty remarkable
W. MASSINGER [3]
Knowledge comes, but w.
lingers TENNYSON [44]
old and new w. mix
admirably BRECHT [17]
price of w. is above rubies BIBLE, OLD
TESTAMENT: JOB [35]
Raphael paints w. EMERSON [63]
road to w. HEIN [2]
serpentine w. BACON, F. [47]
W. ... best ends by the best
means HUTCHESON [1]
w. ... by the awful grace of
God AESCHYLUS [1]
W. crieth without BIBLE, OLD
TESTAMENT: PROVERBS [3]
w. descendeth not from above BIBLE,
NEW TESTAMENT: JAMES [12]
W. hath her excesses MONTAIGNE [19]
w. hears half its applause ELIOT,
G. [22]
w. ... in our mature
years TROLLOPE [6]
w. is better than rubies BIBLE, OLD
TESTAMENT: PROVERBS [16]
w. is conceived for ... mediocre
people STEVENSON, R. L. [13]
W. is justified of her children BIBLE,
NEW TESTAMENT: MATTHEW [85]
W. is like electricity EMERSON [68]
w. is the gray hair unto men BIBLE,
APOCRYPHA: WISDOM OF SOLOMON [7]
W. is the principal thing BIBLE, OLD
TESTAMENT: PROVERBS [6]
W. lies neither in fixity PAZ [5]
w. of this world is foolishness BIBLE,
NEW TESTAMENT: 1 CORINTHIANS [7]
w. ... only after death SOCRATES [14]
where shall w. be found BIBLE, OLD
TESTAMENT: JOB [34]
With the ancient is w. BIBLE, OLD
TESTAMENT: JOB [23]

wise
Be w with speed YOUNG, E. [4]
Be w. today YOUNG. E. [7]
darkly w., and rudely great POPE
[127]
No man is w. enough PLAUTUS [7]
property of a w. person ASTELL [3]
So w. so young SHAKESPEARE:
RICHARD III [10]

To be w. and love SHAKESPEARE:
TROILUS & CRESSIDA [9]
w. and eke to love SPENSER [2]
w., in order to love
wisdom SCHILLER [9]
w. man is strong BIBLE, OLD
TESTAMENT: PROVERBS [71]
w. men are the greatest
fools COWLEY, H. [4]
W. men say nothing SELDEN [11]
want to be the only w. one LA
ROCHEFOUCAULD [20]
Who can be w., amazed SHAKESPEARE:
MACBETH [50]

wisecracking
w. and wit PARKER, D. [19]

wisedoom
what is better than w. CHAUCER
[46]

wisely
men and nations behave w. EBAN [1]

wiser
w. than this fellow SOCRATES [2]

wish
w. was father ... to that
thought SHAKESPEARE: HENRY IV
PT 2 [25]

wished
w. that I had clear POPE [163]

wit
Devise, w.; write, pen SHAKESPEARE:
LOVE'S LABOUR'S LOST [7]
don't screw your w. CIBBER [2]
neither wit, nor words SHAKESPEARE:
JULIUS CAESAR [36]
over-greet a w. CHAUCER [49]
universal monarchy of w. CAREW [1]
w. being well-bred
insolence ARISTOTLE [22]
W. destroys eroticism KING, F. [2]
w. in all languages DRYDEN [4]
W. is a weapon MUIR, F. [1]
w. is nature to advantage
dressed POPE [15]
W. is so shining a quality
CHESTERFIELD [38]
W. is the clash of incongruities HUNT,
L. [10]
W. is the salt of
conversation HAZLITT [9]
W. lies in recognising STAËL [3]
w. of man so well devised BOOK OF
COMMON PRAYER [2]
w. should no more be
sincere CONGREVE [16]
W. that can creep POPE [154]
w.'s end BIBLE, OLD TESTAMENT:
PSALMS [114]
w.'s the noblest frailty SHADWELL
[3]
winding up the watch of his
w. SHAKESPEARE: TEMPEST [12]

Men are the managers of ...
w. KORAN [17]
Most w. have no characters POPE [92]
no need ... to act like 'w.' MITCHELL,
JULIET [2]
not defiled themselves with
w. TAYLOR, J. [2]
proper function of w. ELIOT, G. [19]
superiority of their
w. TOCQUEVILLE [9]
underpaid labor of w. STEINEM [1]
Uneducated clever w. WHITEHEAD [2]
W. and horses and
power KIPLING [28]
w. ... appear to me as
children KEATS [43]
w. are an over-match JOHNSON,
S. [82]
W. ... are best flattered
CHESTERFIELD [14]
w. are born slaves ASTELL [5]
W. are like tricks CONGREVE [11]
W. are most fascinating DIOR [1]
W. are only children CHESTERFIELD
[13]
W. are really much nicer AMIS, K. [2]
W. are stronger than
men STEPHENS [1]
W. ... care ... more for a
marriage BAGEHOT [11]
w. feel just as men BRONTË, C. [7]
W. have dominion over you BIBLE,
APOCRYPHA: 1 ESDRAS [4]
W. have no
sympathy NIGHTINGALE [5]
W. have no wilderness BOGAN [1]
w. in the more conventional
mould BROOKNER [4]
W. know/The way to rear BROWNING,
E. B. [13]
W. must labour to be
beautiful YEATS [20]
W. never have young
minds DELANEY [1]
W. ought to have freedom SACKVILLE-
WEST [1]
W. reminded him of lilies MITCHELL,
E. [1]
W. serve but to keep WYCHERLEY [2]
w. should be struck COWARD [6]
W. ... sit down with
trouble GLASGOW [2]
w. ... touching their
hearts TROLLOPE [7]
W. will not become less
gentle CHILD [3]
W.'s policy hath a
mystical MONTAIGNE [23]
won
Human reason w. KHRUSHCHEV [7]
Things w. are done SHAKESPEARE:
TROILUS & CRESSIDA [2]

wonder
capacity for w. FITZGERALD, F. S. [11]
wonderful
more w. than man SOPHOCLES [1]
O w., wonderful SHAKESPEARE: AS YOU
LIKE IT [22]
things which are too w. BIBLE, OLD
TESTAMENT: PROVERBS [97]
wonderfully
What is so w. made TENNYSON [50]
wonders
write the w. of the
Christian MATHER [1]
wondrous
whatever is truly w. MELVILLE [8]
woo
Come, w. me SHAKESPEARE: AS YOU
LIKE IT [32]
wood
w.'s in trouble HOUSMAN [12]
Where no w. is BIBLE, OLD TESTAMENT:
PROVERBS [82]
woke to find myself in a dark
W. DANTE [1]
woodcock
w. to mine own
springe SHAKESPEARE: HAMLET [158]
woodcocks
springes to catch w. SHAKESPEARE:
HAMLET [38]
woods
Enter these enchanted w. MEREDITH,
G. [11]
If you go down in the w. KENNEDY,
JIMMY [1]
I went to the w. THOREAU [33]
road through the w. KIPLING [73]
Very old are the w. DE LA MARE [2]
w. are lovely, dark FROST, R. [20]
w. decay and fall TENNYSON [182]
woodshed
Something nasty in the
W. GIBBONS [1]
wooed
beautiful ... therefore to be
W. SHAKESPEARE: HENRY VI PT 1 [6]
wooed
ever woman in this humour
W. SHAKESPEARE: RICHARD III [5]
We should be w. SHAKESPEARE:
MIDSUMMER NIGHT'S DREAM [20]
wooing
time I've lost in w. MOORE, T. [8]
wool
Like footsteps upon w. TENNYSON [15]
wool-gathering
summoned your wits from
W. MIDDLETON [2]
Woolworth
live a W. life NICOLSON [1]
word
always time to add a w. GRACIÁN [2]

flowering in a lonely
w. TENNYSON [188]
Give the people a new w. CATHER [10]
How long ... lies in one little
w. SHAKESPEARE: RICHARD II [5]
In the beginning was the W. BIBLE,
NEW TESTAMENT: JOHN [1]
In the w. of no master HORACE [54]
in w. mightier than
they MILTON [154]
Lord, thy w. abideth HYMNS &
CAROLS [55]
Man's w. is God TENNYSON [147]
play upon the w. SHAKESPEARE:
MERCHANT OF VENICE [31]
precious jewel, the W. of
God HENRY VIII [2]
torture one poor w. DRYDEN [44]
w. ... cannot be recalled HORACE
[66]
w. carries far CONRAD [4]
w. fitly spoken BIBLE, OLD TESTAMENT:
PROVERBS [74]
w. is dead DICKINSON, E. [32]
w. is the first small step HOLUB [2]
w. spoken in due season BIBLE, OLD
TESTAMENT: PROVERBS [39]
w./was born in the blood NERUDA [5]
W. was made flesh BIBLE, NEW
TESTAMENT: JOHN [7]
When I use a w. CARROLL [39]
wordes
gloton of w. LANGLAND [3]
words
barren superfluity of w. GARTH [1]
big emotions come from big
w. HEMINGWAY [29]
by thy w. ... justified BIBLE, NEW
TESTAMENT: MATTHEW [92]
Choice w., and measured
speech WORDSWORTH, W. [49]
coiner of sweet w. ARNOLD, M. [21]
common w. on a great
occasion ELIOT, G. [16]
difference between w. and
deeds TOLSTOY [12]
dreamed out in w. MURRAY, L. [3]
Fair w. ... a man shall find WYATT [4]
gotta use w. ELIOT, T. S. [34]
haven't much opinion of
w. GLASGOW [1]
He w. me SHAKESPEARE: ANTONY &
CLEOPATRA [37]
I fear those big w. JOYCE, J. [25]
importance to w. COBBETT [3]
last year's w. ELIOT, T. S. [55]
let thy w. be few BIBLE, OLD
TESTAMENT: ECCLESIASTES [15]
looked at w. HEMINGWAY [19]
make my w. sweet ASHDOWN [2]
manipulation of w. DICK [3]
multiplieth w. without

writes
w. as fast as they can
read HAZLITT [23]

writing
all good w. is *swimming* FITZGERALD,
F. S. [25]
get it in w. LEE, G. R. [1]
itch for w. JUVENAL [14]
no talent for w. BENCHLEY [6]
rest is mere fine w. VERLAINE [5]
True ease in w. POPE [20]
W. ... a mechanic part of
wit ETHEREGE [2]
W. ... a vocation of
unhappiness SIMENON [1]
W. ... different name for
conversation STERNE [8]
w. is like fine wine NAIPAUL [3]
W. is like getting married MURDOCH,
I. [6]
W. is not a profession WELDON [3]
W. ... is the dead letter DERRIDA [1]
W. is turning one's worst
moments DONLEAVY [3]
w. make us chase the writer BARNES,
J. [1]
W. saved me from WALKER [12]
w. that was written BIBLE, OLD
TESTAMENT: DANIEL [8]
w. to be taken seriously LE GUIN [7]

writings
w. I have cast away YEATS [68]

written
No one has ever w. ARTAUD [5]
What I have w. BIBLE, NEW
TESTAMENT: JOHN [66]
What is w. without effort JOHNSON,
S. [157]

wromantic
Cavaliers (Wrong but W.) SELLAR/
YEATMAN [3]

wrong
all his life ... in the w. ROCHESTER [6]
behaves when he is
w. CHESTERTON [47]
hast seen my w. BIBLE, OLD
TESTAMENT: LAMENTATIONS [5]
he done her w. ANONYMOUS [25]
people of/the w. skin JORDAN [3]
redress that w. KINGSLEY [9]
show the dark side of w. GRIFFITH [1]

wrongs
God w. not men anything KORAN [23]
redressing human w. TENNYSON [169]

wrung
w. life dry for your
lips SWINBURNE [6]

Wynken
W., Blynken and Nod FIELD [2]

Xanadu
In X. did Kubla Khan COLERIDGE,
S. T. [4]

xenophobia
X. ... the mass
ideology HOBSBAWM [3]

Xerox
Once the X. copier was
invented YOUNG, A. [1]

yabba
Y. dabba do HANNA [1]

yam
I y. what I yam SEGAR [1]

yankee
one of them is 'Y. Doodle' GRANT,
U. [4]
Y. Doodle came to
town ANONYMOUS [101]
Y. Doodle Dandy COHAN [1]

Yanks
Y. are coming COHAN [3]

Yaptown
Y.-on-the-Hudson HENRY, O. [4]

yawp
sound my barbaric y. WHITMAN [22]

yea
Let your communication be, Y. BIBLE,
NEW TESTAMENT: MATTHEW [31]
Let your y. be yea BIBLE, NEW
TESTAMENT: JAMES [16]

yeah
y. but no LITTLE BRITAIN [3]

year
circle of the golden y. TENNYSON
[63]
pale descending y. THOMSON, J.
(1700–48) [7]

years
Before the beginning of
y. SWINBURNE [3]
what's ten y. AUNG SAN SUU KYI [1]
Y. and years unto years DONNE [16]
y. like great black oxen YEATS [5]

yellow
ought not to dye her hair
y. MENANDER [5]

Yellow Book
put down *The Y.* BETJEMAN [4]

yeoman
y.'s service SHAKESPEARE:
HAMLET [155]

yes
I said y. JOYCE, J. [32]
Y. has one more letter WHARTON [3]

yesterday
believe in y. LENNON/MCCARTNEY [5]
call back y. SHAKESPEARE:
RICHARD II [20]

yesterdays
all our y. have lighted SHAKESPEARE:
MACBETH [97]
cheerful y. WORDSWORTH, W. [103]

yields
never y. by
appointment STENDHAL [3]

ying
Y. tong iddle I po MILLIGAN [2]

yoga
Stand fast in Y. BHAGAVAD-GITA [5]
Y. in Mayfair JUNG [13]

yoke
bear the y. BIBLE, OLD TESTAMENT:
LAMENTATIONS [4]
my y. is easy BIBLE, NEW TESTAMENT:
MATTHEW [87]

yonge
O y. fresshe folkes CHAUCER [13]

Yonghy-Bonghy-Bò
Lived the Y. LEAR [12]

Yorick
Alas, poor Y.. I knew
him SHAKESPEARE: HAMLET [147]

York
Grand old Duke of Y. NURSERY
RHYMES [11]

you
could be y. ADVERTISING SLOGANS
[14]

young
as I was y. and easy THOMAS, D. [11]
compliment him about looking
y. IRVING, W. [8]
crime of being a y. man PITT THE
ELDER [1]
denunciation of the y. SMITH, LOGAN
P. [6]
I have been y. BIBLE, OLD TESTAMENT:
PSALMS [46]
I was y. and foolish YEATS [3]
knew the worst too y. KIPLING [27]
so y. a body ... so old a
head SHAKESPEARE: MERCHANT OF
VENICE [33]
So y., and so untender SHAKESPEARE:
KING LEAR [1]
teach the y. idea THOMSON, J. (1700–
48) [2]
voices of y. people SMITH, LOGAN
P. [4]
Y. blood must have its
course KINGSLEY [6]
Y. men's love then lies SHAKESPEARE:
ROMEO & JULIET [23]
y. ones RICHARD [1]
y. person ... either marries or
dies AUSTEN [24]
yet but y. in deed SHAKESPEARE:
MACBETH [70]

younger
let thy love be y. SHAKESPEARE:
TWELFTH NIGHT [20]

youth
age and y. cannot live
together ANONYMOUS [15]
American ideal is y. MILLER, H. [7]
everybody's y. is a
dream FITZGERALD, F. S. [3]